Neu

Preiswert

Zuverlässig

Dieses neue Taschenbuch ist ein ganz außergewöhnliches Wörterbuch. Sein Inhalt basiert auf den zweisprachigen Wörterbüchern des Verlages Langenscheidt — des bedeutendsten Verlages auf diesem Gebiet. Es enthält über 40 000 Stichwörter, gibt die Aussprache in beiden Teilen in Internationaler Lautschrift und besitzt besondere Anhänge für Eigennamen, Abkürzungen und Maße und Gewichte.

Neu und einzigartig ist die Fülle der grammatischen Informationen: Mehr als 15 000 deutsche Substantive und Verben haben Angaben zur Deklination und Konjugation. Über die unregelmäßigen Verben in beiden Sprachen gibt der Hauptteil und der Anhang zuverlässig Auskunft.

Dieses Wörterbuch ist somit ein modernes und handliches Nachschlagewerk für jeden, der in seinem Beruf, beim Lernen oder Lehren mit der englischen und deutschen Sprache zu tun hat.

LANGENSCHEIDTS
DEUTSCH-ENGLISCHES
ENGLISCH-DEUTSCHES
WÖRTERBUCH

Beide Teile in einem Band

Bearbeitet und herausgegeben
von der
LANGENSCHEIDT-REDAKTION

PUBLISHED BY POCKET BOOKS NEW YORK

LANGENSCHEIDT'S

GERMAN-ENGLISH
ENGLISH-GERMAN
DICTIONARY

Two Volumes in One

Edited by
THE LANGENSCHEIDT
EDITORIAL STAFF

PUBLISHED BY POCKET BOOKS NEW YORK

**POCKET BOOKS, a Simon & Schuster division of
GULF & WESTERN CORPORATION**
1230 Avenue of the Americas, New York, N.Y. 10020

ISBN: 0-671-82782-0

First Pocket Books printing March, 1953

24   23   22   21   20   19   18   17

Trademarks registered in the United States and other countries.

Printed in the U.S.A.

Preface

For over 100 years Langenscheidt's bilingual dictionaries have been an essential tool of the language student. For several decades Langenscheidt's German-English dictionaries have been used in all walks of life as well as in schools.

However, languages are in a constant process of change. To bring you abreast of these changes Langenscheidt has compiled this entirely new dictionary. Many new words which have entered the German and English languages in the last few years have been included in the vocabulary: e.g., Mondfähre, Mehrwertsteuer, Einwegflasche, Antirakete; lunar probe, heart transplant, non-violence.

Langenscheidt's German-English Dictionary contains another new and long desired feature for the English-speaking user: it provides clear answers to questions of declension and conjugation in over 15,000 German noun and verb entries (see pp. 7 to 8).

The phonetic transcription of the German and English headwords follows the principles laid down by the International Phonetic Association (IPA).

In addition to the vocabulary this Dictionary contains special quick-reference sections of proper names — up-to-date with names like Wankel, Mössbauer, Henze —, abbreviations and weights and measures.

Designed for the widest possible variety of uses, this Dictionary, with its more than 40,000 entries in all, will be of great value to students, teachers, and tourists as well as in home and office libraries.

Contents

Arrangement of the Dictionary and Guide for the User

1. Arrangement. Strict alphabetical order has been maintained throughout this Dictionary. The irregular plural forms of English nouns as well as the principal parts (infinitive, preterite, and past participle) of the irregular English and German verbs have also been given in their proper alphabetical order; e.g. *man - men; bite - bit - bitten; beißen - biß - gebissen.*

2. Pronunciation. Pronunciation is given in square brackets by means of the symbols of the International Phonetic Association. No transcription of compounds is given if the parts appear as separate headwords. The German suffixes as given on page 12 are not transcribed unless they are parts of catchwords.

3. Explanatory additions have been printed in italics; e.g. *abstract Inhalt kurz zs.-fassen; Abbau pulling down (of structure); abbauen pull down (structure); durchsichtig glass, etc.*: transparent.

4. Subject Labels. The field of knowledge from which a headword or some of its meanings are taken is, where possible, indicated by figurative or abbreviated labels or by other labels written out in full. A figurative or abbreviated label placed immediately after a headword applies to all translations. Any label preceding an individual translation refers to this only. In Part I, any abbreviated label followed by a colon applies to all following translations. An F placed before a German illustrative phrase or its English equivalent indicates that the phrase in question is colloquial usage. An F: placed before a German phrase applies to that phrase and its translation(s). Figurative labels have always, other labels sometimes, been placed between illustrative phrases and their translations.

5. Translations of similar meanings have been subdivided by commas, the various senses by semicolons.

6. American spelling has been given in the following ways: *theat|re, Am. -er, defen|ce, Am. -se; council(l)or, hono(u)r, judg(e)ment; plough, Am. plow.*

7. Grammatical References in Part I. Parts of speech (adjective, verb, etc.) have been indicated throughout Entries have been subdivided by Arabic numerals to distinguish the various parts of speech.

I. Nouns. The inflectional forms (*genitive singular / nominative plural*) follow immediately after the indication of gender. No forms are given for compounds if the parts appear as separate headwords.

The horizontal stroke replaces that part of the word which remains unchanged in the inflexion: *Affe m (-n/-n); Affäre f (-/-n).*

The sign ⁼ indicates that an Umlaut appears in the inflected form in question. *Blatt n (-[e]s/⁼er).*

II. Verbs. Verbs have been treated in the following ways:

a) *bändigen v/t. (ge-, h):* The past participle of this verb is formed by means of the prefix ge- and the auxiliary verb haben: *er hat gebändigt.*

b) *abfassen v/t. (sep., -ge-, h):* In conjugation the prefix *ab* must be separated from the primary verb *fassen: er faßt ab; er hat abgefaßt.*

c) *verderben v/i. (irr., no -ge-, sein): irr.* following the verb refers the reader to the list of irregular German verbs in the appendix (p. 573) for the principal parts of this particular verb: *es verdarb; es ist verdorben.*

d) *abfallen v/i. (irr. fallen, sep., -ge-, sein):* A reference such as *irr. fallen* indicates that the compound verb *abfallen* is conjugated exactly like the primary verb *fallen* as given in the list of irregular verbs: *er fiel ab; er ist abgefallen.*

e) *sieden v/t. and v/i. ([irr.,] ge-, h):* The square brackets indicate that *sieden* can be treated as a regular or irregular verb: *er siedete or sott; er hat gesiedet or hat gesotten.*

III. Prepositions. Prepositions governing a headword are given in both languages. The grammatical construction following a German preposition is indicated only if the preposition governs two different cases. If a German preposition applies to all translations it is given only with the first whereas its English equivalents are given after each translation: *schützen* .. protect (*gegen*, *vor dat.* against, from), defend (against, from), guard (against, from); shelter (from).

IV. Subdivision. Entries have been subdivided by Arabic numerals

a) to distinguish the various parts of speech *laut* **1.** *adj.* ...; **2.** *adv.* ...; **3.** *prp.* ; **4.** 2 *m* ...;

b) to distinguish between the transitive and intransitive meanings of a verb if these differ in their translations;

c) to show that in case of change of meaning a noun or verb may be differently inflected or conjugated: *Bau m* **1.** (-[e]s/*no pl.*) ...; **2.** (-[e]s/-ten) ...; **3.** (-[e]s/-e) ...; *schwimmen v/i.* (*irr.*, ge-) **1.** (sein) ...; **2.** (h) ...

If grammatical indications come before the subdivision they refer to all translations following: *Alte* (-n/-n) **1.** *m* ...; **2.** *f* ...; *humpeln v/i.* (ge-) **1.** (sein) ...; **2.** (h) ...

8. Grammatical References in Part II. Parts of speech (adjective, verb, etc.) have been indicated only in cases of doubt Entries have been subdivided by Arabic numerals to distinguish the various parts of speech.

a) (~ally) after an English adjective means that the adverb is formed by affixing .ally: *automatic* (~ally) = *automatically*.

b) *irr.* following a verb refers the reader to the list of irregular English verbs in the appendix p. 575) for the principal parts of this particular verb. A reference such as *irr. fall* indicates that the compound verb, e.g. *befall*, is conjugated exactly like the primary verb *fall*.

Symbols and Abbreviations Used in This Dictionary

1. Symbols

The swung dash or tilde (~ 2, ~ 2) serves as a mark of repetition within an entry. The tilde in bold type (~) represents either the complete word at the beginning of the entry or the unchanged part of that word which is followed by a vertical line (|). The simple tilde (~) represents: a) the headword immediately preceding, which itself may contain a tilde in bold type; b) in phonetic transcription, any part of the preceding transcription that remains unchanged.

When the initial letter changes from small to capital or vice versa, the usual tilde is replaced by 2 or 2.

Examples: *abandon* [ə'bændən], ~*ment* [~nmənt = ə'bændənmənt]; *certi|ficate*, ~*fication*, ~*fy*, ~*tude*. *Drama*, ~*tiker*, 2*tisch*; *Haus|flur*, ~*frau*; *fassen*: *sich kurz* ~

□ after an English adjective means that an adverb may be formed regularly from it by adding ...*ly*, or by changing ...*le* into ...*ly*, or ...*y* into ...*ily*; e.g.: *rich* □ = *richly*; *acceptable* □ = *acceptably*; *happy* □ = *happily*.

F *familiar*, familiär; *colloquial usage*, Umgangssprache.

P *low colloquialism*, populär, Sprache des Volkes.

V *vulgar*, vulgär.

† *archaic*, veraltet.

↖ *rare, little used*, selten.

⊞ *scientific term*, wissenschaftlich.

⚘ *botany*, Botanik.

⊕ *engineering*, Technik; *handicraft*, Handwerk.

⚒ *mining*, Bergbau.

⚔ *military term*, militärisch.

⚓ *nautical term*, Schiffahrt.

† *commercial term*, Handelswesen.

🚃 *railway, railroad*, Eisenbahn.

✈ *aviation*, Flugwesen.

✉ *postal affairs*, Postwesen.

♪ *musical term*, Musik.
△ *architecture*, Architektur.
ϟ *electrical engineering*, Elektrotechnik.
⚖ *legal term*, Rechtswissenschaft.

ᚐ *mathematics*, Mathematik.
ϟ *farming*, Landwirtschaft.
⚗ *chemistry*, Chemie.
⚕ *medicine*, Medizin.

2. Abbreviations

a.   *also*, auch.
abbr.   *abbreviation*, Abkürzung.
acc.   *accusative (case)*, Akkusativ.
adj.   *adjective*, Adjektiv.
adv.   *adverb*, Adverb.
allg.   *commonly*, allgemein.
Am.   *American English*, amerikanisches Englisch.
anat.   *anatomy*, Anatomie.
appr.   *approximately*, etwa.
art.   *article*, Artikel.
ast.   *astronomy*, Astronomie.
attr.   *attributively*, attributiv.

biol.   *biology*, Biologie.
Brt.   *British English*, britisches Englisch.
b.s.   *bad sense*, in schlechtem Sinne.
bsd.   *especially*, besonders.

cj.   *conjunction*, Konjunktion.
co.   *comic(al)*, scherzhaft.
coll.   *collectively*, als Sammelwort.
comp.   *comparative*, Komparativ.
contp.   *contemptuously*, verächtlich.

dat.   *dative (case)*, Dativ.
dem.   *demonstrative*, Demonstrativ...

ea.   *one another, each other*, einander.
eccl.   *ecclesiastical*, kirchlich.
e-e, e-e, e-e a(n), eine.
e-m, e-m, e-m to a(n), einem.
e-n, e-n, e-n a(n), einen.
engS.   *more strictly taken*, in engerem Sinne.
e-r, e-r, e-r of a(n), to a(n), einer.
e-s, e-s, e-s of a(n), eines.
esp.   *especially*, besonders.
et., et., et. something, etwas.
etc.   *et cetera, and so on*, und so weiter.

f   *feminine*, weiblich.
fig.   *figuratively*, bildlich.
frz.   *French*, französisch.

gen.   *genitive (case)*, Genitiv.
geogr.   *geography*, Geographie.
geol.   *geology*, Geologie.
geom.   *geometry*, Geometrie.
ger.   *gerund*, Gerundium.
Ggs.   *antonym*, Gegensatz.
gr.   *grammar*, Grammatik.

h   *have*, haben.
hist.   *history*, Geschichte.
hunt.   *hunting*, Jagdwesen.

ichth.   *ichthyology*, Ichthyologie.
impers.   *impersonal*, unpersönlich.
indef.   *indefinite*, Indefinit...
inf.   *infinitive (mood)*, Infinitiv.
int.   *interjection*, Interjektion.
interr.   *interrogative*, Interrogativ...
iro.   *ironically*, ironisch.
irr.   *irregular*, unregelmäßig.

j., j., j. someone, jemand.
j-m, j-m, j-m to s.o. jemandem.
j-n, j-n, j-n someone, jemanden.
j-s, j-s, j-s someone's, jemandes.

konkr.   *concretely*, konkret.

ling.   *linguistics*, Linguistik.
lit.   *literary*, nur in der Schriftsprache vorkommend.

m   *masculine*, männlich.
m-e, m-e, m-e my, meine.
m-r   *of my, to my*, meiner.
metall.   *metallurgy*, Metallurgie.
meteor.   *meteorology*, Meteorologie.
min.   *mineralogy*, Mineralogie.
mot.   *motoring*, Kraftfahrwesen.
mount.   *mountaineering*, Bergsteigerei.
mst   *mostly, usually*, meistens.
myth.   *mythology*, Mythologie.

n   *neuter*, sächlich.
nom.   *nominative (case)*, Nominativ.
npr.   *proper name*, Eigenname.

od.   *or*, oder.
opt.   *optics*, Optik.

orn.	ornithology, Ornithologie.
o.s.	oneself, sich.
P.,	person, Person.
p.	person, Person.
paint.	painting, Malerei.
parl.	parliamentary term, parlamentarischer Ausdruck.
pass.	passive voice, Passiv.
pers.	personal, Personal...
pharm.	pharmacy, Pharmazie.
phls.	philosophy, Philosophie.
phot.	photography, Photographie.
phys.	physics, Physik.
physiol.	physiology, Physiologie.
pl.	plural, Plural.
poet.	poetry, Dichtung.
pol.	politics, Politik.
poss.	possessive, Possessiv...
p.p.	past participle, Partizip Perfekt.
p.pr.	present participle, Partizip Präsens.
pred.	predicative, prädikativ.
pres.	present, Präsens.
pret.	preterit(e), Präteritum.
pron.	pronoun, Pronomen.
prov.	provincialism, Provinzialismus.
prp.	preposition, Präposition.
psych.	psychology, Psychologie.
refl.	reflexive, reflexiv.
rel.	relative, Relativ...
rhet.	rhetoric, Rhetorik.
S., S.	thing, Sache.
s.	see, refer to, siehe.
schott.	Scotch, schottisch.
s-e, s-e, s-e	his, one's, seine.
sep.	separable, abtrennbar.
sg.	singular, Singular.

sl.	slang, Slang.
s-m, s-m, s-m	to his, to one's, seinem.
s-n, s-n, s-n	his, one's, seinen.
s.o., s.o., s.o.	someone, jemand(en).
s-r, s-r, s-r	of his, of one's, to his, to one's, seiner.
s-s, s-s, s-s	of his, of one's, seines.
s.th., s.th., s.th.	something, etwas.
subj.	subjunctive (mood), Konjunktiv.
sup.	superlative, Superlativ.
surv.	surveying, Landvermessung.
tel.	telegraphy, Telegraphie.
teleph.	telephony, Fernsprechwesen.
thea.	theat|re, Am. -er, Theater.
typ.	typography, Typographie.
u., u.	and, und.
univ.	university, Hochschulwesen, Studentensprache.
v/aux.	auxiliary verb, Hilfsverb.
vb.	verb, Verb.
vet.	veterinary medicine, Veterinärmedizin.
vgl.	confer, vergleiche.
v/i.	verb intransitive, intransitives Verb.
v/refl.	verb reflexive, reflexives Verb.
v/t.	verb transitive, transitives Verb.
weitS.	more widely taken, in weiterem Sinne.
z.B.	for example, zum Beispiel.
zo.	zoology, Zoologie.
zs.	together, zusammen.
Zssg(n).	compound word(s), Zusammensetzung(en).

Guide to Pronunciation
for the German-English Part

The length of vowels is indicated by [ː] following the vowel symbol, the stress by ['] preceding the stressed syllable. The glottal stop [ˀ] is the forced stop between one word or syllable and a following one beginning with a vowel, as in *unentbehrlich* [unˀɛntˈbeːrliç].

A. Vowels

[a] as in French *carte*: *Mann* [man].

[aː] as in *father*: *Wagen* ['vaːgən].

[e] as in *bed*: *Edikt* [e'dikt].

[eː] resembles the sound in *day*: *Weg* [veːk].

[ə] unstressed e as in *ago*: *Bitte* ['bitə].

[ɛ] as in *fair*: *männlich* ['mɛnliç], *Geld* [gɛlt].

[ɛː] same sound but long: *zählen* ['tsɛːlən].

[i] as in *it*: *Wind* [vint].

[iː] as in *meet*: *hier* [hiːr].

[ɔ] as in *long*: *Ort* [ɔrt].

[ɔː] same sound but long as in *draw*: *Komfort* [kɔmˈfoːr].

[o] as in *molest*: *Moral* [moˈraːl].

[oː] resembles the English sound in *go* [gou] but without the [u]: *Boot* [boːt].

[øː] as in French *feu*. The sound may be acquired by saying [e] through closely rounded lips: *schön* [ʃøːn].

[ø] same sound but short: *Ökonomie* [økonoˈmiː].

[œ] as in French *neuf*. The sound resembles the English vowel in *her*. Lips, however, must be well rounded as for [ɔ]: *öffnen* ['œfnən].

[u] as in *book*: *Mutter* ['mutər].

[uː] as in *boot*: *Uhr* [uːr].

[y] almost like the French u as in *sur*. It may be acquired by saying [i] through fairly closely rounded lips: *Glück* [glyk].

[yː] same sound but long: *führen* ['fyːrən].

B. Diphthongs

[aɪ] as in *like*: *Mai* [maɪ].

[aʊ] as in *mouse*: *Maus* [maʊs].

[ɔʏ] as in *boy*: *Beute* ['bɔʏtə], *Läufer* ['lɔʏfər].

C. Consonants

[b] as in *better*: *besser* ['bɛsər].

[d] as in *dance*: *du* [duː].

[f] as in *find*: *finden* ['findən], *Vater* ['faːtər], *Philosoph* [filoˈzoːf].

[g] as in *gold*: *Gold* [gɔlt], *Geld* [gɛlt].

[ʒ] as in *measure*: *Genie* [ʒeˈniː], *Journalist* [ʒurnaˈlist].

[h] as in *house* but not aspirated: *Haus* [haʊs].

[ç] an approximation to this sound may be acquired by assuming the mouth-configuration for [i] and emitting a strong current of breath: *Licht* [liçt], *Mönch* [mœnç], *lustig* ['lustiç].

[x] as in Scotch *loch*. Whereas [ç] is pronounced at the front of the mouth, [x] is pronounced in the throat: *Loch* [lɔx].

[j] as in *year*: *ja* [jaː].

[k] as in *kick*: *keck* [kɛk], *Tag* [taːk], *Chronist* [kroˈnist], *Café* [kaˈfeː].

[l] as in *lump*. Pronounced like English initial "clear l": *lassen* ['lasən].

[m] as in *mouse*: *Maus* [maʊs].

[n] as in *not*: *nein* [naɪn].

[ŋ] as in *sing*, *drink*: *singen* ['ziŋən], *trinken* ['triŋkən].

[p] as in *pass*: *Paß* [pas], *Weib* [vaɪp], *obgleich* [ɔpˈglaɪç].

[r] as in *rot*. There are two pronunciations: the frontal or lingual r and the uvular r (the latter unknown in England): *rot* [roːt].

[s] as in *miss*. Unvoiced when final, doubled, or next a voiceless consonant: *Glas* [glaːs], *Masse* ['masə], *Mast* [mast], *naß* [nas].

[z] as in *zero*. S voiced when initial in a word or syllable: *Sohn* [zoːn], *Rose* ['roːzə].

[ʃ] as in *ship*: *Schiff* [ʃif], *Charme* [ʃarm], *Spiel* [ʃpiːl], *Stein* [ʃtain].

[t] as in *tea*: *Tee* [teː], *Thron* [troːn], *Stadt* [ʃtat], *Bad* [baːt], *Findling* ['fintliŋ], *Wind* [vint].

[v] as in *vast*: *Vase* ['vaːzə], *Winter* ['vintər].

[ã, ɛ̃, õ] are nasalized vowels. Examples: *Ensemble* [ã'sãːbəl], *Terrain* [tɛ'rɛ̃ː], *Bonbon* [bõ'bõː].

List of Suffixes

often given without phonetic transcription

-bar	[-baːr]		-ist	[-ist]
-chen	[-çən]		-keit	[-kart]
-d	[-t]		-lich	[-liç]
-de	[-də]		-ling	[-liŋ]
-ei	[-ar]		-losigkeit	[-loːziçkart]
-en	[-ən]		-nis	[-nis]
-end	[-ənt]		-sal	[-zaːl]
-er	[-ər]		-sam	[-zaːm]
-haft	[-haft]		-schaft	[-ʃaft]
-heit	[-hart]		-sieren	[-ziːrən]
-ie	[-iː]		-ste	[-stə]
-ieren	[-iːrən]		-tät	[-tɛːt]
-ig	[-iç]		-tum	[-tuːm]
-ik	[-ik]		-ung	[-uŋ]
-in	[-in]		-ungs-	[-uŋs-]
-isch	[-iʃ]			

Erläuterung der phonetischen Umschrift im englisch-deutschen Teil

A. Vokale und Diphthonge

[ɑ:] reines langes a, wie in Vater, kam, Schwan: *far* [fɑ:], *father* ['fɑ:ðə].

[ʌ] kommt im Deutschen nicht vor. Kurzes dunkles a, bei dem die Lippen nicht gerundet sind. Vorn und offen gebildet: *butter* ['bʌtə], *come* [kʌm], *colour* ['kʌlə], *blood* [blʌd], *flourish* ['flʌriʃ], *twopence* ['tʌpəns].

[æ] heller, ziemlich offener, nicht zu kurzer Laut. Raum zwischen Zunge und Gaumen noch größer als bei ä in Ähre: *fat* [fæt], *man* [mæn].

[ɛə] nicht zu offenes halblanges ä; im Englischen nur vor r, das als ein dem ä nachhallendes ə erscheint: *bare* [bɛə], *pair* [pɛə], *there* [ðɛə].

[ai] Bestandteile: helles, zwischen ɑ: und æ liegendes a und schwächeres offenes i. Die Zunge hebt sich halbwegs zur i-Stellung: *I* [ai], *lie* [lai], *dry* [drai].

[au] Bestandteile: helles, zwischen ɑ: und æ liegendes a und schwächeres offenes u: *house* [haus], *now* [nau].

[ei] halboffenes e, nach i auslautend, indem die Zunge sich halbwegs zur i-Stellung hebt: *date* [deit], *play* [plei], *obey* [ə'bei].

[e] halboffenes kurzes e, etwas geschlossener als das e in Bett: *bed* [bed], *less* [les].

[ə] flüchtiger Gleitlaut, ähnlich dem deutschen flüchtig gesprochenen e in Gelage: *about* [ə'baut], *butter* ['bʌtə], *nation* ['neiʃən], *connect* [kə'nekt].

[i:] langes i wie in lieb, Bibel, aber etwas offener einsetzend als im Deutschen; wird in Südengland doppellautig gesprochen, indem sich die Zunge allmählich zur i-Stellung hebt: *scene* [si:n], *sea* [si:], *feet* [fi:t], *ceiling* ['si:liŋ].

[i] kurzes offenes i wie in bin, mit: *big* [big], *city* ['siti].

[iə] halboffenes halblanges i mit nachhallendem ə: *here* [hiə], *hear* [hiə], *inferior* [in'fiəriə].

[ou] halboffenes langes o, in schwaches u auslautend; keine Rundung der Lippen, kein Heben der Zunge: *note* [nout], *boat* [bout], *below* [bi'lou].

[ɔ:] offener langer, zwischen a und o schwebender Laut: *fall* [fɔ:l], *nought* [nɔ:t], *or* [ɔ:], *before* [bi'fɔ:].

[ɔ] offener kurzer, zwischen a und o schwebender Laut, offener als das o in Motto: *god* [gɔd], *not* [nɔt], *wash* [wɔʃ], *hobby* ['hɔbi].

[ə:] im Deutschen fehlender Laut; offenes langes ö, etwa wie gedehnt gesprochenes ö in öffnen, Mörder; kein Vorstülpen oder Runden der Lippen, kein Heben der Zunge: *word* [wə:d], *girl* [gə:l], *learn* [lə:n], *murmur* ['mə:mə].

[ɔi] Bestandteile: offenes o und schwächeres offenes i. Die Zunge hebt sich halbwegs zur i-Stellung: *voice* [vɔis], *boy* [bɔi], *annoy* [ə'nɔi].

[u:] langes u wie in Buch, doch ohne Lippenrundung; vielfach diphthongisch als halboffenes langes u mit nachhallendem geschlossenen u: *fool* [fu:l], *shoe* [ʃu:], *you* [ju:], *rule* [ru:l], *canoe* [kə'nu:].

[uə] halboffenes halblanges u mit nachhallendem ə: *poor* [puə], *sure* [ʃuə], *allure* [ə'ljuə].

[u] flüchtiges u: *put* [put], *look* [luk], *full* [ful].

Die **Länge eines Vokals** wird durch [:] bezeichnet, z.B. *ask* [ɑ:sk], *astir* [ə'stə:].

Vereinzelt werden auch die folgenden französischen Nasallaute gebraucht: [ã] wie in frz. *blanc*, [ɔ̃] wie in frz. *bonbon* und [ɛ̃] wie in frz. *vin*.

B. Konsonanten

[r] nur vor Vokalen gesprochen. Völlig verschieden vom deutschen Zungenspitzen- oder Zäpfchen-r. Die Zungenspitze bildet mit der oberen Zahnwulst eine Enge, durch die der Ausatmungsstrom mit Stimmton hindurchgetrieben wird, ohne den Laut zu rollen. Am Ende eines Wortes wird r nur bei Bindung mit dem Anlautvokal des folgenden Wortes gesprochen: *rose* [rouz], *pride* [praid], *there is* [ðɛərˈiz].

[ʒ] stimmhaftes sch, wie g in Genie, j in Journal: *azure* [ˈæʒə], *jazz* [dʒæz], *jeep* [dʒiːp], *large* [lɑːdʒ].

[ʃ] stimmloses sch, wie im Deutschen Schnee, rasch: *shake* [ʃeik], *washing* [ˈwɔʃiŋ], *lash* [læʃ].

[θ] im Deutschen nicht vorhandener stimmloser Lispellaut; durch Anlegen der Zunge an die oberen Schneidezähne hervorgebracht: *thin* [θin], *path* [pɑːθ], *method* [ˈmeθəd].

[ð] derselbe Laut wie θ, nur stimmhaft, d.h. mit Stimmton: *there* [ðɛə], *breathe* [briːð], *father* [ˈfɑːðə].

[s] stimmloser Zischlaut, entsprechend dem deutschen ß in Spaß, reißen: *see* [siː], *hats* [hæts], *decide* [diˈsaid].

[z] stimmhafter Zischlaut wie im Deutschen sausen: *zeal* [ziːl], *rise* [raiz], *horizon* [həˈraizn].

[ŋ] wird wie der deutsche Nasenlaut in fangen, singen gebildet: *ring* [riŋ], *singer* [ˈsiŋə].

[ŋk] derselbe Laut mit nachfolgendem k wie im Deutschen senken, Wink: *ink* [iŋk], *tinker* [ˈtiŋkə].

[w] flüchtiges, mit Lippe an Lippe gesprochenes w, aus der Mundstellung für u: gebildet: *will* [wil], *swear* [swɛə], *queen* [kwiːn].

[f] stimmloser Lippenlaut wie im Deutschen flott, Pfeife: *fat* [fæt], *tough* [tʌf], *effort* [ˈefət].

[v] stimmhafter Lippenlaut wie im Deutschen Vase, Ventil: *vein* [vein], *velvet* [ˈvelvit].

[j] flüchtiger zwischen j und i schwebender Laut: *onion* [ˈʌnjən], *yes* [jes], *filial* [ˈfiljəl].

Die Betonung der englischen Wörter wird durch das Zeichen [ˈ] vor der zu betonenden Silbe angegeben, z.B. *onion* [ˈʌnjən]. Sind zwei Silben eines Wortes mit Tonzeichen versehen, so sind beide gleichmäßig zu betonen, z.B. *unsound* [ˈʌnˈsaund].

Um Raum zu sparen, werden die Endung -ed* und das Plural-s** der englischen Stichwörter hier im Vorwort einmal mit Lautschrift gegeben, erscheinen dann aber im Wörterverzeichnis ohne Lautschrift, sofern keine Ausnahmen vorliegen.

* [-d] nach Vokalen und stimmhaften Konsonanten; [-t] nach stimmlosen Konsonanten; [-id] nach auslautendem d und t.

** [-z] nach Vokalen und stimmhaften Konsonanten; [-s] nach stimmlosen Konsonanten.

Numerals

Cardinal Numbers

0	null *nought, zero, cipher*	51	einundfünfzig *fifty-one*
1	eins *one*	60	sechzig *sixty*
2	zwei *two*	61	einundsechzig *sixty-one*
3	drei *three*	70	siebzig *seventy*
4	vier *four*	71	einundsiebzig *seventy-one*
5	fünf *five*	80	achtzig *eighty*
6	sechs *six*	81	einundachtzig *eighty-one*
7	sieben *seven*	90	neunzig *ninety*
8	acht *eight*	91	einundneunzig *ninety-one*
9	neun *nine*	100	hundert *a or one hundred*

0 null *nought, zero, cipher*
1 eins *one*
2 zwei *two*
3 drei *three*
4 vier *four*
5 fünf *five*
6 sechs *six*
7 sieben *seven*
8 acht *eight*
9 neun *nine*
10 zehn *ten*
11 elf *eleven*
12 zwölf *twelve*
13 dreizehn *thirteen*
14 vierzehn *fourteen*
15 fünfzehn *fifteen*
16 sechzehn *sixteen*
17 siebzehn *seventeen*
18 achtzehn *eighteen*
19 neunzehn *nineteen*
20 zwanzig *twenty*
21 einundzwanzig *twenty-one*
22 zweiundzwanzig *twenty-two*
23 dreiundzwanzig *twenty-three*
30 dreißig *thirty*
31 einunddreißig *thirty-one*
40 vierzig *forty*
41 einundvierzig *forty-one*
50 fünfzig *fifty*

51 einundfünfzig *fifty-one*
60 sechzig *sixty*
61 einundsechzig *sixty-one*
70 siebzig *seventy*
71 einundsiebzig *seventy-one*
80 achtzig *eighty*
81 einundachtzig *eighty-one*
90 neunzig *ninety*
91 einundneunzig *ninety-one*
100 hundert *a or one hundred*
101 hundert(und)eins *a hundred and one*
200 zweihundert *two hundred*
300 dreihundert *three hundred*
572 fünfhundert(und)zweiundsiebzig *five hundred and seventy-two*
1000 tausend *a or one thousand*
1972 neunzehnhundertzweiundsiebzig *nineteen hundred and seventy-two*
500000 fünfhunderttausend *five hundred thousand*
1000000 eine Million *a or one million*
2000000 zwei Millionen *two million*
1000000000 eine Milliarde *a or one milliard (Am. billion)*

Ordinal Numbers

1. erste *first (1st)*
2. zweite *second (2nd)*
3. dritte *third (3rd)*
4. vierte *fourth (4th)*
5. fünfte *fifth (5th), etc.*
6. sechste *sixth*
7. siebente *seventh*
8. achte *eighth*
9. neunte *ninth*
10. zehnte *tenth*
11. elfte *eleventh*
12. zwölfte *twelfth*
13. dreizehnte *thirteenth*
14. vierzehnte *fourteenth*
15. fünfzehnte *fifteenth*

16. sechzehnte *sixteenth*
17. siebzehnte *seventeenth*
18. achtzehnte *eighteenth*
19. neunzehnte *nineteenth*
20. zwanzigste *twentieth*
21. einundzwanzigste *twenty-first*
22. zweiundzwanzigste *twenty-second*
23. dreiundzwanzigste *twenty-third*
30. dreißigste *thirtieth*
31. einunddreißigste *thirty-first*
40. vierzigste *fortieth*
41. einundvierzigste *forty-first*
50. fünfzigste *fiftieth*

51. einundfünfzigste *fifty-first*
60. sechzigste *sixtieth*
61. einundsechzigste *sixty-first*
70. siebzigste *seventieth*
71. einundsiebzigste *seventy-first*
80. achtzigste *eightieth*
81. einundachtzigste *eighty-first*
90. neunzigste *ninetieth*
100. hundertste (*one*) *hundredth*
101. hundert(und)erste (*one*) *hundred and first*
200. zweihundertste *two hundredth*

300. dreihundertste *three hundredth*
572. fünfhundert(und)zweiundsiebzigste *five hundred and seventy-second*
1000. tausendste (*one*) *thousandth*
1970. neunzehnhundert(und)siebzigste *nineteen hundred and seventieth*
500000. fünfhunderttausendste *five hundred thousandth*
1000000. millionste (*one*) *millionth*
2000000. zweimillionste *two millionth*

Fractional Numbers and other Numerical Values

$^1/_2$ halb *one* or *a half*
$^1/_2$ eine halbe Meile *half a mile*
$1^1/_2$ anderthalb or eineinhalb *one and a half*
$2^1/_2$ zweieinhalb *two and a half*
$^1/_3$ ein Drittel *one* or *a third*
$^2/_3$ zwei Drittel *two thirds*
$^1/_4$ ein Viertel *one fourth, one* or *a quarter*
$^3/_4$ drei Viertel *three fourths, three quarters*
$1^1/_4$ ein und eine viertel Stunde *one hour and a quarter*
$^1/_5$ ein Fünftel *one* or *a fifth*
$3^4/_5$ drei vier Fünftel *three and four fifths*
0,4 null Komma vier *point four* (*.4*)
2,5 zwei Komma fünf *two point five* (*2.5*)

einfach *single*
    zweifach *double, twofold*
    dreifach *threefold, treble, triple*
    vierfach *fourfold, quadruple*
    fünffach *fivefold, quintuple*

einmal *once*
    zweimal *twice*
    drei-, vier-, fünfmal *three* or *four* or *five times*
    zweimal soviel(e) *twice as much* or *many*

erstens, zweitens, drittens *first(ly), secondly, thirdly; in the first* or *second* or *third place*

$2 \times 3 = 6$ zwei mal drei ist sechs, zwei multipliziert mit drei ist sechs *twice three are* or *make six, two multiplied by three are* or *make six*

$7 + 8 = 15$ sieben plus acht ist fünfzehn *seven plus eight are fifteen*

$10 - 3 = 7$ zehn minus drei ist sieben *ten minus three are seven*

$20 : 5 = 4$ zwanzig (dividiert) durch fünf ist vier *twenty divided by five make four*

PART I

GERMAN-ENGLISH
DICTIONARY

A

Aal *ichth.* [aːl] *m* (-[e]s/-e) eel; '**2-glatt** *adj.* (as) slippery as an eel.

Aas [aːs] *n* 1. (-es/⅝-e) carrion, carcass; 2. *fig.* (-es/Äser) beast; '**⁓geier** *orn. m* vulture.

ab [ap] 1. *prp.* (*dat.*): ⁓ Brüssel from Brussels onwards; ⁓ *Fabrik, Lager etc.* ✝ ex works, warehouse, *etc.*; 2. *prp.* (*dat.*, F *acc.*): ⁓ erstem *or* ersten März from March 1st, on and after March 1st; 3. ✝ *prp.* (*gen.*) less; ⁓ Unkosten less charges; 4. *adv. time:* von jetzt ⁓ from now on, in future; ⁓ *und zu* from time to time, now and then; von da ⁓ from that time forward; *space:* thea. exit, *pl.* exeunt; von da ⁓ from there (on).

abänder|n ['ap⁹-] *v/t.* (*sep.*, -ge-, h) alter, modify; *parl.* amend; '**2ung** *f* alteration, modification; *parl.* amendment (*to bill, etc.*); '**2ungs-antrag** *parl. m* amendment.

abarbeiten ['ap⁹-] *v/t.* (*sep.*, -ge-, h) work off (*debt*); sich ⁓ drudge, toil.

Abart ['ap⁹-] *f* variety.

Abbau *m* 1. (-[e]s/no *pl.*) pulling down, demolition (*of structure*); dismantling (*of machine, etc.*); dismissal, discharge (*of personnel*); reduction (*of staff, prices, etc.*); cut (*of prices, etc.*); 2. ⚒ (-[e]s/-e) working, exploitation; '**2en** *v/t.* (*sep.*, -ge-, h) pull *or* take down, demolish (*structure*); dismantle (*machine, etc.*); dismiss, discharge (*personnel*); reduce (*staff, prices, etc.*); cut (*prices, etc.*); ⚒ work, exploit.

ab|beißen *v/t.* (*irr.* beißen, *sep.*, -ge-, h) bite off; '**⁓bekommen** *v/t.* (*irr.* kommen, *sep.*, no -ge-, h) get off; *s-n Teil or so* ⁓ get one's share; et. ⁓ be hurt, get hurt.

abberuf|en *v/t.* (*irr.* rufen, *sep.*, no -ge-, h) recall; '**2ung** *f* recall.

ab|bestellen *v/t.* (*sep.*, no -ge-, h) countermand, cancel one's order for (*goods, etc.*); cancel one's subscription to, discontinue (*newspaper, etc.*); '**⁓biegen** *v/i.* (*irr.* biegen, *sep.*, -ge-, sein) ρ. turn off; *road:* turn off, bend; nach rechts (links) ⁓ turn right (left); von e-r Straße ⁓ turn off a road.

'**Abbild** *n* likeness; image; '**2en** ['⁓dən] *v/t.* (*sep.*, -ge-, h) figure, represent; sie ist auf der ersten Seite abgebildet her picture is on the front page; '**⁓ung** ['⁓duŋ] *f* picture, illustration.

'**abbinden** *v/t.* (*irr.* binden, *sep.*,

-ge-, h) untie, unbind, remove; ✄ ligate, tie up.

'**Abbitte** *f* apology; ⁓ leisten *or* tun make one's apology (*bei j-m wegen* et. to s.o. for s.th.); '**2n** *v/t.* (*irr.* bitten, *sep.*, -ge-, h): *j-m* et. ⁓ apologize to s.o. for s.th.

'**ab|blasen** *v/t.* (*irr.* blasen, *sep.*, -ge-, h) blow off (*dust, etc.*); call off (*strike, etc.*), cancel; ✕ break off (*attack*); '**⁓blättern** *v/i.* (*sep.*, -ge-, sein) paint, *etc.*: scale, peel (off); ✄ *skin:* desquamate; ♥ shed the leaves; '**⁓blenden** (*sep.*, -ge-, h) 1. *v/t.* screen (*light*); *mot.* dim, dip (*headlights*); 2. *v/i. mot.* dim *or* dip the headlights; *phot.* stop down; '**⁓blitzen** F *v/i.* (*sep.*, -ge-, sein) meet with a rebuff; ⁓ lassen snub; '**⁓brausen** (*sep.*, -ge-) 1. *v/refl.* (h) have a shower(-bath), douche; 2. F *v/i.* (sein) rush off; '**⁓brechen** (*irr.* brechen, *sep.*, -ge-) 1. *v/t.* (h) break off (*a. fig.*); pull down, demolish (*building, etc.*); strike (*tent*); *fig.* stop; *das Lager* ⁓ break up camp, strike tents; 2. *v/i.* (sein) break off; 3. *fig. v/i.* (h) stop; '**⁓bremsen** *v/t.* and *v/i.* (*sep.*, -ge-, h) slow down; brake; '**⁓brennen** (*irr.* brennen, *sep.*, -ge-) 1. *v/t.* (h) burn down (*building, etc.*); let *or* set off (*firework*); 2. *v/i.* (sein) burn away *or* down; *s.* abgebrannt; '**⁓bringen** *v/t.* (*irr.* bringen, *sep.*, -ge-, h) get off; *j-n* ⁓ von argue s.o. out of; dissuade s.o. from; '**⁓bröckeln** *v/i.* (*sep.*, -ge-, sein) crumble (*a. ✝*).

'**Abbruch** *m* pulling down, demolition (*of building, etc.*); rupture (*of relations*); breaking off (*of negotiations, etc.*); *fig.* damage, injury; *j-m* ⁓ tun damage s.o.

'**ab|brühen** *v/t.* (*sep.*, -ge-, h) scald; *s.* abgebrüht; '**⁓bürsten** *v/t.* (*sep.*, -ge-, h) brush off (*dirt, etc.*); brush (*coat, etc.*); '**⁓büßen** *v/t.* (*sep.*, -ge-, h) expiate, atone for (*sin, etc.*); serve (*sentence*). [bet.\

Abc [aːbeˈtseː] *n* (-/-) ABC, alpha-\

'**abdank|en** *v/i.* (*sep.*, -ge-, h) resign; *ruler:* abdicate; '**2ung** *f* (-/-en) resignation, abdication.

'**ab|decken** *v/t.* (*sep.*, -ge-, h) uncover; untile (*roof*); unroof (*building*); clear (*table*); cover; '**⁓dichten** *v/t.* (*sep.*, -ge-, h) make tight; seal up (*window, etc.*); ⊕ pack (*gland, etc.*); '**⁓dienen** *v/t.* (*sep.*, -ge-, h): *s-e Zeit* ⁓ ✕ serve one's time; '**⁓drängen** *v/t.* (*sep.*, -ge-, h) push aside; '**⁓drehen** (*sep.*, -ge-, h)

2*

1. v/t. twist off (wire); turn off (water, gas, etc.); ⚡ switch off (light); **2.** ⚓, ✈ v/i. change one's course; '**~drosseln** mot. v/t. (sep., -ge-, h) throttle.

'**Abdruck** m (-[e]s/~e) impression, print, mark; cast; '**2en** v/t. (sep., -ge-, h) print; publish (article).

'**abdrücken** (sep., -ge-, h) **1.** v/t. fire (gun, etc.); F hug or squeeze affectionately; sich ~ leave an impression or a mark; **2.** v/i. pull the trigger.

Abend ['a:bənt] m (-s/-e) evening; am ~ in the evening, at night; heute abend tonight; morgen (gestern) abend tomorrow (last) night; s. essen; '**~anzug** m evening dress; '**~blatt** n evening paper; '**~brot** n supper, dinner; '**~dämmerung** f (evening) twilight, dusk; '**~essen** n s. Abendbrot; '**~gesellschaft** f evening party; '**~kasse** thea. f box-office; '**~kleid** n evening dress or gown; '**~land** n (-[e]s/no pl.) the Occident; '**2ländisch** adj. ['~lɛndiʃ] western, occidental; '**~mahl** eccl. n (-[e]s/-e) the (Holy) Communion, the Lord's Supper; '**~rot** n evening or sunset glow. [evening.\]

abends adv. ['a:bənts] in the\
'**Abend|schule** f evening school, night-school; '**~sonne** f setting sun; '**~toilette** f evening dress; '**~wind** m evening breeze; '**~zeitung** f evening paper.

Abenteu|er ['a:bəntɔyər] n (-s/-) adventure; '**2erlich** adj. adventurous; fig.: strange; wild, fantastic; '**~rer** ['~ɔyrər] m (-s/-) adventurer.

aber ['a:bər] **1.** adv. again; Tausende und ~ Tausende thousands upon thousands; **2.** cj. but; oder ~ otherwise, (or) else; **3.** int.: ~! now then!; ~, ~! come, come!; ~ nein! no!, on the contrary!; **4.** 2 n (-s/-) but.

'**Aber|glaube** m superstition; 2~gläubisch adj. ['~glɔybiʃ] superstitious.

aberkenn|en ['ap⁹-] v/t. (irr. kennen, sep., no -ge-, h): j-m et. ~ deprive s.o. of s.th. (a. ⚖); dispossess s.o. of s.th.; '**2ung** f (-/-en) deprivation (a. ⚖); dispossession.

aber|malig adj. ['a:bərma:liç] repeated; '**~mals** adv. ['~s] again, once more.

ab|ernten ['ap⁹-] v/t. (sep., -ge-, h) reap, harvest; '**~essen** ['ap⁹-] (irr. essen, sep., -ge-, h) **1.** v/t. clear (plate); **2.** v/i. finish eating; '**~fahren** (irr. fahren, sep., -ge-) **1.** v/i. (sein) leave (nach for), depart (for), start (for); set out or off (for); **2.** v/t. (h) carry or cart away (load).

'**Abfahrt** f departure (nach for), start (for); setting out or off (for); skiing: downhill run; '**~sbahnsteig**

m departure platform; '**~slauf** m skiing: downhill race; '**~ssignal** n starting-signal; '**~szeit** f time of departure; ⚓ a. time of sailing.

'**Abfall** m defection (von from), falling away (from); esp. pol. secession (from); eccl. apostasy (from); often Abfälle pl. waste, refuse, rubbish, Am. a. garbage; ⊕ clippings pl., shavings pl.; at butcher's: offal; '**~eimer** m dust-bin, Am. ash can; '**2en** v/i. (irr. fallen, sep., -ge-, sein) leaves, etc.: fall (off); ground, etc.: slope (down); fig. fall away (von from); esp. pol. secede (from); eccl. apostatize (from); ~ gegen come off badly by comparison with, be inferior to; '**~erzeugnis** n waste product; by-product.

'**abfällig** adj. judgement, etc.: adverse, unfavo(u)rable; remark: disparaging, depreciatory.

'**Abfallprodukt** n by-product; waste product.

'**ab|fangen** v/t. (irr. fangen, sep., -ge-, h) catch; snatch (ball, etc.); intercept (letter, etc.); ⚓, ✈ prop; ✕ check (attack); ✈ flatten out; mot., ✈ right; '**~färben** v/i. (sep., -ge-, h): der Pullover färbt ab the colo(u)r of the pull-over runs (auf acc. on); ~ auf (acc.) influence, affect.

'**abfass|en** v/t. (sep., -ge-, h) compose, write, pen; catch (thief, etc.); '**2ung** f composition; wording.

'**ab|faulen** v/i. (sep., -ge-, sein) rot off; '**~fegen** v/t. (sep., -ge-, h) sweep off; '**~feilen** v/t. (sep., -ge-, h) file off.

abfertig|en ['apfɛrtigən] v/t. (sep., -ge-, h) dispatch (a. ✉); customs: clear; serve, attend to (customer); j-n kurz ~ snub s.o.; '**2ung** f (-/-en) dispatch; customs: clearance; schroffe ~ snub. [(off), discharge.\]

'**abfeuern** v/t. (sep., -ge-, h) fire\
'**abfind|en** v/t. (irr. finden, sep., -ge-, h) satisfy, pay off (creditor); compensate; sich mit et. ~ resign o.s. to s.th.; put up with s.th.; '**2ung** f (-/-en) settlement; satisfaction; compensation; '**2ung(ssumme)** f indemnity; compensation.

'**ab|flachen** v/t. and v/refl. (sep., -ge-, h) flatten; '**~flauen** v/i. (sep., -ge-, sein) wind, etc.: abate; interest, etc.: flag; ✝ business: slacken; '**~fliegen** v/i. (irr. fliegen, sep., -ge-, sein) leave by plane; ✈ take off, start; '**~fließen** v/i. (irr. fließen, sep., -ge-, sein) drain or flow off or away. [parture.\]

'**Abflug** ✈ m take-off, start, de-\
'**Abfluß** m flowing or draining off or away; discharge (a. ⚗); drain (a. fig.); sink; outlet (of lake, etc.).

'**abfordern** v/t. (sep., -ge-, h): j-m et. ~ demand s.th. of or from s.o.

Abfuhr ['apfuːr] *f* (-/-en) removal; *fig.* rebuff.

'abführ|en (*sep.*, -ge-, *h*) **1.** *v/t.* lead off *or* away; march (*prisoner*) off; pay over (*money*) (*an acc.* to); **2.** *v/i.* purge (the bowels), loosen the bowels; **'~end** *adj.* purgative, aperient, laxative; **'2mittel** *n* purgative, aperient, laxative.

'abfüllen *v/t.* (*sep.*, -ge-, *h*) decant; *in Flaschen* ~ bottle; *Bier in Fässer* ~ rack casks with beer.

'Abgabe *f sports:* pass; casting (*of one's vote*); sale (*of shares, etc.*); *mst ~n pl.* taxes *pl.*; rates *pl., Am.* local taxes *pl.*; duties *pl.*; **'2frei** *adj.* tax-free; duty-free; **'2npflichtig** *adj.* taxable; dutiable; liable to tax *or* duty.

'Abgang *m* departure; start; *thea.* exit (*a. fig.*); retirement (*from a job*); loss, wastage; deficiency (*in weight, etc.*); *✝* discharge; *✝* miscarriage; *nach ~ von der Schule* after leaving school.

'abgängig *adj.* missing.

'Abgangszeugnis *n* (school-)leaving certificate, *Am. a.* diploma.

'Abgas *n* waste gas; *esp. mot.* exhaust gas. [toil-worn, worn-out.)

abgearbeitet *adj.* ['apgə'arbəitət])

'abgeben *v/t.* (*irr.* geben, *sep.*, -ge-, *h*) leave (*bei, an dat.* at); hand in (*paper, etc.*); deposit, leave (*luggage*); cast (*one's vote*); *sports:* pass (*ball, etc.*); sell, dispose of (*goods*); give off (*heat, etc.*); *e-e Erklärung* ~ make a statement; *s-e Meinung* ~ express one's opinion (*über acc.* on); *j-m et.* ~ *von et.* give s.o. some of s.th.; *e-n guten Gelehrten* ~ make a good scholar; *sich* ~ *mit* occupy o.s. with *s.th.*; *sie gibt sich gern mit Kindern ab* she loves to be among children.

'abge|brannt *adj.* burnt down; F *fig.* hard up, *sl.* broke; **~brüht** *fig. adj.* ['~bryːt] hardened, callous; **'~droschen** *adj.* trite, hackneyed; **~feimt** *adj.* ['~faimt] cunning, crafty; **~griffen** *adj.* worn; *book:* well-thumbed; **~härtet** *adj.* ['~hertet] hardened (gegen to), inured (to); **~härmt** *adj.* ['~hermt] careworn.

'abgehen (*irr.* gehen, *sep.*, -ge-) **1.** *v/i.* (sein) go off *or* away; leave, start, depart; *letter, etc.:* be dispatched; *post:* go; *thea.* make one's exit; *side-road:* branch off; *goods:* sell; *button, etc.:* come off; *stain, etc.:* come out; *✝* be discharged; (*von e-m Amt*) ~ give up a post; retire; *von der Schule* ~ leave school; ~ *von* digress from (*main subject*); deviate from (*rule*); alter, change (*one's opinion*); relinquish (*plan, etc.*); *diese Eigenschaft geht ihm ab* he lacks this quality; *gut* ~ end well, pass off well; *hiervon geht or gehen*

... *ab ✝* less, minus; **2.** *v/t.* (*h*) measure by steps; patrol.

abge|hetzt *adj.* ['apgəhɛtst] harassed; exhausted; run down; breathless; **~kartet** F *adj.* ['~kartət]: *~e Sache* prearranged affair, put-up job; **'~legen** *adj.* remote, distant; secluded; out-of-the-way; **~macht** *adj.* ['~maxt]: *~l* it's a bargain *or* deal!; **~magert** *adj.* ['~maːgərt] emaciated; **~neigt** *adj.* ['~naikt] disinclined (*dat.* for *s.th.*; *zu tun* to do), averse (to; *from* doing), unwilling (*zu tun* to do); **~nutzt** *adj.* ['~nutst] worn-out.

Abgeordnete ['apgə'ɔrdnətə] *m, f* (-n/-n) deputy, delegate; *in Germany:* member of the Bundestag *or* Landtag; *Brt.* Member of Parliament, *Am.* Representative.

'abgerissen *fig. adj.* ragged; shabby; *style, speech:* abrupt, broken.

'Abgesandte *m, f* (-n/-n) envoy; emissary; ambassador.

'abgeschieden *fig. adj.* isolated, secluded, retired; **'2heit** *f* (-/-en) seclusion; retirement.

'abgeschlossen *adj. flat:* self-contained; training, *etc.*: complete.

abgeschmackt *adj.* ['apgəʃmakt] tasteless; tactless; **'2heit** *f* (-/-en) tastelessness; tactlessness.

'abgesehen *adj.*: ~ *von* apart from, *Am. a.* aside from.

abge|spannt *fig. adj.* ['apgəʃpant] exhausted, tired, run down; **'~standen** *adj.* stale, flat; **'~storben** *adj.* numb; dead; **~stumpft** *adj.* ['~ʃtumpft] blunt(ed); *fig.* indifferent (gegen to); **'~tragen** *adj.* worn-out; threadbare, shabby.

'abgewöhnen *v/t.* (*sep.*, -ge-, *h*): *j-m et.* ~ break *or* cure s.o. of s.th.; *sich das Rauchen* ~ give up smoking.

abgezehrt *adj.* ['apgətseːrt] emaciated, wasted.

'abgießen *v/t.* (*irr.* gießen, *sep.*, -ge-, *h*) pour off; *⚗* decant; *⊕* cast.

'Abglanz *m* reflection (*a. fig.*).

'abgleiten *v/i.* (*irr.* gleiten, *sep.*, -ge-, sein) slip off; slide off; glide)

'Abgott *m* idol. [off.)

abgöttisch *adv.* ['apgœtiʃ]: *j-n* ~ *lieben* idolize *or* worship s.o.; dote (up)on s.o.

'ab|grasen *v/t.* (*sep.*, -ge-, *h*) graze; *fig.* scour; **'~grenzen** *v/t.* (*sep.*, -ge-, *h*) mark off, delimit; demarcate (*a. fig.*); *fig.* define.

'Abgrund *m* abyss; precipice; chasm, gulf; *am Rande des ~s on* the brink of disaster.

'Abguß *m* cast.

'ab|hacken *v/t.* (*sep.*, -ge-, *h*) chop *or* cut off; **'~haken** *fig. v/t.* (*sep.*, -ge-, *h*) tick *or* check off; **'~halten** *v/t.* (*irr.* halten, *sep.*, -ge-, *h*) hold (*meeting, examination, etc.*); keep out (*rain*); *j-n von der Arbeit* ~ keep s.o. from his work; j-n davon ~ et. zu tun keep or restrain s.o. from doing s.th.; et. von j-m ~ keep s.th. away from s.o.; '~handeln v/t. (sep., -ge-, h) discuss, treat; j-m et. ~ bargain s.th. out of s.o.

abhanden adv. [ap'handən]: ~ kommen get lost.

'**Abhandlung** f treatise (über acc. [up]on), dissertation ([up]on, concerning); essay.

'**Abhang** m slope, incline; declivity.

'**abhängen 1.** v/t. (sep., -ge-, h) take down (picture, etc.); 🖼 uncouple; **2.** v/i. (irr. hängen, sep., -ge-, h): ~ von depend (up)on.

abhängig adj. ['apheniç]: ~ von dependent (up)on; '2keit f (-/no pl.) dependence (von [up]on).

ab|härmen v/refl. ['aphermən] (sep., -ge-, h) pine away (über acc. at); '~härten v/t. (sep., -ge-, h) harden (gegen to), inure (to); sich ~ harden o.s. (gegen to), inure o.s. (to); '~hauen (irr. hauen, sep., -ge-) **1.** v/t. (h) cut or chop off; **2.** F v/i. (sein) be off; hau ab! sl. beat it!, scram!; '~häuten v/t. (sep., -ge-, h) skin, flay; '~heben (irr. heben, sep., -ge-, h) **1.** v/t. lift or take off; teleph. lift (receiver); (with)draw (money); sich ~ von stand out against; fig. a. contrast with; **2.** v/i. cut (the cards); teleph. lift the receiver; '~heilen v/i. (sep., -ge-, sein) heal (up); '~helfen v/i. (irr. helfen, sep., -ge-, h): e-m Übel ~ cure or redress an evil; dem ist nicht abzuhelfen there is nothing to be done about it; '~hetzen v/refl. (sep., -ge-, h) tire o.s. out; rush, hurry.

'**Abhilfe** f remedy, redress, relief; ~ schaffen take remedial measures.

'**abhobeln** v/t. (sep., -ge-, h) plane (away, down).

abhold adj. ['aphɔlt] averse (dat. to s.th.); ill-disposed (towards s.o.).

'**ab|holen** v/t. (sep., -ge-, h) fetch; call for, come for; j-n von der Bahn ~ go to meet s.o. at the station; '~holzen v/t. (sep., -ge-, h) fell, cut down (trees); deforest; '~horchen 🖋 v/t. (sep., -ge-, h) auscultate, sound; '~hören v/t. (sep., -ge-, h) listen in to, intercept (telephone conversation); e-n Schüler ~ hear a pupil's lesson.

Abitur [abi'tuːr] n (-s/🔧-e) school-leaving examination (qualifying for university entrance).

'**ab|jagen** v/t. (sep., -ge-, h): j-m et. ~ recover s.th. from s.o.; '~kanzeln F v/t. (sep., -ge-, h) reprimand, F tell s.o. off; '~kaufen v/t. (sep., -ge-, h): j-m et. ~ buy or purchase s.th. from s.o.

Abkehr fig. ['apkeːr] f (-/no pl.) estrangement (von from); withdrawal (from); '2en v/t. (sep., -ge-, h) sweep off; sich ~ von turn away from; fig.: take no further interest in; become estranged from; withdraw from.

'**ab|klingen** v/i. (irr. klingen, sep., -ge-, sein) fade away; pain, etc.: die down; pain, illness: ease off; '~klopfen (sep., -ge-, h) **1.** v/t. knock (dust, etc.) off; dust (coat, etc.); 🎵 sound, percuss; **2.** v/i. conductor: stop the orchestra; '~knicken v/t. (sep., -ge-, h) snap or break off; bend off; '~knöpfen v/t. (sep., -ge-, h) unbutton; F j-m Geld ~ get money out of s.o.; '~kochen (sep., -ge-, h) **1.** v/t. boil; scald (milk); **2.** v/i. cook in the open air (a. ✕); '~kommandieren ✕ v/t. (sep. no -ge-, h) detach, detail; second (officer).

Abkomme ['apkɔmə] m (-n/-n) descendant.

'**abkommen 1.** v/i. (irr. kommen, sep., -ge-, sein) come away, get away or off; von e-r Ansicht ~ change one's opinion; von e-m Thema ~ digress from a topic; vom Wege ~ lose one's way; **2.** 2 n (-s/-) agreement.

abkömm|lich adj. ['apkœmliç] dispensable; available; er ist nicht ~ he cannot be spared; 2ling ['~liŋ] m (-s/-e) descendant.

'**ab|koppeln** v/t. (sep., -ge-, h) uncouple; '~kratzen (sep., -ge-) **1.** v/t. (h) scrape off; **2.** sl. v/i. (sein) kick the bucket; '~kühlen v/t. (sep., -ge-, h) cool; refrigerate; sich ~ cool down (a. fig.).

Abkunft ['apkunft] f (-/🔧=e) descent; origin, extraction; birth.

'**abkürz|en** v/t. (sep., -ge-, h) shorten; abbreviate (word, story, etc.); den Weg ~ take a short cut; '2ung f (-/-en) abridgement; abbreviation; short cut.

'**abladen** v/t. (irr. laden, sep., -ge-, h) unload; dump (rubbish, etc.).

'**Ablage** f place of deposit; filing tray; files pl.; cloak-room.

'**ab|lagern** (sep., -ge-) **1.** v/t. (h) season (wood, wine); age (wine); sich ~ settle; be deposited; **2.** v/i. (sein) wood, wine: season; wine: age; '~lassen (irr. lassen, sep., -ge-, h) **1.** v/t. let (liquid) run off; let off (steam); drain (pond, etc.); **2.** v/i. leave off (von et. [doing] s.th.).

'**Ablauf** m running off; outlet, drain; sports: start; fig. expiration, end; nach ~ von at the end of; '2en (irr. laufen, sep., -ge-) **1.** v/i. (sein) run off; drain off; period of time: expire; ⚓ bill of exchange: fall due; clock, etc.: run down; thread, film: unwind; spool: run out; gut ~ end well; 2. v/t. (h) wear out (shoes); scour (region, etc.); sich die Beine ~ run one's legs off; s. Rang.

'**Ableben** n (-s/ no pl.) death, decease (esp. ⚔, ⚓) demise.

'**ab|lecken** v/t. (sep., -ge-, h) lick (off); '~**legen** (sep., -ge-, h) 1. v/t. take off (garments); leave off (garments); give up, break o.s. of (habit); file (documents, letters, etc.); make (confession, vow); take (oath, examination); Zeugnis ~ bear witness (für to; von of); s. Rechenschaft; 2. v/i. take off one's hat (and) coat.

'**Ableger** ♀ m (-s/-) layer, shoot.

'**ablehn|en** (sep., -ge-, h) 1. v/t. decline, refuse; reject (doctrine, candidate, etc.); turn down (proposal, etc.); 2. v/i. decline; dankend ~ decline with thanks; '~**end** adj. negative; '2**ung** f (-/-en) refusal; rejection.

'**ableit|en** v/t. (sep., -ge-, h) divert (river, etc.); drain off or away (water, etc.); gr., ♙, fig. derive (aus, von from); fig. infer (from); '2**ung** f diversion; drainage; gr., ♙ derivation (a. fig.).

'**ab|lenken** v/t. (sep., -ge-, h) turn aside; divert (suspicion, etc.) (von from); phys., etc.: deflect (rays, etc.); j-n von der Arbeit ~ distract s.o. from his work; '~**lesen** v/t. (irr. lesen, sep., -ge-, h) read (speech, etc.); read (off) (values from instruments); '~**leugnen** v/t. (sep., -ge-, h) deny, disavow, disown.

'**abliefer|n** v/t. (sep., -ge-, h) deliver; hand over; surrender; '2**ung** f delivery.

'**ablöschen** v/t. (sep., -ge-, h) blot (up) (ink); ⊕ temper (steel).

'**ablös|en** v/t. (sep., -ge-, h) detach; take off; ⚔, etc.: relieve; supersede (predecessor in office); discharge (debt); redeem (obligation); sich ~ come off; fig. alternate, take turns; '2**ung** f detachment; ⚔, etc.: relief; fig. supersession; discharge; redemption.

'**abmach|en** v/t. (sep., -ge-, h) remove, detach; fig. settle, arrange (business, etc.); agree (up)on (price, etc.); '2**ung** f (-/-en) arrangement, settlement; agreement.

'**abmager|n** v/i (sep., -ge-, sein) lose flesh; grow lean or thin; '2**ung** f (-/-en) emaciation.

'**abmähen** v/t. (sep., -ge-, h) mow (off); '~**malen** v/t. (sep., -ge-, h) copy.

'**Abmarsch** m start; ⚔ marching off; '2**ieren** v/i. (sep., no -ge-, sein) start; ⚔ march off.

'**abmeld|en** v/t. (sep., -ge-, h): j-n von der Schule ~ give notice of the withdrawal of a pupil (from school); sich polizeilich ~ give notice to the police of one's departure (from

town, etc.); '2**ung** f notice of withdrawal; notice of departure.

'**abmess|en** v/t. (irr. messen, sep., -ge-, h) measure; '2**ung** f (-/-en) measurement.

'**ab|montieren** v/t. (sep., no -ge-, h) disassemble; dismantle, strip (machinery); remove (tyre, etc.); '~**mühen** v/refl. (sep., -ge-, h) drudge, toil; '~**nagen** v/t. (sep., -ge-, h) gnaw off; pick (bone).

Abnahme ['apnaːmə] f (-/✶-n) taking off; removal; ✚ amputation; ✱ taking delivery; ✚ purchase; ✚ sale; ⊕ acceptance (of machine, etc.); administering (of oath); decrease, diminution; loss (of weight).

'**abnehm|en** (irr. nehmen, sep., -ge-, h) 1. v/t. take off; remove; teleph. lift (receiver); ✚ amputate; gather (fruit); ⊕ accept (machine, etc.); j-m et. ~ take s.th. from s.o.; ✚ a. buy or purchase s.th. from s.o.; j-m zuviel ~ overcharge s.o.; 2. v/i. decrease, diminish; decline; lose weight; moon: wane; storm: abate; days: grow shorter; '2**er** ✚ m (-s/-) buyer; customer; consumer.

'**Abneigung** f aversion (gegen to); disinclination (to); dislike (to, of, for); antipathy (against, to).

abnorm adj. [ap'nɔrm] abnormal; anomalous; exceptional; 2**i'tät** f (-/-en) abnormality; anomaly.

'**abnötigen** v/t. (sep., -ge-, h): j-m et. ~ extort s.th. from s.o.

'**ab|nutzen** v/t. and v/refl. (sep., -ge-, h), '~**nützen** v/t. and v/refl. (sep., -ge-, h) wear out; '2**nutzung** f, '2**nützung** f (-/-en) wear (and tear).

Abonn|ement [abon(ə)'mãː] n (-s/ -s) subscription (auf acc. to); ~**ent** [~'nɛnt] m (-en/-en) subscriber; 2**ieren** [~'niːrən] v/t. (no -ge-, h) subscribe to (newspaper); 2**iert** adj. [~'niːrt]: ~ sein auf (acc.) take in (newspaper, etc.).

'**abordn|en** v/t. (sep., -ge-, h) depute, delegate, Am. a. deputize; '2**ung** f delegation, deputation.

Abort [a'bɔrt] m (-[e]s/-e) lavatory, toilet.

'**ab|passen** v/t. (sep., -ge-, h) fit, adjust; watch for, wait for (s.o., opportunity); waylay s.o.; '~**pflücken** v/t. (sep., -ge-, h) pick, pluck (off), gather; '~**plagen** v/refl. (sep., -ge-, h) toil; '~**platzen** v/i. (sep., -ge-, h) burst off; fly off; '~**prallen** v/i. (sep., -ge-, sein) rebound, bounce (off); ricochet; '~**putzen** v/t. (sep., -ge-, h) clean (off, up); wipe off; polish; '~**raten** v/i. (irr. raten, sep., -ge-, h): j-m ~ von dissuade s.o. from, advise s.o. against; '~**räumen** v/t. (sep., -ge-, h) clear (away); '~**reagieren** v/t. (sep., no -ge-, h) work off (one's anger, etc.); sich ~ F a. let off steam.

'**abrechn|en** (*sep.*, *-ge-*, *h*) **1.** *v/t.* deduct; settle (*account*); **2.** *v/i.*: *mit j-m ~* settle with s.o.; *fig.* settle (accounts) with s.o., F get even with s.o.; '**2ung** *f* settlement (of accounts); deduction, discount.

'**Abrede** *f*: *in ~ stellen* deny *or* question *s.th.*

'**abreib|en** *v/t.* (*irr.* reiben, *sep.*, *-ge-*, *h*) rub off; rub down (*body*); polish; '**2ung** *f* rub-down; F *fig.* beating.

'**Abreise** *f* departure (*nach* for); '**2n** *v/i.* (*sep.*, *-ge-*, *sein*) depart (*nach* for), leave (for), start (for), set out (for).

'**abreiß|en** (*irr.* reißen, *sep.*, *-ge-*) **1.** *v/t.* (*h*) tear *or* pull off; pull down (*building*); *s.* abgerissen; **2.** *v/i.* (*sein*) break off; *button, etc.*: come off; '**2kalender** *m* tear-off calendar.

'**ab|richten** *v/t.* (*sep.*, *-ge-*, *h*) train (*animal*), break (*horse*) (in); '**~riegeln** *v/t.* (*sep.*, *-ge-*, *h*) bolt, bar (*door*); block (*road*).

'**Abriß** *m* draft; summary, abstract; (brief) outlines *pl.*; brief survey.

'**ab|rollen** (*sep.*, *-ge-*) *v/t.* (*h*) *and v/i.* (*sein*) unroll; uncoil; unwind, unreel; roll off; '**~rücken** (*sep.*, *-ge-*) **1.** *v/t.* (*h*) move off *or* away (*von* from), remove; **2.** ✕ *v/i.* (*sein*) march off, withdraw.

'**Abruf** *m* call; recall; *auf ~* ✝ on call; '**2en** *v/t.* (*irr.* rufen, *sep.*, *-ge-*, *h*) call off (*a.* ✝), call away; recall; ⚓ call out.

'**ab|runden** *v/t.* (*sep.*, *-ge-*, *h*) round (off); '**~rupfen** *v/t.* (*sep.*, *-ge-*, *h*) pluck off.

abrupt *adj.* [ap'rupt] abrupt.

'**abrüst|en** ✕ *v/i.* (*sep.*, *-ge-*, *h*) disarm; '**2ung** ✕ *f* disarmament.

'**abrutschen** *v/i.* (*sep.*, *-ge-*, *sein*) slip off, glide down; ✈ skid.

'**Absage** *f* cancellation; refusal; '**2n** (*sep.*, *-ge-*, *h*) **1.** *v/t.* cancel, call off; refuse; recall (*invitation*); **2.** *v/i. guest*: decline; *j-m ~* cancel one's appointment with s.o.

'**absägen** *v/t.* (*sep.*, *-ge-*, *h*) saw off; F *fig.* sack s.o.

'**Absatz** *m* stop, pause; *typ.* paragraph; ✝ sale; heel (*of shoe*); landing (*of stairs*); '**2fähig** ✝ *adj.* saleable, marketable; '**~markt** ✝ *m* market, outlet; '**~möglichkeit** ✝ *f* opening, outlet.

'**abschaben** *v/t.* (*sep.*, *-ge-*, *h*) scrape off.

'**abschaff|en** *v/t.* (*sep.*, *-ge-*, *h*) abolish; abrogate (*law*); dismiss (*servants*); '**2ung** *f* (*-/-en*) abolition; abrogation; dismissal.

'**ab|schälen** *v/t.* (*sep.*, *-ge-*, *h*) peel (off), pare; bark (*tree*); '**~schalten** *v/t.* (*sep.*, *-ge-*, *h*) switch off, turn off *or* out; ⚡ disconnect.

'**abschätz|en** *v/t.* (*sep.*, *-ge-*, *h*) esti-

mate; value; assess; '**2ung** *f* valuation; estimate; assessment.

'**Abschaum** *m* (*-[e]s/no pl.*) scum; *fig. a.* dregs *pl.*

'**Abscheu** *m* (*-[e]s/no pl.*) horror (*vor dat.* of), abhorrence (of); loathing (of); disgust (for).

'**abscheuern** *v/t.* (*sep.*, *-ge-*, *h*) scour (off); wear out; chafe, abrade.

abscheulich *adj.* [ap'ʃɔʏlɪç] abominable, detestable, horrid; **2keit** *f* (*-/-en*) detestableness; atrocity.

'**ab|schicken** *v/t.* (*sep.*, *-ge-*, *h*) send off, dispatch; & post; *Am.* mail; '**~schieben** *v/t.* (*irr.* schieben, *sep.*, *-ge-*, *h*) push *or* shove off.

Abschied ['apʃiːt] *m* (*-[e]s/⚓-e*) departure; parting; leave-taking, farewell; dismissal, ✕ discharge; *~ nehmen* take leave (*von* of), bid farewell (to); *j-m den ~ geben* dismiss s.o., ✕ discharge s.o.; *s-n ~ nehmen* resign, retire; '**~feier** *f* farewell party; '**~gesuch** *n* resignation.

'**ab|schießen** *v/t.* (*irr.* schießen, *sep.*, *-ge-*, *h*) shoot off; shoot, discharge, fire (off) (*fire-arm*); launch (*rocket*); kill, shoot; (shoot *or* bring) down (*aircraft*); *s.* Vogel; '**~schinden** *v/refl.* (*irr.* schinden, *sep.*, *-ge-*, *h*) toil and moil, slave, drudge; '**~schirmen** *v/t.* (*sep.*, *-ge-*, *h*) shield (*gegen* from); screen (from), screen off (from); '**~schlachten** *v/t.* (*sep.*, *-ge-*, *h*) slaughter, butcher.

'**Abschlag** ✝ *m* reduction (*in price*); *auf ~* on account; **2en** ['~gən] *v/t.* (*irr.* schlagen, *sep.*, *-ge-*, *h*) knock off, beat off, strike off; cut off (*head*); refuse (*request*); repel (*attack*).

abschlägig *adj.* ['apʃlɛːgɪç] negative; *~e Antwort* refusal, denial.

'**Abschlagszahlung** *f* payment on account; instal(l)ment.

'**abschleifen** *v/t.* (*irr.* schleifen, *sep.*, *-ge-*, *h*) grind off; *fig.* refine, polish.

'**Abschlepp|dienst** *mot. m* towing service, *Am. a.* wrecking service; '**2en** *v/t.* (*sep.*, *-ge-*, *h*) drag off; *mot.* tow off.

'**abschließen** (*irr.* schließen, *sep.*, *-ge-*, *h*) **1.** *v/t.* lock (up); ⊕ seal (up); conclude (*letter, etc.*); settle (*account*); balance (*the books*); effect (*insurance*); contract (*loan*); *fig.* seclude, isolate; *e-n Handel ~* strike a bargain; *sich ~* seclude o.s.; **2.** *v/i.* conclude; '**~d 1.** *adj.* concluding; final; **2.** *adv.* in conclusion.

'**Abschluß** *m* settlement; conclusion; ⊕ seal; '**~prüfung** *f* final examination, finals *pl.*, *Am. a.* graduation; '**~zeugnis** *n* leaving certificate; diploma.

'**ab|schmeicheln** *v/t.* (*sep.*, *-ge-*, *h*): *j-m et. ~* coax s.th. out of s.o.; '**~schmelzen** (*irr.* schmelzen, *sep.*,

-ge-) v/t. (h) and v/i. (sein) melt (off); ⊕ fuse; '~schmieren ⊕ v/t. (sep., -ge-, h) lubricate, grease; '~schnallen v/t. (sep., -ge-, h) unbuckle; take off (ski, etc.); '~schneiden (irr. schneiden, sep., -ge-, h) 1. v/t. cut (off); slice off; den Weg ~ take a short cut; j-m das Wort ~ cut s.o. short; 2. v/i.: gut ~ come out or off well.

'Abschnitt m ⚓ segment; ✝ coupon; typ. section, paragraph; counterfoil, Am. a. stub (of cheque, etc.); stage (of journey); phase (of development); period (of time).

'ab|schöpfen v/t. (sep., -ge-, h) skim (off); '~schrauben v/t. (sep., -ge-, h) unscrew, screw off.

'abschrecken v/t. (sep., -ge-, h) deter (von from); scare away; '~d adj. deterrent; repulsive, forbidding.

'abschreib|en (irr. schreiben, sep., -ge-, h) 1. v/t. copy; write off (debt, etc.); plagiarize; in school: crib; 2. v/i. send a refusal; '2er m copyist; plagiarist; '2ung ✝ f (-/-en) depreciation.

'abschreiten v/t. (irr. schreiten, sep., -ge-, h) pace (off); e-e Ehrenwache ~ inspect a guard of hono(u)r.

'Abschrift f copy, duplicate.

'abschürf|en v/t. (sep., -ge-, h) graze, abrade (skin); '2ung f (-/-en) abrasion.

'Abschuß m discharge (of fire-arm); launching (of rocket); hunt. shooting; shooting down, downing (of aircraft); '~rampe f launching platform.

abschüssig adj. ['apʃʏsɪç] sloping; steep.

'ab|schütteln v/t. (sep., -ge-, h) shake off (a. fig.); fig. get rid of; '~schwächen v/t. (sep., -ge-, h) weaken, lessen, diminish; '~schweifen v/i. (sep., -ge-, sein) deviate; fig. digress; '~schwenken v/i. (sep., -ge-, sein) swerve; ✗ wheel; '~schwören v/i. (irr. schwören, sep., -ge-, h) abjure; forswear; '~segeln v/i. (sep., -ge-, sein) set sail, sail away.

abseh|bar adj. ['apze:ba:r]: in ~er Zeit in the not-too-distant future; '~en (irr. sehen, sep., -ge-, h) 1. v/t. (fore)see; j-m et. ~ learn s.th. by observing s.o.; es abgesehen haben auf (acc.) have an eye on, be aiming at; 2. v/i.: ~ von refrain from; disregard.

abseits ['apzaɪts] 1. adv. aside, apart; football, etc.: off side; 2. prp. (gen.) aside from; off (the road).

'absend|en v/t. (irr. senden, sep., -ge-, h) send off, dispatch; ✍ post, esp. Am. mail; '2er ✍ m sender.

'absengen v/t. (sep., -ge-, h) singe off.

'Absenker ⚘ m (-s/-) layer, shoot.

'absetz|en (sep., -ge-, h) 1. v/t. set or put down, deposit; deduct (sum); take off (hat); remove, dismiss (official); depose, dethrone (king); drop, put down (passenger); ✝ sell (goods); typ. set up (in type); thea.: ein Stück ~ take off a play; 2. v/i. break off, stop, pause; '2ung f (-/-en) deposition; removal, dismissal.

'Absicht f (-/-en) intention, purpose, design; '2lich 1. adj. intentional; 2. adv. on purpose.

'absitzen (irr. sitzen, sep., -ge-) 1. v/i. (sein) rider: dismount; 2. v/t. (h) serve (sentence), do (time).

absolut adj. [apzo'lu:t] absolute.

absolvieren [apzɔl'vi:rən] v/t. (no -ge-, h) absolve; complete (studies); get through, graduate from (school).

'absonder|n v/t. (sep., -ge-, h) separate; ✎ secrete; sich ~ withdraw; '2ung f (-/-en) separation; ✎ secretion.

ab|sorbieren [apzɔr'bi:rən] v/t. (no -ge-, h) absorb; '~speisen fig. v/t. (sep., -ge-, h) put s.o. off.

abspenstig adj. ['apʃpɛnstɪç]: ~ machen entice away (von from).

'absperr|en v/t. (sep., -ge-, h) lock; shut off; bar (way); block (road); turn off (gas, etc.); '2hahn m stopcock.

'ab|spielen v/t. (sep., -ge-, h) play (record, etc.); play back (tape recording); sich ~ happen, take place; '~sprechen v/t. (irr. sprechen, sep., -ge-, h) deny; arrange, agree; '~springen v/i. (irr. springen, sep., -ge-, sein) jump down or off; ✈ jump, bale out, (Am. only) bail out; rebound.

'Absprung m jump; sports: take-off.

'abspülen v/t. (sep., -ge-, h) wash up; rinse.

'abstamm|en v/i. (sep., -ge-, sein) be descended; gr. be derived (both: von from); '2ung f (-/-en) descent; gr. derivation.

'Abstand m distance; interval; ✝ compensation, indemnification; ~ nehmen von desist from.

ab|statten v/t. (sep., -ge-, h): e-n Besuch ~ pay a visit; Dank ~ return or render thanks; '~stauben v/t. (sep., -ge-, h) dust.

'abstech|en (irr. stechen, sep., -ge-, h) 1. v/t. cut (sods); stick (pig, sheep, etc.); stab (animal); 2. v/i. contrast (von with); '2er m (-s/-) excursion, trip; detour.

'ab|stecken v/t. (sep., -ge-, h) unpin, undo; fit, pin (dress); surv. mark out; '~stehen v/i. (irr. stehen, sep., -ge-, h) stand off; stick out, protrude; s. abgestanden; '~steigen v/i. (irr. steigen, sep., -ge-, sein)

descend; alight (von from) (carriage); get off, dismount (from) (horse); put up (in dat. at) (hotel); **˷stellen** v/t. (sep., -ge-, h) put down; stop, turn off (gas, etc.); park (car); fig. put an end to s.th.; **˷stempeln** v/t. (sep., -ge-, h) stamp; **˷sterben** v/i. (irr. sterben, sep.,-ge-, sein) die off; limb: mortify.

Abstieg ['apʃtiːk] m (-[e]s/-e) descent; fig. decline.

abstimm|en (sep., -ge-, h) 1. v/i. vote; 2. v/t. tune in (radio); fig.: harmonize; time; ✝ balance (books); **'˷ung** f voting; vote; tuning.

Abstinenzler [apstiˈnɛntslər] m (-s/-) teetotal(l)er.

'abstoppen (sep., -ge-, h) 1. v/t. stop; slow down; sports: clock, time; 2. v/i. stop.

'abstoßen v/t. (irr. stoßen, sep., -ge-, h) knock off; push off; clear off (goods); fig. repel; sich die Hörner ˷ sow one's wild oats; '˷d fig. adj. repulsive.

abstrakt adj. [apˈstrakt] abstract.

'ab|streichen v/t. (irr. streichen, sep., -ge-, h) take or wipe off; **'˷streifen** v/t. (sep., -ge-, h) strip off; take or pull off (glove, etc.); slip off (dress); wipe (shoes); **'˷streiten** v/t. (irr. streiten, sep., -ge-, h) contest, dispute; deny.

'Abstrich m deduction, cut; ⚕ swab.

'ab|stufen v/t. (sep., -ge-, h) graduate; gradate; **'˷stumpfen** (sep., -ge-) 1. v/t. (h) blunt; fig. dull (mind); 2. fig. v/i. (sein) become dull.

'Absturz m fall; ✈ crash.

'ab|stürzen v/i. (sep., -ge-, sein) fall down; ✈ crash; **'˷suchen** v/t. (sep., -ge-, h) search (nach for); scour or comb (area) (for).

absurd adj. [apˈzurt] absurd, preposterous.

Abszeß ⚕ [apsˈtsɛs] m (Abszesses/Abszesse) abscess.

Abt [apt] m (-[e]s/ͤe) abbot.

'abtakeln ⚓ v/t. (sep.,-ge-, h) unrig, dismantle, strip.

Abtei [apˈtai] f (-/-en) abbey.

Ab|'teil ⬛ n compartment; **'˷teilen** v/t. (sep., -ge-, h) divide; △ partition off; **'˷teilung** f division; **˷'teilung** f department; ward (of hospital); compartment; ⚔ detachment; **˷'teilungsleiter** m head of a department.

abtelegraphieren v/i. (sep., no -ge-, h) cancel a visit, etc. by telegram.

Äbtissin [ɛpˈtisin] f (-/-nen) abbess.

'ab|töten v/t. (sep., -ge-, h) destroy, kill (bacteria, etc.); **'˷tragen** v/t. (irr. tragen, sep., -ge-, h) carry off; pull down (building); wear out (garment); pay (debt).

abträglich adj. ['aptrɛːkliç] injurious, detrimental.

'abtreib|en (irr. treiben, sep., -ge-) 1. v/t. (h) drive away or off; ein Kind ˷ procure abortion; 2. ⚓, ✈ v/i. (sein) drift off; **'˷ung** f (-/-en) abortion.

'abtrennen v/t. (sep., -ge-, h) detach; separate; sever (limbs, etc.); take (trimmings) off (dress).

'abtret|en (irr. treten, sep., -ge-) 1. v/t. (h) wear down (heels); wear out (steps, etc.); fig. cede, transfer; 2. v/i. (sein) retire, withdraw; resign; thea. make one's exit; **'˷er** m (-s/-) doormat; **'˷ung** f (-/-en) cession, transfer.

'ab|trocknen (sep., -ge-) 1. v/t. (h) dry (up); wipe (dry); sich ˷ dry oneself, rub oneself down; 2. v/i. (sein) dry up, become dry; **'˷tropfen** v/i. (sep.,-ge-, sein) liquid: drip; dishes, vegetables: drain.

abtrünnig adj. ['aptrYniç] unfaithful, disloyal; eccl. apostate; **˷e** ['˷gə] m (-n/-n) deserter; eccl. apostate.

'ab|tun v/t. (irr. tun, sep., -ge-, h) take off; settle (matter); fig.: dispose of; dismiss; **˷'urteilen** ['ap˥-] v/t. (sep.,-ge-, h) pass sentence on s.o.; **˷'wägen** v/t. ([irr. wǡgen],sep.,-ge-, h) weigh (out); fig. consider carefully; **'˷wälzen** v/t. (sep., -ge-, h) roll away; fig. shift; **'˷wandeln** v/t. (sep., -ge-, h) vary, modify; **'˷wandern** v/i. (sep., -ge-, sein) wander away; migrate (von from).

'Abwandlung f modification, variation.

'abwarten (sep., -ge-, h) 1. v/t. wait for, await; s-e Zeit ˷ bide one's time; 2. v/i. wait.

abwärts adv. ['apvɛrts] down, downward(s).

'abwaschen v/t. (irr. waschen, sep., -ge-, h) wash (off, away); bathe; sponge off; wash up (dishes, etc.).

'abwechs|eln (sep., -ge-, h) 1. v/t. vary; alternate; 2. v/i. vary; alternate; mit j-m ˷ take turns; **'˷d** adj. alternate.

'Abwechs(e)lung f (-/-en) change; alternation; variation; diversion; zur ˷ for a change.

'Abweg m: auf ˷e geraten go astray; **'˷ig** adj. ['˷giç] erroneous, wrong.

'Abwehr f defen|ce, Am. -se; warding off (of thrust, etc.); **'˷dienst** ⚔ m counter-espionage service; **'˷en** v/t. (sep., -ge-, h) ward off; avert; repulse, repel; ward off (attack, enemy).

'abweich|en v/i. (irr. weichen, sep., -ge-, sein) deviate (von from), swerve (from); differ (from); compass-needle: deviate; **'˷ung** f (-/-en) deviation; difference; deflexion, (Am. only) deflection.

'abweiden v/t. (sep., -ge-, h) graze.

'abweis|en v/t. (irr. weisen, sep., -ge-, h) refuse, reject; repel (a. ⚔);

rebuff; '~end adj. unfriendly, cool; '2ung f refusal, rejection; repulse (a. ⚔); rebuff.

'ab|wenden v/t. ([irr. wenden,] sep., -ge-, h) turn away; avert (disaster, etc.); parry (thrust); sich ~ turn away (von from); '~werfen v/t. (irr. werfen, sep., -ge-, h) throw off; ⚔ drop (bombs); shed, cast (skin, etc.); shed (leaves); yield (profit).

'abwert|en v/t. (sep., -ge-, h) devaluate; '2ung f devaluation.

abwesen|d adj. ['apveːzənt] absent; '2heit f (-/~ -en) absence.

'ab|wickeln v/t. (sep., -ge-, h) unwind, unreel, wind off; transact (business); '~wiegen v/t. (irr. wiegen, sep., -ge-, h) weigh (out) (goods); '~wischen v/t. (sep., -ge-, h) wipe (off); '~würgen v/t. (sep., -ge-, h) strangle, throttle, choke; mot. stall; '~zahlen v/t. (sep., -ge-, h) pay off; pay by instal(l)ments; '~zählen v/t. (sep., -ge-, h) count (out, over).

'Abzahlung f instal(l)ment, payment on account; '~sgeschäft n hire-purchase.

'abzapfen v/t. (sep., -ge-, h) tap, draw off.

'Abzehrung f (-/-en) wasting away, emaciation; ⚕ consumption.

'Abzeichen n badge; ⚔ marking.

'ab|zeichnen v/t. (sep., -ge-, h) copy, draw; mark off; initial; tick off; sich ~ gegen stand out against; '~ziehen (irr. ziehen, sep., -ge-) 1. v/t. (h) take off, remove; 兌 subtract; strip (bed); bottle (wine); phot. print (film); typ. pull (proof); take out (key); das Fell ~ skin (animal); 2. v/i. (sein) go away; ⚔ march off; smoke: escape; thunderstorm, clouds: move on.

'Abzug m departure; ⚔ withdrawal, retreat; ⊕ drain; outlet; deduction (of sum); phot. print; typ. proof (-sheet).

abzüglich prp. (gen.) ['aptsyːkliç] less, minus, deducting.

'Abzugsrohr n waste-pipe.

abzweig|en ['aptsvaɪgən] (sep., -ge-) 1. v/t. (h) branch; divert (money); sich ~ branch off; 2. v/i. (sein) branch off; '2ung f (-/-en) branch; road-junction.

ach int. [ax] oh!, ah!, alas!; ~ so! oh, I see!

Achse ['aksə] f (-/-n) axis; ⊕: axle; shaft; axle(-tree) (of carriage); auf der ~ on the move.

Achsel ['aksəl] f (-/-n) shoulder; die ~n zucken shrug one's shoulders; '~höhle f armpit.

acht[1] [axt] 1. adj. eight; in ~ Tagen today week, this day week; vor ~ Tagen a week ago; 2. 2 f (-/-en) (figure) eight.

Acht[2] [~] f (-/no pl.) ban, outlawry; attention; außer acht lassen dis-

regard; sich in acht nehmen be careful; be on one's guard (vor j-m or et. against s.o. or s.th.); look out (for s.o. or s.th.).

'achtbar adj. respectable.

'achte adj. eighth; 21 ['~əl] n (-s/-) eighth (part).

'achten (ge-, h) 1. v/t. respect, esteem; regard; 2. v/i.: ~ auf (acc.) pay attention to; achte auf meine Worte mark or mind my words; darauf ~, daß see to it that, take care that.

ächten ['ɛçtən] v/t. (ge-, h) outlaw, proscribe; ban.

'Achter m (-s/-) rowing: eight.

achtfach adj. ['axtfax] eightfold.

'achtgeben v/i. (irr. geben, sep., -ge-, h) be careful; pay attention (auf acc. to); take care (of); gib acht! look or watch out!, be careful!

'achtlos adj. inattentive, careless, heedless.

Acht'stundentag m eight-hour day.

'Achtung f (-/no pl.) attention; respect, esteem, regard; ~! look out!, ⚔ attention!; ~ Stufe! mind the step!; '2svoll adj. respectful.

'achtzehn adj. eighteen; ~te adj. ['~tə] eighteenth.

achtzig adj. ['axtsiç] eighty; '~ste adj. eightieth.

ächzen ['ɛçtsən] v/i. (ge-, h) groan, moan.

Acker ['akər] m (-s/⸚) field; '~bau m agriculture; farming; 2bautreibend adj. agricultural, farming; '~geräte n/pl. farm implements pl.; '~land n arable land; '2n v/t. and v/i. (ge-, h) plough, till, Am. plow.

add|ieren [a'diːrən] v/t. (no -ge-, h) add (up); 2tion [adi'tsjoːn] f (-/-en) addition, adding up.

Adel ['aːdəl] m (-s/no pl.) nobility, aristocracy; '2ig adj. noble; '2n v/t. (ge-, h) ennoble (a. fig.); Brt. knight, raise to the peerage; '~stand m nobility; aristocracy; Brt. peerage.

Ader ['aːdər] f (-/-n) ꛭ, wood, etc.: vein; anat.: vein; artery; zur ~ lassen bleed.

adieu int. [a'djøː] good-bye, farewell, adieu, F cheerio.

Adjektiv gr. ['atjɛktiːf] n (-s/-e) adjective.

Adler orn. ['aːdlər] m (-s/-) eagle; '~nase f aquiline nose.

adlig adj. ['aːdliç] noble; 2e ['~gə] m (-n/-n) nobleman, peer.

Admiral ⚓ [atmi'raːl] m (-s/-e, ⸚e) admiral.

adopt|ieren [adɔp'tiːrən] v/t. (no -ge-, h) adopt; 2ivkind [~'tiːf-] n adopted child.

Adressat [adrɛ'saːt] m (-en/-en) addressee; consignee (of goods).

Adreßbuch [a'drɛs-] n directory.

Adress|e [a'drɛsə] f (-/-n) address; direction; per ~ care of (abbr. c/o); **2ieren** [␣'si:rən] v/t. (no -ge-, h) address, direct; ✝ consign; falsch ~ misdirect.

adrett adj. [a'drɛt] smart, neat.

Adverb gr. [at'vɛrp] n (-s/-ien) adverb.

Affäre [a'fɛːrə] f (-/-n) (love) affair; matter, business, incident.

Affe zo. ['afə] m (-n/-n) ape; monkey.

Affekt [a'fɛkt] m (-[e]s/-e) emotion; passion; **2iert** adj. [␣'ti:rt] affected. **'affig** F adj. foppish; affected; silly.

Afrikan|er [afri'kɑːnər] m (-s/-) African; **2isch** adj. African.

After anat. ['aftər] m (-s/-) anus.

Agent [a'gɛnt] m (-en/-en) agent; broker; pol. (secret) agent; ␣**ur** [␣'tuːr] f (-/-en) agency.

aggressiv adj. [agrɛ'siːf] aggressive.

Agio ✝ ['aːʒio] n (-s/no pl.) agio, premium.

Agitator [agi'taːtər] m (-s/-en) agitator. [brooch.\]

Agraffe [a'grafə] f (-/-n) clasp;\

agrarisch adj. [a'graːriʃ] agrarian.

Ägypt|er [ɛ:'gyptər] m (-s/-) Egyptian; **2isch** adj. Egyptian.

ah int. [aː] ah!

aha int. [a'ha] aha!, I see!

Ahle ['aːlə] f (-/-n) awl, pricker; punch.

Ahn [aːn] m (-[e]s, -en/-en) ancestor; ␣**en** pl. a. forefathers pl.

ähneln ['ɛːnəln] v/i. (ge-, h) be like, resemble.

ahnen ['aːnən] v/t. (ge-, h) have a presentiment of or that; suspect; divine.

ähnlich adj. ['ɛːnliç] like, resembling; similar (dat. to); iro.: das sieht ihm ~ that's just like him; **'2keit** f (-/-en) likeness, resemblance; similarity.

Ahnung ['aːnuŋ] f (-/-en) presentiment; foreboding; notion, idea; **'2slos** adj. unsuspecting; **'2svoll** adj. full of misgivings.

Ahorn ['aːhɔrn] m (-s/-e) maple (-tree).

Ähre ❖ ['ɛːrə] f (-/-n) ear, head; spike; ␣n lesen glean.

Akademi|e [akadə'miː] f (-/-n) academy, society; ␣**ker** [␣'deːmikər] m (-s/-) university man, esp. Am. university graduate; **2sch** adj. [␣'deːmiʃ] academic.

Akazie [a'kaːtsjə] f (-/-n) acacia.

akklimatisieren [aklimati'ziːrən] v/t. and v/refl. (no -ge-, h) acclimatize, Am. acclimate.

Akkord [a'kɔrt] m (-[e]s/-e) ♪ chord; ✝: contract; agreement; composition; im ~ ✝ by the piece or job; ␣**arbeit** f piece-work; ␣**arbeiter** m piece-worker; ␣**lohn** m piece-wages pl.

akkredit|ieren [akredi'tiːrən] v/t. (no -ge-, h) accredit (bei to); **2iv** [␣'tiːf] n (-s/-e) credentials pl.; ✝ letter of credit.

Akku F ⊕ ['aku] m (-s/-s), ␣**mulator** ⊕ [␣mu'laːtɔr] m (-s/-en) accumulator, (storage-)battery.

Akkusativ gr. ['akuzatiːf] m (-s/-e) accusative (case). [acrobat.\]

Akrobat [akro'baːt] m (-en/-en)\

Akt [akt] m (-[e]s/-e) act(ion), deed; thea. act; paint. nude.

Akte ['aktə] f (-/-n) document, deed; file; ␣n pl. records pl., papers pl.; deeds pl., documents pl.; files pl.; zu den ␣n to be filed; zu den ␣n legen file; '␣**ndeckel** m folder; '␣**nmappe** f, '␣**ntasche** f portfolio; briefcase, '␣**nzeichen** n reference or file number.

Aktie ✝ ['aktsjə] f (-/-n) share, Am. stock; ␣n besitzen hold shares, Am. hold stock; '␣**nbesitz** m shareholdings pl., Am. stockholdings pl.; '␣**ngesellschaft** f appr. joint-stock company, Am. (stock) corporation; '␣**nkapital** n share-capital, Am. capital stock.

Aktion [ak'tsjoːn] f (-/-en) action; activity; pol., etc.: campaign, drive; ⚔ operation; ␣**är** [␣'nɛːr] m (-s/-e) shareholder, Am. stockholder.

aktiv adj. [ak'tiːf] active.

Aktiv|a ✝ [ak'tiːva] n/pl. assets pl.; ␣**posten** [␣'tiːf-] m asset (a. fig.).

aktuell adj. [aktu'ɛl] current, present-day, up-to-date, topical.

Akust|ik [a'kustik] f (-/no pl.) acoustics sg., pl.; **2isch** adj. acoustic.

akut adj. [a'kuːt] acute.

Akzent [ak'tsɛnt] m (-[e]s/-e) accent; stress; **2uieren** [␣u'iːrən] v/t. (no -ge-, h) accent(uate); stress.

Akzept ✝ [ak'tsɛpt] n (-[e]s/-e) acceptance; ␣**ant** ✝ [␣'tant] m (-en/-en) acceptor; **2ieren** [␣'tiːrən] v/t. (no -ge-, h) accept.

Alarm [a'larm] m (-[e]s/-e) alarm; ~ blasen or schlagen ⚔ sound or give the alarm; ␣**bereitschaft** f: in ~ sein stand by; **2ieren** [␣'miːrən] v/t. (no -ge-, h) alarm.

Alaun ⚗ [a'laun] m (-[e]s/-e) alum.

albern adj. ['albərn] silly, foolish.

Album ['album] n (-s/Alben) album.

Alge ❖ ['algə] f (-/-n) alga, seaweed.

Algebra ⚮ ['algebra] f (-/no pl.) algebra.

Alibi ⚖ ['aːlibi] n (-s/-s) alibi.

Alimente ⚮ [ali'mɛntə] pl. alimony.

Alkohol ['alkohol] m (-s/-e) alcohol; **'2frei** adj. non-alcoholic, esp. Am. soft; ␣**es Restaurant** temperance restaurant; ␣**iker** [␣'hoːlikər] m (-s/-) alcoholic; **2isch** adj. [␣'hoːliʃ] alcoholic; '␣**schmuggler** m liquor-smuggler, Am. bootlegger; '␣**verbot** n prohibition; '␣**vergiftung** f alcoholic poisoning.

all¹ [al] **1.** *pron.* all; ~e everybody; ~es in ~em on the whole; *vor* ~em first of all; **2.** *adj.* all; every, each; any; ~e beide both of them; *auf* ~e *Fälle* in any case, at all events; ~e *Tage* every day; ~e *zwei Minuten* every two minutes.

All² [~] *n* (-s/*no pl.*) *the* universe.
'**alle** F *adj.* all gone; ~ *werden* come to an end; *supplies, etc.*: run out.

Allee [a'le:] *f* (-/-n) avenue; (tree-lined) walk.

allein [a'laɪn] **1.** *adj.* alone; single; unassisted; **2.** *adv.* alone; only; **3.** *cj.* yet, only, but, however; 2be'rechtigung *f* exclusive right; 2be-sitz *m* exclusive possession; 2herr-scher *m* absolute monarch, auto-crat; dictator; ~ig *adj.* only, exclusive, sole; 2sein *n* loneliness, solitariness, solitude; ~stehend *adj.* p.: alone in the world; single; building, etc.: isolated, detached; 2verkauf *m* exclusive sale; monopoly; 2vertreter *m* sole representative or agent; 2vertrieb *m* sole distributors *pl.*

allemal *adv.* ['alə'ma:l] always; *ein für* ~ once (and) for all.

'**allen'falls** *adv.* if need be; possibly, perhaps; at best.

allenthalben † *adv.* ['alənt'halbən] everywhere.

'**aller**|'**best** *adj.* best ... of all, very best; ~dings *adv.* ['~'dɪŋs] indeed; to be sure; ~! certainly!, *Am.* F sure!; '~'erst **1.** *adj.* first ... of all, very first; foremost; **2.** *adv.*: zu ~ first of all.

Allergie *f* [aler'gi:] *f* (-/-n) allergy.
'**aller**|'**hand** *adj.* of all kinds or sorts; F *das ist ja* ~! F I say!; *sl.* that's the limit!; '2'heiligen *n* (-/*no pl.*) All Saints' Day; ~lei *adj.* ['~'laɪ] of all kinds or sorts; '2'lei *n* (-s/-s) medley; '~'letzt **1.** *adj.* last of all, very last; latest (*news, fashion, etc.*); **2.** *adv.*: zu ~ last of all; '~'liebst **1.** *adj.* dearest of all; (most) lovely; **2.** *adv.*: *am* ~en best of all; '~'meist **1.** *adj.* most; **2.** *adv.*: *am* ~en mostly; chiefly; '~'nächst *adj.* very next; '~'neu(e)st *adj.* the very latest; '2'seelen *n* (-/*no pl.*) All Souls' Day; '~'seits *adv.* on all sides; universally; '~'wenigst *adv.*: *am* ~en least of all.

'**alle**|'**samt** *adv.* one and all, all together; '~'zeit *adv.* always, at all times, for ever.

'**all**|'**gegenwärtig** *adj.* omnipresent, ubiquitous; '~ge'mein **1.** *adj.* general; common; universal; **2.** *adv.*: *im* ~en in general, generally; '2ge-'meinheit *f* (-/*no pl.*) generality; universality; general public; 2'heil-mittel *n* panacea, cure-all (*both a. fig.*).

Allianz [ali'ants] *f* (-/-en) alliance.

alli'ier|**en** *v/refl.* (*no* -ge-, h) ally o.s. (*mit* to, with); 2te *m* (-n/-n) ally.

'**all**|'**jährlich 1.** *adj.* annual; **2.** *adv.* annually, every year; '2macht *f* (-/*no pl.*) omnipotence; '~'mächtig *adj.* omnipotent, almighty; ~mäh-lich [~'me:lɪç] **1.** *adj.* gradual; **2.** *adv.* gradually, by degrees.

Allopathie *f* [alopa'ti:] allopathy.
all|**seitig** *adj.* ['alzaɪtɪç] universal; all-round; '2strom *f* m (-[e]s/*no pl.*) alternating current/direct current (*abbr.* A.C./D.C.); '2tag *m* workday; week-day; *fig.* everyday life, daily routine; ~'täglich *adj.* daily; *fig.* common, trivial; '2tags-leben *n* (-s/*no pl.*) everyday life; '~'wissend *adj.* omniscient; '2'wis-senheit *f* (-/*no pl.*) omniscience; '~'wöchentlich *adj.* weekly; '~zu *adv.* (much) too; '~zu'viel *adv.* too much.

Alm [alm] *f* (-/-en) Alpine pasture, alp.

Almosen ['almo:zən] *n* (-s/-) alms; ~ *pl.* alms *pl.*, charity.

Alp|**druck** ['alp-] *m* (-[e]s/~e), '~drücken *n* (-s/*no pl.*) night-mare.

Alpen ['alpən] *pl.* Alps *pl.*
Alphabet [alfa'be:t] *n* (-[e]s/-e) alphabet; 2isch *adj.* alphabetic(al).
'**Alptraum** *m* nightmare.

als *cj.* [als] than; as, like; (in one's capacity) as; but, except; *temporal*: after, when; as; ~ *ob* as if, as though; *so viel* ~ as much as; *er ist zu dumm,* ~ *daß er es verstehen könnte* he is too stupid to under-stand it; ~'bald *adv.* immediately; ~'dann *adv.* then.

also ['alzo] **1.** *adv.* thus, so; **2.** *cj.* therefore, so, consequently; *na* ~! there you are!

alt¹ *adj.* [alt] old; aged; ancient, antique; stale; second-hand.

Alt² *f* [~] *m* (-s/-e) alto, contralto.
Altar [al'ta:r] *m* (-[e]s/~e) altar.
Alteisen ['alt⁹-] *n* scrap-iron.
'**Alte** (-n/-n) **1.** *m* old man; F: *der* ~ the governor; *hist.*: *die* ~n *pl.* the ancients *pl.*; **2.** *f* old woman.
'**Alter** *n* (-s/-) age; old age; seniority; *er ist in meinem* ~ he is my age; *von mittlerem* ~ middle-aged.

älter *adj.* ['eltər] older; senior; *der* ~e *Bruder* the elder brother.

altern ['altərn] *v/i.* (ge-, h, sein) grow old, age.

Alternative [alterna'ti:və] *f* (-/-n) alternative; *keine* ~ *haben* have no choice.

'**Alters**|**grenze** *f* age-limit; retire-ment age; '~heim *n* old people's home; '~rente *f* old-age pension; '2schwach *adj.* decrepit; senile; '~schwäche *f* decrepitude; '~ver-sorgung *f* old-age pension.

Altertum ['altərtu:m] *n* 1. (*-s/no pl.*) antiquity; 2. (*-s/=er*) *mst* Altertümer *pl.* antiquities *pl.*

altertümlich *adj.* ['altərty:mliç] ancient, antique, archaic.

'Altertums|forscher *m* arch(a)eologist; **~kunde** *f* arch(a)eology.

ältest *adj.* ['ɛltəst] oldest; eldest (*sister, etc.*); earliest (*recollections*); '2e *m* (*-n/-n*) elder; senior; mein ~r my eldest (son).

Altistin ♪ [al'tistin] *f* (*-/-nen*) alto-singer, contralto-singer.

altklug *adj.* precocious, forward.

ältlich *adj.* ['ɛltliç] elderly, oldish.

'Alt|material *n* junk, scrap; salvage; **~meister** *m* doyen, dean, F Grand Old Man (*a. sports*); *sports:* ex-champion; '2modisch *adj.* old-fashioned; **~papier** *n* waste paper; **~philologe** *m* classical philologist *or* scholar; **~stadt** *f* old town *or* city; **~warenhändler** *m* second-hand dealer; **~weibersommer** *m* Indian summer; gossamer.

Aluminium 🔬 [alu'mi:njum] *n* (*-s/no pl.*) aluminium, *Am.* aluminum.

am *prp.* [am] = an dem.

Amateur [ama'tø:r] *m* (*-s/-e*) amateur.

Amboß ['ambɔs] *m* (*Ambosses/Ambosse*) anvil.

ambulan|t ⚕ *adj.* [ambu'lant]: ~ Behandelter out-patient; 2z [~ts] *f* (*-/-en*) ambulance.

Ameise ['a:maizə] *f* (*-/-n*) ant; **~nhaufen** *m* ant-hill.

Amerikan|er [ameri'ka:nər] *m* (*-s/-*), **~erin** *f* (*-/-nen*) American; 2isch *adj.* American.

Amme ['amə] *f* (*-/-n*) (wet-)nurse.

Amnestie [amnɛs'ti:] *f* (*-/-n*) amnesty, general pardon.

Amor ['a:mɔr] *m* (*-s/no pl.*) Cupid.

Amortis|ation [amɔrtiza'tsjo:n] *f* (*-/-en*) amortization, redemption; 2ieren [~'zi:rən] *v/t.* (*no -ge-, h*) amortize, redeem; pay off.

Ampel ['ampəl] *f* (*-/-n*) hanging lamp; traffic light.

Amphibie zo. [am'fi:bjə] *f* (*-/-n*) amphibian.

Ampulle [am'pulə] *f* (*-/-n*) ampoule.

Amput|ation ⚕ [amputa'tsjo:n] *f* (*-/-en*) amputation; 2ieren [~'ti:rən] *v/t.* (*no -ge-, h*) amputate; **~ierte** *m* (*-n/-n*) amputee.

Amsel *orn.* ['amzəl] *f* (*-/-n*) black-bird.

Amt [amt] *n* (*-[e]s/=er*) office; post; charge; office, board; official duty, function; (telephone) exchange; 2ieren [~'ti:rən] *v/i.* (*no -ge-, h*) hold office; officiate; '2lich *adj.* official; **~mann** *m* district administrator; *hist.* bailiff.

'Amts|arzt *m* medical officer of health; **~befugnis** *f* competence, authority; **~bereich** *m*, **~bezirk** *m* jurisdiction; **~blatt** *n* gazette; **~eid** *m* oath of office; **~einführung** *f* inauguration; **~führung** *f* administration; **~geheimnis** *n* official secret; **~gericht** *n appr.* district court; **~geschäfte** *n/pl.* official duties *pl.*; **~gewalt** *f* (official) authority; **~handlung** *f* official act; **~niederlegung** *f* (-/~-en) resignation; **~richter** *m appr.* district court judge; **~siegel** *n* official seal; **~vorsteher** *m* head official.

Amulett [amu'lɛt] *n* (*-[e]s/-e*) amulet, charm.

amüs|ant *adj.* [amy'zant] amusing, entertaining; **~ieren** [~'zi:rən] *v/t.* (*no -ge-, h*) amuse, entertain; *sich ~* amuse *or* enjoy o.s., have a good time.

an [an] 1. *prp.* (*dat.*) at; on, upon; in; against; to; by, near, close to; ~ der Themse on the Thames; ~ der Wand on *or* against the wall; es ist ~ dir zu inf. it is up to you to *inf.*; am Leben alive; am 1. März on March 1st; am Morgen in the morning; 2. *prp.* (*acc.*) to; on; on to; at; against; about; bis ~ as far as, up to; 3. *adv.* on; von heute ~ from this day forth, from today; von nun *or* jetzt ~ from now on.

analog *adj.* [ana'lo:k] analogous (*dat. or zu* to, with).

Analphabet [an(?)alfa'be:t] *m* (*-en/-en*) illiterate (person).

Analys|e [ana'ly:zə] *f* (*-/-n*) analysis; 2ieren [~'zi:rən] *v/t.* (*no -ge-, h*) analy|se, *Am.* -ze.

Anämie ⚕ [anɛ'mi:] *f* (*-/-n*) an(a)emia.

Ananas ['ananas] *f* (*-/-, -se*) pine-apple.

Anarchie [anar'çi:] *f* (*-/-n*) anarchy.

Anatom|ie [anato'mi:] *f* (*-/no pl.*) anatomy; 2isch *adj.* [~'to:miʃ] anatomical.

'anbahnen *v/t.* (*sep., -ge-, h*) pave the way for, initiate; open up; *sich ~* be|opening up.

'Anbau *m* 1. ♪ (*-[e]s/no pl.*) cultivation; 2. △ (*-[e]s/-ten*) outbuilding, annex, extension, addition; '2en *v/t.* (*sep., -ge-, h*) ♪ cultivate, grow; △ add (*an acc.* to); **~fläche** ♪ *f* arable land.

'anbehalten *v/t.* (*irr. halten, sep., no -ge-, h*) keep (*garment, etc.*) on.

an'bei ✝ *adv.* enclosed.

'an|beißen (*irr. beißen, sep., -ge-, h*) 1. *v/t.* bite into; 2. *v/i. fish:* bite; **~bellen** *v/t.* (*sep., -ge-, h*) bark at; **~beraumen** [~bəraumən] *v/t.* (*sep., no -ge-, h*) appoint, fix; **~beten** *v/t.* (*sep., -ge-, h*) adore, worship.

'Anbetracht *m: in ~* considering, in consideration of.

'anbetteln v/t. (sep., -ge-, h) beg from, solicit alms of.
'Anbetung f (-/-en) worship, adoration; '2swürdig adj. adorable.
'an|bieten v/t. (irr. bieten, sep., -ge-, h) offer; '~binden v/t. (irr. binden, sep., -ge-, h) bind, tie (up); ~ an (dat., acc.) tie to; s. angebunden; '~blasen v/t. (irr. blasen, sep., -ge-, h) blow at or (up)on.
'Anblick m look; view; sight, aspect; '2en v/t. (sep., -ge-, h) look at; glance at; view; eye.
'an|blinzeln v/t. (sep., -ge-, h) wink at; '~brechen (irr. brechen, sep., -ge-) 1. v/t. (h) break into (provisions, etc.); open (bottle, etc.); 2. v/i. (sein) begin; day: break, dawn; '~brennen (irr. brennen, sep., -ge-) 1. v/t. (h) set on fire; light (cigar, etc.); 2. v/i. (sein) catch fire; burn; '~bringen v/t. (irr. bringen, sep., -ge-, h) bring; fix (an dat. to), attach (to); place; ✝ dispose of (goods); lodge (complaint); s. angebracht.
'Anbruch m (-[e]s/no pl.) beginning; break (of day).
'anbrüllen v/t. (sep., -ge-, h) roar at.
Andacht ['andaxt] f (-/-en) devotion(s pl.); prayers pl.
andächtig adj. ['andɛçtiç] devout.
'andauern v/i. (sep., -ge-, h) last, continue, go on.
'Andenken n (-s/-) memory, remembrance; keepsake, souvenir; zum ~ an (acc.) in memory of.
ander adj. ['andər] other; different; next; opposite; am ~en Tag (on) the next day; e-n Tag um den ~en every other day; ein ~er Freund another friend; nichts ~es nothing else.
andererseits adv. ['andərər'zaɪts] on the other hand.
ändern ['ɛndərn] v/t. (ge-, h) alter; change; ich kann es nicht ~ I can't help it; sich ~ alter; change.
'andern'falls adv. otherwise, else.
anders adv. ['andərs] otherwise; differently (als from); else; j. ~ somebody else; ich kann nicht ~, ich muß weinen I cannot help crying; ~ werden change.
'ander'seits adv. s. andererseits.
'anders'wo adv. elsewhere.
anderthalb adj. ['andərt'halp] one and a half.
'Änderung f (-/-en) change, alteration.
ander|wärts adv. ['andər'vɛrts] elsewhere; '~weitig 1. adj. other; 2. adv. otherwise.
'andeut|en v/t. (sep., -ge-, h) indicate; hint; intimate; imply; suggest; '2ung f intimation; hint; suggestion.
'Andrang m rush; ✿ congestion.
andre adj. ['andrə] s. andere.

'andrehen v/t. (sep., -ge-, h) turn on (gas, etc.); ⚡ switch on (light).
'androh|en v/t. (sep., -ge-, h): j-m et. ~ threaten s.o. with s.th.; '2ung f threat.
aneignen ['an'ʔ-] v/refl. (sep., -ge-, h) appropriate; acquire; adopt; seize; usurp.
aneinander adv. [an'ʔaɪ'nandər] together; '~geraten v/i. (irr. raten, sep., no -ge-, sein) clash (mit with).
anekeln ['an'ʔ-] v/t. (sep., -ge-, h) disgust, sicken.
Anerbieten ['an'ʔ-] n (-s/-) offer.
anerkannt adj. ['an'ʔ-] acknowledged, recognized.
anerkenn|en ['an'ʔ-] v/t. (irr. kennen, sep., no -ge-, h) acknowledge (als as), recognize; appreciate; own (child); hono(u)r (bill); '2ung f (-/-en) acknowledgement; recognition; appreciation.
'anfahr|en (irr. fahren, sep., -ge-) 1. v/t. (sein) start; ⚒ descend; angefahren kommen drive up; 2. v/t. (h) run into; carry, convey; j-n ~ let fly at s.o.; '2t f approach; drive.
'Anfall ⚕ m fit, attack; '2en (irr. fallen, sep., -ge-) 1. v/t. (h) attack; assail; 2. v/i. (sein) accumulate; money: accrue.
anfällig adj. ['anfɛliç] susceptible (für to); prone to (diseases, etc.).
'Anfang m beginning, start, commencement; ~ Mai at the beginning of May, early in May; '2en v/t. and v/i. (irr. fangen, sep., -ge-, h) begin, start, commence.
Anfäng|er ['anfɛŋər] m (-s/-) beginner; '2lich 1. adj. initial; 2. adv. in the beginning.
anfangs adv. ['anfaŋs] in the beginning; '2buchstabe m initial (letter); großer ~ capital letter; '2gründe ['~gryndə] m/pl. elements pl.
'anfassen (sep., -ge-, h) 1. v/t. seize; touch; handle; 2. v/i. lend a hand.
anfecht|bar adj. ['anfɛçtba:r] contestable; '~en v/t. (irr. fechten, sep., -ge-, h) contest, dispute; ⚖ avoid (contract); '2ung f (-/-en) contestation; ⚖ avoidance; fig. temptation.
an|fertigen ['anfɛrtigən] v/t. (sep., -ge-, h) make, manufacture; '~feuchten v/t. (sep., -ge-, h) moisten, wet, damp; '~feuern v/t. (sep., -ge-, h) fire, heat; sports: cheer; fig. encourage; '~flehen v/t. (sep., -ge-, h) implore; '~fliegen ✈ v/t. (irr. fliegen, sep., -ge-, h) approach, head for (airport, etc.); '2flug m ✈ approach (flight); fig. touch, tinge.
'anforder|n v/t. (sep., -ge-, h) demand; request; claim; '2ung f demand; request; claim.
'Anfrage f inquiry; '2n v/i. (sep., -ge-, h) ask (bei j-m s.o.); inquire (bei j-m nach et. of s.o. about s.th.).

an|freunden ['anfrɔʏndən] v/refl.
(sep., -ge-, h): sich ~ mit make
friends with; '~frieren v/i. (irr.
frieren, sep., -ge-, sein) freeze on
(an dat. or acc. to); '~fügen v/t.
(sep., -ge-, h) join, attach (an acc.
to); '~fühlen v/t. (sep., -ge-, h)
feel, touch; sich ~ feel.

Anfuhr ['anfuːr] f (-/-en) conveyance, carriage.

'anführ|en v/t. (sep., -ge-, h) lead;
allege; ✗ command; quote, cite
(authority, passage, etc.); dupe, fool,
trick; '2er m (ring)leader; '2ungs-
zeichen n/pl. quotation marks pl.,
inverted commas pl.

'Angabe f declaration; statement;
instruction; F fig. bragging, show-
ing off.

'angeb|en (irr. geben, sep., -ge-, h)
1. v/t. declare; state; specify; allege;
give (name, reason); † quote (prices);
denounce, inform against; 2.
v/i. cards: deal first; F fig. brag,
show off, Am. blow; '2er m (-s/-)
informer; F braggart, Am. blow-
hard; '~lich adj. ['~pliç] supposed;
pretended, alleged.

'angeboren adj. innate, inborn; ✗
congenital.

'Angebot n offer (a. †); at auction
sale: bid; † supply.

'ange|bracht adj. appropriate, suit-
able; well-timed; '~bunden adj.:
kurz ~ sein be short (gegen with).

'angehen (irr. gehen, sep., -ge-)
1. v/i. (sein) begin; meat, etc.: go
bad, go off; es geht an it will do;
2. v/t. (h): j-n ~ concern s.o.; das
geht dich nichts an that is no business of yours.

'angehör|en v/i. (sep., no -ge-, h)
belong to; 2ige ['~igə] m, f (-/-n):
seine ~n pl. his relations pl.; die
nächsten ~n pl. the next of kin.

Angeklagte ['angəklaːktə] m, f
(-n/-n) the accused; prisoner (at the
bar); defendant.

Angel ['aŋəl] f (-/-n) hinge; fishing-
tackle, fishing-rod.

'angelegen adj.: sich et. ~ sein lassen make s.th. one's business; '2-
heit f business, concern, affair,
matter.

'Angel|gerät n fishing-tackle; '2n
(ge-, h) 1. v/i. fish (nach for), angle
(for) (both a. fig.); ~ in fish (river,
etc.); 2. v/t. fish (trout); '~punkt
fig. n pivot.

'Angel|sachse m Anglo-Saxon; '2-
sächsisch adj. Anglo-Saxon.

'Angelschnur f fishing-line.

'ange|messen adj. suitable, appro-
priate; reasonable; adequate; '~
nehm adj. pleasant, agreeable,
pleasing; sehr ~! glad or pleased to
meet you; ~regt adj. ['~reːkt] stim-
ulated; discussion: animated, lively;
'~sehen adj. respected, esteemed.

'Angesicht n (-[e]s/-er, -e) face,
countenance; von ~ zu ~ face to
face; '2s prp. (gen.) in view of.

angestammt adj. ['angəʃtamt] hereditary, innate.

Angestellte ['angəʃtɛltə] m, f (-n/-n)
employee; die ~n pl. the staff.

'ange|trunken adj. tipsy; '~wandt
adj. ['~vant] applied; '~wiesen
adj.: ~ sein auf (acc.) be dependent
or thrown (up)on.

'angewöhn|en v/t. (sep., -ge-, h):
j-m et. ~ accustom s.o. to s.th.; sich
et. ~ get into the habit of s.th.;
take to (smoking).

'Angewohnheit f custom, habit.

Angina ♂ [aŋ'giːna] f (-/Anginen)
angina; tonsillitis.

'angleichen v/t. (irr. gleichen, sep.,
-ge-, h) assimilate (an acc. to, with),
adjust (to); sich ~ an (acc.) assimilate to or with, adjust or adapt o.s.
to.

Angler ['aŋlər] m (-s/-) angler.

'angliedern v/t. (sep., -ge-, h) join;
annex; affiliate.

Anglist [aŋ'glist] m (-en/-en) professor or student of English, An-
gli(ci)st.

'angreif|en v/t. (irr. greifen, sep.,
-ge-, h) touch; draw upon (capital,
provisions); attack; affect (health,
material); ♠ corrode; exhaust;
'2er m (-s/-) aggressor, assailant.

'angrenzend adj. adjacent; adjoining.

'Angriff m attack, assault; in ~ nehmen set about; '~skrieg m offensive
war; '2slustig adj. aggressive.

Angst [aŋst] f (-/-e) fear; anxiety;
anguish; ich habe ~ I am afraid (vor
dat. of); '~hase m coward.

ängstigen ['ɛŋstigən] v/t. (ge-, h)
frighten, alarm; sich ~ be afraid
(vor dat. of); be alarmed (um about).

ängstlich adj. ['ɛŋstliç] uneasy,
nervous; anxious; afraid; scrupulous; timid; '2keit f (-/no pl.) anxiety; scrupulousness; timidity.

'an|haben v/t. (irr. haben, sep., -ge-,
h) have (garment) on; das kann mir
nichts ~ that can't do me any harm;
'~haften v/i. (sep., -ge-, h) stick,
adhere (dat. to); '~haken v/t. (sep.,
-ge-, h) hook on; tick (off), Am.
check (off) (name, item).

'anhalten (irr. halten, sep., -ge-, h)
1. v/t. stop; j-n ~ zu et. keep s.o. to
s.th.; den Atem ~ hold one's breath;
2. v/i. continue, last; stop; um ein
Mädchen ~ propose to a girl; '~d
adj. continuous; persevering.

'Anhaltspunkt m clue.

'Anhang m appendix, supplement
(to book, etc.); followers pl., adher-
ents pl.

'anhäng|en (sep., -ge-, h) 1. v/t.
hang on; affix, attach, join; add;
couple (on) (coach, vehicle); 2. v/i.

(irr. hängen) adhere to; '2er m (-s/-) adherent, follower; pendant (of necklace, etc.); label, tag; trailer (behind car, etc.).

anhänglich adj. ['anhɛŋliç] devoted, attached; '2keit f (-/no pl.) devotion, attachment.

Anhängsel ['anhɛŋzəl] n (-s/-) appendage.

'anhauchen v/t. (sep., -ge-, h) breathe on; blow (fingers).

'anhäuf|en v/t. and v/refl. (sep., -ge-, h) pile up, accumulate; '2ung f accumulation.

'an|heben v/t. (irr. heben, sep., -ge-, h) lift, raise; '~heften v/t. (sep., -ge-, h) fasten (an acc. to); stitch (to).

an'heim|fallen v/i. (irr. fallen, sep., -ge-, sein): j-m ~ fall to s.o.; ~stellen v/t. (sep., -ge-, h): j-m et. ~ leave s.th. to s.o.

'Anhieb m: auf ~ at the first go.

'Anhöhe f rise, elevation, hill.

'anhören v/t. (sep., -ge-, h) listen to; sich ~ sound.

Anilin ⚗ [ani'li:n] n (-s/no pl.) anilin(e).

'ankämpfen v/i. (sep., -ge-, h): ~ gegen struggle against.

'Ankauf m purchase.

Anker ⚓ ['aŋkər] m (-s/-) anchor; vor ~ gehen cast anchor; '~kette ⚓ f cable; '2n ⚓ v/t. and v/i. (ge-, h) anchor; '~uhr f lever watch.

'anketten v/t. (sep., -ge-, h) chain (an dat. or acc. to).

'Anklage f accusation, charge; ⚖ a. indictment; '2n v/t. (sep., -ge-, h) accuse (gen. or wegen of), charge (with); ⚖ a. indict (for).

'Ankläger m accuser; öffentlicher ⚖ public prosecutor, Am. district attorney.

'anklammern v/t. (sep., -ge-, h) clip s.th. on; sich ~ cling (an dat. or acc. to).

'Anklang m: ~ an (acc.) suggestion of; ~ finden meet with approval.

'an|kleben v/t. (sep., -ge-, h) stick on (an dat. or acc. to); glue on (to); paste on (to); gum on (to); '~kleiden v/t. (sep., -ge-, h) dress; sich ~ dress (o.s.); '~klopfen v/i. (sep., -ge-, h) knock (an acc. at); '~knipsen ⚡ v/t. (sep., -ge-, h) turn or switch on; '~knüpfen (sep., -ge-, h) 1. v/t. tie (an dat. or acc. to); fig. begin; Verbindungen ~ form connexions or (Am. only) connections; 2. v/i. refer (an acc. to); '~kommen v/i. (irr. kommen, sep., -ge-, sein) arrive; ~ auf (acc.) depend (up)on; es darauf ~ lassen run the risk, risk it; darauf kommt es an that is the point; es kommt nicht darauf an it does not matter.

Ankömmling ['ankœmliŋ] m (-s/-e) new-comer, new arrival.

'ankündig|en v/t. (sep., -ge-, h) announce; advertise; '2ung f announcement; advertisement.

Ankunft ['ankunft] f (-/no pl.) arrival.

'an|kurbeln v/t. (sep., -ge-, h) mot. crank up; die Wirtschaft ~ F boost the economy; '~lächeln v/t. (sep., -ge-, h), '~lachen v/t. (sep., -ge-, h) smile at.

'Anlage f construction; installation; ⊕ plant; grounds pl., park; plan, arrangement, layout; enclosure (to letter); ✝ investment; talent; predisposition, tendency; öffentliche ~n pl. public gardens pl.; '~kapital ✝ n invested capital.

'anlangen (sep., -ge-) 1. v/i. (sein) arrive at; 2. v/t. (h) F touch; concern; was mich anlangt as far as I am concerned, (speaking) for myself.

Anlaß ['anlas] m (Anlasses/Anlässe) occasion; ohne allen ~ without any reason.

'anlass|en v/t. (irr. lassen, sep., -ge-, h) F leave or keep (garment, etc.) on; leave (light, etc.) on; ⊕ start, set going; sich gut ~ promise well; '2er mot. m (-s/-) starter.

anläßlich prp. (gen.) ['anlesliç] on the occasion of.

'Anlauf m start, run; '2en (irr. laufen, sep., -ge-) 1. v/i. (sein) run up; start; tarnish, (grow) dim; ~ gegen run against; 2. ⚓ v/t. (h) call or touch at (port).

'an|legen (sep., -ge-, h) 1. v/t. put (an acc. to, against); lay out (garden); invest (money); level (gun); put on (garment); found (town); ⚒ apply (dressing); lay in (provisions); Feuer ~ an (acc.) set fire to; 2. v/i. ⚓: land; moor; ~ auf (acc.) aim at; '~lehnen v/t. (sep., -ge-, h) lean (an acc. against); leave or set (door) ajar; sich ~ an (acc.) lean against or on.

Anleihe ['anlaɪə] f (-/-n) loan.

'anleit|en v/t. (sep., -ge-, h) guide (zu to); instruct (in dat. in); '2ung f guidance, instruction; guide.

'Anliegen n (-s/-) desire, request.

'an|locken v/t. (sep., -ge-, h) allure, entice; decoy; '~machen v/t. (sep., -ge-, h) fasten (an acc. to), fix (to); make, light (fire); ⚡ switch on (light); dress (salad); '~malen v/t. (sep., -ge-, h) paint.

'Anmarsch m approach.

anmaß|en ['anma:sən] v/refl. (sep., -ge-, h) arrogate s.th. to o.s.; assume (right); presume; '~end adj. arrogant; '2ung f (-/-en) arrogance, presumption.

'anmeld|en v/t. (sep., -ge-, h) announce, notify; sich ~ bei make an appointment with; '2ung f announcement, notification.

'anmerk|en v/t. (sep., -ge-, h) mark; note down; j-m et. ~ observe or perceive s.th. in s.o.; '2ung f (-/-en) remark; note; annotation; comment.

'anmessen v/t. (irr. messen, sep., -ge-, h): j-m e-n Anzug ~ measure s.o. for a suit; s. angemessen.

'Anmut f (-/no pl.) grace, charm, loveliness; '2ig adj. charming, graceful, lovely.

'an|nageln v/t. (sep., -ge-, h) nail on (an an acc. to); '~nähen v/t. (sep., -ge-, h) sew on (an an acc. to).

annäher|nd adj. ['annɛː:ɔrnt] approximate; '2ung f (-/-en) approach.

Annahme ['annɑːmə] f (-/-n) acceptance; receiving-office; fig. assumption, supposition.

'annehm|bar adj. acceptable; price: reasonable; '~en (irr. nehmen, sep., -ge-, h) 1. v/t. accept; take; fig.: suppose, take it, Am. guess; assume; contract (habit); adopt (child); parl. pass (bill); sich (gen.) ~ attend to s.th.; befriend s.o.; 2. v/i. accept; '2lichkeit f (-/-en) amenity, agreeableness.

Annexion [anɛk'sjoːn] f (-/-en) annexation.

Annonce [a'nõːsə] f (-/-n) advertisement. [mous.|

anonym adj. [ano'nyːm] anonymous.|

anordn|en ['an?-] v/t. (sep., -ge-, h) order; arrange; direct; '2ung f arrangement; direction; order.

'anpacken v/t. (sep., -ge-, h) seize, grasp; fig. tackle.

'anpass|en v/t. (sep., -ge-, h) fit, adapt, suit; adjust; try or fit (garment) on; sich ~ adapt o.s. (dat. to); '2ung f (-/-en) adaptation; '~ungsfähig adj. adaptable.

'anpflanz|en v/t. (sep., -ge-, h) cultivate, plant; '2ung f cultivation; plantation.

Anprall ['anpral] m (-[e]s/⸚-e) impact; '2en v/i. (sep., -ge-, sein) strike (an acc. against).

'anpreisen v/t. (irr. preisen, sep., -ge-, h) commend, praise; boost, push.

'Anprobe f try-on, fitting.

'an|probieren v/t. (sep., no -ge-, h) try or fit on; '~raten v/t. (irr. raten, sep., -ge-, h) advise; '~rechnen v/t. (sep., -ge-, h) charge; hoch ~ value highly.

'Anrecht n right, title, claim (auf acc. to).

'Anrede f address; '2n v/t. (sep., -ge-, h) address, speak to.

'anreg|en v/t. (sep., -ge-, h) stimulate; suggest; '~end adj. stimulative, stimulating; suggestive; '2ung f stimulation; suggestion.

'Anreiz m incentive; '2en v/t. (sep., -ge-, h) stimulate; incite.

'an|rennen v/i. (irr. rennen, sep., -ge-, sein): ~ gegen run against; angerannt kommen come running; '~richten v/t. (sep., -ge-, h) prepare, dress (food, salad); cause, do (damage).

anrüchig adj. ['anryçiç] disreputable.

anrücken v/i. (sep., -ge-, sein) approach.

Anruf m call (a. teleph.); '2en v/t. (irr. rufen, sep., -ge-, h) call (zum Zeugen to witness); teleph. ring up, F phone, Am. call up; hail (ship); invoke (God, etc.); appeal to (s.o.'s help).

'anrühren v/t. (sep., -ge-, h) touch; mix.

'Ansage f announcement; '2n v/t. (sep., -ge-, h) announce; '~r m (-s/-) announcer; compère, Am. master of ceremonies.

'ansammeln v/t. (sep., -ge-, h) collect, gather; accumulate, amass; sich ~ collect, gather; accumulate.

ansässig adj. ['anzɛsiç] resident.

Ansatz m start.

'an|schaffen v/t. (sep., -ge-, h) procure, provide; purchase; sich et. ~ provide or supply o.s. with s.th.; '~schalten £ v/t. (sep., -ge-, h) connect; switch on (light).

'anschau|en v/t. (sep., -ge-, h) look at, view; '~lich adj. clear, vivid; graphic.

'Anschauung f (-/-en) view; perception; conception; intuition; contemplation; '~smaterial n illustrative material; '~sunterricht ['anʃauuŋs?-] m visual instruction, object-lessons pl.; '~svermögen n intuitive faculty.

'Anschein m (-[e]s/no pl.) appearance; '2end adj. apparent, seeming.

'an|schicken v/refl. (sep., -ge-, h): sich ~, et. zu tun get ready for s.th.; prepare for s.th.; set about doing s.th.; '~schirren ['~ʃirən] v/t. (sep., -ge-, h) harness.

'Anschlag m ⊕ stop, catch; ♪ touch; notice; placard, poster, bill; estimate; calculation; plot; e-n ~ auf j-n verüben make an attempt on s.o.'s life; ~brett ['~k-] n notice-board, Am. bulletin board; 2en ['~gən] (irr. schlagen, sep., -ge-, h) 1. v/t. strike (an dat. or acc. against), knock (against); post up (bill); ♪ touch; level (gun); estimate, rate; 2. v/i. strike (an acc. against), knock (against); dog: bark; ♫ take (effect); food: agree (bei with); ~säule ['~k-] f advertising pillar; ~zettel ['~k-] m notice; placard, poster, bill.

'anschließen v/t. (irr. schließen, sep., -ge-, h) fix with a lock; join, attach, annex; ⊕, ∮ connect; sich j-m ~ join s.o.; sich e-r Meinung ~

follow an opinion; '**_d** *adj.* adjacent (*an acc.* to); subsequent (to).

'**Anschluß** *m* joining; 🚂, ⚡, *teleph., gas, etc.*: connexion, (*Am. only*) connection; **\~ haben an** (*acc.*) 🚂, *boat*: connect with; 🚂 run in connexion with; **\~ finden** make friends (*an acc.* with), F pal up (with); *teleph.*: **\~ bekommen** get through; '**_dose** ⚡ *f* (wall) socket; '**_zug** 🚂 *m* connecting train, connexion.

'**an|schmiegen** *v/refl.* (*sep.*, -ge-, h): **sich \~ an** (*acc.*) nestle to; '**_schmieren** *v/t.* (*sep.*, -ge-, h) (be)smear, grease; F *fig.* cheat; '**_schnallen** *v/t.* (*sep.*, -ge-, h) buckle on; *bitte \~l* ✕ fasten seat-belts, please!; '**_schnauzen** F *v/t.* (*sep.*, -ge-, h) snap at, blow *s.o.* up, *Am. a.* bawl *s.o.* out; '**_schneiden** *v/t.* (*irr. schneiden, sep.*, -ge-, h) cut; broach (*subject*).

'**Anschnitt** *m* first cut *or* slice.

'**an|schrauben** *v/t.* (*sep.*, -ge-, h) screw on (*an dat. or acc.* to); '**_schreiben** *v/t.* (*irr. schreiben, sep.*, -ge-, h) write down; *sports, games:* score; *et. \~ lassen* have s.th. charged to one's account; buy s.th. on credit; '**_schreien** *v/t.* (*irr. schreien, sep.*, -ge-, h) shout at.

'**Anschrift** *f* address.

an|schuldigen ['anʃuldigən] *v/t.* (*sep.*, -ge-, h) accuse, incriminate; '**_schwärzen** *v/t.* (*sep.*, -ge-, h) blacken; *fig. a.* defame.

'**anschwell|en** (*irr. schwellen, sep.*, -ge-) **1.** *v/i.* (sein) swell; increase, rise; **2.** *v/t.* (h) swell; '**2ung** *f* swelling.

anschwemm|en ['anʃvemən] *v/t.* (*sep.*, -ge-, h) wash ashore; *geol.* deposit (*alluvium*); '**2ung** *f* (-/-en) wash; *geol.* alluvial deposits *pl.*, alluvium.

'**ansehen 1.** *v/t.* (*irr. sehen, sep.*, -ge-, h) (take a) look at; view; regard, consider (*als* as); *et. mit \~ witness s.th.*; **\~ für** take for; *man sieht ihm sein Alter nicht an* he does not look his age; **2.** **2** *n* (-s/*no pl.*) authority, prestige; respect; F appearance, aspect.

ansehnlich *adj.* ['anze:nliç] considerable; good-looking.

'**an|seilen** *mount. v/t. and v/refl.* (*sep.*, -ge-, h) rope; '**_sengen** *v/t.* (*sep.*, -ge-, h) singe; '**_setzen** (*sep.*, -ge-, h) **1.** *v/t.* put (*an acc.* to); add (to); fix, appoint (*date*); rate; fix, quote (*prices*); charge; put forth (*leaves, etc.*); put on (*flesh*); put (*food*) on (*to boil*); *Rost \~* rust; **2.** *v/i.* try; start; get ready.

'**Ansicht** *f* (-/-en) sight, view; *fig.* view, opinion; *meiner \~ nach* in my opinion; *zur \~* ↑ on approval; '**_s(post)karte** *f* picture postcard; '**_ssache** *f* matter of opinion.

ansied|eln *v/t. and v/refl.* (*sep.*, -ge-, h) settle; '**2er** *m* settler; '**2lung** *f* settlement.

'**Ansinnen** *n* (-s/-) request, demand.

'**anspann|en** *v/t.* (*sep.*, -ge-, h) stretch; put *or* harness (*horses, etc.*) to the carriage, *etc.*; *fig.* strain, exert; '**2ung** *fig. f* strain, exertion.

'**anspeien** *v/t.* (*irr. speien, sep.*, -ge-, h) spit (up)on *or* at.

'**anspiel|en** *v/t.* (*sep.*, -ge-, h) *cards:* lead; *sports:* lead off; *football:* kick off; **\~ auf** (*acc.*) allude to, hint at; '**2ung** *f* (-/-en) allusion, hint.

'**anspitzen** *v/t.* (*sep.*, -ge-, h) point, sharpen.

'**Ansporn** *m* (-[e]s/⚡ -e) spur; '**2en** *v/t.* (*sep.*, -ge-, h) spur *s.o.* on.

'**Ansprache** *f* address, speech; *e-e \~ halten* deliver an address.

'**ansprechen** *v/t.* (*irr. sprechen, sep.*, -ge-, h) speak to, address; appeal to; '**_d** *adj.* appealing.

'**an|springen** (*irr. springen, sep.*, -ge-) **1.** *v/i.* (sein) *engine:* start; **2.** *v/t.* (h) jump (up)on, leap at; '**_spritzen** *v/t.* (*sep.*, -ge-, h) splash (*j-n mit* et. s.th. on *s.o.*); (be)sprinkle.

'**Anspruch** *m* claim (*a.* 🏛) (*auf acc.* to), pretension (to); 🏛 title (to); **\~ haben auf** (*acc.*) be entitled to; *in \~ nehmen* claim *s.th.*; *Zeit in \~ nehmen* take up time; '**2slos** *adj.* unpretentious; unassuming; '**2svoll** *adj.* pretentious.

'**an|spülen** *v/t.* (*sep.*, -ge-, h) *s. anschwemmen*; '**_stacheln** *v/t.* (*sep.*, -ge-, h) goad (on).

Anstalt ['anʃtalt] *f* (-/-en) establishment, institution; **\~en treffen zu** make arrangements for.

'**Anstand** *m* **1.** (-[e]s/⚡e) *hunt.* stand; objection; **2.** (-[e]s/⚡"e) good manners *pl.*; decency, propriety.

anständig *adj.* ['anʃtendiç] decent; respectable; *price:* fair, handsome; '**2keit** *f* (-/⚡-en) decency.

'**Anstands|gefühl** *n* sense of propriety; tact; '**2los** *adv.* unhesitatingly.

'**anstarren** *v/t.* (*sep.*, -ge-, h) stare *or* gaze at.

anstatt *prp.* (*gen.*) *and cj.* [an'ʃtat] instead of.

'**anstaunen** *v/t.* (*sep.*, -ge-, h) gaze at *s.o. or s.th.* in wonder.

'**ansteck|en** *v/t.* (*sep.*, -ge-, h) pin on; put on (*ring*); 💉 infect; set on fire; kindle (*fire*); light (*candle, etc.*); '**_end** *adj.* infectious; contagious; *fig. a.* catching; '**2ung** 💉 *f* (-/-en) infection; contagion.

'**an|stehen** *v/i.* (*irr. stehen, sep.*, -ge-, h) queue up (*nach* for), *Am.* stand in line (for); '**_steigen** *v/i.* (*irr. steigen, sep.*, -ge-, sein) *ground:* rise, ascend; *fig.* increase.

'**anstell|en** *v/t.* (*sep.*, -ge-, h) engage, employ, hire; make (*ex-*

periments); draw (*comparison*); turn on (*light, etc.*); manage; *sich ~* queue up (*nach for*), *Am.* line up (for); *sich dumm ~* set about *s.th.* stupidly; '**~ig** *adj.* handy, skil(l)ful; '**2ung** *f* place, position, job; employment.

Anstieg ['anʃtiːk] *m* (-[e]s/-e) ascent. '**anstift|en** *v/t.* (*sep., -ge-, h*) instigate; '**2er** *m* instigator; '**2ung** *f* instigation.

'**anstimmen** *v/t.* (*sep., -ge-, h*) strike up (*tune*).

'**Anstoß** *m football*: kick-off; *fig.* impulse; offen|ce, *Am. -se;* ~ *erregen* give offence (*bei* to); ~ *nehmen an* (*dat.*) take offence at; ~ *geben zu et.* start s.th., initiate s.th.; '**2en** (*irr. stoßen, sep., -ge-*) 1. *v/t.* (h) push, knock (*acc. or an against*); nudge; 2. *v/i.* (*sein*) knock (*an acc. against*); border (on, upon; adjoin; 3. *v/i.* (h): *mit der Zunge ~* lisp; *auf j-s Gesundheit ~* drink (to) s.o.'s health; '**2end** *adj.* adjoining. **anstößig** *adj.* ['anʃtøːsiç] shocking.

'**an|strahlen** *v/t.* (*sep., -ge-, h*) illuminate; floodlight (*building, etc.*); *fig.* beam at *s.o.*; '**~streben** *v/t.* (*sep., -ge-, h*) aim at, aspire to, strive for.

'**anstreich|en** *v/t.* (*irr. streichen, sep., -ge-, h*) paint; whitewash; mark; underline (*mistake*); '**2er** *m* (-s/-) house-painter; decorator.

anstreng|en ['anʃtrɛŋən] *v/t.* (*sep., -ge-, h*) exert; try (*eyes*); fatigue; *Prozeß ~* bring an action (*gegen j-n against s.o.*); *sich ~* exert o.s.; '**~end** *adj.* strenuous; trying (*für* to); '**2ung** *f* (-/-en) exertion, strain, effort.

'**Anstrich** *m* paint, colo(u)r; coat (-ing); *fig.*: tinge; air.

'**Ansturm** *m* assault; onset; ~ *auf* (*acc.*) rush for; † run on (*bank*). '**anstürmen** *v/i.* (*sep., -ge-, sein*) storm, rush.

'**Anteil** *m* share, portion; ~ *nehmen an* (*dat.*) take an interest in; sympathize with; **~nahme** ['~naːmə] *f* (-/*no pl.*) sympathy; interest; '**~schein** † *m* share-certificate.

Antenne [an'tɛnə] *f* (-/-n) aerial. **Antialkoholiker** [anti ʔalko'hoːlikər, '~] *m* (-s/-) teetotaller.

antik *adj.* [an'tiːk] antique.

Antilope *zo.* [anti'loːpə] *f* (-/-n) antelope.

Antipathie [antipa'tiː] *f* (-/-n) antipathy.

'**antippen** F *v/t.* (*sep., -ge-, h*) tap. **Antiquar** [anti'kvaːr] *m* (-s/-e) second-hand bookseller; **~iat** [~ar'jaːt] *n* (-[e]s/-e) second-hand bookshop; 2**isch** *adj. and adv.* [~'kvaːriʃ] second-hand.

Antiquitäten [antikvi'tɛːtən] *f/pl.* antiques *pl.*

'**Anti-Rakete** *f* anti-ballistic missile. **antiseptisch** ⚕ *adj.* [anti'zɛptiʃ] antiseptic.

Antlitz ['antlits] *n* (-es/⚕ -e) face, countenance.

Antrag ['antraːk] *m* (-[e]s/⸚e) offer, proposal; application, request; *parl.* motion; ~ *stellen auf* (*acc.*) make an application for; *parl.* put a motion for; '**~steller** *m* (-s/-) applicant; *parl.* mover; ⚖ petitioner.

'**an|treffen** *v/t.* (*irr. treffen, sep., -ge-, h*) meet with, find; '**~treiben** (*irr. treiben, sep., -ge-*) 1. *v/i.* (*sein*) drift ashore; 2. *v/t.* (h) drive (on); *fig.* impel; '**~treten** (*irr. treten, sep., -ge-*) 1. *v/t.* (h) enter upon (*office*); take up (*position*); set out on (*journey*); enter upon. take possession of (*inheritance*); 2. *v/i.* (*sein*) take one's place; ✕ fall in.

'**Antrieb** *m* motive, impulse; ⊕ drive, propulsion.

'**Antritt** *m* (-[e]s/⚕ -e) entrance (*into office*); taking up (*of position*); setting out (*on journey*); entering into possession (*of inheritance*).

'**antun** *v/t.* (*irr. tun, sep., -ge-, h*): *j-m et. ~* do s.th. to s.o.; *sich et. ~* lay hands on o.s.

'**Antwort** *f* (-/-en) answer, reply (*auf acc.* to); '**2en** (*ge-*) 1. *v/i.* answer (*j-m s.o.*), reply (*j-m* to s.o.; *both: auf acc.* to); 2. *v/t.* answer (*auf acc.* to), reply (to); '**~schein** *m* (international) reply coupon.

'**an|vertrauen** *v/t.* (*sep., no -ge-, h*): *j-m et. ~* (en)trust s.o. with s.th., entrust s.th. to s.o.; confide s.th. to s.o.; '**~wachsen** *v/i.* (*irr. wachsen, sep., -ge-, sein*) take root; *fig.* increase; ~ *an* (*acc.*) grow on to.

Anwalt ['anvalt] *m* (-[e]s/⸚e) lawyer; solicitor, *Am.* attorney; counsel; barrister, *Am.* counsel(l)or; *fig.* advocate.

'**Anwandlung** *f* fit; impulse.

'**Anwärter** *m* candidate, aspirant; expectant.

Anwartschaft ['anvartʃaft] *f* (-/-en) expectancy; candidacy; prospect (*auf acc.* of).

'**anweis|en** *v/t.* (*irr. weisen, sep., -ge-, h*) assign; instruct; direct; *s. angewiesen;* '**2ung** *f* assignment; instruction; direction; † : cheque, *Am.* check; draft; *s. Postanweisung.*

'**anwend|en** *v/t.* (*irr. wenden, sep., -ge-, h*) employ, use; apply (*auf acc.* to); *s. angewandt;* '**2ung** *f* application.

'**anwerben** *v/t.* (*irr. werben, sep., -ge-, h*) ✕ enlist, enrol(l); engage.

'**Anwesen** *n* estate; property.

'**anwesen|d** *adj.* present; '**2heit** *f* (-/*no pl.*) presence.

'**Anzahl** *f* (-/*no pl.*) number; quantity.

'anzahl|en v/t. (sep., -ge-, h) pay on account; pay a deposit; **'2ung** f (first) instal(l)ment; deposit.

'anzapfen v/t. (sep., -ge-, h) tap.

'Anzeichen n symptom; sign.

Anzeige ['antsaɪgə] f (-/-n) notice, announcement; ✝ advice; advertisement; ⚏ information; **'2n** v/t. (sep., -ge-, h) announce, notify; ✝ advise; advertise; indicate; ⊕ instrument: indicate, show; thermometer: read (degrees); j-n ∼ denounce s.o., inform against s.o.

'anziehen (irr. ziehen, sep., -ge-, h) 1. v/t. draw, pull; draw (rein); tighten (screw); put on (garment); dress; fig. attract; 2. v/i. draw; prices: rise; **'∼d** adj. attractive, interesting.

'Anziehung f attraction; **'∼skraft** f attractive power; attraction.

'Anzug m 1. (-[e]s/∼e) dress; suit; 2. (-[e]s/no pl.): im ∼ sein storm: be gathering; danger: be impending.

anzüglich adj. ['antsy:klɪç] personal; **'2keit** f (-/-en) personality.

'anzünden v/t. (sep., -ge-, h) light, kindle; strike (match); set (building) on fire.

apathisch adj. [a'pa:tɪʃ] apathetic.

Apfel ['apfəl] m (-s/∼) apple; **'∼mus** n apple-sauce; **'∼sine** [∼'zi:nə] f (-/-n) orange; **'∼wein** m cider.

Apostel [a'pɔstəl] m (-s/-) apostle.

Apostroph [apo'stro:f] m (-s/-e) apostrophe.

Apotheke [apo'te:kə] f (-/-n) chemist's shop, pharmacy, Am. drugstore; **∼r** m (-s/-) chemist, Am. druggist, pharmacist.

Apparat [apa'ra:t] m (-[e]s/-e) apparatus; device; teleph.: am ∼l speaking!; teleph.: am ∼ bleiben hold the line.

Appell [a'pɛl] m (-s/-e) ✕: roll-call; inspection; parade; fig. appeal (an acc. to); **2ieren** [∼'li:rən] v/i. (no -ge-, h) appeal (an acc. to).

Appetit [ape'ti:t] m (-[e]s/-e) appetite; **2lich** adj. appetizing, savo(u)ry, dainty.

Applaus [a'plaʊs] m (-es/**⚏** -e) applause.

Aprikose [apri'ko:zə] f (-/-n) apricot.

April [a'prɪl] m (-[s]/-e) April.

Aquarell [akva'rɛl] n (-s/-e) watercolo(u)r (painting), aquarelle.

Aquarium [a'kva:rium] n (-s/ Aquarien) aquarium.

Äquator [ɛ'kva:tɔr] m (-s/**⚏** -en) equator.

Ära ['ɛ:ra] f (-/**⚏** Ären) era.

Arab|er ['arabər] m (-s/-) Arab; **2isch** adj. [a'ra:bɪʃ] Arabian, Arab(ic).

Arbeit ['arbaɪt] f (-/-en) work; labo(u)r, toil; employment; job;

task; paper; workmanship; bei der ∼ at work; sich an die ∼ machen, an die ∼ gehen set to work; (keine) ∼ haben be in (out of) work; die ∼ niederlegen stop work, down tools; **'2en** (ge-, h) 1. v/i. work; labo(u)r, toil; 2. v/t. work; make.

'Arbeiter m (-s/-) worker; workman, labo(u)rer, hand; **'∼in** f (-/-nen) female worker; working woman, workwoman; **'∼klasse** f working class(es pl.); **'∼partei** f Labo(u)r Party; **'∼schaft** f (-/-en), **'∼stand** m working class(es pl.), labo(u)r.

'Arbeit|geber m (-s/-), **'∼geberin** f (-/-nen) employer; **'∼nehmer** m (-s/-), **'∼nehmerin** f (-/-nen) employee.

'arbeitsam adj. industrious.

'Arbeits|amt n labo(u)r exchange; **'∼anzug** m overall; **'∼beschaffung** f (-/-en) provision of work; **'∼bescheinigung** f certificate of employment; **'∼einkommen** n earned income; **'2fähig** adj. able to work; **'∼gericht** n labo(u)r or industrial court; **'∼kleidung** f working clothes pl.; **'∼kraft** f working power; worker, hand; Arbeitskräfte pl. a. labo(u)r; **'∼leistung** f efficiency; power (of engine); output (of factory); **'∼lohn** m wages pl., pay; **2los** adj. out of work, unemployed; **'∼lose** m (-n/-n): die ∼n pl. the unemployed pl.; **'∼losenunterstützung** f unemployment benefit; ∼ beziehen F be on the dole; **'∼losigkeit** f (-/no pl.) unemployment; **'∼markt** m labo(u)r market; **'∼minister** m Minister of Labour, Am. Secretary of Labor; **'∼nachweis(stelle** f) n employment registry office, Am. labor registry office; **'∼niederlegung** f (-/-en) strike, Am. F a. walkout; **'∼pause** f break, intermission; **'∼platz** m place of work; job; **'∼raum** m workroom; **2scheu** adj. work-shy; **'∼scheu** f aversion to work; **'∼schutzgesetz** n protective labo(u)r law; **'∼tag** m working day, workday; **2unfähig** adj. incapable of working; disabled; **'∼weise** f practice, method of working; **'∼willige** m (-n/-n) non-striker; **'∼zeit** f working time; working hours pl.; **'∼zeug** n tools pl.; **'∼zimmer** n workroom; study.

Archäo|loge [arçəo'lo:gə] m (-n/-n) arch(a)eologist; **'∼logie** [∼o'gi:] f (-/no pl.) arch(a)eology.

Arche ['arçə] f (-/-n) ark.

Architekt [arçi'tɛkt] m (-en/-en) architect; **∼ur** [∼'tu:r] f (-/-en) architecture.

Archiv [ar'çi:f] n (-s/-e) archives pl.; record office.

Areal [are'a:l] n (-s/-e) area.

Arena [a're:na] f (-/Arenen) arena; bullring; (circus-)ring.

arg adj. [ark] bad; wicked; gross. **Ärger** ['ergər] m (-s/no pl.) vexation, annoyance; anger; '2lich adj. vexed, F mad, angry (auf, über acc. at s.th., with s.o.); annoying, vexatious; '2n v/t. (ge-, h) annoy, vex, irritate, fret; bother; sich ~ feel angry or vexed (über acc. at, about s.th.; with s.o.); '~nis n (-ses/-se) scandal, offen|ce, Am. -se.

'Arg|list f (-/no pl.) cunning, craft (-iness); '2listig adj. crafty, cunning; '2los adj. guileless; artless, unsuspecting; '~wohn ['~vo:n] m (-[e]s/no pl.) suspicion; 2wöhnen ['~vø:nən] v/t. (ge-, h) suspect; '2wöhnisch adj. suspicious.

Arie ♪ ['a:rjə] f (-/-n) aria.

Aristokrat [aristo'kra:t] m (-en/-en), ~in f (-/-nen) aristocrat; 2ie [~kra-'ti:] f (-/-n) aristocracy.

Arkade [ar'ka:də] f (-/-n) arcade.

arm[1] adj. [arm] poor.

Arm[2] [~] m (-[e]s/-e) arm; branch (of river, etc.); F: j-n auf den ~ nehmen pull s.o.'s leg.

Armaturenbrett [arma'tu:rənbret] n instrument board, dash-board.

'Arm|band n bracelet; ~banduhr ['armbant?-] f wrist watch; '~bruch m fracture of the arm.

Armee [ar'me:] f (-/-n) army.

Ärmel ['ɛrməl] m (-s/-) sleeve; '~kanal m the (English) Channel.

'Armen|haus n alms-house, Brt. a. workhouse; '~pflege f poor relief; '~pfleger m guardian of the poor; welfare officer; '~unterstützung f poor relief.

ärmlich adj. ['ɛrmliç] s. armselig.

'armselig adj. poor; wretched; miserable; shabby; paltry.

Armut ['armu:t] f (-/no pl.) poverty.

Aroma [a'ro:ma] n (-s/Aromen, Aromata, -s) aroma, flavo(u)r; fragrance.

Arrest [a'rest] m (-es/-e) arrest; confinement; seizure (of goods); detention (of pupil, etc.); ~ bekommen be kept in.

Art [a:rt] f (-/-en) kind, sort; ♀, zo. species; manner, way; nature; manners pl.; breed, race (of animals); auf die(se) ~ in this way; '2en v/i. (ge-, sein): ~ nach take after.

Arterie anat. [ar'te:rjə] f (-/-n) artery.

artig adj. ['a:rtiç] good, well-behaved; civil, polite; '2keit f (-/-en) good behavio(u)r; politeness; civility, a. civilities pl.

Artikel [ar'ti:kəl] m (-s/-) article; commodity.

Artillerie [artilə'ri:] f (-/-n) artillery.

Artist [ar'tist] m (-en/-en), ~in f (-/-nen) circus performer.

Arznei [arts'nai] f (-/-en) medicine, F physic; ~kunde f (-/no pl.) pharmaceutics; ~mittel n medicine, drug.

Arzt [a:rtst] m (-es/"e) doctor, medical man; physician.

Ärztin ['ɛ:rtstin] f (-/-nen) woman or lady doctor.

ärztlich adj. ['ɛ:rtstliç] medical.

As [as] n (-ses/-se) ace.

Asche ['aʃə] f (-/-n) ash(es pl.); '~bahn f sports: cinder-track, mot. dirt-track; '~nbecher m ash-tray; ~nbrödel ['~nbrø:dəl] n (-s/no pl.), ~nputtel ['~nputəl] n 1. (-s/no pl.) Cinderella; 2. (-s/-) drudge.

Ascher|mittwoch m Ash Wednesday.

'asch|grau adj. ash-grey, ashy, Am. ash-gray.

äsen hunt. ['ɛ:zən] v/i. (ge-, h) graze, browse.

Asiat [az'ja:t] m (-en/-en), ~in f (-/-nen) Asiatic, Asian; 2isch adj. Asiatic, Asian.

Asket [as'ke:t] m (-en/-en) ascetic.

Asphalt [as'falt] m (-[e]s/-e) asphalt; 2ieren [~'ti:rən] v/t. (no -ge-, h) asphalt.

aß [a:s] pret. of essen.

Assistent [asis'tent] m (-en/-en), ~in f (-/-nen) assistant.

Ast [ast] m (-es/"e) branch, bough; knot (in timber); '2loch n knot-hole.

Astro|naut [astro'naut] m (-en/-en) astronaut; ~nom [~'no:m] m (-en/-en) astronomer.

Asyl [a'zy:l] n (-s/-e) asylum; fig. sanctuary.

Atelier [atə'lje:] n (-s/-s) studio.

Atem ['a:təm] m (-s/no pl.) breath; außer ~ out of breath; '2los adj. breathless; '~not f difficulty in breathing; '~pause f breathing-space; '~zug m breath, respiration.

Äther ['ɛ:tər] m 1. (-s/no pl.) the ether; 2. ♠ (-s/-) ether; 2isch adj. [ɛ:'te:riʃ] ethereal, etheric.

Athlet [at'le:t] m (-en/-en), ~in f (-/-nen) athlete; ~ik f (-/no pl.) athletics mst sg.; 2isch adj. athletic.

atlantisch adj. [at'lantiʃ] Atlantic.

Atlas ['atlas] m 1. geogr. (-/no pl.) Atlas; 2. (-, -ses/-se, Atlanten) maps: atlas; 3. (-, -ses/-se) textiles: satin.

atmen ['a:tmən] v/i. and v/t. (ge-, h) breathe.

Atmosphär|e [atmo'sfɛ:rə] f (-/-n) atmosphere; 2isch adj. atmospheric.

'Atmung f (-/-en) breathing, respiration.

Atom [a'to:m] n (-s/-e) atom; 2ar adj. [ato'ma:r] atomic; ~bombe f atomic bomb, atom-bomb, A-bomb; ~energie f atomic or nuclear energy; ~forschung f atomic or nuclear research; ~kern m atomic nucleus; ~kraftwerk n nuclear power station; **∼meiler** m atomic pile, nuclear reactor; **∼physiker** m atomic physicist; **∼reaktor** m nuclear reactor, atomic pile; **∼versuch** m atomic test; **∼waffe** f atomic or nuclear weapon; **∼wissenschaftler** m atomic scientist; **∼zeitalter** n atomic age

Attent|at [atɛn'taːt] n (-[e]s/-e) (attempted) assassination; fig. outrage; **∼äter** [∼ɛːtər] m (-s/-) assailant, assassin.

Attest [a'tɛst] n (-es/-e) certificate; **2ieren** [∼'tiːrən] v/t. (no -ge-, h) attest, certify.

Attraktion [atrak'tsjoːn] f (-/-en) attraction.

Attrappe [a'trapə] f (-/-n) dummy.

Attribut [atri'buːt] n (-[e]s/-e) attribute; gr. attributive

ätz|en ['ɛtsən] v/t. (ge-, h) corrode; ⚕ cauterize; etch (metal plate); **∼end** adj. corrosive; caustic (a. fig.); **2ung** f (-/-en) corrosion; ⚕ cauterization; etching.

au int. [au] oh!; ouch!

auch cj. [aux] also, too, likewise; even; ∼ nicht neither, nor; wo ∼ (immer) wher(eso)ever; ist es ∼ wahr? is it really true?

Audienz [audi'ɛnts] f (-/-en) audience, hearing.

auf [auf] 1. prp. (dat.) (up)on; in; at; of; by; ∼ dem Tisch (up)on the table; ∼ dem Markt in the market; ∼ der Universität at the university; ∼ e-m Ball at a ball; 2. prp. (acc.) on; in; at; to; towards (a. ∼ ... zu); up; ∼ deutsch in German; ∼ e-e Entfernung von at a range of; ∼ die Post etc. gehen go to the post-office, etc.; ∼ ein Pfund gehen 20 Schilling 20 shillings go to a pound; es geht ∼ neun it is getting on to nine; ∼ ... hin on the strength of; 3. adv. up(wards); ∼ und ab gehen walk up and down or to and fro; 4. cj.: ∼ daß (in order) that; ∼ daß nicht that not, lest; 5. int.: ∼! up!

auf|arbeiten ['auf⁹-] v/t. (sep., -ge-, h) work off (arrears of work); furbish up; ℉ do up (garments); **∼atmen** fig. ['auf⁹-] v/i. (sep., -ge-, h) breathe again.

Aufbau m (-[e]s/no pl.) building up; construction (of play, etc.); ℉ esp. Am. setup (of organization); mot. body (of car, etc.); **2en** v/t. (sep., -ge-, h) erect, build up; construct.

auf|bauschen v/t. (sep., -ge-, h) puff out; fig. exaggerate; **∼beißen** v/t. (irr. beißen, sep., -ge-, h) crack; **∼bekommen** v/t. (irr. kommen, sep., no -ge-, h) get open (door); be given (a task); **∼bessern** v/t. (sep., -ge-, h) raise (salary); **∼bewahren** v/t. (sep., no -ge-, h) keep; preserve;

∼bieten v/t. (irr. bieten, sep., -ge-, h) summon; exert; ✕ raise; **∼binden** v/t. (irr. binden, sep., -ge-, h) untie; **∼bleiben** v/i. (irr. bleiben, sep., -ge-, sein) sit up; door, etc.: remain open; **∼blenden** (sep., -ge-, h) 1. mot. v/i. turn up the headlights; 2. v/t. fade in (scene); **∼blicken** v/i. (sep., -ge-, h) look up; raise one's eyes; **∼blitzen** v/i. (sep., -ge-, h, sein) flash (up); **∼blühen** v/i. (sep., -ge-, sein) bloom; flourish.

aufbrausen fig. v/i. (sep., -ge-, sein) fly into a passion; **∼d** adj. hot-tempered.

auf|brechen (irr. brechen, sep., -ge-) 1. v/t. (h) break open; force open; 2. v/i. (sein) burst open; set out (nach for); **∼bringen** v/t. (irr. bringen, sep., -ge-, h) raise (money, troops); capture (ship); rouse or irritate s.o.

Aufbruch m departure, start.

auf|bügeln v/t. (sep., -ge-, h) iron; **∼bürden** v/t. (sep., -ge-, h): j-m et. ∼ impose s.th. on s.o.; **∼decken** v/t. (sep., -ge-, h) uncover; spread (cloth); fig. disclose; **∼drängen** v/t. (sep., -ge-, h) force, obtrude (j-m [up]on s.o.); **∼drehen** v/t. (sep., -ge-, h) turn on (gas, etc.).

aufdringlich adj. obtrusive.

Aufdruck m (-[e]s/-e) imprint; surcharge.

aufdrücken v/t. (sep., -ge-, h) impress.

aufeinander adv. [auf⁹ar'nandər] one after or upon another; **2folge** f succession; **∼folgend** adj. successive.

Aufenthalt ['aufɛnthalt] m (-[e]s/-e) stay; residence; delay; ▓ stop; **∼genehmigung** f residence permit. **auferlegen** ['auf⁹ɛrle:gən] v/t. (sep., no -ge-, h) impose (j-m on s.o.).

aufersteh|en ['auf⁹ɛrʃteːən] v/i. (irr. stehen, sep., no -ge-, sein) rise (from the dead); **2ung** f (-/-en) resurrection.

auf|essen ['auf⁹-] v/t. (irr. essen, sep., -ge-, h) eat up; **∼fahren** v/i. (irr. fahren, sep., -ge-, sein) ascend; start up; fig. fly out; ⚓ run aground; mot. drive or run (auf acc. against, into).

Auffahrt f ascent; driving up; approach, drive, Am. driveway; **∼srampe** f ramp.

auf|fallen v/i. (irr. fallen, sep., -ge-, sein) be conspicuous; j-m ∼ strike s.o.; **∼fallend** adj., **∼fällig** adj. striking; conspicuous; flashy. **auffangen** v/t. (irr. fangen, sep., -ge-, h) catch (up); parry (thrust).

auffass|en v/t. (sep., -ge-, h) conceive; comprehend; interpret; **2ung** f conception; interpretation; grasp.

'**auffinden** v/t. (irr. finden, sep., -ge-, h) find, trace, discover, locate.
'**aufforder|n** v/t. (sep., -ge-, h) ask, invite; call (up)on; esp. ⚖ summon; '**2ung** f invitation; esp. ⚖ summons.
'**auffrischen** (sep., -ge-) 1. v/t. (h) freshen up, touch up; brush up (knowledge); revive; 2. v/i. (sein) wind: freshen.
'**aufführ|en** v/t. (sep., -ge-, h) thea. represent, perform, act; enumerate; enter (in list); einzeln ~ specify, Am. itemize; sich ~ behave; '**2ung** f thea. performance; enumeration; entry; specification; conduct.
'**Aufgabe** f task; problem; school: homework; posting, Am. mailing (of letter); booking (of luggage), Am. checking (of baggage); resignation (from office); abandonment; giving up (business); es sich zur ~ machen make it one's business.
'**Aufgang** m ascent; ast. rising; staircase.
'**aufgeben** (irr. geben, sep., -ge-, h) 1. v/t. give up, abandon; resign from (office); insert (advertisement); post, Am. mail (letter); book (luggage), Am. check (baggage); hand in, send (telegram); ✝ give (order); set, Am. assign (homework); set (riddle); 2. v/i. give up or in.
'**Aufgebot** n public notice; ✕ levy; fig. array; banns pl. (of marriage).
'**aufgehen** v/i. (irr. gehen, sep., -ge-, sein) open; ⚤ leave no remainder; sewing: come apart; paste, star, curtain: rise; seed: come up; ~ in (dat.) be merged in; fig. be devoted to (work); in Flammen ~ go up in flames.
aufgeklärt adj. ['aufgəkle:rt] enlightened; '**2heit** f (-/no pl.) enlightenment.
'**Aufgeld** ✝ n agio, premium.
aufge|legt adj. ['aufgəle:kt] disposed (zu for); in the mood (zu inf. for ger., to inf.); gut (schlecht) ~ in a good (bad) humo(u)r; '**~schlossen** fig. adj. open-minded; '**~weckt** fig. adj. ['~vekt] bright.
'**auf|gießen** v/t. (irr. gießen, sep., -ge-, h) pour (on); make (tea); '**~greifen** v/t. (irr. greifen, sep., -ge-, h) snatch up, fig. take up;
'**Aufguß** m infusion. [seize.]
'**auf|haben** (irr. haben, sep., -ge-, h) 1. v/t. have on (hat); have open (door); have to do (task); 2. F v/i.: das Geschäft hat auf the shop is open; '**~haken** v/t. (sep., -ge-, h) unhook; '**~halten** v/t. (irr. halten, sep.,-ge-, h) keep open; stop, detain, delay; hold up (traffic); sich ~ stay; sich ~ bei dwell on; sich ~ mit spend one's time on; '**~hängen** v/t. (irr. hängen, sep., -ge-, h) hang (up); ⊕ suspend.

'**aufheb|en** v/t. (irr. heben, sep., -ge-, h) lift (up), raise; pick up; raise (siege); keep, preserve; cancel, annul, abolish; break off (engagement); break up (meeting); sich ~ neutralize; die Tafel ~ rise from the table; gut aufgehoben sein be well looked after; viel Aufhebens machen make a fuss (von about); '**2ung** f (-/-en) raising; abolition; annulment; breaking up.
'**auf|heitern** v/t. (sep., -ge-, h) cheer up; sich ~ weather: clear up; face: brighten; '**~hellen** v/t. and v/refl. (sep., -ge-, h) brighten.
'**aufhetz|en** v/t. (sep., -ge-, h) incite, instigate s.o.; '**2ung** f (-/-en) instigation, incitement.
'**auf|holen** v/t. (sep., -ge-, h) 1. v/t. make up (for); ⚓ haul up; 2. v/i. gain (gegen on); pull up (to); '**~hören** v/i. (sep., -ge-, h) cease, stop; Am. quit (all: zu tun doing); F: da hört (sich) doch alles auf! that's the limit!, Am. that beats everything!; '**~kaufen** v/t. (sep., -ge-, h) buy up.
'**aufklär|en** v/t. (sep., -ge-, h) clear up; enlighten (über acc. on); ✕ reconnoit|re, Am. -er; sich ~ clear up; '**2ung** f enlightenment; ✕ reconnaissance.
'**auf|kleben** v/t. (sep., -ge-, h) paste on, stick on, affix on; '**~klinken** v/t. (sep., -ge-, h) unlatch; '**~knöpfen** v/t. (sep., -ge-, h) unbutton.
'**aufkommen** 1. v/i. (irr. kommen, sep., -ge-, sein) rise; recover (from illness); come up; come into fashion or use; thought: arise; ~ für st. answer for s.th.; ~ gegen prevail against s.o.; 2. 2 n (-s/no pl.) rise; recovery.
auf|krempeln ['aufkrempəln] v/t. (sep., -ge-, h) turn up, roll up; tuck up; '**~lachen** v/i. (sep., -ge-, h) burst out laughing; '**~laden** v/t. (irr. laden, sep., -ge-, h) load; ⚡ charge.
'**Auflage** f edition (of book); circulation (of newspaper); ⊕ support.
'**auf|lassen** v/t. (irr. lassen, sep., -ge-, h) F leave open (door, etc.); keep on (hat); ⚖ cede; '**~lauern** v/i. (sep., -ge-, h): j-m ~ lie in wait for s.o.
'**Auflauf** m concourse; riot; dish: soufflé; '**2en** v/i. (irr. laufen, sep., -ge-, sein) interest: accrue; ⚓ run aground.
'**auflegen** (sep., -ge-, h) 1. v/t. put on, lay on; apply (auf acc. to); print, publish (book); teleph. hang up; 2. teleph. v/i. ring off.
'**auflehn|en** v/t. (sep., -ge-, h) lean (on); sich ~ lean (on); fig. rebel, revolt (gegen against); '**2ung** f (-/-en) rebellion.

'**auf|lesen** v/t. (irr. lesen, sep., -ge-, h) gather, pick up; '**~leuchten** v/i. (sep., -ge-, h) flash (up); '**~liegen** v/i. (irr. liegen, sep., -ge-, h) lie (auf dat. on).

'**auflös|bar** adj. (dis)soluble; '**~en** v/t. (sep., -ge-, h) undo (knot); break up (meeting); dissolve (salt, etc.; marriage, business, Parliament, etc.); solve (Ä, riddle); disintegrate; fig. aufgelöst upset; '**2ung** f (dis)solution; disintegration.

'**aufmach|en** v/t. (sep., -ge-, h) open; undo (dress, parcel); put up (umbrella); make up, get up; sich ~ wind: rise; set out (nach acc. for); make for; die Tür ~ answer the door; '**2ung** f (-/-en) make-up, get-up.

'**aufmarschieren** v/i. (sep., no -ge-, sein) form into line; ~ lassen ⚔ deploy.

'**aufmerksam** adj. attentive (gegen to); j-n ~ machen auf (acc.) call s.o.'s attention to; '**2keit** f (-/-en) attention; token.

'**aufmuntern** v/t. (sep., -ge-, h) rouse; encourage; cheer up.

Aufnahme ['aufnɑːmə] f (-/-n) taking up (of work); reception; admission; phot.: taking; photograph, shot; shooting (of a film); '**2fähig** adj. capable of absorbing; mind: receptive (für of); '**~gebühr** f admission fee; '**~gerät** n phot. camera; recorder; '**~prüfung** f entrance examination.

'**aufnehmen** v/t. (irr. nehmen, sep., -ge-, h) take up; pick up; take s.o. in; take down (dictation, etc.); take s.th. in (mentally); receive (guests); admit; raise, borrow (money); draw up, record; shoot (film); phot. take (picture); gut (übel) ~ take well (ill); es ~ mit be a match for.

aufopfer|n ['auf²-] v/t. (sep., -ge-, h) sacrifice; '**2ung** f sacrifice.

'**auf|passen** v/i. (sep., -ge-, h) attend (auf acc. to); watch; at school: be attentive; look out; ~ auf (acc.) take care of; '**~platzen** v/i. (sep., -ge-, sein) burst (open); '**~polieren** v/t. (sep., no -ge-, h) polish up; '**~prallen** v/i. (sep., -ge-, sein): auf den Boden ~ strike the ground; '**~pumpen** v/t. (sep., -ge-, h) blow up (tyre, etc.); '**~raffen** v/t. (sep., -ge-, h) snatch up; sich ~ rouse o.s. (zu for); muster up one's energy; '**~räumen** (sep., -ge-, h) 1. v/t. put in order; tidy (up), Am. straighten up; clear away; 2. v/i. tidy up; ~ mit do away with.

'**aufrecht** adj. and adv. upright (a. fig.), erect; '**~erhalten** v/t. (irr. halten, sep., no -ge-, h) maintain, uphold; '**2erhaltung** f (-/no pl.) maintenance.

'**aufregen** v/t. (sep., -ge-, h) stir up,

excite; sich ~ get excited or upset (über acc. about); aufgeregt excited; upset; '**2ung** f excitement, agitation.

'**auf|reiben** v/t. (irr. reiben, sep., -ge-, h) chafe (skin, etc.); fig.: destroy; exhaust, wear s.o. out; '**~reißen** (irr. reißen, sep., -ge-) 1. v/t. (h) rip or tear up or open; fling open (door); open (eyes) wide; 2. v/i. (sein) split open, burst.

'**aufreiz|en** v/t. (sep., -ge-, h) incite, stir up; '**~end** adj. provocative; '**2ung** f instigation.

'**aufrichten** v/t. (sep., -ge-, h) set up, erect; sich ~ stand up; straighten; sit up (in bed).

'**aufrichtig** adj. sincere, candid; '**2keit** f sincerity, cando(u)r.

'**aufriegeln** v/t. (sep., -ge-, h) unbolt.

'**Aufriß** ⚠ m elevation.

'**aufrollen** v/t. and v/refl. (sep., -ge-, h) roll up; unroll.

'**Aufruf** m call, summons; '**2en** v/t. (irr. rufen, sep., -ge-, h) call up; call on s.o.

Aufruhr ['aufruːr] m (-[e]s/-e) uproar, tumult; riot, rebellion.

'**aufrühr|en** v/t. (sep., -ge-, h) stir up; revive; fig. rake up; '**2er** m (-s/-) rebel; '**~erisch** adj. rebellious.

'**Aufrüstung** ⚔ f (re)armament.

'**auf|rütteln** v/t. (sep., -ge-, h) shake up; rouse; '**~sagen** v/t. (sep., -ge-, h) say, repeat; recite.

aufsässig adj. ['aufzɛsiç] rebellious.

'**Aufsatz** m essay; composition; ⊕ top.

'**auf|saugen** v/t. (sep., -ge-, h) suck up; 🜨 absorb; '**~scheuchen** v/t. (sep., -ge-, h) scare (away); disturb; rouse; '**~scheuern** v/t. (sep., -ge-, h) scour; 🜨 chafe; '**~schichten** v/t. (sep., -ge-, h) pile up; '**~schieben** v/t. (irr. schieben, sep., -ge-, h) slide open; fig.: put off; defer, postpone; adjourn.

'**Aufschlag** m striking; impact; additional or extra charge; facing (on coat), lapel (of coat); cuff (on sleeve); turn-up (on trousers); tennis: service; '**2en** ['~gən] (irr. schlagen, sep., -ge-) 1. v/t. (h) open; turn up (sleeve, etc.); take up (abode); pitch (tent); raise (prices); cut (one's knee) open; 2. v/i. (sein) strike, hit; ✝ rise, go up (in price); tennis: serve.

'**auf|schließen** v/t. (irr. schließen, sep., -ge-, h) unlock, open; '**~schlitzen** v/t. (sep., -ge-, h) slit or rip open.

'**Aufschluß** fig. m information.

'**auf|schnallen** v/t. (sep., -ge-, h) unbuckle; '**~schnappen** (sep., -ge-) 1. v/t. (h) snatch; fig. pick up; 2. v/i. (sein) snap open; '**~schnei-**

den (*irr.* schneiden, *sep.*, -ge-, *h*)
1. *v/t.* cut open; cut up (*meat*);
2. *fig. v/i.* brag, boast.

'**Aufschnitt** *m* (slices *pl.* of) cold
meat, *Am.* cold cuts *pl.*

'**auf|schnüren** *v/t.* (*sep.*, -ge-, *h*)
untie; unlace; '**~schrauben** *v/t.*
(*sep.*, -ge-, *h*) screw (*auf acc.* on);
unscrew; '**~schrecken** (*sep.*, -ge-)
1. *v/t.* (*h*) startle; 2. *v/i.* (*irr.*
schrecken, sein) start (up).

'**Aufschrei** *m* shriek, scream; *fig.*
outcry.

'**auf|schreiben** *v/t.* (*irr.* schreiben,
sep., -ge-, *h*) write down; '**~**
schreien *v/i.* (*irr.* schreien, *sep.*,
-ge-, *h*) cry out, scream.

'**Aufschrift** *f* inscription; address,
direction (*on letter*); label.

'**Aufschub** *m* deferment; delay;
adjournment; respite.

'**auf|schürfen** *v/t.* (*sep.*, -ge-, *h*)
graze (*skin*); '**~schwingen** *v/refl.*
(*irr.* schwingen, *sep.*, -ge-, *h*) soar,
rise; *sich zu et.* **~** bring o.s. to do
s.th.

'**Aufschwung** *m fig.* rise, *Am.* up-
swing; ✝ boom.

'**aufsehen** 1. *v/i.* (*irr.* sehen, *sep.*,
-ge-, *h*) look up; 2. **2** *n* (-*s/no pl.*)
sensation; **~ erregen** cause a sensation; '**~erregend** *adj.* sensational.

'**Aufseher** *m* overseer; inspector.

'**aufsetzen** (*sep.*, -ge-, *h*) 1. *v/t.* set
up; put on (*hat, countenance*); draw
up (*document*); *sich* **~** sit up; 2. ✕
v/i. touch down.

'**Aufsicht** *f* (-*/*-en) inspection, supervision; *store:* shopwalker, *Am.* floor-
walker; '**~behörde** *f* board of control; '**~rat** *m* board of directors.

'**auf|sitzen** *v/i.* (*irr.* sitzen, *sep.*,
-ge-, *h*) *rider:* mount; '**~spannen**
v/t. (*sep.*, -ge-, *h*) stretch; put up
(*umbrella*); spread (*sails*); '**~sparen**
v/t. (*sep.*, -ge-, *h*) save; *fig.* reserve;
'**~speichern** *v/t.* (*sep.*, -ge-, *h*)
store up; '**~sperren** *v/t.* (*sep.*, -ge-,
h) open wide; '**~spielen** (*sep.*, -ge-,
h) 1. *v/t.* and *v/i.* strike up; 2. *v/refl.*
show off; *sich* **~ als** set up for; '**~**
spießen *v/t.* (*sep.*, -ge-, *h*) pierce;
with horns: gore; run through,
spear; '**~springen** *v/i.* (*irr.* springen, *sep.*, -ge-, sein) jump up; *door:*
fly open; crack; *skin:* chap; '**~spü-**
ren *v/t.* (*sep.*, -ge-, *h*) hunt up;
track down; '**~stacheln** *fig. v/t.*
(*sep.*, -ge-, *h*) goad; incite, instigate;
'**~stampfen** *v/i.* (*sep.*, -ge-, *h*)
stamp (one's foot).

'**Aufstand** *m* insurrection; rebellion;
uprising, revolt.

aufständisch *adj.* [ˈaʊfʃtɛndɪʃ] rebellious; '**2e** *m* (-*n*/-*n*) insurgent,
rebel.

'**auf|stapeln** *v/t.* (*sep.*, -ge-, *h*) pile
up; ✝ store (up); '**~stechen** *v/t.*
(*irr.* stechen, *sep.*, -ge-, *h*) puncture,

prick open; ✝ lance; '**~stecken** *v/t.*
(*sep.*, -ge-, *h*) pin up; put up (*hair*);
'**~stehen** *v/i.* (*irr.* stehen, *sep.*, -ge-)
1. (sein) stand up; rise, get up; revolt; 2. F (*h*) stand open; '**~steigen**
v/i. (*irr.* steigen, *sep.*, -ge-, sein) rise,
ascend; ✕ take off; *rider:* mount.

'**aufstell|en** *v/t.* (*sep.*, -ge-, *h*) set
up, put up; ✕ draw up; post (*sen-
tries*); make (*assertion*); set (*example*), erect (*column*); set (*trap*);
nominate (*candidate*); draw up
(*bill*); lay down (*rule*); make out
(*list*); set up, establish (*record*);
'**2ung** *f* putting up; drawing up;
erection; nomination; ✝ statement;
list.

'**Aufstieg** [ˈaʊfʃtiːk] *m* (-[e]s/-e)
ascent, *Am. a.* ascension; *fig.* rise.

'**auf|stöbern** *fig. v/t.* (*sep.*, -ge-, *h*)
hunt up; '**~stoßen** (*irr.* stoßen, *sep.*,
-ge-) 1. *v/t.* (*h*) push open; **~ auf**
(*acc.*) knock against; 2. *v/i.* (*h*, sein)
of food: rise, repeat; belch; '**~strei-**
chen *v/t* (*irr.* streichen, *sep.*, -ge-,
h) spread (*butter*).

'**Aufstrich** *m* spread (*for bread*).

'**auf|stützen** *v/t.* (*sep.*, -ge-, *h*) prop
up, support *s.th.*; *sich* **~ auf** (*acc.*)
lean on; '**~suchen** *v/t.* (*sep.*, -ge-, *h*)
visit (*places*); go to see *s.o.*, look
s.o. up.

'**Auftakt** *m* ♪ upbeat; *fig.* prelude,
preliminaries *pl.*

'**auf|tauchen** *v/i.* (*sep.*, -ge-, sein)
emerge, appear, turn up; '**~tauen**
(*sep.*, -ge-) 1. *v/t.* (*h*) thaw; 2. *v/i.*
(sein) thaw (*a. fig.*); '**~teilen** *v/t.*
(*sep.*, -ge-, *h*) divide (up), share.

'**Auftrag** [ˈaʊftraːk] *m* (-[e]s/**~**e)
commission; instruction; mission;
x mandate; ✝ order; **2en** [ˈ**~**ɡən]
v/t. (*irr.* tragen, *sep.*, -ge-, *h*) serve
(up) (*meal*); lay on (*paint*); wear
out (*dress*); *j-m et.* **~** charge *s.o.*
with *s.th.*, '**~geber** [ˈ**~**keːbər] *m* (-*s*/-)
employer; customer; principal; '**~**
erteilung [ˈ**~**ʔɛʀtaɪluŋ] *f* (-/-en)
placing of an order.

'**auf|treffen** *v/i.* (*irr.* treffen, *sep.*,
-ge-, sein) strike, hit; '**~treiben** *v/t.*
(*irr.* treiben, *sep.*, -ge-, *h*) hunt up;
raise (*money*); '**~trennen** *v/t.* (*sep.*,
-ge-, *h*) rip; unstitch (*seam*).

'**auftreten** 1. *v/i.* (*irr.* treten, *sep.*,
-ge-, sein) tread; *thea., witness, etc.:*
appear (*als a.*); behave, act; *difficulties:* arise; 2. **2** *n* (-*s/no pl.*) appearance; occurrence (*of events*);
behavio(u)r.

'**Auftrieb** *m phys. and fig.* buoyancy; ✕ lift; *fig.* impetus.

'**Auftritt** *m thea.* scene (*a. fig.*);
appearance (*of actor*).

'**auf|trumpfen** *fig. v/i.* (*sep.*, -ge-, *h*)
put one's foot down; '**~tun** *v/t.* (*irr.*
tun, *sep.*, -ge-, *h*) open; *sich* **~** open;
chasm: yawn; *society:* form; '**~tür-**
men *v/t.* (*sep.*, -ge-, *h*) pile *or* heap

up; *sich ~* tower up; pile up; *difficulties:* accumulate; **'~wachen** *v/i.* (*sep.,* -ge-, sein) awake, wake up; **'~wachsen** *v/i.* (irr. *wachsen, sep.,* -ge-, sein) grow up.

'Aufwallung *f* ebullition, surge.

Aufwand ['aufvant] *m* (-[e]s/no pl.) expense, expenditure (*an dat.* of); pomp; splendid *or* great display (*of words, etc.*).

'aufwärmen *v/t.* (*sep.,* -ge-, h) warm up.

'Aufwarte|frau *f* charwoman, *Am. a.* cleaning woman; **'2n** *v/i.* (*sep.,* -ge-, h) wait (up)on *s.o.,* attend on *s.o.;* wait (at table).

aufwärts *adv.* ['aufverts] upward(s).

'Aufwartung *f* attendance; visit; *j-m* -s-e ~ *machen* pay one's respects to s.o., call on s.o.

'aufwasch|en *v/t.* (irr. *waschen, sep.,* -ge-, h) wash up; **'2wasser** *n* dish-water.

'auf|wecken *v/t.* (*sep.,* -ge-, h) awake(n), wake (up); **'~weichen** (*sep.,* -ge-) 1. *v/t.* (h) soften; soak; 2. *v/i.* (sein) soften, become soft; **'~weisen** *v/t.* (irr. *weisen, sep.,* -ge-, h) show, exhibit; produce; **'~wenden** *v/t.* ([irr. *wenden*] *sep.,* -ge-, h) spend; *Mühe ~* take pains; **'~werfen** *v/t.* (irr. *werfen, sep.,* -ge-, h) raise (*a. question*).

'aufwert|en *v/t.* (*sep.,* -ge-, h) revalorize; revalue; **'2ung** *f* revalorization; revaluation.

'aufwickeln *v/t. and v/refl.* (*sep.,* -ge-, h) wind up, roll up.

aufwiegel|n ['aufvi:gəln] *v/t.* (*sep.,* -ge-, h) stir up, incite, instigate; **'2ung** *f* (-/-en) instigation.

'aufwiegen *fig. v/t.* (irr. *wiegen, sep.,* -ge-, h) make up for.

Aufwiegler ['aufvi:glər] *m* (-s/-) agitator; instigator.

'aufwirbeln (*sep.,* -ge-) 1. *v/t.* (h) whirl up; raise (*dust*); *fig. viel Staub ~* create a sensation; 2. *v/i.* (sein) whirl up.

'aufwisch|en *v/t.* (*sep.,* -ge-, h) wipe up; **'2lappen** *m* floor-cloth.

'aufwühlen *v/t.* (*sep.,* -ge-, h) turn up; *fig.* stir.

'aufzähl|en *v/t.* (*sep.,* -ge-, h) count up; *fig.* enumerate, *Am. a.* call off; specify, *Am.* itemize; **'2ung** *f* (-/-en) enumeration; specification.

'auf|zäumen *v/t.* (*sep.,* -ge-, h) bridle; **'~zehren** *v/t.* (*sep.,* -ge-, h) consume.

'aufzeichn|en *v/t.* (*sep.,* -ge-, h) draw; note down; record; **'2ung** *f* note; record.

'auf|zeigen *v/t.* (*sep.,* -ge-, h) show; demonstrate; point out (*mistakes, etc.*); disclose; **'~ziehen** (irr. *ziehen, sep.,* -ge-) 1. *v/t.* (h) draw *or* pull up; (pull) open; hoist (*flag*); bring up (*child*); mount (*picture*);

wind (up) (*clock, etc.*); *j-n ~* tease s.o., pull s.o.'s leg; *Saiten auf e-e Violine ~* string a violin; 2. *v/i.* (sein) ⚔ draw up; *storm:* approach.

'Aufzucht *f* rearing, breeding.

'Aufzug *m* ⊕ hoist; lift, *Am.* elevator; *thea.* act; attire; show.

'aufzwingen *v/t.* (irr. *zwingen, sep.,* -ge-, h): *j-m et. ~* force a.th. upon s.o.

Augapfel ['auk⁹-] *m* eyeball.

Auge ['augə] *n* (-s/-n) eye; sight; ⚘ bud; *in meinen ~n* in my view; *im ~ behalten* keep an eye on; keep in mind; *aus den ~n verlieren* lose sight of; *ein ~ zudrücken* turn a blind eye (*bei* to); *ins ~ fallen* strike the eye; *große ~n machen* open one's eyes wide; *unter vier ~n* face to face, privately; *kein ~ zutun* not to get a wink of sleep.

'Augen|arzt *m* oculist, eye-doctor; **'~blick** *m* moment, instant; **'2blicklich** 1. *adj.* instantaneous; momentary; present; 2. *adv.* instant(aneous)ly; at present; **'~braue** *f* eyebrow; **'~entzündung** ⚕ *f* inflammation of the eye; **'~heilkunde** *f* ophthalmology; **'~klinik** *f* ophthalmic hospital; **'~leiden** ⚕ *n* eye-complaint; **'~lid** *n* eyelid; **'~maß** *n*: *ein gutes ~* a sure eye; *nach dem ~* by eye; **'~merk** *n* (-[e]s/no pl.): *sein ~ richten auf* (*acc.*) turn one's attention to; have *s.th.* in view; **'~schein** *m* appearance; *in ~ nehmen* examine, view, inspect; **'2scheinlich** *adj.* evident; **'~wasser** *n* eyewash, eye-lotion; **'~wimper** *f* eyelash; **'~zeuge** *m* eyewitness.

August [au'gust] *m* (-[e]s, - /-e) August.

Auktion [auk'tsjo:n] *f* (-/-en) auction; **~ator** [...o'na:tɔr] *m* (-s/-en) auctioneer.

Aula ['aula] *f* (-/*Aulen,* -s) (assembly) hall, *Am.* auditorium.

aus [aus] 1. *prp.* (*dat.*) out of; from; of; by; for; in; *~ Achtung* out of respect; *~ London kommen* come from London; *~ diesem Grunde* for this reason; *~ Ihrem Brief ersehe ich* I see from your letter; 2. *adv.* out; over; *die Schule ist ~* school is over; F: *von mir ~* for all I care; *auf et. ~ sein* be keen on s.th.; *es ist ~ mit ihm* it is all over with him; *das Spiel ist ~!* the game is up!; *er weiß weder ein noch ~* he is at his wit's end; *on instruments, etc.:* an — *~* on — off.

ausarbeit|en ['aus⁹-] *v/t.* (*sep.,* -ge-, h) work out; elaborate; **'2ung** *f* (-/-en) working-out; elaboration; composition.

aus|arten ['aus⁹-] *v/i.* (*sep.,* -ge-, sein) degenerate; get out of hand; **~atmen** ['aus⁹-] (*sep.,* -ge-, h)

1. v/i. breathe out; **2.** v/t. breathe out; exhale (vapour, etc.); '~bag-gern v/t. (sep., -ge-, h) dredge (river, etc.); excavate (ground).

'Ausbau m (-[e]s/-ten) extension; completion; development; '2en v/t. (sep., -ge-, h) develop; extend; finish, complete; ⊕ dismantle (engine).

'ausbedingen v/t. (irr. bedingen, sep., no -ge-, h) stipulate.

'ausbesser|n v/t. (sep., -ge-, h) mend, repair, Am. F a. fix; '2ung f repair, mending.

'Ausbeut|e f (-/~-n) gain, profit; yield; ⚒ output; '2en v/t. (sep., -ge-, h) exploit; sweat (workers); '~ung f (-/-en) exploitation.

'ausbild|en v/t. (sep., -ge-, h) form, develop; train; instruct, educate; ⚔ drill; '2ung f development; training; instruction; education; ⚔ drill.

'ausbitten v/t. (irr. bitten, sep., -ge-, h): sich et. ~ request s.th.; insist on s.th.

'ausbleiben **1.** v/i. (irr. bleiben, sep., -ge-, sein) stay away, fail to appear; **2.** 2 n (-s/no pl.) non-arrival, non-appearance; absence.

'Ausblick m outlook (auf acc. over, on), view (of), prospect (of); fig. outlook (on).

'aus|bohren v/t. (sep., -ge-, h) bore, drill; '~brechen (irr. brechen, sep., -ge-) **1.** v/t. (h) break out; vomit; **2.** v/i. (sein) break out; fig. burst out (laughing, etc.).

'ausbreit|en v/t. (sep., -ge-, h) spread (out); stretch (out) (arms, wings); display; sich ~ spread; '2ung f (-/~-en) spreading.

'ausbrennen (irr. brennen, sep., -ge-) **1.** v/t. (h) burn out; ⚕ cauter-ize; **2.** v/i. (sein) burn out.

'Ausbruch m outbreak; eruption (of volcano); escape (from prison); outburst (of emotion).

'aus|brüten v/t. (sep., -ge-, h) hatch (a. fig.); '~bürgern v/t. (sep., -ge-, h) denationalize, expatriate.

'Ausdauer f perseverance; '2nd adj. persevering; ♣ perennial.

'ausdehn|en v/t. and v/refl. (sep., -ge-, h) extend (auf acc. to); expand; stretch; '2ung f expansion; exten-sion; extent.

'aus|denken v/t. (irr. denken, sep., -ge-, h) think s.th. out, Am. a. think s.th. up, contrive, devise, invent; imagine; '~dörren v/t. (sep., -ge-, h) dry up; parch; '~drehen v/t. (sep., -ge-, h) turn off (radio, gas); ⚡ turn out, switch off (light).

'Ausdruck m **1.** (-[e]s/no pl.) ex-pression; **2.** (-[e]s/~e) expression; term.

'ausdrück|en v/t. (sep., -ge-, h) press, squeeze (out); stub out (cig-

arette); fig. express; '~lich adj. ex-press, explicit.

'ausdrucks|los adj. inexpressive, expressionless; blank; '~voll adj. expressive, '2weise f mode of ex-pression, style.

'Ausdünstung f (-/-en) exhalation; perspiration; odo(u)r, smell.

auseinander adv. [aus'ar'nandər] asunder, apart; separate(d); ~brin-gen v/t (irr. bringen, sep., -ge-, h) separate, sever; ~gehen v/i. (irr. gehen, sep., -ge-, sein) meeting, crowd break up; opinions: differ; friends part; crowd: disperse; roads: diverge; ~nehmen v/t. (irr. nehmen, sep. -ge-, h) take apart or to pieces; ⊕ disassemble, disman-tle; ~setzen fig. v/t. (sep., -ge-, h) explain; sich mit j-m ~ ♦ compound with s.o., argue with s.o.; have it out with s.o.; sich mit e-m Problem ~ get down to a problem; come to grips with a problem; 2setzung f (-/-en) explanation; discussion; set-tlement (with creditors, etc.); kriege-rische armed conflict.

auserlesen adj. ['aus'-] exquisite, choice, select(ed).

auserwählen ['aus'-] v/t. (sep., no -ge-, h) select, choose.

'ausfahr|en (irr. fahren, sep., -ge-) **1.** v/i. (sein) drive out, go for a drive; ♣ leave (port); **2.** v/t. (h) take (baby) out (in pram); take s.o. for a drive; rut (road); ⚔ lower (undercarriage); '2t f drive; excur-sion; way out, exit (of garage, etc.); gateway, departure.

'Ausfall m falling out; ♦: loss; def-icit; '2en v/i. (irr. fallen, sep., -ge-, sein) fall out; not to take place; turn out, prove; ~ lassen drop; can-cel; die Schule fällt aus there is no school; '2end adj. offensive, insult-ing.

'aus|fasern v/i. (sep., -ge-, sein) ravel out, fray; '~fegen v/t. (sep., -ge- h) sweep (out).

ausfertig|en ['ausfertigən] v/t. (sep., -ge-, h) draw up (document); make out (bill, etc.); issue (passport); '2ung f (-/-en) drawing up; issue; draft; copy; in doppelter ~ in du-plicate. [chen find out; discover.]

ausfindig adj. ['ausfindiç]: ~ ma-]

'Ausflucht f (-/~e) excuse, evasion, shift, subterfuge.

'Ausflug m trip, excursion, outing.

Ausflügler ['ausflyːklər] m (-s/-) excursionist, tripper, tourist.

'Ausfluß m flowing out; discharge (a. ⚕); outlet, outfall.

'aus|fragen v/t. (sep., -ge-, h) inter-rogate, Am. a. quiz; sound; '~fran-sen v/i. (sep., -ge-, sein) fray.

Ausfuhr ♦ ['ausfuːr] f (-/-en) ex-port(ation); '~artikel ♦ m export (article).

'ausführ|bar adj. practicable; ✝ exportable; '~en v/t. (sep., -ge-, h) execute, carry out, perform, Am. a. fill; ✝ export; explain; j-n ~ take s.o. out.

'Ausfuhr|genehmigung f export permit; '~handel m export trade.

'ausführlich 1. adj. detailed; comprehensive; circumstantial; 2. adv. in detail, at (some) length; '2keit f (-/no pl.) minuteness of detail; particularity; comprehensiveness; copiousness.

'Ausführung f execution, performance; workmanship; type, make; explanation; '~sbestimmungen ✝ f/pl. export regulations pl.

'Ausfuhr|verbot n embargo on exports; '~waren f/pl. exports pl.; '~zoll m export duty.

'ausfüllen v/t. (sep., -ge-, h) fill out or up; fill in, complete (form); Am. fill out (blank).

'Ausgabe f distribution; edition (of book); expense, expenditure; issue (of shares, etc.); issuing office.

'Ausgang m going out; exit; way out; outlet; end; result; '~skapital ✝ n original capital; '~spunkt m starting-point; '~sstellung f starting-position.

'ausgeben v/t. (irr. geben, sep., -ge-, h) give out; spend (money); issue (shares, etc.); sich ~ für pass o.s. off for, pretend to be.

'ausge|beult adj. ['ausgɔbɔylt] baggy; ~bombt adj. ['~bɔmpt] bombed out; ~dehnt adj. ['~de:nt] expansive, vast, extensive; ~dient adj. ['~di:nt] worn out; superannuated; retired, pensioned off; ~er Soldat ex-serviceman, veteran; ~fallen fig. adj. odd, queer, unusual.

'ausgehen v/i. (irr. gehen, sep., -ge-, sein) go out; take a walk; end; colour: fade; hair: fall out; money, provisions: run out; uns gehen die Vorräte aus we run out of provisions; darauf ~ aim at; gut etc. ~ turn out well, etc.; leer ~ come away empty-handed; von et. ~ start from s.th.

'ausge|lassen fig. adj. frolicsome, boisterous; '~nommen prp. 1. (acc.) except (for); 2. (nom.): Anwesende ~ present company excepted; ~prägt adj. ['~pre:kt] marked, pronounced; ~rechnet fig. adv. ['~reçnət] just; ~ er he of all people; ~ heute today of all days; '~schlossen fig. adj. impossible.

'ausgestalten v/t. (sep., no -ge-, h) arrange (celebration); et. zu et. ~ develop or turn s.th. into s.th.

'ausge|sucht fig. adj. ['ausgəzu:xt] exquisite, choice; '~wachsen adj. full-grown; ~zeichnet fig. adj. ['~tsaiçnət] excellent.

ausgiebig adj. ['ausgi:biç] abundant, plentiful; meal: substantial.

'ausgießen v/t. (irr. gießen, sep., -ge-, h) pour out.

Ausgleich ['ausglaiç] m (-[e]s/-e) compromise; compensation; ✝ settlement; sports: equalization (of score); tennis: deuce (score of 40 all); '2en v/t. (irr. gleichen, sep., -ge-, h) equalize; compensate (loss); ✝ balance.

'aus|gleiten v/i. (irr. gleiten, sep., -ge-, sein) slip, slide; '~graben v/t. (irr. graben, sep., -ge-, h) dig out or up (a. fig.); excavate; exhume (body).

Ausguck ⚓ ['ausguk] m (-[e]s/-e) look-out.

'Ausguß m sink; '~eimer m slop-pail.

'aus|haken v/t. (sep., -ge-, h) unhook; '~halten (irr. halten, sep., -ge-, h) 1. v/t. endure, bear, stand; ♪ sustain (note); 2. v/i. hold out; last; ~händigen ['~hɛndigən] v/t. (sep., -ge-, h) deliver up, hand over, surrender.

'Aushang m notice, placard, poster.

'aushänge|n 1. v/t. (sep., -ge-, h) hang or put out; unhinge (door); 2. v/i. (irr. hängen, sep., -ge-, h) have been hung or put out; '2-schild n signboard.

aus|harren ['ausharən] v/i. (sep., -ge-, h) persevere; hold out; '~hauchen v/t. (sep., -ge-, h) breathe out, exhale; ~heben v/t. (irr. heben, sep., -ge-, h) dig (trench); unhinge (door); recruit, levy (soldiers); excavate (earth); rob (nest); clean out, raid (nest of criminals); '~helfen v/i. (irr. helfen, sep., -ge-, h) help out.

'Aushilf|e f (temporary) help or assistance; sie hat e-e ~ she has s.o. to help out; '2sweise adv. as a makeshift; temporarily.

'aushöhl|en v/t. (sep., -ge-, h) hollow out; '2ung f hollow.

'aus|holen (sep., -ge-, h) 1. v/i. raise one's hand (as if to strike); weit ~ go far back (in narrating s.th.); 2. v/t. sound, pump s.o.; '~horchen v/t. (sep., -ge-, h) sound, pump s.o.; '~hungern v/t. (sep., -ge-, h) starve (out); '~husten (sep., -ge-, h) cough up; '~kennen v/refl. (irr. kennen, sep., -ge-, h) know one's way (about place); be well versed, be at home (in subject); er kennt sich aus he knows what's what; '~kleiden v/t. (sep., -ge-, h) undress; ⊕ line, coat; sich ~ undress; '~klopfen v/t. (sep., -ge-, h) beat out; dust (garment); knock out (pipe); ~klügeln ['~kly:gəln] v/t. (sep., -ge-, h) work s.th. out; contrive; puzzle s.th. out.

'auskommen 1. v/i. (irr. kommen, sep., -ge-, sein) get out; escape; ~

mit manage with *s.th.*; get on with *s.o.*; ~ *ohne* do without; *mit dem Geld* ~ make both ends meet; 2. 2 *n* (-s/*no pl.*) competence, competency.

'auskundschaften *v/t.* (*sep.*, -ge-, *h*) explore; ✗ reconnoit|re, *Am.* -er, scout.

Auskunft ['aʊskʊnft] *f* (-/⁼e) information; inquiry office, inquiries *pl.*, *Am.* information desk; '~stelle *f* inquiry office, inquiries *pl.*, *Am.* information bureau.

'aus|lachen *v/t.* (*sep.*, -ge-, *h*) laugh at, deride; '~laden *v/t.* (*irr.* laden, *sep.*, -ge-, *h*) unload; discharge (*cargo from ship*); cancel *s.o.'s* invitation, put off (*guest*).

'Auslage *f* display, show (*of goods*); *in der* ~ in the (shop) window; ~*n pl.* expenses *pl.*

'Ausland *n* (-[e]s/*no pl.*): *das* ~ foreign countries *pl.*; *ins* ~, *im* ~ abroad.

Ausländ|er ['aʊslɛndər] *m* (-s/-), '~erin *f* (-/-nen) foreigner; alien; '2isch *adj.* foreign; ♀, *zo.* exotic.

'Auslandskorrespondent *m* foreign correspondent.

'auslass|en *v/t.* (*irr.* lassen, *sep.*, -ge-, *h*) let out (*water*); melt (down) (*butter*); render down (*fat*); let out (*garment*); let down (*hem*); leave out, omit (*word*); cut *s.th.* out; miss or cut out (*meal*); miss (*dance*); *s-n Zorn an j-m* ~ vent one's anger on *s.o.*; *sich* ~ *über* (*acc.*) say *s.th.* about; express one's opinion about; '2ung *f* (-/-en) omission; remark, utterance; '2ungszeichen *gr. n* apostrophe.

'aus|laufen *v/i.* (*irr.* laufen, *sep.*, -ge-, *sein*) run or leak out (*aus et. of s.th.*); leak; end (*in s.th.*); *machine:* run down; ♣ (set) sail; '~leeren *v/t.* (*sep.*, -ge-, *h*) empty; ✸ evacuate (*bowels*).

'ausleg|en *v/t.* (*sep.*, -ge-, *h*) lay out; display (*goods*); explain, interpret; advance (*money*); '2ung *f* (-/-en) explanation, interpretation.

'aus|leihen *v/t.* (*irr.* leihen, *sep.*, -ge-, *h*) lend (out), *esp. Am.* loan; '~lernen *v/i.* (*sep.*, -ge-, *h*) finish one's apprenticeship; *man lernt nie aus* we live and learn.

'Auslese *f* choice, selection; *fig.* pick; '2n *v/t.* (*irr.* lesen, *sep.*, -ge-, *h*) pick out, select; finish reading (*book*).

'ausliefer|n *v/t.* (*sep.*, -ge-, *h*) hand or turn over, deliver (up); extradite (*criminal*); *ausgeliefert sein* (*dat.*) be at the mercy of; '2ung *f* delivery; extradition.

'aus|liegen *v/i.* (*irr.* liegen, *sep.*, -ge-, *h*) be displayed, be on show; '~löschen *v/t.* (*sep.*, -ge-, *h*) put out, switch off (*light*); extinguish (*fire*) (*a. fig.*); efface (*word*); wipe out, erase; '~losen *v/t.* (*sep.*, -ge-, *h*) draw (lots) for.

'auslös|en *v/t.* (*sep.*, -ge-, *h*) ⊕ release; redeem, ransom (*prisoner*); redeem (*from pawn*); *fig.* cause, start; arouse (*applause*); 2er *m* (-s/-) ⊕ release, *esp. phot.* trigger.

'aus|lüften *v/t.* (*sep.*, -ge-, *h*) air, ventilate; '~machen *v/t.* (*sep.*, -ge-, *h*) make out, sight, spot; *sum:* amount to; constitute, make up; put out (*fire*); ⚡ turn out, switch off (*light*); agree on, arrange; settle; *es macht nichts aus* it does not matter; *würde es Ihnen et.* ~, *wenn ...?* would you mind (*ger.*) ...?; '~malen *v/t.* (*sep.*, -ge-, *h*) paint; *sich et.* ~ picture *s.th.* to *o.s.*, imagine *s.th.*

'Ausmaß *n* dimension(*s pl.*), measurement(*s pl.*); *fig.* extent.

aus|mergeln ['aʊsmɛrgəln] *v/t.* (*sep.*, -ge-, *h*) emaciate; exhaust; ~merzen ['~mɛrtsən] *v/t.* (*sep.*, -ge-, *h*) eliminate; eradicate; '~messen *v/t.* (*irr.* messen, *sep.*, -ge-, *h*) measure.

Ausnahm|e ['aʊsnaːmə] *f* (-/-n) exception; '2sweise *adv.* by way of exception; exceptionally.

'ausnehmen *v/t.* (*irr.* nehmen, *sep.*, -ge-, *h*) take out; draw (*fowl*); ⌃ fleece *s.o.*; *fig.* except, exempt; '~d 1. *adj.* exceptional; 2. *adv.* exceedingly.

'aus|nutzen *v/t.* (*sep.*, -ge-, *h*) utilize; take advantage of; *esp.* ⚔, ✗ exploit; '~packen *v/t.* (*sep.*, -ge-, *h*) 1. *v/t.* unpack; 2. ⌃ *fig. v/i.* speak one's mind; '~pfeifen *thea. v/t.* (*irr.* pfeifen, *sep.*, -ge-, *h*) hiss; '~plaudern *v/t.* (*sep.*, -ge-, *h*) blab or let out; '~polstern *v/t.* (*sep.*, -ge-, *h*) stuff, pad; wad; '~probieren *v/t.* (*sep.*, *no* -ge-, *h*) try, test.

Auspuff *mot.* ['aʊspʊf] *m* (-[e]s/-e) exhaust; '~gas *mot. n* exhaust gas; '~rohr *mot. n* exhaust-pipe; '~topf *mot. m* silencer, *Am.* muffler.

'aus|putzen *v/t.* (*sep.*, -ge-, *h*) clean; '~quartieren *v/t.* (*sep.*, *no* -ge-, *h*) dislodge; ✗ billet out; '~radieren *v/t.* (*sep.*, *no* -ge-, *h*) erase; '~rangieren *v/t.* (*sep.*, *no* -ge-, *h*) discard; '~rauben *v/t.* (*sep.*, -ge-, *h*) rob; ransack; '~räumen *v/t.* (*sep.*, -ge-, *h*) empty, clear (out); remove (*furniture*); '~rechnen *v/t.* (*sep.*, -ge-, *h*) calculate, compute; reckon (out), *Am.* figure out or up (*all a. fig.*).

'Ausrede *f* excuse, evasion, subterfuge; '2n (*sep.*, -ge-, *h*) 1. *v/i.* finish speaking; ~ *lassen* hear *s.o.* out; 2. *v/t.*: *j-m et.* ~ dissuade *s.o.* from *s.th.*

'ausreichen *v/i.* (*sep.*, -ge-, *h*) suffice; '~d *adj.* sufficient.

'Ausreise *f* departure; ♣ voyage out.

'ausreiß|en (irr. reißen, sep., -ge-)
1 . v/t. (h) pull or tear out; 2. v/i.
(sein) run away; 'Ler m runaway.
aus|renken ['ausreŋkən] v/t. (sep.,
-ge-, h) dislocate; '~richten v/t.
(sep., -ge-, h) straighten; ⚔ dress;
adjust; deliver (message); do, effect;
accomplish; obtain; arrange (feast);
richte ihr e-n Gruß von mir aus
remember me to her!; ~rotten ['~
rɔtən] v/t. (sep., -ge-, h) root out;
fig. extirpate, exterminate.
'Ausruf m cry; exclamation; '2en
(irr. rufen, sep., -ge-,h) 1. v/i. cry
out, exclaim; 2. v/t. proclaim; '~e-
zeichen n exclamation mark, Am.
a. exclamation point; '~ung f (-/-en)
proclamation; '~ungszeichen n s.
Ausrufezeichen.   [-ge-, h) rest.)
'ausruhen v/i., v/t. and v/refl. (sep.,)
'ausrüst|en v/t. (sep., -ge-, h) fit
out; equip; '2ung f outfit, equipment, fittings pl.   [disseminate.)
'aussäen v/t. (sep., -ge-, h) sow; fig.)
'Aussage f statement; declaration;
tt evidence; gr. predicate; '2n
(sep., -ge-, h) 1. v/t. state, declare;
tt depose; 2. tt v/i. give evidence.
'Aussatz ⚕ m (-es/no pl.) leprosy.
'aus|saugen v/t. (sep., -ge-, h) suck
(out); fig. exhaust (land); '~schal-
ten v/t. (sep., -ge-, h) eliminate; ⚡
cut out, switch off, turn off or out
(light).
Ausschank ['ausʃaŋk] m (-[e]s/ᵘe)
retail (of alcoholic drinks); public
house, F pub.
'Ausschau f (-/no pl.) ~ halten nach
be on the look-out for, watch for.
'ausscheid|en (irr. scheiden, sep.,
-ge-) 1. v/t. (h) separate; 🜍, ⚗,
physiol. eliminate; ⚕ secrete;
2. v/i. (sein) retire; withdraw;
sports: drop out; '2ung f separation; elimination (a. sports); ⚕
secretion.
'aus|schiffen v/t. and v/refl. (sep.,
-ge-, h) disembark; '~schimpfen
v/t. (sep., -ge-, h) scold, tell s.o.
off, berate; ~schirren ['~ʃirən] v/t.
(sep.,-ge-,h) unharness; '~schlach-
ten v/t. (sep., -ge-, h) cut up; can-
nibalize (car, etc.); fig. exploit,
make the most of; '~schlafen (irr.
schlafen, sep., -ge-, h) 1. v/i. sleep
one's fill; 2. v/t. sleep off (effects
of drink, etc.).
'Ausschlag m ⚕ eruption, rash;
deflexion (of pointer); den ~ geben
settle it; 2en ['~gən] (irr. schlagen,
sep., -ge-) 1. v/t. (h) knock or beat
out; line; refuse, decline; 2. v/i.
horse: kick; pointer: deflect; 3. v/i.
(h, sein) bud; 2gebend adj. ['~k-]
decisive.
'ausschließ|en v/t. (irr. schließen,
sep., -ge-, h) shut or lock out; fig.:
exclude; expel; sports: disqualify;
'~lich adj. exclusive.

'Ausschluß m exclusion; expulsion;
sports: disqualification.
'ausschmücken v/t. (sep., -ge-, h)
adorn, decorate; fig. embellish.
'Ausschnitt m cut; décolleté, (low)
neck (of dress); cutting, Am. clip-
ping (from newspaper); fig. part,
section.
'ausschreib|en v/t. (irr. schreiben,
sep., -ge-, h) write out; copy; write
out (word) in full; make out (invoice); announce; advertise; '2ung f
(-/-en) announcement; advertisement.
'ausschreit|en (irr. schreiten, sep.,
-ge-) 1. v/i. (sein) step out, take
long strides; 2. v/t. (h) pace (room),
measure by steps; '2ung f (-/-en)
excess; ~en pl. riots pl.
'Ausschuß m refuse, waste, rubbish; committee, board.
'aus|schütteln v/t. (sep., -ge-, h)
shake out; '~schütten v/t. (sep.,
-ge-, h) pour out; spill; ✝ distribute (dividend); j-m sein Herz ~ pour
out one's heart to s.o.; '~schwär-
men v/i. (sep., -ge-, sein) swarm
out; ~ (lassen) ⚔ extend, deploy.
'ausschweif|end adj. dissolute;
'2ung f (-/-en) debauchery, excess.
'ausschwitzen v/t. (sep., -ge-, h)
exude.
'aussehen 1. v/i. (irr. sehen, sep.,
-ge-, h) look; wie sieht er aus?
what does he look like?; es sieht
nach Regen aus it looks like rain;
2. 2 n (-s/ no pl.) look(s pl.), appearance.
außen adv. ['ausən] (on the) outside; von ~ her from (the) outside;
nach ~ (hin) outward(s); '2auf-
nahme f film: outdoor shot;
'2bordmotor m outboard motor.
'aussenden v/t. (irr. senden,) sep.,
-ge-, h) send out.
'Außen|hafen m outport; '~handel
m foreign trade; '~minister m
foreign minister; Foreign Secretary,
Am. Secretary of State; '~ministe-
rium n foreign ministry; Foreign
Office, Am. State Department;
'~politik f foreign policy; '2poli-
tisch adj. of or referring to foreign
affairs; '~seite f outside, surface;
'~seiter m (-s/-) outsider; '~stände
✝ ['~ʃtɛndə] pl. outstanding debts
pl., Am. accounts pl. receivable;
'~welt f outer or outside world.
außer ['ausər] 1. prp. (dat.) out of;
beside(s), Am. aside from; except;
~ sich sein be beside o.s. (vor Freude
with joy); 2. cj.: ~ daß except that;
~ wenn unless; '~dem cj. besides,
moreover.
äußere ['ɔysərə] 1. adj. exterior,
outer, external, outward; 2. 2 n
(Äußer[e]n/no pl.) exterior, outside,
outward appearance.
'außer|gewöhnlich adj. extra-

ordinary; exceptional; '~halb 1. *prp.* (*gen.*) outside, out of; beyond; 2. *adv.* on the outside.

äußerlich *adj.* ['ɔysərliç] external, outward; '2keit *f* (-/-en) superficiality; formality.

äußern ['ɔysərn] *v/t.* (ge-, h) utter, express; advance; *sich ~ matter*: manifest itself; *p.* express o.s.

'außer'ordentlich *adj.* extraordinary.

äußerst ['ɔysərst] 1. *adj.* outermost; *fig.* utmost, extreme; 2. *adv.* extremely, highly.

außerstande *adj.* [ausər'ʃtandə] unable, not in a position.

'Äußerung *f* (-/-en) utterance, remark.

'aussetz|en (*sep.*, -ge-, h) 1. *v/t.* set or put out; lower (*boat*); promise (*reward*); settle (*pension*); bequeath; expose (*child*); expose (*dat.* to); et. ~ *an* (*dat.*) find fault with; 2. *v/i.* intermit; fail; *activity*: stop; suspend; *mot.* misfire; '2ung *f* (-/-en) exposure (*of child, to weather, etc.*) (*a.* ⚙️).

'Aussicht *f* (-/-en) view (*auf acc.* of); *fig.* prospect (of), chance (of); *in ~ haben* have in prospect; '2slos *adj.* hopeless, desperate; '2sreich *adj.* promising, full of promise.

aussöhn|en ['auszøːnən] *v/t.* (*sep.*, -ge-, h) reconcile *s.o.* (*mit* to *s.th.*, with *s.o.*); *sich ~* reconcile o.s. (to *s.th.*, with *s.o.*); '2ung *f* (-/-en) reconciliation.

'aussondern *v/t.* (*sep.*, -ge-, h) single out; separate.

'aus|spannen (*sep.*, -ge-, h) 1. *v/t.* stretch, extend; F *fig.* steal (*s.o.'s girl friend*); unharness (*draught animal*); 2. *fig. v/i.* (take a) rest, relax; '~speien *v/t. and v/i.* (irr. speien, sep., -ge-, h) spit out.

'aussperr|en *v/t.* (*sep.*, -ge-, h) shut out; lock out (*workmen*); '2ung *f* (-/-en) lock-out.

'aus|spielen (*sep.*, -ge-, h) 1. *v/t.* play (*card*); 2. *v/i.* at cards: lead; *er hat ausgespielt* he is done for; '~spionieren *v/t.* (*sep., no -ge-, h*) spy out. [cent; discussion.]

'Aussprache *f* pronunciation, accent;]

'aussprechen (irr. sprechen, *sep.*, -ge-, h) 1. *v/t.* pronounce, express; *sich ~ für* (*gegen*) declare o.s. for (against); 2. *v/i.* finish speaking.

'Ausspruch *m* utterance; saying; remark.

'aus|spucken *v/i. and v/t.* (*sep.*, -ge-, h) spit out; '~spülen *v/t.* (*sep.*, -ge-, h) rinse.

'Ausstand *m* strike, Am. F a. walkout; *in den ~ treten* go on strike, Am. F a. walk out.

ausstatt|en ['ausʃtatən] *v/t.* (*sep.*, -ge-, h) fit out, equip; furnish; supply (*mit* with); give a dowry to

(*daughter*); get up (*book*); '2ung *f* (-/-en) outfit, equipment; furniture; supply; dowry; get-up (*of book*).

'aus|stechen *v/t.* (irr. stechen, *sep.*, -ge-, h) cut out (*a. fig.*); put out (*eye*); '~stehen *v/t.* (irr. stehen, *sep.*, -ge-, h) 1. *v/i. payments*: be outstanding; 2. *v/t.* endure, bear; '~steigen *v/i.* (irr. steigen, *sep.*, -ge-, sein) get out or off, alight.

'ausstell|en *v/t.* (*sep.*, -ge-, h) exhibit; make out (*invoice*); issue (*document*); draw (*bill*); '2er *m* (-s/-) exhibitor; drawer; '2ung *f* exhibition, show; '2ungsraum *m* show-room.

'aussterben *v/i.* (irr. sterben, *sep.*, -ge-, sein) die out; become extinct.

'Aussteuer *f* trousseau, dowry.

'ausstopfen *v/t.* (*sep.*, -ge-, h) stuff; wad, pad.

'ausstoß|en *v/t.* (irr. stoßen, *sep.*, -ge-, h) thrust out, eject; expel; utter (*cry*); heave (*sigh*); ✂️ cashier; '2ung *f* (-/-en) expulsion.

'aus|strahlen *v/t. and v/i.* (*sep.*, -ge-, h) radiate; '~strecken *v/t.* (*sep.*, -ge-, h) stretch (out); '~streichen *v/t.* (irr. streichen, *sep.*, -ge-, h) strike out; smooth (down); '~streuen *v/t.* (*sep.*, -ge-, h) scatter; spread (*rumours*); '~strömen *v/i.* (*sep.*, -ge-) 1. *v/i.* (sein) stream out; *gas, light*: emanate; *gas, steam*: escape; 2. *v/t.* (h) pour (out); '~suchen *v/t.* (*sep.*, -ge-, h) choose, select.

'Austausch *m* exchange; '2bar *adj.* exchangeable; '2en *v/t.* (*sep.*, -ge-, h) exchange.

'austeil|en *v/t.* (*sep.*, -ge-, h) distribute; deal out (*blows*); '2ung *f* distribution.

Auster *zo.* ['austər] *f* (-/-n) oyster.

'austragen *v/t.* (irr. tragen, *sep.*, -ge-, h) deliver (*letters, etc.*); hold (*contest*).

Austral|ier [au'straːliər] *m* (-s/-) Australian; 2isch *adj.* Australian.

'austreib|en *v/t.* (irr. treiben, *sep.*, -ge-, h) drive out; expel; '2ung *f* (-/-en) expulsion.

'aus|treten (irr. treten, *sep.*, -ge-) 1. *v/t.* (h) tread or stamp out; wear out (*shoes*); wear down (*steps*); 2. *v/i.* (sein) emerge, come out; *river*: overflow its banks; retire (*aus* from); F ease o.s.; ~ *aus* leave (*society, etc.*); '~trinken (irr. trinken, *sep.*, -ge-, h) 1. *v/t.* drink up; empty, drain; 2. *v/i.* finish drinking; '2tritt *m* leaving; retirement; '~trocknen (*sep.*, -ge-) 1. *v/t.* (h) dry up; drain (*land*); parch (*throat, earth*); 2. *v/i.* (sein) dry up.

ausüb|en ['aus?-] *v/t.* (*sep.*, -ge-, h) exercise; practise, Am. -ce (*profession*); exert (*influence*); '2ung *f* practice; exercise.

'**Ausverkauf** ✝ *m* selling off or out (*of stock*); sale; '2t ✝, *thea. adj.* sold out; *theatre notice:* 'full house'.
'**Auswahl** *f* choice; selection; ✝ assortment. [choose, select.]
'**auswählen** *v/t.* (*sep.*, -ge-, *h*)}
'**Auswander|er** *m* emigrant; '2n *v/i.* (*sep.*,-ge-, *sein*) emigrate; '⸤ung *f* emigration.
auswärt|ig *adj.* ['ausvertiç] out-of-town; non-resident; foreign; *das Auswärtige Amt s. Außenministerium*; ⸤s *adv.* ['⸤s] outward(s); out of doors; out of town; abroad; ⸤ **essen** dine out.
'**auswechseln 1.** *v/t.* (*sep.*, -ge-, *h*) exchange; change; replace; **2.** 2 *n* (-s/no *pl.*) exchange; replacement.
'**Ausweg** *m* way out (*a. fig.*); outlet; *fig.* expedient.
'**ausweichen** *v/i.* (*irr. weichen, sep.*, -ge-, *sein*) make way (for); *fig.* evade, avoid; '⸤d *adj.* evasive.
Ausweis ['ausvais] *m* (-es/-e) (bank) return; identity card, *Am.* identification (card); 2en ['⸤zən] *v/t.* (*irr. weisen, sep.*,-ge-,*h*) turn out, expel; evict; deport; show, prove; *sich* ⸤ prove one's identity; '⸤papiere *n/pl.* identity papers *pl.*; ⸤ung ['⸤zuŋ] *f* expulsion; '⸤ungsbefehl *m* expulsion order.
'**ausweiten** *v/t. and v/refl.* (*sep.*, -ge-, *h*) widen, stretch, expand.
'**auswendig 1.** *adj.* outward, outside; **2.** *adv.* outwardly, outside; *fig.* by heart.
'**aus|werfen** *v/t.* (*irr. werfen, sep.*, -ge-, *h*) throw out, cast; eject; *⸗* expectorate; allow (*sum of money*); '⸤werten *v/t.* (*sep.*, -ge-, *h*) evaluate; analyze, interpret; utilize, exploit; '⸤wickeln *v/t.* (*sep.*, -ge-, *h*) unwrap; '⸤wiegen *v/t.* (*irr. wiegen, sep.*, -ge-, *h*) weigh out; '⸤wirken *v/refl.* (*sep.*, -ge-, *h*) take effect, operate; *sich* ⸤ *auf* (*acc.*) affect; '2wirkung *f* effect; '⸤wischen *v/t.* (*sep.*, -ge-, *h*) wipe out, efface; '⸤wringen *v/t.* (*irr. wringen, sep.*, -ge-, *h*) wring out.
'**Auswuchs** *m* excrescence, outgrowth (*a. fig.*), protuberance.
'**Auswurf** *m* *⸗* expectoration; *fig.* refuse, dregs *pl.*
'**aus|zahlen** *v/t.* (*sep.*, -ge-, *h*) pay out; pay *s.o.* off; '⸤zählen *v/t.* (*sep.*, -ge-, *h*) count out.

'**Auszahlung** *f* payment.
'**Auszehrung** *f* (-/-en) consumption.
'**auszeichn|en** *v/t.* (*sep.*, -ge-, *h*) mark (out); *fig.* distinguish (*sich o.s.*); '2ung *f* marking; distinction; hono(u)r; decoration.
'**auszieh|en** (*irr. ziehen, sep.*, -ge-) **1.** *v/t.* (*h*) draw out, extract; take off (*garment*); *sich* ⸤ undress; **2.** *v/i.* (*sein*) set out; move (out), remove, move house; '2platte *f* leaf (*of table*).
'**Auszug** *m* departure; *⸗* marching out; removal; extract, excerpt (*from book*); summary; ✝ statement (of account). [tic, genuine.]
authentisch *adj.* [au'tεntiʃ] authen-
Auto ['auto] *n* (-s/-s) (motor-)car, *Am. a.* automobile; ⸤ **fahren** drive, motor; '⸤bahn *f* motorway, *Am.* highway; *fig.* autobiography; ⸤'bus ['⸤bus] *m* (-ses/-se) (motor-)bus; (motor) coach; '⸤bushaltestelle *f* bus stop; ⸤didakt [⸤di'dakt] *m* (-en/-en) autodidact, self-taught person; '⸤droschke *f* taxi(-cab), *Am.* cab; '⸤fahrer *m* motorist; '⸤gramm *n* autograph; ⸤'grammjäger *m* autograph hunter; '⸤händler *m* car dealer; '⸤kino *n* drive-in cinema; ⸤krat [⸤'krɑːt] *m* (-en/-en) autocrat; ⸤kratie [⸤kra'tiː] *f* (-/-n) autocracy; ⸤mat [⸤'mɑːt] *m* (-en/-en) automaton; slot-machine, vending machine; ⸤'matenrestaurant *n* self-service restaurant, *Am.* automat; ⸤mation ⊕ [⸤ma'tsjoːn] *f* (-/no *pl.*) automation; 2'matisch *adj.* automatic; '⸤mechaniker *m* car mechanic; ⸤mobil [⸤mo'biːl] *n* (-s/-e) *s. Auto*; 2nom *adj.* [⸤'noːm] autonomous; ⸤nomie [⸤'miː] *f* (-/-n) autonomy.
Autor ['autɔr] *m* (-s/-en) author.
'**Autoreparaturwerkstatt** *f* car repair shop, garage. [thor(ess).]
Autorin [au'toːrin] *f* (-/-nen) au-
autori|sieren [autori'ziːrən] *v/t.* (*no* -ge-, *h*) authorize; ⸤tär *adj.* [⸤'tɛːr] authoritarian; 2'tät *f* (-/-en) authority.
'**Auto|straße** *f* motor-road; '⸤vermietung *f* (-/-en) car hire service.
avisieren [avi'ziːrən] *v/t.* (*no* -ge-, *h*) advise.
Axt [akst] *f* (-/¨e) ax(e).
Azetylen ⚗ [atsety'leːn] *n* (-s/no *pl.*) acetylene. [2n *adj.* azure.)
Azur [a'tsuːr] *m* (-s/no *pl.*) azure;}

B

Bach [bax] *m* (-[e]s/¨e) brook, *Am. a.* run. [port.]
Backbord ⚓ ['bak-] *n* (-[e]s/-e)}
Backe ['bakə] *f* (-/-n) cheek.
backen ['bakən] (*irr.*, ge-, *h*) **1.**

v/t. bake; fry; dry (*fruit*); **2.** *v/i.* bake; fry.
'**Backen|bart** *m* (side-)whiskers *pl.*, *Am. a.* sideburns *pl.*; '⸤zahn *⸗* molar (tooth), grind⸗

Bäcker ['bɛkər] *m* (-s/-) baker; ~ei [~'raɪ] *f* (-/-en) baker's (shop), bakery.

'**Back|fisch** *m* fried fish; *fig.* girl in her teens, teenager, *Am. a.* bobby soxer; '~obst *n* dried fruit; ~ofen *m* oven; '~pflaume *f* prune; ~pulver *n* baking-powder; '~stein *m* brick; '~ware *f* baker's ware.

Bad [baːt] *n* (-[e]s/~er) bath; *in river, etc.*: a. bathe; *s.* Badeort; *ein* ~ *nehmen* take *or* have a bath.

Bade|anstalt ['baːdə-] *f* (public swimming) baths *pl.*; '~anzug *m* bathing-costume, bathing-suit; '~hose *f* bathing-drawers *pl.*, (bathing) trunks *pl.*; '~kappe *f* bathing-cap; '~kur *f* spa treatment; ~mantel *m* bathing-gown, *Am.* bathrobe; '~meister *m* bath attendant; swimming-instructor; '²n (ge-, h) 1. *v/t.* bath (*baby, etc.*); bathe (*eyes, etc.*); 2. *v/i.* bath, tub; have *or* take a bath; *in river, etc.*: bathe; ~ *gehen* go swimming; '~ofen *m* geyser, boiler, *Am. a.* water heater; '~ort *m* watering-place; spa; seaside resort; '~salz *n* bath-salt; '~strand *m* bathing-beach; '~tuch *n* bath-towel; '~wanne *f* bath-tub; '~zimmer *n* bathroom.

Bagatell|e [baga'tɛlə] *f* (-/-n) trifle, trifling matter, bagatelle; ²i'sieren *v/t.* (*no* -ge-, h) minimize (the importance of), *Am. a.* play down.

Bagger ['bagər] *m* (-s/-) excavator; dredge(r); '²n *v/i. and v/t.* (ge-, h) excavate; dredge.

Bahn [baːn] *f* (-/-en) course; path; ⚐ railway, *Am.* railroad; *mot.* lane; trajectory (*of bullet, etc.*); *ast.* orbit; *sports*: track, course, lane; *skating*: rink; *bowling*: alley; '²brechend *adj.* pioneer(ing), epoch-making; *art*: avant-gardist; '~damm *m* railway embankment, *Am.* railroad embankment; '²en *v/t.* (ge-, h) clear, open (up) (*way*); *den Weg* ~ *prepare or pave the way* (*dat.* for); *sich e-n Weg* ~ force *or* work *or* elbow one's way; '~hof *m* (railway-)station, *Am.* (railroad-)station; '~linie *f* railway-line, *Am.* railroad line; '~steig *m* platform; '~steigkarte *f* platform ticket; '~übergang *m* level crossing, *Am.* grade crossing.

Bahre ['baːrə] *f* (-/-n) stretcher, litter; bier.

Bai [baɪ] *f* (-/-en) bay; creek.

Baisse ✝ ['bɛːs(ə)] *f* (-/-n) depression (on the market); fall (in prices); *auf* ~ *spekulieren* ✝ bear, speculate for a fall, *Am.* sell short; '~spekulant *m* bear.

Bajonett ⚔ [bajo'nɛt] *n* (-[e]s/-e) bayonet; *das* ~ *aufpflanzen* fix the bayonet.

Bake ['baːkə] *f* (-/-n) ⚓ beacon; ⚑ warning-sign.

Bakterie [bak'teːrjə] *f* (-/-n) bacterium, microbe, germ.

bald *adv.* [balt] soon; shortly; before long; F almost, nearly; early; *so* ~ *als möglich* as soon as possible; ~ *hier*, ~ *dort* now here, now there; ~**ig** *adj.* ['~dɪç] speedy; ~**e Antwort** ✝ early reply.

Baldrian ['baldriaːn] *m* (-s/-e) valerian.

Balg [balk] 1. *m* (-[e]s/~e) skin; body (*of doll*); bellows *pl.*; 2. F *m, n* (-[e]s/~er) brat, urchin; ²en ['balgən] *v/refl.* (ge-, h) scuffle (*um for*), wrestle (for).

Balken ['balkən] *m* (-s/-) beam; rafter.

Balkon [bal'kŏ:; ~'koːn] *m* (-s/-s; -s/-e) balcony; *thea.* dress circle, *Am.* balcony; '~tür *f* French window.

Ball [bal] *m* (-[e]s/~e) ball; *geogr., ast. a.* globe; ball, dance; *auf dem* ~ at the ball.

Ballade [ba'laːdə] *f* (-/-n) ballad.

Ballast ['balast] *m* (-es/*⚆*-e) ballast; *fig.* burden, impediment; dead weight.

'**ballen**[1] *v/t.* (ge-, h) (form into a) ball; clench (*fist*); *sich* ~ (form into a) ball; cluster.

'**Ballen**[2] *m* (-s/-) bale; *anat.* ball; ~ *Papier* ten reams *pl.*

Ballett [ba'lɛt] *n* (-[e]s/-e) ballet; ~**änzer** [ba'lɛttɛntsər] *m* (-s/-) ballet-dancer.

ball|förmig *adj.* ['balfœrmɪç] ball-shaped, globular; '²kleid *n* ball-dress.

Ballon [ba'lŏ:; ~ɔːn] *m* (-s/-s; -s/-s, -e) balloon.

'**Ball|saal** *m* ball-room; '~spiel *n* ball-game, game of ball.

Balsam ['balzaːm] *m* (-s/-e) balsam, balm (*a. fig.*); ²ieren [~'miːrən] *v/t.* (*no* -ge-, h) embalm.

Balz [balts] *f* (-/-en) mating season; display (*by cock-bird*).

Bambus ['bambus] *m* (-ses/-se) bamboo; '~rohr *n* bamboo, cane.

banal *adj.* [ba'naːl] commonplace, banal, trite; trivial; ²ität [~ali'tɛːt] *f* (-/-en) banality; commonplace; triviality.

Banane [ba'naːnə] *f* (-/-n) banana; ~**nstecker** ⚡ *m* banana plug.

Band [bant] 1. *m* (-[e]s/~e) volume; 2. *n* (-[e]s/~er) band; ribbon; tape; *anat.* ligament; 3. *fig. n* (-[e]s/-e) bond, tie; 4. ② *pret. of* binden.

Bandag|e [ban'daːʒə] *f* (-/-n) bandage; ²ieren [~a'ʒiːrən] *v/t.* (*no* -ge-, h) (apply a) bandage.

Bande ['bandə] *f* (-/-n) *billiards*: cushion; *fig.* gang, band.

bändigen ['bɛndigən] *v/t.* (ge-, h)

tame; break in (*horse*); subdue (*a. fig.*); *fig.* restrain, master.

Bandit [ban'di:t] *m* (-en/-en) bandit.

'Band|maß *n* tape measure; '~säge *f* band-saw; '~scheibe *anat. f* intervertebral disc; '~wurm *zo. m* tapeworm.

bang *adj.* [ban], ~e *adj.* ['~ə] anxious (*um* about), uneasy (about), concerned (for); *mir ist ~* I am afraid (*vor dat.* of); *j-m bange machen* frighten *or* scare s.o.; '~en *v/i.* (ge-, h) be anxious *or* worried (*um* about).

Bank [bank] *f* 1. (-/~e) bench; *school*: desk; *F durch die ~* without exception, all through; *auf die lange ~ schieben* put off, postpone; *shelve*; 2. ✝ (-/-en) bank; *Geld auf der ~* money in the bank; '~anweisung *f* cheque, *Am.* check; '~ausweis *m* bank return *or* statement; '~beamte *m* bank clerk *or* official; '~einlage *f* deposit.

Bankett [ban'kɛt] *n* (-[e]s/-e) banquet.

'Bank|geheimnis *n* banker's duty of secrecy; '~geschäft ✝ *n* bank (-ing) transaction, banking operation; '~haus *n* bank(ing-house).

Bankier [bank'je:] *m* (-s/-s) banker.

'Bank|konto *n* bank(ing) account; '~note *f* (bank) note, *Am.* (bank) bill.

bankrott [ban'krɔt] 1. *adj.* bankrupt; 2. ♀ *m* (-[e]s/-e) bankruptcy, insolvency, failure; ~ *machen* fail, go *or* become bankrupt.

'Bankwesen *n* banking.

Bann [ban] *m* (-[e]s/-e) ban; *fig.* spell; *eccl.* excommunication; '♀en *v/t.* (ge-, h) banish (*a. fig.*); exorcize (*devil*); avert (*danger*); *eccl.* excommunicate; spellbind.

Banner ['banər] *n* (-s/-) banner (*a. fig.*); standard; '~träger *m* standard-bearer.

'Bann|fluch *m* anathema; '~meile *f* precincts *pl.*; ⚜ *area around government buildings within which processions and meetings are prohibited.*

bar[1] [ba:r] 1. *adj.*: *e-r Sache ~* destitute *or* devoid of s.th.; *~es Geld* ready money, cash; *~er Unsinn* sheer nonsense; 2. *adv.*: ~ *bezahlen* pay in cash, pay money down.

Bar[2] [~] *f* (-/-s) bar; night-club.

Bär [bɛːr] *m* (-en/-en) bear; *j-m e-n ~en aufbinden* hoax s.o.

Baracke [ba'rakə] *f* (-/-n) barrack; ~nlager *n* hutment.

Barbar [bar'ba:r] *m* (-en/-en) barbarian; ~ei [~ə'rai] *f* (-/-en) barbarism; barbarity; ♀isch [~'ba:riʃ] *adj.* barbarian; barbarous; *art, taste*: barbaric.

'Bar|bestand *m* cash in hand; '~betrag *m* amount in cash.

'Bärenzwinger *m* bear-pit.

barfuß *adj. and adv.* ['ba:r-], ~füßig *adj. and adv.* ['~fy:siç] barefoot.

barg [bark] *pret. of bergen.*

'Bar|geld *n* cash, ready money; '♀geldlos *adj.* cashless; ~er Zahlungsverkehr cashless money transfers *pl.*; ♀häuptig *adj. and adv.* ['~hɔʏptiç] bare-headed, uncovered.

Bariton ♪ ['ba:ritɔn] *m* (-s/-e) baritone. [launch.]

Barkasse ⚓ [bar'kasə] *f* (-/-n)

barmherzig *adj.* [barm'hɛrtsiç] merciful, charitable; *der ~e Samariter* the good Samaritan; ♀e *Schwester* Sister of Mercy *or* Charity; ♀keit *f* (-/-en) mercy, charity.

Barometer [baro'-] *n* barometer.

Baron [ba'ro:n] *m* (-s/-e) baron; ~in *f* (-/-nen) baroness.

Barre ['barə] *f* (-/-n) bar.

Barren ['barən] *m* (-s/-) *metall.* bar, ingot, bullion; *gymnastics*: parallel bars *pl.*

Barriere [bar'jɛːrə] *f* (-/-n) barrier.

Barrikade [bari'ka:də] *f* (-/-n) barricade; ~n *errichten* raise barricades.

barsch *adj.* [barʃ] rude, gruff, rough.

'Bar|schaft *f* (-/-en) ready money, cash; ~scheck ✝ *m* open cheque, *Am.* open check.

barst [barst] *pret. of bersten.*

Bart [ba:rt] *m* (-[e]s/~e) beard; bit (*of key*), *sich e-n ~ wachsen lassen* grow a beard.

bärtig *adj.* ['bɛːrtiç] bearded.

'bartlos *adj.* beardless.

'Barzahlung *f* cash payment; *nur gegen ~* terms strictly cash.

Basis ['ba:zis] *f* (-/Basen) base; *fig.* basis.

Baß ♪ [bas] *m* (Basses/Bässe) bass; '~geige *f* bass-viol.

Bassist [ba'sist] *m* (-en/-en) bass (singer).

Bast [bast] *m* (-es/-e) bast; velvet (*on antlers*).

Bastard ['bastart] *m* (-[e]s/-e) bastard; half-breed; *zo.*, ♀ hybrid.

bast|eln ['bastəln] (ge-, h) 1. *v/t.* build, ♀ rig up; 2. *v/i.* build; '♀er *m* (-s/-) amateur craftsman, do-it-yourself man.

bat [ba:t] *pret. of bitten.*

Bataillon [batal'jo:n] *n* (-s/-e) battalion.

Batist [ba'tist] *m* (-[e]s/-e) cambric.

Batterie ⚡, ⚔ [batə'ri:] *f* (-/-n) battery.

Bau [bau] *m* 1. (-[e]s/*no pl.*) building, construction; build, frame; 2. (-[e]s/-ten) building, edifice; 3. (-[e]s/-e) burrow, den (*a. fig.*), earth.

'Bau|arbeiter *m* workman in the building trade; '~art *f* architecture, style; method of construction; *mot.* type, model.

Bauch [baux] m (-[e]s/⁓e) anat. abdomen, belly; paunch; ship: bottom; '⁓ig adj. big-bellied, bulgy; '⁓landung f belly landing; '⁓redner m ventriloquist; '⁓schmerzen m/pl., '⁓weh n (-s/no pl.) belly-ache, stomach-ache.

bauen ['bauən] (ge-, h) 1. v/t. build, construct; erect, raise; build, make (nest); make (violin, etc.); 2. v/i. build; ⁓ auf (acc.) trust (in); rely or count or depend on.

Bauer ['bauər] 1. m (-n, -s/-n) farmer; peasant, countryman; chess: pawn; 2. n, m (-s/-) (bird-)cage.

Bäuerin ['bɔyərin] f (-/-nen) farmer's wife; peasant woman.

Bauerlaubnis ['bauʔ-] f building permit.

bäuerlich adj. ['bɔyərliç] rural, rustic.

Bauern|fänger contp. ['bauərnfɛŋər] m (-s/-) trickster, confidence man; '⁓haus n farm-house; '⁓hof m farm.

'bau|fällig adj. out of repair, dilapidated; '⁓gerüst n scaffold (-ing); '⁓handwerker m craftsman in the building trade; '⁓herr m owner; '⁓holz n timber, Am. lumber; '⁓jahr n year of construction; ⁓ 1969 1969 model or make; '⁓kasten m box of bricks; '⁓kunst f architecture.

'baulich adj. architectural, structural; in gutem ⁓en Zustand in good repair.

Baum [baum] m (-[e]s/⁓e) tree.

'Baumeister m architect.

baumeln ['bauməln] v/i. (ge-, h) dangle, swing; mit den Beinen ⁓ dangle or swing one's legs.

'Baum|schere f (eine a pair of) pruning-shears pl.; '⁓schule f nursery (of young trees); '⁓stamm m trunk; '⁓wolle f cotton; '⁓wollen adj. (made of) cotton.

'Bau|plan m architect's or building plan; '⁓platz m building plot or site, Am. location; '⁓polizei f Board of Surveyors.

Bausch [bauʃ] m (-es/-e, ⁓e) pad; bolster; wad; in ⁓ und Bogen altogether, wholesale, in the lump; '⁓en v/t. (ge-, h) swell; sich ⁓ bulge, swell out, billow (out).

'Bau|stein m brick, building stone; building block; fig. element; '⁓stelle f building site; '⁓stil m (architectural) style; '⁓stoff m building material; '⁓unternehmer m building contractor; '⁓zaun m hoarding.

Bay|er ['baiər] m (-n/-n) Bavarian; '⁓(e)risch adj. Bavarian.

Bazill|enträger ⁓ [ba'tsilən-] m (germ-)carrier; '⁓us [⁓us] m (-/Bazillen) bacillus, germ.

beabsichtigen [bə'apziçtigən] v/t.

(no -ge-, h) intend, mean, propose (zu tun to do, doing).

be'acht|en v/t. (no -ge-, h) pay attention to; notice; observe; '⁓enswert adj. noteworthy, remarkable; '⁓lich adj. remarkable; considerable; ⁓ung f attention; consideration; notice; observance.

Beamte [bə'amtə] m (-n/-n) official, officer, Am. a. officeholder; functionary; Civil Servant.

be'ängstigend adj. alarming, disquieting.

beanspruch|en [bə'anʃpruxən] v/t. (no -ge-, h) claim, demand; require (efforts, time, space, etc.); ⊕ stress; ⁓ung f (-/-en) claim; demand (gen. on); ⊕ stress, strain.

beanstand|en [bə'anʃtandən] v/t. (no -ge-, h) object to; ⁓ung f (-/-en) objection (gen. to).

beantragen [bə'antra:gən] v/t. (no -ge-, h) apply for; ⁓, parl. move, make a motion; propose.

be'antwort|en v/t. (no -ge-, h) answer (a. fig.), reply to; ⁓ung f (-/-en) answer, reply; in ⁓ (gen.) in answer or reply to.

be'arbeit|en v/t. (no -ge-, h) work; ✗ till; dress (leather); hew (stone); process; ✗ treat; ✗ be in charge of (case); edit, revise (book); adapt (nach from); esp. ♪ arrange; j-n ⁓ work on s.o.; batter s.o.; ⁓ung f (-/-en) working; revision (of book); thea. adaptation; esp. ♪ arrangement; processing; ✗ treatment.

be'argwöhnen v/t. (no -ge-, h) suspect, be suspicious of.

beaufsichtig|en [bə'aufziçtigən] v/t. (no -ge-, h) inspect, superintend, supervise, control; look after (child); ⁓ung f (-/-en) inspection, supervision, control.

be'auftrag|en v/t. (no -ge-, h) commission (zu inf. to inf.), charge (mit with); ⁓te m (-n/-n) commissioner; representative; deputy; proxy.

be'bauen v/t. (no -ge-, h) ▲ build on; ✗ cultivate.

beben ['be:bən] v/i. (ge-, h) shake (vor dat. with), tremble (with); shiver (with); earth: quake.

Becher ['bɛçər] m (-s/-) cup (a. fig.).

Becken ['bɛkən] n (-s/-) basin, Am. a. bowl; ♪ cymbal(s pl.); anat. pelvis.

bedacht adj. [bə'daxt]: ⁓ sein auf (acc.) look after, be concerned about, be careful or mindful of; darauf ⁓ sein zu inf. be anxious to inf.

bedächtig adj. [bə'dɛçtiç] deliberate.

bedang [bə'daŋ] pret. of bedingen.

be'danken v/refl. (no -ge-, h): sich bei j-m für et. ⁓ thank s.o. for s.th.

Bedarf [bə'darf] *m* (-[e]s/*no pl.*) need (*an dat.* of), want (of); ✝ demand (for); ~artikel [bə'darfs⁹-] *m/pl.* necessaries *pl.*, requisites *pl.*

bedauerlich *adj.* [bə'dauərliç] regrettable, deplorable.

be'dauern 1. *v/t.* (*no* -ge-, *h*) feel or be sorry for *s.o.*; pity *s.o.*; regret, deplore *s.th.*; 2. ⚘ *n* (-s/*no pl.*) regret; pity; ~swert *adj.* pitiable, deplorable.

be'deck|en *v/t.* (*no* -ge-, *h*) cover; ✕ escort; ⚓ convoy; ~t *adj.* sky: overcast; ⚘ung *f* cover(ing); ✕ escort; ⚓ convoy.

be'denken 1. *v/t.* (*irr.* denken, *no* -ge-, *h*) consider; think *s.th.* over; *j-n* in *s-m Testament* ~ remember s.o. in one's will; 2. ⚘ *n* (-s/-) consideration; objection; hesitation; scruple; ~los *adj.* unscrupulous.

be'denklich *adj.* doubtful; *character*: a. dubious; *situation, etc.*: dangerous, critical; delicate; risky.

Be'denkzeit *f* time for reflection; *ich gebe dir e-e Stunde* ~ I give you one hour to think it over.

be'deut|en *v/t.* (*no* -ge-, *h*) mean, signify; stand for; ~end *adj.* important, prominent; *sum, etc.* considerable; ~sam *adj.* significant.

Be'deutung *f* meaning, significance; importance; ⚘los *adj.* insignificant; meaningless; ⚘voll *adj.* significant; ~swandel *ling. m* semantic change.

be'dien|en (*no* -ge-, *h*) 1. *v/t.* serve; wait on; ⊕ operate, work (*machine*); ✕ serve (*gun*); answer (*telephone*); *sich* ~ *at table*: help o.s.; 2. *v/i.* serve; wait (at table); *cards*: follow suit; ⚘ung *f* (-/-en) service, *esp.* ✝ attendance; *in restaurant, etc.*: service; waiter, waitress; shop assistant(s *pl.*).

beding|en [bə'diŋən] *v/t.* ([*irr.*,] *no* -ge-, *h*) condition; stipulate; require; cause; imply; ~t *adj.* conditional (*durch on*); restricted; ~ *sein durch* be conditioned by; ⚘ung *f* (-/-en) condition; stipulation; ~en *pl.* ✝ terms *pl.*; ~ungslos *adj.* unconditional.

be'dräng|en *v/t.* (*no* -ge-, *h*) press hard, beset; ⚘nis *f* (-/-se) distress.

be'droh|en *v/t.* (*no* -ge-, *h*) threaten; menace; ~lich *adj.* threatening; ⚘ung *f* threat, menace (*gen.* to).

be'drück|en *v/t.* (*no* -ge-, *h*) oppress; depress; deject; ⚘ung *f* (-/-en) oppression; depression; dejection.

bedungen [bə'duŋən] *p.p.* of bedingen.

be'dürf|en *v/i.* (*irr.* dürfen, *no* -ge-, *h*): *e-r Sache* ~ need or want or require *s.th.*; ⚘nis *n* (-ses/-se) need, want, requirement; *sein* ~ *verrichten* relieve o.s. or nature; ⚘nisan-

stalt [bə'dyrfnis⁹-] *f* public convenience, *Am.* comfort station; ~tig *adj.* needy, poor, indigent.

be'ehren *v/t.* (*no* -ge-, *h*) hono(u)r, favo(u)r; *ich beehre mich zu inf.* I have th. hono(u)r to *inf.*

be'eilen *v. refl.* (*no* -ge-, *h*) hasten, hurry, make haste, *Am.* F a. hustle.

beeindrucken [bə'aindrukən] *v/t.* (*no* -ge- *h*) impress, make an impression on

beeinfluss|en [bə'ainflussən] *v/t.* (*no* -ge-, *h*) influence; affect; *parl.* lobby, ⚘ung *f* (-/-en) influence; *parl.* lobbying

beeinträchtig|en [bə'aintreçtigən] *v/t.* (*no* -ge-, *h*) impair, injure, affect (*adversely*), ⚘ung *f* (-/-en) impairment (*gen* of); injury (to).

be'end|en *v/t.* (*no* -ge-, *h*), ~igen [~igən] *v/t.* (*no* -ge-, *h*) (bring to an) end, finish, terminate; ⚘igung [~iguŋ] *f* (-/-en) ending, termination.

beengt *adj.* [bə'eŋkt] *space:* narrow, confined, cramped; *sich* ~ *fühlen* feel cramped (for room); feel oppressed or uneasy.

be'erben *v/t.* (*no* -ge-, *h*): *j-n* ~ be s.o.'s heir

beerdig|en [bə'eirdigən] *v/t.* (*no* -ge-, *h*) bury, ⚘ung *f* (-/-en) burial, funeral.

Beere ['be:rə] *f* (-/-n) berry.

Beet ✓ [be:t] *n* (-[e]s/-e) bed.

befähig|en [bə'fe:igən] *v/t.* (*no* -ge-, *h*, enable (*zu inf.* to *inf.*); qualify (*für, zu* for); ~t *adj.* [~çt] (*cap*)able, ⚘ung *f* (-/-en) qualification; capacity

befahl [bə'fa:l] *pret.* of befehlen.

befahr|bar *adj.* [bə'fa:rba:r] passable, practicable, trafficable; ⚓ navigable, ~en *v/t.* (*irr.* fahren, *no* -ge-, *h*) drive or travel on; ⚓ navigate (*river*).

be'fallen *v/t.* (*irr.* fallen, *no* -ge-, *h*) attack, befall; *disease:* a. strike; *fear:* seize

be'fangen *adj.* embarrassed; self-conscious, prejudiced (*a.* ⚖); ⚖ bias(s)ed ⚘heit *f* (-/-en) embarrassment self-consciousness; ⚖ bias, prejudice.

be'fassen *v. refl.* (*no* -ge-, *h*): *sich* ~ *mit* occupy o.s. with; engage in; attend to, deal with.

Befehl [bə'fe:l] *m* (-[e]s/-e) command (*über acc.* of); order; ⚘en (*irr.*, *no* -ge-, *h*) 1. *v/t.* command; order; 2. *v/i.* command; ⚘igen [~igən] *v/t.* (*no* -ge-, *h*) command; **Be'fehlshaber** *m* (-s/-) commander(-in-chief, ⚘isch *adj.* imperious.

be'festig|en *v/t.* (*no* -ge-, *h*) fasten (*an dat.* to), fix (to), attach (to); ✕ fortify; *fig.* strengthen; ⚘ung *f* (-/-en) fixing, fastening; ✕ fortification; *fig.* strengthening.

be'feuchten v/t. (no -ge-, h) moisten, damp; wet.

be'finden 1. v/refl. (irr. finden, no -ge-, h) be; **2.** ♀ n (-s/no pl.) (state of) health.

be'flaggen v/t. (no -ge-, h) flag.

be'flecken v/t. (no -ge-, h) spot, stain (a. fig.); fig. sully.

beflissen adj. [bə'flisən] studious; ♀heit f (-/no pl.) studiousness, assiduity.

befohlen [bə'fo:lən] p.p. of befehlen.

be'folg|en v/t. (no -ge-, h) follow, take (advice); obey (rule); adhere to (principle); ♀ung f (-/♀-en) observance (of); adherence (to).

be'förder|n v/t. (no -ge-, h) convey, carry; haul (goods); transport; forward; ✦ ship (a. ⏚); promote (to be) (a. ✗); ♀ung f conveyance, transport(ation), forwarding; promotion; ♀ungsmittel n (means of) transport, Am. (means of) transportation.

be'fragen v/t. (no -ge-, h) question, interview; interrogate.

be'frei|en v/t. (no -ge-, h) (set) free (von from); liberate (nation, mind, etc.) (from); rescue (captive) (from); exempt s.o. (from); deliver s.o. (aus, von from); ♀er m liberator; ♀ung f (-/-en) liberation, deliverance; exemption.

Befremden [bə'fremdən] n (-s/ no pl.) surprise.

befreund|en [bə'frɔyndən] v/refl. (no -ge-, h): sich mit j-m ~ make friends with s.o.; sich mit et. ~ get used to s.th., reconcile o.s. to s.th.; ~et adj. friendly; on friendly terms; ~ sein be friends.

befriedig|en [bə'fri:digən] v/t. (no -ge-, h) satisfy; appease (hunger); meet (expectations, demand); pay off (creditor); ~end adj. satisfactory; ♀ung f (-/-en) satisfaction.

be'fristen v/t. (no -ge-, h) set a time-limit.

be'frucht|en v/t. (no -ge-, h) fertilize; fructify; fecundate; impregnate; ♀ung f (-/-en) fertilization; fructification; fecundation; impregnation.

Befug|nis [bə'fu:knis] f (-/-se) authority, warrant; esp. ♱ competence; ♀t adj. authorized; competent.

be'fühlen v/t. (no -ge-, h) feel; touch, handle, finger.

Be'fund m (-[e]s/-e) result; finding(s pl.); ♱ diagnosis.

be'fürcht|en v/t. (no -ge-, h) fear, apprehend; suspect; ♀ung f (-/-en) fear, apprehension, suspicion.

befürworten [bə'fy:rvɔrtən] v/t. (no -ge-, h) plead for, advocate.

begab|t adj. [bə'ga:pt] gifted, talented; ♀ung [~buŋ] f (-/-en) gift, talent(s pl.).

begann [bə'gan] pret. of beginnen.

be'geben v/t. (irr. geben, no -ge-, h) ✦ negotiate (bill of exchange); sich ~ happen; sich ~ nach go to, make for; sich in Gefahr ~ expose o.s. to danger.

begegn|en [bə'ge:gnən] v/i. (no -ge-, sein) meet s.o. or s.th., meet with; incident: happen to; anticipate, prevent; ♀ung f (-/-en) meeting.

be'gehen v/t. (irr. gehen, no -ge-, h) walk (on); inspect; celebrate (birthday, etc.); commit (crime); make (mistake); ein Unrecht ~ do wrong.

begehr|en [bə'ge:rən] v/t. (no -ge-, h) demand, require; desire, crave (for); long for; ~lich adj. desirous, covetous.

begeister|n [bə'gaistərn] v/t. (no -ge-, h) inspire, fill with enthusiasm; sich ~ für feel enthusiastic about; ♀ung f (-/no pl.) enthusiasm, inspiration.

Be'gier f, ~de [~də] f (-/-n) desire (nach for), appetite (for); concupiscence; ♀ig adj. eager (nach for, auf acc. for; zu inf. to inf.), desirous (nach of; zu inf. to inf.), anxious (zu inf. to inf.).

be'gießen v/t. (irr. gießen, no -ge-, h) water; baste (roasting meat); F wet (bargain).

Beginn [bə'gin] m (-[e]s/no pl.) beginning, start, commencement; origin; ♀en v/t. and v/i. (irr. no -ge-, h) begin, start, commence.

beglaubig|en [bə'glaubigən] v/t. (no -ge-, h) attest, certify; legalize, authenticate; ♀ung f (-/-en) attestation, certification; legalization; ♀ungsschreiben n credentials pl.

be'gleichen v/t. (irr. gleichen, no -ge-, h) pay, settle (bill, debt).

be'gleit|en v/t. (no -ge-, h) accompany (a. ♪ auf dat. on), escort; attend (a. fig.); see (s.o. home, etc.); ♀er m (-s/-) companion, attendant; escort; ♪ accompanist; ♀erscheinung f attendant symptom; ♀schreiben n covering letter; ♀ung f (-/-en) company; attendants pl., retinue (of sovereign, etc.); esp. ✗ escort; ⏚, ✗ convoy; ♪ accompaniment.

be'glückwünschen v/t. (no -ge-, h) congratulate (zu on).

begnadig|en [bə'gna:digən] v/t. (no -ge-, h) pardon; pol. amnesty; ♀ung f (-/-en) pardon; pol. amnesty.

begnügen [bə'gny:gən] v/refl. (no -ge-, h): sich ~ mit content o.s. with, be satisfied with.

begonnen [bə'gɔnən] p.p. of beginnen.

be'graben v/t. (irr. graben, no -ge-, h) bury (a. fig.); inter.

Begräbnis [bə'grɛ:pnis] n (-ses/-se) burial; funeral, obsequies pl.

begradigen [bə'grɑːdigən] *v/t.* (*no -ge-, h*) straighten (*road, frontier, etc.*).

be'greif|en *v/t.* (*irr.* greifen, *no -ge-, h*) comprehend, understand; **~lich** *adj.* comprehensible.

be'grenz|en *v/t.* (*no -ge-, h*) bound, border; *fig.* limit; **2theit** *f* (*-/-en*) limitation (*of knowledge*); narrowness (*of mind*); **2ung** *f* (*-/-en*) boundary; bound, limit; limitation.

Be'griff *m* idea, notion, conception; comprehension; *im ~ sein zu inf.* be about *or* going to *inf.*

be'gründ|en *v/t.* (*no -ge-, h*) establish, found; give reasons for, substantiate (*claim, charge*); **2ung** *f* establishment, foundation; *fig.* substantiation (*of claim or charge*); reason.

be'grüß|en *v/t.* (*no -ge-, h*) greet, welcome; salute; **2ung** *f* (*-/-en*) greeting, welcome; salutation.

begünstig|en [bə'gynstigən] *v/t.* (*no -ge-, h*) favo(u)r; encourage; patronize; **2ung** *f* (*-/-en*) favo(u)r; encouragement; patronage.

begutachten [bə'guːtʔ-] *v/t.* (*no -ge-, h*) give an opinion on; examine; *~ lassen* obtain expert opinion on, submit *s.th.* to an expert.

begütert *adj.* [bə'gyːtərt] wealthy, well-to-do.

be'haart *adj.* hairy.

behäbig *adj.* [bə'hɛːbiç] phlegmatic, comfort-loving; *figure:* portly.

be'haftet *adj.* afflicted (*with disease, etc.*).

behag|en [bə'hɑːgən] **1.** *v/i.* (*no -ge-, h*) please *or* suit *s.o.*; **2.** 2 *n* (*-s/no pl.*) comfort, ease; **~lich** *adj.* [.k-] comfortable; cosy, snug.

be'halten *v/t.* (*irr.* halten, *no -ge-, h*) retain; keep (*für sich* to *o.s.*); remember.

Behälter [bə'hɛltər] *m* (*-s/-*) container, receptacle; box; *for liquid:* reservoir; *for oil, etc.:* tank.

be'hand|eln *v/t.* (*no -ge-, h*) treat; deal with (*a. subject*); ⊕ process; ⚕ treat; dress (*wound*); **2lung** *f* treatment; handling; ⊕ processing.

be'hängen *v/t.* (*no -ge-, h*) hang, drape (*mit with*); *sich ~ mit* cover *or* load *o.s.* with (*jewellery*).

beharr|en [bə'harən] *v/i.* (*no -ge-, h*) persist (*auf dat.* in); **~lich** *adj.* persistent; **2lichkeit** *f* (*-/no pl.*) persistence.

be'hauen *v/t.* (*no -ge-, h*) hew; trim (*wood*).

behaupt|en [bə'hauptən] *v/t.* (*no -ge-, h*) assert; maintain; **2ung** *f* (*-/-en*) assertion; statement.

Behausung [bə'hauzuŋ] *f* (*-/-en*) habitation; lodging.

Be'helf *m* (*-[e]s/-e*) expedient, (make)shift; *s.* Notbehelf; **2en** *v/refl.* (*irr.* helfen, *no -ge-, h*): *sich ~ mit* make shift with; *sich ~ ohne* do without; **~sheim** *n* temporary home.

behend *adj.* [bə'hɛnt], **~e** *adj.* [..də] nimble, agile; smart; **2igkeit** [..d-] *f* (*-/no pl.*) nimbleness, agility; smartness. [lodge, shelter.)

be'herbergen *v/t.* (*no -ge-, h*)

be'herrsch|en *v/t.* (*no -ge-, h*) rule (over), govern, command (*situation, etc.*); have command of (*language*); *sich ~* control *o.s.*; **2er** *m* ruler (*gen.* over, of); **2ung** *f* (*-/-en*) command, control.

beherzigen [bə'hɛrtsigən] *v/t.* (*no -ge-, h*) take to heart, (bear in) mind.

be'hexen *v/t.* (*no -ge-, h*) bewitch.

be'hilflich *adj.*: *j-m ~ sein* help *s.o.* (*bei* in)

be'hindern *v/t.* (*no -ge-, h*) hinder, hamper, impede; handicap; obstruct (*a traffic, etc.*).

Behörde [bə'høːrdə] *f* (*-/-n*) authority, *mst* authorities *pl.*; board; council.

be'hüten *v/t.* (*no -ge-, h*) guard, preserve (*vor dat.* from).

behutsam *adj.* [bə'huːtzɑːm] cautious, careful; **2keit** *f* (*-/no pl.*) caution.

bei *prp.* (*dat.*) *address:* ~ *Schmidt* care of (*abbr.* c/o) Schmidt; *~m Buchhändler* at the bookseller's; ~ *uns* with us; ~ *der Hand nehmen* take by the hand; *ich habe kein Geld ~ mir* I have no money about *or* on me; ~ *der Kirche* near the church; *~ guter Gesundheit* in good health; *wie es ~ Schiller heißt* as Schiller says; *die Schlacht ~ Waterloo* the Battle of Waterloo; ~ *e-m Glase Wein* over a glass of wine; ~ *alledem* for all that; *Stunden nehmen ~* take lessons from *or* with; ~ *günstigem Wetter* weather permitting.

'beibehalten *v/t.* (*irr.* halten, *sep., no -ge-, h*) keep up, retain.

'Beiblatt *n* supplement (*zu* to).

'beibringen *v/t.* (*irr.* bringen, *sep., -ge-, h*) bring forward; produce (*witness, etc.*); *j-m et. ~* impart (*news, etc.*) to *s.o.*; teach *s.o. s.th.*; inflict (*defeat, wound, etc.*) on *s.o.*

Beichte ['baiçtə] *f* (*-/-n*) confession; **2n** *v/t.* *and v/i.* (*ge-, h*) confess.

beide *adj.* ['baidə] both; *nur wir ~* just the two of us; *in ~n Fällen* in either case.

beider|lei *adj.* ['baidərlai] of both kinds; ~ *Geschlechts* of either sex; **'~seitig 1.** *adj.* on both sides; mutual; **2.** *adv.* mutually; **'~seits 1.** *prp.* on both sides (*gen.* of); **2.** *adv.* mutually.

'Beifahrer *m* (*-s/-*) (front-seat) passenger; assistant driver; *motor racing:* co-driver.

'**Beifall** *m* (-[e]s/*no pl.*) approbation; applause; cheers *pl.*

'**beifällig** *adj.* approving; favo(u)rable.

'**Beifallsruf** *m* acclaim; ~e *pl.* cheers *pl.*

'**beifügen** *v/t.* (*sep.*, -ge-, *h*) add; enclose.

'**Beigeschmack** *m* (-[e]s/*no pl.*) slight flavo(u)r; smack (of) (*a. fig.*).

'**Beihilfe** *f* aid; allowance; *for study:* grant; *for project:* subsidy; ᵼᵼᵼ aiding and abetting; *j-m* ~ *leisten* ᵼᵼᵼ aid and abet s.o.

'**beikommen** *v/i.* (*irr. kommen, sep.*, -ge-, *sein*) get at.

Beil [baɪl] *n* (-[e]s/-e) hatchet; chopper; cleaver; ax(e).

'**Beilage** *f* supplement (*to newspaper*); F trimmings *pl.* (*of meal*); vegetables *pl.*

beiläufig *adj.* ['baɪlɔʏfiç] casual; incidental.

'**beileg|en** *v/t.* (*sep.*, -ge-, *h*) add (*dat.* to); enclose; settle (*dispute*); '**2ung** *f* (-/-en) settlement.

Beileid ['baɪlaɪt] *n* condolence; *j-m sein* ~ *bezeigen* condole with s.o. (*zu on, upon*).

'**beiliegen** *v/i.* (*irr. liegen, sep.*, -ge-, *h*) be enclosed (*dat.* with).

'**beimessen** *v/t.* (*irr. messen, sep.*, -ge-, *h*) attribute (*dat.* to), ascribe (to); attach (*importance*) (to).

'**beimisch|en** *v/t.* (*sep.*, -ge-, *h*): e-r *Sache et.* ~ mix s.th. with s.th.; '**2ung** *f* admixture.

Bein [baɪn] *n* (-[e]s/-e) leg; bone.

'**beinah(e)** *adv.* almost, nearly.

'**Beiname** *m* appellation; nickname.

'**Beinbruch** *m* fracture of the leg.

beiordnen ['baɪʔ-] *v/t.* (*sep.*, -ge-, *h*) adjoin; co-ordinate (*a. gr.*).

'**beipflichten** *v/i.* (*sep.*, -ge-, *h*) agree with s.o.; assent to s.th.

'**Beirat** *m* (-[e]s/ᵁᵉ) adviser, counsel(l)or; advisory board.

be'irren *v/t.* (*no -ge-, h*) confuse.

beisammen *adv.* ['baɪ'zamən] together.

'**Beisein** *n* presence; *im* ~ (*gen.*) *or von in the presence of s.o.*, *in s.o.'s* presence.

bei'seite *adv.* aside ‚apart; *Spaß* ~! joking apart!

'**beisetz|en** *v/t.* (*sep.*, -ge-, *h*) bury, inter; '**2ung** *f* (-/-en) burial, funeral.

'**Beisitzer** ᵼᵼᵼ *m* (-s/-) assessor; associate judge; member (*of committee*).

'**Beispiel** *n* example, instance; *zum* ~ *for example or instance;* '**2haft** *adj.* exemplary; '**2los** *adj.* unprecedented, unparalleled; unheard of.

beißen ['baɪsən] (*irr., ge-, h*) **1.** *v/t.* bite; *fleas, etc.:* bite, sting; **2.** *v/i.* bite (*auf acc.* on; *in acc.* into); *fleas, etc.:* bite, sting; *smoke:* bite, burn (*in dat.* in); *pepper, etc.:* bite,

burn (*auf dat.* on); '~d *adj.* biting, pungent (*both a. fig.*); *pepper, etc.:* hot.

'**Beistand** *m* assistance.

'**beistehen** *v/i.* (*irr. stehen, sep.*, -ge-, *h*): *j-m* ~ stand by *or* assist *or* help s.o.

'**beisteuern** *v/t. and v/i.* (*sep.*, -ge-, *h*) contribute (*zu* to).

Beitrag ['baɪtraːk] *m* (-[e]s/ᵁᵉ) contribution; share; subscription, *Am.* dues *pl.*; article (*in newspaper, etc.*).

'**bei|treten** *v/i.* (*irr. treten, sep.*, -ge-, *sein*) join (*political party, etc.*); '**2tritt** *m* joining.

'**Beiwagen** *m* side-car (*of motorcycle*); trailer (*of tram*).

'**Beiwerk** *n* accessories *pl.*

'**beiwohnen** *v/i.* (*sep.*, -ge-, *h*) assist *or* be present at, attend.

bei'zeiten *adv.* early; in good time.

beizen ['baɪtsən] *v/t.* (ge-, *h*) corrode; *metall.* pickle; bate (*hides*); stain (*wood*); ⚕ cauterize; *hunt.* hawk.

bejahen [bə'jaːən] *v/t.* (*no -ge-, h*) answer in the affirmative, affirm; ~d *adj.* affirmative.

be'jahrt *adj.* aged.

Bejahung *f* (-/-en) affirmation, affirmative answer; *fig.* acceptance.

be'jammern *s. beklagen.*

be'kämpfen *v/t.* (*no -ge-, h*) fight (against), combat; *fig.* oppose.

bekannt *adj.* [bə'kant] known (*dat.* to); *j-n mit j-m* ~ *machen* introduce s.o. to s.o.; *2e m, f* (-n/-n) acquaintance, *mst* friend; ~lich *adv.* as you know; ~**machen** *v/t.* (*sep.*, -ge-, *h*) make known; **2machung** *f* (-/-en) publication; public notice; **2schaft** *f* (-/-en) acquaintance.

be'kehr|en *v/t.* (*no -ge-, h*) convert; **2te** *m, f* (-n/-n) convert; **2ung** *f* (-/-en) conversion (*zu* to).

be'kenn|en *v/t.* (*irr. kennen, no -ge-, h*) admit; confess; *sich schuldig* ~ ᵼᵼᵼ plead guilty; *sich* ~ *zu* declare o.s. for; profess *s.th.*; **2tnis** *n* (-ses/-se) confession; creed.

be'klagen *v/t.* (*no -ge-, h*) lament, deplore; *sich* ~ complain (*über acc.* of, about); ~**swert** *adj.* deplorable, pitiable.

Beklagte [bə'klaːktə] *m, f* (-n/-n) *civil case:* defendant, *the* accused.

be'klatschen *v/t.* (*no -ge-, h*) applaud, clap.

be'kleben *v/t.* (*no -ge-, h*) glue or stick *s.th.* on *s.th.*; *mit Etiketten* ~ label *s.th.*; *mit Papier* ~ paste *s.th.* up with paper; *e-e Mauer mit Plakaten* ~ paste (up) posters on a wall.

bekleckern F [bə'klɛkərn] *v/t.* (*no -ge-, h*) stain (*garment*); *sich* ~ soil one's clothes.

be'klecksen *v/t.* (*no -ge-, h*) stain, daub; blot.

be'kleid|en *v/t. (no -ge-, h)* clothe, dress; hold, fill (*office, etc.*); ~ *mit* invest with; 2**ung** *f* clothing, clothes *pl.*

be'klemm|en *v/t. (no -ge-, h)* oppress; 2**ung** *f (-/-en)* oppression; anguish, anxiety.

be'kommen *(irr. kommen, no -ge-)* **1.** *v/t. (h)* get, receive; obtain; get, catch (*illness*); have (*baby*); catch (*train, etc.*); *Zähne* ~ teethe, cut one's teeth; **2.** *v/i. (sein): j-m (gut)* ~ agree with s.o.; *j-m nicht or schlecht* ~ disagree with s.o.

bekömmlich *adj.* [bə'kœmliç] wholesome (*dat.* to).

beköstig|en [bə'kœstigən] *v/t. (no -ge-, h)* board, feed; 2**ung** *f (-/-en)* board(ing).

be'kräftig|en *v/t. (no -ge-, h)* confirm; 2**ung** *f (-/-en)* confirmation.

be'kränzen *v/t. (no -ge-, h)* wreathe; festoon.

be'kritteln *v/t. (no -ge-, h)* carp at, criticize.

be'kümmern *v/t. (no -ge-, h)* afflict, grieve; trouble; *s. kümmern.*

be'laden *v/t. (irr. laden, no -ge-, h)* load; *fig.* burden.

Belag [bə'la:k] *m (-[e]s/ᴗe)* covering; ⊕ coat(ing); surface (*of road*); foil (*of mirror*); ♣ fur (*on tongue*); (slices of) ham, *etc.* (*on bread*); filling (*of roll*).

Belager|er [bə'la:gərər] *m (-s/-)* besieger; 2**n** *v/t. (no -ge-, h)* besiege, beleaguer; ᴗ**ung** *f* siege.

Belang [bə'laŋ] *m (-[e]s/-e)* importance; ᴗ*e pl.* interests *pl.*; 2**en** *v/t. (no -ge-, h)* concern; ⅋⅋ sue; 2**los** *adj.* unimportant; ᴗ**losigkeit** *f (-/-en)* insignificance.

be'lasten *v/t. (no -ge-, h)* load; *fig.* burden; ⅋⅋ incriminate; mortgage (*estate, etc.*); *j-s Konto (mit e-r Summe)* ~ charge *or* debit s.o.'s account (with a sum).

belästig|en [bə'lɛstigən] *v/t. (no -ge-, h)* molest; trouble, bother; 2**ung** *f* molestation; trouble.

Be'lastung *f (-/-en)* load (*a. ⚡, ⊕*); *fig.* burden; ♥ debit; encumbrance; ⅋⅋ incrimination; *erbliche* ~ hereditary taint; ᴗ**szeuge** ⅋⅋ *m* witness for the prosecution.

be'laufen *v/refl. (irr. laufen, no -ge-, h): sich* ~ *auf (acc.)* amount to.

be'lauschen *v/t. (no -ge-, h)* overhear, eavesdrop on *s.o.*

be'leb|en *fig. v/t. (no -ge-, h)* enliven, animate; stimulate; ᴗ**t** *adj. street:* busy, crowded; *stock exchange:* brisk; *conversation:* lively, animated.

Beleg [bə'le:k] *m (-[e]s/-e)* proof; ⅋⅋ (supporting) evidence; document; voucher; 2**en** *v/t. (no -ge-, h)* cover; reserve (*seat, etc.*); prove, verify; *univ.* enrol(l) *or* register for,

Am. a. sign up for (*course of lectures, term*); *ein Brötchen mit et.* ~ put s.th. on a roll, fill a roll with s.th.; ᴗ**schaft** *f (-/-en)* personnel, staff; labo(u)r force; ᴗ**stelle** *f* reference; 2**t** *adj.* engaged, occupied; *hotel, etc.:* full; *voice:* thick, husky; *tongue:* coated, furred; ᴗ*es Brot* (open) sandwich.

be'lehr|en *v/t. (no -ge-, h)* instruct, inform; *sich* ~ *lassen* take advice; ᴗ**end** *adj.* instructive; 2**ung** *f (-/-en)* instruction; information; advice.

beleibt [bə'laɪpt] corpulent, stout, bulky, portly.

beleidig|en [bə'laɪdigən] *v/t. (no -ge-, h)* offend (*s.o.; ear, eye, etc.*); insult; ᴗ**end** *adj.* offensive; insulting; 2**ung** *f (-/-en)* offen|ce, *Am.* -se; insult.

be'lesen *adj.* well-read.

be'leucht|en *v/t. (no -ge-, h)* light (up), illuminate (*a. fig.*); *fig.* shed *or* throw light on; 2**ung** *f (-/-en)* light(ing); illumination; 2**ungskörper** *m* lighting appliance.

Be'lieb|en *n (-s/no pl.)* will, choice; *nach* ~ at will; *es steht in Ihrem* ~ I leave it to you; 2**ig 1.** *adj.* any; *jeder* ᴗ*e* anyone; **2.** *adv.* at pleasure; ~ *viele* as many as you like; 2**t** *adj.* [ᴗpt] popular (*bei* with); ᴗ**theit** *f (-/no pl.)* popularity.

be'liefer|n *v/t. (no -ge-, h)* supply, furnish (*mit* with); 2**ung** *f (-/no pl.)* supply.

bellen ['bɛlən] *v/i. (ge-, h)* bark.

belobigen [bə'lo:bigən] *v/t. (no -ge-, h)* commend, praise.

be'lohn|en *v/t. (no -ge-, h)* reward; recompense; 2**ung** *f (-/-en)* reward; recompense.

be'lügen *v/t. (irr. lügen, no -ge-, h): j-n* ~ lie to s.o.

belustig|en [bə'lustigən] *v/t. (no -ge-, h)* amuse, entertain; *sich* ~ amuse o.s.; 2**ung** *f (-/-en)* amusement, entertainment.

bemächtigen [bə'mɛçtigən] *v/refl. (no -ge-, h): sich e-r Sache* ~ take hold of s.th., seize s.th.; *sich e-r Person* ~ lay hands on s.o., seize s.o.

be'malen *v/t. (no -ge-, h)* cover with paint; paint; daub.

bemängeln [bə'mɛŋəln] *v/t. (no -ge-, h)* find fault with, cavil at.

be'mannen *v/t. (no -ge-, h)* man.

be'merk|bar *adj.* perceptible; ᴗ**en** *v/t. (no -ge-, h)* notice, perceive; remark, mention; ᴗ**enswert** *adj.* remarkable (*wegen* for); 2**ung** *f (-/-en)* remark.

bemitleiden [bə'mitlaɪdən] *v/t. (no -ge-, h)* pity, commiserate (with); ᴗ**swert** *adj.* pitiable.

be'müh|en *v/t. (no -ge-, h)* trouble (*j-n in or wegen et. s.o. about s.th.*);

sich ~ trouble o.s.; endeavo(u)r; *sich um e-e Stelle ~* apply for a position; 2ung *f* (-/-en) trouble; endeavo(u)r, effort.

be'nachbart *adj.* neighbo(u)ring; adjoining, adjacent (to).

benachrichtig|en [bəˈnɑːxrɪçtɪgən] *v/t.* (*no -ge-, h*) inform, notify; ✝ advise; 2ung *f* (-/-en) information; notification; ✝ advice.

benachteilig|en [bəˈnɑːxtaɪlɪgən] *v/t.* (*no -ge-, h*) place *s.o.* at a disadvantage, discriminate against *s.o.*; handicap; *sich benachteiligt fühlen* feel handicapped *or* at a disadvantage; 2ung *f* (-/-en) disadvantage; discrimination; handicap.

be'nehmen 1. *v/refl.* (*irr. nehmen, no -ge-, h*) behave (o.s.); 2. 2 *n* (-s/*no pl.*) behavio(u)r, conduct.

be'neiden *v/t.* (*no -ge-, h*) envy (*j-n um et. s.o. s.th.*); ~swert *adj.* enviable.

be'nennen *v/t.* (*irr. nennen, no -ge-, h*) name.   [rascal; urchin.\

Bengel [ˈbɛŋəl] *m* (-s/-) (little)\

benommen *adj.* [bəˈnɔmən] bemused, dazed, stunned; ~ *sein* be in a daze.

be'nötigen *v/t.* (*no -ge-, h*) need, require, want.

be'nutz|en *v/t.* (*no -ge-, h*) use (*a. patent, etc.*); make use of; avail o.s. of (*opportunity*); take (*tram, etc.*); 2ung *f* use.

Benzin [bɛnˈtsiːn] *n* (-s/-e) ⚙ benzine; *mot.* petrol, F juice, *Am.* gasoline, F gas; ~motor *m* petrol engine, *Am.* gasoline engine; *s.* Tank.

beobacht|en [bəˈʔoːbaxtən] *v/t.* (*no -ge-, h*) observe; watch; *police:* shadow; 2er *m* (-s/-) observer; 2ung *f* (-/-en) observation.

beordern [bəˈʔɔrdərn] *v/t.* (*no -ge-, h*) order, command.

be'packen *v/t.* (*no -ge-, h*) load (*mit with*).   [(*mit with*).\

be'pflanzen *v/t.* (*no -ge-, h*) plant\

bequem *adj.* [bəˈkveːm] convenient, comfortable; *p.:* easy-going; lazy; ~en *v/refl.* (*no -ge-, h*): *sich ~ zu* condescend to; consent to; 2lichkeit *f* (-/-en) convenience; comfort, ease; indolence.

be'rat|en (*irr. raten, no -ge-, h*) 1. *v/t.* advise *s.o.*; consider, debate, discuss *s.th.*; *sich ~ confer* (*mit j-m with s.o.*); *über et. on or about s.th.*); 2. *v/i.* confer; *über et. ~* consider, debate, discuss s.th., confer on *or* about s.th.; 2er *m* (-s/-) adviser, counsel(l)or; consultant; ~schlagen (*no -ge-, h*) 1. *v/i. s. beraten 2*; 2. *v/refl.* confer (*mit j-m with s.o.*; *über et.* on *or* about s.th.); 2ung *f* (-/-en) advice; debate; consultation; conference; 2ungsstelle *f* advisory bureau.

be'raub|en *v/t.* (*no -ge-, h*) rob, deprive (*gen.* of); 2ung *f* (-/-en) robbery, deprivation.

be'rauschen *v/t.* (*no -ge-, h*) intoxicate (*a. fig.*).

be'rechn|en *v/t.* (*no -ge-, h*) calculate; ✝ charge (*zu* at); ~end *adj.* calculating, selfish; 2ung *f* calculation.

berechtig|en [bəˈrɛçtɪgən] *v/t.* (*no -ge-, h*) *j-n ~ zu* entitle s.o. to; authorize s.o. to; ~t *adj.* [~çt] entitled (*zu* to); qualified (to); *claim:* legitimate; 2ung *f* (-/-en) title (*zu* to); authorization.

be'red|en *v/t.* (*no -ge-, h*) talk *s.th.* over; persuade *s.o.*; gossip about *s.o.*; 2samkeit [~tzaːmkaɪt] *f* (-/*no pl.*) eloquence; ~t *adj.* [~t] eloquent (*a. fig.*).

Be'reich *m, n* (-[e]s/-e) area; reach; *fig.* scope, sphere; *science, etc.:* field, province; 2ern *v/t.* (*no -ge-, h*) enrich; *sich ~* enrich o.s.; ~erung *f* (-/-en) enrichment.

be'reif|en *v/t.* (*no -ge-, h*) hoop (*barrel*); tyre, (*Am. only*) tire (*wheel*); 2ung *f* (-/-en) (set of) tyres *pl.*, (*Am. only*) (set of) tires *pl.*

be'reisen *v/t.* (*no -ge-, h*) tour (in), travel (over); *commercial traveller:* cover (*district*).

bereit *adj.* [bəˈraɪt] ready, prepared; ~en *v/t.* (*no -ge-, h*) prepare; give (*joy, trouble, etc.*); ~s *adv.* already; 2schaft *f* (-/-en) readiness; *police:* squad; ~stellen *v/t.* (*sep., -ge-, h*) place *s.th.* ready; provide; 2ung *f* (-/-en) preparation; ~willig *adj.* ready, willing; 2willigkeit *f* (-/*no pl.*) readiness, willingness.

be'reuen *v/t.* (*no -ge-, h*) repent (of); regret, rue.

Berg [bɛrk] *m* (-[e]s/-e) mountain; hill; ~e *pl.* von F heaps *pl.* of, piles *pl.* of; *über den ~ sein* be out of the wood, *Am.* be out of the woods; *über alle ~e* off and away; *die Haare standen ihm zu ~e* his hair stood on end; 2'ab *adv.* downhill (*a. fig.*); 2'an *adv. s.* bergauf; '~arbeiter *m* miner; 2'auf *adv.* uphill (*a. fig.*); '~bahn 🚠 *f* mountain railway; '~bau *m* (-[e]s/*pl.*) mining.

bergen [ˈbɛrgən] *v/t.* (*irr., ge-, h*) save; rescue *s.o.*; ⚓ salvage, salve.

bergig *adj.* [ˈbɛrgɪç] mountainous, hilly.

'Berg|kette *f* mountain chain *or* range; '~mann 🛠 *m* (-[e]s/Bergleute) miner; '~predigt *f* (-/*no pl.*) *the* Sermon on the Mount; '~recht *n* mining laws *pl.*; '~rennen *mot. n* mountain race; '~rücken *m* ridge; '~rutsch *m* landslide, landslip; '~spitze *f* mountain peak; '~steiger *m* (-s/-) mountaineer; '~sturz *m s.* Bergrutsch.

'Bergung f (-/-en) ⚓ salvage; rescue; ~arbeiten ['bɛrguŋs⁹-] f/pl. salvage operations pl.; rescue work.

'Bergwerk n mine; ~saktien ['bɛrkverks⁹-] f/pl. mining shares pl.

Bericht [bə'rɪçt] m (-[e]s/-e) report (über acc. on); account (of); ℒen (no -ge-, h) 1. v/t. report; j-m et. ~ inform s.o. of s.th.; tell s.o. about s.th.; 2. v/i. report (über acc. on); journalist: a. cover (über et. s.th.); ~erstatter m (-s/-) reporter; correspondent; ~erstattung f reporting; report(s pl.).

berichtig|en [bə'rɪçtigən] v/t. (no -ge-, h) correct (s.o.; error, mistake, etc.); put right (mistake); emend (corrupt text); † settle (claim, debt, etc.); ℒung f (-/-en) correction; emendation; settlement.

be'riechen v/t. (irr. riechen, no -ge-, h) smell or sniff at.

Berliner [bɛr'liːnər] 1. m (-s/-) Berliner; 2. adj. (of) Berlin.

Bernstein ['bɛrnʃtam] m amber; schwarzer ~ jet.

bersten ['bɛrstən] v/i. (irr., ge-, sein) burst (fig. vor dat. with).

berüchtigt adj. [bə'rʏçtɪçt] notorious (wegen for), ill-famed.

berücksichtig|en [bə'rʏkzɪçtigən] v/t. (no -ge-, h) take s.th. into consideration, pay regard to s.th.; consider s.o.; ℒung f (-/-en) consideration; regard.

Beruf [bə'ruːf] m (-[e]s/-e) calling; profession; vocation; trade; occupation; ℒen 1. v/t. (irr. rufen, no -ge-, h): j-n zu e-m Amt ~ appoint s.o. to an office; sich auf j-n ~ refer to s.o.; 2. adj. competent; qualified; ℒlich adj. professional; vocational.

Be'rufs|ausbildung f vocational or professional training; ~beratung f vocational guidance; ~kleidung f work clothes pl.; ~krankheit f occupational disease; ~schule f vocational school; ~spieler m sports: professional (player); ℒtätig adj. working; ~tätige [~gə] pl. working people pl.

Be'rufung f (-/-en) appointment (zu to); ℱⱦ appeal (bei dat. to); reference (auf acc. to); ~sgericht n court of appeal.

be'ruhen v/i. (no -ge-, h): ~ auf (dat.) rest or be based on; et. auf sich ~ lassen let a matter rest.

beruhig|en [bə'ruːigən] v/t. (no -ge-, h) quiet, calm; soothe; sich ~ calm down; ℒung f (-/-en) calming (down); soothing; comfort; ℒungsmittel ☞ n sedative.

berühmt adj. [bə'ryːmt] famous (wegen for); celebrated; ℒheit f (-/-en) fame, renown; famous or celebrated person, celebrity; person of note.

be'rühr|en v/t. (no -ge-, h) touch (a. fig.); touch (up)on (subject); ℒung f (-/-en) contact; touch; in ~ kommen mit come into contact with.

be'sag|en v/t. (no -ge-, h) say; mean, signify; ~t adj. [~kt] (afore-)said; above(-mentioned).

besänftigen [bə'zɛnftigən] v/t. (no -ge-, h) appease, calm, soothe.

Be'satz m (-es/~e) trimming; braid.

Be'satzung f ⚔ occupation troops pl.; ⚔ garrison; ⚓, ✈ crew; ~smacht ⚔ f occupying power.

be'schädig|en v/t. (no -ge-, h) damage, injure; ℒung f damage, injury (gen. to).

be'schaffen 1. v/t. (no -ge-, h) procure; provide; raise (money); 2. adj.: gut (schlecht) ~ sein be in good (bad) condition or state; ℒheit f (-/-en) state, condition; properties pl.

beschäftig|en [bə'ʃɛftigən] v/t. (no -ge-, h) employ, occupy; keep busy; sich ~ occupy or busy o.s.; ℒung f (-/-en) employment; occupation.

be'schäm|en v/t. (no -ge-, h) (put to) shame, make s.o. feel ashamed; ~end adj. shameful; humiliating; ~t adj. ashamed (über acc. of); ℒung f (-/-en) shame; humiliation.

beschatten [bə'ʃatən] v/t. (no -ge-, h) shade; fig. shadow s.o., Am. sl. tail s.o.

be'schau|en v/t. (no -ge-, h) look at, view; examine, inspect (goods, etc.); ~lich adj. contemplative, meditative.

Bescheid [bə'ʃaɪt] m (-[e]s/-e) answer; ℱⱦ decision; information (über acc. on, about); ~ geben let s.o. know; ~ bekommen be informed or notified; ~ hinterlassen leave word (bei with, at); ~ wissen be informed, know, F be in the know.

bescheiden adj. [bə'ʃaɪdən] modest, unassuming; ℒheit f (-/no pl.) modesty.

bescheinig|en [bə'ʃaɪnigən] v/i. (no -ge-, h) certify, attest; den Empfang ~ acknowledge receipt; es wird hiermit bescheinigt, daß this is to certify that; ℒung f (-/-en) certification, attestation; certificate; receipt; acknowledgement.

be'schenken v/t. (no -ge-, h): j-n ~ make s.o. a present; j-n mit et. ~ present s.o. with s.th.; j-n reichlich ~ shower s.o. with gifts.

be'scher|en v/t. (no -ge-, h): j-n ~ give s.o. presents (esp. for Christmas); ℒung f (-/-en) presentation of gifts; F fig. mess.

be'schieß|en v/t. (irr. schießen, no -ge-, h) fire or shoot at or on; bombard (a. phys.), shell; ℒung f (-/-en) bombardment.

be'schimpf|en v/t. (no -ge-, h) abuse, insult; call s.o. names; ℒung f (-/-en) abuse; insult, affront.

be'schirmen v/t. (no -ge-, h) shelter, shield, guard, protect (vor dat. from); defend (against).

be'schlafen v/t. (irr. schlafen, no -ge-, h): et. ~ sleep on a matter, take counsel of one's pillow.

Be'schlag m ⊕ metal fitting(s pl.); furnishing(s pl.) (of door, etc.); shoe (of wheel, etc.); (horse)shoe; ⚖ seizure, confiscation; in ~ nehmen, mit ~ belegen seize; ⚖ seize, attach (real estate, salary, etc.); confiscate (goods, etc.); monopolize s.o.'s attention.

be'schlagen 1. v/t. (irr. schlagen, no -ge-, h) cover (mit with); ⊕ fit, mount; shoe (horse); hobnail (shoe); 2. v/i. (irr. schlagen, no -ge-, h) window, wall, etc.: steam up; mirror, etc.: cloud or film over; 3. adj. windows, etc.: steamed-up; fig. well versed (auf, in dat. in).

Beschlagnahme [bə'ʃlaːknaːmə] f (-/-n) seizure; confiscation (of contraband goods, etc.); ⚖ sequestration, distraint (of property); ⚔ requisition (of houses, etc.); embargo, detention (of ship); 2en v/t. (no -ge-, h) seize; attach (real estate); confiscate; ⚖ sequestrate, distrain upon (property); ⚔ requisition; ⚓ embargo.

beschleunig|en [bə'ʃlɔynigən] v/t. (no -ge-, h) mot. accelerate; hasten, speed up; s-e Schritte ~ quicken one's steps; 2ung f (-/-en) acceleration.

be'schließen v/t. (irr. schließen, no -ge-, h) end, close, wind up; resolve, decide.

Be'schluß m decision, resolution, Am. a. resolve; ⚖ decree; 2fähig adj.: ~ sein form or have a quorum; ~fassung f (passing of a) resolution.

be'schmieren v/t. (no -ge-, h) (be)smear (with grease, etc.).

be'schmutzen v/t. (no -ge-, h) soil (a. fig.), dirty; bespatter.

be'schneiden v/t. (irr. schneiden, no -ge-, h) clip, cut; lop (tree); trim, clip (hair, hedge, etc.); dress (vinestock, etc.); fig. cut down, curtail, F slash.

beschönig|en [bə'ʃøːnigən] v/t. (no -ge-, h) gloss over, palliate; 2ung f (-/-en) gloss, palliation.

beschränk|en [bə'ʃrɛŋkən] v/t. (no -ge-, h) confine, limit, restrict, Am. a. curb; sich ~ auf (acc.) confine o.s. to; ~t fig. adj. of limited intelligence; 2ung f (-/-en) limitation, restriction.

be'schreib|en v/t. (irr. schreiben, no -ge-, h) write on (piece of paper, etc.), cover with writing; describe; give a description of; 2ung f (-/-en) description; account.

be'schrift|en v/t. (no -ge-, h) in-

scribe; letter; 2ung f (-/-en) inscription; lettering.

beschuldig|en [bə'ʃuldigən] v/t. (no -ge-, h) accuse (gen. of [doing] s.th.), esp. ⚖ charge (with); 2te [~ktə] m, f (-n/-n) the accused; 2ung f (-/-en) accusation, charge.

Be'schuß m (Beschusses/no pl.) bombardment.

be'schütz|en v/t. (no -ge-, h) protect, shelter, guard (vor dat. from); 2er m (-s/-) protector; 2ung f (-/-en) protection.

be'schwatzen v/t. (no -ge-, h) talk s.o. into (doing) s.th., coax s.o. into (doing s.th.).

Beschwerde [bə'ʃveːrdə] f (-/-n) trouble; ⚕ complaint; complaint (über acc. about); ⚖ objection (gegen to); ~buch n complaints book.

beschwer|en [bə'ʃveːrən] v/t. (no -ge-, h) burden (a. fig.); weight (loose sheets, etc.); lie heavy on (stomach); weigh on (mind, etc.); sich ~ complain (über acc. about, of; bei to); ~lich adj. troublesome.

beschwichtigen [bə'ʃviçtigən] v/t. (no -ge-, h) appease, calm (down), soothe.

be'schwindeln v/t. (no -ge-, h) tell a fib or lie; cheat, F diddle (um out of).

be'schwipst F adj. tipsy.

be'schwör|en v/t. (irr. schwören, no -ge-, h) take an oath on s.th.; implore or entreat s.o.; conjure (up), invoke (spirit); 2ung f (-/-en) conjuration.

be'seelen v/t. (no -ge-, h) animate, inspire.

be'sehen v/t. (irr. sehen, no -ge-, h) look at; inspect; sich et. ~ look at s.th.; inspect s.th.

beseitig|en [bə'zaitigən] v/t. (no -ge-, h) remove, do away with; 2ung f (-/-en) removal.

Besen ['beːzən] m (-s/-) broom; ~stiel m broomstick.

besessen adj. (von by, with) obsessed, possessed (von by, with); wie ~ like mad; 2e m, f (-n/-n) demoniac.

be'setz|en v/t. (no -ge-, h) occupy (seat, table, etc.); fill (post, etc.); man (orchestra); thea. cast (play); ⚔ occupy; trim (dress, etc.); set (crown with jewels, etc.); ~t adj. engaged, occupied; seat: taken; F bus, etc.: full up; hotel: full; teleph. engaged, Am. busy; 2ung f (-/-en) thea. cast; ⚔ occupation.

besichtig|en [bə'ziçtigən] v/t. (no -ge-, h) view, look over; inspect (a. ⚔); visit; 2ung f (-/-en) sightseeing; visit (gen. to); inspection (a. ⚔).

be'sied|eln v/t. (no -ge-, h) colonize, settle; populate; 2lung f (-/-en) colonization, settlement.

be'siegeln v/t. (no -ge-, h) seal (a. fig.).

be'siegen v/t. (no -ge-, h) conquer; defeat, beat (a. sports).

be'sinn|en v/refl. (irr. sinnen, no -ge-, h) reflect, consider; sich ~ auf (acc.) remember, think of; ~lich adj. reflective, contemplative.

Be'sinnung f (-/no pl.) reflection; consideration; consciousness; (wieder) zur ~ kommen recover consciousness; fig. come to one's senses; 2slos adj. unconscious.

Be'sitz m possession; in ~ nehmen, ~ ergreifen von take possession of; 2anzeigend gr. adj. possessive; 2en v/t. (irr. sitzen, no -ge-, h) possess; ~er m (-s/-) possessor, owner, proprietor; den ~ wechseln change hands; ~ergreifung f taking possession (von of), occupation; ~tum n (-s/~er), ~ung f (-/-en) possession; property; estate.

be'sohlen v/t. (no -ge-, h) sole.

besold|en [bə'zɔldən] v/t. (no -ge-, h) pay a salary to (civil servant, etc.); pay (soldier); 2ung f (-/-en) pay; salary.

besonder adj. [bə'zɔndər] particular, special; particular; separate; 2heit f (-/-en) particularity, peculiarity; ~s adv. especially, particularly; chiefly, mainly; separately.

besonnen adj. [bə'zɔnən] sensible, considerate, level-headed; prudent; discreet; 2heit f (-/no pl.) considerateness; prudence; discretion; presence of mind.

be'sorg|en v/t. (no -ge-, h) get (j-m et. s.o. s.th.), procure (s.th. for s.o.); do, manage; 2nis [~knis] f (-/-se) apprehension, fear, anxiety, concern (über acc. about, at); ~niserregend adj. alarming; ~t adj. [~kt] uneasy (um about); worried (about), concerned (about); anxious (um for, about); 2ung f (-/-en) procurement; management; errand; ~en machen go shopping.

be'sprech|en v/t. (irr. sprechen, no -ge-, h) discuss, talk s.th. over; arrange; review (book, etc.); sich ~ mit confer with (über acc. about); 2ung f (-/-en) discussion; review; conference.

be'spritzen v/t. (no -ge-, h) splash, (be)spatter.

besser ['besər] 1. adj. better; superior; 2. adv. better; 2n v/t. (ge-, h) (make) better, improve; reform; sich ~ get or become better, improve, change for the better; mend one's ways; 2ung f (-/-en) improvement; change for the better; reform (of character); ~ improvement, recovery; gute ~! I wish you a speedy recovery!

best [best] 1. adj. best; der erste ~e (just) anybody; ~en Dank thank

you very much; sich von s-r ~en Seite zeigen be on one's best behavio(u)r; 2. adv. best; am ~en best; aufs ~e, ~ens in the best way possible; zum ~en geben recite (poem), tell (story), oblige with (song); j-n zum ~en haben or halten make fun of s.o., F pull s.o.'s leg; ich danke ~ens! thank you very much!

Be'stand m (continued) existence; continuance; stock; † stock-in-trade; † cash in hand; ~ haben be lasting, last.

be'ständig adj. constant, steady; lasting; continual; weather: settled; 2keit f (-/-en) constancy, steadiness; continuance.

Bestand|saufnahme † [bə-'ʃtants⁹-] f stock-taking, Am. inventory; ~teil m component, constituent; element, ingredient; part.

be'stärken v/t. (no -ge-, h) confirm, strengthen, encourage (in dat. in).

bestätig|en [bə'ʃtɛːtigən] v/t. confirm (a. ↱↰ verdict, † order); attest; verify (statement, etc.); ratify (law, treaty); † acknowledge (receipt); 2ung f (-/-en) confirmation; attestation; verification; ratification; acknowledgement.

bestatt|en [bə'ʃtatən] v/t. (no -ge-, h) bury, inter; 2ung f (-/-en) burial, interment; funeral; 2ungsinstitut [bə'ʃtatuŋs⁹-] n undertakers pl.

'Beste 1. n (-n/no pl.) the best (thing); zu deinem ~n in your interest; zum ~n der Armen for the benefit of the poor; das ~ daraus machen make the best of it; 2. m, f (-n/-n): er ist der ~ in s-r Klasse he is the best in his class.

Besteck n (-[e]s/-e) ⚕ (case or set of) surgical instruments pl.; (single set of) knife, fork and spoon; (complete set of) cutlery, Am. a. flatware.

be'stehen 1. v/t. (irr. stehen, no -ge-, h) come off victorious in (combat, etc.); have (adventure); stand, undergo (well) (test, trial); pass (test, examination); 2. v/i. (irr. stehen, no -ge-, h) be, exist; continue, last; ~ auf (dat.) insist (up)on; ~ aus consist of; 3. 2 n (-s/no pl.) existence; continuance; passing.

be'stehlen v/t. (irr. stehlen, no -ge-, h) steal from, rob.

be'steig|en v/t. (irr. steigen, no -ge-, h) climb (up) (mountain, tree, etc.); mount (horse, bicycle, etc.); ascend (throne); get into or on, board (bus, train, plane); 2ung f ascent; accession (to throne).

be'stell|en v/t. (no -ge-, h) order; † a. place an order for; subscribe to (newspaper, etc.); book, reserve (room, seat, etc.); make an appointment with s.o.; send for (taxi, etc.); cultivate, till (soil, etc.); give (message, greetings); *j-n zu sich* ~ send for s.o.; 2ung *f* order; subscription (to); booking, *esp. Am.* reservation; ✗ cultivation; message.

'besten'falls *adv.* at (the) best.

be'steuer|n *v/t.* (*no* -ge-, *h*) tax; 2ung *f* taxation.

besti|alisch *adj.* [bɛst'jɑːliʃ] bestial; brutal; inhuman; *weather, etc.*: ✗ beastly; 2e ['ˌjə] *f* (-/-n) beast; *fig.* brute, beast, inhuman person.

be'stimmen (*no* -ge-, *h*) **1.** *v/t.* determine, decide; fix (*date, place, price, etc.*); appoint (*date, time, place, etc.*); prescribe; define (*species, word, etc.*); *j-n für* or *zu et.* ~ designate *or* intend s.o. for s.th.; **2.** *v/i.*: ~ *über* (*acc.*) dispose of.

be'stimmt **1.** *adj. voice, manner, etc.*: decided, determined, firm; *time, etc.*: appointed, fixed; *point, number, etc.*: certain; *answer, etc.*: positive; *tone, answer, intention, idea*: definite (*a. gr.*); ~ *nach* ♠. ✗ bound for; **2.** *adv.* certainly, surely; 2heit *f* (-/-en) determination, firmness; certainty.

Be'stimmung *f* determination; destination (*of s.o. for the church, etc.*); designation, appointment (*of s.o. as successor, etc.*); definition; *fig.* provision (*in document*); (*amtliche*) ~en *pl.* (official) regulations *pl.*; ~sort [bəˈʃtimuŋsˀ-] *m* destination.

be'straf|en *v/t.* (*no* -ge-, *h*) punish (*wegen, für* for; *mit* with); 2ung *f* (-/-en) punishment.

be'strahl|en *v/t.* (*no* -ge-, *h*) irradiate (*a.* ✗); 2ung *f* irradiation; ✗ ray treatment, radiotherapy.

Be'streb|en *n* (-s/*no pl.*), ~ung *f* (-/-en) effort, endeavo(u)r.

be'streichen *v/t.* (*irr.* streichen, *no* -ge-, *h*) coat, cover; spread; *mit Butter* ~ butter.

be'streiten *v/t.* (*irr.* streiten, *no* -ge-, *h*) contest, dispute, challenge (*point, right, etc.*); deny (*facts, guilt, etc.*); defray (*expenses, etc.*); fill (*programme*).

be'streuen *v/t.* (*no* -ge-, *h*) strew, sprinkle (*mit* with); *mit Mehl* ~ flour; *mit Zucker* ~ sugar.

be'stürmen *v/t.* (*no* -ge-, *h*) storm, assail (*a. fig.*); pester, plague (*s.o. with questions, etc.*).

be'stürz|t *adj.* dismayed, struck with consternation (*über acc.* at); 2ung *f* (-/-en) consternation, dismay.

Besuch [bəˈzuːx] *m* (-[e]s/-e) visit (*gen., bei, in dat.* to); call (*bei* on; *in dat.* at); attendance (*gen.* at) (*lecture, church, etc.*); visitor(s *pl.*), company; 2en *v/t.* (*no* -ge-, *h*) visit; call on, go to see; attend (*school, etc.*); frequent; ~er *m* visitor, caller; ~szeit *f* visiting hours *pl.*

be'tasten *v/t.* (*no* -ge-, *h*) touch, feel, finger; ✗ palpate.

betätigen [bəˈtɛːtigən] *v/t.* (*no* -ge-, *h*) ⊕ operate (*machine, etc.*); put on, apply (*brake*); *sich* ~ *als* act *or* work as; *sich politisch* ~ dabble in politics.

betäub|en [bəˈtɔybən] *v/t.* (*no* -ge-, *h*) stun (*a. fig.*), daze (*by blow, noise, etc.*); deafen (*by noise, etc.*); *slaughtering*: stun (*animal*); ✗ an(a)esthetize; 2ung *f* (-/-en) ✗ an(a)esthetization; ✗ an(a)esthesia; *fig.* stupefaction; 2ungsmittel ✗ *n* narcotic, an(a)esthetic.

beteilig|en [bəˈtailigən] *v/t.* (*no* -ge-, *h*): *j-n* ~ give s.o. a share (*an dat.* in); *sich* ~ take part (*an dat., bei* in), participate (*a.* 2⅓) (in); 2te [ˌçtə] *m, f* (-n/-n) person *or* party concerned; 2ung *f* (-/-en) participation (*a.* 2⅓, ✗), partnership; share, interest (*a.* ✗).

beten ['beːtən] *v/i.* (ge-, *h*) pray (*um* for), say one's prayers; *at table*: say grace

be'teuer|n *v/t.* (*no* -ge-, *h*) protest (*one's innocence*); swear (*to s.th.*; that); 2ung *f* protestation; solemn declaration.

be'titeln *v/t.* (*no* -ge-, *h*) entitle (*book, etc.*); style (*s.o. 'baron', etc.*).

Beton ⊕ [beˈtɔ̃; beˈtɔːn] *m* (-s/-s; -s/-e) concrete.

be'tonen *v/t.* (*no* -ge-, *h*) stress; *fig. a.* emphasize.

betonieren [betoˈniːrən] *v/t.* (*no* -ge-, *h*) concrete.

Be'tonung *f* (-/-en) stress; emphasis.

betör|en [bəˈtøːrən] *v/t.* (*no* -ge-, *h*) dazzle; infatuate, bewitch; 2ung *f* (-/-en) infatuation.

Betracht [bəˈtraxt] *m* (-[e]s/*no pl.*): *in* ~ *ziehen* take into consideration; (*nicht*) *in* ~ *kommen* (not to) come into question; 2en *v/t.* (*no* -ge-, *h*) view; contemplate; *fig. a.* consider.

beträchtlich *adj.* [bəˈtrɛçtliç] considerable.

Be'trachtung *f* (-/-en) view; contemplation; consideration.

Betrag [bəˈtraːk] *m* (-[e]s/ᵘe) amount, sum; 2en [ˌgən] **1.** *v/t.* (*irr.* tragen, *no* -ge-, *h*) amount to; **2.** *v/refl.* (*irr.* tragen, *no* -ge-, *h*) behave (o.s.); **3.** 2 *n* (-s/*no pl.*) behavio(u)r, conduct.

be'trauen *v/t.* (*no* -ge-, *h*): *j-n mit et.* ~ entrust *or* charge s.o. with s.th.

be'trauern *v/t.* (*no* -ge-, *h*) mourn (for, over).

Betreff [bəˈtrɛf] *m* (-[e]s/-e) *at head of letter*: reference; 2en *v/t.* (*irr.* treffen, *no* -ge-, *h*) befall; refer to; concern; *was ... betrifft* as for, as to; 2end *adj.* concerning; *das* ~e *Geschäft* the business referred to *or* in question; 2s *prp.* (*gen.*) concerning; as to.

be'treiben 1. *v/t.* (*irr.* treiben, no -ge-, *h*) carry on (*business, etc.*); pursue (*one's studies*); operate (*railway line, etc.*); 2. 2 *n* (-s/*no pl.*): auf ~ von at *or* by *s.o.'s* instigation.
be'treten 1. *v/t.* (*irr.* treten, no -ge-, *h*) step on; enter (*room, etc.*); 2. *adj.* embarrassed, abashed.
betreu|en [bə'trɔyən] *v/t.* (no -ge-, *h*) look after; attend to; care for; 2ung *f* (-/*no pl.*) care (*gen.* of, for).
Betrieb [bə'tri:p] *m* (-[e]s/-e) working, running, *esp. Am.* operation; business, firm, enterprise; plant, works *sg.*; workshop, *Am. a.* shop; *fig.* bustle; in ~ working; 2sam *adj.* active; industrious.
Be'triebs|anleitung *f* operating instructions *pl.*; ~ausflug *m* firm's outing; ~ferien *pl.* (firm's, works) holiday; ~führer *m s.* Betriebsleiter; ~kapital *n* working capital; ~kosten *pl.* working expenses *pl.*, *Am.* operating costs *pl.* ~leiter *m* (works) manager, superintendent; ~leitung *f* management; ~material *n* working materials *pl.*; ❤ rolling stock; ~rat *m* works council; 2sicher *adj.* safe to operate; foolproof; ~störung *f* breakdown; ~unfall *m* industrial accident, accident while at work.
be'trinken *v/refl.* (*irr.* trinken, no -ge-, *h*) get drunk.
betroffen *adj.* [bə'trɔfən] afflicted (von by), stricken (with); *fig.* disconcerted.
be'trüben *v/t.* (no -ge-, *h*) grieve, afflict.
Be'trug *m* cheat(ing); fraud (*a.* ❤❤); deceit.
be'trüg|en *v/t.* (*irr.* trügen, no -ge-, *h*) deceive; cheat (*a. at games*); defraud; F skin; 2er *m* (-s/-) cheat, deceiver, impostor, confidence man, swindler, trickster; ~erisch *adj.* deceitful, fraudulent.
be'trunken *adj.* drunken; *pred.* drunk; 2e *m* (-n/-n) drunk(en man).
Bett [bɛt] *n* (-[e]s/-en) bed; ~bezug *m* plumeau case; ~decke *f* blanket; bedspread, coverlet.
Bettel|brief ['bɛtəl-] *m* begging letter; ~ei [~'laɪ] *f* (-/-en) begging, mendicancy; 2n *v/i.* (ge-, *h*) beg (um for); ~ gehen go begging; ~stab *m*: an den ~ bringen reduce to beggary.
'Bett|gestell *n* bedstead; 2lägerig *adj.* ['~lɛːgəriç] bedridden, confined to bed, *Am. a.* bedfast; ~laken *n* sheet.
Bettler ['bɛtlər] *m* (-s/-) beggar, *Am. sl.* panhandler.
'Bett|überzug *m* plumeau case; ~uch ['bɛtu:x] *n* sheet; ~vorleger *m* bedside rug; ~wäsche *f* bedlinen; ~zeug *n* bedding.
be'tupfen *v/t.* (no -ge-, *h*) dab.

beug|en ['bɔygən] *v/t.* (ge-, *h*) bend, bow; *fig.* humble, break (*pride*); *gr.* inflect (*word*), decline (*noun, adjective*); sich ~ bend (vor *dat.* to), bow (to); 2ung *f* (-/-en) bending; *gr.* inflection, declension.
Beule ['bɔylə] *f* (-/-n) bump, swelling; boil; *on metal, etc.*: dent.
beunruhig|en [bə'unru:igən] *v/t.* (no -ge-, *h*) disturb, trouble, disquiet, alarm; sich ~ über (*acc.*) be uneasy about, worry about; 2ung *f* (-/*no pl.*) disturbance; alarm; uneasiness.
beurkund|en [bə'u:rkundən] *v/t.* (no -ge-, *h*) attest, certify, authenticate; 2ung *f* (-/-en) attestation, certification, authentication.
beurlaub|en [bə'u:rlaubən] *v/t.* (no -ge-, *h*) give *or* grant *s.o.* leave (of absence); give *s.o.* time off; suspend (*civil servant, etc.*); 2ung *f* (-/-en) leave (of absence); suspension.
beurteil|en [bə'urtaɪlən] *v/t.* (no -ge-, *h*) judge (nach by); 2ung *f* (-/-en) judg(e)ment.
Beute ['bɔytə] *f* (-/*no pl.*) booty, spoil(s *pl.*); loot; prey; *hunt.* bag; *fig.* prey, victim (*gen.* to).
Beutel ['bɔytəl] *m* (-s/-) bag; purse; pouch.
'Beutezug *m* plundering expedition.
bevölker|n [bə'fœlkərn] *v/t.* (no -ge-, *h*) people, populate; 2ung *f* (-/-en) population.
bevollmächtig|en [bə'fɔlmɛçtigən] *v/t.* (no -ge-, *h*) authorize, empower; 2te [~çtə] *m, f* (-n/-n) authorized person *or* agent, deputy; *pol.* plenipotentiary; 2ung *f* (-/-en) authorization.
be'vor *cj.* before.
bevormund|en *fig.* [bə'fo:rmundən] *v/t.* (no -ge-, *h*) patronize, keep in tutelage; 2ung *f* (-/-en) patronizing, tutelage.
be'vorstehen *v/i.* (*irr.* stehen, sep., -ge-, *h*) be approaching, be near; *crisis, etc.*: be imminent; j-m ~ be in store for *s.o.*, await *s.o.*; ~d *adj.* approaching; imminent.
bevorzug|en [bə'fo:rtsu:gən] *v/t.* (no -ge-, *h*) prefer; favo(u)r; ❤❤ privilege; 2ung *f* (-/-en) preference.
be'wach|en *v/t.* (no -ge-, *h*) guard, watch; 2ung *f* (-/-en) guard; escort.
bewaffn|en [bə'vafnən] *v/t.* (no -ge-, *h*) arm; 2ung *f* (-/-en) armament; arms *pl.*
be'wahren *v/t.* (no -ge-, *h*) keep, preserve (*mst fig.*: secret, silence, *etc.*).
be'währen *v/refl.* (no -ge-, *h*) stand the test, prove a success; sich ~ als prove o.s. (as) (*a good teacher, etc.*); sich ~ in prove o.s. efficient in (*one's profession, etc.*); sich nicht ~ prove a failure.

be'wahrheiten v/refl. (no -ge-, h) prove (to be) true; prophecy, etc.: come true.

be'währt adj. friend, etc.: tried; solicitor, etc.: experienced; friendship, etc.: long-standing; remedy, etc.: proved, proven.

Be'währung f z̄ʒ probation; in Zeiten der ~ in times of trial; s. bewähren; ~sfrist z̄ʒ f probation.

bewaldet adj. [bə'valdət] wooded, woody, Am. a. timbered.

bewältigen [bə'vɛltigən] v/t. (no -ge-, h) overcome (obstacle); master (difficulty); accomplish (task).

be'wandert adj. (well) versed (in dat. in), proficient (in); in e-m Fach gut ~ sein have a thorough knowledge of a subject.

be'wässer|n v/t. (no -ge-, h) water (garden, lawn, etc.); irrigate (land, etc.); ung f (-/-en) watering; irrigation.

bewegen[1] [bə've:gən] v/t. (irr., no -ge-, h): j-n ~ zu induce or get s.o. to.

beweg|en[2] [] v/t. and v/refl. (no -ge-, h) move, stir; grund [k-] m motive (gen., für for); lich adj. [k-] movable; p., mind, etc.: agile, versatile; active; lichkeit [k-] f (-/no pl.) mobility; agility, versatility; t adj. [kt] sea: rough, heavy; fig. moved, touched; voice: choked, trembling; life: eventful; times, etc.: stirring, stormy; ung f (-/-en) movement; motion (a. phys.); fig. emotion; in ~ setzen set going or in motion; ungslos adj. motionless, immobile.

be'weinen v/t. (no -ge-, h) weep or cry over; lament (for, over).

Beweis [bə'vais] m (-es/-e) proof (für of); ~e (pl.) evidence (esp. z̄ʒ); en [zən] v/t. (irr. weisen, no -ge-, h) prove; show (interest, etc.); ~führung f argumentation; ~grund m argument; ~material n evidence; ~stück n (piece of) evidence; z̄ʒ exhibit.   [leave it at that.]

be'wenden vb.: es dabei ~ lassen⟩

be'werb|en v/refl. (irr. werben, no -ge-, h): sich ~ um apply for, Am. run for; stand for; compete for (prize); court (woman); er m (-s/-) applicant (um for); candidate; competitor; suitor; ung f application; candidature; competition; courtship; ungsschreiben n (letter of) application.

bewerkstelligen [bə'vɛrkʃtɛligən] v/t. (no -ge-, h) manage, effect, bring about.

be'wert|en v/t. (no -ge-, h) value (auf acc. at; nach by); ung f valuation.

bewillig|en [bə'viligən] v/t. (no -ge-, h) grant, allow; ung f (-/-en) grant, allowance.

be'wirken v/t. (no -ge-, h) cause; bring about, effect.

be'wirt|en v/t. (no -ge-, h) entertain; ~schaften v/t. (no -ge-, h) farm (land); ↗ cultivate (field); manage (farm, etc.); ration (food, etc.); control (foreign exchange, etc.); ung f (-/-en) entertainment; hospitality.

bewog [bə'vo:k] pret. of bewegen[1]; ~en [bə'vo:gən] p.p. of bewegen[1].

be'wohn|en v/t. (no -ge-, h) inhabit, live in; occupy; er m (-s/-) inhabitant; occupant.

bewölk|en [bə'vœlkən] v/refl. (no -ge-, h) sky: cloud up or over; brow: cloud over, darken; ~t adj. sky: clouded, cloudy, overcast; brow: clouded, darkened; ung f (-/no pl.) clouds pl.

be'wunder|n v/t. (no -ge-, h) admire (wegen for); ~nswert adj. admirable; ung f (-/-en) admiration.

bewußt adj. [bə'vust] deliberate, intentional; sich e-r Sache ~ sein be conscious or aware of s.th.; die ~e Sache the matter in question; ~los adj. unconscious; sein n (-s/no pl.) consciousness.

be'zahl|en v/t. (no -ge-, h) 1. v/t. pay; pay for (s.th. purchased); pay off, settle (debt); 2. v/i. pay (für for); ung f payment; settlement.

be'zähmen v/t. (no -ge-, h) tame (animal); restrain (one's anger, etc.); sich ~ control or restrain o.s.

be'zauber|n v/t. (no -ge-, h) bewitch, enchant (a. fig.); fig. charm, fascinate; ung f (-/-en) enchantment, spell; fascination.

be'zeichn|en v/t. (no -ge-, h) mark; describe (als as), call; ~end adj. characteristic, typical (für of); ung f indication (of direction, etc.); mark, sign, symbol; name, designation, denomination.

be'zeugen v/t. (no -ge-, h) z̄ʒ testify to, bear witness to (both a. fig.); attest.

be'zieh|en v/t. (irr. ziehen, no -ge-, h) cover (upholstered furniture, etc.); put cover on (cushion, etc.); move into (flat, etc.); enter (university); draw (salary, pension, etc.); get, be supplied with (goods); take in (newspaper, etc.); sich ~ sky: cloud over; sich ~ auf (acc.) refer to; er m (-s/-) subscriber (gen. to).

Be'ziehung f relation (zu et. to s.th.; zu j-m with s.o.); connexion, (Am. only) connection (zu with); in dieser ~ in this respect; sweise adv. respectively; or rather.

Bezirk [bə'tsirk] m (-[e]s/-e) district, Am. a. precinct; s. Wahlbezirk.

Bezogene † [bə'tso:gənə] m (-n/-n) drawee.

Bezug [bə'tsu:k] m cover(ing), case; purchase (of goods); subscription (*to newspaper*); in ~ auf (*acc.*) with regard *or* reference to, as to; ~ nehmen auf (*acc.*) refer to, make reference to.

be'züglich [bə'tsy:kliç] 1. *adj.* relative, relating (*both: auf acc.* to); 2. *prp.* (*gen.*) regarding, concerning.

Be'zugsbedingungen † *f/pl.* terms *pl.* of delivery

be'zwecken *v/t.* (*no -ge-, h*) aim at; ~ *mιt* intend by.

be'zweifeln *v/t.* (*no -ge-, h*) doubt, question

be'zwing|en *v/t.* (*irr.* zwingen, *no -ge-, h*) conquer (*fortress, mountain, etc.*); overcome, master (*feeling, difficulty, etc.*); sich ~ keep o.s. under control, restrain o.s.; 2ung *f* (*-/-en*) conquest; mastering.

Bibel [bi:bəl] *f* (*-/-n*) Bible.

Biber *zo* ['bi:bər] *m* (*-s/-*) beaver.

Bibliothek [biblio'te:k] *f* (*-/-en*) library, ~ar [~e'ka:r] *m* (*-s/-e*) librarian

biblisch *adj.* ['bi:bliʃ] biblical, scriptural, ~e Geschichte Scripture.

bieder *adj.* ['bi:dər] honest, upright, worthy (*a. iro.*); simple-minded; 2keit *f* (*-/no pl.*) honesty, uprightness; simple-mindedness.

bieg|en ['bi:gən] (*irr.*, ge-) 1. *v/t.* (*h*) bend; 2. *v/refl.* (*h*) bend; sich vor Lachen ~ double up with laughter; 3. *v/i.* (*sein*): um e-e Ecke ~ turn (round) a corner, ~sam *adj.* ['bi:kza:m] *wire, etc.* flexible; *body:* lithe, supple; pliant (*a. fig.*); '2samkeit *f* (*-/no pl.*) flexibility; suppleness; pliability, '2ung *f* (*-/-en*) bend, wind (*of road, river*); curve (*of road, arch*).

Biene *zo* ['bi:nə] *f* (*-/-n*) bee; '~nkönigin *f* queen bee; '~nkorb *m* (bee)hive, '~nschwarm *m* swarm of bees, '~nstock *m* (bee)hive; '~nzucht *f* bee-keeping; '~nzüchter *m* bee-keeper

Bier [bi:r] *n* (*-[e]s/-e*) beer; helles ~ pale beer, ale; *dunkles* ~ dark beer, stout, porter; ~ vom Faß beer on draught, '~brauer *m* brewer; '~brauerei *f* brewery; '~garten *m* beer-garden; '~krug *m* beer-mug, Am. stein

Biest [bi:st] *n* (*-es/-er*) beast, brute.

bieten ['bi:tən] (*irr.*, ge-, *h*) 1. *v/t.* offer; ↑ at auction sale: bid; sich ~ opportunity, etc.: offer itself, arise, occur; 2. ↑ *v/i.* at auction sale: bid.

Bigamie [biga'mi:] *f* (*-/-n*) bigamy.

Bilanz [bi'lants] *f* (*-/-en*) balance; balance-sheet, Am. a. statement; *fig.* result, outcome; die ~ ziehen strike a balance; *fig.* take stock (*of one's life, etc.*).

Bild [bilt] *n* (*-[e]s/-er*) picture; image; illustration; portrait; *fig.* idea, notion; '~bericht *m press:* picture story.

bilden ['bildən] *v/t.* (*ge-, h*) form; shape; *fig.* educate, train (*s.o., mind, etc.*); develop (*mind, etc.*); form, be, constitute (*obstacle, etc.*); sich ~ form; *fig* educate o.s., improve one's mind, sich e-e Meinung ~ form an opinion.

Bilder|buch ['bildər-] *n* picturebook; '~galerie *f* picture-gallery; '~rätsel *n* rebus

'Bild|fläche *f* ↑ auf der ~ erscheinen appear on the scene; F von der ~ verschwinden disappear (from the scene); '~funk *m* radio picture transmission; television; '~hauer *m* (*-s/-*) sculptor, '~hauerei [~'raɪ] *f* (*-/-en*) sculpture; '2lich *adj.* pictorial; *word, etc* figurative; '~nis *n* (*-ses/-se*) portrait, '~röhre *f* picture *or* television tube; '~säule *f* statue; '~schirm *m* (television) screen; '2'schön *adj.* most beautiful; '~seite *f* face, head (*of coin*); '~streifen *m* picture *or* film strip; '~telegraphie *f* (*-/no pl.*) phototelegraphy

'Bildung *f* (*-/-en*) forming, formation (*both a. gr.* of plural, *etc.*); constitution, (*of committee, etc.*); education; culture, (good) breeding. [sg , billiard-table.]

Billard ['biljart] *n* ‹*-s/-e*› billiards)

billig *adj* ['bilıç] just, equitable; fair; *price* reasonable, moderate; *goods:* cheap, inexpensive; *recht und* ~ right and proper, ~en ['~gən] *v/t.* (*ge-, h*) approve of, Am. a. approbate, '2keit *f* (*-/no pl.*) justness, equity, fairness, reasonableness, moderateness, 2ung ['~guŋ] *f* (*-/~-en*) approval, sanction.

Binde ['bində] *f* (*-/-n*) band; tie; ⚕ bandage, (arm-)sling; *s. Damenbinde;* '~gewebe *anat. n* connective tissue, '~glied *n* connecting link; '~haut *anat f* conjunctiva; '~hautentzündung ⚕ *f* conjunctivitis; '2n (*irr*, ge-, *h*) 1. *v/t.* bind, tie (*an acc* to); bind (*book, etc.*); make (*broom, wreath, etc.*); knot (*tie*); sich ~ bind *or* commit *or* engage o.s.; 2. *v/i* bind; unite; ⊕ cement, etc. set, harden; '~strich *m* hyphen; '~wort *gr. n* (*-[e]s/~er*) conjunction

Bindfaden ['bint-] *m* string; packthread.

'Bindung *f* (*-/-en*) binding (*a.* of *ski*); ♪ slur, tie, ligature; *fig.* commitment (*a pol.*); engagement; ~en *pl.* bonds *pl*, ties *pl.*

binnen *prp* (*dat., a. gen.*) ['binən] within; ~ kurzem before long.

'Binnen|gewässer *n* inland water; '~hafen *m* close port; '~handel *m* domestic *or* home trade, Am. domestic commerce; '~land *n* inland, interior; '~verkehr *m* inland traffic *or* transport.

Binse ⚘ ['bɪnzə] f (-/-n) rush; F: *in die ⁓n gehen* go to pot; '⁓nwahrheit f, ⁓nweisheit f truism.

Biochemie [bioçe'mi:] f (-/no pl.) biochemistry.

Biograph|ie [biogra'fi:] f (-/-n) biography; **2isch** adj. [⁓'grɑ:fiʃ] biographic(al).

Biolog|ie [biolo'gi:] f (-/no pl.) biology; **2isch** adj. [⁓'lo:giʃ] biological.

Birke ⚘ ['bɪrkə] f (-/-n) birch(-tree).

Birne ['bɪrnə] f (-/-n) ⚘ pear; ∮ (electric) bulb; fig. sl. nob, Am. bean.

bis [bɪs] 1. prp. (acc.) space: to, as far as; time: till, until, by; zwei ⁓ drei two or three, two to three; ⁓ auf weiteres until further orders, for the meantime; ⁓ vier zählen count up to four; alle ⁓ auf drei all but or except three; 2. cj. till, until.

Bisamratte zo. ['bi:zam-] f muskrat.

Bischof ['bɪʃɔf] m (-s/⁼e) bishop.

bischöflich adj. ['bɪʃøfliç] episcopal.

bisher adv. [bɪs'he:r] hitherto, up to now, so far; ⁓ig adj. until now; hitherto existing; former.

Biß [bɪs] 1. m (Bisses/Bisse) bite; 2. ⚲ pret. of beißen.

bißchen ['bɪsçən] 1. adj.: ein ⁓ a little, (a little) bit of; 2. adv.: ein ⁓ a little (bit).

Bissen ['bɪsən] m (-s/-) mouthful; morsel; bite.

'**bissig** adj. biting (a. fig.); remark: cutting; Achtung, ⁓er Hund! beware of the dog!

Bistum ['bɪstu:m] n (-s/⁼er) bishopric, diocese.

bisweilen adv. [bɪs'vaɪlən] sometimes, at times, now and then.

Bitte ['bɪtə] f (-/-n) request (um for); entreaty; auf j-s ⁓ (hin) at s.o.'s request.

'**bitten** (irr., ge-, h) 1. v/t.: j-n um et. ⁓ ask or beg s.o. for s.th.; j-n um Entschuldigung ⁓ beg s.o.'s pardon; dürfte ich Sie um Feuer ⁓? may I trouble you for a light?; bitte please; (wie) bitte? (I beg your) pardon?; bitte! offering s.th.: (please,) help yourself, (please,) do take some or one; danke (schön) — bitte (sehr)! thank you — not at all, you're welcome, don't mention it, F that's all right; 2. v/i.: um et. ⁓ ask or beg for s.th.

bitter adj. ['bɪtər] bitter (a. fig.); frost: sharp; **2keit** f (-/-en) bitterness; fig. a. acrimony; '⁓lich adv. bitterly.

'**Bitt|gang** eccl. m procession; '⁓schrift f petition; '⁓steller m (-s/-) petitioner.

bläh|en ['blɛ:ən] (ge-, h) 1. v/t. inflate, distend, swell out; belly (out), swell out (sails); sich ⁓ sails: belly (out), swell out; skirt: balloon out; 2. ∮ v/i. cause flatulence; '⁓end ∮ adj. flatulent; '2ung ∮ f (-/-en) flatulence, F wind.

Blam|age [bla'mɑ:ʒə] f (-/-n) disgrace, shame; **2ieren** [⁓'mi:rən] v/t. (no -ge-, h) make a fool of s.o., disgrace; sich ⁓ make a fool of o.s.

blank adj. [blaŋk] shining, shiny, bright; polished; F fig. broke.

blanko † ['blaŋko] 1. adj. form, etc.: blank, not filled in; in blank; 2. adv.: ⁓ verkaufen stock exchange: sell short; '2scheck m blank cheque, Am. blank check; '2unterschrift f blank signature; '2vollmacht f full power of attorney, carte blanche.

Bläschen ∮ ['blɛːsçən] n (-s/-) vesicle, small blister.

Blase ['blɑ:zə] f (-/-n) bubble; blister (a. ∮); anat. bladder; bleb (in glass); ⊕ flaw; '⁓balg m (ein a pair of) bellows pl.; '2n (irr., ge-, h) 1. v/t. blow; blow, sound; play (wind-instrument); 2. v/i. blow.

Blas|instrument ∮ ['blɑ:s-] n wind-instrument; '⁓kapelle f brass band.

blaß adj. [blas] pale (vor dat. with); ⁓ werden turn pale; keine blasse Ahnung not the faintest idea.

Blässe ['blɛsə] f (-/no pl.) paleness.

Blatt [blat] n (-[e]s/⁼er) leaf (of book, ⚘); petal (of flower); leaf, sheet (of paper); ∮ sheet; blade (of oar, saw, airscrew, etc.); sheet (of metal); cards: hand; (news)paper.

Blattern ∮ ['blatərn] pl. smallpox.

blättern ['blɛtərn] v/i. (ge-, h): in e-m Buch ⁓ leaf through a book, thumb a book.

'**Blatternarb|e** f pock-mark; '2ig adj. pock-marked.

'**Blätterteig** m puff paste.

'**Blatt|gold** n gold-leaf, gold-foil; '⁓laus zo. f plant-louse; '⁓pflanze f foliage plant.

blau [blau] 1. adj. blue; F fig. drunk, tight, boozy; ⁓er Fleck bruise; ⁓es Auge black eye; mit e-m ⁓en Auge davonkommen get off cheaply; 2. ⚲ n (-s/no pl.) blue (colo[u]r); Fahrt ins ⁓e mystery tour. [blue.\]

bläuen ['blɔyən] v/t. (ge-, h) (dye)

'**blau|grau** adj. bluish grey; '2jacke ⚓ f bluejacket, sailor.

'**bläulich** adj. bluish.

'**Blausäure** ∩ f (-/no pl.) hydrocyanic or prussic acid.

Blech [blɛç] n (-[e]s/-e) sheet metal; metal sheet, plate; F fig. balderdash, rubbish, Am. sl. a. baloney; '⁓büchse f tin, Am. can; '2ern adj. (of) tin; sound: brassy; sound, voice: tinny; '⁓musik f brass-band music; '⁓waren f/pl. tinware.

Blei [blaɪ] (-[e]s/-e) 1. n lead; 2. F n, m (lead) pencil.

bleiben ['blaɪbən] v/i. (irr., ge-, sein) remain, stay; be left; ruhig ~ keep calm, bei keep to s.th., stick to s.th ; bitte bleiben Sie am Apparat teleph hold the line, please; ~d adj. lasting, permanent; **~lassen** v/t. (irr. lassen, sep., no -ge-, h) leave s.th alone; laß das bleiben! don't do it!; leave it alone!; stop that (noise, etc.)!

bleich adj [blaɪç] pale (vor dat. with), **~en** (ge-) 1. v/t. (h) make pale; bleach, blanch; 2. v/i. (irr., sein) bleach, lose colo(u)r, fade; **'~süchtig** ⚕ adj. chlorotic, green-sick.

'bleiern adj (of) lead, leaden (a.fig.).

'Blei|rohr n lead pipe; **'~soldat** m tin soldier, **~stift** m (lead) pencil; **'~stifthülse** f pencil cap; **'~stift-spitzer** m ~s/-) pencil-sharpener; **'~vergiftung** f f lead-poisoning.

Blend|e [blɛndə] f (-/-n) phot. diaphragm, stop, ⚠ blind or sham window, **~en** (ge-, h) 1. v/t. blind; dazzle (both a. fig.); 2. v/i. light: dazzle the eyes; **~laterne** ['blɛnt-] f dark lantern

blich [blɪç] pret of bleichen 2.

Blick [blɪk] m (-[e]s/-e) glance, look; view (auf acc. of); auf den ersten ~ at first sight; ein böser ~ an evil or angry look; **'2en** v/i. (ge-, h) look, glance (auf acc., nach at); **'~fang** m eye-catcher.

blieb [bli p] pret of bleiben.

blies [bli s] pret of blasen.

blind adj [blint] blind (a. fig.; gegen, für to, vor dat. with); metal: dull, tarnished; window: opaque (with age, dirt); mirror: clouded, dull; cartridge: blank; ~er Alarm false alarm; ~er Passagier stowaway; auf e-m Auge ~ blind in one eye.

'Blinddarm anat. m blind gut; appendix, **~entzündung** ⚕ f appendicitis

Blinde [blɪndə] (-n/-n) 1. m blind man; 2. f blind woman; **~anstalt** ['blɪndən'-] f institute for the blind; **~nheim** n home for the blind; **~nhund** m guide dog, Am. a. seeing-eye dog; **'~nschrift** f braille

'blind|fliegen ✈ (irr. fliegen, sep., -ge-) v/i (h) and v/i. (sein) fly blind or on instruments; **'2flug** ✈ m blind flying or flight; **'2gänger** m ✗ blind shell, dud; F fig. washout; **'2heit** f (~/no pl.) blindness; **~lings** adv. [~lɪŋs] blindly; at random; **'2schleiche** zo. f (-/-n) slow-worm, blind-worm, **~schreiben** v/t. and v/i. (irr. schreiben, sep., -ge-, h) touch-type

blink|en ['blɪŋkən] v/i. (ge-, h) star, light: twinkle; metal, leather, glass, etc.: shine; signal (with lamps),

flash; **'2er** mot. m (-s/-) flashing indicator; **'2feuer** n flashing light.

blinzeln ['blɪntsəln] v/i. (ge-, h) blink (at light, etc.), wink.

Blitz [blɪts] m (-es/-e) lightning; **'~ableiter** m (-s/-) lightning-conductor; **'2en** v/i (ge-, h) flash; es blitzt it is lightening, **~gespräch** teleph. n special priority call; **'~licht** phot n flash-light; **'2schnell** adv. with lightning speed; **'~strahl** m flash of lightning.

Block [blɔk] m 1. (-[e]s/=e) block; slab (of cooking chocolate); block, log (of wood); ingot (of metal); parl., pol., ✚ bloc; 2. (-[e]s/=e, -s) block (of houses), pad, block (of paper); **~ade** ⚓, ⚓ [~'ka:də] f (-/-n) blockade; **~adebrecher** m (-s/-) blockade-runner, **~haus** n log cabin; **2ieren** [~'ki:rən] (no -ge-, h) 1. v/t block (up); lock (wheel); 2. v/i. brakes, etc.: jam.

blöd adj [blø:t], ~e adj. [~'~də] imbecile, stupid, dull, silly; **'2heit** f (-/-en) imbecility, stupidity, dullness; silliness, **'2sinn** m imbecility, rubbish, nonsense , **~sinnig** adj. imbecile, idiotic, stupid, foolish.

blöken ['blø:kən] v/i. (ge-, h) sheep, calf: bleat.

blond adj. [blɔnt] blond, fair (-haired).

bloß [blo:s] 1. adj. bare, naked; mere; ~e Worte mere words; mit dem ~en Auge wahrnehmbar visible to the naked eye; 2. adv. only, merely, simply, just.

Blöße ['blø:sə] f (-/-n) bareness, nakedness; fig weak point or spot; sich e-e ~ geben give o.s. away; lay o.s. open to attack; keine ~ bieten be invulnerable

'bloß|legen v/t. (sep., -ge-, h) lay bare, expose; **~stellen** v/t. (sep., -ge-, h) expose, compromise, unmask; sich ~ compromise o.s.

blühen ['bly:ən] v/i (ge-, h) blossom, flower, bloom, fig. flourish, thrive, prosper; ✚ boom.

Blume ['blu:mə] f (-/-n) flower; wine: bouquet; beer froth.

'Blumen|beet n flower-bed; **'~blatt** n petal, **~händler** m florist; **'~strauß** m bouquet or bunch of flowers; **~topf** m flowerpot; **'~zucht** f floriculture.

Bluse ['blu:zə] f (-/-n) blouse.

Blut [blu:t] n (-[e]s/no pl.) blood; ~ vergießen shed blood; böses ~ machen breed bad blood; **'~andrang** ⚕ m congestion; **'2arm** adj. bloodless, an(a)emic; **'~armut** ⚕ f an(a)emia, **~bad** n carnage, massacre; **'~bank** ⚕ f blood bank; **'~blase** f blood blister; **'~druck** m blood pressure; **2dürstig** adj. ['~dyrstiç] bloodthirsty.

Blüte ['bly:tə] f (-/-n) blossom,

bloom, flower; *esp. fig.* flower; prime, heyday (*of life*).

Blutegel ['bluːtʔeːgəl] *m* (-s/-) leech.

'bluten *v/i.* (ge-, h) bleed (*aus* from); *aus der Nase* ~ bleed at the nose.

Bluterguß ⚕ ['bluːtʔ-] *m* effusion of blood.

'Blütezeit *f* flowering period *or* time; *fig. a.* prime, heyday.

'Blut|gefäß *anat. n* blood-vessel; **~gerinnsel** ⚕ ['-gərinzəl] *n* (-s/-) clot of blood; **~gruppe** *f* blood group; **'~hund** *zo. m* bloodhound.

'blutig *adj.* bloody, blood-stained; *es ist mein ~er Ernst* I am dead serious; *~er Anfänger* mere beginner, F greenhorn.

Blut|körperchen ['bluːtkœrpərçən] *n* (-s/-) blood corpuscle; **'~kreislauf** *m* (blood) circulation; **'~lache** *f* pool of blood; **'2leer** *adj.*, **'2los** *adj.* bloodless; **~probe** *f* blood test; **'~rache** *f* blood feud *or* revenge *or* vengeance, vendetta; **'2rot** *adj.* blood-red; crimson; **2rünstig** *adj.* ['~rynstiç] bloodthirsty; bloody; **~schande** *f* incest; **'~spender** *m* blood-donor; **'2stillend** *adj.* blood-sta(u)nching; **'~sturz** ⚕ *m* h(a)emorrhage; **'2sverwandt** *adj.* related by blood (*mit* to); **'~sverwandtschaft** *f* blood-relationship, consanguinity; **'~übertragung** *f* blood-transfusion; **'~ung** *f* (-/-en) bleeding, h(a)emorrhage; **'2unterlaufen** *adj. eye:* bloodshot; **'~vergießen** *n* bloodshed; **'~vergiftung** *f* blood-poisoning.

Bö [bøː] *f* (-/-en) gust, squall.

Bock [bɔk] *m* (-[e]s/⸚e) *deer, hare, rabbit:* buck; he-goat, F billy-goat; *sheep:* ram; *gymnastics:* buck; *e-n* ~ *schießen* commit a blunder, *sl.* commit a bloomer; *den* ~ *zum Gärtner machen* set the fox to keep the geese; **'2en** *v/i.* (ge-, h) *horse:* buck; *child:* sulk; *p. b* obstinate *or* refractory; *mot.* move jerkily, *Am.* F *a.* buck; **'2ig** *adj.* stubborn, obstinate, pigheaded; **'~sprung** *m* leap-frog; *gymnastics:* vault over the buck; *Bocksprünge machen* caper, cut capers.

Boden ['boːdən] *m* (-s/⸚) ground; ✿ soil; bottom; floor; loft; **'~kammer** *f* garret, attic; **'2los** *adj.* bottomless; *fig.* enormous; unheard-of; **'~personal** ✈ *n* ground personnel *or* staff, *Am.* ground crew; **'~reform** *f* land reform; **'~satz** *m* grounds *pl.*, sediment; **~schätze** ['~ʃɛtsə] *m/pl.* mineral resources *pl.*; **'2ständig** *adj.* native, indigenous.

bog [boːk] *pret. of* biegen.

Bogen ['boːgən] *m* (-s/-, ⸚) bow, bend, curve; ⚛ arc; ⚛ arch; *skiing:* turn; *skating:* curve; sheet (*of* paper); **'2förmig** *adj.* arched; **'~gang** ⚛ *m* arcade; **'~lampe** ⚕ *f* arc-lamp; **'~schütze** *m* archer, bowman.

Bohle ['boːlə] *f* (-/-n) thick plank, board.

Bohne ['boːnə] *f* (-/-n) bean; *grüne* ~*n pl.* French beans *pl., Am.* string beans *pl.*; *weiße* ~*n pl.* haricot beans *pl.*; F *blaue* ~*n pl.* bullets *pl.*; **'~nstange** *f* beanpole (*a.* F *fig.*).

bohnern ['boːnərn] *v/t.* (ge-, h) polish (*floor, etc.*), (bees)wax (*floor*).

bohr|en ['boːrən] (ge-, h) **1.** *v/t.* bore, drill (*hole*); sink, bore (*well, shaft*); bore, cut, drive (*tunnel, etc.*); **2.** *v/i.* drill (*a. dentistry*); bore; **'2er** ⊕ *m* (-s/-) borer, drill.

'böig *adj.* squally, gusty; ✈ bumpy.

Boje ['boːjə] *f* (-/-n) buoy.

Bollwerk ⚔ ['bɔlvɛrk] *n* bastion, bulwark (*a. fig.*).

Bolzen ⊕ ['bɔltsən] *m* (-s/-) bolt.

Bombard|ement [bɔmbardəˈmãː] *n* (-s/-s) bombardment; bombing; shelling; **2ieren** [~ˈdiːrən] *v/t.* (*no* -ge-, h) bomb; shell; bombard (*a. fig.*).

Bombe ['bɔmbə] *f* (-/-n) bomb; *fig.* bomb-shell; **'2nsicher** *adj.* bomb-proof; F *fig.* dead sure; **'~nschaden** *m* bomb damage; **'~r** ✈ ➤ *m* (-s/-) bomber.

Bon ✝ [bɔ̃ː] *m* (-s/-s) coupon; voucher; credit note.

Bonbon [bɔ̃ˈbɔ̃ː] *m, n* (-s/-s) sweet (-meat), bon-bon, F goody, *Am.* candy.

Bonze F ['bɔntsə] *m* (-n/-n) bigwig, *Am. a.* big shot.

Boot [boːt] *n* (-[e]s/-e) boat; **'~shaus** *n* boat-house; **'~smann** *m* (-[e]s/Bootsleute) boatswain.

Bord [bɔrt] *n* (-[e]s/-e) **1.** *n* shelf; **2.** ♣, ⚓ *m: an* ~ on board, aboard (*ship, aircraft, etc.*); *über* ~ overboard; *von* ~ *gehen* go ashore; **'~funker** ♣, ➤ *m* wireless *or* radio operator; **'~stein** *m* kerb, *Am.* curb.

borgen ['bɔrgən] *v/t.* (ge-, h) borrow (*von, bei* from, of); lend, *Am. a.* loan (*j-m et.* s.th. *to* s.o.).

Borke ['bɔrkə] *f* (-/-n) bark (*of tree*).

borniert *adj.* [bɔrˈniːrt] narrow-minded, of restricted intelligence.

Borsalbe ['boːr-] *f* boracic ointment.

Börse ['bœrzə] *f* (-/-n) purse; ✝ stock exchange; stock-market; money-market; **'~nbericht** *m* market report; **'2nfähig** *adj.* stock: negotiable on the stock exchange; **'~nkurs** *m* quotation; **'~nmakler** *m* stock-broker; **'~nnotierung** *f* (official, stock exchange) quotation; **'~npapiere** *n/pl.* listed securities *pl.*; **'~nspekulant** *m* stock-jobber; **'~nzeitung** *f* financial newspaper.

Borst|e ['bɔrstə] f (-/-n) bristle (of hog or brush, etc.); **'2ig** adj. bristly.
Borte ['bɔrtə] f (-/-n) border (of carpet, etc); braid, lace.
'bösartig adj malicious, vicious; ♂ malignant, **2keit** f (-/-en) viciousness, ♂ malignity.
Böschung ['bœʃuŋ] f (-/-en) slope; embankment (of railway); bank (of river)
böse ['bøːzə] **1.** adj. bad, evil, wicked; malevolent, spiteful; angry (über acc. at, about, auf j-n with s.o.); er meint es nicht ~ he means no harm; **2.** ⌂ n (-n/no pl.) evil; **2wicht** ['~viçt] m (-[e]s/-er, -e) villain, rascal.
bos|haft adj. ['bɔːshaft] wicked; spiteful, malicious; **'2heit** f (-/-en) wickedness, ♂ malice; spite.
'böswillig adj malevolent; ~e Absicht ♂ malice prepense; ~es Verlassen ♂ wilful desertion; **'2keit** f (-/-en) malevolence.
bot [boː] pret of bieten.
Botan|ik [boˈtaːnik] f (-/no pl.) botany, **~iker** m (-s/-) botanist; **2isch** adj botanical.
Bote ['boːtə] m (-n/-n) messenger; **'~ngang** m errand; Botengänge machen run errands.
'Botschaft f (-/-en) message; pol. embassy, **~er** m (-s/-) ambassador; in British Commonwealth countries: High Commissioner.
Bottich ['bɔtiç] m (-[e]s/-e) tub; wash-tub brewing: tun. vat.
Bouillon [buˈljõː] f (-/-s) beef tea.
Bowle ['boːlə] f (-/-n) vessel: bowl; cold drink consisting of fruit, hock and champagne or soda-water: appr. punch.
box|en ['bɔksən] **1.** v/i. (ge-, h) box; **2.** v/t (ge-, h) punch s.o.; **3.** ⌂ n (-s/no pl.) boxing, pugilism; **'2er** m (-s/-) boxer, pugilist; **'2handschuh** m boxing-glove; **'2kampf** m boxing-match, bout, fight; **'2sport** m boxing
Boykott [bɔyˈkɔt] (-[e]s/-e) boycott; **2ieren** [.ˈtiːrən] v/t. (no -ge-, h) boycott
brach [braːx] **1.** pret. of brechen; **2.** ♂ adv fallow; uncultivated (both a fig.)
brachte ['braxtə] pret. of bringen.
Branche ♦ ['brãːʃə] f (-/-n) line (of business), trade; branch.
Brand [brant] m (-[e]s/-e) burning, fire, blaze, ♂ gangrene; ⚕, ♂ blight, smut, mildew; **'~blase** f blister, **'~bombe** f incendiary bomb, **2en** ['~dən] v/i. (ge-, h) surge (a fig.), break (an acc., gegen against), **~fleck** m burn; **2ig** adj. ['~diç] ♂ blighted, smutted; ♂ gangrenous; **'~mal** n brand; fig. stigma, blemish; **'2marken** v/t. (ge-, h) brand (animal); fig. brand

or stigmatize s.o.; **'~mauer** f fire (-proof) wall; **~schaden** m damage caused by or loss suffered by fire; **'2schatzen** v/t (ge-, h) lay (town) under contribution sack, pillage; **'~stätte** f, **~stelle** f scene of fire; **'~stifter** m incendiary, Am F a. firebug; **~stiftung** f arson, **~ung** ['~duŋ] f '~-en) sur , surge, breakers pl.; **~wache** f fire-watch; **'~wunde** f burn; scald; **'~zeichen** n brand.
brannte ['brantə] pret. of brennen.
Branntwein ['brantvaɪn] m brandy, spirits pl. whisk(e)y, gin; **'~brennerei** f distillery
braten ['braː tən] **1.** v/t (irr., ge-, h) in oven. roast, grill, in frying-pan: fry; bake (apple), an Spieß . roast on a spit, barbecue **2.** v/i. (irr., ge-, h) roast grill, fry , in der Sonne ~ p. roast or grill in the sun; **3.** 2 m (-s/-) roast meat joint, **2fett** n dripping, **~soße** gravy
'Brat|fisch m fried fish, **~hering** m grilled herring, **~huhn** n roast chicken, **~kartoffeln** pl fried potatoes pl , **~ofen** m (kitchen) oven; **~pfanne** f frying-pan, Am. a. skillet; **~röhre** f Bratofen
Brauch [braux] m [e]s/~e) custom, usage; use, habit practice, **'2bar** adj. p., thing useful; p capable, able; thing serviceable. **'2en** (h) **1.** v/t. (ge- need want, require; take (time); use, **2.** v/aux (no -ge-) du brauchst es nur zu sagen you only have to say so, er hätte nicht zu kommen he need not have come; **'~tum** n (-[e]s/~er) custom; tradition, folklore
Braue ['brauə] f (-/-n) eyebrow.
brau|en ['brauən] v/t (ge-, h) brew; **'2er** m (-s/-) brewer **2erei** [.'rai] f (-/-en) brewery, **'2haus** n brewery.
braun adj. [braun] brown; horse: bay; ~ werden get a tan (on one's skin).
Bräune ['brɔynə] f (-/no pl.) brown colo(u)r; (sun) tan; **2n** (ge-, h) **1.** v/t. make or dye brown; sun: tan; **2.** v/i. tan.
'Braunkohle f brown coal, lignite.
'bräunlich adj brownish.
Brause ['brauzə] f (-/-n) rose, sprinkling-nozzle (of watering can); s. Brausebad, s Brauselimonade; **'~bad** n shower-bath), **'~limonade** f fizzy lemonade, **'2n** v/i. (ge-, h) wind, water, etc roar; rush; have a shower -bath), **~pulver** n effervescent powder
Braut [braut] f (-/~e) fiancée; on wedding-day bride; **'~führer** m best man.
Bräutigam ['brɔytigam] m (-s/-e) fiancé; on wedding-day: bridegroom, Am. a. groom.
'Braut|jungfer f bridesmaid; **'~**

kleid n wedding-dress; '˷kranz m bridal wreath; '˷leute pl., '˷paar n engaged couple; on wedding-day: bride and bridegroom; '˷schleier m bridal veil.

brav adj. [bra:f] honest, upright; good, well-behaved; brave.

bravo int. ['bra:vo] bravo!, well done!

Bravour [bra'vu:r] f (-/no pl.) bravery, courage; brilliance.

Brecheisen ['brɛç?-] n crowbar; (burglar's) jemmy, Am. a. jimmy.

'brechen (irr., ge-) 1. v/t. (h) break; pluck (flower); refract (ray, etc.); fold (sheet of paper); quarry (stone); vomit; die Ehe ˷ commit adultery; sich ˷ break (one's leg, etc.); opt. be refracted; 2. v/i. (h) break; vomit; mit j-m ˷ break with s.o.; 3. v/i. (sein) break, get broken; bones break, fracture.

'Brech|mittel ℰ n emetic; F fig. sickener; ˷reiz m nausea; '˷stange f crowbar, Am. a. pry; '˷ung opt. f (-/-en) refraction.

Brei [braɪ] m (-[e]s/-e) paste; pulp; mash; pap (for babies); made of oatmeal: porridge; (rice, etc.) pudding; '2ig adj. pasty; pulpy; pappy.

breit adj. [braɪt] broad, wide; zehn Meter ˷ ten metres wide; ˷e Schichten der Bevölkerung large sections of or the bulk of the population; '˷beinig 1. adj. with legs wide apart; 2. adv. ˷ gehen straddle.

Breite ['braɪtə] f (-/-n) breadth, width; ast., geogr. latitude; '2n v/t. (ge-, h) spread; vulg. geogr. latitude; '˷ngrad m degree of latitude; '˷nkreis m parallel (of latitude).

'breit|machen v/refl. (sep., -ge-, h) spread o.s.; take up room; '˷schlagen v/t. (irr schlagen, sep., -ge-, h): F j-n ˷ persuade s.o.; F j-n zu et. ˷ talk s.o. into (doing) s.th.; '2seite ⊕ f broadside.

Bremse ['brɛmzə] f (-/-n) zo. gadfly; horse-fly; ⊕ brake; '2n (ge-, h) v/i. brake, put on the brakes; slow down; 2. v/t. brake, put on the brakes to; slow down; fig. curb.

'Brems|klotz m brake-block; ℰ wheelchock, ˷pedal n brake pedal; '˷vorrichtung f brake-mechanism; '˷weg m braking distance.

brenn|bar adj. ['brɛnba:r] combustible, burnable; 2dauer f burning time; '˷en (irr., ge-, h) 1. v/t. burn; distil(l) (brandy); roast (coffee); bake (brick, etc.); 2. v/i. burn; be ablaze, be on fire; wound, eye: smart, burn; nettle: sting; vor Ungeduld ˷ burn with impatience; F darauf ˷ zu inf. be burning to inf.; es brennt! fire!

'Brenn|er m (-s/-) p. distiller; fixture: burner; ˷essel ['brɛnnɛsəl] f

stinging nettle; '˷glas n burning glass; '˷holz n firewood; ˷material n fuel; '˷öl n lamp-oil; fuel-oil; '˷punkt m focus, focal point; in den ˷ rücken bring into focus (a. fig.); im ˷ des Interesses stehen be the focus of interest; '˷schere f curling-tongs pl, ˷spiritus m methylated spirit, '˷stoff m combustible; mot. fuel.

brenzlig ['brɛntsliç] 1. adj. burnt; matter: dangerous; situation precarious; ˷er Geruch burnt smell, smell of burning; 2. adv. es riecht ˷ it smells of burning.

Bresche ['brɛʃə] f (-/-n) breach (a. fig.), gap; in die ˷ springen help s.o. out of a dilemma.

Brett [brɛt] n (-[e]s/-er) board; plank; shelf; spring-board, ˷spiel n game played on a board.

Brezel ['bre:tsəl] f (-/-n) pretzel.

Brief [bri:f] m (-[e]s e) letter; '˷aufschrift f address (on a letter); '˷beschwerer m (-s/-) paperweight; '˷bogen m sheet of notepaper; '˷geheimnis n secrecy of correspondence; ˷karte f correspondence card (with envelope); '˷kasten m letter-box, ˷llar-box; Am. mailbox; 2lich adj and adv. by letter, in writing, ˷marke f (postage) stamp; ˷markensammlung f stamp-collection, öffner m letter-opener; ˷ordner m letter-file; '˷papier n notepaper, ˷porto n postage; '˷post f mail, post; '˷tasche f wallet, Am a billfold; '˷taube f carrier pigeon, homing pigeon, homer; ˷träger m postman, Am. mailman; ˷umschlag m envelope; ˷waage f letter-balance; '˷wechsel m correspondence; '˷zensur f postal censorship.

briet [bri:t] pret. of braten.

Brikett [bri'kɛt] n (-[e]s/-s) briquet (-te).

Brillant [bril'jant] 1. m (-en/-en) brilliant, cut diamond; 2. 2 adj. brilliant; ˷ring m diamond ring.

Brille ['brilə] f (-/-n) (eine a pair of) glasses pl. or spectacles pl., goggles pl.; lavatory seat, ˷nfutteral n spectacle-case; ˷nträger m person who wears glasses.

bringen ['brɪŋən] v/t. (irr., ge-, h) bring; take; see (s.o. home, etc.); put (in order); make (sacrifice); yield (interest); an den Mann ˷ dispose of, get rid of; j-n dazu ˷, et. zu tun make or get s.o. to do s.th.; et. mit sich ˷ involve s.th.; j-n um et. ˷ deprive s.o. of s.th.; j-n zum Lachen ˷ make s.o. laugh.

Brise ['bri:zə] f (-/-n) breeze.

Brit|e ['britə] m (-n/-n) Briton, Am. a. Britisher; die ˷n pl. the British pl.; '2isch adj. British.

bröckeln ['brœkəln] *v/i.* (ge-, h) crumble; become brittle.

Brocken ['brɔkən] **1.** *m* (-s/-) piece; lump (*of earth or stone, etc.*); morsel (*of food*); F ein harter ~ a hard nut; **2.** *2 v/t.* (ge-, h): Brot in die Suppe ~ break bread into soup.

brodeln ['bro:dəln] *v/i.* (ge-, h) bubble, simmer.

Brombeer|e ['brɔm-] *f* blackberry; '~**strauch** *m* blackberry bush.

Bronch|ialkatarrh ☞ [brɔnçi'a:l-katar] *m* bronchial catarrh; '~**ien** *anat. f/pl* bronchi(a) *pl.*; ~**itis** ☞ [~'çi:tis] *f* (-/Bronchitiden) bronchitis.

Bronze ['brõ:sə] *f* (-/-n) bronze; '~**medaille** *f* bronze medal.

Brosche ['brɔʃə] *f* (-/-n) brooch.

broschier|en [brɔ'ʃi:rən] *v/t.* (no -ge-, h) sew, stitch (*book*); ~**t** *adj.* *book* paper-backed, paper-bound; *fabric* figured.

Broschüre [brɔ'ʃy:rə] *f* (-/-n) booklet; brochure; pamphlet.

Brot [bro:t] *n* (-[e]s/-e) bread; loaf; sein ~ verdienen earn one's living; '~**aufstrich** *m* spread.

Brötchen ['brø:tçən] *n* (-s/-) roll.

'**Brot|korb** *m* j-m den ~ höher hängen put s.o. on short allowance; '2**los** *fig. adj.* unemployed; unprofitable; '~**rinde** *f* crust; '~**schneidemaschine** *f* bread-cutter; '~**schnitte** *f* slice of bread; '~**studium** *n* utilitarian study; '~**teig** *m* bread dough.

Bruch [brux] *m* (-[e]s/~e) break(ing); breach; ☞ fracture (*of bones*); ☞ hernia; crack; fold (*in paper*); crease (*in cloth*); split (*in silk*); ☞ fraction; breach (*of promise*); violation (*of oath, etc.*); violation, infringement (*of law, etc.*); '~**band** *n* truss.

brüchig *adj.* ['bryçiç] fragile; brittle, *voice:* cracked.

'**Bruch|landung** ☞ *f* crash-landing; '~**rechnung** *f* fractional arithmetic, F fractions *pl.*; '~**strich** ✗ *m* fraction bar; '~**stück** *n* fragment (*a. fig.*); '~**teil** *m* fraction; im ~ e-r Sekunde in a split second; '~**zahl** *f* fraction(al) number.

Brücke ['brykə] *f* (-/-n) bridge; *carpet:* rug; *sports:* bridge; e-e ~ schlagen über (*acc.*) build *or* throw a bridge across, bridge (*river*); '~**kopf** ✗ *m* bridge-head; '~**npfeiler** *m* pier (*of bridge*).

Bruder ['bru:dər] *m* (-s/~) brother; *eccl.* (lay) brother, friar; '~**krieg** *m* fratricidal *or* civil war; '~**kuß** *m* fraternal kiss.

brüderlich ['bry:dərliç] **1.** *adj.* brotherly, fraternal; **2.** *adv.:* ~ teilen share and share alike; '2**keit** *f* (-/no *pl.*) brotherliness, fraternity.

Brüh|e ['bry:ə] *f* (-/-n) broth; stock;

beef tea; F dirty water; *drink:* F dishwater; '2**heiß** *adj.* scalding hot; '~**würfel** *m* beef cube.

brüllen ['brylən] *v/i.* (ge-, h) roar; bellow; *cattle* low; *bull* bellow; vor Lachen ~ roar with laughter; ~**des Gelächter** roar of laughter.

brumm|en ['brumən] *v/i.* (ge-, h) *p.* speak in a deep voice, mumble; growl (*a. fig.*); *insect* buzz; *engine:* buzz, boom, *fig* grumble, *Am.* F grouch; mir brummt der Schädel my head is buzzing, '2**bär** *fig. m* grumbler, growler, *Am.* F grouch; '2**er** *m* (-s/-) bluebottle; dung-beetle; '~**ig** *adj.* grumbling, *Am.* F grouchy.

brünett *adj.* [bry'net] *woman:* brunette.

Brunft *hunt.* [brunft] *f* (-/~e) rut; '~**zeit** *f* rutting season.

Brunnen ['brunən] *m* (-s/-) well; spring; fountain (*a. fig.*); e-n ~ graben sink a well; '~**wasser** *n* pump-water, well-water.

Brunst [brunst] *f* (-/~e) *zo.* rut (*of male animal*), heat (*of female animal*); lust, sexual desire.

brünstig *adj.* ['brynstiç] *zo.* rutting, in heat; lustful

Brust [brust] *f* (-/~e) chest, *anat.* thorax; breast; (woman's) breast(s *pl.*), bosom; aus voller ~ at the top of one's voice, lustily; '~**bild** *n* half-length portrait

brüsten ['brystən] *v/refl.* (ge-, h) boast, brag.

'**Brust|fell** *anat. n* pleura; '~**fellentzündung** ☞ *f* pleurisy; '~**kasten** *m*, '~**korb** *m* chest, *anat.* thorax; '~**schwimmen** *n* (-s/no *pl.*) breast-stroke

Brüstung ['brystuŋ] *f* (-/-en) balustrade, parapet.

'**Brustwarze** *anat. f* nipple.

Brut [bru:t] *f* (-/-en) brooding, sitting; brood; hatch; fry, spawn (*of fish*); *fig.* F brood, (bad) lot.

brutal *adj.* [bru'ta:l] brutal; 2**ität** [~ali'te:t] *f* (-/-en) brutality.

Brutapparat *zo.* ['bru:t²-] *m* incubator.

brüten ['bry:tən] *v/i.* (ge-, h) brood, sit (*on egg*); incubate; ~ über (*dat.*) brood over.

'**Brutkasten** ☞ *m* incubator.

brutto ✦ *adv.* ['bruto] gross; '2**gewicht** *n* gross weight; '2**registertonne** *f* gross register ton; '2**verdienst** *m* gross earnings *pl.*

Bube ['bu:bə] *m* (-n/-n) boy, lad; knave, rogue; *cards:* knave, jack; '~**nstreich** *m*, '~**nstück** *n* boyish prank; knavish trick.

Buch [bu:x] *n* (-[e]s/~er) book; volume; '~**binder** *m* (book-)binder; '~**drucker** *m* printer; '~**druckerei** [~'rai] *f* printing; printing-office, *Am.* print shop.

Buche ♀ ['buːxə] f (-/-n) beech.

buchen ['buːxən] v/t. (ge-, h) book, reserve (*passage, flight, etc.*); *book-keeping* book (*item, sum*), enter (*transaction*) in the books; et. als *Erfolg* count s.th. as a success.

Bücher|abschluß ✝ ['byːçər-] m closing of or balancing of books; **∼brett** n bookshelf; **∼ei** [∼'raɪ] f (-/-en) library; **∼freund** m book-lover, bibliophil(e); **∼revisor** ✝ m (-s/-en) auditor; accountant; **∼schrank** m bookcase; **∼wurm** m bookworm.

'Buch|fink orn. m chaffinch; **∼hal-ter** m (-s/-) book-keeper; **∼hal-tung** f book-keeping; **∼handel** m book-trade; **∼händler** m book-seller; **∼handlung** f bookshop, Am. bookstore.

Büchse ['byksə] f (-/-n) box; case; tin, Am. can; rifle; **∼nfleisch** n tinned meat, Am. canned meat; **∼nöffner** ['byksən?-] m tin-opener, Am. can opener.

Buchstab|e ['buːxʃtaːbə] m (-n/-n) letter, character; typ. type; **Sieren** [∼a'biːrən] v/t. (no -ge-, h) spell.

buchstäblich ['buːxʃtɛːplɪç] 1. adj. literal; 2. adv. literally; word for word.

Bucht [buxt] f (-/-en) bay; bight; creek, inlet.

'Buchung f (-/-en) booking, reservation; *book-keeping*: entry.

Buckel ['bukəl] 1. m (-s/-) hump, hunch; humpback, hunchback; boss, stud, knob; 2. f (-/-n) boss, stud, knob.

'buckelig adj. s. bucklig.

bücken ['bykən] v/refl. (ge-, h) bend (down), stoop.

bucklig adj. ['buklɪç] humpbacked, hunchbacked.

Bückling ['byklɪŋ] m (-s/-e) bloater, red herring; fig. bow.

Bude ['buːdə] f (-/-n) stall, booth; hut, cabin, Am. shack; F: place; den; (student's, etc.) digs pl.

Budget [by'dʒeː] n (-s/-s) budget.

Büfett [by'feː; by'fɛt] n (-[e]s/-s, -[e]s/-e) sideboard, buffet; buffet, bar, Am. a. counter; kaltes ∼ buffet supper or lunch.

Büffel ['byfəl] m (-s/-) zo. buffalo; F fig. lout, blockhead.

Bug [buːk] m (-[e]s/-e) ♎ bow; ✕ nose; fold; (sharp) crease.

Bügel ['byːgəl] m (-s/-) bow (of spectacles, etc.); handle (of handbag, etc.); coat-hanger; stirrup; **∼brett** n ironing-board; **∼eisen** n (flat-)iron; **∼falte** f crease; **2n** v/t. (ge-, h) iron (shirt, etc.), press (suit, skirt, etc.).

Bühne ['byːnə] f (-/-n) platform (a. ⊕); scaffold; thea. stage; fig.: die ∼ the stage; die politische ∼ the political scene; **∼nanweisungen** ['byː-nən?-] f/pl. stage directions pl.; **∼nbild** n scene(ry); décor; stage design; **∼ndichter** m playwright, dramatist; **∼nlaufbahn** f stage career; **∼nstück** n stage play.

buk [buːk] pret. of backen.

Bull|auge ♎ ['bul-] n porthole, bull's eye; **∼dogge** zo. f bulldog.

Bulle ['bulə] 1. zo. m (-n/-n) bull; 2. eccl. f (-/-n) bull.

Bummel F ['bumǝl] m (-s/-) stroll; spree, pub-crawl, sl binge; **∼ei** [∼'laɪ] f (-/-en) dawdling; negli-gence; **2n** v/i. (ge-) 1. sein) stroll, saunter; pub-crawl; 2. (h) ∼awdle (on way, at work), ∼aste time; **∼streik** m go-slow strike), Am. slowdown; **∼zug** m slow train, Am. way train.

Bummler ['bumlər] m (-s/-) saun-terer, stroller; loafer, Am. F a. bum; dawdler.

Bund [bunt] 1. m (-[e]s/∼e) pol. union, federation, confederacy; (waist-, neck-, wrist)band; 2. n (-[e]s/-e) bundle (of faggots); bundle, truss (of hay or straw); bunch (of radishes, etc.).

Bündel ['byndəl] n (-s/-) bundle, bunch; **2n** v/t. (ge-, h) make into a bundle, bundle up.

Bundes|bahn ['bundəs-] f Federal Railway(s pl.); **∼bank** f Federal Bank; **∼genosse** m ally; **∼ge-richtshof** m Federal Supreme Court; **∼kanzler** m Federal Chan-cellor; **∼ministerium** n Federal Ministry; **∼post** f Federal Postal Administration; **∼präsident** m President of the Federal Republic; **∼rat** m Bundesrat, Upper House of German Parliament; **∼republik** f Federal Republic; **∼staat** m federal state; confederation; **∼tag** m Bundestag, Lower House of German Parliament.

bündig adj. ['byndɪç] style, speech: concise, to the point, terse.

Bündnis ['byntnɪs] n (-ses/-se) alliance; agreement.

Bunker ['buŋkər] m (-s/-) ✕, coal, fuel, etc.: bunker; bin; air-raid shelter; ✕ bunker, pill-box; ♎ (submarine) pen.

bunt adj. [bunt] (multi-)colo(u)red, colo(u)rful; motley; bird, flower, etc.: variegated; bright, gay; fig. mixed, motley; full of variety; **2druck** m colo(u)r-print(ing); **2stift** m colo(u)red pencil, crayon.

Bürde ['byrdə] f (-/-n) burden (a. fig.: für j-n to s.o.), load.

Burg [burk] f (-/-en) castle; fortress; citadel (a. fig.).

Bürge ♎♀ ['byrgə] m (-n/-n) guaran-tor, security, surety, bailsman; sponsor; **2n** v/i. (ge-, h): für j-n ∼ stand guarantee or surety or security for s.o., Am. a. bond s.o.; stand bail for s.o.; vouch *or* answer for s.o.; sponsor s.o.; *für et.* ~ stand security for s.th. guarantee s.th.; vouch *or* answer for s.th.

Bürger ['byrgər] *m* (-s/-) citizen; townsman; ~**krieg** *m* civil war.

'**bürgerlich** *adj.* civic, civil; ~*e Küche* plain cooking; *Verlust der* ~*en Ehrenrechte* loss of civil rights; *Bürgerliches Gesetzbuch* German Civil Code; '2*e m* (-n/-n) commoner.

'**Bürger|meister** *m* mayor; *in Germany*: a. burgomaster; *in Scotland*: provost; '~**recht** *n* civic rights *pl.*; citizenship; ~**schaft** *f* (-/-en) citizens *pl.*; ~**steig** *m* pavement, *Am.* sidewalk; '~**wehr** *f* militia.

Bürgschaft ['byrkʃaft] *f* (-/-en) security; bail; guarantee.

Büro [by'ro:] *n* (-s/-s) office; ~**angestellte** *m, f* (-n/-n) clerk; ~**arbeit** *f* office-work; ~**klammer** *f* paper-clip; ~**krat** [~o'kra:t] *m* (-en/-en) bureaucrat; ~**kratie** [~o-kra'ti:] *f* (-/-n) bureaucracy; red tape; 2**kratisch** *adj.* [~o'kra:tiʃ] bureaucratic; ~**stunden** *f/pl.* office hours *pl.*; ~**vorsteher** *m* head *or* senior clerk.

Bursch [burʃ] *m* (-en/-en), ~**e** ['~ə] *m* (-n/-n) boy, lad, youth; F chap, *Am. a.* guy; *ein übler* ~ a bad lot, F a bad egg.

burschikos *adj.* [burʃi'ko:s] free and easy; *esp. girl*: boyish, unaffected, hearty.

Bürste ['byrstə] *f* (-/-n) brush; '2*n v/t.* (ge-, h) brush.

Busch [buʃ] *m* (-es/⁼e) bush, shrub.

Büschel ['byʃəl] *n* (-s/-) bunch;

tuft, handful (*of hair*); wisp (*of straw or hair*).

'**Busch|holz** *n* brushwood, underwood; '2*ig adj.* hair, *eyebrows, etc.*: bushy, shaggy; covered with bushes *or* scrub, bushy; ~**messer** *n* bush-knife; machete; ~**neger** *m* maroon; '~**werk** *n* bushes *pl.*, shrubbery, *Am. a.* brush.

Busen ['bu:zən] *m* (-s/-) bosom, breast (*esp. of woman*); *fig.* bosom, heart; *geog.* bay, gulf; '~**freund** *m* bosom friend.

Bussard *orn.* ['busart] *m* (-[e]s/-e) buzzard.

Buße ['bu:sə] *f* (-/-n) atonement (*for sins*), penance; repentance; satisfaction; fine; ~ *tun* do penance.

büßen ['by:sən] (ge-, h) 1. *v/t.* expiate, atone for (*sin, crime*); *er mußte es mit s-m Leben* ~ he paid for it with his life; *das sollst du mir* ~*!* you'll pay for that!; 2. *v/i.* atone, pay (*für for*).

'**Büßer** *m* (-s/-) penitent.

'**buß|fertig** *adj.* penitent, repentant, contrite; '2**fertigkeit** *f* (-/no *pl.*) repentance, contrition; '2**tag** *m* day of repentance; *Buß- und Bettag* day of prayer and repentance.

Büste ['bystə] *f* (-/-n) bust; '~**n-halter** *m* (-s/-) brassière, F bra.

Büttenpapier ['bytən-] *n* hand-made paper.

Butter ['butər] *f* (-/no *pl.*) butter; '~**blume** ♀ *f* buttercup; '~**brot** *n* (slice *or* piece of) bread and butter; F: *für ein* ~ for a song; ~**brotpapier** *n* greaseproof paper; '~**dose** *f* butter-dish; '~**faß** *n* butter-churn; '~**milch** *f* buttermilk; '2*n v/i.* (ge-, h) churn.

C

Café [ka'fe:] *n* (-s/-s) café, coffee-house.

Cape [ke:p] *n* (-s/-s) cape.

Ceil|ist ♪ [tʃe'list] *m* (-en/-en) violoncellist, (')cellist; ~**o** ♪ ['~o] *n* (-s/-s, Cellí) violoncello, (')cello.

Celsius ['tselzius]: 5 *Grad* ~ (*abbr.* 5°C) five degrees centigrade.

Chaiselongue [ʃez(ə)'lõ:] *f* (-/-n, -s) chaise longue, lounge, couch.

Champagner [ʃam'panjər] *m* (-s/-) champagne.

Champignon ♀ ['ʃampinjõ] *m* (-s/-s) champignon, (common) mushroom.

Chance ['ʃã:s(ə)] *f* (-/-n) chance; *keine* ~ *haben* not to stand a chance; *sich eine* ~ *entgehen lassen* miss a chance *or* an opportunity; *die* ~*n sind gleich* the chances *or* odds are even.

Chaos ['ka:ɔs] *n* (-/no *pl.*) chaos.

Charakter [ka'raktər] *m* (-s/-e) character; nature; ~**bild** *n* character (sketch); ~**darsteller** *thea. m* character actor; ~**fehler** *m* fault in s.o.'s character; 2**fest** *adj.* of firm *or* strong character; 2**i'sieren** *v/t.* (*no* -ge-, h) characterize, describe (*als acc.* as); ~**i'sierung** *f* (-/-en), ~**istik** [~'ristik] *f* (-/-en) characterization; 2**istisch** *adj.* [~'ristiʃ] characteristic *or* typical (*für of*); 2**lich** *adj.* of *or* concerning (the) character; 2**los** *adj.* characterless, without (strength of) character, spineless; ~**rolle** *thea. f* character role; ~**zug** *m* characteristic, feature, trait.

charm|ant *adj.* [ʃar'mant] charming, winning; 2**e** [ʃarm] *m* (-s/no *pl.*) charm, grace.

Chassis [ʃaˈsiː] n (-/-) mot., radio: frame, chassis.

Chauffeur [ʃɔˈføːr] m (-s/-e) chauffeur, driver

Chaussee [ʃoˈseː] f (-/-n) highway, (high) road

Chauvinismus [ʃoviˈnismus] m (-/ no pl.) jingoism, chauvinism.

Chef [ʃɛf] m (-s/-s) head, chief; ✝ principal, boss, senior partner.

Chemie [çeˈmiː] f (-/no pl.) chemistry, ~faser f chemical fib|re, Am. -er ~ikalien [-iˈkaːljən] f/pl. chemicals pl ~iker ['çeːmikər] m (-s/-) (analytical) chemist; ~isch adj. ['çeː miʃ] chemical.

Chiffre ['ʃifər] f (-/-n) number; cipher, ⚻ advertisement: box number; ~ieren [ʃiˈfriːrən] v/t. (no -ge-, h) ciphe. code (message, etc.); write in code o cipher

Chinese [çiˈneːzə] m (-n/-n) Chinese, contp Chinaman; ~isch adj. Chinese

Chinin ⚕ [çiˈniːn] n (-s/no pl.) quinine

Chirurg [çiˈrurk] m (-en/-en) surgeon; ~ie [-ˈgiː] f (-/-n) surgery; ~isch adj ~giʃ] surgical.

Chlor ⚕ [kloːr] n (-s/no pl.) chlorine; ~en v/t (ge-, h) chlorinate (water), ~kalk ⚕ m chloride of lime

Chloroform ⚕ [kloroˈfɔrm] n (-/no pl.) chloroform, ~ieren ⚗ [-ˈmiː rən] v/t (no -ge-, h) chloroform.

Cholera ⚕ ['koːlərə] f (-/no pl.) cholera

cholerisch adj. [koˈleːriʃ] choleric, irascible

Chor [koːr] m 1. △ a. n (-[e]s/-e, ~e) chancel; choir; (organ-)loft; 2. (-[e]s/~e ⚻ in drama: chorus; singers: choir chorus; piece of music: chorus; ~al [koˈraːl] m (-s/~e) cho-

ral(e); hymn; ~gesang m choral singing, chorus, ~sänger m member of a choir, chorister

Christ [krist] m (-en/-en) Christian; ~baum m Christmas-tree, '~enheit f (-/no pl.) die Christendom; ~entum n (-s/no pl Christianity; '~kind n (-[e]s/no pl Christ-child, Infant Jesus '⚕lich adj Christian.

Chrom [kroːm] n (-s/no pl.) metal: chromium, pigment chrome.

chromatisch ♪, opt adj. [kroˈmaː tiʃ] chromatic

Chronik ['kroːnik] f (-/-en) chronicle.

chronisch adj. ['kroːniʃ] disease: chronic (a fig.).

Chronist [kroˈnist] m (-en/-en) chronicler

chronologisch adj. [kronoˈloːgiʃ] chronological.

circa adv ['tsirka] about, approximately.

Clique ['klikə] f (-/-n) clique, set, group, coterie, '~nwirtschaft f (-/no pl. cliquism

Conférencier [kõfərãˈsjeː] m (-s/-s) compère, Am. master of ceremonies.

Couch [kautʃ] f (-/-es) couch.

Coupé [kuˈpeː] n (-s/-s) mot. coupé; ⚕ 🚃 compartment

Couplet [kuˈpleː] n (-s/-s) comic or music-hall song.

Coupon [kuˈpõ] m (-s/-s) coupon; dividend-warrant, counterfoil.

Courtage [kurˈtaːʒə] f (-/-n) brokerage.

Cousin [kuˈzɛ̃] m (-s/-s), ~e [-ˈiːnə] f (-/-n) cousin.

Creme [krɛːm, kreːm] f (-/-s) cream (a. fig.: only sg.).

Cut [kœt, kat] m (-s/-s), ~away ['kœtəveː, 'katəveː] m (-s/-s) cutaway (coat), morning coat.

D

da [daː] 1. adv. space: there; ~ wo where; hier und ~ here and there; ~ bin ich here I am; ~ haben wir's! there we are!, von ~ an from there; time: ~ erst only then, not till then; von ~ an from that time (on), since then; hier und ~ now and then or again; 2. cj time as, when, while; nun, ~ du es einmal gesagt hast now (that) you have mentioned it; causal as, since, because; ~ ich krank war, konnte ich nicht kommen as or since I was ill I couldn't come.

dabei adv. [daˈbai, when emphatic: 'daːbai] near (at hand), by; about, going (zu inf. to inf.), on the point

(of ger.); besides; nevertheless, yet, for all that; was ist schon ~? what does it matter?; lassen wir es ~ let's leave it at that; ~ bleiben stick to one's point, persist in it.

da'bei|bleiben v/i (irr. bleiben, sep., -ge-, sein) stay with it or them; ~sein v/i. (irr. sein, sep., -ge-, sein) be present or there; ~stehen v/i. (irr. stehen, sep., -ge-, h) stand by or near.

'dableiben v/i. (irr. bleiben, sep., -ge-, sein) stay, remain.

da capo adv. [daˈkaːpo] at opera, etc.: encore.

Dach [dax] n (-[e]s/~er) roof; fig. shelter; '~antenne f roof aerial;

'**∼decker** *m* (-s/-) roofer; tiler; slater; '**∼fenster** *n* skylight; dormer window; '**∼garten** *m* roof-garden; '**∼gesellschaft ✝** *f* holding company; '**∼kammer** *f* attic, garret; '**∼pappe** *f* roofing felt; '**∼rinne** *f* gutter, eaves *pl.*

dachte ['daxtə] *pret. of* denken.

Dachs *zo.* [daks] *m* (-es/-e) badger; '**∼bau** *m* (-[e]s/-e) badger's earth.

'**Dach|sparren** *m* rafter; '**∼stube** *f* attic, garret; '**∼stuhl** *m* roof framework; '**∼ziegel** *m* (roofing) tile.

dadurch [da'durç, *when emphatic:* 'daːdurç] 1. *adv.* for this reason, in this manner *or* way, thus; by it *or* that; 2. *cj.*: ∼ daß owing to (the fact that), because; by ger.

dafür [da'fyːr, *when emphatic:* 'daːfyːr] for it *or* that; instead (of it); in return (for it), in exchange; ∼ sein be in favo(u)r of it; ∼ sein zu *inf.* be for ger., be in favo(u)r of ger.; er kann nichts ∼ it is not his fault; ∼ sorgen, daß see to it that.

Da'fürhalten *n* (-s/*no pl.*): nach meinem ∼ in my opinion.

dagegen [da'geːgən, *when emphatic:* 'daːgeːgən] 1. *adv.* against it *or* that; in comparison with it, compared to it; ∼ sein be against it, be opposed to it; ich habe nichts ∼ I have no objection (to it); 2. *cj.* on the other hand, however.

daheim *adv.* [da'haɪm] at home.

daher [da'heːr, *when emphatic:* 'daːheːr] 1. *adv.* from there; *prefixed to verbs of motion:* along; *fig.* from this, hence; ∼ kam es, daß thus it happened that; 2. *cj.* therefore; that is (the reason) why.

dahin [da'hin, *when emphatic:* 'daːhin] there, to that place; gone, past; *prefixed to verbs of motion:* along; j-n ∼ bringen, daß induce s.o. to *inf.*; m-e Meinung geht ∼, daß my opinion is that.

da'hingestellt *adj.*: es ∼ sein lassen (,ob) leave it undecided (whether).

dahinter *adv.* [da'hintər, *when emphatic:* 'daːhintər] behind it *or* that, at the back of it; es steckt nichts ∼ there is nothing in it.

da'hinterkommen *v/i. (irr. kommen, sep., -ge-, sein)* find out about it.

damalig *adj.* ['daːmaːlic] then, of that time; der ∼e Besitzer the then owner; '∼s *adv.* then, at that time.

Damast [da'mast] *m* (-es/-e) damask.

Dame ['daːmə] *f* (-/-n) lady; *dancing, etc.*: partner; *cards, chess:* queen; *s.* Damespiel; '∼brett *n* draught-board, *Am.* checkerboard.

'**Damen|binde** *f* (woman's) sanitary towel, *Am.* sanitary napkin; '∼**doppel** *n* tennis: women's doubles *pl.*; '∼**einzel** *n* tennis: women's

singles *pl.*; '∼**haft** *adj.* ladylike; '∼**konfektion** *f* ladies' ready-made clothes *pl.*; '∼**mannschaft** *f sports:* women's team; ∼**schneider** *m* ladies' tailor, dressmaker.

'**Damespiel** *n* (game of) draughts *pl.*, *Am.* (game of) checkers *pl.*

damit 1. *adv.* [da'mit, *when emphatic:* 'daːmit] with it *or* that, therewith, herewith; by it *or* that; was will er ∼ sagen? what does he mean by it?; wie steht es ∼? how about it?; ∼ einverstanden sein agree to it; 2. *cj.* (in order) that, in order to *inf.*; so (that); ∼ nicht lest, (so as) to avoid that; for fear that *(all with subjunctive).*

dämlich F *adj.* ['deːmlic] silly, asinine.

Damm [dam] *m* (-[e]s/∼e) dam; dike, dyke; 🜉 embankment; embankment, *Am.* levee *(of river)*; roadway; *fig.* barrier; '∼**bruch** *m* bursting of a dam *or* dike.

dämmer|ig *adj.* ['dɛməric] dusky; '∼**Licht** *n* twilight; '∼**n** *v/i.* (ge-, h) dawn *(a. fig.:* F j-m on s.o.); grow dark *or* dusky; '∼**ung** *f* (-/-en) twilight, dusk; *in the morning:* dawn.

Dämon ['dɛːmɔn] *m* (-s/-en) demon; Lisch *adj.* [dɛ'moːnɪʃ] demoniac(al).

Dampf [dampf] *m* (-[e]s/∼e) steam; vapo(u)r; '∼**bad** *n* vapo(u)r-bath; '∼**boot** *n* steamboat; '∼**en** *v/i.* (ge-, h) steam.

dämpfen ['dɛmpfən] *v/t.* (ge-, h) deaden *(pain, noise, force of blow)*; muffle *(bell, drum, oar)*; damp *(sound, oscillation, fig. enthusiasm)*; ♪ mute *(stringed instrument)*; soften *(colour, voice)*; attenuate *(wave)*; steam *(cloth, food)*; stew *(meat, fruit)*; *fig.* suppress, curb *(emotion).*

'**Dampfer** *m* (-s/-) steamer, steamship.

'**Dämpfer** *m* (-s/-) damper *(a. ♪ of piano)*; ♪ mute *(for violin, etc.).*

'**Dampf|heizung** *f* steam-heating; '∼**kessel** *m* (steam-)boiler; '∼**maschine** *f* steam-engine; '∼**schiff** *n* steamer, steamship; '∼**walze** *f* steam-roller.

danach *adv.* [da'naːx, *when emphatic:* 'daːnaːx] after it *or* that; afterwards; subsequently; accordingly; ich fragte ihn ∼ I asked him about it; iro. er sieht ganz ∼ aus he looks very much like it.

Däne ['dɛːnə] *m* (-n/-n) Dane.

daneben *adv.* [da'neːbən, *when emphatic:* 'daːneːbən] next to it *or* that, beside it *or* that; besides, moreover; beside the mark.

da'nebengehen F *v/i. (irr. gehen, sep., -ge-, sein)* bullet, *etc.*: miss the target *or* mark; *remark, etc.*: miss one's effect, F misfire.

daniederliegen [da'niːdər-] *v/i.*

(irr. liegen, sep., -ge-, h) be laid up (an dat with), trade: be depressed.

dänisch adj ['dɛːniʃ] Danish.

Dank [daŋk] 1. m (-[e]s/no pl.) thanks pl, gratitude; reward; j-m ~ sagen thank s.o.; Gott sei ~! thank God!, 2. 2 prp. (dat.) owing ~ thanks to; '2bar adj. thankful grateful (j-m to s.o.; für for); profitable ~barkeit f (-/no pl.) gratitude. 2en v/i. (ge-, h) thank j-n für et. s.o. for s.th.); danke schön) thank you (very much) danke thank you; [nein, danke n thank you; nichts zu ~ don't mention it. '2enswert adj. thing on can be grateful for; efforts, etc. kind, task, etc.: rewarding, worth-while ~gebet n thanksgiving (prayer), ~schreiben n letter of thanks

dann adv [dan] then; ~ und wann (every now and then).

daran adv [da'ran, when emphatic: 'daːran] a ~ or by, in, on, to) it or that; sich festhalten hold on tight to it; festhalten stick to it; nahe ~ sein zu inf be on the point or verge of ger

da'rangehen v/i. (irr. gehen, sep., -ge-, sein) set to work; set about ger.

darauf adv [da'rauf, when emphatic: daːrauf] space: (on top of) it or that; time thereupon, after it or that, an Tage ~ the day after, the next or following day; zwei Jahre ~ two years later; ~ kommt es an that's what matters; ~hin adv. [daːrauf'hin, when emphatic: 'daːraufhin] thereupon.

daraus adv [da'raus, when emphatic: daːraus] out of it or that, from it or that, ~ folgt hence it follows was ist ~ geworden? what has become of it?; ich mache mir nichts ~ I don't care or mind (about it)

darben ['darbən] v/i. (ge-, h) suffer want, starve

darbiet|en ['daːr-] v/t. (irr. bieten, sep., -ge-, h) offer, present; perform, '2ung f (-/-en) thea., etc.: performance

'darbringen v/t. (irr. bringen, sep., -ge-, h) offer, make (sacrifice).

darein adv [da'rain, when emphatic 'daːrain] into it or that, therein

da'rein|finden v/refl. (irr. finden, sep., -ge-, h) put up with it; ~mischen v/refl (sep., -ge-, h) interfere (with it), ~reden v/i. (sep., -ge-, h) interrupt; fig. interfere.

darin adv [da'rin, when emphatic: 'daːrin] in it or that; therein; es war nichts ~ there was nothing in it or them.

darleg|en ['daːr-] v/t. (sep., -ge-, h)

lay open, expose, disclose; show; explain; demonstrate, point out; '2ung f (-/-en) exposition; explanation; statement

Darlehen [dɑːrleːən] n (-s/-) loan.

Darm [darm] m -[e]s/~e gut, anat. intestine, sausage-)skin Därme pl. intestines pl, bowels pl

'darstell|en v/t (sep., -ge-, h) represent; show, depict, delineate; describe, acting interpret (character, part), represent (character); graphic arts graph, plot (curve, etc.); '2er thea m '-s/-) interpreter (of a part), actor, '2ung f representation, thea performance.

'dartun v/t (irr tun, sep , -ge-, h) prove; demonstrate , set forth.

darüber adv [daːrʏbər, when emphatic 'daːrʏbər] over it or that; across it; in the meantime; ~ werden Jahre vergehen it will take years; wir sind hinweg we got over it; ein Buch schreiben write a book about it.

darum [da'rum, when emphatic: 'daːrum] 1. adv around it or that; er kümmert sich nicht ~ he does not care, es handelt sich ~ zu inf. the point is to inf , 2. cj. therefore, for that reason, ist er nicht gekommen that's the (reason) why he hasn't come

darunter adv [da'runtər, when emphatic 'daːruntər] under it or that; beneath it, among them; less; zwei Jahre und ~ two years and under; was verstehst du ~? what do you understand by it?

das [das] s der

dasein ['daː-] 1. v/i. (irr. sein, sep., -ge-, sein) be there or present; exist; 2. 2 n (-s/no pl.) existence, life; being.

daß cj. [das] that; ~ nicht less; es sei denn, ~ unless; ohne ~ without ger.; nicht ~ ich wüßte not that I know of.

'dastehen v/i. (irr. stehen, sep., -ge-, h) stand (there).

Daten ['daːtən] pl data pl. (a. ⊕), facts pl., particulars pl.; '~verarbeitung f (-/-en) data processing.

datieren [da'tiːrən] v/t. and v/i. (no -ge-, h) date [(case).)

Dativ gr ['daːtiːf] m -s/-e dative)

Dattel ['datəl] f (-/-n) date.

Datum ['daːtum] n (-s/Daten) date.

Dauer ['dauər] f (-/no pl.) length, duration, continuance; auf die ~ in the long run, für die ~ von for a period or term of, von ~ sein last well; '2haft adj peace, etc.: lasting; material, etc durable; colour, dye: fast; ~karte f season ticket, Am. commutation ticket; '~lauf m jog-trot; endurance-run; '2n v/i. (ge-, h) continue, last; take (time); '~welle f permanent wave, F perm.

Daumen ['daumən] m (-s/-) thumb; j-m den ~ halten keep one's fingers crossed (for s.o.); '~abdruck m (-[e]s/~e) thumb-print.

Daune ['daunə] f (-/-n): ~(n pl.) down; '~ndecke f eiderdown (quilt).

davon adv. [da'fɔn, when emphatic: 'daːfɔn] of it or that; thereof; from it or that; off, away; was habe ich ~? what do I get from it?; das kommt ~! it serves you right!

da'von|kommen v/i. (irr. kommen, sep., -ge-, sein) escape, get off; ~laufen v/i. (irr. laufen, sep., -ge-, sein) run away.

davor adv. [da'foːr, when emphatic: 'daːfoːr] space: before it or that, in front of it or that; er fürchtet sich ~ he is afraid of it.

dazu adv. [da'tsuː, when emphatic: 'daːtsuː] to it or that; for it or that; for that purpose; in addition to that; noch ~ at that; ~ gehört Zeit it requires time.

da'zu|gehörig adj. belonging to it; ~kommen v/i. (irr. kommen, sep., -ge-, sein) appear (on the scene); find time.

dazwischen adv. [da'tsviʃən] between (them), in between; ~kommen v/i. (irr. kommen, sep., -ge-, sein) thing: intervene, happen.

Debatt|e [de'batə] f (-/-n) debate; 2ieren [~'tiːrən] (no -ge-, h) 1. v/t. discuss; debate; 2. v/i. debate (über acc. on).

Debüt [de'byː] n (-s/-s) first appearance, début.

dechiffrieren [deʃi'friːrən] v/t. (no -ge-, h) decipher, decode.

Deck ⚓ [dɛk] n (-[e]s/-s, ~e) deck; '~adresse f cover (address); '~bett n feather bed.

Decke ['dɛkə] f (-/-n) cover(ing); blanket; (travel[l]ing) rug; ceiling; '~l m (-s/-) lid, cover (of box or pot, etc.); lid (of piano); (book-)cover; '2n (ge-, h) 1. v/t. cover; den Tisch ~ lay the table; 2. v/i. paint: cover.

'Deck|mantel m cloak, mask, disguise; '~name m assumed name, pseudonym; '~ung f (-/-en) cover; security.

defekt [de'fɛkt] 1. adj. defective, faulty; 2. 2 m (-[e]s/-e) defect, fault.

defin|ieren [defi'niːrən] v/t. (no -ge-, h) define; 2ition [~i'tsjoːn] f (-/-en) definition; ~itiv adj. [~i'tiːf] definite; definitive.

Defizit ✝ ['deːfitsit] n (-s/-e) deficit, deficiency.

Degen ['deːgən] m (-s/-) sword; fencing: épée.

degradieren [degra'diːrən] v/t. (no -ge-, h) degrade, Am. a. demote.

dehn|bar adj. ['deːnbaːr] extensible; elastic; metal: ductile; notion,

etc.: vague; '~en v/t. (ge-, h) extend; stretch; '2ung f (-/-en) extension; stretch(ing).

Deich [daɪç] m (-[e]s/-e) dike, dyke.

Deichsel ['daɪksəl] f (-/-n) pole, shaft.

dein poss. pron. [daɪn] your der (die, das) ~e yours; ich bin ~ I am yours; die Deinen pl. your family; ~erseits adv. ['~ər'zaɪts] for or on your part; '~es'gleichen pron. your like, your (own) kind, F the like(s) of you.

Dekan eccl. and univ. [de'kaːn] m (-s/-e) dean.

Deklam|ation [deklama'tsjoːn] f (-/-en) declamation; reciting; 2ieren [~'miːrən] v/t. and v/i. (no -ge-, h) recite; declaim.

Deklin|ation gr. [deklina'tsjoːn] f (-/-en) declension; 2ieren gr. [~'niːrən] v/t. (no -ge-, h) decline.

Dekor|ateur [dekora'tøːr] m (-s/-e) decorator; window-dresser; thea. scene-painter; ~ation [~'tsjoːn] f (-/-en) decoration; (window-)dressing; thea. scenery; 2ieren [~'riːrən] v/t. (no -ge-, h) decorate; dress (window).

Dekret [de'kreːt] n (-[e]s/-e) decree.

delikat adj. [deli'kaːt] delicate (a. fig.); delicious; fig. ticklish; 2esse [~a'tɛsə] f (-/-n) delicacy; dainty.

Delphin zo. [dɛl'fiːn] m (-s/-e) dolphin.

Dementi [de'mɛnti] n (-s/-s) (formal) denial; 2ieren [~'tiːrən] v/t. (no -ge-, h) deny, give a (formal) denial of.

'dem|entsprechend adv., '~gemäß adv. correspondingly, accordingly; '~nach adv. therefore, hence; accordingly; '~nächst adv. soon, shortly, before long.

demobili'sier|en (no -ge-, h) 1. v/t. demobilize; disarm; 2. v/i. disarm; 2ung f (-/-en) demobilization.

Demokrat [demo'kraːt] m (-en/-en) democrat; ~ie [~a'tiː] f (-/-n) democracy; 2isch adj. [~'kraːtiʃ] democratic.

demolieren [demo'liːrən] v/t. (no -ge-, h) demolish.

Demonstr|ation [demɔnstra'tsjoːn] f (-/-en) demonstration; 2ieren [~'striːrən] v/t. and v/i. (no -ge-, h) demonstrate.

Demont|age [demɔn'taːʒə] f (-/-n) disassembly; dismantling; 2ieren [~'tiːrən] v/t. (no -ge-, h) disassemble; dismantle.

Demut ['deːmuːt] f (-/no pl.) humility, humbleness.

demütig adj. ['deːmyːtiç] humble; ~en ['~gən] v/t. (ge-, h) humble, humiliate.

denk|bar ['dɛŋkbaːr] 1. adj. conceivable; thinkable; imaginable; 2. adv.: ~ einfach most simple;

,~en (*irr.*, ge-, h) 1. *v/i.* think; ~ *an* (*acc.*) think of; remember; ~ *über* (*acc.*) think about; *j-m zu* ~ *geben* set s.o thinking, 2. *v/t.* think; *sich et.* ~ imagine *or* fancy s.th.; *das habe ich mir gedacht* I thought as much, **£mal** *n* monument; memorial; **£schrift** *f* memorandum; memou **£stein** *m* memorial stone; **'~würdig** *adj* memorable; **£zettel** *fig. m* lesson

denn [dɛn] 1. *cj* for; *mehr* ~ *je* more than *ever* 2 *adv.* then; *es sei* ~, *daß* unless, except; *wieso* ~? how so.

dennoch *c* ['dɛnnɔx] yet, still, nevertheless though.

Denunz|iant denun'tsjant] *m* (-en/ -en) informe **.iation** [.'tsjoːn] *f* (-/-en) denunciation; **£ieren** [.'tsiːrən] *v/t* (*no* -ge-, h) inform against, denounc

Depesche [de'pɛʃə] *f* (-/-n) dispatch telegram, F wire; wireless.

deponieren [depo'niːrən] *v/t.* (*no* -ge-, h deposit

Deposit ‡ [depo'ziːtən] *pl.* deposits *pl* **.bank** *f* deposit bank.

der [de r], **die** [diː], **das** [das] 1. *art.* the; 2. *dem pron* that; this; he, she, it die *pi* these, those, they, them, 3 *rel pron.* who, which, that. **'der'artig** *adj* such, of such a kind of this *or* tha kind.

derb *adj* |dɛrp| *cloth*: coarse, rough, *shoes, et.* stout, strong; *ore, etc.*: massive, p sturdy; rough; *food*: coarse, p *manners*: rough, coarse; *way of speaking* blunt, unrefined; *joke* crude *humour*: broad.

der'gleichen *adj.* such, of that kind, *used a u noun*: the like, such a thing *und* and the like; *nichts* ~ nothing of the kind.

der- ['de rjenıgə], **'die-**, **'dasjenige** *dem. pron* he *who*, she *who*, that *which* diejenigen *pl.* those *who*, those *which*

der- [de rzɛlbə], **die-**, **das'selbe** *dem. pron* the same; he, she, it.

Desert|eu [dezer'tøːr] *m* (-s/-e) deserte **.ieren** [.'tiːrən] *v/i.* (*no* -ge-, sein desert.

desgleichen [dɛs'glaıçən] 1. *dem. pron* such thing; 2. *cj.* likewise.

deshalb [dɛshalp] 1. *cj.* for this *or* that reason, therefore; 2. *adv.*: *ich tat es nur* ., *weil* I did it only because

desinfizieren [dɛs?infi'tsiːrən] *v/t.* (*no* -ge h disinfect.

Despot [dɛs po t] *m* (-en/-en) despot, **£isch** *adj* despotic.

destillieren [dɛsti'liːrən] *v/t.* (*no* -ge-, h/ distil

desto *adv* ['dɛsto] (all, so much) the; *besser* all the better; ~ *erstaunter* (all) the more astonished.

deswegen *cj. and adv.* ['dɛs've:gən] *s.* deshalb.

Detail [de'taı] *n* (-s/-s) detail.

Detektiv [detɛk'tiːf] *m* (-s/-e) detective.

deuten ['dɔrtən] (ge-, h) 1. *v/t.* interpret, read (*stars, dream, etc.*); 2. *v/i.*: ~ *auf* (acc) point at.

'deutlich *adj* clear, distinct, plain.

deutsch *adj* [dɔrtʃ] German; **'£e** *m*, *f* (-n/-n) German

'Deutung *f* (-/-en) interpretation, explanation

Devise [de'viːzə] *f* (-/-n) motto; ~*n pl.* † foreign exchange *or* currency.

Dezember [de'tsɛmbər] *m* (-[s]/-) December.

dezent *adj.* [de'tsɛnt] *attire, etc.*: decent, modest, *literature, etc.*: decent; *behaviour* decent, proper; *music, colour* soft, restrained; *lighting, etc.* subdued

Dezernat [detsɛr'naːt] *n* (-[e]s/-e) (administrative) department.

dezimal *adj* [detsı maː.l] decimal; **£bruch** *m* decimal fraction; **£stelle** *f* decimal place

dezi'mieren *v/t.* (*no* -ge-, h) decimate; *fig* a reduce (drastically).

Diadem [dia'de m] *n* (-s/-e) diadem.

Diagnose [dia'gnoːzə] *f* (-/-n) diagnosis.

diagonal *adj* [diago'naːl] diagonal; **£e** *f* (-/-n) diagonal

Dialekt [dia'lɛkt] *m* (-[e]s/-e) dialect; **£isch** *adj* dialectal.

Dialog [dia'lo k] *m* (-[e]s/-e) dialogue, *Am a* dialog

Diamant [dia'mant] *m* (-en/-en) diamond.

Diät [di'ɛːt] *f* (-/*no pl.*) diet; *diät leben* live on a diet.   [yourself.|

dich *pers. pron* [dıç] you; ~(selbst))

dicht [dıçt] 1. *adj* fog, rain, *etc.*: dense; fog, forest, hair thick; *eyebrows*: bushy, thick, *crowd*: thick, dense; *shoe, etc.* (water)tight; 2. *adv.* ~ *an* (*dat.*) *or* bei close to. **'dichten**[1] *v/t.* (ge-, h) make tight. **'dicht|en**[2] *v/t.* 1. *v/t.* compose, write; 2. *v/i* compose *or* write poetry; **'£er** *m* (-s/-) poet; author; **'~erisch** *adj.* poetic(al); **'£kunst** *f* poetry.

'Dichtung[1] ⊕ *f* (-/-en) seal(ing).

'Dichtung[2] *f* (-/-en) poetry; fiction; poem, poetic work.

dick *adj.* [dık] *wall, material, etc.*: thick; *book* thick, bulky; *p.* fat, stout; **'£e** *f* (-/-n) thickness; bulkiness; *p.* fatness, stoutness, **'~fellig** *adj. p.* thick-skinned, **~flüssig** *adj.* thick; viscid, viscous, syrupy; **£icht** ['.ıçt] *n* (-[e]s/-e) thicket, **'£kopf** *m* stubborn person, F pig-headed person; **~leibig** *adj.* ['.laıbıç] corpulent; *fig* bulky.

die [diː] *s.* der.

Dieb [diːp] *m* (-[e]s/-e) thief, *Am.* F a. crook; **~erei** [diːbə'raı] *f* (-/-en) thieving, thievery.

Diebes|bande ['di:bəs-] *f* band of thieves; **'gut** *n* stolen goods *pl.*

dieb|isch adj. ['di:biʃ] thievish; *fig.* malicious; **2stahl** ['di:p-] *m* (-[e]s/ ~e) theft, ⅌ *mst* larceny.

Diele ['di:lə] *f* (-/-n) board, plank; hall, *Am. a.* hallway.

dienen ['di:nən] *v/i.* (ge-, h) serve (*j-m s.o.*; *als* as; *zu* for; *dazu, zu inf.* to *inf.*); womit kann ich ~? what can I do for you?

'Diener *m* (-s/-) (man-, domestic) servant; *fig.* bow (*vor dat.* to); **'~in** *f* (-/-nen) (woman-)servant, maid; **'~schaft** *f* (-/-nen) servants *pl.*

'dienlich adj. useful, convenient; expedient, suitable.

Dienst [di:nst] *m* (-es/-e) service; duty; employment; ~ *haben* be on duty; *im* (*außer*) ~ on (off) duty.

Dienstag ['di:nsta:k] *m* (-[e]s/-e) Tuesday.

'Dienst|alter *n* seniority, length of service; **'2bar** adj. subject (*j-m* to *s.o.*); subservient (to); **'~bote** *m* domestic (servant), *Am.* help; **'2eifrig** adj. (over-)eager (in one's duty); **'2frei** adj. off duty; **~er** *Tag* day off; **'~herr** *m* master; employer; **'~leistung** *f* service; **'2lich** adj. official; **'~mädchen** *n* maid, *Am.* help; **'~mann** *m* (street-)porter; **'~stunden** *f/pl.* office hours *pl.*; **'2tauglich** adj. fit for service *or* duty; **2tuend** adj. ['~tu:ənt] on duty; **'2untauglich** adj. unfit for service *or* duty; **'~weg** *m* official channels *pl.*; **'~wohnung** *f* official residence.

dies [di:s], **~er** ['di:zər], **~e** ['di:zə], **~es** ['di:zəs] adj. and dem. pron. this; *diese pl.* these; *dieser Tage* one of these days; *used as a noun:* this one; he, she, it; *dies pl.* they.

Dieselmotor ['di:zəl-] *m* Diesel engine.

dies|jährig adj. ['di:sjɛ:riç] of this year, this year's; **'~mal** adv. this time; *for* (this) once; **~seits** ['~zaɪts] 1. adv. on this side; 2. *prp.* (*gen.*) on this side of.

Dietrich ['di:triç] *m* (-s/-e) skeleton key; picklock.

Differenz [difə'rɛnts] *f* (-/-en) difference; disagreement.

Diktat [dik'ta:t] *m* (-[e]s/-e) dictation; *nach* ~ at *or* from dictation; **~or** [~ɔr] *m* (-s/-en) dictator; **2orisch** adj. [~a'to:riʃ] dictatorial; **~ur** [~a'tu:r] *f* (-/-en) dictatorship.

dik'tieren *v/t.* and *v/i.* (no -ge-, h) dictate.

Dilettant [dile'tant] *m* (-en/-en) dilettante, dabbler; amateur.

Ding [diŋ] *n* (-[e]s/-e) thing; *guter* ~e in good spirits; *vor allen* ~en first of all, above all.

Diphtherie ⚕ [difte'ri:] *f* (-/-n) diphtheria.

Diplom [di'plo:m] *n* (-[e]s/-e) diploma, certificate.

Diplomat [diplo'ma:t] *m* (-en/-en) diplomat; diplomatist; **~ie** [~a'ti:] *f* (-/no pl.) diplomacy; **2isch** adj. [~'ma:tiʃ] diplomatic (a. fig.).

dir *pers. pron.* [di:r] (to) you.

direkt [di'rɛkt] 1. adj. direct; **~er** *Wagen* 🚃 through carriage, *Am.* through car; 2. adv. direct(ly); **2ion** [~'tsjo:n] *f* (-/-en) direction; management; board of directors; **2or** [di'rɛktɔr] *m* (-s/-en) director; manager; headmaster, *Am.* principal; **2orin** [~'to:rin] *f* (-/-nen) headmistress, *Am.* principal; **2rice** [~'tri:s(ə)] *f* (-/-n) directress; manageress.

Dirig|ent ♪ [diri'gɛnt] *m* (-en/-en) conductor; **2ieren** [~'gi:rən] *v/t.* and *v/i.* (no -ge-, h) conduct.

Dirne ['dirnə] *f* (-/-n) prostitute.

Disharmon|ie ♪ [disharmo'ni:] *f* (-/-n) disharmony, dissonance (*both a. fig.*); **2isch** adj. [~'mo:niʃ] discordant, dissonant.

Diskont ⁜ [dis'kɔnt] *m* (-s/-e) discount; **2ieren** [~'ti:rən] *v/t.* (no -ge-, h) discount.

diskret adj. [dis'kre:t] discreet; **2ion** [~e'tsjo:n] *f* (-/no pl.) discretion.

Disku|ssion [disku'sjo:n] *f* (-/-en) discussion, debate; **2'tieren** (no -ge-, h) 1. *v/t.* discuss, debate; 2. *v/i.:* ~ *über* (*acc.*) have a discussion about, debate (up)on.

dispo|nieren [dispo'ni:rən] *v/i.* (no -ge-, h) make arrangements; plan ahead; dispose (*über acc.* of); **2si-tion** [~zi'tsjo:n] *f* (-/-en) disposition; arrangement; disposal.

Distanz [di'stants] *f* (-/-en) distance (*a. fig.*); **2ieren** [~'ti:rən] *v/refl.* (no -ge-, h): *sich* ~ *von* dis(as)sociate o.s. from.

Distel ⚘ ['distəl] *f* (-/-n) thistle.

Distrikt [di'strikt] *m* (-[e]s/-e) district; region; area.

Disziplin [distsi'pli:n] *f* (-/-en) discipline.

Divid|ende ⁜ [divi'dɛndə] *f* (-/-n) dividend; **2ieren** [~'di:rən] *v/t.* (no -ge-, h) divide (*durch* by).

Diwan ['di:va:n] *m* (-s/-e) divan.

doch [dɔx] 1. *cj.* but, though; however, yet; 2. adv. *in answer to negative question:* yes; *bist du noch nicht fertig?* — ~*!* aren't you ready yet? — yes, I am; *also* ~*!* I knew it!, I was right after all!; *komm* ~ *herein!* do come in!; *nicht* ~*!* I don't!

Docht [dɔxt] *m* (-[e]s/-e) wick.

Dock ⚓ [dɔk] *n* (-[e]s/-s) dock.

Dogge *zo.* ['dɔgə] *f* (-/-n) Great Dane.

Dohle *orn.* ['do:lə] *f* (-/-n) (jack)daw.

Doktor ['dɔktɔr] *m* (-s/-en) doctor.

Dokument [doku'mɛnt] *n* (-[e]s/-e)

document; **g'** instrument; ~arfilm
[',tai:r-] *m* documentary (film).
Dolch [dɔlç] *m* (-[e]s/-e) dagger;
poniard. ~stoß *m* dagger-thrust.
Dollar ['dɔlar] *m* (-s/-s) dollar.
dolmetsch|en ['dɔlmetʃən] *v/i. and
v/t.* (ge-, h' interpret; '2er *m* (-s/-)
interpreter
Dom [do:m] *m* (-[e]s/-e) cathedral.
Domäne [do'mɛ:nə] *f* (-/-n) domain
(a. *fig.*), province.
Domino ['do:mino] (-s/-s) **1.** *m*
domino; **2.** *n* (game of) dominoes
pl.
Donner ['dɔnər] *m* (-s/-) thunder;
'2n *v/i* (ge-, h) thunder (a. *fig.*);
'~schlag *m* thunderclap (a. *fig.*);
'~stag *m* Thursday; '~wetter *n*
thunderstorm; F *fig.* telling off; F:
~! my word!, by Jove!; F zum ~!
F confound it!, *sl.* damn it.
Doppel ['dɔpəl] *n* (-s/-) duplicate;
tennis, etc double, *Am.* doubles
pl.; '~bett *n* double bed; '~decker
m (-s/-) & biplane; double-decker
(bus); '~ehe *f* bigamy; '~gänger
['~gɛnər *m* ı-s/-) double; '~punkt
m colon. ~sinn *m* double meaning,
ambiguity, £sinnig adj. ambiguous,
equivocal. ~stecker & *m* two-way
adapter. '2t **1.** *adj.* double; **2.** *adv.*
doubly, twice. ~zentner *m* quin-
tal; 2züngig adj. ['~tsyŋiç] two-
faced.
Dorf [dɔrf] *n* (-[e]s/-er) village; '~be-
wohner *m* villager.
Dorn [dɔrn *m* **1.** (-[e]s/-en) thorn
(a. *fig.*), prickle, spine; *j-m* ein ~ im
Auge sein be a thorn in s.o.'s flesh
or side. **2.** -[e]s/-e) tongue (of
buckle); spike of running-shoe, etc.);
⊕ punch '2ig adj. thorny (a. *fig.*).
dörr|en ['dœrən] v/t. (ge-, h) dry;
'2fleisch *n* dried meat; '2gemüse
n dried vegetables *pl.*; '2obst *n*
dried fruit
Dorsch *ichth.* [dɔrʃ] *m* (-es/-e)
cod(fish)
dort adv [dɔrt] there; over there;
'~her adv from there; '~hin adv.
there, to that place; '~ig adj. there,
in or of that place
Dose ['do:zə] *f* (-/-n) box; tin, *Am.*
can. ~nöffner ['do:zən⁹-] *m* (-s/-)
tin-opener, *Am* can opener.
Dosis ['do:zis] *f* (-/Dosen) dose (a.
fig.).
dotieren [do'ti:rən] v/t. (no -ge-, h)
endow
Dotter [dɔtər] *m, n* (-s/-) yolk.
Dozent [do'tsɛnt] *m* (-en/-en) (university) lecturer, *Am.* assistant
professor
Drache ['draxə] *m* (-n/-n) dragon;
'~n *m* (-s/-) kite; *fig.* termagant,
shrew, battle-axe.
Dragoner [dra'go:nər] *m* (-s/-) ⚔
dragoon (a. *fig.*).
Draht [drɑ:t] *m* (-[e]s/-e) wire; '2en

v/t. (ge-, h) telegraph, wire; '~ge-
flecht *n* (-[e]s/-e) wire netting;
'~hindernis ⚔ *n* wire entanglement; '2ig adj. p. wiry, '2los adj.
wireless; ~seilbahn *f* funicular
(railway); ~stift *m* wire tack;
'~zieher ¹ *fig. m* (-s/-) wire-puller.
drall adj [dral] *girl, legs, etc.*:
plump; *woman* buxom.
Drama ['drɑ:ma] *n* (-s/Dramen)
drama; ~tiker [dra'mɑ:tikər] *m*
(-s/-) dramatist, 2tisch adj. [dra-
'mɑ:tiʃ] dramatic
dran F adv [dran] *s. daran*; er ist
gut (übel) ~ he's well (badly) off;
ich bin ~ it's my turn.
Drang [draŋ] **1.** *m* (-[e]s/*~e)
pressure, rush; *fig.* urge; **2.** 2 *pret.*
of dringen.
drängen ['drɛŋən] (ge-, h) **1.** *v/t.*
press (a. *fig.*), push; *fig.* urge;
creditor: dun; *sich ~* crowd, throng;
2. *v/i.* press, be pressing or urgent.
drangsalieren [draŋza'li:rən] v/t.
(no -ge-, h) harass, vex, plague.
drastisch adj ['drastiʃ] drastic.
drauf F adv [drauf] *s darauf*; ~ und
dran sein zu *inf* be on the point of
ger.; 2gänger ['~gɛŋər *m* (-s/-)
dare-devil, *Am sl.* a. go-getter.
draus F adv [draus] *s daraus*.
draußen adv ['drausən] outside;
out of doors, abroad; out at sea.
drechs|eln ['drɛksəln] v/t. (ge-, h)
turn (*wood, etc.*); 2ler ['~slər] *m*
(-s/-) turner.
Dreck F [drɛk] *m* (-[e]s/no pl.) dirt;
mud; filth (a. *fig.*); *fig.* trash; F ~
am Stecken haben not to have a
clean slate; F das geht dich einen ~
an that's none of your business;
'2ig adj. dirty; filthy.
Dreh|bank ['dre:-] *f* (-/~e) (turning-)
lathe; '2bar adj. revolving, rotating;
'~bleistift *m* propelling pencil;
'~buch *n* scenario, script; ~bühne
thea. f revolving stage; '2en v/t.
(ge-, h) turn, shoot (*film*); roll
(*cigarette*); es dreht sich darum zu
inf. it is a matter of *ger.*; *sich ~*
turn; '~kreuz *n* turnstile, ~orgel *f*
barrel-organ, ~punkt *m* ⊕ centre
of rotation, *Am* center of rotation,
pivot (a. *fig.*). ~strom & *m* three-
phase current, ~stuhl *m* swivel-
chair; '~tür *f* revolving door; '~ung
f (-/-en) turn; rotation
drei adj. [drai] three; '~beinig adj.
three-legged; '2eck *n* triangle;
'~eckig adj. triangular, ~erlei adj.
['~ər'lai] of three kinds or sorts;
'~fach adj. ['~fax] threefold, treble,
triple; '~farbig adj three-col-
o(u)r(ed); '2fuß *m* tripod; ~jährig
adj. ['~jɛːriç] three-year-old; trien-
nial; '~mal adv. three times; '~ma-
lig adj. done or repeated three
times; three; 2'meilenzone ⊕, **g'**
f three-mile limit; '2rad *n* tricycle;

'**.seitig** adj. three-sided; trilateral; '**.silbig** adj. trisyllabic.

dreißig adj ['draisiç] thirty; '**.ste** adj. thirtieth

dreist adj [draist] bold, audacious; cheeky, saucy, '**2igkeit** f (-/-en) boldness, audacity; cheek, sauciness.

'**drei|stimmig** ♪ adj. for or in three voices, **.tägig** adj. ['..tɛːgiç] three-day; **.teilig** adj. in three parts, tripartite '**.zehn(te)** adj. thirteen(th)

dresch|en ['drɛʃən] v/t. and v/i. (irr., ge-, h) thresh; thrash; '**2flegel** m flail; '**2maschine** f threshing-machine

dressieren [drɛˈsiːrən] v/t. (no -ge-, h) train; break in (horse).

drillen ⚔ ⚒ ['drilən] v/t. (ge-, h) drill.

Drillinge ['drilɪŋə] m/pl. triplets pl.

drin F adv [drin] s. darin.

dringen ['drɪŋən] v/i. (irr., ge-) 1. (sein) durch force one's way through s.th, penetrate or pierce s.th.; **.aus** break forth from s.th.; noise: come from; **.in** (acc.) penetrate into, in j-n. urge or press s.o.; an die Öffentlichkeit **.** get abroad; 2. (h) auf (acc.) insist on, press for; '**.e** adj urgent, pressing; suspicion strong

'**dringlich** adj urgent, pressing; '**2keit** f ¡no pl.) urgency.

drinnen adv. ['drinən] inside; indoors

dritt|e adj ['dritə] third; '**2el** n (-s/-) third, **.ens** adv. thirdly; '**.letzt** adj last but two.

Drog|e ['droːgə] f (-/-n) drug; **.erie** [droːgəˈriː] f (-/-n) chemist's (shop), Am drugstore; **.ist** [droˈgist] m (-en/-en) (retail pharmaceutical) chemist.

drohen ['droːən] v/i. (ge-, h) threaten, menace

Drohne ['droːnə] f (-/-n) zo. drone (a. fig.)

dröhnen ['drøːnən] v/i. (ge-, h) voice, etc resound; cannon, drum, etc.: roar, voice, cannon: boom.

Drohung ['droːʊŋ] f (-/-en) threat, menace

drollig adj ['drɔliç] amusing, quaint, comical

Dromedar zo. [droməˈdaːr] n (-s/-e) dromedary

drosch [drɔːʃ] pret. of dreschen.

Droschke ['drɔʃkə] f (-/-n) taxi (-cab), Am a cab, hack; '**.nkutscher** m cabman, driver, Am. a. hackman

Drossel orn ['drɔsəl] f(-/-n) thrush; '**2n** ⊕ v/t (ge-, h) throttle.

drüben adv. ['dryːbən] over there, yonder

drüber F adv. ['dryːbər] s. darüber.

Druck [druk] m 1. (-[e]s/**e**) pres-

sure; squeeze (of hand, etc.); 2. typ. (-[e]s/-e) print(ing); '**.bogen** m printed sheet; '**.buchstabe** m block letter.

drucken ['drukən] v/t. (ge-, h) print; **.lassen** have s.th. printed, publish.

drücken ['drykən] (ge-, h) 1. v/t. press; squeeze (hand, etc.); force down (prices, wages, etc.); lower (record); press, push (button, etc.). F sich **.** vor (dat.) or von shirk (work, etc.); 2. v/i. shoe: pinch.

'**Drucker** m (-s/-) printer.

'**Drücker** m (-s/-) door-handle; trigger.

Drucker|ei [drukəˈrai] f (-/-en) printing office, Am. printery, print shop; **.schwärze** f printer's or printing-ink.

'**Druck|fehler** m misprint; '**.fehlerverzeichnis** n errata pl.; '**2fertig** adj. ready for press; '**.kammer** f pressurized cabin, **.knopf** m patent fastener, snap-fastener; ⚡ push-button, **.luft** f compressed air; '**.pumpe** f pressure pump; '**.sache(n** pl.) ✉ f printed matter, Am. a. second-class or third-class matter, **.schrift** f block letters; publication; **.taste** f press key.

drum F adv., cj. [drum] s. darum.

drunter F adv. ['druntər] s. darunter.

Drüse anat. ['dryːzə] f (-/-n) gland.

du pers. pron. [duː] you.

Dublette [duˈblɛtə] f (-/-n) duplicate.

ducken ['dukən] v/refl. (ge-, h) duck, crouch; fig. cringe (vor dat. to, before).

Dudelsack ♪ ['duːdəl-] m bagpipes pl.

Duell [duˈɛl] n (-s/-e) duel; **2ieren** [duɛˈliːrən] v/refl. (no -ge-, h) (fight a) duel (mit with).

Duett ♪ [duˈɛt] n (-[e]s/-e) duet.

Duft [duft] m (-[e]s/**e**) scent, fragrance, perfume; '**2en** v/i. (ge-, h) smell, have a scent, be fragrant; '**2end** adj. fragrant; '**2ig** adj. dainty, fragrant.

duld|en ['duldən] (ge-, h) 1. v/t. bear, stand, endure, suffer (pain, grief, etc.); tolerate, put up with; 2. v/i. suffer, **.sam** adj. ['..t-] tolerant; '**2samkeit** f (-/no pl.) tolerance; **2ung** ['..duŋ] f (-/**-**en) toleration, sufferance.

dumm adj. [dum] stupid, dull, Am. F dumb; '**2heit** f (-/-en) stupidity, dullness, stupid or foolish action; '**2kopf** m fool, blockhead, Am. sl. a. dumbbell.

dumpf adj. [dumpf] smell, air, etc.: musty, fusty, atmosphere: stuffy, heavy; sound, sensation, etc.: dull; '**.ig** adj. cellar, etc.: damp, musty.

Düne ['dyːnə] f (-/-n) dune, sandhill.

Dung [duŋ] *m* (-[e]s/*no pl.*) dung, manure.

düngen ['dyŋən] *v/t.* (ge-, h) dung, manure; fertilize; **'2r** *m* (-s/-) *s.* Dung; fertilizer.

dunkel ['dʊŋkəl] 1. *adj.* dark; dim; *fig.* obscure; *idea, etc.:* dim, faint, vague; 2. **2** *n* (-s/*no pl.*) *s.* Dunkelheit.

Dünkel ['dʏŋkəl] *m* (-s/*no pl.*) conceit, arrogance; **'2haft** *adj.* conceited, arrogant.

'Dunkel|heit *f* (-/*no pl.*) darkness (*a. fig.*); *fig.* obscurity; **'~kammer** *phot. f* dark-room; **'2n** *v/i.* (ge-, h) grow dark, darken.

dünn *adj.* [dʏn] *paper, material, voice, etc.:* thin; *hair, population, etc.:* thin, sparse; *liquid:* thin, watery; *air:* rare(fied).

Dunst [dʊnst] *m* (-es/~e) vapo(u)r; haze, mist; fume.

dünsten ['dʏnstən] (ge-, h) 1. *v/t.* steam (*fish, etc.*); stew (*fruit, etc.*); 2. *v/i.* steam.

'dunstig *adj.* vaporous; hazy.

Duplikat [dupli'kɑːt] *n* (-[e]s/-e) duplicate.

Dur ♪ [duːr] *n* (-/-) major.

durch [dʊrç] 1. *prp.* (*acc.*) through; 2. *adv.: die ganze Nacht ~* all night long; *~ und ~* through and through; thoroughly.

durcharbeiten ['dʊrç'-] (sep., -ge-, h) 1. *v/t.* study thoroughly; *sich ~ durch* work through (*book, etc.*); 2. *v/i.* work without a break.

durch'aus *adv.* through and through; thoroughly; by all means; absolutely, quite; **~** *nicht* not at all, by no means.

'durch|biegen *v/t.* (irr. biegen, sep., -ge-, h) bend; deflect (*beam, etc.*); *sich ~* beam, etc.: deflect, sag; **'~blättern** *v/t.* (sep., -ge-, h) glance or skim through (*book, etc.*), Am. thumb through, skim; **'2blick** *m:* **~** *auf* (*acc.*) view through to, vista over, view of; **'~blicken** *v/i.* (sep., -ge-, h) look through; **~** *lassen, daß* give to understand that.

durch|'bluten *v/t.* (*no* -ge-, h) supply with blood; **~'bohren** *v/t.* (*no* -ge-, h) pierce; perforate; *mit Blicken ~* look daggers at *s.o.*

durch'braten *v/t.* (irr. braten, sep., -ge-, h) roast thoroughly; **~brechen** (irr. brechen) 1. ['~brɛçən] *v/i.* (sep., -ge-, sein) break through or apart; 2. ['~] *v/t.* (sep., -ge-, h) break apart or in two; 3. [~'brɛçən] *v/t.* (*no* -ge-, h) break through, breach; run (*blockade*); crash (*sound barrier*); **'~brennen** *v/i.* (irr. brennen, sep., -ge-, sein) *fuse:* blow; *F fig.* run away; *woman:* elope; **'~bringen** *v/t.* (irr. bringen, sep., -ge-, h) bring or get through; dissipate, squander (*money*); **'2bruch** *m* ✕ break-

through; rupture; breach; *fig.* ultimate success.

durch'denken *v/t.* (irr. denken, *no* -ge-, h) think *s.th.* over thoroughly.

'durch|drängen *v/refl.* (sep., -ge-, h) force or push one's way through; **~dringen** (irr. dringen) 1. ['~drɪŋən] *v/i.* (sep., -ge-, sein) penetrate (through); win acceptance (*mit for*) (*proposal*); 2. [~'drɪŋən] *v/t.* (*no* -ge-, h) penetrate, pierce; *water, smell, etc.:* permeate.

durcheinander [dʊrç'aɪ'nandər] 1. *adv.* in confusion or disorder; pell-mell; 2. **2** *n* (-s/-) muddle, mess, confusion; **~bringen** *v/t.* (irr. bringen, sep., -ge-, h) confuse *s.o.*; *fig.* mix (*things*) up; **~werfen** *v/t.* (irr. werfen, sep., -ge-, h) throw into disorder; *fig.* mix up.

durchfahr|en (irr. fahren) 1. ['~faːrən] *v/i.* (sep., -ge-, sein) go or pass or drive through; 2. [~'faːrən] *v/t.* (*no* -ge-, h) go or pass or travel or drive through; traverse (*tract of country, etc.*); **'2t** *f* passage (through); gate(way); *~ verboten!* no thoroughfare!

'Durchfall *m* ♂ diarrh(o)ea; *F fig.* failure, *Am. a.* flunk; **2en** (irr. fallen) 1. ['~falən] *v/i.* (sep., -ge-, sein) fall through; fail, *F* get ploughed (*in examination*); *thea.* be a failure, *sl.* be a flop; **~** *lassen* reject, *F* plough; 2. [~'falən] *v/t.* (*no* -ge-, h) fall or drop through (*space*).

durch'fechten *v/t.* (irr. fechten, sep., -ge-, h) fight or see *s.th.* through; **~finden** *v/refl.* (irr. finden, sep., -ge-, h) find one's way (through).

durch|'flechten *v/t.* (irr. flechten, *no* -ge-, h) interweave, intertwine; **~'forschen** *v/t.* (*no* -ge-, h) search through, investigate; explore (*region, etc.*).

'Durchfuhr † *f* (-/-en) transit.

durchführ|bar *adj.* ['dʊrçfyːrbaːr] practicable, feasible, workable; **~en** *v/t.* (sep., -ge-, h) lead or take through or across; *fig.* carry out or through; realize; **'2ungsbestimmung** *f* (implementing) regulation.

'Durchgang *m* passage; † transit; *sports:* run; **'~sverkehr** *m* through traffic; † transit traffic; **'~szoll** *m* transit duty.

'durchgebraten *adj.* well done.

'durchgehen (irr. gehen, sep., -ge-) 1. *v/i.* (sein) go or walk through; *bill:* pass, be carried; run away or off; abscond; *woman:* elope; *horse:* bolt; 2. *v/t.* (sein) go through (*street, etc.*); 3. *v/t.* (h, sein) go or look or read through (*work, book, etc.*); **'~d** 1. *adj.* continuous; *~er Zug* through train; 2. *adv.* generally; throughout.

durch'geistigt *adj.* spiritual.

'durch|greifen *v/i.* (irr. greifen,

sep., -ge-, *h*) put one's hand through, *fig.* take drastic measures or steps; **~greifend** *adj.* drastic; radical, sweeping; **~halten** (*irr. halten, sep.*, -ge-, *h*) 1. *v/t.* keep up (*pace, etc.*), 2. *v/i.* hold out; **~hauen** *v/t* (*irr. hauen, sep.*, -ge-, *h*) cut or chop through; *fig.* give *s.o.* a good hiding; **~helfen** *v/i.* (*irr. helfen, sep.*, -ge-, *h*) help through (*a. fig.*); **~kämpfen** *v/t.* (*sep.*, -ge-, *h*) fight through, *sich ~* fight one's way through; **~kneten** *v/t.* (*sep.*, -ge-, *h*) knead or work thoroughly; **~kommen** *v/i* (*irr. kommen, sep.*, -ge-, *sein*) come or get or pass through; *sick person:* pull through; *in examination* pass.

durch'kreuzen *v/t.* (*no* -ge-, *h*) cross, foil thwart (*plan, etc.*).

Durch|laß ['dʊrçlas] *m* (*Durch-lasses/Durchlässe*) passage; **²lassen** (*irr lassen, sep.*, -ge-, *h*) let pass, allow to pass, let through; *Wasser leak,* **²lässig** *adj.* pervious (to permeable (to); leaky.

durchlaufen '*irr laufen*) 1. ['~laufən] *v/i. sep.*, -ge-, *sein*) run or pass through 2. [.] *v/t.* (*sep.*, -ge-, *h*) wear out (*shoes, etc.*); 3. [.~'laufən] *v/t.* (*no* -ge, *h*) pass through (*stages, departments, etc.*); *sports:* cover (*distance*)

durch'leben *v/t.* (*no* -ge-, *h*) go or live through

durchlesen *v/t* (*irr. lesen, sep.*, -ge, *h* read through.

durchleuchten (*h*) 1. ['~lɔyçtən] *v/i.* (*sep.*, -ge-) shine through; 2.[. bɔyçtən] *v/t* (*no* -ge-) ⚕ X-ray; *fig.* investigate

durchlöchern [dʊrç'lœçərn] *v/t.* (*no* -ge-, *h*) perforate, make holes into *s.th*

'durchmachen *v/t.* (*sep.*, -ge-, *h*) go through (*difficult times, etc.*); undergo *suffering*).

'Durchmarsch *m* march(ing) through

'Durchmesser *m* (-s/-) diameter.

durch nässen *v/t.* (*no* -ge-, *h*) wet through, soak, drench.

'durch|nehmen *v/t.* (*irr. nehmen, sep.*, -ge, *h*) go through or over (*subject etc.*); **~pausen** *v/t.* (*sep.*, -ge-, *h*) trace, calk (*design, etc.*).

durchqueren [dʊrç'kveːrən] *v/t.* (*no* -ge, *h* cross, traverse.

'durch|rechnen *v/t.* (*sep.*, -ge-, *h*) (re)calculate, check; **²reise** *f* journey or way through; **~reisen** 1. ['~raızən] *v/s.* (*sep.*, -ge-, *sein*) travel or pass through; 2. [.~'raızən] *v/t.* (*no* -ge, *h*) travel over or through or across **~reisende** *m, f* (-n/-n) person travel(l)ing through, *Am. a.* transient, ~ through passenger; '~reißen (*irr. reißen, sep.*, -ge-) 1. *v/i.* (*sein*) tear, break; 2. *v/t.* (*h*) tear

asunder, tear in two; **~schauen** (*h*) 1. ['~ʃauən] *v/i. and v/t.* (*sep.*, -ge-) look through; 2. *fig.* [.~'ʃauən] *v/t.* (*no* -ge-) see through.

'durchscheinen *v/i* (*irr. scheinen, sep.*, -ge-, *h*) shine through; **~d** *adj.* translucent, transparent.

'durchscheuern *v/t* (*sep.*, -ge-, *h*) rub through, **~schießen** (*irr. schießen*) 1. ['~ʃiːsən] *v/s* (*sep.*, -ge-, *h*) shoot through, 2. ['.~] *v/i.* (*sep.*, -ge-, *sein*) *water* shoot or race through; 3. [. 'ʃiːsən] *v/t.* (*no* -ge-, *h*) shoot *s.th.* through, *typ.* space out (*lines*); interleave (*book*).

'Durchschlag *m* colander, strainer; carbon copy, **²en** (*irr schlagen*) 1. ['~ʃlaːgən] *v/t* (*sep.*, -ge-, *h*) break or pass through; strain (*peas, etc.*); *sich ~* get along, make one's way; 2. ['.~] *v/i.* (*sep.*, -ge-, *h*) *typ.* come through, take or have effect; 3. [.~'ʃlaːgən] *v/t* (*no* -ge-, *h*) pierce; *bullet* penetrate; **²end** *adj.* effective, telling, **~papier** ['.~k-] *n* copying pape

durchschneiden *v/t.* (*irr. schneiden, h*) 1. ['.~ʃnaɪdən] (*sep.*, -ge-) cut through; 2. [. 'ʃnaɪdən] (*no* -ge-) cut through, cut in two.

'Durchschnitt *m* cutting through; ⊕ section, profile; ⓐ intersection; *fig.* average, *im* ~ on an average; **²lich** 1. *adj* average, normal; 2. *adv.* on an average, normally; **~swert** *m* averag value

'durch|sehen (*irr sehen, sep.*, -ge-, *h*) 1. *v/i.* see or look through; 2. *v/t.* see or look through *s.th.*; look *s.th.* over, go over *s.th.*; **~sehen** *v/i.* (*sep.*, -ge-, *h*) filter, strain; **~setzen** *v/t.* (*h*) 1. ['~zetsən] (*sep.*, -ge-) put (*plan, etc.*) through, force through; *seinen Kopf ~* have one's way; *sich ~* opinion, *etc* gain acceptance; 2. [.~'zetsən] (*no* -ge-) intersperse.

'Durchsicht *f* looking through or over; examination; correction; *typ.* reading, **²ig** *adj* glass, water, *etc.*: transparent; *fig.* clear, lucid; **~igkeit** *f* (-/*no pl.*) transparency; *fig.* clarity, lucidity

'durch|sickern *v/i.* (*sep.*, -ge-, *sein*) seep or ooze through; *news, etc.*: leak out; **~sieben** *v/t.* (*h*) 1. ['~ziːbən] (*sep.*, -ge-) sieve, sift; bolt (*flour*); 2. [.~'ziːbən] (*no* -ge-) riddle (*with bullets*), **~sprechen** *v/t.* (*irr. sprechen, sep.*, -ge-, *h*) discuss, talk over; **~stechen** *v/t.* (*irr. stechen, h*) 1. ['~ʃteçən] (*sep.*, -ge-) stick (*needle, etc.*) through *s.th.*; stick through *s.th.*, 2. [.~'ʃteçən] (*no* -ge-) pierce; cut through (*dike, etc.*); **~stecken** *v/t.* (*sep.*, -ge-, *h*) pass or stick through

'Durchstich *m* cut(ting).

durch'stöbern *v/t.* (*no* -ge-, *h*) ransack (*room, pockets, etc.*); rum-

6*

mage through (*drawers, papers*, etc.).

'**durchstreichen** v/t. (irr. streichen, sep., -ge-, h) strike or cross out, cancel.

durch'streifen v/t. (no -ge-, h) roam or wander through or over or across.

durch'such|en v/t. (no -ge-, h) search (a, ৯); **2ung** f (-/-en) search.

durchtrieben adj. [durç'tri:bən] cunning, artful; **2heit** f (-/no pl.) cunning, artfulness.

durch'wachen v/t. (no -ge-, h) pass (*the night*) waking.

durch'wachsen adj. bacon: streaky.

durchwandern 1. ['͜vandərn] v/i. (sep., -ge-, sein) walk or pass through; 2. [͜'vandərn] v/t. (no -ge-, h) walk or pass through (*place, area*, etc.).

durch'weben v/t. (no -ge-, h) interweave; fig. a. intersperse.

durchweg adv. ['durçvɛk] throughout, without exception.

durch|weichen 1. ['͜vaiçən] v/i. (sep., -ge-, sein) soak; 2. [͜'vaiçən] v/t. (no -ge-, h) soak, drench; '͜winden v/refl. (irr. winden, sep., -ge-, h) worm or thread one's way through; '͜wühlen (h) 1. fig. ['͜vy:lən] v/refl. (sep., -ge-) work one's way through; 2. [͜'vy:lən] v/t. (no -ge-) rummage; '͜zählen v/t. (sep., -ge-, h) count; '͜ziehen (irr. ziehen) 1. ['͜tsi:ən] v/i. (sep., -ge-, sein) pass or go or come or march through; 2. [͜'] v/t. (sep., -ge-, h) pull (*thread*, etc.) through; 3. [͜'tsi:ən] v/t. (no -ge-, h) go or travel through; scent, etc.: fill, pervade (*room*, etc.).

durch'zucken v/t. (no -ge-, h) flash through.

'**Durchzug** m passage through; draught, Am. draft.

'**durchzwängen** v/refl. (sep., -ge-, h) squeeze o.s. through.

dürfen ['dyrfən] (irr., h) 1. v/i. (ge-): ich darf (nicht) I am (not) allowed to; 2. v/aux. (no -ge-): ich darf inf. I am permitted or allowed to inf.; I may inf.; du darfst nicht inf. you must not inf.; iro.: wenn ich bitten darf if you please.

durfte ['durftə] pret. of dürfen.

dürftig adj. ['dyrftiç] poor; scanty.

dürr adj. [dyr] wood, leaves, etc.: dry; land: barren, arid; p. gaunt, lean, skinny; '**2e** f (-/-n) dryness; barrenness; leanness.

Durst [durst] m (-es/no pl.) thirst (nach for); ͜ haben be thirsty.

dürsten ['dyrstən] v/i. (ge-, h): ͜ nach thirst for.

'**durstig** adj. thirsty (nach for).

Dusche ['duʃə] f (-/-n) shower (-bath); '**2n** v/refl. and v/i. (ge-, h) have a shower(-bath).

Düse ['dy:zə] f (-/-n) ⊕ nozzle; ✈ jet; ͜**nantrieb** ['͜n⁹-] m jet propulsion; mit ͜ jet-propelled; '͜**nflugzeug** n jet(-propelled) aircraft, F jet; '͜**njäger** ✈ m jet fighter.

düster adj. ['dy:stər] dark, gloomy (both a. fig.); light: dim; fig.: sad; depressing; '**2heit** f (-/no pl.), '**2keit** f (-/no pl.) gloom(iness).

Dutzend ['dutsənt] n (-s/-e) dozen; ein ͜ Eier a dozen eggs; ͜e von Leuten dozens of people; '**2weise** adv. by the dozen, in dozens.

Dynam|ik [dy'na:mik] f (-/no pl.) dynamics; **2isch** adj. dynamic(al).

Dynamit [dyna'mi:t] n (-s/no pl.) dynamite.

Dynamo [dy'na:mo] m (-s/-s), ͜**ma-schine** f dynamo, generator.

D-Zug ['de:tsu:k] m express train.

E

Ebbe ['ɛbə] f (-/-n) ebb(-tide); low tide; '**2n** v/i. (ge-, sein) ebb.

eben ['e:bən] 1. adj. even; plain, level; Å plane; zu ͜er Erde on the ground floor, Am. on the first floor; 2. adv. exactly; just; ͜ erst just now; '**2bild** n image, likeness; ͜**bürtig** adj. ['͜byrtiç] of equal birth; j-m ͜ sein be a match for s.o., be s.o.'s equal; '͜**da** adv., '͜**daselbst** adv. at the very (same) place, just there; quoting books: ibidem (abbr. ib., ibid.); '͜**der**, '͜**die**, '͜**das** dem. pron. = '͜**derselbe**, '͜**dieselbe**, '͜**dasselbe** dem. pron. the very (same); '͜

des'wegen adv. for that very reason.

Ebene ['e:bənə] f (-/-n) plain; Å plane; fig. level.

'**eben|erdig** adj. and adv. at street level; on the ground floor, Am. on the first floor; '͜**falls** adv. likewise; '**2holz** n ebony; '͜**maß** n symmetry; harmony; regularity (of features); '͜**mäßig** adj. symmetrical; harmonious; regular; '͜**so** adv. just so; just as ...; likewise; '͜**sosehr** adv., '͜**soviel** adv. just as much; '͜**sowenig** adv. just as little or few (pl.), no more.

Eber zo. ['e:bər] m (-s/-) boar; '~esche ♀ f mountain-ash.

ebnen ['e:bnən] v/t. (ge-, h) level; fig. smooth.

Echo ['ɛço] n (-s/-s) echo.

echt adj [ɛçt] genuine; true; pure; real; colour fast; document: authentic; '2heit f (-/no pl.) genuineness; purity, reality; fastness; authenticity.

Eck [ɛk] n (-[e]s/-e) s. Ecke; '~ball m sports corner-kick; '~e f (-/-n) corner; edge; '2ig adj. angular; fig. awkward, '~platz m corner-seat; '~stein m corner-stone; '~zahn m canine tooth

edel adj ['e:dəl] noble; min. precious; organs of the body: vital; '~denkend adj noble-minded; '2mann m nobleman; '2mut m generosity, '~mütig adj. ['~my:tiç] noble-minded, generous; '2stein m precious stone, gem.

Edikt [e dikt] ʰ (-[e]s/-e) edict.

Efeu ♀ [e fɔy] m (-s/no pl.) ivy.

Effekt [ɛ'fɛkt] m (-[e]s/-e) effect; ~en pl effects pl.; ✝: securities pl.; stocks pl , '~enhandel m dealing in stocks, '~hascherei [~haʃə'raɪ] f (-/-en) claptrap; 2iv adj. [~'ti:v] effective, 2uieren [~u'i:rən] v/t. (no -ge-, h) effect; execute, Am. a. fill; 2voll adj effective, striking.

egal adj [e'gɑ:l] equal; F all the same.

Egge ['ɛgə] f (-/-n) harrow; '2n v/t. (ge-, h) harrow.

Egois|mus [ego'ismus] m (-/Egoismen) ego(t)ism; ~t m (-en/-en) ego-(t)ist; ✝ tisch adj. selfish, ego(t)istic(al)

ehe¹ cj. ['e:ə] before.

Ehe² [~] f(-/-n) marriage; matrimony; '~anbahnung f (-/-en) matrimonial agency, '~brecher m (-s/-) adulterer; '~brecherin f (-/-nen) adulteress; '2brecherisch adj. adulterous, '~bruch m adultery; '~frau f wife; '~gatte m, '~gattin f spouse, '~leute pl. married people pl.; '2lich adj. conjugal; child: legitimate; '~losigkeit f (-/no pl.) celibacy, single life.

ehemal|ig adj. ['e:əma:liç] former, ex-.. , old; '~s adv. formerly.

'Ehe|mann m husband; '~paar n married couple.

'eher adv sooner; rather; more likely; je ~ desto besser the sooner the better

'Ehering m wedding ring.

ehern adj ['e:ərn] brazen, of brass.

'Ehe|scheidung f divorce; '~schließung f -/-en) (contraction of) marriage; '~stand m (-[e]s/no pl.) married state, matrimony; '~stifter m, '~stifterin f (-/-nen) matchmaker; '~vermittlung f s. Eheanbahnung; '~versprechen n promise of mar-

riage; '~vertrag m marriage contract.

Ehrabschneider ['e:rʷapʃnaɪdər] m (-s/-) slanderer.

'ehrbar adj. hono(u)rable, respectable; modest; '2keit f (-/no pl.) respectability, modesty

Ehre ['e:rə] f (-/-n) hono(u)r; zu ~n (gen.) in hono(u)r of; '2n v/t. (ge-, h) hono(u)r; esteem

'ehren|amtlich adj honorary; '2bürger m honorary citizen; '2doktor m honorar doctor; '2erklärung f (full) apology; '2gast m guest of hono(u)r; '2gericht n court of hono(u)r; '~haft adj. hono(u)rable; '2kodex m code of hono(u)r; '2legion f [legioːn] f (-/no pl.) Legion of Hono(u)r; '2mann m man of hono(u)r, '2mitglied n honorary member, '~platz m place of hono(u)r, '2recht n bürgerliche ~e pl. civil rights pl , '2rettung f rehabilitation, '~rührig adj. defamatory; '2sache f affair of hono(u)r; point of hono(u)r, '~voll adj. hono(u)rable; '~wert adj. hono(u)rable; '2wort n (-[e]s/-e) word of hono(u)r.

ehr|erbietig adj. ['e:rʷerbi:tiç] respectful; '2erbietung f (-/-en) reverence; '2furcht f(-/⚤-en) respect; awe; '~furchtgebietend adj. awe-inspiring, awesome, '~fürchtig adj. ['~fyrçtiç] respectful; '2gefühl n (-[e]s/no pl.) sense of hono(u)r; '2geiz m ambition; '~geizig adj. ambitious.

'ehrlich adj. honest; commerce, game: fair; opinion: candid; ~ währt am längsten honesty is the best policy; '2keit f (-/no pl.) honesty; fairness.

'ehrlos adj. dishono(u)rable, infamous; '2igkeit f (-/-en) dishono(u)rable, infamy.

'ehr|sam adj. s. ehrbar; '2ung f (-/-en) hono(u)r (conferred on s.o.); '~vergessen adj dishono(u)rable, infamous; '2verlust ⚤ m (-es/no pl.) loss of civil rights; '~würdig adj. venerable, reverend.

ei¹ int. [aɪ] ah!, indeed!

Ei² [~] n (-[e]s/-er) egg; physiol. ovum.

Eibe ♀ ['aɪbə] f (-/-n) yew(-tree).

Eiche ♀ ['aɪçə] f (-/-n) oak(-tree); ~l ['~l] f (-/-n) ♀ acorn; cards: club; '~lhäher orn. ['~he:ər] m (-s/-) jay.

eichen¹ ['aɪçən] v/t. (ge-, h) ga(u)ge.

eichen² adj. [~] oaken, of oak.

Eich|hörnchen zo. ['aɪçhœrnçən] n (-s/-) squirrel; '~maß n standard.

Eid [aɪt] m (-[e]s/-e) oath; '2brüchig adj.: ~ werden break one's oath.

Eidechse zo. ['aɪdɛksə] f(-/-n) lizard.

eidesstattlich ⚤ adj. ['aɪdəs-] in lieu of (an) oath; ~e Erklärung statutory declaration.

'eidlich 1. adj. sworn; 2. adv. on oath.

'Eidotter m, n yolk.

'Eier|kuchen m omelet(te), pancake; '⁓schale f egg-shell; '⁓stock anat. m ovary; '⁓uhr f egg-timer.

Eifer ['aɪfər] m (-s/no pl.) zeal; eagerness; ardo(u)r; '⁓er m (-s/-) zealot; '⁓sucht f (-/no pl.) jealousy; '2süchtig adj. jealous (auf acc. of).

eifrig adj. ['aɪfrɪç] zealous, eager; ardent.

eigen adj. ['aɪgən] own; particular; strange, odd; in compounds: ...⁓ owned; peculiar (dat. to); '2art f peculiarity, '⁓artig adj. peculiar; singular; 2brötler ['⁓brøːtlər] m (-s/-) odd or eccentric person, crank; '2gewicht n dead weight; ⁓händig adj. and adv. ['⁓hendɪç] with one's own hands; '2heim n house of one's own; homestead; '2heit f (-/-en) peculiarity; oddity; of language: idiom; '2liebe f self-love; '2lob n self-praise; '⁓mächtig adj. arbitrary; 2name m proper name; ⁓nützig adj. ['⁓nytsɪç] self-interested, selfish; '⁓s adv. expressly, specially; on purpose.

'Eigenschaft f (-/-en) quality (of s.o.); property (of s.th.); in s-r ⁓ als in his capacity as; '⁓swort gr. n (-[e]s/⁓er) adjective.

'Eigensinn m (-[e]s/no pl.) obstinacy; '2ig adj. wil(l)ful, obstinate.

'eigentlich 1. adj. proper; actual; true, real; 2. adv. properly (speaking).

'Eigentum n (-s/⁓er) property.

Eigentüm|er ['aɪgəntyːmər] m (-s/-) owner, proprietor; '2lich adj. peculiar; odd; '⁓lichkeit f (-/-en) peculiarity.

'Eigentums|recht n ownership; copyright; '⁓wohnung f freehold flat.

'eigenwillig adj. self-willed; fig. individual.

eign|en ['aɪgnən] v/refl. (ge-, h): sich ⁓ für be suited for; '2ung f (-/-en) aptitude, suitability.

'Eil|bote ⅋ m express messenger; durch ⁓n by special delivery; '⁓brief ⅋ m express letter, Am. special delivery letter.

Eile ['aɪlə] f (-/no pl.) haste, speed; hurry; '2n v/i. (ge-, sein) hasten, make haste; hurry; letter, affair: be urgent; 2nds adv. ['⁓ts] quickly, speedily.

'Eil|fracht f, '⁓gut n express goods pl., Am. fast freight; '2ig adj. hasty, speedy; urgent; es ⁓ haben be in a hurry.

Eimer ['aɪmər] m (-s/-) bucket, pail.

ein [aɪn] 1. adj. one; 2. indef. art. a, an.

einander adv. [aɪ'nandər] one another; each other.

ein|arbeiten ['aɪn⁹-] v/t. (sep., -ge-, h): j-n ⁓ in (acc.) make s.o. acquainted with; '⁓armig adj. ['aɪn⁹-] one-armed; '⁓äschern ['aɪn⁹eʃərn] v/t. (sep., -ge-, h) burn to ashes; cremate (dead body); '2äscherung f (-/-en) cremation; ⁓atmen ['aɪn⁹-] v/t. (sep., -ge-, h) breathe, inhale; ⁓äugig adj. ['aɪn⁹ɔygɪç] one-eyed.

'Einbahnstraße f one-way street.

'einbalsamieren v/t. (sep., no -ge-, h) embalm.

'Einband m (-[e]s/⁓e) binding; cover.

'ein|bauen v/t. (sep., -ge-, h) build in; install (engine, etc.); '⁓behalten v/t. (irr. halten, sep., no -ge-, h) detain; '⁓berufen v/t. (irr. rufen, sep., no -ge-, h) convene; ✕ call up, Am. induct.

'einbett|en v/t. (sep., -ge-, h) embed; '2zimmer n single(-bedded) room.

'einbild|en v/refl. (sep., -ge-, h) fancy, imagine; '2ung f imagination, fancy; conceit.

'einbinden v/t. (irr. binden, sep., -ge-, h) bind (books).

'Einblick m insight (in acc. into).

'einbrechen (irr. brechen, sep., -ge-) 1. v/t. (h) break open; 2. v/i. (sein) break in; of night, etc.: set in; ⁓ in (acc.) break into (house).

'Einbrecher m at night: burglar; by day: housebreaker.

'Einbruch m ✕ invasion; housebreaking, burglary; bei ⁓ der Nacht at nightfall; '⁓(s)diebstahl m house-breaking, burglary.

einbürger|n ['aɪnbyrgərn] v/t. (sep., -ge-, h) naturalize; '2ung f (-/-en) naturalization.

'Ein|buße f loss; '2büßen v/t. (sep., -ge-, h) lose, forfeit.

ein|dämmen ['aɪndɛmən] v/t. (sep., -ge-, h) dam (up); embank (river); fig. check; '⁓deutig adj. unequivocal; clear, plain.

'eindring|en v/i. (irr. dringen, sep., -ge-, sein) enter; penetrate; intrude; ⁓ in (acc.) penetrate (into); force one's way into; invade (country); '⁓lich adj. urgent; 2ling ['⁓lɪŋ] m (-s/-e) intruder; invader.

'Eindruck m (-[e]s/⁓e) impression.

'ein|drücken v/t. (sep., -ge-, h) press in; crush (in) (hat); break (pane); '⁓drucksvoll adj. impressive; ⁓engen ['aɪn⁹-] v/t. (sep., -ge-, h) narrow; fig. limit.

ein|er¹ ['aɪnər], '⁓e, '⁓(e)s indef. pron. one.

Einer² [⁓] m (-s/-) A⁄ unit, digit; rowing: single sculler, skiff.

einerlei ['aɪnər'laɪ] 1. adj. of the same kind; immaterial; es ist mir ⁓ it is all the same to me; 2. 2 n (-s/no pl.) sameness; monotony; humdrum (of one's existence).

einerseits adv. ['aɪnər'zaɪts] on the one hand.

einfach adj. ['aɪnfax] simple; single; plain; meal frugal; ticket: single, Am. one-way; **2heit** f (-/no pl.) simplicity

einfädeln ['aɪnfɛːdəln] v/t. (sep., -ge-, h) thread; fig. start, set on foot; contrive

'**Einfahrt** f entrance, entry.

'**Einfall** m ⚔ invasion; idea, inspiration, **2en** v/i (irr. fallen, sep., -ge-, sein) fall in, collapse; break in (on a conversation), interrupt, cut short; chime in; ♪ join in; invade; j~m ⚓ occur to s.o

Ein|falt ['aɪnfalt] f (-/no pl.) simplicity, silliness, **2fältig** adj. ['~fɛltiç] simple, silly; '~**faltspinsel** m simpleton, Am F sucker.

'**ein|farbig** adj one-colo(u)red, unicolo(u)red, plain; '~**fassen** v/t. (sep., -ge-, h) border; set (precious stone), '~**fassung** f border; setting; '~**fetten** v/t sep, -ge-, h) grease; oil; ~**finden** v/refl. (irr. finden, sep., -ge-, h) appear; arrive; '~**flechten** fig v/t. (irr. flechten, sep., -ge-, h) put in, insert; '~**fließen** v/i. (irr fließer, sep., -ge-, sein) flow in, in (acc.) flow into; ~ **lassen** mention in passing; '~**flößen** v/t. (sep, -ge-, h) infuse.

'**Einfluß** m influx, fig. influence; '**2reich** adj. influential.

ein|förmig adj ['aɪnfœrmiç] uniform, monotonous; '~**frieden** ['~friːdən] v/t (sep., -ge-, h) fence, enclose, **2friedung** f (-/-en) enclosure, '~**frieren** (irr. frieren, sep., -ge-, h) 1. v/i. (sein) freeze (in); 2. v/t. (h) freeze (food); '~**fügen** v/t. (sep., -ge-, h) put in; fig. insert; sich ~ fit in

Einfuhr ['aɪnfuːr] f (-/-en) import(ation), '~**bestimmungen** f/pl. import regulations pl.

'**einführen** v/t (sep., -ge-, h) ✝ import; introduce (s.o., custom); insert; initiate, install (s.o. in an office).

'**Einfuhrwaren** ✝ f/pl. imports pl.

'**Eingabe** f petition; application.

'**Eingang** m entrance; entry; arrival (of goods) nach on receipt; '~**buch** ✝ n book of entries.

'**eingeben** v/t (irr geben, sep., -ge-, h) give, administer (medicine) (dat. to); prompt, suggest (to).

'**einge|bilde** adj imaginary; conceited (auf acc of); '~**boren** adj. native, **2borene** m, f (-/n/-n) native. **Eingebung** ['aɪngeːbuŋ] f (-/-en) suggestion, inspiration.

einge|denk adj. ['aɪngədeŋk] mindful (gen of), '~**fallen** adj. eyes, cheeks: sunken, hollow; emaciated; ~**fleischt** fig. adj. ['~gəflaɪʃt] inveterate; confirmed; ~er Junggeselle confirmed bachelor.

'**eingehen** (irr. gehen, sep., -ge-) 1. v/i. (sein) mail, goods: come in, arrive; ⚓, animal die; cease (to exist); material shrink; ~ auf (acc.) agree to; enter into; 2. v/t. (h, sein) enter into (relationship); contract (marriage); ein Risiko ~ run a risk, esp. Am take a chance; e-n Vergleich ~ come to terms; Verbindlichkeiten ~ incur liabilities; e-e Wette ~ make a bet, eingegangene Gelder n/pl. receipts pl, ~d adj. detailed; thorough; examination. close.

Eingemachte ['aɪngəmaxtə] n (-n/ no pl.) preserves pl , pickles pl.

'**eingemeinden** v/t (sep., no -ge-, h) incorporate (dat into).

'**einge|nommen** adj. partial (für to); prejudiced (gegen against); von sich ~ conceited, **2sandt** ⚓ n (-s/-s) letter to the editor, ~**schnappt** F fig. adj. ['~gəʃnapt] offended, touchy; ~**sessen** adj long-established; **2ständnis** n confession, avowal; ~**stehen** v/t (irr. stehen, sep., no -ge , h) confess, avow.

Eingeweide anat ['aɪngəvaɪdə] pl. viscera pl , intestines pl.; bowels pl.; esp. of animals entrails pl.

'**einge|wöhnen** v/refl. (sep., no -ge-, h) accustom o.s (in acc. to); acclimatize o.s , Am. acclimate o.s.; get used (to)

eingewurzelt adj. ['~gəvurtsəlt] deep-rooted, inveterate.

'**eingießen** v/t (irr. gießen, sep., -ge-, h) pour in or out.

eingleisig adj. ['aɪnglaɪziç] single-track.

'**ein|graben** v/t. (irr. graben, sep., -ge-, h) dig in; bury; engrave; sich ~ ⚔ dig o.s in, entrench o.s.; fig. engrave itself (on one's memory); '~**gravieren** v/t. (sep., no -ge-, h) engrave

'**eingreifen** 1. v/i. (irr. greifen, sep., -ge-, h) intervene; ~ in (acc.) interfere with; encroach on (s.o.'s rights); in die Debatte ~ join in the debate; 2. **2** n (-s/no pl.) intervention.

'**Eingriff** m fig. encroachment; ⚕ operation

'**einhaken** v/t. (sep., -ge-, h) fasten; sich bei j-m take s.o.'s arm.

'**Einhalt** m (-[e]s/no pl.): ~ gebieten (dat.) put a stop to; **2en** fig. (irr. halten, sep., -ge-, h) 1. v/t. observe, keep; 2. v/i. stop, leave off (zu tun doing).

'**ein|hängen** ([irr. hängen] sep., -ge-, h) 1. v/t hang in, hang up, replace (receiver), sich bei j-m take s.o.'s arm, link arms with s.o.; 2. teleph. v/i. hang up; '~**heften** v/t. (sep., -ge-, h) sew or stitch in.

'**einheimisch** adj. native (in dat.

to), indigenous (to) (a. ⚜); ⚜ endemic; *product*: home-grown; '2e *m*, *f* (-n/-n) native; resident.

'Einheit *f* (-/-en) unity; oneness; ♣, *phys.*, ✕ unit; '2lich *adj.* uniform; '~spreis *m* standard price.

'einheizen (*sep.*, -ge-, h) 1. *v/i.* make a fire; 2. *v/t.* heat (*stove*).

einhellig *adj.* ['aɪnhɛlɪç] unanimous.

'einholen (*sep.*, -ge-, h) 1. *v/t.* catch up with, overtake; make up for (*lost time*); make (*inquiries*); take (*order*); seek (*advice*); ask for (*permission*); buy; 2. *v/i.*: ~ gehen go shopping.

'Einhorn *zo.* *n* unicorn.

'einhüllen *v/t.* (*sep.*, -ge-, h) wrap (up *or* in); envelop.

einig *adj.* ['aɪnɪç] united; ~ sein agree; *nicht* ~ sein differ (*über acc.* about); ~e *indef. pron.* ['aɪnɪgə] several; some; ~en ['aɪŋən] *v/t.* (*sep.*, h) unite; *sich* ~ come to terms; ~ermaßen *adv.* ['aɪnɐ'maːsən] in some measure; somewhat; ~es *indef. pron.* ['aɪnɪgəs] some(thing); '2keit *f* (-/no *pl.*) unity; concord; '2ung ['aɪn-] *f* (-/-en) union; agreement.

ein|impfen ['aɪn?-] *v/t.* (*sep.*, -ge-, h) ⚜ inoculate (*a. fig.*); '~jagen *v/t.* (*sep.*, -ge-, h): j-m Furcht ~ scare s.o.

einjährig *adj.* ['aɪnjɛːrɪç] one-year-old; *esp.* ♣ annual; *animal*: yearling.

'ein|kalkulieren *v/t.* (*sep.*, no -ge-, h) take into account, allow for; '~kassieren *v/t.* (*sep.*, no -ge-, h) cash; collect.

'Einkauf *m* purchase; *Einkäufe machen s.* einkaufen 2; '2en (*sep.*, -ge-, h) 1. *v/t.* buy, purchase; 2. *v/i.* make purchases, go shopping.

'Einkäufer *m* buyer.

'Einkaufs|netz *n* string bag; '~preis ✝ *m* purchase price; '~tasche *f* shopping-bag.

'ein|kehren *v/i.* (*sep.*, -ge-, sein) put up *or* stop (*at an inn*); '~kerben *v/t.* (*sep.*, -ge-, h) notch; '~kerkern *v/t.* (*sep.*, -ge-, h) imprison; '~klagen *v/t.* (*sep.*, -ge-, h) sue for; '~klammern *v/t.* (*sep.*, -ge-, h) *typ.* bracket; put in brackets.

'Einklang *m* unison; harmony.

'ein|kleiden *v/t.* (*sep.*, -ge-, h) clothe; fit out; '~klemmen *v/t.* (*sep.*, -ge-, h) squeeze (in); jam; '~klinken (*sep.*, -ge-) 1. *v/t.* (h) latch; 2. *v/i.* (sein) latch; engage; '~knicken (*sep.*, -ge-) *v/t.* (h) *and* *v/i.* (sein) bend in, break; '~kochen (*sep.*, -ge-) 1. *v/t.* (h) preserve; 2. *v/i.* (sein) boil down *or* away.

'Einkommen *n* (-s/-) income, revenue; '~steuer *f* income-tax.

'einkreisen *v/t.* (*sep.*, -ge-, h) encircle.

'Einkünfte ['aɪnkʏnftə] *pl.* income, revenue.

'einlad|en *v/t.* (*irr. laden*, *sep.*, -ge-, h) load (in) (*goods*); *fig.* invite; '2ung *f* invitation.

'Einlage *f* enclosure (*in letter*); ✝ investment; deposit (*of money*); *gambling*: stake; inserted piece; ⚜ arch-support; temporary filling (*of tooth*); '2rn ✝ *v/t.* (*sep.*, -ge-, h) store (up).

Einlaß ['aɪnlas] *m* (*Einlasses/Einlässe*) admission, admittance.

'einlassen *v/t.* (*irr. lassen*, *sep.*, -ge-, h) let in, admit; ~ in (*acc.*) ⊕ imbed in; *sich* ~ in *or* auf (*both acc.*) engage in, enter into.

'ein|laufen *v/i.* (*irr. laufen*, *sep.*, -ge-, sein) come in, arrive; *ship*: enter; *material*: shrink; '~leben *v/refl.* (*sep.*, -ge-, h) accustom o.s. (in *acc.* to).

'einlege|n *v/t.* (*sep.*, -ge-, h) lay *or* put in; insert; ⊕ inlay; deposit (*money*); pickle; preserve (*fruit*); *Berufung* ~ lodge an appeal (*bei* to); *Ehre* ~ mit gain hono(u)r *or* credit by; '2sohle *f* insole, sock.

'einleit|en *v/t.* (*sep.*, -ge-, h) start; introduce; '~end *adj.* introductory; '2ung *f* introduction.

'ein|lenken *fig.* *v/i.* (*sep.*, -ge-, h) come round; '~leuchten *v/i.* (*sep.*, -ge-, h) be evident *or* obvious; '~liefern *v/t.* (*sep.*, -ge-, h) deliver (up); in ein Krankenhaus ~ take to a hospital, *Am.* hospitalize; '~lösen *v/t.* (*sep.*, -ge-, h) ransom (*prisoner*); redeem (*pledge*); ✝ hono(u)r (*bill*); cash (*cheque*); ✝ meet (*bill*); '~machen *v/t.* (*sep.*, -ge-, h) preserve (*fruit*); tin, *Am.* can.

'einmal *adv.* once; one day; *auf* ~ all at once; *es war* ~ once (upon a time) there was; *nicht* ~ not even; '2eins *n* (-/-) multiplication table; '~ig *adj.* single; unique.

'Einmarsch *m* marching in, entry; '2ieren *v/i.* (*sep.*, no -ge-, sein) march in, enter.

'ein|mengen *v/refl.* (*sep.*, -ge-, h), '~mischen *v/refl.* (*sep.*, -ge-, h) meddle, interfere (in *acc.* with), *esp. Am. sl.* butt in.

'Einmündung *f* junction (*of roads*); mouth (*of river*).

einmütig *adj.* ['aɪnmyːtɪç] unanimous; '2keit *f* (-/no *pl.*) unanimity.

Einnahme ['aɪnnaːmə] *f* (-/-n) ✕ taking, capture; *mst* ~n *pl.* takings *pl.*; receipts *pl.*

'einnehmen *v/t.* (*irr. nehmen*, *sep.*, -ge-, h) take (*meal, position, ✕*); ✝ take (*money*); ✕ earn, make (*money*); take up, occupy (*room*); *fig.* captivate; '~d *adj.* taking, engaging, captivating.

'einnicken *v/i.* (*sep.*, -ge-, sein) doze *or* drop off.

Einöde ['aɪnˀ-] f desert, solitude.
ein|ordnen ['aɪnˀ-] v/t. (sep., -ge-, h) arrange in proper order; classify; file (letters, etc.); ~packen v/t. (sep., -ge-, h) pack up; wrap up; '~pferchen v/t (sep., ge-, h) pen in; fig. crowd, ~ram, ~pflanzen v/t. (sep., -ge-, h) plant, fig implant; '~pökeln v/t sep., -ge-, h) pickle, salt; ~prägen v/t (sep., -ge-, h) imprint; impress; sich ~ imprint itself; commit t.h. to one's memory; ~quartieren v/t. (sep., no -ge-, h) quarter, billet; ~rahmen v/t. (sep., -ge-, h) frame; ~räumen fig. v/t. (sep., -ge-, h) grant, concede; ~rechnen v/t sep., -ge-, h) comprise, include; ~reden (sep., -ge-, h) 1. v/t j-m persuade or talk s.o. into (doing) s.th.; 2. v/i.: auf j-n ~ talk insistently to s.o.; '~reichen v/t. sep., -ge-, h) hand in, send in, present, ~reihen v/t. (sep., -ge-, h) insert (unter acc. in); class (with); place (among); sich ~ take one's place.

einreihig adj. ['aɪnraɪç] jacket: single-breasted.
'Einreise f entry; '~erlaubnis f, ~genehmigung f entry permit.
'ein|reißen irr reißen, sep., -ge-) 1. v/t. (h) tear, pull down (building); 2. v/i. (sein) tear, abuse, etc.: spread; ~renken [˙rɛŋkən] v/t. (sep., -ge-, h) ✗ set, fig. set right.
'einricht|en v/t (sep. -ge-, h) establish; equip, arrange; set up (shop); furnish (flat); es ~ manage; sich ~ establish o.s., settle down; economize, sich ~ auf acc.) prepare for; '~ung f establishment; arrangement, esp. Am. setup; equipment; furniture; fittings pl. (of shop); institution.
'ein|rollen v/t. (sep., -ge-, h) roll up or in; sich ~ roll up; curl up; '~rosten v/i. (sep., -ge-, sein) rust; screw, etc. rust in; ~rücken (sep., -ge-) 1. v/i. (sein) enter, march in; ✗ join the army, 2. v/t. (h) insert (advertisement in a paper); typ. indent (line, word, etc.); '~rühren v/t. (sep., -ge-, h) stir (in).
eins adj. [aɪns] one.
'einsam adj. lonely, solitary; '2keit f (/-% -en) loneliness, solitude.
'einsammeln v/t. (sep., -ge-, h) gather; collect.
'Einsatz m inset; insertion (of piece of material); gambling stake, pool; ♪ striking in, entry; employment; engagement (a. ✗); ✗ action, operation; unter ~ s-s Lebens at the risk of one's life.
'ein|saugen v/t. (sep., -ge-, h) suck in; fig. imbibe; ~schalten v/t. (sep., -ge-, h) insert; ⚡ switch or turn on; den ersten Gang ~ mot. go into first or bottom gear; sich ~

intervene; '~schärfen v/t. (sep., -ge-, h) inculcate (dat. upon); '~schätzen v/t. (sep., -ge-, h) assess, appraise, estimate auf acc. at); value (a. fig.); ~schenken v/t. (sep., -ge-, h) pour in or out; ~schicken v/t. (sep., -ge-, h) send in; '~schieben v/t irr schieben, sep., -ge-, h) insert; schiffen v/t. and v/refl. (sep., -ge-, h) ~mbark; '2schiffung f (-/-en) ~mbarkation; '~schlafen v/t. (irr schlafen, sep., -ge-, sein) fall asleep, schläfern ['~ʃlɛ:fərn] v/t. (sep., -ge-, h) lull to sleep; ✗ narcotize.
'Einschlag m striking (of lightning); impact (of missile), fig touch; '2en (irr. schlagen, sep., -ge-, h) ✗ 1. v/t. drive in (nail); break in), smash (in); wrap up; take (road), tuck in (hem, etc.); enter upon career); 2. v/i. shake hands, lightning, missile: strike; fig. be a success, ~cht fail; (wie e-e Bombe) cause a sensation; auf j-n ~ belabour s.o.
einschlägig adj. ['aɪnʃlɛ:gɪç] relevant, pertinent.
'Einschlagpapier n wrapping-paper.
'ein|schleichen v/refl. (irr. schleichen, sep., -ge-, h) creep or sneak in; '~schleppen v/t. (sep., -ge-, h) ⚓ tow in; import (disease), ~schleusen fig. v/t. (sep., -ge-, h) channel or let in; ~schließen v/t. (irr. schließen, sep., -ge-, h) lock in or up; enclose; ✗ surround, ~circle; fig. include; '~schließlich ~rp gen.) inclusive of; including, ~mprising, '~schmeicheln v/refl ~ep , -ge-, h) ingratiate o.s. (bei with , ~schmeichelnd adj. insinuating; '~schmuggeln v/t. sep., -ge-, h) smuggle in; '~schnappen v/i. (sep., -ge-, sein) catch, fig. s. eingeschnappt; '~schneidend fig. adj. incisive, drastic.
'Einschnitt m cut, incision; notch.
'ein|schnüren v/t. (sep., -ge-, h) lace (up); ~schränken [ʃrɛŋkən] v/t. (sep., -ge-, h) restrict, confine; reduce (expenses); sich ~ ~conomize; '2schränkung f (-/-en) restriction; reduction.
'Einschreibe|brief m registered letter; '2n v/t. (irr. schreiben, sep., -ge-, h) enter; book; ~nrol(l); ✗ enlist, enrol(l); ⛪ register; ~ lassen have registered; sich ~ enter one's name.
'einschreiten 1. fig. v/i. (irr. schreiten, sep., -ge-, sein) step in, interpose, intervene; take action (gegen against); 2. 2 n (-s/no pl.) intervention.
'ein|schrumpfen v/i. (sep., -ge-, sein) shrink; '~schüchtern v/t. (sep., -ge-, h) intimidate; bully; '2schüchterung f (-/-en) intim-

idation; '~schulen v/t. (sep., -ge-, h) put to school.

'Einschuß m bullet-hole; ✝ invested capital.

'ein|segnen v/t. (sep., -ge-, h) consecrate; confirm (children); '2segnung f consecration; confirmation.

'einsehen 1. v/t. (irr. sehen, sep., -ge-, h) look into; fig.: see, comprehend; realize; 2. 2 n (-s/no pl.): ein ~ haben show consideration.

'einseifen v/t. (sep., -ge-, h) soap; lather (beard); F fig. humbug (s.o.).

einseitig adj. ['amzartiç] one-sided; ⚔, pol., ⚙ unilateral.

'einsend|en v/t. ([irr. senden], sep., -ge-, h) send in; '2er m (-s/-) sender; contributor (to a paper).

'einsetz|en (sep., -ge-, h) 1. v/t. set or put in; stake (money); insert; institute; instal(l); appoint (s.o.); fig. use, employ; risk (one's life); sich ~ für stand up for; 2. v/i. fever, flood, weather: set in; ♪ strike in; '2ung f (-/-en) insertion; appointment, installation.

'Einsicht f (-/-en) inspection; fig. insight, understanding; judiciousness; '2ig adj. judicious, sensible.

'einsickern v/i. (sep., -ge-, sein) soak in; infiltrate.

'Einsiedler m hermit.

einsilbig adj. ['amzilbiç] monosyllabic, fig taciturn; '2keit f (-/no pl.) taciturnity.

'einsinken v/i. (irr. sinken, sep., -ge-, sein) sink (in).

Einspänn|er m ['amʃpɛnɔr] m (-s/-) one-horse carriage; '2ig adj. one-horse.

'ein|sparen v/t. (sep., -ge-, h) save, economize; '~sperren v/t. (sep., -ge-, h) imprison; lock up, confine; '~springen v/i. (irr. springen, sep., -ge-, sein) ⊕ catch; fig. step in, help out; für j-n ~ substitute for s.o.; '~spritzen v/t. (sep., -ge-, h) inject; '2spritzung f (-/-en) injection.

'Einspruch m objection, protest, veto; appeal; '~srecht n veto.

'einspurig adj. single-track.

einst adv. [amst] once; one or some day.

'Einstand m entry; tennis: deuce.

'ein|stecken v/t. (sep., -ge-, h) put in; pocket; plug in; '~steigen ⚙/i. (irr. steigen, sep., -ge-, sein) get in; ~l 🚃 take your seats!, Am. all aboard!

'einstell|en v/t. (sep., -ge-, h) put in; ⚔ enrol(l), enlist, Am. muster in; engage, employ, Am. a. hire; give up; stop, cease, Am. a. quit (payment, etc.); adjust (mechanism) (auf acc. to); tune in (radio) (to); opt., focus (on) (a. fig.); die Arbeit ~ cease working; strike, Am. a. walk out; sich ~ appear; sich ~ auf (acc.) be

prepared for; adapt o.s. to; '2ung f ⚔ enlistment; engagement; adjustment; focus; (mental) attitude, mentality.

'einstimm|en ♪ v/i. (sep., -ge-, h) join in; '~ig adj. unanimous; '2igkeit f (-/no pl.) unanimity.

einstöckig adj. ['amʃtœkiç] onestoried.

'ein|streuen fig. v/t. (sep., -ge-, h) intersperse; ~studieren v/t. (sep., no -ge-, h) study; thea. rehearse; '~stürmen v/i. (sep., -ge-, sein): auf j-n ~ rush at s.o.; '2sturz m falling in, collapse; '~stürzen v/i. (sep., -ge-, sein) fall in, collapse.

einst'weilen adv. ['amst'vailən] for the present; in the meantime; '~weilig adj. temporary.

'ein|tauschen v/t. (sep., -ge-, h) exchange (gegen for); '~teilen v/t. (sep., -ge-, h) divide (in acc. into); classify; ~teilig adj. one-piece; '2teilung f division; classification.

eintönig adj. ['amtø:niç] monotonous; '2keit f (-/~ -en) monotony.

'Eintopf(gericht n) m hot-pot; stew.

'Eintracht f (-/no pl.) harmony, concord.

einträchtig adj. ['amtrɛçtiç] harmonious.

'eintragen v/t. (irr. tragen, sep., -ge-, h) enter; register; bring in, yield (profit); sich ~ in (acc.) sign.

einträglich adj. ['amtrɛ:kliç] profitable.

'Eintragung f (-/-en) entry; registration.

'ein|treffen v/i. (irr. treffen, sep., -ge-, sein) arrive; happen; come true; '~treiben v/t. (irr. treiben, sep., -ge-, h) drive in or home; collect (debts, taxes); '~treten (irr. treten, sep., -ge-) 1. v/i. (sein) enter; occur, happen, take place; ~ für stand up for; ~ in (acc.) enter into (rights); enter upon (possession); enter (room); join (the army, etc.); 2. v/t. (h) kick in (door); sich et. ~ run s.th. into one's foot.

'Eintritt m entry, entrance; admittance; beginning, setting-in (of winter, etc.); ~ frei! admission free!; ~ verboten! no admittance!; '~sgeld n entrance or admission fee; sports: gate money; '~skarte f admission ticket.

'ein|trocknen v/i. (sep., -ge-, sein) dry (up); '~trüben v/refl. (sep., -ge-, h) become cloudy or overcast; ~üben ['am³-] v/t. (sep., -ge-, h) practi|se, Am. -ce s.th.; train s.o.

einver|leiben ['amferlaibən] v/t. ([sep.] no -ge-, h) incorporate (dat. in); annex (to); F sich et. ~ eat or drink s.th.; '2nehmen n (-s/no pl.) agreement, understanding; in gutem ~ on friendly terms; '~standen *adj.:* ~ *sein* agree; **'ständnis** *n* agreement.

'Einwand *m* (-[e]s/=e) objection (*gegen* to).

'Einwander|er *m* immigrant; **'n** *v/i.* (*sep.*, -ge-, *sein*) immigrate; **'ung** *f* immigration.

'einwandfrei *adj* unobjectionable; perfect; faultless; *alibi* sound.

einwärts *adv* [anverts] inward(s).

'Einwegflasche *f* one-way bottle, non-return bottle.

'einweih|en *v/t.* (*sep.*, -ge-, *h*) *eccl.* consecrate; inaugurate; ~ *in* (*acc.*) initiate *s.o.* into; **ung** *f* (-/-en) consecration; inauguration; initiation.

'einwend|en *v/t.* ([*irr.* wenden,] *sep.*, -ge-, *h*) object; **'ung** *f* objection.

'einwerfen (*irr.* werfen, *sep.*, -ge-, *h*) **1.** *v/t.* throw in (*a. fig.*); smash, break (*window-pane*); post, *Am.* mail (*letter*); interject (*remark*); **2.** *v/i.* *football* throw in.

'einwickel|n *v/t.* (*sep.*, -ge-, *h*) wrap (up), envelop; **'papier** *n* wrapping-paper.

einwillig|en ['ainviligən] *v/i.* (*sep.*, -ge-, *h*) consent, agree (*in acc.* to); **'ung** *f* (-/-en) consent, agreement.

'einwirk|en *v/i.* (*sep.*, -ge-, *h*): ~ *auf* (*acc.*) act (up)on, influence; effect; **'ung** *f* influence; effect.

Einwohner ['ainvo:nər] *m* (-s/-), **'in** *f* (-/-nen) inhabitant, resident.

'Einwurf *m* throwing in; *football:* throw-in; *fig.* objection; slit (*for letters, etc.*); lot (*for coins*).

'Einzahl *gr.* *f* (-/-en) singular (number); **'en** *v/t* (*sep.*, -ge-, *h*) pay in; **'ung** *f* payment; deposit (*at bank*).

einzäunen ['aintsɔynən] *v/t.* (*sep.*, -ge-, *h*) fence in.

Einzel ['aintsəl] *n* (-s/-) *tennis:* single, *Am.* singles *pl.*; **gänger** ['genər] *m* (-s/-) outsider; F lone wolf; **'handel** + *m* retail trade; **'händler** + *m* retailer, retail dealer; **'heit** *f* (-/-en) detail, item; *en pl.* particulars *pl.*, details *pl.*; **'n 1.** *adj.* single; particular; individual; separate; (*of shoes, etc.* odd; *im en* in detail; **2.** *adv.:* ~ *angeben* or *aufführen* specify, *esp. Am.* itemize; **'ne** *m* (-n/-n) *the* individual; **'verkauf** *m* retail sale; **'wesen** *n* individual.

'einziehen (*irr.* ziehen, *sep.*, -ge-) **1.** *v/t.* (*h*) draw in; *esp.* ⊕ retract; ✕ call up, *Am.* draft, induct; ✂ seize, confiscate; make (*inquiries*) (*über acc.* on, about); **2.** *v/i.* (*sein*) enter; move in; *liquid:* soak in; ~ *in* (*acc.*) move into (*flat, etc.*).

einzig *adj.* ['aintsiç] only; single; sole; unique; **'artig** *adj.* unique, singular.

'Einzug *m* entry, entrance; moving in.

'einzwängen *v/t.* (*sep.*, -ge-, *h*) squeeze, jam.

Eis [ais] *n* (-es/no *pl.*) ice; ice-cream; **'bahn** *f* skating-rink, **'bär** *zo. m* polar bear; **'bein** *n* pickled pork shank; **'berg** *m* iceberg; **'decke** *f* sheet of ice; **'diele** *f* ice-cream parlo(u)r.

Eisen ['aizən] *n* (-s/-) iron.

'Eisenbahn *f* railway, *Am.* railroad; *mit der* ~ *by* rail, *by* train, **'er** *m* (-s/-) railwayman; **'fahrt** *f* railway journey; **'knotenpunkt** *m* (railway) junction; **'unglück** *n* railway accident; **'wagen** *m* railway carriage, *Am.* railroad car; coach.

'Eisen|blech *n* sheet-iron; **'erz** *n* iron-ore; **'gießerei** *f* iron-foundry; **'haltig** *adj.* ferruginous; **'hütte** *f* ironworks *sg., pl.*, **'waren** *f/pl.* ironmongery, *esp. Am.* hardware; **'warenhändler** *m* ironmonger, *esp. Am.* hardware dealer.

eisern *adj.* ['aizərn] iron, of iron.

'Eis|gang *m* breaking up of the ice; ice-drift; **'gekühlt** *adj* gəky:lt] iced; **'grau** *adj.* hoary, **'hockey** *n* ice-hockey; **'ig** *adj.* ['aiziç] icy; **'kalt** *adj.* icy (cold); **'kunstlauf** *m* figure-skating; **'lauf** *m*, **'laufen** *n* (-s/no *pl.*) skating; skate; **'läufer** *m* skater; **'meer** *n* polar sea; **'schnellauf** *m* speed-skating; **'scholle** *f* ice-floe; **'schrank** *m s. Kühlschrank;* **'vogel** *orn. m* kingfisher; **'zapfen** *m* icicle; **'zeit** *geol. f* ice-age.

eitel *adj.* ['aitəl] vain (*auf acc.* of); conceited; mere; **'keit** *f* (-/-en) vanity.

Eiter ['aitər] *m* (-s/no *pl.*) matter, pus; **'beule** *f* abscess; **'ig** *adj.* purulent; **'n** *v/i* ge-, *h*) fester, suppurate; **'ung** *f* (-/-en) suppuration.

eitrig *adj.* ['aitriç] purulent.

'Eiweiß *n* (-es/-e) white of egg; 🜊 albumen; **'haltig** 🜊 *adj.* albuminous.

'Eizelle *f* egg-cell, ovum.

Ekel ['e:kəl] **1.** *m* (-s/no *pl.*) disgust (*vor dat.* at), loathing; aversion; 🜊 nausea; **2.** F *n* (-s/-) nasty person; **'erregend** *adj.* nauseating, sickening; **'haft** *adj.*, **'ig** *adj* revolting; *fig.* disgusting; **'n** *v/refl* ge-, *h*): *sich* ~ be nauseated (*vor dat.* at); *fig.* be or feel disgusted (at).

eklig *adj.* ['e:kliç] *s. ekelhaft.*

elasti|sch *adj.* ['elasti∫] elastic; **zität** [tsi'te:rt] *f* (-/no *pl.*) elasticity.

Elch *zo.* [elç] *m* (-[e]s/-e) elk; moose.

Elefant *zo.* [ele'fant] *m* (-en/-en) elephant.

elegan|t adj. [ele'gant] elegant; smart; 2z [...ts] f (-/no pl.) elegance.
elektrifizier|en [elektrifi'tsi:rən] v/t. (no -ge-, h) electrify; 2ung f (-/-en) electrification.
Elektri|ker [e'lɛktrikər] m (-s/-) electrician. 2sch adj. electric(al); 2sieren [. zi:rən] v/t. (no -ge-, h) electrify
Elektrizität [elektritsi'tɛ:t] f (-/no pl.) electricity; ~sgesellschaft f electricity supply company; ~s-werk n (electric) power station, power-house, Am. power plant.
Elektrode [elek'tro:də] f (-/-n) electrode
Elektro|gerät [e'lɛktro-] n electric appliance. ~lyse [..'ly:zə] f (-/-n) electrolysis
Elektron ƒ [e'lɛktron] n (-s/-en) electron. ~engehirn [..'tro:nən-] n electronic brain; ~ik [..'tro:nik] f (-/no pl.) electronics sg.
Elektro'technik f electrical engineering. ~er m electrical engineer.
Element [ele'mɛnt] n (-[e]s/-e) element
elementar adj. [elemen'ta:r] elementary. 2schule elementary or primary school, Am. grade school.
Elend [e lɛnt] 1. n (-[e]s/no pl.) misery, need, distress; 2. 2 adj. miserable, wretched; needy, distressed; ~sviertel n slums pl.
elf[1] [ɛlf] 1. adj. eleven; 2. 2 f (-/-en) eleven (a sports).
Elf[2] [..] m (-en/-en), ~e ['ɛlfə] f (-/-n) elf, fairy.
'Elfenbein n (-[e]s/%-e) ivory; '2ern adj ivory.
Eif'meter m football: penalty kick; ~marke f penalty spot.
'elfte adj eleventh.
Elite [e'li:tə] f (-/-n) élite.
'Ellbogen anat. m (-s/-) elbow.
Elle [ɛlə] f (-/-n) yard; anat. ulna.
Elster orn ['ɛlstər] f (-/-n) magpie.
elter|lich adj. ['ɛltərliç] parental; '2n pl. parents pl.; ~nlos adj. parentless, orphaned; '2nteil m parent. [(-/-n) enamel.]
Email [e'ma:j] n (-s/-s), ~le [..] f)
Emanzipation [emantsipa'tsjo:n] f (-/-en) emancipation.
Embargo [ɛm'bargo] n (-s/-s) embargo
Embolie ♂ [ɛmbo'li:] f (-/-n) embolism
Embryo biol. ['ɛmbryo] m (-s/-s, -nen) embryo.
Emigrant [emi'grant] m (-en/-en) emigrant
empfahl [ɛm'pfa:l] pret. of empfehlen.
Empfang [ɛm'pfaŋ] m (-[e]s/ʷe) reception (a. radio); receipt (of s.th.); nach or bei ~ on receipt; '2en v/t. (irr. fangen, no -ge-, h) receive; welcome; conceive (child).

Empfänger [ɛm'pfɛŋər] m (-s/-) receiver, recipient; payee (of money); addressee (of letter); ✝ consignee (of goods).
em'pfänglich adj. susceptible (für to); 2keit f -/no pl.) susceptibility.
Em'pfangs|dame f receptionist; ~gerät n receiver, receiving set; ~schein m receipt, ~zimmer n reception-room
empfehl|en [ɛm'pfe:lən] v/t. (irr., no -ge-, h) recommend; commend; ~ Sie mich (dat) please remember me to; ~enswert adj. (re)commendable, 2ung f (-/-en) recommendation, compliments pl.
empfinden [ɛm'pfindən] v/t. (irr. finden, no -ge-, h) feel; perceive.
empfindlich adj [ɛm'pfintliç] sensitive (a. phot., ⚡) (für, gegen to); pred. a. susceptible (gegen to); delicate; tender, p.: touchy, sensitive; cold severe; pain, loss, etc.: grievous; pain acute; 2keit f (-/-en) sensitivity; sensibility; touchiness; delicacy.
empfindsam adj [ɛm'pfintza:m] sensitive, sentimental; 2keit f (-/-en) sensitiveness; sentimentality.
Empfindung [ɛm'pfinduŋ] f (-/-en) perception, sensation, sentiment; 2slos adj. insensible; esp. fig. unfeeling; ~svermögen n faculty of perception.
empfohlen [ɛm'pfo:lən] p.p. of empfehlen.
empor adv. [ɛm'po:r] up, upwards.
empören [ɛm'pø:rən] v/t. (no -ge-, h) incense; shock; sich ~ revolt (a. fig.), rebel; grow furious (über acc. at); empört indignant, shocked (both: über acc. at).
em'por|kommen v/i. (irr. kommen, sep., -ge-, sein) rise (in the world); 2kömmling [..kœmliŋ] m (-s/-e) upstart; ~ragen v/i. (sep., -ge-, h) tower, rise; ~steigen v/i. (irr. steigen, sep., -ge-, sein) rise, ascend.
Em'pörung f (-/-en) rebellion, revolt; indignation.
emsig adj. ['ɛmziç] busy, industrious, diligent; 2keit f (-/no pl.) busyness, industry, diligence.
Ende ['ɛndə] n (-s/-n) end; am ~ at or in the end; after all; eventually; zu ~ gehen end; expire; run short; '2n v/i. (ge-, h) end; cease, finish.
end|gültig adj. ['ɛntgyltiç] final, definitive; ~lich adv. finally, at last; ~los adj ['..lo:s] endless; '2punkt m final point; '2runde f sports: final; '2station ⚑ f terminus, Am. terminal; '2summe f (sum) total.
Endung ling. ['ɛnduŋ] f (-/-en) ending, termination.
Endzweck ['ɛnt-] m ultimate object.

Energie [enɛr'giː] f (-/-n) energy; 2los adj. lacking (in) energy.

e'nergisch adj. vigorous; energetic.

eng adj. [ɛŋ] narrow; clothes: tight; close; intimate; im ~eren Sinne strictly speaking.

engagieren [ãga'ʒiːrən] v/t. (no -ge-, h) engage, Am. a. hire.

Enge ['ɛŋə] f (-/-n) narrowness; fig. straits pl.

Engel ['ɛŋəl] m (-s/-) angel.

'engherzig adj. ungenerous, petty.

Engländer ['ɛŋlɛndər] m (-s/-) Englishman; die pl. the English pl.; '~in f (-/-nen) Englishwoman.

englisch adj. ['ɛŋliʃ] English; British.

'Engpaß m defile, narrow pass, Am. a. notch; fig. bottle-neck.

en gros † adv. [ã'groː] wholesale.

En'groshandel † m wholesale trade.

'engstirnig adj. narrow-minded.

Enkel ['ɛŋkəl] m (-s/-) grandchild; grandson; ~in f (-/-nen) granddaughter.

enorm adj. [e'nɔrm] enormous; F fig. tremendous.

Ensemble thea., ♪ [ã'sãːbəl] n (-s/-s) ensemble; company.

entart|en [ɛnt'a:rtən] v/i. (no -ge-, sein) degenerate; 2ung f (-/-en) degeneration.

entbehr|en [ɛnt'be:rən] v/t. (no -ge-, h) lack; miss, want; do without; ~lich adj. dispensable; superfluous; 2ung f (-/-en) want, privation.

ent'bind|en (irr. binden, no -ge-, h) 1. v/t. dispense, release (von from); deliver (of a child); 2. v/i. be confined; 2ung f dispensation, release; delivery; 2ungsheim n maternity hospital.

ent'blöß|en v/t. (no -ge-, h) bare, strip; uncover (head); ~t adj. bare.

ent'deck|en v/t. (no -ge-, h) discover; detect; disclose; ~er m (-s/-) discoverer; 2ung f discovery.

Ente ['ɛntə] f (-/-n) orn. duck; false report; F canard, hoax.

ent'ehr|en v/t. (no -ge-, h) dishono(u)r; 2ung f degradation; rape.

ent'eign|en v/t. (no -ge-, h) expropriate; dispossess; 2ung f expropriation, dispossession.

ent'erben v/t. (no -ge-, h) disinherit.

entern ['ɛntərn] v/t. (ge-, h) board, grapple (ship).

ent'|fachen v/t. (no -ge-, h) kindle; fig. a. rouse (passions); ~'fallen v/i. (irr. fallen, no -ge-, sein): j-m ~ escape s.o.; fig. slip s.o.'s memory; auf j-n ~ fall to s.o.'s share; s. wegfallen; ~'falten v/t. (no -ge-, h) unfold; fig.: develop; display; sich ~ unfold; fig. develop (zu into).

ent'fern|en v/t. (no -ge-, h) remove; sich ~ withdraw; ~t adj. distant,

remote (both a. fig.); 2ung f (-/-en) removal; distance; range, 2ungsmesser phot. m (-s/-) range-finder.

ent'flamm|en (no -ge-) v/t (h) and v/i. (sein) inflame; ~'fliehen v/i. (irr. fliehen, no -ge-, sein) flee, escape (aus or dat. from), ~'fremden v/t. (no -ge-, h) estrange, alienate (j-m from s.o.).

ent'führ|en v/t. (no -ge-, h) abduct, kidnap; run away with; 2er m abductor; kidnap(p)er; 2ung f abduction, kidnap(p)ing.

ent'gegen 1. prp. (dat.) in opposition to, contrary to; against; 2. adv. towards; ~gehen v/i irr. gehen, sep., -ge-, sein) go to meet; ~gesetzt adj. opposite; fig. contrary; ~halten v/t. (irr. halten, sep., -ge-, h) hold out; fig. object; kommen v/i. (irr. kommen, sep. -ge-, sein) come to meet; fig. meet s.o.('s wishes) halfway; 2kommen n (-s/no pl.) obligingness; ~kommend adj. obliging; ~nehmen v/t. (irr. nehmen, sep., -ge-, h) accept, receive; ~sehen v/i. dat.) (irr. sehen, sep., -ge-, h) await; look forward to; ~setzen v/t sep., -ge-, h) oppose; ~stehen v/i irr stehen, sep., -ge-, h) be opposed dat. to); ~strecken v/t. (sep., -ge-, h) hold or stretch out (dat. to); ~treten v/i. (dat.) (irr. treten, sep., -ge-, sein) step up to s.o.; oppose; face (danger).

entgegn|en [ɛnt'ge:gnən] v/i. (no -ge-, h) reply; return; retort; 2ung f (-/-en) reply; retort.

ent'gehen v/i. (irr. gehen, no -ge-, sein) escape.

entgeistert adj. [ɛnt'gaɪstərt] aghast, thunderstruck, flabbergasted.

Entgelt [ɛnt'gɛlt] n (-[e]s/no pl.) recompense; 2en v/t. (irr gelten, no -ge-, h) atone or suffer or pay for.

entgleis|en [ɛnt'glaɪzən] v/i. (no -ge-, sein) run off the rails, be derailed; fig. (make a) slip; 2ung f (-/-en) derailment; fig. slip.

ent'gleiten v/i. (irr. gleiten, no -ge-, sein) slip (dat. from).

ent'halt|en v/t. (irr. halten, no -ge-, h) contain, hold, include; sich ~ (gen.) abstain or refrain from; ~sam adj. abstinent; 2samkeit f (-/no pl.) abstinence; 2ung f abstention.

ent'haupten v/t. (no -ge-, h) behead, decapitate.

ent'hüll|en v/t. (no -ge-, h) uncover; unveil; fig. reveal, disclose; 2ung f (-/-en) uncovering, unveiling; fig. revelation, disclosure.

Enthusias|mus [ɛntʊzi'asmʊs] m (-/no pl.) enthusiasm; ~t m (-en/-en) enthusiast; film, sports: F fan; 2tisch adj. enthusiastic.

ent'kleiden v/t. and v/refl. (no -ge-, h) undress.

ent'kommen 1. *v/i.* (*irr.* kommen, *no* -ge-, sein) escape (*j-m* s.o.; *aus* from), get away *or* off; **2.** ♀ *n* (*-s/no pl.*) escape.

entkräft|en [ent'krɛftən] *v/t.* (*no* -ge-, h) weaken, debilitate; *fig.* refute; ♀ung *f* (*-/-en*) weakening; debility, *fig* refutation.

ent'lad|en *v/t.* (*irr.* laden, *no* -ge-, h) unload, *esp* ∉ discharge; explode; *sich* ∼ *esp* ∉ discharge; *gun:* go off; *anger* vent itself; ♀ung *f* unloading; *esp* ∉ discharge; explosion.

ent'lang 1. *prp* (*dat.; acc.*) along; **2.** *adv* along, *er geht die Straße* ∼ he goes along the street.

ent'larven *v/t* (*no* -ge-, h) unmask; *fig. a* expose

ent'lass|en *v/t.* (*irr.* lassen, *no* -ge-, h) dismiss, discharge; F give *s.o.* the sack, *Am a.* fire; ♀ung *f* (*-/-en*) dismissal, discharge; ♀ungsgesuch *n* resignation

ent'lasten *v/t.* (*no* -ge-, h) unburden; ♀ exonerate, clear (*from suspicion*)

Ent'lastung *f* (*-/-en*) relief; discharge, exoneration; ∼straße *f* by-pass road); ∼szeuge *m* witness for the defen|ce, *Am.* -se.

ent'|laufen *v/i.* (*irr.* laufen, *no* -ge-, sein) run away (*dat.* from); ∼ledigen [∼'le digən] *v/refl.* (*gen.*) (*no* -ge-, h) rid o.s. of *s.th.*, get rid of *s.th.*; acquit o.s. of (*duty*); execute (*orders*); ∼'leeren *v/t.* (*no* -ge-, h) empty [of-the-way.)

ent'legen *adj.* remote, distant, out-)

ent'|lehnen *v/t.* (*no* -ge-, h) borrow (*dat. or aus* from); ∼'locken *v/t.* (*no* -ge-, h) draw, elicit (*dat.* from); ∼'lohnen *v/t* (*no* -ge-, h) pay (off); ∼'lüften *v/t* (*no* -ge-, h) ventilate; ∼militarisieren [∼militari'zi:rən] *v/t.* (*no* -ge- h) demilitarize; ∼mutigen [∼'mu tigən] *v/t.* (*no* -ge-, h) discourage; ∼'nehmen *v/t.* (*irr.* nehmen, *no* -ge- h) take (*dat.* from); ∼ *aus* (with)draw from; *fig.* gather or learn from; ∼'rätseln *v/t.* (*no* -ge-, h) unriddle; ∼'reißen *v/t.* (*irr.* reißen, *no* -ge-, h) snatch away (*dat.* from); ∼'richten *v/t.* (*no* -ge-, h) pay; ∼'rinnen *v/i.* (*irr.* rinnen, *no* -ge-, sein) escape (*dat.* from); ∼'rollen *v/t* (*no* -ge-, h) unroll; ∼'rücken *v/t* (*no* -ge-, h) remove (*dat.* from), carry off *or* away; ∼'rückt *adj.* entranced; lost in thought

ent'rüst|en *v/t.* (*no* -ge-, h) fill with indignation, *sich* ∼ become angry *or* indignant (*über acc.* at *s.th.*, with *s.o.*); ∼et *adj* indignant (*über acc.* at *s.th.*, with *s.o.*); ♀ung *f* indignation.

ent'sag|en *v/i.* (*no* -ge-, h) renounce, resign; ♀ung *f* (*-/-en*) renunciation, resignation.

ent'schädig|en *v/t.* (*no* -ge-, h) indemnify, compensate; ♀ung *f* indemnification, indemnity; compensation.

ent'scheid|en (*irr.* scheiden, *no* -ge-, h) **1.** *v/t.* decide, *sich* ∼ question, etc.: be decided; *p* decide (*für* for; *gegen* against; *über acc.* on); come to a decision, **2.** *v/i.* decide, ∼end *adj.* decisive; crucial; ♀ung *f* decision.

entschieden *adj* [ent'ʃi:dən] decided; determined, resolute; ♀heit *f* (*-/no pl.*) determination.

ent'schließen *v/refl* (*irr.* schließen, *no* -ge-, h) resolve, decide, determine (*zu* on *s.th.*, *zu inf.* to *inf.*), make up one's mind (*zu inf.* to *inf.*).

ent'schlossen *adj* resolute, determined; ♀heit *f* (*-/no pl.*) resoluteness.

ent'schlüpfen *v/i.* (*no* -ge-, sein) escape, slip (*dat* from).

Ent'schluß *m* resolution, resolve, decision, determination.

entschuldig|en [ent'ʃuldigən] *v/t.* (*no* -ge-, h) excuse, *sich* ∼ apologize (*bei* to; *für* for), *sich* ∼ *lassen* beg to be excused, ♀ung *f* (*-/-en*) excuse; apology, *ich bitte* (*Sie*) *um* ∼ I beg your pardon

ent'senden *v/t* (*irr.* senden, *no* -ge-, h) send off, dispatch; delegate, depute.

ent'setz|en 1. *v/t.* (*no* -ge-, h) dismiss (*from a position*); ♀ relieve; frighten; *sich* ∼ be terrified *or* shocked (*über acc.* at); **2.** ♀ *n* (*-/no pl.*) horror, fright, ∼lich *adj.* horrible, dreadful, terrible, shocking.

ent'sinnen *v/refl.* (*gen.*) (*irr.* sinnen, *no* -ge-, h) remember *or* recall *s.o.*, *s.th.*

ent'spann|en *v/t.* (*no* -ge-, h) relax; unbend; *sich* ∼ relax; *political situation:* ease; ♀ung *f* relaxation; *pol.* détente.

ent'sprech|en *v/i.* (*irr.* sprechen, *no* -ge-, h) answer (*description, etc.*); correspond to, meet (*demand*); ∼end *adj.* corresponding; appropriate; ♀ung *f* (*-/-en*) equivalent.

ent'springen *v/i* (*irr.* springen, *no* -ge-, sein) escape (*dat.* from); *river:* rise, *Am.* head; *s* entstehen.

ent'stammen *v/i* (*no* -ge-, sein) be descended from; come from *or* of, originate from.

ent'steh|en *v/i.* (*irr.* stehen. *no* -ge-, sein) arise, originate (*both: aus* from); ♀ung *f* (*-/-en*) origin.

ent'stell|en *v/t* (*no* -ge-, h) disfigure; deface, deform; distort; ♀ung *f* disfigurement; distortion, misrepresentation.

ent'täusch|en *v/t.* (*no* -ge-, h) disappoint; ♀ung *f* disappointment.

ent'thronen *v/t.* (*no* -ge-, h) dethrone.

entvölker|n [ɛnt'fœlkərn] *v/t.* (*no*

-ge-, h) depopulate; 2ung f (-/-en) depopulation.

ent'wachsen v/i. (irr. wachsen, no -ge-, sein) outgrow.

entwaffn|en [ent'vafnən] v/t. (no -ge-, h) disarm; 2ung f (-/-en) disarmament.

ent'warnen v/i. (no -ge-, h) civil defence: sound the all-clear (signal).

ent'wässer|n v/t. (no -ge-, h) drain; 2ung f (-/-en) drainage; ⚓ dehydration.

ent'weder cj.: ~ ... oder either ... or.

ent|'weichen v/i. (irr. weichen, no -ge-, sein) escape (aus from); ~'weihen v/t. (no -ge-, h) desecrate, profane; ~'wenden v/t. (no -ge-, h) pilfer, purloin (j-m et. s.th. from s.o.); ~'werfen v/t. (irr. werfen, no -ge-, h) draft, draw up (document); design; sketch, trace out, outline; plan.

ent'wert|en v/t. (no -ge-, h) depreciate, devaluate; cancel (stamp); 2ung f depreciation, devaluation; cancellation.

ent'wickeln v/t. (no -ge-, h) develop (a. phot.); evolve; sich ~ develop.

Entwicklung [ent'viklun] f (-/-en) development; evolution; ~shilfe f development aid.

ent|'wirren v/t. (no -ge-, h) disentangle, unravel; ~'wischen v/i. (no -ge-, sein) slip away, escape (j-m [from] s.o.; aus from); j-m ~ give s.o. the slip; ~'wöhnen [~'vø:nən] v/t. (no -ge-, h) wean.

Ent'wurf m sketch; design; plan; draft.

ent|'wurzeln v/t. (no -ge-, h) uproot; ~'ziehen v/t. (irr. ziehen, no -ge-, h) deprive (j-m et. s.o. of s.th.); withdraw (dat. from); sich ~ avoid, elude; evade (responsibility); ~'ziffern v/t. (no -ge-, h) decipher, make out; tel. decode.

ent'zück|en 1. v/t. (no -ge-, h) charm, delight; 2. 2 n (-s/no pl.) delight, rapture(s pl.), transport(s pl.).

ent'zückend adj. delightful; charming.

Ent'zug m (-[e]s/no pl.) withdrawal; cancellation (of licence); deprivation.

entzünd|bar adj. [ent'tsyntba:r] (in)flammable; ~en v/t. (no -ge-, h) inflame (a. ⚓), kindle; sich ~ catch fire; ⚓ become inflamed; 2ung f inflammation.

ent'zwei adv. asunder, in two, to pieces; ~en v/t. (no -ge-, h) disunite, set at variance; sich ~ quarrel, fall out (both: mit with); ~gehen v/i. (irr. gehen, sep., -ge-, sein) break, go to pieces; 2ung f (-/-en) disunion.

Enzian ⚘ ['entsja:n] m (-s/-e) gentian.

Enzyklopädie [entsyklope'di:] f (-/-n) (en)cyclop(a)edia.

Epidemie ⚕ [epide'mi:] f (-/-n) epidemic (disease).

Epilog [epi'lo:k] m (-s/-e) epilog(ue).

episch adj. ['e:pif] epic.

Episode [epi'zo:də] f (-/-n) episode.

Epoche [e'pɔxə] f (-/-n) epoch.

Epos ['e:pɔs] n (-/Epen) epic (poem).

er pers. pron. [e:r] he.

erachten [er'-] 1. v/t. (no -ge-, h) consider, think, deem; 2. 2 n (-s/no pl.) opinion; m-s ~s in my opinion.

erbarmen [er'barmən] 1. v/refl. (gen.) (no -ge-, h) pity or commiserate s.o.; 2. 2 n (-s/no pl.) pity, compassion, commiseration; mercy; ~swert adj. pitiable.

erbärmlich adj. [er'bermliç] pitiful, pitiable; miserable; behaviour: mean.

er'barmungslos adj. pitiless, merciless, relentless.

er'bau|en v/t. (no -ge-, h) build (up), construct, raise; fig. edify; 2er m (-s/-) builder; constructor; ~lich adj. edifying; 2ung fig. f (-/-en) edification, Am uplift.

Erbe ['erbə] 1. m (-n/-n) heir; 2. n (-s/no pl.) inheritance, heritage.

er'beben v/i. (no -ge-, sein) tremble, shake, quake.

'erben v/t. (ge-, h) inherit.

er'beuten v/t. (no -ge-, h) capture.

er'bieten v/refl. (irr. bieten, no -ge-, h) offer, volunteer.

'Erbin f (-/-nen) heiress.

er'bitten v/t. (irr. bitten, no -ge-, h) beg or ask for, request, solicit.

er'bitter|n v/t. (no -ge-, h) embitter, exasperate; 2ung f (-/⚓ -en) bitterness, exasperation.

Erbkrankheit ⚕ ['erp-] f hereditary disease.

erblassen [er'blasən] v/i. (no -ge-, sein) grow or turn pale, lose colo(u)r.

Erblasser ⚖ ['erplasər] m (-s/-) testator; '~in f (-/-nen) testatrix.

er'bleichen v/i. (no -ge-, sein) s. erblassen.

erblich adj. ['erpliç] hereditary; '2keit physiol. f (-/no pl.) heredity.

er'blicken v/t. (no -ge-, h) perceive, see; catch sight of.

erblind|en [er'blindən] v/i. (no -ge-, sein) grow blind; 2ung f (-/-en) loss of sight.

er'brechen 1. v/t. (irr. brechen, no -ge-, h) break or force open; vomit; sich ~ ⚕ vomit; 2. 2 n (-s/no pl.) vomiting.

Erbschaft ['erpfaft] f (-/-en) inheritance, heritage.

Erbse ⚘ ['erpsə] f (-/-n) pea; '~nbrei m pease-pudding, Am. pea purée; '~nsuppe f pea-soup.

Erb|stück ['erp-] n heirloom; '~sünde f original sin; '~teil n (portion of an) inheritance.

Erd|arbeiter ['eːrt-] *m* digger, navvy; '⁓ball *m* globe; '⁓beben *n* (-s/-) earthquake; '⁓beere ⚘ *f* strawberry; '⁓boden *m* earth; ground, soil; ⁓e ['eːrdə] *f* (-/⁓, -n) earth; ground, soil; world; '2en ⚘ *v/t.* (*ge-*, *h*) earth, ground.

er'denklich *adj.* imaginable.

Erdgeschoß ['eːrt-] *n* ground-floor, *Am.* first floor.

er'dicht|en *v/t.* (*no -ge-*, *h*) invent, feign; ⁓et *adj.* fictitious.

erdig *adj.* ['eːrdiç] earthy.

Erd|karte ['eːrt-] *f* map of the earth; '⁓kreis *m* earth, world; '⁓kugel *f* globe; '⁓kunde *f* geography; '⁓leitung ⚡ *f* earth-connexion, earth-wire, *Am.* ground wire; '⁓nuß *f* peanut; '⁓öl *n* mineral oil, petroleum

er'dolchen *v/t.* (*no -ge-*, *h*) stab (with a dagger).

Erdreich ['eːrt-] *n* ground, earth.

er'dreisten *v/refl.* (*no -ge-*, *h*) dare, presume

er'drosseln *v/t.* (*no-ge-*, *h*) strangle, throttle.

er'drücken *v/t.* (*no -ge-*, *h*) squeeze or crush to death; ⁓d *fig. adj.* overwhelming.

Erd|rutsch ['eːrt-] *m* landslip; landslide (*a. pol.*); '⁓schicht *f* layer of earth, stratum; '⁓teil *m* part of the world; *geogr.* continent.

er'dulden *v/t.* (*no -ge-*, *h*) suffer, endure.

er'eifern *v/refl.* (*no -ge-*, *h*) get excited, fly into a passion.

er'eignen *v/refl.* (*no -ge-*, *h*) happen, come to pass, occur.

Ereignis [ɛr'aiknis] *n* (-ses/-se) event, occurrence; **2reich** *adj.* eventful.

Eremit [ere'miːt] *m* (-en/-en) hermit, anchorite.

ererbt *adj.* [ɛr'ɛrpt] inherited.

er'fahr|en 1. *v/t.* (*irr. fahren, no -ge-*, *h*) learn; hear; experience; 2. *adj.* experienced, expert, skil(l)-ful; **2ung** *f* (-/-en) experience; practice; skill.

er'fassen *v/t.* (*no -ge-*, *h*) grasp (*a. fig.*), seize, catch; cover; register, record.

er'find|en *v/t.* (*irr. finden, no -ge-*, *h*) invent; **2er** *m* inventor; ⁓erisch *adj.* inventive; **2ung** *f* (-/-en) invention.

Erfolg [ɛr'fɔlk] *m* (-[e]s/-e) success; result; 2en [⁓gən] *v/i.* (*no -ge-*, sein) ensue; follow; happen; **2los** *adj.* [⁓kˌ] unsuccessful; vain; **2-reich** *adj.* [⁓kˌ] successful.

er'forder|lich *adj.* necessary; required; ⁓n *v/t.* (*no -ge-*, *h*) require, demand; **2nis** *n* (-ses/-se) requirement, demand, exigence, exigency.

er'forsch|en *v/t.* (*no -ge-*, *h*) inquire into, investigate; explore

(*country*); **2er** *m* investigator; explorer; **2ung** *f* investigation; exploration.

er'freu|en *v/t.* (*no -ge-*, *h*) please; delight; gratify; rejoice; *sich e-r Sache* ⁓ enjoy s.th.; ⁓lich *adj.* delightful, pleasing, pleasant, gratifying.

er'frier|en *v/i.* (*irr. frieren, no -ge-*, sein) freeze to death; **2ung** *f* (-/-en) frost-bite.

er'frisch|en *v/t.* (*no -ge-*, *h*) refresh; **2ung** *f* (-/-en) refreshment.

er'froren *adj.* limb frost-bitten.

er'füll|en *v/t.* (*no -ge-*, *h*) fill; *fig.* fulfil(l); perform (*mission*); comply with (*s.o.'s wishes*); meet (*requirements*); **2ung** *f* fulfil(l)ment; performance; compliance; **2ungsort** ⚘, ₂⁚ [ɛr'fylʊŋs°-] *m* place of performance (*of contract*).

ergänz|en [ɛr'gɛntsən] *v/t.* (*no -ge-*, *h*) complete, complement; supplement; replenish (*stores, etc.*); ⁓end *adj.* complementary, supplementary; **2ung** *f* (-/-en) completion; supplement; replenishment; *gr.* complement; **2ungsband** *m* (-[e]s/⁓e) supplementary volume.

er'geben 1. *v/t.* (*irr. geben, no -ge-*, *h*) yield, give; prove; *sich* ⁓ surrender; *difficulties* arise; devote o.s. to *s.th.*; *sich* ⁓ *aus* result from; *sich* ⁓ *in* (*acc.*) resign o.s. to; 2. *adj.* devoted (*dat* to); ⁓st *adv.* respectfully; **2heit** *f* (-/*no pl.*) devotion.

Ergeb|nis [ɛr'ge pnis] *n* (-ses/-se) result, outcome; *sports* score; **2ung** [⁓buŋ] *f* (-/-en) resignation; ✕ surrender.

er'gehen *v/i.* (*irr. gehen, no -ge-*, sein) be issued; ⁓ *lassen* issue, publish; *über sich* ⁓ *lassen* suffer, submit to; *wie ist es ihm ergangen?* how did he come off?; *sich* ⁓ *in* (*dat.*) indulge in.

ergiebig *adj.* [ɛr'giːbiç] productive, rich.

er'gießen *v/refl.* (*irr. gießen, no -ge-*, *h*) flow (*in acc.* into; *über acc.* over).

er'götz|en 1. *v/t.* (*no -ge-*, *h*) delight; *sich* ⁓ *an* (*dat.*) delight in; 2. **2** *n* (-s/*no pl.*) delight; ⁓lich *adj.* delightful.

er'greif|en *v/t.* (*irr. greifen, no -ge-*, *h*) seize; grasp; take (*possession, s.o.'s part, measures, etc.*); take to (*flight*); take up (*profession, pen, arms*); *fig.* move, affect, touch; **2ung** *f* (-/⁓ -en) seizure.

Er'griffenheit *f* (-/*no pl.*) emotion.

er'gründen *v/t.* (*no -ge-*, *h*) fathom; *fig.* penetrate, get to the bottom of.

Er'guß *m* outpouring, effusion.

er'haben *adj.* elevated, *fig.* exalted, sublime; ⁓ *sein über* (*acc.*) be above; **2heit** *f* (-/⁓ -en) elevation; *fig.* sublimity.

er'halt|en 1. v/t. (irr. halten, no -ge-, h) get; obtain; receive; preserve, keep; support, maintain; sich ~ von subsist on; 2. adj.: gut ~ in good repair or condition; 2ung f preservation; maintenance.

erhältlich adj. [ɛr'hɛltlɪç] obtainable.

er|'hängen v/t. (no -ge-, h) hang; ~härten v/t. (no -ge-, h) harden; fig. confirm; ~'haschen v/t. (no -ge-, h) snatch, catch.

er'heb|en v/t. (irr. heben, no -ge-, h) lift, raise; elevate; exalt; levy, raise, collect (taxes, etc.); Klage ~ bring an action; sich ~ rise; question, etc.: arise; and fig. adj. elevating; ~lich adj. [~ɔ-] considerable; 2ung f [~buŋ] f (-/-en) elevation; levy (of taxes); revolt; rising ground.

er|'heitern v/t. (no -ge-, h) cheer up, amuse; ~'hellen v/t. (no -ge-, h) light up; fig. clear up; ~'hitzen v/t. (no -ge-, h) heat; sich ~ get or grow hot; ~'hoffen v/t. (no -ge-, h) hope for.

er'höh|en v/t. (no -ge-, h) raise; increase; 2ung f (-/-en) elevation; rise (in prices, wages); advance (in prices); increase.

er'hol|en v/refl. (no -ge-, h) recover; (take a) rest, relax; 2ung f (-/-en) recovery, recreation; relaxation; 2ungsurlaub [ɛr'ho:luŋs⁹-] m holiday, Am. vacation; recreation leave; ⚕ convalescent leave, sickleave.   [(request).]

er'hören v/t. (no -ge-, h) hear; grant⌋

erinner|n [ɛr'ɪnərn] v/t. (no -ge-, h): j-n ~ an (acc.) remind s.o. of; sich ~ (gen.), sich ~ an (acc.) remember s.o. or s.th., recollect s.th.; 2ung f (-/-en) remembrance; recollection; reminder; ~en pl. reminiscences pl.

er'kalten v/i. (no -ge-, sein) cool down (a fig.), get cold.

erkält|en [ɛr'kɛltən] v/refl. (no -ge-, h): sich (sehr) ~ catch (a bad) cold; 2ung f (-/-en) cold.

er'kennen v/t. (irr. kennen, no -ge-, h) recognize (an dat. by); perceive, discern; realize.

er'kenntlich adj. perceptible; sich ~ zeigen show one's appreciation; 2keit f (-/-en) gratitude; appreciation.

Er'kenntnis 1. f perception; realization; 2. ⚖ n (-ses/-se) decision, sentence, finding.

Erker [ˈɛrkər] m (-s/-) bay; '~fenster n bay-window.

er'klär|en v/t. (no -ge-, h) explain; account for; declare, state; sich ~ declare (für for; gegen against); ~lich adj. explainable, explicable; ~t adj. professed, declared; 2ung f explanation; declaration.

er'klingen v/i. (irr. klingen, no -ge-, sein) (re)sound, ring (out).

erkoren adj. [ɛr'ko:rən] (s)elect, chosen.

er'krank|en v/i. (no -ge-, sein) fall ill, be taken ill (an dat. of, with); become affected; 2ung f (-/-en) illness, sickness, falling ill.

er|'kühnen v/refl (no -ge-, h) venture, presume, make bold (zu inf. to inf.); ~'kunden v/t. (no -ge-, h) explore; ⚔ reconnoitre, Am. -er.

erkundig|en [ɛr'kundigən] v/refl. (no -ge-, h) inquire (über acc. after; nach after or for s.o.; about s.th.); 2ung f (-/-en) inquiry.

er|'lahmen fig. v/i. (no -ge-, sein) grow weary, tire; slacken; interest: wane, flag; ~'langen v/t. (no -ge-, h) obtain, get.

Er|laß [ɛr'las] m (Erlasses/Erlasse) dispensation, exemption; remission (of debt, penalty, etc.); edict, decree; 2'lassen v/t. (irr. lassen, no -ge-, h) remit (debt, penalty, etc.); dispense (j-m et. s.o from s.th.); issue (decree); enact (law).

erlauben [ɛr'laubən] v/t. (no -ge-, h) allow, permit, sich et. ~ indulge in s.th.; sich zu inf ✦ beg to inf.

Erlaubnis [ɛr'laupnis] f (-/no pl.) permission, authority; ~schein m permit.

er'läuter|n v/t. (no -ge-, h) explain, illustrate, comment (up)on; 2ung f explanation, illustration; comment.

Erle ⚘ [ˈɛrlə] f (-/-n) alder.

er'leb|en v/t (no -ge-, h) (live to) see; experience; go through; 2nis [~pnis] n (-ses/-se) experience; adventure.

erledig|en [ɛr'le:digən] v/t. (no -ge-, h) dispatch, execute; settle (matter); ~t adj. [~çt] finished, settled; fig. played out; F done for; F: du bist für mich ~ I am through with you; 2ung [~guŋ] f (-/⚹, -en) dispatch; settlement

er'leichter|n v/t. (no -ge-, h) lighten (burden), fig. make easy, facilitate; relieve; 2ung f (-/-en) ease; relief; facilitation; ~en pl facilities pl.

er|'leiden v/t. (irr leiden, no -ge-, h) suffer, endure; sustain (damage, loss); ~'lernen v/t. (no -ge-, h) learn, acquire

er'leucht|en v/t. (no -ge-, h) illuminate; fig enlighten; 2ung f (-/-en) illumination; fig enlightenment.

er'liegen v/i. (irr liegen, no -ge-, sein) succumb (dat to).

erlogen adj. [ɛr'lo:gən] false, untrue.

Erlös [ɛr'lø:s] m (-es/-e) proceeds pl.

erlosch [ɛr'lɔʃ] pret. of erlöschen; ~en 1. p.p. of erlöschen; 2. adj. extinct.

er'löschen v/i. (irr., no -ge-, sein) go out; fig. become extinct; contract: expire.

er'lös|en v/t. (no -ge-, h) redeem;

deliver; 2er *m* (-s/-) redeemer, deliverer; *eccl.* Redeemer, Saviour; 2ung *f* redemption; deliverance.

ermächtig|en [ɛr'mɛçtɪgən] *v/t.* (*no -ge-, h*) authorize; 2ung *f* (-/-en) authorization; authority; warrant.

er'mahn|en *v/t.* (*no -ge-, h*) admonish; 2ung *f* admonition.

er'mangel|n *v/i.* (*no -ge-, h*) be wanting (*gen.* in); 2ung *f* (-/*no pl.*): in ~ (*gen.*) in default of, for want of, failing.

er'mäßig|en *v/t.* (*no -ge-, h*) abate, reduce, cut (down); 2ung *f* (-/-en) abatement, reduction.

er'matt|en (*no -ge-*) 1. *v/t.* (h) fatigue, tire, exhaust; 2. *v/i.* (*sein*) tire, grow weary; *fig.* slacken; 2ung *f* (-/✎ -en) fatigue, exhaustion.

er'messen 1. *v/t.* (*irr. messen, no -ge-, h*) judge; 2. 2 *n* (-s/*no pl.*) judg(e)ment; discretion.

er'mitt|eln *v/t.* (*no -ge-, h*) ascertain, find out; ⚖ investigate; 2(e)lung [~(ə)lʊŋ] *f* (-/-en) ascertainment; inquiry; ⚖ investigation.

er'möglichen *v/t.* (*no -ge-, h*) render *or* make possible.

er'mord|en *v/t.* (*no-ge-, h*) murder; assassinate; 2ung *f* (-/-en) murder; assassination.

er'müd|en (*no -ge-*) 1. *v/t.* (h) tire, fatigue; 2. *v/i.* (*sein*) tire, get tired *or* fatigued; 2ung *f* (-/✎-en) fatigue, tiredness.

er'munter|n *v/t.* (*no -ge-, h*) rouse, encourage; animate; 2ung *f* (-/-en) encouragement, animation.

ermutig|en [ɛr'muːtɪgən] *v/t.* (*no -ge-, h*) encourage; 2ung *f* (-/-en) encouragement.

er'nähr|en *v/t.* (*no -ge-, h*) nourish, feed; support; 2er *m* (-s/-) breadwinner, supporter; 2ung *f* (-/✎-en) nourishment; support; *physiol.* nutrition.

er'nenn|en *v/t.* (*irr. nennen, no -ge-, h*) nominate, appoint; 2ung *f* nomination, appointment.

er'neu|ern *v/t.* (*no -ge-, h*) renew, renovate; revive; 2erung *f* renewal, renovation; revival; ~t *adv.* once more.

erniedrig|en [ɛr'niːdrɪgən] *v/t.* (*no -ge-, h*) degrade; humiliate, humble; 2ung *f* (-/-en) degradation; humiliation.

Ernst [ɛrnst] 1. *m* (-es/*no pl.*) seriousness; earnest(ness); gravity; im ~ in earnest; 2. 2 *adj.* — '2haft *adj.*, '2lich *adj.* serious, earnest; grave.

Ernte ['ɛrntə] *f* (-/-n) harvest; crop; ~'dankfest *n* harvest festival; '2n *v/t.* (*ge-, h*) harvest, gather (in), reap (*a. fig.*).

er'nüchter|n *v/t.* (*no -ge-, h*) (make) sober; *fig.* disillusion; 2ung *f* (-/-en) sobering; *fig.* disillusionment.

Er'ober|er *m* (-s/-) conqueror; 2n *v/t.* (*no -ge-, h*) conquer; ~ung *f* (-/-en) conquest.

er'öffn|en *v/t.* (*no -ge-, h*) open; inaugurate; disclose (*j-m et. s.th. to s.o.*); notify; 2ung *f* opening; inauguration; disclosure.

erörter|n [ɛr'œrtərn] *v/t.* (*no-ge-, h*) discuss; 2ung *f* (-/-en) discussion.

Erpel *orn.* ['ɛrpəl] *m* (-s/-) drake.

erpicht *adj.* [ɛr'pɪçt]: ~ auf (*acc.*) bent *or* intent *or* set *or* keen on.

er'press|en *v/t.* (*no -ge-, h*) extort (*von* from); blackmail; 2er *m* (-s/-), 2erin *f* (-/-nen) extort(ion)er; blackmailer; 2ung *f* (-/-en) extortion; blackmail.

er'proben *v/t.* (*no -ge-, h*) try, test.

erquick|en [ɛr'kvɪkən] *v/t.* (*no -ge-, h*) refresh; 2ung *f* (-/-en) refreshment.

er'raten *v/t.* (*irr. raten, no -ge-, h*) guess, find out; ~'rechnen *v/t.* (*no -ge-, h*) calculate, compute, work out.

erreg|bar *adj.* [ɛr'reːkbaːr] excitable; ~en [~gən] *v/t.* (*no -ge-, h*) excite; cause; 2er [~gər] *m* (-s/-) exciter (*a. ♪*); ♨ germ, virus; 2ung [~gʊŋ] *f* excitation; excitement.

er'reich|bar *adj.* attainable; within reach *or* call; ~en *v/t.* (*no -ge-, h*) reach; *fig.* achieve, attain; catch (*train*); come up to (*certain standard*).

er'rett|en *v/t.* (*no -ge-, h*) rescue; 2ung *f* rescue.

er'richt|en *v/t.* (*no -ge-, h*) set up, erect; establish; 2ung *f* erection; establishment.

er'ring|en *v/t.* (*irr. ringen, no -ge-, h*) gain, obtain; achieve (*success*); ~'röten *v/i.* (*no -ge-, sein*) blush.

Errungenschaft [ɛr'rʊŋənʃaft] *f* (-/-en) acquisition; achievement.

Er'satz *m* (-es/*no pl.*) replacement; substitute; compensation, amends *sg.*, damages *pl.*; indemnification; ~s. Ersatzmann, Ersatzmittel; ~ leisten make amends; ~mann *m* substitute; ~mine *f* refill (*for pencil*); ~mittel *n* substitute, surrogate; ~reifen *mot. m* spare tyre, (*Am. only*) spare tire; ~teil ⊕ *n*, *m* spare (part).

er'schaff|en *v/t.* (*irr. schaffen, no -ge-, h*) create; 2ung *f* (-/*no pl.*) creation.

er'schallen *v/i.* ([*irr. schallen,*] *no -ge-, sein*) (re)sound; ring.

er'schein|en 1. *v/i.* (*irr. scheinen, no -ge-, sein*) appear; 2. 2 *n* (-s/*no pl.*) appearance; 2ung *f* (-/-en) appearance; apparition; vision.

er'schieß|en *v/t.* (*irr. schießen, no -ge-, h*) shoot (dead); ~'schlaffen *v/i.* (*no -ge-, sein*) tire; relax; *fig.* languish, slacken; ~'schlagen *v/t.* (*irr. schlagen, no -ge-, h*) kill, slay;

~'schließen *v/t.* (*irr. schließen, no* -ge-, *h*) open; open up (*new market*); develop (*district*).

er'schöpf|en *v/t.* (*no* -ge-, *h*) exhaust; ₂ung *f* exhaustion.

erschrak [er'ʃraːk] *pret.* of erschrecken 2.

er'schrecken 1. *v/t.* (*no* -ge-, *h*) frighten, scare; 2. *v/i.* (*irr., no* -ge-, *sein*) be frightened (*über acc.* at); ~d *adj.* alarming, startling.

erschrocken [er'ʃrɔkən] 1. *p.p.* of erschrecken 2; 2. *adj.* frightened, terrified.

erschütter|n [er'ʃytərn] *v/t.* (*no* -ge-, *h*) shake; *fig.* shock, move; ₂ung *f* (-/-en) shock; *fig.* emotion; ⚕ concussion; ⊕ percussion.

er'schweren *v/t.* (*no* -ge-, *h*) make more difficult; aggravate.

er'schwing|en *v/t.* (*irr. schwingen, no* -ge-, *h*) afford; ~lich *adj.* within *s.o.'s* means; *prices:* reasonable.

er|'sehen *v/t.* (*irr. sehen, no* -ge-, *h*) see, learn, gather (*all: aus* from); ~'sehnen *v/t.* (*no* -ge-, *h*) long for; ~'setzen *v/t.* (*no* -ge-, *h*) repair; make up for, compensate (for); replace; refund.

er'sichtlich *adj.* evident, obvious.

er'sinnen *v/t.* (*irr. sinnen, no* -ge-, *h*) contrive, devise.

er'spar|en *v/t.* (*no* -ge-, *h*) save; *j-m et.* ~ spare s.o. s.th.; ₂nis *f* (-/-se) saving.

er'sprießlich *adj.* useful, beneficial.

erst [eːrst] 1. *adj.:* der (die, das) ~e the first; 2. *adv.* first; at first; only; not ... till *or* until.

er'starr|en *v/i.* (*no* -ge-, *sein*) stiffen; solidify; congeal; set; grow numb; *fig. blood:* run cold; ~t *adj.* benumbed; ₂ung *f* (-/-en) numbness; solidification; congealment; setting.

erstatt|en [er'ʃtatən] *v/t.* (*no* -ge-, *h*) restore; *s.* ersetzen; Bericht ~ (make a) report; ₂ung *f* (-/-en) restitution.

'Erstaufführung *f thea.* first night *or* performance, premiere; *film:* a. first run.

er'staun|en 1. *v/i.* (*no* -ge-, *sein*) be astonished (*über acc.* at); 2. *v/t.* (*no* -ge-, *h*) astonish; 3. ₂ *n* astonishment; *in* ~ setzen astonish; ~lich *adj.* astonishing, amazing.

er'stechen *v/t.* (*irr. stechen, no* -ge-, *h*) stab.

er'steig|en *v/t.* (*irr. steigen, no* -ge-, *h*) ascend, climb; ₂ung *f* ascent.

erstens *adv.* ['eːrstəns] first, firstly.

er'stick|en (*no* -ge-) *v/t.* (*h*) and *v/i.* (*sein*) choke, suffocate; stifle; ₂ung *f* (-/-en) suffocation. [rate, F A l.\

'erstklassig *adj.* first-class, first-\

er'streben *v/t.* (*no* -ge-, *h*) strive after *or* for; ~swert *adj.* desirable.

er'strecken *v/refl.* (*no* -ge-, *h*) extend; *sich* ~ *über* (*acc.*) cover.

er'suchen 1. *v/t.* (*no* -ge-, *h*) request; 2. ₂ *n* (-s/-) request.

er|'tappen *v/t.* (*no* -ge-, *h*) catch, surprise; *s.* frisch; ~'tönen *v/i.* (*no* -ge-, *sein*) (re)sound.

Ertrag [er'traːk] *m* (-[e]s/-̈e) produce, yield; proceeds *pl.*; returns *pl.*; ⚔ output; ₂en [~gən] *v/t.* (*irr. tragen, no* -ge-, *h*) bear, endure; suffer; stand.

er'träglich *adj.* [er'trɛːkliç] tolerable.

er|'tränken *v/t.* (*no* -ge-, *h*) drown; ~'trinken *v/i.* (*irr. trinken, no* -ge-, *sein*) be drowned, drown; ~'übrigen [er'yːbrigən] *v/t.* (*no* -ge-, *h*) save; spare (*time*); *sich* ~ be unnecessary; ~'wachen *v/i.* (*no* -ge-, *sein*) awake, wake up.

er'wachsen 1. *v/i.* (*irr. wachsen, no* -ge-, *sein*) arise (*aus* from); 2. *adj.* grown-up, adult; ₂e *m, f* (-n/-n) grown-up, adult.

er'wäg|en *v/t.* (*irr. wägen, no* -ge-, *h*) consider, think *s.th.* over; ₂ung *f* (-/-en) consideration.

er'wählen *v/t.* (*no* -ge-, *h*) choose, elect.

er'wähn|en *v/t.* (*no* -ge-, *h*) mention; ₂ung *f* (-/-en) mention.

er'wärmen *v/t.* (*no* -ge-, *h*) warm, heat; *sich* ~ warm (up).

er'wart|en *v/t.* (*no* -ge-, *h*) await, wait for; *fig.* expect; ₂ung *f* expectation.

er|'wecken *v/t.* (*no* -ge-, *h*) wake, rouse; *fig.* awake; cause (*fear*); arouse (*suspicion*); ~'wehren *v/refl.* (*gen.*) (*no* -ge-, *h*) keep *or* ward off; ~'weichen *v/t.* (*no* -ge-, *h*) soften; *fig.* move; ~'weisen *v/t.* (*irr. weisen, no* -ge-, *h*) prove; show (*respect*); render (*service*); do, pay (*honour*); do (*favour*).

er'weiter|n *v/t. and v/refl.* (*no* -ge-, *h*) expand, enlarge, extend, widen; ₂ung *f* (-/-en) expansion, enlargement, extension.

Erwerb [er'verp] *m* (-[e]s/-e) acquisition; living; earnings *pl.*; business; ₂en [~bən] *v/t.* (*irr. werben, no* -ge-, *h*) acquire; gain; earn.

erwerbs|los *adj.* [er'verpsloːs] unemployed; ~tätig *adj.* (gainfully) employed; ~unfähig *adj.* [er'verps?-] incapable of earning one's living; ₂zweig *m* line of business.

Erwerbung [er'verbuŋ] *f* acquisition.

er'wider|n [er'viːdərn] *v/t.* (*no* -ge-, *h*) return; answer, reply; retort; ₂ung *f* (-/-en) return; answer, reply.

er'wischen *v/t.* (*no* -ge-, *h*) catch, trap, get hold of.

er'wünscht *adj.* desired; desirable; welcome.

er'würgen *v/t.* (*no* -ge-, *h*) strangle, throttle.

Erz ⚔ [eːrts] *n* (-es/-e) ore; *poet.* brass.

er'zähl|en *v/t.* (*no* -ge-, *h*) tell; relate; narrate; **2er** *m*, **2erin** *f* (-/-nen) narrator; writer; **2ung** *f* narration; (short) story, narrative.

'Erz|bischof *eccl. m* archbishop; **'~bistum** *eccl. n* archbishopric; **'~engel** *eccl. m* archangel.

er'zeug|en *v/t.* (*no* -ge-, *h*) beget; produce; make, manufacture; **2er** *m* (-s/-) father (*of child*); ✝ producer; **2nis** *n* produce; production; ⊕ product; **2ung** *f* production.

'Erz|feind *m* arch-enemy; **'~herzog** *m* archduke; **'~herzogin** *f* archduchess; **'~herzogtum** *n* archduchy.

er'zieh|en *v/t.* (*irr.* ziehen, *no* -ge-, *h*) bring up, rear; raise; educate; **2er** *m* (-s/-) educator; teacher, tutor; **2rin** *f* (-/-nen) teacher; governess; **~risch** *adj.* educational, pedagogic (-al).

Er'ziehung *f* (-/⚘ -en) upbringing; breeding; education; **~sanstalt** [er'tsiːuŋs⁹-] *f* reformatory, approved school; **~swesen** *n* (-s/*no pl.*) educational matters *pl.* or system.

er|'zielen *v/t.* (*no* -ge-, *h*) obtain; realize (*price*); achieve (*success*); *sports:* score (*points, goal*); **~'zürnen** *v/t.* (*no* -ge-, *h*) make angry, irritate, enrage; **~'zwingen** *v/t.* (*irr.* zwingen, *no* -ge-, *h*) (en)force; compel; extort (*von* from).

es *pers. pron.* [ɛs] 1. *pers.:* it, he, she; *wo ist das Buch?* — *~ ist auf dem Tisch* where is the book? — it is on the table; *das Mädchen blieb stehen, als ~ seine Mutter sah* the girl stopped when she saw her mother; 2. *impers.:* it; *~ gibt* there is, there are; *~ ist kalt* it is cold; *~ klopft* there is a knock at the door.

Esche ⚘ ['ɛʃə] *f* (-/-n) ash(-tree).

Esel *zo.* ['eːzəl] *m* (-s/-) donkey; *esp. fig.* ass; **~ei** [~'laɪ] *f* (-/-en) stupidity, stupid thing, folly; **'~sbrücke** *f at school:* crib, *Am.* pony; **~sohr** ['eːzəls⁹-] *n* dog's ear (*of book*).

Eskorte [ɛs'kɔrtə] *f* (-/-n) ⚔ escort; ⚓ convoy.

Espe ⚘ ['ɛspə] *f* (-/-n) asp(en).

'eßbar *adj.* eatable, edible.

Esse ['ɛsə] *f* (-/-n) chimney.

essen ['ɛsən] 1. *v/i.* (*irr.*, ge-, *h*) eat; *zu Mittag ~* (have) lunch, dine, have dinner; *zu Abend ~* dine, have dinner; *esp. late at night:* sup, have supper; *auswärts ~* eat or dine out; 2. *v/t.* (*irr.*, ge-, *h*) eat; *et. zu Mittag etc. ~* have s.th. for lunch, *etc.*; 3. 2 *n* (-s/-) eating; food; meal; dish; *midday meal:* lunch, dinner; *evening meal:* dinner; *last meal of the day:* supper; **'2szeit** *f* lunch-time; dinner-time; supper-time.

Essenz [ɛ'sɛnts] *f* (-/-en) essence.

Essig ['ɛsɪç] *m* (-s/-e) vinegar; **'~gurke** *f* pickled cucumber, gherkin.

'Eß|löffel *m* soup-spoon; **'~nische** *f* dining alcove, *Am.* dinette; **'~tisch** *m* dining-table; **'~waren** *f/pl.* eatables *pl.*, victuals *pl.*, food; **'~zimmer** *n* dining-room.

etablieren [eta'bliːrən] *v/t.* (*no* -ge-, *h*) establish, set up.

Etage [e'taːʒə] *f* (-/-n) floor, stor(e)y; **~nwohnung** *f* flat, *Am. a.* apartment.

Etappe [e'tapə] *f* (-/-n) ⚔ base; *fig.* stage, leg.

Etat [e'taː] *m* (-s/-s) budget, *parl. the* Estimates *pl.*; **~sjahr** *n* fiscal year. [*or sg.*)

Ethik ['eːtik] *f* (-/⚘ -en) ethics *pl.*)

Etikett [eti'kɛt] *n* (-[e]s/-e, -s) label, ticket; tag; gummed: *Am. a.* sticker; **~e** *f* (-/-n) etiquette; **2ieren** [~'tiːrən] *v/t.* (*no* -ge-, *h*) label.

etliche *indef. pron.* ['ɛtlɪçə] some, several.

Etui [e'tviː] *n* (-s/-s) case.

etwa *adv.* ['ɛtva] perhaps, by chance; about, *Am. a.* around; **~ig** *adj.* ['~⁹ɪç] possible, eventual.

etwas ['ɛtvas] 1. *indef. pron.* something; anything; 2. *adj.* some; any; 3. *adv.* somewhat; 4. 2 *n* (-/-): *das gewisse ~* that certain something.

euch *pers. pron.* [ɔʏç] you; *~* (*selbst*) yourselves.

euer *poss. pron.* ['ɔʏər] your; *der* (*die, das*) eu(e)re yours.

Eule *orn.* ['ɔʏlə] *f* (-/-n) owl; *~n nach Athen tragen* carry coals to Newcastle.

euresgleichen *pron.* ['ɔʏrəs'glaɪçən] people like you, F the likes of you.

Europä|er [ɔʏro'pɛːər] *m* (-s/-) European; **2isch** *adj.* European.

Euter ['ɔʏtər] *n* (-s/-) udder.

evakuieren [evaku'iːrən] *v/t.* (*no* -ge-, *h*) evacuate.

evangeli|sch *adj.* [evaŋ'geːliʃ] evangelic(al); Protestant; Lutheran; **2um** [~jum] *n* (-s/Evangelien) gospel.

eventuell [evɛntu'ɛl] 1. *adj.* possible; 2. *adv.* possibly, perhaps.

ewig *adj.* ['eːvɪç] eternal; everlasting; perpetual; *auf ~* for ever; **'2keit** *f* (-/-en) eternity; F: *seit e-r ~* for ages.

exakt *adj.* [ɛ'ksakt] exact; **2heit** *f* (-/-en) exactitude, exactness; accuracy.

Exam|en [ɛ'ksaːmən] *n* (-s/-, *Examina*) examination, F exam; **2inieren** [~ami'niːrən] *v/t.* (*no* -ge-, *h*) examine.

Exekutive [ɛksəku'tiːvə] *f* (-/*no pl.*) executive power.

Exempel [ɛ'ksɛmpəl] *n* (-s/-) example, instance.

Exemplar [ɛksɛm'plɑːr] n (-s/-e) specimen; copy (of book).

exerzier|en ✕ [ɛksɛr'tsiːrən] v/i. and v/t. (no -ge-, h) drill; **2platz** ✕ m drill-ground, parade-ground.

Exil [ɛ'ksiːl] n (-s/-e) exile.

Existenz [ɛksis'tɛnts] f (-/-en) existence; living, livelihood; **~minimum** n subsistence minimum.

exis|tieren v/i. (no -ge-, h) exist; subsist.

exotisch adj. [ɛ'ksoːtiʃ] exotic.

exped|ieren [ɛkspe'diːrən] v/t. (no -ge-, h) dispatch; **2ition** [ʌi'tsjoːn] f (-/-en) dispatch, forwarding; expedition; † dispatch or forwarding office.

Experiment [ɛksperi'mɛnt] n (-[e]s/-e) experiment; **2ieren** [ʌ'tiːrən] v/i. (no -ge-, h) experiment.

explo|dieren [ɛksplo'diːrən] v/i. (no -ge-, sein) explode, burst; **2sion** [ʌ'zjoːn] f (-/-en) explosion; **~siv** adj. [ʌ'ziːf] explosive.

Export [ɛks'pɔrt] m (-[e]s/-e) export(ation); **2ieren** [ʌ'tiːrən] v/t. (no -ge-, h) export.

extra adj. ['ɛkstra] extra; special; **2blatt** n extra edition (of newspaper), Am. extra.

Extrakt [ɛks'trakt] m (-[e]s/-e) extract.

Extrem [ɛks'treːm] 1. n (-s/-e) extreme; 2. 2 adj. extreme.

Exzellenz [ɛkstsɛ'lɛnts] f (-/-en) Excellency.

exzentrisch adj. [ɛks'tsɛntriʃ] eccentric.

Exzeß [ɛks'tsɛs] m (Exzesses/Exzesse) excess.

F

Fabel ['fɑːbəl] f (-/-n) fable (a. fig.); plot (of story, book, etc.); **2haft** adj. fabulous; marvellous; **2n** v/i. (ge-, h) tell (tall) stories.

Fabrik [fa'briːk] f (-/-en) factory, works sg., pl., mill; **~ant** [ʌi'kant] m (-en/-en) factory-owner, mill-owner; manufacturer; **~arbeit** f factory work; s. Fabrikware; **~arbeiter** m factory worker or hand; **~at** [ʌi'kaːt] n (-[e]s/-e) make; product; **~ationsfehler** [ʌa'tsjoːns-] m flaw; **~besitzer** m factory-owner; **~marke** f trade mark; **~stadt** f factory or industrial town; **~ware** f manufactured article; **~zeichen** n s. Fabrikmarke.

Fach [fax] n (-[e]s/ᵘer) section, compartment, shelf (of bookcase, cupboard, etc.); pigeon-hole (in desk); drawer; fig. subject; s. Fachgebiet; **2arbeiter** m skilled worker; **~arzt** m specialist (für in); **~ausbildung** f professional training; **~ausdruck** m technical term.

fächeln ['fɛçəln] v/t. (ge-, h) fan s.o.

Fächer ['fɛçər] m (-s/-) fan; **2förmig** adj. ['ʌfœrmiç] fan-shaped.

Fach|gebiet n branch, field, province; **~kenntnisse** f/pl. specialized knowledge; **~kreis** m: in ~en among experts; **2kundig** adj. competent, expert; **~literatur** f specialized literature; **~mann** m expert; **2männisch** adj. ['ʌmɛniʃ] expert; **~schule** f technical school; **~werk** 🏛 n framework.

Fackel ['fakəl] f (-/-n) torch; **2n** F v/i. (ge-, h) hesitate, F shilly-shally; **~zug** m torchlight procession.

fad adj. ['faːt], **~e** adj. ['faːdə] food:

insipid, tasteless; stale; p. dull, boring.

Faden ['faːdən] m (-s/ᵘ) thread (a. fig.); fig.: an e-m ~ hängen hang by a thread; **~nudeln** f/pl. vermicelli pl.; **2scheinig** adj. ['ʌʃainiç] threadbare; excuse, etc.: flimsy, thin.

fähig adj. ['fɛːiç] capable (zu inf. of ger.; gen. of); able (to inf.); **2keit** f (-/-en) (cap)ability; talent, faculty.

fahl adj. [faːl] pale, pallid; colour: faded; complexion: leaden, livid.

fahnd|en ['faːndən] v/i. (ge-, h): nach j-m ~ search for s.o.; **2ung** f (-/-en) search.

Fahne ['faːnə] f (-/-n) flag; standard; banner; 𝄞, ✕, fig. colo(u)rs pl.; typ. galley-proof.

Fahnen|eid m oath of allegiance; **~flucht** f desertion; **2flüchtig** adj.: ~ werden desert (the colo[u]rs); **~stange** f flagstaff, Am. a. flagpole.

Fahr|bahn f, **~damm** m roadway.

Fähre ['fɛːrə] f (-/-n) ferry(-boat).

fahren ['faːrən] (irr., ge-) 1. v/i. (sein) driver, vehicle, etc.: drive, go, travel; cyclist: ride, cycle; ⚓ sail; mot. motor; mit der Eisenbahn ~ go by train or rail; spazieren~ go for or take a drive; mit der Hand ~ über (acc.) pass one's hand over; ~ lassen let go or slip; gut (schlecht) ~ bei do or fare well (badly) at or with; er ist gut dabei gefahren he did very well out of it; 2. v/t. (h) carry, convey; drive (car, train, etc.); ride (bicycle, etc.).

Fahrer m (-s/-) driver; **~flucht** f (-/no pl.) hit-and-run offence, Am. hit-and-run offense.

'Fahr|gast *m* passenger; *in taxi:* fare; **~geld** *n* fare; **~gelegenheit** *f* transport facilities *pl.*; **~gestell** *n* *mot.* chassis; ⊕ undercarriage, landing gear; **~karte** *f* ticket; **~kartenschalter** *m* booking-office, *Am.* ticket office; **'2lässig** *adj.* careless, negligent; **~lässigkeit** *f* (-/~-en) carelessness, negligence; **~lehrer** *mot.* *m* driving instructor; **~plan** *m* timetable, *Am.* a. schedule; **'2planmäßig 1.** *adj.* regular, *Am.* scheduled; **2.** *adv.* on time, *Am.* a. on schedule; **~preis** *m* fare; **~rad** *n* bicycle, F bike; **~schein** *m* ticket; **~schule** *mot.* *f* driving school, school of motoring; **~stuhl** *m* lift, *Am.* elevator; **~stuhlführer** *m* lift-boy, lift-man, *Am.* elevator operator; **~stunde** *mot.* *f* driving lesson.

Fahrt [fɑ:rt] *f* (-/-en) ride, drive; journey, voyage, passage; trip; *~ ins Blaue* mystery tour; *in voller ~* (at) full speed.

Fährte ['fɛːrtə] *f* (-/-n) track (a. *fig.*); *auf der falschen ~ sein* be on the wrong track.

'Fahr|vorschrift *f* rule of the road; **~wasser** *n* ⊕ navigable water; *fig.* track; **~weg** *m* roadway; **~zeug** *n* vehicle; ⊕ vessel.

Fakt|or ['faktɔr] *m* (-s/-en) factor; **~otum** [~'to:tum] *n* (-s/-s, Faktoten) factotum; **~ur** † [~'tu:r] *f* (-/-en), **~ura** † [~'tu:ra] *f* (-/Fakturen) invoice.

Fakultät *univ.* [fakul'tɛːt] *f* (-/-en) faculty.

Falke *orn.* ['falkə] *m* (-n/-n) hawk, falcon.

Fall [fal] *m* (-[e]s/⸚e) fall (*of body, stronghold, city, etc.*); *gr.*, *ʦ*, ⸚ case; *gesetzt den ~* suppose; *auf alle Fälle* at all events; *auf jeden ~* in any case, at any rate; *auf keinen ~* on no account, in no case.

Falle ['falə] *f* (-/-n) trap (a. *fig.*); pitfall (a. *fig.*); *e-e ~ stellen* set a trap (*j-m* for s.o.).

fallen ['falən] **1.** *v/i.* (*irr.*, ge-, sein) fall, drop; ⚔ be killed in action; *shot:* be heard; *flood water:* subside; *auf j-n ~* suspicion, *etc.*: fall on s.o.; *~ lassen* drop (*plate, etc.*); **2.** *2 n* (-s/*no pl.*) fall(ing).

fällen ['fɛlən] *v/t.* (ge-, h) fell, cut down (*tree*); ⚔ lower (*bayonet*); *ʦ* pass (*judgement*), give (*decision*).

'fallenlassen *v/t.* (*irr. lassen*, sep., *no* -ge-, h) drop (*plan, claim, etc.*).

fällig *adj.* ['fɛliç] due; payable; **'2keit** *f* (-/⸚-en) maturity; **'2keitstermin** *m* date of maturity.

'Fall|obst *n* windfall; **~reep** ⊕ ['~re:p] *n* (-[e]s/-e) gangway.

falls *cj.* [fals] if; in the event of *ger.*; in case.

'Fall|schirm *m* parachute; **'~**

schirmspringer *m* parachutist; **'~strick** *m* snare; **'~tür** *f* trap door.

falsch [falʃ] **1.** *adj.* false; wrong; *bank-note, etc.:* counterfeit; *money:* base; *bill of exchange, etc.* forged; *p.* deceitful; **2.** *adv.:* ~ *gehen watch:* go wrong; ~ *verbunden!* *teleph.* sorry, wrong number.

fälsch|en ['fɛlʃən] *v/t.* (ge-, h) falsify; forge, fake (*document, etc.*); counterfeit (*bank-note, coin, etc.*); fake (*calculations, etc.*); tamper with (*financial account*); adulterate (*food, wine*); **'2er** *m* (-s/-) forger, faker; adulterator.

'Falsch|geld *n* counterfeit *or* bad *or* base money; **~heit** *f* (-/-en) falseness, falsity; duplicity, deceitfulness; **~meldung** *f* false report; **~münzer** *m* (-s/-) coiner; **~münzerwerkstatt** *f* coiner's den; **'2spielen** *v/i.* (*sep.*, -ge-, h) cheat (at cards); **'2spieler** *m* cardsharper.

'Fälschung *f* (-/-en) forgery; falsification; fake; adulteration.

Falt|boot ['falt-] *n* folding canoe, *Am.* foldboat, faltboat; **~e** ['~ə] *f* (-/-n) fold; pleat (*in skirt, etc.*); crease (*in trousers*); wrinkle (*on face*); **'2en** *v/t.* (ge-, h) fold; clasp *or* join (*one's hands*); **'2ig** *adj.* folded; pleated; wrinkled.

Falz [falts] *m* (-es/-e) fold; rabbet (*for woodworking, etc.*); bookbinding: guard; **'2en** *v/t.* (ge-, h) fold; rabbet.

familiär *adj.* [fami'lɛ:r] familiar; informal.

Familie [fa'mi:ljə] *f* (-/-n) family (a. *zo.*, ♀).

Fa'milien|angelegenheit *f* family affair; **~anschluß** *m:* ~ *haben* live as one of the family; **~nachrichten** *f/pl. in newspaper:* birth, marriage and death announcements *pl.*; **~name** *m* family name, surname, *Am.* a. last name; **~stand** *m* marital status.

Fanati|ker [fa'nɑ:tikər] *m* (-s/-) fanatic; **2sch** *adj.* fanatic(al).

Fanatismus [fana'tismus] *m* (-/*no pl.*) fanaticism.

fand [fant] *pret. of* finden.

Fanfare [fan'fɑ:rə] *f* (-/-n) fanfare, flourish (of trumpets).

Fang [faŋ] *m* (-[e]s/⸚e) capture, catch(ing); *hunt.* bag; **'2en** *v/t.* (*irr.* ge-, h) catch (*animal, ball, thief, etc.*); **~zahn** *m* fang (*of dog, wolf, etc.*); tusk (*of boar*).

Farb|band ['farp-] *n* (typewriter) ribbon; **~e** ['~bə] *f* (-/-n) colo(u)r; paint; dye; complexion; *cards:* suit; **2echt** *adj.* ['farp?-] colo(u)r-fast.

färben ['fɛrbən] *v/t.* (ge-, h) colo-o(u)r (*glass, food, etc.*); dye (*material, hair, Easter eggs, etc.*); tint (*hair,* *paper, glass*); stain (*wood, fabrics, glass, etc.*); *sich ~* take on *or* assume a colo(u)r; *sich rot ~* turn *or* go red.

'farben|blind *adj.* colo(u)r-blind; **'2druck** *m* (-[e]s/-e) colo(u)r print; **'~prächtig** *adj.* splendidly col-o(u)rful.

Färber ['fɛrbər] *m* (-s/-) dyer.

Farb|fernsehen ['farp-] *n* colo(u)r television; **'~film** *m* colo(u)r film; **2ig** *adj.* ['~biç] colo(u)red; *glass:* tinted, stained; *fig.* colo(u)rful; **2los** *adj.* ['~loːs] colo(u)rless; *fig.:* **photographie** *f* colo(u)r photography; **'~stift** *m* colo(u)red pencil; **'~stoff** *m* colo(u)ring matter; **'~ton** *m* tone; shade, tint.

Färbung ['fɛrbʊŋ] *f* (-/-en) colo(u)r-ing (*a. fig.*); shade (*a. fig.*).

Farnkraut ♦ ['farnkraut] *n* fern.

Fasan *orn.* [fa'zaːn] *m* (-[e]s/-e[n]) pheasant.

Fasching ['faʃiŋ] *m* (-s/-e, -s) carni-val.

Fasel|ei [faːzə'laɪ] *f* (-/-en) driv-elling, waffling; twaddle; **'2n** *v/i.* (ge-, h) blather; F waffle.

Faser ['faːzər] *f* (-/-n) anat., ♀, *fig.* fib|re, *Am.* -er; *cotton, wool, etc.:* staple; **'2ig** *adj.* fibrous; **'2n** *v/i.* (ge-, h) *wool:* shed fine hairs.

Faß [fas] *n* (*Fasses/Fässer*) cask, barrel; tub; vat; **'~bier** *n* draught beer.

Fassade ⚠ [fa'saːdə] *f* (-/-n) façade, front (*a. fig.*); **~nkletterer** *m* (-s/-) cat burglar.

fassen ['fasən] (ge-, h) **1.** *v/t.* seize, take hold of; catch, apprehend (*criminal*); hold; *s.* einfassen; *fig.* grasp, understand, believe; pluck up (*courage*); form (*plan*); make (*decision*); *sich ~* compose o.s.; *sich kurz ~* be brief; **2.** *v/i.:* ~ *nach* reach for. [ceivable.]

'faßlich *adj.* comprehensible, con-]

'Fassung *f* (-/-en) setting (*of jewels*); ⚡ socket; *fig.:* composure; draft (-ing); wording, version; *die ~ verlieren* lose one's self-control; *aus der ~ bringen* disconcert; **'~s-kraft** *f* (powers of) comprehension, mental capacity; **'~svermögen** *n* (holding) capacity; *fig. s. Fassungs-kraft.*

fast *adv.* [fast] almost, nearly; ~ *nichts* next to nothing; ~ *nie* hardly ever.

fasten ['fastən] *v/i.* (ge-, h) fast; abstain from food and drink; **'2zeit** *f* Lent.

'Fast|nacht *f* (-/*no pl.*) Shrovetide; carnival; **'~tag** *m* fast-day.

fatal *adj.* [fa'taːl] *situation, etc.:* awkward; *business, etc.:* unfortu-nate; *mistake, etc.:* fatal.

fauchen ['fauxən] *v/i.* (ge-, h) *cat, etc.:* spit; F *p.* spit (*with anger*); *locomotive, etc.:* hiss.

faul *adj.* [faul] *fruit, etc.:* rotten, bad; *fish, meat:* putrid, bad; *fig.* lazy, indolent, idle; fishy; ~*e Aus-rede* lame excuse; **'~en** *v/i.* (ge-, h) rot, go bad, putrefy.

faulenze|n ['faulɛntsən] *v/i.* (ge-, h) idle; laze, loaf; **'2r** *m* (-s/-) idler, sluggard, F lazy-bones.

'Faul|heit *f* (-/*no pl.*) idleness, laziness; **'2ig** *adj.* putrid.

Fäulnis ['fɔʏlnis] *f* (-/*no pl.*) rotten-ness; putrefaction; decay.

'Faul|pelz *m s. Faulenzer;* **'~tier** *n zo.* sloth (*a. fig.*).

Faust [faust] *f* (-/*Fäuste*) fist; *auf eigene ~ on one's own initiative;* **'~hand-schuh** *m* mitt(en); **'~schlag** *m* blow with the fist, punch, *Am.* F *a.* slug.

Favorit [favo'riːt] *m* (-en/-en) favo(u)rite.

Faxe ['faksə] *f* (-/-n): ~*n machen* (play the fool; ~*n schneiden* pull *or* make faces.

Fazit ['faːtsit] *n* (-s/-e, -s) result, upshot; total; *das ~ ziehen* sum *or* total up.

Februar ['feːbruaːr] *m* (-[s]/-e) February.

fecht|en ['fɛçtən] *v/i.* (*irr.*, ge-, h) fight; *fenc.* fence; **'2er** *m* (-s/-) fencer.

Feder ['feːdər] *f* (-/-n) feather; (*ornamental*) plume; pen; ⊕ spring; **'~bett** *n* feather bed; **'~busch** *m* tuft of feathers; plume; **'~gewicht** *n boxing, etc.:* featherweight; **'~hal-ter** *m* (-s/-) penholder; **'~kiel** *m* quill; **'~kraft** *f* elasticity, resilience; **'~krieg** *m* paper war; literary con-troversy; **'2leicht** *adj.* (as) light as a feather; **'~lesen** *n* (-s/*no pl.*): *nicht viel ~s machen mit* make short work of; **'~messer** *n* penknife; **'2n** *v/i.* (ge-, h) be elastic; **'2nd** *adj.* springy, elastic; **'~strich** *m* stroke of the pen; **'~vieh** *n* poultry; **'~zeichnung** *f* pen-and-ink draw-ing.

Fee [feː] *f* (-/-n) fairy.

Fegefeuer ['feːgə-] *n* purgatory.

fegen ['feːgən] *v/t.* (ge-, h) sweep; clean.

Fehde ['feːdə] *f* (-/-n) feud; private war; *in ~ liegen* be at feud; F be at daggers drawn.

Fehl [feːl] *m: ohne ~* without fault *or* blemish; **'~betrag** *m* deficit, deficiency.

fehlen ['feːlən] *v/i.* (ge-, h) be absent; be missing *or* lacking; do wrong; *es fehlt ihm an* (*dat.*) he lacks; *was fehlt Ihnen?* what is the matter with you?; *weit gefehlt!* far off the mark!

Fehler ['feːlər] *m* (-s/-) mistake, error, F slip; fault; ⊕ defect, flaw; **'2frei** *adj.*, **'2los** *adj.* faultless, perfect; ⊕ flawless; **'2haft** *adj.* faulty, defective; incorrect.

'Fehl|geburt *f* miscarriage, abortion; '2gehen v/i. (irr. gehen, sep., -ge-, sein) go wrong; ~griff fig. m mistake, blunder; ~schlag fig. m failure; 2schlagen (irr. schlagen, sep., -ge-, sein) fail, miscarry; ~schuß m miss; 2treten v/i. (irr. treten, sep., -ge-, sein) make a false step; ~tritt m false step; slip; fig. slip, fault; ~urteil ง๒ n error of judg(e)ment; '~zündung mot. f misfire, backfire.

Feier ['faɪər] f (-/-n) ceremony; celebration; festival; festivity; '~abend m finishing or closing time; ~ machen finish, F knock off; '2lich adj. promise, oath, etc.: solemn; act: ceremonial; ~lichkeit f (-/-en) solemnity; ceremony; '2n (ge-, h) 1. v/t. hold (celebration); celebrate, observe (feast, etc.); 2. v/i. celebrate; rest (from work), make holiday; '~tag m holiday; festive day.

feig adj. [faɪk] cowardly.

feige¹ adj. ['faɪgə] cowardly.

Feige² [~] f (-/-n) fig; ~nbaum ♀ m fig-tree; ~nblatt n fig-leaf.

Feig|heit ['faɪkhaɪt] f (-/no pl.) cowardice, cowardliness; ~ling ['~klɪŋ] m (-s/-e) coward.

feil adj. [faɪl] for sale, to be sold; fig. venal; ~bieten v/t. (irr. bieten, sep., -ge-, h) offer for sale.

Feile ['faɪlə] f (-/-n) file; '2n (ge-, h) 1. v/t. file (a. fig.); fig. polish; 2. v/i.: ~ an (dat.) file (at); fig. polish (up).

feilschen ['faɪlʃən] v/i. (ge-, h) bargain (um for), haggle (for, about), Am. a. dicker (about).

fein adj. [faɪn] fine; material, etc.: high-grade; wine, etc.: choice; fabric, etc.: delicate, dainty; manners: polished; p. polite; distinction: subtle.

Feind [faɪnt] m (-[e]s/-e) enemy (a. ✕); '2lich adj. hostile, inimical; ~schaft f (-/-en) enmity; animosity, hostility; '2selig adj. hostile (gegen to); '~seligkeit f (-/-en) hostility; malevolence.

'fein|fühlend adj., '~fühlig adj. sensitive; '2gefühl n sensitiveness; delicacy; '2gehalt m (monetary) standard; '2heit f (-/-en) fineness; delicacy; daintiness; politeness; elegance; '2kost f high-class groceries pl., Am. delicatessen; '2mechanik f precision mechanics; '2schmecker m (-s/-) gourmet, epicure; '~sinnig adj. subtle.

feist adj. [faɪst] fat, stout.

Feld [fɛlt] n (-[e]s/-er) field (a. ✕, ♟, sports); ground, soil; plain; chess: square; ⚡, ⊕ panel, compartment; ins ~ ziehen take the field; '~arbeit f agricultural work; '~bett n camp-bed; '~blume f wild flower; '~dienst ✕ m field service; '~flasche f water-bottle;

'~frucht f fruit of the field; '~geschrei n war-cry, battle-cry; '~herr m general; ~kessel m camp-kettle; '~lazarett ✕ n field-hospital; '~lerche orn. f skylark; '~marschall m Field Marshal; '2marschmäßig ✕ adj. in full marching order; ~maus zo. f field-mouse; '~messer m (land) surveyor; '~post ✕ f army postal service; '~schlacht ✕ f battle; '~stecher m (-s/-) (ein a pair of) field-glasses pl.; '~stuhl m camp-stool; ~webel ['~ve:bəl] m (-s/-) sergeant; '~weg m (field) path; ~zeichen ✕ n standard; '~zug m ✕ campaign (a. fig.), (military) expedition; Am. fig. a. drive.

Felge ['fɛlgə] f (-/-n) felloe (of cart-wheel); rim (of car wheel, etc.).

Fell [fɛl] n (-[e]s/-e) skin, pelt, fur (of dead animal); coat (of cat, etc.); fleece (of sheep).

Fels [fɛls] m (-en/-en), ~en ['~zən] m (-s/-) rock; ~block ['fɛls-] m rock; boulder; 2ig adj. ['~zɪç] rocky.

Fenchel ♀ ['fɛnçəl] m (-s/no pl.) fennel.

Fenster ['fɛnstər] n (-s/-) window; '~brett n window-sill; ~flügel m casement (of casement window); sash (of sash window); '~kreuz n cross-bar(s pl.); '~laden m shutter; '~rahmen m window-frame; '~riegel m window-fastener; '~scheibe f (window-)pane; '~sims m, n window-sill.

Ferien ['fe:rjən] pl. holiday(s pl.), esp. Am. vacation; leave, Am. a. furlough; parl. recess; ง๒ vacation, recess; '~kolonie f children's holiday camp.

Ferkel ['fɛrkəl] n (-s/-) young pig; contp. p. pig.

fern [fɛrn] 1. adj. far (off), distant; remote; 2. adv. far (away); von ~ from a distance.

'Fernamt teleph. n trunk exchange, Am. long-distance exchange.

'fernbleiben 1. v/i. (irr. bleiben, sep., -ge-, sein) remain or stay away (dat. from); 2. 2 n (-s/no pl.) absence (from school, etc.); absenteeism (from work).

Fern|e ['fɛrnə] f (-/-n) distance; remoteness; aus der ~ from or at a distance; '2er 1. adj. farther; fig.: further; future; 2. adv. further (-more), in addition, also; .. liefen ... also ran ...; '~flug ✕ m long-distance flight; '2gelenkt adj. ['~gə-lɛŋkt] missile: guided; aircraft, etc.: remote-control(l)ed; ~gespräch teleph. n trunk call, Am. long-distance call; '2gesteuert adj. s. ferngelenkt; ~glas n binoculars pl.; '2halten v/t. and v/refl. (irr. halten, sep., -ge-, h) keep away (von from); '~heizung f district heating; '~laster F *mot. m* long-distance lorry, *Am.* long haul truck; '⸌lenkung *f* (-/-en) remote control; '⸌liegen *v/i.* (*irr. liegen, sep., -ge-, h*): es liegt mir fern zu *inf.* I am far from *ger.*; '⸌rohr *n* telescope; ⸌schreiber *m* teleprinter, *Am.* teletypewriter; ⸌sehen 1. *n* (-s/no *pl.*) television; 2. 2 *v/i.* (*irr. sehen, sep., -ge-, h*) watch television; '⸌seher *m* television set; *p.* television viewer, televiewer; ⸌sehsendung *f* television broadcast, telecast; '⸌sicht *f* visual range.

'Fernsprech|amt *n* telephone exchange, *Am. a.* central; '⸌anschluß *m* telephone connection; ⸌er *m* telephone; ⸌leitung *f* telephone line; '⸌zelle *f* telephone box.

'fern|stehen *v/i.* (*irr. stehen, sep., -ge-, h*) have no real (point of) contact (*dat.* with); 2steuerung *f s.* Fernlenkung; 2unterricht *m* correspondence course *or* tuition; '2verkehr *m* long-distance traffic.

Ferse ['fɛrzə] *f* (-/-n) heel.

fertig *adj.* ['fɛrtiç] ready, *article, etc.*: finished; *clothing*: ready-made; mit et. ⸌ werden get s.th. finished; mit et. ⸌ sein have finished s.th.; '⸌bringen *v/t.* (*irr. bringen, sep., -ge-, h*) bring about; manage; '2keit *f* (-/-en) dexterity; skill; fluency (*in the spoken language*); '⸌machen *v/t.* (*sep., -ge-, h*) finish, complete; get *s.th.* ready; *fig.* finish, settle *s.o.'s* hash; *sich* ⸌ get ready; '2stellung *f* completion; '2waren *f/pl.* finished goods *pl. or* products *pl.*

fesch F *adj.* [fɛʃ] hat, dress. *etc.*: smart, stylish, chic; dashing.

Fessel ['fɛsəl] *f* (-/-n) chain, fetter, shackle; *vet.* fetlock; *fig.* bond, fetter, tie; '⸌ballon *m* captive balloon; '2n *v/t.* (*ge-, h*) chain, fetter, shackle; *j-n* ⸌ hold *or* arrest s.o.'s attention; fascinate s.o.

fest [fɛst] 1. *adj.* firm; solid; fixed; fast; *principle* firm, strong; *sleep*: sound; *fabric* close; 2. 2 *n* (-es/-e) festival, celebration; holiday, *eccl.* feast; '⸌binden *v/t.* (*irr. binden, sep., -ge-, h*) fasten, tie (*an dat.* to); 2essen *n* banquet, feast; '⸌fahren *v/refl.* (*irr. fahren, sep., -ge-, h*) get stuck; *fig.* reach a deadlock; 2halle *f* (festival) hall; '⸌halten (*irr. halten, sep., -ge-, h*) 1. *v/i.* hold fast *or* tight; ⸌ *an* (*dat.*) adhere *or* keep to; 2. *v/t.* hold on to; hold tight; *sich* ⸌ *an* (*dat.*) hold on to; '⸌igen ['⸌iɡən] *v/t.* (*ge-, h*) consolidate (*one's position, etc.*); strengthen (*friendship, etc.*); stabilize (*currency*); 2igkeit ['⸌ç-] *f* (-/no *pl.*) firmness; solidity; '2land *n* mainland, continent; '⸌legen *v/t.* (*sep., -ge-, h*) fix, set; *sich auf et.* ⸌

commit o.s. to s.th.; ⸌lich *adj.* meal, day, *etc.*: festive; *reception, etc.*: ceremonial; 2lichkeit *f* (-/-en) festivity; festive character; '⸌machen (*sep., -ge-, h*) 1. *v/t.* fix, fasten, attach (*an dat.* to), ⬥ moor; 2. ⬥ *v/i.* moor; put ashore; 2mahl *n* banquet, feast; ⸌nahme ['⸌na:mə] *f* (-/-n) arrest; ⸌nehmen *v/t.* (*irr. nehmen, sep., -ge-, h*) arrest, take into custody; 2rede *f* speech of the day; '⸌setzen *v/t* *sep., -ge-, h*) fix, set; *sich* ⸌ *dust, etc* become ingrained; *p.* settle (down), 2spiel *n* festival; '⸌stehen *v/i.* (*irr stehen, sep., -ge-, h*) stand firm; *fact*: be certain; '⸌stehend *adj.* fixed, stationary; *fact* established; ⸌stellen *v/t.* (*sep., -ge-, h*) establish (*fact, identity, etc.*); ascertain, find out (*fact, s.o.'s whereabouts, etc.*); state; see, perceive (*fact, etc.*); '2stellung *f* establishment; ascertainment; statement; 2tag *m* festive day; festival, holiday; *eccl.* feast; '2ung ⚔ *f* (-/-en) fortress; '2zug *m* festive procession.

fett [fɛt] 1. *adj.* fat; fleshy; *voice*: oily; *land, etc.*: rich; 2. 2 *n* (-[e]s/-e) fat; grease (*a.* ⊕); 2druck *typ. m* bold type; '2fleck *m* grease-spot; '⸌ig *adj.* hair, skin, *etc.* greasy, oily; *fingers, etc.*: greasy; *substance*: fatty.

Fetzen ['fɛtsən] *m* (-s/-) shred; rag, *Am. a.* frazzle; scrap (*of paper*); *in* ⸌ in rags.

feucht *adj.* [fɔyçt] *climate, air, etc.*: damp, moist; *air, zone, etc.* humid; '2igkeit *f* (-/no *pl.*) moisture (*of substance*); dampness (*of place, etc.*); humidity (*of atmosphere, etc.*).

Feuer ['fɔyɛr] *n* (-s/-) fire; light; *fig.* ardo(u)r; ⸌ *fangen* catch fire; *fig.* fall for (*girl*); ⸌alarm *m* fire alarm; '2beständig *adj* fire-proof, fire-resistant; '⸌bestattung *f* cremation; '⸌eifer *m* ardo(u)r; 2fest *adj. s.* feuerbeständig; 2gefährlich *adj.* inflammable; ⸌haken *m* poker; '⸌löscher *m* (-s/-) fire extinguisher; '⸌melder *m* (-s/-) fire-alarm; '2n (*ge-, h*) 1. ⚔ *v/i.* shoot, fire (*auf acc.* at, on); 2. *v/t.* hurl; ⸌probe *fig. f* crucial test; '2rot *adj.* fiery red), (as) red as fire; ⸌sbrunst *f* conflagration; '⸌schiff ⬥ *n* lightship; ⸌schutz *m* fire prevention; ⚔ covering fire; '⸌sgefahr *f* danger *or* risk of fire; 2speiend *adj.*: ⸌er *Berg* volcano; '⸌spritze *f* fire engine; ⸌stein *m* flint; '⸌versicherung *f* fire insurance (*company*); '⸌wache *f* fire station, *Am. a.* firehouse; ⸌wehr *f* fire-brigade, *Am. a.* fire department; '⸌wehrmann *m* fireman; '⸌werk *n* (display of) fireworks *pl.*; '⸌werkskörper *m* firework; '⸌

zange f (e-e a pair of) firetongs pl.; '~zeug n lighter.

feurig adj. ['fɔʏriç] fiery (a. fig.); fig. ardent.

Fiasko [fi'asko] n (-s/-s) (complete) failure, fiasco; sl. flop.

Fibel ['fi:bəl] f (-/-n) spelling-book, primer.

Fichte ♣ ['fiçtə] f (-/-n) spruce; '~nnadel f pine-needle.

fidel adj. [fi'de:l] cheerful, merry, jolly, Am. F a. chipper.

Fieber ['fi:bər] n (-s/-) temperature, fever; ~ haben have or run a temperature; '~anfall m attack or bout of fever; '2haft adj. feverish (a. fig.); febrile; '2krank adj. ill with fever; '~mittel n febrifuge; '2n v/i. (ge-, h) have or run a temperature; ~ nach crave or long for; '~schauer m chill, shivers pl.; '~tabelle f temperature-chart; '~thermometer n clinical thermometer.

fiel [fi:l] pret. of fallen.

Figur [fi'gu:r] f (-/-en) figure; chess: chessman, piece.

figürlich adj. [fi'gy:rliç] meaning, etc.: figurative.

Filet [fi'le:] n (-s/-s) fillet (of beef, pork, etc.).

Filiale [fi'ja:lə] f (-/-n) branch.

Filigran(arbeit f) [fili'gra:n(?-)] n (-s/-e) filigree.

Film [film] m (-[e]s/-e) film, thin coating (of oil, wax, etc.); phot. film; film, (moving) picture, Am. a. motion picture, F movie; e-n ~ einlegen phot. load a camera; '~atelier n film studio; '~aufnahme f filming, shooting (of a film); film (of sporting event, etc.); '2en (ge-, h) 1. v/t. film, shoot (scene, etc.); 2. v/i. film; make a film; '~gesellschaft f film company, Am. motion-picture company; '~kamera f film camera, Am. motion-picture camera; '~regisseur m film director; '~reklame f screen advertising; '~schauspieler m film or screen actor, Am. F movie actor; '~spule f (film) reel; '~streifen m film strip; '~theater n cinema, Am. motion-picture or F movie theater; '~verleih m (-[e]s/-e) film distributors pl.; '~vorführer m projectionist; '~vorstellung f cinema performance, Am. F movie performance.

Filter ['filtər] (-s/-) 1. m (coffee-, etc.) filter; 2. ⊕ n filter; '2n v/t. (ge-, h) filter (water, air, etc.); filtrate (water, impurities, etc.); strain (liquid); '~zigarette f filter-tipped cigarette.

Filz [filts] m (-es/-e) felt; fig. F skinflint; '2ig adj. felt-like; of felt; fig. F niggardly, stingy; '~laus f crab louse.

Finanz|amt [fi'nants?amt] n (inland) revenue office, office of the Inspector of Taxes; ~en f/pl. finances pl.; 2iell adj. [~'tsjel] financial; 2ieren [~'tsi:rən] v/t. (no -ge-, h) finance (scheme, etc.); sponsor (radio programme, etc.); ~lage f financial position; ~mann m financier; ~minister m minister of finance; Chancellor of the Exchequer, Am. Secretary of the Treasury; ~ministerium n ministry of finance; Exchequer, Am. Treasury Department; ~wesen n (-s/no pl.) finances pl.; financial matters pl.

Findelkind ['fɪndəl-] n foundling.

finden ['fɪndən] (irr., ge-, h) 1. v/t. find; discover, come across; find, think, consider; wie ~ Sie ...? how do you like ...?; sich ~ thing: be found; 2. v/i.: ~ zu find one's way to.

'Finder m (-s/-) finder; '~lohn m finder's reward.

'findig adj. resourceful, ingenious.

Findling ['fɪntlɪŋ] m (-s/-e) foundling; geol. erratic block, boulder.

fing [fɪŋ] pret. of fangen.

Finger ['fɪŋər] m (-s/-) finger; sich die ~ verbrennen burn one's fingers; er rührte keinen ~ he lifted no finger; '~abdruck m fingerprint; '~fertigkeit f manual skill; '~hut m thimble; ♣ foxglove; '2n v/i. (ge-, h): ~ nach fumble for; '~spitze f finger-tip; '~spitzengefühl fig. n sure instinct; '~übung ♪ f finger exercise; '~zeig ['~tsaɪk] m (-[e]s/-e) hint, F pointer.

Fink orn. [fɪŋk] m (-en/-en) finch.

finster adj. ['fɪnstər] night, etc.: dark; shadows, wood, etc.: sombre; night, room, etc.: gloomy, murky; person, nature: sullen; thought, etc.: sinister, sombre, gloomy; '2nis f (-/no pl.) darkness, gloom.

Finte ['fɪntə] f (-/-n) feint; fig. a. ruse, trick.

Firma ✝ ['fɪrma] f (-/Firmen) firm, business, company.

firmen eccl. ['fɪrmən] v/t. (ge-, h) confirm.

'Firmen|inhaber m owner of a firm; '~wert m goodwill.

Firn [fɪrn] m (-[e]s/-e) firn, névé.

First ⌂ [fɪrst] m (-es/-e) ridge; '~ziegel m ridge tile.

Fisch [fɪʃ] m (-es/-e) fish; '~dampfer m trawler; '2en v/t. and v/i. (ge-, h) fish; '~er m (-s/-) fisherman; '~erboot n fishing-boat; '~erdorf n fishing-village; '~erei f (-/-en) fishery; fishing; '~fang m fishing; '~geruch m fishy smell; '~gräte f fish-bone; '~grätenmuster n herring-bone pattern; '~händler m fishmonger, Am. fish dealer; '2ig adj. fishy; '~laich m spawn; '~leim m fish-glue; '~mehl n fish-meal; '~schuppe f scale; '~tran m train-oil; '~vergiftung

ſ f fish-poisoning; '**~zucht** f pisci-culture, fish-hatching; '**~zug** m catch, haul, draught (of fish).

fiskalisch adj. [fis'kɑːliʃ] fiscal, governmental.

Fiskus ['fiskus] m (-/⚓ -se, Fisken) Exchequer, esp. Am. Treasury; government.

Fistel ⚕ ['fistəl] f (-/-n) fistual; '**~stimme** ſ f falsetto.

Fittich ['fitiç] m (-[e]s/-e) poet. wing; j-n unter s-e ~e nehmen take s.o. under one's wing.

fix adj. [fiks] salary, price, etc.: fixed; quick clever, smart; e-e ~e Idee an obsession; ein ~er Junge a smart fellow; **Qierbad** phot. [fi-'ksiːrbaːt] n fixing bath; **~ieren** [fi'ksiːrən] v/t. (no -ge-, h) fix (a. phot.); fix one's eyes (auf on), stare at s.o.; '**Qstern** ast. m fixed star; '**Qum** n (-s/Fixa) fixed or basic salary.

flach adj. [flax] roof, etc.: flat; ground, etc.: flat, level, even; water, plate, fig.: shallow; A⃗ plane.

Fläche ['fleçə] ſ (-/-n) surface, A⃗ a. plane; sheet (of water, snow, etc.); geom. area; tract, expanse (of land, etc.); '**~inhalt** A⃗ ['fleçən?-] m (surface) area; '**~nmaß** n square or surface measure.

'**Flach|land** n plain, flat country; '**~rennen** n turf: flat race.

Flachs ⚘ [flaks] m (-es/no pl.) flax.

flackern ['flakərn] v/i. (ge-, h) light, flame, eyes, etc.: flicker, wave; voice: quaver, shake.

Flagge ⚓ ['flagə] ſ (-/-n) flag, colo(u)rs pl.; '**Qn** v/i. (ge-, h) fly or hoist a flag; signal (with flags).

Flak ⚔ [flak] ſ (-/-, -s) anti-aircraft gun; anti-aircraft artillery.

Flamme ['flamə] ſ (-/-n) flame; blaze; '**~nmeer** n sea of flames; '**~nwerfer** ⚔ m (-s/-) flame-thrower.

Flanell [fla'nɛl] m (-s/-e) flannel; **~anzug** m flannel suit; **~hose** f flannel trousers pl., flannels pl.

Flank|e ['flaŋkə] ſ (-/-n) flank (a. A⃗, ⊕, ⚔, mount.); side; **Qieren** [~'kiːrən] v/t. (no -ge-, h) flank.

Flasche ['flaʃə] ſ (-/-n) bottle; flask.

'**Flaschen|bier** n bottled beer; '**~hals** m neck of a bottle; '**~öffner** m (-s/-) bottle-opener; '**~zug** ⊕ m block and tackle.

flatter|haft adj. ['flatərhaft] girl, etc.: fickle, flighty; mind: fickle, volatile; '**~n** v/i. (ge-) 1. (h, sein) bird, butterfly, etc.: flutter (about); bird, bat, etc.: flit (about); 2. (h) hair, flag, garment, etc.: stream, fly; mot. wheel: shimmy, wobble; car steering: judder; 3. (sein): auf den Boden ~ flutter to the ground.

flau adj. [flau] weak, feeble, faint; sentiment, reaction, etc.: lukewarm;

drink: stale; colour: pale, dull; ✝ market, business, etc.: dull, slack; ~e Zeit slack period.

Flaum [flaum] m (-[e]s/no pl.) down, fluff; fuzz.

Flau|s [flaus] m (-es/-e), **~sch** [~ʃ] m (-es/-e) tuft (of wool, etc.); napped coating.

Flausen F ['flauzən] ſ/pl. whims pl., fancies pl., (funny) ideas pl.; F fibs pl.; j-m ~ in den Kopf setzen put funny ideas into s.o.'s head; j-m ~ vormachen tell s.o. fibs.

Flaute ['flautə] ſ (-/-n) ⚓ dead calm; esp. ✝ dullness, slack period.

Flecht|e ['fleçtə] ſ (-/-n) braid, plait (of hair); ⚘ lichen; ⚕ herpes; '**Qen** v/t. (irr. ge-, h) braid, plait (hair, ribbon, etc.); weave (basket, wreath, etc.); wreath (flowers); twist (rope, etc.); '**~werk** n wickerwork.

Fleck [flɛk] m (-[e]s/-e, -en) 1. mark (of dirt, grease, etc.; zo.); spot (of grease, paint, etc.); smear (of oil, blood, etc.); stain (of wine, coffee, etc.); blot (of ink); place, spot; fig. blemish, spot, stain; 2. patch (of material); bootmaking: heel-piece; '**~en** m (-s/-) s. Fleck 1; small (market-)town, townlet; '**~enwasser** n spot or stain remover; '**~fieber** ⚕ n (epidemic) typhus; '**Qig** adj. spotted; stained.

Fledermaus zo. ['fleːdər-] ſ bat.

Flegel ['fleːgəl] m (-s/-) flail; fig. lout, boor; **~ei** [~'lai] ſ (-/-en) rude-ness; loutishness; '**Qhaft** adj. rude-ill-mannered; loutish; '**Qjahre** pl. awkward age.

flehen ['fleːən] 1. v/i. (ge-, h) en-treat, implore (zu j-m s.o.; um et. s.th.); 2. Qn n (-s/no pl.) supplication; imploration, entreaty.

Fleisch [flaiʃ] n (-es/no pl.) flesh; meat; ⚘ pulp; '**~brühe** f meat-broth; beef tea; '**~er** m (-s/-) butcher; **~erei** [~'rai] ſ (-/-en) butcher's (shop), Am. butcher shop; '**~extrakt** m meat extract; '**Qfressend** adj. carnivorous; '**~hackmaschine** f mincing machine, mincer, Am. meat grinder; '**Qig** adj. fleshy; ⚘ pulpy; '**~konserven** ſ/pl. tinned or potted meat, Am. canned meat; '**~kost** f meat (food); '**Qlich** adj. desires, etc.: carnal, fleshly; '**Qlos** adj. meatless; '**~pastete** f meat pie, Am. a. potpie; '**~speise** f meat dish; '**~vergiftung** f meat or ptomaine poisoning; '**~ware** f meat (product); '**~wolf** m s. Fleischhack-maschine.

Fleiß [flais] m (-es/no pl.) diligence, industry; '**Qig** adj. diligent, indus-trious, hard-working.

fletschen ['fletʃən] v/t. (ge-, h): die Zähne ~ animal: bare its teeth; p. bare one's teeth.

Flicken ['flikən] 1. m (-s/-) patch;

2. ♀ v/t. (ge-, h) patch (*dress, tyre, etc.*); repair (*shoe, roof, etc.*); cobble (*shoe*).

'**Flick|schneider** *m* jobbing tailor; '~**schuster** *m* cobbler; '~**werk** *n* (-[e]s/*no pl.*) patchwork.

Flieder ♀ ['fliːdər] *m* (-s/-) lilac.

Fliege ['fliːgə] *f* (-/-n) *zo.* fly; bow-tie.

'**fliegen 1.** v/i. (*irr.*, ge-, sein) fly; go by air; **2.** v/t. (*irr.*, ge-, h) fly, pilot (*aircraft, etc.*); convey (*goods, etc.*) by air; **3.** ♀ *n* (-s/*no pl.*) flying; ✈ *a.* aviation.

Fliegen|fänger ['fliːgənfɛŋər] *m* (-s/-) fly-paper; '~**fenster** *n* fly-screen; '~**gewicht** *n* boxing, *etc.*: flyweight; '~**klappe** *f* fly-flap, *Am.* fly swatter; '~**pilz** ♀ *m* fly agaric.

'**Flieger** *m* (-s/-) flyer; ✈ airman, aviator; pilot; F plane, bomber; *cycling*: sprinter; '~**abwehr** ✕ *f* anti-aircraft defen|ce, *Am.* -se; '~**alarm** ✕ *m* air-raid alarm *or* warn-ing; '~**bombe** ✕ *f* aircraft bomb; '~**offizier** ✕ *m* air-force officer.

flieh|en ['fliːən] (*irr.*, ge-) **1.** v/i. (sein) flee (*vor dat.* from), run away; **2.** v/t. (h) flee, avoid, keep away from; '**2kraft** *phys.* *f* centrifugal force.   [(floor-)tile.\

Fliese ['fliːzə] *f* (-/-n) (wall-)tile;]

Fließ|band ['fliːs-] *n* (-[e]s/*er) con-veyor-belt; assembly-line; '**2en** v/i. (*irr.*, ge-, sein) river, traffic, *etc.*: flow; *tap-water, etc.*: run; '**2end 1.** *adj.* *water*: running; *traffic*: moving; *speech, etc.*: fluent; **2.** *adv.*: ~ **lesen** (*sprechen*) read (speak) fluently; '~**papier** *n* blotting-paper.

Flimmer ['flimər] *m* (-s/-) glimmer, glitter; '**2n** v/i. (ge-, h) glimmer, glitter; *television, film*: flicker; *es flimmert mir vor den Augen* every-thing is dancing in front of my eyes.

flink *adj.* [fliŋk] quick, nimble, brisk.

Flinte ['flintə] *f* (-/-n) shotgun; *die ~ ins Korn werfen* throw up the sponge.

Flirt [flœrt] *m* (-es/-s) flirtation; '**2en** v/i. (ge-, h) flirt (*mit* with).

Flitter ['flitər] *m* (-s/-) tinsel (*a. fig.*), spangle; ~**kram** *m* cheap finery; '~**wochen** *pl.* honeymoon.

flitzen F ['flitsən] v/i. (ge-, sein) whisk, scamper; dash (off, *etc.*).

flocht [flɔxt] *pret. of* flechten.

Flock|e ['flɔkə] *f* (-/-n) flake (*of snow, soap, etc.*); flock (*of wool*); '**2ig** *adj.* fluffy, flaky.

flog [floːk] *pret. of* fliegen.

floh¹ [floː] *pret. of* fliehen.

Floh² *zo.* [~] *m* (-[e]s/*e) flea.

Flor [floːr] *m* (-s/-e) bloom, blos-som; *fig.* bloom, prime; gauze; crêpe, crape.

Florett *fenc.* [flo'rɛt] *n* (-[e]s/-e) foil.

florieren [flo'riːrən] v/i. (*no* -ge-, h)

business, *etc.*: flourish, prosper, thrive.

Floskel ['flɔskəl] *f* (-/-n) flourish; empty phrase.

floß¹ [flɔs] *pret. of* fließen.

Floß² [floːs] *n* (-es/*e) raft, float.

Flosse ['flɔsə] *f* (-/-n) fin; flipper (*of penguin, etc.*).

flöß|en ['flœːsən] v/t. (ge-, h) raft, float (*timber, etc.*); '**2er** *m* (-s/-) rafter, raftsman.

Flöte ♪ ['fløːtə] *f* (-/-n) flute; '**2n** (ge-, h) **1.** v/i. (play the) flute; **2.** v/t. play on the flute.

flott *adj.* [flɔt] ♎ floating, afloat; *pace, etc.*: quick, brisk; *music, etc.*: gay, lively; *dress, etc.*: smart, stylish; *car, etc.*: sporty, racy; *dancer, etc.*: excellent.

Flotte ['flɔtə] *f* (-/-n) ♎ fleet; ✕ navy; '~**nstützpunkt** ✕ *m* naval base.

Flotille ♎ [flɔ'tiljə] *f* (-/-n) flotilla.

Flöz *geol.*, ♀ [fløːts] *n* (-es/-e) seam; layer, stratum.

Fluch [fluːx] *m* (-[e]s/*e) curse, malediction; *eccl.* anathema; curse, swear-word; '**2en** v/i. (ge-, h) swear, curse.

Flucht [fluxt] *f* (-/-en) flight (*vor dat.* from); escape (*aus dat.* from); line (*of windows, etc.*); suite (*of rooms*); flight (*of stairs*).

flücht|en ['flyçtən] (ge-) v/i. (sein) *and* v/refl. (h) flee (*nach, zu* to); run away; escape; '~**ig** *adj.* fugitive (*a. fig.*); *thought, etc.*: fleeting; *fame, etc.*: transient; *p.* careless, super-ficial; ♎ volatile; '**2ling** ['~lɪŋ] *m* (-s/-e) fugitive; *pol.* refugee; '**2-lingslager** *n* refugee camp.

Flug [fluːk] *m* (-[e]s/*e) flight; *im ~(e)* rapidly; quickly; '~**abwehrra-kete** *f* anti-aircraft missile; '~**bahn** *f* trajectory (*of rocket, etc.*); ✈ flight path; '~**ball** *m* tennis, *etc.*: volley; '~**blatt** *n* handbill, leaflet, *Am. a.* flier; '~**boot** ✈ *n* flying-boat; '~**dienst** ✈ *m* air service.

Flügel ['flyːgəl] *m* (-s/-) wing (*a.* ♎, ✈, ✕); blade, vane (*of propeller, etc.*); *s.* Fensterflügel, Türflügel, Lungenflügel; sail (*of windmill, etc.*); ♪ grand piano; '~**fenster** *n* case-ment-window; '**2lahm** *adj.* broken-winged; '~**mann** ✕ *m* marker; flank man; '~**tür** ♎ *f* folding door.

Fluggast ['fluːk-] *m* (air) passenger.

flügge *adj.* ['flygə] fledged; ~ *wer-den* fledge; *fig.* begin to stand on one's own feet.

'**Flug|hafen** *m* airport; '~**linie** *f* ✈ air route; airline; '~**platz** *m* air-field, aerodrome, *Am. a.* airdrome; airport; '~**sand** *geol. m* wind-blown sand; '~**schrift** *f* pamphlet; '~**sicherung** *f* air traffic control; '~**sport** *m* sporting aviation; '~**wesen** *n* aviation, aeronautics.

'Flugzeug n aircraft, aeroplane, F plane, Am. a. airplane; '**~bau** m aircraft construction; '**~führer** m pilot; '**~halle** f hangar; '**~rumpf** m fuselage, body; '**~träger** m aircraft carrier, Am. sl. flattop; '**~unglück** n air crash or disaster.

Flunder ichth. ['flundər] f (-/-n) flounder.

Flunker|ei F [fluŋkə'raɪ] f (-/-en) petty lying, F fib(bing); '**²en** v/i. (ge-, h) F fib, tell fibs.

fluoreszieren [fluores'tsi:rən] v/i. (no -ge-, h) fluoresce.

Flur [flu:r] 1. f (-/-en) field, meadow; poet. lea; 2. m (-[e]s/-e) (entrance-)hall.

Fluß [flus] m (Flusses/Flüsse) river, stream; flow(ing); fig. fluency, flux; **²abwärts** adv. downriver, downstream; **²aufwärts** adv. upriver, upstream; '**~bett** n river bed.

flüssig adj. ['flysiç] fluid, liquid; metal: molten, melted; **✝** money, capital, etc.: available, in hand; style: fluent, flowing; '**²keit** f (-/-en) fluid, liquid; fluidity, liquidity; availability; fluency.

'Fluß|lauf m course of a river; '**~mündung** f mouth of a river; '**~pferd** zo. ~ hippopotamus; '**~schiffahrt** f river navigation or traffic.

flüstern ['flystərn] v/i. and v/t. (ge-, h) whisper.

Flut [flu:t] f (-/-en) flood; high tide, (flood-)tide; fig. flood, torrent, deluge; '**²en** (ge-) 1. v/i. (sein) water, crowd, etc.: flood, surge (über acc. over); 2. v/t. (h) flood (dock, etc.); '**~welle** f tidal wave.

focht [fɔxt] pret. of fechten.

Fohlen zo. ['fo:lən] 1. n (-s/-) foal; male: colt; female: filly; 2. **♀** v/i. (ge-, h) foal.

Folge ['fɔlgə] f (-/-n) sequence, succession (of events); instalment, part (of radio series, etc.); consequence, result; series; set, suit; future; **~n** pl. aftermath.

'folgen v/i. (dat.) (ge-, sein) follow; succeed (j-m s.o.; auf acc. to); follow, ensue (aus from); obey (j-m s.o.); **~dermaßen** adv. ['~dərmɑ:sən] as follows; '**~schwer** adj. of grave consequence, grave.

'folgerichtig adj. logical; consistent.

folger|n ['fɔlgərn] v/t. (ge-, h) infer, conclude, deduce (aus from); '**²ung** f (-/-en) inference, conclusion, deduction.

'folgewidrig adj. illogical; inconsistent.

folglich cj. ['fɔlkliç] therefore, consequently.

folgsam adj. ['fɔlkzɑ:m] obedient; '**²keit** f (-/no pl.) obedience.

Folie ['fo:ljə] f (-/-n) foil.

Folter ['fɔltər] f (-/-n) torture; auf die ~ spannen put to the rack; fig. F a. keep on tenterhooks; '**²n** v/t. (ge-, h) torture, torment; '**~qual** f torture, fig. a. torment.

Fonds **✝** [fõ:] m (-/-) fund (a. fig.); funds pl.

Fontäne [fɔn'tɛ:nə] f (-/-n) fountain.

foppen ['fɔpən] v/t. (ge-, h) tease, F pull s.o.'s leg; hoax, fool.

forcieren [fɔr'si:rən] v/t. (no -ge-, h) force (up).

'Förder|band n (-[e]s/-er) conveyor-belt; '**²lich** adj. conducive (dat. to), promotive (of); '**~korb** **⚒** m cage.

fordern ['fɔrdərn] v/t. (ge-, h) demand; claim (compensation, etc.); ask (price, etc.); challenge (to duel).

fördern ['fœrdərn] v/t. (ge-, h) further, advance, promote; **⚒** haul, raise (coal, etc.); zutage ~ reveal, bring to light.

'Forderung f (-/-en) demand; claim; charge; challenge.

'Förderung f (-/-en) furtherance, advancement, promotion; **⚒** haulage; output. [trout.\]

Forelle ichth. [fo'rɛlə] f (-/-n)

Form [fɔrm] f (-/-en) form; figure, shape; model; **⊕** mo(u)ld; sports: form, condition; **²al** adj. [**~**'mɑ:l] formal; **~alität** [**~**ali'tɛ:t] f (-/-en) formality; **~at** [**~**'mɑ:t] n (-[e]s/-e) size; von ~ of distinction; **~el** [**'~**əl] f (-/-n) formula; **²ell** adj. [**~**'mɛl] formal; '**²en** v/t. (ge-, h) form (object, character, etc.); shape, fashion (wood, metal, etc.); mo(u)ld (clay, character, etc.); '**~enlehre** gr. f accidence; '**~fehler** m informality; **⚖** flaw; **²ieren** [**~**'mi:rən] v/t. (no -ge-, h) form; draw up, line up; sich ~ line up.

förmlich adj. ['fœrmliç] formal; ceremonious; '**²keit** f (-/-en) formality; ceremoniousness.

'formlos adj. formless, shapeless; fig. informal.

Formular [fɔrmu'lɑ:r] n (-s/-e) form, Am. a. blank.

formu'lieren v/t. (no -ge-, h) formulate (question, etc.); word, phrase (question, contract, etc.).

forsch adj. [fɔrʃ] vigorous, energetic; smart, dashing.

forsch|en ['fɔrʃən] v/i. (ge-, h): ~ nach (dat.) search for or after; ~ in (dat.) search (through); '**²er** m (-s/-) researcher, research worker.

'Forschung f (-/-en) research (work); '**~sreise** f (exploring) expedition; '**~sreisende** m explorer.

Forst [fɔrst] m (-es/-e[n]) forest; '**~aufseher** m (forest-)keeper, gamekeeper.

Förster ['fœrstər] m (-s/-) forester; ranger.

'Forst|haus n forester's house; '~revier n forest district; '~wesen n, '~wirtschaft f forestry.

Fort¹ ⚔ [fɔːr] n (-s/-s) fort.

fort² adv. [fɔrt] away, gone; on; gone, lost; in e-m ~ continuously; und so ~ and so on or forth; s. a. weg.

'fort|bestehen v/i. (irr. stehen, sep., no -ge-, h) continue, persist; '~bewegen v/t. (sep., no -ge-, h) move (on, away); sich ~ move, walk; '2dauer f continuance; '~dauern v/i. (sep., -ge-, h) continue, last; '~fahren v/i. (irr. fahren, sep., -ge-) 1. (sein) depart, leave; drive off; 2. (h) continue, keep on (et. zu tun doing s.th.); ~führen v/t. (sep., -ge-, h) continue, carry on; 2gang m departure, leaving; continuance; '~gehen v/i. (irr. gehen, sep., -ge-, sein) go (away), leave; '~geschritten adj. advanced; 2kommen n (-s/no pl.) progress; '~laufend adj. consecutive, continuous; '~pflanzen v/t. (sep., -ge-, h) propagate; sich ~ biol. propagate, reproduce; phys., disease, rumour: be propagated; '2pflanzung f propagation; reproduction; '~reißen v/t. (irr. reißen, sep., -ge-, h) avalanche, etc.: sweep or carry away; '~schaffen v/t. (sep., -ge-, h) get or take away, remove; '~schreiten v/i. (irr. schreiten, sep., -ge-, sein) advance, proceed, progress; '~schreitend adj. progressive; '2schritt m progress; '~schrittlich adj. progressive; '~setzen v/t. (sep., -ge-, h) continue, pursue; 2setzung f (-/-en) continuation, pursuit; ~ folgt to be continued; '~während 1. adj. continual, continuous; perpetual; 2. adv. constantly, always.

Forum ['foːrum] n (-s/Foren, Fora and -s) forum.

Foto... ['foːto] s. Photo...

Foyer [foaˈjeː] n (-s/-s) thea. foyer, Am. and parl. lobby; hotel: foyer, lounge.

Fracht [fraxt] f (-/-en) goods pl.; 🚂 carriage, freight, ⚓, 🚂 freight (-age), cargo; '~brief m ⚓ consignment note, Am., ⚓ bill of lading; ~dampfer m cargo steamer, freighter; '~er m (-s/-) freighter; '2frei adj. carriage or freight paid; '~führer m carrier, Am. a. teamster; '~geld n carriage charges pl., 🚂, ⚓, Am. freight; '~gut n goods pl., freight; '~stück n package.

Frack [frak] m (-[e]s/ᵘe, -s) dress coat, tail-coat, F tails; '~anzug m dress-suit.

Frag|e ['fraːɡə] f (-/-n) question; gr., reth. interrogation; problem, point; e-e ~ stellen ask a question; in ~ stellen question; '~ebogen m questionnaire; form; '2en (ge-, h)

1. v/t. ask; question; es fragt sich, ob it is doubtful whether; 2. v/i. ask; '~er m (-s/-) questioner; '~ewort gr. n (-[e]s/ᵘer) interrogative; '~ezeichen n question-mark, point of interrogation, Am. mst interrogation point; 2lich adj. ['fraːk-] doubtful, uncertain; in question; 2los adv. ['fraːk-] indoubtedly, unquestionably.

Fragment [fragˈment] n (-[e]s/-e) fragment.

fragwürdig adj. ['fraːk-] doubtful, dubious, questionable.

Fraktion parl. [frakˈtsjoːn] f (-/-en) (parliamentary) group.

frank|ieren [fraŋˈkiːrən] v/t. (no -ge-, h) prepay, stamp; ~o adv. ['~o] free; post(age) paid; parcel: carriage paid.

Franse ['franzə] f (-/-n) fringe.

Franz|ose [franˈtsoːzə] m (-n/-n) Frenchman; die ~n pl. the French pl.; ~ösin [~øːzin] f (-/-nen) Frenchwoman; 2ösisch adj. [~øːtʃif] French.

fräs|en ⊕ ['freːzən] v/t. (ge-, h) mill; 2maschine ['freːs-] f milling-machine.

Fraß [fraːs] 1. F m (-es/-e) sl. grub; 2. 2 pret. of fressen.

Fratze ['fratsə] f (-/-n) grimace, F face; ~n schneiden make grimaces.

Frau [frau] f (-/-en) woman; lady; wife; ~ X Mrs X.

'Frauen|arzt m gyn(a)ecologist; '~klinik f hospital for women; '~rechte n/pl. women's rights pl.; '~stimmrecht pol. n women's suffrage; '~zimmer mst contp. n female, woman.

Fräulein ['frɔylaɪn] n (-s/-, F -s) young lady; teacher; shop-assistant; waitress; ~ X Miss X.

'fraulich adj. womanly.

frech adj. [frɛç] impudent, insolent, F saucy, cheeky, Am. F a. sassy, sl. fresh; lie, etc. brazen; thief, etc.: bold, daring; '2heit f (-/-en) impudence, insolence; F sauciness, cheek; boldness.

frei adj. [fraɪ] free (von from, of); position: vacant; field: open; parcel: carriage-paid; journalist, etc.: freelance; liberal; candid, frank; licentious; ~ Haus ✝ franco domicile; ~er Tag day off; im Freien in the open air.

'Frei|bad n open-air bath; '~beuter ['~bɔytər] m (-s/-) freebooter; 2bleibend ✝ adj. price, etc.: subject to alteration; offer: conditional; '~brief m charter; fig. warrant; '~denker m (-s/-) freethinker.

Freier ['fraɪər] m (-s/-) suitor.

'Frei|exemplar n free or presentation copy; '~frau f baroness; '~gabe f release; '2geben (irr. geben, sep., -ge-, h) 1. v/t. release; give (*s.o. an hour, etc.*) off; **2.** *v/i.*: j-m ~ give s.o. time off; '2gebig *adj.* generous, liberal; '~gebigkeit *f* (-/-en) generosity, liberality; '~gepäck *n* free luggage; '2haben *v/i.* (*irr. haben, sep., -ge-, h*) have a holiday; have a day off; '~hafen *m* free port; '2halten *v/t.* (*irr. halten, sep., -ge-, h*) keep free *or* clear; *in restaurant, etc.*: treat; '~handel *m* free trade.

'Freiheit *f* (-/-en) liberty; freedom; *dichterische* ~ poetic licence, *Am.* poetic license.

'Frei|herr *m* baron; '~karte *f* free (*thea. a.* complimentary) ticket; '2lassen *v/t.* (*irr. lassen, sep., -ge-, h*) release, set free *or* at liberty; *gegen Kaution* ~ release on bail; '~lassung *f* (-/-en) release; '~lauf *m* free-wheel.

'freilich *adv.* indeed, certainly, of course; admittedly.

'Frei|lichtbühne *f* open-air stage *or* theat|re, *Am.* -er; '2machen *v/t.* (*sep., -ge-, h*) ✉ prepay, stamp (*letter, etc.*); *sich* ~ undress, take one's clothes off; '~marke *f* stamp; '~maurer *m* freemason; '~maurerei [~'raɪ] *f* (-/*no pl.*) freemasonry; '~mut *m* frankness; '2mütig *adj.* ['~myːtiç] frank; '2schaffend *adj.*: ~er *Künstler* free-lance artist; '~schärler ✗ ['~ʃɛːrlər] *m* (-s/-) volunteer, irregular; '~schein *m* licen|ce, *Am.* -se; '2sinnig *adj.* liberal; '2sprechen *v/t.* (*irr. sprechen, sep., -ge-, h*) *esp. eccl.* absolve (*von* from); ⚖ acquit (*of*); release (*apprentice*) from his articles; '~sprechung *f* (-/-en) *esp. eccl.* absolution; release from articles; ~ '~spruch ⚖ *m* acquittal; '~staat *pol. m* free state; '2stehen *v/i.* (*irr. stehen, sep., -ge-, h*) house, *etc.*: stand empty; *es steht Ihnen frei zu inf.* you are free *or* at liberty to *inf.*; '2stellen *v/t.* (*sep., -ge-, h*): j-n ~ exempt s.o. (*von* from) (*a.* ✗); j-m et. ~ leave s.th. open to s.o.; '~stoß *m* football: free kick; '~tag *m* Friday; '~tod *m* suicide; '2tragend △ *adj.* cantilever; '~treppe *f* outdoor staircase; '2willig **1.** *adj.* voluntary; **2.** *adv. a.* of one's own free will; ~willige ['~viligə] *m* (-n/-n) volunteer; '~zeit *f* free *or* spare *or* leisure time; '2zügig *adj.* ['~tsy:giç] free to move; '~zügigkeit *f* (-/*no pl.*) freedom of movement.

fremd *adj.* [fremt] strange; foreign; alien; extraneous; '~artig *adj.* strange; exotic.

Fremde ['fremdə] **1.** *f* (-/*no pl.*) distant *or* foreign parts; *in der* ~ far away from home, abroad; **2.** *m, f* (-n/-n) stranger; foreigner; '~buch *n* visitors' book; '~führer *m* guide, cicerone; '~nheim *n*

boarding house; ~nindustrie ['fremdən?-] *f* tourist industry; '~nlegion ✗ *f* Foreign Legion; '~nverkehr *m* tourism, tourist traffic; '~nzimmer *n* spare (bed-) room; *tourism:* room.

'Fremd|herrschaft *f* foreign rule; '~körper ⚗ *m* foreign body; '2ländisch *adj.* ['~lendiʃ] foreign, exotic; '~sprache *f* foreign language; '2sprachig *adj.*, '2sprachlich *adj.* foreign-language; '~wort *n* (-[e]s/~er) foreign word.

Frequenz *phys.* [fre'kvɛnts] *f* (-/-en) frequency.

fressen ['fresən] **1.** *v/t.* (*irr., ge-, h*) eat; *beast of prey:* devour; F *p.* devour, gorge; **2.** *v/i.* (*irr., ge-, h*) eat; F *p.* gorge; **3.** 2 *n* (-s/*no pl.*) feed, food.

'Freß|gier *f* voracity, gluttony; '~napf *m* feeding dish.

Freude ['frɔʏdə] *f* (-/-n) joy, gladness; delight; pleasure; ~ *haben an* (*dat.*) find *or* take pleasure in.

'Freuden|botschaft *f* glad tidings *pl.*; '~fest *n* happy occasion; '~feuer *n* bonfire; '~geschrei *n* shouts *pl.* of joy; '~tag *m* day of rejoicing, red-letter day; '~taumel *m* transports *pl.* of joy.

'freud|estrahlend *adj.* radiant with joy; '~ig *adj.* joyful; happy; ~es *Ereignis* happy event; '~los *adj.* ['frɔʏtloːs] joyless, cheerless.

freuen ['frɔʏən] *v/t.* (*ge-, h*): es freut mich, daß I am glad *or* pleased (that); *sich* ~ *über* (*acc.*) be pleased about *or* with, be glad about; *sich* ~ *auf* (*acc.*) look forward to.

Freund [frɔʏnt] *m* (-es/-e) (boy-) friend; '~in ['~dɪn] *f* (-/-nen) (girl-) friend; '2lich *adj.* friendly, kind, nice; cheerful, bright; *climate:* mild; '~lichkeit *f* (-/-en) friendliness, kindness; '~schaft *f* (-/-en) friendship; ~ *schließen* make friends (*mit* with); '2schaftlich *adj.* friendly.

Frevel ['freːfəl] *m* (-s/-) outrage (*an dat., gegen* on), crime (against); '2haft *adj.* wicked, outrageous; impious; '2n *v/i.* (*ge-, h*) commit a crime *or* outrage (*gegen* against).

Frevler ['freːflər] *m* (-s/-) evil-doer, offender; blasphemer.

Friede(n) ['friːdə(n)] *m* (*Friedens/ Frieden*) peace; *im Frieden* in peace-time; *laß mich in Frieden!* leave me alone!

'Friedens|bruch *m* violation of (the) peace; '~stifter *m* peace-maker; '~störer *m* disturber of the peace; '~verhandlungen *f/pl.* peace negotiations *pl.*; '~vertrag *m* peace treaty.

fried|fertig *adj.* ['friːt-] peaceable, peace-loving; '2hof *m* cemetery, graveyard; churchyard; '~lich *adj.*

s. friedfertig; peaceful; '~liebend *adj.* peace-loving.

frieren ['fri:rən] *v/i.* (irr., ge-) 1. (sein) *liquid:* freeze, become frozen; *river, etc.:* freeze (over, up); *window-pane, etc.:* freeze over; 2. (h) be *or* feel cold; mich friert *or* ich friere an den Füßen my feet are cold

Fries △ [fri:s] *m* (-es/-e) frieze.

frisch [friʃ] 1. *adj. food, flowers, etc.:* fresh; *egg* new-laid; *linen, etc.:* clean, auf ~er Tat ertappen catch red-handed, 2. *adv.:* ~ gestrichen! wet paint', *Am* fresh paint!; 2e ['~ə] *f* (-/no *pl.*) freshness.

Friseu|r [fri'zø:r] *m* (-s/-e) hairdresser, (*men's*) barber; ~se [~zə] *f* (-/-n) (woman) hairdresser.

fri'sier|en *v/t.* (no -ge-, h): j-n ~ do *or* dress s.o.'s hair; F: einen Wagen ~ mot tune up *or* soup up *or* hot up a car, sich ~ do one's hair; 2kommode *f* dressing-table; 2salon *m* hairdressing saloon; 2tisch *m s.* Frisierkommode.

Frist [frist] *f* (~-en) (fixed *or* limited) period *or* time; time allowed; term; *fig* prescribed time; *fig* respite, grace; 2en *v/t* (ge-, h): sein Dasein ~ scrape along, scrape a living

Frisur [fri'zu:r] *f* (-/-en) hair-style, hair-do, coiffure

frivol *adj* [fri'vo:l] frivolous, flippant, 2ität [~oli'tɛ:t] *f* (-/-en) frivolity, flippancy

froh *adj* [fro:] joyful, glad; cheerful; happ~, gay (*a. colour*).

fröhlich *adj* ['frø:liç] gay, merry, cheerful, happy, *Am*. F *a.* chipper; 2keit *f* (-/~-en) gaiety, cheerfulness; merriment

froh|'locken *v/i* (no -ge-, h) shout for joy, b~ jubilant; exult (*über acc.* at, in), gloat (over); 2sinn *m* (-[e]s/no *pl*) gaiety, cheerfulness.

fromm *adj* [from] *p.* pious, religious, *life, etc* godly; *prayer, etc.:* devout, *horse, etc.:* docile; ~e Lüge white lie, ~er Wunsch wishful thinking, idle wish.

Frömmelei [frœmə'lai] *f* (-/-en) affected piet~, bigotry.

'Frömmigkeit *f* (-/-en) piety, religiousness; godliness; devoutness.

Fron [fro:n] *f* (-/-en), '~arbeit *f*, '~dienst *hist m* forced *or* compulsory labo(u)r *or* service; *fig.* drudgery

frönen ['frø:nən] *v/i.* (dat.) (ge-, h) indulge in, be a slave to.

Front [front] *f* (-/-en) △ front, façade, face; ✕ front (line); line; *pol.*, ✈, *etc* front.

fror [fro:r] *pret. of* frieren.

Frosch *zo.* [froʃ] *m* (-es/=e) frog; '~perspektive *f* worm's-eye view.

Frost [frost] *m* (-es/=e) frost; chill; '~beule *f* chilblain.

frösteln ['frœstəln] *v/i.* (ge-, h) feel chilly, shiver (with cold).

'frostig *adj* frosty (*a. fig.*); *fig.* cold, frigid, icy

'Frost|salbe ✗ *f* chilblain ointment; '~schaden *m* frost damage; '~schutzmittel *mot n* anti-freezing mixture; '~wetter *n* frosty weather.

frottier|en [fro'ti:rən] *v/t.* (no -ge-, h) rub; 2(hand)tuch *n* Turkish towel.

Frucht [fruxt] *f* (-/=e) & fruit (*a. fig.*); corn; crop; *fig.* reward, result; 2bar *adj* fruitful (*esp. fig.*); fertile (*a. biol.*), '~barkeit *f* (-/no *pl.*) fruitfulness, fertility; '2bringend *adj.* fruit-bearing; *fig.* fruitful; '2en *fig v/i* (ge-, h) be of use; '~knoten *m* ovary; '2los *adj.* fruitless; *fig a* ineffective.

früh [fry:] 1. *adj* early; am ~en Morgen in the early morning; ~es Aufstehen early rising, ~e Anzeichen early symptoms, ~ er former; 2. *adv.* in the morning, aufstehen rise early; heute this morning; morgen ~ tomorrow morning, ~er earlier; formerly, in former times, ~estens at the earliest; '2aufsteher *m* (-s/-) early riser, ~ early bird; '2e *f* (-/no *pl.*): in aller ~ very early in the morning; '2geburt *f* premature birth; premature baby *or* animal; '2gottesdienst *m* early service; '2jahr *n*, 2ling [liŋ] *m* (-s/-e) spring, ~ morgens adv. early in the morning, ~reif *fig. adj.* precocious; '2sport *m* early morning exercises; '2stück *n* breakfast; '~stücken (ge-, h) 1. *v/i.* (have) breakfast, 2. ~ *v/t.* have s.th. for breakfast; '2zug ✕ *m* early train.

Fuchs [fuks] *m* (-es/=e) *zo.* fox (*a. fig.*); *horse* sorrel.

Füchsin *zo* ['fyksin] *f* (-/-nen) she-fox, vixen

'Fuchs|jagd *f* fox-hunt(ing); '~pelz *m* fox-fur; '2rot *adj* foxy-red, sorrel; '~schwanz *m* foxtail; ⊕ pad-saw, ✗ amarant(h); '2teufels'wild *f adj.* mad with rage, F hopping mad

fuchteln ['fuxtəln] *v/i.* (ge-, h): ~ mit (dat.) wave (one's hands) about.

Fuder ['fu:dər] *n* (-s/-) cart-load; tun (of wine) [♩ fugue.]

Fuge ['fu:gə] *f* (-/-n) ⊕ joint; seam;)

füg|en ['fy:gən] *v/refl.* (h) submit, give in, yield (dat , in acc. to); comply (with), ~sam *adj.* ['fy:k-] (com)pliant; manageable.

fühl|bar *adj* ['fy:lba:r] tangible, palpable; *fig.* sensible, noticeable; '~en (ge-, h) 1. *v/t.* feel; be aware of; sich glücklich ~ feel happy; 2. *v/i.*: mit j-m ~ feel for *or* sympathize with s.o.; 2er *m* (-s/-) feeler

(a. fig.); '²ung f (-/-en) touch, contact (a. ⚡); ~ haben be in touch (mit with); ~ verlieren lose touch.

fuhr [fuːr] pret of fahren.

Fuhre ['fuːrə] f (-/-n) cart-load.

führen ['fyːrən] (ge-, h) 1. v/t. lead, guide (blind person, etc.); show (zu dat. to); wield (paint-brush, etc.); ✕ command (regiment, etc.); have, bear (title, etc.); carry on (conversation, etc.); conduct (campaign, etc.); ✝ run (shop, etc.); deal in (goods); lead (life); keep (diary, etc.); 𝄢 try (case); wage (war) (mit, gegen against); ~ durch show round; sich ~ conduct o.s., behave (o.s.); 2. v/i. path, etc. lead, run, go (nach, zu to); sports, etc.: (hold the) lead, be ahead; ~ zu lead to, result in; '~d adj. leading, prominent, Am. a. banner.

'Führer m (-s/-) leader (a. pol., sports); guide(-book); '~raum ✈ m cockpit; '~schein mot. m driving licence, Am. driver's license; '~sitz m mot. driver's seat, ✈ pilot's seat; '~stand 🚂 m (driver's) cab.

'Fuhr|geld n, '~lohn m cartage, carriage; '~mann m (-[e]s/~er, Fuhrleute) carter, carrier, wag(g)oner; driver; '~park m fleet (of lorries), Am. fleet (of trucks).

'Führung f (-/-en) leadership; conduct, management; guidance; conduct, behavio(u)r; sports, etc.: lead; '~szeugnis n certificate of good conduct.

'Fuhr|unternehmer m carrier, haulage contractor, Am. a. trucker, teamster; '~werk n (horse-drawn) vehicle; cart, wag(g)on.

Fülle ['fylə] f (-/no pl.) fullness (a. fig.); corpulence, plumpness, stoutness; fig. wealth, abundance, profusion.

füllen[1] ['fylən] v/t. (ge-, h) fill (a. tooth); stuff (cushion, poultry, etc.).

Füllen[2] zo. [~] n (-s/-) foal; male: colt; female: filly.

'Füll|er F m (-s/-), '~feder(halter m) f fountain-pen; '~horn n horn of plenty; '~ung f (-/-en) filling; panel (of door, etc.).

Fund [funt] m (-[e]s/-e) finding, discovery; find.

Fundament [funda'ment] n (-[e]s/-e) △ foundation; fig. basis.

'Fund|büro n lost-property office; '~gegenstand m object found; '~grube fig. f rich source, mine.

fünf [fynf] five; '²eck n pentagon; '~fach adj. ['~fax] fivefold, quintuple; '²kampf m sports: pentathlon; '²linge ['~liŋə] m/pl. quintuplets pl.; '~te adj. fifth; '²tel ['~[-]) fifth; '~tens adv. fifthly, in the fifth place; '~zehn(te) adj. fifteen(th); '~zig adj. ['~tsiç] fifty; '~zigste adj. fiftieth.

8 SW E II

fungieren [fuŋ'giːrən] v/i. (no -ge-, h): ~ als officiate or act as.

Funk [fuŋk] m (-s/no pl.) radio, wireless; '~anlage f radio or wireless installation or equipment; '~bastler m do-it-yourself radio ham; '~bild n photo-radiogram.

Funke ['fuŋkə] m (-ns/-n) spark; fig. a. glimmer.

'funkeln v/i. (ge-, h) sparkle, glitter; star: twinkle, sparkle.

'Funken[1] esp. fig. m (-s/-) s. Funke.

'funken[2] v/t. (ge-, h) radio, wireless, broadcast.

'Funk|er m (-s/-) radio or wireless operator; '~gerät n radio (communication) set; '~spruch m radio or wireless message; '~station f radio or wireless station; '~stille f radio or wireless silence; '~streifenwagen m radio patrol car.

Funktion [fuŋk'tsjoːn] f (-/-en) function; '~är [~tsjo'nɛːr] m (-s/-e) functionary, official; ²ieren [~o-'niːrən] v/i. (no -ge-, h) function, work.

'Funk|turm m radio or wireless tower; '~verkehr m radio or wireless communication; '~wagen m radio car; '~wesen n (-s/no pl.) radio communication.

für prp. (acc.) [fyːr] for; in exchange or return for; in favo(u)r of; in s.o.'s place; Schritt ~ Schritt step by step; Tag ~ Tag day after day; ich ~ meine Person ... as for me, I ...; das Für und Wider the pros and cons pl.

'Fürbitte f intercession.

Furche ['furçə] f (-/-n) furrow (a. in face); rut; ⊕ groove; '²n v/i. (ge-, h) furrow (a. face); ⊕ groove.

Furcht [furçt] f (-/no pl.) fear, dread; aus ~ vor for fear of; '²bar adj. awful, terrible, dreadful.

fürchten ['fyrçtən] (ge-, h) 1. v/t. fear, dread; sich ~ vor (dat.) be afraid or scared of; 2. v/i.: ~ um fear for.

'fürchterlich adj. s. furchtbar.

'furcht|los adj. fearless; '²losigkeit f (-/no pl.) fearlessness; '~sam adj. timid, timorous; '²samkeit f (-/no pl.) timidity.

Furie fig. ['fuːrjə] f (-/-n) fury.

Furnier ⊕ [fur'niːr] n (-s/-e) veneer; ²en v/t. (no -ge-, h) veneer.

'Für|sorge f care; öffentliche ~ public welfare work; '~sorgeamt n welfare department; '~sorgeerziehung f corrective training for juvenile delinquents; '~sorger m (-s/-) social or welfare worker; '²sorglich adj. considerate, thoughtful, solicitous; '~sprache f intercession (für for, bei with); '~sprecher m intercessor.

Fürst [fyrst] m (-en/-en) prince; sovereign; '~enhaus n dynasty;

'.enstand *m* prince's rank; '.en-
tum *n* (-s/=er) principality; '.lich
1. *adj.* princely (*a. fig.*), royal; *fig.*
magnificent, sumptuous; 2. *adv.*: ~
leben live like a lord *or* king; '.lich-
keiten *f/pl.* royalties *pl.*

Furt [furt] *f* (-/-en) ford.

Furunkel [fu'ruŋkəl] *m* (-s/-) boil,
furuncle.

'Fürwort *gr. n* (-[e]s/=er) pronoun.

Fusel F ['fu:zəl] *m* (-s/-) low-quality
spirits, F rotgut.

Fusion † [fu:'zjo:n] *f* (-/-en) merger,
amalgamation.

Fuß [fu:s] *m* (-es/=e) foot; ~ *fassen*
find a foothold; *fig.* become established; *auf gutem* (*schlechtem*) ~
stehen mit be on good (bad) terms
with; *zu* ~ on foot; *zu* ~ *gehen*
walk; *gut zu* ~ *sein* be a good walker;
'.abstreifer *m* (-s/-) door-scraper,
door-mat; '.angel *f* mantrap;
'.ball *m* (association) football, F
and Am. soccer; '.ballspieler *m*
football player, footballer; '.bank
f footstool; '.bekleidung *f* foot-
wear, footgear; '.boden *m* floor
(-ing); '.bodenbelag *m* floor covering; '.bremse *mot. f* foot-brake;

'.en *v/i.* (ge-, h): ~ *auf* (*dat.*) be
based *or* founded on; '.gänger
['.geŋər] *m* (-s/-) pedestrian; '.ge-
lenk *anat. n* ankle joint; '.note *f*
footnote; '.pfad *m* footpath; '.sack
m foot-muff; '.sohle *anat. f* sole
of the foot; '.soldat *m* foot-
soldier, infantryman; '.spur *f* footprint; track; '.stapfe *f* [.ʃtapfə] *f*
(-/-n) footprint, *fig. a.* footstep;
'.steig *m* footpath; '.tritt *m* kick;
'.wanderung *f* walking tour, hike;
'.weg *m* footpath.

Futter ['futər] *n* 1. (-s/*no pl.*) food,
sl. grub, *Am.* F *a.* chow; feed,
fodder; 2. (-s/-) lining; ⚠ casing.

Futteral [futə'ra:l] *n* (-s/-e) case
(*for spectacles, etc.*); cover (*of umbrella*); sheath (*of knife*).

'Futtermittel *n* feeding stuff.

füttern ['fytərn] *v/t.* (ge-, h) feed;
line (*dress, etc.*); ⚠ case.

'Futter|napf *m* feeding bowl *or*
dish; '.neid *fig. m* (professional)
jealousy; '.stoff *m* lining (material).

'Fütterung *f* (-/-en) feeding; lining;
⚠ casing.

Futur *gr.* [fu'tu:r] *n* (-s/-e) future
(tense).

G

gab [ga:p] *pret. of* geben.

Gabe ['ga:bə] *f* (-/-n) gift, present;
alms; donation; dose; talent.

Gabel ['ga:bəl] *f* (-/-n) fork; '.en
v/refl. (ge-, h) fork, bifurcate; '.ung
f (-/-en) bifurcation.

gackern ['gakərn] *v/i.* (ge-, h)
cackle.

gaffen ['gafən] *v/i.* (ge-, h) gape;
stare.

Gage ['ga:ʒə] *f* (-/-n) salary, pay.

gähnen ['gɛ:nən] 1. *v/i.* (ge-, h)
yawn; 2. *n* (-s/*no pl.*) yawning.

Gala ['gala] *f* (-/*no pl.*) gala; *in* ~ in
full dress.

galant *adj.* [ga'lant] gallant; courteous; erie [.ə'ri:] *f* (-/-n) gallantry;
courtesy.

Galeere [ga'le:rə] *f* (-/-n) galley.

Galerie [galə'ri:] *f* (-/-n) gallery.

Galgen ['galgən] *m* (-s/-) gallows,
gibbet; '.frist *f* respite; '.ge-
sicht *n* gallows-look, hangdog look;
'.humor *m* grim humo(u)r;
'.strick *m*, '.vogel *m* gallows-bird,
hangdog.

Galle *anat.* ['galə] *f* (-/-n) bile (*of
person*); gall (*of animal*) (*a. fig.*);
'.nblase *anat. f* gall-bladder; '.n-
leiden *n* bilious complaint; '.n-
stein *m* gall-stone, bile-stone.

Gallert ['galərt] *n* (-[e]s/-e), ~e
[ga'lertə] *f* (-/-n) gelatine, jelly.

'gallig *fig. adj.* bilious.

Galopp [ga'lɔp] *m* (-s/-, -e) gallop;
canter; ieren [.'pi:rən] *v/i.* (*no
-ge-, sein*) gallop; canter.

galt [galt] *pret. of* gelten.

galvani|sch *adj.* [gal'va:niʃ] gal-
vanic; .sieren [.ani'-] *v/t.* (*no -ge-,
h*) galvanize.

Gang[1] [gaŋ] *m* (-[e]s/=e) walk; *s.*
Gangart; fig. motion; running;
working (*of machine*); errand; way;
course (*of events, of a meal, etc.*);
passage(-way); alley; corridor, gallery; *in vehicle, between seats:* gangway, *esp. Am.* aisle; corridor,
Am. aisle; *fencing:* pass; *anat.* duct;
mot. gear; *erster* (*zweiter, dritter,
vierter*) ~ low *or* bottom (second,
third, top) gear; *in* ~ *bringen or*
setzen set going *or* in motion, *Am.*
operate; *in* ~ *kommen* get going,
get started; *im* ~ *sein* be in motion;
⊕ be working *or* running; *fig.* be
in progress; *in vollem* ~ in full
swing.

gang[2] *adj.* [~]: ~ *und gäbe* customary,
traditional.

'Gang|art *f* gait, walk (*of person*);
pace (*of horse*); bar *adj.* road:
practicable, passable; *money:* current; † *goods:* marketable; *s. gängig.*

Gängelband ['gɛŋəl-] *n* leading-strings *pl.*; *am ~ führen* keep in leading-strings, lead by the nose.

gängig *adj.* ['gɛŋɪç] *money*: current; ✝ *goods* marketable; *~er Ausdruck* current word *or* phrase.

Gans *orn* [gans] *f (-/⸗e)* goose.

Gänse|blümchen ✿ ['gɛnzəbly:mçən] *n (-s/-)* daisy; **'~braten** *m* roast goose; **~feder** *f* goose-quill; **~füßchen** ['~fy:sçən] *n/pl.* quotation marks *pl.*, inverted commas *pl.*; **'~haut** *f* goose-skin; *fig. a.* goose-flesh, *Am. a.* goose pimples *pl.*; **'~klein** *n (-s/no pl.)* (goose-)giblets *pl.*; **'~marsch** *m* single *or* Indian file; **~rich** *orn.* ['~rɪç] *m (-s/-e)* gander; **'~schmalz** *n* goose-grease.

ganz [gants] **1.** *adj.* all; entire, whole; complete, total, full; *den ~en Tag* all day (long); **2.** *adv.* quite; entirely, *etc.* (*s.* 1.); very; *~ Auge (Ohr)* all eyes (ears); *~ und gar* wholly, totally; *~ und gar nicht* not at all; *im ~en* on the whole, generally; in all; ✝ *in the lump*; **'2e** *n (-n/no pl.)* whole; totality; *aufs ~ gehen* go all out, *esp. Am. sl.* go the whole hog.

gänzlich *adj.* ['gɛntslɪç] complete, total, entire

'Ganztagsbeschäftigung *f* full-time job *or* employment.

gar [ga:r] **1.** *adj. food*: done; **2.** *adv.* quite, very; even; *~ nicht* not at all.

Garage [ga'ra:ʒə] *f (-/-n)* garage.

Garantie [garan'ti:] *f (-/-n)* guarantee, warranty, ⷭ guaranty; **2ren** *v/t. (no -ge-, h)* guarantee, warrant.

Garbe ['garbə] *f (-/-n)* sheaf.

Garde ['gardə] *f (-/-n)* guard.

Garderobe [gardə'ro:bə] *f (-/-n)* wardrobe, cloakroom, *Am.* checkroom; *thea* dressing-room; **~nfrau** *f* cloak-room attendant, *Am.* hat-check girl; **~nmarke** *f* check; **~nschrank** *m* wardrobe; **~nständer** *m* coat-stand, hat-stand, hall-stand.

Garderobiere [gardəro'bjɛ:rə] *f (-/-n) s Garderobenfrau*; *thea.* wardrobe mistress.

Gardine [gar'di:nə] *f (-/-n)* curtain.

gär|en ['gɛ:rən] *v/i. (irr., ge-, h, sein)* ferment; **2mittel** *n* ferment.

Garn [garn] *n (-[e]s/-e)* yarn; thread; cotton; net; *j-m ins ~ gehen* fall into s.o.'s snare.

Garnele *zo.* [gar'ne:lə] *f (-/-n)* shrimp.

garnieren [gar'ni:rən] *v/t. (no -ge-, h)* trim; garnish (*esp. a dish*).

Garnison ⚔ [garni'zo:n] *f (-/-en)* garrison, post.

Garnitur [garni'tu:r] *f (-/-en)* trimming; ⊕ fittings *pl.*; set.

garstig *adj.* ['garstɪç] nasty, bad; ugly.

'Gärstoff *m* ferment.

Garten ['gartən] *m (-s/⸗)* garden; **'~anlage** *f* gardens *pl.*, park; **'~ar-**

beit *f* gardening; **'~bau** *m* horticulture; **'~erde** *f* (garden-)mo(u)ld; **'~fest** *n* garden-party, *Am. a.* lawn party; **'~geräte** *n/pl.* gardening-tools *pl.*; **'~stadt** *f* garden city.

Gärtner ['gɛrtnər] *m (-s/-)* gardener; **~ei** [~'raɪ] *f (-/-en)* gardening, horticulture; nursery; **'~in** *f (-/-nen)* gardener.

Gärung ['gɛ:rʊŋ] *f (-/-en)* fermentation.

Gas [ga:s] *n (-es/-e)* gas; *~ geben mot.* open the throttle, *Am.* step on the gas; **'~anstalt** *f* gas-works, *Am. a.* gas plant; **'~behälter** *m* gasometer, *Am* gas tank *or* container; **'~beleuchtung** *f* gaslight; **'~brenner** *m* gas-burner; **2förmig** *adj.* ['~fœrmɪç] gaseous; **'~hahn** *m* gas-tap; **'~herd** *m* gas-stove, *Am.* gas range; **'~leitung** *f* gas-mains *pl.*; **'~messer** *m (-s/-)* gas-meter; **'~ofen** *m* gas-oven; **'~pedal** *mot. n* accelerator (pedal), *Am.* gas pedal.

Gasse ['gasə] *f (-/-n)* lane, by-street, alley(-way); **'~nhauer** *m (-s/-)* street ballad, popular song; **'~njunge** *m* street arab.

Gast [gast] *m (-es/⸗e)* guest; visitor; customer (*of public house, etc.*); *thea.*: guest (artist); guest star; **'~arbeiter** *m* foreign worker; **'~bett** *n* spare bed.

Gäste|buch ['gɛstə-] *n* visitors' book; **'~zimmer** *n* guest-room; spare (bed)room; *s. Gaststube.*

gast|freundlich *adj.* hospitable; **'2freundschaft** *f* hospitality; **'2geber** *m (-s/-)* host; **'2geberin** *f (-/-nen)* hostess; **'2haus** *n*, **'2hof** *m* restaurant; inn, hotel; **'2hörer** *univ. m* guest student, *Am. a.* auditor.

gastieren *thea.* [gas'ti:rən] *v/i. (no -ge-, h)* appear as a guest.

'gast|lich *adj.* hospitable; **'2mahl** *n* feast, banquet; **'2recht** *n* right of *or* to hospitality; **'2rolle** *thea. f* guest part; starring part *or* role; **'2spiel** *thea. n* guest appearance *or* performance, starring (performance); **'2stätte** *f* restaurant; **'2stube** *f* taproom; restaurant; **'2wirt** *m* innkeeper, landlord; **'2wirtin** *f* innkeeper, landlady; **'2wirtschaft** *f* inn, public house, restaurant; **'2zimmer** *n s. Gästezimmer.*

'Gas|uhr *f* gas-meter; **'~werk** *n s. Gasanstalt.*

Gatte ['gatə] *m (-n/-n)* husband; spouse, consort.

Gatter ['gatər] *n (-s/-)* lattice; railing, grating.

'Gattin *f (-/-nen)* wife; spouse, consort.

Gattung ['gatʊŋ] *f (-/-en)* kind; sort; type; species; genus.

gaukeln ['gaʊkəln] *v/i. (ge-, h)* juggle; *birds, etc.*: flutter.

Gaul [gaul] *m* (-[e]s/ᵉe) (old) nag.
Gaumen *anat.* ['gaumən] *m* (-s/-) palate.
Gauner ['gaunər] *m* (-s/-) scoundrel, swindler, sharper, *sl.* crook; **~ei** [~'rai] *f* (-/-en) swindling, cheating, trickery.
Gaze ['ga:zə] *f* (-/-n) gauze.
Gazelle *zo.* [ga'tsɛlə] *f* (-/-n) gazelle.
Geächtete [gə'ɛçtətə] *m*, *f* (-n/-n) outlaw.
Gebäck [gə'bɛk] *n* (-[e]s/-e) baker's goods *pl.*; pastry; fancy cakes *pl.*
ge'backen *p.p. of* backen.
Gebälk [gə'bɛlk] *n* (-[e]s/no *pl.*) framework, timber-work; beams *pl.*
gebar [gə'ba:r] *pret. of* gebären.
Gebärde [gə'bɛ:rdə] *f* (-/-n) gesture; **2n** *v/refl.* (no -ge-, *h*) conduct o.s., behave; **~nspiel** *n* (-[e]s/no *pl.*) gesticulation; dumb show, panto-mime; **~nsprache** *f* language of gestures.
Gebaren [gə'ba:rən] *n* (-s/no *pl.*) conduct, deportment, behavio(u)r.
gebären [gə'bɛ:rən] *v/t.* (irr., no -ge-, *h*) bear, bring forth (*a. fig.*); give birth to.
Ge|bäude [gə'bɔydə] *n* (-s/-) build-ing, edifice, structure; **~bell** [~'bɛl] *n* (-[e]s/no *pl.*) barking.
geben ['ge:bən] *v/t.* (irr., ge-, *h*) give (*j-m* et. s.o. s.th.); present (s.o. with s.th.); put; yield *s.th.*; deal (*cards*); pledge (*one's word*); *von sich ~* emit; utter (*words*); bring up, vomit (*food*); et. (*nichts*) ~ *auf* (*acc.*) set (no) great store by; *sich geschlagen ~* give in; *sich zufrieden ~* content o.s. (*mit* with); *sich zu erkennen ~* make o.s. known; *es gibt* there is, there are; *was gibt es?* what is the matter?; *thea.: gegeben werden* be on.
Gebet [gə'be:t] *n* (-[e]s/-e) prayer.
ge'beten *p.p. of* bitten.
Gebiet [gə'bi:t] *n* (-[e]s/-e) territory; district; region; area; *fig.:* field; province; sphere.
ge'biet|en (irr. bieten, no -ge-, *h*) **1.** *v/t.* order, command; **2.** *v/i.* rule; **2er** *m* (-s/-) master, lord, governor; **2erin** *f* (-/-nen) mistress; **~erisch** *adj.* imperious; commanding.
Gebilde [gə'bildə] *n* (-s/-) form, shape; structure; **2t** *adj.* educated; cultured, cultivated.
Gebirg|e [gə'birgə] *n* (-s/-) moun-tains *pl.*; mountain chain *or* range; **2ig** *adj.* mountainous; **~sbewoh-ner** *m* mountaineer; **~szug** *m* moun-tain range.
Ge'biß *n* (Gebisses/Gebisse) (set of) teeth; (set of) artificial *or* false teeth, denture; *harness:* bit.
ge|'bissen *p.p. of* beißen; **~'blasen** *p.p. of* blasen; **~'blichen** *p.p. of* bleichen 2; **~'blieben** [~'bli:bən] *p.p. of* bleiben; **~blümt** *adj.*

[~'bly:mt] *pattern, design:* flowered; *material:* sprigged; **~'bogen 1.** *p.p. of* biegen; **2.** *adj.* bent, curved; **~boren** [~'bo:rən] **1.** *p.p. of* ge-bären; **2.** *adj.* born; *ein ~er Deut-scher* German by birth; *~e Schmidt* née Smith.
ge'borgen 1. *p.p. of* bergen; **2.** *adj.* safe, sheltered; **2heit** *f* (-/no *pl.*) safety, security.
geborsten [gə'bɔrstən] *p.p. of* ber-sten.
Ge'bot *n* (-[e]s/-e) order; command; bid(ding), offer; *eccl.: die Zehn ~e pl.* the Ten Commandments *pl.*; **2en** *p.p. of* bieten.
ge|bracht [gə'braxt] *p.p. of* bringen; **~brannt** [~'brant] *p.p. of* brennen; **~'braten** *p.p. of* braten.
Ge'brauch *m* **1.** (-[e]s/no *pl.*) use; application; **2.** (-[e]s/~e) usage, practice; custom; **2en** *v/t.* (no -ge-, *h*) use, employ; **2t** *adj. clothes, etc.:* second-hand.
gebräuchlich *adj.* [gə'brɔyçliç] in use; usual, customary.
Ge'brauchs|anweisung *f* direc-tions *pl.* or instructions *pl.* for use; **~artikel** *m* commodity, necessary, requisite; personal article; **2fertig** *adj.* ready for use; *coffee, etc.:* instant; **~muster ↑** *n* sample; registered design.
Ge'braucht|wagen *mot. m* used car; **~waren** *f/pl.* second-hand articles *pl.*
Ge'brechen *n* (-s/-) defect, infir-mity; affliction.
ge'brechlich *adj.* fragile; *p.:* frail, weak; infirm; **2keit** *f* (-/-en) fragility, infirmity.
gebrochen [gə'brɔxən] *p.p. of* bre-chen.
Ge|brüder [gə'bry:dər] *pl.* brothers *pl.*; **~brüll** [~'bryl] *n* (-[e]s/no *pl.*) roaring; lowing (*of cattle*).
Gebühr [gə'by:r] *f* (-/-en) due; duty; charge; rate; fee; *~en pl.* fee(s *pl.*), dues *pl.*; **2en** *v/i.* (no -ge-, *h*) be due (*dat.* to); *sich ~* be proper *or* fitting; **2end** *adj.* due; becoming; proper; **2enfrei** *adj.* free of charge; **2enpflichtig** *adj.* liable to charges, chargeable.
gebunden [gə'bundən] **1.** *p.p. of* binden; **2.** *adj.* bound.
Geburt [gə'bu:rt] *f* (-/-en) birth; **~enkontrolle** *f*, **~enregelung** *f* birth-control; **~enziffer** *f* birth-rate.
gebürtig *adj.* [gə'byrtiç]: *~ aus a* native of.
Ge'burts|anzeige *f* announcement of birth; **~fehler** *m* congenital defect; **~helfer** *m* obstetrician; **~hilfe** *f* obstetrics, midwifery; **~jahr** *n* year of birth; **~land** *n* na-tive country; **~ort** *m* birth-place; **~schein** *m* birth certificate; **~tag** *m*

birthday; **~urkunde** f birth certificate.
Gebüsch [gə'byʃ] n (-es/-e) bushes
pl., undergrowth, thicket.
gedacht [gə'daxt] p.p. of denken.
Gedächtnis [gə'dɛçtnis] n (-ses/-se)
memory; remembrance, recollection; im ~ behalten keep in mind;
zum ~ (gen.) in memory of; **~feier**
f commemoration.
Gedanke [gə'daŋkə] m (-ns/-n)
thought; idea; in ~n (versunken or
verloren) absorbed in thought; sich
~n machen über (acc.) worry about.
Ge'danken|gang m train of thought;
~leser m, **~leserin** f (-/-nen)
thought-reader; **2los** adj. thoughtless; **~strich** m dash; **2voll** adj.
thoughtful, pensive.
Ge|därm [gə'dɛrm] n (-[e]s/-e) mst
pl. entrails pl., bowels pl., intestines
pl.; **~deck** [~'dɛk] n (-[e]s/-e) cover;
menu; ein ~ auflegen lay a place.
gedeihen [gə'daɪən] 1. v/i. (irr., no
-ge-, sein) thrive, prosper; 2. 2 n
(-s/no pl.) thriving, prosperity.
ge'denken 1. v/i. (gen.) (irr. denken,
no -ge-, h) think of; remember,
recollect; commemorate; mention;
~ zu inf. intend to inf.; 2. 2 n (-s/no
pl.) memory, remembrance (an acc.
of).
Ge'denk|feier f commemoration;
~stein m memorial stone; **~tafel** f
commemorative or memorial tablet.
Ge'dicht n (-[e]s/-e) poem.
gediegen adj. [gə'di:gən] solid;
pure; **2heit** f (-/no pl.) solidity;
purity.
gedieh [gə'di:] pret. of gedeihen;
~en p.p. of gedeihen.
Gedräng|e [gə'drɛŋə] n (-s/no pl.)
crowd, throng; **2t** adj. crowded,
packed, crammed; style: concise.
ge|droschen [gə'drɔʃən] p.p. of
dreschen; **~'drückt** fig. adj. depressed; **~drungen** [~'druŋən]
1. p.p. of dringen; 2. adj. compact;
squat, stocky, thickset.
Geduld [gə'dult] f (-/no pl.) patience; **2en** [~dən] v/refl. (no -ge-,
h) have patience; **2ig** adj. [~diç]
patient.
ge|dunsen adj. [gə'dunzən] bloated;
~durft [~'durft] p.p. of dürfen 1;
~ehrt adj. [~'e:rt] hono(u)red; correspondence: Sehr ~er Herr N.! Dear
Sir, Dear Mr N.; **~eignet** adj.
[~'aɪgnət] fit (für, zu, als for s.th.);
suitable (to, for); qualified (for).
Gefahr [gə'fa:r] f (-/-en) danger,
peril; risk; auf eigene ~ at one's
own risk; ~ laufen zu inf. run the
risk of ger.
gefährden [gə'fɛ:rdən] v/t. (no -ge-,
h) endanger; risk.
ge'fahren p.p. of fahren.
gefährlich adj. [gə'fɛ:rliç] dangerous.

ge'fahrlos adj. without risk, safe.
Gefährt|e [gə'fɛ:rtə] m (-en/-en),
~in f (-/-nen) companion, fellow.
Gefälle [gə'fɛlə] n (-s/-) fall, slope,
incline, descent, gradient, esp. Am.
a. grade; fall (of river, etc.).
Ge'fallen 1. m (-s/-) favo(u)r; 2. n
(-s/no pl.): ~ finden an (dat.) take
(a) pleasure in, take a fancy to or
for; 3. 2 v/i. (irr. fallen, no -ge-, h)
please (j-m s.o.); er gefällt mir I
like him; sich et. ~ lassen put up
with s.th.; 4. 2 p.p. of fallen.
gefällig adj. [gə'fɛliç] pleasing,
agreeable; p.: complaisant, obliging;
kind; **2keit** f (-/-\,-en) complai-
sance, kindness; favo(u)r; **~st** adv.
(if you) please.
ge'fangen 1. p.p. of fangen; 2. adj.
captive, imprisoned; **2e** m (-n/-n),
f (-n/-n) prisoner, captive; **2en-
lager** n prison(ers') camp; **2-
nahme** f (-/no pl.) capture; seizure,
arrest; **~nehmen** v/t. (irr. nehmen,
sep., -ge-, h) take prisoner; fig. captivate; **2schaft** f (-/no pl.) captiv-
ity, imprisonment; **~setzen** v/t.
(sep., -ge-, h) put in prison.
Gefängnis [gə'fɛŋnis] n (-ses/-se)
prison, jail, gaol, Am. a. peniten-
tiary; **~direktor** m governor,
warden; **~strafe** f (sentence or term
of) imprisonment; **~wärter** m
warder, gaoler, jailer, (prison)
guard.
Gefäß [gə'fɛ:s] n (-es/-e) vessel.
gefaßt adj. [gə'fast] composed; ~
auf (acc.) prepared for.
Ge|fecht [gə'fɛçt] n (-[e]s/-e) en-
gagement; combat, fight; action;
~fieder [~'fi:dər] n (-s/-) plumage,
feathers pl.
ge|fleckt adj. spotted; **~flochten**
[~'flɔxtən] p.p. of flechten; **~flogen**
[~'flo:gən] p.p. of fliegen; **~flohen**
[~'flo:ən] p.p. of fliehen; **~flossen**
[~'flɔsən] p.p. of fließen.
Ge|'flügel n (-s/no pl.) fowl; poul-
try; **~flüster** [~'flystər] n (-s/no pl.)
whisper(ing).
gefochten [gə'fɔxtən] p.p. of fechten.
Ge'folg|e n (-s/no pl.) retinue,
train, followers pl.; attendants pl.;
~schaft [~kʃaft] f (-/-en) followers
pl.
gefräßig adj. [gə'frɛ:siç] greedy,
voracious; **2keit** f (-/no pl.) greedi-
ness, gluttony, voracity.
ge'fressen p.p. of fressen.
ge'frier|en v/i. (irr. frieren, no -ge-,
sein) congeal, freeze; **2fleisch** n
frozen meat; **2punkt** m freezing-
point; **2schutz(mittel** n) m anti-
freeze.
gefroren [gə'fro:rən] p.p. of frieren;
2e [~ə] n (-n/no pl.) ice-cream.
Gefüge [gə'fy:gə] n (-s/-) structure;
texture.

ge'fügig *adj.* pliant; **2keit** *f* (*-/no pl.*) pliancy.

Gefühl [gə'fy:l] *n* (*-[e]s/-e*) feeling; touch; sense (*für* of); sensation; **2los** *adj.* unfeeling, insensible (*gegen* to); **2sbetont** *adj.* emotional; **2voll** *adj.* (full of) feeling; tender; sentimental.

ge|funden [gə'fundən] *p.p. of finden;* **~gangen** [*~*'gaŋən] *p.p. of gehen.*

ge'geben *p.p. of geben,* **~enfalls** *adv.* in that case; if necessary.

gegen *prp.* (*acc.*) ['ge:gən] space, time: towards; against, *t*'*z* versus; about, *Am.* around; by; compared with; (in exchange) for; *remedy:* for; *freundlich sein ~* be kind to (*-wards*); *~ bar* for cash.

'Gegen|angriff *m* counter-attack; **~antrag** *m* counter-motion; '**~antwort** *f* rejoinder; '**~befehl** *m* counter-order, **~beschuldigung** *f* countercharge, **~besuch** *m* return visit; '**~bewegung** *f* counter-movement; '**~beweis** *m* counter-evidence.

Gegend ['ge:gənt] *f* (*-/-en*) region; area.

'Gegen|dienst *m* return service, service in return; '**~druck** *m* counter-pressure; *fig.* reaction; **2ei'nander** *adv.* against one another *or* each other; **~erklärung** *f* counter-statement; **~forderung** *f* counter-claim; '**~frage** *f* counter-question; '**~geschenk** *n* return present; '**~gewicht** *n* counterbalance, counterpoise; '**~gift** *š n* antidote; '**~kandidat** *m* rival candidate; '**~klage** *f* countercharge; '**~leistung** *f* return (service), equivalent; '**~lichtaufnahme** *phot.* ['gə:gənliçt^?-] *f* back-lighted shot; '**~liebe** *f* requited love; *keine ~ finden* meet with no sympathy *or* enthusiasm; '**~maßnahme** *f* counter-measure; '**~mittel** *n* remedy (*gegen* for), antidote (against, for); '**~partei** *f* opposite party; **~probe** *f* check-test; '**~satz** *m* contrast; opposition; *im ~ zu* in contrast to *or* with, in opposition to; **2sätzlich** *adj.* ['**~**zetsliç] contrary, opposite; '**~seite** *f* opposite side; **2seitig** *adj.* mutual, reciprocal; '**~seitigkeit** *f* (*-/no pl.*): *auf ~ assurance:* mutual; *auf ~ beruhen* be mutual; '**~spieler** *m* games, sports: opponent; antagonist; '**~spionage** *f* counter-espionage; '**~stand** *m* object; subject, topic; '**~strömung** *f* counter-current; '**~stück** *n* counterpart; match; '**~teil** *n* contrary, reverse; *im ~* on the contrary, '**2teilig** *adj.* contrary, opposite; **2'über 1.** *adv.* opposite; **2.** *prp.* (*dat.*) opposite (to); to (*-wards*); as against; face to face with; **~'über** *n* (*-s/-*) vis-à-vis;

2'überstehen *v/i.* (*irr.* stehen, *sep.,* -ge-, h) (*dat.*) be faced with, face; **~'überstellung** *esp. t*'*z f* confrontation; '**~vorschlag** *m* counter-proposal, **~wart** ['**~**vart] *f* (*-/no pl.*) presence; present time; *gr.* present tense; **2wärtig** [**~**'vertiç] **1.** *adj.* present; actual; **2.** *adv.* at present; '**~wehr** *f* defen|ce, *Am.* -se; resistance; '**~wert** *m* equivalent; '**~wind** *m* contrary wind, head wind; '**~wirkung** *f* counter-effect, reaction; '**2zeichnen** *v/t.* (*sep.,* -ge-, h) countersign; '**~zug** *m* counter-move (*a. fig.*); **ᚋ** corresponding train.

ge|gessen [gə'gesən] *p.p. of essen,* **~glichen** [**~**'gliçən] *p.p. of gleichen;* **~'gliedert** *adj.* articulate, jointed; **~'glitten** [**~**'glitən] *p.p. of gleiten;* **~glommen** [**~**'glomən] *p.p. of glimmen.*

Gegner ['ge:gnər] *m* (*-s/-*) adversary, opponent; '**~schaft** *f* (*-/-en*) opposition.

ge|golten [gə'goltən] *p.p. of gelten;* **~goren** [**~**'go:rən] *p.p. of gären;* **~gossen** [**~**'gosən] *p.p. of gießen;* **~graben** *p.p. of graben;* **~griffen** [**~**'grifən] *p.p. of greifen;* **~habt** [**~**'ha:pt] *p.p. of haben.*

Gehalt [gə'halt] **1.** *m* (*-[e]s/-e*) contents *f*.; capacity; merit; **2.** *n* (*-[e]s/**~**er*) salary; **2en** *p.p. of halten;* **2los** [**~**lo:s] *adj* empty; **~sempfänger** [gə'halts^?-] *m* salaried employee *or* worker; **~serhöhung** [gə'halts^?-] *f* rise (in salary), *Am.* raise; **2voll** *adj.* rich; substantial; *wine:* racy.

gehangen [gə'haŋən] *p.p. of hängen 1.*

gehässig *adj.* [gə'hesiç] malicious, spiteful; **2keit** *f* (*-/-en*) malice, spitefulness.

ge'hauen *p.p. of hauen.*

Ge|häuse [gə'hɔyzə] *n* (*-s/-*) case, box; cabinet; shell; core (*of apple, etc.*); **~hege** [**~**'he:gə] *n* (*-s/-*) enclosure.

geheim *adj.* [gə'haɪm] secret; **2dienst** *m* secret service.

Ge'heimnis *n* (*-ses/-se*) secret; mystery; **~krämer** *m* mystery-monger; **2voll** *adj.* mysterious.

Ge'heim|polizei *f* secret police; **~polizist** *m* detective; plain-clothes man; **~schrift** *f* cipher; *tel.* code.

ge'heißen *p.p. of heißen.*

gehen ['ge:ən] *v/i.* (*irr.,* ge-, sein) go; walk; leave; *machine:* go, work; *clock, watch:* go; *merchandise:* sell; *wind:* blow; *paste:* rise; *wie geht es Ihnen?* how are you (getting on)?; *das geht nicht* that won't do; *in sich ~* repent; *wieviel Pfennige ~ auf e-e Mark?* how many pfennigs go to a mark?; *das Fenster geht nach Norden* the window faces *or* looks north; *es geht nichts über* (acc.) there is nothing like; *wenn es nach mir ginge* if I had my way.

Geheul [gə'hɔʏl] n (-[e]s/no pl.) howling.

Ge'hilf|e m (-n/-n), **~in** f (-/-nen) assistant; fig. helpmate.

Ge'hirn n (-[e]s/-e) brain(s pl.); **~erschütterung** ♂ f concussion (of the brain); **~schlag** ♂ m cerebral apoplexy.

gehoben [gə'ho:bən] 1. p.p. of *heben*; 2. adj. speech, style: elevated; **~e Stimmung** elated mood.

Gehöft [gə'hø:ft] n (-[e]s/-e) farm (-stead).

geholfen [gə'hɔlfən] p.p. of *helfen*.

Gehölz [gə'hœlts] n (-es/-e) wood, coppice, copse.

Gehör [gə'hø:r] n (-[e]s/no pl.) hearing; ear; *nach dem ~* by ear; *j-m ~ schenken* lend an ear to s.o.; *sich ~ verschaffen* make o.s. heard.

ge'horchen v/i. (no -ge-, h) obey (j-m s.o.).

ge'hör|en v/i. (no -ge-, h) belong (dat. or zu to); *es gehört sich* it is proper or fit or right or suitable; *das gehört nicht hierher* that's not to the point; **~ig** 1. adj. belonging (dat. or zu to); fit, proper, right; due; F good; 2. adv. duly; F thoroughly.

gehorsam [gə'ho:rza:m] 1. adj. obedient; 2. 2 m (-s/no pl.) obedience.

Geh|steig m, **~weg** m pavement, Am. sidewalk; **~werk** ⊕ n clockwork, works pl.

Geier orn. ['gaɪər] m (-s/-) vulture.

Geige ♪ ['gaɪgə] f (-/-n) violin, F fiddle; *(auf der) ~ spielen* play (on) the violin; **~nbogen** ♪ m (violin-)bow; **~nkasten** ♪ m violin-case; **~r** ♪ m (-s/-), **~rin** ♪ f (-/-nen) violinist.

'Geigerzähler phys. m Geiger counter.

geil adj. [gaɪl] lascivious, wanton; luxuriant.

Geisel ['gaɪzəl] f (-/-n) hostage.

Geiß zo. [gaɪs] f (-/-en) (she-, nanny-)goat; **~blatt** ♀ n (-[e]s/no pl.) honeysuckle, woodbine; **~bock** zo. m he-goat, billy-goat.

Geißel ['gaɪsəl] f (-/-n) whip, lash; fig. scourge; **2n** v/t. (ge-, h) whip, lash; fig. castigate.

Geist [gaɪst] m (-es/-er) spirit; mind, intellect; wit; ghost; sprite. **'Geister|erscheinung** f apparition; **2haft** adj. ghostly.

'geistes|abwesend adj. absentminded; **2arbeiter** m brainworker, white-collar worker; **2blitz** m brain-wave, flash of genius; **2gabe** f talent; **2gegenwart** f presence of mind; **~gegenwärtig** adj. alert; quick-witted; **~gestört** adj. mentally disturbed; **~krank** adj. insane, mentally ill; **2krankheit** f insanity, mental illness; **~schwach** adj. feeble-minded, imbecile; **~verwandt** adj. congenial; **2wissenschaften** f/pl. the Arts pl., the Humanities pl.; **2zustand** m state of mind.

'geistig adj. intellectual, mental; spiritual; **~e Getränke** n/pl. spirits pl.

'geistlich adj. spiritual; clerical; sacred; **2e** m (-n/-n) clergyman; minister; **2keit** f (-/no pl.) clergy. **'geist|los** adj. spiritless; dull; stupid; **~reich** adj., **~voll** adj. ingenious, spirited.

Geiz [gaɪts] m (-es/no pl.) avarice; **~hals** m miser, niggard; **2ig** adj. avaricious, stingy, mean.

Gejammer [gə'jamər] n (-s/no pl.) lamentation(s pl.), wailing.

gekannt [gə'kant] p.p. of *kennen*.

Geklapper [gə'klapər] n (-s/no pl.) rattling.

Geklirr [gə'klir] n (-[e]s/no pl.), **~e** [**~ə**] n (-s/no pl.) clashing, clanking.

ge|klungen [**~'kluŋən**] p.p. of *klingen*; **~'kniffen** p.p. of *kneifen*; **~'kommen** p.p. of *kommen*; **~'konnt** [**~'kɔnt**] p.p. of *können* 1, 2.

Ge|kreisch [gə'kraɪʃ] n (-es/no pl.) screaming, screams pl.; shrieking; **~kritzel** [**~'kritsəl**] n (-s/no pl.) scrawl(ing), scribbling, scribble.

ge|krochen [gə'krɔxən] p.p. of *kriechen*; **~künstelt** adj. [**~'kyn-stəlt**] affected.

Gelächter [gə'lɛçtər] n (-s/-) laughter.

ge'laden p.p. of *laden*.

Ge'lage n (-s/-) feast; drinking-bout.

Gelände [gə'lɛndə] n (-s/-) ground; terrain; country; area; **2gängig** mot. adj. cross-country; **~lauf** m sports: cross-country race or run.

Geländer [gə'lɛndər] n (-s/-) railing, balustrade; banisters pl.

ge'lang pret. of *gelingen*.

ge'langen v/i. (no -ge-, sein): **~ an** (acc.) or *in* (acc.) arrive at, get or come to; **~ zu** attain (to), gain.

ge'lassen 1. p.p. of *lassen*; 2. adj. calm, composed.

Gelatine [ʒela'ti:nə] f (-/no pl.) gelatin(e).

ge'laufen p.p. of *laufen*; **~läufig** adj. [**~'lɔʏfiç**] current; fluent, easy; tongue: voluble; familiar; **~launt** adj. [**~'lɔʏnt**] in a (good, etc.) humo(u)r or Am. mood.

Geläut [gə'lɔʏt] n (-[e]s/-e), **~e** [**~ə**] n (-s/-) ringing (of bells); chimes pl. (of church bells).

gelb adj. [gɛlp] yellow; **~lich** adj. yellowish; **2sucht** ♂ f (-/no pl.) jaundice.

Geld [gɛlt] n (-[e]s/-er) money; im

~ schwimmen be rolling in money; zu ~ machen turn into cash; '~angelegenheit f money-matter; '~anlage f investment; ~ausgabe f expense; ~beutel m purse; '~entwertung f devaluation of the currency; ~erwerb m money-making; ~geber m -s/- financial backer, investor; ~geschäfte n/pl. money transactions pl.; 2gierig adj. greedy for money, avaricious; '~mittel n/pl. ~unds pl., resources pl.; ~schein m bank-note, Am. bill; ~schrank m strong-box, safe; '~sendung f remittance; ~strafe f fine; ~stück n coin; ~tasche f money-bag; notecase, Am. billfold; '~überhang m surplus money; '~umlauf m circulation of money; '~umsatz m turnover (of money); '~verlegenheit f pecuniary embarrassment, ~wechsel m exchange of money, ~wert m (-[e]s/no pl.) value of money, money value.

Gelee [ʒə'le:] n, m -s/-s jelly.

ge'legen 1. p.p. of liegen; **2.** adj. situated, Am. a located; convenient, opportune, 2heit f (-/-en) occasion; opportunity; chance; facility; bei on occasion.

Ge'legenheits|arbeit f casual or odd job, 4m a. chore; ~arbeiter m casual labo(u)rer, odd-job man; ~kauf m bargain.

ge'legentlich 1. adj. occasional; **2.** prp. (gen.) on the occasion of.

ge'lehrig adj. docile, 2igkeit f (-/no pl.) docility, 2samkeit f (-/no pl.) learning; ~t adj. [~t] learned; 2te [~ə] m (-n/-n) learned man, scholar.

Geleise [gə'laızə] n (-s/-) rut, track; ⑯ rails pl., line, esp. Am. tracks pl.

Geleit [gə'laıt] n (-[e]s/-e) escort; attendance; j-m das ~ geben accompany s.o.; 2en v/t. (no -ge-, h) accompany, conduct; escort; ~zug ⚓ m convoy.

Gelenk anat., ⊕, ⚓ [gə'leŋk] n (-[e]s/-e) joint; 2ig adj. pliable, supple.

ge'lernt adj. worker: skilled; trained; ~lesen p.p. of lesen.

Geliebte [gə'li:ptə] (-n/-n) **1.** m lover; **2.** f mistress, sweetheart.

geliehen [gə'li:ən] p.p. of leihen.

ge'linde 1. adj. soft, smooth; gentle; **2.** adv. gelinde gesagt to put it mildly, to say the least.

gelingen [gə'liŋən] **1.** v/i. (irr., no -ge-, sein) succeed; es gelingt mir zu inf. I succeed in ger.; **2.** 2 n (-s/no pl.) success.

ge'litten p.p. of leiden.

gellen ['gɛlən] (ge-) **1.** v/i. shrill; yell; of ears: ring, tingle; **2.** v/t. shrill; yell; '~d adj. shrill, piercing.

ge'loben v/t. (no -ge-, h) vow, promise.

Gelöbnis [gə'lø:pnis] n (-ses/-se) promise, pledge; vow.

ge'logen p.p. of lügen.

gelt|en ['gɛltən] (irr., ge-, h) **1.** v/t. be worth; **2.** v/i. be of value; be valid; go; count; money be current; maxim, etc. hold good or true); et. ~ haben have credit or influence; j-m ~ concern s.o.; für or als pass for, be reputed or thought or supposed to be; ~ für apply to; ~ lassen let pass, allow; ~d machen maintain, assert; s-n Einfluß bei j-m ~d machen bring one's influence to bear on s.o., das gilt nicht that is not fair; that does not count; es galt unser Leben our life was at stake; '2ung f (-/~ -en) validity; value; currency; authority (of person); zur ~ kommen tell; take effect; show; '2ungsbedürfnis n desire to show off. [ise; vow.

Gelübde [gə'lypdə] n -s/- prom-]

gelungen [gə'luŋən] **1.** p.p. of gelingen; **2.** adj. successful; amusing, funny; F: das ist ja ~! that beats everything!

gemächlich adj. [gə'mɛ:çlɪç] comfortable, easy; 2keit f (-/no pl.) ease, comfort.

Gemahl [gə'mɑ:l] m (-[e]s/-e) consort; husband.

ge'mahlen p.p. of mahlen.

Gemälde [gə'mɛ:ldə] n (-s/-) painting, picture; ~galerie f picture-gallery.

gemäß prp. (dat.) [gə'mɛ:s] according to; ~igt adj. moderate; temperate (a. geogr.).

gemein adj. [gə'maın] common; general; low, vulgar, mean, coarse; et. ~ haben mit have s.th. in common with.

Gemeinde [gə'maındə] f (-/-n) community; parish; municipality; eccl. congregation; ~bezirk m district; municipality; ~rat m municipal council; ~steuer f rate, Am. local tax; ~vorstand m district council.

ge'mein|gefährlich adj. dangerous to the public; ~er Mensch public danger, Am. public enemy; 2heit f (-/-en) vulgarity; meanness; mean trick; ~nützig adj. of public utility; 2platz m commonplace; ~sam adj. common; joint; mutual; 2schaft f (-/-en) community; intercourse; ~schaftlich adj. s. gemeinsam; 2schaftsarbeit [gə'maınʃafts'-] f team-work; 2sinn m (-[e]s/no pl.) public spirit; ~verständlich adj. popular; 2wesen n community; 2wohl n public welfare.

Ge'menge n (-s/-) mixture.

ge'messen 1. p.p. of messen; **2.** adj. measured; formal; grave.

Gemetzel [gə'mɛtsəl] n (-s/-) slaughter, massacre.

gemieden [gə'mi:dən] *p.p. of* meiden.

Gemisch [gə'miʃ] *n* (-es/-e) mixture; ♫ compound, composition.

ge|mocht [gə'məxt] *p.p. of* mögen; **molken** [gə'məlkən] *p.p. of* melken.

Gemse *zo.* ['gemzə] *f* (-/-n) chamois.

Gemurmel [gə'murməl] *n* (-s/no *pl.*) murmur(ing).

Gemüse [gə'my:zə] *n* (-s/-) vegetable(s *pl.*); greens *pl.*; **anbau** *m* vegetable gardening, *Am.* truck farming; **garten** *m* kitchen garden; **händler** *m* greengrocer.

gemußt [gə'must] *p.p. of* müssen 1.

Gemüt [gə'my:t] *n* (-[e]s/-er) mind; feeling; soul; heart; disposition; temper; **lich** *adj.* good-natured; genial; comfortable, snug, cosy, cozy; **lichkeit** *f* (-/no *pl.*) snugness, cosiness; easy-going; genial temper.

Ge'müts|art *f* disposition, nature, temper, character; **bewegung** *f* emotion; **krank** *adj.* emotionally disturbed; melancholic, depressed; **krankheit** *f* mental disorder; melancholy; **ruhe** *f* composure; **verfassung** *f*, **zustand** *m* state of mind, humo(u)r.

ge'mütvoll *adj.* emotional; full of feeling.

genannt [gə'nant] *p.p. of* nennen.

genas [gə'nɑːs] *pret. of* genesen.

genau *adj.* [gə'nau] exact, accurate; precise; strict; es nehmen (mit) be particular (about); **eres** full particulars *pl.*; **igkeit** *f* (-/-en) accuracy, exactness; precision; strictness.

genehm *adj.* [gə'ne:m] agreeable, convenient; **igen** [..igən] *v/t.* (*no* -ge-, h) grant; approve (of); **igung** *f* (-/-en) grant; approval; licen|ce, *Am.* -se; permit; permission; consent.

geneigt *adj.* [gə'naikt] well disposed (j-m towards s.o.); inclined (zu to).

General ♫ [gene'rɑːl] *m* (-s/-e, **e**) general; **bevollmächtigte** *m* chief representative *or* agent, **direktor** *m* general manager, managing director; **feldmarschall** ♫ *m* field-marshal, **intendant** *thea. m* (artistic) director, **konsul** *m* consul-general; **konsulat** *n* consulate-general; **leutnant** ♫ *m* lieutenant-general; **major** ♫ *m* major-general; **probe** *thea. f* dress rehearsal; **stab** ♫ *m* general staff; **stabskarte** ♫ *f* ordnance (survey) map, *Am.* strategic map; **streik** *m* general strike; **versammlung** *f* general meeting; **vertreter** *m* general agent; **vollmacht** *f* full power of attorney.

Generation [genəra'tsjo:n] *f* (-/-en) generation.

generell *adj.* [genə'rel] general.

genes|en [gə'ne:zən] **1.** *v/i.* (*irr., no* -ge-, sein) recover (von from); **2.** *p.p. of* 1; **ende** *m, f* (-n/-n) convalescent; **ung** *f* (-/**%** -en) recovery.

genial *adj.* [gen'jɑːl] highly gifted, ingenious; **ität** [..ali'tɛːt] *f* (-/no *pl.*) genius.

Genick [gə'nik] *n* (-[e]s/-e) nape (of the neck), (back of the) neck.

Genie [ʒe'niː] *n* (-s/-s) genius.

ge'nieren *v/t.* (*no* -ge-, h) trouble, bother; sich feel *or* be embarrassed *or* shy; be self-conscious.

genießen [gə'niːsən] *v/t.* (*irr., no* -ge-, h) enjoy; eat; drink; et. take some food *or* refreshments; j-s Vertrauen be in s.o.'s confidence.

Genitiv *gr.* ['ge:nitiːf] *m* (-s/-e) genitive (case); possessive (case).

ge|nommen [gə'nɔmən] *p.p. of* nehmen; **normt** *adj.* standardized; **noß** [..'nɔs] *pret. of* genießen.

Genoss|e [gə'nɔsə] *m* (-n/-n) companion, mate; comrade (*a. pol.*); **en** *p.p. of* genießen; **enschaft** *f* (-/-en) company, association; co(-)operative (society); **in** *f* (-/-nen) (female) companion; comrade (*a. pol.*).

genug *adj.* [gə'nuːk] enough, sufficient.

Genüg|e [gə'ny:gə] *f* (-/no *pl.*): zur enough, sufficiently; **en** *v/i.* (*no* -ge-, h) be enough, suffice; das genügt that will do; j-m satisfy s.o.; **end** *adj.* sufficient; **sam** *adj.* [..k-] easily satisfied; frugal; **samkeit** [..k-] *f* (-/no *pl.*) modesty; frugality.

Genugtuung [gə'nuːktuːuŋ] *f* (-/-en) satisfaction. [gender.]

Genus *gr.* ['ge:nus] *n* (-/Genera)

Genuß [gə'nus] *m* (Genusses/Genüsse) enjoyment; pleasure; use; consumption; taking (of food); *fig.* treat; **mittel** *n* semi-luxury; **sucht** *f* (-/no *pl.*) thirst for pleasure; **süchtig** *adj.* pleasure-seeking.

Geo|graph [geo'grɑːf] *m* (-en/-en) geographer; **graphie** [..a'fiː] *f* (-/no *pl.*) geography; **graphisch** *adj.* [..'grɑːfiʃ] geographic(al); **loge** [..'lo:gə] *m* (-n/-n) geologist; **logie** [..lo'giː] *f* (-/no *pl.*) geology; **logisch** *adj.* [..'lo:giʃ] geologic(al); **metrie** [..me'triː] *f* (-/-n) geometry; **metrisch** *adj.* [..'me:triʃ] geometric(al).

Gepäck [gə'pɛk] *n* (-[e]s/no *pl.*) luggage, ♫ *or Am.* baggage; **annahme** *f* luggage (registration) counter, *Am.* baggage (registration) counter; **aufbewahrung** *f* (-/-en) left-luggage office, *Am.* checkroom; **ausgabe** *f* luggage delivery office, *Am.* baggage room; **netz** *n* luggage-rack, *Am.* baggage rack; ~schein *m* luggage-ticket, *Am.* baggage check; ~träger *m* porter, *Am. a.* redcap; *on bicycle* carrier; ~wagen *m* luggage van, *Am.* baggage car.

ge|pfiffen [gə'pfifən] *p.p. of* pfeifen; ~pflegt *adj.* [~'pfle:kt] *appearance:* well-groomed; *hands, garden, etc.:* well cared-for; *garden, etc.:* well-kept.

Gepflogenheit [gə'pflo:gənhaɪt] *f* (-/-en) habit; custom; usage.

Ge|plapper [gə'plapər] *n* (-s/*no pl.*) babbling, chattering; ~plauder [~'plaudər] *n* (-s/*no pl.*) chatting, small talk; ~polter [~'pɔltər] *n* (-s/*no pl.*) rumble; ~präge [~'prɛ:gə] *n* (-s/-) impression; stamp (*a. fig.*).

ge|priesen [gə'pri:zən] *p.p. of* preisen; ~quollen [~'kvɔlən] *p.p. of* quellen.

gerade [gə'ra:də] 1. *adj.* straight (*a. fig.*); *number, etc.:* even; direct; *bearing* upright, erect; 2. *adv.* just; *er schrieb* ~ he was (just) writing; *nun* ~ now more than ever; *an dem Tage* on that very day; 3. 2 *f* (-n/-n) A straight line; straight (*of race-course*); *linke* (*rechte*) ~ *boxing:* straight left (right); ~'aus *adv.* straight on *or* ahead; ~her'aus *adv.* frankly; ~nwegs *adv.* [~nve:ks] directly; ~stehen *v/i.* (*irr.* stehen, *sep.,* -ge-, *h*) stand erect; ~ *für* answer *for s.th.*; ~wegs *adv.* [~ve:ks] straight, directly; ~'zu *adv.* straight; almost; downright.

ge'rannt *p.p. of* rennen.

Gerassel [gə'rasəl] *n* (-s/*no pl.*) clanking, rattling.

Gerät [gə'rɛ:t] *n* (-[e]s/-e) tool, implement, utensil; ⊕ gear; *teleph., radio:* set; apparatus; equipment; *elektrisches* ~ electric(al) appliance.

ge'raten 1. *v/i.* (*irr.* raten, *no* -ge-, *sein*) come *or* fall *or* get (*an acc.* by, upon; *auf acc.* on, upon; *in acc.* in, into); (*gut*) ~ succeed, turn out well; *in Brand* ~ catch fire; *ins Stocken* ~ come to a standstill; *in Vergessenheit* ~ fall *or* sink into oblivion; *in Zorn* ~ fly into a passion; 2. *p.p. of* raten.

Gerate'wohl *n: aufs* ~ at random.

geräumig *adj.* [gə'rɔʏmɪç] spacious.

Geräusch [gə'rɔʏʃ] *n* (-es/-e) noise; 2los *adj.* noiseless; 2voll *adj.* noisy.

gerb|en ['gɛrbən] *v/t.* (ge-, *h*) tan; '2er *m* (-s/-) tanner; 2erei [~'raɪ] *f* (-/-en) tannery.

ge'recht *adj.* just; righteous; ~ *werden* (*dat.*) do justice to; be fair to; meet; please *s.o.*; fulfil (*requirements*); 2igkeit *f* (-/*no pl.*) justice; righteousness; *j-m* ~ *widerfahren lassen* do s.o. justice.

Ge'rede *n* (-s/*no pl.*) talk; gossip; rumo(u)r.

ge'reizt *adj.* irritable, irritated; 2-heit *f* (-/*no pl.*) irritation.

ge'reuen *v/t.* (*no* -ge-, *h*): *es gereut mich* I repent (of) it, I am sorry for it.

Gericht [gə'rɪçt] *n* (-[e]s/-e) dish, course; *s.* Gerichtshof; *mst rhet. and fig.* tribunal; 2lich *adj.* judicial, legal.

Ge'richts|barkeit *f* (-/-en) jurisdiction; ~bezirk *m* jurisdiction; ~diener *m* (court) usher; ~gebäude *n* court-house; ~hof *m* law-court, court of justice; ~kosten *pl.* (law-)costs *pl.*; ~saal *m* court-room; ~schreiber *m* clerk (of the court); ~stand *m* (legal) domicile; venue; ~tag *m* court-day; ~verfahren *n* legal proceedings *pl.,* lawsuit; ~verhandlung *f* (court) hearing; trial; ~vollzieher *m* (-s/-) (court-)bailiff.

ge|rieben [gə'ri:bən] *p.p. of* reiben. gering *adj.* [gə'rɪŋ] little, small; trifling, slight; mean, low; poor; inferior; ~achten *v/t.* (*sep.,* -ge-, *h*) think little of; disregard; ~er *adj.* inferior less, minor; ~fügig *adj.* insignificant, trifling, slight; ~schätzen *v/t.* (*sep.,* -ge-, *h*) *a.* ringachten; ~schätzig *adj.* disdainful, contemptuous, slighting; 2-schätzung *f* (-/*no pl.*) disdain; disregard; ~st *adj.* least; *nicht im* ~en not in the least.

ge'rinnen *v/i.* (*irr.* rinnen, *no* -ge-, *sein*) curdle (*a. fig.*); congeal; coagulate clot.

Ge'rippe *n* (-s/-) skeleton (*a. fig.*); ⊕ framework.

ge|rissen [gə'rɪsən] 1. *p.p. of* reißen; 2. *fig. adj.* cunning, crafty, smart; ~ritten [~'rɪtən] *p.p. of* reiten.

germanis|ch *adj.* [gɛr'ma:nɪʃ] Germanic, Teutonic; 2t [~a'nɪst] *m* (-en/-en) Germanist, German scholar; student of German.

gern(e) *adv.* ['gɛrn(ə)] willingly, gladly; ~ *haben or mögen* be fond of, like; *er singt* ~ he is fond of singing, he likes to sing.

ge'rochen *p.p. of* riechen.

Geröll [gə'rœl] *n* (-[e]s/-e) boulders *pl.*

geronnen [gə'rɔnən] *p.p. of* rinnen. Gerste ♀ ['gɛrstə] *f* (-/-n) barley; '~nkorn *n* barleycorn; ♂ sty(e).

Gerte ['gɛrtə] *f* (-/-n) switch, twig.

Geruch [gə'rux] *m* (-[e]s/-e) smell, odo(u)r; scent; *fig.* reputation; 2los *adj.* odo(u)rless, scentless; ~ssinn *m* (-[e]s/ *no pl.*) sense of smell.

Gerücht [gə'rʏçt] *n* (-[e]s/-e) rumo(u)r.

ge'ruchtilgend *adj.:* ~es *Mittel* deodorant.

ge'rufen *p.p. of* rufen.

ge'ruhen *v/i.* (*no* -ge-, *h*) deign, condescend, be pleased.

Gerümpel [gə'rympəl] *n* (-*s*/*no pl.*) lumber, junk.

Gerundium *gr.* [gə'rundjum] *n* (-*s*/Gerundien) gerund.

gerungen [gə'ruŋən] *p.p. of* ringen.

Gerüst [gə'ryst] *n* (-[e]*s*/-e) scaffold(ing); stage; trestle.

ge'salzen *p.p. of* salzen.

gesamt *adj.* [gə'zamt] whole, entire, total, all; **2ausgabe** *f* complete edition; **2betrag** *m* sum total; **~deutsch** *adj.* all-German.

gesandt [gə'zant] *p.p. of* senden; **2e** [~ə] *m* (-*n*/-*n*) envoy; **2schaft** *f* (-/-en) legation.

Ge'sang *m* (-[e]*s*/~e) singing; song; **~buch** *eccl. n* hymn-book; **~slehrer** *m* singing-teacher; **~verein** *m* choral society, *Am.* glee club.

Gesäß *anat.* [gə'zɛːs] *n* (-es/-e) seat, buttocks *pl.*, posterior, F bottom, behind.

ge'schaffen *p.p. of* schaffen 1.

Geschäft [gə'ʃɛft] *n* (-[e]*s*/-e) business; transaction; affair; occupation; shop, *Am.* store; **2ig** *adj.* busy, active; **~igkeit** *f* (-/*no pl.*) activity; **2lich** 1. *adj.* business ...; commercial; 2. *adv.* on business.

Ge'schäfts|bericht *m* business report; **~brief** *m* business letter; **~frau** *f* business woman; **~freund** *m* business friend, correspondent; **~führer** *m* manager; **~haus** *n* business firm; office building; **~inhaber** *m* owner *or* holder of a business; shopkeeper; **~jahr** *n* financial *or* business year, *Am.* fiscal year; **~lage** *f* business situation; **~leute** *pl.* businessmen *pl.*; **~mann** *m* businessman; **2mäßig** *adj.* business-like; **~ordnung** *f* standing orders *pl.*; rules *pl.* (of procedure); **~papiere** *n/pl.* commercial papers *pl.*; **~partner** *m* (business) partner; **~räume** *m/pl.* business premises *pl.*; **~reise** *f* business trip; **~reisende** *m* commercial travel(l)er, *Am.* travel(l)ing salesman; **~schluß** *m* closing-time; *nach* ... *a.* after business hours; **~stelle** *f* office; **~träger** *m pol.* chargé d'affaires; **↑** agent, representative; **2tüchtig** *adj.* efficient, smart; **~unternehmen** *n* business enterprise; **~verbindung** *f* business connexion *or* connection; **~viertel** *n* business cent|re, *Am.* -er; *Am.* downtown; shopping cent|re, *Am.* -er; **~zeit** *f* office hours *pl.*, business hours *pl.*; **~zimmer** *n* office, bureau; **~zweig** *m* branch (of business), line (of business).

geschah [gə'ʃaː] *pret. of* geschehen.

geschehen [gə'ʃeːən] 1. *v/i.* (*irr.*, *no* -ge-, *sein*) happen, occur, take place; be done; *es geschieht ihm recht* it serves him right; 2. *p.p. of* 1; 3. **2** *n* (-*s*/-) events *pl.*, happenings *pl.*

gescheit *adj.* [gə'ʃaɪt] clever, intelligent, bright.

Geschenk [gə'ʃɛŋk] *n* (-[e]*s*/-e) present, gift; **~packung** *f* gift-box.

Geschicht|e [gə'ʃiçtə] *f* 1. (-/-*n*) story; tale; *fig.* affair; 2. (-/*no pl.*) history; **2lich** *adj.* historical; **~sforscher** *m*, **~sschreiber** *m* historian.

Ge'schick *n.* 1. (-[e]*s*/-e) fate; destiny; 2. (-[e]*s*/*no pl.*) = **~lichkeit** *f* (-/-en) skill; dexterity; aptitude; **2t** *adj.* skil(l)ful; dexterous; apt; clever.

ge|schieden [gə'ʃiːdən] *p.p. of* scheiden; **~schienen** [~'ʃiːnən] *p.p. of* scheinen.

Geschirr [gə'ʃir] *n* (-[e]*s*/-e) vessel; dishes *pl.*; china; earthenware, crockery; service; *horse:* harness.

ge'schlafen *p.p. of* schlafen; **~'schlagen** *p.p. of* schlagen.

Ge'schlecht *n* (-[e]*s*/-er) sex; kind, species; race; family; generation; *gr.* gender; **2lich** *adj.* sexual.

Ge'schlechts|krankheit ♂ *f* venereal disease; **~reife** *f* puberty; **~teile** *anat. n/pl.* genitals *pl.*; **~trieb** *m* sexual instinct *or* urge; **~verkehr** *m* (-[e]*s*/*no pl.*) sexual intercourse; **~wort** *gr.* *n* (-[e]*s*/~er) article.

ge|schlichen [gə'ʃliçən] *p.p. of* schleichen; **~schliffen** [~'ʃlifən] 1. *p.p. of* schleifen; 2. *adj. jewel:* cut; *fig.* polished; **~schlossen** [~'ʃlɔsən] 1. *p.p. of* schließen; 2. *adj. formation:* close; collective; *a Gesellschaft* private party; **~schlungen** [~'ʃluŋən] *p.p. of* schlingen.

Geschmack [gə'ʃmak] *m* (-[e]*s*/~e, *co.* ~er) taste (*a. fig.*); flavo(u)r; *~ finden an* (*dat.*) take a fancy to; **2los** *adj.* tasteless; *pred. fig.* in bad taste; **~(s)sache** *f* matter of taste; **2voll** *adj.* tasteful; *pred. fig.* in good taste.

ge|schmeidig *adj.* [gə'ʃmaɪdiç] supple, pliant; **~schmissen** [~'ʃmisən] *p.p. of* schmeißen; **~schmolzen** [~'ʃmɔltsən] *p.p. of* schmelzen.

Geschnatter [gə'ʃnatər] *n* (-*s*/*no pl.*) cackling (*of geese*); chatter(ing) (*of girls, etc.*).

ge|schnitten [gə'ʃnitən] *p.p. of* schneiden; **~schoben** [~'ʃoːbən] *p.p. of* schieben; **~scholten** [~'ʃɔltən] *p.p. of* schelten.

Geschöpf [gə'ʃœpf] *n* (-[e]*s*/-e) creature.

ge'schoren *p.p. of* scheren.

Geschoß [gə'ʃɔs] *n* (Geschosses/ Geschosse) projectile; missile; sto-r(e)y, floor.

geschossen [gə'ʃɔsən] *p.p. of* schießen.

Ge'schrei n (-[e]s/no pl.) cries pl.; shouting, fig. noise, fuss.

ge|schrieben [gə'ʃriːbən] p.p. of schreiben, **schrie(e)n** [ˌʃriː(ə)n] p.p. of schreien; **schritten** [ˌʃritən] p.p. of schreiten; **schunden** [ˌʃundən] p.p. of schinden.

Geschütz ✗ [gə'ʃyts] n (-es/-e) gun, cannon, ordnance.

Geschwader ✗ [gə'ʃvaːdər] n (-s/-) ⊕ squadron; ✗ wing, Am. group.

Geschwätz [gə'ʃvɛts] n (-es/no pl.) idle talk, gossip; **2ig** adj. talkative.

geschweige cj. [gə'ʃvaigə]: **~** (denn) not to mention; let alone, much less.

geschwiegen [gə'ʃviːgən] p.p. of schweigen

geschwind adj. [gə'ʃvint] fast, quick, swift; **2igkeit** [ˌdiçkait] f (/-en) quickness; speed, pace; phys. velocity; rate; mit e-r **~** von ... at the rate of ...; **2igkeitsbegrenzung** f speed limit.

Geschwister [gə'ʃvistər] n (-s/-): **~** pl. brother(s pl.) and sister(s pl.).

ge|schwollen [gə'ʃvɔlən] 1. p.p. of schwellen; 2. adj. language: bombastic, pompous; **schwommen** [ˌʃvɔmən] p.p. of schwimmen.

geschworen [gə'ʃvoːrən] p.p. of schwören; **2e** [ˌə] m, f (-n/-n) juror; **die ~n** pl the jury; **2engericht** n jury.

Geschwulst ✗ [gə'ʃvulst] f (/-⸚e) swelling, tumo(u)r.

ge|schwunden [gə'ʃvundən] p.p. of schwinden, **schwungen** [ˌʃvuŋən] p.p. of schwingen.

Geschwür ✗ [gə'ʃvyːr] n (-[e]s/-e) abscess, ulcer.

ge'sehen p.p. of sehen.

Gesell ✗ [gə'zɛl] m (-en/-en), **~e** [ˌə] m (-n/-n) companion, fellow; ⊕ journeyman; **2en** v/refl. (no -ge-, h) associate, come together; sich zu j-m **~** join s.o.; **2ig** adj. social; sociable.

Ge'sellschaft f (/-en) society; company (a. ✝); party; j-m **~** leisten keep s.o company; **~er** m (-s/-) companion; ✝ partner; **~erin** f (/-nen) (lady) companion; ✝ partner; **2lich** adj. social.

Ge'sellschafts|dame f (lady) companion, **reise** f party tour; **spiel** n party or round game; **tanz** m ball-room dance.

gesessen [gə'zɛsən] p.p. of sitzen.

Gesetz [gə'zɛts] n (-es/-e) law; statute, **buch** n code; statute-book; **entwurf** m bill; **eskraft** f legal force; **essammlung** f code; **2gebend** adj. legislative; **geber** m (-s/-) legislator; **gebung** f (/-en) legislation; **2lich** 1. adj. lawful, legal; 2. adv.: **~** geschützt patented, registered; **2los** adj. lawless; **2mäßig** adj. legal; lawful.

ge'setzt 1. adj. sedate, staid; sober;

mature; 2. cj.: **~** den Fall, (daß) ... suppose or supposing (that) ...

ge'setzwidrig adj unlawful, illegal.

Ge'sicht n -[e]s/-er) face; countenance; fig character; zu **~** bekommen catch sight or a glimpse of; set eyes on.

Ge'sichts|ausdruck m (facial) expression, **farbe** f complexion; **kreis** m horizon, **punkt** m point of view, viewpoint, aspect, esp. Am. angle; **zug** m mst Gesichtszüge pl. feature(s pl.), lineament(s pl.).

Ge'sims n ledge

Gesinde [gə'zində] n (-s/-) (domestic) servants pl.; **~l** [ˌl] n (-s/no pl.) rabble, mob.

ge'sinnt adj. in compounds: **...-**minded; wohl **~** well disposed (j-m towards s.o.); **2ung** f (/-en) mind; conviction; sentiment(s pl.); opinions pl.

gesinnungs|los adj. [gə'zinuŋsloːs] unprincipled; **treu** adj. loyal; **2wechsel** m change of opinion; esp. pol. volte-face

ge|sittet adj. [gə'zitət] civilized; well-bred, well-mannered; **soffen** p.p. of saufen, **sogen** [ˌ'zoːgən] p.p. of saugen, **sonnen** [ˌ'zɔnən] 1. p.p. of sinnen, 2. adj. minded, disposed, **sotten** [ˌ'zɔtən] p.p. of sieden; **spalten** p.p of spalten.

Ge'spann n -[e]s/-e) team, Am. a. span; oxen yoke; fig. pair, couple.

ge'spannt adj. tense (a. fig.); rope: tight, taut; fig intent; attention: close; relations strained; **~** sein auf (acc.) be anxious for; auf **~em** Fuß on bad terms; **2heit** f (/-no pl.) tenseness, tension.

Gespenst [gə'ʃpɛnst] n (-es/-er) ghost, spect|re, Am. -er; **2isch** adj. ghostly.

Ge'spiel|e m (-n/-n), **in** f (/-nen) playmate.

gespien [gə'ʃpiːn] p.p. of speien.

Gespinst [gə'ʃpinst] n (-es/-e) web, tissue (both a. fig.); spun yarn.

gesponnen [gə'ʃpɔnən] p.p. of spinnen.

Gespött [gə'ʃpœt] n (-[e]s/no pl.) mockery, derision, ridicule; zum **~** der Leute werden become a laughing-stock.

Gespräch [gə'ʃprɛːç] n (-[e]s/-e) talk; conversation; teleph. call; dialogue; **2ig** adj talkative.

ge|sprochen [gə'ʃprɔxən] p.p. of sprechen; **sprossen** p.p. of sprießen; **sprungen** [ˌ'ʃpruŋən] p.p. of springen.

Gestalt [gə'ʃtalt] f (-/-en) form, figure, shape; stature; **2en** v/t. and v/refl. (no -ge-, h) form, shape; **ung** f (/-en) formation; arrangement, organization.

gestanden [gə'ʃtandən] p.p. of stehen.

ge'ständ|ig *adj.*: ~ sein confess; 2nis [ˌt-] *n* (-ses/-se) confession.

Ge'stank *m* (-[e]s/*no pl.*) stench.

gestatten [gə'ʃtatən] *v/t.* (*no* -ge-, h) allow, permit.

Geste ['gestə] *f* (-/-n) gesture.

ge'stehen (*irr.* stehen, *no* -ge-, h) 1. *v/t.* confess, avow; 2. *v/i.* confess.

Ge|'stein *n* (-[e]s/-e) rock, stone; ~stell [ˌ'ʃtɛl] *n* (-[e]s/-e) stand, rack, shelf; frame; trestle, horse.

gestern *adv.* ['gestərn] yesterday; ~ abend last night.

gestiegen [gə'ʃtiːɡən] *p.p. of* steigen.

Ge'stirn *n* (-[e]s/-e) star; *astr.* constellation; 2t *adj.* starry.

ge|stoben [gə'ʃtoːbən] *p.p. of* stieben; ~stochen [ˌ'ʃtɔxən] *p.p. of* stechen; ~stohlen [ˌ'ʃtoːlən] *p.p. of* stehlen; ~storben [ˌ'ʃtɔrbən] *p.p. of* sterben; ~stoßen *p.p. of* stoßen; ~strichen [ˌ'ʃtriçən] *p.p. of* streichen.

gestrig *adj.* ['gestriç] of yesterday, yesterday's ...

ge'stritten *p.p. of* streiten.

Gestrüpp [gə'ʃtryp] *n* (-[e]s/-e) brushwood; undergrowth.

gestunken [gə'ʃtuŋkən] *p.p. of* stinken.

Gestüt [gə'ʃtyːt] *n* (-[e]s/-e) stud farm; *horses kept for breeding, etc.*: stud.

Gesuch [gə'zuːx] *n* (-[e]s/-e) application, request; petition; 2t *adj.* wanted; sought-after; *politeness*: studied.

gesund *adj.* [gə'zunt] sound, healthy; salubrious; wholesome (*a. fig.*); ~er Menschenverstand common sense; ~en [ˌdən] *v/i.* (*no* -ge-, sein) recover.

Ge'sundheit *f* (-/*no pl.*) health (-iness); wholesomeness (*a. fig.*); auf j-s ~ trinken drink (to) s.o.'s health; 2lich *adj.* sanitary; ~ geht es ihm gut he is in good health.

Ge'sundheits|amt *n* Public Health Department; ~pflege *f* hygiene; public health service; 2schädlich *adj.* injurious to health, unhealthy, unwholesome; ~wesen *n* Public Health; ~zustand *m* state of health, physical condition.

ge|sungen [gə'zuŋən] *p.p. of* singen; ~sunken [ˌ'zuŋkən] *p.p. of* sinken; ~tan [ˌ'taːn] *p.p. of* tun.

Getöse [gə'tøːzə] *n* (-s/*no pl.*) din, noise.

ge'tragen 1. *p.p. of* tragen; 2. *adj.* solemn.

Getränk [gə'trɛŋk] *n* (-[e]s/-e) drink, beverage.

ge'trauen *v/refl.* (*no* -ge-, h) dare, venture.

Getreide [gə'traɪdə] *n* (-s/-) corn, *esp. Am.* grain; cereals *pl.*; ~(an)bau *m* corn-growing, *esp. Am.* grain growing; ~pflanze *f* cereal plant;

~speicher *m* granary, grain silo, *Am.* elevator.

ge'treten *p.p. of* treten.

ge'treu(lich) *adj.* faithful, loyal; true.

Getriebe [gə'triːbə] *n* (-s/-) bustle; ⊕ gear(ing); ⊕ drive.

ge|trieben [gə'triːbən] *p.p. of* treiben; ~troffen [ˌ'trɔfən] *p.p. of* treffen; ~trogen [ˌ'troːgən] *p.p. of* trügen.

ge'trost *adv.* confidently.

ge'trunken *p.p. of* trinken.

Ge|tue [gə'tuːə] *n* (-s/*no pl.*) fuss; ~tümmel [ˌ'tyməl] *n* (-s/-) turmoil; ~viert [ˌ'fiːrt] *n* (-[e]s/-e) square.

Gewächs [gə'vɛks] *n* (-es/-e) growth (*a. ♨*); plant; vintage; ~haus *n* greenhouse, hothouse, conservatory.

ge|'wachsen 1. *p.p. of* wachsen; 2. *adj.*: j-m ~ sein be a match for s.o.; e-r Sache ~ sein be equal to s.th.; sich der Lage ~ zeigen rise to the occasion; ~wagt *adj.* [ˌ'vaːkt] risky; bold; ~wählt *adj.* [ˌ've:lt] *style*: refined; ~'wahr *adj.*: ~ werden (*acc. or gen.*) perceive s.th.; become aware of s.th.; ~ werden, daß become aware that.

Gewähr [gə've:r] *f* (-/*no pl.*) guarantee, warrant, security; 2en *v/t.* (*no* -ge-, h) grant, allow; give, yield, afford; j-n ~ lassen let s.o. have his way; leave s.o. alone; 2leisten *v/t.* (*no* -ge-, h) guarantee.

Ge'wahrsam *m* (-s/-e) custody, safe keeping.

Ge'währsmann *m* informant, source.

Gewalt [gə'valt] *f* (-/-en) power; authority; control; force, violence; höhere ~ act of God; mit ~ by force; ~herrschaft *f* despotism, tyranny; 2ig *adj.* powerful, mighty; vehement; vast; ~maßnahme *f* violent measure; 2sam 1. *adj.* violent; 2. *adv. a.* forcibly; ~ öffnen force open; open by force; ~tat *f* act of violence; 2tätig *adj.* violent.

Gewand [gə'vant] *n* (-[e]s/ᵘer) garment; robe; *esp. eccl.* vestment.

ge'wandt 1. *p.p. of* wenden 2; 2. *adj.* agile, nimble, dexterous, adroit; clever; 2heit *f* (-/*no pl.*) agility, nimbleness; adroitness, dexterity; cleverness.

ge'wann *pret. of* gewinnen.

Gewäsch F [gə'vɛʃ] *n* (-es/*no pl.*) twaddle, nonsense.

ge'waschen *p.p. of* waschen.

Gewässer [gə'vɛsər] *n* (-s/-) water(s *pl.*).

Gewebe [gə've:bə] *n* (-s/-) tissue (*a. anat. and fig.*); fabric, web; texture.

Ge'wehr *n* gun; rifle; ~kolben *m* (rifle-)butt; ~lauf *m* (rifle-, gun-)barrel.

Geweih [gə'vaɪ] n (-[e]s/-e) horns pl., head, antlers pl.

Gewerbe [gə'verbə] n (-s/-) trade, business, industry; **~freiheit** f freedom of trade; **~schein** m trade licen|ce, Am. -se; **~schule** f technical school; **~steuer** f trade tax; **2treibend** adj carrying on a business, engaged in trade; **~treibende** m (-n/-n) tradesman.

gewerb|lich adj. [gə'verplɪç] commercial, industrial; **~smäßig** adj. professional.

Ge'werkschaft f (-/-en) trade(s) union, Am. labor union; **~ler** m (-s/-) trade(s)-unionist; **2lich** adj. trade-union; **~sbund** m Trade Union Congress, Am. Federation of Labor

ge|wesen [gə've:zən] p.p. of sein; **~wichen** [~'vɪçən] p.p. of weichen.

Gewicht [gə'vɪçt] n (-[e]s/-e) weight, Am. f a heft, e-r Sache ~ beimessen attach importance to s.th.; ~ haben carry weight (bei dat. with); ~ legen auf et. lay stress on s.th.; ins ~ fallen be of great weight, count, matter, 2ig adj. weighty (a. fig.).

ge|wiesen [gə'vi:zən] p.p. of weisen; **~willt** adj [~'vɪlt] willing.

Ge|wimmel [gə'vɪməl] n (-s/no pl.) swarm, throng, **~winde** ⊕ [~'vɪndə] n (-s/-) thread.

Gewinn [gə'vɪn] m (-[e]s/-e) gain; ↑ gains pl., profit; lottery ticket: prize; game winnings pl.; **~anteil** m dividend, **~beteiligung** f profit-sharing; **2bringend** adj. profitable; **2en** (irr., no -ge-, h) 1. v/t. win; gain; get, 2. v/i. win; gain; fig. improve, **2end** adj. manner, smile: winning, engaging; **~er** m (-s/-) winner.

Ge'wirr n (-[e]s/-e) tangle, entanglement; streets: maze; voices: confusion.

gewiß [gə'vɪs] 1. adj. certain; ein gewisser Herr N. a certain Mr. N., one Mr. N.; 2. adv.: ~! certainly!, to be sure!, Am. sure!

Ge'wissen n (-s/-) conscience; **2haft** adj. conscientious; **2los** adj. unscrupulous; **~sbisse** m/pl. remorse, pangs pl. of conscience; **~sfrage** f question of conscience.

gewissermaßen adv. [gəvɪsər'ma:sən] to a certain extent.

Ge'wißheit f (-/-en) certainty; certitude.

Gewitter [gə'vɪtər] n (-s/-) (thunder)storm; **2n** v/i. (no -ge-, h): es gewittert there is a thunderstorm; **~regen** m thunder-shower; **~wolke** f thundercloud.

ge|woben [gə'vo:bən] p.p. of weben; **~wogen** 1. p.p. of wägen and wiegen[1]; 2. adj. (dat.) well or kindly disposed towards, favo(u)rably inclined towards.

gewöhnen [gə'vø:nən] v/t. (no -ge-, h) accustom, get used (an acc. to).

Gewohnheit [gə'vo:nhaɪt] f (-/-en) habit; custom; **2smäßig** adj. habitual.

ge'wöhnlich adj. common; ordinary; usual, customary; habitual; common, vulgar.

ge'wohnt adj. customary, habitual; (es) ~ sein zu inf. be accustomed or used to inf.

Gewölbe [gə'vœlbə] n (-s/-) vault.

ge|wonnen [gə'vonən] p.p. of gewinnen; **~worben** [~'vorbən] p.p. of werben; **~worden** [~'vordən] p.p. of werden; **~worfen** [~'vorfən] p.p. of werfen; **~wrungen** [~'vruŋən] p.p. of wringen.

Gewühl [gə'vy:l] n (-[e]s/no pl.) bustle; milling crowd.

gewunden [gə'vundən] 1. p.p. of winden; 2. adj. twisted; winding.

Gewürz [gə'vyrts] n (-es/-e) spice; condiment; **~nelke** ♀ f clove.

ge'wußt p.p. of wissen.

Ge|zeit f: mst ~en pl. tide(s pl.); **~'zeter** n (-s/no pl.) (shrill) clamo(u)r.

ge|'ziert adj. affected; **~zogen** [~'tso:gən] p.p. of ziehen.

Gezwitscher [gə'tsvɪtʃər] n (-s/no pl.) chirping, twitter(ing).

gezwungen [gə'tsvuŋən] 1. p.p. of zwingen; 2. adj. forced, constrained.

Gicht [gɪçt] f (-/no pl.) gout; **2isch** ♂ adj. gouty; **~knoten** ♂ m gouty knot.

Giebel ['gi:bəl] m (-s/-) gable(-end).

Gier [gi:r] f (-/no pl.) greed(iness) (nach for); **2ig** adj. greedy (nach for, of).

'Gießbach m torrent.

gieß|en ['gi:sən] (irr., ge-, h) 1. v/t. pour; ⊕ cast, found; water (flowers); 2. v/i. es gießt it is pouring (with rain); **2er** m (-s/-) founder; **2erei** [~'raɪ] f (-/-en) foundry; **'2kanne** f watering-can or -pot.

Gift [gɪft] n (-[e]s/-e) poison; venom (esp. of snakes) (a. fig.); malice, spite; **2ig** adj. poisonous; venomous; malicious, spiteful; **'~schlange** f venomous or poisonous snake; **'~zahn** m poison-fang.

Gigant [gi'gant] m (-en/-en) giant.

Gimpel orn. ['gɪmpəl] m (-s/-) bullfinch.

ging [gɪŋ] pret. of gehen.

Gipfel ['gɪpfəl] m (-s/-) summit, top; peak; **'~konferenz** pol. f summit meeting or conference; **'2n** v/i. (ge-, h) culminate.

Gips [gɪps] m (-es/-e) min. gypsum; ⊕ plaster (of Paris); **'~abdruck** m, **'~abguß** m plaster cast; **'2en** v/t. (ge-, h) plaster; **'~verband** ♂ m plaster (of Paris) dressing.

Giraffe zo. [gi'rafə] f (-/-n) giraffe.

girieren † [ʒiˈriːrən] *v/t.* (*no* -ge-, h) endorse, indorse (*bill of exchange*).

Girlande [girˈlandə] *f* (-/-n) garland.

Giro † [ˈʒiːro] *n* (-s/-s) endorsement, indorsement; **∼bank** *f* clearing-bank; **∼konto** *n* current account.

girren [ˈgirən] *v/i.* (ge-, h) coo.

Gischt [giʃt] *m* (-es/ɤ -e) *and f* (-/ɤ -en) foam, froth; spray; spindrift.

Gitarre ♪ [giˈtarə] *f* (-/-n) guitar.

Gitter [ˈgitər] *n* (-s/-) grating; lattice; trellis; railing; **∼bett** *n* crib; **∼fenster** *n* lattice-window.

Glacéhandschuh [glaˈseː-] *m* kid glove.

Glanz [glants] *m* (-es/*no pl.*) brightness; lust|re, *Am.* -er; brilliancy; splendo(u)r.

glänzen [ˈglentsən] *v/i.* (ge-, h) glitter, shine; **∼d** *adj.* bright, brilliant; *fig.* splendid.

Glanz|leistung *f* brilliant achievement *or* performance; **∼papier** *n* glazed paper; **∼punkt** *m* highlight; **∼zeit** *f* golden age, heyday.

Glas [glaːs] *n* (-es/ɤer) glass; **∼er** [ˈɤzər] *m* (-s/-) glazier.

gläsern *adj.* [ˈglɛːzərn] of glass; *fig.* glassy.

Glas|glocke *f* (glass) shade *or* cover; globe; bell-glass; **∼hütte** *f* glassworks *sg.*, *pl.*

glasieren [glaˈziːrən] *v/t.* (*no* -ge-, h) glaze; ice, frost (*cake*).

glasig *adj.* [ˈglaːziç] glassy, vitreous.

Glasscheibe *f* pane of glass.

Glasur [glaˈzuːr] *f* (-/-en) glaze, glazing; enamel; icing, frosting (*on cakes*).

glatt [glat] 1. *adj.* smooth (*a. fig.*); even; *lie, etc.*: flat, downright; *road, etc.*: slippery; 2. *adv.* smoothly; evenly; **∼ anliegen** fit closely *or* tightly; **∼ rasiert** clean-shaven; et. **∼ ableugnen** deny s.th. flatly.

Glätte [ˈglɛtə] *f* (-/-n) smoothness; *road, etc.*: slipperiness.

Glatteis *n* glazed frost, icy glaze, *Am.* glaze; F: j-n *aufs* **∼** *führen* lead s.o. up the garden path.

glätten *v/t.* (ge-, h) smooth.

Glatze [ˈglatsə] *f* (-/-n) bald head.

Glaube [ˈglaubə] *m* (-ns/ɤ-n) faith, belief (*an acc.* in); **²n** (ge-, h) 1. *v/t.* believe; think, suppose, *Am. a.* guess; 2. *v/i.* believe (*j-m* s.o.; *an acc.* in).

Glaubens|bekenntnis *n* creed, profession *or* confession of faith; **∼lehre** *f*, **∼satz** *m* dogma, doctrine.

glaubhaft *adj.* [ˈglaup-] credible; plausible; authentic.

gläubig *adj.* [ˈglɔybiç] believing, faithful; **²e** [ˈɤgə] *m*, *f* (-n/-n)

believer; **²er** † [ˈɤgər] *m* (-s/-) creditor.

glaubwürdig *adj.* [ˈglaup-] credible.

gleich [glaiç] 1. *adj.* equal (*an dat.* in); the same; like; even, level; in **∼er Weise** likewise; *zur* **∼en Zeit** at the same time; *es ist mir* **∼** it's all the same to me; *das* **∼e** the same; as much; *er ist nicht* (*mehr*) *der* **∼e** he is not the same man; 2. *adv.* alike, equally; immediately, presently, directly, at once; just; *es ist* **∼ acht** (*Uhr*) it is close on *or* nearly eight (o'clock); **∼altrig** *adj.* [ˈɤaltriç] (of) the same age; **∼artig** *adj.* homogeneous; similar; uniform; **∼bedeutend** *adj.* synonymous; equivalent (to); tantamount (*mit* to); **∼berechtigt** *adj.* having equal rights; **∼bleibend** *adj.* constant, steady; **∼en** *v/i.* (*irr.*, ge-, h) equal; resemble.

gleich|falls *adv.* also, likewise; **∼förmig** *adj.* [ˈɤfœrmiç] uniform; **∼gesinnt** *adj.* like-minded; **²ge-wicht** *n* balance (*a. fig.*); equilibrium, equipoise; *pol.*: **∼** *der Kräfte* balance of power; **∼gültig** *adj.* indifferent (*gegen* to); *es ist mir* **∼** I don't care; **∼**, *was du tust* no matter what you do; **²gültigkeit** *f* indifference; **²heit** *f* (-/-en) equality; likeness; **²klang** *m* unison; consonance, harmony; **∼kommen** *v/i.* (*irr.* kommen, sep., -ge-, sein): e-r Sache **∼** amount to s.th.; *j-m* **∼** equal s.o.; **∼laufend** *adj.* parallel; **∼lautend** *adj.* consonant; identical; **∼machen** *v/t.* (sep., -ge-, h) make equal (*dat.* to), equalize (to *or* with); **²maß** *n* regularity; evenness; *fig.* equilibrium; **∼mäßig** *adj.* equal; regular; constant; even; **²mut** *m* equanimity; calm; **∼mütig** *adj.* even-tempered; calm; **∼namig** *adj.* [ˈɤnaːmiç] of the same name; **²nis** *n* (-ses/-se) parable; *rhet.* simile; **∼sam** *adv.* as it were, so to speak; **∼schalten** *v/t.* (sep., -ge-, h) ⊕ synchronize; *pol.* co-ordinate, unify; **∼seitig** *adj.* equilateral; **∼setzen** *v/t.* (sep., -ge-, h) equate (*dat.* or *mit* with); **∼stehen** *v/i.* (*irr.* stehen, sep., -ge-, h) be equal; **∼stellen** *v/t.* (sep., -ge-, h) equalize, equate (*dat.* with); put *s.o.* on an equal footing (with); **²stellung** *f* equalization, equation; **²strom** ⚡ *f* direct current; **²ung** Ⱥ *f* (-/-en) equation; **∼wertig** *adj.* equivalent, of the same value, of equal value; **∼zeitig** *adj.* simultaneous; synchronous; contemporary.

Gleis [glaɪs] *n* (-es/-e) *s.* Geleise.

gleiten [ˈglaɪtən] *v/i.* (*irr.*, ge-, sein) glide, slide.

Gleit|flug *m* gliding flight, glide, ⚡ volplane; **∼schutzreifen** *m* non-skid tyre, (Am. only) non-skid tire; '~schutz(vorrichtung) f) m anti-skid device.

Gletscher ['glɛtʃər] m (-s/-) glacier; '~spalte f crevasse.

glich [gliç] pret. of gleichen.

Glied [gliːt] n (-[e]s/-er) anat. limb; member (a. anat.); link; ✕ rank, file; ²ern ['~dərn] v/t. (ge-, h) joint, articulate; arrange; divide (in acc. into); ~erung f (-/-en) articulation; arrangement; division; formation; ~maßen ['~tmaːsən] pl. limbs pl., extremities pl.

glimmen ['glimən] v/i. ([irr.,] ge-, h) fire: smo(u)lder (a. fig.); glimmer; glow.

glimpflich ['glimpfliç] 1. adj. lenient, mild; 2. adv.: ~ davonkommen get off lightly.

glitschig adj. ['glitʃiç] slippery.

glitt [glit] pret. of gleiten.

glitzern ['glitsərn] v/i. (ge-, h) glitter, glisten.

Globus ['gloːbus] m (-, -ses/Globen, Globusse) globe.

Glocke ['glɔkə] f (-/-n) bell; shade; (glass) cover.

'Glocken|schlag m stroke of the clock; '~spiel n chime(s pl.); '~stuhl m bell-cage; '~turm m bell tower, belfry.

Glöckner ['glœknər] m (-s/-) bell-ringer.

glomm [glɔm] pret. of glimmen.

Glorie ['gloːrjə] f (-/-n) glory; '~n-schein fig. m halo, aureola.

glorreich adj. ['gloːr-] glorious.

glotzen F ['glɔtsən] v/i. (ge-, h) stare.

Glück [glyk] n (-[e]s/no pl.) fortune; good luck; happiness, bliss, felicity; prosperity; auf. gut ~ on the off chance; ~ haben be lucky, succeed; das ~ haben zu inf. have the good fortune to inf.; j-m ~ wünschen congratulate s.o. (zu on); viel ~! good luck!; zum ~ fortunately; ²bringend adj. lucky.

Glucke orn. ['glukə] f (-/-n) sitting hen. [gen.\
'glücken v/i. (ge-, sein) s. gelin-\

gluckern ['glukərn] v/i. (ge-, h) water, etc. gurgle.

'glücklich adj. fortunate; happy; lucky; '~er'weise adv. fortunately.

'Glücksbringer m (-s/-) mascot.

glück'selig adj. blissful, blessed, happy.

glucksen ['gluksən] v/i. (ge-, h) gurgle.

'Glücks|fall m lucky chance, stroke of (good) luck; '~göttin f Fortune; '~kind n lucky person; '~pfennig m lucky penny; '~pilz m lucky person; '~spiel n game of chance; fig. gamble; '~stern m lucky star; '~tag m happy or lucky day, red-letter day.

'glück|strahlend adj. radiant(ly happy); '²wunsch m congratulation, good wishes pl.; compliments pl.; ~ zum Geburtstag many happy returns (of the day).

Glüh|birne ≠ ['gly:-] f (electric-light) bulb; ²en v/i. (ge-, h) glow; ²end adj. glowing; iron: red-hot; coal: live; fig. ardent, fervid; '²(end)'heiß adj. burning hot; '~lampe f incandescent lamp; '~wein m mulled wine; ~würmchen zo. ['~vyrmçən] n (-s/-) glow-worm.

Glut [gluːt] f (-/-en) heat, glow (a. fig.); glowing fire, embers pl.; fig. ardo(u)r.

Gnade ['gnaːdə] f (-/-n) grace; favo(u)r; mercy; clemency; pardon; ✕ quarter.

'Gnaden|akt m act of grace; '~brot n (-[e]s/no pl.) bread of charity; '~frist f reprieve; '~gesuch n petition for mercy.

gnädig adj. ['gnɛːdiç] gracious; merciful; address: Şe Frau Madam.

Gnom [gnoːm] m (-en/-en) gnome, goblin.

Gobelin [gobə'lɛ̃] m (-s/-s) Gobelin tapestry.

Gold [gɔlt] n (-[e]s/no pl.) gold; '~barren m gold bar, gold ingot, bullion; '~borte f gold lace; ²en adj. ['~dən] gold; fig. golden; '~feder f gold nib; '~fisch m goldfish; '²gelb adj. golden(-yellow); ~gräber ['~grɛːbər] m (-s/-) gold-digger; '~grube f gold-mine; '²haltig adj. gold-bearing, containing gold; ²ig fig. adj. ['~diç] sweet, lovely, Am. F a. cute; '~mine f gold-mine; '~münze f gold coin; '~schmied m goldsmith; '~schnitt m gilt edge; mit ~ gilt-edged; '~stück n gold coin; '~waage f gold-balance; '~währung f gold standard.

Golf¹ geogr. [gɔlf] m (-[e]s/-e) gulf.

Golf² [~] n (-s/no pl.) golf; '~platz m golf-course, (golf-)links pl.; '~schläger m golf-club; '~spiel n golf; '~spieler m golfer.

Gondel ['gɔndəl] f (-/-n) gondola; ✕ mst car.

gönnen ['gœnən] v/t. (ge-, h): j-m et. ~ allow or grant or not to grudge s.o. s.th.

'Gönner m (-s/-) patron; Am. a. sponsor; '²haft adj. patronizing.

gor [goːr] pret. of gären.

Gorilla zo. [go'rila] m (-s/-s) gorilla.

goß [gɔs] pret. of gießen.

Gosse ['gɔsə] f (-/-n) gutter (a. fig.).

Gott [gɔt] m (-es, ✕ -s/-er) God; god, deity; '²ergeben adj. resigned (to the will of God).

'Gottes|dienst eccl. m (divine) service; '²fürchtig adj. godfearing; '~haus n church, chapel; '~läste-

rer m (-s/-) blasphemer; '**~läste-**
rung f blasphemy.

'**Gottheit** f (-/-en) deity, divinity.
Göttin ['gœtin] f (-/-nen) goddess.
göttlich adj. ['gœtliç] divine.
gott|'lob int. thank God or good-
ness!; '**~los** adj. godless; impious;
F fig. deed: unholy, wicked; '2**ver-**
trauen n trust in God.
Götze ['gœtsə] m (-n/-n) idol;
'**~nbild** n idol; '**~ndienst** m idolatry.
Gouvern|ante [guver'nantə] f (-/-n)
governess; **~eur** [~'nø:r] m (-s/-e)
governor.
Grab [grɑːp] n (-[e]s/=er) grave,
tomb, sepulch|re, Am. -er.
Graben ['grɑːbən] 1. m (-s/=) ditch;
✕ trench; 2. 2 v/t. (irr., ge-, h)
dig; animal: burrow.
Grab|gewölbe ['grɑːp-] n vault,
tomb; '**~mal** n monument; tomb,
sepulch|re, Am. -er; '**~rede** f funeral
sermon; funeral oration or address;
'**~schrift** f epitaph; '**~stätte** f
burial-place; grave, tomb; '**~stein**
m tombstone; gravestone.
Grad [grɑːt] m (-[e]s/-e) degree;
grade, rank; 15 ~ Kälte 15 degrees
below zero; '**~einteilung** f graduation; '**~messer** m (-s/-) graduated
scale, graduator; fig. criterion;
'**~netz** n map: grid.
Graf [grɑːf] m (-en/-en) in Britain:
earl; count.
Gräfin ['grɛːfin] f (-/-nen) countess.
'**Grafschaft** f (-/-en) county.
Gram [grɑːm] 1. m (-[e]s/no pl.)
grief, sorrow; 2. 2 adj.: j-m ~
sein bear s.o. ill will or a grudge.
grämen ['grɛːmən] v/t. (ge-, h)
grieve; sich ~ grieve (über acc. at,
for, over).
Gramm [gram] n (-s/-e) gramme,
Am. gram.
Grammati|k [gra'matik] f (-/-en)
grammar; 2**sch** adj. grammatical.
Granat min. [gra'nɑːt] m (-[e]s/-e)
garnet; **~e** ✕ f (-/-n) shell; grenade;
'**~splitter** ✕ m shell-splinter;
'**~trichter** ✕ m shell-crater; '**~wer-**
fer ✕ m (-s/-) mortar.
Granit min. [gra'niːt] m (-s/-e)
granite.
Granne ♀ ['granə] f (-/-n) awn,
beard.
Graphi|k ['grɑːfik] f (-/-en) graphic
arts pl.; '2**sch** adj. graphic(al).
Graphit min. [gra'fiːt] m (-s/-e)
graphite.
Gras ♀ [grɑːs] n (-es/=er) grass;
2**bewachsen** adj. ['~bəvaksən]
grass-grown, grassy; 2**en** ['~zən]
v/i. (ge-, h) graze; '**~halm** m blade
of grass; '**~narbe** f turf, sod;
'**~platz** m grass-plot, green.
grassieren [gra'siːrən] v/i. (no -ge-,
h) rage, prevail.
gräßlich adj. ['grɛsliç] horrible;
hideous, atrocious.

Grassteppe ['grɑːs-] f prairie,
savanna(h).
Grat [grɑːt] m (-[e]s/-e) edge, ridge.
Gräte ['grɛːtə] f (-/-n) (fish-)bone.
Gratifikation [gratifika'tsjoːn] f
(-/-en) gratuity, bonus.
gratis adv. ['grɑːtis] gratis, free of
charge.
Gratul|ant [gratu'lant] m (-en/-en)
congratulator; **~ation** [~'tsjoːn] f
(-/-en) congratulation; 2**ieren** [~
'liːrən] v/i. (no -ge-, h) congratulate
(j-m zu et. s.o. on s.th.); j-m zum
Geburtstag ~ wish s.o. many happy
returns (of the day).
grau adj. [grau] grey, esp. Am. gray.
'**grauen**[1] v/i. (ge-, h) day: dawn.
'**grauen**[2] 1. v/i. (ge-, h): mir graut
vor (dat.) I shudder at, I dread;
2. 2 n (-s/no pl.) horror (vor dat. of);
'**~erregend** adj., '**~haft** adj., '**~voll**
adj. horrible, dreadful.
gräulich adj. ['grɔyliç] greyish, esp.
Am. grayish.
Graupe ['graupə] f (-/-n) (peeled)
barley, pot-barley; '**~ln** 1. f/pl.
sleet; 2. 2 v/i. (ge-, h) sleet.
'**grausam** adj. cruel; '2**keit** f (-/-en)
cruelty.
grausen ['grauzən] 1. v/i. (ge-, h)
s. grauen[2] 1; 2. 2 n (-s/no pl.)
horror (vor dat. of).
'**grausig** adj. horrible. [graver.]
Graveur [gra'vøːr] m (-s/-e) en-]
gravieren [gra'viːrən] v/t. (no -ge-,
h) engrave, **~d** fig. adj. aggravating.
gravitätisch adj. [gravi'tɛːtiʃ] grave;
dignified; solemn; stately.
Grazie ['grɑːtsjə] f (-/-n) grace(fulness).
graziös adj. [gra'tsjøːs] graceful.
greifen ['graifən] (irr., ge-, h) 1. v/t.
seize, grasp, catch hold of; ♪ touch
(string); 2. v/i.: an den Hut ~ touch
one's hat; ~ nach grasp or snatch
at; um sich ~ spread; j-m unter die
Arme ~ give s.o. a helping hand;
zu strengen Mitteln ~ resort to
severe measures; zu den Waffen ~
take up arms.
Greis [grais] m (-es/-e) old man;
2**enhaft** adj. ['~zən-] senile (a. ♣);
'**~in** ['~zin] f (-/-nen) old woman.
grell adj. [grɛl] light: glaring;
colour: loud; sound: shrill.
Grenze ['grɛntsə] f (-/-n) limit;
territory: boundary; state: frontier, borders pl.; e-e ~ ziehen draw
the line; 2**n** v/i. (ge-, h): ~ an (acc.)
border on (a. fig.); fig. verge on;
'2**nlos** adj. boundless.
'**Grenz|fall** m border-line case;
'**~land** n borderland; '**~linie** f
boundary or border line; '**~schutz**
m frontier or border protection;
frontier or border guard; '**~stein** m
boundary stone; '**~übergang** m
frontier or border crossing(-point).
Greuel ['grɔyəl] m (-s/-) horror;

abomination; atrocity; '~tat f atrocity.

Griech|e ['griːçə] m (-n/-n) Greek; '2isch adj. Greek; ⚠, features: Grecian.

griesgrämig adj. ['griːsgrɛːmiç] morose, sullen.

Grieß [griːs] m (-es/-e) gravel (a. ✍), grit; semolina; '~brei m semolina pudding.

Griff [grif] 1. m (-[e]s/-e) grip, grasp, hold; ♪ touch; handle (of knife, etc.); hilt (of sword); 2. 2 pret. of greifen.

Grille ['grilə] f (-/-n) zo. cricket; fig. whim, fancy; '2nhaft adj. whimsical.

Grimasse [gri'masə] f (-/-n) grimace; ~n schneiden pull faces.

Grimm [grim] m (-[e]s/no pl.) fury, rage; '2ig adj. furious, fierce, grim.

Grind [grint] m (-[e]s/-e) scab, scurf.

grinsen ['grinzən] 1. v/i. (ge-, h) grin (über acc. at); sneer (at); 2. 2 n (-s/no pl.) grin; sneer.

Grippe ✍ ['gripə] f (-/-n) influenza, F flu(e), grippe.

grob adj. [grɔp] coarse; gross; rude; work, skin: rough; '2heit f (-/-en) coarseness; grossness; rudeness; ~en pl. rude things pl.

grölen F ['grøːlən] v/t. and v/i. (ge-, h) bawl.

Groll [grɔl] m (-[e]s/no pl.) grudge, ill will; '2en v/i. (ge-, h) thunder: rumble; j-m ~ bear s.o. ill will or a grudge.

Gros¹ ✝ [grɔs] n (-ses/-se) gross.

Gros² [groː] n (-/-) main body.

Groschen ['grɔʃən] m (-s/-) penny.

groß adj. [groːs] great; large; big; figure: tall; huge; fig. great, grand; heat: intense; cold: severe; loss: heavy; die 2en pl. the grown-ups pl.; im ~en wholesale, on a large scale; im ~en (und) ganzen on the whole; ~er Buchstabe capital (letter); das ~e Los the first prize; ich bin kein ~er Tänzer I am not much of a dancer; '~artig adj. great, grand, sublime; first-rate; '2aufnahme f film: close-up.

Größe ['grøːsə] f (-/-n) size; largeness; height, tallness; quantity (esp. ♣); importance: greatness; p. celebrity; thea. star.

'Großeltern pl. grandparents pl.

'großenteils adv. to a large or great extent, largely.

'Größenwahn m megalomania.

'Groß|grundbesitz m large landed property; '~handel ✝ m wholesale trade; '~handelspreis ✝ m wholesale price; '~händler ✝ m wholesale dealer, wholesaler; '~handlung f wholesale business; '~herzog m grand duke; '~industrielle m big industrialist.

Grossist [grɔ'sist] m (-en/-en) s. Großhändler.

groß|jährig adj. ['groːsjɛːriç] of age; ~ werden come of age; '2jährigkeit f (-/no pl.) majority, full (legal) age; '2kaufmann m wholesale merchant; '2kraftwerk ⚡ n superpower station; '2macht f great power; '2maul n braggart; '2mut f (-/no pl.) generosity; ~mütig adj. ['~myːtiç] magnanimous, generous; '2mutter f grandmother; '2neffe m great-nephew, grandnephew; '2nichte f great-niece, grand-niece; '2onkel m great-uncle, grand-uncle; '2schreibung f (-/-en) use of capital letters; capitalization; '~sprecherisch adj. boastful; '~spurig adj. arrogant; '2stadt f large town or city; '~städtisch adj. of or in a large town or city; '2tante f great-aunt, grand-aunt.

größtenteils adv. ['grøːstəntaɪls] mostly, chiefly, mainly.

'groß|tun v/i. (irr. tun, sep., -ge-, h) swagger, boast; sich mit et. ~ boast or brag of or about s.th.; '2vater m grandfather; '2verdiener m (-s/-) big earner; '2wild n big game; '~ziehen v/t. (irr. ziehen, sep., -ge-, h) bring up (child); rear, raise (child, animal); '~zügig adj. ['~tsyːgiç] liberal; generous; broad-minded; planning: a. on a large scale.

grotesk adj. [gro'tesk] grotesque.

Grotte ['grɔtə] f (-/-n) grotto.

grub [gruːp] pret. of graben.

Grübchen ['gryːpçən] n (-s/-) dimple.

Grube ['gruːbə] f (-/-n) pit; ✕ mine, pit.

Grübel|ei [gryːbə'laɪ] f (-/-en) brooding, musing, meditation; 2n ['~ln] v/i. (ge-, h) muse, meditate, ponder (all: über acc. on, over), Am. F a. mull (over).

'Gruben|arbeiter ✕ m miner; '~gas ✕ n fire-damp; '~lampe ✕ f miner's lamp.

Gruft [gruft] f (-/⸚e) tomb, vault.

grün [gryːn] 1. adj. green; ~er Hering fresh herring; ~er junge greenhorn; ~ und blau schlagen beat s.o. black and blue; vom ~en Tisch aus armchair (strategy, etc.); 2. 2 n (-s/no pl.) green; verdure.

Grund [grunt] m (-[e]s/⸚e) ground; soil; bottom (a. fig.); land, estate; foundation; fig.: motive; reason; argument; von ~ auf thoroughly, fundamentally; '~ausbildung f basic instruction; ✕ basic (military) training; '~bedeutung f basic or original meaning; '~bedingung f basic or fundamental condition; '~begriff m fundamental or basic idea; ~e pl. principles pl.; rudiments pl.; '~besitz m land(ed property); '~besitzer *m* landowner; '~buch *n* land register.

gründ|en ['gryndən] *v/t.* (ge-, h) establish; ✝ promote; *sich ~ auf (acc.)* be based *or* founded on; '2er *m* (-s/-) founder; ✝ promoter.

'grund|'falsch *adj.* fundamentally wrong; '2farbe *f* ground-colo(u)r; *opt.* primary colo(u)r; '2fläche *f* base; area (*of room, etc.*); '2gebühr *f* basic rate *or* fee; flat rate; '2gedanke *m* basic *or* fundamental idea; '2gesetz *n* fundamental law; *z* *appr.* constitution; '2kapital ✝ *n* capital (fund); '2lage *f* foundation, basis; '~legend *adj.* fundamental, basic.

gründlich *adj.* ['gryntliç] thorough; *knowledge* profound.

'Grund|linie *f* base-line; '2los *adj.* bottomless, *fig.*: groundless; unfounded; '~mauer *f* foundation-wall. [Thursday.\

Grün'donnerstag *eccl. m* Maundy\

'Grund|regel *f* fundamental rule; '~riß *m* △ ground-plan; outline; compendium; '~satz *m* principle; 2sätzlich ['~zetsliç] 1. *adj.* fundamental; 2. *adv.* in principle; on principle; '~schule *f* elementary *or* primary school; '~stein *m* △ foundation-stone; *fig.* corner-stone; '~steuer *f* land-tax; '~stock *m* basis, foundation; '~stoff *m* element; '~strich *m* down-stroke; '~stück *n* plot (of land); *z* (real) estate; premises *pl.*; '~stücksmakler *m* real estate agent, *Am.* realtor; '~ton *m* ♪ keynote; ground shade.

'Gründung *f* (-/-en) foundation, establishment

'grund|ver'schieden *adj.* entirely different; '2wasser *geol. n* (under-)ground water; '2zahl *gr. f* cardinal number; '2zug *m* main feature, characteristic.

'grünlich *adj.* greenish.

'Grün|schnabel *fig. m* greenhorn; whipper-snapper; '~span *m* (-[e]s/*no pl.*) verdigris.

grunzen ['gruntsən] *v/i. and v/t.* (ge-, h) grunt.

Gruppe ['grupə] *f* (-/-n) group; ✗ section, *Am.* squad; 2ieren [~'piːrən] *v/t.* (*no* -ge-, h) group, arrange in groups; *sich ~* form groups.

Gruselgeschichte ['gruːzəl-] *f* tale of horror, spine-chilling story *or* tale, F creepy story *or* tale.

Gruß [gruːs] *m* (-es/*~e*) salutation; greeting, *esp.* ✗, ⚓ salute; *mst* Grüße *pl* regards *pl.*; respects *pl.*, compliments *pl.*

grüßen ['gryːsən] *v/t.* (ge-, h) greet, *esp.* ✗ salute; hail; ~ *Sie ihn von mir* remember me to him; *j-n ~ lassen* send one's compliments *or* regards to s.o.

9*

Grütze ['grytsə] *f* (-/-n) grits *pl.*, groats *pl.*

guck|en ['gukən] *v/i.* (ge-, h) look; peep, peer; '2loch *n* peep- *or* spy-hole.

Guerilla ✗ [ge'ril(j)a] *f* (-/-s) guer(r)illa war.

gültig *adj.* ['gyltiç] valid; effective, in force; legal; *coin* current; *ticket:* available; '2keit *f* (-/*no pl.*) validity; currency (*of money*); availability (*of ticket*).

Gummi ['gumi] *n, m* (-s/-s) gum; (india-)rubber; '~ball *m* rubber ball; '~band *n* elastic (band); rubber band; '~baum ♀ *m* gum-tree; (india-)rubber tree.

gum'mieren *v/t.* (*no* -ge-, h) gum.

'Gummi|handschuh *m* rubber glove; '~knüppel *m* truncheon, *Am.* club; '~schuhe *m/pl.* rubber shoes *pl.*, *Am* rubbers *pl.*; '~sohle *f* rubber sole, elastic webbing; '~stiefel *m* wellington (boot), *Am* rubber boot; '~zug *m* elastic, elastic webbing.

Gunst [gunst] *f* (-/*no pl.*) favo(u)r, goodwill; *zu ~en (gen.)* in favo(u)r of.

günst|ig *adj.* ['gynstiç] favo(u)rable; *omen* propitious, *im ~sten Fall* at best; *zu ~en Bedingungen* ✝ on easy terms; 2ling ['~liŋ] *m* (-s/-e) favo(u)rite.

Gurgel [gurgəl] *f* (-/-n): *j-m an die ~ springen* leap *or* fly at s.o.'s throat; '2n *v/i.* (ge-, h) ♪ gargle; gurgle

Gurke [gurkə] *f* (-/-n) cucumber; *pickled* gherkin.

gurren [gurən] *v/i.* (ge-, h) coo.

Gurt [gurt] *m* (-[e]s/-e) girdle; *harness:* girth, strap; belt.

Gürtel ['gyrtəl] *m* (-s/-) belt; girdle, *geogr* zone.

Guß [gus] *m* (Gusses/Güsse) ⊕ founding, casting; *typ* fount, *Am.* font; *rain* downpour, shower; '~eisen *n* cast iron; '2eisern *adj.* cast-iron; '~stahl *m* cast steel.

gut[1] [guːt] 1. *adj.* good; *~e Worte* fair words; *~es Wetter* fine weather; *~er Dinge or ~en Mutes* sein be of good cheer; *~e Miene zum bösen Spiel* machen grin and bear it; *~ sol* good!, well done!; *~ werden* get well, heal; *fig.* turn out well; *ganz ~* not bad; *schon ~!* never mind!, all right!; *sei so ~ und ...* (will you) be so kind as to *inf.*; *auf ~ deutsch* in plain German; *j-m ~ sein* love *or* like s.o.; 2. *adv.* well; *ein ~ gehendes Geschäft* a flourishing business; *du hast ~ lachen* it's easy *or* very well for you to laugh; *es ~ haben* be lucky; be well off.

Gut[2] [~] *n* (-[e]s/*~er*) possession, property; (landed) estate; ✝ goods *pl.*

'**Gut|achten** n (-s/-) (expert) opinion; '**~achter** m (-s/-) expert; consultant; '**2artig** adj. good-natured; ✗ benign; '**~dünken** ['~dʏŋkən] n (-s/no pl.): nach ~ at discretion or pleasure.

Gute 1. n (-n/no pl.) the good; **~s** tun do good; **2.** m, f (-n/-n): die **~n** pl. the good pl.

Güte ['gy:tə] f (-/no pl.) goodness; kindness; ✝ class, quality; in ~ amicably; F: meine **~l** good gracious!; haben Sie die ~ zu inf. be so kind as to inf.

'**Güter|abfertigung** f dispatch of goods; **~ '~annahme** f goods office, Am. freight office; '**~bahnhof** m goods station, Am. freight depot or yard; '**~gemeinschaft** ✝✝ f community of property; '**~trennung** ✝✝ f separation of property; '**~verkehr** m goods traffic, Am. freight traffic; '**~wagen** m (goods) wag(g)on, Am. freight car; offener ~ (goods) truck; geschlossener ~ (goods) van, Am. boxcar; '**~zug** m goods train, Am. freight train.

'**gut|gelaunt** adj. good-humo(u)red; '**~gläubig** adj. acting or done in good faith; s. leichtgläubig; '**~haben** v/t. (irr. haben, sep., -ge-, h) have credit for (sum of money); '**2~haben** ✝ n credit (balance); '**~heißen** v/t. (irr. heißen, sep., -ge-, h)

approve (of); '**~herzig** adj. good-natured, kind-hearted.

'**gütig** adj. good, kind(ly).

'**gütlich** adv.: sich ~ einigen settle s.th. amicably; sich ~ tun an (dat.) regale o.s. on.

'**gut|machen** v/t. (sep., -ge-, h) make up for, compensate, repair; '**~mütig** adj. ['~my:tiç] good-natured; '**2mütigkeit** f (-/✗, -en) good nature.

'**Gutsbesitzer** m landowner; owner of an estate.

'**Gut|schein** m credit note, coupon; voucher; '**2schreiben** v/t. (irr. schreiben, sep., -ge-, h): j-m e-n Betrag ~ put a sum to s.o.'s credit; '**~schrift** ✝ f credit(ing).

'**Guts|haus** n farm-house; manor house; '**~herr** m lord of the manor; landowner; '**~hof** m farmyard; estate, farm; '**~verwalter** m (landlord's) manager or steward.

'**gutwillig** adj. willing; obliging.

Gymnasi|albildung [gymnaˈzja:l-] f classical education; '**~ast** [~ast] m (-en/-en) appr. grammar-school boy; '**~um** [~ˈna:zjum] n (-s/Gymnasien) appr. grammar-school.

Gymnasti|k [gymˈnastik] f (-/no pl.) gymnastics pl.; **2sch** adj. gymnastic.

Gynäkologe ✗ [gynɛkoˈlo:gə] m (-n/-n) gyn(a)ecologist.

H

Haar [ha:r] n (-[e]s/-e) hair; sich die **~e** kämmen comb one's hair; sich die **~e** schneiden lassen have one's hair cut; aufs ~ to a hair; um ein ~ by a hair's breadth; '**~ausfall** m loss of hair; '**~bürste** f hairbrush; '**2en** v/i. and v/refl. (ge-, h) lose or shed one's hairs; '**~esbreite** f: um ~ by a hair's breadth; '**2'fein** adj. (as) fine as a hair; fig. subtle; '**~gefäß** anat. n capillary (vessel); '**2ge'nau** adj. exact to a hair; '**2ig** adj. hairy; in compounds: ...-haired; '**2'klein** adv. to the last detail; '**~klemme** f hair grip, Am. bobby pin; '**~nadel** f hairpin; '**~nadelkurve** f hairpin bend; '**~netz** n hair-net; '**~öl** n hair-oil; '**2'scharf 1.** adj. very sharp; fig. very precise; **2.** adv. by a hair's breadth; '**~schneidemaschine** f (e-e a pair of) (hair) clippers pl.; '**~schneider** m barber, (men's) hairdresser; '**~schnitt** m haircut; '**~schwund** m loss of hair; **~spalte'rei** f (-/-en) hair-splitting; '**2sträubend** adj. hair-raising, horrifying; '**~tracht** f hair-style, coiffure; '**~wäsche** f hair-wash,

shampoo; '**~wasser** n hair-lotion; '**~wuchs** m growth of the hair; '**~wuchsmittel** n hair-restorer.

Habe ['ha:bə] f (-/no pl.) property; belongings pl.

haben ['ha:bən] **1.** v/t. (irr., ge-, h) have; F fig.: sich ~ (make a) fuss; etwas (nichts) auf sich ~ be of (no) consequence; unter sich ~ be in control of, command; zu ~ ✝ goods: obtainable, to be had; da ~ wir's / there we are!; **2.** 2 ✝ n (-s/-) credit (side).

Habgier ['ha:p-] f avarice, covetousness; '**2ig** adj. avaricious, covetous.

habhaft adj. ['ha:phaft]: ~ werden (gen.) get hold of; catch, apprehend.

Habicht orn. ['ha:biçt] m (-[e]s/-e) (gos)hawk.

Hab|seligkeiten ['ha:p-] f/pl. property, belongings pl.; '**~sucht** f s. Habgier; '**2süchtig** adj. s. habgierig.

Hacke ['hakə] f (-/-n) ✗ hoe, mattock; (pick)axe; heel.

Hacken ['hakən] **1.** m (-s/-) heel; die ~ zusammenschlagen ✗ click one's heels; **2.** 2 v/t. (ge-, h) ✗

hack (*soil*); mince (*meat*); chop (*wood*).

'**Hackfleisch** *n* minced meat, *Am.* ground meat.

Häcksel ['hɛksəl] *n*, *m* (-s/*no pl.*) chaff, chopped straw.

Hader ['haːdər] *m* (-s/*no pl.*) dispute, quarrel; discord; '**2n** *v/i.* (ge-, h) quarrel (*mit* with).

Hafen ['haːfən] *m* (-s/╵) harbo(u)r; port; '**~anlagen** *f/pl.* docks *pl.*; '**~arbeiter** *m* docker, *Am. a.* long-shoreman; '**~damm** *m* jetty; pier; '**~stadt** *f* seaport.

Hafer ['haːfər] *m* (-s/-) oats *pl.*; '**~brei** *m* (oatmeal) porridge; '**~flocken** *f/pl.* porridge oats *pl.*; '**~grütze** *f* groats *pl.*, grits *pl.*; '**~schleim** *m* gruel.

Haft ⚖ [haft] *f* (-/*no pl.*) custody; detention, confinement; '**2bar** *adj.* responsible, ⚖ liable (*für* for); '**~befehl** *m* warrant of arrest; '**2en** *v/i.* (ge-, h) stick, adhere (*an dat.* to); **~ für** ⚖ answer for, be liable for.

Häftling ['hɛftliŋ] *m* (-s/-e) prisoner.

'**Haftpflicht** ⚖ *f* liability; '**2ig** *adj.* liable (*für* for); '**~versicherung** *f* third-party insurance.

'**Haftung** *f* (-/-en) responsibility, ⚖ liability; *mit beschränkter* **~** limited.

Hagel ['haːgəl] *m* (-s/-) hail; *fig. a.* shower, volley; '**~korn** *n* hailstone; '**2n** *v/i.* (ge-, h) hail (*a. fig.*); '**~schauer** *m* shower of hail, (brief) hailstorm.

hager *adj.* ['haːgər] lean, gaunt; scraggy, lank.

Hahn [haːn] *m* 1. *orn.* (-[e]s/╵e) cock; rooster; 2. ⊕ (-[e]s/╵e, -en) (stop)cock, tap, *Am. a.* faucet; '**~enkampf** *m* cock-fight; '**~enschrei** *m* cock-crow.

Hai *ichth.* [hai] *m* (-[e]s/-e), '**~fisch** *m* shark.

Hain *poet.* [hain] *m* (-[e]s/-e) grove; wood.

häkel|n ['hɛːkəln] *v/t. and v/i.* (ge-, h) crochet; '**2nadel** *f* crochet needle *or* hook.

Haken ['haːkən] 1. *m* (-s/-) hook (*a. boxing*); peg; *fig.* snag, catch; 2. 2 *v/i.* (ge-, h) get stuck, jam.

'**hakig** *adj.* hooked.

halb [halp] 1. *adj.* half; *eine* **~e** *Stunde* half an hour, a half-hour; *eine* **~e** *Flasche Wein* a half-bottle of wine; *ein* **~es** *Jahr* half a year; **~e** *Note* ♩ minim, *Am. a.* half note; **~er** *Ton* ♩ semitone, *Am. a.* half tone; 2. *adv.* half; **~ voll** half full; **~ soviel** half as much; *es schlug* **~** it struck the half-hour.

'**halb|amtlich** *adj.* semi-official; '**2bruder** *m* half-brother; '**2dunkel** *n* semi-darkness; dusk, twilight; '**~er** *prp.* (*gen.*) ['halbər] on account of; for the sake of; '**2fabri-**

kat ⊕ *n* semi-finished product; '**~gar** *adj.* underdone, *Am. a.* rare; '**2gott** *m* demigod; '**2heit** *f* (-/-en) half-measure.

halbieren [hal'biːrən] *v/t.* (*no* -ge-, h) halve, divide in half; ⚖ bisect.

'**Halb|insel** *f* peninsula; '**~jahr** *n* half-year, six months *pl.*; '**2jährig** *adj.* [...jɛːriç] half-year, six months; of six months; '**2jährlich** 1. *adj.* half-yearly; 2. *adv. a.* twice a year; '**~kreis** *m* semicircle; '**~kugel** *f* hemisphere; '**2laut** 1. *adj.* low, subdued; 2. *adv.* in an undertone; '**2mast** *adv.* (at) half-mast, *Am. a.* (at) half-staff; '**~messer** ⚙ *m* (-s/-) radius; '**~mond** *m* half-moon, crescent; '**2part** *adv.*: **~** *machen* go halves, F go fifty-fifty; '**~schuh** *m* (low) shoe; '**~schwester** *f* half-sister; '**~tagsbeschäftigung** *f* part-time job *or* employment; '**2tot** *adj.* half-dead; '**2wegs** *adv.* ['...'veːks] half-way; *fig.* to some extent, tolerably; '**~welt** *f* demi-monde; '**2wüchsig** *adj.* ['...vyːksiç] adolescent, *Am. a.* teen-age; '**~zeit** *f* *sports:* half(-time).

Halde ['haldə] *f* (-/-n) slope; ⚒ dump.

half [half] *pret. of* helfen.

Hälfte ['hɛlftə] *f* (-/-n) half, ⚖ moiety, *die* **~** *von* half of.

Halfter ['halftər] *m*, *n* (-s/-) halter.

Halle ['halə] *f* (-/-n) hall; *hotel:* lounge; *tennis:* covered court; ✈ hangar.

hallen ['halən] *v/i.* (ge-, h) (re)sound, ring, (re-)echo.

'**Hallen|bad** *n* indoor swimming-bath, *Am. a.* natatorium; '**~sport** *m* indoor sports *pl.*

hallo [ha'loː] 1. *int.* hallo!, hello!, hullo!; 2. 2 *fig. n* (-s/-s) hullabaloo.

Halm ♦ [halm] *m* (-[e]s/-e) blade; stem, stalk; straw.

Hals [hals] *m* (-es/╵e) neck; throat; **~** *über Kopf* head over heels; *auf dem* **~e** *haben* have on one's back, be saddled with; *sich den* **~** *verrenken* crane one's neck; '**~abschneider** *fig. m* extortioner, F shark; '**~band** *n* necklace; collar (*for dog, etc.*); '**~entzündung** ⚕ *f* sore throat; '**~kette** *f* necklace; string; chain; '**~kragen** *m* collar; '**~schmerzen** *m/pl.*: **~** *haben* have a sore throat; '**2starrig** *adj.* stubborn, obstinate; '**~tuch** *n* neckerchief; scarf; '**~weite** *f* neck size.

Halt [halt] *m* (-[e]s/-e) hold; foothold, handhold; support (*a. fig.*); *fig.*: stability; security; mainstay.

halt 1. *int.* stop!; ⚔ halt!; 2. F *adv.* just; *das ist* **~** *so* that's the way it is.

'**haltbar** *adj. material, etc.*: durable, lasting; *colour*: fast; *fig. theory, etc.*: tenable.

'**halten** (*irr.*, ge-, h) 1. *v/t.* hold (*fort,*

position, water, etc.); maintain (*position, level, etc.*); keep (*promise, order, animal, etc.*); make, deliver (*speech*); give, deliver (*lecture*); take in (*newspaper*); ~ für regard as, take to be; take for; es ~ mit side with; be fond of; kurz~ keep *s.o.* short; viel (wenig) ~ von think highly (little) of; sich ~ hold out; last; *food:* keep; sich gerade ~ hold o.s. straight; sich gut ~ *in examination, etc.*: do well; *p.* be well preserved; sich ~ an (*acc.*) adhere *or* keep to; **2.** *v/i.* stop, halt; *ice:* bear; *rope, etc.*: stand the strain; ~ zu stick to *or* by; ~ auf (*acc.*) set store by, value; auf sich ~ pay attention to one's appearance; have self-respect.

'**Halte|punkt** *m* 🚑, *etc.*: wayside stop, halt; *shooting:* point of aim; *phys.* critical point; '~r *m* (*-s/-*) keeper; *a.* owner; *devices:* ... holder; '~stelle *f* stop; 🚑 station, stop; '~signal 🚑 *n* stop signal.

halt|los *adj.* ['haltlo:s] *p.* unsteady, unstable; *theory, etc.*: baseless, without foundation; '~machen *v/i.* (*sep.*, -ge-, h) stop, halt; vor nichts ~ stick *or* stop; at nothing; '2ung *f* (*-/-en*) deportment, carriage; pose; *fig.* attitude (*gegenüber towards*); self-control; *stock exchange:* tone.

hämisch *adj.* ['hɛ:miʃ] spiteful, malicious.

Hammel ['haməl] *m* (*-s/-,* ¨) wether; '~fleisch *n* mutton; '~keule *f* leg of mutton; '~rippchen *n* (*-s/-*) mutton chop.

Hammer ['hamər] *m* (*-s/*¨) hammer; (auctioneer's) gavel; unter den ~ kommen come under the hammer.

hämmern ['hɛmərn] (ge-, h) **1.** *v/t.* hammer; **2.** *v/i.* hammer (*a.* an dat. at *door, etc.*); hammer away (*auf dat.* at *piano*); *heart, etc.*: throb (violently), pound.

Hämorrhoiden 💊 [hɛ:mɔro'i:dən] *f/pl.* h(a)emorrhoids *pl.*, piles *pl.*

Hampelmann ['hampəlman] *m* jumping-jack; *fig.* (mere) puppet.

Hamster *zo.* ['hamstər] *m* (*-s/-*) hamster; '2n *v/t. and v/i.* (ge-, h) hoard.

Hand [hant] *f* (*-/*¨e) hand; *j-m die* ~ geben shake hands with s.o.; an ~ (*gen.*) *or* von with the help *or* aid of; aus erster ~ first-hand, at first hand; bei der ~, zur ~ at hand; ~ und Fuß haben be sound, hold water; seine ~ im Spiele haben have a finger in the pie; '~arbeit *f* manual labo(u)r *or* work; (handi)craft; needlework; '~arbeiter *m* manual labo(u)rer; '~bibliothek *f* reference library; '~breit **1.** *f* (*-/-*) hand's breadth; **2.** ♀ *adj.* a hand's breadth across; '~bremse *mot.* *f* hand-brake; '~buch *n* manual, handbook.

Hände|druck ['hɛndə-] *m* (*-[e]s/*¨e)

handshake; '~klatschen *n* (*-s/no pl.*) (hand-)clapping; applause.

Handel ['handəl] *m* **1.** (*-s/no pl.*) commerce; trade; business; market; traffic; transaction, deal, bargain; **2.** (*-s/-*): *Händel pl.* quarrels *pl.*, contention; '2n *v/i.* (ge-, h) act, take action; ✝ trade (*mit with s.o.*, in *goods*), deal (in *goods*); bargain (*um for*), haggle (over); ~ von treat of, deal with; es handelt sich um it concerns, it is a matter of.

'**Handels|abkommen** *n* trade agreement; '~bank *f* commercial bank; '2einig *adj.*: ~ werden come to terms; '~genossenschaft *f* traders' co-operative association; '~gericht *n* commercial court; '~gesellschaft *f* (trading) company; '~haus *n* business house, firm; '~kammer *f* Chamber of Commerce; '~marine *f* mercantile marine; '~minister *m* minister of commerce; President of the Board of Trade, *Am.* Secretary of Commerce; '~ministerium *n* ministry of commerce; Board of Trade, *Am.* Department of Commerce; '~reisende *m* commercial traveller, *Am.* traveling salesman, F drummer; '~schiff *n* merchantman; '~schiffahrt *f* merchant shipping; '~schule *f* commercial school; '~stadt *f* commercial town; '2üblich *adj.* customary in trade; '~vertrag *m* commercial treaty, trade agreement.

'**handeltreibend** *adj.* trading.

'**Hand|feger** *m* (*-s/-*) hand-brush; '~fertigkeit *f* manual skill; 2fest *adj.* sturdy, strong; *fig.* well-founded, sound; '~feuerwaffen *f/pl.* small arms *pl.*; '~fläche *f* flat of the hand, palm; '2gearbeitet *adj.* hand-made; '~geld *n* earnest money; ⚔ bounty; '~gelenk *anat.* *n* wrist; '~gemenge *n* scuffle, mêlée; '~gepäck *n* hand luggage, *Am.* hand baggage; '~granate ⚔ *f* hand-grenade; '2greiflich *adj.* violent; *fig.* tangible, palpable; ~ werden turn violent, *Am. a.* get tough; '~griff *m* grasp; handle, grip; *fig.* manipulation; '~habe *fig. f* handle; '2haben *v/t.* (ge-, h) handle, manage; operate (*machine, etc.*); administer (*law*); '~karren *m* hand-cart; '~koffer *m* suitcase, *Am. a.* valise; '~kuß *m* kiss on the hand; '~langer *m* (*-s/-*) hodman, handy man; *fig.* dog's-body, henchman.

Händler ['hɛndlər] *m* (*-s/-*) dealer, trader.

'**handlich** *adj.* handy; manageable.

Handlung ['handluŋ] *f* (*-/-en*) act, action; deed; *thea.* action, plot; ✝ shop, *Am.* store.

'**Handlungs|bevollmächtigte** *m* proxy; '~gehilfe *m* clerk; shop-assistant, *Am.* salesclerk; '~reisende *m s.* Handelsreisende; '~weise *f* conduct; way of acting.

'Hand|rücken *m* back of the hand; '~schelle *f* handcuff, manacle; '~schlag *m* handshake; '~schreiben *n* autograph letter; '~schrift *f* handwriting; manuscript; '2schriftlich 1. *adj.* hand-written; 2. *adv.* in one's own handwriting; '~schuh *m* glove; '~streich ⚔ *m* surprise attack, coup de main; *im* ~ *nehmen* take by surprise; '~tasche *f* handbag, *Am. a.* purse; '~tuch *n* towel; '~voll *f* (-/-) handful; '~wagen *m* hand-cart; '~werk *n* (handi)craft, trade; '~werker *m* (-s/-) (handi)craftsman, artisan; workman; '~werkzeug *n* (kit of) tools *pl.*; '~wurzel *anat. f* wrist; '~zeichnung *f* drawing.

Hanf ♀ [hanf] *m* (-[e]s/no *pl.*) hemp.

Hang [haŋ] *m* (-[e]s/=e) slope, incline, declivity; hillside; *fig.* inclination, propensity (*zu* for; *zu inf.* to *inf.*); tendency (to).

Hänge|boden ['hɛŋə-] *m* hangingloft; '~brücke △ *f* suspension bridge; '~lampe *f* hanging lamp; '~matte *f* hammock.

hängen ['hɛŋən] 1. *v/i.* (irr., ge-, h) hang, be suspended; adhere, stick, cling (*an dat.* to); ~ *an* (*dat.*) be attached *or* devoted to; 2. *v/t.* (ge-, h) hang, suspend; '~bleiben *v/i.* (irr. bleiben, sep., -ge-, sein) get caught (up) (*an dat.* on, in); *fig.* stick (in the memory).

hänseln ['hɛnzəln] *v/t.* (ge-, h) tease (*wegen* about), F rag.

Hansestadt ['hanzə-] *f* Hanseatic town.

Hanswurst [hans'-] *m* (-es/-e, F ⸗e) merry andrew; Punch; *fig. contp.* clown, buffoon.

Hantel ['hantəl] *f* (-/-n) dumb-bell.

hantieren [han'ti:rən] *v/i.* (no -ge-, h) be busy (*mit* with); work (*an dat.* on).

Happen ['hapən] *m* (-s/-) morsel, mouthful, bite; snack.

Harfe ♪ ['harfə] *f* (-/-n) harp.

Harke ♪ ['harkə] *f* (-/-n) rake; '2n *v/t. and v/i.* (ge-, h) rake.

harmlos *adj.* ['harmlo:s] harmless, innocuous; inoffensive.

Harmon|ie [harmo'ni:] *f* (-/-n) harmony (*a.* ♪); 2ieren *v/i.* (no -ge-, h) harmonize (*mit* with); *fig. a.* be in tune (with); '~ika ♪ [~'mo:nika] *f* (-/-s, Harmoniken) accordion; mouth-organ; 2isch *adj.* [~'mo:niʃ] harmonious.

Harn [harn] *m* (-[e]s/-e) urine; '~blase *anat. f* (urinary) bladder; '2en *v/i.* (ge-, h) pass water, urinate.

Harnisch ['harniʃ] *m* (-es/-e) armo(u)r; *in* ~ *geraten* be up in arms (*über acc.* about).

'Harnröhre *anat. f* urethra.

Harpun|e [har'pu:nə] *f* (-/-n) harpoon; 2ieren [~u'ni:rən] *v/t.* (no -ge-, h) harpoon.

hart [hart] 1. *adj.* hard; *fig. a.* harsh; heavy, severe; 2. *adv.* hard; ~ *arbeiten* work hard.

Härte ['hɛrtə] *f* (-/-n) hardness; *fig. a.* hardship; severity; '2n (ge-, h) 1. *v/t.* harden (*metal*); temper (*steel*); case-harden (*iron, steel*); 2. *v/i. and v/refl.* harden, become *or* grow hard; *steel:* temper.

'Hart|geld *n* coin(s *pl.*), specie; '~gummi *m* hard rubber; † ebonite, vulcanite; '2herzig *adj.* hard-hearted; 2köpfig *adj.* ['~kœpfiç] stubborn, headstrong; 2näckig *adj.* ['~nɛkiç] *p.* obstinate, obdurate; *effort:* dogged, tenacious; ⚔ *ailment:* refractory.

Harz [ha:rts] *n* (-es/-e) resin; ♪ rosin; *mot.* gum; '2ig *adj.* resinous.

Hasardspiel [ha'zart-] *n* game of chance; *fig.* gamble.

haschen ['haʃən] (ge-, h) 1. *v/t.* catch (hold of), snatch; *sich* ~ *children* play tag; 2. *v/i.:* ~ *nach* snatch at; *fig.* strain after (*effect*), fish for (*compliments*).

Hase ['ha:zə] *m* (-n/-n) *zo.* hare; *ein alter* ~ an old hand, an old-timer.

Haselnuß ♀ ['ha:zəlnus] *f* hazelnut.

'Hasen|braten *m* roast hare; '~fuß F *fig. m* coward, F funk; '~panier F *n: das* ~ *ergreifen* take to one's heels; '~scharte ⚔ *f* hare-lip.

Haß [has] *m* (Hasses/no *pl.*) hatred.

'hassen *v/t.* (ge-, h) hate.

häßlich *adj.* ['hɛsliç] ugly; *fig. a.* nasty, unpleasant.

Hast [hast] *f* (-/no *pl.*) hurry, haste; rush; *in wilder* ~ in frantic haste; '2en *v/i.* (ge-, sein) hurry, hasten; rush; '2ig *adj.* hasty, hurried.

hätscheln ['hɛ:tʃəln] *v/t.* (ge-, h) caress, fondle, pet; pamper, coddle.

hatte ['hatə] *pret. of* haben.

Haube ['haubə] *f* (-/-n) bonnet (*a.* ⊕, *mot.*); cap; *orn.* crest, tuft; *mot. Am. a.* hood.

Haubitze ⚔ [hau'bitsə] *f* (-/-n) howitzer.

Hauch [haux] *m* (-[e]s/⸗, -e) breath; *fig.:* waft, whiff (*of perfume, etc.*); touch, tinge (*of irony, etc.*); '2en (ge-, h) 1. *v/i.* breathe; 2. *v/t.* breathe, whisper; *gr.* aspirate.

Haue ['hauə] *f* (-/-n) ✗ hoe, mattock; pick; F hiding, spanking; '2n (irr., ge-, h) 1. *v/t.* hew (*coal, stone*); cut up (*meat*); chop (*wood*); cut (*hole, steps, etc.*); beat (*child*); *sich* ~ (have a) fight; 2. *v/i.:* ~ *nach* cut at, strike out at.

Haufen ['haufən] *m* (-es/-) heap, pile (*both* F *a. fig.*); *fig.* crowd.

häufen ['hɔyfən] *v/t.* (ge-, h) heap

(up), pile (up); accumulate; *sich ~* pile up, accumulate; *fig.* become more frequent, increase.

'häufig *adj.* frequent; **'2keit** *f* (-/*no pl.*) frequency.

'Häufung *fig. f* (-/-en) increase, *fig.* accumulation.

Haupt [haupt] *n* (-[e]s/*ⁿer*) head; *fig.* chief, head, leader; **'~altar** *m* high altar; **'~anschluß** *teleph. m* subscriber's main station; **'~bahn-hof** 🚂 *m* main *or* central station; **'~beruf** *m* full-time occupation; **'~buch** ✝ *n* ledger; **'~darsteller** *thea. m* leading actor; **'~fach** *univ. n* main *or* principal subject, *Am. a.* major; **'~film** *m* feature (film); **'~geschäft** *n* main transaction; main shop; **'~geschäftsstelle** *f* head *or* central office; **'~gewinn** *m* first prize; **'~grund** *m* main reason; **'~handelsartikel** ✝ ['haupthandəls⁹-] *m* staple.

Häuptling ['hɔyptliŋ] *m* (-s/-e) chief(tain).

'Haupt|linie 🚂 *f* main *or* trunk line; **'~mann** ✕ *m* (-[e]s/*Hauptleute*) captain; **'~merkmal** *n* characteristic feature; **'~postamt** *n* general post office, *Am.* main post office; **'~punkt** *m* main *or* cardinal point; **'~quartier** *n* headquarters *sg. or pl.*; **'~rolle** *thea. f* lead(ing part); **'~sache** *f* main thing *or* point; **'2sächlich** *adj.* main, chief, principal; **'~satz** *gr. m* main clause; **'~stadt** *f* capital; **'2städtisch** *adj.* metropolitan; **'~straße** *f* main street; major road; **'~treffer** *m* first prize, jackpot; **'~verkehrs-straße** *f* main road; arterial road; **'~verkehrsstunden** *f/pl.*, **'~verkehrszeit** *f* rush hour(s pl.), peak hour(s *pl.*); **'~versammlung** *f* general meeting; **'~wort** *gr. n* (-[e]s/*ⁿer*) substantive, noun.

Haus [haus] *n* (-es/*ⁿer*) house; building; home, family, household; dynasty; ✝ (business) house, firm; *parl.* House; *nach ~e* home; *zu ~e* at home, F in; **'~angestellte** *f* (-n/-n) (house-)maid; **'~apotheke** *f* (household) medicine-chest; **'~arbeit** *f* housework; **'~arrest** *m* house arrest; **'~arzt** *m* family doctor; **'~aufgaben** *f/pl.* homework, F prep; **'2backen** *fig. adj.* homely; **'~bar** *f* cocktail cabinet; **'~bedarf** *m* household requirements *pl.*; **'~besitzer** *m* house-owner; **'~diener** *m* (man-)servant; *hotel:* porter, boots *sg.*

hausen ['hauzən] *v/i.* (ge-, h) live; play *or* work havoc (*in a place*).

'Haus|flur *m* (entrance-)hall, *esp. Am.* hallway; **'~frau** *f* housewife; **'~halt** *m* household; **'2halten** *v/i.* (irr. *halten*, sep., -ge-, h) be economical (*mit with*), economize (on);

'~hälterin ['~hɛltərin] *f* (-/-nen) housekeeper; **'~halt(s)plan** *parl. m* budget; **'~haltung** *f* housekeeping; household, family; **'~halt-waren** *f/pl.* household articles *pl.*; **'~herr** *m* master of the family; landlord.

hausier|en [hau'zi:rən] *v/i.* (*no -ge-, h*) hawk, peddle (*mit et. s.th.*); *~ gehen* be a hawker *or* pedlar; **2er** *m* (-s/-) hawker, pedlar.

'Haus|kleid *n* house dress; **'~knecht** *m* boots; **'~lehrer** *m* private tutor.

häuslich ['hɔyslɪç] *adj.* domestic; domesticated; **'2keit** *f* (-/*no pl.*) domesticity; family life; home.

'Haus|mädchen *n* (house-)maid; **'~mannskost** *f* plain fare; **'~meister** *m* caretaker; janitor; **'~mittel** *n* popular medicine; **'~ordnung** *f* rules *pl.* of the house; **'~rat** *m* household effects *pl.*; **'~recht** *n* domestic authority; **'~sammlung** *f* house-to-house collection; **'~schlüssel** *m* latchkey; front-door key; **'~schuh** *m* slipper.

Hauss|e ✝ ['ho:s(ə)] *f* (-/-n) rise, boom; **'~ier** [hos'je:] *m* (-s/-s) speculator for a rise, bull.

'Haus|stand *m* household; *e-n ~ gründen* set up house; **'~suchung** ⚖ *f* house search, domiciliary visit, *Am. a.* house check; **'~tier** *n* domestic animal; **'~tür** *f* front door; **'~verwalter** *m* steward; **'~wirt** *m* landlord; **'~wirtin** *f* (-/-nen) landlady.

Haut [haut] *f* (-/*ⁿe*) skin; hide; film; *bis auf die ~* to the skin; *aus der ~ fahren* jump out of one's skin; F *e-e ehrliche ~* an honest soul; **'~abschürfung** 🩹 *f* skin abrasion; **'~arzt** *m* dermatologist; **'~ausschlag** 🩹 *m* rash; **'2eng** *adj. garment:* skin-tight; **'~farbe** *f* complexion.

Hautgout [o'gu] *m* (-s/*no pl.*) high taste.

häutig *adj.* ['hɔytɪç] membranous; covered with skin.

'Haut|krankheit *f* skin disease; **'~pflege** *f* care of the skin; **'~schere** *f* (e-e a pair of) cuticle scissors *pl.*

Havarie ⚓ [hava'ri:] *f* (-/-n) average.

H-Bombe ✕ ['ha:-] *f* H-bomb.

he *int.* [he:] hi!, hi there!; I say!

Hebamme ['he:p⁹amə] *f* midwife.

Hebe|baum ['he:bə-] *m* lever (*for raising heavy objects*); **'~bühne** *mot. f* lifting ramp; **'~eisen** *n* crowbar; **'~kran** *m* lifting crane.

Hebel ⊕ ['he:bəl] *m* (-s/-) lever; **'~arm** *m* lever arm.

heben ['he:bən] *v/t.* (*irr.*, ge-, h) lift (*a. sports*), raise (*a. fig.*); heave (*heavy load*); hoist; recover (*treas-*

ure); raise (*sunken ship*); *fig.* promote, improve, increase; *sich ~* rise, go up.

Hecht *ichth.* [hɛçt] *m* (-[e]s/-e) pike.

Heck [hɛk] *n* (-[e]s/-e, -s) ⚓ stern; *mot.* rear; ✠ tail.

Hecke ['hɛkə] *f* (-/-n) ⚘ hedge; *zo.* brood, hatch; **'2n** *v/t. and v/i.* (ge-, h) breed, hatch; **'~nrose** ⚘ *f* dog-rose. [(hallo!)]

heda *int.* ['he:dɑ:] hi (there)!,

Heer [he:r] *n* (-[e]s/-e) ⚔ army; *fig. a.* host; **'~esdienst** *m* military service; **'~esmacht** *f* military force(s *pl.*); **'~eszug** *m* military expedition; **'~führer** *m* general; **'~lager** *n* (army) camp; **'~schar** *f* army, host; **'~straße** *f* military road; highway; **'~zug** *m s.* Heereszug.

Hefe ['he:fə] *f* (-/-n) yeast; barm.

Heft [hɛft] *n* (-[e]s/-e) dagger, *etc.*: haft; *knife*: handle; *fig.* reins *pl.*; exercise book; *periodical, etc.*: issue, number.

'heft|en *v/t.* (ge-, h) fasten, fix (*an acc.* on to); affix, attach (to); pin on (to); tack, baste (*seam, etc.*); stitch, sew (*book*); **'2faden** *m* basting thread.

'heftig *adj. storm, anger, quarrel, etc.*: violent, fierce; *rain, etc.*: heavy; *pain, etc.*: severe; *speech, desire, etc.*: vehement, passionate; *p.* irascible; **'2keit** *f* (-/-en) violence, fierceness; severity; vehemence; irascibility.

'Heft|klammer *f* paper-clip; **'~pflaster** *n* sticking plaster.

hegen ['he:gən] *v/t.* (ge-, h) preserve (*game*); nurse, tend (*plants*); have, entertain (*feelings*); harbo(u)r (*fears, suspicions, etc.*).

Hehler ⚖ ['he:lər] *m* (-s/-) receiver (of stolen goods); **~ei** [~'raɪ] *f* (-/-en) receiving of stolen goods).

Heide ['haɪdə] 1. *m* (-n/-n) heathen; 2. *f* (-/-n) heath(-land); ⚬ **~kraut** ⚘ *n* heather; **~land** *n* heath(-land).

'Heiden|geld F *n* pots *pl.* of money; **'~lärm** F *m* hullabaloo; **'~spaß** F *m* capital fun; **'~tum** *n* (-s/no *pl.*) heathenism. [(-ish).]

heidnisch *adj.* ['haɪdnɪʃ] heathen|

heikel *adj.* ['haɪkəl] *p.* fastidious, particular; *problem, etc.*: delicate, awkward.

heil [haɪl] 1. *adj. p.* safe, unhurt; whole, sound; 2. 2 *n* (-[e]s/no *pl.*) welfare, benefit; *eccl.* salvation; 3. *int.* hail!

Heiland *eccl.* ['haɪlant] *m* (-[e]s/-e) Saviour, Redeemer.

'Heil|anstalt *f* sanatorium, *Am. a.* sanitarium; **'~bad** *n* medicinal bath; spa; **'2bar** *adj.* curable; **'2en** (ge-) 1. *v/t.* (h) cure, heal; *~ von* cure *s.o.* of; 2. *v/i.* (sein) heal (up); **'~gehilfe** *m* male nurse.

heilig *adj.* ['haɪlɪç] holy; sacred; solemn; **2e** ['~gə] *m, f* (-n/-n) saint; **~en** ['~gən] *v/t.* (ge-, h) sanctify (*a. fig.*), hallow; **'2keit** *f* (-/no *pl.*) holiness; sacredness, sanctity; **~sprechen** *v/t.* (*irr. sprechen, sep., -ge-, h*) canonize; **2sprechung** *f* (-/-en) canonization; **2tum** *n* (-[e]s/=er) sanctuary; sacred relic; **2ung** ['~gʊŋ] *f* (-/-en) sanctification (*a. fig.*), hallowing.

'Heil|kraft *f* healing *or* curative power; **2kräftig** *adj.* healing, curative; **'~kunde** *f* medical science; **'2los** *fig. adj.* confusion: utter, great; **~mittel** *n* remedy, medicament; **'~praktiker** *m* non-medical practitioner; **'~quelle** *f* medicinal spring; **'2sam** *adj.* curative; *fig.* salutary. [(Army.)]

Heilsarmee ['haɪls?-] *f* Salvation

'Heil|ung *f* (-/-en) cure, healing, successful treatment; **'~verfahren** *n* therapy.

heim [haɪm] 1. *adv.* home; 2. 2 *n* (-[e]s/-e) home; hostel; **2arbeit** *f* homework, outwork.

Heimat ['haɪmɑ:t] *f* (-/✠-en) home; own country; native land; **~land** *n* own country, native land; **2lich** *adj.* native; **2los** *adj.* homeless; **'~ort** *m* home town *or* village; **'~vertriebene** *m* expellee.

Heimchen *zo.* ['haɪmçən] *n* (-s/-) cricket.

'heimisch *adj. trade, industry, etc.*: home, local, domestic; ⚘, *zo., etc.*: native, indigenous; *~ werden* settle down; become established; *sich ~ fühlen* feel at home.

Heim|kehr ['haɪmke:r] *f* (-/no *pl.*) return (home), homecoming; **'2kehren** *v/i.* (*sep., -ge-, sein*), **'2kommen** *v/i.* (*irr. kommen, sep., -ge-, sein*) return home.

'heimlich *adj. plan, feeling, etc.*: secret; *meeting, organization, etc.*: clandestine; *glance, movement, etc.*: stealthy, furtive.

'Heim|reise *f* homeward journey; **'2suchen** *v/t.* (*sep., -ge-, h*) disaster, *etc.*: afflict, strike; *ghost* haunt; *God:* visit, punish; **'~tücke** *f* underhand malice, treachery; **2tückisch** *adj.* malicious, treacherous, insidious; **2wärts** *adv.* ['~verts] homeward(s); **'~weg** *m* way home; **'~weh** *n* homesickness, nostalgia; *~ haben* be homesick.

Heirat ['haɪrɑ:t] *f* (-/-en) marriage; **2en** (ge-) 1. *v/t.* marry; 2. *v/i.* marry, get married.

'Heirats|antrag *m* offer *or* proposal of marriage; **'2fähig** *adj.* marriageable; **'~kandidat** *m* possible marriage partner; **'~schwindler** *m* marriage impostor; **'~vermittler** *m* matrimonial agent.

heiser *adj.* ['haɪzər] hoarse; husky; '2keit *f* (-/no *pl.*) hoarseness; huskiness.

heiß *adj.* [haɪs] hot; *fig. a.* passionate, ardent; *mir ist ~* I am or feel hot.

heißen ['haɪsən] (*irr.*, ge-, h) 1. *v/t.*: *e-n Lügner ~* call *s.o.* a liar; *willkommen ~* welcome; 2. *v/i.* be called; mean; *wie ~ Sie?* what is your name?; *was heißt das auf englisch?* what's that in English?

heiter *adj.* ['haɪtər] day, weather: bright; *sky* bright, clear; *p.*, *etc.*: cheerful, gay; serene; '2keit *f* (-/no *pl.*) brightness; cheerfulness, gaiety; serenity.

heiz|en ['haɪtsən] (ge-, h) 1. *v/t.* heat (*room*, *etc.*); light (*stove*); fire (*boiler*); 2. *v/i.* stove, *etc.*: give out heat; turn on the heating; *mit Kohlen ~* burn coal; '2er *m* (-s/-) stoker, fireman; '2kissen *n* electric heating pad; '2körper *m* central heating radiator; *~* heating element; '2material *n* fuel; '2ung *f* (-/-en) heating.

Held [hɛlt] *m* (-en/-en) hero.

'Helden|gedicht *n* epic (poem); '2haft *adj.* heroic, valiant; '~mut *m* heroism, valo(u)r; 2mütig *adj.* ['~my:tiç] heroic; '~tat *f* heroic or valiant deed; '~tod *m* hero's death; '~tum *n* (-[e]s/no *pl.*) heroism.

helfen ['hɛlfən] *v/i.* (*dat.*) (*irr.*, ge-, h) help, assist, aid; *~ gegen* be good for; *sich nicht zu ~ wissen* be helpless.

'Helfer *m* (-s/-) helper, assistant; '~shelfer *m* accomplice.

hell *adj.* [hɛl] sound, voice, light, *etc.*: clear; *light*, *flame*, *etc.*: bright; *hair*: fair; *colour* light; *ale*: pale; '~blau *adj.* light-blue; '~blond *adj.* very fair, '~hörig *adj. p.* quick of hearing; *fig.* perceptive; Δ poorly sound-proofed; '2seher *m* clairvoyant.

Helm [hɛlm] *m* (-[e]s/-e) ⚔ helmet; Δ dome, cupola; ⚓ helm; '~busch *m* plume.

Hemd [hɛmt] *n* (-[e]s/-en) shirt; vest; '~bluse *f* shirt-blouse, *Am.* shirtwaist.

Hemisphäre [he:mi'sfɛːrə] *f* (-/-n) [hemisphere.\

hemm|en ['hɛmən] *v/t.* (ge-, h) check, stop (*movement*, *etc.*); stem (*stream*, *flow of liquid*); hamper (*free movement*, *activity*); be a hindrance to; *psych.* gehemmt sein be inhibited; '2nis *n* (-ses/-se) hindrance, impediment; '2schuh *m* slipper; *fig.* hindrance, F drag (*für acc.* on); '2ung *f* (-/-en) stoppage, check; *psych.*: inhibition.

Hengst *zo.* [hɛŋst] *m* (-es/-e) stallion.

Henkel ['hɛŋkəl] *m* (-s/-) handle, ear.

Henker ['hɛŋkər] *m* (-s/-) hangman, executioner; F: *zum ~!* hang it (all)!

Henne *zo.* ['hɛnə] *f* (-/-n) hen.

her *adv.* [heːr] here; hither; *es ist schon ein Jahr ~, daß ... or seit ...* it is a year since ...; *wie lange ist es ~ seit ... how long is it since ...*; *hinter (dat.) ~ sein* be after; *~ damit!* out with it!

herab *adv.* [hɛ'rap] down, downward; **~lassen** *v/t.* (*irr.* lassen, sep., -ge-, h) let down, lower; *fig. sich ~* condescend; **~lassend** *adj.* condescending; **~setzen** *v/t.* (sep., -ge-, h) take down; *fig.* belittle, disparage *s.o.*); 2setzung *fig. f* (-/-en) reduction; disparagement; **~steigen** *v/i.* (*irr.* steigen, sep., -ge-, sein) climb down, descend; **~würdigen** *v/t.* (sep., -ge-, h) degrade, belittle, abase.

heran *adv.* [hɛ'ran] close, near; up; *nur ~!* come on!; **~bilden** *v/t.* (sep., -ge-, h) train, educate (*zu* as *s.th.*, to be *s.th.*); **~kommen** *v/i.* (*irr.* kommen, sep., -ge-, sein) come or draw near; approach; *~ an (acc.)* come up to *s.o.*; measure up to; **~wachsen** *v/i.* (*irr.* wachsen, sep., -ge-, sein) grow (up) (*zu* into).

herauf *adv.* [hɛ'rauf] up (wards), up here; upstairs; **~beschwören** *v/t.* (*irr.* schwören, sep., no -ge-, h) evoke, call up, conjure up (*spirit*, *etc.*); *fig. a.* bring about, provoke, give rise to (*war*, *etc.*); **~steigen** *v/i.* (*irr.* steigen, sep., -ge-, sein) climb up (here), ascend; **~ziehen** (*irr.* ziehen, sep., -ge-) 1. *v/t.* (h) pull or hitch up (*trousers*, *etc.*); 2. *v/i.* (sein) cloud, *etc.*: come up.

heraus *adv.* [hɛ'raus] out, out here; *zum Fenster ~* out of the window; *~ mit der Sprache!* speak out!; **~bekommen** *v/t.* (*irr.* kommen, sep., no -ge-, h) get out; get (*money*) back; *fig.* find out; **~bringen** *v/t.* (*irr.* bringen, sep., -ge-, h) bring or get out; *thea.* stage; **~finden** *v/t.* (*irr.* finden, sep., -ge-, h) find out; *fig. a.* discover; **2forderer** *m* (-s/-) challenger; **~fordern** *v/t.* (sep., -ge-, h) challenge (*to a fight*); provoke; 2forderung *f* (-/-en) challenge; provocation; **~geben** *v/t.* (*irr.* geben, sep., -ge-, h) 1. *v/t.* surrender; hand over; restore; edit (*periodical*, *etc.*); publish (*book*, *etc.*); issue (*regulations*, *etc.*); 2. *v/i.* give change (*auf acc.* for); **2geber** *m* (-s/-) editor; publisher; **~kommen** *v/i.* (*irr.* kommen, sep., -ge-, sein) come out; *fig. a.* appear, be published; **~nehmen** *v/t.* (*irr.* nehmen, sep., -ge-, h) take out; *sich viel ~* take liberties; **~putzen** *v/t.* (sep., -ge-, h) dress up; *sich ~* dress (o.s.)

up; **~reden** v/refl. (sep., -ge-, h) talk one's way out; **~stellen** v/t. (sep., -ge-, h) put out; fig. emphasize, set forth; sich ~ emerge, turn out; **~strecken** v/t. (sep., -ge-, h) stretch out; put out; **~streichen** v/t. (irr. streichen, sep., -ge-, h) cross out, delete (word, etc.); fig. extol, praise; **~winden** fig. v/refl. (irr. winden, sep., -ge-, h) extricate o.s. (aus from).

herb adj. [hɛrp] fruit, flavour, etc.: tart; wine, etc.: dry; features, etc.: austere; criticism, etc.: harsh; disappointment, etc.: bitter.

herbei adv. [hɛr'baɪ] here; **~!** come here!; **~eilen** [hɛr'baɪ?-] v/i. (sep., -ge-, sein) come hurrying; **~führen** fig. v/t. (sep., -ge-, h) cause, bring about, give rise to; **~schaffen** v/t. (sep., -ge-, h) bring along; procure.

Herberge ['hɛrbɛrgə] f (-/-n) shelter, lodging; inn.

'**Herbheit** f (-/no pl.) tartness; dryness; fig.: austerity; harshness, bitterness.

Herbst [hɛrpst] m (-[e]s/-e) autumn, Am. a. fall.

Herd [hɛːrt] m (-[e]s/-e) hearth, fireplace; stove; fig. seat, focus.

Herde ['hɛːrdə] f (-/-n) herd (of cattle, pigs, etc.) (contp. a. fig.); flock (of sheep, geese, etc.).

herein adv. [hɛ'raɪn] in (here); **~!** come in!; **~brechen** fig. v/i. (irr. brechen, sep., -ge-, sein) night: fall; ~ über (acc.) misfortune, etc.: befall; **~fallen** fig. v/i. (irr. fallen, sep., -ge-, sein) be taken in.

'**her|fallen** v/i. (irr. fallen, sep., -ge-, sein): ~ über (acc.) attack (a. fig.), fall upon; F fig. pull to pieces; '**2-gang** m course of events, details pl.; '**~geben** v/t. (irr. geben, sep., -ge-, h) give up, part with, return; yield; sich ~ zu lend o.s. to; '**~gebracht** fig. adj. traditional; customary; '**~halten** (irr. halten, sep., -ge-, h) 1. v/t. hold out; 2. v/i.: ~ müssen be the one to pay or suffer (für for).

Hering ichth. ['hɛːrɪŋ] m (-s/-e) herring.

'**her|kommen** v/i. (irr. kommen, sep., -ge-, sein) come or get here; come or draw near; ~ von come from; fig. a. be due to, be caused by; **~kömmlich** adj. ['~kœmlɪç] traditional; customary; **2kunft** ['~kunft] f (-/no pl.) origin; birth, descent; '**~leiten** v/t. (sep., -ge-, h) lead here; fig. derive (von from); '**2leitung** fig. f derivation.

Herold ['hɛːrɔlt] m (-[e]s/-e) herald.

Herr [hɛr] m (-n, ⚡-en/-en) lord, master; eccl. the Lord; gentleman; ~ Maier Mr Maier; mein ~ Sir; m-e ~en gentlemen; ~ der Situation master of the situation.

'**Herren|bekleidung** f men's cloth-

ing; '**~einzel** n tennis: men's singles pl.; '**~haus** n manor-house; **2-los** adj. ['.lɔːs] ownerless; '**~reiter** m sports: gentleman-jockey; '**~schneider** m men's tailor; '**~zimmer** n study; smoking-room.

herrichten ['hɛːr-] v/t. (sep., -ge-, h) arrange, prepare.

'**herrisch** adj. imperious, overbearing; voice, etc.: commanding, peremptory.

'**herrlich** adj. excellent, glorious, magnificent, splendid; '**2keit** f (-/-en) glory, splendo(u)r.

'**Herrschaft** f (-/-en) rule, dominion (über acc. of); fig. mastery; master and mistress; m-e ~en! ladies and gentlemen!; **2lich** adj. belonging to a master or landlord; fig. high-class, elegant.

herrsch|en ['hɛrʃən] v/i. (ge-, h) rule (über acc. over); monarch: reign (over); govern; fig. prevail, be; '**2er** m (-s/-) ruler; sovereign, monarch; '**2sucht** f thirst for power; **2süchtig** adj. thirsting for power; imperious.

'**her|rühren** v/i. (sep., -ge-, h): ~ von come from, originate with; '**~sagen** v/t. (sep., -ge-, h) recite; say (prayer); '**~stammen** v/i. (sep., -ge-, h): ~ von or aus be descended from; come from; be derived from; '**~stellen** v/t. (sep., -ge-, h) place here; ✝ make, manufacture, produce; '**2stellung** f (-/-en) manufacture, production.

herüber adv. [hɛ'ryːbər] over (here), across.

herum adv. [hɛ'rum] (a)round; about; **~führen** v/t. (sep., -ge-, h) show a(round); ~ in (dat.) show over; **~lungern** v/i. (sep., -ge-, h) loaf or loiter or hang about; **~reichen** v/t. (sep., -ge-, h) pass or hand round; **~sprechen** v/refl. (irr. sprechen, sep., -ge-, h) get about, spread; **~treiben** v/refl. (irr. treiben, sep., -ge-, h) F gad or knock about.

herunter adv. [hɛ'runtər] down (here); downstairs; von oben ~ down from above; **~bringen** v/t. (irr. bringen, sep., -ge-, h) bring down; fig. a. lower, reduce; **~kommen** v/i. (irr. kommen, sep., -ge-, sein) come down(stairs); fig. come down in the world; deteriorate; **~machen** v/t. (sep., -ge-, h) take down; turn (collar, etc.) down; fig. give s.o. a dressing-down; fig. pull to pieces; **~reißen** v/t. (irr. reißen, sep., -ge-, h) pull or tear down; fig. pull to pieces; **~sein** F fig. v/i. (irr. sein, sep., -ge-, sein) be low in health; **~wirtschaften** v/t. (sep., -ge-, h) run down.

hervor adv. [hɛr'foːr] forth, out; **~bringen** v/t. (irr. bringen, sep.,

-ge-, h) bring out, produce (a. fig.); yield (fruit); fig. utter (word); ~**gehen** v/i. (irr. gehen, sep., -ge-, sein) p. come (aus from); come off (victorious) (from); fact, etc.: emerge (from); be clear or apparent (from); ~**heben** fig. v/t. (irr. heben, sep., -ge-, h) stress, emphasize; give prominence to; ~**holen** v/t. (sep., -ge-, h) produce; ~**ragen** v/i. (sep., -ge-, h) project (über acc. over); fig. tower (above); ~**ragend** adj. projecting, prominent; fig. outstanding, excellent; ~**rufen** v/t. (irr. rufen, sep., -ge-, h) thea. call for; fig. arouse, evoke, ~**stechend** fig. adj. outstanding, striking; conspicuous.

Herz [hɛrts] n (-ens/-en) anat. heart (a. fig.); cards: hearts pl.; fig. courage, spirit; sich ein ~ fassen take heart; mit ganzem ~en whole-heartedly; sich et. zu ~en nehmen take s.th. to heart; es nicht übers ~ bringen zu inf. not to have the heart to inf.; '~**anfall** m heart attack.

'Herzens|brecher m (-s/-) lady-killer; ~**lust** f: nach ~ to one's heart's content; '~**wunsch** m heart's desire.

'herz|ergreifend fig. adj. heart-moving, **2fehler** m cardiac defect; **2gegend** anat. f cardiac region; '~**haft** adj. hearty, good; '~**ig** adj. lovely, Am. a. cute; **2infarkt** ⚕ ['~'infarkt] m (-[e]s/~er) cardiac infarction, '**2klopfen** ⚕ n (-s/no pl.) palpitation, '~**krank** adj. having heart trouble; '~**lich** 1. adj. heartfelt; cordial, hearty; ~**es Beileid** sincere sympathy; 2. adv.: ~ gern with pleasure; '~**los** adj. heartless; unfeeling.

Herzog ['hɛrtso:k] m (-[e]s/~e, -e) duke; '~**in** f (-/-nen) duchess; '~**tum** n (-[e]s/~er) dukedom; duchy.

'Herz|schlag m heartbeat; ~ heart failure; ~**schwäche** ⚕ f cardiac insufficiency; ~**verpflanzung** ⚕ f heart transplant; '**2zerreißend** adj. heart-rending.

Hetze ['hɛtsə] f (-/-n) hurry, rush; instigation (gegen acc. against); baiting (of); '**2en** (ge-) 1. v/t. (h) course (hare); bait (bear, etc.); hound: hunt, chase (animal); fig. hurry, rush; sich ~ hurry, rush; e-n Hund auf j-n ~ set a dog at s.o.; 2. v/i. (h) fig.: cause discord; agitate (gegen against); 3. fig. v/i. (sein) hurry, rush; '~**er** fig. m (-s/-) instigator; agitator; '**2erisch** adj. virulent, inflammatory; '~**jagd** f hunt(ing); fig.: virulent campaign; rush, hurry; '~**presse** f yellow press.

Heu [hɔy] n (-[e]s/no pl.) hay; '~**boden** m hayloft.

Heuchel|ei [hɔyçə'laɪ] f (-/-en) hypocrisy; '**2n** (ge-, h) 1. v/t. sim-

ulate, feign, affect; 2. v/i. feign, dissemble; play the hypocrite.

'Heuchler m (-s/-) hypocrite; '**2isch** adj. hypocritical.

heuer ['hɔyər] 1. adv. this year; 2. ⚓ f (-/-n) pay, wages pl.; '~**n** v/t. (ge-, h) hire; ⚓ engage, sign on (crew), charter (ship).

heulen ['hɔylən] v/i. (ge-, h) wind, etc.: howl; storm, wind, etc.: roar; siren: wail; F p. howl, cry.

'Heu|schnupfen ⚕ m hay-fever; ~**schrecke** zo. ['~ʃrɛkə] f (-/-n) grasshopper, locust.

heut|e adv. ['hɔytə] today; ~ abend this evening, tonight; ~ früh, ~ morgen this morning; ~ in acht Tagen today or this day week; ~ vor acht Tagen a week ago today; '~**ig** adj. this day's, today's; present; ~**zutage** adv. ['hɔyttsuːtaːgə] nowadays, these days.

Hexe ['hɛksə] f (-/-n) witch, sorceress; fig.: hell-cat; hag; '**2n** v/i. (ge-, h) practice witchcraft; F fig. work miracles; '~**nkessel** fig. m inferno; '~**nmeister** m wizard, sorcerer; '~**nschuß** ⚕ m lumbago; ~**rei** [~'raɪ] f (-/-en) witchcraft, sorcery, magic.

Hieb [hiːp] 1. m (-[e]s/-e) blow, stroke; lash, cut (of whip, etc.); a. punch (with fist); fenc. cut; ~e pl. hiding, thrashing; 2. ♀ pret. of hauen.

hielt [hiːlt] pret. of halten.

hier adv. [hiːr] here; in this place; ~ I present!; ~ entlang! this way!

hier|an adv. ['hiːran, when emphatic 'hiːran] at or by in or on or to it or this; ~**auf** adv. ['hiːrauf, when emphatic 'hiːrauf] on it or this; after this or that, then; ~**aus** adv. ['hiːraus, when emphatic 'hiːraus] from or out of it or this; ~**bei** adv. ['hiːrbaɪ, when emphatic 'hiːrbaɪ] here; in this case, in connection with this; ~**durch** adv. ['hiːrdurç, when emphatic 'hiːrdurç] through here; by this, hereby; ~**für** adv. ['hiːrfyːr, when emphatic 'hiːrfyːr] for it or this; ~**her** adv. ['hiːrheːr, when emphatic 'hiːrheːr] here, hither; bis ~ as far as here; ~**in** adv. ['hiːrin, when emphatic 'hiːrin] in it or this; in here; ~**mit** adv. ['hiːrmit, when emphatic 'hiːrmit] with it or this, herewith; ~**nach** adv. ['hiːrnaːx, when emphatic 'hiːrnaːx] after it or this; according to this; ~**über** adv. ['hiːryːbər, when emphatic 'hiːryːbər] over it or this; over here; on this (subject); ~**unter** adv. ['hiːruntər, when emphatic 'hiːruntər] under it or this; among these; by this or that; ~**von** adv. ['hiːrfɔn, when emphatic 'hiːrfɔn] of or from it or this; ~**zu** adv. ['hiːrtsuː, when emphatic 'hiːrtsuː]

with it *or* this; (in addition) to this.

hiesig *adj.* ['hi:ziç] of *or* in this place *or* town, local.

hieß [hi:s] *pret. of* heißen.

Hilfe ['hilfə] *f* (-/-n) help; aid, assistance; succour; relief (*für* to); ~! help!; *mit* ~ *von* with the help *or* aid of; '~ruf *m* shout *or* cry for help.

'**hilf|los** *adj.* helpless; '~reich *adj.* helpful.

'**Hilfs|aktion** *f* relief measures *pl.*; '~arbeiter *m* unskilled worker *or* labo(u)rer; 2bedürftig *adj.* needy, indigent; '~lehrer *m* assistant teacher; ~mittel *n* aid; device; remedy; expedient; '~motor *m*: *Fahrrad mit* ~ motor-assisted bicycle; '~quelle *f* resource; '~schule *f* elementary school for backward children; '~werk *n* relief organization. [berry.]

Himbeere & ['himbeːrə] *f* rasp-]

Himmel ['himəl] *m* (-s/-) sky, heavens *pl.*; *eccl.*, *fig.* heaven; '~bett *n* tester-bed; '2blau *adj.* sky-blue; '~fahrt *eccl. f* ascension (of Christ); Ascension-day; 2schreiend *adj.* crying.

'**Himmels|gegend** *f* region of the sky; cardinal point; '~körper *m* celestial body; '~richtung *f* point of the compass, cardinal point; direction; '~strich *m* region, climate zone.

'**himmlisch** *adj.* celestial, heavenly.

hin *adv.* [hin] there; gone, lost; ~ *und her* to and fro, *Am.* back and forth; ~ *und wieder* now and again *or* then; ~ *und zurück* there and back.

hinab *adv.* [hi'nap] down; ~steigen *v/i.* (*irr.* steigen, *sep.*, *-ge-*, *sein*) climb down, descend.

hinarbeiten ['hinʔ-] *v/i.* (*sep.*, *-ge-*, *h*): ~ *auf* (*acc.*) work for *or* towards.

hinauf *adv.* [hi'nauf] up (there); upstairs; ~gehen *v/i.* (*irr.* gehen, *sep.*, *-ge-*, *sein*) go up(stairs) *or* ~ prices, wages, etc.: go up, rise; ~steigen *v/i.* (*irr.* steigen, *sep.*, *-ge-*, *sein*) climb up, ascend.

hinaus *adv.* [hi'naus] out; ~ *mit euch!* out with you!; *auf (viele) Jahre* ~ for (many) years (to come); ~gehen *v/i.* (*irr.* gehen, *sep.*, *-ge-*, *sein*) go *or* walk out; ~ *über* (*acc.*) go beyond, exceed; ~ *auf* (*acc.*) *window, etc.*: look out on, overlook; *intention, etc.*: drive *or* aim at; ~laufen *v/i.* (*irr.* laufen, *sep.*, *-ge-*, *sein*) run *or* rush out; ~ *auf* (*acc.*) come *or* amount to; ~schieben *fig. v/t.* (*irr.* schieben, *sep.*, *-ge-*, *h*) put off, postpone, defer; ~werfen *v/t.* (*irr.* werfen, *sep.*, *-ge-*, *h*) throw out (*aus* of); turn *or* throw *or* F chuck *s.o.* out.

'**Hin|blick** *m*: *im* ~ *auf* (*acc.*) in view of, with regard to; '2bringen *v/t.* (*irr.* bringen, *sep.*, *-ge-*, *h*) take there; while away, pass (*time*).

hinder|lich *adj.* ['hindərliç] hindering, impeding; *j-m* ~ *sein* be in s.o.'s way; ~n *v/t.* (*ge-*, *h*) hinder, hamper (*bei*, *in dat.* in); ~ *an* (*dat.*) prevent from; 2nis *n* (-ses/-se) hindrance; *sports*: obstacle; *turf*, *etc.*: fence; '2nisrennen *n* obstacle-race.

hin'durch *adv.* through; all through, throughout; across.

hinein *adv.* [hi'nain] in; ~ *mit dir!* in you go!; ~gehen *v/i.* (*irr.* gehen, *sep.*, *-ge-*, *sein*) go in; ~ *in* (*acc.*) go into; *in den Topf gehen ... hinein* the pot holds *or* takes ...

'**Hin|fahrt** *f* journey *or* way there; '2fallen *v/i.* (*irr.* fallen, *sep.*, *-ge-*, *sein*) fall (down); '2fällig *adj. p.* frail; *regulation, etc.*: invalid; ~ *machen* invalidate, render invalid.

hing [hiŋ] *pret. of* hängen 1.

'**Hin|gabe** *f* devotion (*an acc.* to); '2geben *v/t.* (*irr.* geben, *sep.*, *-ge-*, *h*) give up *or* away; *sich* ~ (*dat.*) give o.s. to; devote o.s. to; ~gebung *f* (-/-en) devotion; '2gehen *v/i.* (*irr.* gehen, *sep.*, *-ge-*, *sein*) go *or* walk there; go (*zu* to); *path, etc.*: lead there; lead (*zu* to *a place*); '2halten *v/t.* (*irr.* halten, *sep.*, *-ge-*, *h*) hold out (*object, etc.*); put *s.o.* off.

hinken ['hiŋkən] *v/i.* (*ge-*) **1.** (*h*) limp (*auf dem rechten Fuß* with one's right leg), have a limp; **2.** (*sein*) limp (along).

'**hin|länglich** *adj.* sufficient, adequate; '~legen *v/t.* (*sep.*, *-ge-*, *h*) lay *or* put down; *sich* ~ lie down; '~nehmen *v/t.* (*irr.* nehmen, *sep.*, *-ge-*, *h*) accept, take; put up with; '~raffen *v/t.* (*sep.*, *-ge-*, *h*) *death, etc.*: snatch *s.o.* away, carry *s.o.* off; '~reichen (*sep.*, *-ge-*, *h*) **1.** *v/t.* reach *or* stretch *or* hold out (*dat.* to); **2.** *v/i.* suffice; '~reißen *fig. v/t.* (*irr.* reißen, *sep.*, *-ge-*, *h*) carry away; enrapture, ravish; '~reißend *adj.* ravishing, captivating; '~richten *v/t.* (*sep.*, *-ge-*, *h*) execute, put to death; '2richtung *f* execution; '~setzen *v/t.* (*sep.*, *-ge-*, *h*) set *or* put down; *sich* ~ sit down; '2sicht *f* regard, respect; *in* ~ *auf* (*acc.*) = '~sichtlich *prp.* (*gen.*) with regard to, as to, concerning; '~stellen *v/t.* (*sep.*, *-ge-*, *h*) place; put; put down; *et.* ~ *als* represent s.th. as; make s.th. appear (as).

hintan|setzen [hint'an-] *v/t.* (*sep.*, *-ge-*, *h*) set aside; 2setzung *f* (-/-en) setting aside; ~stellen *v/t.* (*sep.*, *-ge-*, *h*) set aside; 2stellung *f* (-/-en) setting aside.

hinten *adv.* ['hintən] behind, at the

back; in the background; in the rear.

hinter *prp.* ['hintər] **1.** (*dat.*) behind, *Am. a.* back of; ~ *sich lassen* outdistance, **2.** (*acc.*) behind; '2**bein** *n* hind leg; 2**bliebenen** *pl.* [.'bli:bə- nən] *the* bereaved *pl.*; surviving dependants *pl.*; ~'**bringen** *v/t.* (*irr. bringen, no* -ge-, *h*): *j-m et.* ~ inform s.o of s.th. (secretly); ~**ei'nander** *adv.* one after the other; in succession, '2**gedanke** *m* ulterior motive, ~ **gehen** *v/t.* (*irr. ge- hen, no* -ge-, *h*) deceive; *Am.* double- cross; 2'**gehung** *f* (-/-en) deception; '2**grund** *m* background (*a. fig.*); '2**halt** *m* ambush; ~**hältig** *adj.* ['.heltiç] insidious; underhand; '2**haus** *n* back *or* rear building; ~'**her** *adv* behind; afterwards; '2**hof** *m* backyard; '2**kopf** *m* back of the head; ~'**lassen** *v/t.* (*irr. lassen, no* -ge-, *h*) leave (behind); 2'**lassenschaft** *f* (-/-en) property (left), estate, ~'**legen** *v/t.* (*no* -ge-, *h*) deposit, lodge (*bei* with); 2'**legung** *f* (-/-en) deposit(ion); '2**list** *f* deceit; craftiness, insidiousness; '~**listig** *adj.* deceitful, crafty; insidious; '2**mann** *m* ✕ rear-rank man; *fig.*: † subsequent endorser; *pol.* backer; wire-puller, instigator; '2**n** F *m* (-s/-) backside, behind, bottom; '2**rad** *n* rear wheel; ~'**rücks** *adv.* ['.ryks] from behind; *fig.* behind his, *etc* back, '2**seite** *f* back; '2**teil** *n* back (part), rear (part); F *s. Hintern*, ~'**treiben** *v/t.* (*irr. treiben, no* -ge-, *h*) thwart, frustrate; '2**treppe** *f* backstairs *pl.*; '2**tür** *f* back door, ~'**ziehen** ✍ *v/t.* (*irr. ziehen, no* -ge-, *h*) evade (*tax, duty, etc.*); 2'**ziehung** *f* evasion.

hinüber *adv* [hi'ny:bər] over (there), across

Hin- und 'Rückfahrt *f* journey there and back, *Am.* round trip.

hinunter *adv* [hi'nuntər] down (there), downstairs; ~**schlucken** *v/t.* (*sep*, -ge-, *h*) swallow (down); *fig.* swallow

'**Hinweg**[1] *m* way there *or* out.

hinweg[2] *adv* [hin'vɛk] away, off; ~**gehen** *v/i* (*irr. gehen, sep*, -ge- *sein*): ~ *über* (*acc.*) go *or* walk over *or* across, *fig* pass over, ignore; ~**kommen** *v/i.* (*irr. kommen, sep*, -ge-, *sein*) ~ *über* (*acc.*) get over (*a. fig.*); ~**sehen** *v/i.* (*irr. sehen, sep*, -ge-, *h*): ~ *über* (*acc.*) see *or* look over, *fig.* overlook, shut one's eyes to; ~**setzen** *v/refl.* (*sep*, -ge-, *h*): *sich* ~ *über* (*acc.*) ignore, disregard, make light of.

Hin|weis ['hinvais] *m* (-es/-e) reference (*auf acc* to); hint (at); indication (of); '2**weisen** (*irr. weisen, sep*, -ge-, *h*) **1.** *v/t.*: *j-n* ~ *auf* (*acc.*) draw *or* call s.o.'s attention to; **2.** *v/i.*: ~

auf (*acc.*) point at *or* to, indicate (*a. fig.*); *fig.*: point out; hint at; '2**wer- fen** *v/t.* (*irr. werfen, sep*, -ge-, *h*) throw down; *fig.*: dash off (*sketch, etc.*); say *s.th.* casually; '2**wirken** *v/i.* (*sep*, -ge-, *h*): ~ *auf* (*acc.*) work towards; use one's influence to; '2**ziehen** (*irr. ziehen, sep*, -ge-) **1.** *fig. v/t.* (*h*) attract *or* draw there; *sich* ~ *space*: extend (*bis zu* to), stretch (to); *time*: drag on; **2.** *v/i.* (*sein*) go *or* move there; '2**zielen** *fig. v/i.* (*sep*, -ge-, *h*): ~ *auf* (*acc.*) aim *or* drive at.

hin'zu *adv* there; near; in addition; ~**fügen** *v/t* (*sep*, -ge-, *h*) add (*zu* to) (*a. fig.*); 2**fügung** *f* (-/-en) addition; ~**kommen** *v/i.* (*irr. kom- men, sep*, -ge-, *sein*) come up (*zu* to); supervene; be added; *es kommt (noch) hinzu, daß* add to this that, (and) moreover; ~**rechnen** *v/t.* (*sep*, -ge-, *h*) add (*zu* to), include (in, among); ~**setzen** *v/t.* (*sep*, -ge-, *h*) *s. hinzufügen*; ~**treten** *v/i.* (*irr. treten, sep*, -ge-, *sein*) *s. hinzu- kommen*; join; ~**ziehen** *v/t.* (*irr. zie- hen, sep*, -ge-, *h*) call in (*doctor, etc.*).

Hirn [hirn] *n* (-[e]s/-e) *anat.* brain; *fig.* brains *pl*, mind; ~**gespinst** *n* figment of the mind, chimera; '2**los** *fig. adj* brainless, senseless; '~**schale** *anat.* *f* brain-pan, cranium; '~**schlag** ✗ *m* apoplexy; '2**ver- brannt** *adj.* crazy, F crack-brained, cracky.

Hirsch *zo.* [hirʃ] *m* (-es/-e) *species*: deer; stag, hart; '~**geweih** *n* (stag's) antlers *pl.*; '~**kuh** *f* hind; '~**leder** *n* buckskin, deerskin.

Hirse ♀ ['hirzə] *f* (-/-n) millet.

Hirt [hirt] *m* (-en/-en), ~**e** ['.ə] *m* (-n/-n) herdsman; shepherd.

hissen ['hisən] *v/t.* (*ge*-, *h*) hoist, raise (*flag*); ♃ *a.* trice up (*sail*).

Histori|ker [hi'sto:rikər] *m* (-s/-) historian; 2**sch** *adj.* historic(al).

Hitz|e ['hitsə] *f* (-/no *pl.*) heat; '2**ebeständig** *adj.* heat-resistant, heat-proof; '~**ewelle** *f* heat-wave, hot spell; '2**ig** *adj. p.* hot-tempered, hot-headed; *discussion*: heated; '~**kopf** *m* hothead; '~**schlag** ✗ *m* heat-stroke.

hob [ho:p] *pret. of heben.*

Hobel ⊕ ['ho:bəl] *m* (-s/-) plane; '~**bank** *f* carpenter's bench; '2**n** *v/t.* (*ge*-, *h*) plane.

hoch [ho:x] **1.** *adj.* high; *church spire, tree, etc.*: tall; *position, etc.*: high, important; *guest, etc.*: distinguished; *punishment, etc.*: heavy, severe; *age*: great, old; *hohe See* open sea, high seas *pl.*; **2.** *adv.*: ~ *lebe ...!* long live ...! **3.** 2 *n* (-s/-s) cheer; toast; *meteorology*: high (-pressure area).

'**hoch|achten** *v/t.* (*sep*, -ge-, *h*) esteem highly; '2**achtung** *f* high esteem *or* respect; '*~*achtungsvoll 1. *adj.* (most) respectful; 2. *adv. correspondence*: yours faithfully *or* sincerely, *esp. Am.* yours truly; '2adel *m* greater *or* higher nobility; '2amt *eccl. n* high mass; '2antenne *f* overhead aerial; '2bahn *f* elevated *or* overhead railway, *Am.* elevated railroad; '2betrieb *m* intense activity, rush; '2burg *fig. f* stronghold; '*~*deutsch *adj.* High *or* standard German; '2druck *m* high pressure (*a. fig.*); mit *~* arbeiten work at high pressure; '2ebene *f* plateau, tableland; '*~*fahrend *adj.* highhanded, arrogant; '*~*fein *adj.* superfine; '2form *f*: in *~* in top form; '2frequenz *∮ f* high frequency; '2gebirge *n* high mountains *pl.*; '2genuß *m* great enjoyment; '2glanz *m* high polish; '2haus *n* multi-stor(e)y building, skyscraper; '*~*herzig *adj.* nobleminded; generous; '2herzigkeit *f* (-/-en) noble-mindedness; generosity; '2konjunktur ↑ *f* boom, business prosperity; '2land *n* upland(s *pl.*), highlands *pl.*; '2mut *m* arrogance, haughtiness; *~*mütig *adj.* ['*~*my:tiç] arrogant, haughty; *~*näsig F *adj.* ['*~*nɛːziç] stuck-up; '2ofen ⊕ *m* blast-furnace; '*~*rot *adj.* bright red; '2saison *f* peak season, height of the season; '*~*schätzen *v/t.* (*sep.*, -ge-, *h*) esteem highly; '2schule *f* university; academy; '2seefischerei *f* deep-sea fishing; '2sommer *m* midsummer; '2spannung *∮ f* high tension *or* voltage; '2sprung *m sports*: high jump.

höchst [høːçst] 1. *adj.* highest; *fig. a.*: supreme; extreme; 2. *adv.* highly, most, extremely.

Hochstap|elei [hoːxʃtaːpəˈlaɪ] *f* (-/-en) swindling; '*~*ler *m* (-s/-) confidence man, swindler.

höchstens *adv.* ['høːçstəns] at (the) most, at best.

'**Höchst|form** *f sports*: top form; '*~*geschwindigkeit *f* maximum speed; speed limit; '*~*leistung *f sports*: record (performance); ⊕ maximum output (*of machine, etc.*); '*~*lohn *m* maximum wages *pl.*; '*~*maß *n* maximum; '*~*preis *m* maximum price.

'**hoch|trabend** *fig. adj.* high-flown; pompous; '2verrat *m* high treason; '2wald *m* high forest; '2wasser *n* high tide *or* water; flood; '*~*wertig *adj.* high-grade, high-class; '2wild *n* big game; '2wohlgeboren *m* (-s/-) Right Hono(u)rable.

Hochzeit ['hɔxtsaɪt] *f* (-/-en) wedding; marriage; '2lich *adj.* bridal, nuptial; '*~*sgeschenk *n* wedding present; '*~*sreise *f* honeymoon (trip).

Hocke ['hɔkə] *f* (-/-n) *gymnastics*: squat-vault; *skiing*: crouch; '2n *v/i.* (ge-, *h*) squat, crouch; '*~*r *m* (-s/-) stool.

Höcker ['hœkər] *m* (-s/-) *surface, etc.*: bump; camel, *etc.*: hump; *p.* hump, hunch; '2ig *adj. animal*: humped; *p.* humpbacked, hunchbacked; *surface, etc.*: bumpy, rough, uneven.

Hode *anat.* ['hoːdə] *m* (-n/-n), *f* (-/-n), '*~*n *anat. m* (-s/-) testicle.

Hof [hoːf] *m* (-[e]s/⁀e) court(yard)/ farm; king, *etc.*: court; *ast.* halo; j-m den *~* machen court s.o.; '*~*dame *f* lady-in-waiting; '2fähig *adj.* presentable at court.

Hoffart ['hɔfart] *f* (-/*no pl.*) arrogance, haughtiness; pride.

hoffen ['hɔfən] (ge-, *h*) 1. *v/i.* hope (auf acc. for); trust (in); 2. *v/t.*: das Beste *~* hope for the best; '*~*t-lich *adv.* it is to be hoped that, I hope, let's hope.

Hoffnung ['hɔfnuŋ] *f* (-/-en) hope (auf acc. for, of); in der *~* zu *inf.* in the hope of ger., hoping to *inf.*; s-e *~* setzen auf (acc.) pin one's hopes on; '2slos *adj.* hopeless; '2svoll *adj.* hopeful; promising.

'**Hofhund** *m* watch-dog.

höfisch *adj.* ['høːfiʃ] courtly.

höflich *adj.* ['høːfliç] polite, civil, courteous (gegen to); '2keit *f* (-/-en) politeness, civility, courtesy.

'**Hofstaat** *m* royal *or* princely household; suite, retinue.

Höhe ['høːə] *f* (-/-n) height; ✶, ♃, *ast., geogr.* altitude; hill; peak; amount (*of bill, etc.*); size (*of sum, fine, etc.*); level (*of price, etc.*); severity (*of punishment, etc.*); *∮* pitch; in gleicher *~* mit on a level with; auf der *~* sein be up to the mark; in die *~* up(wards).

Hoheit ['hoːhaɪt] *f* (-/-en) *pol.* sovereignty; *title*: Highness; '*~*sgebiet *n* (sovereign) territory; '*~*sgewässer *n/pl.* territorial waters *pl.*; '*~*szeichen *n* national emblem.

'**Höhen|kurort** *m* high-altitude health resort; '*~*luft *f* mountain air; '*~*sonne *f* mountain sun; ☀ ultra-violet lamp; '*~*steuer ✈ *n* elevator; '*~*zug *m* mountain range.

'**Höhepunkt** *m* highest point; *ast., fig.* culmination, zenith; *fig. a.*: climax; summit, peak.

hohl *adj.* [hoːl] hollow (*a. fig.*); cheeks, *etc.*: sunken; hand: cupped; sound: hollow, dull.

Höhle ['høːlə] *f* (-/-n) cave, cavern; den, lair (*of bear, lion, etc.*) (*both a. fig.*); hole, burrow (*of fox, rabbit, etc.*); hollow; cavity.

'**Hohl|maß** *n* dry measure; '*~*raum *m* hollow, cavity; '*~*spiegel *m* concave mirror.

Höhlung ['hø:luŋ] *f* (-/-en) excavation, hollow, cavity.

'**Hohlweg** *m* defile.

Hohn [ho n] *m* (-[e]s/*no pl.*) scorn, disdain, derision.

höhnen ['hø nən] *v/i.* (ge-, h) sneer, jeer, mock, scoff (*über acc.* at).

'**Hohngelächter** *n* scornful *or* derisive laughter.

'**höhnisch** *adj.* scornful; sneering, derisive.

Höker ['hø:kər] *m* (-s/-) hawker, huckster; '**2n** *v/i.* (ge-, h) huckster, hawk about.

holen ['ho:lən] *v/t.* (ge-, h) fetch; go for; a ~ *lassen* send for; draw (*breath*); *sich e-e Krankheit* ~ catch a disease; *sich bei j-m Rat* ~ seek s.o.'s advice

Holländer ['hɔlendər] *m* (-s/-) Dutchman

Hölle ['hœlə] *f* (-/٩-n) hell.

'**Höllen|angst** *fig f* · *e-e* ~ *haben* be in a mortal fright *or* F blue funk; '**~lärm** *fig m* infernal noise; '**~maschine** *f* infernal machine, time bomb, **~pein** F *fig. f* torment of hell

'**höllisch** *adj.* hellish, infernal (*both a. fig.*).

holper|ig *adj.* ['hɔlpəriç] *surface, road, etc* bumpy, rough, uneven; *vehicle, etc* jolty, jerky; *verse, style, etc* rough, jerky; '**~n** (ge-) 1. *v/i.* (sein) *vehicle*: jolt; bump; 2. (h) *vehicle*: jolt, bump; be jolty *or* bumpy.

Holunder ٩ [ho'lundər] *m* (-s/-) elder

Holz [hɔlts] *n* (-es/٠er) wood; timber, *Am.* lumber, '**~bau** ⚠ *m* wooden structure, **~bildhauer** *m* woodcarver, **~blasinstrument** ♪ *n* woodwind instrument; '**~boden** *m* wood(en floor, wood-loft.

hölzern *adj.* ['hœltsərn] wooden; *fig. a* clumsy, awkward.

'**Holz|fäller** *m* (-s/-) woodcutter, woodman, *Am a.* lumberjack, logger, **~hacker** *m* (-s/-) woodchoppe , woodcutter, *Am.* lumberjack, **~händler** *m* wood *or* timber merchant, *Am* lumberman; '**~haus** *n* wooden house, *Am.* frame house; '**2ig** *adj* woody, **~kohle** *f* charcoal; '**~platz** *m* wood *or* timber yard, *Am.* lumberyard, **~schnitt** *m* woodcut, wood-engraving; '**~schnitzer** *m* wood-carver, '**~schuh** *m* wooden shoe, clog, **~stoß** *m* pile *or* stack of wood, stake, **~weg** *fig. m: auf dem* ~ *sein* be on the wrong track; '**~wolle** *f* wood-wool, fine wood shavings *pl., Am a* excelsior.

Homöopath ♪ [homøo'pa:t] *m* (-en/-en) hom(o)opath(ist); **~ie** [~a'ti:] *f* (-/*no pl.*) hom(o)eopathy; **2isch** *adj.* [~'pa:tif] hom(o)eopathic.

Honig ['ho:niç] *m* (-s/-e) honey;

'**~kuchen** *m* honey-cake; gingerbread; '**2süß** *adj.* honey-sweet, honeyed (*a. fig.*); '**~wabe** *f* honeycomb.

Honor|ar [hono'ra:r] *n* (-s/-e) fee; royalties *pl* ; salary; **~atioren** [~a-'tsjo:rən] *pl* notabilities *pl.*; **2ieren** [~'ri:rən] *v/t.* (*no* -ge-, h) fee, pay a fee to; ✦ hono(u)r, meet (*bill of exchange*).

Hopfen ['hɔpfən] *m* (-s/-) ٩ hop; *brewing* hops *pl.*

hops|a *int.* ['hɔpsa] (wh)oops!; upsadaisy!; '**~en** F *v/i.* (ge-, sein) hop, jump.

hörbar *adj.* ['hø:rba:r] audible.

horch|en ['hɔrçən] *v/i.* (ge-, h) listen (*auf acc* to); eavesdrop; '**2er** *m* (-s/-) eavesdropper.

Horde ['hɔrdə] *f* (-/-n) horde, gang.

hör|en ['hø:rən] (ge-, h) 1. *v/t.* hear; listen (in) to (*radio*), attend (*lecture, etc.*); hear, learn; 2. *v/i.* hear (*von dat.* from), listen, *auf* (*acc.*) listen to; *schwer* ~ be hard of hearing; ~ *Sie mal!* look here!, I say!; '**2er** *m* (-s/-) hearer, *radio* listener(-in); *univ.* student; *teleph* receiver; '**2erschaft** *f* (-/-en) audience; '**2gerät** *n* hearing aid; '**~ig** *adj.*: *j-m* ~ *sein* be enslaved to s.o.; '**2igkeit** *f* (-/*no pl*) subjection.

Horizont [hori'tsɔnt] *m* (-[e]s/-e) horizon, skyline, *s-n* ~ *erweitern* broaden one 's mind; *das geht über meinen* that's beyond me; **2al** *adj.* [~'ta:l] horizontal

Hormon [hɔr'mo:n] *n* (-s/-e) hormone

Horn [hɔrn] *n* 1. (-[e]s/٠er) horn (*of bull*), ♪, *mot., etc.* horn; ✕ bugle, peak, 2. (-[e]s/-e) horn, horny matter, **~haut** *f* horny skin; *anat.* cornea (*on eye*).

Hornisse *zo.* [hɔr'nisə] *f* (-/-n) hornet

Hornist ♪ [hɔr'nist] *m* (-en/-en) horn-playe , ✕ bugler.

Horoskop [horo'sko:p] *n* (-s/-e) horoscope, *j-m das* ~ *stellen* cast s.o.'s horoscope

'**Hör|rohr** *n* ear-trumpet; ✂ stethoscope, '**~saal** *m* lecture-hall; '**~spiel** *n* radio play; '**~weite** *f: in* ~ within earshot

Hose ['ho:zə] *f* (-/-n) (*e-e* pair of) trousers *pl. or Am.* pants *pl.*; slacks *pl.*

'**Hosen|klappe** *f* flap; **~latz** [~lats] *m* (-es/٠e) flap, fly; '**~tasche** *f* trouser-pocket, **~träger** *m: (ein Paar)* ~ *pl* (a pair of) braces *pl. or Am.* suspenders *pl.*

Hospital [hɔspi'ta:l] *n* (-s/-e, ٠er) hospital.

Hostie *eccl.* ['hɔstjə] *f* (-/-n) host, consecrated *or* holy wafer.

Hotel [ho'tɛl] *n* (-s/-s) hotel; **~besitzer** *m* hotel owner *or* proprietor;

~gewerbe n hotel industry; ~ier [~'je:] m (-s/-s) hotel-keeper.

Hub ⊕ [hu:p] m (-[e]s/~e) mot. stroke (of piston); lift (of valve, etc.); '~raum mot. m capacity.

hübsch adj. [hypʃ] pretty, nice; good-looking, handsome; attractive.

'**Hubschrauber** ✈ m (-s/-) helicopter.

Huf [hu:f] m (-[e]s/-e) hoof; ~eisen n horseshoe; '~schlag m hoof-beat; (horse's) kick; '~schmied m farrier.

Hüft|e anat. ['hyftə] f (-/-n) hip; esp. zo. haunch; '~gelenk n hipjoint; '~gürtel m girdle; suspender belt, Am. garter belt.

Hügel ['hy:gəl] m (-s/-) hill(ock); '2ig adj hilly.

Huhn orn [hu:n] n (-[e]s/~er) fowl, chicken; hen; junges ~ chicken.

Hühnchen ['hy:nçən] n (-s/-) chicken; ein ~ zu rupfen haben have a bone to pick (mit with).

Hühner|auge ℱ ['hy:nər-] n corn; '~ei n hen's egg; '~hof m poultry-yard, Am. chicken yard; '~hund zo. m pointer, setter; '~leiter f chicken-ladder.

Huld [hult] f (-/no pl.) grace, favo(u)r; 2igen ['~digən] v/i. (dat.) (ge-, h) pay homage to (sovereign, lady, etc.); indulge in (vice, etc.); '~igung f (-/-en) homage; 2reich adj., '2voll adj. gracious.

Hülle ['hylə] f (-/-n) cover(ing), wrapper, letter, balloon, etc.: envelope; book, etc.: jacket; umbrella, etc.: sheath; '2n v/t. (ge-, h) wrap, cover, envelope (a. fig.); sich in Schweigen ~ wrap o.s. in silence.

Hülse ['hylzə] f (-/-n) legume, pod (of leguminous plant); husk, hull (of rice, etc.); skin (of pea, etc.); ⚔ case; '~nfrucht f legume(n); leguminous plant; '~nfrüchte f/pl. pulse.

human adj. [hu'ma:n] humane; 2i-tät [~ni'tɛ:t] f (-/no pl.) humanity.

Hummel zo. ['huməl] f (-/-n) bumble-bee.

Hummer zo. ['humər] m (-s/-) lobster.

Humor [hu'mo:r] m (-s/⚔-e) humo(u)r; '~ist [~o'rist] m (-en/-en) humorist; 2istisch adj. [~o'risti∫] humorous.

humpeln ['humpəln] v/i. (ge-) 1. (sein) hobble (along), limp (along); 2. (h) (have a) limp, walk with a limp.

Hund [hunt] m (-[e]s/-e) zo. dog; ⚒ tub; ast. dog, canis; auf den ~ kommen go to the dogs.

'**Hunde|hütte** f dog-kennel, Am. a. doghouse; '~kuchen m dog-biscuit; '~leine f (dog-)lead or leash; '~peitsche f dog-whip.

hundert ['hundərt] 1. adj. a or one

hundred; 2. 2 n (-s/-e) hundred; fünf vom ~ five per cent; zu ~en by hundreds; '~fach adj., '~fältig adj. hundredfold; 2'jahrfeier f centenary, Am. a. centennial; ~jährig adj. ['~jɛ:riç] centenary, a hundred years old; '~st adj. hundredth.

'**Hunde|sperre** f muzzling-order; '~steuer f dog tax.

Hündi|n zo. ['hyndin] f (-/-nen) bitch, she-dog; '2sch adj. doggish; fig. servile, cringing.

'**hunds|ge'mein** F adj. dirty, mean, scurvy; ~'mise'rabel F adj. rotten, wretched, lousy; '2tage m/pl. dogdays pl.

Hüne ['hy:nə] m (-n/-n) giant.

Hunger ['huŋər] m (-s/no pl.) hunger (fig. nach for); ~ bekommen get hungry; ~ haben be or feel hungry; '~kur f starvation cure; '~leider F m (-s/-) starveling, poor devil; '~lohn m starvation wages pl.; '2n v/i. (ge-, h) hunger (fig. nach after, for); go without food; ~ lassen starve s.o.; '~snot f famine; '~streik m hunger-strike; '~tod m death from starvation; '~tuch fig. n: am ~ nagen have nothing to bite.

'**hungrig** adj. hungry (fig. nach for).

Hupe mot. ['hu:pə] f (-/-n) horn, hooter; klaxon; '2n v/i. (ge-, h) sound one's horn, hoot.

hüpfen ['hypfən] v/i. (ge-, sein) hip, skip; gambol, frisk (about).

Hürde ['hyrdə] f (-/-n) hurdle; fold, pen; '~nrennen n hurdle-race.

Hure ['hu:rə] f (-/-n) whore, prostitute.

hurtig adj. ['hurtiç] quick, swift; agile, nimble.

Husar ⚔ [hu'za:r] m (-en/-en) hussar.

husch int. [huʃ] in or like a flash; shoo!; '~en v/i. (ge-, sein) slip, dart; small animal: scurry, scamper; bat, etc.: flit.

hüsteln ['hy:stəln] 1. v/i. (ge-, h) cough slightly; 2. 2 n (-s/no pl.) slight cough.

husten ['hu:stən] 1. v/i. (ge-, h) cough; 2. 2 m (-s/⚔-) cough.

Hut [hu:t] 1. m (-[e]s/~e) hat; den ~ abnehmen take off one's hat; ~ ab vor (dat.)! hats off to ...!; 2. f (-/no pl.) care, charge, guard; auf der ~ sein be on one's guard (vor dat. against).

hüte|n ['hy:tən] v/t. (ge-, h) guard, protect, keep watch over; keep (secret); tend (sheep, etc.); das Bett ~ be confined to (one's) bed; sich ~ vor (dat.) beware of; '2r m (-s/-) keeper, guardian; herdsman.

'**Hut|futter** n hat-lining; '~krempe f hat-brim; '~macher m (-s/-) hatter; '~nadel f hat-pin.

Hütte ['hytə] f (-/-n) hut; cottage, cabin; ⊕ metallurgical plant; mount.

refuge; **~nwesen** ⊕ *n* metallurgy, metallurgical engineering.

Hyäne *zo.* [hy'ɛ:nə] *f (-/-n)* hy(a)ena.

Hyazinthe ♀ [hya'tsintə] *f (-/-n)* hyacinth. [hydrant.\]

Hydrant [hy'drant] *m (-en/-en)*

Hydrauli|k *phys.* [hy'draulik] *f (-/no pl.)* hydraulics *pl.*; **2sch** *adj.* hydraulic.

Hygien|e [hy'gje:nə] *f (-/no pl.)* hygiene; **2isch** *adj.* hygienic(al).

Hymne ['hymnə] *f (-/-n)* hymn.

Hypno|se [hyp'no:zə] *f (-/-n)* hypnosis; **2tisieren** [~oti'zi:rən] *v/t.* and *v/i. (no -ge-, h)* hypnotize.

Hypochond|er [hypo'xɔndər] *m (-s/-)* hypochondriac; **2risch** *adj.* hypochondriac.

Hypotenuse ♈ [hypote'nu:zə] *f (-/-n)* hypotenuse.

Hypothek [hypo'te:k] *f (-/-en)* mortgage; **e-e ~ aufnehmen** raise a mortgage; **2arisch** *adj.* [~e'ka:riʃ]; **~e Belastung** mortgage.

Hypothe|se [hypo'te:zə] *f (-/-n)* hypothesis; **2tisch** *adj.* hypothetical.

Hyster|ie *psych.* [hyste'ri:] *f (-/-n)* hysteria; **2isch** *psych. adj.* [~'te:riʃ] hysterical.

I

ich [iç] **1.** *pers. pron.* I; **2.** **2** *n (-[s]/-[s])* self; *psych.* the ego.

Ideal [ide'a:l] **1.** *n (-s/-e)* ideal; **2. 2** *adj.* ideal; **2isieren** [~ali'zi:rən] *v/t. (no -ge-, h)* idealize; **~ismus** [~a'lismus] *m (-/Idealismen)* idealism; **~ist** [~a'list] *m (-en/-en)* idealist.

Idee [i'de:] *f (-/-n)* idea, notion.

identi|fizieren [identifi'tsi·rən] *v/t. (no -ge-, h)* identify; *sich* identify o.s.; **~sch** *adj.* [i'dentiʃ] identical; **2tät** [~'tɛ:t] *f (-/no pl.)* identity.

Ideolog|ie [ideolo'gi:] *f (-/-n)* ideology; **2isch** *adj.* [~'lo:giʃ] ideological.

Idiot [idi'o:t] *m (-en/-en)* idiot; **~ie** [~o'ti:] *f (-/-n)* idiocy; **2isch** *adj.* [~'o:tiʃ] idiotic.

Idol [i'do:l] *n (-s/-e)* idol.

Igel *zo.* ['i:gəl] *m (-s/-)* hedgehog.

Ignor|ant [igno'rant] *m (-en/-en)* ignorant person, ignoramus; **~anz** [~ts] *f (-/no pl.)* ignorance; **2ieren** *v/t. (no -ge-, h)* ignore, take no notice of.

ihm *pers. pron.* [i:m] *p.* (to) him; *thing:* (to) it.

ihn *pers. pron.* [i:n] *p.* him; *thing:* it.

'ihnen *pers. pron.* (to) them; *Ihnen sg. and pl.* (to) you.

ihr [i:r] **1.** *pers. pron.: (2nd pl. nom.)* you; *(3rd sg. dat.)* (to) her; **2.** *poss. pron.:* her; their; *Ihr sg. and pl.* your; der *(die, das)* **~e** hers; theirs; der *(die, das)* Ihre *sg. and pl.* yours; **~erseits** ['~ər'zarts] *adv.* on her part; on their part; *Ihrerseits sg. and pl.* on your part; **'~es'gleichen** *pron.* (of) her *or* their kind, her *or* their equal; *Ihresgleichen sg.* (of) your kind, your equal; *pl.* (of) your kind, your equals; **'~et'wegen** *adv.* for her *or* their sake, on her *or* their account; *Ihretwegen sg. or pl.* for your sake, on your account; **'~et-willen** *adv.:* um ~ *s. ihretwegen;*

~ige *poss. pron.* ['~igə]: der *(die, das)* ~ hers; theirs; der *(die, das)* Ihrige yours.

illegitim *adj.* [ilegi'ti:m] illegitimate.

illusorisch *adj.* [ilu'zo:riʃ] illusory, deceptive.

illustrieren [ilu'stri:rən] *v/t. (no -ge-, h)* illustrate.

Iltis *zo.* ['iltis] *m (-ses/-se)* fitchew, polecat.

im *prp.* [im] = *in dem.*

imaginär *adj.* [imagi'nɛ:r] imaginary.

'Imbiß *m* light meal, snack; **'~stube** *f* snack bar.

Imker ['imkər] *m (-s/-)* bee-master, bee-keeper.

immatrikulieren [imatriku'li:rən] *v/t. (no -ge-, h)* matriculate, enrol(l); *sich ~ lassen* matriculate, enrol(l).

immer *adv.* ['imər] always; **~ mehr** more and more; **~ wieder** again *or* time and again; **für ~** for ever, for good; **'2grün** ♀ *n (-s/-e)* evergreen; **'~'hin** *adv.* still, yet; **'~'zu** *adv.* always, continually.

Immobilien [imo'bi:ljən] *pl.* immovables *pl.*, real estate; **~händler** *m s. Grundstücksmakler.*

immun *adj.* [i'mu:n] immune *(gegen* against, from*)*; **2ität** [~uni'tɛ:t] *f (-/no pl.)* immunity.

Imperativ *gr.* ['imperati:f] *m (-s/-e)* imperative (mood).

Imperfekt *gr.* ['imperfekt] *n (-s/-e)* imperfect (tense), past tense.

Imperialis|mus [imperia'lismus] *m (-/no pl.)* imperialism; **~t** *m (-en/-en)* imperialist; **2tisch** *adj.* imperialistic.

impertinent *adj.* [imperti'nent] impertinent, insolent.

impf|en ♣ ['impfən] *v/t. (ge-, h)* vaccinate; inoculate; **'2schein** *m* certificate of vaccination *or* inoculation; **'2stoff** ♣ *m* vaccine;

serum; ²ung f (-/-en) vaccination; inoculation.

imponieren [impo'ni:rən] v/i. (no -ge-, h): j-m ~ impress s.o.

Import ✝ [im'pɔrt] m (-[e]s/-e) import(ation); ~eur ✝ [~'tø:r] m (-s/-e) importer; ²ieren [~'ti:rən] v/t. (no -ge-, h) import.

imposant adj. [impo'zant] imposing, impressive

imprägnieren [imprɛ'gni:rən] v/t. (no -ge-, h) impregnate; (water-) proof (raincoat, etc.).

improvisieren [improvi'zi:rən] v/t. and v/i. (no -ge-, h) improvise.

Im'puls m (-es/-e) impuls; ²iv adj. [~'zi:f] impulsive.   [be able.\

imstande adj. [im'ʃtandə]: ~ sein\

in prp. (dat ; acc.) [in] 1. place: in, at; within; into, in; with names of important towns: in, g'g at, of; with names of villages and less important towns at; im Hause in the house, indoors, in; im ersten Stock on the first floor; ~ der Schule (im Theater) at school (the theat|re, Am. -er); ~ die Schule (~s Theater) to school (the theat|re, Am. -er); ~ England in England; waren Sie schon einmal in England? have you ever been to England?; 2. time: in, at, during; within; ~ drei Tagen (with)in three days; heute ~ vierzehn Tagen today fortnight; im Jahre 1960 in 1960; im Februar in February; im Frühling in (the) spring; ~ der Nacht at night; ~ letzter Zeit lately, of late, recently; 3. mode: ~ großer Eile in great haste; ~ Frieden leben live at peace; ~ Reichweite within reach; 4. condition, state im Alter von fünfzehn Jahren at (the age of) fifteen; ~ Behandlung under treatment.

'Inbegriff m (quint)essence; embodiment, incarnation; paragon; ²en adj. included, inclusive (of).

'Inbrunst f (-/no pl.) ardo(u)r, fervo(u)r.

'inbrünstig adj. ardent, fervent.

in'dem cj. whilst, while; by (ger.); ~ er mich ansah, sagte er looking at me he said.

Inder ['indər] m (-s/-) Indian.

in'des(sen) 1. adv. meanwhile; 2. cj. while; however.

Indianer [in'dja:nər] m (-s/-) (American or Red) Indian.

Indikativ gr. ['indikati:f] m (-s/-e) indicative (mood).

'indirekt adj. indirect.

indisch adj. ['indiʃ] Indian.

'indiskret adj. indiscreet; ²ion [~e'tsjo:n] f (-/-en) indiscretion.

indiskutabel adj. ['indiskuta:bəl] out of the question.

individu|ell adj. [individu'ɛl] individual; ²um [~'vi:duum] n (-s/ Individuen) individual.

10*

Indizienbeweis g'g [in'di:tsjən-] m circumstantial evidence.

Indoss|ament ✝ [indɔsa'ment] n (-s/-e) endorsement, indorsement; ²ieren ✝ [~'si:rən] v/t. (no -ge-, h) indorse, endorse.

Industrialisierung [industriali'zi:ruŋ] f (-/-en) industrialization.

Industrie [indus'tri:] f (-/-n) industry; ~anlage f industrial plant; ~arbeiter m industrial worker; ~ausstellung f industrial exhibition; ~erzeugnis n industrial product; ~gebiet n industrial district or area; ²ll adj [~i'ɛl] industrial; ~lle [~i'ɛlə] m (-n/-n) industrialist; ~staat m industrial country.

ineinander adv. [in'ʔaɪ'nandər] into one another; ~greifen ⊕ v/i. (irr. greifen, sep., -ge-, h) gear into one another, interlock.

infam adj. [in'fɑ:m] infamous.

Infanter|ie ⚔ [infantə'ri:] f (-/-n) infantry, ~ist ⚔ m (-en/-en) infantryman.

Infektion ⚕ [infek'tsjo:n] f (-/-en) infection; ~skrankheit ⚕ f infectious disease.

Infinitiv gr. ['infiniti:f] m (-s/-e) infinitive (mood).

infizieren [infi'tsi:rən] v/t. (no -ge-, h) infect.   [flation.\

Inflation [infla'tsjo:n] f (-/-en) in-\

in'folge prp. (gen.) in consequence of, owing or due to; ~'dessen adv. consequently.

Inform|ation [informa'tsjo:n] f (-/-en) information; ²ieren [~'mi:rən] v/t. (no -ge-, h) inform; falsch ~ misinform.

Ingenieur [inʒe'njø:r] m (-s/-e) engineer.

Ingwer ['iŋvər] m (-s/no pl.) ginger.

Inhaber ['inha:bər] m (-s/-) owner, proprietor (of business or shop); occupant (of flat); keeper (of shop); holder (of office, share, etc.); bearer (of cheque, etc.).

'Inhalt m (-[e]s/-e) contents pl. (of bottle, book, etc.); tenor (of speech); geom. volume; capacity (of vessel).

'Inhalts|angabe f summary; ²los adj. empty, devoid of substance; ²reich adj. full of meaning; life: rich, full; ~verzeichnis n on parcel: list of contents; in book: table of contents.

Initiative [initsja'ti:və] f (-/no pl.) initiative; die ~ ergreifen take the initiative.

Inkasso ✝ [in'kaso] n (-s/-s, Inkassi) collection.

'inkonsequen|t adj. inconsistent; ²z ['~ts] f (-/-en) inconsistency.

In'krafttreten n (-s/no pl.) coming into force, taking effect (of new law, etc.).

'Inland n (-[e]s/no pl.) home (country); inland.

inländisch *adj.* ['inlɛndiʃ] native; inland; home; domestic; *product*: home-made.

Inlett ['inlɛt] *n* (-[e]s/-e) bedtick.

in'mitten *prp.* (*gen.*) in the midst of, amid(st).

'inne|haben *v/t.* (*irr. haben, sep.*, -ge-, *h*) possess, hold (*office, record, etc.*); occupy (*flat*); '~halten *v/i.* (*irr. halten, sep.*, -ge-, *h*) stop, pause.

innen *adv.* ['inən] inside, within; indoors; *nach* ~ inwards.

'Innen|architekt *m* interior decorator; '~ausstattung *f* interior decoration, fittings *pl.*, furnishing; '~minister *m* minister of the interior; Home Secretary, *Am.* Secretary of the Interior; '~ministerium *n* ministry of the interior; Home Office, *Am.* Department of the Interior; '~politik *f* domestic policy; '~seite *f* inner side, inside; '~stadt *f* city, *Am.* downtown.

inner *adj.* ['inər] interior; inner; ⚙, *pol.* internal; **'2e** *n* (-n/*no* pl.) interior; *Minister(ium) des Innern* s. *Innenminister(ium)*; **2eien** [~'raɪən] *f/pl.* offal(s *pl.*); '~halb **1.** *prp.* (*gen.*) within; **2.** *adv.* within, inside; '~lich *adv.* inwardly; *esp.* ⚙ internally.

innig *adj.* ['iniç] intimate, close; affectionate.

Innung ['inuŋ] *f* (-/-en) guild, corporation.

inoffiziell *adj.* ['inʔ-] unofficial.

ins *prp.* [ins] = *in das*.

Insasse ['inzasə] *m* (-n/-n) inmate; occupant, passenger (*of car*).

'Inschrift *f* inscription; legend (*on coin, etc.*).

Insekt *zo.* [in'zɛkt] *n* (-[e]s/-en) insect.

Insel ['inzəl] *f* (-/-n) island; '~bewohner *m* islander.

Inser|at [inzə'raːt] *n* (-[e]s/-e) advertisement, F ad; **2ieren** [~'riːrən] *v/t. and v/i.* (*no* -ge-, *h*) advertise.

insge'heim *adv.* secretly; ~'samt *adv.* altogether.

in'sofern *cj.* so far; ~ *als* in so far as.

insolvent † *adj.* ['inzɔlvɛnt] insolvent.

Inspekt|ion [inspɛk'tsjoːn] *f* (-/-en) inspection; ~or [in'spɛktɔr] *m* (-s/-en) inspector; surveyor; overseer.

inspirieren [inspi'riːrən] *v/t.* (*no* -ge-, *h*) inspire.

inspizieren [inspi'tsiːrən] *v/t.* (*no* -ge-, *h*) inspect (*troops, etc.*); examine (*goods*); survey (*buildings*).

Install|ateur [instala'tøːr] *m* (-s/-e) plumber; (gas- *or* electrical) fitter; **2ieren** [~'liːrən] *v/t.* (*no* -ge-, *h*) install.

instand *adv.* [in'ʃtant]: ~ *halten* keep in good order; keep up; ⊕

maintain; ~ *setzen* repair; **2haltung** *f* maintenance; upkeep.

'inständig *adv.*: *j-n* ~ *bitten* implore *or* beseech s.o.

Instanz [in'stants] *f* (-/-en) authority; ⟹ instance; ~enweg ⟹ *m* stages of appeal; *auf dem* ~ through the prescribed channels.

Instinkt [in'stiŋkt] *m* (-[e]s/-e) instinct; **2iv** *adj.* [~'tiːf] instinctively.

Institut [insti'tuːt] *n* (-[e]s/-e) institute.

Instrument [instru'mɛnt] *n* (-[e]s/-e) instrument.

inszenier|en *esp. thea.* [instse'niːrən] *v/t.* (*no* -ge-, *h*) (put on the) stage; **2ung** *thea.* *f* (-/-en) staging, production.

Integr|ation [integra'tsjoːn] *f* (-/-en) integration; **2ieren** [~'griːrən] *v/t.* (*no* -ge-, *h*) integrate.

intellektuell *adj.* [intelɛktu'ɛl] intellectual, highbrow; **2e** *m* (-n/-n) intellectual, highbrow.

intelligen|t *adj.* [inteli'gɛnt] intelligent; **2z** [~ts] *f* (-/-en) intelligence.

Intendant *thea.* [inten'dant] *m* (-en/-en) director.

intensiv *adj.* [inten'ziːf] intensive; intense.

interess|ant *adj.* [intere'sant] interesting; **2e** [~'rɛsə] *n* (-s/-n) interest (*an dat.*, *für* in); **2engebiet** [~'rɛsən-] *n* field of interest; **2engemeinschaft** [~'rɛsən-] *f* community of interests; combine, pool, trust; **2ent** [~'sɛnt] *m* (-en/-en) interested person *or* party; ⟹ prospective buyer, *esp. Am.* prospect; **~ieren** [~'siːrən] *v/t.* (*no* -ge-, *h*) interest (*für* in); *sich* ~ *für* take an interest in.

intern *adj.* [in'tern] internal; **2at** [~'naːt] *n* (-[e]s/-e) boarding-school.

international *adj.* [internatsjo'naːl] international.

inter|nieren *v/t.* (*no* -ge-, *h*) intern; **2'nierung** *f* (-/-en) internment; **2'nist** ⚕ *m* (-en/-en) internal specialist, *Am.* internist.

inter|pretieren [interpre'tiːrən] *v/t.* (*no* -ge-, *h*) interpret; **2punktion** [~puŋk'tsjoːn] *f* (-/-en) punctuation; **2vall** [~'val] *n* (-s/-e) interval; **~venieren** [~ve'niːrən] *v/i.* (*no* -ge-, *h*) intervene; **2'zonenhandel** *m* interzonal trade; **2'zonenverkehr** *m* interzonal traffic.

intim *adj.* [in'tiːm] intimate (*mit* with); **2ität** [~imi'tɛːt] *f* (-/-en) intimacy.

'intoleran|t *adj.* intolerant; **2z** ['~ts] *f* (-/-en) intolerance.

intransitiv *gr. adj.* ['intranzitiːf] intransitive.

I..trig|e [in'triːgə] *f* (-/-n) intrigue, scheme, plot; **2ieren** [~i'giːrən] *v/i.* (*no* -ge-, *h*) intrigue, scheme, plot.

Invalid|e [inva'li:də] *m* (*-n/-n*) invalid; disabled person; **~enrente** *f* disability pension; **~ität** [~idi-'tɛ:t] *f* (*-/no pl.*) disablement, disability.

Inventar [invɛn'ta:r] *n* (*-s/-e*) inventory, stock.

Inventur ✝ [invɛn'tu:r] *f* (*-/-en*) stock-taking; **~ machen** take stock.

invest|ieren ✝ [invɛs'ti:rən] *v/t.* (*no -ge-, h*) invest; **~ition** ✝ [~i'tsjo:n] *f* (*-/-en*) investment.

inwie'fern *cj.* to what extent; in what way *or* respect; **~'weit** *cj.* how far, to what extent.

in'zwischen *adv.* in the meantime, meanwhile.

Ion *phys.* [i'o:n] *n* (*-s/-en*) ion.

ird|en *adj.* ['irdən] earthen; **~isch** *adj.* earthly; worldly; mortal.

Ire ['i:rə] *m* (*-n/-n*) Irishman; **die ~n** *pl.* the Irish *pl.*

irgend *adv.* ['irgənt] *in compounds:* some; any (*a. negative and in questions*); **wenn ich ~ kann** if I possibly can; **~'ein(e)** *indef. pron. and adj.* some(one); any(one); **~'einer** *indef. pron. s.* irgend jemand; **~'ein(e)s** *indef. pron.* some; any; **~ etwas** *indef. pron.* something; anything; **~ jemand** *indef. pron.* someone; anyone; **~'wann** *adv.* some time (or other); **~'wie** *adv.* somehow; anyhow; **~'wo** *adv.* somewhere; anywhere; **~'wo'her** *adv.* from somewhere; from anywhere; **~'wo'hin** *adv.* somewhere; anywhere.

'irisch *adj.* Irish.

Iron|ie [iro'ni:] *f* (*-/-n*) irony; **⊆isch** *adj.* [i'ro:niʃ] ironic(al).

irre ['irə] **1.** *adj.* confused; ⚕ insane; mad; **2.** ⊆ *f* (*-/no pl.*): **in die ~ gehen** go astray; **3.** ⊆ *m, f* (*-n/-n*) lunatic; mental patient; **wie ein ~** like a madman; **~führen** *v/t.* (*sep., -ge-, h*) lead astray; *fig.* mislead; **~gehen** *v/i.* (*irr. gehen, sep., -ge-, sein*) go astray, stray; lose one's way; **~machen** *v/t.* (*sep., -ge-, h*) puzzle, bewilder; perplex; confuse;

~n 1. *v/i.* (*ge-, h*) err; wander; **2.** *v/refl.* (*ge-, h*) be mistaken (*in dat.* in *s.o.,* about *s.th.*); be wrong.

'Irren|anstalt ⚕ *f* lunatic asylum, mental home *or* hospital; **~arzt** ⚕ *m* alienist, mental specialist; **~haus** ⚕ *n s.* Irrenanstalt.

'irrereden *v/i.* (*sep., -ge-, h*) rave.

'Irr|fahrt *f* wandering; Odyssey; **~garten** *m* labyrinth, maze; **~glaube** *m* erroneous belief; false doctrine, heterodoxy; heresy; **⊆gläubig** *adj.* heterodox; heretical; **⊆ig** *adj.* erroneous, mistaken, false, wrong.

irritieren [iri'ti:rən] *v/t.* (*no -ge-, h*) irritate, annoy; confuse.

'Irr|lehre *f* false doctrine, heterodoxy; heresy; **~licht** *n* will-o'-the-wisp, jack-o'-lantern; **~sinn** *m* insanity; madness; *fig.* fantastic; terrible; **⊆sinnig** *adj.* insane; mad; *fig.* fantastic; terrible; **~sinnige** *m, f* (*-n/-n*) *s.* irre 3; **~tum** *m* (*-s/⁻er*) error, mistake; **im ~ sein** be mistaken; **⊆tümlich** ['~ty:mliç] **1.** *adj.* erroneous; **2.** *adv.* = **⊆tümlicherweise** *adv.* by mistake; mistakenly, erroneously; **~wisch** *m s.* Irrlicht; *p.* flibbertigibbet.

Ischias ⚕ ['iʃias] *f, F a.:* n, *m* (*-/no pl.*) sciatica.

Islam ['islam, is'la:m] *m* (*-s/no pl.*) Islam.

Island|er ['i:slɛndər] *m* (*-s/-*) Icelander; **⊆isch** *adj.* Icelandic.

Isolator ⚡ [izo'la:tɔr] *m* (*-s/-en*) insulator.

Isolier|band ⚡ [izo'li:r-] *n* insulating tape; **⊆en** *v/t.* (*no -ge-, h*) isolate; **~masse** ⚡ *f* insulating compound; **~schicht** ⚡ *f* insulating layer; **~ung** *f* (*-/-en*) isolation (*a. ⚗*); ⚕ quarantine; ⚡ insulation.

Isotop ⚛ *phys.* [izo'to:p] *n* (*-s/-e*) isotope.

Israeli [isra'e:li] *m* (*-s/-s*) Israeli.

Italien|er [ital'je:nər] *m* (*-s/-*) Italian; **⊆isch** *adj.* Italian.

I-Tüpfelchen *fig.* ['i:typfəlçən] *n* (*-s/-*): **bis aufs ~** to a T.

J

ja [ja:] **1.** *adv.* yes; ⚓, *parl.* aye, *Am. parl. a.* yea; **~ doch, ~ freilich** yes, indeed; **to be sure; da ist er ~!** well, there he is!; **ich sagte es Ihnen ~** I told you so; **tut es ~ nicht!** don't you dare do it!; **vergessen Sie es ~ nicht!** be sure not to forget it!; **2.** *cj.:* **~ sogar, ~ selbst** nay (even); **wenn ~** if so; **er ist ~ mein Freund** why, he is my friend; **3.** *int.:* **~, weißt du**

denn nicht, daß why, don't you know that.

Jacht ⚓ [jaxt] *f* (*-/-en*) yacht; **~klub** *m* yacht-club.

Jacke ['jakə] *f* (*-/-n*) jacket.

Jackett [ʒa'kɛt] *n* (*-s/-e, -s*) jacket.

Jagd [ja:kt] *f* (*-/-en*) hunt(ing); *with a gun:* shoot(ing); chase; *s.* Jagdrevier; **auf (die) ~ gehen** go hunting *or* shooting, *Am. a.* be gunning; **~ machen auf (acc.)** hunt after *or* for;

'~aufseher m gamekeeper, Am. game warden; '~bomber ✕ m (-s/-) fighter-bomber; '~büchse f sporting rifle; '~flinte f sporting gun; fowling-piece; '~flugzeug ✕ n fighter (aircraft); '~geschwader ✕ n fighter wing, Am. fighter group; '~gesellschaft f hunting or shooting party; '~haus n shooting-box or -lodge, hunting-box or -lodge; '~hund m hound; '~hütte f shooting-box, hunting-box; '~pächter m game-tenant; '~rennen n steeplechase; '~revier n hunting-ground, shoot; '~schein m shooting licen|ce, Am. -se; '~schloß n hunting seat; '~tasche f game-bag.

jagen ['ja:gən] (ge-, h) 1. v/i. go hunting or shooting, hunt; shoot; rush, dash; 2. v/t. hunt; chase; aus dem Hause ~ turn s.o. out (of doors).

Jäger ['je:gər] m (-s/-) hunter. huntsman, sportsman; ✕ rifleman; '~latein n fig. ~ huntsmen's yarn, tall stories pl. [jaguar.)

Jaguar zo. ['ja:gua:r] m (-s/-e)) jäh adj. [je:] sudden, abrupt; precipitous, steep.

Jahr [ja:r] n (-[e]s/-e) year; ein halbes ~ half a year, six months pl.; einmal im ~ once a year; im ~ 1900 in 1900; mit 18 ~en, im Alter von 18 ~en at (the age of) eighteen; letztes ~ last year; das ganze ~ hindurch or über all the year round; ~'aus adv.: ~, jahrein year in, year out; year after year; '~buch n year-book, annual; ~'ein adv. s. jahraus.

'jahrelang 1. adv. for years; 2. adj.: ~e Erfahrung (many) years of experience.

jähren ['je:rən] v/refl. (ge-, h): es jährt sich heute, daß ... it is a year ago today that ..., it is a year today since ...

'Jahres|abonnement n annual subscription (to magazine, etc.); thea. yearly season ticket; '~abschluß m annual statement of accounts; '~anfang m beginning of the year; zum ~ die besten Wünsche! best wishes for the New Year; '~bericht m annual report; '~einkommen n annual or yearly income; '~ende n end of the year; '~gehalt n annual salary; '~tag m anniversary; '~wechsel m turn of the year; '~zahl f date, year; '~zeit f season, time of the year.

'Jahrgang m volume, year (of periodical, etc.); p. age-group; univ., school: year, class; wine: vintage.

Jahr'hundert n (-s/-e) century; ~feier f centenary, Am. centennial; ~wende f turn of the century.

jährig adj. ['je:riç] one-year-old.

jährlich ['je:rliç] 1. adj. annual, yearly; 2. adv. every year, yearly, once a year.

'Jahr|markt m fair; ~'tausend n (-s/-e) millennium; ~'tausendfeier f millenary; ~'zehnt n (-[e]s/-e) decade.

'Jähzorn m violent (fit of) temper; irascibility; '2ig adj. hot-tempered; irascible.

Jalousie [ʒalu'zi:] f (-/-n) (Venetian) blind, Am. a. window shade.

Jammer ['jamər] m (-s/no pl.) lamentation; misery; es ist ein ~ it is a pity.

jämmerlich adj. ['jemərliç] miserable, wretched; piteous; pitiable (esp. contp.).

jammer|n ['jamərn] v/i. (ge-, h) lament (nach, um for; über acc. over); moan; wail, whine; '~schade adj.: es ist ~ it is a thousand pities, it is a great shame.

Januar ['janua:r] m (-[s]/-e) January.

Japan|er [ja'pa:nər] m (-s/-) Japanese; die ~ pl. the Japanese pl.; 2isch adj. Japanese.

Jargon [ʒar'gõ] m (-s/-s) jargon, cant, slang.

Jasmin ♀ [jas'mi:n] m (-s/-e) jasmin(e), jessamin(e).

'Jastimme parl. f aye, Am. a. yea.

jäten ['je:tən] v/t. (ge-, h) weed.

Jauche ['jauxə] f (-/-n) ♪ liquid manure; sewage.

jauchzen ['jauxtsən] v/i. (ge-, h) exult, rejoice, cheer; vor Freude ~ shout for joy.

jawohl adv. [ja'vo:l] yes; yes, indeed; yes, certainly; that's right; ✕, etc.: yes, Sir!

'Jawort n consent; j-m das ~ geben accept s.o.'s proposal (of marriage).

je [je:] 1. adv. ever, at any time; always; ohne ihn ~ gesehen zu haben without ever having seen him; seit eh und ~ since time immemorial, always; distributive with numerals: ~ zwei two at a time, two each, two by two, by or in twos; sie bekamen ~ zwei Äpfel they received two apples each; für ~ zehn Wörter for every ten words; in Schachteln mit or zu ~ zehn Stück verpackt packed in boxes of ten; 2. cj.: ~ nach Größe according to or depending on size; ~ nachdem it depends; ~ nachdem, was er für richtig hält according as he thinks fit; ~ nachdem, wie er sich fühlt depending on how he feels; ~ mehr, desto besser the more the better; ~ länger, ~ lieber the longer the better; 3. prp.: die Birnen kosten e-e Mark ~ Pfund the pears cost one mark a pound; s. pro.

jede|(r, -s) indef. pron. ['je:də(r, -s)] every; any; of a group: each; of two persons: either; jeder, der whoever; jeden zweiten Tag every other day; '~n'falls adv. at all events, in any case; **˷rmann** *indef. pron.* everyone, everybody; '**˷r'zeit** *adv.* always, at any time; '**˷s'mal** *adv.* each *or* every time; **˷ wenn** whenever.

jedoch *cj.* [je'dɔx] however, yet, nevertheless.

'**jeher** *adv.*: *von or seit* **˷** at all times, always, from time immemorial.

jemals *adv.* ['je:mɑːls] ever, at any time.

jemand *indef. pron.* ['je:mant] someone, somebody; *with questions and negations*: anyone, anybody.

jene|(r, -s) *dem. pron.* ['je:nə(r, -s)] that (one); **jene** *pl.* those *pl.*

jenseitig *adj.* ['jenzaitiç] opposite. '**jenseits 1.** *prp.* (*gen.*) on the other side of, beyond, across; **2.** *adv.* on the other side, beyond; **3.** ♀ *n* (-/no *pl.*) *the* other *or* next world, *the* world to come, *the* beyond.

jetzig *adj.* ['jetsiç] present, existing; *prices, etc.*: current.

jetzt *adv.* [jetst] now, at present; *bis* **˷** until now; so far; *eben* **˷** just now; *erst* **˷** only now; *für* **˷** for the present; *gleich* **˷** at once, right away; *noch* **˷** even now; *von* **˷** *an* from now on.

jeweil|ig *adj.* ['je:vailiç] respective; **˷s** *adv.* ['.˷s] respectively, at a time; from time to time (*esp.* ȿȿ).

Joch [jɔx] *n* (-[e]s/-e) yoke; *in mountains*: col, pass, saddle; ⚓ bay; '**˷bein** *anat. n* cheek-bone.

Jockei ['dʒɔki] *m* (-s/-s) jockey.

Jod ⚗ [jo:t] *n* (-[e]s/no *pl.*) iodine.

jodeln ['jo:dəln] *v/i.* (ge-, h) yodel.

Johanni [jo'hani] *n* (-/no *pl.*), **˷s** [˷s] *n* (-/no *pl.*) Midsummer day; **˷s-beere** *f* currant; *rote* **˷** red currant; **˷stag** *m eccl.* St John's day; Midsummer day.

johlen ['jo:lən] *v/i.* (ge-, h) bawl, yell, howl.

Jolle ⚓ ['jɔlə] *f* (-/-n) jolly-boat, yawl, dinghy.

Jongl|eur [ʒɔ̃'glør] *m* (-s/-e) juggler, **˷ieren** *v/t. and v/i.* (no -ge-, h) juggle.

Journal [ʒur'nɑːl] *n* (-s/-e) journal; newspaper, magazine; diary; ⚓ log-book, **˷ist** [˷a'list] *m* (-en/-en) journalist, *Am. a.* newspaperman.

Jubel ['ju:bəl] *m* (-s/no *pl.*) jubilation, exultation, rejoicing; cheering; '**˷n** *v/i.* (ge-, h) jubilate; exult, rejoice (*über acc.* at).

Jubil|ar [jubi'lɑːr] *m* (-s/-e) person celebrating his jubilee, *etc.*; **˷äum** [˷ɛːum] *n* (-s/ *Jubiläen*) jubilee.

Juchten ['juxtən] *m, n* (-s/no *pl.*), '**˷leder** *n* Russia (leather).

jucken ['jukən] (ge-, h) **1.** *v/i.* itch; **2.** *v/t.* irritate, (make) itch; F *sich* **˷** scratch (o.s.).

Jude ['ju:də] *m* (-n/-n) Jew; **˷n-feindlich** *adj.* anti-Semitic; '**˷n-**

tum *n* (-s/no *pl.*) Judaism; '**˷nverfolgung** *f* persecution of Jews, Jew-baiting; pogrom.

Jüd|in ['jy:din] *f* (-/-nen) Jewess; **˷isch** *adj.* Jewish.

Jugend ['ju:gənt] *f* (-/no *pl.*) youth; '**˷amt** *n* youth welfare department; '**˷buch** *n* book for the young; '**˷freund** *m* friend of one's youth; school-friend; '**˷fürsorge** *f* youth welfare; '**˷gericht** *n* juvenile court; '**˷herberge** *f* youth hostel; '**˷jahre** *n/pl.* early years, youth; '**˷kriminalität** *f* juvenile delinquency; **♀lich** *adj.* youthful, juvenile, young; '**˷liche** *m, f* (-n/-n) young person; juvenile; young man, youth; young girl; teen-ager; '**˷liebe** *f* early *or* first love, calf-love, *Am. a.* puppy love; old sweetheart *or* flame; '**˷schriften** *f/pl.* books for the young; '**˷schutz** *m* protection of children and young people; '**˷streich** *m* youthful prank; '**˷werk** *n* early work (*of author*); **˷e** *pl. a.* juvenilia *pl.*; '**˷zeit** *f* (time *or* days of) youth.

Jugoslav|e [ju:go'slɑːvə] *m* (-en/-en) Jugoslav, Yugoslav, **♀isch** *adj.* Jugoslav, Yugoslav.

Juli ['ju:li] *m* (-[s]/-s) July.

jung *adj.* [juŋ] young; youthful; *peas*: green; *beer, wine*: new; **˷es** Gemüse young *or* early vegetables *pl.*; F *fig.* young people, small fry.

'**Junge 1.** *m* (-n/-n) boy, youngster; lad; fellow, chap, *Am.* guy; *cards*: knave, jack; **2.** *n* (-n/-n) young; puppy (*of dog*); kitten (*of cat*); calf (*of cow, elephant, etc.*); cub (*of beast of prey*); **˷** werfen bring forth young; *ein* **˷s** a young one; '**♀nhaft** *adj.* boyish; '**˷nstreich** *m* boyish prank *or* trick.

jünger ['jyŋər] **1.** *adj.* younger, junior; *er ist drei Jahre* **˷** *als ich* he is my junior by three years, he is three years younger than I; **2.** ♀ *m* (-s/-) disciple.

Jungfer ['juŋfər] *f* (-/-n): *alte* **˷** old maid *or* spinster.

'**Jungfern|fahrt** ⚓ *f* maiden voyage *or* trip; '**˷flug** ✈ *m* maiden flight; '**˷rede** *f* maiden speech.

'**Jung|frau** *f* maid(en), virgin; ♀-**fräulich** *adj.* ['.frɔʏliç] virginal; *fig.* virgin; '**˷fräulichkeit** *f* (-/no *pl.*) virginity, maidenhood; '**˷geselle** *m* bachelor; '**˷gesellenstand** *m* bachelorhood; '**˷gesellin** *f* (-/-nen) bachelor girl.

Jüngling ['jyŋliŋ] *m* (-s/-e) youth, young man.

jüngst [jyŋst] **1.** *adj.* youngest; *time*: (most) recent, latest; *das* ♀e Gericht, *der* ♀e Tag Last Judg(e)ment, Day of Judg(e)ment; **2.** *adv.* recently, lately.

'**jungverheiratet** *adj.* newly married; '♀en *pl. the* newlyweds *pl.*

Juni ['juːni] m (-[s]/-s) June; '∼käfer zo. m cockchafer, June-bug.

junior ['juːnjər] 1. adj. junior; 2. ♀ m (-s/-en) junior (a. sports).

Jura ['juːra] n/pl.: ∼ studieren read or study law.

Jurist [ju'rist] m (-en/-en) lawyer; law-student; ♀isch adj. legal.

Jury [ʒy'riː] f (-/-s) jury.

justier|en ⊕ [jus'tiːrən] v/t. (no -ge-, h) adjust; ♀ung ⊕ f (-/-en) adjustment.

Justiz [ju'stiːts] f (-/no pl.) (administration of) justice; ∼beamte m judicial officer; ∼gebäude n courthouse; ∼inspektor m judicial officer; ∼irrtum m judicial error; ∼minister m minister of justice; Lord Chancellor, Am. Attorney General; ∼ministerium n ministry of justice; Am. Department of Justice; ∼mord m judicial murder.

Juwel [ju've:l] m, n (-s/-en) jewel, gem; ∼en pl. jewel(le)ry; ∼ier [∼e'liːr] m (-s/-e) jewel(l)er.

Jux F [juks] m (-es/-e) (practical) joke, fun, spree, lark; prank.

K

(Compare also C and Z)

Kabel ['kaːbəl] n (-s/-) cable.

Kabeljau ichth. ['kaːbəljau] m (-s/-e, -s) cod(fish).

'**kabeln** v/t. and v/i. (ge-, h) cable.

Kabine [ka'biːnə] f (-/-n) cabin; at hairdresser's, etc.: cubicle; cage (of lift).

Kabinett pol. [kabi'nɛt] n (-s/-e) cabinet, government.

Kabriolett [kabrio'lɛt] n (-s/-e) cabriolet, convertible.

Kachel ['kaxəl] f (-/-n) (Dutch or glazed) tile; '∼ofen m tiled stove.

Kadaver [ka'daːvər] m (-s/-) carcass.

Kadett [ka'dɛt] m (-en/-en) cadet.

Käfer zo. ['kɛːfər] m (-s/-) beetle, chafer.

Kaffee ['kafe, ka'feː] m (-s/-s) coffee; (')∼bohne ♀ f coffee-bean; (')∼kanne f coffee-pot; (')∼mühle f coffee-mill or -grinder; (')∼satz m coffee-grounds pl.; (')∼tasse f coffee-cup.

Käfig ['kɛːfiç] m (-s/-e) cage (a. fig.).

kahl adj. [kaːl] p. bald; tree, etc.: bare; landscape, etc.: barren, bleak; rock, etc.: naked; '♀kopf m baldhead, baldpate; '∼köpfig adj. ['∼kœpfiç] bald(-headed).

Kahn [kaːn] m (-[e]s/∼e) boat; riverbarge; ∼ fahren go boating; '∼fahren n (-s/no pl.) boating.

Kai [kai] m (-s/-e, -s) quay, wharf.

Kaiser ['kaizər] m (-s/-) emperor; '∼krone f imperial crown; '♀lich adj. imperial; '∼reich n, '∼tum n (-[e]s/∼er) empire; '∼würde f imperial status.

Kajüte ⚓ [ka'jyːtə] f (-/-n) cabin.

Kakao [ka'kaːo] m (-s/-s) cocoa; ♀ a. cacao.

Kakt|ee ♀ [kak'teː(ə)] f (-/-n), ∼us ♀ ['∼us] m (-/Kakteen, F Kaktusse) cactus.

Kalauer ['kaːlauər] m (-s/-) stale joke; pun.

Kalb zo. [kalp] n (-[e]s/∼er) calf; ♀en ['∼bən] v/i. (ge-, h) calve; '∼fell n calfskin; '∼fleisch n veal; '∼leder n calf(-leather).

'**Kalbs|braten** m roast veal; '∼keule f leg of veal; '∼leder n s. Kalbleder; '∼nierenbraten m loin of veal.

Kalender [ka'lɛndər] m (-s/-) calendar; almanac; ∼block m dateblock; ∼jahr n calendar year; ∼uhr f calendar watch or clock.

Kali 🜖 ['kaːli] n (-s/-s) potash.

Kaliber [ka'liːbər] n (-s/-) calib|re, Am. -er (a. fig.), bore (of firearm).

Kalk [kalk] m (-[e]s/-e) lime; geol. limestone; ∼brenner m limeburner; '♀en v/t. (ge-, h) whitewash (wall, etc.); ♂ lime (field); ♀ig adj. limy; '∼ofen m limekiln; ∼stein m limestone; '∼steinbruch m limestone quarry.

Kalorie [kalo'riː] f (-/-n) calorie.

kalt adj. [kalt] climate, meal, sweat, etc.: cold; p., manner, etc.: cold, chilly, frigid; mir ist ∼ I am cold; ∼e Küche cold dishes pl. or meat, etc.; j-m die ∼e Schulter zeigen give s.o. the cold shoulder; ∼blütig adj. ['∼blyːtiç] cold-blooded (a. fig.).

Kälte ['kɛltə] f (-/no pl.) cold; chill; coldness, chilliness (both a. fig.); vor ∼ zittern shiver with cold; fünf Grad ∼ five degrees below zero; '∼grad m degree below zero; '∼welle f cold spell.

'**kalt|stellen** fig. v/t. (sep., -ge-, h) shelve, reduce to impotence; '♀welle f cold wave.

kam [kaːm] pret. of kommen.

Kamel zo. [ka'meːl] n (-[e]s/-e) camel; ∼haar n textiles: camel hair.

Kamera phot. ['kaməra] f (-/-s) camera.

Kamerad [kamə'ra:t] *m* (-en/-en) comrade; companion; mate, F pal, chum; **~schaft** *f* (-/-en) comradeship, companionship; **2schaftlich** *adj.* comradely, companionable.

Kamille ♀ [ka'milə] *f* (-/-n) camomile; **~ntee** *m* camomile tea.

Kamin [ka'mi:n] *m* (-s/-e) chimney (*a. mount.*); fireplace, fireside; **~sims** *m, n* mantelpiece; **~vorleger** *m* hearth-rug; **~vorsetzer** *m* (-s/-) fender.

Kamm [kam] *m* (-[e]s/ᵘe) comb; crest (*of bird or wave*); crest, ridge (*of mountain*).

kämmen ['kemən] *v/t.* (ge-, h) comb; *sich (die Haare)* ~ comb one's hair.

Kammer ['kamər] *f* (-/-n) (small) room; closet; *pol.* chamber; board; ⚖ division (*of court*); **~diener** *m* valet; **~frau** *f* lady's maid; **~gericht** ⚖ *n* supreme court; **~herr** *m* chamberlain; **~jäger** *m* vermin exterminator; **~musik** *f* chamber music; **~zofe** *f* chambermaid.

'Kamm|garn *n* worsted (yarn); **~rad** ⊕ *n* cogwheel.

Kampagne [kam'panjə] *f* (-/-n) campaign.

Kampf [kampf] *m* (-[e]s/ᵘe) combat, fight (*a. fig.*); struggle (*a. fig.*); battle (*a. fig.*); *fig.* conflict; *sports:* contest, match; *boxing:* fight, bout; **~bahn** *f sports:* stadium, arena; **2bereit** *adj.* ready for battle.

kämpfen ['kempfən] *v/i.* (ge-, h) fight (*gegen* against; *mit* with; *um* for) (*a. fig.*); struggle (*a. fig.*); *fig.* contend, wrestle (*mit* with).

Kampfer ['kampfər] *m* (-s/*no pl.*) camphor.

Kämpfer ['kempfər] *m* (-s/-) fighter (*a. fig.*); ✕ combatant, warrior.

'Kampf|flugzeug *n* tactical aircraft; **~geist** *m* fighting spirit; **~platz** *m* battlefield; *fig.*, *sports:* arena; **~preis** *m sports:* prize; ✝ cut-throat price; **~richter** *m* referee, judge, umpire; **2unfähig** *adj.* disabled.

kampieren [kam'pi:rən] *v/i.* (no -ge-, h) camp.

Kanal [ka'na:l] *m* (-s/ᵘe) canal; channel (*a.* ⊕, *fig.*); *geogr. the* Channel; sewer, drain; **~isation** [~aliza'tsjo:n] *f* (-/-en) river: canalization; *town, etc.*: sewerage; drainage; **2isieren** [~ali'zi:rən] *v/t.* (no -ge-, h) canalize; sewer.

Kanarienvogel *orn.* [ka'na:rjən-] *m* canary(-bird).

Kandare [kan'da:rə] *f* (-/-n) curb (-bit).

Kandid|at [kandi'da:t] *m* (-en/-en) candidate; applicant; **~atur** [~a'tu:r] *f* (-/-en) candidature, candidacy; **2ieren** [~'di:rən] *v/i.* (no -ge-, h) be a candidate (*für* for);

~ *für* apply for, stand for, *Am.* run for (*office, etc.*).

Känguruh *zo.* ['kenguru:] *n* (-s/-s) kangaroo.

Kaninchen *zo.* [ka'ni:nçən] *n* (-s/-) rabbit; **~bau** *m* rabbit-burrow.

Kanister [ka'nistər] *m* (-s/-) can.

Kanne ['kanə] *f* (-/-n) milk, *etc.*: jug; coffee, tea: pot; oil, milk: can; **~gießer** F *fig. m* political wiseacre.

Kannibal|e [kani'ba:lə] *m* (-n/-n) cannibal; **2isch** *adj.* cannibal.

kannte ['kantə] *pret. of* kennen.

Kanon ♪ ['ka:nɔn] *m* (-s/-s) canon.

Kanon|ade ✕ [kano'na:də] *f* (-/-n) cannonade; **~e** [~'no:nə] *f* (-/-n) ✕ cannon, gun; F *fig.*: big shot; *esp. sports:* ace, crack.

Ka'nonen|boot ✕ *n* gunboat; **~donner** *m* boom of cannon; **~futter** *fig. n* cannon-fodder; **~kugel** *f* cannon-ball; **~rohr** *n* gun barrel.

Kanonier ✕ [kano'ni:r] *m* (-s/-e) gunner.

Kant|e ['kantə] *f* (-/-n) edge; brim; **~en** *m* (-s/-) end of loaf; **2en** *v/t.* (ge-, h) square (*stone, etc.*); set on edge; tilt; edge (*skis*); **2ig** *adj.* angular, edged; square(d).

Kantine [kan'ti:nə] *f* (-/-n) canteen.

Kanu ['ka:nu] *n* (-s/-s) canoe.

Kanüle ⚕ [ka'ny:lə] *f* (-/-n) tubule, cannula.

Kanzel ['kantsəl] *f* (-/-n) *eccl.* pulpit; ✈ cockpit; ✕ (gun-)turret.; **~redner** *m* preacher.

Kanzlei [kants'laı] *f* (-/-en) office.

'Kanzler *m* (-s/-) chancellor.

Kap *geogr.* [kap] *n* (-s/-s) headland.

Kapazität [kapatsi'te:t] *f* (-/-en) capacity; *fig.* authority.

Kapell|e [ka'pelə] *f* (-/-n) *eccl.* chapel; ♪ band; **~meister** *m* bandleader, conductor.

kaper|n ⚓ ['ka:pərn] *v/t.* (ge-, h) capture, seize; **2schiff** *n* privateer.

kapieren F [ka'pi:rən] *v/t.* (no -ge-, h) grasp, get.

Kapital [kapi'ta:l] 1. *n* (-s/-e, -ien) capital, stock, funds *pl.*; ~ *und Zinsen* principal and interest; 2. ♀ *adj.* capital; **~anlage** *f* investment; **~flucht** *f* flight of capital; **~gesellschaft** *f* joint-stock company; **2isieren** [~ali'zi:rən] *v/t.* (no -ge-, h) capitalize; **~ismus** [~a'lismus] *m* (-/*no pl.*) capitalism; **~ist** [~a'list] *m* (-en/-en) capitalist; **~markt** [~'ta:l-] *m* capital market; **~verbrechen** *n* capital crime.

Kapitän [kapi'te:n] *m* (-s/-e) captain; ~ *zur See* naval captain; **~leutnant** *m* (senior) lieutenant.

Kapitel [ka'pitəl] *n* (-s/-) chapter (*a. fig.*).

Kapitul|ation ✕ [kapitula'tsjo:n] *f* (-/-en) capitulation, surrender; **2ieren** [~'li:rən] *v/i.* (no -ge-, h) capitulate, surrender.

Kaplan *eccl.* [ka'plɑ:n] *m* (-s/ᵘe) chaplain.

Kappe ['kapə] *f* (-/-n) cap; hood (*a.* ⊕); bonnet; '2n *v/t.* (ge-, *h*) cut (*cable*); lop, top (*tree*).

Kapriole [kapri'o:lə] *f* (-/-n) *equitation*: capriole; *fig.*: caper; prank.

Kapsel ['kapsəl] *f* (-/-n) case, box; ♀, ♂, *anat., etc.*: capsule.

kaputt *adj.* [ka'put] broken; *elevator, etc.*: out of order; *fruit, etc.*: spoilt; *p.*: ruined; tired out, F fagged out; **~gehen** *v/i.* (*irr. gehen, sep.*, -ge-, *sein*) break, go to pieces; spoil.

Kapuze [ka'pu:tsə] *f* (-/-n) hood; *eccl.* cowl.

Karabiner [kara'bi:nər] *m* (-s/-) carbine.

Karaffe [ka'rafə] *f* (-/-n) carafe (*for wine or water*); decanter (*for liqueur, etc.*).

Karambol|age [karambo'lɑ:ʒə] *f* (-/-n) collision, crash; *billiards*: cannon, *Am. a.* carom; 2ieren *v/i.* (*no* -ge-, *sein*) cannon, *Am. a.* carom; F *fig.* collide.

Karat [ka'rɑ:t] *n* (-[e]s/-e) carat.

Karawane [kara'vɑ:nə] *f* (-/-n) caravan.

Karbid [kar'bi:t] *n* (-[e]s/-e) carbide.

Kardinal *eccl.* [kardi'nɑ:l] *m* (-s/-e) cardinal.

Karfreitag *eccl.* [kɑːr'-] *m* Good Friday.

karg *adj.* [kark] *soil*: meagre; *vegetation*: scant, sparse; *meal*: scanty, meagre, frugal; **~en** ['~gən] *v/i.* (ge-, *h*) *~ mit* be sparing of.

kärglich *adj.* ['kerkliç] scanty, meagre; poor.

kariert *adj.* [ka'ri:rt] check(ed), chequered, *Am.* checkered.

Karik|atur [karika'tu:r] *f* (-/-en) caricature, cartoon; 2ieren [~ki'rən] *v/t.* (*no* -ge-, *h*) caricature, cartoon.

karmesin *adj.* [karme'zi:n] crimson.

Karneval ['karnəval] *m* (-s/-e, -s) Shrovetide, carnival.

Karo ['ka:ro] *n* (-s/-s) square, check; *cards*: diamonds *pl.*

Karosserie *mot.* [karosə'ri:] *f* (-/-n) body.

Karotte ♀ [ka'rɔtə] *f* (-/-n) carrot.

Karpfen *ichth.* ['karpfən] *m* (-s/-) carp.

Karre ['karə] *f* (-/-n) cart; wheelbarrow.

Karriere [kar'jɛ:rə] *f* (-/-n) (successful) career.

Karte ['kartə] *f* (-/-n) card; postcard; map; chart; ticket; menu, bill of fare; list.

Kartei [kar'tai] *f* (-/-en) card-index; **~karte** *f* index-card, filing-card; **~schrank** *m* filing cabinet.

Kartell † [kar'tɛl] *n* (-s/-e) cartel.

'Karten|brief *m* letter-card; **'~haus** *n* ♣ chart-house; *fig.* house of cards; **'~legerin** *f* (-/-nen) fortuneteller from the cards; **'~spiel** *n* card-playing; card-game.

Kartoffel [kar'tɔfəl] *f* (-/-n) potato, F spud; **~brei** *m* mashed potatoes *pl.*; **~käfer** *m* Colorado *or* potato beetle, *Am. a.* potato bug; **~schalen** *f/pl.* potato peelings *pl.*

Karton [kar'tõ:, kar'to:n] *m* (-s/-s, -e) cardboard, pasteboard; cardboard box, carton. [*Kartei.*]

Kartothek [karto'te:k] *f* (-/-en) *s.*]

Karussell [karu'sɛl] *n* (-s/-s, -e) roundabout, merry-go-round, *Am. a.* car(r)ousel.

Karwoche *eccl.* ['kɑːr-] *f* Holy *or* Passion Week.

Käse ['kɛ:zə] *m* (-s/-) cheese.

Kasern|e ✗ [ka'zɛrnə] *f* (-/-n) barracks *pl.*; **~enhof** *m* barrack-yard *or* -square; 2ieren [~'ni:rən] *v/t.* (*no* -ge-, *h*) quarter in barracks, barrack.

'käsig *adj.* cheesy; *complexion*: pale, pasty.

Kasino [ka'zi:no] *n* (-s/-s) casino, club(-house); (officers') mess.

Kasperle ['kasperlə] *m, n* (-s/-) Punch; **'~theater** *n* Punch and Judy show.

Kasse ['kasə] *f* (-/-n) cash-box; till (*in shop, etc.*); cash-desk, pay-desk (*in bank, etc.*); pay-office (*in firm*); *thea., etc.*: box-office, booking-office; cash; *bei* ~ in cash.

'Kassen|abschluß † *m* balancing of the cash (accounts); **'~anweisung** *f* disbursement voucher; **'~bestand** *m* cash in hand; **'~bote** *m* bank messenger; **'~buch** *n* cash book; **'~erfolg** *m* *thea., etc.*: box-office success; **'~patient** ♂ *m* panel patient; **'~schalter** *m* *bank, etc.*: teller's counter.

Kasserolle [kasə'rɔlə] *f* (-/-n) stewpan, casserole.

Kassette [ka'sɛtə] *f* (-/-n) box (*for money, etc.*); casket (*for jewels, etc.*); slip-case (*for books*); *phot.* plateholder.

kassiere|n [ka'si:rən] (*no* -ge-, *h*) **1.** *v/i.* waiter, *etc.*: take the money (*für for*); **2.** *v/t.* take (*sum of money*); collect (*contributions, etc.*); annul; ♯♯ quash (*verdict*); 2r *m* (-s/-) cashier; *bank*: a. teller; collector.

Kastanie ♀ [ka'stɑ:njə] *f* (-/-n) chestnut.

Kasten ['kastən] *m* (-s/², ⸰-) box; chest (*for tools, etc.*); case (*for violin, etc.*); bin (*for bread, etc.*).

Kasus *gr.* ['kɑːsus] *m* (-/-) case.

Katalog [kata'lo:k] *m* (-[e]s/-e) catalogue, *Am. a.* catalog; 2isieren [~ogi'zi:rən] *v/t.* (*no* -ge-, *h*) catalogue, *Am. a.* catalog.

Katarrh ♯♯ [ka'tar] *m* (-s/-e) (common) cold, catarrh.

katastroph|al adj. [katastro'fɑːl] catastrophic, disastrous; 2e [ˌ'stroː-fə] f (-/-n) catastrophe, disaster.

Katechismus eccl. [kate'çismus] m (-/Katechismen) catechism.

Katego|rie [katego'riː] f (-/-n) category; 2risch adj. [ˌ'goːriʃ] categorical.

Kater ['kaːtər] m (-s/-) zo. male cat, tom-cat; fig. s. Katzenjammer.

Katheder [ka'teːdər] n, m (-s/-) lecturing-desk.

Kathedrale [kate'drɑːlə] f (-/-n) [cathedral.\

Katholi|k [kato'liːk] m (-en/-en) (Roman) Catholic; 2sch adj. [ˌ'toːliʃ] (Roman) Catholic.

Kattun [ka'tuːn] m (-s/-e) calico; cotton cloth or fabric; chintz.

Katze zo. ['katsə] f (-/-n) cat; '~n-jammer F fig. m hangover, morning-after feeling.

Kauderwelsch ['kaudərvelʃ] n (-[s]/ no pl.) gibberish, F double Dutch; 2en v/i. (ge-, h) gibber, F talk double Dutch.

kauen ['kauən] v/t. and v/i. (ge-, h) chew.

kauern ['kauərn] (ge-, h) 1. v/i. crouch; squat; 2. v/refl. crouch (down); squat (down); duck (down).

Kauf [kauf] m (-[e]s/=e) purchase; bargain, F good buy; acquisition; purchasing, buying; '~brief m deed of purchase; 2en v/t. (ge-, h) buy, purchase; acquire (by purchase); sich et. ~ buy o.s. s.th., buy s.th. for o.s.

Käufer ['kɔyfər] m (-s/-) buyer, purchaser; customer.

'**Kauf|haus** n department store; '~laden m shop, Am. a. store.

käuflich ['kɔyfliç] 1. adj. for sale; purchasable; fig. open to bribery, bribable; venal; 2. adv.: ~ erwerben (acquire by) purchase; ~ überlassen transfer by way of sale.

'**Kauf|mann** m (-[e]s/Kaufleute) businessman; merchant; trader; dealer, shopkeeper; Am. a. storekeeper; 2männisch adj. ['~meniʃ] commercial, mercantile; '~vertrag m contract of sale.

'**Kaugummi** m chewing-gum.

kaum adv. [kaum] hardly, scarcely, barely; ~ glaublich hard to believe.

'**Kautabak** m chewing-tobacco.

Kaution [kau'tsjoːn] f (-/-en) security, surety; ɟʦ mst bail.

Kautschuk ['kautʃuk] m (-s/-e) caoutchouc, pure rubber.

Kavalier [kava'liːr] m (-s/-e) gentleman; beau, admirer.

Kavallerie ✕ [kavalə'riː] f (-/-n) cavalry, horse.

Kaviar ['kɑːviar] m (-s/-e) caviar(e).

keck adj. [kɛk] bold; impudent, saucy, cheeky; 2heit f (-/-en) boldness; impudence, sauciness, cheekiness.

Kegel ['keːgəl] m (-s/-) games: skittle, pin; esp. A, ⊕ cone; ~ schieben s. kegeln; '~bahn f skittle, alley, Am. bowling alley; 2förmig adj. ['~fœrmiç] conic(al), coniform; tapering; 2n v/i. (ge-, h) play (at) skittles or ninepins, Am. bowl.

Kegler ['keːglər] m (-s/-) skittle-player, Am. bowler.

Kehl|e ['keːlə] f (-/-n) throat; '~kopf anat. m larynx.

Kehre ['keːrə] f (-/-n) (sharp) bend, turn; 2n v/t. (ge-, h) sweep, brush; turn (nach oben upwards); j-m den Rücken ~ turn one's back on s.o.

Kehricht ['keːriçt] m, n (-[e]s/no pl.) sweepings pl., rubbish.

'**Kehrseite** f wrong side, reverse; esp. fig. seamy side.

'**kehrtmachen** v/i. (sep., -ge-, h) turn on one's heel; ✕ turn or face about.

keifen ['kaifən] v/i. (ge-, h) scold, chide.

Keil [kail] m (-[e]s/-e) wedge; gore, gusset; '~e F f (-/no pl.) thrashing, hiding; '~er zo. m (-s/-) wild-boar; ~erei F [ˌ'rai] f (-/-en) row, scrap; 2förmig adj. ['~fœrmiç] wedge-shaped, cuneiform; '~kissen n wedge-shaped bolster; '~schrift f cuneiform characters pl.

Keim [kaim] m (-[e]s/-e) ♀, biol. germ; ♀: seed-plant; shoot; sprout; fig. seeds pl., germ, bud; 2en v/i. (ge-, h) seeds, etc.: germinate; seeds, plants, potatoes, etc.: sprout; fig. b(o)urgeon; 2frei adj. sterilized, sterile; '~träger ✽ m (germ-)carrier; '~zelle f germ-cell.

kein indef. pron. [kain] as adj.: ~(e) no, not any; ~ anderer als none other but; as noun: ~er, ~e, ~(e)s none, no one, nobody; ~er von beiden neither (of the two); ~er von uns none of us; '~esfalls adv., ~eswegs adv. ['ˌ'veːks] by no means, not at all; '~mal adv. not once, not a single time.

Keks [keːks] m, n (-, -es/-, -e) biscuit, Am. cookie; cracker.

Kelch [kɛlç] m (-[e]s/-e) cup, goblet; eccl. chalice, communion-cup; ♀ calyx.

Kelle ['kɛlə] f (-/-n) scoop; ladle; tool: trowel.

Keller ['kɛlər] m (-s/-) cellar; basement; ~ei [ˌ'rai] f (-/-en) wine-vault; '~geschoß n basement; '~meister m cellarman.

Kellner ['kɛlnər] m (-s/-) waiter; '~in f (-/-nen) waitress.

Kelter ['kɛltər] f (-/-n) winepress; 2n v/t. (ge-, h) press.

kenn|en ['kɛnən] v/t. (irr., ge-, h) know, be acquainted with; have knowledge of s.th.; '~enlernen v/t. (sep., -ge-, h) get or come to know;

make *s.o.'s* acquaintance, meet *s.o.*; '2er *m* (-*s*/-) expert; connoisseur; '˷tlich *adj.* recognizable (*an dat.* by); ˷ machen mark; label; '2tnis *f* (-/-se) knowledge; ˷ nehmen von take not(ic)e of; '2zeichen *n* mark, sign; *mot.* registration (number), *Am.* license number; *fig.* hallmark, criterion; '˷zeichnen *v/t.* (ge-, h) mark, characterize.

kentern ⚓ ['kɛntərn] *v/i.* (ge-, sein) capsize, keel over, turn turtle.

Kerbe ['kɛrbə] *f* (-/-n) notch, nick; slot; '2n *v/t.* (ge-, h) notch, nick, indent.

Kerker ['kɛrkər] *m* (-*s*/-) gaol, jail, prison; '˷meister *m* gaoler, jailer.

Kerl F [kɛrl] *m* (-*s*, ⚓ -*es*/-*e*, F -*s*) man; fellow, F chap, bloke, *esp. Am.* guy.

Kern [kɛrn] *m* (-[*e*]*s*/-*e*) kernel (*of nut, etc.*); stone, *Am.* pit (*of cherry, etc.*); pip (*of orange, apple, etc.*); core (*of the earth*); *phys.* nucleus; *fig.* core, heart, crux; *Kern... s. a. Atom...*; '˷energie *f* nuclear energy; '˷forschung *f* nuclear research; '˷gehäuse *n* core; '2ge'sund *adj.* thoroughly healthy, F as sound as a bell; '2ig *adj.* full of pips; *fig.*: pithy; solid; '˷punkt *m* central *or* crucial point; '˷spaltung *f* nuclear fission.

Kerze ['kɛrtsə] *f* (-/-n) candle; '˷n-licht *n* candle-light; '˷nstärke *f* candle-power.

keß F *adj.* [kɛs] pert, jaunty; smart.

Kessel ['kɛsəl] *m* (-*s*/-) kettle; cauldron; boiler; hollow.

Kette ['kɛtə] *f* (-/-n) chain; range (*of mountains, etc.*); necklace; '2n *v/t.* (ge-, h) chain (*an acc.* to).

'Ketten|hund *m* watch-dog; '˷rau-cher *m* chain-smoker; '˷reaktion *f* chain reaction.

Ketzer ['kɛtsər] *m* (-*s*/-) heretic; ˷ei [˷'raɪ] *f* (-/-en) heresy; 2isch *adj.* heretical.

keuch|en ['kɔʏçən] *v/i.* (ge-, h) pant, gasp; '2husten ♣ *m* (w)hooping cough.

Keule ['kɔʏlə] *f* (-/-n) club; leg (*of mutton, pork, etc.*).

keusch *adj.* [kɔʏʃ] chaste, pure; '2heit *f* (-/no *pl.*) chastity, purity.

kichern ['kiçərn] *v/i.* (ge-, h) giggle, titter.

Kiebitz ['ki:bits] *m* (-*es*/-*e*) *orn.* pe(e)wit; F *fig.* kibitzer; '2en F *fig. v/i.* (ge-, h) kibitz.

Kiefer ['ki:fər] 1. *anat. m* (-*s*/-) jaw(-bone); 2. ♀ *f* (-/-n) pine.

Kiel [ki:l] *m* (-[*e*]*s*/-*e*) ⚓ keel; quill; '˷raum *m* bilge, hold; '˷wasser *n* wake (*a. fig.*).

Kieme *zo.* ['ki:mə] *f* (-/-n) gill.

Kies [ki:s] *m* (-*es*/-*e*) gravel; *sl. fig.* dough; '˷el ['˷zəl] *m* (-*s*/-) pebble, flint; '˷weg *m* gravel-walk.

Kilo ['ki:lo] *n* (-*s*/-[*s*]), '˷gramm [kilo'gram] *n* kilogram(me); '˷hertz ['˷hɛrts] *n* (-/no *pl.*) kilocycle per second; '˷meter *m* kilomet|re, *Am.* -er; '˷watt *n* kilowatt.

Kimme ['kimə] *f* (-/-n) notch.

Kind [kint] *n* (-[*e*]*s*/-*er*) child; baby. 'Kinder|arzt *m* p(a)ediatrician; '˷ei [˷'raɪ] *f* (-/-en) childishness; childish trick; trifle; '˷frau *f* nurse; '˷fräulein *n* governess; '˷funk *m* children's program(me); '˷garten *m* kindergarten, nursery school; '˷lähmung ♣ *f* infantile paralysis, polio(myelitis); 2'leicht *adj.* very easy *or* simple, F as easy as winking *or* as ABC; '˷lied *n* children's song; '2los *adj.* childless; '˷mäd-chen *n* nurse(maid); '˷spiel *n* children's game; *ein* ˷ *s. kinderleicht*; '˷stube *f* nursery; *fig.* manners *pl.*, upbringing; '˷wagen *m* perambulator, F pram, *Am.* baby carriage; '˷zeit *f* childhood; '˷zimmer *n* children's room.

'Kindes|alter *n* childhood, infancy; '˷beine *n/pl.*: *von* ˷ *an* from childhood, from a very early age; '˷kind *n* grandchild.

'Kind|heit *f* (-/no *pl.*) childhood; 2isch *adj.* ['˷dɪʃ] childish; '2lich *adj.* childlike.

Kinn *anat.* [kin] *n* (-[*e*]*s*/-*e*) chin; '˷backe *f*, '˷backen *m* (-*s*/-) jaw(-bone); '˷haken *m boxing*: hook to the chin; uppercut; '˷lade *f* jaw(-bone).

Kino ['ki:no] *n* (-*s*/-*s*) cinema, F *the* pictures *pl.*, *Am.* motion-picture theater, F *the* movies *pl.*; *ins* ˷ *gehen* go to the cinema *or* F pictures, *Am.* F go to the movies; '˷besu-cher *m* cinema-goer, *Am.* F moviegoer; '˷vorstellung *f* cinema-show, *Am.* motion-picture show.

Kippe F ['kipə] *f* (-/-n) stub, fag-end, *Am. a.* butt; *auf der* ˷ *stehen or sein* hang in the balance; '2n (ge-) 1. *v/i.* (sein) tip (over), topple (over), tilt (over); 2. *v/t.* (h) tilt, tip over *or* up.

Kirche ['kirçə] *f* (-/-n) church. 'Kirchen|älteste *m* (-*n*/-*n*) church-warden, elder; '˷buch *n* parochial register; '˷diener *m* sacristan, sexton; '˷gemeinde *f* parish; '˷jahr *n* ecclesiastical year; '˷lied *n* hymn; '˷musik *f* sacred music; '˷schiff △ *n* nave; '˷steuer *f* church-rate; '˷stuhl *m* pew; '˷vor-steher *m* churchwarden.

'Kirch|gang *m* church-going; '˷gän-ger ['˷gɛŋər] *m* (-*s*/-) church-goer; '˷hof *m* churchyard; '2lich *adj.* ecclesiastical; '˷spiel *n* parish; '˷turm *m* steeple; '˷weih ['˷vaɪ] *f* (-/-en) parish fair.

Kirsche ['kirʃə] *f* (-/-n) cherry.

Kissen ['kisən] n (-s/-) cushion; pillow; bolster, pad.

Kiste ['kistə] f (-/-n) box, chest; crate.

Kitsch [kitʃ] m (-es/no pl.) trash, rubbish; '2ig adj. shoddy, trashy.

Kitt [kit] m (-[e]s/-e) cement; putty.

Kittel ['kitəl] m (-s/-) overall; smock, frock.

'kitten v/t. (ge-, h) cement; putt.

kitz|cln ['kitsəln] (ge-, h) 1. v/t. tickle; 2. v/i.: meine Nase kitzelt my nose is tickling; '~lig adj. ticklish (a. fig.).

Kladde ['kladə] f (-/-n) rough note-book, waste-book.

klaffen ['klafən] v/i. (ge-, h) gape, yawn.

kläffen ['klefən] v/i. (ge-, h) yap, yelp.

klagbar ʒ̇ʒ̇ adj. ['klɑːkbɑːr] matter, etc.: actionable; debt, etc.: suable.

Klage ['klɑːgə] f (-/-n) complaint; lament; ʒ̇ʒ̇ action, suit; '2n (ge-, h) 1. v/i. complain (über acc. of, about; bei to); lament; ʒ̇ʒ̇ take legal action (gegen against); 2. v/t.: j-m et. ~ complain to s.o. of or about s.th.

Kläger ʒ̇ʒ̇ ['klɛːgər] m (-s/-) plaintiff; complainant.

kläglich adj. ['klɛːkliç] pitiful, piteous, pitiable; cries, etc.: plaintive; condition: wretched, lamentable; performance, result, etc.: miserable, poor; failure, etc.: lamentable, miserable.

klamm [klam] 1. adj. hands, etc.: numb or stiff with cold, clammy; 2. 2 f (-/-en) ravine, gorge, canyon.

Klammer ['klamər] f (-/-n) ⊕ clamp, cramp; (paper-)clip; gr., typ., ⅃ bracket, parenthesis; '2n (ge-, h) 1. v/t. clip together; ʒ̇ʒ̇ close (wound) with clips; sich ~ an (acc.) cling to (a. fig.); 2. v/i. boxing: clinch.

Klang [klaŋ] 1. m (-[e]s/ᵘe) sound, tone (of voice, instrument, etc.); tone (of radio, etc.); clink (of glasses, etc.); ringing (of bells, etc.); timbre; 2. 2 pret. of klingen; '~fülle ⅃ f sonority; '2los adj. toneless; '2voll adj. sonorous.

Klappe ['klapə] f (-/-n) flap; flap, drop leaf (of table, etc.); shoulder strap (of uniform, etc.); tailboard (of lorry, etc.); ⊕, ⚓, anat. valve; ⅃ key; F fig.: bed; trap; '2n (ge-, h) 1. v/t.: nach oben ~ tip up; nach unten ~ lower, put down; 2. v/i. clap, flap; fig. come off well, work out fine, Am. sl. a. click.

Klapper ['klapər] f (-/-n) rattle; '2ig adj. vehicle, etc.: rattly, ramshackle; furniture: rickety; person, horse, etc.: decrepit; '~kasten F m wretched piano; rattletrap; '2n (ge-, h) clatter, rattle (mit et. s.th.); er klapperte vor Kälte mit den Zäh-

---

nen his teeth were chattering with cold; '~schlange zo. f rattlesnake, Am. a. rattler.

'Klapp|kamera phot. f folding camera; '~messer n clasp-knife, jack-knife; '~sitz m tip-up or flap seat; '~stuhl m folding chair; '~tisch m folding table, Am. a. gate-leg(ged) table; '~ult f (klap-pult] n folding desk.

Klaps [klaps] m (-es/-e) smack, slap; '2en v/t. (ge-, h) smack, slap.

klar adj. [klɑːr] clear; bright; transparent, limpid; pure; fig.: clear, distinct; plain; evident, obvious; sich ~ sein über (acc.) be clear about; ~en Kopf bewahren keep a clear head.

klären ['klɛːrən] v/t. (ge-, h) clarify; fig. clarify, clear up, elucidate.

'klar|legen v/t. (sep., -ge-, h), '~stellen v/t. (sep., -ge-, h) clear up.

'Klärung f (-/-en) clarification; fig. a. elucidation.

Klasse ['klasə] f (-/-n) class, category; school: class, form, Am. a. grade; (social) class.

'Klassen|arbeit f (test) paper; '2be-wußt adj. class-conscious; '~be-wußtsein n class-consciousness; '~buch n class-book; '~haß m class-hatred; '~kamerad m classmate; '~kampf m class-war(fare); '~zim-mer n classroom, schoolroom.

klassifizier|en [klasifi'tsiːrən] v/t. (no -ge-, h) classify; 2ung f (-/-en) classification.

Klass|iker ['klasikər] m (-s/-) classic; '2isch adj. classic(al).

klatsch [klatʃ] 1. int. smack!, slap!; 2. 2 m (-es/-e) smack, slap; F fig.: gossip; scandal; '2base ['~bɑːzə] f (-/-n) gossip; '2e f (-/-n) fly-flap; '~en (ge-, h) 1. v/t. fling, hurl; Bei-fall ~ clap, applaud (j-m s.o.) 2. v/i. splash; applaud, clap; F fig. gossip; '~haft adj. gossiping, gossipy; '2maul F n s. Klatschbase; '~naß F adj. soaking wet.

Klaue ['klauə] f (-/-n) claw; paw; fig. clutch.

Klause ['klauzə] f (-/-n) hermitage; cell.

Klausel ʒ̇ʒ̇ ['klauzəl] f (-/-n) clause; proviso; stipulation.

Klaviatur ⅃ [klavja'tuːr] f (-/-en) keyboard, keys pl.

Klavier ⅃ [kla'viːr] n (-s/-e) piano (-forte); '~konzert n piano concert or recital; '~lehrer m piano teacher; '~sessel m music-stool; '~stimmer m (-s/-) piano-tuner; '~stunde f piano-lesson.

kleb|en ['kleːbən] (ge-, h) 1. v/t. glue, paste, stick; 2. v/i. stick, adhere (an dat. to); '~end adj. adhesive; '2epflaster n adhesive or sticking plaster; '~rig adj. adhesive, sticky; '2stoff m adhesive; glue.

Klecks [klɛks] *m* (-es/-e) blot (*of ink*); mark (*of dirt, grease, paint, etc.*); spot (*of grease, paint, etc.*); stain (*of wine, coffee, etc.*); '₂en (ge-) 1. *v/i.* (*h*) make a mark *or* spot *or* stain; 2. *v/i.* (*sein*) *ink, etc.*: blot (down); 3. *v/t.* (*h*): et. auf et. ~ splash *or* spill s.th. on s.th.

Klee ⚘ [kle:] *m* (-s/*no pl.*) clover, trefoil.

Kleid [klart] *n* (-[e]s/-er) garment; dress, frock; gown; ~er *pl.* clothes *pl.*; '₂en [~dən] *v/t.* (ge-, *h*) dress, clothe; *sich* ~ dress (o.s.); j-n gut ~ suit *or* become s.o.

Kleider|ablage ['klaɪdər-] *f* cloak-room, *Am. a.* checkroom; '~bügel *m* coat-hanger; '~bürste *f* clothes-brush; '~haken *m* clothes-peg; '~schrank *m* wardrobe; '~ständer *m* hat and coat stand; '~stoff *m* dress material.

'kleidsam *adj.* becoming.

Kleidung ['klaɪduŋ] *f* (-/-en) clothes *pl.*, clothing; dress; '~sstück *n* piece *or* article of clothing; garment.

Kleie ['klaɪə] *f* (-/-n) bran.

klein [klaɪn] 1. *adj.* little (*only attr.*), small; *fig. a.* trifling, petty; 2. *adv.*: ~ schreiben write with a small (initial) letter; ~ anfangen start in a small *or* modest way; 3. *noun*: von ~ auf from an early age; '₂auto *n* baby *or* small car; '₂bahn *f* narrow-ga(u)ge railway; '₂bildkamera *f* miniature camera; '₂geld *n* (small) change; ~gläubig *adj.* of little faith; '₂handel ⚘ *m* retail trade; '₂händler *m* retailer; '₂heit *f* (-/*no pl.*) smallness, small size; '₂holz *n* firewood, matchwood, kindling.

'Kleinigkeit *f* (-/-en) trifle, triviality; '~skrämer *m* pettifogger.

'Klein|kind *n* infant; '₂laut *adj.* subdued; '₂lich *adj.* paltry; pedantic, fussy; '~mut *m* pusillanimity; despondency; '₂mütig *adj.* ['~my:tiç] pusillanimous; despondent; '₂schneiden *v/t.* (*irr. schneiden, sep., -ge-, h*) cut into small pieces; '~staat *m* small *or* minor state; '~stadt *f* small town; '~städter *m* small-town dweller, *Am. a.* small-towner; '₂städtisch *adj.* small-town, provincial; '~vieh *n* small livestock.

Kleister ['klaɪstər] *m* (-s/-) paste; '₂n *v/t.* (ge-, *h*) paste.

Klemm|e ['klɛmə] *f* (-/-n) ⊕ clamp; ⚡ terminal; F in der ~ sitzen be in a cleft stick, F be in a jam; '₂en *v/t.* (ge-, *h*) jam, squeeze, pinch; '~er *m* (-s/-) pince-nez; '~schraube ⊕ *f* set screw.

Klempner ['klɛmpnər] *m* (-s/-) tin-man, tin-smith, *Am. a.* tinner; plumber.

Klerus ['kle:rus] *m* (-/*no pl.*) clergy.

Klette ['klɛtə] *f* (-/-n) ⚘ bur(r); *fig. a.* leech.

Kletter|er ['klɛtərər] *m* (-s/-) climber; '₂n *v/i.* (ge-, *sein*) climb, clamber (*auf e-n Baum* [up] *a tree*); '~pflanze *f* climber, creeper.

Klient [kli'ɛnt] *m* (-en/-en) client.

Klima ['kli:ma] *n* (-s/-s, -te) climate; *fig. a.* atmosphere; '~anlage *f* air-conditioning plant; ₂tisch *adj.* [~'ma:tiʃ] climatic.

klimpern ['klɪmpərn] *v/i.* (ge-, *h*) jingle, chink (*mit* et. s.th.); F strum *or* tinkle away (*auf acc.* on, at *piano, guitar*).

Klinge ['klɪŋə] *f* (-/-n) blade.

Klingel ['klɪŋəl] *f* (-/-n) bell, hand-bell; '~knopf *m* bell-push; '₂n *v/i.* (ge-, *h*) ring (the bell); doorbell, *etc.*: ring; es *klingelt* the doorbell is ringing; '~zug *m* bell-pull.

klingen ['klɪŋən] *v/i.* (*irr., ge-, h*) sound; bell, metal, *etc.*: ring; glasses, *etc.*: clink; *musical instrument*: speak.

Klini|k ['kli:nɪk] *f* (-/-en) nursing home; private hospital; clinic(al hospital); '₂sch *adj.* clinical.

Klinke ['klɪŋkə] *f* (-/-n) latch; (door-) handle.

Klippe ['klɪpə] *f* (-/-n) cliff; reef; crag; rock; *fig.* rock, hurdle.

klirren ['klɪrən] *v/i.* (ge-, *h*) *window-pane, chain, etc.*: rattle; *chain, swords, etc.*: clank, jangle; *keys, spurs, etc.*: jingle; *glasses, etc.*: clink, chink; *pots, etc.*: clatter; ~ mit rattle, jingle

Klistier ⚕ [klɪ'sti:r] *n* (-s/-e) enema.

Kloake [klo'a:kə] *f* (-/-n) sewer, cesspool (*a. fig.*).

Klob|en ['klo:bən] *m* (-s/-) ⊕ pulley, block; log; '₂ig *adj.* clumsy (*a. fig.*).

klopfen ['klɔpfən] (ge-, *h*) 1. *v/i.* heart, pulse: beat, throb; knock (*at door, etc.*); tap (*on shoulder*); pat (*on cheek*); es *klopft* there's a knock at the door; 2. *v/t.* knock, drive (*nail, etc.*).

Klöppel ['klœpəl] *m* (-s/-) clapper (*of bell*); lacemaking: bobbin; beetle; '~spitze *f* pillow-lace, bone-lace.

Klops [klɔps] *m* (-es/-e) meat ball.

Klosett [klo'zɛt] *n* (-s/-e, -s) lavatory, (water-)closet, W.C., toilet; '~papier *n* toilet-paper.

Kloß [klo:s] *m* (-es/⸚e) earth, clay, *etc.*: clod, lump; *cookery*: dumpling.

Kloster ['klo:stər] *n* (-s/⸚) cloister; monastery; convent, nunnery; '~bruder *m* friar; '~frau *f* nun; '~gelübde *n* monastic vow.

Klotz [klɔts] *m* (-es/⸚e) block, log (*a. fig.*).

Klub [klup] *m* (-s/-s) club; '~kamerad *m* clubmate; '~sessel *m* lounge-chair.

Kluft [kluft] *f* 1. (-/⸚e) gap (*a. fig.*),

crack; cleft; gulf, chasm (*both a. fig.*); 2. F (-/-en) outfit, F togs *pl.*; uniform.

klug *adj.* [klu:k] clever; wise, intelligent, sensible; prudent; shrewd; cunning; '2heit *f* (-/*no pl.*) cleverness; intelligence; prudence; shrewdness; good sense.

Klump|en ['klumpən] *m* (-s/-) lump (*of earth, dough, etc.*); clod (*of earth, etc.*); nugget (*of gold, etc.*); heap; '~fuß *m* club-foot; '2ig *adj.* lumpy; cloddish.

knabbern ['knabərn] (ge-, h) 1. *v/t.* nibble, gnaw; 2. *v/i.* nibble, gnaw (*an dat.* at).

Knabe ['kna:bə] *m* (-n/-n) boy; lad; F alter ~ F old chap.

'**Knaben|alter** *n* boyhood; '~chor *m* boys' choir; '2haft *adj.* boyish.

Knack [knak] *m* (-[e]s/-e) crack, snap, click; '2en (ge-, h) 1. *v/i. wood:* crack; *fire:* crackle; click; 2. *v/t.* crack (*nut, etc.*); F crack open (*safe*); e-e harte Nuß zu ~ haben have a hard nut to crack; ~s [~s] *m* (-es/-e) *s.* Knack; F *fig.* defect; '2sen *v/i.* (ge-, h) *s.* knacken 1.

Knall [knal] *m* (-[e]s/-e) crack, bang (*of shot*); bang (*of explosion*); crack (*of rifle or whip*); report (*of gun*); detonation, explosion, report; '~bonbon *m, n* cracker; '~effekt *fig. m* sensation; '2en *v/i.* (ge-, h) *rifle, whip:* crack; *fireworks, door, etc.:* bang; *gun:* fire; *cork, etc.:* pop; *explosive, etc.:* detonate.

knapp *adj.* [knap] *clothes:* tight, close-fitting; *rations, etc.:* scanty, scarce; *style, etc.:* concise; *lead, victory, etc.:* narrow; *majority, etc.:* bare; mit ~er Not entrinnen have a narrow escape; ~ werden run short; '2e ⚒ *m* (-n/-n) miner; '~halten *v/t.* (*irr. halten, sep., -ge-, h*) keep *s.o.* short; '2heit *f* (-/*no pl.*) scarcity, shortage; conciseness; '~schaft ⚒ *f* (-/-en) miners' society.

Knarre ['knarə] *f* (-/-n) rattle; F rifle, gun; '2n *v/i.* (ge-, h) creak; *voice:* grate.

knattern ['knatərn] *v/i.* (ge-, h) crackle; *machine-gun, etc.:* rattle; *mot.* roar.

Knäuel ['knɔʏəl] *m, n* (-s/-) clew, ball; *fig.* bunch, cluster.

Knauf [knauf] *m* (-[e]s/⸗e) knob; pommel (*of sword*).

Knauser ['knauzər] *m* (-s/-) niggard, miser, skinflint; ~ei [~'raɪ] *f* (-/-en) niggardliness, miserliness; '2ig *adj.* niggardly, stingy; '2n *v/i.* (ge-, h) be stingy.

Knebel ['kne:bəl] *m* (-s/-) gag; '2n *v/t.* (ge-, h) gag; *fig.* muzzle (*press*).

Knecht [knɛçt] *m* (-[e]s/-e) servant; farm-labo(u)rer, farm-hand; slave; '2en *v/t.* (ge-, h) enslave; tyrannize;

subjugate; '~schaft *f* (-/*no pl.*) servitude, slavery.

kneif|en ['knaɪfən] (*irr.*, ge-, h) 1. *v/t.* pinch, nip; 2. *v/i.* pinch; F *fig.* back out, *Am.* F *a.* crawfish; '2er *m* (-s/-) pince-nez; '2zange *f* (e-e a pair of) pincers *pl. or* nippers *pl.*

Kneipe ['knaɪpə] *f* (-/-n) public house, tavern, F pub, *Am. a.* saloon; '2n *v/i.* (ge-, h) carouse, tipple, F booze; '~rei *f* (-/-en) drinking-bout, carousal.

kneten ['kne:tən] *v/t.* (ge-, h) knead (*dough, etc.*); 🖑 *a.* massage (*limb, etc.*).

Knick [knik] *m* (-[e]s/-e) *wall, etc.:* crack; *paper, etc.:* fold, crease; *path, etc.:* bend; '2en *v/t.* (ge-, h) fold, crease; bend; break.

Knicker F ['knikər] *m* (-s/-) *s.* Knauser.

Knicks [kniks] *m* (-es/-e) curts(e)y; e-n ~ machen = '2en *v/i.* (ge-, h) (drop a) curts(e)y (*vor dat.* to).

Knie [kni:] *n* (-s/-) knee; '2fällig *adv.* on one's knees; '~kehle *anat.* *f* hollow of the knee; '2n *v/i.* (ge-, h) kneel, be on one's knees; '~scheibe *anat.* *f* knee-cap, knee-pan; '~strumpf *m* knee-length sock.

Kniff [knif] 1. *m* (-[e]s/-e) crease, fold; *fig.* trick, knack; 2. 2 *pret. of* kneifen; 2(e)lig *adj.* ['~(ə)liç] tricky; intricate.

knipsen ['knipsən] (ge-, h) 1. *v/t.* clip, punch (*ticket, etc.*); F *phot.* take a snapshot of, snap; 2. F *phot. v/i.* take snapshots.

Knirps [knirps] *m* (-es/-e) little man; little chap, F nipper; '2ig *adj.* very small.

knirschen ['knirʃən] *v/i.* (ge-, h) *gravel, snow, etc.:* crunch, grind; *teeth, etc.:* grate; mit den Zähnen ~ grind *or* gnash one's teeth.

knistern ['knistərn] *v/i.* (ge-, h) *woodfire, etc.:* crackle; *dry leaves, silk, etc.:* rustle.

knitter|frei *adj.* ['knitər-] crease-resistant; '2n *v/t. and v/i.* (ge-, h) crease, wrinkle.

Knoblauch 🌿 ['kno:plaux] *m* (-[e]s/*no pl.*) garlic.

Knöchel *anat.* ['knœçəl] *m* (-s/-) knuckle; ankle.

Knoch|en *anat.* ['knɔxən] *m* (-s/-) bone; '~enbruch *m* fracture (of a bone); '2ig *adj.* bony.

Knödel ['knø:dəl] *m* (-s/-) dumpling.

Knolle 🌿 ['knɔlə] *f* (-/-n) tuber; bulb.

Knopf [knɔpf] *m* (-[e]s/⸗e) button; **knöpfen** ['knœpfən] *v/t.* (ge-, h) button.

'**Knopfloch** *n* buttonhole.

Knorpel ['knɔrpəl] *m* (-s/-) cartilage, gristle.

Knorr|en ['knɔrən] *m* (-s/-) knot,

knag, gnarl; '2ig adj. gnarled, knotty.

Knospe ♀ ['knɔspə] f (-/-n) bud; '2n v/i. (ge-, h) (be in) bud.

Knot|en ['knoːtən] 1. m (-s/-) knot (a. fig., ⚓); 2. ♀ v/t. (ge-, h) knot; '‿enpunkt m ⚙ junction; intersection; '2ig adj. knotty.

Knuff F [knuf] m (-[e]s/ᵘe) poke, cuff, nudge; '2en F v/t. (ge-, h) poke, cuff, nudge.

knülle|n ['knylən] v/t. and v/i. (ge-, h) crease, crumple; '2r F m (-s/-) hit.

knüpfen ['knypfən] v/t. (ge-, h) make, tie (knot, etc.); make (net); knot (carpet, etc.); tie (shoe-lace, etc.); strike up (friendship, etc.); attach (condition, etc.) (an acc. to).

Knüppel ['knypəl] m (-s/-) cudgel.

knurren ['knurən] v/i. (ge-, h) growl, snarl; fig. grumble (über acc. at, over about); stomach: rumble.

knusp(e)rig adj. ['knusp(ə)riç] crisp, crunchy

Knute ['knuːtə] f (-/-n) knout.

Knüttel ['knytəl] m (-s/-) cudgel.

Kobold ['koːbɔlt] m (-[e]s/-e) (hob)goblin, imp

Koch [kɔx] m (-[e]s/ᵘe) cook; '‿buch n cookery-book, Am. cookbook; '2en (ge-, h) 1. v/t. boil (water, egg, fish, etc.); cook (meat, vegetables, etc.) (by boiling); make (coffee, tea, etc.); 2. v/i. water, etc.: boil (a. fig.); do the cooking; be a (good, etc.) cook; ‿er m (-s/-) cooker.

Köcher ['kœçər] m (-s/-) quiver.

'Koch|kiste f haybox; '‿löffel m wooden spoon; '‿nische f kitchenette; '‿salz n common salt; '‿topf m pot, saucepan.

Köder ['køːdər] m (-s/-) bait (a. fig.); lure (a fig.); '2n v/t. (ge-, h) bait; lure; fig a decoy.

Kodex ['koːdɛks] m (-es, -/-e, Kodizes) code

Koffer ['kɔfər] m (-s/-) (suit)case; trunk; '‿radio n portable radio (set).

Kognak ['kɔnjak] m (-s/-s, ⚔-e) French brandy, cognac.

Kohl ♀ [koːl] m (-[e]s/-e) cabbage.

Kohle ['koːlə] f (-/-n) coal; charcoal; ∉ carbon; wie auf (glühenden) ‿n sitzer be on tenterhooks.

'Kohlen|bergwerk n coal-mine, coal-pit, colliery; '‿eimer m coal-scuttle; '‿händler m coal-merchant; '‿kasten m coal-box; '‿revier ⚒ n coal-district; '‿säure ⚗ f carbonic acid; '‿stoff ⚗ m carbon

'Kohle|papier n carbon paper; '‿zeichnung f charcoal-drawing.

'Kohl|kopf ♀ m (head of) cabbage; '‿rübe ♀ f Swedish turnip.

Koje ⚓ ['koːjə] f (-/-n) berth, bunk.

Kokain [koka'iːn] n (-s/no pl.) cocaine, sl. coke, snow.

kokett adj. [ko'kɛt] coquettish; 2erie [‿ə'riː] f (-/-n) coquetry, coquettishness; ‿ieren [‿'tiːrən] v/i. (no -ge-, h) coquet, flirt (mit with; a. fig.).

Kokosnuß ♀ ['koːkɔs-] f coconut.

Koks [koːks] m (-es/-e) coke.

Kolben ['kɔlbən] m (-s/-) butt (of rifle); ⊕ piston; '‿stange f piston-rod.

Kolchose [kɔl'çoːzə] f (-/-n) collective farm, kolkhoz.

Kolleg univ [kɔ'leːk] n (-s/-s, -ien) course of lectures; '‿e m (-n/-n) colleague; '‿ium [‿gjum] n (-s/Kollegien) council, board; teaching staff.

Kollekt|e eccl. [kɔ'lɛktə] f (-/-n) collection; '‿ion ✝ [‿'tsjoːn] f (-/-en) collection, range.

Koller ['kɔlər] m (-s/-) vet. staggers pl.; F fig. rage, tantrum; '2n v/i. 1. (h) turkey-cock gobble; pigeon: coo; bowels rumble; vet. have the staggers; 2. (sein) ball, tears, etc.: roll.

kolli|dieren [kɔli'diːrən] v/i. (no -ge-, sein) collide; fig. clash; 2sion [‿'zjoːn] f (-/-en) collision; fig. clash, conflict.

Kölnischwasser ['kœlnɪ∫-] n eau-de-Cologne.

Kolonialwaren [kolo'njaːl-] f/pl. groceries pl, ‿händler m grocer; ‿handlung f grocer's (shop), Am. grocery

Kolon|ie [kolo'niː] f (-/-n) colony; 2isieren [‿i'ziːrən] v/t. (no -ge-, h) colonize

Kolonne [ko'lɔnə] f (-/-n) column; convoy; gang (of workers, etc.).

kolorieren [kolo'riːrən] v/t. (no -ge-, h) colo(u)r.

Kolo|ß [kɔ lɔs] m (Kolosses/Kolosse) colossus; 2ssal adj. [‿'saːl] colossal, huge (both a fig.).

Kombin|ation [kɔmbina'tsjoːn] f (-/-en) combination; overall; ✈ flying-suit; football, etc.: combined attack; 2ieren [‿'niːrən] (no -ge-, h) 1. v/t. combine; 2. v/i. reason, deduce; football, etc.: combine, move.

Kombüse ⚓ [kɔm'byːzə] f (-/-n) galley, caboose.

Komet ast. [ko'meːt] m (-en/-en) comet.

Komfort [kɔm'foːr] m (-s/no pl.) comfort, 2abel adj. [‿r'taːbəl] comfortable.

Komik ['koːmik] f (-/no pl.) humo(u)r, fun(niness); '‿er m (-s/-) comic actor, comedian.

komisch adj. ['koːmi∫] comic(al), funny; fig. funny, odd, queer.

Komitee [komi'teː] n (-s/-s) committee.

Kommand|ant ✕ [kɔman'dant] *m* (-en/-en), **~eur** ✕ [~'døːr] *m* (-s/-e) commander, commanding officer; **2ieren** [~'diːrən] (*no* -ge-, *h*) **1.** *v/i.* order, command, be in command; **2.** *v/t.* ✕ command, be in command of; order; **~itgesellschaft** ✝ [~'ditː-] *f* limited partnership; **~o** [~'mando] *n* (-s/-s) ✕ command, order; order(s *pl.*), directive(s *pl.*); ✕ detachment; **~obrücke** ⚓ *f* navigating bridge.

kommen ['kɔmən] *v/i.* (*irr.*, ge-, sein) come; arrive; **~ lassen** send for *s.o.*, order *s.th.*; *et.* **~ sehen** foresee; *an die Reihe* **~** it is one's turn; **~ auf** (*acc.*) think of, hit upon; remember; *zu dem Schluß* **~**, *daß* decide that; *hinter et.* **~** find *s.th.* out; *um et.* **~** lose *s.th.*; *zu et.* **~** come by *s.th.*; *wieder zu sich* **~** come round *or* to; *wie Sie dazu!* how dare you!

Komment|ar [kɔmɛn'taːr] *m* (-s/-e) commentary, comment; **~ator** [~tɔr] *m* (-s/-en) commentator; **2ieren** [~'tiːrən] *v/t.* (*no* -ge-, *h*) comment on

Kommissar [kɔmi'saːr] *m* (-s/-e) commissioner; superintendent; *pol.* commissar

Kommißbrot F [kɔ'mis-] *n* army *or* ration bread, *Am a.* G.I. bread.

Kommission [kɔmi'sjoːn] *f* (-/-en) commission (*a* ✝); committee; **~är** ✝ [~o'nɛːr] *m* (-s/-e) commission agent

Kommode [kɔ'moːdə] *f* (-/-n) chest of drawers, *Am* bureau.

Kommunis|mus *pol.* [kɔmu'nismus] *m* (-/*no pl*) communism; **~t** *m* (-en/-en) communist; **2tisch** *adj.* communist(ic)

Komöd|iant [kømø'djant] *m* (-en/-en) comedian, *fig* play-actor; **~ie** [~'møːdjə] *f* (-/-n) comedy; **~ spielen** play-act

Kompagnon ✝ [kɔmpan'jõː] *m* (-s/-s) (business-)partner, associate.

Kompanie ✕ [kɔmpa'niː] *f* (-/-n) company

Kompaß ['kɔmpas] *m* (Kompasses/Kompasse) compass.

kompetent *adj.* [kɔmpe'tɛnt] competent

komplett *adj.* [kɔm'plɛt] complete.

Komplex [kɔm'plɛks] *m* (-es/-e) complex (*a. psych.*); block (*of houses*).

Kompliment [kɔmpli'mɛnt] *n* (-[e]s/-e) compliment.

Komplize [kɔm'pliːtsə] *m* (-n/-n) accomplice

komplizier|en [kɔmpli'tsiːrən] *v/t.* (*no* -ge-, *h*) complicate; **~t** *adj.* machine, etc. complicated; *argument, situation, etc.* complex; **~er Bruch** ✂ compound fracture.

Komplott [kɔm'plɔt] *n* (-[e]s/-e) plot, conspiracy.

kompo|nieren ♪ [kɔmpo'niːrən] *v/t. and v/i.* (*no* -ge-, *h*) compose; **2nist** *m* (-en/-en) composer; **2sition** [~zi'tsjoːn] *f* (-/-en) composition.

Kompott [kɔm'pɔt] *n* (-[e]s/-e) compote, stewed fruit, *Am. a.* sauce.

komprimieren [kɔmpri'miːrən] *v/t.* (*no* -ge-, *h*) compress.

Kompromi|ß [kɔmpro'mis] *m* (Kompromisses/Kompromisse) compromise, ♪Blos *adj.* uncompromising; **2ttieren** [~'tiːrən] *v/t.* (*no* -ge-, *h*) compromise

Kondens|ator [kɔndɛn'zaːtɔr] *m* (-s/-en) ⚡ capacitor, condenser (*a.* 📷); **2ieren** [~'ziːrən] *v/t.* (*no* -ge-, *h*) condense

Kondens|milch [kɔn'dɛns-] *f* evaporated milk, **~streifen** ✈ *m* condensation *or* vapo(u)r trail; **~wasser** *n* water of condensation.

Konditor [kɔn'diːtɔr] *m* (-s/-en) confectioner, pastry-cook; **~ei** [~to'raɪ] *f* (-/-en) confectionery, confectioner's (shop); **~elwaren** *f/pl.* confectionery

Konfekt [kɔn'fɛkt] *n* (-[e]s/-e) sweets *pl.*, sweetmeat, *Am. a.* soft candy; chocolates *pl*

Konfektion [kɔnfɛk'tsjoːn] *f* (-/-en) (manufacture of) ready-made clothing; **~sanzug** [kɔnfɛk'tsjoːns-] *m* ready-made suit, **~sgeschäft** *n* ready-made clothes shop.

Konfer|enz [kɔnfe'rɛnts] *f* (-/-en) conference. **2ieren** [~'riːrən] *v/i.* (*no* -ge-, *h*) confer (*uber acc.* on).

Konfession [kɔnfe'sjoːn] *f* (-/-en) confession, creed, denomination; **2ell** *adj.* [~o'nɛl] confessional, denominational, **~sschule** [~'sjoːns-] *f* denominational school

Konfirm|and *eccl.* [kɔnfir'mant] *m* (-en/-en) candidate for confirmation, confirmee, **~ation** [~'tsjoːn] *f* (-/-en) confirmation; **2ieren** [~'miːrən] *v/t.* (*no* -ge-, *h*) confirm.

konfiszieren ⚖ [kɔnfis'tsiːrən] *v/t.* (*no* -ge-, *h*) confiscate, seize.

Konfitüre [kɔnfi'tyːrə] *f* (-/-n) preserve(s *pl.*), (whole-fruit) jam.

Konflikt [kɔn'flikt] *m* (-[e]s/-e) conflict.

konform *adv.* [kɔn'fɔrm]: **~ gehen** *mit* agree *or* concur with.

konfrontieren [kɔnfrɔn'tiːrən] *v/t.* (*no* -ge-, *h*) confront (*mit* with).

konfus *adj.* [kɔn'fuːs] *p., a. ideas:* muddled; *j* muddle-headed.

Kongreß [kɔn'grɛs] *m* (Kongresses/Kongresse) congress; *Am. parl.* Congress, **~halle** *f* congress hall.

König ['køːnɪç] *m* (-s/-e) king; **2lich** *adj.* ['~k-] royal; regal; **~reich** ['~k-] *n* kingdom; **~swürde** ['~ks-] *f* royal dignity, kingship; **~tum** *n* (-s/~er) monarchy; kingship.

Konjug|ation *gr.* [kɔnjuga'tsjoːn] *f*

(-/-en); 2ieren [~'giːrən] v/t. (no -ge-, h) conjugate.

Konjunkt|iv gr. ['kɔnjuŋktiːf] m (-s/-e) subjunctive (mood); ~ur † [~'tuːr] f (-/-en) trade or business cycle; economic or business situation.

konkret adj. [kɔn'kreːt] concrete.

Konkurrent [kɔnku'rɛnt] m (-en/-en) competitor, rival.

Konkurrenz [kɔnku'rɛnts] f (-/-en) competition; competitors pl., rivals pl.; sports: event; 2fähig adj. able to compete; competitive; ~geschäft n rival business or firm; ~kampf m competition.

konkur'rieren v/i. (no -ge-, h) compete (mit with; um for).

Konkurs †, ʀ̃ʀ̃ [kɔn'kurs] m (-es/-e) bankruptcy, insolvency, failure; ~ anmelden file a petition in bankruptcy; in ~ gehen or geraten become insolvent, go bankrupt; ~erklärung ʀ̃ʀ̃ f declaration of insolvency; ~masse ʀ̃ʀ̃ f bankrupt's estate; ~verfahren ʀ̃ʀ̃ n bankruptcy proceedings pl.; ~verwalter ʀ̃ʀ̃ m trustee in bankruptcy; liquidator.

können ['kœnən] 1. v/i. (irr., ge-, h): ich kann nicht I can't, I am not able to; 2. v/t. (irr., ge-, h) know, understand; e-e Sprache ~ know a language, have command of a language; 3. v/aux. (irr., no -ge-, h) be able to inf., be capable of ger.; be allowed or permitted to inf.; es kann sein it may be; du kannst hingehen you may go there; er kann schwimmen he can swim, he knows how to swim; 4. 2 n (-s/no pl.) ability; skill; proficiency.

Konnossement † [kɔnɔsə'mɛnt] n (-[e]s/-e) bill of lading.

konnte ['kɔntə] pret. of können.

konsequen|t adj. [kɔnze'kvɛnt] consistent; 2z [~ts] f (-/-en) consistency; consequence; die ~en ziehen do the only thing one can.

konservativ adj. [kɔnzɛrva'tiːf] conservative.

Konserven [kɔn'zɛrvən] f/pl. tinned or Am. canned foods pl.; ~büchse f, ~dose f tin, Am. can; ~fabrik f tinning factory, esp. Am. cannery.

konservieren [kɔnzɛr'viːrən] v/t. (no -ge-, h) preserve.

Konsonant gr. [kɔnzo'nant] m (-en/-en) consonant.

Konsortium † [kɔn'zɔrtsjum] n (-s/Konsortien) syndicate.

konstruieren [kɔnstru'iːrən] v/t. (no -ge-, h) gr. construe; h, ⊕ construct; design.

Konstruk|teur ⊕ [kɔnstruk'tøːr] m (-s/-e) designer; ~tion ⊕ [~'tsjoːn] f (-/-en) construction; ~tionsfehler ⊕ m constructional defect.

Konsul pol. ['kɔnzul] m (-s/-n) con-

sul; ~at pol. [~'laːt] n (-[e]s/-e) consulate; 2'tieren v/t. (no -ge-, h) consult, seek s.o.'s advice.

Konsum [kɔn'zuːm] m 1. (-s/no pl.) consumption; 2. (-s/-s) co-operative shop, Am. co-operative store, F co-op; 3. (-s/no pl.) consumers' co-operative society, F co-op; ~ent [~u'mɛnt] m (-en/-en) consumer; 2ieren [~u'miːrən] v/t. (no -ge-, h) consume; ~verein m s. Konsum 3.

Kontakt [kɔn'takt] m (-[e]s/-e) contact (a. ⚡); in ~ stehen mit be in contact or touch with.

Kontinent ['kɔntinɛnt] m (-[e]s/-e) continent.

Kontingent [kɔntiŋ'gɛnt] n (-[e]s/-e) × contingent, quota (a. †).

Konto † ['kɔnto] n (-s/Konten, Kontos, Konti) account; '~auszug † m statement of account; ~korrentkonto † [~kɔ'rɛnt-] n current account.

Kontor [kɔn'toːr] n (-s/-e) office; ~ist [~o'rist] m (-en/-en) clerk.

Kontrast [kɔn'trast] m (-es/-e) contrast.

Kontroll|e [kɔn'trɔlə] f (-/-n) control; supervision; check; 2ieren [~'liːrən] v/t. (no -ge-, h) control; supervise; check.

Kontroverse [kɔntro'vɛrzə] f (-/-n) controversy.

konventionell adj. [kɔnvɛntsjo'nɛl] conventional.

Konversation [kɔnvɛrza'tsjoːn] f (-/-en) conversation; ~slexikon n encyclop(a)edia.

Konzentr|ation [kɔntsɛntra'tsjoːn] f (-/-en) concentration; 2ieren [~tri'rən] v/t. (no -ge-, h) concentrate, focus (attention, etc.) (auf acc. on); sich ~ concentrate (auf acc. on).

Konzern † [kɔn'tsɛrn] m (-s/-e) combine, group.

Konzert ♪ [kɔn'tsɛrt] n (-[e]s/-e) concert; recital; concerto; ~saal ♪ m concert-hall.

Konzession [kɔntsɛ'sjoːn] f (-/-en) concession; licen|ce, Am. -se; 2ieren [~o'niːrən] v/t. (no -ge-, h) license.

Kopf [kɔpf] m (-[e]s/-e) head; top; brains pl.; pipe: bowl; ein fähiger ~ a clever fellow; ~ hoch! chin up!; j-m über den ~ wachsen outgrow s.o.; fig. get beyond s.o.; '~arbeit f brain-work; '~bahnhof ✿ m terminus, Am. terminal; '~bedeckung f headgear, headwear.

köpfen ['kœpfən] v/t. (ge-, h) behead, decapitate; football: head (ball).

'Kopf|ende n head; '~hörer m headphone, headset; '~kissen n pillow; '2los adj. headless; fig. confused; '~nicken n (-s/no pl.) nod; '~rechnen n (-s/no pl.) mental arithmetic; '~salat m cabbage-lettuce;

'⁓schmerzen *m/pl.* headache; '⁓sprung *m* header; '⁓tuch *n* scarf; 2'über *adv.* head first, headlong; '⁓weh *n* (-[e]s/-e) *s.* Kopfschmerzen; '⁓zerbrechen *n* (-s/*no pl.*): j-m ⁓ machen puzzle s.o.

Kopie [ko'piː] *f*(-/-n) copy; duplicate; *phot.*, *film:* print; '⁓rstift *m* indelible pencil.

Koppel ['kɔpəl] 1. *f* (-/-n) hounds: couple, *horses.* string; paddock; 2. ⚔ *n* (-s/-) belt; 2n *v/t.* (ge-, h) couple (*a* ⊕, ♂).

Koralle [ko'ralə] *f* (-/-n) coral; ⁓fischer *m* coral-fisher.

Korb [kɔrp] *m* (-[e]s/⁓e) basket; *fig.* refusal, Hahn im ⁓ cock of the walk; '⁓möbel *n/pl.* wicker furniture.

Kordel ['kɔrdəl] *f* (-/-n) string, twine; cord

Korinthe [ko'rintə] *f* (-/-n) currant.

Kork [kɔrk] *m* (-[e]s/-e), '⁓en *m* (-s/-) cork; '⁓(en)zieher *m* (-s/-) corkscrew.

Korn [kɔrn] 1. *n* (-[e]s/⁓er) seed; grain; 2. *n* (-[e]s/-e) corn, cereals *pl.*; 3. *n* (-[e]s/✛-e) front sight; 4. *F m* (-[e]s/-) (German) corn whisky.

körnig *adj.* ['kœrniç] granular; *in compounds* ⁓grained.

Körper ['kœrpər] *m* (-s/-) body (*a. phys.*, ♆), ♙ solid; '⁓bau *m* build, physique, 2behindert *adj.* ['⁓bəhindərt] (physically) disabled, handicapped, ⁓beschaffenheit *f* constitution, physique; '⁓fülle *f* corpulence; ⁓geruch *m* body-odo(u)r; '⁓größe *f* stature; ⁓kraft *f* physical strength, 2lich *adj.* physical; corporal; bodily; '⁓pflege *f* care of the body, hygiene; '⁓schaft *f* (-/-en) body, ⁂ body (corporate), corporation; '⁓verletzung ⁂ *f* bodily harm, physical injury.

korrekt *adj.* [kɔ'rekt] correct; 2or [⁓ɔr] *m* (-s/-en) (proof-)reader; 2ur [⁓'tuːr] *f* (-/-en) correction; 2urbogen *m* proof-sheet.

Korrespond|ent [kɔrespɔn'dent] *m* (-en/-en) correspondent; ⁓enz [⁓ts] *f* (-/-en) correspondence; 2ieren [⁓'diːrən] *v/i.* (*no* -ge-, h) correspond (*mit* with).

korrigieren [kɔri'giːrən] *v/t.* (*no* -ge-, h) correct.

Korsett [kɔr'zet] *n* (-[e]s/-e, -s) corset, stays *pl.*

Kosename ['koːzə-] *m* pet name.

Kosmetik [kɔs'meːtik] *f* (-/*no pl.*) beauty culture; ⁓erin *f* (-/-nen) beautician, cosmetician.

Kost [kɔst] *f* (-/*no pl.*) food, fare; board; diet; 2bar *adj. present, etc.:* costly, expensive; *health, time, etc.:* valuable; *mineral, etc.:* precious.

'kosten¹ *v/t.* (ge-, h) taste, try, sample.

'Kosten² 1. *pl.* cost(s *pl.*); expense(s *pl.*), charges *pl.*; *auf* ⁓ (*gen.*) at the expense of; 2. ♀ *v/t.* (ge-, h) cost; take, require (*time, etc.*); '⁓anschlag *m* estimate, tender; '2frei 1. *adj.* free; 2. *adv.* free of charge; '2los *s.* kostenfrei.

Kost|gänger ['kɔstgeŋər] *m* (-s/-) boarder; '⁓geld *n* board-wages *pl.*

köstlich *adj.* ['kœstliç] delicious.

'Kost|probe *f* taste, sample (*a. fig.*); 2spielig *adj.* ['⁓ʃpiːliç] expensive, costly.

Kostüm [kɔs'tyːm] *n* (-s/-e) costume, dress; suit; ⁓fest *n* fancy-dress ball.

Kot [koːt] *m* (-[e]s/*no pl.*) mud, mire; excrement.

Kotelett [kot(ə)'let] *n* (-[e]s/-s, ✎-e) *pork, veal, lamb* cutlet; *pork, veal, mutton.* chop; ⁓en *pl.* sidewhiskers *pl.*, Am *a* sideburns *pl.*

'Kot|flügel *mot. m* mudguard, Am. *a.* fender, '2ig *adj.* muddy, miry.

Krabbe *zo.* ['krabə] *f* (-/-n) shrimp; crab.

krabbeln ['krabəln] *v/i.* (ge-, sein) crawl.

Krach [krax] *m* (-[e]s/-e, -s) crack, crash (*a.* ✛); quarrel, *fig.* bust-up; F row; ⁓ machen kick up a row; 2en *v/i.* (ge-) 1. (h) *thunder:* crash; *cannon* roar, thunder; 2. (sein) crash (*a.* ✛), smash.

krächzen ['kreçtsən] *v/t. and v/i.* (ge-, h) croak

Kraft [kraft] 1. *f* (-/⁓e) strength; force (*a* ⚔); power (*a.* ♂, ⊕); energy; vigo(u)r; efficacy; *in* ⁓ *sein* (*setzen, treten*) be in (put into, come into) operation or force; *außer* ⁓ *setzen* repeal, abolish (*law*); 2. ♀ *prp* (*gen.*) by virtue of; '⁓anlage ⚙ *f* power plant; '⁓brühe *f* beef tea; '⁓fahrer *m* driver, motorist; '⁓fahrzeug *n* motor vehicle.

kräftig *adj.* ['kreftiç] strong (*a. fig.*), powerful, *fig* nutritious, rich; ⁓en ['⁓gən] (ge-, h) 1. *v/t.* strengthen; 2. *v/i.* give strength.

'kraft|los *adj.* powerless; feeble; weak; '2probe *f* trial of strength; '2rad *n* motor cycle; '2stoff *mot. m* fuel; '2voll *adj.* powerful (*a. fig.*); '2wagen *m* motor vehicle; '2werk ⚡ *n* power station.

Kragen ['kraːgən] *m* (-s/-) collar; '⁓knopf *m* collar-stud, Am. collar button.

Krähe *orn.* ['kreːə] *f* (-/-n) crow; '2n *v/i.* (ge-, h) crow.

Kralle ['kralə] *f* (-/-n) claw (*a. fig.*); talon, clutch.

Kram [kraːm] *m* (-[e]s/*no pl.*) stuff, odds and ends *pl.*; *fig.* affairs *pl.*, business.

Krämer ['kreːmər] *m* (-s/-) shop-keeper.

Krampf ⚔ [krampf] *m* (-[e]s/⸚e) cramp; spasm, convulsion; **ʌader** ⚔ *f* varicose vein; **'⸚haft** *adj.* ⚔ spasmodic, convulsive; *laugh:* forced.

Kran ⊕ [krɑːn] *m* (-[e]s/⸚e, -e) crane.

krank *adj.* [kraŋk] sick; *organ, etc.:* diseased; ~ *sein p.* be ill, *esp. Am.* be sick; *animal:* be sick *or* ill; ~ *werden p.* fall ill *or esp. Am.* sick; *animal:* fall sick; **'⸚e** *m, f* (-n/-n) sick person, patient, invalid.

kränkeln ['krɛŋkəln] *v/i.* (ge-, h) be sickly, be in poor health.

'kranken *fig. v/i.* (ge-, h) suffer (*an dat.* from).

kränken ['krɛŋkən] *v/t.* (ge-, h) offend, injure; wound *or* hurt *s.o.'s* feelings; *sich* ~ feel hurt (*über acc.* at, about).

'Kranken|bett *n* sick-bed; **'ʌgeld** *n* sick-benefit; **'ʌhaus** *n* hospital; **'ʌkasse** *f* health insurance (fund); **'ʌkost** *f* invalid diet; **'ʌlager** *n s. Krankenbett;* **'ʌpflege** *f* nursing; **'ʌpfleger** *m* male nurse; **'ʌschein** *m* medical certificate; **'ʌschwester** *f* (sick-)nurse; **'ʌversicherung** *f* health *or* sickness insurance; **'ʌwagen** *m* ambulance; **'ʌzimmer** *n* sick-room.

'krank|haft *adj.* morbid, pathological; **'⸚heit** *f* (-/-en) illness, sickness; disease.

'Krankheits|erreger ⚔ *m* pathogenic agent; **'ʌerscheinung** *f* symptom (*a. fig.*).

'kränklich *adj.* sickly, ailing.

'Kränkung *f* (-/-en) insult, offen|ce, *Am.* -se.

Kranz [krants] *m* (-es/⸚e) wreath; garland.

Kränzchen *fig.* ['krɛntsçən] *n* (-s/-) tea-party, F hen-party.

kraß *adj.* [kras] crass, gross.

kratzen ['kratsən] (ge-, h) 1. *v/i.* scratch; 2. *v/t.* scratch; skin ~ scratch (o.s.).

kraulen ['kraulən] (ge-) 1. *v/t.* (h) scratch gently; 2. *v/i.* (sein) *sports:* crawl.

kraus *adj.* [kraus] curly, curled; crisp; frizzy; *die Stirn* ~ *ziehen* knit one's brow; **'⸚e** *f* (-/-n) ruff(le), frill.

kräuseln ['krɔyzəln] *v/t.* (ge-, h) curl, crimp (*hair, etc.*); pucker (*lips*); *sich* ~ *hair:* curl; *waves, etc.:* ruffle; *smoke:* curl *or* wreath up.

Kraut 🌿 [kraut] *n* 1. (-[e]s/⸚er) plant; herb; 2. (-[e]s/*no pl.*) tops *pl.*; cabbage; weed.

Krawall [kra'val] *m* (-[e]s/-e) riot; shindy, F row, sl. rumpus.

Krawatte [kra'vatə] *f* (-/-n) (neck-)tie.

Kreatur [krea'tuːr] *f* (-/-en) creature.

Krebs [kreːps] *m* (-es/-e) *zo.* crayfish, *Am. a.* crawfish; *ast.* Cancer, Crab; ⚔ cancer; ~e *pl.* ♈ returns *pl.*

Kredit ♈ [kre'diːt] *m* (-[e]s/-e) credit; *auf* ~ on credit; **⸚fähig** ♈ *adj.* credit-worthy.

Kreide ['kraidə] *f* (-/-n) chalk; *paint.* crayon.

Kreis [krais] *m* (-es/-e) circle (*a. fig.*); *ast.* orbit; ⚡ circuit; district, *Am.* county; *fig.:* sphere; field; range.

kreischen ['kraiʃən] (ge-, h) 1. *v/i.* screech, scream; squeal, shriek; *circular saw, etc.:* grate (on the ear); 2. *v/t.* shriek, screech (*insult, etc.*).

Kreisel ['kraizəl] *m* (-s/-) (whipping-)top; **'ʌkompaß** *m* gyro-compass.

kreisen ['kraizən] *v/i.* (ge-, h) (move in a) circle; revolve, rotate; ✈, *bird:* circle; *bird:* wheel; *blood, money:* circulate.

kreis|förmig *adj.* ['kraisfœrmiç] circular; **⸚lauf** *m physiol., money, etc.:* circulation; *business, trade:* cycle; **⸚laufstörungen** ⚔ *f/pl.* circulatory trouble; **'ʌrund** *adj.* circular; **⸚säge** ⊕ *f* circular saw, *Am. a.* buzz saw; **'⸚verkehr** *m* roundabout (traffic).

Krempe ['krɛmpə] *f* (-/-n) brim (*of hat*).

Krempel F ['krɛmpəl] *m* (-s/*no pl.*) rubbish, stuff, lumber.

krepieren [kre'piːrən] *v/i.* (*no -ge-, sein*) *shell:* burst, explode; *sl.* kick the bucket, peg *or* snuff out; *animal:* die, perish.

Krepp [krɛp] *m* (-s/-s, -e) crêpe; crape; **ʌapier** ['krɛppapiːr] *n* crêpe paper; **'ʌsohle** *f* crêpe(-rubber) sole.

Kreuz [krɔyts] 1. *n* (-es/-e) cross (*a. fig.*); crucifix; *anat.* small of the back; ⚔ sacral region; *cards:* club(s *pl.*); ♪ sharp; *zu* ~*e kriechen* eat humble pie; 2. ♀ *adv.:* ~ *und quer* in all directions; criss-cross.

'kreuzen (ge-, h) 1. *v/t.* cross, fold (*arms, etc.*); ♀, *zo.* cross(-breed), hybridize; *sich* ~ *roads:* cross, intersect; *plans, etc.:* clash; 2. ⚓ *v/i.* cruise.

'Kreuzer ⚓ *m* (-s/-) cruiser.

'Kreuz|fahrer *hist. m* crusader; **'ʌfahrt** *f hist.* crusade; ⚓ cruise; **'ʌfeuer** *n* ✕ cross-fire (*a. fig.*); **⸚igen** ['ʌigən] *v/t.* (ge-, h) crucify; **ʌigung** ['ʌiguŋ] *f* (-/-en) crucifixion; **'ʌotter** *zo. f* common viper; **'ʌritter** *hist. m* knight of the Cross; **'ʌschmerzen** *m/pl.* back ache; **'ʌspinne** *zo. f* garden- *or* cross-spider; **'ʌung** *f* (-/-en) 🛒, *roads, etc.:* crossing, intersection; *roads:* crossroads; ♀, *zo.* cross-breeding, hybridization; **'verhör** ✕ *n* cross-examination; *ins* ~ *nehmen* cross-examine; '○weise *adv.* crosswise, crossways; '○worträtsel *n* crossword (puzzle); '○zug *hist. m* crusade.

kriech|en ['kriːçən] *v/i.* (*irr., ge-, sein*) creep, crawl; *fig.* cringe (*vor dat.* to, before); '○er *contp. m* (-s/-) toady; ○erei *contp.* [○'raɪ] *f* (-/-en) toadyism.

Krieg [kriːk] *m* (-[e]s/-e) war; *im* ~ at war; *s. führen.*

kriegen F ['kriːgən] *v/t.* (ge-, h) catch, seize; get.

Krieg|er ['kriːgər] *m* (-s/-) warrior; '○erdenkmal *n* war memorial; '○erisch *adj.* warlike; militant; '○führend *adj.* belligerent; '○führung *f* warfare.

'**Kriegs|beil** *fig. n: das* ~ *begraben* bury the hatchet; ○beschädigt *adj.* ['○bəʃɛːdiçt] war-disabled; '○beschädigte *m* (-n/-n) disabled ex-serviceman; '○dienst ⚔ *m* war service; '○dienstverweigerer ⚔ *m* (-s/-) conscientious objector; '○erklärung *f* declaration of war; '○flotte *f* naval force; '○gefangene *m* prisoner of war; '○gefangenschaft ⚔ *f* captivity; '○gericht ⚔ *n* court martial; ○gewinnler ['○gəvinlər] *m* (-s/-) war profiteer; '○hafen *m* naval port; '○kamerad *m* wartime comrade; '○list *f* stratagem; '○macht *f* military forces *pl.*; '○minister *hist. m* minister of war; Secretary of State for War, *Am.* Secretary of War; '○ministerium *hist. n* ministry of war; War Office, *Am.* War Department; '○rat *m* council of war; '○schauplatz ⚔ *m* theat|re *or Am.* -er of war; '○schiff *n* warship; '○schule *f* military academy; '○teilnehmer *m* combatant; ex-serviceman, *Am.* veteran; '○treiber *m* (-s/-) warmonger; '○verbrecher *m* war criminal; '○zug *m* (military) expedition, campaign.

Kriminal|beamte [krimiˈnaːl-] *m* criminal investigator, *Am.* plainclothes man; ○film *m* crime film; thriller; ○polizei *f* criminal investigation department; ○roman *m* detective *or* crime novel, thriller, *sl.* whodun(n)it.

kriminell *adj.* [krimiˈnɛl] criminal; ○e *m* (-n/-n) criminal.

Krippe ['kripə] *f* (-/-n) crib, manger; crèche.

Krise ['kriːzə] *f* (-/-n) crisis.

Kristall [krisˈtal] 1. *m* (-s/-e) crystal. 2. *n* (-s/*no pl.*) crystal(-glass); ○isieren [○iˈziːrən] *v/i. and v/refl.* (*no -ge-, h*) crystallize.

Kriti|k [kriˈtiːk] *f* (-/-en) criticism; ♪, *thea.*, *etc.*: review, criticism; *unter aller* ~ beneath contempt; ~ *üben an* (*dat.*) *s. kritisieren;* ○ker ['kriːtikər] *m* (-s/-) critic; *books:* re-

viewer; ○sch *adj.* ['kriːtiʃ] critical (*gegenüber of*); ○sieren [kritiˈziːrən] *v/t.* (*no -ge-, h*) criticize; review (*book*).

kritt|eln ['kritəln] *v/t.* (ge-, h) find fault (*an dat.* with), cavil (at); ○ler ['○lər] *m* (-s/-) fault-finder, caviller.

Kritzel|ei [kritsəˈlaɪ] *f* (-/-en) scrawl(ing), scribble, scribbling; '○n *v/t. and v/i.* (ge-, h) scrawl, scribble.

kroch [krɔx] *pret. of kriechen.*

Krokodil *zo.* [krokoˈdiːl] *n* (-s/-e) crocodile.

Krone ['kroːnə] *f* (-/-n) crown; coronet (*of duke, earl, etc.*).

krönen ['krøːnən] *v/t.* (ge-, h) crown (*zum König king*) (*a. fig.*).

'**Kron|leuchter** *m* chandelier; lust|re, *Am.* -er; electrolier; '○prinz *m* crown prince; '○prinzessin *f* crown princess.

'**Krönung** *f* (-/-en) coronation, crowning; *fig.* climax, culmination.

'**Kronzeuge** ♂♀ *m* chief witness; King's evidence, *Am.* State's evidence.

Kropf 🐦 [krɔpf] goit|re, *Am.* -er.

Kröte *zo.* ['krøːtə] *f* (-/-n) toad.

Krücke ['krykə] *f* (-/-n) crutch.

Krug [kruːk] *m* (-[e]s/*ⸯe*) jug, pitcher; jar; mug; tankard.

Krume ['kruːmə] *f* (-/-n) crumb; ♂ topsoil.

Krümel ['kryːməl] *m* (-s/-) small crumb; '○n *v/t. and v/i.* (ge-, h) crumble.

krumm *adj.* [krum] *ⸯ.* bent, stooping; *limb, nose, etc.:* crooked; *spine:* curved; *deal, business, etc.:* crooked; '○beinig *adj.* bandy- *or* bow-legged.

krümmen ['krymən] *v/t.* (ge-, h) bend (*arm, back, etc.*); crook (*finger, etc.*); curve (*metal sheet, etc.*); *sich* ~ *person, snake, etc.:* writhe; *worm, etc.:* wriggle; *sich vor Schmerzen* ~ writhe with pain; *sich vor Lachen* ~ be convulsed with laughter.

'**Krümmung** *f* (-/-en) *road, etc.:* bend; *arch, road, etc.:* curve; *river, path, etc.:* turn, wind, meander; *earth's surface, spine, etc.:* curvature.

Krüppel ['krypəl] *m* (-s/-) cripple.

Kruste ['krustə] *f* (-/-n) crust.

Kübel ['kyːbəl] *m* (-s/-) tub; pail, bucket.

Kubik|meter [kuˈbiːk-] *n, m* cubic met|re, *Am.* -er; ○wurzel *⅍ f* cube root.

Küche ['kyçə] *f* (-/-n) kitchen; cuisine, cookery; *s. kalt.*

Kuchen ['kuːxən] *m* (-s/-) cake, flan; pastry.

'**Küchen|gerät** *n*, '○geschirr *n* kitchen utensils *pl.*; '○herd *m* (kitchen-)range; cooker, stove; '○schrank *m* kitchen cupboard *or* cabinet; '~zettel *m* bill of fare, menu.

Kuckuck *orn.* ['kukuk] *m* (-s/-e) cuckoo.

Kufe ['ku:fə] *f* (-/-n) ⚔ skid; *sleigh, etc.*: runner.

Küfer ['ky:fər] *m* (-s/-) cooper; cellarman.

Kugel ['ku:gəl] *f* (-/-n) ball; ⚒ bullet; ⚗, *geogr.* sphere; *sports*: shot, weight; 2förmig *adj.* ['~fœrmiç] spherical, ball-shaped, globular; '~gelenk ⊕, *anat.* *n* ball-and-socket joint; '~lager ⊕ *n* ball-bearing; '2n (ge-) 1. *v/i.* (sein) *ball, etc.*: roll; 2. *v/t.* (h) roll (*ball, etc.*); *sich ~ children, etc.*: roll about; F double up (vor with *laughter*); '~schreiber *m* ball(-point)-pen; '~stoßen *n* (-s/no *pl.*) *sports*: putting the shot *or* weight.

Kuh *zo.* [ku:] *f* (-/~e) cow.

kühl *adj.* [ky:l] cool (*a. fig.*); '2anlage *f* cold-storage plant; '2e *f* (-/no *pl.*) cool(ness); '~en *v/t.* (ge-, h) cool (*wine, wound, etc.*); chill (*wine, etc.*); '2er *mot.* *m* (-s/-) radiator; '2raum *m* cold-storage chamber; '2schrank *m* refrigerator, F fridge.

kühn *adj.* [ky:n] bold (*a. fig.*), daring; audacious.

'**Kuhstall** *m* cow-house, byre, *Am. a.* cow barn.

Küken *orn.* ['ky:kən] *n* (-s/-) chick.

kulant ✝ *adj.* [ku'lant] firm, *etc.*: accommodating, obliging; *price, terms, etc.*: fair, easy.

Kulisse [ku'lisə] *f* (-/-n) *thea.* wing, side-scene; *fig.* front; ~n *pl. a.* scenery; hinter den ~n behind the scenes.

Kult [kult] *m* (-[e]s/-e) cult, worship.

kultivieren [kulti'vi:rən] *v/t.* (no -ge-, h) cultivate (*a. fig.*).

Kultur [kul'tu:r] *f* (-/-en) ⚘ cultivation; *fig.*: culture; civilization; 2ell *adj.* [~u'rel] cultural; ~film [~'tu:r-] *m* educational film; ~geschichte *f* history of civilization; ~volk *n* civilized people.

Kultus ['kultus] *m* (-/Kulte) *s. Kult;* '~minister *m* minister of education and cultural affairs; '~ministerium *n* ministry of education and cultural affairs.

Kummer ['kumər] *m* (-s/no *pl.*) grief, sorrow; trouble, worry.

kümmer|lich *adj.* ['kymərliç] life, *etc.*: miserable, wretched; *conditions, etc.*: pitiful, pitiable; *result, etc.*: poor; *resources*: scanty; '~n *v/t.* (ge-, h): es kümmert mich I bother, I worry; *sich ~ um* look after, take care of; *see to*; meddle with.

'**kummervoll** *adj.* sorrowful.

Kump|an F [kum'pa:n] *m* (-s/-e) companion; F mate, chum, *Am.* F *a.*

buddy; ~el ['~pəl] *m* (-s/-, F -s) ⚒ pitman, collier; F work-mate; F *s. Kumpan.*

Kunde ['kundə] 1. *m* (-n/-n) customer, client; 2. *f* (-/-n) knowledge.

Kundgebung ['kunt-] *f* (-/-en) manifestation; *pol.* rally.

kündig|en ['kyndigən] (ge-, h) 1. *v/i.*: j-m ~ give s.o. notice; 2. *v/t.* ✝ call in (*capital*); ⚖ cancel (*contract*); *pol.* denounce (*treaty*); '2ung *f* (-/-en) notice; ✝ calling in; ⚖ cancellation; *pol.* denunciation.

'**Kundschaft** *f* (-/-en) customers *pl.*, clients *pl.*; custom, clientele; '~er ⚒ *m* (-s/-) scout; spy.

künftig ['kynftiç] 1. *adj.* event, years, *etc.*: future; event, programme, *etc.*: coming; life, world, *etc.*: next; 2. *adv.* in future, from now on.

Kunst [kunst] *f* (-/~e) art; skill; ~akademie *f* academy of arts; ~ausstellung *f* art exhibition; ~druck *m* art print(ing); ~dünger *m* artificial manure, fertilizer; 2fertig *adj.* skilful, skilled; ~fertigkeit *f* artistic skill; ~gegenstand *m* objet d'art; 2gerecht *adj.* skilful; professional, expert; ~geschichte *f* history of art; ~gewerbe *n* arts and crafts *pl.*; applied arts *pl.*; ~glied *n* artificial limb; ~griff *m* trick, dodge; artifice, knack; ~händler *m* art-dealer; ~kenner *m* connoisseur of *or* in art; ~leder *n* imitation *or* artificial leather.

Künstler ['kynstlər] *m* (-s/-) artist; *f*, *thea.* performer; '2isch *adj.* artistic.

künstlich *adj.* ['kynstliç] eye, flower, light, *etc.*: artificial; teeth, hair, *etc.*: false; fibres, dyes, *etc.*: synthetic.

'**Kunst|liebhaber** *m* art-lover; '~maler *m* artist, painter; ~reiter *m* equestrian; circus-rider; ~schätze ['~fɛtsə] *m/pl.* art treasures *pl.*; ~seide *f* artificial silk, rayon; ~stück *n* feat, trick, F stunt; ~tischler *m* cabinet-maker; '~verlag *m* art publishers *pl.*; '2voll *adj.* artistic, elaborate; '~werk *n* work of art.

kunterbunt F *fig. adj.* ['kuntər-] higgledy-piggledy.

Kupfer ['kupfər] *n* (-s/no *pl.*) copper; ~geld *n* copper coins *pl.*, F coppers *pl.*; '2n *adj.* (of) copper; '2rot *adj.* copper-colo(u)red; '~stich *m* copper-plate engraving.

Kupon [ku'pö:] *m* (-s/-s) *s. Coupon.*

Kuppe ['kupə] *f* (-/-n) rounded hilltop; *nail*: head.

Kuppel △ ['kupəl] *f* (-/-n) dome, cupola; ~ei ⚖ [~'lai] *f* (-/-en) procuring; '2n (ge-, h) 1. *v/t. s. koppeln*; 2. *mot. v/i.* declutch.

Kuppl|er ['kuplər] *m* (-s/-) pimp, procurer; '~ung *f* (-/-en) ⊕ coupling (*a.* 🚂); *mot.* clutch.

Kur [kuːr] f (-/-en) course of treatment, cure.

Kür [kyːr] f (-/-en) sports: s. Kürlauf; voluntary exercise.

Kuratorium [kura'toːrium] n (-s/ Kuratorien) board of trustees.

Kurbel ⊕ ['kurbəl] f (-/-n) crank, winch, handle; '**2n** (ge-, h) 1. v/t. shoot (film); in die Höhe ~ winch up (load, etc.); wind up (car window, etc.); 2. v/i. crank.

Kürbis ♀ ['kyrbis] m (-ses/-se) pumpkin.

'**Kur|gast** m visitor to or patient at a health resort or spa; '**~haus** n spa hotel.

Kurier [ku'riːr] m (-s/-e) courier, express (messenger).

kurieren [ku'riːrən] v/t. (no -ge-, h) cure.

kurios adj. [kur'joːs] curious, odd, strange, queer. [(skating.)]

'**Kürlauf** m sports: free (roller))

'**Kur|ort** m health resort; spa; '**~-pfuscher** m quack (doctor); **~pfusche'rei** f (-/-en) quackery.

Kurs [kurs] m (-es/-e) ↑ currency; ↑ rate, price; ⊕ and fig. course, course, class; '**~bericht** ↑ m market-report; '**~buch** 🕮 n railway guide, Am. railroad guide.

Kürschner ['kyrʃnər] m (-s/-) furrier.

kursieren [kur'ziːrən] v/i. (no -ge-, h) money, etc.: circulate, be in circulation; rumour, etc.: circulate, be afloat, go about.

Kursivschrift typ. [kur'ziːf-] f italics pl.

Kursus ['kurzus] m (-/Kurse) course, class.

'**Kurs|verlust** ↑ m loss on the stock exchange; '**~wert** ↑ m market value; '**~zettel** ↑ m stock exchange list.

Kurve ['kurvə] f (-/-n) curve; road, etc.: a. bend, turn.

kurz [kurts] 1. adj. space: short; time, etc.: short, brief; ~ und bündig brief, concise; ~e Hose shorts pl.; mit ~en Worten with a few words; den kürzeren ziehen get the worst of it; 2. adv. in short; ~ angebunden sein be curt or sharp; ~ und gut in short, in a word; ~ vor London short of London; sich ~ fassen be brief or concise; in ~em before long, shortly; vor ~em a short time ago; zu ~ kommen come off badly, get a raw deal; um es ~ zu sagen to cut a long story short; '**2arbeit** ↑ f short-time work; '**2arbeiter** ↑ m short-time worker; **~atmig** adj. ['~ʔɑːtmiç] short-winded.

Kürze ['kyrtsə] f (-/no pl.) shortness; brevity; in ~ shortly, before long; '**2n** v/t. (ge-, h) shorten (dress, etc.) (um by); abridge, condense (book, etc.); cut, reduce (expenses, etc.).

'**kurz|er|hand** adv. without hesitation; on the spot; '**2film** m short (film); '**2form** f shortened form; '**~fristig** adj. short-term; ↑ bill, etc.: short-dated; '**2geschichte** f (short) short story; '**~lebig** adj. ['~leːbiç] short-lived; '**2nachrichten** f/pl. news summary.

kürzlich adv. ['kyrtsliç] lately, recently, not long ago.

'**Kurz|schluß** ⚡ m short circuit, F short; '**~schrift** f shorthand, stenography; '**2sichtig** adj. shortsighted, near-sighted; **2'um** adv. in short, in a word.

'**Kürzung** f (-/-en) shortening (of dress, etc.); abridg(e)ment, condensation (of book, etc.); cut, reduction (of expenses, etc.).

'**Kurz|waren** f/pl. haberdashery, Am. dry goods pl., notions pl.; '**~weil** f (-/no pl.) amusement, entertainment; '**2weilig** adj. amusing, entertaining; '**~welle** ⚡ f short wave; radio: short-wave band.

Kusine [ku'ziːnə] f (-/-n) s. Cousine.

Kuß [kus] m (Kusses/Küsse) kiss; '**2echt** adj. kiss-proof.

küssen ['kysən] v/t. and v/i. (ge-, h) kiss.

'**kußfest** adj. s. kußecht.

Küste ['kystə] f (-/-n) coast; shore.

'**Küsten|bewohner** m inhabitant of a coastal region; '**~fischerei** f inshore fishery or fishing; '**~gebiet** n coastal area or region; '**~schiffahrt** f coastal shipping.

Küster eccl. ['kystər] m (-s/-) verger, sexton, sacristan.

Kutsch|bock ['kutʃ-] m coach-box; '**~e** f (-/-n) carriage, coach; '**~en-schlag** m carriage-door, coach-door; '**~er** m (-s/-) coachman; **2ie-ren** [~'tʃiːrən] (no -ge-) 1. v/t. (h) drive s.o. in a coach; 2. v/i. (h) (drive a) coach; 3. v/i. (sein) (drive or ride in a) coach.

Kutte ['kutə] f (-/-n) cowl.

Kutter ⚓ ['kutər] m (-s/-) cutter.

Kuvert [ku'vɛrt; ku'veːr] n (-[e]s/-e; -s/-s) envelope; at table: cover.

Kux ⚒ [kuks] m (-es/-e) mining share.

L

Lab zo. [lɑ:p] n (-[e]s/-e) rennet.
labil adj. [la'bi:l] unstable (a. ⊕, ⚙); phys., ⚛ labile.
Labor [la'bo:r] n (-s/-s, -e) s. Laboratorium; **~ant** [labo'rant] m (-en/-en) laboratory assistant; **~atorium** [labora'to:rjum] n (-s/ Laboratorien) laboratory; ⚳ieren [~o'ri:rən] v/i. (no -ge-, h): ~ an (dat.) labo(u)r under, suffer from.
Labyrinth [laby'rint] n (-[e]s/-e) labyrinth, maze.
Lache ['laxə] f (-/-n) pool, puddle.
lächeln ['leçəln] 1. v/i. (ge-, h) smile (über acc. at); höhnisch ~ sneer (über acc. at); 2. ⚳ n (-s/no pl.) smile; höhnisches ~ sneer.
lachen ['laxən] 1. v/i. (über acc. at); 2. ⚳ n (-s/no pl.) laugh(ter).
lächerlich adj. ['leçərliç] ridiculous, laughable, ludicrous; absurd; derisory, scoffing; ~ machen ridicule; sich ~ machen make a fool of o.s.
Lachs ichth. [laks] m (-es/-e) salmon.
Lack [lak] m (-[e]s/-e) (gum-)lac; varnish; lacquer, enamel; ⚳ieren [la'ki:rən] v/t. (no -ge-, h) lacquer, varnish, enamel; '**~leder** n patent leather; '**~schuhe** m/pl. patent leather shoes pl., F patents pl.
Lade|fähigkeit ['lɑ:də-] f loading capacity; '**~fläche** f loading area; '**~hemmung** ✗ f jam, stoppage; '**~linie** ⚓ f load-line.
laden¹ ['lɑ:dən] v/t. (irr., ge-, h) load; load (gun), charge (a. ⚡); freight, ship; ⚖ cite, summon; invite, ask (guest).
Laden² [~] m (-s/ˮ) shop, Am. store; shutter; '**~besitzer** m s. Ladeninhaber; '**~dieb** m shop-lifter; '**~diebstahl** m shop-lifting; '**~hüter** m drug on the market; '**~inhaber** m shopkeeper, Am. storekeeper; '**~kasse** f till; '**~preis** m selling-price, retail price; '**~schild** n shopsign; '**~schluß** m closing time; nach ~ after hours; '**~tisch** m counter.
'**Lade|platz** m loading-place; '**~rampe** f loading platform or ramp; '**~raum** m loading space; ⚓ hold; '**~schein** ⚓ m bill of lading.
'**Ladung** f (-/-en) loading; load, freight; ⚓ cargo; ⚡ charge (a. of gun); ⚖ summons.
lag [lɑ:k] pret. of liegen.
Lage ['lɑ:gə] f (-/-n) situation, position; site, location (of building); state, condition; attitude; geol. layer, stratum; round (of beer, etc.); in der ~ sein zu inf. be able to inf., be in a position to inf.; versetzen

Sie sich in meine ~ put yourself in my place.
Lager ['lɑ:gər] n (-s/-) couch, bed; den, lair (of wild animals); geol. deposit; ⊕ bearing; warehouse, storehouse, depot; store, stock (✝ pl. a. Läger); ✗, etc.: camp, encampment; auf ~ ✝ on hand, in stock; '**~buch** n stock-book; '**~feuer** n camp-fire; '**~geld** n storage; '**~haus** n warehouse; '⚳n (ge-, h) 1. v/i. lie down, rest; ✗ (en)camp; ✝ be stored; 2. v/t. lay down; ✗ (en)camp; ✝ store, warehouse; sich ~ lie down, rest; '**~platz** m ✝ depot; resting-place; ✗, etc.: camp-site; '**~raum** m store-room; '**~ung** f (-/-en) storage (of goods).
Lagune [la'gu:nə] f (-/-n) lagoon.
lahm adj. [lɑ:m] lame; **~en** v/i. (ge-, h) be lame.
lähmen ['le:mən] v/t. (ge-, h) (make) lame; paraly|se, Am. -ze (a. fig.).
'**lahmlegen** v/t. (sep., -ge-, h) paraly|se, Am. -ze; obstruct.
'**Lähmung** ✗ f (-/-en) paralysis.
Laib [laip] m (-[e]s/-e) loaf.
Laich [laiç] m (-[e]s/-e) spawn; '⚳en v/i. (ge-, h) spawn.
Laie ['laiə] m (-n/-n) layman; amateur; '**~nbühne** f amateur theat|re, Am. -er.
Lakai [la'kai] m (-en/-en) lackey (a. fig.), footman.
Lake ['lɑ:kə] f (-/-n) brine, pickle.
Laken ['lɑ:kən] n (-s/-) sheet.
lallen ['lalən] v/i. and v/t. (ge-, h) stammer; babble.
Lamelle [la'melə] f (-/-n) lamella, lamina; ♧ gill (of mushrooms).
lamentieren [lamen'ti:rən] v/i. (no -ge-, h) lament (um for; über acc. over).
Lamm zo. [lam] n (-[e]s/ˮer) lamb; '**~fell** n lambskin; '⚳fromm adj. (as) gentle or (as) meek as a lamb.
Lampe ['lampə] f (-/-n) lamp.
'**Lampen|fieber** n stage fright; '**~licht** n lamplight; '**~schirm** m lamp-shade.
Lampion [lã'pjõ:] m, n (-s/-s) Chinese lantern.
Land [lant] n (-[e]s/ˮer, poet. -e) land; country; territory; ground, soil; an ~ gehen go ashore; auf dem ~e in the country; aufs ~ gehen go into the country; außer ~es gehen go abroad; zu ~e by land; '**~arbeiter** m farm-hand; '**~besitz** m landed property; ⚖ real estate; '**~besitzer** m landowner, landed proprietor; '**~bevölkerung** f rural population.
Lande|bahn ✈ ['landə-] f runway; '**~deck** ✈ n flight-deck.

land'einwärts *adv.* upcountry, inland.
landen ['landən] (ge-) **1.** *v/i.* (*sein*) land; **2.** *v/t.* (*h*) ⚓ disembark (*troops*); ✈ land, set down (*troops*).
'Landenge *f* neck of land, isthmus.
Landeplatz ✈ ['landə-] *m* landing-field.
Ländereien [lɛndə'raɪən] *pl.* landed property, lands *pl.*, estates *pl.*
Länderspiel ['lɛndər-] *n sports*: international match.
Landes|grenze ['landəs-] *f* frontier, boundary; **'~innere** *n* interior, inland, upcountry; **'~kirche** *f* national church; *Brt.* Established Church; **'~regierung** *f* government; *in Germany*: Land government; **'~sprache** *f* native language, vernacular; **'⁊üblich** *adj.* customary; **'~verrat** *m* treason; **'~verräter** *m* traitor to his country; **'~verteidigung** *f* national defen|ce, *Am.* -se.
'Land|flucht *f* rural exodus; **'~friedensbruch** ⚖ *m* breach of the public peace; **'~gericht** *n appr.* district court; **'~gewinnung** *f* (-/-*en*) reclamation of land; **'~gut** *n* country-seat, estate; **'~haus** *n* country-house, cottage; **'~karte** *f* map; **'~kreis** *m* rural district; **⁊läufig** *adj.* ['~lɔʏfiç] customary, current, common.
ländlich *adj.* ['lɛntliç] rural, rustic.
'Land|maschinen *f/pl.* agricultural *or* farm equipment; **'~partie** *f* picnic, outing, excursion into the country; **'~plage** *iro. f* nuisance; **'~rat** *m* (-[e]s/⁼e) *appr.* district president; **'~ratte** ⚓ *f* landlubber; **'~recht** *n* common law; **'~regen** *m* persistent rain.
'Landschaft *f* (-/-*en*) province, district, region; countryside, scenery; *esp. paint.* landscape; **'⁊lich** *adj.* provincial; scenic (*beauty, etc.*).
'Landsmann *m* (-[e]s/*Landsleute*) (fellow-)countryman, compatriot; *was sind Sie für ein ~?* what's your native country?
'Land|straße *f* highway, high road; **'~streicher** *m* (-s/-) vagabond, tramp, *Am. sl.* hobo; **'~streitkräfte** *f/pl.* land forces *pl.*, *the* Army; ground forces *pl.*; **'~strich** *m* tract of land, region; **'~tag** *m* Landtag, Land parliament.
Landung ['landuŋ] *f* (-/-*en*) ⚓, ✈ landing; disembarkation; arrival; **'~sbrücke** ⚓ *f floating*: landing-stage; pier; **'~ssteg** ⚓ *m* gangway, gang-plank.
'Land|vermesser *m* (-s/-) surveyor; **'~vermessung** *f* land-surveying; **⁊wärts** *adv.* ['~vɛrts] landward(s); **'~weg** *m*: *auf dem ~e* by land; **'~wirt** *m* farmer, agriculturist; **'~wirtschaft** *f* agriculture, farming; **'⁊wirtschaftlich** *adj.* agricultural; *~e Maschinen f/pl. s. Landmaschinen*; **'~zunge** *f* spit.
lang [laŋ] **1.** *adj.* long; *p.* tall; *er machte ein ~es Gesicht* his face fell; **2.** *adv.* long; *e-e Woche ~* for a week; *über kurz oder ~* sooner or later; *~(e) anhaltend* continuous; *~(e) entbehrt* long-missed; *~(e) ersehnt* long-wished-for; *das ist schon ~(e) her* that was a long time ago; *~ und breit* at (full *or* great) length; *noch ~(e) nicht* not for a long time yet; far from *ger.*; *wie ~e lernen Sie schon Englisch?* how long have you been learning English?; **~atmig** *adj.* ['~ɑːtmiç] long-winded; **'~e** *adv. s. lang 2.*
Länge ['lɛŋə] *f* (-/-*n*) length; tallness; *geogr., ast.* longitude; *der ~ nach* (at) full length, lengthwise.
langen ['laŋən] *v/i.* (ge-, *h*) suffice, be enough; *~ nach* reach for.
'Längen|grad *m* degree of longitude; **'~maß** *n* linear measure.
'länger 1. *adj.* longer; *~e Zeit* (for) some time; **2.** *adv.* longer; *ich kann es nicht ~ ertragen* I cannot bear it any longer; *je ~, je lieber* the longer the better.
'Langeweile *f* (-, *Langenweile/no pl.*) boredom, tediousness, ennui.
'lang|fristig *adj.* long-term; **'~jährig** *adj.* of long standing; *~e Erfahrung* (many) years of experience; **'⁊lauf** *m skiing*: cross-country run *or* race.
'länglich *adj.* longish, oblong.
'Langmut *f* (-/*no pl.*) patience, forbearance.
längs [lɛŋs] **1.** *prp.* (*gen., dat.*) along(side of); *~ der Küste fahren* ⚓ (sail along the) coast; **2.** *adv.* lengthwise; **'⁊achse** *f* longitudinal axis.
'lang|sam *adj.* slow; **⁊schläfer** ['~ʃlɛːfər] *m* (-s/-) late riser, lie-abed; **'⁊spielplatte** *f* long-playing record.
längst *adv.* [lɛŋst] long ago *or* since; *ich weiß es ~* I have known it for a long time; **'~ens** *adv.* at the longest; at the latest; at the most.
'lang|stielig *adj.* long-handled; ⚘ long-stemmed, long-stalked; **'⁊streckenlauf** *m* long-distance run *or* race; **'⁊weile** *f* (-, *Langenweile/no pl.*) *s. Langeweile*; **'~weilen** *v/t.* (ge-, *h*) bore; *sich ~* be bored; **'~weilig** *adj.* tedious, boring, dull; *~e Person* bore; **'⁊welle** *f* ⚡ long wave; *radio*: long wave band; **~wierig** *adj.* ['~viːriç] protracted, lengthy; ⚕ lingering.
Lanze ['lantsə] *f* (-/-*n*) spear, lance.
Lappalie [la'pɑːljə] *f* (-/-*n*) trifle.
Lapp|en ['lapən] *m* (-s/-) patch; rag; duster; (dish- *or* floor-)cloth; *anat.*, ⚘ lobe; **'⁊ig** *adj.* flabby.
läppisch *adj.* ['lɛpiʃ] foolish, silly.

Lärche ♀ ['lɛrçə] *f* (-/-n) larch.

Lärm [lɛrm] *m* (-[e]s/*no pl.*) noise; din; ~ *schlagen* give the alarm; **'2en** *v/i.* (ge-, h) make a noise; **'2end** *adj.* noisy.

Larve ['larfə] *f* (-/-n) mask; face (*often iro.*); *zo.* larva, grub.

las [la:s] *pret. of lesen.*

lasch F *adj.* [laʃ] limp, lax.

Lasche ['laʃə] *f* (-/-n) strap; tongue (*of shoe*).

lassen ['lasən] (*irr.*, h) **1.** *v/t.* (ge-) let; leave; *laß das!* don't!; *laß das Weinen!* stop crying!; *ich kann es nicht* ~ I cannot help (doing) it; *sein Leben* ~ *für* sacrifice one's life for; **2.** *v/i.* (ge-): *von et.* ~ desist from s.th., renounce s.th.; do without s.th.; **3.** *v/aux.* (no -ge-) allow, permit, let; make, cause; *drucken* ~ *have s. th.* printed; *gehen* ~ *let s.o. go; ich habe ihn dieses Buch lesen* ~ I have made him read this book; *von sich hören* ~ send word; *er läßt sich nichts sagen* he won't take advice; *es läßt sich nicht leugnen* there is no denying (the fact).

lässig *adj.* ['lɛsiç] indolent, idle; sluggish; careless.

Last [last] *f* (-/-en) load; burden; weight; cargo, freight; *fig.* weight, charge, trouble; *zu* ~*en von* ✝ to the debit of; *j-m zur* ~ *fallen* be a burden to s.o.; *j-m et. zur* ~ *legen* lay s.th. at s.o.'s door *or* to s.o.'s charge; **'~auto** *n s.* Lastkraftwagen.

'lasten *v/i.* (ge-, h): ~ *auf* (*dat.*) weigh *or* press (up)on; **'2aufzug** *m* goods lift, *Am.* freight elevator.

Laster ['lastər] *n* (-s/-) vice.

Lästerer ['lɛstərər] *m* (-s/-) slanderer, backbiter.

'lasterhaft *adj.* vicious; corrupt.

Läster|maul ['lɛstər-] *n s.* Lästerer; **'2n** *v/i.* (ge-, h) slander, calumniate, defame; abuse; **'~ung** *f* (-/-en) slander, calumny.

lästig *adj.* ['lɛstiç] troublesome; annoying; uncomfortable, inconvenient.

'Last|kahn *m* barge, lighter; **'~kraftwagen** *m* lorry, *Am.* truck; **'~schrift** *f* debit; **'~tier** *n* pack animal; **'~wagen** *m s.* Lastkraftwagen.

Latein [la'taɪn] *n* (-s/*no pl.*) Latin; **2isch** *adj.* Latin.

Laterne [la'tɛrnə] *f* (-/-n) lantern; street-lamp; **~npfahl** *m* lamp-post.

latschen F ['la:tʃən] *v/i.* (ge-, sein) shuffle (along).

Latte ['latə] *f* (-/-n) pale; lath; *sports:* bar; **'~nkiste** *f* crate; **'~nverschlag** *m* latticed partition; **'~nzaun** *m* paling, *Am.* picket fence.

Lätzchen ['lɛtsçən] *n* (-s/-) bib, feeder.

lau *adj.* [laʊ] tepid, lukewarm (*a. fig.*).

Laub [laʊp] *n* (-[e]s/*no pl.*) foliage, leaves *pl.*; **'~baum** *m* deciduous tree.

Laube ['laʊbə] *f* (-/-n) arbo(u)r, bower; **'~ngang** *m* arcade.

'Laub|frosch *zo.* *m* tree-frog; **'~säge** *f* fret-saw.

Lauch ♀ [laʊx] *m* (-[e]s/-e) leek.

Lauer ['laʊər] *f* (-/*no pl.*): *auf der* ~ *liegen or sein* lie in wait *or* ambush, be on the look-out; **'2n** *v/i.* (ge-, h) lurk (*auf acc.* for); ~ *auf* (*acc.*) watch for; **'2nd** *adj.* louring, lowering.

Lauf [laʊf] *m* (-[e]s/-e) run(ning); *sports:* a. run, heat; race; current (*of water*); course; barrel (*of gun*); ♪ run; *im* ~ *der Zeit* in (the) course of time; **'~bahn** *f* career; **'~bursche** *m* errand-boy, office-boy; **'~disziplin** *f sports:* running event.

'laufen (*irr.*, ge-) **1.** *v/i.* (sein) run; walk; flow; *time:* pass, go by, elapse; leak; *die Dinge* ~ *lassen* let things slide; *j-n* ~ *lassen* let s.o. go; **2.** *v/t.* (sein, h) run; walk; **'~d** *adj.* running; current; regular; *~en Monats* ✝ instant; *auf dem* ~*en sein* be up to date, be fully informed.

Läufer ['lɔʏfər] *m* (-s/-) runner (*a. carpet*); *chess:* bishop; *football:* half-back.

'Lauf|masche *f* ladder, *Am. a.* run; **'~paß** F *m* sack, *sl.* walking papers *pl.*; **'~planke** ♣ *f* gang-board, gang-plank; **'~schritt** *m:* *im* ~ running; **'~steg** *m* footbridge; ♣ gangway.

Lauge ['laʊgə] *f* (-/-n) lye.

Laun|e ['laʊnə] *f* (-/-n) humo(u)r; mood; temper; caprice, fancy, whim; *guter* ~ in (high) spirits; **'2enhaft** *adj.* capricious; **'2isch** *adj.* moody; wayward.

Laus *zo.* [laʊs] *f* (-/-e) louse; **~bub** ['~buːp] *m* (-en/-en) young scamp, F young devil, rascal.

lausch|en ['laʊʃən] *v/i.* (ge-, h) listen; eavesdrop; **'~ig** *adj.* snug, cosy; peaceful.

laut [laʊt] **1.** *adj.* loud (*a. fig.*); noisy; **2.** *adv.* aloud, loud(ly); (*sprechen Sie*) ~*er!* speak up!; *Am.* louder!; **3.** *prp.* (*gen., dat.*) according to; ✝ as per; **4.** **2** *m* (-[e]s/-e) sound; **'2e** ♪ *f* (-/-n) lute; **'~en** *v/i.* (ge-, h) sound; *words, etc.:* run; read; ~ *auf* (*acc.*) passport, *etc.:* be issued to.

läuten ['lɔʏtən] (ge-, h) **1.** *v/i.* ring; toll; *es läutet* the bell is ringing; **2.** *v/t.* ring; toll.

'lauter *adj.* pure; clear; genuine; sincere; mere, nothing but, only.

läuter|n ['lɔʏtərn] *v/t.* (ge-, h) purify; ⊕ cleanse; refine; **'2ung** *f* (-/-en) purification; refining.

'laut|los *adj.* noiseless; mute; silent; *silence:* hushed; **'2schrift** *f* phonetic transcription; **'2sprecher** *m* loud-speaker; **'2stärke** *f* sound intensity; *radio:* (sound-)volume; **2-stärkeregler** ['‿re:glər] *m* (-s/-) volume control.

'lauwarm *adj.* tepid, lukewarm.

Lava *geol.* ['la:va] *f* (-/Laven) lava.

Lavendel ❧ [la'vɛndəl] *m* (-s/-) lavender.

lavieren [la'vi:rən] *v/i.* (*no* -ge-, *h*, *sein*) ❧ tack (*a. fig.*).

Lawine [la'vi:nə] *f* (-/-n) avalanche.

lax *adj.* [laks] lax, loose; *morals:* a. easy.

Lazarett [latsa'rɛt] *n* (-[e]s/-e) (military) hospital.

leben¹ ['le:bən] (ge-, *h*) **1.** *v/i.* live; be alive; ‿ *Sie wohl!* good-bye!, farewell!; *j-n hochleben lassen* cheer s.o.; *at table:* drink s.o.'s health; *von et.* ‿ live on s.th.; *hier lebt es sich gut* it is pleasant living here; **2.** *v/t.* live (*one's life*).

Leben² [‿] *n* (-s/-) life; stir, animation, bustle; *am* ‿ *bleiben* remain alive, survive; *am* ‿ *erhalten* keep alive; *ein neues* ‿ *beginnen* turn over a new leaf; *ins* ‿ *rufen* call into being; *sein* ‿ *aufs Spiel setzen* risk one's life; *sein* ‿ *lang* all one's life; *ums* ‿ *kommen* lose one's life; perish.

lebendig *adj.* [le'bɛndiç] living; *pred.:* alive; quick; lively.

'Lebens|alter *n* age; **'‿anschauung** *f* outlook on life; **'‿art** *f* manners *pl.*, behavio(u)r; **'‿auffassung** *f* philosophy of life; **'‿bedingungen** *f/pl.* living conditions *pl.*; **'‿beschreibung** *f* life, biography; **'‿dauer** *f* span of life; ⊕ durability; **'2echt** *adj.* true to life; **'‿erfahrung** *f* experience of life; **'2-fähig** *adj.* ☞ *and fig.* viable; **'‿gefahr** *f* danger of life; **‿/** danger (of death)!; *unter* ‿ at the risk of one's life; **'2gefährlich** *adj.* dangerous (to life), perilous; **'‿gefährte** *m* life's companion; **'‿größe** *f* life-size; *in* ‿ at full length; **'‿kraft** *f* vital power, vigo(u)r, vitality; **'2länglich** *adj.* for life, lifelong; **'‿lauf** *m* course of life; personal record, curriculum vitae; **'2lustig** *adj.* gay, merry; **'‿mittel** *pl.* food (-stuffs *pl.*), provisions *pl.*, groceries *pl.*; **'2müde** *adj.* weary or tired of life; **'2notwendig** *adj.* vital, essential; **'‿retter** *m* life-saver, rescuer; **'‿standard** *m* standard of living; **'‿unterhalt** *m* livelihood; *s-n* ‿ *verdienen* earn one's living; **'‿versicherung** *f* life-insurance; **'‿wandel** *m* life, (moral) conduct; **'‿weise** *f* mode of living, habits *pl.*; *gesunde* ‿ regimen; **'‿weisheit** *f* worldly wisdom; **'2wichtig** *adj.* vital, essential; **‿e** *Organe pl.* vitals

pl.; **'‿zeichen** *n* sign of life; **'‿zeit** *f* lifetime; *auf* ‿ for life.

Leber *anat.* ['le:bər] *f* (-/-n) liver; **'‿fleck** *m* mole; **'2krank** *adj.*, **'2-leidend** *adj.* suffering from a liver-complaint; **'‿tran** *m* cod-liver oil; **'‿wurst** *f* liver-sausage, *Am.* liverwurst.

'Lebewesen *n* living being, creature.

Lebe'wohl *n* (-[e]s/-e, -s) farewell.

leb|haft *adj.* ['le:phaft] lively; vivid; spirited; *interest:* keen; *traffic:* busy; **'2kuchen** *m* gingerbread; **'‿los** *adj.* lifeless; **'2zeiten** *pl.:* *zu s-n* ‿ in his lifetime.

lechzen ['lɛçtsən] *v/i.* (ge-, *h*): ‿ *nach* languish *or* yearn *or* pant for.

Leck [lɛk] **1.** *n* (-[e]s/-s) leak; **2.** 2 *adj.* leaky; ‿ *werden* ❧ spring a leak.

lecken ['lɛkən] (ge-, *h*) **1.** *v/t.* lick; **2.** *v/i.* lick; leak.

lecker *adj.* ['lɛkər] dainty; delicious; **'2bissen** *m* dainty, delicacy.

Leder ['le:dər] *n* (-s/-) leather; *in* ‿ *gebunden* leather-bound; **'2n** *adj.* leathern, of leather.

ledig *adj.* ['le:diç] single, unmarried; *child:* illegitimate; **'‿lich** *adv.* ['‿k-] solely, merely.

Lee ❧ [le:] *f* (-/*no pl.*) lee (side).

leer [le:r] **1.** *adj.* empty; vacant; void; vain; blank; **2.** *adv.:* ‿ *laufen* ⊕ idle; **'2e** *f* (-/*no pl.*) emptiness, void (*a. fig.*); *phys.* vacuum; **‿en** *v/t.* (ge-, *h*) empty; clear (out); pour out; **'2gut** ✝ *n* empties *pl.*; **'2lauf** *m* ⊕ idling; *mot.* neutral gear; *fig.* waste of energy; **'‿stehend** *adj.* flat: empty, unoccupied, vacant.

legal *adj.* [le'ga:l] legal, lawful.

Legat [le'ga:t] **1.** *m* (-en/-en) legate; **2.** ꬰ *n* (-[e]s/-e) legacy.

legen ['le:gən] (ge-, *h*) **1.** *v/t.* lay; place, put; *sich* ‿ *wind, etc.:* calm down, abate; cease; *Wert* ‿ *auf* (*acc.*) attach importance to; **2.** *v/i.* hen: lay.

Legende [le'gɛndə] *f* (-/-n) legend.

legieren [le'gi:rən] *v/t.* (*no* -ge-, *h*) ⊕ alloy; *cookery:* thicken (*mit* with).

Legislative [le:gisla'ti:və] *f* (-/-n) legislative body *or* power.

legitim *adj.* [legi'ti:m] legitimate; **‿ieren** [‿i'mi:rən] *v/t.* (*no* -ge-, *h*) legitimate; authorize; *sich* ‿ prove one's identity.

Lehm [le:m] *m* (-[e]s/-e) loam; mud; **'2ig** *adj.* loamy.

Lehn|e ['le:nə] *f* (-/-n) support; arm, back (*of chair*); **'2en** (ge-, *h*) **1.** *v/i.* lean (*an dat.* against); **2.** *v/t.* lean, rest (*an acc., gegen* against); *sich* ‿ *an acc.* lean against; *sich* ‿ *auf* (*acc.*) rest *or* support o.s. (up-)on; *sich aus dem Fenster* ‿ lean out of the window; **'‿sessel** *m*, **'‿stuhl** *m* armchair, easy chair.

Lehrbuch ['leːr-] *n* textbook.
Lehre ['leːrə] *f* (-/-*n*) rule, precept; doctrine; system; science; theory; lesson, warning; moral (*of fable*); instruction, tuition; ⊕ ga(u)ge; ⊕ pattern; *in der ~ sein* be apprenticed (*bei to*); *in die ~ geben* apprentice, article (*both: bei, zu* to); '**2n** *v/t.* (*ge-, h*) teach, instruct; show.
'**Lehrer** *m* (-*s*/-) teacher; master, instructor; '**~in** *f* (-/-*nen*) (lady) teacher; (school)mistress; '**~kolle-gium** *n* staff (of teachers).
'**Lehr|fach** *n* subject; '**~film** *m* instructional film; '**~gang** *m* course (of instruction); '**~geld** *n* premium; '**~herr** *m* master, *sl.* boss; '**~jahre** *n/pl.* (years *pl.* of) apprenticeship; '**~junge** *m s.* Lehrling; '**~körper** *m* teaching staff; *univ.* professorate, faculty; '**~kraft** *f* teacher; professor; '**~ling** *m* (-*s*/-*e*) apprentice; '**~mädchen** *n* girl apprentice; '**~meister** *m* master; '**~methode** *f* method of teaching; '**~plan** *m* curriculum, syllabus; '**2reich** *adj.* instructive; '**~satz** *m* ⊕ theorem; doctrine; *eccl.* dogma; '**~stoff** *m* subject-matter, subject(s *pl.*); '**~stuhl** *m* professorship; '**~vertrag** *m* articles *pl.* of apprenticeship, indenture(s *pl.*); '**~zeit** *f* apprenticeship.
Leib [laɪp] *m* (-[*e*]*s*/-*er*) body; belly, *anat.* abdomen; womb; *bei leben-digem ~* alive; *mit ~ und Seele* body and soul; *sich j-n vom ~e halten* keep s.o. at arm's length; '**~arzt** *m* physician in ordinary, personal physician; '**~chen** *n* (-*s*/-) bodice.
Leibeigen|e ['laɪpˀaɪɡənə] *m* (-*n*/-*n*) bond(s)man, serf; '**~schaft** *f* (-/*no pl.*) bondage, serfdom.
Leibes|erziehung ['laɪbəs-] *f* physical training; '**~frucht** *f* (o)etus; '**~kraft** *f*: *aus Leibeskräften pl.* with all one's might; '**~übung** *f* bodily or physical exercise.
'**Leib|garde** *f* body-guard; '**~ge-richt** *n* favo(u)rite dish; **2haftig** *adj.* [**~**'haftiç]: *der ~e Teufel* the devil incarnate; '**2lich** *adj.* bodily, corpor(e)al; '**~rente** *f* life-annuity; '**~schmerzen** *m/pl.* stomach-ache, belly-ache, ✻ colic; '**~wache** *f* body-guard; '**~wäsche** *f* underwear.
Leiche ['laɪçə] *f* (-/-*n*) (dead) body, corpse.
Leichen|beschauer 🕱 ['laɪçənbə-ʃaʊər] *m* (-*s*/-) *appr.* coroner; '**~be-statter** *m* (-*s*/-) undertaker, *Am. a.* mortician; '**~bittermiene** F *f* woebegone look or countenance; '**2'blaß** *adj.* deadly pale; '**~halle** *f* mortuary; '**~schau** 🕱 *f f* (coroner's) inquest; '**~schauhaus** *n* morgue; '**~tuch** *n* (-[*e*]*s*/=*er*) shroud; '**~verbrennung** *f* cremation; '**~wa-gen** *m* hearse.

Leichnam ['laɪçnaːm] *m* (-[*e*]*s*/-*e*) *s.* Leiche.
leicht [laɪçt] **1.** *adj.* light; easy; slight; *tobacco:* mild; **2.** *adv.: es ~ nehmen* take it easy; '**2athlet** *m* athlete; '**2athletik** *f* athletics *pl.*, *Am.* track and field events *pl.*; '**~fer-tig** *adj.* light(-minded); careless; frivolous, flippant; '**2fertigkeit** *f* levity; carelessness; frivolity, flip-pancy; '**2gewicht** *n* boxing: light-weight; '**2gläubig** *adj.* credulous; '**~hin** *adv.* lightly, casually; **2ig-keit** ['**~**iç-] *f* (-/-*en*) lightness, ease, facility; '**~lebig** *adj.* easy-going; '**2metall** *n* light metal; '**2sinn** *m* (-[*e*]*s*/*no pl.*) frivolity, levity; care-lessness; '**~sinnig** *adj.* light-minded, frivolous; careless; '**~verdaulich** *adj.* easy to digest; '**~verständlich** *adj.* easy to understand.
leid [laɪt] **1.** *adv.*: *es tut mir ~* I am sorry (*um* for), I regret; **2. 2** *n* (-[*e*]*s*/*no pl.*) injury, harm; wrong; grief, sorrow; '**~en** ['**~**dən] (*irr., ge-, h*) **1.** *v/i.* suffer (*an dat.* from); **2.** *v/t.*: (*nicht*) *~ können* (dis)like; **2en** ['**~**dən] *n* (-*s*/-) suffering; ✻ complaint; ailing; **~end** ✻ *adj.* ['**~**dənt] ailing.
'**Leidenschaft** *f* (-/-*en*) passion; '**2lich** *adj.* passionate; ardent; vehe-ment; '**2slos** *adj.* dispassionate.
'**Leidens|gefährte** *m*, '**~gefährtin** *f* fellow-sufferer.
leid|er *adv.* ['**~**dər] unfortunately; *int.* alas!; *~ muß ich inf.* I'm (so) sorry to *inf.*; *ich muß ~ gehen* I am afraid I have to go; '**~ig** *adj.* disagreeable; '**~lich** *adj.* ['**~**laɪt-] tolerable; fairly well; **2tragende** ['laɪt-] *m* (-*n*/-*n*) mourner; *er ist der ~ dabei* he is the one who suf-fers for it; **2wesen** ['laɪt-] *n* (-*s*/*no pl.*): *zu meinem ~* to my regret.
Leier ♪ ['laɪər] *f* (-/-*n*) lyre; '**~ka-sten** *m* barrel-organ; '**~kasten-mann** *m* organ-grinder.
Leih|bibliothek ['laɪ-] *f*, '**~büche-rei** *f* lending *or* circulating library, *Am. a.* rental library; '**2en** *v/t.* (*irr., ge-, h*) lend; borrow (*von* from); '**~gebühr** *f* lending fee(s *pl.*); '**~haus** *n* pawnshop, *Am. a.* loan office; '**2weise** *adv.* as a loan.
Leim [laɪm] *m* (-[*e*]*s*/-*e*) glue; F *aus dem ~ gehen* get out of joint; F: *auf den ~ gehen* fall for it, fall into the trap; '**2en** *v/t.* (*ge-, h*) glue; size.
Lein ♀ [laɪn] *m* (-[*e*]*s*/-*e*) flax.
Leine ['laɪnə] *f* (-/-*n*) line, cord; (dog-)lead, leash.
leinen ['laɪnən] **1.** *adj.* (of) linen; **2. 2** *n* (-*s*/-) linen; *in ~ gebunden* cloth-bound; '**2schuh** *m* canvas shoe.
'**Lein|öl** *n* linseed-oil; '**~samen** *m* linseed; '**~wand** *f* (-/*no pl.*) linen (cloth); *paint.* canvas; *film:* screen.

leise *adj.* ['laɪzə] low, soft; gentle; slight, faint; ~*r stellen* turn down (*radio*).

Leiste ['laɪstə] *f* (-/-*n*) border, ledge; △ fillet; *anat.* groin.

leisten ['laɪstən] *v/t.* (*ge-, h*) do; perform; fulfil(l); take (*oath*); render (*service*); *ich kann mir das ~* I can afford it; **2.** ⊕ *m* (-*s*/-) last; boot-tree, *Am. a.* shoetree; '2-**bruch** ♂ *m* inguinal hernia.

'**Leistung** *f* (-/-*en*) performance; achievement; work(manship); result(s *pl.*); ⊕ capacity; output (*of factory*); benefit (*of insurance company*); '2s**fähig** *adj.* productive; efficient, ⊕ *a.* powerful; '~s**fähigkeit** *f* efficiency; ⊕ productivity; ⊕ capacity, producing-power.

Leit|artikel ['laɪt-] *m* leading article, leader, editorial; '~**bild** *n* image; example.

leiten ['laɪtən] *v/t.* (*ge-, h*) lead, guide; conduct (*a. phys., ♪*); *fig.* direct, run, manage, operate; preside over (*meeting*); '~**d** *adj.* leading; *phys.* conductive; ~*e Stellung* key position.

'**Leiter 1.** *m* (-*s*/-) leader; conductor (*a. phys., ♪*); guide; manager; **2.** *f* (-/-*n*) ladder; '~**in** *f* (-/-*nen*) leader; conductress, guide; manageress; '~**wagen** *m* rack-wag(g)on.

'**Leit|faden** *m* manual, textbook, guide; '~**motiv** ♪ *n* leit-motiv; '~**spruch** *m* motto; '~**tier** *n* leader; '~**ung** *f* (-/-*en*) lead(ing), conducting, guidance; management, direction, administration, *Am. a.* operation; *phys.* conduction; ⚡ lead; circuit; *tel.* line; mains *pl.* (*for gas, water, etc.*); pipeline; *die ~ ist besetzt teleph.* the line is engaged or *Am.* busy.

'**Leitungs|draht** *m* conducting wire, conductor; '~**rohr** *n* conduit(-pipe); main (*for gas, water, etc.*); '~**wasser** *n* (-*s*/=) tap water.

'**Leitwerk** ⚓ *n* tail unit or group, empennage.

Lekt|ion [lɛk'tsjoːn] *f* (-/-*en*) lesson; ~**or** ['lɛktɔr] *m* (-*s*/-*en*) lecturer; reader; ~**üre** [~'tyːrə] *f* **1.** (-/*no pl.*) reading; **2.** (-/-*n*) books *pl.*

Lende *anat.* ['lɛndə] *f* (-/-*n*) loin(s *pl.*).

lenk|bar *adj.* ['lɛŋkbaːr] guidable, manageable, tractable, docile; ⊕ steerable, dirigible; '~**en** *v/t.* (*ge-, h*) direct, guide; turn; rule; govern; drive (*car*); ♨ steer; *Aufmerksamkeit ~ auf* (*acc.*) draw attention to; '2**rad** *mot.* *n* steering wheel; '2-**säule** *mot.* *f* steering column; '2-**stange** *f* handle-bar (*of bicycle*); '2**ung** *mot.* *f* (-/-*en*) steering-gear.

Lenz [lɛnts] *m* (-*es*/-*e*) spring.

Leopard *zo.* [leo'part] *m* (-*en*/-*en*) leopard.

Lepra ♂ ['leːpra] *f* (-/*no pl.*) leprosy.

Lerche *orn.* ['lɛrçə] *f* (-/-*n*) lark.

lern|begierig *adj.* ['lɛrn-] eager to learn, studious; '~**en** *v/t. and v/i.* (*ge-, h*) learn; study.

Lese ['leːzə] *f* (-/-*n*) gathering; *s. Weinlese*; '~**buch** *n* reader; '~**lampe** *f* reading-lamp.

lesen ['leːzən] (*irr., ge-, h*) **1.** *v/t.* read; ♂ gather; *Messe ~ eccl.* say mass; **2.** *v/i.* read; *univ.* (give a) lecture (*über acc.* on); '~**swert** *adj.* worth reading.

'**Leser** *m* (-*s*/-), '~**in** *f* (-/-*nen*) reader; ♂ gatherer; vintager; '2**lich** *adj.* legible; '~**zuschrift** *f* letter to the editor.

'**Lesezeichen** *n* book-mark.

'**Lesung** *parl.* *f* (-/-*en*) reading.

letzt *adj.* [lɛtst] last; final; ultimate; ~*e Nachrichten pl.* latest news *pl.*; ~*e Hand anlegen* put the finishing touches (*an acc.* to); *das ~e* the last thing; *der ~ere* the latter; *der (die, das) Letzte* the last (one); *zu guter Letzt* last but not least; finally; '~**ens** *adv.*, '~**hin** *adv.* lately, of late; '~**lich** *adv. s. letztens*; finally; ultimately.

Leucht|e ['lɔyçtə] *f* (-/-*n*) (*fig.* shining) light, lamp (*a. fig.*), luminary (*a. fig., esp. p.*); '2**en** *v/i.* (*ge-, h*) (give) light, shine (forth); beam, gleam; '~**en** *n* (-*s*/*no pl.*) shining, light, luminosity; '2**end** *adj.* shining, bright; luminous; brilliant (*a. fig.*); '~**er** *m* (-*s*/-) candlestick; *s. Kronleuchter*; '~**feuer** *n* ⚓, ✈, *etc.*: beacon(-light), flare (light); '~**käfer** *zo.* *m* glow-worm; '~**kugel** ✗ *f* Very light; flare; '~**turm** *m* lighthouse; '~**ziffer** *f* luminous figure.

leugnen ['lɔygnən] *v/t.* (*ge-, h*) deny; disavow; contest.

Leukämie ♂ [lɔykɛ'miː] *f* (-/-*n*) leuk(a)emia.

Leumund ['lɔymunt] *m* (-[*e*]*s*/*no pl.*) reputation, repute; character; '~**szeugnis** ♣♣ *n* character reference.

Leute ['lɔytə] *pl.* people *pl.*; persons *pl.*; ✗, *pol.* men *pl.*; *workers*: hands *pl.*; F folks *pl.*; domestics *pl.*, servants *pl.*

Leutnant ✗ ['lɔytnant] *m* (-*s*/-*s*, ✗, -*e*) second lieutenant.

leutselig *adj.* ['lɔytzeːliç] affable.

Lexikon ['lɛksikɔn] *n* (-*s*/*Lexika, Lexiken*) dictionary; encyclop(a)edia.

Libelle *zo.* [li'bɛlə] *f* (-/-*n*) dragon-fly.

liberal *adj.* [libe'raːl] liberal.

Licht [liçt] **1.** *n* (-[*e*]*s*/-*er*) light; brightness; lamp; candle; *hunt.* eye; ~ *machen* ⚡ switch or turn on the light (*pl.*); *das ~ der Welt erblicken* see the light, be born; **2.** 2 *adj.* light, bright; clear; ~*er Augenblick* ♂ lucid interval; '~**anlage** *f* lighting plant; **~bild** n photo (-graph); **~bildervortrag** m slide lecture; **~blick** fig. m bright spot; **~bogen** ⚡ m arc; **²durchlässig** adj. translucent; **²echt** adj. fast (to light), unfading; **²empfindlich** adj. sensitive to light, phot. sensitive; machen sensitize.

lichten v/t (ge-, h) clear (forest); den Anker . ⚓ weigh anchor; sich ~ hair, crowd thin.

lichterloh adv ['lɪçtər'lo:] blazing, in full blaze

'Licht|geschwindigkeit f speed of light; **~hof** m glass-roofed court; patio; halo (a phot.); **'~leitung** f lighting mains pl.; **'~maschine** mot. f dynamo, generator; **'~pause** f blueprint, **~quelle** f light source, source of light, **~reklame** f neon sign; **~schacht** m well; **'~schalter** m (light) switch, **~schein** m gleam of light, **²scheu** adj. shunning the light; **~signal** n light or luminous signal, **~spieltheater** n s. Filmtheater, Kino, **~strahl** m ray or beam of light (a fig.); **²undurchlässig** adj opaque.

'Lichtung f (-/-en) clearing, opening, glade

'Lichtzelle f s. Photozelle.

Lid [li:t] n (-[e]s/-er) eyelid.

lieb adj [li:p] dear; nice, kind; child. good; in letters: ~er Herr N. dear Mr N.; ~er Himmel! good Heavens!, dear me!; es ist mir ~, daß I am glad that; **²chen** n (-s/-) sweetheart

Liebe ['li:bə] f (-/no pl.) love (zu of, for); aus ~ for love; aus ~ zu for the love of; **²n** (ge-, h) 1. v/t. love; be in love with; be fond of, like; 2. v/i. (be in) love; **~nde** m, f (-n/-n): die ~n pl. the lovers pl.

'liebens|wert adj. lovable; charming; **'~würdig** adj. lovable, amiable; das ist sehr ~ von Ihnen that is very kind of you; **²würdigkeit** f (-/-en) amiability, kindness.

'lieber 1. adj. dearer; 2. adv. rather, sooner, haben prefer, like better.

'Liebes|brief m love-letter; '**~dienst** m favo(u)r, kindness; good turn; **~erklärung** f: e-e ~ machen declare one's love; '**~heirat** f love-match; **~kummer** m lover's grief; **~paar** n (courting) couple, lovers pl.; **~verhältnis** n love-affair.

'liebevoll adj. loving, affectionate.

lieb|gewinnen ['li:p-] v/t. (irr. gewinnen, sep., no -ge-, h) get or grow fond of; **'~haben** v/t. (irr. haben, sep., -ge-, h) love, be fond of; **²haber** m (-s/-) lover; beau; fig. amateur; **²haberei** fig. [.'raɪ] f (-/-en) hobby; **²haberpreis** m fancy price; **²haberwert** m sentimental value; **'~kosen** v/t. (no -ge-, h) caress, fondle; **²kosung** f (-/-en) caress;

'~lich adj. lovely, charming, delightful.

Liebling ['li:plɪŋ] m (-s/-e) darling; favo(u)rite; esp. animals: pet; esp. form of address darling, esp. Am. honey; **~sbeschäftigung** f favo(u)rite occupation, hobby.

lieb|los adj. ['li:p-] unkind; careless; **²schaft** f (-/-en) (love-)affair; **²ste** m, f (-n/-n) sweetheart; darling.

Lied [li:t] n (-[e]s/-er) song; tune.

liederlich adj. ['li:dərlɪç] slovenly, disorderly; careless; loose, dissolute.

lief [li:f] pret. of laufen.

Lieferant [li:fə'rant] m (-en/-en) supplier, purveyor; caterer.

Liefer|auto ['li:fər-] n s. Lieferwagen; **²bar** adj. to be delivered; available; **~bedingungen** f/pl. terms pl. of delivery; **~frist** f term of delivery; **²n** v/t (ge-, h) deliver; j-m et. ~ furnish or supply s.o. with s.th.; **~schein** m delivery note; **~ung** f (-/-en) delivery; supply; consignment; instal(l)ment (of book); **~ungsbedingungen** ~/pl. s. Lieferbedingungen; **~wagen** m deliveryvan, Am. delivery wagon.

Liege ['li:gə] f (-/-n) couch; bedchair.

liegen ['li:gən] v/i. (irr., ge-, h) lie; house, etc.: be (situated); room: face; an wem liegt es? whose fault is it? es liegt an or bei ihm zu inf. it is for him to inf.; es liegt daran, daß the reason for it is that; es liegt mir daran zu inf. I am anxious to inf.; es liegt mir nichts daran it does not matter or it is of no consequence to me; **~bleiben** v/i. (irr. bleiben, sep., -ge-, sein) stay in bed; break down (on the road, a. mot., etc.); work, etc.: stand over; fall behind; 🕇 goods: remain on hand; **~lassen** v/t. (irr. lassen, sep., [-ge-,] h) leave; leave behind; leave alone; leave off (work); j-n links ~ ignore s.o., give s.o. the cold shoulder; **²schaften** f/pl. real estate.

'Liege|stuhl m deck-chair; '**~wagen** 🚃 m couchette coach.

lieh [li:] pret. of leihen.

ließ [li:s] pret. of lassen.

Lift [lɪft] m (-[e]s/-e, -s) lift, Am. elevator.

Liga ['li:ga] f (-/Ligen) league.

Likör [li'kø:r] m (-s/-e) liqueur, cordial.

lila adj. ['li:la] lilac.

Lilie 🌸 ['li:ljə] f (-/-n) lily.

Limonade [limo'na:də] f (-/-n) soft drink, fruit-juice; lemonade.

Limousine mot. [limu'zi:nə] f (-/-n) limousine, saloon car, Am. sedan.

lind adj. [lɪnt] soft, gentle; mild.

Linde 🌸 ['lɪndə] f (-/-n) lime(-tree), linden(-tree).

linder|n ['lindərn] v/t. (ge-, h) soften; mitigate; alleviate, soothe; allay, ease (*pain*); **'2ung** f (-/‰-en) softening; mitigation; alleviation; easing.

Lineal [line'a:l] n (-s/-e) ruler.

Linie ['li:njə] f (-/-n) line; **'‿npapier** n ruled paper; **'‿nrichter** m sports: linesman; **'2ntreu** pol. adj.: ‿ sein follow the party line.

lin(i)ieren [li'ni:rən; lini'i:rən] v/t. (no -ge-, h) rule, line.

link adj. [liŋk] left; ‿e Seite left (-hand) side, left; of cloth: wrong side; **'2e** f (-n/-n) the left (hand); pol. the Left (Wing); boxing: the left; **'‿isch** adj. awkward, clumsy.

links adv. on or to the left; **2händer** ['‿hendər] m (-s/-) left-hander, Am. a. southpaw.

Linse ['linzə] f (-/-n) & lentil; opt. lens.

Lippe ['lipə] f (-/-n) lip; **'‿nstift** m lipstick.

liquidieren [likvi'di:rən] v/t. (no -ge-, h) liquidate (a. pol.); wind up (business company); charge (fee).

lispeln ['lispəln] v/i. and v/t. (ge-, h) lisp; whisper.

List [list] f (-/-en) cunning, craft; artifice, ruse, trick; stratagem.

Liste ['listə] f (-/-n) list, roll.

'listig adj. cunning, crafty, sly.

Liter ['li:tər] n, m (-s/-) lit|re, Am. -er.

literarisch adj. [lite'ra:riʃ] literary.

Literatur [litera'tu:r] f (-/-en) literature; **‿beilage** f literary supplement (in newspaper); **‿geschichte** f history of literature; **‿verzeichnis** n bibliography.

litt [lit] pret. of leiden.

Litze ['litsə] f (-/-n) lace, cord, braid; ƒ strand(ed wire).

Livree [li'vre:] f (-/-n) livery.

Lizenz [li'tsents] f (-/-en) licen|ce, Am. -se; **‿inhaber** m licensee.

Lob [lo:p] n (-[e]s/no pl.) praise; commendation; **2en** ['lo:bən] v/t. (ge-, h) praise; **2enswert** adj. ['lo:bəns-] praise-worthy, laudable; **‿gesang** ['lo:p-] m hymn, song of praise; **‿hudelei** [lo:phu:də'lai] f (-/-en) adulation, base flattery.

löblich adj. ['lø:pliç] s. lobenswert.

Lobrede ['lo:p-] f eulogy, panegyric.

Loch [lɔx] n (-[e]s/‿er) hole; **'2en** v/t. (ge-, h) perforate, pierce; punch (ticket, etc.); **'‿er** m (-s/-) punch, perforator; **'‿karte** f punch(ed) card.

Locke ['lɔkə] f (-/-n) curl, ringlet.

'locken¹ v/t. and v/refl. (ge-, h) curl.

'locken² v/t. (ge-, h) hunt.: bait; decoy (a. fig.); fig. allure, entice.

'Locken|kopf m curly head; **‿wickler** ['‿viklər] m (-s/-) curler, roller.

locker adj. ['lɔkər] loose; slack; '‿n

v/t. (ge-, h) loosen; slacken; relax (grip); break up (soil); sich ‿ loosen, (be)come loose; give way; fig. relax.

'lockig adj. curly.

'Lock|mittel n s. Köder; **'‿vogel** m decoy (a. fig.); Am. a. stool pigeon (a. fig.).

lodern ['lo:dərn] v/i. (ge-, h) flare, blaze.

Löffel ['lœfəl] m (-s/-) spoon; ladle; **'2n** v/t. (ge-, h) spoon up; ladle out; **'‿voll** m (-/-) spoonful.

log [lo:k] pret. of lügen.

Loge ['lo:ʒə] f (-/-n) thea. box; freemasonry: lodge; **'‿nschließer** thea. m (-s/-) box-keeper.

logieren [lo'ʒi:rən] v/i. (no -ge-, h) lodge, stay, Am. a. room (all: bei with; in dat. at).

logisch adj. ['lo:giʃ] logical; '‿erweise adv. logically.

Lohn [lo:n] m (-[e]s/‿e) wages pl., pay(ment); hire; fig. reward; **'‿büro** n pay-office; **'‿empfänger** m wage-earner; **'2en** v/t. (ge-, h) compensate, reward; sich ‿ pay; es lohnt sich zu inf. it is worth while ger., it pays to inf.; **'2end** adj. paying; advantageous; fig. rewarding; **'‿erhöhung** f increase in wages, rise, Am. raise; **'‿forderung** f demand for higher wages; **'‿steuer** f tax on wages or salary; **'‿stopp** m (-s/no pl.) wage freeze; **'‿tarif** m wage rate; **'‿tüte** f pay envelope.

lokal [lo'ka:l] **1.** adj. local; **2.** 2 n (-[e]s/-e) locality, place; restaurant; public house, F pub, F local, Am. saloon.

Lokomotiv|e [lokomo'ti:və] f (-/-n) (railway) engine, locomotive; **‿führer** [‿'ti:f-] m engine-driver, Am. engineer.

Lorbeer f ['lɔrbe:r] m (-s/-en) laurel, bay.

Lore ['lo:rə] f (-/-n) lorry, truck.

Los¹ [lo:s] n (-es/-e) lot; lottery ticket; fig. fate, destiny, lot; das Große ‿ ziehen win the first prize, Am. sl. hit the jackpot; durchs ‿ entscheiden decide by lot.

los² [‿] **1.** pred. adj. loose; free; was ist ‿? what is the matter?, F what's up?, Am. F what's cooking?; ‿ sein be rid of; **2.** int.: ‿! go (on or ahead)!

losarbeiten ['lo:s?-] v/i. (sep., -ge-, h) start work(ing).

lösbar adj. ['lø:sba:r] soluble, & a. solvable.

'los|binden v/t. (irr. binden, sep., -ge-, h) untie, loosen; **'‿brechen** (irr. brechen, sep., -ge-) **1.** v/t. (h) break off; **2.** v/i. (sein) break or burst out.

Lösch|blatt ['lœʃ-] n blotting-paper; **'2en** v/t. (ge-, h) extinguish, put out (fire, light); blot out (writing);

erase (*tape recording*); cancel (*debt*); quench (*thirst*); slake (*lime*); ⚓ unload; ~er *m* (-s/-) blotter; '~papier *n* blotting-paper.

lose *adj* ['loːzə] loose.

'Lösegeld *n* ransom.

losen ['loːzən] *v/i.* (ge-, h) cast *or* draw lots (um for).

lösen ['løːzən] *v/t.* (ge-, h) loosen, untie; buy, book (*ticket*); solve (*task, doubt, etc.*); break off (*engagement*); annul (*agreement, etc.*); 🜋 dissolve; *ein Schuß löste sich the* gun went off.

'los|fahren *v/i.* (*irr. fahren, sep.,* -ge-, sein) depart, drive off; '~gehen *v/i.* (*irr gehen, sep., -ge-, sein*) go *or* be off, come off, get loose; *gun:* go off; begin, start; F *auf j-n ~* fly at s.o.; '~haken *v/t.* (*sep., -ge-, h*) unhook, ~kaufen *v/t.* (*sep., -ge-, h*) ransom, redeem, ~ketten *v/t.* (*sep.,* -ge-, h) unchain, '~kommen *v/i.* (*irr. kommen, sep., -ge-, sein*) get loose *or* free, '~lachen *v/i.* (*sep.,* -ge-, h) laugh out; '~lassen *v/t.* (*irr. lassen, sep., -ge-, h*) let go; release

löslich 🜋 *adj.* ['løːsliç] soluble.

'los|lösen *v/t* (*sep., -ge-, h*) loosen, detach, sever, ~machen *v/t.* (*sep.,* -ge-, h) unfasten, loosen; *sich ~* disengage (...s) (von from); '~reißen *v/t.* (*irr reißer, sep., -ge-, h*) tear off; *sich break* away, *esp. fig.* tear o.s. away (*both* von from); '~sagen *v/refl.* (*sep , -ge-, h*) *sich ~* von renounce, ~schlagen (*irr. schlagen, sep , -ge , h*) 1. *v/t.* knock off; 2. *v/i* open the attack; *auf j-n ~* attack s.o.; '~schnallen *v/t.* (*sep.,* -ge-, h) unbuckle, '~schrauben *v/t.* (*sep , -ge-, h*) unscrew, screw off; '~sprechen *v/t* (*irr. sprechen, sep., -ge-, h*) absolve (von of, from); acquit (of); free (from, of); '~stürzen *v/i* (*sep., -ge-, sein*): ~ auf (acc.) rush at

Losung ['loːzuŋ] *f* 1. (-/-en) ✕ password, watchword; *fig.* slogan; 2. *hunt.* (-/*no pl.*) droppings *pl.*, dung.

Lösung ['løːzuŋ] *f* (-/-en) solution; '~smittel *n* solvent.

'los|werden *v/t* (*irr. werden, sep.,* -ge-, sein) get rid of, dispose of; '~ziehen *v/i* (*irr. ziehen, sep., -ge-, sein*) set out, take off, march away.

Lot [loːt] *n* (-[e]s/-e) plumb(-line), plummet

löten ['løːtən] *v/t.* (ge-, h) solder.

Lotse ['loːtsə] *m* (-n/-n) pilot; '2n *v/t* (ge-, h) ⚓ pilot (*a. fig.*).

Lotterie [lɔtəˈriː] *f* (-/-n) lottery; ~gewinn *m* prize; ~los *n* lottery ticket.

Lotto ['lɔto] *n* (-s/-s) numbers pool, lotto.

Löwe *zo.* ['løːvə] *m* (-n/-n) lion.

'Löwen|anteil *m* lion's share; '~maul ♣ *n* (-[e]s/*no pl.*) snapdragon; '~zahn ♣ *m* (-[e]s/*no pl.*) dandelion.

'Löwin *zo. f* (-/-nen) lioness.

loyal *adj.* [loaˈjaːl] loyal.

Luchs *zo.* [luks] *m* (-es/-e) lynx.

Lücke ['lykə] *f* (-/-n) gap; blank, void (*a. fig.*); ~nbüßer *m* stopgap; '2nhaft *adj.* full of gaps; *fig.* defective, incomplete; '2nlos *adj.* without a gap; *fig.* unbroken; complete; ~er Beweis close argument.

lud [luːt] *pret. of* laden.

Luft [luft] *f* (-/-e) air; breeze; breath; *frische ~ schöpfen* take the air; *an die ~ gehen* go for an airing; *aus der ~ gegriffen* (totally) unfounded, fantastic; *es liegt et. in der ~* there is s.th in the wind; *in die ~ fliegen* be blown up, explode; *in die ~ gehen* explode, *sl.* blow one's top; *in die ~ sprengen* blow up; F *j-n an die ~ setzen* turn s.o. out, *Am. sl.* give s.o. the air; *sich or s-n Gefühlen ~ machen* give vent to one's feelings

'Luft|alarm *m* air-raid alarm; '~angriff *m* air raid; ~aufnahme *f* aerial photograph, ~ballon *m* (air-)balloon, ~bild *n* aerial photograph, airview; ~blase *f* air-bubble, ~brücke *f* air-bridge; *for supplies, etc* air-lift.

Lüftchen ['lyftçən] *n* (-s/-) gentle breeze.

'luft|dicht *adj.* air-tight; '2druck *phys. m* (-[e]s/*no pl.*) atmospheric *or* air pressure; '2druckbremse ⊕ *f* air-brake; '~durchlässig *adj.* permeable to air

lüften ['lyftən] (ge-, h) 1. *v/i.* air; 2. *v/t.* air; raise (*hat*); lift (*veil*); disclose (*secret*).

'Luft|fahrt *f* aviation, aeronautics; '~feuchtigkeit *f* atmospheric humidity; '2gekühlt ⊕ *adj.* air-cooled; '~hoheit *f* air sovereignty; '2ig *adj* airy; breezy; flimsy; '~kissen *n* air-cushion; '~klappe *f* air-valve; '~korridor *m* air corridor; '~krankheit *f* airsickness; '~krieg *m* aerial warfare; '~kurort *m* climatic health resort; '~landetruppen *f/pl* airborne troops *pl.*; '2leer *adj* void of air, evacuated; ~er Raum vacuum; '~linie *f* air line, bee-line; '~loch *n* ✈ air-pocket; vent(-hole); '~post *f* air mail; '~pumpe *f* air-pump; '~raum *m* airspace; '~röhre *anat. f* windpipe, trachea; '~schacht *m* air-shaft, '~schaukel *f* swing-boat; '~schiff *n* airship; '~schloß *n* castle in the air *or* in Spain; '~schutz *m* air-raid protection; '~schutzkeller *m* air-raid shelter; '~sprünge [~ʃpryŋə] *m/pl.: ~ machen* cut capers *pl.*; gambol; '~stützpunkt ✕ *m* air base.

'**Lüftung** *f* (-/-en) airing; ventilation.

'**Luft|veränderung** *f* change of air; '**~verkehr** *m* air-traffic; '**~verkehrsgesellschaft** *f* air transport company, airway, *Am.* airline; '**~verteidigung** ✗ *f* air defen|ce, *Am.* -se; '**~waffe** ✗ *f* air force; '**~weg** *m* airway; *auf dem* **~** by air; '**~zug** *m* draught, *Am.* draft.

Lüge ['lyːɡə] *f* (-/-n) lie, falsehood; *j-n* **~n** *strafen* give the lie to s.o.

'**lügen** *v/i.* (*irr.*, ge-, h) (tell a) lie; '**~haft** *adj.* lying, mendacious; untrue, false.

Lügner ['lyːɡnər] *m* (-s/-), '**~in** *f* (-/-nen) liar; '**~isch** *adj. s.* **lügenhaft.**

Luke ['luːkə] *f* (-/-n) dormer- *or* garret-window; hatch.

Lümmel ['lyməl] *m* (-s/-) lout, boor; saucy fellow; '**~n** *v/refl.* (ge-, h) loll, lounge, sprawl.

Lump [lump] *m* (-en/-en) ragamuffin, beggar; cad, *Am. sl.* rat, heel; scoundrel.

'**Lumpen 1.** *m* (-s/-) rag; **2.** ♀ *vb.*: *sich nicht* **~** *lassen* come down handsomely; '**~pack** *n* rabble, riffraff; '**~sammler** *m* rag-picker.

'**lumpig** *adj.* ragged; *fig.*: shabby, paltry; mean.

Lunge ['luŋə] *f* (-/-n) *anat.* lungs *pl.*; *of animals:* a. lights *pl.*

'**Lungen|entzündung** ✿ *f* pneumonia; '**~flügel** *anat. m* lung; '**❷krank** ✿ *adj.* suffering from consumption, consumptive; '**~kranke** ✿ *m, f* consumptive (patient); '**~krankheit** ✿ *f* lung-disease; '**~schwindsucht** ✿ *f* (pulmonary) consumption.

lungern ['luŋərn] *v/i.* (ge-, h) *s. herumlungern.*

Lupe ['luːpə] *f* (-/-n) magnifying-glass; *unter die* **~** *nehmen* scrutinize, take a good look at.

Lust [lust] *f* (-/-e) pleasure, delight; desire; lust; **~** *haben zu inf.* have a mind to *inf.*, feel like *ger.*; *haben Sie* **~** *auszugehen?* would you like to go out?

lüstern *adj.* ['lystərn] desirous (*nach* of), greedy (of, for); lewd, lascivious, lecherous.

'**lustig** *adj.* merry, gay; jolly, cheerful; amusing, funny; *sich* **~** *machen über* (*acc.*) make fun of; '**❷keit** *f* (-/no *pl.*) gaiety, mirth; jollity, cheerfulness; fun.

Lüstling ['lystliŋ] *m* (-s/-e) voluptuary, libertine.

'**lust|los** *adj.* dull, spiritless; ✝ flat; '**❷mord** *m* rape and murder; '**❷spiel** *n* comedy.

lutschen ['lutʃən] *v/i. and v/t.* (ge-, h) suck.

Luv ⚓ [luːf] *f* (-/no *pl.*) luff, windward.

luxuriös *adj.* [luksuˈrjøːs] luxurious.

Luxus ['luksus] *m* (-/no *pl.*) luxury (*a. fig.*); '**~artikel** *m* luxury; '**~ausgabe** *f* de luxe edition (*of books*); '**~ware** *f* luxury (article); fancy goods *pl.*

Lymph|drüse *anat.* ['lymf-] *f* lymphatic gland; '**~e** *f* (-/-n) lymph; ✿ vaccine; '**~gefäß** *anat. n* lymphatic vessel.

lynchen ['lynçən] *v/t.* (ge-, h) lynch.

Lyrik ['lyːrik] *f* (-/no *pl.*) lyric verses *pl.*, lyrics *pl.*; '**~er** *m* (-s/-) lyric poet.

'**lyrisch** *adj.* lyric; lyrical (*a. fig.*).

M

Maat ⚓ [maːt] *m* (-[e]s/-e[n]) (ship's) mate.

Mache F ['maxə] *f* (-/no *pl.*) make-believe, window-dressing, *sl.* eyewash; *et. in der* **~** *haben* have s.th. in hand.

machen ['maxən] (ge-, h) **1.** *v/t.* make; do; produce, manufacture; give (*appetite, etc.*); sit for, undergo (*examination*); come *or* amount to; make (*happy, etc.*); *was macht das* (*aus*)? what does that matter?; *das macht nichts!* never mind!, that's (quite) all right!; *da(gegen) kann man nichts* **~** that cannot be helped; *ich mache mir nichts daraus* I don't care about it; *mach, daß du fortkommst!* off with you!; *j-n* **~** *lassen, was er will* let s.o. do as he pleases; *sich* **~** *an* (*acc.*) go *or* set

about; *sich et.* **~** *lassen* have s.th. made; **2.** F *v/i.: na, mach schon!* hurry up!; '**❷schaften** *f/pl.* machinations *pl.*

Macht [maxt] *f* (-/-e) power; might; authority; control (*über acc.* of); *an der* **~** *pol.* in power; '**~befugnis** *f* authority, power; '**~haber** *pol. m* (-s/-) ruler.

mächtig *adj.* ['mɛçtiç] powerful (*a. fig.*); mighty; immense, huge; **~** *sein* (*gen.*) be master of *s.th.*; have command of (*language*).

'**Macht|kampf** *m* struggle for power; '**❷los** *adj.* powerless; '**~politik** *f* power politics *sg.*; policy of the strong hand; '**~spruch** *m* authoritative decision; '**❷voll** *adj.* powerful (*a. fig.*); '**~vollkommenheit** *f* authority; '**~wort** *n* (-[e]s/-e) word of command; *ein ~ sprechen* put one's foot down.

'Machwerk *n* concoction, F put-up job; *elendes ~* bungling work.

Mädchen ['mɛːtçən] *n* (-s/-) girl; maid(-servant); *~ für alles* maid of all work; *fig. a.* jack of all trades; **'2haft** *adj.* girlish; **'~name** *m* girl's name; maiden name; **'~schule** *f* girls' school.

Made *zo.* ['maːdə] *f* (-/-n) maggot, mite; *fruit:* worm.

Mädel ['mɛːdəl] *n* (-s/-, F -s) girl, lass(ie).

madig *adj.* ['maːdiç] maggoty, full of mites; *fruit:* wormeaten.

Magazin [magaˈtsiːn] *n* (-s/-e) store, warehouse; $\times$ *in rifle, periodical:* magazine.

Magd [maːkt] *f* (-/-e) maid(-servant).

Magen ['maːgən] *m* (-s/-, *a.* -) stomach, F tummy; *animals:* maw; **'~beschwerden** *f/pl.* stomach *or* gastric trouble, indigestion; **'~bitter** *m* (-s/-) bitters *pl.*; **'~geschwür** $\mathscr{H}$ *n* gastric ulcer; **'~krampf** $\mathscr{H}$ *m* stomach cramp; **'~krebs** $\mathscr{H}$ *m* stomach cancer; **'~leiden** *n* gastric complaint; **'~säure** *f* gastric acid.

mager *adj.* ['maːgər] meag|re, *Am.* -er (*a. fig.*); *p., animal, meat:* lean, *Am. a.* scrawny; **'2milch** *f* skim milk.

Magie [maˈgiː] *f* (-/*no pl.*) magic; **~r** ['maːgjər] *m* (-s/-) magician.

magisch *adj.* ['maːgiʃ] magic(al).

Magistrat [magisˈtraːt] *m* (-[e]s/-e) municipal *or* town council.

Magnet [maˈgneːt] *m* (-[e]s, -en/ -e[n]) magnet (*a. fig.*); lodestone; **2isch** *adj.* magnetic; **2isieren** [~etiˈziːrən] *v/t.* (*no -ge-, h*) magnetize; **~nadel** [~ˈgneːt-] *f* magnetic needle.

Mahagoni [mahaˈgoːni] *n* (-s/*no pl.*) mahogany (wood).

mähen ['mɛːən] *v/t.* (ge-, h) cut, mow, reap.

Mahl [maːl] *n* (-[e]s/uer, -e) meal, repast.

'mahlen (*irr.*, ge-, h) **1.** *v/t.* grind, mill; **2.** *v/i. tyres:* spin.

'Mahlzeit *f s.* Mahl; F feed.

Mähne ['mɛːnə] *f* (-/-n) mane.

mahn|en ['maːnən] *v/t.* (ge-, h) remind, admonish (*both: an acc. of*); *j-n wegen e-r Schuld ~* press s.o. for payment, dun s.o.; **'2mal** *n* (-[e]s/-e) memorial; **'2ung** *f* (-/-en) admonition; $\dagger$ reminder, dunning; **'2zettel** *m* reminder.

Mai [mai] *m* (-[e]s, -/-e) May; **'~baum** *m* maypole; **~glöckchen** $\mathfrak{P}$ ['~glœkçən] *n* (-s/-) lily of the valley; **'~käfer** *zo. m* cockchafer, may-beetle, may-bug.

Mais $\mathfrak{P}$ [mais] *m* (-es/-e) maize, Indian corn, *Am.* corn.

Majestät [majesˈtɛːt] *f* (-/-en) majesty; **2isch** *adj.* majestic; **~s-beleidigung** *f* lese-majesty.

Major $\times$ [maˈjoːr] *m* (-s/-e) major.

Makel ['maːkəl] *m* (-s/-) stain, spot; *fig. a.* blemish, fault; **'2los** *adj.* stainless, spotless; *fig. a.* unblemished, faultless, immaculate.

mäkeln F ['mɛːkəln] *v/i.* (ge-, h) find fault (*an dat.* with), carp (at), F pick (at).

Makler $\dagger$ ['maːklər] *m* (-s/-) broker; **'~gebühr** $\dagger$ *f* brokerage.

Makulatur $\oplus$ [makulaˈtuːr] *f* (-/-en) waste paper.

Mal[1] [maːl] *n* (-[e]s/-e, uer) mark, sign; *sports:* start(ing-point), goal; spot, stain; mole.

Mal[2] [~] **1.** *n* (-[e]s/-e) time; *für dieses ~* this time; *zum ersten ~* for the first time; *mit e-m ~e* all at once, all of a sudden; **2.** $\mathfrak{Q}$ *adv.* times, multiplied by; *drei ~ fünf ist fünfzehn* three times five is *or* are fifteen; F *s. einmal.*

'malen *v/t.* (ge-, h) paint; portray.

'Maler *m* (-s/-) painter; artist; **~ei** [~ˈrai] *f* (-/-en) painting; **2isch** *adj.* pictorial, painting; *fig.* picturesque.

'Malkasten *m* paint-box.

'malnehmen $\mathfrak{P}$ *v/t.* (*irr. nehmen, sep., -ge-, h*) multiply (*mit* by).

Malz [malts] *n* (-es/*no pl.*) malt; **'~bier** *n* malt beer.

Mama [maˈmaː, F 'mama] *f* (-/-s) mamma, mammy, F ma, *Am.* F *a.* mummy, mom.

man *indef. pron.* [man] one, you, we; they, people; *~ sagte mir* I was told. [manager.\]

Manager ['menidʒər] *m* (-s/-)|

manch [manç], **'~er**, **~e**, **~es** *adj. and indef. pron.* many a; **~e** *pl.* some, several; **~erlei** *adj.* ['~ərˈlai] diverse, different; all sorts of, ... of several sorts; *auf ~e Art* in various ways; *used as a noun:* many *or* various things; **'~mal** *adv.* sometimes, at times.

Mandant $\mathfrak{z}\mathfrak{z}$ [manˈdant] *m* (-en/-en) client.

Mandarine $\mathfrak{P}$ [mandaˈriːnə] *f* (-/-n) tangerine.

Mandat [manˈdaːt] *n* (-[e]s/-e) authorization; $\mathfrak{z}\mathfrak{z}$ brief; *pol.* mandate; *parl.* seat.

Mandel ['mandəl] *f* (-/-n) $\mathfrak{P}$ almond; *anat.* tonsil; **'~baum** $\mathfrak{P}$ *m* almond-tree; **~entzündung** $\mathscr{H}$ *f* tonsillitis.

Manege [maˈnɛːʒə] *f* (-/-n) (circus-) ring, manège.

Mangel[1] ['maŋəl] *m* **1.** (-s/*no pl.*) want, lack, deficiency; shortage; penury; *aus ~ an* for want of; *~ leiden an* (*dat.*) be in want of; **2.** (-s/u) defect, shortcoming.

Mangel[2] [~] *f* (-/-n) mangle; calender.

'mangelhaft adj. defective; deficient; unsatisfactory; 'Qigkeit f (-/no pl.) defectiveness; deficiency.

'mangeln[1] v/i. (ge-, h): es mangelt an Brot there is a lack or shortage of bread, bread is lacking or wanting; es mangelt ihm an (dat.) he is in need of or short of or wanting in, he wants or lacks.

'mangeln[2] v/t. (ge-, h) mangle (clothes, etc.); ⊕ calender (cloth, paper).

'mangels prp. (gen.) for lack or want of, esp. ₤₤ in default of.

'Mangelware ⸸ f scarce commodity; goods pl in short supply.

Manie [ma'ni:] f (-/-n) mania.

Manier [ma'ni:r] f (-/-en) manner; Qlich adj well-behaved; polite, mannerly [manifesto.]

Manifest [mani'fest] n (-es/-e)]

Mann [man] m (-[e]s/⸗er) man; husband.

'mannbar adj. marriageable; 'Q-keit f (-/no pl.) puberty, manhood.

Männchen ['mɛnçən] n (-s/-) little man; zo male, birds: cock.

'Mannes|alter n virile age, manhood, ⸗kraft f virility.

mannig|fach ['maniç-], ⸗fal-tig adj manifold, various, diverse; 'Qfaltigkeit f (-/no pl.) manifold-ness, variety, diversity.

männlich adj ['mɛnliç] male; gr. masculine, fig manly; 'Qkeit f (-/no pl) manhood, virility.

'Mannschaft f (-/-en) (body of) men; ⚓ crew, sports: team, side; ⸗führer m sports: captain; ⸗s-geist m (-es/no pl.) sports: team spirit.

Manöv|er [ma'nø:vər] n (-s/-) ma-nœuvre, Am maneuver; Qrieren [⸗'vri:rən] v/i (no -ge-, h) manœu-vre, Am maneuver.

Mansarde [man'zardə] f (-/-n) attic, garret; ⸗nfenster n dormer-window.

mansche|n F ['manʃən] (ge-, h) 1. v/t. mix, work; 2. v/i. dabble (in dat. in); Qrei F f (-/-en) mixing, F mess, dabbling

Manschette [man'ʃɛtə] f (-/-n) cuff; ⸗nknopf m cuff-link.

Mantel ['mantəl] m (-s/⸗) coat; over-coat, greatcoat; cloak, mantle (both a. fig.); ⊕ case, jacket; (outer) cover (of tyre).

Manuskript [manu'skript] n (-[e]s/-e) manuscript; typ. copy.

Mappe ['mapə] f (-/-n) portfolio, brief-case, folder; s. a. Schreib-mappe, Schulmappe.

Märchen ['mɛ:rçən] n (-s/-) fairy-tale; fig. (cock-and-bull) story, fib; ⸗buch n book of fairy-tales; 'Qhaft adj. fabulous (a. fig.).

Marder zo. ['mardər] m (-s/-) mar-ten.

Marine [ma'ri:nə] f (-/-n) marine; ✕ navy, naval forces pl.; ⸗minister m minister of naval affairs; First Lord of the Admiralty, Am. Secre-tary of the Navy; ⸗ministerium n ministry of naval affairs; the Ad-miralty, Am. Department of the Navy.

marinieren [mari'ni:rən] v/t. (no -ge-, h) pickle, marinade.

Marionette [mario'nɛtə] f (-/-n) puppet, marionette; ⸗ntheater n puppet-show.

Mark [mark] 1. f (-/-) coin: mark; 2. n (-[e]s/no pl.) anat. marrow; ♦ pith; fig. core

markant adj. [mar'kant] character-istic; striking; (well-)marked.

Marke ['markə] f (-/-n) mark, sign, token; ✉, etc. stamp; ⸸ brand, trade-mark; coupon; ⸗nartikel ⸸ m branded or proprietary article.

mar'kier|en (no -ge-, h) 1. v/t. mark (a. sports); brand (cattle, goods, etc.); 2. F fig. v/i. put it on; Qung f (-/-en) mark(ing).

'markig adj marrowy; fig. pithy.

Markise [mar'ki:zə] f (-/-n) blind, (window-)awning.

'Markstein m boundary-stone, land-mark (a fig.).

Markt [markt] m (-[e]s/⸗e) ⸸ mar-ket; s. Marktplatz; fair; auf den ⸗ bringen ⸸ put on the market; '⸗flecken m small market-town; '⸗platz m market-place; ⸗schreier m (-s/-) quack, puffer.

Marmelade [marmə'la:də] f (-/-n) jam; marmalade (made of oranges).

Marmor ['marmɔr] m (-s/-e) marble; Qieren [⸗o'ri:rən] v/t. (no -ge-, h) marble, vein, grain; Qn adj. [⸗ɔrn] (of) marble. [whim, caprice.]

Marotte [ma'rɔtə] f (-/-n) fancy,]

Marsch [marʃ] 1. m (-es/⸗e) march (a. ♪); 2. f (-/-en) marsh, fen.

Marschall ['marʃal] m (-s/⸗e) mar-shal.

'Marsch|befehl ✕ m marching orders pl.; Qieren [⸗'ʃi:rən] v/i. (no -ge-, sein) march; '⸗land n marshy land.

Marter ['martər] f (-/-n) torment, torture; 'Qn v/t. (ge-, h) torment, torture; '⸗pfahl m stake.

Märtyrer ['mɛrtyrər] m (-s/-) mar-tyr; '⸗tod m martyr's death; '⸗tum n (-s/no pl.) martyrdom.

Marxis|mus m [mar'ksismus] m (-/no pl.) Marxism; ⸗t pol. m (-en/-en) Marxian, Marxist; Qtisch pol. adj. Marxian, Marxist.

März [mɛrts] m (-[e]s/-e) March.

Marzipan [martsi'pa:n] n, ⸸ m (-s/-e) marzipan, marchpane.

Masche ['maʃə] f (-/-n) mesh; knit-ting: stitch; F fig. trick, line; 'Qn-fest adj. ladder-proof, Am. run-proof.

12*

Maschine [ma'ʃiːnə] f (-/-n) machine; engine.
maschinell adj. [maʃi'nɛl] mechanical; ~e Bearbeitung machining.
Ma'schinen|bau ⊕ m (-[e]s/no pl.) mechanical engineering; ~gewehr ✗ n machine-gun; 2mäßig adj. mechanical; automatic; ~pistole ✗ f sub-machine-gun; ~schaden m engine trouble; ~schlosser m (engine) fitter; ~schreiberin f (-/-nen) typist; ~schrift f typescript.
Maschin|erie [maʃinə'riː] f (-/-n) machinery; ~ist [~'nist] m (-en/-en) machinist.
Masern ✗ ['maːzərn] pl. measles pl.
Mask|e ['maskə] f (-/-n) mask (a. fig.); ~enball m fancy-dress or masked ball; ~erade [~'raːdə] f (-/-n) masquerade; 2ieren [~'kiːrən] v/t. (no -ge-, h) mask; sich ~ put on a mask; dress o.s. up (als as).
Maß [maːs] 1. n (-es/-e) measure; proportion; fig. moderation; ~e pl. und Gewichte pl. weights and measures pl.; ~e pl. room, etc.: measurements pl.; 2. f (-/-[e]) appr. quart (of beer); 3. 2 pret. of messen.
Massage [ma'saːʒə] f (-/-n) massage.
'**Maßanzug** m tailor-made or bespoke suit, Am. a. custom(-made) suit.
Masse ['masə] f (-/-n) mass; bulk; substance; multitude; crowd; ✗ assets pl., estate; die breite ~ the rank and file; F e-e ~ a lot of, F lots pl. or heaps pl. of.
'**Maßeinheit** f measuring unit.
'**Massen|flucht** f stampede; '~grab n common grave; ~güter ✝ ['~gyːtər] n/pl. bulk goods pl.; '2haft adj. abundant; '~produktion ✝ f mass production; '~versammlung f mass meeting, Am. a. rally; '2weise adv. in masses, in large numbers.
Masseu|r [ma'søːr] m (-s/-e) masseur; ~se [~zə] f (-/-n) masseuse.
'**maß|gebend** adj. standard; authoritative, decisive; board: competent; circles: influential, leading; '~halten v/i. (irr. halten, sep., -ge-, h) keep within limits, be moderate.
mas'sieren v/t. (no -ge-, h) massage, knead.
'**massig** adj. massy, bulky; solid.
mäßig adj. ['mɛːsiç] moderate; food, etc.: frugal; ✝ price: moderate, reasonable; result, etc.: poor; ~en ['~gən] v/t. (ge-, h) moderate; sich ~ moderate or restrain o.s.; '2ung f (-/-en) moderation; restraint.
massiv [ma'siːf] 1. adj. massive, solid; 2. 2 geol. n (-s/-e) massif.
'**Maß|krug** m beer-mug, Am. a. stein; '2los adj. immoderate; boundless; exorbitant, excessive;

extravagant; ~nahme ['~naːmə] f (-/-n) measure, step, action; '2regeln v/t. (ge-, h) reprimand; inflict disciplinary punishment on; '~schneider m bespoke or Am. custom tailor; '~stab m measure, rule(r); maps, etc.: scale; fig. yardstick, standard; '2voll adj. moderate.
Mast[1] ✿ [mast] m (-es/-e[n]) mast.
Mast[2] ✗ [~] f (-/-en) fattening; mast, food; '~darm anat. m rectum.
mästen ['mɛstən] v/t. (ge-, h) fatten, feed; stuff (geese, etc.).
'**Mastkorb** ✿ m mast-head, crowsnest.
Material [mater'jaːl] n (-s/-ien) material; substance; stock, stores pl.; fig.: material, information; evidence; ~ismus phls. [~a'lismus] m (-/no pl.) materialism; ~ist [~a'list] m (-en/-en) materialist; 2istisch adj. [~a'listiʃ] materialistic.
Materie [ma'teːrjə] f (-/-n) matter (a. fig.), stuff; fig. subject; 2ll adj. [~er'jɛl] material.
Mathemati|k [matema'tiːk] f (-/no pl.) mathematics sg.; ~ker [~'maːtikər] m (-s/-) mathematician; 2sch adj. [~'maːtiʃ] mathematical.
Matinee thea. [mati'neː] f (-/-n) morning performance.
Matratze [ma'tratsə] f (-/-n) mattress.
Matrone [ma'troːnə] f (-/-n) matron; 2nhaft adj. matronly.
Matrose ✿ [ma'troːzə] m (-n/-n) sailor, seaman.
Matsch [matʃ] m (-es/no pl.), ~e F ['~ə] f (-/no pl.) pulp, squash; mud, slush; '2ig adj. pulpy, squashy; muddy, slushy.
matt adj. [mat] faint, feeble; voice, etc.: faint; eye, colour, etc.: dim; colour, light, ✝ stock exchange, style, etc.: dull; metal: tarnished; gold, etc.: dead, dull; chess: mated; ⚡ bulb: non-glare; ~ geschliffen glass: ground, frosted, matted; ~ setzen at chess: (check)mate s.o.
Matte ['matə] f (-/-n) mat.
'**Mattigkeit** f (-/no pl.) exhaustion, feebleness; faintness.
'**Mattscheibe** f phot. focus(s)ing screen; television: screen.
Mauer ['mauər] f (-/-n) wall; ~blümchen fig. ['~blyːmçən] n (-s/-) wall-flower; '2n (ge-, h) 1. v/i. make a wall, lay bricks; 2. v/t. build (in stone or brick); '~stein m brick; '~werk n masonry, brickwork.
Maul [maul] n (-[e]s/-er) mouth; sl.: halt's ~! shut up!; '2en F v/i. (ge-, h) sulk, pout; '~esel zo. m mule, hinny; '2en F v/i. sulk, pout; '~held F m braggart; '~korb m muzzle; '~schelle F f box on the ear; '~tier zo. n mule;

'⁓wurf zo. m mole; '⁓wurfshügel m molehill.

Maurer ['maʊrər] m (-s/-) bricklayer, mason; '⁓meister m master mason; '⁓polier m bricklayers' foreman.

Maus zo. [maʊs] f (-/⁓e) mouse; ⁓efalle ['⁓ɔə-] f mousetrap; 2en ['⁓zən] (ge-, h) 1. v/i. catch mice; 2. F v/t. pinch, pilfer, F swipe.

Mauser ['maʊzər] f (-/no pl.) mo(u)lt(ing); in der ⁓ sein be mo(u)lting; '2n v/refl. (ge-, h) mo(u)lt.

Maximum ['maksimʊm] n (-s/Maxima) maximum.

Mayonnaise [majo'nɛːzə] f (-/-n) mayonnaise.

Mechani|k [me'ça:nik] f 1. (-/no pl.) mechanics mst sg.; 2. ⊕ (-/-en) mechanism; ⁓ker m (-s/-) mechanic; 2sch adj. mechanical; 2sieren [⁓ani'ziːrən] v/t. (no -ge-, h) mechanize; ⁓smus ⊕ [⁓a'nɪsmʊs] m (-/Mechanismen) mechanism; clock, watch, etc. works pl.

meckern ['mekərn] v/i. (ge-, h) bleat; fig. grumble (über acc. over, at, about), carp (at); nag (at); sl. grouse, Am sl. gripe.

Medaill|e [me'daljə] f (-/-n) medal; ⁓on [⁓'jõː] n (-s/-s) medallion; locket.

Medikament [medika'ment] n (-[e]s/-e) medicament, medicine.

Medizin [medi'tsiːn] f 1. (-/no pl.) (science of) medicine; 2. (-/-en) medicine, F physic; ⁓er m (-s/-) medical man; medical student; 2isch adj. medical; medicinal.

Meer [meːr] n (-[e]s/-e) sea (a. fig.), ocean; '⁓busen m gulf, bay; '⁓enge f strait(s pl.); '⁓esspiegel m sea level; '⁓rettich ⚕ m horse-radish; '⁓schweinchen zo. n guinea-pig.

Mehl [meːl] n (-[e]s/-e) flour; meal; '⁓brei m pap; '2ig adj. floury, mealy, farinaceous; '⁓speise f sweet dish, pudding; '⁓suppe f gruel.

mehr [meːr] 1. adj. more; er hat ⁓ Geld als ich he has (got) more money than I; 2. adv. more; nicht ⁓ no more, no longer, not any longer; ich habe nichts ⁓ I have nothing left; '2arbeit f additional work; overtime; '2ausgaben f/pl. additional expenditure; '2betrag m surplus; '⁓deutig adj. ambiguous; '2einnahme(n pl.) f additional receipts pl.; '⁓en v/t. (ge-, h) augment, increase; sich ⁓ multiply, grow; '⁓ere adj. and indef. pron. several, some; '⁓fach 1. adj. manifold, repeated; 2. adv. repeatedly, several times; '2gebot n higher bid; '2heit f (-/-en) majority, plurality; '2kosten pl. additional expense; '⁓malig adj. repeated, reiterated;

⁓mals adv. ['⁓maːls] several times, repeatedly; '⁓sprachig adj. polyglot; '⁓stimmig ♪ adj.: ⁓er Gesang part-song; '2verbrauch m excess consumption; '2wertsteuer ✝ f (-/no pl.) value-added tax; '2zahl f majority; gr. plural (form); die ⁓ (gen.) most of.

melden ['mɛldən] v/t. (irr., ge-, h) avoid, shun, keep away from.

Meile ['maɪlə] f (-/-n) mile; '⁓nstein m milestone.

mein poss. pron. [maɪn] my; der (die, das) ⁓e my; die 2en pl. my family, F my people or folks pl.; ich habe das ⁓e getan I have done all I can; die Damen und Herren! Ladies and Gentlemen!

Meineid ⚖ ['maɪn⁹-] m perjury; '2ig adj. perjured.

meinen ['maɪnən] v/t. (ge-, h) think, believe, be of (the) opinion, Am. a. reckon, guess; say; mean; wie ⁓ Sie das? what do you mean by that?; ⁓ Sie das ernst? do you (really) mean it?; es gut ⁓ mean well.

meinetwegen adv. ['maɪnət'-] for my sake; on my behalf; because of me, on my account; for all I care; I don't mind or care.

'**Meinung** f (-/-en) opinion (über acc., von about, of); die öffentliche ⁓ (the) public opinion; meiner ⁓ nach in my opinion, to my mind; j-m (gehörig) die ⁓ sagen give s.o. a piece of one's mind; '⁓saustausch ['maɪnʊŋ⁹-] m exchange of views (über acc. on); '⁓sverschiedenheit f difference of opinion (über acc. on); disagreement.

Meise orn. ['maɪzə] f (-/-n) titmouse.

Meißel ['maɪsəl] m (-s/-) chisel; '2n v/t. and v/i. (ge-, h) chisel; carve.

meist [maɪst] 1. adj. most; die ⁓en Leute most people; die ⁓e Zeit most of one's time; 2. adv.: s. meistens; am ⁓en most (of all); '2bietende ['⁓biːtəndə] m (-n/-n) highest bidder; ⁓ens adv. ['⁓əns], '⁓enteils adv. mostly, in most cases; usually.

Meister ['maɪstər] m (-s/-) master, sl. boss; sports: champion; '2haft 1. adj. masterly; 2. adv. in a masterly manner or way; '2n v/t. (ge-, h) master; '⁓schaft f 1. (-/no pl.) mastery, 2. (-/-en) sports: championship, title; '⁓stück n, '⁓werk n masterpiece.

'**Meistgebot** n highest bid, best offer.

Melanchol|ie [melaŋko'liː] f (-/-n) melancholy; 2isch adj. [⁓'koːliʃ] melancholy; ⁓ sein F have the blues.

Melde|amt ['mɛldə-] n registration office; '⁓liste f sports: list of entries; '2n v/t. (ge-, h) announce; j-m et. ⁓ inform s.o. of s.th.; officially: notify s.th. to s.o.; j-n ⁓

enter s.o.'s name (*für, zu* for); *sich* ~ report o.s. (*bei* to); *school, etc.*: put up one's hand; answer the telephone; enter (one's name) (*für, zu* for *examination, etc.*); *sich* ~ *zu* apply for; *sich auf ein Inserat* ~ answer an advertisement.

'**Meldung** *f* (-/-en) information, advice; announcement; report; registration; application; *sports*: entry.

melke|n ['mɛlkən] *v/t.* ((*irr.,*] ge-, h) milk; '2**r** *m* (-s/-) milker.

Melod|ie ♩ [melo'di:] *f* (-/-n) melody; tune, air; 2**isch** *adj.* [~'lo:diʃ] melodious, tuneful.

Melone [me'lo:nə] *f* (-/-n) ⚜ melon; F bowler(-hat), *Am.* derby.

Membran [mɛm'bra:n] *f* (-/-en), ~**e** *f* (-/-n) membrane; *teleph. a.* diaphragm.

Memme F ['mɛmə] *f* (-/-n) coward; poltroon.

Memoiren [memo'a:rən] *pl.* memoirs *pl.*

Menagerie [menaʒə'ri:] *f* (-/-n) menagerie.

Menge ['mɛŋə] *f* (-/-n) quantity; amount; multitude; crowd; *in großer* ~ in abundance; *persons, animals*: in crowds; *e-e* ~ *Geld* plenty of money, F lots *pl.* of money; *e-e* ~ *Bücher* a great many books; '2**n** *v/t.* (ge-, h) mix, blend; *sich* ~ mix (*unter acc.* with), mingle (with); *sich* ~ *in* (*acc.*) meddle *or* interfere with.

Mensch [mɛnʃ] *m* (-en/-en) human being; man; person, individual; *die* ~**en** *pl.* people *pl.*, the world, mankind; *kein* ~ nobody.

'**Menschen|affe** *zo. m* anthropoid ape; ~**alter** *n* generation, age; '~**feind** *m* misanthropist; 2**feindlich** *adj.* misanthropic; '~**fresser** *m* (-s/-) cannibal, man-eater; '~**freund** *m* philanthropist; '2~**freundlich** *adj.* philanthropic; '2~**gedenken** *n* (-s/no pl.): *seit* ~ from time immemorial, within the memory of man; '~**geschlecht** *n* human race, mankind; '~**haß** *m* misanthropy; '~**kenner** *m* judge of men *or* human nature; '~**kenntnis** *f* knowledge of human nature; '~**leben** *n* human life; '2**leer** *adj.* deserted; '**liebe** *f* philanthropy; '~**menge** *f* crowd (of people), throng; '2**möglich** *adj.* humanly possible; '~**raub** *m* kidnap(p)ing; '~**rechte** *n/pl.* human rights *pl.*; '2**scheu** *adj.* unsociable, shy; '~**seele** *f*: *keine* ~ not a living soul; '~**verstand** *m* human understanding; *gesunder* ~ common sense, F horse sense; '~**würde** *f* dignity of man.

'**Menschheit** *f* (-/no pl.) human race, mankind.

'**menschlich** *adj.* human; *fig.* humane; '2**keit** *f* (-/no pl.) human nature; humanity, humaneness.

Mentalität [mɛntali'tɛ:t] *f* (-/-en) mentality.

merk|bar *adj.* ['mɛrkbɑ:r] *s.* merklich; 2**blatt** *n* leaflet, instructional pamphlet; '~**en** (ge-, h) 1. *v/i.*: ~ *auf* (*acc.*) pay attention to, listen to; 2. *v/t.* notice, perceive, find out, discover; *sich et.* ~ remember s.th.; bear s.th. in mind; '~**lich** *adj.* noticeable, perceptible; 2**mal** *n* (-[e]s/-e) mark, sign; characteristic, feature.

'**merkwürdig** *adj.* noteworthy, remarkable; strange, odd, curious; ~**erweise** *adv.* ['~gər'~] strange to say, strangely enough; 2**keit** *f* (-/-en) remarkableness; curiosity; peculiarity.

meßbar *adj.* ['mɛsbɑ:r] measurable.

Messe ['mɛsə] *f* (-/-n) ♱ fair; *eccl.* mass; ⚓, ♱ mess.

messen ['mɛsən] *v/t.* (*irr.,* ge-, h) measure; ⚓ sound; *sich mit j-m* ~ compete with s.o.; *sich nicht mit j-m* ~ *können* be no match for s.o.; *gemessen an* (*dat.*) measured against, compared with.

Messer ['mɛsər] *n* (-s/-) knife; ⚕ scalpel; *bis aufs* ~ to the knife; *auf des* ~**s** *Schneide* on a razor-edge *or* razor's edge; ~**griff** *m* knife-handle; '~**held** *m* stabber; ~**klinge** *f* knife-blade; ~**schmied** *m* cutler; ~**schneide** *f* knife-edge; ~**stecher** *m* (-s/-) stabber; ~**stecherei** [~ʃtɛçə'raɪ] *f* (-/-en) knifing, knife-battle; '~**stich** *m* stab with a knife.

Messing ['mɛsiŋ] *n* (-s/no pl.) brass; '~**blech** *n* sheet-brass.

'**Meß|instrument** *n* measuring instrument; '~**latte** *f* surveyor's rod; ~**tisch** *m* surveyor's *or* plane table.

Metall [me'tal] *n* (-s/-e) metal; ~**arbeiter** *m* metal worker; 2**en** *adj.* (of) metal, metallic; ~**geld** *n* coin(s *pl.*), specie; ~**glanz** *m* metallic lust|re, *Am.* -er; 2**haltig** *adj.* metalliferous; ~**industrie** *f* metallurgical industry; ~**waren** *f/pl.* hardware.

Meteor *ast.* [mete'o:r] *m* (-s/-e) meteor; ~**ologe** [~oro'lo:gə] *m* (-n/-n) meteorologist; ~**ologie** [~orolo'gi:] *f* (-/no pl.) meteorology.

Meter ['me:tər] *n, m* (-s/-) met|re, *Am.* -er; '~**maß** *n* tape-measure.

Method|e [me'to:də] *f* (-/-n) method; ⊕ *a.* technique; 2**isch** *adj.* methodical. [metropolis.]

Metropole [metro'po:lə] *f* (-/-n)]

Metzel|ei [mɛtsə'laɪ] *f* (-/-en) slaughter, massacre; '2**n** *v/t.* (ge-, h) butcher, slaughter, massacre.

Metzger ['mɛtsgər] *m* (-s/-) butcher; ~**ei** [~'raɪ] *f* (-/-en) butcher's (shop).

Meuchel|mord ['mɔʏçəl-] *m* assassination; '~**mörder** *m* assassin.

Meute ['mɔʏtə] f (-/-n) pack of hounds; fig. gang; ~rei [~'raɪ] f (-/-en) mutiny; '~rer m (-s/-) mutineer; '2risch adj. mutinous; '2rn v/i. (ge-, h) mutiny (gegen against).

mich pers. pron. [miç] me; ~ (selbst) myself.

mied [miːt] pret. of meiden.

Mieder ['miːdər] n (-s/-) bodice; corset; '~waren f/pl. corsetry.

Miene ['miːnə] f (-/-n) countenance, air; feature; gute ~ zum bösen Spiel machen grin and bear it; ~ machen zu inf. offer or threaten to inf.

mies F adj. [miːs] miserable, poor; out of sorts, seedy.

Miet|e ['miːtə] f (-/-n) rent; hire; zur ~ wohnen live in lodgings, be a tenant; '2en v/t. (ge-, h) rent (land, building, etc.); hire (horse, etc.); (take on) lease (land, etc.), ♻, ✈; charter; '~er m (-s/-) tenant; lodger, Am. a. roomer; ⚖ lessee; '2frei adj. rent-free; '~shaus n block of flats, Am. apartment house; '~vertrag m tenancy agreement; lease; '~wohnung f lodgings pl., flat, Am. apartment.

Migräne ✠ [mi'grɛːnə] f (-/-n) migraine, megrim; sick headache.

Mikrophon [mikro'foːn] n (-s/-e) microphone, F mike.

Mikroskop [mikro'skoːp] n (-s/-e) microscope; 2isch adj. microscopic(al).

Milbe zo. ['milbə] f (-/-n) mite.

Milch [milç] f (-/no pl.) milk; milt, soft roe (of fish); '~bar f milk-bar; '~bart fig. m stripling; '~brötchen n (French) roll; '~gesicht n baby face; '~glas n frosted glass; '2ig adj. milky; '~kanne f milk-can; '~kuh f milk cow (a. fig.); '~mädchen F n milkmaid, dairymaid; '~mann F m milkman, dairyman; '~pulver n milk-powder; '~reis m rice-milk; '~straße ast. f Milky Way, Galaxy; '~wirtschaft f dairy-farm(ing); '~zahn m milk-tooth.

mild [milt] 1. adj. weather, punishment, etc.: mild; air, weather, light, etc.: soft; wine, etc.: smooth; reprimand, etc.: gentle; 2. adv.: et. ~ beurteilen take a lenient view of s. th.

milde ['mildə] 1. adj. s. mild 1; 2. adv.: ~ gesagt to put it mildly; 3. 2 f (-/no pl.) mildness; softness; smoothness; gentleness.

milder|n ['mildərn] v/t. (ge-, h) soften, mitigate; soothe, alleviate (pain, etc.); ~de Umstände ⚖ extenuating circumstances; '2ung f (-/-en) softening, mitigation; alleviation.

'mild|herzig adj. charitable; '2herzigkeit f (-/no pl.) charitableness;

'~tätig adj. charitable; '2tätigkeit f charity.

Milieu [mil'jøː] n (-s/-s) surroundings pl., environment; class, circles pl.; local colo(u)r.

Militär [mili'tɛːr] 1. n (-s/no pl.) military, armed forces pl.; army; 2. m (-s/-s) military man, soldier; ~attaché [~ataʃe:] m (-s/-s) military attaché; ~dienst m military service; 2isch adj. military; ~musik f military music; ~regierung f military government; ~zeit f (-/no pl.) term of military service.

Miliz ⚔ [mi'liːts] f (-/-en) militia; ~soldat ⚔ m militiaman.

Milliarde [mil'jardə] f (-/-n) thousand millions, milliard, Am. billion.

Millimeter [mili'-] n, m millimet|re, Am. -er.

Million [mil'joːn] f (-/-en) million; ~är [~o'nɛːr] m (-s/-e) millionaire.

Milz anat. [milts] f (-/-en) spleen, milt.

minder ['mindər] 1. adv. less; nicht ~ no less, likewise; 2. adj. less(er); smaller; minor; inferior; '~begabt adj. less gifted; ~bemittelt adj. ['~bəmitəlt] of moderate means; 2betrag m deficit, shortage; '2einnahme f shortfall in receipts; '2gewicht n short weight; '2heit f (-/-en) minority; '~jährig adj. ['~jɛːriç] under age, minor; '2jährigkeit f (-/no pl.) minority; '~n v/t. and v/refl. (ge-, h) diminish, lessen, decrease; '2ung f (-/-en) decrease, diminution; '~wertig adj. inferior, of inferior quality; '2wertigkeit f (-/no pl.) inferiority; ✝ inferior quality; '2wertigkeitskomplex m inferiority complex.

mindest adj. ['mindəst] least; slightest; minimum; nicht die ~e Aussicht not the slightest chance; nicht im ~en not in the least, by no means; zum ~en at least; '2alter n minimum age; '2anforderungen f/pl. minimum requirements pl.; '2betrag m lowest amount; '2einkommen n minimum income; '~ens adv. at least; '2gebot n lowest bid; '2lohn m minimum wage; '2maß n minimum; auf ein ~ herabsetzen minimize; '2preis m minimum price.

Mine ['miːnə] f (-/-n) ⚔, ⚓, ⚒ mine; pencil: lead; ball-point-pen: refill.

Mineral [minə'raːl] n (-s/-e, -ien) mineral; 2isch adj. mineral; ~ogie [~alo'giː] f (-/no pl.) mineralogy; ~wasser n (-s/⸗) mineral water.

Miniatur [minia'tuːr] f (-/-en) miniature; ~gemälde n miniature.

Minirock ['mini-] m miniskirt.

Minister [mi'nistər] m (-s/-) minister; Secretary (of State), Am. Secretary; ~ium [~'te:rjum] n (-s/Mi-nisterien) ministry; Office, Am. Department; ~präsident m prime minister, premier; in Germany, etc.: minister president; ~rat m (-[e]s/~e) cabinet council.

minus adv. ['mi:nus] minus, less, deducting.

Minute [mi'nu:tə] f (-/-n) minute; ~nzeiger m minute-hand.

mir pers. pron. [mi:r] (to) me.

Misch|ehe ['miʃ?-] f mixed marriage; intermarriage; '2en v/t. (ge-, h) mix, mingle; blend (coffee, tobacco, etc.); alloy (metal); shuffle (cards); sich ~ in (acc.) interfere in; join in (conversation); sich ~ unter (acc.) mix or mingle with (the crowd); ~ling ['~liŋ] m (-s/-e) half-breed, half-caste; &, zo. hybrid; ~masch F ['~maʃ] m (-es/-e) hotch-potch, jumble; '~ung f (-/-en) mixture; blend; alloy.

miß|achten [mis'-] v/t. (no -ge-, h) disregard, ignore, neglect; slight, despise; '2achtung f disregard, neglect; '~behagen 1. v/i. (no -ge-, h) displease; 2. 2 n discomfort, uneasiness; '2bildung f malformation, deformity; ~'billigen v/t. (no -ge-, h) disapprove (of); '2billigung f disapproval; '2brauch m abuse; misuse; ~'brauchen v/t. (no -ge-, h) abuse; misuse; ~bräuchlich adj. ['~brɔʏçliç] abusive; improper; ~'deuten v/t. (no -ge-, h) misinterpret; '2deutung f misinterpretation.

missen ['misən] v/t. (ge-, h) miss; do without, dispense with.

'Miß|erfolg m failure; fiasco; '~ernte f bad harvest, crop failure.

Misse|tat ['misə-] f misdeed; crime; '~täter m evil-doer, offender; criminal.

miß|'fallen v/i. (irr. fallen, no -ge-, h): j-m ~ displease s.o.; '2fallen n (-s/no pl.) displeasure, dislike; '~fällig 1. adj. displeasing; shocking; disparaging; 2. adv.: sich ~ äußern über (acc.) speak ill of; '2geburt f monster, freak (of nature), deformity; '2geschick n bad luck, misfortune; mishap; ~gestimmt fig. adj. ['~gəʃtimt] s. mißmutig; ~'glücken v/i. (no -ge-, sein) fail; ~'gönnen v/t. (no -ge-, h): j-m et. ~ envy or grudge s.o. s.th.; '2griff m mistake, blunder; '2gunst f envy, jealousy; '~günstig adj. envious, jealous; ~'handeln v/t. (no -ge-, h) ill-treat; maul, sl. manhandle; 2'handlung f ill-treatment; mauling, sl. manhandling; ½½ assault and battery; '2heirat f misalliance; '~hellig adj. dissonant, dissentient; '2helligkeit f (-/-en) dissonance, dissension, discord.

Mission [mis'jo:n] f (-/-en) mission

(a. pol. and fig.); ~ar [~o'na:r] m (-s/-e) missionary.

'Miß|klang m dissonance, discord (both a. fig.); '~kredit fig. m (-[e]s/no pl.) discredit; in ~ bringen bring discredit upon s.o.

miß|'lang pret. of mißlingen; '~lich adj. awkward; unpleasant; ~liebig adj. ['~li:biç] unpopular; ~lingen [~'liŋən] v/i. (irr., no -ge-, sein) fail; 2'lingen n (-s/no pl.) failure; '2mut m ill humo(u)r; discontent; '~mutig adj. ill-humo(u)red; discontented; ~'raten 1. v/i. (irr. raten, no -ge-, sein) fail; turn out badly; 2. adj. wayward; ill-bred; '2stand m nuisance; grievance; '2stimmung f ill humo(u)r; '2ton m (-[e]s/~e) dissonance, discord (both a. fig.); ~'trauen v/i. (no -ge-, h): j-m distrust or mistrust s.o.; 2'trauen n (-s/no pl.) distrust, mistrust; ~'trauisch adj. distrustful; suspicious; 2ver-gnügen n (-s/no pl.) ¹ispleasure; '~vergnügt adj. displeased; discontented; '2verhältnis n disproportion; incongruity; 2verständnis n misunderstanding; dissension; '~verstehen v/t. (irr. stehen, no -ge-, h) misunderstand, mistake (intention, etc.); '2wirtschaft f maladministration, mismanagement.

Mist [mist] m (-es/-e) dung, manure; dirt; F fig. trash, rubbish; '~beet n hotbed.

Mistel ⚘ ['mistəl] f (-/-n) mistletoe.

'Mist|gabel f dung-fork; '~haufen m dung-hill.

mit [mit] 1. prp. (dat.) with; ~ 20 Jahren at (the age of) twenty; ~ e-m Schlage at a blow; ~ Gewalt by force; ~ der Bahn by train; 2. adv. also, too; ~ dabeisein be there too, be (one) of the party.

Mit|arbeiter ['mit?-] m co-worker; writing, art, etc.: collaborator; colleague; newspaper, etc. contributor (an dat. to); '2benutzen v/t. (sep., no -ge-, h) use jointly or in common; '~besitzer m joint owner; '~bestimmungsrecht n right of co-determination; '~bewerber m competitor; '~bewohner m co-inhabitant, fellow-lodger; '2brin-gen v/t. (irr. bringen, sep., -ge-, h) bring along (with one); ~bringsel ['~briŋzəl] n (-s/-) little present; '~bürger m fellow-citizen; 2ein-ander adv. [mit?ai'nandər] together, jointly; with each other, with one another; ~empfinden ['mit?-] n (-s/no pl.) sympathy; ~erbe ['mit?-] m co-heir; ~esser ⚘ ['mit?-] m (-s/-) blackhead; '2fah-ren v/i. (irr. fahren, sep., -ge-, sein): mit j-m ~ drive or go with s.o.; j-n ~ lassen give s.o. a lift; '2fühlen *v/i.* (*sep.*, -ge-, h) sympathize (*mit* with); '⁲**geben** *v/t.* (*irr. geben, sep.*, -ge-, h) give along (*dat.* with); '~**gefühl** *n* sympathy; '⁲**gehen** *v/i.* (*irr. gehen, sep.*, -ge-, *sein*): mit *j-m* ~ go with s.o.; ~**gift** *f* (-/-en) dowry, marriage portion.

'**Mitglied** *n* member; '~**erversammlung** *f* general meeting; '~**erzahl** *f* membership; '~**sbeitrag** *m* subscription; '~**schaft** *f* (-/no *pl.*) membership.

mit|'**hin** *adv.* consequently, therefore; ⁲**inhaber** ['mit?-] *m* copartner; '⁲**kämpfer** *m* fellow-combatant; '~**kommen** *v/i.* (*irr. kommen, sep.*, -ge-, *sein*) come along (*mit* with); *fig.* be able to follow; '⁲**läufer** *pol. m* nominal member; *contp.* trimmer.

'**Mitleid** *n* (-[e]s/no *pl.*) compassion, pity; sympathy; *aus* ~ out of pity; ~ *haben mit* have or take pity on; '~**enschaft** *f* (-/no *pl.*): in ~ ziehen affect; implicate, involve; damage; '⁲**ig** *adj.* compassionate, pitiful; ⁲(s)**los** ['~t-] pitiless, merciless; ⁲(s)**voll** *adj.* ['~t-] pitiful, compassionate.

'**mit**|**machen** (*sep.*, -ge-, h) **1.** *v/i.* make one of the party; take part in, participate in; follow, go with (*fashion*); go through (*hardships*); '⁲**mensch** *m* fellow creature; '~**nehmen** *v/t.* (*irr. nehmen, sep.*, -ge-, h) take along (with one); *fig.* exhaust, wear out; *j-n* (*im Auto*) ~ give s.o. a lift; ~**nichten** *adv.* ['~niçtən] by no means, not at all; '~**rechnen** *v/t.* (*sep.*, -ge-, h) include (in the account); *nicht* ~ leave out of account; *nicht mitgerechnet* not counting; '~**reden** (*sep.*, -ge-, h) **1.** *v/i.* join in the conversation; **2.** *v/t.*: *ein Wort or Wörtchen mitzureden haben* have a say (*bei* in); '~**reißen** *v/t.* (*irr. reißen, sep.*, -ge-, h) tear or drag along; *fig.* sweep along.

'**Mitschuld** *f* complicity (*an dat.* in); '⁲**ig** *adj.* accessary (*an dat.* to *crime*); '~**ige** *m* accessary, accomplice.

'**Mitschüler** *m* schoolfellow.

'**mitspiel**|**en** (*sep.*, -ge-, h) **1.** *v/i.* play (*bei* with); *sports:* be on the team; *thea.* appear, star (*in a play*); join in a game; *matter:* be involved; *j-m arg or übel* ~ play s.o. a nasty trick; **2.** *fig. v/t.* join in (*game*); '⁲**er** *m* partner.

'**Mittag** *m* midday, noon; *heute* ⁲ at noon today; *zu* ~ *essen* lunch, dine; '~**essen** *n* lunch(eon), dinner; '⁲s *adv.* at noon.

'**Mittags**|**pause** *f* lunch hour; '~**ruhe** *f* midday rest; '~**schlaf** *m*, '~**schläfchen** *n* after-dinner nap, siesta; '~**stunde** *f* noon; '~**tisch**

fig. m lunch, dinner; '~**zeit** *f* noontide; lunch-time, dinner-time.

Mitte ['mitə] *f* (-/-n) middle; cent|re, *Am.* -er; *die goldene* ~ the golden or happy mean; *aus unserer* ~ from among us; ~ *Juli* in the middle of July; ~ *Dreißig* in the middle of one's thirties.

'**mitteil**|**en** *v/t.* (*sep.*, -ge-, h): *j-m et.* ~ communicate s.th. to s.o.; impart s.th. to s.o.; inform s.o. of s.th.; make s.th. known to s.o.; '~**sam** *adj.* communicative; '⁲**ung** *f* (-/-en) communication; information; communiqué.

'**Mittel** ['mitəl] *n* (-s/-) means *sg.*, way; remedy (*gegen* for); average; &, mean; *phys.* medium; ~ *pl. a.* means *pl.*, funds *pl.*, money; ~ *pl. und Wege* ways and means *pl.*; '~**alter** *n* Middle Ages *pl.*; '⁲**alterlich** *adj.* medi(a)eval; ⁲**bar** *adj.* mediate, indirect; '~**ding** *n*: *ein* ~ zwischen ... *und* ... something between ... and ...; '~**finger** *m* middle finger; '~**gebirge** *n* highlands *pl.*; '⁲**groß** *adj.* of medium height; medium-sized; '~**läufer** *m* *sports:* centre half back, *Am.* center half back; '⁲**los** *adj.* without means, destitute; '⁲**mäßig** *adj.* middling; mediocre; '~**mäßigkeit** *f* (-/no *pl.*) mediocrity; '~**punkt** *m* cent|re, *Am.* -er; *fig. a.* focus; '⁲s *prp.* (*gen.*) by (means of), through; '~**schule** *f* intermediate school, *Am.* high school; '~**smann** *m* (-[e]s/=er, *Mittelsleute*) mediator, go-between; '~**stand** *m* middle classes *pl.*; '~**stürmer** *m* *sports:* centre forward, *Am.* center forward; '~**weg** *fig. m* middle course; '~**wort** *gr. n* (-[e]s/=er) participle.

mitten *adv.* ['mitən]: ~ *in* or *an* or *auf* or *unter* (*acc.; dat.*) in the midst or middle of; ~ *entzwei* right in two; ~ *im Winter* in the depth of winter; ~ *in der Nacht* in the middle or dead of night; ~ *ins Herz* right into the heart; ~'**drin** F *adv.* right in the middle; ~'**durch** F *adv.* right through or across.

Mitter|**nacht** ['mitər-] *f* midnight; *um* ~ at midnight; '⁲**nächtig** *adj.* ['~neçtiç], '⁲**nächtlich** *adj.* midnight.

Mittler ['mitlər] **1.** *m* (-s/-) mediator, intercessor; **2.** ⁲ *adj.* middle, central; average, medium; '⁲'**weile** *adv.* meanwhile, (in the) meantime.

Mittwoch *m* (-[e]s/-e) Wednesday; '⁲s *adv.* on Wednesday(s), every Wednesday.

mit|'**unter** *adv.* now and then, sometimes; '~**verantwortlich** *adj.* jointly responsible; '⁲**welt** *f* (-/no *pl.*): *die* ~ our, *etc.* contemporaries *pl.*

'mitwirk|en *v/i.* (*sep.*, -ge-, *h*) co-operate (*bei* in), contribute (to), take part (in); '²ende *m* (-*n*/-*n*) *thea.* performer, actor, player (*a. J.*); die ~*n pl.* the cast; '²ung *f* (-/*no pl.*) co(-)operation, contribution.

'Mitwisser *m* (-*s*/-) confidant; ²**½** accessary.   [rechnen.\]

'mitzählen *v/t.* (*sep.*, -ge-, *h*) s. mit-|

Mix|becher ['miks-] *m* (cocktail-)shaker; '²en *v/t.* (ge-, *h*) mix; ~tur [~'tu:r] *f* (-/-*en*) mixture.

Möbel ['mø:bəl] *n* (-*s*/-) piece of furniture, ~ *pl.* furniture; '~händ-ler *m* furniture-dealer; '~spedi-teur *m* furniture-remover; '~stück *n* piece of furniture; '~tischler *m* cabinet-maker; '~wagen *m* pan-technicon, *Am.* furniture truck.

mobil *adj.* [mo'bi:l] **½** mobile; F active, nimble; ~ machen **½** mobi-lize; ²**½**ar [~il'ja:r] *n* (-*s*/-*e*) furni-ture; movables *pl.*; ~isieren [~ili-'zi:rən] *v/t.* (*no* -ge-, *h*) **½** mobilize; **†** realize (*property, etc.*); ²ma-chung **½** [mo'bi:lmaxuŋ] *f* (-/-*en*) mobilization.

möblieren [mø'bli:rən] *v/t.* (*no* -ge-, *h*) furnish; möbliertes Zimmer furnished room, F bed-sitter.

mochte ['mɔxtə] *pret.* of mögen.

Mode ['mo:də] *f* (-/-*n*) fashion, vogue; use, custom; die neueste ~ the latest fashion; in ~ in fashion *or* vogue; aus der ~ kommen grow *or* go out of fashion; die ~ bestimmen set the fashion; die ~ mitmachen follow the fashion; '~artikel *m/pl.* fancy goods *pl.*, novelties *pl.*; '~far-be *f* fashionable colo(u)r.

Modell [mo'dɛl] *n* (-*s*/-*e*) ⊕, *fashion, paint.*: model; pattern, design; ⊕ mo(u)ld; *j-m* ~ stehen *paint.* pose for s.o.; '~eisenbahn *f* model rail-way; ²ieren [~'li:rən] *v/t.* (*no* -ge-, *h*) model, mo(u)ld, fashion.

'Moden|schau *f* dress parade, fashion-show; '~zeitung *f* fashion magazine.

Moder ['mo:dər] *m* (-*s*/*no pl.*) must, putrefaction; '~geruch *m* musty smell; '²ig *adj.* musty, putrid.

modern¹ ['mo:dərn] *v/i.* (ge-, *h*) putrefy, rot, decay.

modern² *adj.* [mo'dɛrn] modern; progressive; up-to-date; fashion-able; ~isieren [~i'zi:rən] *v/t.* (*no* -ge-, *h*) modernize, bring up to date.

'Mode|salon *m* fashion house; '~schmuck *m* costume jewel(le)ry; '~waren *f/pl.* fancy goods *pl.*; '~zeichner *m* fashion-designer.

modifizieren [modifi'tsi:rən] *v/t.* (*no* -ge-, *h*) modify.

modisch *adj.* ['mo:diʃ] fashionable, stylish.   [liner.\]

Modistin [mo'distin] *f* (-/-*nen*) mil-|

Mogel|ei F [mo:gə'lai] *f* (-/-*en*) cheat; '²n F *v/i.* (ge-, *h*) cheat.

mögen ['mø:gən] (*irr.*, *h*) 1. *v/i.* (ge-) be willing; ich mag nicht I don't like to; 2. *v/t.* (ge-) want, wish; like, be fond of; nicht ~ dislike; not to be keen on (*food, etc.*); lieber ~ like better, prefer; 3. *v/aux.* (*no* -ge-) may, might; ich möchte wissen I should like to know; ich möchte lieber gehen I would rather go; das mag (wohl) sein that's (well) pos-sible; wo er auch sein mag wherever he may be; mag er sagen, was er will let him say what he likes.

möglich ['mø:kliç] 1. *adj.* possible; practicable, feasible; market, crim-inal, etc.: potential; alle ~en all sorts of; alles ~e all sorts of things; sein ~stes tun do one's utmost *or* level best; nicht ~! you don't say (so)!; so bald etc. wie ~ = 2. *adv.*: ~st bald etc. as soon, etc., as possible; '~er'weise *adv.* possibly, if pos-sible; perhaps; ²keit *f* (-/-*en*) pos-sibility; chance; nach ~ if possible.

Mohammedan|er [mohame'da:-nər] *m* (-*s*/-) Muslim, Moslem, Mohammedan; ²isch *adj.* Muslim, Moslem, Mohammedan.

Mohn [mo:n] *m* (-[*e*]*s*/-*e*) poppy.

Möhre **♣** ['mø:rə] *f* (-/-*n*) carrot.

Mohrrübe **♣** ['mo:r-] *f* carrot.

Molch *zo.* [mɔlç] *m* (-[*e*]*s*/-*e*) sala-mander; newt.

Mole ⊕ ['mo:lə] *f* (-/-*n*) mole, jetty.

molk [mɔlk] *pret.* of melken.

Molkerei [mɔlkə'rai] *f* (-/-*en*) dairy; ~produkte *n/pl.* dairy products *pl.*

Moll ♪ [mɔl] *n* (-/-) minor (key).

mollig F *adj.* ['mɔliç] snug, cosy; plump, rounded.

Moment [mo'ment] (-[*e*]*s*/-*e*) 1. *m* moment, instant; im ~ at the moment; 2. *n* motive; fact(or); ⊕ momentum; **⊕** impulse (*a. fig.*); ²an [~'ta:n] 1. *adj.* momentary; 2. *adv.* at the moment, for the time being; ~aufnahme *phot. f* snapshot, instantaneous photograph.

Monarch [mo'narç] *m* (-*en*/-*en*) monarch; ~ie [~çi:] *f* (-/-*n*) mon-archy.

Monat ['mo:nat] *m* (-[*e*]*s*/-*e*) month; '²elang 1. *adj.* lasting for months; 2. *adv.* for months; '²lich 1. *adj.* monthly; 2. *adv.* monthly, a month.

Mönch [mœnç] *m* (-[*e*]*s*/-*e*) monk, friar.

'Mönchs|kloster *n* monastery; '~kutte *f* (monk's) frock; '~leben *n* monastic life; '~orden *m* monastic order; '~zelle *f* monk's cell.

Mond [mo:nt] *m* (-[*e*]*s*/-*e*) moon; hinter dem ~ leben be behind the times; '~fähre *f* lunar module; '~finsternis *f* lunar eclipse; '²hell *adj.* moonlit; '~schein *m* (-[*e*]*s*/*no pl.*) moonlight; '~sichel *f* crescent; '²süchtig *adj.* moonstruck.

Mono|log [mono'lo:k] *m* (-*s*/-*e*)

monologue, *Am. a.* monolog;
soliloquy; ⹁'pol † *n* (-s/-e) monopoly; ⍁polisieren [⹁ɔli'ziːrən] *v/t.*
(no -ge-, h) monopolize; ⍁'ton *adj.*
monotonous; ⹁tonie [⹁to'niː] *f*
(-/-n) monotony.

Monstrum ['mɔnstrum] *n* (-s/Mon-
stren, Monstra) monster.

Montag ['moːnˌ] *m* Monday; ⍁s
adv. on Monday(s), every Monday.

Montage ⊕ [mɔn'taːʒə] *f* (-/-n)
mounting, fitting; setting up; as-
semblage, assembly.

Montan|industrie [mɔn'taːnˌ] *f*
coal and steel industries *pl.*; ⹁union
f European Coal and Steel Community.

Mont|eur [mɔn'tøːr] *m* (-s/-e) ⊕
fitter, assembler; *esp. mot.*, ⚔
mechanic; ⹁euranzug *m* overall;
⍁ieren [⹁'tiːrən] *v/t.* (no -ge-, h)
mount, fit; set up; assemble; ⹁ur
⚔ [⹁'tuːr] *f* (-/-en) regimentals *pl.*

Moor [moːr] *n* (-[e]s/-e) bog; swamp;
'⹁bad *n* mud-bath; ⍁ig *adj.* boggy,
marshy.

Moos ⚘ [moːs] *n* (-es/-e) moss; '⍁ig
adj. mossy.

Moped *mot.* ['moːpet] *n* (-s/-s)
moped.

Mops *zo.* [mɔps] *m* (-es/⍁e) pug;
⍁en *v/t.* (ge-, h) F pilfer, pinch; *sl.:*
sich ⹁ be bored stiff.

Moral [mo'raːl] *f* (-/⚔ -en) morality; morals *pl.*; moral; ⚔, *etc.:*
morale; ⍁isch *adj.* moral; ⍁isieren
[⹁ali'ziːrən] *v/i.* (no -ge-, h) moral-
ize.

Morast [mo'rast] *m* (-es/-e, ⚔e)
slough, morass; *s.* Moor; mire, mud;
⍁ig *adj.* marshy, muddy, miry.

Mord [mɔrt] *m* (-[e]s/-e) murder
(an dat. of); e-n ⹁ begehen commit
murder; '⹁anschlag *m* murderous
assault; ⍁en *v/i.* (ge-, h)
commit murder(s).

Mörder ['mœrdər] *m* (-s/-) murderer; ⍁isch *adj.* murderous;
climate, etc.: deadly; † *competition:*
cut-throat.

'Mord|gier *f* lust of murder, blood-
thirstiness; '⍁gierig *adj.* bloodthirsty; '⹁kommission *f* homicide
squad; '⹁prozeß ɪ⍁ *m* murder trial.

'Mords|angst † *f* blue funk, *sl.*
mortal fear; '⹁glück F *n* stupendous
luck; '⹁kerl F *m* devil of a fellow;
'⹁spek'takel F *m* hullabaloo.

Morgen ['mɔrgən] 1. *m* (-s/-) morning; *measure:* acre; *am* ⹁ *s.* morgens;
2. ⚘ *adv.* tomorrow; ⹁ früh (abend)
tomorrow morning (evening or
night); ⹁ *in acht Tagen* tomorrow
week; '⹁ausgabe *f* morning edition; '⹁blatt *n* morning paper;
'⹁dämmerung *f* dawn, daybreak;
'⹁gebet *n* morning prayer; '⹁gym-
nastik *f* morning exercises *pl.*;
'⹁land *n* (-[e]s/no pl.) Orient, East;

'⹁rock *m* peignoir, dressing-gown,
wrapper (for woman); '⹁röte *f*
dawn; ⍁s *adv.* in the morning; '⹁
zeitung *f* morning paper.

'morgig *adj.* of tomorrow.

Morphium *pharm.* ['mɔrfium] *n*
(-s/no pl.) morphia, morphine.

morsch *adj.* [mɔrʃ] rotten, decayed;
brittle.

Mörser ['mœrzər] *m* (-s/-) mortar
(a. ⚔).

Mörtel ['mœrtəl] *m* (-s/-) mortar.

Mosaik [moza'iːk] *n* (-s/-en) mosaic;
⹁fußboden *m* mosaic or tessellated
pavement.

Moschee [mɔ'ʃeː] *f* (-/-n) mosque.

Moschus ['mɔʃus] *m* (-/no pl.) musk.

Moskito *zo.* [mɔs'kiːto] *m* (-s/-s)
mosquito; ⹁netz *n* mosquito-net.

Moslem ['mɔslem] *m* (-s/-s) Mus-
lim, Moslem.

Most [mɔst] *m* (-es/-e) must, grape-
juice; *of apples:* cider; *of pears:*
perry.

Mostrich ['mɔstriç] *m* (-[e]s/no pl.)
mustard.

Motiv [mo'tiːf] *n* (-s/-e) motive,
reason; *paint.*, ♪ motif; ⍁ieren
[⹁i'viːrən] *v/t.* (no -ge-, h) motivate.

Motor ['moːtɔr] *m* (-s/-en) engine,
esp. ⚔ motor; '⹁boot *n* motor boat;
'⹁defekt *m* engine or ⚔ motor
trouble; '⹁haube *f* bonnet, *Am.*
hood; ⍁isieren [motori'ziːrən] *v/t.*
(no -ge-, h) motorize; ⹁isierung
[motori'ziːruŋ] *f* (-/no pl.) motor-
ization; '⹁rad *n* motor (bi)cycle;
'⹁radfahrer *m* motor cyclist; '⹁rol-
ler *m* (motor) scooter; '⹁sport *m*
motoring.

Motte *zo.* ['mɔtə] *f* (-/-n) moth.

'Motten|kugel *f* moth-ball; '⍁si-
cher *adj.* mothproof; '⍁zerfressen
adj. moth-eaten.

Motto ['mɔto] *n* (-s/-s) motto.

Möwe *orn.* ['møːvə] *f* (-/-n) sea-gull,
(sea-)mew.

Mücke *zo.* ['mykə] *f* (-/-n) midge,
gnat, mosquito; *aus e-r* ⹁ *e-n Elefanten machen* make a mountain
out of a molehill; '⹁nstich *m* gnat-
bite.

Mucker ['mukər] *m* (-s/-) bigot,
hypocrite.

müd|e *adj.* ['myːdə] tired, weary;
e-r Sache ⹁ *sein* be weary or tired
of s.th.; ⍁igkeit *f* (-/no pl.) tired-
ness, weariness.

Muff [muf] *m* 1. (-[e]s/-e) muff;
2. (-[e]s/no pl.) mo(u)ldy or musty
smell; '⹁e ⊕ *f* (-/-n) sleeve, socket;
⍁eln F *v/i.* (ge-, h) munch; mumble; '⍁ig *adj.* smell, *etc.:* musty,
fusty; *air:* close; *fig.* sulky, sullen.

Mühe ['myːə] *f* (-/-n) trouble, pains
pl.; (nicht) der ⹁ *wert* (not) worth
while; *j-m* ⹁ *machen* give s.o.
trouble; *sich* ⹁ *geben* take pains
(mit over, with s.th.); '⍁los *adj.*

effortless, easy; '2n v/refl. (ge-, h) take pains, work hard; '2voll adj. troublesome, hard; laborious.

Mühle ['my:lə] f (-/-n) mill.

'**Müh|sal** f (-/-e) toil, trouble; hardship; '2sam, '2selig 1. adj. toilsome, troublesome; difficult; 2. adv. laboriously; with difficulty.

Mulatte [mu'latə] m (-n/-n) mulatto.

Mulde ['muldə] f (-/-n) trough; depression, hollow.

Mull [mul] m (-[e]s/-e) mull.

Müll [myl] m (-[e]s/no pl.) dust, rubbish, refuse, Am. a. garbage; '~abfuhr f removal of refuse; '~eimer m dust-bin, Am. garbage can.

Müller ['mylər] m (-s/-) miller.

'**Müll|fahrer** m dust-man, Am. garbage collector; '~haufen m dust-heap; '~kasten m s. Mülleimer; '~kutscher m s. Müllfahrer; '~wagen m dust-cart, Am. garbage cart.

Multipli|kation Å [multiplika-'tsjo:n] f (-/-en) multiplication; 2zieren Å [~'tsi:rən] v/t. (no -ge-, h) multiply (mit by).

Mumie ['mu:mjə] f (-/-n) mummy.

Mumps ♂ [mumps] m, F f (-/no pl.) mumps.

Mund [munt] m (-[e]s/=er) mouth; den ~ halten hold one's tongue; den ~voll nehmen talk big; sich den ~ verbrennen put one's foot in it; nicht auf den ~ gefallen sein have a ready or glib tongue; j-m über den ~ fahren cut s.o. short; '~art f dialect; '2artlich adj. dialectal.

Mündel ['myndəl] m, n (-s/-), girl: a. f (-/-n) ward, pupil; '2sicher adj.: ~e Papiere n/pl. ♱ gilt-edged securities pl.

münden ['myndən] v/i. (ge-, h): ~ in (acc.) river, etc.: fall or flow into; street, etc.: run into.

'**mund|faul** adj. too lazy to speak; '~gerecht adj. palatable (a. fig.); '2harmonika ♪ f mouth-organ; '2höhle anat. f oral cavity.

mündig ⚖ adj. ['myndiç] of age; ~ werden come of age; '2keit f (-/no pl.) majority.

mündlich ['myntliç] 1. adj. oral, verbal; 2. adv. a. by word of mouth.

'**Mund|pflege** f oral hygiene; '~raub ⚖ m theft of comestibles; '~stück n mouthpiece (of musical instrument, etc.); tip (of cigarette); '2tot adj.: ~ machen silence or gag s.o.

'**Mündung** f (-/-en) mouth; a. estuary (of river); muzzle (of fire-arms).

'**Mund|vorrat** m provisions pl., victuals pl.; '~wasser n (-s/=) mouth-wash, gargle; '~werk F fig. n: ein gutes ~ haben have the gift of the gab.

Munition [muni'tsjo:n] f (-/-en) ammunition.

munkeln F ['muŋkəln] (ge-, h) 1. v/i. whisper; 2. v/t. whisper, rumo(u)r; man munkelt there is a rumo(u)r afloat. (lively; merry.)

munter adj. ['muntər] awake; fig.:)

Münz|e ['myntsə] f (-/-n) coin; (small) change; medal; mint; für bare ~ nehmen take at face value; j-m et. mit gleicher ~ heimzahlen pay s.o. back in his own coin; '~einheit f (monetary) unit, standard of currency; '2en v/t. (ge-, h) coin, mint; gemünzt sein auf (acc.) be meant for, be aimed at; '~fernsprecher teleph. m coin-box telephone; '~fuß m standard (of coinage); '~wesen n monetary system.

mürbe adj. ['myrbə] tender; pastry, etc.: crisp, short; meat: well-cooked; material: brittle; F fig. worn-out, demoralized; F j-n~ machen break s.o.'s resistance; F ~ werden give in.

Murmel ['murməl] f (-/-n) marble; '2n v/t. and v/i. (ge-, h) mumble, murmur; '~tier zo. n marmot.

murren ['murən] v/i. (ge-, h) grumble, F grouch (both: über acc. at, over, about).

mürrisch adj. ['myriʃ] surly, sullen.

Mus [mu:s] n (-es/-e) pap; stewed fruit.

Muschel ['muʃəl] f (-/-n) zo.: mussel; shell, conch; teleph. ear-piece.

Museum [mu'ze:um] n (-s/Museen) museum.

Musik [mu'zi:k] f (-/no pl.) music; ~alienhandlung [~i'ka:ljən-] f music-shop; 2alisch [~i'ka:-liʃ] musical; ~ant [~i'kant] m (-en/-en) musician; ~automat m juke-box; ~er ['mu:zikər] m (-s/-) musician; bandsman; '~instrument n musical instrument; '~lehrer m music-master; '~stunde f music-lesson; ~truhe f radio-gram(ophone), Am. radio-phonograph.

musizieren [muzi'tsi:rən] v/i. (no -ge-, h) make or have music.

Muskat ♚ [mus'ka:t] m (-[e]s/-e) nutmeg; ~nuß ♚ f nutmeg.

Muskel ['muskəl] m (-s/-n) muscle; '~kater F m stiffness and soreness, Am. a. charley horse; '~kraft f muscular strength; '~zerrung ⚕ f pulled muscle.

Muskul|atur [muskula'tu:r] f (-/-en) muscular system, muscles pl.; 2ös adj. [~'lø:s] muscular, brawny.

Muß [mus] n (-/no pl.) necessity; es ist ein ~ it is a must.

Muße ['mu:sə] f (-/no pl.) leisure; spare time; mit ~ at one's leisure.

Musselin [musə'li:n] m (-s/-e) muslin.

müssen ['mysən] (irr., h) 1. v/i. (ge-): ich muß I must; 2. v/aux. (no -ge-): ich muß I must, I have to;

I am obliged or compelled or forced to; I am bound to; *ich habe gehen ~* I had to go; *ich müßte (eigentlich) wissen* I ought to know.

müßig *adj.* ['myːsiç] idle; superfluous; useless; '**gang** *m* idleness, laziness; '**gänger** ['ɡɛŋər] *m* (-s/-) idler, loafer; lazy-bones.

mußte ['mustə] *pret. of* müssen.

Muster ['mustər] *n* (-s/-) model; example, paragon; design, pattern; specimen; sample; '**betrieb** *m* model factory *or* farm; '**gatte** *m* model husband; '**gültig, **haft 1. *adj.* model, exemplary, perfect; 2. *adv.: sich ~ benehmen* be on one's best behavio(u)r; '**kollektion** ✝ *f* range of samples; '**n** *v/t.* (ge-, h) examine; eye; inspect, review; figure, pattern (*fabric, etc.*); '**schutz** *m* protection of patterns and designs; '**ung** *f* (-/-en) examination; review; pattern (*of fabric, etc.*); '**werk** *n* standard work.

Mut [muːt] *m* (-[e]s/*no pl.*) courage; spirit; pluck; *~ fassen* pluck up courage, summon one's courage; *den ~ sinken lassen* lose courage or heart; *guten ~(e)s sein* be of good cheer; '**ig** *adj.* courageous, plucky; '**los** *adj.* discouraged; despondent; '**losigkeit** *f* (-/*no pl.*) discouragement; despondency; **maßen** ['maːsən] *v/t.* (ge-, h) suppose, guess, surmise; **maßlich** *adj.* presumable; supposed; *heir:* presumptive; '**maßung** *f* (-/-en) supposition, surmise; *bloße ~en pl.* guesswork.

Mutter ['mutər] *f* 1. (-/⸗) mother; 2. ⊕ (-/-n) nut; '**brust** *f* mother's breast; '**leib** *m* womb.

mütterlich *adj.* ['mytərliç] motherly; maternal; **erseits** *adv.* ['ɛr-'tsaɪts] on *or* from one's mother's side; *uncle, etc.:* maternal.

'**Mutter**|**liebe** *f* motherly love; '**los** *adj.* motherless; '**mal** *n* birth-mark, mole; '**milch** *f* mother's milk; '**schaft** *f* (-/*no pl.*) maternity, motherhood; **seelenal'lein** *adj.* all *or* utterly alone; **söhnchen** ['zøːnçən] *n* (-s/-) milksop, *sl.* sissy; '**sprache** *f* mother tongue; '**witz** *m* (-es/*no pl.*) mother wit.

'**Mutwill**|**e** *m* wantonness; mischievousness; '**ig** *adj.* wanton; mischievous; wilful.

Mütze ['mytsə] *f* (-/-n) cap.

Myrrhe ['myrə] *f* (-/-n) myrrh.

Myrte ♀ ['myrtə] *f* (-/-n) myrtle.

mysteri|**ös** *adj.* [myster'jøːs] mysterious; **um** [~'teːrjum] *n* (-s/ *Mysterien*) mystery.

Mystifi|**kation** [mystifika'tsjoːn] *f* (-/-en) mystification; **zieren** [~'tsiːrən] *v/t.* (no -ge-, h) mystify.

Mysti|**k** ['mystik] *f* (-/*no pl.*) mysticism; '**sch** *adj.* mystic(al).

Myth|**e** ['myːtə] *f* (-/-n) myth; '**isch** *adj.* mythic; *esp. fig.* mythical; **ologie** [mytolo'giː] *f* (-/-n) mythology; **ologisch** *adj.* [myto-'loːgiʃ] mythological; **os** ['~ɔs] *m* (-/*Mythen*), **us** ['~us] *m* (-/*Mythen*) myth.

N

na *int.* [na] now!, then!, well!, *Am. a.* hey!

Nabe ['naːbə] *f* (-/-n) hub.

Nabel *anat.* ['naːbəl] *m* (-s/-) navel.

nach [naːx] 1. *prp.* (*dat.*) *direction, striving:* after; to(wards), for (*a. ~ ... hin or zu*); *succession:* after; *time:* after, past; *manner, measure, example:* according to; *~ Gewicht* by weight; *~ deutschem Geld in German money;* e-r *~ dem andern* one by one; *fünf Minuten ~ eins* five minutes past one; 2. *adv.* after; *~ und ~* little by little, gradually; *~ wie vor* now as before, still.

nachahm|**en** ['naːxˀaːmən] *v/t.* (*sep., -ge-, h*) imitate, copy; counterfeit; '**ens'wert** *adj.* worthy of imitation, exemplary; '**er** *m* (-s/-) imitator; '**ung** *f* (-/-en) imitation; copy; counterfeit, fake.

Nachbar ['naːxbaːr] *m* (-n, -s/-n), '**in** *f* (-/-nen) neighbo(u)r; '**~-**

schaft *f* (-/-en) neighbo(u)rhood, vicinity.

'**Nachbehandlung** ⚕ *f* after-treatment.

'**nachbestell**|**en** *v/t.* (*sep., no -ge-, h*) repeat one's order for *s.th.*; '**ung** *f* repeat (order).

'**nachbeten** *v/t.* (*sep., -ge-, h*) echo.

'**Nachbildung** *f* copy, imitation; replica; dummy.

'**nachblicken** *v/i.* (*sep., -ge-, h*) look after.

nachdem *cj.* [naːx'deːm] after, when; *je ~* according as.

'**nachdenk**|**en** *v/i.* (*irr. denken, sep., -ge-, h*) think (*über acc.* over, about); reflect, meditate (*über acc.* on); '**en** *n* (-s/*no pl.*) reflection, meditation; musing; '**lich** *adj.* meditative, reflecting; pensive.

'**Nachdichtung** *f* free version.

'**Nachdruck** *m* 1. (-[e]s/*no pl.*) stress, emphasis; 2. *typ.* (-[e]s/-e) reprint; *unlawfully*: piracy, pirated edition; *lit.* (*sep.*, -ge-, *h*) reprint; *unlawfully*: pirate.

nachdrücklich ['naːxdryklɪç] **1.** *adj.* emphatic, energetic; forcible; positive; **2.** *adv.* ~ betonen emphasize.

nacheifern ['naːx⁹-] *v/i.* (*sep.*, -ge-, *h*) emulate *s.o.*

nacheinander *adv.* [naːx⁹aɪ'nandər] one after another, successively; by *or* in turns.

nachempfinden ['naːx⁹-] *v/t.* (*irr.* empfinden, *sep.*, no -ge-, *h*) s. nachfühlen.

nacherzähl|en ['naːx⁹-] *v/t.* (*sep.*, no -ge-, *h*) repeat; retell; *dem Englischen nacherzählt* adapted from the English; **2ung** ['naːx⁹-] *f* repetition, story retold, reproduction.

'**Nachfolge** *f* succession; **2n** *v/i.* (*sep.*, -ge-, sein) follow *s.o.*; *j-m im Amt* ~ succeed *s.o.* in his office; '~r *m* (-*s*/-) follower; successor.

'**nachforsch|en** *v/i.* (*sep.*, -ge-, *h*) investigate, search for; '**2ung** *f* investigation, inquiry, search.

'**Nachfrage** *f* inquiry; † demand; **2n** *v/i.* (*sep.*, -ge-, *h*) inquire (*nach* after).

'**nach|fühlen** *v/t.* (*sep.*, -ge-, *h*): *es j-m* ~ feel *or* sympathize with *s.o.*; '~**füllen** *v/t.* (*sep.*, -ge-, *h*) fill up, refill; '~**geben** *v/i.* (*irr.* geben, *sep.*, -ge-, *h*) give way (*dat.* to); *fig.* give in, yield (to); **2gebühr** & *f* surcharge; '~**gehen** *v/i.* (*irr.* gehen, *sep.*, -ge-, sein) follow (*s.o.*, *business*, *trade*, *etc.*); pursue (*pleasure*); attend to (*business*); investigate *s.th.*; *watch* be slow; **2geschmack** *m* (-[*e*]*s*/no *pl.*) after-taste.

nachgiebig *adj.* ['naːxgiːbɪç] elastic, flexible; *fig.* a. yielding, compliant; '**2keit** *f* (-/-en) flexibility; compliance.

'**nachgrübeln** *v/i.* (*sep.*, -ge-, *h*) ponder, brood (*both:* über *acc.* over), muse (on).

nachhaltig *adj.* ['naːxhaltɪç] lasting, enduring.

nach'her *adv.* afterwards; then; *bis* ~*l* see you later!, so long!

'**Nachhilfe** *f* help, assistance; '~**lehrer** *m* coach, private tutor; '~**unterricht** *m* private lesson(s *pl.*), coaching.

'**nach|holen** *v/t.* (*sep.*, -ge-, *h*) make up for, make good; '**2hut** ✗ *f* (-/-en) rear(-guard); *die* ~ *bilden* bring up the rear (*a. fig.*); '~**jagen** *v/i.* (*sep.*, -ge-, sein) chase *or* pursue *s.o.*; '~**klingen** *v/i.* (*irr.* klingen, *sep.*, -ge-, *h*) resound, echo.

'**Nachkomme** *m* (-*n*/-*n*) descendant; ~*n pl. esp.* ₰ issue; **2n** *v/i.* (*irr.* kommen, *sep.*, -ge-, sein) follow; come later; obey (*order*); meet (*liabilities*); '~**nschaft** *f* (-/-en) descendants *pl.*, *esp.* ₰ issue.

'**Nachkriegs...** post-war.

Nachlaß ['naːxlas] *m* (*Nachlasses*/*Nachlasse*, *Nachlässe*) † reduction, discount; assets *pl.*, estate, inheritance (*of deceased*).

'**nachlassen** (*irr.* lassen, *sep.*, -ge-, *h*) **1.** *v/t.* reduce (*price*); **2.** *v/i.* deteriorate; slacken, relax; diminish; *pain, rain, etc.* abate; *storm:* calm down; *strength* wane; *interest:* flag.

'**nachlässig** *adj.* careless, negligent.

'**nach|laufen** *v/i.* (*irr.* laufen, *sep.*, -ge-, sein) run (*dat.* after); '~**lesen** *v/t.* (*irr.* lesen, *sep.*, -ge-, *h*) *in book:* look up; ✗ glean; '~**liefern** † *v/t.* (*sep.*, -ge-, *h*) deliver subsequently; repeat delivery of; '~**lösen** *v/t.* (*sep.*, -ge-, *h*): *e-e Fahrkarte* ~ take a supplementary ticket; buy a ticket en route; '~**machen** *v/t.* (*sep.*, -ge-, *h*) imitate (*j-m et. s.o.* in *s.th.*); copy; counterfeit, forge; '~**messen** *v/t.* (*irr.* messen, *sep.*, -ge-, *h*) measure again.

'**Nachmittag** *m* afternoon; **2s** *adv.* in the afternoon; '~**svorstellung** *thea. f* matinée.

Nach|nahme ['naːxnaːmə] *f* (-/-n) cash on delivery, *Am.* collect on delivery; *per* ~ *schicken* send C.O.D.; '~**name** *m* surname, last name; '~**porto** & *n* surcharge.

'**nach|prüfen** *v/t.* (*sep.*, -ge-, *h*) verify; check; '~**rechnen** *v/t.* (*sep.*, -ge-, *h*) reckon *or* again; check (*bill*).

'**Nachrede** *f*: *üble* ~ ₰ defamation (of character); *oral:* slander, *written:* libel; **2n** *v/t.* (*sep.*, -ge-, *h*): *j-m Übles* ~ slander *s.o.*

Nachricht ['naːxrɪçt] *f* (-/-en) news; message; report; information, notice; ~ *geben s. benachrichtigen*; '~**enagentur** *f* news agency; '~**endienst** *m* news service; ✗ intelligence service; '~**ensprecher** *m* newscaster; '~**enwesen** *n* (-*s*/no *pl.*) communications *pl.*

'**nachrücken** *v/i.* (*sep.*, -ge-, sein) move along.

'**Nach|ruf** *m* obituary (notice); '~**ruhm** *m* posthumous fame.

'**nachsagen** *v/t.* (*sep.*, -ge-, *h*) repeat; *man sagt ihm nach, daß he is said to inf.*

'**Nachsaison** *f* dead *or* off season.

'**nachschicken** *v/t.* (*sep.*, -ge-, *h*) s. nachsenden.

'**nachschlage|n** *v/t.* (*irr.* schlagen, *sep.*, -ge-, *h*) consult (*book*); look up (*word*); **2werk** *n* reference-book.

'**Nach|schlüssel** *m* skeleton key; '~**schrift** *f* in *letter:* postscript; '~**schub** *esp.* ✗ *m* supplies *pl.*; '~**schubweg** ✗ *m* supply line.

'**nach|sehen** (*irr.* sehen, *sep.*, -ge-, *h*) **1.** *v/i.* look after; ~, *ob* (go and) see whether; **2.** *v/t.* look after; examine, inspect; check; overhaul (*machine*); *s. nachschlagen*; *j-m et.* ~ indulge s.o. in s.th.; '**~senden** *v/t.* ([*irr. senden*,] *sep.*, *-ge-*, *h*) send after; send on, forward (*letter*) (*j-m* to s.o.).

'**Nachsicht** *f* indulgence; '**2ig** *adj.*, '**2svoll** *adj.* indulgent, forbearing.

'**Nachsilbe** *gr. f* suffix.

'**nach|sinnen** *v/i.* (*irr. sinnen*, *sep.*, *-ge-*, *h*) muse, meditate (*über acc.* [*up*]on); '**~sitzen** *v/i.* (*irr. sitzen*, *sep.*, *-ge-*, *h*) pupil: be kept in.

'**Nach|sommer** *m* St. Martin's summer, *esp. Am.* Indian summer; '**~speise** *f* dessert; '**~spiel** *fig. n* sequel.

'**nach|spionieren** *v/i.* (*sep.*, *no -ge-*, *h*) spy (*dat. on*); '**~sprechen** (*irr. sprechen*, *sep.*, *-ge-*, *h*) repeat; '**~spülen** *v/t.* (*sep.*, *-ge-*, *h*) rinse; '**~spüren** *v/i.* (*sep.*, *-ge-*, *h*) (*dat.*) track, trace.

nächst [nɛːçst] **1.** *adj. succession*, *time*: next; *distance*, *relation*: nearest; **2.** *prp.* (*dat.*) next to, next after; '**2'beste** *m, f, n* (*-n/-n*): der (*die*) ~ anyone; *das* ~ anything; er fragte den ~*n* he asked the next person he met.

'**nachstehen** *v/i.* (*irr. stehen*, *sep.*, *-ge-*, *h*): *j-m in nichts* ~ be in no way inferior to s.o.

'**nachstell|en** (*sep.*, *-ge-*, *h*) **1.** *v/t.* place behind; put back (*watch*); ⊕ adjust (*screw*, *etc.*); '**2ung** *fig. f* persecution.

'**Nächstenliebe** *f* charity.

'**nächstens** *adv.* shortly, (very) soon, before long.

'**nach|streben** *v/i.* (*sep.*, *-ge-*, *h*) *s. nacheifern*; '**~suchen** *v/i.* (*sep.*, *-ge-*, *h*): ~ *um* apply for, seek.

Nacht [naxt] *f* (*-/⸚e*) night; *bei* ~, *des* ~*s s. nachts*; '**~arbeit** *f* nightwork; '**~asyl** *n* night-shelter; '**~ausgabe** *f* night edition (*of newspaper*); '**~dienst** *m* night-duty.

'**Nachteil** *m* disadvantage, drawback; *im* ~ *sein* be at a disadvantage; '**2ig** *adj.* disadvantageous.

'**Nacht|essen** *n* supper; '**~falter** *zo. m* (*-s/-*) moth; '**~gebet** *n* evening prayer; '**~geschirr** *n* chamberpot; '**~hemd** *n* night-gown, *Am. a.* night robe; *for men*: nightshirt.

Nachtigall *orn.* ['naxtigal] *f* (*-/-en*) nightingale.

'**Nachtisch** *m* (*-es/no pl.*) sweet, dessert.

'**Nachtlager** *n* (*a*) lodging for the night; bed.

nächtlich *adj.* ['nɛçtliç] nightly, nocturnal.

'**Nacht|lokal** *n* night-club; '**~mahl** *n* supper; '**~portier** *m* night-porter; '**~quartier** *n* night-quarters *pl.*

Nachtrag ['naːxtraːk] *m* (*-[e]s/⸚e*) supplement; '**2en** *v/t.* (*irr. tragen*, *sep.*, *-ge-*, *h*) carry (*j-m et. s.th. after s.o.*); add; † post up (*ledger*); *j-m et.* ~ bear s.o. a grudge; '**2end** *adj.* unforgiving, resentful.

nachträglich *adj.* ['naːxtrɛːkliç] additional; subsequent.

nachts *adv.* [naxts] at *or* by night.

'**Nacht|schicht** *f* night-shift; '**2-schlafend** *adj.*: *zu* ~*er Zeit* in the middle of the night; '**~schwärmer** *fig. m* night-reveller; '**~tisch** *m* bedside table; '**~topf** *m* chamberpot; '**~vorstellung** *thea. f* night performance; '**~wache** *f* nightwatch; '**~wächter** *m* (night-) watchman; '**~wandler** ['~vandlər] *m* (*-s/-*) sleep-walker; '**~zeug** *n* night-things *pl.*

'**nachwachsen** *v/i.* (*irr. wachsen*, *sep.*, *-ge-*, *sein*) grow again.

'**Nachwahl** *parl. f* by-election.

Nachweis ['naːxvaɪs] *m* (*-es/-e*) proof, evidence; '**2bar** *adj.* demonstrable; traceable; **2en** ['~zən] *v/t.* (*irr. weisen*, *sep.*, *-ge-*, *h*) point out, show; trace; prove; '**2lich** *adj. s. nachweisbar*.

'**Nach|welt** *f* posterity; '**~wirkung** *f* after-effect; consequences *pl.*; aftermath; '**~wort** *n* (*-[e]s/-e*) epilog(ue); '**~wuchs** *m* (*-[e]s/no pl.*) rising generation.

'**nach|zahlen** *v/t.* (*sep.*, *-ge-*, *h*) pay in addition; '**~zählen** *v/t.* (*sep.*, *-ge-*, *h*) count over (again), check; '**2zahlung** *f* additional payment.

Nachzügler ['naːxtsyːklər] *m* (*-s/-*) straggler, late-comer.

Nacken ['nakən] *m* (*-s/-*) nape (of the neck), neck.

nackt *adj.* [nakt] naked, nude; bare (*a. fig.*); *young birds*: unfledged; *truth*: plain.

Nadel ['naːdəl] *f* (*-/-n*) needle; pin; brooch; '**~arbeit** *f* needlework; '**~baum** ♣ *m* conifer(ous tree); '**~stich** *m* prick; stitch; *fig.* pin-prick.

Nagel ['naːgəl] *m* (*-s/⸚*) *anat.*, ⊕ nail; *of wood*: peg; spike; stud; *die Arbeit brennt mir auf den Nägeln* it's a rush job; '**~haut** *f* cuticle; '**~lack** *m* nail varnish; '**2n** *v/t.* (*ge-*, *h*) nail (*an or auf acc. to*); '**~necessaire** ['~nesɛsɛːr] *n* (*-s/-s*) manicure-case; '**2neu** F *adj.* bran(d)-new; '**~pflege** *f* manicure.

nage|n ['naːgən] (*ge-*, *h*) **1.** *v/i.* gnaw; ~ *an* (*dat.*) gnaw at; pick (*bone*); **2.** *v/t.* gnaw; '**2tier** *zo. n* rodent, gnawer.

nah *adj.* [naː] near, close (*bei* to); nearby; *danger*: imminent.

Näharbeit ['nɛːʔ-] *f* needlework, sewing.

'**Nahaufnahme** *f film*: close-up.

nahe *adj.* ['naːə] *s. nah.*

Nähe ['nɛːə] *f* (-/*no pl.*) nearness, proximity; vicinity; *in der* ~ close by.

'nahe|gehen *v/i.* (*irr.* gehen, *sep.*, -*ge*-, *sein*) (*dat.*) affect, grieve; '~**kommen** *v/i.* (*irr.* kommen, *sep.*, -*ge*-, *sein*) (*dat.*) approach; get at (*truth*); '~**legen** *v/t.* (*sep.*, -*ge*-, h) suggest; '~**liegen** *v/i.* (*irr.* liegen, *sep.*, -*ge*-, h) suggest itself, be obvious.

nahen ['naːən] **1.** *v/i.* (ge-, sein) approach; **2.** *v/refl.* (ge-, h) approach (*j-m* s.o.).

nähen ['nɛːən] *v/t. and v/i.* (ge-, h) sew, stitch.

näher *adj.* ['nɛːər] nearer, closer; *road* shorter; *das Nähere* (further) particulars *pl or* details *pl.*

'Näherin *f* (-/-nen) seamstress.

'nähern *v/t.* (ge-, h) approach (*dat.* to); *sich* approach (*j-m* s.o.).

'nahe'zu *adv* nearly, almost.

'Nähgarn *n* (sewing-)cotton.

'Nahkampf ⚔ *m* close combat.

nahm [nɑ m] *pret of* nehmen.

'Näh|maschine *f* sewing-machine; '~**nadel** *f* (sewing-)needle.

nähren ['nɛːrən] *v/t.* (ge-, h) nourish (*a fig.*), feed; nurse (*child*); *sich* vor live *or* feed on.

nahrhaft *adj.* ['naːrhaft] nutritious, nourishing

'Nahrung *f* ~/*no pl.*) food, nourishment, nutriment.

'Nahrungs|aufnahme *f* intake of food; ~**mittel** *n/pl.* food(-stuff), victuals *pl*

'Nährwert *m* nutritive value.

Naht [nɑ t] *f* -/-e) seam; ⚕ suture.

'Nahverkehr *m* local traffic.

'Nähzeug *n* sewing-kit.

naiv *adj.* [na'i f] naïve, naive, simple; **2ität** [naivi'tɛːt] *f* (-/*no pl.*) naïvete, naivety, simplicity.

Name ['nɑ mə] *m* (-ns/-n) name; *im* ~*n* (*gen*) on behalf of; *dem* ~*n nach* nominal(ly), in name only; *dem* ~*n nach kennen* know by name; *die Dinge beim rechten* ~*n nennen* call a spade a spade; *darf ich um Ihren* ~*n bitten?* may I ask your name?

'namen|los *adj.* nameless, anonymous; *fig.* unutterable; '~**s 1.** *adv.* named, by the name of, called; **2.** *prp.* (*gen*) in the name of.

'Namens|tag *m* name-day; '~**vetter** *m* name sake ; ~**zug** *m* signature.

namentlich ['nɑ məntliç] **1.** *adj.* nominal; **2.** *adv.* by name; especially, in particular.

'namhaft *adj.* notable; considerable; *machen* name.

nämlich [nɛ mliç] **1.** *adj.* the same; **2.** *adv* namely, that is (to say).

nannte ['nantə] *pret. of* nennen.

Napf [napf] *m* (-[e]s/-e) bowl, basin.

Narb|e ['narbə] *f* (-/-n) scar; '2**ig** *adj.* scarred; *leather*: grained.

Narko|se ⚕ [nar'koːzə] *f* (-/-n) narcosis; **2tisieren** [~oti'ziːrən] *v/t.* (*no* -ge-, h) narcotize.

Narr [nar] *m* (-en/-en) fool; jester; *zum* ~*en halten* = '2**en** *v/t.* (ge-, h) make a fool of, fool.

'Narren|haus F *n* madhouse; '~**kappe** *f* fool's-cap; '2**sicher** *adj.* foolproof.

'Narrheit *f* (-/-en) folly.

Närrin ['nɛrin] *f* (-/-nen) fool, foolish woman.

'närrisch *adj.* foolish, silly; odd.

Narzisse ♀ [nar'tsisə] *f* (-/-n) narcissus; *gelbe* daffodil.

nasal *adj.* [na'zɑːl] nasal; ~*e Sprechweise* twang.

nasch|en ['naʃən] (ge-, h) **1.** *v/i.* nibble (*an dat.* at); *gern* ~ have a sweet tooth; **2.** *v/t.* nibble; eat *s.th.* on the sly; **2erei en** [~'raiən] *f/pl.* dainties *pl*, sweets *pl.*; '~**haft** *adj.* fond of dainties *or* sweets.

Nase ['nɑːzə] *f* (-/-n) nose; *die* ~ *rümpfen* turn up one's nose (*über acc.* at).

näseln ['nɛːzəln] *v/i.* (ge-, h) speak through the nose, nasalize; snuffle.

'Nasen|bluten *n* (-s/*no pl.*) nosebleeding, '~**loch** *n* nostril; '~**spitze** *f* tip of the nose.

naseweis *adj.* ['nɑːzəvais] pert, saucy.

nasführen ['nɑːs-] *v/t.* (ge-, h) fool, dupe.

Nashorn *zo.* ['nɑːs-] *n* rhinoceros.

naß *adj* [nas] wet; damp, moist.

Nässe ['nɛsə] *f* (-/*no pl.*) wet(ness); moisture; ⚗ humidity; '2**n** (ge-, h) **1.** *v/t.* wet; moisten; **2.** ⚕ *v/i.* discharge

'naßkalt *adj.* damp and cold, raw.

Nation [na'tsjoːn] *f* (-/-en) nation.

national *adj.* [natsjo'nɑːl] national; **2hymne** *f* national anthem; **2ismus** [~a lismus] *m* (-/*Nationalismen*) nationalism; **2ität** [~ali'tɛːt] *f* (-/-en) nationality; **2mannschaft** *f* national team.

Natter ['natər] *f* (-/-n) *zo.* adder, viper; *fig* serpent.

Natur [na tu r] *f* **1.** (-/*no pl.*) nature; **2.** (-/-en) constitution; temper(ament), disposition, nature; *von* ~ by nature

Naturalien [natu'rɑːljən] *pl.* natural produce *sg.*; *in* ~ in kind.

naturalisieren [naturali'ziːrən] *v/t.* (*no* -ge , h) naturalize.

Naturalismus [natura'lismus] *m* (-/*no pl*) naturalism.

Naturanlage [na'tuːr⁹-] *f* (natural) disposition

Naturell [natu'rel] *n* (-s/-e) natural disposition, nature, temper.

Na'tur|ereignis *n*, ~**erscheinung** *f* phenomenon; ~**forscher** *m* naturalist, scientist; ²gemäß *adj.* natural; ~geschichte *f* natural history; ~gesetz *n* law of nature, natural law; ²getreu *adj.* true to nature; life-like; ~kunde *f* (natural) science.

natürlich [na'ty:rliç] 1. *adj.* natural; genuine; innate; unaffected; 2. *adv.* naturally, of course.

Na'tur|produkte *n/pl.* natural products *pl.* or produce *sg.*; ~schutz *m* wild-life conservation; ~schutzgebiet *n*, ~schutzpark *m* national park, wild-life (p)reserve; ~trieb *m* instinct; ~wissenschaft *f* (natural) science; ~wissenschaftler *m* (natural) scientist.

Nebel ['ne:bəl] *m* (-s/-) fog; mist; haze; smoke; ²haft *fig. adj.* nebulous, hazy, dim; '~horn *n* fog-horn.

neben *prp.* (*dat.*; *acc.*) ['ne:bən] beside, by (the side of); near to; against, compared with; apart *or Am. a.* aside from, besides.

neben|'an *adv.* next door; close by; ²anschluß *teleph.* ['ne:bən²-] *m* extension (line); ²arbeit ['ne-bən²-] *f* extra work; ²ausgaben ['ne:bən²-] *f/pl.* incidental expenses *pl.*, extras *pl.*; ²ausgang ['ne:bən²-] *m* side-exit, side-door; ²bedeutung *f* secondary meaning, connotation; ~'bei *adv.* by the way; besides; ²beruf *m* side-line; '~beruflich *adv.* as a side-line; in one's spare time; ²beschäftigung *f s.* Nebenberuf; ²buhler ['~bu:lər] *m* (-s/-) rival; ~ei'nander *adv.* side by side; ~ bestehen co-exist; ²eingang ['ne:bən²-] *m* side-entrance; ²einkünfte ['ne:bən²-] *pl.*, ²einnahmen ['ne:bən²-] *f/pl.* casual emoluments *pl.*, extra income; ²erscheinung ['ne:bən²-] *f* accompaniment; '²fach *n* subsidiary subject, *Am.* minor (subject); ²fluß *m* tributary (river); ²gebäude *n* annex(e); outhouse; ²geräusch *n* radio: atmospherics *pl.*, interference, jamming; '²gleis *n* siding, side-track; '²handlung *thea. f* underplot; '²haus *n* adjoining house; ~'her *adv.*, ~'hin *adv.* by his *or* her side; *s.* nebenbei; '²kläger *m* co-plaintiff; '²kosten *pl.* extras *pl.*; '²mann *m* person next to one; '²produkt *n* by-product; '²rolle *f* minor part (*a. thea.*); '²sache *f* minor matter, side issue; '~sächlich *adj.* subordinate, incidental, unimportant; '²satz *gr. m* subordinate clause; '~stehend *adj.* in the margin; '²stelle *f* branch; agency; *teleph.* extension; '²straße *f* by-street, by-road; '²strecke *f* branch line; '²tisch *m* next table; '²tür *f* side-door; '²verdienst *m* incidental *or* extra earnings *pl.*; '²zimmer *n* adjoining room.

'neblig *adj.* foggy, misty, hazy.

nebst *prp.* (*dat.*) [ne:pst] together with, besides; including.

neck|en ['nɛkən] *v/t.* (ge-, h) tease, banter, *sl.* kid; ²erei ['~'raɪ] *f* (-/-en) teasing, banter; '~isch *adj.* playful; droll, funny.

Neffe ['nɛfə] *m* (-n/-n) nephew.

negativ [nega'ti:f] 1. *adj.* negative; 2. ² *n* (-s/-e) negative.

Neger ['ne:gər] *m* (-s/-) negro; '~in *f* (-/-nen) negress.

nehmen ['ne:mən] *v/t.* (*irr.*, ge-, h) take; receive; charge (*money*); zu sich ~ take, have (*meal*); *j-m* et. ~ take s.th. from s.o.; *ein Ende* ~ come to an end; *es sich nicht* ~ *lassen zu inf.* insist upon *ger.*; *streng genommen* strictly speaking.

Neid [naɪt] *m* (-[e]s/no *pl.*) envy; ²en ['naɪdən] *v/t.* (ge-, h): *j-m* et. ~ envy s.o. s.th.; ~er ['~dər] *m* (-s/-) envious person; ~hammel ['~dɪʃ] *m* dog in the manger; ²isch *adj.* ['~dɪʃ] envious (*auf acc.* of); ²los *adj.* ['naɪt-] ungrudging.

Neige ['naɪgə] *f* (-/-n) decline; *barrel:* dregs *pl.*; *glass* heeltap; *zur* ~ *gehen* (be on the) decline; *esp.* ✝ run short; ²n (ge-, h) 1. *v/t. and v/refl.* bend, incline; 2. *v/i.*: *er neigt zu Übertreibungen* he is given to exaggeration.

'Neigung *f* (-/-en) inclination (*a. fig.*); slope, incline.

nein *adv.* [naɪn] no.

Nektar ['nɛkta:r] *m* (-s/no *pl.*) nectar.

Nelke ['nɛlkə] *f* (-/-n) carnation, pink; *spice* clove.

nennen ['nɛnən] *v/t.* (*irr.*, ge-, h) name; call, term; mention; nominate (*candidate*); *sports:* enter (für for); *sich* ... ~ be called ...; '~swert *adj.* worth mentioning.

'Nenn|er *m* (-s/-) denominator; '~ung *f* (-/-en) naming; mentioning; nomination (*of candidates*); *sports:* entry; '~wert *m* nominal *or* face value; *zum* ~ ✝ at par.

Neon ['ne:ɔn] *n* (-s/no *pl.*) neon; '~röhre *f* neon tube.

Nerv [nɛrf] *m* (-s/-en) nerve; *j-m auf die* ~*en fallen or gehen* get on s.o.'s nerves.

'Nerven|arzt *m* neurologist; '²aufreibend *adj.* trying; '~heilanstalt *f* mental hospital; '~kitzel *m* (-s/no *pl.*) thrill, sensation; '²krank *adj.* neurotic; '²leidend *adj.* neuropathic, neurotic; '~schwäche *f* nervous debility; '²stärkend *adj.* tonic; '~system *n* nervous system; '~zusammenbruch *m* nervous breakdown.

nerv|ig *adj.* ['nɛrviç] sinewy; ~ös *adj.* [~'vø:s] nervous; ²osität [~ozi'te:t] *f* (-/no *pl.*) nervousness.

Nerz *zo.* [nɛrts] *m* (-es/-e) mink.

Nessel ⚭ ['nɛsəl] f (-/-n) nettle.
Nest [nɛst] n (-es/-er) nest; F fig. bed; F fig. hick or one-horse town.
nett adj. [nɛt] nice; neat, pretty, Am. a. cute; pleasant; kind.
netto ↑ adv. ['nɛto] net, clear.
Netz [nɛts] n (-es/-e) net; fig. network; '~anschluß ⚡ m mains connection, power supply; '~haut anat. f retina; '~spannung ⚡ f mains voltage.

neu adj. [nɔy] new; fresh; recent; modern; ~ere Sprachen modern languages; ~este Nachrichten latest news; von ~em anew, afresh; ein ~es Leben beginnen turn over a new leaf; was gibt es Neues? what is the news?, Am. what is new?
'Neu|anschaffung f (-/-en) recent acquisition; '2artig adj. novel; '~auflage typ. f, '~ausgabe typ. f new edition; reprint; '~bau m (-[e]s/-ten) new building; '2bearbeitet adj. revised; '~e m (-n/-n) new man; new-comer; novice; '2entdeckt adj. recently discovered.
neuer|dings adv. ['nɔyər'dɪŋs] of late, recently; '2er m (-s/-) innovator.
Neuerscheinung ['nɔy?-] f new book or publication.
'Neuerung f (-/-en) innovation.
'neu|geboren adj. new-born; '~gestalten v/t. (sep., -ge-, h) reorganize; '2gestaltung f reorganization; '2gier f, 2gierde ['~də] f (-/no pl.) curiosity, inquisitiveness; ~gierig adj. curious (auf acc. about, of), inquisitive, sl. nos(e)y; ich bin ~, ob I wonder whether or if; '2heit f (-/-en) newness, freshness; novelty.
'Neuigkeit f (-/-en) (e-e a piece of) news.
'Neu|jahr n New Year('s Day); '~land n (-[e]s/no pl.): ~ erschließen break fresh ground (a. fig.); '2lich adv. the other day, recently; '~ling m (-s/-e) novice; contp. greenhorn; '2modisch adj. fashionable; '~mond m (-[e]s/no pl.) new moon.
neun adj. [nɔyn] nine; '~te adj. ninth; '2tel n (-s/-) ninth part; '~tens adv. ninthly; '~zehn adj. nineteen; '~zehnte adj. nineteenth; '~zig adj. ['~tsɪç] ninety; '~zigste adj. ninetieth.
'Neu|philologe m student or teacher of modern languages; '~regelung f reorganization, rearrangement.
neutr|al adj. [nɔy'traːl] neutral; 2alität [~ali'tɛːt] f (-/no pl.) neutrality; '2um gr. ['nɔytrum] n (-s/Neutra, Neutren) neuter.
'neu|vermählt adj. newly married; die 2en pl. the newly-weds pl.; '2wahl parl. f new election; '~wertig adj. as good as new; '2zeit f (-/no pl.) modern times pl.

nicht adv. [nɪçt] not; auch ~ nor; ~ anziehend unattractive; ~ besser no better; ~ bevollmächtigt noncommissioned; ~ einlösbar ↑ inconvertible; ~ erscheinen fail to attend.
'Nicht|achtung f disregard; '2amtlich adj. unofficial; '~angriffspakt pol. m non-aggression pact; '~annahme f non-acceptance; '~befolgung f non-observance.
Nichte ['nɪçtə] f (-/-n) niece.
'nichtig adj. null, void; invalid; vain, futile; für ~ erklären declare null and void, annul; '2keit f (-/-en) ztz nullity; vanity, futility.
'Nichtraucher m non-smoker.
nichts [nɪçts] 1. indef. pron. nothing, naught, not anything; 2. 2 n (-/no pl.) nothing(ness); fig.: nonentity; void; '~ahnend adj. unsuspecting; '~destoweniger adv. nevertheless; '~nutzig adj. ['~nutsɪç] good-for-nothing, worthless; '~sagend adj. insignificant; 2tuer ['~tuːər] m (-s/-) idler; '~würdig adj. vile, base, infamous.
'Nicht|vorhandensein n absence; lack; '~wissen n ignorance.
nick|en ['nɪkən] v/i. (ge-, h) nod; bow; '2erchen F n (-s/-): ein ~ machen take a nap, have one's forty winks.
nie adv. [niː] never, at no time.
nieder ['niːdər] 1. adj. low; base, mean, vulgar; value, rank: inferior; 2. adv. down.
'Nieder|gang m decline; '2gedrückt adj. dejected, downcast; '2gehen v/i. (irr. gehen, sep., -ge-, sein) go down; ✈ descend; storm: break; '2geschlagen adj. dejected, downcast; '2hauen v/t. (irr. hauen, sep., -ge-, h) cut down; '2kommen v/i. (irr. kommen, sep., -ge-, sein) be confined; be delivered (mit of); ~kunft ['~kunft] f (-/~e) confinement, delivery; '~lage f defeat; ↑ warehouse; branch; '2lassen v/t. (irr. lassen, sep., -ge-, h) let down; sich ~ settle (down); bird: alight; sit down; establish o.s.; settle (in dat. at); '~lassung f (-/-en) establishment; settlement; branch, agency; '2legen v/t. (sep., -ge-, h) lay or put down; resign (position); retire from (business); abdicate; die Arbeit ~ (go on) strike, down tools, Am. F a. walk out; sich ~ lie down, go to bed; '2machen v/t. (sep., -ge-, h) cut down; massacre; '~schlag m 🜄 precipitate; sediment; precipitation (of rain, etc.); radioactive: fall-out; boxing: knockdown, knock-out; '2schlagen v/t. (irr. schlagen, sep., -ge-, h) knock down; boxing: a. floor; cast down (eyes); suppress; put down, crush (rebellion); ztz quash; sich ~

precipitate; '2schmettern *fig.*
v/t. (*sep.*, -ge-, h) crush; '2setzen
v/t. (*sep.*, -ge-, h) set *or* put down;
sich ~ sit down; *birds:* perch, alight;
'2strecken *v/t.* (*sep.*, -ge-, h) lay
low, strike to the ground, floor;
'2trächtig *adj.* base, mean; F
beastly; '~ung *f* (-/-en) lowlands *pl.*
niedlich *adj.* ['ni:tliç] neat, nice,
pretty, *Am. a.* cute.
Niednagel ['ni:t-] *m* agnail, hang-
nail.
niedrig *adj.* ['ni:driç] low (*a. fig.*);
moderate; *fig.* mean, base.
niemals *adv.* ['ni:ma:ls] never, at
no time.
niemand *indef. pron.* ['ni:mant]
nobody, no one, none; '2sland *n*
(-[e]s/*no pl.*) no man's land.
Niere ['ni:rə] *f* (-/-n) kidney; '~n-
braten *m* loin of veal.
niesel|n F ['ni:zəln] *v/i.* (ge-, h)
drizzle; '2regen F *m* drizzle.
niesen ['ni:zən] *v/i.* (ge-, h) sneeze.
Niet ⊕ [ni:t] *m* (-[e]s/-e) rivet; '~e *f*
(-/-n) lottery: blank; F *fig.* wash-
out; '2en ⊕ *v/t.* (ge-, h) rivet.
Nilpferd *zo.* ['ni:l-] *n* hippopotamus.
nimmer *adv.* ['nimər] never; '~
mehr *adv.* nevermore; '2satt *m*
(-, -[e]s/-e) glutton; 2'wiedersehen F *n:* auf ~ never to meet
again; *er verschwand auf ~* he left
for good.   [*dat.* at).\
nippen ['nipən] *v/i.* (ge-, h) sip (*an*)
Nipp|es ['nipəs] *pl.*, '~sachen *pl.*
(k)nick-(k)nacks *pl.*
nirgend|s *adv.* ['nirgənts], '~(s)'wo
adv. nowhere.
Nische ['ni:ʃə] *f* (-/-n) niche, recess.
nisten ['nistən] *v/i.* (ge-, h) nest.
Niveau [ni'vo:] *n* (-s/-s) level; *fig. a.*
standard.
nivellieren [nive'li:rən] *v/t.* (*no*
-ge-, h) level, grade.
Nixe ['niksə] *f* (-/-n) water-nymph,
mermaid.
noch [nɔx] **1.** *adv.* still; yet; ~ *ein*
another, one more; ~ *einmal* once
more *or* again; ~ *etwas* something
more; ~ *etwas?* anything else?; ~
heute this very day; ~ *immer* still;
~ *nicht* not yet; ~ *nie* never before;
~ *so* ever so; ~ *im 19. Jahrhundert*
as late as the 19th century; *es wird*
~ *2 Jahre dauern* it will take two
more *or* another two years; **2.** *cj.*:
s. weder; ~malig *adj.* ['~ma:liç]
repeated; ~mals *adv.* ['~ma:ls]
once more *or* again.
Nomad|e [no'ma:də] *m* (-n/-n)
nomad; 2isch *adj.* nomadic.
Nominativ *gr.* ['no:minati:f] *m*
(-s/-e) nominative (case).
nominieren [nomi'ni:rən] *v/t.* (*no*
-ge-, h) nominate.

13*

Nonne ['nɔnə] *f* (-/-n) nun; '~n-
kloster *n* nunnery, convent.
Nord *geogr.* [nɔrt], ~en ['~dən] *m*
(-s/*no pl.*) north; 2isch *adj.* ['~diʃ]
northern.
nördlich *adj.* ['nœrtliç] northern,
northerly.
'**Nord|licht** *n* northern lights *pl.*;
~'ost(en *m*) north-east; '~pol *m*
North Pole; 2wärts ['~vɛrts]
northward(s), north; ~'west(en *m*)
north-west.
nörg|eln ['nœrgəln] *v/i.* (ge-, h)
nag, carp (*an dat.* at); grumble;
2ler ['~lər] *m* (-s/-) faultfinder,
grumbler.
Norm [nɔrm] *f* (-/-en) standard;
rule; norm.
normal *adj.* [nɔr'ma:l] normal;
regular; *measure, weight, time:*
standard; ~isieren [~ali'zi:rən]
v/refl. (*no* -ge-, h) return to normal.
'**norm|en** *v/t.* (ge-, h), ~ieren
[~'mi:rən] *v/t.* (*no* -ge-, h) stand-
ardize.
Not [no:t] *f* (-/⁓e) need, want; necessity; difficulty, trouble; misery;
danger, emergency, distress (*a.* ⚓);
~ *leiden* suffer privations; *in* ~ *ge-*
raten become destitute, get into
trouble; *in* ~ *sein* be in trouble; *zur*
~ at a pinch; *es tut not, daß* it is necessary that.
Notar [no'ta:r] *m* (-s/-e) (public)
notary.
'**Not|ausgang** *m* emergency exit;
~behelf *m* makeshift, expedient,
stopgap, ~bremse *f* emergency
brake; ~brücke *f* temporary
bridge; ~durft ['~durft] *f* (-/*no pl.*):
s-e ~ verrichten relieve o.s.; '2dürf-
tig *adj.* scanty, poor; temporary.
Note ['no:tə] *f* (-/-n) note (*a.* ♩);
pol. note, memorandum; *school:*
mark.
'**Noten|bank** ✝ *f* bank of issue; '~
schlüssel ♩ *m* clef; '~system ♩ *n*
staff.
'**Not|fall** *m* case of need, emergency;
'2falls *adv.* if necessary; '2gedrun-
gen *adv.* of necessity, needs.
notier|en [no'ti:rən] *v/t.* (*no* -ge-, h)
make a note of, note (down); ✝
quote, 2ung ✝ *f* (-/-en) quotation.
nötig *adj.* ['nø:tiç] necessary; ~ *ha-*
ben need, ~en ['~gən] *v/t.* (ge-, h)
force, oblige, compel; press, urge
(*guest*); '~enfalls *adv.* if necessary;
'2ung *f* (-/-en) compulsion; pressing; ⁿ⁺ intimidation.
Notiz [no'ti:ts] *f* (-/-en) notice; note,
memorandum; ~ *nehmen von* take
notice of; pay attention to; *keine* ~
nehmen von ignore; *sich* ~en *ma-*
chen take notes; ~block *m* pad,
Am. a. scratch pad; ~buch *n* note-
book.
'**Not|lage** *f* distress; emergency;
'2landen ✈ *v/i.* (-ge-, sein) make

a forced or emergency landing; '~landung ✈ f forced or emergency landing; 'Qleidend adj. needy, destitute; distressed; 'Qlösung f expedient; '~lüge f white lie.

notorisch adj. [no'to:riʃ] notorious.

'Not|ruf teleph. m emergency call; '~signal n emergency or distress signal; '~sitz mot. m dick(e)y(-seat), Am. a. rumble seat; '~stand m emergency; '~standsarbeiten f/pl. relief works pl.; '~standsgebiet n distressed area; '~standsgesetze n/pl. emergency laws pl.; '~verband m first-aid dressing; '~verordnung f emergency decree; '~wehr f self-defen|ce, Am. -se; 'Qwendig adj. necessary; '~wendigkeit f (-/-en) necessity; '~zucht f (-/no pl.) rape.

Novelle [no'vɛlə] f (-/-n) short story, novella; parl. amendment.

November [no'vɛmbər] m (-[s]/-) November.

Nu [nu:] m (-/no pl.): im ~ in no time.

Nuance [ny'ɑ̃:sə] f (-/-n) shade.

nüchtern adj. ['nyçtərn] empty, fasting, sober (a. fig.); matter-of-fact; writings: jejune; prosaic; cool; plain; 'Qheit f (-/no pl.) sobriety; fig. soberness.

Nudel ['nu:dəl] f (-/-n) noodle.

null [nul] 1. adj. null; nil; tennis: love; ~ und nichtig null and void; 2. Q f (-/-en) nought, cipher (a. fig.); zero; 'Qpunkt m zero.

numerieren [numə'ri:rən] v/t. (no -ge-, h) number; numerierter Platz reserved seat.

Nummer ['numər] f (-/-n) number

(a. newspaper, thea.); size (of shoes, etc.); thea. turn; sports: event; '~nschild mot. n number-plate.

nun [nu:n] 1. adv. now, at present; then; ~? well?; ~ also well then; 2. int. now then!; '~mehr adv. now.

nur adv. [nu:r] only; (nothing) but; merely; ~ noch only.

Nuß [nus] f (-/Nüsse) nut; '~kern m kernel; '~knacker m (-s/-) nut-cracker; '~schale f nutshell.

Nüstern ['ny:stərn] f/pl. nostrils pl.

nutz adj. [nuts] s. nütze; 'Qanwendung f practical application; '~bar adj. useful; '~bringend adj. profitable.

nütze adj. ['nytsə] useful; zu nichts ~ sein be of no use, be good for nothing.

Nutzen ['nutsən] 1. m (-s/-) use; profit, gain; advantage; utility; 2. Q v/i. and v/t. (ge-, h) s. nützen.

nützen ['nytsən] (ge-, h) 1. v/i.: zu et. ~ be of use or useful for s.th.; j-m ~ serve s.o.; es nützt nichts zu inf. it is no use ger.; 2. v/t. use, make use of; put to account; avail o.s. of, seize (opportunity).

'Nutz|holz n timber; '~leistung f capacity.

nützlich adj. ['nytsliç] useful, of use; advantageous.

'nutz|los adj. useless; Qnießer ['~ni:sər] m (-s/-) usufructuary; 'Qnießung f (-/-en) usufruct.

'Nutzung f (-/-en) using, utilization.

Nylon ['nailɔn] n (-s/no pl.) nylon; ~strümpfe ['~ʃtrympfə] m/pl. nylons pl., nylon stockings pl.

Nymphe ['nymfə] f (-/-n) nymph.

O

o int. [o:] oh!, ah!; ~ weh! alas!, oh dear (me)!

Oase [o'ɑ:zə] f (-/-n) oasis.

ob cj. [ɔp] whether, if; als ~ as if, as though.

Obacht ['o:baxt] f (-/no pl.): ~ geben auf (acc.) pay attention to, take care of, heed.

Obdach ['ɔpdax] n (-[e]s/no pl.) shelter, lodging; 'Qlos adj. unsheltered, homeless; '~lose m, f (-n/-n) homeless person; '~losenasyl n casual ward.

Obdu|ktion ✚ [ɔpduk'tsjo:n] f (-/-en) post-mortem (examination), autopsy; Qzieren ✚ [~'tsi:rən] v/t. (no -ge-, h) perform an autopsy on.

oben adv. ['o:bən] above; mountain: at the top; house: upstairs; on the surface; von ~ from above; von ~ bis unten from top to bottom;

von ~ herab behandeln treat haughtily; '~'an adv. at the top; '~'auf adv. on the top; on the surface; ~drein adv. ['~'drain] into the bargain, at that; '~erwähnt adj. ['o:bən ʔɛr'vɛ:nt], '~genannt adj. above-mentioned, aforesaid; '~'hin adv. superficially, perfunctorily.

ober ['o:bər] 1. adj. upper, higher; fig. a. superior; 2. Q m (-s/-) (head) waiter; German cards: queen.

Ober|arm ['o:bər ʔ-] m upper arm; ~arzt ['o:bər ʔ-] m head physician; ~aufseher ['o:bər ʔ-] m superintendent; ~aufsicht ['o:bər ʔ-] f superintendence; '~befehl ✕ m supreme command; '~befehlshaber ✕ m commander-in-chief; '~bekleidung f outer garments pl., outer wear; '~bürgermeister m chief burgomaster; Lord Mayor;

'~deck ⚓ n upper deck; '~fläche f surface; 2flächlich adj. ['~fleçliç] superficial; fig. a. shallow; '2halb prp. (gen.) above; '~hand fig. f: die ~ gewinnen über (acc.) get the upper hand of; '~haupt n head, chief; '~haus Brt. parl. n House of Lords; '~hemd n shirt; '~herrschaft f supremacy.

'Oberin f (-/-nen) eccl. Mother Superior; at hospital: matron.

ober|irdisch adj. ['o:bər⁹-] overground, above ground; ⚡ overhead; '2kellner m head waiter; '2kiefer anat. m upper jaw; '2körper m upper part of the body; '2land n upland; '2lauf m upper course (of river); '2leder n upper; '2leitung f chief management; ⚡ overhead wires pl.; '2leutnant ⚔ m (Am. first) lieutenant; '2licht n skylight; '2lippe f upper lip; '2schenkel m thigh; '2schule f secondary school, Am. a. high school.

'oberst 1. adj. uppermost, topmost, top; highest (a. fig.); fig. chief, principal; rank, etc.: supreme; 2. ♀ ⚔ m (-en, -s/-en, -e) colonel.

'Ober|'staatsanwalt ⚖ m chief public prosecutor; '~stimme ♪ f treble, soprano.

'Oberst'leutnant ⚔ m lieutenant-colonel.

'Ober|tasse f cup; '~wasser fig. n: ~ bekommen get the upper hand.

obgleich cj. [ɔp'glaiç] (al)though.

'Obhut f (-/no pl.) care, guard; protection; custody; in (seine) ~ nehmen take care or charge of.

obig adj. ['o:biç] above(-mentioned), aforesaid.

Objekt [ɔp'jɛkt] n (-[e]s/-e) object (a. gr.); project; ✝ a. transaction.

objektiv [ɔpjɛk'ti:f] 1. adj. objective; impartial, detached, actual, practical; 2. ♀ n (-s/-e) object-glass, objective; phot. lens; 2ität [~ivi-'tɛ:t] f (-/no pl.) objectivity; impartiality.

obligat adj. [obli'gɑ:t] obligatory; indispensable, inevitable; 2ion f [~a'tsjo:n] f (-/-en) bond, debenture; ~orisch adj. [~a'to:riʃ] obligatory (für on), compulsory, mandatory.

'Obmann m chairman; ⚖ foreman (of jury); umpire; ✝ shop-steward, spokesman.

Oboe ♪ [o'bo:ə] f (-/-n) oboe, hautboy.

Obrigkeit ['o:briçkait] f (-/-en) the authorities pl.; government; '2lich adj. magisterial, official; '~sstaat m authoritarian state.

ob'schon cj. (al)though.

Observatorium ast. [ɔpzɛrva'to:r-jum] n (-s/Observatorien) observatory.

Obst [o:pst] n (-es/no pl.) fruit;
'~bau m fruit-culture, fruit-growing; '~baum m fruit-tree; '~ernte f fruit-gathering; fruit-crop; '~garten m orchard; '~händler m fruiterer, Am. fruitseller; '~züchter m fruiter, fruit-grower.

obszön adj. [ɔps'tsø:n] obscene, filthy.

ob'wohl cj. (al)though.

Ochse zo ['ɔksə] m (-n/-n) ox; bullock; ~nfleisch n beef.

öde ['ø:də] 1. adj. deserted, desolate; waste; fig. dull, tedious; 2. ♀ f (-/-n) desert, solitude; fig. dullness, tedium.

oder cj. ['o:dər] or.

Ofen ['o:fən] m (-s/⸚) stove; oven; kiln; furnace; '~heizung f heating by stove; '~rohr n stove-pipe.

offen adj. ['ɔfən] open (a. fig.); position: vacant; hostility: overt; fig. frank, outspoken.

'offen'bar 1. adj. obvious, evident, apparent; 2. adv. a. it seems that; ~en [ɔfən'-] v/t. (no -ge-, h) reveal, disclose; manifest; sich j-m ~ open one's heart to s.o.; 2ung [ɔfən'-] f (-/-en) manifestation; revelation; 2ungseid ⚖ [ɔfən'bɑ:ruŋs⁹-] m oath of manifestation.

'Offenheit fig. f (-/no pl.) openness, frankness.

'offen|herzig adj. open-hearted, sincere; frank; '~kundig adj. public; notorious; '~sichtlich adj. manifest, evident, obvious.

offensiv adj. [ɔfɛn'zi:f] offensive; 2e [~və] f (-/-n) offensive.

'offenstehen v/i. (irr. stehen, sep., -ge-, h) stand open; ✝ bill: be outstanding; fig. be open (j-m to s.o.); es steht ihm offen zu inf. he is free or at liberty to inf.

öffentlich ['œfəntliç] 1. adj. public; ~es Ärgernis public nuisance; ~er Dienst Civil Service; 2. adv. publicly, in public; ~ auftreten make a public appearance; '2keit f (-/no pl.) publicity; the public; in aller ~ in public.

offerieren [ɔfə'ri:rən] v/t. (no -ge-, h) offer.

Offerte [ɔ'fɛrtə] f (-/-n) offer; tender.

offiziell adj. [ɔfi'tsjɛl] official.

Offizier ⚔ [ɔfi'tsi:r] m (-s/-e) (commissioned) officer; ~skorps ⚔ [~sko:r] n (-/-) body of officers, the officers pl.; ~smesse f ⚔ officers' mess; ⚓ a. wardroom.

offiziös adj. [ɔfi'tsjø:s] officious, semi-official.

öffn|en ['œfnən] v/t. (ge-, h) open; a. uncork (bottle); ⚕ dissect (body); sich ~ open; '2er m (-s/-) opener; '2ung f (-/-en) opening, aperture; '2ungszeiten f/pl. hours pl. of opening, business hours pl.

oft adv. [ɔft] often, frequently.

öfters adv. ['œftərs] s. oft.
'oftmal|ig adj. frequent, repeated; '~s adv. s. oft.
oh int. [o:] o(h)!
ohne ['o:nə] 1. prp. (acc.) without; 2. cj.: ~ daß, ~ zu inf. without ger.; ~'dies adv. anyhow, anyway; ~'glei- chen adv. unequal(l)ed, matchless; ~'hin adv. s. ohnedies.
'Ohn|macht f (-/-en) powerlessness; impotence; ~ faint, unconscious- ness; in ~ fallen faint, swoon; ~machtsanfall ~ ['o:nmaxts°-] m fainting fit, swoon; '2mächtig adj. powerless; impotent; ~ uncon- scious; ~ werden faint, swoon.
Ohr [o:r] n (-[e]s/-en) ear; fig. a. hearing; ein ~ haben für have an ear for; ganz ~ sein be all ears; F j-n übers ~ hauen cheat s.o., sl. do s.o. (in the eye); bis über die ~en up to the ears or eyes.
Öhr [ø:r] n (-[e]s/-e) eye (of needle).
'Ohren|arzt m aurist, ear specialist; '2betäubend adj. deafening; '~lei- den n ear-complaint; '~schmalz n ear-wax; '~schmaus m treat for the ears; '~schmerzen m/pl. ear- ache; '~zeuge m ear-witness.
'Ohr|feige f box on the ear(s), slap in the face (a. fig.); '2feigen v/t. (ge-, h): j-n ~ box s.o.'s ear(s), slap s.o.'s face; '~läppchen ['~lɛpçən] n (-s/-) lobe of ear; '~ring m ear- ring.
Ökonom|ie [økono'mi:] f (-/-n) economy; 2isch adj. [~'no:miʃ] economical.
Oktav [ɔk'ta:f] n (-s/-e) octavo; ~e ♪ [~və] f (-/-n) octave.
Oktober [ɔk'to:bər] m (-[s]/-) October.
Okul|ar opt. [oku'la:r] n (-s/-e) eye- piece, ocular; 2ieren ✕ v/t. (no -ge-, h) inoculate, graft.
Öl [ø:l] n (-[e]s/-e) oil; ~ ins Feuer gießen add fuel to the flames; ~ auf die Wogen gießen pour oil on the (troubled) waters; '~baum ♀ m olive-tree; '~berg eccl. m (-[e]s/no pl.) Mount of Olives; '2en v/t. (ge-, h) oil; ⊕ a. lubricate; '~farbe f oil-colo(u)r, oil-paint; '~gemälde n oil-painting; '~heizung f oil heating; '2ig adj. oily (a. fig.).
Olive ♀ [o'li:və] f (-/-n) olive; ~nbaum ♀ m olive-tree; 2grün adj. olive(-green).
Öl|male'rei f oil-painting; '~quelle f oil-spring, gusher; oil-well; '~ung f (-/-en) oiling; ⊕ a. lubrication; Letzte ~ eccl. extreme unction.
Olympi|ade [olym'pja:də] f (-/-n) Olympiad; a. Olympic Games pl.; 2sch adj. [o'lympiʃ] Olympic; Olym- pische Spiele pl. Olympic Games pl.
'Ölzweig m olive-branch.
Omelett [ɔm(ə)'lɛt] n (-[e]s/-e, -s), ~e [~'lɛt] f (-/-n) omelet(te).

Om|en ['o:mən] n (-s/-, Omina) omen, augury; 2inös adj. [omi'nø:s] ominous.
Omnibus ['ɔmnibus] m (-ses/-se) (omni)bus; (motor-)coach; '~halte- stelle f bus-stop.
Onkel ['ɔŋkəl] m (-s/-, F -s) uncle.
Oper ['o:pər] f (-/-n) ♪ opera; opera- house.
Operat|eur [opəra'tø:r] m (-s/-e) operator; ✕ surgeon; ~ion [~'tsjo:n] f (-/-en) operation; ~ions- saal ✕ m operating room, Am. surgery; 2iv ✕ adj. [~'ti:f] operative.
Operette ♪ [opə'rɛtə] f (-/-n) operetta.
operieren [opə'ri:rən] (no -ge-, h) 1. v/t.: j-n ~ ✕ operate (up)on s.o. (wegen for); 2. ✕, ✕ v/i. operate; sich ~ lassen undergo an opera- tion.
'Opern|glas n, ~gucker F ['~gukər] m (-s/-) opera-glass(es pl.); '~haus n opera-house; '~sänger m opera- singer, operatic singer; '~text m libretto, book (of an opera).
Opfer ['ɔpfər] n (-s/-) sacrifice; offering; victim (a. fig.); ein ~ brin- gen make a sacrifice; j-m zum ~ fallen be victimized by s.o.; '~gabe f offering; '2n (ge-, h) 1. v/t. sacri- fice; immolate; sich für et. ~ sacri- fice o.s. for s.th.; 2. v/i. (make a) sacrifice (dat. to); '~stätte f place of sacrifice; '~tod m sacrifice of one's life; '~ung f (-/-en) sacrificing, sacrifice; immolation.
Opium ['o:pjum] n (-s/no pl.) opium.
opponieren [ɔpo'ni:rən] v/i. (no -ge-, h) be opposed (gegen to), resist.
Opposition [ɔpozi'tsjo:n] f (-/-en) opposition (a. parl.); ~führer parl. m opposition leader; ~spartei parl. f opposition party.
Optik ['ɔptik] f (-/-%-en) optics; phot. lens system; fig. aspect; '~er m (-s/-) optician.
Optim|ismus [ɔpti'mismus] m (-/no pl.) optimism; ~ist m (-en/-en) optimist; 2istisch adj. optimis- tic.
'optisch adj. optic(al); ~e Täu- schung optical illusion.
Orakel [o'ra:kəl] n (-s/-) oracle; 2haft adj. oracular; 2n v/i. (no -ge-, h) speak oracularly; '~spruch m oracle.
Orange [o'rãːʒə] f (-/-n) orange; 2farben adj. orange(-colo[u]red); ~nbaum ♀ m orange-tree.
Oratorium ♪ [ora'to:rjum] n (-s/ Oratorien) oratorio.
Orchester ♪ [ɔr'kɛstər] n (-s/-) orchestra.
Orchidee ♀ [ɔrçi'de:ə] f (-/-n) orchid.

Orden ['ɔrdən] *m* (-s/-) order (*a. eccl.*); order, medal, decoration.

'**Ordens|band** *n* ribbon (of an order); '**~bruder** *eccl. m* brother, friar; '**~gelübde** *eccl. n* monastic vow; '**~schwester** *eccl. f* sister, nun; '**~verleihung** *f* conferring (of) an order.

ordentlich *adj.* ['ɔrdentliç] tidy; orderly; proper; regular; respectable; good, sound; **~er** *Professor univ.* professor in ordinary.

ordinär *adj.* [ɔrdi'nɛːr] common, vulgar, low.

ordn|en ['ɔrdnən] *v/t.* (ge-, h) put in order; arrange, fix (up); settle (*a.* † *liabilities*); '**2er** *m* (-s/-) *at festival, etc.*: steward; *for papers, etc.*: file.

'**Ordnung** *f* (-/-en) order; arrangement; system; rules *pl.*, regulations *pl.*; class; *in* ~ *bringen* put in order.

'**ordnungs|gemäß**, '**~mäßig 1.** *adj.* orderly, regular; **2.** *adv.* duly; '**2ruf** *parl. m* call to order; '**2strafe** *f* disciplinary penalty; fine; '**~widrig** *adj.* contrary to order, irregular; '**2zahl** *f* ordinal number.

Ordonnanz ⚔ [ɔrdɔ'nants] *f* (-/-en) orderly.

Organ [ɔr'gaːn] *n* (-s/-e) organ.

Organisat|ion [ɔrganiza'tsjoːn] *f* (-/-en) organization; **~ionstalent** *n* organizing ability; **~or** [~'zaːtɔr] *m* (-s/-en) organizer; **2orisch** *adj.* [~a'toːriʃ] organizational, organizing.

or'ganisch *adj.* organic.

organi'sieren *v/t.* (no -ge-, h) organize; *sl.* scrounge; (*nicht*) *organisiert(er Arbeiter)* (non-)unionist.

Organismus [ɔrga'nismus] *m* (-/*Organismen*) organism; **#** *a.* system.

Organist ♪ [ɔrga'nist] *m* (-en/-en) organist.

Orgel ♪ ['ɔrgəl] *f* (-/-n) organ, *Am. a.* pipe organ; '**~bauer** *m* organbuilder; '**~pfeife** *f* organ-pipe; '**~spieler** ♪ *m* organist.

Orgie ['ɔrgjə] *f* (-/-n) orgy.

Oriental|e [orien'taːlə] *m* (-n/-n) oriental; **2isch** *adj.* oriental.

orientier|en [orien'tiːrən] *v/t.* (no -ge-, h) inform, instruct; *sich* ~ orient(ate) o.s. (*a. fig.*); inform o.s. (*über acc.* of); *gut orientiert sein über* (*acc.*) be well informed about, be familiar with; **2ung** *f* (-/-en) orientation; *fig. a.* information; *die* ~ *verlieren* lose one's bearings.

Origin|al [origi'naːl] **1.** *n* (-s/-e) original; **2.** **2** *adj.* original; **~alität** [~ali'tɛːt] *f* (-/-en) originality; **2ell** *adj.* [~'nɛl] original; design, *etc.*: ingenious.

Orkan [ɔr'kaːn] *m* (-[e]s/-e) hurricane; typhoon; **2artig** *adj.* storm; violent; *applause*: thunderous, frenzied.

Ornat [ɔr'naːt] *m* (-[e]s/-e) robe(s *pl.*), vestment.

Ort [ɔrt] *m* (-[e]s/-e) place; site; spot, point; locality; place, village, town; ~ *der Handlung thea.* scene (of action); *an* ~ *und Stelle* on the spot; *höher(e)n* ~*(e)s* at higher quarters; '**2en** *v/t.* (ge-, h) locate.

ortho|dox *adj.* [ɔrto'dɔks] orthodox; **2graphie** [~gra'fiː] *f* (-/-n) orthography; **~graphisch** *adj.* ['~'graːfiʃ] orthographic(al); **2päde** [~'pɛːdə] *m* (-n/-n) orthop(a)edist; **2pädie** [~'pɛːdiː] *f* (-/no pl.*) orthop(a)edics, orthop(a)edy; **~pädisch** *adj.* [~'pɛːdiʃ] orthop(a)edic.

örtlich *adj.* ['œrtliç] local; **#** *a.* topical; **2keit** *f* (-/-en) locality.

'**Orts|angabe** *f* statement of place; '**2ansässig** *adj.* resident, local; **~ansässige** ['~gə] *m* (-n/-n) resident; '**~beschreibung** *f* topography; '**~besichtigung** *f* local inspection.

'**Ortschaft** *f* (-/-en) place, village.

'**Orts|gespräch** *teleph. n* local call; '**~kenntnis** *f* knowledge of a place; '**2kundig** *adj.* familiar with the locality; '**~name** *m* place-name; '**~verkehr** *m* local traffic; '**~zeit** *f* local time.

Öse ['øːzə] *f* (-/-n) eye, loop; eyelet (*of shoe*).

Ost *geogr.* [ɔst] east; '**~en** *m* (-s/no pl.*) east; *der Ferne* (*Nahe*) ~ the Far (Near) East.

ostentativ *adj.* [ɔstenta'tiːf] ostentatious.

Oster|ei ['oːstər⁹-] *n* Easter egg; '**~fest** *n* Easter; '**~hase** *m* Easter bunny *or* rabbit; '**~lamm** *n* paschal lamb; '**~n** *n* (-/-) Easter.

Österreich|er ['øːstaraiçər] *m* (-s/-) Austrian; '**2isch** *adj.* Austrian.

östlich ['œstliç] **1.** *adj.* eastern; *wind, etc.*: easterly; **2.** *adv.*: ~ *von* east of.

ost|wärts *adv.* ['ɔstverts] eastward(s); '**2wind** *m* east(erly) wind.

Otter *zo.* ['ɔtər] **1.** *m* (-s/-) otter; **2.** *f* (-/-n) adder, viper.

Ouvertüre ♪ [uver'tyːrə] *f* (-/-n) overture.

oval [o'vaːl] **1.** *adj.* oval; **2.** **2** *n* (-s/-e) oval.

Ovation [ova'tsjoːn] *f* (-/-en) ovation; *j-m* ~*en bereiten* give s.o. ovations.

Oxyd 🔬 [ɔ'ksyːt] *n* (-[e]s/-e) oxide; **2ieren** [~y'diːrən] (no -ge-) **1.** *v/t.* (h) oxidize; **2.** *v/i.* (sein) oxidize.

Ozean ['oːtsea:n] *m* (-s/-e) ocean.

P

Paar [pɑːr] 1. *n* (-[e]s/-e) pair; couple; 2. ♀ *adj.*: ein ~ a few, some; *j-m* ein ~ Zeilen schreiben drop s.o. a few lines; '2en *v/t.* (ge-, h) pair, couple; mate (*animals*); sich ~ (form a) pair; *animals*: mate; *fig.* join, unite; '~lauf *m sports*: pair-skating; '~läufer *m sports*: pair-skater; '2mal *adv.*: ein ~ several *or* a few times; '~ung *f* (-/-en) coupling; mating, copulation; *fig.* union; '2weise *adv.* in pairs *or* couples, by twos.

Pacht [paxt] *f* (-/-en) lease, tenure, tenancy; *money payment*: rent; '2en *v/t.* (ge-, h) (take on) lease; rent.

Pächter ['pɛçtər] *m* (-s/-), '~in *f* (-/-nen) lessee, lease-holder; tenant.

'**Pacht|ertrag** *m* rental; '~geld *n* rent; '~gut *n* farm; '~vertrag *m* lease; '2weise *adv.* on lease.

Pack [pak] 1. *m* (-[e]s/-e, ⸚e) s. *Packen*²; 2. *n* (-[e]s/*no pl.*) rabble.

Päckchen ['pɛkçən] *n* (-s/-) small parcel, *Am. a.* package; ein ~ Zigaretten a pack(et) of cigarettes.

packen¹ ['pakən] (ge-, h) 1. *v/t.* pack (up); seize, grip, grasp, clutch; collar; *fig.* grip, thrill; F *pack dich!* F clear out!, *sl.* beat it!; 2. *v/i.* pack (up); 3. 2 *n* (-s/*no pl.*) packing.

Packen² [⸚] *m* (-s/-) pack(et), parcel; bale.

'**Packer** *m* (-s/-) packer; '~ei [⸚'raɪ] *f* 1. (-/-en) packing-room; 2. (-/*no pl.*) packing.

'**Pack|esel** *fig. m* drudge; '~material *n* packing materials *pl.*; '~papier *n* packing-paper, brown paper; '~pferd *n* pack-horse; '~ung *f* (-/-en) pack(age); packet; ℱ pack; e-e ~ Zigaretten a pack(et) of cigarettes; '~wagen *m s. Gepäckwagen.*

Pädagog|e [pɛda'goːgə] *m* (-n/-n) pedagog(ue), education(al)ist; '~ik *f* (-/*no pl.*) pedagogics, pedagogy; 2isch *adj.* pedagogic(al).

Paddel ['padəl] *n* (-s/-) paddle; '~boot *n* canoe; '2n *v/i.* (ge-, h, sein) paddle, canoe.

Page ['paːʒə] *m* (-n/-n) page.

pah *int.* [pɑː] pah!, pooh!, pshaw!

Paket [pa'keːt] *n* (-[e]s/-e) parcel, packet, package; '~annahme ⸚ *f* parcel counter; '~karte ⸚ *f* dispatch-note; '~post *f* parcel post; '~zustellung ⸚ *f* parcel delivery.

Pakt [pakt] *m* (-[e]s/-e) pact; agreement; treaty.

Palast [pa'last] *m* (-es/⸚e) palace.

Palm|e ⸚ ['palmə] *f* (-/-n) palm (-tree); '~öl *n* palm-oil; '~sonntag *eccl. m* Palm Sunday.

panieren [pa'niːrən] *v/t.* (*no* -ge-, h) crumb.

Pani|k ['paːnik] *f* (-/-en) panic; stampede; '2sch *adj.* panic; *von* ~em Schrecken erfaßt panic-stricken.

Panne ['panə] *f* (-/-n) breakdown, *mot. a.* engine trouble; *tyres*: puncture; *fig.* blunder.

panschen ['panʃən] (ge-, h) 1. *v/i.* splash (about); 2. *v/t.* adulterate (*wine, etc.*).

Panther *zo.* ['pantər] *m* (-s/-) panther.

Pantine [pan'tiːnə] *f* (-/-n) clog.

Pantoffel [pan'tɔfəl] *m* (-s/-n, F -) slipper; *unter dem* ~ *stehen* be henpecked; '~held F *m* henpecked husband.

pantschen ['pantʃən] *v/i. and v/t.* (ge-, h) *s. panschen.*

Panzer ['pantsər] *m* (-s/-) armo(u)r; ✗ tank; *zo.* shell; '~abwehr ✗ *f* anti-tank defen|ce, *Am.* -se; '~glas *n* bullet-proof glass; '~hemd *n* coat of mail; '~kreuzer ✗ *m* armo(u)red cruiser; '2n *v/t.* (ge-, h) armo(u)r; '~platte *f* armo(u)r-plate; '~schiff ✗ *n* ironclad; '~schrank *m* safe; '~ung *f* (-/-en) armo(u)r-plating; '~wagen *m* armo(u)red car; ✗ tank.

Papa [pa'pɑː, F 'papa] *m* (-s/-s) papa, F pa, dad(dy), *Am. a.* pop.

Papagei *orn.* [papa'gaɪ] *m* (-[e]s, -en/-e[n]) parrot.

Papier [pa'piːr] *n* (-s/-e) paper; ~e *pl.* papers *pl.*, documents *pl.*; papers *pl.*, identity card; ein Bogen ~ a sheet of paper; '2en *adj.* (of) paper; *fig.* dull; '~fabrik *f* paper-mill; '~geld *n* (-[e]s/*no pl.*) paper-money; bank-notes *pl.*, *Am.* bills *pl.*; '~korb *m* waste-paper-basket; '~schnitzel *f* or *m*/*pl.* scraps *pl.* of paper; '~tüte *f* paper-bag; '~waren *f*/*pl.* stationery.

'**Papp|band** *m* (-[e]s/⸚e) paperback; '~deckel *m* pasteboard, cardboard.

Pappe ['papə] *f* (-/-n) pasteboard, cardboard.

Pappel ⸚ ['papəl] *f* (-/-n) poplar.

päppeln F ['pɛpəln] *v/t.* (ge-, h) feed (with pap).

papp|en F ['papən] (ge-, h) 1. *v/t.* paste; 2. *v/i.* stick; '1g *adj.* sticky; '2karton *m*, '2schachtel *f* cardboard box, carton.

Papst [paːpst] *m* (-es/⸚e) pope.

päpstlich *adj.* ['pɛːpstliç] papal.

Papsttum *n* (-s/*no pl.*) papacy.

Parade [pa'rɑːdə] *f* (-/-n) parade; ✗ review; *fencing*: parry.

Paradies [para'diːs] *n* (-es/-e) paradise; 2isch *fig. adj.* [⸚'diːzɪʃ] heavenly, delightful.

paradox *adj.* [para'dɔks] paradoxical.

Paragraph [para'grɑːf] m (-en, -s/-en) article, section; paragraph; section-mark.

parallel adj. [para'leːl] parallel; 2e f (-/-n) parallel.

Paralys|e [para'lyːzə] f (-/-n) paralysis; 2ieren ⚔ [ˌy'ziːrən] v/t. (no -ge-, h) paralyse.

Parasit [para'ziːt] m (-en/-en) parasite.

Parenthese [paren'teːzə] f (-/-n) parenthesis.

Parforcejagd [par'fɔrs-] f hunt (-ing) on horseback (with hounds), after hares: coursing.

Parfüm [par'fyːm] n (-s/-e, -s) perfume, scent; ˌerie [ˌyməˈriː] f (-/-n) perfumery; 2ieren [ˌy'miːrən] v/t. (no -ge-, h) perfume, scent.

pari ↑ adv. ['paːri] par; al ˌ at par.

parieren [pa'riːrən] (no -ge-, h) 1. v/t. fencing: parry (a. fig.); pull up (horse); 2. v/i. obey (j-m s.o.).

Park [park] m (-s/-s, -e) park; 'ˌanlage f park; 'ˌaufseher m parkkeeper; '2en (ge-, h) 1. v/i. park; ˌ verboten! no parking!; 2. v/t. park.

Parkett [par'ket] n (-[e]s/-e) parquet; thea. (orchestra) stalls pl., esp. Am. orchestra or parquet.

'Park|gebühr f parking-fee; 'ˌlicht n parking light; 'ˌplatz m (car-) park, parking lot; 'ˌuhr mot. f parking meter.

Parlament [parla'ment] n (-[e]s/-e) parliament; 2arisch adj. [ˌˈtaːriʃ] parliamentary.

Parodie [paro'diː] f (-/-n) parody; 2ren v/t. (no -ge-, h) parody.

Parole [pa'roːlə] f (-/-n) ⚔ password, watchword; fig. slogan.

Partei [par'tai] f (-/-en) party (a. pol.); j-s ˌ ergreifen take s.o.'s part, side with s.o.; ˌapparat pol. m party machinery; ˌgänger [ˌgeŋər] m (-s/-) partisan; 2isch adj., 2lich adj. partial (für to); prejudiced (gegen against); 2los pol. adj. independent; ˌmitglied pol. n party member; ˌprogramm pol. n platform; ˌtag pol. m convention; ˌzugehörigkeit pol. f party membership.

Parterre [par'ter] n (-s/-s) ground floor, Am. first floor; thea.: pit, Am. parterre, Am. parquet circle.

Partie [par'tiː] f (-/-n) ↑ part, lot; outing, excursion; cards, etc.: game; ♪ part; marriage: match.

Partitur ♪ [parti'tuːr] f (-/-en) score.

Partizip gr. [parti'tsiːp] n (-s/-ien) participle.

Partner ['partnər] m (-s/-), 'ˌin f (-/-nen) partner; film: a. co-star; 'ˌschaft f (-/-en) partnership.

Parzelle [par'tselə] f (-/-n) plot, lot, allotment.

Paß [pas] m (Passes/Pässe) pass;

passage; football, etc.: pass; passport.

Passage [pa'saːʒə] f (-/-n) passage; arcade.

Passagier [pasa'ʒiːr] m (-s/-e) passenger, in taxis: a. fare; ˌflugzeug n air liner.

Passah ['pasa] n (-s/no pl.), 'ˌfest n Passover.

Passant [pa'sant] m (-en/-en), ˌin f (-/-nen) passer-by.

'Paßbild n passport photo(graph).

passen ['pasən] (ge-, h) 1. v/i. fit (j-m s.o.; auf acc. or für or zu et. s.th.); suit (j-m s.o.), be convenient; cards, football: pass; ˌ zu go with, match (with); 2. v/refl. be fit or proper; 'ˌd adj. fit, suitable; convenient (für for).

passier|bar adj. [pa'siːrbaːr] passable, practicable; ˌen (no -ge-) 1. v/i. (sein) happen; 2. v/t. (h) pass (over or through); 2schein m pass, permit.

Passion [pa'sjoːn] f (-/-en) passion; hobby; eccl. Passion.

passiv ['pasiːf] 1. adj. passive; 2. 2 gr. n (-s/⚔ -e) passive (voice); 2a ✝ [pa'siːva] pl. liabilities pl.

Paste ['pastə] f (-/-n) paste.

Pastell [pa'stel] n (-[e]s/-e) pastel.

Pastete [pa'steːtə] f (-/-n) pie; ˌnbäcker m pastry-cook.

Pate ['paːtə] m (-n/-n) godfather; godchild; 2. f (-/-n) godmother; 'ˌnkind n godchild; 'ˌnschaft f (-/-en) sponsorship.

Patent [pa'tent] n (-[e]s/-e) patent; ✕ commission; ein ˌ anmelden apply for a patent; ˌamt n Patent Office; ˌanwalt m patent agent; 2ieren [ˌ'tiːrən] v/t. (no -ge-, h) patent; et. ˌ lassen take out a patent for s.th.; ˌinhaber m patentee; ˌurkunde f letters patent.

Patient [pa'tsjent] m (-en/-en), ˌin f (-/-nen) patient.

Patin ['paːtin] f (-/-nen) godmother.

Patriot [patri'oːt] m (-en/-en), ˌin f (-/-nen) patriot.

Patron [pa'troːn] m (-s/-e) patron, protector; contp. fellow, bloke, customer; ˌat [ˌo'naːt] n (-[e]s/-e) patronage; ˌe [pa'troːnə] f (-/-n) cartridge, Am. a. shell.

Patrouill|e [pa'truljə] f (-/-n) patrol; 2ieren ✕ [ˌ'jiːrən] v/i. (no -ge-, h) patrol.

Patsch|e F fig. ['patʃə] f (-/no pl.): in der ˌ sitzen be in a fix or scrape; '2n F (ge-) 1. v/i. (h, sein) splash; 2. v/t. (h) slap; '2naß adj. dripping wet, drenched.

patzig F adj. ['patsiç] snappish.

Pauke ♪ ['paukə] f (-/-n) kettledrum; '2n F v/i. and v/t. (ge-, h) school: cram.

Pauschal|e [pau'ʃaːlə] f (-/-n), ˌsumme f lump sum.

Pause ['pauzə] f (-/-n) pause, stop, interval; *school*: break, *Am.* recess; *thea.* interval, *Am.* intermission; ♪ rest; *drawing*: tracing; '2n v/t. (ge-, h) trace; '2nlos adj. uninterrupted, incessant; '∼nzeichen n *wireless*: interval signal.

pau'sieren v/i. (no -ge-, h) pause.

Pavian zo. ['pɑːviaːn] m (-s/-e) baboon.

Pavillon ['paviljõ] m (-s/-s) pavilion.

Pazifist [patsi'fist] m (-en/-en) pacif(ic)ist.

Pech [pɛç] n 1. (-[e]s /-e) pitch; 2. F *fig.* (-[e]s/no pl.) bad luck; '∼strähne F f run of bad luck; '∼vogel F m unlucky fellow.

pedantisch adj. [pe'dantiʃ] pedantic; punctilious, meticulous.

Pegel ['peːgəl] m (-s/-) water-ga(u)ge.

peilen ['paɪlən] v/t. (ge-, h) sound (*depth*); take the bearings of (*coast*).

Pein [paɪn] f (-/no pl.) torment, torture, anguish; 2igen ['∼igən] v/t. (ge-, h) torment; 2iger ['∼igər] m (-s/-) tormentor.

'peinlich adj. painful, embarrassing; particular, scrupulous, meticulous.

Peitsche ['paɪtʃə] f (-/-n) whip; '2n v/t. (ge-, h) whip; '∼nhieb m lash.

Pelikan orn. ['peːlikaːn] m (-s/-e) pelican.

Pell|e ['pɛlə] f (-/-n) skin, peel; '2en v/t. (ge-, h) skin, peel; '∼kartoffeln f/pl. potatoes pl. (boiled) in their jackets or skins.

Pelz [pɛlts] m (-es/-e) fur; *garment*: mst furs pl.; '2gefüttert adj. fur-lined; '∼händler m furrier; '∼handschuh m furred glove; '2ig adj. furry; ♪ *tongue*: furred; '∼mantel m fur coat; '∼stiefel m fur-lined boot; '∼tiere n/pl. fur-covered animals pl.

Pendel ['pɛndəl] n (-s/-) pendulum; '2n v/i. (ge-, h) oscillate, swing; ⛟ shuttle, *Am.* commute; '∼tür f swing-door; '∼verkehr ⛟ m shuttle service.

Pension [pã'sjõː, pɑn'zjoːn] f (-/-en) (old-age) pension, retired pay; board; boarding-house; ∼är [∼'nɛːr] m (-s/-e) (old-age) pensioner; boarder; ∼at [∼o'naːt] n (-[e]s/-e) boarding-school; 2ieren [∼o'niːrən] v/t. (no -ge-, h) pension (off); sich ∼ lassen retire; ∼sgast m boarder.

Pensum ['pɛnzum] n (-s/Pensen, Pensa) task, lesson.

perfekt 1. adj. [pɛr'fɛkt] perfect; *agreement*: settled; 2. 2 gr. ['∼] n (-[e]s/-e) perfect (tense).

Pergament [pɛrga'mɛnt] n (-[e]s/-e) parchment.

Period|e [per'joːdə] f (-/-n) period; ♪ periods pl.; 2isch adj. periodic (-al).

Peripherie [perife'riː] f (-/-n)

circumference; outskirts pl. (of *town*).

Perle ['pɛrlə] f (-/-n) pearl; *of glass*: bead; '2n v/i. (ge-, h) sparkle; '∼kette f pearl necklace; '∼nschnur f string of pearls or beads.

'Perl|muschel zo. f pearl-oyster; ∼mutt ['∼mut] n (-s/no pl.), ∼'mutter f (-/no pl.) mother-of-pearl.

Person [pɛr'zoːn] f (-/-en) person; *thea.* character.

Personal [pɛrzo'naːl] n (-s/no pl.) staff, personnel; ∼abteilung f personnel office; ∼angaben f/pl. personal data pl.; ∼ausweis m identity card; ∼chef m personnel officer or manager or director; ∼ien [∼jən] pl. particulars pl., personal data pl.; ∼pronomen gr. n personal pronoun.

Per'sonen|verzeichnis n list of persons; *thea.* dramatis personae pl.; ∼wagen m ⛟ (passenger-)carriage or *Am.* car, coach; *mot.* (motor-)car; ∼zug ⛟ m passenger train.

personifizieren [pɛrzonifi'tsiːrən] v/t. (no -ge-, h) personify.

persönlich adj. [pɛr'zøːnliç] personal; *opinion, letter*: a. private; 2keit f (-/-en) personality; personage.

Perücke [pe'rykə] f (-/-n) wig.

Pest ⚕ [pɛst] f (-/no pl.) plague.

Petersilie ♀ [petər'ziːljə] f (-/-n) parsley.

Petroleum [pe'troːleum] n (-s/no pl.) petroleum; *for lighting, etc.*: paraffin, *esp. Am.* kerosene.

Pfad [pfaːt] m (-[e]s/-e) path, track; '∼finder m boy scout; '∼finderin f (-/-nen) girl guide, *Am.* girl scout.

Pfahl [pfaːl] m (-[e]s/∸e) stake, pale, pile.

Pfand [pfant] n (-[e]s/∸er) pledge; ✝ deposit, security; *real estate*: mortgage; *game*: forfeit; '∼brief ✝ m debenture (bond).

pfänden ⚖ ['pfɛndən] v/t. (ge-, h) seize *s.th.*; distrain upon *s.o.* or *s.th.*

'Pfand|haus n s. Leihhaus; '∼leiher m (-s/-) pawnbroker; '∼schein m pawn-ticket.

'Pfändung ⚖ f (-/-en) seizure; distraint.

Pfann|e ['pfanə] f (-/-n) pan; '∼kuchen m pancake.

Pfarr|bezirk ['pfar-] m parish; '∼er m (-s/-) parson; *Church of England*: rector, vicar; *dissenters*: minister; '∼gemeinde f parish; '∼haus n parsonage; *Church of England*: rectory, vicarage; '∼kirche f parish church; '∼stelle f (church) living.

Pfau orn. [pfau] m (-[e]s/-en) peacock.

Pfeffer ['pfɛfər] m (-s/-) pepper; '∼gurke f gherkin; '2ig adj. peppery; '∼kuchen m gingerbread;

~minze ♀ ['~mintsə] f (-/no pl.) peppermint; '**~minzplätzchen** n peppermint; '**~2n** v/t. (ge-, h) pepper; '**~streuer** m (-s/-) pepperbox, pepper-caster, pepper-caster.

Pfeife ['pfaɪfə] f (-/-n) whistle; ✕ fife; pipe (of organ, etc.); (tobacco-) pipe; '**~2n** (irr., ge-, h) **1.** v/i. whistle (dat. to, for); radio: howl; pipe; **2.** v/t. whistle; pipe; '**~nkopf** m pipe-bowl.

Pfeil [pfaɪl] m (-[e]s/-e) arrow.

Pfeiler ['pfaɪlər] m (-s/-) pillar (a. fig.); pier (of bridge, etc.).

'**pfeil'schnell** adj. (as) swift as an arrow; '**2spitze** f arrow-head.

Pfennig ['pfɛniç] m (-[e]s/-e) coin: pfennig; fig. penny, farthing.

Pferch [pfɛrç] m (-[e]s/-e) fold, pen; '**2en** v/t. (ge-, h) fold, pen; fig. cram.

Pferd zo. [pfe:rt] n (-[e]s/-e) horse; zu ~e on horseback.

Pferde|geschirr ['pfe:rdə-] n harness; '**~koppel** f (-/-n) paddock, Am. a. corral; '**~rennen** n horserace; '**~schwanz** m horse's tail; hair-style: pony-tail; '**~stall** m stable; '**~stärke** ⊕ f horsepower.

pfiff[1] [pfif] pret. of pfeifen.

Pfiff[2] m (-[e]s/-e) whistle; fig. trick; '**2ig** adj. cunning, artful.

Pfingst|en eccl. ['pfiŋstən] n (-/-), '**~fest** eccl. n Whitsun(tide); '**~'montag** eccl. m Whit Monday; '**~rose** ♀ f peony; '**~'sonntag** eccl. m Whit Sunday.

Pfirsich ['pfirziç] m (-[e]s/-e) peach.

Pflanze ['pflantsə] f (-/-n) plant; '**2en** v/t. (ge-, h) plant, set; pot; '**~enfaser** f vegetable fib|re, Am. -er; '**2enfett** n vegetable fat; '**2enfressend** adj. herbivorous; '**~er** m (-s/-) planter; '**~ung** f (-/-en) plantation.

Pflaster ['pflastər] n (-s/-) plaster; road: pavement; '**~er** m (-s/-) paver, pavio(u)r; '**2n** v/t. (ge-, h) ✖ plaster; pave (road); '**~stein** m paving-stone; cobble.

Pflaume ['pflaumə] f (-/-n) plum; dried: prune.

Pflege ['pfle:gə] f (-/-n) care; ✖ nursing; cultivation (of art, garden, etc.); ⊕ maintenance; in ~ geben put out (child) to nurse; in ~ nehmen take charge of; '**2bedürftig** adj. needing care; '**befohlene** ['~bəfo:lənə] m, f (-n/-n) charge; '**~eltern** pl. foster-parents pl.; '**~heim** ✖ n nursing home; '**~kind** n foster-child; '**2n** (ge-, h) **1.** v/t. take care of; attend (to); foster (child); ✖ nurse; maintain; cultivate (art, garden); **2.** v/i.: ~ zu inf. be accustomed or used or wont to inf., be in the habit of ger.; sie pflegte zu sagen she used to say; '**~r** m (-s/-) fosterer; ✖ male nurse;

trustee; ✖½ guardian, curator; '**~rin** f (-/-nen) nurse.

Pflicht [pfliçt] f (-/-en) duty (gegen to); obligation; '**2bewußt** adj. conscious of one's duty; '**2eifrig** adj.zealous; '**~erfüllung** f performance of one's duty; '**~fach** n school, univ.: compulsory subject; '**~gefühl** n sense of duty; '**2gemäß** adj. dutiful; '**2getreu** adj. dutiful, loyal; '**2schuldig** adj. in duty bound; '**2vergessen** adj. undutiful, disloyal; '**~verteidiger** ✖½ m assigned counsel.

Pflock [pflɔk] m (-[e]s/~e) plug, peg.

pflücken ['pflykən] v/t. (ge-, h) pick, gather, pluck.

Pflug [pflu:k] m (-[e]s/~e) plough, Am. plow.

pflügen ['pfly:gən] v/t. and v/i. (ge-, h) plough, Am. plow.

Pforte ['pfɔrtə] f (-/-n) gate, door.

Pförtner ['pfœrtnər] m (-s/-) gatekeeper, door-keeper, porter, janitor.

Pfosten ['pfɔstən] m (-s/-) post.

Pfote ['pfo:tə] f (-/-n) paw.

Pfropf [pfrɔpf] m (-[e]s/-e) s. Pfropfen.

'**Pfropfen 1.** m (-s/-) stopper; cork; plug; ✖ clot (of blood); **2.** ✖ v/t. (ge-, h) stopper; cork; fig. cram; ✖ graft.

Pfründe eccl. ['pfryndə] f (-/-n) prebend; benefice, (church) living.

Pfuhl [pfu:l] m (-[e]s/-e) pool, puddle; fig. sink, slough.

pfui int. [pfui] fie!, for shame!

Pfund [pfunt] n (-[e]s/-e) pound; '**2ig** F adj. ['~diç] great, Am. swell; '**2weise** adv. by the pound.

pfusch|en F ['pfuʃən] (ge-, h) **1.** v/i. bungle; **2.** v/t. bungle, botch; '**2erei** F [~'raɪ] f (-/-en) bungle, botch.

Pfütze ['pfytsə] f (-/-n) puddle, pool.

Phänomen [fɛno'me:n] n (-s/-e) phenomenon; '**2al** adj. [~e'na:l] phenomenal.

Phantasie [fanta'zi:] f (-/-n) imagination, fancy; vision; ♪ fantasia; '**2ren** (no -ge-, h) **1.** v/i. dream; ramble; ✖ be delirious or raving; ♪ improvise; **2.** v/t. dream; ♪ improvise.

Phantast [fan'tast] m (-en/-en) visionary, dreamer; '**2isch** adj. fantastic; F great, terrific.

Phase ['fa:zə] f (-/-n) phase (a. ✖), stage.

Philanthrop [filan'tro:p] m (-en/-en) philanthropist.

Philolog|e [filo'lo:gə] m (-n/-n), '**~in** f (-/-nen) philologist; '**~ie** [~o'gi:] f (-/-n) philology.

Philosoph [filo'zo:f] m (-en/-en) philosopher; '**~ie** [~o'fi:] f (-/-n) philosophy; '**2ieren** [~o'ti:rən] v/i. (no -ge-, h) philosophize (über acc. on); '**2isch** adj. [~'zo:fiʃ] philosophical.

Phlegma ['flegma] *n* (-s/no *pl.*) phlegm; **2tisch** *adj.* [~'mɑ:tɪʃ] phlegmatic.

phonetisch *adj.* [fo'ne:tiʃ] phonetic.

Phosphor ♫ ['fɔsfɔr] *m* (-s/no *pl.*) phosphorus.

Photo F ['fo:to] **1.** *n* (-s/-s) photo; **2.** *m* (-s/-s) ~ '.apparat *m* camera.

Photograph [foto'grɑ:f] *m* (-en/-en) photographer; ~ie [~a'fi:] *f* **1.** (-/-n) photograph, F: photo, picture; **2.** (-/no *pl.*) *as an art*: photography; **2ieren** [~a'fi:rən] (*no* -ge-, *h*) **1.** *v/t.* photograph; take a picture of; *sich* ~ *lassen* have one's photo(graph) taken; **2.** *v/i.* photograph; **2isch** *adj.* [~'grɑ:fiʃ] photographic.

Photo|kopie *f* photostat; **~ko'piergerät** *n* photostat; **'~zelle** *f* photoelectric cell.

Phrase ['frɑ:zə] *f* (-/-n) phrase.

Physik [fy'zi:k] *f* (-/no *pl.*) physics *sg.*; **2alisch** *adj.* [~i'kɑ:liʃ] physical; **~er** ['fy:zikər] *m* (-s/-) physicist.

physisch *adj.* ['fy:ziʃ] physical.

Pian|ist [pia'nist] *m* (-en/-en) pianist; **~o** [pi'ɑ:no] *n* (-s/-s) piano.

Picke ⊕ ['pikə] *f* (-/-n) pick(axe).

Pickel ['pikəl] *m* (-s/-) ⚘ pimple; ⊕ pick(axe); ice-pick; **2ig** *adj.* pimpled, pimply.

picken ['pikən] *v/i. and v/t.* (ge-, *h*) pick, peck.

picklig *adj.* ['pikliç] *s. pickelig.*

Picknick ['piknik] *n* (-s/-e, -s) picnic.

piekfein F *adj.* ['pi:k'-] smart, tiptop, slap-up.

piep(s)en ['pi:p(s)ən] *v/i.* (ge-, *h*) cheep, chirp, peep; squeak.

Pietät [pie'tɛ:t] *f* (-/no *pl.*) reverence; piety; **2los** *adj.* irreverent; **2voll** *adj.* reverent.

Pik [pi:k] **1.** *m* (-s/-s) peak; **2.** F *m* (-s/-e): e-n ~ *auf j-n haben* bear s.o. a grudge; **3.** *n* (-s/-s) *cards*: spade(s *pl.*).

pikant *adj.* [pi'kant] piquant, spicy (*both a. fig.*); *das Pikante* the piquancy.

Pike ['pi:kə] *f* (-/-n) pike; *von der* ~ *auf dienen* rise from the ranks.

Pilger ['pilgər] *m* (-s/-) pilgrim; **'~fahrt** *f* pilgrimage; **2n** *v/i.* (ge-, *sein*) go on *or* make a pilgrimage; wander.

Pille ['pilə] *f* (-/-n) pill.

Pilot [pi'lo:t] *m* (-en/-en) pilot.

Pilz ♧ [pilts] *m* (-es/-e) fungus, *edible*: mushroom, *inedible*: toadstool.

pimp(e)lig F *adj.* ['pimp(ə)liç] sickly; effeminate.

Pinguin *orn.* ['piŋguiːn] *m* (-s/-e) penguin.

Pinsel ['pinzəl] *m* (-s/-) brush; F *fig.* simpleton; **2n** *v/t. and v/i.* (ge-, *h*) paint; daub; **'~strich** *m* stroke of the brush.

Pinzette [pin'tsetə] *f* (-/-n) (e-e a pair of) tweezers *pl.*

Pionier [pio'ni:r] *m* (-s/-e) pioneer, *Am. a.* trail blazer; ✗ engineer.

Pirat [pi'rɑ:t] *m* (-en/-en) pirate.

Pirsch *hunt.* [pirʃ] *f* (-/no *pl.*) deerstalking, *Am. a.* still hunt.

Piste ['pistə] *f* (-/-n) *skiing, etc.*: course; ✈ runway.

Pistole [pis'to:lə] *f* (-/-n) pistol, *Am.* F *a.* gun, rod; **~ntasche** *f* holster.

placieren [pla'si:rən] *v/t.* (*no* -ge-, *h*) place; *sich* ~ *sports*: be placed (*second, etc.*).

Plackerei F [plakə'raɪ] *f* (-/-en) drudgery.

plädieren [plɛ'di:rən] *v/i.* (*no* -ge-, *h*) plead (*für* for).

Plädoyer ⚖ [plɛdoa'je:] *n* (-s/-s) pleading.

Plage ['plɑ:gə] *f* (-/-n) trouble, nuisance, F plague; torment; **2n** *v/t.* (ge-, *h*) torment; trouble, bother; F plague; *sich* ~ toil, drudge.

Plagiat [plag'jɑ:t] *n* (-[e]s/-e) plagiarism; *ein* ~ *begehen* plagiarize.

Plakat [pla'kɑ:t] *n* (-[e]s/-e) poster, placard, bill; **~säule** *f* advertisement pillar.

Plakette [pla'kɛtə] *f* (-/-n) plaque.

Plan [plɑ:n] *m* (-[e]s/ᵘe) plan; design, intention; scheme.

Plane ['plɑ:nə] *f* (-/-n) awning, tilt.

'planen *v/t.* (ge-, *h*) plan; scheme.

Planet [pla'ne:t] *m* (-en/-en) planet.

planieren ⊕ [pla'ni:rən] *v/t.* (*no* -ge-, *h*) level.

Planke ['plaŋkə] *f* (-/-n) plank, board.

plänkeln ['plɛŋkəln] *v/i.* (ge-, *h*) skirmish (*a. fig.*).

'plan|los 1. *adj.* planless, aimless, desultory; **2.** *adv.* at random; **'~mäßig 1.** *adj.* systematic, planned; **2.** *adv.* as planned.

planschen ['planʃən] *v/i.* (ge-, *h*) splash, paddle.

Plantage [plan'tɑ:ʒə] *f* (-/-n) plantation.

Plapper|maul F ['plapər-] *n* chatterbox; **'2n** F *v/i.* (ge-, *h*) chatter, prattle, babble.

plärren ['plɛrən] *v/i. and v/t.* (ge-, *h*) blubber; bawl.

Plasti|k [plastik] **1.** *f* (-/no *pl.*) plastic art; **2.** *f* (-/-en) sculpture; ⚘ plastic; **3.** ⊕ *n* (-s/-s) plastic; **'2sch** *adj.* plastic; three-dimensional.

Platin [pla'ti:n] *n* (-s/no *pl.*) platinum.

plätschern ['plɛtʃərn] *v/i.* (ge-, *h*) dabble, splash; *water*: ripple, murmur.

platt *adj.* [plat] flat, level, even; *fig.* trivial, commonplace, trite; F *fig.* flabbergasted.

Plättbrett ['plɛt-] *n* ironing-board.

Platte ['platə] f (-/-n) plate; dish; sheet (of metal, etc.); flag, slab (of stone); mountain: ledge; top (of table); tray, salver; disc, record; F fig. bald pate; kalte ~ cold meat.

plätten ['plɛtən] v/t. (ge-, h) iron.

'Platten|spieler m record-player; **'~teller** m turn-table.

'Platt|form f platform; **'~fuß** m & flat-foot; F mot. flat; **'~heit** fig. f (-/-en) triviality; commonplace, platitude, Am. sl. a. bromide.

Platz [plats] m (-es/=e) place; spot, Am. a. point; room, space; site; seat; square; round: circus; sports: ground; tennis: court; ~ behalten remain seated; ~ machen make way or room (dat. for); ~ nehmen take a seat, sit down, Am. a. have a seat; ist hier noch ~? is this seat taken or engaged or occupied?; den dritten ~ belegen sports: be placed third, come in third; '~anweiserin f (-/-nen) usherette.

Plätzchen ['plɛtsçən] n (-s/-) snug place; spot; biscuit, Am. cookie.

'platzen v/i. (ge-, sein) burst; explode; crack, split.

'Platz|patrone f blank cartridge; **'~regen** m downpour.

Plauder|ei [plaudə'rai] f (-/-en) chat; talk; small talk; '**~n** v/i. (ge-, h) (have a) chat (mit with), talk (to); chatter.

plauz int. [plauts] bang!

Pleite F ['plaitə] 1. f (-/-n) smash; fig. failure; 2. ♀ F adj. (dead) broke, Am. sl. bust.

Plissee [pli'se:] n (-s/-s) pleating; **~rock** m pleated skirt.

Plomb|e ['plɔmbə] f (-/-n) (lead) seal; stopping, filling (of tooth); **♀ieren** [~'bi:rən] v/t. (no -ge-, h) seal; stop, fill (tooth).

plötzlich adj. ['plœtsliç] sudden.

plump adj. [plump] clumsy; **~s** int. plump, plop; '**~sen** v/i. (ge-, sein) plump, plop, flop.

Plunder F ['plundər] m (-s/no pl.) lumber, rubbish, junk.

plündern ['plyndərn] (ge-, h) 1. v/t. plunder, pillage, loot, sack; 2. v/i. plunder, loot.

Plural gr. ['plu:ra:l] m (-s/-e) plural (number).

plus adv. [plus] plus.

Plusquamperfekt gr. ['pluskvamperfɛkt] n (-s/-e) pluperfect (tense), past perfect.

Pöbel ['pø:bəl] m (-s/no pl.) mob, rabble; '♀haft adj. low, vulgar.

pochen ['pɔxən] v/i. (ge-, h) knock, rap, tap; heart: beat, throb, thump; auf sein Recht ~ stand on one's rights.

Pocke & ['pɔkə] f (-/-n) pock; '~n pl. smallpox; '♀nnarbig adj. pock-marked.

Podest [po'dɛst] n, m (-es/-e) pedestal (a. fig.).

Podium ['po:dium] n (-s/Podien) podium, platform, stage.

Poesie [poe'zi:] f (-/-n) poetry.

Poet [po'e:t] m (-en/-en) poet; **♀isch** adj. poetic(al).

Pointe [po'ɛ:tə] f (-/-n) point.

Pokal [po'ka:l] m (-s/-e) goblet; sports: cup; **~endspiel** n sports: cup final; **~spiel** n football: cup-tie.

Pökel|fleisch ['pø:kəl-] n salted meat; '**♀n** v/t. (ge-, h) pickle, salt.

Pol [po:l] m (-s/-e) pole; ≠ a. terminal; **♀ar** adj. [po'la:r] polar (a. ≠).

Pole ['po:lə] m (-n/-n) Pole.

Polemi|k [po'le:mik] f (-/-en) polemic(s pl.); **♀sch** adj. polemic (-al); **♀sieren** [~mi'zi:rən] v/i. (no -ge-, h) polemize.

Police [po'li:s(ə)] f (-/-n) policy.

Polier ⊕ [po'li:r] m (-s/-e) foreman; **♀en** v/t. (no-ge-, h) polish, burnish; furbish.

Politi|k [poli'ti:k] f (-/~-en) policy, politics sg., pl.; **~ker** [po'li:tikər] m (-s/-) politician; statesman; **♀sch** adj. [po'li:tiʃ] political; **♀sieren** [~iti'zi:rən] v/i. (no -ge-, h) talk politics.

Politur [poli'tu:r] f (-/-en) polish; lust|re, Am. -er, finish.

Polizei [poli'tsai] f (-/~-en) police; **~beamte** m police officer; **~knüppel** m truncheon, Am. club; **~kommissar** m inspector; **♀lich** adj. (of or by the) police; **~präsident** m president of police; Brt. Chief Constable, Am. Chief of Police; **~präsidium** n police headquarters pl.; **~revier** n police-station; police precinct; **~schutz** m: unter ~ under police guard; **~streife** f police patrol; police squad; **~stunde** f (-/no pl.) closing-time; **~verordnung** f police regulation(s pl.); **~wache** f police-station.

Polizist [poli'tsist] m (-en/-en) policeman, constable, sl. bobby, cop; **~in** f (-/-nen) policewoman.

polnisch adj. ['pɔlniʃ] Polish.

Polster ['pɔlstər] m (-s/-) pad; cushion; bolster; s. Polsterung; '**~möbel** n/pl. upholstered furniture; upholstery; '**♀n** v/t. (ge-, h) upholster, stuff; pad, wad; '**~sessel** m, '**~stuhl** m upholstered chair; '**~ung** f (-/-en) padding, stuffing; upholstery.

poltern ['pɔltərn] v/i. (ge-, h) make a row; rumble; p. bluster.

Polytechnikum [poly'tɛçnikum] n (-s/Polytechnika, Polytechniken) polytechnic (school).

Pommes frites [pɔm'frit] pl. chips pl., Am. French fried potatoes pl.

Pomp [pɔmp] m (-[e]s/no pl.) pomp, splendo(u)r; '**♀haft** adj., **♀ös** adj. [~'pø:s] pompous, splendid.

Pony ['pɔni] 1. zo. n (-s/-s) pony;
2. m (-s/-s) hairstyle: bang, fringe.
popul|är adj. [popu'lɛ:r] popular;
ßarität [~ari'tɛ:t] f (-/no pl.)
popularity.
Por|e ['po:rə] f (-/-n) pore; ßös adj.
[po'rø:s] porous; permeable.
Portemonnaie [pɔrtmɔ'nɛ:] n (-s/-s)
purse.
Portier [pɔr'tje:] m (-s/-s) s. Pförtner.
Portion [pɔr'tsjo:n] f (-/-en) portion, share; ✕ ration; helping, serving; zwei ~en Kaffee coffee for two.
Porto ['pɔrto] n (-s/-s, Porti) postage; ßfrei adj. post-free; prepaid,
esp. Am. postpaid; ßpflichtig adj.
subject to postage.
Porträt [pɔr'trɛ:; ~t] n (-s/-s;
-[e]s/-e) portrait, likeness; ßieren
[~ɛ'ti:rən] v/t. (no -ge-, h) portray.
Portugies|e [pɔrtu'gi:zə] m (-n/-n)
Portuguese; die ~n pl. the Portuguese pl.; ßisch adj. Portuguese.
Porzellan [pɔrtsɛ'la:n] n (-s/-e)
porcelain, china.
Posaune [po'zaunə] f (-/-n) ♪
trombone; fig. trumpet.
Pose ['po:zə] f (-/-n) pose, attitude;
fig. a. air.
Position [pozi'tsjo:n] f (-/-en)
position; social standing; ♣ station.
positiv adj. [po'zi:tif] positive.
Positur [pozi'tu:r] f (-/-en) posture;
sich in ~ setzen strike an attitude.
Posse thea. ['pɔsə] f (-/-n) farce.
ßPossen m (-s/-) trick, prank; ßhaft
adj. farcical, comical; ßreißer m
(-s/-) buffoon, clown.
possessiv gr. adj. ['pɔsɛsi:f] possessive.
pos'sierlich adj. droll, funny.
Post [pɔst] f (-/-en) post, Am. mail;
mail, letters pl.; post office; mit
der ersten ~ by the first delivery;
ßamt n post office; ßanschrift f
mailing address; ßanweisung f
postal order; ßbeamte m post-
office clerk; ßbote m postman,
Am. mailman; ßdampfer m
packet-boat.
Posten ['pɔstən] m (-s/-) post, place,
station; job; ✕ sentry, sentinel;
item; entry; goods: lot, parcel.
ßPostfach n post-office box.
pos'tieren v/t. (no -ge-, h) post,
station, place; sich ~ station o.s.
ßPost|karte f postcard, with printed
postage stamp: Am. a. postal card;
ßkutsche f stage-coach; ßlagernd
adj. to be (kept until) called for,
poste restante, Am. (in care of)
general delivery; ßleitzahl f post-
code; ßminister m minister of
post; Brt. and Am. Postmaster
General; ßpaket n postal parcel;
ßschalter m (post-office) window;
ßscheck m postal cheque, Am.
postal check; ßschließfach n

post-office box; ßsparbuch n
post-office savings-book; ßstem-
pel m postmark; ßwendend adv.
by return of post; ßwertzeichen
n (postage) stamp; ßzug 🚂 m
mail-train.
Pracht [praxt] f (-/⚡ -en, ⁿe) splen-
do(u)r, magnificence; luxury.
prächtig adj. ['prɛçtiç] splendid,
magnificent; gorgeous; grand.
ßprachtvoll adj. s. prächtig.
Prädikat [predi'ka:t] n (-[e]s/-e) gr.
predicate; school, etc.: mark.
prägen ['prɛ:gən] v/t. (ge-, h)
stamp; coin (word, coin).
prahlen ['pra:lən] v/i. (ge-, h) brag,
boast (mit of); ~ mit show off s.th.
ßPrahler m (-s/-) boaster, braggart;
ßei [~'rai] f (-/-en) boasting,
bragging; ßisch adj. boastful;
ostentatious.
Prakti|kant [prakti'kant] m (-en/-en)
probationer; ßker m (-s/-) practical man; expert; ßkum ['~kum] n
(-s/Praktika, Praktiken) practical
course; ßsch adj. practical; useful;
handy; ~er Arzt general practitioner;
ßzieren ⚕, ⚖ [~'tsi:rən] v/i. (no
-ge-, h) practi|se, Am. -ce medicine
or the law.   [prelate.]
Prälat eccl. [prɛ'la:t] m (-en/-en)⎪
Praline [pra'li:nə] f (-/-n): ~n pl.
chocolates pl.
prall adj [pral] tight; plump; sun:
blazing, ßen v/i. (ge-, sein) bounce
or bound (auf acc., gegen against).
Prämi|e ['prɛ:mjə] f (-/-n) ✝
premium; prize; bonus; ß(i)eren
[prɛ'mi:rən, prɛmi'i:rən] v/t. (no
-ge-, h) award a prize to.
prang|en ['praŋən] v/i. (ge-, h)
shine, make a show; ßer m (-s/-)
pillory.
Pranke ['praŋkə] f (-/-n) paw.
pränumerando adv. [prɛ:numə-
'rando] beforehand, in advance.
Präpa|rat [prɛpa'ra:t] n (-[e]s/-e)
preparation; microscopy: slide;
ßrieren v/t. (no -ge-, h) prepare.
Präposition gr. [prɛpozi'tsjo:n] f
(-/-en) preposition.
Prärie [prɛ'ri:] f (-/-n) prairie.
Präsens gr ['prɛ:zɛns] n (-/Präsen-
tia, Präsenzien) present (tense).
Präsi|dent [prɛzi'dɛnt] m (-en/-en)
president; chairman; ßdieren v/i.
(no -ge-, h) preside (über acc. over);
be in the chair; ßdium [~'zi:djum]
n (-s/Präsidien) presidency, chair.
prasseln ['prasəln] v/i. (ge-, h)
fire: crackle; rain: patter.
prassen ['prasən] v/i. (ge-, h) feast,
carouse.
Präteritum gr. [prɛ'te:ritum] n
(-s/Präterita) preterite (tense); past
tense.
Praxis ['praksis] f 1. (-/no pl.)
practice; 2. (-/Praxen) practice (of
doctor or lawyer).

Präzedenzfall [pretse'dents-] *m* precedent; ᵇⁱˢ *a.* case-law.

präzis *adj.* [pre'tsi:s], ⸰e *adj.* [⸰zə] precise.

predig|en ['pre:digən] *v/i. and v/t.* (ge-, *h*) preach; '⸰er *m* (-s/-) preacher; clergyman; ⸰t ['⸰diçt] *f* (-/-en) sermon (*a. fig.*); *fig.* lecture.

Preis [praɪs] *m* (-es/-e) price; cost; *competition:* prize; award; reward; praise; *um jeden* ⸰ at any price *or* cost; '⸰ausschreiben *n* (-s/-) competition.

preisen ['praɪzən] *v/t.* (*irr.*, ge-, *h*) praise.

'**Preis|erhöhung** *f* rise *or* increase in price(s); '⸰gabe *f* abandonment; revelation (*of secret*); ⸰geben *v/t.* (*irr.* geben, *sep.*, -ge-, *h*) abandon; reveal, give away (*secret*); disclose, expose; '⸰gekrönt *adj.* prize-winning, prize (*novel, etc.*); '⸰gericht *n* jury; '⸰lage *f* range of prices; '⸰liste *f* price-list; ⸰nachlaß *m* price cut; discount, ⸰richter *m* judge, umpire; ⸰schießen *n* (-s/-) shooting-match; '⸰stopp *m* (-s/no pl.) price freeze; ⸰träger *m* prize-winner; ⸰wert *adj.*: ⸰ sein be a bargain.

prell|en ['prelən] *v/t.* (ge-, *h*) *fig.* cheat, defraud (*um of*); sich et. ⸰ ᶠ contuse *or* bruise s.th.; '⸰ung ᶠ (-/-en) contusion.

Premier|e *thea.* [prəm'je:rə] *f* (-/-n) première, first night; ⸰minister [⸰'je:-] *m* prime minister.

Presse ['presə] *f* **1.** (-/-n) ⊕, *typ.* press; squeezer; **2.** (-/no pl.) *newspapers generally: the* press; ⸰amt *n* public relations office; ⸰freiheit *f* freedom of the press; ⸰meldung *f* news item; '⸰n *v/t.* (ge-, *h*) press; squeeze; '⸰photograph *m* press-photographer; ⸰vertreter *m* reporter; public relations officer.

Preßluft ['pres-] *f* (-/no pl.) compressed air.

Prestige [pres'ti:ʒə] *n* (-s/no pl.) prestige; ⸰ *verlieren a.* lose face.

Preuß|e ['prɔYsə] *m* (-n/-n) Prussian; '⸰isch *adj.* Prussian.

prickeln ['prikəln] *v/i.* (ge-, *h*) prick(le), tickle; itch; *fingers:* tingle.

Priem [pri:m] *m* (-[e]s/-e) quid.

pries [pri:s] *pret. of* preisen.

Priester ['pri:stər] *m* (-s/-) priest; '⸰in *f* (-/-nen) priestess; '⸰lich *adj.* priestly; sacerdotal; '⸰rock *m* cassock.

prim|a *f adj.* ['pri:ma] first-rate, F A 1; ✝ *a.* prime; F swell; ⸰är *adj.* [pri'me:r] primary.

Primel ᵏ ['pri:məl] *f* (-/-n) primrose.

Prinz [prints] *m* (-en/-en) prince; ⸰essin [⸰'tsesin] *f* (-/-nen) princess; '⸰gemahl *m* prince consort.

Prinzip [prin'tsi:p] *n* (-s/-ien)

principle; *aus* ⸰ on principle; *im* ⸰ in principle, basically.

Priorität [priori'te:t] *f* **1.** (-/-en) priority; **2.** (-/no pl.) *time:* priority.

Prise ['pri:zə] *f* (-/-n) ⚓ prize; e-e ⸰ a pinch of (*salt, snuff*).

Prisma ['prisma] *n* (-s/Prismen) prism.

Pritsche ['pritʃə] *f* (-/-n) bat; plank-bed.

privat *adj.* [pri'va:t] private; ⸰adresse *f* home address; ⸰mann *m* (-[e]s/Privatmänner, Privatleute) private person *or* gentleman; ⸰patient ᶠ *m* paying patient; ⸰person *f* private person; ⸰schule *f* private school.

Privileg [privi'le:k] *n* (-[e]s/-ien, -e) privilege.

pro *prp.* [pro:] per; ⸰ *Jahr* per annum; ⸰ *Kopf* per head; ⸰ *Stück* a piece.

Probe ['pro:bə] *f* (-/-n) experiment; trial, test; *metall.* assay; sample; specimen; proof; probation; check; *thea.* rehearsal; audition; *auf* ⸰ on probation, on trial; *auf die* ⸰ *stellen* (put to the) test; '⸰abzug *typ.*, *phot. m* proof; '⸰exemplar *n* specimen copy; '⸰fahrt ᶠ ⚓ trial trip; *mot.* trial run; '⸰flug *m* test *or* trial flight; '⸰n *v/t.* (ge-, *h*) exercise; *thea.* rehearse; '⸰nummer *f* specimen copy *or* number; '⸰seite *typ. f* specimen page; '⸰sendung *f* goods on approval; ⸰weise *adv.* on trial; *p. a.* on probation; '⸰zeit *f* time of probation.

probieren [pro'bi:rən] *v/t.* (*no* -ge-, *h*) try, test; taste (*food.*)

Problem [pro'ble:m] *n* (-s/-e) problem; ⸰atisch *adj.* [⸰e'ma:tiʃ] problematic(al).

Produkt [pro'dukt] *n* (-[e]s/-e) product (*a. Aᵣ*); ᵃ produce; result; ⸰ion [⸰'tsjo:n] *f* (-/-en) production; output; ⸰iv *adj.* [⸰'ti:f] productive.

Produz|ent [produ'tsent] *m* (-en/-en) producer; ⸰ieren [⸰'tsi:rən] *v/t.* (*no* -ge-, *h*) produce; sich ⸰ perform; *contp.* show off.

professionell *adj.* [profesio'nel] professional, by trade.

Profess|or [pro'fesɔr] *m* (-s/-en) professor; ⸰ur [⸰'su:r] *f* (-/-en) professorship, chair.

Profi ['pro:fi] *m* (-s/-s) *sports:* professional, F pro. [*on tyre:* tread.)

Profil [pro'fi:l] *n* (-s/-e) profile;)

Profit [pro'fi:t] *m* (-[e]s/-e) profit; ⸰ieren [⸰'ti:rən] *v/i.* (*no* -ge-, *h*) profit (*von* by).

Prognose [pro'gno:zə] *f* (-/-n) ᵃ prognosis; *meteor.* forecast.

Programm [pro'gram] *n* (-s/-e) program(me); *politisches* ⸰ political program(me), *Am.* platform.

Projektion [projek'tsjo:n] *f* (-/-en) projection; ⸰sapparat [projek-'tsjo:ns⸰-] *m* projector.

proklamieren [prokla'mi:rən] *v/t.* (*no* -ge-, *h*) proclaim.

Prokur|a ✝ [pro'ku:ra] *f* (-/*Prokuren*) procuration; **~ist** [~ku'rist] *m* (-en/-en) confidential clerk.

Proletari|er [prole'ta:rjər] *m* (-s/-) proletarian, **2sch** *adj.* proletarian.

Prolog [pro'lo:k] *m* (-[e]s/-e) prolog(ue).

prominen|t *adj.* [promi'nent] prominent; **2z** [~ts] *f* (-/*no pl.*) notables *pl.*, celebrities *pl* ; high society.

Promo|tion *univ.* [promo'tsjo:n] *f* (-/-en) graduation; **2vieren** [~'vi:rən] *v/i.* (*no* -ge-, *h*) graduate (*an dat.* from), take one's degree.

Pronomen *gr.* [pro'no:mɛn] *n* (-s/-, *Pronomina*) pronoun.

Propeller [pro'pɛlər] *m* (-s/-) ✈, ⚓ (screw-)propeller, screw; ⚓ airscrew.

Prophe|t [pro'fe:t] *m* (-en/-en) prophet, **2tisch** *adj.* prophetic; **2zeien** [~'tsaiən] *v/t.* (*no* -ge-, *h*) prophesy, predict, foretell; **~'zeiung** *f* (-/-en) prophecy; prediction.

Proportion [propor'tsjo:n] *f* (-/-en) proportion

Prosa ['pro:za] *f* (-/*no pl.*) prose.

prosit *int.* ['pro:zit] your health!, here's to you!, cheers!

Prospekt [pro'spɛkt] *m* (-[e]s/-e) prospectus; brochure, leaflet, folder.

prost *int.* [pro:st] *s.* prosit.

Prostituierte [prostitu'i:rtə] *f* (-n/-n) prostitute

Protest [pro'tɛst] *m* (-es/-e) protest; **~ einlegen** *or* **erheben gegen** (enter *a*) protest against.

Protestant *eccl.* [protɛs'tant] *m* (-en/-en) Protestant; **2isch** *adj.* Protestant.

protes'tieren *v/i.* (*no* -ge-, *h*): **gegen et. ~** protest against s.th., object to s.th.

Prothese 🦷 [pro'te:zə] *f* (-/-n) pro(s)thesis; *dentistry:* a. denture; artificial limb.

Protokoll [proto'kɔl] *n* (-s/-e) record, minutes *pl.* (*of meeting*); *diplomacy:* protocol; *das* **~ aufnehmen** take down the minutes; *das* **~ führen** keep the minutes; *zu* **~ geben** ⚖ depose, state in evidence; *zu* **~ nehmen** take down, record; **2ieren** [~'li:rən] (*no* -ge-, *h*) **1.** *v/t.* record, take down (on record); **2.** *v/i.* keep the minutes.

Protz *contp.* [prɔts] *m* (-en, -es/-e[n]) braggart, ⊢ show-off; **2en** *v/i.* (ge-, *h*) show off (*mit dat.* with); **2ig** *adj.* ostentatious, showy.

Proviant [pro'vjant] *m* (-s/⚓-e) provisions *pl.*, victuals *pl.*

Provinz [pro'vints] *f* (-/-en) province; *fig. the* provinces *pl.*; **2ial** *adj.* [~'tsja:l], **2iell** *adj.* [~'tsjɛl] provincial.

Provis|ion ✝ [provi'zjo:n] *f* (-/-en) commission; **2orisch** *adj.* [~'zo:riʃ] provisional, temporary.

provozieren [provo'tsi:rən] *v/t.* (*no* -ge-, *h*) provoke.

Prozent [pro'tsɛnt] *n* (-[e]s/-e) per cent; **~satz** *m* percentage; proportion; **2ual** *adj.* [~'u'a:l] percental; **~er Anteil** percentage.

Prozeß [pro'tsɛs] *m* (Prozesses/Prozesse) process; ⚖: action, lawsuit; trial; (legal) proceedings *pl.*; **e-n ~ gewinnen** win one's case; **gegen j-n anstrengen** bring an action against s.o., sue s.o.; **j-m den ~ machen** try s.o., put s.o. on trial; **kurzen ~ machen mit** make short work of.

prozessieren [protsɛ'si:rən] *v/i.* (*no* -ge-, *h*) **mit j-m ~** go to law against s.o., have the law of s.o.

Prozession [protsɛ'sjo:n] *f* (-/-en) procession

prüde *adj.* ['pry:də] prudish.

prüf|en ['pry:fən] *v/t.* (ge-, *h*) examine; try, test; quiz; check, verify; **~end** *adj. look:* searching, scrutinizing; **2er** *m* (-s/-) examiner; **2ling** *m* (-s/-e) examinee; **2stein** *fig. m* touchstone; **2ung** *f* (-/-en) examination; *school, etc.:* a. ⊢ exam; test; quiz; verification, checking, check-up; **e-e ~ machen** go in for *or* sit for *or* take an examination.

'Prüfungs|arbeit *f*, **~aufgabe** *f* examination-paper; **~ausschuß** *m*, **~kommission** *f* board of examiners.

Prügel ['pry:gəl] **1.** *m* (-s/-) cudgel, club, stick; **2.** ⊢ *fig. pl.* beating, thrashing; **~ei** ⊢ [~'lai] *f* (-/-en) fight, row; **~knabe** *m* scapegoat; **2n** ⊢ *v/t.* (ge-, *h*) cudgel, flog; beat (up), thrash; *sich* **~** (have a) fight.

Prunk [pruŋk] *m* (-[e]s/*no pl.*) splendo(u)r; pomp, show; **2en** *v/i.* (ge-, *h*) make a show (*mit of*), show off (*mit et.* s.th.); **2voll** *adj.* splendid, gorgeous.

Psalm *eccl.* [psalm] *m* (-s/-en) psalm.

Pseudonym [psɔydo'ny:m] *n* (-s/-e) pseudonym.

pst *int.* [pst] hush!

Psychi|ater [psyçi'a:tər] *m* (-s/-) psychiatrist, alienist; **2sch** *adj.* ['psy:çiʃ] psychic(al).

Psycho|analyse [psyço°ana'ly:zə] *f* (-/*no pl.*) psychoanalysis; **~analytiker** [~'tikər] *m* (-s/-) psychoanalist; **~loge** [~'lo:gə] *m* (-n/-n) psychologist; **~se** [~'ço:zə] *f* (-/-n) psychosis; panic.

Pubertät [puber'tɛ:t] *f* (-/*no pl.*) puberty.

Publikum ['pu:blikum] *n* (-s/*no pl.*) *the* public; audience; spectators *pl.*, crowd; readers *pl.*

publiz|ieren [publi'tsi:rən] *v/t.* (*no*

-ge-, h) publish; ²ist m (-en/-en) publicist; journalist.

Pudding ['puding] m (-s/-e, -s) cream.

Pudel zo. ['pu:dəl] m (-s/-) poodle; '²naß F adj. dripping wet, drenched.

Puder ['pu:dər] m (-s/-) powder; '∼dose f powder-box; compact; '²n v/t. (ge-, h) powder; sich ∼ powder o.s. or one's face; '∼quaste f powder-puff; '∼zucker m powdered sugar.

Puff F [puf] m (-[e]s/∼e, -e) poke, nudge; '²en (ge-, h) 1. F v/t. nudge; 2. v/i. pop; '∼er ⚙ m (-s/-) buffer.

Pullover [pu'lo:vər] m (-s/-) pullover, sweater.

Puls ⚕ [puls] m (-es/-e) pulse; '∼ader anat. f artery; ²ieren [∼'zi:rən] v/i. (no -ge-, h) pulsate, throb; '∼schlag ⚕ m pulsation.

Pult [pult] n (-[e]s/-e) desk.

Pulv|er ['pulfər] n (-s/-) powder; gunpowder; F fig cash, sl. brass, dough; '²erig adj. powdery; ²erisieren [∼vəri'zi:rən] v/t. (no -ge-, h) pulverize; ²rig adj. ['∼friç] powdery.

Pump F [pump] m (-[e]s/-e): auf ∼ on tick; '∼e f (-/-n) pump; '²en (ge-, h) 1. v/i. pump; 2. v/t. pump; F fig.: give s.th. on tick; borrow (et. von j-m s.th. from s.o.).

Punkt [puŋkt] m (-[e]s/-e) point (a. fig.); dot; typ., gr. full stop, period; spot, place; fig item; article, clause (of agreement), der springende ∼ the point; toter ∼ deadlock, dead end; wunder ∼ tender subject, sore point; ∼ zehn Uhr on the stroke of ten, at 10 (o'clock) sharp; in vielen ∼en on many points, in many respects; nach ∼en siegen sports. win on points; ²ieren [∼'ti:rən] v/t. (no -ge-, h) dot, point; ⚕ puncture, tap; drawing, painting stipple.

pünktlich adj. ['pyŋktliç] punctual; ∼ sein be on time; '²keit f (-/no pl.) punctuality.

Punsch [punʃ] m (-es/-e) punch.

Pupille anat. [pu'pilə] f (-/-n) pupil.

Puppe ['pupə] f (-/-n) doll (a. fig.); puppet (a. fig.); tailoring: dummy; zo. chrysalis, pupa; '∼nspiel n puppet-show; '∼nstube f doll's room; '∼nwagen m doll's pram, Am. doll carriage or buggy.

pur adj. [pu:r] pure, sheer.

Püree [py're:] n (-s/-s) purée, mash.

Purpur ['purpur] m (-s/no pl.) purple; '²farben adj., '²n adj., ²rot adj. purple.

Purzel|baum ['purtsəl-] m somersault; e-n ∼ schlagen turn a somersault; '²n v/i. (ge-, sein) tumble.

Puste F ['pu:stə] f (-/no pl.) breath; ihm ging die ∼ aus he got out of breath.

Pustel ⚕ ['pustəl] f (-/-n) pustule, pimple.

pusten ['pu:stən] v/i. (ge-, h) puff, pant; blow.

Pute orn. ['pu:tə] f (-/-n) turkey (-hen); '∼r orn. m (-s/-) turkey (-cock); '²r'rot adj. (as) red as a turkey-cock.

Putsch [putʃ] m (-es/-e) putsch, insurrection; riot; '²en v/i. (ge-, h) revolt, riot.

Putz [puts] m (-es/-e) on garments: finery; ornaments pl.; trimming; △ roughcast, plaster; '²en v/t. (ge-, h) clean, cleanse; polish, wipe; adorn; snuff (candle); polish, Am. shine (shoes); sich ∼ smarten or dress o.s. up; sich die Nase ∼ blow or wipe one's nose; sich die Zähne ∼ brush one's teeth; '∼frau f charwoman, Am. a. scrubwoman; '²ig adj. droll, funny; '∼lappen m cleaning rag; '∼zeug n cleaning utensils pl.

Pyjama [pi'dʒa:ma] m (-s/-s) (ein a suit of) pyjamas pl. or Am. a. pajamas pl.

Pyramide [pyra'mi:də] f (-/-n) pyramid (a. Å); ✕ stack (of rifles); ²nförmig adj. [∼nfœrmiç] pyramidal.

Q

Quacksalber ['kvakzalbər] m (-s/-) quack (doctor); ∼ei F [∼'raı] f (-/-en) quackery; '²n v/i. (ge-, h) (play the) quack.

Quadrat [kva'dra:t] n (-[e]s/-e) square; 2 Fuß im ∼ 2 feet square; ins ∼ erheben square; ²isch adj. square; Å equation quadratic; ∼meile f square mile; ∼meter n, m square met|re, Am. -er; ∼wurzel Å f square root; ∼zahl Å f square number.

quaken ['kva:kən] v/i. (ge-, h) duck: quack; frog: croak.

quäken ['kvɛ:kən] v/i. (ge-, h) squeak.

Quäker ['kvɛ:kər] m (-s/-) Quaker, member of the Society of Friends.

Qual [kva:l] f (-/-en) pain; torment; agony.

quälen ['kvɛ:lən] v/t. (ge-, h) torment (a. fig.); torture; agonize; fig. bother, pester; sich ∼ toil, drudge.

Qualifikation [kvalifika'tsjoːn] *f* (-/-en) qualification.

qualifizieren [kvalifi'tsiːrən] *v/t. and v/refl.* (no -ge-, h) qualify (*zu* for).

Qualit|ät [kvali'tɛːt] *f* (-/-en) quality; **2ativ** [‿a'tiːf] **1.** *adj.* qualitative; **2.** *adv.* as to quality. **Quali'täts|arbeit** *f* work of high quality; **stahl** *m* high-grade steel; **ware** *f* high-grade *or* quality goods *pl.*

Qualm [kvalm] *m* (-[e]s/*no pl.*) dense smoke; fumes *pl.*; vapo(u)r, steam; **2en** (ge-, h) **1.** *v/i.* smoke, give out vapo(u)r *or* fumes; F *p.* smoke heavily; **2.** F *v/t.* puff (away) at (*cigar, pipe, etc.*); **2ig** *adj.* smoky.

'qualvoll *adj.* very painful; *pain:* excruciating; *fig.* agonizing, harrowing.

Quantit|ät [kvanti'tɛːt] *f* (-/-en) quantity; **2ativ** [‿a'tiːf] **1.** *adj.* quantitative; **2.** *adv.* as to quantity. **Quantum** ['kvantum] *n* (-s/Quanten) quantity, amount; quantum (*a. phys.*).

Quarantäne [karan'tɛːnə] *f* (-/-n) quarantine; *in ~ legen* (put in) quarantine. [curd(s *pl.*).\
Quark [kvark] *m* (-[e]s/*no pl.*)/ **Quartal** [kvar'taːl] *n* (-s/-e) quarter (of a year); *univ.* term.

Quartett [kvar'tɛt] *n* (-[e]s/-e) *f* quartet(te); *cards:* four.

Quartier [kvar'tiːr] *n* (-s/-e) accommodation; ✕ quarters *pl.*, billet.

Quaste ['kvastə] *f* (-/-n) tassel; (powder-)puff.

Quatsch F [kvatʃ] *m* (-es/*no pl.*) nonsense, fudge, *sl.* bosh, rot, *Am. sl. a.* baloney; **2en** F *v/i.* (ge-, h) twaddle, blether, *sl.* talk rot; (have a) chat; **kopf** F *m* twaddler.

Quecksilber ['kvɛk-] *n* mercury, quicksilver.

Quelle ['kvɛlə] *f* (-/-n) spring, source (*a. fig.*); *oil:* well; *fig.* fountain, origin; **2n** *v/i.* (irr., ge-, sein) gush, well; **nangabe** ['kvɛlənʔ-] *f*

mention of sources used; **n-forschung** *f* original research.

Quengel|ei F [kvɛŋə'laɪ] *f* (-/-en) grumbling, whining; nagging; **2n** F *v/i.* (ge-, h) grumble, whine; nag.

quer *adv.* [kveːr] crossways, crosswise; F *fig.* wrong; F *~ gehen* go wrong; *~ über* (*acc.*) across.

'Quer|e *f* (-/*no pl.*): *der ~ nach* crossways, crosswise; F *j-m in die kommen* cross s.o.'s path; *fig.* thwart s.o.'s plans; **frage** *f* cross-question; **kopf** *fig. m* wrongheaded fellow; **2schießen** F *v/i.* (irr. schießen, sep., -ge-, h) try to foil s.o.'s plans; **schiff** △ *n* transept; **schläger** ✕ *m* ricochet; **schnitt** *m* cross-section (*a. fig.*); **'straße** *f* cross-road; *zweite ~ rechts* second turning to the right; **treiber** *m* (-s/-) schemer; **treibe'rei** *f* (-/-en) intriguing, machination.

Querulant [kveru'lant] *m* (-en/-en) querulous person, grumbler, *Am. sl. a.* griper.

quetsch|en ['kvɛtʃən] *v/t.* (ge-, h) squeeze; ❦ bruise, contuse; *sich den Finger ~* jam one's finger; **'2ung** ❦ *f* (-/-en), **'2wunde** ❦ *f* bruise, contusion.

quick *adj.* [kvik] lively, brisk.

quieken ['kviːkən] *v/i.* (ge-, h) squeak, squeal.

quietsch|en ['kviːtʃən] *v/i.* (ge-, h) squeak, squeal; *door-hinge, etc.:* creak, squeak; *brakes, etc.:* screech; **ver'gnügt** F *adj.* (as) jolly as a sandboy.

Quirl [kvirl] *m* (-[e]s/-e) twirlingstick; **2en** *v/t.* (ge-, h) twirl.

quitt *adj.* [kvit]: *~ sein mit j-m* be quits *or* even with s.o.; *jetzt sind wir ~* that leaves us even; **ieren** [‿'tiːrən] *v/t.* (no -ge-, h) receipt (*bill, etc.*); quit, abandon (*post, etc.*); **'2ung** *f* (-/-en) receipt; *fig.* answer; *gegen ~* against receipt.

quoll [kvɔl] *pret. of* quellen.

Quot|e ['kvoːtə] *f* (-/-n) quota; share, portion; **ient** Å [kvo'tsjɛnt] *m* (-en/-en) quotient.

R

Rabatt ✝ [ra'bat] *m* (-[e]s/-e) discount, rebate.

Rabe *orn.* ['raːbə] *m* (-n/-n) raven; **2n'schwarz** F *adj.* raven, jet-black.

rabiat *adj.* [ra'bjaːt] rabid, violent.

Rache ['raxə] *f* (-/*no pl.*) revenge, vengeance; retaliation.

Rachen *anat.* ['raxən] *m* (-s/-) throat, pharynx; jaws *pl.*

rächen ['rɛçən] *v/t.* (ge-, h) avenge,

revenge; *sich ~ an* (*dat.*) revenge o.s. *or* be revenged on.

'Rachen|höhle *anat. f* pharynx; **katarrh** ❦ *m* cold in the throat.

'rach|gierig *adj.*, **süchtig** *adj.* revengeful, vindictive.

Rad [raːt] *n* (-[e]s/‿er) wheel; (bi)cycle, F bike; (*ein*) *~ schlagen peacock:* spread its tail; *sports:* turn cart-wheels; *unter die Räder*

kommen go to the dogs; **'⁓achse** f axle(-tree).

Radar ['rɑːdɑːr, rɑ'dɑːr] m, n (-s/-s) radar.

Radau F [ra'dau] m (-s/no pl.) row, racket, hubbub.

radebrechen ['rɑːdə-] v/t. (ge-, h) speak (language) badly, murder (language).

radeln ['rɑːdəln] v/i. (ge-, sein) cycle, pedal, F bike.

Rädelsführer ['rɛːdəls-] m ringleader.

Räderwerk ⊕ ['rɛːdər-] n gearing.

'rad|fahren v/i. (irr. fahren, sep., -ge-, sein) cycle, (ride a) bicycle, pedal, F bike; **'⁓fahrer** m cyclist, Am. a. cycler or wheelman.

radier|en [ra'diːrən] v/t. (no -ge-, h) rub out, erase; art: etch; **⁓gummi** m (india-)rubber, esp. Am. eraser; **⁓messer** n eraser; **⁓ung** f (-/-en) etching.

Radieschen 🌹 [ra'diːsçən] n (-s/-) (red) radish.

radikal adj. [radi'kɑːl] radical.

Radio ['rɑːdjo] n (-s/-s) radio, wireless; im ⁓ on the radio, on the air; **⁓aktiv** phys. adj. [radjoak'tiːf] radio(-)active; **⁓er** Niederschlag fall-out; **'⁓apparat** m radio or wireless (set).

Radium 🜀 ['rɑːdjum] n (-s/no pl.) radium.

Radius ⚕ ['rɑːdjus] m (-/Radien) radius.

'Rad|kappe f hub cap; **'⁓kranz** m rim; **'⁓rennbahn** f cycling track; **'⁓rennen** n cycle race; **'⁓sport** m cycling; **'⁓spur** f rut, track.

raffen ['rafən] v/t. (ge-, h) snatch up; gather (dress).

raffiniert adj. [rafi'niːrt] refined; fig. clever, cunning.

ragen ['rɑːgən] v/i. (ge-, h) tower, loom.

Ragout [ra'guː] n (-s/-s) ragout, stew, hash.

Rahe ⚓ ['rɑːə] f (-/-n) yard.

Rahm [rɑːm] m (-[e]s/no pl.) cream.

Rahmen ['rɑːmən] 1. m (-s/-) frame; fig.: frame, background, setting; scope; aus dem ⁓ fallen be out of place; 2. ⚒ v/t. (ge-, h) frame.

Rakete [ra'keːtə] f (-/-n) rocket; e-e ⁓ abfeuern or starten launch a rocket; dreistufige ⁓ three-stage rocket; **⁓nantrieb** [ra'keːtən⁻] m rocket propulsion; mit ⁓ rocket-propelled; **⁓nflugzeug** n rocket (-propelled) plane; **⁓ntriebwerk** n propulsion unit.

Ramm|bär ⊕ ['ram⁻] m, **'⁓bock** m, **'⁓e** f (-/-n) ram(mer); **'⁓en** v/t. (ge-, h) ram.

Rampe ['rampə] f (-/-n) ramp, ascent; **'⁓nlicht** n footlights pl.; fig. limelight.

Ramsch [ramʃ] m (-es/⚖-e) junk,

trash; im ⁓ kaufen buy in the lump; **'⁓verkauf** m jumble-sale; **'⁓ware** f job lot.

Rand [rant] m (-[e]s/⁓er) edge, brink (a. fig.); fig. verge; border; brim (of hat, cup, etc.); rim (of plate, etc.); margin (of book, etc.); lip (of wound); Ränder pl. under the eyes: rings pl., circles pl.; vor Freude außer ⁓ und Band geraten be beside o.s. with joy; er kommt damit nicht zu ⁓e he can't manage it; **'⁓bemerkung** f marginal note; fig. comment.

rang¹ [raŋ] pret. of ringen.

Rang² [⁓] m (-[e]s/⁓e) rank, order; ✕ rank; position; thea. tier; erster ⁓ thea. dress-circle, Am. first balcony; zweiter ⁓ thea. upper circle, Am. second balcony; ersten ⁓es first-class, first-rate; j-m den ⁓ ablaufen get the start or better of s.o.

Range ['raŋə] m (-n/-n), f (-/-n) rascal, romp.

rangieren [rã'ʒiːrən] (no -ge-, h) 1. 🚂 v/t. shunt, Am. a. switch; 2. fig. v/i. rank.

'Rang|liste f sports, etc.: ranking list; ✕ army-list, navy or air-force list; **'⁓ordnung** f order of precedence.

Ranke 🌹 ['raŋkə] f (-/-n) tendril; runner.

Ränke ['rɛŋkə] m/pl. intrigues pl.

'ranken v/refl. (ge-, h) creep, climb.

rann [ran] pret. of rinnen.

rannte ['rantə] pret. of rennen.

Ranzen ['rantsən] m (-s/-) knapsack; satchel.

ranzig adj. ['rantsiç] rancid, rank.

Rappe zo. ['rapə] m (-n/-n) black horse.

rar adj. [rɑːr] rare, scarce.

Rarität [rari'tɛːt] f (-/-en) rarity; curiosity, curio.

rasch adj. [raʃ] quick, swift, brisk; hasty; prompt.

rascheln ['raʃəln] v/i. (ge-, h) rustle.

rasen¹ ['rɑːzən] v/i. (ge-) 1. (h) rage, storm; rave; 2. (sein) race, speed; **'⁓d** adj. raving; frenzied; speed: tearing; pains: agonizing; headache: splitting; j-n ⁓ machen drive s.o. mad.

Rasen² [⁓] m (-s/-) grass; lawn; turf; **'⁓platz** m lawn, grass-plot.

Raserei F [rɑːzə'raɪ] f (-/-en) rage, fury; frenzy, madness; F mot. scorching; j-n zur ⁓ bringen drive s.o. mad.

Rasier|apparat [ra'ziːr⁻] m (safety) razor; **⁓en** v/t. (no -ge-, h) shave; sich ⁓ (lassen get a) shave; **⁓klinge** f razor-blade; **⁓messer** n razor; **⁓pinsel** m shaving-brush; **⁓seife** f shaving-soap; **⁓wasser** n after-shave lotion; **⁓zeug** n shaving kit.

Rasse ['rasə] f (-/-n) race; zo. breed.

rasseln ['rasəln] v/i. (ge-, h) rattle.

'Rassen|frage f (-/no pl.) racial
issue; '_kampf m race conflict;
'_problem n racial issue; '_schran-
ke f colo(u)r bar; '_trennung f
(-/no pl.) racial segregation; '_un-
ruhen f/pl. race riots pl.

'rasserein adj. thoroughbred, pure-
bred.

'rassig adj. thoroughbred; fig. racy.

Rast [rast] f (-/-en) rest, repose;
break, pause; '2en v/i. (ge-, h) rest,
repose; '2los adj. restless; '_platz
m resting-place; mot. picnic area.

Rat [ra:t] m 1. (-[e]s/no pl.) advice,
counsel; suggestion; fig. way out;
zu _e ziehen consult; j-n um _ fragen
ask s.o.'s advice; 2. (-[e]s/\ue)
council, board; council(l)or, alderman.

Rate ['ra:tə] f (-/-n) instal(l)ment
(a. ✝); auf _n ✝ on hire-purchase.

'raten (irr., ge-, h) 1. v/i. advise,
counsel (j-m zu inf. s.o. to inf.);
2. v/t. guess, divine.

'raten|weise adv. by instal(l)ments;
'2zahlung ✝ f payment by instal(l)-
ments.

'Rat|geber m (-s/-) adviser, coun-
sel(l)or; '_haus n town hall, Am. a.
city hall.

ratifizieren [ratifi'tsi:rən] v/t. (no
-ge-, h) ratify.

Ration [ra'tsjo:n] f (-/-en) ration,
allowance; 2ell adj. [_o'nel] rational; efficient; economical; 2ieren
[_o'ni:rən] v/t. (no -ge-, h) ration.

'rat|los adj. puzzled, perplexed, at
a loss; '_sam adj. advisable; expedient; '2schlag m (piece of)
advice, counsel.

Rätsel ['rɛ:tsəl] n (-s/-) riddle,
puzzle; enigma, mystery; '2haft
adj. puzzling; enigmatic(al), mysterious.

Ratte zo. ['ratə] f (-/-n) rat.

rattern ['ratərn] v/i. (ge-, h, sein)
rattle, clatter.

Raub [raup] m (-[e]s/no pl.) robbery; kidnap(p)ing; piracy (of intellectual property); booty, spoils
pl.; '_bau m (-[e]s/no pl.): _ treiben
⚒ exhaust the land; ⚒ rob a mine;
_ treiben mit undermine (one's
health); 2en ['_bən] v/t. (ge-, h)
rob, take by force, steal; kidnap;
j-m et. _ rob or deprive s.o. of s.th.

Räuber ['rɔybər] m (-s/-) robber;
'_bande f gang of robbers; '2isch
adj. rapacious, predatory.

'Raub|fisch ichth. m fish of prey;
'_gier f rapacity; '2gierig adj.
rapacious; '_mord m murder with
robbery; '_mörder m murderer
and robber; '_tier zo. n beast of
prey; '_überfall m hold-up, armed
robbery; '_vogel orn. m bird of
prey; '_zug m raid.

Rauch [raux] m (-[e]s/no pl.) smoke;
fume; '2en (ge-, h) 1. v/i. smoke;

fume; p. (have a) smoke; 2. v/t.
smoke (cigarette); '_er m (-s/-)
smoker; s. Raucherabteil.

Räucheraal ['rɔyçər?-] m smoked
eel.

Raucherabteil 🚬 ['rauxər?-] n
smoking-car(riage), smoking-com-
partment, smoker.

'Räucher|hering m red or smoked
herring, kipper; '2n (ge-, h) 1. v/t.
smoke, cure (meat, fish); 2. v/i.
burn incense.

'Rauch|fahne f trail of smoke;
'_fang m chimney, flue; '_fleisch
n smoked meat; '2ig adj. smoky;
'_tabak m tobacco; '_waren f/pl.
tobacco products pl.; furs pl.;
'_zimmer n smoking-room.

Räud|e ['rɔydə] f (-/-n) mange,
scab; '2ig adj. mangy, scabby.

Rauf|bold contp. ['raufbɔlt] m
(-[e]s/-e) brawler, rowdy, Am. sl.
tough; '2en (ge-, h) 1. v/t. pluck,
pull; sich die Haare _ tear one's
hair; 2. v/i. fight, scuffle; _erei
[_ə'rai] f (-/-en) fight, scuffle.

rauh adj. [rau] rough; rugged;
weather: inclement, raw; voice:
hoarse; fig.: harsh; coarse, rude; F:
in _en Mengen galore; '2reif m
(-[e]s/no pl.) hoar-frost, poet.
rime.

Raum [raum] m (-[e]s/\ue) room,
space; expanse; area; room; premises pl.; '_anzug m space suit.

räumen ['rɔymən] v/t. (ge-, h)
remove, clear (away); leave, give
up, esp. 🅇 evacuate; vacate (flat).

'Raum|fahrt f astronautics; '_flug
m space flight; '_inhalt m volume,
capacity; '_kapsel f capsule.

räumlich adj. ['rɔymliç] relating to
space, of space, spatial.

'Raum|meter n, m cubic met|re,
Am. -er; '_schiff n space craft or
ship; '_sonde f space probe;
'_station f space station.

'Räumung f (-/-en) clearing, removal; esp. ✝ clearance; vacating
(of flat), by force: eviction; 🅇 eva-
cuation (of town); '_sverkauf ✝ m
clearance sale.

raunen ['raunən] (ge-, h) 1. v/i.
whisper, murmur; 2. v/t. whisper,
murmur; man raunt rumo(u)r has
it.

Raupe zo. ['raupə] f (-/-n) caterpillar; '_nschlepper ⊕ m caterpillar tractor.

raus int. [raus] get out!, sl. beat it!,
scram!

Rausch [rauʃ] m (-es/\ue) intoxica-
tion, drunkenness; fig. frenzy,
transport(s pl.); e-n _ haben be
drunk; '2en v/i. (ge-) 1. (h) leaves,
rain, silk: rustle; water, wind: rush;
surf: roar; applause: thunder;
2. (sein) movement: sweep; '_gift n
narcotic (drug), F dope.

räuspern ['rɔyspərn] v/refl. (ge-, h) clear one's throat.

Razzia ['ratsja] f (-/Razzien) raid, round-up

reagieren [rea'giːrən] v/i. (no -ge-, h) react (auf acc. [up]on; to); fig. and ⊕ a. respond (to).

Reaktion [reak'tsjoːn] f (-/-en) reaction (a. pol.); fig. a. response (auf acc. to); **~är** [~o'nɛːr] 1. m (-s/-e) reactionary; 2. ⚥ adj. reactionary.

Reaktor phys. [re'aktɔr] m (-s/-en) (nuclear) reactor, atomic pile.

real adj. [re'aːl] real; concrete; **~isieren** [reali'ziːrən] v/t. (no -ge-, h) realize, **Qismus** [rea'lismus] m (-/no pl.) realism, **~istisch** adj. [rea'listiʃ] realistic; **Qität** [reali'tɛːt] f (-/-en) reality; **Qschule** f non-classical secondary school.

Rebe f ['reːbə] f (-/-n) vine.

Rebell [re'bel] m (-en/-en) rebel; **Qieren** [~'liːrən] v/i. (no -ge-, h) rebel, revolt, rise; **Qisch** adj. rebellious.

Reb|huhn orn. ['rep-] n partridge; **~laus** zo. ['reːp-] f vine-fretter, phylloxera, **~stock** ⚥ ['reːp-] m vine.

Rechen ['reçən] m (-s/-) rake; grid.

Rechen|aufgabe ['reçən-] f sum, (arithmetical) problem; **~fehler** m arithmetical error, miscalculation; **~maschine** f calculating-machine; **~schaft** f (-/no pl.): ~ ablegen give or render an account (über acc. of), account or answer (for); zur ~ ziehen call to account (wegen for); **~schieber** ⚥ m slide-rule.

rechne|n ['reçnən] (ge-, h) 1. v/t. reckon, calculate; estimate, value; charge; ~ zu rank with or among(st); 2. v/i. count; ~ auf (acc.) or mit count or reckon or rely (up)on; **~risch** adj. arithmetical.

'Rechnung f (-/-en) calculation, sum, reckoning; account, bill; invoice (of goods); in restaurant: bill, Am. check; score; auf ~ on account; ~ legen render an account (über acc. of); e-r Sache ~ tragen make allowance for s.th.; es geht auf meine ~ in restaurants: it is my treat, Am. F this is on me; **~sprüfer** m auditor.

recht[1] [reçt] 1. adj. right; real; legitimate; right, correct; zur ~en Zeit in due time, at the right moment; ein ~er Narr a regular fool; mir ist es ~ I don't mind; ~ haben be right; j-m ~ geben agree with s.o.; 2. adv. right(ly), well; very; rather; really; correctly; ganz ~! quite (so)!; es geschieht ihm ~ it serves him right; ~ gern gladly, with pleasure; ~ gut quite good or well; ich weiß nicht ~ I wonder.

Recht[2] [~] n (-[e]s/-e) right (auf

acc. to), title (to), claim (on), interest (in); privilege; power, authority; ⚥ law; justice; ~ sprechen administer justice; mit ~ justly.

'Rechte f (-n/-n) right hand; boxing: right; pol. the Right.

Rechteck ['reçt°-] n (-[e]s/-e) rectangle; **Qig** adj. rectangular.

recht|fertigen ['reçtfertigən] v/t. (ge-, h) justify, defend, vindicate; **Qfertigung** f (-/-en) justification; vindication, defen|ce, Am. -se; **~gläubig** adj. orthodox; **~haberisch** adj. ['~haːbəriʃ] dogmatic; **~lich** adj. legal, lawful, legitimate; honest, righteous; **~los** adj. without rights, outlawed; **Qlosigkeit** f (-/no pl.) outlawry; **~mäßig** adj. legal, lawful, legitimate; **Qmäßigkeit** f (-/no pl.) legality, legitimacy.

rechts adv. [reçts] on or to the right (hand)

'Rechts|anspruch m legal right or claim (auf acc. on, to); title (to); **~anwalt** m lawyer, solicitor; barrister, Am. attorney (at law); **~außen** m (-/-) football: outside right; **~beistand** m legal adviser, counsel.

'recht|schaffen 1. adj. honest, righteous; 2. adv. thoroughly, downright, F awfully; **Qschreibung** f (-/-en) orthography, spelling.

'Rechts|fall m case, cause; **~frage** f question of law; issue of law; **~gelehrte** m jurist, lawyer; **Qgültig** adj. s rechtskräftig; **~kraft** f (-/no pl.) legal force or validity; **Qkräftig** adj. valid, legal; judgement: final; **~kurve** f right-hand bend; **~lage** f legal position or status; **~mittel** n legal remedy; **~nachfolger** m assign, assignee; **~person** f legal personality; **~pflege** f administration of justice, judicature.

'Rechtsprechung f (-/-en) jurisdiction.

'Rechts|schutz m legal protection; **~spruch** m legal decision; judg(e)-ment; sentence, verdict (of jury); **~steuerung** mot. f (-/-en) right-hand drive; **~streit** m action, lawsuit; **~verfahren** n (legal) proceedings pl.; **~verkehr** mot. m right-hand traffic; **~verletzung** f infringement; **~vertreter** m s. Rechtsbeistand; **~weg** m: den ~ beschreiten take legal action, go to law; unter Ausschluß des ~es eliminating legal proceedings; **Qwidrig** adj. illegal, unlawful; **~wissenschaft** f jurisprudence.

'recht|wink(e)lig adj. right-angled; **~zeitig** 1. adj. punctual; opportune; 2. adv. in (due) time, punctually, Am. on time.

Reck [rɛk] n (-[e]s/-e) sports: horizontal bar.

recken ['rɛkən] v/t. (ge-, h) stretch; sich ~ stretch o.s.

Redakt|eur [redak'tø:r] m (-s/-e) editor; ~ion [ˌ'tsjo:n] f (-/-en) editorship; editing, wording; editorial staff, editors pl.; editor's or editorial office; **Sionell** adj. [ˌtsjo'nɛl] editorial.

Rede ['re:də] f (-/-n) speech; oration; language; talk, conversation; discourse; direkte ~ gr. direct speech; indirekte ~ gr. reported or indirect speech; e-e ~ halten make or deliver a speech; zur ~ stellen call to account (wegen for); davon ist nicht die ~ that is not the point; davon kann keine ~ sein that's out of the question; es ist nicht der ~ wert it is not worth speaking of; **Sgewandt** adj. eloquent; **~kunst** f rhetoric; **Sn** (ge-, h) 1. v/t. speak; talk; 2. v/i. speak (mit to); talk (to), chat (with); discuss (über et. s.th.); sie läßt nicht mit sich ~ she won't listen to reason.

Redensart ['re:dənsˌ?-] f phrase, expression; idiom; proverb, saying.

redigieren [redi'gi:rən] v/t. (no -ge-, h) edit; revise.

redlich ['re:tlɪç] 1. adj. honest, upright; sincere; 2. adv.: sich ~ bemühen take great pains.

Redner ['re:dnər] m (-s/-) speaker; orator; **~bühne** f platform; **Sisch** adj. oratorical, rhetorical; **~pult** n speaker's desk.

redselig adj. ['re:tze:lɪç] talkative.

reduzieren [redu'tsi:rən] v/t. (no -ge-, h) reduce (auf acc. to).

Reede ⚓ ['re:də] f (-/-n) roads pl., roadstead; **~r** m (-s/-) shipowner; **~rei** f (-/-en) shipping company or firm.

reell [re'ɛl] 1. adj. respectable, honest; business firm: solid; goods: good; offer: real; 2. adv.: ~ bedient werden get good value for one's money.

Refer|at [refe'ra:t] n (-[e]s/-e) report; lecture; paper; ein ~ halten esp. univ. read a paper; **~endar** [ˌɛn'da:r] m (-s/-e) r̃ᵗ̃ junior lawyer; at school: junior teacher; **~ent** [ˌ'rɛnt] m (-en/-en) reporter, speaker; **~enz** [ˌ'rɛnts] f (-/-en) reference; **Sieren** [ˌ'ri:rən] v/i. (no -ge-, h) report (über acc. [up]on); (give a) lecture (on); esp. univ. read a paper (on).

reflektieren [reflɛk'ti:rən] (no -ge-, h) 1. phys. v/t. reflect; 2. v/i. reflect (über acc. [up]on); ~ auf (acc.) ✝ think of buying; be interested in.

Reflex [re'flɛks] m (-es/-e) phys. reflection or reflexion; ⚕ reflex (action); **Sᵢv** gr. adj. [ˌ'ksi:f] reflexive.

Reform [re'fɔrm] f (-/-en) reform; **~er** m (-s/-) reformer; **Sieren** [ˌ'mi:rən] v/t. (no -ge-, h) reform.

Refrain [rə'frɛ̃] m (-s/-s) refrain, chorus, burden.

Regal [re'ga:l] n (-s/-e) shelf.

rege adj. ['re:gə] active, brisk, lively; busy.

Regel ['re:gəl] f (-/-n) rule; regulation; standard; physiol. menstruation; menses pl.; in der ~ as a rule; **Slos** adj. irregular; disorderly; **Smäßig** adj. regular; **Sn** v/t. (ge-, h) regulate, control; arrange, settle; put in order; **Srecht** adj. regular; **~ung** f (-/-en) regulation, control; arrangement, settlement; **Swidrig** adj. contrary to the rules, irregular; abnormal; sports: foul.

regen[1] ['re:gən] v/t. and v/refl. (ge-, h) move, stir.

Regen[2] [ˌ] m (-s/-) rain; vom ~ in die Traufe kommen jump out of the frying-pan into the fire, get from bad to worse; **Sarm** adj. dry; **~bogen** m rainbow; **~bogenhaut** anat. f iris; **Sdicht** adj. rain-proof; **~guß** m downpour; **~mantel** m waterproof, raincoat, mac(k)intosh, F mac; **Sreich** adj. rainy; **~schauer** m shower (of rain); **~schirm** m umbrella; **~tag** m rainy day; **~tropfen** m raindrop; **~wasser** n rain-water; **~wetter** n rainy weather; **~wolke** f rain-cloud; **~wurm** zo. m earthworm, Am. a. angleworm; **~zeit** f rainy season.

Regie [re'ʒi:] f (-/-n) management; thea., film: direction; unter der ~ von directed by.

regier|en [re'gi:rən] (no -ge-, h) 1. v/i. reign; 2. v/t. govern (a. gr.), rule; **Sung** f (-/-en) government, Am. administration; reign.

Re'gierungs|antritt m accession (to the throne); **~beamte** m government official; Brt. Civil Servant; **~bezirk** m administrative district; **~gebäude** n government offices pl.

Regiment [regi'mɛnt] n 1. (-[e]s/-e) government, rule; 2. ✕ (-[e]s/-er) regiment.

Regisseur [reʒi'sø:r] m (-s/-e) thea. stage manager, director; film: director.

Regist|er [re'gɪstər] n (-s/-) register (a. ♪), record; index; **~ratur** [ˌra-'tu:r] f (-/-en) registry; registration.

registrier|en [regɪs'tri:rən] v/t. (no -ge-, h) register, record; **Skasse** f cash register.

reglos adj. ['re:klo:s] motionless.

regne|n ['re:gnən] v/i. (ge-, h) rain; es regnet in Strömen it is pouring with rain; **~risch** adj. rainy.

Regreß r̃ᵗ̃ ✝ [re'grɛs] m (Regresses/Regresse) recourse; **Spflichtig** r̃ᵗ̃, ✝ adj. liable to recourse.

regulär adj. [regu'lɛ:r] regular.

regulier|bar *adj.* [regu'li:rba:r] adjustable, controllable; **~en** *v/t.* (*no -ge-, h*) regulate, adjust; control.

Regung *f* [re'gun] *f* (-/-en) movement, motion; emotion; impulse; **2slos** *adj.* motionless.

Reh *zo.* [re:] *n* (-[e]s/-e) deer, roe; *female:* doe.

rehabilitieren [rehabili'ti:rən] *v/t.* (*no -ge-, h*) rehabilitate.

'Reh|bock *zo. m* roebuck; **2braun** *adj.*, **2farben** *adj.* fawn-colo(u)red; **~geiß** *zo. f* doe; **~kalb** *zo. n*, **~kitz** *zo.* ['~kits] *n* (-es/-e) fawn.

Reib|e ['raibə] *f* (-/-n), **~eisen** ['raip-] *n* grater.

reib|en ['raibən] (*irr.*, ge-, h) 1. *v/t.* rub (an *dat.* [up]on); 2. *v/t.* rub, grate; pulverize; *wund* ~ chafe, gall; **2erei** F *fig.* ['~'rai] *f* (-/-en) (constant) friction; **2ung** *f* (-/-en) friction; **~ungslos** *adj.* frictionless; *fig.* smooth.

reich[1] *adj.* [raiç] rich (an *dat.* in); wealthy; ample, abundant, copious.

Reich[2] [~] *n* (-es/-e) empire; kingdom (*of animals, vegetables, minerals*); *poet.*, *rhet.*, *fig.* realm.

reichen ['raiçən] (ge-, h) 1. *v/t.* offer; serve (*food*); *j-m et.* ~ hand or pass s.th. to s.o.; *sich die Hände* ~ join hands; 2. *v/i.* reach; extend; suffice; *das reicht!* that will do!

reich|haltig *adj.* ['raiçhaltiç] rich; abundant, copious; **~lich** 1. *adj.* ample, abundant, copious, plentiful; ~ *Zeit* plenty of time; 2. F *adv.* rather, fairly, F pretty, plenty; **2tum** *m* (-s/-er) riches *pl.*; wealth (an *dat* of).

'Reichweite *f* reach; ⚔ range; *in* ~ within reach, near at hand.

reif[1] *adj.* [raif] ripe, mature.

Reif[2] [~] *m* (-[e]s/*no pl.*) white or hoar-frost, *poet.* rime.

'Reife *f* (-/*no pl.*) ripeness, maturity.

'reifen[1] *v/i.* (ge-, h) (*sein*) ripen, mature; 2. (h): *es hat gereift* there is a white or hoar-frost.

'Reifen[2] *m* (-s/-) hoop; ring; tyre, (*Am. only*) tire; *as ornament*: circlet; ~ *wechseln mot.* change tyres; **~panne** *mot. f* puncture, *Am.* a blowout.

'Reife|prüfung *f s.* Abitur; **~zeugnis** *n s.* Abschlußzeugnis.

'reiflich *adj.* mature, careful.

Reihe ['raiə] *f* (-/-n) row; line; rank; series; number; *thea.* row, tier; *der* ~ *nach* by turns; *ich bin an der* ~ *it is my turn.*

'Reihen|folge *f* succession, sequence; *alphabetische* ~ alphabetical order; **~haus** *n* terrace-house, *Am.* row house; **2weise** *adv.* in rows.

Reiher *orn.* ['raiər] *m* (-s/-) heron.

Reim [raim] *m* (-[e]s/-e) rhyme; **2en** (ge-, h) 1. *v/i.* rhyme; 2. *v/t.* and *v/refl.* rhyme (*auf acc.* with).

rein *adj.* [rain] pure; clean; clear; ~ *e Wahrheit* plain truth; **2ertrag** *m* net proceeds *pl.*; **2fall** F *m* letdown; **2gewicht** *n* net weight; **2gewinn** *m* net profit; **2heit** *f* (-/*no pl.*) purity; cleanness.

'reinig|en *v/t.* (ge-, h) clean(se); *fig.* purify; **2ung** *f* (-/-en) clean(s)-ing; *fig.* purification; cleaners *pl.*; *chemische* ~ dry cleaning; **2ungs-mittel** *n* detergent, cleanser.

'rein|lich *adj.* clean; cleanly; neat, tidy; **2machefrau** *f* charwoman; **~rassig** *adj.* pedigree, thoroughbred, *esp. Am.* purebred; **2schrift** *f* fair copy.

Reis[1] ♀ [rais] *m* (-es/-e) rice.

Reis[2] ♀ [~] *n* (-es/-er) twig, sprig.

Reise ['raizə] *f* (-/-n) journey; ⚓, ~ voyage; travel; tour; trip; passage; **~büro** *n* travel agency *or* bureau; **~decke** *f* travel(l)ing-rug; **2fertig** *adj.* ready to start; **~füh-rer** *m* guide(-book); **~gepäck** *n* luggage, *Am.* baggage; **~gesell-schaft** *f* tourist party; **~kosten** *pl.* travel(l)ing-expenses *pl.*; **~leiter** *m* courier; **2n** *v/i.* (ge-, sein) travel, journey; ~ *nach* go to; *ins Ausland* ~ go abroad; **~nde** *m, f* (-n/-n) (*commercial*) travel(l)er; *in trains:* passenger; *for pleasure:* tourist; **~necessaire** f '~nesesε:r] *n* (-s/-s) dressing-case; **~paß** *m* passport; **~scheck** *m* traveller's cheque, *Am.* traveler's check; **~schreibma-schine** *f* portable typewriter; **~tasche** *f* travel(l)ing-bag, *Am.* grip(sack).

Reisig ['raiziç] *n* (-s/*no pl.*) brush-wood.

Reißbrett ['rais-] *n* drawing-board.

reißen ['raisən] 1. *v/t.* (*irr.*, ge-, h) tear; pull; *an dat.* ~ seize; *sich* ~ scratch o.s. (*an dat.* with); *sich* ~ *um* scramble for; 2. *v/i.* (*irr.*, ge-, sein) break; burst; split; tear; *mir riß die Geduld* I lost (all) patience; 3. 2 F ✚ *n* (-s/*no pl.*) rheumatism; **~d** *adj.* rapid; *animal:* rapacious; *pain:* acute; **~en** *Absatz finden* sell like hot cakes.

'Reiß|er F *m* (-s/-) draw, box-office success; thriller; **~feder** *f* drawing-pen; **~leine** *f* ✈ rip-cord; **~nagel** *m s.* Reißzwecke; **~schiene** *f* (T-)square; **~verschluß** *m* zip-fastener, zipper, *Am.* a. slide fastener; **~zeug** *n* drawing instruments *pl.*; **~zwecke** *f* drawing-pin, *Am.* thumbtack.

Reit|anzug ['rait-] *m* riding-dress; **~bahn** *f* riding-school, manège; riding-track; **2en** (*irr.*, ge-) 1. *v/i.* (*sein*) ride, go on horseback; 2. *v/t.* (*h*) ride; **~er** *m* (-s/-) rider, horse-man; ✕, *police:* trooper; *filing:* tab; **~erei** *f* (-/-en) cavalry; **~erin** *f* (-/-nen) horsewoman; **~gerte** *f* riding-whip; '**∼hose** f (riding-) breeches pl.; '**∼knecht** m groom; '**∼kunst** f horsemanship; '**∼lehrer** m riding master; '**∼peitsche** f riding-whip; '**∼pferd** zo. n riding-horse, saddle-horse; '**∼schule** f riding-school; '**∼stiefel** m/pl. riding-boots pl.; '**∼weg** m bridle-path.

Reiz [raits] m (-es/-e) irritation; charm, attraction; allurement; '**2-bar** adj. sensitive; irritable, excitable, Am. sore; '**2en** (ge-, h) 1. v/t. irritate (a. 𝒔); excite; provoke; nettle; stimulate, rouse; entice, (al)lure, tempt, charm, attract; 2. v/i. cards: bid; '**2end** adj. charming, attractive; Am. cute; lovely; '**2los** adj. unattractive; '**∼mittel** n stimulus; 𝒔 stimulant; '**∼ung** f (-/-en) irritation; provocation; '**2-voll** adj. charming, attractive.

rekeln F ['re:kəln] v/refl. (ge-, h) loll, lounge, sprawl.

Reklamation [reklama'tsjo:n] f (-/-en) claim; complaint, protest.

Reklame [re'kla:mə] f (-/-n) advertising; advertisement, F ad; publicity; **∼** machen advertise; **∼** machen für et. advertise s.th.

rekla'mieren (no -ge-, h) 1. v/t. (re)claim; 2. v/i. complain (wegen about).

Rekonvaleszen|t [rekɔnvales'tsɛnt] m (-en/-en), **∼tin** f (-/-nen) convalescent; **∼z** [∼ts] f (-/no pl.) convalescence.

Rekord [re'kɔrt] m (-[e]s/-e) sports, etc.: record.

Rekrut 𝒳 [re'kru:t] m (-en/-en) recruit; **2ieren** 𝒳 [∼u'ti:rən] v/t. (no -ge-, h) recruit.

Rektor ['rɛktɔr] m (-s/-en) headmaster, rector, Am. principal; univ. chancellor, rector, Am. president.

relativ adj. [rela'ti:f] relative.

Relief [rel'jɛf] n (-s/-s, -e) relief.

Religi|on [reli'gjo:n] f (-/-en) religion; **2ös** adj. [∼ø:s] religious; pious, devout; **∼osität** [∼ozi'tɛ:t] f (-/no pl.) religiousness; piety.

Reling ⚓ ['re:liŋ] f (-/-s, -e) rail.

Reliquie [re'li:kvjə] f (-/-n) relic.

Ren zo. [rɛn; re:n] n (-s/-s; -s/-e) reindeer.

Renn|bahn ['rɛn-] f racecourse, Am. race track, horse-racing: a. the turf; mot. speedway; '**∼boot** n racing boat, racer.

rennen ['rɛnən] 1. v/i. (irr., gesein) run; race; 2. v/t. (irr., ge-, h): j-n zu Boden **∼** run s.o. down; 3. 2 n (-s/-) run(ning); race; heat.

'**Renn|fahrer** m mot. racing driver, racer; racing cyclist; '**∼läufer** m ski racer; '**∼mannschaft** f racecrew; '**∼pferd** zo. n racehorse, racer; '**∼rad** n racing bicycle, racer; '**∼sport** m racing; horse-racing: a. the turf; '**∼stall** m racing stable;

'**∼strecke** f racecourse, Am. race track; mot. speedway; distance (to be run); '**∼wagen** m racing car, racer.

renommiert adj. [renɔ'mi:rt] famous, noted (wegen for).

renovieren [reno'vi:rən] v/t. (no -ge-, h) renovate, repair; redecorate (interior of house).

rent|abel adj. [rɛn'ta:bəl] profitable, paying; **2e** f (-/-n) income, revenue; annuity; (old-age) pension; rent; **2enempfänger** ['rɛntən⁹-] m s. Rentner; rentier.

Rentier zo. ['rɛn-] n s. Ren.

rentieren [rɛn'ti:rən] v/refl. (no -ge-, h) pay.

Rentner ['rɛntnər] m (-s/-) (old-age) pensioner.

Reparatur [repara'tu:r] f (-/-en) repair; **∼werkstatt** f repair-shop; mot. a. garage, service station.

repa'rieren v/t. (no -ge-, h) repair, Am. F fix.

Report|age [repɔr'ta:ʒə] f (-/-n) reporting, commentary, coverage; **∼er** [re'pɔrtər] m (-s/-) reporter.

Repräsent|ant [reprezɛn'tant] m (-en/-en) representative; **∼antenhaus** Am. parl. n House of Representatives; **2ieren** (no -ge-, h) 1. v/t. represent; 2. v/i. cut a fine figure.

Repressalie [reprɛ'sa:ljə] f (-/-n) reprisal.

reproduzieren [reprodu'tsi:rən] v/t. (no -ge-, h) reproduce.

Reptil zo. [rɛp'ti:l] n (-s/-ien, ♦ -e) reptile.

Republik [repu'bli:k] f (-/-en) republic; **∼aner** pol. [∼i'ka:nər] m (-s/-) republican; **2anisch** adj. [∼i'ka:niʃ] republican.

Reserve [re'zɛrvə] f (-/-n) reserve; **∼rad** mot. n spare wheel.

reser'vier|en v/t. (no -ge-, h) reserve; **∼** lassen book (seat, etc.); **∼t** adj. reserved (a. fig.).

Resid|enz [rezi'dɛnts] f (-/-en) residence; **2ieren** v/i. (no -ge-, h) reside.

resignieren [rezi'gni:rən] v/i. (no -ge-, h) resign.

Respekt [re'spɛkt] m (-[e]s/no pl.) respect; **2ieren** [∼'ti:rən] v/t. (no -ge-, h) respect; **2los** adj. irreverent, disrespectful; **2voll** adj. respectful.

Ressort [rɛ'so:r] n (-s/-s) department; province.

Rest [rɛst] m (-es/-e, ♦ -er) rest, remainder; residue (a. 🔥); esp. ♦ remnant (of cloth); leftover (of food); das gab ihm den **∼** that finished him (off).

Restaurant [rɛsto'rɑ̃:] n (-s/-s) restaurant.

'**Rest|bestand** m remnant; '**∼betrag** m remainder, balance; '**2lich** adj. remaining; '**2los** adv. com-

pletely; entirely; **'~zahlung** f payment of balance; final payment.
Resultat [rezul'ta:t] n (-[e]s/-e) result, outcome; *sports:* score.
retten ['rɛtən] v/t. (ge-, h) save; deliver, rescue.
Rettich ♀ ['rɛtiç] m (-s/-e) radish.
'Rettung f (-/-en) rescue; deliverance; escape.
'Rettungs|boot n lifeboat; **'~gürtel** m lifebelt; **'2los** adj. irretrievable, past help *or* hope, beyond recovery; **'~mannschaft** f rescue party; **~ring** m life-buoy.
Reu|e ['rɔʏə] f (-/no pl.) repentance (*über acc.* of), remorse (at); **'2en** v/t. (ge-, h): et. reut mich I repent (of) s.th.; **'2evoll** adj. repentant; **2(müt)ig** adj. ['~(my:t)iç] repentant.
Revanche [re'vãː∫(ə)] f (-/-n) revenge; **~spiel** n return match.
revan'chieren v/refl. (no -ge-, h) take *or* have one's revenge (*an dat.* on); return (*für* er. s.th.).
Revers 1. [re'vɛːr] n, m (-/-) lapel (*of coat*); **2.** [re'vɛrs] m (-es/-e) declaration; ♣ bond.
revidieren [revi'diːrən] v/t. (no -ge-, h) revise; check; ♣ audit.
Revier [re'viːr] n (-s/-e) district, quarter; *s. Jagdrevier.*
Revision [revi'zjoːn] f (-/-en) revision (*a. typ.*); ♣ audit; ♣ appeal; **~ einlegen** ♣ lodge an appeal.
Revolt|e [re'vɔltə] f (-/-n) revolt, uprising; **2ieren** [~'tiːrən] v/i. (no -ge-, h) revolt, rise (in revolt).
Revolution [revolu'tsjoːn] f (-/-en) revolution; **~är** [~o'nɛːr] **1.** m (-s/-e) revolutionary; **2.** ♀ adj. revolutionary.
Revolver [re'vɔlvər] m (-s/-) revolver, *Am.* F a. gun.
Revue [rə'vyː] f (-/-n) review; *thea.* revue, (musical) show; **~ passieren lassen** pass in review.
Rezens|ent [retsɛn'zɛnt] m (-en/-en) critic, reviewer; **2ieren** v/t. (no -ge-, h) review, criticize; **~ion** [~'zjoːn] f (-/-en) review, critique.
Rezept [re'tsɛpt] n (-[e]s/-e) ♣ prescription; *cooking:* recipe (*a. fig.*).
Rhabarber ♀ [ra'barbər] m (-s/no pl.) rhubarb.
rhetorisch adj. [re'toːri∫] rhetorical.
rheumati|sch ♣ adj. [rɔʏ'maːti∫] rheumatic; **2smus** ♣ [~a'tismus] m (-/Rheumatismen) rheumatism.
rhythm|isch adj. ['rʏtmi∫] rhythmic(al); **2us** ['~us] m (-/Rhythmen) rhythm.
richten ['riçtən] v/t. (ge-, h) set right, arrange, adjust; level, point (*gun*) (*auf acc.* at); direct (*gegen* at); ♣ judge; execute; *zugrunde* ~ ruin, destroy; *in die Höhe* ~ raise, lift up; *sich* ~ *nach* conform to, act according to; take one's bearings from;

gr. agree with; depend on; *price:* be determined by; *ich richte mich nach Ihnen* I leave it to you.
'Richter m (-s/-) judge; **'2lich** adj. judicial; **'~spruch** m judg(e)ment, sentence.
'richtig 1. adj. right, correct, accurate; proper; true; just; *ein ~er Londoner* a regular cockney; **2.** adv.: ~ *gehen clock:* go right; **'2keit** f (-/no pl.) correctness; accuracy; justness; **'~stellen** v/t. (sep., -ge-, h) put *or* set right, rectify.
'Richt|linien f/pl. (general) directions pl., rules pl.; **'~preis** ♣ m standard price; **'~schnur** f ⊕ plumb-line; *fig.* rule (of conduct), guiding principle.
'Richtung f (-/-en) direction; course, way; *fig.* line; **~anzeiger** *mot.* ['riçtuŋs9-] m (-s/-) flashing indicator, trafficator; **2weisend** adj. directive, leading, guiding.
'Richtwaage ⊕ f level.
rieb [riːp] *pret. of reiben.*
riechen ['riːçən] (*irr.*, ge-, h) **1.** v/i. smell (*nach* of; *an dat.* at); sniff (*an dat.* at); **2.** v/t. smell; sniff.
rief [riːf] *pret. of rufen.*
riefeln ⊕ ['riːfəln] v/t. (ge-, h) flute, groove.
Riegel ['riːgəl] m (-s/-) bar, bolt; bar, cake (*of soap*); bar (*of chocolate*).
Riemen ['riːmən] m (-s/-) strap, thong; belt; ⚓ oar.
Ries [riːs] n (-es/-e) ream.
Riese ['riːzə] m (-n/-n) giant.
rieseln ['riːzəln] v/i. (ge-) **1.** (*sein*) *small stream:* purl, ripple; trickle; **2.** (h): *es rieselt* it drizzles.
ries|engroß adj. ['riːzən'-], **~enhaft** adj., **~ig** adj. gigantic, huge; **'2in** f (-/-nen) giantess.
riet [riːt] *pret. of raten.*
Riff [rif] n (-[e]s/-e) reef.
Rille ['rilə] f (-/-n) groove; ⊕ *a.* flute.
Rimesse ♣ [ri'mɛsə] f (-/-n) remittance.
Rind *zo.* [rint] n (-[e]s/-er) ox; cow; neat; ~*er pl.* (horned) cattle *pl.*; *zwanzig* ~*er* twenty head of cattle.
Rinde ['rində] f (-/-n) ♀ bark; rind (*of fruit, bacon, cheese*); crust (*of bread*).
'Rinder|braten m roast beef; **'~herde** f herd of cattle; **'~hirt** m cowherd, *Am.* cowboy.
'Rind|fleisch n beef; **'~(s)leder** n neat's-leather, cow-hide; **'~vieh** n (horned) cattle *pl.*, neat *pl.*
Ring [riŋ] m (-[e]s/-e) ring; circle; link (*of chain*); ♣ ring, pool, trust, *Am.* F combine; **'~bahn** f circular railway.
ringel|n ['riŋəln] v/refl. (ge-, h) curl, coil; **2natter** *zo.* f ringsnake.

ring|en ['riŋən] (*irr.*, ge-, h) **1.** *v/i.* wrestle; struggle (*um* for); *nach Atem* ~ gasp (for breath); **2.** *v/t.* wring (*hands, washing*); '⁰er *m* (-s/-) wrestler.

ring|förmig *adj.* ['riŋfœrmiç] annular, ring-like; '⁰kampf *m* sports: wrestling(-match); '⁰richter *m* boxing: referee.

rings *adv.* [riŋs] around; '⁀he'rum *adv.*, '⁀'um *adv.*, '⁀um'her *adv.* round about, all (a)round.

Rinn|e ['rinə] *f* (-/-n) groove, channel; gutter (*of roof or street*); gully; '⁰en *v/i.* (*irr.*, ge- , sein) run, flow; drip; leak; '⁀sal *n* ['⁀za:l] *n* (-[e]s/-e) watercourse, streamlet; '⁀stein *m* gutter; sink (*of kitchen unit*).

Rippe ['ripə] *f* (-/-n) rib; ⚠ groin; bar (*of chocolate*); '⁰n *v/t.* (ge-, h) rib; '⁀nfell *anat.* *n* pleura; '⁀nfell-entzündung ⚕ *f* pleurisy; '⁀n-stoß *m* dig in the ribs; nudge.

Risiko ['ri:ziko] *n* (-s/-s, *Risiken*) risk; *ein* ~ *eingehen* take a risk.

risk|ant *adj.* [ris'kant] risky; '⁀ieren *v/t.* (*no* -ge-, h) risk.

Riß [ris] **1.** *m* (*Risses/Risse*) rent, tear; split (*a. fig.*); crack; *in skin:* chap; scratch; ⊕ draft, plan; *fig.* rupture; **2.** ⁰ *pret. of reißen*.

rissig *adj.* ['risiç] full of rents; *skin, etc.:* chappy; ~ *werden* crack.

Rist [rist] *m* (-es/-e) instep; back of the hand; wrist.

Ritt [rit] **1.** *m* (-[e]s/-e) ride; **2.** ⁰ *pret. of reiten*.

'**Ritter** *m* (-s/-) knight; *zum* ~ *schlagen* knight; '⁀gut *n* manor; '⁰lich *adj.* knightly, chivalrous; '⁀lich-keit *f* (-/-en) gallantry, chivalry.

rittlings *adv.* ['ritliŋs] astride (*auf e-m Pferd* a horse).

Ritz [rits] *m* (-es/-e) crack, chink; scratch; '⁀e *f* (-/-n) crack, chink; fissure; '⁰en *v/t.* (ge-, h) scratch; cut.

Rival|e [ri'va:lə] *m* (-n/-n), '⁀in *f* (-/-nen) rival; '⁰isieren [⁀ali'zi:rən] *v/i.* (*no* -ge-, h) rival (*mit j-m* s.o.); '⁀ität [⁀ali'tε:t] *f* (-/-en) rivalry.

Rizinusöl ['ri:tsinusʔ-] *n* (-[e]s/*no pl.*) castor oil.

Robbe *zo.* ['rɔbə] *f* (-/-n) seal.

Robe ['ro:bə] *f* (-/-n) gown; robe.

Roboter ['rɔbɔtər] *m* (-s/-) robot.

robust *adj.* [ro'bust] robust, sturdy, vigorous.

roch [rɔx] *pret. of riechen.*

röcheln ['rœçəln] (ge-, h) **1.** *v/i.* rattle; **2.** *v/t.* gasp out (*words*).

Rock [rɔk] *m* (-[e]s/⁀e) skirt; coat; jacket; '⁀schoß *m* coat-tail.

Rodel|bahn ['ro:dəl-] *f* toboggan-run; '⁰n *v/i.* (ge-, h, sein) toboggan, *Am. a.* coast; '⁀schlitten *m* sled(ge), toboggan.

roden ['ro:dən] *v/t.* (ge-, h) clear (*land*); root up, stub (*roots*).

Rogen *ichth.* ['ro:gən] *m* (-s/-) roe, spawn.

Roggen ♦ ['rɔgən] *m* (-s/-) rye.

roh *adj.* [ro:] raw; *fig.:* rough, rude; cruel, brutal; *oil, metal:* crude; '⁰bau *m* (-[e]s/-ten) rough brickwork; '⁰eisen *n* pig-iron.

Roheit ['ro:hart] *f* (-/-en) rawness; roughness (*a. fig.*); *fig.:* rudeness; brutality.

'**Roh|ling** *m* (-s/-e) brute, ruffian; '⁀material *n* raw material; '⁀produkt *n* raw product.

Rohr [ro:r] *n* (-[e]s/-e) tube, pipe; duct; ♦: reed; cane.

Röhre ['rø:rə] *f* (-/-n) tube, pipe; duct; *radio:* valve, *Am.* (electron) tube.

'**Rohr|leger** *m* (-s/-) pipe fitter, plumber; '⁀leitung *f* plumbing, pipeline; '⁀post *f* pneumatic dispatch *or* tube; '⁀stock *m* cane; '⁀zucker *m* cane-sugar.

'**Rohstoff** *m* raw material.

Rolladen ['rɔlla:dən] *m* (-s/⁼, -) rolling shutter.

'**Rollbahn** ✈ *f* taxiway, taxi-strip.

Rolle ['rɔlə] *f* (-/-n) roll; roller; coil (*of rope, etc.*); pulley; *beneath furniture:* cast|or, -er; mangle; *thea.* part, role; *fig.* figure; ~ *Garn* reel of cotton, *Am.* spool of thread; *das spielt keine* ~ that doesn't matter, it makes no difference; *Geld spielt keine* ~ money (is) no object; *aus der* ~ *fallen* forget o.s.

'**rollen** (ge-) **1.** *v/i.* (sein) roll; ✈ taxi; **2.** *v/t.* (h) roll; wheel; mangle (*laundry*).

'**Rollenbesetzung** *thea.* *f* cast.

'**Roller** *m* (-s/-) *children's toy:* scooter; *mot.* (motor) scooter.

'**Roll|feld** ✈ *n* manœuvring area, *Am.* maneuvering area; '⁀film *phot.* *m* roll film; '⁀kragen *m* turtle neck; '⁀schrank *m* roll-fronted cabinet; '⁀schuh *m* roller-skate; '⁀schuhbahn *f* roller-skating rink; '⁀stuhl *m* wheel chair; '⁀treppe *f* escalator; '⁀wagen *m* lorry, truck.

Roman [ro'ma:n] *m* (-s/-e) novel, (work of) fiction; *novel of adventure and fig.:* romance; '⁀ist [⁀a'nist] *m* (-en/-en) Romance scholar *or* student; '⁀schriftsteller *m* novelist.

Romanti|k [ro'mantik] *f* (-/*no pl.*) romanticism; ⁰sch *adj.* romantic.

Röm|er ['rø:mər] *m* (-s/-) Roman; '⁰isch *adj.* Roman.

röntgen ['rœntgən] *v/t.* (ge-, h) X-ray; '⁰aufnahme *f*, '⁰bild *n* X-ray; '⁰strahlen *m/pl.* X-rays *pl.*

rosa *adj.* ['ro:za] pink.

Rose ['ro:zə] *f* (-/-n) ♦ rose; ⚕ erysipelas.

'**Rosen|kohl** ♦ *m* Brussels sprouts *pl.*; '⁀kranz *eccl.* *m* rosary; '⁰rot *adj.* rose-colo(u)red, rosy; '~stock & *m* (-[e]s/~e) rose-bush.

'rosig *adj.* rosy (*a. fig.*), rose-colo(u)red, roseate.

Rosine [ro'zi:nə] *f* (-/-n) raisin.

Roß *zo.* [rɔs] *n* (*Rosses/Rosse*, F *Rösser*) horse, *poet.* steed; '~haar *n* horsehair.

Rost [rɔst] *m* 1. (-es/*no pl.*) rust; 2. (-es/-e) grate; gridiron; grill; '~braten *m* roast joint.

'rosten *v/i.* (ge-, h, sein) rust.

rösten ['rœstən] *v/t.* (ge-, h) roast, grill; toast (*bread*); fry (*potatoes*).

'Rost|fleck *m* rust-stain; *in cloth:* iron-mo(u)ld; 'Qfrei *adj.* rustless, rustproof; *esp. steel:* stainless; 'Qig *adj.* rusty, corroded.

rot [ro:t] 1. *adj.* red; 2. Q *n* (-s/-, F -s) red.

Rotationsmaschine *typ.* [rota-'tsjo:ns-] *f* rotary printing machine.

'rot|backig *adj.* ruddy; '~blond *adj.* sandy.

Röte ['rø:tə] *f* (-/*no pl.*) redness, red (colo[u]r); blush; 'Qn *v/t.* (ge-, h) redden; paint or dye red; *sich* ~ redden; flush, blush.

'rot|gelb *adj.* reddish yellow; '~glühend *adj.* red-hot; 'Qhaut *f* red-skin.

rotieren [ro'ti:rən] *v/i.* (*no* -ge-, h) rotate, revolve.

Rot|käppchen ['ro:tkɛpçən] *n* (-s/-) Little Red Riding Hood; '~kehlchen *orn.* *n* (-s/-) robin (redbreast).

rötlich *adj.* ['rø:tliç] reddish.

'Rot|stift *m* red crayon or pencil; '~tanne & *f* spruce (fir).

Rotte ['rɔtə] *f* (-/-n) band, gang.

'Rot|wein *m* red wine; claret; '~wild *zo.* *n* red deer.

Rouleau [ru'lo:] *n* (-s/-s) *s.* Rollladen; blind, *Am.* (window) shade.

Route ['ru:tə] *f* (-/-n) route.

Routine [ru'ti:nə] *f* (-/*no pl.*) routine, practice.

Rübe & ['ry:bə] *f* (-/-n) beet; *weiße* ~ (Swedish) turnip, *Am. a.* rutabaga; *rote* ~ red beet, beet(root); *gelbe* ~ carrot.

Rubin [ru'bi:n] *m* (-s/-e) ruby.

ruch|bar *adj.* ['ru:xba:r]: ~ *werden* become known, get about or abroad; '~los *adj.* wicked, profligate.

Ruck [ruk] *m* (-[e]s/-e) jerk, *Am.* F yank; jolt (*of vehicle*).

Rück|antwort ['ryk?-] *f* reply; *Postkarte mit* ~ reply postcard; *mit bezahlter* ~ *telegram:* reply paid; 'Qbezüglich *gr. adj.* reflexive; '~blick *m* retrospect(ive view) (*auf acc.* at); reminiscences *pl.*

rücken[1] ['rykən] (ge-) 1. *v/t.* (h) move, shift; 2. *v/i.* (sein) move; *näher* ~ near, approach.

Rücken[2] [~] *m* (-s/-) back; ridge (*of mountain*); '~deckung *fig. f* backing, support; '~lehne *f* back

(*of chair, etc.*); '~mark *anat. n* spinal cord; '~schmerzen *m/pl.* pain in the back, back ache; '~schwimmen *n* (-s/*no pl.*) back-stroke swimming; '~wind *m* following or tail wind; '~wirbel *anat. m* dorsal vertebra.

Rück|erstattung ['ryk?-] *f* restitution; refund (*of money*), reimbursement (*of expenses*); '~fahrkarte *f* return (ticket), *Am. a.* round-trip ticket; '~fahrt *f* return journey or voyage; *auf der* ~ on the way back; '~fall *m* relapse; 'Qfällig *adj.:* ~ *werden* relapse; '~flug *m* return flight; '~frage *f* further inquiry; '~gabe *f* return, restitution; '~gang *fig. m* retrogression; † recession, decline; 'Qgängig *adj.* retrograde; ~ *machen* cancel; '~grat *anat. n* (-[e]s/-e) spine, backbone (*both a. fig.*); '~halt *m* support; 'Qhaltlos *adj.* unreserved, frank; '~hand *f* (-/*no pl.*) *tennis:* backhand (stroke); '~kauf *m* repurchase; '~kehr ['~ke:r] *f* (-/*no pl.*) return; '~kopp(e)lung *f f* (-/-en) feedback; '~lage *f* reserve(s *pl.*); savings *pl.*; Qläufig *fig. adj.* ['~lɔyfiç] retrograde; '~licht *mot. n* tail-light, tail-lamp, rear-light; 'Qlings *adv.* backwards; from behind; '~marsch *m* march back or home; retreat; '~porto & *n* return postage; '~reise *f* return journey, journey back or home.

'Rucksack *m* knapsack, ruck-sack.

'Rück|schlag *m* backstroke; *fig.* setback; '~schluß *m* conclusion, inference; '~schritt *fig. m* retrogression, set-back; *pol.* reaction; '~seite *f* back, reverse; *a.* tail (*of coin*); '~sendung *f* return; '~sicht *f* respect, regard, consideration (*auf j-n* for s.o.); 'Qsichtslos *adj.* inconsiderate (*gegen of*), regardless (of); ruthless; reckless; ~es *Fahren mot.* reckless driving; 'Qsichtsvoll *adj.* regardful (*gegen of*); considerate, thoughtful; '~sitz *mot. m* back-seat; '~spiegel *mot. m* rearview mirror; '~spiel *n sports:* return match; '~sprache *f* consultation; ~ *nehmen mit* consult (*lawyer*), consult with (*fellow workers*); nach ~ *mit* on consultation with; '~stand *m* arrears *pl.*; backlog; *f*, residue; *im* ~ *sein mit* be in arrears or behind with; 'Qständig *fig. adj.* old-fashioned, backward; ~e *Miete* arrears of rent; '~stoß *m* recoil; kick (*of gun*); '~strahler *m* (-s/-) rear reflector, cat's eye; '~tritt *m* withdrawal, retreat; resignation; '~tritt-bremse *f* back-pedal brake, *Am.* coaster brake; '~versicherung *f* reinsurance; Qwärts *adv.* ['~vɛrts] back, backward(s); '~wärtsgang *mot.* m reverse (gear); '**~weg** m way back, return.

'**ruckweise** *adv.* by jerks.

'**rück|wirkend** *adj.* reacting; $\frac{z_{1}}{z_{2}}$, *etc.*: retroactive, retrospective; '2**wirkung** f reaction; '2**zahlung** f repayment; '2**zug** m retreat.

Rüde ['ry:də] 1. *zo.* m (-n/-n) male dog *or* fox *or* wolf; large hound; 2. 2 *adj.* rude, coarse, brutal.

Rudel ['ru:dəl] n (-s/-) troop; pack (*of wolves*); herd (*of deer*).

Ruder ['ru:dər] n (-s/-) oar; rudder (*a.* $\nleftarrow$); helm; '**~boot** n row(ing)-boat; '**~er** m (-s/-) rower, oarsman; '**~fahrt** f row; '2**n** (ge-) 1. *v/i.* (h, sein) row; 2. *v/t.* (h) row; **~regatta** ['~regata] f (-/*Ruderregatten*) boat race, regatta; '**~sport** m rowing.

Ruf [ru:f] m (-[e]s/-e) call; cry, shout; summons, *univ.* call; reputation, repute; fame; standing, credit; '2**en** (*irr.*, ge-, h) 1. *v/i.* call; cry, shout; 2. *v/t.* call: *lassen* send for.

'**Ruf|name** m Christian *or* first name; '**~nummer** f telephone number; '**~weite** f (-/*no pl.*): in ~ within call *or* earshot.

Rüge ['ry:gə] f (-/-n) rebuke, censure, reprimand; '2**n** *v/t.* (ge-, h) rebuke, censure, blame.

Ruhe ['ru:ə] f (-/*no pl.*) rest, repose; sleep; quiet, calm; tranquillity; silence; peace; composure; *sich zur* ~ *setzen* retire; ~*l* quiet!, silence!; *immer mit der* ~*l* take it easy!; *lassen Sie mich in* ~*l* let me alone!; '2**bedürftig** *adj.*: ~ *sein* want *or* need rest; '**~gehalt** n pension; '2**los** *adj.* restless; '2**n** *v/i.* (ge-, h) rest, repose; sleep; *laß die Vergangenheit* ~*l* let bygones be bygones!; '**~pause** f pause; lull; '**~platz** m resting-place; '**~stand** m (-[e]s/*no pl.*) retirement; *im* ~ retired; *in den* ~ *treten* retire; *in den* ~ *versetzen* superannuate, pension off, retire; '**~stätte** f: *letzte* ~ last resting-place; '**~störer** m (-s/-) disturber of the peace, peacebreaker; '**~störung** f disturbance (of the peace), disorderly behavio(u)r, riot.

'**ruhig** *adj.* quiet; *mind, water*: tranquil, calm; silent; ⊕ smooth.

Ruhm [ru:m] m (-[e]s/*no pl.*) glory; fame, renown.

rühm|en ['ry:mən] *v/t.* (ge-, h) praise, glorify; *sich e-r Sache* ~ boast of s.th.; '**~lich** *adj.* glorious, laudable.

'**ruhm|los** *adj.* inglorious; '**~reich** *adj.* glorious.

Ruhr ⚕ [ru:r] f (-/*no pl.*) dysentery.

Rühr|ei ['ry:r⁹-] n scrambled egg; '2**en** (ge-, h) 1. *v/t.* stir, move; *fig.* touch, move, affect; *sich* ~ stir, move, bustle; 2. *v/i.*: *an et.* ~ touch s.th.; *wir wollen nicht daran* ~ let sleeping dogs lie; '2**end**

adj. touching, moving; '2**ig** *adj.* active, busy; enterprising; nimble; '2**selig** *adj.* sentimental; '**~ung** f (-/*no pl.*) emotion, feeling.

Ruin [ru'i:n] m (-s/*no pl.*) ruin; decay; **~e** f (-/-n) ruin(s *pl.*); *fig.* ruin, wreck; 2**ieren** [rui'ni:rən] *v/t.* (*no -ge-*, h) ruin; destroy, wreck; spoil; *sich* ~ ruin o.s.

rülpsen ['rylpsən] *v/i.* (ge-, h) belch.

Rumän|e [ru'mɛ:nə] m (-n/-n) Ro(u)manian; 2**isch** *adj.* Ro(u)manian.

Rummel f ['ruməl] m (-s/*no pl.*) hurly-burly, row; bustle; revel; *in publicity* f ballyhoo; '**~platz** m fun fair, amusement park.

rumoren [ru'mo:rən] *v/i.* (*no -ge-*, h) make a noise *or* row; *bowels*: rumble

Rumpel|kammer f ['rumpəl-] f lumber-room; '2**n** f *v/i.* (ge-, h, sein) rumble.

Rumpf [rumpf] m (-[e]s/¨e) *anat.* trunk, body; torso (*of statue*); ⚓ hull, frame, body; ✈ fuselage, body.

rümpfen ['rympfən] *v/t.* (ge-, h): *die Nase* ~ turn up one's nose, sniff (*über acc. at*).

rund [runt] 1. *adj.* round (*a. fig.*); circular; 2. *adv.* about; '2**blick** m panorama, view all (a)round; 2**e** ['rundə] f (-/-n) round; *sports*: lap; *boxing* round; round, patrol; beat (*of policeman*); *in der or die* ~ (a)round; **~en** ['~dən] *v/refl.* (ge-, h) (grow) round; '2**fahrt** f drive round (*town, etc.*); *s. Rundreise*; '2**flug** m circuit (*über of*); '2**frage** f inquiry, poll.

'**Rundfunk** m broadcast(ing); broadcasting service; broadcasting company; radio, wireless; *im* ~ over the wireless, on the radio *or* air; '**~anstalt** f broadcasting company; '**~ansager** m (radio) announcer; '**~gerät** n radio *or* wireless set; '**~gesellschaft** f broadcasting company; '**~hörer** m listener(-in); ~ *pl. a.* (radio) audience; '**~programm** n broadcast *or* radio program(me); '**~sender** m broadcast transmitter; broadcasting *or* radio station; '**~sendung** f broadcast; '**~sprecher** m broadcaster, broadcast speaker, (radio) announcer; '2**station** f broadcasting *or* radio station; '**~übertragung** f radio transmission, broadcast(ing); broadcast (*of programme*).

'**Rund|gang** m tour, round, circuit; '**~gesang** m glee, catch; '2**he'raus** *adv.* in plain words, frankly, plainly; '2**he'rum** *adv.* round about, all (a)round; '2**lich** *adj.* roundish; rotund, plump; '**~reise** f circular tour *or* trip, sight-seeing trip, *Am. a.* round trip; '**~schau** f panorama;

newspaper: review; '**~schreiben** n circular (letter); '**²weg** adv. flatly, plainly.

Runz|el ['runtsəl] f (-/-n) wrinkle; '**²elig** adj. wrinkled; '**²eln** v/t. (ge-, h) wrinkle; *die Stirn ~ knit one's brows, frown;* '**²lig** adj. wrinkled.

Rüpel ['ry:pəl] m (-s/-) boor, lout; '**²haft** adj. coarse, boorish, rude.

rupfen ['rupfən] v/t. (ge-, h) pull up *or* out, pick; pluck *(fowl)* (a. fig.).

ruppig adj. ['rupiç] ragged, shabby; fig. rude.

Rüsche ['ry:ʃə] f (-/-n) ruffle, frill.

Ruß [ru:s] m (-es/no pl.) soot.

Russe ['rusə] m (-n/-n) Russian.

Rüssel ['rysəl] m (-s/-) trunk *(of elefant)*; snout *(of pig).*

'**ruß|en** v/i. (ge-, h) smoke; '**~ig** adj. sooty.

'**russisch** adj. Russian.

---

rüsten ['rystən] (ge-, h) **1.** v/t. *and* v/refl. prepare, get ready (*zu* for); **2.** esp. ✗ v/i. arm.

rüstig adj. ['rystiç] vigorous, strong; '**²keit** f (-/no pl.) vigo(u)r.

'**Rüstung** f (-/-en) preparations pl.; ✗ arming, armament; armo(u)r; **~sindustrie** ['rystuŋs²-] f armament industry.

'**Rüstzeug** n (set of) tools pl., implements pl.; fig. equipment.

Rute ['ru:tə] f (-/-n) rod; switch; *fox's tail:* brush.

Rutsch [rutʃ] m (-es/-e) (land)slide; F short trip; '**~bahn** f, **~e** f (-/-n) slide, chute; '**²en** v/i. (ge-, sein) glide, slide; slip; *vehicle:* skid; '**²ig** adj. slippery.

rütteln ['rytəln] (ge-, h) **1.** v/t. shake, jog; jolt; **2.** v/i. shake, jog; *car:* jolt; *an der Tür ~ rattle at the door; daran ist nicht zu ~ that's a fact.*

S

Saal [za:l] m (-[e]s/Säle) hall.

Saat [za:t] f (-/-en) sowing; standing *or* growing crops pl.; seed (a. fig.); '**~feld** n cornfield; '**~gut** n (-[e]s/no pl.) seeds pl.; '**~kartoffel** f seed-potato.

Sabbat ['zabat] m (-s/-e) Sabbath.

sabbern ['zabərn] v/i. (ge-, h) slaver, slobber, *Am. a.* drool; twaddle, *Am. sl. a.* drool.

Säbel ['zɛ:bəl] m (-s/-) sab|re, *Am.* -er; *mit dem ~ rasseln pol.* rattle the sabre; '**~beine** n/pl. bandy legs pl.; '**²beinig** adj. bandy-legged; '**~hieb** m sabre-cut; '**²n** F fig. v/t. (ge-, h) hack.

Sabot|age [zabo'ta:ʒə] f (-/-n) sabotage; **~eur** [~ø:r] m (-s/-e) saboteur; **²ieren** v/t. (no -ge-, h) sabotage.

Sach|bearbeiter ['zax-] m (-s/-) official in charge; *social work:* case worker; '**~beschädigung** f damage to property; '**²dienlich** adj. relevant, pertinent; useful, helpful.

'**Sache** f (-/-n) thing; affair, matter, concern; ✗ case; point; issue; **~n** pl. things pl.; *beschlossene ~* foregone conclusion; *e-e ~ für sich a matter apart; (nicht) zur ~ gehörig* (ir)relevant, pred. a. to (off) the point; *bei der ~ bleiben* stick to the point; *gemeinsame ~ machen mit* make common cause with.

'**sach|gemäß** adj. appropriate, proper; '**²kenntnis** f expert knowledge; '**~kundig** adj. s. sachverständig; '**²lage** f state of affairs, situation; '**~lich 1.** adj. relevant,

pertinent, pred. a. to the point; matter-of-fact, business-like; unbias(s)ed; objective; **2.** adv.: *~ einwandfrei od. richtig* factually correct.

sächlich gr. adj. ['zɛçliç] neuter.

'**Sachlichkeit** f (-/no pl.) objectivity; impartiality; matter-of-factness.

'**Sach|register** n (subject) index; '**~schaden** m damage to property.

Sachse ['zaksə] m (-n/-n) Saxon.

sächsisch adj. ['zɛksiʃ] Saxon.

sacht adj. [zaxt] soft, gentle; slow.

Sach|verhalt ['zaxfɛrhalt] m (-[e]s/-e) facts pl. (of the case); '**²verständig** adj. expert; '**~verständige** m (-n/-n) expert, authority; ⅔ expert witness; '**~wert** m real value.

Sack [zak] m (-[e]s/²e) sack; bag; *mit ~ und Pack* with bag and baggage; '**~gasse** f blind alley, cul-de-sac, impasse (a. fig.), Am. a. dead end (a. fig.); fig. deadlock; '**~leinwand** f sackcloth.

Sadis|mus [za'dismus] m (-/no pl.) sadism; **~t** m (-en/-en) sadist; **²tisch** adj. sadistic.

säen ['zɛ:ən] v/t. *and* v/i. (ge-, h) sow (a. fig.).

Saffian ['zafja:n] m (-s/no pl.) morocco.

Saft [zaft] m (-[e]s/²e) juice *(of vegetables or fruits)*; sap *(of plants)* (a. fig.); '**²ig** adj. fruits, etc.: juicy; meadow, etc.: lush; *plants:* sappy (a. fig.); joke, etc.: spicy, coarse; '**²los** adj. juiceless; sapless (a. fig.).

Sage ['za:gə] f (-/-n) legend, myth; *die ~ geht* the story goes.

Säge ['zɛːgə] *f* (-/-n) saw; **∼blatt** *n* saw-blade; **∼bock** *m* saw-horse, *Am. a.* sawbuck; **∼fisch** *ichth. m* sawfish; **∼mehl** *n* sawdust.

sagen ['zaːgən] (ge-, h) **1.** *v/t.* say; *j-m et.* ∼ tell s.o. s.th., say s.th. to s.o.; *j-m* ∼ *lassen,* daß send s.o. word that; *er läßt sich nichts* ∼ he will not listen to reason; *das hat nichts zu* ∼ that doesn't matter; *j-m gute Nacht* ∼ bid s.o. good night; **2.** *v/i.* say; *es ist nicht zu* ∼ it is incredible *or* fantastic; *wenn ich so* ∼ *darf* if I may express myself in these terms; *sage und schreibe* believe it or not; no less than, as much as.

'sägen *v/t. and v/i.* (ge-, h) saw.

'sagenhaft *adj.* legendary, mythical; F *fig.* fabulous, incredible.

Säge|späne ['zɛːgəʃpɛːnə] *m/pl.* sawdust; **∼werk** *n* sawmill.

sah [zaː] *pret. of* sehen.

Sahne ['zaːnə] *f* (-/no *pl.*) cream.

Saison [zɛˈzõ:] *f* (-/-s) season; 2**bedingt** *adj* seasonal.

Saite ['zaɪtə] *f* (-/-n) string, chord (a. *fig.*), **∼ninstrument** ['zaɪtɛn⁹-] *n* stringed instrument.

Sakko ['zako] *m, n* (-s/-s) lounge coat; **∼anzug** *m* lounge suit.

Sakristei [zakrisˈtaɪ] *f* (-/-en) sacristy, vestry.

Salat [zaˈlaːt] *m* (-[e]s/-e) salad; ⚘ lettuce.

Salb|e ['zalbə] *f* (-/-n) ointment; 2**en** *v/t* (ge-, h) rub with ointment; anoint; **∼ung** *f* (-/-en) anointing, unction (a. *fig.*); 2**ungsvoll** *fig. adj.* unctuous.

saldieren ✝ [zalˈdiːrən] *v/t.* (no -ge-, h) balance, settle.

Saldo ✝ ['zaldo] *m* (-s/Salden, Saldos, Saldi) balance; *den* ∼ *ziehen* strike the balance; **∼vortrag** ✝ *m* balance carried down.

Saline [zaˈliːnə] *f* (-/-n) salt-pit, salt-works.

Salmiak 🜍 [zalˈmjak] *m, n* (-s/no *pl.*) sal-ammoniac, ammonium chloride; **∼geist** *m* (-es/no *pl.*) liquid ammonia.

Salon [zaˈlõ:] *m* (-s/-s) drawing-room, *Am. a.* parlor; ⚓ saloon; 2**fähig** *adj.* presentable; 2**löwe** *fig. m* lady's man, carpet-knight; **∼wagen** 🚂 *m* salooncar, saloon carriage, *Am.* parlor car.

Salpeter 🜍 [zalˈpeːtər] *m* (-s/no *pl.*) saltpet|re *Am.* -er; nit|re, *Am.* -er.

Salto ['zalto] *m* (-s/-s, Salti) somersault; ∼ *mortale* break-neck leap; *e-n* ∼ *schlagen* turn a somersault.

Salut [zaˈluːt] *m* (-[e]s/-e) salute; ∼ *schießen* fire a salute; ∼ **ieren** [∼uˈtiːrən] *v/i.* (no -ge-, h) (stand at the) salute.

Salve ['zalvə] *f* (-/-n) volley; ⚓ broadside; salute.

Salz [zalts] *n* (-es/-e) salt; **∼bergwerk** *n* salt-mine; 2**en** *v/t.* (irr.) ge-, h) salt; **∼faß** *n,* **∼fäßchen** ['∼fɛsçən] *n* (-s/-) salt-cellar; **∼gurke** *f* pickled cucumber; 2**haltig** *adj.* saline, saliferous; **∼hering** *m* pickled herring; 2**ig** *adj.* salt(y); *s.* salzhaltig; **∼säure** 🜍 *f* hydrochloric *or* muriatic acid; **∼wasser** *n* (-s/⸚) salt water, brine; **∼werk** *n* salt-works, saltern.

Same ['zaːmə] *m* (-ns/-n), **∼n** *m* (-s/-) ⚘ seed (a. *fig.*); *biol.* sperm, semen; **∼nkorn** 🜍 *n* grain of seed.

Sammel|büchse ['zaməl-] *f* collecting-box; **∼lager** *n* collecting point; *refugees, etc.:* assembly camp; 2**n** (ge-, h) **1.** *v/t.* gather; collect (*stamps, etc.*); *sich* ∼ gather; *fig.:* concentrate; compose o.s.; **2.** *v/i.* collect money (*für for*) **∼platz** *m* meeting-place, place of appointment; ⚔, ⚓ rendezvous.

Samml|er ['zamlər] *m* (-s/-) collector; **∼ung** *f* **1.** (-/-en) collection; **2.** *fig.* (-/no *pl.*) composure; concentration.

Samstag ['zams-] *m* Saturday.

samt¹ [zamt] **1.** *adv.:* ∼ *und sonders* one and all; **2.** *prp.* (*dat.*) together *or* along with.

Samt² [∼] *m* (-[e]s/-e) velvet.

sämtlich ['zɛmtlɪç] **1.** *adj.* all (together); complete; **2.** *adv.* all (together *or* of them).

Sanatorium [zanaˈtoːrjum] *n* (-s/ Sanatorien) sanatorium, *Am. a.* sanitarium.

Sand [zant] *m* (-[e]s/-e) sand; *j-m* ∼ *in die Augen streuen* throw dust into s.o.'s eyes; *im* ∼ *verlaufen* end in smoke, come to nothing.

Sandale [zanˈdaːlə] *f* (-/-n) sandal.

'Sand|bahn *f sports:* dirt-track; **∼bank** *f* sandbank; **∼boden** *m* sandy soil; **∼grube** *f* sand-pit; 2**ig** *adj.* ['∼dɪç] sandy; **∼korn** *n* grain of sand; **∼mann** *fig. m* (-[e]s/no *pl.*) sandman, dustman; **∼papier** *n* sandpaper; **∼sack** *m* sand-bag; **∼stein** *m* sandstone.

sandte ['zantə] *pret. of* senden.

'Sand|torte *f* Madeira cake; **∼uhr** *f* sand-glass; **∼wüste** *f* sandy desert.

sanft [zanft] *adj.* soft; gentle, mild; smooth; *slope, death, etc.:* easy; ∼*er Zwang* non-violent coercion; *mit* ∼*er Stimme* softly, gently; **∼mütig** *adj.* ['∼myːtɪç] gentle, mild; meek.

sang [zaŋ] *pret. of* singen.

Sänger ['zɛŋər] *m* (-s/-) singer.

Sanguini|ker [zaŋguˈiːnikər] *m* (-s/-) sanguine person; 2**sch** *adj.* sanguine.

sanier|en [zaˈniːrən] *v/t.* (no -ge-, h) improve the sanitary conditions of; *esp.* ✝: reorganize; readjust; 2**ung** *f* (-/-en) sanitation; *esp.* ✝: reorganization; readjustment.

sanitär adj. [zani'tɛːr] sanitary.

Sanität|er [zani'tɛːtər] m (-s/-) ambulance man; ✗ medical orderly.

sank [zaŋk] pret. of sinken.

Sankt [zaŋkt] Saint, St.

sann [zan] pret. of sinnen.

Sard|elle ichth. [zar'dɛlə] f (-/-n) anchovy; **~ine** ichth. [~'iːnə] f (-/-n) sardine.

Sarg [zark] m (-[e]s/ː̈e) coffin, Am. a. casket; **~deckel** m coffin-lid.

Sarkas|mus [zar'kasmus] m (-/ Sarkasmen) sarcasm; **2tisch** adj. [~tiʃ] sarcastic.

saß [zaːs] pret. of sitzen.

Satan ['zaːtan] m (-s/-e) Satan; fig. devil; **2isch** fig. adj. [za'taːniʃ] satanic.

Satellit ast., pol. [zate'liːt] m (-en/-en) satellite; **~enstaat** pol. m satellite state.

Satin [sa'tɛ̃ː] m (-s/-s) satin; sateen.

Satir|e [za'tiːrə] f (-/-n) satire; **~iker** [~ikər] m (-s/-) satirist; **2isch** adj. [~iʃ] satiric(al).

satt adj. [zat] satisfied, satiated, full; colour: deep, rich; sich ~ essen eat one's fill; ich bin ~ I have had enough; F et. ~ haben be tired or sick of s.th., sl. be fed up with s.th.

Sattel ['zatəl] m (-s/ː̈) saddle; **~gurt** m girth; **2n** v/t. (ge-, h) saddle.

'Sattheit f (-/no pl.) satiety, fullness; richness, intensity (of colours).

sättig|en ['zɛtigən] (ge-, h) 1. v/t. satisfy, satiate; ✎, phys. saturate; 2. v/i. food: be substantial; **2ung** f (-/-en) satiation; ✎, fig. saturation.

Sattler ['zatlər] m (-s/-) saddler; **~ei** [~'rai] f (-/-en) saddlery.

'sattsam adv. sufficiently.

Satz [zats] m (-es/ː̈e) gr. sentence, clause; phls. maxim; ♪ proposition, theorem; ♪ movement; tennis, etc.: set; typ. setting, composition; sediment, dregs pl., grounds pl.; rate (of prices, etc.); set (of stamps, tools, etc.); leap, bound.

'Satzung f (-/-en) statute, by-law; **2sgemäß** adj. statutory.

'Satzzeichen gr. n punctuation mark.

Sau [zau] f 1. (-/ː̈e) zo. sow; fig. contp. filthy swine; 2. hunt. (-/-en) wild sow.

sauber adj. ['zaubər] clean; neat (a. fig.), tidy; attitude: decent; iro. fine, nice; **2keit** f (-/no pl.) clean-(li)ness; tidiness, neatness; decency (of attitude).

säuber|n ['zɔybərn] v/t. (ge-, h) clean(se); tidy, clean up (room, etc.); clear (von of); purge (of, from) (a. fig., pol.); **2ungsaktion** pol. f purge.

sauer ['zauər] 1. adj. sour (a. fig.), acid (a. ✎); cucumber: pickled; task, etc.: hard, painful; fig. morose,

surly; 2. adv.: ~ reagieren auf et. take s.th. in bad part.

säuer|lich adj. ['zɔyərliç] sourish, acidulous; **~n** v/t. (ge-, h) (make) sour, acidify (a. ✎); leaven (dough).

'Sauer|stoff ✎ m (-[e]s/no pl.) oxygen; **~teig** m leaven.

saufen ['zaufən] v/t. and v/i. (irr., ge-, h) animals: drink; F p. sl. soak, lush.

Säufer F ['zɔyfər] m (-s/-) sot, sl. soak.

saugen ['zaugən] ([irr.,] ge-, h) 1. v/i. suck (an et. s.th.); 2. v/t. suck.

säuge|n ['zɔygən] v/t. (ge-, h) suckle, nurse; **2tier** n mammal.

Säugling ['zɔyklin] m (-s/-e) baby, suckling; **~sheim** n baby-farm, baby-nursery.

'Saug|papier n absorbent paper; **~pumpe** f suction-pump; **~wirkung** f suction-effect.

Säule ['zɔylə] f (-/-n) ✎, anat. column (a. of smoke, mercury, etc.); pillar, support (both a. fig.); **~ngang** m colonnade; **~nhalle** f pillared hall; portico.

Saum [zaum] m (-[e]s/ː̈e) seam, hem; border, edge.

säum|en ['zɔymən] v/t. (ge-, h) hem; border, edge; die Straßen ~ line the streets; **~ig** adj. payer: dilatory.

'Saum|pfad m mule-track; **~tier** n sumpter-mule.

Säure ['zɔyrə] f (-/-n) sourness; acidity (a. ♪ of stomach); ✎ acid.

Saure'gurkenzeit f silly or slack season.

säuseln ['zɔyzəln] (ge-, h) 1. v/i. leaves, wind: rustle, whisper; 2. v/t. p. say airily, purr.

sausen ['zauzən] v/i. (ge-) 1. (sein) F rush, dash; bullet, etc.: whiz(z), whistle; 2. (h) wind: whistle, sough.

'Saustall m pigsty; F fig. a. horrid mess.

Saxophon ♪ [zakso'foːn] n (-s/-e) saxophone.

Schab|e ['ʃaːbə] f (-/-n) zo. cockroach; ⊕ s. Schabeisen; **~efleisch** n scraped meat; **~eisen** ⊕ n scraper, shaving-tool; **~emesser** ⊕ n scraping-knife; **2en** v/t. (ge-, h) scrape (a. ⊕); grate, rasp; scratch; **~er** ⊕ m (-s/-) scraper.

Schabernack ['ʃaːbərnak] m (-[e]s/ -e) practical joke, hoax, prank.

schäbig adj. ['ʃɛːbiç] shabby (a. fig.), F seedy, Am. F a. dowdy, tacky; fig. mean.

Schablone [ʃa'bloːnə] f (-/-n) model, pattern; stencil; fig.: routine; cliché; **2nhaft** adj., **2nmäßig** adj. according to pattern; fig.: mechanical; attr. a. routine.

Schach [ʃax] n (-s/-s) chess; **~!** check!; ~ und matt! checkmate!;

matic art, *the* drama; '~steller *m* (-s/-) showman.

Scheck ✦ [ʃɛk] *m* (-s/-s) cheque, *Am.* check; '~buch *n*, '~heft *n* chequebook, *Am.* checkbook.

'**scheckig** *adj.* spotted; *horse*: piebald.

scheel [ʃeːl] **1.** *adj.* squint-eyed, cross-eyed; *fig.* jealous, envious; **2.** *adv.*: j-n ~ ansehen look askance at s.o.

Scheffel ['ʃɛfəl] *m* (-s/-) bushel; '~n *v/t.* (ge-, h) amass (*money*, *etc.*).

Scheibe ['ʃaɪbə] *f* (-/-n) disk, disc (*a. of sun, moon*); *esp. ast.* orb; slice (*of bread, etc.*); pane (*of window*); *shooting*: target; '~nhonig *m* honey in combs; '~nwischer *mot. m* (-s/-) wind-screen wiper, *Am.* windshield wiper.

Scheide ['ʃaɪdə] *f* (-/-n) *sword, etc.*: sheath, scabbard; border, boundary; '~münze *f* small coin; '2n (*irr.*, ge-) **1.** *v/t.* (h) separate; ⚛ analyse; ⚖ divorce; *sich* ~ *lassen von* ⚖ divorce (*one's husband or wife*); **2.** *v/i.* (sein) depart; part (*von* with); *aus dem Dienst* ~ retire from service; *aus dem Leben* ~ depart from this life; '~wand *f* partition; '~weg *fig. m* cross-roads *sg.*

'**Scheidung** *f* (-/-en) separation; ⚖ divorce; '~sgrund ⚖ *m* ground for divorce; '~sklage ⚖ *f* divorce-suit; *die* ~ *einreichen* file a petition for divorce.

Schein [ʃaɪn] *m* **1.** (-[e]s/*no pl.*) shine; *sun, lamp, etc.*: light; *fire*: blaze; *fig.* appearance; **2.** (-[e]s/-e) certificate; receipt; bill; (bank-) note; '2bar *adj.* seeming, apparent; '2en *v/i.* (*irr.*, ge-, h) shine; *fig.* seem, appear, look; '~grund *m* pretext, preten|ce, *Am.* -se; '2heilig *adj.* sanctimonious, hypocritical; '~tod ☠ *m* suspended animation; '2tot *adj.* in a state of suspended animation; '~werfer *m* (-s/-) reflector, projector; ⚔, ⚓, searchlight; *mot.* headlight; *thea.* spotlight.

Scheit [ʃaɪt] *n* (-[e]s/-e) log, billet.
Scheitel ['ʃaɪtəl] *m* (-s/-) crown *or* top of the head; *hair*: parting; summit, peak; *esp.* ⚛ vertex; '2n *v/t.* (ge-, h) part (*hair*).

Scheiterhaufen ['ʃaɪtər-] *m* (funeral) pile; stake.

'**scheitern** *v/i.* (ge-, sein) ⚓ run aground, be wrecked; *fig.* fail, miscarry.   [box on the ear.]

Schelle ['ʃɛlə] *f* (-/-n) (little) bell;⟩
'**Schellfisch** *ichth. m* (-/-) haddock.

Schelm [ʃɛlm] *m* (-[e]s/-e) rogue; '~enstreich *m* roguish trick; '2isch *adj.* roguish, arch.

Schelte ['ʃɛltə] *f* (-/-n) scolding; '2n (*irr.*, ge-, h) **1.** *v/t.* scold, rebuke; **2.** *v/i.* scold.

Schema ['ʃeːma] *n* (-s/-s, -ta, *Schemen*) scheme; model, pattern; arrangement; 2tisch *adj.* [ʃeˈmaːtiʃ] schematic.

Schemel ['ʃeːməl] *m* (-s/-) stool.
Schemen ['ʃeːmən] *m* (-s/-) phantom, shadow; '2haft *adj.* shadowy.

Schenke ['ʃɛŋkə] *f* (-/-n) public house, F pub; tavern, inn.

Schenkel ['ʃɛŋkəl] *m* (-s/-) *anat.* thigh; *anat.* shank; *triangle, etc.*: leg; ⚛ *angle*: side.

schenken ['ʃɛŋkən] *v/t.* (ge-, h) give; remit (*penalty, etc.*); j-m et. ~ give s.o. s.th., present s.o. with s.th., make s.o. a present of s.th.

'**Schenkung** ⚖ *f* (-/-en) donation; ~surkunde ⚖ ['ʃɛŋkuŋs?-] *f* deed of gift.

Scherbe ['ʃɛrbə] *f* (-/-n), '~n *m* (-s/-) (broken) piece, fragment.

Schere ['ʃeːrə] *f* (-/-n) (e-e a pair of) scissors *pl.*; *zo.* crab, *etc.*: claw; '2n *v/t.* **1.** (*irr.*, ge-, h) shear (*a. sheep*), clip; shave (*beard*); cut (*hair*); clip, prune (*hedge*); **2.** (ge-, h): *sich um et.* ~ trouble about s.th.; '~nschleifer *m* (-s/-) knife-grinder; ~rei [ˌ~ˈraɪ] *f* (-/-en) trouble, bother.

Scherz [ʃɛrts] *m* (-es/-e) jest, joke; ~ *beiseite* joking apart; *im* ~, *zum* ~ in jest *or* joke; ~ *treiben mit* make fun of; '2en *v/i.* (ge-, h) jest, joke; '2haft *adj.* joking, sportive.

scheu [ʃɔʏ] **1.** *adj.* shy, bashful, timid; *horse*: skittish; ~ *machen* frighten; **2.** 2 *f* (-/*no pl.*) shyness; timidity; aversion (*vor dat.* to).

scheuchen ['ʃɔʏçən] *v/t.* (ge-, h) scare, frighten (away).

'**scheuen** (ge-, h) **1.** *v/i.* shy (*vor dat.* at), take fright (at); **2.** *v/t.* shun, avoid; fear; *sich* ~ *vor* (*dat.*) shy at, be afraid of.

Scheuer|lappen ['ʃɔʏər-] *m* scouring-cloth, floor-cloth; '~leiste *f* skirting-board; '2n (ge-, h) **1.** *v/t.* scour, scrub; chafe; **2.** *v/i.* chafe.
'**Scheuklappe** *f* blinker, *Am. a.* blinder.

Scheune ['ʃɔʏnə] *f* (-/-n) barn.
Scheusal ['ʃɔʏzaːl] *n* (-[e]s/-e) monster.

scheußlich *adj.* ['ʃɔʏslɪç] hideous, atrocious (F *a. fig.*), abominable (F *a. fig.*); '2keit *f* **1.** (-/*no pl.*) hideousness; **2.** (-/-en) abomination; atrocity.

Schi [ʃiː] *m* (-s/-er) *etc. s.* Ski, *etc.*
Schicht [ʃɪçt] *f* (-/-en) layer; *geol.* stratum (*a. fig.*); *at work*: shift; (social) class, rank, walk of life; '2en *v/t.* (ge-, h) arrange *or* put in layers, pile up; classify; '2weise *adv.* in layers; *work*: in shifts.

Schick [ʃɪk] **1.** *m* (-[e]s/*no pl.*) chic, elegance, style; **2.** 2 *adj.* chic, stylish, fashionable.

schicken ['ʃɪkən] *v/t.* (ge-, h) send

(*nach, zu* to); remit (*money*); *nach j-m* ~ send for s.o.; *sich* ~ *für* become, suit, befit *s.o.*; *sich* ~ *in* put up with, resign o.s. to *s.th.*

'schicklich *adj.* becoming, proper, seemly; '2keit *f* (-/*no pl.*) propriety, seemliness.

'Schicksal *n* (-[e]s/-e) fate, destiny.

Schiebe|dach *mot.* ['ʃiːbə-] *n* sliding roof; '~fenster *n* sash-window; '2n (*irr.*, ge-, h) 1. *v/t.* push, shove; shift (*blame*) (*auf acc.* on to); F *fig.* sell on the black market; 2. F *fig. v/i.* profiteer; '~r *m* (-s/-) bolt (*of door*); ⊕ slide; *fig.* profiteer, black marketeer, *sl.* spiv; '~tür *f* sliding door.

'Schiebung *fig. f* (-/-en) black marketeering, profiteering; put-up job.

schied [ʃiːt] *pret. of* scheiden.

Schieds|gericht ['ʃiːts-] *n* court of arbitration, arbitration committee; '~richter *m* arbitrator; *tennis, etc.*: umpire; *football, etc.*: referee; '2richterlich *adj.* arbitral; '~spruch *m* award, arbitration.

schief [ʃiːf] 1. *adj.* sloping, slanting, oblique; *face, mouth*: wry; *fig.* false, wrong; ~e *Ebene* ⚛ inclined plane; 2. *adv.: j-n* ~ *ansehen* look askance at s.o.

Schiefer ['ʃiːfər] *m* (-s/-) slate; splinter; '~stift *m* slate-pencil; '~tafel *f* slate.

'schiefgehen *v/i.* (*irr. gehen, sep.*, -ge-, sein) go wrong or awry.

schielen ['ʃiːlən] *v/i.* (ge-, h) squint, be cross-eyed; ~ *auf* (*acc.*) squint at; leer at.

schien [ʃiːn] *pret. of* scheinen.

Schienbein ['ʃiːn-] *n* shin(-bone), tibia.

Schiene ['ʃiːnə] *f* (-/-n) 🚋, *etc.*: rail; 🩹 splint; '2n 🩹 *v/t.* (ge-, h) splint.

schießen ['ʃiːsən] (*irr.*, ge-) 1. *v/t.* (h) shoot; *tot* ~ shoot dead; *ein Tor* ~ score (a goal); *Salut* ~ fire a salute; 2. *v/i.* (h): *auf j-n* ~ shoot or fire at; *gut* ~ be a good shot; 3. *v/i.* (sein) shoot, dart, rush.

'Schieß|pulver *n* gunpowder; '~scharte *f* ⚔ loop-hole, embrasure; '~scheibe *f* target; '~stand *m* shooting-gallery or -range.

Schiff [ʃif] *n* (-[e]s/-e) ⚓ ship, vessel; ⛪ *church:* nave.

Schiffahrt ['ʃifaːrt] *f* (-/-en) navigation.

'schiff|bar *adj.* navigable; '2bau *m* shipbuilding; '2bauer *m* (-s/-) shipbuilder; '2bruch *m* shipwreck (*a. fig.*); ~ *erleiden* be shipwrecked; *fig.* make or suffer shipwreck; '~brüchig *adj.* shipwrecked; '2brücke *f* pontoon-bridge; '~en *v/i.* (ge-, sein) navigate, sail; '2er

15*

m (-s/-) sailor; boatman; navigator; skipper.

'Schiffs|junge *m* cabin-boy; '~kapitän *m* (sea-)captain; '~ladung *f* shipload; cargo; '~makler *m* shipbroker; '~mannschaft *f* crew; '~raum *m* hold; tonnage; '~werft *f* shipyard, *esp.* ⚔ dockyard, *Am. a.* navy yard.

Schikan|e [ʃiˈkaːnə] *f* (-/-n) vexation, nasty trick; 2ieren [~kaˈniːrən] *v/t.* (*no -ge-*, h) vex, ride.

Schild [ʃilt] 1. ⚔ *m* (-[e]s/-e) shield, buckler; 2. *n* (-[e]s/-er) shop, *etc.:* sign(board), facia; name-plate; *traffic:* signpost; label; *cap:* peak; '~drüse *anat. f* thyroid gland.

'Schilder|haus ⚔ *n* sentry-box; '~maler *m* sign-painter; '2n *v/t.* (ge-, h) describe, delineate; '~ung *f* (-/-en) description, delineation.

'Schild|kröte *zo. f* tortoise; turtle; '~wache ⚔ *f* sentinel, sentry.

Schilf 🌿 [ʃilf] *n* (-[e]s/-e) reed; '2ig *adj.* reedy; '~rohr *n* reed.

schillern ['ʃilərn] *v/i.* (ge-, h) show changing colo(u)rs; be iridescent.

Schimmel ['ʃiməl] *m* 1. *zo.* (-s/-) white horse; 2. ♦ (-s/*no pl.*) mo(u)ld, mildew; '2ig *adj.* mo(u)ldy, musty; '2n *v/i.* (ge-, h) become mo(u)ldy, *Am. a.* mo(u)ld.

Schimmer ['ʃimər] *m* (-s/*no pl.*) glimmer, gleam (*a. fig.*); '2n *v/i.* (ge-, h) glimmer, gleam.

Schimpanse *zo.* [ʃimˈpanzə] *m* (-n/-n) chimpanzee.

Schimpf [ʃimpf] *m* (-[e]s/-e) insult; disgrace; *mit* ~ *und Schande* ignominiously; '2en (ge-, h) 1. *v/i.* rail (*über acc., auf acc.* at, against); 2. *v/t.* scold; *j-n Lügner* ~ call s.o. a liar; '2lich *adj.* disgraceful (*für* to), ignominious (to); '~name *m* abusive name; '~wort *n* term of abuse; ~e *pl. a.* invectives *pl.*

Schindel ['ʃindəl] *f* (-/-n) shingle.

schinden ['ʃindən] *v/t.* (*irr.*, ge-, h) flay, skin (*rabbit, etc.*); sweat (*worker*); *sich* ~ drudge, slave, sweat.

'Schinder *m* (-s/-) knacker; *fig.* sweater, slave-driver; ~ei *fig.* [~ˈrai] *f* (-/-en) sweating; drudgery, grind.

Schinken ['ʃiŋkən] *m* (-s/-) ham.

Schippe ['ʃipə] *f* (-/-n) shovel; '2n *v/t.* (ge-, h) shovel.

Schirm [ʃirm] *m* (-[e]s/-e) umbrella; parasol, sunshade; *wind, television, etc.:* screen; *lamp:* shade; *cap:* peak, visor; '~futteral *n* umbrella-case; '~herr *m* protector; patron; '~herrschaft *f* protectorate; patronage; *unter der* ~ *von event:* under the auspices of; '~mütze *f* peaked cap; '~ständer *m* umbrella-stand.

Schlacht ⚔ [ʃlaxt] *f* (-/-en) battle (*bei* of); '~bank *f* shambles; '2en *v/t.* (ge-, h) slaughter, butcher.

Schlächter ['ʃlɛçtər] m (-s/-) butcher.

'Schlacht|feld ✗ n battle-field; **'~haus** n, **'~hof** m slaughter-house, abattoir; **'~kreuzer** ⚓ m battle-cruiser; **'~plan** m ✗ plan of action (a. fig.); **'~schiff** ⚓ n battleship; **'~vieh** n slaughter cattle.

Schlack|e ['ʃlakə] f (-/-n) wood, coal: cinder; metall. dross (a. fig.), slag; geol. scoria; **'2ig** adj. drossy, slaggy; F weather: slushy.

Schlaf [ʃlaːf] m (-[e]s/no pl.) sleep; im ~(e) in one's sleep; e-n leichten (festen) ~ haben be a light (sound) sleeper; in tiefem ~e liegen be fast asleep; **'~abteil** 🚂 n sleeping-compartment; **'~anzug** m (ein a pair of) pyjamas pl. or Am. pajamas pl.

Schläfchen ['ʃlɛːfçən] n (-s/-) doze, nap, F forty winks pl.; ein ~ machen take a nap, F have one's forty winks.

'Schlafdecke f blanket.

Schläfe ['ʃlɛːfə] f (-/-n) temple.

'schlafen v/i. (irr., ge-, h) sleep; ~ gehen, sich ~ legen go to bed.

schlaff adj. [ʃlaf] slack, loose; muscles, etc.: flabby, flaccid; plant, etc.: limp; discipline, morals, etc.: lax; **'2heit** f (-/no pl.) slackness; flabbiness; limpness; fig. laxity.

'Schlaf|gelegenheit f sleeping accommodation; **'~kammer** f bed-room; **'~krankheit** 🐛 f sleeping-sickness; **'~lied** n lullaby; **'2los** adj. sleepless; **'~losigkeit** f (-/no pl.) sleeplessness, ⚕ insomnia; **'~mittel** 🧪 n soporific; **'~mütze** f nightcap; fig. sleepyhead.

schläfrig adj. ['ʃlɛːfrɪç] sleepy, drowsy; **'2keit** f (-/no pl.) sleepiness, drowsiness.

'Schlaf|rock m dressing-gown, Am. a. robe; **'~saal** m dormitory; **'~sack** m sleeping-bag; **'~stelle** f sleeping-place; night's lodging; **'~tablette** 🧪 f sleeping-tablet; **'2trunken** adj. very drowsy; **'~wagen** 🚂 m sleeping-car(riage), Am. a. sleeper; **~wandler** ['~vandlər] m (-s/-) sleep-walker, somnambulist; **~zimmer** n bedroom.

Schlag [ʃlaːk] m (-[e]s/~e) blow (a. fig.); stroke (of clock, piston) (a. tennis, etc.); slap (with palm of hand); punch (with fist); kick (of horse's hoof); ∮ shock; beat (of heart or pulse); clap (of thunder); warbling (of bird); door (of carriage); ⚕ apoplexy; fig. race, kind, sort; breed (esp. of animals); Schläge bekommen get a beating; ~ sechs Uhr on the stroke of six; **'~ader** anat. f artery; **'~anfall** 🐛 m (stroke of) apoplexy, stroke; **'2artig 1.** adj. sudden, abrupt; **2.** adv. all of a sudden; **'~baum** m turnpike.

schlagen ['ʃlaːɡən] (irr., ge-, h) **1.** v/t. strike, beat, hit; punch; slap;

beat, defeat; fell (trees); fight (battle); Alarm ~ sound the alarm; zu Boden ~ knock down; in den Wind ~ cast or fling to the winds; sich ~ (have a) fight; sich et. aus dem Kopf or Sinn ~ put s.th. out of one's mind, dismiss s.th. from one's mind; **2.** v/i. strike, beat; heart, pulse: beat, throb; clock: strike; bird: warble; das schlägt nicht in mein Fach that is not in my line; um sich ~ lay about one; **'~d** fig. adj. striking.

Schlager ['ʃlaːɡər] m (-s/-) ♪ song hit; thea. hit, draw, box-office success; book: best seller.

Schläger ['ʃlɛːɡər] m (-s/-) rowdy, hooligan; cricket, etc.: batsman; horse: kicker; cricket, etc.: bat; golf: club; tennis, etc.: racket; hockey, etc.: stick; **~ei** [~'raɪ] f (-/-en) tussle, fight.

'schlag|fertig fig. adj. quick at repartee; **~e** Antwort repartee; **'2fertigkeit** fig. f (-/no pl.) quickness at repartee; **'2instrument** ♪ n percussion instrument; **'2kraft** f (-/no pl.) striking power (a. ✗); **'2loch** n pot-hole; **'2mann** m rowing: stroke; **'2ring** m knuckle-duster, Am. a. brass knuckles pl.; **'2sahne** f whipped cream; **'2schatten** m cast shadow; **'2seite** ⚓ f list; ~ haben ⚓ list; F fig. be half-seas-over; **'2uhr** f striking clock; **'2werk** n clock: striking mechanism; **'2wort** n catchword, slogan; **'2zeile** f headline; banner headline, Am. banner; **'2zeug** ♪ n in orchestra: percussion instruments pl.; in band: drums pl., percussion; **'2zeuger** ♪ m (-s/-) in orchestra: percussionist; in band: drummer.

schlaksig adj. ['ʃlaːksɪç] gawky.

Schlamm [ʃlam] m (-[e]s/✗, -e) mud, mire; **'~bad** n mud-bath; **'2ig** adj. muddy, miry.

Schlämmkreide ['ʃlɛm-] f (-/no pl.) whit(en)ing.

Schlamp|e ['ʃlampə] f (-/-n) slut, slattern; **'2ig** adj. slovenly, slipshod.

schlang [ʃlaŋ] pret. of schlingen.

Schlange ['ʃlaŋə] f (-/-n) zo. snake, rhet. serpent (a. fig.); fig.: snake in the grass; queue, Am. a. line; ~ stehen queue up (um for), Am. line up (for).

schlängeln ['ʃlɛŋəln] v/refl. (ge-, h): sich ~ durch person: worm one's way or o.s. through; path, river, etc.: wind (one's way) through, meander through.

'Schlangenlinie f serpentine line.

schlank adj. [ʃlaŋk] slender, slim; **'2heit** f (-/no pl.) slenderness, slimness; **'2heitskur** f: e-e ~ machen slim.

schlapp F adj. [ʃlap] tired, exhausted,

worn out; '≗e F *f* (-/-n) reverse, set-back; defeat; '‿machen F *v/i.* (sep., -ge-, h) break down, faint.

schlau *adj.* [ʃlau] sly, cunning; crafty, clever, F cute.

Schlauch [ʃlaux] *m* (-[e]s/≗e) tube; hose; *car, etc.*: inner tube; '‿boot *n* rubber dinghy, pneumatic boat.

Schlaufe ['ʃlaufə] *f* (-/-n) loop.

schlecht [ʃlɛçt] 1. *adj.* bad; wicked; poor; *temper* ill; *quality*: inferior; ‿e Laune haben be in a bad temper; ‿e Aussichten poor prospects; ‿e Zeiten hard times; *mir ist* ‿ I feel sick; 2. *adv.* badly, ill; '‿erdings *adv.* ['‿ər'dɪŋs] absolutely, downright, utterly; '‿gelaunt *adj.* ['‿gəlaunt] ill-humo(u)red, in a bad temper; '‿'hin *adv.* plainly, simply; '2igkeit *f* (-/-en) badness; wickedness; ‿en *pl.* base acts *pl.*, mean tricks *pl.*; '‿machen *v/t.* (sep., -ge-, h) run down, backbite; ‿weg *adv.* ['‿vɛk] plainly, simply.

schleich|en ['ʃlaɪçən] *v/i.* (irr., ge-, sein) creep (*a. fig.*); sneak, steal; '2er *m* (-s/-) creeper; *fig.* sneak; '2handel *m* illicit trade; smuggling, contraband; '2händler *m* smuggler, contrabandist; black marketeer; '2weg *m* secret path.

Schleier ['ʃlaɪər] *m* (-s/-) veil (*a. fig.*); *mist a.* haze; *den* ‿ *nehmen* take the veil; '2haft *fig. adj.* mysterious, inexplicable.

Schleife ['ʃlaɪfə] *f* (-/-n) loop (*a.* ⚒); slip-knot, bow; *wreath*: streamer; loop, horse-shoe bend.

'schleif|en ['ʃlaɪfən] 1. *v/t.* (irr., ge-, h) whet (*knife, etc.*); cut (*glass, precious stones*); polish (*a. fig.*); 2. *v/t.* (ge-, h) ♪ slur; drag, trail; ✗ raze (*fortress, etc.*); 3. *v/i.* (ge-, h) drag, trail; '2stein *m* grindstone, whetstone.

Schleim [ʃlaɪm] *m* (-[e]s/-e) slime; ♪ mucus, phlegm; '‿haut *anat. f* mucous membrane; '2ig *adj.* slimy (*a. fig.*); mucous.

schlemm|en ['ʃlɛmən] *v/i.* (ge-, h) feast, gormandize; '2er *m* (-s/-) glutton, gormandizer; 2erei [‿'raɪ] *f* (-/-en) feasting; gluttony.

schlen|dern ['ʃlɛndərn] *v/i.* (ge-, sein) stroll, saunter; 2drian ['‿driːaːn] *m* (-[e]s/*no pl.*) jogtrot; beaten track.

schlenkern ['ʃlɛŋkərn] (ge-, h) 1. *v/t.* dangle, swing; 2. *v/i.*: *mit den Armen* ‿ swing one's arms.

Schlepp|dampfer ['ʃlɛp-] *m* steam tug, tug(boat); '‿e *f* (-/-n) train (*of woman's dress*); '2en (ge-, h) 1. *v/t.* carry with difficulty, haul, *Am.* F *a.* tote; ⚓, ⚒, *mot.* tow, haul; ⚓ tug; ✝ tout (*customers*); *sich* ‿ drag o.s.; 2. *v/i.* dress: drag, trail; '2end *adj.* *speech*: drawling; *gait*: shuffling; *style*: heavy; con-

versation, *etc.*: tedious; '‿er ⚓ *m* (-s/-) steam tug, tug(boat); '‿tau *n* tow(ing)-rope; *ins* ‿ *nehmen* take in or on tow (*a. fig.*).

Schleuder ['ʃlɔʏdər] *f* (-/-n) sling, catapult (*a.* ✗), *Am. a.* slingshot; spin drier; '2n (ge-, h) 1. *v/t.* fling, hurl (*a. fig.*); sling, catapult (*a.* ✗); spin-dry (*washing*), 2. *mot.* *v/i.* skid; '‿preis ✝ *m* ruinous or give-away price, *zu* ‿en dirt-cheap.

schleunig *adj.* ['ʃlɔʏnɪç] prompt, speedy, quick

Schleuse ['ʃlɔʏzə] *f* (-/-n) lock, sluice; '2n *v/t.* (ge-, h) lock (*boat*) (up or down); *fig.* manœuvre, *Am.* maneuver

schlich [ʃlɪç] *pret. of* schleichen.

schlicht *adj.* [ʃlɪçt] plain, simple; modest, unpretentious; *hair*: smooth, sleek; '‿en *fig. v/t.* (ge-, h) settle, adjust; settle by arbitration; '2er *fig. m* (-s/-) mediator; arbitrator.

schlief [ʃliːf] *pret. of* schlafen.

schließ|en ['ʃliːsən] (*irr.*, ge-, h) 1. *v/t.* shut, close; shut down (*factory, etc.*); shut up (*shop*); contract (*marriage*); conclude (*treaty, speech, etc.*); *parl* close (*debate*); *in die Arme* ‿ clasp in one's arms; *in sich* ‿ comprise, include; *Freundschaft* ‿ make friends (*mit with*); 2. *v/i.* shut, close; *school*: break up; *aus et.* ‿ *auf* (*acc.*) infer or conclude *s.th.* from s.th.; '2fach ☏ *n* post-office box, '‿lich *adv.* finally, eventually; at last; after all.

Schliff [ʃlɪf] 1. *m* (-[e]s/-e) polish (*a. fig.*); *precious stones, glass*: cut; 2. 2 *pret of* schleifen 1.

schlimm [ʃlɪm] 1. *adj.* bad; evil, wicked, nasty; serious; F ✗ bad, sore; ‿er worse; *am* ‿sten, *das* 2ste the worst; *es wird immer* ‿er things are going from bad to worse; 2. *adv.*: ‿ *daran sein* be badly off; '‿sten'falls *adv* at (the) worst.

Schling|e ['ʃlɪŋə] *f* (-/-n) loop, sling (*a.* ♪); noose; coil (*of wire or rope*); *hunt.* snare (*a. fig.*); *den Kopf in die* ‿ *stecken* put one's head in the noose; '‿el *m* (-s/-) rascal, naughty boy; '2en *v/t.* (*irr.*, ge-, h) wind, twist; plait; *die Arme* ‿ *um* (*acc.*) fling one's arms round; *sich um et.* ‿ wind round, '‿pflanze ♀ *f* creeper, climber

Schlips [ʃlɪps] *m* (-es/-e) (neck)tie.

Schlitten ['ʃlɪtən] *m* (-s/-) sled(ge); sleigh, *sports* toboggan.

'Schlittschuh *m* skate; ‿ *laufen* skate, '‿läufer *m* skater.

Schlitz [ʃlɪts] *m* (-es/-e) slit, slash; slot; '2en *v/t.* (ge-, h) slit, slash.

Schloß [ʃlɔs] 1. *n* (Schlosses/Schlösser) lock (*of door, gun, etc.*); castle; palace; *ins* ‿ *fallen door*: snap to;

hinter ~ *und Riegel* behind prison bars; **2.** ♀ *pret. of schließen.*
Schlosser ['ʃlɔsər] *m* (-*s*/-) locksmith; mechanic, fitter.
Schlot [ʃlo:t] *m* (-[e]*s*/-e, ⸚e) chimney; flue; ⚓, 🚂 funnel; '**~feger** *m* (-*s*/-) chimney-sweep(er).
schlotter|ig *adj.* ['ʃlɔtəriç] shaky, tottery; loose; '**~n** *v/i.* (ge-, *h*) *garment*: hang loosely; *p.* shake, tremble (*both*: *vor dat.* with).
Schlucht [ʃluxt] *f* (-/-en) gorge, mountain cleft; ravine, *Am. a.* gulch.
schluchzen ['ʃluxtsən] *v/i.* (ge-, *h*) sob.
Schluck [ʃluk] *m* (-[e]*s*/-e, ⸚e) draught, swallow; mouthful, sip; '**~auf** *m* (-*s*/*no pl.*) hiccup(s *pl.*).
'**schlucken 1.** *v/t. and v/i.* (ge-, *h*) swallow (*a. fig.*); **2.** ♀ *m* (-*s*/*no pl.*) hiccup(s *pl.*).
schlug [ʃlu:k] *pret. of schlagen.*
Schlummer ['ʃlumər] *m* (-*s*/*no pl.*) slumber; '**♀n** *v/i.* (ge-, *h*) slumber.
Schlund [ʃlunt] *m* (-[e]*s*/⸚e) *anat.* pharynx; *fig.* abyss, chasm, gulf.
schlüpf|en ['ʃlypfən] *v/i.* (ge-, *sein*) slip, slide; *in die Kleider* ~ slip on one's clothes; *aus den Kleidern* ~ slip out of *or* slip off one's clothes; '**♀er** *m* (-*s*/-) (*ein* a pair of) knickers *pl. or* drawers *pl. or* F panties *pl.*; briefs *pl.*
Schlupfloch ['ʃlupf-] *n* loop-hole.
'**schlüpfrig** *adj.* slippery; *fig.* lascivious.
'**Schlupfwinkel** *m* hiding-place.
schlurfen ['ʃlurfən] *v/i.* (ge-, *sein*) shuffle, drag one's feet.
schlürfen ['ʃlyrfən] *v/t. and v/i.* (ge-, *h*) drink *or* eat noisily; sip.
Schluß [ʃlus] *m* (*Schlusses*/*Schlüsse*) close, end; conclusion; *parl.* closing (*of debate*).
Schlüssel ['ʃlysəl] *m* (-*s*/-) key (*zu* of; *fig.* to); ♪ clef; *fig.*: code; quota; '**~bart** *m* key-bit; '**~bein** *anat. n* collar-bone, clavicle; '**~bund** *m, n* (-[e]*s*/-e) bunch of keys; '**~industrie** *fig. f* key industry; '**~loch** *n* keyhole; '**~ring** *m* key-ring.
'**Schluß|folgerung** *f* conclusion, inference; '**~formel** *f in letter*: complimentary close.
schlüssig *adj.* ['ʃlysiç] *evidence*: conclusive; *sich* ~ *werden* make up one's mind (*über acc.* about).
'**Schluß|licht** *n* 🚂, *mot., etc.*: taillight; *sports*: last runner; bottom club; '**~runde** *f sports*: final; '**~schein** ✝ *m* contract-note.
Schmach [ʃma:x] *f* (-/*no pl.*) disgrace; insult; humiliation.
schmachten ['ʃmaxtən] *v/i.* (ge-, *h*) languish (*nach* for), pine (for).
schmächtig *adj.* ['ʃmɛçtiç] slender, slim; *ein* **~er** *Junge* a (mere) slip of a boy.
'**schmachvoll** *adj.* disgraceful; humiliating.
schmackhaft *adj.* ['ʃmakhaft] palatable, savo(u)ry.
schmäh|en ['ʃmɛ:ən] *v/t.* (ge-, *h*) abuse, revile; decry, disparage; slander, defame; '**~lich** *adj.* ignominious, disgraceful; '**♀schrift** *f* libel, lampoon; '**♀ung** *f* (-/-en) abuse; slander, defamation.
schmal *adj.* [ʃma:l] narrow; *figure*: slender, slim; *face*: thin; *fig.* poor, scanty.
schmäler|n ['ʃmɛ:lərn] *v/t.* (ge-, *h*) curtail; impair; belittle; '**♀ung** *f* (-/-en) curtailment; impairment; detraction.
'**Schmal|film** *phot. m* substandard film; '**~spur** 🚂 *f* narrow ga(u)ge; '**~spurbahn** 🚂 *f* narrow-ga(u)ge railway; '**♀spurig** 🚂 *adj.* narrow-ga(u)ge.
Schmalz [ʃmalts] *n* (-*es*/-e) grease; lard; '**♀ig** *adj.* greasy; lardy; F *fig.* soppy, sentimental.
schmarotz|en [ʃma'rɔtsən] *v/i.* (*no* -ge-, *h*) sponge (*bei* on); **♀er** *m* (-*s*/-) ⚘, *zo.* parasite; *fig. a.* sponge.
Schmarre F ['ʃmarə] *f* (-/-n) slash, cut; scar.
Schmatz [ʃmats] *m* (-*es*/-e) smack, loud kiss; '**♀en** *v/i.* (ge-, *h*) smack (*mit den Lippen* one's lips); eat noisily.
Schmaus [ʃmaʊs] *m* (-*es*/⸚e) feast, banquet; *fig.* treat; **♀en** ['~zən] *v/i.* (ge-, *h*) feast, banquet.
schmecken ['ʃmɛkən] (ge-, *h*) **1.** *v/t.* taste, sample; **2.** *v/i.*: ~ *nach* taste *or* smack of (*both a. fig.*); *dieser Wein schmeckt mir* I like *or* enjoy this wine.
Schmeichel|ei [ʃmaɪçə'laɪ] *f* (-/-en) flattery; cajolery; '**♀haft** *adj.* flattering; '**♀n** *v/i.* (ge-, *h*): *j-m* ~ flatter s.o.; cajole s.o.
Schmeichler ['ʃmaɪçlər] *m* (-*s*/-) flatterer; '**♀isch** *adj.* flattering; cajoling.
schmeiß|en F ['ʃmaɪsən] (*irr.*, ge-, *h*) **1.** *v/t.* throw, fling, hurl; slam, bang (*door*); **2.** *v/i.*: *mit Geld um sich* ~ squander one's money; '**♀fliege** *zo. f* blowfly, bluebottle.
Schmelz [ʃmɛlts] *m* **1.** (-*es*/-e) enamel; **2.** *fig.* (-*es*/*no pl.*) bloom; ♪ sweetness, mellowness; '**♀en** (*irr.*, ge-) **1.** *v/i.* (*sein*) melt (*a. fig.*); liquefy; *fig.* melt away, dwindle; **2.** *v/t.* (*h*) melt; smelt, fuse (*ore, etc.*); liquefy; **~erei** [~'raɪ] *f* (-/-en), '**~hütte** *f* foundry; '**~ofen** *m* smelting furnace; '**~tiegel** *m* melting-pot, crucible.
Schmerbauch ['ʃme:r-] *m* paunch, pot-belly, F corporation, *Am. sl. a.* bay window.
Schmerz [ʃmɛrts] *m* (-*es*/-en) pain (*a. fig.*); ache; *fig.* grief, sorrow;

'²en (ge-, h) 1. v/i. pain (a. fig.), hurt; ache; 2. v/t. pain (a. fig.); hurt; fig grieve, afflict; '²haft adj. painful, '²lich adj. painful, grievous; '²lindernd adj. soothing; '²los adj. painless

Schmetter|ling zo. ['ʃmɛtərliŋ] m (-s/-e) butterfly; '²n (ge-, h) 1. v/t. dash (zu Boden to the ground; in Stücke to pieces); 2. v/i. crash; trumpet, etc.: bray, blare; bird: warble

Schmied [ʃmiːt] m (-[e]s/-e) (black-)smith, ~e ['~də] f (-/-n) forge, smithy, ~eeisen ['~da⁹-] n wrought iron; ~ehammer m sledge(-hammer); ²en ['~dən] v/t. (ge-, h) forge; make, devise, hatch (plans).

schmiegen ['ʃmiːgən] v/refl. (ge-, h) nestle (an ac to).

schmiegsam adj. ['ʃmiːkzaːm] pliant, flexible, supple (a. fig.); '²keit f (-/no pl.) pliancy, flexibility; suppleness (a. fig.).

Schmier|e ['ʃmiːrə] f (-/-n) grease; thea. contp troop of strolling players, sl penny gaff; '²en v/t. (ge-, h) smear, ⊕ grease, oil, lubricate; butter (bread); spread (butter, etc.); scrawl, scribble; painter: daub; ~enkomödiant ['~komødjant] m (-en/-en) strolling actor, barnstormer, sl ham (actor); ~erei [~'rai] f (-/-en) scrawl; paint. daub; '²ig adj. greasy; dirty; fig.: filthy; F smarmy; ~mittel ⊕ n lubricant.

Schminke ['ʃmiŋkə] f (-/-n) make-up (a thea.), paint; rouge; thea. grease-paint, '²n v/t. and v/refl. (ge-, h) paint, make up; rouge (o.s.); put on lipstick.

Schmirgel ['ʃmirgəl] m (-s/no pl.) emery; '²n v/t. (ge-, h) (rub with) emery, ~papier n emery-paper.

Schmiß [ʃmis] 1. m (Schmisses/ Schmisse) gash, cut; (duelling-) scar; 2. F m (Schmisses/no pl.) verve, go, Am. sl. a. pep; 3. ② pret. of schmeißen.

schmoll|en ['ʃmɔlən] v/i. (ge-, h) sulk, pout; '²winkel m sulking-corner.

schmolz [ʃmɔlts] pret. of schmelzen.

Schmor|braten ['ʃmoːr-] m stewed meat; '²en v/t. and v/i. (ge-, h) stew (a fig.).

Schmuck [ʃmuk] 1. m (-[e]s/⁎-e) ornament; decoration; jewel(le)ry, jewels pl.; 2. ② adj. neat, smart, spruce, trim.

schmücken ['ʃmykən] v/t. (ge-, h) adorn, trim; decorate.

'schmuck|los adj. unadorned; plain; '²sachen f/pl jewel(le)ry, jewels pl.

Schmuggel ['ʃmugəl] m (-s/no pl.), ~ei [~'lai] f (-/-en) smuggling; '²n v/t. and v/i. (ge-, h) smuggle; '²ware f contraband, smuggled goods pl.

Schmuggler ['ʃmuglər] m (-s/-) smuggler.

schmunzeln ['ʃmuntsəln] v/i. (ge-, h) smile amusedly

Schmutz [ʃmuts] m (-es/no pl.) dirt; filth; fig a smut; '²en v/i. (ge-, h) soil, get dirty; ~fink fig m mudlark; '~fleck m smudge, stain; fig. blemish, '²ig adj dirty; filthy; fig. a. mean, shabby

Schnabel ['ʃnaːbəl] m (-s/⁎) bill, esp. bird of prey beak.

Schnalle ['ʃnalə] f (-/-n) buckle; '²n v/t (ge-, h) buckle; strap.

schnalzen ['ʃnaltsən] v/i. (ge-, h): mit den Fingern snap one's fingers; mit der Zunge click one's tongue.

schnappen ['ʃnapən] (ge-, h) 1. v/i. lid, spring, etc snap; lock catch; nach ac ~ snap or snatch at; nach Luft ~ gasp for breath; 2. F v/t. catch, sl nab (criminal).

'Schnapp|messer n flick-knife; '~schloß ⊢ spring-lock; '~schuß phot. m snapshot

Schnaps [ʃnaps] m (-es/⁎e) strong liquor, Am hard liquor; brandy; ein (Glas) ~ a dram

schnarch|en ⊢ ['ʃnarçən] v/i. (ge-, h) snore; '²er m (-s/-) snorer.

schnarren ['ʃnarən] v/i. (ge-, h) rattle; jar

schnattern ['ʃnatərn] v/i. (ge-, h) cackle; fig a chatter, gabble.

schnauben ['ʃnaubən] (ge-, h) 1. v/i. snort; vor Wut ~ foam with rage; 2. v/t. sich die Nase ~ blow one's nose.

schnaufen ['ʃnaufən] v/i. (ge-, h) pant, puff, blow, wheeze.

Schnauz|bart ['ʃnauts-] m m(o)ustache; ~e f (-/-n) snout, muzzle; ⊕ nozzle; teapot, etc spout; sl. fig. potato-trap; '²en ⊢ v/i. (ge-, h) jaw.

Schnecke zo. ['ʃnɛkə] f (-/-n) snail; slug; ~nhaus n snail's shell; '~ntempo n im ~ at a snail's pace.

Schnee [ʃneː] m (-s/no pl.) snow; '~ball m snowball; '~ballschlacht f pelting-match with snowballs; ²bedeckt adj. [~'bədɛkt] snow-covered, mountain-top: snow-capped; '²blind adj. snow-blind; '~blindheit f snow-blindness; '~brille f (e-e a pair of) snow-goggles pl.; '~fall m snow-fall; '~flocke f snow-flake; '~gestöber n (-s/-) snow-storm; ~glöckchen ⚘ ['~glœkçən] n (-s/-) snowdrop; '~grenze f snow-line; '~mann m snow man; '~pflug m snow-plough, Am. snowplow; '~schuh m snow-shoe; '~sturm m snow-storm, blizzard; '~wehe f (-/-n) snow-drift; '²weiß adj. snow-white.

Schneid ⊢ [ʃnart] m (-[e]s/no pl.) pluck, dash, sl. guts pl.

Schneide ['ʃnardə] f (-/-n) edge; '~mühle f sawmill; '²n (irr., ge-, h)

1. v/t. cut; carve (meat); pare, clip (finger-nails, etc.); 2. v/i. cut.

'Schneider m (-s/-) tailor; ~ei [~'raɪ] f 1. (-/no pl.) tailoring; dressmaking; 2. (-/-en) tailor's shop; dressmaker's shop; '~in f (-/-nen) dressmaker; '~meister m master tailor; 'ℒn (ge-, h) 1. v/i. tailor; do tailoring; do dressmaking; 2. v/t. make, tailor.

'Schneidezahn m incisor.

'schneidig fig. adj. plucky; dashing, keen; smart, Am. sl. a. nifty.

schneien ['ʃnaɪən] v/i. (ge-, h) snow.

schnell [ʃnɛl] 1. adj. quick, fast; rapid; swift, speedy; reply, etc.: prompt; sudden; 2. adv.: ~ fahren drive fast; ~ handeln act promptly or without delay; (mach) ~! be quick!, hurry up!

Schnelläufer ['ʃnɛlⁿɔʏfər] m sprinter; speed skater.

'schnell|en (ge-) v/t. (h) and v/i. (sein) jerk; 'ℒfeuer ✕ n rapid fire; 'ℒhefter m (-s/-) folder.

'Schnelligkeit f (-/no pl.) quickness, fastness; rapidity; swiftness; promptness; speed, velocity.

'Schnell|imbiß m snack (bar); '~imbißstube f snack bar; '~kraft f (-/no pl.) elasticity; '~verfahren n t½ summary proceeding; ⊕ high-speed process; '~zug 🚂 m fast train, express (train).

schneuzen ['ʃnɔʏtsən] v/refl. (ge-, h) blow one's nose.

schniegeln ['ʃniːɡəln] v/refl. (ge-, h) dress or smarten or spruce (o.s.) up.

Schnipp|chen ['ʃnɪpçən] n: F j-m ein ~ schlagen outwit or overreach s.o.; 'ℒisch adj. pert, snappish, Am. F a. snippy.

Schnitt [ʃnɪt] m 1. m (-[e]s/-e) cut; dress, etc.: cut, make, style; pattern; book: edge; ⋏ (inter)section; fig.: average; F profit; ℒ pret. of schneiden; '~blumen f/pl. cut flowers pl.; '~e f (-/-n) slice; '~er m (-s/-) reaper, mower; '~fläche ⋏ f section(al plane); 'ℒig adj. streamline(d); '~muster n pattern; '~punkt m (point of) intersection; '~wunde f cut, gash.

Schnitzel ['ʃnɪtsəl] 1. n (-s/-) schnitzel; 2. F n, m (-s/-) chip; paper: scrap; ~ pl. ⊕ parings pl., shavings pl.; paper: a. clippings pl.; 'ℒn v/t. (ge-, h) chip, shred; whittle.

schnitzen ['ʃnɪtsən] v/t. (ge-, h) carve, cut (in wood).

'Schnitzer m (-s/-) carver; F fig. blunder, Am. sl. a. boner; ~ei [~'raɪ] f 1. (-/-en) carving, carved work; 2. (-/no pl.) carving.

schnöde adj. ['ʃnøːdə] contemptuous; disgraceful; base, vile; ~r Mammon filthy lucre.

Schnörkel ['ʃnœrkəl] m (-s/-) flourish (a. fig.), scroll (a. 🔺).

schnorr|en F ['ʃnɔrən] v/t. and v/i. (ge-, h) cadge; 'ℒer m (-s/-) cadger.

schnüffel|n ['ʃnyfəln] v/i. (ge-, h) sniff, nose (both: an dat. at); fig. nose about, Am. F a. snoop around; 'ℒer fig. m (-s/-) spy, Am. F a. snoop; F sleuth(-hound).

Schnuller ['ʃnʊlər] m (-s/-) dummy, comforter.

Schnulze F ['ʃnʊltsə] f (-/-n) sentimental song or film or play, F tearjerker.

Schnupf|en ['ʃnʊpfən] 1. m (-s/-) cold, catarrh; 2. ♀ v/i. (ge-, h) take snuff; '~er m (-s/-) snuff-taker; '~tabak m snuff.

schnuppe F adj. ['ʃnʊpə]: das ist mir ~ I don't care (F a damn); '~rn v/i. (ge-, h) sniff, nose (both: an dat. at).

Schnur [ʃnuːr] f (-/ℒe, ✎-en) cord; string, twine; line; ✍ flex.

Schnür|band ['ʃnyːr-] n lace; '~chen ['~çən] n (-s/-): wie am ~ like clockwork; 'ℒen (ge-, h) lace (up); (bind with) cord, tie up.

'schnurgerade adj. dead straight.

Schnurr|bart ['ʃnuːr-] m m(o)ustache; 'ℒen (ge-, h) 1. v/i. wheel, etc.: whir(r); cat: purr (a. fig.); F fig. cadge; 2. F fig. v/t. cadge.

Schnür|senkel ['ʃnyːrzɛŋkəl] m (-s/-) shoe-lace, shoe-string; '~stiefel m lace-boot.

schnurstracks adv. ['ʃnuːr'ʃtraks] direct, straight; on the spot, at once, sl. straight away.

schob [ʃoːp] pret. of schieben.

Schober ['ʃoːbər] m (-s/-) rick, stack.

Schock [ʃɔk] 1. n (-[e]s/-e) three-score; 2. ⊛ m (-[e]s/-s, ✎-e) shock; 'ℒieren [~'kiːrən] v/t. (no -ge-, h) shock, scandalize.

Schokolade [ʃoko'laːdə] f (-/-n) chocolate.

scholl [ʃɔl] pret. of schallen.

Scholle ['ʃɔlə] f (-/-n) clod (of earth), poet. glebe; floe (of ice); ichth. plaice.

schon adv. [ʃoːn] already; ~ lange for a long time; ~ gut! all right!; ~ der Name the bare name; hast du ~ einmal ...? have you ever ...?; mußt du ~ gehen? need you go yet?; ~ um 8 Uhr as early as 8 o'clock.

schön [ʃøːn] 1. adj. beautiful; man: handsome (a. fig.); weather: fair, fine (a. iro.); das ~e Geschlecht the fair sex; die ~en Künste the fine arts; ~e Literatur belles-lettres pl.; 2. adv.: ~ warm nice and warm; du hast mich ~ erschreckt you gave me quite a start.

schonen ['ʃoːnən] v/t. (ge-, h) spare (j-n s.o.; j-s Leben s.o.'s life); take

care of; husband (*strength, etc.*);
sich ~ take care of o.s., look after
o.s.

'**Schönheit** *f* 1. (-/*no pl.*) beauty;
of woman: a. pulchritude; 2. (-/-*en*)
beauty; beautiful woman, belle;
'**~spflege** *f* beauty treatment.

'**schöntun** *v/i.* (*irr. tun, sep., -ge-, h*)
flatter (*j-m s.o.*); flirt (*dat.* with).

'**Schonung** *f* 1. (-/*no pl.*) mercy;
sparing, forbearance; careful treatment; 2. (-/-*en*) tree-nursery;
'**2slos** *adj.* unsparing, merciless,
relentless.

Schopf [ʃɔpf] *m* (-[e]s/⁼e) tuft; *orn.*
a. crest.

schöpfen ['ʃœpfən] *v/t.* (*ge-, h*)
scoop, ladle; draw (*water at well*);
draw, take (*breath*); take (*courage*);
neue Hoffnung ~ gather fresh hope;
Verdacht ~ become suspicious.

'**Schöpf|er** *m* (-*s*/-) creator; '**2e-**
risch *adj.* creative; '**~ung** *f* (-/-*en*)
creation.

schor [ʃoːr] *pret. of* scheren.

Schorf [ʃɔrf] *m* (-[e]s/-*e*) scurf;
scab, crust; '**2ig** *adj.* scurfy; scabby.

Schornstein ['ʃɔrn-] *m* chimney;
⚓, 🚂 funnel; '**~feger** *m* (-*s*/-)
chimney-sweep(er).

Schoß 1. [ʃoːs] *m* (-es/⁼e) lap; womb;
coat: tail; 2. 2 [ʃɔs] *pret. of* schießen.

Schote ⚓ 1. ['ʃoːtə] *f* (-/-*n*) pod, husk.

Schott|e ['ʃɔtə] *m* (-*n*/-*n*) Scot,
Scotchman, Scotsman; *die ~n pl.*
the Scotch *pl.*; '**~er** *m* (-*s*/-) gravel;
(road-)metal; '**2isch** *adj.* Scotch,
Scottish.

schräg [ʃrɛːk] 1. *adj.* oblique, slanting; sloping; 2. *adv.:* ~ *gegenüber*
diagonally across (*von* from).

schrak [ʃraːk] *pret. of* schrecken 2.

Schramme ['ʃramə] *f* (-/-*n*) scratch;
skin: a. abrasion; '**2n** *v/t.* (*ge-, h*)
scratch; graze, abrade (*skin*).

Schrank [ʃraŋk] *m* (-[e]s/⁼e) cupboard, *esp. Am.* closet; wardrobe.

'**Schranke** *f* (-/-*n*) barrier (*a. fig.*);
🚂 *a.* (railway-)gate; ⚖️ bar; *~n pl.*
fig. bounds *pl.*, limits *pl.*; '**2nlos**
fig. adj. boundless; unbridled; '**~n-**
wärter 🚂 *m* gate-keeper.

'**Schrankkoffer** *m* wardrobe trunk.

Schraube ['ʃraubə] *f* (-/-*n*) ⊕ screw;
⚓ screw(-propeller); '**2n** *v/t.* (*ge-,*
h) screw.

'**Schrauben|dampfer** ⚓ *m* screw
(steamer); '**~mutter** ⊕ *f* nut;
'**~schlüssel** ⊕ *m* spanner, wrench;
'**~zieher** ⊕ *m* screwdriver.

Schraubstock ⊕ ['ʃraup-] *m* vice,
Am. vise.

Schrebergarten ['ʃreːbər-] *m* allotment garden.

Schreck [ʃrek] *m* (-[e]s/-*e*) fright,
terror; consternation; '**~bild** *n*
bugbear; '**~en** *m* (-*s*/-) fright, terror;
consternation; '**2en** (*ge-*) 1. *v/t.* (h)
frighten; scare; 2. *v/i.* (*irr., sein*):

only in compounds; '**~ensbotschaft**
f alarming *or* terrible news; '**~ens-**
herrschaft *f* reign of terror; '**2haft**
adj. fearful, timid; '**2lich** *adj.* terrible, dreadful (*both a.* F *fig.*);
'**~schuß** *m* scare shot; *fig.* warning
shot.

Schrei [ʃrai] *m* (-[e]s/-*e*) cry; shout;
scream.

schreiben ['ʃraibən] 1. *v/t. and v/i.*
(*irr., ge-, h*) write (*j-m to s.o.; über*
acc. on); *mit der Maschine ~*
type(write); 2. *v/t.* (*irr., ge-, h*)
spell; 3. 2 *n* (-*s*/-) letter.

'**Schreiber** *m* (-*s*/-) writer; secretary, clerk.

schreib|faul *adj.* ['ʃraip-] lazy in
writing; '**2feder** *f* pen; '**2fehler** *m*
mistake in writing *or* spelling, slip
of the pen; '**2heft** *n* exercise-book;
'**2mappe** *f* writing-case; '**2ma-**
schine *f* typewriter; (*mit der*) ~
schreiben type(write); '**2material**
n writing-materials *pl.*, stationery;
'**2papier** *n* writing-paper; '**2-**
schrift *typ.* *f* script; '**2tisch** *m*
(writing-)desk; **2ung** ['~buŋ] *f*
(-/-*en*) spelling; '**2unterlage** *f*
desk pad; '**2waren** *f/pl.* writing-
materials *pl.*, stationery; '**2waren-**
händler *m* stationer; '**2zeug** *n*
writing-materials *pl.*

'**schreien** (*irr., ge-, h*) 1. *v/t.* shout;
scream; 2. *v/i.* cry (out) (*vor dat.*
with *pain, etc.*; *nach* for *bread,*
etc.); shout (*vor* with); scream
(with); '**~d** *adj. colour:* loud; *injus-*
tice: flagrant.

schreiten ['ʃraitən] *v/i.* (*irr., ge-,*
sein) step, stride (*über acc.* across);
fig. proceed (*zu* to).

schrie [ʃriː] *pret. of* schreien.

schrieb [ʃriːp] *pret. of* schreiben.

Schrift [ʃrift] *f* (-/-*en*) (hand-)
writing, hand; *typ.* type; character,
letter; writing; publication; *die*
Heilige ~ the (Holy) Scriptures *pl.*;
'**~art** *f* type; '**2deutsch** *adj.*
literary German; '**~führer** *m*
secretary; '**~leiter** *m* editor; '**2lich**
1. *adj.* written, in writing; 2. *adv.*
in writing; '**~satz** *m* ⚖️ pleadings
pl.; *typ.* composition, type-setting;
'**~setzer** *m* compositor, type-setter;
'**~sprache** *f* literary language;
'**~steller** *m* (-*s*/-) author, writer;
'**~stück** *n* piece of writing, paper,
document; '**~tum** *n* (-*s*/*no pl.*)
literature; '**~wechsel** *m* exchange
of letters, correspondence; '**~zei-**
chen *n* character, letter.

schrill *adj.* [ʃril] shrill, piercing.

Schritt [ʃrit] 1. *m* (-[e]s/-*e*) step
(*a. fig.*); pace (*a. fig.*); *~e unter-*
nehmen take steps; 2. 2 *pret. of*
schreiten; '**~macher** *m* (-*s*/-) *sports:*
pace-maker; '**2weise** 1. *adj.* gradual;
2. *adv. a.* step by step.

schroff *adj.* [ʃrɔf] rugged, jagged;

steep, precipitous; *fig.* harsh, gruff; ~er Widerspruch glaring contradiction.

schröpfen ['ʃrœpfən] *v/t.* (ge-, h) $\mathcal{S}^{\!g}$ cup; *fig.* milk, fleece.

Schrot [ʃroːt] *m, n* (-[e]s/-e) crushed grain; small shot; '~brot *n* wholemeal bread; '~flinte *f* shotgun.

Schrott [ʃrɔt] *m* (-[e]s/-e) scrap (-iron *or* -metal).

schrubben ['ʃrubən] *v/t.* (ge-, h) scrub.

Schrulle ['ʃrulə] *f* (-/-n) whim, fad.

schrumpf|en ['ʃrumpfən] *v/i.* (ge-, sein) shrink (a ⊕, ⊕, *fig.*); 'Qung *f* (-/-en) shrinking; shrinkage.

Schub [ʃuːp] *m* (-[e]s/-e) push, shove; *phys.*, ⊕ thrust; *bread, people, etc.* batch; '~fach *n* drawer; '~karren *m* wheelbarrow; '~kasten *m* drawer; '~kraft *phys.*, ⊕ *f* thrust; '~lade *f* (-/-n) drawer.

Schubs F [ʃups] *m* (-es/-e) push; 'Qen F *v/t* (ge-, h) push.

schüchtern *adj.* ['ʃʏçtərn] shy, bashful, timid; *girl:* coy; 'Qheit *f* (-/no *pl.*) shyness, bashfulness, timidity; coyness (*of girl*).

schuf [ʃuːf] *pret. of* **schaffen** 1.

Schuft [ʃuft] *m* (-[e]s/-e) scoundrel, rascal; cad; 'Qen F *v/i.* (ge-, h) drudge, slave, plod; 'Qig *adj.* scoundrelly, rascally; caddish.

Schuh [ʃuː] *m* (-[e]s/-e) shoe; *j-m et. in die ~e schieben* put the blame for s.th. on s.o.; *wissen, wo der ~ drückt* know where the shoe pinches; '~anzieher *m* (-s/-) shoehorn; '~band *n* shoe-lace *or* -string; '~creme *f* shoe-cream, shoe-polish; '~geschäft *n* shoe-shop; '~löffel *m* shoehorn; '~macher *m* (-s/-) shoemaker; '~putzer *m* (-s/-) shoeblack, *Am. a.* shoeshine; '~sohle *f* sole; '~spanner *m* (-s/-) shoetree; '~werk *n*, '~zeug F *n* foot-wear, boots and shoes *pl.*

'Schul|amt *n* school-board; '~arbeit *f* homework; '~bank *f* (school-)desk; '~beispiel *n* test-case, typical example; '~besuch *m* (-[e]s/no *pl.*) attendance at school; '~bildung *f* education; *höhere* ~ secondary education; '~buch *n* school-book.

Schuld [ʃult] *f* 1. (-/no *pl.*) guilt; fault, blame; *es ist s-e* ~ it is his fault, he is to blame for it; 2. (-/-en) debt; *~en machen* contract *or* incur debts; 'Qbewußt *adj.* conscious of one's guilt; Qen ['~dən] *v/t.* (ge-, h): *j-m et.* ~ owe s.o. s.th.; *j-m Dank* ~ be indebted to s.o. (*für* for); Qhaft *adj.* ['~haft] culpable.

'Schuldiener *m* school attendant *or* porter.

schuldig *adj.* ['ʃuldiç] guilty (*e-r Sache of* s.th.); *respect, etc.*: due; *j-m et.* ~ *sein* owe s.o. s.th.; *Dank* ~ *sein* be indebted *to s.o.* (*für* for);

für ~ *befinden* $\frac{1}{2}\frac{1}{2}$ find guilty; Qe ['~gə] *m, f* (-/-n) guilty person; culprit; 'Qkeit *f* (-/no *pl.*) duty, obligation.

'Schuldirektor *m* headmaster, *Am. a.* principal.

'schuld|los *adj.* guiltless, innocent; 'Qlosigkeit *f* (-/no *pl.*) guiltlessness, innocence; Qner ['~dnər] *m* (-s/-) debtor; 'Qschein *m* evidence of debt, certificate of indebtedness, IOU (= I owe you); 'Qverschreibung *f* bond, debt certificate.

Schule ['ʃuːlə] *f* (-/-n) school; *höhere* ~ secondary school, *Am. a.* high school; *auf or in der* ~ at school; *in die* ~ *gehen* go to school; 'Qn *v/t.* (ge-, h) train, school; *pol.* indoctrinate.

Schüler ['ʃyːlər] *m* (-s/-) schoolboy, pupil; *phls., etc.:* disciple; '~austausch *m* exchange of pupils; '~in *f* (-/-nen) schoolgirl.

'Schul|ferien *pl.* holidays *pl.*, vacation; '~fernsehen *n* educational TV; '~funk *m* educational broadcast; '~gebäude *n* school(house); '~geld *n* school fee(s *pl.*), tuition; '~hof *m* playground, *Am. a.* schoolyard; '~kamerad *m* schoolfellow; '~lehrer *m* schoolmaster, teacher; '~mappe *f* satchel; 'Qmeistern *v/t.* (ge-, h) censure pedantically; '~ordnung *f* school regulations *pl.*; 'Qpflichtig *adj.* schoolable; '~rat *m* supervisor of schools, school inspector; '~schiff *n* training-ship; '~schluß *m* end of school; end of term; '~schwänzer *m* (-s/-) truant; '~stunde *f* lesson.

Schulter ['ʃultər] *f* (-/-n) shoulder; '~blatt *anat.* *n* shoulder-blade; 'Qn *v/t.* (ge-, h) shoulder.

'Schul|unterricht *m* school, lessons *pl.*; school instruction; '~versäumnis *f* (-/no *pl.*) absence from school; '~wesen *n* educational system; '~zeugnis *n* report.

schummeln F ['ʃuməln] *v/i.* (ge-, h) cheat, *Am.* F *a.* chisel.

Schund [ʃunt] 1. *m* (-[e]s/no *pl.*) trash, rubbish (*both a. fig.*); 2. Q *pret. of* **schinden**; '~literatur *f* trashy literature; '~roman *m* trashy novel, *Am. a.* dime novel.

Schupp|e ['ʃupə] *f* (-/-n) scale; *~n pl. on head:* dandruff; '~en 1. *m* (-s/-) shed; *mot.* garage; ✈ hangar; 2. Q *v/t.* (ge-, h) scale (*fish*); *sich* ~ *skin:* scale off; 'Qig *adj.* scaly.

Schür|eisen ['ʃyːrʔ-] *n* poker; 'Qen *v/t.* (ge-, h) poke; stoke; *fig.* fan, foment.

schürfen ['ʃʏrfən] (ge-, h) 1. ⛏ *v/i.* prospect (*nach* for); 2. *v/t.* ⛏ prospect for; *sich den Arm* ~ graze one's arm.

Schurk|e ['ʃurkə] *m* (-n/-n) scoundrel, knave; '~erei [~'raɪ] *f* (-/-en)

rascality, knavish trick; '2isch adj.
scoundrelly, knavish.
Schürze ['ʃyrtsə] f (-/-n) apron;
children: pinafore; '2n v/t. (ge-, h)
tuck up (*skirt*); tie (*knot*); purse
(*lips*); '~njäger m skirt-chaser, Am.
sl. wolf.
Schuß [ʃus] m (Schusses/Schüsse)
shot (a. *sports*); *ammunition*: round;
sound: report; charge; *wine, etc.*:
dash (a. *fig.*); in ~ sein be in full
swing, be in full working order.
Schüssel ['ʃysəl] f (-/-n) basin (*for
water, etc.*); bowl, dish, tureen
(*for soup, vegetables, etc.*).
'**Schuß|waffe** f fire-arm; '~weite f
range; '~wunde f gunshot wound.
Schuster ['ʃuːstər] m (-s/-) shoemaker; '2n fig. v/i. (ge-, h) s. pfuschen.
Schutt [ʃut] m (-[e]s/no pl.) rubbish,
refuse; rubble, debris.
Schüttel|frost ['ʃytəl-] m shiver-
ing-fit; '2n v/t. (ge-, h) shake; den
Kopf ~ shake one's head; j-m die
Hand ~ shake hands with s.o.
schütten ['ʃytən] (ge-, h) 1. v/t.
pour; spill (*auf acc. on*); 2. v/i.:
es schüttet it is pouring with rain.
Schutz [ʃuts] m (-es/no pl.) protection (gegen, vor dat. against),
defen|ce, Am. -se (against, from);
shelter (from); safeguard; cover;
'~brille f (e-e a pair of) goggles pl.
Schütze ['ʃytsə] m (-n/-n) marksman,
shot; ✕ rifleman; '2n v/t. (ge-, h)
protect (gegen, vor dat. against,
from), defend (against, from),
guard (against, from); shelter
(from); safeguard (*rights, etc.*).
Schutzengel ['ʃuts?-] m guardian
angel.
'**Schützen|graben** ✕ m trench;
'~könig m champion shot.
'**Schutz|haft** 🕮 f protective cus-
tody; '~heilige m patron saint;
'~herr m patron, protector; '2imp-
fung 🖋 f protective inoculation;
smallpox: vaccination.
Schützling ['ʃytslɪŋ] m (-s/-e) pro-
tégé, female: protégée.
'**schutz|los** adj. unprotected; de-
fen|celess, Am. -seless; '2mann m
(-[e]s/~er, Schutzleute) policeman,
(police) constable, sl. bobby, sl. cop;
'2marke f trade mark, brand; '2-
mittel n preservative; 🖋 prophylactic; '2patron m patron saint;
'2umschlag m (dust-)jacket, wrapper; '~zoll m protective duty.
Schwabe ['ʃvaːbə] m (-n/-n) Swabian.
schwäbisch adj. ['ʃvɛːbiʃ] Swabian.
schwach adj. [ʃvax] *resistance, team,
knees* (a. *fig.*), *eyes, heart, voice,
character, tea, gr. verb*, 🕇 *demand,
etc.*: weak; *person, etc.*: infirm;
person, recollection, etc.: feeble;
sound, light, hope, idea, etc.: faint;

consolation, attendance, etc.: poor;
light, recollection, etc.: dim; *resemblance*: remote; *das ~e Geschlecht*
the weaker sex; ~e Seite weak point
or side.
Schwäche ['ʃvɛçə] f (-/-n) weakness
(a. *fig.*); infirmity; *fig.* foible; e-e ~
haben für have a weakness for; '2n
v/t. (ge-, h) weaken (a. *fig.*); impair
(*health*).
'**Schwach|heit** f (-/-en) weakness;
fig. a. frailty; '~kopf m simpleton,
soft(y), Am. F a. sap(head); 2köp-
fig adj. ['~kœpfiç] weak-headed,
soft, Am. sl. a. sappy.
schwäch|lich adj. ['ʃvɛçliç] weakly,
feeble; delicate, frail; '2ling m
(-s/-e) weakling (a. *fig.*).
'**schwach|sinnig** adj. weak- *or*
feeble-minded; '2strom ⚡ m
(-[e]s/no pl.) weak current.
Schwadron ✕ [ʃva'droːn] f (-/-en)
squadron; 2ieren [~o'niːrən] v/t.
(no -ge-, h) swagger, vapo(u)r.
Schwager ['ʃvaːgər] m (-s/~) broth-
er-in-law.
Schwägerin ['ʃvɛːgərin] f (-/-nen)
sister-in-law. [swallow.\]
Schwalbe orn. ['ʃvalbə] f (-/-n)\
Schwall [ʃval] m (-[e]s/-e) swell,
flood; *words*: torrent.
Schwamm [ʃvam] 1. m (-[e]s/~e)
sponge; 🍄 fungus; 🖋 dry-rot; 2. 2
pret. of schwimmen; '2ig adj.
spongy; *face, etc.*: bloated.
Schwan orn. [ʃvaːn] m (-[e]s/~e)
swan.
schwand [ʃvant] pret. of schwinden.
schwang [ʃvaŋ] pret. of schwingen.
schwanger adj. ['ʃvaŋər] pregnant,
with child, in the family way.
schwängern ['ʃvɛŋərn] v/t. (ge-, h)
get with child, impregnate (a. *fig.*).
'**Schwangerschaft** f (-/-en) preg-
nancy.
schwanken ['ʃvaŋkən] v/i. (ge-)
1. (h) *earth, etc.*: shake, rock; 🕇
prices: fluctuate; *branches, etc.*:
sway; *fig.* waver, oscillate, vacillate;
2. (sein) stagger, totter.
Schwanz [ʃvants] m (-es/~e) tail (a.
✕, ast.); *fig.* train.
schwänz|eln ['ʃvɛntsəln] v/i. (ge-, h)
wag one's tail; *fig.* fawn (um [up]on);
'~en v/t. (ge-, h) cut (*lecture, etc.*);
die Schule ~ play truant, Am. a.
play hooky.
Schwarm [ʃvarm] m (-[e]s/~e) *bees,
etc.*: swarm; *birds*: a. flight, flock;
fish: school, schoal; *birds, girls,
etc.*: bevy; F *fig.* fancy, craze; p.:
idol, hero; flame.
schwärmen ['ʃvɛrmən] v/i. (ge-, h)
bees, etc.: swarm; *fig.*: revel; rave
(von about, of), gush (over); ~ für
be wild about, adore s.o.
'**Schwärmer** m (-s/-) enthusiast;
esp. eccl. fanatic; visionary; *fireworks*: cracker, squib; *zo.* hawk-

moth; **~ei** [~'raɪ] *f* (-/-en) enthusiasm (*für* for); idolization; ecstasy; *esp. eccl.* fanaticism; **'2isch** *adj.* enthusiastic; gushing, raving; adoring; *esp. eccl.* fanatic(al).

Schwarte ['ʃvartə] *f* (-/-n) bacon: rind; F *fig.* old book.

schwarz *adj.* [ʃvarts] black (*a. fig.*); dark; dirty; **~es Brett** notice-board, *Am.* bulletin board; **~es Brot** brown bread; **~er Mann** bog(e)y; **~er Markt** black market; **~ auf weiß** in black and white; *auf die* **~e** *Liste setzen* blacklist; **'2arbeit** *f* illicit work; **'2brot** *n* brown bread; **'2e** *m, f* (-n/-n) black.

Schwärze ['ʃvɛrtsə] *f* (-/no *pl.*) blackness (*a. fig.*); darkness; **'2n** *v/t.* (ge-, h) blacken.

'schwarz|fahren F *v/i.* (*irr. fahren, sep.*, -ge-, *sein*) travel without a ticket; *mot.* drive without a licence; **'2fahrer** *m* fare-dodger; *mot.* person driving without a licence; **'2fahrt** *f* ride without a ticket; *mot.* drive without a licence; **'2handel** *m* illicit trade, black marketeering; **'2händler** *m* black marketeer; **'2hörer** *m* listener without a licence.

'schwärzlich *adj.* blackish.

'Schwarz|markt *m* black market; **'~seher** *m* pessimist; *TV:* viewer without a licence; **'~sender** *m* pirate broadcasting station; **~'weißfilm** *m* black-and-white film.

schwatzen ['ʃvatsən] *v/i.* (ge-, h) chat; chatter, tattle.

schwätz|en ['ʃvɛtsən] *v/i.* (ge-, h) *s. schwatzen*; **'2er** *m* (-s/-) chatterbox; tattler, prattler; gossip.

'schwatzhaft *adj.* talkative, garrulous.

Schwebe *fig.* ['ʃve:bə] *f* (-/no *pl.*): *in der* **~** *sein* be in suspense; *law, rule, etc.*: be in abeyance; **'~bahn** *f* aerial railway *or* ropeway; **'2n** *v/i.* (ge-, h) be suspended; *bird:* hover (*a. fig.*); glide; *fig.* be pending (*a. ɡ̊ɡ̊*); *in Gefahr* **~** be in danger.

Schwed|e ['ʃve:də] *m* (-n/-n) Swede; **'2isch** *adj.* Swedish.

Schwefel ['ʃve:fəl] *m* (-s/no *pl.*) sulphur, *Am. a.* sulfur; **'~säure** *f* (-/no *pl.*) sulphuric acid, *Am. a.* sulfuric acid.

Schweif [ʃvaɪf] *m* (-[e]s/-e) tail (*a. ast.*); *fig.* train; **'2en** (ge-) 1. *v/i.* (*sein*) rove, ramble; 2. ⊕ *v/t.* (h) curve; scallop.

schweigen ['ʃvaɪɡən] 1. *v/i.* (*irr.*, ge-, h) be silent; 2. 2 *n* (-s/no *pl.*) silence; **'~d** *adj.* silent.

schweigsam *adj.* ['ʃvaɪkza:m] taciturn; **'2keit** *f* (-/no *pl.*) taciturnity.

Schwein [ʃvaɪn] *n* 1. (-[e]s/-e) *zo.* pig, hog, swine (*all a. contp. fig.*); 2. F (-[e]s/no *pl.*): **~** *haben* be lucky.

'Schweine|braten *m* roast pork;

'~fleisch *n* pork; **'~hund** F *contp. m* swine; **~rei** [~'raɪ] *f* (-/-en) mess; dirty trick; smut(ty story); **'~stall** *m* pigsty (*a. fig.*).

'schweinisch *fig. adj.* swinish; smutty.

'Schweinsleder *n* pigskin.

Schweiß [ʃvaɪs] *m* (-es/-e) sweat, perspiration; **'2en** ⊕ *v/t.* (ge-, h) weld; **'~er** ⊕ *m* (-s/-) welder; **'~fuß** *m* perspiring foot; **'2ig** *adj.* sweaty, damp with sweat.

Schweizer ['ʃvaɪtsər] *m* (-s/-) Swiss; *on farm:* dairyman.

schwelen ['ʃve:lən] *v/i.* (ge-, h) smo(u)lder (*a. fig.*).

schwelg|en ['ʃvɛlɡən] *v/i.* (ge-, h) lead a luxurious life; revel; *fig.* revel (*in dat.* in); **'2er** *m* (-s/-) revel(l)er; epicure; **2erei** [~'raɪ] *f* (-/-en) revel(ry), feasting; **'~erisch** *adj.* luxurious; revel(l)ing.

Schwell|e ['ʃve:lə] *f* (-/-n) sill, threshold (*a. fig.*); 🚂 sleeper, *Am.* tie; **'2en** 1. *v/i.* (*irr.*, ge-, *sein*) swell (out); 2. *v/t.* (ge-, h) swell; **'~ung** *f* (-/-en) swelling.

Schwemme ['ʃvɛmə] *f* (-/-n) watering-place; horse-pond; *at tavern, etc.:* taproom; ☂ glut (*of fruit, etc.*).

Schwengel ['ʃvɛŋəl] *m* (-s/-) clapper (*of bell*); handle (*of pump*).

schwenk|en ['ʃvɛŋkən] (ge-) 1. *v/t.* (h) swing; wave (*hat, etc.*); brandish (*stick, etc.*); rinse (*washing*); 2. *v/i.* (*sein*) turn, wheel; **'2ung** *f* (-/-en) turn; *fig.* change of mind.

schwer [ʃve:r] 1. *adj.* heavy; *problem, etc.*: hard, difficult; *illness, mistake, etc.*: serious; *punishment, etc.*: severe; *fault, etc.*: grave; *wine, cigar, etc.*: strong; **~e** *Zeiten* hard times; *2 Pfund* **~** *sein* weigh two pounds; 2. *adv.*: **~** *arbeiten* work hard; **~** *hören* be hard of hearing; **'2e** *f* (-/no *pl.*) heaviness; *phys.* gravity (*a. fig.*); severity; **'~fällig** *adj.* heavy, slow; clumsy; **'2gewicht** *n sports:* heavy-weight; *fig.* main emphasis; **'2gewichtler** *m* (-s/-) *sports:* heavy-weight; **'~hörig** *adj.* hard of hearing; **'2industrie** *f* heavy industry; **'2kraft** *phys. f* (-/no *pl.*) gravity; **'~lich** *adv.* hardly, scarcely; **'2mut** *f* (-/no *pl.*) melancholy; **'~mütig** *adj.* ['~my:tɪç] melancholy; **'2punkt** *m* centre of gravity, *Am.* center of gravity; *fig.*: crucial point; emphasis.

Schwert [ʃve:rt] *n* (-[e]s/-er) sword.

'Schwer|verbrecher *m* felon; **'2verdaulich** *adj.* indigestible, heavy; **'2verständlich** *adj.* difficult *or* hard to understand; **'2verwundet** *adj.* seriously wounded; **'2wiegend** *fig. adj.* weighty, momentous.

Schwester ['ʃvɛstər] *f* (-/-n) sister; nurse.

schwieg [ʃviːk] *pret. of* schweigen.

Schwieger|eltern ['ʃviːgər-] *pl.* parents-in-law *pl.*; '~mutter *f* mother-in-law; '~sohn *m* son-in-law; '~tochter *f* daughter-in-law; '~vater *m* father-in-law.

Schwiel|e ['ʃviːlə] *f* (-/-n) callosity; 'Qig *adj.* callous.

schwierig *adj.* ['ʃviːriç] difficult, hard; 'Qkeit *f* (-/-en) difficulty, trouble.

Schwimm|bad ['ʃvɪm-] *n* swimming-bath, *Am.* swimming pool; 'Qen *v/i.* (*irr.*, ge-) 1. (*sein*) swim; *thing*: float; *ich bin über den Fluß geschwommen* I swam across the river; *in Geld ~* be rolling in money; 2. (*h*) swim; *ich habe lange unter Wasser geschwommen* I swam under water for a long time; '~gürtel *m* swimming-belt; lifebelt; '~haut *f* web; '~lehrer *m* swimming-instructor; '~weste *f* life-jacket.

Schwindel ['ʃvɪndəl] *m* (-s/no *pl.*) $\mathscr{F}$ vertigo, giddiness, dizziness; F *fig.*: swindle, humbug, *sl.* eyewash; cheat, fraud; '~anfall $\mathscr{F}$ *m* fit of dizziness; 'Qerregend *adj.* dizzy (*a. fig.*); '~firma † *f* long firm, *Am.* wildcat firm; 'Qn *v/i.* (ge-, *h*) cheat, humbug, swindle.

schwinden ['ʃvɪndən] *v/i.* (*irr.*, ge-, *sein*) dwindle, grow less; *strength, colour, etc.*: fade.

'**Schwindl|er** *m* (-s/-) swindler, cheat, humbug; liar; 'Qig $\mathscr{F}$ *adj.* giddy, dizzy.

Schwind|sucht $\mathscr{F}$ ['ʃvɪnt-] *f* (-/no *pl.*) consumption; 'Qsüchtig $\mathscr{F}$ *adj.* consumptive.

Schwing|e ['ʃvɪŋə] *f* (-/-n) wing, *poet.* pinion; swingle; 'Qen (*irr.*, ge-, *h*) 1. *v/t.* swing; brandish (*weapon*); swingle (*flax*); 2. *v/i.* swing; $\oplus$ oscillate; *sound, etc.*: vibrate; '~ung *f* (-/-en) oscillation; vibration.

Schwips F [ʃvɪps] *m* (-es/-e): e-n ~ *haben* be tipsy, have had a drop too much.

schwirren ['ʃvɪrən] *v/i.* (ge-) 1. (*sein*) whir(r); *arrow, etc.*: whiz(z); *insects*: buzz; *rumours, etc.*: buzz, circulate; 2. (*h*): *mir schwirrt der Kopf* my head is buzzing.

'**Schwitz|bad** *n* sweating-bath, hot-air bath, vapo(u)r bath; 'Qen (ge-, *h*) 1. *v/i.* sweat, perspire; 2. F *fig. v/t.*: *Blut und Wasser ~* be in great anxiety.

schwoll [ʃvɔl] *pret. of* schwellen.

schwor [ʃvoːr] *pret. of* schwören.

schwören ['ʃvøːrən] (*irr.*, ge-) 1. *v/t.* swear; e-n *Meineid ~* commit perjury; *j-m Rache ~* vow vengeance against s.o.; 2. *v/i.* swear (*bei by*);

~ *auf* (*acc.*) have great belief in, F swear by.

schwül *adj.* [ʃvyːl] sultry, oppressively hot; 'Qe *f* (-/no *pl.*) sultriness.

Schwulst [ʃvʊlst] *m* (-es/-̈e) bombast.

schwülstig *adj.* ['ʃvʏlstɪç] bombastic, turgid.

Schwund [ʃvʊnt] *m* (-[e]s/no *pl.*) dwindling; *wireless, etc.*: fading; $\mathscr{F}$ atrophy.

Schwung [ʃvʊŋ] *m* (-[e]s/-̈e) swing; *fig.* verve, go; flight (*of imagination*); buoyancy; 'Qhaft † *adj.* flourishing, brisk; '~rad $\oplus$ *n* fly-wheel; *watch, clock*: balance-wheel; 'Qvoll *adj.* full of energy *or* verve; *attack, translation, etc.*: spirited; *style, etc.*: racy.

Schwur [ʃvuːr] *m* (-[e]s/-̈e) oath; '~gericht ⚖ *n England, Wales*: *appr.* court of assize.

sechs [zɛks] 1. *adj.* six; 2. Q *f* (-/-en) six; 'Qeck *n* (-[e]s/-e) hexagon; '~eckig *adj.* hexagonal; '~fach *adj.* sixfold, sextuple; '~mal *adv.* six times; '~monatig *adj.* lasting *or* of six months, six-months ...; '~monatlich 1. *adj.* six-monthly; 2. *adv.* every six months; '~stündig *adj.* ['~ʃtʏndɪç] lasting *or* of six hours, six-hour ...; 2'tagerennen *n* *cycling*: six-day race; '~tägig *adj.* ['~tɛːgɪç] lasting *or* of six days.

sechs|te *adj.* ['zɛkstə] sixth; 'Qtel *n* (-s/-) sixth (part); '~tens *adv.* sixthly, in the sixth place.

sech|zehn(te) *adj.* ['zɛç-] sixteen(th); '~zig *adj.* ['~tsɪç] sixty; '~zigste *adj.* sixtieth.

See [zeː] 1. *m* (-s/-n) lake; 2. *f* (-/no *pl.*) sea; *an die ~ gehen* go to the seaside; *in ~ gehen or stechen* put to sea; *auf ~ at sea*; *auf hoher ~* on the high seas; *zur ~ gehen* go to sea; 3. *f* (-/-n) sea, billow; '~bad *n* seaside resort; '~fahrer *m* sailor, navigator; '~fahrt *f* navigation; voyage; 'Qfest *adj.* seaworthy; *~ sein* be a good sailor; '~gang *m* (motion of the) sea; '~hafen *m* seaport; '~handel † *m* maritime trade; '~herrschaft *f* naval supremacy; '~hund *zo.* *m* seal; 'Qkrank *adj.* seasick; '~krankheit *f* (-/no *pl.*) seasickness; '~krieg *m* naval war(fare).

Seele ['zeːlə] *f* (-/-n) soul (*a. fig.*); *mit or von ganzer ~* with all one's heart.

'**Seelen|größe** *f* (-/no *pl.*) greatness of soul *or* mind; '~heil *n* salvation, spiritual welfare; 'Qlos *adj.* soulless; '~qual *f* anguish of mind, (mental) agony; '~ruhe *f* peace of mind; coolness.

'**seelisch** *adj.* psychic(al), mental.

'**Seelsorge** *f* (-/no *pl.*) cure of souls;

ministerial work; '**~r** *m* (-s/-) pastor, minister.

'**See|macht** *f* naval power; '**~mann** *m* (-[e]s/*Seeleute*) seaman, sailor; '**~meile** *f* nautical mile; '**~not** *f* (-/*no pl.*) distress (at sea); '**~räuber** *m* pirate; **~räuberei** [~'raɪ] *f* (-/-en) piracy; '**~recht** *n* maritime law; **~reise** *f* voyage; '**~schiff** *n* sea-going ship; '**~schlacht** *f* naval battle; '**~schlange** *f* sea serpent; '**~sieg** *m* naval victory; '**~stadt** *f* seaside town; '**~streitkräfte** *f/pl.* naval forces *pl.*; '**2tüchtig** *adj.* seaworthy; '**~warte** *f* naval observatory; '**~weg** *m* sea-route; *auf dem* **~** by sea; '**~wesen** *n* (-s/*no pl.*) maritime *or* naval affairs *pl.*

Segel ['ze:gəl] *n* (-s/-) sail; *unter* **~** *gehen* set sail; '**~boot** *n* sailing-boat, *Am.* sailboat; *sports:* yacht; '**~fliegen** *n* (-s/*no pl.*) gliding, soaring; '**~flug** *m* gliding flight, glide; '**~flugzeug** *n* glider; '**2n** (ge-) 1. *v/i.* (h, sein) sail; *sports:* yacht; 2. *v/t.* (h) sail; '**~schiff** *n* sailing-ship, sailing-vessel; '**~sport** *m* yachting; '**~tuch** *n* (-[e]s/-e) sail-cloth, canvas.

Segen ['ze:gən] *m* (-s/-) blessing (*a. fig.*), *esp. eccl.* benediction; '**2s-reich** *adj.* blessed.

Segler ['ze:glər] *m* (-s/-) sailing-vessel, sailing-ship; *fast, good, etc.* sailer; yachtsman.

segn|en ['ze:gnən] *v/t.* (ge-, h) bless; '**2ung** *f* (-/-en) *s.* Segen.

sehen ['ze:ən] (*irr.*, ge-, h) 1. *v/i.* see; *gut* **~** have good eyes; **~** *auf* (*acc.*) look at; be particular about; **~** *nach* look for; look after; 2. *v/t.* see; notice; watch, observe; '**~swert** *adj.* worth seeing; '**2swürdigkeit** *f* (-/-en) object of interest, curiosity; **~en** *pl.* sights *pl.* (*of a place*).

Seher ['ze:ər] *m* (-s/-) seer, prophet; '**~blick** *m* (-[e]s/*no pl.*) prophetic vision; '**~gabe** *f* (-/*no pl.*) gift of prophecy.

'**Seh|fehler** *m* visual defect; '**~kraft** *f* vision, eyesight.

Sehne ['ze:nə] *f* (-/-n) *anat.* sinew, tendon; string (*of bow*); ♃ chord.

'**sehnen** *v/refl.* (ge-, h) long (*nach* for), yearn (for, after); *sich danach* **~** *zu inf.* be longing to *inf.*

'**Sehnerv** *anat. m* visual *or* optic nerve.

'**sehnig** *adj.* sinewy (*a. fig.*), stringy.

'**sehn|lich** *adj.* longing; ardent; passionate; '**2sucht** *f* longing, yearning; '**~süchtig** *adj.*, '**~suchts-voll** *adj.* longing, yearning; *eyes, etc.:a.* wistful.

sehr *adv.* [ze:r] *before adj. and adv.:* very, most; *with vb.:* (very) much, greatly.

'**Seh|rohr** ⚓ *n* periscope; '**~weite** *f*

range of sight, visual range; *in* **~** within eyeshot *or* sight.

seicht *adj.* [zaɪçt] shallow; *fig. a.* superficial.

Seide ['zaɪdə] *f* (-/-n) silk.

'**seiden** *adj.* silk, silken (*a. fig.*); '**2flor** *m* silk gauze; '**2glanz** *m* silky lust[re, *Am.* -er; '**2händler** *m* mercer; '**2papier** *n* tissue(-paper); '**2raupe** *zo.* *f* silkworm; '**2spinnerei** *f* silk-spinning mill; '**2stoff** *m* silk cloth *or* fabric.

'**seidig** *adj.* silky.

Seife ['zaɪfə] *f* (-/-n) soap.

'**Seifen|blase** *f* soap-bubble; '**~ki-stenrennen** *n* soap-box derby; '**~lauge** *f* (soap-)suds *pl.*; '**~pulver** *n* soap-powder; '**~schale** *f* soap-dish; '**~schaum** *m* lather.

'**seifig** *adj.* soapy.

seih|en ['zaɪən] *v/t.* (ge-, h) strain, filter; '**2er** *m* (-s/-) strainer, colander.

Seil [zaɪl] *n* (-[e]s/-e) rope; '**~bahn** *f* funicular *or* cable railway; '**~er** *m* (-s/-) rope-maker; '**~tänzer** *m* rope-dancer.

sein¹ [zaɪn] 1. *v/i.* (*irr.*, ge-, sein) be; exist; 2. **2** *n* (-s/*no pl.*) being; existence.

sein² *poss. pron.* [~] his, her, its (*in accordance with gender of possessor*); der (die, das) **~e** his, hers, its; **~** *Glück machen* make one's fortune; *die Seinen pl.* his family *or* people.

'**seiner'|seits** *adv.* for his part; '**~zeit** *adv.* then, at that time; in those days.

'**seines'gleichen** *pron.* his equal(s *pl.*); *j-n wie* **~** *behandeln* treat *s.o.* as one's equal; *er hat nicht* **~** he has no equal; there is no one like him.

seit [zaɪt] 1. *prp.* (*dat.*): **~** *1945 since* 1945; **~** *drei Wochen* for three weeks; 2. *cj.* since; *es ist ein Jahr her*, **~** ... it is a year now since ...; **~dem** [~'de:m] 1. *adv.* since *or* from that time, ever since; 2. *cj.* since.

Seite ['zaɪtə] *f* (-/-n) side (*a. fig.*); flank (*a.* ✕, △); page (*of book*).

'**Seiten|ansicht** *f* profile, side-view; '**~blick** *m* side-glance; '**~flügel** △ *m* wing; '**~hieb** *fig. m* innuendo, sarcastic remark; '**2s** *prp.* (*gen.*) on the part of; by; '**~schiff** △ *n* *church:* aisle; '**~sprung** *fig. m* extra-marital adventure; '**~straße** *f* bystreet; '**~stück** *fig. n* counterpart (*zu of*); '**~weg** *m* by-way.

seit'her *adv.* since (then, that time).

'**seit|lich** *adj.* lateral; **~wärts** *adv.* ['~vɛrts] sideways; aside.

Sekret|är [zekre'tɛ:r] *m* (-s/-e) secretary; bureau; **~ariat** [~ari'a:t] *n* (-[e]s/-e) secretary's office; secretariat(e); **~ärin** *f* (-/-nen) secretary.

Sekt [zɛkt] *m* (-[e]s/-e) champagne.

Sekt|e ['zɛktə] *f* (-/-n) sect; ~ierer [~'ti:rər] *m* (-s/-) sectarian.

Sektor ['zɛktɔr] *m* (-s/-en) Å, ✕, *pol.* sector; *fig.* field, branch.

Sekunde [ze'kundə] *f* (-/-n) second; ~nbruchteil *m* split second; ~nzeiger *m* second-hand.

selb *adj.* [zɛlp] same; ~er F *pron.* ['~bər] *s. selbst 1.*

selbst [zɛlpst] 1. *pron.* self; personally; *ich* ~ I myself; *von* ~ *p.* of one's own accord; *thing:* by itself, automatically; 2. *adv.* even; 3. 2 *n* (-/*no pl.*) (one's own) self; ego.

selbständig *adj.* ['zɛlpʃtɛndiç] independent; *sich* ~ *machen* set up for o.s.; '2keit *f* (-/*no pl.*) independence.

'Selbst|anlasser *mot. m* self-starter; '~anschluß *teleph. m* automatic connection; '~bedienungsladen *m* self-service shop; '~beherrschung *f* self-command, self-control; '~bestimmung *f* self-determination; '~betrug *m* self-deception; '2bewußt *adj.* self-confident, self-reliant; '~bewußtsein *n* self-confidence, self-reliance; '~binder *m* (-s/-) tie; '~erhaltung *f* self-preservation; '~erkenntnis *f* self-knowledge; '~erniedrigung *f* self-abasement; '2gefällig *adj.* (self-)complacent; '~gefälligkeit *f* (-/*no pl.*) self-complacency; '~gefühl *n* (-[e]s/*no pl.*) self-reliance; 2gemacht *adj.* ['~gəmaxt] homemade; '2gerecht *adj.* self-righteous; '~gespräch *n* soliloquy, monolog(ue); '2herrlich 1. *adj.* high-handed, autocratic(al); 2. *adv.* with a high hand; '~hilfe *f* self-help; '~kostenpreis ✝ *m* cost price; '~laut *gr. m* vowel; '2los *adj.* unselfish, disinterested; '~mord *m* suicide; '~mörder *m* suicide; '2mörderisch *adj.* suicidal; '2sicher *adj.* self-confident, self-assured; '~sucht *f* (-/*no pl.*) selfishness, ego(t)ism; '2süchtig *adj.* selfish, ego(t)istic(al); '2tätig ⊕ *adj.* self-acting, automatic; '~täuschung *f* self-deception; '~überwindung *f* (-/*no pl.*) self-conquest; '~unterricht *m* self-instruction; '~verleugnung *f* self-denial; '~versorger *m* (-s/-) self-supporter; '2verständlich 1. *adj.* self-evident, obvious; 2. *adv.* of course, naturally; ~ *l a.* by all means!; '~verständlichkeit *f* 1. (-/*no pl.*) matter of course; 2. (-/*no pl.*) matter-of-factness; '~verteidigung *f* self-defen|ce, *Am.* -se; '~vertrauen *n* self-confidence, self-reliance; '~verwaltung *f* self-government, autonomy; '2zufrieden *adj.* self-satisfied; '~zufriedenheit *f* self-satisfaction; '~zweck *m* (-[e]s/*no pl.*) end in itself.

selig *adj.* ['ze:liç] *eccl.* blessed; late, deceased; *fig.* blissful, overjoyed; '2keit *fig. f* (-/-en) bliss, very great joy.

Sellerie ⚕ ['zɛləri:] *m* (-s/-[s]), *f* (-/-) celery.

selten ['zɛltən] 1. *adj.* rare; scarce; 2. *adv.* rarely, seldom; '2heit *f* (-/-en) rarity, scarcity; rarity, curio(sity); '2heitswert *m* (-[e]s/*no pl.*) scarcity value.

Selterswasser ['zɛltərs-] *n* (-s/⸗) seltzer (water), soda-water.

seltsam *adj.* ['zɛltza:m] strange, odd.

Semester *univ.* [ze'mɛstər] *n* (-s/-) term.

Semikolon *gr.* [zemi'ko:lɔn] *n* (-s/-s, Semikola) semicolon.

Seminar [zemi'na:r] *n* (-s/-e) *univ.* seminar; seminary (*for priests*).

Senat [ze'na:t] *m* (-[e]s/-e) senate; *parl.* Senate.

send|en ['zɛndən] *v/t.* 1. (*irr.*, *ge-*, *h*) send; forward; 2. (*ge-*, *h*) transmit; broadcast, *Am. a.* radio(broadcast); telecast; '2er *m* (-s/-) transmitter, broadcasting station. 'Sende|raum *m* (broadcasting) studio; '~zeichen *n* interval signal.

Sendung *f* (-/-en) ✝ consignment, shipment; broadcast; telecast; *fig.* mission. [⚥).]

Senf [zɛnf] *m* (-[e]s/-e) mustard (*a.*)

sengen ['zɛŋən] *v/t.* (*ge-*, *h*) singe; scorch; ~ *d adj.* heat parching.

senil *adj.* [ze'ni:l] senile; 2ität [~ili'tɛ:t] *f* (-/*no pl.*) senility. senior *adj.* ['ze:niɔr] senior.

Senk|blei ['zɛŋk-] *n* ⚒ plumb, plummet; ✦ *a.* sounding-lead; '2e *geogr. f* (-/-n) depression, hollow; '2en *v/t.* (*ge-*, *h*) lower; sink (*a. voice*); let down; bow (*head*); cut *prices, etc.*); *sich* ~ *land, buildings, etc.*: sink, subside; *ceiling, etc.*: sag; '~fuß ⚕ *m* flat-foot; '~fußeinlage *f* arch support; '~grube *f* cesspool; '2recht *adj.* vertical, *esp.* Å perpendicular; '~ung *f* (-/-en) *geogr.* depression, hollow; lowering, reduction (*of prices*); ⚒ sedimentation.

Sensation [zɛnza'tsjo:n] *f* (-/-en) sensation; 2ell *adj.* [~'nɛl] sensational; '~slust *f* (-/*no pl.*) sensationalism; '~spresse *f* yellow press.

Sense ['zɛnzə] *f* (-/-n) scythe.

sensi|bel *adj.* [~'zi:bəl] sensitive; 2bilität [~ibili'tɛ:t] *f* (-/*no pl.*) sensitiveness.

sentimental *adj.* [zɛntimen'ta:l] sentimental; 2ität [~ali'tɛ:t] *f* (-/-en) sentim·ntality.

September [zɛp'tɛmbər] *m* (-[s]/-) September.

Serenade ♪ [zere'nɑːdə] f (-/-n) serenade.

Serie ['zeːrjə] f (-/-n) series; set; *billiards*: break; '**2nmäßig 1.** *adj.* standard; **2.** *adv.*: ~ *herstellen* produce in mass; '**~nproduktion** f mass production.

seriös *adj.* [ze'rjøːs] serious; trustworthy, reliable.

Serum ['zeːrum] n (-s/Seren, Sera) serum.

Service[1] [zər'viːs] n (-s/-) service, set.

Service[2] ['zœːrvis] m, n (-/-s) service.

servier|en [zɛr'viːrən] v/t. (no -ge-, h) serve; **2wagen** m trolley(-table).

Serviette [zɛr'vjɛtə] f (-/-n) (table-) napkin.

Sessel ['zɛsəl] m (-s/-) armchair, easy chair; '**~lift** m chair-lift.

seßhaft *adj.* ['zɛshaft] settled, established; resident.

Setzei ['zɛtsʔ-] n fried egg.

'**setzen** (ge-) **1.** v/t. (h) set, place, put; *typ.* compose; ♂ plant; erect, raise (*monument*); stake (*money*) (*auf acc.* on); *sich* ~ sit down, take a seat; *bird*: perch; *foundations of house, sediment, etc.*: settle; **2.** v/i. (h): ~ *auf* (*acc.*) back (*horse, etc.*); **3.** v/i. (sein): ~ *über* (*acc.*) leap (*wall, etc.*); clear (*hurdle, etc.*); take (*ditch, etc.*).

'**Setzer** *typ.* m (-s/-) compositor, type-setter; **~ei** *typ.* [~'raɪ] f (-/-en) composing-room.

Seuche ['zɔʏçə] f (-/-n) epidemic (disease).

seufz|en ['zɔʏftsən] v/i. (ge-, h) sigh; '**2er** m (-s/-) sigh.

sexuell *adj.* [zɛksu'ɛl] sexual.

sezieren [ze'tsiːrən] v/t. (no -ge-, h) dissect (*a. fig.*).

sich *refl. pron.* [ziç] oneself; *sg.* himself, herself, itself; *pl.* themselves; *sg.* yourself, *pl.* yourselves; each other, one another; *sie blickte* ~ *um* she looked about her.

Sichel ['ziçəl] f (-/-n) sickle; *s.* Mondsichel.

sicher ['ziçər] **1.** *adj.* secure (*vor dat.* from), safe (from); proof (against); *hand*: steady; certain, sure; positive; *aus* ~*er Quelle* from a reliable source; *e-r Sache* ~ *sein* be sure of s.th.; **2.** *adv.* s. sicherlich; *um* ~ *zu gehen* to be on the safe side, to make sure.

'**Sicherheit** f (-/-en) security; safety, surety, certainty; positiveness; assurance (*of manner*); *in* ~ *bringen* place in safety; '**~snadel** f safety-pin; '**~sschloß** n safety-lock.

'**sicher|lich** *adv.* surely, certainly; undoubtedly; *er wird* ~ *kommen* he is sure to come; '**~n** v/t. (ge-, h) secure (*a.* ⚔, ⊕); guarantee (*a.* ↑); protect, safeguard; *sich et.* ~ secure

(*prize, seat, etc.*); '**~stellen** v/t. (*sep.*, -ge-, h) secure; '**2ung** f (-/-en) securing; safeguard(ing); ↑ security, guaranty; ⊕ safety device; ⚡ fuse.

Sicht [ziçt] f (-/no pl.) visibility; view; *in* ~ *kommen* come in(to) view *or* sight; *auf lange* ~ in the long run; *auf or bei* ~ ↑ at sight; '**2bar** *adj.* visible; '**2en** v/t. (ge-, h) ♣ sight; *fig.* sift; '**2lich** *adv.* visibly; '**~vermerk** m visé, visa (*on passport*).

sickern ['zikərn] v/i. (ge-, sein) trickle, ooze, seep.

sie *pers. pron.* [ziː] *nom.*: *sg.* she, *pl.* they; *acc.*: *sg.* her, *pl.* them; *Sie* *nom. and acc.*: *sg. and pl.* you.

Sieb [ziːp] n (-[e]s/-e) sieve; riddle (*for soil, gravel, etc.*).

sieben[1] ['ziːbən] v/t. (ge-, h) sieve, sift; riddle.

sieben[2] [~] **1.** *adj.* seven; **2.** ♀ f (-/-) (number) seven; *böse* ~ shrew, vixen; '**~fach** *adj.* sevenfold; '**~mal** *adv.* seven times; '**2'sachen** F f/pl. belongings pl., F traps pl.; '**~te** *adj.* seventh; '**2tel** n (-s/-) seventh (part); '**~tens** *adv.* seventhly, in the seventh place.

sieb|zehn(te) *adj.* ['ziːp-] seventeen(th); '**~zig** *adj.* [~'tsiç] seventy; '**~zigste** *adj.* seventieth.

siech *adj.* [ziːç] sickly; '**2tum** n (-s/no pl.) sickliness, lingering illness.

Siedehitze ['ziːdə-] f boiling-heat.

siedeln ['ziːdəln] v/i. (ge-, h) settle; *Am. a.* homestead.

siede|n ['ziːdən] v/t. and v/i. ([irr.,] ge-, h) boil, simmer; '**2punkt** m boiling-point (*a. fig.*).

Siedler ['ziːdlər] m (-s/-) settler; *Am. a.* homesteader; '**~stelle** f settler's holding; *Am. a.* homestead.

'**Siedlung** f (-/-en) settlement; housing estate.

Sieg [ziːk] m (-[e]s/-e) victory (*über acc.* over); *sports*: a. win; *den* ~ *davontragen* win the day, be victorious.

Siegel ['ziːgəl] n (-s/-) seal (*a. fig.*); signet; '**~lack** m sealing-wax; '**2n** v/t. (ge-, h) seal; '**~ring** m signet-ring.

sieg|en ['ziːgən] v/i. (ge-, h) be victorious (*über acc.* over), conquer s.o.; *sports*: win; '**2er** m (-s/-) conqueror, *rhet.* victor; *sports*: winner. **Siegeszeichen** ['ziːgəs-] n trophy. '**siegreich** *adj.* victorious, triumphant.

Signal [zi'gnɑːl] n (-s/-e) signal; **2isieren** [~ali'ziːrən] v/t. (no -ge-, h) signal.

Silbe ['zilbə] f (-/-n) syllable; '**~ntrennung** f syllabi(fi)cation.

Silber ['zilbər] n (-s/no pl.) silver; *s. Tafelsilber*; '**2n** *adj.* (of) silver;

'_zeug F n silver plate, Am. a. silverware.

Silhouette [zilu'ɛtə] f (-/-n) silhouette; skyline.

Silvester [zil'vɛstər] n (-s/-), _abend m new-year's eve.

simpel ['zimpəl] 1. adj. plain, simple; stupid, silly; 2. ♀ m (-s/-) simpleton

Sims [zims] m, n (-es/-e) ledge; sill (of window); mantelshelf (of fireplace); shelf; ⚠ cornice.

Simul|ant [zimu'lant] m (-en/-en) esp. ✕, ♣ malingerer; 2ieren (no -ge-, h) 1. v/t. sham, feign, simulate (illness, etc.); 2. v/i. sham, feign; esp. ✕, ♣ malinger.

Sinfonie ♪ [zinfo'ni:] f (-/-n) symphony.

sing|en ['ziŋən] v/t. and v/i. (irr., ge-, h) sing; vom Blatt _ sing at sight; nach Noten _ sing from music; '2sang F m (-[e]s/no pl.) singsong; '2spiel n musical comedy; '2stimme ♪ f vocal part.

Singular gr ['ziŋgula:r] m (-s/-e) singular (number).

'Singvogel m song-bird, songster.

sinken ['ziŋkən] v/i. (irr., ge-, sein) sink; ship a founder, go down; ✝ prices fall, drop, go down; den Mut _ lassen lose courage.

Sinn [zin] m (-[e]s/-e) sense; taste (für for); tendency; sense, meaning; von _en sein be out of one's senses; im _ haben have in mind; in gewissem _e in a sense; '_bild n symbol, emblem; '2bildlich adj. symbolic(al), emblematic; '2en v/i. (irr., ge-, h): auf Rache _ meditate revenge.

'Sinnen|lust f sensuality; '_mensch m sensualist; '_rausch m intoxication of the senses.

sinnentstellend adj. ['zin?-] garbling, distorting.   [world.]

'Sinnenwelt f (-/no pl.) material)

'Sinnes|änderung f change of mind; '_art f disposition, mentality; '_organ n sense-organ; '_täuschung f illusion, hallucination.

'sinn|lich adj. sensual; material; '2lichkeit f (-/no pl.) sensuality; '_los adj. senseless; futile, useless; '2losigkeit f (-/-en) senselessness; futility, uselessness; '_reich adj. ingenious; '_verwandt adj. synonymous.

Sipp|e ['zipə] f (-/-n) tribe; (blood-) relations pl.; family; '_schaft contp. f (-/-en) relations pl.; fig. clan, clique; die ganze _ the whole lot.

Sirene [zi're:nə] f (-/-n) siren.

Sirup ['zi:rup] m (-s/-e) syrup, Am. sirup; treacle, molasses sg.

Sitte ['zitə] f (-/-n) custom; habit; usage; _n pl. morals pl.; manners pl.

'Sitten|bild n, '_gemälde n genre (-painting); fig. picture of manners and morals; '_gesetz n moral law; '_lehre f ethics pl.; '2los adj. immoral; '_losigkeit f (-/-no ge-) immorality; '_polizei f appr. vice squad; '_prediger m moralizer; '_richter fig m censor, moralizer; '2streng adj. puritanic(al).

'sittlich adj. moral; '2keit f (-/no pl.) morality; '2keitsverbrechen n sexual crime

'sittsam adj. modest; '2keit f (-/no pl.) modesty.

Situation [zitua'tsjo:n] f (-/-en) situation.

Sitz [zits] m (-es/-e) seat (a. fig.); fit (of dress, etc.).

'sitzen v/i. (irr., ge-, h) sit, be seated; dress, etc.: fit; blow, etc.: tell; F fig. do time; _ bleiben remain seated, keep one's seat; '_bleiben v/i. (irr. bleiben, sep., -ge-, sein) girl at dance· F be a wallflower; girl: be left on the shelf; at school: not to get one's remove; _ auf (dat.) be left with (goods) on one's hands; '_d adj.: _e Tätigkeit sedentary work; '_lassen v/t. (irr. lassen, sep., [no] -ge-, h) leave s.o. in the lurch, let s.o. down; girl: jilt (lover); leave (girl) high and dry; auf sich _ pocket (insult, etc.).

'Sitz|gelegenheit f seating accommodation, seat(s pl.); _ bieten für seat; '_platz m seat; '_streik m sit-down or stay-in strike.

'Sitzung f (-/-en) sitting (a. parl., paint.); meeting, conference; '_periode f session.

Skala ['ska:la] f (-/Skalen, Skalas) scale (a. ♪); dial (of radio set); fig. gamut; gleitende . sliding scale.

Skandal [skan'da:l] m (-s/-e) scandal; row, riot; 2ös adj. [_a'lø:s] scandalous

Skelett [ske'lɛt] n (-[e]s/-e) skeleton.

Skep|sis ['skɛpsis] f (-/no pl.) scepticism, Am. a. skepticism; _tiker ['_tikər] m (-s/-) sceptic, Am. a. skeptic; '2tisch adj. sceptical, Am. a. skeptical.

Ski [ʃi:] m (-s/-er, ✍-, ⚲-) ski; _ laufen or fahren ski; '_fahrer m, '_läufer m skier; '_lift m ski-lift; '_sport m (-[e]s/no pl.) skiing.

Skizz|e ['skitsə] f (-/-n) sketch (a. fig.); 2ieren [_'tsi:rən] v/t. (no -ge-, h) sketch, outline (both a. fig.).

Sklav|e ['skla:və] m (-n/-n) slave (a. fig.); '_enhandel m slave-trade; '_enhändler m slave-trader; _e'rei f (-/-en) slavery; '2isch adj. slavish.

Skonto ✝ ['skɔnto] m, n (-s/-s, ✍ Skonti) discount.

Skrupel [skru:pəl] m (-s/-) scruple; '2los adj. unscrupulous.

Skulptur [skulp'tu:r] f (-/-en) sculpture.

Slalom ['slɑːlɔm] m (-s/-s) skiing, etc.: slalom.

Slaw|e ['slɑːvə] m (-n/-n) Slav; **'2isch** adj. Slav(onic).

Smaragd [sma'rakt] m (-[e]s/-e) emerald; **2grün** adj. emerald.

Smoking ['smoːkiŋ] m (-s/-s) dinner-jacket, Am. a. tuxedo, F tux.

so [zoː] 1. adv. so, thus; like this or that; as; ~ ein such a; ~ ... wie as ... as; nicht ~ ... wie not so ... as; ~ oder ~ by hook or by crook; 2. cj. so, therefore, consequently; ~ daß so that; bald cj. [zoː'-]: ~ (als) as soon as.

Socke ['zɔkə] f (-/-n) sock; 'l m (-s/-) ⚓ pedestal, socle; socket (of lamp); 'n m (-s/-) sock; nhalter m/pl. suspenders pl., Am. garters pl.

Sodawasser ['zoːda-] n (-s/u) soda(-water).

Sodbrennen ⚡ ['zoːt-] n (-s/no pl.) heartburn.

soeben adv. [zoː'-] just (now).

Sofa ['zoːfa] n (-s/-s) sofa.

sofern cj. [zoː'-] if, provided that; ~ nicht unless.

soff [zɔf] pret. of saufen.

sofort adv. [zoː'-] at once, immediately, directly, right or straight away; ig adj. immediate, prompt.

Sog [zoːk] 1. m (-[e]s/-e) suction; ⚓ wake (a. fig.), undertow; 2. ⚓ pret. of saugen.

so|gar adv. [zoː'-] even; genannt adj. ['zoː-] so-called; gleich adv. [zoː'-] s. sofort.

Sohle ['zoːlə] f (-/-n) sole; bottom (of valley, etc.); ⚒ floor.

Sohn [zoːn] m (-[e]s/e) son.

solange cj. [zoː'-]: ~ (als) so or as long as. [such.]

solch pron. [zɔlç] such; als ~e(r) as]

Sold ⚔ [zɔlt] m (-[e]s/-e) pay.

Soldat [zɔl'daːt] m (-en/-en) soldier; der unbekannte ~ the Unknown Warrior or Soldier.

Söldner ['zœldnər] m (-s/-) mercenary.

Sole ['zoːlə] f (-/-n) brine, salt water.

solid adj. [zoː'liːt] solid (a. fig.); basis, etc.: sound; ✝ firm, etc.: sound, solvent; prices: reasonable, fair; p. steady, staid, respectable.

solidarisch adj. [zoli'daːriʃ]: sich ~ erklären mit declare one's solidarity with.

solide adj. [zoː'liːdə] s. solid.

Solist [zoː'list] m (-en/-en) soloist.

Soll ✝ [zɔl] n (-[s]/-[s]) debit; (output) target.

'sollen (h) 1. v/i. (ge-): ich sollte (eigentlich) I ought to; 2. v/aux. (irr., no -ge-): er soll he shall; he is to; he is said to; ich sollte I should; er sollte (eigentlich) zu Hause sein he ought to be at home; er sollte seinen Vater niemals wiedersehen he was never to see his father again.

Solo ['zoːlo] n (-s/-s, Soli) solo.

somit cj. [zoː'-] thus; consequently.

Sommer ['zɔmər] m (-s/-) summer; 'frische f (-/-n) summer-holidays pl.; summer-resort; '2lich adj. summer-like, summer(l)y; 'sprosse f freckle; '2sprossig adj. freckled; 'wohnung f summer residence, Am. cottage, summer house; 'zeit f 1. (-/-en) season: summertime; 2. (-/no pl.) summer time, Am. daylight-saving time.

Sonate ♩ [zoː'nɑːtə] f (-/-n) sonata.

Sonde ['zɔndə] f (-/-n) probe.

Sonder|angebot ['zɔndər-] n special offer; 'ausgabe f special (edition); '2bar adj. strange, odd; 'beilage f inset, supplement (of newspaper); 'berichterstatter m special correspondent; '2lich 1. adj. special, peculiar; 2. adv.: nicht ~ not particularly; 'ling m (-s/-e) crank, odd person; '2n 1. cj. but; nicht nur, ~ auch not only, but (also); 2. v/t. (ge-, h): die Spreu vom Weizen ~ sift the chaff from the wheat; 'recht n privilege; 'zug ⚙ m special (train).

sondieren [zɔn'diːrən] (no -ge-, h) 1. v/t. ⚡ probe (a. fig.); 2. fig. v/i. make tentative inquiries.

Sonn|abend ['zɔn⁹-] m (-s/-e) Saturday; 'e f (-/-n) sun; '2en v/t. (ge-, h) (expose to the) sun; sich ~ sun o.s. (a. fig. in dat. in), bask in the sun.

'Sonnen|aufgang m sunrise; 'bad n sun-bath; 'brand m sunburn; 'bräune f sunburn, tan, Am. (sun) tan; 'brille f (-e-a pair of) sunglasses pl.; 'finsternis f solar eclipse; 'fleck m sun-spot; '2klar fig. adj. (as) clear as daylight; 'licht n (-[e]s/no pl.) sunlight; 'schein m (-[e]s/no pl.) sunshine; 'schirm m sunshade, parasol; 'segel n awning; 'seite f sunny side (a. fig.); 'stich ⚡ m sunstroke; 'strahl m sunbeam; 'uhr f sun-dial; 'untergang m sunset, sundown; '2verbrannt adj. sunburnt, tanned; 'wende f solstice.

'sonnig adj. sunny (a. fig.).

'Sonntag m Sunday.

'Sonntags|anzug m Sunday suit or best; 'fahrer mot. contp. m Sunday driver; 'kind n person born on a Sunday; fig. person born under a lucky star; 'rückfahrkarte ⚙ f week-end ticket; 'ruhe f Sunday rest; 'staat F co. m (-[e]s/no pl.) Sunday go-to-meeting clothes pl.

sonor adj. [zoː'noːr] sonorous.

sqnst [zɔnst] 1. adv. otherwise, with pron. else; usually, normally; wer ~? who else?; wie ~ as usual; ~ nichts nothing else; 2. cj. otherwise, or else; 'ig adj. other; 'wie adv.

in some other way; '‿wo adv. elsewhere, somewhere else.

Sopran ♪ [zo'praːn] m (-s/-e) soprano; sopranist; ‿istin ♪ [‿a'nistin] f (-/-nen) soprano, sopranist.

Sorge ['zɔrgə] f (-/-n) care; sorrow; uneasiness, anxiety; ‿ tragen für take care of; sich ‿n machen um be anxious or worried about; mach dir keine ‿n don't worry.

'sorgen (ge-, h) 1. v/i.: ‿ für care for, provide for; take care of, attend to; dafür ‿, daß take care that; 2. v/refl.: sich ‿ um be anxious or worried about; '‿frei adj., '‿los adj. carefree, free from care; '‿voll adj. full of cares; face: worried, troubled.

Sorg|falt ['zɔrkfalt] f (-/no pl.) care(fulness); ♀fältig adj. ['‿fɛltiç] careful; ♀lich adj. careful, anxious; '♀los adj. carefree; thoughtless; negligent; careless; '♀sam adj. careful.

Sort|e ['zɔrtə] f (-/-n) sort, kind, species, Am. a. stripe; ♀ieren [‿'tiːrən] v/t. (no -ge-, h) (as)sort; arrange; ‿iment [‿i'mɛnt] n (-[e]s/-e) assortment.

Soße ['zoːsə] f (-/-n) sauce; gravy.

sott [zɔt] pret. of sieden.

Souffl|eurkasten thea. [su'fløːr-] m prompt-box; promter's box; ‿euse thea. [‿zə] f (-/-n) prompter; ♀ieren thea. (no -ge-, h) v/i. prompt (j-m s.o.); 2. v/t. prompt.

Souverän [suvə'rɛːn] 1. m (-s/-e) sovereign; 2. ♀ adj. sovereign; fig. superior; ‿ität [‿ɛni'tɛːt] f (-/no pl.) sovereignty.

so|viel [zo'-] 1. cj. so or as far as; ‿ich weiß so far as I know; 2. adv.: doppelt ‿ twice as much; ‿weit 1. cj.: ‿ es mich betrifft in so far as it concerns me, so far as I am concerned; 2. adv.: ‿ ganz gut not bad (for a start); ‿wieso adv. [zovi'zoː] in any case, anyhow, anyway.

Sowjet [zɔ'vjɛt] m (-s/-s) Soviet; ♀isch adj. Soviet.

sowohl cj. [zo'-]: ‿ ... als (auch) ... both ... and ..., ... as well as ...

sozial adj. [zo'tsjaːl] social; ♀demokrat m social democrat; ‿isieren [‿ali'ziːrən] v/t. (no -ge-, h) socialize; ♀isierung [‿ali'ziːruŋ] f (-/-en) socialization; ♀ist [‿a'list] m (-en/-en) socialist; ‿istisch adj. [‿a'listiʃ] socialist.

Sozius ['zoːtsjus] m (-/-se) † partner; mot. pillion-rider; '‿sitz mot. m pillion.

sozusagen adv. [zotsu'zaːgən] so to speak, as it were.

Spachtel ['ʃpaxtəl] m (-s/-), f (-/-n) spatula.

spähe|n ['ʃpɛːən] v/i. (ge-, h) look

out (nach for); peer; '♀r m (-s/-) look-out; ⚔ scout.

Spalier [ʃpa'liːr] n (-s/-e) trellis, espalier; fig. lane; ‿ bilden form a lane.

Spalt [ʃpalt] m (-[e]s/-e) crack, split, rift, crevice, fissure; '‿e f (-/-n) s. Spalt; typ. column; 'ℓen v/t. ([irr.,] ge-, h) split (a. fig. hairs); cleave (block of wood, etc.); sich ‿ split (up); '‿ung f (-/-en) splitting, cleavage; fig. split; eccl. schism.

Span [ʃpaːn] m (-[e]s/‿e) chip, shaving, splinter.

Spange ['ʃpaŋə] f (-/-n) clasp; buckle; clip; slide (in hair); strap (of shoes); bracelet.

Span|ier ['ʃpaːnjər] m (-s/-) Spaniard; '♀isch adj. Spanish.

Spann [ʃpan] 1. m (-[e]s/-e) instep; 2. ♀ pret. of spinnen; '‿e f (-/-n) span; ✂, orn. spread (of wings); † margin; 'ℓen (ge-, h) 1. v/t. stretch (rope, muscles, etc.); cock (rifle); bend (bow, etc.); tighten (spring, etc.); vor den Wagen ‿ harness to the carriage; s. gespannt; 2. v/i. be (too) tight; 'ℓend adj. exciting, thrilling, gripping; '‿kraft f (-/no pl.) elasticity; fig. energy; '‿ung f (-/-en) tension (a. fig.); ⚡ voltage; ⊕ strain, stress; △ span; fig. close attention.

Spar|büchse ['ʃpaːr-] f money-box; 'ℓen (ge-, h) 1. v/t. save (money, strength, etc.); put by; 2. v/i. save; economize, cut down expenses; ‿ mit be chary of (praise, etc.); '‿er m (-s/-) saver.

Spargel ♀ ['ʃpargəl] m (-s/-) asparagus.

'Spar|kasse f savings-bank; '‿konto n savings-account.

spärlich adj. ['ʃpɛːrliç] crop, dress, etc.: scanty; population, etc.: sparse; hair: thin.

Sparren ['ʃparən] m (-s/-) rafter, spar.

'sparsam 1. adj. saving, economical (mit of); 2. adv.: ‿ leben lead a frugal life, economize; ‿ umgehen mit use sparingly, be frugal of; '♀keit f (-/no pl.) economy, frugality.

Spaß [ʃpaːs] m (-es/‿e) joke, jest; fun, lark; amusement; aus or im or zum ‿ in fun; ‿ beiseite joking apart; er hat nur ‿ gemacht he was only joking; 'ℓen v/i. (ge-, h) joke, jest, make fun; damit ist nicht zu ‿ that is no joking matter; '♀haft adj., '♀ig adj. facetious, waggish; funny; '‿macher m (-s/-), '‿vogel m wag, joker.

spät [ʃpɛːt] 1. adj. late; advanced; zu ‿ too late; am ‿en Nachmittag late in the afternoon; wie ‿ ist es? what time is it?; 2. adv. late; er kommt 5 Minuten zu ‿ he is five minutes late (zu for); ~ in der Nacht late at night.

Spaten ['ʃpɑːtən] m (-s/-) spade.

'späte|r 1. adj. later; **2.** adv. later on; afterward(s); früher oder ~ sooner or later; **~stens** adv. ['~stəns] at the latest.

Spatz orn. [ʃpats] m (-en, -es/-en) sparrow.

spazieren [ʃpa'tsiːrən] v/i. (no -ge-, sein) walk, stroll; **~fahren** (irr. fahren, sep., -ge-) **1.** v/i. (sein) go for a drive; **2.** v/t. (h) take for a drive; take (baby) out (in pram); **~gehen** v/i. (irr. gehen, sep., -ge-, sein) go for a walk.

Spa'zier|fahrt f drive, ride; **~gang** m walk, stroll; e-n ~ machen go for a walk; **~gänger** [~genər] m (-s/-) walker, stroller; **~weg** m walk.

Speck [ʃpek] m (-[e]s/-e) bacon.

Spedi|teur [ʃpedi'tøːr] m (-s/-e) forwarding agent; (furniture) remover; **~tion** [~'tsjoːn] f (-/-en) forwarding agent or agency.

Speer [ʃpeːr] m (-[e]s/-e) spear; sports: javelin; **'~werfen** n (-s/no pl.) javelin-throw(ing); **'~werfer** m (-s/-) javelin-thrower.

Speiche ['ʃpaɪçə] f (-/-n) spoke.

Speichel ['ʃpaɪçəl] m (-s/no pl.) spit(tle), saliva; **'~lecker** fig. m (-s/-) lickspittle, toady.

Speicher ['ʃpaɪçər] m (-s/-) granary; warehouse; garret, attic.

speien ['ʃpaɪən] (irr., ge-, h) **1.** v/t. spit out (blood, etc.); volcano, etc.: belch (fire, etc.); **2.** v/i. spit; vomit, be sick.

Speise ['ʃpaɪzə] f (-/-n) food, nourishment; meal; dish; **'~eis** n ice-cream; **'~kammer** f larder, pantry; **'~karte** f bill of fare, menu; **'2n** (ge-, h) **1.** v/i. s. essen 1; at restaurants: take one's meals; **2.** v/t. feed; ⊕, ≠ ⚙ supply (mit with); **'~nfolge** f menu; **'~röhre** anat. f gullet, (o)esophagus; **'~saal** m dining-hall; **'~schrank** m (meat-)safe; **'~wagen** ⚙ m dining-car, diner; **'~zimmer** n dining-room.

Spektakel F [ʃpek'tɑːkəl] m (-s/-) noise, din.

Spekul|ant [ʃpeku'lant] m (-en/-en) speculator; **~ation** [~a'tsjoːn] f (-/-en) speculation; ≠ a. venture; **2ieren** [~'liːrən] v/i. (no -ge-, h) speculate (auf acc. on).

Spelunke [ʃpe'luŋkə] f (-/-n) den; drinking-den, Am. F a. dive.

Spende ['ʃpendə] f (-/-n) gift; alms pl.; contribution; **'2n** v/t. (ge-, h) give; donate (money to charity, blood, etc.); eccl. administer (sacraments); bestow (praise) (dat. on); **'~r** m (-s/-) giver; donor.

spen'dieren v/t. (no -ge-, h): j-m et. ~ treat s.o. to s.th., stand s.o. s.th.

Sperling orn. ['ʃperlɪŋ] m (-s/-e) sparrow.

Sperr|e ['ʃperə] f (-/-n) barrier; ⚙ barrier, Am. gate; toll-bar; ⊕ lock(ing device), detent; barricade; ✝, ♻ embargo; ⚓ blockade; sports: suspension; **'2en** (ge-, h) **1.** v/t. close; ✝, ♻ embargo; cut off (gas supply, electricity, etc.); stop (cheque, etc.); sports: suspend; **2.** v/i. jam, be stuck; **'~holz** n plywood; **'~konto** ✝ n blocked account; **'~kreis** ≠ m wave-trap; **'~sitz** thea. m stalls pl., Am. orchestra; **'~ung** f (-/-en) closing; stoppage (of cheque, etc.); ✝, ♻ embargo; ⚓ blockade; **'~zone** f prohibited area.

Spesen ['ʃpeːzən] pl. expenses pl., charges pl.

Spezial|ausbildung [ʃpe'tsjɑːl?~] f special training; **~fach** n special(i)ty; **~geschäft** ✝ n one-line shop, Am. specialty store; **2isieren** [~ali'ziːrən] v/refl. (no -ge-, h) specialize (auf acc. in); **~ist** [~a'list] m (-en/-en) specialist; **~ität** [~ali'tɛːt] f (-/-en) special(i)ty.

speziell adj. [ʃpe'tsjɛl] specific, special, particular.

spezifisch adj. [ʃpe'tsiːfiʃ]: ~es Gewicht specific gravity.

Sphäre ['sfɛːrə] f (-/-n) sphere (a. fig.).

Spick|aal ['ʃpik~] m smoked eel; **'2en** (ge-, h) **1.** v/t. lard; fig. (inter)lard (mit with); F: j-n ~ grease s.o.'s palm; **2.** F fig. v/i. crib.

spie [ʃpiː] pret. of speien.

Spiegel ['ʃpiːgəl] m (-s/-) mirror (a. fig.), looking-glass; **'~bild** n reflected image; **'2blank** adj. mirror-like; **'~ei** ['ʃpiːgəl?-] n fried egg; **'2glatt** adj. water: glassy, unrippled; road, etc.: very slippery; **'2n** (ge-, h) **1.** v/i. shine; **2.** v/refl. be reflected; **'~schrift** f mirror-writing.

Spieg(e)lung ['ʃpiːg(ə)luŋ] f (-/-en) reflection, reflexion; mirage.

Spiel [ʃpiːl] n (-[e]s/-e) play (a. fig.); game (a. fig.); match; ♪ playing; ein ~ Karten a pack of playing-cards, Am. a. a deck; auf dem ~ stehen be at stake; aufs ~ setzen jeopardize, stake; **'~art** ♈, zo. f variety; **'~ball** m tennis: game ball; billiards: red ball; fig. plaything, sport; **'~bank** f (-/-en) gaming-house; **'2en** (ge-, h) **1.** v/i. play; gamble; mit play with; fig. a. toy with; **2.** v/t. play (tennis, violin, etc.); thea. act, play (part); mit j-m Schach ~ play s.o. at chess; den Höflichen ~ do the polite; **'2end** fig. adv. easily; **'~er** m (-s/-) player; gambler; **'~erei** f (-/-en) pastime; child's amusement; **'~ergebnis** n sports: result, score; **'~feld** n sports: (playing-)field; pitch; **'~film** m feature film or picture; '~gefährte m playfellow, playmate; '~karte f playing-card; '~leiter m thea. stage manager; cinematography: director; sports: referee; '~marke f counter, sl. chip; '~plan m thea., etc.: program(me); repertory; '~platz m playground; '~raum fig. m play, scope; '~regel f rule (of the game); '~sachen f/pl playthings pl., toys pl.; '~schuld f gambling-debt; '~schule f infant-school, kindergarten; '~tisch m card-table; gambling-table; '~uhr f musical box, Am music box; '~verderber m (-s/-) spoil-sport, killjoy, wet blanket; '~waren f/pl. playthings pl., toys pl.; '~zeit f thea. season; sports: time of play; '~zeug n toy(s pl.), playthings(s pl.).

Spieß [ʃpi:s] m (-es/-e) spear, pike; spit; den ~ umdrehen turn the tables; '~bürger m bourgeois, Philistine, Am. a. Babbit; 2bürgerlich adj. bourgeois, Philistine; '~er m (-s/-) s. Spießbürger; '~geselle m accomplice; '~ruten f/pl.: ~ laufen run the gauntlet (a. fig.).

spinal adj. [ʃpi'na:l]: ~e Kinderlähmung ♣ infantile paralysis, poliomyelitis, F polio.

Spinat ♥ [ʃpi'na:t] m (-[e]s/-e) spinach.

Spind [ʃpint] n, m (-[e]s/-e) wardrobe, cupboard; ✕, sports, etc.: locker.

Spindel ['ʃpindəl] f (-/-n) spindle; '2'dürr adj. (as) thin as a lath.

Spinn|e zo. ['ʃpinə] f (-/-n) spider; '2en (irr., ge-, h) 1. v/t. spin (a. fig.); hatch (plot, etc.); 2. v/i. cat: purr; F fig. be crazy, sl. be nuts; '~engewebe n cobweb; '~er m (-s/-) spinner; F fig. silly; ~e'rei f (-/-en) spinning; spinning-mill; '~maschine f spinning-machine; '~webe f (-/-n) cobweb.

Spion [ʃpi'o:n] m (-s/-e) spy, intelligencer; fig. judas; ~age [~o'na:ʒə] f (-/no pl.) espionage; 2ieren [~o'ni:rən] v/i. (no -ge-, h) (play the) spy.

Spiral|e [ʃpi'ra:lə] f (-/-n) spiral (a. ♣), helix; 2förmig adj. [~fœrmiç] spiral, helical.

Spirituosen [ʃpiritu'o:zən] pl. spirits pl.

Spiritus ['ʃpi:ritus] m (-/-se) spirit, alcohol; '~kocher m (-s/-) spirit stove.

Spital [ʃpi'ta:l] n (-s/⁻er) hospital; alms-house; home for the aged.

spitz [ʃpits] 1. adj. pointed (a. fig.); ♣ angle: acute; fig. poignant; ~e Zunge sharp tongue; ~ zulaufen taper (off); '2bube m thief; rogue, rascal (both a. co.); 2büberei [~by:bə'raɪ] f (-/-en) roguery, ras-

cality (both a. co.); ~bübisch adj. ['~by:biʃ] eyes, smile, etc.: roguish.

'Spitz|e f (-/-n) point (of pencil, weapon, jaw, etc.); tip (of nose, finger, etc.); nib (of tool, etc.); spire; head (of enterprise, etc.); lace; an der ~ liegen sports: be in the lead; j-m die ~ bieten make head against s.o.; auf die ~ treiben carry to an extreme; '~el m (-s/-) (common) informer; '2en v/t. (ge-, h) point, sharpen; den Mund ~ purse (up) one's lips; die Ohren ~ prick up one's ears (a. fig.).

'Spitzen|leistung f top performance; ⊕ maximum capacity; '~lohn m top wages pl.

'spitz|findig adj. subtle, captious; '2findigkeit f (-/-en) subtlety, captiousness; '2hacke f pickax(e), pick; '~ig adj. pointed; fig. a. poignant; '2marke typ. f head(ing); 2name m nickname.

Splitter ['ʃplitər] m (-s/-) splinter, shiver; chip; '2frei adj. glass: shatterproof; '2ig adj. splintery; '2n v/i. (ge-, h, sein) splinter, shiver; '2'nackt F adj. stark naked, Am. a. mother-naked; '~partei pol. f splinter party.

spontan adj. [ʃpɔn'ta:n] spontaneous.

sporadisch adj. [ʃpo'ra:diʃ] sporadic.

Sporn [ʃpɔrn] m (-[e]s/Sporen) spur; die Sporen geben put or set spurs to (horse); sich die Sporen verdienen win one's spurs; '2en v/t. (ge-, h) spur.

Sport [ʃpɔrt] m (-[e]s/✤-e) sport; fig. hobby; ~ treiben go in for sports; '~ausrüstung f sports equipment; '~geschäft n sporting-goods shop; '~kleidung f sport clothes pl., sportswear; '~lehrer m games-master; '2lich adj. sporting, sportsmanlike; figure: athletic; '~nachrichten f/pl. sports news sg., pl.; '~platz m sports field; stadium.

Spott [ʃpɔt] m (-[e]s/no pl.) mockery; derision; scorn; (s-n) ~ treiben mit make sport of; '2'billig F adj. dirtcheap.

Spötte|lei [ʃpœtə'laɪ] f (-/-en) raillery, sneer, jeer; '2ln v/i. (ge-, h) sneer (über acc. at), jeer (at).

'spotten v/i. (ge-, h) mock (über acc. at); jeer (at); jeder Beschreibung ~ beggar description.

Spötter ['ʃpœtər] m (-s/-) mocker, scoffer; ~ei [~'raɪ] f (-/-en) mockery.

'spöttisch adj. mocking, sneering, ironical.

'Spott|name m nickname; '~preis m ridiculous price; für e-n ~ for a mere song; '~schrift f lampoon, satire.

sprach [ʃpra:x] pret. of sprechen.

'Sprache f (-/-n) speech; language

(a. fig.); diction; zur ~ bringen bring up, broach; zur ~ kommen come up (for discussion).

'Sprach|eigentümlichkeit f idiom; '~fehler ∦ m impediment (in one's speech); '~führer m language guide; '~gebrauch m usage; '~gefühl n (-[e]s/no pl.) linguistic instinct; 2kundig adj. ['~kundiç] versed in languages; '~lehre f grammar; '~lehrer m teacher of languages; 2lich adj. linguistic; grammatical; '~los adj. speechless; '~rohr n speaking-trumpet, megaphone; fig.: mouthpiece; organ; '~schatz m vocabulary; '~störung ∦ f impediment (in one's speech); '~wissenschaft f philology, science of language; linguistics pl.; '~wissenschaftler m philologist; linguist; 2wissenschaftlich adj. philological; linguistic.

sprang [ʃpraŋ] pret. of springen.

Sprech|chor ['ʃpreç-] m speaking chorus; 2en (irr., ge-, h) 1. v/t. speak (language, truth, etc.); ɪ̃ɪ̃ pronounce (judgement); say (prayer); j-n zu ~ wünschen wish to see s.o.; j-n schuldig ~ pronounce s.o. guilty; F Bände ~ speak volumes (für for); 2. v/i. speak; talk (both: mit to, with; über acc., von of, about); er ist nicht zu ~ you cannot see him; '~er m (-s/-) speaker; radio: announcer; spokesman; '~fehler m slip of the tongue; '~stunde f consulting-hours pl.; '~übung f exercise in speaking; '~zimmer n consulting-room, surgery.

spreizen ['ʃpraɪtsən] v/t. (ge-, h) spread (out); a. straddle (legs); sich ~ pretend to be unwilling.

Spreng|bombe ✕ ['ʃpreŋ-] f high-explosive bomb, demolition bomb; '~el eccl. m (-s/-) diocese, see; parish; 2en (ge-) 1. v/t. (h) sprinkle, water (road, lawn, etc.); blow up, blast (bridge, rocks, etc.); burst open (door, etc.); spring (mine, etc.); gambling: break (bank); break up (meeting, etc.); 2. v/i. (sein) gallop; '~stoff m explosive; '~ung f (-/-en) blowing-up, blasting; explosion; '~wagen m water(ing)-cart.

Sprenkel ['ʃpreŋkəl] m (-s/-) speckle, spot; 2n v/t. (ge-, h) speckle, spot.

Spreu [ʃprɔʏ] f (-/no pl.) chaff; s. sondern 2.

Sprich|wort ['ʃpriç-] n (-[e]s/=er) proverb, adage; 2wörtlich adj. proverbial (a. fig.).

sprießen ['ʃpriːsən] v/i. (irr., ge-, sein) sprout; germinate.

Spring|brunnen ['ʃpriŋ-] m fountain; 2en v/i. (irr., ge-, sein) jump, leap; ball, etc.: bounce; swimming: dive; burst, crack, break; in die Augen ~ strike the eye; ~ über (acc.)

jump (over), leap, clear; '~er m (-s/-) jumper; swimming: diver; chess: knight; '~flut f spring tide.

Sprit [ʃprit] m (-[e]s/-e) spirit, alcohol; F mot. fuel, petrol, sl. juice, Am. gasoline, F gas.

Spritz|e ['ʃpritsə] f (-/-n) syringe (a. ✍), squirt; ⊕ fire-engine; j-m e-e ~ geben ∦ give s.o. an injection; 2en (ge-) 1. v/t. (h) sprinkle, water (road, lawn, etc.); splash (water, etc.) (über acc. on, over); 2. v/i. (h) splash; pen: splutter; 3. v/i. (sein) F fig. dash, flit; ~ aus blood, etc.: spurt or spout from (wound, etc.); '~er m (-s/-) splash; '~tour F f: e-e ~ machen go for a spin.

spröde adj. ['ʃprøːdə] glass, etc.: brittle; skin: chapped, chappy; esp. girl: prudish, prim, coy.

Sproß [ʃprɔs] 1. m (Sprosses/Sprosse) ✍ shoot, sprout, scion (a. fig.); fig. offspring; 2. ⌀ pret. of sprießen.

Sprosse ['ʃprɔsə] f (-/-n) rung, round, step.

Sprößling ['ʃprœslɪŋ] m (-s/-e) ✍ s. Sproß 1.; co. son.

Spruch [ʃprux] m (-[e]s/=e) saying; dictum; ɪ̃ɪ̃ sentence; ɪ̃ɪ̃ verdict; '~band n banner; 2reif adj. ripe for decision.

Sprudel ['ʃpruːdəl] m (-s/-) mineral water; 2n v/i. (ge-) 1. (h) bubble, effervesce; 2. (sein): ~ aus or von gush from.

sprüh|en ['ʃpryːən] (ge-) 1. v/t. (h) spray, sprinkle (liquid); throw off (sparks); Feuer ~ eyes: flash fire; 2. v/i. (h): ~ vor sparkle with (wit, etc.); es sprüht it is drizzling; 3. v/i. (sein) sparks: fly; '2regen m drizzle.

Sprung [ʃpruŋ] m (-[e]s/=e) jump, leap, bound; swimming: dive; crack, fissure; '~brett n sports: spring-board; fig. stepping-stone; '~feder f spiral spring.

Spuck|e F ['ʃpukə] f (-/no pl.) spit(tle); 2en (ge-, h) 1. v/t. spit (out) (blood, etc.); 2. v/i. spit; engine: splutter; '~napf m spittoon, Am. a. cuspidor.

Spuk [ʃpuːk] m (-[e]s/-e) apparition, ghost, co. spook; F fig. noise; 2en v/i. (ge-, h): ~ in (dat.) haunt (a place); hier spukt es this place is haunted.

Spule ['ʃpuːlə] f (-/-n) spool, reel; bobbin; ∮ coil; 2n v/t. (ge-, h) spool, reel.

spülen ['ʃpyːlən] (ge-, h) 1. v/t. rinse (clothes, mouth, cup, etc.); wash up (dishes, etc.); an Land ~ wash ashore; 2. v/i. flush the toilet.

Spund [ʃpunt] m (-[e]s/=e) bung; plug; '~loch n bunghole.

Spur [ʃpuːr] f (-/-en) trace (a. fig.); track (a. fig.); print (a. fig.); rut (of wheels); j-m auf der ~ sein be on s.o.'s track.

spür|en ['ʃpyːrən] v/t. (ge-, h) feel; sense; perceive; 'Ωsinn m (-[e]s/no pl.) scent; fig. a. flair (für for).
Spurweite ᚛ f ga(u)ge.
sputen ['ʃpuːtən] v/refl. (ge-, h) make haste, hurry up.
Staat [ʃtaːt] m 1. F (-[e]s/no pl.) pomp, state; finery; ~ machen mit make a parade of; 2. (-[e]s/-en) state; government; '~enbund m (-[e]s/-ᵉe) confederacy, confederation; 'Ωenlos adj stateless; 'Ωlich adj. state, national; political; public.
'Staats|angehörige m, f (-n/-n) national, citizen, esp. Brt. subject; '~angehörigkeit f (-/no pl.) nationality, citizenship; '~anwalt ⚥ m public prosecutor, Am. prosecuting attorney; '~beamte m Civil Servant, Am a. public servant; '~begräbnis n state or national funeral; '~besuch m official or state visit; '~bürger m citizen; '~bürgerkunde f (-/no pl.) civics sg.; '~bürgerschaft f (-/-en) citizenship; '~dienst m Civil Service; 'Ωeigen adj. state-owned; '~feind m public enemy; 'Ωfeindlich adj subversive; '~gewalt f (-/no pl.) supreme power; '~haushalt m budget; '~hoheit f (-/no pl.) sovereignty, '~kasse f treasury, Brt. exchequer; '~klugheit f political wisdom; '~kunst f (-/no pl.) statesmanship; '~mann m statesman, Ωmännisch adj. ['~mɛnɪʃ] statesmanlike; '~oberhaupt n head of (the) state; '~papiere n/pl. Government securities pl.; '~rat m Privy Council; '~recht n public law; '~schatz m s. Staatskasse; '~schulden f/pl. national debt; '~sekretär m under-secretary of state; '~streich m coup d'état; '~trauer f national mourning; '~vertrag m treaty; '~wesen n polity; '~wirtschaft f public sector of the economy; '~wissenschaft f political science; '~wohl n public weal.
Stab [ʃtaːp] m (-[e]s/-ᵉe) staff (a. fig.); bar (of metal, wood); crosier, staff (of bishop); wand (of magician); relay-race, ᛋ conducting: baton; pole-vaulting. pole.
stabil adj. [ʃtaˈbiːl] stable (a. ✝); health. robust.
stabilisier|en [ʃtabiliˈziːrən] v/t. (no -ge-, h) stabilize (a. ✝); Ωung f (-/-en) stabilization (a. ✝).
stach [ʃtaːx] pret. of stechen.
Stachel ['ʃtaxəl] m (-s/-n) prickle (of plant, hedgehog, etc.); sting (of bee, etc.); tongue (of buckle); spike (of sports shoe); fig.: sting; goad; '~beere ᚛ f gooseberry; '~draht m barbed wire; 'Ωig adj. prickly, thorny.
'stachlig adj. s. stachelig.

Stadi|on ['ʃtaːdjɔn] n (-s/Stadien) stadium; '~um ['~um] n (-s/Stadien) stage, phase.
Stadt [ʃtat] f (-/-ᵉe) town; city.
Städt|chen ['ʃtɛːtçən] n (-s/-) small town; '~ebau m (-[e]s/no pl.) town-planning; '~er m (-s/-) townsman; ~ pl. townspeople pl.
'Stadt|gebiet n urban area; '~gespräch n teleph. local call; fig. town talk, talk of the town; '~haus n town house.
städtisch adj. ['ʃtɛːtiʃ] municipal.
'Stadt|plan m city map; plan (of a town); '~planung f town-planning; '~rand m outskirts pl. (of a town); '~rat m (-[e]s/-ᵉe) town council; town council(l)or; '~teil m, '~viertel n quarter.
Staffel ['ʃtafəl] f (-/-n) relay, relay-race; '~ei paint. ['~laɪ] f (-/-en) easel; '~lauf m relay-race; 'Ωn v/t. (ge-, h) graduate (taxes, etc.); stagger (hours of work, etc.).
Stahl¹ [ʃtaːl] m (-[e]s/-ᵉe, -e) steel.
stahl² [~] pret. of stehlen.
stählen ['ʃtɛːlən] v/t. (ge-, h) ⊕ harden (a. fig.), temper.
'Stahl|feder f steel pen; steel spring; '~kammer f strong-room; '~stich m steel engraving.
stak [ʃtaːk] pret. of stecken 2.
Stall [ʃtal] m (-[e]s/-ᵉe stable (a. fig.); cow-house, cowshed; pigsty, Am. a. pigpen; shed; '~knecht m stableman; '~ung f (-/-en) stabling; ~en pl. stables pl.
Stamm [ʃtam] m (-[e]s/-ᵉe ᚛ stem (a. gr.), trunk; fig.: race; stock; family; tribe; '~aktie ✝ f ordinary share, Am. common stock; '~baum m family or genealogical tree, pedigree (a. zo.); '~buch n album; book that contains the births, deaths, and marriages in a family; zo. stud-book; 'Ωeln (ge-, h) 1. v/t. stammer (out); 2. v/i. stammer; '~eltern pl. ancestors pl., first parents pl.; 'Ωen v/i. (ge-, sein): ~ von or aus come from (town, etc.), Am. a. hail from; date from (certain time); gr. be derived from; aus gutem Haus ~ be of good family; '~gast m regular customer or guest, F regular.
stämmig adj. ['ʃtɛmiç] stocky; thickset, squat(ty).
'Stamm|kapital ✝ n share capital, Am. capital stock; '~kneipe F f one's favo(u)rite pub, local; '~kunde m regular customer, patron; '~tisch m table reserved for regular guests; ~utter ['ʃtammutər] f (-/-ᵉ) ancestress; '~vater m ancestor; Ωverwandt adj. cognate, kindred; pred. of the same race.
stampfen ['ʃtampfən] (ge-) 1. v/t. (h) mash (potatoes, etc.); aus dem Boden ~ conjure up; 2. v/i. (h) stamp (one's foot); horse: paw;

3. *v/i.* (*sein*): ~ *durch* plod through; ⚓ pitch through.

Stand [ʃtant] **1.** *m* (-[e]s/⸚e) stand (-ing), standing *or* upright position; footing, foothold; *s. Standplatz*; stall; *fig.*: level; state; station, rank, status; class; profession; reading (*of thermometer, etc.*); *ast.* position; *sports*: score; *auf den neuesten* ~ *bringen* bring up to date; *e-n schweren* ~ *haben* have a hard time (of it); **2.** ♀ *pret. of stehen*.

Standarte [ʃtan'dartə] *f* (-/-n) standard, banner.

'**Standbild** *n* statue.

Ständchen ['ʃtɛntçən] *n* (-s/-) serenade; *j-m ein* ~ *bringen* serenade s.o.

Ständer ['ʃtɛndər] *m* (-s/-) stand; post, pillar, standard.

'**Standes|amt** *n* registry (office), register office; '**♀amtlich** *adj.*: ~*e Trauung* civil marriage; '**~beamte** *m* registrar; '**~dünkel** *m* pride of place; '**♀gemäß** *adj.*, '**♀mäßig** *adj.* in accordance with one's rank; '**~person** *f* person of rank *or* position; '**~unterschied** *m* social difference.

'**standhaft** *adj.* steadfast; firm; constant; ~ *bleiben* stand pat; resist temptation; '**♀igkeit** *f* (-/*no pl.*) steadfastness; firmness.

'**standhalten** *v/i.* (*irr. halten, sep.*, -ge-, *h*) hold one's ground; *j-m or e-r Sache* ~ resist s.o. *or* s.th.

ständig *adj.* ['ʃtɛndiç] permanent; constant; *income, etc.*: fixed.

'**Stand|ort** *m* position (*of ship, etc.*); ⚔ garrison, post; '**~platz** *m* stand; '**~punkt** *fig. m* point of view, standpoint, angle, *Am. a.* slant; '**~quartier** ⚔ *n* fixed quarters *pl.*; '**~recht** ⚔ *n* martial law; '**~uhr** *f* grandfather's clock.

Stange ['ʃtaŋə] *f* (-/-n) pole; rod, bar (*of iron, etc.*); staff (*of flag*); *Anzug or Kleid von der* ~ *sl.* reach-me-down, *Am.* F hand-me-down.

stank [ʃtaŋk] *pret. of stinken*.

Stänker|(er) *contp.* ['ʃtɛŋkər(ər)] *m* (-s/-) mischief-maker, quarrel(l)er; '**♀n** F *v/i.* (ge-, *h*) make mischief.

Stanniol [ʃta'njoːl] *n* (-s/-e) tin foil.

Stanze ['ʃtantsə] *f* (-/-n) stanza; ⊕ punch, stamp, die; '**♀n** ⊕ *v/t.* (ge-, *h*) punch, stamp.

Stapel ['ʃtaːpəl] *m* (-s/-) pile, stack; ⚓ stocks *pl.*; *vom or von* ~ *lassen* ⚓ launch; *vom or von* ~ *laufen* ⚓ be launched; '**~lauf** ⚓ *m* launch; '**♀n** *v/t.* (ge-, *h*) pile (up), stack; '**~platz** *m* dump; emporium.

stapfen ['ʃtapfən] *v/i.* (ge-, *sein*) plod (*durch* through).

Star 1. [ʃtaːr] *m* (-[e]s/-e) *orn.* starling; ⚕ cataract; *j-m den* ~ *stechen* open s.o.'s eyes; **2.** [staːr] *m* (-s/-s) *thea., etc.*: star.

starb [ʃtarp] *pret. of sterben*.

stark [ʃtark] **1.** *adj.* strong (*a. fig.*); stout, corpulent; *fig.*: intense; large; ~*e Erkältung* bad cold; ~*er Raucher* heavy smoker; ~*e Seite* strong point, forte; **2.** *adv.* very much; ~ *erkältet sein* have a bad cold; ~ *übertrieben* grossly exaggerated.

Stärke ['ʃtɛrkə] *f* (-/-n) strength (*a. fig.*); stoutness, corpulence; *fig.*: intensity; largeness; strong point, forte; ⚗ starch; '**♀n** *v/t.* (ge-, *h*) strengthen (*a. fig.*); starch (*linen, etc.*); *sich* ~ take some refreshment(s).

'**Starkstrom** ⚡ *m* heavy current.

'**Stärkung** *f* (-/-en) strengthening; *fig. a.* refreshment; '**~smittel** *n* restorative; ⚕ *a.* tonic.

starr [ʃtar] **1.** *adj.* rigid (*a. fig.*), stiff; *gaze*: fixed; ~ *vor* (*dat.*) numb with (*cold, etc.*); transfixed with (*horror, etc.*); dumbfounded with (*amazement, etc.*); **2.** *adv.*: *j-n* ~ *ansehen* stare at s.o.; '**~en** *v/i.* (ge-, *h*) stare (*auf acc.* at); *vor Schmutz* ~ be covered with dirt; '**♀heit** *f* (-/*no pl.*) rigidity (*a. fig.*), stiffness; '**♀kopf** *m* stubborn *or* obstinate fellow; **~köpfig** *adj.* ['~kœpfiç] stubborn, obstinate; '**♀krampf** ⚕ *m* (-[e]s/*no pl.*) tetanus; '**♀sinn** *m* (-[e]s/*no pl.*) stubbornness, obstinacy; '**~sinnig** *adj.* stubborn, obstinate.

Start [ʃtart] *m* (-[e]s/-s, ⸚-e) start (*a. fig.*); ✈ take-off; '**~bahn** ✈ *f* runway; '**♀bereit** *adj.* ready to start; ✈ ready to take off; '**♀en** (ge-) **1.** *v/i.* (*sein*) start; ✈ take off; **2.** *v/t.* (*h*) start; *fig. a.* launch; '**~er** *m* (-s/-) *sports*: starter; '**~platz** *m* starting-place.

Station [ʃta'tsjoːn] *f* (-/-en) station; ward (*of hospital*); (*gegen*) *freie* ~ board and lodging (found); ~ *machen* break one's journey; **~svorsteher** 🚂 *m* station-master, *Am. a.* station agent.

Statist [ʃta'tist] *m* (-en/-en) *thea.* supernumerary (actor), F super; *film*: extra; **~ik** *f* (-/-en) statistics *pl., sg.*; **~iker** *m* (-s/-) statistician; **♀isch** *adj.* statistic(al).

Stativ [ʃta'tiːf] *n* (-s/-e) tripod.

Statt [ʃtat] **1.** *f* (-/*no pl.*): *an Eides* ~ in lieu of an oath; *an Kindes* ~ *annehmen* adopt; **2.** ♀ *prp.* (*gen.*) instead of; ~ *zu inf.* instead of *ger.*; ~ *meiner* in my place.

Stätte ['ʃtɛtə] *f* (-/-n) place, spot; scene (*of events*).

'**statt|finden** *v/i.* (*irr. finden, sep.*, -ge-, *h*) take place, happen; '**~haft** *adj.* admissible, allowable; legal.

'**Statthalter** *m* (-s/-) governor.

'**stattlich** *adj.* stately; impressive; *sum of money, etc.*: considerable.

Statue ['ʃtaːtuə] *f* (-/-n) statue.

statuieren [ʃtatu'iːrən] *v/t.* (*no* -ge-,

h): ein Exempel ~ make an example (an dat. of).

Statur [ʃta'tuːr] f (-/-en) stature, size.

Statut [ʃta'tuːt] n (-[e]s/-en) statute; ~en pl. regulations pl.; ✝ articles pl. of association.

Staub [ʃtaup] m (-[e]s/⊕ -e, ~e) dust; powder.

Staubecken ['ʃtau⁹-] n reservoir.

stauben ['ʃtaubən] v/i. (ge-, h) give off dust, make or raise a dust.

stäuben ['ʃtɔybən] (ge-, h) 1. v/t. dust; 2. v/i. spray.

'**Staub|faden** ♀ m filament; ⒚ig adj. ['~biç] dusty; '~sauger ['~p-] m (-s/-) vacuum cleaner; ~tuch ['~p-] n (-[e]s/~er) duster.

stauchen ⊕ ['ʃtauxən] v/t. (ge-, h) upset, jolt.

'**Staudamm** m dam.

Staude ♀ ['ʃtaudə] f (-/-n) perennial (plant); head (of lettuce).

stau|en ['ʃtauən] v/t. (ge-, h) dam (up) (river, etc.); ⚓ stow; sich ~ waters, etc.: be dammed (up), vehicles: be jammed; '⒉er ⚓ m (-s/-) stevedore.

staunen ['ʃtaunən] 1. v/i. (ge-, h) be astonished (über acc. at); 2. ⒉ n (-s/no pl.) astonishment; '~swert adj. astonishing. [temper.)

Staupe vet. ['ʃtaupə] f (-/-n) dis-)

'**Stau|see** m reservoir; '~ung f (-/-en) damming (up) (of water); stoppage; ✇ congestion (a. of traffic); jam; ⚓ stowage.

stechen ['ʃtɛçən] (irr., ge-, h) 1. v/t. prick; insect, etc.: sting; flea, mosquito, etc.: bite; card: take, trump (other card); ⊕ engrave (in or auf acc. on); cut (lawn, etc.); sich in den Finger ~ prick one's finger; 2. v/i. prick; stab (nach at); insect, etc.: sting; flea, mosquito, etc.: bite; sun: burn; j-m in die Augen ~ strike s.o.'s eye; '~d adj. pain, look, etc.: piercing; pain: stabbing.

Steck|brief ⒤ ['ʃtɛk-] m warrant of apprehension; '⒉brieflich ⒤ adv.: er wird ~ gesucht a warrant is out against him; '~dose ∮ f (wall) socket; '⒉en 1. v/t. (ge-, h) put; esp. ⊕ insert (in acc. into); F stick; pin (an acc. to, on); ✄ set, plant; 2. v/i. [irr.,] ge-, h) be; stick, be stuck; tief in Schulden ~ be deeply in debt; '~en m (-s/-) stick; '⒉en-bleiben v/i. (irr. bleiben, sep., -ge-, sein) get stuck; speaker, etc.: break down; '~enpferd n hobby-horse; fig. hobby; '~er ∮ m (-s/-) plug; '~kontakt ∮ m s. Steckdose; '~na-del f pin.

Steg [ʃteːk] m (-[e]s/-e) foot-bridge; ⚓ landing-stage; '~reif m (-[e]s/-e): aus dem ~ extempore, offhand (both a. attr.); aus dem ~ sprechen extemporize, F ad-lib.

stehen ['ʃteːən] v/i. (irr., ge-, h) stand; be; be written; dress: suit, become (j-m s.o.); ~ vor be faced with; gut ~ mit be on good terms with; es kam ihm or ihn teuer zu ~ it cost him dearly; wie steht's mit ...? what about ...?; wie steht das Spiel? what's the score?; ~ bleiben remain standing; '~bleiben v/i. (irr. bleiben, sep., -ge-, sein) stand (still), stop; leave off reading, etc.; '~lassen v/t. (irr. lassen, sep., [no] -ge-, h) turn one's back (up)on; leave (meal) untouched; leave (behind), forget; leave alone.

'**Steher** m (-s/-) sports: stayer.

'**Steh|kragen** m stand-up collar; '~lampe f standard lamp; '~leiter f (e-e a pair of) steps pl., step-ladder.

stehlen ['ʃteːlən] (irr., ge-, h) 1. v/t. steal; j-m Geld ~ steal s.o.'s money; 2. v/i. steal.

'**Stehplatz** m standing-room; '~in-haber m Am. F standee; in bus, etc.: straphanger.

steif adj. [ʃtaif] stiff (a. fig.); numb (vor Kälte with cold); '~halten v/t. (irr. halten, sep. -ge-, h): F die Ohren ~ keep a stiff upper lip.

Steig [ʃtaik] m (-[e]s/-e) steep path; '~bügel m stirrup.

steigen ['ʃtaigən] 1. v/i. (irr., ge-, sein) flood, barometer, spirits, prices, etc.: rise; mists, etc.: ascend; blood, tension, etc.: mount; prices, etc.: increase; auf e-n Baum ~ climb a tree; 2. ⒉ n (-s/no pl.) rise; fig. a. increase.

steigern ['ʃtaigərn] v/t. (ge-, h) raise; increase; enhance; gr. compare.

'**Steigerung** f (-/-en) raising; increase; enhancement; gr. comparison; '~sstufe gr. f degree of comparison.

Steigung ['ʃtaiguŋ] f (-/-en) rise, gradient, ascent, grade.

steil adj. [ʃtail] steep; precipitous.

Stein [ʃtain] m (-[e]s/-e) stone (a. ♀, ✍), Am. F a. rock; s. Edel⒉, '⒉alt F adj. (as) old as the hills; '~bruch m quarry; '~druck m 1. (-[e]s/no pl.) lithography; 2. (-[e]s/-e) lithograph; '~drucker m lithographer; '⒉ern adj. stone-..., of stone; fig. stony; '~gut n (-[e]s/-e) crockery, stoneware, earthenware; '⒉ig adj. stony; '⒉igen ['~gən] v/t. (ge-, h) stone; '~igung ['~guŋ] f (-/-en) stoning; '~kohle f mineral coal; pit-coal; '~metz ['~mɛts] m (-en/ -en) stonemason; '~obst n stone-fruit; '⒉reich F adj. immensely rich; '~salz n (-es/no pl.) rock-salt; '~setzer m (-s/-) pavio(u)r; '~wurf m throwing of a stone; fig. stone's throw; '~zeit f (-/no pl.) stone age.

Steiß [ʃtais] m (-es/-e) buttocks pl., rump; '~bein anat. n coccyx.

Stelldichein co. ['ʃtɛldiçᵍaın] n (-[s]/-[s]) meeting, appointment, rendezvous, Am. F a. date.

Stelle ['ʃtɛlə] f (-/-n) place; spot; point; employment, situation, post, place, F job; agency, authority; passage (of book, etc.); freie ~ vacancy; an deiner ~ in your place, if I were you; auf der ~ on the spot; zur ~ sein be present.

'stellen v/t. (ge-, h) put, place, set, stand; regulate (watch, etc.); set (watch, trap, task, etc.); stop (thief, etc.); hunt down (criminal); furnish, supply, provide; Bedingungen ~ make conditions; e-e Falle ~ a. lay a snare; sich ~ give o.s. up (to the police); stand, place o.s. (somewhere); sich krank ~ feign or pretend to be ill.

'Stellen|angebot n position offered, vacancy, ~gesuch n application for a post; 2weise adv. here and there, sporadically.

'Stellung f (-/-en) position, posture; position, situation, (place of) employment; position, rank, status; arrangement (a. gr.); ✕ position; ~ nehmen give one's opinion (zu on), comment (on); ~nahme ['~naːmə] f (-/-n) attitude (zu to[wards]); opinion (on); comment (on); 2slos adj. unemployed.

'stellvertret|end adj. vicarious, representative; acting, deputy; ~er Vorsitzender vice-chairman, deputy chairman; 2er m representative; deputy; proxy; 2ung f representation; substitution; proxy.

Stelz|bein contp. ['ʃtɛlts-] n wooden leg; ~e f (-/-n) stilt; 2en mst iro. v/i. (ge-, sein) stalk.

stemmen ['ʃtɛmən] v/t. (ge-, h) lift (weight); sich ~ press (gegen against); fig. resist or oppose s.th.

Stempel ['ʃtɛmpəl] m (-s/-) stamp; ⊕ piston; ♀ pistil; '~geld F n the dole; '~kissen n ink-pad; '2n (ge-, h) 1. v/t. stamp; hallmark (gold, silver); 2. v/i. F: ~ gehen be on the dole.

Stengel ♀ ['ʃtɛŋəl] m (-s/-) stalk, stem.

Steno F ['ʃteno] f (-/no pl.) s. Stenographie; '~gramm n (-s/-e) stenograph; ~graph [~'graːf] m (-en/-en) stenographer; ~graphie [~a'fiː] f (-/-n) stenography, shorthand; 2graphieren [~a'fiːrən] (no -ge-, h) 1. v/t. take down in shorthand; 2. v/i. know shorthand; 2graphisch [~'graːfiʃ] 1. adj. shorthand, stenographic; 2. adv. in shorthand; ~typistin [~ty'pistin] f (-/-nen) shorthand-typist.

Stepp|decke ['ʃtɛp-] f quilt, Am. a. comforter; '2en (ge-, h) 1. v/t. quilt; stitch; 2. v/i. tap-dance.

Sterbe|bett ['ʃtɛrbə-] n deathbed; '~fall m (case of) death; '~kasse f burial-fund.

'sterben 1. v/i. (irr., ge-, sein) die (a. fig.) (an dat. of); esp. ♣♣ decease; 2. ♀ n (-s/no pl.): im ~ liegen be dying.

sterblich ['ʃtɛrplıç] 1. adj. mortal; 2. adv.: ~ verliebt sein be desperately in love (in acc with); '2keit f (-/no pl.) mortality; '2keitsziffer f death-rate, mortality.

stereotyp adj [stereo'tyːp] typ. stereotyped (a. fig.); ~ieren typ. [~y'piːrən] v/t. (no -ge-, h) stereotype.

steril adj. [ʃte'riːl] sterile; ~isieren [~ili'ziːrən] v/t. (no -ge-, h) sterilize.

Stern [ʃtɛrn] m (-[e]s/-e) star (a. fig.); '~bild ast. n constellation; '~deuter m (-s/-) astrologer; '~deutung f astrology, ~enbanner n Star-Spangled Banner, Stars and Stripes pl., Old Glory; '~fahrt mot. f motor rally; '~gucker F m (-s/-) star-gazer; '2hell adj. starry, starlit; '~himmel m (-s/no pl.) starry sky; ~kunde f (-/no pl.) astronomy; '~schnuppe f (-/-n) shooting star; '~warte f observatory.

stet adj. [ʃteːt], '~ig adj. continual, constant; steady; '2igkeit f (-/no pl.) constancy, continuity; steadiness; ~s adv always; constantly.

Steuer ['ʃtɔʏər] 1. n (-s/-) ♣♣ helm, rudder, steering-wheel; 2. f (-/-n) tax; duty; rate, local tax; '~amt n s. Finanzamt; '~beamte m revenue officer; '~berater m (-s/-) tax adviser; 2bord ♣♣ n (-[e]s/-e) starboard; ~erhebung f levy of taxes; '~erklärung f tax-return; '~ermäßigung f tax allowance; '2frei adj tax-free; goods: duty-free; '~freiheit f (-/no pl.) exemption from taxes, ~hinterziehung f tax-evasion; '~jahr n fiscal year; '~klasse f tax-bracket; '~knüppel ✈ m control lever or stick; '~mann m (-[e]s/~er, Steuerleute) ♣♣ helmsman, steersman, Am. a. wheelsman; coxwain (a. rowing); '2n (ge-) 1. v/t. (h) ♣♣, ✈ steer, navigate, pilot; ⊕ control; fig. direct, control; 2. v/i. (h) check s.th.; 3. v/i. (sein): ~ in (acc.) ♣♣ enter (harbour, etc.); ~ nach ♣♣ be bound for; '2pflichtig adj. taxable; goods: dutiable; '~rad n steering-wheel; '~ruder ♣♣ n helm, rudder; '~satz m rate of assessment; '~ung f (-/-en) ♣♣, ✈ steering; ⊕, ∮ control (a. fig.); ✈ controls pl.; ~veranlagung f tax assessment; '~zahler m (-s/-) taxpayer; ratepayer.

Steven ♣♣ ['ʃteːvən] m (-s/-) stem; stern-post.

Stich [ʃtıç] m (-[e]s/-e) prick (of needle, etc.); sting (of insect, etc.);

stab (of knife, etc.); sewing: stitch; cards: trick; ⊕ engraving; ⚟ stab; ~ halten hold water; im ~ lassen abandon, desert, forsake.

Stichel|ei ['ʃtiçə'laɪ] f (-/-en) gibe, jeer; **'2n** fig. v/i. (ge-, h) gibe (gegen at), jeer (at).

'Stich|flamme f flash; **'2haltig** adj. valid, sound; ~ sein hold water; **'~probe** f random test or sample, Am. a. spot check; **'~tag** m fixed day; **'~wahl** f second ballot; **'~wort** n 1. typ. (-[e]s/-er) head-word; 2. thea. (-[e]s/-e) cue; **'~wunde** f stab.

sticken ['ʃtikən] v/t. and v/i. (ge-, h) embroider.

'Stick|garn n embroidery floss; **'~husten** ⚕ m (w)hooping cough; **'2ig** adj. stuffy, close; **'~stoff** ⚗ m (-[e]s/no pl.) nitrogen.

stieben ['ʃtiːbən] v/i. ([irr.,] ge-, h, sein) sparks, etc.: fly about.

Stief... ['ʃtiːf-] step...

Stiefel ['ʃtiːfəl] m (-s/-) boot; **'~knecht** m bootjack; **'~schaft** m leg of a boot.

'Stief|mutter f (-/⁻) stepmother; **~mütterchen** ⚘ ['~mytərçən] n (-s/-) pansy; **'~vater** m stepfather.

stieg [ʃtiːk] pret. of steigen.

Stiel [ʃtiːl] m (-[e]s/-e) handle; helve (of weapon, tool); haft (of axe); stick (of broom); ⚘ stalk.

Stier [ʃtiːr] 1. zo. m (-[e]s/-e) bull; 2. ⚥ adj. staring; **'2en** v/i. (ge-, h) stare (auf acc. at); **'~kampf** m bull-fight.

stieß [ʃtiːs] pret. of stoßen.

Stift [ʃtift] 1. m (-[e]s/-e) pin; peg; tack; pencil, crayon; F fig.: young-ster; apprentice; 2. n (-[e]s/-e, -er) charitable institution; **'2en** v/t. (ge-, h) endow, give, Am. a. donate; found; fig. cause; make (mischief, peace); **'~er** m (-s/-) donor; found-er; fig. author; **'~ung** f (-/-en) (charitable) endowment, donation; foundation.

Stil [ʃtiːl] m (-[e]s/-e) style (a. fig.); **'2gerecht** adj. stylish; **2isieren** [ʃtili'ziːrən] v/t. (no -ge-, h) stylize; **2istisch** adj. [ʃti'listiʃ] stylistic.

still adj. [ʃtil] still, quiet; silent; ♱ dull, slack; secret; ~! silence!; im ~en secretly; ~er Gesellschafter ♱ sleeping or silent partner; der 2e Ozean the Pacific (Ocean); '2e f (-/no pl.) stillness, quiet(ness); silence; in aller ~ quietly, silently; privately; **2eben** paint. ['ʃtilleːbən] n (-s/-) still life; **~egen** ['ʃtille:gən] v/t. (sep., -ge-, h) shut down (fac-tory, etc.); stop (traffic); **'~en** v/t. (ge-, h) soothe (pain); appease (ap-petite); quench (thirst); sta(u)nch (blood); nurse (baby); **'~halten** v/i. (irr. halten, sep., -ge-, h) keep still; **~iegen** ['ʃtilliːgən] v/i.

(irr. liegen, sep., -ge-, h) factory, etc.: be shut down; traffic: be suspended; machines, etc.: be idle.

stillos adj. ['ʃtiːllo:s] without style.

'stillschweigen 1. v/i. (irr. schwei-gen, sep., -ge-, h) be silent; ~ zu et. ignore s.th.; 2. ⚥ n (-s/no pl.) silence; secrecy; ~ bewahren ob-serve secrecy; et. mit ~ übergehen pass s.th. over in silence; **'~d** adj. silent; agreement, etc.: tacit.

'Still|stand m (-[e]s/no pl.) standstill; fig.: stagnation (a. ♱); deadlock; **2stehen** v/i. (irr. stehen, sep., -ge-, h) stop; be at a standstill; still-gestanden! ✕ attention!

'Stil|möbel n/pl. period furniture; **2voll** adj. stylish.

Stimm|band anat. ['ʃtim-] n (-[e]s/⁻er) vocal c(h)ord; **'2berech-tigt** adj. entitled to vote; **'~e** f (-/-n) voice (a. ♪, fig.); vote; comment; ♪ part; **'2en** (ge-, h) 1. v/t. tune (piano, etc.); j-n fröhlich ~ put s.o. in a merry mood; 2. v/i. be true or right; sum, etc.: be correct; ~ für vote for; **'~enmehrheit** f majority or plurality of votes; **'~enthaltung** f abstention; **'~enzählung** f count-ing of votes; **'~gabel** ♪ f tuning-fork; **'~recht** n right to vote; pol. franchise; **'~ung** f (-/-en) ♪ tune; fig. mood, humo(u)r; **2ungsvoll** adj. impressive; **'~zettel** m ballot, voting-paper.

stinken ['ʃtinkən] v/i. (irr., ge-, h) stink (nach of); F fig. be fishy.

Stipendium univ. [ʃti'pendjum] n (-s/Stipendien) scholarship; ex-hibition.

stippen ['ʃtipən] v/t. (ge-, h) dip, steep; **2visite** F f flying visit.

Stirn [ʃtirn] f (-/-en) forehead, brow; fig. face, cheek; j-m die ~ bieten make head against s.o.; s. runzeln; **'~runzeln** n (-s/no pl.) frown(ing).

stob [ʃto:p] pret. of stieben.

stöbern F ['ʃtø:bərn] v/i. (ge-, h) rummage (about) (in dat. in).

stochern ['ʃtɔxərn] v/i. (ge-, h): ~ in (dat.) poke (fire); pick (teeth).

Stock [ʃtɔk] m 1. (-[e]s/⁻e) stick; cane; ♪ baton; beehive; ⚥ stock; 2. (-[e]s/-) stor(e)y, floor; im ersten ~ on the first floor, Am. on the sec-ond floor; **'2be'trunken** F adj. dead drunk; **'2'blind** F adj. stone-blind; **'2'dunkel** F adj. pitch-dark.

Stöckelschuh ['ʃtœkəl-] m high-heeled shoe.

'stocken v/i. (ge-, h) stop; liquid: stagnate (a. fig.); speaker: break down; voice: falter; traffic: be blocked; ihm stockte das Blut his blood curdled.

'Stock|engländer F m thorough or true-born Englishman; **'2'finster** F adj. pitch-dark; **'~fleck** m spot of mildew; '♀(**fleck**)**ig** adj. foxy, mildewy; '♀'**nüchtern** F adj. (as) sober as a judge; '**schnupfen** ♂ m chronic rhinitis; '♀'**taub** F adj. stone-deaf; '**ung** f (-/-en) stop (-page); stagnation (of liquid) (a. fig.); block (of traffic); '**werk** n stor(e)y, floor.

Stoff [ʃtɔf] m (-[e]s/-e) matter, substance; material, fabric, textile; material, stuff; fig.: subject(-matter); food; '♀**lich** adj. material.

stöhnen ['ʃtø:nən] v/i. (ge-, h) groan, moan.

Stolle ['ʃtɔlə] f (-/-n) loaf-shaped Christmas cake; '**n** m (-s/-) s. Stolle; ⚒ tunnel, gallery (a. ⚒).

stolpern ['ʃtɔlpərn] v/i. (ge-, sein) stumble (über acc. over), trip (over) (both a. fig.).

stolz [ʃtɔlts] 1. adj. proud (auf acc. of) (a. fig.); haughty; 2. ♀ m (-es/no pl.) pride (auf acc. in); haughtiness; **ieren** [**'tsi:rən**] v/i. (no -ge-, sein) strut, flaunt.

stopfen ['ʃtɔpfən] (ge-, h) 1. v/t. stuff; fill (pipe); cram (poultry, etc.); darn (sock, etc.); j-m den Mund ~ stop s.o.'s mouth; 2. ⚕ v/i. cause constipation.

'**Stopf**|**garn** n darning-yarn; '**na-del** f darning-needle.

Stoppel ['ʃtɔpəl] f (-/-n) stubble; '**bart** F m stubbly beard; '♀**ig** adj. stubbly.

stopp|**en** ['ʃtɔpən] (ge-, h) 1. v/t. stop; time, F clock; 2. v/i. stop; '♀**licht** mot. n stop-light; '♀**uhr** f stop-watch.

Stöpsel ['ʃtœpsəl] m (-s/-) stopper, cork; plug (a. ⚡); F fig. whipper-snapper; '♀**n** v/t. (ge-, h) stopper, cork; plug (up).

Storch orn. [ʃtɔrç] m (-[e]s/≈e) stork.

stör|**en** ['ʃtø:rən] (ge-, h) 1. v/t. disturb; trouble; radio: jam (reception); lassen Sie sich nicht ~! I don't let me disturb you!; darf ich Sie kurz ~? may I trouble you for a minute?; 2. v/i. be intruding; be in the way; '♀**fried** [**'fri:t**] m (-[e]s/-e) troublemaker; intruder.

störr|**ig** adj. ['ʃtœriç], '**isch** adj. stubborn, obstinate; a. horse: restive.

'**Störung** f (-/-en) disturbance; trouble (a. ⊕); breakdown; radio: jamming, interference.

Stoß [ʃto:s] m (-es/≈e) push, shove; thrust (a. fencing); kick; butt; shock; knock, strike; blow; swimming, billiards: stroke; jolt (of car, etc.); pile, stock, heap; '**dämpfer** mot. m shock-absorber; '♀**en** (irr., ge-) 1. v/t. (h) push, shove; thrust (weapon, etc.); kick; butt; knock, strike; pound (pepper, etc.); sich ~ an (dat.) strike or knock against; fig. take offence at; 2. v/i. (h) thrust

(nach at); kick (at); butt (at); goat, etc.: butt; car: jolt; ~an (acc.) adjoin, border on; 3. v/i. (sein): F ~ auf (acc.) come across; meet with (opposition, etc.); ~ gegen or an (acc.) knock or strike against.

'**Stoß**|**seufzer** m ejaculation; '**stange** mot. f bumper; '♀**weise** adv. by jerks; by fits and starts; '**zahn** m tusk.

stottern ['ʃtɔtərn] (ge-, h) 1. v/t. stutter (out); stammer; 2. v/i. stutter; stammer; F mot. conk (out).

Straf|**anstalt** ['ʃtra:fʔ-] f penal institution; prison; Am. penitentiary; '**arbeit** f imposition, F impo(t); '♀**bar** adj. punishable, penal; '**e** f (-/-n) punishment; ⚖, ⚑, sports, fig. penalty; fine; bei ~ von on or under pain of; zur ~ as a punishment; '♀**en** v/t. (ge-, h) punish.

straff adj. [ʃtraf] tight; rope: a. taut; fig. strict, rigid.

'**straf**|**fällig** adj. liable to prosecution; '♀**gesetz** n penal law; '♀**gesetzbuch** n penal code.

sträf|**lich** adj. ['ʃtrɛ:fliç] culpable; reprehensible; inexcusable; ♀**ling** ['**lɪŋ**] m (-s/-e) convict; Am. sl. a. lag.

'**straf**|**los** adj. unpunished; '♀**losig-keit** f (-/no pl.) impunity; '♀**porto** n surcharge; '♀**predigt** f severe lecture; j-m e-e ~ halten lecture s.o. severely; '♀**prozeß** m criminal action; '♀**raum** m football: penalty area; '♀**stoß** m football: penalty kick; '♀**verfahren** n criminal proceedings pl.

Strahl [ʃtra:l] m (-[e]s/-en) ray (a. fig.); beam; flash (of lightning, etc.); jet (of water, etc.); '♀**en** v/i. (ge-, h) radiate; shine (vor dat. with); fig. beam (vor dat. with), shine (with); '**ung** f (-/-en) radiation, rays pl.

Strähne ['ʃtrɛ:nə] f (-/-n) lock, strand (of hair); skein, hank (of yarn); fig stretch.

stramm adj. [ʃtram] tight; rope: a. taut; stalwart; soldier: smart.

strampeln ['ʃtrampəln] v/i. (ge-, h) kick.

Strand [ʃtrant] m (-[e]s/⚓, -e, ≈e) beach; '**anzug** m beach-suit; ♀**en** ['**dən**] v/i. (ge-, sein) ⚓ strand, run ashore; fig. fail, founder; '**gut** n stranded goods pl.; fig. wreckage; '**korb** m roofed wicker chair for use on the beach; **promenade** ['**pro-mənɑ:də**] f (-/-n) promenade, Am. boardwalk.

Strang [ʃtraŋ] m (-[e]s/≈e) cord (a. anat.); rope; halter (for hanging s.o.); trace (of harness); ⚒ track; über die Stränge schlagen kick over the traces.

Strapaz|**e** [ʃtra'pɑ:tsə] f (-/-n) fatigue; toil; ♀**ieren** [**a'tsi:rən**] v/t.

(no -ge-, h) fatigue, strain (a. fig.); wear out (fabric, etc.); 2ierfähig adj. [͜ə'tsiːr-] long-lasting; 2iös adj. [͜ə'tsjøːs] fatiguing.

Straße ['ʃtraːsə] f (-/-n) road, highway; street (of town, etc.); strait; auf der ~ on the road; in the street.

'Straßen|anzug m lounge-suit, Am. business suit; '~bahn f tram(way), tram-line, Am. street railway; streetcar line; s. Straßenbahnwagen; '~bahnhaltestelle f tram stop, Am. streetcar stop; '~bahnwagen m tram(-car), Am. streetcar; '~beleuchtung f street lighting; '~damm m roadway; '~händler m hawker; '~junge m street arab, Am. street Arab; '~kehrer m (-s/-) scavenger, street orderly; '~kreuzung f crossing, cross roads; '~reinigung f street-cleaning, scavenging; '~rennen n road-race.

strategisch adj. [ʃtra'teːgiʃ] strategic(al).

sträuben ['ʃtrɔʏbən] v/t. (ge-, h) ruffle up (its feathers, etc.); sich ~ hair: stand on end; sich ~ gegen kick against or at.

Strauch [ʃtraux] m (-[e]s/⁎er) shrub; bush.

straucheln ['ʃtrauxəln] v/i. (ge-, sein) stumble (über acc. over, at), trip (over) (both a. fig.).

Strauß [ʃtraus] m 1. orn. (-es/-e) ostrich; 2. (-es/⁎e) bunch (of flowers), bouquet; strife, combat.

Strebe ['ʃtreːbə] f (-/-n) strut, support, brace.

'streben 1. v/i. (ge-, h): ~ nach strive for or after, aspire to or after; 2. 2 n (-s/no pl.) striving (nach for, after), aspiration (for, after); effort, endeavo(u)r.

'Streber m (-s/-) pusher, careerist; at school: sl. swot.

strebsam adj. ['ʃtreːpzaːm] assiduous; ambitious; 2keit f (-/no pl.) assiduity; ambition.

Strecke ['ʃtrɛkə] f (-/-n) stretch; route; tract, extent; distance (a. sports); course; 🎗, etc.: section, line; hunt. bag; zur ~ bringen hunt. bag, hunt down (a. fig.); 2n v/t. (ge-, h) stretch, extend; dilute (fluid); sich ~ stretch (o.s.); die Waffen ~ lay down one's arms; fig. a. give in.

Streich [ʃtraɪç] m (-[e]s/-e) stroke; blow; fig. trick, prank; j-m e-n ~ spielen play a trick on s.o.; 2eln ['͜əln] v/t. (ge-, h) stroke; caress; pat; '2en (irr., ge-) 1. v/t. (h) rub; spread (butter, etc.); paint; strike out, delete, cancel (a. fig.); strike, lower (flag, sail); 2. v/i. (sein) prowl (um round); 3. v/i. (h): mit der Hand über et. ~ pass one's hand over s.th.; '~holz n match; '~instrument ♪ n stringed instrument;

'~orchester n string band; '~riemen m strop.

Streif [ʃtraɪf] m (-[e]s/-e) s. Streifen; '~band n (-[e]s/⁎er) wrapper; '~e f (-/-n) patrol; patrolman; raid.

'streifen (ge-) 1. v/t. (h) stripe, streak; graze, touch lightly in passing, brush; touch (up)on (subject); 2. v/i. (sein): ~ durch rove, wander through; 3. v/i. (h): ~ an (acc.) graze, brush; fig. border or verge on; 4. 2 m (-s/-) strip; stripe; streak.

'streif|ig adj. striped; '2licht n sidelight; '2schuß ⚔ m grazing shot; '2zug m ramble; ⚔ raid.

Streik [ʃtraɪk] m (-[e]s/-s) strike, Am. F a. walkout; in den ~ treten go on strike, Am. F a. walk out; '~brecher m (-s/-) strike-breaker, blackleg, scab; '2en v/i. (ge-, h) (be on) strike; go on strike, Am. F a. walk out; '~ende ['͜əndə] m, f (-n/-n) striker; '~posten m picket.

Streit [ʃtraɪt] m (-[e]s/-e) quarrel; dispute; conflict; ♛ litigation; '2bar adj. pugnacious; '2en v/i. and v/refl. (irr., ge-, h) quarrel (mit with; wegen for; über acc. about); '~frage f controversy, (point of) issue; '2ig adj. debatable, controversial; j-m et. ~ machen dispute s.o.'s right to s.th.; '~igkeiten f/pl. quarrels pl.; disputes pl.; '~kräfte ⚔ ['͜krɛftə] f/pl. (military or armed) forces pl.; '2lustig adj. pugnacious, aggressive; '2süchtig adj. quarrelsome; pugnacious.

streng [ʃtrɛŋ] 1. adj. severe; stern; strict; austere; discipline, etc.: rigorous; weather, climate: inclement; examination: stiff; 2. adv.: ~ vertraulich in strict confidence; '2e f (-/no pl.) s. streng 1: severity; sternness; strictness; austerity; rigo(u)r; inclemency; stiffness; '~genommen adv. strictly speaking; '~gläubig adj. orthodox.

Streu [ʃtrɔʏ] f (-/-en) litter; '2en v/t. (ge-, h) strew, scatter; '~zucker m castor sugar.

Strich [ʃtriç] 1. m (-[e]s/-e) stroke; line; dash; tract (of land); j-m e-n ~ durch die Rechnung machen queer s.o.'s pitch; 2. 2 pret. of streichen; '~regen m local shower; '2weise adv. here and there.

Strick [ʃtrik] m (-[e]s/-e) cord; rope; halter, rope (for hanging s.o.); F fig. (young) rascal; '2en v/t. and v/i. (ge-, h) knit; '~garn n knitting-yarn; '~jacke f cardigan, jersey; '~leiter f rope-ladder; '~nadel f knitting-needle; '~waren f/pl. knit-wear; '~zeug n knitting(-things pl.).

Striemen ['ʃtriːmən] m (-s/-) weal, wale.

Strippe F ['ʃtripə] f (-/-n) band; string; shoe-lace; an der ~ hängen be on the phone.

stritt [ʃtrit] *pret. of* streiten; '~ig *adj.* debatable, controversial; ~er Punkt (point of) issue.

Stroh [ʃtroː] *n* (-[e]s/*no pl.*) straw; thatch; '~dach *n* thatch(ed roof); '~halm *m* straw; *nach e-m* ~ *greifen* catch at a straw; '~hut *m* straw hat; '~mann *m* man of straw; scarecrow; *fig.* dummy; '~sack *m* straw mattress; '~witwe F *f* grass widow.

Strolch [ʃtrɔlç] *m* (-[e]s/-e) scamp, F vagabond; 'Sen *v/i.* (ge-, sein): ~ *durch* rove

Strom [ʃtroːm] *m* (-[e]s/*=e) stream (*a. fig.*); (large) river; ℰ current (*a. fig.*); *es regnet in Strömen* it is pouring with rain; 'S'ab(wärts) *adv.* down-stream; 'S'auf(wärts) *adv.* up-stream.

strömen ['ʃtrøːmən] *v/i.* (ge-, sein) stream; flow, run; *rain:* pour; *people:* stream, pour (*aus* out of; *in* acc. into).

'Strom|kreis ℰ *m* circuit; '~linienform *f* (-/*no pl.*) streamline shape; 'Slinienförmig *adj.* streamline(d); '~schnelle *f* (-/-n) rapid, *Am. a.* riffle; '~sperre ℰ *f* stoppage of current.

'Strömung *f* (-/-en) current; *fig. a.* trend, tendency.

'Stromzähler ℰ *m* electric meter.

Strophe ['ʃtroːfə] *f* (-/-n) stanza, verse.

strotzen ['ʃtrɔtsən] *v/i.* (ge-, h): ~ *von* abound in; teem with (*blunders, etc.*); burst with (*health, etc.*).

Strudel ['ʃtruːdəl] *m* (-s/-) eddy, whirlpool; *fig.* whirl; 'Sn *v/i.* (ge-, h) swirl, whirl.   [ture.\

Struktur [ʃtrukˈtuːr] *f* (-/-en) struc-

Strumpf [ʃtrumpf] *m* (-[e]s/*=e) stocking; '~band *n* (-[e]s/*=er) garter; '~halter *m* (-s/-) suspender, *Am.* garter; '~waren *f/pl.* hosiery.

struppig *adj.* ['ʃtrupiç] *hair:* rough, shaggy; *dog, etc.:* shaggy.

Stube ['ʃtuːbə] *f* (-/-n) room.

'Stuben|hocker *fig. m* (-s/-) stay-at-home; '~mädchen *n* chambermaid; 'Srein *adj.* house-trained.

Stück [ʃtyk] *n* (-[e]s/-e) piece (*a.* ♪); fragment; head (*of cattle*); lump (*of sugar*); *thea.* play; *aus freien ~en* of one's own accord; *in ~e gehen or schlagen* break to pieces; '~arbeit *f* piece-work; 'Sweise *adv.* piece by piece; (by) piecemeal; ✝ by the piece; '~werk *fig. n* patchwork.

Student [ʃtuˈdɛnt] *m* (-en/-en), ~in *f* (-/-nen) student, undergraduate.

Studie ['ʃtuːdjə] *f* (-/-n) study (*über acc.*, *zu* of, in) (*a. art, literature*); *paint, etc.:* sketch; '~nrat *m* (-[e]s/*=e) *appr.* secondary-school teacher; '~nreise *f* study trip.

studier|en [ʃtuˈdiːrən] (*no* -ge-, h) 1. *v/t.* study, read (*law, etc.*); 2. *v/i.*

study; be a student; 'Szimmer *n* study.

Studium ['ʃtuːdjum] *n* (-s/Studien) study (*a fig.*); studies *pl.*

Stufe ['ʃtuːfə] *f* (-/-n) step; *fig.*: degree, grade; stage.

'Stufen|folge *fig. f* gradation; '~leiter *f* step-ladder; *fig.* scale; 'Sweise 1. *adj.* gradual; 2. *adv.* gradually, by degrees.

Stuhl [ʃtuːl] *m* (-[e]s/*=e) chair, seat; *in a church* pew; *weaving:* loom; ℰ *s. Stuhlgang;* '~bein *n* leg of a chair; '~gang ℰ *m* (-[e]s/*no pl.*) stool; motion; '~lehne *f* back of a chair.

stülpen ['ʃtylpən] *v/t.* (ge-, h) put (*über acc.* over); clap (*hat*) (*auf acc.* on).

stumm *adj.* [ʃtum] dumb, mute; *fig. a.* silent; *gr.* silent, mute.

Stummel ['ʃtuməl] *m* (-s/-) stump; stub.

'Stummfilm *m* silent film.

Stümper F ['ʃtympər] *m* (-s/-) bungler, ~ei F [~ˈrai] *f* (-/-en) bungling, bungle; 'Shaft *adj.* bungling; 'Sn F *v/i.* (ge-, h) bungle, botch.

stumpf [ʃtumpf] 1. *adj.* blunt; Ƙ *angle* obtuse; *senses:* dull, obtuse; apathetic; 2. 2 *m* (-[e]s/*=e) stump, stub; *mit ~ und Stiel* root and branch; 'Ssinn *m* (-[e]s/*no pl.*) stupidity, dul(l)ness; '~sinnig *adj.* stupid, dull.

Stunde ['ʃtundə] *f* (-/-n) hour; lesson, *Am a* period; 'Sn *v/t.* (ge-, h) grant respite for.

'Stunden|kilometer *m* kilometre per hour, *Am.* kilometer per hour; 'Slang 1. *adj.*: *nach ~em Warten* after hours of waiting; 2. *adv.* for hours (and hours); '~lohn *m* hourly wage; '~plan *m* time-table, *Am* schedule; 'Sweise 1. *adj.*: ~ *Beschäftigung* part-time employment; 2. *adv* by the hour; '~zeiger *m* hour-hand

stündlich ['ʃtyntliç] 1. *adj.* hourly; 2. *adv.* hourly, every hour; at any hour.

'Stundung *f* (-/-en) respite.

stur F *adj.* [ʃtuːr] *gaze:* fixed, staring; *p.* pigheaded, mulish.

Sturm [ʃturm] *m* (-[e]s/*=e) storm (*a. fig.*); ✿ gale.

stürm|en ['ʃtyrmən] (ge-) 1. *v/t.* (h) Ӿ storm (*a. fig.*); 2. *v/i.* (h) *wind:* storm, rage; *es stürmt* it is stormy weather; 3. *v/i.* (sein) rush; 'Ser *m* (-s/-) *football, etc.:* forward; '~isch *adj.* stormy; *fig.*: impetuous; tumultuous.

'Sturm|schritt Ӿ *m* double-quick step; '~trupp Ӿ *m* storming-party; '~wind *m* storm-wind.

Sturz [ʃturts] *m* (-es/*=e) fall, tumble; overthrow (*of government, etc.*);

fig. ruin; † slump; '**~bach** *m* torrent.

stürzen ['ʃtyrtsən] (ge-) 1. *v/i.* (sein) (have a) fall, tumble; *fig.* rush, plunge (*in acc.* into); 2. *v/t.* (h) throw; overthrow (*government, etc.*); *fig.* plunge (*in acc.* into), precipitate (into); *j-n ins Unglück* ~ ruin s.o.; *sich in Schulden* ~ plunge into debt.

'**Sturz|flug** ✶ *m* (nose)dive; '**~helm** *m* crash-helmet.

Stute *zo.* ['ʃtuːtə] *f* (-/-n) mare.

Stütze ['ʃtytsə] *f* (-/-n) support, prop, stay (*all a. fig.*).

stutzen ['ʃtutsən] (ge-, h) 1. *v/t.* cut (*hedge*); crop (*ears, tail, hair*); clip (*hedge, wing*); trim (*hair, beard, hedge*); dock (*tail*); lop (*tree*); 2. *v/i.* start (*bei* at); stop dead *or* short.

'**stützen** *v/t.* (ge-, h) support, prop, stay (*all a. fig.*); ~ *auf* (*acc.*) base *or* found on; *sich* ~ *auf* (*acc.*) lean on; *fig.* rely (*up*)on; *argument, etc.*: be based on.

'**Stutz|er** *m* (-s/-) dandy, fop, *Am. a.* dude; '**2ig** *adj.* suspicious; ~ *machen* make suspicious.

'**Stütz|pfeiler** ▲ *m* abutment; '**~punkt** *m* *phys.* fulcrum; ✕ base.

Subjekt [zup'jɛkt] *n* (-[e]s/-e) *gr.* subject; *contp.* individual; **2iv** *adj.* [~'tiːf] subjective; **~ivität** [~ivi'tɛːt] *f* (-/no pl.) subjectivity.

Substantiv *gr.* ['zupstantiːf] *n* (-s/-e) noun, substantive; **2isch** *gr. adj.* ['~viʃ] substantival.

Substanz [zup'stants] *f* (-/-en) substance (*a. fig.*).

subtra|hieren Ⓐ [zuptra'hiːrən] *v/t.* (no -ge-, h) subtract; **2ktion** Ⓐ [~k'tsjoːn] *f* (-/-en) subtraction.

Such|dienst ['zuːx-] *m* tracing service; '**~e** *f* (-/no pl.) search (*nach* for); *auf der* ~ *nach* in search of; '**2en** (ge-, h) 1. *v/t.* seek (*advice, etc.*); search for; look for; *Sie haben hier nichts zu* ~ you have no business to be here; 2. *v/i.:* ~ *nach* seek for *or* after; search for; look for; '**~er** *phot. m* (-s/-) view-finder.

Sucht [zuxt] *f* (-/-e) mania (*nach* for), rage (for), addiction (to).

süchtig *adj.* ['zyçtiç] having a mania (*nach* for); ~ *sein* be a drug addict; **2e** ['~gə] *m, f* (-n/-n) drug addict *or* fiend.

Süd *geogr.* [zyːt], **~en** ['~dən] *m* (-s/no pl.) south; '**~früchte** ['zyːt-fryçtə] *f/pl.* fruits from the south; '**2lich** 1. *adj.* south(ern); southerly; 2. *adv.:* ~ *von* (to) the south of; **~ost** *geogr.*, **~osten** *m* (-s/no pl.) south-east; **2östlich** *adj.* south-east(ern); '**~pol** *geogr. m* (-s/no pl.) South Pole; **2wärts** *adv.* ['~verts] southward(s); '**~west** *geogr.*, '**~westen** *m* (-s/no pl.) south-west;

2'westlich *adj.* south-west(ern); '**~wind** *m* south wind.

süffig F *adj.* ['zyfiç] palatable, tasty.

suggerieren [zugeˈriːrən] *v/t.* (no -ge-, h) suggest.

suggestiv *adj.* [zugesˈtiːf] suggestive.

Sühne ['zyːnə] *f* (-/-n) expiation, atonement; '**2n** *v/t.* (ge-, h) expiate, atone for.

Sülze ['zyltsə] *f* (-/-n) jellied meat.

summ|arisch *adj.* [zuˈmaːriʃ] summary (*a. ✞*); '**2e** *f* (-/-n) sum (*a. fig.*); (sum) total; amount.

'**summen** (ge-, h) 1. *v/i.* bees, *etc.*: buzz, hum; 2. *v/t.* hum (*song, etc.*).

sum'mieren *v/t.* (no -ge-, h) sum *or* add up; *sich* ~ run up.

Sumpf [zumpf] *m* (-[e]s/-e) swamp, bog, marsh; '**2ig** *adj.* swampy, boggy, marshy.

Sünd|e ['zyndə] *f* (-/-n) sin (*a. fig.*); '**~enbock** F *m* scapegoat; '**~er** *m* (-s/-) sinner; **2haft** ['~t-] 1. *adj.* sinful; 2. *adv.:* F ~ *teuer* awfully expensive; **2ig** ['~diç] *adj.* sinful; **2igen** ['~digən] *v/i.* (ge-, h) commit a) sin.

Superlativ ['zuːperlatiːf] *m* (-s/-e) *gr.* superlative degree; *in ~en sprechen* speak in superlatives.

Suppe ['zupə] *f* (-/-n) soup; broth.

'**Suppen|löffel** *m* soup-spoon; '**~schöpfer** *m* soup ladle; '**~schüssel** *f* tureen; '**~teller** *m* soup-plate.

surren ['zurən] *v/i.* (ge-, h) whir(r); *insects:* buzz.

Surrogat [zuroˈgaːt] *n* (-[e]s/-e) substitute.

suspendieren [zuspenˈdiːrən] *v/t.* (no -ge-, h) suspend.

süß *adj.* [zyːs] sweet (*a. fig.*); '**2e** *f* (-/no pl.) sweetness; '**2en** (ge-, h) sweeten; '**2igkeiten** *pl.* sweets *pl.*, sweetmeats *pl.*, *Am. a.* candy; '**~lich** *adj.* sweetish; mawkish (*a. fig.*); '**2stoff** *m* saccharin(e); '**2-wasser** *n* (-s/-) fresh water.

Symbol [zymˈboːl] *n* (-s/-e) symbol; **~ik** *f* (-/no pl.) symbolism; **2isch** *adj.* symbolic(al).

Symmetr|ie [zymeˈtriː] *f* (-/-n) symmetry; **2isch** *adj.* [~ˈmeːtriʃ] symmetric(al).

Sympath|ie [zympaˈtiː] *f* (-/-n) liking; **2isch** *adj.* [~ˈpaːtiʃ] likable; *er ist mir* ~ I like him; **2isieren** [~iˈziːrən] *v/i.* (no -ge-, h) sympathize (*mit* with).

Symphonie ♪ [zymfoˈniː] *f* (-/-n) symphony; **~orchester** *n* symphony orchestra.

Symptom [zympˈtoːm] *n* (-s/-e) symptom; **2atisch** *adj.* [~oˈmaːtiʃ] symptomatic (*für* of).

Synagoge [zynaˈgoːgə] *f* (-/-n) synagogue.

synchronisieren [zynkroniˈziːrən] *v/t.* (no -ge-, h) synchronize; dub.

Syndik|at [zyndi'ka:t] *n* (-[e]s/-e) syndicate; **~us** ['zyndikus] *m* (-/-se, *Syndizi*) syndic.

Synkope ♪ [zyn'ko:pə] *f* (-/-n) syncope.

synonym [zyno'ny:m] **1.** *adj.* synonymous; **2.** ♀*n* (-s/-e) synonym.

Syntax *gr.* ['zyntaks] *f* (-/-en) syntax.

synthetisch *adj.* [zyn'te:tiʃ] synthetic.

System [zys'te:m] *n* (-s/-e) system; scheme; **2atisch** *adj.* [~e'ma:tiʃ] systematic(al), methodic(al).

Szene [tsse nə] *f* (-/-n) scene (*a. fig.*); in ~ setzen stage; **~rie** [stsenə'ri:] *f* (-/-n) scenery.

T

Tabak ['ta:bak, 'tabak, ta'bak] *m* (-s/-e) tobacco; **~händler** *m* tobacconist; (')**~sbeutel** *m* tobacco-pouch; (')**~sdose** *f* snuff-box; (')**~waren** *pl.* tobacco products *pl.*, F smokes *pl.*

tabellarisch [tabe'la:riʃ] **1.** *adj.* tabular. **2.** *adv.* in tabular form.

Tabelle [ta'belə] *f* (-/-n) table; schedule.

Tablett [ta'blɛt] *n* (-[e]s/-e, -s) tray; *of metal* salver; **~e** *pharm. f* (-/-n) tablet; lozenge.

Tachometer [taxo'-] *n, m* (-s/-) ⊕ tachometer, *mot. a.* speedometer.

Tadel ['ta:dəl] *m* (-s/-) blame; censure, reprimand, rebuke, reproof; reproach; *at school:* bad mark; **'2los** *adj.* faultless, blameless; excellent, splendid; **'2n** *v/t.* (*ge-, h*) blame (*wegen for*); censure, reprimand, rebuke, reprove; scold; find fault with.

Tafel ['ta:fəl] *f* (-/-n) table; plate (*a. book illustration*); slab; *on houses, etc.:* tablet, plaque; slate; blackboard, signboard, notice-board, *Am.* billboard; cake, bar (*of chocolate, etc.*); dinner-table; dinner; **2förmig** *adj.* ['~fœrmiç] tabular, **~geschirr** *n* dinner-service, dinner-set; **'~land** *n* tableland, plateau; **'2n** *v/i.* (*ge-, h*) dine; feast, banquet; **'~service** *n s. Tafelgeschirr*, **~silber** *n* silver plate, *Am.* silverware.

Täf(e)lung ['te:f(ə)luŋ] *f* (-/-en) wainscot, panelling.

Taft [taft] *m* (-[e]s/-e) taffeta.

Tag [ta:k] *m* (-[e]s/-e) day; *officially:* a. date; *am or bei* ~e by day; *e-s* ~es one day; *den ganzen* ~ all day long; ~ *für* ~ day by day; *über* ~e ⚒ aboveground, *unter* ~e ⚒ underground; *heute vor acht* ~en a week ago; *heute in acht (vierzehn)* ~en today *or* this day week (fortnight), a week (fortnight) today; *denkwürdiger or freudiger* ~ red-letter day; *freier* ~ day off; *guten* ~! how do you do?; good morning!; good afternoon!; F hallo!, hullo!, *Am.* hello!; *am hellichten* ~e in broad daylight; *es wird* ~ it dawns; *an den*

~ *bringen (kommen)* bring (come) to light; *bis auf den heutigen* ~ to this day; ♀*aus adv.:* ~, *tagein* day in, day out.

Tage|blatt [ta:gə-] *n* daily (paper); **'~buch** *n* journal, diary

tagein *adv.* [ta k ain] *s tagaus.*

tage|lang *adv.* ['ta:gə-] day after day, for days together; **'2lohn** *m* day's *or* daily wages *pl.*, **2löhner** ['~lø:nər] *m* (-s/-) day-labo(u)rer; **~n** *v/i.* (*ge-, h*) dawn; hold a meeting, meet, sit, ⚖ be in session; **'2reise** *f* day's journey.

Tages|anbruch ['ta:gəs⁹-] *m* daybreak, dawn, bei ~ at daybreak *or* dawn, **~befehl** ⚔ *m* order of the day; **~bericht** *m* daily report, bulletin, **~einnahme** ✝ *f* receipts *pl. or* takings *pl* of the day; **'~gespräch** *n* topic of the day; **'~kasse** *f thea* box-office, booking-office; *s. Tageseinnahme*, **~kurs** ✝ *m* current rate, *stock exchange* quotation of the day; **~licht** *n* daylight; **'~ordnung** *f* order of the day, agenda, *das ist an der* ~ that is the order of the day, that is quite common, **~presse** *f* daily press; **'~zeit** *f* time of day, daytime; *zu jeder* ~ at any hour, at any time of the day, **~zeitung** *f* daily (paper).

tage|weise *adv.* ['ta:gə-] by the day; **'2werk** *r* day's work, man-day.

täglich *adj.* ['te: kliç] daily.

tags *adv.* [ta:ks] . *darauf* the following day, the day after; ~ *zuvor* (on) the previous day, the day before

'Tagschicht *f* day shift.

tagsüber *adv.* ['ta:ks⁹-] during the day, in the day-time.

Tagung [ta:guŋ] *f* (-/-en) meeting.

Taille [taljə] *f* (-/-n) waist; bodice (*of dress*).

Takel ⚓ ['ta:kəl] *n* (-s/-) tackle, **~age** ⚓ [takə'la:ʒə] *f* (-/-n) rigging, tackle, **'2n** *v/t.* (*ge-, h*) rig (*ship*); **'~werk** ⚓ *n s. Takelage.*

Takt [takt] *m* **1.** (-[e]s/-e) ♪ time, measure; bar; *mot.* stroke; *den* ~ *halten* ♪ keep time; *den* ~ *schlagen* ♪ beat time; **2.** (-[e]s/*no pl.*) tact; **'2fest** *adj.* steady in keeping time;

fig. firm; '⹁ik ✕ *f* (-/-en) tactics *pl. and sg.* (*a. fig.*); '⹁iker *m* (-s/-) tactician; '2isch *adj.* tactical; '2los *adj.* tactless; '⹁stock *m* baton; '⹁strich *♪ m* bar; '2voll *adj.* tactful.

Tal [tɑːl] *n* (-[e]s/ᵘer) valley, *poet. a.* dale; *enges* ⹁ glen.

Talar [taˈlɑːr] *m* (-s/-e) ₃½, *eccl., univ.* gown; ₃½ robe.

Talent [taˈlɛnt] *n* (-[e]s/-e) talent, gift, aptitude, ability; 2iert *adj.* [⹁'tiːrt] talented, gifted.

'Talfahrt *f* downhill journey; ♄ passage downstream.

Talg [talk] *m* (-[e]s/-e) suet; *melted:* tallow; '⹁drüse *anat. f* sebaceous gland; 2ig *adj.* ['⹁ɡiç] suety; tallowish, tallowy; '⹁licht *n* tallow candle.

Talisman ['tɑːlisman] *m* (-s/-e) talisman, (good-luck) charm.

'Talsperre *f* barrage, dam.

Tampon [tã'põː, 'tampɔn] *m* (-s/-s) tampon, plug.

Tang ♃ [taŋ] *m* (-[e]s/-e) seaweed.

Tank [taŋk] *m* (-[e]s/-s, -e) tank; 2en *v/i.* (ge-, h) get (some) petrol, *Am.* get (some) gasoline; '⹁er ⚓ *m* (-s/-) tanker; '⹁stelle *f* petrol station, *Am.* gas or filling station; '⹁wagen *m mot.* tank truck, *Am. a.* gasoline truck, tank trailer; ⹁ tank-car; ⹁wart ['⹁vart] *m* (-[e]s/-e) pump attendant.

Tanne ♃ ['tanə] *f* (-/-n) fir(-tree).

'Tannen|baum *m* fir-tree; '⹁nadel *f* fir-needle; '⹁zapfen *m* fir-cone.

Tante ['tantə] *f* (-/-n) aunt.

Tantieme [tã'tjɛːmə] *f* (-/-n) royalty, percentage, share in profits.

Tanz [tants] *m* (-es/ᵘe) dance.

tänzeln ['tɛntsəln] *v/i.* (ge-, h, sein) dance, trip, frisk.

'tanzen (ge-) *v/i.* (h, sein) and *v/t.* (h) dance.

Tänzer ['tɛntsər] *m* (-s/-), '⹁in *f* (-/-nen) dancer; *thea.* ballet-dancer; partner.

'Tanz|lehrer *m* dancing-master; '⹁musik *f* dance-music; '⹁saal *m* dancing-room, ball-room, dance-hall; '⹁schule *f* dancing-school; '⹁stunde *f* dancing-lesson.

Tapete [ta'peːtə] *f* (-/-n) wallpaper, paper-hangings *pl.*

tapezier|en [tape'tsiːrən] *v/t.* (no -ge-, h) paper; 2er *m* (-s/-) paper-hanger; upholsterer.

tapfer *adj.* ['tapfər] brave; valiant, heroic; courageous; '2keit *f* (-/no *pl.*) bravery, valo(u)r; heroism; courage.

tappen ['tapən] *v/i.* (ge-, sein) grope (about), fumble.   [awkward.\
täppisch *adj.* ['tɛpiʃ] clumsy,\
tapsen ['tapsən] *v/i.* (ge-, sein) walk clumsily.

Tara ♰ ['tɑːra] *f* (-/Taren) tare.

Tarif [ta'riːf] *m* (-s/-e) tariff, (table of) rates *pl.*, price-list; 2lich *adv.* according to tariff; '⹁lohn *m* standard wage(s *pl.*); ⹁vertrag *m* collective or wage agreement.

tarn|en ['tarnən] *v/t.* (ge-, h) camouflage; *esp. fig.* disguise; 2ung *f* (-/-en) camouflage.

Tasche ['taʃə] *f* (-/-n) pocket (of *garment*); (hand)bag; pouch; *s. Aktentasche, Schultasche.*

'Taschen|buch *n* pocket-book; '⹁dieb *m* pickpocket, *Am. sl.* dip; '⹁geld *n* pocket-money; *monthly:* allowance; '⹁lampe *f* (electric) torch, *esp. Am.* flashlight; '⹁messer *n* pocket-knife; '⹁spielerei *f* juggle(ry); '⹁tuch *n* (pocket) handkerchief; '⹁uhr *f* (pocket-)watch; '⹁wörterbuch *n* pocket dictionary.

Tasse ['tasə] *f* (-/-n) cup.

Tastatur [tasta'tuːr] *f* (-/-en) keyboard, keys *pl.*

Tast|e ['tastə] *f* (-/-n) key; 2en (ge-, h) 1. *v/i.* touch; grope (*nach* for, after), fumble (for); 2. *v/t.* touch, feel; *sich* ⹁ feel *or* grope one's way; '⹁sinn *m* (-[e]s/no *pl.*) sense of touch.

Tat [tɑːt] 1. *f* (-/-en) action, act, deed; offen|ce, *Am.* -se, crime; *in der* ⹁ indeed, in fact, as a matter of fact, really; *auf frischer* ⹁ *ertappen* catch *s.o.* red-handed; *zur* ⹁ *schreiten* proceed to action; *in die* ⹁ *umsetzen* implement, carry into effect; 2. ♀ *pret. of tun;* '⹁bestand ₃½ *m* facts *pl.* of the case; 2enlos *adj.* inactive, idle.

Täter ['tɛːtər] *m* (-s/-) perpetrator; offender, culprit.

tätig *adj.* ['tɛːtiç] active; busy; ⹁ *sein bei* work at; be employed with; ⹁en ♰ ['⹁ɡən] *v/t.* (ge-, h) effect, transact; conclude; 2keit *f* (-/-en) activity; occupation, business, job; profession.

'Tat|kraft *f* (-/no *pl.*) energy; enterprise; 2kräftig *adj.* energetic, active.

tätlich *adj.* ['tɛːtliç] violent; ⹁ *werden gegen* assault; 2keiten *f/pl.* (acts *pl.* of) violence; ₃½ assault (and battery).

Tatort ₃½ ['tɑːt?-] *m* (-[e]s/-e) place *or* scene of a crime.

tätowieren [tɛto'viːrən] *v/t.* (no -ge-, h) tattoo.

'Tat|sache *f* (matter of) fact; '⹁sachenbericht *m* factual or documentary report, matter-of-fact account; 2sächlich *adj.* actual, real.   [pat.\
tätscheln ['tɛtʃəln] *v/t.* (ge-, h) pet,\
Tatze ['tatsə] *f* (-/-n) paw, claw.

Tau[1] [tau] *n* (-[e]s/-e) rope, cable.

Tau[2] [⹁] *m* (-[e]s/no *pl.*) dew.

taub *adj.* [taup] deaf (*fig.: gegen* to); *fingers, etc.:* benumbed, numb; *nut:*

deaf, empty; *rock*: dead; ~es Ei
addle egg; *auf e-m Ohr* ~ *sein* be
deaf of or in one ear.

Taube orn. ['taubə] f (-/-n) pigeon;
'~nschlag m pigeon-house.

'**Taub|heit** f (-/no pl.) deafness;
numbness; '2stumm adj. deaf and
dumb; '~stumme m, f (-n/-n) deaf
mute.

tauch|en ['tauxən] (ge-) **1.** v/t.
(h) dip, plunge; **2.** v/i. (h, sein) dive,
plunge; dip; *submarine*: submerge;
'2er m (-s/-) diver; '2sieder m (-s/-)
immersion heater.

tauen ['tauən] v/i. (ge-) **1.** (h, sein):
der Schnee or es taut the snow or
it is thawing; *der Schnee ist von
den Dächern getaut* the snow has
melted off the roofs; **2.** (h): *es taut*
dew is falling.

Taufe ['taufə] f (-/-n) baptism,
christening; '2n v/t. (ge-, h) baptize,
christen.

Täufling ['tɔʏfliŋ] m (-s/-e) child or
person to be baptized.

'**Tauf|name** m Christian name, Am.
a. given name; '~pate **1.** m godfather; **2.** f godmother; '~patin f
godmother; '~schein m certificate
of baptism.

taug|en ['taugən] v/i. (ge-, h) be
good, be fit, be of use (*all*: zu for);
(zu) nichts ~ be good for nothing,
be no good, be of no use; '2enichts
m (-, -es/-e) good-for-nothing, Am.
sl. dead beat; ~lich adj. ['tauk-]
good, fit, useful (*all*: für, zu for, to
inf.); able; ✕, ⚓ able-bodied.

Taumel ['tauməl] m (-s/no pl.)
giddiness; rapture, ecstasy; '2ig
adj. reeling; giddy; '2n v/i. (ge-,
sein) reel, stagger; be giddy.

Tausch [tauʃ] m (-es/-e) exchange;
barter; '2en v/t. (ge-, h) exchange;
barter (*gegen* for).

täuschen ['tɔʏʃən] v/t. (ge-, h)
deceive, delude, mislead (on purpose); cheat; *sich* ~ deceive o.s.; be
mistaken; *sich* ~ *lassen* let o.s. be
deceived; '~d adj. deceptive, delu-
sive; *resemblance*: striking.

'**Tauschhandel** m barter.

'**Täuschung** f (-/-en) deception,
delusion.

tausend adj. ['tauzənt] a thousand;
'~fach adj. thousandfold; '2fuß zo.
m, 2füß(l)er zo. [' ~fy:s(l)ər] m
(-s/-) millepede, milliped(e), Am. a.
wireworm; '~st adj. thousandth;
'2stel n (-s/-) thousandth (part).

'**Tau|tropfen** m dew-drop; '~wetter
n thaw.

Taxameter [taksa'-] m taximeter.

Taxe ['taksə] f (-/-n) rate; fee;
estimate; *s. Taxi.*

Taxi ['taksi] n (-[s]/-[s]) taxi(-cab),
cab, Am. a. hack.

ta'xieren v/t. (no -ge-, h) rate,
estimate; *officially*: value, appraise.

'**Taxistand** m cabstand.

Technik ['tɛçnik] f **1.** (-/no pl.)
technology; engineering; **2.** (-/-en)
skill, workmanship; technique,
practice; ♪ execution; '~er m (-s/-)
(technical) engineer; technician;
~um [' ~um] n (-s/Technika, Tech-
niken) technical school.

'**technisch** adj. technical; ~e Hochschule school of technology.

Tee [te:] m (-s/-s) tea; '~büchse f
tea-caddy; '~gebäck n scones pl.,
biscuits pl., Am. a. cookies pl.;
'~kanne f teapot; '~kessel m tea-
kettle; '~löffel m tea-spoon.

Teer [te:r] m (-[e]s/-e) tar; '2en v/t.
(ge-, h) tar.

'**Tee|rose** ⚘ f tea-rose; '~sieb n
tea-strainer; '~tasse f teacup;
'~wärmer m (-s/-) tea-cosy.

Teich [taiç] m (-[e]s/-e) pool,
pond.

Teig [taik] m (-[e]s/-e) dough, paste;
2ig adj. [' ~giç] doughy, pasty;
'~waren f/pl. farinaceous food;
noodles pl.

Teil [tail] m, n (-[e]s/-e) part; portion, share; component; ⚖ party;
zum ~ partly, in part; *ich für mein
~ ...* for my part I ...; '2bar adj.
divisible; '~chen n (-s/-) particle;
'2en v/t. (ge-, h) divide; fig. share;
'2haben v/i. (irr. haben, sep., -ge-,
h) participate, (have a) share (*both*:
an dat. in); '~haber m (-s/-)
partner; ~nahme [' ~na:mə] f (-/no
pl.) participation (an dat. in); fig.:
interest (in); sympathy (with);
2nahmslos adj. [' ~na:mslo:s] indifferent, unconcerned; passive;
apathetic; '2nahmslosigkeit f
(-/no pl.) indifference; passiveness;
apathy; 2nehmen v/i. (irr. nehmen,
sep., -ge-, h): ~ an (dat.) take part or
participate in; join in; be present
at, attend at; fig. sympathize with;
'~nehmer m (-s/-) participant;
member; *univ., etc.*: student; con-
testant; *sports*: competitor; *teleph.*
subscriber; 2s adv. [~s] partly;
'~strecke f section; stage, leg; 🚋
fare stage; '~ung f (-/-en) division;
'2weise adv. partly, partially, in
part; '~zahlung f (payment by)
instal(l)ments.

Teint [tɛ̃:] m (-s/-s) complexion.

Tele|fon [tele'fo:n] n (-s/-e) etc. s.
Telephon, etc.; ~graf [~'gra:f] m
(-en/-en) etc. s. *Telegraph, etc.*;
~gramm [~'gram] n (-s/-e) telegram, wire; *overseas*: cable(gram).

Telegraph [tele'gra:f] m (-en/-en)
telegraph; ~enamt [~ən'-] n telegraph office; 2ieren [~a'fi:rən] v/t.
and v/i. (no -ge-, h) telegraph, wire;
overseas: cable; 2isch [~'gra:fiʃ]
1. adj. telegraphic; **2.** adv. by telegram, by wire; by cable; ~ist
[~a'fist] m (-en/-en), ~istin f (-/-nen)

telegraph operator, telegrapher, telegraphist.

Teleobjektiv *phot.* ['te:le-] *n* telephoto lens.

Telephon [tele'fo:n] *n* (-s/-e) telephone, F phone; *am ~ on the* (tele)phone; *ans ~ gehen* answer the (tele)phone; *~ haben* be on the (tele)phone; *~anschluß m* telephone connexion *or* connection; *~buch n* (tele)phone directory; *~gespräch n* (tele)phone call; conversation *or* chat over the (tele-) phone; *~hörer m* (telephone) receiver, handset; *2ieren* [~o'ni:rən] *v/i.* (*no -ge-*, *h*) telephone, F phone; *mit j-m ~ ring s.o. up, Am.* call **s.o.** up; *2isch adv.* [~'fo:nɪʃ] by (tele)phone, over the (tele)phone; *~ist* [~o'nɪst] *m* (-en/-en), *~istin f* (-/-nen) (telephone) operator, telephonist; *~vermittlung f s. Telephonzentrale; *~zelle f* telephone kiosk *or* box, call-box, *Am.* telephone booth; *~zentrale f* (telephone) exchange.

Teleskop *opt.* [tele'sko:p] *n* (-s/-e) telescope.

Teller ['tɛlər] *m* (-s/-) plate.

Tempel ['tɛmpəl] *m* (-s/-) temple.

Temperament [tɛmpəra'mɛnt] *n* (-[e]s/-e) temper(ament); *fig.* spirit(s *pl.*); *2los adj.* spiritless; *2voll adj.* (high-)spirited.

Temperatur [tɛmpəra'tu:r] *f* (-/-en) temperature; *j-s ~ messen* take s.o.'s temperature.

Tempo ['tɛmpo] *n* (-s/-s, *Tempi*) time; pace; speed; rate.

Tendenz [tɛn'dɛnts] *f* (-/-en) tendency; trend; *2iös adj.* [~'tsjø:s] tendentious.

Tennis ['tɛnɪs] *n* (-/*no pl.*) (lawn) tennis; *~ball m* tennis-ball; *'~platz m* tennis-court; *'~schläger m* (tennis-)racket; *'~spieler m* tennis player; *'~turnier n* tennis tournament.

Tenor *♪* [te'no:r] *m* (-s/*=e) tenor.

Teppich ['tɛpɪç] *m* (-s/-e) carpet; *'~kehrmaschine f* carpet-sweeper.

Termin [tɛr'mi:n] *m* (-s/-e) appointed time *or* day; 🕰, 🕇 date, term; *sports:* fixture; *äußerster ~* final date, dead(-)line; *~geschäfte* 🕇 *n/pl.* futures *pl.*; *~kalender m* appointment book *or* pad; *Am.* calendar; *~liste* 🕇 *f* causelist, *Am.* calendar.

Terpentin [tɛrpɛn'ti:n] *n* (-s/-e) turpentine.

Terrain [tɛ'rɛ̃:] *n* (-s/-s) ground; plot; building site.

Terrasse [tɛ'rasə] *f* (-/-n) terrace; *2förmig adj.* [~nfœrmɪç] terraced, in terraces.

Terrine [tɛ'ri:nə] *f* (-/-n) tureen.

Territorium [tɛri'to:rjum] *n* (-s/*Territorien*) territory.

Terror ['tɛror] *m* (-s/*no pl.*) terror; *2isieren* [~ori'zi:rən] *v/t.* (*no -ge-*, *h*) terrorize.

Terz *♪* [tɛrts] *f* (-/-en) third; *~ett* ♪ [~'tsɛt] *n* (-[e]s/-e) trio.

Testament [tɛsta'mɛnt] *n* (-[e]s/-e) (last) will, (*often:* last will and) testament; *eccl.* Testament; *2arisch* [~'ta:rɪʃ] 1. *adj.* testamentary; 2. *adv.* by will; *~svollstrecker m* (-s/-) executor; *officially:* administrator.

testen ['tɛstən] *v/t.* (ge-, h) test.

teuer *adj.* ['tɔyər] dear (*a. fig.*), expensive; *wie ~ ist es?* how much is it?

Teufel ['tɔyfəl] *m* (-s/-) devil; *der ~* the Devil, Satan; *zum ~! F* dickens!, hang it!; *wer zum ~? F* who the devil *or* deuce?; *der ~ ist los* the fat's in the fire; *scher dich zum ~! F* go to hell!, go to blazes!; *~ei* [~'laɪ] *f* (-/-en) devilment, mischief, devilry, *Am.* deviltry; *'~skerl F m* devil of a fellow.

'teuflisch *adj.* devilish, diabolic(al).

Text [tɛkst] *m* (-es/-e) text; words *pl.* (*of song*); book, libretto (*of opera*); *~buch n* book; libretto.

Textil|ien [tɛks'ti:ljən] *pl.*, *~waren pl.* textile fabrics *pl.*, textiles *pl.*

'textlich *adv.* concerning the text.

Theater [te'a:tər] *n* 1. (-s/-) theat|re, *Am.* -er; stage; 2. F (-s/*no pl.*) playacting; *~besucher m* playgoer; *~karte f* theatre ticket; *~kasse f* box-office; *~stück n* play; *~vorstellung f* theatrical performance; *~zettel m* playbill.

theatralisch *adj.* [tea'tra:lɪʃ] theatrical, stagy.

Theke ['te:kə] *f* (-/-n) *at inn:* bar, *Am. a.* counter; *at shop:* counter.

Thema ['te:ma] *n* (-s/*Themen, Themata*) theme, subject; topic (*of discussion*).

Theolog|e [teo'lo:gə] *m* (-n/-n) theologian, divine; *~ie* [~o'gi:] *f* (-/-n) theology.

Theoret|iker [teo're:tikər] *m* (-s/-) theorist; *2isch adj.* theoretic(al).

Theorie [teo'ri:] *f* (-/-n) theory.

Therapie ⚕ [tera'pi:] *f* (-/-n) therapy. [spa.]

Thermalbad [tɛr'ma:l-] *n* thermal]

Thermometer [tɛrmo'-] *n* (-s/-) thermometer; *~stand m* (thermometer) reading.

Thermosflasche ['tɛrmɔs-] *f* vacuum bottle *or* flask, thermos (flask).

These ['te:zə] *f* (-/-n) thesis.

Thrombose ⚕ [trɔm'bo:zə] *f* (-/-n) thrombosis.

Thron [tro:n] *m* (-[e]s/-e) throne; *~besteigung f* accession to the throne; *~erbe m* heir to the throne, heir apparent; *'~folge f* succession to the throne; *'~folger m* (-s/-) successor to the throne; *~rede parl. f* Queen's *or* King's Speech.

Thunfisch *ichth.* ['tuːn-] *m* tunny, tuna.

Tick F [tik] *m* (-[e]s/-s, -e) crotchet, fancy, kink; e-n ~ haben have a bee in one's bonnet.

ticken ['tikən] *v/i.* (ge-, h) tick.

tief [tiːf] **1.** *adj.* deep (*a. fig.*); *fig.*: profound; low; *im ~sten Winter* in the dead *or* depth of winter; **2.** *adv.*: *bis ~ in die Nacht* far into the night; *das läßt ~ blicken* that speaks volumes; *zu ~ singen* sing flat; **3.** ♀ *meteor. n* (-[e]s/-s) depression, low(-pressure area); '♀bau *m* civil *or* underground engineering; '♀druckgebiet *meteor. n s. Tief*; '♀e *f* (-/-n) depth (*a. fig.*); *fig.* profundity; '♀ebene *f* low plain, lowland; '♀enschärfe *phot. f* depth of focus; '♀flug *m* low-level flight; '♀gang ♣ *m* draught, *Am.* draft; ~gebeugt *fig. adj.* ['~gəbɔʏkt] deeply afflicted, bowed down; ~gekühlt *adj.* deep-frozen; '~greifend *adj.* fundamental, radical; ♀land *n* lowland(s *pl.*); '~liegend *adj. eyes*: sunken; *fig.* deep-seated; ♀schlag *m boxing*: low hit; '~schürfend *fig. adj.* profound; thorough; '♀see *f* deep sea; '~sinnig *adj.* thoughtful, pensive; F melancholy; ♀stand *m* (-[e]s/*no pl.*) low level.

Tiegel ['tiːgəl] *m* (-s/-) saucepan, stew-pan; ⊕ crucible.

Tier [tiːr] *n* (-[e]s/-e) animal; beast; brute; *großes ~ fig. sl.* bigwig, big bug, *Am.* big shot; '~arzt *m* veterinary (surgeon), F vet, *Am. a.* veterinarian; '~garten *m* zoological gardens *pl.*, zoo; '~heilkunde *f* veterinary medicine; '♀isch *adj.* animal; *fig.* bestial, brutish, savage; '~kreis *ast. m* zodiac; ~quälerei [~kvɛːlə'raɪ] *f* (-/-en) cruelty to animals; '~reich *n* (-[e]s/*no pl.*) animal kingdom; '~schutzverein *m* Society for the Prevention of Cruelty to Animals.

Tiger *zo.* ['tiːgər] *m* (-s/-) tiger; '~in *zo. f* (-/-nen) tigress.

tilg|en ['tilgən] *v/t.* (ge-, h) extinguish; efface; wipe *or* blot out, erase; *fig.* obliterate; annul, cancel; discharge, pay (*debt*); redeem (*mortgage, etc.*); '♀ung *f* (-/-en) extinction; extermination; cancel(l)ing; discharge, payment; redemption.

Tinktur [tiŋk'tuːr] *f* (-/-en) tincture. [*sitzen* F be in a scrape.\]

Tinte ['tintə] *f* (-/-n) ink; *in der ~*\

'Tinten|faß *n* ink-pot, *desk*: inkwell; '~fisch *ichth. m* cuttle-fish; '~fleck *m*, '~klecks *m* (ink-)blot; '~stift *m* indelible pencil.

Tip [tip] *m* (-s/-s) hint, tip; '♀pen (ge-, h) **1.** *v/i.* F type; *fig.* guess; *j-m auf die Schulter ~* tap s.o. on his shoulder; **2.** *v/t.* tip; foretell, predict; F type.

Tiroler [ti'roːlər] **1.** *m* (-s/-) Tyrolese; **2.** *adj.* Tyrolese.

Tisch [tiʃ] *m* (-es/-e) table; *bei ~* at table; *den ~ decken* lay the table *or* cloth, set the table; *reinen ~ machen* make a clean sweep (*damit of it*); *zu ~ bitten* invite *or* ask to dinner *or* supper; *bitte zu ~!* dinner is ready!; '~decke *f* table-cloth; '♀fertig *adj. food*: ready-prepared; '~gast *m* guest; '~gebet *n*: *das ~ sprechen* say grace; '~gesellschaft *f* dinner-party; '~gespräch *n* table-talk; '~lampe *f* table-lamp; desk lamp.

Tischler ['tiʃlər] *m* (-s/-) joiner; carpenter; cabinet-maker; ~ei [~'raɪ] *f* (-/-en) joinery; joiner's workshop.

'Tisch|platte *f* top (of a table), table top; leaf (*of extending table*); '~rede *f* toast, after-dinner speech; '~tennis *n* table tennis, ping-pong; '~tuch *n* table-cloth; '~zeit *f* dinner-time.

Titan [ti'taːn] *m* (-en/-en) Titan; ♀isch *adj.* titanic.

Titel ['tiːtəl] *m* (-s/-) title; e-n ~ (*inne*)*haben sports*: hold a title; '~bild *n* frontispiece; cover picture (*of magazine, etc.*); '~blatt *n* title-page; cover (*of magazine*); '~halter *m* (-s/-) *sports*: title-holder; '~kampf *m boxing*: title fight; '~rolle *thea. f* title-role.

titulieren [titu'liːrən] *v/t.* (*no -ge-*, h) style, call, address as.

Toast [toːst] *m* (-es/-e, -s) toast (*a. fig.*).

tob|en ['toːbən] *v/i.* (ge-, h) rage, rave, storm, bluster; *children*: romp; ♀sucht ✽ ['toːp-] *f* (-/*no pl.*) raving madness, frenzy; ~süchtig *adj.* ['toːp-] raving mad, frantic.

Tochter ['tɔxtər] *f* (-/-) daughter; '~gesellschaft ♱ *f* subsidiary company.

Tod [toːt] *m* (-[e]s/✽-e) death; ♱ decease.

Todes|angst ['toːdəs-] *f* mortal agony; *fig.* mortal fear; *Todesängste ausstehen* be scared to death, be frightened out of one's wits; '~anzeige *f* obituary (notice); '~fall *m* (case of) death; *Todesfälle pl.* deaths *pl.*, ✗ casualties *pl.*; '~kampf *m* death throes *pl.*, mortal agony; '~strafe *f* capital punishment, death penalty; *bei ~ verboten* forbidden on *or* under pain *or* penalty of death; '~ursache *f* cause of death; '~urteil *n* death *or* capital sentence, death-warrant.

'Tod|feind *m* deadly *or* mortal enemy; '♀krank *adj.* dangerously ill.

tödlich *adj.* ['tøːtliç] deadly; fatal; *wound*: *a.* mortal.

'tod|'müde *adj.* dead tired; '~

'schick F *adj.* dashing, gorgeous; '‿'sicher F *adj.* cock-sure; '2sünde *f* deadly *or* mortal sin.

Toilette [toa'lɛtə] *f* (-/-n) dress(ing): toilet; lavatory, gentlemen's *or* ladies' room, *esp. Am.* toilet.

Toi'letten|artikel *m/pl.* toilet articles *pl.*, *Am. a.* toiletry; ‿papier *n* toilet-paper; ‿tisch *m* toilet (-table), dressing-table, *Am. a.* dresser.

toleran|t *adj.* [tole'rant] tolerant (gegen of); 2z [‿ts] *f* 1. (-/no pl.) tolerance, toleration (*esp. eccl.*); 2. ⊕ (-/-en) tolerance, allowance.

toll [tɔl] 1. *adj.* (raving) mad, frantic; mad, crazy, wild (*all a. fig.*); fantastic; noise, etc.: frightful, *F* awful; *das ist ja* ‿ F that's (just) great; 2. *adv.*: es ‿ treiben carry on like mad; *es zu* ‿ *treiben* go too far; '‿en *v/i.* (ge-, h, sein) *children*: romp; '2haus *fig. n* bedlam; '2heit *f* (-/-en) madness; mad trick; '‿kühn *adj.* foolhardy, rash; '2wut *vet. f* rabies.

Tolpatsch F ['tɔlpatʃ] *m* (-es/-e) awkward *or* clumsy fellow; '2ig F *adj.* awkward, clumsy.

Tölpel F ['tœlpəl] *m* (-s/-) awkward *or* clumsy fellow; boob(y).

Tomate F [to'ma:tə] *f* (-/-n) tomato.

Ton¹ [to:n] *m* (-[e]s/-e) clay.

Ton² [‿] *m* (-[e]s/‿e) sound; ♪ tone (*a. of language*); ♪ *single*: note; accent, stress; *fig.* tone; *paint.* tone, tint, shade; *guter* ‿ good form; *den* ‿ *angeben* set the fashion; *zum guten* ‿ *gehören* be the fashion; *große Töne reden or F spucken F* talk big, boast; '‿abnehmer *m* pick-up; '2angebend *adj.* setting the fashion, leading; '‿arm *m* pick-up arm (*of record-player*); '‿art ♪ *f* key; '‿band *n* recording tape; '‿bandgerät *n* tape recorder.

tönen ['tø:nən] (ge-, h) 1. *v/i.* sound, ring; 2. *v/t.* tint, tone, shade.

tönern *adj.* ['tø:nərn] (of) clay, earthen.

'Ton|fall *m in speaking*: intonation, accent; '‿film *m* sound film; '‿lage *f* pitch; '‿leiter ♪ *f* scale, gamut; '2los *adj.* soundless; *fig.* toneless; '‿meister *m* sound engineer.

Tonne ['tɔnə] *f* (-/-n) *large*: tun; *smaller*: barrel, cask; ⊕ *measure of weight*: ton.

'Tonsilbe *gr. f* accented syllable.

Tonsur [tɔn'zu:r] *f* (-/-en) tonsure.

'Tönung *paint. f* (-/-en) tint, tinge, shade.

'Tonwaren *f/pl. s.* Töpferware.

Topf [tɔpf] *m* (-[e]s/‿e) pot.

Töpfer ['tœpfər] *m* (-s/-) potter; stove-fitter; '‿ei [‿'raɪ] *f* (-/-en) pottery; '‿ware *f* pottery, earthenware, crockery.

topp¹ *int.* [tɔp] done!, agreed!

Topp² ♣ [‿] *m* (-s/-e, -s) top, masthead.

Tor¹ [to:r] *n* (-[e]s/-e) gate; gateway (*a. fig.*); *football*: goal; *skiing*: gate.

Tor² [‿] *m* (-en/-en) fool.

Torf [tɔrf] *m* (-[e]s/no pl.) peat.

Torheit ['to:rhaɪt] *f* (-/-en) folly.

'Torhüter *m* gate-keeper; *sports*: goalkeeper.

töricht *adj.* ['tø:rɪçt] foolish, silly.

Törin ['tø:rin] *f* (-/-nen) fool(ish woman).

torkeln ['tɔrkəln] *v/i.* (ge-, h, sein) reel, stagger, totter.

'Tor|latte *f sports*: cross-bar; '‿lauf *m skiing*: slalom; '‿linie *f sports*: goal-line.

Tornister [tɔr'nistər] *m* (-s/-) knapsack; satchel.

torpedieren [tɔrpe'di:rən] *v/t.* (no -ge-, h) torpedo (*a. fig.*).

Torpedo [tɔr'pe:do] *m* (-s/-s) torpedo; ‿boot *n* torpedo-boat.

'Tor|pfosten *m* gate-post; *sports*: goal-post; '‿schuß *m* shot at the goal; '‿schütze *m sports*: scorer.

Torte ['tɔrtə] *f* (-/-n) fancy cake, *Am.* layer cake; tart, *Am.* pie.

Tortur [tɔr'tu:r] *f* (-/-en) torture; *fig.* ordeal.

'Tor|wart ['to:rvart] *m* (-[e]s/-e) *sports*: goalkeeper; '‿weg *m* gateway.

tosen ['to:zən] *v/i.* (ge-, h, sein) roar, rage; '‿d *adj.* applause: thunderous.

tot *adj.* [to:t] dead (*a. fig.*); deceased; ‿er Punkt ⊕ dead cent|re, *Am.* -er; *fig.*: deadlock; fatigue; ‿es Rennen *sports*: dead heat.

total *adj.* [to'ta:l] total, complete.

'tot|arbeiten *v/refl.* (sep., -ge-, h) work o.s. to death; '2e (-n/-n) 1. *m* dead man; (dead) body, corpse; *die* ‿n *pl.* the dead *pl.*, the deceased *pl. or* departed *pl.*; ⚔ casualties *pl.*; 2. *f* dead woman.

töten ['tø:tən] *v/t.* (ge-, h) kill; destroy; murder; deaden (*nerve, etc.*).

'Toten|bett *n* deathbed; '2blaß *adj.* deadly *or* deathly pale; '‿blässe *f* deadly paleness *or* pallor; '2bleich *adj. s.* totenblaß; ‿gräber ['‿grɛ:bər] *m* (-s/-) grave-digger (*a. zo.*); '‿hemd *n* shroud; '‿kopf *m* death's-head (*a. zo.*); *emblem of death*: *a.* skull and cross-bones; '‿liste *f* death-roll (*a.* ⚔), *esp.* ⚔ casualty list; '‿maske *f* death-mask; '‿messe *eccl. f* mass for the dead; requiem; '‿schädel *m* death's-head, skull; '‿schein *m* death certificate; '2still *adj.* (as) still as the grave; '‿stille *f* dead(ly) silence, deathly stillness.

'tot|geboren *adj.* still-born; '2geburt *f* still birth; '‿lachen *v/refl.* (sep., -ge-, h) die of laughing.

Toto ['to:to] *m*, F *a. n* (-s/-s) football pools *pl.*

'tot|schießen *v/t.* (*irr. schießen, sep.*, -ge-, *h*) shoot dead, kill; 'Qschlag g̱t̲ *m* manslaughter, homicide; '‿schlagen *v/t.* (*irr. schlagen, sep.*, -ge-, *h*) kill (*a. time*), slay; '‿schweigen *v/t.* (*irr. schweigen, sep.*, -ge-, *h*) hush up; '‿stechen *v/t.* (*irr. stechen, sep.*, -ge-, *h*) stab to death; '‿stellen *v/refl.* (*sep.*, -ge-, *h*) feign death.

'Tötung *f* (-/-en) killing, slaying; g̱t̲ homicide; *fahrlässige* ‿ g̱t̲ manslaughter.

Tour [tu:r] *f* (-/-en) tour; excursion, trip; ⊕ turn, revolution; *auf* ‿*en kommen mot.* pick up speed; '‿enwagen *mot. m* touring car.

Tourist [tu'rist] *m* (-en/-en), ‿in *f* (-/-nen) tourist.

Tournee [tur'ne:] *f* (-/-s, -n) tour.

Trab [tra:p] *m* (-[e]s/no *pl.*) trot.

Trabant [tra'bant] *m* (-en/-en) satellite.

trab|en ['tra:bən] *v/i.* (ge-, *h*, sein) trot; Qrennen ['tra:p-] *n* trotting race.

Tracht [traxt] *f* (-/-en) dress, costume; uniform; fashion; load; e-e (*gehörige*) ‿ *Prügel* a (sound) thrashing; '2en *v/i.* (ge-, *h*): ‿ *nach et.* strive for; *j-m nach dem Leben* ‿ seek s.o.'s life.

trächtig *adj.* ['trɛçtiç] (big) with young, pregnant.   [tradition.]

Tradition [tradi'tsjo:n] *f* (-/-en)

traf [tra:f] *pret. of* treffen.

Trag|bahre ['tra:k-] *f* stretcher, litter; '2bar *adj.* portable; *dress:* wearable; *fig.:* bearable; reasonable; ‿e ['‿gə] *f* (-/-n) hand-barrow; *s. Tragbahre.*

träge *adj.* ['trɛ:gə] lazy, indolent; *phys.* inert (*a. fig.*).

tragen ['tra:gən] (*irr.*, ge-, *h*) 1. *v/t.* carry; bear (*costs, name, responsibility, etc.*); bear, endure; support; bear, yield (*fruit,* ⊕ *interest, etc.*); wear (*dress, etc.*); *bei sich* ‿ have about one; *sich* ‿ *material:* wear well; *zur Schau* ‿ show off; 2. *v/i. tree:* bear, yield; *gun, voice:* carry; *ice:* bear.

Träger ['trɛ:gər] *m* (-s/-) carrier; porter (*of luggage*); holder, bearer (*of name, licence, etc.*); wearer (*of dress*); (shoulder-)strap (*of slip, etc.*); ⊕ support; △ girder.

Trag|fähigkeit ['tra:k-] *f* carrying or load capacity; ⊕ tonnage; '‿fläche *f*, '‿flügel *m* wing, plane.

Trägheit ['trɛ:khait] *f* (-/no *pl.*) laziness, indolence; *phys.* inertia (*a. fig.*).

tragisch *adj.* ['tra:giʃ] tragic (*a. fig.*); *fig.* tragical.

Tragödie [tra'gø:djə] *f* (-/-n) tragedy.

Trag|riemen ['tra:k-] *m* (carrying) strap; sling (*of gun*); '‿tier *n* pack animal; '‿tüte *f* carrier-bag; '‿weite *f* range; *fig.* import(ance), consequences *pl.*; *von großer* ‿ of great moment.

Train|er ['trɛ:nər] *m* (-s/-) trainer; coach; Qieren [‿'ni:rən] (*no* -ge-, *h*) 1. *v/t.* train; coach; 2. *v/i.* train; ‿ing ['‿iŋ] *n* (-s/-s) training; '‿ingsanzug *m sports:* track suit.

traktieren [trak'ti:rən] *v/t.* (*no* -ge-, *h*) treat (badly).

Traktor ⊕ ['traktɔr] *m* (-s/-en) tractor.

trällern ['trɛlərn] *v/t. and v/i.* (ge-, *h*) troll.

trampe|ln ['trampəln] *v/i.* (ge-, *h*) trample, stamp; 'Qpfad *m* beaten track.

Tran [tra:n] *m* (-[e]s/e-) train-oil, whale-oil.

Träne ['trɛ:nə] *f* (-/-n) tear; *in* ‿*n ausbrechen* burst into tears; '2n *v/i.* (ge-, *h*) water; '‿ngas *n* tear-gas.

Trank [traŋk] 1. *m* (-[e]s/⁀e) drink, beverage; ⚕ potion; 2. Q *pret. of* trinken.

Tränke ['trɛŋkə] *f* (-/-n) watering-place; '2n *v/t.* (ge-, *h*) water (*animals*); soak, impregnate (*material*).

Trans|formator ⚡ [transfɔr'ma:tɔr] *m* (-s/-en) transformer; ‿fusion ⚕ [‿u'zjo:n] *f* (-/-en) transfusion.

Transistorradio [tran'zistɔr-] *n* transistor radio *or* set.

transitiv *gr. adj.* ['tranzitiːf] transitive.

transparent [transpa'rent] 1. *adj.* transparent; 2. Q *n* (-[e]s/e-) transparency; *in political processions, etc.:* banner.

transpirieren [transpi'ri:rən] *v/i.* (*no* -ge-, *h*) perspire.

Transplantation ⚕ [transplanta'tsjo:n] *f* transplant (operation).

Transport [trans'pɔrt] *m* (-[e]s/e-) transport(ation), conveyance, carriage; Qabel *adj.* [‿'ta:bəl] (trans-)portable; ‿er *m* (-s/-) ⚓, ✈ (troop-)transport; ✈ transport (aircraft *or* plane); Qfähig *adj.* transportable, *sick person:* as transferable; Qieren [‿'ti:rən] *v/t.* (*no* -ge-, *h*) transport, convey, carry; ‿unternehmen *n* carrier.

Trapez [tra'pe:ts] *n* (-es/-e) Ⓐ trapezium, *Am.* trapezoid; *gymnastics:* trapeze.

trappeln ['trapəln] *v/i.* (ge-, sein) *horse:* clatter; *children, etc.:* patter.

Trass|ant ✝ [tra'sant] *m* (-en/-en) drawer; ‿at ✝ [‿'sa:t] *m* (-en/-en) drawee; ‿e ⊕ *f* (-/-n) line; Qieren [‿'si:rən] *v/t.* (*no* -ge-, *h*) ⊕ lay *or* trace out; ‿ *auf* (*acc.*) ✝ draw on.

trat [traːt] *pret. of* treten.

Tratte ✝ ['tratə] *f* (-/-n) draft.

Traube ['traubə] *f* (-/-n) bunch of grapes; grape; cluster; **'∿nsaft** *m* grape-juice; **'∿nzucker** *m* grape-sugar, glucose.

trauen ['trauən] (ge-, h) **1.** *v/t.* marry; *sich ∿ lassen* get married; **2.** *v/i.* trust (*j-m* s.o.), confide (*dat.* in); *ich traute meinen Ohren nicht* I could not believe my ears.

Trauer ['trauər] *f* (-/no pl.) sorrow, affliction; *for dead person:* mourning; **'∿botschaft** *f* sad news; **'∿fall** *m* death; **∿feier** *f* funeral ceremonies *pl.*, obsequies *pl.*; **'∿flor** *m* mourning-crape; **∿geleit** *n* funeral procession; **∿gottesdienst** *m* funeral service; **'∿kleid** *n* mourning (-dress); **'∿marsch** *m* funeral march; **'2n** *v/i.* (ge-, h) mourn (*um* for); be in mourning; **'∿spiel** *n* tragedy; **'∿weide** ♀ *f* weeping willow; **'∿zug** *m* funeral procession.

Traufe ['traufə] *f* (-/-n) eaves *pl.*; gutter; *s. Regen².*

träufeln ['trɔʏfəln] *v/t.* (ge-, h) drop, drip, trickle. [cosy, snug.\

traulich *adj.* ['trauliç] intimate;\

Traum [traum] *m* (-[e]s/∿e) dream (*a. fig.*); reverie; *das fällt mir nicht im ∿ ein!* I would not dream of (doing) it!; **'∿bild** *n* vision; **'∿deuter** *m* (-s/-) dream-reader.

träum|en ['trɔʏmən] *v/i. and v/t.* (ge-, h) dream; **'2er** *m* (-s/-) dreamer (*a. fig.*); **2erei** [∿'raɪ] *f* (-/-en) dreaming; *fig. a.* reverie (*a. ♪*), day-dream, musing; **'∿erisch** *adj.* dreamy; musing.

traurig *adj.* ['trauriç] sad (*über acc.* at), *Am.* F blue; wretched.

'Trau|ring *m* wedding-ring; **'∿schein** *m* marriage certificate *or* lines *pl.*; **'∿ung** *f* (-/-en) marriage, wedding; **'∿zeuge** *m* witness to a marriage.

Trecker ⊕ ['trekər] *m* (-s/-) tractor.

Treff [tref] *n* (-s/-s) *cards:* club(s *pl.*).

treffen¹ ['trefən] (*irr.*, ge-) **1.** *v/t.* (h) hit (*a. fig.*), strike; concern, *disadvantageously:* affect; meet; *nicht ∿ miss*; *e-e Entscheidung ∿* come to a decision; *Maßnahmen ∿* take measures *or* steps; *Vorkehrungen ∿* take precautions *or* measures; *sich ∿* happen; meet; gather, assemble; *a.* have an appointment (*mit* with), *Am.* have a date (with); *das trifft sich gut!* that's lucky!, how fortunate!; *sich getroffen fühlen* feel hurt; *wen trifft die Schuld?* who is to blame?; *das Los traf ihn* the lot fell on him; *du bist gut getroffen paint., phot.* this is a good likeness of you; *vom Blitz getroffen* struck by lightning; **2.** *v/i.* (h) hit; **3.** *v/i.* (sein): *∿ auf* (*acc.*) meet with; encounter (*a. ⊗*).

Treffen² [∿] *n* (-s/-) meeting; rally; gathering; ✕ encounter; **'2d** *adj.* remark: appropriate, to the point.

'Treff|er *m* (-s/-) hit (*a. fig.*); prize; **'∿punkt** *m* meeting-place.

Treibeis ['traɪp∿-] *n* drift-ice.

treiben¹ ['traɪbən] (*irr.*, ge-) **1.** *v/t.* (h) drive; ⊕ put in motion, propel; drift (*smoke, snow*); put forth (*leaves*); force (*plants*); *fig.* impel, urge, press (*j-n zu inf.* s.o. to *inf.*); carry on (*business, trade*); *Musik* (*Sport*) *∿* go in for music (sports); *Sprachen ∿* study languages; *es zu weit ∿* go too far; *wenn er es weiterhin so treibt* if he carries *or* goes on like that; *was treibst du da?* what are you doing there?; **2.** *v/i.* (sein) drive; float, drift; **3.** *v/i.* (h) ♀ shoot; *dough:* ferment, work.

Treiben² [∿] *n* (-s/no pl.) driving; doings *pl.*, goings-on *pl.*; *geschäftiges ∿* bustle; **'2d** *adj.: ∿e Kraft** driving force.

Treib|haus ['traɪp-] *n* hothouse; **'∿holz** *n* drift-wood; **'∿jagd** *f* battue; **'∿riemen** *m* driving-belt; **'∿stoff** *m* fuel; propell|ant, -ent (*of rocket*).

trenn|en ['trenən] *v/t.* (ge-, h) separate, sever; rip (*seam*); *teleph., ⚡* cut off, disconnect; isolate, segregate; *sich ∿* separate (*von* from), part (*from or with s.o.*); with *s.th.*); **'2schärfe** *f radio:* selectivity; **'2ung** *f* (-/-en) separation; disconne|xion, -ction; segregation (*of races, etc.*); **'2(ungs)wand** *f* partition (wall). [(-bit.)\

Trense ['trenzə] *f* (-/-n) snaffle\

Treppe ['trepə] *f* (-/-n) staircase, stairway, (e-e a flight *or* pair of) stairs *pl.*; *zwei ∿n hoch* on the second floor, *Am.* on the third floor.

'Treppen|absatz *m* landing; **'∿geländer** *n* banisters *pl.*; **'∿haus** *n* staircase; **'∿stufe** *f* stair, step.

Tresor [tre'zoːr] *m* (-s/-e) safe; *bank:* strong-room, vault.

treten ['treːtən] (*irr.*, ge-) **1.** *v/i.* (h) tread, step (*j-n or j-m auf die Zehen* on s.o.'s toes); **2.** *v/i.* (sein) tread, step (*j-m auf die Zehen* on s.o.'s toes); walk; *ins Haus ∿* enter the house; *j-m unter die Augen ∿* appear before s.o., face s.o.; *j-m zu nahe ∿* offend s.o.; *zu j-m ∿* step *or* walk up to s.o.; *über die Ufer ∿* overflow its banks; **3.** *v/t.* (h) tread; kick; *mit Füßen ∿* trample upon.

treu *adj.* [trɔʏ] faithful, loyal; **'2bruch** *m* breach of faith, perfidy; **'2e** *f* (-/no pl.) fidelity, faith(fulness), loyalty; **2händer** ['∿hɛndər] *m* (-s/-) trustee; **'∿herzig** *adj.* guileless; ingenuous, simpleminded; **'∿los** *adj.* faithless (*gegen* to), disloyal (to); perfidious.

Tribüne [tri'by:nə] f (-/-n) platform; *sports, etc.*: (grand) stand.
Tribut [tri'bu:t] m (-[e]s/-e) tribute.
Trichter ['triçtər] m (-s/-) funnel; *made by bomb, shell, etc.*: crater; horn (*of wind instruments, etc.*).
Trick [trik] m (-s/-e, -s) trick; '~film m animation, animated cartoon.
Trieb [tri:p] 1. m (-[e]s/-e) ♀ sprout, (new) shoot; driving force; impulse; instinct; (sexual) urge; desire; 2. ♀ *pret. of* treiben; '~feder f main-spring; *fig.* driving force, motive; '~kraft f motive power; *fig.* driving force, motive; '~wagen ⚙ m rail-car, rail-motor; '~werk ⊕ n gear (drive), (driving) mechanism, transmission; engine.
triefen ['tri:fən] v/i. ([irr.,] ge-, h) drip (von with); *eye*: run.
triftig adj. ['triftiç] valid.
Trigonometrie Å [trigonome'tri:] f (-/no pl.) trigonometry.
Trikot [tri'ko:] (-s/-s) 1. m stockinet; 2. n tights pl.; vest; ~agen [~o'ta:-ʒən] f/pl. hosiery.
Triller ♪ ['trilər] m (-s/-) trill, shake, quaver; '♀n ♪ v/i. and v/t. (ge-, h) trill, shake, quaver; *bird*: a. warble.
trink|bar adj. ['triŋkba:r] drinkable; '♀becher m drinking-cup; '~en (irr., ge-, h) 1. v/t. drink; take, have (tea, etc.); 2. v/i. drink; ~ auf (acc.) drink to, toast; '♀er m (-s/-) drinker; drunkard; '♀gelage n drinking-bout; '♀geld n tip, gratuity; j-m e-e Mark ~ geben tip s.o. one mark; '♀glas n drinking-glass; '♀halle f at spa: pump-room; '♀kur f: e-e ~ machen drink the waters; '♀spruch m toast; '♀wasser n (-s/no pl.) drinking-water.
Trio ['tri:o] n (-s/-s) trio (a. ♪).
trippeln ['tripəln] v/i. (ge-, sein) trip.
Tritt [trit] m (-[e]s/-e) tread, step; footprint; *noise*: footfall, (foot)step; kick; ⊕ treadle; s. Trittbrett, Trittleiter; im (falschen) ~ in (out of) step; ~ halten keep step; '~brett n step, footboard; *mot.* running-board; '~leiter f stepladder, (e-e a pair or set of) steps pl.
Triumph [tri'umf] m (-[e]s/-e) triumph; ♀al adj. [~'fa:l] triumphant; ~bogen m triumphal arch; ♀ieren [~'fi:rən] v/i. (no -ge-, h) triumph (über acc. over).
trocken adj. ['trokən] dry (a. fig.); *soil, land*: arid; '♀dock ⚓ n dry dock; '♀haube f (hood of) hairdrier; '♀heit f (-/no pl.) dryness; drought, aridity; '~legen v/t. (sep., -ge-, h) dry up; drain (land); change the napkins (Am. change the diapers of (baby); '♀obst n dried fruit.

trocknen ['troknən] (ge-) 1. v/i. (sein) dry; 2. v/t. (h) dry.
Troddel ['trodəl] f (-/-n) tassel.
Trödel F ['trø:dəl] m (-s/no pl.) second-hand articles pl.; lumber, Am. junk; rubbish; '♀n F fig. v/i. (ge-, h) dawdle, loiter.
Trödler ['trø:dlər] m (-s/-) second-hand dealer, Am. junk dealer, junkman; fig. dawdler, loiterer.
troff [trof] pret. of triefen.
Trog¹ [tro:k] m (-[e]s/⁼e) trough.
trog² [~] pret. of trügen.
Trommel ['troməl] f (-/-n) drum; ⊕ a. cylinder, barrel; '~fell n drumskin; anat. ear-drum; '♀n v/i. and v/t. (ge-, h) drum.
Trommler ['tromlər] m (-s/-) drummer.
Trompete [trom'pe:tə] f (-/-n) trumpet; ♀n v/i. and v/t. (no -ge-, h) trumpet; ~r m (-s/-) trumpeter.
Tropen ['tro:pən]: die ~ pl. the tropics pl.
Tropf F [tropf] m (-[e]s/⁼e) simpleton; armer ~ poor wretch.
tröpfeln ['trœpfəln] (ge-) 1. v/i. (h) drop, drip, trickle; tap: a. leak; es tröpfelt rain: a few drops are falling; 2. v/i. (sein): ~ aus or von trickle or drip from; 3. v/t. (h) drop, drip.
tropfen¹ ['tropfən] (ge-) 1. v/i. (h) drop, drip, trickle; tap: a. leak; candle: gutter; 2. v/i. (sein): ~ aus or von trickle or drip from; 3. v/t. (h) drop, drip.
Tropfen² [~] m (-s/-) drop; ein ~ auf den heißen Stein a drop in the ocean or bucket; ♀förmig adj. ['~fœrmiç] drop-shaped; '♀weise adv. drop by drop, by drops.
Trophäe [tro'fɛ:ə] f (-/-n) trophy.
tropisch adj. ['tro:piʃ] tropical.
Trosse ['trosə] f (-/-n) cable; ♀ a. hawser.
Trost [tro:st] m (-es/no pl.) comfort, consolation; das ist ein schlechter ~ that is cold comfort; du bist wohl nicht (recht) bei ~! F you must be out of your mind!
tröst|en ['trø:stən] v/t. (ge-, h) console, comfort; sich ~ console o.s. (mit with); ~ Sie sich! be of good comfort!, cheer up!; '~lich adj. comforting.
'trost|los adj. disconsolate, inconsolable; land, etc.: desolate; fig. wretched; '♀losigkeit f (-/no pl.) desolation; fig. wretchedness; '♀-preis m consolation prize, booby prize; '~reich adj. consolatory, comforting.
Trott [trot] m (-[e]s/-e) trot; F fig. jogtrot, routine; '~el F m (-s/-) idiot, fool, ninny; '♀en v/i. (ge-, sein) trot.
trotz [trots] 1. prp. (gen.) in spite of, despite; ~ alledem for all that; 2. ♀ m (-es/no pl.) defiance; obsti-

(-s/-) remnant, *Am.* F *a.* holdover; ~ *pl. a.* remains *pl.*

'**Überblick** *fig. m* survey, general view (*both:* über *acc.* of).

über|'**blicken** *v/t. (no -ge-, h)* overlook; *fig.* survey, have a general view of; ~'**bringen** *v/t. (irr. bringen, no -ge-, h)* deliver; 2'**bringer** *m (-s/-)* bearer; ~'**brücken** *v/t. (no -ge-, h)* bridge; *fig.* bridge over *s.th.*; ~'**dachen** *v/t. (no -ge-, h)* roof over; ~'**dauern** *v/t. (no -ge-, h)* outlast, outlive; ~'**denken** *v/t. (irr. denken, no -ge-, h)* think *s.th.* over.

über'**dies** *adv.* besides, moreover. **über**'**drehen** *v/t. (no -ge-, h)* overwind (*watch, etc.*); strip (*screw*).

'**Überdruck** *m* 1. (-[e]s/-e) overprint; & *a.* surcharge; 2. ⊕ (-[e]s/ue) overpressure.

Über|'**druß** ['y:bərdrus] *m (Überdrusses/no pl.)* satiety; *bis zum* ~ to satiety; 2**drüssig** *adj.* (*gen.*) ['~ysiç] disgusted with, weary *or* sick of.

Übereif|**er** ['y:bər⁹-] *m* over-zeal; 2**rig** *adj.* ['y:bər⁹-] over-zealous.

über'**eilen** *v/t. (no -ge-, h)* precipitate, rush; *sich* ~ hurry too much; ~t *adj.* precipitate, rash.

übereinander *adv.* [y:bər⁹aɪ'nandər] one upon the other; ~**schlagen** *v/t. (irr. schlagen, sep., -ge-, h)* cross (*one's legs*).

über'**ein**|**kommen** *v/i. (irr. kommen, sep., -ge-, sein)* agree; 2**kommen** *n (-s/-)*, 2**kunft** [~kunft] *f (-/ue)* agreement; ~**stimmen** *v/i. (sep., -ge-, h) p.* agree (*with* with); *thing:* correspond (*with, to*); 2**stimmung** *f* agreement; correspondence; *in* ~ *mit* in agreement *or* accordance with.

über|**fahren** 1. ['~faːrən] *v/i. (irr. fahren, sep., -ge-, sein)* cross; 2. [~'faːrən] *v/t. (irr. fahren, no -ge-, h)* run over; disregard (*traffic sign, etc.*); 2**fahrt** *f* passage; crossing.

'**Überfall** *m* ✗ surprise; ✗ invasion (*auf acc.* of); ✗ raid; hold-up; assault [up]on).

über'**fallen** *v/t. (irr. fallen, no -ge-, h)* ✗ surprise; ✗ invade; ✗ raid; hold up; assault.

'**über**|**fällig** *adj.* overdue; 2**fallkommando** *n* flying squad, *Am.* riot squad.

über'**fliegen** *v/t. (irr. fliegen, no -ge-, h)* fly over *or* across; *fig.* glance over, skim (through); *den Atlantik* ~ fly (across) the Atlantic.

'**überfließen** *v/i. (irr. fließen, sep., -ge-, sein)* overflow.

über'**flügeln** *v/t. (no -ge-, h)* ✗ outflank; *fig.* outstrip, surpass.

'**Überfluß** *m* (*Überflusses/no pl.*) abundance (*an dat.* of); superfluity (of); ~ *haben an* (*dat.*) abound in;

'2**flüssig** *adj.* superfluous; redundant.

über'**fluten** *v/t. (no -ge-, h)* overflow, flood (*a. fig.*).

'**Überfracht** *f* excess freight.

über|**führen** *v/t.* 1. ['~fyːrən] (*sep., -ge-, h*) convey (*dead body*); 2. [~'fyːrən] (*no -ge-, h*) s. 1; ฐ convict (*gen.* of); 2**führung** *f (-/-en)* conveyance (*of dead body*); bridge, *Am.* overpass; ฐ conviction (*gen.* of). [*dat.* of).]

'**Überfülle** *f* superabundance (*an*)

über|**füllen** *v/t. (no -ge-, h)* overfill; cram; overcrowd; *sich den Magen* ~ glut *o.s.*; ~'**füttern** *v/t. (no -ge-, h)* overfeed.

'**Übergabe** *f* delivery; handing over; surrender (*a.* ✗).

'**Übergang** *m* bridge; ॠ crossing; *fig.* transition (*a.* ♪); *esp.* ฐ devolution; ~**sstadium** *n* transition stage.

über|'**geben** *v/t. (irr. geben, no -ge-, h)* deliver up; hand over; surrender (*a.* ✗); *sich* ~ vomit, be sick; ~**gehen** 1. ['~geːən] *v/i. (irr. gehen, sep., -ge-, sein)* pass over; *work, duties:* devolve (*auf acc.* [up]on); ~ *in* (*acc.*) pass into; ~ *zu et.* proceed to *s.th.*; 2. [~'geːən] *v/t. (irr. gehen, no -ge-, h)* pass over, ignore.

'**Übergewicht** *n* (-[e]s/no pl.) overweight; *fig. a.* preponderance (*über acc.* over).

über'**gießen** *v/t. (irr. gießen, no -ge-, h): mit Wasser* ~ pour water over *s.th.; mit Fett* ~ baste (*roasting meat*).

'**über**|**greifen** *v/i. (irr. greifen, sep., -ge-, h):* ~ *auf* (*acc.*) encroach (up)on (*s.o.'s rights*); *fire, epidemic, etc.:* spread to; 2**griff** *m* encroachment (*auf acc.* [up]on), inroad (on); ~**haben** F *v/t. (irr. haben, sep., -ge-, h)* have (*coat, etc.*) on; *fig.* have enough of, *sl.* be fed up with.

über'**handnehmen** *v/i. (irr. nehmen, sep., -ge-, h)* be rampant, grow *or* wax rife.

'**überhängen** 1. *v/i. (irr. hängen, sep., -ge-, h)* overhang; 2. *v/t. (sep., -ge-, h)* put (*coat, etc.*) round one's shoulders; sling (*rifle*) over one's shoulder.

über'**häufen** *v/t. (no -ge-, h):* ~ *mit* swamp with (*letters, work, etc.*); overwhelm with (*inquiries, etc.*).

über'**haupt** *adv.: wer will denn* ~, *daß er kommt?* who wants him to come anyhow?; *wenn* ~ if at all; ~ *nicht* not at all; ~ *kein* no ... whatever.

überheblich *adj.* [y:bər'heːpliç] presumptuous, arrogant; 2**keit** *f* (-/~-en) presumption, arrogance.

über|'**hitzen** *v/t. (no -ge-, h)* overheat (*a.* ✝); ⊕ superheat; ~'**holen** *v/t. (no -ge-, h)* overtake (*a. mot.*);

esp. sports: outstrip (a. fig.); over-
haul, esp. Am. a. service; ~'holt
adj. outmoded; pred. a. out of date;
~'hören v/t. (no -ge-, h) fail to
hear, miss; ignore.

'überirdisch adj. supernatural; un-
earthly.

'überkippen v/i. (sep., -ge-, sein) p.
overbalance, lose one's balance.

über'kleben v/t. (no -ge-, h) paste
over.

'Überkleidung f outer garments pl.

'überklug adj. would-be wise,
sapient.

'überkochen v/i. (sep., -ge-, sein)
boil over; F leicht ~ be very irritable.

über'kommen v/t. (irr. kommen,
no -ge-, h): Furcht überkam ihn he
was seized with fear; ~'laden v/t.
(irr. laden, no -ge-, h) overload;
overcharge (battery, picture, etc.).

'Überland|flug m cross-country
flight; ~zentrale ∮ f long-distance
power-station.

über'lassen v/t. (irr. lassen, no
-ge-, h): j-m et. ~ let s.o. have s.th.;
fig. leave s.th. to s.o.; j-n sich selbst
~ leave s.o. to himself; j-n s-m
Schicksal ~ leave or abandon s.o. to
his fate; ~'lasten v/t. (no -ge-, h)
overload; fig. overburden.

über'laufen 1. ['~laufən] v/i. (irr.
laufen, sep., -ge-, sein) run over;
boil over; ✕ desert (zu to);
2. [~'laufən] v/t. (irr. laufen, no
-ge-, h): es überlief mich kalt a
shudder passed over me; überlaufen
werden von doctor, etc.: be besieged
by (patients, etc.); 3. adj. [~'laufən]
place, profession, etc.: overcrowded;
'2läufer m ✕ deserter; pol. renegade, turncoat.

'überlaut adj. too loud.

über'leben (no -ge-, h) 1. v/t.
survive, outlive; 2. v/i. survive; 2de
m, f (-n/-n) survivor.

'überlebensgroß adj. bigger than
life-size(d).

überlebt adj. [y:bər'le:pt] outmoded, disused, out of date.

'überlegen[1] F v/t. (sep., -ge-, h)
give (child) a spanking.

über'legen[2] 1. v/t. and v/refl. (no
-ge-, h) consider, reflect upon,
think about; ich will es mir ~ I will
think it over; es sich anders ~ change
one's mind; 2. v/i. (no -ge-, h): er
überlegt noch he hasn't made up
his mind yet; 3. adj. superior (dat.
to; an dat. in); 2enheit f (-/no pl.)
superiority; preponderance; ~t adj.
[~kt] deliberate; prudent; 2ung
[~gʊŋ] f (-/-en) consideration,
reflection; nach reiflicher ~ after
mature deliberation.

über'lesen v/t. (irr. lesen, no -ge-, h)
read s.th. through quickly, run over
s.th.; overlook.

über'liefer|n v/t. (no -ge-, h) hand
down or on (dat. to); 2ung f tradition.

über'listen v/t. (no -ge-, h) outwit,
F outsmart.

'Über|macht f (-/no pl.) superiority;
esp. ✕ superior forces pl.; in der ~
sein be superior in numbers;
'2mächtig adj. superior.

über'malen v/t. (no -ge-, h) paint
out; ~'mannen v/t. (no -ge-, h)
overpower, overcome, overwhelm
(all. a. fig.).

'Über|maß n (-es/no pl.) excess (an
dat. of); '2mäßig 1. adj. excessive;
immoderate; 2. adv. excessively,
Am. a. overly; ~ trinken drink to
excess.

'Übermensch m superman; '2lich
adj. superhuman.

über'mitt|eln v/t. (no -ge-, h) trans-
mit; convey; 2lung f (-/-en) transmission; conveyance.

'übermorgen adv. the day after
tomorrow.

über'müd|et adj. overtired; 2ung f
(-/⚆-en) overfatigue.

'Über|mut m wantonness; frolic-
someness; 2mütig adj. ['~my:tiç]
wanton; frolicsome.

'übernächst adj. the next but one;
~e Woche the week after next.

über'nacht|en v/i. (no -ge-, h) stay
overnight (bei at a friend's [house],
with friends), spend the night (at,
with); 2ung f (-/-en) spending the
night; ~ und Frühstück bed and
breakfast.

Übernahme ['y:bərnɑːmə] f (-/-n)
field of application s. übernehmen 1:
taking over; undertaking; assumption; adoption.

'übernatürlich adj. supernatural.

übernehmen v/t. 1. [~'ne:mən] (irr.
nehmen, no -ge-, h) take over (business, etc.); undertake (responsibility,
etc.); take (lead, risk, etc.); assume
(direction of business, office, etc.);
adopt (idea, custom, etc.); sich ~
overreach o.s.; 2. ✕ ['~ne:mən] (irr.
nehmen, sep., -ge-, h) slope, shoul
der (arms).

'über|ordnen v/t. (sep., -ge-, h):
j-n j-m ~ set s.o. over s.o.; '~par-
teilich adj. non-partisan; '2pro-
duktion f over-production.

über'prüf|en v/t. (no -ge-, h)
reconsider; verify; check; review;
screen s.o.; 2ung f reconsideration;
checking; review.

über'queren v/t. (no -ge-, h) cross;
~'ragen v/t. (no -ge-, h) tower
above (a. fig.), overtop; fig. surpass.

überrasch|en [y:bər'raʃən] v/t. (no
-ge-, h) surprise; catch (bei at, in);
2ung f (-/-en) surprise.

über'red|en v/t. (no -ge-, h) per-
suade (zu inf. to inf., into ger.);

talk (into *ger.*); 2ung *f* (-/%-en)
persuasion.

über'reich|en *v/t.* (*no* -ge-, h)
present; 2ung *f* (-/%-en) presentation.

über|'reizen *v/t.* (*no* -ge-, h) over-
excite; ~'reizt *adj.* overstrung;
~'rennen *v/t.* (*irr. rennen, no* -ge-,
h) overrun.

'Überrest *m* remainder; ~e *pl.*
remains *pl.*; sterbliche ~e *pl.* mortal
remains *pl.*

über|'rump|eln *v/t.* (*no* -ge-, h)
(take by) surprise; 2(e)lung *f*
(-/%-en) surprise.

über|'rund|en *v/t.* (*no* -ge-, h)
sports: lap; *fig.* surpass; 2ung *f*
(-/-en) lapping.

übersät *adj.* [y:bər'zɛ:t] studded,
dotted.

über|'sättig|en *v/t.* (*no* -ge-, h)
surfeit (*a. fig.*); ⫯ supersaturate;
2ung *f* (-/-en) surfeit (*a. fig.*); ⫯
supersaturation.

'Überschallgeschwindigkeit *f* su-
personic speed.

über|'schatten *v/t.* (*no* -ge-, h)
overshadow (*a. fig.*); ~'schätzen
v/t. (*no* -ge-, h) overrate, overesti-
mate.

'Überschlag *m gymnastics:* somersault; ⚡ loop; ⚡ flashover; *fig.*
estimate, approximate calculation;
2en (*irr. schlagen*) 1. ['~ʃla·gən] *v/t.*
(*sep.,* -ge-, h) cross (*one's legs*);
2. [~'ʃla·gən] *v/i.* (*sep.,* -ge-, *sein*)
voice: become high-pitched; 3.
[~'ʃla·gən] *v/t.* (*no* -ge-, h) skip
(*page, etc.*); make a rough estimate
of (*cost, etc.*); *sich* ~ fall head over
heels; *car, etc.:* (be) turn(ed) over;
⚡ loop the loop; *voice:* become
high-pitched; *sich* ~ *vor* (*dat.*) outdo
(*one's friendliness, etc.*); 4. *adj.*
[~'ʃla·gən] lukewarm, tepid.

'überschnappen *v/i.* (*sep.,* -ge-,
sein) *voice:* become high-pitched;
F *p.* go mad, turn crazy.

über|'schneiden *v/refl.* (*irr. schnei-
den, no* -ge-, h) overlap; intersect;
~'schreiben *v/t.* (*irr. schreiben, no*
-ge-, h) superscribe, entitle; make
s.th. over (*dat.* to); ~'schreiten
v/t. (*irr. schreiten, no* -ge-, h) cross;
transgress (*limit, bound*); infringe
(*rule, etc.*); exceed (*speed limit, one's
instructions, etc.*); *sie hat die* 40 *bereits überschritten* she is on the
wrong side of 40.

'Über|schrift *f* heading, title;
headline; '~schuh *m* overshoe.

'Über|schuß *m* surplus, excess;
profit; 2schüssig *adj.* ['~ʃysiç]
surplus, excess.

über'schütten *v/t.* (*no* -ge-, h): ~
mit pour (*water, etc.*) on; *fig.:* overwhelm with (*inquiries, etc.*); shower
(*gifts, etc.*) upon.

überschwemm|en [y:bər'ʃvemən]

v/t. (*no* -ge-, h) inundate, flood
(*both a. fig.*); 2ung *f* (-/-en) inunda-
tion, flood(ing).

überschwenglich *adj.* ['y:bər-
ʃveŋliç] effusive, gushy.

'Übersee: *nach* ~ gehen go overseas; '~dampfer ⚓ *m* transoceanic
steamer; '~handel *m* (-s/*no pl.*)
oversea(s) trade.

über'sehen *v/t.* (*irr. sehen, no* -ge-,
h) survey; overlook (*printer's error,
etc.*); *fig.* ignore, disregard.

über'send|en *v/t.* ([*irr. senden,*] *no*
-ge-, h) send, transmit; consign;
2ung *f* sending, transmission; ⚡
consignment.

über|'setzen[1] (*sep.,* -ge-, h) 1. *v/i.* (*sein*)
cross; 2. *v/t.* (h) ferry.

über'setz|en[2] *v/t.* (*no* -ge-, h)
translate (*in acc.* into), render (into);
⊕ gear; 2er *m* (-s/-) translator;
2ung *f* (-/-en) translation (*aus
from; in acc.* into); rendering; ⊕
gear(ing), transmission.

'Übersicht *f* (-/-en) survey (*über
acc.* of); summary; 2lich *adj.*
clear(ly arranged).

über|siedeln ['y:bərzi:dəln] *v/i.*
(*sep.,* -ge-, *sein*) *and* [~'zi:dəln] *v/i.*
(*no* -ge-, *sein*) remove (*nach* to);
2siedelung [~'zi:dəluŋ] *f* (-/-en),
2siedlung ['~zi:dluŋ, ~'zi:dluŋ] *f*
(-/-en) removal (*nach* to).

'übersinnlich *adj.* transcendental;
forces: psychic.

über'spann|en *v/t.* (*no* -ge-, h)
cover (*mit* with); *den Bogen* ~ go
too far; *fig.* 2t *adj.* extravagant; *p.*
eccentric; *claims, etc.:* exaggerated;
2theit *f* (-/%-en) extravagance;
eccentricity.

über'spitzt *adj.* oversubtle; exaggerated.

überspringen 1. ['~ʃpriŋən] *v/i.*
(*irr. springen, sep.,* -ge-, *sein*) ⚡
spark: jump; *in a speech, etc.:* ~ *von*
... *zu* ... jump *or* skip from (*one
subject* to) (*another*); 2. [~'ʃpriŋən]
v/t. (*irr. springen, no* -ge-, h) jump,
clear; skip (*page, etc.*); jump (*class*).

überstehen (*irr. stehen*) 1. ['~ʃte:ən]
v/i. (*sep.,* -ge-, h) jut (*out or* forth),
project; 2. [~'ʃte:ən] *v/t.* (*no* -ge-, h)
survive (*misfortune, etc.*); weather
(*crisis*); get over (*illness*).

über|'steigen *v/t.* (*irr. steigen, no*
-ge-, h) climb over; *fig.* exceed;
~'stimmen *v/t.* (*no* -ge-, h) out-
vote, vote down.

'überstreifen *v/t.* (*sep.,* -ge-, h)
slip *s.th.* over.

überströmen 1. ['~ʃtrø:mən] *v/i.*
(*sep.,* -ge-, *sein*) overflow (*vor dat.*
with); 2. [~'ʃtrø:mən] *v/t.* (*no* -ge-,
h) flood, inundate.

'Überstunden *f/pl.* overtime; ~
machen work overtime.

über'stürz|en *v/t.* (*no* -ge-, h)
rush, hurry (up *or* on); *sich* ~ act

rashly; *events*: follow in rapid succession; ~t *adj.* precipitate, rash; 2ung *f* (-/~-en) precipitancy.

über|'teuern *v/t. (no -ge-, h)* overcharge; ~'**tölpeln** *v/t. (no -ge-, h)* dupe, take in; ~'**tönen** *v/t. (no -ge-, h)* drown.

Übertrag ✝ ['y:bərtra:k] *m* (-[e]s/ ~e) carrying forward; sum carried forward.

über'trag|bar *adj.* transferable; ✝ negotiable; 🦠 communicable; ~**en** [~gən] 1. *v/t. (irr. tragen, no -ge-, h)* ✝ carry forward; make over (*property*) (*auf acc.* to); 🦠 transfuse (*blood*); delegate (*rights, etc.*) (*dat.* to); render (*book, etc.*) (*in acc.* into); transcribe (*s.th. written in shorthand*); 🦠, ⊕, *phys., radio*: transmit; *radio*: a. broadcast; *im Fernsehen* ~ televise; *ihm wurde eine wichtige Mission* ~ he was charged with an important mission; 2. *adj.* figurative; 2ung [~gʊŋ] *f* (-/-en) *field of application s.* übertragen 1: carrying forward; making over; transfusion; delegation; rendering; free translation; transcription; transmission; broadcast; ~ *im Fernsehen* telecast.

über'treffen *v/t. (irr. treffen, no -ge-, h)* excel *s.o.* (*an dat.* in; *in dat.* in, at); surpass (in), exceed (in).

über'treib|en (*irr. treiben, no -ge-, h*) 1. *v/t.* overdo; exaggerate, overstate; 2. *v/i.* exaggerate, draw the long bow; 2ung *f* (-/-en) exaggeration, overstatement.

'übertreten[1] *v/i. (irr. treten, sep., -ge-, sein) sports*: cross the take-off line; *fig.* go over (*zu* to); *zum Katholizismus* ~ turn Roman Catholic.

über'tret|en[2] *v/t. (irr. treten, no -ge-, h)* transgress, violate, infringe (*law, etc.*); *sich den Fuß* ~ sprain one's ankle; 2ung *f* (-/-en) transgression, violation, infringement.

'Übertritt *m* going over (*zu* to); *eccl.* conversion (to).

übervölker|n [y:bər'fœlkərn] *v/t. (no -ge-, h)* over-populate; 2ung *f* (-/~-en) over-population.

über'vorteilen *v/t. (no -ge-, h)* overreach, F do.

über'wach|en *v/t. (no -ge-, h)* supervise, superintend; control; *police*: keep under surveillance, shadow; 2ung *f* (-/~-en) supervision, superintendence; control; surveillance.

überwältigen [y:bər'vɛltigən] *v/t. (no -ge-, h)* overcome, overpower, overwhelm (*all a. fig.*); ~d *fig. adj.* overwhelming.

über'weis|en *v/t. (irr. weisen, no -ge-, h)* remit (*money*) (*dat. or an acc.* to); (*zur Entscheidung etc.*) ~ refer (to); 2ung *f* (-/-en) remittance;

reference (*an acc.* to); *parl.* devolution.

überwerfen (*irr. werfen*) 1. ['~vɛr-fən] *v/t. (sep., -ge-, h)* slip (*coat*) on; 2. [~'vɛrfən] *v/refl. (no -ge-, h)* fall out (*mit* with).

über|'wiegen (*irr. wiegen, no -ge-, h*) 1. *v/t.* outweigh; 2. *v/i.* preponderate; predominate; ~'**wiegend** *adj.* preponderant; predominant; ~**winden** *v/t. (irr. winden, no -ge-, h)* overcome (*a. fig.*); subdue; *sich* ~ *zu inf.* bring o.s. to *inf.*; ~'**wintern** *v/i. (no -ge-, h)* (pass the) winter.

'Über|wurf *m* wrap; '~**zahl** *f* (-/~-en) numerical superiority; *in der* ~ superior in numbers; 2**zählig** *adj.* ['~tsɛ:liç] supernumerary; surplus.

über'zeug|en *v/t. (no -ge-, h)* convince (*von* of); satisfy (of); 2ung *f* (-/-en) conviction.

überziehe|n *v/t.* (*irr. ziehen*) 1. ['~tsi:ən] (*sep., -ge-, h*) put on; 2. [~'tsi:ən] (*no -ge-, h*) cover; put clean sheets on (*bed*); ✝ overdraw (*account*); *sich* ~ *sky*: become overcast; '2**r** *m* (-s/-) overcoat, topcoat.

'Überzug *m* cover; case, tick; ⊕ coat(ing). [ary; normal.]

üblich *adj.* ['y:pliç] usual, custom-|

U-Boot ⚓, ✕ ['u:-] *n* submarine, *in Germany*: a. U-boat.

übrig *adj.* ['y:briç] left, remaining; *die* ~**e** *Welt* the rest of the world; *die* ~**en** *pl.* the others *pl.*, the rest; *im* ~**en** for the rest; by the way; *haben have s.th.* left; *keine Zeit* ~ *haben have* no time to spare; *etwas* ~ *haben für* care for, have a soft spot for; *ein* ~**es** *tun* go out of one's way; '~**bleiben** *v/i. (irr. bleiben, sep., -ge-, sein)* be left; remain; *es blieb ihm nichts anderes übrig* he had no (other) alternative (*als* but); ~**ens** *adv.* ['~gəns] by the way; '~**lassen** *v/t. (irr. lassen, sep., -ge-, h)* leave; *viel zu wünschen* ~ leave much to be desired.

'Übung *f* (-/-en) exercise; practice; drill; '~**shang** *m* skiing: nursery slope.

Ufer ['u:fər] *n* (-s/-) shore (*of sea, lake*); bank (*of river, etc.*).

Uhr [u:r] *f* (-/-en) clock; watch; *um vier* ~ at four o'clock; '~**armband** *n* (-[e]s/~er) watch-strap; '~**feder** *f* watch-spring; '~**macher** *m* (-s/-) watch-maker; '~**werk** *n* clockwork; watch-work; '~**zeiger** *m* hand (*of clock or watch*); '~**zeigersinn** *m* (-[e]s/*no pl.*): *im* ~ clockwise; *entgegen dem* ~ counter-clockwise.

Uhu *orn.* ['u:hu:] *m* (-s/-s) eagle-owl.

Ulk [ulk] *m* (-[e]s/-e) fun, lark; '2**en** *v/i. (ge-, h)* (sky)lark, joke; '2**ig** *adj.* funny.

Ulme ♣ ['ulmə] *f* (-/-n) elm.

Ultimatum [ulti'ma:tum] *n* (-s/*Ul-*|

timaten, -s) ultimatum; *j-m ein ~ stellen* deliver an ultimatum to s.o.

Ultimo † ['ultimo] *m* (-s/-s) last day of the month.

Ultrakurzwelle *phys.* [ultra'-] *f* ultra-short wave, very-high-frequency wave.

um [um] **1.** *prp.* (*acc.*) round, about; *~ vier Uhr* at four o'clock; *~ sein Leben laufen* run for one's life; et. *~ einen Meter verfehlen* miss s.th. by a metre; et. *~ zwei Mark verkaufen* sell s.th. at two marks; **2.** *prp.* (*gen.*): *~ seinetwillen* for his sake; **3.** *cj.*: *~ so besser* all the better, so much the better; *~ so mehr* (*weniger*) all the more (less); *~ zu* (in order) to; **4.** *adv.*: *er drehte sich ~* he turned round.

um|ändern ['um9-] *v/t.* (*sep.*, *-ge-*, *h*) change, alter; *~arbeiten* ['um9-] *v/t.* (*sep.*, *-ge-*, *h*) make over (*coat*, *etc.*); revise (*book*, *etc.*); *~ zu* make into.

um'arm|en *v/t.* (*no -ge-*, *h*) hug, embrace; *sich ~* embrace; **Qung** *f* (-/-en) embrace, hug.

'Umbau *m* (-[e]s/-e, -ten) rebuilding; reconstruction; **Qen** *v/t.* (*sep.*, *-ge-*, *h*) rebuild; reconstruct.

'umbiegen *v/t.* (*irr. biegen*, *sep.*, *-ge-*, *h*) bend; turn up *or* down.

'umbild|en *v/t.* (*sep.*, *-ge-*, *h*) remodel, reconstruct; reorganize, reform; reshuffle (*cabinet*); **Qung** *f* (-/-en) remodel(l)ing, reconstruction; reorganization, *pol.* reshuffle.

'um|binden *v/t.* (*irr. binden*, *sep.*, *-ge-*, *h*) put on (*apron*, *etc.*); *~blättern* (*sep.*, *-ge-*, *h*) **1.** *v/t.* turn over; **2.** *v/i.* turn over the page; *~brechen* *v/t.* (*irr. brechen*) **1.** ↯ ['~brεçən] (*sep.*, *-ge-*, *h*) dig, break up (*ground*); **2.** *typ.* [~'brεçən] (*no -ge-*, *h*) make up; *~bringen* *v/t.* (*irr. bringen*, *sep.*, *-ge-*, *h*) kill; *sich ~* kill o.s.; **'Qbruch** *m typ.* make-up; *fig.*: upheaval; radical change; *'~buchen* *v/t.* (*sep.*, *-ge-*, *h*) † transfer *or* switch to another account; book for another date; *'~disponieren* *v/i.* (*sep.*, *no -ge-*, *h*) change one's plans.

'umdreh|en *v/t.* (*sep.*, *-ge-*, *h*) turn; *s. Spieß*; *sich ~* turn round; **Qung** [um'-] *f* (-/-en) turn; *phys.*, ⊕ rotation, revolution.

um|fahren (*irr. fahren*) **1.** ['~fɑːrən] *v/t.* (*sep.*, *-ge-*, *h*) run down; **2.** ['~fɑːrən] *v/i.* (*sep.*, *-ge-*, *sein*) go a roundabout way; **3.** [~'fɑːrən] *v/t.* (*no -ge-*, *h*) drive round; ⊕ sail round; ⊕ double (*cape*); *~fallen* *v/i.* (*irr. fallen*, *sep.*, *-ge-*, *sein*) fall; collapse; *tot ~* drop dead.

'Umfang *m* (-[e]s/*no pl.*) circumference, circuit; perimeter; girth (*of body, tree, etc.*); *fig.*: extent; volume; *in großem ~* on a large

scale; **'Qreich** *adj.* extensive; voluminous; spacious.

um'fassen *v/t.* (*no -ge-*, *h*) clasp; embrace (*a. fig.*); ✗ envelop; *fig.* comprise, cover, comprehend; *~d* *adj.* comprehensive, extensive; sweeping, drastic.

'umform|en *v/t.* (*sep.*, *-ge-*, *h*) remodel, recast, transform (*a. ⚡*); ⚡ convert; **'Qer** ⚡ *m* (-s/-) transformer; converter.

'Umfrage *f* poll; *öffentliche ~* public opinion poll.

'Umgang *m* **1.** (-[e]s/≈e) ⚛ gallery, ambulatory; *eccl.* procession (*round the fields, etc.*); **2.** (-[e]s/*no pl.*) intercourse (*mit* with); company; *~ haben mit* associate with.

umgänglich *adj.* ['umgɛŋlɪç] sociable, companionable, affable.

'Umgangs|formen *f/pl.* manners *pl.*; *~sprache* *f* colloquial usage; *in der deutschen ~* in colloquial German.

um'garnen *v/t.* (*no -ge-*, *h*) ensnare.

um'geb|en 1. *v/t.* (*irr. geben*, *no -ge-*, *h*) surround; *mit e-r Mauer ~* wall in; **2.** *adj.* surrounded (*von* with, *by*) (*a. fig.*); **Qung** *f* (-/-en) environs *pl.* (*of town, etc.*); surroundings *pl.*, environment (*of place, person, etc.*).

umgeh|en (*irr. gehen*) **1.** ['~geːən] *v/i.* (*sep.*, *-ge-*, *sein*) make a detour; *rumour*, *etc.*: go about, be afloat; *ghost*: walk; *~ mit* use *s.th.*; deal with *s.o.*; keep company with; *ein Gespenst soll im Schlosse ~* the castle is said to be haunted; **2.** [~'geːən] *v/t.* (*no -ge-*, *h*) go round; ✗ flank; bypass (*town, etc.*); *fig.* avoid, evade; circumvent, elude (*law, etc.*); *~end* *adj.* immediate; **Qungsstraße** [um'geːʊŋs-] *f* bypass.

umgekehrt ['umgəkeːrt] **1.** *adj.* reverse; inverse, inverted; *in ~er Reihenfolge* in reverse order; *im ~en Verhältnis zu* in inverse proportion to; **2.** *adv.* vice versa.

'umgraben *v/t.* (*irr. graben*, *sep.*, *-ge-*, *h*) dig (up).

um'grenzen *v/t.* (*no -ge-*, *h*) encircle; enclose; *fig.* circumscribe, limit.

'umgruppier|en *v/t.* (*sep.*, *no -ge-*, *h*) regroup; **Qung** *f* (-/-en) regrouping.

'um|haben F *v/t.* (*irr. haben*, *sep.*, *-ge-*, *h*) have (*coat, etc.*) on; **'Qhang** *m* wrap; cape; *'~hängen* *v/t.* (*sep.*, *-ge-*, *h*) rehang (*pictures*); sling (*rifle*) over one's shoulder; *sich den Mantel ~* put one's coat round one's shoulders; *'~hauen* *v/t.* (*irr. hauen*, *sep.*, *-ge-*, *h*) fell, cut down; F: *die Nachricht hat mich umgehauen* I was bowled over by the news.

um'her|blicken v/i. (sep., -ge-, h) look about (one); **~streifen** v/i. (sep., -ge-, sein) rove.

um'hinkönnen v/i. (irr. können, sep., -ge-, h): ich kann nicht umhin, zu sagen I cannot help saying.

um'hüll|en v/t. (no -ge-, h) wrap up (mit in), envelop (in); **2ung** f (-/-en) wrapping, wrapper, envelopment.

Umkehr ['umke:r] f (-/no pl.) return; **2en** (sep., -ge-) 1. v/i. (sein) return, turn back; 2. v/t. (h) turn out (one's pocket, etc.); invert (a. ♪); reverse (a. ♬, ♩); **~ung** f (-/-en) reversal; inversion.

'umkippen (sep., -ge-) 1. v/t. (h) upset, tilt; 2. v/i. (sein) upset, tilt (over); F faint.

um'klammer|n v/t. (no -ge-, h) clasp; boxing: clinch; **2ung** f (-/-en) clasp; boxing: clinch.

'umkleid|en v/refl. (sep., -ge-, h) change (one's clothes); **2eraum** m dressing-room.

'umkommen v/i. (irr. kommen, sep., -ge-, sein) be killed (bei in), die (in), perish (in); vor Langeweile ~ die of boredom.

'Umkreis m (-es/no pl.) ♬ circumscribed circle; im ~ von within a radius of. [round.]

um'kreisen v/t. (no -ge-, h) circle)

'um|krempeln v/t. (sep., -ge-, h) tuck up (shirt-sleeves, etc.); change (plan, etc.); (völlig) ~ turn s.th. inside out; **~laden** v/t. (irr. laden, sep., -ge-, h) reload; ♥, ⚓ transship.

'Umlauf m circulation; phys., ⊕ rotation; circular (letter); in ~ setzen or bringen circulate, put into circulation; im ~ sein circulate, be in circulation; rumours: a. be afloat; außer ~ setzen withdraw from circulation; **~bahn** f orbit; **2en** (irr. laufen) 1. ['~laufən] v/t. (sep., -ge-, h) knock over; 2. ['~laufən] v/i. (sep., -ge-, sein) circulate; make a detour; 3. [~'laufən] v/t. (no -ge-, h) run round.

'Umlege|kragen m turn-down collar; **2n** v/t. (sep., -ge-, h) lay down; ⊕ throw (lever); storm, etc.: beat down (wheat, etc.); re-lay (cable, etc.); put (coat, etc.) round one's shoulders; apportion (costs, etc.); fig. sl. do s.o. in.

'umleit|en v/t. (sep., -ge-, h) divert; **2ung** f diversion, detour.

'umliegend adj. surrounding; circumjacent.

um'nacht|et adj.: geistig ~ mentally deranged; **2ung** f (-/~-en): geistige ~ mental derangement.

'um|packen v/t. (sep., -ge-, h) repack; **~pflanzen** v/t. 1. ['~pflantsən] (sep., -ge-, h) transplant; 2. [~'pflantsən] (no -ge-, h): ~ mit

plant s.th. round with; **~pflügen** v/t. (sep., -ge-, h) plough, Am. plow.

um'rahmen v/t. (no -ge-, h) frame; musikalisch ~ put into a musical setting.

umrand|en [um'randən] v/t. (no -ge-, h) edge, border; **2ung** f (-/-en) edge, border.

um'ranken v/t. (no -ge-, h) twine (mit with).

'umrechn|en v/t. (sep., -ge-, h) convert (in acc. into); **'2ung** f (-/no pl.) conversion; **'2ungskurs** m rate of exchange.

umreißen v/t. (irr. reißen) 1. ['~raisən] (sep., -ge-, h) pull down; knock s.o. over; 2. [~'raisən] (no -ge-, h) outline. [round (a. fig.).]

um'ringen v/t. (no -ge-, h) sur-)

'Um|riß m outline (a. fig.), contour; **'2rühren** v/t. (sep., -ge-, h) stir; **'2satteln** (sep., -ge-, h) 1. v/t. resaddle; 2. F fig. v/i. change one's studies or occupation; ~ von ... auf (acc.) change from ... to ...; **'~satz** ♥ m turnover; sales pl.; return(s pl.); stock exchange: business done.

'umschalt|en (sep., -ge-, h) 1. v/t. ⊕ change over; ≴ commutate; ⊕ switch; 2. ♬, ⊕ v/i. switch over; **'2er** m ⊕ change-over switch; ≴ commutator; **2ung** f (-/-en) ⊕ change-over; ≴ commutation.

'Umschau f (-/no pl.): ~ halten nach look out for, be on the look-out for; **'2en** v/refl. (sep., -ge-, h) look round (nach for); look about (for) (a. fig.), look about one.

'umschicht|en v/t. (sep., -ge-, h) pile afresh; fig. regroup (a. ♥); **'~ig** adv. by or in turns; **2ung** fig. f (-/-en) regrouping; soziale **~en** pl. social upheavals pl.

um'schiff|en v/t. (no -ge-, h) circumnavigate; double (cape); **2ung** f (-/~-en) circumnavigation; doubling.

'Umschlag m envelope; cover, wrapper; jacket; turn-up, Am. a. cuff (of trousers); ≴ compress; ≴ poultice; trans-shipment (of goods); fig. change, turn; **'2en** (irr. schlagen, sep., -ge-) 1. v/t. (h) knock s.o. down; cut down, fell (tree); turn (leaf); turn up (sleeves, etc.); turn down (collar); trans-ship (goods); 2. v/i. (sein) turn over, upset; ⚓ capsize, upset; wine, etc.: turn sour; fig. turn (in acc. into); **'~hafen** m port of trans-shipment.

um'schließen v/t. (irr. schließen, no -ge-, h) embrace, surround (a. ✕), enclose; ✕ invest; **'schlingen** v/t. (irr. schlingen, no -ge-, h) embrace.

'um|schmeißen F v/t. (irr. schmeißen, sep., -ge-, h) s. umstoßen; **'~**

schnallen v/t. (sep., -ge-, h) buckle on.

umschreib|en v/t. (irr. schreiben) 1. ['ˌʃraibən] (sep., -ge-, h) rewrite; transfer (property, etc.) (auf acc. to); 2. [ˌˈʃraibən] (no -ge-, h) ⓐ circumscribe; paraphrase; ²ung f (-/-en) 1. ['ˌʃraibuŋ] rewriting; transfer (auf acc. to); 2. [ˌˈʃraibuŋ] ⓐ circumscription; paraphrase.

'Umschrift f circumscription; phonetics: transcription.

'umschütten v/t. (sep., -ge-, h) pour into another vessel; spill.

'Um|schweife pl.: ~ machen beat about the bush; ohne ~ pointblank; **'²schwenken** fig. v/i. (sep., -ge-, sein) veer or turn round; **'~schwung** fig. m revolution; revulsion (of public feeling, etc.); change (in the weather, etc.); reversal (of opinion, etc.).

um'segel|n v/t. (no -ge-, h) sail round; double (cape); circumnavigate (globe, world); ²(e)lung f (-/-en) sailing round (world, etc.); doubling; circumnavigation.

'um|sehen v/refl. (irr. sehen, sep., -ge-, h) look round (nach for); look about (for) (a. fig.), look about one; **'~sein** f v/i. (irr. sein, sep., -ge-, sein) time: be up; holidays, etc.: be over; **'~setzen** v/t. (sep., -ge-, h) transpose (a. ♪); ♀ transplant; ✝ turn over; spend (money) (in acc. on books, etc.); in die Tat ~ realize, convert into fact.

'Umsicht f (-/no pl.) circumspection; **'²ig** adj. circumspect.

'umsied|eln (sep., -ge-) 1. v/t. (h) resettle; 2. v/i. (sein) (re)move (nach, in acc. to); **'²lung** f (-/ꜗ -en) resettlement; evacuation; removal.

um'sonst adv. gratis, free of charge; in vain; to no purpose; nicht ~ not without good reason.

umspann|en v/t. 1. ['ˌʃpanən] (sep., -ge-, h) change (horses); ⚡ transform; 2. [ˌˈʃpanən] (no -ge-, h) span; fig. a. embrace; **'²er** ⚡ m (-s/-) transformer.

'umspringen v/i. (irr. springen, sep., -ge-, sein) shift, veer (round); ~ mit treat badly, etc.

'Umstand m circumstance; fact, detail; unter diesen Umständen in or under the circumstances; unter keinen Umständen in or under no circumstances, on no account; unter Umständen possibly; ohne Umstände without ceremony; in anderen Umständen sein be in the family way.

umständlich adj. ['umʃtentliç] story, etc.: long-winded; method, etc.: roundabout; p. fussy; das ist (mir) viel zu ~ that is far too much trouble (for me); **'²keit** f (-/ꜗ -en) long-windedness; fussiness.

'Umstands|kleid n maternity robe; **'~wort** gr. n (-[e]s/ꜗer) adverb.

'umstehend 1. adj.: auf der ~en Seite overleaf; 2. adv. overleaf; **²en** ['ˌdən] pl. the bystanders pl.

'Umsteige|karte f transfer; **'²n** v/i. (irr. steigen, sep., -ge-, sein) change (nach for); 🚋 a. change ʃtrains (for). **Umsteigkarte** ['umʃtaik-] f s. Umsteigekarte.

umstell|en v/t. 1. ['ˌʃtelən] (sep., -ge-, h) transpose (a. gr.); shift (furniture) about or round; convert (currency, production) (auf acc. to); sich ~ change one's attitude; accommodate o.s. to new conditions; adapt o.s. (auf acc. to); 2. [ˌˈʃtelən] (no -ge-, h) surround; ²ung ['ˌʃteluŋ] f transposition; fig.: conversion; adaptation; change.

'um|stimmen v/t. (sep., -ge-, h) tune to another pitch; j-n ~ change s.o.'s mind, bring s.o. round; **'~stoßen** v/t. (irr. stoßen, sep., -ge-, h) knock over; upset; fig. annul; ⚖ overrule, reverse; upset (plan).

um|stricken fig. v/t. (no -ge-, h) ensnare; **~stritten** adj. [ˌˈʃtritən] disputed, contested; controversial.

'Um|sturz m subversion, overturn; **'²stürzen** (sep., -ge-) 1. v/t. (h) upset, overturn (a. fig.); fig. subvert; 2. v/i. (sein) upset, overturn; fall down; **²stürzlerisch** adj. ['ˌləriʃ] subversive.

'Umtausch m (-es/ꜗ -e) exchange; ✝ conversion (of currency, etc.); **'²en** v/t. (sep., -ge-, h) exchange (gegen for); ✝ convert.

'umtun F v/t. (irr. tun, sep., -ge-, h) put (coat, etc.) round one's shoulders; sich ~ nach look about for.

'umwälz|en v/t. (sep., -ge-, h) roll round; fig. revolutionize; **'~end** adj. revolutionary; **'²ung** fig. f (-/-en) revolution, upheaval.

'umwand|eln v/t. (sep., -ge-, h) transform (in acc. into); ⚡, ✝ convert (into); ⚡ commute (into); **'²lung** f transformation; ⚡, ✝ conversion; ⚡ commutation.

'um|wechseln v/t. (sep., -ge-, h) change; **'²weg** m roundabout way or route; detour; auf ~en in a roundabout way; **'~wehen** v/t. (sep., -ge-, h) blow down or over; **'²welt** f (-/ꜗ -en) environment; **'~wenden** 1. v/t. (sep., -ge-, h) turn over; 2. v/refl. ([irr. wenden], sep., -ge-, h) look round (nach for).

um'werben v/t. (irr. werben, no -ge-, h) court, woo.

'umwerfen v/t. (irr. werfen, sep., -ge-, h) upset (a. fig.), overturn; sich e-n Mantel ~ throw a coat round one's shoulders.

um|'wickeln v/t. (no -ge-, h): et. mit Draht ~ wind wire round s.th.;

~wölken [~'vœlkən] v/refl. (no -ge-, h) cloud over (a. fig.); **~zäunen** [~'tsɔynən] v/t. (no -ge-, h) fence (in).

umziehen (irr. ziehen) 1. ['~tsi:ən] v/i. (sep., -ge-, sein) (re)move (nach to); move house; 2. ['~tsi:ən] v/refl. (sep., -ge-, h) change (one's clothes); 3. [~'tsi:ən] v/refl. (no -ge-, h) cloud over.

umzingeln [um'tsiŋəln] v/t. (no -ge-, h) surround, encircle.

'Umzug m procession; move (nach to), removal (to); change of residence.

unab|änderlich adj. [un°ap'ɛndərliç] unalterable; **~hängig** ['~heŋiç] 1. adj. independent (von of); 2. adv.: ~ von irrespective of; **'2hängigkeit** f (-/no pl.) independence (von of); **~kömmlich** adj. ['~kœmliç]: er ist im Moment ~ we cannot spare him at the moment, we cannot do without him at the moment; **~lässig** adj. incessant, unremitting; **~sehbar** adj. [~'ze:ba:r] incalculable; in ~er Ferne in a distant future; **'~sichtlich** adj. unintentional, inadvertent; **~wendbar** adj. [~'vɛntba:r] inevitable, inescapable.

unachtsam adj. ['un°-] careless, heedless; **'2keit** f (-/~-en) carelessness, heedlessness.

unähnlich adj. ['un°-] unlike, dissimilar (dat. to).

unan|fechtbar adj. [un°an'-] unimpeachable, unchallengeable, incontestable; **'~gebracht** adj. inappropriate; pred. a. out of place; **'~gefochten** 1. adj. undisputed; unchallenged; 2. adv. without any hindrance; **'~gemessen** adj. unsuitable; improper; inadequate; **'~genehm** adj. disagreeable, unpleasant; awkward; troublesome; **~'nehmbar** adj. unacceptable (für to); **'2nehmlichkeit** f (-/-en) unpleasantness; awkwardness; troublesomeness; **~en** pl. trouble, inconvenience; **'~sehnlich** adj. unsightly; plain; **'~ständig** adj. indecent; obscene; **'2ständigkeit** f (-/-en) indecency; obscenity; **~'tastbar** adj. unimpeachable; inviolable.

unappetitlich adj. ['un°-] food, etc.: unappetizing; sight, etc.: distasteful, ugly.

Unart ['un°-] 1. f bad habit; 2. m (-[e]s/-e) naughty child; **'2ig** adj. naughty; **'~igkeit** f (-/-en) naughty behavio(u)r, naughtiness.

unauf|dringlich adj. ['un°auf-] unobtrusive; unostentatious; **~fällig** adj. inconspicuous; unobtrusive; **~findbar** adj. [~'fintba:r] undiscoverable, untraceable; **~gefordert** ['~gəfordərt] 1. adj. un-

asked; 2. adv. without being asked, of one's own accord; **~'hörlich** adj. incessant, continuous, uninterrupted; **'~merksam** adj. inattentive; **'2merksamkeit** f (-/-en) inattention, inattentiveness; **'~richtig** adj. insincere; **'2richtigkeit** f (-/-en) insincerity; **~schiebbar** adj. [~'ʃi:pba:r] urgent; ~ sein brook no delay.

unaus|bleiblich adj. [un°aus'blaipliç] inevitable; das war ~ that was bound to happen; **~'führbar** adj. impracticable; **~geglichen** ['~gəgliçən] unbalanced (a. ♥); **~'löschlich** adj. indelible; fig. a. inextinguishable; **~'sprechlich** adj. unutterable; unspeakable; inexpressible; **~'stehlich** adj. unbearable, insupportable.

'unbarmherzig adj. merciless, unmerciful; **'2keit** f (-/no pl.) mercilessness, unmercifulness.

unbe|absichtigt adj. ['unbə°apziçtiçt] unintentional, undesigned; **'~achtet** adj. unnoticed; **~anstandet** adj. ['unbə°-] unopposed, not objected to; **'~baut** adj. ♪ untilled; land: undeveloped; **'~dacht** adj. inconsiderate; imprudent; **~'denklich** 1. adj. unobjectionable; 2. adv. without hesitation; **'~deutend** adj. insignificant; slight; **'~dingt** 1. adj. unconditional; obedience, etc.: implicit; 2. adv. by all means; under any circumstances; **~'fahrbar** adj. impracticable, impassable; **'~fangen** adj. unprejudiced, unbias(s)ed; ingenuous; unembarrassed; **~'friedigend** adj. unsatisfactory; **~'friedigt** adj. ['~çt] dissatisfied; disappointed; **'~fugt** adj. unauthorized; incompetent; **'2fugte** m (-n/-n) unauthorized person; ~n ist der Zutritt verboten! no trespassing!; **'~gabt** adj. untalented; **~'greiflich** adj. inconceivable, incomprehensible; **~'grenzt** adj. unlimited; boundless; **~'gründet** adj. unfounded; **'2hagen** n uneasiness; discomfort; **'~haglich** adj. uneasy; uncomfortable; **~'helligt** adj. [~'hɛliçt] unmolested; **~'herrscht** adj. lacking self-control; **'2herrschtheit** f (-/no pl.) lack of self-control; **~'hindert** adj. unhindered, free; **~'holfen** adj. ['~bəholfən] clumsy, awkward; **'2holfenheit** f (-/no pl.) clumsiness, awkwardness; **~'irrt** adj. unswerving; **'~kannt** adj. unknown; ~e Größe ♠ unknown quantity (a. fig.); **~'kümmert** adj. unconcerned (um, wegen about); careless (of, about); **'~lebt** adj. inanimate; street, etc.: unfrequented; **'~lehrbar** adj.: sein take no advice; **'~liebt** adj. unpopular; sich ~ machen get o.s. disliked; **'~mannt** adj. unmanned;

'**_merkt** adj. unnoticed; '**_mittelt** adj. impecunious, without means; '**_nommen** adj. [**_**'nɔmən]: es bleibt ihm **_** zu inf. he is at liberty to inf.; '**_nutzt** adj. unused; '**_quem** adj. uncomfortable; inconvenient; '**2quemlichkeit** f lack of comfort; inconvenience; '**_rechtigt** adj. unauthorized; unjustified; **_schadet** prp. (gen.) without prejudice to; **_schädigt** adj. ['**_**çt] uninjured, undamaged; '**_scheiden** adj. immodest; **_scholten** adj. ['**_**ʃɔltən] blameless, irreproachable; '**_schränkt** adj. unrestricted; absolute; **_schreiblich** adj. ['**_**ʃraipliç] indescribable; '**sehen** adv. unseen; without inspection; '**_setzt** adj. unoccupied; vacant; **_siegbar** adj. [**_**'zi:kbɑ:r] invincible; '**_sonnen** adj. thoughtless, imprudent; rash; **2sonnenheit** f (-/-en) thoughtlessness, rashness; '**_ständig** adj. inconstant; unsteady; weather: changeable, unsettled (a. ✦); p. erratic; '**2ständigkeit** f (-/no pl.) inconstancy; changeability; **_stätigt** adj. ['**_**çt] unconfirmed; letter, etc.: unacknowledged; **_stechlich** adj. incorruptible, unbribable; **2'stechlichkeit** f (-/no pl.) incorruptibility; '**_stimmt** adj. indeterminate (a. ♌); indefinite (a. gr.); uncertain; feeling, etc.: vague; '**2stimmtheit** f (-/no pl.) indeterminateness, indetermination; indefiniteness; uncertainty; vagueness; **_streitbar** adj. incontestable; indisputable; '**_stritten** adj. uncontested, undisputed; **_teiligt** adj. unconcerned (an dat. in); indifferent; **_trächtlich** adj. inconsiderable, insignificant; [flexible.)

unbeugsam adj. [un'bɔykza:m] in-) '**unbe|wacht** adj. unwatched, unguarded (a. fig.); '**_waffnet** adj. unarmed; eye: naked; **_weglich** adj. immovable; motionless; '**_wiesen** adj. unproven; '**_wohnt** adj. uninhabited; unoccupied, vacant; '**_wußt** adj. unconscious; '**_zähmbar** adj. indomitable.

'**Un|bilden** pl.: **_** der Witterung inclemency of the weather; '**_bildung** f lack of education.

'**un|billig** adj. unfair; '**_blutig** 1. adj. bloodless; 2. adv. without bloodshed.

unbotmäßig adj. ['unbo:t-] insubordinate; '**2keit** f (-/-en) insubordination.

'**un|brauchbar** adj. useless; '**_christlich** adj. unchristian.

und cj. [unt] and; F: na **_**? so what?

'**Undank** m ingratitude; '**2bar** adj. ungrateful (gegen to); task, etc.: thankless; '**_barkeit** f ingratitude, ungratefulness; fig. thanklessness.

un|'denkbar adj. unthinkable; inconceivable; **_kdenklich** adj.: seit **_**en Zeiten from time immemorial; '**_deutlich** adj. indistinct; speech: a. inarticulate; fig. vague, indistinct; '**_deutsch** adj. un-German; '**_dicht** adj. leaky; '**2ding** n: es wäre ein **_**, zu behaupten, daß ... it would be absurd to claim that ...

'**unduldsam** adj. intolerant; '**2keit** f intolerance.

undurch|'dringlich adj. impenetrable; countenance: impassive; '**_führbar** adj. impracticable; '**_lässig** adj. impervious, impermeable; '**_sichtig** adj. opaque; fig. mysterious.

uneben adj. ['un²-] ground: uneven, broken; way, etc.: bumpy; '**2heit** f 1. (-/no pl.) unevenness; 2. (-/-en) bump.

un|echt adj. ['un²-] jewellery, etc.: imitation; hair, teeth, etc.: false; money, jewellery, etc.: counterfeit; picture, etc.: fake; Ⓐ fraction: improper; '**_ehelich** adj. illegitimate.

Unehr|e ['un²-] f dishono(u)r; j-m **_** machen discredit s.o.; '**2enhaft** adj. dishono(u)rable; '**2lich** adj. dishonest; '**_lichkeit** f dishonesty.

uneigennützig adj. ['un²-] disinterested, unselfish.

uneinig adj. ['un²-]: **_** sein be at variance (mit with); disagree (über acc. on); '**2keit** f variance, disagreement.

un|ein'nehmbar adj. impregnable; '**_empfänglich** adj. insusceptible (für of, to).

unempfindlich adj. ['un²-] insensitive (gegen to); '**2keit** f insensitiveness (gegen to).

un'endlich 1. adj. endless, infinite (both a. fig.); 2. adv. infinitely (a. fig.); **_** lang endless; **_** viel no end of (money, etc.); '**2keit** f (-/no pl.) endlessness, infinitude; infinity (all a. fig.).

unent|behrlich adj. [un²ɛnt'be:rliç] indispensable; **_geltlich** 1. adj gratuitous, gratis; 2. adv. gratis, free of charge; '**_rinnbar** adj. ineluctable; '**_schieden** 1. adj. undecided; **_** enden game: end in a draw or tie; 2. ♌ n (-s/-) draw, tie; '**_schlossen** adj. irresolute; '**2schlossenheit** f irresoluteness, irresolution; **_schuldbar** adj. inexcusable; **_wegt** adv. [**_**'ve:kt] untiringly; continuously; '**_wirrbar** adj. inextricable.

uner|bittlich adj. [un²ɛr'bitliç] inexorable; fact: stubborn; '**_fahren** adj. inexperienced; **_findlich** adj. [**_**'fintliç] incomprehensible; '**_forschlich** adj. inscrutable; '**_freulich** adj. unpleasant; '**_füllbar** adj. unrealizable; '**_giebig** adj. unproductive (an dat. of); '**_heb**-

lich *adj.* irrelevant (*für* to); inconsiderable; **~hört** *adj.* **1.** ['~hø:rt] unheard; **2.** [~'hø:rt] unheard-of; outrageous; '**~kannt** *adj.* unrecognized; **~'klärlich** *adj.* inexplicable; **~läßlich** *adj.* [~'lɛsliç] indispensable (*für* to, for); **~laubt** *adj.* ['~laʊpt] unauthorized; illegal, illicit; *~e Handlung* ⚖ tort; **~ledigt** *adj.* ['~le:diçt] unsettled (*a.* ✝); **~meßlich** *adj.* [~'mɛsliç] immeasurable, immense; **~müdlich** *adj.* [~'my:tliç] *p.* indefatigable, untiring; *efforts, etc.*: untiring, unremitting; '**~quicklich** *adj.* unpleasant, unedifying; **~'reichbar** *adj.* inattainable; inaccessible; *pred. a.* above *or* beyond *or* out of reach; **~'reicht** *adj.* unrival(l)ed, unequal(l)ed; **~sättlich** *adj.* [~'zɛtliç] insatiable, insatiate; **~'schöpflich** *adj.* inexhaustible.

unerschrocken *adj.* ['unˀ-] intrepid, fearless; '**2heit** *f* (-/*no pl.*) intrepidity, fearlessness.

uner|schütterlich *adj.* [unˀɛr'ʃytərliç] unshakable; **~'schwinglich** *adj. price*: prohibitive; *pred. a.* above *or* beyond *or* out of reach (*für* of); **~'setzlich** *adj.* irreplaceable; *loss, etc.*: irreparable; **~'träglich** *adj.* intolerable, unbearable; '**~wartet** *adj.* unexpected; '**~wünscht** *adj.* undesirable, undesired.

'**unfähig** *adj.* incapable (*zu inf.* of *ger.*); unable (to *inf.*); inefficient; '**2keit** *f* incapability (*zu inf.* of *ger.*); inability (to *inf.*); inefficiency.

'**Unfall** *m* accident; *e-n ~ haben* meet with *or* have an accident; '**~station** *f* emergency ward; '**~versicherung** *f* accident insurance.

un'faßlich *adj.* incomprehensible, inconceivable; *das ist mir ~* that is beyond me.

un'fehlbar **1.** *adj.* infallible (*a. eccl.*); *decision, etc.*: unimpeachable; *instinct, etc.*: unfailing; **2.** *adv.* without fail; inevitably; **2keit** *f* (-/*no pl.*) infallibility.

'**un|fein** *adj.* indelicate; *pred. a.* lacking in refinement; '**~fern** *prp.* (*gen. or von*) not far from; '**~fertig** *adj.* unfinished; *fig. a.* half-baked; **~flätig** *adj.* ['~flɛ:tiç] dirty, filthy.

'**unfolgsam** *adj.* disobedient; '**2keit** *f* disobedience.

un|förmig *adj.* ['unfœrmiç] misshapen; shapeless; '**~frankiert** *adj.* unstamped; '**~frei** *adj.* not free; ✉ unstamped; '**~freiwillig** *adj.* involuntary; *humour*: unconscious; '**~freundlich** *adj.* unfriendly (*zu* with), unkind (to); *climate, weather*: inclement; *room, day*: cheerless; '**2friede(n)** *m* discord.

'**unfruchtbar** *adj.* unfruitful; sterile; '**2keit** *f* (-/*no pl.*) unfruitfulness; sterility.

Unfug ['unfu:k] *m* (-[e]*s*/*no pl.*) mischief.

Ungar ['uŋgar] *m* (-*n*/-*n*) Hungarian; '**2isch** *adj.* Hungarian.

'**ungastlich** *adj.* inhospitable.

unge|achtet *prp.* (*gen.*) ['ungəˀaxtət] regardless of; despite; **~ahnt** *adj.* ['ungəˀ-] undreamt-of; unexpected; **~bärdig** *adj.* ['~bɛ:rdiç] unruly; '**~beten** *adj.* uninvited, unasked; *~er Gast* intruder, *sl.* gate-crasher; '**~bildet** *adj.* uneducated; '**~bräuchlich** *adj.* unusual; '**~braucht** *adj.* unused; '**~bührlich** *adj.* improper, undue, unseemly; '**~bunden** *adj. book*: unbound; *fig.*: free; single; '**~deckt** *adj. table*: unlaid; *sports*, ⚔, ✝: uncovered; *paper currency*: fiduciary.

'**Ungeduld** *f* impatience; '**2ig** *adj.* impatient.

'**ungeeignet** *adj.* unfit (*für* for *s.th.*, to do *s.th.*); *p. a.* unqualified; *moment*: inopportune.

ungefähr ['ungəfɛ:r] **1.** *adj.* approximate, rough; **2.** *adv.* approximately, roughly, about, *Am.* F *a.* around; *von ~* by chance; '**~det** *adj.* unendangered, safe; '**~lich** *adj.* harmless; *pred. a.* not dangerous.

'**unge|fällig** *adj.* disobliging; '**~halten** *adj.* displeased (*über acc.* at); '**~hemmt** **1.** *adj.* unchecked; **2.** *adv.* without restraint; '**~heuchelt** *adj.* unfeigned.

ungeheuer ['ungəhɔʏər] **1.** *adj.* vast, huge, enormous; **2.** **2** *n* (-*s*/-) monster; **~lich** *adj.* [~'hɔʏərliç] monstrous.

'**ungehobelt** *adj.* not planed; *fig.* uncouth, rough.

'**ungehörig** *adj.* undue, improper; '**2keit** *f* (-/⁓-*en*) impropriety.

'**ungehorsam** **1.** *adj.* disobedient; **2.** **2** *m* disobedience.

'**unge|künstelt** *adj.* unaffected; '**~kürzt** *adj.* unabridged.

'**ungelegen** *adj.* inconvenient, inopportune; '**2heiten** *f*/*pl.* inconvenience; trouble; *j-m ~ machen* put s.o. to inconvenience.

'**unge|lehrig** *adj.* indocile; '**~lenk** *adj.* awkward, clumsy; '**~lernt** *adj.* unskilled; '**~mütlich** *adj.* uncomfortable; *room*: *a.* cheerless; *p.* nasty; '**~nannt** *adj.* unnamed; *p.* anonymous.

'**ungenau** *adj.* inaccurate, inexact; '**2igkeit** *f* inaccuracy, inexactness.

'**ungeniert** *adj.* free and easy, unceremonious; undisturbed.

unge|nießbar *adj.* ['ungəni:sba:r] uneatable; undrinkable; F *p.* unbearable, *pred. a.* in a bad humo(u)r; '**~nügend** *adj.* insufficient; '**~pflegt** *adj.* unkempt; '**~rade** *adj.* odd; '**~raten** *adj.* spoilt, undutiful.

'**ungerecht** *adj.* unjust (*gegen* to); '**2igkeit** *f* (-/-en) injustice.

'**un|gern** *adv.* unwillingly, grudgingly; reluctantly; **~geschehen** *adj.*: ~ *machen* undo *s.th.*

'**Ungeschick** *n* (-[e]s/*no pl.*), '**~lichkeit** *f* awkwardness, clumsiness, maladroitness; '**2t** *adj.* awkward, clumsy, maladroit.

unge|schlacht *adj.* ['ungəʃlaxt] hulking; uncouth; '**~schliffen** *adj.* unpolished, rough (*both a. fig.*); '**~schminkt** *adj.* not made up; *fig.* unvarnished.

'**ungesetzlich** *adj.* illegal, unlawful, illicit; '**2keit** *f* (-/-en) illegality, unlawfulness.

'**unge|sittet** *adj.* uncivilized; unmannerly; '**~stört** *adj.* undisturbed, uninterrupted; '**~straft 1.** *adj.* unpunished; **2.** *adv.* with impunity; ~ *davonkommen* get off *or* escape scot-free.

ungestüm ['ungə∫ty:m] **1.** *adj.* impetuous; violent; **2.** 2 *n* (-[e]s/*no pl.*) impetuosity; violence.

'**unge|sund** *adj. climate:* unhealthy; *appearance: a.* unwholesome; *food:* unwholesome; '**~teilt** *adj.* undivided (*a. fig.*); **~trübt** *adj.* ['~try:pt] untroubled; unmixed; 2tüm ['~ty:m] *n* (-[e]s/-e) monster; **~übt** *adj.* ['~⁹y:pt] untrained; inexperienced; '**~waschen** *adj.* unwashed.

'**ungewiß** *adj.* uncertain; *j-n im ungewissen lassen* keep *s.o.* in suspense; '**2heit** *f* (-/⸜-en) uncertainty; suspense.

'**unge|wöhnlich** *adj.* unusual, uncommon; '**~wohnt** *adj.* unaccustomed; unusual; '**~zählt** *adj.* numberless, countless; 2ziefer ['~tsi:fər] *n* (-s/-) vermin; '**~ziemend** *adj.* improper, unseemly; '**~zogen** *adj.* ill-bred, rude, uncivil; *child:* naughty; '**~zügelt** *adj.* unbridled.

'**ungezwungen** *adj.* unaffected, easy; '**2heit** *f* (-/⸜-en) unaffectedness, ease, easiness.

'**Unglaube(n)** *m* unbelief, disbelief.

'**ungläubig** *adj.* incredulous, unbelieving (*a. eccl.*); infidel; '**2e** *m, f* unbeliever; infidel.

unglaub|lich *adj.* [un'glauplɪç] incredible; '**~würdig** *adj. p.* untrustworthy; *thing:* incredible; **~e** *Geschichte* cock-and-bull story.

'**ungleich 1.** *adj.* unequal, different; uneven; unlike; **2.** *adv.* (by) far, much; '**~artig** *adj.* heterogeneous; '**2heit** *f* difference, inequality; unevenness; unlikeness; '**~mäßig** *adj.* uneven; irregular.

'**Unglück** *n* (-[e]s/⸜-e) misfortune; bad *or* ill luck; accident; calamity, disaster; misery; '**2lich** *adj.* unfortunate, unlucky, unhappy; 2'**licher**'**weise** *adv.* unfortunately,

unluckily; '**2selig** *adj.* unfortunate; disastrous.

'**Unglücks|fall** *m* misadventure; accident; '**~rabe** F *m* unlucky fellow.

'**Un|gnade** *f* (-/*no pl.*) disgrace, disfavo(u)r; *in ~ fallen bei* fall into disgrace with, incur *s.o.'s* disfavo(u)r; **2gnädig** *adj.* ungracious, unkind.

'**ungültig** *adj.* invalid; *ticket:* not available; *money:* not current; ⸘⸙ (null and) void; '**2keit** *f* invalidity, ⸘⸙ *a.* voidness.

'**Un|gunst** *f* disfavo(u)r; inclemency (*of weather*); *zu meinen* **~en** *to my disadvantage;* '**2günstig** *adj.* unfavo(u)rable; disadvantageous.

'**un|gut** *adj.*: **~es** *Gefühl* misgiving; *nichts für ~l* no offen/ce, *Am.* -se!; '**~haltbar** *adj. shot:* unstoppable; *theory, etc.*: untenable; '**~handlich** *adj.* unwieldy, bulky.

'**Unheil** *n* mischief; disaster, calamity; '**2bar** *adj.* incurable; '**2voll** *adj.* sinister, ominous.

'**unheimlich 1.** *adj.* uncanny (*a. fig.*), weird; sinister; F *fig.* tremendous, terrific; **2.** F *fig. adv.*: ~ *viel* heaps of, an awful lot of.

'**unhöflich** *adj.* impolite, uncivil; '**2keit** *f* impoliteness, incivility.

Unhold ['unhɔlt] *m* (-[e]s/-e) fiend.

'**un|hörbar** *adj.* inaudible; '**~hygienisch** *adj.* unsanitary, insanitary.

Uni ['uni] *f* (-/-s) F varsity.

Uniform [uni'fɔrm] *f* (-/-en) uniform.

Unikum ['u:nikum] *n* (-s/*Unika*, -s) unique (thing); queer fellow.

uninteress|ant *adj.* ['un⁹-] uninteresting, boring; queer fellow.

'**~iert** *adj.* uninterested (*an dat.* in).

Universität [univerzi'tɛ:t] *f* (-/-en) university.

Universum [uni'verzum] *n* (-s/*no pl.*) universe.

Unke ['uŋkə] *f* (-/-n) *zo.* fire-bellied toad; F *fig.* croaker; '**2n** F *v/i.* (ge-, *h*) croak.

'**unkennt|lich** *adj.* unrecognizable; '**2lichkeit** *f* (-/*no pl.*): *bis zur ~* past all recognition; '**2nis** *f* (-/*no pl.*) ignorance.

'**unklar** *adj.* not clear; *meaning, etc.*: obscure; *answer, etc.*: vague; *im* **~en** *sein* be in the dark (*über acc.* about); '**2heit** *f* want of clearness; vagueness; obscurity.

'**unklug** *adj.* imprudent, unwise.

'**Unkosten** *pl.* cost(s *pl.*), expenses *pl.*; *sich in (große)* ~ *stürzen* go to great expense.

'**Unkraut** *n* weed.

un|kündbar *adj.* ['unkyntba:r] *loan, etc.*: irredeemable; *employment:* permanent; **~kundig** *adj.* ['~kundiç] ignorant (*gen.* of); '**~längst**

adv. lately, recently, the other day; '⸚lauter *adj. competition*: unfair; '⸚leidlich *adj.* intolerable, insufferable; '⸚leserlich *adj.* illegible; ⸚leugbar *adj.* ['⸚bɪkbɑːr] undeniable; '⸚logisch *adj.* illogical; '⸚lösbar *adj.* unsolvable, insoluble. 'Unlust *f* (-/*no pl.*) reluctance (*zu inf.* to *inf.*); '⸚ig *adj.* reluctant. 'un|manierlich *adj.* unmannerly; '⸚männlich *adj.* unmanly; ⸚maßgeblich *adj.* ['⸚geːpliç]: *nach m-r* ⸚en Meinung in my humble opinion; '⸚mäßig *adj.* immoderate; intemperate; '2menge *f* enormous *or* vast quantity *or* number. 'Unmensch *m* monster, brute; '2lich *adj.* inhuman, brutal; '⸚lichkeit *f* inhumanity, brutality. 'un|mißverständlich *adj.* unmistakable; '⸚mittelbar *adj.* immediate, direct; '⸚möbliert *adj.* unfurnished; '⸚modern *adj.* unfashionable, outmoded. 'unmöglich *adj.* impossible; '2keit *f* impossibility. 'Unmoral *f* immorality; '2isch *adj.* immoral. 'unmündig *adj.* under age. 'un|musikalisch *adj.* unmusical; '2mut *m* (-[e]s/*no pl.*) displeasure (*über acc.* at, over); '⸚nachahmlich *adj.* inimitable; '⸚nachgiebig *adj.* unyielding; '⸚nachsichtig *adj.* strict, severe; inexorable; '⸚nahbar *adj.* inaccessible, unapproachable; '⸚natürlich *adj.* unnatural; affected; '⸚nötig *adj.* unnecessary, needless; '⸚nütz *adj.* useless; ⸚ordentlich *adj.* ['un⁹-] untidy; *room, etc.*: *a.* disorderly; 2ordnung ['un⁹-] *f* disorder, mess. 'unpartei|isch *adj.* impartial, unbias(s)ed; '2ische *m* (-n/-n) referee; umpire; '2lichkeit *f* impartiality. 'un|passend *adj.* unsuitable; improper; inappropriate; '⸚passierbar *adj.* impassable. unpäßlich *adj.* ['unpeslɪç] indisposed, unwell; '2keit *f* (-/-en) indisposition. 'un|persönlich *adj.* impersonal (*a. gr.*); '⸚politisch *adj.* unpolitical; '⸚praktisch *adj.* unpractical, *Am. a.* impractical; '2rat *m* (-[e]s/*no pl.*) filth; rubbish; ⸚ *wittern* smell a rat. 'unrecht 1. *adj.* wrong; ⸚ *haben* be wrong; *j-m* ⸚ *tun* wrong s.o.; 2. 2 *n* (-[e]s/*no pl.*): *mit or zu* ⸚ wrongly; *ihm ist* ⸚ *geschehen* he has been wronged; '⸚mäßig *adj.* unlawful; '2mäßigkeit *f* unlawfulness. 'unreell *adj.* dishonest; unfair. 'unregelmäßig *adj.* irregular (*a. gr.*); '2keit *f* (-/-en) irregularity. 'unreif *adj.* unripe, immature (*both a. fig.*); '2e *f* unripeness, immaturity (*both a. fig.*).

'un|rein *adj.* impure (*a. eccl.*); unclean (*a. fig.*); '⸚reinlich *adj.* uncleanly; ⸚rettbar *adv.*: ⸚ *verloren* irretrievably lost; '⸚richtig *adj.* incorrect, wrong. Unruh ['unruː] *f* (-/-en) balance (-wheel); '⸚e *f* (-/-n) restlessness, unrest (*a. pol.*); uneasiness; disquiet(ude); flurry; alarm; ⸚n *pl.* disturbances *pl.*, riots *pl.*; '2ig *adj.* restless; uneasy; *sea*: rough, choppy. 'unrühmlich *adj.* inglorious. uns *pers. pron.* [uns] us; *dat.*: *a.* to us; ⸚ (*selbst*) ourselves, *after prp.*: us; *ein Freund von* ⸚ a friend of ours. 'un|sachgemäß *adj.* inexpert; '⸚sachlich *adj.* not objective; personal; ⸚säglich *adj.* [⸚ˈzeːkliç] unspeakable; untold; '⸚sanft *adj.* ungentle; '⸚sauber *adj.* dirty; *fig. a.* unfair (*a. sports*); '⸚schädlich *adj.* innocuous, harmless; '⸚scharf *adj.* blurred; *pred. a.* out of focus; ⸚schätzbar *adj.* inestimable, invaluable; '⸚scheinbar *adj.* plain, *Am. a.* homely. 'unschicklich *adj.* improper, indecent; '2keit *f* (-/-en) impropriety, indecency. unschlüssig *adj.* ['unʃlysiç] irresolute; '2keit *f* (-/*no pl.*) irresoluteness, irresolution. 'un|schmackhaft *adj.* insipid; unpalatable, unsavo(u)ry; '⸚schön *adj.* unlovely, unsightly; *fig. a.* unpleasant. 'Unschuld *f* (-/*no pl.*) innocence; '2ig *adj.* innocent (*an dat.* of). 'unselbständig *adj.* dependent (on others); '2keit *f* (lack of in)dependence. unser ['unzər] 1. *poss. pron.* our; *der (die, das)* ⸚e ours; *die* ⸚en *pl.* our relations *pl.*; 2. *pers. pron.* of us; *wir waren* ⸚ *drei* there were three of us. 'unsicher *adj.* unsteady; unsafe, insecure; uncertain; '2heit *f* unsteadiness; insecurity, unsafeness; uncertainty. 'unsichtbar *adj.* invisible. 'Unsinn *m* (-[e]s/*no pl.*) nonsense; '2ig *adj.* nonsensical. 'Unsitt|e *f* bad habit; abuse; '2lich *adj.* immoral; indecent (*a. 🡒*); '⸚lichkeit *f* (-/-en) immorality. 'un|solid(e) *adj. p.* easy-going; *life*: dissipated; 🡒 unreliable; '⸚sozial *adj.* unsocial, antisocial; '⸚sportlich *adj.* unsportsmanlike; unfair (*gegenüber* to). 'unstatthaft *adj.* inadmissible. 'unsterblich *adj.* immortal. Un'sterblichkeit *f* immortality. 'un|stet *adj.* unsteady; *character, life*: unsettled; 2stimmigkeit ['⸚ʃtimiçkait] *f* (-/-en) discrepancy; dissension; '⸚sträflich *adj.* blameless; '∟streitig adj. incontestable; '∟sympathisch adj. disagreeable; er ist mir ∼ I don't like him; '∟tätig adj. inactive; idle.

'untauglich adj. unfit (a. ✕); unsuitable; '2keit f (-/no pl.) unfitness (a. ✕).

un'teilbar adj. indivisible.

unten adv. ['untən] below; downstairs; von oben bis ∼ from top to bottom.

unter ['untər] 1. prp. (dat.; acc.) below, under; among; ∼ anderem among other things; ∼ zehn Mark (for) less than ten marks; ∼ Null below zero; ∼ aller Kritik beneath contempt; ∼ diesem Gesichtspunkt from this point of view; 2. adj. lower; inferior; die ∼en Räume the downstair(s) rooms.

Unter|abteilung ['untər⁹-] f subdivision; ∼arm ['untər⁹-] m forearm; '∟bau m (-[e]s/-ten) ⚠ substructure (a. ⬡), foundation.

unter|'bieten v/t. (irr. bieten, no -ge-, h) underbid; ✝ undercut, undersell (competitor); lower (record); ∼'binden v/t. (irr. binden, no -ge-, h) ⚙ ligature; fig. stop; ∼'bleiben v/i. (irr. bleiben, no -ge-, sein) remain undone; not to take place.

unter'brech|en v/t. (irr. brechen, no -ge-, h) interrupt (a. ⚡); break, Am. a. stop over; ⚡ break (circuit); 2ung f (-/-en) interruption, break, Am. a. stopover. [mit.]

unter'breiten v/t. (no -ge-, h) sub-]

'unterbring|en v/t. (irr. bringen, sep., -ge-, h) place (a. ✝); accommodate, lodge; '2ung f (-/-en) accommodation; ✝ placement.

unterdessen adv. [untər'desən] (in the) meantime, meanwhile.

unter'drück|en v/t. (no -ge-, h) oppress (subjects, etc.); repress (revolt, sneeze, etc.); suppress (rising, truth, yawn, etc.); put down (rebellion, etc.); 2ung f (-/-en) oppression; repression; suppression; putting down.

unterernähr|t adj. ['untər⁹-] underfed, undernourished; '2ung f (-/no pl.) underfeeding, malnutrition.

Unter'führung f subway, Am. underpass.

'Untergang m (-[e]s/⚡ ∼e) ast. setting; ⚓ sinking; fig. ruin.

Unter'gebene m (-n/-n) inferior, subordinate; contp. underling.

'untergehen v/i. (irr. gehen, sep., -ge-, sein) ast. set; ⚓ sink, founder; fig. be ruined.

untergeordnet adj. ['untərgə⁹ordnət] subordinate; importance: secondary.

'Untergewicht n (-[e]s/no pl.) underweight.

unter'graben fig. v/t. (irr. graben, no -ge-, h) undermine.

'Untergrund m (-[e]s/no pl.) subsoil; '∟bahn f underground (railway), in London: tube; Am. subway; '∟bewegung f underground movement.

'unterhalb prp. (gen.) below, underneath.

'Unterhalt m (-[e]s/no pl.) support, subsistence, livelihood; maintenance.

unter'halt|en v/t. (irr. halten, no -ge-, h) maintain; support; entertain, amuse; sich ∼ converse (mit with; über acc. on, about), talk (with; on, about); sich gut ∼ enjoy o.s.; 2ung f maintenance, upkeep; conversation, talk; entertainment.

'Unterhändler m negotiator; ✕ Parlementaire.

'Unter|haus parl. n (-es/no pl.) House of Commons; '∟hemd n vest, undershirt; '∟holz n (-es/no pl.) underwood, brushwood; '∟hose f (e-e a pair of) drawers pl., pants pl.; '2irdisch adj. subterranean, underground (both a. fig.).

unter'joch|en v/t. (no -ge-, h) subjugate, subdue; 2ung f (-/-en) subjugation.

'Unter|kiefer m lower jaw; '∟kleid n slip; '∟kleidung f underclothes pl., underclothing, underwear.

'unterkommen 1. v/i. (irr. kommen, sep., -ge-, sein) find accommodation; find employment; 2. 2 n (-s/⚡ -) accommodation; employment, situation.

'unter'kriegen F v/t. (sep., -ge-, h) bring to heel; sich nicht ∼ lassen not to knuckle down or under; 2kunft ['∟kunft] f (-/⚡e) accommodation, lodging; ✕ quarters pl.; '2lage f base; pad; fig.: voucher; ∼n pl. documents pl.; data pl.

unter'lass|en v/t. (irr. lassen, no -ge-, h) omit (zu tun doing, to do); neglect (to do, doing); fail (to do); 2ung f (-/-en) omission; neglect; failure; 2ungssünde f sin of omission.

'unterlegen¹ v/t. (sep., -ge-, h) lay or put under; give (another meaning).

unter'legen² adj. inferior (dat. to); 2e m (-n/-n) loser; underdog; 2heit f (-/no pl.) inferiority.

'Unterleib m abdomen, belly.

unter'liegen v/i. (irr. liegen, no -ge-, sein) be overcome (dat. by); be defeated (by), sports: a. lose (to); fig.: be subject to; be liable to; es unterliegt keinem Zweifel, daß ... there is no doubt that ...

'Unter|lippe f lower lip; '∟mieter m subtenant, lodger, Am. a. roomer.

unter'nehmen 1. v/t. (irr. nehmen, no -ge-, h) undertake; take (steps);

2. 2 *n* (-s/-) enterprise; ✝ *a.* business; ✖ operation.

unter'nehm|end *adj.* enterprising; 2er ✝ *m* (-s/-) entrepreneur; contractor; employer; 2ung *f* (-/-en) enterprise, undertaking; ✖ operation; ~ungslustig *adj.* enterprising.

'Unter|offizier ✖ *m* non-commissioned officer; '2ordnen *v/t.* (*sep.*, -ge-, *h*) subordinate (*dat.* to); *sich* ~ submit (to).

Unter'redung *f* (-/-en) conversation, conference.

Unterricht ['untərrıçt] *m* (-[e]s/✎-e) instruction, lessons *pl.*

unter'richten *v/t.* (*no* -ge-, *h*): ~ *in* (*dat.*) instruct in, teach (*English, etc.*); ~ *von* inform *s.o.* of.

'Unterrichts|ministerium *n* ministry of education; '~stunde *f* lesson, (teaching) period; '~wesen *n* (-s/*no pl.*) education; teaching.

'Unterrock *m* slip.

unter'sagen *v/t.* (*no* -ge-, *h*) forbid (*j-m et.* s.o. to do s.th.).

'Untersatz *m* stand; saucer.

unter'schätzen *v/t.* (*no* -ge-, *h*) undervalue; underestimate, underrate.

unter'scheid|en *v/t.* and *v/i.* (*irr. scheiden, no* -ge-, *h*) distinguish (*zwischen* between; *von* from); *sich* ~ differ (*von* from); 2ung *f* distinction.

'Unterschenkel *m* shank.

'unterschieb|en *v/t.* (*irr. schieben, sep.*, -ge-, *h*) push under; *fig.*: attribute (*dat.* to); substitute (*statt* for); '2ung *f* substitution.

Unterschied ['untərʃiːt] *m* (-[e]s/-e) difference; distinction; *zum* ~ *von* in distinction from *or* to; '2lich *adj.* different; differential; variable, varying; '2slos *adj.* indiscriminate; undiscriminating.

unter'schlag|en *v/t.* (*irr. schlagen, no* -ge-, *h*) embezzle; suppress (*truth, etc.*); 2ung *f* (-/-en) embezzlement; suppression.

'Unterschlupf *m* (-[e]s/ᵘe, -e) shelter, refuge.

unter'schreiben *v/t.* and *v/i.* (*irr. schreiben, no* -ge-, *h*) sign.

'Unterschrift *f* signature.

'Untersee|boot ⚓, ✖ *n* s. U-Boot; '~kabel *n* submarine cable.

unter'setzt *adj.* thick-set, squat.

unterst *adj.* ['untərst] lowest, undermost.

'Unterstand ✖ *m* shelter, dug-out.

unter'stehen *v/i.* (*irr. stehen, no* -ge-, *h*) **1.** *v/i.* (*dat.*) be subordinate to; be subject to (*law, etc.*); **2.** *v/refl.* dare; *untersteh dich!* don't you dare!; ~stellen *v/t.* **1.** ['~ʃtelən] (*sep.*, -ge-, *h*) put *or* under; garage (*car*); *sich* ~ take shelter (*vor dat.* from); **2.** [~'ʃtelən] (*no* -ge-, *h*) (pre)suppose, assume; impute (*dat.*

to); *j-m* ~ ✖ put (*troops, etc.*) under s.o.'s command; 2'stellung *f* (-/-en) assumption, supposition; imputation; ~'streichen *v/t.* (*irr. streichen, no* -ge-, *h*) underline, underscore (*both a. fig.*).

unter'stütz|en *v/t.* (*no* -ge-, *h*) support; back up; 2ung *f* (-/-en) support (*a.* ✖); assistance, aid; relief.

unter'such|en *v/t.* (*no* -ge-, *h*) examine (*a.* 🗗); inquire into, investigate (*a.* 🗗🗗); explore; 🗗🗗 try; analy|se, *Am.* -ze (*a.* 🗗); 2ung *f* (-/-en) examination (*a.* 🗗); inquiry (*gen.* into), investigation (*a.* 🗗🗗); exploration; analysis (*a.* 🗗).

Unter'suchungs|gefangene *m* prisoner on remand; ~gefängnis *n* remand prison; ~haft *f* detention on remand; ~richter *m* investigating judge.

Untertan ['untərtaːn] *m* (-s, -en/-en) subject.

untertänig *adj.* ['untərtɛːnıç] submissive.

'Unter|tasse *f* saucer; '2tauchen (*sep.*, -ge-) **1.** *v/i.* (*sein*) dive, dip; duck; *fig.* disappear; **2.** *v/t.* (*h*) duck.

'Unterteil *n, m* lower part.

unter'teil|en *v/t.* (*no* -ge-, *h*) subdivide; 2ung *f* subdivision.

'Unter|titel *m* subheading; subtitle; *a.* caption (*of film*); '~ton *m* undertone; '2vermieten *v/t.* (*no* -ge-, *h*) sublet.

unter'wander|n *pol. v/t.* (*no* -ge-, *h*) infiltrate; 2ung *pol. f* infiltration.

'Unterwäsche *f s.* Unterkleidung.

unterwegs *adv.* [untər've:ks] on the *or* one's way.

unter'weis|en *v/t.* (*irr. weisen, no* -ge-, *h*) instruct (*in dat.* in); 2ung *f* instruction.

'Unterwelt *f* underworld (*a. fig.*).

unter'werf|en *v/t.* (*irr. werfen, no* -ge-, *h*) subdue (*dat.* to), subjugate (to); subject (to); submit (to); *sich* ~ submit (to); 2ung *f* (-/-en) subjugation; subjection; submission (*unter acc.* to).

unterworfen *adj.* [untər'vɔrfən] subject (*dat.* to).

unterwürfig *adj.* [untər'vyrfıç] submissive; subservient; 2keit *f* (-/*no pl.*) submissiveness; subservience.

unter'zeichn|en *v/t.* (*no* -ge-, *h*) sign; 2er *m* signer, *the* undersigned; subscriber (*gen.* to); signatory (*gen.* to treaty); 2erstaat *m* signatory state; 2ete *m, f* (-n/-n) *the* undersigned; 2ung *f* signature, signing.

unterziehen *v/t.* (*irr. ziehen*) **1.** ['~tsiːən] (*sep.*, -ge-, *h*) put on underneath; **2.** [~'tsiːən] (*no* -ge-, *h*) subject (*dat.* to); *sich e-r Operation* ~ undergo an operation; *sich e-r Prüfung* ~ go in *or* sit for an examination; *sich der Mühe* ~ *zu inf.* take the trouble to *inf.*

'**Untiefe** f shallow, shoal.
'**Untier** n monster (a. fig.).
un|tilgbar adj. [un'tilkbɑːr] indelible; † government annuities: irredeemable; ~'**tragbar** adj. unbearable, intolerable; costs: prohibitive; ~'**trennbar** adj. inseparable.
'**untreu** adj. untrue (dat. to), disloyal (to); husband, wife: unfaithful (to); '~e f disloyalty; unfaithfulness, infidelity.
un'tröstlich adj. inconsolable, disconsolate; ~**trüglich** adj. [~'tryːklɪç] infallible, unerring.
'**Untugend** f vice, bad habit.
un|über'legt adj. ['un⁹yːbər-] inconsiderate, thoughtless; '~**sichtlich** adj. badly arranged; difficult to survey; involved; mot. corner: blind; ~'**trefflich** adj. unsurpassable; ~**windlich** adj. [~'vintlɪç] invincible; fortress: impregnable; obstacle, etc.: insurmountable; difficulties, etc.: insuperable.
unum|gänglich adj. [un⁹um'gɛŋlɪç] absolutely necessary; ~**schränkt** adj. [~'ʃrɛŋkt] absolute; ~**stößlich** adj. [~'ʃtøːsliç] irrefutable; incontestable; irrevocable; ~**wunden** adj. ['~vundən] frank, plain.
ununterbrochen adj. ['un⁹untərbrɔxən] uninterrupted; incessant.
unver|'änderlich adj. unchangeable; invariable; ~'**antwortlich** adj. irresponsible, inexcusable; ~'**besserlich** adj. incorrigible; '~**bindlich** adj. not binding or obligatory; answer, etc.: non-committal; ~**blümt** adj. [~'blyːmt] plain, blunt; ~**bürgt** adj. [~'byrkt] unwarranted; news: unconfirmed; '~**dächtig** adj. unsuspected; '~**daulich** adj. indigestible (a. fig.); '~**dient** adj. undeserved; '~**dorben** adj. unspoiled, unspoilt; fig.: uncorrupted; pure, innocent; ~**drossen** adj. indefatigable, unflagging; '~**dünnt** adj. undiluted, Am. a. straight; ~'**einbar** adj. incompatible; '~**fälscht** adj. unadulterated; fig. genuine; ~**fänglich** adj. ['~fɛŋlɪç] not captious; ~**froren** adj. ['~froːrən] unabashed, impudent; '2**frorenheit** f (-/-en) impudence, F cheek; ~**gänglich** adj. imperishable; ~'**geßlich** adj. unforgettable; ~'**gleichlich** adj. incomparable; '~**hältnismäßig** adj. disproportionate; '~**heiratet** adj. unmarried, single; '~**hofft** adj. unhoped-for, unexpected; '~**hohlen** adj. unconcealed; '~**käuflich** adj. unsal(e)able; not for sale; ~'**kennbar** adj. unmistakable; '~**letzbar** adj. invulnerable; fig. a. inviolable; ~**meidlich** adj. [~'maitlɪç] inevitable; '~**mindert** adj. undiminished; '~**mittelt** adj. abrupt.

'**Unvermögen** n (-s/no pl.) inability; impotence; '2d adj. impecunious, without means.
'**unvermutet** adj. unexpected.
'**Unver|nunft** f unreasonableness, absurdity; '2**nünftig** adj. unreasonable, absurd; '2**richteterdinge** adv. without having achieved one's object.
'**unverschämt** adj. impudent, impertinent; '2**heit** f (-/-en) impudence, impertinence.
'**unver|schuldet** adj. not in debt; through no fault of mine, etc.; '~**sehens** adv. unawares, suddenly, all of a sudden; ~**sehrt** adj. ['~zeːrt] uninjured; '~**söhnlich** adj. implacable, irreconcilable; '~**sorgt** adj. unprovided for; '2**stand** m injudiciousness; folly, stupidity; '~**ständig** adj. injudicious; foolish; '~**ständlich** adj. unintelligible; incomprehensible; das ist mir ~ that is beyond me; '~**sucht** adj.: nichts ~ lassen leave nothing undone; '~**träglich** adj. unsociable; quarrelsome; '~**wandt** adj. steadfast; ~**wundbar** adj. [~'vuntbɑːr] invulnerable; ~**wüstlich** adj. [~'vyːstlɪç] indestructible; fig. irrepressible; ~**zagt** adj. ['~tsaːkt] intrepid, undaunted; ~'**zeihlich** adj. unpardonable; ~'**zinslich** adj. bearing no interest; non-interest-bearing; ~**züglich** adj. [~'tsyːklɪç] immediate, instant.
'**unvollendet** adj. unfinished.
'**unvollkommen** adj. imperfect; '2**heit** f imperfection.
'**unvollständig** adj. incomplete; '2**keit** f (-/no pl.) incompleteness.
'**unvorbereitet** adj. unprepared; extempore.
'**unvoreingenommen** adj. unbias(s)ed, unprejudiced; '2**heit** f freedom from prejudice.
'**unvor|hergesehen** adj. unforeseen; ~**schriftsmäßig** adj. irregular.
'**unvorsichtig** adj. incautious; imprudent; '2**keit** f incautiousness; imprudence.
'**unvor|stellbar** adj. unimaginable; '~**teilhaft** adj. unprofitable; dress, etc.: unbecoming.
'**unwahr** adj. untrue; '2**heit** f untruth.
'**unwahrscheinlich** adj. improbable, unlikely; '2**keit** f (-/-en) improbability, unlikelihood.
'**un|wegsam** adj. pathless, impassable; '~**weit** prp. (gen. or von) not far from; '2**wesen** n (-s/no pl.) nuisance; sein ~ treiben be up to one's tricks; '~**wesentlich** adj. unessential, immaterial (für to); '2**wetter** n thunderstorm; '~**wichtig** adj. unimportant, insignificant.
unwider|legbar adj. [unviːdər'leːk-

ba:r] irrefutable; **~'ruflich** *adj.* irrevocable (*a.* ✝).

unwider'stehlich *adj.* irresistible; 2keit *f* (-/*no pl.*) irresistibility.

unwieder'bringlich *adj.* irretrievable.

'Unwille *m* (-ns/*no pl.*), **~en** *m* (-s/*no pl.*) indignation (*über acc.* at), displeasure (at, over); 2ig *adj.* indignant (*über acc.* at), displeased (at, with); unwilling; **'2kürlich** *adj.* involuntary.

'unwirklich *adj.* unreal.

'unwirksam *adj.* ineffective, inefficient; *laws, rules, etc.*: inoperative; 🧬 inactive; **'2keit** *f* (-/*no pl.*) ineffectiveness, inefficiency; 🧬 inactivity.

unwirsch *adj.* ['unvirʃ] testy.

'unwirt|lich *adj.* inhospitable, desolate; **'~schaftlich** *adj.* uneconomic(al).

'unwissen|d *adj.* ignorant; **'2heit** *f* (-/*no pl.*) ignorance; **'~tlich** *adj.* unwitting, unknowing.

'unwohl *adj.* unwell, indisposed; **'2sein** *n* (-s/*no pl.*) indisposition.

'unwürdig *adj.* unworthy (*gen.* of).

un|zählig *adj.* [un'tsɛːlɪç] innumerable; **'2zart** *adj.* indelicate.

Unze ['untsə] *f* (-/-n) ounce.

'Unzeit *f*: *zur* ~ inopportunely; **'2-gemäß** *adj.* old-fashioned; inopportune; **'2ig** *adj.* untimely; unseasonable; *fruit*: unripe.

unzer|'brechlich *adj.* unbreakable; **~'reißbar** *adj.* untearable; **~'stör-bar** *adj.* indestructible; **~'trenn-lich** *adj.* inseparable.

'un|ziemlich *adj.* unseemly; **'2-zucht** *f* (-/*no pl.*) lewdness; ♊ sexual offen|ce, *Am.* -se; **'~züchtig** *adj.* lewd; obscene.

'unzufrieden *adj.* discontented (*mit* with), dissatisfied (with, at); **'2heit** *f* discontent, dissatisfaction.

'unzugänglich *adj.* inaccessible.

'unzulänglich *adj.* ['untsulɛnlɪç] insufficient; **'2keit** *f* (-/-en) insufficiency; shortcoming.

'unzulässig *adj.* inadmissible; *esp.* ♊ *influence*: undue.

'unzurechnungsfähig *adj.* irresponsible; **'2keit** *f* irresponsibility.

'unzu|reichend *adj.* insufficient; **'~sammenhängend** *adj.* incoherent; **'~träglich** *adj.* unwholesome; **'~treffend** *adj.* incorrect; inapplicable (*auf acc.* to).

'unzuverlässig *adj.* unreliable, untrustworthy; *friend*: *a.* uncertain; **'2keit** *f* unreliability, untrustworthiness.

'unzweckmäßig *adj.* inexpedient; **'2keit** *f* inexpediency.

'un|zweideutig *adj.* unequivocal; unambiguous; **'~zweifelhaft 1.** *adj.* undoubted, undubitable; **2.** *adv.* doubtless.

üppig *adj.* ['ypɪç] 🌿 luxuriant, exuberant, opulent; *food*: luxurious, opulent; *figure*: voluptuous; **'2keit** *f* (-/🜹-en) luxuriance, luxuriancy, exuberance; voluptuousness.

ur|alt *adj.* ['uːrʔalt] very old; (as) old as the hills; **2aufführung** ['uːrʔ-] *f* world première.

Uran [u'raːn] *n* (-s/*no pl.*) uranium.

urbar *adj.* ['uːrbaːr] arable, cultivable; ~ *machen* reclaim; **'2ma-chung** *f* (-/-en) reclamation.

'Ur|bevölkerung *f* aborigines *pl.*; **'~bild** *n* original, prototype; **'2-eigen** *adj.* one's very own; **'~enkel** *m* great-grandson; **'~großeltern** *pl.* great-grandparents *pl.*; **'~groß-mutter** *f* great-grandmother; **'~großvater** *m* great-grandfather.

'Urheber *m* (-s/-) author; **'~recht** *n* copyright (*an dat.* in); **'~schaft** *f* (-/*no pl.*) authorship.

Urin [u'riːn] *m* (-s/-e) urine; **2ieren** [.i'niːrən] *v/i.* (*no* -ge-, *h*) urinate.

'Urkund|e *f* document; deed; **'~en-fälschung** *f* forgery of documents; **2lich** *adj.* ['.tlɪç] documentary.

Urlaub ['uːrlaup] *m* (-[e]s/-e) léave (of absence) (*a.* ✂); holiday(s *pl.*), *esp. Am.* vacation; **~er** ['.bər] *m* (-s/-) holiday-maker, *esp. Am.* vacationist, vacationer.

Urne ['urnə] *f* (-/-n) urn; ballotbox.

'ur|plötzlich 1. *adj.* very sudden, abrupt; **2.** *adv.* all of a sudden; **'2sache** *f* cause; reason; *keine* ~! don't mention it, *Am. a.* you are welcome; **'~sächlich** *adj.* causal; **'2schrift** *f* original (text); **'2-sprung** *m* origin, source; **'~sprünglich** *adj.* ['.ʃprʏŋlɪç] original; **'2stoff** *m* primary matter.

Urteil ['urtaɪl] *n* (-s/-e) judg(e)-ment; ♊ *a.* sentence; *meinem* ~ *nach* in my judg(e)ment; *sich ein* ~ *bilden* form a judg(e)ment (*über acc.* of, on); **'2en** *v/i.* (ge-, *h*) judge (*über acc.* of; *nach* by, from); **'~s-kraft** *f* (-/🜹-e) discernment.

'Ur|text *m* original (text); **'~wald** *m* primeval or virgin forest; **2-wüchsig** *adj.* ['.vyːksɪç] original; *fig.*: natural; rough; **'~zeit** *f* primitive times *pl.*

Utensilien [uten'ziːljən] *pl.* utensils *pl.*

Utop|ie [uto'piː] *f* (-/-n) Utopia; **2isch** *adj.* [u'toːpiʃ] Utopian, utopian.

V

Vagabund [vaga'bunt] *m* (-en/-en) vagabond, vagrant, tramp, *Am.* hobo, F bum.

Vakuum ['vɑːkuʔum] *n* (-s/*Vakua, Vakuen*) vacuum.

Valuta ✝ [va'luːta] *f* (-/*Valuten*) value; currency.

Vanille [va'niljə] *f* (-/*no pl.*) vanilla.

variabel *adj.* [vari'ɑːbəl] variable.

Varia|nte [vari'antə] *f* (-/-n) variant; **~tion** [~'tsjoːn] *f* (-/-en) variation.

Varieté [varie'teː] *n* (-s/-s), **~theater** *n* variety theatre, music-hall, *Am.* vaudeville theater.

variieren [vari'iːrən] *v/i.* and *v/t.* (*no -ge-, h*) vary.

Vase ['vɑːzə] *f* (-/-n) vase.

Vater ['fɑːtər] *m* (-s/ᵁ) father; **~land** *n* native country *or* land, mother country; **'~landsliebe** *f* patriotism.

väterlich *adj.* ['fɛːtərliç] fatherly, paternal.

'Vater|schaft *f* (-/*no pl.*) paternity, fatherhood; **'~unser** *eccl. n* (-s/-) Lord's Prayer.

Vati ['fɑːti] *m* (-s/-s) dad(dy).

Veget|arier [vege'tɑːrjər] *m* (-s/-) vegetarian; **~arisch** *adj.* vegetarian; **~ation** [~a'tsjoːn] *f* (-/-en) vegetation; **~ieren** [~'tiːrən] *v/i.* (*no -ge-, h*) vegetate.

Veilchen ♦ ['faɪlçən] *n* (-s/-) violet.

Vene *anat.* ['veːnə] *f* (-/-n) vein.

Ventil [vɛn'tiːl] *n* (-s/-e) valve (*a. ♪*); ♪ stop (*of organ*); *fig.* vent, outlet; **~ation** [~ila'tsjoːn] *f* (-/-en) ventilation; **~ator** [~i'lɑːtər] *m* (-s/-en) ventilator, fan.

verab|folgen [fɛr'ap-] *v/t.* (*no -ge-, h*) deliver; give; ⊕ administer (*medicine*); **~reden** *v/t.* (*no -ge-, h*) agree upon, arrange; appoint, fix (*time, place*); sich ~ make an appointment, *Am.* F (have a) date; **Qredung** *f* (-/-en) agreement; arrangement; appointment, *Am.* F date; **~reichen** *v/t.* (*no -ge-, h*) s. *verabfolgen*; **~scheuen** *v/t.* (*no -ge-, h*) abhor, detest, loathe; **~schieden** [~'ʃiːdən] *v/t.* (*no -ge-, h*) dismiss; retire (*officer*); ✕ discharge (*troops*); *parl.* pass (*bill*); sich ~ take leave (von of), say good-bye (to); **Qschiedung** *f* (-/-en) dismissal; discharge; passing.

ver|'ac͟ten *v/t.* (*no -ge-, h*) despise; **~ächtlich** *adj.* [~'ɛçtliç] contemptuous; contemptible; **Q'achtung** *f* contempt; **~allgemeinern** [~ʔalgə'maɪnərn] *v/t.* (*no -ge-, h*) generalize; **~altet** *adj.* antiquated, obsolete, out of date.

Veranda [ve'randa] *f* (-/*Veranden*) veranda(h), *Am. a.* porch.

veränder|lich *adj.* [fɛr'endərliç] changeable; variable (*a. ♣, gr.*); **~n** *v/t.* and *v/refl.* (*no -ge-, h*) alter, change; vary; **Qung** *f* change, alteration (*in dat.* in; *an dat.* to); variation.

verängstigt *adj.* [fɛr'ɛŋstiçt] intimidated, scared.

ver'anlag|en *v/t.* (*no -ge-, h*) of *taxation*: assess; **~t** *adj.* [~kt] talented; **Qung** [~gʊŋ] *f* (-/-en) assessment; *fig.* talent(s *pl.*); ✂ predisposition.

ver'anlass|en *v/t.* (*no -ge-, h*) cause, occasion; arrange; **Qung** *f* (-/-en) occasion, cause; *auf m-e* ~ at my request *or* suggestion.

ver|'anschaulichen *v/t.* (*no -ge-, h*) illustrate; **~'anschlagen** *v/t.* (*no -ge-, h*) rate, value, estimate (*all: auf acc.* at).

ver'anstalt|en *v/t.* (*no -ge-, h*) arrange, organize; give (*concert, ball, etc.*); **Qung** *f* (-/-en) arrangement; *sports:* event, meeting, *Am.* meet.

ver'antwort|en *v/t.* (*no -ge-, h*) take the responsibility for; account for; **~lich** *adj.* responsible; *j-n* ~ *machen für* hold s.o. responsible for.

Ver'antwortung *f* (-/-en) responsibility; *die* ~ *tragen* be responsible; *zur* ~ *ziehen* call to account; **Qslos** *adj.* irresponsible.

ver|'arbeiten *v/t.* (*no -ge-, h*) work up; ⊕ process, manufacture (*both: zu* into); digest (*food*) (*a. fig.*); **~'ärgern** *v/t.* (*no -ge-, h*) vex, annoy.

ver'arm|en *v/i.* (*no -ge-, sein*) become poor; **~t** *adj.* impoverished.

ver|'ausgaben *v/t.* (*no -ge-, h*) spend (*money*); sich ~ run short of money; *fig.* spend o.s.; **~'äußern** *v/t.* (*no -ge-, h*) sell; alienate.

Verb *gr.* [vɛrp] *n* (-s/-en) verb.

Ver'band *m* (-[e]s/ᵁe) ♣ dressing, bandage; association, union; ✕ formation, unit; **~(s)kasten** *m* first-aid box; **~(s)zeug** *n* dressing (material).

ver'bann|en *v/t.* (*no -ge-, h*) banish (*a. fig.*), exile; **Qung** *f* (-/-en) banishment, exile.

ver|barrikadieren [fɛrbarika'diːrən] *v/t.* (*no -ge-, h*) barricade; block (*street, etc.*); **~'bergen** *v/t.* (*irr. bergen, no -ge-, h*) conceal, hide.

ver'besser|n *v/t.* (*no -ge-, h*) improve; correct; **Qung** *f* improvement; correction.

ver'beug|en *v/refl.* (*no -ge-, h*) bow (*vor dat.* to); **Qung** *f* bow.

ver|'biegen *v/t.* (*irr. biegen, no*

-ge-, h) bend, twist, distort; ~
'bieten v/t. (irr. bieten, no -ge-, h)
forbid, prohibit; ~'billigen v/t.
(no -ge-, h) reduce in price,
cheapen.

ver'bind|en v/t. (irr. binden, no
-ge-, h) ✄ dress; tie (together);
bind (up); link (mit to); join, unite,
combine; connect (a. teleph.);
teleph. put s.o. through (mit to);
j-m die Augen ~ blindfold s.o.; sich
~ join, unite, combine (a. ♊️); ich
bin Ihnen sehr verbunden I am
greatly obliged to you; falsch verbunden! teleph. wrong number!;
~lich adj. [~tlıç] obligatory; obliging; 2lichkeit f (-/-en) obligation,
liability; obligingness, civility.

Ver'bindung f union; alliance;
combination; association (of ideas);
connexion, (Am. only) connection
(a. teleph., 🚿, ⚗️, ⊕); relation;
communication (a. teleph.); 🜍
compound; geschäftliche ~ business relations pl.; teleph.: ~ bekommen (haben) get (be) through;
die ~ verlieren mit lose touch with;
in ~ bleiben (treten) keep (get) in
touch (mit with); sich in ~ setzen
mit communicate with, esp. Am.
contact s.o.; ~sstraße f communication road, feeder road; ~stür f
communication door.

ver'bissen adj. [fɛr'bisən] dogged;
crabbed; ~'bitten v/refl. (irr. bitten,
no -ge-, h): das verbitte ich mir!
I won't suffer or stand that!

ver'bitter|n v/t. (no -ge-, h) em-
bitter; 2ung f (-/%-en) bitterness
(of heart).

verblassen [fɛr'blasən] v/i. (no
-ge-, sein) fade (a. fig.).

Verbleib [fɛr'blaıp] m (-[e]s/no pl.)
whereabouts sg., pl.; 2en [~bən] v/i.
(irr. bleiben, no -ge-, sein) be left,
remain.

ver'blend|en v/t. (no -ge-, h) △
face (wall, etc.); fig. blind, delude;
2ung f (-/%-en) △ facing; fig.
blindness, delusion. [faded.]

verblichen adj. [fɛr'blıçən] colour:)

verblüff|en [fɛr'blyfən] v/t. (no
-ge-, h) amaze; perplex; puzzle;
dumbfound; 2ung f (-/%-en)
amazement, perplexity.

ver|'blühen v/i. (no -ge-, sein) fade,
wither; ~'bluten v/i. (no -ge-, sein)
bleed to death.

ver'borgen adj. hidden; secret;
2heit f (-/no pl.) concealment,
secrecy.

Verbot [fɛr'bo:t] n (-[e]s/-e) prohibition; 2en adj. forbidden, pro-
hibited; Rauchen ~ no smoking.

Ver'brauch m (-[e]s/%-e) consumption (an dat. of); 2en v/t. (no
-ge-, h) consume, use up; wear out;
~er m (-s/-) consumer; 2t adj. air:
stale; p. worn out.

ver'brechen 1. v/t. (irr. brechen,
no -ge-, h) commit; was hat er ver-
brochen? what is his offen|ce, Am.
-se?, what has he done?; 2. ♀ n
(-s/-) crime, offen|ce, Am. -se.

Ver'brecher m (-s/-) criminal;
2isch adj. criminal; ~tum n (-s/no
pl.) criminality.

ver'breit|en v/t. (no -ge-, h) spread,
diffuse; shed (light, warmth, happiness); sich ~ spread; sich ~ über
(acc.) enlarge (up)on (theme); ~ern
v/t. and v/refl. (no -ge-, h) widen,
broaden; 2ung f (-/%-en) spread
(-ing), diffusion.

ver'brenn|en (irr. brennen, no -ge-)
1. v/i. (sein) burn; 2. v/t. (h) burn
(up); cremate (corpse); 2ung f
(-/-en) burning, combustion;
cremation (of corpse); wound: burn.

ver'bringen v/t. (irr. bringen, no
-ge-, h) spend, pass.

verbrüder|n [fɛr'bry:dərn] v/refl.
(no -ge-, h) fraternize; 2ung f
(-/-en) fraternization.

ver|'brühen v/t. (no -ge-, h) scald;
sich ~ scald o.s.; ~'buchen v/t.
(no -ge-, h) book.

Verbum gr. ['vɛrbum] n (-s/Verba)
verb.

verbünden [fɛr'byndən] v/refl. (no
-ge-, h) ally o.s. (mit to, with).

Verbundenheit [fɛr'bundənhaıt] f
(-/no pl.) bonds pl., ties pl.; solidarity; affection.

Ver'bündete m, f (-n/-n) ally, con-
federate; die ~n pl. the allies pl.

ver|'bürgen v/t. (no -ge-, h) guar-
antee, warrant; sich ~ für answer
or vouch for; ~'büßen v/t. (no -ge-,
h): e-e Strafe ~ serve a sentence,
serve (one's) time.

Verdacht [fɛr'daxt] m (-[e]s/no pl.)
suspicion; in ~ haben suspect.

verdächtig adj. [fɛr'dɛçtıç] sus-
pected (gen. of); pred. suspect;
suspicious; ~en [~gən] v/t. (no
-ge-, h) suspect s.o. (gen. of); cast
suspicion on; 2ung [~guŋ] f (-/-en)
suspicion; insinuation.

verdamm|en [fɛr'damən] v/t. (no
-ge-, h) condemn, damn (a. eccl.);
2nis f (-/no pl.) damnation; ~t
1. adj. damned; F: ~! damn (it)!,
confound it!; 2. F adv.: ~ kalt
beastly cold; 2ung f (-/%-en) con-
demnation, damnation.

ver|'dampfen (no -ge-) v/t. (h) and
v/i. (sein) evaporate; ~'danken v/t.
(no -ge-, h): j-m et. ~ owe s.th. to
s.o.

verdarb [fɛr'darp] pret. of verderben.

verdau|en [fɛr'dauən] v/t. (no -ge-,
h) digest; ~lich adj. digestible;
leicht ~ easy to digest, light; 2ung
f (-/no pl.) digestion; 2ungsstö-
rung f indigestion.

Ver'deck n (-[e]s/-e) ⚓ deck;

hood (of carriage, car, etc.); top (of vehicle); 2en v/t. (no -ge-, h) cover; conceal, hide.

ver|'denken v/t. (irr. denken, no -ge-, h): ich kann es ihm nicht ~, daß I cannot blame him for ger.

Verderb [fɛr'dɛrp] m (-[e]s/no pl.) ruin; 2en [∼bən] 1. v/i. (irr., no -ge-, sein) spoil (a. fig.); rot; meat, etc.: go bad; fig. perish; 2. v/t. (irr., no -ge-, h) spoil; fig. a.: corrupt; ruin; er will es mit niemandem ~ he tries to please everybody; sich den Magen ~ upset one's stomach; ~en [∼bən] n (-s/no pl.) ruin; 2lich adj. [∼pliç] pernicious; food: perishable; ~nis [∼pnis] f (-/∼-se) corruption; depravity; 2t adj. [∼pt] corrupted, depraved.

ver|'deutlichen v/t. (no -ge-, h) make plain or clear; ~'dichten v/t. (no -ge-, h) condense; sich ~ condense; suspicion: grow stronger; ~'dicken v/t. and v/refl. (no -ge-, h) thicken; ~'dienen v/t. (no -ge-, h) merit, deserve; earn (money).

Ver'dienst (-es/-e) 1. m gain, profit; earnings pl.; 2. n merit; es ist sein ~, daß it is owing to him that; 2voll adj. meritorious, deserving; ~spanne ✝ f profit margin.

ver|'dient adj. p. of merit; (well-) deserved; sich ~ gemacht haben um deserve well of; ~'dolmetschen v/t. (no -ge-, h) interpret (a. fig.); ~'doppeln v/t. and v/refl. (no -ge-, h) double.

verdorben [fɛr'dɔrbən] 1. p.p. of verderben; 2. adj. meat: tainted; stomach: disordered, upset; fig. corrupt, depraved.

ver|'dorren [fɛr'dɔrən] v/i. (no -ge-, sein) wither (up); ~'drängen v/t. (no -ge-, h) push away, thrust aside; fig. displace; psych. repress; ~'drehen v/t. (no -ge-, h) distort, twist (both a. fig.); roll (eyes); fig. pervert; j-m den Kopf ~ turn s.o.'s head; ~'dreht F fig. adj. crazy; ~'dreifachen v/t. and v/refl. (no -ge-, h) triple.

verdrieß|en [fɛr'dri:sən] v/t. (irr., no -ge-, h) vex, annoy; ~lich adj. vexed, annoyed; sulky; thing: annoying.

ver|droß [fɛr'drɔs] pret. of verdrießen; ~'drossen [∼'drɔsən] 1. p.p. of verdrießen; 2. adj. sulky; listless.

ver'drucken typ. v/t. (no -ge-, h) misprint.

Verdruß [fɛr'drus] m (Verdrusses/∼ Verdrusse) vexation, annoyance.

ver|'dummen (no -ge-) 1. v/t. (h) make stupid; 2. v/i. (sein) become stupid.

ver|'dunk|eln v/t. (no -ge-, h) darken, obscure (both a. fig.); black out (window); sich ~ darken;

2(e)lung f (-/∼-en) darkening; obscuration; black-out; ⚖ collusion.

ver|'dünnen v/t. (no -ge-, h) thin; dilute (liquid); ~'dunsten v/i. (no -ge-, sein) volatilize, evaporate; ~'dursten v/i. (no -ge-, sein) die of thirst; ~'dutzt adj. [∼'dutst] nonplussed.

ver|'ed|eln v/t. (no -ge-, h) ennoble; refine; improve; ✿ graft; process (raw materials); 2(e)lung f (-/∼-en) refinement; improvement; processing.

ver|'ehr|en v/t. (no -ge-, h) revere, venerate; worship; admire, adore; 2er m (-s/-) worship(p)er; admirer, adorer; 2ung f (-/∼-en) reverence, veneration; worship; adoration.

vereidigen [fɛr'aɪdɪgən] v/t. (no -ge-, h) swear (witness); at entrance into office: swear s.o. in.

Verein [fɛr'aɪn] m (-[e]s/-e) union; society, association; club.

ver|'einbar adj. compatible (mit with), consistent (with); ~en v/t. (no -ge-, h) agree upon, arrange; 2ung f (-/-en) agreement, arrangement.

ver|'einen v/t. (no -ge-, h) s. vereinigen.

ver|'einfach|en v/t. (no -ge-, h) simplify; 2ung f (-/-en) simplification.

ver|'einheitlichen v/t. (no -ge-, h) unify, standardize.

ver|'einig|en v/t. (no -ge-, h) unite, join; associate; sich ~ unite, join; associate o.s.; 2ung f 1. (-/∼-en) union; 2. (-/-en) union; society, association.

ver|'ein|samen v/i. (no -ge-, sein) grow lonely or solitary; ~zelt adj. isolated; sporadic.

ver|'eiteln v/t. (no -ge-, h) frustrate; ~'ekeln v/t. (no -ge-, h): er hat mir das Essen verekelt he spoilt my appetite; ~'enden v/i. (no -ge-, sein) animals: die, perish; ~enge(r)n [∼'eŋə(r)n] v/t. and v/refl. (no -ge-, h) narrow.

ver|'erb|en v/t. (no -ge-, h) leave, bequeath; biol. transmit; sich ~ be hereditary; sich ~ auf (acc.) descend (up)on; 2ung f (-/∼-en) biol. transmission; physiol. heredity; 2ungslehre f genetics.

ver|'ewig|en [fɛr'e:vɪgən] v/t. (no -ge-, h) perpetuate; ~t adj. [∼çt] deceased, late.

ver|'fahren 1. v/i. (irr. fahren, no -ge-, sein) proceed; ~ mit deal with; 2. v/t. (irr. fahren, no -ge-, h) mismanage, muddle, bungle; sich ~ miss one's way; 3. 2 n (-s/-) procedure; proceeding(s pl. ⚖); ⊕ process.

Ver'fall m (-[e]s/no pl.) decay, decline; dilapidation (of house, etc.);

$_\text{g's}^\text{g's}$ forfeiture; expiration; maturity (*of bill of exchange*); **£en 1.** *v/i.* (*irr.* fallen, *no* -ge-, sein) decay; *house*: dilapidate; *document*, *etc.*: expire; *pawn*: become forfeited; *right*: lapse; *bill of exchange*: fall due; *sick person*: waste away; ~ auf (*acc.*) hit upon (*idea*, *etc.*); ~ in (*acc.*) fall into; j-m ~ become s.o.'s slave; **2.** *adj.* ruinous; addicted (*dat.* to *drugs*, *etc.*); **~serscheinung** [fɛr'fals⁹-] *f* symptom of decline; **~tag** *m* day of payment.

ver|'fälschen *v/t.* (*no* -ge-, h) falsify; adulterate (*wine*, *etc.*); **~fäng-lich** *adj.* [~'fɛŋliç] *question*: captious, insidious; risky; embarrassing; **~färben** *v/refl.* (*no* -ge-, h) change colo(u)r.

ver|'fass|en *v/t.* (*no* -ge-, h) compose, write; **£er** *m* (-s/-) author.

Ver|'fassung *f* state, condition; *pol.* constitution; disposition (*of mind*); **£smäßig** *adj.* constitutional; **£s-widrig** *adj.* unconstitutional.

ver|'faul|en *v/i.* (*no* -ge-, sein) rot, decay; **~fechten** *v/t.* (*irr.* fechten, *no* -ge-, h) defend, advocate.

ver|'fehl|en *v/t.* (*no* -ge-, h) miss; **£ung** *f* (-/-en) offen|ce, *Am.* -se.

ver|'feinden [fɛr'faɪndən] *v/t.* (*no* -ge-, h) make enemies of; *sich* ~ mit make an enemy of; **~feinern** [~'faɪnərn] *v/t. and v/refl.* (*no* -ge-, h) refine; **~fertigen** [~'fɛrtɪgən] *v/t.* (*no* -ge-, h) make, manufacture, compose.

ver|'film|en *v/t.* (*no* -ge-, h) film, screen; **£ung** *f* (-/-en) film-version.

ver|'finstern *v/t.* (*no* -ge-, h) darken, obscure; *sich* ~ darken; **~flachen** (*no* -ge-) *v/i.* (sein *and* v/refl.* (h) (become) shallow (a. *fig.*); **~flechten** *v/t.* (*irr.* flechten, *no* -ge-, h) interlace; *fig.* involve; **~fliegen** (*irr.* fliegen, *no* -ge-) **1.** *v/i.* (sein) evaporate; *time*: fly; *fig.* vanish; **2.** *v/refl.* (h) *bird*: stray; $_\text{\sphericalangle}^\text{\sphericalangle}$ lose one's bearings, get lost; **~fließen** *v/i.* (*irr.* fließen, *no* -ge-, sein) *colours*: blend; *time*: elapse; **~flossen** *adj.* [~'flɔsən] *time*: past; F ein ~er Freund a late friend, an ex-friend.

ver|'fluch|en *v/t.* (*no* -ge-, h) curse, *Am.* F cuss; **~t** *adj.* damned; **~!** damn (it)!, confound it!

ver|'flüchtigen [fɛr'flʏçtɪgən] *v/t.* (*no* -ge-, h) volatilize; *sich* ~ evaporate (a. *fig.*); F *fig.* vanish; **~flüssigen** [~'flʏsɪgən] *v/t. and v/refl.* (*no* -ge-, h) liquefy.

ver|'folg|en *v/t.* (*no* -ge-, h) pursue; persecute; follow (*tracks*); trace; *thoughts*, *dream*: haunt; *gerichtlich* ~ prosecute; **£er** *m* (-s/-) pursuer; persecutor; **£ung** *f* (-/-en) pursuit; persecution; pursuance; *gericht-*

liche ~ prosecution; **£ungswahn** $^\text{x}$ *m* persecution mania.

ver|'frachten [fɛr'fraxtən] *v/t.* (*no* -ge-, h) freight, *Am.* a. ship (*goods*); **∯** ship; F j-n ~ in (*acc.*) bundle s.o. in(to) (*train*, *etc.*); **~froren** *adj.* chilled through; **~früht** *adj.* premature.

verfüg|bar *adj.* [fɛr'fy:kbaːr] available; **~en** [~gən] (*no* -ge-, h) **1.** *v/t.* decree, order; **2.** *v/i.*: ~ über (*acc.*) have at one's disposal; dispose of; **£ung** [~guŋ] *f* (-/-en) decree, order; disposal; j-m zur ~ stehen (*stellen*) be (place) at s.o.'s disposal.

ver|'führ|en *v/t.* (*no* -ge-, h) seduce; **£er** *m* (-s/-) seducer; **~erisch** *adj.* seductive; enticing, tempting; **£ung** *f* seduction.

vergangen *adj.* [fɛr'gaŋən] gone, past; *im* ~en *Jahr* last year; **£heit** *f* (-/-en) past; *gr.* past tense.

vergänglich *adj.* [fɛr'gɛnliç] transient, transitory.

vergas|en [fɛr'gaːzən] *v/t.* (*no* -ge-, h) gasify; gas *s.o.*; **£er** *mot.* *m* (-s/-) carburet(t)or.

vergaß [fɛr'gaːs] *pret.* of vergessen.

ver|'geb|en *v/t.* (*irr.* geben, *no* -ge-, h) give away (*an* j-n to s.o.); confer (on), bestow (on); place (*order*); forgive; *sich* et. ~ compromise one's dignity; **~ens** *adv.* [~s] in vain; **~lich** [~pliç] **1.** *adj.* vain; **2.** *adv.* in vain; **£ung** [~buŋ] *f* (-/⁹-en) bestowal, conferment (*both*: *an* *acc.* on); forgiveness, pardon.

vergegenwärtigen [fɛrge'gɛnˈvɛrtɪgən] *v/t.* (*no* -ge-, h) represent; *sich et.* ~ visualize s.th.

ver|'gehen 1. *v/i.* (*irr.* gehen, *no* -ge-, sein) pass (away); fade (away); ~ *vor* (*dat.*) die of; **2.** *v/refl.* (*irr.* gehen, *no* -ge-, h): *sich an* j-m ~ assault s.o.; violate s.o.; *sich gegen das Gesetz* ~ offend against or violate the law; **3.** **£** *n* (-s/-) offen|ce, *Am.* -se.

ver|'gelt|en *v/t.* (*irr.* gelten, *no* -ge-, h) repay, requite; reward; retaliate; **£ung** *f* (-/-en) requital; retaliation, retribution.

vergessen [fɛr'gɛsən] **1.** *v/t.* (*irr.*, *no* -ge-, h) forget; leave; **2.** *p.p.* of **1**; **£heit** *f* (-/*no pl.*): *in* ~ geraten sink *or* fall into oblivion.

vergeßlich *adj.* [fɛr'gɛsliç] forgetful.

vergeud|en [fɛr'gɔʏdən] *v/t.* (*no* -ge-, h) dissipate, squander, waste (*time*, *money*); **£ung** *f* (-/⁹-en) waste.

vergewaltig|en [fɛrgə'valtɪgən] *v/t.* (*no* -ge-, h) violate; rape; **£ung** *f* (-/-en) violation; rape.

ver|gewissern [fɛrgə'wɪsərn] *v/refl.* (*no* -ge-, h) make sure (e-r *Sache* of s.th.); ~'gießen v/t. (irr. gießen, no -ge-, h) shed (tears, blood); spill (liquid).

ver'gift|en v/t. (no -ge-, h) poison (a. fig.); sich ~ take poison; 2ung f (-/-en) poisoning.

Vergißmeinnicht ♀ [fɛr'gɪsmaɪn-nɪçt] n (-[e]s/-[e]) forget-me-not.

vergittern [fɛr'gɪtərn] v/t. (no -ge-, h) grate.

Vergleich [fɛr'glaɪç] m (-[e]s/-e) comparison; ⚖: agreement; compromise, composition; 2bar adj. comparable (mit to); 2en v/t. (irr. gleichen, no -ge-, h) compare (mit with, to); sich ~ mit ⚖ come to terms with; verglichen mit as against, compared to; 2sweise adv. comparatively.

vergnügen [fɛr'gny:gən] 1. v/t. (no -ge-, h) amuse; sich ~ enjoy o.s.; 2. 2 n (-s/-) pleasure, enjoyment; entertainment; ~ finden an (dat.) take pleasure in; viel ~! I have a good time! [gay.)

vergnügt adj. [fɛr'gny:kt] merry,)

Ver'gnügung f (-/-en) pleasure, amusement, entertainment; ~s-reise f pleasure-trip, tour; 2s-süchtig adj. pleasure-seeking.

ver|golden [fɛr'gɔldən] v/t. (no -ge-, h) gild; ~göttern fig. [~'gœtərn] v/t. (no -ge-, h) idolize, adore; ~graben v/t. (irr. graben, no -ge-, h) bury (a. fig.); sich ~ bury o.s.; ~greifen v/refl. (irr. greifen, no -ge-, h) sprain (one's hand, etc.); sich ~ an (dat.) lay (violent) hands on, attack, assault; embezzle (money); encroach upon (s.o.'s property); ~griffen adj. [~'grɪfən] goods: sold out; book: out of print.

vergrößer|n [fɛr'grø:sərn] v/t. (no -ge-, h) enlarge (a. phot.); opt. magnify; sich ~ enlarge; 2ung f 1. (-/-en) phot. enlargement; opt. magnification; 2. (-/-en) enlargement; increase; extension; 2ungs-glas n magnifying glass.

Vergünstigung [fɛr'gynstɪguŋ] f (-/-en) privilege.

vergüt|en [fɛr'gy:tən] v/t. (no -ge-, h) compensate (j-m et. s.o. for s.th.); reimburse (money spent); 2ung f (-/-en) compensation; reimbursement.

ver'haft|en v/t. (no -ge-, h) arrest; 2ung f (-/-en) arrest.

ver'halten 1. v/t. (irr. halten, no -ge-, h) keep back; catch or hold (one's breath); suppress, check; sich ~ thing: be; p. behave; sich ruhig ~ keep quiet; 2. 2 n (-s/no pl.) behavio(u)r, conduct.

Verhältnis [fɛr'hɛltnɪs] n (-ses/-se) proportion, rate; relation(s pl.) (zu with); F liaison, love-affair; F mistress; ~se pl. conditions pl., circumstances pl.; means pl.; 2mäßig

adv. in proportion; comparatively; ~wort gr. n (-[e]s/~er) preposition.

Ver'haltungsmaßregeln f/pl. instructions pl.

ver'hand|eln (no -ge-, h) 1. v/i. negotiate, treat (über acc., wegen for); ⚖ try (über et. s.th.); 2. v/t. discuss; 2lung f negotiation; discussion; ⚖ trial, proceedings pl.

ver'häng|en v/t. (no -ge-, h) cover (over), hang; inflict (punishment) (über acc. upon); 2nis n (-ses/-se) fate; ~nisvoll adj. fatal; disastrous.

ver|härmt [fɛr'hɛrmt] care-worn; ~harren [~'harən] v/i. (no -ge-, h, sein) persist (auf dat., bei, in dat. in), stick (to); ~'härten v/t. and v/refl. (no -ge-, h) harden; ~haßt adj. [~'hast] hated; hateful, odious; ~'hätscheln v/t. (no -ge-, h) coddle, pamper, spoil; ~'hauen v/t. (irr. hauen, no -ge-, h) thrash.

verheer|en [fɛr'he:rən] v/t. (no -ge-, h) devastate, ravage, lay waste; ~end fig. adj. disastrous; 2ung f (-/-en) devastation.

ver|hehlen [fɛr'he:lən] v/t. (no -ge-, h) s. verheimlichen; ~'heilen v/i. (no -ge-, sein) heal (up).

ver'heimlich|en v/t. (no -ge-, h) hide, conceal; 2ung f (-/~-en) concealment.

ver'heirat|en v/t. (no -ge-, h) marry (mit to); sich ~ marry; 2ung f (-/~-en) marriage.

ver'heiß|en v/t. (irr. heißen, no -ge-, h) promise; 2ung f (-/-en) promise; ~ungsvoll adj. promising.

ver'helfen v/i. (irr. helfen, no -ge-, h): j-m zu et. ~ help s.o. to s.th.

ver'herrlich|en v/t. (no -ge-, h) glorify; 2ung f (-/~-en) glorification.

ver|'hetzen v/t. (no -ge-, h) instigate; ~'hexen v/t. (no -ge-, h) bewitch.

ver'hinder|n v/t. (no -ge-, h) prevent; 2ung f (-/~-en) prevention.

ver'höhn|en v/t. (no -ge-, h) deride, mock (at), taunt; 2ung f (-/-en) derision, mockery.

Verhör ⚖ [fɛr'hø:r] n (-[e]s/-e) interrogation, questioning (of prisoners, etc.); examination; 2en v/t. (no -ge-, h) examine, hear; interrogate; sich ~ hear it wrong.

ver|'hüllen v/t. (no -ge-, h) cover, veil; ~'hungern v/i. (no -ge-, sein) starve; ~'hüten v/t. (no -ge-, h) prevent.

ver'irr|en v/refl. (no -ge-, h) go astray, lose one's way; ~t adj.: ~es Schaf stray sheep; 2ung fig. f (-/-en) aberration; error.

ver'jagen v/t. (no -ge-, h) drive away.

verjähr|en ⚖ [fɛr'jɛ:rən] v/i. (no -ge-, sein) become prescriptive;

ꭴung f (-/-en) limitation, (negative) prescription.

verjüngen [fɛr'jyŋən] v/t. (no -ge-, h) make young again, rejuvenate; reduce (scale); sich ~ grow young again, rejuvenate; taper off.

Ver'kauf m sale; ꭴen v/t. (no -ge-, h) sell; zu ~ for sale; sich gut ~ sell well.

Ver'käuf|er m seller; vendor; shop-assistant, salesman, Am. a. (sales-)clerk; ~erin f (-/-nen) seller; vendor; shop-assistant, saleswoman, shop girl, Am. a. (sales)clerk; ꭴlich adj. sal(e)able; for sale.

Ver'kaufs|automat m slot-machine, vending machine; ~schlager m best seller.

Verkehr [fɛr'keːr] m (-[e]s/~-e) traffic; transport(ation); communication; correspondence; ⚓, ⛴, ✈, etc.: service; commerce, trade; intercourse (a. sexually); aus dem ~ ziehen withdraw from service; withdraw (money) from circulation; ꭴen (no -ge-, h) 1. v/t. convert (in acc. into), turn (into); 2. v/i. ship, bus, etc.: run, ply (zwischen dat. between); bei j-m ~ go to or visit s.o.'s house; ~ in (dat.) frequent (public house, etc.); ~ mit associate or mix with; have (sexual) intercourse with.

Ver'kehrs|ader f arterial road; ~ampel f traffic lights pl., traffic signal; ~büro n tourist bureau; ~flugzeug n air liner; ~insel f refuge, island; ~minister m minister of transport; ~mittel n (means of) conveyance or transport, Am. transportation; ~polizist m traffic policeman or constable, sl. traffic cop; ꭴreich adj. congested with traffic, busy; ~schild n traffic sign; ~schutzmann m s. Verkehrs-polizist; ~stauung f, ~stockung f traffic block, traffic jam; ~störung f interruption of traffic; ⛴, etc.: breakdown; ~straße f thoroughfare; ~teilnehmer m road user; ~unfall m traffic accident; ~verein m tourist agency; ~verhältnisse f/pl. traffic conditions pl.; ~vorschrift f traffic regulation; ~wesen n (-s/no pl.) traffic; ~zeichen n traffic sign.

ver'kehrt adj. inverted, upside down; fig. wrong; ~'kennen v/t. (irr. kennen, no -ge-, h) mistake; misunderstand, misjudge.

Ver'kettung f (-/-en) concatenation (a. fig.).

ver'klagen ⚖ v/t. (no -ge-, h) sue (auf acc., wegen for); bring an action against s.o.; ~'kleben v/t. (no -ge-, h) paste s.th. up.

ver'kleid|en v/t. (no -ge-, h) disguise; ⊕: line; face; wainscot; encase; sich ~ disguise o.s.; ꭴung f

(-/-en) disguise; ⊕: lining; facing; panel(l)ing, wainscot(t)ing.

verkleiner|n [fɛr'klaınərn] v/t. (no -ge-, h) make smaller, reduce, diminish; fig. belittle, derogate; ꭴung f (-/-en) reduction, diminution; fig. derogation.

ver'|klingen v/i. (irr. klingen, no -ge-, sein) die away; ~knöchern [~'knœçərn] (no -ge-) 1. v/t. (h) ossify; 2. v/i. (sein) ossify; fig. a. fossilize; ~'knoten v/t. (no -ge-, h) knot; ~'knüpfen v/t. (no -ge-, h) knot or tie (together); fig. connect, combine; ~'kohlen (no -ge-) 1. v/t. (h) carbonize; char; F: j-n ~ pull s.o.'s leg; 2. v/i. (sein) char; ~'kommen 1. v/i. (irr. kommen, no -ge-, sein) decay; p.: go downhill or to the dogs; become demoralized; 2. adj. decayed; depraved, corrupt; ~'korken v/t. (no -ge-, h) cork (up).

ver'körper|n v/t. (no -ge-, h) personify, embody; represent; esp. thea. impersonate; ꭴung f (-/-en) personification, embodiment; impersonation.

ver'|krachen F v/refl. (no -ge-, h) fall out (mit with); ~'krampft adj. cramped; ~'kriechen v/refl. (irr. kriechen, no -ge-, h) hide; ~'krümmt adj. crooked; ~krüppelt adj. [~'krypəlt] crippled; stunted; ~krustet adj. [~'krustət] (en)crusted; caked; ~'kühlen v/refl. (no -ge-, h) catch (a) cold.

ver'kümmer|n v/i. (no -ge-, sein) ♀, ♣ become stunted; ♣ atrophy; fig. waste away; ꭴt adj. stunted; atrophied; rudimentary (a. biol.).

verkünd|en [fɛr'kyndən] v/t. (no -ge-, h), ~igen v/t. (no -ge-, h) announce; publish, proclaim; pronounce (judgement); ꭴigung f, ꭴung f (-/-en) announcement; proclamation; pronouncement.

ver'|kuppeln v/t. (no -ge-, h) ⊕ couple; fig. pander; ~'kürzen v/t. (no -ge-, h) shorten; abridge; beguile (time, etc.); ~'lachen v/t. (no -ge-, h) laugh at; ~'laden v/t. (irr. laden, no -ge-, h) load; ship; 🚂 entrain (esp. troops).

Verlag [fɛr'laːk] m (-[e]s/-e) publishing house, the publishers pl.; im ~ von published by.

ver'lagern v/t. (no -ge-, h) displace, shift; sich ~ shift.

Ver'lags|buchhändler m publisher; ~buchhandlung f publishing house; ~recht n copyright.

ver'langen 1. v/t. (no -ge-, h) demand; require; desire; 2. v/i. (no -ge-, h): ~ nach ask for; long for; 3. n (-s/~-) desire; longing (nach for); demand, request; auf ~ by request, ✝ on demand; auf ~ von at the request of, at s.o.'s request.

verlänger|n [fɛr'lɛŋərn] v/t. (no

-ge-, *h*) lengthen; prolong, extend; **2ung** *f* (-/-en) lengthening; prolongation, extension.
ver'langsamen *v/t.* (*no* -ge-, *h*) slacken, slow down.
ver'lassen *v/t.* (*irr.* lassen, *no* -ge-, *h*) leave; forsake, abandon, desert; *sich* ~ *auf* (*acc.*) rely on; **2heit** *f* (-/*no pl.*) abandonment; loneliness.
verläßlich *adj.* [fɛr'lɛsliç] reliable.
Ver'lauf *m* lapse, course (*of time*); progress, development (*of matter*); course (*of disease, etc.*); *im* ~ (*gen.*) *or von* in the course of; *e-n schlimmen* ~ *nehmen* take a bad turn; **2en** (*irr.* laufen, *no* -ge-) **1.** *v/i.* (*sein*) *time*: pass, elapse; *matter*: take its course; turn out, develop; *road, etc.*: run, extend; **2.** *v/refl.* (*h*) lose one's way, go astray; *crowd*: disperse; *water*: subside.
ver'lauten *v/i.* (*no* -ge-, *sein*): ~ *lassen* give to understand, hint; *wie verlautet* as reported.
ver'leb|en *v/t.* (*no* -ge-, *h*) spend, pass; **~t** *adj.* [~pt] worn out.
ver'leg|en 1. *v/t.* (*no* -ge-, *h*) mislay; transfer, shift, remove; ⊕ lay (*cable, etc.*); bar (*road*); put off, postpone; publish (*book*); *sich* ~ *auf* (*acc.*) apply o.s. to; **2.** *adj.* embarrassed; at a loss (*um* for *answer, etc.*); **2enheit** *f* (-/⁓-en) embarrassment; difficulty; predicament; **2er** *m* (-s/-) publisher; **2ung** (-/-en) transfer, removal; ⊕ laying; *time*: postponement.
ver'leiden *v/t.* (*no* -ge-, *h*) *s.* verekeln.
ver'leih|en *v/t.* (*irr.* leihen, *no* -ge-, *h*) lend, *Am. a.* loan; hire *or* let out; bestow (*right, etc.*) (*j-m* on s.o.); award (*price*); **2ung** *f* (-/-en) lending, loan; bestowal.
ver|'leiten *v/t.* (*no* -ge-, *h*) mislead; induce; seduce; ⚖ suborn; **~'lernen** *v/t.* (*no* -ge-, *h*) unlearn, forget; **~'lesen** *v/t.* (*irr.* lesen, *no* -ge-, *h*) read out; call (*names*) over; pick (*vegetables, etc.*); *sich* ~ read wrong.
verletz|en [fɛr'lɛtsən] *v/t.* (*no* -ge-, *h*) hurt, injure; *fig. a.*: offend; violate; **~end** *adj.* offensive; **2te** [~tə] *m, f* (-n/-n) injured person; *die* ~*n pl.* the injured *pl.*; **2ung** *f* (-/-en) hurt, injury, wound; *fig.* violation.
ver'leugn|en *v/t.* (*no* -ge-, *h*) deny; disown; renounce (*belief, principle, etc.*); *sich* ~ *lassen* have o.s. denied (*vor j-m* to s.o.); **2ung** *f* (-/-en) denial; renunciation.
verleumd|en [fɛr'lɔymdən] *v/t.* (*no* -ge-, *h*) slander, defame; **~erisch** *adj.* slanderous; **2ung** *f* (-/-en) slander, defamation, *in writing*: libel.
ver'lieb|en *v/refl.* (*no* -ge-, *h*): *sich* ~ *in* (*acc.*) fall in love with; **~t** *adj.* [~pt] in love (*in acc.* with); amorous; **2theit** *f* (-/⁓-en) amorousness.
verlieren [fɛr'li:rən] (*irr., no* -ge-, *h*) **1.** *v/t.* lose; shed (*leaves, etc.*); *sich* ~ lose o.s.; disappear; **2.** *v/i.* lose.
ver'lob|en *v/t.* (*no* -ge-, *h*) engage (*mit* to); *sich* ~ become engaged; **2te** [~ptə] (-n/-n) **1.** *m* fiancé; *die* ~*n pl.* the engaged couple *sg.*; **2.** *f* fiancée; **2ung** [~buŋ] *f* (-/-en) engagement.
ver'lock|en *v/t.* (*no* -ge-, *h*) allure, entice; tempt; **~end** *adj.* tempting; **2ung** *f* (-/-en) allurement, enticement.
verlogen *adj.* [fɛr'lo:gən] mendacious; **2heit** *f* (-/⁓-en) mendacity.
verlor [fɛr'lo:r] *pret. of* verlieren; **~en 1.** *p.p. of* verlieren; **2.** *adj.* lost; *fig.* forlorn; ~*e Eier* poached eggs; **~engehen** *v/i.* (*irr.* gehen, *sep.*, -ge-, *sein*) be lost.
ver'los|en *v/t.* (*no* -ge-, *h*) raffle; **2ung** *f* (-/-en) lottery, raffle.
ver'löten *v/t.* (*no* -ge-, *h*) solder.
Verlust [fɛr'lust] *m* (-es/-e) loss; **~e** *pl.* ⚔ casualties *pl.*
ver'machen *v/t.* (*no* -ge-, *h*) bequeath, leave *s.th.* (*dat.* to).
Vermächtnis [fɛr'mɛçtnis] *n* (-ses/-se) will; legacy, bequest.
vermähl|en [fɛr'mɛ:lən] *v/t.* (*no* -ge-, *h*) marry (*mit* to); *sich* ~ (*mit*) marry (*s.o.*); **2ung** *f* (-/-en) wedding, marriage.
ver'mehr|en *v/t.* (*no* -ge-, *h*) increase (*um* by), augment; multiply; add to; *durch Zucht* ~ propagate; breed; *sich* ~ increase, augment; multiply (*a. biol.*); propagate (itself), *zo.* breed; **2ung** *f* (-/⁓-en) increase; addition (*gen.* to); propagation.
ver'meid|en *v/t.* (*irr.* meiden, *no* -ge-, *h*) avoid; **2ung** *f* (-/⁓-en) avoidance.
ver|meintlich *adj.* [fɛr'maɪntliç] supposed; **~'mengen** *v/t.* (*no* -ge-, *h*) mix, mingle, blend.
Vermerk [fɛr'mɛrk] *m* (-[e]s/-e) note, entry; **2en** *v/t.* (*no* -ge-, *h*) note down, record.
ver'mess|en 1. *v/t.* (*irr.* messen, *no* -ge-, *h*) measure; survey (*land*); **2.** *adj.* presumptuous; **2enheit** *f* (-/⁓-en) presumption; **2ung** *f* (-/-en) measurement; survey (*of land*).
ver'miete|n *v/t.* (*no* -ge-, *h*) let, *esp. Am.* rent; hire (out); ⚖ lease; *zu* ~ on *or* for hire; *Haus zu* ~ house to (be) let; **2r** *m* landlord, ⚖ lessor; letter, hirer.
ver'mindern *v/t.* (*no* -ge-, *h*) diminish, lessen; reduce, cut.
ver'misch|en *v/t.* (*no* -ge-, *h*) mix, mingle, blend; **~t** *adj.* mixed; *news,*

etc.: miscellaneous; 2ung *f* (-/~-en) mixture.

ver'mis|sen *v/t.* (*no* -ge-, *h*) miss; ~ßt *adj.* [~'mist] missing; 2ßte *m, f* (-*n*/-*n*) missing person; *die* ~*n pl.* the missing *pl.*

vermitt|eln [fɛr'mitəln] (*no* -ge-, *h*) 1. *v/t.* mediate (*settlement, peace*); procure, get; give (*impression, etc.*); impart (*knowledge*) (*j-m* to *s.o.*); 2. *v/i.* mediate (*zwischen dat.* between); intercede (*bei* with, *für* for), intervene; 2ler *m* mediator; go-between; ✝ agent; 2ung *f* (-/-en) mediation; intercession; intervention; *teleph.* (telephone) exchange.

ver'modern *v/i.* (*no* -ge-, *sein*) mo(u)lder, decay, rot.

ver'mögen 1. *v/t.* (*irr.* mögen, *no* -ge-, *h*): ~ *zu inf.* be able to *inf.*; *et.* ~ *bei j-m* have influence with s.o.; 2. 2*n* (-*s*/-) ability, power; property; fortune; means *pl.*; 𝔤𝔱 assets *pl.*; ~d *adj.* wealthy; *pred.* well off; 2sverhältnisse *pl.* pecuniary circumstances *pl.*

vermut|en [fɛr'muːtən] *v/t.* (*no* -ge-, *h*) suppose, presume, *Am. a.* guess; conjecture, surmise; ~lich 1. *adj.* presumable; 2. *adv.* presumably; I suppose; 2ung *f* (-/-en) supposition, presumption; conjecture, surmise.

vernachlässig|en [fɛr'naːxlɛsigən] *v/t.* (*no* -ge-, *h*) neglect; 2ung *f* (-/~-en) neglect(ing).

ver'narben *v/i.* (*no* -ge-, *sein*) cicatrize, scar over. [with.]

ver'narrt *adj.:* ~ *in* (*acc.*) infatuated)

ver'nehm|en *v/t.* (*irr.* nehmen, *no* -ge-, *h*) hear, learn; examine, interrogate; ~lich *adj.* audible, distinct; 2ung 𝔤𝔱 *f* (-/-en) interrogation; questioning; examination.

ver'neig|en *v/refl.* (*no* -ge-, *h*) bow (*vor dat.* to); 2ung *f* bow.

vernein|en [fɛr'naɪnən] (*no* -ge-, *h*) 1. *v/t.* answer in the negative; deny; 2. *v/i.* answer in the negative; ~end *adj.* negative; 2ung *f* (-/-en) negation; denial; *gr.* negative.

vernicht|en [fɛr'nɪçtən] *v/t.* (*no* -ge-, *h*) annihilate; destroy; dash (*hopes*); ~end *adj.* destructive (*a. fig.*); *look*: withering; *criticism*: scathing; *defeat, reply*: crushing; 2ung *f* (-/~-en) annihilation; destruction.

ver|nickeln [fɛr'nikəln] *v/t.* (*no* -ge-, *h*) nickel(-plate); ~'nieten *v/t.* (*no* -ge-, *h*) rivet.

Vernunft [fɛr'nunft] *f* (-/*no pl.*) reason; ~ *annehmen* listen to *or* hear reason; *j-n zur* ~ *bringen* bring s.o. to reason *or* to his senses.

vernünftig *adj.* [fɛr'nynftiç] rational; reasonable; sensible.

ver'öden (*no* -ge-) 1. *v/t.* (*h*) make

desolate; 2. *v/i.* (*sein*) become desolate.

ver'öffentlich|en *v/t.* (*no* -ge-, *h*) publish; 2ung *f* (-/-en) publication.

ver'ordn|en *v/t.* (*no* -ge-, *h*) decree; order (*a.* 𝔤𝔱); 𝔤 prescribe (*j-m* to *or* for s.o.); 2ung *f* decree, order; 𝔤 prescription.

ver'pachten *v/t.* (*no* -ge-, *h*) rent, 𝔤𝔱 lease (*building, land*).

Ver'pächter *m* landlord, 𝔤𝔱 lessor.

ver'pack|en *v/t.* (*no* -ge-, *h*) pack (up); wrap up; 2ung *f* packing (material); wrapping.

ver|'passen *v/t.* (*no* -ge-, *h*) miss (*train, opportunity, etc.*); ~'patzen F [~'patsən] *v/t.* (*no* -ge-, *h*) *s.* verpfuschen; ~'pesten *v/t.* (*no* -ge-, *h*) *fumes*: contaminate (*the air*); ~'pfänden *v/t.* (*no* -ge-, *h*) pawn, pledge (*a. fig.*); mortgage.

ver'pflanz|en *v/t.* (*no* -ge-, *h*) transplant (*a.* 𝔤); 2ung *f* transplantation; 𝔤 *a.* transplant.

ver'pfleg|en *v/t.* (*no* -ge-, *h*) board; supply with food, victual; 2ung *f* (-/~-en) board; food-supply; provisions *pl.*

ver'pflicht|en *v/t.* (*no* -ge-, *h*) oblige; engage; 2ung *f* (-/-en) obligation, duty; ✝, 𝔤𝔱 liability; engagement, commitment.

ver'pfusch|en F *v/t.* (*no* -ge-, *h*) bungle, botch; make a mess of; ~t *adj. life*: ruined, wrecked.

ver|pönt *adj.* [fɛr'pøːnt] taboo; ~'prügeln F *v/t.* (*no* -ge-, *h*) thrash, flog, F wallop; ~'puffen *fig. v/i.* (*no* -ge-, *sein*) fizzle out.

Ver'putz △ *m* (-es/~-e) plaster; 2en △ *v/t.* (*no* -ge-, *h*) plaster.

ver|quicken [fɛr'kvikən] *v/t.* (*no* -ge-, *h*) mix up; ~'quollen *adj. wood*: warped; *face*: bloated; *eyes*: swollen; ~'rammeln [~'raməln] *v/t.* (*no* -ge-, *h*) bar(ricade).

Verrat [fɛr'raːt] *m* (-[e]s/*no pl.*) betrayal (*an dat.* of); treachery (to); 𝔤𝔱 treason (to); 2en *v/t.* (*irr.* raten, *no* -ge-, *h*) betray, give s.o. away; give away (*secret*); *sich* ~ betray o.s., give o.s. away.

Verräter [fɛr'rɛːtər] *m* (-*s*/-) traitor (*an dat.* to); 2isch *adj.* treacherous; *fig.* telltale.

ver'rechn|en *v/t.* (*no* -ge-, *h*) reckon up; charge; settle; set off (*mit* against); account for; ~ *mit* offset against; *sich* ~ miscalculate, make a mistake (*a. fig.*); *fig.* be mistaken; *sich um e-e Mark* ~ be one mark out; 2ung *f* settlement; clearing; booking *or* charging (*to account*); 2ungsscheck *m* collection-only cheque *or Am.* check.

ver'regnet *adj.* rainy, rain-spoilt.

ver'reis|en *v/i.* (*no* -ge-, *sein*) go on a journey; ~t *adj.* out of town; (*geschäftlich*) ~ away (on business).

verrenk|en v/t. (no -ge-, h) ✗: wrench; dislocate; luxate; sich et. ~ ✗ dislocate or luxate s.th.; sich den Hals ~ crane one's neck; 2ung ✗ f (-/-en) dislocation, luxation.

ver|'richten v/t. (no -ge-, h) do, perform; execute; sein Gebet ~ say one's prayer(s); ~'riegeln v/t. (no -ge-, h) bolt, bar.

verringer|n [fɛr'rɪŋərn] v/t. (no -ge-, h) diminish, lessen; reduce, cut; sich ~ diminish, lessen; 2ung f (-/-en) diminution; reduction, cut.

ver|'rosten v/i. (no -ge-, sein) rust; ~rotten [~'rɔtən] v/i. (no -ge-, sein) rot.

ver'rück|en v/t. (no -ge-, h) displace, (re)move, shift; ~t adj. mad, crazy (both a. fig.: nach about); wie ~ like mad; j-n ~ machen drive s.o. mad; 2te (-n/-n) 1. m lunatic, madman; 2. f lunatic, madwoman; 2theit f (-/-en) madness; foolish action; craze.

Ver'ruf m (-[e]s/no pl.): in ~ bringen bring discredit (up)on; in ~ kommen get into discredit; 2en adj. ill-reputed, ill-famed.

ver'rutsch|en v/i. (no -ge-, sein) slip; ~t adj. not straight.

Vers [fɛrs] m (-es/-e) verse.

ver'sag|en 1. v/t. (no -ge-, h) refuse, deny (j-m et. s.o. s.th.); sich et. ~ deny o.s. s.th.; 2. v/i. (no -ge-, h) fail, break down; gun: misfire; 3. 2 n (-s/no pl.) failure. [ure.\
Ver'sager m (-s/-) misfire; p. fail-\
ver'salzen v/t. ([irr. salzen,] no -ge-, h) oversalt; F fig. spoil.

ver'samm|eln v/t. (no -ge-, h) assemble; sich ~ assemble, meet; 2lung f assembly, meeting.

Versand [fɛr'zant] m (-[e]s/no pl.) dispatch, Am. a. shipment; mailing; ~ ins Ausland a. export(ation); ~abteilung f forwarding department; ~geschäft n, ~haus n mailorder business or firm or house.

ver'säum|en v/t. (no -ge-, h) neglect (one's duty, etc.); miss (opportunity, etc.); lose (time); ~ zu inf. fail or omit to inf.; 2nis n (-ses/-se) neglect, omission, failure.

ver|'schachern F v/t. (no -ge-, h) barter (away); ~'schaffen v/t. (no -ge-, h) procure, get; sich ~ obtain, get; raise (money); sich Respekt ~ make o.s. respected; ~'schämt adj. bashful; ~'schanzen v/refl. (no -ge-, h) entrench o.s.; sich ~ hinter (dat.) (take) shelter behind; ~'schärfen v/t. (no -ge-, h) heighten, intensify; aggravate; sich ~ get worse; ~'scheiden v/i. (irr. scheiden, no -ge-, sein) pass away; ~'schenken v/t. (no -ge-, h) give s.th. away; make a present of; ~'scherzen v/t. and v/refl. (no

-ge-, h) forfeit; ~'scheuchen v/t. (no -ge-, h) frighten or scare away; fig. banish; ~'schicken v/t. (no -ge-, h) send (away), dispatch, forward.

ver'schieb|en v/t. (irr. schieben, no -ge-, h) displace, shift, (re)move; 🚂 shunt; put off, postpone; F fig. ✝ sell underhand; sich ~ shift; 2ung f shift(ing); postponement.

verschieden adj. [fɛr'ʃiːdən] different (von from); dissimilar, unlike; aus ~en Gründen for various or several reasons; Verschiedenes various things pl., esp. ✝ sundries pl.; ~artig adj. of a different kind, various; 2heit f (-/-en) difference; diversity, variety; ~tlich adv. repeatedly; at times.

ver'schiff|en v/t. (no -ge-, h) ship; 2ung f (-/⚹-en) shipment.

ver|'schimmeln v/i. (no -ge-, sein) get mo(u)ldy, Am. mo(u)ld; ~'schlafen 1. v/t. (irr. schlafen, no -ge-, h) miss by sleeping; sleep (afternoon, etc.) away; sleep off (headache, etc.); 2. v/i. (irr. schlafen, no -ge-, h) oversleep (o.s.); 3. adj. sleepy, drowsy.

Ver'schlag m shed; box; crate; 2en [~gən] 1. v/t. (irr. schlagen, no -ge-, h) board up; nail up; es verschlug ihm die Sprache it dum(b)-founded him; 2. adj. cunning; eyes: a. shifty, ~enheit f (-/no pl.) cunning.

verschlechter|n [fɛr'ʃlɛçtərn] v/t. (no -ge-, h) deteriorate, make worse; sich ~ deteriorate, get worse; 2ung f (-/⚹, -en) deterioration; change for the worse.

ver'schleiern v/t. (no -ge-, h) veil (a. fig.).

Verschleiß [fɛr'ʃlaɪs] m (-es/⚹, -e) wear (and tear); 2en v/t. ([irr.,] no -ge-, h) wear out.

ver|'schleppen v/t. (no -ge-, h) carry off; pol. displace (person); abduct, kidnap; delay, protract; neglect (disease); ~'schleudern v/t. (no -ge-, h) dissipate, waste; ✝ sell at a loss, sell dirt-cheap; ~'schließen v/t. (irr. schließen, no -ge-, h) shut, close; lock (door); lock up (house).

verschlimmern [fɛr'ʃlɪmərn] v/t. (no -ge-, h) make worse, aggravate; sich ~ get worse.

ver'schlingen v/t. (irr. schlingen, no -ge-, h) devour; wolf (down) (one's food); intertwine, entwine, interlace; sich ~ intertwine, entwine, interlace.

verschli|ß [fɛr'ʃlɪs] pret. of verschleißen; ~ssen [~sən] p.p. of verschleißen.

verschlossen adj. [fɛr'ʃlɔsən] closed, shut; fig. reserved; 2heit f (-/no pl.) reserve.

ver'schlucken v/t. (no -ge-, h) swallow (up); sich ~ swallow the wrong way.

Ver'schluß m lock; clasp; lid; plug; stopper (of bottle); seal; fastener, fastening; phot. shutter; unter ~ under lock and key.

ver|'schmachten v/i. (no -ge-, sein) languish, pine away; vor Durst ~ die or be dying of thirst, be parched with thirst; ~'schmähen v/t. (no -ge-, h) disdain, scorn.

ver'schmelz|en (irr. schmelzen, no -ge-) v/t. (h) and v/i. (sein) melt, fuse (a. fig.); blend; fig.: amalgamate; merge (mit in, into); 2ung f (-/~-en) fusion; † merger; fig. amalgamation.

ver|'schmerzen v/t. (no -ge-, h) get over (the loss of); ~'schmieren v/t. (no -ge-, h) smear (over); blur; ~schmitzt adj. [~'ʃmitst] cunning; roguish; arch; ~'schmutzen (no -ge-) 1. v/t. (h) soil, dirty; pollute (water); 2. v/i. (sein) get dirty; ~'schnaufen F v/i. and v/refl. (no -ge-, h) stop for breath; ~'schneiden v/t. (irr. schneiden, no -ge-, h) cut badly; blend (wine, etc.); geld, castrate; ~'schneit adj. covered with snow; mountains: a. snow-capped; roofs: a. snow-covered.

Ver'schnitt m (-[e]s/no pl.) blend.

ver'schnupf|en F fig. v/t. (no -ge-, h) nettle, pique; ~t ⚕ adj.: ~ sein have a cold.

ver|'schnüren v/t. (no -ge-, h) tie up, cord; ~schollen adj. [~'ʃɔlən] not heard of again; missing; ⚖ presumed dead; ~'schonen v/t. (no -ge-, h) spare; j-n mit et. ~ spare s.o. s.th.

verschöne|(r)n [fɛr'ʃøːnə(r)n] v/t. (no -ge-, h) embellish, beautify; 2rung f (-/-en) embellishment.

ver|schossen adj. [fɛr'ʃɔsən] colour: faded; F ~ sein in (acc.) be madly in love with; ~schränken [~'ʃrɛŋkən] v/t. (no -ge-, h) cross, fold (one's arms).

ver'schreib|en v/t. (irr. schreiben, no -ge-, h) use up (in writing); ⚕ prescribe (j-m for s.o.); ⚖ assign (j-m to s.o.); sich ~ make a slip of the pen; sich e-r Sache ~ devote o.s. to s.th.; 2ung f (-/-en) assignment; prescription.

ver|schroben adj. [fɛr'ʃroːbən] eccentric, queer, odd; ~'schrotten v/t. (no -ge-, h) scrap; ~schüchtert adj. [~'ʃʏçtərt] intimidated.

ver'schulden 1. v/t. (no -ge-, h) be guilty of; be the cause of; 2. 2 n (-s/no pl.) fault.

ver|'schuldet adj. indebted, in debt; ~'schütten v/t. (no -ge-, h) spill (liquid); block (up) (road); bury s.o. alive; ~schwägert adj. [~'ʃvɛːgərt] related by marriage;

~'schweigen v/t. (irr. schweigen, no -ge-, h) conceal (j-m et. s.th. from s.o.).

verschwend|en [fɛr'ʃvɛndən] v/t. (no -ge-, h) waste, squander (an acc. on); lavish (on); 2er m (-s/-) spendthrift, prodigal; ~erisch adj. prodigal, lavish (both: mit of); wasteful; 2ung f (-/~-en) waste; extravagance.

verschwiegen adj. [fɛr'ʃviːgən] discreet; place: secret, secluded; 2heit f (-/no pl.) discretion; secrecy.

ver|'schwimmen v/i. (irr. schwimmen, no -ge-, sein) become indistinct or blurred; ~'schwinden v/i. (irr. schwinden, no -ge-, sein) disappear, vanish; F verschwinde! go away!, sl. beat it!; 2'schwinden n (-s/no pl.) disappearance; ~schwommen adj. [~'ʃvɔmən] vague (a. fig.); blurred; fig. woolly.

ver'schwör|en v/refl. (irr. schwören, no -ge-, h) conspire; 2er m (-s/-) conspirator; 2ung f (-/-en) conspiracy, plot.

ver'sehen 1. v/t. (irr. sehen, no -ge-, h) fill (an office); look after (house, etc.); mit et. ~ furnish or supply with; sich ~ make a mistake; ehe man sich's versieht all of a sudden; 2. 2 n (-s/-) oversight, mistake, slip; aus ~ = ~tlich adv. by mistake; inadvertently.

Versehrte [fɛr'zeːrtə] m (-n/-n) disabled person.

ver'send|en v/t. ([irr. senden,] no -ge-, h) send, dispatch, forward, Am. ship; by water: ship; ins Ausland ~ a. export; 2ung f (-/~-en) dispatch, shipment, forwarding.

ver|'sengen v/t. (no -ge-, h) singe, scorch; ~'senken v/t. (no -ge-, h) sink; sich ~ in (acc.) immerse o.s. in; ~sessen adj. [~'zɛsən]: ~ auf (acc.) bent on, mad after.

ver'setz|en v/t. (no -ge-, h) displace, remove; transfer (officer); at school: remove, move up, Am. promote; transplant (tree, etc.); pawn, pledge; F fig. stand (lover, etc.) up; ~ in (acc.) put or place into (situation, condition); j-m e-n Schlag ~ give or deal s.o. a blow; in Angst ~ frighten or terrify s.o.; in den Ruhestand ~ pension s.o. off, retire s.o.; versetzt werden be transferred; at school: go up; ~ Sie sich in m-e Lage put or place yourself in my position; Wein mit Wasser ~ mix wine with water, add water to wine; et. ~ reply s.th.; 2ung f (-/-en) removal; transfer; at school: remove, Am. promotion.

ver'seuch|en v/t. (no -ge-, h) infect; contaminate; 2ung f (-/~-en) infection; contamination.

ver'sicher|n v/t. (no -ge-, h) assure

(a. one's life); protest, affirm; insure (one's property or life); sich ~ insure or assure o.s.; sich ~ (, daß) make sure (that); ~te m, f (-n/-n) insurant, the insured or assured, policy-holder; ~ung f assurance, affirmation; insurance; (life-)assurance; insurance company.

Ver'sicherungs|gesellschaft f insurance company, ~police f, ~schein m policy of assurance, insurance policy.

ver|'sickern v/i. (no -ge-, sein) trickle away; ~'siegeln v/t. (no -ge-, h) seal (up); ~'siegen v/i. (no -ge-, sein) dry up, run dry; ~'silbern v/t. (no -ge-, h) silver; F fig. realize, convert into cash; ~'sinken v/i. (irr. sinken, no -ge-, sein) sink; s. versunken; ~'sinnbildlichen v/t. (no -ge-, h) symbolize.

Version [vɛr'zjoːn] f (-/-en) version.
'Versmaß n met|re, Am. -er.
versöhn|en [fɛr'zøːnən] v/t. (no -ge-, h) reconcile (mit to, with); sich (wieder) ~ become reconciled; ~lich adj. conciliatory; ~ung f (-/-en) reconciliation.

ver'sorg|en v/t. (no -ge-, h) provide (mit with), supply (with); take care of, look after; ~t adj. [~kt] provided for; ~ung [~guŋ] f (-/-en) providing (mit with), supplying (with); supply, provision.

ver'spät|en v/refl. (no -ge-, h) be late; ~et adj. belated, late, Am. tardy; ~ung f (-/-en) lateness, Am. tardiness; ~ haben be late; mit 2 Stunden ~ two hours behind schedule.

ver|'speisen v/t. (no -ge-, h) eat (up); ~'sperren v/t. (no -ge-, h) lock (up); bar, block (up), obstruct (a. view); ~'spielen v/t. (no -ge-, h) at cards, etc.: lose (money); ~'spielt adj. playful; ~'spotten v/t. (no -ge-, h) scoff at, mock (at), deride, ridicule; ~'sprechen v/t. (irr. sprechen, no -ge-, h) promise; sich ~ make a mistake in speaking; sich viel ~ von expect much of; 2'sprechen n (-s/~) promise; ~'sprühen v/t. (no -ge-, h) spray; ~'spüren v/t. (no -ge-, h) feel; perceive, be conscious of.

ver'staatlich|en v/t. (no -ge-, h) nationalize; ~ung f (-/-en) nationalization.

Verstand [fɛr'ʃtant] m (-[e]s/no pl.) understanding; intelligence, intellect, brains pl.; mind, wits pl.; reason; (common) sense.

Verstandes|kraft [fɛr'ʃtandəs-] f intellectual power or faculty; 2mäßig adj. rational; intellectual; ~mensch m matter-of-fact person.

verständ|ig adj. [fɛr'ʃtɛndiç] intelligent; reasonable, sensible; judi-

cious; ~igen [~gən] v/t. (no -ge-, h) inform (von of), notify (of); sich mit j-m ~ make o.s. understood to s.o.; come to an understanding with s.o.; 2igung [~guŋ] f (-/~ -en) information; understanding, agreement; teleph. communication; ~lich adj. [~tliç] intelligible; understandable; j-m et. ~ machen make s.th. clear to s.o.; sich ~ machen make o.s. understood.

Verständnis [fɛr'ʃtɛntnis] n (-ses/~ -se) comprehension, understanding; insight; appreciation (für of); ~ haben für appreciate; 2los adj. uncomprehending; look, etc.: blank; unappreciative; 2voll adj. understanding; appreciative; sympathetic; look: knowing.

ver'stärk|en v/t. (no -ge-, h) strengthen, reinforce (a. ⊕, ✗); amplify (radio signals, etc.); intensify; 2er m (-s/-) in radio, etc.: amplifier; 2ung f (-/~ -en) strengthening, reinforcement (a. ✗); amplification; intensification.

ver'staub|en v/i. (no -ge-, sein) get dusty; ~t adj. [~pt] dusty.

ver'stauch|en ✗ v/t. (no -ge-, h) sprain; sich den Fuß ~ sprain one's foot; 2ung ✗ f (-/-en) sprain.

ver'stauen v/t. (no -ge-, h) stow away.

Versteck [fɛr'ʃtɛk] n (-[e]s/-e) hiding-place; for gangsters, etc.: Am. F a. hide-out; ~ spielen play at hide-and-seek; 2en v/t. (no -ge-, h) hide, conceal; sich ~ hide.

ver'stehen v/t. (irr. stehen, no -ge-, h) understand, see, F get; comprehend; realize; know (language); es ~ zu inf. know how to inf.; Spaß ~ take a joke; zu ~ geben intimate; ~ Sie? do you see?; ich ~! I see!; verstanden? (do you) understand?, F (do you) get me?; falsch ~ misunderstand; ~ Sie mich recht! don't misunderstand me!; was ~ Sie unter (dat.)? what do you mean or understand by ...?; er versteht et. davon he knows a thing or two about it; sich ~ understand one another; sich ~ auf (acc.) know well, be an expert at or in; sich mit j-m gut ~ get on well with s.o.; es versteht sich von selbst it goes without saying.

ver'steifen v/t. (no -ge-, h) ⊕ strut, brace; stiffen; sich ~ stiffen; sich ~ auf (acc.) make a point of, insist on.

ver'steiger|n v/t. (no -ge-, h) (sell by or Am. at) auction; 2ung f (-/-en) (sale by or Am. at) auction, auction-sale.

ver'steinern (no -ge-) v/t. (h) and v/i. (sein) turn into stone, petrify (both a. fig.).

ver'stell|bar adj. adjustable; ~en v/t. (no -ge-, h) shift; adjust; disarrange; bar, block (up), obstruct; disguise (*voice*, etc.); sich ~ play or act a part; dissemble, feign; 2ung *f* (-/~-en) disguise; dissimulation.

ver|'steuern *v/t.* (*no* -ge-, *h*) pay duty or tax on; ~stiegen *fig. adj.* [~'ʃtiːɡən] eccentric.

ver'stimm|en *v/t.* (*no* -ge-, *h*) put out of tune; *fig.* put out of humo(u)r; ~t *adj.* out of tune; *fig.* out of humo(u)r, F cross; 2ung *f* ill humo(u)r; disagreement; ill feeling.

ver'stockt *adj.* stubborn, obdurate; 2heit *f* (-/*no pl.*) obduracy.

verstohlen *adj.* [fer'ʃtoːlən] furtive.

ver'stopf|en *v/t.* (*no* -ge-, *h*) stop (up); clog, block (up), obstruct; jam, block (*passage*, *street*); ⚕ constipate; 2ung ⚕ *f* (-/~-en) constipation.

verstorben *adj.* [fer'ʃtɔrbən] late, deceased; 2e *m, f* (-n/-n) *the* deceased, Am. ⚕ *a.* decedent; die ~n *pl.* the deceased *pl.*, the departed *pl.*

ver'stört *adj.* scared; distracted, bewildered; 2heit *f* (-/*no pl.*) distraction, bewilderment.

Ver'stoß *m* offen|ce, *Am.* -se; contravention (*gegen* of *law*); infringement (*on trade name*, etc.); blunder; 2en (*irr.* stoßen, *no* -ge-, *h*) 1. *v/t.* expel (*aus* from); repudiate, disown (*wife*, *child*, etc.); 2. *v/i.*: ~ gegen offend against; contravene (*law*); infringe (*rule*, etc.).

ver|'streichen (*irr.* streichen, *no* -ge-) 1. *v/i.* (sein) *time*: pass, elapse; expire; 2. *v/t.* (*h*) spread (*butter*, etc.); ~'streuen *v/t.* (*no* -ge-, *h*) scatter.

verstümmel|n [fer'ʃtyməln] *v/t.* (*no* -ge-, *h*) mutilate; garble (*text*, etc.); 2ung *f* (-/~-en) mutilation.

ver'stummen *v/i.* (*no* -ge-, sein) grow silent or dumb.

Verstümmlung [fer'ʃtymluŋ] *f* (-/-en) mutilation.

Versuch [fer'zuːx] *m* (-[e]s/-e) attempt, trial; *phys.*, etc.: experiment; e-n ~ machen mit give *s.o.* or *s.th.* a trial; try one's hand at *s.th.*, have a go at *s.th.*; 2en *v/t.* (*no* -ge-, *h*) try, attempt; taste; j-n ~ tempt *s.o.*; es ~ mit give *s.o.* or *s.th.* a trial.

Ver'suchs|anstalt *f* research institute; ~kaninchen *fig. n* guinea-pig; 2weise *adv.* by way of trial or (an) experiment; on trial; ~zweck *m*: zu ~en *pl.* for experimental purposes *pl.*

Ver'suchung *f* (-/-en) temptation; j-n in ~ bringen tempt *s.o.*; in ~ sein be tempted.

ver|'sündigen *v/refl.* (*no* -ge-, *h*) sin (*an that.* against); ~sunken *fig. adj.* [~'zuŋkən]: ~ in (*acc.*) absorbed

or lost in; ~'süßen *v/t.* (*no* -ge-, *h*) sweeten.

ver'tag|en *v/t.* (*no* -ge-, *h*) adjourn; *parl.* prorogue; sich ~ adjourn, *Am.* -a. recess; 2ung *f* adjournment; *parl.* prorogation.

ver'tauschen *v/t.* (*no* -ge-, *h*) exchange (*mit* for).

verteidig|en [fer'taɪdiɡən] *v/t.* (*no* -ge-, *h*) defend; sich ~ defend o.s.; 2er *m* (-s/-) defender; ⚽ *fig.* advocate; ⚽ counsel for the defen|ce, *Am.* -se, *Am.* attorney for the defendant or defense; *football*: fullback; 2ung *f* (-/~-en) defen|ce, *Am.* -se.

Ver'teidigungs|bündnis *n* defensive alliance; ~minister *m* minister of defence; *Brt.* Minister of Defence, *Am.* Secretary of Defense; ~ministerium *n* ministry of defence; *Brt.* Ministry of Defence, *Am.* Department of Defense.

ver'teil|en *v/t.* (*no* -ge-, *h*) distribute; spread (*colour*, etc.); 2er *m* (-s/-) distributor; 2ung *f* (-/~-en) distribution.

ver'teuern *v/t.* (*no* -ge-, *h*) raise or increase the price of.

ver'tief|en *v/t.* (*no* -ge-, *h*) deepen (*a. fig.*); sich ~ deepen; sich ~ in (*acc.*) plunge in(to); become absorbed in; 2ung *f* (-/-en) hollow, cavity; recess.

vertikal *adj.* [verti'kaːl] vertical.

ver'tilg|en *v/t.* (*no* -ge-, *h*) exterminate; F consume, eat (up) (*food*); 2ung *f* (-/~-en) extermination.

ver'tonen ♪ *v/t.* (*no* -ge-, *h*) set to music.

Vertrag [fer'traːk] *m* (-[e]s/~e) agreement, contract; *pol.* treaty; 2en [~ɡən] *v/t.* (*irr.* tragen, *no* -ge-, *h*) endure, bear, stand; diese Speise kann ich nicht ~ this food does not agree with me; sich ~ things: be compatible or consistent; *colours*: harmonize; *p.*: agree; get on with one another; sich wieder ~ be reconciled, make it up; 2lich [~kliç] 1. *adj.* contractual, stipulated; 2. *adv.* as stipulated; ~ verpflichtet sein be bound by contract; sich ~ verpflichten contract (*zu* for *s.th.*; *zu inf.* to *inf.*).

verträglich *adj.* [fer'trɛːkliç] sociable.

Ver'trags|bruch *m* breach of contract; 2brüchig *adj.*: ~ werden commit a breach of contract; ~entwurf *m* draft agreement; ~partner *m* party to a contract.

ver'trauen 1. *v/i.* (*no* -ge-, *h*) trust (j-m *s.o.*); ~ auf (*acc.*) trust or confide in; 2. 2 *n* (-s/*no pl.*) confidence, trust; im ~ confidentially, between you and me; ~erweckend *adj.* inspiring confidence; promising.

Ver'trauens|bruch *m* breach or

betrayal of trust; ~frage *parl. f:
die ~ stellen* put the question of
confidence; ~mann *m* (-[e]s/~er,
Vertrauensleute) spokesman; shop-
steward; confidential agent; ~
sache *f: das ist ~* that is a matter
of confidence; ~stellung *f* position
of trust; 2voll *adj.* trustful, trusting; ~votum *parl. n* vote of confidence; 2würdig *adj.* trustworthy,
reliable.

ver'traulich *adj.* confidential, in
confidence; intimate, familiar; 2-
keit *f* (-/-en) confidence; intimacy,
familiarity.

ver'traut *adj.* intimate, familiar;
2e (-n/-n) 1. *m* confidant, intimate
friend; 2. *f* confidante, intimate
friend; 2heit *f* (-/~-en) familiarity.

ver'treib|en *v/t.* (*irr. treiben, no
-ge-, h*) drive away; expel (*aus*
from); turn out; † sell, distribute
(*goods*); *sich die Zeit ~* pass one's
time, kill time; 2ung *f* (-/~-en)
expulsion.

ver'tret|en *v/t.* (*irr. treten, no -ge-,
h*) represent (*s.o., firm, etc.*); substitute for *s.o.*; attend to, look after
(*s.o.'s interests*); hold (*view*); *parl.*
sit for (*borough*); answer for *s.th.*;
j-s Sache ~ ⚖ plead s.o.'s case or
cause; *sich den Fuß ~* sprain one's
foot; F *sich die Beine ~* stretch
one's legs; 2er *m* (-s/-) representative; ✝ *a.* agent; proxy, agent;
substitute, deputy; exponent; (sales)
representative; door-to-door salesman; commercial travel(l)er, *esp.
Am.* travel(l)ing salesman; 2ung *f*
(-/-en) representation (*a. pol.*); ✝
agency; *in office:* substitution; *in ~*
by proxy; *gen.:* acting for.

Vertrieb ✝ [fer'tri:p] *m* (-[e]s/-e)
sale; distribution; ~ene [~bǝnǝ] *m, f*
(-n/-n) expellee.

ver'trocknen *v/i.* (*no -ge-, sein*)
dry up; ~trödeln F *v/t.* (*no -ge-, h*)
dawdle away, waste (*time*); ~trö-
sten *v/t.* (*no -ge-, h*) put off; ~tu-
schen F *v/t.* (*no -ge-, h*) hush up;
~übeln *v/t.* (*no -ge-, h*) take *s.th.*
amiss; ~üben *v/t.* (*no -ge-, h*) commit, perpetrate.

ver'unglück|en *v/i.* (*no -ge-, sein*)
meet with *or* have an accident; F
fig. fail, go wrong; *tödlich ~* be
killed in an accident; 2te *m, f* (-n/-n)
casualty.

verun|reinigen [fer'unrainigǝn]
v/t. (*no -ge-, h*) soil, dirty; defile;
contaminate (*air*); pollute (*water*);
~stalten [~ʃtaltǝn] *v/t.* (*no -ge-, h*)
disfigure.

ver'untreu|en *v/t.* (*no -ge-, h*) em-
bezzle; 2ung *f* (-/-en) embezzle-
ment.

ver'ursachen *v/t.* (*no -ge-, h*) cause.
ver'urteil|en *v/t.* (*no -ge-, h*) con-
demn (*zu* to) (*a. fig.*), sentence (to);

convict (*wegen of*); 2te *m, f* (-n/-n)
convict; 2ung *f* (-/-en) condemna-
tion (*a. fig.*), conviction.

ver|vielfältigen [fer'fi:lfɛltigǝn] *v/t.*
(*no -ge-, h*) manifold; ~vollkomm-
nen [~'fɔlkɔmnǝn] *v/t.* (*no -ge-, h*)
perfect; *sich ~* perfect o.s.

vervollständig|en [fer'fɔlʃtendigǝn]
v/t. (*no -ge-, h*) complete; 2ung *f*
(-/~-en) completion.

ver|'wachsen 1. *v/i.* (*irr. wachsen,
no -ge-, sein*): *miteinander ~* grow
together; 2. *adj.* deformed;
humpbacked, hunchbacked; ~
'wackeln *phot. v/t.* (*no -ge-, h*)
blur.

ver'wahr|en *v/t.* (*no -ge-, h*) keep;
sich ~ gegen protest against; ~lost
adj. [~lo:st] *child, garden, etc.:*
uncared-for, neglected; degenerate;
2ung *f* keeping; charge; custody;
fig. protest; *j-m et. in ~ geben* give
s.th. into s.o.'s charge; *in ~ nehmen*
take charge of.

verwaist *adj.* [fɛr'vaist] orphan(ed);
fig. deserted.

ver'walt|en *v/t.* (*no -ge-, h*) ad-
minister, manage; 2er *m* (-s/-) administrator, manager; steward (*of
estate*); 2ung *f* (-/-en) administration; management.

ver'wand|eln *v/t.* (*no -ge-, h*)
change, turn, transform; *sich ~*
change (*all: in acc. into*); 2lung *f*
(-/-en) change; transformation.

verwandt *adj.* [fɛr'vant] related
(*mit* to); *languages, tribes, etc.:*
kindred; *languages, sciences:* cognate (*with*); *pred.* akin (*to*) (*a. fig.*);
2e *m, f* (-n/-n) relative, relation;
2schaft *f* (-/-en) relationship; relations *pl.*; *geistige ~* congeniality.

ver'warn|en *v/t.* (*no -ge-, h*) cau-
tion; 2ung *f* caution.

ver'wässern *v/t.* (*no -ge-, h*) water
(down), dilute; *fig.* water down,
dilute.

ver'wechs|eln *v/t.* (*no -ge-, h*)
mistake (*mit for*); confound, mix
up, confuse (*all: mit with*); 2(e)-
lung *f* (-/-en) mistake; confusion.

verwegen *adj.* [fɛr've:gǝn] daring,
bold, audacious; 2heit *f* (-/~-en)
boldness, audacity, daring.

ver|'wehren *v/t.* (*no -ge-, h*): *j-m
et. ~* (de)bar s.o. from (doing) s.th.;
den Zutritt ~ deny *or* refuse admittance (*zu* to); ~'weichlicht *adj.* effeminate, soft.

ver'weiger|n *v/t.* (*no -ge-, h*) deny,
refuse; disobey (*order*); 2ung *f*
denial, refusal.

ver'weilen *v/i.* (*no -ge-, h*) stay,
linger; *bei et. ~* dwell (up)on s.th.

Verweis [fɛr'vais] *m* (-es/-e) reprimand; rebuke, reproof; reference
(*auf acc.* to); 2en [~zǝn] *v/t.* (*irr.
weisen, no -ge-, h*): *j-n des Landes ~*
expel s.o. from Germany, *etc.*;

j-m et. ~ reprimand s.o. for s.th.;
j-n ~ *auf (acc.)* or *an (acc.)* refer s.o.
to.

ver'welken *v/i.* (*no -ge-, sein*) fade,
wither (up).

ver'wend|en *v/t.* ([*irr.* wenden,] *no*
-ge-, h) employ, use; apply (*für*
for); spend (*time, etc.*) (*auf acc.*
on); *sich bei j-m* ~ *für* intercede
with s.o. for; 2ung *f* (*-/₊-en*) use,
employment; application; *keine* ~
haben für have no use for.

ver'werf|en *v/t.* (*irr.* werfen, *no*
-ge-, h) reject; ₊₊ quash (*verdict*);
₊lich *adj.* abominable.

ver'werten *v/t.* (*no -ge-, h*) turn to
account, utilize.

verwes|en [fɛr'veːzən] *v/i.* (*no -ge-,*
sein) rot, decay; 2ung *f* (*-/₊-en*)
decay.

ver'wick|eln *v/t.* (*no -ge-, h*) entan-
gle (*in acc.* in); *sich* ~ entangle o.s.
(in) (*a. fig.*); ₊elt *fig. adj.* complicated; 2(e)lung *f* (*-/-en*) entanglement; *fig. a.* complication.

ver'wilder|n *v/i.* (*no -ge-, sein*) run
wild; ₊t *adj.* garden, *etc.*: uncultivated, weed-grown; *fig.* wild, unruly.

ver'winden *v/t.* (*irr.* winden, *no*
-ge-, h) get over *s.th.*

ver'wirklich|en *v/t.* (*no -ge-, h*)
realize; *sich* ~ be realized, *esp. Am.*
materialize; come true; 2ung *f*
(*-/₊-en*) realization.

ver'wirr|en *v/t.* (*no -ge-, h*) entan-
gle; *j-n* ~ confuse s.o.; embarrass
s.o.; ₊t *fig. adj.* confused; embarrassed; 2ung *fig. f* (*-/-en*) confusion.

ver'wischen *v/t.* (*no -ge-, h*) wipe *or*
blot out; efface (*a. fig.*); blur,
obscure; cover up (*one's tracks*).

ver'witter|n *geol. v/i.* (*no -ge-, sein*)
weather; ₊t *adj. geol.* weathered;
weather-beaten (*a. fig.*).

ver'witwet *adj.* widowed.

verwöhn|en [fɛr'vøːnən] *v/t.* (*no*
-ge-, h) spoil; ₊t *adj.* fastidious,
particular.

verworren *adj.* [fɛr'vɔrən] *ideas,*
etc.: confused; *situation, plot*: intricate.

ver'wund|bar *adj.* [fɛr'vʊntbaːr]
vulnerable (*a. fig.*); ₊en [₊dən] *v/t.*
(*no -ge-, h*) wound.

ver'wunder|lich *adj.* astonishing;
2ung *f* (*-/₊-en*) astonishment.

Ver'wund|ete ⚔ *m* (*-n/-n*) wounded
(soldier), casualty; ₊ung *f* (*-/-en*)
wound, injury.

ver'wünsch|en *v/t.* (*no -ge-, h*)
curse; 2ung *f* (*-/-en*) curse.

ver'wüst|en *v/t.* (*no -ge-, h*) lay
waste, devastate, ravage (*a. fig.*);
2ung *f* (*-/-en*) devastation, ravage.

verzag|en [fɛr'tsaːgən] *v/i.* (*no -ge-,*
h) despond (*an dat.* of); ₊t *adj.* [₊kt]
despondent; 2theit [₊kt-] *f* (*-/no*
pl.) desponden|ce, -cy.

ver|'zählen *v/refl.* (*no -ge-, h*)
miscount; ₊zärteln [₊'tsɛːrtəln]
v/t. (*no -ge-, h*) coddle, pamper;
₊'zaubern *v/t.* (*no -ge-, h*) bewitch,
enchant, charm; ₊'zehren *v/t.* (*no*
-ge-, h) consume (*a. fig.*).

ver'zeichn|en *v/t.* (*no -ge-, h*) note
down; record; list; *fig.* distort; ~
können, zu ~ *haben* score (*success,*
etc.); ₊et *paint. adj.* out of drawing;
2is *n* (*-ses/-se*) list, catalog(ue);
register; inventory; index (*of book*);
table, schedule.

verzeih|en [fɛr'tsaɪən] (*irr., no -ge-,*
h) **1.** *v/i.* pardon, forgive; ~ *Sie!*
I beg your pardon!; excuse me!;
sorry!; **2.** *v/t.* pardon, forgive (*j-m*
et. s.o. s.th.); ₊lich *adj.* pardonable;
2ung *f* (*-/no pl.*) pardon; ₊l I beg
your pardon!, sorry!

ver'zerr|en *v/t.* (*no -ge-, h*) distort;
sich ~ become distorted; 2ung *f*
distortion.

ver'zetteln *v/t.* (*no -ge-, h*) enter on
cards; *sich* ~ fritter away one's
energies.

Verzicht [fɛr'tsɪçt] *m* (*-[e]s/-e*)
renunciation (*auf acc.* of); 2en *v/i.*
(*no -ge-, h*) renounce (*auf* et. s.th.);
do without (s.th.).

verzieh [fɛr'tsiː] *pret. of* verzeihen.

ver'ziehen¹ (*irr.* ziehen, *no -ge-*)
1. *v/i.* (*sein*) (re)move (*nach* to);
2. *v/t.* (*h*) spoil (*child*); distort; *das*
Gesicht ~ make a wry face, screw
up one's face, grimace; *ohne e-e*
Miene zu ~ without betraying the
least emotion; *sich* ~ *wood*: warp;
crowd, clouds: disperse; *storm,*
clouds: blow over; F disappear.

ver'ziehen² *p.p. of* verzeihen.

ver'zier|en *v/t.* (*no -ge-, h*) adorn,
decorate; 2ung *f* (*-/-en*) decoration;
ornament.

verzins|en [fɛr'tsɪnzən] *v/t.* (*no*
-ge-, h) pay interest on; *sich* ~ yield
interest; 2ung *f* (*-/₊-en*) interest.

ver'zöger|n *v/t.* (*no -ge-, h*) delay,
retard; *sich* ~ be delayed; 2ung *f*
(*-/-en*) delay, retardation.

ver'zollen *v/t.* (*no -ge-, h*) pay duty
on; *haben Sie* et. *zu* ~? have you
anything to declare?

verzück|t *adj.* [fɛr'tsʏkt] ecstatic,
enraptured; 2ung *f* (*-/₊-en*)
ecstasy, rapture; *in* ~ *geraten* go
into ecstasies (*wegen* over).

Ver'zug *m* (*-[e]s/no pl.*) delay; ⚔
default; *in* ~ *geraten* ⚔ come in
default; *im* ~ *sein* (be in) default.

ver'zweif|eln *v/i.* (*no -ge-, h, sein*)
despair (*an dat.* of); *es ist zum Ver-*
zweifeln it is enough to drive one
mad; ₊elt *adj.* hopeless; desperate;
2lung [₊luŋ] *f* (*-/no pl.*) despair;
j-n zur ~ *bringen* drive s.o. to despair.

verzweig|en [fɛr'tsvaɪgən] *v/refl.*
(*no -ge-, h*) ramify; *trees*: branch
(out); *road*: branch; *business firm,*

etc.: branch out; **2ung** *f* (-/-en) ramification; branching.

verzwickt *adj.* [fer'tsvikt] intricate, complicated.

Veteran [vete'ra:n] *m* (-en/-en) ✕ veteran (*a. fig.*), ex-serviceman.

Veterinär [veteri'nɛ:r] *m* (-s/-e) veterinary (surgeon), F vet.

Veto ['ve:to] *n* (-s/-s) veto; *ein ~ einlegen gegen* put a veto on, veto *s.th.*

Vetter ['fɛtər] *m* (-s/-n) cousin; **˜nwirtschaft** *f* (-/*no pl.*) nepotism.

vibrieren [vi'bri:rən] *v/i.* (*no -ge-, h*) vibrate.

Vieh [fi:] *n* (-[e]s/*no pl.*) livestock, cattle; animal, brute, beast; F *fig.* brute, beast; **˜bestand** *m* livestock; **˜händler** *m* cattle-dealer; **˜hof** *m* stockyard; **2isch** *adj.* bestial, beastly, brutal; **˜wagen 🚃** *m* stock-car; **˜weide** *f* pasture; **˜zucht** *f* stock-farming, cattle-breeding; **˜züchter** *m* stock-breeder, stock-farmer, cattle-breeder, *Am. a.* rancher.

viel [fi:l] **1.** *adj.* much; *˜e pl.* many; a lot (of), lots of; plenty of (*cake, money, room, time, etc.*); *das ˜e Geld* all that money; *seine ˜en Geschäfte pl.* his numerous affairs *pl.*; *sehr ˜* a great many *pl.*; *ziemlich ˜* a good deal of; *ziemlich ˜e pl.* a good many *pl.*; *˜ zuviel* far too much; *sehr ˜* a great *or* good deal; **2.** *adv.* much; *˜ besser* much *or* a good deal *or* a lot better; *et. ˜ lieber tun* prefer to do *s.th.*

viel|beschäftigt *adj.* ['fi:lbəʃeftiçt] very busy; **˜deutig** *adj.* ambiguous; **˜erlei** *adj.* ['˜ərlai] of many kinds, many kinds of; multifarious; **˜fach** ['˜fax] **1.** *adj.* multiple; **2.** *adv.* in many cases, frequently; **˜fältig** *adj.* ['˜fɛltiç] multiple, manifold, multifarious; **˜leicht** *adv.* perhaps, maybe; **˜mals** *adv.* ['˜ma:ls] *ich danke Ihnen ~* many thanks, thank you very much; *sie läßt* (*dich*) *~ grüßen* she sends you her kind regards; *ich bitte ~ um Entschuldigung* I am very sorry, I do beg your pardon; **˜mehr** *cj.* rather; **˜sagend** *adj.* significant, suggestive; **˜seitig** *adj.* ['˜zaitiç] many-sided, versatile; **˜versprechend** *adj.* (very) promising.

vier *adj.* [fi:r] four; *zu ~t* four of us *or* them; *auf allen ˜en* on all fours; *unter ~ Augen* confidentially, privately; *um halb ~* at half past three; **˜beinig** *adj.* four-legged; **2eck** *n* square, quadrangle; **˜eckig** *adj.* square, quadrangular; **˜erlei** *adj.* ['˜ər'lai] of four different kinds, four kinds of; **˜fach** *adj.* ['˜fax] fourfold; *~e Ausfertigung* four copies; **2füßer** *zo.* ['˜fy:sər] *m* (-s/-) quadruped; **˜füßig** *adj.* ['˜fy:siç]

four-footed; *zo.* quadruped; **2füßler** *zo.* ['˜fy:slər] *m* (-s/-) quadruped; **˜händig** *♪ adv.* ['˜hɛndiç]: *~ spielen* play a duet; **˜jährig** *adj.* ['˜jɛ:riç] four-year-old, of four; **2linge** ['˜liŋə] *m/pl.* quadruplets *pl.*, F quads *pl.*; **˜mal** *adv.* four times; **˜schrötig** *adj.* ['˜ʃrø:tiç] square-built, thickset; **˜seitig** *adj.* ['˜zaitiç] four-sided; Å quadrilateral; **2sitzer** *esp. mot. m* (-s/-) four-seater; **˜stöckig** *adj.* ['˜ʃtœkiç] four-storeyed, four-storied; **2takt-motor** *mot. m* four-stroke engine; **˜te** *adj.* fourth; **˜teilen** *v/t.* (*ge-, h*) quarter.

Viertel ['firtəl] *n* (-s/-) fourth (part); quarter; *~ fünf,* (*ein*) *~ nach vier* a quarter past four; *drei ~ vier* a quarter to four; **˜jahr** *n* three months *pl.*, quarter (of a year); **2jährlich, 2jährlich 1.** *adj.* quarterly; **2.** *adv.* every three months, quarterly; **˜note** *f ♪* crotchet, *Am. a.* quarter note; **˜pfund** *n,* **˜pfund** *n* quarter of a pound; **˜stunde** *f* quarter of an hour, *Am.* quarter hour.

vier|tens *adv.* ['fi:rtəns] fourthly; **2'vierteltakt** *♪ m* common time.

vierzehn *adj.* ['firtse:n] fourteen; *~ Tage pl.* a fortnight, *Am.* two weeks *pl.*; **˜te** *adj.* fourteenth.

vierzig *adj.* ['firtsiç] forty; **˜ste** *adj.* fortieth.

Vikar *eccl.* [vi'ka:r] *m* (-s/-e) curate; vicar.

Villa ['vila] *f* (-/Villen) villa.

violett *adj.* [vio'lɛt] violet.

Violine *♪* [vio'li:nə] *f* (-/-n) violin.

Viper *zo.* ['vi:pər] *f* (-/-n) viper.

virtuos *adj.* [virtu'o:s] masterly; **2e** [˜zə] *m* (-n/-n), **2in** [˜zin] *f* (-/-nen) virtuoso; **2ität** [˜ozi'tɛ:t] *f* (-/*no pl.*) virtuosity.

Virus 🦠 ['vi:rus] *n, m* (-/Viren) virus.

Vision [vi'zjo:n] *f* (-/-en) vision.

Visitation [vizita'tsjo:n] *f* (-/-en) search; inspection.

Visite 🩺 [vi'zi:tə] *f* (-/-n) visit; **˜nkarte** *f* visiting-card, *Am.* calling card.

Visum ['vi:zum] *n* (-s/Visa, Visen) visa, visé.

Vitalität [vitali'tɛ:t] *f* (-/*no pl.*) vitality. [min.)

Vitamin [vita'mi:n] *n* (-s/-e) vita-

Vize|kanzler ['fi:tsə-] *m* vice-chancellor; **˜könig** *m* viceroy; **˜konsul** *m* vice-consul; **˜präsident** *m* vice-president.

Vogel ['fo:gəl] *m* (-s/Ü) bird; F *e-n ~ haben* have a bee in one's bonnet, *sl.* have bats in the belfry; *den ~ abschießen* carry off the prize, *Am. sl.* take the cake; **˜bauer** *n, m* (-s/-) bird-cage; **˜flinte** *f* fowling-piece; **2frei** *adj.* outlawed; **˜futter** *n* food for birds, bird-seed; **˜kunde**

f (-/no *pl.*) ornithology; '~**liebhaber** *m* bird-fancier; '~**nest** *n* bird's nest, bird-nest; '~**perspektive** *f* (-/no *pl.*), '~**schau** *f* (-/no *pl.*) bird's-eye view; '~**scheuche** *f* (-/-n) scarecrow (*a. fig.*); ~'**Strauß-Politik** *f* ostrich policy; ~ betreiben hide one's head in the sand (like an ostrich); '~**warte** *f* ornithological station; '~**zug** *m* passage *or* migration of birds.

Vokab|el [vo'ka:bəl] *f* (-/-n) word; ~**ular** [~abu'la:r] *n* (-s/-e) vocabulary.

Vokal *ling.* [vo'ka:l] *m* (-s/-e) vowel.

Volk [fɔlk] *n* **1.** (-[e]s/~er) people; nation; swarm (*of bees*); covey (*of partridges*); **2.** (-[e]s/no *pl.*) populace, *the* common people; *contp. the* common *or* vulgar herd; *der Mann aus dem* ~*e* the man in the street *or Am.* on the street.

Völker|bund ['fœlkər-] *m* (-[e]s/no *pl.*) League of Nations; '~**kunde** *f* (-/no *pl.*) ethnology; '~**recht** *n* (-[e]s/no *pl.*) international law, law of nations; '~**wanderung** *f* age of national migrations.

'**Volks|abstimmung** *pol. f* plebiscite; '~**ausgabe** *f* popular edition (*of book*); '~**bücherei** *f* free *or* public library; '~**charakter** *m* national character; '~**dichter** *m* popular *or* national poet; '~**entscheid** *pol.* ['~ʃaɪt] *m* (-[e]s/-e) referendum; plebiscite; '~**fest** *n* fun fair, amusement park *or* grounds *pl.*; public merry-making; national festival; '~**gunst** *f* popularity; '~**herrschaft** *f* democracy; '~**hochschule** *f* adult education (courses *pl.*); '~**lied** *n* folk-song; '~**menge** *f* crowd (of people), multitude; '~**partei** *f* people's party; '~**republik** *f* people's republic; '~**schule** *f* elementary *or* primary school, *Am. a.* grade school; '~**schullehrer** *m* elementary *or* primary teacher, *Am.* grade teacher; '~**sprache** *f* vernacular; '~**stamm** *m* tribe, race; '~**stück** *thea. n* folk-play; '~**tanz** *m* folk-dance; '~**tracht** *f* national costume; **2tümlich** *adj.* ['~ty:mlɪç] national; popular; '~**versammlung** *f* public meeting; '~**vertreter** *parl. m* deputy, representative; member of parliament; *Brt.* Member of Parliament, *Am.* Representative; '~**vertretung** *parl. f* representation of the people; parliament; '~**wirt** *m* (political) economist; '~**wirtschaft** *f* economics, political economy; ~**wirtschaftler** ['~tlər] *m* (-s/-) *s.* Volkswirt; '~**zählung** *f* census.

voll [fɔl] **1.** *adj.* full; filled; whole, complete, entire; *figure, face:* full; round; *figure:* buxom; ~*er Knospen* full of buds; *aus* ~*em Halse* at the top of one's voice; *aus* ~*em Herzen* from the bottom of one's heart; *in* ~*er Blüte* in full blossom; *in* ~*er Fahrt* at full speed; *mit* ~*en Händen* lavishly, liberally; *mit* ~*em Recht* with perfect right; *um das Unglück* ~*zumachen* to make things worse; **2.** *adv.* fully, in full; ~ *und ganz* fully, entirely; *j-n nicht für* ~ *ansehen or nehmen* have a poor opinion of s.o., think little of s.o.

'**voll|auf** *adv.*, ~'**auf** *adv.* abundantly, amply, F plenty; '~**automatisch** *adj.* fully automatic; '**2bad** *n* bath; '**2bart** *m* beard; '**2beschäftigung** *f* full employment; '**2besitz** *m* full possession; '**2blut(pferd)** *zo. n* thoroughbred (horse); ~'**bringen** *v/t.* (*irr.* bringen, *no* -ge-, *h*) accomplish, achieve; perform; '**2dampf** *m* full steam; F: *mit* ~ *a/or* in full blast; '~**enden** *v/t.* (*no* -ge-, *h*) finish, complete; ~'**endet** *adj.* perfect; ~**ends** *adv.* ['~ɛnts] entirely, wholly, altogether; **2'endung** *f* (-/~-en) finishing, completion; *fig.* perfection.

Völlerei [fœlə'raɪ] *f* (-/~-en) gluttony.

voll|'führen *v/t.* (*no* -ge-, *h*) execute, carry out; '~**füllen** *v/t.* (*sep.*, -ge-, *h*) fill (up); '**2gas** *mot. n:* ~ *geben* open the throttle; *mit* ~ with the throttle full open; at full speed; ~**gepfropft** *adj.* ['~gəpfrɔpft] crammed, packed; '~**gießen** *v/t.* (*irr.* gießen, *sep.*, -ge-, *h*) fill (up); '**2gummi** *n, m* solid rubber.

völlig *adj.* ['fœlɪç] entire, complete; *silence, calm, etc.:* dead.

voll|jährig *adj.* ['fɔljɛ:rɪç]: ~ *sein* be of age; ~ *werden* come of age; '**2jährigkeit** *f* (-/no *pl.*) majority; '~**kommen** *adj.* perfect; **2'kommenheit** *f* (-/~-en) perfection; '**2kornbrot** *n* whole-meal bread; '~**machen** *v/t.* (*sep.*, -ge-, *h*) fill (up); F soil, dirty; *um das Unglück vollzumachen* to make things worse; '**2macht** *f* (-/-en) full power, authority; ₰ power of attorney; ~ *haben* be authorized; '**2matrose** ⚓ *m* able-bodied seaman; '**2milch** *f* whole milk; '**2mond** *m* full moon; '~**packen** *v/t.* (*sep.*, -ge-, *h*) stuff, cram; '**2pension** *f* (-/-en) full board; '~**schenken** *v/t.* (*sep.*, -ge-, *h*) fill (up); '~**schlank** *adj.* stout, corpulent; '~**ständig** *adj.* complete; '~**stopfen** *v/t.* (*sep.*, -ge-, *h*) stuff, cram; *sich* ~ stuff o.s.; *sich die Taschen* ~ stuff one's pockets; ~'**strecken** *v/t.* (*no* -ge-, *h*) execute; **2'streckung** *f* (-/-en) execution; '~**tönend** *adj.* sonorous, rich; '**2treffer** *m* direct hit; '**2versammlung** *f* plenary meeting *or* assembly; General Assembly (*of the United Nations*); '~**wertig** *adj.* equivalent,

equal in value; full; '~zählig adj.
complete; ~'ziehen v/t. (irr. ziehen,
no -ge-, h) execute; consummate
(marriage); sich ~ take place;
♀ziehung f (-/~-en), ♀zug m
(-[e]s/no pl.) execution.

Volontär [volɔn'tɛːr] m (-s/-e) unpaid
assistant.

Volt ≠ [vɔlt] n (-, -[e]s/-) volt.

Volumen [vo'luːmən] n (-s/-, Vo-
lumina) volume.

vom [fɔm] = von dem

von prp. (dat.) [fɔn] space, time:
from; instead of gen.: of; passive:
by; ~ Hamburg from Hamburg;
~ nun an from now on; ~ morgen an
from tomorrow (on), beginning
tomorrow; ein Freund ~ mir a
friend of mine; die Einrichtung ~
Schulen the erection of schools; ~
dem or vom Apfel essen eat (some)
of the apple; der Herzog ~ Edinburgh the Duke of Edinburgh; ein
Gedicht ~ Schiller a poem by
Schiller; ~ selbst by itself; ~ selbst,
~ sich aus by oneself; ~ drei Meter
Länge three metres long; ein Betrag
~ 300 Mark a sum of 300 marks;
e-e Stadt ~ 10 000 Einwohnern a
town of 10,000 inhabitants; reden ~
talk of or about s.th.; speak on
(scientific subject); ~ mir aus as far
as I am concerned; I don't mind,
for all I care; das ist nett ~ ihm that
is nice of him; ich habe ~ ihm gehört I have heard of him; ~statten
adv. [~'ʃtatən]: gut ~ gehen go well.

vor prp. (dat.; acc.) [foːr] space: in
front of, before; time: before; ~
langer Zeit a long time ago; ~ einigen Tagen a few days ago; (heute) ~
acht Tagen a week ago (today); am
Tage ~ (on) the day before, on the
eve of; 5 Minuten ~ 12 five minutes
to twelve, Am. five minutes of
twelve; fig. at the eleventh hour;
~ der Tür stehen be imminent,
be close at hand; ~ e-m Hintergrund
against a background; ~ Zeugen in
the presence of witnesses; ~ allen
Dingen above all; (dicht) ~ dem
Untergang stehen be on the brink
or verge of ruin; ~ Hunger sterben
die of hunger; ~ Kälte zittern
tremble with cold; ~ schützen (verstecken) protect (hide) from or
against; ~ sich gehen take place, pass
off; ~ sich hin lächeln smile to o.s.;
sich fürchten ~ be afraid of, fear.

Vor|abend['foːrʔ-] m eve; '~ahnung
f presentiment, foreboding.

voran adv. [fo'ran] at the head (dat.
of), in front (of), before; Kopf ~
head first; ~gehen v/i. (irr. gehen,
sep., -ge-, sein) lead the way;
precede; ~kommen v/i. (irr. kommen, sep., -ge-, sein) make progress; fig. get on (in life).

Voran|schlag ['foːrʔan-] m (rough)

estimate; '~zeige f advance notice;
film: trailer.

vorarbeite|n ['foːrʔ-] v/t. and v/i.
(sep., -ge-, h) work in advance;
'♀r m foreman.

voraus adv. [fo'raus] in front (dat.
of), ahead (of); im ~ in advance,
beforehand; ~bestellen v/t. (sep.,
no -ge-, h) s. vorbestellen; ~bezah-
len v/t. (sep., no -ge-, h) pay in
advance, prepay; ~gehen v/i. (irr.
gehen, sep., -ge-, sein) go on before;
s. vorangehen; ♀sage f prediction;
prophecy; forecast (of weather);
~sagen v/t. (sep., -ge-, h) foretell,
predict; prophesy; forecast (weather,
etc.); ~schicken v/t. (sep., -ge-, h)
send on in advance; fig. mention
beforehand, premise; ~sehen v/t.
(irr. sehen, sep., -ge-, h) foresee; ~
setzen v/t. (sep., -ge-, h) (pre)sup-
pose, presume, assume; vorausgesetzt, daß provided that; ♀setzung
f (-/-en) (pre)supposition, assumption; prerequisite; ♀sicht f fore-
sight; aller ~ nach in all probability;
~sichtlich adj. presumable, prob-
able, likely; ♀zahlung f advance
payment or instal(l)ment.

'Vor|bedacht 1. m (-[e]s/no pl.): mit
~ deliberately, on purpose; 2. ♀ adj.
premeditated; '~bedeutung f foreboding, omen, portent; '~bedin-
gung f prerequisite.

Vorbehalt ['foːrbəhalt] m (-[e]s/-e)
reservation, reserve; '♀en 1. v/t.
(irr. halten, sep., no -ge-, h): sich
~ reserve (right, etc.); 2. adj.: Än-
derungen ~ subject to change (without notice); '♀los adj. unreserved,
unconditional.

vorbei adv. [fɔr'bai] space: along,
by, past (all: an dat. s.o., s.th.); time:
over, gone; 3 Uhr ~ past three
(o'clock); ~fahren v/i. (irr. fahren,
sep., -ge-, sein) drive past; ~gehen
v/i. (irr. gehen, sep., -ge-, sein) pass,
go by; pain: pass (off); storm:
blow over; ~ an (dat.) pass; im
Vorbeigehen in passing; ~kommen
v/i. (irr. kommen, sep., -ge-, sein)
pass by; F drop in; F ~ an (dat.)
get past (obstacle, etc.); ~lassen v/t.
(irr. lassen, sep., -ge-, h) let
pass.

'Vorbemerkung f preliminary remark or note.

'vorbereit|en v/t. (sep., no -ge-, h)
prepare (für, auf acc. for); '♀ung f
preparation (für, auf acc. for).

'Vorbesprechung f preliminary discussion or talk.

'vor|bestellen v/t. (sep., no -ge-, h)
order in advance; book (room, etc.);
'~bestraft adj. previously con-
victed.

'vorbeug|en v/i. (sep., -ge-, h) 1. v/i.
prevent (e-r Sache s.th.); 2. v/t.
and v/refl. bend forward; '~end

adj. preventive; ⚕ *a.* prophylactic; 'Ωung *f* prevention.

'**Vorbild** *n* model; pattern; example; prototype; 'Ωlich *adj.* exemplary; ~ung ['~duŋ] *f* preparatory training.

'**vor|bringen** *v/t.* (*irr.* bringen, *sep.*, -ge-, h) bring forward, produce; advance (*opinion*); ᵗᵗᵗ prefer (*charge*); utter, say, state; '~datieren *v/t.* (*sep.*, *no* -ge-, h) post-date.

vorder *adj.* ['fɔrdər] front, fore.

'**Vorder|achse** *f* front axle; '~ansicht *f* front view; '~bein *n* foreleg; '~fuß *m* forefoot; '~grund *m* foreground (*a. fig.*); '~haus *n* front building; '~mann *m* man in front (*of s.o.*); '~rad *n* front wheel; ~radantrieb *mot.* ['fɔrdərra:t?-] *m* front-wheel drive; '~seite *f* front (side); obverse (*of coin*); '~sitz *m* front seat; 'Ωst *adj.* foremost; '~teil *n, m* front (part); '~tür *f* front door; '~zahn *m* front tooth; '~zimmer *n* front room.

'**vordrängen** *v/refl.* (*sep.*, -ge-, h) press *or* push forward.

'**vordring|en** *v/i.* (*irr.* dringen, *sep.*, -ge-, sein) advance; '~lich *adj.* urgent. \u2003\u2003\u2003\u2003\u2003\u2003\u2003[blank.]

'**Vordruck** *m* (-[e]s/-e) form, *Am. a.*]

voreilig *adj.* ['fo:r?-] hasty, rash, precipitate; ~e *Schlüsse ziehen* jump to conclusions.

voreingenommen *adj.* ['fo:r?-] prejudiced, bias(s)ed; 'Ωheit *f* (-/*no pl.*) prejudice, bias.

vor|enthalten ['fo:r?-] *v/t.* (*irr.* halten, *sep.*, *no* -ge-, h) keep back, withhold (*j-m et. s.th.* from *s.o.*); Ωentscheidung ['fo:r?-] *f* preliminary decision; '~erst *adv.* ['fo:r?-] for the present, for the time being.

Vorfahr ['fo:rfa:r] *m* (-en/-en) ancestor.

'**vorfahr|en** *v/i.* (*irr.* fahren, *sep.*, -ge-, sein) drive up; pass; *den Wagen* ~ *lassen* order the car; 'Ωt(**recht** *n*) *f* right of way, priority.

'**Vorfall** *m* incident, occurrence, event; 'Ωen *v/i.* (*irr.* fallen, *sep.*, -ge-, sein) happen, occur.

'**vorfinden** *v/t.* (*irr.* finden, *sep.*, -ge-, h) find.

'**Vorfreude** *f* anticipated joy.

'**vorführ|en** *v/t.* (*sep.*, -ge-, h) bring forward, produce; bring (*dat.* before); show, display, exhibit; demonstrate (*use of s.th.*); show, present (*film*); 'Ωer *m* projectionist (*in cinema theatre*); 'Ωung *f* presentation, showing; ⊕ demonstration; ᵗᵗᵗ production (*of prisoner*); *thea.*, *film*: performance.

'**Vor|gabe** *f sports*: handicap; *athletics*: stagger; *golf*, *etc.*: odds *pl.*; '~gang *m* incident, occurrence, event; *facts pl.*; file, record(*s pl.*); *biol.*, ⊕ process; ~gänger ['~gɛŋər]

m (-s/-), '~gängerin *f* (-/-nen) predecessor; '~garten *m* front garden.

'**vorgeben** *v/t.* (*irr.* geben, *sep.*, -ge-, h) *sports*: give (*j-m s.o.*); *fig.* pretend, allege.

'**Vor|gebirge** *n* promontory, cape, headland; foot-hills *pl.*; '~gefühl *n* presentiment, foreboding.

'**vorgehen 1.** *v/i.* (*irr.* gehen, *sep.*, -ge-, sein) ⚔ advance; F lead the way; go on before; *watch*, *clock*: be fast, gain (*fünf Minuten* five minutes); take precedence (*dat.* of, over), be more important (than); take action, act; proceed (*a.* ᵗᵗᵗ gegen against); go on, happen, take place; **2.** Ω *n* (-*s/no pl.*) action, proceeding.

'**Vor|geschmack** *m* (-[e]s/*no pl.*) foretaste; '~gesetzte ['~gəzɛtstə] *m* (-n/-n) superior; *esp. Am.* F boss; 'Ωgestern *adv.* the day before yesterday; 'Ωgreifen *v/i.* (*irr.* greifen, *sep.*, -ge-, h) anticipate (*j-m* or e-r *Sache s.o.* or *s.th.*).

'**vorhaben 1.** *v/t.* (*irr.* haben, *sep.*, -ge-, h) intend, mean; be going to *do s.th.*; *nichts* ~ be at a loose end; *haben Sie heute abend et. vor?* have you anything on tonight?; *was hat er jetzt wieder vor?* what is he up to now?; *was hast du mit ihm vor?* what are you going to *do with* him?; **2.** Ω *n* (-*s*/-) intention, purpose, ᵗᵗᵗ intent; plan; project.

'**Vorhalle** *f* vestibule, (entrance-) hall; lobby; porch.

'**vorhalt|en** (*irr.* halten, *sep.*, -ge-, h) **1.** *v/t.*: *j-m et.* ~ hold s.th. before s.o.; *fig.* reproach s.o. with s.th.; **2.** *v/i.* last; 'Ωung *f* remonstrance; *j-m* ~en machen remonstrate with s.o. (*wegen* on).

vorhanden *adj.* [for'handən] at hand, present; available (*a.* ✝); ✝ on hand, in stock; ~ *sein* exist; Ω~ *sein n* presence, existence.

'**Vor|hang** *m* curtain; '~hänge-schloß *n* padlock.

'**vorher** *adv.* before, previously; in advance, beforehand.

vor'her|bestellen *v/t.* (*sep.*, *no* -ge-, h) *s.* vorbestellen; ~bestimmen *v/t.* (*sep.*, *no* -ge-, h) determine beforehand, predetermine; ~gehen *v/i.* (*irr.* gehen, *sep.*, -ge-, sein) precede; ~ig *adj.* preceding, previous.

'**Vorherr|schaft** *f* predominance; 'Ωschen *v/i.* (*sep.*, -ge-, h) predominate, prevail; 'Ωschend *adj.* predominant, prevailing.

Vor'her|sage *f s.* Voraussage; Ωsagen *v/t.* (*sep.*, -ge-, h) *s.* voraussagen; Ωsehen *v/t.* (*irr.* sehen, *sep.*, -ge-, h) foresee; Ωwissen *v/t.* (*irr.* wissen, *sep.*, -ge-, h) know beforehand, foreknow.

'vor|hin *adv.*, ~'hin *adv.* a short while ago, just now.

'Vor|hof *m* outer court, forecourt; *anat.* auricle (*of heart*); '~hut ✕ *f* vanguard.

'vor|ig *adj.* last; ~jährig *adj.* ['~je:riç] of last year, last year's.

'Vor|kämpfer *m* champion, pioneer; '~kehrung *f* (-/-en) precaution; ~en treffen take precautions; '~kenntnisse *f/pl.* preliminary or basic knowledge (*in dat.* of); mit guten ~n in (*dat.*) well grounded in.

'vorkommen **1.** *v/i.* (*irr.* kommen, *sep.*, -ge-, *sein*) be found; occur, happen; es kommt mir vor it seems to me; **2.** 2 *n* (-s/-) occurrence.

'Vor|kommnis *n* (-ses/-se) occurrence; event; '~kriegszeit *f* prewar times *pl.*

'vorlad|en ᵷⁱᶜ *v/t.* (*irr.* laden, *sep.*, -ge-, h) summon; '~ung ᵷⁱᶜ *f* summons.

'Vorlage *f* copy; pattern; *parl.* bill; presentation; production (*of document*); football: pass.

'vorlassen *v/t.* (*irr.* lassen, *sep.*, -ge-, h) let *s.o.* pass, allow *s.o.* to pass; admit.

'Vorläuf|er *m*, '~erin *f* (-/-nen) forerunner; '2ig **1.** *adj.* provisional, temporary; **2.** *adv.* provisionally, temporarily; for the present, for the time being.

'vorlaut *adj.* forward, pert.

'Vorleben *n* past (life), antecedents*pl.*

'vorlege|n *v/t.* (*sep.*, -ge-, h) put (lock) on; produce (*document*); submit (*plans, etc. for discussion, etc.*); propose (*plan, etc.*); present (*bill, etc.*); j-m et. ~ lay or place or put *s.th.* before *s.o.*; show *s.o. s.th.*; *at table:* help *s.o.* to *s.th.*; j-m eine Frage ~ put a question to *s.o.*; sich ~ lean forward; '2r *m* (-s/-) rug.

'vorles|en *v/t.* (*irr.* lesen, *sep.*, -ge-, h) read aloud; j-m et. ~ read (out) *s.th.* to *s.o.*; '2ung *f* lecture (*über acc.* on; *vor dat.* to); e-e ~ halten (give) a lecture.

'vorletzt *adj.* last but one; ~e Nacht the night before last.

'Vorlieb|e *f* (-/*no pl.*) predilection, preference; 2nehmen [~'li:p-] *v/i.* (*irr.* nehmen, *sep.*, -ge-, h) be satisfied (*mit* with); ~ mit dem, was da ist *at meals:* take pot luck.

'vorliegen *v/i.* (*irr.* liegen, *sep.*, -ge-, h) lie before *s.o.*; be there, exist; da muß ein Irrtum ~ there must be a mistake; was liegt gegen ihn vor? what is the charge against him?; '~d *adj.* present, in question.

'vor|lügen *v/t.* (*irr.* lügen, *sep.*, -ge-, h): j-m et. ~ tell *s.o.* lies; '~machen *v/t.* (*sep.*, -ge-, h): j-m et. ~ show *s.o.* how to do *s.th.*; *fig.* impose upon *s.o.*; sich (selbst) et. ~ fool *o.s.*

'Vormacht *f* (-/✕ ⁼e), '~stellung *f* predominance; supremacy; hegemony.

'Vormarsch ✕ *m* advance.

'vormerken *v/t.* (*sep.*, -ge-, h) note down, make a note of; reserve; sich ~ lassen für put one's name down for.

'Vormittag *m* morning, forenoon; '2s *adv.* in the morning.

'Vormund *m* (-[e]s/-e, ⁼er) guardian; '~schaft *f* (-/-en) guardianship.

vorn *adv.* [fɔrn] in front; nach ~ forward; von ~ from the front; ich sah sie von ~ I saw her face; von ~ anfangen begin at the beginning; noch einmal von ~ anfangen begin anew, make a new start.

'Vorname *m* Christian name, first name, *Am. a.* given name.

vornehm ['fo:rne:m] **1.** *adj.* of (superior) rank, distinguished; aristocratic; noble; fashionable; ~e Gesinnung high character; **2.** *adv.*: ~ tun give *o.s.* airs; '~en *v/t.* (*irr.* nehmen, *sep.*, -ge-, h) take *s.th.* in hand; deal with; make (*changes, etc.*); take up (*book*); F sich j-n ~ take *s.o.* to task (wegen for, about); sich ~ resolve (up)on *s.th.*; resolve (*zu inf.* to *inf.*), make up one's mind (*zu inf.* to *inf.*); sich vorgenommen haben *a.* be determined (*zu inf.* to *inf.*); '2heit *f* (-/*no pl.*) refinement; elegance; high-mindedness.

'vorn|herein *adv.*, ~he'rein *adv.*: von ~ from the first *or* start *or* beginning.

Vorort ['fo:rʔ-] *m* (-[e]s/-e) suburb; '~(s)verkehr *m* suburban traffic; '~(s)zug *m* local (train).

'Vor|posten *m* outpost (*a.* ✕); '~rang *m* (-[e]s/*no pl.*) precedence (*vor dat.* of, over), priority (over); '~rat *m* store, stock (*an dat.* of); Vorräte *pl. a.* provisions *pl.*, supplies *pl.*; 2rätig *adj.* ['~rε:tiç] available; ✝ *a.* on hand, in stock; '2rechnen *v/t.* (*sep.*, -ge-, h) reckon up (j-m to *s.o.*); '~recht *n* privilege; '~rede *f* preface, introduction; '~redner *m* previous speaker; '~richtung ⊕ *f* contrivance, device; 2rücken (*sep.*, -ge-) **1.** *v/t.* (h) move (*chair, etc.*) forward; **2.** *v/i.* (*sein*) advance; '~runde *f* sports: preliminary round; '~sagen *v/i.* (*sep.*, -ge-, h): j-m ~ prompt *s.o.*; '~saison *f* off *or* dead season; '~satz *m* intention, purpose, design; 2sätzlich *adj.* ['~zetslic] intentional, deliberate; ~er Mord ᵷⁱᶜ wil(l)ful murder; '~schein *m*: zum ~ bringen bring forward, produce; zum ~ kommen appear, turn up; '2schieben *v/t.* (*irr.* schieben, *sep.*, -ge-, h) push *s.th.* forward; slip (*bolt*); *s.* vorschützen; '2schießen *v/t.* (*irr.* schießen, *sep.*, -ge-, *h*) advance (*money*).

'**Vorschlag** *m* proposition, proposal; suggestion; offer; 2en ['~gən] *v/t.* (*irr.* schlagen, *sep.*, -ge-, *h*) propose; suggest; offer.

'**Vor|schlußrunde** *f sports*: semifinal; 2schnell *adj.* hasty, rash; 2schreiben *v/t.* (*irr.* schreiben, *sep.*, -ge-, *h*): j-m et. ~ write s.th. out for s.o.; *fig.* prescribe.

'**Vorschrift** *f* direction, instruction; prescription (*esp.* 🐾); order (*a.* 🐾); regulation(s *pl.*); 2smäßig *adj.* according to regulations; ~e *Kleidung* regulation dress; 2swidrig *adj. and adv.* contrary to regulations.

'**Vor|schub** *m*: ~ leisten (*dat.*) countenance (*fraud, etc.*); further, encourage; ⚖ aid and abet; '~schule *f* preparatory school; '~schuß *m* advance; *for barrister*: retaining fee, retainer; 2schützen *v/t.* (*sep.*, -ge-, *h*) pretend, plead (*sickness, etc. as excuse*); 2schweben *v/i.* (*sep.*, -ge-, *h*): mir schwebt et. vor I have s.th. in mind.

'**vorseh|en** *v/t.* (*irr.* sehen, *sep.*, -ge-, *h*) plan; design; ⚖ provide; sich ~ take care, be careful; sich ~ vor (*dat.*) guard against; 2ung *f* (-/~-en) providence.

'**vorsetzen** *v/t.* (*sep.*, -ge-, *h*) put forward; place *or* put *or* set before, offer.

'**Vorsicht** *f* caution; care; ~! caution!, danger!; look out!, be careful!; ⚠, *Glas!* Glass, with care!; ~, *Stufe!* mind the step!; 2ig *adj.* cautious; careful; ~! F steady!

'**vorsichts|halber** *adv.* as a precaution; 2maßnahme *f*, 2maßregel *f* precaution(ary measure); ~n treffen take precautions.

'**Vorsilbe** *gr. f* prefix.

'**vorsingen** *v/t.* (*irr.* singen, *sep.*, -ge-, *h*): j-m et. ~ sing s.th. to s.o.

'**Vorsitz** *m* (-es/*no pl.*) chair, presidency; den ~ führen *or* haben be in the chair, preside (*bei* over; at); den ~ übernehmen take the chair; ~ende ['~əndə] (-n/-n) 1. *m* chairman, president; 2. *f* chairwoman.

'**Vorsorg|e** *f* (-/*no pl.*) provision, providence; precaution; ~ treffen make provision; 2en *v/i.* (*sep.*, -ge-, *h*) provide; 2lich ['~kliç] 1. *adj.* precautionary; 2. *adv.* as a precaution.

'**Vorspeise** *f* appetizer, hors d'œuvre.

'**vorspieg|eln** *v/t.* (*sep.*, -ge-, *h*) pretend; j-m et. ~ delude s.o. (*with false hopes, etc.*); 2(e)lung *f* preten|ce, *Am.* -se.

'**Vorspiel** *n* prelude; 2en *v/t.* (*sep.*, -ge-, *h*): j-m et. ~ play s.th. to s.o.

'**vor|sprechen** *v/t.* (*irr.* sprechen, *sep.*, -ge-, *h*) 1. *v/t.* pronounce (*j-m et.*

s.th. *to* *or* for s.o.); 2. *v/i.* call (*bei on s.o.*; at *an office*); *thea.* audition; '~springen *v/i.* (*irr.* springen, *sep.*, -ge-, *sein*) jump forward; project; 2sprung *m* △ projection; *sports*: lead; *fig.* start, advantage (*vor dat.* of); 2stadt *f* suburb; '~städtisch *adj.* suburban; 2stand *m* board of directors, managing directors *pl.*

'**vorsteh|en** *v/i.* (*irr.* stehen, *sep.*, -ge-, *h*) project, protrude; *fig.*: direct; manage (*both*: e-r *Sache* s.th.); 2er *m* director, manager; head, chief.

'**vorstell|en** *v/t.* (*sep.*, -ge-, *h*) put forward; put (*clock*) on; introduce (*j-n j-m s.o. to s.o.*); mean, stand for; represent; sich ~ *bei* have an interview with; sich et. ~ imagine *or* fancy s.th.; 2ung *f* introduction, presentation; interview (*of applicant for post*); *thea.* performance; *fig.*: remonstrance; idea, conception; imagination; 2ungsvermögen *n* imagination.

'**Vor|stoß** ✕ *m* thrust, advance; '~strafe *f* previous conviction; 2strecken *v/t.* (*sep.*, -ge-, *h*) thrust out, stretch forward; advance (*money*); '~stufe *f* first step *or* stage; '2täuschen *v/t.* (*sep.*, -ge-, *h*) feign, pretend.

Vorteil ['fɔrtail] *m* advantage (*a. sports*); profit; *tennis*: (ad)vantage; 2haft *adj.* advantageous (*für* to), profitable (to).

Vortrag ['fo:rtra:k] *m* (-[e]s/~e) performance; execution (*esp.* ♪); recitation (*of poem*); ♪ recital; lecture; report; ♣ balance carried forward; e-n ~ halten (give a) lecture (*über acc.* on); 2en *v/t.* (*irr.* tragen, *sep.*, -ge-, *h*) ♣ carry forward; report on; recite (*poem*); perform, *esp.* ♪ execute; lecture on; state, express (*opinion*); ~ende ['~gəndə] *m* (-n/-n) performer; lecturer; speaker.

vor|trefflich *adj.* [fo:r'trɛfliç] excellent; '~treten *v/i.* (*irr.* treten, *sep.*, -ge-, *sein*) step forward; *fig.* project, protrude, stick out; 2tritt *m* (-[e]s/*no pl.*) precedence.

vorüber *adv.* ['fo:ry:bər] *space*: by, past; *time*: gone by, over; ~gehen *v/i.* (*irr.* gehen, *sep.*, -ge-, *sein*) pass, go by; ~gehend *adj.* passing; temporary; 2gehende [~də] *m* (-n/-n) passer-by; ~ziehen *v/i.* (*irr.* ziehen, *sep.*, -ge-, *sein*) march past, pass by; *storm*: blow over.

Vor|übung ['fo:r?-] *f* preliminary practice; ~untersuchung ⚖ ['fo:r?-] *f* preliminary inquiry.

Vorurteil ['fo:r?-] *n* prejudice; '2slos *adj.* unprejudiced, unbias(s)ed.

'**Vor|verkauf** *thea. m* booking in advance; *im* ~ bookable (*bei* at);

¹**Ɔverlegen** v/t. (sep., no -ge-, h) advance; **~wand** m (-[e]s/⸚e) pretext, preten|ce, Am. -se.

vorwärts adv. ['fo:rverts] forward, onward, on; **~l** go ahead!; **'~kommen** v/i. (irr. kommen, sep., -ge-, sein) (make) progress; fig. make one's way, get on (in life).

vorweg adv. [for'vek] beforehand; **~nehmen** v/t. (irr. nehmen, sep., -ge-, h) anticipate.

vor|weisen v/t. (irr. weisen, sep., -ge-, h) produce, show; **'~werfen** v/t. (irr. werfen, sep., -ge-, h) throw or cast before; j-m et. ~ reproach s.o. with s.th.; **'~wiegend 1.** adj. predominant, preponderant; **2.** adv. predominantly, chiefly, mainly, mostly; **'~witzig** adj. forward, pert; inquisitive.

'Vorwort n (-[e]s/-e) preface (by author); foreword.

'Vorwurf m reproach; subject (of drama, etc.); j-m e-n ~ or Vorwürfe machen reproach s.o. (wegen with); **'Ɔsvoll** adj. reproachful.

'vor|zählen v/t. (sep., -ge-, h) enu-

merate, count out (both: j-m to s.o.); **'Ɔzeichen** n omen; **'~zeichnen** v/t. (sep., -ge-, h): j-m et. ~ draw or sketch s.th. for s.o.; show s.o. how to draw s.th.; fig. mark out, destine; **'~zeigen** v/t. (sep., -ge-, h) produce, show.

'Vorzeit f antiquity; in literature often: times of old, days of yore; **Ɔig** adj. premature.

'vor|ziehen v/t. (irr. ziehen, sep., -ge-, h) draw forth; draw (curtains); fig. prefer; **Ɔzimmer** n antechamber, anteroom; waiting-room; **'Ɔzug** fig. m preference; advantage; merit; priority; **~züglich** adj. [~'tsy:kliç] excellent, superior, exquisite.

'Vorzugs|aktie f preference share or stock, Am. preferred stock; **'~preis** m special price; **Ɔweise** adv. preferably; chiefly.

Votum ['vo:tum] n (-s/Voten, Vota) vote.

vulgär adj. [vul'gɛ:r] vulgar.

Vulkan [vul'ka:n] m (-s/-e) volcano; **Ɔisch** adj. volcanic.

W

Waag|e ['va:gə] f (-/-n) balance, (e-e a pair of) scales pl.; die ~ halten (dat.) counterbalance; **Ɔerecht** adj., **Ɔrecht** adj. ['va:k-] horizontal, level; **~schale** ['va:k-] f scale.

Wabe ['va:bə] f (-/-n) honeycomb.

wach adj. [vax] awake; hell~ wide awake; ~ werden awake, wake up; **'Ɔe** f (-/-n) watch; guard; guardhouse, guardroom; police-station; sentry, sentinel; ~ haben be on guard; ~ halten keep watch; **'~en** v/i. (ge-, h) (keep) watch (über acc. over); sit up (bei with); **'Ɔhund** m watch-dog.

Wacholder ♀ [va'xɔldər] m (-s/-) juniper.

'wach|rufen v/t. (irr. rufen, sep., -ge-, h) rouse, evoke; **'~rütteln** v/t. (sep., -ge-, h) rouse (up); fig. rouse, shake up.

Wachs [vaks] n (-es/-e) wax.

'wachsam adj. watchful, vigilant; **'Ɔkeit** f (-/no pl.) watchfulness, vigilance.

wachsen¹ ['vaksən] v/i. (irr., ge-, sein) grow; fig. increase.

wachsen² [~] v/t. (ge-, h) wax.

wächsern adj. ['veksərn] wax; fig. waxen, waxy.

'Wachs|kerze f, **'~licht** n wax candle; **'~tuch** n waxcloth, oilcloth.

Wachstum ['vakstu:m] n (-s/no pl.) growth; fig. increase.

Wächte mount. ['veçtə] f (-/-n) cornice.

Wachtel orn. ['vaxtəl] f (-/-n) quail.

Wächter ['veçtər] m (-s/-) watcher, guard(ian); watchman.

'Wacht|meister m sergeant; **'~turm** m watch-tower.

wackel|ig adj. ['vakəliç] shaky (a. fig.), tottery; furniture, etc.: rickety; tooth, etc.: loose; **'Ɔkontakt** ⚡ m loose connexion or (Am. only) connection; **'~n** v/i. (ge-, h) shake; table, etc.: wobble; tooth, etc.: loose; tail, etc.: wag; ~ mit wag s.th.

wacker adj. ['vakər] honest, upright; brave, gallant.

wacklig adj. ['vakliç] s. wackelig.

Wade ['va:də] f (-/-n) calf; **'~nbein** anat. n fibula.

Waffe ['vafə] f (-/-n) weapon (a. fig.); ~n pl. a. arms pl.

Waffel ['vafəl] f (-/-n) waffle; wafer.

'Waffen|fabrik f armaments factory, Am. a. armory; **'~gattung** f arm; **'~gewalt** f (-/no pl.): mit ~ by force of arms; **'Ɔlos** adj. weaponless, unarmed; **'~schein** m firearm certificate, Am. gun license; **'~stillstand** m armistice (a. fig.), truce.

Wage|hals ['va:gəhals] m daredevil; **Ɔhalsig** adj. daring, foolhardy; attr. a. daredevil; **'~mut** m daring

wagen[1] ['vɑ:gən] v/t. (ge-, h) venture; risk, dare; sich ~ venture (an acc. [up]on).

Wagen[2] [~] m (-s/-, ⁿ) carriage (a. ⚙); Am. ⚙ car; ⚙ coach; wag(g)on; cart; car; lorry, truck; van.

wägen ['vɛ:gən] v/t. ([irr.,] ge-, h) weigh (a. fig.).

Wagen|heber m (-s/-) (lifting) jack; '~park m (-[e]s/no pl.) fleet of vehicles; '~schmiere f grease; '~spur f rut.

Waggon ⚙ [va'gõ:] m (-s/-s) (railway) carriage, Am. (railroad) car.

wag|halsig adj. ['vɑ:khalsiç] s. wagehalsig; '~nis n (-ses/-se) venture, risk.

Wahl [vɑ:l] f (-/-en) choice; alternative; selection; pol. election; e-e ~ treffen make a choice; s-e ~ treffen take one's choice; ich hatte keine (andere) ~ I had no choice.

wählbar adj. ['vɛ:lbaːr] eligible; '2keit f (-/no pl.) eligibility.

wahl|berechtigt adj. ['vɑ:lbərɛçtiçt] entitled to vote; '2beteiligung f percentage of voting, F turn-out; '2bezirk m constituency.

wählen (ge-, h) 1. v/t. choose; pol. elect; teleph. dial; 2. v/i. choose, take one's choice; teleph. dial (the number).

Wahlergebnis n election return.

Wähler m (-s/-) elector, voter; '2isch adj. particular (in dat. in, about, as to); nice (about), fastidious, F choosy; '~schaft f (-/-en) constituency, electorate.

Wahl|fach n optional subject, Am. a. elective; '2fähig adj. having a vote; eligible; '~gang m ballot; '~kampf m election campaign; '~kreis m constituency; '~lokal n polling station; '2los adj. indiscriminate; '~recht n (-[e]s/no pl.) franchise; '~rede f electoral speech.

'Wählscheibe teleph. f dial.

'Wahl|spruch m device, motto; '~stimme f vote; '~urne f ballotbox; '~versammlung f electoral rally; '~zelle f polling-booth; '~zettel m ballot, voting-paper.

Wahn [vɑ:n] m (-[e]s/no pl.) delusion, illusion; mania; '~sinn m (-[e]s/no pl.) insanity, madness (both a. fig.); '2sinnig adj. insane, mad (vor dat. with) (both a. fig.); ~sinnige ['~gə] m (-n/-n) madman, lunatic; '~vorstellung f delusion, hallucination; '~witz m (-es/no pl.) madness, insanity; '2witzig adj. mad, insane.

wahr adj. [vɑ:r] true; real; genuine; '~en v/t. (ge-, h) safeguard (interests, etc.); maintain (one's dignity); den Schein ~ keep up or save appearances.

währen ['vɛ:rən] v/i. (ge-, h) last, continue.

während 1. prp. (gen.) during; pending; 2. cj. while, whilst; while, whereas.

'wahrhaft adv. really, truly, indeed; ~ig ['~'haftiç] 1. adj. truthful, veracious; 2. adv. really, truly, indeed.

'Wahrheit f (-/-en) truth; in ~ in truth; j-m die ~ sagen give s.o. a piece of one's mind; '2getreu adj. true, faithful; '~sliebe f (-/no pl.) truthfulness, veracity; '2sliebend adj. truthful, veracious.

'wahr|lich adv. truly, really; '~nehmbar adj. perceivable, perceptible; '~nehmen v/t. (irr. nehmen, sep., -ge-, h) perceive, notice, avail o.s. of (opportunity); safeguard (interests); '2nehmung f (-/-en) perception, observation; '~sagen v/i. (sep., -ge-, h) tell or read fortunes; sich ~ lassen have one's fortune told; '2sagerin f (-/-nen) fortuneteller; '~scheinlich 1. adj. probable; likely; 2. adv.: ich werde ~ gehen I am likely to go; 2'scheinlichkeit f (-/⁓-en) probability, likelihood; aller ~ nach in all probability or likelihood.

'Wahrung f (-/no pl.) maintenance; safeguarding.

Währung ['vɛ:ruŋ] f (-/-en) currency; standard; '~sreform f currency or monetary reform.

'Wahrzeichen n landmark.

Waise ['vaizə] f (-/-n) orphan; '~nhaus n orphanage.

Wal zo. [vɑ:l] m (-[e]s/-e) whale.

Wald [valt] m (-[e]s/ⁿer) wood, forest; '~brand m forest fire; 2ig adj. ['~diç] wooded, woody; 2reich adj. ['~t-] rich in forests; '~ung ['~duŋ] f (-/-en) forest.

Walfänger ['vɑ:lfɛŋər] m (-s/-) whaler.

walken ['valkən] v/t. (ge-, h) full (cloth); mill (cloth, leather).

Wall [val] m (-[e]s/ⁿe) ✕ rampart (a. fig.); dam; mound.

Wallach ['valax] m (-[e]s/-e) gelding.

wallen ['valən] v/i. (ge-, h, sein) hair, articles of dress, etc.: flow; simmer; boil (a. fig.).

wall|fahren ['valfɑ:rən] v/i. (ge-, sein) (go on a) pilgrimage; '2fahrer m pilgrim; '2fahrt f pilgrimage; '~fahrten v/i. (ge-, sein) (go on a) pilgrimage.

'Wallung f (-/-en) ebullition; ✍ congestion; (Blut) in ~ bringen make s.o.'s blood boil, enrage.

Walnuß ['val-] f walnut; '~baum ♣ m walnut(-tree).

Walroß zo. ['val-] n walrus.

walten ['valtən] v/i. (ge-, h): s-s Amtes ~ attend to one's duties; Gnade ~ lassen show mercy.

Walze ['valtsə] f (-/-n) roller, cylinder; ⊕ *a.* roll; ⊕, ♪ barrel; '2n *v/t.* (ge-, h) roll (*a.* ⊕).

wälzen ['veltsən] *v/t.* (ge-, h) roll; roll (*problem*) round in one's mind; shift (*blame*) (*auf acc.* [up]on); *sich* ~ roll; wallow (*in mud, etc.*); welter (*in blood, etc.*).

Walzer ♪ ['valtsər] *m* (-s/-) waltz.

Wand [vant] 1. *f* (-/ᵉe) wall; partition; 2. 2 *pret. of* winden.

Wandel ['vandəl] *m* (-s/*no pl.*) change; '2bar *adj.* changeable; variable; '~gang *m*, '~halle *f* lobby; '2n (ge-) 1. *v/i.* (sein) walk; 2. *v/refl.* (h) change.

Wander|er ['vandərər] *m* (-s/-) wanderer; hiker; '~leben *n* (-s/*no pl.*) vagrant life; '2n *v/i.* (ge-, sein) wander; hike; '~niere ♪ *f* floating kidney; '~prediger *m* itinerant preacher; '~preis *m* challenge trophy; '~schaft *f* (-/*no pl.*) wanderings *pl.*; *auf (der)* ~ *on the* tramp; '~ung *f* (-/-en) walking-tour; hike.

'Wand|gemälde *n* mural (painting); '~kalender *m* wall-calendar; '~karte *f* wall-map.

Wandlung ['vandluŋ] *f* (-/-en) change, transformation; *eccl.* transubstantiation; ♄ redhibition.

'Wand|schirm *m* folding-screen; '~schrank *m* wall-cupboard; '~spiegel *m* wall-mirror; '~tafel *f* blackboard; '~teppich *m* tapestry; '~uhr *f* wall-clock.

wandte ['vantə] *pret. of* wenden 2.

Wange ['vaŋə] *f* (-/-n) cheek.

Wankel|mut ['vaŋkəlmuːt] *m* fickleness, inconstancy; 2mütig *adj.* ['~myˑtiç] fickle, inconstant.

wanken ['vaŋkən] *v/i.* (ge-, h, sein) totter, stagger (*a. fig.*); house, *etc.*: rock; *fig.* waver.

wann *adv.* [van] when; *s. dann*; *seit* ~? how long?, since when?

Wanne ['vanə] *f* (-/-n) tub; bath (-tub), F tub; '~bad *n* bath, F tub.

Wanze *zo.* ['vantsə] *f* (-/-n) bug, *Am. a.* bedbug.

Wappen ['vapən] *n* (-s/-) (coat of) arms *pl.*; '~kunde *f* (-/*no pl.*) heraldry; '~schild *m, n* escutcheon; '~tier *n* heraldic animal.

wappnen *fig.* ['vapnən] *v/refl.* (ge-, h): *sich* ~ *gegen* be prepared for; *sich mit Geduld* ~ have patience.

war [vaːr] *pret. of* sein¹.

warb [varp] *pret. of* werben.

Ware ['vaːrə] *f* (-/-n) commodity, article of trade; ~n *pl. a.* goods *pl.*, merchandise, wares *pl.*

'Waren|aufzug *m* hoist; '~bestand *m* stock (on hand); '~haus *n* department store; '~lager *n* stock; warehouse, *Am. a.* stock room; '~probe *f* sample; '~zeichen *n* trade mark.

warf [varf] *pret. of* werfen.

warm *adj.* [varm] warm (*a. fig.*); *meal:* hot; *schön* ~ nice and warm.

Wärme ['vermə] *f* (-/♄ -n) warmth; *phys.* heat; '~grad *m* degree of heat; '2n *v/t.* (ge-, h) warm; *sich die Füße* ~ warm one's feet.

'Wärmflasche *f* hot-water bottle.

'warmherzig *adj.* warm-hearted.

'Warm|wasser|heizung *f* hot-water heating; '~versorgung *f* hot-water supply.

warn|en ['varnən] *v/t.* (ge-, h) warn (*vor dat.* of, against), caution (against); '2signal *n* danger-signal (*a. fig.*); '2streik *m* token strike; '2ung *f* (-/-en) warning, caution; 2ungstafel ['varnuŋs-] *f* notice-board.

Warte *fig.* ['vartə] *f* (-/-n) point of view.

warten ['vartən] *v/i.* (ge-, h) wait (*auf acc.* for); be in store (for *s.o.*); *j-n* ~ *lassen* keep s.o. waiting.

Wärter ['vertər] *m* (-s/-) attendant; keeper; (*male*) nurse.

'Warte|saal *m*, '~zimmer *n* waiting-room.

Wartung ⊕ ['vartuŋ] *f* (-/♄ -en) maintenance.

warum *adv.* [va'rum] why.

Warze ['vartsə] *f* (-/-n) wart; nipple.

was [vas] 1. *interr. pron.* what; ~ *kostet das Buch?* how much is this book?; F ~ *rennst du denn so* (*schnell*)? why are you running like this?; ~ *für (ein)* ...! what a(n) ...!; ~ *für ein* ...? what ...?; 2. *rel. pron.* what; ~ (*auch immer*), *alles* ~ what(so)ever; ..., ~ *ihn völlig kalt ließ* ... which left him quite cold; 3. F *indef. pron.* something; *ich will dir mal* ~ *sagen* I'll tell you what.

wasch|bar *adj.* ['vaʃbaːr] washable; '2becken *n* wash-basin, *Am.* wash-bowl.

Wäsche ['veʃə] *f* (-/-n) wash(ing); laundry; linen (*a. fig.*); underwear; *in der* ~ *sein* be at the wash; *sie hat heute große* ~ she has a large wash today.

waschecht *adj.* ['vaʃ⁹-] washable; *colour:* *a.* fast; *fig.* dyed-in-the-wool.

'Wäsche|klammer *f* clothes-peg, clothes-pin; '~leine *f* clothes-line.

'waschen *v/t.* (irr., ge-, h) wash; *sich* ~ (have a) wash; *sich das Haar or den Kopf* ~ wash *or* shampoo one's hair *or* head; *sich gut* ~ (*lassen*) wash well.

Wäscher|ei [veʃə'raɪ] *f* (-/-en) laundry; '~in *f* (-/-nen) washer-woman, laundress.

'Wäscheschrank *m* linen closet.

'Wasch|frau *f s.* Wäscherin; '~haus *n* wash-house; '~kessel *m* copper; '~korb *m* clothes-basket;

'**~küche** f wash-house; '**~lappen** m face-cloth, Am. washrag, wash-cloth; '**~maschine** f washing machine, washer; '**~pulver** n washing powder; '**~raum** m lavatory, Am. a. washroom; '**~schüssel** f wash-basin; '**~tag** m wash(ing)-day; '**~ung** f (-/-en) ♂ wash; ablution; '**~weib** contp. n gossip; '**~wanne** f wash-tub.

Wasser ['vasər] n (-s/-, ⁀) water; ~ lassen make water; zu ~ und zu Land(e) by sea and land; '**~ball** m 1. beach-ball; water-polo ball; 2. (-[e]s/no pl.) water-polo; '**~ballspiel** n 1. (-[e]s/no pl.) water-polo; 2. water-polo match; '**~behälter** m reservoir, water-tank; '**~blase** ✝ f water-blister; '**~dampf** m steam; '2**dicht** adj. waterproof; water-tight; '**~eimer** m water-pail, bucket; '**~fall** m waterfall, cascade; cataract; '**~farbe** f water-colo(u)r; '**~flugzeug** n waterplane, seaplane; '**~glas** n 1. tumbler; 2. ♠ (-es/no pl.) water-glass; '**~graben** m ditch; '**~hahn** m tap, Am. a. faucet; '**~hose** f waterspout.

wässerig ['vesəriç] ['vesəriç] watery, washy (a. fig.); j-m den Mund ~ machen make water s.o.'s mouth water.

'**Wasser|kanne** f water-jug, ewer; '**~kessel** m kettle; '**~klosett** n water-closet, W.C.; '**~kraft** f water-power; '**~kraftwerk** n hydroelectric power station or plant, water-power station; '**~krug** m water-jug, ewer; '**~kur** f water-cure, hydropathy; '**~lauf** m water-course; '**~leitung** f water-supply; '**~leitungsrohr** n water-pipe; '**~mangel** m shortage of water; '2**n** v/i. (ge-, h) alight on water; splash down. (salted herring, etc.).\

wässern ['vesərn] v/t. (ge-, h) soak/
'**Wasser|pflanze** f aquatic plant; '**~rinne** f gutter; '**~rohr** n water-pipe; '**~schaden** m damage caused by water; '**~scheide** f watershed, Am. a. divide; '2**scheu** adj. afraid of water; '**~schlauch** m water-hose; '**~spiegel** m water-level; '**~sport** m aquatic sports pl.; '**~spülung** f (-/-en) flushing (system); '**~stand** m water-level; '**~standsanzeiger** ['vasərʃtants?-] m water-gauge; '**~stiefel** m/pl. waders pl.; '**~stoff** ♠ m (-[e]s/no pl.) hydrogen; '**~stoffbombe** f hydrogen bomb, H-bomb; '**~strahl** m jet of water; '**~straße** f waterway; '**~tier** n aquatic animal; '**~verdrängung** f (-/-en) displacement; '**~versorgung** f water-supply; '**~waage** f spirit-level, water-level; '**~weg** m waterway; auf dem ~ by water; '**~welle** f water-wave; '**~werk** n waterworks sg., pl.; '**~zeichen** n watermark.

wäßrig adj. ['vesriç] s. wässerig.
waten ['vaːtən] v/i. (ge-, sein) wade.
watscheln ['vaːtʃəln] v/i. (ge-, sein, h) waddle.
Watt ♂ [vat] n (-s/-) watt.
Watt|e ['vatə] f (-/-n) cotton-wool; surgical cotton; wadding; '**~ebausch** m wad; 2**ieren** [~'tiːrən] v/t. wad, pad.
weben ['veːbən] v/t. and v/i. ([irr.] ge-, h) weave.
'**Weber** m (-s/-) weaver; '**~ei** [~'raɪ] f 1. (-/no pl.) weaving; 2. (-/-en) weaving-mill.
Webstuhl ['veːpʃtuːl] m loom.
Wechsel ['veksəl] m (-s/-) change; allowance; ✝ bill (of exchange); hunt. runway; eigener ~ ✝ promissory note; '**~beziehung** f correlation; '**~fälle** ['~fɛlə] pl. vicissitudes pl.; '**~fieber** ♂ n (-s/no pl.) intermittent fever; malaria; '**~frist** ✝ f usance; '**~geld** n change; '**~kurs** m rate of exchange; '**~makler** ✝ m bill-broker; '2**n** (ge-, h) 1. v/t. change; vary; exchange (words, etc.); den Besitzer ~ change hands; die Kleider ~ change (one's clothes); 2. v/i. change; vary; alternate; '**~nehmer** ✝ m (-s/-) payee; 2**seitig** adj. ['~zaɪtiç] mutual, reciprocal; '**~strom** ♂ m alternating current; '**~stube** f exchange office; 2**weise** adv. alternately, by or in turns; '**~wirkung** f interaction.
wecke|n ['vekən] v/t. (ge-, h) wake (up), waken; arouse (a. fig.); '2**r** m (-s/-) alarm-clock.
wedeln ['veːdəln] v/i. (ge-, h): ~ mit wag (tail).
weder cj. ['veːdər]: ~ ... noch neither ... nor.
Weg[1] [veːk] m (-[e]s/-e) way (a. fig.); road (a. fig.); path; route; walk; auf halbem ~ half-way; am ~e by the roadside; aus dem ~e gehen steer clear of; aus dem ~e räumen remove (a. fig.); in die ~e leiten set on foot, initiate.
weg[2] adv. [vek] away, off; gone; geh ~ be off (with you)!; ~ mit ihm! off with him!; Hände ~! hands off!; F ich muß ~ I must be off; F ganz ~ sein be quite beside o.s.; '**~bleiben** F v/i. (irr. bleiben, sep., -ge-, sein) stay away; be omitted; '**~bringen** v/t. (irr. bringen, sep., -ge-, h) take away; a. remove (things).
wegen prp. (gen.) ['veːgən] because of, on account of, owing to.
weg|fahren ['vek-] (irr. fahren, sep., -ge-) 1. v/t. (h) remove; cart away; 2. v/i. (sein) leave; '**~fallen** v/i. (irr. fallen, sep., -ge-, sein) be omitted; be abolished; '2**gang** m (-[e]s/no pl.) going away, departure; '**~gehen** v/i. (irr. gehen, sep., -ge-, sein) go away or off; merchandise:

sell; '**~haben** F *v/t.* (*irr.* haben, *sep.*, *-ge-*, h): e-n ~ be tight; have a screw loose; er hat noch nicht weg, wie man es machen muß he hasn't got the knack of it yet; '**~jagen** *v/t.* (*sep.*, *-ge-*, h) drive away; '**~kommen** F *v/i.* (*irr.* kommen, *sep.*, *-ge-*, sein) get away; be missing; gut (schlecht) ~ come off well (badly); mach, daß du wegkommst! be off (with you)!; '**~lassen** *v/t.* (*irr.* lassen, *sep.*, *-ge-*, h) let s.o. go; leave out, omit; '**~laufen** *v/i.* (*irr.* laufen, *sep.*, *-ge-*, sein) run away; '**~legen** *v/t.* (*sep.*, *-ge-*, h) put away; '**~machen** F *v/t.* (*sep.*, *-ge-*, h) remove; *a.* take out (stains); '**~müssen** *v/i.* (*irr.* müssen 1, *sep.*, *-ge-*, h): ich muß weg I must be off; **2nahme** ['~nɑ:mə] *f* (-/-n) taking (away); '**~nehmen** *v/t.* (*irr.* nehmen, *sep.*, *-ge-*, h) take up, occupy (time, space); j-m et. ~ take s.th. away from s.o.; '**~raffen** fig. *v/t.* (*sep.*, *-ge-*, h) carry off.

Wegrand ['ve:k-] *m* wayside.
weg|räumen ['vɛk-] *v/t.* (*sep.*, *-ge-*, h) clear away, remove; '**~schaffen** *v/t.* (*sep.*, *-ge-*, h) remove; '**~schikken** *v/t.* (*sep.*, *-ge-*, h) send away or off; '**~sehen** *v/i.* (*irr.* sehen, *sep.*, *-ge-*, h) look away; ~ über (*acc.*) overlook, shut one's eyes to; '**~setzen** *v/t.* (*sep.*, *-ge-*, h) put away; sich ~ über (*acc.*) disregard, ignore; '**~streichen** *v/t.* (*irr.* streichen, *sep.*, *-ge-*, h) strike off or out; '**~tun** *v/t.* (*irr.* tun, *sep.*, *-ge-*, h) put away or aside.

Wegweiser ['ve:kvaɪzər] *m* (-s/-) signpost, finger-post; fig. guide.
weg|wenden ['vɛk-] *v/t.* ([*irr.* wenden,] *sep.*, *-ge-*, h) turn away, avert (one's eyes); sich ~ turn away; '**~werfen** *v/t.* (*irr.* werfen, *sep.*, *-ge-*, h) throw away; '**~werfend** adj. disparaging; '**~wischen** *v/t.* (*sep.*, *-ge-*, h) wipe off; '**~ziehen** (*irr.* ziehen, *sep.*, *-ge-*) 1. *v/t.* (h) pull or draw away; 2. *v/i.* (sein) (re)move.

weh [ve:] 1. adj. sore; 2. adv.: ~ tun ache, hurt; j-m ~ tun pain or hurt s.o.; fig. a. grieve s.o.; sich ~ tun hurt o.s.; mir tut der Finger ~ my finger hurts.
Wehen[1] ♀ ['ve:ən] *f/pl.* labo(u)r, travail.
wehen[2] [~] (ge-, h) 1. *v/t.* blow; 2. *v/i.* blow; es weht ein starker Wind it is blowing hard.
weh|klagen *v/i.* (ge-, h) lament (um for, over); '**~leidig** adj. snivel(l)ing; voice: plaintive; '**~mut** *f* (-/no pl.) wistfulness; '**~mütig** adj. '**~my**-tiç] wistful.
Wehr [ve:r] 1. *f* (-/-en): sich zur ~ setzen offer resistance (gegen to), show fight; 2. *n* (-[e]s/-e) weir;

'**~dienst** ⚔ *m* military service; '**2en** *v/refl.* (ge-, h) defend o.s.; offer resistance (gegen to); '**2fähig** ⚔ adj. able-bodied; '**2los** adj. defenceless, Am. defenseless; '**~pflicht** ⚔ *f* (-/no pl.) compulsory military service, conscription; '**2-pflichtig** ⚔ adj. liable to military service.

Weib [vaɪp] *n* (-[e]s/-er) woman; wife; '**~chen** zo. *n* (-/-) female.
Weiber|feind ['vaɪbər-] *m* womanhater; '**~held** contp. *m* ladies' man; '**~volk** F *n* (-[e]s/no pl.) womenfolk.
weib|isch adj. ['vaɪbiʃ] womanish, effeminate; '**~lich** adj. ['~p-] female; gr. feminine; womanly, feminine.
weich adj. [vaɪç] soft (a. fig.); meat, etc.: tender; egg: soft-boiled; ~ werden soften; fig. relent.
Weiche[1] 🚂 ['vaɪçə] *f* (-/-n) switch; ~n pl. points pl.
Weiche[2] anat. ['~] *f* (-/-n) flank, side.
weichen[1] ['vaɪçən] *v/i.* (*irr.*, ge-, sein) give way, yield (dat. to); nicht von der Stelle ~ not to budge an inch; j-m nicht von der Seite ~ stick to s.o.
weichen[2] [~] *v/i.* (ge-, h, sein) soak.
'**Weichensteller** 🚂 *m* (-s/-) pointsman, switch-man.
'**weich|herzig** adj. soft-hearted, tender-hearted; '**~lich** adj. somewhat soft; fig. effeminate; '**2ling** ['~liŋ] *m* (-s/-e) weakling, milksop, molly(-coddle), sl. sissy; '**2tier** *n* mollusc.

Weide[1] ♀ ['vaɪdə] *f* (-/-n) willow.
Weide[2] ♀ [~] *f* (-/-n) pasture; auf der ~ out at grass; '**~land** *n* pasture(-land); '**2n** (ge-, h) 1. *v/t.* feed, pasture, graze; sich ~ an (dat.) gloat over; feast on; 2. *v/i.* pasture, graze.
'**Weiden|korb** *m* wicker basket, osier basket; '**~rute** *f* osier switch.
weidmännisch hunt. adj. ['vaɪtmɛniʃ] sportsmanlike.
weiger|n ['vaɪgərn] *v/refl.* (ge-, h) refuse, decline; '**2ung** *f* (-/-en) refusal.
Weihe eccl. ['vaɪə] *f* (-/-n) consecration; ordination; '**2n** eccl. *v/t.* (ge-, h) consecrate; j-n zum Priester ~ ordain s.o. priest.
Weiher ['vaɪər] *m* (-s/-) pond.
'**weihevoll** adj. solemn.
Weihnachten ['vaɪnaxtən] *n* (-s/no pl.) Christmas, Xmas.
'**Weihnachts|abend** *m* Christmas eve; '**~baum** *m* Christmas-tree; '**~ferien** pl. Christmas holidays pl.; '**~fest** *n* Christmas; '**~geschenk** *n* Christmas present; '**~gratifikation** *f* Christmas bonus; '**~karte** *f* Christmas card; '**~lied** *n* carol, Christmas hymn; '**~mann** *m* Father Christmas, Santa Claus; '**~markt** *m* Christmas fair; '**~zeit** *f*

(-/no pl.) Christmas(-tide) (in Germany beginning on the first Advent Sunday).

'Weih|rauch eccl. m incense; '∼wasser eccl. n (-s/no pl.) holy water.

weil cj. [vaɪl] because, since, as.

Weil|chen ['vaɪlçən] n (-s/-): ein ∼ a little while, a spell; '∼e f (-/no pl.): e-e ∼ a while.

Wein [vaɪn] m (-[e]s/-e) wine; ♀ vine; wilder ∼ ♀ Virginia creeper; '∼bau m (-[e]s/no pl.) vine-growing, viticulture; '∼beere f grape; '∼berg m vineyard; '∼blatt n vine-leaf.

wein|en ['vaɪnən] v/i. (ge-, h) weep (um, vor dat. for), cry (vor dat. for joy, etc., with hunger, etc.); '∼erlich adj. tearful, lachrymose; whining.

'Wein|ernte f vintage; '∼essig m vinegar; '∼faß n wine-cask; '∼flasche f wine-bottle; '∼geist m (-[e]s/-e) spirit(s pl.) of wine; '∼glas n wineglass; '∼handlung f wine-merchant's shop; '∼karte f wine-list; '∼keller m wine-vault; '∼kelter f winepress; '∼kenner m connoisseur of or in wines.

'Weinkrampf ⋅ m paroxysm of weeping.

'Wein|kühler m wine-cooler; '∼lese f vintage; '∼presse f winepress; '∼ranke f vine-tendril; '∼rebe f vine; '²rot adj. claret-colo(u)red; '∼stock m vine; '∼traube f grape, bunch of grapes.

weise[1] ['vaɪzə] 1. adj. wise; sage; 2. ♀ m (-n/-n) wise man, sage.

Weise[2] [∼] f (-/-n) ♪ melody, tune; fig. manner, way; auf diese ∼ in this way.

weisen ['vaɪzən] (irr., ge-, h) 1. v/t.: j-m die Tür ∼ show s.o. the door; von der Schule ∼ expel from school; von sich ∼ reject (idea, etc.); deny (charge, etc.); 2. v/i.: auf (acc.) point at or to.

Weis|heit ['vaɪshaɪt] f (-/∼-en) wisdom; am Ende s-r ∼ sein be at one's wit's end; '∼heitszahn m wisdom-tooth; '²machen v/t. (sep., -ge-, h): j-m et. ∼ make s.o. believe s.th.

weiß adj. [vaɪs] white; '²blech n tin(-plate); '²brot n white bread; '²e m (-n/-n) white (man); '∼en v/t. (ge-, h) whitewash; '∼glühend adj. white-hot, incandescent; '²kohl m white cabbage; '∼lich adj. whitish; '²waren pl. linen goods pl.; '²wein m white wine.

Weisung ['vaɪzʊŋ] f (-/-en) direction, directive.

weit [vaɪt] 1. adj. distant (von from); world, garment: wide; area, etc.: vast; garment: loose; journey, way: long; conscience: elastic; 2. adv.: ∼ entfernt far away; ∼ entfernt von a. a long distance from; fig. far from;

∼ und breit far and wide; ∼ über sechzig (Jahre alt) well over sixty; bei ∼em (by) far; von ∼em from a distance.

weit|ab adv. ['vaɪt-] far away (von from); '∼aus adv. (by) far, much; '²blick m (-[e]s/no pl.) far-sightedness; '∼blickend adj. far-sighted, far-seeing; '∼en v/t. and v/refl. (ge-, h) widen.

'weiter 1. adj. particulars, etc.: further; charges, etc.: additional, extra; ∼e fünf Wochen another five weeks; bis auf ∼es until further notice; ohne ∼es without any hesitation; off-hand; 2. adv. furthermore, moreover; ∼! go on; nichts ∼ nothing more; und so ∼ and so on; bis hierher und nicht ∼ so far and no farther; '²e n (-n/no pl.) the rest; further details pl.

'weiter|befördern v/t. (sep., no -ge-, h) forward; '∼bestehen v/i. (irr. stehen, sep., no -ge-, h) continue to exist, survive; '∼bilden v/t. (sep., -ge-, h) give s.o. further education; sich ∼ improve one's knowledge; continue one's education; '∼geben v/t. (irr. geben, sep., -ge-, h) pass (dat., an acc. to); '∼gehen v/i. (irr. gehen, sep., -ge-, sein) pass or move on, walk along; fig. continue, go on; '∼hin adv. in (the) future; furthermore; et. ∼ tun continue doing or to do s.th.; '∼kommen v/i. (irr. kommen, sep., -ge-, sein) get on; '∼können v/i. (irr. können, sep., -ge-, h) be able to go on; '∼leben v/i. (sep., -ge-, h) live on, survive (a. fig.); '∼machen v/t. and v/i. (sep., -ge-, h) carry on.

'weit|gehend adj. powers: large; support: generous; '∼gereist adj. travel(l)ed; '∼greifend adj. far-reaching; '∼herzig adj. broad-minded; '∼hin adv. far off; '∼läufig ['∼ɔyfɪç] 1. adj. house, etc.: spacious; story, etc.: detailed; relative: distant; 2. adv.: ∼ erzählen (tell in) detail; er ist ∼ verwandt mit mir he is a distant relative of mine; '∼reichend adj. far-reaching; '∼schweifig adj. diffuse, prolix; '∼sichtig adj. ⋅ far-sighted; fig. a. far-seeing; '²sichtigkeit ⋅ f (-/∼-en) far-sightedness; '²sprung m (-[e]s/no pl.) long jump, Am. broad jump; '∼tragend adj. ⋅ long-range; fig. far-reaching; '∼verbreitet adj. widespread.

Weizen ♀ ['vaɪtsən] m (-s/-) wheat; '∼brot n wheaten bread; '∼mehl n wheaten flour.

welch [vɛlç] 1. interr. pron. what; which; ∼er? which one?; ∼er von beiden? which of the two?; 2. rel. pron. who, that; which, that; 3. f indef. pron.: es gibt ∼e, die sagen, daß ... there are some who say that ...; *es sollen viele Ausländer hier sein, hast du schon ~e gesehen?* many foreigners are said to be here, have you seen any yet?

welk *adj.* [velk] faded, withered; *skin:* flabby, flaccid; '~en *v/i.* (ge-, sein) fade, wither.

Wellblech ['vɛlblɛç] *n* corrugated iron.

Welle [velə] *f* (-/-n) wave (*a. fig.*); ⊕ shaft.

wellen *v/t. and v/refl.* (ge-, h) wave; '2bereich ∮ *m* wave-range; '~förmig *adj.* ['~fœrmiç] undulating, undulatory; '2länge ∮ *f* wave-length; '2linie *f* wavy line; '2reiten *n* (-s/no *pl.*) surf-riding.

'wellig *adj.* wavy.

'Wellpappe *f* corrugated cardboard *or* paper.

Welt [vɛlt] *f* (-/-en) world; *die ganze* ~ the whole world, all the world; *auf der* ~ in the world, *auf der ganzen* ~ all over the world; *zur* ~ *bringen* give birth to, bring into the world.

'Welt|all *n* universe, cosmos; '~anschauung *f* Weltanschauung; '~ausstellung *f* world fair; '2bekannt *adj.* known all over the world; '2berühmt *adj.* world-famous; '2bürger *m* cosmopolite; '2erschütternd *adj.* world-shaking; '2fremd *adj.* wordly innocent; '~friede(n) *m* universal peace; '~geschichte *f* (-/no *pl.*) universal history; '2gewandt *adj.* knowing the ways of the world; '~handel ∮ *m* (-s/no *pl.*) world trade; '~karte *f* map of the world; '2klug *adj.* wordly-wise; '~krieg *m* world war; *der zweite* ~ World War II; '2lage *f* international situation; '~lauf *m* course of the world; '2lich 1. *adj.* wordly; secular, temporal; 2. *adv.*: ~ *gesinnt* wordly-minded; '~literatur *f* world literature; '~macht *f* world-power; 2männisch *adj.* ['~menif] man-of-the-world; '~markt *m* (-[e]s/no *pl.*) world market; '~meer *n* ocean; '~meister *m* world champion; '~meisterschaft *f* world championship; '~raum *m* (-[e]s/no *pl.*) (outer) space; '~reich *n* universal empire; *das Britische* ~ the British Empire; '~reise *f* journey round the world; '~rekord *m* world record; '~ruf *m* (-[e]s/no *pl.*) world-wide reputation; '~schmerz *m* Weltschmerz; '~sprache *f* world *or* universal language; '~stadt *f* metropolis; '2weit *adj.* world-wide; '~wunder *n* wonder of the world.

Wende ['vɛndə] *f* (-/-n) turn (*a. swimming*); *fig. a.* turning-point; '~kreis *m geogr.* tropic; *mot.* turning-circle.

Wendeltreppe ['vɛndəl-] *f* winding

staircase, (e-e a flight of) winding stairs *pl.*, spiral staircase.

'Wende|marke *f sports*: turning-point; '2n 1. *v/t.* (ge-, h) turn (*coat, etc.*); turn (*hay*) about; 2. *v/refl.* [*irr.*] (ge-, h): *sich ~ an* (*acc.*) turn to; address o.s. to; apply to (*wegen* for); 3. *v/i.* (ge-, h) ⊕, *mot.* turn; *bitte ~!* please turn over!; '~punkt *m* turning-point.

'wend|ig *adj.* nimble, agile (*both a. fig.*); *mot.*, ⊕ easily steerable; *mot.* flexible; '2ung *f* (-/-en) turn (*a. fig.*); ✗ facing; *fig.*: change; expression; idiom.

wenig ['ve:niç] 1. *adj.* little; ~e *pl.* few *pl.*; ~er less; ~er *pl.* fewer; *ein klein* ~ *Geduld* a little bit of patience; *das* ~e the little; 2. *adv.* little; ~er less; ∦ *a. minus*; *am* ~sten least (of all); '2keit *f* (-/-en): *meine* ~ my humble self; ~stens *adv.* ['~stəns] at least.

wenn *cj.* [vɛn] when; if; ~ ... *nicht* if ... not, unless; ~ *auch* (al)though, even though; ~ *nun* ...? what if ...?; *und* ~ *nun* ...? what if ... ?; *wie wäre es,* ~ *wir jetzt heimgingen?* what about going home now?

wer [ve:r] 1. *interr. pron.* who; which; ~ *von euch?* which of you?; 2. *rel. pron.* who; ~ *auch* (immer) who(so)ever; 3. F *indef. pron.* somebody; anybody; *ist schon* ~ *gekommen?* has anybody come yet?

Werbe|abteilung ['vɛrbə-] *f* advertising *or* publicity department; '~film *m* advertising film.

'werb|en (*irr.*, ge-, h) 1. *v/t.* canvass (*votes, subscribers, etc.*); ✗ recruit, enlist; 2. *v/i.*: ~ *für* advertise, *Am. a.* advertize; make propaganda for; canvass for; '2ung *f* (-/-en) advertising, publicity, *Am. a.* advertizing; propaganda; canvassing; ✗ enlistment, recruiting.

Werdegang ['ve:rdə-] *m* career; ⊕ process of manufacture.

'werden 1. *v/i.* (*irr.*, ge-, sein) become, get; grow; turn (*pale, sour, etc.*); *was ist aus ihm geworden?* what has become of him?; *was will er* (*einmal*) ~? what is he going to be?; 2. 2 *n* (-s/no *pl.*): *noch im* ~ *sein* be in embryo.

werfen ['vɛrfən] (*irr.*, ge-, h) 1. *v/t.* throw (*nach at*); *zo.* throw (*young*); cast (*shadow, glance, etc.*); *Falten* ~ fall in folds; set badly; 2. *v/i.* throw; *zo.* litter; ~ *mit* throw (*auf acc., nach at*).

Werft ⊕ [vɛrft] *f* (-/-en) shipyard, dockyard.

Werk [vɛrk] *n* (-[e]s/-e) work; act; ⊕ works *pl.*; works *sg., pl.*, factory; *das* ~ *e-s Augenblicks* the work of a moment; *zu* ~ *e gehen* proceed; '~bank ⊕ *f* work-bench; '~meister *m* foreman; ~statt ['~ʃtat] *f*

(-/=en) workshop; '~tag m work-day; '2tätig adj. working; '~zeug n tool; implement; instrument. Wermut ['ve:rmu:t] m (-[e]s/no pl.) ♀ wormwood; verm(o)uth.

wert [ve:rt] 1. adj. worth; worthy (gen. of); ~, getan zu werden worth doing; 2. ♀ m (-[e]s/-e) value (a. ♣, ♏, phys., fig.); worth (a. fig.); Brief-marken im ~ von 2 Schilling 2 shillings' worth of stamps; großen ~ legen auf (acc.) set a high value (up)on.

'Wert|brief m money-letter; '2en v/t. (ge-, h) value; appraise; '~ge-genstand m article of value; '2los adj. worthless, valueless; '~pa-piere n/pl. securities pl.; '~sachen pl. valuables pl.; '~ung f (-/-en) valuation; appraisal; sports: score; '2voll adj. valuable, precious.

Wesen ['ve:zən] n 1. (-s/no pl.) entity, essence; nature, character; viel ~s machen um make a fuss of; 2. (-s/-) being; creature; '2los adj. unreal; '2tlich adj. essential, sub-stantial.

weshalb [ves'halp] 1. interr. pron. why; 2. cj. that's why.

Wespe zo. ['vespə] f (-/-n) wasp.

West geogr. [vest] west; '~en m (-s/no pl.) west; the West.

Weste ['vestə] f (-/-n) waistcoat, ♣ and Am. vest; e-e reine ~ haben have a clean slate.

'west|lich adj. west; westerly; western; '2wind m west(erly) wind.

Wett|bewerb ['vetbəverp] m (-[e]s/-e) competition (a. ♣); '2büro n betting office; '~e f (-/-n) wager, bet; e-e ~ eingehen lay or make a bet; '~eifer m emulation, rivalry; '2eifern v/i. (ge-, h) vie (mit with; in dat. in; um for); '2en v/i. (ge-, h) 1. v/t. wager, bet; 2. v/i.: mit j-m um et. ~ wager or bet s.o. s.th.; ~ auf (acc.) wager or bet on, back.

Wetter1 ['vetər] n (-s/-) weather.

Wetter2 [~] m (-s/-) better.

'Wetter|bericht m weather-fore-cast; '2fest adj. weather-proof; '~karte f weather-chart; '~lage f weather-conditions pl.; '~leuchten n (-s/no pl.) sheet-lightning; '~vor-hersage f (-/-n) weather-forecast; '~warte f weather-station.

'Wett|kampf m contest, competi-tion; '~kämpfer m contestant; '~lauf m race; '~läufer m racer, runner; '2machen v/t. (sep., -ge-, h) make up for; '~rennen n race; '~rüsten n (-s/no pl.) armament race; '~spiel n match, game; '~streit m contest. [sharpen.]

wetzen ['vetsən] v/t. (ge-, h) whet,∫ wich [viç] pret. of weichen1.

Wichse ['viksə] f 1. (-/-n) blacking; polish; 2. F fig. (-/no pl.) thrashing; '2n v/t. (ge-, h) black; polish.

wichtig adj. ['viçtiç] important; sich ~ machen show off; '2keit f (-/♣-en) importance; 2tuer ['~tu:-ər] m (-s/-) pompous fellow; '~tue-risch adj. pompous.

Wickel ['vikəl] m (-s/-) roll(er); ♣: compress; packing; '2n v/t. (ge-, h) wind; swaddle (baby); wrap.

Widder zo. ['vidər] m (-s/-) ram.

wider prp. (acc.) ['vi:dər] against, contrary to; '~borstig adj. cross-grained; '~fahren v/i. (irr. fahren, no -ge-, sein) happen (dat. to); '2haken m barb; 2hall ['~hal] m (-[e]s/-e) echo, reverberation; fig. response; retraction; '~hallen v/i. (sep., -ge-, h) (re-)echo (von with), resound (with); '~legen v/t. (no -ge-, h) refute, disprove; '~lich adj. repug-nant, repulsive; disgusting; '~na-türlich adj. unnatural; '~recht-lich adj. illegal, unlawful; '2rede f contradiction; '2ruf m ♣ revoca-tion; retraction; '~rufen v/t. (irr. rufen, no -ge-, h) revoke; retract (a. ♣); '~ruflich adj. revocable; 2sa-cher ['~zaxər] m (-s/-) adversary; '2schein m reflection; '~setzen v/refl. (no -ge-, h): sich e-r Sache ~ oppose or resist s.th.; '~setzlich adj. refractory; insubordinate; '~sinnig adj. absurd; '~spenstig adj. ['~∫penstiç] refractory; '2spenstig-keit f (-/♣-en) refractoriness; '~spiegeln v/t. (sep., -ge-, h) reflect (a. fig.); sich ~ in (dat.) be reflected in; '~sprechen v/i. (irr. sprechen, no -ge-, h): j-m ~ con-tradict s.o.; '2spruch m contradic-tion; opposition; im ~ zu in con-tradiction to; '~sprüchlich adj. ['~∫pry:çliç] contradictory; '~spruchslos 1. adj. uncontradicted; 2. adv. without contradiction; '2stand m resistance (a. ♀); op-position; ~ leisten offer resistance (dat. to); auf heftigen ~ stoßen meet with stiff opposition; '~stands-fähig adj. resistant (a. ♣); '~ste-hen v/i. (irr. stehen, no -ge-, h) resist (e-r Sache s.th.); '~streben v/i. (no -ge-, h): es widerstrebt mir, dies zu tun I hate doing or to do that, I am reluctant to do that; '~strebend adv. reluctantly; '2-streit m (-[e]s/♣ -e) antagonism; fig. conflict; '~wärtig adj. ['~vertiç] unpleasant, disagreeable; disgust-ing; '2wille m aversion (gegen to, for, from); dislike (to, of, for); disgust (at, for); reluctance, un-willingness; '~willig adj. reluctant, unwilling.

widm|en ['vitmən] v/t. (ge-, h) dedicate; 2ung f (-/-en) dedica-tion.

widrig adj. ['vi:driç] adverse; ~en-falls adv. ['~gən'-] failing which, in default of which.

wie [vi:] 1. *adv.* how; ~ *alt ist er?* what is his age?; ~ *spät ist es?* what is the time?; 2. *cj.*: *ein Mann* ~ *er* a man such as he, a man like him; ~ *er dies hörte* hearing this; *ich hörte,* ~ *er es sagte* I heard him saying so.

wieder *adv.* ['vi:dər] again, anew; *immer* ~ again and again; 2'**aufbau** *m* (-[e]s/*no pl.*) reconstruction; rebuilding; ~'**aufbauen** *v/t.* (*sep.,* -ge-, *h*) reconstruct; ~'**aufleben** *v/i.* (*sep.,* -ge-, *sein*) revive; 2'**aufleben** *n* (-s/*no pl.*) revival; 2'**aufnahme** *f* resumption; ~'**aufnehmen** *v/t.* (*irr. nehmen, sep.,* -ge-, *h*) resume; 2'**beginn** *m* recommencement; re-opening; ~**bekommen** *v/t.* (*irr. kommen, sep., no* -ge-, *h*) get back; '~**beleben** *v/t.* (*sep., no* -ge-, *h*) resurrect; 2**belebung** *f* (-/-en) revival; *fig. a.* resurrection; 2**belebungsversuch** *m* attempt at resuscitation; ~**bringen** *v/t.* (*irr. bringen, sep.,* -ge-, *h*) bring back; restore, give back; ~'**einsetzen** *v/t.* (*sep.,* -ge-, *h*) restore; ~'**einstellen** *v/t.* (*sep.,* -ge-, *h*) re-engage; 2**er'greifung** *f* reseizure; ~'**erkennen** *v/t.* (*irr. kennen, sep., no* -ge-, *h*) recognize (*an dat.* by); ~'**erstatten** *v/t.* (*sep., no* -ge-, *h*) restore; reimburse, refund (*money*); ~'**geben** *v/t.* (*irr. geben, sep.,* -ge-, *h*) give back, return; render, reproduce; ~'**gutmachen** *v/t.* (*sep.,* -ge-, *h*) make up for; 2'**gutmachung** *f* (-/-en) reparation; ~'**herstellen** *v/t.* (*sep.,* -ge-, *h*) restore; ~**holen** *v/t.* (*h*) [. ~'ho:lən] (*no* -ge-) repeat; 2. ['~ho:lən] (*sep.,* -ge-) fetch back; 2'**holung** *f* (-/-en) repetition; ~**käuen** ['~kɔyən] (*sep.,* -ge-, *h*) 1. *v/i.* ruminate, chew the cud; 2. F *fig. v/t.* repeat over and over; 2**kehr** ['~ke:r] *f* (-/*no pl.*) return; recurrence; ~**kehren** *v/i.* (*sep.,* -ge-, *sein*) return; recur; ~**kommen** *v/i.* (*irr. kommen, sep.,* -ge-, *sein*) come back, return; '~**sehen** *v/t.* and *v/refl.* (*irr. sehen, sep.,* -ge-, *h*) see or meet again; 2**sehen** *n* (-s/*no pl.*) meeting again; *auf* ~*l* good-bye!; '~**tun** *v/t.* (*irr. tun, sep.,* -ge-, *h*) do again, repeat; '~**um** *adv.* again, anew; '~**vereinigen** *v/t.* (*sep., no* -ge-, *h*) reunite; 2**vereinigung** *f* reunion; *pol.* reunification; '2**verheiratung** *f* remarriage; 2**verkäufer** *m* reseller; retailer; '2**wahl** *f* re-election; '~**wählen** *v/t.* (*sep.,* -ge-, *h*) re-elect; 2'**zulassung** *f* readmission.

Wiege ['vi:gə] *f* (-/-n) cradle.

wiegen[1] ['vi:gən] *v/t.* and *v/i.* (*irr.,* ge-, *h*) weigh.

wiegen[2] ~ *v/t.* (ge-, *h*) rock; *in Sicherheit* ~ rock in security, lull into (a false sense of) security.

'**Wiegenlied** *n* lullaby.

wiehern ['vi:ərn] *v/i.* (ge-, *h*) neigh.

Wiener ['vi:nər] *m* (-s/-) Viennese; 2**isch** *adj.* Viennese.

wies [vi:s] *pret. of weisen.*

Wiese ['vi:zə] *f* (-/-n) meadow.

wie'so *interr. pron.* why; why so.

wie'viel *adv.* how much; ~ *pl.* how many *pl.*; ~**te** *adv.* [.~tə]: *den* ~**ten haben wir heute?** what's the date today?

wild [vilt] 1. *adj.* wild; savage; ~*es Fleisch* ⚕ proud flesh; ~*e Ehe* concubinage; ~*er Streik* ✝ wildcat strike; 2. 2 *n* (-[e]s/*no pl.*) game. '**Wild**|**bach** *m* torrent; ~**bret** ['~bret] *n* (-s/*no pl.*) game; venison.

Wilde ['vildə] *m* (-n/-n) savage.

Wilder|**er** ['vildərər] *m* (-s/-) poacher; 2**n** *v/i.* (ge-, *h*) poach.

'**Wild**|**fleisch** *n s.* Wildbret; '2**fremd** F *adj.* quite strange; '~**hüter** *m* gamekeeper; '~**leder** *n* buckskin; '2**ledern** *adj.* buckskin; doeskin; '~**nis** *f* (-/-se) wilderness, wild (*a. fig.*); '~**schwein** *n* wildboar.

Wille ['vilə] *m* (-ns/⚕-n) will; *s-n* ~*n durchsetzen* have one's way; *gegen s-n* ~*n* against one's will; *j-m s-n* ~*n lassen* let s.o. have his (own) way; 2**nlos** *adj.* lacking will-power.

'**Willens**|**freiheit** *f* (-/*no pl.*) freedom of (the) will; '~**kraft** *f* (-/*no pl.*) will-power; '~**schwäche** *f* (-/*no pl.*) weak will; '2**stark** *adj.* strong-willed; '~**stärke** *f* (-/*no pl.*) strong will, will-power.

'**will**|**ig** *adj.* willing, ready; '~**kommen** *adj.* welcome; 2**kür** ['~ky:r] *f* (-/*no pl.*) arbitrariness; '~**kürlich** *adj.* arbitrary.

wimmeln ['viməln] *v/i.* (ge-, *h*) swarm (*von* with), teem (with).

wimmern ['vimərn] *v/i.* (ge-, *h*) whimper, whine.

Wimpel ['vimpəl] *m* (-s/-) pennant, pennon, streamer.

Wimper ['vimpər] *f* (-/-n) eyelash.

Wind [vint] *m* (-[e]s/-e) wind; '~**beutel** *m* cream-puff; F *fig.* windbag.

Winde ['vində] *f* (-/-n) windlass, reel.

Windel ['vindəl] *f* (-/-n) diaper, (baby's) napkin; ~*n pl. a.* swaddling-clothes *pl.*

'**winden** *v/t.* (*irr.,* ge-, *h*) wind; twist, twirl; make, bind (*wreath*); *sich* ~ *vor* (*dat.*) writhe with.

'**Wind**|**hose** *f* whirlwind, tornado; '~**hund** *m* greyhound; 2**ig** *adj.* ['~diç] windy; F *fig. excuse:* thin, lame; '~**mühle** *f* windmill; '~**pokken** *f pl.* chicken-pox; '~**richtung** *f* direction of the wind; '~**rose** ⚓ *f* compass card; '~**schutzscheibe** *f* wind-screen, *Am.* windshield; '~**stärke** *f* wind veloc-

ity; '**Ꝙstill** adj. calm; '**⁀stille** f calm; '**⁀stoß** m blast of wind, gust.
'**Windung** f (-/-en) winding, turn; bend (of way, etc.); coil (of snake, etc.).
Wink [viŋk] m (-[e]s/-e) sign; wave; wink; fig.: hint; tip.
Winkel ['viŋkəl] m (-s/-) ⅋ angle; corner, nook; '**⁀zug** m subterfuge, trick, shift.
'**winken** v/i. (ge-, h) make a sign; beckon; mit dem Taschentuch ⁓ wave one's handkerchief.
winklig adj. ['viŋkliç] s. winkelig.
winseln ['vinzəln] v/i. (ge-, h) whimper, whine.
Winter ['vintər] m (-s/-) winter; im ⁓ in winter; '**Ꝙlich** adj. wintry; '**⁀schlaf** m hibernation; '**⁀sport** m winter sports pl.
Winzer ['vintsər] m (-s/-) vine-dresser; vine-grower; vintager.
winzig adj. ['vintsiç] tiny, diminutive.
Wipfel ['vipfəl] m (-s/-) top.
Wippe ['vipə] f (-/-n) seesaw; '**Ꝙn** v/i. (ge-, h) seesaw.
wir pers. pron. [vi:r] we; ⁓ drei the three of us.
Wirbel ['virbəl] m (-s/-) whirl, swirl; eddy; flurry (of blows, etc.); anat. vertebra; '**Ꝙig** adj. giddy, vertiginous; wild; '**Ꝙn** v/i. (ge-, h) whirl; drums: roll; '**⁀säule** anat. f spinal or vertebral column; '**⁀sturm** m cyclone, tornado, Am. a. twister; '**⁀tier** n vertebrate; '**⁀wind** m whirlwind (a. fig.).
wirk|en ['virkən] (ge-, h) 1. v/t. knit, weave; work (wonders) 2. v/i.: ⁓ als act or function as; ⁓ auf (acc.) produce an impression on; beruhigend ⁓ have a soothing effect; '**⁀lich** adj. real, actual; true, genuine; '**Ꝙlichkeit** f (-/-en) reality; in ⁓ in reality; '**⁀sam** adj. effective, efficacious; '**Ꝙsamkeit** f (-/⁜-en) effectiveness; efficacy; '**Ꝙung** f (-/-en) effect.
'**Wirkungs|kreis** m sphere or field of activity; '**Ꝙlos** adj. ineffective, inefficacious; '**⁀losigkeit** f (-/no pl.) ineffectiveness, inefficacy; '**Ꝙvoll** adj. s. wirksam.
wirr adj. [vir] confused; speech: incoherent; hair: dishevel(l)ed; '**Ꝙen** pl. disorders pl.; troubles pl.; **Ꝙwarr** ['⁀var] m (-s/no pl.) confusion, muddle.
Wirsingkohl ['virziŋ-] m (-[e]s/no pl.) savoy.
Wirt [virt] m (-[e]s/-e) host; landlord; innkeeper.
'**Wirtschaft** f (-/-en) housekeeping; economy; trade and industry; economics pl.; s. Wirtshaus; F mess; '**Ꝙen** v/i. (ge-, h) keep house; economize; F bustle (about); '**⁀erin**

f (-/-nen) housekeeper; '**Ꝙlich** adj. economic; economical.
'**Wirtschafts|geld** n housekeeping money; '**⁀jahr** n financial year; '**⁀krise** f economic crisis; '**⁀politik** f economic policy; '**⁀prüfer** m (-s/-) chartered accountant, Am. certified public accountant.
'**Wirtshaus** n public house, F pub.
Wisch [viʃ] m (-es/-e) wisp (of straw, etc.); contp. scrap of paper; '**Ꝙen** v/t. (ge-, h) wipe.
wispern ['vispərn] v/t. and v/i. (ge-, h) whisper.
Wiß|begierde ['vis-] f (-/no pl.) thirst for knowledge; '**Ꝙbegierig** adj. eager for knowledge.
wissen ['visən] 1. v/t. (irr., ge-, h) know; man kann nie ⁓ you never know, you never can tell; 2. Ꝙ n (-s/no pl.) knowledge; meines ⁓s to my knowledge, as far as I know.
'**Wissenschaft** f (-/-en) science; knowledge; '**⁀ler** m (-s/-) scholar; scientist; researcher; '**Ꝙlich** adj. scientific.
'**Wissens|drang** m (-[e]s/no pl.) urge or thirst for knowledge; '**Ꝙwert** adj. worth knowing.
'**wissentlich** adj. knowing, conscious.
wittern ['vitərn] v/t. (ge-, h) scent, smell; fig. a. suspect.
'**Witterung** f (-/⁜-en) weather; hunt. scent; **⁀sverhältnisse** ['⁀sfərhɛltnisə] pl. meteorological conditions pl. [m (-s/-) widower.]
Witwe ['vitvə] f (-/-n) widow; '**⁀r**)
Witz [vits] m 1. (-es/no pl.) wit; 2. (-es/-e) joke; ⁓e reißen crack jokes; '**⁀blatt** n comic paper; '**Ꝙig** adj. witty; funny.
wo [vo:] 1. adv. where?; 2. cj.: F ach ⁓! nonsense!
wob [vo:p] pret. of weben.
wo'bei adv. at what?; at which; in doing so.
Woche ['voxə] f (-/-n) week; heute in e-r ⁓ today week.
'**Wochen|bett** n childbed; '**⁀blatt** n weekly (paper); '**⁀ende** n weekend; '**Ꝙlang** 1. adj.: nach ⁓em Warten after (many) weeks of waiting; 2. adv. for weeks; '**⁀lohn** m weekly pay or wages pl.; '**⁀markt** m weekly market; '**⁀schau** f news-reel; '**⁀tag** m week-day.
wöchentlich ['vœçəntliç] 1. adj. weekly; 2. adv. weekly, every week; einmal ⁓ once a week.
Wöchnerin ['vœçnərin] f (-/-nen) woman in childbed.
wo'durch adv. by what?, how?; by which, whereby; **⁀für** adv. for what?, what ... for?; (in return) for which. [gen¹.]
wog [vo:k] pret. of wägen and wie-)
Woge ['vo:gə] f (-/-n) wave (a. fig.), billow; die ⁓n glätten pour oil on

troubled waters; '**2n** v/i. (ge-, h) surge (a. fig.), billow; wheat: a. wave; heave.

wo|'her adv. from where?, where ... from?; ~ wissen Sie das? how do you (come to) know that?; ~'**hin** adv. where (... to)?

wohl [vo:l] **1.** adv. well; sich nicht ~ fühlen be unwell; ~ oder übel willy-nilly; leben Sie ~l farewell!; er wird ~ reich sein he is rich, I suppose; **2.** 2 n (-[e]s/no pl.): ~ und Wehe weal and woe; auf Ihr ~l your health!, here is to you!

'**Wohl|befinden** n well-being; good health; '~**behagen** n comfort, ease; '2**behalten** adv. safe; '2**bekannt** adj. well-known; '~**ergehen** n (-s/no pl.) welfare, prosperity; 2**er- zogen** adj. ['~ɛrtso:gən] well-bred, well-behaved; '~**fahrt** f (-/no pl.) welfare; public assistance; '~**ge- fallen** n (-s/no pl.) pleasure; sein ~ haben an (dat.) take delight in; '2**gemeint** adj. well-meant, well-intentioned; 2**gemut** adj. ['~gə- mu:t] cheerful; 2**genährt** ['~] well-fed; '~**geruch** m scent, perfume; '2**gesinnt** adj. well-disposed (j-m towards s.o.); '2**habend** adj. well-to-do; '2**ig** adj. comfortable; cosy, snug; '~**klang** m (-[e]s/no pl.) melodious sound, harmony; '2**klingend** adj. melodious, harmonious; '~**laut** m s. Wohlklang; '~**leben** n (-s/no pl.) luxury; 2**riechend** adj. fragrant; 2**schmeckend** savo(u)ry; '~**sein** n well-being; good health; '~**stand** m (-[e]s/no pl.) prosperity, wealth; '~**tat** f kindness, charity; fig. comfort, treat; '~**täter** m benefactor; '2**tätig** adj. charitable, beneficent; '~**tä- tigkeit** f charity; 2**tuend** adj. ['~tu:- ənt] pleasant, comfortable; '2**tun** v/i. (irr. tun, sep., -ge-, h) do good; '2**verdient** adj. well-deserved; p. of great merit; '~**wollen** n (-s/no pl.) goodwill; benevolence; favo(u)r; '2**wollen** v/i. (sep., -ge-, h) be well-disposed (j-m towards s.o.)

wohn|en ['vo:nən] v/i. (ge-, h) live (in dat. in, at; bei j-m with s.o.); reside (in, at; with); '2**haus** n dwelling-house; block of flats, Am. apartment house; '~**haft** adj. resident, living; '~**lich** adj. comfortable; cosy, snug; '2**ort** m dwelling-place, residence; esp. ɪɪɪ domicile; '2**sitz** m residence; mit ~ in resident in or at; ohne festen ~ without fixed abode; '2**ung** f (-/-en) dwelling, habitation; flat, Am. apartment.

'**Wohnungs|amt** n housing office; '~**not** f housing shortage; '~**pro- blem** n housing problem.

'**Wohn|wagen** m caravan, trailer; '~**zimmer** n sitting-room, esp. Am. living room.

wölb|en ['vœlbən] v/t. (ge-, h) vault; arch; sich ~ arch; '2**ung** f (-/-en) vault, arch; curvature.

Wolf zo. [vɔlf] m (-[e]s/ⁿe) wolf.

Wolke ['vɔlkə] f (-/-n) cloud.

'**Wolken|bruch** m cloud-burst; '~**kratzer** m (-s/-) skyscraper; '2**los** adj. cloudless.

'**wolkig** adj. cloudy, clouded.

Woll|decke ['vɔl-] f blanket; '~**e** f (-/-n) wool.

wollen[1] ['vɔlən] (h) **1.** v/t. (ge-) wish, desire; want; lieber ~ prefer; nicht ~ refuse; er weiß, was er will he knows his mind; **2.** v/i. (ge-): ich will schon, aber ... I want to, but ...; **3.** v/aux. (no-ge-) be willing; intend, be going to; be about to; lieber ~ prefer; nicht ~ refuse; er hat nicht gehen ~ he refused to go.

wollen[2] adj. [~] wooll(l)en; '~**ig** adj. wool(l)y; '2**stoff** m wool(l)en.

Wol|lust ['vɔlust] f (-/ⁿe) voluptuousness; 2**lüstig** adj. ['~lystiç] voluptuous.

'**Wollwaren** pl. wool(l)en goods pl.

wo|'mit adv. with what?, what ... with?; with which; ~'**möglich** adv. perhaps, maybe.

Wonn|e ['vɔnə] f (-/-n) delight, bliss; '2**ig** adj. delightful, blissful.

wo|ran adv. [vo:'ran]: ~ denkst du? what are you thinking of?; ich weiß nicht, ~ ich mit ihm bin I don't know what to make of him; ~ liegt es, daß ...? how is it that ...?; ~'**rauf** adv. on what?, what ... on?; whereupon, after which; ~ wartest du? what are you waiting for?; ~'**raus** adv. from what?; what ... of?; from which; ~**rin** adv. [~'rin] in what?; in which.

Wort [vɔrt] n **1.** (-[e]s/ⁿer) word; er kann seine Wörter noch nicht he hasn't learnt his words yet; **2.** (-[e]s/-e) word; term, expression; ums ~ bitten ask permission to speak; das ~ ergreifen begin to speak; parl. rise to speak, address the House, esp. Am. take the floor; das ~ führen be the spokesman; ~ halten keep one's word; '2**brüchig** adj.: er ist ~ geworden he has broken his word.

Wörter|buch ['vœrtər-] n dictionary; '~**verzeichnis** n vocabulary, list of words.

'**Wort|führer** m spokesman; '2**ge- treu** adj. literal; 2**karg** adj. taciturn; ~**klauberei** [~klaubə'raɪ] f (-/-en) word-splitting; '~**laut** m (-[e]s/no pl.) wording; text. [eral.]

wörtlich adj. ['vœrtliç] verbal, lit-'

'**Wort|schatz** m (-es/no pl.) vocabulary; '~**schwall** m (-[e]s/no pl.) verbiage; '~**spiel** n pun (über acc., mit [up]on), play upon words; '~**stellung** gr. f word order, order of words; '~**stamm** ling. m stem; '~**streit** m, '~**wechsel** m dispute.

wo|rüber adv. [vo:'ry:bər] over or upon what?, what ... over or about or on?; over or upon which, about which; **~rum** adv. [~'rum] about what?, what ... about?; about or for which; ~ handelt es sich? what is it about?; **~runter** adv. [~'runtər] under or among what?, what ... under?; under or among which; **~von** adv. of or from what?, what ... from or of?; about what?, what ... about?; of or from which; **~vor** adv. of what?, what ... of?; of which; **~zu** adv. for what?, what ... for?; for which.

Wrack [vrak] n (-[e]s/-e, -s) ⚓ wreck (a. fig.).

wrang [vraŋ] pret. of wringen.

wring|en ['vriŋən] v/t. (irr., ge-, h) wring; **~maschine** f wringing-machine.

Wucher ['vu:xər] m (-s/no pl.) usury; ~ treiben practise usury; **~er** m (-s/-) usurer; **~gewinn** m excess profit; **~isch** adj. usurious; **2n** v/i. (ge-, h) grow exuberantly; **~ung** f (-/-en) 🌿 exuberant growth; 🌿 growth; **~zinsen** m/pl. usurious interest.

Wuchs [vu:ks] 1. m (-es/no pl.) growth, figure, shape; stature; 2. ♀ pret. of wachsen.

Wucht [vuxt] f (-/~, -en) weight; force; **2ig** adj. heavy.

Wühl|arbeit fig. ['vy:l-] f insidious agitation, subversive activity; **2en** v/i. (ge-, h) dig; pig: root; fig. agitate; ~ in (dat.) rummage (about) in; **~er** m (-s/-) agitator.

Wulst [vulst] m (-es/~e), f (-/~e) pad; bulge; 🔺 roll(-mo[u]lding); ⊕ bead; **2ig** adj. lips: thick.

wund adj. [vunt] sore; **~e Stelle** sore; **~er Punkt** tender spot; **2e** ['~də] f (-/-n) wound; alte **~n** wieder aufreißen reopen old sores.

Wunder ['vundər] n (-s/-) miracle; fig. a. wonder, marvel; ~ wirken pills, etc.: work marvels; kein ~, wenn man bedenkt ... no wonder, considering ...; **2bar** adj. miraculous; fig. a. wonderful, marvel(l)ous; **~kind** n infant prodigy; **2lich** adj. queer, odd; **2n** v/t. (ge-, h) surprise, astonish; sich ~ be surprised or astonished (über acc. at); **2schön** adj. very beautiful; **~tat** f wonder, miracle; **~täter** m wonder-worker; **2tätig** adj. wonder-working; **2voll** adj. wonderful; **~werk** n marvel, wonder.

'Wund|fieber ♂ n wound-fever; **~starrkrampf** ♂ m tetanus.

Wunsch [vunʃ] m (-es/~e) wish, desire; request; auf ~ by or on request; if desired; nach ~ as desired; mit den besten Wünschen zum Fest with the compliments of the season.

Wünschelrute ['vynʃəl-] f divin-

ing-rod, dowsing-rod; **~ngänger** ['~gɛnər] m (-s/-) diviner, dowser.

wünschen ['vynʃən] v/t. (ge-, h) wish, desire; wie Sie ~ as you wish; was ~ Sie? what can I do for you?; **~swert** adj. desirable.

'wunsch|gemäß adv. as requested or desired, according to one's wishes; **2zettel** m list of wishes.

wurde ['vurdə] pret. of werden.

Würde ['vyrdə] f (-/-n) dignity; unter seiner ~ beneath one's dignity; **2los** adj. undignified; **~nträger** m dignitary; **2voll** adj. dignified; grave.

'würdig adj. worthy (gen. of); dignified; grave; **~en** ['~gən] v/t. (ge-, h) appreciate, value; mention hono(u)rably; laud, praise; j-n keines Blickes ~ ignore s.o. completely; **2ung** ['~guŋ] f (-/-en) appreciation, valuation.

Wurf [wurf] m (-[e]s/~e) throw, cast; zo. litter.

Würfel ['vyrfəl] m (-s/-) die; cube (a. 🔺); **~becher** m dice-box; **2n** v/i. (ge-, h) (play) dice; **~spiel** n game of dice; **~zucker** m lump sugar.

'Wurfgeschoß n missile, projec-tile.

würgen ['vyrgən] (ge-, h) 1. v/t. choke, strangle; 2. v/i. choke; retch.

Wurm zo. [vurm] m (-[e]s/~er) worm; **2en** F v/t. (ge-, h) vex; rankle (j-n in s.o.'s mind); **2stichig** adj. worm-eaten.

Wurst [vurst] f (-/~e) sausage; F das ist mir ganz ~ I don't care a rap.

Würstchen ['vyrstçən] n (-s/-) sausage; heißes ~ hot sausage, Am. hot dog.

Würze ['vyrtsə] f (-/-n) seasoning, flavo(u)r; spice, condiment; fig. salt.

Wurzel ['vurtsəl] f (-/-n) root (a. gr., 🔺); ~ schlagen strike or take root (a. fig.); **2n** v/i. (ge-, h) (strike or take) root; ~ in (dat.) take one's root in, be rooted in.

'würz|en v/t. (ge-, h) spice, season, flavo(u)r; **~ig** adj. spicy, well-seasoned, aromatic.

wusch [vu:ʃ] pret. of waschen.

wußte ['vustə] pret. of wissen.

Wust F [vu:st] m (-es/no pl.) tangled mass; rubbish; mess.

wüst adj. [vy:st] desert, waste; confused; wild, dissolute; rude; **2e** f (-/-n) desert, waste; **2ling** ['~liŋ] m (-s/-e) debauchee, libertine, rake.

Wut [vu:t] f (-/no pl.) rage, fury; in ~ in a rage; **~anfall** m fit of rage.

wüten ['vy:tən] v/i. (ge-, h) rage (a. fig.); **~d** adj. furious, enraged (über acc. at; auf acc. with), esp. Am. F a. mad (über acc., auf acc. at).

Wüterich ['vy:tərɪç] m (-[e]s/-e) berserker; bloodthirsty man.

'wutschnaubend adj. foaming with rage.

X, Y

X-Beine ['iks-] *n/pl.* knock-knees *pl.*; **'X-beinig** *adj.* knock-kneed.

x-beliebig *adj.* [iksbə'li:biç] any (... you please); jede(r, -s) ∼e ... any ...

x-mal *adv.* ['iks-] many times, *sl.* umpteen times.

X-Strahlen ['iks-] *m/pl.* X-rays *pl.*

x-te *adj.* ['ikstə]: zum ∼n Male for the umpteenth time.

Xylophon ♪ [ksylo'fo:n] *n* (-s/-e) xylophone.

Yacht ⚓ [jaxt] *f* (-/-en) yacht.

Z

Zacke ['tsakə] *f* (-/-n) *s.* Zacken.

'Zacken 1. *m* (-s/-) (sharp) point; prong; tooth (*of comb, saw, rake*); jag (*of rock*); **2.** ⚢ *v/t.* (ge-, h) indent, notch; jag.

'zackig *adj.* indented; notched; *rock:* jagged; pointed; ✗ F *fig.* smart.

zaghaft *adj.* ['tsa:khaft] timid; **'⚢igkeit** *f* (-/no *pl.*) timidity.

zäh *adj.* [tsɛ:] tough, tenacious (*both a. fig.*); *liquid:* viscid, viscous; *fig.* dogged; **'∼flüssig** *adj.* viscid, viscous, sticky; **'⚢igkeit** *f* (-/no *pl.*) toughness, tenacity (*both a. fig.*); viscosity; *fig.* doggedness.

Zahl [tsa:l] *f* (-/-en) number; figure, cipher; **'⚢bar** *adj.* payable.

'zählbar *adj.* countable.

zahlen ['tsa:lən] (ge-, h) **1.** *v/i.* pay; *at restaurant:* ∼ (, bitte)! the bill, please!, Am. the check, please!; **2.** *v/t.* pay.

zählen ['tsɛ:lən] (ge-, h) **1.** *v/t.* count, number; ∼ zu count or number among; **2.** *v/i.* count; ∼ auf (*acc.*) count (up)on, rely (up)on.

'Zahlen|lotto *n* *s.* Lotto; **'⚢mäßig 1.** *adj.* numerical; **2.** *adv.:* j-m ∼ überlegen sein outnumber s.o.

'Zähler *m* (-s/-) counter; 𝄐 numerator; *for gas, etc.:* meter.

'Zahl|karte *f* money-order form (*for paying direct into the postal cheque account*); **'⚢los** *adj.* numberless, innumerable, countless; **'∼meister** ✗ *m* paymaster; **'⚢reich 1.** *adj.* numerous; **2.** *adv.* in great number; **'∼tag** *m* pay-day; **'∼ung** *f* (-/-en) payment.

'Zählung *f* (-/-en) counting.

'Zahlungs|anweisung *f* order to pay; **'∼aufforderung** *f* request for payment; **'∼bedingungen** *f/pl.* terms *pl.* of payment; **'∼befehl** *m* order to pay; **'∼einstellung** *f* suspension of payment; **'⚢fähig** *adj.* solvent; **'∼fähigkeit** *f* solvency; **'∼frist** *f* term for payment; **'∼mittel** *n* currency; gesetzliches ∼ legal tender; **'∼schwierigkeiten** *f/pl.* financial *or* pecuniary difficulties

pl.; **'∼termin** *m* date of payment; **'⚢unfähig** *adj.* insolvent; **'∼unfähigkeit** *f* insolvency.

'Zahlwort *gr.* *n* (-[e]s/∼er) numeral.

zahm *adj.* [tsa:m] tame (*a. fig.*), domestic(ated).

zähm|en ['tsɛ:mən] *v/t.* (ge-, h) tame (*a. fig.*), domesticate; **'⚢ung** *f* (-/∼-en) taming (*a. fig.*), domestication.

Zahn [tsa:n] *m* (-[e]s/∼e) tooth; ⊕ tooth, cog; *Zähne bekommen* cut one's teeth; **'∼arzt** *m* dentist, dental surgeon; **'∼bürste** *f* toothbrush; **'∼creme** *f* tooth-paste; **'⚢en** *v/i.* (ge-, h) teethe, cut one's teeth; **'∼ersatz** *m* denture; **∼fäule** 𝄐 ['∼fɔylə] *f* (-/no *pl.*) dental caries; **'∼fleisch** *n* gums *pl.*; **'∼füllung** *f* filling, stopping; **'∼geschwür** 𝄐 *n* gumboil; **'∼heilkunde** *f* dentistry; **'⚢los** *adj.* toothless; **'∼lücke** *f* gap between the teeth; **∼pasta** ['∼pasta] *f* (-/Zahnpasten), **'∼paste** *f* toothpaste; **'∼rad** *n* cog-wheel; **∼radbahn** *f* rack-railway; **'∼schmerzen** *m/pl.* toothache; **'∼stocher** *m* (-s/-) toothpick.

Zange ['tsaŋə] *f* (-/-n) (e-e a pair of) tongs *pl.* or pliers *pl.* or pincers *pl.*; 𝄐, zo. forceps *sg.*, *pl.*

Zank [tsaŋk] *m* (-[e]s/no *pl.*) quarrel, F row; **'∼apfel** *m* bone of contention; **'⚢en** (ge-, h) **1.** *v/i.* scold (mit j-m s.o.); **2.** *v/refl.* quarrel, wrangle.

zänkisch *adj.* ['tsɛŋkiʃ] quarrelsome.

Zäpfchen ['tsɛpfçən] *n* (-s/-) small peg; *anat.* uvula.

Zapfen ['tsapfən] **1.** *m* (-s/-) plug; peg, pin; bung (*of barrel*); pivot; ⚘ cone; **2.** ⚢ *v/t.* (ge-, h) tap; **'∼streich** ✗ *m* tattoo, retreat, Am. *a.* taps *pl.*

'Zapf|hahn *m* tap, Am. faucet; **'∼säule** *mot.* *f* petrol pump.

zappel|ig *adj.* ['tsapəliç] fidgety; **'∼n** *v/i.* (ge-, h) struggle; fidget.

zart *adj.* [tsa:rt] tender; soft; gentle; delicate; **'∼fühlend** *adj.* delicate; **'⚢gefühl** *n* (-[e]s/no *pl.*) delicacy (of feeling).

zärtlich adj. ['tsɛːrtliç] tender; fond, loving; '2**keit** f 1. (-/no pl.) tenderness; fondness; 2. (-/-en) caress.

Zauber ['tsaubər] m (-s/-) spell, charm, magic (all a. fig.); fig.: enchantment; glamo(u)r; ~**ei** [~'rai] f (-/-en) magic, sorcery; witchcraft; conjuring; '~**er** m (-s/-) sorcerer, magician; conjurer; '~**flöte** f magic flute; '~**formel** f spell; '2**haft** adj. magic(al); fig. enchanting; '~**in** f (-/-nen) sorceress, witch; fig. enchantress; '~**kraft** f magic power; '~**kunststück** n conjuring trick; '2**n** (ge-, h) 1. v/i. practise magic or witchcraft; do conjuring tricks; 2. v/t. conjure; '~**spruch** m spell; '~**stab** m (magic) wand; '~**wort** n (-[e]s/-er) magic word, spell.

zaudern ['tsaudərn] v/i. (ge-, h) hesitate; linger, delay.

Zaum [tsaum] m (-[e]s/ue) bridle; im ~ halten keep in check.

zäumen ['tsɔymən] v/t. (ge-, h) bridle.

'**Zaumzeug** n bridle.

Zaun [tsaun] m (-[e]s/ue) fence; '~**gast** m deadhead; '~**könig** orn. m wren; '~**pfahl** m pale.

Zebra zo. ['tseːbra] n (-s/-s) zebra; '~**streifen** m zebra crossing.

Zech|e ['tsɛçə] f (-/-n) score, reckoning, bill; ✕ mine; coal-pit, colliery; F die ~ bezahlen foot the bill, F stand treat; '2**en** v/i. (ge-, h) carouse, tipple; '~**gelage** n carousal, carouse; '~**preller** m (-s/-) bilk(er).

Zeh [tse:] m (-[e]s/-en), '~**e** f (-/-n) toe; '~**enspitze** f point or tip of the toe; auf ~n on tiptoe.

zehn adj. [tse:n] ten; '2**er** m (-s/-) ten; coin: F ten-pfennig piece; ~**fach** adj. ['~fax] tenfold; '~**jährig** adj. ['~jɛːriç] ten-year-old, of ten (years); '2**kampf** m sports: decathlon; '~**mal** adv. ten times; ~**te** ['~tə] 1. adj. tenth; 2. 2 ✝ m (-n/-n) tithe; 2**tel** ['~təl] n (-s/-) tenth (part); '~**tens** adv. ['~təns] tenthly.

zehren ['tse:rən] v/i. (ge-, h) make thin; ~ von live on s.th.; fig. live off (the capital); ~ an prey (up)on (one's mind); undermine (one's health).

Zeichen ['tsaiçən] n (-s/-) sign; token; mark; indication, symptom; signal; zum ~ (gen.) in sign of, as a sign of; '~**block** m drawing-block; '~**brett** n drawing-board; '~**lehrer** m drawing-master; '~**papier** n drawing-paper; '~**setzung** gr. f (-/no pl.) punctuation; '~**sprache** f sign-language; '~**stift** m pencil, crayon; '~**trickfilm** m animation, animated cartoon; '~**unterricht** m drawing-lessons pl.

zeichn|en ['tsaiçnən] (ge-, h) 1. v/t.

draw (plan, etc.); design (pattern); mark; sign; subscribe (sum of money) (zu to); subscribe for (shares); 2. v/i. draw; sie zeichnet gut she draws well; '2**er** m (-s/-) draftsman, draughtsman; designer; subscriber (gen. for shares); '2**ung** f (-/-en) drawing; design; illustration; zo. marking (of skin, etc.); subscription.

Zeige|finger ['tsaigə-] m forefinger, index (finger); '2**n** (ge-, h) 1. v/t. show; point out; indicate; demonstrate; sich ~ appear; 2. v/i.: ~ auf (acc.) point at; ~ nach point to; '~**r** m (-s/-) hand (of clock, etc.); pointer (of dial, etc.); '~**stock** m pointer.

Zeile ['tsailə] f (-/-n) line; row; j-m ein paar ~n schreiben drop s.o. a line or a few lines. [siskin.]

Zeisig orn. ['tsaiziç] m (-[e]s/-e)|

Zeit [tsait] f (-/-en) time; epoch, era, age; period, space (of time); term; freie ~ spare time; mit der ~ in the course of time; von ~ zu ~ from time to time; vor langer ~ long ago, a long time ago; zur ~ (gen.) in the time of; at (the) present; zu meiner ~ in my time; zu s-r ~ in due course (of time); das hat ~ there is plenty of time for that; es ist höchste ~ it is high time; j-m ~ lassen give s.o. time; laß dir ~ take your time!; sich die ~ vertreiben pass the time, kill time.

'**Zeit|abschnitt** m epoch, period; '~**alter** n age; '~**angabe** f exact date and hour; date; '~**aufnahme** phot. f time-exposure; '~**dauer** f length of time, period (of time); '~**enfolge** gr. f sequence of tenses; '~**geist** m (-es/no pl.) spirit of the time(s), zeitgeist; '2**gemäß** adj. modern, up-to-date; '~**genosse** m contemporary; 2**genössisch** adj. ['~gənœsiʃ] contemporary; '~**geschichte** f contemporary history; '~**gewinn** m gain of time; '2**ig** 1. adj. early; 2. adv. on time; '~**karte** f season-ticket, Am. commutation ticket; '~**lang** f: e-e ~ for some time, for a while; 2'**lebens** adv. for life, all one's life; '2**lich** 1. adj. temporal; 2. adv. as to time; ~ zusammenfallen coincide; '2**los** adj. timeless; '~**lupe** phot. f slow motion; '~**lupenaufnahme** phot. f slow-motion picture; '2**nah** adj. current, up-to-date; '~**ordnung** f chronological order; '~**punkt** m moment; time; date; '~**rafferaufnahme** phot. f time-lapse photography; '2**raubend** adj. time-consuming; pred. a. taking up much time; '~**raum** m space (of time), period; '~**rechnung** f chronology; era; '~**schrift** f journal, periodical, magazine; review; '~**tafel** f chronological table.

'Zeitung f (-/-en) (news)paper, journal.

'Zeitungs|abonnement n subscription to a paper; '~artikel m newspaper article; '~ausschnitt m (press or newspaper) cutting, (Am. only) (newspaper) clipping; ~kiosk ['~kiɔsk] m (-[e]s/-e) news-stand; '~notiz f press item; '~papier n newsprint; '~verkäufer m newsvendor; news-boy, news-man; '~wesen n journalism, the press.

'Zeit|verlust m loss of time; '~verschwendung f waste of time; ~vertreib ['~fɛrtraɪp] m (-[e]s/-e) pastime; zum ~ to pass the time; 2weilig adj. ['~vaɪlɪç] temporary; '2weise adv. for a time; at times, occasionally; '~wort gr. n (-[e]s/⁼er) verb; '~zeichen n time-signal.

Zell|e ['tsɛlə] f (-/-n) cell; '~stoff m, ~ulose ⊕ [~u'lo:zə] f (-/-n) cellulose.

Zelt [tsɛlt] n (-[e]s/-e) tent; 2en v/i. (ge-, h) camp; '~leinwand f canvas; '~platz m camping-ground.

Zement [tse'mɛnt] m (-[e]s/-e) cement; 2ieren [~'ti:rən] v/t. (no -ge-, h) cement.

Zenit [tse'ni:t] m (-[e]s/no pl.) zenith (a. fig.).

zens|ieren [tsɛn'zi:rən] v/t. (no -ge-, h) censor (book, etc.); at school: mark, Am. a. grade; 2or ['~ɔr] m (-s/-en) censor; 2ur [~'zu:r] f 1. (-/no pl.) censorship; 2. (-/-en) at school: mark, Am. a. grade; (school) report, Am. report card.

Zentimeter [tsɛnti'-] n, m centimetre, Am. -er.

Zentner ['tsɛntnər] m (-s/-) (Brt. appr.) hundredweight.

zentral adj. [tsɛn'traːl] central; 2e f (-/-n) central office; teleph. (telephone) exchange, Am. a. central; 2heizung f central heating.

Zentrum ['tsɛntrum] n (-s/Zentren) cent|re, Am. -er. [Am. -er.]

Zepter ['tsɛptər] n (-s/-) scept|re,

zer|beißen [tsɛr'-] v/t. (irr. beißen, no -ge-, h) bite to pieces; ~bersten v/i. (irr. bersten, no -ge-, sein) burst asunder.

zer'brech|en (irr. brechen, no -ge-) 1. v/t. (h) break (to pieces); sich den Kopf ~ rack one's brains; 2. v/i. (sein) break; ~lich adj. breakable, fragile.

zer|'bröckeln v/t. (h) and v/i. (sein) (no -ge-) crumble; ~'drücken v/t. (no -ge-, h) crush; crease (dress).

Zeremon|ie [tseremo'ni:, ~'mo:njə] f (-/-n) ceremony; 2iell adj. [~o'njɛl] ceremonial; ~iell n (-s/-e) ceremonial.

zer'fahren adj. road: rutted; p.: flighty, giddy; scatter-brained; absent-minded.

Zer'fall m (-[e]s/no pl.) ruin, decay;

disintegration; 2en v/i. (irr. fallen, no -ge-, sein) fall to pieces, decay; disintegrate; in mehrere Teile ~ fall into several parts.

zer|'fetzen v/t. (no -ge-, h) tear in or to pieces; ~'fleischen v/t. (no -ge-, h) mangle; lacerate; ~'fließen v/i. (irr. fließen, no -ge-, sein) melt (away); ink, etc.: run; ~'fressen v/t. (irr. fressen, no -ge-, h) eat away; ⚗ corrode; ~'gehen v/i. (irr. gehen, no -ge-, sein) melt, dissolve; ~'gliedern v/t. (no -ge-, h) dismember; anat. dissect; fig. analy|se, Am. -ze; ~'hacken v/t. (no -ge-, h) cut (in)to pieces; mince; chop (up) (wood, meat); ~'kauen v/t. (no -ge-, h) chew; ~'kleinern v/t. (no -ge-, h) mince (meat); chop up (wood); grind.

zer'knirsch|t adj. contrite; 2ung f (-/⚙-en) contrition.

zer|'knittern v/t. (no -ge-, h) (c)rumple, wrinkle, crease; ~'knüllen v/t. (no -ge-, h) crumple up (sheet of paper); ~'kratzen v/t. (no -ge-, h) scratch; ~'krümeln v/t. (no -ge-, h) crumble; ~'lassen v/t. (irr. lassen, no -ge-, h) melt; ~'legen v/t. (no -ge-, h) take apart or to pieces; carve (joint); ⚗, gr., fig. analy|se, Am. -ze; ~'lumpt adj. ragged, tattered; ~'mahlen v/t. (irr. mahlen, no -ge-, h) grind; ~malmen [~'malmən] v/t. (no -ge-, h) crush; crunch; ~'mürben v/t. (no -ge-, h) wear down or out; ~'platzen v/i. (no -ge-, sein) burst; explode; ~'quetschen v/t. (no -ge-, h) crush, squash; mash (esp. potatoes).

Zerrbild ['tsɛr-] n caricature.

zer|'reiben v/t. (irr. reiben, no -ge-, h) rub to powder, grind down, pulverize; ~'reißen (irr. reißen, no -ge-) 1. v/t. (h) tear, rip up; in Stücke ~ tear to pieces; 2. v/i. (sein) tear; rope, string: break.

zerren ['tsɛrən] (ge-, h) 1. v/t. tug, pull; drag; ⚙ strain; 2. v/i.: ~ an (dat.) pull at.

zer'rinnen v/i. (irr. rinnen, no -ge-, sein) melt away; fig. vanish.

'Zerrung ⚙ f (-/-en) strain.

zer|'rütten [tsɛr'rytən] v/t. (no -ge-, h) derange, unsettle; disorganize; ruin, shatter (one's health or nerves); wreck (marriage); ~'sägen v/t. (no -ge-, h) saw up; ~'schellen [~'ʃɛlən] v/i. (no -ge-, sein) be dashed or smashed; ♣ be wrecked; ⚡ crash; ~'schlagen 1. v/t. (irr. schlagen, no -ge-, h) break or smash (to pieces); sich ~ come to nothing; 2. adj. battered; fig. knocked up; ~'schmettern v/t. (no -ge-, h) smash, dash, shatter; ~'schneiden v/t. (irr. schneiden, no -ge-, h) cut in two; cut up, cut to pieces.

zer'setz|en v/t. and v/refl. (no -ge-, h) decompose; **2ung** f (-/%-en) decomposition.

zer'spalten v/t. ([irr. spalten,] no -ge-, h) cleave, split; **~'splittern** (no -ge-) **1.** v/t. (h) split (up), splinter; fritter away (one's energy, etc.); **2.** v/i. (sein) split (up), splinter, **~'sprengen** v/t. (no -ge-, h) burst (asunder); disperse (crowd); **~'springen** v/i. (irr. springen, no -ge-, sein) burst, glass: crack, mein Kopf zerspringt mir I've got a splitting headache. **~'stampfen** v/t. (no -ge-, h) crush, pound.

zer'stäub|en v/t. (no -ge-, h) spray; **2er** m (-s -) sprayer, atomizer.

zer'stör|en v/t. (no -ge-, h) destroy; **2er** m (-s/-) destroyer (a. ⚓); **2ung** f destruction.

zer'streu|en v/t. (no -ge-, h) disperse, scatter; dissipate (doubt, etc.); fig. divert; sich ~ disperse, scatter, fig. amuse o.s.; **~t** fig. adj. absent(-minded); **2theit** f (-/%-en) absent-mindedness, **2ung** f **1.** (-/ -en) dispersion; diversion, amusement; **2.** phys. (-/no pl.) dispersion (of light).

zerstückeln [tser'ʃtykəln] v/t. (no -ge-, h) cut up, cut (in)to pieces; dismember (body, etc.).

zer'teilen v/t. and v/refl. (no -ge-, h) divide (in acc. into); **~'trennen** v/t. (no -ge-, h) rip (up) (dress); **~'treten** v/t. (irr. treten, no -ge-, h) tread down; crush; tread or stamp out (fire); **~'trümmern** v/t. (no -ge-, h) smash.

Zerwürfnis [tser'vyrfnis] n (-ses/ -se) dissension, discord.

Zettel ['tsetəl] m (-s/-) slip (of paper), scrap of paper; note; ticket; label, sticker; tag; s. Anschlagzettel; s. Theaterzettel; **'~kartei** f, **'~kasten** m card index.

Zeug [tsɔyk] n (-[e]s/-e) stuff (a. fig. contp.), material; cloth; tools pl.; things pl.

Zeuge ['tsɔygə] m (-n/-n) witness; **'2n** (ge-, h) **1.** v/i. witness; ⚖ give evidence; für (gegen, von) et. ~ testify for (against, of) s.th.; ~ von be evidence of, bespeak (courage, etc.); **2.** v/t. beget.

'Zeugen|aussage ⚖ f testimony, evidence; **'~bank** f (-/"~e) witness-box, Am. witness stand.

Zeugin ['tsɔygin] f (-/-nen) (female) witness.

Zeugnis ['tsɔyknis] n (-ses/-se) ⚖ testimony, evidence; certificate; (school) report, Am. report card.

Zeugung ['tsɔyguŋ] f (-/-en) procreation; **'2sfähig** adj. capable of begetting; **'2skraft** f generative power; **'2sunfähig** adj. ['tsɔy-guŋs-] impotent.

Zick|lein zo. ['tsiklain] n (-s/-) kid;

~zack ['~tsak] m (-[e]s/-e) zigzag; im ~ fahren etc. zigzag.

Ziege zo. ['tsi:gə] f (-/-n) (she-)goat, nanny-(goat).

Ziegel ['tsi:gəl] m (-s/-) brick; tile (of roof), **~dach** n tiled roof; **~ei** [~'lai] f (~-en) brickworks sg., pl., brickyard, **~stein** m brick.

'Ziegen|bock zo. m he-goat; **'~fell** n goatskin, **~hirt** m goatherd; **'~leder** n kid(-leather); **'~peter** ⚕ m (-s/-) mumps

Ziehbrunnen ['tsi:-] m draw-well.

ziehen ['tsi:ən] (irr. ge-) **1.** v/t. (h) pull, draw, draw (line, weapon, lots, conclusion, etc.), drag; ✚ cultivate; zo. breed, take off (hat); dig (ditch); draw, extract (tooth); ⚗ extract (root of number), Blasen ~ ⚕ raise blisters, e-n Vergleich ~ draw or make a comparison; j-n ins Vertrauen ~ take s.o. into one's confidence; in Erwägung ~ take into consideration, in die Länge ~ draw out; fig. protract, Nutzen ~ aus derive profit or benefit from; an sich ~ draw to one, Aufmerksamkeit etc. auf sich ~ attract attention, etc.; et. nach sich ~ entail or involve s.th.; **2.** v/i. (h) pull (an dat. at); chimney, cigar, etc.: draw; puff (an e-r Zigarre at a cigar); tea: infuse, draw; play draw (large audiences); F ✚ goods draw (customers), take; es zieht there is a draught, Am. there is a draft; **3.** v/i. (sein) move, go; march, (re)move (nach to); birds migrate, **4.** v/refl. (h) extend, stretch, run, wood: warp; sich in die Länge drag on.

'Zieh|harmonika ♪ f accordion; **'~ung** f (-/-en) drawing (of lots).

Ziel [tsi:l] n (-[e]s/-e) aim (a. fig.); mark, sports winning-post, goal (a. fig.), target; ✕ objective; destination (of voyage); fig. end, purpose, target, object(ive); term; sein ~ erreichen gain one's end(s pl.); über das ~ hinausschießen overshoot the mark; zum ~e führen succeed, be successful; sich zum ~ setzen zu inf. aim at ger., Am. aim to inf.; **'~band** n sports tape; **'2-bewußt** adj. purposeful; **'2en** v/i. (ge-, h) (take) aim (auf acc. at); **'~fernrohr** n telescopic sight; **'2-los** adj. aimless, purposeless; **'~scheibe** f target, butt; ~ des Spottes butt or target (of derision); **'2-strebig** adj. purposive.

ziemlich ['tsi:mliç] **1.** adj. fair, tolerable; considerable; **2.** adv. pretty, fairly, tolerably, rather; about.

Zier [tsi:r] f (-/no pl.), **~de** ['~də] f (-/-n) ornament; fig. a. hono(u)r (für to); **'2en** v/t. (ge-, h) ornament, adorn, decorate; sich ~ be affected; esp. of woman: be prudish; refuse; '2lich *adj.* delicate; neat; graceful, elegant; '_lichkeit *f* (-/_-en) delicacy; neatness; gracefulness, elegance; '_pflanze *f* ornamental plant.

Ziffer ['tsifər] *f* (-/-n) figure, digit; '_blatt *n* dial(-plate), face.

Zigarette [tsiga'retə] *f* (-/-n) cigaret(te); _automat [_n⁹-] *m* cigarette slot-machine; _netui [_n⁹-] *n* cigarette-case; _nspitze *f* cigarette-holder; _nstummel *m* stub, *Am. a.* butt.

Zigarre [tsi'garə] *f* (-/-n) cigar.

Zigeuner [tsi'gɔynər] *m* (-s/-), _inf (-/-nen) gipsy, gypsy.

Zimmer ['tsimər] *n* (-s/-) room; apartment; '_antenne *f* radio, *etc.*: indoor aerial, *Am. a.* indoor antenna; '_einrichtung *f* furniture; '_flucht *f* suite (of rooms); '_mädchen *n* chamber-maid; '_mann *m* (-[e]s/Zimmerleute) carpenter; '2n (ge-, h) 1. *v/t.* carpenter; *fig.* frame; 2. *v/i.* carpenter; '_pflanze *f* indoor plant; '_vermieterin *f* (-/-nen) landlady.

zimperlich *adj.* ['tsimpərliç] prim; prudish; affected.

Zimt [tsimt] *m* (-[e]s/-e) cinnamon.

Zink [tsiŋk] *n* (-[e]s/no pl.) zinc; '_blech *n* sheet zinc.

Zinke ['tsiŋkə] *f* (-/-n) prong; tooth (of comb or fork); '_n *m* (-s/-) s. Zinke.

Zinn [tsin] *n* (-[e]s/no pl.) tin.

Zinne ['tsinə] *f* (-/-n) ⚔ pinnacle; ⚔ battlement.

Zinnober [tsi'no:bər] *m* (-s/-) cinnabar; 2rot *adj.* vermilion.

Zins [tsins] *m* (-es/-en) rent; tribute; *mst* _en *pl.* interest; _en *tragen* yield *or* bear interest; '2bringend *adj.* bearing interest; _eszins ['_zəs-] *m* compound interest; '2frei *adj.* rent-free; free of interest; '_fuß *m*, '_satz *m* rate of interest.

Zipf|el ['tsipfəl] *m* (-s/-) tip, point, end; corner (of handkerchief, *etc.*); lappet (of garment); '2elig *adj.* having points *or* ends; '_elmütze *f* jelly-bag cap; nightcap.

Zirkel ['tsirkəl] *m* (-s/-) circle (a. fig.); ⚔ (ein a pair of) compasses pl. *or* dividers pl.

zirkulieren [tsirku'li:rən] *v/i.* (no -ge-, h) circulate.

Zirkus ['tsirkus] *m* (-/-se) circus.

zirpen ['tsirpən] *v/i.* (ge-, h) chirp, cheep.

zisch|eln ['tsiʃəln] *v/t. and v/i.* (ge-, h) whisper; '_en *v/i.* (ge-, h) hiss; whiz(z).

ziselieren [tsize'li:rən] *v/t.* (no -ge-, h) chase.

Zit|at [tsi'ta:t] *n* (-[e]s/-e) quotation; 2ieren [_'ti:rən] *v/t.* (no -ge-, h) summon; quote.

Zitrone [tsi'tro:nə] *f* (-/-n) lemon;

_nlimonade *f* lemonade; lemon squash; _npresse *f* lemon-squeezer; _nsaft *m* lemon juice.

zittern ['tsitərn] *v/i.* (ge-, h) tremble, shake (vor *dat.* with).

zivil [tsi'vi:l] 1. *adj.* civil; civilian; *price:* reasonable; 2. 2 *n* (-s/no pl.) civilians *pl.*; *s.* Zivilkleidung; 2bevölkerung *f* civilian population, civilians *pl.*; 2lsation [_iliza'tsjo:n] *f* (-/_-en) civilization; _isieren [_ili'zi:rən] *v/t.* (no -ge-, h) civilize; 2ist [_i'list] *m* (-en/-en) civilian; 2kleidung *f* civilian *or* plain clothes *pl.*

Zofe ['tso:fə] *f* (-/-n) lady's maid.

zog ['tso:k] *pret. of* ziehen.

zögern ['tsø:gərn] 1. *v/i.* (ge-, h) hesitate; linger; delay; 2. 2 *n* (-s/no pl.) hesitation; delay.

Zögling ['tsø:kliŋ] *m* (-s/-e) pupil.

Zoll [tsɔl] *m* 1. (-[e]s/-) inch; 2. (-[e]s/-e) customs *pl.*, duty; *the* Customs *pl.*; '_abfertigung *f* customs clearance; '_amt *n* customhouse; '_beamte *m* customs officer; '_behörde *f the* Customs *pl.*; '_erklärung *f* customs declaration; '2frei *adj.* duty-free; '_kontrolle *f* customs examination; '2pflichtig *adj.* liable to duty; '_stock *m* footrule; '_tarif *m* tariff.

Zone ['tso:nə] *f* (-/-n) zone.

Zoo [tso] *m* (-[s]/-s) zoo.

Zoolog|e [tso⁹o'lo:gə] *m* (-n/-n) zoologist; _ie [_o'gi:] *f* (-/no pl.) zoology; 2isch *adj.* [_'lo:giʃ] zoological

Zopf [tsɔpf] *m* (-[e]s/_e) plait, tress; pigtail; *alter* _ antiquated ways *pl. or* custom.

Zorn [tsɔrn] *m* (-[e]s/no pl.) anger; '2ig *adj.* angry (auf j-n with s.o.; auf et. at s.th.).

Zote ['tso:tə] *f* (-/-n) filthy *or* smutty joke, obscenity.

Zott|el ['tsɔtəl] *f* (-/-n) tuft (of hair); tassel; '2(e)lig *adj.* shaggy.

zu [tsu:] 1. *prp.* (dat.) direction: to, towards, up to; at, in; on; in addition to, along with; purpose: for; _ *Beginn* at the beginning *or* outset; _ *Weihnachten* at Christmas; *zum ersten Mal* for the first time; _ *e-m ... Preise* at a ... price; _ *meinem Erstaunen* to my surprise; _ *Tausenden* by thousands; _ *Wasser* by water; _ *zweien* by twos; *zum Beispiel* for example; 2. *adv.* too; direction: towards, to; F closed, shut; *with inf.:* to; *ich habe* _ *arbeiten* I have to work.

'zubauen *v/t.* (sep., -ge-, h) build up *or* in; block.

Zubehör ['tsu:bəhø:r] *n, m* (-[e]s/-e) appurtenances *pl.*, fittings *pl.*, *Am.* F fixings *pl.*; *esp.* ⊕ accessories *pl.*

'zubereit|en *v/t.* (sep., no -ge-, h) prepare; '2ung *f* preparation.

'zu|billigen v/t. (sep., -ge-, h) grant; '\binden v/t. (irr. binden, sep., -ge-, h) tie up; '\blinzeln v/i. (sep., -ge-, h) wink at s.o.; '\bringen v/t. (irr. bringen, sep., -ge-, h) pass, spend (time).

Zucht [tsuxt] f 1. (-/no pl.) discipline; breeding, rearing; rearing of bees, etc.: culture; ♀ cultivation; 2. (-/-en) breed, race; '\bulle zo. m bull (for breeding).

züchten ['tsyçtən] v/t. (ge-, h) breed (animals); grow, cultivate (plants); '2er m (-s/-) breeder (of animals); grower (of plants).

'Zucht|haus n penitentiary; punishment: penal servitude; \häusler ['\hɔʏslər] m (-s/-) convict; '\hengst zo. m stud-horse, stallion.

züchtig adj. ['tsyçtiç] chaste, modest; \en ['\gən] v/t. (ge-, h) flog.

'zucht|los adj. undisciplined; '2losigkeit f (-/\-en) want of discipline; '2stute zo. f brood-mare.

zucken ['tsukən] v/i. (ge-, h) jerk; move convulsively, twitch (all: mit et. s.th.); with pain: wince; lightning: flash.

zücken ['tsykən] v/t. (ge-, h) draw (sword); F pull out (purse, pencil).

Zucker ['tsukər] m (-s/no pl.) sugar; '\dose f sugar-basin, Am. sugar bowl; '\erbse ♀ f green pea; '\guß m icing, frosting; '\hut m sugar-loaf; '2ig adj. sugary; '2krank adj. diabetic; '2n v/t. (ge-, h) sugar; '\rohr n sugar-cane; '\rübe ♀ f sugar-beet; '2süß adj. (as) sweet as sugar; '\wasser n sugared water; '\zange f (e-a pair of) sugar-tongs pl.

zuckrig adj. ['tsukriç] sugary.

'Zuckung ♀ f (-/-en) convulsion.

'zudecken v/t. (sep., -ge-, h) cover (up).

zudem adv. [tsu'de:m] besides, moreover.

'zu|drehen v/t. (sep., -ge-, h) turn off (tap); j-m den Rücken ~ turn one's back on s.o.; '\dringlich adj. importunate, obtrusive; '\drücken v/t. (sep., -ge-, h) close, shut; '\erkennen v/t. (irr. kennen, sep., no -ge-, h) award (a. ♏); adjudge (dat. to) (a. ♏).

zuerst adv. [tsu'-] first (of all); at first; er kam ~ an he was the first to arrive.

'zufahr|en v/i. (irr. fahren, sep., -ge-, sein) drive on; ~ auf (acc.) drive to (-wards); fig. rush at s.o.; '2t f approach; drive, Am. driveway; '2tsstraße f approach (road).

'Zufall m chance, accident; durch ~ by chance, by accident; '2en v/i. (irr. fallen, sep., -ge-, sein) eyes: be closing (with sleep); door: shut (of) itself; j-m ~ fall to s.o.('s share).

'zufällig 1. adj. accidental; attr. chance; casual; 2. adv. accidentally, by chance.

'zufassen v/i. (sep., -ge-, h) seize (hold of) s.th.; (mit) ~ lend or give a hand.

'Zuflucht f (-/\-ue) refuge, shelter, resort; s-e ~ nehmen zu have recourse to s.th., take refuge in s.th.

'Zufluß m afflux; influx (a. ♥); affluent, tributary (of river); ♥ supply.

'zuflüstern v/t. (sep., -ge-, h): j-m et. ~ whisper s.th. to s.o.

zufolge prp. (gen.; dat.) [tsu'fɔlgə] according to.

zufrieden adj. [tsu'-] content(ed), satisfied; 2heit f (-/no pl.) contentment, satisfaction; \lassen v/t. (irr. lassen, sep., -ge-, h) let s.o. alone; \stellen v/t. (sep., -ge-, h) satisfy, \stellend adj. satisfactory.

'zu|frieren v/i. (irr. frieren, sep., -ge-, sein) freeze up or over; '\fügen v/t. (sep., -ge-, h) add; do, cause; inflict (wound, etc.) (j-m [up]on s.o.); 2fuhr ['\fuːr] f (-/-en) supply; supplies pl.; influx; '\führen v/t. (sep., -ge-, h) carry, lead, bring; ⊕ feed; supply (a. ⊕).

Zug [tsu:k] m (-[e]s/ue) draw(ing), pull(ing); ⊕ traction; ♀ expedition, campaign; procession; migration (of birds); drift (of clouds); range (of mountains); ♏ train; feature; trait (of character); bent, tendency, trend; draught, Am. draft (of air); at chess: move; drinking: draught, Am. draft; at cigarette, etc.: puff.

'Zu|gabe f addition; extra; thea. encore; '\gang m entrance; access; approach; 2gänglich adj. ['\genlic] accessible (für to); '2geben v/t. (irr. geben, sep., -ge-, h) add; fig.: allow; confess; admit.

zugegen adj. [tsu'-] present (bei at.).

'zugehen v/i. (irr. gehen, sep., -ge-, sein) door, etc.: close, shut; p. move on, walk faster; happen; auf j-n ~ go up to s.o., move or walk towards s.o.

'Zugehörigkeit f (-/no pl.) membership (zu to) (society, etc.); belonging (to).

Zügel ['tsy:gəl] m (-s/-) rein; bridle (a. fig.); '2los adj. unbridled; fig.: unrestrained; licentious; '2n v/t. (ge-, h) rein (in); fig. bridle, check.

'Zuge|ständnis n concession; '2-stehen v/t. (irr. stehen, sep., -ge-, h) concede.

'zugetan adj. attached (dat. to).

'Zugführer ♏ m guard, Am. conductor. [-ge-, h) add.\

'zugießen v/t. (irr. gießen, sep.,)

zug|ig adj. ['tsu:giç] draughty, Am. drafty; 2kraft ['\k-] f ⊕ traction; fig. attraction, draw, appeal; \kräftig adj. ['\k-]: ~ sein be a draw.

zugleich *adv.* [tsu'-] at the same time; together.

'Zug|luft *f* (-/no *pl.*) draught, *Am.* draft; **~maschine** *f* traction-engine, tractor; **~pflaster** 𝒩 *n* blister.

'zu|greifen *v/i.* (*irr.* greifen, *sep.*, -ge-, *h*) grasp *or* grab at *s.th.*; *at table:* help o.s.; lend a hand; **'2griff** *m* grip, clutch.

zugrunde *adv.* [tsu'grundə]: ~ gehen perish; ~ richten ruin.

'Zugtier *n* draught animal, *Am.* draft animal.

zu|gunsten *prp.* (*gen.*) [tsu'gunstən] in favo(u)r of; **~gute** *adv.*: j-m et. ~ halten give s.o. credit for s.th.; ~ kommen be for the benefit (*dat.* of).

'Zugvogel *m* bird of passage.

'zuhalten *v/t.* (*irr.* halten, *sep.*, -ge-, *h*) hold (*door*) to; *sich die Ohren* ~ stop one's ears. [home.)

Zuhause [tsu'hauzə] *n* (-/no *pl.*))

'zu|heilen *v/i.* (*sep.*, -ge-, *sein*) heal up, skin over; **'~hören** *v/i.* (*sep.*, -ge-, *h*) listen (*dat.* to).

'Zuhörer *m* hearer, listener; ~ *pl.* audience; **~schaft** *f* (-/⧖-en) audience.

'zu|jubeln *v/i.* (*sep.*, -ge-, *h*) cheer; **'~kleben** *v/t.* (*sep.*, -ge-, *h*) paste *or* glue up; gum (*letter*) down; **'~knallen** *v/t.* (*sep.*, -ge-, *h*) bang, slam (*door, etc.*); **'~knöpfen** *v/t.* (*sep.*, -ge-, *h*) button (up); **'~kommen** *v/i.* (*irr.* kommen, *sep.*, -ge-, *sein*): *auf j-n* ~ come up to s.o.; *j-m* ~ be due to s.o.; *j-m et.* ~ lassen let s.o. have s.th.; send s.o. s.th.; **'~korken** *v/t.* (*sep.*, -ge-, *h*) cork (up).

Zu|kunft ['tsu:kunft] *f* (-/no *pl.*) future; *gr.* future (tense); **'2künftig 1.** *adj.* future; *~er Vater* father-to-be; **2.** *adv.* in future.

'zu|lächeln *v/i.* (*sep.*, -ge-, *h*) smile at *or* (up)on; **'2lage** *f* extra pay, increase; rise, *Am.* raise (*in salary or wages*); **'~langen** *v/i.* (*sep.*, -ge-, *h*) *at table:* help o.s.; **'~lassen** *v/t.* (*irr.* lassen, *sep.*, -ge-, *h*) leave (*door*) shut; keep closed; *fig.:* admit *s.o.*; license; allow, suffer; admit of (*only one interpretation, etc.*); **'~lässig** *adj.* admissible, allowable; **'2lassung** *f* (-/-en) admission; permission; licen|ce, *Am.* -se.

'zulegen *v/t.* (*sep.*, -ge-, *h*) add; F *sich et.* ~ get o.s. s.th.

zuleide *adv.* [tsu'laɪdə]: *j-m et.* ~ tun do s.o. harm, harm *or* hurt s.o.

'zuleiten *v/t.* (*sep.*, -ge-, *h*) let in (*water, etc.*); conduct to; pass on to s.o.

zu|letzt *adv.* [tsu'-] finally, at last; *er kam* ~ *an* he was the last to arrive; **~liebe** *adv.*: *j-m* ~ for s.o.'s sake.

zum *prp.* [tsum] = *zu dem.*

'zumachen *v/t.* (*sep.*, -ge-, *h*) close, shut; button (up) (*coat*); fasten.

zumal *cj.* [tsu'-] especially, particularly. [up.)

'zumauern *v/t.* (*sep.*, -ge-, *h*) wall)

zumut|en ['tsu:mu:tən] *v/t.* (*sep.*, -ge-, *h*): *j-m et.* ~ expect s.th. of s.o.; *sich zuviel* ~ overtask o.s., overtax one's strength, *etc.*; **'2ung** *f* (-/-en) exacting demand, exaction; *fig.* impudence.

zunächst [tsu'-] **1.** *prp.* (*dat.*) next to; **2.** *adv.* first of all; for the present.

'zu|nageln *v/t.* (*sep.*, -ge-, *h*) nail up; **'~nähen** *v/t.* (*sep.*, -ge-, *h*) sew up; **2nahme** ['~nɑ:mə] *f* (-/-n) increase, growth; **'2name** *m* surname.

zünden ['tsyndən] *v/i.* (ge-, *h*) kindle; *esp. mot.* ignite; *fig.* arouse enthusiasm.

'Zünd|holz ['tsynt-] *n* match; **'~kerze** *mot.* *f* spark(ing)-plug, *Am.* spark plug; **'~schlüssel** *mot.* *m* ignition key; **'~schnur** *f* fuse; **'~stoff** *fig.* *m* fuel; **'~ung** *mot.* ['~duŋ] *f* (-/-en) ignition.

'zunehmen *v/i.* (*irr.* nehmen, *sep.*, -ge-, *h*) increase (*an dat.* in); grow; put on weight; *moon:* wax; *days:* grow longer.

'zuneig|en (*sep.*, -ge-, *h*) **1.** *v/i.* incline to(wards); **2.** *v/refl.* incline to(wards); *sich dem Ende* ~ draw to a close; **'2ung** *f* (-/⧖-en) affection.

Zunft [tsunft] *f* (-/⧖e) guild, corporation.

Zunge ['tsuŋə] *f* (-/-n) tongue.

züngeln ['tsyŋəln] *v/i.* (ge-, *h*) play with its tongue; *flame:* lick.

'zungen|fertig *adj.* voluble; **'2fertigkeit** *f* (-/no *pl.*) volubility; **'2spitze** *f* tip of the tongue.

zunichte *adv.* [tsu'niçtə]: ~ machen *or* werden bring *or* come to nothing.

'zunicken *v/i.* (*sep.*, -ge-, *h*) nod to.

zu|nutze *adv.* [tsu'nutsə]: *sich et.* ~ machen turn s.th. to account, utilize s.th.; **~oberst** *adv.* at the top, uppermost.

zupfen ['tsupfən] **1.** *v/t.* pull, tug, twitch; **2.** *v/i.* pull, tug, twitch (*all: an dat.* at).

zur *prp.* [tsu:r] = *zu der.*

'zurechnungsfähig *adj.* of sound mind; ⚖ responsible; **'2keit** ⚖ *f* (-/no *pl.*) responsibility.

zurecht|finden [tsu'-] *v/refl.* (*irr.* finden, *sep.*, -ge-, *h*) find one's way; **~kommen** *v/i.* (*irr.* kommen, *sep.*, -ge-, *sein*) arrive in time; ~ (*mit*) get on (well) (with); manage *s.th.*; **~legen** *v/t.* (*sep.*, -ge-, *h*) arrange; *sich e-e Sache* ~ think s.th. out; **~machen** *v/t.* (*sep.*, -ge-, *h*) get ready, prepare, *Am.* F fix; adapt (*für* to, for *purpose*); *sich* ~ of *woman*: make (o.s.) up; ~weisen *v/t.* (*irr.* weisen, *sep.*, -ge-, *h*) reprimand; 2weisung *f* reprimand.

'zu|reden *v/i.* (*sep.*, -ge-, *h*): j-m ~ try to persuade s.o.; encourage s.o.; '~reiten *v/t.* (*irr.* reiten, *sep.*, -ge-, *h*) break in; '~riegeln *v/t.* (*sep.*, -ge-, *h*) bolt (up).

zürnen ['tsyrnən] *v/i.* (ge-, *h*) be angry (j-m with s.o.).

zurück *adv.* [tsu'ryk] back; backward(s); behind; ~behalten *v/t.* (*irr.* halten, *sep.*, no -ge-, *h*) keep back, retain; ~bekommen *v/t.* (*irr.* kommen, *sep.*, no -ge-, *h*) get back; ~bleiben *v/i.* (*irr.* bleiben, *sep.*, -ge-, *sein*) remain *or* stay behind; fall behind, lag; ~blicken *v/i.* (*sep.*, -ge-, *h*) look back; ~bringen *v/t.* (*irr.* bringen, *sep.*, -ge-, *h*) bring back; ~datieren *v/t.* (*sep.*, no -ge-, *h*) date back, antedate; ~drängen *v/t.* (*sep.*, -ge-, *h*) push back; *fig.* repress; ~erobern *v/t.* (*sep.*, no -ge-, *h*) reconquer; ~erstatten *v/t.* (*sep.*, no -ge-, *h*) restore, return; refund (*expenses*); ~fahren (*irr.* fahren, *sep.*, -ge-) 1. *v/i.* (*sein*) drive back; *fig.* start; 2. *v/t.* (*h*) drive back; ~fordern *v/t.* (*sep.*, -ge-, *h*) reclaim; ~führen *v/t.* (*sep.*, -ge-, *h*) lead back; ~ auf (*acc.*) reduce to (*rule, etc.*); refer to (*cause, etc.*); ~geben *v/t.* (*irr.* geben, *sep.*, -ge-, *h*) give back, return, restore; ~gehen *v/i.* (*irr.* gehen, *sep.*, -ge-, *sein*) go back; return; ~gezogen *adj.* retired; ~greifen *fig. v/i.* (*irr.* greifen, *sep.*, -ge-, *h*): ~ auf (*acc.*) fall back (up)on; ~halten (*irr.* halten, *sep.*, -ge-, *h*) 1. *v/t.* hold back; 2. *v/i.*: ~ mit keep back; ~haltend *adj.* reserved; ~haltung *f* (-/~-en) reserve; ~kehren *v/i.* (*sep.*, -ge-, *sein*) return; ~kommen *v/i.* (*irr.* kommen, *sep.*, -ge-, *sein*) come back; return (*fig. auf acc.* to); ~lassen *v/t.* (*irr.* lassen, *sep.*, -ge-, *h*) leave (behind); ~legen *v/t.* (*sep.*, -ge-, *h*) lay aside; cover (*distance, way*); ~nehmen *v/t.* (*irr.* nehmen, *sep.*, -ge-, *h*) take back; withdraw, retract (*words, etc.*); ~prallen *v/i.* (*sep.*, -ge-, *sein*) rebound; start; ~rufen *v/t.* (*irr.* rufen, *sep.*, -ge-, *h*) call back; sich ins Gedächtnis ~ recall; ~schicken *v/t.* (*sep.*, -ge-, *h*) send back; ~schlagen (*irr.* schlagen, *sep.*, -ge-, *h*) 1. *v/t.* drive (*ball*) back; repel (*enemy*); turn down (*blanket*); 2. *v/i.* strike back; ~schrecken *v/i.* (*sep.*, -ge-, *sein*) 1. (*irr.* schrecken) shrink back (*vor dat.* from *spectacle, etc.*); 2. shrink (*vor dat.* from *work, etc.*); ~setzen *v/t.* (*sep.*, -ge-, *h*) put back; *fig.* slight, neglect; ~stellen *v/t.* (*sep.*, -ge-, *h*) put back (*a. clock*); *fig.* defer, postpone; ~strahlen *v/t.* (*sep.*, -ge-, *h*) reflect;

~streifen *v/t.* (*sep.*, -ge-, *h*) turn *or* tuck up (*sleeve*); ~treten *v/i.* (*irr.* treten, *sep.*, -ge-, *sein*) step *or* stand back; *fig.*: recede; resign; withdraw; ~weichen *v/i.* (*irr.* weichen, *sep.*, -ge-, *sein*) fall back; recede (*a. fig.*); ~weisen *v/t.* (*irr.* weisen, *sep.*, -ge-, *h*) decline, reject; repel (*attack*); ~zahlen *v/t.* (*sep.*, -ge-, *h*) pay back (*a. fig.*); ~ziehen (*irr.* ziehen, *sep.*, -ge-) 1. *v/t.* (*h*) draw back; *fig.* withdraw; sich ~ retire, withdraw; ✗ retreat; 2. *v/i.* (*sein*) move *or* march back.

'Zuruf *m* call; 2en *v/t.* (*irr.* rufen, *sep.*, -ge-, *h*) call (out), shout (j-m et. s.th. to s.o.).

'Zusage *f* promise; assent; 2n (*sep.*, -ge-, *h*) 1. *v/t.* promise; 2. *v/i.* promise to come; j-m ~ food, *etc.*; agree with s.o.; accept s.o.'s invitation; suit s.o.

zusammen *adv.* [tsu'zamən] together; at the same time; alles ~ (all) in all; ~ betragen amount to, total (up to); 2arbeit *f* (-/no *pl.*) co-operation; team-work; ~arbeiten *v/i.* (*sep.*, -ge-, *h*) work together; co-operate; ~beißen *v/t.* (*irr.* beißen, *sep.*, -ge-, *h*): die Zähne ~ set one's teeth; ~brechen *v/i.* (*irr.* brechen, *sep.*, -ge-, *sein*) break down; collapse; 2bruch *m* breakdown; collapse; ~drücken *v/t.* (*sep.*, -ge-, *h*) compress, press together; ~fahren *fig. v/i.* (*irr.* fahren, *sep.*, -ge-, *sein*) start (*bei at*; *vor dat.* with); ~fallen *v/i.* (*irr.* fallen, *sep.*, -ge-, *sein*) fall in, collapse; coincide; ~falten *v/t.* (*sep.*, -ge-, *h*) fold up; ~fassen *v/t.* (*sep.*, -ge-, *h*) summarize, sum up; 2fassung *f* (-/-en) summary; ~fügen *v/t.* (*sep.*, -ge-, *h*) join (together); ~halten (*irr.* halten, *sep.*, -ge-, *h*) 1. *v/t.* hold together; 2. *v/i.* hold together; *friends*: F stick together; 2hang *m* coherence, coherency, connection; context; ~hängen (*sep.*, -ge-, *h*) 1. *v/i.* (*irr.* hängen) cohere; *fig.* be connected; 2. *v/t.* hang together; ~klappen *v/t.* (*sep.*, -ge-, *h*) fold up; close (*clasp-knife*); ~kommen *v/i.* (*irr.* kommen, *sep.*, -ge-, *sein*) meet; 2kunft [~kunft] *f* (-/~e) meeting; ~laufen *v/i.* (*irr.* laufen, *sep.*, -ge-, *sein*) run *or* crowd together; ✗ converge; *milk*: curdle; ~legen *v/t.* (*sep.*, -ge-, *h*) lay together; fold up; club (*money*) (together); ~nehmen *fig. v/t.* (*irr.* nehmen, *sep.*, -ge-, *h*) collect (*one's wits*); sich ~ be on one's good behavio(u)r; pull o.s. together; ~packen *v/t.* (*sep.*, -ge-, *h*) pack up; ~passen *v/i.* (*sep.*, -ge-, *h*) match, harmonize; ~rechnen *v/t.* (*sep.*, -ge-, *h*) add up; ~reißen F *v/refl.* (*irr.* reißen, *sep.*, -ge-, *h*) pull o.s. together; ~rollen *v/t. and v/refl.* (*sep., -ge-, h*) coil (up); **~rotten** *v/refl.* (*sep., -ge-, h*) band together; **~rücken** (*sep., -ge-*) **1.** *v/t.* (*h*) move together; **2.** *v/i.* (*sein*) close up; **~schlagen** (*irr. schlagen, sep., -ge-*) **1.** *v/t.* (*h*) clap (*hands*) (together); F smash to pieces; beat *s.o.* up; **2.** *v/i.* (*sein*): **~** *über* (*dat.*) close over; **~schließen** *v/refl.* (*irr. schließen, sep., -ge-, h*) join; unite; **2schluß** *m* union; **~schrumpfen** *v/i.* (*sep., -ge-, sein*) shrivel (up), shrink; **~setzen** *v/t.* (*sep., -ge-, h*) put together; compose; compound (*a. ~, word*); ⊕ assemble; *sich* **~** *aus* consist of; **2setzung** *f* (*-/-en*) composition; compound; ⊕ assembly; **~stellen** *v/t.* (*sep., -ge-, h*) put together; compile; combine; **2stoß** *m* collision (*a. fig.*); ✕ encounter; *fig.* clash; **~stoßen** *v/i.* (*irr. stoßen, sep., -ge-, sein*) collide (*a. fig.*); adjoin; *fig.* clash; **~** *mit* knock (*heads, etc.*) together; **~stürzen** *v/i.* (*sep., -ge-, sein*) collapse; *house, etc.*: fall in; **~tragen** *v/t.* (*irr. tragen, sep., -ge-, h*) collect; compile (*notes*); **~treffen** *v/i.* (*irr. treffen, sep., -ge-, sein*) meet; coincide; **2treffen** *n* (*-s/no pl.*) meeting; encounter (*of enemies*); coincidence; **~treten** *v/i.* (*irr. treten, sep., -ge-, sein*) meet; *parl. a.* convene; **~wirken** *v/i.* (*sep., -ge-, h*) co-operate; **2wirken** *n* (*-s/no pl.*) co-operation; **~zählen** *v/t.* (*sep., -ge-, h*) add up, count up; **~ziehen** *v/t.* (*irr. ziehen, sep., -ge-, h*) draw together; contract; concentrate (*troops*); *sich* **~** contract.

'Zusatz *m* addition; admixture, *metall.* alloy; supplement.

zusätzlich *adj.* ['tsuːzɛtslɪç] additional.

'zuschau|en *v/i.* (*sep., -ge-, h*) look on (*e-r Sache dat.*); *j-m* **~** watch *s.o.* (*bei* sth. doing sth.); **'2er** *m* (*-s/-*) spectator, looker-on, onlooker; **2erraum** *thea. m* auditorium.

'zuschicken *v/t.* (*sep., -ge-, h*) send (*dat.* to); mail; consign (*goods*).

'Zuschlag *m* addition; extra charge; excess fare; ✆ surcharge; *at auction:* knocking down; **2en** ['~gən] (*irr. schlagen, sep., -ge-*) **1.** *v/i.* (*h*) strike; **2.** *v/i.* (*sein*) *door:* slam (to); **3.** *v/t.* (*h*) bang, slam (*door*) (to); *at auction:* knock down (*dat.* to).

'zu|schließen *v/t.* (*irr. schließen, sep., -ge-, h*) lock (up); **'~schnallen** *v/t.* (*sep., -ge-, h*) buckle (up); **'~schnappen** (*sep., -ge-*) **1.** *v/i.* (*h*) *dog:* snap; **2.** *v/i.* (*sein*) *door:* snap to; **'~schneiden** *v/t.* (*irr. schneiden, sep., -ge-, h*) cut up; cut (*suit*) (to size); **'2schnitt** *m* (*-[e]s/~-e*) cut; style; **'~schnüren** *v/t.* (*sep., -ge-, h*) lace up; cord up; **'~schrauben** *v/t.*

(*sep., -ge-, h*) screw up or tight; **'~schreiben** *v/t.* (*irr. schreiben, sep., -ge-, h*): *j-m* et. **~** ascribe or attribute sth. to s.o.; **'2schrift** *f* letter.

'Zu|schuß *m* allowance; subsidy, grant (*of government*); **'2schütten** *v/t.* (*sep., -ge-, h*) fill up (*ditch*); F add; **'2sehen** *v/i.* (*irr. sehen, sep., -ge-, h*) *s.* zuschauen; **~**, *daß* see (to it) that; **2sehends** *adv.* ['~ts] visibly; **'2senden** *v/t.* [(*irr. senden,*] *sep., -ge-, h*) *s.* zuschicken; **'2setzen** (*sep., -ge-, h*) **1.** *v/t.* add; lose (*money*); **2.** *v/i.* lose money; *j-m* **~** press s.o. hard.

'zusicher|n *v/t.* (*sep., -ge-, h*): *j-m* et. **~** assure s.o. of sth.; promise s.o. sth.; **'2ung** *f* promise, assurance.

'zu|spielen *v/t.* (*sep., -ge-, h*) *sports:* pass (*ball*) (*dat.* to) **'~spitzen** *v/t.* (*sep., -ge-, h*) point; *sich* **~** taper (off); *fig.* come to a crisis; **'2spruch** *m* (*-[e]s/no pl.*) encouragement; consolation; ✝ custom; **'2stand** *m* condition; state; *in gutem* **~** *house:* in good repair.

'zustande *adv.* [tsuˈʃtandə]: **~** bringen bring about; **~** kommen come about; *nicht* **~** kommen not to come off.

'zuständig *adj.* competent; **'2keit** *f* (*-/-en*) competence.

zustatten *adv.* [tsuˈʃtatən]: *j-m* **~** kommen be useful to s.o.

'zustehen *v/i.* (*irr. stehen, sep., -ge-, h*) be due (*dat.* to).

'zustell|en *v/t.* (*sep., -ge-, h*) deliver (*a.* ✆); ⚖ serve (*j-m* on s.o.); **'2ung** *f* delivery; ⚖ service.

'zustimm|en *v/i.* (*sep., -ge-, h*) agree (*dat.:* to *s.th.*; *with s.o.*); consent (*to s.th.*); **'2ung** *f* consent.

'zustoßen *fig. v/i.* (*irr. stoßen, sep., -ge-, sein*): *j-m* **~** happen to s.o.

zutage *adv.* [tsuˈtaːgə]: **~** treten come to light.

Zutaten ['tsuːtaːtən] *f/pl.* ingredients *pl.* (*of food*); trimmings *pl.* (*of dress*). [fall to s.o.'s share.]

zuteil *adv.* [tsuˈtaɪl]: *j-m* **~** werden]

'zuteil|en *v/t.* (*sep., -ge-, h*) allot, apportion; **'2ung** *f* allotment, apportionment; ration.

'zutragen *v/refl.* (*irr. tragen, sep., -ge-, h*) happen.

'zutrauen **1.** *v/t.* (*sep., -ge-, h*): *j-m* et. **~** credit s.o. with sth.; *sich zuviel* **~** overrate o.s.; **2.** *2 n* (*-s/no pl.*) confidence (*zu in*).

'zutraulich *adj.* confiding, trustful, trusting; *animal:* friendly, tame.

'zutreffen *v/i.* (*irr. treffen, sep., -ge-, h*) be right, be true; **~** *auf* (*acc.*) be true of; **'~d** *adj.* right, correct; applicable.

'**zutrinken** v/i. (irr. trinken, sep., -ge-, h): j-m ~ drink to s.o.

'**Zutritt** m (-[e]s/no pl.) access; admission; ~ verboten! no admittance! [bottom.)

zuunterst adv. [tsu'-] right at the)

zuverlässig adj. ['tsu:ferlɛsiç] reliable; certain; '2keit f (-/no pl.) reliability; certainty.

Zuversicht ['tsu:ferziçt] f (-/no pl.) confidence; '2lich adj. confident.

zuviel adv. [tsu'-] too much; e-r ~ one too many.

zuvor adv. [tsu'-] before, previously; first; ~kommen v/i. (irr. kommen, sep., -ge-, sein): j-m ~ anticipate s.o.; e-r Sache ~ anticipate or prevent s.th.; ~kommend adj. obliging; courteous.

Zuwachs ['tsu:vaks] m (-es/no pl.) increase; '2en v/i. (irr. wachsen, sep., -ge-, sein) become overgrown; wound: close.

zu|wege adv. [tsu've:gə]: ~ bringen bring about; ~weilen adv. sometimes.

'**zu|weisen** v/t. (irr. weisen, sep., -ge-, h) assign; '~wenden v/t. ([irr. wenden], sep., -ge-, h) (dat.) turn to(wards); fig.: give; bestow on; sich ~ (dat.) turn to(wards).

zuwenig adv. [tsu'-] too little.

'**zuwerfen** v/t. (irr. werfen, sep., -ge-, h) fill up (pit); slam (door (to); j-m ~ throw (ball, etc.) to s.o.; cast (look) at s.o.

zuwider prp. (dat.) [tsu'-] contrary to, against; repugnant, distasteful; ~handeln v/i. (sep., -ge-, h) (dat.) act contrary or in opposition to; esp. ₰₰ contravene; 2handlung ₰₰ f contravention.

'**zu|winken** v/i. (sep., -ge-, h) (dat.) wave to; beckon to; '~zahlen v/t. (sep., -ge-, h) pay extra; '~zählen v/t. (sep., -ge-, h) add; '~ziehen (irr. ziehen, sep., -ge-) 1. v/t. (h) draw together; draw (curtains); consult (doctor, etc.); sich ~ incur (s.o.'s displeasure, etc.); ₰ catch (disease); 2. v/i. (sein) move in; ~züglich prp. (gen.) ['~tsy:k-] plus.

Zwang [tsvaŋ] 1. m (-[e]s/⁒ ⁒e) compulsion, coercion; constraint; ₰₰ duress(e); force; sich ~ antun check or restrain o.s.; 2. 2 pret. of zwingen.

zwängen ['tsvɛŋən] v/t. (ge-,h) press, force.

'**zwanglos** fig. adj. free and easy, informal; '2igkeit f (-/-en) ease, informality.

'**Zwangs|arbeit** f hard labo(u)r; '~jacke f strait waistcoat or jacket; '~lage f embarrassing situation; 2läufig fig. adj. ['~lɔyf-] necessary; '~maßnahme f coercive measure; '~vollstreckung ₰₰ f distraint, execution; '~vorstellung ₰ f

obsession, hallucination; '2weise adv. by force; '~wirtschaft f (-/⁒ -en) controlled economy.

zwanzig adj. ['tsvantsiç] twenty; ~ste adj. ['~stə] twentieth.

zwar cj. [tsvɑːr] indeed, it is true; und ~ and that, that is.

Zweck [tsvɛk] m (-[e]s/-e) aim, end, object, purpose; design; keinen ~ haben be of no use; s-n ~ erfüllen answer its purpose; zu dem ~ (gen.) for the purpose of; '2dienlich adj. serviceable, useful, expedient.

Zwecke ['tsvɛkə] f (-/-n) tack; drawing-pin, Am. thumbtack.

'**zweck|los** adj. aimless, purposeless, useless; '~mäßig adj. expedient, suitable; '2mäßigkeit f (-/no pl.) expediency.

zwei adj. [tsvaɪ] two; '~beinig adj. two-legged; '2bettzimmer n double (bedroom); ~deutig adj. ['~dɔy-tiç] ambiguous; suggestive; ~erlei adj. ['~ɔr'laɪ] of two kinds, two kinds of; ~fach adj. ['~fax] double, twofold.

Zweifel ['tsvaɪfəl] m (-s/-) doubt; '2haft adj. doubtful, dubious; '2los adj. doubtless; '2n v/i. (ge-, h) doubt (an e-r Sache s.th.; an j-m s.o.).

Zweig [tsvaɪk] m (-[e]s/-e) branch (a. fig.); kleiner ~ twig; '~geschäft n, '~niederlassung f, '~stelle f branch.

zwei|jährig adj. ['tsvaɪjɛːriç] two-year-old, of two (years); '2kampf m duel, single combat; '~mal adv. twice; '~malig adj. (twice) repeated; ~motorig adj. ['~moːtoːriç] two- or twin-engined; '~reihig adj. having two rows; suit: double-breasted; '~schneidig adj. double- or two-edged (both a. fig.); '~seitig adj. two-sided; contract, etc.: bilateral; fabric: reversible, '2sitzer esp. mot. m (-s/-) two-seater; '~sprachig adj. bilingual; '~stimmig adj. for two voices; ~stöckig adj. ['~ʃtøkiç] two-stor|eyed, -ied; '~stufig ⊕ adj. two-stage; ~stündig adj. ['~ʃtyndiç] of or lasting two hours, two-hour.

zweit adj. [tsvaɪt] second; ein ~er another; aus ~er Hand second-hand; zu ~ by twos; wir sind zu ~ there are two of us. [engine.)

'**Zweitaktmotor** mot. m two-stroke)

'**zweitbest** adj. second-best.

'**zweiteilig** adj. garment: two-piece.

zweitens adv. ['tsvaɪtəns] secondly.

'**zweitklassig** adj. second-class, second-rate.

Zwerchfell anat. ['tsvɛrç-] n diaphragm.

Zwerg [tsvɛrk] m (-[e]s/-e) dwarf; 2enhaft adj. ['~gən-] dwarfish.

Zwetsch(g)e ['tsvɛtʃ(g)ə] f (-/-n) plum.

Zwick|el ['tsvikǝl] *m* (-s/-) *sewing*: gusset; **'≈en** *v/t. and v/i.* (ge-, *h*) pinch, nip; **'≈er** *m* (-s/-) (*ein* a pair of) eye-glasses *pl.*, pince-nez; **'≈mühle** *fig. f* dilemma, quandary, fix.

Zwieback ['tsvi:bak] *m* (-[e]s/≈e, -e) rusk, zwieback.

Zwiebel ['tsvi:bǝl] *f* (-/-n) onion; bulb (*of flowers, etc.*).

Zwie|gespräch ['tsvi:-] *n* dialog(ue); **'≈licht** *n* (-[e]s/*no pl.*) twilight; **'≈spalt** *m* (-[e]s/-e, ≈e) disunion; conflict; **≈spältig** *adj.* ['≈ʃpɛltiç] disunited; *emotions*: conflicting; **'≈tracht** *f* (-/*no pl.*) discord.

Zwilling|e ['tsviliŋǝ] *m/pl.* twins *pl.*; **'≈sbruder** *m* twin brother; **'≈sschwester** *f* twin sister.

Zwinge ['tsviŋǝ] *f* (-/-n) ferrule (*of stick, etc.*); ⊕ clamp; **'≈n** *v/t.* (*irr.*, ge-, *h*) compel, constrain; force; **'≈nd** *adj.* forcible; *arguments*: cogent, compelling; imperative; **'≈r** *m* (-s/-) outer court; kennel(s *pl.*); bear-pit.

zwinkern ['tsviŋkǝrn] *v/i.* (ge-, *h*) wink, blink.

Zwirn [tsvirn] *m* (-[e]s/-e) thread, cotton; **'≈sfaden** *m* thread.

zwischen *prp.* (*dat.*; *acc.*) ['tsviʃǝn] between (*two*); among (*several*); **'≈bilanz** ✝ *f* interim balance; **'≈deck** ♆ *n* steerage; **'≈durch** ⌐ *adv.* in between; for a change; **'≈ergebnis** *n* provisional result; **'≈fall** *m* incident; **'≈händler** ✝ *m* middleman; **'≈landung** ✈ *f* intermediate landing, stop, *Am. a.* stopover; (*Flug*) *ohne* ≈ non-stop (flight);

'≈pause *f* interval, intermission; **'≈prüfung** *f* intermediate examination; **'≈raum** *m* space, interval; **'≈ruf** *m* (loud) interruption; **'≈spiel** *n* interlude; **'≈staatlich** *adj.* international; *Am. between States*: interstate; **'≈station** *f* intermediate station; **'≈stecker** ≴ *m* adapter; **'≈stück** *n* intermediate piece, connexion, (*Am. only*) connection; **'≈stufe** *f* intermediate stage; **'≈wand** *f* partition (wall); **'≈zeit** *f* interval; *in der* ≈ in the meantime.

Zwist [tsvist] *m* (-es/-e), **'≈igkeit** *f* (-/-en) discord; disunion; quarrel.

zwitschern ['tsvitʃǝrn] *v/i.* (ge-, *h*) twitter, chirp.

Zwitter ['tsvitǝr] *m* (-s/-) hermaphrodite.

zwölf *adj.* [tsvœlf] twelve; *um* ≈ (*Uhr*) at twelve (o'clock); (*um*) ≈ *Uhr mittags* (at) noon; (*um*) ≈ *Uhr nachts* (at) midnight; **≈'finger-darm** *anat. m* duodenum; **≈te** *adj.* ['≈tǝ] twelfth.

Zyankali [tsyan'kɑ:li] *n* (-s/*no pl.*) potassium cyanide.

Zyklus ['tsy:klus, 'tsyk-] *m* (-/*Zyklen*) cycle; course, set (*of lectures, etc.*).

Zylind|er [tsi'lindǝr, tsy'-] *m* (-s/-) ♂, ⊕ cylinder; chimney (*of lamp*); top hat; **≈risch** *adj.* [≈driʃ] cylindrical.

Zyni|ker ['tsy:nikǝr] *m* (-s/-) cynic; **'≈sch** *adj.* cynical; **≈smus** [tsy-'nismus] *m* (-/*Zynismen*) cynicism.

Zypresse ♆ [tsy'presǝ] *f* (-/-n) cypress.

Zyste ♂ ['tsystǝ] *f* (-/-n) cyst.

PART II

ENGLISH-GERMAN
DICTIONARY

A

a [ei, ə] *Artikel:* ein(e); per, pro, je; *all of a* size alle gleich groß; *twice a week* zweimal wöchentlich.

A 1 F [ei'wʌn] Ia, prima.

aback [ə'bæk] rückwärts; *taken ~ fig.* überrascht, verblüfft, bestürzt.

abandon [ə'bændən] auf-, preisgeben; verlassen; überlassen; **~ed** verworfen; **~ment** [~nmənt] Auf-, Preisgabe *f;* Unbeherrschtheit *f.*

abase [ə'beis] erniedrigen, demütigen; **~ment** [~smənt] Erniedrigung *f.*

abash [ə'bæʃ] beschämen, verlegen machen; **~ment** [~ʃmənt] Verlegenheit *f.*

abate [ə'beit] *v/t.* verringern; *Mißstand* abstellen; *v/i.* abnehmen, nachlassen; **~ment** [~tmənt] Verminderung *f;* Abschaffung *f.*

abattoir ['æbətwa:] Schlachthaus *n.*

abb|ess ['æbis] Äbtissin *f;* **~ey** ['æbi] Abtei *f;* **~ot** ['æbət] Abt *m.*

abbreviat|e [ə'bri:vieit] (ab)kürzen; **~ion** [əbri:vi'eiʃən] Abkürzung *f.*

ABC ['eibi:'si:] Abc *n,* Alphabet *n.*

ABC weapons *pl.* ABC-Waffen *f/pl.*

abdicat|e ['æbdikeit] entsagen (*dat.*); abdanken; **~ion** [æbdi-'keiʃən] Verzicht *m;* Abdankung *f.*

abdomen ['æbdəmen] Unterleib *m,* Bauch *m.*

abduct [æb'dʌkt] entführen.

aberration [æbə'reiʃən] Abweichung *f; fig.* Verirrung *f.*

abet [ə'bet] aufhetzen; anstiften; unterstützen; **~tor** [~tə] Anstifter *m;* (Helfers)Helfer *m.*

abeyance [ə'beiəns] Unentschiedenheit *f; in ~* 𝔯𝔯 in der Schwebe.

abhor [əb'hɔ:] verabscheuen; **~rence** [əb'hɔrəns] Abscheu *m (of* vor *dat.);* **~rent** [~nt] zuwider (*to dat.*); abstoßend.

abide [ə'baid] (*irr.*) *v/i.* bleiben (*by* bei); *v/t.* erwarten; (v)ertragen.

ability [ə'biliti] Fähigkeit *f.*

abject □ ['æbdʒekt] verächtlich, gemein.

abjure [əb'dʒuə] abschwören; entsagen (*dat.*).

able □ ['eibl] fähig, geschickt; *be ~* imstande sein, können; **~-bodied** kräftig.

abnegat|e ['æbnigeit] ableugnen; verzichten auf (*acc.*); **~ion** [æbni-'geiʃən] Ableugnung *f;* Verzicht *m.*

abnormal □ ['æb'nɔ:məl] abnorm.

aboard [ə'bɔ:d] ⚓ an Bord (*gen.*); *all ~! Am.* ⚓ *etc.* einsteigen!

abode [ə'boud] 1. *pret. u. p.p. von* abide; 2. Aufenthalt *m;* Wohnung *f.*

aboli|sh [ə'bɔliʃ] abschaffen, aufheben; **~tion** [æbə'liʃən] Abschaffung *f,* Aufhebung *f;* **~tionist** [~nist] Gegner *m* der Sklaverei.

A-bomb ['eibɔm] = *atomic bomb.*

abomina|ble □ [ə'bɔminəbl] abscheulich; **~te** [~neit] verabscheuen; **~tion** [əbɔmi'neiʃən] Abscheu *m.*

aboriginal □ [æbə'ridʒənl] einheimisch; Ur...

abortion ⚕ [ə'bɔ:ʃən] Fehlgeburt *f;* Abtreibung *f.*

abortive □ [ə'bɔ:tiv] vorzeitig; erfolglos, fehlgeschlagen; verkümmert.

abound [ə'baund] reichlich vorhanden sein; Überfluß haben (*in* an *dat.*).

about [ə'baut] 1. *prp.* um (...herum); bei; im Begriff; über (*acc.*); *I had no money ~* me ich hatte kein Geld bei mir; *what are you ~?* was macht ihr da? 2. *adv.* herum, umher; in der Nähe; etwa; ungefähr um, gegen; *bring ~* zustande bringen.

above [ə'bʌv] 1. *prp.* über; *fig.* erhaben über; *~ all* vor allem; *~ ground fig.* am Leben; 2. *adv.* oben; darüber; 3. *adj.* obig.

abreact [æbri'ækt] abreagieren.

abreast [ə'brest] nebeneinander.

abridg|e [ə'bridʒ] (ver)kürzen; **~e)ment** [~dʒmənt] (Ver)Kürzung *f;* Auszug *m.*

abroad [ə'brɔ:d] im (ins) Ausland; überall(hin); *there is a report ~* es geht das Gerücht; *all ~* ganz im Irrtum.

abrogate ['æbrougeit] aufheben.

abrupt □ [ə'brʌpt] jäh; zs.-hanglos; schroff.

abscess ⚕ ['æbsis] Geschwür *n.*

abscond [əb'skɔnd] sich davonmachen.

absence ['æbsəns] Abwesenheit *f;* Mangel *m;* *~ of mind* Zerstreutheit *f.*

absent 1. □ ['æbsənt] abwesend; nicht vorhanden; 2. [æb'sent]: *~ o.s.* fernbleiben; **~-minded** □ ['æbsənt'maindid] zerstreut, geistesabwesend.

absolut|e □ ['æbsəlu:t] absolut; unumschränkt; vollkommen; unvermischt; unbedingt; *~ion* [æbsə-'lu:ʃən] Lossprechung *f.*

absolve [əb'zɔlv] frei-, lossprechen.

absorb [əb'sɔ:b] aufsaugen; *fig.* ganz in Anspruch nehmen.

absorption [əb'sɔ:pʃən] Aufsaugung *f; fig.* Vertieftsein *n.*

abstain [əb'stein] sich enthalten.

abstemious □ [æb'sti:mjəs] enthaltsam; mäßig.

abstention [æb'stenʃən] Enthaltung f.

abstinen|ce ['æbstinəns] Enthaltsamkeit f; ~t ⁅ [~nt] enthaltsam.

abstract 1. ['æbstrækt] abstrakt; **2.** [~] Auszug m; gr. Abstraktum n; **3.** [æb'strækt] abstrahieren; ablenken; entwenden; Inhalt kurz zs.-fassen; ~ed □ zerstreut; ~ion [~kʃən] Abstraktion f; (abstrakter) Begriff.

abstruse [æb'stru:s] fig. dunkel, schwer verständlich; tiefgründig.

absurd [əb'sə:d] absurd, sinnwidrig; lächerlich.

abundan|ce [ə'bʌndəns] Überfluß m; Fülle f, Überschwang m; ~t ⁅ [~nt] reich(lich).

abus|e 1. [ə'bju:s] Mißbrauch m; Beschimpfung f; **2.** [~u:z] mißbrauchen, beschimpfen; ~ive □ [~u:siv] schimpfend; Schimpf...

abut [ə'bʌt] (an)grenzen (upon ...).

abyss [ə'bis] Abgrund m.

academic|(al □) [ækə'demik(əl)] akademisch; ~ian [ækædə'miʃən] Akademiemitglied n.

academy [ə'kædəmi] Akademie f.

accede [æk'si:d] ~ to beitreten (dat.); Amt antreten; Thron besteigen

accelerat|e [æk'seləreit] beschleunigen; fig ankurbeln; ~or [ək'seləreitə] Gaspedal n.

accent 1. ['æksənt] Akzent m (a. gr.); **2.** [æk'sent] v/t akzentuieren, betonen; ~uate [~tjueit] akzentuieren, betonen.

accept [ək'sept] annehmen; † akzeptieren, hinnehmen; ~able □ [~təbl] annehmbar; ~ance [~əns] Annahme f; † Akzept n.

access ['ækses] Zugang m; ♣ Anfall m; easy of ~ zugänglich; ~ road Zufahrtstraße f; ~ary [æk'sesəri] Mitwisser(in), Mitschuldige(r m) f; = accessory 2, ~ible □ [~səbl] zugänglich, ~ion [~eʃən] Antritt m (to gen.); Eintritt m (to in acc.); ~ to the throne Thronbesteigung f.

accessory [æk'sesəri] 1. □ zusätzlich; 2. Zubehörteil n.

accident ['æksidənt] Zufall m; Un(glücks)fall m, ~al □ [æksi'dentl] zufällig, nebensächlich.

acclaim [ə'kleim] j-m zujubeln.

acclamation [æklə'meiʃən] Zuruf m.

acclimatize [ə'klaimətaiz] akklimatisieren, eingewöhnen.

acclivity [ə'kliviti] Steigung f; Böschung f.

accommodat|e [ə'kɔmədeit] anpassen; unterbringen; Streit schlichten; versorgen; j-m aushelfen (with mit Geld); ~ion [əkɔmə'deiʃən] Anpassung f; Aushilfe f; Bequemlich-

keit f; Unterkunft f; Beilegung f; seating ~ Sitzgelegenheit f; ~ train Am. Personenzug m.

accompan|iment [ə'kʌmpənimənt] Begleitung f; ~y [ə'kʌmpəni] begleiten; accompanied with verbunden mit

accomplice [ə'kɔmplis] Komplice m.

accomplish [ə'kɔmpliʃ] vollenden; ausführen; ~ed vollendet, perfekt; ~ment [~ʃmənt] Vollendung f; Ausführung f; Tat f, Leistung f; Talent n

accord [ə'kɔːd] 1. Übereinstimmung f; with one ~ einstimmig; 2. v/i übereinstimmen; v/t gewähren; ~ance [~dəns] Übereinstimmung f, ~ant □ [~nt] übereinstimmend, ~ing [~diŋ]: ~ to gemäß (dat.); ~ingly [~li] demgemäß

accost [ə'kɔst] j-n bsd. auf der Straße ansprechen

account [ə'kaunt] 1. Rechnung f; Berechnung f, ✝ Konto n; Rechenschaft f; Bericht m; of no ~ ohne Bedeutung, on no ~ auf keinen Fall; on ~ of wegen, take into ~, take ~ of in Betracht ziehen, berücksichtigen; turn to ~ ausnutzen, keep ~s die Bücher führen; call to ~ zur Rechenschaft ziehen, give a good ~ of o.s. sich bewähren, make ~ of Wert auf et. (acc.) legen, 2. v/t: ~ for Rechenschaft über et (acc) ablegen; (sich) erklären, be much ~ed of hoch geachtet sein; v/t ansehen als; ~able □ [~təbl] verantwortlich, erklärlich; ~ant [~ənt] Buchhalter m; chartered ~, Am certified public ~ vereidigter Bücherrevisor; ~ing [~tiŋ] Buchführung f.

accredit [ə'kredit] beglaubigen.

accrue [ə'kru:] erwachsen (from aus).

accumulat|e [ə'kju:mjuleit] (sich) (an)häufen, ansammeln; ~ion [əkju:mju'leiʃən] Anhäufung f.

accura|cy ['ækjurəsi] Genauigkeit f; ~te □ [~rit] genau, richtig.

accurs|ed [ə'kə:sid], ~t [~st] verflucht, verwunscht

accus|ation [ækju(:)'zeiʃən] Anklage f, Beschuldigung f; ~ative gr. [ə'kju:zətiv] a ~ case Akkusativ m; ~e [ə'kju:z] anklagen, beschuldigen; ~er [~zə] Kläger(in).

accustom [ə'kʌstəm] gewöhnen (to an acc); ~ed gewohnt, üblich; gewöhnt (to an acc , zu inf.).

ace [eis] As n (a. fig.); ~ in the hole Am. ⁅ fig. Trumpf m in Reserve; within an ~ um ein Haar.

acerbity [ə'sə:biti] Herbheit f.

acet|ic [ə'si:tik] essigsauer; ~ify [ə'setitai] säuern.

ache [eik] 1. schmerzen; sich sehnen (for nach; to do zu tun); 2. anhaltende Schmerzen m/pl.

achieve [ə'tʃiːv] ausführen; errei- chen; **~ment** [~vmənt] Ausführ- rung f; Leistung f.

acid ['æsid] 1. sauer; 2. Säure f; **~ity** [ə'siditi] Säure f.

acknowledg|e [ək'nɔlidʒ] anerken- nen; zugeben; ✝ bestätigen; **~(e)- ment** [~dʒmənt] Anerkennung f; Bestätigung f; Eingeständnis n.

acme ['ækmi] Gipfel m; ✍ Krisis f.

acorn ♀ ['eikɔːn] Eichel f.

acoustics [ə'kuːstiks] pl. Akustik f.

acquaint [ə'kweint] bekannt ma- chen; j-m mitteilen; be **~ed with** kennen; **~ance** [~təns] Bekannt- schaft f; Bekannte(r m) f.

acquiesce [ækwi'es] (in) hinnehmen (acc.); einwilligen (in acc.).

acquire [ə'kwaiə] erwerben; **~ment** [~əmənt] Fertigkeit f.

acquisition [ækwi'ziʃən] Erwer- bung f; Errungenschaft f.

acquit [ə'kwit] freisprechen; **~ o.s.** of Pflicht erfüllen; **~ o.s. well** s-e Sache gut machen; **~tal** [~tl] Frei- sprechung f, Freispruch m; **~tance** [~təns] Tilgung f.

acre ['eikə] Morgen m (4047 qm).

acrid ['ækrid] scharf, beißend.

across [ə'krɔs] 1. adv. hin-, herüber; (quer) durch; drüben; überkreuz; 2. prp. (quer) über (acc.); jenseits (gen.), über (dat.); **come ~, run ~** stoßen auf (acc.).

act [ækt] 1. v/i. handeln; sich be- nehmen; wirken; funktionieren; thea. spielen; v/t. thea. spielen; 2. Handlung f, Tat f; thea. Akt m; Gesetz n; Beschluß m; Urkunde f, Vertrag m; **~ing** ['æktin] 1. Han- deln n; thea. Spiel(en) n; 2. tätig, amtierend.

action ['ækʃən] Handlung f (a. thea.); Tätigkeit f; Tat f; Wir- kung f; Klage f, Prozeß m; Gang m (Pferd etc.); Gefecht n; Mechanis- mus m; **take ~** Schritte unter- nehmen.

activ|e □ ['æktiv] aktiv; tätig; rüh- rig, wirksam; ✝ lebhaft; **~ity** [æk- 'tiviti] Tätigkeit f; Betriebsamkeit f; bsd. ✝ Lebhaftigkeit f.

act|or ['æktə] Schauspieler m; **~ress** ['æktris] Schauspielerin f.

actual □ ['æktjuəl] wirklich, tat- sächlich, eigentlich.

actuate ['æktjueit] in Gang bringen.

acute □ [ə'kjuːt] spitz; scharf(sin- nig); brennend (Frage); ✍ akut.

ad F [æd] = advertisement.

adamant fig. ['ædəmənt] unerbitt- lich.

adapt [ə'dæpt] anpassen (to, for dat.); Text bearbeiten (from nach); zurechtmachen; **~ation** [ædæp- 'teiʃən] Anpassung f, Bearbeitung f.

add [æd] v/t. hinzufügen; addieren; v/i.: **~ to** vermehren; hinzukom- men zu.

addict ['ædikt] Süchtige(r m) f; **~ed** [ə'diktid] ergeben (to dat.); **~ to** e-m Laster verfallen.

addition [ə'diʃən] Hinzufügen n; Zusatz m; An-, Ausbau m; Addi- tion f; **in ~** außerdem; **in ~ to** außer, zu; **~al** [~nl] zusätzlich.

address [ə'dres] 1. Worte richten (to an acc.); sprechen zu; 2. Adresse f; Ansprache f; Anstand m, Manieren f/pl.; **pay one's ~es to a lady** e-r Dame den Hof machen; **~ee** [ædre'siː] Adressat m, Empfänger m.

adept ['ædept] 1. erfahren; ge- schickt; 2. Eingeweihte(r m) f; Kenner m.

adequa|cy ['ædikwəsi] Angemes- senheit f; **~te** □ [~kwit] ange- messen.

adhere [əd'hiə] (to) haften (an dat.); fig. festhalten (an dat.); **~nce** [~rəns] Anhaften n, Festhalten n; **~nt** [~nt] Anhänger(in).

adhesion [əd'hiːʒən] = adherence; fig. Einwilligung f.

adhesive [əd'hiːsiv] 1. □ klebend; **~ plaster, ~ tape** Heftpflaster n; 2. Klebstoff m.

adjacent □ [ə'dʒeisənt] (to) anlie- gend (dat.); anstoßend (an acc.); benachbart.

adjective gr. ['ædʒiktiv] Adjektiv n, Eigenschaftswort n.

adjoin [ə'dʒɔin] angrenzen an (acc.).

adjourn [ə'dʒəːn] aufschieben; (v/i. sich) vertagen; **~ment** [~nmənt] Aufschub m; Vertagung f.

adjudge [ə'dʒʌdʒ] zuerkennen; verurteilen.

adjust [ə'dʒʌst] in Ordnung brin- gen; anpassen; Streit schlichten; Mechanismus u. fig. einstellen (to auf acc.); **~ment** [~tmənt] Anordnung f; Einstellung f; Schlichtung f.

administ|er [əd'ministə] verwalten; spenden; ✍ verabfolgen; **~ justice** Recht sprechen; **~ration** [ədminis- 'treiʃən] Verwaltung f; Regierung f; bsd. Am. Amtsperiode f e-s Präsi- denten; **~rative** [əd'ministrətiv] Verwaltungs...; **~rator** [~reitə] Verwalter m.

admir|able □ ['ædmərəbl] bewun- dernswert; (vor)trefflich; **~ation** [ædmə'reiʃən] Bewunderung f; **~e** [əd'maiə] bewundern; verehren.

admiss|ible [əd'misəbl] zulässig; **~ion** [~ʃən] Zulassung f; F Ein- tritt(sgeld n) m; Eingeständnis n.

admit [əd'mit] v/t. (her)einlassen (to, into in acc.), eintreten lassen; zulassen (to zu); zugeben; **~tance** [~təns] Einlaß m, Zutritt m.

admixture [əd'mikstʃə] Beimi- schung f, Zusatz m.

admon|ish [əd'mɔniʃ] ermahnen; warnen (of, against vor dat.); **~ition** [ædmə'niʃən] Ermahnung f; War- nung f.

ado [ə'duː] Getue *n*; Lärm *m*; Mühe *f*.

adolescen|ce [ædou'lesns] Adoleszenz *f*, Reifezeit *f*; **∼t** [∼nt] **1.** jugendlich, heranwachsend; **2.** Jugendliche(r *m*) *f*.

adopt [ə'dɔpt] adoptieren; sich aneignen; **∼ion** [∼pʃən] Annahme *f*.

ador|able [ə'dɔːrəbl] verehrungswürdig; **∼ation** [ædɔː'reiʃən] Anbetung *f*; **∼e** [ə'dɔː] anbeten.

adorn [ə'dɔːn] schmücken, zieren; **∼ment** [∼nmənt] Schmuck *m*.

adroit [ə'drɔit] gewandt.

adult ['ædʌlt] **1.** erwachsen; **2.** Erwachsene(r *m*) *f*.

adulter|ate [ə'dʌltəreit] (ver)fälschen; **∼er** [∼rə] Ehebrecher *m*; **∼ess** [∼ris] Ehebrecherin *f*; **∼ous** □ [∼rəs] ehebrecherisch; **∼y** [∼ri] Ehebruch *m*.

advance [əd'vɑːns] **1.** *v/i.* vorrücken, vorgehen; steigen; Fortschritte machen; *v/t.* vorrücken; vorbringen; vorausbezahlen; vorschießen; (be)fördern; *Preis* erhöhen; beschleunigen; **2.** Vorrücken *n*; Fortschritt *m*; Angebot *n*; Vorschuß *m*; Erhöhung *f*; **in ∼** im voraus; **∼d** vor-, fortgeschritten; **in years** in vorgerücktem Alter; **∼ment** [∼smənt] Förderung *f*; Fortschritt *m*.

advantage [əd'vɑːntidʒ] Vorteil *m*; Überlegenheit *f*; Gewinn *m*; **take ∼ of** ausnutzen; **∼ous** □ [ædvən'teidʒəs] vorteilhaft.

adventur|e [əd'ventʃə] Abenteuer *n*, Wagnis *n*; Spekulation *f*; **∼er** [∼rə] Abenteurer *m*; Spekulant *m*; **∼ous** □ [∼rəs] abenteuerlich; wagemutig.

adverb *gr.* ['ædvəːb] Adverb *n*, Umstandswort *n*.

advers|ary ['ædvəsəri] Gegner *m*, Feind *m*; **∼e** □ ['ædvəːs] widrig; feindlich; ungünstig, nachteilig (**to** für); **∼ity** [əd'vəːsiti] Unglück *n*.

advertis|e ['ædvətaiz] ankündigen; inserieren; Reklame machen (für); **∼ement** [əd'vəːtismənt] Ankündigung *f*, Inserat *n*; Reklame *f*; **∼ing** ['ædvətaiziŋ] Reklame *f*, Werbung *f*; **∼ agency** Annoncenbüro *n*; **∼ designer** Reklamezeichner *m*; **∼ film** Reklamefilm *m*; **screen ∼** Filmreklame *f*.

advice [əd'vais] Rat(schlag) *m*; (*mst pl.*) Nachricht *f*, Meldung *f*; **take medical ∼** e-n Arzt zu Rate ziehen.

advis|able □ [əd'vaizəbl] ratsam; **∼e** [əd'vaiz] *v/t. j-n* beraten; *j-m* raten; ✝ benachrichtigen, avisieren; *v/i.* (sich) beraten; **∼er** [∼zə] Ratgeber(in).

advocate 1. ['ædvəkit] Anwalt *m*; Fürsprecher *m*; **2.** [∼keit] verteidigen, befürworten.

aerial ['ɛəriəl] **1.** □ luftig; Luft...; **∼ view** Luftaufnahme *f*; **2.** *Radio, Fernsehen:* Antenne *f*.

aero|... ['ɛərou] Luft...; **∼cab** *Am.* F ['ɛərəkæb] Lufttaxi *n* (*Hubschrauber als Zubringer*); **∼drome** [∼droum] Flugplatz *m*; **∼naut** [∼nɔːt] Luftschiffer *m*; **∼nautics** [ɛərə'nɔːtiks] *pl.* Luftfahrt *f*; **∼plane** ['ɛərəplein] Flugzeug *n*; **∼stat** ['ɛəroustæt] Luftballon *m*.

aesthetic [iːs'θetik] ästhetisch; **∼s** *sg.* Ästhetik *f*.

afar [ə'fɑː] fern, weit (weg).

affable □ ['æfəbl] leutselig.

affair [ə'fɛə] Geschäft *n*; Angelegenheit *f*; Sache *f*; F Ding *n*; Liebschaft *f*.

affect [ə'fekt] (ein- *od.* sich aus-)wirken auf (*acc.*); (be)rühren; *Gesundheit* angreifen; gern mögen; vortäuschen, nachahmen; **∼ation** [æfek'teiʃən] Vorliebe *f*; Ziererei *f*; Verstellung *f*; **∼ed** □ gerührt; befallen (*von Krankheit*); angegriffen (*Augen etc.*); geziert, affektiert; **∼ion** [∼kʃən] Gemütszustand *m*; (Zu)Neigung *f*; Erkrankung *f*; **∼ionate** □ [∼ʃnit] liebevoll.

affidavit [æfi'deivit] *schriftliche* beeidigte Erklärung.

affiliate [ə'filieit] *als Mitglied* aufnehmen; angliedern; **∼d company** Tochtergesellschaft *f*.

affinity [ə'finiti] *fig.* (geistige) Verwandtschaft *f*; ⚗ Affinität *f*.

affirm [ə'fəːm] bejahen; behaupten; bestätigen; **∼ation** [æfə'meiʃən] Behauptung *f*; Bestätigung *f*; **∼ative** [ə'fəːmətiv] **1.** □ bejahend; **2.:** **answer in the ∼** bejahen.

affix [ə'fiks] (to) anheften (an *acc.*); befestigen (an *dat.*); *Siegel* aufdrücken (*dat.*); bei-, zufügen (*dat.*).

afflict [ə'flikt] betrüben; plagen; **∼ion** [∼kʃən] Betrübnis *f*; Leiden *n*.

affluen|ce ['æfluəns] Überfluß *m*; Wohlstand *m*; **∼t** [∼nt] **1.** □ reich (-lich); **∼ society** Wohlstandsgesellschaft *f*. **2.** Nebenfluß *m*.

afford [ə'fɔːd] liefern; erschwingen; **I can ∼ it** ich kann es mir leisten.

affront [ə'frʌnt] **1.** beleidigen; trotzen (*dat.*); **2.** Beleidigung *f*.

afield [ə'fiːld] im Felde; (weit) weg.

afloat [ə'flout] ⚓ *u.* *fig.* flott; schwimmend; auf See; umlaufend; **set ∼** flottmachen; *fig.* in Umlauf setzen.

afraid [ə'freid] bange; **be ∼ of** sich fürchten *od.* Angst haben vor (*dat.*).

afresh [ə'freʃ] von neuem.

African ['æfrikən] **1.** afrikanisch; **2.** Afrikaner(in); *Am. a.* Neger(in).

after ['ɑːftə] **1.** *adv.* hinterher; nachher; **2.** *prp.* nach; hinter (... her); **∼ all** schließlich (doch); **3.** *cj.* nachdem; **4.** *adj.* später; Nach...; **∼crop** Nachernte *f*; **∼glow** Abendrot *n*; **∼math** [∼əmæθ]

Nachwirkung(en pl.) f, Folgen f/pl.;
~noon [~ə'nu:n] Nachmittag m; **~-season** Nachsaison f; **~-taste** Nachgeschmack m; **~-thought** nachträglicher Einfall; **~wards** [~əwədz] nachher; später.

again [ə'gen] wieder(um); ferner; dagegen; ~ and ~ time and ~ immer wieder; as much ~ noch einmal soviel.

against [ə'genst] gegen; räumlich: gegen; an, vor (dat. od. acc.); fig. in Erwartung (gen.), für; as ~ verglichen mit.

age [eidʒ] 1. (Lebens)Alter n; Zeit (-alter n) f; Menschenalter n; (old) ~ Greisenalter n; of ~ mündig; over ~ zu alt; under ~ unmündig; wait for ~ s F e-e Ewigkeit warten; 2. alt werden od. machen; **~d** ['eidʒid] alt; [eidʒd]: ~ twenty 20 Jahre alt.

agency ['eidʒənsi] Tätigkeit f; Vermittlung f; Agentur f, Büro n.

agenda [ə'dʒendə] Tagesordnung f.

agent ['eidʒənt] Handelnde(r m) f; Agent m; wirkende Kraft, Agens n.

age-worn ['eidʒwɔ:n] altersschwach.

agglomerate [ə'glɔməreit] (sich) zs.-ballen; (sich) (an)häufen.

agglutinate [ə'glu:tineit] zs.-, an-, verkleben.

aggrandize [ə'grændaiz] vergrößern; erhöhen.

aggravate ['ægrəveit] erschweren; verschlimmern; F ärgern.

aggregate 1. ['ægrigeit] (sich) anhäufen; vereinigen (to mit); sich belaufen auf (acc.); 2. □ [~git] gehäuft; gesamt; 3. [~] Anhäufung f; Aggregat n.

aggress|ion [ə'greʃən] Angriff m; **~or** [~esə] Angreifer m.

aggrieve [ə'gri:v] kränken; schädigen.   [setzt.]

aghast [ə'gɑ:st] entgeistert, ent-)

agil|e □ ['ædʒail] flink, behend; **~ity** [ə'dʒiliti] Behendigkeit f.

agitat|e ['ædʒiteit] v/t. bewegen, schütteln; fig. erregen; erörtern; v/i. agitieren; **~ion** [ædʒi'teiʃən] Bewegung f, Erschütterung f; Aufregung f; Agitation f; **~or** ['ædʒiteitə] Agitator m, Aufwiegler m.

ago [ə'gou]: a year ~ vor e-m Jahr.

agonize ['ægənaiz] (sich) quälen.

agony ['ægəni] Qual f, Pein f; Ringen n; Todeskampf m.

agree [ə'gri:] v/i. übereinstimmen; sich vertragen; einig werden (on, upon über acc.); übereinkommen, ~ to zustimmen (dat.); einverstanden sein mit; **~able** □ [ə'griəbl] (to) angenehm (für); übereinstimmend (mit); **~ment** [ə'gri:mənt] Übereinstimmung f; Vereinbarung f, Abkommen n; Vertrag m.

agricultur|al [ægri'kʌltʃərəl] land-

---

wirtschaftlich; **~e** ['ægrikʌltʃə] Landwirtschaft f; **~ist** [ægri'kʌltʃərist] Landwirt m.

aground ⚓ [ə'graund] gestrandet; run ~ stranden, auflaufen.

ague 🞂 ['eigju:] Wechselfieber n; Schüttelfrost m.

ahead [ə'hed] vorwärts; voraus; vorn; straight ~ geradeaus.

aid [eid] 1. helfen (dat.; in bei et.); fördern; 2. Hilfe f, Unterstützung f.

ail [eil] v/i. kränkeln; v/t. schmerzen, weh(e) tun (dat.); what ~s him? was fehlt ihm?; **~ing** ['eiliŋ] leidend; **~ment** ['eilmənt] Leiden n.

aim [eim] 1. v/i. zielen (at auf acc.); ~ at fig. streben nach; ~ to do bsd. Am. beabsichtigen od. versuchen zu tun, tun wollen; v/t. ~ at Waffe etc. richten auf od. gegen (acc.); 2. Ziel n; Absicht f; **~less** □ ['eimlis] ziellos.

air[1] [ɛə] 1. Luft f; Luftzug m; by ~ auf dem Luftwege; in the open ~ im Freien; be in the ~ fig. in der Luft liegen; ungewiß sein; on the ~ im Rundfunk (senden), be on (off) the ~ in (außer) Betrieb sein (Sender); put on the ~ im Rundfunk senden; 2. (aus)lüften; fig. an die Öffentlichkeit bringen; erörtern.

air[2] [~] Miene f; Aussehen n; give o.s. ~s vornehm tun.

air[3] ♪ [~] Arie f, Weise f, Melodie f.

air|-base ✕ ['ɛəbeis] Luftstützpunkt m; **~-bed** Luftmatratze f; **~borne** ✈ in der Luft (Flugzeug); ✕ Luftlande...; **~-brake** Druckluftbremse f; **~-conditioned** mit Klimaanlage; **~craft** Flugzeug (-e pl.) n; **~field** ✈ Flugplatz m; **~-force** ✕ Luftwaffe f; **~-hostess** ✈ Stewardess f; **~-jacket** Schwimmweste f; **~-lift** Luftbrücke f; **~-liner** ✈ Verkehrsflugzeug n; **~-mail** Luftpost f; **~-man** ['ɛəmæn] Flieger m; **~-plane** Am. Flugzeug n; **~-pocket** Luftloch n; **~-port** ✈ Flughafen m; **~-raid** ✕ Luftangriff m; **~-raid precautions** pl. Luftschutz m; **~-raid shelter** Luftschutzraum m; **~-route** ✈ Luftweg m; **~-tight** luftdicht; ~ case sl. todsicherer Fall; **~-tube** Luftschlauch m; **~ umbrella** ✕ Luftsicherung f; **~-way** ✈ Luftverkehrslinie f.

airy □ ['ɛəri] luftig; leicht(fertig).

aisle 🏛 [ail] Seitenschiff n; Gang m.

ajar [ə'dʒɑ:] halb offen, angelehnt.

akin [ə'kin] verwandt (to mit).

alacrity [ə'lækriti] Munterkeit f; Bereitwilligkeit f, Eifer m.

alarm [ə'lɑ:m] 1. Alarm(zeichen n) m; Angst f; 2. alarmieren; beunruhigen; **~-clock** Wecker m.

albuminous [æl'bju:minəs] eiweißartig, -haltig.

alcohol ['ælkəhɔl] Alkohol m; **~ic**

[ˈælkəˈhɔlik] alkoholisch; **~ism** [ˈæl-kəhɔlizəm] Alkoholvergiftung f.

alcove [ˈælkouv] Nische f; Laube f.

alderman [ˈɔːldəmən] Stadtrat m.

ale [eil] Ale n (Art engl. Bier).

alert [əˈləːt] 1. ☐ wachsam; munter; 2. Alarm(bereitschaft f) m; on the ~ auf der Hut; in Alarmbereitschaft.

alibi [ˈælibai] Alibi n; Am. F Entschuldigung f; Ausrede f.

alien [ˈeiljən] 1. fremd, ausländisch; 2. Ausländer(in); **~able** [~nəbl] veräußerlich; **~ate** [~neit] veräußern; fig. entfremden (from dat.); **~ist** [~nist] Irrenarzt m, Psychiater m.

alight [əˈlait] 1. brennend; erhellt; 2. ab-, aussteigen; ⚡ niedergehen, landen; sich niederlassen.

align [əˈlain] (sich) ausrichten (with nach); surv. abstecken; ~ o.s. with sich anschließen an (acc.).

alike [əˈlaik] 1. adj. gleich, ähnlich; 2. adv. gleich; ebenso.

aliment [ˈælimənt] Nahrung f; **~ary** [æliˈmentəri] nahrhaft; ~ canal Verdauungskanal m.

alimony ⚡ [ˈæliməni] Unterhalt m.

alive [əˈlaiv] lebendig; in Kraft, gültig; empfänglich (to für); lebhaft; belebt (with von).

all [ɔːl] 1. adj. all; ganz; jede(r, -s); for ~ that dessenungeachtet, trotzdem; 2. pron. alles; alle pl.; at ~ gar, überhaupt; not at ~ durchaus nicht; for ~ (that) I care meinetwegen; for ~ I know soviel ich weiß; 3. adv. ganz, völlig; ~ at once auf einmal; the better desto besser; ~ but beinahe, fast; ~ in Am. F fertig, ganz erledigt; ~ right (alles) in Ordnung.

all-American [ɔːləˈmerikən] rein amerikanisch; die ganzen USA vertretend.

allay [əˈlei] beruhigen; lindern.

alleg|ation [æleˈgeiʃən] unerwiesene Behauptung; **~e** [əˈledʒ] behaupten; **~ed** angeblich.

allegiance [əˈliːdʒəns] Lehnspflicht f; (Untertanen)Treue f.

alleviate [əˈliːvieit] erleichtern, lindern.

alley [ˈæli] Allee f; Gäßchen n; Gang m; bsd. Am. schmale Zufahrtsstraße.

alliance [əˈlaiəns] Bündnis n.

allocat|e [ˈæləkeit] zuteilen, anweisen; **~ion** [æləˈkeiʃən] Zuteilung f.

allot [əˈlɔt] zuweisen; **~ment** [~mənt] Zuteilung f; Los n; Parzelle f.

allow [əˈlau] erlauben; bewilligen, gewähren; zugeben; ab-, anrechnen; vergüten; ~ for berücksichtigen; **~able** ☐ [əˈlauəbl] erlaubt, zulässig; **~ance** [~əns] Erlaubnis f; Bewilligung f; Taschengeld n; Zuschuß m; Vergütung f; Nachsicht f;

make ~ for s.th. et. in Betracht ziehen.

alloy 1. [ˈælɔi] Legierung f; 2. [əˈlɔi] legieren; fig. verunedeln.

all-red [ˈɔːlˈred] rein britisch.

all-round [ˈɔːlˈraund] zu allem brauchbar; vielseitig.

all-star Am. [ˈɔːlˈstɑː] Sport u. thea.: aus den besten (Schau)Spielern bestehend.

allude [əˈluːd] anspielen (to auf acc.).

allure [əˈljuə] (an-, ver)locken; **~ment** [~mənt] Verlockung f.

allusion [əˈluːʒən] Anspielung f.

ally 1. [əˈlai] (sich) vereinigen, verbünden (to, with mit); 2. [ˈælai] Verbündete(r m) f, Bundesgenosse m; the Allies pl. die Alliierten pl.

almanac [ˈɔːlmənæk] Almanach m.

almighty [ɔːlˈmaiti] 1. ☐ allmächtig; 2 ♀ Allmächtige(r) m.

almond ♀ [ˈɑːmənd] Mandel f.

almoner [ˈɑːmənə] Krankenhausfürsorger(in).

almost [ˈɔːlmoust] fast, beinahe.

alms [ɑːmz] sg. u. pl. Almosen n; **~house** [ˈɑːmzhaus] Armenhaus n.

aloft [əˈlɔft] (hoch) (dr)oben.

alone [əˈloun] allein; let od. leave ~ in Ruhe od. bleiben lassen; let ~ ... abgesehen von ...

along [əˈlɔŋ] 1. adv. weiter, vorwärts, her; mit, bei (sich); all ~ die ganze Zeit; ~ with zs. mit; get ~ with you! F scher dich weg!; 2. prp. entlang, längs; **~side** [~ˈsaid] Seite an Seite; neben.

aloof [əˈluːf] fern; weitab; stand ~ abseits stehen.

aloud [əˈlaud] laut; hörbar.

alp [ælp] Alp(e) f; ⚡s pl. Alpen pl.

already [ɔːlˈredi] bereits, schon.

also [ˈɔːlsou] auch; ferner.

altar [ˈɔːltə] Altar m.

alter [ˈɔːltə] (sich) (ver)ändern; abumändern; **~ation** [ɔːltəˈreiʃən] Änderung f (to an dat.).

alternat|e 1. [ˈɔːltəːneit] abwechseln (lassen); alternating current ⚡ Wechselstrom m; 2. ☐ [ɔːlˈtəːnit] abwechselnd; 3. [~] Am. Stellvertreter m; **~ion** [ɔːltəːˈneiʃən] Abwechslung f; Wechsel m; **~ive** [ɔːlˈtəːnativ] 1. ☐ nur eine Wahl zwischen zwei Möglichkeiten lassend; 2. Alternative f; Wahl f; Möglichkeit f.

although [ɔːlˈðou] obgleich.

altitude [ˈæltitjuːd] Höhe f.

altogether [ɔːltəˈgeðə] im ganzen (genommen), alles in allem; gänzlich.

aluminium [æljuˈminjəm] Aluminium n.

aluminum Am. [əˈluːminəm] = aluminium.

always [ˈɔːlwəz] immer, stets.

am [æm; im Satz əm] 1. sg. pres. von be.

amalgamate [ə'mælgəmeit] amalgamieren; (sich) verschmelzen.
amass [ə'mæs] (an-, auf)häufen.
amateur ['æmətə:] Amateur *m*; Liebhaber *m*; Dilettant *m*.
amaz|e [ə'meiz] in Staunen setzen, verblüffen; **~ement** [~zmənt] Staunen *n*, Verblüffung *f*; **~ing** □ [~ziŋ] erstaunlich, verblüffend.
ambassador [æm'bæsədə] Botschafter *m*, Gesandte(r) *m*.
amber ['æmbə] Bernstein *m*.
ambigu|ity [æmbi'gju(:)iti] Zwei-, Vieldeutigkeit *f*; **~ous** □ [æm'bigjuəs] zwei-, vieldeutig; doppelsinnig.
ambitio|n [æm'biʃən] Ehrgeiz *m*; Streben *n* (*of* nach); **~us** □ [~ʃəs] ehrgeizig; begierig (*of*, *for* nach).
amble ['æmbl] 1. Paßgang *m*; 2. im Paßgang gehen *od.* reiten; schlendern.
ambulance ['æmbjuləns] Feldlazarett *n*; Krankenwagen *m*; **~ station** Sanitätswache *f*, Unfallstation *f*.
ambus|cade [æmbəs'keid], **~h** ['æmbuʃ] 1. Hinterhalt *m*; *be od. lie in ambush for s.o.* j-m auflauern; 2. auflauern (*dat.*); überfallen.
ameliorate [ə'mi:ljəreit] *v/t.* verbessern; *v/i.* besser werden.
amend [ə'mend] (sich) (ver)bessern; berichtigen; *Gesetz* (ab)ändern; **~ment** [~dmənt] Besserung *f*; *parl.* Berichtigung *f*; *parl.* Änderungsantrag *m*; *Am.* Zusatzartikel *m* zur Verfassung der USA; **~s** *sg.* (Schaden)Ersatz *m*.
amenity [ə'mi:niti] Annehmlichkeit *f*; Anmut *f*; *amenities pl.* angenehmes Wesen.
American [ə'merikən] 1. amerikanisch; **~ cloth** Wachstuch *n*; **~ plan** Hotelzimmervermietung *mit voller Verpflegung*; 2. Amerikaner(in); **~ism** [~nizəm] Amerikanismus *m*; **~ize** [~naiz] (sich) amerikanisieren.
amiable □ ['eimjəbl] liebenswürdig, freundlich.
amicable □ ['æmikəbl] freundschaftlich; gütlich.
amid(st) [ə'mid(st)] inmitten (*gen.*); (mitten) unter; mitten in (*dat.*).
amiss [ə'mis] verkehrt; übel; ungelegen; *take ~* übelnehmen.
amity ['æmiti] Freundschaft *f*.
ammonia [ə'mounjə] Ammoniak *n*.
ammunition [æmju'niʃən] Munition *f*.
amnesty ['æmnesti] 1. Amnestie *f* (*Straferlaß*); 2. begnadigen.
among(st) [ə'mʌŋ(st)] (mitten) unter, zwischen. [in *acc.*).]
amorous □ ['æmərəs] verliebt (*of*]
amount [ə'maunt] 1. (*to*) sich belaufen (auf *acc.*); hinauslaufen (auf *acc.*); 2. Betrag *m*, (Gesamt-)

Summe *f*; Menge *f*; Bedeutung *f*, Wert *m*.
amour [ə'muə] Liebschaft *f*; **~-propre** Selbstachtung *f*; Eitelkeit *f*.
ample □ ['æmpl] weit, groß; geräumig; reichlich.
ampli|fication [æmplifi'keiʃən] Erweiterung *f*; *rhet.* weitere Ausführung; *phys.* Verstärkung *f*; **~fier** ['æmplifaiə] *Radio:* Verstärker *m*; **~fy** [~fai] erweitern; verstärken; weiter ausführen; **~tude** [~itju:d] Umfang *m*, Weite *f*, Fülle *f*.
amputate ['æmpjuteit] amputieren.
amuse [ə'mju:z] amüsieren; unterhalten; belustigen; **~ment** [~mənt] Unterhaltung *f*; Zeitvertreib *m*.
an [æn, ən] *Artikel:* ein(e).
an(a)emia [ə'ni:mjə] Blutarmut *f*.
an(a)esthetic [ænis'θetik] 1. betäubend, Narkose...; 2. Betäubungsmittel *n*.
analog|ous □ [ə'næləgəs] analog, ähnlich; **~y** [~dʒi] Ähnlichkeit *f*, Analogie *f*.
analys|e ['ænəlaiz] analysieren; zerlegen; **~is** [ə'næləsis] Analyse *f*.
anarchy ['ænəki] Anarchie *f*, Gesetzlosigkeit *f*; Zügellosigkeit *f*.
anatom|ize [ə'nætəmaiz] zergliedern; **~y** [~mi] Anatomie *f*; Zergliederung *f*, Analyse *f*.
ancest|or ['ænsistə] Vorfahr *m*, Ahn *m*; **~ral** [æn'sestrəl] angestammt; **~ress** ['ænsistris] Ahne *f*; **~ry** [~ri] Abstammung *f*; Ahnen *m/pl.*
anchor ['æŋkə] 1. Anker *m*; *at ~* vor Anker; 2. (ver)ankern; **~age** [~əridʒ] Ankerplatz *m*.
anchovy ['æntʃəvi] Sardelle *f*.
ancient ['einʃənt] 1. alt, antik; uralt; 2. *the ~s pl. hist.* die Alten, die antiken Klassiker.
and [ænd, ənd] und.
anew [ə'nju:] von neuem.
angel ['eindʒəl] Engel *m*; **~ic(al** □) [æn'dʒelik(əl)] engelgleich.
anger ['æŋgə] 1. Zorn *m*, Ärger *m* (*at* über *acc.*); 2. erzürnen, ärgern.
angina [æn'dʒainə] Angina *f*, Halsentzündung *f*.
angle ['æŋgl] 1. Winkel *m*; *fig.* Standpunkt *m*; 2. angeln (*for* nach).
Anglican ['æŋglikən] 1. anglikanisch; *Am. a.* englisch; 2. Anglikaner(in).
Anglo-Saxon ['æŋglou'sæksən] 1. Angelsachse *m*; 2. angelsächsisch.
angry ['æŋgri] zornig, böse (*a. ~*) (*with s.o.*, *at s.th.* über, auf *acc.*).
anguish ['æŋgwiʃ] Pein *f*, (Seelen-) Qual *f*, Schmerz *m*.
angular □ ['æŋgjulə] winkelig; Winkel...; *fig.* eckig.
animadver|sion [ænimæd'və:ʃən]

Verweis *m*, Tadel *m*; ~t [~ː:t] tadeln, kritisieren.

animal ['ænɪməl] 1. Tier *n*; 2. tierisch.

animat|e ['ænɪmeit] beleben; beseelen; aufmuntern; ~ion [æni'meiʃən] Leben *n* (und Treiben *n*), Lebhaftigkeit *f*, Munterkeit *f*.

animosity [æni'mɔsiti] Feindseligkeit *f*.

ankle ['æŋkl] Fußknöchel *m*.

annals ['ænlz] *pl.* Jahrbücher *n/pl.*

annex 1. [ə'neks] anhängen; annektieren; 2. ['æneks] Anhang *m*; Anbau *m*; ~ation [ænek'seiʃən] Annexion *f*, Aneignung *f*; Einverleibung *f*.

annihilate [ə'naiəleit] vernichten; = *annul.*

anniversary [æni'vəːsəri] Jahrestag *m*; Jahresfeier *f*.

annotat|e ['ænouteit] mit Anmerkungen versehen; kommentieren; ~ion [ænou'teiʃən] Kommentieren *n*; Anmerkung *f*.

announce [ə'nauns] ankündigen; ansagen; ~ment [~smənt] Ankündigung *f*; Ansage *f*; *Radio:* Durchsage *f*; Anzeige *f*; ~r [~ə] *Radio:* Ansager *m*.

annoy [ə'nɔi] ärgern; belästigen; ~ance [ə'nɔiəns] Störung *f*; Plage *f*; Ärgernis *n*.

annual ['ænjuəl] 1. □ jährlich; Jahres...; 2. einjährige Pflanze; Jahrbuch *n*. [Rente *f*.]

annuity [ə'njuː(ː)iti] (Jahres-)]

annul [ə'nʌl] für ungültig erklären, annullieren; ~ment [~lmənt] Aufhebung *f*.

anodyne ⚕ ['ænoudain] 1. schmerzstillend; 2. schmerzstillendes Mittel.

anoint [ə'nɔint] salben.

anomalous □ [ə'nɔmələs] anomal, unregelmäßig, regelwidrig.

anonymous □ [ə'nɔniməs] anonym, ungenannt.

another [ə'nʌðə] ein anderer; ein zweiter; noch ein.

answer ['ɑːnsə] 1. *v/t. et.* beantworten; *j-m* antworten; entsprechen (*dat.*); *Zweck* erfüllen; *dem Steuer* gehorchen; *e-r Vorladung* Folge leisten; ~ *the bell od. door* (die Haustür) aufmachen; *v/i.* antworten (*to s.o.* j-m; *to a question* auf e-e Frage); entsprechen (*to dat.*); Erfolg haben; sich lohnen; ~ *for* einstehen für; bürgen für; 2. Antwort *f* (*to auf acc.*); ~able □ [~ərəbl] verantwortlich.

ant [ænt] Ameise *f*.

antagonis|m [æn'tægənizəm] Widerstreit *m*; Widerstand *m*; Feindschaft *f*; ~t [~ist] Gegner(in).

antagonize [æn'tægənaiz] ankämpfen gegen; sich *j-n* zum Feind machen.

antecedent [ænti'siːdənt] 1. □ vor-

hergehend; früher (*to* als); 2. Vorhergehende(s) *n*.

anterior [æn'tiəriə] vorhergehend; früher (*to* als); vorder.

ante-room ['æntirum] Vorzimmer *n*.

anthem ['ænθəm] Hymne *f*.

anti|... ['ænti] Gegen...; gegen ... eingestellt *od.* wirkend; ~aircraft Fliegerabwehr...; ~biotic [~baiˈɔtik] Antibiotikum *n*.

antic ['æntik] Posse *f*; ~s *pl.* Mätzchen *n/pl.*; (tolle) Sprünge *m/pl.*

anticipat|e [æn'tisipeit] vorwegnehmen; zuvorkommen (*dat.*); voraussehen, ahnen; erwarten; ~ion [æntisi'peiʃən] Vorwegnahme *f*; Zuvorkommen *n*; Voraussicht *f*; Erwartung *f*; *in* ~ im voraus.

antidote ['æntidout] Gegengift *n*.

antipathy [æn'tipəθi] Abneigung *f*.

antiqua|ry ['æntikwəri] Altertumsforscher *m*; Antiquitätensammler *m*, -händler *m*; ~ted [~kweitid] veraltet, überlebt.

antiqu|e [æn'tiːk] 1. □ antik, alt (-modisch); 2. alter Kunstgegenstand; ~ity [æn'tikwiti] Altertum *n*; Vorzeit *f*.

antiseptic [ænti'septik] 1. antiseptisch; 2. antiseptisches Mittel.

antlers ['æntləz] *pl.* Geweih *n*.

anvil ['ænvil] Amboß *m*.

anxiety [æŋ'zaiəti] Angst *f*; *fig.* Sorge *f* (*for* um); ⚕ Beklemmung *f*.

anxious □ ['æŋkʃəs] ängstlich, besorgt (*about* um, wegen); begierig, gespannt (*for* auf *acc.*); bemüht (*for* um).

any ['eni] 1. *pron.* (irgend)einer; einige *pl.*; (irgend)welcher; (irgend) etwas; jeder (beliebige); *not* ~ keiner; 2. *adv.* irgend(wie); ~**body** (irgend) jemand; jeder; ~**how** irgendwie; jedenfalls; ~**one** = *anybody*; ~**thing** (irgend) etwas, alles; ~ *but* alles andere als; ~**way** = *anyhow*; ohnehin; ~**where** irgendwo(hin); überall.

apart [ə'pɑːt] einzeln; getrennt; für sich; beiseite; ~ *from* abgesehen von.

apartheid *pol.* [ə'pɑːtheit] Apartheid *f*, Rassentrennung(spolitik) *f*.

apartment [ə'pɑːtmənt] Zimmer *n*, *Am. a.* Wohnung *f*; ~ *house Am.* Mietshaus *n*.

apathetic [æpə'θetik] apathisch, gleichgültig.

ape [eip] 1. Affe *m*; 2. nachäffen.

aperient [ə'piəriənt] Abführmittel *n*.

aperture ['æpətjuə] Öffnung *f*.

apiary ['eipjəri] Bienenhaus *n*.

apiculture ['eipikʌltʃə] Bienenzucht *f*.

apiece [ə'piːs] (für) das Stück; je.

apish □ ['eipiʃ] affig; äffisch.

apolog|etic [əpɔlə'dʒetik] (~ally) verteidigend; rechtfertigend; entschuldigend; ~ize [ə'pɔlədʒaiz] sich

entschuldigen (for wegen; to bei);
~y [~dʒi] Entschuldigung f; Rechtfertigung f; F Notbehelf m.

apoplexy ['æpəpleksi] Schlag(anfall) m.

apostate [ə'postit] Abtrünnige(r m)f.

apostle [ə'posl] Apostel m.

apostroph|e [ə'postrəfi] Anrede f;
Apostroph m; ~ize [~faiz] anreden,
sich wenden an (acc.).

appal [ə'po:l] erschrecken.

apparatus [æpə'reitəs] Apparat m,
Vorrichtung f, Gerät n.

apparel [ə'pærəl] 1. Kleidung f;
2. (be)kleiden.

appar|ent ⌐ [ə'pærənt] anschei-
nend; offenbar; ~ition [æpə'riʃən]
Erscheinung f; Gespenst n.

appeal [ə'pi:l] 1. (to) ⅟₂ appellieren
(an acc.); sich berufen (auf e-n Zeugen); sich wenden (an acc.); wirken
(auf acc.); Anklang finden (bei);
~ to the country parl Neuwahlen
ausschreiben; 2. ⅟₂ Revision f, Be-
rufung(sklage) f; ⅟₂ Rechtsmittel
n; fig. Appell m (to an acc.); Wirkung f, Reiz m; ~ for mercy ⅟₂
Gnadengesuch n; ~ing ⌐ [~liŋ]
flehend; ansprechend.

appear [ə'piə] (er)scheinen; sich
zeigen; öffentlich auftreten; ~ance
[~ərəns] Erscheinen n, Auftreten
n; Äußere(s) n, Erscheinung f; Anschein m; ~s pl. äußerer Schein;
to od. by all ~s allem Anschein
nach.

appease [ə'pi:z] beruhigen; beschwichtigen; stillen; mildern;
beilegen.

appellant [ə'pelənt] 1. appellierend;
2. Appellant(in), Berufungskläger
(-in).

append [ə'pend] anhängen; hinzu-,
beifügen; ~age [~didʒ] Anhang m;
Anhängsel n; Zubehör n, m;
~icitis [əpendi'saitis] Blinddarm-
entzündung f; ~ix [ə'pendiks] Anhang m; a. vermiform ~ ☞ Wurm-
fortsatz m, Blinddarm m.

appertain [æpə'tein] gehören (to
zu).

appetite ['æpitait] (for) Appetit m
(auf acc.); fig. Verlangen n (nach).

appetizing ['æpitaiziŋ] appetit-
anregend.

applaud [ə'plo:d] applaudieren,
Beifall spenden; loben.

applause [ə'plo:z] Applaus m, Beifall m.

apple ['æpl] Apfel m; ~cart Apfel-
karren m; upset s.o.'s ~ F j-s Pläne
über den Haufen werfen; ~pie ge-
deckter Apfelkuchen; in ~ order F
in schönster Ordnung; ~sauce
Apfelmus n; Am. sl. Schmus m,
Quatsch m.

appliance [ə'plaiəns] Vorrichtung
f; Gerät n; Mittel n.

applica|ble ['æplikəbl] anwendbar

(to auf acc.); ~nt [~ənt] Bittsteller
(-in); Bewerber(in) (for um); ~tion
[æpli'keiʃən] (to) Auf-, Anlegung f
(auf acc.); Anwendung f (auf acc.);
Bedeutung f (für); Gesuch n (for
um); Bewerbung f.

apply [ə'plai] v/t. (to) (auf)legen (auf
acc.); anwenden (auf acc.); verwenden (für); ~ o.s. to sich widmen (dat.);
v/i. (to) passen, sich anwenden
lassen (auf acc.); gelten (für); sich
wenden (an acc.); (for) sich bewerben (um); nachsuchen (um).

appoint [ə'point] bestimmen; festsetzen; verabreden; ernennen (s.o.
governor j-n zum ...); berufen (to
auf e-n Posten); well ~ed gut ein-
gerichtet; ~ment [~tmənt] Bestimmung f; Stelldichein n; Verabredung f; Ernennung f, Berufung f; Stelle f; ~s pl. Ausstattung f, Einrichtung f.

apportion [ə'po:ʃən] ver-, zuteilen;
~ment [~nmənt] Verteilung f.

apprais|al [ə'preizəl] Abschätzung
f; ~e [ə'preiz] abschätzen, taxieren.

apprecia|ble ⌐ [ə'pri:ʃəbl] (ab-)
schätzbar; merkbar; ~te [~ʃieit] v/t.
schätzen; würdigen, dankbar sein
für; v/i. im Werte steigen; ~tion
[əpri:ʃi'eiʃən] Schätzung f, Würdi-
gung f; Verständnis n (of für); Einsicht f; Dankbarkeit f; Aufwer-
tung f.

apprehen|d [æpri'hend] ergreifen;
fassen, begreifen; befürchten; ~
sion [~nʃən] Ergreifung f, Fest-
nahme f; Fassungskraft f, Auffassung f; Besorgnis f; ~sive ⌐ [~n-
siv] schnell begreifend (of acc.);
ängstlich; besorgt (of, for um,
wegen; that daß).

apprentice [ə'prentis] 1. Lehrling
m; 2. in die Lehre geben (to dat.);
~ship [~iʃip] Lehrzeit f; Lehre
f.

approach [ə'proutʃ] 1. v/i. näher-
kommen, sich nähern; v/t. sich
nähern (dat.), herangehen od.
herantreten an (acc.); 2. Annähe-
rung f; fig. Herangehen n; Methode
f; Zutritt m; Auffahrt f.

approbation [æprə'beiʃən] Billi-
gung f, Beifall m.

appropriat|e 1. [ə'prouprieit] sich
aneignen; verwenden; parl. bewilligen; 2. ⌐ [~iit] (to) angemessen
(dat.); passend (für); eigen (dat.);
~ion [əproupri'eiʃən] Aneignung f;
Verwendung f.

approv|al [ə'pru:vəl] Billigung f,
Beifall m; ~e [~u:v] billigen, anerkennen; (~ o.s. sich) erweisen als;
~ed ⌐ bewährt.

approximate 1. [ə'proksimeit] sich
nähern; 2. ⌐ [~mit] annähernd;
ungefähr; nahe.

apricot ['eiprikot] Aprikose f.

April ['eiprəl] April m.

apron ['eiprən] Schürze *f*; ~string Schürzenband *n*; be tied to one's wife's (mother's) ~s *fig.* unterm Pantoffel stehen (der Mutter am Rockzipfel) hängen;

apt □ [æpt] geeignet, passend; begabt; ~ to geneigt zu; ~itude ['æptitju:d], ~ness ['æptnis] Neigung *f* (to zu); Befähigung *f*.

aquatic [ə'kwætik] Wasserpflanze *f*; ~s *pl.* Wassersport *m*.

aque|duct ['ækwidʌkt] Aquädukt *m*, Wasserleitung *f*; ~ous □ ['eikwiəs] wässerig.

aquiline ['ækwilain] Adler...; gebogen; ~ nose Adlernase *f*.

Arab ['ærəb] Araber(in), ~ic [~bik] 1. arabisch; 2. Arabisch *n*.

arable ['ærəbl] pflügbar; Acker...

arbit|er ['a:bitə] Schiedsrichter *m*; *fig.* Gebieter *m*; ~rariness [~trərinis] Willkür *f*; ~rary □ [~trəri] willkürlich; eigenmächtig; ~rate [~reit] entscheiden, schlichten; ~ration [a:bi'treiʃən] Schiedsspruch *m*; Entscheidung *f*; ~rator *z'* ['a:bitreitə] Schiedsrichter *m*.

arbo(u)r ['a:bə] Laube *f*.

arc *ast.*, *Å etc* [a:k] (*$ Licht-) Bogen *m*; ~ade [a:'keid] Arkade *f*; Bogen-, Laubengang *m*.

arch¹ [a:tʃ] 1. Bogen *m*; Gewölbe *n*; 2. (sich) wölben; überwölben.

arch² [~] erst; schlimmst; Haupt...; Erz...

arch³ □ [~] schelmisch.

archaic [a:'keiik] (~ally) veraltet.

archangel ['a:keindʒəl] Erzengel *m*.

archbishop ['a:tʃ'biʃəp] Erzbischof *m*.

archer ['a:tʃə] Bogenschütze *m*; ~y [~əri] Bogenschießen *n*.

architect ['a:kitekt] Architekt *m*; Urheber(in), Schöpfer(in), ~onic [a:kitek'tonik] (~ally) architektonisch; *fig.* aufbauend; ~ure ['a:kitektʃə] Architektur *f*, Baukunst *f*.

archives ['a:kaivz] *pl.* Archiv *n*.

archway ['a:tʃwei] Bogengang *m*.

arc|-lamp ['a:klæmp], ~-light *$* Bogenlampe *f*.

arctic ['a:ktik] 1. arktisch, nördlich; Nord...; Polar...; 2. *Am.* wasserdichter Überschuh.

arden|cy ['a:dənsi] Hitze *f*, Glut *f*; Innigkeit *f*; ~t □ [~nt] *mst fig.* heiß, glühend; *fig.* feurig; eifrig.

ardo(u)r ['a:də] *fig.* Glut *f*; Eifer *m*.

arduous □ ['a:djuəs] mühsam; zäh.

are [a:; *im Satz* ə] *pres. pl. u. 2. sg.* von be.

area ['eəriə] Areal *n*; (Boden-) Fläche *f*; Flächenraum *m*; Gegend *f*; Gebiet *n*; Bereich *m*.

Argentine ['a:dʒəntain] 1. argentinisch; 2. Argentinier(in); the ~ Argentinien *n*.

argue ['a:gju:] *v/t.* erörtern; beweisen; begründen; einwenden; ~

s.o. into j-n zu *et.* bereden; *v/i.* streiten; Einwendungen machen.

argument ['a:gjumənt] Beweis (-grund) *m*; Streit(frage *f*) *m*; Erörterung *f*; Thema *n*; ~ation [a:gjumen'teiʃən] Beweisführung *f*.

arid ['ærid] dürr, trocken (*a. fig.*).

arise [ə'raiz] [*irr.*] sich erheben (*a. fig.*); ent~, erstehen (*from* aus); ~n [ə'rizn] *p.p von* arise.

aristocra|cy [æris'tokrəsi] Aristokratie *f* (*a. fig.*), Adel *m*; ~t ['æristəkræt] Aristokrat(in); ~tic(al □) [æristə'krætik(əl)] aristokratisch.

arithmetic [ə'riθmətik] Rechnen *n*.

ark [a:k] Arche *f*.

arm¹ [a:m] Arm *m*; Armlehne *f*; keep *s.o.* at ~'s length sich j-n vom Leibe halten; infant in ~s Säugling *m*.

arm² [~] 1. Waffe *f* (*mst pl.*); Waffengattung *f*; be (*all*) up in ~s in vollem Aufruhr sein; in Harnisch geraten; 2. (sich) (be)waffnen; (aus)rüsten; ⊕ armieren.

armada [a:'ma:də] Kriegsflotte *f*.

arma|ment ['a:məmənt] (Kriegsaus)Rüstung *f*; Kriegsmacht *f*; ~ race Wettrüsten *n*; ~ture ['a:mtjuə] Rüstung *f*; *Å, phys.* Armatur *f*.

armchair ['a:m'tʃeə] Lehnstuhl *m*, Sessel *m*.

armistice ['a:mistis] Waffenstillstand *m* (*a. fig.*).

armo(u)r ['a:mə] 1. ⚔ Rüstung *f*, Panzer *m* (*a. fig.*, *zo.*); 2. panzern; ~ed car Panzerwagen *m*; ~y ['a:məri] Rüstkammer *f* (*a. fig.*); *Am.* Rüstungsbetrieb *m*, Waffenfabrik *f*.

armpit ['a:mpit] Achselhöhle *f*.

army ['a:mi] Heer *n*, Armee *f*; *fig.* Menge *f*; ~ chaplain Militärgeistliche(r) *m*.

arose [ə'rouz] *pret. von* arise.

around [ə'raund] 1. *adv.* rund(her)um; *Am.* F hier herum; 2. *prp.* um ... her(um); *bsd. Am.* F ungefähr, etwa (*bei Zahlenangaben*).

arouse [ə'rauz] aufwecken; *fig.* aufrütteln; erregen.

arraign [ə'rein] vor Gericht stellen, anklagen; *fig.* rügen.

arrange [ə'reindʒ] (an)ordnen, *bsd. ♪* einrichten; festsetzen; *Streit* schlichten; vereinbaren; erledigen; ~ment [~dʒmənt] Anordnung *f*; Disposition *f*; Übereinkommen *n*; Vorkehrung *f*; ♪ Arrangement *n*.

array [ə'rei] 1. (Schlacht)Ordnung *f*; *fig.* Aufgebot *n*; 2. ordnen, aufstellen; aufbieten; kleiden, putzen.

arrear [ə'riə] *mst pl.* Rückstand *m*, *bsd.* Schulden *f/pl.*

arrest [ə'rest] 1. Verhaftung *f*; Haft *f*; Beschlagnahme *f*; 2. verhaften; beschlagnahmen; anhalten; hemmen.

arriv|al [ə'raivəl] Ankunft *f*; Auftreten *n*; Ankömmling *m*; ~s *pl.* angekommene Personen f/pl., Züge m/pl., Schiffe n/pl.; ~e [ə'raiv] (an-)kommen, eintreffen; erscheinen; eintreten (Ereignis); ~ at erreichen (acc.).

arroga|nce ['ærəgəns] Anmaßung f; Überheblichkeit f; ~nt ' [~nt] anmaßend; überheblich; ~te ['ærou-geit] sich et. anmaßen.

arrow ['ærou] Pfeil m; ~-head Pfeilspitze f; ~y ['æroui] pfeilartig.

arsenal ['ɑːsinl] Zeughaus n.

arsenic ['ɑːsnik] Arsen(ik) n.

arson ♭♭ ['ɑːsn] Brandstiftung f.

art [ɑːt] Kunst f; fig. List f; Kniff m; ~s pl. Geisteswissenschaften f/pl.; Faculty of ♭s philosophische Fakultät f.

arter|ial [ɑː'tiəriəl] Pulsader...; ~ road Hauptstraße f; ~y ['ɑːtəri] Arterie f, Pulsader f; fig. Verkehrsader f. [schmitzt.]

artful ☐ ['ɑːtful] schlau, ver-

article ['ɑːtikl] Artikel m; fig. Punkt m; ~d to in in der Lehre bei.

articulat|e 1. ['ɑːtikjuleit] deutlich (aus)sprechen; Knochen zs.-fügen; 2. ☐ [~lit] deutlich, gegliedert; ~ion [ɑːtikju'leiʃən] deutliche Aussprache; anat. Gelenkfügung f.

artific|e ☐ ['ɑːtifis] Kunstgriff m, List f; ~ial ☐ [ɑːti'fiʃəl] künstlich; Kunst...; ~ person ♭♭ juristische Person.

artillery [ɑː'tiləri] Artillerie f; ~man Artillerist m.

artisan [ɑːti'zæn] Handwerker m.

artist ['ɑːtist] Künstler(in); ~e [ɑː'tiːst] Artist(in); ~ic(al) [ɑː-'tistik(əl)] künstlerisch; Kunst...

artless ☐ ['ɑːtlis] ungekünstelt, schlicht; arglos.

as [æz, əz] 1. adv. so; (ebenso) wie; (in der Eigenschaft) als; ~ big ~ so groß wie; ~ well ebensogut; auch; ~ well ~ sowohl... als auch; 2. cj. (so-)wie; ebenso; (zu der Zeit) als, während; da, weil, indem; sofern; ~ it were sozusagen; such ~ to derart, daß; ~ for, ~ to was (an)betrifft; ~ from von... an.

ascend [ə'send] v/i. (auf-, empor-, hinauf)steigen; zeitlich: zurückgehen (to bis zu); v/t. be-, ersteigen; hinaufsteigen; Fluß etc. hinauffahren; ~ancy, ~ency [~dənsi] Überlegenheit f, Einfluß m; Herrschaft f.

ascension [ə'senʃən] Aufsteigen n (bsd. ast.); Am. a. Aufstieg m (e-s Ballons etc.); ♭ (Day) Himmelfahrt(stag m) f.

ascent [ə'sent] Aufstieg m; Besteigung f; Steigung f; Aufgang m.

ascertain [æsə'tein] ermitteln.

ascetic [ə'setik] (~ally) asketisch.

ascribe [ə'skraib] zuschreiben.

aseptic ♯ [æ'septik] 1. aseptisch; 2. aseptisches Mittel.

ash¹ [æʃ] ♀ Esche f; Eschenholz n.

ash² [~], mst. pl. ~es ['æʃiz] Asche f; Ash Wednesday Aschermittwoch m.

ashamed [ə'ʃeimd] beschämt; be ~ of sich e-r Sache od. j-s schämen.

ash can Am. ['æʃkæn] ~ dust-bin.

ashen ['æʃn] Aschen...; aschfahl.

ashore [ə'ʃɔː] am od. ans Ufer od. Land; run ~, be driven ~ stranden.

ash|-pan ['æʃpæn] Asch(en)kasten m; ~-tray Asch(en)becher m.

ashy ['æʃi] aschig; aschgrau.

Asiatic [eiʃi'ætik] 1. asiatisch; 2. Asiat(in).

aside [ə'said] 1. beiseite (a. thea.); abseits; seitwärts; ~ from Am. abgesehen von; 2. thea. Aparte n.

ask [ɑːsk] v/t. fragen (s.th. nach et.); verlangen (of, from s.o. von j-m); bitten (s.o. [for] s.th. j. um et.; that darum, daß); erbitten; ~ (s.o.) a question (j-m) e-e Frage stellen; v/i.: ~ for bitten um, fragen nach; he ~ed for it od. for trouble er wollte es ja so haben; to be had for the ~ing umsonst zu haben.

askance [əs'kæns], **askew** [əs'kjuː] von der Seite, seitwärts; schief.

asleep [ə'sliːp] schlafend; in den Schlaf; eingeschlafen, be ~ schlafen; fall ~ einschlafen.

asparagus ♀ [əs'pærəgəs] Spargel m.

aspect ['æspekt] Äußere n; Aussicht f, Lage f; Aspekt m, Seite f, Gesichtspunkt m.

asperity [æs'periti] Rauheit f; Unebenheit f; fig. Schroffheit f.

asphalt ['æsfælt] 1. Asphalt m; 2. asphaltieren.

aspic ['æspik] Aspik m, Sülze f.

aspir|ant [əs'paiərənt] Bewerber (-in); ~ate ling. ['æspəreit] aspirieren; ~ation [æspə'reiʃən] Aspiration f; Bestrebung f; ~e [əs'paiə] streben, trachten (to, after, at nach).

ass [æs] Esel m.

assail [ə'seil] angreifen, überfallen (a. fig.); befallen (Zweifel etc.); ~ant [~lənt] Angreifer(in).

assassin [ə'sæsin] (Meuchel)Mörder(in); ~ate [~neit] (meuchlings) ermorden; ~ation [əsæsi'neiʃən] Meuchelmord m.

assault [ə'sɔːlt] 1. Angriff m (a. fig.); 2. anfallen; ♭♭ tätlich angreifen od. beleidigen; ✗ bestürmen (a. fig.).

assay [ə'sei] 1. (Erz-, Metall-) Probe f; 2. v/t. untersuchen; v/i. Am. Edelmetall enthalten.

assembl|age [ə'semblidʒ] (An-) Sammlung f; ⊕ Montage f; ~e [ə'sembl] (sich) versammeln; zs.-berufen; ⊕ montieren; ~y [~li] Versammlung f; Gesellschaft f; ⊕ Montage f; ~ line ⊕ Fließband n; ~ man pol. Abgeordnete(r) m.

22*

assent [ə'sent] **1.** Zustimmung f; **2.** (to) zustimmen (dat.); billigen.

assert [ə'sə:t] (sich) behaupten; **~ion** [ə'sə:ʃən] Behauptung f; Erklärung f; Geltendmachung f.

assess [ə'ses] besteuern; zur Steuer veranlagen (at mit); **~able** □ [~əbl] steuerpflichtig; **~ment** [~smənt] (Steuer)Veranlagung f; Steuer f.

asset [' æset] ✚ Aktivposten m; fig. Gut n, Gewinn m; **~s** pl. Vermögen n; ✝ Aktiva pl.; ✝✝ Konkursmasse f.

asseverate [ə'sevəreit] beteuern.

assiduous [[ə'sidjuəs] emsig, fleißig; aufmerksam.

assign [ə'sain] an–, zuweisen; bestimmen; zuschreiben; **~ation** [æsig'neiʃən] Verabredung f, Stelldichein n; — **~ment** [ə'sainmənt] An–, Zuweisung f; bsd. Am. Auftrag m; ✝✝ Übertragung f.

assimilat|e [ə'simileit] (sich) angleichen (to, with dat.); **~ion** [əsimi'leiʃən] Assimilation f, Angleichung f.

assist [ə'sist] j–m beistehen, helfen; unterstützen; **~ance** [~təns] Beistand m; Hilfe f; **~ant** [~nt] **1.** behilflich; **2.** Assistent(in).

assize [ə'saiz] (Schwur)Gerichtssitzung f; **~s** pl. periodisches Geschworenengericht.

associa|te 1. [ə'souʃieit] (sich) zugesellen (with dat.), (sich) vereinigen; Umgang haben (with mit); **2.** [~ʃiit] verbunden; **3.** [~] (Amts)Genosse m; Teilhaber m; **~tion** [əsousi'eiʃən] Vereinigung f, Verbindung f; Handels- etc. Gesellschaft f; Genossenschaft f; Verein m.

assort [ə'sɔ:t] v/t. sortieren, zs.-stellen; v/i. passen (with zu); **~ment** [~mənt] Sortieren n; ✝ Sortiment n, Auswahl f.

assum|e [ə'sju:m] annehmen; vorgeben; übernehmen; **~ption** [ə'sʌmpʃən] Annahme f; Übernahme f; eccl. ♀ (Day) Mariä Himmelfahrt f.

assur|ance [ə'ʃuərəns] Zu–, Versicherung f; Zuversicht f; Sicherheit f, Gewißheit f; Selbstsicherheit f; Dreistigkeit f; (Leben) ver)sichern; sicherstellen; **~ed 1.** (adv. **~edly** [~ridli]) sicher; dreist; **2.** Versicherte(r m) f.

asthma ['æsmə] Asthma n.

astir [ə'stə:] auf (den Beinen); in Bewegung, rege.

astonish [əs'tɔniʃ] in Erstaunen setzen; verwundern; befremden; be **~ed** erstaunt sein (at über acc.); **~ing** □ [~ʃiŋ] erstaunlich; **~ment** [~mənt] (Er)Staunen n; Verwunderung f.

astound [əs'taund] verblüffen.

astray [əs'trei] vom (rechten) Wege

ab (a. fig.); irre; go **~** sich verlaufen, fehlgehen.

astride [əs'traid] mit gespreizten Beinen; rittlings (of auf dat.).

astringent ⚕ [əs'trindʒənt] **1.** □ zs.-ziehend; **2.** zs.-ziehendes Mittel.

astro|logy [əs'trɔlədʒi] Astrologie f; **~naut** ['æstrənɔ:t] Astronaut m, Raumfahrer m; **~nomer** [əs'trɔnəmə] Astronom m; **~nomy** [~mi] Astronomie f.

astute [əs'tju:t] scharfsinnig; schlau; **~ness** [~tnis] Scharfsinn m.

asunder [ə'sʌndə] auseinander; entzwei.

asylum [ə'sailəm] Asyl n.

at [æt; unbetont ət] prp. an; auf; aus; bei; für; in; mit; nach; über; um; von; vor; zu; **~** school in der Schule; **~** the age of im Alter von.

ate [et] pret. von eat **1.**

atheism ['eiθiizm] Atheismus m.

athlet|e ['æθli:t] (bsd. Leicht-) Athlet m; **~ic(al** [~[ə]θ'letik(əl)] athletisch; **~ics** pl. (bsd. Leicht-) Athletik f.

Atlantic [ət'læntik] **1.** atlantisch; **2.** a. **~** Ocean Atlantik m.

atmospher|e ['ætməsfiə] Atmosphäre f (a. fig.); **~ic(al** □) [ætməs'ferik(əl)] atmosphärisch.

atom ⚛ ['ætəm] Atom n (a. fig.); **~ic** [ə'tɔmik] atomartig, Atom...; atomistisch; **~ age** Atomzeitalter n; **~** (a. atom) bomb Atombombe f; **~ pile** Atomreaktor m; **~ic-powered** durch Atomkraft betrieben; **~ize** ['ætəmaiz] in Atome auflösen; atomisieren; **~izer** [~zə] Zerstäuber m.

atone [ə'toun]: **~ for** büßen für et.; **~ment** [~mənt] Buße f; Sühne f.

atroci|ous [ə'trouʃəs] scheußlich, gräßlich; grausam; **~ty** [ə'trɔsiti] Scheußlichkeit f, Gräßlichkeit f; Grausamkeit f.

attach [ə'tætʃ] v/t. (to) anheften (an, acc.), befestigen (an dat.); Wert, Wichtigkeit etc. beilegen (dat.); ✝✝ j–n verhaften; et. beschlagnahmen; **~ o.s.** to sich anschließen an (acc.); **~ed:** **~** to gehörig zu; j–m zugetan, ergeben; **~ment** [~mənt] Befestigung f; Bindung f (to, for an acc.); Anhänglichkeit f (an acc.), Neigung f (zu); Anhängsel n (to gen.); ✝✝ Verhaftung f; Beschlagnahme f.

attack [ə'tæk] **1.** angreifen (a. fig.); befallen (Krankheit); Arbeit in Angriff nehmen; **2.** Angriff m; ✗ Anfall m; Inangriffnahme f.

attain [ə'tein] v/t. Ziel erreichen; v/i. **~** to gelangen zu; **~ment** [~nmənt] Erreichung f; fig. Aneignung f; **~s** pl. Kenntnisse f/pl.; Fertigkeiten f/pl.

attempt [ə'tempt] **1.** versuchen; **2.** Versuch m; Attentat n.

attend [ə'tend] v/t. begleiten; bedienen; pflegen; ✠ behandeln; *j-m* aufwarten; beiwohnen (*dat.*); *Vorlesung etc.* besuchen; *v/i.* achten, hören (*to auf acc.*); anwesend sein (*at bei*); ~ to erledigen; **~ance** [~dəns] Begleitung *f*; Aufwartung *f*; Pflege *f*; ✠ Behandlung *f*; Gefolge *n*; Anwesenheit *f* (*at bei*); Besuch *m* (*der Schule etc.*); Besucher(zahl *f*) *m/pl.*; Publikum *n*; *be in ~* zu Diensten stehen; **~ant** [~nt] **1.** begleitend (*on, upon acc.*); anwesend (*at bei*); **2.** Diener(in); Begleiter(in); Wärter(in); Besucher(in) (*at gen.*); ⊕ Bedienungsmann *m*; **~s** *pl.* Dienerschaft *f*.

atten|tion [ə'tenʃən] Aufmerksamkeit *f* (*a. fig.*); ~! ✗ Achtung!; **~ive** [~ntiv] aufmerksam.

attest [ə'test] bezeugen; beglaubigen; *bsd.* ✗ vereidigen.

attic ['ætik] Dachstube *f*. [dung *f.*\]

attire [ə'taiə] **1.** kleiden; **2.** Klei-\]

attitude ['ætitju:d] (Ein)Stellung *f*; Haltung *f*; *fig.* Stellungnahme *f*.

attorney [ə'tə:ni] Bevollmächtigte(r) *m*; *Am.* Rechtsanwalt *m*; *power of ~* Vollmacht *f*; ⚖ *General* Generalstaats- *od.* Kronanwalt *m*, *Am.* Justizminister *m*.

attract [ə'trækt] anziehen, *Aufmerksamkeit* erregen; *fig.* reizen; **~ion** [~kʃən] Anziehung(skraft) *f*; *fig.* Reiz *m*; Zugartikel *m*; *thea.* Zugstück *n*; **~ive** [~ktiv] anziehend; reizvoll; zugkräftig; **~iveness** [~vnis] Reiz *m*.

attribute 1. [ə'tribju(:)t] beimessen, zuschreiben; zurückführen (*to auf acc.*); **2.** ['ætribju:t] Attribut *n* (*a. gr.*), Eigenschaft *f*, Merkmal *n*.

attune [ə'tju:n] (ab)stimmen.

auburn ['ɔ:bən] kastanienbraun.

auction ['ɔ:kʃən] **1.** Auktion *f*; *sell by ~, put up for ~* versteigern; **2.** *mst* ~ *off* versteigern; **~eer** [ɔ:kʃə'niə] Auktionator *m*.

audaci|ous [ɔ:'deiʃəs] kühn; unverschämt; **~ty** [ɔ:'dæsiti] Kühnheit *f*; Unverschämtheit *f*.

audible □ ['ɔ:dəbl] hörbar; Hör...

audience ['ɔ:djəns] Publikum *n*, Zuhörerschaft *f*; Leserkreis *m*; Audienz *f*; Gehör *n*; *give ~ to* Gehör schenken (*dat.*).

audit ['ɔ:dit] **1.** Rechnungsprüfung *f*; **2.** *Rechnungen* prüfen; **~or** [~tə] Hörer *m*; Rechnungs-, Buchprüfer *m*; **~orium** [ɔ:di'tɔ:riəm] Hörsaal *m*; *Am.* Vortrags-, Konzertsaal *m*.

auger ⊕ ['ɔ:gə] großer Bohrer.

aught [ɔ:t] (irgend) etwas; *for ~ I care* meinetwegen; *for ~ I know* soviel ich weiß.

augment [ɔ:g'ment] vergrößern; **~ation** [ɔ:gmen'teiʃən] Vermehrung *f*, Vergrößerung *f*; Zusatz *m*.

augur ['ɔ:gə] **1.** Augur *m*; **2.** weissagen, voraussagen (*well Gutes, ill*

Übles)}; **~y** ['ɔ:gjuri] Prophezeiung *f*; An-, Vorzeichen *n*; Vorahnung *f*.

August[1] ['ɔ:gəst] *Monat* August *m*.

august[2] □ [ɔ:'gʌst] erhaben.

aunt [ɑ:nt] Tante *f*.

auspic|e ['ɔ:spis] Vorzeichen *n*; **~s** *pl.* Auspizien *pl.*; Schirmherrschaft *f*; **~ious** □ [ɔ:'spiʃəs] günstig.

auster|e □ [ɔs'tiə] streng; herb; hart; einfach; **~ity** [ɔs'teriti] Strenge *f*; Härte *f*; Einfachheit *f*.

Australian [ɔs'treiljən] **1.** australisch; **2.** Australier(in).

Austrian ['ɔstriən] **1.** österreichisch; **2.** Österreicher(in).

authentic [ɔ:'θentik] (~*ally*) authentisch; zuverlässig; echt.

author ['ɔ:θə] Urheber(in); Autor (-in); Verfasser(in); **~itative** □ [ɔ:'θɔritətiv] maßgebend; gebieterisch; zuverlässig; **~ity** [ɔ:'θɔriti] Autorität *f*; (Amts)Gewalt *f*, Vollmacht *f*; Einfluß *m* (*over auf acc.*); Ansehen *n*; Glaubwürdigkeit *f*; Quelle *f*; Fachmann *m*; Behörde *f* (*mst pl.*); *on the ~ of auf j-s Zeugnis hin*; **~ize** ['ɔ:θəraiz] *j-n* autorisieren, bevollmächtigen; *et.* gutheißen; **~ship** ['ɔ:əʃip] Urheberschaft *f*.

autocar ['ɔ:touka:] Kraftwagen *m*.

autocra|cy [ɔ:'tɔkrəsi] Autokratie *f*; **~tic(al** □) [ɔ:tə'krætik(əl)] autokratisch, despotisch.

autogiro ✈ [ɔ:tou'dʒaiərou] Autogiro *n*, Tragschrauber *m*.

autograph ['ɔ:təgra:f] Autogramm *n*. [Restaurant *n.*\]

automat ['ɔ:təmæt] Automaten-\]

automat|ic [ɔ:tə'mætik] (~*ally*) **1.** automatisch; ~ *machine* (Verkaufs)Automat *m*; **2.** *Am.* Selbstladepistole *f*, -gewehr *n*; **~ion** [~'meiʃən] Automation *f*; **~on** *fig.* [ɔ:'tɔmətən] Roboter *m*.

automobile *bsd. Am.* ['ɔ:təməbi:l] Automobil *n*.

autonomy [ɔ:'tɔnəmi] Autonomie *f*.

autumn ['ɔ:təm] Herbst *m*; **~al** □ [ɔ:'tʌmnəl] herbstlich; Herbst...

auxiliary [ɔ:g'ziljəri] helfend; Hilfs...

avail [ə'veil] **1.** nützen, helfen; ~ *o.s. of sich e-r S. bedienen*; **2.** Nutzen *m*; *of no ~* nutzlos; **~able** □ [~əbl] benutzbar; verfügbar; *pred.* erhältlich, vorhanden; gültig.

avalanche ['ævəla:nʃ] Lawine *f*.

avaric|e ['ævəris] Geiz *m*; Habsucht *f*; **~ious** □ [ævə'riʃəs] geizig; habgierig.

avenge [ə'vendʒ] rächen, *et.* ahnden; **~r** [~dʒə] Rächer(in).

avenue ['ævinju:] Allee *f*; Prachtstraße *f*; *fig.* Weg *m*, Straße *f*.

aver [ə'və:] behaupten.

average ['ævəridʒ] **1.** Durchschnitt *m*; ⚓ Havarie *f*; **2.** □ durchschnittlich; Durchschnitts...; **3.** durchschnittlich schätzen (*at* auf *acc.*); durchschnittlich betragen *od.* arbeiten *etc.*

avers|e □ [ə'vəːs] abgeneigt (*to*, *from dat.*); widerwillig; **~ion** [ə'vəːʃən] Widerwille *m.*

avert [ə'vəːt] abwenden (*a. fig.*).

aviat|ion 🛪 [eivi'eiʃən] Fliegen *n*; Flugwesen *n*; Luftfahrt *f*; **~or** ['eivieitə] Flieger *m.*

avid □ ['ævid] gierig (*of* nach; *for* auf *acc.*).

avoid [ə'vɔid] (ver)meiden; *j-m* ausweichen; 🛪 anfechten; ungültig machen; **~ance** [~dəns] Vermeidung *f.*

avouch [ə'vautʃ] verbürgen, bestätigen; — *avow.*

avow [ə'vau] bekennen, (ein)gestehen; anerkennen; **~al** [ə'vauəl] Bekenntnis *n*, (Ein)Geständnis *n*; **~edly** [ə'vauidli] eingestandenermaßen.

await [ə'weit] erwarten (*a. fig.*).

awake [ə'weik] 1. wach, munter; *be ~ to* sich *e-r S.* bewußt sein; 2. [*irr.*] *v/t.* (*mst* **~n** [~kən]) (er-) wecken; *v/i.* erwachen; gewahr werden (*to s.th.* et.).

award [ə'wɔːd] 1. Urteil *n*, Spruch *m*; Belohnung *f*; Preis *m*; 2. zuerkennen, *Orden etc.* verleihen.

aware [ə'wɛə]: *be ~* wissen (*of von od. acc.*), sich bewußt sein (*of gen.*); *become ~ of et.* gewahr werden, merken.

away [ə'wei] (hin)weg; fort; immer weiter, darauflos; *~ back Am.* F (schon) damals, weit zurück.

awe [ɔː] 1. Ehrfurcht *f*, Scheu *f* (*of* vor *dat.*); 2. (Ehr)Furcht einflößen (*dat.*).

awful □ ['ɔːful] ehrfurchtgebietend; furchtbar; F *fig.* schrecklich.

awhile [ə'wail] e-e Weile.

awkward □ ['ɔːkwəd] ungeschickt, unbeholfen; linkisch; unangenehm; dumm, ungünstig, unpraktisch.

awl [ɔːl] Ahle *f*, Pfriem *m.*

awning ['ɔːniŋ] Plane *f*; Markise *f.*

awoke [ə'wouk] *pret. u. p.p. von awake* 2.

awry [ə'rai] schief; *fig.* verkehrt.

ax(e) [æks] Axt *f*, Beil *n.*

axis ['æksis], *pl.* **axes** ['æksiːz] Achse *f.*

axle ⊕ ['æksl] *a.* **~tree** (Rad-) Achse *f*, Welle *f.*

ay(e) [ai] Ja *n*; *parl.* Jastimme *f*; *the ~s have it* die Mehrheit ist dafür.

azure ['æʒə] azurn, azurblau.

B

babble ['bæbl] 1. stammeln; (nach-) plappern; schwatzen; plätschern (*Bach*); 2. Geplapper *n*; Geschwätz *n.*

baboon zo. [bə'buːn] Pavian *m.*

baby ['beibi] 1. Säugling *m*, kleines Kind, Baby *n*; *Am. sl.* Süße *f* (*Mädchen*); 2. Baby...; Kinder...; klein; **~hood** [~ihud] frühe Kindheit.

bachelor ['bætʃələ] Junggeselle *m*; *univ.* Bakkalaureus *m* (*Grad*).

back [bæk] 1. Rücken *m*; Rückseite *f*; Rücklehne *f*; Hinterende *n*; *Fußball*: Verteidiger *m*; 2. *adj.* Hinter..., Rück..; hinter; rückwärtig; entlegen; rückläufig; rückständig; 3. *adv.* zurück; 4. *v/t.* mit e-m Rücken versehen; unterstützen; hinten anstoßen an (*acc.*); zurückbewegen; wetten *od.* setzen auf (*acc.*); ✝ indossieren; *v/i.* sich rückwärts bewegen, zurückgehen *od.* zurückfahren; ~ **alley** *Am.* finstere Seitengasse; **~bite** ['bækbait] [*irr.* (*bite*)] verleumden; **~bone** Rückgrat *n*; **~er** ['bækə] Unterstützer (-in); ✝ Indossierer *m*; Wetter(in); **~fire** *mot.* Frühzündung *f*; **~ ground** Hintergrund *m*; **~number** alte Nummer (*e-r Zeitung*); **~**

pedal rückwärtstreten (*Radfahren*); **~ing brake** Rücktrittbremse *f*; **~side** Hinter-, Rückseite *f*; **~slapper** *Am.* [~slæpə] plump vertraulicher Mensch; **~slide** [*irr.* (*slide*)] rückfällig werden; **~stairs** Hintertreppe *f*; **~stop** *Am.* Baseball: Gitter *n hinter* dem Fänger; Schießstand: Kugelfang *m*; **~stroke** Rückenschwimmen *n*; **~talk** *Am.* freche Antworten; **~track** *Am.* F *fig.* e-n Rückzieher machen; **~ward** ['bækwəd] 1. *adj.* Rück(wärts)...; langsam; zurückgeblieben, rückständig; zurückhaltend; 2. *adv.* (*a.* **~wards** [~dz]) rückwärts, zurück; **~water** Stauwasser *n*; gelegene Waldgebiete; *fig.* Provinz *f*; **~woodsman** Hinterwäldler *m.*

bacon ['beikən] Speck *m.*

bacteri|ologist [bæktiəri'ɔlədʒist] Bakteriologe *m*; **~um** [bæk'tiəriəm], *pl.* **~a** [~iə] Bakterie *f.*

bad □ [bæd] schlecht, böse, schlimm; falsch (*Münze*); faul (*Schuld*); *he is ~ly off* er ist übel dran; *~ly wounded* schwerverwundet; *want ~ly* F dringend brauchen; *be in ~ with Am.* F in Ungnade bei.

bade [beid] *pret. von bid* 1.

badge [bædʒ] Ab-, Kennzeichen *n*.

badger ['bædʒə] 1. *zo*. Dachs *m*; 2. hetzen, plagen, quälen.

badlands *Am*. ['bædlændz] *pl*. Ödland *n*.

badness ['bædnis] schlechte Beschaffenheit; Schlechtigkeit *f*.

baffle ['bæfl] *j-n* verwirren; *Plan etc*. vereiteln, durchkreuzen.

bag [bæg] 1. Beutel *m*, Sack *m*; Tüte *f*; Tasche *f*; ~ *and baggage* mit Sack und Pack; 2. in e-n Beutel *etc*. tun, einsacken; *hunt*. zur Strecke bringen; (sich) bauschen.

baggage *Am*. ['bægidʒ] (Reise-)Gepäck *n*; ~ **car** *Am*. 🚋 Gepäckwagen *m*; ~ **check** *Am*. Gepäckschein *m*.

bagpipe ['bægpaip] Dudelsack *m*.

bail [beil] 1. Bürge *m*; Bürgschaft *f*; Kaution *f*; *admit to* ~ 🏛 gegen Bürgschaft freilassen; 2. bürgen für; ~ *out j-n* freibürgen; ✈ mit dem Fallschirm abspringen.

bailiff ['beilif] Gerichtsdiener *m*; (Guts)Verwalter *m*; Amtmann *m*.

bait [beit] 1. Köder *m*; *fig*. Lockung *f*; 2. *v/t*. *Falle etc*. beködern; *hunt*. hetzen; *fig*. quälen; reizen; *v/i*. rasten; einkehren.

bak|e [beik] 1. backen; braten; *Ziegel* brennen; (aus)dörren; 2. *Am*. gesellige Zusammenkunft; **~er** ['beikə] Bäcker *m*; **~ery** [~əri] Bäckerei *f*; **~ing-powder** [~kiŋpaudə] Backpulver *n*.

balance ['bæləns] 1. Waage *f*; Gleichgewicht *n* (*a. fig*.); Harmonie *f*; † Bilanz *f*, Saldo *m*, Überschuß *m*; Restbetrag *m*; F Rest *m*; ~ *of a wheel* Unruh(e) *f der Uhr*; ~ *of power pol*. Kräftegleichgewicht *n*; ~ *of trade* (Außen-)Handelsbilanz *f*; 2. *v/t*. (ab-, er)wägen; im Gleichgewicht halten; ausgleichen; † bilanzieren; saldieren; *v/i*. balancieren; sich ausgleichen.

balcony ['bælkəni] Balkon *m*.

bald [bɔːld] kahl; *fig*. nackt; dürftig.

bale † [beil] Ballen *m*.

baleful □ ['beilful] verderblich; unheilvoll.

balk [bɔːk] 1. (Furchen)Rain *m*; Balken *m*; Hemmnis *n*; 2. *v/t*. (ver)hindern; enttäuschen; vereiteln; *v/i*. stutzen, scheuen.

ball[1] [bɔːl] 1. Ball *m*; Kugel *f*; (Hand-, Fuß)Ballen *m*; Knäuel *m*, *n*; Kloß *m*; *Sport*. Wurf *m*; *keep the* ~ *rolling* das Gespräch in Gang halten; *play* ~ *Am*. F mitmachen; 2. (sich) (zs.-)ballen.

ball[2] [~] Ball *m*, Tanzgesellschaft *f*.

ballad ['bæləd] Ballade *f*; Lied *n*.

ballast ['bæləst] 1. Ballast *m*; 🚋 Schotter *m*, Bettung *f*; 2. mit Ballast beladen; 🚋 beschottern, betten.

ball-bearing(s *pl*.) ⊕ ['bɔːl-'bɛəriŋ(z)] Kugellager *n*.

ballet ['bælei] Ballett *n*.

balloon [bə'luːn] 1. Ballon *m*; 2. im Ballon aufsteigen; sich blähen; **~ist** [~nist] Ballonfahrer *m*.

ballot ['bælət] 1. Wahlzettel *m*; (geheime) Wahl; 2. (geheim) abstimmen; ~ *for* losen um; **~box** Wahlurne *f*.

ball(-point) pen ['bɔːl(point)pen] Kugelschreiber *m*.

ball-room ['bɔːlrum] Ballsaal *m*.

balm [baːm] Balsam *m*; *fig*. Trost *m*.

balmy □ ['baːmi] balsamisch (*a. fig*.).

baloney *Am*. *sl*. [bə'louni] Quatsch *m*.

balsam ['bɔːlsəm] Balsam *m*.

balustrade [bæləs'treid] Balustrade *f*, Brüstung *f*; Geländer *n*.

bamboo [bæm'buː] Bambus *m*.

bamboozle F [bæm'buːzl] beschwindeln.

ban [bæn] 1. Bann *m*; Acht *f*; (amtliches) Verbot; 2. verbieten.

banal [bə'naːl] banal, abgedroschen.

banana [bə'naːnə] Banane *f*.

band [bænd] 1. Band *n*; Streifen *m*; Schar *f*; ♪ Kapelle *f*; 2. zs.-binden; ~ *o.s.* sich zs.-tun *od*. zs.-rotten.

bandage ['bændidʒ] 1. Binde *f*; Verband *m*; 2. bandagieren; verbinden.

bandbox ['bændbɔks] Hutschachtel *f*.

bandit ['bændit] Bandit *m*.

band|-master ['bændmaːstə] Kapellmeister *m*; **~stand** Musikpavillon *m*; ~ **wagon** *Am*. Wagen *m* mit Musikkapelle; *jump on the* ~ sich der erfolgversprechenden Sache anschließen.

bandy ['bændi] *Worte etc*. wechseln; **~-legged** säbelbeinig.

bane [bein] Ruin *m*; **~ful** □ ['beinful] verderblich.

bang [bæŋ] 1. Knall *m*; Ponyfrisur *f*; 2. dröhnend (zu)schlagen; **~up** *Am*. *sl*. ['bæŋ'ʌp] Klasse, prima.

banish ['bæniʃ] verbannen; **~ment** [~ʃmənt] Verbannung *f*.

banisters ['bænistəz] *pl*. Treppengeländer *n*.

bank [bæŋk] 1. Damm *m*; Ufer *n*; (Spiel-, Sand-, Wolken- *etc*.)Bank *f*; ~ *of issue* Notenbank *f*; 2. *v/t*. eindämmen; † *Geld* auf die Bank legen; ✈ in die Kurve bringen; *v/i*. Bankgeschäfte machen; ein Bankkonto haben; ✈ in die Kurve gehen; ~ *on* sich verlassen auf (*acc*.); **~bill** ['bæŋkbil] Bankwechsel *m*; *Am*. *s*. banknote; **~er** [~kə] Bankier *m*; **~ing** [~kiŋ] Bankgeschäft *n*; Bankwesen *n*; *attr*. Bank...; **~note** Banknote *f*; Kassenschein *m*; **~**

rate Diskontsatz *m*; **~rupt** [.krɔpt] **1.** Bankrotteur *m*; **2.** bankrott; **3.** bankrott machen; **~ruptcy** [.tsi] Bankrott *m*, Konkurs *m*.

banner ['bænə] Banner *n*; Fahne *f*.

banns [bænz] *pl* Aufgebot *n*.

banquet ['bæŋkwit] **1.** Festmahl *n*; **2.** *v/t.* festlich bewirten; *v/i.* tafeln.

banter ['bæntə] necken, hänseln.

baptism ['bæptizəm] Taufe *f*.

baptist ['bæptist] Täufer *m*.

baptize ['bæp'taiz] taufen.

bar [baː] **1.** Stange *f*; Stab *m*; Barren *m*; Riegel *m*; Schranke *f*; Sandbank *f*; *fig* Hindernis *n*; ✕ Spange *f*; ♪ Takt(strich) *m*; (Gerichts)Schranke *f*; *fig* Urteil *n*; Anwaltschaft *f*; Bar *f im Hotel etc.*; **2.** verriegeln, (ver-, ab)sperren; verwehren, einsperren; (ver)hindern; ausschließen

barb [baːb] Widerhaken *m*; **~ed wire** Stacheldraht *m*

barbar|ian [baːˈbɛəriən] **1.** barbarisch; **2.** Barbar(in); **~ous** □ ['baːbərəs] barbarisch; roh; grausam.

barbecue ['baːbikjuː] **1.** großer Bratrost; *Am.* Essen *n* (bei dem Tiere ganz gebraten werden); **2.** im ganzen braten.

barber ['baːbə] (Herren)Friseur *m*.

bare [bɛə] **1.** nackt, bloß, kahl; bar, leer; arm, entblößt, **2.** entblößen, ~**faced** [['bɛəfeist] frech; ~**foot**, ~**footed** barfuß, ~**headed** barhäuptig, ~**ly** ['bɛəli] kaum

bargain ['baːgin] **1.** Geschäft *n*; Handel *m*, Kauf *m*; vorteilhafter Kauf; *a (dead)* ~ spottbillig; *it's a* ~! *I* abgemacht!, *into the* ~ obendrein; **2.** handeln, übereinkommen.

barge [baːdʒ] Flußboot *n*, Lastkahn *m*; Hausboot *n*; ~**man** ['baːdʒmən] Kahnführer *m*

bark¹ [baːk] **1.** Borke *f*, Rinde *f*; **2.** abrinden; *Haut* abschürfen.

bark² [.] **1.** bellen; **2.** Bellen *n*.

bar-keeper ['baːkiːpə] Barbesitzer *m*; Barkellner *m*

barley ['baːli] Gerste *f*; Graupe *f*.

barn [baːn] Scheune *f*; *bsd. Am.* (Vieh)Stall *m*; ~**storm** *Am. pol.* ['baːnstɔːm] herumreisen u. (Wahl-) Reden halten

barometer [bəˈrɔmitə] Barometer *n*.

baron ['bærən] Baron *m*, Freiherr *m*; ~**ess** [.nis] Baronin *f*.

barrack(s *pl.*) ['bærək(s)] (Miets-) Kaserne *f*

barrage ['bæraːʒ] Staudamm *m*.

barrel ['bærəl] **1.** Faß *n*, Tonne *f*; *Gewehr- etc* Lauf *m*; ⊕ Trommel *f*; Walze *f*; **2.** in Fässer füllen; ~**organ** ♪ Drehorgel *f*.

barren [['bærən] unfruchtbar; dürr, trocken; tot (*Kapital*).

barricade [bæriˈkeid] **1.** Barrikade *f*; **2.** verbarrikadieren; sperren.

barrier ['bæriə] Schranke *f (a. fig.)*; Barriere *f*, Sperre *f*; Hindernis *n*.

barrister ['bæristə] (plädierender) Rechtsanwalt, Barrister *m*.

barrow¹ ['bærou] Trage *f*; Karre *f*.

barrow² [.] Hügelgrab *n*, Tumulus *m*.

barter ['baːtə] **1.** Tausch(handel) *m*; **2.** tauschen (*for gegen*); *F* schachern.

base¹ □ [beis] gemein; unecht.

base² [.] **1.** Basis *f*; Grundlage *f*; Fundament *n*; Fuß *m*; ♠ Base *f*; Stützpunkt *m*; **2.** gründen, stützen.

base|ball ['beisbɔːl] Baseball *m*; ~**born** von niedriger Abkunft; unehelich; ~**less** ['beislis] grundlos; ~**ment** ['beismənt] Fundament *n*; Kellergeschoß *n*.

baseness ['beisnis] Gemeinheit *f*.

bashful □ ['bæʃful] schüchtern.

basic ['beisik] (.ally) grundlegend; Grund...; ♠ basisch

basin ['beisn] Becken *n*; Schüssel *f*; Tal-, Wasser-, Hafenbecken *n*.

bas|is ['beisis], *pl.* ~**es** ['beisiːz] Basis *f*; Grundlage *f*; ✕, ♣ Stützpunkt *m*.

bask [baːsk] sich sonnen (*a. fig.*).

basket ['baːskit] Korb *m*; ~**ball** Korbball(spiel *n*) *m*; ~ **dinner**, ~ **supper** *Am.* Picknick *n*.

bass ♪ [beis] Baß *m*.

basso ♪ ['bæsou] Baß(sänger) *m*.

bastard ['bæstəd] **1.** □ unehelich; unecht; Bastard.. ; **2.** Bastard *m*.

baste¹ [beist] *Braten* begießen; durchprügeln.

baste² [.] lose nähen, (an)heften.

bat¹ [bæt] Fledermaus *f*; *as blind as a* ~ stockblind

bat² [.] *Sport* **1.** Schlagholz *n*; Schläger *m*; **2.** *den Ball* schlagen.

batch [bætʃ] Schub *m Brote (a. fig.)*; Stoß *m Briefe etc. (a. fig.)*.

bate [beit] verringern; verhalten.

bath [baːθ] **1.** Bad *n*; ♀ *chair* Rollstuhl *m*; **2.** baden.

bathe [beið] baden.

bathing ['beiðiŋ] Baden *n*, Bad *n*; *attr.* Bade...; ~**suit** Badeanzug *m*.

bath|robe *Am.* ['baːθroub] Bademantel *m*; ~**room** Badezimmer *n*; ~**sheet** Badelaken *n*; ~**towel** Badetuch *n*; ~**tub** Badewanne *f*.

batiste † [bæˈtiːst] Batist *m*.

baton ['bætən] Stab *m*; Taktstock *m*.

battalion ✕ [bəˈtæljən] Bataillon *n*.

batten ['bætn] **1.** Latte *f*; **2.** sich mästen.

batter ['bætə] **1.** *Sport*: Schläger *m*; Rührteig *m*; **2.** heftig schlagen; verbeulen; ~ *down od. in Tür* einschlagen; ~**y** [.əri] Schlägerei *f*; Batterie *f*; ⚡ Akku *m*; *fig.* Satz *m*; *assault and* ~ ✕ tätlicher Angriff.

battle ['bætl] **1.** Schlacht *f (of bei)*;

2. streiten, kämpfen; ~ax(e)
Streitaxt f; F Xanthippe f; ~field
Schlachtfeld n; ~ments [~lmənts]
pl. Zinnen f/pl.; ~plane ✕ Kriegs-
flugzeug n; ~ship ✕ Schlacht-
schiff n.

Bavarian [bə'veəriən] 1. bay(e)-
risch; 2. Bayer(in).

bawdy ['bɔːdi] unzüchtig.

bawl [bɔːl] brüllen; johlen, grölen;
~ out auf~, losbrüllen.

bay[1] [bei] 1. rotbraun; 2. Braune(r)
m (Pferd).

bay[2] [~] Bai f, Bucht f; Erker m.

bay[3] [~] Lorbeer m.

bay[4] [~] 1. bellen, anschlagen;
2. stand at ~ sich verzweifelt
wehren; bring to ~ Wild etc. stellen.

bayonet ✕ ['beiənit] 1. Bajonett n;
2. mit dem Bajonett niederstoßen.

bayou Am. ['baiu:] sumpfiges
Nebenarm.

bay window ['bei'windou] Erker-
fenster n; Am. sl. Vorbau m
(Bauch).

baza(a)r [bə'zɑː] Basar m.

be [biː, bi] (irr.) 1. v/i. sein; there
is od. are es gibt; here you are again!
da haben wir's wieder!; ~ about beschäftigt sein mit; ~ at s.th. et.
vorhaben; ~ off aus sein; sich fortmachen; 2. v/aux.1 ~ reading beim
Lesen sein, gerade lesen; I am to
inform you ich soll Ihnen mitteilen;
3. v/aux. mit p.p. zur Bildung des
Passivs: werden.

beach [biːtʃ] 1. Strand m; 2. ⊕ auf
den Strand setzen od. ziehen;
~comber ['biːtʃkoumə] fig. Nichtstuer m.

beacon ['biːkən] Blinklicht n;
Leuchtfeuer n, Leuchtturm m.

bead [biːd] Perle f; Tropfen m;
Visier-Korn n; ~s pl. a. Rosenkranz m.

beak [biːk] Schnabel m; Tülle f.

beaker ['biːkə] Becher(glas n) m.

beam [biːm] 1. Balken m; Waage-
balken m; Strahl m; Glanz m;
Radio: Richtstrahl m; 2. (aus-)
strahlen.

bean [biːn] Bohne f; Am. sl. Birne f
(Kopf); full of ~s F lebensprühend.

bear[1] [beə] Bär m; ✝ Baissier m.

bear[2] [~] (irr.) v/t. tragen; hervorbringen, gebären; Liebe etc. hegen;
ertragen; ~ down überwältigen; ~
out unterstützen, bestätigen; v/i.
tragen; fruchtbar od. trächtig sein;
leiden, dulden; ~ up standhalten,
fest bleiben; ~ (up)on einwirken auf
(acc.); bring to ~ zur Anwendung
bringen, einwirken lassen, Druck
etc. ausüben.

beard [biəd] 1. Bart m; ♀ Granne f;
2. v/t. j-m entgegentreten, trotzen.

bearer ['beərə] Träger(in); Über-
bringer(in), Wechsel-Inhaber(in).

bearing ['beəriŋ] (Er)Tragen n;

Betragen n; Beziehung f; Richtung f.

beast [biːst] Vieh n, Tier n; Bestie
f; ~ly ['biːstli] viehisch; scheußlich.

beat [biːt] 1. (irr.) v/t. schlagen;
prügeln; besiegen, Am. F j-m zuvorkommen; übertreffen; Am. F
betrügen; ~ it! Am. sl. hau ab!;
~ the band Am. F wichtig od.
großartig sein; ~ a retreat den
Rückzug antreten; ~ one's way Am.
F sich durchschlagen; ~ up auf-
treiben; v/i. schlagen; ~ about the
bush wie die Katze um den heißen
Brei herumgehen; 2. Schlag m;
♪ Takt(schlag) m; Pulsschlag m;
Runde f, Revier n e-s Schutz-
mannes etc.; Am. sensationelle
Erstmeldung e-r Zeitung; 3. F baff,
verblüfft; ~en ['biːtn] p.p. von
beat 1; (aus)getreten (Weg).

beatitude [biː(ː)'ætitjuːd] (Glück-)
Seligkeit f.

beatnik ['biːtnik] Beatnik m, junger
Antikonformist und Bohemien.

beau [bou] Stutzer m; Anbeter m.

beautiful □ ['bjuːtəful] schön.

beautify ['bjuːtifai] verschönern.

beauty ['bjuːti] Schönheit f; Sleeping ♀ Dornrös-chen n; ~ parlo(u)r,
~ shop Schönheitssalon m.

beaver ['biːvə] Biber m; Biberpelz m.

becalm [bi'kɑːm] beruhigen.

became [bi'keim] pret. von become.

because [bi'kɔz] weil; ~ of wegen.

beckon ['bekən] (j-m zu)winken.

becom|e [bi'kʌm] (irr.) v/i. werden
(of aus); v/t. anstehen, ziemen
(dat.); sich schicken für; kleiden
(Hut etc.); ~ing □ [~miŋ] passend;
schicklich; kleidsam.

bed [bed] 1. Bett n; Lager n e-s
Tieres; ♀ Beet n; Unterlage f;
2. betten.

bed-clothes ['bedklouðz] pl. Bett-
wäsche f.

bedding ['bediŋ] Bettzeug n; Streu f.

bedevil [bi'devl] behexen; quälen.

bedlam ['bedləm] Tollhaus n.

bed|rid(den) ['bedrid(n)] bett-
lägerig; ~room Schlafzimmer n;
~spread Bett-, Tagesdecke f;
~stead Bettstelle f; ~time Schla-
fenszeit f.

bee [biː] zo. Biene f; Am. nachbar-
liches Treffen; Wettbewerb m;
have a ~ in one's bonnet F e-e fixe
Idee haben.

beech ♀ [biːtʃ] Buche f; ~nut Buch-
ecker f.

beef [biːf] 1. Rindfleisch n; 2. Am.
F nörgeln; ~tea Fleischbrühe f;
~y ['biːfi] fleischig; kräftig.

bee|hive ['biːhaiv] Bienenkorb m,
-stock m; ~keeper Bienenzüchter
m; ~line kürzester Weg; make a
~ for Am. schnurstracks losgehen
auf (acc.).

been [biːn, bin] *p.p. von* be.

beer [biə] Bier *n*; *small* ~ Dünnbier *n*. [Bete *f*.]

beet ⚶ [biːt] (Runkel)Rübe *f*,

beetle[1] ['biːtl] Käfer *m*.

beetle[2] [~] 1. überhängend; buschig (*Brauen*); 2. *v/i*. überhängen.

beetroot ['biːtruːt] rote Rübe.

befall [bi'fɔːl] [*irr.* (*fall*)] *v/t.* zustoßen (*dat.*); *v/i.* sich ereignen.

befit [bi'fit] sich schicken für.

before [bi'fɔː] 1. *adv. Raum:* vorn; voran; *Zeit* vorher, früher; schon (früher); 2. *cj.* bevor, ehe, bis; 3. *prp.* vor; **~hand** vorher, zuvor; voraus (*with dat.*).

befriend [bi'frend] sich *j-m* freundlich erweisen.

beg [beg] *v/t. et.* erbetteln; erbitten (*of* von); *j-n* bitten; ~ *the question* um den Kern der Frage herumgehen; *v/i* betteln; bitten; betteln gehen, sich gestatten.

began [bi'gæn] *pret. von* begin.

beget [bi'get] [*irr* (*get*)] (er)zeugen.

beggar ['begə] 1. Bettler(in); F Kerl *m*, zum Bettler machen; *fig.* übertreffen; *it ~s all description* es spottet jeder Beschreibung.

begin [bi'gin] [*irr*] beginnen (*at* bei, *mit*); **~ner** [~nə] Anfänger(in); **~ning** [~niŋ] Beginn *m*, Anfang *m*.

begone [bi'gɔn] fort!, F pack dich!

begot [bi'gɔt] *pret. von* beget; **~ten** [~tn] 1. *p.p. von* beget; 2. *adj.* erzeugt.

begrudge [bi'grʌdʒ] mißgönnen.

beguile [bi'gail] täuschen; betrügen (*of, out of* um); *Zeit* vertreiben.

begun [bi'gʌn] *p.p. von* begin.

behalf [bi'hɑːf] *on od.* in ~ *of* im Namen von; um (*gen.*) willen.

behav|e [bi'heiv] sich benehmen; **~io(u)r** [~vjə] Benehmen *n*, Betragen *n*.

behead [bi'hed] enthaupten.

behind [bi'haind] 1. *adv.* hinten; dahinter; zurück; 2. *prp.* hinter; **~hand** zurück, im Rückstand.

behold [bi'hould] [*irr* (*hold*)] 1. erblicken; 2. *siehe* (*da*)!; **~en** [~dən] verpflichtet, verbunden.

behoof [bi'huːf] *to* (*for, on*) (*the*) ~ *of in j-s* Interesse, um *j-s* willen.

behoove *Am* [bi'huːv] = behove.

behove [bi'houv] *it* ~*s s.o. to inf.* es ist *j-s* Pflicht, zu *inf.*

being ['biːiŋ] Da)Sein *n*; Wesen *n*; *in* ~ lebend, wirklich(vorhanden).

belabo(u)r c [bi'leibə] verbleuen.

belated [bi'leitid] verspätet.

belch [beltʃ] 1. rülpsen; ausspeien; 2. Rülpsen *n*, Ausbruch *m*.

beleaguer [bi'liːgə] belagern.

belfry ['belfri] Glockenturm *m*, **~stuhl** *m*. [2. Belgier(in).\]

Belgian ['beldʒən] 1. belgisch;\]

belie [bi'lai] Lügen strafen.

belief [bi'liːf] Glaube *m* (*in an acc.*).

believable [bi'liːvəbl] glaubhaft.

believe [bi'liːv] glauben (*in an acc.*); **~r** [~və] Gläubige(r *m*) *f*.

belittle *fig.* [bi'litl] verkleinern.

bell [bel] Glocke *f*, Klingel *f*; **~boy** *Am.* ['belbɔi] Hotelpage *m*.

belle [bel] Schöne *f*, Schönheit *f*.

belles-lettres ['bel'letr] *pl.* Belletristik *f*, schöne Literatur.

bellhop *Am. sl.* ['belhɔp] Hotelpage *m*.

bellied ['belid] bauchig.

belligerent [bi'lidʒərənt] 1. kriegführend; 2. kriegführendes Land.

bellow ['belou] 1. ˈbrüllen; 2. Gebrüll *n*; **~s** *pl* Blasebalg *m*.

belly ['beli] 1. Bauch *m*; 2. (sich) bauchen; (an)schwellen.

belong [bi'lɔŋ] an)gehören; ~ *to* gehören *dat. od.* zu; sich gehören für; *j-m* gebühren; **~ings** [~niŋz] *pl.* Habseligkeiten *f/pl.*

beloved [bi'lʌvd] 1. geliebt; 2. Geliebte(r *m*) *f*.

below [bi'lou] 1. *adv.* unten; 2. *prp.* unter.

belt [belt] 1. Gürtel *m*; ⚔ Koppel *n*; Zone *f*, Bezirk *m*; ⊕ Treibriemen *m*; 2. umgürten; ~ *out Am.* F herausschmettern, loslegen (*singen*).

bemoan [bi'moun] betrauern, beklagen.

bench [bentʃ] Bank *f*; Richterbank *f*; Gerichtshof *m*; Arbeitstisch *m*.

bend [bend] 1. Biegung *f*, Kurve *f*; ⚓ Seemannsknoten *m*; 2. [*irr.*] (sich) biegen; *Geist etc.* richten (*to, on auf acc.*); (sich) beugen; sich neigen (*to vor dat.*).

beneath [bi'niːθ] = below.

benediction [beni'dikʃən] Segen *m*.

benefact|ion [beni'fækʃən] Wohltat *f*; **~or** ['benifæktə] Wohltäter *m*.

beneficen|ce [bi'nefisəns] Wohltätigkeit *f*; **~t** [~nt] wohltätig.

beneficial [beni'fiʃəl] wohltuend; zuträglich, nützlich.

benefit ['benifit] 1. Wohltat *f*; Nutzen *m*, Vorteil *m*; Wohltätigkeitsveranstaltung *f*, Wohlfahrts-) Unterstützung *f*; 2. nützen; begünstigen; Nutzen ziehen.

benevolen|ce [bi'nevələns] Wohlwollen *n*; **~t** [~nt] wohlwollend; gütig, mildherzig.

benign [bi'nain] freundlich, gütig; zuträglich; ⚕ gutartig.

bent [bent] 1. *pret. u. p.p. von* bend 2; ~ *on versessen auf* (*acc.*); 2. Hang *m*; Neigung *f*.

benzene ⚗ ['benziːn] Benzol *n*.

benzine ⚗ ['benziːn] Benzin *n*.

bequeath [bi'kwiːð] vermachen.

bequest [bi'kwest] Vermächtnis *n*.

bereave [bi'riːv] [*irr.*] berauben.

bereft [bi'reft] *pret. u. p.p. von* bereave.

beret ['berei] Baskenmütze *f*.

berry ['beri] Beere f.

berth [bə:θ] 1. ♏ Ankergrund m; Koje f; fig. (gute) Stelle; 2. vor Anker gehen.

beseech [bi'si:tʃ] [irr.] ersuchen; bitten; um et. bitten; flehen.

beset [bi'set] [irr. (set)] umgeben; bedrängen; verfolgen.

beside prp. [bi'said] neben; weitab von; ~ o.s. außer sich (with vor); ~ the point, ~ the question nicht zur Sache gehörig; ~s [‿dz] 1. adv. außerdem; 2. prp. abgesehen von, außer.

besiege [bi'si:dʒ] belagern.

besmear [bi'smiə] beschmieren.

besom ['bizəm] (Reisig)Besen m.

besought [bi'sɔ:t] pret. u. p.p. von beseech.

bespatter [bi'spætə] (be)spritzen.

bespeak [bi'spi:k] [irr. (speak)] vorbestellen; verraten, (an)zeigen; bespoke tailor Maßschneider m.

best [best] 1. adj. best; höchst; größt, meist; ~ man Brautführer m; 2. adv. am besten, aufs beste; 3. Beste(r m, -s n) f, Besten pl.; to the ~ of ... nach bestem ...; make the ~ of tun, was man kann, mit; at ~ im besten Falle.

bestial ['bestjəl] tierisch, viehisch.

bestow [bi'stou] geben, schenken, verleihen (on, upon dat.).

bet [bet] 1. Wette f; 2. [irr.] wetten; you ~ F sicherlich.

betake [bi'teik] [irr. (take)]: ~ o.s. to sich begeben nach; fig. s-e Zuflucht nehmen zu.

bethink [bi'θiŋk] [irr. (think)]: ~ o.s. sich besinnen (of auf acc.); ~ o.s. to inf. sich in den Kopf setzen zu inf.

betimes [bi'taimz] beizeiten.

betray [bi'trei] verraten (a. fig.); verleiten; ~er [‿iə] Verräter(in).

betrothal [bi'trouðəl] Verlobung f.

better ['betə] 1. adj. besser; he is ~ es geht ihm besser; 2. Bessere(s) n; ~s pl. Höherstehenden pl., Vorgesetzten pl.; get the ~ of die Oberhand gewinnen über (acc.); überwinden; 3. adv. besser; mehr; so much the ~ desto besser; you had ~ go es wäre besser, wenn du gingest; 4. v/t. (ver)bessern; v/i. sich bessern; ~ment [‿əmənt] Verbesserung f.

between [bi'twi:n] ⟨a. betwixt [bi'twikst]⟩ 1. adv. dazwischen; 2. prp. zwischen, unter.

bevel ['bevəl] schräg, schief.

beverage ['bevəridʒ] Getränk n.

bevy ['bevi] Schwarm m; Schar f.

bewail [bi'weil] be-, wehklagen.

beware [bi'weə] sich hüten (of vor).

bewilder [bi'wildə] irremachen; verwirren; bestürzt machen; ~ment [‿əmənt] Verwirrung f; Bestürzung f.

bewitch [bi'witʃ] bezaubern, behexen.

beyond [bi'jɔnd] 1. adv. darüber hinaus; 2. prp. jenseits, über (... hinaus); mehr als; außer.

bi... [bai] zwei ...

bias ['baiəs] 1. adj. u. adv. schief, schräg; 2. Neigung f; Vorurteil n; 3. beeinflussen; ~sed befangen.

bib [bib] (Sabber)Lätzchen n.

Bible ['baibl] Bibel f.

biblical ☐ ['biblikəl] biblisch; Bibel...

bibliography [bibli'ɔgrəfi] Bibliographie f.

bicarbonate ♏ [bai'ka:bənit] doppeltkohlensaures Natron.

biceps ['baiseps] Bizeps m.

bicker ['bikə] (sich) zanken; flakkern; plätschern; prasseln.

bicycle ['baisikl] 1. Fahrrad n; 2. radfahren, radeln.

bid [bid] 1. [irr.] gebieten, befehlen; (ent)bieten; Karten: reizen; ~ fair versprechen; ~ farewell Lebewohl sagen; 2. Gebot n, Angebot n; ~den ['bidn] p.p. von bid 1.

bide [baid] [irr.]: ~ one's time den rechten Augenblick abwarten.

biennial [bai'eniəl] zweijährig.

bier [biə] (Toten)Bahre f.

big [big] groß; erwachsen; schwanger; F wichtig(tuerisch); ~ business Großunternehmertum n; ~ shot F hohes Tier; ~ stick Am. Macht (-entfaltung) f; talk ~ den Mund vollnehmen.

bigamy ['bigəmi] Doppelehe f.

bigot ['bigət] Frömmler(in); blinder Anhänger; ~ry [‿tri] Frömmelei f.

bigwig F ['bigwig] hohes Tier (P.).

bike F [baik] (Fahr)Rad n.

bilateral ☐ [bai'lætərəl] zweiseitig.

bile [bail] Galle f (a. fig.).

bilious ☐ ['biljəs] gallig (a. fig.).

bill¹ [bil] Schnabel m; Spitze f.

bill² [‿] 1. Gesetzentwurf m; Klage-, Rechtsschrift f; a. ~ of exchange Wechsel m; Zettel m; Am. Banknote f; ~ of fare Speisekarte f; ~ of lading Seefrachtbrief m, Konnossement n; ~ of sale Kaufvertrag m; ♀ of Rights englische Freiheitsurkunde (1689); Am. die ersten 10 Zusatzartikel zur Verfassung der USA; 2. (durch Anschlag) ankündigen.

billboard Am. ['bilbɔ:d] Anschlagbrett n.

billfold Am. ['bilfould] Brieftasche f für Papiergeld.

billiards ['biljədz] pl. od. sg. Billiard(spiel) n.

billion ['biljən] Billion f; Am. Milliarde f.

billow ['bilou] 1. Woge f (a. fig.); 2. wogen; ~y [‿oui] wogend.

billy Am. ['bili] (Gummi)Knüppel m.

bin [bin] Kasten *m*, Behälter *m*.

bind [baind] [*irr.*] *v/t.* (an-, ein-, um-, auf-, fest-, ver)binden; verpflichten; *Handel* abschließen; *Saum* einfassen; *v/i.* binden; **~er** ['baində] Binder *m*; Binde *f*; **~ing** [⁓diŋ] 1. bindend; 2. Binden *n*; Einband *m*; Einfassung *f*.

binocular [bi'nɔkjulə] *mst* **~s** *pl.* Feldstecher *m*, Fern-, Opernglas *n*.

biography [bai'ɔgrəfi] Biographie *f*.

biology [bai'ɔlədʒi] Biologie *f*.

biped *zo.* ['baiped] Zweifüßer *m*.

birch [bə:tʃ] 1. ♀ Birke *f*; (Birken-) Rute *f*; 2. mit der Rute züchtigen.

bird [bə:d] Vogel *m*; **~'s-eye** ['bə:dzai]: **~** view Vogelperspektive *f*.

birth [bə:θ] Geburt *f*; Ursprung *m*; Entstehung *f*; Herkunft *f*; *bring to ~* entstehen lassen, veranlassen; *give ~ to* gebären, zur Welt bringen; **~ control** Geburtenregelung *f*; **~day** ['bə:θdei] Geburtstag *m*; **~place** Geburtsort *m*.

biscuit ['biskit] Zwieback *m*; Keks *m*, *n*, Biskuit *n* (*Porzellan*).

bishop ['biʃəp] Bischof *m*; Läufer *m* *im Schach*; **~ric** [⁓prik] Bistum *n*.

bison *zo.* ['baisn] Wisent *m*.

bit [bit] 1. Bißchen *n*, Stückchen *n*; Gebiß *n am Zaum*; *Schlüssel*-Bart *m*; *a* (*little*) **~** ein (kleines) bißchen; 2. zäumen; zügeln; 3. *pret. von* bite 2.

bitch [bitʃ] Hündin *f*; V Hure *f*.

bite [bait] 1. Beißen *n*; Biß *m*; Bissen *m*; ⊕ Fassen *n*; 2. [*irr.*] (an)beißen; brennen (*Pfeffer*); schneiden (*Kälte*); ⊕ fassen; *fig.* verletzen.

bitten ['bitn] *p.p. von* bite 2.

bitter ['bitə] 1. ⌐ bitter; streng; *fig.* verbittert; 2. **~s** *pl.* Magenbitter *m*.

biz F [biz] Geschäft *n*.

blab F [blæb] (aus)schwatzen.

black [blæk] 1. ⌐ schwarz; dunkel; finster; **~** eye blaues Auge; 2. schwärzen; wichsen; **~** out verdunkeln; 3. Schwarz *n*; Schwärze *f*; Schwarze(r *m*) *f* (*Neger*); **~amoor** ['blækəmuə] Neger *m*; **~berry** Brombeere *f*; **~bird** Amsel *f*; **~board** Wandtafel *f*; **~en** [⁓kən] *v/t.* schwärzen; *fig.* anschwärzen; *v/i.* schwarz werden; **~guard** ['blægɑ:d] 1. Lump *m*, Schuft *m*; 2. ⌐ schuftig; **~head** ♂ Mitesser *m*; **~ing** [⁓kiŋ] Schuhwichse *f*; **~ish** ⌐ [⁓iʃ] schwärzlich; **~jack** 1. *bsd. Am.* Totschläger *m* (*Instrument*); 2. niederknüppeln; **~leg** Betrüger *m*; **~letter** *typ.* Fraktur *f*; **~mail** 1. Erpressung *f*; 2. *j-n* erpressen; **~ market** schwarzer Markt; **~ness** [⁓knis] Schwärze *f*; **~out** Verdunkelung *f*; **~ pudding** Blutwurst *f*; **~smith** Grobschmied *m*.

bladder *anat.* ['blædə] Blase *f*.

blade [bleid] Blatt *n*, ♀ Halm *m*; *Säge-*, *Schulter-* etc. Blatt *n*; Propellerflügel *m*; Klinge *f*.

blame [bleim] 1. Tadel *m*; Schuld *f*; 2. tadeln; *be to ~ for* schuld sein an (*dat.*); **~ful** ['bleimful] tadelnswert; **~less** ⌐ [⁓mlis] tadellos.

blanch [blɑ:ntʃ] bleichen; erbleichen (lassen); **~** over beschönigen.

bland ⌐ [blænd] mild, sanft.

blank [blæŋk] 1. ⌐ blank; leer; unausgefüllt; unbeschrieben; ✝ Blanko...; verdutzt; **~** cartridge ✕ Platzpatrone *f*; 2. Weiße *n*; Leere *f*; leerer Raum; Lücke *f*; unbeschriebenes Blatt, Formular *n*; Niete *f*.

blanket ['blæŋkit] 1. Wolldecke *f*; *wet ~* *fig.* Dämpfer *m*; Spielverderber *m*; 2. (mit e-r Wolldecke) zudecken; 3. *Am.* umfassend, Gesamt...

blare [bleə] schmettern; grölen.

blasphem|e [blæs'fi:m] lästern (*against* über *acc.*); **~y** ['blæsfimi] Gotteslästerung *f*.

blast [blɑ:st] 1. Windstoß *m*; Ton *m e-s Blasinstruments*; ⊕ Gebläse (-luft *f*) *n*; Luftdruck *m e-r Explosion*; ♀ Meltau *m*; 2. (in die Luft) sprengen; zerstören (*a. fig.*); **~** (*it*)! verdammt; **~furnace** ⊕ ['blɑ:st'fə:nis] Hochofen *m*.

blatant ⌐ ['bleitənt] lärmend.

blather *Am.* ['blæðə] schwätzen.

blaze [bleiz] 1. Flamme(n *pl.*) *f*; Feuer *n*; **~s** *pl. sl.* Teufel *m*, Hölle *f*; heller Schein; *fig.* Ausbruch *m*; *go to ~s!* zum Teufel mit dir!; 2. *v/i.* brennen, flammen, lodern; leuchten; *v/t.* **~** abroad ausposaunen; **~r** ['bleizə] Blazer *m*.

blazon ['bleizn] Wappen(kunde *f*)*n*.

bleach [bli:tʃ] bleichen; **~er** ['bli:tʃə] Bleicher(in); *mst* **~s** *pl. Am.* nichtüberdachte Zuschauerplätze.

bleak ⌐ [bli:k] öde, kahl; rauh; *fig.* trüb, freudlos, finster.

blear [bliə] 1. trüb; 2. trüben; **~eyed** ['bliəraid] triefäugig.

bleat [bli:t] 1. Blöken *n*; 2. blöken.

bleb [bleb] Bläs-chen, Pustel *f*.

bled [bled] *pret. u. p.p. von* bleed.

bleed [bli:d] [*irr.*] *v/i.* bluten; *v/t.* zur Ader lassen; *fig.* schröpfen; **~ing** ['bli:diŋ] 1. Bluten *n*; Aderlaß *m*; 2. *sl.* verflixt.

blemish ['blemiʃ] 1. Fehler *m*; Makel *m*, Schande *f*; 2. verunstalten; brandmarken.

blench [blentʃ] *v/i.* zurückschrecken; *v/t.* die Augen schließen vor.

blend [blend] 1. [*irr.*] (sich) (ver)mischen; *Wein etc.* verschneiden; 2. Mischung *f*; ✝ Verschnitt *m*.

blent [blent] *pret. u. p.p. von* blend 1.

bless [bles] segnen; preisen; be-

glücken; ~ me! herrje!; ~ed □ [pret. u. p.p. blest; adj. 'blesid] glückselig; gesegnet; ~ing [~siŋ] Segen m.

blew [blu:] pret. von blow² u. blow³1.

blight [blait] 1. ♀ Mehltau m; fig. Gifthauch m; 2. vernichten.

blind □ [blaind] 1. blind (fig. to gegen); geheim; nicht erkennbar; ~ alley Sackgasse f; ~ly fig. blindlings; 2. Blende f; Fenster-Vorhang m, Jalousie f; Am. Versteck n; Vorwand m; 3. blenden; verblenden (to gegen); abblenden; ~fold ['blaindfould] 1. blindlings; 2. j-m die Augen verbinden; ~worm Blindschleiche f.

blink [bliŋk] 1. Blinzeln n; Schimmer m; 2. v/i. blinzeln; blinken; schimmern; v/t. absichtlich übersehen; ~er ['bliŋkə] Scheuklappe f.

bliss [blis] Seligkeit f, Wonne f.

blister ['blistə] 1. Blase f (auf der Haut, im Lack); Zugpflaster n; 2. Blasen bekommen od. ziehen (auf dat.).

blithe □ mst poet. [blaið] lustig.

blizzard ['blizəd] Schneesturm m.

bloat [blout] aufblasen; aufschwellen; ~er ['bloutə] Bückling m.

block [blok] 1. (Häuser-, Schreib-etc.)Block m; Klotz m; Druckstock m; Verstopfung f, Stockung f; 2. formen; verhindern; ~ in entwerfen, skizzieren; mst ~ up (ab-, ver-) sperren; blockieren.

blockade [blo'keid] 1. Blockade f; 2. blockieren.

block|head ['blokhed] Dummkopf m; ~ letters Druckschrift f.

blond(e f) [blond] 1. blond; 2. Blondine f.

blood [blʌd] Blut n; fig. Blut n; Abstammung f; in cold ~ kalten Blutes, kaltblütig; ~-curdling ['blʌdkə:dliŋ] haarsträubend; ~horse Vollblutpferd n; ~shed Blutvergießen n; ~shot blutunterlaufen; ~thirsty blutdürstig; ~vessel Blutgefäß n; ~y □ ['blʌdi] blutig; blutdürstig.

bloom [blu:m] 1. Blüte f; Reif m auf Früchten; fig. Schmelz m; 2. (er-) blühen (a. fig.).

blossom ['blosəm] 1. Blüte f; 2. blühen.

blot [blot] 1. Klecks m; fig. Makel m; 2. v/t. beklecksen, beflecken; (ab-) löschen; ausstreichen; v/i. klecksen.

blotch [blotʃ] Pustel f; Fleck m.

blotter ['blotə] Löscher m; Am. Protokollbuch n. [Löschpapier n.]

blotting-paper ['blotiŋpeipə]]

blouse [blauz] Bluse f.

blow¹ [blou] Schlag m, Stoß m.

blow² [~] irr.] blühen.

blow³ [~] 1. [irr.] v/i. blasen; wehen; schnaufen; ~ up in die Luft fliegen; v/t. (weg- etc.)blasen; wehen; ♪

durchbrennen; ~ one's nose sich die Nase putzen; ~ up sprengen; 2. Blasen n, Wehen n; ~er ['blouə] Bläser m.

blown [bloun] p.p. von blow² und blow³ 1.

blow|-out mot. ['blouaut] Reifenpanne f; ~pipe Gebläsebrenner m.

bludgeon ['blʌdʒən] Knüppel m.

blue [blu:] 1. □ blau; F trüb, schwermütig; 2. Blau n; 3. blau färben; blauen; ~bird ['blu:bə:d] amerikanische Singdrossel; ~ laws Am. strenge (puritanische) Gesetze; ~s [blu:z] pl. Trübsinn m; ♪ Blues m.

bluff [blʌf] 1. □ schroff; steil; derb; 2. Steilufer n; Irreführung f; 3. bluffen, irreführen.

bluish ['blu(:)iʃ] bläulich.

blunder ['blʌndə] 1. Fehler m, Schnitzer m; 2. e-n Fehler machen; stolpern; stümpern; verpfuschen.

blunt [blʌnt] 1. □ stumpf (a. fig.); plump, grob, derb; 2. abstumpfen.

blur [blə:] 1. Fleck(en) m; fig. Verschwommenheit f; 2. v/t. beflecken; verwischen; Sinn trüben.

blush [blʌʃ] 1. Schamröte f; Erröten n; flüchtiger Blick; 2. erröten; (sich) röten.

bluster ['blʌstə] 1. Brausen n, Getöse n; Prahlerei f; 2. brausen; prahlen.

boar [bo:] Eber m; hunt. Keiler m.

board [bo:d] 1. (Anschlag)Brett n; Konferenztisch m; Ausschuß m; Gremium n; Behörde f; Verpflegung f; Pappe f; on ~ a train Am. in e-m Zug; ♀ of Trade Handelsministerium n; 2. v/t. dielen, verschalen; beköstigen; an Bord gehen; ♣ entern; bsd. Am. einsteigen in (ein Fahr- od. Flugzeug); v/i. in Kost sein; ~er ['bo:də] Kostgänger(in); Internatsschüler(in); ~ing-house ['bo:diŋhaus] Pension f; ~ing-school ['bo:diŋsku:l] Internatsschule f; ~walk bsd. Am. Strandpromenade f.

boast [boust] 1. Prahlerei f; 2. (of, about) sich rühmen (gen.), prahlen (mit); ~ful □ ['boustful] prahlerisch.

boat [bout] 1. Boot n; Schiff n; ~ing ['boutiŋ] Bootfahrt f.

bob [bob] 1. Quaste f; Ruck m; Knicks m; Schopf m; sl. Schilling m; 2. v/t. Haar stutzen; ~bed hair Bubikopf m; v/i. springen, tanzen; knicksen.

bobbin ['bobin] Spule f (a. ♀).

bobble Am. F ['bobl] Fehler m.

bobby sl. ['bobi] Schupo m, Polizist m.

bobsleigh ['bobslei] Bob(sleigh) m (Rennschlitten).

bode¹ [boud] prophezeien.

bode² [~] pret. von bide.

bodice ['bɔdis] Mieder n; Taille f.
bodily ['bɔdili] körperlich.
body ['bɔdi] Körper m, Leib m; Leichnam m; Körperschaft f; Hauptteil m; mot. Karosserie f; ✗ Truppenkörper m; ~guard Leibwache f.
Boer ['bouə] Bure m; attr. Buren...
bog [bɔg] 1. Sumpf m, Moor n; 2. im Schlamm versenken.
boggle ['bɔgl] stutzen; pfuschen.
bogus ['bougəs] falsch; Schwindel...
boil [bɔil] 1. kochen, sieden; (sich) kondensieren; 2. Sieden n; Beule f, Geschwür n; ~er ['bɔilə] (Dampf-)Kessel m.
boisterous □ ['bɔistərəs] ungestüm; heftig, laut; lärmend.
bold □ [bould] kühn; keck, dreist; steil; typ. fett; make ~ sich erkühnen; ~ness ['bouldnis] Kühnheit f; Keckheit f, Dreistigkeit f.
bolster ['boulstə] 1. Kopfkeil m; Unterlage f; 2. polstern; (unter-)stützen.
bolt [boult] 1. Bolzen m; Riegel m; Blitz(strahl) m; Ausreißen n; 2. adv. ~ upright kerzengerade; 3. v/t. verriegeln; F hinunterschlingen; sieben; v/i. eilen; durchgehen (Pferd); Am. pol. abtrünnig werden; ~er ['boultə] Ausreißer(in).
bomb [bɔm] 1. Bombe f; 2. mit Bomben belegen.
bombard [bɔm'ba:d] bombardieren.
bombastic [bɔm'bæstik] schwülstig.
bomb-proof ['bɔmpru:f] bombensicher.
bond [bɔnd] Band n; Fessel f; Bündnis n; Schuldschein m; ✝ Obligation f; in ~ ✝ unter Zollverschluß; ~age ['bɔndidʒ] Hörigkeit f; Knechtschaft f; ~(s)man [~d(z)mən] Leibeigene(r) m.
bone [boun] 1. Knochen m; Gräte f; ~s pl. a. Gebeine n/pl.; ~ of contention Zankapfel m; make no ~s about F nicht lange fackeln mit; 2. die Knochen auslösen (aus); aus-, entgräten.
bonfire ['bɔnfaiə] Freudenfeuer n.
bonnet ['bɔnit] Haube f, Schute(nhut m) f; ⊕ (Motor)Haube f.
bonus ✝ ['bounəs] Prämie f; Gratifikation f; Zulage f.
bony ['bouni] knöchern; knochig.
boob Am. [bu:b] Dummkopf m.
booby ['bu:bi] Tölpel m.
book [buk] 1. Buch n; Heft n; Liste f; Block m; 2. buchen; eintragen; Fahrkarte etc. lösen; ~ a Platz etc. bestellen; Gepäck aufgeben; ~burner Am. F ['bukbə:nə] intoleranter Mensch; ~case Bücherschrank m; ~ing-clerk ['bukiŋkla:k] Schalterbeamt|e(r) m, -in f; ~ing-office ['bukiŋɔfis] Fahrkartenausgabe f, -schalter m; thea.

Kasse f; ~ish □ [~iʃ] gelehrt; ~keeping Buchführung f; ~let ['buklit] Büchlein n; Broschüre f; ~seller Buchhändler m.
boom¹ [bu:m] 1. ✝ Aufschwung m, Hochkonjunktur f, Hausse f; Reklamerummel m; 2. in die Höhe treiben od. gehen; für et. Reklame machen.
boom² [~] brummen; dröhnen.
boon¹ [bu:n] Segen m, Wohltat f.
boon² [~] freundlich, munter.
boor fig. [buə] Bauer m, Lümmel m; ~ish □ ['buəriʃ] bäuerisch, lümmel-, flegelhaft.
boost [bu:st] heben; verstärken (a. ∉); Reklame machen.
boot¹ [bu:t]: to ~ obendrein.
boot² [~] Stiefel m; Kofferraum m; ~black Am. ['bu:tblæk] = shoe-black; ~ee ['bu:ti:] Damen-Halbstiefel m.
booth [bu:ð] (Markt- etc.)Bude f; Wahlzelle f; Am. Fernsprechzelle f.
boot|lace ['bu:tleis] Schnürsenkel m; ~legger Am. [~legə] Alkoholschmuggler m.
booty ['bu:ti] Beute f, Raub m.
border ['bɔ:də] 1. Rand m, Saum m; Grenze f; Einfassung f; Rabatte f; 2. einfassen; grenzen (upon an acc.).
bore¹ [bɔ:] 1. Bohrloch n, Kaliber n; fig. langweiliger Mensch; Plage f; 2. bohren; langweilen; belästigen.
bore² [~] pret. von bear².
born [bɔ:n] p.p. von bear² gebären.
borne [bɔ:n] p.p. von bear² tragen.
borough ['bʌrə] Stadt(teil m) f; Am. a. Wahlbezirk m von New York City; municipal ~ Stadtgemeinde f.
borrow ['bɔrou] borgen, entleihen.
bosom ['buzəm] Busen m; fig. Schoß m.
boss F [bɔs] 1. Boss m, Chef m; bsd. Am. pol. (Partei)Bonze m; 2. leiten; ~y Am. F ['bɔsi] tyrannisch, herrisch.
botany ['bɔtəni] Botanik f.
botch [bɔtʃ] 1. Flicken m; Flickwerk n; 2. flicken; verpfuschen.
both [bouθ] beide(s); ~ ... and sowohl ... als (auch).
bother F ['bɔðə] 1. Plage f; 2. (sich) plagen, (sich) quälen.
bottle ['bɔtl] 1. Flasche f; 2. auf Flaschen ziehen.
bottom ['bɔtəm] 1. Boden m, Grund m; Grundfläche f; Fuß m, Ende n; F Hintern m; fig. Wesen n, Kern m; at the ~ ganz unten; fig. im Grunde; 2. grundlegend, Grund...
bough [bau] Ast m, Zweig m.
bought [bɔ:t] pret. u. p.p. von buy.
boulder ['bouldə] Geröllblock m.
bounce [bauns] 1. Sprung m, Rückprall m; F Aufschneiderei f; Auftrieb m; 2. (hoch)springen; F aufschneiden; ~r ['baunsə] F Mordskerl m; Am. sl. Rausschmeißer m.

bound¹ [baund] **1.** *pret. u. p.p von bind*; **2.** *adj.* verpflichtet; bestimmt, unterwegs (*for nach*).

bound² [~] **1.** Grenze *f*, Schranke *f*; **2.** begrenzen; beschränken.

bound³ [~] **1.** Sprung *m*; **2.** (hoch-)springen; an-, abprallen.

boundary ['baundəri] Grenze *f*.

boundless □ ['baundlis] grenzenlos.

bount|eous □ ['bauntiəs], **~iful** □ [~iful] freigebig; reichlich

bounty ['baunti] Freigebigkeit *f*; Spende *f*; † Prämie *f*.

bouquet [bukei] Bukett *n*, Strauß *m*; Blume *f des Weines*.

bout [baut] *Fecht-*Gang *m*; *Tanz-*Tour *f*; ✗ Anfall *m*; Kraftprobe *f*.

bow¹ [bau] **1.** Verbeugung *f*; **2.** *v/i.* sich (ver)beugen; *v/t.* biegen; beugen.

bow² ⚓ [~] Bug *m*.

bow³ [bou] **1.** Bogen *m*; Schleife *f*; **2.** geigen.

bowdlerize ['baudləraiz] *Text* von anstößigen Stellen reinigen.

bowels ['bauəlz] *pl.* Eingeweide *n*; *das Innere*; *fig.* Herz *n*.

bower ['bauə] Laube *f*.

bowl¹ [boul] Schale *f*, Schüssel *f*; *Pfeifen-*Kopf *m*.

bowl² [~] **1.** Kugel *f*; **~s** *pl.* Bowling *n*; **2.** *v/t.* Ball *etc.* werfen; *v/i.* rollen; kegeln.

box¹ [boks] Buchsbaum *m*; Büchse *f*, Schachtel *f*, Kasten *m*; Koffer *m*; ⊕ Gehäuse *n*; *thea.* Loge *f*; *Abteilung f*; **2.** in Kästen *etc.* tun.

box² [~] **1.** boxen; **2.** ~ *on the ear* Ohrfeige *f*.

Boxing-Day ['boksiŋdei] zweiter Weihnachtsfeiertag.

box|-keeper ['bokski:pə] Logenschließer(in); **~office** Theaterkasse *f*.

boy [boi] Junge *m*, junger Mann; Bursche *m* (*a. Diener*); **~friend** Freund *m*; **~ scout** Pfadfinder *m*; **~hood** ['boihud] Knabenalter *n*; **~ish** □ ['boiiʃ] knabenhaft; kindisch.

brace [breis] **1.** ⊕ Strebe *f*; Stützbalken *m*; Klammer *f*; Paar *n* (*Wild, Geflügel*); **~s** *pl.* Hosenträger *m/pl.*; **2.** absteifen; verankern; (an)spannen; *fig.* stärken.

bracelet ['breislit] Armband *n*.

bracket ['brækit] **1.** ⚐ Konsole *f*; Winkelstütze *f*; *typ.* Klammer *f*; *Leuchter-*Arm *m*; *lower income* ~ niedrige Einkommensstufe; **2.** einklammern; *fig.* gleichstellen.

brackish ['brækiʃ] brackig, salzig.

brag [bræg] **1.** Prahlerei *f*; **2.** prahlen. [**2.** □ prahlerisch.]

braggart ['brægət] **1.** Prahler *m*;

braid [breid] **1.** *Haar-*Flechte *f*; Borte *f*; Tresse *f*; **2.** flechten; mit Borte besetzen.

brain [brein] **1.** Gehirn *n*; Kopf *m*

(*fig. mst ~s = Verstand*); **2.** *j-m* den Schädel einschlagen; **~pan** ['breinpæn] Hirnschale *f*; **~(s)** trust *Am.* [~n(z)trast] Expertenrat *m* (*mst pol.*); **~wave** F Geistesblitz *m*.

brake [breik] **1.** ⊕ Bremse *f*; **2.** bremsen; **~(s)man** ⚙ ['breik(s)-mən] Bremser *m*; *Am.* Schaffner *m*.

bramble ['bræmbl] Brombeerstrauch *m*.

bran [bræn] Kleie *f*.

branch [braːntʃ] **1.** Zweig *m*; Fach *n*; Linie *f des Stammbaumes*; Zweigstelle *f*; **2.** sich ver-, abzweigen.

brand [brænd] **1.** (Feuer)Brand *m*; Brandmal *n*; Marke *f*; Sorte *f*; **2.** einbrennen; brandmarken.

brandish ['brændiʃ] schwingen.

bran(d)-new ['bræn(d)'nju:] nagelneu.

brandy ['brændi] Kognak *m*; Weinbrand *m*.

brass [braːs] Messing *n*; F Unverschämtheit *f*; **~ band** Blechblaskapelle *f*; **~ knuckles** *pl. Am.* Schlagring *m*.

brassière ['bræsiə] Büstenhalter *m*.

brave [breiv] **1.** tapfer; prächtig; **2.** trotzen; mutig begegnen (*dat.*); **~ry** ['breivəri] Tapferkeit *f*; Pracht *f*.

brawl [bro:l] **1.** Krakeel *m*, Krawall *m*; **2.** krakeelen, Krawall machen.

brawny ['bro:ni] muskulös.

bray¹ [brei] **1.** Eselsschrei *m*; **2.** schreien; schmettern; dröhnen.

bray² [~] (zer)stoßen, zerreiben.

brazen □ ['breizn] bronzen; metallisch; *a.* **~faced** unverschämt.

Brazilian [brə'ziljən] **1.** brasilianisch; **2.** Brasilianer(in).

breach [bri:tʃ] **1.** Bruch *m*; *fig.* Verletzung *f*; ✗ Bresche *f*; **2.** e-e Bresche schlagen in (*acc.*).

bread [bred] Brot *n*; *know which side one's* ~ *is buttered* s-n Vorteil (er)kennen.

breadth [bredθ] Breite *f*, Weite *f*, Größe *f des Geistes*; *Tuch-*Bahn *f*.

break [breik] **1.** Bruch *m*; Lücke *f*; Pause *f*; Absatz *m*; † *Am.* (Preis-)Rückgang *m*; *Tages-*Anbruch *m*; *a bad* ~ F e-e Dummheit; Pech *n*; *a lucky* ~ Glück *n*; **2.** [*irr.*] *v/t.* (zer)brechen; unterbrechen; übertreten; *Tier* abrichten; *Bank* sprengen; *Brief* erbrechen; *Tür* aufbrechen; abbrechen; *Vorrat* anbrechen; *Nachricht* schonend mitteilen; ruinieren; ~ *up* zerbrechen; auflösen; *v/i.* (zer)brechen; aus-, los-, an-, auf-, hervorbrechen; umschlagen (*Wetter*); ~ *away* sich losreißen; ~ *down* zs.-brechen; steckenbleiben; versagen; **~able** ['breikəbl] zerbrechlich; **~age** [~kidʒ] (*a.* † *Waren*)Bruch *m*; **~down** Zs.-bruch *m*; Maschinen-

schaden *m*; *mot.* Panne *f*; **~fast**
['brekfəst] **1.** Frühstück *n*; **2.** früh-
stücken; **~up** ['breik'ʌp] Verfall
m; Auflösung *f*; Schulschluß *m*;
~water ['~kwɔːtə] Wellenbrecher
m.

breast [brest] Brust *f*; Busen *m*;
Herz *n*; *make a clean ~ of s.th. et.*
offen gestehen; **~-stroke** ['brest-
strouk] Brustschwimmen *n.*

breath [breθ] Atem(zug) *m*; Hauch
m; *waste one's ~* s-e Worte verschwenden; **~e** [briːð] *v/i.* atmen;
fig. leben; *v/t.* (aus-, ein)atmen;
hauchen; flüstern; **~less** □ ['breθ-
lis] atemlos.

bred [bred] *pret. u. p.p. von*
breed 2.

breeches ['britʃiz] *pl.* Knie-, Reit-
hosen *f/pl.*

breed [briːd] **1.** Zucht *f*; Rasse *f*;
Herkunft *f*; *Am.* Mischling *m bsd.*
weiß-indianisch; **2.** [*irr*] *v/t.* erzeugen; auf-, erziehen; züchten; *v/i.*
sich fortpflanzen; **~er** [*~*'riːdə] Er-
zeuger(in); Züchter(in); **~ing** [~diŋ]
Erziehung *f*; Bildung *f*; (Tier-)
Zucht *f.*

breez|e [briːz] Brise *f*; **~y** ['briːzi]
windig, luftig; frisch, flott.

brethren ['breðrin] *pl.* Brüder *m/pl.*

brevity ['breviti] Kürze *f.*

brew [bruː] **1.** *v/t. u. v/i.* brauen;
zubereiten; *fig.* anzetteln; **2.** Gebräu *n*; **~ery** ['bruəri] Brauerei *f.*

briar ['braiə] = brier.

brib|e [braib] **1.** Bestechung(sgeld
n, -geschenk *n*) *f*; **2.** bestechen;
~ery ['braibəri] Bestechung *f.*

brick [brik] **1.** Ziegel(stein) *m*; *drop*
a ~ sl. ins Fettnäpfchen treten;
2. mauern; **~layer** ['brikleiə] Maurer *m*; **~works** *sg.* Ziegelei *f.*

bridal □ ['braidl] bräutlich; Braut-
...; *~ procession* Brautzug *m.*

bride [braid] Braut *f*; Neuvermählte
f; **~groom** ['braidgrum] Bräutigam
m, Neuvermählte(r) *m*; **~smaid**
[~dzmeid] Brautjungfer *f.*

bridge [bridʒ] **1.** Brücke *f*; **2.** e-e
Brücke schlagen über (*acc.*); *fig.*
überbrücken.

bridle ['braidl] **1.** Zaum *m*; Zügel
m; **2.** *v/t.* (auf)zäumen; zügeln; *v/i.*
a. ~ up den Kopf zurückwerfen;
~-path, **~-road** Reitweg *m.*

brief [briːf] **1.** □ kurz, bündig; **2.** rtg.
schriftliche Instruktion; *hold a ~*
for einstehen für; **~-case** ['briːf-
keis] Aktenmappe *f.*

brier ♣ ['braiə] Dorn-, Hagebutten-
strauch *m*, wilde Rose.

brigade ⚔ [bri'geid] Brigade *f.*

bright □ [brait] hell, glänzend, klar;
lebhaft; gescheit; **~en** ['braitn] *v/t.*
auf-, erhellen; polieren; aufheitern;
v/i. sich aufhellen; **~ness** [~nis]
Helligkeit *f*; Glanz *m*; Klarheit *f*;
Heiterkeit *f*; Aufgewecktheit *f.*

brillian|ce, **~cy** ['briljəns, ~si]
Glanz *m*; **~t** [~nt] **1.** □ glänzend;
prächtig; **2.** Brillant *m.*

brim [brim] **1.** Rand *m*; Krempe *f*;
2. bis zum Rande füllen *od.* voll
sein; **~full**, **~-ful** ['brim'ful] ganz
voll; **~stone** † ['brimstən] Schwefel
m.

brindle(d) ['brindl(d)] scheckig.

brine [brain] Salzwasser *n*, Sole *f.*

bring [briŋ] [*irr*.] bringen; *j.* veranlassen; *Klage* erheben; *Grund etc.*
vorbringen; *~ about*, *~ to* pass zustande bringen; *~ down Preis* herabsetzen; *~ forth* hervorbringen; gebären; *~ home to j.* überzeugen; *~*
round wieder zu sich bringen; *~ up*
auf-, erziehen.

brink [briŋk] Rand *m.*

brisk □ [brisk] lebhaft, munter;
frisch; flink; belebend.

bristl|e ['brisl] **1.** Borste *f*; **2.** (sich)
sträuben; hochfahren, zornig wer-
den; *~ with fig.* starren von; **~ed**,
~y [~li] gesträubt; struppig.

British ['britiʃ] britisch; *the ~ pl.* die
Briten *pl.*; **~er** *bsd. Am.* [~ʃə] Ein-
wohner(in) Großbritanniens.

brittle ['britl] zerbrechlich, spröde.

broach [broutʃ] *Faß* anzapfen; vorbringen; *Thema* anschneiden.

broad □ [brɔːd] breit; weit; hell
(*Tag*); deutlich (*Wink etc.*); derb
(*Witz*); allgemein; weitherzig, liberal; **~cast** ['brɔːdkaːst] **1.** weitverbreitet; **2.** [*irr.* (cast)] weit verbreiten; *Radio*: senden; **3.** Rundfunk
(-sendung *f*) *m*; **~cloth** feiner
Wollstoff; **~-minded** großzügig.

brocade † [brə'keid] Brokat *m.*

broil [brɔil] **1.** Lärm *m*, Streit *m*;
2. auf dem Rost braten; *fig.*
schmoren.

broke [brouk] **1.** *pret. von break* 2;
2. *sl.* pleite, ohne e-n Pfennig; **~n**
['broukən] **1.** *p.p. von break* 2; **2.** :
~ health zerrüttete Gesundheit.

broker ['broukə] Altwarenhändler
m; Zwangsversteigerer *m*; Makler
m.

bronc(h)o *Am.* ['brɔŋkou] (halb-)
wildes Pferd; **~-buster** [~oubastə]
Zureiter *m.*

bronze [brɔnz] **1.** Bronze *f*; **2.** bronzen, Bronze...; **3.** bronzieren.

brooch [broutʃ] Brosche *f*; Spange *f.*

brood [bruːd] **1.** Brut *f*; *attr.*
Zucht...; **2.** brüten (*a. fig.*); **~er**
Am. ['bruːdə] Brutkasten *m.*

brook [bruk] Bach *m.*

broom [brum] Besen *m*; **~stick**
['brumstik] Besenstiel *m.*

broth [brɔθ] Fleischbrühe *f.*

brothel ['brɔθl] Bordell *n.*

brother ['brʌðə] Bruder *m*; **~(s) and**
sister(s) Geschwister *pl.*; **~hood**
[~hud] Bruderschaft *f*; **~-in-law**
[~ərinlɔː] Schwager *m*; **~ly** [~əli]
brüderlich.

brought [brɔːt] *pret. u. p.p. von* bring.

brow [brau] (Augen)Braue *f*; Stirn *f*; Rand *m* e-s *Steilhanges*; **~beat** ['braubiːt] *[irr. (beat)]* einschüchtern; tyrannisieren.

brown [braun] 1. braun; 2. Braun *n*; 3. (sich) bräunen.

browse [brauz] 1. Grasen *n*; *fig.* Schmökern *n*; 2. grasen, weiden; *fig.* schmökern.

bruise [bruːz] 1. Quetschung *f*; 2. (zer)quetschen.

brunt [brʌnt] Hauptstoß *m*, (volle) Wucht; *das* Schwerste.

brush [brʌʃ] 1. Bürste *f*; Pinsel *m*; *Fuchs*-Rute *f*; Scharmützel *n*; Unterholz *n*; 2. *v/t.* (ab-, aus)bürsten; streifen; *j.* abbürsten; **~ up** wieder aufbürsten, *fig.* auffrischen; *v/i.* bürsten; (davon)stürzen; **~** *against* s.o. *j.* streifen; **~wood** ['brʌʃwud] Gestrüpp *n*, Unterholz *n*.

brusque [brusk] brüsk, barsch.

Brussels sprouts ♀ ['brʌsl'sprauts] *pl.* Rosenkohl *m*.

brut|al ['bruːtl] viehisch; roh, gemein; **~ality** [bruːˈtæliti] Brutalität *f*, Roheit *f*; **~e** [bruːt] 1. tierisch; unvernünftig; gefühllos; 2. Vieh *n*; F Untier *n*, Scheusal *n*.

bubble ['bʌbl] 1. Blase *f*; Schwindel *m*; 2. sieden; sprudeln.

buccaneer [bʌkəˈniə] Seeräuber *m*.

buck [bʌk] 1. *zo.* Bock *m*; Stutzer *m*; *Am. sl.* Dollar *m*; 2. *v/i.* bocken; **~** *for Am.* sich bemühen um; **~ up** F sich zs.-reißen; *v/t. Am.* F sich stemmen gegen; *Am.* F die Oberhand gewinnen wollen über *et.*

bucket ['bʌkit] Eimer *m*, Kübel *m*.

buckle ['bʌkl] 1. Schnalle *f*; 2. *v/t.* (an-, auf-, um-, zu)schnallen; *v/i.* ⊕ sich (ver)biegen; **~** *to a task* sich ernsthaft an eine Aufgabe machen.

buck|shot *hunt.* ['bʌkʃɔt] Rehposten *m*; **~skin** Wildleder *n*.

bud [bʌd] 1. Knospe *f*; *fig.* Keim *m*; 2. *v/t.* ✿ veredeln; *v/i.* knospen.

buddy *Am.* F ['bʌdi] Kamerad *m*.

budge [bʌdʒ] (sich) bewegen.

budget ['bʌdʒit] Vorrat *m*; Staatshaushalt *m*; *draft* Haushaltsplan *m*.

buff [bʌf] 1. Ochsenleder *n*; Lederfarbe *f*; 2. lederfarben.

buffalo *zo.* ['bʌfəlou] Büffel *m*.

buffer ⊛ ['bʌfə] Puffer *m*; Prellbock *m*.

buffet¹ ['bʌfit] 1. Puff *m*, Stoß *m*, Schlag *m*; 2. puffen, schlagen; kämpfen.

buffet² [~] Büfett *n*; Anrichte *f*.

buffet³ ['bufei] Büfett *n*, Theke *f*; Tisch *m* mit Speisen u. Getränken; Erfrischungsraum *m*.

buffoon [bʌˈfuːn] Possenreißer *m*.

bug [bʌg] Wanze *f*; *Am.* Insekt *n*, Käfer *m*; *Am. sl.* Defekt *m*, Fehler *m*; *big* **~** *sl.* hohes Tier.

bugle ['bjuːgl] Wald-, Signalhorn *n*.

build [bild] 1. *[irr.]* bauen; errichten; 2. Bauart *f*; Schnitt *m*; **~er** ['bildə] Erbauer *m*, Baumeister *m*; **~ing** [~diŋ] Erbauen *n*; Bau *m*, Gebäude *n*; *attr.* Bau...

built [bilt] *pret. u. p.p. von* build 1.

bulb [bʌlb] ♀ Zwiebel *f*, Knolle *f*; (Glüh)Birne *f*.

bulge [bʌldʒ] 1. (Aus)Bauchung *f*; Anschwellung *f*; 2. sich (aus)bauchen; (an)schwellen; hervorquellen.

bulk [bʌlk] Umfang *m*; Masse *f*; Hauptteil *m*; ⚓ Ladung *f*; *in* **~** lose; *in großer Menge*; **~y** [~ki] umfangreich; unhandlich; ❧ sperrig.

bull¹ [bul] 1. Bulle *m*, Stier *m*; ✝ *sl.* Haussier *m*; 2. ✝ *die Kurse* treiben.

bull² [~] *päpstliche* Bulle.

bulldog ['buldɔg] Bulldogge *f*.

bulldoze *Am.* F ['buldouz] terrorisieren; **~r** ⊕ [~zə] Bulldozer *m*, Planierraupe *f*.

bullet ['bulit] Kugel *f*, Geschoß *n*.

bulletin ['bulitin] Tagesbericht *m*; **~ board** *Am.* Schwarzes Brett.

bullion ['buljən] Gold-, Silberbarren *m*; Gold-, Silberlitze *f*.

bully ['buli] 1. Maulheld *m*; Tyrann *m*; 2. prahlerisch; *Am.* F prima; 3. einschüchtern; tyrannisieren.

bulwark *mst fig.* ['bulwək] Bollwerk *n*.

bum *Am.* F [bʌm] 1. Nichtstuer *m*, Vagabund *m*; 2. *v/t.* nassauern.

bumble-bee ['bʌmblbiː] Hummel *f*.

bump [bʌmp] 1. Schlag *m*, Beule *f*; *fig.* Sinn *m* (*or für*); 2. (zs.-)stoßen; holpern; *Rudern...* überholen.

bumper [~] volles Glas (*Wein*); F *et.* Riesiges; *mot.* Stoßstange *f*; **~** *crop* Rekordernte *f*; **~** *house thea.* volles Haus.

bun [bʌn] Rosinenbrötchen *n*; *Haar*-Knoten *m*.

bunch [bʌntʃ] 1. Bund *n*; Büschel *n*; Haufen *m*; **~** *of grapes* Weintraube *f*; 2. (zs.-)bündeln; bauschen.

bundle ['bʌndl] 1. Bündel *n*, Bund *n*; 2. *v/t. a.* **~ up** (zs.-)bündeln.

bung [bʌŋ] Spund *m*.

bungalow ['bʌŋgəlou] Bungalow *m* (*einstöckiges Haus*).

bungle ['bʌŋgl] 1. Pfuscherei *f*; 2. (ver)pfuschen.

bunion ⚕ ['bʌnjən] entzündeter Fußballen.

bunk¹ *Am. sl.* [bʌŋk] Quatsch *m*.

bunk² [~] Schlafkoje *f*.

bunny ['bʌni] Kaninchen *n*.

buoy ⚓ [bɔi] 1. Boje *f*; 2. *Fahrwasser* betonnen; *mst* **~ up** *fig.* aufrechterhalten; **~ant** ☐ ['bɔiənt] schwimmfähig; hebend; spannkräftig; *fig.* heiter.

burden ['bəːdn] 1. Last *f*; Bürde *f*; ⚓ Ladung *f*; ⊕ Tragfähigkeit *f*;

2. beladen; belasten; **~some** [**~n**som] lästig, drückend.

bureau [bjuə'rou] Büro n, Geschäftszimmer n; Schreibpult n; Am. Kommode f; **~cracy** [**~'rɔ**krəsi] Bürokratie f.

burg Am. Ⓕ [bɔ:g] Stadt f.

burgess ['bɔ:dʒis] Bürger m.

burglar ['bɔ:glə] Einbrecher m; **~y** [**~əri**] Einbruch(sdiebstahl) m.

burial ['beriəl] Begräbnis n.

burlesque [bɔ:'lesk] 1. possenhaft; 2. Burleske f, Posse f; 3. parodieren.

burly ['bɔ:li] stämmig, kräftig.

burn [bɔ:n] 1. Brandwunde f; Brandmal n; 2. [irr.] (ver-, an-)brennen; **~er** ['bɔ:nə] Brenner m.

burnish ['bɔ:niʃ] polieren, glätten.

burnt [bɔ:nt] pret. u. p.p. von burn 2.

burrow ['bʌrou] 1. Höhle f, Bau m; 2. (sich ein-, ver)graben.

burst [bɔ:st] 1. Bersten n; Krach m; Riß m; Ausbruch m; 2. [irr.] v/i. bersten, platzen; zerspringen; explodieren; **~** from sich losreißen von; **~** forth, **~** out hervorbrechen; **~** into tears in Tränen ausbrechen; v/t. (zer)sprengen

bury ['beri] be-, vergraben; beerdigen; verbergen

bus Ⓕ [bʌs] (Omni)Bus m; **~** boy Am. Kellnergehilfe m

bush [buʃ] Busch m; Gebüsch n.

bushel ['buʃl] Scheffel m (36,37 Liter).

bushy ['buʃi] buschig.

business ['biznis] Geschäft n; Beschäftigung f; Beruf m; Angelegenheit f; Aufgabe f; **†** Handel m; **~** of the day Tagesordnung f, on **~** geschäftlich, have no **~** to inf. nicht befugt sein zu inf.; mind one's own **~** sich um s-e eigenen Angelegenheiten kümmern; **~hours** pl Geschäftszeit f; **~like** geschäftsmäßig; sachlich; **~man** Geschäftsmann m; **~tour**, **~trip** Geschäftsreise f.

bust¹ [bʌst] Büste f.

bust² Am. Ⓕ [**~**] Bankrott m.

bustle ['bʌsl] 1. Geschäftigkeit f; geschäftiges Treiben f; 2. v/i. (umher)wirtschaften; hasten; v/t. hetzen, jagen.

busy □ ['bizi] 1. beschäftigt; geschäftig; fleißig (at bei, an dat.); lebhaft; Am. teleph. besetzt; 2. (mst **~** o.s. sich) beschäftigen (with, in, at, about, ger. mit).

but [bʌt, bət] 1. cj. aber, jedoch, sondern; a. **~** that wenn nicht; indessen; 2. prp. außer; the last **~** one der vorletzte; the next **~** one der übernächste; **~** for wenn nicht ... gewesen wäre; ohne; 3. nach Negation: der (die od. das) nicht; there is

no one **~** knows es gibt niemand, der nicht wüßte; 4. adv. nur; **~** just soeben, eben erst; **~** now erst jetzt; all **~** fast, nahe daran; nothing **~** nur; I cannot **~** inf. ich kann nur inf.

butcher ['butʃə] 1. Schlächter m, Fleischer m, Metzger m; fig Mörder m; 2. (fig. ab-, hin)schlachten; **~y** [**~əri**] Schlächterei f; Schlachthaus n.

butler ['bʌtlə] Butler m; Kellermeister m.

butt [bʌt] 1. Stoß m; a. **~** end (dikkes) Ende e-s Baumes etc.; Stummel m, Kippe f; Gewehr-Kolben m; Schießstand m; (End)Ziel n; fig. Zielscheibe f; 2. (mit dem Kopf) stoßen.

butter ['bʌtə] 1. Butter f; Ⓕ Schmeichelei f; 2. mit Butter bestreichen; **~cup** Butterblume f; **~fingered** tolpatschig; **~fly** Schmetterling m; **~y** [**~əri**] 1. butter(art)ig; Butter...; 2. Speisekammer f.

buttocks ['bʌtəks] pl. Gesäß n.

button ['bʌtn] 1. Knopf m; Knospe f; 2. an-, zuknöpfen.

buttress ['bʌtris] 1. Strebepfeiler m; fig. Stütze f; 2. (unter)stützen.

buxom ['bʌksəm] drall, stramm.

buy [bai] [irr.] v/t. (an-, ein)kaufen (from bei); **~er** ['baiə] (Ein)Käufer (-in).

buzz [bʌz] 1. Gesumm n; Geflüster n; **~** saw Am. Kreissäge f; 2. v/i. summen; surren; **~** about herumschwirren, herumeilen.

buzzard ['bʌzəd] Bussard m.

by [bai] 1. prp. Raum: bei; an, neben; Richtung: durch, über; an (dat.) entlang od. vorbei; Zeit: an, bei; spätestens bis, bis zu; Urheber, Ursache: von, durch (bsd. beim pass.); Mittel, Werkzeug: durch, mit; Art u. Weise: bei; Schwur: bei; Maß: um, bei; Richtschnur: gemäß, bei; **~** the dozen dutzendweise; **~** o.s. allein; **~** land zu Lande; **~** rail per Bahn; day **~** day Tag für Tag; **~** twos zu zweien; 2. adv. dabei; vorbei; beiseite; **~** and **~** nächstens, bald; nach und nach; **~** the **~** nebenbei bemerkt; **~** and large Am. im großen und ganzen; 3. adj. Neben...; Seiten...; **~election** ['baiilekʃən] Nachwahl f; **~gone** vergangen; **~law** Ortsstatut n; **~s** pl. Satzung f, Statuten n/pl.; **~line** Am. Verfasserangabe f zu e-m Artikel; **~name** Bei-, Spitzname m; **~pass** Umgehungsstraße f; **~path** Seitenpfad m; **~product** Nebenprodukt n; **~road** Seitenweg m; **~stander** Zuschauer m; **~street** Neben-, Seitenstraße f; **~way** Seitenweg m; **~word** Sprichwort n; Inbegriff m; be a **~** for sprichwörtlich bekannt sein wegen.

C

cab [kæb] Droschke *f*, Mietwagen *m*, Taxi *n*; 🚢 Führerstand *m*.

cabbage ♀ ['kæbidʒ] Kohl *m*.

cabin ['kæbin] **1.** Hütte *f*; ⚓ Kabine *f*, Kajüte *f*; Kammer *f*; **2.** einpferchen; **~-boy** Schiffsjunge *m*; **~ cruiser** ⚓ Kabinenkreuzer *m*.

cabinet ['kæbinit] Kabinett *n*, Ministerrat *m*; Schrank *m*, Vitrine *f*; (Radio)Gehäuse *n*; **~ council** Kabinettssitzung *f*; **~-maker** Kunsttischler *m*.

cable ['keibl] **1.** Kabel *n*; ⚓ Ankertau *n*; **2.** *tel.* kabeln; **~-car** Kabine *f*, Gondel *f*; Drahtseilbahn *f*; **~gram** [~lgræm] Kabeltelegramm *n*.

cabman ['kæbmən] Droschkenkutscher *m*, Taxifahrer *m*.

caboose [kə'bu:s] ⚓ Kombüse *f*; *Am.* 🚂 Eisenbahnerwagen *m* am Güterzug.

cab-stand ['kæbstænd] Taxi-, Droschkenstand *m*.

cacao ♀ [kə'ka:ou] Kakaobaum *m*, -bohne *f*.

cackle ['kækl] **1.** Gegacker *n*, Geschnatter *n*; **2.** gackern, schnattern.

cad F [kæd] Prolet *m*; Kerl *m*.

cadaverous [kə'dævərəs] leichenhaft; leichenblaß.

cadence ♪ ['keidəns] Kadenz *f*; Tonfall *m*; Rhythmus *m*.

cadet [kə'det] Kadett *m*.

café ['kæfei] Café *n*.

cafeteria *bsd. Am.* [kæfi'tiəriə] Restaurant *n* mit Selbstbedienung.

cage [keidʒ] **1.** Käfig *m*; Kriegsgefangenenlager *n*; ⚒ Förderkorb *m*; **2.** einsperren.

cagey ⚛ *bsd. Am.* F ['keidʒi] gerissen, raffiniert.

cajole [kə'dʒoul] *j-m* schmeicheln; *j-n* beschwatzen.

cake [keik] **1.** Kuchen *m*; Tafel *f* Schokolade, Riegel *m* Seife *etc.*; **2.** zs.-backen.

calami|tous □ [kə'læmitəs] elend; katastrophal; **~ty** [~ti] Elend *n*, Unglück *n*; Katastrophe *f*.

calcify ['kælsifai] (sich) verkalken.

calculat|e ['kælkjuleit] *v/t.* kalkulieren; be-, aus-, errechnen; *v/i.* rechnen (*on, upon* auf *acc.*); *Am.* F vermuten; **~ion** [kælkju'leiʃən] Kalkulation *f*, Berechnung *f*; Voranschlag *m*; Überlegung *f*.

caldron ['kɔ:ldrən] Kessel *m*.

calendar ['kælində] **1.** Kalender *m*; Liste *f*; **2.** registrieren.

calf [ka:f], *pl.* **calves** [ka:vz] Kalb *n*; Wade *f*; *a.* **~-leather** ['ka:fleðə] Kalbleder *n*; **~-skin** Kalbfell *n*.

calibre ['kælibə] Kaliber *n*.

calico ✝ ['kælikou] Kaliko *m*.

call [kɔ:l] **1.** Ruf *m*; *teleph.* Anruf *m*,

Gespräch *n*; *fig.* Berufung *f* (*to* in *ein Amt*; *auf e-n Lehrstuhl*); Aufruf *m*; Aufforderung *f*; Signal *n*; Forderung *f*; Besuch *m*; Nachfrage *f* (*for* nach); Kündigung *f v. Geldern*; **on ~** ✝ auf Abruf; **2.** *v/t.* (herbei-)rufen; (an)rufen; (ein)berufen; *Am. Baseball: Spiel* abbrechen; *fig.* berufen (*to* in *ein Amt*); nennen; wecken; *Aufmerksamkeit* lenken (*to* auf *acc.*); be **~ed** heißen; **~ s.o. names** j. beschimpfen, beleidigen; **~ down** *bsd. Am.* F anpfeifen; **~ in** *Geld* kündigen; **~ over** *Namen* verlesen; **~ up** aufrufen; *teleph.* anrufen; *v/i.* rufen; *teleph.* anrufen; vorsprechen (*at* an *e-m Ort*; *on s.o.* bei j-m); **~ at** *a port* et-n Hafen anlaufen; **~ for** rufen nach; *et.* fordern; abholen; *to be* (*left till*) **~ed for** postlagernd; **~ on** sich an j. wenden (*for* wegen); *j.* berufen, auffordern (*to inf.* zu); **~-box** ['kɔ:lbɔks] Fernsprechzelle *f*; **~er** ['kɔ:lə] *teleph.* Anrufer(in); Besucher(in).

calling ['kɔ:liŋ] Rufen *n*; Berufung *f*; Beruf *m*; **~-card** *Am.* Visitenkarte *f*.

call-office ['kɔ:lɔfis] Fernsprechstelle *f*.

callous □ ['kæləs] schwielig; *fig.* dickfellig; herzlos.

callow ['kælou] nackt (*ungefiedert*); *fig.* unerfahren.

calm [ka:m] **1.** □ still, ruhig; **2.** (Wind)Stille *f*, Ruhe *f*; **3.** (*~ down sich*) beruhigen; besänftigen.

calori|c *phys.* [kə'lɔrik] Wärme *f*; **~e** *phys.* ['kæləri] Wärmeeinheit *f*.

column|iate [kə'lʌmnieit] verleumden; **~iation** [kəlʌmni'eiʃən], **~y** ['kæləmni] Verleumdung *f*.

calve [ka:v] kalben; **~s** [ka:vz] *pl. von* calf.

cambric ✝ ['keimbrik] Batist *m*.

came [keim] *pret. von* come.

camel *zo.*, ⚓ ['kæməl] Kamel *n*.

camera ['kæmərə] Kamera *f*; *in* **~** 🔒 unter Ausschluß der Öffentlichkeit.

camomile ♀ ['kæməmail] Kamille *f*.

camouflage ⚔ ['kæmuflɑ:ʒ] **1.** Tarnung *f*; **2.** tarnen.

camp [kæmp] **1.** Lager *n*; ⚔ Feldlager *n*; **~ bed** Feldbett *n*; **2.** lagern; **~ out** zelten.

campaign [kæm'pein] **1.** Feldzug *m*; **2.** e-n Feldzug mitmachen *od.* führen.

camphor ['kæmfə] Kampfer *m*.

campus *Am.* ['kæmpəs] Universitätsgelände *n*.

can¹ [kæn] [*irr.*] *v/aux.* können, fähig sein zu; dürfen.

can² [~] **1.** Kanne *f*; *Am.* Büchse *f*; **2.** *Am.* in Büchsen konservieren.

Canadian [kə'neidjən] 1. kanadisch; 2. Kanadier(in).

canal [kə'næl] Kanal *m* (*a. ☆*).

canard [kæ'nɑ:d] (Zeitungs)Ente *f*.

canary [kə'neəri] Kanarienvogel *m*.

cancel ['kænsəl] (durch)streichen; entwerten; absagen; *a.* ~ out *fig.* aufheben; *be* ~*led* ausfallen.

cancer *ast.*, *☆* ['kænsə] Krebs *m*; ~ous [~ərəs] krebsartig.

candid □ ['kændid] aufrichtig; offen.

candidate ['kændidit] Kandidat *m* (*for* für), Bewerber *m* (*for* um).

candied ['kændid] kandiert.

candle ['kændl] Licht *n*, Kerze *f*; *burn the* ~ *at both ends* mit s-n Kräften Raubbau treiben; ~**stick** Leuchter *m*.

cando(u)r ['kændə] Aufrichtigkeit *f*.

candy ['kændi] 1. Kandis(zucker) *m*; *Am.* Süßigkeiten *f/pl.*; 2. *v/t.* kandieren.

cane [kein] 1. ♀ Rohr *n*; (Rohr-)Stock *m*; 2. prügeln.

canine ['keinain] Hunde...

canker ['kæŋkə] *☆* Mundkrebs *m*; ♀ Brand *m*.

canned *Am.* [kænd] Büchsen...

cannery *Am.* ['kænəri] Konservenfabrik *f*.

cannibal ['kænibəl] Kannibale *m*.

cannon ['kænən] Kanone *f*.

cannot ['kænɔt] nicht können *etc.*; *s. can¹.*

canoe [kə'nu:] Kanu *n*; Paddelboot *n*.

canon ['kænən] Kanon *m*; Regel *f*; Richtschnur *f*; ~**ize** [~naiz] heiligsprechen.

canopy ['kænəpi] Baldachin *m*; *fig.* Dach *n*; ⊕ Überdachung *f*.

cant¹ [kænt] 1. Schrägung *f*; Stoß *m*; 2. kippen; kanten.

cant² [~] 1. Zunftsprache *f*; Gewäsch *n*; scheinheiliges Gerede *f*; 2. zunftmäßig *od.* scheinheilig reden.

can't F [kɑ:nt] = *cannot.*

cantankerous F □ [kən'tæŋkərəs] zänkisch, mürrisch.

canteen [kæn'ti:n] ✕ Feldflasche *f*; Kantine *f*; ✕ Kochgeschirr *n*; Besteckkasten *m*.

canton 1. ['kæntən] Bezirk *m*; 2. ✕ [kən'tu:n] (sich) einquartieren.

canvas ['kænvəs] Segeltuch *n*; Zelt (-*e pl.*) *n*; Zeltbahn *f*; Segel *n/pl.*; *paint.* Leinwand *f*; Gemälde *n*.

canvass [~] 1. (Stimmen)Werbung *f*; *Am. a.* Wahlnachprüfung *f*; 2. *v/t.* erörtern; *v/i.* (Stimmen, *a.* Kunden) werben.

caoutchouc ['kautʃuk] Kautschuk *m*.

cap [kæp] 1. Kappe *f*; Mütze *f*; Haube *f*; ⊕ Aufsatz *m*; Zündhütchen *n*; *set one's* ~ *at* sich e-n Mann angeln (*Frau*); 2. mit e-r Kappe *etc.* bedecken; *fig.* krönen; F übertreffen; die Mütze abnehmen.

capab|ility [keipə'biliti] Fähigkeit *f*; ~**le** ['keipəbl] fähig (*of* zu).

capaci|ous □ [kə'peiʃəs] geräumig; ~**ty** [kə'pæsiti] Inhalt *m*; Aufnahmefähigkeit *f*; *geistige* (*od.* ⊕ Leistungs)Fähigkeit *f* (*for ger.* zu *inf.*); Stellung *f*; *in my* ~ *as* in meiner Eigenschaft als.

cape¹ [keip] Kap *n*, Vorgebirge *n*.

cape² [~] Cape *n*, Umhang *m*.

caper ['keipə] 1. Kapriole *f*, Luftsprung *m*; *cut* ~*s* = 2. Kapriolen *od.* Sprünge machen.

capital ['kæpitl] 1. □ Kapital...; todeswürdig, Todes...; hauptsächlich, Haupt...; vortrefflich; ~ *crime* Kapitalverbrechen *n*; ~ *punishment* Todesstrafe *f*; 2. Hauptstadt *f*; Kapital *n*; *mst* ~ *letter* Großbuchstabe *m*; ~**ism** [~təlizəm] Kapitalismus *m*; ~**ize** [kə'pitəlaiz] kapitalisieren.

capitulate [kə'pitjuleit] kapitulieren (*to vor dat.*).

capric|e [kə'pri:s] **Laune** *f*; ~**ious** □ [~ʃəs] kapriziös, launisch.

Capricorn *ast.* ['kæprikɔ:n] Steinbock *m*.

capsize [kæp'saiz] *v/i.* kentern; *v/t.* zum Kentern bringen.

capsule ['kæpsju:l] Kapsel *f*.

captain ['kæptin] Führer *m*; Feldherr *m*; ♠ Kapitän *m*; ✕ Hauptmann *m*.

caption ['kæpʃən] 1. Überschrift *f*; Titel *m*; *Film:* Untertitel *m*; 2. *v/t. Am.* mit Überschrift *etc.* versehen.

captious □ ['kæpʃəs] spitzfindig.

captiv|ate ['kæptiveit] *fig.* gefangennehmen, fesseln; ~**e** ['kæptiv] 1. gefangen, gefesselt; 2. Gefangene(r *m*) *f*; ~**ity** [kæp'tiviti] Gefangenschaft *f*.

capture ['kæptʃə] 1. Eroberung *f*; Gefangennahme *f*; 2. (ein)fangen; erobern; erbeuten; ♠ kapern.

car [kɑ:] Auto *n*; (Eisenbahn-, Straßenbahn)Wagen *m*; Ballonkorb *m*; *Luftschiff*-Gondel *f*; Kabine *f* e-s *Aufzugs*.

caramel ['kærəmel] Karamel *m*; Karamelle *f*.

caravan ['kærəvæn] Karawane *f*; Wohnwagen *m*.

caraway ♀ ['kærəwei] Kümmel *m*.

carbine ['kɑ:bain] Karabiner *m*.

carbohydrate ♫ ['kɑ:bou'haidreit] Kohle(n)hydrat *n*.

carbon ['kɑ:bən] ♫ Kohlenstoff *m*; ~ *copy* Brief-Durchschlag *m*; ~ *paper* Kohlepapier *n*.

carburet(t)or *mot.* ['kɑ:bjuretə] Vergaser *m*.

car|case, *mst* ~**cass** ['kɑ:kəs] (Tier-) Kadaver *m*; *Fleischerei:* Rumpf *m*.

card [kɑ:d] Karte *f*; *have a* ~ *up*

one's sleeve et. in petto haben;
~board ['ka:dbɔ:d] Kartonpapier
n; Pappe f; **~ box** Pappkarton m.
cardigan ['ka:digən] Wolljacke f.
cardinal] ['ka:dinl] **1.** Haupt...;
hochrot; **~ number** Grundzahl f; **2.**
Kardinal m.
card-index ['ka:dindeks] Kartei f.
card-sharper ['ka:dʃa:pə] Falsch-
spieler m.
care [kɛə] **1.** Sorge f; Sorgfalt f,
Obhut f, Pflege f; medical ~ ärzt-
liche Behandlung; ~ of (abbr. c/o) ...
per Adresse, bei ...; take ~ of
acht(geb)en auf (acc.); with ~! Vorsicht!; **2.** Lust haben (to inf. zu);
~ for sorgen für; sich kümmern um;
sich etwas machen aus; I don't ~!
F meinetwegen!; I couldn't ~ less F
es ist mir völlig egal; well ~d-for
gepflegt.   [bahn f; **2.** rasen.]
career [kə'riə] **1.** Karriere f; Lauf-}
carefree ['kɛəfri:] sorgenfrei.
careful ['kɛəful] besorgt (for um),
achtsam (of auf acc.); vorsichtig;
sorgfältig; **~ness** [~lnis] Sorgsam-
keit f; Vorsicht f; Sorgfalt f.
careless] ['kɛəlis] sorglos; nachlässig; unachtsam; leichtsinnig;
~ness [~snis] Sorglosigkeit f; Nachlässigkeit f.
caress [kə'res] **1.** Liebkosung f;
2. liebkosen; fig. schmeicheln.
caretaker ['kɛəteikə] Wärter(in)
(Haus)Verwalter(in).
care-worn ['kɛəwɔ:n] abgehärmt.
carfare Am. ['ka:fɛə] Fahrgeld n.
cargo ♣ ['ka:gou] Ladung f.
caricature ['kærikə'tjuə] **1.** Karikatur f; **2.** karikieren.
carmine ['ka:main] Karmin(rot) n.
carn|al ['ka:nl] fleischlich; sinn-
lich; **~ation** [ka:'neiʃn] **1.** Fleisch-
ton m; ♣ Nelke f; **2.** blaßrot.
carnival ['ka:nivəl] Karneval m.
carnivorous [ka:'nivərəs] fleisch-
fressend.
carol ['kærəl] **1.** Weihnachtslied n;
2. Weihnachtslieder singen.
carous|e [kə'rauz] **1.** a. **~al** [~əl]
(Trink)Gelage n; **2.** zechen.
carp [ka:p] Karpfen m.
carpent|er ['ka:pintə] Zimmer-
mann m; **~ry** [~tri] Zimmerhand-
werk n; Zimmermannsarbeit f.
carpet ['ka:pit] **1.** Teppich m;
bring on the ~ aufs Tapet bringen;
2. mit e-m Teppich belegen; **~bag**
Reisetasche f; **~bagger** [~tbægə]
politischer Abenteurer.
carriage ['kæridʒ] Beförderung f,
Transport m; Fracht f; Wagen m;
Fuhr-, Frachtlohn m; Haltung f;
Benehmen n; **~drive** Anfahrt f
(vor e-m Hause); **~free**, **~paid**
frachtfrei; **~way** Fahrbahn f.
carrier ['kæriə] Fuhrmann m;
Spediteur m; Träger m; Gepäckträger m; **~pigeon** Brieftaube f.

carrion ['kæriən] Aas n; attr. Aas...
carrot ['kærət] Mohrrübe f.
carry ['kæri] **1.** v/t. wohin bringen,
führen, tragen (a. v/i.), fahren, befördern; (bei sich) haben; Ansicht
durchsetzen; Gewinn, Preis davontragen; Zahlen übertragen; Ernte,
Zinsen tragen; Mauer etc. weiter-
führen; Benehmen fortsetzen; Antrag, Kandidaten durchbringen; ✕
erobern; be carried angenommen
werden (Antrag); durchkommen
(Kandidat); ~ the day den Sieg
davontragen; ~ forward od. over ⚁
übertragen; ~ on fortsetzen, weiter-
führen; Geschäft etc. betreiben; ~
out od. through durchführen; **2.**
Trag-, Schußweite f.
cart [ka:t] **1.** Karren m; Wagen m;
put the ~ before the horse fig. das
Pferd beim Schwanz aufzäumen;
2. karren, fahren; **~age** ['ka:tidʒ]
Fahren n; Fuhrlohn m.
carter ['ka:tə] Fuhrmann m.
cartilage ['ka:tilidʒ] Knorpel m.
carton ['ka:tən] Karton m.
cartoon [ka:'tu:n] paint. Karton m;
⊕ Musterzeichnung f; Karikatur f;
Zeichentrickfilm m; **~ist** [~nist]
Karikaturist m.
cartridge ['ka:tridʒ] Patrone f;
~paper Zeichenpapier n.
cart-wheel ['ka:twi:l] Wagenrad n;
Am. Silberdollar m; turn ~s rad-
schlagen.
carve [ka:v] Fleisch vorschneiden,
zerlegen; schnitzen; meißeln; **~r**
['ka:və] (Bild)Schnitzer m; Vor-
schneider m; Vorlegemesser n.
carving ['ka:viŋ] Schnitzerei f.
cascade [kæs'keid] Wasserfall m.
case¹ [keis] m Behälter m; Kiste f;
Etui n; Gehäuse n; Schachtel f;
Fach n; typ. Setzkasten m; **2.** (ein-)
stecken; ver-, umkleiden.
case² ⚖ Fall m (a. gr., ♣, ♟); gr.
Kasus m; ♣ a. Kranke(r m f); Am.
F komischer Kauz; ♟ Schriftsatz
m; Hauptargument n; Sache f, Angelegenheit f.
case-harden ⊕ ['keishɑ:dn] hart-
gießen; **~ed** fig. hartgesotten.
case-history ['keishistəri] Vor-
geschichte f; Krankengeschichte f.
casement ['keismənt] Fensterflügel
m; **~ window** Flügelfenster n.
cash [kæʃ] **1.** Bargeld n, Kasse f;
~ down, for ~ gegen bar; ~ on delivery Lieferung f gegen bar; (per)
Nachnahme f; ~ register Registrierkasse f; **2.** einkassieren, einlösen; **~book** ['kæʃbuk] Kassa-
buch n; **~ier** [kæ'ʃiə] Kassierer(in).
casing ['keisiŋ] Überzug m, Gehäuse n, Futteral n; △ Verkleidung f.
cask [ka:sk] Faß n.
casket ['ka:skit] Kassette f; Am.
Sarg m.

casserole ['kæsəroul] Kasserolle f.

cassock eccl. ['kæsək] Soutane f.

cast [kɑːst] 1. Wurf m; ⊕ Guß (-form f) m; Abguß m, Abdruck m; Schattierung f, Anflug m; Form f, Art f; ♣ Auswerfen n von Senkblei etc.; thea. (Rollen)Besetzung f; 2. [irr.] v/t. (ab-, aus-, hin-, um-, weg)werfen; zo. Haut etc. abwerfen; Zähne etc. verlieren; verwerfen; gestalten; ⊕ gießen; a. ~ up aus-, zs.-rechnen; thea. Rolle besetzen; Rolle übertragen (to dat.); be ~ in a lawsuit ⚖ e-n Prozeß verlieren; ~ lots losen (for um); ~ in one's lot with s.o. j-s Los teilen; be ~ down niedergeschlagen sein; v/i. sich gießen lassen; ⊕ sich (ver)werfen; ~ about for sinnen auf (acc.); sich et. überlegen.

castanet [kæstə'net] Kastagnette f.

castaway ['kɑːstəwei] 1. verworfen, ♣ schiffbrüchig; 2. Verworfene(r m) f; Schiffbrüchige(r m) f.

caste [kɑːst] Kaste f (a. fig.).

castigate ['kæstigeit] züchtigen; fig. geißeln.

cast iron ['kɑːst'aiən] Gußeisen n; **cast-iron** gußeisern.

castle ['kɑːsl] Burg f, Schloß n; Schach: Turm m.

castor¹ ['kɑːstə] ~ oil Rizinusöl f.

castor² [,,] Laufrolle f unter Möbeln; (Salz-, Zucker- etc.) Streuer m.

castrate [kæs'treit] kastrieren.

cast steel ['kɑːststiːl] Gußstahl m; **cast-steel** aus Gußstahl.

casual ☐ ['kæʒjuəl] zufällig; gelegentlich; F lässig; **~ty** [,,lti] Unfall m; ✕ Verlust m.

cat [kæt] Katze f; ~ burglar Fassadenkletterer m.

catalogue, Am. **~g** ['kætələɡ] 1. Katalog m; Am. univ. Vorlesungsverzeichnis n; 2. katalogisieren.

catapult ['kætəpʌlt] Schleuder f; ✕ Katapult m. n.

cataract ['kætərækt] Katarakt m, Wasserfall m; ✱ grauer Star.

catarrh [kə'tɑː] Katarrh m; Schnupfen m.

catastrophe [kə'tæstrəfi] Katastrophe f.

catch [kætʃ] 1. Fang m; Beute f, fig. Vorteil m; ♪ Rundgesang m; Kniff m; ⊕ Haken m, Griff m, Klinke f; 2. [irr.] v/t. fassen, F kriegen; fangen, ergreifen; ertappen; Blick etc. auffangen; Zug etc. erreichen; bekommen; sich Krankheit zuziehen, holen; fig. erfassen; ~ (a) cold sich erkälten; ~ s.o.'s eye j-m ins Auge fallen; ~ up auffangen; F j. unterbrechen; einholen; 3. v/i. sich verfangen, hängenbleiben; fassen, einschnappen (Schloß etc.); ~ on F Anklang finden; Am. F kapieren; ~ up with ⊈, einholen; **~all** ['kætʃɔːl] Am.

Platz m od. Behälter m für alles mögliche (a. fig. u. attr.); **~er** [,,/ə] Fänger(in); **~ing** [,,/iŋ] packend; ansteckend; **~line** Schlagzeile f; **~word** Schlagwort n; Stichwort n.

catechism ['kætikizəm] Katechismus m.

categor|ical ☐ [kæti'gorikəl] kategorisch; **~y** ['kætigəri] Kategorie f.

cater ['keitə]: ~ for Lebensmittel liefern für; fig. sorgen für; **~ing** [,,əriŋ] Verpflegung f.

caterpillar ['kætəpilə] zo. Raupe f; ⊕ Raupe(nschlepper m) f.

catgut ['kætɡʌt] Darmsaite f.

cathedral [kə'θiːdrəl] Dom m, Kathedrale f.

Catholic ['kæθəlik] 1. katholisch; 2. Katholik(in).

catkin ♀ ['kætkin] Kätzchen n.

cattish fig. ['kætiʃ] falsch.

cattle ['kætl] Vieh n; **~-breeding** Viehzucht f; **~-plague** vet. Rinderpest f.   [catch 2.]

caught [kɔːt] pret. u. p.p. von

ca(u)ldron ['kɔːldrən] Kessel m.

cauliflower ♀ ['kɔliflauə] Blumenkohl m.

caulk ♣ [kɔːk] kalfatern (abdichten).

caus|al [,,'kɔːzəl] ursächlich; **~e** [kɔːz] 1. Ursache f, Grund m; ⚖ Klage(grund m) f; Prozeß m; Angelegenheit f, Sache f; 2. verursachen, veranlassen; **~eless** ☐ ['kɔːzlis] grundlos.

causeway ['kɔːzwei] Damm m.

caustic ⚗ ['kɔːstik] (~ally) ätzend; fig. beißend, scharf.

caution ['kɔːʃən] 1. Vorsicht f; Warnung f; Verwarnung f; ~ money Kaution f; 2. warnen; verwarnen.

cautious ☐ ['kɔːʃəs] behutsam, vorsichtig; **~ness** [,,snis] Behutsamkeit f, Vorsicht f.

cavalry ✕ ['kævəlri] Reiterei f.

cave [keiv] 1. Höhle f; 2. v/i. ~ in einstürzen; klein beigeben.

cavern ['kævən] Höhle f; **~ous** fig. [,,nəs] hohl.

cavil ['kævil] 1. Krittelei f; 2. kritteln (at, about an dat.).

cavity ['kæviti] Höhle f; Loch n.

cavort Am. F [kə'vɔːt] sich aufbäumen, umherspringen.

caw [kɔː] 1. krächzen; 2. Krächzen n.

cayuse Am. F ['kaijuːs] kleines (Indianer)Pferd.

cease [siːs] v/i. (from) aufhören (mit), ablassen (von); v/t. aufhören mit; **~less** ☐ ['siːslis] unaufhörlich.

cede [siːd] abtreten, überlassen.

ceiling ['siːliŋ] Zimmer-Decke f; fig. Höchstgrenze f; ~ price Höchstpreis m.

celebrat|e ['selibreit] feiern; **~ed** gefeiert, berühmt (for wegen); **~ion** [seli'breiʃən] Feier f.

celebrity [si'lebriti] Berühmtheit f.

celerity [si'leriti] Geschwindigkeit f.

celery ♦ ['seləri] Sellerie m, f.

celestial] [si'lestjəl] himmlisch.

celibacy ['selibəsi] Ehelosigkeit f.

cell [sel] allg. Zelle f; ⚡ Element n.

cellar ['selə] Keller m.

cement [si'ment] 1. Zement m; Kitt m; 2. zementieren; (ver)kitten.

cemetery ['semitri] Friedhof m.

censor ['sensə] 1. Zensor m; 2. zensieren; ~ious] [sen'sɔːriəs] kritisch; kritt(e)lig; ~ship ['sensəʃip] Zensur f; Zensoramt n.

censure ['sensə] 1. Tadel m; Verweis m; 2. tadeln.

census ['sensəs] Volkszählung f.

cent [sent] Hundert n; Am. Cent m = ¹/₁₀₀ Dollar; per ~ Prozent n.

centenary [sen'tiːnəri] Hundertjahrfeier f.

centennial [sen'tenjəl] 1. hundertjährig; 2. hundertjähriges Jubiläum.

centi|grade ['sentigreid]: 10 degrees ~ 10 Grad Celsius; ~metre, Am. ~meter Zentimeter n, m; ~pede zo. [..ipiːd] Hundertfüßler m.

central] ['sentrəl] zentral; ~ heating Zentralheizung f; ~ office, ⚡ ~ station Zentrale f; ~ize [..laiz] zentralisieren.

cent|re, Am. ~er ['sentə] 1. Zentrum n, Mittelpunkt m; 2. zentral; 3. (sich) konzentrieren; zentralisieren; zentrieren.

century ['sentʃuri] Jahrhundert n.

cereal ['siəriəl] 1. Getreide...; 2. Getreide(pflanze f) n; Hafer-, Weizenflocken f/pl.; Corn-flakes pl.

cerebral anat. ['seribrəl] Gehirn...

ceremon|ial [seri'mounjəl] 1. □ a. ~ious] [..jəs] zeremoniell; förmlich; 2. Zeremoniell n; ~y ['seriməni] Zeremonie f; Feierlichkeit f; Förmlichkeit(en pl.) f.

certain] ['səːtn] sicher, gewiß; zuverlässig; bestimmt; gewisse(r, -s); ~ty [..nti] Sicherheit f, Gewißheit f; Zuverlässigkeit f.

certi|ficate [sə'tifikit] Zeugnis n, Schein m; ~ of birth Geburtsurkunde f; medical ~ ärztliches Attest; [..keit] bescheinigen; ~fication [səːtifi'keiʃən] Bescheinigung f; ~fy ['səːtifai] et. bescheinigen; bezeugen; ~tude [..itjuːd] Gewißheit f.

cessation [se'seiʃən] Aufhören n.

cession ['seʃən] Abtretung f.

cesspool ['sespuːl] Senkgrube f.

chafe [tʃeif] v/t. reiben; wundreiben; erzürnen; v/i. sich scheuern; sich wundreiben; toben.

chaff [tʃaːf] 1. Spreu f; Häcksel n; F Neckerei f; 2. zu Häcksel schneiden; F necken.

chaffer ['tʃæfə] feilschen.

chaffinch ['tʃæfintʃ] Buchfink m.

chagrin ['ʃægrin] 1. Ärger m; 2. ärgern.

chain [tʃein] 1. Kette f; fig. Fessel f; ~ store bsd. Am. Kettenladen m, Zweiggeschäft n; 2. (an)ketten; fig. fesseln.

chair [tʃɛə] Stuhl m; Lehrstuhl m; Vorsitz m; be in the ~ den Vorsitz führen; ~man ['tʃɛəmən] Vorsitzende(r) m; Präsident m.

chalice ['tʃælis] Kelch m.

chalk [tʃɔːk] 1. Kreide f; 2. mit Kreide (be)zeichnen; mst ~ up ankreiden; ~ out entwerfen.

challenge ['tʃælindʒ] 1. Herausforderung f; ✗ Anruf m; bsd. ⚖ Ablehnung f; 2. herausfordern; anrufen; ablehnen; anzweifeln.

chamber ['tʃeimbə] parl., zo., ♀, ⊕, Am. Kammer f; ~s pl. Geschäftsräume m/pl.; ~maid Zimmermädchen n.

chamois ['ʃæmwaː] 1. Gemse f; a. ~-leather [oft a. 'ʃæmiledə] Wildleder n; 2. chamois (gelbbraun).

champagne [ʃæm'pein] Champagner m.

champion ['tʃæmpjən] 1. Vorkämpfer m, Verfechter m; Verteidiger m; Sport. Meister m; 2. verteidigen; kämpfen für; fig. stützen; 3. großartig; ~ship Meisterschaft f.

chance [tʃaːns] 1. Zufall m; Schicksal n; Glück(sfall m) n; Chance f; Aussicht f (of auf acc.); (günstige) Gelegenheit; Möglichkeit f; by ~ zufällig; take a ~, take one's ~ es darauf ankommen lassen; 2. zufällig; gelegentlich; 3. v/i. geschehen; sich ereignen; ~ upon stoßen auf (acc.); v/t. F wagen.

chancellor ['tʃaːnsələ] Kanzler m.

chancery ['tʃaːnsəri] Kanzleigericht n; fig. in ~ in der Klemme.

chandelier [ʃændi'liə] Lüster m.

chandler ['tʃaːndlə] Krämer m.

change [tʃeindʒ] 1. Veränderung f, Wechsel m, Abwechs(e)lung f; Tausch m; Wechselgeld n; Kleingeld n; 2. v/t. (ver)ändern; (aus-) wechseln, (aus-, ver)tauschen (for gegen); ~ trains umsteigen; v/i. sich ändern, wechseln; sich umziehen; ~able] ['tʃeindʒəbl] veränderlich; ~less] [..dʒlis] unveränderlich; ~ling [..liŋ] Wechselbalg m; ~ over Umstellung f.

channel ['tʃænl] 1. Kanal m; Flußbett n; Rinne f; fig. Weg m; 2. furchen; aushöhlen.

chant [tʃaːnt] 1. (Kirchen)Gesang m; fig. Singsang m; 2. singen.

chaos ['keiɔs] Chaos n.

chap¹ [tʃæp] 1. Riß m, Sprung m; 2. rissig machen od. werden.

chap² F [..] Bursche m, Kerl m, Junge m.

chap³ [~] Kinnbacken *m*; ~s *pl.* Maul *n*; ⊕ Backen *f/pl.*

chapel ['tʃæpəl] Kapelle *f*; Gottesdienst *m*.

chaplain ['tʃæplin] Kaplan *m*.

chapter ['tʃæptə] Kapitel *n*; *Am.* Orts-, Untergruppe *f* e-r *Vereinigung*.

char [tʃɑː] verkohlen.

character ['kæriktə] Charakter *m*; Merkmal *n*; Schrift(zeichen *n*) *f*; Sinnesart *f*; Persönlichkeit *f*; Original *n*; *thea.*, *Roman*: Person *f*; Rang *m*, Würde *f*; (*bsd. guter*) Ruf; Zeugnis *n*; **.istic** [kæriktə'ristik] **1.** (~ally) charakteristisch (*of* für); **2.** Kennzeichen *n*; **.ize** ['kæriktəraiz] charakterisieren.

charcoal ['tʃɑːkoul] Holzkohle *f*.

charge [tʃɑːdʒ] **1.** Ladung *f*; *fig.* Last *f* (*on* für); Verwahrung *f*; Obhut *f*; Schützling *m*; Mündel *m*, *f*, *n*; Amt *n*, Stelle *f*; Auftrag *m*; Befehl *m*; Angriff *m*; Ermahnung *f*; Beschuldigung *f*, Anklage *f*; Preis *m*, Forderung *f*; ~s *pl.* † Kosten *pl.*; be *in* ~ *of* et. in Verwahrung haben; mit *et.* beauftragt sein; für *et.* sorgen; **2.** *v/t.* laden; beladen, belasten; beauftragen; *et.* einschärfen, befehlen; ermahnen; beschuldigen, anklagen (*with gen.*); zuschreiben (*on*, *upon dat.*); fordern, verlangen; an-, berechnen, in Rechnung stellen (*to dat.*); angreifen (*a. v/i.*); behaupten.

chariot *poet. od. hist.* ['tʃæriət] Streit-, Triumphwagen *m*.

charitable ['tʃæritəbl] mild(tätig), wohltätig.

charity ['tʃæriti] Nächstenliebe *f*; Wohltätigkeit *f*; Güte *f*; Nachsicht *f*; milde Gabe.

charlatan ['ʃɑːlətən] Marktschreier *m*.

charm [tʃɑːm] **1.** Zauber *m*; *fig.* Reiz *m*; **2.** bezaubern; *fig.* entzücken; **.ing** ['tʃɑːmiŋ] bezaubernd.

chart [tʃɑːt] **1.** ⚓ Seekarte *f*; Tabelle *f*; **2.** auf e-r Karte einzeichnen.

charter ['tʃɑːtə] **1.** Urkunde *f*; Freibrief *m*; Patent *n*; Frachtvertrag *m*; **2.** privilegieren; ⚓, ✈ chartern, mieten.

charwoman ['tʃɑːwumən] Putz-, Reinemachefrau *f*.

chary [ ] ['tʃɛəri] vorsichtig.

chase [tʃeis] **1.** Jagd *f*; Verfolgung *f*; gejagtes Wild; **2.** jagen, hetzen; Jagd machen auf (*acc.*).

chasm ['kæzəm] Kluft *f* (*a. fig.*); Lücke *f*.

chaste [ ] [tʃeist] rein, keusch, unschuldig; schlicht (*Stil.*).

chastise [tʃæs'taiz] züchtigen.

chastity ['tʃæstiti] Keuschheit *f*.

chat [tʃæt] **1.** Geplauder *n*, Plauderei *f*; **2.** plaudern.

chattels ['tʃætlz] *pl. mst goods and* ~ Hab *n* und Gut *n*; Vermögen *n*.

chatter ['tʃætə] **1.** plappern; schnattern; klappern; **2.** Geplapper *n*; **.box** F Plaudertasche *f*; **.er** [~ərə] Schwätzer(in).

chatty ['tʃæti] gesprächig.

chauffeur ['ʃoufə] Chauffeur *m*.

chaw *sl.* [tʃɔː] kauen; ~ *up Am. mst fig.* fix und fertig machen.

cheap □ [tʃiːp] billig; *fig.* gemein; **.en** ['tʃiːpən] (sich) verbilligen; *fig.* herabsetzen.

cheat [tʃiːt] **1.** Betrug *m*, Schwindel *m*; Betrüger(in); **2.** betrügen.

check [tʃek] **1.** Schach(stellung *f*) *n*; Hemmnis *n* (*on* für); Zwang *m*, Aufsicht *f*; Kontrolle *f* (*on gen.*); Kontrollmarke *f*; *Am.* (Gepäck-)Schein *m*; *Am.* † = cheque; *Am.* Rechnung *f* im *Restaurant*; karierter Stoff; **2.** *v/i.* an-, innehalten; *Am.* e-n Scheck ausstellen; ~ *in Am.* (in e-m Hotel) absteigen; ~ *out Am.* das Hotel verlassen (*nach Bezahlung der Rechnung*); *v/t.* hemmen; kontrollieren; nachprüfen; *Kleider* in der Garderobe abgeben; *Am.* *Gepäck* aufgeben; **.er** ['tʃekə] Aufsichtsbeamte(r) *m*; ~s *pl. Am.* Damespiel *n*; **.ing-room** [~kiŋrum] *Am.* Gepäckaufbewahrung *f*; **.mate 1.** Schachmatt *n*; **2.** matt setzen; ~*up Am.* scharfe Kontrolle.

cheek [tʃiːk] Backe *f*, Wange *f*; F Unverschämtheit *f*; **cheeky** ['tʃiːki] frech.

cheer [tʃiə] **1.** Stimmung *f*, Fröhlichkeit *f*; Hoch(ruf *m n*); Beifall(sruf) *m*; Speisen *f/pl.*, Mahl *n*; three ~s! dreimal hoch!; **2.** *v/t. a.* ~ *up* aufheitern; mit Beifall begrüßen; *a.* ~ *on* anspornen; *v/i.* hoch rufen; jauchzen; *a.* ~ *up* Mut fassen; **.ful** □ ['tʃiəful] heiter; **.io** F [~ri'ou] mach's gut!, tschüs!; prosit!; **.less** □ [~lis] freudlos; **.y** □ [~əri] heiter, froh.

cheese [tʃiːz] Käse *m*.

chef [ʃef] Küchenchef *m*.

chemical ['kemikəl] **1.** □ chemisch; **2.** ~s *pl.* Chemikalien *pl.*

chemise [ʃi'miːz] (Frauen)Hemd *n*.

chemist ['kemist] Chemiker(in); Apotheker *m*; Drogist *m*; **.ry** [~tri] Chemie *f*.

cheque † [tʃek] Scheck *m*; crossed ~ Verrechnungsscheck *m*.

chequer ['tʃekə] **1.** *mst* ~s *pl.* Karomuster *n*; **2.** karieren; ~ed gewürfelt; *fig.* bunt.

cherish ['tʃeriʃ] hegen, pflegen.

cherry ['tʃeri] Kirsche *f*.

chess [tʃes] Schach(spiel) *n*; ~**board** ['tʃesbɔːd] Schachbrett *n*; ~**man** Schachfigur *f*.

chest [tʃest] Kiste *f*, Lade *f*; *anat.* Brustkasten *m*; ~ *of drawers* Kommode *f*.

chestnut ['tʃesnʌt] 1. ⚘ Kastanie f;
F alter Witz; 2. kastanienbraun.

chevy F ['tʃevi] 1. Hetzjagd f;
Barlaufspiel n; 2. hetzen, jagen.

chew [tʃuː] kauen; sinnen; ~ the
fact od rag Am sl. die Sache
durchkauen, ~ing-gum ['tʃu(:)ıŋ-
gʌm] Kaugummi m.

chicane [ʃi'kein] 1. Schikane f;
2. schikanieren

chicken ['tʃikin] Hühnchen n, Küken n; ~-hearted furchtsam, feige;
~-pox ⚕ [ˌnpɒks] Windpocken
f/pl.

chid [tʃid] pret. u. p.p. von chide.
~den ['tʃidn] p.p von chide.

chide lit [tʃaid] [irr.] schelten.

chief [tʃiːf] 1. ⎾ oberst; Ober...;
Haupt ˌ; hauptsächlich; ~ clerk
Bürovorsteher m; 2. Oberhaupt n,
Chef m; Häuptling m; ...-in-~
Ober...; ~tain ['tʃiːftən] Häuptling
m.

chilblain ['tʃilblein] Frostbeule f.

child [tʃaild] Kind n; from a ~ von
Kindheiˌ an, with ~ schwanger;
~birth [ˌtʃaildbə:θ] Niederkunft f;
~hood [ˌdhud] Kindheit f; ~ish
[ˌdiʃ] kindlich kindisch; ~like
kindlich, ~ren [ˈtʃildrən] pl. v child.

chill [tʃil] 1. eisig, frostig; 2. Frost
m, Kälte f, ⚕ Fieberfrost m; Erkältung f, 3. v/t erkalten lassen;
abkühlen; v/i erkalten; erstarren;
~y ['tʃili] kalt, frostig.

chime [tʃaim] 1. Glockenspiel n;
Geläut n, fig Einklang m; 2. läuten;
fig. harmonieren, übereinstimmen.

chimney ['tʃimni] Schornstein m;
Rauchfang m, Lampen-Zylinder m;
~-sweep(er) Schornsteinfeger m.

chin [tʃin] Kinn n; take it on the ~
Am. F es standhaft ertragen; 2.: ~
o.s. Am e-n Klimmzug machen.

china ['tʃainə] Porzellan n.

Chinese [tʃai'niːz] 1. chinesisch;
2. Chinese(ɪ pl) m, Chinesin f.

chink [tʃiŋk] Ritz m, Spalt m.

chip [tʃip] 1 Schnitzel n, Stückchen
n; Span m, Glas- etc Splitter m;
Spielmarke f; have a ~ on one's
shoulder Am F aggressiv sein; ~s pl.
Pommes frites pl , 2. v/t. schnitzeln; an-, abschlagen; v/i. ab-
bröckeln; ~muck ['tʃipmʌk], ~
munk [ˌʌŋk] nordamerikanisches
gestreiftes Eichhörnchen.

chirp [tʃə:p] 1. zirpen; zwitschern;
2. Gezirp n.

chisel ['tʃizl] 1. Meißel m; 2. meißeln; sl (be)mogeln.

chit-chat ['tʃitʃæt] Geplauder n.

chivalr|ous ['ʃivəlrəs] ritterlich;
~y [ˌri] Ritterschaft f, Rittertum f;
Ritterlichkeit f

chive ⚘ [tʃaiv] Schnittlauch m.

chlor|ine ['klɔːriːn] Chlor n; ~o-
form ['klɔːrəfɔːm] 1. Chloroform n;
2. chloroformieren.

chocolate ['tʃɔkəlit] Schokolade f.

choice [tʃɔis] 1. Wahl f; Auswahl f;
2. ⎕ auserlesen, vorzüglich.

choir ['kwaiə] Chor m.

choke [tʃouk] 1. v/t. (er)würgen,
(a. v/i.) ersticken; ⚡ (ab)drosseln;
(ver)stopfen; mst ~ down hinunter-
würgen; 2. Erstickungsanfall m; ⊕
Würgung f; mot. Choke m, Starter-
klappe f.

choose [tʃuːz] [irr.] (aus)wählen;
~ to inf. vorziehen zu inf.

chop [tʃɔp] 1. Hieb m; Kotelett n;
~s pl. Maul n, Rachen m; ⊕
Backen f/pl.; 2. v/t. hauen, hacken;
zerhacken; austauschen; v/i. wechseln; ~per ['tʃɔpə] Hackmesser n;
~py [ˌpi] unstet; unruhig (See);
böig (Wind).

choral ⎕ ['kɔːrəl] chormäßig;
Chor...; ~(e) ♪ [kɔ'rɑːl] Choral m.

chord [kɔːd] Saite f; ♪ Akkord m.

chore Am. [tʃɔː] Hausarbeit f (mst
pl.).

chorus ['kɔːrəs] 1. Chor m; Kehrreim m; 2. im Chor singen od.
sprechen.

chose [tʃouz] pret. von choose; ~n
['tʃouzn] p.p von choose.

chow Am. sl. [tʃau] Essen n.

Christ [kraist] Christus m.

christen ['krisn] taufen; ~ing
[ˌniŋ] Taufe f; attr. Tauf...

Christian ['kristjən] 1. ⎕ christ-
lich; ~ name Vor-, Taufname m;
2. Christ(in); ~ity [kristi'æniti]
Christentum n.

Christmas ['krisməs] Weihnachten n.

chromium ['kroumjəm] Chrom n
(Metall); ~-plated verchromt.

chronic ['krɔnik] (~ally) chronisch
(mst ⚕⚕), dauernd, sl. ekelhaft; ~le
[ˌkl] 1. Chronik f; 2. aufzeichnen.

chronolog|ical ⎕ [krɔnə'lɔdʒikəl]
chronologisch; ~y [krə'nɔlədʒi]
Zeitrechnung f; Zeitfolge f.

chubby F ['tʃabi] rundlich; paus-
bäckig; plump (a. fig.).

chuck¹ [tʃʌk] 1. Glucken n; my ~l
mein Täubchen!; 2. glucken.

chuck² F [ˌ] 1. schmeißen; 2. (Hinaus)Wurf m.

chuckle ['tʃʌkl] kichern, glucksen.

chum F [tʃʌm] 1 (Stuben)Kame-
rad m; 2. zs.-wohnen.

chump F [tʃʌmp] Holzklotz m.

chunk F [tʃʌŋk] Klotz m.

church [tʃə:tʃ] Kirche f; attr.
Kirch(en)...; ~ service Gottesdienst
m; ~warden ['tʃə:tʃ'wɔːdn] Kir-
chenvorsteher m; ~yard Kirchhof
m.

churl [tʃə:l] Grobian m; Flegel m;
~ish ⎕ ['tʃə:liʃ] grob, flegelhaft.

churn [tʃə:n] 1. Butterfaß n; 2. but-
tern; aufwühlen.

chute [ʃuːt] Stromschnelle f; Gleit-,
Rutschbahn f; Fallschirm m.

cider ['saidə] Apfelmost *m*.

cigar [si'gɑ:] Zigarre *f*.

cigarette [sigə'ret] Zigarette *f*; **~-case** Zigarettenetui *n*.

cigar-holder [si'gɑ:houldə] Zigarrenspitze *f*.

cilia ['siliə] *pl*. (Augen)Wimpern *f/pl*.

cinch *Am. sl*. [sintʃ] sichere Sache.

cincture ['siŋktʃə] Gürtel *m*, Gurt *m*.

cinder ['sində] Schlacke *f*; **~s** *pl*. Asche *f*; **2ella** [sində'relə] Aschenbrödel *n*; **~-path** *Sport*: Aschenbahn *f*.

cine-camera ['sini'kæmərə] Filmkamera *f*.

cinema ['sinəmə] Kino *n*; Film *m*.

cinnamon ['sinəmən] Zimt *m*.

cipher ['saifə] 1. Ziffer *f*; Null *f* (*a. fig*.); Geheimschrift *f*, Chiffre *f*; 2. chiffrieren; (aus)rechnen.

circle ['sə:kl] 1. Kreis *m*; *Bekannten- etc*. Kreis *m*; Kreislauf *m*; *thea*. Rang *m*; Ring *m*; 2. (um)kreisen.

circuit ['sə:kit] Kreislauf *m*; *⚡* Stromkreis *m*; Rundreise *f*; Gerichtsbezirk *m*; *✈* Rundflug *m*; **short ~** *⚡* Kurzschluß *m*; **~ous** □ [sə(:)'kju(:)itəs] weitschweifig; Um...

circular ['sə:kjulə] 1. □ kreisförmig; Kreis...; **~ letter** Rundschreiben *n*; **~ note** *✝* Kreditbrief *m*; 2. Rundschreiben *n*; Laufzettel *m*.

circulat|e ['sə:kjuleit] *v/i*. umlaufen, zirkulieren; *v/t*. in Umlauf setzen; **~ing** [~tiŋ]: **~ library** Leihbücherei *f*; **~ion** [sə:kju'leiʃən] Zirkulation *f*, Kreislauf *m*; *fig*. Umlauf *m*; Verbreitung *f*; *Zeitungs*-Auflage *f*.

circum|... ['sə:kəm] (her)um; **~ference** [sə'kʌmfərəns] (Kreis-)Umfang *m*, Peripherie *f*; **~jacent** [sə:kəm'dʒeisənt] umliegend; **~locution** [~mlə'kju:ʃən] Umständlichkeit *f*; Weitschweifigkeit *f*; **~navigate** [~m'nævigeit] umschiffen; **~scribe** ['sə:kəmskraib] *A* umschreiben; *fig*. begrenzen; **~spect** □ [~spekt] um-, vorsichtig; **~stance** [~stəns] Umstand *m* (**~s** *pl. a*. Verhältnisse *n/pl*.); Einzelheit *f*; Umständlichkeit *f*; **~stantial** □ [sə:kəm'stænʃəl] umständlich; **~ evidence** *⚌* Indizienbeweis *m*; **~vent** [~m'vent] überlisten; vereiteln.

circus ['sə:kəs] Zirkus *m*; (runder) Platz.

cistern ['sistən] Wasserbehälter *m*.

cit|ation [sai'teiʃən] Vorladung *f*; Anführung *f*, Zitat *n*; *Am*. öffentliche Ehrung; **~e** [sait] *⚌* vorladen; anführen; zitieren.

citizen ['sitizn] (Staats)Bürger(in); Städter(in); **~ship** [~nʃip] Bürgerrecht *n*, Staatsangehörigkeit *f*.

citron ['sitrən] Zitrone *f*.

city ['siti] 1. Stadt *f*; **the 2** die City, das Geschäftsviertel; 2. städtisch, Stadt...; **2 article** Börsen-, Handelsbericht *m*; **~ editor** *Am*. Lokalredakteur *m*; **~ hall** *Am*. Rathaus *n*; **~ manager** *Am*. Oberstadtdirektor *m*.

civic ['sivik] (staats)bürgerlich; städtisch; **~s** *sg*. Staatsbürgerkunde *f*.

civil □ ['sivl] bürgerlich, Bürger...; zivil; **~⚌** zivilrechtlich; höflich; **2 Servant** Verwaltungsbeamt|e(r) *m*, -in *f*; **2 Service** Staatsdienst *m*; **~ian** ⚔ [si'viljən] Zivilist *m*; **~ity** [~liti] Höflichkeit *f*; **~ization** [sivilai'zeiʃən] Zivilisation *f*, Kultur *f*; **~ize** ['sivilaiz] zivilisieren.

clad [klæd] 1. *pret. u. p.p. von* **clothe**; 2. *adj*. gekleidet.

claim [kleim] 1. Anspruch *m*; Anrecht *n* (**to** auf *acc*.); Forderung *f*; *Am*. Parzelle *f*; 2. beanspruchen; fordern; sich berufen auf (*acc*.); **~ to be sich ausgeben für; ~ant** ['kleimənt] Beanspruchende(r *m*) *f*; *⚌* Kläger *m*.

clairvoyant(e) [klɛə'vɔiənt] Hellseher(in).

clamber ['klæmbə] klettern.

clammy □ ['klæmi] feuchtkalt, klamm.

clamo(u)r ['klæmə] 1. Geschrei *n*, Lärm *m*; 2. schreien (**for** nach).

clamp ⊕ [klæmp] 1. Klammer *f*; 2. verklammern; befestigen.

clan [klæn] Clan *m*, Sippe *f* (*a. fig*.).

clandestine □ [klæn'destin] heimlich; Geheim...

clang [klæŋ] 1. Klang *m*, Geklirr *n*; 2. schallen; klirren (lassen).

clank [klæŋk] 1. Gerassel *n*, Geklirr *n*; 2. rasseln, klirren (mit).

clap [klæp] 1. Klatschen *n*; Schlag *m*, Klaps *m*; 2. schlagen (mit); klatschen; **~board** *Am*. ['klæpbɔ:d] Schaltbrett *n*; **~trap** Effekthascherei *f*.

claret ['klærət] roter Bordeaux; *allg*. Rotwein *m*; Weinrot *n*; *sl*. Blut *n*.

clarify ['klærifai] *v/t*. (ab)klären; *fig*. klären; *v/i*. sich klären.

clarity ['klæriti] Klarheit *f*.

clash [klæʃ] 1. Geklirr *n*; Zs.-stoß *m*; Widerstreit *m*; 2. klirren (mit); zs.-stoßen.

clasp [klɑ:sp] 1. Haken *m*, Klammer *f*; Schnalle *f*; Spange *f*; *fig*. Umklammerung *f*; Umarmung *f*; 2. *v/t*. an-, zuhaken; *fig*. umklammern; umfassen; *v/i*. festhalten; **~-knife** ['klɑ:sp'naif] Taschenmesser *n*.

class [klɑ:s] 1. Klasse *f*; Stand *m*; (Unterrichts)Stunde *f*; Kurs *m*; *Am. univ*. Jahrgang *m*; 2. (in Klassen) einteilen, einordnen.

classic ['klæsik] Klassiker *m*; **~s**

pl. die alten Sprachen; ~(al □) [~k(ə)l] klassisch.

classi|fication [klæsifi'keiʃən] Klassifizierung *f*; Einteilung *f*; ~fy ['klæsifai] klassifizieren, einstufen.

clatter ['klætə] 1. Geklapper *n*; 2. klappern (mit); *fig.* schwatzen.

clause [klɔːz] Klausel *f*, Bestimmung *f*; *gr.* (Neben)Satz *m*.

claw [klɔː] 1. Klaue *f*, Kralle *f*, Pfote *f*; *Krebs*-Schere *f*; 2. (zer-) kratzen; (um)krallen.

clay [klei] Ton *m*; *fig.* Erde *f*.

clean [kliːn] 1. *adj.* □ rein; sauber; 2. *adv.* rein, völlig; 3. reinigen (of von); sich waschen lassen (*Stoff etc.*); ~ **up** aufräumen; ~**er** ['kliːnə] Reiniger *m*; *mst* ~**s** *pl.* (chemische) Reinigung; ~**ing** [.niŋ] Reinigung *f*; ~**liness** ['klenlinis] Reinlichkeit *f*; ~**ly** 1. *adv* ['kliːnli] rein; sauber; 2. *adj.* ['klenli] reinlich; ~**se** [klenz] reinigen; säubern.

clear [kliə] 1. □ klar; hell, rein; *fig.* rein (from von); frei (of von); ganz, voll; † rein, netto; 2. *v/t.* er-, aufhellen; (auf)klären; reinigen (of, from von); *Wald* lichten, roden; wegräumen (*a.* ~ **away** *od.* **off**); *Hindernis* nehmen; *Rechnung* bezahlen; † (aus)klarieren; verzollen; *f* freisprechen; befreien; rechtfertigen (from von); *v/i. a.* ~ **up** sich aufhellen; sich verziehen; ~**ance** ['kliərəns] Aufklärung *f*; Freilegung *f*; Räumung *f*; † Abrechnung *f*, ♣, † Verzollung *f*; ~**ing** [.riŋ] Aufklärung *f*; Lichtung *f*, Rodung *f*; † Ab-, Verrechnung *f*; ♀ **House** Ab-, Verrechnungsstelle *f*.

cleave[1] [kliːv] [*irr.*] (sich) spalten; *Wasser, Luft* (zer)teilen.

cleave[2] [.] *fig* festhalten (to an *dat.*); treu bleiben (*dat.*).

cleaver ['kliːvə] Hackmesser *n*.

clef ♪ [klef] Schlüssel *m*.

cleft [kleft] 1. Spalte *f*; Sprung *m*, Riß *m*; 2. *pret. u. p.p. von* cleave[1].

clemen|cy ['klemənsi] Milde *f*; ~**t** □ [.nt] mild

clench [klentʃ] *Lippen etc.* fest zs.-pressen, *Zähne* zs.-beißen; *Faust* ballen; festhalten.

clergy ['kləːdʒi] Geistlichkeit *f*; ~**man** Geistliche(r) *m*.

clerical ['klerikəl] 1. □ geistlich; Schreib(er). ; 2. Geistliche(r) *m*.

clerk [klɑːk] Schreiber(in); Büroangestellte(r *m*) *f*; Sekretär(in); † kaufmännische(r) Angestellte(r); *Am.* Verkäufer(in); Küster *m*.

clever □ ['klevə] gescheit; geschickt.

clew [kluː] Knäuel *m*, *n*; = clue.

click [klik] 1. Knacken *n*; ⊕ Sperrhaken *m*, -klinke *f*; 2. knacken; zu-, einschnappen; klappen.

client ['klaiənt] Klient(in); Kund|e

m, -in *f*; ~**ele** [kliːɑːn'teil] Kundschaft *f*.

cliff [klif] Klippe *f*; Felsen *m*.

climate ['klaimit] Klima *n*.

climax ['klaimæks] 1. *rhet.* Steigerung *f*; Gipfel *m*, Höhepunkt *m*; 2. (sich) steigern.

climb [klaim] (er)klettern, (er-) klimmen, (er)steigen; ~**er** ['klaimə] Kletterer *m*, Bergsteiger(in); ♀ Streber(in); ♣ Kletterpflanze *f*; ~**ing** [.miŋ] Klettern *n*; *attr.* Kletter...

clinch [klintʃ] 1. ⊕ Vernietung *f*; Festhalten *n*; *Boxen:* Umklammerung *f*; 2. *v/t.* vernieten; festmachen; *s. clench*; *v/i.* festhalten.

cling [kliŋ] [*irr.*] (to) festhalten (an *dat.*), sich klammern (an *acc.*); sich (an)schmiegen (an *acc.*); *j-m* anhängen.

clinic ['klinik] Klinik *f*; klinisches Praktikum; ~**al** □ [.kəl] klinisch.

clink [kliŋk] 1. Geklirr *n*; 2. klingen, klirren (lassen); klimpern mit; ~**er** ['kliŋkə] Klinker(stein) *m*.

clip[1] [klip] 1. Schur *f*; at one ~ *Am.* *f* auf einmal; 2. ab-, aus-, beschneiden; *Schafe etc.* scheren.

clip[2] [.] Klammer *f*; Spange *f*.

clipp|er ['klipə]: (*a. pair of*) ~**s** *pl.* Haarschneide-, Schermaschine *f*; Klipper *m*; ♣ Schnellsegler *m*; ✈ Verkehrsflugzeug *n*; ~**ings** [.piŋz] *pl.* Abfälle *m/pl.*; Zeitungs- *etc.* Ausschnitte *m/pl.*

cloak [klouk] 1. Mantel *m*; 2. *fig.* bemänteln, verhüllen; ~**room** ['kloukrum] Garderobe(nraum *m*) *f*; Toilette *f*; ⚅ Gepäckabgabe *f*.

clock [klɔk] Schlag-, *Wand*-Uhr *f*; ~**wise** ['klɔkwaiz] im Uhrzeigersinn; ~**work** Uhrwerk *n*; like ~ wie am Schnürchen.

clod [klɔd] Erdklumpen *m*; *a.* ~**hopper** (Bauern)Tölpel *m*.

clog [klɔg] 1. Klotz *m*; Holzschuh *m*, Pantine *f*; 2. belasten; hemmen; (sich) verstopfen.

cloister ['klɔistə] Kreuzgang *m*; Kloster *n*.

close 1. □ [klous] geschlossen; verborgen; verschwiegen; knapp, eng; begrenzt; nah, eng; bündig; dicht; gedrängt; schwül; knickerig; genau; fest (*Griff*); ~ **by**, ~ **to** dicht bei; ~ **fight**, ~ **quarters** *pl.* Handgemenge *n*, Nahkampf *m*; ~(**ed**) *season*, ~ *time hunt.* Schonzeit *f*; *sail* ~ *to the wind fig.* sich hart an der Grenze des Erlaubten bewegen; 2. [klouz] Schluß *m*; Abschluß *m*; [klous] Einfriedung *f*; Hof *m*; 3. [klouz] *v/t.* (ab-, ein-, ver-, zu-) schließen; beschließen; *v/i.* (sich) schließen; abschließen; handgemein werden; ~ *in* hereinbrechen (*Nacht*); kürzer werden (*Tage*); ~ *on* (*prp.*) sich schließen um, umfassen; **~ness** ['klousnis] Genauigkeit *f*, Geschlossenheit *f*.

closet [klɔzit] **1.** Kabinett *n*; (Wand)Schrank *m*; = water-~; **2.**: be ~ed with mit *j-m* e-e geheime Beratung haben. [nahme *f*.]

close-up ['klousʌp] *Film:* Großauf-/

closure ['klouʒə] Verschluß *m*; *parl.* (Antrag *m* auf) Schluß *m* e-r *Debatte*.

clot [klɔt] **1.** Klümpchen *n*; **2.** zu Klümpchen gerinnen (lassen).

cloth [klɔθ] Stoff *m*, Tuch *n*; Tischtuch *n*; Kleidung *f*, Amts-Tracht *f*; *the ~* F der geistliche Stand; *lay the ~* den Tisch decken; **~-binding** Leineneinband *m*; **~-bound** in Leinen gebunden.

clothe [klouð] [*irr.*] (an-, be)kleiden; einkleiden.

clothes [klouðz] *pl.* Kleider *n/pl.*; Kleidung *f*; Anzug *m*; Wäsche *f*; **~-basket** ['klouðzbɑ:skit] Waschkorb *m*; **~-line** Wäscheleine *f*; **~-peg** Kleiderhaken *m*; Wäscheklammer *f*; **~-pln** *bsd. Am.* Wäscheklammer *f*; **~-press** Kleider-, Wäscheschrank *m*.

clothier ['klouðiə] Tuch-, Kleiderhändler *m*.

clothing ['klouðiŋ] Kleidung *f*.

cloud [klaud] **1.** Wolke *f* (*a. fig.*); Trübung *f*; Schatten *m*; **2.** (sich) be-, umwölken (*a. fig.*); **~-burst** ['klaudbə:st] Wolkenbruch *m*; **~-less** □ [~dlis] wolkenlos; **~y** | [~di] wolkig; Wolken...; trüb; unklar.

clout [klaut] Lappen *m*; F Kopfnuß *f*.

clove¹ [klouv] (Gewürz)Nelke *f*.

clove² [~] *pret. von cleave*¹; **~n** ['klouvn] **1.** *p.p. von cleave*¹; **2.** *adj.* gespalten.

clover ♃ ['klouvə] Klee *m*.

clown [klaun] Hanswurst *m*; Tölpel *m*; **~ish** | ['klauniʃ] bäurisch; plump; clownhaft.

cloy [klɔi] übersättigen, überladen.

club [klʌb] **1.** Keule *f*; (Gummi-) Knüppel *m*; Klub *m*; **~s** *pl.* Karten: Kreuz *n*; **2.** *v/t.* mit e-r Keule schlagen; *v/i.* sich zs.-tun; **~-foot** ['klʌbfut] Klumpfuß *m*.

clue [klu:] Anhaltspunkt *m*, Fingerzeig *m*.

clump [klʌmp] **1.** Klumpen *m*; Baum-Gruppe *f*; **2.** trampeln; zs.-drängen.

clumsy □ ['klʌmzi] unbeholfen, ungeschickt; plump.

clung [klʌŋ] *pret. u. p.p. von cling*.

cluster ['klʌstə] **1.** Traube *f*; Büschel *n*; Haufen *m*; **2.** büschelweise wachsen; (sich) zs.-drängen.

clutch [klʌtʃ] **1.** Griff *m*; ⊕ Kupplung *f*; Klaue *f*; **2.** (er)greifen.

clutter ['klʌtə] **1.** Wirrwarr *m*; **2.** durch-ea.-rennen; durch-ea.-bringen.

coach [koutʃ] **1.** Kutsche *f*; ⛟ Wagen *m*; Reisebus *m*; Einpauker *m*; Trainer *m*; **2.** in e-r Kutsche fahren; (ein)pauken; trainieren; **~man** ['koutʃmən] Kutscher *m*.

coagulate [kou'ægjuleit] gerinnen (lassen).

coal [koul] **1.** (Stein)Kohle *f*; *carry ~s to Newcastle* Eulen nach Athen tragen; **2.** ⚓ (be)kohlen.

coalesce [kouə'les] zs.-wachsen; sich vereinigen.

coalition [kouə'liʃən] Verbindung *f*; Bund *m*, Koalition *f*.

coal-pit ['koulpit] Kohlengrube *f*.

coarse □ [kɔ:s] grob; ungeschliffen.

coast [koust] **1.** Küste *f*; *bsd. Am.* Rodelbahn *f*; **2.** die Küste entlangfahren; im Freilauf fahren; rodeln; **~er** ['koustə] *Am.* Rodelschlitten *m*; ⚓ Küstenfahrer *m*.

coat [kout] **1.** Jackett *n*, Jacke *f*, Rock *m*; Mantel *m*; Pelz *m*, Gefieder *n*; Überzug *m*; *~ of arms* Wappen(schild *m*, *n*) *n*; **2.** überziehen; anstreichen; **~-hanger** ['kouthæŋə] Kleiderbügel *m*; **~ing** ['koutiŋ] Überzug *m*; Anstrich *m*; Mantelstoff *m*.

coax [kouks] schmeicheln (*dat.*); beschwatzen (*into* zu).

cob [kɔb] kleines starkes Pferd; Schwan *m*; *Am.* Maiskolben *m*.

cobbler ['kɔblə] Schuhmacher *m*; Stümper *m*.

cobweb ['kɔbweb] Spinn(en)gewebe *n*.

cock [kɔk] **1.** Hahn *m*; Anführer *m*; Heuhaufen *m*; **2.** *a.* ~ *up* aufrichten; *Gewehrhahn* spannen.

cockade [kɔ'keid] Kokarde *f*.

cockatoo [kɔkə'tu:] Kakadu *m*.

cockboat ⚓ ['kɔkbout] Jolle *f*.

cockchafer ['kɔktʃeifə] Maikäfer *m*.

cock|-eyed *sl.* ['kɔkaid] schieläugig; *Am.* blau (*betrunken*); **~-horse** Steckenpferd *n*.

cockney ['kɔkni] waschechter Londoner.

cockpit ['kɔkpit] Kampfplatz *m* für Hähne; ⚓ Raumdeck *n*; ✈ Führerraum *m*, Kanzel *f*.

cockroach *zo.* ['kɔkroutʃ] Schabe *f*.

cock|sure F ['kɔk'ʃuə] absolut sicher; überheblich; **~tail** Cocktail *m*; **~y** □ F ['kɔki] selbstbewußt; frech.

coco ['koukou] Kokospalme *f*.

cocoa ['koukou] Kakao *m*.

coco-nut ['koukənʌt] Kokosnuß *f*.

cocoon [kə'ku:n] Seiden-Kokon *m*.

cod [kɔd] Kabeljau *m*.

coddle ['kɔdl] verhätscheln.

code [koud] **1.** Gesetzbuch *n*; Kodex *m*; Telegramm-, Signal-Schlüssel *m*; **2.** chiffrieren.

codger F ['kɔdʒə] komischer Kauz.

cod-liver ['kɔdlivə]: ~ *oil* Lebertran *m*.

co-ed *Am.* F ['kou'ed] Schülerin *f*
e-r Koedukationsschule, *allg.* Studentin *f.*

coerc|e [kou'ə:s] (er)zwingen; ~ion
[kou'ə:ʃən] Zwang *m.*

coeval [kou'i:vəl] gleichzeitig;
gleichalt(e)rig.

coexist ['kouig'zist] gleichzeitig
bestehen

coffee ['kɔfi] Kaffee *m*; ~-pot Kaf-
feekanne *f*, ~-room Speisesaal *m*
e-s Hotels, ~-set Kaffeeservice *n.*

coffer ['kɔfə] (Geld)Kasten *m.*

coffin ['kɔfin] Sarg *m.*

cogent ['koudʒənt] zwingend.

cogitate ['kɔdʒiteit] *v/i.* nachdenken; *v/t* (er)sinnen.

cognate ['kɔgneit] verwandt.

cognition [kɔg'niʃən] Erkenntnis *f.*

cognizable ['kɔgnizəbl] erkennbar.

coheir ['kou eə] Miterbe *m.*

coheren|ce [kou'hiərəns] Zs.-hang
m; ~t [~nt] zs-hängend.

cohesi|on [kou'hi:ʒən] Kohäsion *f*;
~ve [~i:siv] (fest) zs.-hängend.

coiff|eur [kwa:'fə:] Friseur *m*; ~ure
[~'fjuə] Frisur *f.*

coil [kɔil] 1. *a.* ~ up aufwickeln;
(sich) zs.-rollen; 2. Rolle *f*, Spirale
f; Wicklung *f*; ∮ Spule *f*; Windung
f; ⊕ (Rohr)Schlange *f.*

coin [kɔin] 1. Münze *f*; 2. prägen
(*a. fig.*); münzen; ~age ['kɔinidʒ]
Prägung *f*; Geld *n*, Münze *f.*

coincide [kouin'said] zs.-treffen;
übereinstimmen; ~nce [kou'insi-
dəns] Zs.-treffen *n*; *fig.* Übereinstimmung *f*

coke [kouk] Koks *m* (*a. sl.* = Kokain*); Am.* F Coca-Cola *n*, *f.*

cold [kould] 1. ~ kalt; 2. Kälte *f*,
Frost *m*; Erkältung *f*; ~ness
['kouldnis] Kälte *f.*

coleslaw *Am.* ['koulslɔ:] Kraut-
salat *m.*

colic ∮ ['kɔlik] Kolik *f.*

collaborat|e [kə'læbəreit] zs.-ar-
beiten; ~ion [kəlæbə'reiʃən] Zs.-,
Mitarbeit *f*; *in* ~ gemeinsam.

collaps|e [kə'læps] 1. zs.-, einfallen;
zs.-brechen; 2. Zs.-bruch *m*; ~ible
[~əbl] zs.-klappbar.

collar ['kɔlə] 1. Kragen *m*; Halsband
n; Kum(me)t *n*; ⊕ Lager *n*; 2. beim
Kragen packen, *Fleisch* zs.-rollen;
~-bone Schlüsselbein *n*; ~-stud
Kragenknopf *m.*

collate [kɔ'leit] *Texte* vergleichen.

collateral [kɔ'lætərəl] 1. ⬡ parallel
laufend; Seiten..., Neben...; indirekt; 2. Seitenverwandte(r *m*) *f.*

colleague ['kɔli:g] Kollege *m*, -in *f.*

collect 1. *eccl.* ['kɔlekt] Kollekte *f*;
2. *v/t.* [kə'lekt] (ein)sammeln; *Gedanken etc.* sammeln; einkassieren;
abholen; *v/i.* sich (ver)sammeln;
~ed *fig.* gefaßt; ~ion [~kʃən]
Sammlung *f*; Einziehung *f*; ~ive
[~ktiv] gesammelt; Sammel...; ~

bargaining   Tarifverhandlungen
f|*pl.*; ~ively [~vli] insgesamt; zs.-
fassend; ~or [~tə] Sammler *m*;
Steuereinnehmer *m*; ⑯ Fahrkarten-
abnehmer *m*; ∮ Stromabnehmer
m.

college ['kɔlidʒ] College *n* (*Teil e-r
Universität*); höhere Schule *od.*
Lehranstalt *f*; Hochschule *f*; Aka-
demie *f*; Kollegium *n.*

collide [kə'laid] zs.-stoßen.

collie ['kɔli] Collie *m*, schottischer
Schäferhund.

collier ['kɔliə] Bergmann *m*; ⚓
Kohlenschiff *n*; ~y ['kɔljəri] Kohlengrube *f.*

collision [kə'liʒən] Zs.-stoß *m.*

colloquial ⬡ [kə'loukwiəl] umgangs-
sprachlich, familiär.

colloquy ['kɔləkwi] Gespräch *n.*

colon *typ.* ['koulən] Doppelpunkt *m.*

colonel ✕ ['kə:nl] Oberst *m.*

coloni|al [kə'lounjəl] Kolonial...;
~alism *pol.* [~lizəm] Kolonialismus
m; ~ze ['kɔlənaiz] kolonisieren;
(sich) ansiedeln; besiedeln.

colony ['kɔləni] Kolonie *f*; Siedlung *f.*

colossal ⬡ [kə'lɔsəl] kolossal.

colo(u)r ['kʌlə] 1. Farbe *f*; *fig.*
Färbung *f*; Anschein *m*; Vorwand
m; ~s *pl.* ✕ Fahne *f*, Flagge *f*; 2. *v/t.*
färben; anstreichen; *fig.* beschönigen; *v/i.* sich (ver)färben; erröten;
~-bar Rassenschranke *f*; ~ed ge-
färbt, farbig; ~ man Farbige(r) *m*;
~ful [~əful] farbenreich, -freu-
dig; lebhaft; ~ing [~əriŋ] Färbung
f; Farbton *m*; *fig.* Beschönigung *f*;
~less ⬡ [~əlis] farblos; ~ line *bsd.*
Am. Rassenschranke *f.*

colt [koult] Hengstfüllen *n*; *fig.*
Neuling *m.*

column ['kɔləm] Säule *f*; *typ.* Spalte
f; ✕ Kolonne *f*; ~ist *Am.* [~mnist]
Kolumnist *m.*

comb [koum] 1. Kamm *m*; ⊕
Hechel *f*; 2. *v/t.* kämmen; striegeln;
Flachs hecheln.

combat ['kɔmbət] 1. Kampf *m*;
single ~ Zweikampf *m*; 2. (be-)
kämpfen; ~ant [~tənt] Kämpfer *m.*

combin|ation [kɔmbi'neiʃən] Ver-
bindung *f*; *mst* ~s *pl.* Hemdhose *f*;
~e [kəm'bain] (sich) verbinden,
vereinigen.

combust|ible [kəm'bʌstəbl] 1.
brennbar; 2. ~s *pl.* Brennmaterial *n*;
mot. Betriebsstoff *m*; ~ion [~tʃən]
Verbrennung *f.*

come [kʌm] [*irr.*] kommen; *to* ~
künftig, kommend; ~ about zutragen; ~ across auf *j. od. et.* stoßen;
~ at erreichen; ~ by vorbeikommen;
zu et. kommen; ~ down herunterkommen (*a. fig.*); *Am.* F erkranken
(*with an dat.*); ~ for abholen; ~ off
davonkommen; losgehen (*Knopf*);
ausfallen (*Haare etc.*); stattfinden;

~ round vorbeikommen (*bsd. zu Besuch*); wiederkehren; F zu sich kommen; *fig.* einlenken; **~ to** *adv.* dazukommen; ♣ beidrehen; *prp.* betragen; **~ up to** entsprechen (*dat.*); es *j-m* gleichtun; *Stand, Maß* erreichen; **~back** ['kʌmbæk] Wiederkehr *f*, Comeback *n*; *Am. sl.* schlagfertige Antwort.

comedian [kə'mi:djən] Schauspieler(in); Komiker(in); Lustspieldichter *m*.

comedy ['kɔmidi] Lustspiel *n*.

comeliness ['kʌmlinis] Anmut *f*.

comfort ['kʌmfət] **1.** Bequemlichkeit *f*; Behaglichkeit *f*; Trost *m*; *fig.* Beistand *m*; Erquickung *f*; **2.** trösten; erquicken; beleben; **~able** ⌐ [~təbl] behaglich, bequem; tröstlich; **~er** [~tə] Tröster *m*; *fig.* wollenes Halstuch; Schnuller *m*; *Am.* Steppdecke *f*; **~less** ☐ [~tlis] unbehaglich; trostlos; **~ station** *Am.* Bedürfnisanstalt *f*.

comic(al ⌐) ['kɔmik(əl)] komisch; lustig, drollig.

coming ['kʌmiŋ] **1.** kommend; künftig; **2.** Kommen *n*.

comma ['kɔmə] Komma *n*.

command [kə'mɑːnd] **1.** Herrschaft *f*, Beherrschung *f* (*a. fig.*); Befehl *m*; ✕ Kommando *n*; be (have) at ~ zur Verfügung stehen (haben); **2.** befehlen; ✕ kommandieren; verfügen über (*acc.*); beherrschen; **~er** [~də] Kommandeur *m*, Befehlshaber *m*; ♣ Fregattenkapitän *m*; **~er-in-chief** [~ərin-'tʃiːf] Oberbefehlshaber *m*; **~ment** [~dmənt] Gebot *n*.

commemorat|e [kə'meməreit] gedenken (*gen.*), feiern; **~ion** [kəmemə'reiʃən] Gedächtnisfeier *f*.

commence [kə'mens] anfangen, beginnen; **~ment** [~smənt] Anfang *m*. [loben; anvertrauen.]

commend [kə'mend] empfehlen;]

commensurable [kə'menʃərəbl] vergleichbar (*with, to* mit).

comment ['kɔment] **1.** Kommentar *m*; Erläuterung *f*; An-, Bemerkung *f*; **2.** (*upon*) erläutern (*acc.*); sich auslassen (über *acc.*); **~ary** ['kɔməntəri] Kommentar *m*; **~ator** ['kɔmenteitə] Kommentator *m*; *Radio:* Berichterstatter *m*.

commerc|e [kə'məˑɔ(:)s] Handel *m*; Verkehr *m*; **~ial** ⌐ [kə'məˑɔ:ʃəl] **1.** kaufmännisch; Handels...; Geschäfts...; gewerbsmäßig; **~ traveller** Handlungsreisende(r) *m*; **2.** *bsd. Am.* Radio, Fernsehen: kommerzielle (Werbe)Sendung.

commiseration [kəmizə'reiʃən] Mitleid *n* (*for* mit).

commissary ['kɔmisəri] Kommissar *m*; ✕ Intendanturbeamte(r) *m*.

commission [kə'miʃən] **1.** Auftrag *m*; Übertragung *f von Macht etc.*;

Begehung *f e-s Verbrechens*; Provision *f*; Kommission *f*; (Offiziers-) Patent *n*; **2.** beauftragen; bevollmächtigen; ✕ bestellen; ♣ in Dienst stellen; **~er** [~ʃnə] Bevollmächtigte(r *m*) *f*; Kommissar *m*.

commit [kə'mit] anvertrauen; übergeben, überweisen; *Tat* begehen; bloßstellen; ~ (*o.s.* sich) verpflichten; ~ (*to prison*) in Untersuchungshaft nehmen; **~ment** [~tmənt], **~tal** [~tl] Überweisung *f*; Verpflichtung *f*; Verübung *f*; **~tee** [~ti] Ausschuß *m*, Komitee *n*.

commodity [kə'mɔditi] Ware *f* (*mst pl.*), Gebrauchsartikel *m*.

common ['kɔmən] **1.** ☐ (all)gemein; gewöhnlich; gemeinschaftlich; öffentlich; gemein (*niedrig*); ♀ Council Gemeinderat *m*; **2.** Gemeindewiese *f*; *in* ~ gemeinsam; *in* ~ *with fig.* genau wie; **~er** [~nə] Bürger *m*, Gemeine(r) *m*; Mitglied *n* des Unterhauses; **~ law** Gewohnheitsrecht *n*; ♀ **Market** Gemeinsamer Markt; **~place 1.** Gemeinplatz *m*; **2.** gewöhnlich; F abgedroschen; **~s** *pl.* das gemeine Volk; Gemeinschaftsverpflegung *f*; (*mst House of*) ♀ Unterhaus *n*; **~ sense** gesunder Menschenverstand; **~wealth** [~nwelθ] Gemeinwesen *n*, Staat *m*; *bsd.* Republik *f*; the British ♀ das Commonwealth.

commotion [kə'mouʃən] Erschütterung *f*; Aufruhr *m*; Aufregung *f*.

communal ☐ ['kɔmjunl] gemeinschaftlich; Gemeinde...

commune 1. [kə'mjuːn] sich vertraulich besprechen; **2.** ['kɔmjuːn] Gemeinde *f*.

communicat|e [kə'mjuːnikeit] *v/t.* mitteilen; *v/i.* das Abendmahl nehmen, kommunizieren; in Verbindung stehen; **~ion** [kəmjuːni'keiʃən] Mitteilung *f*; Verbindung *f*; **~ive** [kə'mjuːnikətiv] gesprächig.

communion [kə'mjuːnjən] Gemeinschaft *f*; *eccl.* Kommunion *f*, Abendmahl *n*.

communis|m ['kɔmjunizəm] Kommunismus *m*; **~t** [~ist] **1.** Kommunist(in); **2.** kommunistisch.

community [kə'mjuːniti] Gemeinschaft *f*; Gemeinde *f*; Staat *m*.

commut|ation [kɔmju(:)'teiʃən] Vertauschung *f*; Umwandlung *f*; Ablösung *f*; Strafmilderung *f*; **~ ticket** *Am.* Dauerkarte *f*; **~e** [kə'mjuːt] ablösen; Strafe (mildernd) umwandeln; *Am.* pendeln *im Arbeitsverkehr*.

compact 1. ['kɔmpækt] Vertrag *m*; **2.** [kəm'pækt] *adj.* dicht, fest; knapp, bündig; *v/t.* fest verbinden.

companion [kəm'pænjən] Gefährt|e *m*, -in *f*; Gesellschafter(in); **~able** [~nəbl] gesellig; **~ship** [~ʃip] Gesellschaft *f*.

company ['kʌmpəni] Gesellschaft f; Kompanie f; Handelsgesellschaft f; Genossenschaft f; ⚓ Mannschaft f; *thea.* Truppe f; *have* ~ Gäste haben; *keep* ~ *with* verkehren mit.

compar|able [['kɔmpərəbl] vergleichbar; **~ative** [kəm'pærətiv] **1.** □ vergleichend; verhältnismäßig; **2.** *a.* ~ *degree gr.* Komparativ m; **~e** [~'pɛə] **1.** *beyond* ~, *without* ~, *past* ~ unvergleichlich; **2.** *v/t.* vergleichen, gleichstellen (*to* mit); *v/i.* sich vergleichen (lassen); **~ison** [~'pærisn] Vergleich(ung f) m.

compartment [kəm'pɑːtmənt] Abteilung f, ▲ Fach n; 🚢 Abteil n.

compass ['kʌmpəs] **1.** Bereich m; ♪ Umfang m; Kompaß m; *oft pair of* ~*es pl.* Zirkel m; **2.** herumgehen um; einschließen; erreichen; planen.

compassion [kəm'pæʃən] Mitleid n; **~ate** [[~nit] mitleidig.

compatible [kəm'pætəbl] vereinbar, verträglich; schicklich.

compatriot [kəm'pætriət] Landsmann m.

compel [kəm'pel] (er)zwingen.

compensat|e ['kɔmpenseit] *j-n* entschädigen, *et.* ersetzen; ausgleichen; **~ion** [kɔmpen'seiʃən] Ersatz m; Ausgleich(ung f) m; Entschädigung f; *Am.* Vergütung f (*Gehalt*).

compère ['kɔmpɛə] **1.** Conférencier m; **2.** ansagen (bei).

compete [kəm'piːt] sich mitbewerben (*for* um), konkurrieren.

competen|ce, ~cy ['kɔmpitəns, ~si] Befugnis f, Zuständigkeit f; Auskommen n; **~t** [[~nt] hinreichend; (leistungs)fähig, fachkundig; berechtigt, zuständig.

competit|ion [kɔmpi'tiʃən] Mitbewerbung f, Wettbewerb m; ♥ Konkurrenz f; **~ive** [kəm'petitiv] wetteifernd; **~or** [~'petitə] Mitbewerber (-in); Konkurrent(in).

compile [kəm'pail] zs.-tragen, zs.-stellen (*from* aus); sammeln.

complacen|ce, ~cy [kəm'pleisns, ~si] Selbstzufriedenheit f.

complain [kəm'plein] (sich be-)klagen; *amt* [~nənt] Kläger(in); **~t** [~nt] Klage f, Beschwerde f; 🐟 Leiden n.

complaisan|ce [kəm'pleizənz] Gefälligkeit f; Entgegenkommen n; **~t** [[~nt] gefällig; entgegenkommend.

complement 1. ['kɔmplimənt] Ergänzung f; volle Anzahl f; **2.** [~ment] ergänzen

complet|e [kəm'pliːt] **1.** □ vollständig, ganz; vollkommen; **2.** vervollständigen; vervollkommnen; abschließen; **~ion** [~'iːʃən] Vervollständigung f; Abschluß m; Erfüllung f.

complex ['kɔmpleks] **1.** □ zs.-gesetzt; *fig.* kompliziert; **2.** Gesamtheit f, Komplex m; **~ion** [kəm'plekʃən] Aussehen n; Charakter m, Zug m; Gesichtsfarbe f, Teint m; **~ity** [~'ksiti] Kompliziertheit f.

complian|ce [kəm'plaians] Einwilligung f; Einverständnis n; *in* ~ *with* gemäß; **~t** □ [~nt] gefällig.

complicate ['kɔmplikeit] komplizieren, erschweren.

complicity [kəm'plisiti] Mitschuld f (*in an dat.*).

compliment 1. ['kɔmplimənt] Kompliment n; Schmeichelei f; Gruß m; **2.** [~ment] *v/t.* (*on*) beglückwünschen; *j-m* Komplimente machen (über *acc.*); **~ary** [kɔmpli'mentəri] höflich.

comply [kəm'plai] sich fügen; nachkommen, entsprechen (*with dat.*).

component [kəm'pounənt] **1.** Bestandteil m; **2.** zs.-setzend.

compos|e [kəm'pouz] zs.-setzen; komponieren, verfassen; ordnen; beruhigen; *typ.* setzen; **~ed** □ ruhig, gesetzt; **~er** [~zə] Komponist(in); Verfasser(in); **~ition** [kɔmpə'ziʃən] Zs.-setzung f; Abfassung f; Komposition f; (Schrift-) Satz m; Aufsatz m; ♦ Vergleich m; **~t** ['kɔmpost] Kompost m; **~ure** [kəm'pouʒə] Fassung f, Gemütsruhe f.

compound 1. ['kɔmpaund] zs.-gesetzt; ~ *interest* Zinseszinsen m/pl.; **2.** Zs.-setzung f, Verbindung f; **3.** [kəm'paund] *v/t.* zs.-setzen; *Streit* beilegen; *v/i.* sich einigen.

comprehend [kɔmpri'hend] umfassen; begreifen, verstehen.

comprehen|sible □ [kɔmpri'hensəbl] verständlich; **~sion** [~ʃən] Verständnis n; Fassungskraft f; Umfang m; **~sive** □ [~nsiv] umfassend.

compress [kəm'pres] zs.-drücken; ~*ed air* Druckluft f; **~ion** [~'eʃən] *phys.* Verdichtung f; ⊕ Druck m.

comprise [kəm'praiz] in sich fassen, einschließen, enthalten.

compromise ['kɔmprəmaiz] **1.** Kompromiß m, n; **2.** *v/t. Streit* beilegen; bloßstellen; *v/i.* e-n Kompromiß schließen.

compuls|ion [kəm'pʌlʃən] Zwang m; **~ory** [~'lsəri] obligatorisch; Zwangs...; Pflicht...

compunction [kəm'pʌŋkʃən] Gewissensbisse m/pl.; Reue f; Bedenken n.

comput|ation [kɔmpju(ː)'teiʃən] (Be)Rechnung f; **~e** [kəm'pjuːt] (be-, er)rechnen; schätzen; **~er** [~tə] Computer m.

comrade ['kɔmrid] Kamerad m.

con[1] *abbr.* [kɔn] = *contra.*

con² *Am. sl.* [~] **1.:** ~ *man* = *confidence man*; **2.** 'reinlegen (*betrügen*).

conceal [kən'si:l] verbergen; *fig.* verhehlen, verheimlichen, verschweigen.

concede [kən'si:d] zugestehen; einräumen, gewähren, nachgeben.

conceit [kən'si:t] Einbildung *f*; spitzfindiger Gedanke; übertriebenes sprachliches Bild; ~ed 1 eingebildet (of auf *acc.*).

conceiv|able [kən'si:vəbl] denkbar; begreiflich; ~e [kən'si:v] *v/i.* empfangen (*schwanger werden*); sich denken (of *acc.*); *v/t.* Kind empfangen; sich denken; aussinnen.

concentrate ['kɔnsentreit] (sich) zs.-ziehen, sich konzentrieren.

conception [kən'sepʃən] Begreifen *n*; Vorstellung *f*, Begriff *m*, Idee *f*; *biol.* Empfängnis *f*.

concern [kən'sə:n] **1.** Angelegenheit *f*; Interesse *n*; Sorge *f*; Beziehung *f* (with zu); ✝ Geschäft *n*, (industrielles) Unternehmen; **2.** betreffen, angehen, interessieren; ~ *o.s. about od. for* sich kümmern um; *be ~ed in* Betracht kommen; ~ed □ interessiert; beteiligt (in an *dat.*); bekümmert; ~ing *prp* [~niŋ] betreffend, über, wegen, hinsichtlich.

concert 1. ['kɔnsət] Konzert *n*; **2.** [~sə(:)t] Einverständnis *n*; **3.** [kən'sə:t] sich einigen, verabreden; ~ed gemeinsam; ♩ mehrstimmig.

concession [kən'seʃən] Zugeständnis *n*; Erlaubnis *f*. [räumend.]

concessive [kən'sesiv] einräumend.)

conciliat|e [kən'silieit] aus-, versöhnen; ausgleichen; ~or [~tə] Vermittler *m*; ~ory [~iətəri] versöhnlich, vermittelnd.

concise [kən'sais] kurz, bündig, knapp; ~ness [~snis] Kürze *f*.

conclude [kən'klu:d] schließen, beschließen; abschließen; folgern; sich entscheiden; *to be ~d* Schluß folgt.

conclusi|on [kən'klu:ʒən] Schluß *m*, Ende *n*; Abschluß *m*; Folgerung *f*; Beschluß *m*; ~ve] [~'klu:siv] schlüssig; endgültig.

concoct [kən'kɔkt] zs.-brauen; *fig.* aussinnen; ~ion [~kʃən] Gebräu *n*; *fig.* Erfindung *f*.

concord ['kɔnkɔ:d] Eintracht *f*; Übereinstimmung *f* (a. *gr.*); ♩ Harmonie *f*; ~ant [kən'kɔ:dənt] übereinstimmend; einstimmig; harmonisch.

concourse ['kɔnkɔ:s] Zusammen-, Auflauf *m*; Menge *f*; *Am.* Bahnhofs-, Schalterhalle *f*.

concrete [kən'kri:t] konkret; Beton...; **2.** [~] Beton *m*; **3.** [kən'kri:t] *zu e-r Masse verbinden*; ['kɔnkri:t] betonieren.

concur [kən'kə:] zs.-treffen, zs.-wirken; übereinstimmen; ~rence [~-'kʌrəns] Zusammentreffen *n*; Übereinstimmung *f*; Mitwirkung *f*.

concussion [kən'kʌʃən]: ~ *of the brain* Gehirnerschütterung *f*.

condemn [kən'dem] verdammen; verurteilen; verwerfen; *Kranke* aufgeben; beschlagnahmen; ~ation [kɔndem'neiʃən] Verurteilung *f*; Verdammung *f*; Verwerfung *f*.

condens|ation [kɔnden'seiʃən] Verdichtung *f*; ~e [kən'dens] (sich) verdichten; ⊕ kondensieren; zs.-drängen; ~er [~sə] ⊕ Kondensator *m*.

condescen|d [kɔndi'send] sich herablassen; geruhen; ~sion [~nʃən] Herablassung *f*.

condiment ['kɔndimənt] Würze *f*.

condition [kən'diʃən] **1.** Zustand *m*, Stand *m*; Stellung *f*, Bedingung *f*; ~s *pl.* Verhältnisse *n/pl.*; **2.** bedingen; in e-n bestimmten Zustand bringen; ~al □ [~nl] bedingt (on, upon durch); Bedingungs...; ~ clause *gr.* Bedingungssatz *m*; ~ mood *gr.* Konditional *m*.

condol|e [kən'doul] kondolieren (with *dat.*); ~ence [~ləns] Beileid *n*.

conduc|e [kən'dju:s] führen, dienen; ~ive [~siv] dienlich, förderlich.

conduct 1. ['kɔndəkt] Führung *f*; Verhalten *n*, Betragen *n*; **2.** [kən'dʌkt] führen; ♩ dirigieren; ~ion [~kʃən] Leitung *f*; ~or [~ktə] Führer *m*; Leiter *m*; Schaffner *m*; ♩ Dirigent *m*; ⚡ Blitzableiter *m*.

conduit ['kɔndit] (Leitungs-) Röhre *f*.

cone [koun] Kegel *m*; ♀ Zapfen *m*.

confabulation [kɔnfæbju'leiʃən] Plauderei *f*.

confection [kən'fekʃən] Konfekt *n*; ~er [~ʃnə] Konditor *m*; ~ery [~ʃəri] Konfekt *n*; Konditorei *f*; *bsd. Am.* Süßwarengeschäft *n*.

confedera|cy [kən'fedərəsi] Bündnis *n*; *the* ⚋ *bsd. Am.* die 11 Südstaaten *bei der Sezession 1860—61*; ~te 1. [~rit] verbündet; 2. [~] Bundesgenosse *m*; 3. [~reit] (sich) verbünden; ~tion [kənfedə'reiʃən] Bund *m*, Bündnis *n*; *the* ⚋ *bsd. Am.* die Staatenkonföderation *f* von 1781—1789.

confer [kən'fə:] *v/t.* übertragen, verleihen; *v/i.* sich besprechen; ~ence ['kɔnfərəns] Konferenz *f*.

confess [kən'fes] bekennen, gestehen; beichten; ~ion [~'feʃən] Geständnis *n*; Bekenntnis *n*; Beichte *f*; ~ional [~nl] Beichtstuhl *m*; ~or [~esə] Bekenner *m*; Beichtvater *m*.

confide [kən'faid] *v/t.* anvertrauen; *v/i.* vertrauen (*in* auf *acc.*); ~nce ['kɔnfidəns] Vertrauen *n*; Zuversicht *f*; ~nce man Schwindler *m*;

Hochstapler *m*; **~nce trick** Bauern-
fängerei *f*; **~nt**) [~nt] vertrauend;
zuversichtlich; **~ntial** [kɔnfi-
'denʃəl] vertraulich.

confine [kən'fain] begrenzen; beschränken; einsperren; be **~d**
niederkommen (*of* mit); be **~d to**
bed das Bett hüten müssen; **~ment**
[~nmənt] Haft *f*; Beschränkung *f*;
Entbindung *f*.

confirm [kən'fə:m] (be)kräftigen;
bestätigen; konfirmieren; firmen;
~ation [kɔnfə'meiʃən] Bestätigung
f; *eccl.* Konfirmation *f*; *eccl.* Fir-
mung *f*.

confiscat|e ['kɔnfiskeit] beschlag-
nahmen; **~ion** [kɔnfis'keiʃən] Beschlagnahme *f*. [ßer Brand.]

conflagration [kɔnflə'greiʃən] gro-
conflict 1. ['kɔnflikt] Konflikt *m*;
2. [kən'flikt] im Konflikt stehen.

conflu|ence [kən'fluəns], **~x** [~ʌks]
Zs.-fluß *m*; Auflauf *m*; **~ent** [~luənt]
1. zs.-fließend, zs.-laufend; **2.** Zu-,
Nebenfluß *m*.

conform [kən'fɔ:m] (sich) anpassen; **~able**) [~məbl] (to) übereinstimmend (mit); entsprechend
(*dat.*); nachgiebig (gegen); **~ity** [~-
miti] Übereinstimmung *f*.

confound [kən'faund] vermengen;
verwechseln; *j-n* verwirren; **~** *it!* F
verdammt!; **~ed**) F verdammt.

confront [kən'frʌnt] gegenüberstellen; entgegentreten (*dat.*).

confus|e [kən'fju:z] verwechseln;
verwirren; **~ion** [~u:ʒən] Verwirrung *f*; Verwechs(e)lung *f*.

confut|ation [kɔnfju:'teiʃən] Wider-
legung *f*; **~e** [kən'fju:t] widerlegen.

congeal [kən'dʒi:l] erstarren (lassen); gerinnen (lassen).

congenial [kən'dʒi:njəl] (geistes-)
verwandt (*with dat.*); zusagend.

congenital [kən'dʒenitl] angeboren.

congestion [kən'dʒestʃən] (Blut-)
Andrang *m*; Stauung *f*; **traffic ~**
Verkehrsstockung *f*.

conglomeration [kɔnglɔmə'reiʃən]
Anhäufung *f*; Konglomerat *n*.

congratulat|e [kən'grætjuleit] be-
glückwünschen; *j-m* gratulieren;
~ion [kɔngrætju'leiʃən] Glück-
wunsch *m*.

congregat|e ['kɔŋgrigeit] (sich)
(ver)sammeln; **~ion** [kɔŋgri'geiʃən]
Versammlung *f*; *eccl.* Gemeinde *f*.

congress ['kɔŋgres] Kongreß *m*;
2 Kongreß *m*, *gesetzgebende Körperschaft der USA*; 2**man**, 2**woman**
Am. pol. Mitglied *n* des Repräsen-
tantenhauses.

congruous) ['kɔŋgruəs] angemessen (to für); übereinstimmend,
folgerichtig.

conifer ['kounifə] Nadelholzbaum
m.

conjecture [kən'dʒektʃə] **1.** Mut-
maßung *f*; **2.** mutmaßen.

conjoin [kən'dʒɔin] (sich) verbinden; **~t** ['kɔndʒɔint] verbunden.

conjugal) ['kɔndʒugəl] ehelich.

conjugat|e *gr.* ['kɔndʒugeit] kon-
jugieren, beugen; **~ion** *gr.* [kɔndʒu-
'geiʃən] Konjugation *f*, Beugung *f*.

conjunction [kən'dʒʌŋkʃən] Verbindung *f*; Zs.-treffen *n*; *gr.* Konjunktion *f*.

conjunctivitis [kəndʒʌŋkti'vaitis]
Bindehautentzündung *f*.

conjure[1] [kən'dʒuə] beschwören,
inständig bitten.

conjur|e[2] ['kʌndʒə] *v/t.* beschwö-
ren; *et. wohin* zaubern; *v/i.* zaubern;
~er [~ərə] Zauber|er *m*, -in *f*;
Taschenspieler(in); **~ing-trick**
[~riŋtrik] Zauberkunststück *n*; **~or**
[~rə] = *conjurer.*

connect [kə'nekt] (sich) verbinden;
ⅇ schalten; **~ed**) verbunden;
zs.-hängend (*Rede etc.*); be **~ with**
in Verbindung stehen mit *j-m*;
~ion [~kʃən] = *connexion.*

connexion [kə'nekʃən] Verbindung
f; **ⅇ** Schaltung *f*; Anschluß *m* (*a.*
📧, **ⅇ**); Zs.-hang *m*; Verwandtschaft
f.

connive [kə'naiv]: **~** *at* ein Auge zudrücken bei.

connoisseur [kɔni'sə:] Kenner(in).

connubial) [kə'nju:bjəl] ehelich.

conquer ['kɔŋkə] erobern; (be)sie-
gen; **~or** [~ərə] Eroberer *m*; Sieger
m.

conquest ['kɔŋkwest] Eroberung *f*;
Errungenschaft *f*; Sieg *m*.

conscience ['kɔnʃəns] Gewissen *n*.

conscientious) [kɔnʃi'enʃəs] gewissenhaft; Gewissens...; **~** *objector*
Kriegsdienstverweigerer *m* aus
Überzeugung; **~ness** [~snis] Ge-
wissenhaftigkeit *f*.

conscious) ['kɔnʃəs] bewußt; be **~**
of sich bewußt sein (*gen.*); **~ness**
[~snis] Bewußtsein *n*.

conscript ✗ ['kɔnskript] Wehr-
pflichtige(r) *m*; **~ion** ✗ [kən'skrip-
ʃən] Einberufung *f*.

consecrat|e ['kɔnsikreit] weihen,
einsegnen; heiligen; widmen; **~ion**
[kɔnsi'kreiʃən] Weihung *f*, Ein-
segnung *f*; Heiligung *f*.

consecutive) [kən'sekjutiv] auf-
ea.-folgend; fortlaufend.

consent [kən'sent] **1.** Zustimmung *f*;
2. einwilligen, zustimmen (*dat.*).

consequen|ce ['kɔnsikwəns] (to)
Folge *f*, Konsequenz *f* (für); Wirkung *f*, Einfluß *m* (auf *acc.*); Bedeutung *f* (für); **~t** [~nt] **1.** folgend;
2. Folge(rung) *f*; **~tial**) [~konsi-
'kwenʃəl] sich ergebend (on aus);
folgerichtig; wichtigtuerisch; **~tly**
['kɔnsikwəntli] folglich, daher.

conserv|ation [kɔnsə(:)'veiʃən] Er-
haltung *f*; **~ative**) [kən'sə:vətiv]
1. erhaltend (*of acc.*); konservativ;
vorsichtig; **2.** Konservative(r) *m*;

~atory [kɔn'sə:vətri] Treib-, Gewächshaus n; ♪ Konservatorium n; **~e** [kən'sə:v] erhalten.

consider [kən'sidə] v/t. betrachten; erwägen; überlegen; in Betracht ziehen; berücksichtigen; meinen, glauben; v/i überlegen; all things ~ed wenn man alles in Betracht zieht; **~able** [~ərəbl] ansehnlich, beträchtlich; **~ably** [~li] bedeutend, ziemlich, (sehr) viel; **~ate** □ [~rit] rücksichtsvoll; **~ation** [kənsidə'reiʃən] Betrachtung f, Erwägung f, Überlegung f; Rücksicht f; Wichtigkeit f; Entschädigung f; Entgelt n; be under ~ erwogen werden; in Betracht kommen; on no ~ unter keinen Umständen; **~ing** □ [kən'sidəriŋ] 1. prp. in Anbetracht (gen.); 2. F adv. den Umständen entsprechend

consign [kən'sain] übergeben, überliefern; anvertrauen; ✝ konsignieren; **~ment** ✝ [~nmənt] Übersendung f; Konsignation f.

consist [kən'sist] bestehen (of aus); in Einklang stehen (with mit); **~ence, ~ency** [~təns, ~si] Festigkeit(sgrad m) f; Übereinstimmung f; Konsequenz f; **~ent** [~nt] fest; übereinstimmend, vereinbar (with mit); konsequent

consol|ation [kɔnsə'leiʃən] Trost m; **~e** [kən'soul] trösten.

consolidate [kən'sɔlideit] festigen, fig. vereinigen; zs.-legen.

consonan|ce [kɔnsənəns] Konsonanz f; Übereinstimmung f; **~t** [~nt] 1. □ übereinstimmend; 2. gr. Konsonant m, Mitlaut m.

consort ['kɔnsɔːt] Gemahl(in); ⚓ Geleitschiff n

conspicuous □ [kən'spikjuəs] sichtbar; auffallend; hervorragend; make o.s. ~ sich auffällig benehmen.

conspir|acy [kən'spirəsi] Verschwörung f; **~ator** [~ə'eitə] Verschwörer m; **~e** [~'spaiə] sich verschwören.

constab|le ['kʌnstəbl] Polizist m; Schutzmann m; **~ulary** [kən'stæbjuləri] Polizei(truppe) f.

constan|cy ['kɔnstənsi] Standhaftigkeit f; Beständigkeit f; **~t** □ [~nt] beständig, fest; unveränderlich; treu.

consternation [kɔnstə(:)'neiʃən] Bestürzung f.

constipation ✿ [kɔnsti'peiʃən] Verstopfung f.

constituen|cy [kən'stitjuənsi] Wählerschaft f; Wahlkreis m; **~t** [~nt] 1. wesentlich; Grund..., Bestand...; konstituierend; 2. wesentlicher Bestandteil; Wähler m.

constitut|e [kən'stitjuːt] ein-, errichten; ernennen; bilden, ausmachen; **~ion** [kɔnsti'tjuːʃən] Ein-, Errichtung f; Bildung f; Körper-

bau m; Verfassung f; **~ional** □ [~nl] konstitutionell; natürlich; verfassungsmäßig.

constrain [kən'strein] zwingen; et. erzwingen; **~t** [~nt] Zwang m.

constrict [kən'strikt] zs.-ziehen; **~ion** [~kʃən] Zs.-ziehung f.

constringent [kən'strindʒənt] zs.-ziehend

construct [kən'strʌkt] bauen, errichten; fig. bilden; **~ion** [~kʃən] Konstruktion f; Bau m; Auslegung f; **~ive** [~ktiv] aufbauend, schöpferisch, konstruktiv, positiv; Bau...; **~or** [~tə] Erbauer m, Konstrukteur m

construe [kən'struː] gr. konstruieren; auslegen, auffassen; übersetzen.

consul ['kɔnsəl] Konsul m; **~general** Generalkonsul m; **~ate** [~sjulit] Konsulat n (a. Gebäude).

consult [kən'sʌlt] v/t. konsultieren, um Rat fragen; in e-m Buch nachschlagen; v/i. sich beraten; **~ation** [kɔnsəl'teiʃən] Konsultation f, Beratung f; Rücksprache f; ~ hour Sprechstunde f; **~ative** [kən'sʌltətiv] beratend.

consume [kən'sjuːm] v/t. verzehren; verbrauchen; vergeuden; **~r** [~mə] Verbraucher m; Abnehmer m.

consummate 1. □ [kən'sʌmit] vollendet; 2. ['kɔnsʌmeit] vollenden.

consumpti|on [kən'sʌmpʃən] Verbrauch m; ✿ Schwindsucht f; **~ve** □ [~ptiv] verzehrend; ✿ schwindsüchtig.

contact ['kɔntækt] Berührung f; Kontakt m; ~ lenses pl. Haft-, Kontaktschalen f/pl.; 2. [kən'tækt] Fühlung nehmen mit.

contagi|on ✿ [kən'teidʒən] Ansteckung f; Verseuchung f; Seuche f; **~ous** [~əs] ansteckend.

contain [kən'tein] (ent)halten, (um-)fassen; ~ o.s. an sich halten; **~er** [~nə] Behälter m; Großbehälter m (im Frachtverkehr).

contaminat|e [kən'tæmineit] verunreinigen; fig. anstecken, vergiften; verseuchen; **~ion** [kɔntæmi'neiʃən] Verunreinigung f; (radioaktive) Verseuchung.

contemplat|e fig. ['kɔntempleit] betrachten; beabsichtigen; **~ion** [kɔntəm'pleiʃən] Betrachtung f; Nachsinnen n; **~ive** □ ['kɔntempleitiv] nachdenklich; [kən'templətiv] beschaulich.

contempora|neous □ [kəntempə'reinjəs] gleichzeitig; **~ry** [kən'tempərəri] 1. zeitgenössisch; gleichzeitig; 2. Zeitgenoss|e m, -in f.

contempt [kən'tempt] Verachtung f; **~ible** [~təbl] verachtenswert; **~uous** □ [~tjuəs] geringschätzig (of gegen); verächtlich.

contend [kən'tend] *v/i.* streiten, ringen (*for* um); *v/t.* behaupten.
content [kən'tent] **1.** zufrieden; **2.** befriedigen; ~ *o.s.* sich begnügen; **3.** Zufriedenheit *f; to one's heart's* ~ nach Herzenslust; ['kɔntent] Umfang *m;* Gehalt *m;* ~*s pl.* stofflicher Inhalt; ~**ed**] [kən'tentid] zufrieden; genügsam.
contention [kən'tenʃən] (Wort-) Streit *m;* Wetteifer *m.*
contentment [kən'tentmənt] Zufriedenheit *f,* Genügsamkeit *f.*
contest 1. ['kɔntest] Streit *m;* Wettkampf *m;* **2.** [kən'test] (be)streiten, anfechten; um *et.* streiten. [*m.*]
context ['kɔntekst] Zusammenhang]
contiguous [kən'tigjuəs] anstoßend (*to an acc.*); benachbart.
continent ['kɔntinənt] **1.**] enthaltsam; mäßig; **2.** Kontinent *m,* Erdteil *m;* Festland *n;* ~**al** [kɔnti'nentl] **1.** kontinental; Kontinental...; **2.** Kontinentaleuropäer(in).
contingen|cy [kən'tindʒənsi] Zufälligkeit *f;* Zufall *m;* Möglichkeit *f;* ~**t** [~nt] **1.** zufällig; möglich (*to* bei); **2.** ✕ Kontingent *n.*
continu|al] [kən'tinjuəl] fortwährend, unaufhörlich; ~**ance** [~əns] (Fort)Dauer *f;* ~**ation** [kəntinju-'eiʃən] Fortsetzung *f;* Fortdauer *f;* ~ *school* Fortbildungsschule *f;* ~**e** [kən'tinju(:)] *v/t.* fortsetzen; beibehalten; *to be* ~*d* Fortsetzung folgt; *v/i.* fortdauern; fortfahren; ~**ity** [kɔnti'nju(:)iti] Kontinuität *f; Film:* Drehbuch *n; Radio* verbindende Worte; ~ *girl* Skriptgirl *n;* ~**ous** □ [kən'tinjuəs] ununterbrochen.
contort [kən'tɔ:t] verdrehen; verzerren; ~**ion** [~ɔ:ʃən] Verdrehung *f;* Verzerrung *f.*
contour ['kɔntuə] Umriß *m.*
contra ['kɔntrə] wider.
contraband ['kɔntrəbænd] Schmuggelware *f;* Schleichhandel *m; attr.* Schmuggel...
contraceptive [kɔntrə'septiv] **1.** empfängnisverhütend; **2.** empfängnisverhütendes Mittel.
contract 1. ['kɔntrækt] *v/t.* zusammenziehen; sich *et.* zuziehen; *Schulden* machen; *Heirat etc.* (ab)schließen; *v/i.* einschrumpfen; e-n Vertrag schließen; sich verpflichten; **2.** [kən'trækt] Kontrakt *m,* Vertrag *m;* ~**ion** [kən'trækʃən] Zs.-ziehung *f; gr.* Kurzform *f;* ~**or** [~ktə] Unternehmer *m;* Lieferant *m.*
contradict [kɔntrə'dikt] widersprechen (*dat.*); ~**ion** [~kʃən] Widerspruch *m;* ~**ory** □ [~ktəri] (sich) widersprechend.
contrar|iety [kɔntrə'raiəti] Widerspruch *m;* Widrigkeit *f;* ~**y** ['kɔntrəri] **1.** entgegengesetzt; widrig; ~ *to* zuwider (*dat.*); gegen; **2.** Gegenteil *n; on the* ~ im Gegenteil.

contrast 1. ['kɔntrɑ:st] Gegensatz *m;* **2.** [kən'trɑ:st] *v/t.* gegenüberstellen; vergleichen; *v/i* sich unterscheiden, abstechen (*with* von).
contribut|e [kən'tribju(:)t] beitragen, beisteuern; ~**ion** [kɔntri'bju-ʃən] Beitrag *m;* ~**or** [kən'tribjutə] Beitragende(r *m*) *f;* Mitarbeiter(in) an e-r *Zeitung;* ~**ory** [~əri] beitragend.
contrit|e □ ['kɔntrait] reuevoll; ~**ion** [kən'triʃən] Zerknirschung *f.*
contriv|ance [kən'traivəns] Erfindung *f;* Plan *m;* Vorrichtung *f;* Kunstgriff *m;* Scharfsinn *m;* ~**e** [kən'traiv] *v/t.* ersinnen; planen; zuwegebringen; *v/i.* es fertig bringen (*to inf.* zu *inf.*); ~**er** [~və] Erfinder(in).
control [kən'troul] **1.** Kontrolle *f,* Aufsicht *f;* Befehl *m;* Zwang *m;* Gewalt *f;* Zwangswirtschaft *f;* Kontrollvorrichtung *f;* Steuerung *f;* ~ *board* ⊕ Schaltbrett *n;* **2.** einschränken; kontrollieren; beaufsichtigen, überwachen; beherrschen; (nach)prüfen; beherrschen; regeln; ✈ steuern (*a. fig. dat.*); ~**ler** [~lə] Kontrolleur *m,* Aufseher *m;* Leiter *m;* Rechnungsprüfer *m.*
controver|sial] [kɔntrə'və:ʃəl] umstritten; streitsüchtig; ⚖ ungehorsam. ~**sy** [~si] Streit(frage *f*) *m;* ~**t** [~ə:t] bestreiten.
contumacious □ [kɔntju(:)'meiʃəs] widerspenstig; ⚖ ungehorsam.
contumely ['kɔntju(:)mli] Beschimpfung *f;* Schmach *f.*
contuse ⚕ [kən'tju:z] quetschen.
convalesce [kɔnvə'les] genesen; ~**nce** [~sns] Genesung *f;* ~**nt** [~nt] **1.** □ genesend; **2.** Genesende(r *m*) *f.*
convene [kən'vi:n] (sich) versammeln; zs.-rufen; ⚖ vorladen.
convenien|ce [kən'vi:njəns] Bequemlichkeit *f;* Angemessenheit *f;* Vorteil *m;* Klosett *n; at your earliest* ~ möglichst bald; ~**t**] [~nt] bequem; passend; brauchbar.
convent ['kɔnvənt] (Nonnen)Kloster *n;* ~**ion** [kən'venʃən] Versammlung *f;* Konvention *f,* Übereinkommen *n;* Vertrag *m;* Herkommen *n;* ~**ional** [~nl] vertraglich; herkömmlich, konventionell.
converge [kən'və:dʒ] konvergieren, zs.-laufen (lassen).
convers|ant [kən'və:sənt] vertraut; ~**ation** [kɔnvə'seiʃən] Gespräch *n,* Unterhaltung *f;* ~**ational** [~nl] Unterhaltungs...; umgangssprachlich; ~**e 1.** □ ['kɔnvə:s] umgekehrt; **2.** [kən'və:s] sich unterhalten; ~**ion** [~ʃən] Um-, Verwandlung *f;* ⊕, ⚡ Umformung *f; eccl.* Bekehrung *f; pol.* Meinungswechsel *m,* Übertritt *m;* ✝ Konvertierung *f;* Umstellung *f* e-r *Währung etc.*

convert 1. ['kɔnvəːt] Bekehrte(r m) f, Konvertit m; **2.** [kən'vəːt] (sich) um-, verwandeln; ⊕, ⚡ umformen; eccl. bekehren; ✝ konvertieren; Währung etc. umstellen; **~er** ⊕, ⚡ [~tə] Umformer m; **~ible 1.** □ [~təbl] um-, verwandelbar; ✝ konvertierbar; **2.** mot. Kabrio(lett) n.

convey [kən'vei] befördern, bringen, schaffen; übermitteln; mitteilen; ausdrücken; übertragen; **~ance** [~iəns] Beförderung f; ✝ Spedition f; Übermittlung f; Verkehrsmittel n; Fuhrwerk n; Übertragung f; **~er, ~or** ⊕ [~eiə] a. ~ belt Förderband n.

convict 1. ['kɔnvikt] Sträfling m; **2.** [kən'vikt] j-n überführen; **~ion** [~kʃən] ʃt̩ Überführung f; Überzeugung f (of von).

convince [kən'vins] überzeugen.

convivial □ [kən'viviəl] festlich; gesellig.

convocation [kɔnvə'keiʃən] Einberufung f; Versammlung f.

convoke [kən'vouk] einberufen.

convoy ['kɔnvɔi] **1.** Geleit n; Geleitzug m; (Geleit)Schutz m; **2.** geleiten.

convuls|ion [kən'vʌlʃən] Zuckung f, Krampf m; **~ive** □ [~lsiv] krampfhaft, -artig, konvulsiv.

coo [kuː] girren, gurren.

cook [kuk] **1.** Koch m; Köchin f; **2.** kochen; Bericht etc. frisieren; **~book** Am. ['kukbuk] Kochbuch n; **~ery** ['kukəri] Kochen n; Kochkunst f; **~ie** Am. ['kuki] Plätzchen n; **~ing** [~iŋ] Küche f (Kochweise); **~y** Am. ['kuki] = cookie.

cool [kuːl] **1.** □ kühl; fig. kaltblütig, gelassen; unverfroren; **2.** Kühle f; **3.** (sich) abkühlen.

coolness ['kuːlnis] Kühle f (a. fig.); Kaltblütigkeit f.

coon Am. F [kuːn] zo. Waschbär m; Neger m; (schlauer) Bursche.

coop [kuːp] **1.** Hühnerkorb m; **2.** ~ up od. in einsperren.

co-op F [kou'ɔp] = co-operative (store).

cooper ['kuːpə] Böttcher m, Küfer m.

co(-)operat|e [kou'ɔpəreit] mitwirken; zs.-arbeiten; **~ion** [kouɔpə-'reiʃən] Mitwirkung f; Zs.-arbeit f; **~ive** [kou'ɔpərətiv] zs.-wirkend; ~ society Konsumverein m; ~ store Konsum(vereinsladen) m; **~or** [~reitə] Mitarbeiter m.

co-ordinat|e 1. □ [kou'ɔːdnit] gleichgeordnet; **2.** [~dineit] koordinieren, gleichordnen; auf-ea. einstellen; **~ion** [kouɔːdi'neiʃən] Gleichordnung f, -schaltung f.

copartner ['kou'paːtnə] Teilhaber m.

cope [koup]: ~ with sich messen mit, fertig werden mit.

copious □ ['koupjəs] reich(lich); weitschweifig; **~ness** [~snis] Fülle f.

copper¹ ['kɔpə] **1.** Kupfer n; Kupfermünze f; **2.** kupfern; Kupfer...

copper² sl. [~] Polyp m (Polizist).

coppice, copse ['kɔpis, kɔps] Unterholz n, Dickicht n.

copy ['kɔpi] **1.** Kopie f; Nachbildung f; Abschrift f; Durchschlag m; Muster n; Exemplar n e-s Buches; Zeitungs-Nummer f; druckfertiges Manuskript; fair od. clean ~ Reinschrift f; **2.** kopieren; abschreiben; nachbilden, nachahmen; **~book** Schreibheft n; **~ing** [~iŋ] Kopier...; **~ist** [~ist] Abschreiber m; Nachahmer m; **~right** Verlagsrecht n, Copyright n.

coral ['kɔrəl] Koralle f.

cord [kɔːd] **1.** Schnur f, Strick m; anat. Strang m; **2.** (zu)schnüren, binden; **~ed** ['kɔːdid] gerippt.

cordial ['kɔːdjəl] **1.** □ herzlich; herzstärkend; **2.** (Magen)Likör m; **~ity** [kɔːdi'æliti] Herzlichkeit f.

cordon ['kɔːdn] **1.** Postenkette f; **2.** ~ off abriegeln, absperren.

corduroy ['kɔːdərɔi] Kord m; **~s** pl. Kordhosen f/pl.; ~ road Knüppeldamm m.

core [kɔː] **1.** Kerngehäuse n; fig. Herz n; Kern m; **2.** entkernen.

cork [kɔːk] **1.** Kork m; **2.** (ver)korken; **~ing** Am. F ['kɔːkiŋ] fabelhaft, prima; **~jacket** Schwimmweste f; **~screw** Kork(en)zieher m.

corn [kɔːn] **1.** Korn n; Getreide n; a. Indian ~ Am. Mais m; ✗ Hühnerauge n; **2.** einpökeln.

corner ['kɔːnə] **1.** Ecke f, Winkel m; Kurve f; fig. Enge f; ✝ Aufkäufer-Ring m; **2.** Eck...; **3.** in die Ecke (fig. Enge) treiben; ✝ aufkaufen; **~ed** ...eckig.

cornet ♪ ['kɔːnit] (kleines) Horn n.

cornice △ ['kɔːnis] Gesims n.

corn|-juice Am. sl. ['kɔːndʒuːs] Maisschnaps m; **~pone** Am. ['kɔːnpoun] Maisbrot n; **~stalk** Am. Getreidehalm m; Am. Maisstengel m; **~starch** Am. Maisstärke f.

coron|ation [kɔrə'neiʃən] Krönung f; **~er** ['kɔrənə] Leichenbeschauer m; **~et** [~nit] Adelskrone f.

corpor|al ['kɔːpərəl] **1.** □ körperlich; **2.** ✗ Korporal m; **~ation** [kɔːpə'reiʃən] Körperschaft f, Innung f, Zunft f; Stadtverwaltung f; Am. Aktiengesellschaft f.

corpse [kɔːps] Leichnam m.

corpulen|ce, ~cy ['kɔːpjuləns, ~si] Beleibtheit f; **~t** [~nt] beleibt.

corral Am. [kɔː'raːl] **1.** Einzäunung f; **2.** zs.-pferchen, einsperren.

correct [kə'rekt] **1.** adj. □ korrekt, richtig; **2.** v/t. korrigieren; zurechtweisen; strafen; **~ion** [~kʃən] Berichtigung f; Verweis m; Strafe f;

Korrektur f; house of ~ Besserungs-
anstalt f.
correlate ['kɔrileit] in Wechselbe-
ziehung stehen od. bringen.
correspond [kɔris'pɔnd] entsprechen (with, to dat); korrespondie-
ren; ~ence [~dəns] Übereinstimmung f; Briefwechsel m; ~ent [~nt]
1.] entsprechend; 2. Briefschrei-
ber(in); Korrespondent(in).
corridor ['kɔridɔ:] Korridor m;
Gang m; ~ train D-Zug m.
corrigible ['kɔridʒəbl] verbesser-
lich; zu verbessern(d).
corroborate [kə'rɔbəreit] stärken;
bestätigen.
corro|de [kə'roud] zerfressen; weg-
ätzen; ~sion [~ouʒən] Ätzen n,
Zerfressen n; ⊕ Korrosion f; Rost
m; ~sive [~ousiv] 1.] zerfressend,
ätzend; 2. Ätzmittel n.
corrugate ['kɔrugeit] runzeln; ⊕
riefen; ~d iron Wellblech f.
corrupt [kə'rʌpt] 1. verdorben;
verderbt; bestechlich; 2. v/t. verderben; bestechen; anstecken; v/i.
(ver)faulen, verderben; ~ible □
[~təbl] verderblich; bestechlich;
~ion [~ʃən] Verderben n; Verdor-
benheit f; Fäulnis f; Bestechung f.
corsage [kɔ:'sɑ:ʒ] Taille f, Mieder
n; Am. Ansteckblume(n pl.) f.
corset ['kɔ:sit] Korsett n.
coruscate ['kɔrəskeit] funkeln.
co-signatory ['kou'signətəri] 1. mit-
unterzeichnend; 2. Mitunterzeich-
ner m.
cosmetic [kɔz'metik] 1. kosme-
tisch; 2. Schönheitsmittel n; Kosmetik f; ~ian [kɔzme'tiʃən] Kos-
metiker(in).
cosmonaut ['kɔzmənɔ:t] Kosmo-
naut m, Weltraumfahrer m.
cosmopolit|an [kɔzmə'pɔlitən], ~e
[kɔz'mɔpəlait] 1. kosmopolitisch;
2. Weltbürger(in).
cost [kɔst] 1. Preis m; Kosten pl.;
Schaden m; first od. prime ~ An-
schaffungskosten pl.; 2. [irr.] kosten.
costl|iness ['kɔstlinis] Kostbarkeit
f; ~y ['kɔstli] kostbar; kostspielig.
costume ['kɔstju:m] Kostüm n;
Kleidung f; Tracht f.
cosy ['kouzi] 1.] behaglich, gemütlich; 2. = tea-cosy.
cot [kɔt] Feldbett n; ⚓ Hängematte
f mit Rahmen, Koje f; Kinderbett n.
cottage ['kɔtidʒ] Hütte f; kleines
Landhaus, Sommerhaus n; ~ cheese
Am. Quark(käse) m; ~ piano Piani-
no n; ~r [~dʒə] Häusler m; Hütten-
bewohner m; Am. Sommergast m.
cotton ['kɔtn] 1. Baumwolle f; ✝
Kattun m; Näh-Garn n; 2. baum-
wollen; Baumwoll-; ~ wool Watte
f; 3. F sich vertragen; sich anschließen; ~-wood ⚘ e-e amerikanische Pappel.

couch [kautʃ] 1. Lager n; Couch f,
Sofa n, Liege f; Schicht f; 2. v/t.
Meinung etc. ausdrücken; Schriftsatz etc. abfassen; ✒ Star stechen;
v/i. sich (nieder)legen; versteckt
liegen; kauern.
cough [kɔf] 1. Husten m; 2. husten.
could [kud] pret. von can[1].
coulee Am. ['ku:li] (trockenes)
Bachbett.
council ['kaunsl] Rat(sversammlung
f) m; ~(l)or [~silə] Ratsmitglied n,
Stadtrat m.
counsel ['kaunsəl] 1. Beratung f;
Rat(schlag) m; ⚖ Anwalt m; ~ for
the defense Verteidiger m; ~ for the
prosecution Anklagevertreter m;
2. j-n beraten; j-m raten; ~(l)or
[~slə] Ratgeber(in); Anwalt m;
Am. Rechtsbeistand m.
count[1] [kaunt] 1. Rechnung f;
Zahl f; ⚖ Anklagepunkt m; 2. v/t.
zählen; rechnen; dazurechnen; fig.
halten für; v/i. zählen; rechnen;
gelten (for little wenig).
count[2] [~] nichtbritischer Graf.
count-down ['kauntdaun] Count-
down m, n, Startzählung f (beim
Raketenstart).
countenance ['kauntinəns] 1. Gesicht n; Fassung f; Unterstützung
f; 2. begünstigen, unterstützen.
counter[1] ['kauntə] Zähler m, Zähl-
apparat m; Spielmarke f; Zahl-
pfennig m; Ladentisch m; Schalter
m.
counter[2] [~] 1. entgegen, zuwider
(to dat.); Gegen...; 2. Gegenschlag
m; 3. Gegenmaßnahmen treffen.
counteract [kauntə'rækt] zuwider-
handeln (dat.).
counterbalance 1. ['kauntəbæləns]
Gegengewicht n; 2. [kauntə'bæləns]
aufwiegen; ↑ ausgleichen.
counter-espionage ['kauntər'espiə-
na:ʒ] Spionageabwehr f.
counterfeit ['kauntəfit] 1.] nachgemacht; falsch, unecht; 2. Nachahmung f; Fälschung f; Falschgeld n; 3. nachmachen; fälschen;
heucheln.
counterfoil ['kauntəfɔil] Kontrollabschnitt m.
countermand [kauntə'mɑ:nd]
1. Gegenbefehl m; Widerruf m;
2. widerrufen; abbestellen.
counter-move fig. ['kauntəmu:v]
Gegenzug m, -maßnahme f.
counterpane ['kauntəpein] Bett-
decke f.
counterpart ['kauntəpɑ:t] Gegenstück n.
counterpoise ['kauntəpɔiz] 1. Gegengewicht n; 2. das Gleichgewicht
halten (dat.) (a. fig.), ausbalancie-
ren.
countersign ['kauntəsain] 1. Ge-
genzeichen n; ⚔ Losung(swort n)
f; 2. gegenzeichnen.

countervail ['kauntəveil] aufwiegen.

countess ['kauntis] Gräfin f.

counting-house ['kauntiŋhaus] Kontor n.

countless ['kauntlis] zahllos.

countrified ['kʌntrifaid] ländlich; bäurisch.

country ['kʌntri] 1. Land n; Gegend f; Heimatland n; 2. Land(s)..., ländlich; **~man** Landmann m (Bauer); Landsmann m; **~side** Gegend f; Land(bevölkerung f) n.

county ['kaunti] Grafschaft f, Kreis m; **~ seat** Am. = **~ town** Kreisstadt f.

coup [ku:] Schlag m, Streich m.

couple ['kʌpl] 1. Paar n; Koppel f; 2. (ver)koppeln; ⊕ kuppeln; (sich) paaren; **~r** [.lə] Radio: Köppler m.

coupling ['kʌpliŋ] Kupplung f; Radio: Kopplung f; attr. Kupplungs...

coupon ['ku:pɔn] Abschnitt m.

courage ['kʌridʒ] Mut m; **~ous** □ [kə'reidʒəs] mutig, beherzt.

courier ['kuriə] Kurier m, Eilbote m; Reiseführer m.

course [kɔ:s] 1. Lauf m, Gang m; Weg m; ♣, fig. Kurs m; Rennbahn f; Gang m (Speisen); Kursus m; univ. Vorlesung f; Ordnung f, Folge f; of ~ selbstverständlich; 2. v/t. hetzen; jagen; v/i. rennen.

court [kɔ:t] Hof m; Hofgesellschaft f; Gericht(shof m) n; General ♀ Am. gesetzgebende Versammlung; pay (one's) **~ to** j-m den Hof machen; 2. j-m den Hof machen; werben um; **~day** ['kɔ:tdei] Gerichtstag m; **~eous** □ ['kə:tjəs] höflich; **~esy** ['kə:tisi] Höflichkeit f; Gefälligkeit f; **~house** ['kɔ:thaus] Gerichtsgebäude n; Am. a. Amtshaus n e-s Kreises; **~ier** ['kɔ:tjə] Höfling m; **~ly** ['kɔ:tli] höfisch; höflich; **~ martial** ⚔ Kriegs-, Militärgericht n; **~-martial** ⚔ ['kɔ:t'ma:ʃəl] vor ein Kriegs- od. Militärgericht stellen; **~ room** Gerichtssaal m; **~ship** ['kɔ:tʃip] Werbung f; **~yard** Hof m.

cousin ['kʌzn] Vetter m; Base f.

cove [kouv] 1. Bucht f; fig. Obdach n.

covenant ['kʌvinənt] 1. ⚖ Vertrag m; Bund m; 2. v/t. geloben; v/i. übereinkommen.

cover ['kʌvə] 1. Decke f; Deckel m; Umschlag m; Hülle f; Deckung f; Schutz m; Dickicht n; Deckmantel m; Decke f, Mantel m (Bereifung); 2. (be-, zu)decken; einschlagen; einwickeln; verbergen, verdecken; schützen; Weg zurücklegen; ⊕ decken; mit e-r Schußwaffe zielen nach; ⚔ Gelände bestreichen; umfassen; fig. erfassen; Zeitung: berichten über (acc.); **~age** [.əridʒ]

Berichterstattung f (of über acc.); **~ing** [.riŋ] Decke f; Bett-Bezug m; Überzug m; Bekleidung f; Bedachung f.

covert ['kʌvət] 1. □ ['kʌvət] heimlich, versteckt; 2. ['kʌvə] Schutz m; Versteck n; Dickicht n.

covet ['kʌvit] begehren; **~ous** □ [.təs] (be)gierig; habsüchtig.

cow¹ [kau] Kuh f.

cow² [.] einschüchtern, ducken.

coward ['kauəd] 1. □ feig; 2. Feigling m; **~ice** [.dis] Feigheit f; **~ly** [.dli] feig(e).

cow|boy ['kauboi] Cowboy m (berittener Rinderhirt); **~catcher** Am. 🚂 Schienenräumer m.

cower ['kauə] kauern; sich ducken.

cow|herd ['kauhə:d] Kuhhirt m; **~hide** 1. Rind(s)leder n; 2. peitschen; **~house** Kuhstall m.

cowl [kaul] Mönchskutte f; Kapuze f; Schornsteinkappe f.

cow|man ['kaumən] Melker m; Am. Viehzüchter m; **~puncher** Am. F ['kaupʌntʃə] Rinderhirt m; **~shed** Kuhstall m; **~slip** ⅋ Schlüsselblume f; Am. Sumpfdotterblume f.

coxcomb ['kɔkskəum] Geck m.

coxswain ['kɔkswein, ♣ mst 'kɔksn] Bootsführer m; Steuermann m.

coy □ [koi] schüchtern; spröde.

crab [kræb] Krabbe f, Taschenkrebs m; ⊕ Winde f; F Querkopf m.

crab-louse ['kræblaus] Filzlaus f.

crack [kræk] 1. Krach m; Riß m, Sprung m; F derber Schlag; Versuch m; Witz m; 2. F erstklassig; 3. v/t. (zer)sprengen; knallen mit et.; (auf)knacken; **~ a joke** e-n Witz reißen; v/i. platzen, springen; knallen; umschlagen (Stimme); sich bersten; F verdreht; **~er** ['krækə] Knallbonbon m; Am. Schwärmer m; Am. Keks m (ungesüßt); **~le** [.kl] knattern, knistern; **~up** Zs.-stoß m; ☀ Bruchlandung f.

cradle ['kreidl] 1. Wiege f; Kindheit f (a. fig.); 2. (ein)wiegen.

craft [kra:ft] Handwerk n, Gewerbe n; Schiff(e pl.) n; Gerissenheit f; **~sman** ['kra:ftsmən] (Kunst)Handwerker m; **~y** □ ['kra:fti] gerissen, raffiniert.

crag [kræg] Klippe f, Felsspitze f.

cram [kræm] (voll)stopfen; nudeln, mästen; F (ein)pauken.

cramp [kræmp] 1. Krampf m; ⊕ Klammer f; fig. Fessel f; 2. verkrampfen; einengen, hemmen.

cranberry ['krænbəri] Preiselbeere f.

crane [krein] 1. Kranich m; ⊕ Kran m; 2. (den Hals) recken; **~fly** zo. ['kreinflai] Schnake f.

crank [kræŋk] 1. Kurbel f; Schwengel m; Wortspiel n; Schrulle f; komischer Kauz; fixe Idee; 2. (an-)kurbeln; **~-shaft** ⊕ ['kræŋkʃɑ:ft]

Kurbelwelle f; ~y [~ki] wacklig; launisch; verschroben.

cranny ['kræni] Riß m, Ritze f.

crape [kreip] Krepp m, Flor m.

craps Am. [kræps] pl. Würfelspiel.

crash [kræʃ] **1.** Krach m (a. ♥); ✈ Absturz m; **2.** v/i. krachen; einstürzen; ✈ abstürzen; mot. zs.-stoßen; fahren, fliegen, stürzen (into in, auf acc.); v/t. zerschmettern; **3.** Am. F blitzschnell ausgeführt; ~-helmet ['kræʃhelmit] Sturzhelm m; ~-landing Bruchlandung f.

crate [kreit] Lattenkiste f.

crater ['kreitə] Krater m; Trichter m.

crave [kreiv] v/t. dringend bitten od. flehen um; v/i. sich sehnen.

craven ['kreivən] feig.

crawfish ['krɔːfiʃ] **1.** Krebs m; **2.** Am. F sich drücken.

crawl [krɔːl] **1.** Kriechen n; **2.** kriechen; schleichen; wimmeln; kribbeln; Schwimmen: kraulen; it makes one's flesh ~ man bekommt e-e Gänsehaut davon.

crayfish ['kreifiʃ] Flußkrebs m.

crayon ['kreiən] Zeichenstift m, bsd. Pastellstift m; Pastell(gemälde) n.

craz|e [kreiz] Verrücktheit f; F Fimmel m; be the ~ Mode sein; ~y ['kreizi] baufällig; verrückt (for, about nach).

creak [kriːk] knarren.

cream [kriːm] **1.** Rahm m, Sahne f; Creme f; Auslese f; das Beste; **2.** den Rahm abschöpfen; ~ery ['kriːməri] Molkerei f; Milchgeschäft n; ~y [~mi] sahnig.

crease [kriːs] **1.** (Bügel)Falte f; **2.** (sich) kniffen, (sich) falten.

creat|e [kri(ː)'eit] (er)schaffen; thea. e-e Rolle gestalten; verursachen; erzeugen; ernennen; ~ion [~'eiʃən] Schöpfung f; Ernennung f; ~ive [~'eitiv] schöpferisch; ~or [~tə] Schöpfer m; ~ure ['kriːtʃə] Geschöpf n; Kreatur f.

creden|ce ['kriːdəns] Glaube m; ~tials [~'denʃəlz] pl. Beglaubigungsschreiben n; Unterlagen f/pl.

credible ɟ ['kredəbl] glaubwürdig; glaubhaft.

credit ['kredit] **1.** Glaube(n) m; Ruf m, Ansehen n; Guthaben n; ♥ Kredit n; ♦ Kredit m; Einfluß m; Verdienst n, Ehre f; Am. Schule: (Anrechnungs)Punkt m; **2.** j-m glauben; j-m trauen; ♦ gutschreiben; ~ s.o. with s.th. j-m et. zutrauen; ~able ɟ [~təbl] achtbar; ehrenvoll (to für); ~or [~tə] Gläubiger m.

credulous □ ['kredjuləs] leichtgläubig.

creed [kriːd] Glaubensbekenntnis n.

creek [kriːk] Bucht f; Am. Bach m.

creel [kriːl] Fischkorb m.

creep [kriːp] [irr.] kriechen; fig. (sich ein)schleichen; kribbeln; it makes my flesh ~ ich bekomme e-e Gänsehaut davon; ~er ['kriːpə] Kriecher(in); Kletterpflanze f.

cremator|ium [kremə'tɔːriəm], bsd. Am. ~y ['krematəri] Krematorium n.

crept [krept] pret. u. p.p. von creep.

crescent ['kresnt] **1.** zunehmend; halbmondförmig; **2.** Halbmond m; ♀ City Am. New Orleans.

cress ♀ [kres] Kresse f.

crest [krest] Hahnen-, Berg- etc. Kamm m; Mähne f; Federbusch m; Heraldik: family ~ Familienwappen n; ~-fallen ['krestfɔːlən] niedergeschlagen.

crevasse [kri'væs] (Gletscher)Spalte f; Am. Deichbruch m.

crevice ['krevis] Riß m, Spalte f.

crew¹ [kruː] Schar f; ⚓, ✈ Mannschaft f.

crew² [~] pret. von crow 2.

crib [krib] **1.** Krippe f; Kinderbett (-stelle f) n; F Schule Klatsche f; bsd. Am. Behälter m; **2.** einsperren; F mausen; F abschreiben.

crick [krik] Krampf m; ~ in the neck steifer Hals.

cricket ['krikit] zo. Grille f; Sport: Kricket n; not ~ F nicht fair.

crime [kraim] Verbrechen n.

criminal ['kriminl] **1.** verbrecherisch; Kriminal..., Straf...; **2.** Verbrecher(in); ~ity [krimi'næliti] Strafbarkeit f; Verbrechertum n.

crimp [krimp] kräuseln.

crimson ['krimzn] karmesin(rot).

cringe [krindʒ] sich ducken.

crinkle ['kriŋkl] **1.** Windung f; Falte f; **2.** (sich) winden; (sich) kräuseln.

cripple ['kripl] **1.** Krüppel m; Lahme(r m) f; **2.** verkrüppeln; fig. lähmen.

cris|is ['kraisis], pl. ~es [~siːz] Krisis f, Krise f, Wende-, Höhepunkt m.

crisp [krisp] **1.** kraus; knusperig; frisch; klar; steif; **2.** (sich) kräuseln; knusperig machen od. werden; **3.** ~s pl., a. potato ~s pl. Kartoffelchips pl.

criss-cross ['kriskrɔs] **1.** Kreuzzeichen n; **2.** (durch)kreuzen.

criteri|on [krai'tiəriən], pl. ~a [~riə] Kennzeichen n, Prüfstein m.

criti|c ['kritik] Kritiker(in); ~cal □ [~kəl] kritisch; bedenklich; ~cism [~isizəm] Kritik f (of an dat.); ~cize [~saiz] kritisieren; beurteilen; tadeln; ~que [kri'tiːk] kritischer Essay; die Kritik.

croak [krouk] krächzen; quaken.

crochet ['krouʃei] **1.** Häkelei f; **2.** häkeln.

crock [krɔk] irdener Topf; ~ery ['krɔkəri] Töpferware f.

crocodile zo. ['krɔkədail] Krokodil n.

crone F [kroun] altes Weib.

crony F ['krouni] alter Freund.

crook [kruk] 1. Krümmung f; Haken m; Hirtenstab m; sl. Gauner m; 2. (sich) krümmen; (sich) (ver)biegen; ~ed ['krukid] krumm; bucklig; unehrlich; [krukt] Krück...

croon [kruːn] schmalzig singen; summen; ~er ['kruːnə] Schnulzensänger m.

crop [krɔp] 1. Kropf m; Peitschenstiel m; Reitpeitsche f; Ernte f; kurzer Haarschnitt; 2. (ab-, be-) schneiden; (ab)ernten; Acker bebauen; ~ up fig. auftauchen.

cross [krɔs] 1. Kreuz n (a. fig. Leiden); Kreuzung f; 2. □ sich kreuzend; quer (liegend, laufend etc.); ärgerlich, verdrießlich; entgegengesetzt; Kreuz..., Quer...; 3. v/t. kreuzen; durchstreichen; fig. durchkreuzen; überqueren; in den Weg kommen (dat.); ~ o.s. sich bekreuzigen; keep one's fingers ~ed den Daumen halten; v/i. sich kreuzen; ~bar ['krɔsbaː] Fußball: Torlatte f; ~breed (Rassen)Kreuzung f; ~country querfeldein; ~examination Kreuzverhör n; ~eyed schieläugig; ~ing [~siŋ] Kreuzung f; Übergang m; -fahrt f; ~road Querstraße f; ~roads pl. od. sg. Kreuzweg m; ~section Querschnitt m; ~wise kreuzweise; ~word (puzzle) Kreuzworträtsel n.

crotchet ['krɔtʃit] Haken m; ♪ Viertelnote f; wunderlicher Einfall.

crouch [krautʃ] 1. sich ducken; 2. Hockstellung f.

crow [krou] 1. Krähe f; Krähen n; eat ~ Am. F zu Kreuze kriechen; 2. [irr.] krähen; triumphieren; ~bar ['kroubaː] Brecheisen n.

crowd [kraud] 1. Haufen m, Menge f; Gedränge n; F Bande f; 2. (sich) drängen; (über)füllen; wimmeln.

crown [kraun] 1. Krone f; Kranz m; Gipfel m; Scheitel m; 2. krönen; Zahn überkronen; to ~ all zu guter Letzt, zu allem Überfluß.

cruci|al [['kruːʃəl] entscheidend; kritisch; ~ble ['kruːsibl] Schmelztiegel m; ~fixion [kruːsi'fikʃən] Kreuzigung f; ~fy ['kruːsifai] kreuzigen.

crude □ [kruːd] roh; unfertig; unreif; unfein; grob; Roh...; grell.

cruel □ ['kruəl] grausam; hart; fig. blutig; ~ty [~lti] Grausamkeit f.

cruet ['kruː(ː)it] (Essig-, Öl)Fläschchen n.

cruise ♔ [kruːz] 1. Kreuzfahrt f, Seereise f; 2. kreuzen; ~r ['kruːzə]

♔ Kreuzer m; Jacht f; Am. Funkstreifenwagen m.

crumb [krʌm] 1. Krume f; Brocken m; 2. panieren; zerkrümeln; ~le ['krʌmbl] (zer)bröckeln; fig. zugrunde gehen.

crumple ['krʌmpl] v/t. zerknittern; fig. vernichten; v/i. (sich) knüllen.

crunch [krʌntʃ] (zer)kauen; zermalmen; knirschen.

crusade [kruː'seid] Kreuzzug m (a. fig.); ~r [~də] Kreuzfahrer m.

crush [krʌʃ] 1. Druck m; Gedränge n; (Frucht)Saft m; Am. sl. Schwarm m; have a ~ on s.o. in j-n verliebt od. verschossen sein; 2. v/t. (zer-, aus)quetschen; zermalmen; fig. vernichten; v/i. sich drängen; ~ barrier ['krʌʃbæriə] Absperrgitter n.

crust [krʌst] 1. Kruste f; Rinde f; Am. sl. Frechheit f; 2. (sich) beüberkrusten, verharschen; ~y □ ['krʌsti] krustig; fig. mürrisch.

crutch [krʌtʃ] Krücke f.

cry [krai] 1. Schrei m; Geschrei n; Ruf m; Weinen n; Gebell n; 2. schreien; (aus)rufen; weinen; ~ for verlangen nach.

crypt [kript] Gruft f; ~ic ['kriptik] verborgen, geheim.

crystal ['kristl] Kristall m, n; Am. Uhrglas n; ~line [~təlain] kristallen; ~lize [~aiz] kristallisieren.

cub [kʌb] 1. Junge(s) n; Flegel m; Anfänger m; 2. (Junge) werfen.

cub|e ♪ [kjuːb] Würfel m; Kubikzahl f; ~ root Kubikwurzel f; ~ic(al □) ['kjuːbik(əl)] würfelförmig; kubisch; Kubik...

cuckoo ['kuku] Kuckuck m.

cucumber ['kjuːkəmbə] Gurke f; as cool as a ~ fig. eiskalt, gelassen.

cud [kʌd] wiedergekäutes Futter; chew the ~ wiederkäuen; fig. überlegen.

cuddle ['kʌdl] v/t. (ver)hätscheln.

cudgel ['kʌdʒəl] 1. Knüttel m; 2. (ver)prügeln.

cue [kjuː] Billard-Queue n; Stichwort n; Wink m.

cuff [kʌf] 1. Manschette f; Handschelle f; (Armel-, Am. a. Hosen-) Aufschlag m; Faust-Schlag m; 2. puffen, schlagen.

cuisine [kwi(ː)'ziːn] Küche f (Art zu kochen).

culminate ['kʌlmineit] gipfeln.

culpable □ ['kʌlpəbl] strafbar.

culprit ['kʌlprit] Angeklagte(r m) f; Schuldige(r m) f, Missetäter(in).

cultivat|e ['kʌltiveit] kultivieren; an-, bebauen; ausbilden; pflegen; ~ion [kʌlti'veiʃən] (An-, Acker)Bau m; Ausbildung f; Pflege f; Zucht f; ~or ['kʌltiveitə] Landwirt m; Züchter m; ♪ Kultivator m (Maschine).

cultural □ ['kʌltʃərəl] kulturell.
culture ['kʌltʃə] Kultur *f*; Pflege *f*;
Zucht *f*; ⚹ kultiviert.
cumb|er ['kʌmbə] überladen; be-
lasten; ⚹ersome [⚹əsəm], ⚹rous □
[⚹brəs] lästig; schwerfällig.
cumulative [['kju:mjulətiv] (an-,
auf)häufend; Zusatz...
cunning ['kʌniŋ] **1.** □ schlau,
listig; geschickt; *Am.* reizend;
2. List *f*, Schlauheit *f*; Geschicklichkeit *f*.
cup [kʌp] Becher *m*, Schale *f*, Tasse
f; Kelch *m*; *Sport* Pokal *m*; ⚹**board**
['kʌbəd] (Speise- *etc.*)Schrank *m*.
cupidity [kju(:)'piditi] Habgier *f*.
cupola ['kju:pələ] Kuppel *f*.
cur [kə:] Köter *m*; Schurke *m*,
Halunke *m*.
curable ['kjuərəbl] heilbar.
carate ['kjuərit] Hilfsgeistliche(r)
m.
curb [kə:b] **1.** Kinnkette *f*; Kandare
f (*a. fig.*); *a.* ⚹**stone** ['kə:bstoun]
Bordschwelle *f*; **2.** an die Kandare
nehmen (*a. fig.*); *fig.* zügeln;
⚹**market** *Am Börse* Freiverkehr
m; ⚹**roof** Mansardendach *n*.
curd [kə:d] **1.** Quark *m*; **2.** (*mst* ⚹**le**
['kə:dl]) gerinnen (lassen).
cure [kjuə] **1.** Kur *f*; Heilmittel *n*;
Seelsorge *f*; Pfarre *f*; **2.** heilen;
pökeln; räuchern; trocknen
curfew ['kə:fju:] Abendglocke *f*;
pol. Ausgehverbot *n*; ⚹**bell** Abendglocke *f*.
curio ['kjuəriou] Rarität *f*; ⚹**sity**
[kjuəri'ositi] Neugier *f*; Rarität *f*;
⚹**us** □ ['kjuəriəs] neugierig; genau;
seltsam, merkwürdig
curl [kə:l] **1.** Locke *f*; **2.** (sich)
kräuseln; (sich) locken; (sich) ringeln; ⚹**y** ['kə:li] gekräuselt; lockig.
currant ['kʌrənt] Johannisbeere *f*;
a. dried ⚹ Korinthe *f*.
curren|cy ['kʌrənsi] Umlauf *m*; ✝
Lauffrist *f*; Kurs *m*, Währung *f*;
⚹**t** [⚹nt] **1.** □ umlaufend; ✝ kur-
sierend (*Geld*); allgemein (bekannt);
laufend (*Jahr etc.*); **2.** Strom *m*
(*a. ⚡*); Strömung *f* (*a. fig.*); Luft-
Zug *m*.
curricul|um [kə'rikjuləm], *pl.* ⚹**a**
[⚹lə] Lehr-, Stundenplan *m*; ⚹**um
vitae** [⚹əm'vaiti:] Lebenslauf *m*.
curry[1] ['kʌri] Curry *m, n*.
curry[2] [⚹] Leder zurichten; *Pferd*
striegeln.
curse [kə:s] **1.** Fluch *m*; **2.** (ver)flu-
chen; strafen; ⚹**d** □ ['kə:sid] ver-
flucht.
curt □ [kə:t] kurz; knapp; barsch.
curtail [kə:'teil] beschneiden; *fig.*
beschränken; kürzen (*of* um).
curtain ['kə:tn] **1.** Vorhang *m*; Gardine *f*; **2.** verhängen, verschleiern;
⚹**lecture** F Gardinenpredigt *f*.
curts(e)y ['kə:tsi] **1.** Knicks *m*;
m; **2.** knicksen (*to* vor).

curvature ['kə:vətʃə] (Ver)Krüm-
mung *f*.
curve [kə:v] **1.** Kurve *f*; Krümmung
f; **2.** (sich) krümmen; (sich) biegen.
cushion ['kuʃən] **1.** Kissen *n*; Polster *n*; *Billard*-Bande *f*; **2.** polstern.
cuss *Am.* F [kʌs] **1.** Nichtsnutz *m*;
2. fluchen.
custody ['kʌstədi] Haft *f*; (Ob)Hut *f*.
custom ['kʌstəm] Gewohnheit *f*,
Brauch *m*; Sitte *f*; Kundschaft *f*;
⚹**s** *pl.* Zoll *m*; ⚹**ary** [[⚹məri] gewöhnlich, üblich; ⚹**er** [⚹mə]
Kund|e *m*, -in *f*; F Bursche *m*;
⚹**house** Zollamt *n*; ⚹**made** *Am.*
maßgearbeitet.
cut [kʌt] **1.** Schnitt *m*; Hieb *m*;
Stich *m*; (Schnitt)Wunde *f*; Einschnitt *m*; Graben *m*; Kürzung *f*;
Ausschnitt *m*; Wegabkürzung *f*
(*mst* short-⚹); Holz-Schnitt *m*;
Kupfer-Stich *m*; Schliff *m*; Schnitte
f, Scheibe *f*; Karten-Abheben *n*;
Küche: cold ⚹s *pl.* Aufschnitt *m*;
give *s.o.* the ⚹ (direct) F j. schneiden; **2.** [*irr.*] *v/t.* schneiden; schnitzen; gravieren; ab-, an-, auf-, aus-,
be-, durch-, zer-, zuschneiden; *Edelstein etc.* schleifen; *Karten* abheben;
j. beim Begegnen schneiden; ⚹ *teeth*
zahnen; ⚹ short *j.* unterbrechen; ⚹
back einschränken; ⚹ down fällen;
mähen; beschneiden; *Preis* drük-
ken; ⚹ out ausschneiden; *Am.* Vieh
aussondern *aus der Herde*; *fig. j.* aus-
stechen; ⚹ ausschalten; be ⚹ out for
das Zeug zu e-r S. haben; *v/i.* ⚹
in sich einschieben; **3.** *adj.* geschnitten *etc.*, *s. cut* 2.
cute □ F [kju:t] schlau; *Am.* reizend.
cuticle ['kju:tikl] Oberhaut *f*; ⚹
scissors *pl.* Hautschere *f*.
cutlery ['kʌtləri] Messerschmiede-
arbeit *f*; Stahlwaren *f/pl.*; Be-
stecke *n/pl.*
cutlet ['kʌtlit] Kotelett *n*; Schnitzel
n.
cut|-off *Am.* ['kʌtɔ:f] Abkürzung
f (*Straße, Weg*); ⚹**out** *mot.*
Auspuffklappe *f*; ⚡ Sicherung *f*;
Ausschalter *m*; *Am.* Ausschneide-
bogen *m*, -bild *n*; ⚹**purse** Taschen-
dieb *m*; ⚹**ter** ['kʌtə] Schneidende(r
m) *f*; Schnitzer *m*; Zuschneider(in)
Film: Cutter *m*; ⊕ Schneidezeug *n*,
-maschine *f*; ⚓ Kutter *m*; *Am.*
leichter Schlitten; ⚹**throat** Hals-
abschneider *m*; Meuchelmörder *m*;
⚹**ting** ['kʌtiŋ] **1.** □ schneidend;
scharf; ⊕ Schneid..., Fräs...;
2. Schneiden *m*; ✚ *etc.* Einschnitt
m; ♀ Steckling *m*; *Zeitungs*-Aus-
schnitt *m*; ⚹**s** *pl.* Schnipsel *m*, *n/pl.*;
⊕ Späne *m/pl.*
cycl|e ['saikl] **1.** Zyklus *m*; Kreis
(-lauf) *m*; Periode *f*; ⊕ Arbeitsgang

m; Fahrrad *n*; **2.** radfahren; **~ist** [⌐list] Radfahrer(in).
cyclone ['saikloun] Wirbelsturm *m*.
cylinder ['silində] Zylinder *m*, Walze *f*; ⊕ Trommel *f*.
cymbal ♩ ['simbəl] Becken *n*.
cynic ['sinik] **1.** *a*. **~al** □ [~kəl] zynisch; **2.** Zyniker *m*.

cypress ♣ ['saipris] Zypresse *f*.
cyst ✻ [sist] Blase *f*; Sackgeschwulst *f*; **~itis** ✻ [sis'taitis] Blasenentzündung *f*.
Czech [tʃek] **1.** Tschech|e *m*, -in *f*; **2.** tschechisch.
Czechoslovak ['tʃekou'slouvæk] **1.** Tschechoslowak|e *m*, -in *f*; **2.** tschechoslowakisch.

D

dab [dæb] **1.** Klaps *m*; Tupf(en) *m*, Klecks *m*; **2.** klapsen; (be)tupfen.
dabble ['dæbl] bespritzen; plätschern; (hinein)pfuschen.
dad F [dæd], **~dy** F ['dædi] Papa *m*.
daddy-longlegs F *zo.* ['dædi'lɔŋlegz] Schnake *f*; *Am.* Weberknecht *m*.
daffodil ♣ ['dæfədil] gelbe Narzisse.
daft F [dɑ:ft] blöde, doof.
dagger ['dægə] Dolch *m*; *be at* **~s** *drawn fig.* auf Kriegsfuß stehen.
dago *Am. sl.* ['deigou] *contp. für* Spanier, Portugiese, *mst* Italiener.
daily ['deili] **1.** täglich; **2.** Tageszeitung *f*.
dainty ['deinti] **1.** □ lecker; zart, fein; wählerisch; **2.** Leckerei *f*.
dairy ['dɛəri] Molkerei *f*, Milchwirtschaft *f*; Milchgeschäft *n*; ~**cattle** Milchvieh *n*; **~man** Milchhändler *m*.
daisy ♣ ['deizi] Gänseblümchen *n*.
dale [deil] Tal *n*.
dalliance ['dæliəns] Trödelei *f*; Liebelei *f*; **~y** ['dæli] vertrödeln; schäkern.
dam [dæm] **1.** Mutter *f von Tieren*; Deich *m*, Damm *m*; **2.** (ab)dämmen.
damage ['dæmidʒ] **1.** Schaden *m*; **~s** *pl.* ⚖ Schadenersatz *m*; **2.** (be-)schädigen.
damask ['dæməsk] Damast *m*.
dame [deim] Dame *f*; *sl.* Weib *n*.
damn [dæm] verdammen; verurteilen; **~ation** [dæm'neiʃən] Verdammung *f*.
damp [dæmp] **1.** feucht, dunstig; **2.** Feuchtigkeit *f*, Dunst *m*; Gedrücktheit *f*; **3.** *a.* **~en** ['dæmpən] anfeuchten; dämpfen; niederdrükken; **~er** [~pə] Dämpfer *m*.
dance [dɑ:ns] **1.** Tanz *m*; Ball *m*; **2.** tanzen (lassen); **~er** ['dɑ:nsə] Tänzer(in); **~ing** [~siŋ] Tanzen *n*; *attr.* Tanz ... [zahn *m*.]
dandelion ♣ ['dændilaiən] Löwen-)
dandle *sl.* ['dændl] wiegen, schaukeln.
dandruff ['dændrəf] (Kopf)Schuppen *f/pl.*

dandy ['dændi] **1.** Stutzer *m*; F erstklassige Sache; **2.** *Am.* F prima.
Dane [dein] Dän|e *m*, -in *f*.
danger ['deindʒə] Gefahr *f*; **~ous** □ [~dʒrəs] gefährlich; **~signal** ⚑ Notsignal *n*.
dangle ['dæŋgl] baumeln (lassen); schlenkern (mit); *fig.* schwanken.
Danish ['deiniʃ] dänisch.
dank [dæŋk] dunstig, feucht.
Danubian [dæ'nju:bjən] Donau...
dapper □ F ['dæpə] nett; behend.
dapple ['dæpl] sprenkeln; **~d** scheckig; **~grey** Apfelschimmel *m*.
dar|e [dɛə] *v/i.* es wagen; *v/t.* *et.* wagen; *j-n* herausfordern; *j-m* trotzen; **~e-devil** ['dɛədevl] Draufgänger *m*; **~ing** ⟨ ['dɛəriŋ] **1.** verwegen; **2.** Verwegenheit *f*.
dark [dɑ:k] **1.** □ dunkel; brünett; schwerverständlich; geheim(nisvoll); trüb(selig); **2.** Dunkel(heit *f*) *n*; *before (after)* ~ vor (nach) Einbruch der Dunkelheit; **2 Ages** *pl. das* frühe Mittelalter; **~en** ['dɑ:kən] (sich) (ver)dunkeln; (sich) verfinstern; **~ness** ['dɑ:knis] Dunkelheit *f*, Finsternis *f*; **~y** F ['dɑ:ki] Schwarze(r *m f*).)
darling ['dɑ:liŋ] **1.** Liebling *m*; **2.** Lieblings...; geliebt.
darn [dɑ:n] stopfen; ausbessern.
dart [dɑ:t] **1.** Wurfspieß *m*; Wurfpfeil *m*; Sprung *m*, Satz *m*; **~s** *pl.* Wurfpfeilspiel *n*; **2.** *v/t.* schleudern; *v/i. fig.* schießen, (sich) stürzen.
dash [dæʃ] **1.** Schlag *m*, (Zs.-)Stoß *m*; Klatschen *n*; Schwung *m*; Ansturm *m*; *fig.* Anflug *m*; Prise *f*; Schuß *m Rum etc.*; Feder-Strich *m*; Gedankenstrich *m*; **2.** *v/t.* schlagen, werfen, schleudern; zerschmettern; vernichten; (be)spritzen; vermengen; verwirren; *v/i.* stoßen, schlagen; stürzen; stürmen; jagen; **~board** *mot.* ['dæʃbɔ:d] Armaturenbrett *n*; **~ing** □ ['dæʃiŋ] schneidig, forsch; flott, F fesch.
dastardly ['dæstədli] heimtückisch; feig.
data ['deitə] *pl., Am. a. sg.* Angaben

f/pl.; Tatsachen f/pl.; Unterlagen f/pl.; Daten pl.

date [deit] **1.** ♀ Dattel f; Datum n; Zeit f; Termin m; Am. F Verabredung f; Freund(in); out of ~ veraltet, unmodern; up to ~ zeitgemäß, modern; auf dem laufenden; **2.** datieren; Am. F sich verabreden.

dative gr. ['deitiv] a. ~ case Dativ m.

daub [dɔːb] (be)schmieren; (be)klecksen.

daughter ['dɔːtə] Tochter f; ~-in-law [~ərinlɔː] Schwiegertochter f.

daunt [dɔːnt] entmutigen; ~less ['dɔːntlis] furchtlos, unerschrocken.

daw orn. [dɔː] Dohle f.

dawdle F ['dɔːdl] (ver)trödeln.

dawn [dɔːn] **1.** Dämmerung f; fig. Morgenrot n; **2.** dämmern, tagen; it ~ed upon him fig. es wurde ihm langsam klar.

day [dei] Tag m; oft ~s pl. (Lebens-) Zeit f; ~ off dienst-freier Tag; carry od. win the ~ den Sieg davontragen; the other ~ neulich; this ~ week heute in einer Woche; heute vor einer Woche; let's call it a ~ machen wir Schluß für heute; ~break ['deibreik] Tagesanbruch m; ~-labo(u)rer Tagelöhner m; ~-star Morgenstern m.

daze [deiz] blenden; betäuben.

dazzle ['dæzl] blenden; ⊕ tarnen.

dead [ded] **1.** tot; unempfindlich (to für); matt (Farbe etc.); blind (Fenster etc.); erloschen (Feuer); schal (Getränk); tief (Schlaf); † tot (Kapital etc.); ~ bargain Spottpreis m; ~ letter unzustellbarer Brief; ~ loss Totalverlust m; a ~ shot ein Meisterschütze; ~ wall blinde Mauer; ~ wood Reisig n; Am. Plunder m; **2.** adv. gänzlich, völlig, total; durchaus; genau, (haar)scharf; ~ against gerade od. ganz und gar (ent)gegen; **3.** the ~ der Tote; die Toten pl.; Totenstille f; in the ~ of winter im tiefsten Winter; in the ~ of night mitten in der Nacht; ~en ['dedn] abstumpfen; dämpfen; (ab)schwächen; ~-end Sackgasse f (a. fig.); ~-line Am. Sperrlinie f im Gefängnis; Schlußtermin m; Stichtag m; ~-lock Stockung f; fig. toter Punkt; ~ly ['dedli] tödlich.

deaf [def] taub; ~en ['defn] taub machen; betäuben.

deal [diːl] **1.** Teil m; Menge f; Kartengeben n; F Geschäft n; Abmachung f; a good ~ ziemlich viel; a great ~ sehr viel; **2.** [irr.] v/t. (aus-, ver-, zu)teilen; Karten geben; e-n Schlag versetzen; v/i. handeln (in mit e-r Ware); ~ out austeilen, verabfolgen; verkehren; ~ with sich befassen mit, behandeln; ~er ['diːlə] Händler m; Kartengeber m; ~ing ['diːliŋ] mst

~s pl. Handlungsweise f; Verfahren n; Verkehr m; ~t [delt] pret. u p.p. von deal 2.

dean [diːn] Dekan m.

dear [diə] **1.** □ teuer; lieb; **2.** Liebling m; herziges Geschöpf; **3.** o(h) ~!, ~ me! F du liebe Zeit!; ach herrje!

death [deθ] Tod m; Todesfall m; ~-bed ['deθbed] Sterbebett n; ~-duty Erbschaftssteuer f; ~less ['deθlis] unsterblich; ~ly [~li] tödlich; ~-rate Sterblichkeitsziffer f; ~-warrant Todesurteil n.

debar [di'bɑː] ausschließen; hindern.

debarkation [diːbɑːˈkeiʃən] Ausschiffung f.

debase [di'beis] verschlechtern; erniedrigen; verfälschen.

debat|able [di'beitəbl] strittig; umstritten; ~e [di'beit] **1.** Debatte f; **2.** debattieren; erörtern; überlegen.

debauch [di'bɔːtʃ] **1.** Ausschweifung f; **2.** verderben; verführen.

debilitate [di'biliteit] schwächen.

debit † ['debit] **1.** Debet n, Schuld f; **2.** j-n belasten; debitieren.

debris ['debriː] Trümmer pl.

debt [det] Schuld f; ~or ['detə] Schuldner(in).

debunk ['diː'bʌŋk] den Nimbus nehmen (dat.).

début ['deibuː] Debüt n.

decade ['dekeid] Jahrzehnt n.

decadence ['dekədəns] Verfall m.

decamp [di'kæmp] aufbrechen; ausreißen; ~ment [~pmənt] Aufbruch m.

decant [di'kænt] abgießen; umfüllen; ~er [~tə] Karaffe f.

decapitate [di'kæpiteit] enthaupten; Am. F fig. absägen (entlassen).

decay [di'kei] **1.** Verfall m; Fäulnis f; **2.** verfallen; (ver)faulen.

decease bsd. ⚖ [di'siːs] **1.** Ableben n; **2.** sterben.

deceit [di'siːt] Täuschung f; Betrug m; ~ful □ [~tful] (be)trügerisch.

deceive [di'siːv] betrügen; täuschen; verleiten; ~r [~və] Betrüger(in).

December [di'sembə] Dezember m.

decen|cy ['diːsnsi] Anstand m; ~t □ [~nt] anständig; F annehmbar, nett.

deception [di'sepʃən] Täuschung f.

decide [di'said] (sich) entscheiden; bestimmen; ~d □ entschieden; bestimmt; entschlossen.

decimal ['desiməl] Dezimalbruch m; attr. Dezimal...

decipher [di'saifə] entziffern.

decis|ion [di'siʒən] Entscheidung f; ⚖ Urteil n; Entschluß m; Entschlossenheit f; ~ve □ [di'saisiv] entscheidend; entschieden.

deck [dek] **1.** ♣ Deck *n*; *Am.* Pack *m* Spielkarten; on ~ *Am.* F da(bei), bereit; **2.** *rhet.* schmücken; **~chair** ['dek'tʃeə] Liegestuhl *m*.

declaim [di'kleim] vortragen; (sich er)eifern.

declar|able [di'kleərəbl] steuer-, zollpflichtig; **~ation** [deklə'reiʃən] Erklärung *f*; *Zoll*-Deklaration *f*; **~e** [di'kleə] (sich) erklären; behaupten; deklarieren.

declension [di'klenʃən] Abfall *m* (*Neigung*); Verfall *m*; *gr.* Deklination *f*.

declin|ation [dekli'neiʃən] Neigung *f*; Abweichung *f*; **~e** [di'klain] **1.** Abnahme *f*; Niedergang *m*; Verfall *m*; **2.** *v/t.* neigen, biegen; *gr.* deklinieren; ablehnen; *v/i.* sich neigen; abnehmen; verfallen.

declivity [di'kliviti] Abhang *m*.

declutch *mot.* ['di:'klʌtʃ] auskuppeln.

decode *tel.* ['di:'koud] entschlüsseln.

decompose [di:kəm'pouz] zerlegen; (sich) zersetzen; verwesen.

decontrol ['di:kən'troul] *Waren, Handel* freigeben.

decorat|e ['dekəreit] (ver)zieren; schmücken; **~ion** [dekə'reiʃən] Verzierung *f*; Schmuck *m*; Orden(sauszeichnung *f*) *m*; ⁓ *Day Am.* Heldengedenktag *m*; **~ive** ['dekərətiv] dekorativ; Zier...; **~or** [~reitə] Dekorateur *m*, Maler *m*.

decor|ous [~'dekərəs] anständig; **~um** [di'kɔ:rəm] Anstand *m*.

decoy [di'kɔi] **1.** Lockvogel *m* (*a. fig.*); Köder *m*; **2.** ködern; locken.

decrease 1. ['di:kri:s] Abnahme *f*; **2.** [di:'kri:s] (sich) vermindern.

decree [di'kri:] **1.** Dekret *n*, Verordnung *f*, Erlaß *m*; ♏ Entscheid *m*; **2.** beschließen; verordnen, verfügen.

decrepit [di'krepit] altersschwach.

decry [di'krai] in Verruf bringen.

dedicat|e ['dedikeit] widmen; **~ion** [dedi'keiʃən] Widmung *f*.

deduce [di'dju:s] ableiten; folgern.

deduct [di'dʌkt] abziehen; **~ion** [~kʃən] Abzug *m*; ✝ Rabatt *m*; Schlußfolgerung *f*.

deed [di:d] **1.** Tat *f*; Heldentat *f*; Urkunde *f*; **2.** *Am.* urkundlich übertragen (*to auf acc.*).

deem [di:m] *v/t.* halten für; *v/i.* denken, urteilen (*of über acc.*).

deep [di:p] **1.** ⌐ tief; gründlich; schlau; vertieft; dunkel (*a. fig.*); verborgen; **2.** Tiefe *f*; *poet.* Meer *n*; **~en** ['di:pən] (sich) vertiefen; (sich) verstärken; **~-freeze 1.** tiefkühlen; **2.** Tiefkühlfach *n*, -truhe *f*; **~ness** ['di:pnis] Tiefe *f*.

deer [diə] Rotwild *n*; Hirsch *m*.

deface [di'feis] entstellen; unkenntlich machen; ausstreichen.

defalcation [di:fæl'keiʃən] Unterschlagung *f*.

defam|ation [defə'meiʃən] Verleumdung *f*; **~e** [di'feim] verleumden; verunglimpfen.

default [di'fɔ:lt] **1.** Nichterscheinen *n vor Gericht*; Säumigkeit *f*; Verzug *m*; *in* ~ *of* which widrigenfalls; **2.** *s-n etc.* Verbindlichkeiten nicht nachkommen.

defeat [di'fi:t] **1.** Niederlage *f*; Besiegung *f*; Vereitelung *f*; **2.** ⚔ besiegen; vereiteln; vernichten.

defect [di'fekt] Mangel *m*; Fehler *m*; **~ive** ⌐ [~tiv] mangelhaft; unvollständig; fehlerhaft.

defen|ce, *Am.* **~se** [di'fens] Verteidigung *f*; Schutzmaßnahme *f*; *witness for the* ~ Entlastungszeuge *m*; **~celess,** *Am.* **~seless** [~slis] schutzlos, wehrlos.

defend [di'fend] verteidigen; schützen (*from vor dat.*); **~ant** [~dənt] Angeklagte(r *m*) *f*; Beklagte(r *m*) *f*; **~er** [~də] Verteidiger(in).

defensive [di'fensiv] Defensive *f*; *attr.* Verteidigungs...

defer [di'fə:] auf-, verschieben; *Am.* ⚔ zurückstellen; sich fügen; nachgeben; *payment on* ~*red terms* Ratenzahlung *f*; **~ence** ['defərəns] Ehrerbietung *f*; Nachgiebigkeit *f*; **~ential** ⌐ [defə'renʃəl] ehrerbietig.

defian|ce [di'faiəns] Herausforderung *f*; Trotz *m*; **~t** ⌐ [~t] herausfordernd; trotzig.

deficien|cy [di'fiʃənsi] Unzulänglichkeit *f*; Mangel *m*; ⁓ *deficit*; **~t** ⌐ [~nt] mangelhaft; unzureichend.

deficit ['defisit] Fehlbetrag *m*.

defile 1. ['di:fail] Engpaß *m*; **2.** [di'fail] *v/i.* vorbeiziehen; *v/t.* beflecken; schänden.

defin|e [di'fain] definieren; erklären; genau bestimmen; **~ite** ⌐ ['definit] bestimmt; deutlich; genau; **~ition** [defi'niʃən] (Begriffs-)Bestimmung *f*; Erklärung *f*; **~itive** ⌐ [di'finitiv] bestimmt; entscheidend; endgültig.

deflect [di'flekt] ablenken; abweichen.

deform [di'fɔ:m] entstellen, verunstalten; **~ed** verwachsen; **~ity** [~miti] Unförmigkeit *f*; Mißgestalt *f*.

defraud [di'frɔ:d] betrügen (*of um*).

defray [di'frei] *Kosten* bestreiten.

defroster *mot.* [di:'frɔstə] Entfroster *m*.

deft ⌐ [deft] gewandt, flink.

defunct [di'fʌŋkt] verstorben.

defy [di'fai] herausfordern; trotzen.

degenerate 1. [di'dʒenəreit] entarten; **2.** [~rit] entartet.

degrad|ation [degrə'deiʃən] Absetzung *f*; **~e** [di'greid] *v/t.* absetzen; erniedrigen; demütigen.

degree [di'gri:] Grad *m*; *fig.* Stufe *f*,

Schritt m; Rang m, Stand m; by ∼s allmählich; in no ∼ in keiner Weise; in some ∼ einigermaßen; take one's ∼ sein Abschlußexamen machen.

dehydrated [di:'haidreitid] Trocken...

deify ['di:ifai] vergöttern; vergöttlichen.

deign [dein] geruhen; gewähren.

deity ['di:iti] Gottheit f.

deject [di'dʒekt] entmutigen; ∼ed ☐ niedergeschlagen; ∼ion [∼kʃən] Niedergeschlagenheit f.

delay [di'lei] 1. Aufschub m; Verzögerung f; 2. v/t. aufschieben; verzögern; v/i. zögern; trödeln.

delega|te 1. ['deligeit] abordnen; übertragen; 2. [∼git] Abgeordnete(r m) f; ∼tion [deli'geiʃən] Abordnung f; Am. parl. die Kongreßabgeordneten m/pl. e-s Staates.

deliberat|e 1. [di'libareit] v/t. überlegen, erwägen; v/i. nachdenken; beraten; 2. ☐ [∼rit] bedachtsam; wohlüberlegt; vorsätzlich; ∼ion [diliba'reiʃən] Überlegung f; Beratung f; Bedächtigkeit f.

delica|cy ['delikəsi] Wohlgeschmack m; Leckerbissen m; Zartheit f; Schwächlichkeit f; Feinfühligkeit f; ∼te [∼kit] schmackhaft; lecker; zart; fein; schwach; heikel; empfindlich; feinfühlig; wählerisch; ∼tessen [delika'tesn] Feinkost(geschäft n) f.

delicious [di'liʃəs] köstlich.

delight [di'lait] 1. Lust f, Freude f, Wonne f; 2. entzücken; (sich) erfreuen (in an dat.); ∼ to inf. Freude daran finden, zu inf.; ∼ful [∼tful] entzückend. [schildern.]

delineate [di'linieit] entwerfen;]

delinquen|cy [di'liŋkwənsi] Vergehen n; Kriminalität f; Pflichtvergessenheit f; ∼t [∼nt] 1. straffällig; pflichtvergessen; 2. Verbrecher(in).

deliri|ous ☐ [di'liriəs] wahnsinnig; ∼um [∼iəm] Fieberwahn m.

deliver [di'livə] befreien; über-, aus-, abliefern; Botschaft ausrichten; äußern; Rede etc. vortragen, halten; ✗ entbinden; Schlag führen; werfen; ∼ance [∼ərəns] Befreiung f; (Meinungs)Äußerung f; ∼er [∼rə] Befreier(in); Überbringer(in); ∼y [∼ri] ✗ Entbindung f; (Ab)Lieferung f; ♭ Zustellung f; Übergabe f; Vortrag m; Wurf m; special ∼ Lieferung f durch Eilboten; ∼y-truck, ∼y-van Lieferwagen m.

dell [del] kleines Tal.

delude [di'lu:d] täuschen; verleiten.

deluge ['delju:dʒ] 1. Überschwemmung f; 2. überschwemmen.

delus|ion [di'lu:ʒən] Täuschung f, Verblendung f; Wahn m; ∼ive ☐ [∼u:siv] (be)trügerisch; täuschend.

demand [di'ma:nd] 1. Verlangen n; Forderung f; Bedarf m; ✝ Nachfrage f; ♫ Rechtsanspruch m; 2. verlangen, fordern; fragen (nach).

demean [di'mi:n]: ∼ o.s. sich benehmen; sich erniedrigen; ∼o(u)r [∼nə] Benehmen n.

demented [di'mentid] wahnsinnig.

demerit [di:'merit] Fehler m.

demesne [di'mein] Besitz m.

demi... ['demi] Halb..., halb...

demijohn ['demidʒɔn] große Korbflasche, Glasballon m.

demilitarize ['di:'militəraiz] entmilitarisieren.

demise [di'maiz] 1. Ableben n; 2. vermachen.

demobilize [di:'moubilaiz] demobilisieren.

democra|cy [di'mɔkrəsi] Demokratie f; ∼t ['deməkræt] Demokrat(in); ∼tic(al) [demə'krætik(əl)] demokratisch

demolish [di'mɔliʃ] nieder-, abreißen; zerstören.

demon ['di:mən] Dämon m; Teufel m.

demonstrat|e ['demənstreit] anschaulich darstellen; beweisen; demonstrieren; ∼ion [deməns'treiʃən] Demonstration f; anschauliche Darstellung, Beweis m; (Gefühls)-Äußerung f; ∼ive ☐ [di'mɔnstrətiv] überzeugend; demonstrativ; ausdrucksvoll; auffällig, überschwenglich.

demote [di:'mout] degradieren.

demur [di'mə:] 1. Einwendung f; 2. Einwendungen erheben.

demure [di'mjuə] ernst; prüde.

den [den] Höhle f; Grube f; sl. Bude f.

denial [di'naiəl] Leugnen n; Verneinung f; abschlägige Antwort.

denizen ['denizn] Bewohner m.

denominat|e [di'nɔmineit] (be)nennen; ∼ion [dinɔmi'neiʃən] Benennung f; Klasse f; Sekte f, Konfession f.

denote [di'nout] bezeichnen; bedeuten

denounce [di'nauns] anzeigen; brandmarken; Vertrag kündigen.

dens|e [dens] dicht, dick (Nebel); beschränkt; ∼ity [di'densiti] Dichte f; Dichtigkeit f.

dent [dent] 1. Kerbe f; Beule f; 2. ver-, einbeulen.

dent|al ['dentl] Zahn...; ∼ surgeon Zahnarzt m; ∼ist [∼tist] Zahnarzt m.

denunciat|ion [dinʌnsi'eiʃən] Anzeige f; Kündigung f; ∼or [di'nʌnsieitə] Denunziant m.

deny [di'nai] verleugnen; verweigern, abschlagen; j-n abweisen.

depart [di'pa:t] v/i. abreisen, abfahren; abstehen, (ab)weichen;

verscheiden; **~ment** [~tmənt] Abteilung f; Bezirk m; ✝ Branche f; *Am.* Ministerium n; State ♀ *Am.* Außenministerium n; **~ store** Warenhaus n; **~ure** [~tʃə] Abreise f, ♒, ♣ Abfahrt f; Abweichung f.

depend [di'pend]: **~** *(up)on* abhängen von; angewiesen sein auf *(acc.)*; sich verlassen auf *(acc.)*; it **~s** F es kommt (ganz) darauf an; **~able** [~dəbl] zuverlässig; **~ant** [~ənt] Abhängige(r m) f; Angehörige(r m) f; **~ence** [~dəns] Abhängigkeit f; Vertrauen n; **~ency** [~si] Schutzgebiet n; **~ent** [~nt] 1. ┆ *(on)* abhängig (von); angewiesen auf *acc.*); 2. *Am.* = dependant.

depict [di'pikt] darstellen; schildern.

deplete [di'pliːt] (ent)leeren; *fig.* erschöpfen.

deplor|able □ [di'plɔːrəbl] beklagenswert; kläglich; jämmerlich; **~e** [di'plɔː] beklagen, bedauern.

deponent ᚥ [di'pounənt] vereidigter Zeuge. [entvölkern.)

depopulate [diː'pɔpjuleit] (sich))

deport [di'pɔːt] *Ausländer* abschieben; verbannen; **~** *o.s.* sich benehmen; **~ment** [~tmənt] Benehmen n.

depose [di'pouz] absetzen; ᚥ (eidlich) aussagen.

deposit [di'pɔzit] 1. Ablagerung f; Lager n; ✝ Depot n; *Bank-*Einlage f; Pfand n; Hinterlegung f; 2. (nieder-, ab-, hin)legen; *Geld* einlegen, einzahlen; hinterlegen; (sich) ablagern; **~ion** [depə'ziʃən] Ablagerung f; eidliche Zeugenaussage; Absetzung f; **~or** [di'pɔzitə] Hinterleger m, Einzahler m; Kontoinhaber m.

depot ['depou] Depot n; Lagerhaus n; *Am.* Bahnhof m.

deprave [di'preiv] *sittlich* verderben.

deprecate ['deprikeit] ablehnen.

depreciate [di'priːʃieit] herabsetzen; geringschätzen; entwerten.

depredation [depri'deiʃən] Plünderung f.

depress [di'pres] niederdrücken; *Preise etc.* senken, drücken; bedrücken; **~ed** *fig.* niedergeschlagen; **~ion** [~eʃən] Senkung f; Niedergeschlagenheit f; ✝ Flaute f, Wirtschaftskrise f; ♀ Schwäche f; Sinken n.

deprive [di'praiv] berauben; entziehen; ausschließen (of von).

depth [depθ] Tiefe f; *attr.* Tiefen...

deput|ation [depju(ː)'teiʃən] Abordnung f; **~e** [di'pjuːt] abordnen; **~y** ['depjuti] Abgeordnete(r m) f; Stellvertreter m, Beauftragte(r) m.

derail ♒ [di'reil] *v/i.* entgleisen; *v/t.* zum Entgleisen bringen.

derange [di'reindʒ] in Unordnung bringen; stören; zerrütten; *(mentally)* **~d** geistesgestört; a **~d** *stomach* eine Magenverstimmung.

derelict ['derilikt] 1. verlassen; *bsd. Am.* nachlässig; 2. herrenloses Gut; Wrack n; **~ion** [deri'likʃən] Verlassen n; Vernachlässigung f.

deri|de [di'raid] verlachen, verspotten; **~sion** [di'riʒən] Verspottung f; **~sive** ┃] [di'raisiv] spöttisch.

deriv|ation [deri'veiʃən] Ableitung f; Herkunft f; **~e** [di'raiv] herleiten; *Nutzen etc.* ziehen *(from* aus).

derogat|e ['derəgeit] schmälern *(from acc.)*; **~ion** [derə'geiʃən] Beeinträchtigung f; Herabwürdigung f; **~ory** □ [di'rɔgətəri] *(to)* nachteilig *(dat.,* für); herabwürdigend.

derrick ['derik] ⊕ Drehkran m; ♣ Ladebaum m; ⚒ Bohrturm m.

descend [di'send] (her-, hin)absteigen, herabkommen; sinken; ♔ niedergehen; **~** *(up)on* herfallen über *(acc.)*; einfallen in *(acc.)*; (ab)stammen; **~ant** [~dənt] Nachkomme m.

descent [di'sent] Herabsteigen n; Abstieg m; Sinken n; Gefälle n; feindlicher Einfall; Landung f; Abstammung f; Abhang m.

describe [dis'kraib] beschreiben.

description [dis'kripʃən] Beschreibung f, Schilderung f; F Art f.

descry [dis'krai] wahrnehmen.

desecrate ['desikreit] entweihen.

desegregate *Am.* [diː'segrigeit] die Rassentrennung aufheben in *(dat.)*.

desert[1] ['dezət] 1. verlassen; wüst, öde; Wüsten...; 2. Wüste f.

desert[2] [di'zəːt] *v/t.* verlassen; *v/i.* ausreißen; desertieren.

desert[3] [di'zəːt] Verdienst n.

desert|er [di'zəːtə] Fahnenflüchtige(r) m; **~ion** [~ɔːʃən] Verlassen n; Fahnenflucht f.

deserve [di'zəːv] verdienen; sich verdient machen *(of* um); **~ing** [~viŋ] würdig *(of gen.)*; verdienstvoll.

design [di'zain] 1. Plan m; Entwurf m; Vorhaben n, Absicht f; Zeichnung f, Muster n; 2. ersinnen; zeichnen, entwerfen; planen; bestimmen.

designat|e ['dezigneit] bezeichnen; ernennnen, bestimmen; **~ion** [dezig'neiʃən] Bezeichnung f; Bestimmung f, Ernennung f.

designer [di'zainə] (Muster)Zeichner(in); Konstrukteur m.

desir|able □ [di'zaiərəbl] wünschenswert; angenehm; **~e** [di'zaiə] 1. Wunsch m; Verlangen n; 2. verlangen, wünschen; **~ous** □ [~rəs] begierig.

desist [di'zist] abstehen, ablassen.

desk [desk] Pult n; Schreibtisch m.

desolat|e 1. ['desəleit] verwüsten; 2. □ [~lit] einsam; verlassen; öde; **~ion** [desə'leiʃən] Verwüstung f; Einöde f; Verlassenheit f.

despair [dis'pɛə] 1. Verzweiflung f;

2. verzweifeln (of an dat.); ~ing
□ [~riŋ] verzweifelt.
despatch [dis'pætʃ] = dispatch.
desperat|e adj. [['despərit] ver-
zweifelt; hoffnungslos; F schrecklich; ~ion [despə'reiʃən] Verzweiflung f; Raserei f.
despicable □ ['despikəbl] verächtlich.
despise [dis'paiz] verachten.
despite [dis'pait] 1. Verachtung f;
Trotz m; Bosheit f; in ~ of zum
Trotz, trotz; 2. prp. a. ~ of trotz.
despoil [dis'poil] berauben (of gen.).
despond [dis'pond] verzagen, verzweifeln; ~ency [~dənsi] Verzagt-
heit f; ~ent [~nt] verzagt.
despot ['despot] Despot m, Tyrann
m; ~ism [~pətizəm] Despotismus
m.
dessert [di'zə:t] Nachtisch m, Dessert n; Am. Süßspeise f.
destin|ation [desti'neiʃən] Be-
stimmung(sort m) f; ~e ['destin]
bestimmen; ~y [~ni] Schicksal n.
destitute □ ['destitju:t] mittellos,
notleidend; entblößt (of von).
destroy [dis'troi] zerstören, vernichten; töten; unschädlich machen; ~er [~ɔiə] Zerstörer(in).
destruct|ion [dis'trʌkʃən] Zerstö-
rung f; Tötung f; ~ive □ [~ktiv]
zerstörend; vernichtend (of, to
acc.); ~or [~tə] (Müll)Verbren-
nungsofen m.
desultory □ ['desəltəri] unstet;
planlos; oberflächlich.
detach [di'tætʃ] losmachen, (ab-)
lösen; absondern; ✕ (ab)komman-
dieren; ~ed einzeln (stehend); unbeeinflußt; ~ment [~ʃmənt] Los-
lösung f; Trennung f; ✕ Abteilung f.
detail ['di:teil] 1. Einzelheit f; ein-
gehende Darstellung; ✕ Kom-
mando n; in ~ ausführlich; 2. genau
schildern; ✕ abkommandieren.
detain [di'tein] zurück-, auf-, abhalten; j-n in Haft behalten.
detect [di'tekt] entdecken; (auf-)
finden; ~ion [~kʃən] Entdeckung f;
~ive [~ktiv] Detektiv m; ~ story, ~
novel Kriminalroman m.
detention [di'tenʃən] Vorenthal-
tung f; Zurück-, Abhaltung f;
Haft f. [von).]
deter [di'tə:] abschrecken (from
detergent [di'tə:dʒənt] 1. reini-
gend; 2. Reinigungsmittel n.
deteriorat|e [di'tiəriəreit] (sich)
verschlechtern; entarten; ~ion
[ditiəriə'reiʃən] Verschlechterung f.
determin|ation [ditə:mi'neiʃən]
Bestimmung f; Entschlossenheit f;
Entscheidung f; Entschluß m; ~e
[di'tə:min] v/t. bestimmen; entscheiden; veranlassen; Strafe festsetzen; beendigen; v/i. sich entschließen; ~ed entschlossen.

deterrent [di'terənt] 1. abschrek-
kend; 2. Abschreckungsmittel n;
nuclear ~ pol. atomare Abschrek-
kung.
detest [di'test] verabscheuen; ~able
□ [~təbl] abscheulich; ~ation [di:-
tes'teiʃən] Abscheu m.
dethrone [di'θroun] entthronen.
detonate ['detouneit] explodieren
(lassen).
detour, détour ['deituə] 1. Umweg m; Umleitung f; 2. e-n Umweg machen.
detract [di'trækt]: ~ from s.th. et.
beeinträchtigen, schmälern; ~ion
[~kʃən] Verleumdung f; Herabset-
zung f.
detriment ['detrimənt] Schaden m.
deuce [dju:s] Zwei f im Spiel;
Tennis: Einstand m; F Teufel m;
the ~! zum Teufel!
devalu|ation [di:vælju'eiʃən] Ab-
wertung f; ~e ['di:'vælju:] abwer-
ten.
devastat|e ['devəsteit] verwüsten;
~ion [devəs'teiʃən] Verwüstung f.
develop [di'veləp] (sich) entwickeln;
(sich) entfalten; (sich) erweitern;
Gelände erschließen; ausbauen;
Am. (~ʃia) zeigen; ~ment [~pmənt]
Entwicklung f, Entfaltung f; Erweiterung f; Ausbau m.
deviat|e ['di:vieit] abweichen; ~ion
[di:vi'eiʃən] Abweichung f.
device [di'vais] Plan m; Kniff m;
Erfindung f; Vorrichtung f; Muster n; Wahlspruch m; leave s.o. to
his own ~s j. sich selbst überlassen.
devil ['devl] 1. Teufel m (a. fig.);
⚖ Hilfsanwalt m; Laufbursche m;
2. v/t. Gericht stark pfeffern; Am.
plagen, quälen; ~ish □ [~liʃ] teuflisch; ~(t)ry [~l(t)ri] Teufelei f.
devious □ ['di:viəs] abwegig.
devise [di'vaiz] 1. ⚖ Vermachen n;
Vermächtnis n; 2. ersinnen; ⚖ vermachen.
devoid [di'void] ~ of bar (gen.), ohne.
devot|e [di'vout] weihen, widmen;
~ed [ergeben; zärtlich; ~ion
[~ouʃən] Ergebenheit f; Hingebung
f; Frömmigkeit f; ~s pl. Andacht f.
devour [di'vauə] verschlingen.
devout [[di'vaut] andächtig,
fromm; innig.
dew [dju:] 1. Tau m; 2. tauen; ~y
['dju:i] betaut; taufrisch.
dexter|ity [deks'teriti] Gewandtheit
f; ~ous [['dekstərəs] gewandt.
diabolic(al □) [daiə'bɔlik(əl)] teuflisch.
diagnose ['daiəgnouz] diagnosti-
zieren, erkennen.
diagram ['daiəgræm] graphische
Darstellung; Schema n, Plan m.
dial ['daiəl] 1. Sonnenuhr f; Zifferblatt n; teleph. Wähl(er)scheibe f;
Radio: Skala f; 2. teleph. wählen.
dialect ['daiəlekt] Mundart f.

dialo|gue, *Am. a.* **~g** ['daiəlɔg] Dialog *m*, Gespräch *n*.

dial-tone *teleph.* ['daiəltoun] Amtszeichen *n*.

diameter [dai'æmitə] Durchmesser *m*.

diamond ['daiəmənd] Diamant *m*; Rhombus *m*; *Am. Baseball*: Spielfeld *n*; *Karten* Karo *n*.

diaper ['daiəpə] 1. Windel *f*; 2. *Am.* Baby trockenlegen, wickeln.

diaphragm ['daiəfræm] Zwerchfell *n*; *opt.* Blende *f*; *teleph.* Membran(e) *f*.

diarrh(o)ea ✠ [daiə'riə] Durchfall *m*.

diary ['daiəri] Tagebuch *n*.

dice [dais] 1. *pl. von* die²; 2. würfeln; **~box** ['daisbɔks] Würfelbecher *m*.

dick *Am. sl* [dik] Detektiv *m*.

dicker *Am.* F ['dikə] (ver)schachern.

dick(e)y ['diki] 1. *sl.* schlecht, schlimm; 2. F Notsitz *m*; Hemdenbrust *f*; *a.* **~-bird** Piepvögelchen *n*.

dictat|e 1. ['dikteit] Diktat *n*, Vorschrift *f*; Gebot *n*; 2. [dik'teit] diktieren; *fig.* vorschreiben; **~ion** [~'eiʃən] Diktat *m*; Vorschrift *f*; **~orship** [~eitəʃip] Diktatur *f*.

diction ['dikʃən] Ausdruck(sweise *f*) *m*, Stil *m*; **~ary** [~nri] Wörterbuch *n*.

did [did] *pret. von* do.

die¹ [dai] sterben, umkommen; untergehen; absterben; F schmachten; *~ away* ersterben; verhallen (*Ton*); sich verlieren (*Farbe*); verlöschen (*Licht*); *~ down* hinsiechen; (dahin)schwinden; erlöschen.

die² [~], *pl.* **dice** [dais] Würfel *m*; *pl.* **dies** [daiz] ⊕ Preßform *f*; Münz-Stempel *m*; *lower* ~ Matrize *f*.

die-hard ['daiha:d] Reaktionär *m*.

diet ['daiət] 1. Diät *f*; Nahrung *f*, Kost *f*; Landtag *m*; 2. *v/t.* Diät vorschreiben; beköstigen; *v/i.* diät leben.

differ ['difə] sich unterscheiden; anderer Meinung sein (*with, from* als); abweichen; **~ence** ['difrəns] Unterschied *m*; A, ✦ Differenz *f*; Meinungsverschiedenheit *f*; **~ent** □ [~nt] verschieden; anders, andere(r, -s) (*from* als); **~entiate** [difə'renʃieit] (sich) unterscheiden.

difficult ['difikəlt] schwierig; **~y** [~ti] Schwierigkeit *f*.

diffiden|ce ['difidəns] Schüchternheit *f*; **~t** □ [~t] schüchtern.

diffus|e 1. *fig.* [di'fju:z] verbreiten; 2. □ [~:s] weitverbreitet, zerstreut (*bsd. Licht*); weitschweifig; **~ion** [~:ʒən] Verbreitung *f*.

dig [dig] 1. [*irr.*] (um-, aus)graben; wühlen (*in in dat.*); 2. (Aus)Grabung(sstelle) *f*; *~s pl.* F Bude *f*, Einzelzimmer *n*; F Stoß *m*, Puff *m*.

digest 1. [di'dʒest] *v/t.* ordnen; verdauen (*a. fig. = überdenken*; *verwinden*); *v/i.* verdaut werden; 2. ['daidʒest] Abriß *m*; Auslese *f*, Auswahl *f*; ⅛ Gesetzsammlung *f*; **~ible** [di'dʒestəbl] verdaulich; **~ion** [~tʃən] Verdauung *f*; **~ive** [~tiv] Verdauungsmittel *n*.

digg|er ['digə] (*bsd.* Gold)Gräber *m*; *sl.* Australier *m*; **~ings** F ['diginz] *pl.* Bude *f* (*Wohnung*); *Am.* Goldmine(n *pl.*) *f*.

dign|ified □ ['dignifaid] würdevoll; würdig; **~y** [~fai] Würde verleihen (*dat.*); (be)ehren; *fig.* adeln.

dignit|ary □ ['dignitəri] Würdenträger *m*; **~y** [~ti] Würde *f*.

digress [dai'gres] abschweifen.

dike [daik] 1. Deich *m*; Damm *m*; Graben *m*; 2. eindeichen; eindämmen. [(lassen).]

dilapidate [di'læpideit] verfallen]

dilat|e [dai'leit] (sich) ausdehnen; *Augen* weit öffnen; **~ory** ['dilətəri] aufschiebend; saumselig.

diligen|ce ['dilidʒəns] Fleiß *m*; **~t** □ [~nt] fleißig, emsig.

dilute [dai'lju:t] 1. verdünnen; verwässern; 2. verdünnt.

dim [dim] 1. □ trüb; dunkel; matt; 2. (sich) verdunkeln; abblenden; (sich) trüben; matt werden.

dime *Am.* [daim] Zehncentstück *n*.

dimension [di'menʃən] Abmessung *f*; *~s pl. a.* Ausmaß *n*.

dimin|ish [di'miniʃ] (sich) vermindern; abnehmen; **~ution** [dimi-'nju:ʃən] Verminderung *f*; Abnahme *f*; **~utive** □ [di'minjutiv] winzig.

dimple ['dimpl] 1. Grübchen *n*; 2. Grübchen bekommen.

din [din] Getöse *n*, Lärm *m*.

dine [dain] (zu Mittag) speisen; bewirten; **~r** ['dainə] Speisende(r *m*) *f*; (Mittags)Gast *m*; 🍴 *bsd. Am.* Speisewagen *m*; *Am.* Restaurant *n*.

dingle ['dingl] Waldschlucht *f*.

dingy □ ['dindʒi] schmutzig.

dining-car 🍴 ['dainiŋka:] Speisewagen *m*; **~-room** Speisezimmer *n*.

dinner ['dinə] (Mittag-, Abend-) Essen *n*; Festessen *n*; **~-jacket** Smoking *m*; **~-pail** *Am.* Essenträger *m* (*Gerät*); **~-party** Tischgesellschaft *f*; **~-service**, **~-set** Tafelgeschirr *n*.

dint [dint] 1. Beule *f*; *by ~ of* kraft, vermöge (*gen.*); 2. ver-, einbeulen.

dip [dip] 1. *v/t.* (ein)tauchen; senken; schöpfen; abblenden; *v/i.* (unter)tauchen, untersinken; sich neigen; sich senken; 2. Eintauchen *n*; F kurzes Bad; Senkung *f*, Neigung *f*. [rie *f*.]

diphtheria ✠ [dif'θiəriə] Diphthe-]

diploma [di'ploumə] Diplom *n*; **~cy** [~əsi] Diplomatie *f*; **~tic(al** □) [diplə'mætik(əl)] diplomatisch; **~tist** [di'ploumətist] Diplomat(in).

dipper ['dipə] Schöpfkelle *f*; *Am. Great od. Big* ≳ *ast.* der Große Bär.

dire ['daiə] gräßlich, schrecklich.

direct [di'rekt] 1. direkt; gerade; unmittelbar; offen, aufrichtig; deutlich; ~ current ≠ Gleichstrom m; ~ train durchgehender Zug; 2. adv. geradeswegs; = ~ly 3. richten; lenken, steuern; leiten; anordnen; j-n (an)weisen; Brief adressieren; ~ion [~kʃən] Richtung f; Gegend f; Leitung f; Anordnung f; Adresse f; Vorstand m; ~ion-finder [~nfaində] Radio. (Funk)Peiler m; Peil-(funk)empfänger m; ~ion-indicator mot. Fahrtrichtungsanzeiger m; ✗ Kursweiser m; ~ive [~ktiv] richtungweisend; leitend; ~ly [~tli] 1. adv. sofort; 2. cj. sobald, als.

director [di'rektə] Direktor m; Film: Regisseur m; board of ~s Aufsichtsrat m; ~ate [~ərit] Direktion f; ~y [~ri] Adreßbuch n; telephone ~ Telephonbuch n.

dirge [də:dʒ] Klage(lied n) f.

dirigible ['diridʒəbl] 1. lenkbar; 2. lenkbares Luftschiff.

dirt [də:t] Schmutz m; (lockere) Erde; ~-cheap F ['də:t'tʃi:p] spottbillig; ~y ['də:ti] 1. schmutzig (a. fig.); 2. beschmutzen; besudeln.

disability [disə'biliti] Unfähigkeit f.

disable [dis'eibl] (dienst-, kampf-)unfähig machen; ~d dienst-, kampfunfähig; körperbehindert; kriegsbeschädigt.

disabuse [disə'bju:z] e-s Besseren belehren (of über acc.).

disadvantage [disəd'vɑ:ntidʒ] Nachteil m; Schaden m; ~ous [disædvɑ:n'teidʒəs] nachteilig, ungünstig.

disagree [disə'gri:] nicht übereinstimmen; uneinig sein; nicht bekommen (with s.o. j-m); ~able □ [~riəbl] unangenehm; ~ment [~ri:mənt] Verschiedenheit f; Unstimmigkeit f; Meinungsverschiedenheit f.

disappear [disə'piə] verschwinden; ~ance [~ərəns] Verschwinden n.

disappoint [disə'pɔint] enttäuschen; vereiteln; j. im Stich lassen; ~ment [~tmənt] Enttäuschung f; Vereitelung f. [Mißbilligung f.]

disapprobation [disæprou'beiʃən]

disapprov|al [disə'pru:vəl] Mißbilligung f; ~e ['disə'pru:v] mißbilligen (of et.).

disarm [dis'ɑ:m] v/t. entwaffnen (a. fig.); v/i. abrüsten; ~ament [~məmənt] Entwaffnung f; Abrüstung f.

disarrange ['dise'reindʒ] in Unordnung bringen, verwirren.

disarray ['disə'rei] 1. Unordnung f; 2. in Unordnung bringen.

disast|er [di'zɑ:stə] Unglück(sfall m) n, Katastrophe f; ~rous □ [~trəs] unheilvoll; katastrophal.

disband [dis'bænd] entlassen; auflösen.

disbelieve ['disbi'li:v] nicht glauben.

disburse [dis'bə:s] auszahlen.

disc [disk] = disk.

discard 1. [dis'kɑ:d] Karten, Kleid etc. ablegen; entlassen; 2. ['diskɑ:d] Karten Abwerfen n; bsd. Am. Abfall(haufen) m.

discern [di'sə:n] unterscheiden; erkennen; beurteilen; ~ing [~niŋ] kritisch, scharfsichtig; ~ment [~nmənt] Einsicht f; Scharfsinn m.

discharge [dis'tʃɑ:dʒ] 1. v/t. ent-, ab-, ausladen; entlasten, entbinden; abfeuern; Flüssigkeit absondern; Amt versehen; Pflicht etc erfüllen; Zorn etc. auslassep (on an dat.); Schuld tilgen; quittieren; Wechsel einlösen; entlassen; freisprechen; v/i. sich entladen; eitern; 2. Entladung f; Abfeuern n; Ausströmen n; Ausfluß m, Eiter(ung f) m; Entlassung f; Entlastung f; Bezahlung f; Quittung f; Erfüllung f e-r Pflicht.

disciple [di'saipl] Schüler m; Jünger m.

discipline ['disiplin] 1. Disziplin f, Zucht f; Erziehung f; Züchtigung f; 2. erziehen; schulen; bestrafen.

disclaim [dis'kleim] (ab)leugnen; ablehnen; verzichten auf (acc.).

disclose [dis'klouz] aufdecken; erschließen, offenbaren, enthüllen.

discolo(u)r [dis'kʌlə] (sich) verfärben.

discomfiture [dis'kʌmfitʃə] Niederlage f; Verwirrung f; Vereitelung f.

discomfort [dis'kʌmfət] 1. Unbehagen n; 2. j-m Unbehagen verursachen.

discompose [diskəm'pouz] beunruhigen.

disconcert [diskən'sə:t] außer Fassung bringen; vereiteln.

disconnect ['diskə'nekt] trennen (a. ≠); ⊕ auskuppeln; ≠ ab-, ausschalten; ~ed □ zs.-hanglos.

disconsolate □ [dis'kɔnsəlit] trostlos.

discontent ['diskən'tent] Unzufriedenheit f; ~ed □ mißvergnügt, unzufrieden.

discontinue ['diskən'tinju(:)] aufgeben, aufhören mit; unterbrechen.

discord ['diskɔ:d], ~ance [dis'kɔ:dəns] Uneinigkeit f; ♪ Mißklang m.

discount ['diskaunt] 1. ✦ Diskont m; Abzug m, Rabatt m; 2. ✦ diskontieren; abrechnen; fig. absehen von; Nachricht mit Vorsicht aufnehmen; beeinträchtigen; ~enance [dis'kauntinəns] mißbilligen; entmutigen.

discourage [dis'kʌridʒ] entmutigen;

abschrecken; **~ment** [~dʒmənt] Entmutigung *f*; Schwierigkeit *f*.

discourse [dis'kɔ:s] 1. Rede *f*; Abhandlung *f*; Predigt *f*; 2. reden, sprechen; e-n Vortrag halten.

discourte|ous ☐ [dis'kɔ:tjəs] unhöflich; **~sy** [~tisi] Unhöflichkeit *f*.

discover [dis'kʌvə] entdecken; ausfindig machen; **~y** [~əri] Entdeckung *f*.

discredit [dis'kredit] 1. schlechter Ruf; Unglaubwürdigkeit *f*; 2. nicht glauben; in Mißkredit bringen.

discreet ☐ [dis'kri:t] besonnen, vorsichtig; klug; verschwiegen.

discrepancy [dis'krepənsi] Widerspruch *m*; Unstimmigkeit *f*.

discretion [dis'kreʃən] Besonnenheit *f*, Klugheit *f*; Takt *m*; Verschwiegenheit *f*; Belieben *n*; *age (od. years) of* **~** Strafmündigkeit *f* (*14 Jahre*); *surrender at* **~** sich auf Gnade und Ungnade ergeben.

discriminat|e [dis'krimineit] unterscheiden; **~** *against* benachteiligen; **~ing** ☐ [~tiŋ] unterscheidend; scharfsinnig; urteilsfähig; **~ion** [diskrimi'neiʃən] Unterscheidung *f*; unterschiedliche (*bsd.* nachteilige) Behandlung; Urteilskraft *f*.

discuss [dis'kʌs] erörtern, besprechen; **~ion** [~ʌʃən] Erörterung *f*.

disdain [dis'dein] 1. Verachtung *f*; 2. geringschätzen, verachten; verschmähen.

disease [di'zi:z] Krankheit *f*; **~d** krank.

disembark [disim'bɑ:k] *v/t.* ausschiffen; *v/i.* landen, an Land gehen.

disengage [disin'geidʒ] (sich) freimachen; **~** lösen; ⊕ loskuppeln.

disentangle [disin'tæŋgl] entwirren; *fig.* freimachen (*from* von).

disfavo(u)r [dis'feivə] 1. Mißfallen *n*, Ungnade *f*; 2. nicht mögen.

disfigure [dis'figə] entstellen.

disgorge [dis'gɔ:dʒ] ausspeien.

disgrace [dis'greis] 1. Ungnade *f*; Schande *f*; 2. in Ungnade fallen lassen; *j-n* entehren; **~ful** ☐ [~sful] schimpflich.

disguise [dis'gaiz] 1. verkleiden; *Stimme* verstellen; verhehlen; 2. Verkleidung *f*; Verstellung *f*; Maske *f*.

disgust [dis'gʌst] 1. Ekel *m*; 2. anekeln; **~ing** ☐ [~tiŋ] ekelhaft.

dish [diʃ] 1. Schüssel *f*, Platte *f*; Gericht *n* (*Speise*); *the* **~es** Geschirr; 2. anrichten; *mst* **~** *up* auftischen; **~-cloth** ['diʃklɔθ] Geschirrspültuch *n*.

dishearten [dis'hɑ:tn] entmutigen.

dishevel(l)ed [di'ʃevəld] zerzaust.

dishonest ☐ [dis'ɔnist] unehrlich, unredlich; **~y** [~ti] Unredlichkeit *f*.

dishono(u)r [dis'ɔnə] 1. Unehre *f*,

Schande *f*; 2. entehren; schänden; *Wechsel* nicht honorieren; **~able** ☐ [~ərəbl] entehrend; ehrlos.

dish|-pan *Am.* ['diʃpæn] Spülschüssel *f*; **~rag** **~** *dish-cloth*; **~water** Spülwasser *n*.

disillusion [disi'lu:ʒən] 1. Ernüchterung *f*, Enttäuschung *f*; 2. ernüchtern, enttäuschen.

disinclined ['disin'klaind] abgeneigt.

disinfect [disin'fekt] desinfizieren; **~ant** [~tənt] Desinfektionsmittel *n*.

disintegrate [dis'intigreit] (sich) auflösen, (sich) zersetzen.

disinterested [dis'intristid] uneigennützig, selbstlos.

disk [disk] Scheibe *f*; Platte *f*; Schallplatte *f*; **~ brake** *mot.* Scheibenbremse *f*; **~ jockey** Ansager *m* e-r Schallplattensendung.

dislike [dis'laik] 1. Abneigung *f*; Widerwille *m*; 2. nicht mögen.

dislocate ['disləkeit] aus den Fugen bringen, verrenken; verlagern.

dislodge [dis'lɔdʒ] vertreiben, verjagen; umquartieren.

disloyal ['dis'lɔiəl] treulos.

dismal ['dizməl] trüb(selig); öde; trostlos, elend.

dismantl|e [dis'mæntl] abbrechen, niederreißen; ♣ abtakeln; ⊕ demontieren; **~ing** [~liŋ] Demontage *f*

dismay [dis'mei] 1. Schrecken *m*; Bestürzung *f*; 2. *v/t.* erschrecken.

dismember [dis'membə] zerstückeln

dismiss [dis'mis] *v/t.* entlassen, wegschicken; ablehnen; *Thema etc.* fallen lassen; ⅞ abweisen; **~al** [~səl] Entlassung *f*; Aufgabe *f*; ⅞ Abweichung *f*.

dismount ['dis'maunt] *v/t.* aus dem Sattel werfen; demontieren; ⊕ aus-ea -nehmen; *v/i.* absteigen.

disobedien|ce [disə'bi:djəns] Ungehorsam *m*; **~t** ☐ [~nt] ungehorsam.

disobey ['disə'bei] ungehorsam sein.

disoblige ['disə'blaidʒ] ungefällig sein gegen; kränken.

disorder [dis'ɔ:də] 1. Unordnung *f*; Aufruhr *m*; ♣ Störung *f*; 2. in Unordnung bringen; stören; zerrütten; **~ly** [~əli] unordentlich; ordnungswidrig; unruhig; aufrührerisch.

disorganize [dis'ɔ:gənaiz] zerrütten.

disown [dis'oun] nicht anerkennen, verleugnen; ablehnen.

disparage [dis'pæridʒ] verächtlich machen, herabsetzen.

disparity [dis'pæriti] Ungleichheit *f*.

dispassionate ☐ [dis'pæʃnit] leidenschaftslos; unparteiisch.

dispatch [dis'pætʃ] **1.** (schnelle) Erledigung; (schnelle) Absendung; Abfertigung *f*; Eile *f*; Depesche *f*; **2.** (schnell) abmachen, erledigen (*a. fig.* = *töten*); abfertigen; (eilig) absenden.

dispel [dis'pel] vertreiben, zerstreuen.

dispensa|ble [dis'pensəbl] entbehrlich; **~ry** [~əri] Apotheke *f*; **~tion** [dispen'seiʃən] Austeilung *f*; Befreiung *f* (*with* von); *göttliche* Fügung.

dispense [dis'pens] *v/t.* austeilen; *Gesetze* handhaben; *Arzneien* anfertigen und ausgeben; befreien.

disperse [dis'pə:s] (sich) zerstreuen; auseinandergehen.

dispirit [di'spirit] entmutigen.

displace [dis'pleis] verschieben; absetzen; ersetzen; verdrängen.

display [dis'plei] **1.** Entfaltung *f*; Aufwand *m*; Schaustellung *f*; *Schaufenster*-Auslage *f*; **2.** entfalten; zur Schau stellen; zeigen.

displeas|e [dis'pli:z] *j-m* mißfallen; **~ed** ungehalten; **~ure** [~leʒə] Mißfallen *n*; Verdruß *m*.

dispos|al [dis'pouzəl] Anordnung *f*; Verfügung(srecht *n*) *f*; Beseitigung *f*; Veräußerung *f*; Übergabe *f*; **~e** [~ouz] *v/t.* (an)ordnen, einrichten; geneigt machen, veranlassen; *v/i.* **~ of** verfügen über (*acc.*); erledigen; verwenden; veräußern; unterbringen; beseitigen; **~ed** geneigt; ...gesinnt; **~ition** [dispə'ziʃən] Disposition *f*; Anordnung *f*; Neigung *f*; Sinnesart *f*; Verfügung *f*.

dispossess ['dispə'zes] (of) vertreiben (aus *od.* von); berauben (*gen.*).

dispraise [dis'preiz] tadeln.

disproof ['dis'pru:f] Widerlegung *f*.

disproportionate [disprə'pɔ:ʃnit] unverhältnismäßig.

disprove ['dis'pru:v] widerlegen.

dispute [dis'pju:t] **1.** Streit(igkeit *f*) *m*; Rechtsstreit *m*; *beyond* (*all*) **~** *past* **~** zweifellos; **2.** (be)streiten.

disqualify [dis'kwɔlifai] unfähig *od.* untauglich machen; für untauglich erklären.

disquiet [dis'kwaiət] beunruhigen.

disregard ['disri'gɑ:d] **1.** Nicht(be)-achtung *f*; **2.** unbeachtet lassen.

disreput|able [dis'repjutəbl] schimpflich; verrufen; **~e** ['disri-'pju:t] übler Ruf; Schande *f*.

disrespect ['disris'pekt] Nichtachtung *f*; Respektlosigkeit *f*; **~ful** [~ful] respektlos; unhöflich.

disroot [dis'ru:t] entwurzeln.

disrupt [dis'rʌpt] zerreißen; spalten.

dissatis|faction ['dissætis'fækʃən] Unzufriedenheit *f*; **~factory** [~ktəri] unbefriedigend; **~fy** ['dis'sætis-fai] nicht befriedigen; *j-m* mißfallen.

25*

dissect [di'sekt] zerlegen; zergliedern.

dissemble [di'sembl] *v/t.* verhehlen; *v/i.* sich verstellen, heucheln.

dissen|sion [di'senʃən] Zwietracht *f*; Streit *m*, Uneinigkeit *f*; **~t** [~nt] **1.** abweichende Meinung; Nichtzugehörigkeit *f* zur Staatskirche; **2.** andrer Meinung sein (*from* als).

dissimilar ☐ ['di'similə] (to) unähnlich (*dat.*); verschieden (von).

dissimulation [disimju'leiʃən] Verstellung *f*, Heuchelei *f*.

dissipat|e ['disipeit] (sich) zerstreuen; verschwenden; **~ion** [dis-'peiʃən] Zerstreuung *f*; Verschwendung *f*; ausschweifendes Leben.

dissociate [di'souʃieit] trennen; **~ o.s.** sich distanzieren, abrücken.

dissoluble [di'sɔljubl] (auf)lösbar.

dissolut|e ☐ ['disəlu:t] liederlich, ausschweifend; **~ion** [disə'lu:ʃən] Auflösung *f*; Zerstörung *f*; Tod *m*.

dissolve [di'zɔlv] *v/t.* (auf)lösen; schmelzen; *v/i.* sich auflösen; vergehen.

dissonant ['disənənt] ♪ mißtönend; abweichend; uneinig.

dissuade [di'sweid] *j-m* abraten.

distan|ce ['distəns] **1.** Abstand *m*, Entfernung *f*; Ferne *f*; Strecke *f*; Zurückhaltung *f*; *at a* **~** von weitem; *in e-r gewissen Entfernung*; weit weg; *keep s.o. at a* **~** *j-m* gegenüber reserviert sein; **2.** hinter sich lassen; **~t** ☐ [~nt] entfernt; fern; zurückhaltend; Fern...; **~** *control* Fernsteuerung *f*.

distaste [dis'teist] Widerwille *m*; Abneigung *f*; **~ful** [~tful] widerwärtig; ärgerlich.

distemper [dis'tempə] Krankheit *f* (*bsd. von Tieren*); (Hunde)Staupe *f*.

distend [dis'tend] (sich) ausdehnen; (auf)blähen; (sich) weiten.

distil [dis'til] herabtröpfeln (lassen); **~** destillieren; **~lery** [~əri] Branntweinbrennerei *f*.

distinct ☐ [dis'tiŋkt] verschieden; getrennt; deutlich, klar; **~ion** [~kʃən] Unterscheidung *f*; Unterschied *m*; Auszeichnung *f*; Rang *m*; **~ive** [~ktiv] unterscheidend; apart; kennzeichnend, bezeichnend.

distinguish [dis'tiŋgwiʃ] unterscheiden; auszeichnen; **~ed** berühmt, ausgezeichnet; vornehm.

distort [dis'tɔ:t] verdrehen; verzerren.

distract ['dis'trækt] ablenken, zerstreuen; beunruhigen; verwirren; verrückt machen; **~ion** [~kʃən] Zerstreutheit *f*; Verwirrung *f*; Wahnsinn *m*; Zerstreuung *f*.

distraught [dis'trɔ:t] verwirrt, bestürzt.

distress [dis'tres] **1.** Qual *f*; Elend *n*, Not *f*; Erschöpfung *f*; **2.** in Not bringing; quälen; erschöpfen; **~ed** in Not befindlich; bekümmert; **~** *area* Notstandsgebiet *n*.

distribut|e [dis'tribju(:)t] verteilen; einteilen; verbreiten; **~ion** [distri-'bju:ʃən] Verteilung *f*; *Film*-Verleih *m*; Verbreitung *f*; Einteilung *f*.

district ['distrikt] Bezirk *m*; Gegend *f*.

distrust [dis'trʌst] **1.** Mißtrauen *n*; **2.** mißtrauen (*dat.*); **~ful** □ [**~**tful] mißtrauisch; **~** (*of o.s.*) schüchtern.

disturb [dis'tə:b] beunruhigen; stören; **~ance** [**~**bəns] Störung *f*; Unruhe *f*; Aufruhr *m*; **~** *of the peace* ᵗᵗᵗ öffentliche Ruhestörung; **~er** [**~**bə] Störenfried *m*, Unruhestifter *m*.

disunite ['disju:'nait] (sich) trennen.

disuse ['dis'ju:z] nicht mehr gebrauchen.

ditch [ditʃ] Graben *m*.

ditto ['ditou] dito, desgleichen.

divan [di'væn] Diwan *m*; **~-bed** [*oft* 'daivænbed] Bettcouch *f*, Liege *f*.

dive [daiv] **1.** (unter)tauchen; *vom Sprungbrett* springen; e-n Sturzflug machen; eindringen in (*acc.*); **2.** *Schwimmen:* Springen *m*; (Kopf-) Sprung *m*; Sturzflug *m*; Kellerlokal *n*; *Am.* F Kaschemme *f*; **~r** ['daivə] Taucher *m*.

diverge [dai'və:dʒ] aus-ea.-laufen; abweichen; **~nce** [**~**dʒəns] Abweichung *f*; **~nt** □ [**~**nt] (von-ea.-)abweichend.

divers ['daivə(:)z] mehrere.

divers|e □ [dai'və:s] verschieden; mannigfaltig; **~ion** [**~**ə:ʃən] Ablenkung *f*; Zeitvertreib *m*; **~ity** [**~**ə:siti] Verschiedenheit *f*; Mannigfaltigkeit *f*.

divert [dai'və:t] ablenken; *j-n* zerstreuen; unterhalten; *Verkehr* umleiten.

divest [dai'vest] entkleiden (*a.fig.*).

divid|e [di'vaid] **1.** *v/t.* teilen; trennen; einteilen; Å dividieren (*by* durch); *v/i.* sich teilen; zerfallen; Å aufgehen; sich trennen *od.* auflösen; **2.** Wasserscheide *f*; **~end** ['dividend] Dividende *f*.

divine [di'vain] **1.** □ göttlich; **~** *service* Gottesdienst *m*; **2.** Geistliche(r) *m*; **3.** weissagen; ahnen.

diving ['daiviŋ] Kunstspringen *n*; *attr.* Taucher...

divinity [di'viniti] Gottheit *f*; Göttlichkeit *f*; Theologie *f*.

divis|ible □ [di'vizəbl] teilbar; **~ion** [**~**iʒən] Teilung *f*; Trennung *f*; Abteilung *f*; ✕, Å Division *f*.

divorce [di'və:s] **1.** (Ehe)Scheidung *f*; **2.** *Ehe* scheiden; sich scheiden lassen.

divulge [dai'vʌldʒ] ausplaudern; verbreiten; bekanntmachen.

dixie ✕ *sl.* ['diksi] Kochgeschirr *n*;

Feldkessel *m*; ♀ *Am.* die Südstaaten *pl.*; **♀crat** *Am. pol.* opponierender Südstaatendemokrat.

dizz|iness ['dizinis] Schwindel *m*; **~y** [['dizi] schwind(e)lig.

do [du:] [*irr.*] *v/t.* tun; machen; (zu)bereiten; *Rolle, Stück* spielen; **~** *London sl.* London besichtigen; *have done reading* fertig sein mit Lesen; **~** *in* F um die Ecke bringen; **~** *into* übersetzen in; **~** *over* überstreifen, -ziehen; **~** *up* instand setzen; einpacken; *v/i.* tun; handeln; sich benehmen; sich befinden; genügen; *that will* **~** das genügt; *how ~ you ~?* guten Tag!, Wie geht's?; **~** *well* s-e Sache gut machen; gute Geschäfte machen; **~** *away with* weg-, abschaffen; *I could* **~** *with* ... ich könnte ... brauchen *od.* vertragen; **~** *without* fertig werden ohne; **~** *be quick* beeile dich doch; *~ you like London?* — *I* **~** gefällt Ihnen London? — Ja.

docil|e ['dousail] gelehrig; fügsam; **~ity** [dou'siliti] Gelehrigkeit *f*.

dock¹ [dɔk] stutzen; *fig.* kürzen.

dock² [**~**] **1.** ⚓ Dock *n*; *bsd. Am.* Kai *m*, Pier *m*; ᵗᵗᵗ Anklagebank *f*; **2.** ⚓ docken.

dockyard ['dɔkjɑ:d] Werft *f*.

doctor ['dɔktə] **1.** Doktor *m*; Arzt *m*; **2.** Fverarzten; F *fig.* (ver)fälschen.

doctrine ['dɔktrin] Lehre *f*; Dogma *n*.

document 1. ['dɔkjumənt] Urkunde *f*; **2.** [**~**ment] beurkunden.

dodge [dɔdʒ] **1.** Seitensprung *m*; Kniff *m*, Winkelzug *m*; **2.** *fig.* irreführen; ausweichen; Winkelzüge machen; **~r** ['dɔdʒə] Schieber(in); *Am.* Hand-, Reklamezettel *m*; *Am.* Maisbrot *n*, -kuchen *m*.

doe [dou] Hirschkuh *f*; Reh *n*; Häsin *f*.

dog [dɔg] **1.** Hund *m*; Haken *m*, Klammer *f*; **2.** nachspüren (*dat.*).

dogged [['dɔgid] verbissen.

dogma ['dɔgmə] Dogma *n*; Glaubenslehre *f*; **~tic(al** □) [dɔg'mætik(əl)] dogmatisch; bestimmt; **~tism** ['dɔgmətizəm] Selbstherrlichkeit *f*.

dog's-ear F ['dɔgziə] Eselsohr *n im Buch*.

dog-tired F ['dɔg'taiəd] hundemüde.

doings ['du(:)iŋz] *pl.* Dinge *n/pl.*; Begebenheiten *f/pl.*; Treiben *n*; Betragen *n*.

dole [doul] **1.** Spende *f*; F Erwerbslosenunterstützung *f*; **2.** verteilen.

doleful □ ['doulful] trübselig.

doll [dɔl] Puppe *f*.

dollar ['dɔlə] Dollar *m*.

dolly ['dɔli] Püppchen *n*.

dolorous □ ['dɔlərəs] schmerzhaft; traurig.

dolphin ['dɔlfin] Delphin *m*.

dolt [doult] Tölpel *m*.

domain [də'mein] Domäne f; fig. Gebiet n; Bereich m.

dome [doum] Kuppel f; ⊕ Haube f; ~d gewölbt.

Domesday Book ['du:mzdei'buk] Reichsgrundbuch n Englands.

domestic [də'mestik] 1. (~ally) häuslich; inländisch; einheimisch; zahm; ~ animal Haustier n; 2. Dienstbote m; ~s pl. Haushaltsartikel m/pl.; ~ate [~keit] zähmen.

domicile ['dɔmisail] Wohnsitz m; ~d wohnhaft.

domin|ant ['dɔminənt] (vor)herrschend; ~ate [~neit] (be)herrschen; ~ation [dɔmi'neiʃən] Herrschaft f; ~eer [~'niə] (despotisch) herrschen; ~eering [~'əriŋ] herrisch, tyrannisch; überheblich.

dominion [də'minjən] Herrschaft f; Gebiet n; ♀ Dominion n (im Brt. Commonwealth).

don [dɔn] anziehen; Hut aufsetzen.

donat|e Am. [dou'neit] schenken; stiften; ~ion [~'eiʃən] Schenkung f.

done [dʌn] 1. p.p. von do; 2. adj. abgemacht; fertig; gar gekocht.

donkey ['dɔŋki] zo. Esel m; attr. Hilfs-.

donor ['dounə] (☤ Blut)Spender m.

doom [du:m] 1. Schicksal n, Verhängnis n; 2. verurteilen, verdammen.

door [dɔ:] Tür f, Tor n; next ~ nebenan; ~handle ['dɔ:hændl] Türgriff m; ~keeper, Am. ~man Pförtner m; Portier m; ~way Türöffnung f; Torweg m; ~yard Am. Vorhof m, Vorgarten m.

dope [doup] 1. Schmiere f; bsd. ⚡ Lack m; Aufputschmittel n; Rauschgift n; Am. sl. Geheimtip m; 2. lackieren; sl. betäuben; aufpulvern; Am. sl. herauskriegen.

dormant mst fig. ['dɔ:mənt] schlafend, ruhend; unbenutzt; ♱ tot.

dormer(-window) ['dɔ:mə('windou)] Dachfenster n.

dormitory ['dɔ:mitri] Schlafsaal m; bsd. Am. Studenten(wohn)heim n.

dose [dous] 1. Dosis f, Portion f; 2. j-m e-e Medizin geben.

dot [dɔt] 1. Punkt m, Fleck m; 2. punktieren, tüpfeln; fig. verstreuen.

dot|e [dout]: ~ (up)on vernarrt sein in (acc.); ~ing ['doutiŋ] vernarrt.

double] ['dʌbl] 1. doppelt; zu zweien; gekrümmt; zweideutig; 2. Doppelte(s) n; Doppelgänger(in) f; Tennis: Doppel(spiel) n; 3. v/t. verdoppeln; a. ~ up zs.-legen; et. umfahren, umsegeln; ~d up zs.-gekrümmt; v/i. sich verdoppeln; a. ~ back e-n Haken schlagen (Hase); ~breasted zweireihig (Jackett); ~cross sl. Partner betrügen; ~dealing Doppelzüngigkeit f; ~edged zweischneidig; ~entry doppelte Buchführung;

~feature Am. Doppelprogramm n im Kino; ~header Am. Baseball: Doppelspiel n; ~park Am. verboten in zweiter Reihe parken.

doubt [daut] 1. v/i zweifeln; v/t. bezweifeln; mißtrauen (dat.); 2. Zweifel m; no ~ ohne Zweifel; ~ful □ ['dautful] zweifelhaft; ~fulness [~lnis] Zweifelhaftigkeit f; ~less ['dautlis] ohne Zweifel.

douche [du:ʃ] 1. Dusche f; Irrigator m; 2. duschen; spülen.

dough [dou] Teig m; ~boy Am. F ['doubɔi] Landser m; ~nut Schmalzgebackenes.

dove [dʌv] Taube f; fig. Täubchen n.

dowel ⊕ ['dauəl] Dübel m.

down¹ [daun] Daune f; Flaum m; Düne f; ~s pl. Höhenrücken m.

down² [~] 1. adv. nieder; her-, hinunter, ab; abwärts; unten; be ~ upon F über j-n herfallen; 2. prp. herab, hinab, her-, hinunter; ~ the river flußabwärts; ~ adj nach unten gerichtet; ~ platform Abfahrtsbahnsteig m (London); ~ train Zug m von London (fort); 4. v/t. niederwerfen; herunterholen; ~cast ['daunkɑ:st] niedergeschlagen; ~easter Am. Neuengländer m bsd. von Maine; ~fall Fall m, Sturz m; Verfall m; ~hearted niedergeschlagen; ~hill bergab; ~pour Regenguß m; ~right 1. adv. geradezu, durchaus; völlig; 2. adj. ehrlich; plump (Benehmen); richtig, glatt (Lüge etc.); ~stairs die Treppe hinunter, (nach) unten; ~stream stromabwärts; ~town bsd. Am. Hauptgeschäftsviertel n; ~ward(s) ['daunwəd(z)] abwärts (gerichtet).

downy ['dauni] flaumig; sl. gerissen.

dowry ['dauəri] Mitgift f (a. fig.).

doze [douz] 1. dösen; 2. Schläfchen n.

dozen ['dʌzn] Dutzend n.

drab [dræb] gelblichgrau; eintönig.

draft [drɑ:ft] 1. Entwurf m; ♱ Tratte f; Abhebung f; ✗ (Sonder-) Kommando n; Einberufung f; = draught; 2. entwerfen; aufsetzen; ✗ abkommandieren; Am. einziehen; ~ee Am. ✗ [~f'ti:] Dienstpflichtige(r) m; ~sman ['drɑ:ftsmən] (technischer) Zeichner; Verfasser m, Entwerfer m.

drag [dræg] 1. Schleppnetz n; Schleife f für Lasten; Egge f; 2. v/t. schleppen, ziehen; v/i. (sich) schleifen; (mit e-m Schleppnetz) fischen;   [Libelle f.]

dragon ['drægən] Drache m; ~fly]

drain [drein] 1. Abfluß(graben m, -rohr n) m; F Schluck m; 2. v/t. entwässern; Glas leeren; a. ~ off abziehen; verzehren; v/i. ablaufen; ~age ['dreinidʒ] Abfluß m; Entwässerung(sanlage) f.

drake [dreik] Enterich m.

dram [dræm] Schluck m; fig. Schnaps m.

drama ['drɑːmə] Drama n; ~tic [drəˈmætik] (~ally) dramatisch; ~tist ['dræmətist] Dramatiker m; ~tize [~taiz] dramatisieren.

drank [dræŋk] pret. von drink 2.

drape [dreip] 1. drapieren; in Falten legen; 2. mst ~s pl. Vorhänge m/pl.; ~ry ['dreipəri] Tuchhandel m; Tuchwaren f/pl.; Faltenwurf m.

drastic ['dræstik] (~ally) drastisch.

draught [drɑːft] Zug m (Ziehen; Fischzug; Zugluft; Schluck); ⚓ Tiefgang m; ~s pl. Damespiel n; s. draft; ~ beer Faßbier n; ~-horse ['drɑːfthɔːs] Zugpferd n; ~sman [~tsmən] Damestein m; = draftsman; ~y [~ti] zugig.

draw [drɔː] 1. [irr.] ziehen; an-, auf-, ein-, zuziehen; (sich) zs.-ziehen; in die Länge ziehen; dehnen; herausziehen, herauslocken; entnehmen; Geld abheben; anlocken, anziehen; abzapfen; ausfischen; Geflügel ausnehmen; zeichnen; entwerfen; Urkunde abfassen; unentschieden spielen; Luft schöpfen; ~ near heranrücken; ~ out in die Länge ziehen; ~ up ab-, verfassen; ~ (up)on ✝ (e-n Wechsel) ziehen auf (acc.); fig. in Anspruch nehmen; 2. Zug m (Ziehen); Lotterie: Ziehung f; Los n; Sport: unentschiedenes Spiel; F Zugstück n, -artikel m; ~back ['drɔːbæk] Nachteil m; Hindernis n; ✝ Rückzoll m; Am. Rückzahlung f; ~er ['drɔːə] Ziehende(r m) f; Zeichner m; ✝ Aussteller m, Trassant m; [drɔː] Schublade f; (a pair of) ~s pl. (eine) Unterhose; (ein) Schlüpfer m; mst chest of ~s Kommode f.

drawing ['drɔːiŋ] Ziehen n; Zeichnen n; Zeichnung f; ~-account Girokonto n; ~-board Reißbrett n; ~-room Gesellschaftszimmer n.

drawn [drɔːn] 1. p.p. von draw 1; 2. adj. unentschieden; verzerrt.

dread [dred] 1. Furcht f; Schrecken m; 2. (sich) fürchten; ~ful □ ['dredful] schrecklich; furchtbar.

dream [driːm] 1. Traum m; 2. [irr.] träumen; ~er ['driːmə] Träumer (-in); ~t [dremt] pret. u. p.p. von dream 2; ~y □ ['driːmi] träumerisch; verträumt.

dreary □ ['driəri] traurig; öde.

dredge [dredʒ] 1. Schleppnetz n; Bagger(maschine f) m; 2. (aus-)baggern.

dregs [dregz] pl. Bodensatz m, Hefe f.

drench [drentʃ] 1. (Regen)Guß m; 2. durchnässen; fig. baden.

dress [dres] 1. Anzug m; Kleidung f; Kleid n; 2. an-, ein-, zurichten; ✕ (sich) richten; zurechtmachen; (sich) ankleiden; putzen; ✍ verbinden; frisieren; ~circle thea. ['dresˈsəːkl] erster Rang; ~er [~sə] Anrichte f; Am. Frisiertoilette f.

dressing ['dresiŋ] An-, Zurichten n; Ankleiden n; Verband m; Appretur f; Küche: Soße f; Füllung f; ~s pl. ✍ Verbandzeug n; ~ down Standpauke f; ~gown Morgenrock m; ~table Frisiertisch m.

dress|maker ['dresmeikə] Schneiderin f; ~parade Modenschau f.

drew ['druː] pret. von draw 1.

dribble ['dribl] tröpfeln, träufeln (lassen); geifern; Fußball: dribbeln.

dried [draid] getrocknet; Dörr...

drift [drift] 1. (Dahin)Treiben n; fig. Lauf m; fig. Hang m; Zweck m; (Schnee-, Sand)Wehe f; 2. v/t. (zs.-)treiben, (zu-)wehen); v/i. (dahin)treiben; sich anhäufen.

drill [dril] 1. Drillbohrer m; Furche f; ✍ Drill-, Sämaschine f; ✕ Exerzieren n (a. fig.); 2. bohren; ✕ (ein)exerzieren (a. fig.).

drink [driŋk] 1. Trunk m; (geistiges) Getränk n; 2. [irr.] trinken.

drip [drip] 1. Tröpfeln n; Traufe f; 2. tröpfeln (lassen); triefen; ~-dry shirt ['drip'drai ʃəːt] bügelfreies Hemd; ~ping [~piŋ] Bratenfett n.

drive [draiv] 1. (Spazier)Fahrt f; Auffahrt f, Fahrweg m; ⊕ Antrieb m; fig. (Auf)Trieb m; Drang m; Unternehmen n, Feldzug m; Am. Sammelaktion f; 2. [irr.] v/t. (an-, ein)treiben; Geschäft betreiben; fahren; lenken; zwingen; vertreiben; v/i. treiben; fahren; ~ at hinzielen auf.

drive-in Am. ['draiv'in] 1. mst attr. Auto...; ~ cinema Autokino n; 2. Autokino n; Autorestaurant n.

drivel ['drivl] 1. geifern; faseln; 2. Geifer m; Faselei f.

driven ['drivn] p.p. von drive 2.

driver ['draivə] Treiber m; mot. Fahrer m, Chauffeur m; 🚂 Führer m.

driving| licence ['draiviŋ laisəns] Führerschein m; ~ school Fahrschule f.

drizzle ['drizl] 1. Sprühregen m; 2. sprühen, nieseln.

drone [droun] 1. zo. Drohne f; fig. Faulenzer m; 2. summen; dröhnen.

droop [druːp] v/t. sinken lassen; v/i. schlaff niederhängen; den Kopf hängen lassen; (ver)welken; schwinden.

drop [drɔp] 1. Tropfen m; Fruchtbonbon m, n; Fall m; Falltür f; thea. Vorhang m; get (have) the ~ on Am. F zuvorkommen; 2. v/t. tropfen (lassen); niederlassen; fallen lassen; Brief einwerfen; Fahrgast absetzen; senken; ~ s.o. a few lines pl. j-m ein paar Zeilen schreiben; v/i. tropfen; (herab)fallen; um-, hinsinken; ~ in unerwartet sein.

dropsy ⚥ ['drɔpsi] Wassersucht f.

drought [draut], **drouth** [drauθ] Trockenheit f, Dürre f.

drove [drouv] **1.** Trift f Rinder; Herde f (a. fig.); **2.** pret. von drive 2.

drown [draun] v/t. ertränken; überschwemmen; fig. übertäuben; übertönen; v/i. ertrinken.

drowse [drauz] schlummern, schläfrig sein od. machen; ~y ['drauzi] schläfrig; einschläfernd.

drudge [drʌdʒ] **1.** fig. Sklave m, Packesel m, Kuli m; **2.** sich (ab-) placken.

drug [drʌg] **1.** Droge f, Arzneiware f; Rauschgift n; unverkäufliche Ware; **2.** mit (schädlichen) Zutaten versetzen; Arznei od. Rauschgift geben (dat.) od. nehmen; ~gist ['drʌgist] Drogist m; Apotheker m; ~store Am. Drugstore m.

drum [drʌm] **1.** Trommel f; Trommelfell n; **2.** trommeln; ~mer ['drʌmə] Trommler m; bsd. Am. F Vertreter m.

drunk [drʌŋk] **1.** p.p. von drink 2; **2.** adj. (be)trunken; get ~ sich betrinken; ~ard ['drʌŋkəd] Trinker m, Säufer m; ~en adj. [~kən] (be-) trunken.

dry [drai] **1.** ☐ trocken; herb (Wein); F durstig; F antialkoholisch; ~ goods pl. Am. F Kurzwaren f/pl.; **2.** Am. F Alkoholgegner m; **3.** trocknen; dörren; ~ up austrocknen; verdunsten; ~-clean ['drai'kli:n] chemisch reinigen; ~-nurse Kinderfrau f.

dual ☐ ['dju:(:)əl] doppelt; Doppel...

dubious ☐ ['dju:bjəs] zweifelhaft.

duchess ['dʌtʃis] Herzogin f.

duck [dʌk] **1.** zo. Ente f; Am. sl. Kerl m; Verbeugung f; Ducken n; (Segel)Leinen n; F Liebling m; **2.** (unter)tauchen; (sich) ducken; Am. j-m ausweichen.

duckling ['dʌkliŋ] Entchen n.

dude Am. [dju:d] Geck m; ~ ranch Am. Vergnügungsfarm f.

dudgeon ['dʌdʒən] Groll m.

due [dju:] **1.** schuldig; gebührend; gehörig; fällig; in ~ time zur rechten Zeit; be ~ to j-m gebühren; herrühren od. kommen von; be ~ to inf. sollen, müssen; Am. im Begriff sein zu; **2.** adv. ♠ gerade; genau; **3.** Schuldigkeit f; Recht n, Anspruch m; Lohn m; mst ~s pl. Abgabe(n pl.) f, Gebühr(en pl.) f; Beitrag m. **2.** sich duellieren.]

duel ['dju:(:)əl] **1.** Zweikampf m;{

dug [dʌg] pret. u. p.p. von dig 1.

duke [dju:k] Herzog m; ~dom ['dju:kdəm] Herzogtum n; Herzogswürde f.

dull [dʌl] **1.** ☐ dumm; träge;

schwerfällig; stumpf(sinnig); matt (Auge etc.); schwach (Gehör); langweilig; teilnahmslos; dumpf; trüb; ✝ flau; **2.** stumpf machen; fig. abstumpfen; (sich) trüben; ~ness ['dʌlnis] Stumpfsinn m; Dummheit f; Schwerfälligkeit f; Mattheit f; Langweiligkeit f; Teilnahmslosigkeit f; Trübheit f; Flauheit f.

duly adv. ['dju:li] gehörig; richtig.

dumb ☐ [dʌm] stumm; sprachlos; Am. F doof, blöd; ~founded [dʌm'faundid] sprachlos; ~-waiter ['dʌm'weitə] Drehtisch m; Am. Speisenaufzug m.

dummy ['dʌmi] Attrappe f; Schein m, Schwindel m; fig. Strohmann m; Statist m; attr. Schein...; Schwindel...

dump [dʌmp] **1.** v/t. auskippen; Schutt etc. abladen; Waren zu Schleuderpreisen ausführen; v/i. hinplumpsen; **2.** Klumpen m; Plumps m; Schuttabladestelle f; ⚔ Munitionslager n; ~ing ✝ ['dʌmpiŋ] Schleuderausfuhr f; ~s pl. (down) in the ~ F niedergeschlagen.

dun [dʌn] mahnen, drängen.

dunce [dʌns] Dummkopf m.

dune [dju:n] Düne f.

dung [dʌŋ] **1.** Dung m; **2.** düngen.

dungeon ['dʌndʒən] Kerker m.

dunk Am. F [dʌŋk] (ein)tunken.

dupe [dju:p] anführen, täuschen.

duplex ⊕ ['dju:pleks] attr. Doppel...; Am. Zweifamilienhaus n.

duplic|ate 1. ['dju:plikit] doppelt; **2.** [~] Duplikat n; **3.** [~keit] doppelt ausfertigen; ~ity [dju:(')plisiti] Doppelzüngigkeit f.

dura|ble ☐ ['djuərəbl] dauerhaft; ~tion [djuə'reiʃən] Dauer f.

duress(e) [djuə'res] Zwang m.

during prp. ['djuəriŋ] während.

dusk [dʌsk] Halbdunkel n, Dämmerung f; ~y ☐ ['dʌski] dämmerig, düster (a. fig.); schwärzlich.

dust [dʌst] **1.** Staub m; **2.** abstauben; bestreuen; ~bin ['dʌstbin] Mülleimer m; ~ bowl Am. Sandstaub-u. Dürregebiet n im Westen der USA; ~-cart Müllwagen m; ~er [~tə] Staublappen m, -wedel m; Am. Staubmantel m; ~-jacket Am. Schutzumschlag m e-s Buches; ~man Müllabfuhrmann m; ~y ☐ [~ti] staubig.

Dutch [dʌtʃ] **1.** holländisch; ~ treat Am. F getrennte Rechnung; **2.** Holländisch n; the ~ die Holländer pl.

duty ['dju:ti] Pflicht f; Ehrerbietung f; Abgabe f, Zoll m; Dienst m; off ~ dienstfrei; ~-free zollfrei.

dwarf [dwɔ:f] **1.** Zwerg m; **2.** in der Entwicklung hindern; verkleinern.

dwell [dwel] [irr.] wohnen; verweilen (on, upon bei); ~ (up)on bestehen auf (acc.); ~ing ['dweliŋ] Wohnung f.

dwelt [dwelt] *pret. u. p.p. von* dwell.
dwindle ['dwindl] (dahin)schwinden, abnehmen; (herab)sinken.
dye [dai] 1. Farbe *f; of deepest ~ fig.* schlimmster Art; 2. färben.
dying ['daiiŋ] 1. □ sterbend; Sterbe...; 2. Sterben *n.*

dynam|ic [dai'næmik] dynamisch, kraftgeladen; **~ics** [~ks] *mst sg.* Dynamik *f;* **~ite** ['dainəmait] 1. Dynamit *n;* 2. mit Dynamit sprengen.
dysentery ♂ ['disntri] Ruhr *f.*
dyspepsia ♂ [dis'pepsiə] Verdauungsstörung *f.*

E

each [i:tʃ] jede(r, -s); ~ other einander, sich.
eager □ ['i:gə] (be)gierig; eifrig; **~ness** ['i:gənis] Begierde *f;* Eifer *m.*
eagle ['i:gl] Adler *m; Am.* Zehndollarstück *n;* **~-eyed** scharfsichtig.
ear [iə] Ähre *f;* Ohr *n;* Öhr *n,* Henkel *m; keep an ~ to the ground bsd. Am.* aufpassen, was die Leute sagen *od.* denken; **~drum** ['iədrʌm] Trommelfell *n.*
earl [ə:l] *englischer* Graf.
early ['ə:li] früh; Früh...; Anfangs-...; erst; bald(ig); *as ~ as* schon in *(dat.).* [nen.]
ear-mark ['iəmɑːk] (kenn)zeich-]
earn [ə:n] verdienen; einbringen.
earnest ['ə:nist] 1. □ ernst(lich, -haft); ernstgemeint; 2. Ernst *m.*
earnings ['ə:niŋz] Einkommen *n.*
ear|piece *teleph.* ['iəpi:s] Hörmuschel *f;* **~shot** Hörweite *f.*
earth [ə:θ] 1. Erde *f;* Land *n;* 2. *v/t. ℰ* erden; **~en** ['ə:θən] irden; **~enware** [~nwɛə] 1. Töpferware *f;* Steingut *n;* 2. irden; **~ing** *ℰ* ['ə:θiŋ] Erdung *f;* **~ly** ['ə:θli] irdisch; **~quake** Erdbeben *n;* **~worm** Regenwurm *m.*
ease [i:z] 1. Bequemlichkeit *f,* Behagen *n;* Ruhe *f;* Ungezwungenheit *f;* Leichtigkeit *f; at ~* bequem, behaglich; 2. *v/t.* erleichtern; lindern; beruhigen; bequem(er) machen; *v/i.* sich entspannen *(Lage).*
easel ['i:zl] Staffelei *f.*
easiness ['i:zinis] = ease 1.
east [i:st] 1. Ost(en *m*); Orient *m; the* ♀ *Am.* die Oststaaten *der USA;* 2. Ost...; östlich; ostwärts.
Easter ['i:stə] Ostern *n; attr.* Oster...
easter|ly ['i:stəli] östlich; Ost...; nach Osten; **~n** [~ən] = easterly; orientalisch; **~ner** [~nə] Ostländer (-in); Orientale *m,* -in *f;* ♀ *Am.* Oststaatler(in).
eastward(s) ['i:stwəd(z)] ostwärts.
easy ['i:zi] □ leicht; bequem; frei von Schmerzen; ruhig; willig; ungezwungen; *in ~ circumstances* wohlhabend; *on ~ street Am.* in guten Verhältnissen; *take it ~!* immer mit der Ruhe!; **~ chair** Klubsessel *m;* **~-going** *fig.* bequem.

eat [i:t] 1. [*irr.*] essen; (zer)fressen; 2. **~s** *pl. Am. sl.* Essen *n,* Eßwaren *f/pl.;* **~ables** ['i:təblz] *pl.* Eßwaren *f/pl.;* **~en** ['i:tn] *p.p. von* eat 1.
eaves [i:vz] *pl.* Dachrinne *f,* Traufe *f;* **~drop** ['i:vzdrɔp] (er)lauschen; horchen.
ebb [eb] 1. Ebbe *f; fig.* Abnahme *f;* Verfall *m;* 2. verebben; *fig.* abnehmen, sinken; **~tide** ['eb'taid] Ebbe *f.*
ebony ['ebəni] Ebenholz *n.*
ebullition [ebə'liʃən] Überschäumen *n;* Aufbrausen *n.*
eccentric [ik'sentrik] 1. exzentrisch; *fig.* überspannt; 2. Sonderling *m.*
ecclesiastic [ikli:zi'æstik] Geistliche(r) *m;* **~al** □ [~kəl] geistlich, kirchlich.
echo ['ekou] 1. Echo *n;* 2. widerhallen; *fig.* echoen, nachsprechen.
eclipse [i'klips] 1. Finsternis *f;* 2. (sich) verfinstern, verdunkeln.
econom|ic(al □) [i:kə'nɔmik(əl)] haushälterisch; wirtschaftlich; Wirtschafts...; **~ics** [~ks] *sg* Volkswirtschaft(slehre) *f;* **~ist** [i(:)'kɔnəmist] Volkswirt *m;* **~ize** [~maiz] sparsam wirtschaften (mit); **~y** [~mi] Wirtschaft *f;* Wirtschaftlichkeit *f;* Einsparung *f; political ~* Volkswirtschaft(slehre) *f.*
ecsta|sy ['ekstəsi] Ekstase *f,* Verzückung *f;* **~tic** [eks'tætik] (~ally) verzückt.
eddy ['edi] 1. Wirbel *m;* 2. wirbeln.
edge [edʒ] 1. Schneide *f;* Schärfe *f;* Rand *m;* Kante *f; Tisch-Ecke f; be on ~* nervös sein; *have the ~ on s.o. bsd. Am.* F j-m über sein; 2. schärfen; (um)säumen; (sich) drängen; **~ways, ~wise** ['edʒweiz, 'edʒwaiz] seitwärts; von der Seite.
edging ['edʒiŋ] Einfassung *f;* Rand)
edgy ['edʒi] scharf; F nervös. [*m.*]
edible ['edibl] eßbar.
edict ['i:dikt] Edikt *n.*
edifice ['edifis] Gebäude *n.*
edifying □ ['edifaiiŋ] erbaulich.
edit ['edit] *Text* herausgeben, redigieren; *Zeitung* als Herausgeber leiten; **~ion** [i'diʃən] *Buch*-Ausgabe *f;* Auflage *f;* **~or** ['editə] Herausgeber *m;* Redakteur *m;* **~orial**

[edi'tɔ:riəl] Leitartikel *m*; *attr.* Redaktions...; **~orship** ['editəʃip] Schriftleitung *f*, Redaktion *f*.

educat|e ['edju(:)keit] erziehen; unterrichten; **~ion** [edju(:)'keiʃən] Erziehung *f*; (Aus)Bildung *f*; Erziehungs-, Schulwesen *n*; Ministry of ♀ Unterrichtsministerium *n*; **~ional** □ [~nl] erzieherisch; Erziehungs...; Bildungs...; **~or** ['edju:keitə] Erzieher *m*.

eel [i:l] Aal *m*

efface [i'feis] auslöschen; *fig.* tilgen.

effect [i'fekt] 1. Wirkung *f*; Folge *f*; ⊕ Leistung *f*; **~s** *pl.* Effekten *pl.*; Habseligkeiten *f/pl.*; be of **~** Wirkung haben; take **~** in Kraft treten; in **~** in der Tat; to the **~** des Inhalts; 2. bewirken, ausführen; **~ive** □ [~tiv] wirkend; wirksam; eindrucksvoll; wirklich vorhanden; ⊕ nutzbar; **~ date** Tag *m* des Inkrafttretens; **~ual** □ [~tjuəl] wirksam, kräftig.

effeminate □ [i'feminit] verweichlicht; weibisch.

effervesce [efə'ves] (auf)brausen; **~nt** [~snt] sprudelnd, schäumend.

effete [e'fi:t] verbraucht; entkräftet.

efficacy ['efikəsi] Wirksamkeit *f*, Kraft *f*.

efficien|cy [i'fiʃənsi] Leistung(sfähigkeit) *f*; **~ expert** *Am.* Rationalisierungsfachmann *m*; **~t** □ [~nt] wirksam; leistungsfähig; tüchtig.

efflorescence [əflɔ:'resns] Blütezeit *f*; ⅋ Beschlag *m*.

effluence ['efluəns] Ausfluß *m*.

effort ['efət] Anstrengung *f*, Bemühung *f* (at um); Mühe *f*.

effrontery [e'frʌntəri] Frechheit *f*.

effulgent [e'fʌldʒənt] glänzend.

effus|ion [i'fju:ʒən] Erguß *m*; **~ive** □ [~:siv] überschwenglich.

egg¹ [eg] *mst* **~ on** aufreizen.

egg² [~] Ei *n*; put all one's **~s** in one basket alles auf eine Karte setzen; as sure as **~s** is **~s** F todsicher; **~-cup** ['egkʌp] Eierbecher *m*; **~head** *Am. sl.* Intellektuelle(r) *m*.

egotism ['egoutizəm] Selbstgefälligkeit *f*.

egregious *iro.* □ [i'gri:dʒəs] ungeheuer.

egress ['i:gres] Ausgang *m*; Ausweg *m*.

Egyptian [i'dʒipʃən] 1. ägyptisch; 2. Ägypter(in).

eider ['aidə]: **~ down** Eiderdaunen *f/pl.*; Daunendecke *f*.

eight [eit] 1. acht; 2. Acht *f*; behind the **~ ball** *Am.* in der (die) Klemme; **~een** ['ei'ti:n] achtzehn; **~eenth** [~nθ] achtzehnt; **~fold** ['eitfould] achtfach; **~h** [eitθ] 1. achte(r, -s); 2. Achtel *n*; **~hly** ['eitθli] achtens; **~ieth** ['eitiiθ] achtzigste(r, -s); **~y** ['eiti] achtzig.

either ['aiðə] 1. *adj. u. pron.* einer

von beiden; beide; 2. *cj.* **~ ... or** entweder ... oder; not (...) **~** auch nicht.

ejaculate [i'dʒækjuleit] Worte, Flüssigkeit ausstoßen.

eject [i(:)'dʒekt] ausstoßen; vertreiben, ausweisen; entsetzen (*e-s Amtes*).

eke [i:k]: **~ out** ergänzen; verlängern; sich mit *et.* durchhelfen.

el *Am.* F [el] = **elevated** railroad.

elaborat|e 1. □ [i'læbərit] sorgfältig ausgearbeitet; kompliziert; 2. [~reit] sorgfältig ausarbeiten; **~eness** [~ritnis], **~ion** [ilæbə'reiʃən] sorgfältige Ausarbeitung.

elapse [i'læps] verfließen, verstreichen.

elastic [i'læstik] 1. (**~ally**) dehnbar; spannkräftig; 2. Gummiband *n*; **~ity** [elæs'tisiti] Elastizität *f*, Dehnbarkeit *f*; Spannkraft *f*.

elate [i'leit] (er)heben, ermutigen, froh erregen; stolz machen; **~d** in gehobener Stimmung, freudig erregt (at über *acc.*; with durch).

elbow ['elbou] 1. Ellbogen *m*, Biegung *f*; ⊕ Knie *n*; at one's **~** nahe, bei der Hand; out at **~s** *fig.* heruntergekommen; 2. mit den Ellbogen (weg)stoßen; **~ out** verdrängen; **~-grease** F Armschmalz *n* (*Kraftanstrengung*).

elder ['eldə] 1. älter; 2. der, die Ältere; (Kirchen)Älteste(r) *m*; ♀ Holunder *m*; **~ly** [~əli] ältlich.

eldest ['eldist] älteste(r, -s).

elect [i'lekt] 1. (aus)gewählt; 2. (aus)er)wählen; **~ion** [~kʃən] Wahl *f*; **~ive** [~ktiv] 1. □ wählend; gewählt; Wahl...; *Am.* fakultativ; 2. *Am.* Wahlfach *n*; **~or** [~tə] Wähler *m*; *Am.* Wahlmann *m*; Kurfürst *m*; **~oral** [~rəl] Wahl..., Wähler...; **~ college** *Am.* Wahlmänner *m/pl.*; **~orate** [~rit] Wähler(schaft *f*) *m/pl.*

electric|(al □) [i'lektrik(əl)] elektrisch; Elektro...; *fig.* faszinierend; **~al engineer** Elektrotechniker *m*; **~ blue** stahlblau; **~ chair** elektrischer Stuhl; **~ian** [ilek'triʃən] Elektriker *m*; **~ity** [~isiti] Elektrizität *f*.

electri|fy [i'lektrifai], **~ze** [~raiz] elektrifizieren; elektrisieren.

electro|cute [i'lektrəkju:t] auf dem elektrischen Stuhl hinrichten; durch elektrischen Strom töten; **~metallurgy** Elektrometallurgie *f*.

electron [i'lektrɔn] Elektron *n*; **~-ray tube** magisches Auge.

electro|plate [i'lektroupleit] galvanisch versilbern; **~type** galvanischer Druck; Galvano *n*.

elegan|ce ['eligəns] Eleganz *f*; Anmut *f*; **~t** □ [~nt] elegant; geschmackvoll; *Am.* erstklassig.

element ['elimənt] Element *n*; Urstoff *m*; (Grund)Bestandteil *m*; **~s** *pl.* Anfangsgründe *m/pl.*; **~al** □

[eli'mentl] elementar; wesentlich; ~ary [~təri] **1.** ⌐ elementar; An- fangs...; ~ **school** Volks-, Grund- schule f; **2.** *elementaries* pl. An- fangsgründe m/pl.

elephant ['elifənt] Elefant m.

elevat|e ['eliveit] erhöhen; *fig.* er- heben; ~ed erhaben; ~ (*railroad*) Am. Hochbahn f; ~ion [eli'veiʃən] Erhebung f, Erhöhung f; Höhe f; Erhabenheit f; ~or ⊕ ['eliveitə] Aufzug m; Am. Fahrstuhl m; ≍ Höhenruder n; (*grain*) ~ Am. Ge- treidespeicher m.

eleven [i'levn] **1.** elf f; **2.** Elf f; ~th [~nθ] elfte(r, -s).

elf [elf] Elf(e f) m, Kobold m; Zwerg m.

elicit [i'lisit] hervorlocken, heraus- holen.

eligible ⌐ ['elidʒəbl] geeignet, an- nehmbar; passend.

eliminat|e [i'limineit] aussondern, ausscheiden; ausmerzen; ~ion [ili- mi'neiʃən] Aussonderung f; Aus- scheidung f.

élite [ei'li:t] Elite f; Auslese f.

elk *zo* [elk] Elch m.

ellipse ⅄ [i'lips] Ellipse f.

elm ♀ [elm] Ulme f, Rüster f.

elocution [elə'kju:ʃən] Vortrag(s- kunst, -sweise f) m.

elongate ['i:lɔŋgeit] verlängern.

elope [i'loup] entlaufen, durchge- hen.

eloquen|ce ['eləkwəns] Beredsam- keit f; ~t [~nt] beredt.

else [els] sonst, andere(r, -s), weiter; ~where ['elswεə] anderswo(hin).

elucidat|e [i'lu:sideit] erläutern; ~ion [i:lu:si'deiʃən] Aufklärung f.

elude [i'lu:d] geschickt umgehen; ausweichen, sich entziehen (*dat.*).

elus|ive [i'lu:siv] schwer faßbar; ~ory [~səri] trügerisch.

emaciate [i'meiʃieit] abzehren, aus- mergeln.

emanat|e ['eməneit] ausströmen; ausgehen (*from* von); ~ion [em- 'neiʃən] Ausströmen n; *fig.* Aus- strahlung f.

emancipat|e [i'mænsipeit] emanzi- pieren, befreien; ~ion [imænsi- 'peiʃən] Emanzipation f; Befrei- ung f.

embalm [im'ba:m] (ein)balsamie- ren; *be* ~ed *in* fortleben in (*dat.*).

embankment [im'bæŋkmənt] Ein- dämmung f; Deich m; (Bahn-) Damm m; Uferstraße f, Kai m.

embargo [em'ba:gou] (Hafen-, Handels)Sperre f, Beschlagnah- me f.

embark [im'ba:k] (sich) einschiffen (*for* nach); *Geld* anlegen; sich ein- lassen (*in, on, upon* in, auf *acc.*).

embarrass [im'bærəs] (be)hindern; verwirren; in (Geld)Verlegenheit bringen; verwickeln; ~ing □ [~siŋ]

unangenehm; unbequem; ~ment [~smənt] (Geld)Verlegenheit f; Schwierigkeit f.

embassy ['embəsi] Botschaft f; Ge- sandtschaft f.

embed [im'bed] (ein)betten, la- gern.

embellish [im'beliʃ] verschönern; ausschmücken. [Asche.\ ]

embers ['embəz] pl. glühende\ **embezzle** [im'bezl] unterschlagen; ~ment [~mənt] Unterschlagung f.

embitter [im'bitə] verbittern.

emblazon [im'bleizən] mit e-m Wappenbild bemalen; *fig.* verherr- lichen.

emblem ['embləm] Sinnbild n; Wahrzeichen n.

embody [im'bɔdi] verkörpern; ver- einigen; einverleiben (*in dat.*).

embolden [im'bouldən] ermutigen.

embolism ✠ ['embəlizəm] Em- bolie f.

embosom [im'buzəm] ins Herz schließen; ~ed *with* umgeben von.

emboss [im'bɔs] bossieren; *mit dem Hammer* treiben.

embrace [im'breis] **1.** (sich) um- armen; umfassen; *Beruf etc.* er- greifen; *Angebot* annehmen; **2.** Umarmung f.

embroider [im'brɔidə] sticken; aus- schmücken; ~y [~əri] Stickerei f.

embroil [im'brɔil] (in Streit) ver- wickeln; verwirren.

emendation [i:men'deiʃən] Ver- besserung f.

emerald ['emərəld] Smaragd m.

emerge [i'mə:dʒ] auftauchen; her- vorgehen; sich erheben; sich zei- gen; ~ncy [~dʒənsi] unerwartetes Ereignis; Notfall m; *attr.* Not...; ~ **brake** Notbremse f; ~ **call** Notruf m; ~ **exit** Notausgang m; ~ **man** *Sport:* Ersatzmann m; ~nt [~nt] auftauchend, entstehend; ~ **countries** Entwicklungsländer n/pl.

emersion [i(:)'mə:ʃən] Auftauchen n.

emigra|nt ['emigrənt] **1.** auswan- dernd; **2.** Auswanderer m; ~te [~reit] auswandern; ~tion [emi- 'greiʃən] Auswanderung f.

eminen|ce ['eminəns] (An)Höhe f; Auszeichnung f; hohe Stellung; Eminenz f (*Titel*); ~t □ [~nt] *fig.* ausgezeichnet, hervorragend; ~tly [~tli] ganz besonders.

emissary ['emisəri] Emissär m.

emit [i'mit] von sich geben; aus- senden, ausströmen; ✦ ausgeben.

emolument [i'mɔljumənt] Ver- gütung f; ~s pl. Einkünfte pl.

emotion [i'mouʃən] (Gemüts-)Be- wegung f; Gefühl(sregung f) n; Rührung f; ~al [~nl] gefühls- mäßig; gefühlvoll, gefühlsbetont; ~less [~nlis] gefühllos, kühl.

emperor ['empərə] Kaiser m.

empha|sis ['emfəsis] Nachdruck m; ~size [~saiz] nachdrücklich betonen; ~tic [im'fætik] (~ally) nachdrücklich; ausgesprochen.

empire ['empaiə] (Kaiser)Reich n; Herrschaft f; the British 2 das britische Weltreich.

empirical □ [em'pirikəl] erfahrungsgemäß.

employ [im'plɔi] 1. beschäftigen, anstellen; an-, verwenden, gebrauchen; 2. Beschäftigung f; in the ~ of angestellt bei; ~ee [emplɔi'i:] Angestellte(r m) f; Arbeitnehmer(in); ~er [im'plɔiə] Arbeitgeber m; ✝ Auftraggeber m; ~ment [~mənt] Beschäftigung f; Arbeit f; ~ agency Stellenvermittlungsbüro n; 2 Exchange Arbeitsamt n.

empower [im'pauə] ermächtigen; befähigen.

empress ['empris] Kaiserin f.

empt|iness ['emptinis] Leere f; Hohlheit f; ~y □ ['empti] 1. leer; fig. hohl; 2. (sich) (aus-, ent)leeren.

emul|ate ['emjuleit] wetteifern mit; nacheifern, es gleichtun (dat.); ~ation [emju'leiʃən] Wetteifer m.

enable [i'neibl] befähigen, es j-m ermöglichen; ermächtigen.

enact [i'nækt] verfügen, verordnen; Gesetz erlassen; thea. spielen.

enamel [i'næməl] 1. Email(le f) n, (Zahn)Schmelz m; Glasur f; Lack m; 2. emaillieren; glasieren.

enamo(u)r [i'næmə] verliebt machen; ~ed of verliebt in.

encamp ⚔ [in'kæmp] (sich) lagern.

encase [in'keis] einschließen.

enchain [in'tʃein] anketten; fesseln.

enchant [in'tʃɑːnt] bezaubern; ~ment [~tmənt] Bezauberung f; Zauber m; ~ress [~tris] Zauberin f.

encircle [in'sɔːkl] einkreisen.

enclos|e [in'klouz] einzäunen; einschließen; beifügen; ~ure [~ouʒə] Einzäunung f; eingehegtes Grundstück; Bei-, Anlage f zu e-m Brief.

encompass [in'kʌmpəs] umgeben.

encore thea. [ɔŋ'kɔː] 1. um e-e Zugabe bitten; 2. Zugabe f.

encounter [in'kauntə] 1. Begegnung f; Gefecht n; 2. begegnen (dat.); auf Schwierigkeiten etc. stoßen; mit j-m zs.-stoßen.

encourage [in'kʌridʒ] ermutigen; fördern; ~ment [~dʒmənt] Ermutigung f; Unterstützung f.

encroach [in'kroutʃ] (on, upon) eingreifen, eindringen (in acc.); beschränken (acc.); mißbrauchen (acc.); ~ment [~ʃmənt] Ein-, Übergriff m.

encumb|er [in'kʌmbə] belasten; (be)hindern; ~rance [~brəns] Last f; fig. Hindernis n; Schuldenlast f; without ~ ohne (Familien)Anhang.

encyclop(a)edia [ensaiklou'piːdjə]

Enzyklopädie f, Konversationslexikon n.

end [end] 1. Ende n; Ziel n, Zweck m; no ~ of unendlich viel(e), unzählige; in the ~ am Ende, auf die Dauer; on ~ aufrecht; stand on ~ zu Berge stehen; to no ~ vergebens; go off the deep ~ fig. in die Luft gehen; make both ~s meet gerade auskommen; 2. enden, beend(ig)en.

endanger [in'deindʒə] gefährden.

endear [in'diə] teuer machen; ~ment [~əmənt] Liebkosung f, Zärtlichkeit f.

endeavo(u)r [in'devə] 1. Bestreben n, Bemühung f; 2. sich bemühen.

end|ing ['endiŋ] Ende n; Schluß m; gr. Endung f; ~less □ ['endlis] endlos, unendlich; ⊕ ohne Ende.

endorse [in'dɔːs] ✝ indossieren; et. vermerken (on auf der Rückseite e-r Urkunde); gutheißen; ~ment [~smənt] Aufschrift f; ✝ Indossament n.

endow [in'dau] ausstatten; ~ment [~aumənt] Ausstattung f; Stiftung f.

endue fig. [in'djuː] (be)kleiden.

endur|ance [in'djuərəns] (Aus-)Dauer f; Ertragen n; ~e [in'djuə] (aus)dauern; ertragen.

enema ✍ ['enimə] Klistier(spritze f) n.

enemy ['enimi] 1. Feind m; the 2 der Teufel; 2. feindlich.

energ|etic [enə'dʒetik] (~ally) energisch; ~y ['enədʒi] Energie f.

enervate ['enəːveit] entnerven.

enfeeble [in'fiːbl] schwächen.

enfold [in'fould] einhüllen; umfassen.

enforce [in'fɔːs] erzwingen; aufzwingen (upon dat.); bestehen auf (dat.); durchführen; ~ment [~smənt] Erzwingung f; Geltendmachung f; Durchführung f.

enfranchise [in'fræntʃaiz] das Wahlrecht verleihen (dat.); Sklaven befreien.

engage [in'geidʒ] v/t. anstellen; verpflichten; mieten; in Anspruch nehmen; ⚔ angreifen; be ~d verlobt sein (to mit); beschäftigt sein (in mit); besetzt sein; ~ the clutch einkuppeln; v/i. sich verpflichten, versprechen, garantieren; sich beschäftigen (in mit); ⚔ angreifen; ⊕ greifen (Zahnräder); ~ment [~dʒmənt] Verpflichtung f; Verlobung f; Verabredung f; Beschäftigung f; ⚔ Gefecht n; Einrücken n e-s Ganges etc.

engaging □ [in'geidʒiŋ] einnehmend.

engender fig. [in'dʒendə] erzeugen.

engine ['endʒin] Maschine f, Motor m; 🚂 Lokomotive f; ~driver Lokomotivführer m.

engineer [endʒi'niə] 1. Ingenieur m,

Techniker *m*; **Maschinist** *m*; *Am.*
Lokomotivführer *m*; ✗ Pionier *m*;
2. Ingenieur sein; bauen; **~ing**
[~ɔriŋ] **1.** Maschinenbau *m*; Inge-
nieurwesen *n*; **2.** technisch; Ingenieur...

English ['iŋgliʃ] **1.** englisch; **2.** Englisch *n*; the ~ *pl.* die Engländer *pl.*;
in plain ~ *fig.* unverblümt; **~man**
Engländer *m*.

engrav|e [in'greiv] gravieren, ste-
chen; *fig.* einprägen; **~er** [~və]
Graveur *m*; **~ing** [~viŋ] (Kupfer-,
Stahl)Stich *m*; Holzschnitt *m*.

engross [in'grous] an sich ziehen;
ganz in Anspruch nehmen.

engulf *fig* [in'gʌlf] verschlingen.

enhance [in'hɑːns] erhöhen.

enigma [i'nigmə] Rätsel *n*; **~tic(al**
▢) [enig'mætik(əl)] rätselhaft.

enjoin [in'dʒɔin] auferlegen (*on j-m*).

enjoy [in'dʒɔi] sich erfreuen an
(*dat.*); genießen; *did you* ~ *it*? hat
es Ihnen gefallen?; ~ *o.s.* sich amüsieren; *I* ~ *my dinner* es schmeckt
mir; **~able** [~əbl] genußreich, erfreulich; **~ment** [~imənt] Genuß
m, Freude *f*.

enlarge [in'lɑːdʒ] (sich) erweitern,
ausdehnen; vergrößern; **~ment**
[~dʒmənt] Erweiterung *f*; Vergrößerung *f*.

enlighten [in'laitn] *fig.* erleuchten;
j-n aufklären; **~ment** [~nmənt]
Aufklärung *f*.

enlist [in'list] *v/t.* ✗ anwerben; gewinnen; **~ed men** *pl. Am.* ✗ Unter-
offiziere *pl.* und Mannschaften *pl.*;
v/i. sich freiwillig melden.

enliven [in'laivn] beleben.

enmity ['enmiti] Feindschaft *f*.

ennoble [i'noubl] adeln; veredeln.

enorm|ity [i'nɔːmiti] Ungeheuer-
lichkeit *f*; **~ous** ▢ [~məs] ungeheuer.

enough [i'nʌf] genug.

enquire [in'kwaiə] = *inquire*.

enrage [in'reidʒ] wütend machen;
~d wütend (*at* über *acc.*).

enrapture [in'ræptʃə] entzücken.

enrich [in'ritʃ] be-, anreichern.

enrol(l) [in'roul] *in e-e* Liste eintragen; ✗ anwerben; aufnehmen;
~ment [~lmənt] Eintragung *f*; *bsd.*
✗ Anwerbung *f*, Einstellung *f*;
Aufnahme *f*; Verzeichnis *n*; Schü-
ler-, Studenten-, Teilnehmerzahl *f*.

ensign ['ensain] Fahne *f*; Flagge *f*;
Abzeichen *n*; ⚓ *Am.* ['ensn] Leutnant *m* zur See.

enslave [in'sleiv] versklaven; **~ment**
[~vmənt] Versklavung *f*.

ensnare *fig.* [in'snɛə] verführen.

ensue [in'sjuː] folgen, sich ergeben.

ensure [in'ʃuə] sichern.

entail [in'teil] **1.** zur Folge haben;
als unveräußerliches Gut vererben;
2. (Übertragung *f* als) unveräußerliches Gut.

entangle [in'tæŋgl] verwickeln; **~-
ment** [~lmənt] Verwicklung *f*; ✗
*Draht-*Verhau *m*.

enter ['entə] *v/t.* (ein)treten in (*acc.*);
betreten; einsteigen, einfahren *etc.*
in (*acc.*); eindringen in (*acc.*); eintragen, ✝ buchen; *Protest* einbringen; aufnehmen; melden; ~ *s.o. at
school* j-n zur Schule anmelden; *v/i.*
eintreten; sich einschreiben; *Sport:*
sich melden; aufgenommen werden;
~ *into fig.* eingehen auf (*acc.*); ~
(*up*)*on Amt etc.* antreten; sich einlassen auf (*acc.*).

enterpris|e ['entəpraiz] Unterneh-
men *n*; Unternehmungslust *f*;
~ing ▢ [~ziŋ] unternehmungslustig.

entertain [entə'tein] unterhalten;
bewirten; in Erwägung ziehen;
Meinung etc. hegen; **~er** [~ə] Gastgeber *m*; Unterhaltungskünstler *m*;
~ment [~nmənt] Unterhaltung *f*;
Bewirtung *f*; Fest *n*, Gesellschaft *f*.

enthral(l) *fig.* [in'θrɔːl] bezaubern.

enthrone [in'θroun] auf den Thron
setzen.

enthusias|m [in'θjuːziæzəm] Be-
geisterung *f*; **~t** [~æst] Schwärmer
(-in); **~tic** [inθjuːzi'æstik] (~ally)
begeistert (*at, about* von).

entice [in'tais] (ver)locken; **~-
ment** [~smənt] Verlockung *f*, Reiz
m.

entire ▢ [in'taiə] ganz; vollständig;
ungeteilt; **~ly** [~əli] völlig; lediglich; **~ty** [~əti] Gesamtheit *f*.

entitle [in'taitl] betiteln; berechtigen.

entity ['entiti] Wesen *n*; Dasein *n*.

entrails ['entreilz] *pl.* Eingeweide
n/*pl.*; Innere(s) *n*.

entrance ['entrəns] Ein-, Zutritt *m*;
Einfahrt *f*, Eingang *m*; Einlaß *m*.

entrap [in'træp] (ein)fangen; verleiten.

entreat [in'triːt] bitten, ersuchen;
et. erbitten; **~y** [~ti] Bitte *f*, Gesuch *n*.

entrench ✗ [in'trentʃ] (mit *od.* in
Gräben) verschanzen.

entrust [in'trʌst] anvertrauen (*s. th.
to s.o.* j-m et.); betrauen.

entry ['entri] Eintritt *m*; Eingang
m; ⚖ Besitzantritt *m* (*on, upon
gen.*); Eintragung *f*; *Sport* Meldung *f*; ~ *permit* Einreisegenehmi-
gung *f*; *book-keeping by double
(single)* ~ doppelte (einfache) Buchführung.

enumerate [i'njuːməreit] aufzäh-
len.

enunciate [i'nʌnsieit] verkünden;
Lehrsatz aufstellen; aussprechen.

envelop [in'veləp] einhüllen; einwickeln; umgeben; ✗ einkreisen;
~e ['enviloup] Briefumschlag *m*; **~-
ment** [in'veləpmənt] Umhüllung *f*.

envi|able ▢ ['enviəbl] beneidens-
wert; **~ous** ▢ [~iəs] neidisch.

environ [in'vaiərən] umgeben; **~ment** [‿nmənt] Umgebung f e-r Person; **~s** ['envirənz] pl. Umgebung f e-r Stadt.

envisage [in'vizidʒ] sich et. vorstellen.

envoy ['envɔi] Gesandte(r) m; Bote m.

envy ['envi] 1. Neid m; 2. beneiden.

epic ['epik] 1. episch; 2. Epos n.

epicure ['epikjuə] Feinschmecker m.

epidemic [epi'demik] 1. (‿ally) seuchenartig; **~ disease** = 2. Seuche f.

epidermis [epi'də:mis] Oberhaut f.

epilepsy ['epilepsi] Epilepsie f.

epilogue ['epilɔg] Nachwort n.

episcopa|cy [i'piskəpəsi] bischöfliche Verfassung; **~l** [‿əl] bischöflich; **~te** [‿pit] Bischofswürde f; Bistum n.

epist|le [i'pisl] Epistel f; **~olary** [‿stəlari] brieflich; Brief...

epitaph ['epita:f] Grabschrift f.

epitome [i'pitəmi] Auszug m, Abriß m.

epoch ['i:pɔk] Epoche f.

equable [‿'ekwəbl] gleichförmig, gleichmäßig; fig. gleichmütig.

equal ['i:kwəl] 1. [gleich, gleichmäßig; **~ to** fig gewachsen (dat.); 2. Gleiche(r m) f; 3. gleichen (dat.); **~ity** [i(:)'kwɔliti] Gleichheit f; **~ization** [i:kwəlai'zeiʃən] Gleichstellung f; Ausgleich m; **~ize** [i:kwəlaiz] gleichmachen, gleichstellen; ausgleichen.

equanimity [i:kwə'nimiti] Gleichmut m.

equat|ion [i'kweiʃən] Ausgleich m; A̋ Gleichung f; **~or** [‿eitə] Aquator m.

equestrian [i'kwestriən] Reiter m.

equilibrium [i:kwi'libriəm] Gleichgewicht n; Ausgleich m.

equip [i'kwip] ausrüsten; **~ment** [‿pmənt] Ausrüstung f; Einrichtung f.

equipoise ['ekwipɔiz] Gleichgewicht n; Gegengewicht n.

equity ['ekwiti] Billigkeit f; equities pl. ✝ Aktien f/pl.

equivalent [i'kwivələnt] 1. gleichwertig; gleichbedeutend (to mit); 2. Aquivalent n, Gegenwert m.

equivoca|l [[i'kwivəkəl] zweideutig, zweifelhaft; **~te** [‿keit] zweideutig reden.

era ['iərə] Zeitrechnung f; -alter n.

eradicate [i'rædikeit] ausrotten.

eras|e [i'reiz] ausradieren, ausstreichen; auslöschen; **~er** [‿zə] Radiergummi m; **~ure** [i'reiʒə] Ausradieren n; radierte Stelle.

ere [eə] 1. cj. ehe, bevor; 2. prp. vor.

erect [i'rekt] 1. [aufrecht; 2. aufrichten; Denkmal etc. errichten; aufstellen; **~ion** [‿kʃən] Auf-, Errichtung f; Gebäude n.

eremite ['erimait] Einsiedler m.

ermine zo. ['ə:min] Hermelin n.

erosion [i'rouʒən] Zerfressen n; Auswaschung f.

erotic [i'rɔtik] 1. erotisch; 2. erotisches Gedicht; **~ism** [‿isizəm] Erotik f.

err [ə:] (sich) irren; fehlen, sündigen.

errand ['erənd] Botengang m, Auftrag m; **~-boy** Laufbursche m.

errant [['erənt] (umher)irrend.

errat|ic [i'rætik] (‿ally) wandernd; unberechenbar; **~um** [e'ra:təm], pl. **~a** [‿tə] Druckfehler m.

erroneous [i'rounjəs] irrig.

error ['erə] Irrtum m, Fehler m; **~s excepted** Irrtümer vorbehalten.

erudit|e ['eru(:)dait] gelehrt; **~ion** [eru(:)'diʃən] Gelehrsamkeit f.

erupt [i'rʌpt] ausbrechen (Vulkan); durchbrechen (Zähne); **~ion** [‿pʃən] Vulkan-Ausbruch m; ✝ Hautausschlag m.

escalat|ion [eskə'leiʃən] Eskalation f (stufenweise Steigerung); **~or** ['eskəleitə] Rolltreppe f.

escap|ade [eskə'peid] toller Streich; **~e** [is'keip] 1. entschlüpfen, entgehen; entkommen, entrinnen; entweichen; j-m entfallen; 2. Entrinnen n; Entweichen n; Flucht f.

eschew [is'tʃu:] (ver)meiden.

escort 1. ['eskɔ:t] Eskorte f; Geleit n; 2. [is'kɔ:t] eskortieren, geleiten.

escutcheon [is'kʌtʃən] Wappenschild m, n; Namenschild n.

especial [is'peʃəl] besonder; vorzüglich; **~ly** [‿li] besonders.

espionage [espiə'na:ʒ] Spionage f.

espresso [es'presou] Espresso m (Kaffee); **~ bar**, **~ café** Espressobar f.

espy [is'pai] erspähen.

esquire [is'kwaiə] Landedelmann m, Gutsbesitzer m; auf Briefen: John Smith Esq. Herrn J. S.

essay 1. [e'sei] versuchen; probieren; 2. ['esei] Versuch m; Aufsatz m, kurze Abhandlung, Essay m, n.

essen|ce ['esns] Wesen n e-r Sache; Extrakt m; Essenz f; **~tial** [i'senʃəl] 1. ☐ (to für) wesentlich; wichtig; 2. Wesentliche(s) n.

establish [is'tæbliʃ] festsetzen; errichten, gründen; einrichten; einsetzen; o.s. sich niederlassen; **~ed Church** Staatskirche f; **~ment** [‿ʃmənt] Festsetzung f; Gründung f; Er-, Einrichtung f; (bsd. großer) Haushalt; Anstalt f; Firma f.

estate [is'teit] Grundstück n; Grundbesitz m, Gut n; Besitz m; (Konkurs)Masse f, Nachlaß m; Stand m; real **~** Liegenschaften pl.; housing **~** Wohnsiedlung f; **~ agent** Grundstücksmakler m; **~ car** Kombiwagen m; **~ duty** Nachlaßsteuer f.

esteem [is'ti:m] 1. Achtung f, Ansehen n (with bei); 2. (hoch)achten, (hoch)schätzen; erachten für.

estimable ['estimǝbl] schätzenswert.

estimat|e 1. ['estimeit] (ab)schätzen; veranschlagen; **2.** [..mit] Schätzung f; (Vor)Anschlag m; **~ion** [esti'meiʃǝn] Schätzung f; Meinung f; Achtung f.

estrange [is'treindʒ] entfremden.

estuary ['estjuǝri] (den Gezeiten ausgesetzte) weite Flußmündung.

etch [etʃ] ätzen, radieren.

etern|al [i(:)'tǝ:nl] immerwährend, ewig; **~ity** [..niti] Ewigkeit f.

ether ['i:θǝ] Äther m; **~eal** [i(:)'θiǝriǝl] ätherisch (a fig.).

ethic|al ['eθikǝl] sittlich, ethisch; **~s** [..ks] sg. Sittenlehre f, Ethik f.

etiquette [eti'ket] Etikette f.

etymology [eti'mɔlǝdʒi] Etymologie f, Wortableitung f.

Eucharist ['ju:kǝrist] Abendmahl n.

euphemism ['ju:fimizǝm] beschönigender Ausdruck.

European [juǝrǝ'pi(:)ǝn] **1.** europäisch; **2.** Europäer(in).

evacuate [i'vækjueit] entleeren; evakuieren; Land etc. räumen.

evade [i'veid] (geschickt) ausweichen (dat.); umgehen.

evaluate [i'væljueit] zahlenmäßig bestimmen, auswerten; berechnen.

evanescent [i:vǝ'nesnt] (ver)schwindend.   [evangelisch.)

evangelic|al ☐] [i:væn'dʒelik(ǝl)]

evaporat|e [i'væpǝreit] verdunsten, verdampfen (lassen); **~ion** [ivæpǝ-'reiʃǝn] Verdunstung f, Verdampfung f.

evasi|on [i'veiʒǝn] Umgehung f; Ausflucht f; **~ve**] [i'veisiv] ausweichend; be ~ ausweichen.

eve [i:v] Vorabend m; Vortag m; on the ~ of unmittelbar vor (dat.), am Vorabend (gen.).

even [i:vǝn] **1.** adj. ☐ eben, gleich; gleichmäßig; ausgeglichen; glatt; gerade (Zahl); unparteiisch; get ~ with s.o. fig. mit j-m abrechnen; **2.** adv. selbst, sogar, auch; not ~ nicht einmal; ~ though, ~ if wenn auch; **3.** ebnen, glätten; gleichstellen; **~-handed** unparteiisch.

evening [i'vi:niŋ] Abend m; ~ dress Gesellschaftsanzug m; Frack m, Smoking m; Abendkleid n.

evenness ['i:vǝnnis] Ebenheit f; Geradheit f; Gleichmäßigkeit f; Unparteilichkeit f; Seelenruhe f.

evensong ['i:vǝnsɔŋ] Abendgottesdienst m.

event [i'vent] Ereignis n; Vorfall m; fig. Ausgang m; sportliche Veranstaltung; athletic ~s pl. Leichtathletikwettkämpfe m/pl.; at all ~s auf alle Fälle; in the ~ of im Falle (gen.); **~ful** [..tful] ereignisreich.

eventual ☐ [i'ventjuǝl] etwaig, möglich; schließlich; **~ly** am Ende; im Laufe der Zeit; gegebenenfalls.

ever ['evǝ] je, jemals; immer; ~ so noch so (sehr); as soon as ~ I can sobald ich nur irgend kann; ~ after, ~ since von der Zeit an; ~ and anon von Zeit zu Zeit; for ~ für immer, auf ewig; Briefschluß yours ~ stets Dein ...; **~glade** Am. Sumpfsteppe f; **~green** 1. immergrün; 2. immergrüne Pflanze; **~lasting**] [evǝ-'lɑ:stiŋ] ewig; dauerhaft; **~more** ['evǝ'mɔ:] immerfort.

every ['evri] jede(r, -s); alle(s); ~ now and then dann und wann; ~ one of them jeder von ihnen; ~ other day einen Tag um den anderen, jeden zweiten Tag; **~body** jeder (-mann); **~day** Alltags...; **~one** jeder(mann); **~thing** alles; **~where** überall.

evict [i(:)'vikt] exmittieren; ausweisen.

eviden|ce [i'evidǝns] **1.** Beweis(material n) m; ⅍ Zeugnis n; Zeuge m; in ~ als Beweis; deutlich sichtbar; **2.** beweisen; **~t**] [..nt] augenscheinlich, offenbar, klar.

evil ['i:vl] **1.** ☐ übel, schlimm, böse; the ♀ One der Böse (Teufel); **2.** Übel n, Böse(s) n; **~-minded** ['i:vl'maindid] übelgesinnt, boshaft.

evince [i'vins] zeigen, bekunden.

evoke [i'vouk] (herauf)beschwören.

evolution [i:vǝ'lu:ʃǝn] Entwicklung f; ⚔ Entfaltung f e-r Formation.

evolve [i'vɔlv] (sich) entwickeln.

ewe [ju:] Mutterschaf n.

ex [eks] prp. ✝ ab Fabrik etc.; Börse: ohne; aus.

ex-... [..] ehemalig, früher.

exact [ig'zækt] **1.** ☐ genau; pünktlich; **2.** Zahlung eintreiben; fordern; **~ing** [..tiŋ] streng, genau; **~itude** [..itju:d]; **~ness** [..tnis] Genauigkeit f; Pünktlichkeit f.

exaggerate [ig'zædʒǝreit] übertreiben.

exalt [ig'zɔ:lt] erhöhen, erheben; verherrlichen; **~ation** [egzɔ:l'teiʃǝn] Erhöhung f, Erhebung f; Höhe f; Verzückung f.

exam Schul-sl. [ig'zæm] Examen n.

examin|ation [igzæmi'neiʃǝn] Examen n, Prüfung f; Untersuchung f; Vernehmung f; **~e** [ig'zæmin] untersuchen; prüfen, verhören.

example [ig'zɑ:mpl] Beispiel n; Vorbild n, Muster n; for ~ zum Beispiel.

exasperate [ig'zɑ:spǝreit] erbittern; ärgern; verschlimmern.

excavate ['ekskǝveit] ausgraben, ausheben, ausschachten.

exceed [ik'si:d] überschreiten; übertreffen; zu weit gehen; **~ing** ☐ [..diŋ] übermäßig; **~ingly** [..ŋli] außerordentlich, überaus.

excel [ik'sel] *v/t.* übertreffen; *v/i.* sich auszeichnen; **~lence** ['eksələns] Vortrefflichkeit *f*; hervorragende Leistung; Vorzug *m*; **~lency** [~si] Exzellenz *f*; **~lent** □ [~nt] vortrefflich

except [ik'sept] **1.** ausnehmen; *et.* einwenden; **2.** *prp.* ausgenommen, außer; **~** *for* abgesehen von; **~ing** *prp.* [~tiŋ] ausgenommen; **~ion** [~pʃən] Ausnahme *f*; Einwendung *f* (*to* gegen); *by way of* **~** ausnahmsweise; *take* **~** *to* Anstoß nehmen an (*dat.*); **~ional** [~nl] außergewöhnlich; **~ionally** [~nəli] un-, außergewöhnlich.

excerpt ['eksə:pt] Auszug *m*.

excess [ik'ses] Übermaß *n*; Überschuß *m*; Ausschweifung *f*; *attr.* Mehr...; **~** *fare* Zuschlag *m*; **~** *luggage* Übergewicht *n* (*Gepäck*); **~** *postage* Nachgebühr *f*; **~ive** □ [~siv] übermäßig, übertrieben.

exchange [iks'tʃeindʒ] **1.** (aus-, ein-, um)tauschen (*for* gegen); wechseln; **2.** (Aus-, Um)Tausch *m*; (*bsd.* Geld)Wechsel *m*; *a. bill of* **~** Wechsel *m*; *a.* ♀ Börse *f*; Fernsprechamt *n*; *foreign* **~**(*s pl.*) Devisen *f/pl.*; (*rate of*) **~** Wechselkurs *m*.

exchequer [iks'tʃekə] Schatzamt *n*; Staatskasse *f*; *Chancellor of the* ♀ (britischer) Schatzkanzler, Finanzminister *m*.

excise[1] [ek'saiz] indirekte Steuer; Verbrauchssteuer *f*.

excise[2] [~] (her)ausschneiden.

excit|able [ik'saitəbl] reizbar; **~e** [ik'sait] er-, anregen; reizen; **~ement** [~tmənt] Auf-, Erregung *f*; Reizung *f*; **~ing** [~tiŋ] erregend.

exclaim [iks'kleim] ausrufen; eifern.

exclamation [eksklə'meiʃən] Ausruf(ung *f*) *m*; **~s** *pl.* Geschrei *n*; *note of* **~**, *point of* **~**, **~** *mark* Ausrufezeichen *n*.

exclude [iks'klu:d] ausschließen.

exclusi|on [iks'klu:ʒən] Ausschließung *f*, Ausschluß *m*; **~ve** □ [~:siv] ausschließlich; sich abschließend; **~** *of* abgesehen von, ohne.

excommunicat|e [ekskə'mju:nikeit] exkommunizieren; **~ion** ['ekskəmju:ni'keiʃən] Kirchenbann *m*.

excrement ['ekskrimənt] Kot *m*.

excrete [eks'kri:t] ausscheiden.

excruciat|e [iks'kru:ʃieit] martern; **~ing** □ [~tiŋ] qualvoll.

exculpate ['ekskʌlpeit] entschuldigen; rechtfertigen; freisprechen (*from* von).

excursion [iks'kə:ʃən] Ausflug *m*; Abstecher *m*.

excursive □ [eks'kə:siv] abschweifend.

excus|able □ [iks'kju:zəbl] entschuldbar; **~e 1.** [iks'kju:z] ent-

schuldigen; **~** *s.o. s.th.* j-m et. erlassen; **2.** [~u:s] Entschuldigung *f*.

exeat ['eksiæt] *Schule etc.*: Urlaub *m*.

execra|ble □ ['eksikrəbl] abscheulich; **~te** ['eksikreit] verwünschen.

execut|e ['eksikju:t] ausführen; vollziehen; ♪ vortragen; hinrichten; *Testament* vollstrecken; **~ion** [eksi'kju:ʃən] Ausführung *f*; Vollziehung *f*; (Zwangs)Vollstreckung *f*; Hinrichtung *f*; ♪ Vortrag *m*; *put od.* *carry a plan into* **~** e-n Plan ausführen *od.* verwirklichen; **~ioner** [~ʃnə] Scharfrichter *m*; **~ive** [~'zekjutiv] **1.** □ vollziehend; **~** *committee* Vorstand *m*; **2.** vollziehende Gewalt; *Am.* Staats-Präsident *m*; ✝ Geschäftsführer *m*; **~or** [~tə] (Testaments)Vollstrecker *m*.

exemplary [ig'zempləri] vorbildlich.

exemplify [ig'zemplifai] durch Beispiele belegen; veranschaulichen.

exempt [ig'zempt] **1.** befreit, frei; **2.** ausnehmen, befreien.

exercise ['eksəsaiz] **1.** Übung *f*; Ausübung *f*; *Schule:* Übungsarbeit *f*; Leibesübung *f*; *take* **~** sich Bewegung machen; *Am.* **~s** *pl.* Feierlichkeit(en *pl.*) *f*; ✗ Manöver *n*; **2.** üben; ausüben; (sich) Bewegung machen; exerzieren.

exert [ig'zə:t] *Einfluß etc.* ausüben; **~** *o.s.* sich anstrengen *od.* bemühen; **~ion** [~ʒən] Ausübung *f etc.*

exhale [eks'heil] ausdünsten, ausatmen; aushauchen; *Gefühlen* Luft machen.

exhaust [ig'zɔ:st] **1.** erschöpfen; entleeren; auspumpen; **2.** ⊕ Abgas *n*, Abdampf *m*; Auspuff *m*; **~** *box* Auspufftopf *m*; **~** *pipe* Auspuffrohr *n*; **~ed** erschöpft (*a. fig.*); vergriffen (*Auflage*); **~ion** [~tʃən] Erschöpfung *f*; **~ive** □ [~tiv] erschöpfend.

exhibit [ig'zibit] **1.** ausstellen; zeigen, darlegen; aufweisen; **2.** Ausstellungsstück *n*; Beweisstück *n*; **~ion** [eksi'biʃən] Ausstellung *f*; Darlegung *f*; Zurschaustellung *f*; Stipendium *n*.

exhilarate [ig'ziləreit] erheitern.

exhort [ig'zɔ:t] ermahnen.

exigen|ce, -cy ['eksidʒəns, ~si] dringende Not; Erfordernis *n*; **~t** [~nt] dringlich; anspruchsvoll.

exile ['eksail] **1.** Verbannung *f*, Exil *n*; Verbannte(r *m*) *f*; **2.** verbannen.

exist [ig'zist] existieren, vorhanden sein; leben; **~ence** [~təns] Existenz *f*, Dasein *n*, Vorhandensein *n*; Leben *n*; *in* **~** **~ent** [~nt] vorhanden.

exit ['eksit] **1.** Abgang *m*; Tod *m*; Ausgang *m*; **2.** *thea.* (geht) ab.

exodus ['eksədəs] Auszug *m*.

exonerate [ig'zɔnəreit] *fig.* entla-

sten, entbinden, befreien; rechtfertigen.

exorbitant ☐ [ig'zɔ:bitənt] maßlos,
übermäßig.

exorci|se, **~ze** ['eksɔ:saiz] *Geister*
beschwören, austreiben (*from* aus);
befreien (*of* von).

exotic [eg'zɔtik] ausländisch, exotisch; fremdländisch.

expan|d [iks'pænd] (sich) ausbrei-
ten; (sich) ausdehnen; (sich) erweitern; *Abkürzungen* (voll) ausschreiben; freundlich *od.* heiter
werden; **~se** [~ns], **~sion** [~nʃən]
Ausdehnung *f*; Weite *f*; Breite *f*;
~sive [~nsiv] ausdehnungsfähig;
ausgedehnt, weit; *fig.* mitteilsam.

expatiate [eks'peiʃieit] sich weitläufig auslassen (*on* uber *acc.*).

expatriate [eks'pætrieit] ausbür-
gern.

expect [iks'pekt] erwarten; F annehmen; *be ~ing* ein Kind erwar-
ten; **~ant** [~tənt] **1.** erwartend (*of*
acc.); *~ mother* werdende Mutter;
2. Anwärter *m*; **~ation** [ekspek-
'teiʃən] Erwartung *f*; Aussicht *f*.

expectorate [eks'pektəreit] *Schleim*
etc. aushusten, auswerfen.

expedi|ent [iks'pi:djənt] **1.** ☐
zweckmäßig; berechnend; **2.** Mittel *n*; (Not)Behelf *m*; **~tion** [ekspi-
'diʃən] Eile *f*; ✕ Feldzug *m*; (For-
schungs)Reise *f*; **~tious** ⌐ [~ʃəs]
schnell, eilig, flink.

expel [iks'pel] (hin)ausstoßen; vertreiben, verjagen; ausschließen.

expen|d [iks'pend] *Geld* ausgeben;
aufwenden; verbrauchen; **~diture**
[~ditʃə] Ausgabe *f*; Aufwand *m*;
~se [iks'pens] Ausgabe *f*; Kosten
pl.; *~s pl.* Unkosten *pl*, Auslagen
f/pl.; *at the ~ of* auf Kosten (*gen.*);
at any ~ um jeden Preis; *at the*
~ of Geld ausgeben für; **~se account**
Spesenrechnung *f*; **~sive** ⌐ [~siv]
kostspielig, teuer.

experience [iks'piəriəns] **1.** Erfahrung *f*; Erlebnis *n*; **2.** erfahren, erleben; **~d** erfahren.

experiment 1. [iks'perimənt] Versuch *m*; **2.** [~iment] experimentie-
ren; **~al** [eksperi'mentl] Versuchs...; erfahrungsmäßig.

expert ['ekspə:t] **1.** | [*pred.* eks-
'pə:t] erfahren, geschickt; fach-
männisch; **2.** Fachmann *m*; Sach-
verständige(r *m*) *f*.

expiate ['ekspieit] büßen, sühnen.

expir|ation [ekspai'reiʃən] Ausat-
mung *f*; Ablauf *m*, Ende *n*; **~e**
[iks'paiə] ausatmen; verscheiden;
ablaufen; ✝ verfallen; erlöschen.

explain [iks'plein] erklären, erläutern; *Gründe* auseinandersetzen; *~*
away wegdiskutieren.

explanat|ion [eksplə'neiʃən] Erklä-
rung *f*; Erläuterung *f*; **~ory** ☐
[iks'plænətəri] erklärend.

explicable ['eksplikəbl] erklärlich.
explicit ⌐ [iks'plisit] deutlich.

explode [iks'ploud] explodieren (lassen); ausbrechen; platzen (*with*
vor).

exploit 1. ['eksplɔit] Heldentat *f*;
2. [iks'plɔit] ausbeuten; **~ation**
[eksplɔi'teiʃən] Ausbeutung *f*.

explor|ation [eksplɔ:'reiʃən] Er-
forschung *f*; **~e** [iks'plɔ:] erforschen; **~er** [~ɔ:rə] (Er)Forscher *m*;
Forschungsreisende(r) *m*.

explosi|on [iks'plouʒən] Explosion
f; Ausbruch *m*; **~ve** [~ousiv] **1.** ☐
explosiv; **2.** Sprengstoff *m*.

exponent [eks'pounənt] Exponent
m; Vertreter *m*.

export 1. [eks'pɔ:t] ausführen;
2. ['ekspɔ:t] Ausfuhr(artikel *m*) *f*;
~ation [ekspɔ:'teiʃən] Ausfuhr *f*.

expos|e [iks'pouz] aussetzen; *phot.*
belichten; ausstellen; entlarven;
bloßstellen; **~ition** [ekspə'ziʃən]
Ausstellung *f*; Erklärung *f*.

expostulate [iks'pɔstjuleit] protestieren; *~ with j-m* Vorhaltungen
machen.

exposure [iks'pouʒə] Aussetzen *n*;
Ausgesetztsein *n*; Aufdeckung *f*;
Enthüllung *f*, Entlarvung *f*; *phot.*
Belichtung *f*; Bild *n*; Lage *f e-s*
Hauses; *~ meter* Belichtungsmesser
m. [legen.]

expound [iks'paund] erklären, aus-)

express [iks'pres] **1.** | ausdrück-
lich, deutlich; Expreß..., Eil...; *~*
company Am. Transportfirma *f*;
~ highway Schnellverkehrsstraße *f*;
2. Eilbote *m*; *a. ~ train* Schnellzug
m; *by ~* = **3.** *adv.* durch Eilboten;
als Eilgut; **4.** äußern, ausdrücken;
auspressen; **~ion** [~eʃən] Ausdruck
m; **~ive** ⌐ [~esiv] ausdrückend (*of*
acc.); ausdrucksvoll; **~ly** [~sli] ausdrücklich, eigens; **~way** *Am.* Autobahn *f*. [eignen.]

expropriate [eks'prouprieit] ent-)

expuls|ion [iks'pʌlʃən] Vertreibung
f; **~ve** [~lsiv] (aus)treibend.

expunge [eks'pʌndʒ] streichen.

expurgate ['ekspə:geit] säubern.

exquisite ☐ ['ekskwizit] auserlesen,
vorzüglich; fein; heftig, scharf.

extant [eks'tænt] (noch) vorhanden.

extempor|aneous ⌐ [ekstempə-
'reinjəs], **~ary** [iks'tempərəri], *a.*
[eks'tempəri] aus dem Stegreif
(vorgetragen).

extend [iks'tend] *v/t.* ausdehnen;
ausstrecken; erweitern; verlängern;
Gunst etc. erweisen; ✕ (aus)schwär-
men lassen; *v/i.* sich erstrecken.

extensi|on [iks'tenʃən] Ausdehnung
f; Erweiterung *f*; Verlängerung *f*;
Aus-, Anbau *m*; *teleph.* Nebenan-
schluß *m*; *~ cord* ⚡ Verlängerungs-
schnur *f*; *University* ♎ Volkshochschule *f*; **~ve** ☐ [~nsiv] ausgedehnt,
umfassend.

extent [iks'tent] Ausdehnung *f*, Weite *f*, Größe *f*, Umfang *m*; Grad *m*; to the ~ of bis zum Betrage von; to some ~ einigermaßen.

extenuate [eks'tenjueit] abschwächen, mildern, beschönigen.

exterior [eks'tiəriə] 1. äußerlich; Außen..; außerhalb; 2. Äußere(s) *n*; *Film* Außenaufnahme *f*.

exterminate [eks'tə:mineit] ausrotten, vertilgen.

external [eks'tə:nl] 1. □ äußere(r, -s), äußerlich; Außen...; 2. ~s *pl*. Äußere(s) *n*; *fig.* Äußerlichkeiten *f*/*pl*.

extinct [iks'tiŋkt] erloschen; ausgestorben.

extinguish [iks'tiŋgwiʃ] (aus)löschen; vernichten.

extirpate ['ekstə:peit] ausrotten; ⚕ *Organ etc.* entfernen.

extol [iks'tɔl] erheben, preisen.

extort [iks'tɔ:t] erpressen; abnötigen (*from dat.*); ~ion [~ʃən] Erpressung *f*.

extra ['ekstrə] 1. Extra...; außer...; Neben...; Sonder...; ~ *pay* Zulage *f*; 2. *adv.* besonders; außerdem; 3. *et.* Zusätzliches; Zuschlag *m*; Extrablatt *n*; *thea.*, *Film*: Statist(in).

extract 1. ['ekstrækt] Auszug *m*; 2. [iks'trækt] (heraus)ziehen; herauslocken; ab~, herleiten; ~ion [~kʃən] (Heraus)Ziehen *n*; Herkunft *f*.

extradit|e ['ekstrədait] *Verbrecher* ausliefern (lassen); ~ion [ekstrə-'diʃən] Auslieferung *f*.

extraordinary □ [iks'trɔ:dnri]

außerordentlich; Extra...; ungewöhnlich; *envoy* ~ außerordentlicher Gesandter.

extra student ['ekstrə'stju:dənt] Gasthörer(in).

extravagan|ce [iks'trævigəns] Übertriebenheit *f*; Überspanntheit *f*; Verschwendung *f*, Extravaganz *f*; ~t □ [~nt] übertrieben, überspannt; verschwenderisch; extravagant.

extrem|e [iks'tri:m] 1. □ äußerst, größt, höchst; sehr streng; außergewöhnlich; 2. Äußerste(s) *n*; Extrem *n*; höchster Grad; ~ity [~remiti] Äußerste(s) *n*; höchste Not; äußerste Maßnahme; *extremities pl.* Gliedmaßen *pl.*

extricate ['ekstrikeit] herauswinden, herausziehen; befreien; ⚕ entwickeln.

extrude [eks'tru:d] ausstoßen.

exuberan|ce [ig'zju:bərəns] Überfluß *m*; Überschwenglichkeit *f*; ~t □ [~nt] reichlich; üppig; überschwenglich.

exult [ig'zʌlt] frohlocken.

eye [ai] 1. Auge *n*; Blick *m*; Öhr *n*; Öse *f*; up to the ~s in work bis über die Ohren in Arbeit; with an ~ to mit Rücksicht auf (*acc.*); mit der Absicht zu; 2. ansehen; mustern; ~ball ['aibɔ:l] Augapfel *m*; ~brow Augenbraue *f*; ~d ~äugig; ~glass Augenglas *n*; (*a pair of*) ~es *pl.* (ein) Kneifer; (e-e) Brille; ~lash Augenwimper *f*; ~lid Augenlid *n*; ~sight Augen(licht *n*) *pl.*; Sehkraft *f*; ~witness Augenzeug|e *m*, -in *f*.

fable ['feibl] Fabel *f*; Mythen *pl.*, Legenden *pl.*; Lüge *f*.

fabric ['fæbrik] Bau *m*, Gebäude *n*; Struktur *f*; Gewebe *n*, Stoff *m*; ~ate [~keit] fabrizieren (*mst fig.* = erdichten, fälschen).

fabulous ⊐ ['fæbjuləs] legendär; sagen-, fabelhaft.

façade ⚕ [fə'sɑ:d] Fassade *f*.

face [feis] 1. Gesicht *n*; Anblick *m*; *fig.* Stirn *f*, Unverschämtheit *f*; (Ober)Fläche *f*; Vorderseite *f*; Zifferblatt *n*; ~ to ~ with Auge in Auge mit; *save one's* ~ das Gesicht wahren; *on the* ~ of it auf den ersten Blick; *set one's* ~ *against* sich gegen *et.* stemmen; 2. *v/t.* ansehen; gegenüberstehen (*dat.*); (hinaus)gehen auf (*acc.*); die Stirn bieten (*dat.*); einfassen; ⚕ bekleiden; *v/i.* ~ *about* sich umdrehen; ~cloth ['feisklɔθ] Waschlappen *m*.

facetious □ [fə'si:ʃəs] witzig.

facil|e ['fæsail] leicht; gewandt; ~itate [fə'siliteit] erleichtern; ~ity [~ti] Leichtigkeit *f*; Gewandtheit *f*; *mst facilities pl.* Erleichterung(en *pl.*) *f*, Möglichkeit(en *pl.*) *f*, Gelegenheit(en *pl.*) *f*.

facing ['feisiŋ] ⊕ Verkleidung *f*; ~s *pl. Schneiderei:* Besatz *m*.

fact [fækt] Tatsache *f*; Wirklichkeit *f*; Wahrheit *f*; Tat *f*. [keit *f*.]

faction ['fækʃən] Partei *f*; Uneinig-]

factitious ⊐ [fæk'tiʃəs] künstlich.

factor ['fæktə] *fig.* Umstand *m*, Moment *n*, Faktor *m*; Agent *m*; Verwalter *m*; ~y [~əri] Fabrik *f*.

faculty ['fækəlti] Fähigkeit *f*; Kraft *f*; *fig.* Gabe *f*; *univ.* Fakultät *f*.

fad F *fig.* [fæd] Steckenpferd *n*.

fade [feid] (ver)welken (lassen), verblassen; schwinden; *Radio:* ~ *in* einblenden.

fag F [fæg] *v/i.* sich placken; *v/t.* erschöpfen, mürbe machen.

fail [feil] **1.** *v/i.* versagen, mißlingen, fehlschlagen; versäumen; versiegen; nachlassen; Bankrott machen; durchfallen (*Kandidat*); he ~ed to do es mißlang ihm zu tun; he can-not ~ to er muß (einfach); *v/t.* im Stich lassen, verlassen; versäumen; **2.** *without* ~ unfehlbar; ~**ing** ['feiliŋ] Fehler *m*, Schwäche *f*; ~**ure** [~ljə] Fehlen *n*; Ausbleiben *n*; Fehlschlag *m*; Mißerfolg *m*; Verfall *m*; Ver-säumnis *n*; Bankrott *m*; Versager *m* (*P.*).

faint [feint] **1.** □ schwach, matt; **2.** schwach werden; in Ohnmacht fallen (*with* vor); **3.** Ohnmacht *f*; ~**-hearted** □ ['feint'hɑːtid] ver-zagt.

fair¹ [fɛə] **1.** *adj.* gerecht, ehrlich, anständig, fair; ordentlich; schön (*Wetter*), günstig (*Wind*); reich-lich; blond; hellhäutig; freundlich; sauber, in Reinschrift; schön (*Frau*); **2.** *adv.* gerecht, ehrlich, anständig, fair; in Reinschrift; di-rekt.

fair² [~] (Jahr)Markt *m*, Messe *f*.

fair|ly ['fɛəli] ziemlich; völlig; ~**ness** ['fɛənis] Schönheit *f*; Blond-heit *f*; Gerechtigkeit *f*; Redlichkeit *f*; Billigkeit *f*; ~**way** ⏚ Fahrwasser *n*.

fairy ['fɛəri] Fee *f*; Zauberin *f*; Elf(e *f*) *m*; ⏚land Feen-, Märchen-land *n*; ~**tale** Märchen *n*.

faith [feiθ] Glaube *m*; Vertrauen *n*; Treue *f*; ~**ful** □ ['feiθful] treu; ehrlich; yours ~ly Ihr ergebener; ~**less** □ ['feiθlis] treulos; ungläu-big.

fake *sl.* [feik] **1.** Schwindel *m*; Fälschung *f*; Schwindler *m*; **2.** *a.* ~ up fälschen.

falcon ['fɔːlkən] Falke *m*.

fall [fɔːl] **1.** Fall(en *n*) *m*; Sturz *m*; Verfall *m*; Einsturz *m*; *Am.* Herbst *m*; Sinken *n der Preise etc.*; Fällen *n*; Wasserfall *m* (*mst pl.*); Sen-kung *f*, Abhang *m*; **2.** *irr.* fallen; ab-, einfallen; sinken; sich legen (*Wind*); in e-n Zustand verfallen; ~ back zurückweichen; ~ back (up)on zurückkommen auf; ~ ill *od.* sick krank werden; ~ in love with sich verlieben in (*acc.*); ~ out sich entzweien; sich zutragen; ~ short knapp werden (of an *dat.*); ~ short of zurückbleiben hinter (*dat.*); ~ to sich machen an (*acc.*).

fallacious □ [fə'leiʃəs] trüge-risch.

fallacy ['fæləsi] Täuschung *f*.

fallen ['fɔːlən] *p.p. von* fall 2.

fall guy *Am. sl.* ['fɔːl'gai] *der* Lackierte, *der* Dumme.

fallible □ ['fæləbl] fehlbar.

falling ['fɔːliŋ] Fallen *n*; ~ **sickness**

Fallsucht *f*; ~ **star** Sternschnuppe *f*.

fallow ['fælou] *zo.* falb; ⚲ brach (-liegend).

false □ [fɔːls] falsch; ~**hood** ['fɔːlshud], ~**ness** [~snis] Falsch-heit *f*.

falsi|fication ['fɔːlsifi'keiʃən] (Ver-)Fälschung *f*; ~**fy** ['fɔːlsifai] (ver-)fälschen; ~**ty** [~iti] Falschheit *f*.

falter ['fɔːltə] schwanken; stocken (*Stimme*); stammeln; *fig.* zaudern.

fame [feim] Ruf *m*, Ruhm *m*; ~**d** [~md] berühmt (for wegen).

familiar [fə'miljə] **1.** □ vertraut; gewohnt; familiär; **2.** Vertraute(r *m*) *f*; ~**ity** [fəmili'æriti] Vertraut-heit *f*; (plumpe) Vertraulichkeit; ~**ize** [fə'miljəraiz] vertraut machen.

family ['fæmili] **1.** Familie *f*; **2.** Fa-milien..., Haus...; in the ~ way in anderen Umständen; ~ allowance Kinderzulage *f*; ~ tree Stamm-baum *m*.

fami|ne ['fæmin] Hungersnot *f*; Mangel *m* (of an *dat.*); ~**sh** [~iʃ] (aus-, ver)hungern.

famous □ ['feiməs] berühmt.

fan¹ [fæn] **1.** Fächer *m*; Ventilator *m*; **2.** (an)fächeln; an-, *fig.* ent-fachen.

fan² F [~] *Sport- etc.* Fanatiker *m*, Liebhaber *m*; *Radio:* Bastler *m*; ...narr *m*, ...fex *m*.

fanatic [fə'nætik] **1.** *a.* ~**al** □ [~kəl] fanatisch; **2.** Fanatiker(in).

fanciful □ ['fænsiful] phantastisch.

fancy ['fænsi] **1.** Phantasie *f*; Ein-bildung(skraft) *f*; Schrulle *f*; Vor-liebe *f*; Liebhaberei *f*; **2.** Phanta-sie...; Liebhaber...; Luxus...; Mo-de...; ~ *ball* Maskenball *m*; ~ *goods pl.* Modewaren *f/pl.*; **3.** sich ein-bilden; Gefallen finden an (*dat.*); just ~! denken Sie nur!; ~**work** feine Handarbeit, Stickerei *f*.

fang [fæŋ] Fangzahn *m*; Giftzahn *m*.

fantas|tic [fæn'tæstik] (~*ally*) phan-tastisch; ~**y** ['fæntəsi] Phantasie *f*.

far [fɑː] **1.** *adj.* fern, entfernt; weit; **2.** *adv.* fern; weit; (sehr) viel; as ~ as bis; in so ~ as insofern als; ~**away** ['fɑːrəwei] weit entfernt.

fare [fɛə] **1.** Fahrgeld *n*; Fahrgast *m*; Verpflegung *f*, Kost *f*; **2.** *gut* leben; he ~d well es (er)ging ihm gut; ~**well** ['fɛə'wel] **1.** lebe(n Sie) wohl!; **2.** Abschied *m*, Lebewohl *n*.

far|-fetched *fig.* ['fɑː'fetʃt] weit her-geholt, gesucht; ~ **gone** F fertig (*todkrank, betrunken etc.*).

farm [fɑːm] **1.** Bauernhof *m*, -gut *n*, Gehöft *n*, Farm *f*; Züchterei *f*; chicken ~ Hühnerfarm *f*; **2.** (ver-)pachten; *Land* bewirtschaften; ~**er** ['fɑːmə] Landwirt *m*; Pächter *m*; ~**hand** Landarbeiter(in); ~**house** Bauern-, Gutshaus *n*; ~**ing** ['fɑːmiŋ]

1. Acker...; landwirtschaftlich; 2. Landwirtschaft *f*; ~stead Gehöft *n*; ~yard Wirtschaftshof *m e-s Bauernguts*.

far-off ['fɑːɔːf] entfernt, fern; ~sighted *fig.* weitblickend.

farthe|r ['fɑːðə] *comp. von far*; ~st ['fɑːðist] *sup. von far*.

fascinat|e ['fæsineit] bezaubern; ~ion [fæsi'neiʃən] Zauber *m*, Reiz *m*.

fashion ['fæʃən] Mode *f*; Art *f*; feine Lebensart; Form *f*; Schnitt *m*; *in (out of)* ~ (un)modern; 2. gestalten; *Kleid* machen; ~able □ ['fæʃnəbl] modern, elegant.

fast[1] [fɑːst] schnell; fest; treu; waschecht; flott; *be* ~ vorgehen (*Uhr*).

fast[2] [~] 1. Fasten *n*; 2. fasten.

fasten ['fɑːsn] *v/t.* befestigen; anheften; fest (zu)machen; zubinden; *Augen etc.* heften (*on, upon auf acc.*); *v/i.* schließen (*Tür*); ~ *upon fig.* sich klammern an (*acc.*); ~er [~nə] Verschluß *m*; Klammer *f*.

fastidious ᵒ [fæs'tidiəs] anspruchsvoll, heikel, wählerisch, verwöhnt.

fat [fæt] 1. □ fett; dick; fettig; 2. Fett *n*; 3. fett machen *od.* werden; mästen.

fatal □ ['feitl] verhängnisvoll (*to* für); Schicksals...; tödlich; ~ity [fə'tæliti] Verhängnis *n*; Unglücks-, Todesfall *m*; Todesopfer *n*.

fate [feit] Schicksal *n*; Verhängnis *n*.

father ['fɑːðə] 1. Vater *m*; 2. der Urheber sein von; ~hood [~əhud] Vaterschaft *f*; ~-in-law [~ərinlɔː] Schwiegervater *m*; ~less [~əlis] vaterlos; ~ly [~li] väterlich.

fathom ['fæðəm] 1. Klafter *f* (*Maß*); ♣ Faden *m*; 2. ♣ loten; *fig.* ergründen; ~less [~mlis] unergründlich.

fatigue [fə'tiːg] 1. Ermüdung *f*; Strapaze *f*; 2. ermüden; strapazieren.

fat|ness ['fætnis] Fettigkeit *f*; Fettheit *f*; ~ten ['fætn] fett machen *od.* werden; mästen; *Boden* düngen.

fatuous □ ['fætjuəs] albern.

faucet *Am.* ['fɔːsit] (Zapf)Hahn *m*.

fault [fɔːlt] Fehler *m*; Defekt *m*; Schuld *f*; *find* ~ *with et.* auszusetzen haben an (*dat.*); *be at* ~ auf falscher Fährte sein; ~-finder ['fɔːltfaində] Nörgler *m*; ~less □ [~tlis] fehlerfrei, tadellos; ~y □ [~ti] mangelhaft.

favo(u)r ['feivə] 1. Gunst(bezeigung) *f*; Gefallen *m*; Begünstigung *f*; *in* ~ *of* zugunsten von *od. gen.*; *do s.o. a* ~ j-m e-n Gefallen tun; 2. begünstigen; beehren; ~able □ [~rəbl] günstig; ~ite [~rit] Günstling *m*; Liebling *m*; *Sport:* Favorit *m*; *attr.* Lieblings...

fawn[1] [fɔːn] 1. *zo.* (Dam)Kitz *n*; Rehbraun *n*; 2. (Kitze) setzen.

fawn[2] [~] schwänzeln (*Hund*); kriechen (*upon vor*).

faze *bsd. Am.* F [feiz] durcheinanderbringen.

fear [fiə] 1. Furcht *f* (*of vor dat.*); Befürchtung *f*; Angst *f*; 2. (be-)fürchten; sich fürchten vor (*dat.*); ~ful □ [~fiəful] furchtsam; furchtbar; ~less □ ['fiəlis] furchtlos.

feasible ['fiːzəbl] ausführbar.

feast [fiːst] 1. Fest *n*; Feiertag *m*; Festmahl *n*, Schmaus *m*; 2. *v/t.* festlich bewirten; *v/i.* sich ergötzen; schmausen. [stück *n.*]

feat [fiːt] (Helden)Tat *f*; Kunst-∫

feather ['feðə] 1. Feder *f*; *a.* ~s Gefieder *n*; *show the white* ~ F sich feige zeigen; *in high* ~ in gehobener Stimmung; 2. mit Federn schmücken; ~bed *n. Feder*-Unterbett *n*; 2. verwöhnen; ~brained, ~headed unbesonnen; albern; ~ed be-, gefiedert; ~y [~əri] feder(art)ig.

feature ['fiːtʃə] 1. (Gesichts-, Grund-, Haupt-, Charakter)Zug *m*; (charakteristisches) Merkmal; *Radio:* Feature *n*; *Am.* Bericht *m*, Artikel *m*; ~s *pl.* Gesicht *n*; Charakter *m*; 2. kennzeichnen; sich auszeichnen durch; groß aufziehen; *Film:* in der Hauptrolle zeigen; ~ film Haupt-, Spielfilm *m*.

February ['februəri] Februar *m*.

fecund ['fiːkənd] fruchtbar.

fed [fed] *pret. u. p.p. von* feed 2.

federa|l ['fedərəl] Bundes...; ~lize [~laiz] (sich) verbünden; ~tion [fedə'reiʃən] Staatenbund *m*; Vereinigung *f*; Verband *m*.

fee [fiː] 1. Gebühr *f*; Honorar *n*; Trinkgeld *n*; 2. bezahlen.

feeble □ ['fiːbl] schwach.

feed [fiːd] 1. Futter *n*; Nahrung *f*; Fütterung *f*; ⊕ Zuführung *f*, Speisung *f*; 2. [*irr.*] *v/t.* füttern; speisen (*a.* ⊕), nähren; weiden; *Material etc.* zuführen; *be fed up with et. od. j-n* satt haben; *well fed* wohlgenährt; *v/i.* (fr)essen; sich nähren; ~er ['fiːdə] Fütterer *m*; *Am.* Viehmäster *m*; Esser(in); ~er road Zubringer(straße *f*) *m*; ~ing-bottle ['fiːdiŋbɔtl] Saugflasche *f*.

feel [fiːl] 1. [*irr.*] (sich) fühlen; befühlen; empfinden; sich anfühlen; *I* ~ *like doing* ich möchte am liebsten tun; 2. Gefühl *n*; Empfindung *f*; ~er ['fiːlə] Fühler *m*; ~ing ['fiːliŋ] 1. ᵒ (mit)fühlend; gefühlvoll; 2. Gefühl *n*; Meinung *f*.

feet [fiːt] *pl. von* foot 1.

feign [fein] heucheln; vorgeben.

feint [feint] Verstellung *f*; Finte *f*.

felicit|ate [fi'lisiteit] beglückwünschen; ~ous □ [~təs] glücklich; ~y [~ti] Glück(seligkeit *f*) *n*.

fell [fel] 1. *pret. von* fall 2; 2. niederschlagen; fällen.

felloe ['felou] (Rad)Felge f.

fellow ['felou] Gefährt|e m, -in f, Kamerad(in); Gleiche(r, -s); Gegenstück n; univ. Fellow m, Mitglied n e-s College; Bursche m, Mensch m; attr. Mit...; old ~ F alter Junge; the ~ of a glove der andere Handschuh; **~country-man** Landsmann m; **~ship** [~ouʃip] Gemeinschaft f; Kameradschaft f; Mitgliedschaft f.

felly ['feli] (Rad)Felge f.

felon ['felən] Verbrecher m; **~y** [~ni] Kapitalverbrechen n.

felt¹ [felt] pret. u. p.p. von feel 1.

felt² [~] 1. Filz m; 2. (be)filzen.

female ['fi:meil] 1. weiblich; 2. Weib n; zo. Weibchen n.

feminine ['feminin] weiblich; weibisch.

fen [fen] Fenn n, Moor n; Marsch f.

fence [fens] 1. Zaun m; Fechtkunst f; sl. Hehler(nest n) m; sit on the ~ abwarten; 2. v/t. a. ~ in ein-, umzäunen; schützen; v/i. fechten; sl. hehlen.

fencing ['fensiŋ] Einfriedung f; Fechten n; attr. Fecht...

fend [fend]: ~ off abwehren; **~er** ['fendə] Schutzvorrichtung f; Schutzblech n; Kamingitter n, -vorsetzer m; Stoßfänger m.

fennel ♀ ['fenl] Fenchel m.

ferment 1. ['fə:ment] Ferment n; Gärung f; 2. [fə(:)'ment] gären (lassen); **~ation** [fə:men'teiʃən] Gärung f.

fern [fə:n] Farn(kraut n) m.

feroci|ous [fə'rouʃəs] wild; grausam; **~ty** [fə'rɔsiti] Wildheit f.

ferret ['ferit] 1. zo. Frettchen n; fig. Spürhund m; 2. (umher)stöbern; ~ out aufstöbern.

ferry ['feri] 1. Fähre f; 2. übersetzen; **~boat** Fährboot n, Fähre f; **~man** Fährmann m.

fertil|e ['fə:tail] fruchtbar; reich (of, in an dat.); **~ity** [fə:'tiliti] Fruchtbarkeit f (a. fig.); **~ize** ['fə:tilaiz] fruchtbar machen; befruchten; düngen; **~izer** [~zə] Düngemittel n.

ferven|cy ['fə:vənsi] Glut f; Inbrunst f; **~t** [~nt] heiß; inbrünstig, glühend; leidenschaftlich.

fervo(u)r ['fə:və] Glut f; Inbrunst f.

festal ['festl] festlich.

fester ['festə] eitern; verfaulen.

festiv|al ['festəvl] Fest n; Feier f; Festspiele npl.; **~e** [ ] [~tiv] festlich; **~ity** [fes'tiviti] Festlichkeit f.

festoon [fes'tu:n] Girlande f.

fetch [fetʃ] holen; Preis erzielen; Seufzer ausstoßen; **~ing** [ ] F ['fetʃiŋ] reizend.

fetid ['fetid] stinkend.

fetter ['fetə] 1. Fessel f; 2. fesseln.

feud [fju:d] Fehde f; Leh(e)n n;

~al [ ] ['fju:dl] lehnbar; Lehns...; **~alism** [~dəlizəm] Lehnswesen n.

fever ['fi:və] Fieber n; **~ish** [ ] [~əriʃ] fieb(e)rig; fig. fieberhaft.

few [fju:] wenige; a ~ ein paar; quite a ~, a good ~ e-e ganze Menge.

fiancé [fi'ã:nsei] Verlobte(r) m; **~e** [~] Verlobte f.

fiat ['faiæt] Befehl m; ~ money Am. Papiergeld n (ohne Deckung).

fib F [fib] 1. Flunkerei f, Schwindelei f; 2. schwindeln, flunkern.

fib|re, Am. **~er** ['faibə] Faser f; Charakter m; **~rous** [ ] ['faibrəs] faserig.

fickle ['fikl] wankelmütig; unbeständig; **~ness** [~lnis] Wankelmut m.

fiction ['fikʃən] Erfindung f; Roman-, Unterhaltungsliteratur f; **~al** [ ] [~nl] erdichtet; Roman...

fictitious [ ] [fik'tiʃəs] erfunden.

fiddle F ['fidl] 1. Geige f, Fiedel f; 2. fiedeln; tändeln; **~r** [~lə] Geiger (-in) **~stick** Fiedelbogen m; **~sl** fig. dummes Zeug!

fidelity [fi'deliti] Treue f; Genauigkeit f.

fidget F ['fidʒit] 1. nervöse Unruhe; 2. nervös machen od. sein; **~y** [~ti] kribbelig. }

fie [fai] pfui! [kribbelig.}

field [fi:ld] Feld n; (Spiel)Platz m; Arbeitsfeld n; Gebiet n; Bereich m; hold the ~ das Feld behaupten; **~day** ['fi:lddei] ✕ Felddienstübung f; Parade f; fig. großer Tag; Am. (Schul)Sportfest n; Am. Exkursionstag m; ~ events pl. Sport: Sprung- u. Wurfwettkämpfe m/pl.; **~glass(es** pl.) Feldstecher m; **~-officer** Stabsoffizier m; **~sports** pl. Jagen n u. Fischen n.

fiend [fi:nd] böser Feind, Teufel m; **~ish** [ ] ['fi:ndiʃ] teuflisch, boshaft.

fierce [ ] [fiəs] wild; grimmig; **~ness** ['fiəsnis] Wildheit f; Grimm m.

fiery [ ] ['faiəri] feurig; hitzig.

fif|teen ['fif'ti:n] fünfzehn; **~teenth** [~nθ] fünfzehnte(r, -s); **~th** [fifθ] 1. fünfte(r, -s); 2. Fünftel n; **~thly** ['fifθli] fünftens; **~tieth** ['fiftiiθ] fünfzigste(r, -s); **~ty** [~ti] fünfzig; **~ty-fifty** F halb und halb.

fig [fig] Feige f; F Zustand m.

fight [fait] 1. Kampf m; Kampflust f; show ~ sich zur Wehr setzen; 2. [irr.] v/t. bekämpfen; erkämpfen; v/i. kämpfen, sich schlagen; **~er** ['faitə] Kämpfer m, Streiter m; ✕ Jagdflugzeug n; **~ing** ['faitiŋ] Kampf m.

figurative [ ] ['figjurətiv] bildlich.

figure ['figə] 1. Figur f; Gestalt f; Ziffer f; Preis m; be good at ~s gut im Rechnen sein; 2. v/t. abbilden; darstellen; sich et. vorstellen; beziffern; ~ up od. out berechnen; v/i. erscheinen; e-e Rolle spielen (as)

als); ~ on *Am. et.* überdenken;
~**-skating** [~əskeitiŋ] Eiskunst-
lauf *m.*

filament ['filəmənt] Faden *m*, Faser
f; ⚙ Staubfaden *m*; ⚡ Glüh-, Heiz-
faden *m.*

filbert ⚙ ['filbə(ː)t] Haselnuß *f.*

filch [filtʃ] stibitzen (*from dat.*).

file[1] [fail] 1. Akte *f*, Ordner *m*;
Ablage *f*; Reihe *f*; ⚔ Rotte *f*; on
~ bei den Akten; 2. *v/t.* aufreihen;
Briefe etc. einordnen; ablegen; einreichen; *v/i.* hinter-ea. marschieren.

file[2] [~] 1. Feile *f*; 2. feilen.

filial □ ['filjəl] kindlich, Kindes...

filibuster ['filibʌstə] 1. *Am.* Ob-
struktion(spolitiker *m*) *f*; 2. *Am.*
Obstruktion treiben.

fill [fil] 1. (sich) füllen; an-, aus-, erfüllen; *Am. Auftrag* ausführen;
~ *in Formular* ausfüllen; 2. Fülle *f*,
Genüge *f*; Füllung *f.*

fillet ['filit] Haarband *n*; Lenden-
braten *m*; Roulade *f*; *bsd.* △ Band *n.*

filling ['filiŋ] Füllung *f*; ~ **station**
Am. Tankstelle *f.*

fillip ['filip] Nasenstüber *m.*

filly ['fili] (Stuten)Füllen *n*; *fig.*
wilde Hummel.

film [film] 1. Häutchen *n*; Mem-
bran(e) *f*; Film *m*; Trübung *f des
Auges*; Nebelschleier *m*; *take od.*
shoot a ~ e-n Film drehen; 2. (sich)
verschleiern; (ver)filmen.

filter ['filtə] 1. Filter *m*; 2. filtern.

filth [filθ] Schmutz *m*; ~**y** □ ['filθi]
schmutzig; *fig.* unflätig.

filtrate ['filtreit] filtrieren.

fin [fin] Flosse *f* (*a. sl.* = Hand).

final ['fainl] 1. □ letzte(r, -s);
endlich; schließlich; End...; endgültig; 2. Schlußprüfung *f*; *Sport:*
Schlußrunde *f*, Endspiel *n.*

financ|e [fai'næns] 1. Finanzwesen
n; ~**s** *pl.* Finanzen *pl.*; 2. *v/t.* finan-
zieren; *v/i.* Geldgeschäfte machen;
~**ial** □ [~nʃəl] finanziell; ~**ier**
[~nsiə] Finanzmann *m*; Geldgeber
m.

finch *orn.* [fintʃ] Fink *m.*

find [faind] 1. [*irr.*] finden; (an-)
treffen; auf-, herausfinden; *schuldig
etc.* befinden; beschaffen; versorgen; *all found* freie Station; 2. Fund
m; ~**ings** ['faindiŋz] *pl.* Befund *m*;
Urteil *n.*

fine[1] □ [fain] 1. schön; fein; ver-
feinert; rein; spitz, dünn, scharf;
geziert; vornehm; 2. *adv.* gut, be-
stens.

fine[2] [~] 1. Geldstrafe *f*; 2. zu e-r
Geldstrafe verurteilen.

fineness ['fainnis] Fein-, Zart-,
Schönheit *f*, Eleganz *f*; Genauigkeit *f.*

finery ['fainəri] Glanz *m*; Putz *m*;
Staat *m.*

finger ['fiŋgə] 1. Finger *m*; 2. be-
tasten, (herum)fingern an (*dat.*);

~**language** Zeichensprache *f*;
~**nail** Fingernagel *m*; ~**print**
Fingerabdruck *m.*

fini|cal □ ['finikəl], ~**cking** [~kiŋ],
~**kin** [~in] geziert; wählerisch.

finish ['finiʃ] 1. *v/t.* beenden, vollenden; fertigstellen; abschließen; vervollkommnen; erledigen; *v/i.* enden; 2. Vollendung *f*, letzter
Schliff (*a. fig.*); Schluß *m.*

finite □ ['fainait] endlich, begrenzt.

fink *Am. sl.* [fiŋk] Streikbrecher *m.*

Finn [fin] Finn|e *m*, -in *f*; ~**ish**
['finiʃ] finnisch.

fir [fəː] (Weiß)Tanne *f*; Fichte *f*;
~**cone** ['fəːkoun] Tannenzapfen *m.*

fire ['faiə] 1. Feuer *n*; on ~ in Brand,
in Flammen; 2. *v/t.* an-, entzünden;
fig. anfeuern; abfeuern; *Ziegel etc.*
brennen; F 'rausschmeißen (*entlassen*); heizen; *v/i.* Feuer fangen
(*a. fig.*); feuern; ~**alarm** ['faiər-
əlɑːm] Feuermelder *m*; ~**brigade**
Feuerwehr *f*; ~**bug** *Am.* F Brandstifter *m*; ~**cracker** Frosch *m*
(*Feuerwerkskörper*); ~ **department**
Am. Feuerwehr *f*; ~**engine** ['faiər-
endʒin] (Feuer)Spritze *f*; ~**escape**
[~riskeip] Rettungsgerät *n*; Not-
treppe *f*; ~**extinguisher** [~rik-
stiŋwiʃə] Feuerlöscher *m*; ~**man**
Feuerwehrmann *m*; Heizer *m*;
~**place** Herd *m*; Kamin *m*; ~**plug**
Hydrant *m*; ~**proof** feuerfest;
~**screen** Ofenschirm *m*; ~**side**
Herd *m*; Kamin *m*; ~**station**
Feuerwache *f*; ~**wood** Brennholz *n*;
~**works** *pl.* Feuerwerk *n.*

firing ['faiəriŋ] Heizung *f*; Feuerung *f.*

firm [fəːm] 1. □ fest; derb; standhaft; 2. Firma *f*; ~**ness** ['fəːmnis]
Festigkeit *f.*

first [fəːst] 1. *adj.* erste(r, -s); be-
ste(r, -s); 2. *adv.* erstens; zuerst;
~ *of all* an erster Stelle; zu aller-
erst; 3. Erste(r, -s); ~ *of exchange*
† Primawechsel *m*; *at* ~ zuerst,
anfangs; *from the* ~ von Anfang
an; ~**born** ['fəːstboːn] erstgeboren;
~ **class** 1. Klasse *f* (*e-s Verkehrsmit-
tels*); ~**class** erstklassig; ~**ly** [~tli]
erstlich; erstens; ~ **name** Vorname *m*; Beiname *m*; ~ **papers** *Am.*
vorläufige Einbürgerungspapiere;
~**rate** ersten Ranges; erstklassig.

firth [fəːθ] Förde *f*; (Flut)Mün-
dung *f.*

fish [fiʃ] 1. Fisch(e *pl.*) *m*; F Kerl *m*;
2. fischen, angeln; haschen; ~**bone**
['fiʃboun] Gräte *f.*

fisher ['fiʃə], ~**man** Fischer *m*;
~**y** [~əri] Fischerei *f.*

fishing ['fiʃiŋ] Fischen *n*; ~**line**
Angelschnur *f*; ~**tackle** Angel-
gerät *n*. [händler *m.*]

fishmonger ['fiʃmʌŋgə] Fisch-)

fiss|ion ⚛ ['fiʃən] Spaltung *f*; ~**ure**
['fiʃə] Spalt *m*; Riß *m.*

fist [fist] Faust *f*; F Klaue *f*; **~icuffs** ['fistikʌfs] *pl.* Faustschläge *m/pl.*

fit¹ [fit] **1.** □ geeignet, passend; tauglich; *Sport:* in (guter) Form; bereit; **2.** *v/t.* passen für *od. dat.*; anpassen, passend machen; befähigen; geeignet machen (*for*, to für, zu); *a. ~ on* anprobieren; ausstatten; *~ out* ausrüsten; *~ up* einrichten; montieren; *v/i.* passen; sich schikken; sitzen (*Kleid*); **3.** Sitz *m* (*Kleid*).

fit² [~] Anfall *m*; ⚓ Ausbruch *m*; Anwandlung *f*; *by ~s and starts* ruckweise; *give s.o. a ~* j-n hochbringen; j-m e-n Schock versetzen.

fit|ful □ ['fitful] ruckartig; *fig.* unstet; **~ness** ['fitnis] Schicklichkeit *f*; Tauglichkeit *f*; **~ter** ['fitə] Monteur *m*; Installateur *m*; **~ting** ['fitiŋ] **1.** passend; **2.** Montage *f*; Anprobe *f*; **~s** *pl.* Einrichtung *f*; Armaturen *f/pl.*

five [faiv] **1.** fünf; **2.** Fünf *f*.

fix [fiks] **1.** *v/t.* befestigen, anheften; fixieren; *Augen etc.* heften, richten; fesseln; aufstellen; bestimmen, festsetzen; *bsd. Am.* richten, *Bett etc.* machen; *~ o.s.* sich niederlassen; *~ up* in Ordnung bringen, arrangieren; *v/i.* fest werden; *~ on* sich entschließen für; **2.** F Klemme *f*; *Am.* Zustand *m*; **~ed** fest; bestimmt; starr; **~ing** ['fiksiŋ] Befestigen *n*; Instandsetzen *n*; Fixieren *n*; Aufstellen *n*, Montieren *n*; Besatz *m*, Versteifung *f*; *Am.* **~s** *pl.* Zubehör *n*, Extraausrüstung *f*; **~ture** [~stʃə] fest angebrachtes Zubehörteil, feste Anlage; Inventarstück *n*; *lighting ~* Beleuchtungskörper *m*.

fizz [fiz] **1.** zischen, sprudeln; **2.** Zischen *n*; F Schampus *m* (*Sekt*).

flabbergast F ['flæbəgɑ:st] verblüffen; *be ~ed* baff *od.* platt sein.

flabby □ ['flæbi] schlaff, schlapp.

flag [flæg] **1.** Flagge *f*; Fahne *f*; Fliese *f*; Schwertlilie *f*; **2.** beflaggen; durch Flaggen signalisieren; mit Fliesen belegen; ermatten; mutlos werden; **~day** ['flægdei] Opfertag *m*; *Flag Day Am.* Tag *m* des Sternenbanners (*14. Juni*).

flagitious [flə'dʒiʃəs] schändlich.

flagrant [['fleigrənt] abscheulich; berüchtigt, offenkundig.

flag|staff ['flægstɑ:f] Fahnenstange *f*; **~stone** Fliese *f*.

flair [flɛə] Spürsinn *m*, feine Nase.

flake [fleik] **1.** Flocke *f*; Schicht *f*; **2.** (sich) flocken; abblättern.

flame [fleim] **1.** Flamme *f*, Feuer *n*; *fig.* Hitze *f*; **2.** flammen, lodern.

flank [flæŋk] **1.** Flanke *f*; Weiche *f* der *Tiere*; **2.** flankieren.

flannel ['flænl] Flanell *m*; Waschlappen *m*; **~s** *pl.* Flanellhose *f*.

flap [flæp] **1.** (Ohr)Läppchen *n*;

Rockschoß *m*; *Hut-*Krempe *f*; Klappe *f*; Klaps *m*; (Flügel)Schlag *m*; **2.** *v/t.* klatschen(d schlagen); *v/i.* lose herabhängen; flattern.

flare [flɛə] **1.** flackern; sich nach außen erweitern, sich bauschen; *~ up* aufflammen; *fig.* aufbrausen; **2.** flackerndes Licht; Lichtsignal *n*.

flash [flæʃ] **1.** aufgedonnert; unecht; Gauner...; **2.** Blitz *m*; *fig.* Aufblitzen *n*; *bsd. Am. Zeitung:* kurze Meldung; *in a ~* im Nu; *~ of wit* Geistesblitz *m*; **3.** (auf)blitzen; auflodern (lassen); *Blick etc.* werfen; flitzen; funken, telegraphieren; *it ~ed on me* mir kam plötzlich der Gedanke; **~back** ['flæʃbæk] *Film:* Rückblende *f*; **~light** *phot.* Blitzlicht *n*; Blinklicht *n*; Taschenlampe *f*; **~y** □ [~ʃi] auffallend.

flask [flɑ:sk] Taschen-, Reiseflasche *f*.

flat [flæt] **1.** □ flach, platt; schal; ♪ flau; klar; glatt; ♪ um e-n halben Ton erniedrigt; *~ price* Einheitspreis *m*; **2.** *adv.* glatt; völlig; *fall ~* danebengehen; *sing ~* zu tief singen; **3.** Fläche *f*, Ebene *f*; Flachland *n*; Untiefe *f*; (Miet)Wohnung *f*; ♪ B *n*; F Simpel *m*; *mot. sl.* Plattfuß *m*; **~foot** ['flætfut] Plattfuß *m*; *Am. sl.* Polyp *m* (*Polizist*); **~footed** plattfüßig; *Am.* F *fig.* stur, eisern; **~iron** Plätteisen *n*; **~ness** [~tnis] Flachheit *f*; Plattheit *f*; ♱ Flauheit *f*; **~ten** [~tn] (sich) ab-, verflachen.

flatter ['flætə] schmeicheln (*dat.*); **~er** [~ərə] Schmeichler(in); **~y** [~ri] Schmeichelei *f*.

flavo(u)r ['fleivə] **1.** Geschmack *m*; Aroma *n*; Blume *f* (*Wein*); *fig.* Beigeschmack *m*; Würze *f*; **2.** würzen; **~less** [~əlis] geschmacklos, fad.

flaw [flɔ:] **1.** Sprung *m*, Riß *m*; Fehler *m*; ♧ Bö *f*; **2.** zerbrechen; beschädigen; **~less** □ ['flɔ:lis] fehlerlos.

flax ⚘ [flæks] Flachs *m*, Lein *m*.

flay [flei] die Haut abziehen (*dat.*).

flea [fli:] Floh *m*.

fled [fled] *pret. u. p.p. von* flee.

fledge [fledʒ] *v/i.* flügge werden; *v/t.* befiedern; **~(e)ling** ['fledʒliŋ] Küken *n* (*a. fig.*); Grünschnabel *m*.

flee [fli:] (*irr.*) fliehen; meiden.

fleec|e [fli:s] **1.** Vlies *n*; **2.** scheren; prellen; **~y** ['fli:si] wollig.

fleer [fliə] höhnen (*at* über *acc.*).

fleet [fli:t] **1.** □ schnell; **2.** Flotte *f*; ♀ *Street* die (Londoner) Presse.

flesh [fleʃ] **1.** *lebendiges* Fleisch; *fig.* Fleisch(eslust *f*) *n*; **2.** *hunt.* Blut kosten lassen; **~ly** ['fleʃli] fleischlich; irdisch; **~y** [~i] fleischig; fett.

flew [flu:] *pret. von* fly 2.

flexib|ility [fleksə'biliti] Biegsamkeit *f*; **~le** □ ['fleksəbl] flexibel, biegsam; *fig.* anpassungsfähig.

flick [flik] schnippen; schnellen.

flicker ['flikə] 1. flackern; flattern; flimmern; 2. Flackern *n*, Flimmern *n*; Flattern *n*; *Am.* Buntspecht *m*.

flier ['flaiə] = flyer.

flight [flait] Flucht *f*; Flug *m* (*a. fig.*); Schwarm *m*; ⚔, ⚒ Kette *f*; (~ of stairs Treppen)Flucht *f*; put to ~ in die Flucht schlagen; ~y □ ['flaiti] flüchtig; leichtsinnig.

flimsy ['flimzi] dünn, locker; schwach; *fig.* fadenscheinig.

flinch [flintʃ] zurückweichen; zukken.

fling [fliŋ] 1. Wurf *m*; Schlag *m*; have one's ~ sich austoben; 2. [*irr.*] *v/i.* eilen; ausschlagen (*Pferd*); *fig.* toben; *v/t.* werfen, schleudern; ~ o.s. sich stürzen; ~ open aufreißen.

flint [flint] Kiesel *m*; Feuerstein *m*.

flip [flip] 1. Klaps *m*; Ruck *m*; 2. schnippen; klapsen; (umher-)flitzen.

flippan|cy ['flipənsi] Leichtfertigkeit *f*; ~t □ [~nt] leichtfertig; vorlaut.

flirt [flə:t] 1. Kokette *f*; Weiberheld *m*; 2. flirten, kokettieren; = flip 2; ~ation [flə:'teiʃən] Flirt *m*.

flit [flit] flitzen; wandern; umziehen.

flivver *Am. sl.* ['flivə] 1. Nuckelpinne *f* (*billiges Auto*); 2. mißlingen.

float [flout] 1. Schwimmer *m*; Floß *n*; Plattformwagen *m*; 2. *v/t.* überfluten; flößen; tragen (*Wasser*); ⚓ flott machen, fig. in Gang bringen; ✝ gründen; verbreiten; *v/i.* schwimmen, treiben; schweben; umlaufen.

flock [flɔk] 1. Herde *f* (*a. fig.*); Schar *f*; 2. sich scharen; zs.-strömen.

floe [flou] (treibende) Eisscholle.

flog [flɔg] peitschen; prügeln.

flood [flʌd] 1. *a.* ~tide Flut *f*; Überschwemmung *f*; 2. überfluten, überschwemmen; ~gate ['flʌdgeit] Schleusentor *n*; ~light ⚡ Flutlicht *n*.

floor [flɔ:] 1. Fußboden *m*; Stock (-werk *n*) *m*; ✝ Tenne *f*; ~ leader *Am.* Fraktionsvorsitzende(r) *m*; ~ show Nachtklubvorstellung *f*; take the ~ das Wort ergreifen; 2. dielen; zu Boden schlagen; verblüffen; ~cloth ['flɔ:klɔθ] Putzlappen *m*; ~ing ['flɔ:riŋ] Dielung *f*; Fußboden *m*; ~lamp Stehlampe *f*; ~walker *Am.* ['flɔ:wɔ:kə] = shopwalker.

flop [flɔp] 1. schlagen; flattern; (hin)plumpsen (lassen); *Am.* versagen; 2. Plumps *m*; Versager *m*; ~house *Am. sl.* Penne *f*.

florid □ ['flɔrid] blühend.

florin ['flɔrin] Zweischillingstück *n*.

florist ['flɔrist] Blumenhändler *m*.

floss [flɔs] Florettseide *f*.

flounce[1] [flauns] Volant *m*.

flounce[2] [~] stürzen; zappeln.

flounder[1] *ichth.* ['flaundə] Flunder *f*.

flounder[2] [~] sich (ab)mühen.

flour ['flauə] (feines) Mehl.

flourish ['flʌriʃ] 1. Schnörkel *m*; Schwingen *n*; ♪ Tusch *m*; 2. *v/i.* blühen, gedeihen; *v/t.* schwingen.

flout [flaut] (ver)spotten.

flow [flou] 1. Fluß *m*; Flut *f*; 2. fließen, fluten; wallen.

flower ['flauə] 1. Blume *f*; Blüte *f* (*a. fig.*); Zierde *f*; 2. blühen; ~pot Blumentopf *m*; ~y [~əri] blumig.

flown [floun] *p.p. von* fly 2.

flubdub *Am. sl.* ['flʌbdʌb] Geschwätz *n*.

fluctuat|e ['flʌktjueit] schwanken; ~ion [flʌktju'eiʃən] Schwankung *f*.

flu(e) *F* [flu:] = influenza.

flue [flu:] Kaminrohr *n*; Heizrohr *n*.

fluen|cy *fig.* ['flu(:)ənsi] Fluß *m*; ~t □ [~nt] fließend, geläufig (*Rede*).

fluff [flʌf] 1. Flaum *m*; Flocke *f*; *fig.* Schnitzer *m*; 2. *Kissen* aufschütteln; *Federn* aufplustern (*Vogel*); ~y ['flʌfi] flaumig; flockig.

fluid ['flu(:)id] 1. flüssig; 2. Flüssigkeit *f*.

flung [flʌŋ] *pret. u. p.p. von* fling 2.

flunk *Am.* F *fig.* [flʌŋk] durchfallen (lassen).

flunk(e)y ['flʌŋki] Lakai *m*.

fluorescent [fluə'resnt] fluoreszierend.

flurry ['flʌri] Nervosität *f*; Bö *f*; *Am. a.* (Regen)Schauer *m*; Schneegestöber *n*.

flush [flʌʃ] 1. ⊕ in gleicher Ebene; reichlich; (über)voll; 2. Erröten *n*; Übermut *m*; Fülle *f*; Wachstum *n*; *fig.* Blüte *f*; Spülung *f*; *Karten:* Flöte *f*; 3. über-, durchfluten; (aus)spülen; strömen; sprießen (lassen); erröten (machen); übermütig machen; aufjagen.

fluster ['flʌstə] 1. Aufregung *f*; 2. *v/t.* aufregen.

flute [flu:t] 1. ♪ Flöte *f*; Falte *f*; 2. (auf der) Flöte spielen; riefeln; fälteln.

flutter ['flʌtə] 1. Geflatter *n*; Erregung *f*; *F* Spekulation *f*; 2. *v/t.* aufregen; *v/i.* flattern.

flux [flʌks] *fig.* Fluß *m*; ⚕ Ausfluß *m*.

fly [flai] 1. *zo.* Fliege *f*; Flug *m*; *Am. Baseball:* hochgeschlagener Ball; Droschke *f*; 2. [*irr.*] (*a. fig.*) fliegen (lassen); entfliehen (*Zeit*); ⚒ führen; *Flagge* hissen; fliehen; ~ überfliegen; ~ at herfallen über; ~ into a passion *od.* rage in Zorn geraten.

flyer ['flaiə] Flieger *m*; Renner *m*; take a ~ *Am.* F Vermögen riskieren.

fly-flap ['flaiflæp] Fliegenklatsche *f*.

flying ['flaiiŋ] fliegend; Flug...; ~ squad Überfallkommando *n*.

fly-|over ['flaiouvə] (Straßen)Überführung *f*; ~weight Boxen: Fliegengewicht *n*; ~-wheel Schwungrad *n*.

foal [foul] 1. Fohlen *n*; 2. fohlen.

foam [foum] 1. Schaum *m*; 2. schäumen, ~y ['foumi] schaumig.

focus ['foukəs] 1. Brennpunkt *m*; 2. (sich) im Brennpunkt vereinigen; *opt.* einstellen (*a. fig.*); konzentrieren

fodder ['fɔdə] (Trocken)Futter *n*.

foe *poet* [fou] Feind *m*, Gegner *m*.

fog [fɔg] 1. (dichter) Nebel; *fig.* Umnebelung *f*; *phot.* Schleier *m*; 2. *mst fig.* umnebeln; *phot.* verschleiern.

fogey F ['fougi]: old ~ komischer alter Kauz.

foggy [['fɔgi] neb(e)lig; *fig.* nebelhaft.

fogy *Am* ['fougi] = fogey.

foible *fig* ['fɔibl] Schwäche *f*.

foil[1] [fɔil] Folie *f*; Hintergrund *m*.

foil[2] [~] 1. vereiteln; 2. Florett *n*.

fold[1] [fould] 1. Schafhürde *f*; *fig.* Herde *f*, 2. einpferchen.

fold[3] [~] 1. Falte *f*; Falz *m*; 2. ...fach, ...fältig, 3. *v/t.* falten; falzen; *Arme* kreuzen, (*up*) einwickeln; *v/i.* sich falten, *Am.* F eingehen; ~er ['fouldə] Mappe *f*, Schnellhefter *m*; Faltprospekt *m*.

folding ['fouldiŋ] zs.-legbar; Klapp...; ~-bed Feldbett *n*; ~-boat Faltboot *n*, ~-door(s *pl.*) Flügeltür *f*; ~-screen spanische Wand; ~-seat Klappsitz *m*.

foliage ['fouliidʒ] Laub(werk) *n*.

folk [fouk] *pl* Leute *pl.*; ~s *pl.* Leute *pl.* (F a *Angehörige*); ~lore ['fouklɔ:] Volkskunde *f*; Volkssagen *f/pl.*; ~song Volkslied *n*.

follow ['fɔlou] folgen (*dat.*); folgen auf (*acc.*), be~, verfolgen; *s-m Beruf etc* nachgehen; ~er ['~ouə] Nachfolger(in); Verfolger(in); Anhänger(in), ~ing ['~ouiŋ] Anhängerschaft *f*, Gefolge *n*.

folly ['fɔli] Torheit *f*; Narrheit *f*.

foment [fou'ment] *j-m* warme Umschläge machen, *Unruhe* stiften.

fond [[fɔnd] zärtlich; vernarrt (*of* in *acc.*); be ~ of gern haben, lieben; ~le ['fɔndl] liebkosen; streicheln; (ver)hätscheln; ~ness ['~dnis] Zärtlichkeit *f*; Vorliebe *f*.

font [fɔnt] Taufstein *m*; *Am.* Quelle *f*.

food [fu:d] Speise *f*, Nahrung *f*; Futter *n*; Lebensmittel *n/pl.*; ~-stuff ['fu:dstʌf] Nahrungsmittel *n*.

fool [fu:l] 1. Narr *m*, Tor *m*; Hanswurst *m*, make a ~ of *s.o.* j-n zum Narren halten; make a ~ of *o.s.* sich lächerlich machen; 2. *Am.* F närrisch, dumm; 3. *v/t.* narren; prellen (*out of* um *et.*); ~ away F vertrödeln; *v/i.* albern; (herum)spielen; ~ (a)round *bsd. Am.* Zeit vertrödeln.

fool|ery ['fu:ləri] Torheit *f*; ~hardy

☐ ['fu:lha:di] tollkühn; ~ish ☐ ['fu:liʃ] töricht; ~ishness [~ʃnis] Torheit *f*; ~proof kinderleicht.

foot [fut] 1. *pl* feet [fi:t] Fuß *m* (*a. Maß*); Fußende *n*; ⊻ Infanterie *f*; on ~ zu Fuß; im Gange, in Gang; 2. *v/t. mst* ~ up addieren; ~ the bill F die Rechnung bezahlen; *v/i.* ~ it zu Fuß gehen; ~board ['futbɔ:d] Trittbrett *n*; ~boy Page *m*; ~fall Tritt *m*, Schritt *m*; ~gear Schuhwerk *n*; ~hold fester Stand; *fig.* Halt *m*.

footing ['futiŋ] Halt *m*, Stand *m*; Grundlage *f*, Basis *f*; Stellung *f*; fester Fuß; Verhältnis *n*; ⊻ Zustand *m*; Endsumme *f*; be on a friendly ~ with *s.o.* ein gutes Verhältnis zu j-m haben; lose one's ~ ausgleiten

foot|lights *thea.* ['futlaits] *pl.* Rampenlicht(er *pl.*) *n*; Bühne *f*; ~man Diener *m*, ~passenger Fußgänger (-in), ~path Fußpfad *m*; ~print Fußstapfe *f*, -spur *f*; ~sore fußkrank; ~step Fußstapfe *f*, Spur *f*; ~stool Fußbank *f*; ~wear = footgear.

fop [fɔp] Geck *m*, Fatzke *m*.

for [fɔ:, fər, fə] 1. *prp. mst* für; *Zweck*, *Ziel*, *Richtung* zu; nach; *warten*, *hoffen etc* auf (*acc.*); *sich sehnen etc.* nach; *Grund*, *Anlaß* aus, vor (*dat.*), wegen, *Zeitdauer* ~ three days drei Tage (lang), seit drei Tagen; *Entfernung* I walked ~ a mile ich ging eine Meile (weit), *Austausch*: (an-) statt; *in der Eigenschaft* als; I ~ one ich zum Beispiel; ~ sure sicher!, gewiß!; 2. *cj* denn.

forage ['fɔridʒ] 1. Futter *n*; 2. (nach Futter) suchen.

foray ['fɔrei] räuberischer Einfall.

forbear[1] [fɔ:'bɛə] [*irr.* (bear)] *v/t.* unterlassen; *v/i* sich enthalten (*from gen.*) Geduld haben.

forbear[3] ['fɔ:bɛə] Vorfahr *m*.

forbid [fə'bid] [*irr.* (bid)] verbieten; hindern; ~ding ☐ [~diŋ] abstoßend.

force [fɔ:s] 1. *mst* Kraft *f*, Gewalt *f*; Nachdruck *m*; Zwang *m*; Heer *n*; Streitmacht *f*; the ~ die Polizei; armed ~s ⊻ Streitkräfte *f/pl.*; come (put) in ~ in Kraft treten (setzen); 2. zwingen, nötigen; erzwingen; aufzwingen; Gewalt antun (*dat.*,); beschleunigen; aufbrechen; künstlich reif machen; ~ open aufbrechen; ~d: ~ landing Notlandung *f*; ~ loan Zwangsanleihe *f*; ~ march Eilmarsch *m*; ~ful ['fɔ:sful] kräftig; eindringlich.

forceps ⚕ ['fɔ:seps] Zange *f*.

forcible [['fɔ:səbl] gewaltsam; Zwangs...; eindringlich; wirksam.

ford [fɔ:d] 1. Furt *f*; 2. durchwaten.

fore [fɔ:] 1. *adv.* vorn; 2. Vorderteil *m*, *n*; bring (come) to the ~ zum

Vorschein bringen (kommen); **3.** *adj.* vorder; Vorder...; **~bode** [fɔ:-'boud] vorhersagen; ahnen; **~boding** [~diŋ] (böses) Vorzeichen; Ahnung *f*; **~cast** ['fɔ:kɑ:st] **1.** Vorhersage *f*; **2.** [*irr.* (*cast*)] vorhersehen; voraussagen; **~father** Vorfahr *m*; **~finger** Zeigefinger *m*; **~foot** Vorderfuß *m*; **~go** [fɔ:'gou] [*irr.* (*go*)] vorangehen; **~gone** [fɔ:-'gɔn, *adj.* 'fɔ:gɔn] von vornherein feststehend; **~ conclusion** Selbstverständlichkeit *f*; **~ground** Vordergrund *m*; **~head** ['fɔrid] Stirn *f*.

foreign ['fɔrin] fremd; ausländisch; auswärtig; **~er** [~nə] Ausländer(in), Fremde(r *m*) *f*; **♀ Office** Außenministerium *n*; **~ policy** Außenpolitik *f*; **~ trade** Außenhandel *m*.

fore|knowledge ['fɔ:'nɔlidʒ] Vorherwissen *n*; **~leg** ['fɔ:leg] Vorderbein *n*; **~lock** Stirnhaar *n*; *fig.* Schopf *m*; **~man** **§Ẑ** Obmann *m*; Vorarbeiter *m*, (Werk)Meister *m*; **⚒** Steiger *m*; **~most** vorderst, erst; **~name** Vorname *m*; **~noon** Vormittag *m*; **~runner** Vorläufer *m*, Vorbote *m*; **~see** [fɔ:'si:] [*irr.* (*see*)] vorhersehen; **~shadow** ankündigen; **~sight** ['fɔ:sait] Voraussicht *f*; Vorsorge *f*.

forest ['fɔrist] **1.** Wald *m* (*a. fig.*), Forst *m*; **2.** aufforsten.

forestall [fɔ:'stɔ:l] *et.* vereiteln; *j-m* zuvorkommen.

forest|er ['fɔristə] Förster *m*; Waldarbeiter *m*; **~ry** [~tri] Forstwirtschaft *f*; Waldgebiet *n*.

fore|taste ['fɔ:teist] Vorgeschmack *m*; **~tell** [fɔ:'tel] [*irr.* (*tell*)] vorhersagen; vorbedeuten; **~thought** ['fɔ:θɔ:t] Vorbedacht *m*; **~woman** Aufseherin *f*; Vorarbeiterin *f*; **~word** Vorwort *n*.

forfeit ['fɔ:fit] **1.** Verwirkung *f*; Strafe *f*; Pfand *n*; **2.** verwirken; einbüßen; **~able** [~təbl] verwirkbar.

forge¹ [fɔ:dʒ] *mst* **~ ahead** sich vor(wärts)arbeiten.

forge² [~] **1.** Schmiede *f*; **2.** schmieden (*fig. ersinnen*); fälschen; **~ry** ['fɔ:dʒəri] Fälschung *f*.

forget [fə'get] [*irr.*] vergessen; **~ful** ⬜ [~tful] vergeßlich; **~me-not** ⚘ Vergißmeinnicht *n*.

forgiv|e [fə'giv] [*irr.* (*give*)] vergeben, verzeihen; *Schuld* erlassen; **~eness** [~vnis] Verzeihung *f*; **~ing** ⬜ [~viŋ] versöhnlich; nachsichtig.

forgo [fɔ:'gou] [*irr.* (*go*)] verzichten auf (*acc.*); aufgeben.

forgot [fə'gɔt] *pret. von* forget; **~ten** [~tn] *p.p. von* forget.

fork [fɔ:k] **1.** Gabel *f*; **2.** (sich) gabeln; **~lift** ['fɔ:klift] Gabelstapler *m*.

forlorn [fə'lɔ:n] verloren, verlassen.

form [fɔ:m] **1.** Form *f*; Gestalt *f*; Formalität *f*; Formular *n*; (Schul-)Bank *f*; *Schul*-Klasse *f*; Kondition

f; geistige Verfassung; **2.** (sich) formen, (sich) bilden, gestalten; **✕** (sich) aufstellen.

formal ⬜ ['fɔ:məl] förmlich; formell; äußerlich; **~ity** [fɔ:'mæliti] Förmlichkeit *f*, Formalität *f*.

format|ion [fɔ:'meiʃən] Bildung *f*; **~ve** ['fɔ:mətiv] bildend; gestaltend; **~ years** *pl.* Entwicklungsjahre *n/pl.*

former ['fɔ:mə] vorig, früher; ehemalig, vergangen; erstere(r, -s); jene(r, -s), **~ly** [~əli] ehemals, früher.

formidable ⬜ ['fɔ:midəbl] furchtbar, schrecklich; ungeheuer.

formula ['fɔ:mjulə] Formel *f*; **♈** Rezept *n*; **~te** [~leit] formulieren.

forsake [fə'seik] [*irr.*] aufgeben; verlassen; **~n** [~kən] *p.p. von* forsake.

forsook [fə'suk] *pret. von* forsake.

forsooth *iro.* [fə'su:θ] wahrlich.

forswear [fɔ:'swɛə] [*irr.* (*swear*)] abschwören. [werk *n*) *f*.]

fort ✕ [fɔ:t] Fort *n*, Festungs-)

forth [fɔ:θ] vor(wärts); voran; heraus, hinaus, hervor; weiter, fort(an); **~coming** [fɔ:θ'kamiŋ] erscheinend; bereit; bevorstehend; F entgegenkommend; **~with** ['fɔ:θ'wiθ] sogleich.

fortieth ['fɔ:tiiθ] **1.** vierzigste(r, -s); Vierzigstel *n*.

forti|fication [fɔ:tifi'keiʃən] Befestigung *f*; **~fy** ['fɔ:tifai] ✕ befestigen; *fig.* (ver)stärken; **~tude** [~itju:d] Seelenstärke *f*; Tapferkeit *f*.

fortnight ['fɔ:tnait] vierzehn Tage.

fortress ['fɔ:tris] Festung *f*.

fortuitous ⬜ [fɔ:'tju(:)itəs] zufällig.

fortunate ['fɔ:tʃnit] glücklich; **~ly** [~tli] glücklicherweise.

fortune ['fɔ:tʃən] Glück *n*; Schicksal *n*; Zufall *m*; Vermögen *n*; **~teller** Wahrsager(in).

forty ['fɔ:ti] **1.** vierzig; **~niner** *Am. kalifornischer Goldsucher von 1849*; **~ winks** *pl.* F Nickerchen *n*; **2.** Vierzig *f*.

forward ['fɔ:wəd] **1.** *adj.* vorder; bereit(willig); fortschrittlich; vorwitzig, keck; **2.** *adv.* vor(wärts); **3.** *Fußball*: Stürmer *m*; **4.** (be)fördern; (ab-, ver)senden.

forwarding-agent ['fɔ:wədiŋei-dʒənt] Spediteur *m*.

foster ['fɔstə] **1.** *fig.* nähren, pflegen; **~ up** aufziehen; **2.** Pflege...

fought [fɔ:t] *pret. u. p.p. von* fight 2.

foul [faul] **1.** ⬜ widerwärtig; schmutzig (*a. fig.*); unehrlich; regelwidrig; übelriechend; faul, verdorben; widrig; schlecht (*Wetter*); *fall ~ of* mit *dem Gesetz* in Konflikt kommen; **2.** Zs.-stoß *m*; *Sport*: regelwidriges Spiel; *through fair and ~* durch dick und dünn; **3.** beschmutzen; (sich) verwickeln.

found [faund] **1.** *pret. u. p.p. von* find 1; **2.** (be)gründen; stiften; ⊕ gießen.

foundation [faun'deiʃən] Gründung *f*; Stiftung *f*; Fundament *n*.

founder ['faundə] **1.** (Be)Gründer (-in), Stifter(in); Gießer *m*; **2.** *v/i.* scheitern; lahmen.

foundling ['faundliŋ] Findling *m*.

foundry ⊕ ['faundri] Gießerei *f*.

fountain ['fauntin] Quelle *f*; Springbrunnen *m*; **~pen** Füllfederhalter *m*.

four [fɔː] **1.** vier; **2.** Vier *f*; *Sport*: Vierer *m*; **~-flusher** *Am. sl.* ['fɔː'flʌʃə] Hochstapler *m*; **~square** viereckig; *fig.* unerschütterlich; **~-stroke** *mot.* Viertakt...; **~teen** ['fɔː'tiːn] vierzehn; **~teenth** [‿nθ] vierzehnte(r, -s); **~th** [fɔːθ] **1.** vierte(r, -s); **2.** Viertel *n*; **~thly** ['fɔːθli] viertens.

fowl [faul] Geflügel *n*; Huhn *n*; Vogel *m*; **~ing-piece** ['faulinpiːs] Vogelflinte *f*.

fox [fɔks] **1.** Fuchs *m*; **2.** überlisten; **~glove** ♀ ['fɔksglʌv] Fingerhut *m*; **~y** ['fɔksi] fuchsartig; schlau.

fraction ['frækʃən] Bruch(teil) *m*.

fracture ['fræktʃə] **1.** (*bsd.* Knochen)Bruch *m*; **2.** brechen.

fragile ['frædʒail] zerbrechlich.

fragment ['frægmənt] Bruchstück *n*.

fragran|ce ['freigrəns] Wohlgeruch *m*, Duft *m*; **~t** [‿nt] wohlriechend.

frail [freil] ge-, zerbrechlich; schwach; **~ty** *fig.* ['freilti] Schwäche *f*.

frame [freim] **1.** Rahmen *m*; Gerippe *n*; Gerüst *n*; (Brillen)Gestell *n*; Körper *m*; (An)Ordnung *f*; *phot.* (Einzel)Bild *n*; ✗ Frühbeetkasten *m*; **~ of mind** Gemütsverfassung *f*; **2.** bilden, formen, bauen; entwerfen; (ein)rahmen, sich entwickeln; **~house** ['freimhaus] Holzhaus *n*; **~up** *bsd. Am.* F abgekartetes Spiel; **~work** ⊕ Gerippe *n*; Rahmen *m*; *fig.* Bau *m*.

franchise ♇ ['fræntʃaiz] Wahlrecht *n*; Bürgerrecht *n*; *bsd. Am.* Konzession *f*.

frank [fræŋk] **1.**] frei(mütig), offen; **2.** *Brief* maschinell frankieren.

frankfurter ['fræŋkfətə] Frankfurter Würstchen.

frankness ['fræŋknis] Offenheit *f*.

frantic ['fræntik] (**~ally**) wahnsinnig.

fratern|al [frə'təːnl] brüderlich; **~ity** [‿niti] Brüderlichkeit *f*; Brüderschaft *f*; *Am. univ.* Verbindung *f*.

fraud [frɔːd] Betrug *m*; F Schwindel *m*; **~ulent** □ ['frɔːdjulənt] betrügerisch.

fray [frei] **1.** (sich) abnutzen; (sich) durchscheuern; **2.** Schlägerei *f*.

frazzle *bsd. Am.* F ['fræzl] **1.** Fetzen *m/pl.*; **2.** zerfetzen.

freak [friːk] Einfall *m*, Laune *f*.

freckle ['frekl] Sommersprosse *f*.

free [friː] **1.**] *allg.* frei; freigebig (of mit); freiwillig; he is ~ to *inf.* es steht ihm frei, zu *inf.*; ~ and easy zwanglos; sorglos; make ~ sich Freiheiten erlauben; set ~ freilassen; **2.** befreien; freilassen, *et.* freimachen; **~booter** ['friːbuːtə] Freibeuter *m*; **~dom** ['friːdəm] Freiheit *f*; freie Benutzung; Offenheit *f*; Zwanglosigkeit *f* (plumpe) Vertraulichkeit; ~ of a city (Ehren-) Bürgerrecht *n*; **~holder** Grundeigentümer *m*; **~man** freier Mann; Vollbürger *m*; **~mason** Freimaurer *m*; **~wheel** Freilauf *m*.

freez|e [friːz] [*irr.*] *v/i.* (ge)frieren; erstarren; *v/t.* gefrieren lassen; **~er** ['friːzə] Eismaschine *f*; Gefriermaschine *f*; Gefriertruhe *f*; **~ing** □ [‿ziŋ] eisig; **~-point** Gefrierpunkt *m*.

freight [freit] **1.** Fracht(geld *n*) *f*; *attr. Am.* Güter...; **2.** be-, verfrachten; **~car** *Am.* ⊠ ['freitkɑː] Güterwagen *m*; **~train** *Am.* Güterzug *m*.

French [frentʃ] **1.** französisch; take ~ leave heimlich weggehen; ~ window Balkon-, Verandatür *f*; **2.** Französisch *n*; the ~ *pl.* die Franzosen *pl.*; **~man** ['frentʃmən] Franzose *m*.

frenz|ied ['frenzid] wahnsinnig; **~y** [‿zi] Wahnsinn *m*.

frequen|cy ['friːkwənsi] Häufigkeit *f*; ⚡ Frequenz *f*; **~t 1.** □ [‿nt] häufig; **2.** [fri'kwent] (oft) besuchen.

fresh] [freʃ] frisch; neu; unerfahren; *Am.* F frech; ~ water Süßwasser *n*; **~en** ['freʃn] frisch machen *od.* werden; **~et** [‿ʃit] Hochwasser *n*; *fig.* Flut *f*; **~man** *univ.* Student *m* im ersten Jahr; **~ness** [‿ʃnis] Frische *f*; Neuheit *f*; Unerfahrenheit *f*; **~water** Süßwasser...; ~ college *Am.* drittrangiges College.

fret [fret] **1.** Aufregung *f*; Ärger *m*; ♪ Bund *m*, Griffleiste *f*; **2.** zerfressen; (sich) ärgern; (sich) grämen; ~ away, ~ out aufreiben.

fretful] ['fretful] ärgerlich.

fret-saw ['fretsɔː] Laubsäge *f*.

fretwork ['fretwəːk] (geschnitztes) Gitterwerk; Laubsägearbeit *f*.

friar ['fraiə] Mönch *m*.

friction ['frikʃən] Reibung *f* (*a. fig.*).

Friday ['fraidi] Freitag *m*.

fridge F [fridʒ] Kühlschrank *m*.

friend [frend] Freund(in); Bekannte(r *m*) *f*; **~ly** ['frendli] freund(schaft)lich; **~ship** [‿dʃip] Freundschaft *f*.

frigate ⚓ ['frigit] Fregatte *f*.

frig(e) F [fridʒ] = *fridge*.

fright [frait] Schreck(en) *m*; *fig.* Vogelscheuche *f*; ~en ['fraitn] erschrecken; ~ed *at od.* of bange vor (*dat.*); ~ful □ [~tful] schrecklich.

frigid □ ['fridʒid] kalt, frostig.

frill [fril] Krause *f*, Rüsche *f*.

fringe [frindʒ] **1.** Franse *f*; Rand *m*; *a.* ~s *pl.* Ponyfrisur *f*; **2.** mit Fransen besetzen.

frippery ['fripəri] Flitterkram *m*.

Frisian ['friziən] friesisch.

frisk [frisk] **1.** ᒐ Luftsprung *m*; **2.** hüpfen; *sl. nach Waffen etc.* durchsuchen; ~y □ ['friski] munter.

fritter ['fritə] **1.** Pfannkuchen *m*, Krapfen *m*; **2.** ~ *away* verzetteln.

frivol|ity [fri'voliti] Frivolität *f*, Leichtfertigkeit *f*; ~ous □ ['frivələs] nichtig; leichtfertig.

frizzle ['frizl] *a.* ~ *up* (sich) kräuseln; *Küche:* brutzeln.

fro [frou]: *to and* ~ hin und her.

frock [frok] Kutte *f*; *Frauen-*Kleid *n*; Kittel *m*; Gehrock *m*.

frog [frog] Frosch *m*.

frolic ['frolik] **1.** Fröhlichkeit *f*; Scherz *m*; **2.** scherzen, spaßen; ~some □ [~ksəm] lustig, fröhlich.

from [from, frəm] von; aus, von ... her; von ... (an); aus, vor, wegen; nach, gemäß; *defend* ~ schützen vor (*dat.*); ~ *amidst* mitten aus.

front [frʌnt] **1.** Stirn *f*; Vorderseite *f*; ✕ Front *f*; Hemdbrust *f*; Strandpromenade *f*; Kühnheit *f*, Frechheit *f*; *in* ~ vorn; *in* ~ *of* räumlich vor; **2.** Vorder...; **3.** *a.* ~ *on,* ~ *towards* die Front haben nach; gegenüberstehen, gegenübertreten (*dat.*); ~al ['frʌntl] Stirn...; Front...; Vorder...; ~ *door* Haustür *f*; ~ier [~tjə] Grenze *f*, *bsd. Am. hist.* Grenze zum Wilden Westen; *attr.* Grenz...; ~iersman [~zmən] Grenzbewohner *m*; *fig.* Pionier *m*; ~ispiece [~tispiːs] ⚙ Vorderseite *f*; *typ.* Titelbild *n*; ~ *man fig.* Aushängeschild *n*; ~page *Zeitung:* Titelseite *f*; ~wheel drive *mot.* Vorderradantrieb *m*.

frost [frost] **1.** Frost *m*; *a. hoar* ~, *white* ~ Reif *m*; **2.** (mit Zucker) bestreuen; glasieren; mattieren; ~ed glass Milchglas *n*; ~bite ᒐ ['frostbait] Erfrierung *f*; ~y □ [~ti] frostig; bereift.

froth [froθ] **1.** Schaum *m*; **2.** schäumen; zu Schaum schlagen; ~y □ ['froθi] schaumig; *fig.* seicht.

frown [fraun] **1.** Stirnrunzeln *n*; finsterer Blick; **2.** *v/i.* die Stirn runzeln; finster blicken.

frow|sty □ ['frausti], ~zy ['frauzi] moderig; schlampig.

froze [frouz] *pret. von* freeze; ~n ['frouzn] **1.** *p.p. von* freeze; **2.** *adj.* (eis)kalt; (ein)gefroren.

frugal □ ['fruːgəl] mäßig; sparsam.

fruit [fruːt] **1.** Frucht *f*; Früchte *pl.*; Obst *n*; **2.** Frucht tragen; ~erer ['fruːtərə] Obsthändler *m*; ~ful □ [~tful] fruchtbar; ~less □ [~tlis] unfruchtbar.

frustrat|e [frʌs'treit] vereiteln; enttäuschen; ~ion [~eiʃən] Vereitelung *f*; Enttäuschung *f*.

fry [frai] **1.** Gebratene(s) *n*; Fischbrut *f*; **2.** braten, backen; ~ing-pan ['fraiiŋpæn] Bratpfanne *f*.

fuchsia ♀ ['fjuːʃə] Fuchsie *f*.

fudge [fʌdʒ] **1.** F zurechtpfuschen; **2.** Unsinn *m*; Weichkaramelle *f*.

fuel ['fjuəl] **1.** Brennmaterial *n*; *Betriebs-, mot.* Kraftstoff *m*; **2.** *mot.* tanken.

fugitive ['fjuːdʒitiv] **1.** flüchtig (*a. fig.*); **2.** Flüchtling *m*.

fulfil(l) [ful'fil] erfüllen; vollziehen; ~ment [~lmənt] Erfüllung *f*.

full [ful] **1.** □ *allg.* voll; Voll...; vollständig, völlig; reichlich; ausführlich; *of* ~ *age* volljährig; **2.** *adv.* völlig, ganz; genau; **3.** Ganze(s) *n*; Höhepunkt *m*; *in* ~ völlig; ausführlich; *to the* ~ vollständig; ~blooded ['ful'blʌdid] vollblütig; kräftig; reinrassig; ~dress Gesellschaftsanzug *m*; ~dress formell, Gala...; *Am.* ausführlich; ~fledged ['ful'fledʒd] flügge; voll ausgewachsen; ~stop Punkt *m*.

ful(l)ness ['fulnis] Fülle *f*.

full-time ['fultaim] vollbeschäftigt; Voll...

fulminate *fig.* ['fʌlmineit] wettern.

fumble ['fʌmbl] tasten; fummeln.

fume [fjuːm] **1.** Dunst *m*, Dampf *m*; **2.** rauchen; aufgebracht sein.

fumigate ['fjuːmigeit] ausräuchern, desinfizieren.

fun [fʌn] Scherz *m*, Spaß *m*; *make* ~ *of* sich lustig machen über (*acc.*).

function ['fʌŋkʃn] **1.** Funktion *f*; Beruf *m*; Tätigkeit *f*; Aufgabe *f*; Feierlichkeit *f*; **2.** funktionieren; ~ary [~ʃnəri] Beamte(r) *m*; Funktionär *m*.

fund [fʌnd] **1.** Fonds *m*; ~s *pl.* Staatspapiere *n/pl.*; Geld(mittel *n/pl.*) *n*; Vorrat *m*; **2.** Schuld fundieren; *Geld* anlegen.

fundamental □ [fʌndə'mentl] **1.** grundlegend; Grund...; **2.** ~s *pl.* Grundlage *f*, ~züge *m/pl.*, ~begriffe *m/pl.*

funer|al ['fjuːnərəl] Beerdigung *f*; *attr.* Trauer..., Begräbnis...; ~eal □ [fjuː(ː)'niəriəl] traurig, düster.

fun-fair ['fʌnfɛə] Rummelplatz *m*.

funicular [fjuː(ː)'nikjulə] **1.** Seil...; **2.** *a.* ~ *railway* (Draht)Seilbahn *f*.

funnel ['fʌnl] Trichter *m*; Rauchfang *m*; ⚓, 🚂 Schornstein *m*.

funnies *Am.* ['fʌniz] *pl.* Comics *pl.* (*primitive Bildserien*).

funny □ ['fʌni] spaßig, komisch.

fur [fəː] 1. Pelz *m*; Belag *m der Zunge*; Kesselstein *m*; ~s *pl.* Pelzwaren *pl.*; 2. mit Pelz besetzen *od.* füttern.

furbish ['fəːbiʃ] putzen, polieren.

furious ['fjuəriəs] wütend; wild.

furl [fəːl] zs.-rollen; zs.-klappen.

furlough ✗ ['fəːlou] Urlaub *m*.

furnace ['fəːnis] Schmelz-, Hochofen *m*; (Heiz)Kessel *m*; Feuerung *f*.

furnish ['fəːniʃ] versehen (*with* mit); *et.* liefern; möblieren; ausstatten.

furniture ['fəːnitʃə] Möbel *pl.*, Einrichtung *f*; Ausstattung *f*; sectional ~ Anbaumöbel *pl.*

furrier ['fʌriə] Kürschner *m*.

furrow ['fʌrou] 1. Furche *f*; 2. furchen.

further ['fəːðə] 1. *adj. u. adv.* ferner, weiter; 2. fördern; ~ance [~ərəns] Förderung *f*; ~more [~ɔ'mɔː] ferner, überdies; ~most [~ɔmoust] weitest.

furthest ['fəːðist] = *furthermost.*

furtive □ ['fəːtiv] verstohlen.

fury ['fjuəri] Raserei *f*, Wut *f*; Furie *f*.

fuse [fjuːz] 1. (ver)schmelzen; ∉ durchbrennen; ausgehen (*Licht*); ✗ mit Zünder versehen; 2. ∉ (Schmelz)Sicherung *f*; ✗ Zünder *m*.

fuselage ['fjuːzilɑːʒ] (Flugzeug-)Rumpf *m*.

fusion ['fjuːʒən] Schmelzen *n*; Verschmelzung *f*, Fusion *f*; ~ **bomb** ✗ Wasserstoffbombe *f*.

fuss F [fʌs] 1. Lärm *m*; Wesen *n*, Getue *n*; 2. viel Aufhebens machen (*about* um, von); (sich) aufregen.

fusty ['fʌsti] muffig; *fig.* verstaubt.

futile ['fjuːtail] nutzlos, nichtig.

future ['fjuːtʃə] 1. (zu)künftig; 2. Zukunft *f*; *gr.* Futur *n*, Zukunft *f*; ~s *pl.* ✝ Termingeschäfte *n/pl.*

fuzz [fʌz] 1. feiner Flaum; Fussel *f*; 2. fusseln, (zer)fasern.

G

gab F [gæb] Geschwätz *n*; *the gift of the ~* ein gutes Mundwerk.

gabardine ['gæbədiːn] Gabardine *m* (*Wollstoff*).

gabble ['gæbl] 1. Geschnatter *n*, Geschwätz *n*; 2. schnattern, schwatzen.

gaberdine ['gæbədiːn] Kaftan *m*; = *gabardine.*

gable ['geibl] Giebel *m*.

gad F [gæd]: ~ *about* sich herumtreiben.

gadfly *zo.* ['gædflai] Bremse *f*.

gadget *sl.* ['gædʒit] Dings *n*, Apparat *m*; Kniff *m*, Pfiff *m*.

gag [gæg] 1. Knebel *m*; Witz *m*; 2. knebeln; *pol.* mundtot machen.

gage¹ [geidʒ] Pfand *m*.

gage² [~] = *gauge.*

gaiety ['geiəti] Fröhlichkeit *f*.

gaily ['geili] *adv. von gay.*

gain [gein] 1. Gewinn *m*; Vorteil *m*; 2. *v/t.* gewinnen; erreichen; bekommen; *v/i.* vorgehen (*Uhr*); ~ *in* zunehmen an (*acc.*); ~ful ['~ful] ['geinful] einträglich.

gait [geit] Gang(art *f m*) *m*; Schritt *m*.

gaiter ['geitə] Gamasche *f*.

gal *Am. sl.* [gæl] Mädel *m*.

gale [geil] Sturm *m*; steife Brise.

gall [gɔːl] 1. Galle *f*; ✾ Wolf *m*; Pein *f*; *bsd. Am. sl.* Frechheit *f*; 2. wundreiben; ärgern.

gallant ['gælənt] 1. □ stattlich, tapfer; galant, höflich; 2. Kavalier *m*; 3. galant sein; ~ry [~tri] Tapferkeit *f*; Galanterie *f*.

gallery ['gæləri] Galerie *f*; Empore *f*.

galley ['gæli] ✠ Galeere *f*; ✠ Kombüse *f*; ~proof Korrekturfahne *f*.

gallon ['gælən] Gallone *f* (4,54 Liter, *Am.* 3,78 *Liter*).

gallop ['gæləp] 1. Galopp *m*; 2. galoppieren (lassen).

gallows ['gælouz] *sg.* Galgen *m*.

galore [gə'lɔː] in Menge.

gamble ['gæmbl] (um Geld) spielen; 2. F Glücksspiel *n*; ~r [~lə] Spieler(in).

gambol ['gæmbəl] 1. Luftsprung *m*; 2. (fröhlich) hüpfen, tanzen.

game [geim] 1. Spiel *n*; Scherz *m*; Wild *n*; 2. F entschlossen; furchtlos; 3. spielen; ~keeper ['geimkiːpə] Wildhüter *m*; ~licence Jagdschein *m*; ~ster ['geimstə] Spieler(in).

gander ['gændə] Gänserich *m*.

gang [gæŋ] 1. Trupp *m*; Bande *f*; 2. ~ *up* sich zs.-rotten *od.* zs.-tun; ~board ✠ ['gæŋbɔːd] Laufplanke *f*.

gangster *Am.* ['gæŋstə] Gangster *m*.

gangway ['gæŋwei] (Durch)Gang *m*; ✠ Fallreep *n*; ✠ Laufplanke *f*.

gaol [dʒeil], ~bird ['dʒeilbɔːd], ~er ['dʒeilə] *s. jail etc.*

gap [gæp] Lücke *f*; Kluft *f*; Spalte *f*.

gape [geip] gähnen; klaffen; gaffen.

garage ['gærɑːʒ] 1. Garage *f*; Autowerkstatt *f*; 2. *Auto* einstellen.

garb [gɑːb] Gewand *n*, Tracht *f*.

garbage ['gɑːbidʒ] Abfall *m*;

Schund *m*; ~ can *Am.* Mülltonne *f*; ~ pail Mülleimer *m*.

garden ['gɑːdn] **1.** Garten *m*; **2.** Gartenbau treiben; ~er [~nə] Gärtner(in); ~ing [~niŋ] Gartenarbeit *f*.

gargle ['gɑːgl] **1.** gurgeln; **2.** Gurgelwasser *n*.

garish □ ['geəriʃ] grell, auffallend.

garland ['gɑːlənd] Girlande *f*.

garlic ♠ ['gɑːlik] Knoblauch *m*.

garment ['gɑːmənt] Gewand *n*.

garnish ['gɑːniʃ] garnieren, zieren.

garret ['gærət] Dachstube *f*.

garrison ⚔ ['gærisn] **1.** Besatzung *f*; Garnison *f*; **2.** mit e-r Besatzung belegen. [haft.]

garrulous □ ['gærʊləs] schwatz-]

garter ['gɑːtə] Strumpfband *n*; *Am.* Socken-, Strumpfhalter *m*.

gas [gæs] **1.** Gas *n*; *Am.* = gasoline; **2.** *v/t.* vergasen; *v/i.* F faseln; ~eous ['geiziəs] gasförmig.

gash [gæʃ] **1.** klaffende Wunde; Hieb *m*; Riß *m*; **2.** tief (ein)schneiden in (*acc.*).

gas|**-light** ['gæslait] Gasbeleuchtung *f*, ~meter Gasuhr *f*; ~olene, ~oline *Am. mot.* ['gæsəliːn] Benzin *n*.

gasp [gɑːsp] **1.** Keuchen *n*; **2.** keuchen; nach Luft schnappen.

gas|**sed** [gæst] gasvergiftet; ~stove ['gæs'stouv] Gasofen *m*, -herd *m*; ~works ['gæswɔːks] *sg.* Gaswerk *n*, -anstalt *f*.

gener|**osity** [dʒenə'rɔsiti] Großmut *f*; Großzügigkeit *f*; ~ous ['dʒenərəs] großmütig, großzügig.

gat *Am. sl.* [gæt] Revolver *m*.

gate [geit] Tor *n*; Pforte *f*; Sperre *f*; ~man ['geitmən] Schrankenwärter *m*; ~way Tor(weg *m*) *n*, Einfahrt *f*.

gather ['gæðə] **1.** *v/t.* (ein-, ver-)sammeln; ernten; pflücken; schließen (from aus); zs.-ziehen; kräuseln; ~ speed schneller werden; *v/i.* sich (ver)sammeln; sich vergrößern; ✿ *u. fig.* reifen; **2.** Falte *f*; ~ing [~riŋ] Versammlung *f*; Zs.-kunft *f*.

gaudy □ ['gɔːdi] grell; protzig.

gauge [geidʒ] **1.** (Normal)Maß *n*; Maßstab *m*; ⊕ Lehre *f*; 🚃 Spurweite *f*; Meßgerät *n*; **2.** eichen; (aus)messen; *fig.* abschätzen.

gaunt □ [gɔːnt] hager; finster.

gauntlet ['gɔːntlit] *fig.* Fehdehandschuh *m*; run the ~ Spießruten laufen.

gauze [gɔːz] Gaze *f*.

gave [geiv] *pret. von* give.

gavel *Am.* ['gævl] Hammer *m des Versammlungsleiters od. Auktionators.*

gawk F [gɔːk] Tölpel *m*; ~y [gɔːki] tölpisch.

gay □ [gei] lustig, heiter; bunt, lebhaft, glänzend.

gaze [geiz] **1.** starrer *od.* aufmerksamer Blick; **2.** starren.

gazette [gə'zet] **1.** Amtsblatt *n*; **2.** amtlich bekanntgeben.

gear [giə] **1.** ⊕ Getriebe *n*; *mot.* Gang *m*; Mechanismus *m*; Gerät *n*; in ~ mit eingelegtem Gang; in Betrieb; out of ~ im Leerlauf; außer Betrieb; landing ~ ✈ Fahrgestell *n*; steering ~ ⚓ Ruderanlage *f*; *mot.* Lenkung *f*; **2.** einschalten; ⊕ greifen; ~ing [giəriŋ] (Zahnrad-)Getriebe *n*; Übersetzung *f*; ~lever, *bsd. Am.* ~shift Schalthebel *m*.

gee [dʒiː] **1.** *Kindersprache:* Hottehü *n* (*Pferd*); **2.** *Fuhrmannsruf:* hü! hott!; *Am.* nanu!, so was!

geese [giːs] *pl. von* goose.

gem [dʒem] Edelstein *m*; Gemme *f*; *fig.* Glanzstück *n*.

gender *gr.* ['dʒendə] Genus *n*, Geschlecht *n*.

general ['dʒenərəl] **1.** □ allgemein; gewöhnlich; Haupt..., General...; ~ election allgemeine Wahlen; **2.** ⚔ General *m*; Feldherr *m*; ~ity [dʒenə'ræliti] Allgemeinheit *f*; die große Masse; ~ize ['dʒenərəlaiz] verallgemeinern; ~ly [~li] im allgemeinen, überhaupt; gewöhnlich.

generat|**e** ['dʒenəreit] erzeugen; ~ion [dʒenə'reiʃən] (Er)Zeugung *f*; Generation *f*; Menschenalter *n*; ~or ['dʒenəreitə] Erzeuger *m*; ⊕ Generator *m*; *bsd. Am. mot.* Lichtmaschine *f*.

genial □, ['dʒiːnjəl] freundlich; anregend; gemütlich (*Person*); heiter.

genitive *gr.* ['dʒenitiv] *a.* ~ case Genitiv *m*.

genius ['dʒiːnjəs] Geist *m*; Genie *n*.

gent F [dʒent] Herr *m*.

genteel □ [dʒen'tiːl] vornehm; elegant.

gentile ['dʒentail] **1.** heidnisch, nichtjüdisch; **2.** Heide *m*, -in *f*.

gentle □ ['dʒentl] sanft, mild; zahm; leise, sacht; vornehm; ~man Herr *m*; Gentleman *m*; ~manlike, ~manly [~li] gebildet; vornehm; ~ness [~lnis] Sanftheit *f*; Milde *f*, Güte *f*, Sanftmut *f*.

gentry ['dʒentri] niederer Adel; gebildete Stände *m/pl.*

genuine □ ['dʒenjuin] echt; aufrichtig.

geography [dʒi'ɔgrəfi] Geographie *f*.

geology [dʒi'ɔlədʒi] Geologie *f*.

geometry [dʒi'ɔmitri] Geometrie *f*.

germ [dʒəːm] **1.** Keim *m*; **2.** keimen.

German[1] ['dʒəːmən] **1.** deutsch; **2.** Deutsche(r *m*) *f*; Deutsch *n*.

german[2] [~] brother ~ leiblicher Bruder; ~e [dʒəː'mein] (to) verwandt (mit); entsprechend (*dat.*).

germinate ['dʒəːmineit] keimen.

gesticulat|e [dʒes'tikjuleit] gestikulieren; ~ion [dʒestikju'leiʃən] Gebärdenspiel n.

gesture ['dʒestʃə] Geste f, Gebärde f.

get [get] [irr.] v/t. erhalten, bekommen, F kriegen; besorgen; holen; bringen; erwerben; verdienen; ergreifen, fassen; (veran)lassen; mit adv. mst bringen, machen; have got haben; ~ one's hair cut sich das Haar schneiden lassen; ~ by heart auswendig lernen; v/i. gelangen, geraten, kommen, gehen; werden; ~ ready sich fertig machen; ~ about auf den Beinen sein; ~ abroad bekannt werden; ~ ahead vorwärtskommen; ~ at (heran-) kommen an ... (acc.); zu et. kommen; ~ away wegkommen; sich fortmachen; ~ in einsteigen; ~ on with s.o. mit j-m auskommen; ~ out aussteigen; ~ to hear (know, learn) erfahren; ~ up aufstehen; ~-up ['getʌp] Aufmachung f; Am. F Unternehmungsgeist m.

ghastly ['gɑːstli] gräßlich; schrecklich; (toten)bleich; gespenstisch.

gherkin ['gəːkin] Gewürzgurke f.

ghost [goust] Geist m, Gespenst n; fig. Spur f; ~like ['goustlaik], ~ly [~li] geisterhaft.

giant ['dʒaiənt] 1. riesig; 2.Riese m.

gibber ['dʒibə] kauderwelschen; ~ish ['gibəriʃ] Kauderwelsch n.

gibbet ['dʒibit] 1. Galgen m; 2. hängen.

gibe [dʒaib] verspotten, aufziehen.

giblets ['dʒiblits] pl. Gänseklein n.

gidd|iness ['gidinis] ⚓ Schwindel m; Unbeständigkeit f; Leichtsinn m; ~y □ ['gidi] schwind(e)lig; leichtfertig; unbeständig; albern.

gift [gift] Gabe f; Geschenk n; Talent n; ~ed ['giftid] begabt.

gigantic [dʒai'gæntik] (~ally) riesenhaft, riesig, gigantisch.

giggle ['gigl] 1. kichern; 2. Gekicher n.

gild [gild] [irr.] vergolden; verschönen; ~ed youth Jeunesse f dorée.

gill [gil] ichth. Kieme f; ⚘ Lamelle f.

gilt [gilt] 1. pret. u. p.p. von gild; 2. Vergoldung f.

gimmick Am. sl. ['gimik] Trick m.

gin [dʒin] Gin m (Wacholderschnaps); Schlinge f; ⊕ Entkörnungsmaschine f.

ginger ['dʒindʒə] 1. Ingwer m; Lebhaftigkeit f; 2. ~ up in Schwung bringen; 3. hellrot, rötlich-gelb; ~bread Pfefferkuchen m; ~ly [~əli] zimperlich; sachte.

gipsy ['dʒipsi] Zigeuner(in).

gird [gəːd] sticheln; [irr.] (um)gürten; umgeben.

girder ⊕ ['gəːdə] Tragbalken m.

girdle ['gəːdl] 1. Gürtel m; Hüfthalter m, -gürtel m; 2. umgürten.

girl [gəːl] Mädchen n; ♀ Guide ['gəːlgaid] Pfadfinderin f; ~hood ['gəːlhud] Mädchenzeit f; Mädchenjahre n/pl.; ~ish ['gəːliʃ] mädchenhaft; ~y Am. F ['gəːli] mit spärlich bekleideten Mädchen (Magazin, Varieté etc.).

girt [gəːt] pret. u. p.p. von gird.

girth [gəːθ] (Sattel)Gurt m; Umfang m.

gist [dʒist] das Wesentliche.

give [giv] [irr.] v/t. geben; ab-, übergeben; her-, hingeben; überlassen; zum besten geben; schenken; gewähren; von sich geben; ergeben; ~ birth to zur Welt bringen; ~ away verschenken; F verraten; ~ forth von sich geben; herausgeben; ~ in einreichen; ~ up Geschäft etc. aufgeben; j-n ausliefern; v/i. mst ~ in nachgeben; weichen; ~ into, ~ (up)on hinausgehen auf (acc.) (Fenster etc.); ~ out aufhören; versagen; ~ and take [givən'teik] (Meinungs)Austausch m; Kompromiß m, n; ~away ['givəwei] Preisgabe f; ~ show od. program bsd. Am. Radio, Fernsehen öffentliches Preisraten; ~n ['givn] 1. p.p. von give; 2. ~ to ergeben (dat.).

glaci|al □ [gleisjəl] eisig; Eis...; Gletscher...; ~er ['glæsjə] Gletscher m.

glad □ [glæd] froh, erfreut; erfreulich; ~ly gern; ~den ['glædn] erfreuen.

glade [gleid] Lichtung f; Am. sumpfige Niederung.

gladness ['glædnis] Freude f.

glair [glɛə] Eiweiß n.

glamo|rous ['glæmərəs] bezaubernd; ~(u)r ['glæmə] 1. Zauber m, Glanz m, Reiz m; 2. bezaubern.

glance [glɑːns] 1. Schimmer m, Blitz m; flüchtiger Blick; 2. hinweggleiten; mst ~ off abprallen; blitzen; glänzen; ~ at flüchtig ansehen; anspielen auf (acc.).

gland anat. [glænd] Drüse f.

glare [glɛə] 1. grelles Licht; wilder, starrer Blick; 2. grell leuchten; wild blicken; (at an)starren.

glass [glɑːs] 1. Glas n; Spiegel m; Opern-, Fernglas n; Barometer n; (a pair of) ~es pl. (eine) Brille; 2. gläsern; Glas...; 3. verglasen; ~-case ['glɑːskeis] Vitrine f; Schaukasten m; ~-house Treibhaus n; ✕ sl. Bau m; ~y [~si] gläsern; glasig.

glaz|e [gleiz] 1. Glasur f; 2. v/t. verglasen; glasieren; polieren; v/i. trüb(e) od. glasig werden (Auge); ~ier ['gleizjə] Glaser m.

gleam [gliːm] 1. Schimmer m, Schein m; 2. schimmern.

glean [gli:n] v/t. sammeln; v/i. Ähren lesen.

glee [gli:] Fröhlichkeit f; mehrstimmiges Lied; ~ club Gesangverein m.

glen [glen] Bergschlucht f.

glib [glib] glatt, zungenfertig.

glid|e [glaid] 1. Gleiten n; ✈ Gleitflug m; 2. (dahin)gleiten (lassen); e-n Gleitflug machen; ~er ['glaidə] Segelflugzeug n.

glimmer ['glimə] 1. Schimmer m; min. Glimmer m; 2. schimmern.

glimpse [glimps] 1. flüchtiger Blick (of auf acc.); Schimmer m; flüchtiger Eindruck; 2. flüchtig (er)blikken.

glint [glint] 1. blitzen, glitzern; 2. Lichtschein m.

glisten ['glisn], **glitter** ['glitə] glitzern, glänzen.

gloat [glout]: ~ (up)on od. over sich weiden an (dat.).

globe [gloub] (Erd)Kugel f; Globus m.

gloom [glu:m], **~iness** ['glu:minis] Düsterkeit f, Dunkelheit f; Schwermut f; ~y □ ['glu:mi] dunkel, düster; schwermütig; verdrießlich.

glori|fy ['glɔ:rifai] verherrlichen; **~ous** □ [~iəs] herrlich; glorreich.

glory ['glɔ:ri] 1. Ruhm m; Herrlichkeit f, Pracht f; Glorienschein m; 2. frohlocken; stolz sein.

gloss [glɔs] 1. Glosse f, Bemerkung f; Glanz m; 2. Glossen machen (zu); Glanz geben (dat.); ~ over beschönigen.

glossary ['glɔsəri] Wörterverzeichnis n.

glossy □ ['glɔsi] glänzend, blank.

glove [glʌv] Handschuh m.

glow [glou] 1. Glühen n; Glut f; 2. glühen.

glower ['glauə] finster blicken.

glow-worm ['glouwə:m] Glühwürmchen n.

glucose ['glu:kous] Traubenzucker m.

glue [glu:] 1. Leim m; 2. leimen.

glum □ [glʌm] mürrisch.

glut [glʌt] überfüllen.

glutinous □ ['glu:tinəs] klebrig.

glutton ['glʌtn] Unersättliche(r m) f; Vielfraß m; **~ous** □ [~nəs] gefräßig; **~y** [~ni] Gefräßigkeit f.

G-man Am. F ['dʒi:mæn] FBI-Agent m.

gnarl [na:l] Knorren m, Ast m.

gnash [næʃ] knirschen (mit).

gnat [næt] (Stech)Mücke f.

gnaw [nɔ:] (zer)nagen; (zer)fressen.

gnome [noum] Erdgeist m, Gnom m.

go [gou] 1. [irr.] allg. gehen, fahren; vergehen (Zeit); werden; führen (to nach); sich wenden (to an); funktionieren, arbeiten; passen; kaputtgehen; let ~ loslassen; ~

shares teilen; ~ to od. and see besuchen; ~ at losgehen auf (acc.); ~ between vermitteln (zwischen); ~ by sich richten nach; ~ for gehen nach, holen; ~ for a walk, etc. einen Spaziergang etc. machen; ~ in for an examination e-e Prüfung machen; ~ on weitergehen; fortfahren; ~ through durchgehen; durchmachen; ~ without sich behelfen ohne; 2. F Mode f; Schwung m, Schneid m; on the ~ auf den Beinen; im Gange; it is no ~ es geht nicht; in one ~ auf Anhieb; have a ~ at es versuchen mit.

goad [goud] 1. Stachelstock m; fig. Ansporn m; 2. fig. anstacheln.

go-ahead F ['gouəhed] 1. zielstrebig; unternehmungslustig; 2. bsd. Am. F Erlaubnis f zum Weitermachen.

goal [goul] Mal n; Ziel n; Fußball: Tor n; **~keeper** ['goulki:pə] Torwart m.

goat [gout] Ziege f, Geiß f.

gob [gɔb] V Schleimklumpen m; F Maul n; Am. F Blaujacke f (Matrose).

gobble ['gɔbl] gierig verschlingen, **~dygook** Am. sl. [~ldiguk] Amts-, Berufsjargon m; Geschwafel n; ~r [~lə] Vielfraß m; Truthahn m.

go-between ['goubitwi:n] Vermittler(in).

goblet ['gɔblit] Kelchglas n; Pokal m.

goblin ['gɔblin] Kobold m, Gnom m.

god, eccl. 2 [gɔd] Gott m; fig. Abgott m; **~child** ['gɔdtʃaild] Patenkind n; **~dess** ['gɔdis] Göttin f; **~father** Pate m; **~head** Gottheit f; **~less** ['gɔdlis] gottlos; **~like** gottähnlich; göttlich; **~ly** [~li] gottesfürchtig; fromm; **~mother** Patin f.

go-getter Am. sl. ['gou'getə] Draufgänger m.

goggle ['gɔgl] 1. glotzen; 2. **~s** pl. Schutzbrille f.

going ['gouiŋ] 1. gehend; im Gange (befindlich); be ~ to inf. im Begriff sein zu inf., gleich tun wollen od. werden; 2. Gehen n; Vorwärtskommen n; Straßenzustand m; Geschwindigkeit f, Leistung f; **~s-on** F [~ŋz'ɔn] pl. Treiben n.

gold [gould] 1. Gold n; 2. golden; **~digger** Am. ['goulddigə] Goldgräber m; **~en** mst fig. [~dən] golden, goldgelb; **~finch** zo. Stieglitz m; **~smith** Goldschmied m.

golf [gɔlf] 1. Golf(spiel) n; 2. Golf spielen; **~course** ['gɔlfkɔ:s], **~links** pl. Golfplatz m.

gondola ['gɔndələ] Gondel f.

gone [gɔn] 1. p.p. von go 1; 2. adj. fort; F futsch; vergangen; tot; F hoffnungslos.

good [gud] 1. allg. gut; artig; gütig;

† zahlungsfähig; gründlich; **~** *at geschickt in* (*dat.*); 2. Gute(s) *n*; Wohl *n*, Beste(s) *n*; **~s** *pl.* Waren *f/pl.*; Güter *n/pl.*; *that's no* **~** *das nützt nichts; for* **~** für immer; **~by(e) 1.** [gud'bai] Lebewohl *n*; **2.** ['gud'bai] (auf) Wiedersehen!; **♀ Friday** Karfreitag *m*; **~ly** ['gudli] anmutig, hübsch; *fig.* ansehnlich; **~natured** gutmütig; **~ness** [~nis] Güte *f*; *das Beste*; *thank* **~!** Gott sei Dank!; **~will** Wohlwollen *n*; **†** Kundschaft *f*; **†** Firmenwert *m*.

goody ['gudi] Bonbon *m, n.*

goon *Am. sl.* [gu:n] bestellter Schläger *bsd. für Streik*, Dummkopf *m.*

goose [gu:s], *pl.* **geese** [gi:s] Gans *f* (*a. fig.*); Bügeleisen *n.*

gooseberry ['guzbəri] Stachelbeere *f.*

goose|-flesh ['gu:sfleʃ], *Am.* **~pimples** *pl. fig.* Gänsehaut *f.*

gopher *bsd. Am.* ['goufə] Erdeichhörnchen *n.*

gore [gɔ:] **1.** (geronnenes) Blut; *Schneiderei:* Keil *m*; **2.** durchbohren, aufspießen.

gorge [gɔ:dʒ] **1.** Kehle *f*, Schlund *m*; enge (Fels)Schlucht; **2.** (ver-)schlingen, (sich) vollstopfen.

gorgeous ['gɔ:dʒəs] prächtig.

gory] ['gɔ:ri] blutig.

gospel [gɔspəl] Evangelium *n.*

gossip ['gɔsip] **1.** Geschwätz *n*; Klatschbase *f*; **2.** schwatzen.

got [gɔt] *pret. u. p.p. von* get.

Gothic ['gɔθik] gotisch; *fig.* barbarisch.

gotten *Am.* ['gɔtn] *p.p. von* get.

gouge [gaudʒ] **1.** ⊕ Hohlmeißel *m*; **2.** ausmeißeln; *Am.* F betrügen.

gourd ♣ [guəd] Kürbis *m.*

gout ♣ [gaut] Gicht *f.*

govern ['gʌvən] *v/t.* regieren, beherrschen; lenken, leiten; *v/i.* herrschen; **~ess** [~nis] Erzieherin *f*; **~ment** ['gʌvnmənt] Regierung(sform) *f*; Leitung *f*; Herrschaft *f* (*of* über *acc.*); Ministerium *n*; Statthalterschaft *f*; *attr.* Staats...; **~mental** [gʌvən'mentl] Regierungs...; **~or** ['gʌvənə] Gouverneur *m*; Direktor *m*, Präsident *m*; F Alte(r) *m* (*Vater, Chef*).

gown [gaun] **1.** (Frauen)Kleid *n*; Robe *f*, Talar *m*; **2.** kleiden.

grab F [græb] **1.** grapsen; an sich reißen, packen; **2.** plötzlicher Griff; ⊕ Greifer *m*; **~bag** *bsd. Am.* Glückstopf *m.*

grace [greis] **1.** Gnade *f*; Gunst *f*; (Gnaden)Frist *f*; Grazie *f*, Anmut *f*; Anstand *m*; Zier(de) *f*; Reiz *m*; Tischgebet *n*; *Your* ♀ Euer Gnaden; **2.** zieren, schmücken; begünstigen, auszeichnen; **~ful**] ['greisful] anmutig; **~fulness** [~nis] Anmut *f.*

gracious □ ['greiʃəs] gnädig.

gradation [grə'deiʃən] Abstufung *f.*

grade [greid] **1.** Grad *m*, Rang *m*; Stufe *f*; Qualität *f*; *bsd. Am.* = gradient; *Am. Schule:* Klasse *f*, Note *f*; *make the* **~** *Am.* Erfolg haben; **~ crossing** *bsd. Am.* schienengleicher Bahnübergang; **~(d) school** *bsd. Am.* Grundschule *f*; **2.** abstufen; einstufen; ⊕ planieren.

gradient 🚂 *etc.* ['greidjənt] Steigung *f.*

gradua|l [□ ['grædjuəl] stufenweise, allmählich; **~te 1.** [~ueit] graduieren; (sich) abstufen; die Abschlußprüfung machen; promovieren; **2.** *univ.* [~uit] Graduierte(r *m*) *f*; **~tion** [grædju'eiʃən] Gradeinteilung *f*; Abschlußprüfung *f*; Promotion *f.*

graft [gra:ft] **1.** ♂ Pfropfreis *n*; *Am.* Schiebung *f*; **2.** ♂ pfropfen; ♂ verpflanzen; *Am. fig.* schieben.

grain [grein] (Samen)Korn *n*; Getreide *n*; Gefüge *n*; *fig.* Natur *f*; Gran *n* (*Gewicht*).

gram [græm] = **gramme**.

gramma|r ['græmə] Grammatik *f*; **~r-school** höhere Schule, Gymnasium *n*; *Am. a.* Mittelschule *f*; **~tical** □ [grə'mætikəl] grammati(kali)sch.

gramme [græm] Gramm *n.*

granary ['grænəri] Kornspeicher *m.*

grand □ [grænd] **1.** *fig.* großartig; erhaben; groß; Groß..., Haupt...; **~ stand** *Sport* (Haupt-)Tribüne *f*; **2.** ♪ *a.* **~ piano** Flügel *m*; *Am. sl.* tausend Dollar *pl.*; **~child** ['græntʃaild] Enkel(in); **~eur** [~ndʒə] Größe *f*, Hoheit *f*; Erhabenheit *f*; **~father** Großvater *m.*

grandiose □ ['grændious] großartig.

grand|mother ['grænmʌðə] Großmutter *f*; **~parents** [~npɛərənts] *pl.* Großeltern *pl.*

grange [greindʒ] Gehöft *n*; Gut *n*; *Am. Name für* Farmerorganisation *f.*

granny F ['græni] Oma *f.*

grant [gra:nt] **1.** Gewährung *f*; Unterstützung *f*; Stipendium *n*; **2.** gewähren; bewilligen; verleihen; zugestehen; ⚖ übertragen; *take for* **~ed** als selbstverständlich annehmen.

granul|ate ['grænjuleit] (sich) körnen; **~e** [~ju:l] Körnchen *n.*

grape [greip] Weinbeere *f*, -traube *f*; **~fruit** ♣ ['greipfru:t] Pampelmuse *f.*

graph [græf] graphische Darstellung; **~ic(al** □) ['græfik(əl)] graphisch; anschaulich; *graphic arts pl.* Graphik *f*; **~ite** *min.* [~fait] Graphit *m.*

grapple ['græpl] entern; packen; ringen.

grasp [grɑːsp] **1.** Griff *m*; Bereich *m*; Beherrschung *f*; Fassungskraft *f*; **2.** (er)greifen, packen; begreifen.

grass [grɑːs] Gras *n*; Rasen *m*; *send to* ~ auf die Weide schicken; **~hopper** ['grɑːʃhɔpə] Heuschrecke *f*; ~ **roots** *pl. Am. pol* die landwirtschaftlichen Bezirke, *die* Landbevölkerung; **~widow(er)** F Strohwitwe(r *m*) *f*; ~**y** [~si] grasig; Gras...

grate [greit] **1.** (Kamin)Gitter *n*; (Feuer)Rost *m*; **2.** (zer)reiben; *mit et.* knirschen; *fig.* verletzen.

grateful [ˈgreitful] dankbar.

grater [ˈgreitə] Reibeisen *n*.

grati|fication [grætifiˈkeiʃən] Befriedigung *f*; Freude *f*; ~**fy** [ˈgrætifai] erfreuen; befriedigen.

grating [ˈgreitiŋ] **1.** schrill; unangenehm; **2.** Gitter(werk) *n*.

gratitude [ˈgrætitjuːd] Dankbarkeit *f*.

gratuit|ous [grəˈtjuː(ː)itəs] unentgeltlich; freiwillig; ~**y** [~ti] Abfindung *f*; Gratifikation *f*; Trinkgeld *n*.

grave [greiv] **1.** ernst; (ge)wichtig; gemessen; **2.** Grab *n*; **3.** [*irr.*] *mst fig.* (ein)graben; ~**digger** [ˈgreivdigə] Totengräber *m*.

gravel [ˈgrævəl] **1.** Kies *m*; Harngrieß *m*; **2.** mit Kies bedecken.

graven [ˈgreivən] *p.p. von* grave 3.

graveyard [ˈgreivjɑːd] Kirchhof *m*.

gravitation [græviˈteiʃən] Schwerkraft *f*; *fig.* Hang *m*.

gravity [ˈgræviti] Schwere *f*; Wichtigkeit *f*; Ernst *m*; Schwerkraft *f*.

gravy [ˈgreivi] Fleischsaft *m*, Bratensoße *f*.

gray *bsd. Am.* [grei] = grau.

graze [greiz] (ab)weiden; (ab)grasen; streifen, schrammen.

grease 1. [griːs] Fett *n*; Schmiere *f*; **2.** [griːz] (be)schmieren.

greasy [ˈgriːzi] fettig; schmierig.

great [greit] *allg.* groß; Groß...; F großartig; ~**coat** [ˈgreitˈkout] Überzieher *m*; ~**grandchild** Urenkel(in); ~**grandfather** Urgroßvater *m*; ~**ly** [~tli] sehr; ~**ness** [~tnis] Größe *f*; Stärke *f*.

greed [griːd] Gier *f*; ~**y** [~] [ˈgriːdi] (be)gierig (of, for nach); habgierig.

Greek [griːk] **1.** griechisch; **2.** Grieche *m*, -in *f*; Griechisch *n*.

green [griːn] **1.** grün (*a. fig.*); frisch (*Fisch etc.*); neu; Grün...; **2.** Grün *n*; Rasen *m*; Wiese *f*; ~**s** *pl.* frisches Gemüse; ~**back** *Am.* [ˈgriːnbæk] Dollarnote *f*; ~**grocer** Gemüsehändler(in); ~**grocery** Gemüsehandlung *f*; ~**horn** Grünschnabel *m*; ~**house** Gewächshaus *n*; ~**ish** [~niʃ] grünlich; ~**sickness** Bleichsucht *f*.

greet [griːt] (be)grüßen; ~**ing** [ˈgriːtiŋ] Begrüßung *f*; Gruß *m*.

grenade [griˈneid] Granate *f*.

grew [gruː] *pret. von* grow.

grey [grei] **1.** grau; **2.** Grau *n*; **3.** grau machen *od.* werden; ~**hound** [ˈgreihaund] Windhund *m*.

grid [grid] Gitter *n*; Netz *n*; *Am.* Fußball: Spielfeld *n*; ~**iron** [ˈgridaiən] (Brat)Rost *m*.

grief [griːf] Gram *m*, Kummer *m*; *come to* ~ zu Schaden kommen.

griev|ance [ˈgriːvəns] Beschwerde *f*; Mißstand *m*; ~**e** [griːv] kränken; (sich) grämen; ~**ous** [ˈgriːvəs] kränkend, schmerzlich; schlimm.

grill [gril] **1.** grillen; braten (*a. fig.*); **2.** Bratrost *m*, Grill *m*; gegrilltes Fleisch; *a.* ~**room** Grillroom *m*.

grim [grim] grimmig; schrecklich.

grimace [griˈmeis] **1.** Fratze *f*, Grimasse *f*; **2.** Grimassen schneiden.

grim|e [graim] Schmutz *m*; Ruß *m*; ~**y** [ˈgraimi] schmutzig; rußig.

grin [grin] **1.** Grinsen *n*; **2.** grinsen.

grind [graind] **1.** [*irr.*] (zer)reiben; mahlen; schleifen; *Leierkasten etc.* drehen; *fig.* schinden; *mit den Zähnen* knirschen; **2.** Schinderei *f*; ~**stone** [ˈgraindstoun] Schleif-, Mühlstein *m*.

grip [grip] **1.** packen, fassen (*a. fig.*); **2.** Griff *m*; Gewalt *f*; Herrschaft *f*; *Am.* = gripsack.

gripe [graip] Griff *m*; ~**s** *pl.* Kolik *f*; *bsd. Am.* Beschwerden *f/pl.*

gripsack *Am.* [ˈgripsæk] Handtasche *f*, ~köfferchen *n*.

grisly [ˈgrizli] gräßlich, schrecklich.

gristle [ˈgrisl] Knorpel *m*.

grit [grit] **1.** Kies *m*; Sand(stein) *m*; *fig.* Mut *m*; **2.** knirschen (mit).

grizzly [ˈgrizli] **1.** grau; **2.** Graubär *m*.

groan [groun] seufzen, stöhnen.

grocer [ˈgrousə] Lebensmittelhändler *m*; ~**ies** [~əriz] *pl.* Lebensmittel *n/pl.*; ~**y** [~] [ˈgrousəri] Lebensmittelgeschäft *n*.

groceteria *Am.* [grousiˈtiəriə] Selbstbedienungsladen *m*.

groggy [ˈgrɔgi] taumelig; wackelig.

groin *anat.* [grɔin] Leistengegend *f*.

groom [grum] **1.** Reit-, Stallknecht *m*; Bräutigam *m*; **2.** pflegen; *Am. pol. Kandidaten* lancieren.

groove [gruːv] **1.** Rinne *f*, Nut *f*; *fig.* Gewohnheit *f*; **2.** nuten, falzen.

grope [group] (be)tasten, tappen.

gross [grous] **1.** dick; grob; derb; Brutto...; **2.** Gros *n* (*12 Dutzend*); *in the* ~ im ganzen.

grotto [ˈgrɔtou] Grotte *f*.

grouch *Am.* F [grautʃ] **1.** quengeln, meckern; **2.** Griesgram *m*; schlechte Laune; ~**y** [ˈgrautʃi] quenglig.

ground[1] [graund] 1. *pret. u. p.p. von* grind 1; 2. ~ *glass* Mattglas *n*.

ground[2] [graund] 1. *mst* Grund *m*; Boden *n*; Gebiet *n*; *Spiel- etc.* Platz *m*; *Beweg- etc.* Grund *m*; ⚡ Erde *f*; ~*s* pl. Grundstück *n*, Park(s *pl.*) *m*, Gärten *m/pl.*; *Kaffee-* Satz *m*; *on the* ~(*s*) *of* auf Grund (*gen.*); *stand od. hold od. keep one's* ~ sich behaupten; 2. niederlegen; (be)gründen; *j-m* die Anfangs- gründe beibringen; ⚡ erden; ~*floor* ['graund'flɔ:] Erdgeschoß *n*; ~*hog* [~dhɔg] *bsd. Am.* Murmel- tier *n*; ~*less* □ [~dlis] grundlos; ~*staff* ✗ Bodenpersonal *n*; ~*work* Grundlage *f*.

group [gru:p] 1. Gruppe *f*; 2. (sich) gruppieren.

grove [grouv] Hain *m*; Gehölz *n*.

grovel *mst fig.* ['grɔvl] kriechen.

grow [grou] (*irr.*) *v/i.* wachsen; werden; *v/t.* ⚡ anpflanzen, an- bauen; ~*er* ['grouə] Bauer *m*, Züchter *m*.

growl [graul] knurren, brummen; ~*er* ['graulə] *fig.* Brummbär *m*; *Am. sl.* Bierkrug *m*.

grow|**n** [groun] 1. *p.p. von* grow; 2. *adj.* erwachsen; bewachsen; ~**n-up** ['grounʌp] 1. erwachsen; 2. Erwachsene(r *m*) *f*; ~**th** [grouθ] Wachstum *n*; (An)Wachsen *n*; Ent- wicklung *f*; Wuchs *m*; Gewächs *n*, Erzeugnis *n*.

grub [grʌb] 1. Raupe *f*, Larve *f*, Made *f*; *contp.* Prolet *m*; 2. graben; sich abmühen; ~**by** ['grʌbi] schmie- rig.

grudge [grʌdʒ] 1. Groll *m*; 2. miß- gönnen; ungern geben *od.* tun *etc.*

gruel [gruəl] Haferschleim *m*.

gruff [grʌf] grob, schroff, barsch.

grumble ['grʌmbl] murren; (g)rol- len; ~*r fig.* [~lə] Brummbär *m*.

grunt [grʌnt] grunzen.

guarant|**ee** [gærən'ti:] 1. Bürge *m*; = *guaranty*; 2. bürgen für; ~**or** [~'tɔ:] Bürge *m*; ~**y** ['gærənti] Bürg- schaft *f*, Garantie *f*; Gewähr *f*.

guard [ga:d] 1. Wacht *f*; ✗ Wache *f*; Wächter *m*, Wärter *m*; ⊕ Schaffner *m*; Schutz(vorrichtung *f*) *m*; 2*s pl.* Garde *f*; *be on* (*off*) *one's* ~ (nicht) auf der Hut sein; 2. *v/t.* bewachen, (be)schützen (*from vor dat.*); *v/i.* sich hüten (*against vor dat.*); ~**ian** ['ga:djən] Hüter *m*, Wächter *m*; ✗✗ Vormund *m*; *attr.* Schutz...; ~**ianship** [~nʃip] Obhut *f*; Vor- mundschaft *f*.

guess [ges] 1. Vermutung *f*; 2. ver- muten; (er)raten; *Am.* denken.

guest [gest] Gast *m*; ~**house** ['gesthaus] (Hotel)Pension *f*, Frem- denheim *n*; ~**room** Gast-, Frem- denzimmer *n*.

guffaw [gʌ'fɔ:] schallendes Ge- lächter.

guidance ['gaidəns] Führung *f*; (An)Leitung *f*.

guide [gaid] 1. Führer *m*; ⊕ Füh- rung *f*; *attr.* Führungs...; 2. leiten; führen; lenken; ~**book** ['gaidbuk] Reiseführer *m*; ~**post** Wegweiser *m*.

guild [gild] Gilde *f*, Innung *f*; 2**hall** ['gild'hɔ:l] Rathaus *n* (*Lon- don*).

guile [gail] Arglist *f*; ~**ful** □ ['gailful] arglistig; ~**less** □ ['gaillis] arglos.

guilt [gilt] Schuld *f*; Strafbarkeit *f*; ~**less** □ ['giltlis] schuldlos; un- kundig; ~**y** □ [~ti] schuldig; straf- bar.

guinea ['gini] Guinee *f* (*21 Schil- ling*); ~**pig** Meerschweinchen *n*.

guise [gaiz] Erscheinung *f*, Gestalt *f*; Maske *f*.

guitar ♪ [gi'ta:] Gitarre *f*.

gulch *Am.* [gʌlʃ] tiefe Schlucht.

gulf [gʌlf] Meerbusen *m*, Golf *m*; Abgrund *m*; Strudel *m*.

gull [gʌl] 1. Möwe *f*; Tölpel *m*; 2. übertölpeln; verleiten (*into* zu).

gullet ['gʌlit] Speiseröhre *f*; Gur- gel *f*.

gulp [gʌlp] Schluck *m*; Schlucken *n*.

gum [gʌm] 1. *a.* ~*s pl.* Zahnfleisch *n*; Gummi *n*; Klebstoff *m*; ~*s pl. Am.* Gummischuhe *m/pl.*; 2. gummie- ren; zukleben.

gun [gʌn] 1. Gewehr *n*; Flinte *f*; Geschütz *n*, Kanone *f*; *Am.* Re- volver *m*; *big* ~ F *fig.* hohes Tier; 2. *Am.* auf die Jagd gehen; ~**boat** ['gʌnbout] Kanonenboot *n*; ~**licence** Waffenschein *m*; ~**man** *Am.* Gangster *m*; ~**ner** ✗✗ [' gʌnə] Kanonier *m*; ~**powder** Schießpulver *n*; ~**smith** Büchsen- macher *m*.

gurgle ['gə:gl] gluckern, gur- geln.

gush [gʌʃ] 1. Guß *m*; *fig.* Erguß *m*; 2. (sich) ergießen, schießen (*from* aus); *fig.* schwärmen; ~**er** ['gʌʃə] *fig.* Schwärmer(in); Ölquelle *f*.

gust [gʌst] Windstoß *m*, Bö *f*.

gut [gʌt] Darm *m*; ♪ Darmsaite *f*; ~*s pl.* Eingeweide *n/pl.*; *das* In- nere; *fig.* Mut *m*.

gutter ['gʌtə] Dachrinne *f*; Gosse *f* (*a. fig.*), Rinnstein *m*.

guy [gai] 1. Halteseil *n*; F Vogel- scheuche *f*; *Am.* F Kerl *m*; 2. ver- albern.

guzzle ['gʌzl] saufen; fressen.

gymnas|**ium** [dʒim'neizjəm] Turn- halle *f*, -platz *m*; ~**tics** [~'næstiks] *pl.* Turnen *n*; Gymnastik *f*.

gypsy *bsd. Am.* ['dʒipsi] = gipsy.

gyrate [dʒaiə'reit] kreisen; wir- beln.

gyroplane ['dʒaiərəplein] Hub- schrauber *m*.

H

haberdasher ['hæbədæʃə] Kurz-
warenhändler *m*; *Am.* Herrenarti-
kelhändler *m*; ~y [~əri] Kurzwaren
(-geschäft *n*) *f/pl.*; *Am.* Herren-
artikel *m/pl.*

habit ['hæbit] **1.** (An)Gewohnheit
f; Verfassung *f*; Kleid(ung *f*) *n*;
fall od. get into bad ~s schlechte
Gewohnheiten annehmen; **2.** (an-)
kleiden; ~able [~təbl] bewohnbar;
~ation [hæbi'teiʃən] Wohnung *f*.

habitual [ ]hə'bitjuəl] gewohnt,
gewöhnlich; Gewohnheits...

hack [hæk] **1.** Hieb *m*; Einkerbung
f; Miet-, Arbeitspferd *n* (*a. fig.*);
a. ~ writer literarischer Lohn-
schreiber *m*; **2.** (zer)hacken.

hackneyed *fig.* ['hæknid] abgedroschen.

had [hæd] *pret. u. p.p. von* have.

haddock ['hædək] Schellfisch *m*.

h(a)emorrhage ['hemərid3] Blut-
sturz *m*.

hag [hæg] (*mst fig.* alte) Hexe.

haggard □ ['hægəd] verstört; hager.

haggle ['hægl] feilschen, schachern.

hail [heil] **1.** Hagel *m*; Anruf *m*;
2. (nieder)hageln (lassen); anrufen;
(be)grüßen; ~ *from* stammen aus;
~**stone** ['heilstoun] Hagelkorn *n*;
~**storm** Hagelschauer *m*.

hair [hεə] Haar *n*; ~**breadth**
['hεəbredθ] Haaresbreite *f*; ~**cut**
Haarschnitt *m*; ~**do** *Am.* Frisur *f*;
~**dresser** (*bsd.* Damen)Friseur *m*;
~**drier** [~draiə] Trockenhaube *f*;
Fön *m*; ~**less** [~hεəlis] ohne Haare,
kahl; ~**pin** Haarnadel *f*; ~**raising**
['hεəreizin] haarsträubend; ~**splitting** Haarspalterei *f*; ~**y** [~hεəri]
haarig.

hale [heil] gesund, frisch, rüstig.

half [hɑ:f] **1.** *pl.* halves [hɑ:vz]
Hälfte *f*; *by halves* nur halb; *go
halves* halbpart machen, teilen
2. halb; ~ *a crown* eine halbe
Krone; ~**back** ['hɑ:f'bæk] *Fußball:* Läufer *m*; ~**breed** ['hɑ:f-
bri:d] Halbblut *n*; ~**caste** Halbblut *n*; ~**hearted** ['hɑ:f'hɑ:tid]
lustlos, lau; ~**length** Brustbild *n*;
~**penny** ['heipni] halber Penny;
~**time** ['hɑ:f'taim] *Sport:* Halb-
zeit *f*; ~**way** halbwegs; ~**witted**
einfältig, idiotisch.

halibut *ichth.* ['hælibət] Heilbutt *m*.

hall [hɔ:l] Halle *f*; Saal *m*; Vorraum
m; Flur *m*; Diele *f*; Herren-, Gutshaus *n*; *univ.* Speisesaal *m*; ~ *of
residence* Studentenwohnheim *n*.

halloo [hə'lu:] (hallo) rufen.

hallow ['hælou] heiligen, weihen;
♀mas [~oumæs] Allerheiligenfest *n*.

halo ['heilou] *ast.* Hof *m*; Heiligenschein *m*.

halt [hɔ:lt] **1.** Halt(estelle *f*) *m*;
Stillstand *m*; **2.** (an)halten; *mst fig.*
hinken; schwanken.

halter ['hɔ:ltə] Halfter *f*; Strick *m*.

halve [hɑ:v] halbieren; ~s [hɑ:vz]
pl. von half 1.

ham [hæm] Schenkel *m*; Schinken
m.

hamburger *Am.* ['hæmbə:gə] Frikadelle *f*; mit Frikadelle belegtes
Brötchen.

hamlet ['hæmlit] Weiler *m*.

hammer ['hæmə] **1.** Hammer *m*;
2. (be)hämmern.

hammock ['hæmək] Hängematte *f*.

hamper ['hæmpə] **1.** Geschenk-,
Eßkorb *m*; **2.** verstricken; behin-
dern.

hamster *zo.* ['hæmstə] Hamster *m*.

hand [hænd] **1.** Hand *f* (*a. fig.*);
Handschrift *f*; Handbreite *f*;
(Uhr)Zeiger *m*; Mann *m*, Arbeiter
m; *Karten:* Blatt *n*; at ~ bei der
Hand; nahe bevorstehend; at first ~
aus erster Hand; a good (poor) ~ at
(un)geschickt in (*dat.*); and glove
ein Herz und eine Seele; change ~s
den Besitzer wechseln; lend a ~
(mit) anfassen; off ~ aus dem Handgelenk *od.* Stegreif; on ~ ↑ vorrätig, auf Lager; *Am.* zur
Stelle, bereit; on one's ~s auf dem
Halse; on the one ~ einerseits; on
the other ~ andererseits; ~ to ~
Mann gegen Mann; come to ~
sich bieten; einlaufen (*Briefe*) **2.**
reichen; ~ about herumreichen; ~
down vererben; ~ in einhändigen;
einreichen; ~ over aushändigen;
~**bag** ['hændbæg] Handtasche *f*;
~**bill** Hand-, Reklamezettel *m*;
~**brake** ⊕ Handbremse *f*; ~**cuff**
Handfessel *f*; ~**ful** [~dful] Hand-
voll *f*; F Plage *f*; ~**glass** Hand-
spiegel *m*; Leselupe *f*.

handicap ['hændikæp] **1.** Handikap
n; Vorgaberennen *n*, Vorgabespiel
n; (Extra)Belastung *f*; **2.** (extra)
belasten; beeinträchtigen.

handi|craft ['hændikrɑ:ft] Hand-
werk *n*; Handfertigkeit *f*; ~**crafts-
man** Handwerker *m*; ~**work** Handarbeit *f*; Werk *n*.

handkerchief ['hæŋkətʃi(:)f] Taschentuch *n*; Halstuch *n*.

handle ['hændl] **1.** Griff *m*; Stiel *m*;
Henkel *m*; Pumpen- *etc.* Schwengel
m; *fig.* Handhabe *f*; fly off the ~ F
platzen vor Wut; **2.** anfassen; handhaben; behandeln; ~**bar** Lenk-
stange *f e-s Fahrrades*.

hand|-luggage ['hændlʌgid3]
Handgepäck *n*; ~**made** handgear-
beitet; ~**me-downs** *Am.* F *pl.* Fer-
tigkleidung *f*; getragene Kleider *pl.*;
~**rail** Geländer *n*; ~**shake** Hände-

druck m; ~some □ ['hænsəm] ansehnlich; hübsch; anständig; ~work Handarbeit f; ~writing Handschrift f; ~y □ ['hændi] geschickt; handlich; zur Hand.

hang [hæŋ] 1. [irr.] v/t. hängen; auf-, einhängen; verhängen; (pret. u. p.p. mst ~ed) (er)hängen; hängen lassen; Tapete ankleben; v/i. hängen; schweben; sich neigen; ~ about (Am. around) herumlungern; sich an j-n hängen; ~ back sich zurückhalten; ~ on sich klammern an (acc.); fig. hängen an (dat.); 2. Hang m; Fall m e-r Gardine etc.; F Wesen n; F fig. Kniff m; Dreh m.

hangar ['hæŋə] Flugzeughalle f.

hang-dog ['hæŋdɔg] Armesünder...

hanger ['hæŋə] Aufhänger m; Hirschfänger m; ~-on fig. ['~ər'ɔn] Klette f.

hanging ['hæŋiŋ] 1. Hänge...; 2. ~s pl. Behang m; Tapeten f/pl.

hangman ['hæŋmən] Henker m.

hang-nail ♂ ['hæŋneil] Niednagel m.

hang-over sl. ['hæŋouvə] Katzenjammer m, Kater m.

hanker ['hæŋkə] sich sehnen.

hap|hazard ['hæp'hæzəd] 1. Zufall m; at ~ aufs Geratewohl; 2. zufällig; ~less □ ['hæplis] unglücklich.

happen ['hæpən] sich ereignen, geschehen; he ~ed to be at home er war zufällig zu Hause; ~ (up)on zufällig treffen auf (acc.); ~ in Am. F hereinschneien; ~ing ['hæpniŋ] Ereignis n.

happi|ly ['hæpili] glücklicherweise; ~ness [~inis] Glück(seligkeit f) n.

happy □ ['hæpi] allg. glücklich; beglückt; erfreut; erfreulich; geschickt; treffend; F angeheitert; ~-go-lucky F unbekümmert.

harangue [hə'ræŋ] 1. Ansprache f, Rede f; 2. v/t. feierlich anreden.

harass ['hærəs] belästigen, quälen.

harbo(u)r ['ha:bə] 1. Hafen m; Zufluchtsort m; 2. (be)herbergen; Rache etc. hegen; ankern; ~age [~əridʒ] Herberge f; Zuflucht f.

hard [ha:d] 1. adj. allg. hart; schwer; mühselig; streng; ausdauernd; fleißig; heftig; Am. stark (Spirituosen); ~ of hearing schwerhörig; 2. adv. stark; tüchtig; mit Mühe; ~ by nahe bei; ~ up in Not; ~-boiled ['ha:d'bɔild] hartgesotten; Am. gerissen; ~ cash Bargeld n; klingende Münze; ~en ['ha:dn] härten; hart machen od. werden; (sich) abhärten; fig. (sich) verhärten; † sich festigen (Preise); ~-headed nüchtern denkend; ~-hearted □ hartherzig; ~ihood ['ha:dihud] Kühnheit f; ~iness [~inis] Widerstandsfähigkeit f, Härte f; ~ly ['ha:dli] kaum; streng;

mit Mühe; ~ness ['ha:dnis] Härte f; Schwierigkeit f; Not f; ~pan Am. harter Boden, fig. Grundlage f; ~ship ['ha:dʃip] Bedrängnis f, Not f; Härte f; ~ware Eisenwaren f/pl.; ~y □ ['ha:di] kühn; widerstandsfähig, hart; abgehärtet; winterfest (Pflanze).

hare [hɛə] Hase m; ~bell ♀ ['hɛəbel] Glockenblume f; ~brained zerfahren; ~lip anat. ['hɛə'lip] Hasenscharte f.

hark [ha:k] horchen (to auf acc.).

harlot ['ha:lət] Hure f.

harm [ha:m] 1. Schaden m; Unrecht n, Böse(s) n; 2. beschädigen, verletzen; schaden, Leid zufügen (dat.); ~ful □ ['ha:mful] schädlich; ~less □ ['ha:mlis] harmlos; unschädlich.

harmon|ic [ha:'mɔnik] (~ally), ~ious □ [ha:'mounjəs] harmonisch; ~ize ['ha:mənaiz] v/t. in Einklang bringen; v/i. harmonieren; ~y [~ni] Harmonie f.

harness ['ha:nis] 1. Harnisch m; Zug-Geschirr n; die in ~ in den Sielen sterben; 2. anschirren; bändigen; Wasserkraft nutzbar machen.

harp [ha:p] 1. Harfe f; 2. Harfe spielen; ~ (up)on herumreiten auf (dat.). 2. harpunieren.

harpoon [ha:'pu:n] 1. Harpune f;

harrow ♂ ['hærou] 1. Egge f; 2. eggen; fig. quälen, martern.

harry ['hæri] plündern; quälen.

harsh □ [ha:ʃ] rauh; herb; grell; streng; schroff; barsch.

hart zo. [ha:t] Hirsch m.

harvest ['ha:vist] 1. Ernte(zeit) f; Ertrag m; 2. ernten; einbringen.

has [hæz] 3. sg. pres. von have.

hash [hæʃ] 1. gehacktes Fleisch; Am. F Essen n, Fraß m; fig. Mischmasch m; 2. (zer)hacken.

hast|e [heist] Eile f; Hast f; make ~ (sich be)eilen; ~en ['heisn] (sich be)eilen; j-n antreiben; et. beschleunigen; ~y □ ['heisti] (vor-)eilig; hastig; hitzig, heftig.

hat [hæt] Hut m.

hatch [hætʃ] 1. Brut f, Hecke f; ⚓, ⚒ Luke f; serving ~ Durchreiche f; 2. (aus)brüten (a. fig.).

hatchet ['hætʃit] Beil n.

hatchway ⚓ ['hætʃwei] Luke f.

hat|e [heit] 1. Haß m; 2. hassen; ~ful □ ['heitful] verhaßt; abscheulich; ~red ['heitrid] Haß m.

haught|iness ['hɔ:tinis] Stolz m; Hochmut m; ~y □ ['hɔ:ti] stolz; hochmütig.

haul [hɔ:l] 1. Ziehen n; (Fisch-)Zug m; Am. Transport(weg) m; 2. ziehen; schleppen; transportieren; ⚒ fördern; ⚓ abdrehen; ~ down one's flag die Flagge streichen; fig. sich geschlagen geben.

haunch [hɔ:ntʃ] Hüfte *f*; Keule *f von Wild*.

haunt [hɔ:nt] **1.** Aufenthaltsort *m*; Schlupfwinkel *m*; **2.** oft besuchen; heimsuchen; verfolgen; spuken in (*dat.*).

have [hæv] [*irr.*] *v/t.* haben; bekommen; *Mahlzeit* einnehmen; lassen; ~ *to do tun müssen*; *I ~ my hair cut* ich lasse mir das Haar schneiden; *he will ~ it that ...* er behauptet, daß ...; *I had better go* es wäre besser, wenn ich ginge; *I had rather go* ich möchte lieber gehen; ~ *about one* bei *od.* an sich haben; ~ *on* anhaben; ~ *it out with* sich auseinandersetzen mit; *v/aux.* haben; *bei v/i.* oft sein; ~ *come* gekommen sein.

haven ['heivn] Hafen *m* (*a. fig.*).

havoc ['hævək] Verwüstung *f*; *make ~ of, play ~ with od. among* verwüsten; übel zurichten.

haw ♀ [hɔ:] Hagebutte *f*.

Hawaiian [hɑ:'waiiən] **1.** hawaiisch; **2.** Hawaiier(in).

hawk [hɔ:k] **1.** Habicht *m*; Falke *m*; **2.** sich räuspern; hausieren mit.

hawthorn ♀ ['hɔ:θɔ:n] Weißdorn *m*.

hay [hei] **1.** Heu *n*; **2.** heuen; **~cock** ['heikɔk] Heuhaufen *m*; **~fever** Heuschnupfen *m*; **~loft** Heuboden *m*; **~maker** *bsd. Am.* K.o.-Schlag *m*; **~rick** = haycock; **~seed** *bsd. Am.* F Bauerntölpel *m*; **~stack** = haycock.

hazard ['hæzəd] **1.** Zufall *m*; Gefahr *f*, Wagnis *n*; Hasard(spiel) *n*; **2.** wagen; **~ous** [[~dəs] gewagt.

haze [heiz] Dunst *m*; **2.** ♠ *u. Am.* schinden; F schurigeln.

hazel ['heizl] **1.** ♀ Hasel(staude) *f*; **2.** nußbraun; **~nut** Haselnuß *f*.

hazy [['heizi] dunstig; *fig.* unklar.

H-bomb ☢ ['eitʃbɔm] H-Bombe *f*, Wasserstoffbombe *f*.

he [hi:] **1.** er; ~ *who* derjenige, welcher; **2.** Mann *m*; *zo.* Männchen *n*; **3.** *adj. in Zssgn.* männlich, ...männchen *n*; **~-goat** Ziegenbock *m*.

head [hed] **1.** *allg.* Kopf *m* (*a. fig.*); Haupt *n* (*a. fig.*); *nach Zahlwort:* Mann *m* (*a. pl.*); Stück *n* (*a. pl.*); Leiter(in); Chef *m*; Kopfende *n e-s Bettes etc.*; Kopfseite *f e-r Münze*; Gipfel *m*; Quelle *f*; *Schiffs-*Vorderteil *n*; Hauptpunkt *m*, Abschnitt *m*; Überschrift *f*; *come to a ~* eitern (*Geschwür*); *fig.* sich zuspitzen, zur Entscheidung kommen; *get it into one's ~ that ...* es sich in den Kopf setzen, daß; ~ *over heels* Hals über Kopf; **2.** erst; Ober...; Haupt...; **3.** *v/t.* (an)führen; an der Spitze von *et.* stehen; vorausgehen (*dat.*); mit e-r Überschrift versehen; *v/i.* ♠ zusteuern (*for auf acc.*); *Am.* entspringen (*Fluß*); **~ache** ['hedeik] Kopfweh *n*; ~

dress Kopfputz *m*; Frisur *f*; **~gear** Kopfbedeckung *f*; Zaumzeug *n*; **~ing** ['hedin] Brief-, Titelkopf *m*, Rubrik *f*; Überschrift *f*, Titel *m*; *Sport:* Kopfball *m*; **~land** ['hedlənd] Vorgebirge *n*; **~light** *mot.* Scheinwerfer(licht *n*) *m*; **~line** Überschrift *f*; Schlagzeile *f*; ~*s pl. Radio:* das Wichtigste in Kürze; **~long 1.** *adj.* ungestüm; **2.** *adv.* kopfüber; **~master** Direktor *m e-r Schule*; **~phone** *Radio* Kopfhörer *m*; **~quarters** *pl.* ✕ Hauptquartier *n*; Zentral(stell)e *f*; **~strong** halsstarrig; **~waters** *pl.* Quellgebiet *n*; **~way** Fortschritt(e *pl.*) *m*; *make ~* vorwärtskommen; **~word** Stichwort *n e-s Wörterbuchs*; **~y** [['hedi] ungestüm; voreilig; zu Kopfe steigend.

heal [hi:l] heilen; ~ *up* zuheilen.

health [helθ] Gesundheit *f*; **~ful** [['helθful] gesund; heilsam; **~resort** Kurort *m*; **~y** [['helθi] gesund.

heap [hi:p] **1.** Haufe(n) *m*; **2.** *a.* ~ *up* (auf)häufen; überhäufen.

hear [hiə] [*irr.*] hören; erfahren; anhören; *j-m* zuhören; erhören; *Zeugen* verhören; *Lektion* abhören; **~d** [hə:d] *pret. u. p.p. von hear*; **~er** ['hiərə] (Zu)Hörer(in); **~ing** [~riŋ] Gehör *n*; Audienz *f*; ✕ Verhör *n*; Hörweite *f*; **~say** Hörensagen *n*.

hearse [hə:s] Leichenwagen *m*.

heart [hɑ:t] *allg.* Herz *n* (*a. fig.*); Innere(s) *n*; Kern *m*; *fig.* Schatz *m*; *by ~* auswendig; *out of ~* mutlos; *lay to ~* sich zu Herzen nehmen; *lose ~* den Mut verlieren; *take ~* sich ein Herz fassen; **~ache** ['hɑ:teik] Kummer *m*; **~break** Herzeleid *n*; **~breaking** [~kiŋ] herzzerbrechend; **~broken** gebrochenen Herzens; **~burn** Sodbrennen *n*; **~en** ['hɑ:tn] ermutigen; **~failure** ☢ Herzversagen *n*; **~felt** innig, tief empfunden.

hearth [hɑ:θ] Herd *m* (*a. fig.*).

heart|less [['hɑ:tlis] herzlos; **~rending** ['hɑ:trendiŋ] herzzerreißend; ~ **transplant** Herzverpflanzung *f*; **~y** ['hɑ:ti] herzlich; aufrichtig; gesund; herzhaft.

heat [hi:t] **1.** *allg.* Hitze *f*; Wärme *f*; Eifer *m*; *Sport:* Gang *m*, einzelner Lauf; *zo.* Läufigkeit *f*; **2.** heizen; (sich) erhitzen (*a. fig.*); **~er** ⊕ ['hi:tə] Erhitzer *m*; Ofen *m*.

heath [hi:θ] Heide *f*; ♀ Heidekraut *n*.

heathen ['hi:ðən] **1.** Heid|e *m*, -in *f*; **2.** heidnisch.

heather ♀ ['heðə] Heide(kraut *n*) *f*.

heat|ing ['hi:tiŋ] Heizung *f*; *attr.* Heiz...; ~ **lightning** *Am.* Wetterleuchten *n*.

heave [hi:v] **1.** Heben *n*; Übelkeit *f*;

2. [irr.] v/t. heben; schwellen; *Seufzer* ausstoßen; *Anker* lichten; v/i. sich heben, wogen, schwellen.

heaven ['hevn] Himmel m; **~ly** [~nli] himmlisch.

heaviness ['hevinis] Schwere f, Druck m; Schwerfälligkeit f; Schwermut f.

heavy □ ['hevi] allg. schwer; schwermütig; schwerfällig; trüb; drückend; heftig (*Regen etc.*); unwegsam (*Straße*); Schwer...; **~current** ⚡ Starkstrom m; **~handed** ungeschickt; **~hearted** niedergeschlagen; **~weight** *Boxen*: Schwergewicht n.

heckle ['hekl] durch Zwischenfragen in die Enge treiben.

hectic ⚕ ['hektik] hektisch (*auszehrend*; *sl.* fieberhaft erregt).

hedge [hedʒ] **1.** Hecke f; **2.** v/t. einhegen, einzäunen; umgeben; **~up sperren**; v/i. sich decken; sich nicht festlegen; **~hog** zo. ['hedʒhɔg] Igel m; Am. Stachelschwein n; **~row** Hecke f.

heed [hi:d] **1.** Beachtung f, Aufmerksamkeit f; take ~ of, give od. pay ~ to achtgeben auf (acc.), beachten; **2.** beachten, achten auf (acc.); **~less** □ ['hi:dlis] unachtsam; unbekümmert (of um).

heel [hi:l] **1.** Ferse f; Absatz m; Am. sl. Lump m; head over ~s Hals über Kopf; down at ~ mit schiefen Absätzen; fig. abgerissen; schlampig; **2.** mit e-m Absatz versehen; **~ed** Am. F finanzstark; Am. sl. pol. ['hi:ld] Befehlsempfänger m.

heft [heft] Gewicht n; Am. F Hauptteil m.

heifer ['hefə] Färse f (junge Kuh).

height [hait] Höhe f; Höhepunkt m; **~en** ['haitn] erhöhen; vergrößern.

heinous □ ['heinəs] abscheulich.

heir [ɛə] Erbe m; ~ apparent rechtmäßiger Erbe; **~ess** ['ɛəris] Erbin f; **~loom** ['ɛəlu:m] Erbstück n.

held [held] pret. u. p.p. von hold 2.

helibus Am. F ['helibʌs] Lufttaxi n.

helicopter ♣ ['helikɔptə] Hubschrauber m.

hell [hel] Hölle f; attr. Höllen...; what the ~ ...? F was zum Teufel ...?; raise ~ Krach machen; **~bent** ['helbent] Am. sl. unweigerlich entschlossen; **~ish** □ ['heliʃ] höllisch.

hello ['he'lou] hallo!

helm ♣ [helm] (Steuer)Ruder n.

helmet ['helmit] Helm m.

helmsman ♣ ['helmzmən] Steuermann m.

help [help] **1.** allg. Hilfe f; (Hilfs-) Mittel n; (Dienst)Mädchen n; **2.** v/t. (ab)helfen (dat.); unterlassen; bei Tisch geben, reichen;

~ o.s. sich bedienen, zulangen; I could not ~ laughing ich konnte nicht umhin zu lachen; v/i. helfen, dienen; **~er** ['helpə] Helfer(in), Gehilf|e m, -in f; **~ful** □ ['helpful] hilfreich; nützlich; **~ing** [~piŋ] Portion f; **~less** □ ['helplis] hilflos; **~lessness** [~snis] Hilflosigkeit f; **~mate, ~meet** Gehilf|e m, -in f; Gattin f.

helter-skelter ['heltə'skeltə] holterdiepolter.

helve [helv] Stiel m, Griff m.

Helvetian [hel'vi:ʃjən] Helvetier (-in); attr. Schweizer...

hem [hem] **1.** Saum m; **2.** v/t. säumen; ~ in einschließen; v/i. sich räuspern.

hemisphere ['hemisfiə] Halbkugel f.

hem-line ['hemlain] Kleid: Saum m.

hemlock ♀ ['hemlɔk] Schierling m; **~tree** Schierlingstanne f.

hemp [hemp] Hanf m.

hemstitch ['hemstitʃ] Hohlsaum m.

hen [hen] Henne f; *Vogel*-Weibchen n.

hence [hens] weg; hieraus; daher; von jetzt an; a year ~ heute übers Jahr; **~forth** [hens'fɔ:θ], **~forward** [~'fɔ:wəd] von nun an.

hen|-coop ['henku:p] Hühnerstall m; **~pecked** unter dem Pantoffel (stehend).

hep Am. sl. [hep]: to be ~ to kennen; **~cat** Am. sl. ['hepkæt] Eingeweihte(r m) f; Jazzfanatiker(in).

her [hɔ:, hə] sie; ihr; ihr(e).

herald ['herəld] **1.** Herold m; **2.** (sich) ankündigen; ~ in einführen; **~ry** [~dri] Wappenkunde f, Heraldik f.

herb [hə:b] Kraut n; **~age** ['hə:bidʒ] Gras n; Weide f; **~ivorous** [hə:'bivərəs] pflanzenfressend.

herd [hə:d] **1.** Herde f (a. fig.); **2.** v/t. Vieh hüten; v/i. a. ~ together in e-r Herde leben; zs.- hausen; **~er** ['hə:də], **~sman** ['hə:dzmən] Hirt m.

here [hiə] hier; hierher; ~'s to ...! auf das Wohl von ...!

here|after [hiər'a:ftə] **1.** künftig; **2.** Zukunft f; **~by** ['hiə'bai] hierdurch.

heredit|ary [hi'reditəri] erblich; Erb...; **~y** [~ti] Erblichkeit f.

here|in ['hiər'in] hierin; **~of** [hiər-'ɔv] hiervon.

heresy ['herəsi] Ketzerei f.

heretic ['herətik] Ketzer(in).

here|tofore ['hiətu'fɔ:] bis jetzt; ehemals; **~upon** ['hiərə'pɔn] hierauf; **~with** hiermit.

heritage ['heritidʒ] Erbschaft f.

hermit ['hə:mit] Einsiedler m.

hero ['hiərou] Held m; **~ic(al** □) [hi'rouik(əl)] heroisch; heldenhaft;

Helden...; **~ine** ['herouin] Heldin f; **~ism** [~izəm] Heldenmut m, -tum n.

heron zo. ['herən] Reiher m.

herring ichth. ['heriŋ] Hering m.

hers [həːz] der (die, das) ihrige; ihr.

herself [həːˈself] (sie, ihr, sich) selbst; sich; of ~ von selbst; by ~ allein.

hesitat|e ['heziteit] zögern, unschlüssig sein; Bedenken tragen; **~ion** [hezi'teiʃən] Zögern n; Unschlüssigkeit f; Bedenken n.

hew [hjuː] [irr.] hauen, hacken; **~n** [hjuːn] p.p. von hew.

hey [hei] ei!; hei!; he!, heda!

heyday ['heidei] 1. heisa!; oho!; 2. fig. Höhepunkt m, Blüte f.

hi [hai] he!, heda!; hallo!

hicc|ough, ~up ['hikʌp] 1. Schlukken m; 2. schlucken; den Schlukken haben.

hid [hid] pret. u. p.p. von hide 2; **~den** ['hidn] p.p. von hide 2.

hide [haid] 1. Haut f; 2. [irr.] (sich) verbergen, verstecken; **~and-seek** ['haidənd'siːk] Versteckspiel n.

hidebound fig. ['haidbaund] engherzig.

hideous □ ['hidiəs] scheußlich.

hiding ['haidiŋ] F Tracht f Prügel; Verbergen n; **~place** Versteck n.

hi-fi Am. ['hai'fai] = high-fidelity.

high [hai] 1. adj. □ allg. hoch; vornehm; gut, edel (Charakter); stolz; hochtrabend; angegangen (Fleisch); extrem; stark; üppig, flott (Leben); Hoch...; Ober...; with a ~ hand arrogant, anmaßend; in ~ spirits in gehobener Stimmung, guter Laune; ~ life die vornehme Welt; ~ time höchste Zeit; ~ words heftige Worte; 2. meteor. Hoch n; bsd. Am. für Zssgn wie high school, etc.; 3. adv. hoch; sehr, mächtig; **~ball** Am. ['haibɔːl] Whisky m mit Soda; **~bred** vornehm erzogen; **~brow** F 1. Intellektuelle(r m) f; 2. betont intellektuell; **~class** erstklassig; **~fidelity** mit höchster Wiedergabetreue, Hi-Fi; **~grade** hochwertig; **~handed** anmaßend; **~land** ['hailənd] Hochland n; **~lights** pl. fig. Höhepunkte m/pl.; **~ly** ['haili] hoch; sehr; speak ~ of s.o. j-n loben; **~minded** hochherzig; **~ness** ['hainis] Höhe f; fig. Hoheit f; **~pitched** schrill (Ton); steil (Dach); **~power**: ~ station Großkraftwerk n; **~road** Landstraße f; **~school** höhere Schule; **~strung** überempfindlich; ~ tea frühes Abendessen mit Tee u. Fleisch etc.; **~water** Hochwasser n; **~way** Landstraße f; Eig. Weg m; ~ code Straßenverkehrsordnung f; **~wayman** Straßenräuber m.

hike F [haik] 1. wandern; 2. Wanderung f; bsd. Am. F Erhöhung f (Preis etc.); **~r** ['haikə] Wanderer m.

hilarious □ [hi'lɛəriəs] ausgelassen.

hill [hil] Hügel m, Berg m; **~billy** Am. F ['hilbili] Hinterwäldler m; **~ock** ['hilɔk] kleiner Hügel; **~side** ['hil'said] Hang m; **~y** ['hili] hügelig.

hilt [hilt] Griff m (bsd. am Degen).

him [him] ihn; ihm; den, dem(jenigen); **~self** [him'self] (er, ihm, ihn, sich) selbst; sich; of ~ von selbst; by ~ allein.

hind[1] zo. [haind] Hirschkuh f.

hind[2] [~] Hinter...; **~er** 1. ['haində] hintere(r, -s); Hinter...; 2. ['hində] v/t. hindern (from an dat.); hemmen; **~most** ['haindmoust] hinterst, letzt.

hindrance ['hindrəns] Hindernis n.

hinge [hindʒ] 1. Türangel f; Scharnier n; fig. Angelpunkt m; 2. ~ upon fig. abhängen von.

hint [hint] 1. Wink m; Anspielung f; 2. andeuten; anspielen (at auf acc.).

hinterland ['hintəlænd] Hinterland n.   [butte f.]

hip [hip] anat. Hüfte f; & Hage-)

hippopotamus zo. [hipə'pɔtəməs] Flußpferd n.

hire ['haiə] 1. Miete f; Entgelt m, n, Lohn m; 2. mieten; j-n anstellen; ~ out vermieten.

his [hiz] sein(e); der (die, das) seinige.

hiss [his] v/i. zischen; zischeln; v/t. a. ~ off auszischen, auspfeifen.

histor|ian [his'tɔːriən] Historiker m; **~ic(al** □) [his'tɔrik(əl)] historisch, geschichtlich; Geschichts...; **~y** ['histəri] Geschichte f.

hit [hit] 1. Schlag m, Stoß m; fig. (Seiten)Hieb m; (Glücks)Treffer m; thea., ♪ Schlager m; 2. [irr.] schlagen, stoßen; treffen; auf et. stoßen; Am. F eintreffen in (dat.) ~ s.o. a blow j-m e-n Schlag versetzen; ~ it off with F sich vertragen mit; ~ (up)on (zufällig) kommen od. stoßen od. verfallen auf (acc.).

hitch [hitʃ] 1. Ruck m; ♣ Knoten m; fig. Haken m, Hindernis n; 2. rükken; (sich) festmachen, festhaken; hängenbleiben; rutschen; **~hike** F ['hitʃhaik] per Anhalter fahren.

hither lit. ['hiðə] hierher; **~to** bisher.

hive [haiv] 1. Bienenstock m; Bienenschwarm m; fig. Schwarm m; 2. ~ up aufspeichern; zs.-wohnen.

hoard [hɔːd] 1. Vorrat m, Schatz m; 2. a. ~ up aufhäufen; horten.

hoarfrost ['hɔː'frɔst] (Rauh)Reif m.

hoarse □ [hɔːs] heiser, rauh.

hoary ['hɔːri] (alters)grau.

hoax [houks] 1. Täuschung f; Falschmeldung f; 2. foppen.

hob [hɔb] = hobgoblin; raise ~ bsd. Am. F Krach schlagen.

hobble ['hɔbl] 1. Hinken n, Humpeln n; F Klemme f, Patsche f; 2. v/i. humpeln, hinken (a. fig.); v/t. an den Füßen fesseln.

hobby ['hɔbi] fig. Steckenpferd n, Hobby n; **~-horse** Steckenpferd n; Schaukelpferd n.

hobgoblin ['hɔbgɔblin] Kobold m.

hobo Am. sl. ['houbou] Landstreicher m.

hock¹ [hɔk] Rheinwein m.

hock² zo. [~] Sprunggelenk n.

hod [hɔd] Mörteltrog m.

hoe ✓ [hou] 1. Hacke f; 2. hacken.

hog [hɔg] 1. Schwein n (a. fig.); 2. Mähne stutzen; mot. drauflos rasen; **~gish** □ ['hɔgiʃ] schweinisch; gefräßig.

hoist [hɔist] 1. Aufzug m; 2. hochziehen, hissen.

hokum sl. ['houkəm] Mätzchen n/pl.; Kitsch m; Humbug m.

hold [hould] 1. Halten n; Halt m, Griff m, Gewalt f, Einfluß m; ⚓ Lade-, Frachtraum m; catch (od. get, lay, take, seize) ~ of erfassen, ergreifen, sich aneignen; keep ~ of festhalten; 2. [irr.] v/t. allg. halten; fest-, aufhalten; enthalten; fig. behalten; Versammlung etc. abhalten; (inne)haben; Ansicht vertreten; Gedanken etc. hegen; halten für; glauben; behaupten; ~ one's ground, ~ one's own sich behaupten; ~ the line teleph. am Apparat bleiben; ~ on et. (an s-m Platz fest)halten; ~ over aufschieben; ~ up aufrecht halten; (unter-)stützen, aufhalten; (räuberisch) überfallen; v/i. (fest)halten; gelten; sich bewähren; standhalten; ~ forth Reden halten; ~ good od. true gelten, sich bestätigen; ~ off sich fernhalten; ~ on ausharren; fortdauern, sich festhalten; teleph. am Apparat bleiben; ~ to festhalten an (dat.), ~ up sich (aufrecht) halten; **~er** ['houldə] Pächter m; Halter m (Gerät), Besitz m; Inhaber(in) (bsd. ✝); **~ing** [~diŋ] Halten n; Halt m; Pachtgut n, Besitz m; ~ company Dachgesellschaft f; **~-over** Am. Rest m; **~-up** Raubüberfall m; Stauung f, Stockung f.

hole [houl] 1. Loch n; Höhle f; F fig. Klemme f; pick ~s in bekritteln; 2. aushöhlen, durchlöchern.

holiday ['hɔlədi] Feiertag m; freier Tag; ~s pl Ferien pl., Urlaub m; **~-maker** Urlauber(in).

holler Am. F ['hɔlə] laut rufen.

hollow ['hɔlou] 1. □ hohl; leer; falsch, 2. Höhle f, (Aus)Höhlung f; Land-Senke f; 3. aushöhlen.

holly ♀ ['hɔli] Stechpalme f.

holster ['houlstə] Pistolentasche f.

holy ['houli] heilig; ♀ Thursday Gründonnerstag m; ~ water Weihwasser n; ♀ Week Karwoche f.

homage ['hɔmidʒ] Huldigung f; do od. pay od. render ~ huldigen (to dat.).

home [houm] 1. Heim n; Haus n, Wohnung f; Heimat f; Mal n; at ~ zu Hause; 2. adj. (ein)heimisch, inländisch; wirkungsvoll; tüchtig (Schlag etc.); ♀ Office Innenministerium n; ~ rule Selbstregierung f; ♀ Secretary Innenminister m; ~ trade Binnenhandel m; 3. adv. heim, nach Hause; an die richtige Stelle; gründlich; hit od. strike ~ den rechten Fleck treffen; ♀ Counties die Grafschaften um London; **~ economics** Am. Hauswirtschaftslehre f; **~-felt** ['houmfelt] tief empfunden; **~less** ['houmlis] heimatlos; **~like** anheimelnd, gemütlich; **~ly** [~li] anheimelnd, häuslich; fig. hausbacken; schlicht; anspruchslos; reizlos; **~-made** selbstgemacht; Hausmacher...; **~sickness** Heimweh n; **~stead** Anwesen n; ~ team Sport: Gastgeber m/pl.; **~ward(s)** ['houmwəd(z)] heimwärts (gerichtet); Heim...; **~work** Hausaufgabe(n pl.) f, Schularbeiten f/pl.

homicide ['hɔmisaid] Totschlag m; Mord m; Totschläger(in).

homogeneous □ [hɔmə'dʒiːnjəs] homogen, gleichartig.

hone ⊕ [houn] 1. Abziehstein m; 2. Rasiermesser abziehen.

honest □ ['ɔnist] ehrlich, rechtschaffen; aufrichtig; echt; **~y** [~ti] Ehrlichkeit f, Rechtschaffenheit f; Aufrichtigkeit f.

honey ['hʌni] Honig m; fig. Liebling m; **~comb** [~koum] (Honig-)Wabe f; **~ed** ['hʌnid] honigsüß; **~moon** 1. Flitterwochen f/pl.; 2. die Flitterwochen verleben.

honk mot. [hɔŋk] hupen, tuten.

honky-tonk Am. sl. ['hɔŋkitɔŋk] Spelunke f.

honorary ['ɔnərəri] Ehren...; ehrenamtlich.

hono(u)r ['ɔnə] 1. Ehre f; Achtung f; Würde f; fig. Zierde f; Your ♀ Euer Gnaden; 2. (be)ehren; ✝ honorieren; **~able** □ ['ɔnərəbl] ehrenvoll; redlich; ehrbar; ehrenwert.

hood [hud] 1. Kapuze f; mot. Verdeck n; Am. (Motor)Haube f; ⊕ Kappe f; 2. mit e-r Kappe etc. bekleiden; ein-, verhüllen.

hoodlum Am. F ['huːdləm] Strolch m.

hoodoo bsd. Am. ['huːduː] Unglücksbringer m; Pech n (Unglück).

hoodwink ['hudwiŋk] täuschen.

hooey Am. sl. ['huːi] Quatsch m.

hoof [huːf] Huf m; Klaue f.

hook [huk] 1. (bsd. Angel)Haken m; Sichel f; by ~ or by crook so oder so;

2. (sich) (zu-, fest)haken; angeln (a. fig.); ~y ['huki] 1. hakig; 2.: play ~ Am. sl. (die Schule) schwänzen.

hoop [hu:p] 1. Faß- etc. Reif(en) m; ⊕ Ring m; 2. Fässer binden.

hooping-cough ♣ ['hu:piŋkɔf] Keuchhusten m.

hoot [hu:t] 1. Geschrei n; 2. v/i. heulen; johlen; mot. hupen; v/t. auspfeifen, auszischen.

Hoover ['hu:və] 1. Staubsauger m; 2. (mit e-m Staubsauger) saugen.

hop [hɔp] 1. ♀ Hopfen m; Sprung m; F Tanzerei f; 2. hüpfen, springen (über acc.).

hope [houp] 1. Hoffnung f; 2. hoffen (for auf acc.); ~ in vertrauen auf (acc.); ~ful [['houpful] hoffnungsvoll; ~less [['houplis] hoffnungslos; verzweifelt.

horde [hɔːd] Horde f.

horizon [hə'raizn] Horizont m.

horn [hɔːn] Horn n; Schalltrichter m; mot Hupe f; ~s pl. Geweih n; ~ of plenty Füllhorn n.

hornet zo ['hɔːnit] Hornisse f.

horn|swoggle Am. sl. ['hɔːnswɔgl] j-n reinlegen; ~y ['hɔːni] hornig; schwielig.

horr|ible [['hɔrəbl] entsetzlich; scheußlich, ~id □ ['hɔrid] gräßlich, abscheulich; schrecklich; ~ify [~ifai] erschrecken; entsetzen; ~or ['hɔrə] Entsetzen n, Schauder m; Schrecken m; Greuel m.

horse [hɔːs] zo. Pferd n; Reiterei f; Bock m, Gestell n; ~back ['hɔːsbæk]: on ~ zu Pferde; ~hair Roßhaar n; ~laugh F wieherndes Lachen; ~man Reiter m; ~manship [~ʃip] Reitkunst f; ~ opera Am. drittklassiger Wildwestfilm; ~power Pferdestärke f; ~radish Meerrettich m; ~shoe Hufeisen n.

horticulture ['hɔːtikʌltʃə] Gartenbau m.

hose [houz] Schlauch m; Strumpfhose f; coll. Strümpfe m/pl.

hosiery['houʒəri]Strumpfwaren f/pl.

hospitable [['hɔspitəbl] gastfrei.

hospital ['hɔspitl] Krankenhaus n; ✗ Lazarett n; ~ity [hɔspi'tæliti] Gastfreundschaft f, Gastlichkeit f.

host [houst] Wirt m; Gastgeber m; fig. Heer n; Schwarm m; eccl Hostie f.

hostage ['hɔstidʒ] Geisel m, f.

hostel ['hɔstəl] Herberge f; univ. Studenten(wohn)heim n.

hostess ['houstis] Wirtin f; Gastgeberin f; = air ~.

hostil|e [['hɔstail] feindlich (gesinnt); ~ity [hɔs'tiliti] Feindseligkeit f (to gegen).

hot [hɔt] heiß; scharf; beißend; hitzig, heftig; eifrig; warm (Speise, Fährte); Am. sl. falsch (Scheck); gestohlen; radioaktiv; ~bed ['hɔtbed] Mistbeet n; fig. Brutstätte f.

hotchpotch ['hɔtʃpɔtʃ] Mischmasch m; Gemüsesuppe f. [chen.] hot dog F ['hɔt 'dɔg] heißes Würst-]

hotel [hou'tel] Hotel n.

hot|head ['hɔthed] Hitzkopf m; ~house Treibhaus n; ~pot Irish Stew n; ~rod Am. sl. mot. frisiertes altes Auto; ~spur Hitzkopf m.

hound [haund] 1. Jagd-, Spürhund m; fig. Hund m; 2. jagen, hetzen

hour ['auə] Stunde f; Zeit f, Uhr f; ~ly ['auəli] stündlich.

house 1. [haus] allg. Haus n; the ♀ das Unterhaus; die Börse; 2. [hauz] v/t. unterbringen; v/i. hausen; ~agent ['hauseidʒənt] Häusermakler m; ~breaker ['hausbreikə] Abbrucharbeiter m; ~hold Haushalt m; attr. Haushalts...; Haus...; ~holder Hausherr m; ~keeper Haushälterin f; ~keeping Haushaltung f; ~maid Hausmädchen n; ~warming ['hauswɔːmiŋ] Einzugsfeier f; ~wife ['hauswaif] Hausfrau f; ['hazif] Nähtäschchen n; ~wifery ['hauswifəri] Haushaltung f; ~work Haus(halts)arbeit f/pl.

housing ['hauziŋ] Unterbringung f; Wohnung f; ~ estate Wohnsiedlung f.

hove [houv] pret. u. p.p. von heave 2.

hovel ['hɔvəl] Schuppen m; Hütte f.

hover ['hɔvə] schweben; lungern; fig. schwanken; ~craft Luftkissenfahrzeug n.

how [hau] wie; ~ do you do? Begrüßungsformel bei der Vorstellung; ~ about ...? wie steht's mit ...? ~ever [hau'evə] 1. adv. wie auch (immer); wenn auch noch so ...; 2. cj. jedoch.

howl [haul] 1. heulen, brüllen; 2. Geheul n; ~er ['haulə] Heuler m; sl. grober Fehler.

hub [hʌb] (Rad)Nabe f; fig. Mittel-, Angelpunkt m.

hubbub ['hʌbʌb] Tumult m, Lärm m.

hub(by) F ['hʌb(i)] (Ehe)Mann m.

huckleberry ♀ ['hʌklberi] amerikanische Heidelbeere.

huckster ['hʌkstə] Hausierer(in).

huddle ['hʌdl] 1. a. ~ together (sich) zs.-drängen, zs.-pressen; ~ (o.s.) up sich zs.-kauern; 2. Gewirr n, Wirrwarr m. [cry Zetergeschrei n.]

hue [hju:] Farbe f; Hetze f; ~ and]

huff [hʌf] 1. üble Laune; 2. v/t. grob anfahren; beleidigen; v/i. wütend werden; schmollen.

hug [hʌg] 1. Umarmung f; 2. an sich drücken, umarmen; fig. festhalten an (dat.); sich dicht am Weg etc. halten.

huge □ [hju:dʒ] ungeheuer, riesig; ~ness ['hju:dʒnis] ungeheure Größe.

hulk fig. [hʌlk] Klotz m.

hull [hʌl] 1. ♣ Schale *f*; Hülse *f*; ⚓ Rumpf *m*; 2. enthülsen; schälen.

hullabaloo [hʌləbə'luː] Lärm *m*.

hullo ['hʌ'lou] hallo (*bsd. teleph.*).

hum [hʌm] summen; brumme(l)n; *make things* ~ F Schwung in die Sache bringen.

human ['hjuːmən] 1. □ menschlich; ~ly nach menschlichem Ermessen; 2. F Mensch *m*; ~e □ [hju(ː)'mein] human, menschenfreundlich; ~i-tarian [hju(ː)mæni'tɛəriən] 1. Menschenfreund *m*; 2. menschenfreundlich; ~ity [hju(ː)'mæniti] menschliche Natur; Menschheit *f*; Humanität *f*; ~kind ['hjuːmən'kaind] Menschengeschlecht *n*.

humble ['hʌmbl] 1. □ demütig; bescheiden; 2. erniedrigen; demütigen.

humble-bee ['hʌmblbiː] Hummel *f*.

humbleness ['hʌmblnis] Demut *f*.

humbug ['hʌmbʌg] 1. (be)schwindeln; 2. Schwindel *m*.

humdinger *Am. sl.* [hʌm'diŋə] Mordskerl *m*, -sache *f*.

humdrum ['hʌmdrʌm] eintönig.

humid ['hjuːmid] feucht, naß; ~ity [hju(ː)'miditi] Feuchtigkeit *f*.

humiliat|e [hju(ː)'milieit] erniedrigen, demütigen; ~ion [hju(ː)mili-'ei[ən] Erniedrigung *f*, Demütigung *f*.

humility [hju(ː)'militi] Demut *f*.

humming F ['hʌmiŋ] mächtig, gewaltig; ~bird *zo.* Kolibri *m*.

humorous □ ['hjuːmərəs] humoristisch, humorvoll; spaßig.

humo(u)r ['hjuːmə] 1. Laune *f*, Stimmung *f*; Humor *m*; *das* Spaßige; ⚔ *hist.* Körpersaft *m*; *out of* ~ schlecht gelaunt; 2. *j-m* s-n Willen lassen; eingehen auf (*acc.*).

hump [hʌmp] 1. Höcker *m*, Buckel *m*; 2. krümmen; ärgern, verdrießen; ~ o.s. *Am. sl.* sich dranhalten; ~back ['hʌmpbæk] — *hunchback*.

hunch [hʌntʃ] 1. Höcker *m*; großes Stück; *Am.* F Ahnung *f*; 2. *a.* ~ *out,* ~ *up* krümmen; ~back ['hʌntʃbæk] Bucklige(r *m*) *f*.

hundred ['hʌndrəd] 1. hundert; 2. Hundert *n*; ~th [~dθ] 1. hundertste; 2. Hundertstel *n*; ~weight *englischer Zentner* (*50,8 kg*).

hung [hʌŋ] 1. *pret. u. p.p. von hang* 1; 2. *adj.* abgehangen (*Fleisch*).

Hungarian [hʌŋ'gɛəriən] 1. ungarisch; 2. Ungar(in); Ungarisch *n*.

hunger ['hʌŋgə] 1. Hunger *m* (*a. fig.*; *for* nach); 2. *v/i.* hungern (*for, after* nach); *v/t.* durch Hunger zwingen (*into* zu).

hungry □ ['hʌŋgri] hungrig.

hunk F ['hʌŋk] dickes Stück.

hunt [hʌnt] 1. Jagd *f* (*for* nach); Jagd(revier *n*) *f*; Jagd(gesellschaft) *f*; 2. jagen; *Revier* bejagen; hetzen; ~ *out od. up* aufspüren; ~ *for,* ~ *after*

Jagd machen auf (*acc.*); ~er ['hʌntə] Jäger *m*; Jagdpferd *n*; ~ing [~tiŋ] Jagen *n*; Verfolgung *f*; *attr.* Jagd...; ~ing-ground Jagdrevier *n*; ~sman [~tsmən] Jäger *m*; Rüdemann *m* (*Meutenführer*).

hurdle ['həːdl] Hürde *f* (*a. fig.*); ~r [~lə] Hürdenläufer(in); ~race Hürdenrennen *n*.

hurl [həːl] 1. Schleudern *n*; 2. schleudern; *Worte* ausstoßen.

hurricane ['hʌrikən] Orkan *m*.

hurried □ ['hʌrid] eilig; übereilt.

hurry ['hʌri] 1. (große) Eile, Hast *f*; *be in a* ~ es eilig haben; *not ... in a* ~ F nicht so bald, nicht so leicht; 2. *v/t.* (an)treiben; drängen; *et.* beschleunigen; eilig schicken *od.* bringen; *v/i.* eilen, hasten; ~ *up* sich beeilen.

hurt [həːt] 1. Verletzung *f*; Schaden *m*; 2. [*irr.*] verletzen (*a. fig.*); weh tun (*dat.*); schaden (*dat.*).

husband ['hʌzbənd] 1. (Ehe)Mann *m*; 2. haushalten mit; verwalten; ~man Landwirt *m*; ~ry [~dri] Landwirtschaft *f*, Ackerbau *m*.

hush [hʌʃ] 1. still! 2. Stille *f*; 3. *v/t.* zum Schweigen bringen; beruhigen; *Stimme* dämpfen; ~ *up* vertuschen; *v/i.* still sein; ~-money ['hʌʃmʌni] Schweigegeld *n*.

husk [hʌsk] 1. ♣ Hülse *f*, Schote *f*; Schale *f* (*a. fig.*); 2. enthülsen; ~y ['hʌski] 1. □ hülsig; trocken; heiser; F stramm, stämmig; 2. F stämmiger Kerl.

hussy ['hʌsi] Flittchen *n*; Range *f*.

hustle ['hʌsl] 1. *v/t.* (an)rempeln; stoßen; drängen; *v/i.* (sich) drängen; eilen; *bsd. Am.* mit Hochdruck arbeiten; 2. Hochbetrieb *m*; Rührigkeit *f*; ~ *and bustle* Gedränge und Gehetze *n*.

hut [hʌt] Hütte *f*; ⚔ Baracke *f*.

hutch [hʌtʃ] Kasten *m*; *bsd. Ka-ninchen-*Stall *m* (*a. fig.*); Trog *m*.

hyacinth ♣ ['haiəsinθ] Hyazinthe *f*.

hyaena *zo.* [hai'iːnə] Hyäne *f*.

hybrid ⚏ ['haibrid] Bastard *m*, Mischling *m*; Kreuzung *f*; *attr.* Bastard...; Zwitter...; ~ize [~daiz] kreuzen.

hydrant ['haidrənt] Hydrant *m*.

hydro|... ⚏ ['haidrou] Wasser...; ~carbon Kohlenwasserstoff *m*; ~chloric acid [~rə'klɔrikæsid] Salzsäure *f*; ~gen [~ridʒən] Wasserstoff *m*; ~gen bomb Wasserstoffbombe *f*; ~pathy [hai'drɔpəθi] Wasserheilkunde *f*, Wasserkur *f*; ~phobia [haidrə'foubjə] Wasserscheu *f*; ⚔ Tollwut *f*; ~plane ['haidrouplein] Wasserflugzeug *n*; (Motor)Gleitboot *n*, Rennboot *n*.

hyena *zo.* [hai'iːnə] Hyäne *f*.

hygiene ['haidʒiːn] Hygiene *f*.

hymn [him] 1. Hymne *f*; Lobgesang *m*; Kirchenlied *n*; 2. preisen.

hyphen ['haifən] **1.** Bindestrich *m*; **2.** mit Bindestrich schreiben *od.* verbinden; **~ated** [␣neitid] mit Bindestrich geschrieben; **~** Americans *pl.* Halb-Amerikaner *m/pl.* (*z. B.* German-Americans). [ren.)

hypnotize ['hipnətaiz] hypnotisie-}

hypo|chondriac [haipou'kɔndriæk] Hypochonder *m*; **~crisy** [hi'pɔ-

krəsi] Heuchelei *f*; **~crite** ['hipə-krit] Heuchler(in); Scheinheilige(r *m*) *f*; **~critical** □ [hipə'kritikəl] heuchlerisch; **~thesis** [hai'pɔθisis] Hypothese *f*.

hyster|ia ♂ [his'tiəriə] Hysterie *f*; **~ical** □ [␣'terikəl] hysterisch; **~ics** [␣ks] *pl.* hysterischer Anfall; *go into ~* hysterisch werden.

I

I [ai] ich.

ice [ais] **1.** Eis *n*; **2.** gefrieren lassen; *a. ~ up* vereisen; *Kuchen* mit Zuckerguß überziehen; in Eis kühlen; **~age** [␣'aiseidʒ] Eiszeit *f*; **~berg** ['aisbəːg] Eisberg *m* (*a. fig.*); **~bound** vereist; eingefroren; **~box** Eisschrank *m*; *Am. a.* Kühlschrank *m*; **~cream** Speiseeis *n*; **~floe** Eisscholle *f*.

icicle ['aisikl] Eiszapfen *m*.

icing ['aisiŋ] Zuckerguß *m*; Vereisung *f*.

icy □ ['aisi] eisig (*a. fig.*); vereist.

idea [ai'diə] Idee *f*; Begriff *m*; Vorstellung *f*; Gedanke *m*; Meinung *f*; Ahnung *f*; Plan *m*; **~l** [␣əl] **1.** □ ideell; eingebildet; ideal; **2.** Ideal *n*.

identi|cal □ [ai'dentikəl] identisch, gleich(bedeutend); **~fication** [aidentifi'keiʃən] Identifizierung *f*; Ausweis *m*; **~fy** [ai'dentifai] identifizieren; ausweisen; erkennen; **~ty** [␣iti] Identität *f*; Persönlichkeit *f*; Eigenart *f*; **~** card Personalausweis *m*, Kennkarte *f*; **~** disk ✕ Erkennungsmarke *f*.

ideological □ [aidiə'lɔdʒikəl] ideologisch.

idiom ['idiəm] Idiom *n*; Mundart *f*; Redewendung *f*.

idiot ['idiət] Idiot(in), Schwachsinnige(r *m*) *f*; **~ic** [idi'ɔtik] (*~ally*) blödsinnig.

idle ['aidl] **1.** □ müßig, untätig; träg, faul; unnütz; nichtig; *~ hours pl.* Mußestunden *f/pl.*; **2.** *v/t. mst ~ away* vertrödeln; *v/i.* faulenzen; ⊕ leer laufen; **~ness** ['aidlnis] Muße *f*; Trägheit *f*; Nichtigkeit *f*; **~r** ['aidlə] Müßiggänger(in).

idol ['aidl] Idol *n*, Götzenbild *n*; *fig.* Abgott *m*; **~atrous** □ [ai'dɔlə-trəs] abgöttisch; **~atry** [␣ri] Abgötterei *f*; Vergötterung *f*; **~ize** ['aidəlaiz] vergöttern.

dyl ['idil] Idyll(e *f*) *n*.

if [if] **1.** wenn, falls; ob; **2.** Wenn *n*; **~fy** *Am.* F ['ifi] zweifelhaft.

ignit|e [ig'nait] (sich) entzünden; zünden; **~ion** [ig'niʃən] 🔧 Entzündung *f*; *mot.* Zündung *f*.

ignoble □ [ig'noubl] unedel; niedrig, gemein.

ignominious □ [ignə'miniəs] schändlich, schimpflich.

ignor|ance ['ignərəns] Unwissenheit *f*; **~ant** [␣nt] unwissend; unkundig; **~e** [ig'nɔː] ignorieren, nicht beachten; ♯'♯ verwerfen.

ill [il] **1.** *adj. u. adv.* übel, böse; schlimm, schlecht; krank; *adv.* kaum; *fall ~*, *be taken ~* krank werden; **2.** Übel *n*; Übel(s) *n*, Böse(s) *n.* **ill|-advised** □ ['iləd'vaizd] schlecht beraten; unbesonnen, unklug; **~bred** ungebildet, ungezogen; **~** breeding schlechtes Benehmen.

illegal □ [i'liːgəl] ungesetzlich.

illegible □ [i'ledʒəbl] unleserlich.

illegitimate □ [ili'dʒitimit] illegitim; unrechtmäßig; unehelich.

ill|-favo(u)red ['il'feivəd] häßlich; **~humo(u)red** übellaunig.

illiberal □ [i'libərəl] engstirnig; intolerant; knauserig.

illicit □ [i'lisit] unerlaubt.

illiterate □ [i'litərit] **1.** ungelehrt, ungebildet; **2.** Analphabet(in).

ill|-judged ['il'dʒʌdʒd] unklug, unvernünftig; **~mannered** ungezogen; mit schlechten Umgangsformen; **~natured** □ boshaft, bösartig.

illness ['ilnis] Krankheit *f*.

illogical □ [i'lɔdʒikəl] unlogisch.

ill|-starred ['il'staːd] unglücklich; **~tempered** schlecht gelaunt; **~timed** ungelegen; **~treat** mißhandeln.

illuminat|e [i'ljuːmineit] be-, erleuchten (*a. fig.*); erläutern; aufklären; **~ing** [␣tiŋ] Leucht...; *fig.* aufschlußreich; **~ion** [iljuːmi'nei-ʃən] Er-, Beleuchtung *f*; Erläuterung *f*; Aufklärung *f*.

ill-use ['il'juːz] mißhandeln.

illus|ion [i'luːʒən] Illusion *f*, Täuschung *f*; **~ive** [i'luːsiv], **~ory** □ [␣səri] illusorisch, täuschend.

illustrat|e ['iləstreit] illustrieren; erläutern; bebildern; **~ion** [iləs-'treiʃən] Erläuterung *f*; Illustration *f*; **~ive** □ ['iləstreitiv] erläuternd.

illustrious □ [i'lʌstriəs] berühmt.

ill will ['il'wil] Feindschaft f.

image ['imidʒ] Bild n; Standbild n; Ebenbild n; Vorstellung f; ~ry [~dʒəri] Bilder n/pl.; Bildersprache f, Metaphorik f.

imagin|able ['i'mædʒinəbl] denkbar; ~ary [~əri] eingebildet; ~ation [imædʒi'neiʃən] Einbildung(skraft) f; ~ative ['i'mædʒinətiv] ideen-, einfallsreich; ~e [i'mædʒin] sich et. einbilden od. vorstellen od. denken.

imbecile ['imbisi:l] 1. geistesschwach; 2. Schwachsinnige(r m) f.

imbibe [im'baib] einsaugen; fig. sich zu eigen machen.

imbue [im'bju:] (durch)tränken; tief färben; fig. erfüllen.

imitat|e ['imiteit] nachahmen; imitieren; ~ion [imi'teiʃən] 1. Nachahmung f; 2. künstlich, Kunst...

immaculate □ [i'mækjulit] unbefleckt, rein; fehlerlos.

immaterial □ [imə'tiəriəl] unkörperlich; unwesentlich (to für).

immature [imə'tjuə] unreif.

immeasurable □ [i'meʒərəbl] unermeßlich.

immediate □ [i'mi:djət] unmittelbar; unverzüglich, sofortig; ~ly [~tli] 1. adv. sofort; 2. cj. gleich nachdem.

immense □ [i'mens] ungeheuer.

immerse [i'mə:s] (ein-, unter)tauchen; fig. ~ o.s. in sich versenken od. vertiefen in (acc.).

immigra|nt ['imigrənt] Einwanderer(in); ~te [~greit] v/i. einwandern; v/t. ansiedeln (into in dat.); ~tion [imi'greiʃən] Einwanderung f.

imminent □ ['iminənt] bevorstehend, drohend.

immobile [i'moubail] unbeweglich.

immoderate □ [i'mɔdərit] maßlos.

immodest □ [i'mɔdist] unbescheiden; unanständig.

immoral □ [i'mɔrəl] unmoralisch.

immortal [i'mɔ:tl] 1. □ unsterblich; 2. Unsterbliche(r m) f; ~ity [imɔ:'tæliti] Unsterblichkeit f.

immovable [i'mu:vəbl] 1. □ unbeweglich; unerschütterlich; 2. ~s pl. Immobilien pl.

immun|e & # u. fig. [i'mju:n] immun, gefeit (from gegen); ~ity [~niti] Immunität f, Freiheit f (from von); Unempfänglichkeit f (für).

immutable □ [i'mju:təbl] unveränderlich.

imp [imp] Teufelchen n; Schelm m.

impact ['impækt] (Zs.-)Stoß m; Anprall m; Einwirkung f.

impair [im'pɛə] schwächen; (ver)mindern; beeinträchtigen.

impart [im'pa:t] verleihen; weitergeben.

impartial [im'pa:ʃəl] unparteiisch; ~ity ['impa:ʃi'æliti] Unparteilichkeit f, Objektivität f.

impassable □ [im'pa:səbl] ungangbar, unpassierbar.

impassible □ [im'pæsibl] unempfindlich; gefühllos (to gegen).

impassioned [im'pæʃənd] leidenschaftlich.

impassive □ [im'pæsiv] unempfindlich; teilnahmslos; heiter.

impatien|ce [im'peiʃəns] Ungeduld f; ~t □ [~nt] ungeduldig.

impeach [im'pi:tʃ] anklagen (of, with gen.); anfechten, anzweifeln.

impeccable □ [im'pekəbl] sündlos; makellos, einwandfrei.

impede [im'pi:d] (ver)hindern.

impediment [im'pedimənt] Hindernis n.

impel [im'pel] (an)treiben.

impend [im'pend] hängen, schweben; bevorstehen, drohen.

impenetrable □ [im'penitrəbl] undurchdringlich; fig. unergründlich; fig. unzugänglich (to dat.).

impenitent □ [im'penitənt] unbußfertig, verstockt.

imperative [im'perətiv] 1. □ notwendig, dringend, unbedingt erforderlich; befehlend; gebieterisch; gr. imperativisch; 2. Befehl m; a. ~ mood gr. Imperativ m, Befehlsform f. [unmerklich.]

imperceptible □ [impə'septəbl]

imperfect [im'pə:fikt] 1. □ unvollkommen; unvollendet; 2. a. ~ tense gr. Imperfekt n.

imperial □ [im'piəriəl] kaiserlich; Reichs...; majestätisch; großartig; ~ism [~lizəm] Imperialismus m, Weltmachtpolitik f.

imperil [im'peril] gefährden.

imperious □ [im'piəriəs] gebieterisch, anmaßend; dringend.

imperishable □ [im'periʃəbl] unvergänglich.

impermeable □ [im'pə:mjəbl] undurchdringlich, undurchlässig.

impersonal □ [im'pə:snl] unpersönlich.

impersonate [im'pə:səneit] verkörpern; thea. darstellen.

impertinen|ce [im'pə:tinəns] Unverschämtheit f; Nebensächlichkeit f; ~t □ [~nt] unverschämt; ungehörig; nebensächlich.

imperturbable □ [impə(:)'tə:bəbl] unerschütterlich.

impervious □ [im'pə:vjəs] unzugänglich (to für); undurchlässig.

impetu|ous □ [im'petjuəs] ungestüm, heftig; ~s ['impitəs] Antrieb m.

impiety [im'paiəti] Gottlosigkeit f.

impinge [im'pindʒ] v/i. (ver)stoßen (on, upon, against gegen).

impious □ ['impiəs] gottlos; pietätlos; frevelhaft.

implacable □ [im'plækəbl] unversöhnlich, unerbittlich.

implant [im'pla:nt] einpflanzen.

implement 1. ['implimənt] Werkzeug *n*; Gerät *n*; **2.** [~iment] ausführen.

implicat|e ['implikeit] verwickeln; in sich schließen; ~ion [impli'keiʃən] Verwick(e)lung *f*; Folgerung *f*.

implicit [[im'plisit] mit eingeschlossen; blind (*Glaube etc.*).

implore [im'plɔ:] (an-, er)flehen.

imply [im'plai] mit einbegreifen, enthalten; bedeuten; andeuten.

impolite [[impə'lait] unhöflich.

impolitic [[im'politik] unklug.

import 1. ['impɔ:t] Bedeutung *f*; Wichtigkeit *f*; Einfuhr *f*; ~s *pl*. Einfuhrwaren *f/pl.*; **2.** [im'pɔ:t] einführen; bedeuten; ~ance [~təns] Wichtigkeit *f*; ~ant □ [~nt] wichtig; wichtigtuerisch; ~ation [impɔ:-'teiʃən] Einfuhr(waren *f/pl.*) *f*.

importun|ate □ [im'pɔ:tjunit] lästig; zudringlich; ~e [im'pɔ:tju:n] dringend bitten; belästigen.

impos|e [im'pouz] *v/t.* auf(er)legen, aufbürden (*on, upon dat.*); *v/i.* ~ upon *j-m* imponieren; *j-n* täuschen; ~ition [impə'ziʃən] Auf(er)legung *f*; Steuer *f*; Strafarbeit *f*; Betrügerei *f*.

impossib|ility [impɔsə'biliti] Unmöglichkeit *f*; ~le □ [im'pɔsəbl] unmöglich.

impost|or [im'pɔstə] Betrüger *m*; ~ure [~tʃə] Betrug *m*.

impoten|ce [im'impətəns] Unfähigkeit *f*; Machtlosigkeit *f*; ~t [~nt] unvermögend, machtlos, schwach.

impoverish [im'pɔvəriʃ] arm machen; *Boden* auslaugen.

impracticable □ [im'præktikəbl] undurchführbar; unwegsam.

impractical [im'præktikəl] unpraktisch; theoretisch; unnütz.

imprecate ['imprikeit] *Böses* herabwünschen (*upon auf acc.*).

impregn|able □ [im'pregnəbl] uneinnehmbar; unwiderstehlich; ~ate ['impregneit] schwängern; ⚗ sättigen; ⊕ imprägnieren.

impress 1. ['impres] (Ab-, Ein-)Druck *m*; *fig.* Stempel *m*; **2.** [im'pres] eindrücken, prägen; *Kraft etc.* übertragen; *Gedanken etc.* einprägen (*on dat.*); *j-n* beeindrucken; *j-n mit et.* erfüllen; ~ion [~eʃən] Eindruck *m*; *typ.* Abdruck *m*; Abzug *m*; Auflage *f*; *be under the* ~ *that* den Eindruck haben, daß; ~ive □ [~esiv] eindrucksvoll.

imprint 1. [im'print] aufdrücken, prägen; *fig.* einprägen (*on, in dat.*); **2.** ['imprint] Eindruck *m*; Stempel *m* (*a. fig.*); *typ.* Druckvermerk *m*.

imprison [im'prizn] inhaftieren, ~ment [~nment] Haft *f*; Gefängnis (-strafe *f*) *n*.

improbable □ [im'prɔbəbl] unwahrscheinlich.

improper □ [im'prɔpə] ungeeignet, unpassend; falsch; unanständig.

impropriety [imprə'praiəti] Ungehörigkeit *f*; Unanständigkeit *f*.

improve [im'pru:v] *v/t.* verbessern; veredeln; aus-, benutzen; *v/i.* sich (ver)bessern; ~ *upon* vervollkommnen; ~ment [~vmənt] Verbesserung *f*, Vervollkommnung *f*; Fortschritt *m* (*on, upon gegenüber dat.*).

improvise ['imprəvaiz] improvisieren.

imprudent □ [im'pru:dənt] unklug.

impuden|ce ['impjudəns] Unverschämtheit *f*, Frechheit *f*; ~t [[~nt] unverschämt, frech.

impuls|e ['impʌls], ~ion [im'pʌl-ʃən] Impuls *m*, (An)Stoß *m*; *fig.* (An)Trieb *m*; ~ive □ [~siv] (an-)treibend; *fig.* impulsiv; rasch (handelnd).

impunity [im'pju:niti] Straflosigkeit *f*; *with* ~ ungestraft.

impure □ [im'pjuə] unrein (*a. fig.*); unkeusch.

imput|ation [impju(:)'teiʃən] Beschuldigung *f*; ~e [im'pju:t] zurechnen, beimessen; *zur Last legen*.

in [in] **1.** *prp. allg.* in (*dat.*); *engS.*: (~ *the morning,* ~ *number,* ~ *itself, professor* ~ *the university*) *an* (*dat.*); (~ *the street,* ~ *English*) auf (*dat.*); (~ *this manner*) auf (*acc.*); (*coat* ~ *velvet*) aus; (~ *Shakespeare,* ~ *the daytime,* ~ *crossing the road*) bei; (*engaged* ~ *reading,* ~ *a word*) mit; (~ *my opinion*) nach; (*rejoice* ~ *s.th.*) über (*acc.*); (~ *the circumstances,* ~ *the reign of, one* ~ *ten*) unter (*dat.*); (*cry out* ~ *alarm*) vor (*dat.*); (*grouped* ~ *tens, speak* ~ *reply,* ~ *excuse,* ~ *honour of*) zu; ~ *1949* im Jahre 1949; ~ *that* ... insofern als, weil; **2.** *adv.* drin(nen); herein; hinein; *be* ~ *for et.* zu erwarten haben; *e-e Prüfung etc.* vor sich haben; *F be well* ~ *with* sich gut mit *j-m* stehen; **3.** *adj.* hereinkommend; Innen...

inability [inə'biliti] Unfähigkeit *f*.

inaccessible □ [inæk'sesəbl] unzugänglich. [unrichtig.]

inaccurate □ [in'ækjurit] ungenau;]

inactiv|e □ [in'æktiv] untätig; ♥ lustlos; ⚗ unwirksam; ~ity [inæk-'tiviti] Untätig-, Lustlosigkeit *f*.

inadequate □ [in'ædikwit] unangemessen; unzulänglich.

inadmissible □ [inəd'misəbl] unzulässig.

inadvertent □ [inəd'və:tənt] unachtsam; unbeabsichtigt, versehentlich.

inalienable □ [in'eiljənəbl] unveräußerlich.

inane [[i'nein] *fig.* leer; albern.

inanimate □ [in'ænimit] leblos; *fig.* unbelebt; geistlos, langweilig.

inapproachable [inə'proutʃəbl] unnahbar, unzugänglich.

inappropriate □ [inə'proupriit] unangebracht, unpassend.

inapt □ [in'æpt] ungeeignet, untauglich; ungeschickt; unpassend.

inarticulate ⌐ [inɑː'tikjulit] undeutlich; schwer zu verstehen(d); undeutlich sprechend.

inasmuch [inəz'mʌtʃ]: ~ *as* insofern als. [merksam.]

inattentive □ [inə'tentiv] unauf-⌐

inaudible □ [in'ɔːdəbl] unhörbar.

inaugura|l [i'nɔːgjurəl] Antrittsrede *f*; *attr*. Antritts...; **~te** [~reit] (feierlich) einführen, einweihen; beginnen; **~tion** [inɔːgju'reiʃən] Einführung *f*, Einweihung *f*; 2 *Day Am*. Amtseinführung *f* des neugewählten Präsidenten der USA.

inborn [in'bɔːn] angeboren.

incalculable ⌐ [in'kælkjuləbl] unberechenbar; unzählig.

incandescent [inkæn'desnt] weiß glühend; Glüh...

incapa|ble ⌐ [in'keipəbl] unfähig, ungeeignet (*of* zu); **~citate** [inkə'pæsiteit] unfähig machen; **~city** [~ti] Unfähigkeit *f*.

incarnate [in'kɑːnit] Fleisch geworden; *fig*. verkörpert.

incautious □ [in'kɔːʃəs] unvorsichtig.

incendiary [in'sendjəri] **1.** brandstifterisch; *fig*. aufwieglerisch; **2.** Brandstifter *m*; Aufwiegler *m*.

incense[1] ['insens] Weihrauch *m*.

incense[2] [in'sens] in Wut bringen.

incentive [in'sentiv] Antrieb *m*.

incessant □ [in'sesnt] unaufhörlich.

incest ['insest] Blutschande *f*.

inch [intʃ] Zoll *m* (*2,54 cm*); *fig*. *ein* bißchen; *by* ~*es* allmählich; *every* ~ ganz (u. gar).

inciden|ce ['insidəns] Vorkommen *n*; Wirkung *f*; **~t** [~nt] **1.** (*to*) vorkommend(bei), eigen (*dat*.); **2.** Zu-, Vor-, Zwischenfall *m*; Nebenumstand *m*; **~tal** ⌐ [insi'dentl] zufällig, gelegentlich; Neben...; *be* ~ *to* gehören zu; **~ly** nebenbei.

incinerate [in'sinəreit] einäschern; *Müll* verbrennen.

incis|e [in'saiz] einschneiden; **~ion** [in'siʒən] Einschnitt *m*; **~ive** ⌐ [in'saisiv] (ein)schneidend, scharf; **~or** [~aizə] Schneidezahn *m*.

incite [in'sait] anspornen, anregen, anstiften; **~ment** [~tmənt] Anregung *f*; Ansporn *m*; Anstiftung *f*.

inclement [in'klemənt] rauh.

inclin|ation [inkli'neiʃən] Neigung *f* (*a. fig.*); **~e** [in'klain] **1.** *v/i*. sich neigen (*a. fig.*); ~ *to fig*. zu et. neigen; *v/t*. neigen; geneigt machen; **2.** Neigung *f*, Abhang *m*.

inclos|e [in'klouz], **~ure** [~ouʒə] *s*. *enclose*, *enclosure*.

inclu|de [in'kluːd] einschließen; enthalten; **~sive** ⌐ [~uːsiv] einschließlich; alles einbegriffen; *be* ~ *of* einschließen; ~ *terms pl*. Pauschalpreis *m*.

incoheren|ce [inkou'hiərəns, ~si] Zs.-hangslosigkeit *f*; Inkonsequenz *f*; **~t** □ [~nt] unzs.-hängend; inkonsequent.

income ['inkəm] Einkommen *n*; **~-tax** Einkommensteuer *f*.

incommode [inkə'moud] belästigen.

incommunica|do *bsd. Am*. [inkəmjuː'niˈkɑːdou] ohne Verbindung mit der Außenwelt; **~tive** ⌐ [inkə'mjuːniˈkətiv] nicht mitteilsam, verschlossen.

incomparable □ [in'kɔmpərəbl] unvergleichlich.

incompatible □ [inkəm'pætəbl] unvereinbar; unverträglich.

incompetent [in'kɔmpitənt] unfähig; unzuständig, unbefugt.

incomplete □ [inkəm'pliːt] unvollständig; unvollkommen.

incomprehensible □ [inkɔmpri'hensəbl] unbegreiflich.

inconceivable □ [inkən'siːvəbl] unbegreiflich, unfaßbar.

incongruous □ [in'kɔŋgruəs] nicht übereinstimmend; unpassend.

inconsequent □ [in'kɔnsikwənt] inkonsequent, folgewidrig; **~ial** [inkɔnsi'kwenʃəl] unbedeutend; = *inconsequent*.

inconsidera|ble □ [inkən'sidərəbl] unbedeutend; **~te** □ [~rit] unüberlegt; rücksichtslos.

inconsisten|cy [inkən'sistənsi] Unvereinbarkeit *f*; Inkonsequenz *f*; **~t** □ [~nt] unvereinbar; widerspruchsvoll; inkonsequent.

inconsolable □ [inkən'souləbl] untröstlich.

inconstant □ [in'kɔnstənt] unbeständig; veränderlich.

incontinent □ [in'kɔntinənt] unmäßig; ausschweifend.

inconvenien|ce [inkən'viːnjəns] **1.** Unbequemlichkeit *f*; Unannehmlichkeit *f*; **2.** belästigen; **~t** □ [~nt] unbequem; ungelegen; lästig.

incorporat|e 1. [in'kɔːpəreit] einverleiben (*into dat*.); (sich) vereinigen; *als Mitglied* aufnehmen; *als Körperschaft* eintragen; **2.** [~rit] einverleibt; vereinigt; **~ed** (*amtlich*) eingetragen; **~ion** [inkɔːpə'reiʃən] Einverleibung *f*; Verbindung *f*. [fehlerhaft; ungehörig.]

incorrect □ [inkə'rekt] unrichtig;⌐

incorrigible □ [in'kɔridʒəbl] unverbesserlich.

increas|e 1. [in'kriːs] *v/i*. zunehmen; sich vergrößern *od*. vermehren; *v/t*. vermehren, vergrößern; erhöhen; **2.** ['inkriːs] Zunahme *f*; Vergrößerung *f*; Zuwachs *m*; **~ingly** [in'kriːsiŋli] zunehmend, immer (*mit folgendem comp.*); ~ *difficult* immer schwieriger.

incredible □ [in'kredəbl] unglaublich.

incredul|ity [inkri'dju:liti] Unglaube *m*; **~ous** □ [in'kredjuləs] ungläubig, skeptisch.

incriminate [in'krimineit] beschuldigen; belasten.

incrustation [inkrʌs'teiʃən] Verkrustung *f*; Kruste *f*; ⊕ Belag *m*.

incub|ate ['inkjubeit] (aus)brüten; **~ator** [‿tə] Brutapparat *m*.

inculcate ['inkʌlkeit] einschärfen (*upon dat.*).

incumbent [in'kʌmbənt] obliegend; *be ~ on s.o.* j-m obliegen.

incur [in'kə:] sich *et.* zuziehen; geraten in (*acc.*); *Verpflichtung* eingehen; *Verlust* erleiden.

incurable [in'kjuərəbl] 1. □ unheilbar; 2. Unheilbare(r *m*) *f*.

incurious [in'kjuəriəs] gleichgültig, uninteressiert.

incursion [in'kə:ʃən] *feindlicher* Einfall.

indebted [in'detid] verschuldet; *fig.* (zu Dank) verpflichtet.

indecen|cy [in'di:snsi] Unanständigkeit *f*; **~t** □ [‿nt] unanständig.

indecis|ion [indi'siʒən] Unentschlossenheit *f*; **~ve** □ [‿'saisiv] nicht entscheidend; unbestimmt.

indecorous □ [in'dekərəs] unpassend; ungehörig.

indeed [in'di:d] 1. *adv.* in der Tat, tatsächlich; wirklich; allerdings; 2. *int.* so?; nicht möglich!

indefatigable □ [indi'fætigəbl] unermüdlich.

indefensible □ [indi'fensəbl] unhaltbar.

indefinite □ [in'definit] unbestimmt; unbeschränkt; ungenau.

indelible □ [in'delibl] untilgbar.

indelicate [in'delikit] unfein; taktlos.

indemni|fy [in'demnifai] sicherstellen; *j-m* Straflosigkeit zusichern; entschädigen; **~ty** [‿iti] Sicherstellung *f*; Straflosigkeit *f*; Entschädigung *f*.

indent 1. [in'dent] einkerben, auszacken; eindrücken; *typ. Vertrag* mit Doppel ausfertigen; **~** *upon s.o. for s.th.* ✝ et. bei j-m bestellen; 2. ['indent] Kerbe *f*; Vertiefung *f*; ✝ Auslandsauftrag *m*; = *indenture*; **~ation** [inden'teiʃən] Einkerbung *f*; Einschnitt *m*; **~ure** [in'dentʃə] 1. Vertrag *m*; Lehrbrief *m*; 2. vertraglich verpflichten.

independen|ce [indi'pendəns] Unabhängigkeit *f*; Selbständigkeit *f*; Auskommen *n*; ♀ *Day Am.* Unabhängigkeitstag *m* (4. Juli); **~t** □ [‿nt] unabhängig; selbständig.

indescribable □ [indis'kraibəbl] unbeschreiblich.

indestructible □ [indis'trʌktəbl] unzerstörbar.

indeterminate □ [indi'tə:minit] unbestimmt.

index ['indeks] 1. (An)Zeiger *m*; Anzeichen *n*; Zeigefinger *m*; Index *m*; (Inhalts-, Namen-, Sach)Verzeichnis *n*; 2. *Buch* mit e-m Index versehen.

Indian ['indjən] 1. indisch; indianisch; 2. Inder(in); *a. Red ~* Indianer(in); **~ corn** Mais *m*; **~ file:** *in ~* im Gänsemarsch; **~ pudding** *Am.* Maismehlpudding *m*; **~ summer** Altweiber-, Nachsommer *m*.

Indiarubber ['indjə'rabə] Radiergummi *m*.

indicat|e [in'indikeit] (an)zeigen; hinweisen auf (*acc.*); andeuten; **~ion** [indi'keiʃən] Anzeige *f*; Anzeichen *n*; Andeutung *f*; **~ive** [in'dikətiv] *a.* **~** *mood gr.* Indikativ *m*; **~or** ['indikeitə] Anzeiger *m* (*a.* ⊕); *mot.* Blinker *m*.

indict [in'dait] anklagen (*for wegen*); **~ment** [‿tmənt] Anklage *f*.

indifferen|ce [in'difrəns] Gleichgültigkeit *f*; **~t** □ [‿nt] gleichgültig (*to gegen*); unparteiisch; (nur) mäßig; unwesentlich; unbedeutend.

indigenous [in'didʒinəs] eingeboren, einheimisch.

indigent □ ['indidʒənt] arm.

indigest|ible □ [indi'dʒestəbl] unverdaulich; **~ion** [‿tʃən] Verdauungsstörung *f*, Magenverstimmung *f*.

indign|ant □ [in'dignənt] entrüstet, empört, ungehalten; **~ation** [indig'neiʃən] Entrüstung *f*; **~ity** [in'digniti] Beleidigung *f*.

indirect □ [indi'rekt] indirekt; nicht direkt; *gr. a.* abhängig.

indiscre|et □ [indis'kri:t] unbesonnen; unachtsam; indiskret; **~tion** [‿reʃən] Unachtsamkeit *f*; Unbesonnenheit *f*; Indiskretion *f*.

indiscriminate □ [indis'kriminit] unterschieds-, wahllos.

indispensable □ [indis'pensəbl] unentbehrlich, unerläßlich.

indispos|ed [indis'pouzd] unpäßlich; abgeneigt; **~ition** [indispə-'ziʃən] Abneigung *f* (*to gegen*); Unpäßlichkeit *f*.

indisputable □ [indis'pju:təbl] unbestreitbar, unstreitig.

indistinct □ [indis'tiŋkt] undeutlich; unklar.

indistinguishable □ [indis'tiŋgwiʃəbl] nicht zu unterscheiden(d).

indite [in'dait] ab-, verfassen.

individual [indi'vidjuəl] 1. □ persönlich, individuell; besondere(r, -s); einzeln; Einzel...; 2. Individuum *n*; **~ism** [‿lizəm] Individualismus *m*; **~ist** [‿ist] Individualist *m*; **~ity** [individju'æliti] Individualität *f*.

indivisible □ [indi'vizəbl] unteilbar.

indolen|ce ['indələns] Trägheit *f*;

~t □ [~nt] indolent, träge, lässig; *⚓* schmerzlos.

indomitable □ [in'dɔmitəbl] unbezähmbar.

indoor ['indɔ:] im Hause (befindlich); Haus..., Zimmer..., *Sport:* Hallen...; **~s** ['in'dɔ:z] zu Hause; im *od.* ins Haus.

indorse [in'dɔ:s] = *endorse etc.*

induce [in'dju:s] veranlassen; **~ment** [~smənt] Anlaß *m*, Antrieb *m.*

induct [in'dʌkt] einführen; **~ion** [~kʃən] Einführung *f*, Einsetzung *f in Amt, Pfründe; ⚡* Induktion *f.*

indulge [in'dʌldʒ] nachsichtig sein gegen *j-n*; *j-m* nachgeben; **~** *with j-n* erfreuen mit; **~** *(o.s.) in s.th.* sich et. gönnen; sich e-r S. hin- *od.* ergeben; **~nce** [~dʒəns] Nachsicht *f*; Nachgiebigkeit *f*; Sichgehenlassen *n*; Vergünstigung *f*; **~nt** □ [~nt] nachsichtig.

industri|al □ [in'dʌstriəl] gewerbetreibend, gewerblich; industriell; Gewerbe...; Industrie...; **~** *area* Industriebezirk *m*; **~** *estate* Industriegebiet *n e-r Stadt;* **~** *school* Gewerbeschule *f*; **~alist** [~list] Industrielle(r) *m*; **~alize** [~laiz] industrialisieren; **~ous** □ [~iəs] fleißig.

industry ['indəstri] Fleiß *m*; Gewerbe *n*; Industrie *f.*

inebriate [i'ni:brieit] betrunken machen; **2.** [~iit] Trunkenbold *m.*

ineffable □ [in'efəbl] unaussprechlich.

ineffect|ive [ini'fektiv], **~ual** □ [~tjuəl] unwirksam, fruchtlos.

inefficient □ [ini'fiʃənt] wirkungslos; (leistungs)unfähig.

inelegant □ [in'eligənt] unelegant, geschmacklos.

ineligible □ [in'elidʒəbl] nicht wählbar; ungeeignet; *bsd.* ⚔ untauglich.

inept □ [i'nept] unpassend; albern.

inequality [ini(:)'kwɔliti] Ungleichheit *f*; Ungleichmäßigkeit *f*; Unebenheit *f.*

inequitable □ [in'ekwitəbl] unbillig.

inert □ [i'nə:t] träge; **~ia** [i'nə:ʃjə], **~ness** [i'nə:tnis] Trägheit *f.*

inescapable [inis'keipəbl] unentrinnbar.

inessential ['ini'senʃəl] unwesentlich (*to* für).

inestimable □ [in'estiməbl] unschätzbar.

inevitab|le □ [in'evitəbl] unvermeidlich; **~ly** [~li] unweigerlich.

inexact □ [inig'zækt] ungenau.

inexcusable □ [iniks'kju:zəbl] unentschuldbar.

inexhaustible □ [inig'zɔ:stəbl] unerschöpflich; unermüdlich.

inexorable □ [in'eksərəbl] unerbittlich.

inexpedient □ [iniks'pi:djənt] unzweckmäßig, unpassend.

inexpensive □ [iniks'pensiv] nicht teuer, billig, preiswert.

inexperience [iniks'piəriəns] Unerfahrenheit *f*; **~d** [~st] unerfahren.

inexpert □ [iniks'pə:t] unerfahren.

inexplicable □ [in'eksplikəbl] unerklärlich.

inexpressi|ble □ [iniks'presəbl] unaussprechlich; **~ve** [~siv] ausdruckslos.

inextinguishable □ [iniks'tiŋgwiʃəbl] unauslöschlich.

inextricable □ [in'ekstrikəbl] unentwirrbar.

infallible □ [in'fæləbl] unfehlbar.

infam|ous □ ['infəməs] ehrlos; schändlich; verrufen; **~y** [~mi] Ehrlosigkeit *f*; Schande *f*; Niedertracht *f.*

infan|cy ['infənsi] Kindheit *f*; 🏛 Minderjährigkeit *f*; **~t** [~nt] Säugling *m*; (kleines) Kind; Minderjährige(r *m*) *f.*

infanti|le ['infəntail], **~ne** [~ain] kindlich; Kindes..., Kinder...; kindisch.

infantry ⚔ ['infəntri] Infanterie *f.*

infatuate [in'fætjueit] betören; **~d** vernarrt (*with in acc.*).

infect [in'fekt] anstecken (*a. fig.*); infizieren, verseuchen, verpesten; **~ion** [~kʃən] Ansteckung *f*; **~ious** □ [~ʃəs], **~ive** [~ktiv] ansteckend; Ansteckungs...

infer [in'fə:] folgern, schließen; **~ence** ['infərəns] Folgerung *f.*

inferior [in'fiəriə] **1.** untere(r, -s); minderwertig; **~** *to* niedriger *od.* geringer als; untergeordnet (*dat.*); unterlegen (*dat.*); **2.** Geringere(r *m*) *f*; Untergebene(r *m*) *f*; **~ity** [infiəri-'ɔriti] geringerer Wert *od.* Stand; Unterlegenheit *f*; Minderwertigkeit *f.*

infern|al □ [in'fə:nl] höllisch; **~o** [~nou] Inferno *n*, Hölle *f.*

infertile [in'fə:tail] unfruchtbar.

infest [in'fest] heimsuchen; verseuchen; *fig.* überschwemmen.

infidelity [infi'deliti] Unglaube *m*; Untreue *f* (*to* gegen).

infiltrate ['infiltreit] *v/t.* durchdringen; *v/i.* durchsickern, eindringen.

infinite □ ['infinit] unendlich.

infinitive [in'finitiv] *a.* **~** *mood gr.* Infinitiv *m*, Nennform *f.*

infinity [in'finiti] Unendlichkeit *f.*

infirm □ [in'fə:m] kraftlos, schwach; **~ary** [~məri] Krankenhaus *n*; **~ity** [~miti] Schwäche *f* (*a. fig.*); Gebrechen *n.*

inflame [in'fleim] entflammen (*mst fig.*); (sich) entzünden (*a. fig. u. ⚓*).

inflamma|ble □ [in'flæməbl] entzündlich; feuergefährlich; **~tion** [inflə'meiʃən] Entzündung *f*; **~tory** [inflə'meiʃən]

inflate [in'flæmətəri] entzündlich; *fig.* aufrührerisch; hetzerisch; Hetz...

inflat|e [in'fleit] aufblasen, aufblähen (*a. fig.*); **~ion** [~eiʃən] Aufblähung *f*; † Inflation *f*; *fig.* Aufgeblasenheit *f*.

inflect [in'flekt] biegen; *gr.* flektieren, beugen.

inflexi|ble [in'fleksəbl] unbiegsam; *fig.* unbeugsam; **~on** [~kʃən] Biegung *f*; *gr.* Flexion *f*, Beugung *f*; Modulation *f*.

inflict [in'flikt] auferlegen; zufügen; *Hieb* versetzen; *Strafe* verhängen; **~ion** [~kʃən] Auferlegung *f*; Zufügung *f*; Plage *f*.

influen|ce ['influəns] 1. Einfluß *m*; 2. beeinflussen; **~tial** [influ'enʃəl] einflußreich.

influenza ✗ [influ'enzə] Grippe *f*.

influx ['inflʌks] Einströmen *n*; *fig.* Zufluß *m*, (Zu)Strom *m*.

inform [in'fɔ:m] *v/t.* benachrichtigen, unterrichten (*of* von); *v/i.* anzeigen (*against* s.o. *j.*); **~al** [~əml] formlos, zwanglos; **~ality** [infɔ:'mæliti] Formlosigkeit *f*; Formfehler *m*; **~ation** [infə'meiʃən] Auskunft *f*; Nachricht *f*, Information *f*; **~ative** [in'fɔ:mətiv] informatorisch; lehrreich; mitteilsam; **~er** [in'fɔ:mə] Denunziant *m*; Spitzel *m*.

infrequent [in'fri:kwənt] selten.

infringe [in'frindʒ] *a.* **~ upon** *Vertrag etc.* verletzen; übertreten.

infuriate [in'fjuərieit] wütend machen.

infuse [in'fju:z] einflößen; aufgießen.

ingen|ious ☐ [in'dʒi:njəs] geist-, sinnreich; erfinderisch; raffiniert; genial; **~uity** [indʒi'nju(:)iti] Genialität *f*; **~uous** ☐ [in'dʒenjuəs] freimütig; unbefangen, naiv.

ingot ['iŋgət] *Gold- etc.* Barren *m*.

ingrati|ate [in'greiʃieit]: **~** *o.s.* sich beliebt machen (*with* bei); **~tude** [~rætitju:d] Undankbarkeit *f*.

ingredient [in'gri:djənt] Bestandteil *m*.

ingrowing ['ingrouiŋ] nach innen wachsend; eingewachsen.

inhabit [in'hæbit] bewohnen; **~able** [~təbl] bewohnbar; **~ant** [~ənt] Bewohner(in), Einwohner(in).

inhal|ation [inhə'leiʃən] Einatmung *f*; **~e** [in'heil] einatmen.

inherent ☐ [in'hiərənt] anhaftend; innewohnend, angeboren (*in dat.*).

inherit [in'herit] (er)erben; **~ance** [~təns] Erbteil *n*, Erbe *n*; Erbschaft *f*; *biol.* Vererbung *f*.

inhibit [in'hibit] (ver)hindern; verbieten; zurückhalten; **~ion** [inhi-'biʃən] Hemmung *f*; Verbot *n*.

inhospitable ☐ [in'hɔspitəbl] ungastlich, unwirtlich.

inhuman ☐ [in'hju:mən] unmenschlich.

inimical ☐ [i'nimikəl] feindlich; schädlich.

inimitable ☐ [i'nimitəbl] unnachahmlich.

iniquity [i'nikwiti] Ungerechtigkeit *f*; Schlechtigkeit *f*.

initia|l [i'niʃəl] 1. ☐ Anfangs...; anfänglich; 2. Anfangsbuchstabe *m*; **~te 1.** [~ʃiit] Eingeweihte(r *m*) *f*; 2. [~ʃieit] beginnen; anbahnen; einführen, einweihen; **~tion** [iniʃi'eiʃən] Einleitung *f*; Einführung *f*; Einweihung *f*; **~ fee** *bsd. Am.* Aufnahmegebühr *f* (*Vereinigung*); **~tive** [i'niʃiətiv] Initiative *f*; einleitender Schritt, Entschlußkraft *f*; Unternehmungsgeist *m*; Volksbegehren *n*; **~tor** [~eitə] Initiator *m*, Urheber *m*.

inject [in'dʒekt] einspritzen; **~ion** [~kʃən] Injektion *f*, Spritze *f*.

injudicious ☐ [indʒu(:)'diʃəs] unverständig, unklug, unüberlegt.

injunction [in'dʒʌŋkʃən] gerichtliche Verfügung; ausdrücklicher Befehl.

injur|e ['indʒə] (be)schädigen; schaden (*dat.*); verletzen; beleidigen; **~ious** [in'dʒuəriəs] schädlich; ungerecht; beleidigend; **~y** ['indʒəri] Unrecht *n*; Schaden *m*; Verletzung *f*; Beleidigung *f*.

injustice [in'dʒʌstis] Ungerechtigkeit *f*; Unrecht *n*.

ink [iŋk] 1. Tinte *f*; *mst printer's* Druckerschwärze *f*; *attr.* Tinten...; 2. (mit Tinte) schwärzen; beklecksen.

inkling ['iŋkliŋ] Andeutung *f*; dunkle *od.* leise Ahnung.

ink|pot ['iŋkpɔt] Tintenfaß *n*; **~stand** Schreibzeug *n*; **~y** ['iŋki] tintig; Tinten...; tintenschwarz.

inland 1. ['inlənd] inländisch; Binnen...; 2. [~] Landesinnere(s) *n*, Binnenland *n*; 3. [in'lænd] landeinwärts.

inlay 1. ['in'lei] (*irr. (lay)*) einlegen; 2. ['inlei] Einlage *f*; Einlegearbeit *f*.

inlet ['inlet] Bucht *f*; Einlaß *m*.

inmate ['inmeit] Insass|e *m*, -in *f*; Hausgenoss|e *m*, -in *f*.

inmost ['inmoust] innerst.

inn [in] Gasthof *m*, Wirtshaus *n*.

innate ☐ ['i'neit] angeboren.

inner ['inə] inner, inwendig; geheim; **~most** innerst; geheimst.

innervate ['inə:veit] Nervenkraft geben (*dat.*); kräftigen.

innings ['iniŋz] *Sport:* Dransein *n*.

innkeeper ['inki:pə] Gastwirt(in).

innocen|ce ['inəsns] Unschuld *f*; Harmlosigkeit *f*; Einfalt *f*; **~t** [~t] 1. ☐ unschuldig; harmlos; 2. Unschuldige(r *m*) *f*; Einfältige(r *m*) *f*.

innocuous ☐ [i'nɔkjuəs] harmlos.

innovation [inou'veiʃən] Neuerung *f*.

innoxious ☐ [i'nɔkʃəs] unschädlich.

innuendo [inju(:)'endou] Andeutung *f*

innumerable □ [i'nju:mərəbl] unzählbar, unzählig.

inoccupation ['inɔkju'peiʃən] Beschäftigungslosigkeit *f*.

inoculate [i nɔkjuleit] (ein)impfen.

inoffensive [inə'fensiv] harmlos.

inofficial [inə'fiʃəl] inoffiziell.

inoperative [in'ɔpərətiv] unwirksam

inopportune [in'ɔpətju:n] unangebracht, zur Unzeit.

inordinate [i'nɔ:dinit] unmäßig.

in-patient ['inpeiʃənt] Krankenhauspatient *m*, stationärer Patient.

inquest [inkwest] Untersuchung *f*; *coroner's* Leichenschau *f*.

inquir|e [in'kwaiə] fragen, sich erkundigen (*of* bei *j-m*); ~ *into* untersuchen, **~ing** [~əriŋ] forschend; **~y** [~ri] Erkundigung *f*, Nachfrage *f*; Untersuchung *f*; Ermittlung *f*.

inquisit|ion [inkwi'ziʃən] Untersuchung *f*, **~ive** □ [in'kwizitiv] neugierig, wißbegierig.

inroad ['inroud] *feindlicher* Einfall; Ein-, Übergriff *m*.

insan|e [in'sein] wahnsinnig; **~ity** [in'sæniti] Wahnsinn *m*.

insatia|ble [in'seiʃjəbl], **~te** [~ʃiit] unersättlich (*of* nach).

inscribe [in'skraib] ein-, auf-, beschreiben, beschriften; *fig.* einprägen (*in, on dat.*); *Buch* widmen.

inscription [in'skripʃən] In-, Aufschrift *f*; ➜ Eintragung *f*.

inscrutable □ [in'skru:təbl] unerforschlich, unergründlich.

insect ['insekt] Insekt *n*; **~icide** [in'sektisaid] Insektengift *n*.

insecure [insi'kjuə] unsicher.

insens|ate [in'senseit] gefühllos; unvernünftig, **~ible** □ [~səbl] unempfindlich; bewußtlos; unmerklich; gleichgültig, **~itive** [~sitiv] unempfindlich.

inseparable □ [in'separəbl] untrennbar; unzertrennlich.

insert 1. [in'sə:t] einsetzen, einschalten, einfügen; (hinein)stecken; *Münze* einwerfen; inserieren; 2. ['insə:t] Bei-, Einlage *f*; **~ion** [in'sə:ʃən] Einsetzung *f*, Einfügung *f*, Eintragung *f*; Einwurf *m e-r Münze*; Anzeige *f*, Inserat *n*.

inshore ⏚ ['in'ʃɔ:] an *od.* nahe der Küste (befindlich) Küsten...

inside [in'said] 1. Innenseite *f*; Innere(s) *n*; *turn* ~ *out* umkrempeln; auf den Kopf stellen; 2. *adj.* inner, inwendig; Innen...; 3. *adv.* im Innern; 4. *prp.* innerhalb.

insidious □ [in'sidiəs] heimtückkisch.

insight ['insait] Einsicht *f*, Einblick *m*.

insignia [in'signiə] *pl.* Abzeichen *n/pl.*, Insignien *pl.*

insignificant [insig'nifikənt] bedeutungslos; unbedeutend.

insincere [insin'siə] unaufrichtig.

insinuat|e [in'sinjueit] unbemerkt hineinbringen; zu verstehen geben; andeuten; **~ion** [insinju'eiʃən] Einschmeichelung *f*; Anspielung *f*, Andeutung *f*; Wink *m*

insipid [in'sipid] geschmacklos, fad.

insist [in'sist] ~ (*up*)*on* bestehen auf (*dat.*); dringen auf (*acc*); **~ence** [~təns] Bestehen *n*; Beharrlichkeit *f*; Drängen *n*; **~ent** □ [~nt] beharrlich; eindringlich

insolent □ [in'solənt] unverschämt.

insoluble □ [in'sɔljubl] unlöslich.

insolvent [in'sɔlvənt] zahlungsunfähig. [keit *f*.]

insomnia [in'sɔmniə] Schlaflosig-]

insomuch [insou'mʌtʃ] ~ *that* dermaßen *od.* so sehr, daß

inspect [in'spekt] untersuchen, prüfen, nachsehen; **~ion** [~kʃən] Prüfung *f*, Untersuchung *f*; Inspektion *f*; **~or** [~ktə] Aufsichtsbeamte(r) *m*.

inspir|ation [inspə reiʃən] Einatmung *f*; Eingebung *f*; Begeisterung *f*; **~e** [in'spaiə] einatmen; *fig.* eingeben, erfüllen; *j-n* begeistern.

install [in'stɔ:l] einsetzen; (sich) niederlassen; ⊕ installieren; **~ation** [instə'leiʃən] Einsetzung *f*; ⊕ Installation *f*, Einrichtung *f*; ⚡ etc. Anlage *f*.

instal(l)ment [in'stɔ:lmənt] Rate *f*; Teil-, Ratenzahlung *f*; (Teil)Lieferung *f*; Fortsetzung *f*.

instance ['instəns] Ersuchen *n*; Beispiel *n*; (besonderer) Fall; ⚖ Instanz *f*; *for* ~ zum Beispiel.

instant □ [in'stənt] 1. dringend; sofortig; *on the 10th* ~ am 10. dieses Monats; 2. Augenblick *m*; **~aneous** □ [instən'teinjəs] augenblicklich; Moment...; **~ly** [in'stəntli] sogleich.

instead [in'sted] dafür; ~ *of* anstatt.

instep ['instep] Spann *m*.

instigat|e ['instigeit] anstiften; aufhetzen; **~or** [~tə] Anstifter *m*, Hetzer *m*.

instil(l) [in'stil] einträufeln; *fig.* einflößen (*into dat.*).

instinct ['instiŋkt] Instinkt *m*; **~ive** □ [in'stiŋktiv] instinktiv.

institut|e ['institju:t] 1. Institut *n*; 2. einsetzen, stiften, einrichten; anverordnen; **~ion** [insti'tju:ʃən] Einsetzung *f*, Einrichtung *f*; An-, Verordnung *f*; Satzung *f*; Institut(ion *f*) *n*; Gesellschaft *f*; Anstalt *f*; **~ional** [~nl] Instituts..., Anstalts...

instruct [in'strʌkt] unterrichten; belehren; *j-n* anweisen; **~ion** [~kʃən] Vorschrift *f*; Unterweisung *f*; Anweisung *f*; **~ive** □ [~ktiv] lehrreich; **~or** [~tə] Lehrer *m*; Ausbilder *m*; *Am. univ.* Dozent *m*.

instrument ['instrumənt] Instru-

ment *n*, Werkzeug *n* (*a. fig.*); ⁓
Urkunde *f*; ⁓al □ [instru'mentl]
als Werkzeug dienend; dienlich; ♪
Instrumental...; ⁓ality [instrumen-
'tæliti] Mitwirkung *f*, Mittel *n*.

insubordinat|e [insə'bɔ:dnit] auf-
sässig; ⁓ion ['insəbɔ:di'neiʃən] Auf-
lehnung *f*.

insubstantial [insəb'stænʃəl] unwirklich; gebrechlich.

insufferable] [in'sʌfərəbl] unerträglich, unausstehlich.

insufficient □ [insə'fiʃənt] unzulänglich, ungenügend.

insula|r □ ['insjulə] Insel...; *fig.*
engstirnig; ⁓te [⁓leit] isolieren;
⁓tion [insju'leiʃən] Isolierung *f*.

insult 1. ['insʌlt] Beleidigung *f*;
2. [in'sʌlt] beleidigen.

insupportable] [insə'pɔ:təbl] unerträglich, unausstehlich.

insur|ance [in'ʃuərəns] Versiche-
rung *f*; *attr.* Versicherungs...;
⁓ance policy Versicherungspolice
f, -schein *m*; ⁓e [in'ʃuə] versichern;
insurgent [in'sə:dʒənt] 1. aufrührerisch; 2. Aufrührer *m*.

insurmountable □ [insə(:)'maun-
təbl] unübersteigbar, *fig.* unüberwindlich.

insurrection [insə'rekʃən] Aufstand
m, Empörung *f*.

intact [in'tækt] unberührt; unversehrt.

intangible □ [in'tændʒəbl] unfühl-
bar; unfaßbar; unantastbar.

integ|ral □ ['intigrəl] ganz, voll-
ständig; wesentlich; ⁓rate [⁓reit]
ergänzen; zs.-tun; einfügen; ⁓rity
[in'tegriti] Vollständigkeit *f*; Redlichkeit *f*, Integrität *f*.

intellect [in'telekt] Verstand *m*;
konkr. die Intelligenz *f*; ⁓ual [inti-
'lektjuəl] 1. □ intellektuell; Ver-
standes...; geistig; verständig; 2. In-
tellektuelle(r *m*) *f*.

intelligence [in'telidʒəns] Intelligenz *f*; Verstand *m*; Verständnis *n*;
Nachricht *f*, Auskunft *f*; ⁓ department Nachrichtendienst *m*.

intellig|ent] [in'telidʒənt] intelli-
gent; klug; ⁓ible □ [⁓dʒəbl] verständlich (*to* für).

intempera|nce [in'tempərəns] Un-
mäßigkeit *f*; Trunksucht *f*; ⁓te □
[⁓rit] unmäßig; zügellos; unbe-
herrscht; trunksüchtig.

intend [in'tend] beabsichtigen, wollen; ⁓ for bestimmen für *od.* zu;
⁓ed 1. absichtlich; beabsichtigt, *a.*
zukünftig; 2. F Verlobte(r *m*) *f*.

intense □ [in'tens] intensiv; ange-
strengt; heftig; kräftig (*Farbe*).

intensify [in'tensifai] (sich) verstärken *od.* steigern.

intensity [in'tensiti] Intensität *f*.

intent [in'tent] 1. □ gespannt; bedacht; beschäftigt (*on* mit); 2. Absicht *f*; Vorhaben *n*; *to all* ⁓s *and*

purposes in jeder Hinsicht; ⁓ion
[⁓nʃən] Absicht *f*; Zweck *m*; ⁓ional
□ [⁓nl] absichtlich; ⁓ness [⁓ntnis]
gespannte Aufmerksamkeit; Eifer
m.

inter [in'tə:] beerdigen, begraben.

inter... ['intə(:)] zwischen; Zwischen...; gegenseitig, einander.

interact [intər'ækt] sich gegenseitig
beeinflussen.

intercede [intə(:)'si:d] vermitteln.

intercept [intə(:)'sept] ab-, auffangen; abhören; unter-
brechen; ⁓ion [⁓pʃən] Ab-, Auffangen *n*; Ab-, Mithören *n*; Unterbrechung *f*; Aufhalten *n*.

intercess|ion [intə'seʃən] Fürbitte
f; ⁓or [⁓esə] Fürsprecher *m*.

interchange 1. [intə(:)'tʃeindʒ] *v/t.*
austauschen, auswechseln; *v/i.* abwechseln; 2. ['intə(:)'tʃeindʒ] Austausch *m*; Abwechs(e)lung *f*.

intercourse ['intə(:)kɔ:s] Verkehr *m*.

interdict 1. [intə(:)'dikt] untersagen,
verbieten (*s.th. to s.o.* j-m et.; *s.o.
from doing* j-m zu tun); 2. ['intə(:)-
dikt], ⁓ion [intə(:)'dikʃən] Verbot
n; Interdikt *n*.

interest ['intrist] 1. Interesse *n*;
Anziehungskraft *f*; Bedeutung *f*;
Nutzen *m*; † Anteil *m*, Beteiligung
f, Kapital *n*; Zins(en *pl.*) *m*; ⁓s *pl.*
Interessenten *m/pl.*, Kreise *m/pl.*;
take an ⁓ *in* sich interessieren für;
return a blow with ⁓ noch heftiger
zurückschlagen; *banking* ⁓s *pl.*
Bankkreise *m/pl.*; 2. *allg.* interessieren (*in* für *et.*); ⁓ing [⁓tiŋ]
interessant.

interfere [intə'fiə] sich einmischen
(*with in acc.*); vermitteln; (*ea.*)
stören; ⁓nce [⁓rəns] Einmischung
f; Beeinträchtigung *f*; Störung *f*.

interim ['intərim] 1. Zwischenzeit
f; 2. vorläufig; Interims...

interior [in'tiəriə] 1. □ inner; inner-
lich; Innen...; ⁓ decorator Innen-
architekt *m*; Maler *m*, Tapezierer
m; 2. Innere(s) *n*; Interieur *n*; *pl.*
innere Angelegenheiten; *Department of the* ☉ *Am.* Innenministerium *n*.

interjection [intə(:)'dʒekʃən] Ausruf *m*.

interlace [intə(:)'leis] *v/t.* durch-
flechten, -weben; *v/i.* sich kreuzen.

interlock [intə(:)'lɔk] in-ea.-greifen;
in-ea.-schlingen; in-ea.-haken.

interlocut|ion [intə(:)lou'kju:ʃən]
Unterredung *f*; ⁓or [⁓ə(:)'lɔkjutə]
Gesprächspartner *m*.

interlope [intə(:)'loup] sich ein-
drängen; ⁓r ['intə(:)loupə] Eindringling *m*.

interlude ['intə(:)lu:d] Zwischen-
spiel *n*; Zwischenzeit *f*; ⁓s *of bright
weather* zeitweilig schön.

intermarriage [intə(:)'mæridʒ]
Mischehe *f*.

intermeddle [intə(:)'medl] sich einmischen (*with, in* in *acc.*).
intermedia|ry [intə(:)'mi:djəri] **1.** = *intermediate*; vermittelnd; **2.** Vermittler *m*; **~te** □ [~ət] in der Mitte liegend; Mittel..., Zwischen ; *~-range ballistic missile* Mittelstreckenrakete *f*; *~ school Am* Mittelschule *f*.
interment [in'tə:mənt] Beerdigung *f*
interminable □ [in'tə:minəbl] endlos, unendlich.
intermingle [intə(:)'miŋgl] (sich) vermischen
intermission [intə(:)'miʃən] Aussetzen *n*, Unterbrechung *f*; Pause *f*.
intermit [intə(:)'mit] unterbrechen, aussetzen, **~tent** □ [~tənt] aussetzend; *~ fever* ⚕ Wechselfieber *n*.
intermix [intə(:)'miks] (sich) vermischen
intern¹ [in tə:n] internieren.
intern² ['intə:n] Assistenzarzt *m*.
internal [in'tə:nl] inner(lich); inländisch
international □ [intə(:)'næʃənl] international; *~ law* Völkerrecht *n*.
interphone ['intəfoun] Haustelephon *n*; *Am.* ✈ Bordsprechanlage *f*.
interpolate [in'tə:pouleit] einschieben
interpose [intə(:)'pouz] *v/t. Veto* einlegen, *Wort* einwerfen; *v/i.* dazwischentreten; vermitteln.
interpret [in'tə:prit] auslegen, erklären, interpretieren; (ver)dolmetschen; darstellen; **~ation** [intə:pri'teiʃən] Auslegung *f*; Darstellung *f*; **~er** [in'tə:pritə] Ausleger (-in); Dolmetscher(in); Interpret (-in).
interrogat|e [in'terəgeit] (be-, aus-) fragen, verhören; **~ion** [interə'geiʃən] (Be-, Aus)Fragen *n*, Verhör(en) *n*; Frage *f*; *note od. mark od. point of ~* Fragezeichen *n*; **~ive** □ [intə'rɔgətiv] fragend; Frage...
interrupt [intə'rʌpt] unterbrechen; **~ion** [~pʃən] Unterbrechung *f*.
intersect [intə(:)'sekt] (sich) schneiden; **~ion** [~kʃən] Durchschnitt *m*; Schnittpunkt *m*; *Straßen- etc.* Kreuzung *f*.
intersperse [intə(:)'spə:s] einstreuen; untermengen, durchsetzen.
interstate *Am.* [intə(:)'steit] zwischenstaatlich.
intertwine [intə(:)'twain] verflechten.
interval ['intəvəl] Zwischenraum *m*; Pause *f*; (Zeit)Abstand *m*.
interven|e [intə(:)'vi:n] dazwischenkommen; sich einmischen; einschreiten; dazwischenliegen; **~tion** [~'venʃən] Dazwischenkommen *n*; Einmischung *f*; Vermitt(e)lung *f*.

interview ['intəvju:] **1.** Zusammenkunft *f*, Unterredung *f*; Interview *n*; **2.** interviewen.
intestine [in'testin] **1.** inner; **2.** Darm *m*; *~s pl* Eingeweide *n/pl*.
intima|cy ['intiməsi] Intimität *f*, Vertraulichkeit *f*; **~te** **1.** [~meit] bekanntgeben; zu verstehen geben; **2.** □ [~mit] intim; **3.** [~] Vertraute(r *m*) *f*; **~tion** [inti'meiʃən] Andeutung *f*, Wink *m*; Ankündigung *f*.
intimidate [in'timideit] einschüchtern.
into *prp.* ['intu, *vor Konsonant* 'intə] in (*acc.*), in ... hinein.
intolera|ble □ [in'tɔlərəbl] unerträglich; **~nt** □ [~ənt] unduldsam, intolerant.
intonation [intou'neiʃən] Anstimmen *n*; *gr.* Intonation *f*, Tonfall *m*.
intoxica|nt [in'tɔksikənt] **1.** berauschend; **2.** berauschendes Getränk; **~te** [~keit] berauschen (*a. fig.*); **~tion** [intɔksi'keiʃən] Rausch *m* (*a. fig.*).
intractable □ [in'træktəbl] unlenksam, störrisch; schwer zu bändigen(d).
intransitive □ *gr.* [in'trænsitiv] intransitiv.
intrastate *Am.* [intrə'steit] innerstaatlich.
intrench [in'trentʃ] = *entrench*.
intrepid [in'trepid] unerschrocken.
intricate □ ['intrikit] verwickelt.
intrigue [in'tri:g] **1.** Ränkespiel *n*, Intrige *f*; (Liebes)Verhältnis *n*; **2.** *v/i.* Ränke schmieden, intrigieren; ein (Liebes)Verhältnis haben; *v/t.* neugierig machen; **~r** [~gə] Intrigant(in).
intrinsic(al □) [in'trinsik(əl)] inner(lich); wirklich, wahr.
introduc|e [intrə'dju:s] einführen (*a. fig.*); bekannt machen (*to* mit), vorstellen (*to j-m*); einleiten; **~tion** [~'dʌkʃən] Einführung *f*; Einleitung *f*; Vorstellung *f*; *letter of ~* Empfehlungsschreiben *n*; **~tory** [~ktəri] einleitend, einführend.
introspection [introu'spekʃən] Selbstprüfung *f*; Selbstbetrachtung *f*.
introvert **1.** [introu'və:t] einwärtskehren; **2.** *psych.* ['introuvə:t] nach innen gekehrter Mensch.
intru|de [in'tru:d] hineinzwängen; (sich) ein- *od.* aufdrängen; **~der** [~də] Eindringling *m*; **~sion** [~u:ʒən] Eindringen *n*; Auf-, Zudringlichkeit *f*; **~sive** □ [~u:siv] zudringlich.
intrust [in'trʌst] = *entrust*.
intuition [intju(:)'iʃən] unmittelbare Erkenntnis, Intuition *f*.
inundate ['inʌndeit] überschwemmen.
inure [i'njuə] gewöhnen (*to* an *acc.*).
invade [in'veid] eindringen in, ein-

fallen in (acc.); fig. befallen; ~r [~də] Angreifer m; Eindringling m.
invalid¹ ['invəlid] 1. dienstunfähig; kränklich; 2. Invalide m.
invalid² [in'vælid] (rechts)ungültig; ~ate [~deit] entkräften; g̃ ungültig machen. [schätzbar.]
invaluable ☐ [in'væljuəbl] un-
invariab|le ☐ [in'vɛəriəbl] unver-änderlich; ~ly [~li] ausnahmslos.
invasion [in'veiʒən] Einfall m, An-griff m, Invasion f; Eingriff m; ⚔ Anfall m.
invective [in'vektiv] Schmähung f, Schimpfrede f, Schimpfwort n.
inveigh [in'vei] schimpfen (against über, auf acc.).
inveigle [in'viːgl] verleiten.
invent [in'vent] erfinden; ~ion [~nʃən] Erfindung(sgabe) f; ~ive ☐ [~ntiv] erfinderisch; ~or [~tə] Er-finder(in); ~ory ['invəntri] 1. In-ventar n; Inventur f; 2. inventari-sieren.
invers|e ☐ ['in'vəːs] umgekehrt; ~ion [in'vəːʃən] Umkehrung f; gr. Inversion f.
invert [in'vəːt] umkehren; umstel-len; ~ed commas pl. Anführungs-zeichen n/pl.
invest [in'vest] investieren, anlegen; bekleiden; ausstatten; umgeben (with von); ⚔ belagern.
investigat|e [in'vestigeit] erfor-schen; untersuchen; nachforschen; ~ion [investi'geiʃən] Erforschung f; Untersuchung f; Nachforschung f; ~or [in'vestigeitə] Untersuchen-de(r m) f.
invest|ment ✝ [in'vestmənt] Kapi-talanlage f; Investition f; ~or [~tə] Geldgeber m.
inveterate [in'vetərit] eingewur-zelt.
invidious ☐ [in'vidiəs] verhaßt; ge-hässig; beneidenswert.
invigorate [in'vigəreit] kräftigen.
invincible ☐ [in'vinsəbl] unbesieg-bar; unüberwindlich.
inviola|ble ☐ [in'vaiələbl] unver-letzlich; ~te [~lit] unverletzt.
invisible [in'vizəbl] unsichtbar.
invit|ation [invi'teiʃən] Einladung f, Aufforderung f; ~e [in'vait] ein-laden; auffordern; (an)locken.
invoice ✝ ['invois] Faktura f, Wa-renrechnung f.
invoke [in'vouk] anrufen; zu Hilfe rufen (acc.); sich berufen auf (acc.); Geist heraufbeschwören.
involuntary [in'vɔləntəri] un-freiwillig; unwillkürlich.
involve [in'vɔlv] verwickeln, hinein-ziehen; in sich schließen, enthalten; mit sich bringen; ~ment [~vmənt] Verwicklung f; (bsd. Geld)Schwie-rigkeit f.
invulnerable ☐ [in'vʌlnərəbl] un-verwundbar; fig. unanfechtbar.

inward ['inwəd] 1. ☐ inner(lich); 2. adv. mst ~s einwärts; nach innen; 3. ~s pl. Eingeweide n/pl.
iodine ['aiədiːn] Jod n.
IOU ['aiou'juː] (= I owe you) Schuld-schein m.
irascible ☐ [i'ræsibl] jähzornig.
irate [ai'reit] zornig, wütend.
iridescent [iri'desnt] schillernd.
iris ['aiəris] anat. Regenbogenhaut f, Iris f; ♀ Schwertlilie f.
Irish ['aiəriʃ] 1. irisch; 2. Irisch n; the ~ pl. die Iren pl.; ~man Ire m.
irksome ['əːksəm] lästig, ermüdend.
iron ['aiən] 1. Eisen n; a. flat~ Bügeleisen n; ~s pl. Fesseln f/pl.; strike while the ~ is hot fig. das Eisen schmieden, solange es heiß ist; 2. eisern (a. fig.); Eisen...; 3. bügeln; in Eisen legen; ~bound eisenbeschlagen; felsig; unbeug-sam; ~clad 1. gepanzert; 2. Panzer-schiff n; ~ curtain pol. eiserner Vor-hang; ~hearted fig. hartherzig.
ironic(al ☐) [ai'rɔnik(əl)] ironisch, spöttisch.
iron|ing ['aiəniŋ] Plätten n, Bügeln n; attr. Plätt..., Bügel...; ~ lung ⚔ eiserne Lunge; ~monger Eisenhändler m; ~mongery [~əri] Eisenwaren f/pl.; ~mo(u)ld Rost-fleck m; ~work schmiedeeiserne Arbeit; ~works mst ag. Eisenhütte f.
irony¹ ['aiəni] eisenartig, -haltig.
irony² ['aiərəni] Ironie f.
irradiant [i'reidjənt] strahlend (with vor Freude etc.).
irradiate [i'reidieit] bestrahlen (a. ♀); fig. aufklären; strahlen lassen.
irrational [i'ræʃənl] unvernünftig.
irreclaimable ☐ [iri'kleiməbl] un-verbesserlich.
irrecognizable ☐ [i'rekəgnaizəbl] nicht (wieder)erkennbar.
irreconcilable ☐ [i'rekənsailəbl] unversöhnlich; unvereinbar.
irrecoverable ☐ [iri'kʌvərəbl] un-ersetzlich; unwiederbringlich.
irredeemable ☐ [iri'diːməbl] un-kündbar; nicht einlösbar; uner-setzlich.
irrefutable ☐ [i'refjutəbl] unwider-leglich, unwiderlegbar.
irregular ☐ [i'regjulə] unregel-mäßig, regelwidrig; ungleichmäßig.
irrelevant ☐ [i'relivənt] nicht zur Sache gehörig; unzutreffend; un-erheblich, belanglos (to für).
irreligious ☐ [iri'lidʒəs] gottlos.
irremediable ☐ [iri'miːdiəbl] un-heilbar; unersetzlich.
irremovable ☐ [iri'muːvəbl] nicht entfernbar; unabsetzbar.
irreparable ☐ [i'repərəbl] nicht wieder gutzumachen(d).
irreplaceable ☐ [iri'pleisəbl] uner-setzlich.
irrepressible ☐ [iri'presəbl] un-unterdrückbar; unbezähmbar.

irreproachable □ [iri'proutʃəbl] einwandfrei, untadelig.

irresistible □ [iri'zistəbl] unwiderstehlich

irresolute □ [i'rezəlu:t] unentschlossen

irrespective □ [iris'pektiv] (of) rücksichtslos (gegen); ohne Rücksicht (auf acc); unabhängig (von).

irresponsible [iris'pɔnsəbl] unverantwortlich; verantwortungslos.

irretrievable [iri'tri:vəbl] unwiederbringlich, unersetzlich; nicht wieder gutzumachen(d).

irreverent [i'revərənt] respektlos, ehrfurchtslos

irrevocable [i'revəkəbl] unwiderruflich, unabänderlich, endgültig.

irrigate ['irigeit] bewässern.

irrita|ble ['iritəbl] reizbar; ~nt [~ənt] Reizmittel n; ~te [~teit] reizen, ärgern; ~ting □ [~tiŋ] aufreizend, ärgerlich (Sache); ~tion [iri'teiʃən] Reizung f; Gereiztheit f, Ärger m

irrupt|ion [i'rʌpʃən] Einbruch m (mst fig.), ~ive [~ptiv] (her)einbrechend

is [iz] 3 sg pres. von be.

island [ailənd] Insel f; Verkehrsinsel f, ~er [Inselbewohner(in).

isle [ail] Insel f; ~t ['ailit] Inselchen n.

isolat|e ['aisəleit] absondern; isolieren, ~ed abgeschieden; ~ion [aisə'leiʃən] Isolierung f, Absonderung f, ~ward ⚕ Isolierstation f; ~ionist Am. pol. [~ʃnist] Isolationist m.

issue ['isju:, Am. 'iʃu:] 1. Heraus-

kommen n, Herausfließen n; Abfluß m; Ausgang m; Nachkommen (-schaft f) m/pl.; fig. Ausgang m, Ergebnis n; Streitfrage f; Ausgabe f v. Material etc., Erlaß m v. Befehlen; Ausgabe f, Exemplar n; Nummer f e-r Zeitung; ~ in law Rechtsfrage f; be at ~ uneinig sein; point at ~ strittiger Punkt; 2. v/i. herauskommen; herkommen, entspringen; endigen (in in acc.); v/t. von sich geben; Material etc. ausgeben; Befehl erlassen; Buch herausgeben.

isthmus ['isməs] Landenge f.

it [it] 1. es; nach prp. da... (z.B. by ~ dadurch; for ~ dafür); 2. das gewisse Etwas.

Italian [i'tæljən] 1. italienisch; 2. Italiener(in); Italienisch n.

italics typ. [i'tæliks] Kursivschrift f.

itch [itʃ] 1. 🦠 Krätze f; Jucken n; Verlangen n; 2. jucken; be ~ing to inf. darauf brennen, zu inf.; have an ~ing palm raffgierig sein; ~ing ['itʃiŋ] Jucken n; fig Gelüste n.

item ['aitem] 1. desgleichen; 2. Einzelheit f, Punkt m; Posten m; (Zeitungs)Artikel m; ~ize [~maiz] einzeln angeben od. aufführen.

iterate ['itəreit] wiederholen.

itiner|ant [i'tinərənt] reisend; umherziehend; Reise...; ~ary [ai-'tinərəri] Reiseroute f, -plan m; Reisebericht m; attr. Reise...

its [its] sein(e); dessen, deren.

itself [it'self] (es, sich) selbst; sich; of ~ von selbst; in ~ in sich, an sich; by ~ für sich allein, besonders.

ivory ['aivəri] Elfenbein n.

ivy ♀ ['aivi] Efeu m.

J

jab F [dʒæb] 1. stechen; stoßen; 2. Stich m, Stoß m.

jabber ['dʒæbə] plappern.

jack [dʒæk] 1. Hebevorrichtung f, bsd. Wagenheber m; Malkugel f beim Bowlspiel; ⚓ Gösch f, kleine Flagge; Karten: Bube m; 2. a. ~ up aufbocken [Handlanger m.)

jackal ['dʒækɔ:l] zo. Schakal m; fig.)

jack|ass ['dʒækæs] Esel m (a. fig.); ~boots Reitstiefel m/pl.; hohe Wasserstiefel m/pl ; ~daw orn. Dohle f.

jacket ['dʒækit] Jacke f; ⊕ Mantel m; Schutzumschlag m e-s Buches.

jack|-knife ['dʒæknaif] (großes) Klappmesser n; ♀ of all trades Hansdampf m in allen Gassen; ♀ of all work Faktotum n; ~pot Poker: Einsatz m; hit the ~ Am. F großes Glück haben.

jade [dʒeid] (Schind)Mähre f, Klepper m; contp. Frauenzimmer n.

jag [dʒæg] Zacken m; sl. Sauferei f; ~ged ['dʒægid] zackig; gekerbt; bsd. Am. sl. voll (betrunken).

jaguar zo. ['dʒægjuə] Jaguar m.

jail [dʒeil] 1. Kerker m; 2. einkerkern; ~bird ['dʒeilbə:d] F Knastbruder m; Galgenvogel m; ~er ['dʒeilə] Kerkermeister m.

jalop(p)y bsd. Am. F mot. ⚡ [dʒə-'lɔpi] Kiste f.

jam¹ [dʒæm] Marmelade f.

jam² [~] 1. Gedränge n; ⊕ Hemmung f; Radio Störung f; traffic ~ Verkehrsstockung f; be in a ~ sl. in der Klemme sein; 2. (sich) (fest-, ver)klemmen; pressen, quetschen; versperren; Radio stören; ~ the brakes mit aller Kraft bremsen.

jamboree [dʒæmbə'ri:] (bsd. Pfadfinder)Treffen n; sl. Vergnügen n, Fez m.

jangle ['dʒæŋgl] schrillen (lassen); laut streiten, keifen.

janitor ['dʒænitə] Portier m.

January ['dʒænjuəri] Januar m.

Japanese [dʒæpə'niːz] 1. japanisch; 2. Japaner(in); Japanisch n; the ~ pl. die Japaner pl.

jar [dʒɑː] 1. Krug m; Topf m; Glas n; Knarren n, Mißton m; Streit m; mißliche Lage; 2. knarren; unangenehm berühren; erzittern (lassen); streiten.

jaundice ['dʒɔːndis] Gelbsucht f; ~d [..st] ↯ gelbsüchtig; fig. neidisch.

jaunt [dʒɔːnt] 1. Ausflug m, Spritztour f; 2. e-n Ausflug machen; ~y □ ['dʒɔːnti] munter; flott.

javelin ['dʒævlin] Wurfspeer m.

jaw [dʒɔː] Kinnbacken m, Kiefer m; ~s pl. Rachen m; Maul n; Schlund m; ⊕ Backen f/pl.; ~bone ['dʒɔːboun] Kieferknochen m.

jay orn. [dʒei] Eichelhäher m; ~walker Am. F ['dʒeiwɔːkə] achtlos die Straße überquerender Fußgänger.

jazz [dʒæz] 1. Jazz m; 2. F grell.

jealous □ ['dʒeləs] eifersüchtig; besorgt (of um); neidisch; ~y [~si] Eifersucht f; Neid m.

jeans [dʒiːnz] pl. Jeans pl., Niet(en)hose f.

jeep [dʒiːp] Jeep m.

jeer [dʒiə] 1. Spott m, Spötterei f; 2. spotten (at über acc.); (ver)höhnen.

jejune □ [dʒi'dʒuːn] nüchtern, fad.

jelly ['dʒeli] 1. Gallert(e f) n; Gelee n; 2. gelieren; ~fish zo. Qualle f.

jeopardize ['dʒepədaiz] gefährden.

jerk [dʒɜːk] 1. Ruck m; (Muskel-)Krampf m; 2. rucken od. zerren (an dat.); schnellen; schleudern; ~water Am. ['dʒɜːkwɔːtə] 1. 🚂 Nebenbahn f; 2. F klein, unbedeutend; ~y ['dʒɜːki] 1. ruckartig; holperig; 2. Am. luftgetrocknetes Rindfleisch.

jersey ['dʒɜːzi] Wollpullover m; wollenes Unterhemd.

jest [dʒest] 1. Spaß m; 2. scherzen; ~er ['dʒestə] Spaßmacher m.

jet [dʒet] 1. (Wasser-, Gas)Strahl m; Strahlrohr n; ⊕ Düse f; Düsenflugzeug n; Düsenmotor m; 2. hervorsprudeln; ~-propelled ['dʒetprəpeld] mit Düsenantrieb.

jetty ⚓ ['dʒeti] Mole f; Pier m.

Jew [dʒuː] Jude m; attr. Juden...

jewel ['dʒuːəl] Juwel m, n; ~(l)er [~lə] Juwelier m; ~(le)ry [~lri] Juwelen pl., Schmuck m.

Jew|ess ['dʒu(ː)is] Jüdin f; ~ish ['dʒu(ː)iʃ] jüdisch.

jib ⚓ [dʒib] Klüver m.

jibe Am. F [dʒaib] zustimmen.

jiffy F ['dʒifi] Augenblick m.

jig-saw ['dʒigsɔː] Laubsägema-

schine f; ~ puzzle Zusammensetzspiel n.

jilt [dʒilt] 1. Kokette f; 2. Liebhaber versetzen.

Jim [dʒim] ~ Crow Am. Neger m; Am. Rassentrennung f.

jingle ['dʒiŋgl] 1. Geklingel n; 2. klingeln, klimpern (mit).

jitney Am. sl. ['dʒitni] 5-Cent-Stück n; billiger Omnibus.

jive Am. sl. [dʒaiv] heiße Jazzmusik; Jazzjargon m.

job [dʒɔb] 1. (Stück n) Arbeit f; Sache f, Aufgabe f; Beruf m; Stellung f; by the ~ stückweise; im Akkord; ~ lot F Ramschware f; ~ work Akkordarbeit f; 2. v/t. Pferd etc. (ver)mieten; ✝ vermitteln; v/i. im Akkord arbeiten; Maklergeschäfte machen; ~ber ['dʒɔbə] Akkordarbeiter m; Makler m; Schieber m.

jockey ['dʒɔki] 1. Jockei m; 2. prellen.

jocose □ [dʒə'kous] scherzhaft, spaßig.

jocular □ ['dʒɔkjulə] lustig; spaßig.

jocund □ ['dʒɔkənd] lustig, fröhlich.

jog [dʒɔg] 1. Stoß(en n) m; Rütteln n; Trott m; 2. v/t. (an)stoßen, (auf-)rütteln; v/i. mst ~ along, ~ on dahintrotten, dahinschlendern.

John [dʒɔn]: ~ Bull John Bull (der Engländer); ~ Hancock Am. F Friedrich Wilhelm m (Unterschrift).

join [dʒɔin] 1. v/t. verbinden, zs.-fügen (to mit); sich vereinigen mit, sich gesellen zu; eintreten in (acc.); ~ battle den Kampf beginnen; ~ hands die Hände falten; sich die Hände reichen (a. fig.); v/i. sich verbinden, sich vereinigen; ~ in mitmachen bei; ~ up Soldat werden; 2. Verbindung(sstelle) f.

joiner ['dʒɔinə] Tischler m; ~y [~əri] Tischlerhandwerk n; Tischlerarbeit f.

joint [dʒɔint] 1. Verbindung(sstelle) f; Scharnier n; anat. Gelenk n; ☘ Knoten m; Braten m; Am. sl. Spelunke f; put out of ~ verrenken; 2. □ gemeinsam; Mit...; ~ heir Miterbe m; ~ stock ✝ Aktienkapital n; 3. zs.-fügen; zerlegen; ~ed ['dʒɔintid] gegliedert; Glieder...; ~-stock ✝ Aktien...; ~ company Aktiengesellschaft f.

jok|e [dʒouk] 1. Scherz m, Spaß m; practical ~ Streich m; 2. v/i. scherzen; schäkern; v/t. necken (about mit); ~er ['dʒoukə] Spaßvogel m; Karten: Joker m; Am. versteckte Klausel; ~y □ ['dʒouki] spaßig.

jolly ['dʒɔli] lustig, fidel; F nett.

jolt [dʒɔlt] 1. stoßen, rütteln; holpern; 2. Stoß m; Rütteln n.

Jonathan ['dʒɔnəθən]: Brother ~ der Amerikaner.

josh *Am. sl.* [dʒɔʃ] **1.** Ulk *m*; **2.** aufziehen, auf die Schippe nehmen.

jostle ['dʒɔsl] **1.** anrennen; zs.-stoßen; **2.** Stoß *m*; Zs.-Stoß *m*.

jot [dʒɔt] **1.** Jota *n*, Pünktchen *n*; **2.** ~ *down* notieren.

journal [ˈdʒəːnl] Journal *n*; Tagebuch *n*; Tageszeitung *f*; Zeitschrift *f*; ⊕ Wellenzapfen *m*; ~**ism** [ˈdʒəː-nəlizəm] Journalismus *m*.

journey [ˈdʒəːni] **1.** Reise *f*; Fahrt *f*; **2.** reisen, ~**man** Geselle *m*.

jovial   [ˈdʒouvjəl] heiter; gemütlich.

joy [dʒɔi] Freude *f*; Fröhlichkeit *f*; ~**ful** [ˈdʒɔiful] freudig; erfreut; fröhlich; ~**less** [ˈdʒɔilis] freudlos; unerfreulich; ~**ous** □ [ˈdʒɔiəs] freudig, fröhlich

jubil|ant [ˈdʒuːbilənt] jubilierend, frohlockend, ~**ate** [~leit] jubeln; ~**ee** [~li] Jubiläum *n*.

judge [dʒʌdʒ] **1.** Richter *m*; Schiedsrichter *m*, Beurteiler(in), Kenner(in); **2.** *v/i.* urteilen (*of über acc.*); *v/t* richten, aburteilen; beurteilen (*by nach*); ansehen als.

judg(e)ment [ˈdʒʌdʒmənt] Urteil *n*; Urteilsspruch *m*; Urteilskraft *f*; Einsicht *f*; Meinung *f*; *göttliches* (Straf)Gericht, *Day of ꝺ*, ꝺ *Day* Jüngstes Gericht.

judicature [ˈdʒuːdikətʃə] Gerichtshof *m*; Rechtspflege *f*.

judicial [dʒu(ː)ˈdiʃəl] gerichtlich; Gerichts ~, kritisch; unparteiisch.

judicious [dʒu(ː)ˈdiʃəs] verständig, klug, ~**ness** [~snis] Einsicht *f*.

jug [dʒʌg] Krug *m*, Kanne *f*.

juggle [ˈdʒʌgl] **1.** Trick *m*; Schwindel *m*, **2.** jonglieren (*a. fig.*); verfälschen; betrügen; ~**r** [~ə] Jongleur *m*, Taschenspieler(in).

Jugoslav [ˈjuːgouˈslɑːv] **1.** Jugoslaw|e *m*, -in *f*; **2.** jugoslawisch.

juic|e [dʒuːs] Saft *m*; *sl. mot.* Sprit *m*, Gas *m*, ~**y** □ [ˈdʒuːsi] saftig; F interessant   [sikautomat *m.*]

juke-box *Am.* F [ˈdʒuːkbɔks] Mu-⌍

julep [ˈdʒuːlep] *süßes* (Arznei)Getränk, *bsd. Am. alkoholisches* Eisgetränk

July [dʒu(ː)ˈlai] Juli *m*.

jumble [ˈdʒʌmbl] **1.** Durcheinander *n*; **2.** *v/t* durch-ea.-werfen; ~**sale** Wohltätigkeitsbasar *m*.

jump [dʒʌmp] **1.** Sprung *m*; ~**s** *pl.*

nervöses Zs.-fahren; *high* (*long*) ~ Hoch- (Weit)Sprung *m*; *get* (*have*) *the* ~ *on Am.* F zuvorkommen; **2.** *v/i.* (auf)springen; ~ *at* sich stürzen auf (*acc.*); ~ *to conclusions* übereilte Schlüsse ziehen; *v/t.* hinwegspringen über (*acc.*); überspringen; springen lassen; ~**er** [ˈdʒʌmpə] Springer *m*; Jumper *m*; ~**y** [~pi] nervös.

junct|ion [ˈdʒʌŋkʃən] Verbindung *f*; Kreuzung *f*; 🚉 Knotenpunkt *m*; ~**ure** [~ktʃə] Verbindungspunkt *m*, -stelle *f*; (kritischer) Zeitpunkt; *at this* ~ bei diesem Stand der Dinge.

June [dʒuːn] Juni *m*.

jungle [ˈdʒʌŋgl] Dschungel *m, n, f*.

junior [ˈdʒuːnjə] **1.** jünger (*to* als); *Am. univ* der Unterstufe (angehörend); ~ *high school Am.* Oberschule *f* mit Klassen 7, 8, 9; **2.** Jüngere(r *m*) *f*; *Am.* (Ober)Schüler *m od.* Student *m* im 3. Jahr; F Kleine(r) *m*

junk [dʒʌŋk] ⚓ Dschunke *f*; Plunder *m*, alter Kram.

junket [ˈdʒʌŋkit] Quarkspeise *f*; *Am.* Party *f*; Vergnügungsfahrt *f*.

juris|diction   [dʒuərisˈdikʃən] Rechtsprechung *f*; Gerichtsbarkeit *f*; Gerichtsbezirk *m*; ~**prudence** [ˈdʒuərispruːdəns] Rechtswissenschaft *f*.

juror [ˈdʒuərə] Geschworene(r) *m*.

jury [ˈdʒuəri] *die* Geschworenen *pl.*; Jury *f*, Preisgericht *n*; ~**man** Geschworene(r) *m*.

just □ [dʒʌst] **1.** *adj.* gerecht; rechtschaffen; **2.** *adv.* richtig; genau; (so)eben; nur; ~ *now* eben *od.* gerade jetzt.

justice [ˈdʒʌstis] Gerechtigkeit *f*; Richter *m*; Recht *n*; Rechtsverfahren *n*; *court of* ~ Gericht(shof *m*) *n*.

justification [dʒʌstifiˈkeiʃən] Rechtfertigung *f*.

justify [ˈdʒʌstifai] rechtfertigen.

justly [ˈdʒʌstli] mit Recht.

justness [ˈdʒʌstnis] Gerechtigkeit *f*, Billigkeit *f*; Rechtmäßigkeit *f*; Richtigkeit *f*.

jut [dʒʌt] *a.* ~ *out* hervorragen.

juvenile [ˈdʒuːvinail] **1.** jung, jugendlich; Jugend...; **2.** junger Mensch.

K

kale [keil] (*bsd.* Kraus-, Grün)Kohl *m*; *Am. sl.* Moos *n* (*Geld*).

kangaroo [kæŋgə'ru:] Känguruh *n*.

keel ⚓ [ki:l] 1. Kiel *m*; 2. ~ over kieloben legen *od* liegen; umschlagen.

keen [[ki:n] scharf (*a. fig.*); eifrig, heftig, stark, groß (*Appetit etc.*); ~ on F scharf *od* erpicht auf *acc.*; be ~ on *hunting* ein leidenschaftlicher Jäger sein; ~edged [ki:nedʒd] scharfgeschliffen; ~ness ['ki:nnis] Schärfe *f*; Heftigkeit *f*; Scharfsinn *m*.

keep [ki:p] 1. (Lebens)Unterhalt *m*; for ~s F für immer; 2. [*irr.*] *v/t.* *allg.* halten, behalten, unterhalten; (er-)halten, einhalten, (ab)halten, *Buch, Ware etc* führen, *Bett etc.* hüten; fest-, aufhalten, (bei)behalten; (auf)bewahren; ~ s.o. *company* j-m Gesellschaft leisten; ~ *company* with verkehren mit; ~ one's temper sich beherrschen; ~ *time* richtig gehen (*Uhr*), ♪, ✗ Takt, Schritt halten; ~ s.o. *waiting* j-n warten lassen; ~ *away* fernhalten; ~ s.th. *from* s.o j-m et vorenthalten; ~ *in* zurückhalten; *Schüler* nachsitzen lassen; ~ *on Kleid* anbehalten, *Hut* aufbehalten; ~ *up* aufrechterhalten; (*Mut*) bewahren, in Ordnung halten; hindern, zu Bett zu gehen; aufbleiben lassen; ~ *it up* (es) durchhalten; *v/i* sich halten, bleiben; F sich aufhalten; ~ *doing* immer wieder tun; ~ *away* sich fernhalten; ~ *from* sich enthalten (*gen.*); ~ *off* sich fernhalten; ~ *on talking* fortfahren zu sprechen; ~ *to* sich halten an (*acc*); ~ *up* sich aufrecht halten, sich aufrechterhalten; ~ *up with Schritt* halten mit; ~ *up with the Joneses* es den Nachbarn gleichtun.

keep|er ['ki:pə] Wärter *m*, Wächter *m*, Aufseher *m*; Verwalter *m*; Inhaber *m*; ~ing ['ki:piŋ] Verwahrung *f*; Obhut *f*, Gewahrsam *m*, *n*; Unterhalt *m*; be *in* (out *of*) ~ with ... (nicht) übereinstimmen mit ...; ~sake [ki:pseik] Andenken *n*.

keg [keg] Fäßchen *n*.

kennel ['kenl] Gosse *f*, Rinnstein *m*; Hundehütte *f*, -zwinger *m*.

kept [kept] *pret. u. p.p. von* keep 2.

kerb [kə:b], ~stone ['kə:bstoun] = curb *etc*

kerchief ['kə:tʃif] (Kopf)Tuch *n*.

kernel ['kə:nl] Kern *m* (*a. fig.*); Hafer-, Mais- *etc.* Korn *n*.

kettle ['ketl] Kessel *m*; ~drum ♪ Kesselpauke *f*.

key [ki:] 1. Schlüssel *m* (*a. fig.*); ⚒ Schlüssel zum; ⊕ Keil *m*; Schraubenschlüssel *m*; *Klavieretc.* Taste *f*; ♪ Taste *f*, Druck-

knopf *m*; ♪ Tonart *f*; *fig.* Ton *m*; 2. ~ up ♪ stimmen; erhöhen; *fig.* in erhöhte Spannung versetzen; ~board ['ki:bɔ:d] Klaviatur *f*, Tastatur *f*; ~hole Schlüsselloch *n*; ~man Schlüsselfigur *f*; ~money Ablösung *f* (*für e-e Wohnung*); ~note ♪ Grundton *m*; ~stone Schlußstein *m*; *fig.* Grundlage *f*.

kibitzer *Am.* F ['kibitsə] Kiebitz *m*, Besserwisser *m*.

kick [kik] 1. (Fuß)Tritt *m*; Stoß *m*; Schwung *m*; F Nervenkitzel *m*; get a ~ out of F Spaß finden an (*dat.*); 2. *v/t.* (mit dem Fuß) stoßen *od.* treten; *Fußball:* schießen; ~ out F hinauswerfen; *v/i.* (hinten) ausschlagen; stoßen (*Gewehr*); sich auflehnen; ~ *in with Am. sl.* Geld 'reinbuttern; ~ *off Fußball* anstoßen; ~back *bsd. Am.* F ['kikbæk] Rückzahlung *f*; ~er ['kikə] Fußballspieler *m*.

kid [kid] 1. Zicklein *n*; *sl.* Kind *n*; Ziegenleder *n*; 2. *sl.* foppen; ~dy *sl.* ['kidi] Kind *n*; ~ *glove* Glacéhandschuh *m* (*a. fig.*); ~glove sanft, zart.

kidnap ['kidnæp] entführen; ~(p)er [~pə] Kindesentführer *m*, Kidnapper *m*.

kidney ['kidni] *anat.* Niere *f*; F Art *f*; ~ *bean* ♀ weiße Bohne.

kill [kil] 1. töten (*a. fig.*); *fig.* vernichten; *parl.* zu Fall bringen; ~ *off* abschlachten; ~ *time* die Zeit totschlagen; 2. Tötung *f*; Jagdbeute *f*; ~er ['kilə] Totschläger *m*; ~ing ['kiliŋ] 1. ☐ mörderisch; F komisch; 2. *Am.* F *finanzieller* Volltreffer.

kiln [kiln] Brenn-, Darrofen *m*.

kilo|gram(me) ['kiləgræm] Kilogramm *n*; ~metre, *Am.* ~meter Kilometer *m*.

kilt [kilt] Kilt *m*, Schottenrock *m*.

kin [kin] (Bluts)Verwandtschaft *f*.

kind [kaind] 1. ☐ gütig, freundlich; 2. Art *f*, Gattung *f*, Geschlecht *n*; Art und Weise *f*; pay in ~ in Naturalien zahlen; *fig.* mit gleicher Münze heimzahlen.

kindergarten ['kindəgɑːtn] Kindergarten *m*.

kind-hearted ['kaind'hɑːtid] gütig.

kindle ['kindl] anzünden; (sich) entzünden (*a. fig.*).

kindling ['kindliŋ] Kleinholz *n*.

kind|ly ['kaindli] freundlich, günstig; ~ness ['kaindnis] Güte *f*, Freundlichkeit *f*; Gefälligkeit *f*.

kindred ['kindrid] 1. verwandt, gleichartig; 2. Verwandtschaft *f*.

king [kiŋ] König *m* (*a. fig. u. im Schach, Kartenspiel*); ~dom ['kiŋdəm] Königreich *n*; *bsd.* ♀, *zo.* Reich *n*, Gebiet *n*; *eccl.* Reich *n* Gottes; ~like ['kiŋlaik], ~ly [~li] königlich; ~size F ['kiŋsaiz] überlang, übergroß.

kink [kiŋk] Schlinge *f*, Knoten *m*; *fig.* Schrulle *f*, Fimmel *m*.

kin|ship ['kinʃip] Verwandtschaft *f*; ~sman ['kinzmən] Verwandte(r) *m*.

kipper ['kipə] Räucherhering *m* Bückling *m*; *sl* Kerl *m*.

kiss [kis] 1. Kuß *m*; 2. (sich) küssen.

kit [kit] Ausrüstung *f* (*a.* ✕ *u.* *Sport*); Handwerkszeug *n*, Werkzeug *n*; ~bag ['kitbæg] ✕ Tornister *m*; Seesack *m*; Reisetasche *f*.

kitchen ['kitʃin] Küche *f*; ~ette [kitʃi'net] Kochnische *f*; ~garden ['kitʃin'gɑ:dn] Gemüsegarten *m*.

kite [kait] Papier-Drachen *m*.

kitten ['kitn] Kätzchen *n*.

Klan *Am.* [klæn] Ku-Klux-Klan *m*; ~sman ['klænzmən] Mitglied *n* des Ku-Klux-Klan.

knack [næk] Kniff *m*, Dreh *m*; Geschicklichkeit *f*.   [Rucksack *m*.]

knapsack ['næpsæk] Tornister *m*;]

knave [neiv] Schurke *m*; Kartenspiel Bube *m*; ~ry ['neivəri] Gaunerei *f*.

knead [ni:d] kneten; massieren.

knee [ni:] Knie *n*; ⊕ Kniestück *n*; ~cap ['ni:kæp] Kniescheibe *f*; ~deep bis an die Knie (reichend); ~joint Kniegelenk *n*; ~l [ni:l] [*irr.*] knien (*to vor dat.*).

knell [nel] Totenglocke *f*.

knelt [nelt] *pret. u. p.p. von* kneel.

knew [nju:] *pret. von* know.

knicker|bockers ['nikəbɔkəz] *pl.* Knickerbocker *pl.*, Kniehosen *f/pl.*; ~s F ['nikəz] *pl.* Schlüpfer *m*; = knickerbockers.

knick-knack ['niknæk] Spielerei *f*; Nippsache *f*.

knife [naif] 1. *pl.* knives [naivz] Messer *n*; 2. schneiden; (er)stechen.

knight [nait] 1. Ritter *m*; Springer *m* im *Schach*; 2. zum Ritter schlagen; ~errant ['nait'erənt] fahrender Ritter; ~hood ['naithud] Rittertum *n*; Ritterschaft *f*; ~ly ['naitli] ritterlich.

knit [nit] [*irr.*] stricken; (ver)knüp-

fen; (sich) eng verbinden; ~ the brows die Stirn runzeln; ~ting ['nitiŋ] Stricken *n*; Strickzeug *n*; *attr.* Strick...

knives [naivz] *pl. von* knife 1.

knob [nɔb] Knopf *m*; Buckel *m*; Brocken *m*.

knock [nɔk] 1. Schlag *m*; Anklopfen *n*; *mot.* Klopfen *n*; 2. *v/i.* klopfen; pochen; stoßen; schlagen; ~ about F sich herumtreiben; *v/t.* klopfen, stoßen, schlagen; *Am. sl.* bekritteln, schlechtmachen; ~ about herumstoßen, übel zurichten; ~ down niederschlagen; *Auktion:* zuschlagen; ⊕ aus-ea.-nehmen; be ~ed down überfahren werden; ~ off aufhören mit; F zs.-hauen (*schnell erledigen*); *Summe* abziehen; ~ out Boxen: k.o. schlagen; ~er ['nɔkə] Klopfende(r) *m*; Türklopfer *m*; *Am. sl.* Kritikaster *m*; ~kneed ['nɔkni:d] x-beinig; *fig.* hinkend; ~out Boxen: Knockout *m*, K.o. *m*; *sl.* tolle Sache *od.* Person.

knoll[1] [noul] kleiner Erdhügel.

knoll[2] [~] (*bsd. zu Grabe*) läuten.

knot [nɔt] 1. Knoten *m*, Knorren *m*; Seemeile *f*; Schleife *f*, Band *n* (*a. fig.*).; Schwierigkeit *f*; 2. (ver)knoten, (ver)knüpfen (*a. fig.*); *Stirn* runzeln; verwickeln; ~ty ['nɔti] knotig; knorrig; *fig.* verwickelt.

know [nou] [*irr.*] wissen; (er)kennen; erfahren; ~ French Französisch können; come to ~ erfahren; get to ~ kennenlernen; ~ one's business, ~ the ropes, ~ a thing or two, ~ what's what sich auskennen, Erfahrung haben; you ~ (*am Ende des Satzes*) nämlich; ~ing [~] ['nouiŋ] erfahren; klug; schlau; verständnisvoll; wissentlich; ~ledge ['nɔlidʒ] Kenntnis(se *pl.*) *f*; Wissen *n*; to my ~ meines Wissens; ~n [noun] *p.p. von* know; come to be ~ bekannt werden; make ~ bekanntmachen.

knuckle ['nʌkl] 1. Knöchel *m*; 2. ~ down, ~ under nachgeben.

Kremlin ['kremlin] der Kreml.

Ku-Klux-Klan *Am.* ['kju:klʌks'klæn] Geheimbund in den USA.

L

label ['leibl] 1. Zettel *m*, Etikett *n*; Aufschrift *f*; Schildchen *n*; Bezeichnung *f*; 2. etikettieren, beschriften; *fig.* abstempeln (*as* als).

laboratory [lə'bɔrətəri] Laboratorium *n*; ~ *assistant* Laborant(in).

laborious] [lə'bɔːriəs] mühsam; arbeitsam; schwerfällig (*Stil*).

labo(u)r ['leibə] 1. Arbeit *f*; Mühe

f; (Geburts)Wehen *f/pl.*; Arbeiter *m/pl.*; *Ministry of* ⚥ Arbeitsministerium *n*; *hard* ~ Zwangsarbeit *f*; 2. Arbeiter...; Arbeits...; 3. *v/i.* arbeiten; sich abmühen; ~ *under* leiden unter (*dat.*), zu kämpfen haben mit; *v/t.* ausarbeiten; ~ed schwerfällig (*Stil*); mühsam (*Atem etc.*); ~er [~ərə] ungelernter Arbeiter; ⚥ *Ex-change* Arbeitsamt *n*; *Labour*

Party *pol.* Labour Party *f*; **labor union** *Am.* Gewerkschaft *f*.

lace [leis] **1.** Spitze *f*; Borte *f*; Schnur *f*; **2.** (zu)schnüren; mit Spitze *etc.* besetzen; *Schnur* durchziehen; ~ *(into) s.o.* j-n verprügeln.

lacerate ['læsəreit] zerreißen; *fig.* quälen.

lack [læk] **1.** Fehlen *n*, Mangel *m*; **2.** *v/t.* ermangeln (*gen.*); he ~s money es fehlt ihm an Geld; *v/i.* be ~ing fehlen, mangeln; ~lustre ['læklʌstə] glanzlos, matt.

laconic [lə'kɔnik] (~ally) lakonisch, wortkarg, kurz und prägnant.

lacquer ['lækə] **1.** Lack *m*; **2.** lakkieren.

lad [læd] Bursche *m*, Junge *m*.

ladder ['lædə] Leiter *f*; Laufmasche *f*; ~-**proof** maschenfest (*Strumpf etc.*).

laden ['leidn] beladen.

lading ['leidiŋ] Ladung *f*, Fracht *f*.

ladle ['leidl] **1.** Schöpflöffel *m*, Kelle *f*; **2.** ~ *out Suppe* austeilen.

lady ['leidi] Dame *f*; Lady *f*; Herrin *f*; ~ *doctor* Ärztin *f*; ~**bird** Marienkäfer *m*; ~**like** damenhaft; ~**love** Geliebte *f*; ~**ship** [~iʃip]: her ~ die gnädige Frau; *Your* ♀ gnädige Frau, Euer Gnaden.

lag [læg] **1.** zögern; *a.* ~ *behind* zurückbleiben; **2.** Verzögerung *f*.

lager (beer) ['lɑːgə(biə)] Lagerbier *n*.

laggard ['lægəd] Nachzügler *m*.

lagoon [lə'guːn] Lagune *f*.

laid [leid] *pret. u. p.p. von* lay³ 2; ~ *up* bettlägerig (*with* mit, wegen).

lain [lein] *p.p. von* lie² 2.

lair [lɛə] Lager *n e-s wilden Tieres*.

laity ['leiiti] Laien *m/pl.*

lake [leik] See *m*; rote Pigmentfarbe.

lamb [læm] **1.** Lamm *n*; **2.** lammen.

lambent ['læmbənt] leckend; züngelnd (*Flamme*); funkelnd.

lamb|kin ['læmkin] Lämmchen *n*; ~**like** lammfromm.

lame [leim] **1.** □ lahm (*a. fig.* = mangelhaft), **2.** lähmen.

lament [lə'ment] **1.** Wehklage *f*; **2.** (be)klagen, trauern; ~**able** □ ['læməntəbl] beklagenswert; kläglich; ~**ation** [læmən'teiʃən] Wehklage *f*.

lamp [læmp] Lampe *f*; *fig.* Leuchte *f*.

lampoon [læm'puːn] **1.** Schmähschrift *f*; **2.** schmähen.

lamp-post ['læmppoust] Laternenpfahl *m*.

lampshade ['læmpʃeid] Lampenschirm *m*.

lance [lɑːns] **1.** Lanze *f*; Speer *m*; **2.** ⚕ aufschneiden; ~**corporal** ✕ ['lɑːns'kɔːpərəl] Gefreite(r) *m*.

land [lænd] **1.** Land *n*; Grundstück *n*; *by* ~ auf dem Landweg; ~**s** *pl.*

Ländereien *f/pl.*; **2.** landen; ⚓ löschen; *Preis* gewinnen; ~**agent** ['lændeidʒənt] Grundstücksmakler *m*; Gutsverwalter *m*; ~**ed** grundbesitzend; Land..., Grund...; ~**holder** Grundbesitzer(in).

landing ['lændiŋ] Landung *f*; Treppenabsatz *m*; Anlegestelle *f*; ~**field** ✖ Landebahn *f*; ~**gear** Fahrgestell *n*; ~**stage** Landungsbrücke *f*.

land|lady ['lænleidi] Vermieterin *f*, Wirtin *f*; ~**lord** [~lɔːd] Vermieter *m*; Wirt *m*; Haus-, Grundbesitzer *m*; ~**lubber** ⚓ *contp.* Landratte *f*; ~**mark** Grenz-, Markstein *m* (*a. fig.*); Wahrzeichen *n*; ~**owner** Grundbesitzer(in). ~**scape** ['lænskeip] Landschaft *f*; ~**slide** Erdrutsch *m* (*a. pol.*); *a Democratic* ~ ein Erdrutsch zugunsten der Demokraten; ~**slip** *konkr.* Erdrutsch *m*.

lane [lein] Feldweg *m*; Gasse *f*; Spalier *n*; *mot.* Fahrbahn *f*, Spur *f*.

language ['læŋgwidʒ] Sprache *f*; *strong* ~ Kraftausdrücke *m/pl.*

languid □ ['læŋgwid] matt; träg.

languish ['læŋgwiʃ] matt werden; schmachten; dahinsiechen.

languor ['læŋgə] Mattigkeit *f*; Schmachten *n*; Stille *f*.

lank □ [læŋk] schmächtig, dünn; schlicht; ~**y** □ ['læŋki] schlaksig.

lantern ['læntən] Laterne *f*; ~**slide** Dia(positiv) *n*, Lichtbild *n*.

lap [læp] **1.** Schoß *m*; ⊕ Vorstoß *m*; Runde *f*; **2.** über-ea.-legen; (ein)hüllen; (auf)lecken; schlürfen; plätschern (gegen) (*Wellen*).

lapel [lə'pel] Aufschlag *m am Rock*.

lapse [læps] **1.** Verlauf *m der Zeit*; Verfallen *n*; Versehen *n*; **2.** (ver)fallen; verfließen; fehlen.

larceny ['lɑːsni] Diebstahl *m*.

larch ♦ [lɑːtʃ] Lärche *f*.

lard [lɑːd] **1.** (Schweine)Schmalz *n*; **2.** spicken (*a. fig.*); ~**er** ['lɑːdə] Speisekammer *f*.

large □ [lɑːdʒ] groß; weit; reichlich; weitherzig; flott; Groß...; *at* ~ auf freiem Fuß; ausführlich; als Ganzes; ~**ly** ['lɑːdʒli] zum großen Teil, weitgehend; ~**minded** weitherzig; ~**ness** ['lɑːdʒnis] Größe *f*; Weite *f*; ~**sized** groß(formatig).

lariat *Am.* ['læriət] Lasso *n*, *m*.

lark [lɑːk] *orn.* Lerche *f*; *fig.* Streich *m*.

larkspur ♦ ['lɑːkspə:] Rittersporn *m*.

larva *zo.* ['lɑːvə] Larve *f*, Puppe *f*.

larynx *anat.* ['læriŋks] Kehlkopf *m*.

lascivious □ [lə'siviəs] lüstern.

lash [læʃ] **1.** Peitsche(nschnur) *f*; Hieb *m*; Wimper *f*; **2.** peitschen; *fig.* geißeln; schlagen; anbinden.

lass, ~ie [læs, 'læsi] Mädchen *n*.

lassitude ['læsitjuːd] Mattigkeit *f*, Abgespanntheit *f*; Desinteresse *n*.

last[1] [lɑːst] 1. adj. letzt; vorig; äußerst; geringst; ~ but one vorletzt; ~ night gestern abend; 2. Letzte(r m, -s n) f; Ende n; at ~ zuletzt, endlich; 3. adv. zuletzt; ~, but not least nicht zuletzt.

last[2] [~] dauern; halten (Farbe); ausreichen; ausdauern.

last[3] [~] (Schuhmacher)Leisten m.

lasting ⅃ ['lɑːstiŋ] dauerhaft; beständig.

lastly ['lɑːstli] zuletzt, schließlich.

latch [lætʃ] 1. Klinke f, Drücker m; Druckschloß n; 2. ein-, zuklinken.

late [leit] spät; (kürzlich) verstorben; ehemalig; jüngst; at (the) ~st spätestens; as ~ as noch (in dat.); of ~ letzthin; ~r on später; be ~ (zu) spät kommen; ~ly ['leitli] kürzlich.

latent ['leitənt] verborgen, latent; gebunden (Wärme etc.).

lateral ⅃ ['lætərəl] seitlich; Seiten...

lath [lɑːθ] 1. Latte f; 2. belatten.

lathe ⊕ [leið] Drehbank f; Lade f.

lather ['lɑːðə] 1. (Seifen)Schaum m; 2. v/t. einseifen; v/i. schäumen.

Latin ['lætin] 1. lateinisch; 2. Latein n.

latitude ['lætitjuːd] Breite f; fig. Umfang m, Weite f; Spielraum m.

latter ['lætə] neuer; der (die, das) letztere; ~ly [~əli] neuerdings.

lattice ['lætis] a. ~work Gitter n.

laud [lɔːd] loben, preisen; ~able □ ['lɔːdəbl] lobenswert, löblich.

laugh [lɑːf] 1. Gelächter n, Lachen n; 2. lachen; ~ at j-n auslachen; he ~s best who ~s last wer zuletzt lacht, lacht am besten; ~able □ ['lɑːfəbl] lächerlich; ~ter ['lɑːftə] Gelächter n, Lachen n.

launch [lɔːntʃ] 1. ⅃ Stapellauf m; Barkasse f; 2. vom Stapel laufen lassen; Boot aussetzen; schleudern (a. fig.); Schläge versetzen; Rakete starten, abschießen; fig. in Gang bringen; ~ing-pad ['lɔːntʃiŋpæd] (Raketen)Abschußrampe f.

launderette [lɔːndəˈret] Selbstbedienungswaschsalon m.

laund|ress ['lɔːndris] Wäscherin f; ~ry [~ri] Waschanstalt f; Wäsche f.

laurel ♀ ['lɔrəl] Lorbeer m (a. fig.).

lavatory ['lævətəri] Waschraum m; Toilette f; public ~ Bedürfnisanstalt f.

lavender ♀ ['lævində] Lavendel m.

lavish ['lævif] 1. ⅃ freigebig, verschwenderisch; 2. verschwenden.

law [lɔː] Gesetz n; (Spiel)Regel f; Recht(swissenschaft f) n; Gericht(sverfahren) n; go to ~ vor Gericht gehen; lay down the ~ den Ton angeben; ~-abiding ['lɔːəbaidiŋ] friedlich; ~-court Gericht(shof m) n; ~ful □ ['lɔːful] gesetzlich; gültig; ~less □ ['lɔːlis] gesetzlos; ungesetzlich; zügellos.

lawn [lɔːn] Rasen(platz) m; Batist m.

law|suit ['lɔːsjuːt] Prozeß m; ~yer ['lɔːjə] Jurist m; (Rechts)Anwalt m.

lax □ [læks] locker; schlaff (a. fig.); lasch; ~ative ⅌ ['læksətiv] 1. abführend; 2. Abführmittel n.

lay[1] [lei] pret. von lie[2] 2.

lay[2] [~] weltlich; Laien...

lay[3] [~] 1. Lage f, Richtung f; 2. [irr.] v/t. legen; umlegen; Plan etc. ersinnen; stellen, setzen; Tisch decken; lindern; besänftigen; auferlegen; Summe wetten; ~ before s.o. j-m vorlegen; ~ in einlagern, sich eindecken mit; ~ low niederwerfen; ~ open darlegen; ~ out auslegen; Garten etc. anlegen; ~ up Vorräte hinlegen, sammeln; be laid up ans Bett gefesselt sein; ~ with belegen mit; v/i. (Eier) legen; a. ~ a wager wetten.

lay-by ['leibai] Park-, Rastplatz m an e-r Fernstraße.

layer ['leiə] Lage f, Schicht f.

layman ['leimən] Laie m.

lay|off ['leiɔf] Arbeitsunterbrechung f; ~out Anlage f; Plan m.

lazy □ ['leizi] faul.

lead[1] [led] Blei n; ⅃ Lot n, Senkblei n; typ. Durchschuß m.

lead[2] [liːd] 1. Führung f, Leitung f; Beispiel n; thea. Hauptrolle f; Kartenspiel: Vorhand f; ⅌ Leitung f; Hunde-Leine f; 2. [irr.] v/t. (an-)führen, leiten; bewegen (to zu); Karte ausspielen; ~ on (ver)locken; v/i. vorangehen; ~ off den Anfang machen; ~ up to überleiten zu.

leaden ['ledn] bleiern (a. fig.); Blei...

leader ['liːdə] (An)Führer(in), Leiter(in); Erste(r) m; Leitartikel m; ~ship [~ʃip] Führerschaft f.

leading ['liːdiŋ] 1. leitend; Leit...; Haupt...; 2. Leitung f, Führung f.

leaf [liːf], pl. **leaves** [liːvz] Blatt n; Tür- etc. Flügel m; Tisch-Platte f; ~let ['liːflit] Blättchen n; Flug-, Merkblatt n; ~y ['liːfi] belaubt.

league [liːg] 1. Liga f (a. hist. u. Sport); Bund m; mst poet. Meile f; 2. (sich) verbünden.

leak [liːk] 1. Leck n; 2. leck sein; tropfen; ~ out durchsickern; ~age ['liːkidʒ] Lecken n; ⅌ Leckage f; Verlust m (a. fig.), Schwund m; Durchsickern n; ~y ['liːki] leck; undicht.

lean [liːn] 1. [irr.] (sich) (an)lehnen; (sich) stützen; (sich) (hin)neigen; 2. mager; 3. mageres Fleisch.

leant [lent] pret. u. p.p. von lean 1.

leap [liːp] 1. Sprung m; 2. [irr.] (über)springen; ~t [lept] pret. u. p.p. von leap 2; ~-year ['liːpjə] Schaltjahr n.

learn [lɜːn] [irr.] lernen; erfahren, hören; ~ from ersehen aus; ~ed ['lɜːnid] gelehrt; ~er ['lɜːnə] Anfänger(in); **∼ing** ['lɔːniŋ] Lernen *n*; Gelehrsamkeit *f*; **∼t** [lɔːnt] *pret. u. p.p. von learn.*

lease [liːs] 1. Verpachtung *f*, Vermietung *f*; Pacht *f*, Miete *f*; Pacht-, Mietvertrag *m*; 2. (ver-)pachten, (ver)mieten.

leash [liːʃ] 1. Koppelleine *f*; Koppel *f* (3 *Hunde etc.*); 2. koppeln.

least [liːst] 1. *adj.* kleinst, geringst; wenigst, mindest; 2. *adv. a.* **∼** of all am wenigsten; at **∼** wenigstens; 3. *das* Mindeste, *das* Wenigste; *to* say *the* **∼** gelinde gesagt.

leather ['leðə] 1. Leder *n* (*fig. Haut*); 2. *a.* **∼n** ledern; Leder...

leave [liːv] 1. Erlaubnis *f*; *a.* **∼** of absence Urlaub *m*; Abschied *m*; 2. [*irr.*] *v/t.* (ver)lassen; zurück-, hinterlassen; übriglassen; überlassen; **∼** off aufhören (mit); *Kleid* ablegen; *v/i.* ablassen; weggehen, abreisen (*for* nach).

leaven ['levn] Sauerteig *m*; Hefe *f*.

leaves [liːvz] *pl. von leaf*; Laub *n*.

leavings ['liːviŋz] *pl.* Überbleibsel *n/pl.*

lecherous ['letʃərəs] wollüstig.

lecture ['lektʃə] 1. Vorlesung *f*, Vortrag *m*; Strafpredigt *f*; 2. *v/i.* Vorlesungen *od.* Vorträge halten; *v/t.* abkanzeln; **∼r** [∼ərə] Vortragende(r *m*) *f*; *univ.* Dozent(in).

led [led] *pret. u. p.p. von lead²* 1.

ledge [ledʒ] Leiste *f*; Sims *m*, *n*; Riff *n*.

ledger † ['ledʒə] Hauptbuch *n*.

leech *zo.* [liːtʃ] Blutegel *m*; *fig.* Schmarotzer *m*.

leek ♦ [liːk] Lauch *m*, Porree *m*.

leer [liə] (lüsterner *od.* finsterer) Seitenblick *m*; 2. schielen (*at* nach).

lees [liːz] *pl.* Bodensatz *m*, Hefe *f*.

lee|ward ♣ ['liːwəd] leewärts; **∼way** ['liːwei] ♣ Abtrift *f*; *make* up **∼** *fig.* Versäumtes nachholen.

left¹ [left] *pret. u. p.p. von leave* 2.

left² [∼] 1. link(s); 2. Linke *f*; **∼handed** [ˌ'left'hændid] linkshändig; linkisch.

left|-luggage office ['left'lʌgidʒɔfis] Gepäckaufbewahrung(sstelle) *f*; **∼overs** *pl.* Speisereste *m/pl.*

leg [leg] Bein *n*; Keule *f*; (Stiefel-) Schaft *m*; ♣ Schenkel *m*; *pull s.o.'s* **∼** j-n auf den Arm nehmen (*hänseln*).

legacy ['legəsi] Vermächtnis *n*.

legal □ ['liːgəl] gesetzlich; rechtsgültig; juristisch; Rechts...; **∼ize** [ˌ∼laiz] rechtskräftig machen; beurkunden.

legation [li'geiʃən] Gesandtschaft *f*.

legend ['ledʒənd] Legende *f*; **∼ary** [ˌ∼dəri] legendär, sagenhaft.

leggings ['leginz] *pl.* Gamaschen *f/pl.*

legible □ ['ledʒəbl] leserlich.

legionary ['liːdʒənəri] Legionär *m*.

legislat|ion [ledʒis'leiʃən] Gesetz-

gebung *f*; **∼ive** ['ledʒislətiv] gesetzgebend; **∼or** [ˌ∼leitə] Gesetzgeber *m*.

legitima|cy [li'dʒitiməsi] Rechtmäßigkeit *f*; **∼te** 1. [ˌ∼meit] legitimieren; 2. [ˌ∼mit] rechtmäßig.

leisure ['leʒə] Muße *f*; *at your* **∼** wenn es Ihnen paßt; **∼ly** [ˌ∼li] gemächlich.

lemon ['lemən] Zitrone *f*; **∼ade** [lemə'neid] Limonade *f*; **∼** squash Zitronenwasser *n*.

lend [lend] [*irr.*] (ver-, aus)leihen; *Hilfe* leisten, gewähren.

length [leŋθ] Länge *f*; Strecke *f*; (Zeit)Dauer *f*; *at* **∼** endlich, zuletzt; *go all* **∼s** aufs Ganze gehen; **∼en** ['leŋθən] (sich) verlängern, (sich) ausdehnen; **∼wise** [ˌ∼θwaiz] der Länge nach; **∼y** □ [ˌ∼θi] sehr lang.

lenient □ ['liːnjənt] mild, nachsichtig.

lens *opt.* [lenz] Linse *f*.

lent¹ [lent] *pret. u. p.p. von lend.*

Lent² [∼] Fasten *pl.*, Fastenzeit *f*.

leopard ['lepəd] Leopard *m*.

lep|rosy ✠ ['leprəsi] Aussatz *m*, Lepra *f*; **∼ous** [ˌ∼əs] aussätzig.

less [les] 1. *adj. u. adv.* kleiner, geringer; weniger; 2. *prp.* minus.

lessen ['lesn] *v/t.* vermindern, schmälern; *v/i.* abnehmen.

lesser ['lesə] kleiner; geringer.

lesson ['lesn] Lektion *f*; Aufgabe *f*; (Unterrichts)Stunde *f*; Lehre *f*; **∼s** *pl.* Unterricht *m*.

lest [lest] damit nicht, daß nicht.

let [let] [*irr.*] lassen; vermieten, verpachten; **∼** *alone* in Ruhe lassen; geschweige denn; **∼** *down* j-n im Stich lassen; **∼** *go* loslassen; **∼** *into* einweihen in (*acc.*); **∼** *off* abschießen; *j-n* laufen lassen; **∼** *out* hinauslassen; ausplaudern; vermieten; **∼** *up* aufhören.

lethal □ ['liːθəl] tödlich; Todes...

lethargy ['leθədʒi] Lethargie *f*.

letter ['letə] 1. Buchstabe *m*; Type *f*; Brief *m*; **∼s** *pl.* Literatur *f*, Wissenschaft *f*; *attr.* Brief...; *to the* **∼** buchstäblich; 2. beschriften, betiteln; **∼-box** Briefkasten *m*; **∼card** Kartenbrief *m*; **∼carrier** *Am.* Briefträger *m*; **∼case** Brieftasche *f*; **∼cover** Briefumschlag *m*; **∼ed** (literarisch) gebildet; **∼file** Briefordner *m*; **∼ing** [ˌ∼riŋ] Beschriftung *f*; **∼press** Kopierpresse *f*.

lettuce ♦ ['letis] Lattich *m*, Salat *m*.

leuk(a)emia ✠ [ljuː'kiːmiə] Leukämie *f*.

levee¹ ['levi] Morgenempfang *m*.

levee² *Am.* [∼] Uferdamm *m*.

level ['levl] 1. waag(e)recht, eben; gleich; ausgeglichen; *my* **∼** *best* mein möglichstes; **∼** *crossing* 🚃 schienengleicher Übergang; 2. ebene Fläche; (gleiche) Höhe, Niveau n, Stand m; fig. Maßstab m; Wasserwaage f; sea ~ Meeresspiegel m; on the ~ F offen, aufrichtig; 3. v/t. gleichmachen, ebnen; fig. anpassen; richten, zielen mit; ~ up erhöhen; v/i. ~ at, against zielen auf (acc.); ~headed vernünftig, nüchtern.

lever ['li:və] Hebel m; Hebestange f; ~age ['~əridʒ] Hebelkraft f.

levity ['leviti] Leichtfertigkeit f.

levy ['levi] 1. Erhebung f von Steuern; ✗ Aushebung f; Aufgebot n; 2. Steuern erheben; ✗ ausheben.

lewd [lu:d] liederlich, unzüchtig.

liability [laiə'biliti] Verantwortlichkeit f; ⚖ Haftpflicht f; Verpflichtung f; fig. Hang m; liabilities pl. Verbindlichkeiten f/pl., ✝ Passiva pl.

liable □ ['laiəbl] verantwortlich; haftpflichtig; verpflichtet; ausgesetzt (to dat.); be ~ to neigen zu.

liar ['laiə] Lügner(in).

libel ['laibəl] 1. Schmähschrift f; Verleumdung f; 2. schmähen; verunglimpfen.

liberal ['libərəl] 1. □ liberal (a. pol.); freigebig; reichlich; freisinnig; 2. Liberale(r) m; ~ity [libə-'ræliti] Freigebigkeit f; Freisinnigkeit f.

liberat|e ['libəreit] befreien; freilassen; ~ion [libə'reiʃən] Befreiung f; ~or ['libəreitə] Befreier m.

libertine ['libə(:)tain] Wüstling m.

liberty ['libəti] Freiheit f; take liberties sich Freiheiten erlauben; be at ~ frei sein.

librar|ian [lai'brɛəriən] Bibliothekar(in); ~y ['laibrəri] Bibliothek f.

lice [lais] pl. von louse.

licen|ce, Am. ~se ['laisəns] 1. Lizenz f; Erlaubnis f; Konzession f; Freiheit f; Zügellosigkeit f; driving ~ Führerschein m; 2. lizenzieren, berechtigen; et. genehmigen; ~see [laisən'si:] Lizenznehmer m.

licentious [lai'senʃəs] unzüchtig; ausschweifend.

lichen ❀, ⚕ ['laikən] Flechte f.

lick [lik] 1. Lecken n; Salzlecke f; F Schlag m; 2. (be)lecken; F verdreschen; übertreffen; ~ the dust im Staub kriechen; fallen; geschlagen werden; ~ into shape zurechtstutzen.

licorice ['likəris] Lakritze f.

lid [lid] Deckel m; (Augen)Lid n.

lie[1] [lai] 1. Lüge f; give s.o. the ~ j-n Lügen strafen; 2. lügen.

lie[2] [~] 1. Lage f; 2. [irr.] liegen; ~ by still-, brachliegen; ~ down sich niederlegen; ~ in wait for j-m auflauern; let sleeping dogs ~ F. daran rühren wir lieber nicht; ~down [lai'daun] Nickerchen n; ~in: have a ~ sich gründlich ausschlafen.

lien ⚖ ['liən] Pfandrecht n.

lieu [lju:]: in ~ of (an)statt.

lieutenant [lef'tenənt; ⚓ le'tenənt; Am. lu:'tenənt] Leutnant m; Statthalter m; ~commander ⚓ Korvettenkapitän m.

life [laif], pl. lives [laivz] Leben n; Menschenleben n; Lebensbeschreibung f; for ~ auf Lebenszeit; for one's ~, for dear ~ ums (liebe) Leben; to the ~ naturgetreu; ~ sentence lebenslängliche Zuchthausstrafe; ~ assurance Lebensversicherung f; ~belt ['laifbelt] Rettungsgürtel m; ~boat Rettungsboot n; ~guard Leibwache f; Bademärter m am Strand; ~ insurance Lebensversicherung f; ~jacket ⚓ Schwimmweste f; ~less □ ['laiflis] leblos; matt (a. fig.); ~like lebenswahr; ~long lebenslänglich; ~preserver 4m. ['laif-prizə:və] Schwimmgürtel m; Totschläger m (Stock mit Bleikopf); ~time Lebenszeit f.

lift [lift] 1. Heben n; phys., ✈ Auftrieb m; fig. Erhebung f; Fahrstuhl m; give s.o. a ~ j-m helfen; j-n (im Auto) mitnehmen; 2. v/t (auf)heben; erheben; beseitigen; sl. klauen, stehlen; v/i. sich heben.

ligature ['ligətʃuə] Binde f; ⚕ Verband m.

light[1] [lait] 1. Licht n (a. fig.); Fenster n; Aspekt m, Gesichtspunkt m; Feuer n; Glanz m; fig. Leuchte f; ~s pl. Fähigkeiten f/pl; will you give me a ~ darf ich Sie im Feuer bitten; put a ~ to anzünden; 2. licht, hell; blond; 3. [irr.] v/t. oft ~ up be-, erleuchten; anzünden; v/i. mst ~ up aufleuchten; ~ out Am. sl. schnell losziehen, abhauen.

light[2] [~] 1. adj. u. adv. leicht (a. fig.); ~ current ⚡ Schwachstrom m; make ~ of et. leicht nehmen; 2. ~ (up)on stoßen od. fallen auf (acc.), geraten an (acc.); sich niederlassen auf (dat.).

lighten ['laitn] blitzen; (sich) erhellen; leichter machen; (sich) erleichtern.

lighter ['laitə] Anzünder m; (Taschen)Feuerzeug n; ⚓ L(e)ichter m.

light|-headed ['lait'hedid] wirr im Kopf, irr; ~hearted [['~ha:tid] leichtherzig; fröhlich; ~house ['laithaus] Leuchtturm m.

lighting ['laitiŋ] Beleuchtung f; Anzünden n.

light|-minded ['lait'maindid] leichtsinnig; ~ness ['laitnis] Leichtigkeit f; Leichtsinn m.

lightning ['laitniŋ] Blitz m; ~ bug Am. zo. Leuchtkäfer m; ~conductor, ~rod ⚡ Blitzableiter m.

light-weight ['laitweit] Sport: Leichtgewicht n.

like [laik] 1. gleich; ähnlich; wie; such ~ dergleichen; feel ~ F sich aufgelegt fühlen zu *et.*; ~ *that* so; *what is he* ~*?* wie sieht er aus?; wie ist er?; 2. Gleiche *m, f, n*; ~*s pl.* Neigungen *f/pl.*; *his* ~ seinesgleichen; *the* ~ der-, desgleichen; 3. mögen, gern haben; *how do you* ~ *London?* wie gefällt Ihnen L.?; *I should* ~ *to know* ich möchte wissen.

like|lihood ['laiklihud] Wahrscheinlichkeit *f*; ~**ly** ['laikli] wahrscheinlich; geeignet; *he is* ~ *to die* er wird wahrscheinlich sterben.

like|n ['laikən] vergleichen (*to* mit); ~**ness** ['laiknis] Ähnlichkeit *f*; (Ab-)Bild *n*; Gestalt *f*; ~**wise** ['laikwaiz] gleich-, ebenfalls.

liking ['laikiŋ] (*for*) Neigung *f* (für, zu), Gefallen *n* (*an dat.*).

lilac ['lailək] 1. lila; 2. ♀ Flieder *m*.

lily ♀ ['lili] Lilie *f*; ~ *of the valley* Maiglöckchen *n*; ~**-white** schneeweiß.

limb [lim] *Körper*-Glied *n*; Ast *m*.

limber ['limbə] 1. biegsam, geschmeidig; 2.: ~ *up* (sich) lockern.

lime [laim] Kalk *m*; Vogelleim *m*; ♀ Limone *f*; ♀ Linde *f*; ~**light** ['laimlait] Kalklicht *n*; *thea.* Scheinwerfer(licht *n*) *m*; *fig.* Mittelpunkt *m* des öffentlichen Interesses.

limit ['limit] 1. Grenze *f*; *in* (*off*) ~*s* Zutritt gestattet (verboten) (*to* für); *that is the* ~*! F* das ist der Gipfel!; das ist (doch) die Höhe!; *go the* ~ *Am.* F bis zum Äußersten gehen; 2. begrenzen; beschränken (*to auf acc.*); ~**ation** [limi'teiʃən] Begrenzung *f*, Beschränkung *f*; *fig.* Grenze *f*; *i̯s* Verjährung *f*; ~**ed**: ~ *(liability) company* Gesellschaft *f* mit beschränkter Haftung; ~ *in time* befristet; ~**less** □ [~tlis] grenzenlos.

limp [limp] 1. hinken; 2. Hinken *n*; 3. schlaff; weich.

limpid □ ['limpid] klar, durchsichtig.

line [lain] 1. Linie *f*; Reihe *f*, Zeile *f*; Vers *m*; Strich *m*; Falte *f*, Furche *f*; (Menschen)Schlange *f*; Folge *f*; Verkehrsgesellschaft *f*; Eisenbahnlinie *f*; Strecke *f*; *tel.* Leitung *f*; Branche *f*, Fach *n*; Leine *f*, Schnur *f*; Äquator *m*; Richtung *f*; ✗ Linie(ntruppe) *f*; Front *f*; ~*s pl.* Richtlinien *f/pl.*; Grundlage *f*; ~ *of conduct* Lebensweise *f*; *hard* ~*s pl.* hartes Los, Pech *n*; *in* ~ *with* in Übereinstimmung mit; *stand in* ~ Schlange stehen; *draw the* ~ *fig.* nicht mehr mitmachen; *hold the* ~ *teleph.* am Apparat bleiben; 2. *v/t.* liniieren; aufstellen; *Weg etc.* säumen, einfassen; *Kleid* füttern; ~ *out* entwerfen; *v/i.* ~ *up* sich auf-, anstellen.

linea|ge ['liniidʒ] Abstammung *f*; Familie *f*; Stammbaum *m*; ~**l** □ [~iəl] gerade, direkt (*Nachkomme*

etc.); ~**ment** [~əmənt] (Gesichts-)Zug *m*; ~**r** ['liniə] geradlinig.

linen ['linin] 1. Leinen *n*, Leinwand *f*; Wäsche *f*; 2. leinen; ~**closet,** ~**cupboard** Wäscheschrank *m*; ~**draper** [~ndreipə] Weißwarenhändler *m*, Wäschegeschäft *n*.

liner ['lainə] Linienschiff *n*, Passagierdampfer *m*; Verkehrsflugzeug *n*.

linger ['liŋgə] zögern; (ver)weilen; sich aufhalten; sich hinziehen; dahinsiechen; ~ *at,* ~ *about* sich herumdrücken an *od.* bei (*dat.*).

lingerie ['lɛ̃:nʒəri:] Damenunterwäsche *f*   [Einreibemittel *n.*\
liniment ⚕ ['linimənt] Liniment *n,*]

lining ['lainiŋ] *Kleider- etc.* Futter *n*; Besatz *m*; ⊕ Verkleidung *f*.

link [liŋk] ⊕ *Ketten*-Glied *n*, Gelenk *n*; Manschettenknopf *m*; *fig.* Bindeglied *n*; 2. (sich) verbinden.

links [liŋks] *pl.* Dünen *f/pl.*; *a. golf-*~. Golf(spiel)platz *m*.

linseed ['linsi:d] Leinsame(n) *m*; ~ *oil* Leinöl *n*.

lion ['laiən] Löwe *m*; *fig.* Größe *f*, Berühmtheit *f*; ~**ess** [~nis] Löwin *f*.

lip [lip] Lippe *f*; Rand *m*; *sl.* Unverschämtheit *f*; ~**stick** ['lipstik] Lippenstift *m*.

liquefy ['likwifai] schmelzen.

liquid ['likwid] 1. flüssig; † liquid; klar (*Luft etc.*); 2. Flüssigkeit *f*.

liquidat|e ['likwideit] † liquidieren; bezahlen, tilgen; 2. *fig.* Abwicklung *f*, Liquidation *f*.

liquor ['likə] Flüssigkeit *f*; Alkohol *m*, alkoholisches Getränk.

liquorice ['likəris] Lakritze *f*.

lisp [lisp] 1. Lispeln *n*; 2. lispeln.

list [list] 1. Liste *f*, Verzeichnis *n*; Leiste *f*; Webkante *f*; 2. (in e-e Liste) eintragen; verzeichnen.

listen ['lisn] (*to*) lauschen, horchen (auf *acc.*); anhören (*acc.*), zuhören (*dat.*); hören (auf *acc.*); ~ *in teleph., Radio* (mit)hören (*to acc.*); ~**er** [~nə] Zuhörer(in); *a.* ~-*in* (Rundfunk)Hörer(in).

listless □ ['listlis] gleichgültig; lustlos.

lists [lists] *pl.* Schranken *f/pl.*

lit [lit] *pret. u. p.p. von light*[1] 3.

literal ['litərəl] buchstäblich; am Buchstaben klebend; wörtlich.

litera|ry [~] ['litərəri] literarisch; Literatur...; Schrift...; ~**ture** [~ritʃə] Literatur *f*.

lithe [laið] geschmeidig, wendig.

lithography [li'θɔgrəfi] Lithographie *f*, Steindruck *m*.

litigation [liti'geiʃən] Prozeß *m*.

lit|re, *Am.* ~**er** ['li:tə] Liter *n, m*.

litter ['litə] 1. Sänfte *f*; Tragbahre *f*; Streu *f*; Abfall *m*; Unordnung *f*; Wurf *m junger Tiere*; 2. ~ *down* mit Streu versehen; ~ *up* in Unordnung bringen; *Junge* werfen; ~**basket,** ~**bin** Abfallkorb *m*.

little ['litl] **1.** adj. klein; gering(fügig); wenig; a ~ one ein Kleines (Kind); **2.** adv. wenig; **3.** Kleinigkeit f; a ~ ein bißchen; by ~ nach und nach; not a ~ nicht wenig.

live 1. [liv] allg. leben; wohnen; ~ to see erleben; ~ s.th. down et. durch guten Lebenswandel vergessen machen; . through durchmachen, durchstehen, überleben; ~ up to s-m Ruf gerecht werden, s-n Grundsätzen gemäß leben; Versprechen halten; **2.** [laiv] lebendig; richtig; aktuell; glühend; ≴ scharf (Munition); ∉ stromführend; Radio Direkt. , Original. , **lihood** ['laivlihud] Unterhalt m; **.liness** [~inis] Lebhaftigkeit f; **~ly** ['laivli] lebhaft; lebendig; aufregend; schnell; bewegt.

liver anat. ['livə] Leber f.

livery ['livəri] Livree f; (Amts-) Tracht f; at ~ in Futter (stehen etc.).

live|s [laivz] pl. von life; **~stock** ['laivstɔk] Vieh(bestand m) n.

livid ['livid] bläulich; fahl; F wild.

living ['livin] **1.** lebend(ig); the ~ image of das genaue Ebenbild gen.; **2.** Leben n; Lebensweise f; Lebensunterhalt m; eccl. Pfründe f; **~room** Wohnzimmer n.

lizard zo. ['lizəd] Eidechse f.

load [loud] **1.** Last f; Ladung f; **2.** (be)laden; fig. überhäufen; überladen; **~ing** ['loudin] Laden n; Ladung f, Fracht f; attr. Lade-.

loaf [louf] **1.** pl. **loaves** [louvz] Brot-Laib m; (Zucker)Hut m; **2.** herumlungern.

loafer ['loufə] Bummler m.

loam [loum] Lehm m, Ackerkrume f.

loan [loun] **1.** Anleihe f, Darlehen n; Leihen n; Leihgabe f; on ~ leihweise; **2.** bsd. Am. ausleihen.

loath] [louθ] abgeneigt; **~e** [louð] sich ekeln vor (dat.); verabscheuen; **~ing** ['louðin] Ekel m; **~some** □ ['louðsəm] ekelhaft; verhaßt.

loaves [louvz] pl. von loaf 1.

lobby ['lɔbi] **1.** Vorhalle f; parl. Wandelgang m; thea. Foyer n; **2.** parl. s-n Einfluß geltend machen.

lobe anat., ⚕ [loub] Lappen m.

lobster ['lɔbstə] Hummer m.

local ['loukəl] **1.** örtlich; Orts-...; lokal; ~ government Gemeindeverwaltung f; ~ Zeitung Lokalnachricht f; 🚂 a. ~ train Vorortzug m; F Wirtshaus n (am Ort); **.ity** [lou'kæliti] Örtlichkeit f; Lage f; **~ize** ['loukəlaiz] lokalisieren.

locat|e [lou'keit] v/t. versetzen, verlegen, unterbringen; ausfindig machen; Am. an-, festlegen; be ~d gelegen sein; wohnen; v/i. sich niederlassen; **.ion** [~ei∫ən] Lage f; Niederlassung f; Am. Anweisung f von Land; angewiesenes Land; Ort

m; Film: Gelände n für Außenaufnahmen.

loch schott. [lɔk] See m; Bucht f.

lock [lɔk] **1.** Tür-, Gewehr- etc. Schloß n; Schleuse(nkammer) f; ⊕ Sperrvorrichtung f; Stauung f; Locke f; Wollflocke f; **2.** (ver-) schließen (a. fig.), absperren; sich verschließen lassen; ⊕ blockieren, sperren; greifen; umschließen; ~ s.o. in j-n einsperren; ~ up wegschließen; abschließen; einsperren; Geld fest anlegen.

lock|er ['lɔkə] Schrank m, Kasten m; **.et** ['lɔkit] Medaillon n; **~out** Aussperrung f von Arbeitern; **~smith** Schlosser m; **~-up 1.** Haftzelle f; ✝ zinslose Kapitalanlage; **2.** verschließbar.

loco Am. sl. ['loukou] verrückt.

locomot|ion [loukə'mou∫ən] Fortbewegung(sfähigkeit) f; **.ive** ['loukəmoutiv] **1.** sich fortbewegend; beweglich; **2.** a. ~ engine Lokomotive f.

locust ['loukəst] zo. Heuschrecke f; ♀ unechte Akazie.

lode|star ['loudsta:] Leitstern m (a. fig.); **~stone** Magnet(eisenstein) m.

lodg|e [lɔdʒ] **1.** Häus-chen n; (Forst-, Park-, Pförtner)Haus n; Portierloge f; Freimaurer-Loge f; **2.** v/t. beherbergen, aufnehmen; Geld hinterlegen; Klage einreichen; Hieb versetzen; v/i. (bsd zur Miete) wohnen; logieren; **~er** ['lɔdʒə] (Unter)Mieter(in); **~ing** ['lɔdʒin] Unterkunft f; **~s** pl. möbliertes Zimmer; Wohnung f.

loft [lɔ:ft] (Dach)Boden m; Empore f; **~y** □ ['lɔfti] hoch; erhaben; stolz.

log [lɔg] Klotz m; Block m; gefällter Baumstamm; ⚓ Log n; **~-cabin** ['lɔgkæbin] Blockhaus n; **~gerhead** ['lɔgəhed]: be at ~s sich in den Haaren liegen; **~-house**, **~-hut** Blockhaus n.

logic ['lɔdʒik] Logik f; **~al** □ [~kəl] logisch.

logroll bsd. Am. pol. ['lɔgroul] (sich) gegenseitig in die Hände arbeiten.

loin [lɔin] Lende(nstück n) f.

loiter ['lɔitə] trödeln, schlendern.

loll [lɔl] (sich) strecken; (sich) rekeln; ~ about herumlungern.

lone|liness ['lounlinis] Einsamkeit f; **~ly**, **~ly** ['lounli], **~some**] ['lounsəm] einsam.

long¹ [lɔŋ] **1.** Länge f; before ~ binnen kurzem; for ~ lange; take ~ lange brauchen od. dauern; **2.** adj. lang; langfristig; langsam; in the ~ run am Ende; auf die Dauer; be ~ lange dauern od. brauchen; **3.** adv. lang(e); so ~! bis dann! (auf Wiedersehen); (no) ~er (nicht) länger od. mehr.

long² [ˌ] sich sehnen (*for* nach).

long|-distance['lɔŋ'distəns]Fern..., Weit...; ~evity [lɔn'dʒeviti] Langlebigkeit *f*; langes Leben; ~hand ['lɔŋhænd] Langschrift *f*.

longing ['lɔŋiŋ] 1. | sehnsüchtig; 2. Sehnsucht *f*; Verlangen *n*.

longitude geogr. ['lɔndʒitjuːd] Länge *f*.

long|-shore-man ['lɔŋʃɔːmən] Hafenarbeiter*m*; ~-sighted['lɔŋ'saitid] weitsichtig; ~-standing seit langer Zeit bestehend, alt; ~-suffering 1. langmütig; 2. Langmut *f*; ~-term ['lɔŋtəːm] langfristig; ~-winded □ ['lɔŋ'windid] langatmig.

look [luk] 1. Blick *m*; Anblick *m*; *oft* ~*s pl.* Aussehen *n; have a* ~ *at s.th.* sich et. ansehen; *I don't like the* ~ *of it* es gefällt mir nicht; 2. *v/i.* sehen, blicken (*at,* on *auf acc.,* nach); zusehen, *daß od. wie* ...; nachsehen, *wer etc.* ...; *krank etc.* aussehen; *nach e-r Richtung liegen;* ~ *after* sehen nach, sich kümmern um; versorgen; nachsehen, nachblicken (*dat.*); ~ *at* ansehen; ~ *for* erwarten; suchen; ~ *forward to* sich freuen auf (*acc.*); ~ *in als Besucher* hereinschauen (*on bei*); ~ *into* prüfen; erforschen; ~ *on* zuschauen (*dat.*);betrachten (*as als*); liegen zu, gehen auf (*acc.*) (*Fenster*); ~ *out* vorsehen; ~ *(up)on fig.* ansehen (*as als*); *v/t.* ~ *disdain* verächtlich blicken; ~ *over et.* durchsehen; *j-n* mustern; ~ *up et.* nachschlagen.

looker-on ['lukər'ɔn] Zuschauer(in).

looking-glass ['lukiŋglɑːs] Spiegel *m.*

look-out ['luk'aut] Ausguck *m,* Ausblick *m,* Aussicht *f* (*a. fig.*); *that is my* ~ F das ist meine Sache.

loom [luːm] 1. Webstuhl *m*; 2. undeutlich zu sehen sein, sich abzeichnen.

loop [luːp] 1. Schlinge *f,* Schleife *f,* Öse *f*; 2. *v/t.* in Schleifen legen; schlingen; *v/i.* e-e Schleife machen; sich winden; ~hole ['luːphoul] Guck-, Schlupfloch *n*; ✕ Schießscharte *f.*

loose [luːs] 1. □ *allg.* lose, locker; schlaff; weit; frei; un-zs.-hängend; ungenau; liederlich; 2. lösen; aufbinden; lockern; ~n ['luːsn] (sich) lösen, (sich) lockern.

loot [luːt] 1. plündern; 2. Beute *f.*

lop [lɔp] *Baum* beschneiden; stutzen; schlaff herunterhängen (lassen); ~-sided ['lɔp'saidid] schief, einseitig.

loquacious □ [lou'kweiʃəs] geschwätzig.

lord [lɔːd] Herr *m*; Gebieter *m*; Magnat *m*; Lord *m*; *the* ⅔ *der Herr* (*Gott*); *my* ~ [mi'lɔːd] Mylord, Euer Gnaden; *the* ⅔*'s Prayer das* Vaterunser; *the* ⅔*'s Supper das* Abendmahl; ~ly ['lɔːdli] vornehm, edel; großartig; hochmütig; ~ship ['lɔːdʃip] Lordschaft *f* (*Titel*).

lore [lɔː] Lehre *f,* Kunde *f.*

lorry ['lɔri] Last(kraft)wagen *m,* LKW *m*; 🚋 Lore *f.*

lose [luːz] [*irr.*] *v/t.* verlieren; vergeuden; verpassen; abnehmen; ~ *o.s.* sich verirren; *v/i.* verlieren; nachgehen (*Uhr*).

loss [lɔs] Verlust *m*; Schaden *m*; *at a* ~ in Verlegenheit; außerstande.

lost [lɔst] *pret. u. p.p. von* lose; *be* ~ verlorengehen; verschwunden sein; *fig.* versunken sein; ~-*property office* Fundbüro *n.*

lot [lɔt] Los *n* (*a. fig.*); Anteil *m*; ⚓ Partie *f*; Posten *m*; F Menge *f*; Parzelle *f*; *Am.* Filmi Ateliergelände *n; a* ~ *of people* F eine Menge Leute; *draw* ~*s* losen; *fall to s.o.'s* ~ j-m zufallen.

loth [loθ] s. loath.

lotion ['louʃən] (Haut)Wasser *n.*

lottery ['lɔtəri] Lotterie *f.*

loud [laud] laud (*a. adv.*); *fig.* schreiend, grell; ~-speaker ['laud'spiːkə] Lautsprecher *m.*

lounge [laundʒ] 1. sich rekeln; faulenzen; 2. Bummel *m*; Wohnzimmer *n,* -diele *f*; Gesellschaftsraum *m e-s Hotels*; *thea.* Foyer *n*; Chaiselongue *f*; ~-chair ['laundʒ'tʃɛə] Klubsessel *m*; ~-suit Straßenanzug *m.*

lour ['lauə] finster blicken *od.* aussehen; die Stirn runzeln.

lous|e [laus], *pl.* lice [lais] Laus *f*; ~y ['lauzi] verlaust; lausig; Lause...

lout [laut] Tölpel *m,* Lümmel *m.*

lovable □ ['lʌvəbl] liebenswürdig, liebenswert.

love [lʌv] 1. Liebe *f* (*of, a. for, to, towards* zu); Liebschaft *f*; Angebetete *f*; Liebling *m* (*als Anrede*); liebe Grüße *m*|*pl.*; *Sport:* nichts, null; *attr.* Liebes...; *give od. send one's* ~ *to s.o.* j-n freundlichst grüßen (lassen); *in* ~ *with* verliebt in (*acc.*); *fall in* ~ *with* sich verlieben in (*acc.*); *make* ~ *to* werben um; 2. lieben; gern haben; ~ *to do* gern tun; ~-affair ['lʌvəfɛə] Liebschaft *f*; ~ly ['lʌvli] lieblich; entzückend; reizend; ~r ['lʌvə] Liebhaber *m*; *fig.* Verehrer(in), Liebhaber(in).

loving □ ['lʌviŋ] liebevoll.

low¹ [lou] 1. niedrig; tief; gering; leise; *fig.* niedergeschlagen; schwach; gemein; ~*est bid* Mindestgebot *n*; 2. *meteor.* Tief(druckgebiet) *n*; *bsd. Am.* Tiefstand *m,* -punkt *m.*

low² [ˌ] brüllen, muhen (*Rind*).

low-brow F ['loubrau] 1. geistig anspruchslos, spießig; 2. Spießer *m,* Banause *m.*

lower¹ ['louə] 1. niedriger; tiefer; geringer; leiser; untere(r, -s); Unter...; 2. v/t. nieder-, herunterlassen; senken; erniedrigen; abschwächen; *Preis etc.* herabsetzen; v/i. fallen, sinken.

lower² ['lauə] s. *lour.*

low|land ['loulənd] Tiefland *n;* **~liness** ['loulinis] Demut *f;* **~ly** ['louli] demütig; bescheiden; **~~necked** (tief) ausgeschnitten (*Kleid*); **~-spirited** niedergeschlagen. [Treue *f.*\

loyal □ ['lɔiəl] treu; **~ty** [~lti] f.

lozenge ['lɔzindʒ] Pastille *f.*

lubber ['lʌbə] Tölpel *m,* Stoffel *m.*

lubric|ant ['lu:brikənt] Schmiermittel *n;* **~ate.** [~keit] schmieren; **~ation** [lu:bri'keiʃən] Schmieren *n,* ⊕ Ölung *f.*

lucid □ ['lu:sid] leuchtend, klar.

luck [lʌk] Glück(sfall *m*) *n;* Geschick *n; good ~* Glück *n; bad ~,* *hard ~, ill ~* Unglück *n,* Pech *n; worse ~* unglücklicherweise; **~ily** ['lʌkili] glücklicherweise, zum Glück; **~y** □ ['lʌki] glücklich; *Glücks...; be ~* Glück haben.

lucr|ative □ ['lu:krətiv] einträglich; **~e** ['lu:kə] Gewinn(sucht *f*) *m.*

ludicrous □ ['lu:dikrəs] lächerlich.

lug [lʌg] zerren, schleppen.

luge [lu:ʒ] 1. Rodelschlitten *m;* 2. rodeln.

luggage ['lʌgidʒ] Gepäck *n;* **~-carrier** Gepäckträger *m am Fahrrad;* **~-office** 🞓 Gepäckschalter *m;* **~-rack** Gepäcknetz *n;* **~-ticket** Gepäckschein *m.*

lugubrious □ [lu:'gju:briəs] traurig.

lukewarm ['lu:kwɔ:m] lau (*a. fig.*).

lull [lʌl] 1. einlullen; (sich) beruhigen; 2. (Wind)Stille *f;* Ruhepause *f.*

lullaby ['lʌləbai] Wiegenlied *n.*

lumbago 🞓 [lʌm'beigou] Hexenschuß *m.*

lumber ['lʌmbə] 1. Bau-, Nutzholz *n;* Gerümpel *n;* 2. v/t. a. **~ up** vollstopfen; v/i. rumpeln, poltern; sich (dahin)schleppen; **~er** [~ərə], **~jack**, **~man** Holzfäller *m,* -arbeiter *m;* **~-mill** Sägewerk *n;* **~-room** Rumpelkammer *f;* **~-yard** Holzplatz *m,* -lager *n.*

lumin|ary ['lu:minəri] Himmelskörper *m;* Leuchtkörper *m; fig.* Leuchte *f;* **~ous** □ [~nəs] leuchtend; Licht...; Leucht...; *fig.* lichtvoll.

lump [lʌmp] 1. Klumpen *m; fig.* Klotz *m;* Beule *f;* Stück *n Zucker etc.; in the ~* in Bausch und Bogen; **~ sugar** Würfelzucker *m; ~ sum*

Pauschalsumme *f;* 2. v/t. zs.-werfen, zs.-fassen; v/i. Klumpen bilden; **~ish** ['lʌmpiʃ] schwerfällig; **~y** □ [~pi] klumpig.

lunacy ['lu:nəsi] Wahnsinn *m.*

lunar ['lu:nə] Mond...

lunatic ['lu:nətik] 1. irr-, wahnsinnig; 2. Irre(r *m*) *f;* Wahnsinnige(r *m*) *f;* Geistesgestörte(r *m*) *f;* **~ asylum** Irrenhaus *n,* -anstalt *f.*

lunch|(eon) [lʌntʃ, 'lʌntʃən] 1. Lunch *m,* Mittagessen *n;* zweites Frühstück; 2. zu Mittag essen; *j-m* ein Mittagessen geben; **~-hour** Mittagszeit *f,* -pause *f.*

lung *anat.* [lʌŋ] Lunge(nflügel *m*) *f; the ~s pl.* die Lunge.

lunge [lʌndʒ] 1. *Fechten:* Ausfall *m;* 2. v/i. ausfallen (*at gegen*); (dahin-)stürmen; v/t. stoßen.

lupin(e) ♀ ['lu:pin] Lupine *f.*

lurch [lə:tʃ] 1. taumeln, torkeln; 2.: *leave in the ~* im Stich lassen.

lure [ljuə] 1. Köder *m; fig.* Lockung *f;* 2. ködern, (an)locken.

lurid □ ['ljuərid] unheimlich; erschreckend, schockierend; düster, finster.

lurk [lə:k] lauern; versteckt liegen.

luscious □ ['lʌʃəs] köstlich; üppig; süß(lich), widerlich.

lust [lʌst] (sinnliche) Begierde; *fig.* Gier *f,* Sucht *f.*

lust|re, Am. ~er ['lʌstə] Glanz *m;* Kronleuchter *m;* **~rous** □ [~trəs] glänzend.

lusty □ ['lʌsti] rüstig; *fig.* lebhaft, kräftig.

lute¹ ♪ [lu:t] Laute *f.*

lute² [~] 1. Kitt *m;* 2. (ver)kitten.

Lutheran ['lu:θərən] lutherisch.

luxate 🞓 ['lʌkseit] verrenken.

luxur|iant □ [lʌg'zjuəriənt] üppig; **~ious** [~iəs] luxuriös, üppig; **~y** ['lʌkʃəri] Luxus *m,* Üppigkeit *f;* Luxusartikel *m;* Genußmittel *n.*

lyceum [lai'siəm] Vortragsraum *m; bsd. Am.* Volkshochschule *f.*

lye [lai] Lauge *f.*

lying ['laiiŋ] 1. *p.pr. von* lie¹ 2 *u.* lie² 2; 2. *adj.* lügnerisch; **~-in** [~'in] Wochenbett *n;* **~ hospital** Entbindungsheim *n.*

lymph 🞓 [limf] Lymphe *f.*

lynch [lintʃ] lynchen; **~-law** ['lintʃlɔ:] Lynchjustiz *f.*

lynx *zo.* [liŋks] Luchs *m.*

lyric ['lirik] 1. lyrisch; 2. lyrisches Gedicht; **~s** *pl.* (Lied)Text *m (bsd. e-s Musicals);* Lyrik *f;* **~al** □ [~kəl] lyrisch, gefühlvoll; schwärmerisch, begeistert.

M

ma'am [mæm] Majestät *f* (*Anrede für die Königin*); Hoheit *f* (*Anrede für Prinzessinnen*); F [məm] gnä' Frau *f* (*von Dienstboten verwendete Anrede*).

macaroni [mækə'rouni] Makkaroni *pl.*

macaroon [mækə'ruːn] Makrone *f.*

machin|ation [mæki'neiʃən] Anschlag *m*; ~s *pl.* Ränke *pl.*; ~e [mə'ʃiːn] 1. Maschine *f*; Mechanismus *m* (*a. fig.*); 2. maschinell herstellen *od.* (be)arbeiten; ~e-made maschinell hergestellt; ~ery [~nəri] Maschinen *f/pl.*; Maschinerie *f*; ~ist [~nist] Maschinist *m*; Maschinennäherin *f.*

mackerel *ichth.* ['mækrəl] Makrele *f.*

mackinow *Am.* ['mækinɔ:] Stutzer *m* (*Kleidungsstück*).

mackintosh ['mækintɔʃ] Regenmantel *m.*

mad ☐ [mæd] wahnsinnig; toll (-wütig); *fig.* wild; F wütend; go ~ verrückt werden; drive ~ verrückt machen.

madam ['mædəm] gnädige Frau, gnädiges Fräulein (*Anrede*).

mad|cap ['mædkæp] 1. toll; 2. Tollkopf *m*; Wildfang *m*; ~den ['mædn] toll *od.* rasend machen.

made [meid] *pret. u. p.p. von* make 1.

made-up ['meid'ʌp] zurechtgemacht; erfunden; fertig; ~ clothes *pl.* Konfektion *f.*

mad|house ['mædhaus] Irrenhaus *n*; ~man Wahnsinnige(r) *m*; ~ness ['mædnis] Wahnsinn *m*; (Toll)Wut *f.*

magazine [mægə'ziːn] Magazin *n*; (Munitions)Lager *n*; Zeitschrift *f.*

maggot *zo.* ['mægət] Made *f.*

magic ['mædʒik] 1. *a.* ~al [~kəl] magisch; Zauber...; 2. Zauberei *f*; *fig.* Zauber *m*; ~ian [mə'dʒiʃən] Zauberer *m.*

magistra|cy ['mædʒistrəsi] Richteramt *n*; *die Richter m/pl.*; ~te [~rit] (Polizei-, Friedens)Richter *m.*

magnanimous ☐ [mæg'næniməs] großmütig.

magnet ['mægnit] Magnet *m*; ~ic [mæg'netik] (~ally) magnetisch.

magni|ficence [mæg'nifisns] Pracht *f*, Herrlichkeit *f*; ~ficent [~nt] prächtig, herrlich; ~fy ['mægnifai] vergrößern; ~tude [~itjuːd] Größe *f*, Wichtigkeit *f.*

magpie *orn.* ['mægpai] Elster *f.*

mahagony [mə'hɔgəni] Mahagoni (-holz) *n.*

maid [meid] *lit.* Mädchen *n*; (Dienst)Mädchen *n*; old ~ alte

Jungfer; ~ of all work Mädchen *n* für alles; ~ of honour Ehren-, Hofdame *f.*

maiden ['meidn] 1. = maid; 2. jungfräulich; unverheiratet; *fig.* Jungfern..., Erstlings...; *name* Mädchenname *m* e-r Frau; ~head Jungfräulichkeit *f*; ~hood [~hud] Mädchenjahre *n/pl.*; ~ly [~nli] jungfräulich, mädchenhaft.

mail[1] [meil] (Ketten)Panzer *m.*

mail[2] [~] 1. Post(dienst *m*) *f*; Post(sendung) *f*; 2. *Am.* mit der Post schicken, aufgeben; ~able *Am.* ['meiləbl] postversandfähig; ~bag Briefträger-, Posttasche *f*; Postsack *m*; ~box *bsd* *Am* Briefkasten *m*; ~carrier *Am* Briefträger *m*; ~man *Am* Briefträger *m*; ~order firm, *bsd* *Am* ~order house (Post)Versandgeschäft *n.*

maim [meim] verstümmeln.

main [mein] 1. Haupt...; hauptsächlich; by ~ force mit voller Kraft; 2. Hauptrohr *n*, -leitung *f*; ~s *pl.* ∉ (Strom)Netz *n*, in the ~ in der Hauptsache, im wesentlichen; ~land ['meinlənd] Festland *n*; ~ly [~li] hauptsächlich; ~spring Uhrfeder *f*; *fig.* Haupttriebfeder *f*; ~stay ⚓ Großtag *n*; *fig.* Hauptstütze *f* 2 Street *Am.* Hauptstraße *f*; 2 Streeter *Am.* Kleinstadtbewohner *m.*

maintain [men'tein] (aufrecht)erhalten; beibehalten; (unter)stützen; unterhalten; behaupten.

maintenance ['meintinəns] Erhaltung *f*, Unterhalt *m*; ⊕ Wartung *f.*

maize [meiz] Mais *m.*

majest|ic [mə'dʒestik] (~ally) majestätisch; ~y ['mædʒisti] Majestät *f*; Würde *f*, Hoheit *f.*

major ['meidʒə] 1. größer; wichtig(er); mündig; ♪ Dur *n*; ~ key Dur-Tonart *f*; ~ league *Am.* Baseball: Oberliga *f*; 2. ⚔ Major *m*; Mündige(r *m*) *f*; *Am. univ.* Hauptfach *n*; ~general ⚔ Generalmajor *m*; ~ity [mə'dʒɔriti] Mehrheit *f*; Mündigkeit *f*; Majorsrang *m.*

make [meik] 1. [*irr*] *v/t. allg.* machen; verfertigen, fabrizieren; bilden; (aus)machen; ergeben; (veran)lassen; gewinnen, verdienen; sich erweisen als, abgeben; Regel *etc.* aufstellen; Frieden *etc.* schließen; e-e Rede halten; good wieder gutmachen; wahr machen; do you ~ one of us? machen Sie mit?; ~ port ⚓ den Hafen anlaufen; ~ way vorwärtskommen; ~ into verarbeiten zu; ~ out ausfindig machen; erkennen; verstehen; entziffern; Rechnung *etc.* ausstellen; ~ over übertragen; ~ up ergänzen; vervoll-

ständigen; zs.-stellen; bilden, ausmachen, *Streit* beilegen; zurechtmachen, schminken; = ~ up for
(*v/i.*); ~ up one's mind sich entschließen; *v/i.* sich begeben;
gehen; ~ away with beseitigen;
Geld vertun; ~ for zugehen auf
(*acc.*); sich aufmachen nach; ~ off
sich fortmachen; ~ up sich zurechtmachen; sich schminken; ~ up for
nach-, aufholen; für *et.* entschädigen; 2. Mach~, Bauart *f*; Bau *m des
Körpers*; Form *f*; Fabrikat *n*, Erzeugnis *n*; ~believe ['meikbili:v]
Schein *m*, Vorwand *m*, Verstellung
f; ~r ['meikə] Hersteller *m*; ♀
Schöpfer *m* (*Gott*); ~shift 1. Notbehelf *m*, 2. behelfsmäßig; ~up
typ. Umbruch *m*; *fig.* Charakter *m*;
Schminke *f*, Make-up *n*.

maladjustment ['mælə'dʒʌstmənt]
mangelhafte Anpassung.

maladministration ['mælədmi-
nis'treiʃən] schlechte Verwaltung.

malady ['mælədi] Krankheit *f*.

malcontent ['mælkəntent] 1. unzufrieden; 2. Unzufriedene(r) *m*.

male [meil] 1. männlich; 2. Mann
m; *zo.* Männchen *n*.

malediction [mæli'dikʃən] Fluch
m.

malefactor ['mælifæktə] Übeltäter
m.

malevolen|ce [mə'levələns] Bös-
willigkeit *f*; ~t □ [~nt] böswillig.

malice ['mælis] Bosheit *f*; Groll *m*.

malicious □ [mə'liʃəs] boshaft;
böswillig, ~ness [~snis] Bosheit *f*.

malign [mə'lain] 1. □ schädlich;
2. verleumden; ~ant □ [mə-
'lignənt] böswillig; ☞ bösartig;
~ity [~niti] Bosheit *f*; Schaden-
freude *f*; *bsd.* ☞ Bösartigkeit *f*.

malleable ['mæliəbl] hämmerbar;
fig. geschmeidig.

mallet ['mælit] Schlegel *m*.

malnutrition ['mælnju(:)'triʃən]
Unterernährung *f*.

malodorous □ [mæ'loudərəs] übelriechend.

malpractice ['mæl'præktis] Übel-
tat *f*; ☞ falsche Behandlung.

malt [mɔ:lt] Malz *n*.

maltreat [mæl'tri:t] schlecht behandeln, mißhandeln.

mam(m)a [mə'mɑ:] Mama *f*.

mammal ['mæməl] Säugetier *n*.

mammoth ['mæməθ] riesig.

mammy F ['mæmi] Mami *f*; *Am.*
farbiges Kindermädchen.

man [mæn, *in Zssgn* ...mən] 1. *pl.*
men [men] Mann *m*; Mensch(en
pl.) *m*; Menschheit *f*; Diener *m*;
Schach: Figur *f*; Damestein *m*;
2. männlich; 3. ☒, ⚓ bemannen;
~ o.s. sich ermannen.

manage ['mænidʒ] *v/t.* handhaben;
verwalten, leiten; *Menschen, Tiere*
lenken; mit *j-m* fertig werden; *et.*

fertigbringen; ~ to *inf.* es fertigbringen, zu *inf.*; *v/i.* die Aufsicht
haben, die Geschäfte führen; auskommen; F es schaffen; ~able □
[~dʒəbl] handlich; lenksam; ~ment
[~dʒmənt] Verwaltung *f*, Leitung *f*,
Direktion *f*, Geschäftsführung *f*;
geschickte Behandlung; ~r [~dʒə]
Leiter *m*, Direktor *m*; Regisseur *m*;
Manager *m*; ~ress [~əres] Leiterin
f, Direktorin *f*.

managing ['mænidʒiŋ] geschäfts-
führend; Betriebs...; ~ clerk Ge-
schäftsführer *m*, Prokurist *m*.

mandat|e ['mændeit] Mandat *n*;
Befehl *m*; Auftrag *m*; Vollmacht *f*;
~ory [~dətəri] befehlend.

mane [mein] Mähne *f*.

maneuver [mə'nu:və] = *manoeuvre*.

manful □ ['mænful] mannhaft.

mange *vet.* [meindʒ] Räude *f*.

manger ['meindʒə] Krippe *f*.

mangle ['mæŋgl] 1. Wringmaschine
f; Wäschemangel *f*; 2. mangeln;
wringen; zerstückeln; *fig.* verstümmeln.

mangy ['meindʒi] räudig; *fig.*
schäbig.

manhood ['mænhud] Mannesalter
n; Männlichkeit *f*; die Männer *m/pl.*

mania ['meinjə] Wahnsinn *m*;
Sucht *f*, Manie *f*; ~c ['meiniæk]
1. Wahnsinnige(r *m*) *f*; 2. wahnsinnig.

manicure ['mænikjuə] 1. Maniküre
f; 2. maniküren.

manifest ['mænifest] 1. □ offenbar;
2. ⚓ Ladungsverzeichnis *n*; 3. *v/t.*
offenbaren; kundtun; ~ation
[mænifes'teiʃən] Offenbarung *f*;
Kundgebung *f*; ~o [mæni'festou]
Manifest *n*.

manifold □ ['mænifould] 1. mannigfaltig; 2. vervielfältigen.

manipulat|e [mə'nipjuleit] (ge-
schickt) handhaben; ~ion [mənipju-
pju'leiʃən] Handhabung *f*, Behandlung *f*, Verfahren *n*; Kniff *m*.

man|kind [mæn'kaind] die Mensch-
heit; ['mænkaind] die Männer *m/pl.*;
~ly ['mænli] männlich; mannhaft.

manner ['mænə] Art *f*, Weise *f*;
Stil(art *f*) *m*; Manier *f*; ~s *pl.* Manieren *f/pl.*, Sitten *f/pl.*; *in a* ~
gewissermaßen, ~ed [~əd] ...gear-
tet; gekünstelt; ~ly [~əli] manier-
lich, gesittet.

manoeuvre, *Am. a.* **maneuver**
[mə'nu:və] 1. Manöver *n* (*a. fig.*);
2. manövrieren (lassen).

man-of-war ⚓ ['mænəv'wɔ:]
Kriegsschiff *n*.

manor ['mænə] Rittergut *n*; *lord of
the* ~ Gutsherr *m*; ~house Herr-
schaftshaus *n*, Herrensitz *m*; Schloß
n.

manpower ['mænpauə] Men-
schenpotential *n*; Arbeitskräfte *f/pl.*

man-servant ['mænsəːvənt] Diener *m*.

mansion ['mænʃən] (herrschaftliches) Wohnhaus.

manslaughter ℟ ['mænslɔːtə] Totschlag *m*, fahrlässige Tötung.

mantel|piece ['mæntlpiːs], ~shelf Kaminsims *m*, -platte *f*.

mantle ['mæntl] 1. Mantel *m*; *fig.* Hülle *f*; Glühstrumpf *m*; 2. *v/t.* verhüllen; *v/i.* sich röten (*Gesicht*).

manual ['mænjuəl] 1. ☐ Hand...; mit der Hand (gemacht); 2. Handbuch *n*. [brik *f*.]

manufactory [mænju'fæktəri] Fabrik}

manufactur|e [mænju'fæktʃə] 1. Fabrikation *f*; Fabrikat *n*; 2. fabrizieren; verarbeiten; ~er [~ərə] Fabrikant *m*; ~ing [~riŋ] Fabrik...; Gewerbe...; Industrie...

manure [mə'njuə] 1. Dünger *m*; 2. düngen.

manuscript ['mænjuskript] Manuskript *n*; Handschrift *f*.

many ['meni] 1. viele; ~ a manche(*r*, -s); be one too ~ for s.o. j-m überlegen sein; 2. Menge *f*; a good ~, a great ~ ziemlich viele, sehr viele.

map [mæp] 1. (Land)Karte *f*; 2. aufzeichnen; ~ out planen; einteilen.

maple ⅋ ['meipl] Ahorn *m*.

mar [maː] schädigen; verderben.

maraud [mə'rɔːd] plündern.

marble ['maːbl] 1. Marmor *m*; Murmel *f*; 2. marmorn.

March¹ [maːtʃ] März *m*.

march² [~] 1. Marsch *m*; Fortschritt *m*; Gang *m der Ereignisse etc.*; 2. marschieren (lassen); *fig.* vorwärtsschreiten.

marchioness ['maːʃənis] Marquise *f*.

mare [meə] Stute *f*; ~'s nest *fig.* Schwindel *m*; (Zeitungs)Ente *f*.

marg|arine ['maːdʒə'riːn], *a.* ~e F [maːdʒ] Margarine *f*.

margin ['maːdʒin] Rand *m*; Grenze *f*; Spielraum *m*; Verdienst-, Gewinn-, Handelsspanne *f*; ~al [~nl] am Rande (befindlich); Rand...; ~ note Randbemerkung *f*.

marine [mə'riːn] Marineinfanterist *m*; Marine *f*; *paint.* Seestück *n*; *attr.* See...; Marine...; Schiffs...; ~r ['mærinə] Seemann *m*.

marital [☐ 'mæritl] ehelich, Ehe...

maritime ['mæritaim] an der See liegend *od.* lebend; See...; Küsten-...; Schiffahrt(s)...

mark¹ [maːk] Mark *f* (*Geldstück*).

mark² [~] 1. Marke *f*, Merkmal *n*, Zeichen *n*; ✝ Preiszettel *m*; Fabrik-, Schutzmarke *f*; (Körper)Mal *n*; Norm *f*; *Schule:* Zensur *f*, Note *f*, Punkt *m*; *Sport:* Startlinie *f*; Ziel *n*; a man of ~ ein Mann von Bedeutung; *fig.* up to the ~ auf der Höhe;

beside the ~, wide of the ~ den Kern der Sache verfehlend; unrichtig; 2. *v/t.* (be)zeichnen, markieren; *Sport:* anschreiben; kennzeichnen; be(ob)achten; sich *et.* merken; ~ off abtrennen; ~ out bezeichnen; abstecken; ~ time auf der Stelle treten; *v/i.* achtgeben; ~ed ☐ auffallend; merklich; ausgeprägt.

market ['maːkit] 1. Markt(platz) *m*; Handel *m*; ✝ Absatz *m*; in the ~ auf dem Markt; play the ~ *Am. sl.* an der Börse spekulieren; 2. *v/t.* auf den Markt bringen, verkaufen; *v/i.* einkaufen gehen; ~able ☐ [~təbl] marktfähig, -gängig; ~ing [~tiŋ] ✝ Marketing *n*, Absatzpolitik *f*; Marktbesuch *m*.

marksman ['maːksmən] (guter) Schütze.

marmalade ['maːməleid] Orangenmarmelade *f*.

maroon [mə'ruːn] 1. kastanienbraun; 2. auf e-r einsamen Insel aussetzen; 3. Leuchtrakete *f*.

marquee [maː'kiː] (großes) Zelt.

marquis ['maːkwis] Marquis *m*.

marriage ['mæridʒ] Heirat *f*, Ehe (-stand *m*) *f*; Hochzeit *f*; civil ~ standesamtliche Trauung; ~able ☐ [~dʒəbl] heiratsfähig; ~ articles *pl.* Ehevertrag *m*; ~ lines *pl.* Trauschein *m*; ~ portion Mitgift *f*.

married ['mærid] verheiratet; ehelich; Ehe...; ~ couple Ehepaar *n*.

marrow ['mærou] Mark *n*; *fig.* Kern *m*, Beste(s) *n*; ~y [~oui] markig.

marry ['mæri] *v/t.* (sich ver)heiraten; *eccl.* trauen; *v/i.* (sich ver)heiraten.

marsh [maːʃ] Sumpf *m*, Morast *m*.

marshal ['maːʃəl] 1. Marschall *m*; *hist.* Hofmarschall *m*; Zeremonienmeister *m*; *Am.* Bezirkspolizeichef *m*; Leiter *m* der Feuerwehr; 2. ordnen; führen; zs.-stellen.

marshy ['maːʃi] sumpfig.

mart [maːt] Markt *m*; Auktionsraum *m*.

marten *zo.* ['maːtin] Marder *m*.

martial ☐ ['maːʃəl] kriegerisch; Kriegs...; ~ law Stand-, Kriegsrecht *n*.

martyr ['maːtə] 1. Märtyrer(in) (*to gen.*); 2. (zu Tode) martern.

marvel ['maːvel] 1. Wunder *n*; 2. sich wundern; ~lous ☐ ['maːviləs] wunderbar, erstaunlich.

mascot ['mæskət] Maskottchen *n*.

masculine ['maːskjulin] männlich.

mash [mæʃ] 1. Gemisch *n*; Maische *f*; Mengfutter *n*; 2. mischen; zerdrücken; (ein)maischen; ~ed potatoes *pl.* Kartoffelbrei *m*.

mask [maːsk] 1. Maske *f*; 2. maskieren; *fig.* verbergen; tarnen; ~ed: ~ ball Maskenball *m*.

mason ['meisn] Steinmetz *m*; Maurer *m*; Freimaurer *m*; ~ry [~nri] Mauerwerk *n*.

masque [mɑːsk] Maskenspiel *n*.

masquerade [mæskə'reid] **1.** Maskenball *m*; Verkleidung *f*; **2.** *fig.* sich maskieren.

mass [mæs] **1.** *eccl.* Messe *f*; Masse *f*; Menge *f*; ~ *meeting* Massenversammlung *f*; **2.** (sich) (an)sammeln.

massacre ['mæsəkə] **1.** Blutbad *n*; **2.** niedermetzeln.

massage ['mæsɑːʒ] **1.** Massage *f*; **2.** massieren.

massif ['mæsiːf] (Gebirgs)Massiv *n*.

massive ['mæsiv] massiv; schwer.

mast ⚓ [mɑːst] Mast *m*.

master ['mɑːstə] **1.** Meister *m*; Herr *m* (*a. fig.*); Gebieter *m*; Lehrer *m*; Kapitän *m* *e-s Handelsschiffs*; *Anrede:* (junger) Herr; *univ.* Rektor *m* *e-s College*; ♀ *of Arts* Magister *m* Artium; ♀ *of Ceremonies* Conférencier *m*; **2.** Meister...; *fig.* führend; **3.** Herr sein *od.* werden über (*acc.*); *Sprache etc* meistern, beherrschen; ~**builder** Baumeister *m*; ~**ful** □ [~sful] herrisch; meisterhaft; ~**key** Hauptschlüssel *f*; ~**ly** [~əli] meisterhaft, ~**piece** Meisterstück *n*; ~**ship** [~əʃip] Meisterschaft *f*; Herrschaft *f*; Lehramt *n*; ~**y** [~əri] Herrschaft *f*; Vorrang *m*; Oberhand *f*; Meisterschaft *f*; Beherrschung *f*.

masticate ['mæstikeit] kauen.

mastiff ['mæstif] englische Dogge.

mat [mæt] **1.** Matte *f*; Deckchen *n*; Unterlage *f*, **2.** *fig.* bedecken; (sich) verflechten, **3.** mattiert, matt.

match¹ [mætʃ] Streichholz *n*.

match² [~] **1.** Gleiche(r *m*, -s *n*) *f*; Partie *f*; Wettspiel *n*, -kampf *m*; Heirat *f*; *be a ~ for j-m* gewachsen sein; *meet one's ~* s-n Meister finden; **2.** *v/t* anpassen; passen zu; *et.* Passendes finden *od.* geben zu; *es* aufnehmen mit; verheiraten; *well ~ed* zs.-passend; *v/i.* zs.-passen; *to ~* dazu passend; ~**less** □ ['mætʃlis] unvergleichlich, ohnegleichen; ~**maker** Ehestifter(in).

mate¹ [meit] *Schach:* matt (setzen).

mate² [~] **1.** Gefährt|e *m*, -in *f*; Kamerad(in); Gatt|e *m*, -in *f*; Männchen *n*, Weibchen *n* *von Tieren*; Gehilf|e *m*, -in *f*; ⚓ Maat *m*; **2.** (sich) verheiraten; (sich) paaren.

material □ [mə'tiəriəl] **1.** materiell; körperlich; materialistisch; wesentlich, **2.** Material *n*, Stoff *m*; Werkstoff *m*; *writing ~s pl.* Schreibmaterial(ien *pl.*) *n*.

matern|al [mə'təːnl] mütterlich; Mutter...; mütterlicherseits; ~**ity** [~niti] Mutterschaft *f*; Mütterlichkeit *f*; *mst ~ hospital* Entbindungsanstalt *f*.

mathematic|ian [mæθimə'tiʃən] Mathematiker *m*; ~**s** [~'mætiks] *mst sg.* Mathematik *f*.

matriculate [mə'trikjuleit] (sich) immatrikulieren (lassen).

matrimon|ial □ [mætri'mounjəl] ehelich; Ehe...; ~**y** ['mætriməni] Ehe(stand *m*) *f*.

matrix ['meitriks] Matrize *f*.

matron ['meitrən] Matrone *f*; Hausmutter *f*; Oberin *f*.

matter ['mætə] **1.** Materie *f*, Stoff *m*; ⚕ Eiter *m*; Gegenstand *m*; Ursache *f*; Sache *f*; Angelegenheit *f*, Geschäft *n*; *printed ~* ✉ Drucksache *f*; *what's the ~?* was gibt es?; *what's the ~ with you?* was fehlt Ihnen?; *no ~* es hat nichts zu sagen; *no ~ who* gleichgültig wer; *~ of course* Selbstverständlichkeit *f*; *for that ~, for the ~ of that* was dies betrifft; *~ of fact* Tatsache *f*; **2.** von Bedeutung sein; *it does not ~* es macht nichts; *~-of-fact* tatsächlich; sachlich.

mattress ['mætris] Matratze *f*.

matur|e [mə'tjuə] **1.** □ reif; reiflich; ✝ fällig; **2.** reifen; zur Reife bringen; ✝ fällig werden; ~**ity** [~əriti] Reife *f*; ✝ Fälligkeit *f*.

maudlin □ ['mɔːdlin] rührselig.

maul [mɔːl] beschädigen; *fig.* heruntermachen; roh umgehen mit.

Maundy Thursday *eccl.* ['mɔːndi 'θəːzdi] Gründonnerstag *m*.

mauve [mouv] **1.** Malvenfarbe *f*; **2.** hellviolett.

maw [mɔː] *Tier-*Magen *m*; Rachen *m*.

mawkish □ ['mɔːkiʃ] rührselig, sentimental.

maxim ['mæksim] Grundsatz *m*; ~**um** [~əm] Höchstmaß *n*, -stand *m*, -betrag *m*; *attr.* Höchst...

May¹ [mei] Mai *m*.

may² [~] *[irr.]* mag, kann, darf.

maybe *Am.* ['meibiː] vielleicht.

may|-beetle *zo.* ['meibiːtl], ~**bug** Maikäfer *m*.

May Day ['meidei] der 1. Mai.

mayor [mεə] Bürgermeister *m*.

maypole ['meipoul] Maibaum *m*.

maz|e [meiz] Irrgarten *m*, Labyrinth *n*; *fig.* Wirrnis *f*; *in a ~* ~**ed** [meizd] bestürzt, verwirrt; ~**y** □ ['meizi] labyrinthisch; wirr.

me [miː; mi] mich; mir; *F* ich.

mead [miːd] Met *m*; *poet.* = *meadow*.

meadow ['medou] Wiese *f*.

meag|re, *Am.* ~**er** □ ['miːgə] mager, dürr; dürftig.

meal [miːl] Mahl(zeit *f*) *n*; Mehl *n*.

mean¹ □ [miːn] gemein, niedrig, gering; armselig; knauserig.

mean² [~] **1.** mittler, mittelmäßig; Durchschnitts...; *in the ~ time* inzwischen; **2.** Mitte *f*; ~**s** *pl.* (Geld)Mittel *n/pl.*; (*a. sg.*) Mittel *n*; *by all ~s* jedenfalls; *by no ~s* keineswegs; *by ~s of* mittels (*gen.*).

mean³ [~] *[irr.]* meinen; beabsich-

tigen; bestimmen; bedeuten; ~
well (*ill*) es gut (schlecht) meinen.
meaning ['mi:niŋ] **1.** ☐ bedeut-
sam; **2.** Sinn *m*, Bedeutung *f*; ~**less**
[~lis] bedeutungslos; sinnlos.
meant [ment] *pret. u. p.p. von*
mean[3].
mean|time ['mi:n'taim], ~**while**
mittlerweile, inzwischen.
measles ⚕ ['mi:zlz] *sg.* Masern *pl.*
measure ['meʒə] **1.** Maß *n*; ♪ Takt
m; Maßregel *f*; ~ *of capacity* Hohl-
maß *n*; *beyond* ~ über alle Maßen;
in a great ~ großenteils; *made to* ~
nach Maß gemacht; **2.** (ab-, aus-,
ver)messen; *j-m* Maß nehmen; ~ *up*
Am. heranreichen; ~**less** ☐ [~lis]
unermeßlich; ~**ment** [~əmənt]
Messung *f*; Maß *n*.
meat [mi:t] Fleisch *n*; *fig.* Gehalt *m*;
~ **tea** reiches Abendessen mit Tee;
~**y** ['mi:ti] fleischig; *fig.* gehaltvoll.
mechanic [mi'kænik] Handwerker
m; Mechaniker *m*; ~**al** [~kəl]
mechanisch; Maschinen...; ~**ian**
[mekə'niʃən] Mechaniker *m*; ~**s**
[mi'kæniks] *mst sg.* Mechanik *f*.
mechan|ism ['mekənizəm] Me-
chanismus *m*; ~**ize** [~naiz] mecha-
nisieren; ✕ motorisieren.
medal ['medl] Medaille *f*; Orden
m.
meddle ['medl] sich einmischen
(*with, in* in *acc.*); ~**some** [~lsəm]
zu-, aufdringlich.
mediaeval ☐ [medi'i:vəl] mittelal-
terlich.
media|l ['mi:djəl], ~**n** [~ən]
Mittel..., in der Mitte (befindlich).
mediat|e ['mi:dieit] vermitteln;
~**ion** [mi:di'eiʃən] Vermittlung *f*;
~**or** ['mi:dieitə] Vermittler *m*.
medical ☐ ['medikəl] medizinisch,
ärztlich; ~ *certificate* Kranken-
schein *m*, Attest *n*; ~ *evidence* ärzt-
liches Gutachten; ~ *man* Arzt *m*,
Mediziner *m*; ~ *supervision* ärzt-
liche Aufsicht.
medicate ['medikeit] medizinisch
behandeln; mit Arzneistoff versehen; ~*d bath* medizinisches Bad.
medicin|al ☐ [me'disinl] medizi-
nisch; heilend, heilsam; ~**e** ['med-
sin] Medizin *f*.
medieval ☐ [medi'i:vəl] = *mediaeval*.
mediocre ['mi:dioukə] mittelmäßig.
meditat|e ['mediteit] *v/i.* nachden-
ken, überlegen; *v/t.* sinnen auf
(*acc.*); erwägen; ~**ion** [medi'teiʃən]
Nachdenken *n*; innere Betrachtung;
~**ive** ☐ ['meditətiv] nachdenklich,
meditativ.
Mediterranean [meditə'reinjən]
Mittelmeer *n*; *attr.* Mittelmeer...
medium ['mi:djəm] **1.** Mitte *f*;
Mittel *n*; Vermittlung *f*; Medium
n; *Lebens*-Element *n*; **2.** mittler;
Mittel..., Durchschnitts...

medley ['medli] Gemisch *n*; ♪ Pot-
pourri *n*.
meek ☐ [mi:k] sanft-, demütig;
~**ness** ['mi:knis] Sanft-, Demut *f*.
meerschaum ['miəʃəm] Meer-
schaum(pfeife *f*) *m*.
meet[1] [mi:t] passend; schicklich.
meet[2] [~] [*irr.*] *v/t.* treffen; begegnen (*dat.*); abholen; stoßen auf
den Gegner; Wunsch etc. befriedigen; *e-r Verpflichtung* nachkommen; *Am. j-m* vorgestellt werden;
go to ~ *s.o.* j-m entgegengehen; *v/i.*
sich treffen; zs.-stoßen; sich versammeln; ~ *with* stoßen auf (*acc.*);
erleiden; ~**ing** ['mi:tiŋ] Begegnung
f; (Zs.-)Treffen *n*, Versammlung *f*;
Tagung *f*.
melancholy ['melənkəli] **1.** Schwermut *f*; **2.** melancholisch.
meliorate ['mi:ljəreit] (sich) verbessern.
mellow ['melou] **1.** ☐ mürbe; reif;
weich; mild; **2.** reifen (lassen);
weich machen *od.* werden; (sich)
mildern.
melo|dious ☐ [mi'loudjəs] melo-
disch; ~**dramatic** [meloudrə-
'mætik] melodramatisch; ~**dy**
['melədi] Melodie *f*; Lied *n*.
melon ⚘ ['melən] Melone *f*.
melt [melt] (zer)schmelzen; *fig.* zer-
fließen; *Gefühl* erweichen.
member ['membə] (Mit)Glied *n*;
parl. Abgeordnete(r *m*) *f*; ~**ship**
[~ʃip] Mitgliedschaft *f*; Mitgliederzahl *f*.
membrane ['membrein] Mem-
bran(e) *f*, Häutchen *n*. [*n*.]
memento [mi'mentou] Andenken
memo ['mi:mou] = *memorandum.*
memoir ['memwa:] Denkschrift *f*;
~**s** *pl.* Memoiren *pl.*
memorable ☐ ['memərəbl] denk-
würdig.
memorandum [memə'rændəm]
Notiz *f*; *pol.* Note *f*; Schriftsatz *m*.
memorial [mi'mɔ:riəl] Denkmal *n*;
Gedenkzeichen *n*; Denkschrift *f*,
Eingabe *f*; *attr.* Gedächtnis..., Gedenk...
memorize ['meməraiz] auswendig
lernen, memorieren.
memory ['meməri] Gedächtnis *n*;
Erinnerung *f*; Andenken *n*; *commit
to* ~ dem Gedächtnis einprägen;
in ~ *of* zum Andenken an (*acc.*).
men [men] *pl. von man* 1; Mannschaft *f*.
menace ['menəs] **1.** (be)drohen;
2. Gefahr *f*; Drohung *f*.
mend [mend] **1.** *v/t.* (ver)bessern;
ausbessern, flicken; besser machen;
~ *one's ways* sich bessern; *v/i.* sich
bessern; **2.** Flicken *m*; *on the* ~ auf
dem Wege der Besserung.
mendacious ☐ [men'deiʃəs] lügnerisch, verlogen.
mendicant ['mendikənt] **1.** bet-

telnd; Bettel...; 2. Bettler m; Bettel-
mönch m

menial contp ['mi:njəl] 1. □ knech-
tisch; niedrig, 2. Knecht m; Lakai m.

meningitis ♂ [menin'dʒaitis] Hirn-
hautentzündung f, Meningitis f.

mental ['mentl] geistig; Geistes...; , arithmetic Kopfrechnen n;
~ity [men'tæliti] Mentalität f.

mention [menʃən] 1. Erwähnung f;
2. erwähnen, don't ~ it! bitte!

menu ['menju:] Speisenfolge f,
Menü n, Speisekarte f.

mercantile ['mə:kəntail] kaufmännisch, Handels

mercenary ['mə:sinəri] 1. □ feil,
käuflich gedungen; gewinnsüch-
tig; 2. ⚔ Söldner m.

mercer ['mə:sə] Seidenwaren-,
Stoffhändler m

merchandise ['mə:tʃəndaiz] Wa-
re(n pl.) f

merchant [mə:tʃənt] 1. Kaufmann
m; Am (Klein) Händler m; 2. Handels. , Kaufmanns ; law ~ Han-
delsrecht n ~man Handelsschiff n.

merci|ful ['mə:siful] barmher-
zig, ~less [~ilis] unbarmherzig.

mercury [mə: kjuri] Quecksilber n.

mercy [mə:si] Barmherzigkeit f;
Gnade f, be at s.o.'s ~ in j-s Gewalt sein

mere [miə] rein, lauter; bloß;
~ly ['miəli] bloß, lediglich, allein.

meretricious [meri'triʃəs] aufdringlich, kitschig

merge [mə dʒ] verschmelzen (in
mit), ~r [mə dʒə] Verschmelzung f.

meridian [mə'ridiən] geogr. Meridian m, fig Gipfel m; attr. Mittags..

merit [merit] 1. Verdienst n; Wert
m; Vorzug m, bsd ğ̌ḡ ~s pl. Haupt-
punkte m/pl , Wesen n e-r Sache;
make a ~ of als Verdienst ansehen;
2. fig verdienen, ~orious □
[meri'tɔ:riəs] verdienstvoll.

mermaid [mə meid] Nixe f.

merriment [merimənt] Lustigkeit
f; Belustigung f

merry ['meri] lustig, fröhlich;
make lustig sein, ~andrew
Hanswurst m, ~go-round Karussell n; ~making [~imeikiŋ] Lustbarkeit f

mesh [meʃ] 1. Masche f; fig. oft ~es
pl. Netz n, be in ⊕ (in-ea.-)grei-
fen; 2. in e-m Netz fangen

mess¹ [mes] 1. Unordnung f;
Schmutz m, ᴀ Schweinerei f; F Patsche f, make a ~ of verpfuschen; 2.
v/t. in Unordnung bringen; verpfuschen; v/i. about herummurksen.

mess² [..] Kasino n, Messe f.

message [mesidʒ] Botschaft f; go
on a ~, e-m Besorgung machen.

messenger ['mesindʒə] Bote m.

Messieurs, mst Messrs. ['mesəz]
(die) Herren m/pl.; Firma f.

---

met [met] pret. u. p.p. von meet².

metal ['metl] 1. Metall n; Schotter
m; 2. beschottern, ~lic [mi'tælik]
(~ally) metallisch; Metall ; ~lurgy
[me'tælədʒi] Hüttenkunde f.

metamorphose[metə'mɔ:fouz] verwandeln, umgestalten

metaphor ['metəfə] Metapher f.

meteor ['mi:tjə] Meteor m (a. fig.);
~ology [mi:tjə'rɔlədʒi] Meteorologie f, Wetterkunde f.

meter ['mi:tə] Messer m, Zähler m;
Am. = metre.

methinks † [mi'θiŋks] mich dünkt.

method ['meθəd] Methode f; Art
u. Weise f; Verfahren n; Ordnung
f, System n; ~ic(al) [mi'θɔ-
dik(əl)] methodisch.

methought [mi'θɔ:t] pret. von
methinks.

meticulous □ [mi'tikjuləs] peinlich
genau.

met|re, Am. ~er ['mi:tə] Meter n,
m; Versmaß n.

metric ['metrik] (~ally) metrisch;
~ system Dezimalsystem n.

metropol|is [mi'trɔpəlis] Haupt-
stadt f, Metropole f, ~tan [metrə-
'pɔlitən] hauptstädtisch

mettle ['metl] Feuereifer m, Mut m;
be on one's ~ sein Bestes tun.

mews [mju:z] Stallung f; daraus
entstandene Garagen f/pl. od. Wohn-
häuser n/pl.

Mexican ['meksikən] 1. mexika-
nisch; 2. Mexikaner(in).

miaow [mi(:)'au] miauen; mauzen.

mice [mais] pl. von mouse

Michaelmas ['miklməs] Michaelis
(-tag m) n (29 September)

micro... ['maikrou] klein , Klein...

micro|phone [maikrəfoun] Mikro-
phon n; ~scope Mikroskop n.

mid [mid] mittler, Mitt(el) .; in ~
air mitten in der Luft; in ~ winter
mitten im Winter, ~day ['midei]
1. Mittag m; 2. mittägig, Mittags...

middle ['midl] 1. Mitte f, Hüften
f/pl.; 2. mittler, Mittel ; ♀ Ages
pl. Mittelalter n, ~aged von mittlerem Alter; ~class Mittelstands-
...; ~ class(es pl.) Mittelstand m;
~man Mittelsmann m; ~ name
zweiter Vorname m; ~sized mittel-
groß; ~weight Boxen: Mittelge-
wicht n.

middling † ['midliŋ] mittelmäßig;
leidlich; Mittel...

middy F ['midi] = midshipman.

midge [midʒ] Mücke f; ~t ['midʒit]
Zwerg m, Knirps m

mid|land ['midlənd] 1. binnenlän-
disch; 2. the ♀s pl. Mittelengland n;
~most mittelste(r, -s); ~night
Mitternacht f; ~riff ['midrif]
Zwerchfell n; ~shipman Leutnant
m zur See; Am. Oberfähnrich m
zur See; ~st [midst] Mitte f; in the
~ of inmitten (gen.); ~summer

Sommersonnenwende *f*; Hochsommer *m*; **~way** 1. halber Weg; *Am.* Schaubudenstraße *f*; 2. *adj.* in der Mitte befindlich; 3. *adv.* auf halbem Wege, **~wife** Hebamme *f*; **~wifery** ['midwifəri] Geburtshilfe *f*; **~winter** Wintersonnenwende *f*; Mitte *f* des Winters.

mien [miːn] Miene *f*.

might [mait] 1. Macht *f*, Gewalt *f*, Kraft *f*, *with ~ and main* mit aller Gewalt 2. *pret von* may²; **~y** □ ['maiti] mächtig, gewaltig.

migrat|e [mai'greit] (aus)wandern; **~ion** [~iʃən] Wanderung *f*; **~ory** ['maigrətəri] wandernd; Zug...

mild [maild] mild, sanft; gelind. **~ew** ◊ ['mildjuː] Mehltau *m*. **mildness** [~mildnis] Milde *f*.

mile [mail] Meile *f* (1609.33 *m*).

mil(e)age [maildʒ] Laufzeit *f in Meilen*, Meilenstand *m e-s Autos*; Kilometergeld *n*

milestone ['mailstoun] Meilenstein *m*.

milit|ary ['militəri] 1. □ militärisch; Kriegs ; ♀ *Government* Militärregierung *f*; 2. das Militär; **~ia** [m~liʃə] Land-, Bürgerwehr *f*.

milk [milk] 1. Milch *f*; *it's no use crying over spilt* geschehen ist geschehe , 2. *v/t* melken; *v/i.* Milch geben, **~maid** [milkmeid] Melkerin *f*, Milchmädchen *n*; **~man** Milchmann *m*, **~powder** Milchpulver *n*, **~shake** Milchmischgetränk *n*, **~sop** Weichling *m*; **~y** ['milki] milchig, Milch...; ♀ *Way* Milchstraße *f*

mill¹ [mil] 1. Mühle *f*; Fabrik *f*, Spinnerei *f*, 2. mahlen; ⊕ fräsen; *Geld* prägen , *Münze* rändeln.

mill² *Am* [ ] ¹⁄₁₀₀₀ Dollar *m*.

millepede *zo* ['milipiːd] Tausendfüß(l)e *m*

miller ['milə] Müller *m*; ⊕ Fräsmaschine *f*

millet ♀ ['milit] Hirse *f*.

milline: ['milinə] Putzmacherin *f*, Modist. *f*, **~y** [~əri] Putz-, Modewaren(geschäf *n*) *pl.*

million ['miljən] Million *f*; **~aire** [miljə nɛə] Millionär(in); **~th** ['miljənθ] 1. millionste(r, -s); 2. Millionstel *n*

mill-pond ['milpɔnd] Mühlteich *m*; **~stone** Mühlstein *m*.

milt [milt] Milch *f der Fische*.

mimic ['mimik] 1. mimisch; Schein , 2. Mime *m*; 3. nachahmen, nachäffen; **~ry** [~kri] Nachahmung *f*, *zo* Angleichung *f*.

mince [mins] 1. *v/t* zerhacken; *he does not ~ matters* er nimmt kein Blatt vor den Mund; *v/i.* sich zieren; 2. *a ~d meat* Hackfleisch *n*; **~meat** ['minsmiːt] *e-e* Tortenfüllung, **~pie** Torte *f* aus mincemeat; **~r** [~sə] Fleischwolf *m*.

mincing-machine ['minsiŋməʃiːn] = mincer.

mind [maind] 1. Sinn *m*, Gemüt *n*; Geist *m*, Verstand *m*; Meinung *f*; Absicht *f*; Neigung *f*, Lust *f*; Gedächtnis *n*; Sorge *f*; *to my ~* meiner Ansicht nach; *out of one's ~*, *not in one's right ~* von Sinnen; *change one's ~* sich anders besinnen; *bear s.th. in ~* (immer) an et denken; *have (half) a ~ to* (beinahe) Lust haben zu; *have s th on one's ~* et. auf dem Herzen haben; *make up one's ~* sich entschließen; 2. merken *od.* achten auf (*acc*); sich kümmern um; etwas (einzuwenden) haben gegen; *~! gib acht!*, *never ~! macht nichts!*; *~ the step! Achtung, Stufe!*; *I don't ~* (*it*) ich habe nichts dagegen; *do you . if I smoke?* dürfte es Sie, wenn ich rauche? *would you ~ taking off your hat?* würden Sie bitte den Hut abnehmen?; *~ your own business!* kümmern Sie sich um Ihre Angelegenheiten!; **~ful** ['maindful] (*of*) eingedenk (*gen.*); achtsam (auf *acc*).

mine¹ [main] 1. der (die, das) meinige; mein; 2. die Mein(ig)en *pl.*

mine² [~] 1. Bergwerk *n*, Grube *f*; *fig.* Fundgrube *f*; ✗ Mine *f*; 2. *v/i.* graben, minieren, *v/t* graben; ✗ fördern; ✗ unterminieren; ✗ verminen, **~r** [mainə] Bergmann *m*.

mineral ['minərəl] 1. Mineral *n*; **~s** *pl.* Mineralwasser *n*, 2. mineralisch.

mingle ['miŋgl] (ver)mischen; sich mischen *od.* mengen (*with* unter).

miniature ['minjətʃə] 1. Miniatur (-gemälde *n*) *f*; 2. in Miniatur; Miniatur. , Klein...; **~ camera** Kleinbildkamera *f*

minikin ['minikin] 1. winzig; geziert; 2. Knirps *m*

minim|ize ['minimaiz] möglichst klein machen; *fig* verringern; **~um** [~məm] Minimun *n*, Mindestmaß *n*; Mindestbetrag *m*; *attr.* Mindest...

mining ['mainiŋ] Bergbau *m*; *attr.* Berg(bau) , Gruben .

minion ['minjən] Günstling *m*; *fig.* Lakai *m*

miniskirt ['miniskəːt] Minirock *m*.

minister ['ministə] 1. Diener *m*; *fig.* Werkzeug *n*, Geistliche(r) *m*; Minister *m*; Gesandte(r) *m*; 2. *v/t.* darreichen, *v/i.* dienen; Gottesdienst halten

ministry ['ministri] geistliches Amt; Ministerium *n*, Regierung *f*.

mink *zo* [miŋk] Nerz *m*

minor ['mainə] 1. kleiner, geringer, weniger bedeutend; ♪ Moll *n*; AA-moll *n*; 2. Minderjährige(r *m*) *f*; *Am. univ* Nebenfach *n*; **~ity** [mai'nɔriti] Minderheit *f*; Unmündigkeit *f*.

minster ['minstə] Münster *n*.

minstrel ['minstrəl] Minnesänger m; ~s pl. Negersänger m/pl.

mint [mint] 1. ♀ Minze f; Münze f; fig. Goldgrube f; a ~ of money e-e Menge Geld; 2. münzen, prägen.

minuet ♪ [minju'et] Menuett n.

minus ['mainəs] 1. prp. weniger; F ohne; 2. adj. negativ.

minute 1. ⸗ [mai'nju:t] sehr klein, winzig; unbedeutend; sehr genau; 2. ['minit] Minute f; Augenblick m; ~s pl. Protokoll n; ~ness [mai-'nju:tnis] Kleinheit f; Genauigkeit f.

mirac|le ['mirəkl] Wunder n; ~ulous ⸗ [mi'rækjuləs] wunderbar.

mirage ['mira:ʒ] Luftspiegelung f.

mire ['maiə] 1. Sumpf m; Kot m, Schlamm m; 2. mit Schlamm od. Schmutz bedecken.

mirror ['mirə] 1. Spiegel m; 2. (wider)spiegeln (a. fig.).

mirth [mə:θ] Fröhlichkeit f; ~ful □ ['mə:θful] fröhlich; ~less □ ['mə:θ-lis] freudlos.

miry ['maiəri] kotig.

mis... [mis] miß..., übel, falsch.

misadventure ['misəd'ventʃə] Mißgeschick n, Unfall m.

misanthrop|e ['mizənθroup], ~ist [mi'zænθrəpist] Menschenfeind m.

misapply ['misə'plai] falsch anwenden.   [mißverstehen.]

misapprehend ['misæpri'hend]⸗

misappropriate ['misə'prouprieit] unterschlagen, veruntreuen.

misbehave ['misbi'heiv] sich schlecht benehmen.

misbelief ['misbi'li:f] Irrglaube m.

miscalculate ['miskælkjuleit] falsch (be)rechnen.

miscarr|iage [mis'kæridʒ] Mißlingen n; Verlust m v. Briefen; Fehlgeburt f; ~ of justice Fehlspruch m; ~y [~ri] mißlingen; verlorengehen (Brief); fehlgebären.

miscellan|eous □ [misi'leinjəs] ge-, vermischt; vielseitig; ~y [mi-'seləni] Gemisch n; Sammelband m.

mischief ['mistʃif] Schaden m, Unfug m; Mutwille m, Übermut m; ~-maker Unheilstifter(in).

mischievous ⸗ ['mistʃivəs] schädlich; boshaft, mutwillig.

misconceive ['miskən'si:v] falsch auffassen od. verstehen.

misconduct 1. [mis'kɔndʌkt] schlechtes Benehmen; Ehebruch m; schlechte Verwaltung; 2. ['miskən-'dʌkt] schlecht verwalten; ~ o.s. sich schlecht benehmen; e-n Fehltritt begehen.

misconstrue ['miskən'stru:] mißdeuten.

miscreant ['miskriənt] Schurke m.

misdeed ['mis'di:d] Missetat f.

misdemeano(u)r ⸗ [misdi'mi:nə] Vergehen n.

misdirect ['misdi'rekt] irreleiten; an die falsche Adresse richten.

misdoing ['misdu(:)iŋ] Vergehen n (mst pl.).

mise en scène thea. ['mi:zã:n'sein] Inszenierung f.

miser ['maizə] Geizhals m.

miserable ⸗ ['mizərəbl] elend; unglücklich, erbärmlich.

miserly ['maizəli] geizig, filzig.

misery ['mizəri] Elend n, Not f.

misfit ['misfit] schlecht passendes Stück (Kleid, Stiefel etc.); Einzelgänger m, Eigenbrötler m.

misfortune [mis'fɔ:tʃən] Unglück(sfall m) n; Mißgeschick n.

misgiving [mis'giviŋ] böse Ahnung, Befürchtung f.

misguide ['mis'gaid] irreleiten.

mishap ['mishæp] Unfall m; mot. Panne f.

misinform ['misin'fɔ:m] falsch unterrichten.   [deuten.]

misinterpret ['misin'tə:prit] miß-⸗

mislay [mis'lei] [irr. (lay)] verlegen.

mislead [mis'li:d] [irr. (lead)] irreführen; verleiten.

mismanage ['mis'mænidʒ] schlecht verwalten.

misplace ['mis'pleis] falsch stellen, verstellen; verlegen; falsch anbringen.

misprint 1. [mis'print] verdrucken; 2. ['mis'print] Druckfehler m.

misread ['mis'ri:d] [irr. (read)] falsch lesen od. deuten.

misrepresent ['misrepri'zent]falsch darstellen, verdrehen.

miss[1] [mis] mst ♀ Fräulein n.

miss[2] [~] 1. Verlust m; Fehlschuß m, -stoß m, -wurf m; 2. v/t. (ver-)missen; verfehlen; verpassen; auslassen; übersehen; überhören; v/i. fehlen (nicht treffen); fehlgehen.

misshapen ['mis'ʃeipən] verunstaltet; mißgestaltet.

missile ['misail] (Wurf)Geschoß n; Rakete f.

missing ['misiŋ] fehlend; ✕ vermißt; be ~ fehlen; vermißt werden.

mission ['miʃən] Sendung f; Auftrag m; Berufung f, Lebensziel n; Gesandtschaft f; eccl., pol. Mission f; ~ary ['miʃnəri] Missionar m; attr. Missions...

missive ['misiv] Sendschreiben n.

mis-spell ['mis'spel] [irr. (spell)] falsch buchstabieren od. schreiben.

mis-spend ['mis'spend] [irr. (spend)] falsch verwenden; vergeuden.

mist [mist] 1. Nebel m; 2. (um)nebeln; sich trüben; beschlagen.

mistake [mis'teik] 1. [irr. (take)] sich irren in (dat.), verkennen; mißverstehen; verwechseln (for mit); be ~n sich irren; 2. Irrtum m; Versehen n; Fehler m; ~n □ [~kən] irrig, falsch (verstanden).

mister ['mistə] Herr *m* (*abbr.* **Mr.**).

mistletoe ♀ ['misltou] Mistel *f*.

mistress ['mistris] Herrin *f*; Hausfrau *f*; Lehrerin *f*; Geliebte *f*; Meisterin *f*.

mistrust ['mis'trʌst] **1.** mißtrauen (*dat.*); **2.** Mißtrauen *n*; ~ful □ [~tful] mißtrauisch.

misty ['misti] neb(e)lig; unklar.

misunderstand ['misʌndə'stænd] [*irr.* (*stand*)] mißverstehen; ~ing [~diŋ] Mißverständnis *n*.

misus|age [mis'ju:zidʒ] Mißhandlung *f*; ~e **1.** ['mis'ju:z] mißbrauchen, mißhandeln; **2.** [~u:s] Mißbrauch *m*.

mite [mait] *zo.* Milbe *f*; Heller *m*; *fig.* Scherflein *n*; Knirps *m*.

mitigate ['mitigeit] mildern, lindern (*a. fig.*).

mit|re, *Am.* ~**er** ['maitə] Bischofsmütze *f*.

mitt [mit] *Baseball*-Handschuh *m*; F Boxhandschuh *m*; = **mitten.**

mitten ['mitn] Fausthandschuh *m*; Halbhandschuh *m* (*ohne Finger*); *Am. sl.* Tatze *f* (*Hand*).

mix [miks] (sich) (ver)mischen; verkehren (*with* mit); ~ed gemischt; *fig.* zweifelhaft; ~ *up* durch-ea.-bringen, be ~ed up with in e-e S. verwickelt sein; ~ture ['mikstʃə] Mischung *f*.

moan [moun] **1.** Stöhnen *n*; **2.** stöhnen.

moat [mout] Burg-, Stadtgraben *m*.

mob [mɔb] **1.** Pöbel *m*; **2.** anpöbeln.

mobil|e ['moubail] beweglich; ⚔ mobil; ~ization ⚔ [moubilai'zeiʃən] Mobilmachung *f*; ~ize ⚔ ['moubilaiz] mobil machen.

moccasin ['mɔkəsin] weiches Leder; Mokassin *m* (*Schuh*).

mock [mɔk] **1.** Spott *m*; **2.** Schein...; falsch, nachgemacht; **3.** *v/t.* verspotten; nachmachen; täuschen; *v/i.* spotten (*at* über *acc.*); ~ery ['mɔkəri] Spötterei *f*, Gespött *n*; Äfferei *f*.

mocking-bird *orn.* ['mɔkiŋbə:d] Spottdrossel *f*.

mode [moud] Art und Weise *f*; (Erscheinungs)Form *f*; Sitte *f*; Mode *f*.

model ['mɔdl] **1.** Modell *n*; Muster *n*; *fig.* Vorbild *n*; Vorführdame *f*; *attr.* Muster...; **2.** modellieren; (ab)formen; *fig.* modeln, bilden.

moderat|e 1. □ [~'mɔdərit] (mittel-)mäßig, **2.** [~reit] (sich) mäßigen; ~ion [mɔdə'reiʃən] Mäßigung *f*; Mäßigkeit *f*.

modern ['mɔdən] modern, neu; ~ize [~ə(:)naiz] (sich) modernisieren.

modest □ ['mɔdist] bescheiden; anständig; ~y [~ti] Bescheidenheit *f*.

modi|fication [mɔdifi'keiʃən] Ab-,

Veränderung *f*; Einschränkung *f*; ~fy ['mɔdifai] (ab)ändern; mildern.

mods [mɔdz] *pl.* Halbstarke *m/pl.*

modulate ['mɔdjuleit] modulieren.

moiety ['mɔiəti] Hälfte *f*; Teil *m*.

moist [mɔist] feucht, naß; ~en ['mɔisn] be-, anfeuchten; ~ure ['mɔistʃə] Feuchtigkeit *f*.

molar ['moulə] Backenzahn *m*.

molasses [mə'læsiz] Melasse *f*; Sirup *m*.

mole¹ *zo.* [moul] Maulwurf *m*.

mole² [~] Muttermal *n*.

mole³ [~] Mole *f*, Hafendamm *m*.

molecule ['mɔlikju:l] Molekül *n*.

molehill ['moulhil] Maulwurfshügel *m*; *make a mountain out of a* ~ aus e-r Mücke e-n Elefanten machen.

molest [mou'lest] belästigen.

mollify ['mɔlifai] besänftigen.

mollycoddle ['mɔlikɔdl] **1.** Weichling *m*, Muttersöhnchen *n*; **2.** verzärteln.

molten ['moultən] geschmolzen.

moment ['moumənt] Augenblick *m*; Bedeutung *f*; = *momentum*; ~ary □ [~təri] augenblicklich; vorübergehend; ~ous [mou'mentəs] (ge)wichtig, bedeutend; ~um *phys.* [~təm] Moment *n*; Triebkraft *f*.

monarch ['mɔnək] Monarch(in); ~y [~ki] Monarchie *f*.

monastery ['mɔnəstəri] (Mönchs-) Kloster *n*.

Monday ['mʌndi] Montag *m*.

monetary ['mʌnitəri] Geld...

money ['mʌni] Geld *n*; *ready* ~ Bargeld *n*; ~-box Sparbüchse *f*; ~-changer [~tʃeindʒə] (Geld-) Wechsler *m*; ~-order Postanweisung *f*.

monger ['mʌŋgə] ...händler *m*, ...krämer *m*.

mongrel ['mʌŋgrəl] Mischling *m*, Bastard *m*; *attr.* Bastard...

monitor ['mɔnitə] ⊕ Monitor *m*; (Klassen)Ordner *m*.

monk [mʌŋk] Mönch *m*.

monkey ['mʌŋki] **1.** *zo.* Affe *m* (*a. fig.*); ⊕ Rammblock *m*; *put s.o.'s* ~ *up* F j-n auf die Palme bringen; ~ *business Am. sl.* fauler Zauber; **2.** F (herum)albern, ~ *with* herummurksen an (*dat.*); ~**wrench** ⊕ Engländer *m* (*Schraubenschlüssel*); *throw a* ~ *in s.th. Am. sl.* et. über den Haufen werfen.

monkish ['mʌŋkiʃ] mönchisch.

mono|... ['mɔnou] ein(fach)...; ~cle ['mɔnɔkl] Monokel *n*; ~gamy [mɔ-'nɔgəmi] Einehe *f*; ~logue ['mɔnəlɔg] Monolog *m*; ~polist [mə'nɔpəlist] Monopolist *m*; ~polize [~laiz] monopolisieren; *fig.* an sich reißen; ~poly [~li] Monopol *n* (*of auf acc.*); ~tonous □ [~'tɔnəs] monoton, eintönig; ~tony [~ni] Monotonie *f*.

monsoon [mɔn'suːn] Monsun m.

monster ['mɔnstə] Ungeheuer n (a. fig.); Monstrum n; attr. Riesen...

monstro|sity [mɔns'trɔsiti] Ungeheuer(lichkeit f) n; ~us □ ['mɔnstrəs] ungeheuer(lich); gräßlich.

month [mʌnθ] Monat m; this day ~ heute in e-m Monat; ~ly ['mʌnθli] 1. monatlich; Monats...; 2. Monatsschrift f.

monument ['mɔnjumənt] Denkmal n; ~al □ [mɔnju'mentl] monumental; Gedenk...; großartig.

mood [muːd] Stimmung f, Laune f; ~y □ ['muːdi] launisch; schwermütig; übellaunig.

moon [muːn] 1. Mond m; once in a blue ~ F alle Jubeljahre einmal; 2. mst ~ about F herumdösen; ~light ['muːnlait] Mondlicht n, -schein m; ~lit mondhell; ~struck mondsüchtig.

Moor[1] [muə] Maure m; Mohr m.

moor[2] [~] Ödland n, Heideland n.

moor[3] [~] (sich) vertäuen; ~ings [['muəriŋz] pl. Vertäuungen f/pl.

moose zo. [muːz] a. ~-deer amerikanischer Elch.

moot [muːt]: ~ point Streitpunkt m.

mop [mɔp] 1. Mop m; (Haar)Wust m; 2. auf-, abwischen.

mope [moup] den Kopf hängen lassen.

moral ['mɔrəl] 1. □ Moral...; moralisch; 2. Moral f; Nutzanwendung f; ~s pl. Sitten f/pl.; ~e [mɔ'rɑːl] bsd. ⚔ Moral f, Haltung f; ~ity [mə'ræliti] Moralität f; Sittlichkeit f, Moral f; ~ize ['mɔrəlaiz] moralisieren.

morass [mə'ræs] Morast m, Sumpf m.

morbid □ ['mɔːbid] krankhaft.

more [mɔː] mehr; once ~ noch einmal, wieder; so much od. all the ~ um so mehr; no ~ nicht mehr.

morel ♄ [mɔ'rel] Morchel f.

moreover [mɔː'rouvə] überdies, weiter, ferner.

morgue [mɔːg] Leichenschauhaus n; Archiv n.

moribund ['mɔribʌnd] im Sterben (liegend), dem Tode geweiht.

morning ['mɔːniŋ] Morgen m; Vormittag m; tomorrow ~ morgen früh; ~ dress Tagesgesellschaftsanzug m. [m) f.]

moron ['mɔːrɔn] Schwachsinnige(r]

morose □ [mə'rous] mürrisch.

morph|ia ['mɔːfjə], ~ine ['mɔːfiːn] Morphium n.

morsel ['mɔːsəl] Bissen m; Stückchen n, das bißchen.

mortal ['mɔːtl] 1. □ sterblich; tödlich; Tod(es)...; 2. Sterbliche(r m) f; ~ity [mɔː'tæliti] Sterblichkeit f.

mortar ['mɔːtə] Mörser m; Mörtel m.

mortgag|e ['mɔːgidʒ] 1. Pfandgut n; Hypothek f; 2. verpfänden; ~ee [mɔːgə'dʒiː] Hypothekengläubiger m; ~er ['mɔːgidʒə], ~or [mɔːgə'dʒɔː] Hypothekenschuldner m.

mortician Am. [mɔː'tiʃən] Leichenbestatter m.

morti|fication [mɔːtifi'keiʃən] Kasteiung f; Kränkung f; ~fy ['mɔːtifai] kasteien; kränken.

mortise ['mɔːtis], ~ce ⊕ ['mɔːtis] Zapfenloch n.

mortuary ['mɔːtjuəri] Leichenhalle f.

mosaic [mə'zeiik] Mosaik n.

mosque [mɔsk] Moschee f.

mosquito zo. [məs'kiːtou] Moskito m. [moosig.]

moss [mɔs] Moos n; ~y ['mɔsi]]

most [moust] 1. adj. □ meist; 2. adv. meist, am meisten; höchst; 3. das meiste; die meisten; Höchste(s) n; at (the) ~ höchstens; make the ~ of möglichst ausnutzen; ~ly ['moustli] meistens.

moth [mɔθ] Motte f; ~-eaten ['mɔθiːtn] mottenzerfressen.

mother ['mʌðə] 1. Mutter f; 2. bemuttern; ~ country Vaterland n; Mutterland n; ~hood [~hud] Mutterschaft f; ~-in-law [~rinlɔː] Schwiegermutter f; ~ly [~li] mütterlich; ~-of-pearl [~rəv'pəːl] Perlmutter f; ~-tongue Muttersprache f.

motif [mou'tiːf] (Leit)Motiv n.

motion ['mouʃən] 1. Bewegung f; Gang m (a. ⊕); parl. Antrag m; 2. v/t. durch Gebärden auffordern od. andeuten; v/i. winken; ~less [~nlis] bewegungslos; ~ picture Film m.

motivate ['moutiveit] motivieren, begründen.

motive ['moutiv] 1. bewegend; 2. Motiv n, Beweggrund m; 3. veranlassen; ~less [~vlis] grundlos.

motley ['mɔtli] (bunt)scheckig.

motor ['moutə] 1. Motor m; treibende Kraft; Automobil n; ⚓ Muskel m; 2. motorisch, bewegend; Motor...; Kraft...; Auto...; 3. (im) Auto fahren; ~-assisted [~ərə'sistid] mit Hilfsmotor; ~ bicycle, ~bike = motor cycle; ~ boat Motorboot n; ~ bus Autobus m; ~cade Am. [~keid] Autokolonne f; ~-car Auto(mobil) n; ~ coach Reisebus m; ~ cycle Motorrad n; ~ing [~əriŋ] Autofahren n; ~ist [~rist] Kraftfahrer(in); ~ize [~raiz] motorisieren; ~ launch Motorbarkasse f; ~-road, ~way Autobahn f.

mottled ['mɔtld] gefleckt.

mo(u)ld [mould] 1. Gartenerde f; Schimmel m, Moder m; (Guß)Form f (a. fig.); Abdruck m; Art f; 2. formen, gießen (on, upon nach).

mo(u)lder ['mouldə] zerfallen.

mo(u)lding △ ['mouldiŋ] Fries m.

mo(u)ldy ['mouldi] schimm(e)lig, dumpfig mod(e)rig.

mo(u)lt [moult] (*fig.* sich) mausern.

mound [maund] Erdhügel m, -wall m.

mount [maunt] 1. Berg m; Reitpferd n, 2. v/i. (empor)steigen; aufsteigen (*Reiter*); v/t. be-, ersteigen; beritten machen; montieren; aufziehen, aufkleben; *Edelstein* fassen.

mountain ['mauntin] 1. Berg m; ~s *pl.* Gebirge n; 2. Berg..., Gebirgs. ~eer [maunti'niə] Bergbewohner(in); Bergsteiger(in); ~ous ['mauntinəs] bergig, gebirgig.

mountebank ['mauntibæŋk]Marktschreier m, Scharlatan m.

mourn [mɔ:n] (be)trauern; ~er ['mɔ:nə] Leidtragende(r m) f; ~ful □ ['mɔ:nful] Trauer..., traurig; ~ing ['mɔ:niŋ] Trauer f; *attr.* Trauer [Maus f.\
mouse [maus], *pl.* mice [mais]

moustache [məs'ta:ʃ] Schnurrbart m.

mouth [mauθ], *pl.* ~s [mauðz]Mund m; Maul n; Mündung f; Öffnung f; ~ful ['mauθful] Mundvoll m; ~organ Mundharmonika f; ~piece Mundstück n; *fig.* Sprachrohr n.

move [mu:v] 1. v/t. *allg.* bewegen; in Bewegung setzen; (weg)rücken; (an)treiben, *Leidenschaft* erregen; *seelisch* rühren; beantragen; ~ heaven and earth Himmel und Hölle in Bewegung setzen; v/i. sich (fort)bewegen; sich rühren; *Schach:* ziehen, (um)ziehen (*Mieter*); ~ for s.th. et. beantragen; ~ in einziehen; ~ on weitergehen; ~ out ausziehen; 2. Bewegung f; *Schach:* Zug m; *fig.* Schritt m; on the ~ in Bewegung; make a ~ die Tafel aufheben; ~ment ['mu:vmənt] Bewegung f; ♩ Tempo n; ♩ Satz m; ⊕ (Geh-) Werk n.

movies F ['mu:viz] *pl.* Kino n.

moving ['mu:viŋ] bewegend; beweglich; ~ staircase Rolltreppe f.

mow [mou] [*irr.*] mähen; ~er ['mouə] Mäher(in); ~ing machine ['mouiŋməʃi:n] Mähmaschine f; ~n [moun] *p.p. von* mow.

much [mʌtʃ] 1. *adj.* viel; 2. *adv.* sehr; viel; bei weitem; fast; ~ as I would like so gern wie ich möchte; I thought as ~ das dachte ich mir; make ~ of viel Wesens machen von; I am not ~ of a dancer ich bin kein großer Tänzer.

muck [mʌk] Mist m (F *a. fig.*); ~rake ['mʌkreik] 1. Mistgabel f; ~ ~r; 2. im Schmutz wühlen; ~raker [~kə] *Am.* Korruptionsschnüffler m.

mucus ['mju:kəs] (Nasen)Schleim m.

mud [mʌd] Schlamm m; Kot m; ~dle ['mʌdl] 1. v/t. verwirren; a. ~ up, ~ together durcheinanderbringen; F benebeln; v/i. stümpern; ~ through F sich durchwursteln; 2. Wirrwarr m; F Wurstelei f; ~dy ['mʌdi] schlammig; trüb; ~guard Kotflügel m.

muff [mʌf] Muff m.

muffin ['mʌfin] Muffin n (*heißes Teegebäck*).

muffle ['mʌfl] oft ~ up ein-, umhüllen, umwickeln; *Stimme etc.* dämpfen; ~r [~lə] Halstuch n; Boxhandschuh m; *mot.* Auspufftopf m.

mug [mʌg] Krug m; Becher m.

muggy ['mʌgi] schwül.

mugwump *Am. iro.* ['mʌgwʌmp] großes Tier (*Person*); *pol.* Unabhängige(r) m.

mulatto [mju(:)'lætou] Mulatt|e m, -in f.

mulberry ['mʌlbəri] Maulbeere f.

mule [mju:l] Maultier n, -esel m; störrischer Mensch; ~teer [mju:li-'tiə] Maultiertreiber m.

mull¹ [mʌl] Mull m.

mull² [~]: ~ over überdenken.

mulled [mʌld]: ~ wine Glühwein m.

mulligan *Am.* F ['mʌligən] Eintopf m aus Resten.

mullion ['mʌliən] Fensterpfosten m.

multi|farious □ [mʌlti'fɛəriəs] mannigfaltig; ~form ['mʌltifɔ:m] vielförmig; ~ple [~ipl] 1. vielfach; 2. Vielfache(s) n; ~plication [mʌlti-tipli'keiʃən] Vervielfältigung f, Vermehrung f; Multiplikation f; *compound (simple)* ~ Großes (Kleines) Einmaleins; ~ table Einmaleins n; ~plicity [~i'plisiti] Vielfalt f; ~ply ['mʌltiplai] (sich) vervielfältigen; multiplizieren; ~tude [~itju:d] Vielheit f, Menge f; ~tudinous [mʌlti-'tju:dinəs] zahlreich.

mum [mʌm] still.

mumble ['mʌmbl] murmeln, nuscheln; mummeln (*mühsam essen*).

mummery *contp.* ['mʌməri] Mummenschanz m.

mummify ['mʌmifai] mumifizieren.

mummy¹ ['mʌmi] Mumie f.

mummy² F [~] Mami f, Mutti f.

mumps ⚕ [mʌmps] *sg.* Ziegenpeter m, Mumps m.

munch [mʌntʃ] mit vollen Backen (fr)essen, mampfen.

mundane □ ['mʌndein] weltlich.

municipal □ [mju(:)'nisipəl] städtisch, Gemeinde..., Stadt...; ~ity [mju(:)nisi'pæliti] Stadtbezirk m; Stadtverwaltung f.

munificen|ce [mju(:)'nifisns] Freigebigkeit f; ~t [~nt] freigebig.

munitions [mju(:)'niʃənz] *pl.* Munition f.

mural ['mjuərəl] Mauer...

murder ['mə:də] 1. Mord m; 2. (er-)

morden; *fig.* verhunzen; ~er [~ərə]
Mörder *m*; ~ess [~ris] Mörderin *f*;
~ous] [~rəs] mörderisch.

murky] ['mə:ki] dunkel, finster.

murmur ['mə:mə] 1. Gemurmel *n*;
Murren *n*; 2. murmeln; murren.

murrain ['mʌrin] Viehseuche *f*.

musc|le ['mʌsl] 1. Muskel *m*; 2. ~ *in*
Am. sl. sich rücksichtslos eindrän-
gen; ~le-bound mit Muskelkater;
be ~ Muskelkater haben; ~ular
['mʌskjulə] Muskel. .; muskulös.

Muse¹ [mju:z] Muse *f*.

muse² [~] (nach)sinnen, grübeln.

museum [mju(:)'ziəm] Museum *n*.

mush [mʌʃ] Brei *m*, Mus *n*; *Am.*
Polenta *f*, Maisbrei *m*.

mushroom ['mʌʃrum] 1. Pilz *m*,
bsd. Champignon *m*; 2. rasch wachsen; ~ *up* in die Höhe schießen.

music ['mju:zik] Musik *f*; Musik-
stück *n*; Noten *f/pl.*; *set to* ~ ver-
tonen; ~al [.kəl] musikalisch;
Musik. .; wohlklingend; ~ *box*
Spieldose *f*; ~ box 4*m.* Spieldose *f*;
~hall Varieté(theater) *n*; ~ian
[mju(:)'ziʃən] Musiker(in); ~stand
Notenständer *m*; ~stool Klavier-
stuhl *m*.

musk [mʌsk] Moschus *m*, Bisam *m*;
~deer *zo.* ['mʌsk'diə] Moschus-
tier *n*.

musket ['mʌskit] Muskete *f*.

musk-rat *zo.* ['mʌskræt] Bisamratte *f*.

muslin ['mʌzlin] Musselin *m*.

musquash ['mʌskwɔʃ] Bisamratte *f*;
Bisampelz *m*.

muss *bsd. Am.* F [mʌs] Durcheinander *n*.

mussel ['mʌsl] (Mies)Muschel *f*.

must¹ [mʌst] 1. muß(te); darf;
durfte; *I* ~ *not* ich darf nicht; 2.
Muß *n*.

must² [~] Schimmel *m*, Moder *m*.

must³ [~] Most *m*.

mustach|e *Am.* [məs'tæʃ], ~io *Am.*
[məs'tɑ:ʃou] = moustache.

mustard ['mʌstəd] Senf *m*.

muster ['mʌstə] 1. ⚔ Musterung *f*;
fig. Heerschau *f*; 2. ⚔ mustern;
aufbieten, aufbringen.

musty ['mʌsti] mod(e)rig, muffig.

muta|ble] ['mju:təbl] veränder-
lich; wankelmütig; ~tion [mju(:)-
'teiʃən] Veränderung *f*.

mute [mju:t] 1.] stumm; 2. Stum-
me(r *m*) *f*; Statist(in); 3. dämpfen.

mutilate ['mju:tileit] verstümmeln.

mutin|eer [mju:ti'niə] Meuterer *m*;
~ous] ['mju:tinəs] meuterisch;
~y [~ni] 1. Meuterei *f*; 2. meu-
tern.

mutter ['mʌtə] 1. Gemurmel *n*;
Gemurre *n*; 2. murmeln; murren.

mutton ['mʌtn] Hammelfleisch *n*;
leg of ~ Hammelkeule *f*; ~ *chop*
Hammelkotelett *n*.

mutual] ['mju:tjuəl] gegenseitig;
gemeinsam.

muzzle ['mʌzl] 1. Maul *n*, Schnauze
f; Mündung *f* e-r *Feuerwaffe*;
Maulkorb *m*; 2. e-n Maulkorb anlegen (*dat.*); *fig.* den Mund stopfen
(*dat.*).

my [mai] mein(e).

myrrh ⚕ [mə:] Myrrhe *f*.

myrtle ⚕ [mə:tl] Myrte *f*.

myself [mai'self] (ich) selbst; mir;
mich; *by* ~ allein.

myster|ious] [mis'tiəriəs] ge-
heimnisvoll, mysteriös; ~y ['mistəri]
Mysterium *n*; Geheimnis *n*; Rätsel
n.

mysti|c ['mistik] 1. *a.* ~cal □
[~kəl] mystisch, geheimnisvoll; 2.
Mystiker *m*; ~fy [~ifai] mystifizie-
ren, täuschen.

myth [miθ] Mythe *f*, Mythos *m*,
Sage *f*.

N

nab *sl.* [næb] schnappen, erwischen.

nacre ['neikə] Perlmutter *f*.

nadir ['neidiə] *ast.* Nadir *m* (*Fuß-
punkt*); *fig.* tiefster Stand.

nag [næg] 1. F Klepper *m*; 2. *v/i.*
nörgeln, quengeln; *v/t.* bekritteln.

nail [neil] 1. (Finger-, Zehen)Nagel
m; ⊕ Nagel *m*; *zo.* Kralle *f*, Klaue
f; 2. (an-, fest)nageln; *Augen etc.*
heften (*to auf acc.*); ~scissors
['neilsizəz] *pl.* Nagelschere *f*; ~
varnish Nagellack *m*.

naïve] [nɑ:'i:v], **naive** □ [neiv]
naiv; ungekünstelt.

naked □ ['neikid] nackt, bloß; kahl;
fig. unverhüllt; *poet.* schutzlos;

~ness [~dnis] Nacktheit *f*, Blöße *f*;
Kahlheit *f*; Schutzlosigkeit *f*; *fig.*
Unverhülltheit *f*.

name [neim] 1. Name *m*; Ruf *m*;
of od. by the ~ *of* ... namens ...;
call s.o. ~s j-n beschimpfen; 2. (be-)
nennen; erwähnen; ernennen; ~
less] ['neimlis] namenlos; unbekannt; ~ly [~li] nämlich; ~plate
Namens-, Tür-, Firmenschild *n*;
~sake ['neimseik] Namensvetter *m*.

nanny ['næni] Kindermädchen *n*;
~goat Ziege *f*.

nap [næp] 1. *Tuch-*Noppe *f*; Schläfchen *n*; *have od. take a* ~ ein
Nickerchen machen; 2. schlummern.

nape [neip] *mst* ~ *of the neck* Genick *n*

nap|kin ['næpkin] Serviette *f*; Windel *f*; *mst sanitary* ~ *Am.* Monatsbinde *f*; **~py** F ['næpi] Windel *f*.

narcosis [nɑː'kousis] Narkose *f*.

narcotic [nɑː'kɔtik] **1.** (*~ally*) narkotisch; **2.** Betäubungsmittel *n*.

narrat|e [næ'reit] erzählen; **~ion** [~'eiʃən] Erzählung *f*; **~ive** ['nærətiv] **1.** erzählend; **2.** Erzählung *f*; **~or** [næ'reitə] Erzähler *m*.

narrow ['nærou] **1.** eng; schmal; beschränkt; knapp (*Mehrheit, Entkommen*); engherzig; **2.** ~s *pl.* Engpaß *m*; Meerenge *f*; **3.** (sich) verengen; beschränken; einengen; *Maschen* abnehmen; **~chested** schmalbrüstig, **~minded** ☐ engherzig; **~ness** [~ounis] Enge *f*; Beschränktheit *f* (*a. fig.*); Engherzigkeit *f*.

nary *Am.* F ['nɛəri] kein.

nasal ⸢ ['neizəl] nasal; Nasen...

nasty ['nɑːsti] schmutzig; garstig; eklig, widerlich; häßlich; unflätig; ungemütlich

natal ['neitl] Geburts...

nation ['neiʃən] Nation *f*, Volk *n*.

national ['næʃənl] **1.** ☐ national; Volks..., Staats...; **2.** Staatsangehörige(r *m*) *f*; **~ity** [næʃə'næliti] Nationalität *f*; **~ize** ['næʃnəlaiz] naturalisieren, einbürgern; verstaatlichen

nation-wide ['neiʃənwaid] die ganze Nation umfassend.

native ['neitiv] **1.** ☐ angeboren; heimatlich, Heimat...; eingeboren; einheimisch; ~ *language* Muttersprache *f*; **2.** Eingeborene(r *m*) *f*; **~born** (im Lande) geboren, einheimisch

nativity [nə'tiviti] Geburt *f*.

natter F ['nætə] plaudern.

natural ⸢ ['nætʃrəl] natürlich; *engS.* angeboren; ungezwungen; unehelich (*Kind*); ~ *science* Naturwissenschaft *f*; **~ist** [~list] Naturalist *m*; Naturforscher *m*; Tierhändler *m*; **~ize** [~laiz] einbürgern; **~ness** [~lnis] Natürlichkeit *f*.

nature ['neitʃə] Natur *f*.

naught [nɔːt] Null *f*; set *at* ~ für nichts achten; **~y** ☐ ['nɔːti] unartig.

nause|a ['nɔːsjə] Übelkeit *f*; Ekel *m*; **~ate** ['nɔːsieit] *v/i.* Ekel empfinden; *v/t.* verabscheuen; *be* ~*d* sich ekeln; **~ous** ⸢ ['nɔːsjəs] ekelhaft.

nautical ['nɔːtikəl] nautisch; See...

naval ⚓ ['neivəl] See..., Marine...; ~ *base* Flottenstützpunkt *m*.

nave¹ ⸢ [neiv] (Kirchen)Schiff *n*.

nave² [~] *Rad*-Nabe *f*.

navel ['neivəl] Nabel *m*; Mitte *f*.

naviga|ble ⸢ ['nævigəbl] schiffbar; fahrbar; lenkbar; **~te** [~'geit] *v/i.* schiffen, fahren; *v/t. See etc.* befahren; steuern; **~tion** [nævi'geiʃən]

Schiffahrt *f*; Navigation *f*; **~tor** ['nævigeitə] Seefahrer *m*.

navy ['neivi] (Kriegs)Marine *f*.

nay † [nei] nein; nein vielmehr.

near [niə] **1.** *adj.* nahe; gerade (*Weg*); nahe verwandt; verwandt; vertraut; genau; knapp; knauserig; ~ *at hand* dicht dabei; **2.** *adv.* nahe; **3.** *prp.* nahe (*dat.*), nahe bei *od.* an; **4.** sich nähern (*dat.*); **~by** ['niəbai] in der Nähe (gelegen); nah; **~ly** ['niəli] nahe; fast, beinahe; genau; **~ness** ['niənis] Nähe *f*; **~sighted** kurzsichtig.

neat ☐ [niːt] nett; niedlich; geschickt; ordentlich; sauber; rein; **~ness** ['niːtnis] Nettigkeit *f*; Sauberkeit *f*; Zierlichkeit *f*.

nebulous ☐ ['nebjuləs] neblig.

necess|ary ☐ ['nesisəri] **1.** notwendig; unvermeidlich; **2.** *mst necessaries pl.* Bedürfnisse *n/pl.*; **~itate** [ni'sesiteit] *et.* erfordern; zwingen; **~ity** [~ti] Notwendigkeit *f*; Zwang *m*; Not *f*.

neck [nek] **1.** (*a. Flaschen*)Hals *m*; Nacken *m*; Genick *n*; Ausschnitt *m* (*Kleid*); ~ *and* ~ Kopf an Kopf; ~ *or nothing* F alles oder nichts; **2.** *sl.* sich abknutschen; **~band** ['nekbænd] Halsbund *m*; **~erchief** ['nekətʃif] Halstuch *n*; **~lace** ['neklis], **~let** [~lit] Halskette *f*; **~tie** Krawatte *f*.

necromancy ['nekroumænsi] Zauberei *f*.

née [nei] *bei Frauennamen:* geborene.

need [niːd] **1.** Not *f*; Notwendigkeit *f*; Bedürfnis *n*; Mangel *m*, Bedarf *m*; *be od.* stand in ~ *of* brauchen; **2.** nötig haben, brauchen; bedürfen (*gen.*); müssen; **~ful** ['niːdful] notwendig.

needle ['niːdl] **1.** Nadel *f*; Zeiger *m*; **2.** nähen; *bsd. Am.* irritieren; anstacheln.

needless ☐ ['niːdlis] unnötig.

needle|woman ['niːdlwumən] Näherin *f*; **~work** Handarbeit *f*.

needy ☐ ['niːdi] bedürftig, arm.

nefarious ☐ [ni'fɛəriəs] schändlich.

negat|e [ni'geit] verneinen; **~ion** [~'eiʃən] Verneinung *f*; Nichts *n*; **~ive** ['negətiv] **1.** ☐ negativ; verneinend; **2.** Verneinung *f*; *phot.* Negativ *n*; **3.** ablehnen.

neglect [ni'glekt] **1.** Vernachlässigung *f*; Nachlässigkeit *f*; **2.** vernachlässigen; **~ful** ☐ [~tful] nachlässig.

negligen|ce ['neglidʒəns] Nachlässigkeit *f*; **~t** ☐ [~nt] nachlässig.

negligible ['neglidʒəbl] nebensächlich; unbedeutend.

negotia|te [ni'gouʃieit] verhandeln (über *acc.*); zustande bringen; bewältigen; *Wechsel* begeben; **~tion** [nigouʃi'eiʃən] Begebung *f e-s Wechsels etc.*; Ver-, Unterhandlung *f*; Bewältigung *f*; **~tor** [ni'gouʃieitə] Unterhändler *m*.

negr|ess ['ni:gris] Negerin *f*; **~o** [~rou], *pl* **~oes** Neger *m*.

neigh [nei] 1. Wiehern *n*; 2. wiehern.

neighbo(u)r ['neibə] Nachbar(in); Nächste(r *m*) *f*; **~hood** [~hud] Nachbarschaft *f*; **~ing** [~riŋ] benachbart; **~ly** [~əli] nachbarlich, freundlich; **~ship** [~əʃip] Nachbarschaft *f*.

neither ['naiðə] 1. keiner (von beiden); 2. **~ ... nor** weder ... noch ...; not ... **~** auch nicht.

nephew ['nevju(:)] Neffe *m*.

nerve [nə:v] 1. Nerv *m*; Sehne *f*; *Blatt*-Rippe *f*; Kraft *f*, Mut *m*; Dreistigkeit *f*, get on one's **~s** e-m auf die Nerven gehen; 2. kräftigen; ermutigen; **~less** [~'nə:vlis] kraftlos.

nervous □ ['nə:vəs] Nerven...; nervig, kräftig; nervös; **~ness** [~snis] Nervigkeit *f*; Nervosität *f*.

nest [nest] 1. Nest *n* (*a. fig.*); 2. nisten; **~le** ['nesl] *v/i*. (sich ein-) nisten; sich (an)schmiegen; *v/t.* schmiegen.

net¹ [net] 1. Netz *n*; 2. mit e-m Netz fangen *od.* umgeben.

net² [~] 1. netto; Rein...; 2. netto einbringen.

nether ['neðə] nieder; Unter...

nettle ['netl] 1. ♀ Nessel *f*; 2. ärgern.

network ['netwə:k] (Straßen-, Kanal- *etc.*)Netz *n*; Sendergruppe *f*.

neurosis ♂ [njuə'rousis] Neurose *f*.

neuter ['nju:tə] 1. geschlechtslos; 2. geschlechtsloses Tier; *gr.* Neutrum *n*.

neutral ['nju:trəl] 1. neutral; unparteiisch; 2. Neutrale(r *m*) *f*; Null(punkt *m*) *f*; Leerlauf(stellung *f*) *m*; **~ity** [nju(:)'træliti] Neutralität *f*; **~ize** ['nju:trəlaiz] neutralisieren.

neutron *phys.* ['nju:trɔn] Neutron *n*.

never ['nevə] nie(mals); gar nicht; **~more** [~'mɔ:] nie wieder; **~theless** [nevəðə'les] nichtsdestoweniger.

new [nju:] neu; frisch; unerfahren; **~comer** ['nju:kʌmə] Ankömmling *m*; **~ly** ['nju:li] neulich; neu.

news [nju:z] *mst sg.* Neuigkeit(en *pl.*) *f*, Nachricht(en *pl*) *f*; **~agent** ['nju:zeidʒənt] Zeitungshändler *m*; **~boy** Zeitungsausträger *m*; **~butcher** *Am. sl* Zeitungsverkäufer *m*; **~cast** *Radio* Nachrichten *f/pl.*; **~monger** Neuigkeitskrämer *m*; **~paper** Zeitung *f*; *attr.* Zeitungs...; **~print** Zeitungspapier *n*; **~reel** *Film* Wochenschau *f*; **~room** Leszimmer *n*; *Am. Zeitung*: Nachrichtenredaktion *f*; **~stall**, *Am.* **~stand** Zeitungskiosk *m*.

new year ['nju:'jə:] *das* neue Jahr; *New Year's Day* Neujahr(stag *m*) *n*; *New Year's Eve* Silvester *m*.

next [nekst] 1. *adj.* nächst; **~ but one** *der* übernächste; **~ door to fig.* beinahe; *to* **~** (*dat.*); 2. *adv.* zunächst, gleich darauf; nächstens.

nibble ['nibl] *v/t.* knabbern an (*dat.*); *v/i.* **~ at** nagen *od.* knabbern an (*dat.*); (*herum*)kritteln an (*dat.*).

nice [nais] fein; wählerisch; peinlich (*genau*); heikel; nett; niedlich; hübsch; **~ly** ['naisli] *F* (*sehr*) gut; **~ty** ['naisiti] Feinheit *f*; Genauigkeit *f*; Spitzfindigkeit *f*.

niche [nitʃ] Nische *f*.

nick [nik] 1. Kerbe *f*; *in the* **~** *of time* gerade zur rechten Zeit; 2. (ein)kerben; *sl. j-n* schnappen.

nickel ['nikl] 1. *min.* Nickel *m* (*Am. a. Fünfcentstück*); 2. vernickeln.

nick-nack ['niknæk] = *knick-knack*.

nickname ['nikneim] 1. Spitzname *m*; 2. e-n Spitznamen geben (*dat.*).

niece [ni:s] Nichte *f*.

nifty *Am. sl.* ['nifti] elegant; stinkend.

niggard ['nigəd] Geizhals *m*; **~ly** [~dli] geizig, knauserig; karg.

nigger *F mst contp* ['nigə] Nigger *m* (*Neger*); **~ in the woodpile** *Am. sl.* *der* Haken an der Sache.

night [nait] Nacht *f*; Abend *m*; *by* **~**, *in the* **~**, *at* **~** nachts; **~cap** ['naitkæp] Nachtmütze *f*; Nachttrunk *m*; **~club** Nachtlokal *n*; **~dress** (*Damen*)Nachthemd *n*; **~fall** Einbruch *m der* Nacht; **~gown** = *night-dress*; **~ingale** *orn.* [~naitiŋgeil] Nachtigall *f*; **~ly** ['naitli] nächtlich; jede Nacht; **~mare** Alptraum *m*; **~shirt** (*Herren*)Nachthemd *n*; **~spot** *Am.* Nachtlokal *n*; **~y** ['naiti] *F* (*Damen-od.Kinder*)Nachthemd *n*.

nil [nil] *bsd. Sport* nichts, null.

nimble ['nimbl] flink, behend.

nimbus ['nimbəs] Nimbus *m*, Heiligenschein *m*; Regenwolke *f*.

nine [nain] 1. neun; 2. Neun *f*; **~pins** ['nainpinz] *pl.* Kegel(spiel *n*) *m/pl.*; **~teen** ['nain'ti:n] neunzehn; **~ty** ['nainti] neunzig.

ninny *F* ['nini] Dummkopf *m*.

ninth [nainθ] 1. neunte(r, -s); 2. Neuntel *n*; **~ly** ['nainθli] neuntens.

nip [nip] 1. Kniff *m*; scharfer Frost; Schlückchen *n*; 2. zwicken; schneiden (*Kälte*); *sl.* flitzen; nippen; **~ in the bud** im Keime ersticken.

nipper ['nipə] Krebsschere *f*; (*a pair of*) **~s** *pl.* (eine) (Kneif)Zange.

nipple ['nipl] Brustwarze *f*.

Nisei *Am.* ['ni:'sei] (*a. pl.*) Japaner *m, geboren in den USA*.

nit|re, *Am.* **~er** ♂ ['naitə] Salpeter *m*.

nitrogen ['naitridʒən] Stickstoff *m*.

no [nou] 1. *adj.* kein; *in ~ time* im Nu; *~ one* keiner; 2. *adv.* nein; nicht; 3. Nein *n*.

nobility [nou'biliti] Adel *m* (*a. fig.*).

noble ['noubl] 1. ‖ adlig; edel, vornehm; vortrefflich; 2. Adlige(r *m*) *f*; *~man* Adlige(r) *m*; *~minded* edelmütig; *~ness* [ʌlnis] Adel *m*; Würde *f*.

nobody ['noubədi] niemand.

nocturnal [nɔk'tə:nl] Nacht...

nod [nɔd] 1. nicken; schlafen; (sich) neigen; *~ding acquaintance* oberflächliche Bekanntschaft; 2. Nicken *n*; Wink *m*.

node [noud] Knoten *m* (*a. & u. ast.*); ✳ Überbein *n*.

noise [nɔiz] 1. Lärm *m*; Geräusch *n*; Geschrei *n*; *big ~ bsd. Am.* F großes Tier (*Person*); 2. *~ abroad* ausschreien; *~less* □ ['nɔizlis] geräuschlos.

noisome ['nɔisəm] schädlich; widerlich.

noisy □ ['nɔizi] geräuschvoll, lärmend; aufdringlich (*Farbe*).

nomin|al ‖ ['nɔminl] nominell; (nur) dem Namen nach (vorhanden); namentlich; *~ value* Nennwert *m*; *~ate* [ʌneit] ernennen; zur Wahl vorschlagen; *~ation* [nɔmi'neiʃən] Ernennung *f*; Vorschlagsrecht *n*.

nominative ['nɔminətiv] *a. ~ case* gr. Nominativ *m*.

non [nɔn] *in Zssgn:* nicht, un..., Nicht...

nonage ['nounidʒ] Minderjährigkeit *f*.

non-alcoholic ['nɔnælkə'hɔlik] alkoholfrei.

nonce [nɔns]: *for the ~* nur für diesen Fall.

non-commissioned ['nɔnkə'miʃənd] nicht bevollmächtigt; *~ officer* ✕ Unteroffizier *m*.

non-committal ['nɔnkə'mitl] unverbindlich.

non-compliance ['nɔnkəm'plaiəns] Zuwiderhandlung *f*, Verstoß *m*.

non-conductor ⚡ ['nɔnkəndʌktə] Nichtleiter *m*.

nonconformist ['nɔnkən'fɔ:mist] Dissident(in), Freikirchler(in).

nondescript ['nɔndiskript] unbestimmbar; schwer zu beschreiben(d).

none [nʌn] 1. keine(r, -s); nichts; 2. keineswegs, gar nicht; *~ the less* nichtsdestoweniger.

nonentity [nɔ'nentiti] Nichtsein *n*; Unding *n*; Nichts *n*; *fig.* Null *f*.

non-existence ['nɔnig'zistəns] Nicht(da)sein *n*.

non-fiction ['nɔn'fikʃən] Sachbücher *n/pl.*

nonpareil ['nɔnpərəl] Unvergleichliche(r *m*, -s *n*) *f*.

non-party ['nɔn'pɑ:ti] parteilos.

non-performance ⚖ ['nɔnpə-'fɔ:məns] Nichterfüllung *f*.

nonplus ['nɔn'plʌs] 1. Verlegenheit *f*; 2. in Verlegenheit bringen.

non-resident ['nɔn'rezidənt] nicht im Haus *od.* am Ort wohnend.

nonsens|e ['nɔnsəns] Unsinn *m*; *~ical* □ [nɔn'sensikəl] unsinnig.

non-skid ['nɔn'skid] rutschfest.

non-smoker ['nɔn'smoukə] Nichtraucher *m*.

non-stop ⊙, ✈ ['nɔn'stɔp] durchgehend; Ohnehalt...

non-union ['nɔn'ju:njən] nicht organisiert (*Arbeiter*).

non-violence ['nɔn'vaiələns] (Politik *f* der) Gewaltlosigkeit *f*.

noodle ['nu:dl] Nudel *f*.

nook [nuk] Ecke *f*, Winkel *m*.

noon [nu:n] Mittag *m*; *attr.* Mittags...; *~day* ['nu:ndei], *~tide*, *~time* = *noon*.

noose [nu:s] 1. Schlinge *f*; 2. (mit der Schlinge) fangen; schlingen.

nope *Am.* F [noup] nein.

nor [nɔ:] noch; auch nicht.

norm [nɔ:m] Norm *f*, Regel *f*; Muster *n*; Maßstab *m*; *~al* □ ['nɔ:məl] normal; *~alize* [ʌlaiz] normalisieren; normen.

north [nɔ:θ] 1. Nord(en *m*); 2. nördlich; Nord...; *~east* ['nɔ:r'i:st] 1. Nordost *m*; 2. *a. ~eastern* [ʌtən] nordöstlich; *~erly* ['nɔ:ðəli], *~ern* [ʌən] nördlich; Nord..; *~erner* [ʌnə] Nordländer(in); *Am.* Nordstaatler(in); *~ward(s)* ['nɔ:θwəd(z)] *adv.* nördlich; nordwärts; *~west* ['nɔ:'west] 1. Nordwest *m*; 2. *a. ~western* [ʌtən] nordwestlich.

Norwegian [nɔ:'wi:dʒən] 1. norwegisch; 2. Norweger(in); Norwegisch *n*.

nose [nouz] 1. Nase *f*; Spitze *f*; Schnauze *f*; 2. *v/t.* riechen; *~ one's way* vorsichtig fahren; *v/i* schnüffeln; *~dive* ✈ ['nouzdaiv] Sturzflug *m*; *~gay* ['nouzgei] Blumenstrauß *m*.

nostalgia [nɔs'tældʒiə] Heimweh *n*, Sehnsucht *f*.

nostril ['nɔstril] Nasenloch *n*, Nüster *f*.

nostrum ['nɔstrəm] Geheimmittel *n*; Patentlösung *f*.

nosy F ['nouzi] neugierig.

not [nɔt] nicht.

notable ['noutəbl] 1. □ bemerkenswert; 2. angesehene Person.

notary ['noutəri] *oft ~ public* Notar *m*. [*f.*\]

notation [nou'teiʃən] Bezeichnung‿

notch [nɔtʃ] 1. Kerbe *f*, Einschnitt *m*; Scharte *f*; *Am.* Engpaß *m*, Hohlweg *m*; 2. einkerben.

note [nout] 1. Zeichen *n*; Notiz *f*; Anmerkung *f*; Briefchen *n*; (*bsd.* Schuld)Schein *m*; Note *f*; Ton *m*; Ruf *m*; Beachtung *f*; *take ~s* sich

Notizen machen; 2. be(ob)achten; besonders erwähnen; a. ~ down notieren; mit Anmerkungen versehen; ~book ['noutbuk] Notizbuch n; ~d bekannt; berüchtigt; ~paper Briefpapier n; ~worthy beachtenswert.

nothing ['nʌθiŋ] 1. nichts; 2. Nichts n; Null f; for ~ umsonst; good for ~ untauglich; bring (come) to ~ zunichte machen (werden).

notice ['noutis] 1. Notiz f; Nachricht f, Bekanntmachung f; Kündigung f; Warnung f; Beachtung f; at short ~ kurzfristig; give ~ that bekanntgeben, daß; give a week's ~ acht Tage vorher kündigen; take ~ of Notiz nehmen von; without ~ fristlos; 2. bemerken; be(ob)achten; ~able [~~~əbl] wahrnehmbar; bemerkenswert.

noti|fication [noutifi'keiʃən] Anzeige f; Meldung f; Bekanntmachung f; ~fy ['noutifai] et. anzeigen, melden; bekanntmachen.

notion ['nouʃən] Begriff m, Vorstellung f; Absicht f; ~s pl. Am. Kurzwaren f/pl.

notorious [nou'tɔːriəs] all-, weltbekannt; notorisch; berüchtigt.

notwithstanding prp. [nɔtwiθ-'stændiŋ] ungeachtet, trotz (gen.).

nought [nɔːt] Null f, Nichts n.

noun gr. [naun] Hauptwort n.

nourish ['nʌriʃ] (er)nähren; fig. hegen; ~ing [~iŋ] nahrhaft; ~ment [~mənt] Nahrung(smittel n) f.

novel ['nɔvəl] 1. neu; ungewöhnlich; 2. Roman m; ~ist [~list] Romanschriftsteller(in), Romancier m; ~ty [~lti] Neuheit f.

November [nou'vembə] November m.

novice ['nɔvis] Neuling m; eccl. Novize m, f.

now [nau] 1. nun, jetzt; eben; just ~ soeben; ~ and again od. then dann u. wann; 2. cj. a. ~ that nun da.

nowadays ['nauədeiz] heutzutage.

nowhere ['nouwɛə] nirgends.

noxious ['nɔkʃəs] schädlich.

nozzle ['nɔzl] ⊕ Düse f; Tülle f.

nuance [nju(ː)'ãːns] Nuance f, Schattierung f.

nub [nʌb] Knubbe(n m) f; Am. F springender Punkt in e-r Sache.

nucle|ar ['njuːkliə] Kern...; ~ reactor Kernreaktor m; ~ research (Atom-)Kernforschung f; ~us [~iəs] Kern m.

nude [njuːd] 1. nackt; 2. paint. Akt m.

nudge F [nʌdʒ] 1. j-n heimlich anstoßen; 2. Rippenstoß m.

nugget ['nʌgit] (bsd. Gold)Klumpen m.

nuisance ['njuːsns] Mißstand m;

Ärgernis n; Unfug m; fig. Plage f; what a ~! wie ärgerlich!; make o.s. od. be a ~ lästig fallen.

null [nʌl] nichtig; nichtssagend; ~ and void null u. nichtig; ~ify ['nʌlifai] zunichte machen; aufheben, ungültig machen; ~ity [~iti] Nichtigkeit f, Ungültigkeit f.

numb [nʌm] 1. starr; taub (empfindungslos); 2. starr od. taub machen; ~ed erstarrt.

number ['nʌmbə] 1. Nummer f; (An)Zahl f; Heft n, Lieferung f, Nummer f e-s Werkes; without ~ zahllos; in ~ an der Zahl; 2. zählen; numerieren; ~less [~əlis] zahllos; ~plate mot. Nummernschild n.

numera|l ['njuːmərəl] 1. Zahl...; 2. Ziffer f; ~tion [njuːməˈreiʃən] Zählung f; Numerierung f.

numerical □ [njuˈ(ː)merikəl] zahlenmäßig; Zahl...

numerous □ ['njuːmərəs] zahlreich.

numskull F ['nʌmskʌl] Dummkopf m.

nun [nʌn] Nonne f; orn. Blaumeise f.

nunnery ['nʌnəri] Nonnenkloster n.

nuptial ['nʌpʃəl] 1. Hochzeits..., Ehe...; 2. ~s pl. Hochzeit f.

nurse [nəːs] 1. Kindermädchen n, Säuglingsschwester f; a. wet-Amme f; (Kranken)Pflegerin f, (Kranken)Schwester f; at ~ in Pflege; put out to ~ in Pflege geben; 2. stillen, nähren; großziehen; pflegen; hätscheln; ~ling ['nəːsliŋ] Säugling m; Pflegling m; ~maid ['nəːsmeid] Kindermädchen n; ~ry ['nəːsri] Kinderzimmer n; ♪ Pflanzschule f; ~ rhymes pl. Kinderlieder n/pl., -reime m/pl.; ~ school Kindergarten m; ~ slopes pl. Ski: Idiotenhügel m/pl.

nursing ['nəːsiŋ] Stillen n; (Kranken)Pflege f; ~ bottle Saugflasche f; ~ home Privatklinik f.

nursling ['nəːsliŋ] = nurseling.

nurture ['nəːtʃə] 1. Pflege f; Erziehung f; 2. aufziehen; nähren.

nut [nʌt] Nuß f; ⊕ (Schrauben-) Mutter f; sl. verrückter Kerl; ~s pl. Nußkohle f; ~cracker ['nʌtkrækə] Nußknacker m; ~meg ['nʌtmeg] Muskatnuß f.

nutriment ['njuːtrimənt] Nahrung f.

nutri|tion [njuˈ(ː)triʃən] Ernährung f; Nahrung f; ~tious [~əs], ~tive □ ['njuːtritiv] nahrhaft; Ernährungs...

nut|shell ['nʌtʃel] Nußschale f; in a ~ in aller Kürze; ~ty ['nʌti] nußreich; nußartig; sl. verrückt.

nylon ['nailən] Nylon n; ~s pl. Nylonstrümpfe m/pl.

nymph [nimf] Nymphe f.

O

o [ou] **1.** oh!; ach!; **2.** (in Telefonnummern) Null f.

oaf [ouf] Dummkopf m; Tölpel m.

oak [ouk] Eiche f.

oar [ɔ:] **1.** Ruder n; **2.** rudern; **~sman** ['ɔ:zmən] Ruderer m.

oas|is [ou'eisis], pl. **~es** [ou'eisi:z] Oase f (a. fig.).

oat [out] mst **~s** pl. Hafer m; feel one's **~s** Am. F groß in Form sein; sich wichtig vorkommen; sow one's wild **~s** sich austoben.

oath [ouθ], pl. **~s** [ouðz] Eid m; Schwur m; Fluch m; take (make, swear) an **~** e-n Eid leisten, schwören.

oatmeal ['outmi:l] Haferflocken f/pl.

obdurate □ ['ɔbdjurit] verstockt.

obedien|ce [ə'bi:djəns] Gehorsam m; **~t** □ [**~**nt] gehorsam.

obeisance [ou'beisəns] Ehrerbietung f; Verbeugung f; do **~** huldigen.

obesity [ou'bi:siti] Fettleibigkeit f.

obey [ə'bei] gehorchen (dat.); Befehl etc. befolgen, Folge leisten (dat.).

obituary [ə'bitjuəri] Totenliste f; Todesanzeige f; Nachruf m; attr. Todes...; Toten...

object 1. ['ɔbdʒikt] Gegenstand m; Ziel n, fig. Zweck m; Objekt n (a. gr.); **2.** [əb'dʒekt] v/t. einwenden (to gegen); v/i. et. dagegen haben (to ger. daß).

objection [əb'dʒekʃən] Einwand m; **~able** □ [**~**nəbl] nicht einwandfrei; unangenehm.

objective [əb'dʒektiv] **1.** □ objektiv, sachlich; **2.** ✕ Ziel n.

object-lens opt. ['ɔbdʒiktlenz] Objektiv n.

obligat|ion [ɔbli'geiʃən] Verpflichtung f; ✦ Schuldverschreibung f; be under (an) **~** to s o j-m zu Dank verpflichtet sein; be under **~** to inf. die Verpflichtung haben, zu inf.; **~ory** [ɔ'bligətəri] verpflichtend; verbindlich.

oblig|e [ə'blaidʒ] (zu Dank) verpflichten, nötigen; **~** s.o. j-m e-n Gefallen tun; much **~**d sehr verbunden; danke bestens; **~ing** □ [**~**dʒiŋ] verbindlich, hilfsbereit, gefällig.

oblique □ [ə'bli:k] schief, schräg.

obliterate [ə'blitəreit] auslöschen, tilgen (a. fig.); Schrift ausstreichen; Briefmarken entwerten.

oblivi|on [ə'bliviən] Vergessen(heit f) n; **~ous** □ [**~**iəs] vergeßlich.

oblong ['ɔblɔŋ] länglich; rechteckig.

obnoxious □ [əb'nɔkʃəs] anstößig; widerwärtig, verhaßt.

obscene □ [ɔb'si:n] unanständig.

obscur|e [əb'skjuə] **1.** □ dunkel (a. fig.); unbekannt; **2.** verdunkeln; **~ity** [**~**riti] Dunkel...heit f (a. fig.); Unbekanntheit f; Niedrigkeit f der Geburt.

obsequies ['ɔbsikwiz] pl. Leichenbegängnis n, Trauerfeier f.

obsequious □ [əb'si:kwiəs] unterwürfig (to gegen).

observ|able □ [əb'zə:vəbl] bemerkbar; bemerkenswert; **~ance** [**~**əns] Befolgung f; Brauch m; **~ant** □ [**~**nt] beobachtend; achtsam; **~ation** [ɔbzə:(')veiʃən] Beobachtung f; Bemerkung f; attr. Beobachtungs...; Aussichts...; **~atory** [əb'zə:vətri] Sternwarte f; **~e** [əb'zə:v] v/t. be(ob)achten; acht(geb)en auf (acc.); bemerken; v/i. sich äußern.

obsess [əb'ses] heimsuchen, quälen; **~ed** by od. with besessen von; **~ion** [**~**eʃən] Besessenheit f.

obsolete ['ɔbsəli:t] veraltet.

obstacle ['ɔbstəkl] Hindernis n.

obstina|cy ['ɔbstinəsi] Hartnäckigkeit f; **~te** □ [**~**nit] halsstarrig; eigensinnig; hartnäckig.

obstruct [əb'strʌkt] verstopfen, versperren; hindern; **~ion** [**~**kʃən] Verstopfung f; Hemmung f, Hindernis n; **~ive** □ [**~**ktiv] hinderlich.

obtain [əb'tein] v/t. erlangen, erhalten, erreichen, bekommen; v/i. sich erhalten (haben); **~able** □ [**~**nəbl] erhältlich.

obtru|de [əb'tru:d] (sich) aufdrängen (on dat.); **~sive** □ [**~**u:siv] aufdringlich. [schwerfällig.]

obtuse □ [əb'tju:s] stumpf(sinnig);

obviate ['ɔbvieit] vorbeugen (dat.).

obvious □ ['ɔbviəs] offensichtlich, augenfällig, einleuchtend.

occasion [ə'keiʒən] **1.** Gelegenheit f; Anlaß m; Veranlassung f; F (festliches) Ereignis; on the **~** of anläßlich (gen.); **2.** veranlassen; **~al** □ [**~**nl] gelegentlich; Gelegenheits...

occident ['ɔksidənt] Westen m; Okzident m, Abendland n; **~al** □ [ɔksi'dentl] abendländisch, westlich.

occult □ [ɔ'kʌlt] geheim, verborgen; magisch, okkult.

occup|ant [ɔ'kjupənt] Besitzergreifer(in); Bewohner(in); **~ation** [ɔkju-'peiʃən] Besitz(ergreifung f) m; ✕ Besetzung f; Beruf m; Beschäftigung f; **~y** ['ɔkjupai] einnehmen, in Besitz nehmen, ✕ besetzen; besitzen; innehaben; in Anspruch nehmen; beschäftigen.

occur [ɔ'kə:] vorkommen; sich ereignen; it **~**red to me es fiel mir ein; **~rence** [ə'kʌrəns] Vorkommen n; Vorfall m, Ereignis n.

ocean ['ouʃən] Ozean *m*, Meer *n*.

o'clock [ə'klɔk] Uhr (*bei Zeitangaben*); five ~ fünf Uhr.

October [ɔk'toubə] Oktober *m*.

ocul|ar [['ɔkjulə] Augen...; ~ist [~list] Augenarzt *m*.

odd □ [ɔd] ungerade (*Zahl*); einzeln; und einige *od.* etwas darüber; überzählig; gelegentlich; sonderbar, merkwürdig; ~ity ['ɔditi] Seltsamkeit *f*; ~s [ɔdz] *oft sg.* (Gewinn)Chancen *f/pl.*; Wahrscheinlichkeit *f*; Vorteil *m*; Vorgabe *f*, Handikap *n*; Verschiedenheit *f*; Unterschied *m*; Streit *m*; be at ~ with s.o. mit j-m im Streit sein; nicht übereinstimmen mit j-m; ~ and ends Reste *m/pl.*; Krimskrams *m*.

ode [oud] Ode *f* (*Gedicht*).

odious □ ['oudjəs] verhaßt; ekelhaft.

odo(u)r ['oudə] Geruch *m*; Duft *m*.

of *prp.* [ɔv, əv] *allg.* von; *Ort:* bei (*the battle ~ Quebec*); um (*cheat s.o. ~ s.th.*); aus (~ *charity*); vor (*dat.*) (*afraid ~*); auf (*acc.*) (*proud ~*); über (*acc.*) (*ashamed ~*); nach (*smell ~ roses; desirous ~*); an (*acc.*) (*think ~ s.th.*); nimble ~ foot leichtfüßig.

off [ɔːf, ɔf] **1.** *adv.* weg; ab; herunter; aus (*vorbei*); *Zeit:* hin (*3 months ~*); ~ and on ab und an; hin und her; be ~ fort sein, weg sein; *engS.:* abgesperrt; zu sein (*Hahn etc.*); aus sein; well etc. ~ gut etc. daran; **2.** *prp.* von ... (weg, ab, herunter); frei von, ohne; unweit(*gen.*), neben(♣ auf der Höhe von; **3.** *adj.* entfernt(er); abseitsliegend; Neben...; arbeits-, dienstfrei; † ~ shade Fehlfarbe *f*; **4.** *int.* weg!, fort!, raus!

offal ['ɔfəl] Abfall *m*; Schund *m*; ~s *pl.* Fleischerei: Innereien *f/pl.*

offen|ce, *Am.* ~se [ə'fens] Angriff *m*; Beleidigung *f*, Kränkung *f*; Ärgernis *n*, Anstoß *m*; Vergehen *n*; **~d** [ə'fend] *v/t.* beleidigen, verletzen; ärgern; *v/i.* sich vergehen; **~er** [~də] Übel-, Missetäter(in); Straffällige(r *m*) *f*; first ~ noch nicht Vorbestrafte(r *m*) *f*.

offensive [ə'fensiv] **1.** □ beleidigend; anstößig; ekelhaft; Offensiv..., Angriffs...; **2.** Offensive *f*.

offer ['ɔfə] **1.** Angebot *n*, Anerbieten *n*; ~ of marriage Heiratsantrag *m*; **2.** *v/t.* anbieten; *Preis, Möglichkeit etc.* bieten; *Gebet, Opfer* darbringen; versuchen; zeigen; *Widerstand* leisten; *v/i.* sich bieten; **~ing** ['ɔfəriŋ] Opfer *n*; Anerbieten *n*, Angebot *n*.

off-hand ['ɔːf'hænd] aus dem Handgelenk *od.* Stegreif, unvorbereitet; ungezwungen, frei.

office ['ɔfis] Büro *n*; Geschäftsstelle

f; Ministerium *n*; Amt *n*, Pflicht *f*; ~s *pl.* Hilfe *f*; booking-~ Schalter *m*; box-~ (*Theater- etc.*)Kasse *f*; Divine ♀ Gottesdienst *m*; ~r [~sə] Beamt|e(r) *m*, -in *f*; ⚔ Offizier *m*.

official [ə'fiʃəl] **1.** □ offiziell, amtlich; Amts...; **2.** Beamt(er) *m*.

officiate [ə'fiʃieit] amtieren.

officious □ [ə'fiʃəs] aufdringlich, übereifrig; offiziös, halbamtlich.

off|-licence ['ɔːflaisəns] Schankrecht *n* über die Straße; **~print** Sonderdruck *m*; **~set** ausgleichen; **~shoot** Sproß *m*; Ausläufer *m*; **~side** ['ɔːf'said] *Sport:* abseits; **~spring** ['ɔːfspriŋ] Nachkomme(n-schaft *f*) *m*; Ergebnis *n*.

often ['ɔːfn] oft(mals), häufig.

ogle ['ougl] liebäugeln (mit).

ogre ['ougə] Menschenfresser *m*.

oh [ou] oh!; ach!

oil [ɔil] **1.** Öl *n*; Erdöl *n*, Petroleum *n*; **2.** ölen; (*a. fig.*) schmieren; **~cloth** ['ɔilklɔθ] Wachstuch *n*; **~skin** Öleinwand *f*; ~s *pl.* Ölzeug *n*; **~y** □ ['ɔili] ölig (*a. fig.*); fettig; schmierig (*a. fig.*).

ointment ['ɔintmənt] Salbe *f*.

O.K., okay F ['ou'kei] **1.** richtig, stimmt!; gut, in Ordnung; **2.** annehmen, gutheißen.

old [ould] alt; altbekannt; althergebracht; erfahren; ~ age (das) Alter; days of ~ alte Zeiten *f/pl.*; **~age** ['ouldeidʒ] Alters...; **~-fashioned** ['ould'fæʃənd] altmodisch; altväterlich; ♀ Glory Sternenbanner *n*; **~ish** ['ouldiʃ] ältlich.

olfactory *anat.* [ɔl'fæktəri] Geruchs...

olive ['ɔliv] ♀ Olive *f*; Olivgrün *n*.

Olympic Games [ou'limpik 'geimz] Olympische Spiele *pl.*

ominous □ ['ɔminəs] unheilvoll.

omission [ou'miʃən] Unterlassung *f*; Auslassung *f*.

omit [ou'mit] unterlassen; auslassen.

omnipoten|ce [ɔm'nipətəns] Allmacht *f*; **~t** □ [~nt] allmächtig.

omniscient □ [ɔm'nisiənt] allwissend.

on [ɔn] **1.** *prp. mst* auf; *engS.:* an (~ *the wall*, ~ *the Thames*); auf ... (los), nach ... (hin) (*march ~ London*); auf ... (hin) (~ *his authority*); *Zeit:* an (~ *the 1st of April*); (gleich) nach, bei (~ *his arrival*); über (*acc.*) (*talk ~ a subject*); nach (~ *this model*); get ~ a train bsd. Am. in en-Zug einsteigen; ~ hearing it als ich etc. es hörte; **2.** *adv.* darauf; auf (*keep one's hat ~*), an (*have a coat ~*); voraus, vorwärts; weiter (*and so ~*); be ~ im Gange sein; auf sein (*Hahn etc.*); an sein (*Licht etc.*); **3.** *int.* drauf!, ran!

once [wʌns] **1.** *adv.* einmal; einst (-mals); at ~ (so)gleich, sofort; zugleich; ~ *for all* ein für allemal; ~ *in a while* dann und wann; *this* ~ dieses eine Mal; 2. *cj. a.* ~ *that* sobald.

one [wʌn] 1. ein; einzig; eine(r), ein; eins; man; ~ *day* eines Tages; 2. Eine(r) *m*; Eins *f*; *the little* ~*s pl.* die Kleinen *pl.*; ~ *another* einander; *at* ~ einig; *by* ~ einzeln; *I for* ~ ich für meinen Teil.

onerous □ ['ɔnərəs] lästig.

one|self [wʌn'self] (man) selbst, sich; ~**sided** ['wʌn'saidid] einseitig; ~**way** ['wʌnwei]: ~ *street* Einbahnstraße *f*.

onion [ˈʌnjən] Zwiebel *f*.

onlooker [ˈɔnlukə] Zuschauer(in).

only ['ounli] 1. *adj* einzig; 2. *adv.* nur; bloß; erst; ~ *yesterday* erst gestern; 3. *cj.* ~ *(that)* nur daß.

onrush [ˈɔnrʌʃ] Ansturm *m*.

onset ['ɔnset], **onslaught** ['ɔnslɔːt] Angriff *m*; *bsd. fig.* Anfall *m*; Anfang *m*.

onward ['ɔnwəd] 1. *adj.* fortschreitend; 2. *a.* ~*s adv.* vorwärts, weiter.

ooze [uːz] 1. Schlamm *m*; 2. *v/i.* (durch)sickern; ~ *away* schwinden; *v/t.* ausströmen, ausschwitzen.

opaque □ [ou'peik] undurchsichtig.

open ['oupən] 1. *allg* offen; geöffnet, auf; frei (*Feld etc.*); öffentlich; offenstehend, unentschieden; aufrichtig; zugänglich (*to dat.*); aufgeschlossen (*to gegenüber*); mild (*Wetter*); 2. *in the ~ (air)* im Freien; *come out into the ~ fig* an die Öffentlichkeit treten; 3. *v/t* öffnen; eröffnen (*a. fig.*); *v/i.* (sich) öffnen; anfangen; ~ *into* führen in (*acc.*) (*Tür etc.*); ~ *on to* hinausgehen auf (*acc.*) (*Fenster etc.*); ~ *out* sich ausbreiten; ~**air** ['oupn'ɛə] im Freien (stattfindend), Freilicht..., Frei(luft)...; ~**armed** ['oupn'ɑːmd] herzlich, warm; ~**er** ['oupnə] (Er-)Öffner(in); (Dosen)Öffner *m*; ~**eyed** ['oupn'aid] wach; mit offenen Augen; aufmerksam; ~**handed** ['oupn'hændid] freigebig, großzügig; ~**hearted** ['oupnhɑːtid] offen(herzig), aufrichtig; ~**ing** ['oupniŋ] (Er)Öffnung *f*; Gelegenheit *f*; *attr.* Eröffnungs...; ~**minded** *fig.* ['oupn'maindid] aufgeschlossen. (*pl.*) Opernglas *n*.

opera ['ɔpərə] Oper *f*; ~**glass(es)**

operat|e ['ɔpəreit] *v/t.* 💉 operieren; *bsd. Am.* in Gang bringen; *Maschine* bedienen; *Unternehmen* leiten; *v/i.* (ein)wirken; sich auswirken; arbeiten; ⚔, 💉, ✈ operieren; ~**ion** [ɔpə-ˈreiʃən] Wirkung *f*; Tätigkeit *f*; ✈, ⚔, 💉 Operation *f*; *be in* ~ in Betrieb sein; in Kraft sein; ~**ive** ['ɔpərətiv] 1. □ wirksam, tätig, praktisch; 💉 operativ; 2. Arbeiter *m*; ~**or** [~reitə] Operateur *m*; Telephonist(in); ⊕ Maschinist *m*.

opin|e [ou'pain] meinen; ~**ion** [əˈpinjən] Meinung *f*; Ansicht *f*; Stellungnahme *f*; Gutachten *n*; *in my* ~ meines Erachtens.

opponent [ə'pounənt] Gegner *m*.

opportun|e □ ['ɔpətjuːn] passend; rechtzeitig; günstig; ~**ity** [ɔpəˈtjuː-niti] (günstige) Gelegenheit.

oppos|e [ə'pouz] entgegen-, gegenüberstellen; bekämpfen; ~**ed** entgegengesetzt; *be* ~ *to* gegen sein; ~**ite** ['ɔpəzit] 1. □ gegenüberliegend; entgegengesetzt; 2. *prp. u. adv.* gegenüber; 3. Gegenteil *n*; ~**ition** [ɔpəˈziʃən] Gegenüberstehen *n*; Widerstand *m*; Gegensatz *m*; Widerspruch *m*, -streit *m*; ✚ Konkurrenz *f*; Opposition *f*.

oppress [ə'pres] be-, unterdrücken; ~**ion** [~eʃən] Unterdrückung *f*; Druck *m*; Bedrängnis *f*, Bedrücktheit *f*; ~**ive** □ [~esiv] (be)drückend; gewaltsam.

optic ['ɔptik] Augen..., Seh...; ~**al** □ [~kəl] optisch; ~**ian** [ɔp'tiʃən] Optiker *m*.

optimism ['ɔptimizəm] Optimismus *m*.

option ['ɔpʃən] Wahl(freiheit) *f*; ✚ Vorkaufsrecht *n*, Option *f*; ~**al** □ [~nl] freigestellt, wahlfrei.

opulence ['ɔpjuləns] Reichtum *m*.

or [ɔː] oder; ~ *else* sonst, wo nicht.

oracular □ [ɔ'rækjulə] orakelhaft.

oral □ ['ɔːrəl] mündlich, Mund...

orange ['ɔrindʒ] 1. Orange(farbe) *f*; Apfelsine *f*; 2. orangefarben; ~**ade** ['ɔrindʒ'eid] Orangenlimonade *f*.

orat|ion [ɔː'reiʃən] Rede *f*; ~**or** ['ɔrətə] Redner *m*; ~**ory** [~ɔri] Redekunst *f*, Rhetorik *f*; Kapelle *f*.

orb [ɔːb] Ball *m*; *fig.* Himmelskörper *m*; *poet.* Augapfel *m*; ~**it** ['ɔːbit] 1. Planetenbahn *f*; Kreis-, Umlaufbahn *f*; Auge(nhöhle *f*) *n*; 2. sich in e-r Umlaufbahn bewegen.

orchard ['ɔːtʃəd] Obstgarten *m*.

orchestra [' ɔːkistrə] Orchester *n*.

orchid ⚘ ['ɔːkid] Orchidee *f*.

ordain [ɔː'dein] an-, verordnen; bestimmen; *Priester* ordinieren.

ordeal *fig.* [ɔː'diːl] schwere Prüfung.

order ['ɔːdə] 1. Ordnung *f*; Anordnung *f*; Befehl *m*; Regel *f*; ✚ Auftrag *m*; Zahlungsanweisung *f*; Klasse *f*, Rang *m*; Orden *m* (*a. eccl.*); *take (holy)* ~*s* in den geistlichen Stand treten; *in* ~ *to inf.* um zu *inf.*; *in* ~ *that* damit; *make to* ~ auf Bestellung anfertigen; *standing* ~*s pl. parl.* Geschäftsordnung *f*; 2. (an)ordnen; befehlen; ✚ bestellen; *j-n* beordern; ~**ly** ['ɔːdəli] 1. ordentlich; ruhig; regelmäßig; 2. ⚔ Ordonnanz *f*; ⚔ Bursche *m*; Krankenpfleger *m*.

ordinal ['ɔːdinl] 1. Ordnungs...; 2. *a.* ~ *number* Ordnungszahl *f*.

ordinance ['ɔːdinəns] Verordnung *f*.

ordinary □ ['ɔːdnri] gewöhnlich.
ordnance ✗, ⚓ ['ɔːdnəns] Artillerie f, Geschütze n/pl.; Feldzeugwesen n.
ordure ['ɔːdjuə] Kot m, Schmutz m.
ore [ɔː] Erz n.
organ ['ɔːgən] ♪ Orgel f; Organ n; **~grinder** [~graɪndə] Leierkastenmann m; **~ic** [ɔː'gænik] (~ally) organisch; **~ization** [ɔːgənai'zeiʃən] Organisation f; **~ize** ['ɔːgənaiz] organisieren; **~izer** [~zə] Organisator(in).
orgy ['ɔːdʒi] Ausschweifung f.
orient ['ɔːrient] 1. Osten m; Orient m, Morgenland n; 2. orientieren; **~al** [ɔːri'entl] 1. □ östlich; orientalisch; 2. Orientale m, -in f; **~ate** ['ɔːrienteit] orientieren.
orifice ['ɔrifis] Mündung f; Öffnung f.
origin ['ɔridʒin] Ursprung m; Anfang m; Herkunft f.
original [ə'ridʒənl] 1. □ ursprünglich; originell; Original...; ♱ Stamm...; 2. Original n; **~ity** [əridʒi'næliti] Originalität f; **~ly** [ə'ridʒnəli] originell; ursprünglich; zuerst, anfangs, anfänglich.
originat|e [ə'ridʒineit] v/t. hervorbringen, schaffen; v/i. entstehen; **~or** [~tə] Urheber m.
ornament 1. ['ɔːnəmənt] Verzierung f; fig. Zierde f; 2. [~ment] verzieren; schmücken; **~al** □ [ɔːnə'mentl] zierend; schmückend.
ornate □ [ɔː'neit] reich verziert; überladen.
orphan ['ɔːfən] 1. Waise f; 2. a. **~ed** verwaist; **~age** [~nidʒ] Waisenhaus n.
orthodox □ ['ɔːθədɔks] rechtgläubig; üblich; anerkannt.
oscillate ['ɔsileit] schwingen; fig. schwanken.
osier ⚘ ['ouʒə] Korbweide f.
osprey orn. ['ɔspri] Fischadler m.
ossify ['ɔsifai] verknöchern.
ostensible □ [ɔs'tensəbl] angeblich.
ostentatio|n [ɔstən'teiʃən] Zurschaustellung f; Protzerei f; **~us** □ [~ʃəs] prahlend, prahlerisch.
ostler ['ɔslə] Stallknecht m.
ostracize ['ɔstrəsaiz] verbannen; ächten.
ostrich orn. ['ɔstritʃ] Strauß m.
other ['ʌðə] andere(r, -s); the ~ day neulich; the ~ morning neulich morgens; every ~ day einen Tag um den anderen, jeden zweiten Tag; **~wise** ['ʌðəwaiz] anders; sonst.
otter zo. ['ɔtə] Otter(pelz) m.
ought [ɔːt] sollte; you ~ to have done it Sie hätten es tun sollen.
ounce [auns] Unze f (= 28,35 g).
our ['auə] unser; **~s** ['auəz] der (die, das) unsrige; unsere(r, -s); pred. unser; **~selves** [auə'selvz] wir selbst; uns (selbst).

oust [aust] verdrängen, vertreiben, hinauswerfen; e-s Amtes entheben.
out [aut] 1. adv. aus; hinaus, heraus; draußen; außerhalb; (bis) zu Ende; be ~ with böse sein mit; ~ and ~ durch und durch; ~ and about wieder auf den Beinen; way ~ Ausgang m; 2. Am. F Ausweg m; the ~s pl. parl. die Opposition; 3. ♱ übernormal, Über...(Größe); 4. prp. ~ of aus, aus ... heraus; außerhalb; außer; aus, von.
out|balance [aut'bæləns] schwerer wiegen als; **~bid** [~'bid] [irr. (bid)] überbieten; **~board** ['autbɔːd] Außenbord...; **~break** [~breik] Ausbruch m; **~building** [~bildiŋ] Nebengebäude n; **~burst** [~bəːst] Ausbruch m; **~cast** [~kɑːst] 1. ausgestoßen; 2. Ausgestoßene(r m) f; **~come** [~kʌm] Ergebnis n; **~cry** [~krai] Aufschrei m, Schrei m der Entrüstung; **~dated** [aut'deitid] zeitlich überholt; **~distance** [~'distəns] überholen; **~do** [~'duː] [irr. (do)] übertreffen; **~door** adj. ['autdɔː], **~doors** adv. [~'dɔːz] Außen...; draußen, außer dem Hause; im Freien.
outer ['autə] äußer; Außen...; **~most** ['autəmoust] äußerst.
out|fit ['autfit] Ausrüstung f, Ausstattung f; Am. Haufen m, Trupp m, (Arbeits)Gruppe f; **~going** [~gouiŋ] 1. weg-, abgehend; 2. Ausgehen n; **~s** pl. Ausgaben f/pl.; **~grow** [aut'grou] [irr. (grow)] herauswachsen aus; hinauswachsen über (acc.); **~house** ['authaus] Nebengebäude n; Am. Außenbort m.
outing ['autiŋ] Ausflug m, Tour f.
out|last [aut'lɑːst] überdauern; **~law** ['autlɔː] 1. Geächtete(r m) f; 2. ächten; **~lay** [~lei] Geld-Auslage(n pl.) f; **~let** [~let] Auslaß m; Ausgang m; Abfluß m; **~line** [~lain] 1. Umriß m; Überblick m; Skizze f; 2. umreißen; skizzieren; **~live** [aut'liv] überleben; **~look** ['autluk] Ausblick m (a. fig.); Auffassung f; **~lying** [~laiiŋ] entlegen; **~match** [aut'mætʃ] weit übertreffen; **~number** [~'nʌmbə] an Zahl übertreffen; **~patient** ♰ ['autpeiʃənt] ambulanter Patient; **~post** [~poust] Vorposten m; **~pouring** [~pɔːriŋ] Erguß m (a. fig.); **~put** [~put] Produktion f, Ertrag m.
outrage ['autreidʒ] 1. Gewalttätigkeit f; Attentat n; Beleidigung f; 2. gröblich verletzen; Gewalt antun (dat.); **~ous** [aut'reidʒəs] abscheulich; empörend; gewalttätig.
out|reach [aut'riːtʃ] weiter reichen als; **~right** [adj. 'autrait, adv. aut-'rait] gerade heraus; völlig; **~run** [~'rʌn] [irr. (run)] schneller laufen als; hinausgehen über (acc.); **~set**

['autset] Anfang m; Aufbruch m;
~shine [aut'ʃain] [irr (shine)] über-
strahlen; ~side ['aut'said] 1. Au-
ßenseite f; fig Äußerste(s) n; at
the ~ höchstens; 2. Außen. .; außen-
stehend; äußerst (Preis); 3. (nach)
(dr)außen; 4. prp außerhalb; ~
sider [~də] Außenseiter(in), -ste-
hende(r m) f; ~size [~saiz] Über-
größe f; ~skirts [~skə:ts] pl Außen-
bezirke m/pl., (Stadt)Rand m;
~smart Am. F [aut'sma:t] übervorteilen; ~spoken [~spoukən] frei-
mütig; ~spread [aut'spred] ausgestreckt, ausgebreitet; ~standing
[aut'stændiŋ] hervorragend (a. fig.);
ausstehend (Schuld), offenstehend
(Frage); ~stretched [autstretʃt] =
outspread; ~strip [aut'strip] überholen (a. fig.).

outward ['autwəd] 1. äußer(lich);
nach (dr)außen gerichtet; 2. adv.
mst ~s auswärts, nach (dr)außen;
~ly [~dli] äußerlich; an der Ober-
fläche.

out|weigh [aut'wei] überwiegen,
~wit [~'wit] überlisten; ~worn
['autwɔ:n] erschöpft; fig. abgegrif-
fen; überholt.

oval ['ouvəl] 1. oval; 2. Oval n.

oven ['ʌvn] Backofen m.

over ['ouvə] 1. adv über; hin-, herüber; drüben; übermäßig; zu
darüber; von Anfang bis zu Ende;
noch einmal; and above neben,
zusätzlich zu; (all) again noch
einmal (von vorn); against gegenüber (dat.); all ~ ganz und gar;
~ and ~ again immer wieder; read ~
durchlesen; 2. prp über; all ~ the
town durch die ganze od. in der
ganzen Stadt.

over|act ['ouvər'ækt] übertreiben;
~all [~rɔ:l] 1. Arbeitsanzug m,
-kittel m; Kittel(schürze) m; 2. gesamt, Gesamt , ~awe [ouvər'ɔ:]
einschüchtern; ~balance [ouvə-
'bæləns] 1. Übergewicht n; 2. umkippen; überwiegen; ~bearing □
[~'bɛəriŋ] anmaßend; ~board □
['ouvəbɔ:d] über Bord; ~cast
[~ka:st] bewölkt; ~charge [~-
'tʃa:dʒ] 1. überladen; überfordern;
2. Überladung f; Überforderung f;
~coat [~kout] Mantel m; ~come
[ouvə'kʌm][irr (come)] überwinden,
überwältigen; ~crowd [~'kraud]
überfüllen; ~do [~'du:] [irr. (do)]
zu viel tun; übertreiben; zu sehr
kochen; überanstrengen; ~draw
['ouvə'drɔ:] [irr (draw)] übertreiben; † Konto überziehen; ~dress
[~'dres] (sich) übertrieben anziehen;
~due [~'dju:] (über)fällig; ~eat
[~'i:t] [irr. (eat)]: ~ o.s. sich
überessen; ~flow 1. [ouvə'flou]
[irr.(flow)] v/t. überfluten; v/i überfließen; 2. ['ouvəflou] Überschwemmung f; Überfüllung f; ~grow

[~'grou] [irr. (grow)] v/t. überwu-
chern; v/i. zu sehr wachsen; ~
hang 1. [~'hæŋ] [irr (hang)] v/t.
über (acc.) hängen; v/i überhängen; 2. [~hæŋ] Überhang m; ~
haul [ouvə'hɔ:l] überholen; ~
head 1. adv. ['ouvə'hed] (dr)o-
ben; 2. adj. [~hed] Ober...; †
allgemein (Unkosten); 3. ~s pl. †
allgemeine Unkosten pl.; ~hear
[ouvə'hiə] [irr. (hear)] belauschen;
~joyed [~'dʒɔid] überglücklich;
~lap [~'læp] v/t. übergreifen auf
(acc.); überschneiden; v/i inein-
andergreifen, überlappen; ~lay
[~'lei] [irr. (lay)] belegen; ⊕ über-
lagern; ~leaf ['ouvə'li:f] umseitig;
~load [~'loud] überladen; ~look
[ouvə'luk] übersehen; beaufsichtigen; ~master [~'ma:stə] überwältigen; ~much [ouvə'mʌtʃ]zu viel;
~night [~'nait] 1. am Vorabend;
über Nacht; 2. Nacht nächtlich;
Übernachtungs..; ~pay [~'pei] [irr.
(pay)] zu viel bezahlen für; ~peopled
[ouvə'pi:pld] überschuß m; ~plus
['ouvəplʌs] Überschuß m, ~power
[ouvə'pauə] überwältigen; ~rate
['ouvə'reit] überschätzen; ~reach
[ouvə'ri:tʃ] übervorteilen; ~ o.s. sich
übernehmen; ~ride fig [~'raid]
[irr. (ride)] sich hinwegsetzen über
(acc.); umstoßen; ~rule [~'ru:l]
überstimmen; ⚖ verwerfen; ~run
[~'rʌn] [irr (run)] überrennen;
überziehen; überlaufen; bedecken;
~sea ['ouvə'si:] 1. a ~ s überseeisch;
Übersee...; 2. ~ s in od nach Übersee; ~see [~'si:] [irr (see)] beaufsichtigen; ~seer [~siə] Aufseher m;
~shadow [ouvə'ʃædou] überschat-
ten; ~sight ['ouvəsait] Versehen n;
~sleep [~'sli:p] [irr (sleep)] verschlafen; ~state [~steit] übertreiben; ~statement [~tmənt] Übertreibung f; ~strain 1. [~'strein]
(sich) überanstrengen; fig. übertreiben; 2. [~.strein] Überanstren-
gung f.

overt ['ouvə:t] offen(kundig).

over|take [ouvə'teik] [irr (take)]
einholen; j-n überraschen; ~tax
['ouvə'tæks] zu hoch besteuern; fig.
überschätzen; übermäßig in Anspruch nehmen; ~throw 1. [ouvə-
'θrou] [irr. (throw)] (um)stürzen (a.
fig.); vernichten; 2. ['ouvəθrou]
Sturz m; Vernichtung f; ~time
[~taim] Überstunden f/pl.

overture ['ouvətjuə] ♪ Ouvertüre f;
Vorspiel n; Vorschlag m, Antrag
m.

over|turn [ouvə'tə:n] (um)stürzen;
~value ['ouvə'vælju:] zu hoch ein-
schätzen; ~weening [ouvə'wi:niŋ]
eingebildet; ~weight ['ouvəweit]
Übergewicht n; ~whelm [ouvə-
'welm] überschütten (a. fig.); überwältigen; ~work ['ouvə'wə:k] 1.

Überarbeitung *f*; **2.** [*irr.* (*work*)] sich überarbeiten; **~wrought** [*~'rɔ:t*] überarbeitet; überreizt.

owe [ou] *Geld, Dank etc.* schulden, schuldig sein; verdanken.

owing ['ouiŋ] schuldig; **~ to** infolge.

owl *orn.* [aul] Eule *f.*

own [oun] **1.** eigen; richtig; einzig, innig geliebt; **2.** *my* **~** mein Eigentum; *a house of one's* **~** ein eigenes Haus; *hold one's* **~** standhalten;

3. besitzen; zugeben; anerkennen; sich bekennen (*to zu*).

owner['ounə]Eigentümer(in); **~ship** ['ounəʃip] Eigentum(srecht) *n.*

ox [ɔks], *pl.* **oxen** ['ɔksən] Ochse *m*; Rind *n.*

oxid|ation [ɔksi'deiʃən] Oxydation *f*, Oxydierung *f*; **~e** ['ɔksaid] Oxyd *n*; **~ize** ['ɔksidaiz] oxydieren.

oxygen [ɔksidʒən] Sauerstoff *m.*

oyster ['ɔistə] Auster *f.*

ozone [ˈouzoun] Ozon *n.*

P

pace [peis] **1.** Schritt *m*; Gang *m*; Tempo *n*; **2.** *v/t.* abschreiten; *v/i.* (einher)schreiten; (im) Paß gehen.

pacific [pə'sifik] (*~ally*) friedlich; *the* ♀ (*Ocean*) der Pazifik, der Pazifische *od.* Stille Ozean; **~ation** [pæsifi'keiʃən] Beruhigung *f.*

pacify ['pæsifai] beruhigen.

pack [pæk] **1.** Pack(en) *m*; Paket *n*; Ballen *m*; Spiel *n Karten*; Meute *f*; Rotte *f*, Bande *f*; Packung *f*; **2.** *v/t. oft* **~** *up* (zs.-, ver-, ein)packen; *a.* **~** *off* fortjagen; *Am.* F (bei sich) tragen (*als Gepäck etc.*); bepacken, vollstopfen; ⊕ dichten; *v/i. oft* **~** *up* packen, sich packen (lassen); **~age** ['pækidʒ] Pack *m*, Ballen *m*; *bsd. Am.* Paket *n*; Packung *f*; Frachtstück *n*; **~er** ['pækə] Packer(in); *Am* Konservenfabrikant *m*; **~et** ['pækit] Paket *n*; Päckchen *n*; *a.* **~boat** Postschiff *n.*

packing ['pækiŋ] Packen *m*; Verpackung *f*; **~ house** *Am.* (*bsd.* Fleisch)Konservenfabrik *f.*

packthread ['pækθred] Bindfaden *m.*

pact [pækt] Vertrag *m*, Pakt *m.*

pad [pæd] **1.** Polster *n*; *Sport:* Beinschutz *m*; Schreibblock *m*; Stempelkissen *n*; (Abschuß)Rampe *f*; **2.** (aus)polstern; **~ding** ['pædiŋ] Polsterung *f*; *fig.* Lückenbüßer *m.*

paddle ['pædl] **1.** Paddel(ruder) *n*; ⛴ (Rad)Schaufel *f*; **2.** paddeln; planschen; **~wheel** Schaufelrad *n.*

paddock ['pædək] (Pferde)Koppel *f*; *Sport* Sattelplatz *m.*

padlock ['pædlɔk] Vorhängeschloß *n.*

pagan ['peigən] **1.** heidnisch; **2.** Heid|e *m*, -in *f.*

page[1] [peidʒ] **1.** Buch-Seite *f*; *fig.* Buch *n*; **2.** paginieren.

page[2] [*~*] **1.** (Hotel)Page *m*; *Am.* Amtsdiener *m*; **2.** *Am.* (durch e-n Pagen) holen lassen.

pageant ['pædʒənt] historisches Festspiel; festlicher Umzug.

paid [peid] *pret. u. p.p. von* pay 2.

pail [peil] Eimer *m.*

pain [pein] **1.** Pein *f*, Schmerz *m*; Strafe *f*; **~s** *pl.* Leiden *n/pl.*; Mühe *f*; *on od. under* **~** *of death* bei Todesstrafe; *be in* **~** leiden; *take* **~s** sich Mühe geben; **2.** *j-m* weh tun; **~ful** □ ['peinful] schmerzhaft, schmerzlich; peinlich; mühevoll; **~less** □ ['peinlis] schmerzlos; **~staking** [['peinzteikiŋ] fleißig.

paint [peint] **1.** Farbe *f*; Schminke *f*; Anstrich *m*; **2.** (be)malen; anstreichen; (sich) schminken; **~brush** ['peintbraʃ] Malerpinsel *m*; **~er** [*~tə*] Maler(in); **~ing** [*~tiŋ*] Malen *n*; Malerei *f*; Gemälde *n.*

pair [pɛə] **1.** Paar *n*; *a* **~** *of scissors* eine Schere; **2.** (sich) paaren; zs.-passen; *a.* **~** *off* paarweise weggehen.

pal *sl.* [pæl] Kumpel *m*, Kamerad *m.*

palace ['pælis] Palast *m.*

palatable [['pælətəbl] schmackhaft. [schmack *m* (*a. fig.*).]

palate ['pælit] Gaumen *m*; Ge-]

pale[1] [peil] **1.** blaß, bleich; fahl; **~** *ale* helles Bier; **2.** (er)bleichen.

pale[2] [*~*] Pfahl *m*; *fig.* Grenzen *f/pl.*

paleness ['peilnis] Blässe *f.*

palisade [pæli'seid] **1.** Palisade *f*; Staket *n*; **~s** *pl. Am.* Steilufer *n*; **2.** umpfählen.

pall [pɔ:l] schal werden; **~** (*up*)*on j-n* langweilen.

pallet ['pælit] Strohsack *m.*

palliat|e ['pælieit] bemänteln; lindern; **~ive** [*~iətiv*] Linderungsmittel *n.*

pall|id □ ['pælid] blaß; **~idness** [*~dnis*], **~or** ['pælə] Blässe *f.*

palm [pɑ:m] **1.** Handfläche *f*; ♀ Palme *f*; **2.** in der Hand verbergen; **~** *s.th. off upon s.o.* j-m *et.* andrehen; **~tree** ['pɑ:mtri:] Palme *f.*

palpable [['pælpəbl] fühlbar; *fig.* handgreiflich, klar, eindeutig.

palpitat|e [['pælpiteit] klopfen (*Herz*); **~ion** [pælpi'teiʃən] Herzklopfen *n.*

palsy ['pɔ:lzi] 1. Lähmung *f*; *fig.* Ohnmacht *f*; 2. *fig.* lähmen.

palter ['pɔ:ltə] sein Spiel treiben.

paltry ['pɔ:ltri] erbärmlich.

pamper ['pæmpə] verzärteln.

pamphlet ['pæmflit] Flugschrift *f*.

pan [pæn] Pfanne *f*; Tiegel *m*.

pan... [~] all..., gesamt...; pan..., Pan.

panacea [pænə'siə] Allheilmittel *n*.

pancake ['pænkeik] Pfannkuchen *m*; . landing ⚓ Bumslandung *f*.

pandemonium *fig* [pændi'mounjəm] Höllen[lärm *m*) *f*.

pander [pændə] 1. Vorschub leisten (*to dat.*); kuppeln; 2. Kuppler *m*

pane [pein] (Fenster)Scheibe *f*.

panegyric [pæni'dʒirik] Lobrede *f*.

panel [pænl] 1. ⚙ Fach *n*; Tür-Füllung *f*, ⚙ Geschworenen(liste *f*) *m/pl*.; Diskussionsteilnehmer *m/pl*.; Kassenarztliste *f*; 2. täfeln.

pang [pæŋ] plötzlicher Schmerz, Weh *n*; *fig* Angst *f*, Qual *f*.

panhandle ['pænhændl] 1. Pfannenstiel *m*, *Am* schmaler Fortsatz *e-s Staatsgebiets*; 2. *Am.* F betteln

panic ['pænik] 1. panisch; 2. Panik *f*.

pansy ⚘ ['pænzi] Stiefmütterchen *n*.

pant [pænt] *nach Luft* schnappen; keuchen, klopfen (*Herz*); lechzen (*for, after nach*)

panther ['pænθə] Panther *m*.

panties F ['pæntiz] (Damen)Schlüpfer *m*; (Kinder)Hös-chen *n*.

pantry ['pæntri] Vorratskammer *f*.

pants [pænts] *pl* Hose *f*; † lange Pap [pæp] Brei *m* [Unterhose.]

papa [pə pɑ] Papa *m*.

papal [peipəl] päpstlich.

paper [peipə] 1. Papier *n*; Zeitung *f*; Prüfungsaufgabe *f*; Vortrag *m*, Aufsatz *m*, *s pl* (Ausweis)Papiere *n/pl*.; 2. tapezieren, ~back Taschenbuch *n*, Paperback *n*; ~bag Tüte *f*; ~clip Büroklammer *f*; ~fastener Musterklammer *f*; ~hanger 'apezierer *m*; ~mill Papierfabrik *f*; ~weight Briefbeschwerer *m*.

pappy [pæpi] breiig.

par [pɑ:] † Nennwert *m*, Pari *n*; at ~ zum Nennwert; be on a ~ with gleich *oa* ebenbürtig sein (*dat.*).

parable ['pærəbl] Gleichnis *n*.

parachute ['pærəʃu:t] Fallschirm *m*; ~ist [~tist] Fallschirmspringer(in).

parade [pə'reid] 1. ✕ (Truppen-)Parade *f*; Zurschaustellung *f*; Promenade *f*; (Um)Zug *m*; *programme* ~ *Radio* Programmvorschau *f*; *make a . of et.* zur Schau stellen; 2. ✕ antreten (lassen); ✕ vorbeimarschieren (lassen); ✕ zur Schau stellen; ~ground ✕ Exerzier-, Paradeplatz *m*.

paradise ['pærədais] Paradies *n*.

paragon ['pærəgən] Vorbild *n*; Muster *n*.

paragraph ['pærəgrɑ:f] Absatz *m*; Paragraph(zeichen *n*) *m*; kurze Zeitungsnotiz

parallel ['pærəlel] 1. parallel; 2. Parallele *f* (*a . fig.*); Gegenstück *n*; Vergleich *m*; *without (a)* ~ ohnegleichen; 3. vergleichen; entsprechen; gleichen; parallel laufen (mit).

paraly|se ['pærəlaiz] lähmen; *fig.* unwirksam machen, ~sis ⚕ [pə'rælisis] Paralyse *f*, Lähmung *f*.

paramount ['pærəmaunt] oberst, höchst, hervorragend, größer, höher stehend (*to als*)

parapet ['pærəpit] ✕ Brustwehr *f*; Brüstung *f*, Geländer *n*

paraphernalia [pærəfə neiljə] *pl.* Ausrüstung *f*, Zubehör *n*, *m*.

parasite ['pærəsait] Schmarotzer *m*.

parasol [pær. ~ l] Sonnenschirm *m*.

paratroops ⚔ ['pærətru:ps] Luftlandetruppen *f/pl*

parboil ['pɑ:bɔil] ankochen.

parcel ['pɑ:sl] 1. Paket *n*; Parzelle *f*; 2. ~ out aus , aufteilen

parch [pɑ:tʃ] rösten, (aus)dörren.

parchment ['pɑ:tʃmənt] Pergament *n*

pard *Am sl* [pɑ:d] Partner *m*.

pardon ['pɑ:dn] 1. Verzeihung *f*; ⚖ Begnadigung *f*; 2. verzeihen; *f*. begnadigen, ~able [[~əbl] verzeihlich.

pare [pɛə] (be)schneiden (*a. fig.*); schälen

parent ['pɛərənt] Vater *m*, Mutter *f*; *fig.* Ursache *f*, ~s *pl* Eltern *pl*.; ~age [~tidʒ] Herkunft *f*; ~al [pə'rentl] elterlich

parenthe|sis [pə renθisis], *pl.* ~ses [~si:z] Einschaltung *f*; *typ.* (runde) Klammer

paring ['pɛəriŋ] Schälen *n*, Abschneiden *n*, ~s *pl.* Schalen *f/pl*., Schnipsel *m/pl*

parish ['pæriʃ] 1. Kirchspiel *n*, Gemeinde *f*; 2. Pfarr , Gemeinde...; ~ council Gemeinderat *m*; ~ioner [pə'riʃənə] Pfarrkind *n*, Gemeindemitglied *n*.

parity ['pæriti] Gleichheit *f*.

park [pɑ:k] 1. Park *m*, Anlagen *f/pl*.; Naturschutzgebiet *n*; *mst car* ~ Parkplatz *m*, 2. *mot.* parken; ~ing *mot.* ['pɑ:kiŋ] Parken *n*; ~ing lot Parkplatz *m*; ~ing meter Parkuhr *f*.

parlance ['pɑ:ləns] Ausdrucksweise *f*

parley ['pɑ:li] 1. Unterhandlung *f*; 2. unterhandeln, sich besprechen.

parliament ['pɑ:ləmənt] Parlament *n*; ~arian [pɑ:ləmen'tɛəriən] Parlamentarier(in); ~ary [pɑ:lə'mentəri] parlamentarisch; Parlaments...

parlo(u)r ['pɑːlə] Wohnzimmer n; Empfangs-, Sprechzimmer n; beauty ~ bsd. Am. Schönheitssalon m; ~ car 🚗 Am. Salonwagen m; ~maid Stubenmädchen n.

parochial □ [pə'roukjəl] Pfarr...; Gemeinde...; fig. engstirnig, beschränkt.

parole [pə'roul] **1.** 🇹 mündlich; **2.** ✕ Parole f; Ehrenwort n; put on ~ = **3.** 🇹 bsd. Am. bedingt freilassen.

parquet ['pɑːkei] Parkett(fußboden m) n; Am. thea. Parkett n.

parrot ['pærət] **1.** orn. Papagei m (a. fig.); **2.** (nach)plappern.

parry ['pæri] abwehren, parieren.

parsimonious □ [pɑːsi'mounjəs] sparsam, karg; knauserig.

parsley 🌿 ['pɑːsli] Petersilie f.

parson ['pɑːsn] Pfarrer m; ~age [~nidʒ] Pfarrei f; Pfarrhaus n.

part [pɑːt] **1.** Teil m; Anteil m; Partei f; thea. fig. Rolle f; 🎵 Einzel-Stimme f; Gegend f; a man of ~s ein fähiger Mensch; take ~ in s.th. an e-r Sache teilnehmen; take in good (bad) ~ gut (übel) aufnehmen; for my (own) ~ meinerseits; in ~ teilweise; on the ~ of von seiten (gen.); on my ~ meinerseits; **2.** adv. teils; **3.** v/t. (ab-, ein-, zer)teilen; Haar scheiteln; ~ company sich trennen (with von); v/i. sich trennen (with von); scheiden.

partake [pɑː'teik] [irr. (take)] teilnehmen, teilhaben; ~ of Mahlzeit einnehmen; grenzen an (acc.).

partial □ ['pɑːʃəl] Teil...; teilweise; partiell; parteiisch; eingenommen (to von, für); ~ity [pɑːʃi'æliti] Parteilichkeit f; Vorliebe f.

particip|ant [pɑː'tisipənt] Teilnehmer(in); ~ate [~peit] teilnehmen; ~ation [pɑːtisi'peiʃən] Teilnahme f.

participle gr. ['pɑːtsipl] Partizip n, Mittelwort n.

particle ['pɑːtikl] Teilchen n.

particular □ [pə'tikjulə] **1.** □ mst besonder; einzeln; Sonder...; genau; eigen; wählerisch; **2.** Einzelheit f; Umstand m; in ~ insbesondere; ~ity [pətikju'læriti] Besonderheit f; Ausführlichkeit f; Eigenheit f; ~ly [pə'tikjuləli] besonders.

parting ['pɑːtiŋ] **1.** Trennung f; Teilung f; Abschied m; Haar-Scheitel m; ~ of the ways bsd. fig. Scheideweg m; **2.** Abschieds...

partisan [pɑːti'zæn] Parteigänger (-in); ✕ Partisan m; attr. Partei...

partition [pɑː'tiʃən] **1.** Teilung f; Scheidewand f; Verschlag m, Fach n; **2.** mst ~ off (ab)teilen.

partly ['pɑːtli] teilweise, zum Teil.

partner ['pɑːtnə] **1.** Partner(in); **2.** (sich) zs.-tun mit, zs.-arbeiten mit; ~ship [~ʃip] Teilhaber-, Part-

nerschaft f; 🕆 Handelsgesellschaft f.

part-owner ['pɑːtounə] Miteigentümer(in).

partridge orn. ['pɑːtridʒ] Rebhuhn n.

part-time ['pɑːttaim] **1.** adj. Teilzeit..., Halbtags...; **2.** adv. halbtags.

party ['pɑːti] Partei f; ✕ Trupp m, Kommando n; Party f, Gesellschaft f; Beteiligte(r) m; co. Type f, Individuum n; ~ line pol. Parteilinie f, -direktive f.

pass [pɑːs] **1.** Paß m, Ausweis m; Passierschein m; Bestehen n e-s Examens; univ. gewöhnlicher Grad; (kritische) Lage; Fußball: Paß m; Bestreichung f, Strich m; (Gebirgs-) Paß m, Durchgang m; Karten: Passen n; free ~ Freikarte f; **2.** v/i. passieren, geschehen; hingenommen werden; Karten: passen; (vorbei)gehen, (vorbei)kommen, (vorbei)fahren; vergehen (Zeit); sich verwandeln; angenommen werden (Banknoten); bekannt sein; vergehen; aussterben; a. ~ away sterben; durchkommen (Gesetz; Prüfling); ~ for gelten als; ~ off vonstatten gehen; ~ out F ohnmächtig werden; come to ~ geschehen; bring to ~ bewirken; v/t. vorbeigehen od. vorbeikommen od. vorbeifahren an (dat.); passieren; kommen od. fahren durch; verbringen; reichen, geben; Bemerkung machen, von sich geben; Banknoten in Umlauf bringen; Gesetz durchbringen, annehmen; Prüfung durchkommen lassen; Prüfung bestehen; (hinaus-)gehen über (acc.); Urteil abgeben; Meinung äußern; bewegen; streichen mit; Ball zuspielen; Truppen vorbeimarschieren lassen; ~able □ ['pɑːsəbl] passierbar; gangbar, gültig (Geld); leidlich.

passage ['pæsidʒ] Durchgang m, Durchfahrt f; Überfahrt f; Durchreise f; Korridor m, Gang m; Weg m; Annahme f e-s Gesetzes; 🎵 Passage f; Text-Stelle f; bird of ~ Zugvogel m.

passbook 🕆 ['pɑːsbuk] Sparbuch n.

passenger ['pæsindʒə] Passagier m, Fahr-, Fluggast m, Reisende(r m) n f.

passer-by ['pɑːsə'bai] Vorübergehende(r m) f, Passant(in).

passion ['pæʃən] Leidenschaft f; (Gefühls)Ausbruch m; Zorn m; 🙎 eccl. Passion f; be in a ~ zornig sein; in ~ 🇹 im Affekt; 🙎 Week eccl. Karwoche f; ~ate □ [~nit] leidenschaftlich.

passive □ ['pæsiv] passiv (a. gr.); teilnahmslos; untätig.

passport ['pɑːspɔːt] (Reise)Paß m.

password ✕ ['pɑːswəːd] Losung f.

past [pɑːst] **1.** adj. vergangen; gr. Vergangenheits...; früher; for some

time ~ seit einiger Zeit; ~ tense gr.
Vergangenheit f; 2. adv. vorbei;
3. prp. nach, über; über ... (acc.)
hinaus; an ... (dat.) vorbei; half ~
two halb drei; ~ endurance unerträglich; ~ hope hoffnungslos;
4. Vergangenheit f (a. gr.).
paste [peist] 1. Teig m; Kleister m;
Paste f; 2. (be)kleben; **~board**
['peistbɔːd] Pappe f; attr. Papp...
pastel [pæs tel] Pastell(bild) n.
pasteurize ['pæstəraiz] pasteurisie-
ren, keimfrei machen.
pastime ['pɑːstaim] Zeitvertreib m.
pastor ['pɑːstə] Pastor m; Seel-
sorger m; **~al** □ [~ərəl] Hirten...;
pastoral
pastry ['peistri] Tortengebäck n,
Konditorwaren f/pl.; Pasteten f/pl.;
~cook Pastetenbäcker m, Konditor m
pasture ['pɑːstʃə] 1. Vieh-Weide f;
Futter n; 2. (ab)weiden.
pat [pæt] 1. Klaps m; Portion f
Butter; 2. tätscheln; klopfen; 3. gelegen, gerade recht; bereit.
patch [pætʃ] 1. Fleck m; Flicken m;
Stück n Land; ✠ Pflaster n; 2. flik-
ken; **~work** ['pætʃwəːk] Flickwerk
n.
pate F [peit] Schädel m.
patent ['peitənt, Am. 'pætənt] 1. offenkundig, patentiert; Patent...;
letters ['pætənt] pl. Freibrief m;
~ leather Lackleder n; 2. Patent n;
Privileg n, Freibrief m; ~ agent
Patentanwalt m; 3. patentieren;
~ee [peitən'tiː] Patentinhaber m.
patern|al [pə'təːnl] väterlich;
~ity [~nti] Vaterschaft f.
path [pɑːθ], pl. **~s** [pɑːðz] Pfad m;
Weg m
pathetic [pə'θetik] (~ally) pathe-
tisch; rührend, ergreifend.
pathos ['peiθɔs] Pathos n.
patien|ce ['peiʃəns] Geduld f; Aus-
dauer f, Patience f (Kartenspiel);
~t [~nt] 1. □ geduldig; 2. Pa-
tient(in)
patio Am ['pætiou] Innenhof m,
Patio m
patrimony ['pætriməni] väterliches
Erbteil
patriot ['peitriət] Patriot(in).
patrol ⚔ [pə'troul] 1. Patrouille f,
Streife f, ~ wagon Am. Polizei-
gefangenenwagen m; 2. (ab)pa-
trouillieren, **~man** [~lmæn] pa-
trouillierender Polizist; Pannen-
helfer m e-s Automobilclubs.
patron ['peitrən] (Schutz)Patron m;
Gönner m, Kunde m; **~age** [~pætrə-
nidʒ] Gönnerschaft f; Kundschaft f;
Schutz m, **~ize** [~naiz] beschützen;
begünstigen, Kunde sein bei; gön-
nerhaft behandeln.
patter ['pætə] v/i. platschen; trappeln; v/t. (her)plappern.
pattern ['pætən] 1. Muster n (a.

fig.); Modell n; 2. formen (after, on
nach).
paunch ['pɔːntʃ] Wanst m.
pauper ['pɔːpə] Fürsorgeempfän-
ger(in); **~ize** [~əraiz] arm machen.
pause [pɔːz] 1. Pause f; 2. pausie-
ren.
pave [peiv] pflastern; fig. Weg bahnen; **~ment** ['peivmənt] Bürgersteig m, Gehweg m; Pflaster n.
paw [pɔː] 1. Pfote f, Tatze f; 2. scharren; F befingern; rauh behandeln.
pawn [pɔːn] 1. Bauer m im Schach;
Pfand n; in od. at ~ verpfändet; 2.
verpfänden; **~broker** ['pɔːnbroukə]
Pfandleiher m; **~shop** Leihhaus n.
pay [pei] 1. (Be)Zahlung f; Sold m,
Lohn m; 2. [irr.] v/t (be)zahlen;
(be)lohnen; sich lohnen für; Ehre
etc. erweisen; Besuch abstatten; ~
attention od. heed to achtgeben auf
(acc.); ~ down bar bezahlen; ~ off j-n
bezahlen u. entlassen; j-n voll
auszahlen; v/i. zahlen; sich lohnen;
~ for (für) et. bezahlen; **~able**
['peiəbl] zahlbar; fällig; **~day**
Zahltag m; **~ee** ✝ [pei'iː] Zahlungs-
empfänger m; **~ing** ['peiiŋ] loh-
nend; **~master** Zahlmeister m;
~ment ['peimənt] (Be)Zahlung f;
Lohn m, Sold m; **~off** Abrechnung
f (a. fig.); Am F Höhepunkt m;
~roll Lohnliste f.
pea ♀ [piː] Erbse f.
peace [piːs] Frieden m, Ruhe f; at ~
friedlich; **~able** ['piːsəbl] fried-
liebend, friedlich, **~ful** ['piːsful]
friedlich; **~maker** Friedensstif-
ter(in).
peach ♀ [piːtʃ] Pfirsich(baum) m.
pea|cock orn. ['piːkɔk] Pfau(hahn)
m; **~hen** orn. ['piːhen] Pfauhenne f.
peak [piːk] Spitze f; Gipfel m;
Mützen-Schirm m; attr Spitzen...;
Höchst..., f [~t] piːk] spitz.
peal [piːl] 1. Geläut n; Glockenspiel n; Dröhnen n; ~s of laughter
dröhnendes Gelächter; 2. erschallen (lassen); laut verkünden; dröhnen.
peanut ['piːnʌt] Erdnuß f.
pear ♀ [pɛə] Birne f.
pearl [pəːl] 1. Perle f (a. fig.); attr.
Perl(en)...; 2. tropfen, perlen; **~y**
['pəːli] perlenartig.
peasant ['pezənt] 1. Bauer m;
2. bäuerlich; **~ry** [~tri] Landvolk n.
peat [piːt] Torf m
pebble['pebl] Kiesel(stein) m.
peck [pek] 1. Viertelscheffel m
(9,087 Liter); fig Menge f; 2. pik-
ken, hacken (at nach).
peculate ['pekjuleit] unterschlagen.
peculiar [pi'kjuːljə] eigen(tümlich); besonder; seltsam; **~ity**
[pikjuːli'æriti] Eigenheit f; Eigentümlichkeit f
pecuniary [pi'kjuːnjəri] Geld...
pedagog|ics [pedə'gɔdʒiks] mst sg.

Pädagogik *f*; **~ue** ['pedəgɔg] Pädagoge *m*; Lehrer *m*.

pedal ['pedl] 1. Pedal *n*; 2. Fuß...; 3. *Radfahren*: fahren, treten.

pedantic [pi'dæntik] (**~ally**) pedantisch.

peddle ['pedl] hausieren (mit); **~r** *Am.* [**~**ə] = *pedlar*.

pedestal ['pedistl] Sockel *m* (*a. fig.*).

pedestrian [pi'destriən] 1. zu Fuß; nüchtern; 2. Fußgänger(in); **~** *crossing* Fußgängerübergang *m*.

pedigree ['pedigri:] Stammbaum *m*.

pedlar ['pedlə] Hausierer *m*.

peek [pi:k] 1. spähen, gucken, lugen; 2. flüchtiger Blick.

peel [pi:l] 1. Schale *f*; Rinde *f*; 2. *a.* **~** *off* *v/t.* (ab)schälen; *Kleid* abstreifen; *v/i.* sich (ab)schälen.

peep [pi:p] 1. verstohlener Blick, Piepen *n*; 2. (verstohlen) gucken; *a.* **~** *out* (hervor)gucken (*a. fig.*); piepen; **~hole** ['pi:phoul] Guckloch *n*.

peer [piə] 1. spähen, lugen; **~** *at* angucken; 2. Gleiche(r *m*) *f*; Pair *m*; **~less** □ ['piəlis] unvergleichlich.

peevish □ ['pi:viʃ] verdrießlich.

peg [peg] 1. Stöpsel *m*, Dübel *m*, Pflock *m*; *Kleider*-Haken *m*; ♪ Wirbel *m*; *Wäsche*-Klammer *f*; *fig.* Aufhänger *m*; *take s.o. down a* **~** *or two j-n* demütigen; 2. festpflöcken; *Grenze* abstecken; **~** *away od. along* F darauflosarbeiten; **~top** ['pegtɔp] Kreisel *m*.

pelican *orn.* ['pelikən] Pelikan *m*.

pellet ['pelit] Kügelchen *n*; Pille *f*; Schrotkorn *n*.

pell-mell ['pel'mel] durcheinander.

pelt [pelt] 1. Fell *n*; ✝ rohe Haut; 2. *v/t.* bewerfen; *v/i.* niederprasseln.

pelvis *anat.* ['pelvis] Becken *n*.

pen [pen] 1. (Schreib)Feder *f*; Hürde *f*; 2. schreiben; [*irr.*] einpferchen.

penal □ ['pi:nl] Straf...; strafbar; **~** *code* Strafgesetzbuch *n*; **~** *servitude* Zuchthausstrafe *f*; **~ize** ['pi:nəlaiz] bestrafen; **~ty** ['penlti] Strafe *f*; *Sport*: Strafpunkt *m*; **~** *area Fußball*: Strafraum *m*; **~** *kick Fußball*: Freistoß *m*.

penance ['penəns] Buße *f*.

pence [pens] *pl. von penny*.

pencil ['pensl] 1. Bleistift *m*; 2. zeichnen; (mit Bleistift) anzeichnen *od.* anstreichen; *Augenbrauen* nachziehen; **~sharpener** Bleistiftspitzer *m*.

pendant ['pendənt] Anhänger *m*.

pending ['pendiŋ] 1. ⚖ schwebend; 2. *prp.* während; bis zu.

pendulum ['pendjuləm] Pendel *n*.

penetra|ble □ ['penitrəbl] durchdringbar; **~te** [**~**reit] durchdringen; ergründen; eindringen (in *acc.*); vordringen (*to* bis zu); **~tion** [peni-

'treiʃən] Durch-, Eindringen *n*; Scharfsinn *m*; **~tive** □ ['penitrətiv] durchdringend (*a. fig.*); eindringlich; scharfsinnig.

pen-friend ['penfrend] Brieffreund (-in).

penguin *orn.* ['peŋgwin] Pinguin *m*.

penholder ['penhouldə] Federhalter *m*.

peninsula [pi'ninsjulə] Halbinsel *f*.

peniten|ce ['penitəns] Buße *f*, Reue *f*; **~t** 1. □ reuig, bußfertig; 2. Büßer(in); **~tiary** [peni'tenʃəri] Besserungsanstalt *f*; *Am.* Zuchthaus *n*.

pen|knife ['pennaif] Taschenmesser *n*; **~man** Schönschreiber *m*; Schriftsteller *m*; **~name** Schriftstellername *m*, Pseudonym *n*.

pennant ⚓ ['penənt] Wimpel *m*.

penniless □ ['penilis] ohne Geld.

penny ['peni], *pl. mst* **pence** [pens] (englischer) Penny (¹/₁₂ *Schilling*); *Am.* Cent *m*; Kleinigkeit *f*; **~weight** englisches Pennygewicht (1¹/₂ *Gramm*).

pension ['penʃən] 1. Pension *f*, Ruhegehalt *n*; 2. *oft* **~** *off* pensionieren; **~ary**, **~er** [**~**nəri, **~**nə] Pensionär(in).

pensive □ ['pensiv] gedankenvoll.

pent [pent] *pret. u. p.p. von pen* 2; **~up** aufgestaut (*Zorn etc.*).

Pentecost ['pentikɔst] Pfingsten *n*.

penthouse ['penthaus] Schutzdach *n*; Dachwohnung *f* *auf e-m Hochhaus.*

penu|rious □ [pi'njuəriəs] geizig; **~ry** ['penjuri] Armut *f*; Mangel *m*.

people ['pi:pl] 1. Volk *n*, Nation *f*; *coll.* die Leute *pl.*; man; 2. bevölkern.

pepper ['pepə] 1. Pfeffer *m*; 2. pfeffern; **~mint** ♣ Pfefferminze *f*; **~y** □ [**~**əri] pfefferig; *fig.* hitzig.

per [pə:] per, durch, für; laut; je.

perambulat|e [pə'ræmbjuleit] (durch)wandern; bereisen; **~or** ['præmbjuleitə] Kinderwagen *m*.

perceive [pə'si:v] (be)merken, wahrnehmen; empfinden; erkennen.

per cent [pə'sent] Prozent *n*.

percentage [pə'sentidʒ] Prozentsatz *m*; Prozente *n/pl.*; *fig.* Teil *m*.

percept|ible □ [pə'septəbl] wahrnehmbar; **~ion** [**~**pʃən] Wahrnehmung(svermögen *n*) *f*; Erkenntnis *f*; Auffassung(skraft) *f*.

perch [pə:tʃ] 1. *ichth.* Barsch *m*; Rute *f* (5,029 *m*); (Sitz)Stange *f* *für Vögel*; 2. (sich) setzen; sitzen.

perchance [pə'tʃɑ:ns] zufällig; vielleicht.

percolate ['pə:kəleit] durchtropfen, durchsickern (lassen); sickern.

percussion [pə:'kaʃən] Schlag *m*; Erschütterung *f*; ♫ Abklopfen *n*.

perdition [pə:'diʃən] Verderben *n*.

peregrination [perigri'neiʃən] Wanderschaft *f*; Wanderung *f*.

peremptory ☐ [pə'remptəri] bestimmt; zwingend; rechthaberisch.

perennial [pə'renjəl] dauernd; immerwährend; ♀ perennierend.

perfect 1. ['pə:fikt] ☐ vollkommen; vollendet; gänzlich, völlig; **2.** [~] a. ~ tense gr. Perfekt n; **3.** [pə-'fekt] vervollkommnen; vollenden; **~ion** [~kʃən] Vollendung f; Vollkommenheit f; fig. Gipfel m.

perfidious [pə:'fidiəs] treulos (to gegen), verräterisch.

perfidy ['pə:fidi] Treulosigkeit f.

perforate ['pə:fəreit] durchlöchern.

perforce [pə'fɔ:s] notgedrungen.

perform [pə'fɔ:m] verrichten; ausführen; tun; Pflicht etc. erfüllen; thea., ♪ aufführen, spielen, vortragen (a. v/i.); **~ance** [~məns] Verrichtung f; thea. Aufführung f; Vortrag m; Leistung f; **~er** [~mə] Vortragende(r m) f.

perfume 1. ['pə:fju:m] Wohlgeruch m; Parfüm n; **2.** [pə'fju:m] parfümieren; **~ry** [~məri] Parfümerie(n pl.) f.

perfunctory ☐ [pə'fʌŋktəri] mechanisch; oberflächlich.

perhaps [pə'hæps, præps] vielleicht.

peril ['peril] **1.** Gefahr f; **2.** gefährden; **~ous** [[~ləs] gefährlich.

period ['piəriəd] Periode f; Zeitraum m; gr. Punkt m; langer Satz; (Unterrichts)Stunde f; mst ~s pl. ✿ Periode f; **~ic** [piəri'ɔdik] periodisch; **~ical** [~kəl] **1.** ☐ periodisch; **2.** Zeitschrift f.

perish ['periʃ] umkommen, zugrunde gehen; **~able** ☐ [~əbl] vergänglich; leicht verderblich; **~ing** ☐ [~ʃiŋ] vernichtend, tödlich.

periwig ['periwig] Perücke f.

perjure ['pə:dʒə]: ~ o.s. falsch schwören; **~y** [~əri] Meineid m.

perk F [pə:k] v/i. mst ~ up selbstbewußt auftreten; sich wieder erholen; v/t. recken; ~ o.s. (up) sich putzen.

perky [['pə:ki] keck, dreist; flott.

perm F [pə:m] **1.** Dauerwelle f; **2.** j-m Dauerwellen machen.

permanen|ce ['pə:mənəns] Dauer f; **~t** [[~nt] dauernd, ständig; dauerhaft; Dauer...; ~ wave Dauerwelle f.

permea|ble ☐ [pə'mjəbl] durchlässig; **~te** ['pə:mieit] durchdringen; eindringen.

permissi|ble ☐ [pə'misəbl] zulässig; **~on** [~iʃən] Erlaubnis f.

permit 1. [pə'mit] erlauben, gestatten; **2.** ['pə:mit] Erlaubnis f, Genehmigung f; Passierschein m.

pernicious ☐ [pə:'niʃəs] verderblich; ✿ bösartig.

perpendicular ☐ [pə:pən'dikjulə] senkrecht; aufrecht; steil.

perpetrate ['pə:pitreit] verüben.

perpetu|al ☐ [pə'petjuəl] fort-

während, ewig; **~ate** [~ueit] verewigen.

perplex [pə'pleks] verwirren; **~ity** [~siti] Verwirrung f.

perquisites ['pə:kwizits] pl. Nebeneinkünfte pl.

persecut|e ['pə:sikju:t] verfolgen; **~ion** [pə:si'kju:ʃən] Verfolgung f; **~or** ['pə:sikju:tə] Verfolger m.

persever|ance [pə:si'viərəns] Beharrlichkeit f, Ausdauer f; **~e** [pə:-si'viə] beharren; aushalten.

persist [pə'sist] beharren (in auf dat.); **~ence, ~ency** [~təns, ~si] Beharrlichkeit f; **~ent** ☐ [~nt] beharrlich.

person ['pə:sn] Person f (a. gr.); Persönlichkeit f; thea. Rolle f; **~age** [~nidʒ] Persönlichkeit f; thea. Charakter m; **~al** [[~nl] persönlich (a. gr.); attr. Personal...; Privat...; eigen; **~ality** [pə:sə'næliti] Persönlichkeit f; **~alities** pl. persönliche Bemerkungen f/pl.; **~ate** ['pə:səneit] darstellen; sich ausgeben für; **~ify** [pə:'sɔnifai] verkörpern; **~nel** [pə:sə'nel] Personal n.

perspective [pə'spektiv] Perspektive f; Ausblick m, Fernsicht f.

perspex ['pə:speks] Plexiglas n.

perspicuous [[pə'spikjuəs] klar.

perspir|ation [pə:spə'reiʃən] Schwitzen n; Schweiß m; **~e** [pəs-'paiə] (aus)schwitzen.

persua|de [pə'sweid] überreden; überzeugen; **~sion** [~eiʒən] Überredung f; Überzeugung f; Glaube m; **~sive** ☐ [~eisiv] überredend, überzeugend. [weis.]

pert ☐ [pə:t] keck, vorlaut, nase-)

pertain [pə:'tein] (to) gehören (dat. od. zu); betreffen (acc.).

pertinacious ☐ [pə:ti'neiʃəs] hartnäckig, zäh.

pertinent ☐ ['pə:tinənt] sachdienlich, -gemäß; zur Sache gehörig.

perturb [pə'tə:b] beunruhigen; stören.

perus|al [pə'ru:zəl] sorgfältige Durchsicht; **~e** [~u:z] durchlesen; prüfen.

pervade [pə:'veid] durchdringen.

pervers|e ☐ [pə'və:s] verkehrt; ✿ pervers; eigensinnig; vertrackt (Sache); **~ion** [~:ʃən] Verdrehung f; Abkehr f; **~ity** [~:siti] Verkehrtheit f; ✿ Perversität f; Eigensinn m.

pervert 1. [pə'və:t] verdrehen; verführen; **2.** ✿ ['pə:və:t] perverser Mensch.

pessimism ['pesimizəm] Pessimismus m.

pest [pest] Pest f; Plage f; Schädling m; **~er** ['pestə] belästigen.

pestl|iferous ☐ [pes'tifərəs] krankheiterregend; **~ence** ['pestiləns] Seuche f, bsd. Pest f; **~ent** [~nt] gefährlich; co. verdammt; **~ential**

□ ['pesti'lenʃəl] pestartig; verderbenbringend.

pet [pet] 1. üble Laune; zahmes Tier; Liebling m; 2. Lieblings...; ~ dog Schoßhund m; ~ name Kosename m; 3. (ver)hätscheln; knutschen.

petal ⚥ ['petl] Blütenblatt n.

petition [pi'tiʃən] 1. Bitte f; Bittschrift f, Eingabe f; 2. bitten, ersuchen; e-e Eingabe machen.

petrify ['petrifai] versteinern.

petrol mot. ['petrəl] Benzin n; ~ station Tankstelle f.

petticoat ['petikout] Unterrock m.

pettish □ ['petiʃ] launisch.

petty □ ['peti] klein, geringfügig.

petulant ['petjulənt] gereizt.

pew [pju:] Kirchensitz m, -bank f.

pewter ['pju:tə] Zinn(gefäße n/pl.) n.

phantasm ['fæntæzəm] Trugbild n.

phantom ['fæntəm] Phantom n, Trugbild n; Gespenst n.

Pharisee ['færisi:] Pharisäer m.

pharmacy ['fɑːməsi] Pharmazie f; Apotheke f.   [Phasen.]

phase [feiz] Phase f; ~d [feizd] in|

pheasant orn. ['feznt] Fasan m.

phenomen|on [fi'nɔminən], pl. ~a [~nə] Phänomen n, Erscheinung f.

phial ['faiəl] Phiole f, Fläschchen n.

philander [fi'lændə] flirten.

philanthropist [fi'lænθrəpist] Menschenfreund(in).

philolog|ist [fi'lɔlədʒist] Philolog|e m, -in f; ~y [~dʒi] Philologie f.

philosoph|er [fi'lɔsəfə] Philosoph m; ~ize [~faiz] philosophieren; ~y [~fi] Philosophie f.

phlegm [flem] Schleim m; Phlegma n.

phone F [foun] s. telephone.

phonetics [fou'netiks] pl. Phonetik f, Lautbildungslehre f.

phon(e)y Am. sl. ['founi] 1. Fälschung f; Schwindler m; 2. unecht.

phosphorus ['fɔsfərəs] Phosphor m.

photograph ['foutəgrɑ:f] 1. Photographie f (Bild); 2. photographieren; ~er [fə'tɔgrəfə] Photograph (-in); ~y [~fi] Photographie f.

phrase [freiz] 1. (Rede)Wendung f, Redensart f, Ausdruck m; 2. ausdrücken.

physic|al □ ['fizikəl] physisch; körperlich; physikalisch; ~ education, ~ training Leibeserziehung f; ~ian [fi'ziʃən] Arzt m; ~ist ['fizisist] Physiker m; ~s [~iks] sg. Physik f.

physique [fi'zi:k] Körperbau m.

piano ['pjænou] Klavier n.

piazza [pi'ætsə] Piazza f, (Markt-)Platz m; Am. große Veranda.

pick [pik] Auswahl f; = pickaxe; 2. auf-, wegnehmen; pflücken; (herum)stochern; in der Nase bohren; abnagen; Schloß knacken; Streit suchen; auswählen; (auf-)picken; bestehlen; ~ out auswählen

heraussuchen; ~ up aufreißen, aufbrechen; aufnehmen, auflesen; sich e-e Fremdsprache aneignen; erfassen; (im Auto) mitnehmen, abholen; Täter ergreifen; gesund werden; ~-a-back ['pikəbæk] huckepack; ~axe Spitzhacke f.

picket ['pikit] 1. Pfahl m; ✕ Feldwache f; Streikposten m; 2. einpfählen; an e-n Pfahl binden; mit Streikposten besetzen.

picking ['pikiŋ] Picken n, Pflücken n; Abfall m; mst ~s pl. Nebengewinn m.

pickle ['pikl] 1. Pökel m; Eingepökelte(s) n, Pickles pl.; F mißliche Lage; 2. (ein)pökeln; ~d herring Salzhering m.

pick|lock ['piklɔk] Dietrich m; ~pocket Taschendieb m; ~up Ansteigen n; Tonabnehmer m; Kleinlieferwagen m; sl. Straßenbekanntschaft f.

picnic ['piknik] Picknick n.

pictorial [pik'tɔ:riəl] 1. □ malerisch; illustriert; 2. Illustrierte f.

picture ['piktʃə] 1. Bild n, Gemälde n; et. Bildschönes; ~s pl. F Kino n; attr. Bilder...; put s.o. in the ~ j. ins Bild setzen; j. informieren; 2. (aus-)malen; sich et. ausmalen; ~ postcard Ansichtskarte f; ~sque [piktʃə'resk] malerisch.

pie [pai] Pastete f; Obsttorte f.

piebald ['paibɔ:ld] (bunt)scheckig.

piece [pi:s] 1. Stück n; Geschütz n; Gewehr n; Teil n e-s Services; Schach- etc. Figur f; a ~ of advice ein Rat; a ~ of news e-e Neuigkeit; of a ~ gleichmäßig; give s.o. a ~ of one's mind j-m gründlich die Meinung sagen; take to ~s zerlegen; 2. a. ~ up flicken, ausbessern; ~ together zs.-stellen, -setzen, -stücken, -flicken; ~ out ausfüllen; ~meal ['pi:smi:l] stückweise; ~work Akkordarbeit f.

pieplant Am. ['paiplɑ:nt] Rhabarber m.

pier [piə] Pfeiler m; Wellenbrecher m; Pier m, f, Hafendamm m, Mole f, Landungsbrücke f.

pierce [piəs] durchbohren; durchdringen; eindringen (in acc.).

piety ['paiəti] Frömmigkeit f; Pietät f.

pig [pig] Ferkel n; Schwein n.

pigeon ['pidʒin] Taube f; ~hole 1. Fach n; 2. in ein Fach legen.

pig|headed ['pig'hedid] dickköpfig; ~-iron ['pigaiən] Roheisen n; ~skin Schweinsleder n; ~sty Schweinestall m; ~tail (Haar)Zopf m.

pike [paik] ✕ Pike f; Spitze f; ichth. Hecht m; Schlagbaum m; gebührenpflichtige Straße.

pile [pail] 1. (Scheiter)Haufen m; Stoß m (Holz); großes Gebäude; ⚡ Batterie f; Pfahl m; Haar n;

Noppe *f*; ~s *pl.* ♣ Hämorrhoiden *f/pl.*; (*atomic*) ~ *phys.* Atommeiler *m*, Reaktor *m*; 2. *oft* ~ *up*, ~ *on* auf-, anhäufen, aufschichten.

pilfer ['pilfə] mausen, stibitzen.

pilgrim ['pilgrim] Pilger *m*; ~**age** [~midʒ] Pilgerfahrt *f*.

pill [pil] Pille *f*.

pillage ['pilidʒ] 1. Plünderung *f*; 2. plündern.

pillar ['pilə] Pfeiler *m*, Ständer *m*; Säule *f*; ~**box** Briefkasten *m*.

pillion *mot* ['piljən] Soziussitz *m*.

pillory ['piləri] 1. Pranger *m*; 2. an den Pranger stellen; anprangern.

pillow ['pilou] (Kopf)Kissen *n*; ~**case**, ~**slip** (Kissen)Bezug *m*.

pilot ['pailət] 1. ✈ Pilot *m*; ⚓ Lotse *m*; *fig.* Führer *m*; 2. lotsen, steuern; ~**balloon** Versuchsballon *m*.

pimp [pimp] 1. Kuppler(in); 2. kuppeln.

pin [pin] 1. (Steck-, Krawatten-, Hut- *etc.*)Nadel *f*; Reißnagel *m*; Pflock *m*; ♪ Wirbel *m*; Kegel *m*; 2. (an)heften; befestigen; *fig.* festnageln

pinafore ['pinəfɔ:] Schürze *f*.

pincers ['pinsəz] *pl.* Kneifzange *f*.

pinch [pintʃ] 1. Kniff *m*; Prise *f* (*Tabak etc.*); Druck *m*, Not *f*; 2. *v/t.* kneifen, zwicken; F klauen; *v/i.* drücken; in Not sein; knausern.

pinch-hit *Am.* ['pintʃhit] einspringen (*for* für).

pincushion ['pinkuʃin] Nadelkissen *n*.

pine [pain] 1. ♀ Kiefer *f*, Föhre *f*; 2. sich abhärmen; sich sehnen, schmachten; ~**apple** ♀ ['painæpl] Ananas *f*; ~**cone** Kiefernzapfen *m*.

pinion ['pinjən] 1. Flügel(spitze *f*) *m*; Schwungfeder *f*; ⊕ Ritzel *n* (*Antriebsrad*); 2. die Flügel beschneiden (*dat.*); *fig.* fesseln.

pink [piŋk] 1. ♀ Nelke *f*; Rosa *n*; *fig.* Gipfel *m*; 2. rosa(farben).

pin-money ['pinmʌni] Nadelgeld *n*.

pinnacle ['pinəkl] △ Zinne *f*, Spitztürmchen *n*; (Berg)Spitze *f*; *fig.* Gipfel *m*.

pint [paint] Pinte *f* (*0,57 od. Am. 0,47 Liter*).

pioneer [paiə'niə] 1. Pionier *m* (*a.* ✕); 2. den Weg bahnen (für).

pious [['paiəs] fromm, religiös; pflichtgetreu.

pip [pip] *vet.* Pips *m*; *sl.* miese Laune; Obstkern *m*; Auge *n auf Würfeln etc.*; ✕ Stern *m* (*Rangabzeichen*).

pipe [paip] 1. Rohr *n*, Röhre *f*; Pfeife *f* (*a. ♪*); Flöte *f*; Lied *n e-s Vogels*; Luftröhre *f*; Pipe *f* (*Weinfaß = 477,3 Liter*); 2. pfeifen; quieken; ~**layer** ['paipleiə] Rohrleger *m*; *Am. pol.* Drahtzieher *m*;

~**line** Ölleitung *f*, Pipeline *f*; ~**r** ['paipə] Pfeifer *m*.

piping ['paipiŋ] 1. pfeifend; schrill (*Stimme*); ~ *hot* siedend heiß; 2. Rohrnetz *n*; *Schneiderei:* Paspel *f*.

piquant [['pi:kənt] pikant.

pique [pi:k] 1. Groll (*m*); 2. *j-n* reizen; ~ *o.s. on* sich brüsten mit.

pira|cy ['paiərəsi] Seeräuberei *f*; Raubdruck *m von Büchern*; ~**te** [~rit] 1. Seeräuber(schiff *n*) *m*; Raubdrucker *m*; 2. unerlaubt nachdrucken.

pistol ['pistl] Pistole *f*.

piston ⊕ ['pistən] Kolben *m*; ~**rod** Kolbenstange *f*; ~**stroke** Kolbenhub *m*.

pit [pit] 1. Grube *f* (*a.* ✕, *anat.*); ♪ Miete *f*; *thea.* Parterre *n*; Pockennarbe *f*; (Tier)Falle *f*; *Am. Börse:* Maklerstand *m*; *Am. Obst-*Stein *m*; 2. ♪ einmieten; mit Narben bedecken.

pitch [pitʃ] 1. Pech *n*; Stand(platz) *m*; Tonhöhe *f*; Grad *m*, Stufe *f*; Steigung *f*, Neigung *f*; Wurf *m*; ⚓ Stampfen *f*; 2. *v/t.* werfen; schleudern; *Zelt etc.* aufschlagen; ♪ stimmen (*a. fig.*); ~ *too high fig. Ziel etc.* zu hoch stecken; *v/i.* ✕ (sich) lagern; fallen; ⚓ stampfen; ~ *into* F herfallen über (*acc.*).

pitcher ['pitʃə] Krug *m*.

pitchfork ['pitʃfɔ:k] Heu-, Mistgabel *f*; ♪ Stimmgabel *f*.

piteous [['pitiəs] kläglich.

pitfall ['pitfɔ:l] Fallgrube *f*, Falle *f*.

pith [piθ] Mark *n*; *fig.* Kern *m*; Kraft *f*; ~**y** [['piθi] markig, kernig.

pitiable [['pitiəbl] erbärmlich.

pitiful [['pitiful] mitleidig; erbärmlich, jämmerlich (*a. contp.*).

pitiless [['pitilis] unbarmherzig.

pittance ['pitəns] Hungerlohn *m*.

pity ['piti] 1. Mitleid *n* (on mit); *it is a* ~ es ist schade; 2. bemitleiden.

pivot ['pivət] 1. ⊕ Zapfen *m*; (Tür-) Angel *f*; *fig.* Drehpunkt *m*; 2. sich drehen (on, upon um) [verrückt.]

pixilated *Am.* F ['piksileitid] leicht]

placable [['plækəbl] versöhnlich.

placard ['plæka:d] 1. Plakat *n*; 2. anschlagen; mit e-m Plakat bekleben.

place [pleis] 1. Platz *m*; Ort *m*; Stadt *f*; Stelle *f*; Stätte *f*; Stellung *f*; Aufgabe *f*; Anwesen *n*, Haus *n*, Wohnung *f*; ~ *of delivery* ✦ Erfüllungsort *m*; *give* ~ *to j-m* Platz machen; *in* ~ *of* an Stelle (*gen.*); *out of* ~ fehl am Platz; 2. stellen, legen, setzen; *j-n* anstellen; *Auftrag* erteilen; *I can't place him fig.* ich weiß nicht, wo ich ihn hintun soll (*identifizieren*).

placid [['plæsid] sanft; ruhig.

plagiar|ism ['pleidʒjərizəm] Plagiat *n*; ~**ize** [~raiz] abschreiben.

plague [pleig] 1. Plage *f*; Seuche *f*;
Pest *f*; 2. plagen, quälen.

plaice *ichth.* [pleis] Scholle *f*.

plaid [plæd] *schottisches* Plaid.

plain [plein] 1. flach, eben; klar;
deutlich; rein; einfach, schlicht;
unscheinbar; offen, ehrlich; einfarbig; 2. *adv.* klar, deutlich;
3. Ebene *f*, Fläche *f*; bsd. *Am.*
Prärie *f*; ~clothes man ['plein-
klouðz mən] Geheimpolizist *m*;
~ dealing ehrliche Handlungsweise; ~dealing ehrlich.

plainsman ['pleinzmən] Flachland-
bewohner *m*; *Am.* Präriebewohner
m.

plaint|iff *t's* ['pleintif] Kläger(in);
~ive □ [~iv] traurig, klagend.

plait [plæt, *Am.* pleit] 1. *Haar- etc.*
Flechte *f*; Zopf *m*; 2. flechten.

plan [plæn] 1. Plan *m*; 2. e-n Plan
machen von od. zu; *fig.* planen.

plane [plein] 1. flach, eben; 2. Ebene
f, Fläche *f*; ~ Tragfläche *f*; Flugzeug *n*; *fig.* Stufe *f*; ⊕ Hobel *m*;
3. ebnen; (ab)hobeln; ~ fliegen.

plank [plæŋk] 1. Planke *f*, Bohle *f*,
Diele *f*; *Am. pol.* Programm-
punkt *m*; 2. dielen; verschalen; ~
down *sl.*, *Am.* F Geld auf den Tisch
legen.

plant [plɑːnt] 1. Pflanze *f*; ⊕ Anlage *f*; Fabrik *f*; 2. (an-, ein)pflan-
zen (*a fig.*); (auf)stellen; anlegen;
Schlag verpassen; bepflanzen; besiedeln; ~ation [plæn'teiʃən] Pflan-
zung *f* (*a. fig.*); Plantage *f*; Be-
siedelung *f*; ~er ['plɑːntə] Pflanzer
m.

plaque [plɑːk] Platte *f*; Gedenk-
tafel *f*.

plash [plæʃ] platschen.

plaster ['plɑːstə] 1. *pharm.* Pflaster
n; ⊕ Putz *m*; *mst* ~ of Paris Gips
m, Stuck *m*; 2. bepflastern; verputzen.

plastic ['plæstik] 1. (~ally) plastisch;
Plastik...; 2. *oft* ~s *pl.* Plastik(material) *n*, Kunststoff *m*.

plat [plæt] *s.* plait; *s.* plot 1.

plate [pleit] 1. *allg.* Platte *f*; Bild-
Tafel *f*; Schild *n*; *Kupfer-*Stich *m*;
Tafelsilber *n*; Teller *m*; *Am.* Baseball: (Schlag)Mal *n*; ⊕ Grobblech
n; 2. plattieren; ~, ⊕ panzern.

platform ['plætfɔːm] Plattform *f*;
geogr. Hochebene *f*; ⑯ Bahnsteig
m; *Am. bsd.* Plattform *f am Wagen-
ende*; Rednerbühne *f*; *pol.* Partei-
programm *n*; *bsd. Am. pol.* Aktions-
programm *n im Wahlkampf*.

platinum *min.* ['plætinəm] Platin *n*.

platitude *fig.* ['plætitjuːd] Plattheit *f*.

platoon ⚔ [plə'tuːn] Zug *m*.

plat(t)en ['plætən] (Schreibma-
schinen)Walze *f*.

platter ['plætə] (Servier)Platte *f*.

plaudit ['plɔːdit] Beifall *m*.

plausible □ ['plɔːzəbl] glaubhaft.

play [plei] 1. Spiel *n*; Schauspiel *n*;
⊕ Spiel *n*, Gang *m*; Spielraum *m*;
2. spielen; ⊕ laufen; ~ upon einwirken auf (*acc.*); .. off *fig.* ausspielen (against gegen); ~ed out
erledigt; ~bill ['pleibil] Theaterzettel *m*; ~book *thea* Textbuch *n*;
~boy Playboy *m*; ~er ['pleiə]
(Schau)Spieler(in); ~piano elektrisches Klavier; ~fellow Spiel-
gefährt|e *m*, -in *f*; ~ful [~ful]
spielerisch, scherzhaft; ~goer
['pleigouə] Theaterbesucher(in);
~ground Spielplatz *m*; Schulhof *m*;
~house Schauspielhaus *n*; *Am.*
Miniaturhaus *n für Kinder*; ~mate
s. playfellow; ~thing Spielzeug *n*;
~wright Bühnenautor *m*, Dramatiker *m*.

plea [pliː] *t's* Einspruch *m*; Aus-
rede *f*; Gesuch *n*; on the ~ of od.
that unter dem Vorwand (*gen.*) od.
daß.

plead [pliːd] *v/i.* plädieren; ~ for
für *j-n* sprechen; sich einsetzen für;
~ guilty sich schuldig bekennen;
v/t. Sache vertreten; als Beweis anführen; ~er *t's* ['pliːdə] Verteidiger
m; ~ing [~diŋ] Schriftsatz *m*.

pleasant □ ['pleznt] angenehm;
erfreulich; ~ry [~tri] Scherz *m*,
Spaß *m*.

please [pliːz] *v/i.* gefallen; belieben;
if you ~ *iro.* stellen Sie sich vor;
~ come in! bitte, treten Sie ein!
v/t. j-m gefallen, angenehm sein;
befriedigen; ~ yourself tun Sie, was
Ihnen gefällt; be ..d to do *et.* gerne
tun; be ..d with Vergnügen haben
an (*dat.*); ..d erfreut; zufrieden.

pleasing □ ['pliːziŋ] angenehm.

pleasure ['pleʒə] Vergnügen *n*,
Freude *f*; Belieben *n*; *attr.* Vergnügungs...; *at* .. nach Belieben;
~ground (Vergnügungs)Park *m*.

pleat [pliːt] 1. (Plissee)Falte *f*;
2. fälteln, plissieren.

pledge [pledʒ] 1. Pfand *n*; Zutrinken *n*; Gelöbnis *n*; 2. verpfänden;
j-m zutrinken; he ..d himself er
gelobte.

plenary ['pliːnəri] Voll...

plenipotentiary [plenipə'tenʃəri]
Bevollmächtigte(r *m*) *f* [reichlich.\
plenteous □ *poet* ['plentjəs] voll,]

plentiful □ ['plentiful] reichlich.

plenty ['plenti] 1. Fülle *f*, Überfluß
m; ~ of reichlich; 2. F reichlich.

pliable □ ['plaiəbl] biegsam; *fig.*
geschmeidig, nachgiebig.

pliancy ['plaiənsi] Biegsamkeit *f*.

pliers ['plaiəz] *pl.* (a pair of ~ *pl.*
eine) (Draht-, Kombi)Zange.

plight [plait] 1. Ehre, Wort verpfänden; verloben; 2. Gelöbnis *n*;
Zustand *m*, (Not)Lage *f*.

plod [plɔd] *a.* ~ along, ~ on sich
dahinschleppen; sich plagen, schuf-
ten.

plot [plɔt] **1.** Platz m; Parzelle f; Plan m; Komplott n, Anschlag m; Intrige f; Handlung f e-s Dramas etc.; **2.** v/t. aufzeichnen; planen, anzetteln; v/i. intrigieren.

plough, *Am. mst* **plow** [plau] **1.** Pflug m; **2.** pflügen; (a. fig.) furchen; **~man** ['plaumən] Pflüger m; **~share** ['plauʃeə] Pflugschar f.

pluck [plʌk] **1.** Mut m, Schneid m, f; Innereien f/pl.; Zug m, Ruck m; **2.** pflücken; Vogel rupfen (a. fig.); reißen; **~ at** zerren an; **~ up courage** Mut fassen; **~.y** F ['plʌki] mutig.

plug [plʌg] **1.** Pflock m; Dübel m; Stöpsel m; ⚡ Stecker m; Zahn-Plombe f; Priem m (Tabak); Am. Radio: Reklamehinweis m; alter Gaul; **~ socket** Steckdose f; **2.** v/t. zu-, verstopfen; Zahn plombieren; stöpseln; Am. F im Rundfunk etc. Reklame machen für et.

plum [plʌm] Pflaume f; Rosine f (a. fig.).

plumage ['plu:midʒ] Gefieder n.

plumb [plʌm] **1.** lotrecht; gerade; richtig; **2.** (Blei)Lot n; **3.** v/t. lotrecht machen; loten; sondieren (a. fig.); F Wasser- od. Gasleitungen legen in; v/i. F als Rohrleger arbeiten; **~er** ['plʌmə] Klempner m, Installateur m; **~ing** [~miŋ] Klempnerarbeit f; Rohrleitungen f/pl.

plume [plu:m] **1.** Feder f; Federbusch m; **2.** mit Federn schmücken; die Federn putzen; **~ o.s.** on sich brüsten mit.

plummet ['plʌmit] Senkblei n.

plump [plʌmp] **1.** adj. drall, prall, mollig; F glatt (Absage etc.); **2.** (hin)plumpsen (lassen); **3.** Plumps m; **4.** F adv. geradeswegs.

plum pudding ['plʌm'pudiŋ] Plumpudding m.

plunder ['plʌndə] **1.** Plünderung f; Raub m, Beute f, **2.** plündern.

plunge [plʌndʒ] **1.** (Unter)Tauchen n; (Kopf)Sprung m; Sturz m; make o.d. take the ~ den entscheidenden Schritt tun; **2.** (unter-)tauchen; (sich) stürzen (into in acc.); Schwert etc. stoßen; ⚓ stampfen.

plunk [plʌŋk] v/t. Saite zupfen; et. hinplumpsen lassen, hinwerfen; v/i. (hin)plumpsen, fallen.

pluperfect gr. ['plu:'pə:fikt] Plusquamperfekt n.

plural gr. ['pluərəl] Plural m, Mehrzahl f; **~ity** [pluə'ræliti] Vielheit f, Mehrheit f; Mehrzahl f.

plus [plʌs] **1.** prp. plus; **2.** adj. positiv; **3.** Plus n; Mehr n.

plush [plʌʃ] Plüsch m.

ply [plai] **1.** Lage f Tuch etc.; Strähne f; fig. Neigung f; **2.** v/t. fleißig anwenden; j-m zusetzen, j-n überhäufen; v/i. regelmäßig fahren; **~wood** ['plaiwud] Sperrholz n.

---

pneumatic [nju(:)'mætik] **1.** (~ally) Luft...; pneumatisch; **2.** Luftreifen m.

pneumonia ♣ [nju(:)'mounjə] Lungenentzündung f.

poach [poutʃ] wildern; Erde zertreten; **~ed eggs** pl. verlorene Eier n/pl.

poacher ['poutʃə] Wilddieb m.

pock ♣ [pɔk] Pocke f, Blatter f.

pocket ['pɔkit] **1.** Tasche f; ✶ Luft-Loch n; **2.** einstecken (a. fig.); Am. pol. Gesetzesvorlage nicht unterschreiben; Gefühl unterdrücken; **3.** Taschen...; **~book** Notizbuch n; Brieftasche f; Am. Geldbeutel m; Taschenbuch n.

pod ♀ [pɔd] Hülse f, Schale f, Schote f.

poem ['pouim] Gedicht n.

poet ['pouit] Dichter m; **~ess** [~tis] Dichterin f; **~ic(al**)) [pou'etik(əl)] dichterisch; **~ics** [~ks] sg. Poetik f; **~ry** ['pouitri] Dichtkunst f; Dichtung f, coll. Dichtungen f/pl.

poignan|cy ['pɔinənsi] Schärfe f; **~t** [~nt] scharf; fig. eindringlich.

point [pɔint] **1.** Spitze f; Pointe f; Landspitze f; gr. ⚡, ♣, phys. etc. Punkt m; Fleck m, Stelle f; ♠ Kompaßstrich m; Auge n auf Karten etc.; Grad m; (springender) Punkt; Zweck m; fig. Eigenschaft f; **~s** pl. ♒ Weichen f/pl.; ~ of view Stand-, Gesichtspunkt m; the ~ is that ... die Sache ist die, daß ...; make a ~ of s.th. auf et bestehen; in ~ of Hinsicht auf (acc.); off od. beside the ~ nicht zur Sache (gehörig); on the ~ of ger im Begriff zu inf.; win on ~s nach Punkten siegen; to the ~ zur Sache (gehörig); **2.** v/t. (zu)spitzen; oft out zeigen, hinweisen auf (acc.); punktieren; ~ at Waffe etc. richten auf (acc.); v/i. ~ at weisen auf (acc.); to nach e-r Richtung weisen; **~ed** ['pɔintid] spitz(ig), Spitz...; fig. scharf; **~er** [~tə] Zeiger m; Zeigestock m; Hühnerhund m; **~less** [~tlis] stumpf; witzlos; zwecklos.

poise [pɔiz] **1.** Gleichgewicht n; Haltung f; **2.** v/t. im Gleichgewicht erhalten; Kopf etc. tragen, halten; v/i. schweben.

poison ['pɔizn] **1.** Gift n; **2.** vergiften; **~ous** □ [~nəs] giftig (a. fig.).

poke [pouk] **1.** Stoß m, Puff m; **2.** v/t. stoßen; schüren, Nase etc. in et. stecken; **~ fun** at sich über j-n lustig machen; v/i. stoßen; stochern.

poker ['poukə] Feuerhaken m.

poky ['pouki] eng; schäbig; erbärmlich. [m.]

polar ['poulə] polar; **~ bear** Eisbär

Pole[1] [poul] Pole m, Polin f.

pole[2] [~] Pol m; Stange f, Mast m; Deichsel f; (Sprung)Stab m.

polecat *zo.* ['poulkæt] Iltis *m*; *Am.* Skunk *m*.

polemic [po'lemik], *a.* **~al** □ [~kəl] polemisch; feindselig.

pole-star ['poulsta:] Polarstern *m*; *fig.* Leitstern *m*.

police [po'li:s] 1. Polizei *f*; 2. überwachen; **~man** Polizist *m*; **~office** Polizeipräsidium *n*; **~officer** Polizeibeamte(r) *m*, Polizist *m*; **~station** Polizeiwache *f*.

policy ['polisi] Politik *f*; (Welt-) Klugheit *f*; Police *f*; *Am.* Zahlenlotto *n*

polio(myelitis) *≈* ['pouliou(maiə'laitis)] spinale Kinderlähmung.

Polish¹ ['poulif] polnisch.

polish² ['polif] 1. Politur *f*; *fig.* Schliff *m*; 2. polieren; *fig.* verfeinern.

polite □ [pə'lait] artig, höflich; fein; **~ness** [~tnis] Höflichkeit *f*.

politic [['politik] politisch; schlau; **~al** [[pə'litikəl] politisch; staatlich; Staats..; **~ian** [poli'tifən] Politiker *m*; **~s** ['politiks] *oft sg.* Staatswissenschaft *f*, Politik *f*.

polka ['polkə] Polka *f*; **~ dot** *Am.* Punktmuster *n auf Stoff*.

poll [poul] 1. Wählerliste *f*; Stimmenzählung *f*; Wahl *f*; Stimmenzahl *f*; Umfrage *f*; *co.* Kopf *m*; 2. *v/t.* Stimmen erhalten; *v/i.* wählen; **~book** ['poulbuk] Wählerliste *f*.

pollen *♀* ['polin] Blütenstaub *m*.

polling-district ['pouliŋdistrikt] Wahlbezirk *m*.

poll-tax ['poultæks] Kopfsteuer *f*.

pollute [pə'lu:t] beschmutzen, beflecken; entweihen.

polyp(e) *zo.* ['polip], **~us** *≈* [~pəs] Polyp *m*.

pommel ['pʌml] 1. *Degen-*, *Sattel*-Knopf *m*; 2. knuffen, schlagen.

pomp [pomp] Pomp *m*, Gepränge *n*.

pompous □ ['pompəs] prunkvoll; hochtrabend; pompös.

pond [pond] Teich *m*, Weiher *m*.

ponder ['pondə] *v/t.* erwägen; *v/i.* nachdenken; **~able** [~ərəbl] wägbar; **~ous** □ [~rəs] schwer(fällig).

pontiff ['pontif] Hohepriester *m*; Papst *m*.

pontoon *✗* [pon'tu:n] Ponton *m*; **~bridge** Schiffsbrücke *f*.

pony ['pouni] Pony *n*, Pferdchen *n*.

poodle ['pu:dl] Pudel *m*.

pool [pu:l] 1. Teich *m*; Pfütze *f*, Lache *f*; (Schwimm)Becken *n*; (Spiel)Einsatz *m*; *†* Ring *m*, Kartell *n*; **~ room** *Am.* Billardspielhalle *f*; Wettannahmestelle *f*; 2. *†* zu e-m Ring vereinigen; *Gelder* zs.-werfen.

poop *♩* [pu:p] Heck *n*; Achterhütte *f*.

poor [[puə] arm(selig); dürftig; schlecht; **~house** ['puəhaus] Armenhaus *n*; **~law** *🕀* Armenrecht

---

n; **~ly** [~li] 1. *adj.* unpäßlich; 2. *adv.* dürftig; **~ness** ['puənis] Armut *f*.

pop¹ [pop] 1. Knall *m*; F Sprudel *m*; F Schampus *m*; 2. *v/t.* knallen lassen; *Am. Mais* rösten; schnell *wohin* tun, stecken; *v/i.* puffen, knallen; *mit adv.* huschen; **~** *in* hereinplatzen.

pop² F [~] 1. populär, beliebt; 2. Schlager *m*; volkstümliche Musik.

pop³ *Am.* F [~] Papa *m*, alter Herr.

popcorn *Am.* ['popko:n] Puffmais *m*.

pope [poup] Papst *m*.

poplar *♀* ['poplə] Pappel *f*.

poppy *♀* ['popi] Mohn *m*; **~cock** *Am.* F Quatsch *m*.

popu|lace ['popjuləs] Pöbel *m*; **~lar** □ [~lə] Volks...; volkstümlich, populär; **~larity** [popju'læriti] Popularität *f*.

populat|e ['popjuleit] bevölkern; **~ion** [popju'leifən] Bevölkerung *f*.

populous □ ['popjuləs] volkreich.

porcelain ['po:slin] Porzellan *n*.

porch [po:tf] Vorhalle *f*, Portal *n*; *Am.* Veranda *f*.

porcupine *zo.* ['po:kjupain] Stachelschwein *n*.

pore [po:] 1. Pore *f*; 2. *fig.* brüten.

pork [po:k] Schweinefleisch *n*; **~ barrel** *Am. sl.* ['po:kbærəl] *politisch berechnete* Geldzuwendung *der Regierung*; **~y** F ['po:ki] 1. fett, dick; 2. *Am.* = porcupine.

porous □ ['po:rəs] porös.

porpoise *ichth.* ['po:pəs] Tümmler *m*.

porridge ['poridʒ] Haferbrei *m*.

port [po:t] 1. Hafen *m*; *♩* (Pfort-, Lade)Luke *f*; *♩* Backbord *n*; Portwein *m*; 2. *♩* das Ruder nach der Backbordseite umlegen.

portable ['po:təbl] transportabel.

portal ['po:tl] Portal *n*, Tor *n*.

portend [po:'tend] vorbedeuten.

portent ['po:tent] *(bsd. üble)* Vorbedeutung; Wunder *n*; **~ous** □ [po:'tentəs] unheilvoll; wunderbar.

porter ['po:tə] Pförtner *m*; (Gepäck)Träger *m*; Porterbier *n*.

portion ['po:fən] 1. (An)Teil *m*; Portion *f Essen*; Erbteil *n*; Aussteuer *f*; *fig.* Los *n*; 2. teilen; ausstatten.

portly ['po:tli] stattlich.

portmanteau [po:t'mæntou] Handkoffer *m*. [nis *n*.]

portrait ['po:trit] Porträt *n*, Bild-]

portray [po:'trei] (ab)malen, porträtieren; schildern; **~al** [~eiəl] Porträtieren *n*; Schilderung *f*.

pose [pouz] 1. Pose *f*; 2. (sich) in Positur setzen; F sich hinstellen (*as* als); *Frage* aufwerfen.

posh *sl.* [pof] schick, erstklassig.

position [pə'zifən] Lage *f*, Stellung *f* (*a. fig.*); Stand *m*; *fig.* Standpunkt *m*.

positive ['pozstiv] 1. □ bestimmt, ausdrücklich; feststehend, sicher; unbedingt; positiv; überzeugt; rechthaberisch; 2. *das* Bestimmte; *gr.* Positiv *m*; *phot.* Positiv *n*.

possess [pə'zes] besitzen; beherrschen; *fig.* erfüllen; ~ *o.s. of et.* in Besitz nehmen; ~**ed** besessen; ~**ion** [~eʃən] Besitz *m*; *fig.* Besessenheit *f*; ~**ive** *gr.* [~esiv] 1. besitzanzeigend; ~ *case* Genitiv *m*; 2. Possessivpronomen *n*, besitzanzeigendes Fürwort; Genitiv ~; ~**or** [~sə] Besitzer *m*.

possib|ility [posə'biliti] Möglichkeit *f*; ~**le** ['posəbl] möglich; ~**ly** [~li] möglicherweise, vielleicht; *if I* ~ *can* wenn ich irgend kann.

post [poust] 1. Pfosten *m*; Posten *m*; Stelle *f*, Amt *n*; Post *f*; ~ *exchange Am.* ✕ Einkaufsstelle *f*; 2. *v/t.* Plakat *etc.* anschlagen; postieren; eintragen; zur Post geben; per Post senden; ~ *up j-n* informieren; *v/i.* (dahin)eilen.

postage ['poustidʒ] Porto *n*; ~ **stamp** Briefmarke *f*.

postal □ ['poustəl] 1. postalisch; Post...; ~ *order* Postanweisung *f*; 2. *a.* ~ **card** *Am.* Postkarte *f*.

postcard ['poustkɑːd] Postkarte *f*.

poster ['poustə] Plakat *n*, Anschlag *m*.

posterior [pos'tiəriə] 1. □ später (*to als*); hinter; 2. Hinterteil *n*.

posterity [pos'teriti] Nachwelt *f*; Nachkommenschaft *f*.

post-free ['poust'friː] portofrei.

post-graduate ['poust'grædjuit] 1. nach beendigter Studienzeit; 2. Doktorand *m*.

post-haste ['poust'heist] eilig(st).

posthumous] ['postjuməs] nachgeboren; hinterlassen.

post|man ['poustmən] Briefträger *m*; ~**mark** 1. Poststempel *m*; 2. abstempeln; ~**master** Postamtsvorsteher *m*.

post-mortem ['poust'mɔːtem] 1. nach dem Tode; 2. Leichenschau *f*.

post|(-)office ['poust'ɔfis] Postamt *n*; ~ **box** Post(schließ)fach *n*; ~ **paid** frankiert.

postpone [poust'poun] ver-, aufschieben; ~**ment** [~nmənt] Aufschub *m*. [tum *n*.]

postscript ['pousskript] Postskrip-]

postulate 1. ['postjulit] Forderung *f*; 2. [~leit] fordern; (als gegeben) voraussetzen.

posture ['postʃə] 1. Stellung *f*, Haltung *f des Körpers*; 2. (sich) zurechtstellen; posieren.

post-war ['poust'wɔː] Nachkriegs...

posy ['pouzi] Blumenstrauß *m*.

pot [pot] 1. Topf *m*; Kanne *f*; Tiegel *m*; 2. in e-n Topf tun; einlegen.

potation [pou'teiʃən] *mst ~pl.* Trinken *n*, Zecherei *f*; Trunk *m*.

potato [pə'teitou], *pl.* ~**es** Kartoffel *f*.

pot-belly ['potbeli] Schmerbauch *m*.

poten|cy ['poutənsi] Macht *f*; Stärke *f*; ~**t** [~nt] mächtig; stark; ~**tial** [po'tenʃəl] 1. potentiell; möglich; 2. Leistungsfähigkeit *f*.

pother ['poðə] Aufregung *f*.

pot|-herb ['pothəːb] Küchenkraut *n*; ~**house** Kneipe *f*.

potion ['pouʃən] (Arznei)Trank *m*.

potter[1] ['potə]: ~ *about* herumwerkeln.

potter[2] [~] Töpfer *m*; ~**y** [~ri] Töpferei *f*; Töpferware(n *pl.*) *f*.

pouch [pautʃ] 1. Tasche *f*; Beutel *m*; 2. einstecken; (sich) beuteln.

poulterer ['poultərə] Geflügelhändler *m*.

poultice ✚ ['poultis] Packung *f*.

poultry ['poultri] Geflügel *n*.

pounce [pauns] 1. Stoß *m*, Sprung *m*; 2. sich stürzen (*on, upon auf acc.*).

pound [paund] 1. Pfund *n*; ~ (*sterling*) Pfund *n* Sterling (*abbr.* £ = 20 *shillings*); Pfandstall *m*; Tierasyl *n*; 2. (zer)stoßen; stampfen; schlagen.

pounder ['paundə] ...pfünder *m*.

pour [pɔː] *v/t.* gießen, schütten; ~ *out Getränk* eingießen; *v/i.* sich ergießen, strömen; *it never rains but it ~s fig.* ein Unglück kommt selten allein.

pout [paut] 1. Schmollen *n*; 2. *v/t.* Lippen aufwerfen; *v/i.* schmollen.

poverty ['povəti] Armut *f*.

powder ['paudə] 1. Pulver *n*; Puder *m*; 2. pulverisieren; (sich) pudern; bestreuen; ~**box** Puderdose *f*.

power ['pauə] Kraft *f*; Macht *f*, Gewalt *f*; ⚖ Vollmacht *f*; ⚡ Potenz *f*; *in* ~ an der Macht, im Amt; ~**current** Starkstrom *m*; ~**ful** □ ['pauəful] mächtig, kräftig; wirksam; ~**less** ['pauəlis] macht-, kraftlos; ~**plant** *s. power-station*; ~ **politics** *oft sg.* Machtpolitik *f*; ~**station** Kraftwerk *n*.

powwow ['pauwau] Medizinmann *m*; *Am.* F Versammlung *f*.

practica|ble □ ['præktikəbl] ausführbar; gangbar (*Weg*); brauchbar; ~**l** □ [~əl] praktisch; tatsächlich; eigentlich; sachlich; ~ *joke* Schabernack *m*; ~**lly** [~li] so gut wie.

practice ['præktis] 1. Praxis *f*; Übung *f*; Gewohnheit *f*; Brauch *m*; Praktik *f*; *put into* ~ in die Praxis umsetzen; 2. *Am.* = *practise*.

practise [~] *v/t.* in die Praxis umsetzen; ausüben; betreiben; üben; *v/i.* (sich) üben; praktizieren; ~ *upon j-s Schwäche* ausnutzen; ~**d** geübt (*P.*).

practitioner [præk'tiʃnə] *a. general* ~ praktischer Arzt; Rechtsanwalt *m.*

prairie *Am.* ['prɛəri] Grasebene *f*; Prärie *f*; ~schooner *Am.* Planwagen *m.*

praise [preiz] 1. Preis *m*, Lob *n*; 2. loben, preisen.

praiseworthy □ ['preizwə:ði] lobenswert

pram F [præm] Kinderwagen *m.*

prance [pra:ns] sich bäumen; paradieren, einherstolzieren.

prank [præŋk] Possen *m*, Streich *m.*

prate [preit] 1. Geschwätz *n*; 2. schwatzen, plappern.

prattle ['prætl] *s.* prate.

pray [prei] beten; (er)bitten; bitte!

prayer [prɛə] Gebet *n*; Bitte *f*; *oft* ~s *pl.* Andacht *f*; Lord's 2 Vaterunser *n*; ~book ['prɛəbuk] Gebetbuch *n*

pre... [pri:; pri] vor(her)...; Vor...; früher.

preach [pri:tʃ] predigen; ~er ['pri:tʃə] Prediger(in).

preamble [pri:'æmbl] Einleitung *f.*

precarious [pri'kɛəriəs] unsicher.

precaution [pri'kɔ:ʃən] Vorsicht(smaßregel) *f*; ~ary [~ʃnəri] vorbeugend.

precede [pri(:)'si:d] voraus-, vorangehen (dat.); ~nce, ~ncy [~dəns, ~si] Vortritt *m*, Vorrang *m*; ~nt ['presidənt] Präzedenzfall *m.*

precept ['pri:sept] Vorschrift *f*, Regel *f*; ~or [pri'septə] Lehrer *m.*

precinct ['pri:siŋkt] Bezirk *m*, *bsd. Am.* Wahlbezirk *m*, -kreis *m*; ~s *pl.* Umgebung *f*; Bereich *m*; Grenze *f*; *pedestrian* ~ Fußgängerzone *f.*

precious ['preʃəs] 1. □ kostbar; edel; F arg, gewaltig, schön; 2. F *adv.* recht, äußerst.

precipi|ce ['presipis] Abgrund *m*; ~tate 1. [pri'sipiteit] (hinab)stürzen; ⚗ fällen; überstürzen; 2. □ [~tit] übereilt, hastig; 3. [~] ⚗ Niederschlag *m*; ~tation [prisipi-'teiʃən] Sturz *m*; Überstürzung *f*, Hast *f*, ⚗ Niederschlag(en *n*) *m*; ~tous [pri'sipitəs] steil, jäh.

précis ['preisi:] gedrängte Übersicht, Zs.-fassung *f.*

precis|e [pri'sais] genau; ~ion [~'siʒən] Genauigkeit *f*; Präzision *f.*

preclude [pri'klu:d] ausschließen; vorbeugen (dat.); j-n hindern.

precocious □ [pri'kouʃəs] frühreif; altklug.

preconceive ['pri:kən'si:v] vorher ausdenken; ~d vorgefaßt (Meinung).

preconception ['pri:kən'sepʃən] vorgefaßte Meinung.   [m.)

precursor [pri(:)'kə:sə] Vorläufer)

predatory ['predətəri] räuberisch.

predecessor ['pri:disesə] Vorgänger *m.*

predestin|ate   [pri(:)'destineit]

vorherbestimmen; ~ed [~nd] auserkoren.

predetermine ['pri:di'tə:min] vorher festsetzen; vorherbestimmen.

predicament [pri'dikəmənt] (mißliche) Lage.

predicate 1. ['predikeit] aussagen; 2. *gr.* [~kit] Prädikat *n*, Satzaussage *f.*

predict [pri'dikt] vorhersagen; ~ion [~kʃən] Prophezeiung *f.*

predilection [pri:di'lekʃən] Vorliebe *f.*

predispos|e ['pri:dis'pouz] vorher geneigt *od.* empfänglich machen (to für); ~ition [~spə'ziʃən] Geneigtheit *f*; *bsd.* ⚘ Anfälligkeit *f* (to für).

predomina|nce [pri'dɔminəns] Vorherrschaft *f*; Übergewicht *n*; Vormacht(stellung) *f*; ~nt □ [~nt] vorherrschend; ~te [~neit] die Oberhand haben; vorherrschen.

pre-eminent □ [pri(:)'eminənt] hervorragend.

pre-emption [pri(:)'empʃən] Vorkauf(srecht *n*) *m.*

pre-exist ['pri:ig'zist] vorher dasein.

prefabricate ['pri:'fæbrikeit] vorfabrizieren.

preface ['prefis] 1. Vorrede *f*, Vorwort *n*, Einleitung *f*; 2. einleiten.

prefect ['pri:fekt] Präfekt *m*; *Schule:* Vertrauensschüler *m*, Klassensprecher *m.*

prefer [pri'fə:] vorziehen; *Gesuch etc.* vorbringen; *Klage* einreichen; befördern; ~able □ ['prefərəbl] (to) vorzuziehen(d) (dat.); vorzüglicher (als); ~ably [~li] vorzugsweise; besser; ~ence [~rəns] Vorliebe *f*; Vorzug *m*; ~ential □ [prefə'renʃəl] bevorzugt; Vorzugs...; ~ment [pri'fə:mənt] Beförderung *f.*

prefix ['pri:fiks] Präfix *n*, Vorsilbe *f.*

pregnan|cy ['pregnənsi] Schwangerschaft *f*; *fig.* Fruchtbarkeit *f*; Bedeutungsreichtum *m*; ~t □ [~nt] schwanger; *fig.* fruchtbar, inhaltsvoll.

prejud|ge ['pri:'dʒʌdʒ] vorher (ver-)urteilen; ~ice ['predʒudis] 1. Voreingenommenheit *f*; Vorurteil *n*; Schaden *m*; 2. voreinnehmen; benachteiligen; *e-r S.* Abbruch tun; ~d (vor)eingenommen; ~icial □ [predʒu'diʃəl] nachteilig.

prelate ['prelit] Prälat *m.*

preliminary [pri'liminəri] 1. □ vorläufig; einleitend; Vor...; 2. Einleitung *f.*

prelude ♪ ['prelju:d] Vorspiel *n.*

premature □ [premə'tjuə] *fig.* frühreif; vorzeitig; vorschnell.

premeditat|e [pri(:)'mediteit] vorher überlegen; ~ion [pri(:)medi-'teiʃən] Vorbedacht *m.*

premier ['premjə] **1.** erst; **2.** Premierminister *m*.

premises ['premisiz] *pl.* (Gebäude *pl.* mit) Grundstück *n*, Anwesen *n*; Lokal *n*.

premium ['pri:mjəm] Prämie *f*; Anzahlung *f*; † Agio *n*; Versicherungsprämie *f*; Lehrgeld *n*; *at a* ~ über pari; sehr gesucht.

premonition [pri:mə'niʃən] Warnung *f*; (Vor)Ahnung *f*.

preoccup|ied [pri(:)'ɔkjupaid] in Gedanken verloren; ~y [~pai] vorher in Besitz nehmen; ausschließlich beschäftigen; in Anspruch nehmen.

prep F [prep] = *preparation*, *preparatory school*.

preparat|ion [prepə'reiʃən] Vorbereitung *f*; Zubereitung *f*; ~ory □ [pri'pærətəri] vorbereitend; ~ (*school*) Vorschule *f*.

prepare [pri'pɛə] *v/t.* vorbereiten; zurechtmachen; (zu)bereiten; (aus-)rüsten; *v/i.* sich vorbereiten; sich anschicken; ~d □ bereit.

prepay ['pri:'pei] [*irr.* (*pay*)] vorausbezahlen; frankieren.

prepondera|nce [pri'pɔndərəns] Übergewicht *n*; ~nt □ [~nt] überwiegend; ~te [~reit] überwiegen.

preposition *gr.* [prepə'ziʃən] Präposition *f*, Verhältniswort *n*.

prepossess [pri:pə'zes] günstig stimmen; ~ing □ [~siŋ] einnehmend.

preposterous [pri'pɔstərəs] widersinnig, albern; grotesk.

prerequisite ['pri:'rekwizit] Vorbedingung *f*, Voraussetzung *f*.

prerogative [pri'rɔgətiv] Vorrecht *n*.

presage ['presidʒ] **1.** Vorbedeutung *f*; Ahnung *f*; **2.** vorbedeuten; ahnen; prophezeien.

prescribe [pris'kraib] vorschreiben; ~ verschreiben.

prescription [pris'kripʃən] Vorschrift *f*, Verordnung *f*; ~ Rezept *n*.

presence ['prezns] Gegenwart *f*; Anwesenheit *f*; Erscheinung *f*; ~ *of mind* Geistesgegenwart *f*.

present[1] ['preznt] **1.** □ gegenwärtig; anwesend, vorhanden; jetzig; laufend (*Jahr etc.*); vorliegend (*Fall etc.*); ~ *tense* gr. Präsens *n*; **2.** Gegenwart *f*, *gr. a.* Präsens *n*; Geschenk *n*; *at* ~ jetzt; *for the* ~ einstweilen.

present[2] [pri'zent] präsentieren; (dar)bieten; (vor)zeigen; *j-n* vorstellen; vorschlagen; (über)reichen; (be)schenken.

presentation [prezen'teiʃən] Dar-, Vorstellung *f*; Ein-, Überreichung *f*; Schenkung *f*; Vorzeigen *n*, Vorlage *f*.

presentiment [pri'zentimənt] Vorgefühl *n*, Ahnung *f*.

presently ['prezntli] sogleich, bald (darauf), alsbald; *Am.* zur Zeit.

preservati|on [prezə(:)'veiʃən] Bewahrung *f*, Erhaltung *f*; ~ve [pri'zə:vətiv] **1.** bewahrend; **2.** Schutz-, Konservierungsmittel *n*.

preserve [pri'zə:v] **1.** bewahren, behüten; erhalten; einmachen; *Wild* hegen; **2.** *hunt* Gehege *n* (*a. fig.*); *mst* ~ *pl.* Eingemachte(s) *n*. [ren (over bei).]

preside [pri'zaid] den Vorsitz führen;

presiden|cy ['prezidənsi] Vorsitz *m*; Präsidentschaft *f*; ~t [~nt] Präsident *m*, Vorsitzende(r) *m*; *Am.* † Direktor *m*.

press [pres] **1.** Druck *m der Hand*; (Wein- *etc.*)Presse *f*; *die Presse* (*Zeitungen*); Druckerei *f*; Verlag *m*; Druck(en *n*) *m*; *a. printing-*~ Druckerpresse *f*; Menge *f*; *fig.* Druck *m*, Last *f*, Andrang *m*; Schrank *m*; **2.** *v/t.* (aus)pressen; drücken; lasten auf (*dat.*); (be)drängen; dringen auf (*acc.*); aufdrängen (*on dat.*); bügeln; *be* ~*ed for time* es eilig haben; *v/i.* drücken; (sich) drängen; ~ *for* sich eifrig bemühen um; ~ *on* weitereilen; ~ (*up*)*on* eindringen auf (*acc.*); ~ *agency* Nachrichtenbüro *n*; ~ *agent* Reklameagent *m*; ~ *button* Druckknopf *m*; ~ing □ ['presiŋ] dringend; ~ure ['preʃə] Druck *m* (*a. fig.*); Drang(sal *f*) *m*.

prestige [pres'ti:ʒ] Prestige *n*.

presum|able □ [pri'zju:məbl] vermutlich; ~e [pri'zju:m] *v/t.* annehmen; vermuten; voraussetzen; *v/i.* vermuten; sich erdreisten; anmaßend sein; ~ (*up*)*on* pochen auf (*acc.*); ausnutzen, mißbrauchen.

presumpt|ion [pri'zʌmpʃən] Mutmaßung *f*; Wahrscheinlichkeit *f*; Anmaßung *f*; ~ive □ [~ptiv] mutmaßlich; ~uous □ [~tjuəs] überheblich; vermessen.

presuppos|e [pri:sə'pouz] voraussetzen; ~ition [pri:sʌpə'ziʃən] Voraussetzung *f*.

preten|ce, *Am.* ~se [pri'tens] Vortäuschung *f*; Vorwand *m*; Schein *m*, Verstellung *f*.

pretend [pri'tend] vorgeben; vortäuschen; heucheln; Anspruch erheben (*to auf acc.*); ~ed □ angeblich.

pretension [pri'tenʃən] Anspruch *m* (*to auf acc.*); Anmaßung *f*.

preterit(e) *gr.* ['pretərit] Präteritum *n*, Vergangenheitsform *f*.

pretext ['pri:tekst] Vorwand *m*.

pretty ['priti] **1.** □ hübsch, niedlich; nett; **2.** *adv.* ziemlich.

prevail [pri'veil] die Oberhand haben *od.* gewinnen; (vor)herrschen; maßgebend *od.* ausschlaggebend sein; ~ (*up*)*on s.o.* j-n dazu bewegen; *et.* zu tun; ~ing □ [~liŋ] (vor)herrschend.

prevalent □ ['prevələnt] vorherrschend, weit verbreitet.
prevaricate [pri'værikeit] Ausflüchte machen.
prevent [pri'vent] verhüten, e-r S.
vorbeugen; j-n hindern; ~ion [~-
ʃən] Verhinderung f; Verhütung
f; ~ive [~ntiv] 1. □ vorbeugend;
2. Schutzmittel n.
preview ['pri:vju:] Vorschau f;
Vorbesichtigung f.
previous [['pri:vjəs] vorhergehend; vorläufig; Vor...; ~' to vor
(dat.); ~ly [~sli] vorher, früher.
pre-war ['pri:'wɔ:] Vorkriegs...
prey [prei] 1. Raub m, Beute f;
beast of ~ Raubtier n; bird of ~ Raub-
vogel m; be a ~ to geplagt werden
von; 2. ~ (up)on rauben, plündern;
fressen; fig. nagen an (dat.).
price [prais] 1. Preis m; Lohn m;
2. Waren auszeichnen; die Preise
festsetzen für; (ab)schätzen; ~less
['praislis] unschätzbar; unbezahl-
bar.
prick [prik] 1. Stich m; Stachel m
(a. fig.); 2. v/t. (durch)stechen; fig.
peinigen; a. ~ out Muster punktieren; ~ up one's ears die Ohren
spitzen; v/i. stechen; ~le ['prikl]
Stachel m, Dorn m; ~ly [~li] stachelig.
pride [praid] 1. Stolz m; Hochmut
m; take ~ in stolz sein auf (acc.);
2. ~ o.s. sich brüsten (on, upon mit).
priest [pri:st] Priester m.
prig [prig] Tugendbold m, selbst-
gerechter Mensch; Pedant m.
prim [[prim] steif; zimperlich.
primacy ['praiməsi] Vorrang m;
~rily [~ərili] in erster Linie; ~ry
□ [~ri] 1. ursprünglich; hauptsächlich; Ur...; Anfangs..., Haupt...;
Elementar...; höchst; ́, ҂ Pri-
mär.. ; 2. a ~ meeting Am. Wahl-
versammlung f; ~ry school Ele-
mentar-, Grundschule f.
prime [praim] 1. □ erst; wichtigst;
Haupt , vorzüglich(st); ~ cost ҂
Selbstkosten pl.; ~ minister Mini-
sterpräsident m; ~ number Prim-
zahl f; 2. fig Blüte(zeit) f; Beste(s)
n; höchste Vollkommenheit; 3. v/t.
vorbereiten; Pumpe anlassen; in-
struieren; F vollaufen lassen (betrunken machen); paint. grundieren.
primer ['praimə] Fibel f, Elemen-
tarbuch n   [lich; Ur...]
primeval [prai'mi:vəl] uranfäng-
primitive ['primitiv] 1. □ erst, ursprünglich, Stamm...; primitiv;
2. gr Stammwort n.
primrose ♀ ['primrouz] Primel f.
prince [prins] Fürst m; Prinz m;
~ss [prin'ses, vor npr. 'prinses]
Fürstin f; Prinzessin f.
principal ['prinsəpəl] 1. □ erst,
hauptsächlich(st); Haupt...; ~ parts
pl. gr. Stammformen f/pl. des vb.;

2. Hauptperson f; Vorsteher m;
bsd. Am. (Schul)Direktor m, Rektor
m; ✝ Chef m; ҂҂ Hauptschuldige(r)
m; ✝ Kapital n; ~ity [prinsi'pæliti]
Fürstentum n.
principle ['prinsəpl] Prinzip n;
Grund(satz) m; Ursprung m; on ~
grundsätzlich, aus Prinzip.
print [print] 1. Druck m; (Finger-
etc.)Abdruck m; bedruckter Kattun, Druckstoff m; Stich m; phot.
Abzug m; Am. Zeitungsdrucksache
f; out of ~ vergriffen; 2. (ab-, auf-,
be)drucken; phot. kopieren; fig.
einprägen (on dat.); in Druckbuch-
staben schreiben; ~er ['printə]
(Buch)Drucker m.
printing ['printiŋ] Druck m;
Drucken n; phot. Abziehen n, Kopieren n; ~ink Druckerschwärze f;
~-office (Buch)Druckerei f;
~-press Druckerpresse f.
prior ['praiə] 1. früher, älter (to
als); 2. adv. ~ to vor (dat.); 3. eccl.
Prior m; ~ity [prai'ɔriti] Priorität f;
Vorrang m; Vorfahrtsrecht n.
prism ['prizəm] Prisma n.
prison ['prizn] Gefängnis n; ~er
[~nə] Gefangene(r m) f, Häftling m;
take s.o. ~ j-n gefangennehmen.
privacy ['praivəsi] Zurückgezogenheit f; Geheimhaltung f.
private ['praivit] 1. □ privat; Privat...; persönlich; vertraulich; geheim; 2. ✕ (gewöhnlicher) Soldat;
in ~ privatim; im geheimen.
privation [prai'veiʃən] Mangel m,
Entbehrung f.
privilege ['privilidʒ] 1. Privileg n;
Vorrecht n; 2. bevorrechten.
privy ['privi] 1. □ ~ to eingeweiht in
(acc.); ♀ Council Staatsrat m; ♀
Councillor Geheimer Rat; ♀ Seal
Geheimsiegel n; 2. ҂҂ Mitinteres-
sent m (to an dat.); Abort m.
prize [praiz] 1. Preis m, Prämie f;
✤ Beute f; (Lotterie)Gewinn m;
2. preisgekrönt, Preis.. ; 3. (hoch-)
schätzen; aufbrechen (öffnen); ~
fighter ['praizfaitə] Berufsboxer m.
pro [prou] für
probability [prɔbə'biliti] Wahrscheinlichkeit f; ~le □ ['prɔbəbl]
wahrscheinlich.
probation [prə'beiʃən] Probe f,
Probezeit f; ҂҂ Bewährungsfrist f;
~ officer Bewährungshelfer m.
probe [proub] 1. ⚕ Sonde f; fig.
Untersuchung f; lunar ~ Mond-
sonde f; 2. a. ~ into sondieren;
untersuchen.
probity ['proubiti] Redlichkeit f.
problem ['prɔbləm] Problem n; ƛ
Aufgabe f; ~atic(al □) ['prɔbli-
'mætik(əl)] problematisch, zweifelhaft.   [n; Handlungsweise f.]
procedure [prə'si:dʒə] Verfahren
proceed [prə'si:d] weitergehen;
fortfahren; vor sich gehen; vor-

gehen; *univ.* promovieren; ~ *from von od.* aus *et.* kommen; ausgehen von; ~ *to zu et.* übergehen; ~ing [~diŋ] Vorgehen *n*; Handlung *f*; ~s *pl.* Verfahren *n*; Verhandlungen *f/pl.*, (Tätigkeits)Bericht *m*; ~s ['prousi:dz] *pl.* Ertrag *m*, Gewinn *m*.

process ['prouses] 1. Fortschreiten *n*, Fortgang *m*; Vorgang *m*; Verlauf *m der Zeit*; Prozeß *m*, Verfahren *n*; in ~ im Gange; *in* ~ *of construction* im Bau (befindlich); 2. gerichtlich belangen; ⊕ bearbeiten; ~ion [prə'seʃən] Prozession *f*.

proclaim [prə'kleim] proklamieren; erklären; ausrufen.

proclamation [prɔklə'meiʃən] Proklamation *f*; Bekanntmachung *f*; Erklärung *f*.

proclivity [prə'kliviti] Neigung *f*.

procrastinate [prou'kræstineit] zaudern.

procreate ['proukrieit] (er)zeugen.

procurat|ion [prɔkjuə'reiʃən] Vollmacht *f*; ✝ Prokura *f*; ~or ['prɔkjuəreitə] Bevollmächtigte(r) *m*.

procure [prə'kjuə] *v/t.* be-, verschaffen; *v/i.* Kuppelei treiben.

prod [prɔd] 1. Stich *m*; Stoß *m*; *fig.* Ansporn *m*; 2. stechen; stoßen; *fig.* anstacheln.

prodigal ['prɔdigəl] 1. □ verschwenderisch; the ~ son der verlorene Sohn; 2. Verschwender(in).

prodig|ious □ [prə'didʒəs] erstaunlich, ungeheuer; ~y ['prɔdidʒi] Wunder *n* (*a. fig.*); Ungeheuer *n*; *oft infant* ~ Wunderkind *n*.

produce 1. [prə'dju:s] vorbringen, vorführen, vorlegen; beibringen; hervorbringen; produzieren, erzeugen; *Zinsen etc.* (ein)bringen; ✗ verlängern; *Film etc.* herausbringen; 2. ['prɔdju:s] (Natur)Erzeugnis(se *pl.*) *n*, Produkt *n*; Ertrag *m*; ~r [prə'dju:sə] Erzeuger *m*, Hersteller *m*; *Film:* Produzent *m*; *thea.* Regisseur *m*.

product ['prɔdəkt] Produkt *n*, Erzeugnis *n*; ~ion [prə'dʌkʃən] Hervorbringung *f*; Vorlegung *f*, Beibringung *f*; Produktion *f*, Erzeugung *f*; *thea.* Herausbringen *n*; Erzeugnis *n*; ~ive □ [~ktiv] schöpferisch; produktiv, erzeugend; ertragreich; fruchtbar; ~iveness [~vnis], ~ivity [prɔdʌk'tiviti] Produktivität *f*.

prof *Am.* F [prɔf] Professor *m*.

profan|ation [prɔfə'neiʃən] Entweihung *f*; ~e [prə'fein] 1. □ profan; weltlich; uneingeweiht; gottlos; 2. entweihen; ~ity [~'fæniti] Gottlosigkeit *f*; Fluchen *m*.

profess [prə'fes] (sich) bekennen (zu); erklären; *Reue etc.* bekunden; *Beruf* ausüben; lehren; ~ed □ erklärt; angeblich; *Berufs...*; ~ion

[~eʃən] Bekenntnis *n*; Erklärung *f*; Beruf *m*; ~ional [~nl] 1. □ *Berufs...*; Amts...; berufsmäßig; freiberuflich; ~ *men* Akademiker *m/pl.*; 2. Fachmann *m*; *Sport:* Berufsspieler *m*; Berufskünstler *m*; ~or [~esə] Professor *m*.

proffer ['prɔfə] 1. anbieten; 2. Anerbieten *n*.

proficien|cy [prə'fiʃənsi] Tüchtigkeit *f*; ~t [~nt] 1. □ tüchtig; bewandert; 2. Meister *m*.

profile ['proufail] Profil *n*.

profit ['prɔfit] 1. Vorteil *m*, Nutzen *m*, Gewinn *m*; 2. *v/t. j-m* Nutzen bringen; *v/i.* ~ *by* Nutzen ziehen aus; ausnutzen; ~able □ [~təbl] nützlich, vorteilhaft, einträglich; ~eer [prɔfi'tiə] 1. Schiebergeschäfte machen; 2. Profitmacher *m*, Schieber *m*; ~sharing ['prɔfitʃɛəriŋ] Gewinnbeteiligung *f*.

profligate ['prɔfligit] 1. □ liederlich; 2. liederlicher Mensch.

profound □ [prə'faund] tief; tiefgründig; gründlich; *fig.* dunkel.

profundity [prə'fʌnditi] Tiefe *f*.

profus|e □ [prə'fju:s] verschwenderisch; übermäßig, überreich; ~ion *fig.* [~u:ʒən] Überfluß *m*.

progen|itor [prou'dʒenitə] Vorfahr *m*, Ahn *m*; ~y ['prɔdʒini] Nachkommen(schaft *f*) *m/pl.*; Brut *f*.

prognos|is ♂ [prɔg'nousis], *pl.* ~es [~si:z] Prognose *f*.

prognostication [prəgnɔsti'keiʃən] Vorhersage *f*.

program(me) ['prougræm] Programm *n*.

progress 1. ['prougres] Fortschritt(e *pl.*) *m*; Vorrücken *n* (*a.* ✗); Fortgang *m*; *in* ~ im Gang; 2. [prə'gres] fortschreiten; ~ion [prə'greʃən] Fortschreiten *n*; ✗ Reihe *f*; ~ive [~esiv] 1. □ fortschreitend; fortschrittlich; 2. *pol.* Fortschrittler *m*.

prohibit [prə'hibit] verbieten; verhindern; ~ion [proui'biʃən] Verbot *n*; Prohibition *f*; ~ionist [~ʃnist] *bsd. Am.* Prohibitionist *m*; ~ive □ [prə'hibitiv] verbietend; Sperr...; unerschwinglich.

project 1. ['prɔdʒekt] Projekt *n*; Vorhaben *n*, Plan *m*; 2. [prə'dʒekt] *v/t.* planen; (ent)werfen; ✗ projizieren; *v/i.* vorspringen; ~ile ['prɔdʒiktail] Projektil *n*, Geschoß *n*; ~ion [prə'dʒekʃən] Werfen *n*; Entwurf *m*; Vorsprung *m*; ✗, *aus.*, *phot.* Projektion *f*; ~or [~ktə] ✝ Gründer *m*; *opt.* Projektor *m*.

proletarian [proule'tɛəriən] 1. proletarisch; 2. Proletarier(in).

prolific [prə'lifik] (~ally) fruchtbar.

prolix □ ['prouliks] weitschweifig.

prolo|gue, *Am. a.* ~g ['proulɔg] Prolog *m*.

prolong [prə'lɔŋ] verlängern.

promenade [prɔmi'nɑ:d] **1.** Promenade *f*; **2.** promenieren.

prominent ['prɔminənt] hervorragend (*a fig*.); *fig.* prominent.

promiscuous [prɔ'miskjuəs] unordentlich, verworren; gemeinsam; unterschiedslos

promis|e [prɔmis] **1.** Versprechen *n*; *fig.* Aussicht *f*; **2.** versprechen; **~ing** [.siŋ] vielversprechend; **~sory** [.səri] versprechend; **~ note** ✝ Eigenwechsel *m*.

promontory ['prɔmən try] Vorgebirge *n*

promot|e [prə'mout] *et.* fördern; *j-n* befördern, *bsd Am. Schule:* versetzen, *parl* unterstützen; ✝ gründen; *bsd Am Verkauf durch Werbung* steigern, **~ion** [.ou∫ən] Förderung *f*; Beförderung *f*; ✝ Gründung *f*

prompt [prɔmpt] **1.** □ schnell; bereit(willig), sofortig; pünktlich; **2.** *j-n* veranlassen; *Gedanken* eingeben; *j-m* vorsagen, soufflieren; **~er** ['prɔmptə] Souffleu|r *m*, -se *f*; **~ness** [.tnis] Schnelligkeit *f*; Bereitschaft *f*

promulgate ['prɔməlgeit] verkünden, verbreiten

prone [proun] mit dem Gesicht nach unter (liegend); hingestreckt; **~ to** *fig* geneigt od neigend zu.

prong [prɔŋ] Zinke *f*; Spitze *f*.

pronoun *gr* ['prounaun] Pronomen *n*, Fürwor n

pronounce [prə'nauns] aussprechen, verkunden, erklären (für).

pronto *Am* ['prɔntou] sofort.

pronunciation [prənʌnsi'ei∫ən] Ausspruche *f*

proof [pru f] **1.** Beweis *m*; Probe *f*, Versuch *m*, *typ* Korrekturbogen *m*; *typ., phot* Probeabzug *m*; **2.** fest; *in Zssgn* ..fest, ...dicht, ...sicher; **~reader** *typ*. ['pru:fri:də] Korrektor *m*

prop [prɔp] **1.** Stütze *f* (*a. fig*.); **2.** *a.* **~ up** (unter)stutzen.

propaga|te [prɔpəgeit] (sich) fortpflanzen , verbreiten, **~tion** [prɔpə'gei∫ən] Fortpflanzung *f*; Verbreitung *f*

propel [prə'pel] (vorwärts-, an-) treiben **~ler** [.lə] Propeller *m*, (*Schiffs-*, *Luft*)Schraube *f*.

propensity [prə'pensiti] Neigung *f*.

proper ['prɔpə] eigen(tümlich); eigentlich , passend, richtig; anständig, **~ty** [.əti] Eigentum *n*, Besitz *m*, Vermögen *n*; Eigenschaft *f*

prophe|cy ['prɔfisi] Prophezeiung*f*; **~sy** [.sai] prophezeien.

prophet [prɔfit] Prophet *m*.

propi|tiate [prə'pi∫ieit] günstig stimmen, versöhnen; **~tious** □ [.∫əs] gnädig; günstig.

proportion [prə'pɔ:∫ən] **1.** Verhältnis *n*; Gleichmaß *n*; (An)Teil *m*;

~s *pl.* (Aus)Maße *n/pl.*; **2.** in ein Verhältnis bringen; **~al** □ [.nl] im Verhältnis (*to zu*); **~ate** □ [.∫nit] angemessen

propos|al [prə'pouzəl] Vorschlag *m*, (*a.* Heirats)Antrag *m*; Angebot *n*; Plan *m*; **~e** [.ouz] *v/t* vorschlagen; e-n Toast ausbringen auf (*acc.*); **~** *to o.s.* sich vornehmen; *v/i.* beabsichtigen; anhalten (*to um*); **~ition** [prɔpə'zi∫ən] Vorschlag *m*, Antrag *m*; Behauptung *f*, Problem *n*.

propound [prə paund] *Frage etc.* vorlegen; vorschlagen

propriet|ary [prə'praiətəri] Eigentümer...; Eigentums ; Besitz(er)...; gesetzlich geschützt (*bsd Arzneimittel*); **~or** [.tə] Eigentümer *m*; **~y** [.ti] Richtigkeit *f*; Schicklichkeit *f*; *the proprieties pl.* die Anstandsformen *f/pl*   [*m.*]

propulsion ⊕ [prə pʌl∫ən] Antrieb]

prorate *Am.* [prou'reit] anteilmäßig verteilen.

prosaic [prou'zeiik] (.ally) *fig.* prosaisch (*nüchtern, trocken*).

proscribe [prous'kraib] ächten.

proscription [prous'krip∫ən] Achtung *f*; Acht *f*; Verbannung *f*.

prose [prouz] **1.** Prosa *f*; **2.** prosaisch.

prosecut|e ['prɔsikju:t] (*a.* gerichtlich) verfolgen; *Gewerbe etc.* betreiben; verklagen, **~ion** [prɔsi'kju:∫ən] Verfolgung *f e-s Plans etc*; Betreiben *n e-s Gewerbes etc*; gerichtliche Verfolgung; **~or** *ź* ['prɔsikju:tə] Kläger *m*; Anklagevertreter *m*; *public* **~** Staatsanwalt *m*

prospect 1. ['prɔspekt] Aussicht *f* (*a. fig*.); Anblick *m*, ✝ Interessent *m*; **2.** [prə'spekt] ৯ schürfen; bohren (*for nach Öl*); **~ive** [.tiv] vorausblickend, voraussichtlich; **~us** [.təs] (Werbe)Prospekt *m*

prosper ['prɔspə] *v/i* Erfolg haben, gedeihen, blühen, *v/t* begünstigen, segnen; **~ity** [prɔs periti] Gedeihen *n*; Wohlstand *m*; Glück *n*; *fig.* Blüte *f*; **~ous** □ ['prɔspərəs] glücklich, gedeihlich; *fig.* blühend; günstig.

prostitute ['prɔstitju:t] **1.** Dirne *f*; **2.** zur Dirne machen; (der Schande) preisgeben, feilbieter (*a. fig*.).

prostrat|e 1. ['prɔstreit] hingestreckt; erschöpft; danniederliegend; demütig; gebrochen, **2.** [prɔs'treit] niederwerfen, *fig* niederschmettern; entkräften; **~ion** [.ei∫ən] Niederwerfung *f*; Fußfall *m*; *fig.* Demütigung *f*; Entkräftung *f*

prosy *fig.* ['prouzi] prosaisch; langweilig.

protagonist [prou'tægənist] *thea.* Hauptfigur *f*; *fig.* Vorkämpfer(in).

protect [prə'tekt] (be)schützen; **~ion** [.k∫ən] Schutz *m*; Wirtschaftsschutz *m*, Schutzzoll *m*; **~ive**

[„ktiv] schützend; Schutz...; ~ duty
Schutzzoll m; ~or [„tə] (Be)Schüt-
zer m; Schutz~, Schirmherr m;
~orate [„ərit] Protektorat n.

protest 1. ['proutest] Protest m;
Einspruch m; 2. [prə'test] beteuern; protestieren; reklamieren.
Protestant ['prɔtistənt] 1. prote-
stantisch; 2. Protestant(in).
protestation [proutes'teiʃən] Be-
teuerung f; Verwahrung f.
protocol ['proutəkɔl] 1. Protokoll n;
2. protokollieren.
prototype ['proutətaip] Urbild n;
Prototyp m, Modell n.
protract [prə'trækt] in die Länge
ziehen, hinziehen.
protru|de [prə'tru:d] (sich) (her-)
vorstrecken; (her)vorstehen, (her-)
vortreten (lassen); ~sion [„u:ʒən]
Vorstrecken n; (Her)Vorstehen n,
(Her)Vortreten n.
protuberance [prə'tju:bərəns] Hervortreten n; Auswuchs m, Höcker
m.
proud [praud] stolz (of auf acc.).
prove [pru:v] v/t. be~, er~, nachweisen; prüfen; erleben, erfahren;
v/i. sich herausstellen od. erweisen
(als); ausfallen; ~n ['pru:vən] er-
wiesen; bewährt.
provenance ['prɔvinəns] Herkunft f.
provender ['prɔvində] Futter n.
proverb ['prɔvəb] Sprichwort n.
provide [prə'vaid] v/t. besorgen,
beschaffen, liefern; bereitstellen;
versehen, versorgen; ⚖ vorsehen,
festsetzen; v/i. (vor)sorgen; ~d
(that) vorausgesetzt, daß; sofern.
providen|ce ['prɔvidəns] Vorsehung
f; Voraussicht f; Vorsorge f; ~t □
[„nt] vorausblickend; vorsorglich;
haushälterisch; ~tial □ [prɔvi'den-
ʃəl] durch die göttliche Vorsehung
bewirkt; glücklich.
provider [prə'vaidə] Ernährer m
der Familie; Lieferant m.
provinc|e ['prɔvins] Provinz f; fig.
Gebiet n; Aufgabe f; ~ial [prə'vin-
ʃəl] 1. provinziell; kleinstädtisch;
2. Provinzbewohner(in).
provision [prə'viʒən] Beschaffung f;
Vorsorge f; ⚖ Bestimmung f; Vorkehrung f, Maßnahme f; Vorrat m;
~s pl. Proviant m, Lebensmittel
pl.; ~al □ [„nl] provisorisch.
proviso [prə'vaizou] Vorbehalt m.
provocat|ion [prɔvə'keiʃən] Her-
ausforderung f; ~ive [prə'vɔkətiv]
herausfordernd; (auf)reizend.
provoke [prə'vouk] auf~, anreizen;
herausfordern.
provost ['prɔvəst] Leiter m e-s
College; schott. Bürgermeister m;
✕ [prə'vou]: ~ marshal Kommandeur m der Militärpolizei.
prow ⚓ [prau] Bug m, Vorschiff
n.
prowess ['prauis] Tapferkeit f.

prowl [praul] 1. v/i. umherstreifen;
v/t. durchstreifen; 2. Umherstreifen n; ~ car Am ['praulka:] Strei-
fenwagen m der Polizei.
proximity [prɔk'simiti] Nähe f.
proxy ['prɔksi] Stellvertreter m;
Stellvertretung f; Vollmacht f;
by ~ in Vertretung.
prude [pru:d] Prüde f, Spröde f;
Zimperliese f.
pruden|ce ['pru:dəns] Klugheit f,
Vorsicht f; ~t □ [„nt] klug, vorsichtig.
prud|ery ['pru:dəri] Prüderie f,
Sprödigkeit f, Zimperlichkeit f;
~ish □ [„diʃ] prüde, zimperlich,
spröde.
prune [pru:n] 1. Backpflaume f;
2. ✂ beschneiden (a. fig.); a. ~
away, ~ off wegschneiden.
prurient □ ['pruəriənt] geil, lüstern.
pry [prai] 1. neugierig gucken; ~
into s-e Nase stecken in (acc.); ~
open aufbrechen; ~ up hochheben;
2. Hebel(bewegung f) m.
psalm [sɑːm] Psalm m.
pseudo|... ['psju:dou] Pseudo...,
falsch; ~nym [„dənim] Deckname
m.
psychiatr|ist [sai'kaiətrist] Psychia-
ter m (Nervenarzt); ~y [„ri] Psychia-
trie f.
psychic(al □) ['saikik(əl)] psy-
chisch, seelisch.
psycholog|ical □ [saikə'lɔdʒikəl]
psychologisch; ~ist [sai'kɔlədʒist]
Psycholog|e m, -in f; ~y [„dʒi]
Psychologie f (Seelenkunde).
pub F [pʌb] Kneipe f, Wirtschaft f.
puberty ['pju:bəti] Pubertät f.
public ['pʌblik] 1. [öffentlich;
staatlich, Staats...; allbekannt; ~
spirit Gemeinsinn m; 2. Publikum
n; Öffentlichkeit f; ~an [„kən]
Gastwirt m; ~ation [pʌbli'keiʃən]
Bekanntmachung f; Veröffentli-
chung f; Verlagswerk n; ~ monthly
Monatsschrift f; ~ house Wirtshaus n; ~ity [pʌb'lisiti] Öffentlichkeit f; Propaganda f, Reklame f,
Werbung f; ~ library Volksbüche-
rei f; ~ relations pl Verhältnis n
zur Öffentlichkeit, Public Relations
pl.; ~ school Public School f, Internatsschule f.
publish ['pʌbliʃ] bekanntmachen,
veröffentlichen, Buch etc. herausgeben, verlegen, ~ing house Verlag
m; ~er [„ʃə] Herausgeber m, Verleger m; ~s pl. Verlag(sanstalt f) m.
pucker ['pʌkə] 1. Falte f; 2. falten;
Falten werfen; runzeln.
pudding ['pudin] Pudding m; Süßspeise f; Auflauf m; Wurst f;
black ~ Blutwurst f.
puddle ['pʌdl] Pfütze f.
pudent ['pju:dənt] verschämt.
puerile □ ['pjuərail] kindisch.
puff [pʌf] 1. Hauch m; Zug m beim

Rauchen; (Dampf-, Rauch)Wölkchen *n*; Puderquaste *f*; (aufdringliche) Reklame; **2.** *v/t.* (auf)blasen, pusten; paffen; anpreisen; ~ *out* sich (auf)blähen; *up Preise* hochtreiben; ~*ed up fig.* aufgeblasen; ~*ed eyes* geschwollene Augen; *v/i.* paffen; pusten; **~-paste** ['pʌfpeist] Blätterteig *m*; **~y** ['pʌfi] böig; kurzatmig; geschwollen; dick; bauschig.

pug [pʌg], **~-dog** ['pʌgdɔg] Mops *m*.

pugnacious [pʌg'neiʃəs] kämpferisch; kampflustig; streitsüchtig.

pug-nose ['pʌgnouz] Stupsnase *f*.

puissant ['pjuː(i)snt] mächtig.

puke [pjuːk] (sich) erbrechen.

pull [pul] **1.** Zug *m*; Ruck *m*; *typ.* Abzug *m*; Ruderpartie *f*; Griff *m*; Vorteil *m*; **2.** ziehen; zerren; reißen; zupfen; pflücken; rudern; ~ *about* hin- u. herzerren; ~ *down* niederreißen; ~ *in* einfahren (*Zug*); ~ *off* zustande bringen; *Preis* erringen; ~ *out* heraus-, hinausfahren; ausscheren; ~ *round* wiederherstellen; ~ *through j-n* durchbringen; ~ *o.s. together* sich zs.-nehmen; ~ *up Wagen* anhalten; halten; ~ *up with*, ~ *up to* einholen.

pulley ⊕ ['puli] Rolle *f*; Flaschenzug *m*; Riemenscheibe *f*.

pull|-over ['pulouvə] Pullover *m*; **~-up** Halteplatz *m*, Raststätte *f*.

pulp [pʌlp] Brei *m*; *Frucht-, Zahn-*Mark *n*; ⊕ Papierbrei *m*; *a.* ~ *magazine Am.* Schundillustrierte *f*.

pulpit ['pulpit] Kanzel *f*.

pulpy ['pʌlpi] breiig; fleischig.

puls|ate ['pʌl'seit] pulsieren; schlagen; **~e** [pʌls] Puls(schlag) *m*.

pulverize ['pʌlvəraiz] *v/t.* pulverisieren; *v/i* zu Staub werden.

pumice ['pʌmis] Bimsstein *m*.

pump [pʌmp] **1.** Pumpe *f*; Pumps *m*; **2.** pumpen; F *j-n* aushorchen.

pumpkin ♀ ['pʌmpkin] Kürbis *m*.

pun [pʌn] **1.** Wortspiel *n*; **2.** ein Wortspiel machen.

Punch[1] [pʌntʃ] Kasperle *n, m*.

punch[2] [~] **1.** ⊕ Punze(n *m*) *f*, Locheisen *n*, Locher *m*; Lochzange *f*; (Faust)Schlag *m*; Punsch *m*; **2.** punzen, durchbohren; lochen; knuffen, puffen; *Am.* Vieh treiben, hüten.

puncher ['pʌntʃə] Locheisen *n*; Locher *m*; F Schläger *m*; *Am.* Cowboy *m*.

punctilious [pʌŋk'tiliəs] peinlich (genau), spitzfindig; förmlich.

punctual ['pʌŋktjuəl] pünktlich; **~ity** [pʌŋktju'æliti] Pünktlichkeit *f*.

punctuat|e ['pʌŋktjueit] (inter-)punktieren; *fig.* unterbrechen; **~ion** *gr.* [pʌŋktju'eiʃən] Interpunktion *f*.

puncture ['pʌŋktʃə] **1.** Punktur *f*;

Stich *m*; Reifenpanne *f*; **2.** (durch-)stechen; platzen (*Luftreifen*).

pungen|cy ['pʌndʒənsi] Schärfe *f*; **~t** [~nt] stechend, beißend, scharf.

punish ['pʌniʃ] (be)strafen; **~able** □ [~ʃəbl] strafbar; **~ment** [~ʃmənt] Strafe *f*, Bestrafung *f*.

punk *Am.* [pʌŋk] Zunderholz *n*; Zündmasse *f*; F *fig.* Mist *m*, Käse *m*.

puny □ ['pjuːni] winzig; schwächlich.

pupa *zo.* ['pjuːpə] Puppe *f*.

pupil ['pjuːpl] *anat.* Pupille *f*; Schüler(in); Mündel *m, n*.

puppet ['pʌpit] Marionette *f* (*a. fig.*); **~-show** Puppenspiel *n*.

pup(py) [pʌp], ['pʌpi] Welpe *m*, junger Hund; *fig.* Laffe *m*, Schnösel *m*.

purchase ['pəːtʃəs] **1.** (An-, Ein-)Kauf *m*; Erwerb(ung *f*) *m*; Anschaffung *f*; ⊕ Hebevorrichtung *f*; *fig.* Ansatzpunkt *m*; *make* ~*s* Einkäufe machen; **2.** kaufen; *fig.* erkaufen; anschaffen; ⊕ aufwinden; **~r** [~sə] Käufer(in).

pure □ [pjuə] *allg.* rein; *engS.*: lauter; echt; gediegen; theoretisch; **~-bred** *Am.* ['pjuəbred] reinrassig.

purgat|ive ✠ ['pəːgətiv] **1.** abführend; **2.** Abführmittel *n*; **~ory** [~təri] Fegefeuer *n*.

purge [pəːdʒ] **1.** ✠ Abführmittel *n*; *pol.* Säuberung *f*; **2.** *mst fig.* reinigen; *pol.* säubern; ✠ abführen.

purify ['pjuərifai] reinigen; läutern.

Puritan ['pjuəritən] **1.** Puritaner (-in); **2.** puritanisch.

purity ['pjuəriti] Reinheit *f* (*a. fig.*).

purl [pəːl] murmeln (*Bach*).

purlieus ['pəːljuːz] *pl.* Umgebung *f*.

purloin [pəː'lɔin] entwenden.

purple ['pəːpl] **1.** purpurn, purpurrot; **2.** Purpur *m*; **3.** (sich) purpurn färben.

purport ['pəːpət] **1.** Sinn *m*; Inhalt *m*; **2.** besagen; beabsichtigen; vorgeben.

purpose ['pəːpəs] **1.** Vorsatz *m*; Absicht *f*, Zweck *m*; Entschlußkraft *f*; *for the* ~ *of ger.* um zu *inf.*; *on* ~ absichtlich; *to no* ~ zwecklos, vergebens; **2.** vorhaben, bezwecken; **~ful** [~sful] zweckmäßig; absichtlich; zielbewußt; **~less** □ [~slis] zwecklos; ziellos; **~ly** [~li] vorsätzlich.

purr [pəː] schnurren (*Katze*).

purse [pəːs] **1.** Börse *f*, Geldbeutel *m*; Geld(preis *m*) *n*; *public* ~ Staatssäckel *m*; **2.** *oft* ~ *up Mund* spitzen; *Stirn* runzeln; *Augen* zs.-kneifen.

pursuan|ce [pə'sjuː(ə)ns] Verfolgung *f*; *in* ~ *of* zufolge (*dat.*); **~t** □ [~nt]: ~ *to* zufolge, gemäß, entsprechend (*dat.*).

pursu|e [pə'sjuː] verfolgen (*a. fig.*); streben nach; *e-m Beruf etc.* nachgehen; fortsetzen, fortfahren; **~er**

[ˌju(ː)ə] Verfolger(in); ˌit [ˌjuːt] Verfolgung f; mst ˌs pl. Beschäftigung f.

purvey [pəˈvei] Lebensmittel liefern; ˌor [ˌeiə] Lieferant m.

pus [pʌs] Eiter m.

push [puʃ] 1. (An-, Vor)Stoß m; Schub m; Druck m; Notfall m; Energie f; Unternehmungsgeist m; Elan m; 2. stoßen; schieben; drängen; Knopf drücken; (an)treiben; a. ˌ through durchführen; Anspruch etc. durchdrücken; ˌ s.th. on s.o. j-m et. aufdrängen; ˌ one's way sich durch- od. vordrängen; ˌ along, ˌ on, ˌ forward weitermachen, -gehen, -fahren etc.; ˌbutton ⚓ ['puʃbʌtn] Druckknopf m; ˌover Am. fig. Kinderspiel n; leicht zu beeinflussender Mensch.

pusillanimous ☐ [pjuːsiˈlæniməs] kleinmütig.

puss [pus] Kätzchen n, Katze f (a. fig. = Mädchen); ˌy ['pusi], a. ˌcat Mieze f, Kätzchen n; ˌyfoot Am. F leisetreten, sich zurückhalten.

put [put] (irr.) v/t. setzen, legen, stellen, stecken, tun, machen; Frage stellen, vorlegen; werfen; ausdrücken, sagen; ˌ about Gerüchte etc. verbreiten; ⚓ wenden; ˌ across sl. drehen, schaukeln; ˌ back zurückstellen; ˌ by Geld zurücklegen; ˌ down niederlegen, -setzen, -werfen; aussteigen lassen; notieren; zuschreiben (to dat.); unterdrücken; ˌ forth Kräfte aufbieten; Knospen etc. treiben; ˌ forward Meinung etc. vorbringen; ˌ o.s. forward sich hervortun; ˌ in hinein-, hereinst(r)ecken; Anspruch erheben; Gesuch einreichen; Urkunde vorlegen; anstellen; ˌ off auf-, verschieben; vertrösten; abbringen; hindern; fig. ablegen; ˌ on Kleid anziehen, Hut aufsetzen; fig. annehmen; an-, einschalten;

vergrößern; ˌ on airs sich aufspielen; ˌ on weight zunehmen; ˌ out ausmachen, (aus)löschen; verrenken; (her)ausstrecken; verwirren; j-m Ungelegenheiten bereiten; Kraft aufbieten; Geld ausleihen; ˌ right in Ordnung bringen; ˌ through teleph. verbinden (to mit); ˌ to hinzufügen; ˌ to death hinrichten; ˌ to the rack od. torture auf die Folter spannen; ˌ up aufstellen etc.; errichten, bauen; Waren anbieten; Miete erhöhen; ver-, wegpacken; Widerstand leisten; Kampf liefern; Gäste unterbringen; Bekanntmachung anschlagen; v/i. ˌ off, ˌ out, ˌ to sea ⚓ auslaufen; ˌ in ⚓ einlaufen; ˌ up at einkehren od. absteigen in (dat.); ˌ up for sich bewerben um; ˌ up with sich gefallen lassen; sich abfinden mit.

putrefy ['pjuːtrifai] (ver)faulen.

putrid ☐ ['pjuːtrid] faul, verdorben; sl. scheußlich, saumäßig; ˌity [pjuːˈtriditi] Fäulnis f.

putty ['pʌti] 1. Kitt m; 2. kitten.

puzzle ['pʌzl] 1. schwierige Aufgabe, Rätsel n; Verwirrung f; Geduldspiel n; 2. v/t. irremachen; j-m Kopfzerbrechen machen; ˌ out austüfteln; v/i. sich den Kopf zerbrechen; ˌheaded konfus.

pygm|(a)ean [pigˈmiːən] zwerghaft; ˌy ['pigmi] Zwerg m; attr. zwerghaft.

pyjamas [pəˈdʒɑːməz] pl. Schlafanzug m.

pyramid ['pirəmid] Pyramide f; ˌal ☐ [piˈræmidl] pyramidal.

pyre ['paiə] Scheiterhaufen m.

pyrotechnic|(al ☐) [pairouˈteknik(əl)] pyrotechnisch, Feuerwerks...; ˌs pl. Feuerwerk n (a. fig.).

Pythagorean [paiθægəˈriː(ː)ən] 1. pythagoreisch; 2. Pythagoreer m.

pyx eccl. [piks] Monstranz f.

Q

quack [kwæk] 1. Quaken n; Scharlatan m; Quacksalber m, Kurpfuscher m; Marktschreier m; 2. quacksalberisch; 3. quaken; quacksalben (an dat.); ˌery ['kwækəri] Quacksalberei f.

quadrangle ['kwɔdræŋgl] Viereck n; Innenhof m e-s College.

quadrennial ☐ [kwɔˈdreniəl] vierjährig; vierjährlich.

quadru|ped ['kwɔdruped] Vierfüßer m; ˌple [ˌpl] 1. ☐ vierfach; 2. (sich) vervierfachen; ˌplets [ˌlits] pl. Vierlinge m/pl.

quagmire ['kwægmaiə] Sumpf (-land n) m, Moor n.

quail[1] orn. [kweil] Wachtel f.

quail[2] [ˌ] verzagen; beben.

quaint ☐ [kweint] anheimelnd, malerisch; putzig, seltsam.

quake [kweik] 1. beben, zittern (with, for vor dat.); 2. Erdbeben n.

Quaker ['kweikə] Quäker m.

quali|fication [kwɔlifiˈkeiʃən] (erforderliche) Befähigung; Einschränkung f; gr. nähere Bestimmung; ˌfy ['kwɔlifai] v/t. befähigen; (be-) nennen; gr. näher bestimmen; ein-

schränken, mäßigen; mildern; v/i.
seine Befähigung nachweisen; ~ty
[.iti] Eigenschaft f, Beschaffenheit
f; ✝ Qualität f; vornehmer Stand.

qualm [kwɔːm] plötzliche Übelkeit;
Zweifel m; Bedenken n.

quandary ['kwɔndəri] verzwickte
Lage, Verlegenheit f.

quantity ['kwɔntiti] Quantität f,
Menge f; großer Teil.

quantum ['kwɔntəm] Menge f,
Größe f, Quantum n; Anteil m.

quarantine ['kwɔrəntiːn] 1. Quarantäne f; 2. unter Quarantäne
stellen.

quarrel ['kwɔrəl] 1. Zank m, Streit
m; 2. (sich) zanken, streiten; ~
some □ [.Isəm] zänkisch; streitsüchtig.

quarry ['kwɔri] 1. Steinbruch m;
fig. Fundgrube f; (Jagd)Beute f;
2. Steine brechen; fig. stöbern.

quart [kwɔːt] Quart n (1,136 l).

quarter ['kwɔːtə] 1. Viertel n, vierter Teil; bsd. Viertelstunde f; Vier-
teljahr n, Quartal n; Viertelzentner
m; Am. 25 Cent; Keule f, Viertel n
e-s geschlachteten Tieres; Stadtvier-
tel n; (Himmels)Richtung f, Gegend f; ✗ Gnade f, Pardon m; ~s
pl. Quartier n (a ✗), Unterkunft f;
fig. Kreise m/pl ; live in close ~s
beengt wohnen; at close ~s dicht
aufeinander; come to close ~s handgemein werden; 2. vierteln, vier-
teilen; beherbergen; ✗ einquartieren; ~back Am. Sport Abwehr-
spieler m; ~day Quartalstag m;
~deck Achterdeck n; ~ly [.əli]
1. vierteljährlich; 2. Vierteljahres-
schrift f; ~master ✗ Quartiermei-
ster m.
[n.]
quartet(te) ♪ [kwɔːˈtet] Quartett]

quarto ['kwɔːtou] Quart(format) n.

quash ✗ [kwɔʃ] aufheben, verwerfen; unterdrücken.

quasi ['kwɑːzi(ː)] gleichsam, sozusagen; Quasi..., Schein...

quaver ['kweivə] 1. Zittern n; ♪
Triller m; 2. mit zitternder Stimme
sprechen od. singen; trillern.

quay [kiː] Kai m; Uferstraße f.

queasy □ ['kwiːzi] empfindlich
(Magen, Gewissen); heikel, mäkelig; ekelhaft.

queen [kwiːn] Königin f; ~ bee
Bienenkönigin f; ~like ['kwiːnlaik],
~ly [.li] wie eine Königin, königlich.

queer [kwiə] sonderbar, seltsam;
wunderlich; komisch; homo-
sexuell.

quench [kwentʃ] fig. Durst etc. löschen, stillen; kühlen; Aufruhr
unterdrücken.

querulous □ ['kweruləs] quengelig,
mürrisch, verdrossen.

query ['kwiəri] 1. Frage(zeichen n)
f; 2. (be)fragen; (be~, an)zweifeln.

quest [kwest] 1. Suche(n n) f, Nach-
forschen n; 2. suchen, forschen.

question ['kwestʃən] 1. Frage f;
Problem n; Untersuchung f; Streitfrage f; Zweifel m; Sache f, Angelegenheit f; beyond (all) ~ ohne
Frage; in ~ fraglich; call in ~ anzweifeln; that is out of the ~ das
steht außer od. kommt nicht in
Frage; 2. befragen; bezweifeln;
~able □ [.nəbl] fraglich; fragwürdig; ~er [.nə] Fragende(r m) f;
~mark Fragezeichen n; ~naire
[kwestiə'nɛə] Fragebogen m.

queue [kjuː] 1. Reihe f v. Personen
etc., Schlange f; Zopf m; 2. mst ~
up (in e-r Reihe) anstehen, Schlange
stehen.

quibble ['kwibl] 1. Wortspiel n;
Spitzfindigkeit f; Ausflucht f; 2. fig.
ausweichen; witzeln.

quick [kwik] 1. schnell, rasch; voreilig; lebhaft; gescheit; beweglich;
lebendig; scharf (Gehör etc.); 2. lebendes Fleisch; the ~ die Leben-
den; to the ~ (bis) ins Fleisch; fig.
(bis) ins Herz, tief; cut s.o. to the ~
j-n aufs empfindlichste kränken; ~en
['kwikən] v/t. beleben; beschleunigen; v/i. aufleben; sich regen; ~ly
[.kli] schnell, rasch; ~ness [.knis]
Lebhaftigkeit f; Schnelligkeit f;
Voreiligkeit f; Schärfe f des Ver-
standes etc.; ~sand Triebsand m;
~set ⚘ Setzling m, bsd Hagedorn
m; a. ~ hedge lebende Hecke; ~
sighted scharfsichtig; ~silver min.
Quecksilber n; ~witted schlag-
fertig.

quid¹ [kwid] Priem m (Kautabak).

quid² sl. [.] Pfund n Sterling.

quiescen|ce [kwai'esns] Ruhe f,
Stille f; ~t □ [.nt] ruhend; fig.
ruhig, still.

quiet ['kwaiət] 1. □ ruhig, still;
2. Ruhe f; on the ~ (sl. on the q.t.)
unter der Hand, im stillen; 3. a. ~
down (sich) beruhigen; ~ness
[.tnis], ~ude ['kwaiitjuːd] Ruhe f,
Stille f.

quill [kwil] 1. Federkiel m; fig. Feder f; Stachel m des Igels etc.;
2. rund fälteln; ~ing ['kwilin]
Rüsche f, Krause f; ~pen Gänse-
feder f zum Schreiben.

quilt [kwilt] 1. Steppdecke f;
2. steppen; wattieren.

quince ⚘ [kwins] Quitte f.

quinine pharm. [kwi'niːn, Am.
'kwainain] Chinin n.

quinquennial □ [kwiŋ'kweniəl]
fünfjährig; fünfjährlich.

quinsy ✗ ['kwinzi] Mandelentzündung f.

quintal ['kwintl] (Doppel)Zentner
m.

quintessence [kwin'tesns] Quint-
essenz f, Kern m, Inbegriff m.

quintuple ['kwintjupl] 1. □ fünffach; 2. (sich) verfünffachen; ~ts [~lits] pl Fünflinge m/pl.

quip [kwip] Stich(elei f) m; Witz (-wort n) m; Spitzfindigkeit f.

quirk [kwə:k] Spitzfindigkeit f; Witz(elei f) m; Kniff m; Schnörkel m; Eigentümlichkeit f; ▲ Hohlkehle f

quisling ['kwizliŋ] Quisling m, Kollaborateur m.

quit [kwit] 1. v/t. verlassen; aufgeben; Am aufhören (mit); vergelten; Schuld tilgen; v/i. aufhören; ausziehen (Mieter); give notice to ~ kündigen; 2. quitt; frei, los.

quite [kwait] ganz, gänzlich; recht; durchaus; ~ a hero ein wirklicher Held; . (so)!, ~ that! ganz recht; ~ the thing F große Mode.

quittance ['kwitəns] Quittung f.

quitter Am. F ['kwitə] Drückeberger m.

quiver¹ ['kwivə] zittern, beben.

quiver² [~] Köcher m.

quiz [kwiz] 1. Prüfung f, Test m; Quiz n; belustigter Blick; 2. (aus-)fragen; prüfen; necken, foppen; anstarren, beäugen; ~zical □ ['kwizikəl] spöttisch; komisch.

quoit [kɔit] Wurfring m; ~s pl. Wurfringspiel n.

Quonset Am. ['kwonsit] a. ~ hut Wellblechbaracke f.

quorum parl. ['kwɔːrəm] beschlußfähige Mitgliederzahl.

quota ['kwoutə] Quote f, Anteil m, Kontingent n.

quotation [kwou'teiʃən] Anführung f, Zitat n; † Preisnotierung f; Kostenvoranschlag m; ~marks pl. Anführungszeichen n/pl.

quote [kwout] anführen, zitieren; † berechnen, notieren (at mit).

quotient ▲ ['kwouʃənt] Quotient m.

quoth † [kwouθ] ~ I sagte ich; ~ he sagte er.

quotidian [kwɔ'tidiən] (all)täglich.

R

rabbi ['ræbai] Rabbiner m.

rabbit ['ræbit] Kaninchen n.

rabble ['ræbl] Pöbel(haufen) m.

rabid ['ræbid] tollwütig (Tier); fig. wild, wütend.

rabies vet ['reibiːz] Tollwut f.

raccoon [rə'kuːn] = racoon.

race [reis] 1. Geschlecht n, Stamm m; Rasse f, Schlag m; Lauf m (a. fig.); Wettrennen n; Strömung f; ~s pl Pferderennen n; 2. rennen; rasen; um die Wette laufen (mit); ⊕ leer laufen; ~course ['reiskɔːs] Rennbahn f, -strecke f; ~horse Rennpferd n; ~r ['reisə] Rennpferd n; Rennboot n; Rennwagen)

racial ['reiʃəl] Rassen... [m.]

racing ['reisiŋ] Rennsport n; attr. Renn.

rack [ræk] 1. Gestell n; Kleiderständer m; Gepäcknetz n; Raufe f, Futtergestell n; Folter(bank) f; go to ~ and ruin völlig zugrunde gehen; 2. strecken; foltern, quälen (a. fig.); ~ one's brains sich den Kopf zermartern.

racket ['rækit] 1. Tennis-Schläger m; Lärm m; Trubel m; Am. F Schwindel(geschäft n) m; Strapaze f; 2. lärmen; sich amüsieren; ~eer Am. [ræki'tiə] Erpresser m; ~eering Am. [~əriŋ] Erpresserwesen n; ~y ['rækiti] ausgelassen.

racoon zo. [rə'kuːn] Waschbär m.

racy ['reisi] kraftvoll, lebendig; stark; würzig; urwüchsig.

radar ['reidə] Radar(gerät) n.

radian|ce ['reidjəns, ~si]

Strahlen n; ~t □ [~nt] strahlend, leuchtend.

radiat|e ['reidieit] (aus)strahlen; strahlenförmig ausgehen; ~ion [reidi'eiʃən] (Aus)Strahlung f; ~or ['reidieitə] Heizkörper m; mot. Kühler m.

radical ['rædikəl] 1. □ Wurzel..., Grund...; gründlich; eingewurzelt; pol. radikal; 2. pol. Radikale(r m) f.

radio ['reidiou] 1. Radio n; Funk (-spruch) m; ~ drama, ~ play Hörspiel n; ~ set Radiogerät n; 2. funken; ~('~)active radioaktiv; ~graph [~ougrɑːf] 1. Röntgenbild n; 2. ein Röntgenbild machen von; ~telegram Funktelegramm n; ~therapy Strahlen-, Röntgentherapie f.

radish ♀ ['rædiʃ] Rettich m; (red) ~ Radieschen n.

radius ['reidjəs] Radius m.

raffle ['ræfl] 1. Tombola f, Verlosung f; 2. verlosen.

raft [rɑːft] 1. Floß n; 2. flößen; ~er ['rɑːftə] ⊕ (Dach)Sparren m.

rag¹ [ræg] Lumpen m; Fetzen m; Lappen m.

rag² sl. [~] 1. Unfug m; Radau m; 2. Unfug treiben (mit); j-n aufziehen; j-n beschimpfen; herumtollen, Radau machen.

ragamuffin ['rægəmʌfin] Lumpenkerl m; Gassenjunge m.

rage [reidʒ] 1. Wut f, Zorn m; Raserei f; Sucht f, Gier f (for nach); Manie f; Ekstase f; it is all the ~ es ist allgemein Mode; 2. wüten, rasen.

rag-fair ['rægfɛə] Trödelmarkt m.
ragged ☐ ['rægid] rauh; zottig; zackig; zerlumpt.
ragman ['rægmən] Lumpensammler m.
raid [reid] 1. (feindlicher) Überfall, Streifzug m; (Luft)Angriff m; Razzia f; 2. einbrechen in (acc.); überfallen.
rail¹ [reil] schimpfen.
rail² [˷] 1. Geländer n; Stange f; 🚂 Schiene f; off the ˷s entgleist; fig. in Unordnung; by ˷ per Bahn; 2. a. ˷ in, ˷ off mit e-m Geländer umgeben.
railing ['reilin], a. ˷s pl. Geländer n; Staket n.
raillery ['reiləri] Spötterei f.
railroad Am. ['reilroud] Eisenbahn f. (˷man Eisenbahner m.)
railway ['reilwei] Eisenbahn f.)
rain [rein] 1. Regen m; 2. regnen; ˷bow ['reinbou] Regenbogen m; ˷coat Regenmantel m; ˷fall Regenmenge f; ˷proof 1. regendicht; 2. Regenmantel m; ˷y ☐ ['reini] regnerisch; Regen...; a ˷ day fig. Notzeiten f/pl.
raise [reiz] ˷ up heben; (oft fig.) erheben; errichten; erhöhen (a. fig.); Geld etc aufbringen; Anleihe aufnehmen; verursachen; fig. erwecken; anstiften; züchten, ziehen; Belagerung etc aufheben.
raisin ['reizn] Rosine f.
rake [reik] 1. Rechen m, Harke f; Wüstling m; Lebemann m; 2. v/t (zs.-)harken; zs.-scharren; fig. (durch)stöbern; ˷ off Am. sl. ['reikɔf] Schwindelprofit m.
rakish ☐ ['reikiʃ] schnittig; liederlich, ausschweifend; verwegen; salopp.
rally ['ræli] 1. Sammeln n; Treffen n; Am. Massenversammlung f; Erholung f; mot Rallye f; 2. (sich ver)sammeln; sich erholen; necken.
ram [ræm] 1. zo., ast. Widder m; ⊕, ⚓ Ramme f; 2. (fest)rammen; ⚓ rammen.
rambl|e ['ræmbl] 1. Streifzug m; 2. umherstreifen; abschweifen; ˷er [˷lə] Wanderer m; ♣ Kletterrose f; ˷ing [˷liŋ] weitläufig.
ramify ['ræmifai] (sich) verzweigen.
ramp [ræmp] Rampe f; ˷ant ☐ ['ræmpənt] wuchernd; fig. zügellos.
rampart ['ræmpɑːt] Wall m.
ramshackle ['ræmʃækl] wack(e)lig.
ran [ræn] pret. von run 1.
ranch [rɑːntʃ, Am. ræntʃ] Ranch f, Viehfarm f; ˷er ['rɑːntʃə, Am. 'ræntʃə], ˷man Rancher m, Viehzüchter m; Farmer m.
rancid ☐ ['rænsid] ranzig.
ranco(u)r ['ræŋkə] Groll m, Haß m.
random ['rændəm] 1. at ˷ aufs Geratewohl, blindlings; 2. ziel-, wahllos; zufällig.

rang [ræŋ] pret. von ring 2.
range [reindʒ] 1. Reihe f; (Berg-)Kette f; ⚡ Kollektion f, Sortiment n; Herd m; Raum m; Umfang m, Bereich m; Reichweite f; Schußweite f; (ausgedehnte) Fläche f; Schießstand m; 2. v/t. (ein)reihen, ordnen; Gebiet etc. durchstreifen; ⚓ längs et. fahren; v/i. in e-r Reihe od. Linie stehen; (umher-) streifen; sich erstrecken, reichen; ˷r ['reindʒə] Förster m; Aufseher m e-s Parks; Am. Förster m; ⚔ Nahkampfspezialist m.
rank [ræŋk] 1. Reihe f, Linie f; ⚔ Glied n; Klasse f; Rang m, Stand m; the ˷s pl., the ˷ and file die Mannschaften f/pl.; fig. die große Masse; 2. v/t. (ein)reihen, (ein-) ordnen; v/i. sich reihen, sich ordnen; gehören (with zu); e-e Stelle einnehmen (above über dat.); ˷ as gelten als; 3. üppig; ranzig; stinkend.
rankle fig. ['ræŋkl] nagen.
ransack ['rænsæk] durchwühlen, durchstöbern, durchsuchen; ausrauben.
ransom ['rænsəm] 1. Lösegeld n; Auslösung f; 2. loskaufen; erlösen.
rant [rænt] 1. Schwulst m; 2. Phrasen dreschen; mit Pathos vortragen.
rap [ræp] 1. Klaps m; Klopfen n; fig. Heller m; 2. schlagen, klopfen.
rapaci|ous ☐ [rə'peiʃəs] raubgierig; ˷ty [rə'pæsiti] Raubgier f.
rape [reip] 1. Raub m; Entführung f; Notzucht f, Vergewaltigung f; ♣ Raps m; 2. rauben; vergewaltigen.
rapid ['ræpid] 1. ☐ schnell, reißend, rapid(e); steil; 2. ˷s pl. Stromschnelle(n pl.) f; ˷ity [rə'piditi] Schnelligkeit f.
rapprochement pol. [ræ'prɔʃmɑ̃ː] Wiederannäherung f.
rapt [ræpt] entzückt; versunken; ˷ure ['ræptʃə] Entzücken n; go into ˷s in Entzücken geraten.
rare ☐ [rɛə] selten; phys. dünn.
rarebit ['rɛəbit]: Welsh ˷ geröstete Käseschnitte.
rarefy ['rɛərifai] (sich) verdünnen.
rarity ['rɛəriti] Seltenheit f; Dünnheit f.
rascal ['rɑːskəl] Schuft m; co. Gauner m; ˷ity [rɑːs'kæliti] Schurkerei f; ˷ly ['rɑːskəli] schuftig; erbärmlich.
rash¹ ☐ [ræʃ] hastig, vorschnell; übereilt; unbesonnen; waghalsig.
rash² 🞸 [˷] Hautausschlag m.
rasher ['ræʃə] Speckschnitte f.
rasp [rɑːsp] 1. Raspel f; 2. raspeln; j-m weh(e) tun; kratzen; krächzen.
raspberry ['rɑːzbəri] Himbeere f.
rat [ræt] zo. Ratte f; pol. Überläufer m; smell a ˷ Lunte od. den Braten riechen; ˷s! Quatsch!
rate [reit] 1. Verhältnis n, Maß n,

Satz m; Rate f; Preis m, Gebühr f; Taxe f; (Gemeinde)Abgabe f, Steuer f; Grad m, Rang m; bsd. ⚓ Klasse f; Geschwindigkeit f; at any ~ auf jeden Fall; ~ of exchange (Umrechnungs)Kurs m; ~ of interest Zinsfuß m; 2. (ein)schätzen; besteuern; ~ among rechnen, zählen zu (dat.); ausschelten.

rather ['rɑːðə] eher, lieber; vielmehr; besser gesagt; ziemlich; ~! F und ob!, I had od. would ~ do ich möchte lieber tun.

ratify ['rætifai] ratifizieren.

rating ['reitin] Schätzung f; Steuersatz m; ⚓ Dienstgrad m; ⚓ (Segel-) Klasse f; Matrose m; Schelte(n n) f.

ratio & etc. ['reiʃiou] Verhältnis n.

ration ['ræʃən] 1. Ration f, Zuteilung f; 2. rationieren.

rational [['ræʃənl] vernunftgemäß; vernünftig, (a. &) rational; ~ity ['ræʃə'næliti] Vernunft(mäßigkeit) f; ~ize ['ræʃnəlaiz] rationalisieren, wirtschaftlich gestalten.

rat race ['ræt 'reis] sinnlose Hetze; rücksichtsloses Aufstiegsstreben.

ratten ['rætn] sabotieren.

rattle ['rætl] 1. Gerassel n; Geklapper n, Geplapper n; Klapper f; (Todes)Röcheln n; 2. rasseln (mit); klappern, plappern; röcheln; ~ off herunterrasseln; ~-brain, ~-pate Hohl-, Wirrkopf m; ~-snake Klapperschlange f; ~-trap fig. Klapperkasten m (Fahrzeug).

rattling ['rætlin] 1. adj. rasselnd; fig. scharf (Tempo); 2. adv. sehr, äußerst.

raucous ['rɔːkəs] heiser, rauh.

ravage ['rævidʒ] 1. Verwüstung f; 2. verwüsten; plündern.

rave [reiv] rasen, toben; schwärmen (about, of von).

ravel ['rævəl] v/t. verwickeln; ~ (out) auftrennen; fig. entwirren; v/i. a. ~ out ausfasern, aufgehen.

raven orn ['reivn] Rabe m.

raven|ing ['rævnin], ~ous □ ['rævinəs] gefräßig; heißhungrig; raubgierig.

ravine [rə'viːn] Hohlweg m; Schlucht f.

ravings ['reivinz] pl. Delirien n/pl.

ravish ['ræviʃ] entzücken; vergewaltigen, rauben; ~ing □ ['~ʃin] hinreißend, entzückend; ~ment ['~ʃmənt] Schändung f; Entzücken n.

raw [[rɔː] roh; Roh...; wund; rauh (Wetter); ungeübt, unerfahren; ~-boned ['rɔːbound] knochig, hager; ~ hide Rohleder n.

ray [rei] Strahl m; fig. Schimmer m.

rayon ['reiɔn] Kunstseide f.

raze [reiz] Haus etc. abreißen; Festung schleifen; tilgen.

razor ['reizə] Rasiermesser n; Ra-

sierapparat m; ~-blade Rasierklinge f; ~-edge fig. des Messers Schneide f, kritische Lage.

razz Am. sl. [ræz] aufziehen.

re... [riː] wieder...; zurück...; neu...; um...

reach [riːtʃ] 1. Ausstrecken n; Griff m; Reichweite f; Fassungskraft f, Horizont m; Flußstrecke f; beyond ~, out of ~ unerreichbar; within easy ~ leicht erreichbar; 2. v/i. reichen; langen, greifen; sich erstrecken; v/t. (hin-, her)reichen, (hin-, her)langen; ausstrecken; erreichen.

react [ri(ː)'ækt] reagieren (to auf acc.); (ein)wirken (on, upon auf acc.); sich auflehnen (against gegen).

reaction [ri(ː)'ækʃən] Reaktion f (a. pol.); ~ary ['~əri] 1. reaktionär; 2. Reaktionär(in).

reactor phys. [ri(ː)'æktə] Reaktor m.

read 1. [riːd] [irr.] lesen; deuten; (an)zeigen (Thermometer); studieren; sich gut etc. lesen; lauten; ~ to s.o. j-m vorlesen; 2. [red] pret. u. p.p. von 1; 3. [~] adj. belesen; ~able □ ['riːdəbl] lesbar; leserlich; lesenswert; ~er ['riːdə] (Vor)Leser(in); typ. Korrektor m; Lektor m; univ. Dozent m; Lesebuch n.

readi|ly ['redili] adv. gleich, leicht; gern; ~ness ['~inis] Bereitschaft f; Bereitwilligkeit f; Schnelligkeit f.

reading ['riːdin] Lesen n; Lesung f (a. parl.); Stand m des Thermometers; Belesenheit f; Lektüre f; Lesart f; Auffassung f; attr. Lese...

readjust ['riːə'dʒʌst] wieder in Ordnung bringen; wieder anpassen; ~ment ['~tmənt] Wiederanpassung f; Neuordnung f.

ready ~ ['redi] bereit, fertig; bereitwillig; im Begriff (to do zu tun); schnell; gewandt; leicht; zur Hand; ✝ bar; ~ for use gebrauchsfertig; make od. get ~ (sich) fertig machen; ~-made fertig, Konfektions...

reagent ⚗ [ri(ː)'eidʒənt] Reagens n.

real [[riəl] wirklich, tatsächlich, real; echt; ~ estate Grundbesitz m, Immobilien pl.; ~ism ['riəlizəm] Realismus m; ~istic [riə'listik] (~ally) realistisch; sachlich; wirklichkeitsnah; ~ity [ri(ː)'æliti] Wirklichkeit f; ~ization [riəlai'zeiʃən] Verwirklichung f; Erkenntnis f; ✝ Realisierung f; ~ize ['riəlaiz] sich klarmachen; erkennen; verwirklichen; realisieren, zu Geld machen; ~ly ['~li] wirklich, in der Tat.

realm [relm] Königreich n; Reich n.

realt|or Am. ['riəltə] Grundstücksmakler m; ~y ⚖ ['~ti] Grundeigentum n.

reap [riːp] Korn schneiden; Feld

mähen; *fig.* ernten; ~er ['ri:pə]
Schnitter(in); Mähmaschine *f*.

reappear ['ri:ə'piə] wieder erscheinen.

rear [riə] **1.** *v/t.* auf-, großziehen;
züchten; *v/i.* sich aufrichten;
2. Rück-, Hinterseite *f*; *mot.*, ⚓
Heck *n*; ✕ Nachhut *f*, *at the ~ of*,
in (the) ~ of hinter *(dat* ;3. Hinter...,
Nach...; ~ *wheel drive* Hinterradantrieb *m*; ~admiral ⚓ ['riə'ædmərəl] Konteradmiral *m*;
~guard ✕ Nachhut *f*; ~lamp
mot. Schlußlicht *n*.

rearm ['ri:'a:m] (wieder)aufrüsten;
~ament [~'məmənt] Aufrüstung *f*.

rearmost ['riəmoust] hinterst.

rearward ['riəwəd] **1.** *adj.* rückwärtig; **2.** *adv. a. ~s* rückwärts.

reason ['ri:zn] **1.** Vernunft *f*; Verstand *m*; Recht *n*, Billigkeit *f*; Ursache *f*, Grund *m*, *by ~ of* wegen;
for this ~ aus diesem Grund; *listen
to ~* Vernunft annehmen; *it stands
to ~ that* es leuchtet ein, daß; **2.**
v/i. vernünftig lenken; schließen;
urteilen; argumentieren; *v/t. a.
~ out* durchdenken; *~ away* fortdisputieren; *~ s.o. into (out of)
s.th.* j-m et. ein- (aus)reden;
~able [~'nəbl] vernünftig; billig;
angemessen; leidlich.

reassure [ri:ə'ʃuə] wieder versichern; (wieder) beruhigen.

rebate ['ri:beit] ↑ Rabatt *m*, Abzug
m; Rückzahlung *f*.

rebel 1. ['rebl] Rebell *m*; Aufrührer
m; **2.** [~] rebellisch, **3.** [ri'bel] sich
auflehnen, ~lion [~ljən] Empörung
f; ~lious [~jəs] *rebel* 2.

rebirth ['ri:'bə:θ] Wiedergeburt *f*.

rebound [ri'baund] **1.** zurückprallen; **2.** Rückprall *m*, Rückschlag *m*.

rebuff [ri'bʌf] **1.** Zurück-, Abweisung *f*; **2.** zurück-, abweisen.

rebuild ['ri:'bild] [*irr.* (build)] wieder (auf)bauen.

rebuke [ri'bju:k] **1.** Tadel *m*;
2. tadeln.

rebut [ri'bʌt] zurückweisen.

recall [ri'kɔ:l] **1.** Zurückrufung *f*;
Abberufung *f*, Widerruf *m*; *beyond
~ past ~* unwiderruflich; **2.** zurückrufen; ab(be)rufen; (sich) erinnern an *(acc.)*; widerrufen; ↑
Kapital kündigen.

recapitulate [ri:kə'pitjuleit] kurz
wiederholen, *~s.*-fassen.

recapture ['ri:'kæptʃə] wieder (gefangen)nehmen; ✕ zurückerobern.

recast ['ri:'ka:st] [*irr. (cast)*] ⊕ umgießen; umformen, neu gestalten.

recede [ri(:)'si:d] zurücktreten.

receipt [ri'si:t] **1.** Empfang *m*;
Eingang *m v. Waren*; Quittung *f*;
(Koch)Rezept *n*; *~s pl.* Einnahmen
f/pl.; **2.** quittieren.

receiv|able [ri'si:vəbl] annehmbar;
↑ noch zu fordern(d), ausstehend;

~e [ri'si:v] empfangen; erhalten,
bekommen; aufnehmen; annehmen; anerkennen; ~ed anerkannt;
~er [~və] Empfänger *m*; *teleph.*
Hörer *m*; Hehler *m*; *Steuer- etc.*
Einnehmer *m*; *official ~* ⚖ Masseverwalter *m*.

recent □ ['ri:snt] neu; frisch; modern; ~ *events pl. die jüngsten Ereignisse *n/pl.*; ~ly [~tli] neulich,
vor kurzem.

receptacle [ri'septəkl] Behälter *m*.

reception [ri'sepʃən] Aufnahme *f*
(a. fig.), *(a. Radio)*Empfang *m*;
Annahme *f*; ~ist [~nist] Empfangsdame *f*, -herr *m*; ~room Empfangszimmer *n*.

receptive □ [ri'septiv] empfänglich, aufnahmefähig *(of für)*.

recess [ri'ses] Pause *f*; *bsd. parl.*
Ferien *pl.*; (entlegener) Winkel;
Nische *f*; ~es *pl. fig.* Tiefe(n *pl.*) *f*;
~ion [~'seʃən] Zurückziehen *n*, Zurücktreten *n*; ↑ Konjunkturrückgang *m*, rückläufige Bewegung.

recipe ['resipi] Rezept *n*.

recipient [ri'sipiənt] Empfänger(in).

reciproc|al [ri'siprəkəl] wechsel-,
gegenseitig; ~ate [~keit] *v/i.* sich
erkenntlich zeigen; ⊕ sich hin- und
herbewegen; *v/t. Glückwünsche etc.*
erwidern; ~ity [resi'prositi] Gegenseitigkeit *f*.

recit|al [ri'saitl] Bericht *m*; Erzählung *f*; ♪ (Solo)Vortrag *m*, Konzert *n*; ~ation [resi'teiʃən] Hersagen *n*; Vortrag *m*; ~e [ri'sait] vortragen; aufsagen; berichten.

reckless □ ['reklis] unbekümmert;
rücksichtslos; leichtsinnig.

reckon ['rekən] *v/t.* rechnen; *a. ~
for*, *~ as* schätzen als, halten für; *~
up* zs.-zählen; *v/i.* rechnen, denken,
vermuten; *~ (up)on* sich verlassen
auf *(acc.)*; ~ing ['rekniŋ] Rechnen
n; (Ab-, Be)Rechnung *f*.

reclaim [ri'kleim] wiedergewinnen;
j-n bessern; zivilisieren; urbar
machen.

recline [ri'klain] (sich) (zurück-)
lehnen; ~ *upon fig.* sich stützen auf.

recluse [ri'klu:s] Einsiedler(in).

recogni|tion [rekəg'niʃən] Anerkennung *f*; Wiedererkennen *n*; ~ze
['rekəgnaiz] anerkennen; (wieder-)
erkennen.

recoil [ri'koil] **1.** zurückprallen;
2. Rückstoß *m*, -lauf *m*.

recollect[1] [rekə'lekt] sich erinnern
an *(acc.)*.

re-collect[2] ['ri:kə'lekt] wieder sammeln; ~ *o.s.* sich fassen.

recollection [rekə'lekʃən] Erinnerung *f (of an acc.)*; Gedächtnis *n*.

recommend [rekə'mend] empfehlen; ~ation [rekəmen'deiʃən] Empfehlung *f*; Vorschlag *m*.

recompense ['rekəmpens] **1.** Belohnung *f*, Vergeltung *f*; Ersatz *m*;

2. belohnen, vergelten; entschädigen; ersetzen.

reconcil|e ['rekənsail] aus-, versöhnen; in Einklang bringen; schlichten; **~iation** [rekənsili'eiʃən] Ver-, Aussöhnung f.

recondition ['ri:kən'diʃən] wieder herrichten; ⊕ überholen.

reconn|aissance ⚔ [ri'konisəns] Aufklärung f, Erkundung f; fig. Übersicht f; **~oitre**, Am. **~oiter** [rekə'noitə] erkunden, auskundschaften.

reconsider ['ri:kən'sidə] wieder erwägen; nochmals überlegen.

reconstitute ['ri:'konstitju:t] wiederherstellen.

reconstruct ['ri:kəns'trʌkt] wiederaufbauen; **~ion** [~kʃən] Wiederaufbau m, Wiederherstellung f.

reconvert ['ri:kən'və:t] umstellen.

record 1. ['rekɔːd] Aufzeichnung f; ⚖ Protokoll n; schriftlicher Bericht; Ruf m, Leumund m; Wiedergabe f; Schallplatte f; Sport: Rekord m; place on ~ schriftlich niederlegen; ♀ Office Staatsarchiv n; off the ~ Am. inoffiziell; **2.** [ri'kɔːd] auf-, verzeichnen; auf Schallplatte etc. aufnehmen; **~er** [~də] Registrator m; Stadtrichter m; Aufnahmegerät n, bsd. Tonbandgerät n; ♪ Blockflöte f; **~ing** [~diŋ] Radio: Aufzeichnung f, Aufnahme f; **~-player** Plattenspieler m.

recount [ri'kaunt] erzählen.

recoup [ri'ku:p] j-n entschädigen (for für); et. wieder einbringen.

recourse [ri'kɔːs] Zuflucht f; have ~ to s-e Zuflucht nehmen zu.

recover [ri'kʌvə] v/t. wiedererlangen, wiederfinden; wieder einbringen, wiedergutmachen; Schulden etc. eintreiben; be ~ed wiederhergestellt sein; v/i. sich erholen; genesen; **~y** [~əri] Wiedererlangung f; Wiederherstellung f; Genesung f; Erholung f.

recreat|e ['rekrieit] v/t. erfrischen; v/i. a. ~ o.s. sich erholen; **~ion** [rekri'eiʃən] Erholung(spause) f.

recrimination [rikrimi'neiʃən] Gegenbeschuldigung f; Gegenklage f.

recruit [ri'kru:t] **1.** Rekrut m; fig. Neuling m; **2.** erneuern, ergänzen; Truppe rekrutieren; ⚔ Rekruten ausheben; sich erholen.

rectangle △ ['rektæŋgl] Rechteck n.

recti|fy ['rektifai] berichtigen; verbessern; ⚡, Radio gleichrichten; **~tude** [~itju:d] Geradheit f.

rector ['rektə] Pfarrer m; Rektor m; **~y** [~əri] Pfarre(i) f; Pfarrhaus n.

recumbent [ri'kʌmbənt] liegend.

recuperate [ri'kju:pəreit] wiederherstellen; sich erholen.

recur [ri'kə:] zurück-, wiederkehren (to zu), zurückkommen (to auf acc.); ~ to j-m wieder einfallen; **~rence**

[ri'kʌrəns] Wieder-, Rückkehr f; **~rent** □ [~nt] wiederkehrend.

red [red] **1.** rot; ~ heat Rotglut f; ~ herring Bückling m; ~ tape Amtsschimmel m; **2.** Rot n; (bsd. pol.) Rote(r m) f; be in the ~ Am. F in Schulden stecken.

red|breast ['redbrest] a. robin ~ Rotkehlchen n; **~cap** Militärpolizist m; Am. Gepäckträger m; **~den** ['redn] (sich) röten; erröten; **~dish** ['rediʃ] rötlich.

redecorate ['ri:'dekəreit] Zimmer renovieren (lassen).

redeem [ri'di:m] zurück-, loskaufen; ablösen; Versprechen einlösen; büßen; entschädigen für; erlösen; **~er** eccl. [~mə] Erlöser m, Heiland m.

redemption [ri'dempʃən] Rückkauf m; Auslösung f; Erlösung f.

red|-handed ['red'hændid] catch od. take s.o. ~ j-n auf frischer Tat ertappen; **~head** Rotschopf m; Hitzkopf m; **~-headed** rothaarig; **~-hot** rotglühend; fig. hitzig; ♀ **Indian** Indianer(in); **~-letter day** Festtag m; fig. Freuden-, Glückstag m; **~ness** ['rednis] Röte f.

redolent ['redoulənt] duftend.

redouble [ri'dʌbl] (sich) verdoppeln.

redoubt ⚔ [ri'daut] Redoute f; **~able** rhet. [~təbl] furchtbar.

redound [ri'daund]: ~ to beitragen od. gereichen od. führen zu.

redress [ri'dres] **1.** Abhilfe f; Wiedergutmachung f; ⚖ Entschädigung f; **2.** abhelfen (dat.); wiedergutmachen.

red|-tapism ['red'teipizəm] Bürokratismus m; **~tapist** [~ist] Bürokrat m.

reduc|e [ri'dju:s] fig. zurückführen, bringen (to auf, in acc., zu); verwandeln (to in acc.); verringern, vermindern; einschränken; Preise herabsetzen; (be)zwingen; ⚡, 🔬 reduzieren; ⚕ einrenken; ~ to writing schriftlich niederlegen; **~tion** [ri'dʌkʃən] Reduktion f; Verwandlung f; Herabsetzung f, (Preis)Nachlaß m, Rabatt m; Verminderung f; Verkleinerung f; ⚕ Einrenkung f.

redundant □ [ri'dʌndənt] überflüssig; übermäßig; weitschweifig.

reed [ri:d] Schilfrohr n; Rohrflöte f.

re-education ['ri:edju(:)'keiʃən] Umschulung f, Umerziehung f.

reef [ri:f] (Felsen)Riff n; ♣ Reff n.

reefer ['ri:fə] Seemannsjacke f; Am. sl. Marihuana-Zigarette f.

reek [ri:k] **1.** Rauch m, Dampf m; Dunst m; **2.** rauchen, dampfen (with von); unangenehm riechen.

reel [ri:l] **1.** Haspel f; (Garn-, Film)Rolle f, Spule f; **2.** v/t. haspeln; wickeln, spulen; v/i. wirbeln; schwanken; taumeln.

re-elect ['ri:i'lekt] wiederwählen.
re-enter [ri:'entə] wieder eintreten (in *acc.*).
re-establish [ri:is'tæbliʃ] wiederherstellen.
refection [ri'fekʃən] Erfrischung *f.*
refer [ri'fə:]: ~ *to* ver-, überweisen an (*acc.*); sich beziehen auf (*acc.*); erwähnen (*acc.*); zuordnen (*dat.*); befragen (*acc.*), nachschlagen in (*dat.*); zurückführen auf (*acc.*); zuschreiben (*dat.*); ~ee [refə'ri:] Schiedsrichter *m*; *Boxen:* Ringrichter *m*; ~ence ['refrəns] Referenz *f*, Empfehlung *f*, Zeugnis *n*; Verweisung *f*; Bezugnahme *f*; Anspielung *f*; Beziehung *f*; Auskunft (-geber *m*) *f*; in *od.* with ~ to in betreff (*gen.*), in bezug auf (*acc.*); ~ *book* Nachschlagewerk *n*; ~ *library* Handbibliothek *f*; ~ *number* Aktenzeichen *n*; *make* ~ *to et.* erwähnen.
referendum [refə'rendəm] Volksentscheid *m.*
refill 1. ['ri:fil] Nachfüllung *f*; Ersatzfüllung *f*; **2.** ['ri:'fil] (sich) wieder füllen, auffüllen.
refine [ri'fain] (sich) verfeinern *od.* veredeln; ⊕ raffinieren; (sich) läutern (*a. fig.*); klügeln; ~ (*up*)*on et.* verfeinern, verbessern; ~ment [~nmənt] Verfeinerung *f*, Vered(e)-lung *f*; Läuterung *f*; Feinheit *f*; Bildung *f*; Spitzfindigkeit *f*; ~ry [~nəri] ⊕ Raffinerie *f*; *metall.* (Eisen)Hütte *f.*
refit ⚓ ['ri:'fit] *v/t.* ausbessern; neu ausrüsten; *v/i.* ausgebessert werden.
reflect [ri'flekt] *v/t.* zurückwerfen, reflektieren; zurückstrahlen, widerspiegeln (*a. fig.*); zum Ausdruck bringen; *v/i.* ~ (*up*)*on* nachdenken über (*acc.*); sich abfällig äußern über (*acc.*); ein schlechtes Licht werfen auf (*acc.*); ~ion [~kʃən] Zurückstrahlung *f*, Widerspiegelung *f*; Reflex *m*; Spiegelbild *n*; Überlegung *f*; Gedanke *m*; abfällige Bemerkung *f*; Makel *m*; ~ive [~ktiv] zurückstrahlend; nachdenklich.
reflex ⚓ ['ri:fleks] **1.** Reflex...; **2.** Widerschein *m*, Reflex *m* (*a. physiol.*).
reflexive □ [ri'fleksiv] zurückwirkend; *gr.* reflexiv, rückbezüglich.
reforest [ri:'fɔrist] aufforsten.
reform¹ [ri'fɔ:m] **1.** Verbesserung *f*, Reform *f*; **2.** verbessern, reformieren; (sich) bessern.
re-form² ['ri:'fɔ:m] (sich) neu bilden; ~ sich wieder formieren.
reform|ation [refə'meiʃən] Umgestaltung *f*; Besserung *f*; *eccl.* ♀ Reformation *f*; ~atory [ri'fɔ:mətəri] **1.** bessernd; **2.** Besserungsanstalt *f*; ~er [ri'fɔ:mə] *eccl.* Reformator *m*; *bsd. pol.* Reformer *m.*

refract|ion [ri'frækʃən] Strahlenbrechung *f*; ~ory □ [~ktəri] widerspenstig; hartnäckig; ⊕ feuerfest.
refrain [ri'frein] **1.** sich enthalten (*from gen.*), unterlassen (*from acc.*); **2.** Kehrreim *m*, Refrain *m.*
refresh [ri'freʃ] (sich) erfrischen; auffrischen; ~ment [~ʃmənt] Erfrischung *f* (*a. Getränk etc.*).
refrigerat|e [ri'fridʒəreit] kühlen; ~or [~tə] Kühlschrank *m*, -raum *m*; ~ *car* Kühlwagen *m.*
refuel ['ri:'fjuəl] tanken.
refuge ['refju:dʒ] Zuflucht(sstätte) *f*; *a. street-*~ Verkehrsinsel *f*; ~e [refju:(')dʒi:] Flüchtling *m*; ~ *camp* Flüchtlingslager *n.*
refulgent □ [ri'fʌldʒənt] strahlend.
refund [ri:'fʌnd] zurückzahlen.
refurbish ['ri:'fə:biʃ] aufpolieren.
refusal [ri'fju:zəl] abschlägige Antwort; (Ver)Weigerung *f*; Vorkaufsrecht *n* (*of auf acc.*).
refuse¹ [ri'fju:z] *v/t.* verweigern; abweisen, ablehnen; scheuen vor (*dat.*); *v/i.* sich weigern; scheuen (*Pferd*). [fall *m*, Müll *m.*]
refuse² ['refju:s] Ausschuß *m*; Ab-⌋
refute [ri'fju:t] widerlegen.
regain [ri'gein] wiedergewinnen.
regal □ ['ri:gəl] königlich; Königs...
regale [ri'geil] *v/t.* festlich bewirten; *v/i.* schwelgen (*on in dat.*).
regard [ri'gɑ:d] **1.** fester Blick; (Hoch)Achtung *f*, Rücksicht *f*; Beziehung *f*; with ~ to im Hinblick auf (*acc.*); *kind* ~s herzliche Grüße; **2.** ansehen; betrachten; betreffen; *as* ~s ... was ... anbetrifft; ~ing [~diŋ] hinsichtlich (*gen.*); ~less [~dlis]: ~ *of* ohne Rücksicht auf (*acc.*).
regenerat|e [ri'dʒenəreit] (sich) erneuern; (sich) regenerieren; (sich) neu bilden; *f.* [~rit] wiedergeboren.
regent ['ri:dʒənt] **1.** herrschend; **2.** Regent *m.*
regiment ⚔ ['redʒimənt] **1.** Regiment *n*; **2.** [~mənt] organisieren; ~als ⚔ [redʒi'mentlz] *pl.* Uniform *f.*
region ['ri:dʒən] Gegend *f*, Gebiet *n*; *fig.* Bereich *m*; ~al □ [~nl] örtlich; Orts...
register ['redʒistə] **1.** Register *n*, Verzeichnis *n*; ⊕ Schieber *m*, Ventil *n*; ♪ Register *n*; Zählwerk *n*; *cash* ~ Registrierkasse *f*; **2.** registrieren *od.* eintragen (lassen); (an-)zeigen, auf-, verzeichnen; *Postsache* einschreiben (lassen), *Gepäck* aufgeben; sich *polizeilich* melden.
registr|ar [redʒis'trɑ:] Registrator *m*; Standesbeamte(r) *m*; ~ation [~reiʃən] Eintragung *f*; ~ *fee* Anmeldegebühr *f*; ~y ['redʒistri] Eintragung *f*; Registratur *f*; Register *n*; ~ *office* Standesamt *n.*
regress, ~ion ['ri:gres, ri'greʃən] Rückkehr *f*; *fig.* Rückgang *m.*

regret [ri'gret] 1. Bedauern *n*; Schmerz *m*; 2. bedauern; *Verlust* beklagen; **.ful** [~tful] bedauernd; **.fully** [~li] mit Bedauern; **.table** □ [~təbl] bedauerlich.

regular □ ['regjulə] regelmäßig; regelrecht, richtig; ordentlich; pünktlich; **.ity** regulär; **.ity** [regju-'læriti] Regelmäßigkeit *f*; Richtigkeit *f*, Ordnung *f*.

regulat|e ['regjuleit] regeln, ordnen, regulieren; **.ion** [regju'leiʃən] 1. Regulierung *f*; Vorschrift *f*, Bestimmung *f*; 2. vorschriftsmäßig.

rehash *fig.* ['ri:'hæʃ] 1. wieder durchkauen *od.* aufwärmen; 2. Aufguß *m*.

rehears|al [ri'hə:səl] *thea.*, ♪ Probe *f*; Wiederholung *f*; **.e** [ri'hə:s] *thea.* proben; wiederholen; aufsagen.

reign [rein] 1. Regierung *f*; *fig.* Herrschaft *f*; 2. herrschen, regieren.

reimburse [ri:im'bə:s] *j-n* entschädigen; *Kosten* wiedererstatten.

rein [rein] 1. Zügel *m*; 2. zügeln.

reindeer *zo.* ['reindiə] Ren(tier)*n*.

reinforce [ri:in'fɔ:s] verstärken; **.ment** [~smənt] Verstärkung *f*.

reinstate ['ri:in'steit] wieder einsetzen; wieder instand setzen.

reinsure ['ri:in'ʃuə] rückversichern.

reiterate [ri:'itəreit] (dauernd) wiederholen.

reject [ri'dʒekt] ver-, wegwerfen; ablehnen, ausschlagen; zurückweisen; **.ion** [~kʃən] Verwerfung *f*; Ablehnung *f*; Zurückweisung *f*.

rejoic|e [ri'dʒɔis] *v/t.* erfreuen; *v/i.* sich freuen (*at, in* über *acc.*); **.ing** [~siŋ] 1. □ freudig; 2. *oft* **.s** *pl.* Freude(nfest *n*) *f*.

rejoin ['ri:'dʒɔin] (sich) wieder vereinigen (mit); wieder zurückkehren zu; [ri'dʒɔin] erwidern.

rejuvenate [ri'dʒu:vineit] verjüngen. [entzünden.)

rekindle ['ri:'kindl] (sich) wieder)

relapse [ri'læps] 1. Rückfall *m*; 2. zurückfallen, rückfällig werden.

relate [ri'leit] *v/t.* erzählen; in Beziehung bringen; *v/i.* sich beziehen (*to* auf *acc.*); **.d** verwandt (*to* mit).

relation [ri'leiʃən] Erzählung *f*; Beziehung *f*; Verhältnis *n*; Verwandtschaft *f*; Verwandte(r *m*) *f*; *in* ~ *to* in bezug auf (*acc.*); **.ship** [~nʃip] Verwandtschaft *f*; Beziehung *f*.

relative ['relətiv] 1. □ bezüglich (*to* gen.); *gr.* relativ; verhältnismäßig; entsprechend; 2. *gr.* Relativpronomen *n*; Verwandte(r *m*) *f*.

relax [ri'læks] (sich) lockern; mildern; nachlassen (in dat.); (sich) entspannen, ausspannen; milder werden; **.ation** [ri:læk'seiʃən] Lockerung *f*; Nachlassen *n*; Entspannung *f*, Erholung *f*.

relay¹ 1. [ri'lei] frisches Gespann; Ablösung *f*; ['ri:'lei] ∉ Relais *n*; *Radio:* Übertragung *f*; 2. [~] *Radio:* übertragen.

re-lay² ['ri:'lei] *Kabel etc.* neu verlegen.

relay-race ['ri:leireis] *Sport:* Staffellauf *m*.

release [ri'li:s] 1. Freilassung *f*; *fig.* Befreiung *f*; Freigabe *f*; *Film: oft* *first* ~ Uraufführung *f*; ⊕, *phot.* Auslöser *m*; 2. freilassen; erlösen; freigeben; *Recht* aufgeben, übertragen; *Film* uraufführen; ⊕ auslösen.

relegate ['religeit] verbannen; verweisen (*to* an *acc.*).

relent [ri'lent] sich erweichen lassen; **.less** □ [~tlis] unbarmherzig.

relevant ['relivənt] sachdienlich; zutreffend; wichtig, erheblich.

reliab|ility [rilaiə'biliti] Zuverlässigkeit *f*, **.le** □ [ri'laiəbl] zuverlässig.

reliance [ri'laiəns] Ver-, Zutrauen *n*; Verlaß *m*.

relic ['relik] Überrest *m*; Reliquie *f*; **.t** [~kt] Witwe *f*.

relief [ri'li:f] Erleichterung *f*; (angenehme) Unterbrechung; Unterstützung *f*; ✕ Ablösung *f*; ✕ Entsatz *m*; Hilfe *f*; △ etc. Relief *n*; **.works** *pl.* Notstandsarbeiten *f/pl.*

relieve [ri'li:v] erleichtern; mildern, lindern; *Arme etc.* unterstützen; ✕ ablösen; ✕ entsetzen; ☱ (ab)helfen (dat.); befreien; hervortreten lassen; (angenehm) unterbrechen.

religion [ri'lidʒən] Religion *f*; Ordensleben *n*; *fig.* Ehrensache *f*.

religious □ [ri'lidʒəs] Religions...; religiös; *eccl.* Ordens...; gewissenhaft.

relinquish [ri'liŋkwiʃ] aufgeben; verzichten auf (*acc.*); loslassen.

relish ['reliʃ] 1. (Bei)Geschmack *m*; Würze *f*; Genuß *m*; 2. gern essen; Geschmack finden an (dat.); schmackhaft machen.

reluctan|ce [ri'lʌktəns] Widerstreben *n*; *bsd. phys.* Widerstand *m*; **.t** □ [~nt] widerstrebend, widerwillig.

rely [ri'lai]: ~ (up)on sich verlassen (auf *acc.*), bauen auf (*acc.*).

remain [ri'mein] 1. (ver)bleiben; übrigbleiben; 2. **.s** *pl.* Überbleibsel *n/pl.*, Überreste *m/pl.*; sterbliche Reste *m/pl.*; **.der** [~ndə] Rest *m*.

remand [ri'mɑ:nd] 1. (☱ in die Untersuchungshaft) zurückschicken; 2. (Zurücksendung *f* in die) Untersuchungshaft *f*; *prisoner on* ~ Untersuchungsgefangene(r *m*) *f*; ~ *home* Jugendstrafanstalt *f*.

remark [ri'mɑ:k] 1. Beachtung *f*; Bemerkung *f*; 2. *v/t.* bemerken; *v/i.* sich äußern; **.able** □ [~kəbl] bemerkenswert; merkwürdig.

remedy ['remidi] **1.** (Heil-, Hilfs-, Gegen-, Rechts)Mittel *n*; (Ab-) Hilfe *f*; **2.** heilen; abhelfen (*dat.*).

rememb|er [ri'membə] sich erinnern an (*acc.*); denken an (*acc.*); beherzigen; ～ me to her grüße sie von mir; ～rance [˶brəns] Erinnerung *f*; Gedächtnis *n*; Andenken *n*; ～s *pl.* Empfehlungen *f/pl.*, Grüße *m/pl.*

remind [ri'maind] erinnern (*of an acc.*); ～er [˶də] Mahnung *f*.

reminiscen|ce [remi'nisns] Erinnerung *f*; ～t □ [˶nt] (sich) erinnernd.

remiss □ [ri'mis] schlaff, (nach-)lässig; ～ion [˶ʃən] *Sünden*-Vergebung *f*; Erlassung *f v. Strafe etc.*; Nachlassen *n*.

remit [ri'mit] *Sünden* vergeben; *Schuld etc.* erlassen; nachlassen in (*dat.*); überweisen; ～tance [˶təns] (Geld)Sendung *f*; ✝ Rimesse *f*.

remnant ['remnənt] (Über)Rest *m*.

remodel ['ri:'mɔdl] umbilden.

remonstra|nce [ri'mɔnstrəns] Vorstellung *f*, Einwendung *f*; ～te [˶treit] Vorstellungen machen (*on über acc.*; *with s.o.* j-m); einwenden.

remorse [ri'mɔːs] Gewissensbisse *m/pl.*; ～less □ [˶slis] hart(herzig).

remote □ [ri'mout] entfernt, entlegen; ～ness [˶tnis] Entfernung *f*.

remov|al [ri'muːvəl] Entfernen *n*; Beseitigung *f*; Umzug *m*; Entlassung *f*; ～ van Möbelwagen *m*; ～e [˶uːv] **1.** *v/t.* entfernen; wegräumen, wegrücken; beseitigen; entlassen; *v/i.* (aus-, um-, ver)ziehen; **2.** Entfernung *f*; Grad *m*; *Schule:* Versetzung *f*; Abteilung *f e-r Klasse*; ～er [˶və] (Möbel)Spediteur *m*.

remunerat|e [ri'mjuːnəreit] (be-) lohnen; entschädigen; ～ive □ [˶rətiv] lohnend.

Renaissance [rə'neisəns] Renaissance *f*.

renascen|ce [ri'næsns] Wiedergeburt *f*; Renaissance *f*; ～t [˶nt] wieder wachsend.

rend [rend] [*irr.*] (zer)reißen.

render ['rendə] wieder-, zurückgeben; *Dienst etc.* leisten; *Ehre etc.* erweisen; *Dank* abstatten; übersetzen; ♪ vortragen; darstellen, interpretieren; *Grund* angeben; ✝ *Rechnung* überreichen; übergeben; machen (zu); *Fett* auslassen; ～ing [˶əriŋ] Wiedergabe *f*; Interpretation *f*; Übersetzung *f*, Wiedergabe *f*; △ Rohbewurf *m*.

rendition [ren'diʃən] Wiedergabe *f*.

renegade ['renigeid] Abtrünnige(r *m*) *f*.

renew [ri'njuː]erneuern; ～al [˶u(ː)əl] Erneuerung *f*.

renounce [ri'nauns] entsagen (*dat.*); verzichten auf (*acc.*); verleugnen.

renovate ['renouveit] erneuern.

renown [ri'naun] Ruhm *m*, Ansehen *n*; ～ed [˶nd] berühmt, namhaft.

rent[1] [rent] **1.** *pret. u. p.p. von* rend; **2.** Riß *m*; Spalte *f*.

rent[2] [˶] **1.** Miete *f*; Pacht *f*; **2.** (ver)mieten, (ver)pachten; ～al ['rentl] (Einkommen *n* aus) Miete *f od.* Pacht *f*.

renunciation [rinʌnsi'eiʃən] Entsagung *f*; Verzicht *m* (*of auf acc.*).

repair[1] [ri'pɛə] **1.** Ausbesserung *f*, Reparatur *f*; ～s *pl.* Instandsetzungsarbeiten *f/pl.*; ～ shop Reparaturwerkstatt *f*; *in good* ～ in gutem (baulichen) Zustand, gut erhalten; *out of* ～ baufällig; **2.** reparieren, ausbessern; erneuern; wiedergutmachen.

repair[2] [˶] ～ *to* sich begeben nach.

reparation [repə'reiʃən] Ersatz *m*; Entschädigung *f*; *make* ～s *pol.* Reparationen leisten.

repartee [repɑː'tiː] schlagfertige Antwort; Schlagfertigkeit *f*.

repast [ri'pɑːst] Mahl(zeit *f*) *n*.

repay [ri:'pei] [*irr.* (pay)] *et.* zurückzahlen; *fig.* erwidern; *et.* vergelten; *j-n* entschädigen; ～ment [˶eimənt] Rückzahlung *f*.

repeal [ri'piːl] **1.** Aufhebung *f von Gesetzen*; **2.** aufheben, widerrufen.

repeat [ri'piːt] **1.** (sich) wiederholen; aufsagen; nachliefern; aufstoßen (*Essen*); **2.** Wiederholung *f*; ♪ *oft* ～ *order* Nachbestellung *f*; ♪ Wiederholungszeichen *n*.

repel [ri'pel] zurückstoßen, zurücktreiben, zurückweisen; *fig.* abstoßen.

repent [ri'pent] bereuen; ～ance [˶təns] Reue *f*; ～ant [˶nt] reuig.

repercussion [riːpəː'kʌʃən] Rückprall *m*; *fig.* Rückwirkung *f*.

repertory ['repətəri] *thea.* Repertoire *n*; *fig.* Fundgrube *f*.

repetition [repi'tiʃən] Wiederholung *f*; Aufsagen *n*; Nachbildung *f*.

replace [ri'pleis] wieder hinstellen *od.* einsetzen; ersetzen; *an j-s* Stelle treten; ～ment [˶smənt] Ersatz *m*.

replant ['ri:'plɑːnt] umpflanzen.

replenish [ri'pleniʃ] wieder auffüllen; ～ment [˶mənt] Auffüllung*f*; Ergänzung *f*.

replete [ri'pliːt] angefüllt, voll.

replica ['replikə] Nachbildung *f*.

reply [ri'plai] **1.** antworten, erwidern (*to auf acc.*); **2.** Erwiderung *f*.

report [ri'pɔːt] **1.** Bericht *m*; Gerücht *n*; *guter* Ruf; Knall *m*; *school* ～ (Schul)Zeugnis *n*; **2.** berichten (*über acc.*); (sich) melden; anzeigen; ～er [˶tə] Berichterstatter(in).

repos|e [ri'pouz] **1.** *allg.* Ruhe *f*; **2.** *v/t.* ausruhen; (aus)ruhen lassen; ～ *trust etc. in* Vertrauen *etc.* setzen

auf (*acc.*); *v/i. a.* ~ *o.s.* (sich) ausruhen; ruhen; beruhen (*on* auf
dat.); ~itory [ri'pɔzitəri] Verwah-
rungsort *m*; Warenlager *n*; *fig.*
Fundgrube *f*.

reprehend [repri'hend] tadeln.

represent [repri'zent] darstellen;
verkörpern; *thea* aufführen; schildern; bezeichnen (*as* als); vertreten; ~ation [reprizən'teiʃən] Darstellung *f*; *thea* Aufführung *f*; Vorstellung *f*; Vertretung *f*; ~ative □
[repri'zentətiv] 1. dar-, vorstellend
(*of acc.*); vorbildlich; (stell)vertre-
tend; *parl.* repräsentativ; typisch;
2. Vertreter(in); *House of* ~s *Am.
parl.* Repräsentantenhaus *n*.

repress [ri'pres] unterdrücken;
~ion [~eʃən] Unterdrückung *f*.

reprieve [ri'pri:v] 1. (Gnaden)Frist
f; Aufschub *m*; 2. *j-m* Aufschub *od.*
eine Gnadenfrist gewähren.

reprimand ['reprima:nd] 1. Verweis *m*; 2. *j-m* e-n Verweis geben.

reprisal [ri'praizəl] Repressalie *f*.

reproach [ri'prəutʃ] 1. Vorwurf *m*;
Schande *f*; 2. vorwerfen (*s.o. with
s.th.* j-m et.); Vorwürfe machen;
~ful □ [~sful] vorwurfsvoll.

reprobate ['reproubeit] 1. verkom-
men, verderbt; 2. verkommenes
Subjekt; 3. mißbilligen; verdammen.

reproduc|e [ri:prə'dju:s] wieder-
erzeugen; (sich) fortpflanzen; wiedergeben, reproduzieren; ~tion
[~'dakʃən] Wiedererzeugung *f*;
Fortpflanzung *f*; Reproduktion *f*.

reproof [ri'pru:f] Vorwurf *m*, Tadel *m*.

reprov|al [ri'pru:vəl] Tadel *m*,
Rüge *f*; ~e [~u:v] tadeln, rügen.

reptile *zo.* ['reptail] Reptil *n*.

republic [ri'pʌblik] Republik *f*; ~an
[~kən] 1. republikanisch; 2. Repu-
blikaner(in).

repudiate [ri'pju:dieit] nicht anerkennen; ab-, zurückweisen.

repugnan|ce [ri'pʌgnəns] Abnei-
gung *f*, Widerwille *m*; ~t □ [~nt]
abstoßend; widerwärtig.

repuls|e [ri'pʌls] 1. Zurück-, Ab-
weisung *f*; 2. zurück-, abweisen;
~ive □ [~siv] abstoßend; widerwärtig.

reput|able □ ['repjutəbl] achtbar,
ehrbar, anständig; ~ation [repju(:)-
'teiʃən] (*bsd.* guter) Ruf, Ansehen
n; ~e [ri:'pju:t] 1. Ruf *m*; 2. halten
für; ~ed vermeintlich; angeblich.

request [ri'kwest] 1. Gesuch *n*,
Bitte *f*; Ersuchen *n*; † Nachfrage *f*;
by ~, *on* ~ auf Wunsch; *in (great)* ~
(sehr) gesucht, begehrt; ~ *stop* Be-
darfshaltestelle *f*; 2. um et. bitten
od. ersuchen; *j-n* bitten; *et.* erbitten.

require [ri'kwaiə] verlangen, fordern; brauchen, erfordern; ~d er-

forderlich; ~ment [~əmənt] (An-)
Forderung *f*; Erfordernis *n*.

requisit|e ['rekwizit] 1. erforder-
lich; 2. Erfordernis *n*; Bedarfs-,
Gebrauchsartikel *m*; *toilet* ~s *pl.*
Toilettenartikel *m/pl* ~ion [rekwi-
'ziʃən] 1. Anforderung *f*; ✗ Requisition *f*; 2. anfordern; ✗ requirie-
ren.

requital [ri'kwaitl] Vergeltung *f*.

requite [ri'kwait] *j-m et.* vergelten.

rescind [ri'sind] aufheben.

rescission [ri'siʒən] Aufhebung *f*.

rescue ['reskju:] 1. Rettung *f*; (ʒ̵ʒ̵
gewaltsame) Befreiung; 2. retten;
(ʒ̵ʒ̵ gewaltsam) befreien.

research [ri'sə:tʃ] Forschung *f*;
Untersuchung *f*; Nachforschung *f*;
~er [~ʃə] Forscher *m*.

resembl|ance [ri'zembləns] Ähn-
lichkeit *f* (*to* mit); ~e [ri'zembl]
gleichen, ähnlich sein (*dat.*).

resent [ri'zent] übelnehmen; ~ful
□ [~tful] übelnehmerisch; ärgerlich; ~ment [~tmənt] Ärger *m*;
Groll *m*.

reservation [rezə'veiʃən] Vorbehalt
m; *Am.* Indianerreservation *f*; Vor-
bestellung *f von Zimmern etc.*

reserve [ri'zə:v] 1. Vorrat *m*; ✝
Rücklage *f*; Reserve *f* (*a. fig.*, ✗);
Zurückhaltung *f*, Verschlossenheit
f; Vorsicht *f*; Vorbehalt *m*; *Sport:*
Ersatzmann *m*; 2. aufbewahren,
aufsparen; reservieren; zurücklegen; *Platz etc.* reservieren; ~d □
fig. zurückhaltend, reserviert.

reservoir ['rezəvwa:] Behälter *m*
für Wasser etc.; Sammel-, Staubek-
ken *n*; *fig.* Reservoir *n*.

reside [ri'zaid] wohnen; (orts)an-
sässig sein; ~ *in* innewohnen (*dat.*);
~nce ['rezidəns] Wohnen *n*; Orts-
ansässigkeit *f*; (Wohn)Sitz *m*; Re-
sidenz *f*; ~ *permit* Aufenthaltsge-
nehmigung *f*; ~nt [~nt] 1. wohnhaft; ortsansässig; 2. Ortsansässi-
ge(r *m*) *f*, Einwohner(in).

residu|al [ri'zidjual] übrigbleibend;
~e ['rezidju:] Rest *m*; Rückstand *m*;
ʒ̵ʒ̵ Reinnachlaß *m*.

resign [ri'zain] *v/t.* aufgeben; *Amt*
niederlegen; überlassen; ~ *o.s. to*
sich ergeben in (*acc.*), sich abfinden
mit; *v/i.* zurücktreten; ~ation [re-
zig'neiʃən] Rücktritt *m*; Ergebung
f; Entlassungsgesuch *n*; ~ed □ ergeben, resigniert.

resilien|ce [ri'ziliəns] Elastizität *f*;
~t [~nt] elastisch, *fig.* spannkräftig.

resin ['rezin] 1. Harz *n*; 2. harzen.

resist [ri'zist] widerstehen (*dat.*);
sich widersetzen (*dat.*); ~ance
[~təns] Widerstand *m*; *attr.* Widerstands...; *line of least* ~ Weg *m* des
geringsten Widerstands; ~ant [~nt]
widerstehend; widerstandsfähig.

resolut|e □ ['rezəlu:t] entschlossen;
~ion [rezə'lu:ʃən] (Auf)Lösung *f*;

Entschluß *m*; Entschlossenheit *f*; Resolution *f*.

resolve [ri'zɔlv] **1.** *v/t.* auflösen; *fig.* lösen; *Zweifel etc.* beheben; entscheiden; *v/i. a.* ~ *o.s.* sich auflösen; beschließen; ~ (*up*)*on* sich entschließen zu; **2.** Entschluß *m*; *Am.* Beschluß *m*; ~d □ entschlossen.

resonan|ce ['reznəns] Resonanz *f*; ~t □ [~nt] nach-, widerhallend.

resort [ri'zɔːt] **1.** Zuflucht *f*; Besuch *m*; Aufenthalt(sort) *m*; Erholungsort *m*; *health* ~ Kurort *m*; *seaside* ~ Seebad *n*; *summer* ~ Sommerfrische *f*; **2.** ~ *to* oft besuchen; seine Zuflucht nehmen zu. [sen).\

resound [ri'zaund] widerhallen(las-\

resource [ri'sɔːs] *natürlicher* Reichtum; Hilfsquelle *f*, -mittel *n*; Zuflucht *f*; Findigkeit *f*; Zeitvertreib *m*, Entspannung *f*; ~**ful** □ [~sful] findig.

respect [ris'pekt] **1.** Rücksicht *f* (*to*, *of* auf *acc.*); Beziehung *f*; Achtung *f*; ~*s pl.* Empfehlungen *f/pl.*; **2.** *v/t.* (hoch)achten; Rücksicht nehmen auf (*acc.*); betreffen; ~**able** □ [~təbl] achtbar; ansehnlich; anständig; *bsd.* ↑ solid; ~**ful** □ [~tful] ehrerbietig; *yours* ~*ly* hochachtungsvoll; ~**ing** [~tiŋ] hinsichtlich (*gen.*); ~**ive** □ [~iv] jeweilig; we went to our ~ places wir gingen jeder an seinen Platz; ~**ively** [~vli] beziehungsweise; je.

respirat|ion [respə'reiʃən] Atmen *n*; Atemzug *m*; ~**or** ['respəreitə] Atemfilter *m*; ✠ Atemgerät *n*; Gasmaske *f*.

respire [ris'paiə] atmen; aufatmen.

respite ['respait] Frist *f*; Stundung *f*.

resplendent □ [ris'plendənt] glänzend.

respond [ris'pɔnd] antworten, erwidern; ~ *to* reagieren auf (*acc.*).

response [ris'pɔns] Antwort *f*, Erwiderung *f*; *fig.* Reaktion *f*.

responsi|bility [rispɔnsə'biliti] Verantwortlichkeit *f*; Verantwortung *f*; ↑ Zahlungsfähigkeit *f*; ~**ble** [ris'pɔnsəbl] verantwortlich; verantwortungsvoll; ↑ zahlungsfähig.

rest [rest] **1.** Rest *m*; Ruhe *f*; Rast *f*; Schlaf *m*; *fig.* Tod *m*; Stütze *f*; Pause *f*; **2.** *v/i.* ruhen, rasten; schlafen; (sich) lehnen, sich stützen (*on* auf *acc.*); ~ (*up*)*on fig.* beruhen auf (*dat.*); *in e-m Zustand* bleiben; *v/t.* (aus)ruhen lassen; stützen.

restaurant ['restərɔːŋ, ~rɔnt] Gaststätte *f*.

rest-cure ✠ ['restkjuə] Liegekur *f*.

restful ['restful] ruhig, geruhsam.

resting-place ['restiŋpleis] Ruheplatz *m*, -stätte *f*.

restitution [resti'tjuːʃən] Wiederherstellung *f*; Rückerstattung *f*.

restive □ ['restiv] widerspenstig.

restless ['restlis] ruhelos; rastlos; unruhig; ~**ness** [~snis] Ruhelosigkeit *f*; Rastlosigkeit *f*; Unruhe *f*.

restorat|ion [restə'reiʃən] Wiederherstellung *f*; Wiedereinsetzung *f*; Rekonstruktion *f*, Nachbildung *f*; ~**ive** [ris'tɔrətiv] **1.** stärkend; **2.** Stärkungsmittel *n*.

restore [ris'tɔː] wiederherstellen; wiedereinsetzen (*to* in *acc.*); wiedergeben; ~ *to health* wieder gesund machen.

restrain [ris'trein] zurückhalten (*from* von); in Schranken halten; unterdrücken; einsperren; ~**t** [~nt] Zurückhaltung *f*; Beschränkung *f*, Zwang *m*; Zwangshaft *f*.

restrict [ris'trikt] be-, einschränken; ~**ion** [~kʃən] Be-, Einschränkung *f*; Vorbehalt *m*.

result [ri'zʌlt] **1.** Ergebnis *n*, Folge *f*, Resultat *n*; **2.** folgen, sich ergeben (*from* aus); ~ *in* hinauslaufen auf (*acc.*), zur Folge haben.

resum|e [ri'zjuːm] wiedernehmen, -erlangen; wiederaufnehmen; zs.-fassen; ~**ption** [ri'zʌmpʃən] Zurücknahme *f*; Wiederaufnahme *f*.

resurgent [ri'sə:dʒənt] sich wiedererhebend, wieder aufkommend.

resurrection [rezə'rekʃən] Wiederaufleben *n*; ♀ *eccl.* (Wieder)Auferstehung *f*.

resuscitate [ri'sʌsiteit] wiedererwecken, wiederbeleben.

retail 1. ['riːteil] Einzelhandel *m*; *by* ~ im Einzelverkauf; **2.** [~] Einzelhandels..., Detail...; **3.** [ri:'teil] im kleinen verkaufen; ~**er** [~lə] Einzelhändler(in).

retain [ri'tein] behalten (*a. fig.*); zurück-, festhalten; beibehalten; *Anwalt* nehmen.

retaliat|e [ri'tælieit] *v/t. Unrecht* vergelten, *v/i.* sich rächen; ~**ion** [ritæli'eiʃən] Vergeltung *f*.

retard [ri'tɑːd] verzögern; aufhalten; verspäten.

retention [ri'tenʃən] Zurück-, Behalten *n*; Beibehaltung *f*.

reticent ['retisənt] verschwiegen; schweigsam; zurückhaltend.

retinue ['retinju] Gefolge *n*.

retir|e [ri'taiə] *v/t.* zurückziehen; pensionieren; *v/i.* sich zurückziehen; zurück-, abtreten; in den Ruhestand treten; ~**ed** □ zurückgezogen; im Ruhestand (lebend); entlegen; ~ *pay* Pension *f*; ~**ement** [~əmənt] Sichzurückziehen *n*; Aus-, Rücktritt *m*; Ruhestand *m*; Zurückgezogenheit *f*; ~**ing** [~əriŋ] zurückhaltend; schüchtern; ~ *pension* Ruhegehalt *n*.

retort [ri'tɔːt] **1.** Erwiderung *f*; ♂ Retorte *f*; **2.** erwidern.

retouch ['riː'tʌtʃ] *et.* überarbeiten; *phot.* retuschieren.

retrace [ri'treis] zurückverfolgen; ~ one's steps zurückgehen.

retract [ri'trækt] (sich) zurückziehen; ⊕ einziehen; widerrufen.

retread ['ri:tred] 1. *Reifen* runderneuern; 2. runderneuerter Reifen.

retreat [ri'tri:t] 1. Rückzug m; Zurückgezogenheit f; Zuflucht(sort m) f; ✕ Zapfenstreich m; beat a ~ fig. es aufgeben; 2. sich zurückziehen; fig. zurücktreten.

retrench [ri'trentʃ] (sich) einschränken; kürzen; *Wort etc.* streichen; ✕ verschanzen.

retribution [retri'bju:ʃən] Vergeltung f.

retrieve [ri'tri:v] wiederbekommen; wiederherstellen; wiedergutmachen; hunt. apportieren.

retro|... ['retrou] (zu)rück...; **~active** [retrou'æktiv] rückwirkend; **~grade** ['retrougreid] 1. rückläufig; 2. zurückgehen; **~gression** [retrou'greʃən] Rück-, Niedergang m; **~spect** ['retrouspekt] Rückblick m; **~spective** [retrou'spektiv] zurückblickend; rückwirkend.

retry ⅍ ['ri:'trai] *Prozeß* wiederaufnehmen.

return [ri'tə:n] 1. Rückkehr f; Wiederkehr f; parl. Wiederwahl f; oft ~s pl. ✛ Gewinn m, Ertrag m; Umsatz m; ⅍ Rückfall m; Rückgabe f, Rückzahlung f; Vergeltung f; Erwiderung f; Gegenleistung f; Dank m; amtlicher Bericht; Wahlergebnis n; Steuererklärung f; ✛ Rückfahrkarte f; attr Rück- .; many happy ~s of the day herzliche Glückwünsche zum Geburtstag; in ~ dafür; als Ersatz (for für); by ~ (of post) postwendend; ~ ticket Rückfahrkarte f; 2. v/i. zurückkehren; wiederkehren; v/t zurückgeben; zurücktun; zurückzahlen; zurücksenden; *Dank* abstatten; erwidern; berichten, angeben; parl. wählen; *Gewinn* abwerfen.

reunification pol. ['ri:ju:nifi'keiʃən] Wiedervereinigung f.

reunion ['ri:'ju:njən] Wiedervereinigung f; Treffen n, Zs.-kunft f.

reval|**orization** ✛ [ri:vælərai'zeiʃən] Aufwertung f; **~uation** [ˌ:lju-'eiʃən] Neubewertung f.

revamp ⊕ ['ri:'væmp] vorschuhen; Am. F aufmöbeln; erneuern.

reveal [ri'vi:l] enthüllen; offenbaren; ~ing [ˌiŋ] aufschlußreich.

revel ['revl] 1. Lustbarkeit f; Gelage n; 2. ausgelassen sein; schwelgen; zechen.

revelation [revi'leiʃən] Enthüllung f; Offenbarung f.

revel|(l)**er** ['revlə] Feiernde(r m) f; Zecher m; **~ry** [ˌlri] Gelage n; Lustbarkeit f, Rummel m; Orgie f.

revenge [ri'vendʒ] 1. Rache f; Sport: Revanche f; 2. rächen; **~ful** ☐ [ˌdʒful] rachsüchtig; **~r** [ˌdʒə] Rächer(in).

revenue ['revinju:] Einkommen n; ~s pl. Einkünfte pl.; ~ board, ~ office Finanzamt n.

reverberate [ri'və:bəreit] zurückwerfen; zurückstrahlen; widerhallen.

revere [ri'viə] (ver)ehren; **~nce** ['revərəns] 1. Verehrung f; Ehrfurcht f; 2. (ver)ehren; **~nd** [ˌnd] 1. ehrwürdig; 2. Geistliche(r) m.

reverent(**ial**) ☐ ['revərənt, revə'renʃəl] ehrerbietig, ehrfurchtsvoll.

reverie ['revəri] Träumerei f.

revers|**al** [ri'və:səl] Umkehrung f; Umschwung m; ⅍ Umstoßung f; ⊕ Umsteuerung f; ~e [ˌə:s] 1. Gegenteil n; Kehrseite f; Rückschlag m; 2. umgekehrt; Rück(wärts)...; ~ (gear) mot. Rückwärtsgang m; ~ side linke Stoff-Seite; 3. umkehren, umdrehen; *Urteil* umstoßen; ⊕ umsteuern; ~ion [ˌə:ʃən] Umkehrung f; Rückkehr f; ⅍ Heimfall m; biol. Rückartung f.

revert [ri'və:t] um-, zurückkehren; biol. zurückarten; *Blick* wenden.

review [ri'vju:] 1. Nachprüfung f; ⅍ Revision f; ✕, ⚓ Parade f; Rückblick m; Überblick m; Rezension f; Zeitschrift f; pass s.th. in ~ et. Revue passieren lassen; 2. (über-, nach)prüfen; zurückblicken auf (acc.); überblicken; ✕, ⚓ besichtigen; rezensieren; **~er** [ˌu(:)ə] Rezensent m. [fen.]

revile [ri'vail] schmähen, beschimpfen.

revis|**e** [ri'vaiz] überarbeiten, durchsehen, revidieren; **~ion** [ri'viʒən] Revision f; Überarbeitung f.

reviv|**al** [ri'vaivl] Wiederbelebung f; Wiederaufleben n, Wiederaufblühen n; Erneuerung f; fig. Erweckung f; ~e [ˌaiv] wiederbeleben; wieder aufleben (lassen); erneuern; wieder aufblühen.

revocation [revə'keiʃən] Widerruf m; Aufhebung f.

revoke [ri'vouk] v/t. widerrufen; v/i. *Karten* nicht bedienen.

revolt [ri'voult] 1. Revolte f, Empörung f; Aufruhr m; 2. v/i. sich empören; abfallen; v/t. fig. abstoßen.

revolution [revə'lu:ʃən] Umwälzung f, Umdrehung f; pol. Revolution f; **~ary** [ˌʃnəri] 1. revolutionär; 2. a. **~ist** [ˌʃnist] Revolutionär(in); **~ize** [ˌʃnaiz] aufwiegeln; umgestalten.

revolv|**e** [ri'vɔlv] v/i. sich drehen (about, round um); v/t. umdrehen; fig. erwägen; **~ing** [ˌviŋ] sich drehend; Dreh...

revue thea. [ri'vju:] Revue f; Kabarett n.

revulsion [ri'vʌlʃən] fig. Umschwung m; 💢 Ableitung f.

reward [ri'wɔːd] **1.** Belohnung *f*; Vergeltung *f*; **2.** belohnen; vergelten.

rewrite ['riː'rait] [*irr.* (write)] neu (*od.* um)schreiben.

rhapsody ['ræpsədi] Rhapsodie *f*; *fig.* Schwärmerei *f*; Wortschwall *m*.

rhetoric ['retərik] Rhetorik *f*.

rheumatism ✞ ['ruːmətizəm] Rheumatismus *m*.

rhubarb ♦ ['ruːbaːb] Rhabarber *m*.

rhyme [raim] **1.** Reim *m* (*to* auf *acc.*); Vers *m*; *without ~ or reason* ohne Sinn u. Verstand; **2.** (sich) reimen.

rhythm ['riðəm] Rhythmus *m*; **~ic(al** □) ['riðmik(əl)] rhythmisch.

Rialto *Am.* [ri'æltou] Theaterviertel *n e-r* Stadt, *bsd. in New York*.

rib [rib] **1.** Rippe *f*; **2.** rippen; *sl.* aufziehen, necken.

ribald ['ribəld] lästerlich; unflätig; **~ry** [~dri] Zoten *f/pl.*; derbe Späße *m/pl.*

ribbon ['ribən] Band *n*; Streifen *m*; **~s** *pl.* Fetzen *m/pl.*; Zügel *m/pl.*; *~ building*, *~ development* Reihenbau *m*.

rice [rais] Reis *m*.

rich □ [ritʃ] reich (*in* an *dat.*); reichlich; prächtig; kostbar; ergiebig, fruchtbar; voll (*Ton*); schwer (*Speise, Wein, Duft*); satt (*Farbe*); **~es** ['ritʃiz] *pl.* Reichtum *m*, Reichtümer *m/pl.*; **~ness** [~ʃnis] Reichtum *m*; Fülle *f*.

rick ✗ [rik] (Heu)Schober *m*.

ricket|s ['rikits] *sg. od. pl.* Rachitis *f*; **~y** [~ti] rachitisch; wack(e)lig (*Möbel*).

rid [rid] [*irr.*] befreien, frei machen (*of* von); *get ~ of* loswerden.

ridden ['ridn] **1.** *p.p. von* ride 2; **2.** *in Zssgn*: bedrückt *od.* geplagt von ...

riddle ['ridl] **1.** Rätsel *n*; grobes Sieb; **2.** sieben; durchlöchern.

ride [raid] **1.** Ritt *m*; Fahrt *f*; Reitweg *m*; **2.** [*irr.*] *v/i.* reiten; rittlings sitzen; fahren; treiben; schweben; liegen; *v/t.* Pferd *etc.* reiten; *Land* durchreiten, **~r** ['raidə] Reiter(in) *f*; Fahrende(r *m*) *f*.

ridge [ridʒ] **1.** (Gebirgs)Kamm *m*, Grat *m*; ⚓ First *m*; ✗ Rain *m*; **2.** (sich) furchen.

ridicul|e ['ridikjuːl] **1.** Hohn *m*, Spott *m*; **2.** lächerlich machen; **~ous** □ [ri'dikjuləs] lächerlich.

riding ['raidiŋ] Reiten *n*; *attr.* Reit... [*~ with* voll von.]

rife □ [raif] häufig; vorherrschend;}

riff-raff ['rifræf] Gesindel *n*.

rifle ['raifl] **1.** Gewehr *n*; **2.** (aus)plündern; **~man** ✗ Schütze *m*.

rift [rift] Riß *m*, Sprung *m*; Spalte *f*.

rig¹ [rig] **1.** Markt *etc.* manipulieren; **2.** Schwindelmanöver *n*.

rig² [~] **1.** ⚓ Takelung *f*; F Aufma-

chung *f*; **2.** auftakeln; *~ s.o. out* j-n versorgen *od.* ausrüsten; j-n herausputzen *od.* herrichten; **~ging** ⚓ ['rigiŋ] Takelage *f*.

right [rait] **1.** □ recht; richtig; recht (*Ggs. left*); *be ~* recht haben; *all ~!* alles in Ordnung!; ganz recht!; *put od. set ~* in Ordnung bringen; berichtigen; **2.** *adv.* recht, richtig; gerade; direkt; ganz (und gar); *~ away* sogleich; *~ on* geradeaus; **3.** Recht *n*; Rechte *f*, rechte Seite *od.* Hand; *the ~s and wrongs* der wahre Sachverhalt; *by ~ of* auf Grund (*gen.*); *on od. to the ~* rechts; *~ of way* Wegerecht *n*; Vorfahrt(srecht *n*) *f*; **4.** *j-m* Recht verschaffen; *et.* in Ordnung bringen; ⚓ (sich) aufrichten; **~down** ['rait'daun] regelrecht, ausgemacht; wirklich; **~eous** □ ['raitʃəs] rechtschaffen; **~ful** □ ['raitful] recht(mäßig); gerecht.

rigid □ ['ridʒid] starr; *fig. a.* streng, hart; **~ity** [ri'dʒiditi] Starrheit *f*; Strenge *f*, Härte *f*.

rigmarole ['rigməroul] Geschwätz *n*.

rigor ✞ ['raigɔː] Fieberfrost *m*.

rigo(u)r ['rigə] Strenge *f*, Härte *f*.

rigorous □ ['rigərəs] streng, rigoros.

rim [rim] **1.** Felge *f*; Radkranz *m*; Rand *m*; **2.** rändern; einfassen.

rime [raim] Reim *m*; Rauhreif *m*.

rind [raind] Rinde *f*, Schale *f*; *Speck*-Schwarte *f*.

ring¹ [riŋ] **1.** Klang *m*; Geläut(e) *n*; Klingeln *n*; Rufzeichen *n*; Anruf *m*; *give s.o. a ~* j-n anrufen; **2.** [*irr.*] läuten; klingen (lassen); erschallen (*with* von); *~ again* widerhallen; *~ off teleph.* das Gespräch beenden; *~ the bell* klingeln; *~ s.o. up* j-n *od.* bei j-m anrufen.

ring² [~] **1.** Ring *m*; Kreis *m*; **2.** beringen; *mst ~ in*, *~ round*, *~ about* umringen; **~leader** ['riŋliːdə] Rädelsführer *m*; **~let** [~lit] (Ringel)Locke *f*.

rink [riŋk] Eisbahn *f*; Rollschuhbahn *f*.

rinse [rins] *oft ~ out* (aus)spülen.

riot ['raiət] **1.** Tumult *m*; Aufruhr *m*; Orgie *f* (*a. fig.*); *run ~* durchgehen; (sich aus)toben; **2.** Krawall machen, im Aufruhr sein; toben; schwelgen; **~er** [~tə] Aufrührer(in); Randalierer *m*; **~ous** □ [~təs] aufrührerisch; lärmend; liederlich (*Leben*).

rip [rip] **1.** Riß *m*; **2.** (auf)trennen; (auf-, zer)reißen; (dahin)sausen.

ripe □ [raip] reif; **~n** ['raipən] reifen; **~ness** ['raipnis] Reife *f*.

ripple ['ripl] **1.** kleine Welle; Kräuselung *f*; Geriesel *n*; **2.** (sich) kräuseln; rieseln.

rise [raiz] **1.** (An-, Auf)Steigen *n*;

Anschwellen *n*; (Preis-, Gehalts-) Erhöhung *f*; *fig.* Aufstieg *m*; Steigung *f*; Anhöhe *f*; Ursprung *m*; take (one's) ~ entstehen; entspringen; **2.** [*irr.*] sich erheben, aufstehen; die Sitzung schließen; steigen; aufsteigen (*a. fig.*); auferstehen; aufgehen (*Sonne, Samen*); anschwellen; sich empören; entspringen (*Fluß*); ~ to sich e-r Lage gewachsen zeigen; **~n** ['rizn] *p.p. von* rise 2; **~r** ['raizə]: early ~ Frühaufsteher(in).

rising ['raiziŋ] **1.** (Auf)Steigen *n*; Steigung *f*; *ast.* Aufgang *m*; Aufstand *m*; **2.** heranwachsend (*Generation*).

risk [risk] **1.** Gefahr *f*, Wagnis *n*; † Risiko *n*; run the ~ Gefahr laufen; **2.** wagen, riskieren; **~y** □ ['riski] gefährlich, gewagt.

rit|e [rait] Ritus *m*, Brauch *m*; **~ual** ['ritjuəl] **1.** rituell; **2.** Ritual *n*.

rival ['raivəl] **1.** Nebenbuhler(in); Rivale *m*; **2.** rivalisierend; † Konkurrenz...; **3.** wetteifern (mit); **~ry** [~lri] Rivalität *f*; Wetteifer *m*.

rive [raiv] [*irr.*] (sich) spalten; **~n** ['rivən] *p.p. von* rive.

river ['rivə] Fluß *m*; Strom *m* (*a. fig.*); **~side 1.** Flußufer *n*; **2.** am Wasser (gelegen).

rivet ['rivit] **1.** ⊕ Niet(e *f*) *m*; **2.** (ver)nieten; *fig.* heften (to an *acc.*; on, upon auf *acc.*); fesseln.

rivulet ['rivjulit] Bach *m*, Flüßchen *n*.

road [roud] Straße *f* (*a. fig.*), Weg *m*; *Am.* = railroad; mst **~s** pl. ⊕ Reede *f*; **~stead** ⊕ ['roudsted] Reede *f*; **~ster** [~tə] Roadster *m*, offener Sportwagen; **~way** Fahrbahn *f*.

roam [roum] *v/i.* umherstreifen, wandern; *v/t.* durchstreifen.

roar [rɔː] **1.** brüllen; brausen, tosen, donnern; **2.** Gebrüll *n*; Brausen *n*; Krachen *n*, Getöse *n*; brüllendes Gelächter.

roast [roust] **1.** rösten, braten; **2.** geröstet; gebraten; ~ meat Braten *m*.

rob [rɔb] (be)rauben; **~ber** ['rɔbə] Räuber *m*; **~bery** [~əri] Raub (-überfall) *m*; Räuberei *f*.

robe [roub] (Amts)Robe *f*, Talar *m*; (Staats)Kleid *n*; *Am.* Morgenrock *m*.

robin *orn.* ['rɔbin] Rotkehlchen *n*.

robust □ [rə'bʌst] robust, kräftig.

rock [rɔk] **1.** Felsen *m*; Klippe *f*; Gestein *n*; Zuckerstange *f*; ~ crystal Bergkristall *m*; **2.** schaukeln; (ein)wiegen.

rocker ['rɔkə] Kufe *f*; *Am.* Schaukelstuhl *m*; Rocker *m*, Halbstarke(r) *m*.

rocket ['rɔkit] Rakete *f*; *attr.* Ra-

keten...; **~-powered** mit Raketenantrieb; **~ry** [~tri] Raketentechnik*f*.

rocking-chair ['rɔkiŋtʃeə] Schaukelstuhl *m*.

rocky ['rɔki] felsig; Felsen...

rod [rɔd] Rute *f*; Stab *m*; ⊕ Stange *f*; Meßrute *f* (5½ *yards*); *Am. sl.* Pistole *f*.

rode [roud] *pret. von* ride 2.

rodent ['roudənt] Nagetier *n*.

rodeo *Am.* [rou'deiou] Rodeo *m*; Zusammentreiben *n*; Cowboyturnier *n*.

roe¹ [rou] Reh *n*.

roe² *ichth.* [~] *a.* hard ~ Rogen *m*; soft ~ Milch *f*.

rogu|e [roug] Schurke *m*; Schelm *m*; **~ish** ['rougiʃ] schurkisch; schelmisch.

roister ['rɔistə] krakeelen.

role, rôle *thea.* [roul] Rolle *f* (*a.fig.*).

roll [roul] **1.** Rolle *f*; ⊕ Walze *f*; Brötchen *n*, Semmel *f*; Verzeichnis *n*; Urkunde *f*; (Donner)Rollen *n*; (Trommel)Wirbel *m*; ⊕ Schlingern *n*; **2.** *v/t.* rollen; wälzen; walzen; *Zigarette* drehen; ~ up zs.-rollen; einwickeln; *v/i.* rollen; sich wälzen; wirbeln (*Trommel*); ⊕ schlingern; **~-call** ['roulkɔːl] Appell *m*; **~er** ['roulə] Rolle *f*, Walze *f*; Sturzwelle *f*; ~ coaster *Am.* Achterbahn *f*; ~ skate Rollschuh *m*.

rollicking ['rɔlikiŋ] übermütig.

rolling ['rouliŋ] rollend; Roll..., Walz...; ~ mill ⊕ Walzwerk *n*.

Roman ['roumən] **1.** römisch; **2.** Römer(in); mst ℒ *typ.* Antiqua *f*.

romance¹ [rə'mæns] **1.** (Ritter-, Vers)Roman *m*; Abenteuer-, Liebesroman *m*; Romanze *f* (*a. fig.*); *fig.* Märchen *n*; Romantik *f*; **2.** *fig.* aufschneiden.

Romance² *ling.* [~]: ~ languages romanische Sprachen *f/pl.*

romancer [rə'mænsə] Romanschreiber(in); Aufschneider(in).

Romanesque [roumə'nesk] **1.** romanisch; **2.** romanischer Baustil.

romantic [rə'mæntik] (~ally) romantisch; ~ism [~isizəm] Romantik *f*; ~ist [~ist] Romantiker(in).

romp [rɔmp] **1.** Range *f*, Wildfang *m*; Balgerei *f*; **2.** sich balgen, toben; **~er(s)** ['rɔmpə(z)] Spielanzug *m*.

rood [ruːd] Kruzifix *n*; Viertelmorgen *m* (10,117 *Ar*).

roof [ruːf] **1.** Dach *n*; ~ of the mouth Gaumen *m*; **2.** *a.* ~ over überdachen; **~ing** ['ruːfiŋ] **1.** Bedachung*f*; **2.** Dach...; ~ felt Dachpappe *f*.

rook [ruk] **1.** *Schach:* Turm *m*; *fig.* Gauner *m*; *orn.* Saatkrähe *f*; **2.** betrügen.

room [rum] **1.** Raum *m*; Platz *m*; Zimmer *n*; Möglichkeit *f*; **~s** pl. Wohnung *f*; in my ~ an meiner Stelle; **2.** *Am.* wohnen; **~er** ['rumə] *bsd. Am.* Untermieter(in); **~ing-house** ['ruminhaus] *bsd. Am.* Miets-, Logierhaus *n*; **~mate** Stubenkamerad *m*; **~y** □ ['rumi] geräumig.

roost [ru:st] 1. Schlafplatz *m e-s Vogels*; Hühnerstange *f*; Hühnerstall *m*; 2. sich (zum Schlaf) niederhocken; *fig.* übernachten; **~er** ['ru:stə] Haushahn *m*.

root [ru:t] 1. Wurzel *f*; 2. (ein)wurzeln; (auf)wühlen; **~** for *Am. sl.* Stimmung machen für; **~** out ausrotten; **~** out *od.* up ausgraben; **~ed** ['ru:tid] eingewurzelt; **~er** *Am. sl.* ['ru:tə] Fanatiker *m für et.*

rope [roup] 1. Tau *n*, Seil *n*; Strick *m*; Schnur *f Perlen etc.*; *be at the end of one's* **~** *f* mit s-m Latein zu Ende sein; *know the* **~** *s* sich auskennen; 2. mit e-m Seil befestigen *od.* (*mst* **~** *in od.* off *od.* out) absperren; anseilen; **~way** ['roupwei] Seilbahn *f*.

ropy ['roupi] klebrig, zähflüssig.

rosary *eccl.* ['rouzəri] Rosenkranz *m*.

rose¹ [rouz] ♣ Rose *f*; (Gießkannen)Brause *f*; Rosenrot *n*.

rose² [~] *pret von* rise 2.

rosebud ['rouzbʌd] Rosenknospe *f*; *Am.* hübsches Mädchen; Debütantin *f*.

rosin ['rozin] (Geigen)Harz *n*.

rostrum ['rostrəm] Rednertribüne *f*.

rosy ['rouzi] rosig.

rot [rot] 1. Fäulnis *f*; *sl.* Quatsch *m*; 2. *v/t.* faulen lassen; Quatsch machen mit *j-m*; *v/i.* verfaulen, vermodern.

rota|ry ['routəri] drehend; Rotations..; **~te** [rou'teit] (sich) drehen, (ab)wechseln; **~tion** [~eiʃən] Umdrehung *f*; Kreislauf *m*; Abwechs(e)lung *f*; **~tory** ['routətəri] *s. rotary*; abwechselnd.

rote [rout] *by* auswendig.

rotten ['rotn] verfault, faul(ig); mod(e)rig, morsch (*alle a. fig.*); *sl.* saumäßig, dreckig.

rotund [rou'tʌnd] rund; voll (*Stimme*); hochtrabend.

rouge [ru:ʒ] 1. Rouge *n*; Silberputzmittel *n*; 2. Rouge auflegen (auf *acc.*).

rough [rʌf] 1. □ rauh; roh; grob; *fig.* ungehobelt; ungefähr (*Schätzung*); **~** and ready grob (gearbeitet); Not..., Behelfs.. ; **~** copy roher Entwurf; 2. Rauhe *n*, Grobe *n*; Lümmel *m*; 3. (an-, auf)rauhen; **~** it sich mühsam durchschlagen; **~cast** ['rʌfka:st] 1. ⊕ Rohputz *m*; 2. unfertig; 3. ⊕ roh verputzen; roh entwerfen; **~en** ['rʌfən] rauh machen *od.* werden; **~neck** *Am. sl.* Rabauke *m*; **~ness** [~nis] Rauheit *f*; Roheit *f*; Grobheit *f*; **~shod**: *ride* **~** *over* rücksichtslos behandeln.

round [raund] 1. □ rund; voll (*Stimme etc.*); flott (*Gangart*); abgerundet (*Stil*); unverblümt; **~**game Gesellschaftsspiel *n*; **~** trip Rundreise *f*; 2. *adv* rund~, ringsum(her); *a.* **~** about in der Runde; *all* **~** ringsum; *fig.* ohne Unterschied; *all the year* **~** das ganze Jahr hindurch; 3. *prp.* um herum; 4. Rund *n*, Kreis *m*; Runde *f*; Kreislauf *m*; (Leiter)Sprosse *f*; Rundgesang *m*; *Lach- etc.*Salve *f*; *100* **~**s ✗ 100 Schuß; 5. *v/t.* runden; herumgehen *od.* herumfahren um; **~** off abrunden; **~** up einkreisen; *v/i.* sich runden; sich umdrehen; **~about** ['raundəbaut] 1. umschweifig; 2. Umweg *m*; Karussell *n*; Kreisverkehr *m*; **~ish** [~diʃ] rundlich; **~up** Einkreisung *f*; Razzia *f*.

rous|e [rauz] *v/t.* wecken; ermuntern; aufjagen; (auf)reizen; **~** *o.s.* sich aufraffen; *v/i.* aufwachen; **~ing** ['rauziŋ] brausend (*Beifall etc.*).

roustabout 4*m* [ˈraustəbaut] ungelernter (*mst* Hafen)Arbeiter.

rout [raut] 1. Rotte *f*; wilde Flucht; *a. put to* **~** vernichtend schlagen; 2. aufwühlen.

route [ru:t, ✗ *a.* raut] Weg *m*; ✗ Marschroute *f*.

routine [ru:'ti:n] 1. Routine *f*; 2. üblich; Routine...

rove [rouv] umherstreifen, umherwandern.

row¹ [rou] 1. Reihe *f*; Ruderfahrt *f*; 2. rudern.

row² ♣[rau] 1. Spektakel *m*; Krach *m*; Schlägerei *f*; 2. ausschimpfen.

row-boat ['roubout] Ruderboot *n*.

rower ['rouə] Ruder|er *m*, -in *f*.

royal ['roiəl] königlich; prächtig; **~ty** [~lti] Königtum *n*, -reich *n*; Königswürde *f*; königliche Persönlichkeit; Lantieme *f*.

rub [rʌb] 1. Reiben *n*; Schwierigkeit *f*, *fig.* Stichelei *f*, Unannehmlichkeit *f*; 2. *v/t.* reiben; (ab)wischen; (wund)scheuern; schleifen; **~** down abreiben; **~** in einreiben; *fig.* betonen; **~** off abreiben; **~** out auslöschen; **~** up auffrischen; verreiben; *v/i.* sich reiben; *fig.* **~** along *od.* on *od.* through sich durchschlagen.

rubber ['rʌbə] 1. Gummi *n, m*; Radiergummi *m*; Masseur *m*; Wischtuch *n*; *Whist* Robber *m*; **~**s *pl. Am.* Gummischuhe *m/pl.*; 2. Gummi...; **~** check *Am. sl.* geplatzter Scheck; **~neck** *Am. sl.* 1. Gaffer(in); 2. sich den Hals verrenken; mithören; **~** stamp Gummistempel *m*; *Am.* F *fig.* Nachbeter *m*; **~stamp** automatisch gutheißen.

rubbish ['rʌbiʃ] Schutt *m*; Abfall *m*; Kehricht *m*; *fig.* Schund *m*; Unsinn *m*.

rubble ['rʌbl] Schutt *m*.

rube *Am.sl.* [ru:b] Bauernlümmel *m.*

ruby ['ru:bi] Rubin(rot *n*) *m.*

rucksack ['ruksæk] Rucksack *m.*

rudder ['rʌdə] ⏚ (Steuer)Ruder *n*; ✈ Seitenruder *n.*

rudd|iness ['rʌdinis] Röte *f*; ~**y** ['rʌdi] rot; rotbäckig.

rude □ [ru:d] unhöflich; unanständig; heftig, unsanft; ungebildet; einfach, kunstlos; robust; roh.

rudiment *biol.* ['ru:dimənt] Ansatz *m*; ~**s** *pl.* Anfangsgründe *m/pl.*

rueful □ ['ru:ful] reuig; traurig.

ruff [rʌf] Halskrause *f.*

ruffian ['rʌfjən] Rohling *m*; Raufbold *m*; Schurke *m.*

ruffle ['rʌfl] 1. Krause *f*, Rüsche *f*; Kräuseln *n*; *fig.* Unruhe *f*; 2. kräuseln; zerdrücken; zerknüllen; *fig.* aus der Ruhe bringen; stören.

rug [rʌg] (Reise-, Woll)Decke *f*; Vorleger *m*, Brücke *f*; ~**ged** □ ['rʌgid] rauh (*a. fig.*); uneben; gefurcht.

ruin [ruin] 1. Ruin *m*, Zs.-bruch *m*; Untergang *m*; *mst* ~**s** *pl.* Ruine(n *pl.*) *f*, Trümmer *pl.*; 2. ruinieren; zugrunde richten; zerstören; verderben; ~**ous** □ ['ruinəs] ruinenhaft, verfallen; verderblich, ruinös.

rul|e [ru:l] 1. Regel *f*; Vorschrift *f*; Ordnung *f*; Satzung *f*; Herrschaft *f*; Lineal *n*; *as a* ~ in der Regel; ~**(s)** *of the road* Straßenverkehrsordnung *f*; 2. *v/t.* regeln; leiten; beherrschen; verfügen; liniieren; ~ *out* ausschließen; *v/i.* herrschen; ~**er** ['ru:lə] Herrscher(in); Lineal *n.*

rum [rʌm] Rum *m*; *Am.* Alkohol *m.*

Rumanian [ru(:)'meinjən] 1. rumänisch; 2. Rumän|e *m*, -in *f*; Rumänisch *n.*

rumble ['rʌmbl] 1. Rumpeln *n*; *a.* ~**-seat** *Am. mot.* Notsitz *m*; *Am.* F Fehde *f* zwischen Gangsterbanden; 2. rumpeln, rasseln; grollen (*Donner*).

rumina|nt ['ru:minənt] 1. wiederkäuend; 2. Wiederkäuer *m*; ~**te** [~neit] wiederkäuen; *fig.* nachsinnen.

rummage ['rʌmidʒ] 1. Durchsuchung *f*; Ramsch *m*, Restwaren *f/pl.*; 2. *v/t.* durchsuchen, durchstöbern, durchwühlen; *v/i.* wühlen.

rumo(u)r ['ru:mə] 1. Gerücht *n*; 2. (als Gerücht) verbreiten; *it is* ~*ed* es geht das Gerücht. [*m.*\]

rump *anat.* [rʌmp] Steiß *m*; Rumpf|

rumple ['rʌmpl] zerknittern; zerren, (zer)zausen.

rum-runner *Am.* ['rʌmrʌnə] Alkoholschmuggler *m.*

run [rʌn] 1. (*irr.*) *v/i. allg.* laufen; rennen (*Mensch, Tier*); eilen; zerlaufen (*Farbe etc.*); umgehen (*Gerücht etc.*); lauten (*Text*); gehen (*Melodie*); ✈ sich stellen (*Preis*); ~ *across s.o.* j-m in die Arme laufen;

~ *away* davonlaufen; ~ *down* ablaufen (*Uhr etc.*); *fig.* herunterkommen; ~ *dry* aus-, vertrocknen; ~ *for parl.* kandidieren für; ~ *into* geraten in (*acc.*); werden zu; *j-m* in die Arme laufen; ~ *low* zur Neige gehen; ~ *mad* verrückt werden; ~ *off* weglaufen; ~ *on* fortfahren; ~ *out*, ~ *short* zu Ende gehen; ~ *through* durchmachen; durchlesen; ~ *to* sich belaufen auf (*acc.*); sich entwickeln zu; ~ *up* to sich belaufen auf (*acc.*); *v/t. Strecke* durchlaufen; *Weg* einschlagen; laufen lassen; *Hand etc.* gleiten lassen; stecken, stoßen; transportieren; *Flut* ergießen; *Geschäft* betreiben, leiten; *hunt.* verfolgen, hetzen; um die Wette rennen mit; schmuggeln; heften; ~ *the blockade* die Blockade brechen; ~ *down* umrennen; zur Strecke bringen; *fig.* schlecht machen; heruntërwirtschaften; *be* ~ *down* abgearbeitet sein; ~ *errands* Botengänge machen; ~ *in mot.* einfahren; F *Verbrecher* einbuchten; ~ *off* ablaufen lassen; ~ *out* hinausjagen; ~ *over* überfahren; *Text* überfliegen; ~ *s.o. through* j-n durchbohren; ~ *up Preis, Rechnung etc.* emportreiben; *Rechnung etc.* auflaufen lassen; 2. Laufen *n*, Rennen *n*, Lauf *m*; Verlauf *m*; Fahrt *f e-s Schiffes*; Reihe *f*; Folge *f*; Serie *f*; Reise *f*, Ausflug *m*; ✈ *Andrang m*; Ansturm *m*; *Am.* Bach *m*; *Am.* Laufmasche *f*; *Vieh*-Trift *f*; freie Benutzung; Art *f*, Schlag *m*; *the common* ~ die große Masse; *have a* ~ *of 20 nights thea.* 20mal nacheinander gegeben werden; *in the long* ~ auf die Dauer, am Ende; *in the short* ~ fürs nächste.

run|about *mot.* ['rʌnəbaut] kleiner (Sport)Wagen *m*; ~**away** Ausreißer *m.*

rune [ru:n] Rune *f.*

rung[1] [rʌŋ] *p.p. von* ring 2.

rung[2] [~] (Leiter)Sprosse *f* (*a. fig.*).

run-in ['rʌn'in] *Sport:* Einlauf *m*; *Am.* F Krach *m*, Zs.-stoß *m* (*Streit*).

run|let ['rʌnlit], ~**nel** ['rʌnl] Rinnsal *n*; Rinnstein *m.*

runner ['rʌnə] Läufer *m*; Bote *m*; (Schlitten)Kufe *f*; Schieber *m am Schirm*; ♀ Ausläufer *m*; ~**up** [~ər'ʌp] *Sport:* Zweitbeste(r *m*) *f*, Zweite(r *m*) *f.*

running ['rʌniŋ] 1. laufend; *two days* ~ zwei Tage nacheinander; ~ *hand* Kurrentschrift *f*; 2. Rennen *n*; ~**-board** *mot.* Trittbrett *n.*

runt [rʌnt] *zo.* Zwergrind *n*; *fig.* Zwerg *m*; *attr.* Zwerg...

runway ['rʌnwei] ✈ Rollbahn *f*; *hunt.* Wechsel *m*; Holzrutsche *f*; ~ *watching* Ansitzjagd *f.*

rupture ['rʌptʃə] 1. Bruch *m* (*a.* ✻); 2. brechen; sprengen.

rural □ ['ruərəl] ländlich; Land...

ruse [ru:z] List *f*, Kniff *m*.

rush [rʌʃ] 1. ♀ Binse *f*; Jagen *n*, Hetzen *n*, Stürmen *n*; (An)Sturm *m*; Andrang *m*; ✝ stürmische Nachfrage; ~ hour(s *pl.*) Hauptverkehrszeit *f*; 2. *v/i.* stürzen, jagen, hetzen, stürmen; ~ at sich stürzen auf (*acc.*); ~ into print *et.* überstürzt veröffentlichen; *v/t.* jagen, hetzen; drängen; ✕ *u. fig.* stürmen; *sl.* neppen.

russet ['rʌsit] braunrot; grob.

Russian ['rʌʃən] 1. russisch; 2. Russ|e *m*, -in *f*; Russisch *n*.

rust [rʌst] 1. Rost *m*; 2. (ver-, ein-) rosten (lassen) (*a. fig.*).

rustic ['rʌstik] 1. (~ally) ländlich; bäurisch; Bauer...; 2. Bauer *m*.

rustle ['rʌsl] 1. rascheln (mit *od.* in *dat.*); rauschen; *Am.* F sich ranhalten; *Vieh* stehlen; 2. Rascheln *n*.

rust|less ['rʌstlis] rostfrei; ~y [~ti] rostig; eingerostet (*a. fig.*); verschossen (*Stoff*); rostfarben.

rut [rʌt] Wagenspur *f*; *bsd. fig.* ausgefahrenes Geleise; *hunt.* Brunst *f*, Brunft *f*.

ruthless □ ['ru:θlis] unbarmherzig; rücksichts-, skrupellos.

rutted ['rʌtid] ausgefahren (*Weg*).

rutty ['rʌti] ausgefahren (*Weg*).

rye ♀ [rai] Roggen *m*.

S

sable ['seibl] Zobel(pelz) *m*; Schwarz *n*. [2. sabotieren.\

sabotage ['sæbətɑ:ʒ] 1. Sabotage *f*;\

sabre ['seibə] Säbel *m*.

sack [sæk] 1. Plünderung *f*; Sack *m*; *Am.* Tüte *f*; Sackkleid *n*; Sakko *m*, *n*; give (get) the ~ F entlassen (werden); den Laufpaß geben (bekommen); 2. plündern; einsacken; F rausschmeißen; *j-m* den Laufpaß geben; ~cloth ['sækklɔθ], ~ing ['sækiŋ] Sackleinwand *f*.

sacrament *eccl.* ['sækrəmənt] Sakrament *n*.

sacred □ ['seikrid] heilig; geistlich.

sacrifice ['sækrifais] 1. Opfer *n*; at a ~ ✝ mit Verlust; 2. opfern; ✝ mit Verlust verkaufen.

sacrileg|e ['sækrilidʒ] Kirchenraub *m*, -schändung *f*; Sakrileg *n*; ~ious □ [sækri'lidʒəs] frevelhaft.

sad □ [sæd] traurig; jämmerlich, kläglich; schlimm, arg; dunkel.

sadden ['sædn] (sich) betrüben.

saddle ['sædl] 1. Sattel *m*; 2. satteln; *fig.* belasten; ~r [~lə] Sattler *m*.

sadism ['sædizəm] Sadismus *m*.

sadness ['sædnis] Traurigkeit *f*, Trauer *f*, Schwermut *f*.

safe [seif] 1. □ *allg.* sicher; unversehrt; zuverlässig; 2. Safe *m*, *n*, Geldschrank *m*; Speiseschrank *m*; ~-blower *Am.* ['seifblouə] Geldschrankknacker *m*; ~ conduct freies Geleit; Geleitbrief *m*; ~ guard 1. Schutz *m*; 2. sichern, schützen.

safety ['seifti] Sicherheit *f*; ~belt *mot.* Sicherheitsgurt *m*; ~ island Verkehrsinsel *f*; ~lock Sicherheitsschloß *n*; ~pin Sicherheitsnadel *f*; ~ razor Rasierapparat *m*.

saffron ['sæfrən] Safran(gelb *n*) *m*.

sag [sæg] durchsacken; ⊕ durchhängen; ⚓ (ab)sacken (*a. fig.*).

sagaci|ous □ [sə'geiʃəs] scharfsinnig; ~ty [sə'gæsiti] Scharfsinn *m*.

sage [seidʒ] 1. □ klug, weise; 2. Weise(r) *m*; ♀ Salbei *m*, *f*.

said [sed] *pret. u. p.p. von say* 1.

sail [seil] 1. Segel *n*; Fahrt *f*; Windmühlenflügel *m*; (Segel-) Schiff(e *pl.*) *n*; set ~ in See stechen; 2. *v/i.* (ab)segeln, fahren; *fig.* schweben; *j-m* den Laufpaß *Schiff* führen; ~boat *Am.* ['seilbout] Segelboot *n*; ~er ['seilə] Segler *m* (*Schiff*); ~ing-ship ['seiliŋʃip], ~ing-vessel [~ŋvesl] Segelschiff *n*; ~or ['seilə] Seemann *m*, Matrose *m*; be a good (bad) ~ (nicht) seefest sein; ~plane Segelflugzeug *n*.

saint [seint] 1. Heilige(r *m*) *f*; [*vor npr.* snt] Sankt...; 2. heiligsprechen; ~ly ['seintli] *adj.* heilig, fromm.

saith † *od. poet.* [seθ] *3. sg. pres. von say* 1.

sake [seik]: for the ~ of um ... (*gen.*) willen; for my ~ meinetwegen; for God's ~ um Gottes willen.

salad ['sæləd] Salat *m*.

salary ['sæləri] 1. Besoldung *f*, Gehalt *n*; 2. besolden; ~earner [~ɪə:nə] Gehaltsempfänger(in).

sale [seil] (Aus)Verkauf *m*; Absatz *m*; Auktion *f*; for ~, on ~ zum Verkauf, zu verkaufen, verkäuflich.

sal(e)able ['seiləbl] verkäuflich.

sales|man ['seilzmən] Verkäufer *m*; ~woman Verkäuferin *f*.

salient □ ['seiljənt] vorspringend; *fig.* hervorragend, hervortretend; Haupt...

saline ['seilain] salzig; Salz...

saliva [sə'laivə] Speichel *m*.

sallow ['sælou] blaß; gelblich.

sally ['sæli] 1. ✕ Ausbruch *m*; witziger Einfall; 2. *a.* ~ out ✕ ausbrechen; ~ forth, ~ out sich aufmachen.

salmon *ichth.* ['sæmən] Lachs *m*, Salm *m*.

saloon [sə'lu:n] Salon *m*; (Gesellschafts)Saal *m*; erste Klasse *auf Schiffen*; *Am.* Kneipe *f*.

salt [sɔ:lt] **1.** Salz *n*; *fig.* Würze *f*; *old* ~ alter Seebär; **2.** salzig; gesalzen; Salz...; Pökel...; **3.** (ein)salzen; pökeln; **~cellar** ['sɔ:ltselə] Salzfäßchen *n*; **~petre**, *Am.* **~peter** [ˌtpi:tə] Salpeter *m*; **~water** Salzwasser...; **~y** [ˌti] salzig.

salubrious ☐ [sə'lu:briəs], **salutary** ☐ ['sæljutəri] heilsam, gesund.

salut|ation [sælju(:)'teiʃən] Gruß *m*, Begrüßung *f*; Anrede *f*; **~e** [sə'lu:t] **1.** Gruß *m*; *co.* Kuß *m*; ✕ Salut *m*; **2.** (be)grüßen; ✕ salutieren.

salvage ['sælvidʒ] **1.** Bergung(sgut *n*) *f*; Bergegeld *n*; **2.** bergen.

salvation [sæl'veiʃən] Erlösung *f*; (Seelen)Heil *n*; *fig.* Rettung *f*; ♀ *Army* Heilsarmee *f*.

salve[1] [sælv] retten, bergen.

salve[2] [sɑ:v] **1.** Salbe *f*; *fig.* Balsam *m*; **2.** *mst fig.* (ein)salben; beruhigen.

salvo ['sælvou] Vorbehalt *m*; ✕ Salve *f* (*fig. Beifall*).

same [seim]: *the* ~ der-, die-, dasselbe; *all the* ~ trotzdem; *it is all the* ~ *to* me es ist mir (ganz) gleich.

samp *Am.* [sæmp] grobgemahlener Mais.

sample ['sɑ:mpl] **1.** Probe *f*, Muster *n*; **2.** bemustern; (aus)probieren.

sanatorium [sænə'tɔ:riəm] (*bsd.* Lungen)Sanatorium *n*; Luftkurort *m*.

sanct|ify ['sæŋktifai] heiligen; weihen; **~imonious** ☐ [sæŋkti'mounjəs] scheinheilig; **~ion** ['sæŋkʃən] **1.** Sanktion *f*; Bestätigung *f*; Genehmigung *f*; Zwangsmaßnahme *f*; **2.** bestätigen, genehmigen; **~ity** [ˌktiti] Heiligkeit *f*; **~uary** [ˌtjuəri] Heiligtum *n*; *das* Allerheiligste; Asyl *n*, Freistätte *f*.

sand [sænd] **1.** Sand *m*; **~s** *pl.* Sand (-massen *f/pl.*) *m*; Sandwüste *f*; Sandbank *f*; **2.** mit Sand bestreuen.

sandal ['sændl] Sandale *f*.

sand|-glass ['sændglɑ:s] Sanduhr *f*; **~hill** Sanddüne *f*; **~piper** *orn.* Flußuferläufer *m*.

sandwich ['sænwidʒ] **1.** Sandwich *n*; **2.** *a.* ~ *in* einlegen, einklemmen.

sandy ['sændi] sandig; sandfarben.

sane [sein] geistig gesund; vernünftig (*Antwort etc.*).

sang [sæŋ] *pret. von* sing.

sanguin|ary ☐ ['sæŋgwinəri] blutdürstig; blutig; **~e** [ˌwin] leichtblütig; zuversichtlich; vollblütig.

sanitarium *Am.* [sæni'teəriəm] = *sanatorium*.

sanitary ☐ ['sænitəri] Gesundheits...; gesundheitlich; ⊕ Sanitär...; ~ *towel* Damenbinde *f*.

sanit|ation [sæni'teiʃən] Gesund-

heitspflege *f*; sanitäre Einrichtung; **~y** ['sæniti] gesunder Verstand.

sank [sæŋk] *pret. von* sink **1**.

Santa Claus [sæntə'klɔ:z] Nikolaus *m*.

sap [sæp] **1.** ♀ Saft *m*; *fig.* Lebenskraft *f*; ✕ Sappe *f*; **2.** untergraben (*a. fig.*); *sl.* büffeln; **~less** ['sæplis] saft-, kraftlos; **~ling** [ˌliŋ] junger Baum; *fig* Grünschnabel *m*.

sapphire *min* ['sæfaiə] Saphir *m*.

sappy ['sæpi] saftig; *fig.* kraftvoll.

sarcasm ['sɑ:kæzəm] bitterer Spott.

sardine *ichth.* [sɑ:'di:n] Sardine *f*.

sash [sæʃ] Schärpe *f*; Fensterrahmen *m* [fenster *n*.)

sash-window ['sæʃwindou] Schie-)

sat [sæt] *pret. u. p.p. von* sit.

Satan ['seitən] Satan *m*.

satchel ['sætʃəl] Schulmappe *f*.

sate [seit] (über)sättigen.

sateen [sæ'ti:n] Satin *m*.

satellite ['sætəlait] Satellit(enstaat) *m*.

satiate ['seiʃieit] (über)sättigen.

satin ['sætin] Seidensatin *m*.

satir|e ['sætaiə] Satire *f*; **~ist** ['sætərist] Satiriker *m*; **~ize** [ˌraiz] verspotten

satisfaction [sætis'fækʃən] Befriedigung *f*; Genugtuung *f*; Zufriedenheit *f*, Sühne *f*; Gewißheit *f*.

satisfactory [sætis'fæktəri] befriedigend, zufriedenstellend.

satisfy ['sætisfai] befriedigen; genügen (*dat.*); zufriedenstellen; überzeugen; *Zweifel* beheben.

saturate ⚗ *u. fig.* ['sætʃəreit] sättigen.

Saturday ['sætədi] Sonnabend *m*, Samstag *m*.

saturnine ['sætə:nain] düster, finster.

sauce [sɔ:s] **1.** (*oft kalte*) Soße; *Am.* Kompott *n*; *fig.* Würze *f*; F Frechheit *f*; **2.** würzen; F frech werden zu *j-m*; **~boat** ['sɔ:sbout] Soßenschüssel *f*; **~pan** Kochtopf *m*; Kasserolle *f*; **~r** ['sɔ:sə] Untertasse *f*.

saucy F ['sɔ:si] frech; dreist.

saunter ['sɔ:ntə] **1.** Schlendern *n*; Bummel *m*; **2.** (umher)schlendern; bummeln

sausage ['sɔsidʒ] Wurst *f*.

savage ['sævidʒ] **1.** ☐ wild; roh, grausam; **2.** Wilde(r *m*) *f*; *fig.* Barbar *m*; **~ry** [ˌdʒəri] Wildheit *f*; Barbarei *f*.

savant ['sævənt] Gelehrte(r) *m*.

save [seiv] **1.** retten; erlösen; bewahren; (er)sparen; schonen; **2.** *rhet. prp. u. cj.* außer; ~ *for* bis auf (*acc.*); ~ *that* nur daß.

saver ['seivə] Retter(in); Sparer(in).

saving ['seiviŋ] **1.** ☐ sparsam; **2.** Rettung *f*; **~s** *pl.* Ersparnisse *f/pl.*

savings|-bank ['seiviŋzbæŋk] Sparkasse *f*; **~deposit** Spareinlage *f*.

savio(u)r ['seivjə] Retter m; Saviour eccl. Heiland m.

savo(u)r ['seivə] 1. Geschmack m; fig. Beigeschmack m; 2. fig. schmecken, riechen (of nach).

savo(u)ry¹] ['seivəri] schmackhaft; appetitlich; pikant.

savo(u)ry² ⚘ [~] Bohnenkraut n.

saw¹ [sɔ:] pret. von see.

saw² [~] Spruch m.

saw³ [~] 1. [irr.] sägen; 2. Säge f; ~dust ['sɔ:dʌst] Sägespäne m/pl.; ~mill Sägewerk n; ~n [sɔ:n] p.p. von saw³ 1.

Saxon ['sæksn] 1. sächsisch; ling. oft germanisch; 2. Sachse m, Sächsin f.

say [sei] 1. [irr.] sagen; hersagen; berichten; ~ grace das Tischgebet sprechen; that is to ~ das heißt; you don't ~ sol was Sie nicht sagen!; I ~ sag(en Sie) mal; ich muß schon sagen; he is said to be .. er soll ... sein; no sooner said than done gesagt, getan; 2. Rede f, Wort n; it is my ~ now jetzt ist die Reihe zu reden an mir; have a od. some (no) ~ in s.th. et. (nichts) zu sagen haben bei et.; ~ing ['seiiŋ] Rede f; Redensart f; Ausspruch m; it goes without ~ es versteht sich von selbst.

scab [skæb] ⚘, ♥ Schorf m; vet. Räude f; sl. Streikbrecher m.

scabbard ['skæbəd] Säbel-Scheidef.

scabrous ['skeibrəs] heikel.

scaffold ['skæfəld] (Bau)Gerüst n; Schafott n; ~ing [~diŋ] (Bau)Gerüst n.

scald [skɔ:ld] 1. Verbrühung f; 2. verbrühen; Milch abkochen.

scale¹ [skeil] 1. Schuppe f; Kesselstein m; ⚙ Zahnstein m; Waagschale f; (a pair of) ~s pl. (eine) Waage; 2. (sich) abschuppen, ablösen; ⊕ Kesselstein abklopfen; Zähne vom Zahnstein reinigen; wiegen.

scale² [~] 1. Stufenleiter f; ♪ Tonleiter f; Skala f; Maßstab m; fig. Ausmaß n; 2. ersteigen; ~ up (down) maßstabsgetreu vergrößern (verkleinern).

scallop ['skɔləp] 1. zo. Kammuschel f; ⊕ Langette f; 2. ausbogen.

scalp [skælp] 1. Kopfhaut f; Skalp m; 2. skalpieren.

scaly ['skeili] schuppig; voll Kesselstein.

scamp [skæmp] 1. Taugenichts m; 2. pfuschen; ~er ['skæmpə] 1. (umher)tollen; hetzen; 2. fig. Hetzjagdf.

scan [skæn] Verse skandieren; absuchen; fig. überfliegen.

scandal ['skændl] Skandal m; Ärgernis n; Schande f; Klatsch m; ~ize [~dəlaiz] Anstoß erregen bei j-m; ~ous [~ləs] skandalös, anstößig; schimpflich; klatschhaft.

Scandinavian [skændi'neivjən]

1. skandinavisch; 2. Skandinavier (-in).

scant lit. [skænt] 1. knapp, kärglich; 2. knausern mit, sparen an (dat.); ~y □ ['skænti] knapp, spärlich, kärglich, dürftig.

scape|goat ['skeipgout] Sündenbock m; ~grace [~greis] Taugenichts m.

scar [ska:] 1. Narbe f; fig. (Schand-) Fleck m, Makel m; Klippe f; 2. v/t. schrammen; v/i. vernarben.

scarc|e [skeəs] knapp; rar; selten; ~ely ['skeəsli] kaum; ~ity [~siti] Mangel m; Knappheit f; Teuerung f.

scare [skeə] 1. er-, aufschrecken; verscheuchen; ~d verstört; ängstlich; 2. Panik f; ~crow ['skeəkrou] Vogelscheuche f (a. fig.); ~head (-ing) Riesenschlagzeile f.

scarf [ska:f], pl. ~s, scarves [~fs, ska:vz] Schal m; Hals-, Kopftuch n; Krawatte f; ⚔ Schärpe f.

scarlet ['ska:lit] 1. Scharlach(rot n) m; 2. scharlachrot; ~ fever ♂ Scharlach m; ~ runner ♀ Feuerbohne f.

scarred [ska:d] narbig.

scarves [ska:vz] pl. von scarf.

scathing fig. ['skeiðiŋ] vernichtend.

scatter ['skætə] (sich) zerstreuen; aus-, verstreuen; (sich) verstreuen.

scavenger ['skævindʒə] Straßenkehrer m.

scenario [si'na:riou] Film: Drehbuch n.

scene [si:n] Szene f; Bühne(nbild n) f; Schauplatz m; ~s pl. Kulissen f/pl.; ~ry ['si:nəri] Szenerie f; Bühnenausstattung f; Landschaft f.

scent [sent] 1. (Wohl)Geruch m; Duft m; Parfüm n; hunt. Witterung(svermögen n) f; Fährte f; 2. wittern; parfümieren; ~less ['sentlis] geruchlos.

sceptic ['skeptik] Skeptiker(in); ~al □ [~kəl] skeptisch.

scept|re, Am. ~er ['septə] Zepter n.

schedule ['ʃedju:l, Am. skedju:l] 1. Verzeichnis n; Tabelle f; Am. Fahrplan m; on ~ fahrplanmäßig; 2. auf-, verzeichnen; festsetzen.

scheme [ski:m] 1. Schema n; Zs.-stellung f; Plan m; 2. v/t. planen; v/i. Pläne machen; Ränke schmieden.

schism ['sizəm] (Kirchen)Spaltung f.

scholar ['skɔlə] Gelehrte(r) m; univ. Stipendiat m; † Schüler(in); ~ly adj. [~əli] gelehrt; ~ship [~ʃip] Gelehrsamkeit f; Wissenschaftlichkeit f; univ. Stipendium n.

scholastic [skə'læstik] 1. (~ally) phls. scholastisch; schulmäßig; Schul...; 2. phls. Scholastiker m.

school [sku:l] 1. Schwarm m; Schule f (a. fig.); univ. Fakultät f;

Disziplin f; Hochschule f; at ~ auf od. in der Schule; 2. schulen, erziehen; ~boy ['sku:lbɔi] Schüler m; ~fellow Mitschüler(in); ~girl Schülerin f; ~ing [~liŋ] (Schul-)Ausbildung f; ~master Lehrer m (bsd. e-r höheren Schule); ~mate Mitschüler(in); ~mistress Lehrerin f (bsd. e-r höheren Schule); ~teacher (bsd. Volksschul)Lehrer (-in).

schooner ['sku:nə] ♣ Schoner m; Am. großes Bierglas; = prairieschooner.

science ['saiəns] Wissenschaft f; Naturwissenschaft(en pl.) f; Technik f.

scientific [saiən'tifik] (~ally) (engS. natur)wissenschaftlich; kunstgerecht.

scientist ['saiəntist] (bsd. Natur-) Wissenschaftler m.

scintillate ['sintileit] funkeln.

scion ['saiən] Sproß m, Sprößling m.

scissors ['sizəz] pl. (a pair of ~ pl. eine) Schere.

scoff [skɔf] 1. Spott m; 2. spotten.

scold [skould] 1. zänkisches Weib; 2. (aus)schelten, schimpfen.

scon(e) [skɔn] weiches Teegebäck.

scoop [sku:p] 1. Schaufel f, Schippe f; Schöpfeimer m, -kelle f; F Coup m, gutes Geschäft; F Exklusivmeldung f; 2. (aus)schaufeln; einscheffeln.

scooter ['sku:tə] (Kinder)Roller m; Motorroller m.

scope [skoup] Bereich m; geistiger Gesichtskreis; Spielraum m.

scorch [skɔ:tʃ] v/t. versengen, verbrennen; v/i. F (dahin)rasen.

score [skɔ:] 1. Kerbe f; Zeche f, Rechnung f; 20 Stück; Sport: Punktzahl f; (Tor)Stand m; Grund m; ♪ Partitur f; ~s of viele; four ~ achtzig; run up ~s Schulden machen; on the ~ of wegen (gen.); 2. (ein)kerben; anschreiben; Sport: (Punkte) machen; Fußball: ein Tor schießen; gewinnen; instrumentieren; Am. F scharfe Kritik üben an (dat.).

scorn [skɔ:n] 1. Verachtung f; Spott m; 2. verachten; verschmähen; ~ful □ ['skɔ:nful] verächtlich.

Scotch [skɔtʃ] 1.schottisch; 2.Schottisch n; die Schotten pl.; ~man ['skɔtʃmən] Schotte m.

scot-free ['skɔt'fri:] straflos.

Scots [skɔts], ~man ['skɔtsmən] = Scotch(man).

scoundrel ['skaundrəl] Schurke m.

scour ['skauə] v/t. scheuern; reinigen; durchstreifen, absuchen; v/i. eilen.

scourge [skə:dʒ] 1. Geißel f; 2. geißeln.

scout [skaut] 1. Späher m, Kundschafter m; ♣ Aufklärungsfahrzeug

n; ⚡ Aufklärer m; mot. Mitglied n der Straßenwacht; (Boy) ⚡ Pfadfinder m; ~ party ⚡ Spähtrupp m; 2. (aus)kundschaften, spähen; verächtlich zurückweisen.

scowl [skaul] 1. finsteres Gesicht; 2. finster blicken.

scrabble ['skræbl] (be)kritzeln; scharren; krabbeln.

scrag fig. [skræg] Gerippe n (dürrer Mensch etc.).

scramble ['skræmbl] 1. klettern; sich balgen (for um); ~d eggs pl. Rührei n; 2. Kletterei f; Balgerei f.

scrap [skræp] 1. Stückchen n; (Zeitungs)Ausschnitt m, Bild n zum Einkleben; Altmaterial m; Schrott m; ~s pl. Reste m/pl.; 2. ausrangieren; verschrotten; ~book ['skræpbuk] Sammelalbum n.

scrap|e [skreip] 1. Kratzen n, Scharren n; Kratzfuß m; Not f, Klemme f; 2. schrap(p)en; (ab-)schaben; (ab)kratzen; scharren; (entlang)streifen; ~er ['skreipə] Kratzeisen n.

scrap|-heap ['skræphi:p] Abfall-, Schrotthaufen m; ~iron Alteisen n, Schrott m.

scratch [skrætʃ] 1. Schramme f; Sport: Startlinie f; 2. zs.-gewürfelt; Zufalls...; Sport: ohne Vorgabe; 3. (zer)kratzen; (zer)schrammen; parl. u. Sport: streichen; ~ out ausstreichen.

scrawl [skrɔ:l] 1. kritzeln; 2. Gekritzel n.

scrawny Am. F ['skrɔ:ni] dürr.

scream [skri:m] 1. Schrei m; Gekreisch n; he is a ~ F er ist zum Schreien komisch; 2. schreien, kreischen.

screech [skri:tʃ] s. scream; ~owl orn. ['skri:tʃaul] Käuzchen n.

screen [skri:n] 1. Wand-, Ofen-, Schutzschirm m; fig. Schleier m; (Film)Leinwand f; der Film; Sandsieb n; (Fliegen)Gitter m; 2. (ab-)schirmen; (be)schützen; ⚡ tarnen; auf der Leinwand zeigen; verfilmen; (durch)sieben; ~ play Drehbuch n; Fernsehfilm m.

screw [skru:] 1. Schraube f; ⚡ Propeller m; 2. (fest)schrauben; fig. bedrängen; ver~, umdrehen; ~ up festschrauben; ~ up one's courage Mut fassen; ~ball Am. sl. ['skru:bɔ:l] komischer Kauz; ~driver Schraubenzieher m; ~jack Wagenheber m; ~propeller Schiffs-, Flugzeugschraube f.

scribble ['skribl] 1. Gekritzel n; 2. kritzeln. [skimp etc.]

scrimp [skrimp], ~y ['skrimpi] s.)

scrip ✝ [skrip] Interimsschein(e pl.) m.

script [skript] Schrift f; Schreibschrift f; Manuskript n; Film: Drehbuch n.

Scripture ['skriptʃə] *mst the Holy* ~*s pl.* die Heilige Schrift.
scroll [skroul] Schriftrolle *f*, Liste*f*; ♠ Schnecke *f*; Schnörkel *m*.
scrub [skrʌb] **1.** Gestrüpp *n*; Zwerg *m*; *Am. Sport* zweite (Spieler-) Garnitur; **2.** schrubben, scheuern.
scrubby ['skrʌbi] struppig; schäbig.
scrup|le ['skru:pl] **1.** Skrupel *m*, Zweifel *m*, Bedenken *n*; **2.** Bedenken haben; ~**ulous** ⌐ [~pjuləs] (allzu) bedenklich; gewissenhaft; ängstlich.
scrutin|ize ['skru:tinaiz] (genau) prüfen; ~**y** [~ni] forschender Blick; genaue (*bsd.* Wahl)Prüfung.
scud [skʌd] **1.** (Dahin)Jagen *n*; (dahintreibende) Wolkenfetzen *m/pl.*; Bö *f*; **2.** eilen, jagen, gleiten.
scuff [skʌf] schlurfen, schlorren.
scuffle ['skʌfl] **1.** Balgerei *f*, Rauferei *f*; **2.** sich balgen, raufen.
scull ⚓ [skʌl] **1.** kurzes Ruder; **2.** rudern, skullen.
scullery ['skʌləri] Spülküche *f*.
sculptor ['skʌlptə] Bildhauer *m*.
sculpture ['skʌlptʃə] **1.** Plastik *f*; Bildhauerkunst *f*, Skulptur *f*; **2.** (heraus)meißeln, formen.
scum *fig.* [skʌm] (Ab)Schaum *m*.
scurf [skə:f] (Haut)Schuppen *f/pl.*
scurrilous ['skʌriləs] gemein.
scurry ['skʌri] hasten, rennen.
scurvy ⚕ ['skə:vi] Skorbut *m*.
scurvy² [~] (hunds)gemein.
scuttle ['skʌtl] **1.** Kohlenbehälter *m*; **2.** eilen; *fig.* sich drücken.
scythe ⚯ [saið] Sense *f*.
sea [si:] See *f*, Meer *n* (*a. fig.*); hohe Welle; *at* ~ auf See; *fig.* ratlos; ~**board** ['si:bɔ:d] Küste(ngebiet *n*) *f*; ~**coast** Küste *f*; ~**faring** ['si:fɛəriŋ] seefahrend; ~**food** eßbare Seefische *m/pl.*; Meeresfrüchte *pl.*; ~**going** Hochsee...; ~**gull** (See)Möwe *f*.
seal [si:l] **1.** *zo.* Seehund *m*, Robbe *f*; Siegel *n*; Stempel *m*; Bestätigung *f*; **2.** versiegeln; *fig.* besiegeln; ~ *up* (fest) verschließen; ⊕ abdichten.
sea-level ['si:levl] Meeresspiegel *m*.
sealing-wax ['si:liŋwæks] Siegellack *m*.
seam [si:m] **1.** Saum *m*; (*a.* ⊕) Naht *f*; ⊕ Fuge *f*; *geol.* Flöz *n*; Narbe *f*; **2.** schrammen; furchen.
seaman ['si:mən] Seemann *m*, Matrose *m*.
seamstress ['semstris] Näherin *f*.
sea|-plane ['si:plein] Wasserflugzeug *n*; ~**power** Seemacht *f*.
sear [siə] **1.** dürr, welk; **2.** austrocknen, versengen; ✶ brennen; *fig.* verhärten.
search [sə:tʃ] **1.** Suchen *n*, Forschen *n*; Unter-, Durchsuchung *f*; *in* ~ *of* auf der Suche nach; **2.** *v/t.* durchuntersuchen; ✶ sondieren; erfor-

schen; durchdringen; *v/i.* suchen, forschen (*for* nach); ~ *into* ergründen; ~**ing** ⬜ ['sə:tʃiŋ] forschend, prüfend; eingehend (*Prüfung etc.*); ~**light** (Such)Scheinwerfer *m*; ~**warrant** ⚖ Haussuchungsbefehl *m*.
sea|-shore ['si:'ʃɔ:] Seeküste *f*; ~**sick** seekrank; ~**side** Strand *m*, Küste *f*; ~ *place*, ~ *resort* Seebad *n*; *go to the* ~ an die See gehen.
season ['si:zn] **1.** Jahreszeit *f*; (rechte) Zeit; Saison *f*; F *für* ~**-ticket**; *cherries are in* ~ jetzt ist Kirschenzeit; *out of* ~ zur Unzeit; *with the compliments of the* ~ mit den besten Wünschen zum Fest; **2.** *v/t.* reifen (lassen); würzen; abhärten (*to* gegen); *v/i.* ablagern; ~**able** ⬜ [~nəbl] zeitgemäß; rechtzeitig; ~**al** ⬜ ['si:zənl] Saison...; periodisch; ~**ing** ['si:zniŋ] Würze *f*; ~**-ticket** ⚄ Zeitkarte *f*; *thea.* Abonnement *n*.
seat [si:t] **1.** Sitz *m* (*a. fig.*); Sessel *m*, Stuhl *m*, Bank *f*; Sitz)Platz *m*; Landsitz *m*; Gesäß *n*; Schauplatz *m*; **2.** (hin)setzen; *e-n* Hosenboden einsetzen in (*acc.*); fassen, Sitzplätze haben für; *be* ~*ed* sitzen, sich setzen; ...sitzig; *be* ~*ed* sitzen, sich setzen; ~**-belt** ⚙ ['si:tbelt] Sicherheitsgurt *m*.
sea|-urchin *zo.* ['si:'ə:tʃin] Seeigel *m*; ~**ward** ['si:wəd] **1.** *adj* seewärts gerichtet; **2.** *adv. a.* ~*s* seewärts; ~**weed** ⚘ (See)Tang *m*; ~**worthy** seetüchtig.
secede [si'si:d] sich trennen.
secession [si'seʃən] Lossagung *f*; Abfall *m*; ~**ist** [~ʃnist] Abtrünnige(r *m*) *f*.
seclu|de [si'klu:d] abschließen, absondern; ~**ded** einsam; zurückgezogen; abgelegen; ~**sion** [~u:ʒən] Abgeschlossen-, Abgeschiedenheit *f*.
second ['sekənd] **1.** ⬜ zweite(r, -s); nächste(r, -s); geringer (*to* als); *on* ~ *thoughts* bei genauerer Überlegung; **2.** Zweite(r, -s); Sekundant *m*; Beistand *m*; Sekunde *f*; ~*s pl.* Waren *pl.* zweiter Wahl; **3.** sekundieren (*dat.*); unterstützen; ~**ary** ⬜ [~dəri] sekundär; untergeordnet; Neben...; Hilfs-; Sekundär...; ~**ary school** höhere Schule; weiterführende Schule; ~**-hand** aus zweiter Hand; gebraucht; antiquarisch; ~**ly** [~dli] zweitens; ~**-rate** zweiten Ranges; zweitklassig.
secre|cy ['si:krisi] Heimlichkeit *f*; Verschwiegenheit *f*; ~**t** [~it] **1.** ⬜ geheim; Geheim...; verschwiegen; verborgen; **2.** Geheimnis *n*; *in* ~ insgeheim; *be in the* ~, *be taken into the* ~ eingeweiht sein.
secretary ['sekrətri] Schriftführer *m*; Sekretär(in) *f*; ♀ *of State* Staats-

sekretär *m*, Minister *m*; *Am.* Außen-
minister *m*.

secret|e [si'kri:t] verbergen; ab-
sondern; **~ion** [~i:ʃən] Absonde-
rung *f*; **~ive** [~:tiv] *fig.* verschlossen; geheimtuerisch.

section ['sekʃən] ✖ Sektion *f*;
(Durch)Schnitt *m*; Teil *m*; Abschnitt *m*, Paragraph *m*; *typ.* Absatz *m*; Abteilung *f*; Gruppe *f*.

secular ['sekjulə] weltlich.

secur|e [si'kjuə] 1. sicher; 2. (sich
et.) sichern, schützen; festmachen;
~ity [~riti] Sicherheit *f*; Sorglosigkeit *f*; Gewißheit *f*; Schutz *m*;
Kaution *f*; *securities pl.* Wert-
papiere *n/pl.*

sedan [si'dæn] Limousine *f*; *a.*
~-chair Sänfte *f*.

sedate [ ] [si'deit] gesetzt; ruhig.

sedative *mst* ✖ ['sedətiv] 1. beruhi-
gend; 2. Beruhigungsmittel *n*.

sedentary □ ['sedntəri] sitzend;
seßhaft.

sediment ['sedimənt] (Boden)Satz
m; *geol.* Ablagerung *f*.

sediti|on [si'diʃən] Aufruhr *m*; **~ous**
□ [~ʃəs] aufrührerisch.

seduc|e [si'dju:s] verführen; **~tion**
[si'dʌkʃən] Verführung *f*; **~tive** □
[~ktiv] verführerisch.

sedulous [ ] ['sedjuləs] emsig.

see¹ [si:] [*irr.*] *v/i.* sehen; *fig.* einsehen; *I* ~ ich verstehe; ~ *about*
s.th. sich um et. kümmern; ~ *through*
s.o. od. s.th. j-n *od.* et. durch-
schauen; ~ *to* achten auf (*acc.*); *v/t.*
sehen; beobachten; einsehen; sorgen (*daß et. geschieht*); besuchen;
Arzt aufsuchen; ~ *s.o. home* j-n nach
Hause begleiten; ~ *off Besuch etc.*
wegbringen; ~ *out Besuch* hinaus-
begleiten; *et.* zu Ende erleben; ~
s.th. through et. durchhalten; ~ *s.o.
through* j-m durchhelfen; *live to* ~
erleben.

see² [ ] (erz)bischöflicher Stuhl.

seed [si:d] 1. Same(n) *m*, Saat(gut *n*)
f; (Obst)Kern *m*; Keim *m* (*a. fig.*);
go od. run to ~ in Samen schießen;
fig. herunterkommen; 2. *v/t.* (be-)
säen; entkernen; *v/i.* in Samen
schießen; **~less** ['si:dlis] kernlos
(*Obst*); **~ling** [~liŋ] Sämling *m*;
~y ['si:di] schäbig; F elend.

seek [si:k] [*irr.*] suchen (nach); begehren; trachten nach.

seem [si:m] (er)scheinen; **~ing** □
['si:miŋ] anscheinend; scheinbar;
~ly ['si:mli] schicklich.

seen [si:n] *p.p. von* see¹.

seep [si:p] durchsickern, tropfen.

seer ['si(:)ə] Seher(in), Prophet(in).

seesaw ['si:so:] 1. Wippen *n*; Wippe
f, Wippschaukel *f*; 2. wippen; *fig.*
schwanken.

seethe [si:ð] sieden, kochen.

segment ['segmənt] Abschnitt *m*.

segregat|e ['segrigeit] absondern,

trennen; **~ion** [segri'geiʃən] Ab-
sonderung *f*; Rassentrennung *f*.

seiz|e [si:z] ergreifen, fassen; mit
Beschlag belegen; *fig* erfassen; *a.*
~ *upon* sich *e-r S. od.* j-s bemächti-
gen; **~ure** ['si:ʒə] Ergreifung *f*, *a.*
Beschlagnahme *f*; ✖ plötzlicher
Anfall.

seldom *adv.* ['seldəm] selten.

select [si'lekt] 1. auswählen, aus-
lesen, aussuchen; 2. auserwählt;
erlesen; exklusiv; **~ion** [~kʃən]
Auswahl *f*, Auslese *f*; **~man** *Am.*
Stadtrat *m in den Neuenglandstaa-
ten.*

self [self] 1. *pl.* selves [selvz] Selbst
n, Ich *n*; Persönlichkeit *f*; 2. *pron.*
selbst; ✝ *od.* F = *myself etc.*; 3. *adj.*
⚘ einfarbig; **~-centered** ['self-
'sentəd] egozentrisch; **~-command**
Selbstbeherrschung *f*; **~-conceit**
Eigendünkel *m*; **~-conceited** dün-
kelhaft; **~-confidence** Selbstver-
trauen *n*; **~-conscious** befangen,
gehemmt; *fig.* verschlossen;
~-contained (in sich)
abgeschlossen; *fig.* verschlossen;
~-control Selbstbeherrschung *f*;
~-defence, *Am.* **~-defense** Selbst-
verteidigung *f*; *in* ~ in (der) Not-
wehr; **~-denial** Selbstverleugnung
f; **~-employed** selbständig (*Handwerker etc.*); **~-evident** selbstverständlich; **~-government** Selbst-
verwaltung *f*, Autonomie *f*; **~-in-
dulgent** bequem; zügellos; **~-in-
terest** Eigennutz *m*; **~-ish** [~fiʃ]
selbstsüchtig; **~-possession** Selbstbeherrschung *f*; **~-reliant** [~ri-
'laiənt] selbstsicher; **~-righteous**
selbstgerecht; **~-seeking** [~'si:kiŋ]
eigennützig; **~-willed** eigenwillig.

sell [sel] [*irr.*] *v/t.* verkaufen (*a. fig.*);
Am. aufschwatzen; *v/i.* handeln,
gehen (*Ware*); ~ *off*, ~ *out* ✝ ausver-
kaufen; **~er** ['selə] Verkäufer *m*;
good etc., ~ ✝ gut *etc.* gehende Ware.

selves [selvz] *pl. von* self 1.

semblance ['sembləns] Anschein
m; Gestalt *f*.

semi|... ['semi] halb...; Halb...;
~colon Strichpunkt *m*; **~detached
house** Doppelhaus(hälfte *f*) *n*;
~-final *Sport*: Vorschlußrunde *f*.

seminary ['seminəri] (Priester)Se-
minar *n*; *fig.* Schule *f*.

sempstress ['sempstris] Näherin *f*.

senate ['senit] Senat *m*.

senator ['senətə] Senator *m*.

send [send] [*irr.*] senden, schicken;
(*mit adj. od. p.pr.*) machen; ~ *for*
kommen lassen, holen (lassen); ~
forth aussenden; veröffentlichen;
~ *in* einsenden; einreichen; ~ *up* in
die Höhe treiben; ~ *word* mitteilen.

senil|e ['si:nail] greisenhaft, senil;
~ity [si'niliti] Greisenalter *n*.

senior ['si:njə] 1. älter; dienstälter;
Ober...; ~ *partner* ✝ Chef *m*;
2. Ältere(r) *m*; Dienstältere(r) *m*;

Senior *m*; *he is my ~ by a year* er ist ein Jahr älter als ich; **~ity** [si:ni-'oriti] höheres Alter *od.* Dienstalter.

sensation [sen'seiʃən] (Sinnes-) Empfindung *f*, Gefühl *n*; Eindruck *m*; Sensation *f*; **~al** □ [~nl] Empfindungs...; sensationell.

sense [sens] **1.** *allg.* Sinn *m* (*of* für); Empfindung *f*, Gefühl *n*; Verstand *m*; Bedeutung *f*; Ansicht *f*; *in* (*out of*) *one's ~s* bei (von) Sinnen; *bring s.o. to his ~s* j-n zur Vernunft bringen; *make ~* Sinn haben (*S.*); *talk ~* vernünftig reden; **2.** spüren.

senseless □ ['senslis] sinnlos; bewußtlos; gefühllos; **~ness** [~snis] Sinnlosigkeit *f*; Bewußt-, Gefühllosigkeit *f*.

sensibility [sensi'biliti] Sensibilität *f*, Empfindungsvermögen *n*; Empfindlichkeit *f*; **sensibilities** *pl.* Empfindsamkeit *f*, Zartgefühl *n*.

sensible □ ['sensəbl] verständig, vernünftig; empfänglich (*of* für); fühlbar; *be ~ of sich e-r S.* bewußt sein; *et.* empfinden.

sensitiv|e □ ['sensitiv] empfindlich (*to* für); Empfindungs...; feinfühlig; **~eness** [~vnis], **~ity** [sensi-'tiviti] Empfindlichkeit *f* (*to* für).

sensual □ ['sensjuəl] sinnlich.

sensuous □ ['sensjuəs] sinnlich; Sinnes...; sinnenfreudig.

sent [sent] *pret. u. p.p. von* send.

sentence ['sentəns] **1.** Urteil *n*; *gr.* Satz *m*; *serve one's ~* s-e Strafe absitzen; **2.** verurteilen.

sententious □ [sen'tenʃəs] sentenziös; salbungsvoll; salbaderisch.

sentient ['senʃənt] empfindend.

sentiment ['sentimənt] (seelische) Empfindung, Gefühl *n*; Meinung *f*; *s. sentimentality;* **~al** □ [senti'mentl] empfindsam; sentimental; **~ality** [sentimen'tæliti] Sentimentalität *f*.

sent|inel ['sentinl], **~ry** [~tri] Schildwache *f*, Posten *m*.

separa|ble □ ['sepərəbl] trennbar; **~te 1.** □ ['seprit] (ab)getrennt, gesondert, besonder, separat, für sich; **2.** ['sepəreit] (sich) trennen; (sich) absondern; (sich) scheiden; **~tion** [sepə'reiʃən] Trennung *f*, Scheidung *f.*

sepsis ['sepsis] Sepsis *f*, Blutvergiftung *f.*   [*m.*]

September [səp'tembə] September)

septic ['septik] septisch.

sepul|chral [si'pʌlkrəl] Grab...; Toten...; *fig.* düster; **~chre** ['sepəlkə] Grab(stätte *f*) *n*; **~ture** [~ltʃə] Begräbnis *n.*

sequel ['si:kwəl] Folge *f*; Nachspiel *n*; (Roman)Fortsetzung *f.*

sequen|ce ['si:kwəns] Aufeinander-, Reihenfolge *f*; *Film:* Szene *f*; *~ of tenses gr.* Zeitenfolge *f*; **~t** [~nt] aufeinanderfolgend.

sequestrate [si'kwestreit] *Eigentum* einziehen; beschlagnahmen.

serenade [seri'neid] **1.** *♪* Serenade *f*, Ständchen *n*; **2.** *j-m* ein Ständchen bringen.

seren|e □ [si'ri:n] klar, heiter; ruhig; **~ity** [si'reniti] Heiterkeit *f*; Ruhe *f.*

serf [sə:f] Leibeigene(r *m*) *f*, Hörige(r *m*) *f*; *fig.* Sklave *m.*

sergeant ['sa:dʒənt] ✗ Feldwebel *m*, Wachtmeister *m*; (Polizei)Wachtmeister *m.*

serial □ ['siəriəl] **1.** fortlaufend, reihenweise, Serien...; Fortsetzungs...; **2.** Fortsetzungsroman *m.*

series ['siəriz] *sg. u. pl.* Reihe *f*; Serie *f*; Folge *f*; *biol.* Gruppe *f.*

serious □ ['siəriəs] *allg.* ernst; ernsthaft, ernstlich; *be ~* es im Ernst meinen; **~ness** [~snis] Ernst (-haftigkeit *f*) *m.*

sermon ['sə:mən] (*iro.* Straf)Predigt *f.*

serpent ['sə:pənt] Schlange *f*; **~ine** [~tain] schlangengleich, -förmig; Serpentinen...

serum ['siərəm] Serum *n.*

servant ['sə:vənt] Diener(in); *a. domestic ~* Dienstbote *m*, Bedienstete(r *m*) *f*; Dienstmädchen *n.*

serve [sə:v] **1.** *v/t.* dienen (*dat.*); *Zeit* abdienen; bedienen; *Speisen* reichen; *Speisen* auftragen; behandeln; nützen, dienlich sein (*dat.*); *Zweck* erfüllen; *Tennis:* angeben; (*it*) *~s him right* (das) geschieht ihm recht; *s. sentence;* *~ out et.* austeilen; *v/i.* dienen (*a.* ✗; *as, for* als, zu); bedienen; nützen, zweckmäßig sein; *~ at table* servieren; **2.** *Tennis:* Aufschlag *m.*

service ['sə:vis] **1.** Dienst *m*; Bedienung *f*; Gefälligkeit *f*; *a. divine ~* Gottesdienst *m*; Betrieb *m*; Verkehr *m*; Nutzen *m*; Gang *m von Speisen;* Service *n*; *♪* Zustellung *f*; *Tennis:* Aufschlag *m*; *be at s.o.'s ~* j-m zu Diensten stehen; **2.** ⊕ warten, pflegen; **~able** □ [~əbl] dienlich, nützlich; benutzbar; strapazierfähig; **~ station** Tankstelle *f*; Werkstatt *f.*

servil|e □ ['sə:vail] sklavisch (*a. fig.*); unterwürfig; kriecherisch; **~ity** [sə:'viliti] Unterwürfigkeit *f*, Kriecherei *f.*

serving ['sə:viŋ] Portion *f.*

servitude ['sə:vitju:d] Knechtschaft *f*; Sklaverei *f.*

session ['seʃən] (*a.* Gerichts)Sitzung *f*; *be in ~* tagen.

set [set] **1.** [*irr.*] *v/t.* setzen; stellen; legen; zurechtstellen, (ein)richten, ordnen; *Aufgabe, Wecker* stellen; *Messer* abziehen; *Edelstein* fassen; festsetzen; erstarren lassen; *Haar* legen; *✗ Knochenbruch* einrichten; *~ s.o. laughing* j-n zum Lachen

bringen; ~ *an example* ein Beispiel
geben; ~ *sail* Segel setzen; ~ *one's
teeth* die Zähne zs.-beißen; ~ *aside*
beiseite stellen *od* legen; *fig.* verwerfen; ~ *at ease* beruhigen; ~ *at
rest* beruhigen, *Frage* entscheiden;
~ *store by* Wert legen auf (*acc.*); ~
forth darlegen; *off* hervorheben;
anrechnen; ~ *up* auf-, er-, einrichten; aufstellen, *j-n* etablieren; *v/i.
ast.* untergehen; gerinnen, fest
werden; laufen (*Flut etc.*); sitzen
(*Kleid etc.*); ~ *about s.th.* sich an et.
machen; ~ *about s o.* F über j-n
herfallen; ~ *forth* aufbrechen; ~
off aufbrechen; ~ (*up*)*on* anfangen;
angreifen; ~ *out* aufbrechen; ~ *to*
sich daran machen; ~ *up* sich niederlassen; ~ *up for* sich aufspielen
als; **2.** fest; starr, festgesetzt, bestimmt; vorgeschrieben; ~ (*up*)*on*
versessen auf (*acc.*); ~ *with* besetzt
mit; *Barometer* ~ *fair* beständig;
hard ~ in großer Not; ~ *speech*
wohlüberlegte Rede; **3.** Reihe *f*,
Folge *f*, Serie *f*, Sammlung *f*, Satz
m; Garnitur *f*; Service *n*; *Radio*-
Gerät *n*; ✦ Kollektion *f*; Gesellschaft *f*; Sippschaft *f*; ⚡ Setzling
m; *Tennis* Satz *m*; Neigung *f*;
Richtung *f*, Sitz *m e-s Kleides etc.*;
poet. Untergang *m der Sonne*; *thea.*
Bühnenausstattung *f*.

set|-back ['setbæk] *fig.* Rückschlag
m; **~down** *fig.* Dämpfer *m*; **~off**
Kontrast *m*; *fig.* Ausgleich *m*.

settee [se'ti:] *kleines* Sofa.

setting ['setiŋ] Setzen *n*; Einrichten
n; Fassung *f e-s Edelsteins*; Lage *f*;
Schauplatz *m*; Umgebung *f*; *thea.*
Ausstattung *f*, *fig.* Umrahmung *f*;
⚡ Komposition *f*; (*Sonnen- etc.*)
Untergang *m*, ⊕ Einstellung *f*.

settle ['setl] **1.** Sitzbank *f*; **2.** *v/t.*
(fest)setzen; *Kind etc.* versorgen,
ausstatten; *j-n* etablieren; regeln;
Geschäft abschließen, abmachen,
erledigen; *Frage* entscheiden; *Rechnung* begleichen; ordnen, beruhigen; *Streit* beilegen; *Rente* aussetzen; ansiedeln; *Land* besiedeln;
v/i. sich senken (*Haus*); *oft* ~ *down*
sich niederlassen; *a.* in sich einrichten; sich legen (*Wut etc.*);
beständig werden (*Wetter*); sich
entschließen; ~ *down to* sich widmen (*dat.*); **~d** fest; beständig;
auf Rechnungen: bezahlt; **~ment**
[~lmənt] Erledigung *f*; Überein-
kunft *f*; (Be)Siedlung *f*; ⚖ (Eigen-
tums)Übertragung *f*; **~r** [~lə]
Siedler *m*.

set|-to F ['set'tu:] Kampf *m*; Schlä-
gerei *f*; **~up** F Aufbau *m*; *Am. sl.*
abgekartete Sache.

seven ['sevn] **1.** sieben; **2.** Sieben *f*;
~teen(th) [~n'ti:n(θ)] siebzehn
(-te[r, -s]); **~th** [~nθ] **1.** ⬚ sieb(en)-
te(r, -s); **2.** Sieb(en)tel *n*; **~thly**

33*

[~θli] sieb(en)tens; **~tieth** [~ntiiθ]
siebzigste(r, -s); **~ty** [~ti] **1.** siebzig;
2. Siebzig *f*.

sever ['sevə] (sich) trennen; (auf-)
lösen; zerreißen.

several ⬚ ['sevrəl] mehrere, verschiedene; einige; einzeln; besonder; getrennt; **~ly** [~li] besonders,
einzeln.

severance ['sevərəns] Trennung *f*.

sever|e ⬚ [si'viə] streng; rauh
(*Wetter*); hart (*Winter*); scharf
(*Tadel*); ernst (*Mühe*); heftig
(*Schmerz etc.*); schlimm, schwer
(*Unfall etc.*); **~ity** [si'veriti] Strenge
f, Härte *f*, Schwere *f*; Ernst *m*.

sew [sou] [*irr.*] nähen; heften.

sewage ['sju:(:)idʒ] Abwasser *n*.

sewer¹ ['souə] Näherin *f*.

sewer² ['sjuə] Abwasserkanal *m*;
~age [~əridʒ] Kanalisation *f*.

sew|ing ['souiŋ] Nähen *n*; Nähe-
rei *f*; *attr.* Näh...; **~n** [soun] *p.p.
von sew.*

sex [seks] Geschlecht *n*.

sexton ['sekstən] Küster *m*, Totengräber *m*.

sexual ⬚ ['seksjuəl] geschlechtlich;
Geschlechts...; sexuell, Sexual...

shabby ⬚ ['ʃæbi] schäbig; gemein.

shack *Am.* [ʃæk] Hütte *f*, Bude *f*.

shackle ['ʃækl] **1.** Fessel *f* (*fig. mst
pl.*); **2.** fesseln.

shade [ʃeid] **1.** Schatten *m*, Dunkel *n*
(*a. fig.*); *Lampen- etc* Schirm *m*;
Schattierung *f*; *Am.* Rouleau *n*;
fig. Spur *f*, Kleinigkeit *f*; **2.** beschatten; verdunkeln (*a. fig.*); ab-
schirmen; schützen; schattieren; ~
away, ~ *off* allmählich übergehen
(lassen) (*into* in *acc.*).

shadow ['ʃædou] **1.** Schatten *m* (*a.
fig.*); Phantom *n*, Spur *f*, Kleinigkeit *f*; **2.** beschatten; *mst* ~ *forth
od. out*) andeuten; versinnbildlichen;
j-n beschatten, überwachen; **~y**
[~oui] schattig, dunkel; schatten-
haft; wesenlos.

shady ['ʃeidi] schattenspendend;
schattig; dunkel; F zweifelhaft.

shaft [ʃɑ:ft] Schaft *m*; Stiel *m*;
Pfeil *m* (*a. fig.*); *poet* Strahl *m*; ⊕
Welle *f*; Deichsel *f*; ⚒ Schacht *m*.

shaggy ['ʃægi] zottig.

shake [ʃeik] **1.** [*irr.*] *v/t.* schütteln,
rütteln; erschüttern; ~ *down* her-
unterschütteln; *Stroh etc.* hin-
schütten; ~ *hands* sich die Hände
geben *od.* schütteln; ~ *up Bett* aufschütteln; *fig.* aufrütteln; *v/i.* zittern, beben, wackeln, wanken (*with*
vor *dat.*); ⚡ trillern; **2.** Schütteln *n*;
Erschütterung *f*; Beben *n*, ⚡ Triller *m*; **~down** ['ʃeik'daun] **1.** Not-
lager *n*; *Am. sl.* Erpressung *f*; **2.**
adj.: ~ *cruise* ⚓ Probefahrt *f*;
~hands *pl.* Händedruck *m*; **~n**
['ʃeikən] **1.** *p.p. von* shake; **2.** *adj.*
erschüttert.

shaky □ ['ʃeiki] wack(e)lig (*a. fig.*); (sch)wankend; zitternd, zitterig.

shall [ʃæl] [*irr.*] *v*/*aux.* soll; werde.

shallow ['ʃæləu] **1.** seicht; flach; *fig.* oberflächlich; **2.** Untiefe *f*; **3.** (sich) verflachen.

sham [ʃæm] **1.** falsch; Schein...; **2.** Trug *m*; Täuschung *f*; Schwindler(in); **3.** *v*/*t.* vortäuschen; *v*/*i.* sich verstellen; simulieren; ~ **ill** (-ness) sich krank stellen.

shamble ['ʃæmbl] watscheln; ~s *pl. od. sg.* Schlachthaus *n*; *fig.* Schlachtfeld *n*.

shame [ʃeim] **1.** Scham *f*; Schande *f*; *for* ~, *l*, ~ *on you*! pfui, schäm dich!; *put to* ~ beschämen; **2.** beschämen; *j-m* Schande machen; **~faced** ['ʃeimfeist] schamhaft, schüchtern; **~ful** [~ful] schändlich, beschämend; **~less** □ ['ʃeimlis] schamlos.

shampoo [ʃæm'pu:] **1.** Shampoo *n*; Haarwäsche *f*; **2.** *Haare* waschen.

shamrock ['ʃæmrɔk] Kleeblatt *n*.

shank [ʃæŋk] (Unter)Schenkel *m*; ⚓ Stiel *m*; (⚓ Anker)Schaft *m*.

shanty ['ʃænti] Hütte *f*, Bude *f*.

shape [ʃeip] **1.** Gestalt *f*, Form *f* (*a. fig.*); Art *f*; **2.** *v*/*t.* gestalten, formen, bilden; anpassen (*to dat.*); *v*/*i.* sich entwickeln; **~d** ...förmig; **~less** ['ʃeiplis] formlos; **~ly** [~li] wohlgestaltet.

share [ʃeə] **1.** (An)Teil *m*; Beitrag *m*; † Aktie *f*; ⚒ Kux *m*; *have a* ~ *in* teilhaben an (*dat.*); *go* ~*s* teilen; **2.** *v*/*t.* teilen; *v*/*i.* teilhaben (*in an dat.*); **~cropper** *Am.* ['ʃeəkrɔpə] *kleiner* Farmpächter; **~holder** † Aktionär(in).

shark [ʃa:k] *ichth.* Hai(fisch) *m*; Gauner *m*; *Am. sl.* Kanone *f* (*Experte*).

sharp [ʃa:p] **1.** □ *allg.* scharf (*a. fig.*); spitz; schneidend, stechend; schrill; hitzig; schnell; pfiffig, schlau, gerissen; *C* ~ ♪ Cis *n*; **2.** *adv.* ♪ zu hoch; F pünktlich; *look* ~! (mach) schnell!; **3.** ♪ Kreuz *n*; durch ein Kreuz erhöhte Note; F Gauner *m*; **~en** ['ʃa:pən] (ver-)schärfen; spitzen; **~ener** ['ʃa:pnə] *Messer*-Schärfer *m*; *Bleistift*-Spitzer *m*; **~er** ['ʃa:pə] Gauner *m*; **~ness** ['ʃa:pnis] Schärfe *f* (*a. fig.*); **~set** ['ʃa:p'set] hungrig; erpicht; **~sighted** scharfsichtig; **~witted** scharfsinnig.

shatter ['ʃætə] zerschmettern, zerschlagen; *Nerven etc.* zerrütten.

shave [ʃeiv] **1.** [*irr.*] (sich) rasieren; (ab)schälen; haarscharf vorbeigehen *od.* vorbeifahren *od.* vorbeikommen an (*dat.*); **2.** Rasieren *n*, Rasur *f*; *have a* ~ sich rasieren (lassen); *a close* ~ ein Entkommen mit knapper Not; **~n** ['ʃeivn] *p.p. von* shave 1.

shaving ['ʃeiviŋ] **1.** Rasieren *n*; ~*s pl.* (*bsd.* Hobel)Späne *m*/*pl.*; **2.** Rasier...

shawl [ʃɔ:l] Schal *m*, Kopftuch *n*.

she [ʃi:] **1.** sie; **2.** Sie *f*; *zo.* Weibchen *n*; **3.** *adj. in Zssgn:* weiblich, ...weibchen *n*; ~*dog* Hündin *f*.

sheaf [ʃi:f], *pl.* **sheaves** [ʃi:vz] Garbe *f*; Bündel *n*.

shear [ʃiə] **1.** [*irr.*] scheren; *fig.* rupfen; **2.** ~*s pl.* große Schere.

sheath [ʃi:θ] Scheide *f*; **~e** [ʃi:ð] (in die Scheide) stecken; einhüllen; ⊕ bekleiden, belegen.

sheaves [ʃi:vz] *pl. von* sheaf.

shebang *Am. sl.* [ʃə'bæŋ] Bude *f*, Laden *m*.

shed[1] [ʃed] [*irr.*] aus-, vergießen; verbreiten; *Blätter etc.* abwerfen.

shed[2] [~] Schuppen *m*; Stall *m*.

sheen [ʃi:n] Glanz *m* (*bsd. Stoff*).

sheep [ʃi:p] Schaf(e *pl.*) *n*; Schafleder *n*; ~*cot* ['ʃi:pkɔt] = sheepfold; ~*dog* Schäferhund *m*; ~*fold* Schafhürde *f*; ~*ish* □ ['ʃi:piʃ] blöd(e), einfältig; ~*man* *Am.* Schafzüchter *m*; ~*skin* Schaffell *n*; Schafleder *n*; F Diplom *n*.

sheer [ʃiə] rein; glatt; *Am.* hauchdünn, steil; senkrecht; direkt.

sheet [ʃi:t] Bett-, Leintuch *n*, Laken *n*, (*Glas- etc.*)Platte *f*; ⊕ ...blech *n*; Blatt *n*, Bogen *m Papier*; weite Fläche (*Wasser etc.*); ⚓ Schot(e) *f*; *the rain came down in* ~*s* es regnete in Strömen; ~ *iron* Eisenblech *n*; ~ **lightning** ['ʃi:t-laitniŋ] Wetterleuchten *n*.

shelf [ʃelf], *pl.* **shelves** [ʃelvz] Brett *n*, Regal *n*, Fach *n*; Riff *n*; *on the* ~ *fig.* ausrangiert.

shell [ʃel] **1.** Schale *f*, Hülse *f*, Muschel *f*; Gehäuse *n*; Gerippe *n* e-s *Hauses*; ✗ Granate *f*; **2.** schälen, enthülsen; ✗ bombardieren; ~**fire** ['ʃelfaiə] Granatfeuer *n*; ~**fish** *zo.* Schalentier *n*; ~**proof** bombensicher.

shelter ['ʃeltə] **1.** Schuppen *m*; Schutz-, Obdach *n*; *fig.* Schutz *m*, Schirm *m*; **2.** *v*/*t.* (be)schützen; (be)schirmen; Zuflucht gewähren (*dat.*); *v*/*i.* *a. take* ~ Schutz suchen.

shelve [ʃelv] mit Brettern *od.* Regalen versehen; auf ein Brett stellen; *fig.* zu den Akten legen; beiseite legen; sich allmählich neigen.

shelves [ʃelvz] *pl. von* shelf.

shenanigan *Am.* F [ʃi'nænigən] Gaunerei *f*; Humbug *m*.

shepherd ['ʃepəd] **1.** Schäfer *m*, Hirt *m*; **2.** (be)hüten; leiten.

sherbet ['ʃə:bət] Brauselimonade *f*; (*Art*) (Speise)Eis *n*.

shield [ʃi:ld] **1.** (Schutz)Schild *m*; Wappenschild *m*, *n*; **2.** (be)schirmen (*from vor dat.*, *gegen*).

shift [ʃift] **1.** Veränderung *f*, Verschiebung f, Wechsel m; Notbehelf m; List f, Kniff m; Ausflucht f; (Arbeits)Schicht f, make .. es möglich machen (to inf zu inf); sich behelfen, sich durchschlagen; 2. v/t. (ver-, weg)schieben, (ab)wechseln; verändern; Platz, Szene verlegen, verlagern; v/i wechseln, sich verlagern; sich behelfen; for o.s. sich selbst helfen; ~less] ['ʃiftlis] hilflos, faul; ~y] [..ti] fig. gerissen; unzuverlässig.

shilling ['ʃiliŋ] *englischer* Schilling.

shin [ʃin] 1. *a* ~bone Schienbein n; 2. ~ up hinaufklettern.

shine [ʃain] 1. Schein m; Glanz m; 2. [irr] v/i scheinen, leuchten; fig. glänzen, strahlen; v/t blank putzen.

shingle ['ʃiŋgl] Schindel f; Am. F (Aushänge)Schild n; Strandkiesel m/pl.; ~s pl ✠ Gürtelrose f.

shiny [ ] ['ʃaini] blank, glänzend.

ship [ʃip] 1. Schiff n, Am. F Flugzeug n; 2. an Bord nehmen od. bringen; verschiffen, versenden; ✠ heuern; ~board ['ʃipbɔːd]: on ~ ✠ an Bord; ~ment ['ʃipmənt] Verschiffung f; Versand m; Schiffsladung f; ~owner Reeder m; ~ping ['ʃipiŋ] Verschiffung f; Schiffe n/pl., Flotte f; attr Schiffs. .; Verschiffungs..., Verlade ; ~wreck 1. Schiffbruch m; 2. scheitern (lassen); ~wrecked schiffbrüchig; ~yard Schiffswerft f. [schaft f.]

shire ['ʃaiə, *in Zssgn* .ʃiə] Graf-[

shirk [ʃəːk] sich drücken (um *et.*); ~er ['ʃəːkə] Drückeberger m.

shirt [ʃəːt] Herrenhemd n; a. ~waist Am. Hemdbluse f; ~sleeve ['ʃəːtsliːv] 1. Hemdsärmel m; 2. hemdsärmelig; informell; ~ diplomacy bsd. Am. offene Diplomatie.

shiver ['ʃivə] 1. Splitter m; Schauer m; 2. zersplittern; schau(d)ern; (er)zittern; frösteln; ~y [.əri] fröstelnd.

shoal [ʃoul] 1. Schwarm m, Schar f; Untiefe f; 2. flacher werden; 3. seicht.

shock [ʃɔk] 1. Garbenhaufen m; (Haar)Schopf m; Stoß m; Anstoß m; Erschütterung f, Schlag m; ✠ (Nerven)Schock m; 2. fig. verletzen; empören, Anstoß erregen bei; erschüttern; ~ing ['ʃɔkiŋ] anstößig; empörend; haarsträubend.

shod [ʃɔd] *pret. u. p.p. von* shoe 2.

shoddy ['ʃɔdi] 1. Reißwolle f; fig. Schund m; Am. Protz m; 2. falsch; minderwertig; Am. protzig.

shoe [ʃuː] 1. Schuh m; Hufeisen n; 2. [irr.] beschuhen; beschlagen; ~black ['ʃuːblæk] Schuhputzer m; ~blacking Schuhwichse f; ~horn Schuhanzieher m; ~lace Schnürsenkel m; ~maker Schuhmacher m; ~string Schnürsenkel m.

shone [ʃɔn] *pret. u. p.p. von* shine 2.

shook [ʃuk] *pret. von* shake 1.

shoot [ʃuːt] 1. fig. Schuß m; ⚘ Schößling m; 2. [irr] v/t. (ab-)schießen; erschießen, werfen, stoßen; Film aufnehmen, drehen; fig. unter e-r Brücke etc hindurchschießen, über et hinwegschießen, ⚘ treiben; ✠ (ein)spritzen; v/i. schießen; stechen (Schmerz); daherschießen; stürzen, a ~ forth ✠ ausschlagen; ~ ahead vorwärtsschießen; ~er ['ʃuːtə] Schütze m.

shooting ['ʃuːtiŋ] 1. Schießen n; Schießerei f; Jagd f, Film Dreharbeiten f/pl.; 2. stechend (Schmerz); ~gallery Schießstand m, ~bude f; ~range Schießplatz m; ~ star Sternschnuppe f.

shop [ʃɔp] 1. Laden m, Geschäft n; Werkstatt f, Betrieb m, talk ~ fachsimpeln; 2. mst go ~ping ~inkaufen gehen; ~assistant ['ʃɔpəsistənt] Verkäufer(in); ~keeper Ladeninhaber(in); ~lifter ['ʃɔpliftə] Ladendieb m; ~man ~adengehilfe m; ~per ['ʃɔpə] Käufer(in); ~ping ['ʃɔpiŋ] Einkaufen n; attr Einkaufs...; ~ centre Einkaufszentrum n; ~steward Betriebsrat m; ~walker ['ʃɔpwɔːkə] Aufsichtsherr m, ~dame f; ~window Schaufenster n.

shore [ʃɔː] 1. Küste f, Ufer n; Strand m; Stütze f; on ~ an Land; 2. ~ up abstützen.

shorn [ʃɔːn] *p.p. von* shear 1.

short [ʃɔːt] 1. *adj.* kurz (*a. fig.*); klein; knapp; mürbe (*Gebäck*), wortkarg; in ~ kurz(um); ~ of knapp an (*dat.*); 2. *adv.* ~ of abgesehen von; come od. fall ~ of nicht erreichen; cut ~ plötzlich unterbrechen; run ~ (of) ausgehen (*Vorräte*); stop ~ of zurückschrecken vor (*dat.*); ~age ['ʃɔːtidʒ] Fehlbetrag m; Gewichtsverlust m; Knappheit f; ~coming Unzulänglichkeit f; Fehler m; Mangel m; ~ cut Abkürzungsweg m; ~dated ✝ auf kurze Sicht; ~en ['ʃɔːtn] v/t. ab-, verkürzen; v/i. kürzer werden; ~ening [.niŋ] Backfett n; ~hand Kurzschrift f; ~ typist Stenotypistin f; ~ly ['ʃɔːtli] *adv.* kurz; bald; ~ness ['ʃɔːtnis] Kürze f; Mangel m; ~sighted kurzsichtig; ~term kurzfristig; ~winded kurzatmig.

shot [ʃɔt] 1. *pret. u. p.p. von* shoot 2; 2. Schuß m; Geschoß n, Kugel f; Schrot(korn) n; Schußweite f; Schütze m; Sport Stoß m, Schlag m; Wurf m; phot., Film. Aufnahme f; ✠ Spritze f; have a ~ at et. versuchen; not by a long ~ F noch lange nicht; big ~ F großes Tier; ~gun ['ʃɔtgʌn] Schrotflinte f; ~ marriage Am. F Mußheirat f.

should [ʃud, ʃəd] *pret. von* shall.

shoulder ['∫ouldə] 1. Schulter f (a. v. Tieren; fig. Vorsprung); Achsel f; 2. auf die Schulter od. fig. auf sich nehmen; ✗ schultern; drängen; ~blade anat. Schulterblatt n; ~strap Träger m am Kleid; ✗ Schulter-, Achselstück n.

shout [∫aut] 1. lauter Schrei od. Ruf; Geschrei n; 2. laut schreien.

shove [∫ʌv] 1. Schub m, Stoß m; 2. schieben, stoßen.

shovel ['∫ʌvl] 1. Schaufel f; 2. schaufeln.

show [∫ou] 1. [irr.] v/t. zeigen; ausstellen; erweisen; beweisen; ~ in hereinführen; ~ off zur Geltung bringen; ~ out hinausgeleiten; ~ round herumführen; ~ up hinaufführen; entlarven; v/i. a. ~ up sich zeigen; zu sehen sein; ~ off angeben, prahlen, sich aufspielen; 2. Schau(stellung) f; Ausstellung f; Auf-, Vorführung f; Anschein m; on ~ zu besichtigen; ~ business ['∫oubiznis] Unterhaltungsindustrie f; Schaugeschäft n; ~case Schaukasten m, Vitrine f; ~down Aufdecken n der Karten (bsd. Am. a. fig.); fig. Kraftprobe f.

shower ['∫auə] 1. (Regen)Schauer m; Dusche f; fig. Fülle f; 2. v/t. herabschütten (a. fig.); überschütten; v/i. sich ergießen; ~y ['∫auəri] regnerisch.

show|n [∫oun] p.p. von show 1; ~room ['∫ourum] Ausstellungsraum m; ~window Schaufenster n; ~y □ ['∫oui] prächtig; protzig.

shrank [∫ræŋk] pret. von shrink.

shred [∫red] 1. Stückchen n; Schnitz(el n) m; Fetzen m (a. fig.); 2. [irr.] (zer)schnitzeln; zerfetzen.

shrew [∫ru:] zänkisches Weib.

shrewd □ ['∫ru:d] scharfsinnig schlau.

shriek [∫ri:k] 1. (Angst)Schrei m; Gekreisch n; 2. kreischen, schreien.

shrill [∫ril] 1. □ schrill, gellend; 2. schreien, gellen; schrillen.

shrimp [∫rimp] zo. Krabbe f; fig. Knirps m. [m.]

shrine [∫rain] Schrein m; Altar]

shrink [∫riŋk] [irr.] (ein-, zs.-) schrumpfen (lassen); einlaufen; sich zurückziehen; zurückschrecken (from, at vor dat.); ~age ['∫riŋkidʒ] Einlaufen n, Zs.-schrumpfen n; Schrumpfung f; fig. Verminderung f.

shrivel ['∫rivl] einschrumpfen (lassen).

shroud [∫raud] 1. Leichentuch n; fig. Gewand n; 2. in ein Leichentuch einhüllen; fig. hüllen.

Shrove|tide ['∫rouvtaid] Fastnachtszeit f; ~Tuesday Fastnachtsdienstag m.

shrub [∫rʌb] Strauch m; Busch m; ~bery ['∫rʌbəri] Gebüsch n.

shrug [∫rʌg] 1. (die Achseln) zucken; 2. Achselzucken n.

shrunk [∫rʌŋk] p.p. von shrink; ~en ['∫rʌŋkən] adj. (ein)geschrumpft.

shuck bsd. Am. [∫ʌk] 1. Hülse f, Schote f; ~s! F Quatsch! 2. enthülsen.

shudder ['∫ʌdə] 1. schaudern; (er-) beben; 2. Schauder m.

shuffle ['∫ʌfl] 1. schieben; Karten: mischen; schlurfen; Ausflüchte machen; ~ off von sich schieben; abstreifen; 2. Schieben n; Mischen n; Schlurfen n; Ausflucht f; Schiebung f.

shun [∫ʌn] (ver)meiden.

shunt [∫ʌnt] 1. ⚙ Rangieren n; ⚙ Weiche f; ⚡ Nebenschluß m; 2. ⚙ rangieren; ⚡ nebenschließen; fig. verschieben

shut [∫ʌt] [irr.] (sich) schließen; zumachen; ~ down Betrieb schließen; ~ up ein-, verschließen; einsperren; ~ up! F halt den Mund!; ~ter ['∫ʌtə] Fensterladen m; phot. Verschluß m.

shuttle ['∫ʌtl] 1. ⊕ Schiffchen n; Pendelverkehr m; 2. pendeln.

shy [∫ai] 1. □ scheu; schüchtern; 2. (zurück)scheuen (at vor dat.).

shyness ['∫ainis] Schüchternheit f; Scheu f.

shyster sl., bsd. Am. ['∫aistə] gerissener Kerl; Winkeladvokat m.

Siberian [sai'biəriən] 1. sibirisch; 2. Sibirier(in).

sick [sik] krank (of an dat.; with vor dat.); übel; überdrüssig; be ~ for sich sehnen nach; be ~ of genug haben von; go ~, report ~ sich krank melden; ~benefit ['sikbenifit] Krankengeld n; ~en ['sikn] v/i. krank werden; kränkeln; ~ at sich ekeln vor (dat.); v/t. krank machen; anekeln.

sickle ['sikl] Sichel f.

sick|-leave ['sikli:v] Krankheitsurlaub m; ~ly [~li] kränklich; schwächlich; bleich, blaß; ungesund (Klima); ekelhaft; matt (Lächeln); ~ness ['siknis] Krankheit f; Übelkeit f.

side [said] 1. allg. Seite f; ~ by ~ Seite an Seite; take ~ with Partei ergreifen für; 2. Seiten...; Neben...; 3. Partei ergreifen (with für); ~board ['saidbɔ:d] Anrichte(tisch m) f, Sideboard n; ~car mot. Beiwagen m; ~d ...seitig; ~light Streiflicht n; ~long 1. adv. seitwärts; 2. adj. seitlich; Seiten...; ~stroke Seitenschwimmen n; ~track 1. ⚙ Nebengleis n; 2. auf ein Nebengleis schieben; bsd. Am. fig. aufschieben; beiseite schieben; ~walk bsd. Am. Bürgersteig m; ~ward(s) [~wəd(z)], ~ways seitlich; seitwärts.

siding ⚙ ['saidiŋ] Nebengleis n.

sidle ['saidl] seitwärts gehen.

siege [si:dʒ] Belagerung *f*; *lay ~ to* belagern.

sieve [siv] 1. Sieb *n*; 2. (durch-) sieben.

sift [sift] sieben; *fig.* sichten; prüfen.

sigh [sai] 1. Seufzer *m*; 2. seufzen; sich sehnen (*after, for* nach).

sight [sait] 1. Sehvermögen *n*, Sehkraft *f*; *fig.* Auge *n*; Anblick *m*; Visier *n*; Sicht *f*; *~s pl.* Sehenswürdigkeiten *f/pl.*; *at ~, on ~* a. on ~ beim Anblick; *♪* vom Blatt; *♱* nach Sicht; *catch ~ of* erblicken, zu Gesicht bekommen; *lose ~ of* aus den Augen verlieren; *within ~* in Sicht; *know by ~* vom Sehen kennen; 2. sichten; (an)visieren; *~ed* ['saitid] *...sichtig*; *~ly* ['saitli] ansehnlich, stattlich; *~seeing* ['saitsiːiŋ] Besichtigung *f* von Sehenswürdigkeiten; *~seer* Tourist(in).

sign [sain] 1. Zeichen *n*; Wink *m*; Schild *n*; *in ~ of* zum Zeichen (*gen.*); 2. *v/i.* winken, Zeichen geben; *v/t.* (unter)zeichnen, unterschreiben.

signal ['signl] 1. Signal *n*; Zeichen *n*; 2. □ bemerkenswert, außerordentlich; 3. signalisieren; *~ize* [*~nəlaiz*] auszeichnen; = *signal* 3.

signat|ory ['signətəri] 1. Unterzeichner *m*; 2. unterzeichnend; *~ powers pl.* Signatarmächte *f/pl.*; *~ure* [*~nitʃə*] Signatur *f*; Unterschrift *f*; *~ tune Radio:* Kennmelodie *f*.

sign|board ['sainbɔːd] (Aushänge-) Schild *n*; *~er* ['sainə] Unterzeichner(in).

signet ['signit] Siegel *n*.

signific|ance [sig'nifikəns] Bedeutung *f*; *~ant* □ [*~nt*] bedeutsam; bezeichnend (*of* für); *~ation* [signifi'keiʃən] Bedeutung *f*.

signify ['signifai] bezeichnen, andeuten; kundgeben; bedeuten.

signpost ['sainpoust] Wegweiser *m*.

silence ['sailəns] 1. (Still)Schweigen *n*; Stille *f*, Ruhe *f*; *~!* Ruhe! put *od.* reduce to ~ = 2. zum Schweigen bringen; *~r* [*~sə*] ⊕ Schalldämpfer *m*; *mot.* Auspufftopf *m*.

silent □ ['sailənt] still; schweigend; schweigsam; stumm; *~ partner †* stiller Teilhaber.

silk [silk] Seide *f*; *attr.* Seiden...; *~en* □ ['silkən] seiden; *~stocking Am.* vornehm; *~worm* Seidenraupe *f*; *~y* [*~ki*] seid(enart)ig.

sill [sil] Schwelle *f*; Fensterbrett *n*.

silly □ ['sili] albern, töricht.

silt [silt] 1. Schlamm *m*; 2. *mst ~ up* verschlammen.

silver ['silvə] 1. Silber *n*; 2. silbern; Silber...; 3. versilbern; silberig *od.* silberweiß werden (lassen); *~ware Am.* Tafelsilber *n*; *~y* [*~əri*] silberglänzend; silberhell.

similar □ ['similə] ähnlich, gleich; *~ity* [simi'læriti] Ähnlichkeit *f*.

simile ['simili] Gleichnis *n*.

similitude [si'militjuːd] Gestalt *f*; Ebenbild *n*; Gleichnis *n*.

simmer ['simə] sieden *od.* brodeln (lassen); *fig.* kochen, gären (*Gefühl, Aufstand*); *~ down* ruhig(er) werden.

simper ['simpə] 1. einfältiges Lächeln; 2. einfältig lächeln.

simple □ ['simpl] einfach; schlicht; einfältig; arglos; *~hearted, ~minded* arglos, naiv; *~ton* [*~ltən*] Einfaltspinsel *m*.

simpli|city [sim'plisiti] Einfachheit *f*; Klarheit *f*; Schlichtheit *f*; Einfalt *f*; *~fication* [simplifi'keiʃən] Vereinfachung *f*; *~fy* ['simplifai] vereinfachen.

simply ['simpli] einfach; bloß.

simulate ['simjuleit] vortäuschen; (er)heucheln; sich tarnen als.

simultaneous □ [siməl'teinjəs] gleichzeitig.

sin [sin] 1. Sünde *f*; 2. sündigen.

since [sins] 1. *prp.* seit; 2. *adv.* seitdem; 3. *cj.* seit(dem); da (ja).

sincer|e □ [sin'siə] aufrichtig; *Yours ~ly* Ihr ergebener; *~ity* [*~'seriti*] Aufrichtigkeit *f*.

sinew ['sinjuː] Sehne *f*; *fig. mst. ~s pl.* Nerven(kraft *f*) *m/pl.*; Seele *f*; *~y* [*~ju(ː)i*] sehnig; nervig, stark.

sinful □ ['sinful] sündig, sündhaft, böse.

sing [siŋ] 1. [*irr.*] singen; besingen; *~ to s.o.* j-m vorsingen.

singe [sindʒ] (ver)sengen.

singer ['siŋə] Sänger(in).

singing ['siŋiŋ] Gesang *m*, Singen *n*; *~ bird* Singvogel *m*.

single ['siŋgl] 1. □ einzig; einzeln; Einzel...; einfach; ledig, unverheiratet; *book-keeping by ~ entry* einfache Buchführung; *~ file* Gänsemarsch *m*; 2. einfache Fahrkarte; *mst ~s sg. Tennis:* Einzel *n*; 3. *~ out* auswählen, aussuchen; *~breasted* einreihig (*Jacke etc.*); *~engined ✈* einmotorig; *~handed* eigenhändig, allein; *~hearted* □, *~minded* □ aufrichtig; zielstrebig; *~t* [*~lit*] Unterhemd *n*; *~track* eingleisig.

singular ['siŋgjulə] 1. □ einzigartig; eigenartig; sonderbar; 2. *a. ~ number gr.* Singular *m*, Einzahl *f*; *~ity* [siŋgju'leriti] Einzigartigkeit *f*; Sonderbarkeit *f*.

sinister □ ['sinistə] unheilvoll; böse.

sink [siŋk] 1. [*irr.*] *v/i.* sinken; nieder-, unter-, versinken; sich senken; eindringen; erliegen; *v/t.* (ver)senken; *Brunnen* bohren; *Geld* festlegen; *Namen etc.* aufgeben; 2. Ausguß *m*; *~ing* ['siŋkiŋ] (Ver-) Sinken *n*; Versenken *n*; *✚* Schwäche(gefühl *n*) *f*; Senkung *f*; *†*

Tilgung f; ~ fund (Schulden)Tilgungsfonds m.

sinless ['sinlis] sündenlos, -frei.

sinner ['sinə] Sünder(in).

sinuous □ ['sinjuəs] gewunden.

sip [sip] 1. Schlückchen n; 2. schlürfen; nippen; langsam trinken.

sir [sə:] Herr m; ♀ Sir (Titel).

sire ['saiə] mst poet. Vater m; Vorfahr m; zo. Vater(tier n) m.

siren ['saiərin] Sirene f.

sirloin ['sə:loin] Lendenstück n.

sissy Am. ['sisi] Weichling m.

sister ['sistə] (a. Ordens-, Ober-) Schwester f; ~hood [~əhud] Schwesternschaft f; ~-in-law [~ərinlɔ:] Schwägerin f; ~ly [~əli] schwesterlich.

sit [sit] (irr.) v/i. sitzen; Sitzung halten, tagen; fig. liegen; ~ down sich setzen; ~ up aufrecht sitzen; aufbleiben; v/t. setzen; sitzen auf (dat.).

site [sait] Lage f; (Bau)Platz m.

sitting ['sitiŋ] Sitzung f; ~-room Wohnzimmer n.

situat|ed ['sitjueitid] gelegen; be ~ liegen, gelegen sein; ~ion [sitju-'eiʃən] Lage f; Stellung f.

six [siks] 1. sechs; 2. Sechs f; ~teen ['siks'ti:n] sechzehn; ~teenth [~nθ] sechzehnte(r, -s); ~th [siksθ] 1. sechste(r, -s); 2. Sechstel n; ~thly ['siksθli] sechstens; ~tieth [~stii:θ] sechzigste(r, -s); ~ty [~ti] 1. sechzig; 2. Sechzig f.

size [saiz] 1. Größe f; Format n; 2. nach der Größe ordnen; ~ up F j-n abschätzen; ~d von ... Größe.

siz(e)able □ ['saizəbl] ziemlich groß.

sizzle ['sizl] zischen; knistern; brutzeln; sizzling hot glühend heiß.

skat|e [skeit] 1. Schlittschuh m; roller-~ Rollschuh m; 2. Schlittod. Rollschuh laufen; ~er ['skeitə] Schlittschuh-, Rollschuhläufer(in).

skedaddle F [ski'dædl] abhauen.

skeesicks Am. F ['ski:ziks] Nichtsnutz m.

skein [skein] Strähne f, Docke f.

skeleton ['skelitn] Skelett n; Gerippe n; Gestell n; attr. Skelett...; ✕ Stamm...; ~ key Nachschlüssel m.

skeptic ['skeptik] s. sceptic.

sketch [sketʃ] 1. Skizze f; Entwurf m; Umriß m; 2. skizzieren, entwerfen.

ski [ski:] 1. pl. a. ski Schi m, Ski m; 2. Schi od. Ski laufen.

skid [skid] 1. Hemmschuh m, Bremsklotz m; ✕ (Gleit)Kufe f; Rutschen n; mot. Schleudern n; 2. v/t. hemmen; v/i. (aus)rutschen.

skiddoo Am. sl. [ski'du:] abhauen.

ski|er ['ski:ə] Schi-, Skiläufer(in); ~ing ['ski:iŋ] Schi-, Skilauf(en n) m.

skilful □ ['skilful] geschickt; kundig.

skill [skil] Geschicklichkeit f, Fertigkeit f; ~ed [skild] geschickt; gelernt; ~ worker Facharbeiter m.

skillful Am. ['skilful] s. skilful.

skim [skim] 1. abschöpfen; abrahmen; dahingleiten über (acc.); Buch überfliegen; ~ through durchblättern; 2. ~ milk Magermilch f.

skimp [skimp] j-n knapp halten; sparen (mit et.); ~y □ ['skimpi] knapp, dürftig.

skin [skin] 1. Haut f; Fell n; Schale f; 2. v/t. (ent)häuten; abbalgen; schälen; ~ off F abstreifen; v/i. a. ~ over zuheilen; ~-deep ['skin'di:p] (nur) oberflächlich; ~flint Knicker m; ~ny [~ni] mager.

skip [skip] 1. Sprung m; 2. v/i. hüpfen, springen; seilhüpfen; v/t. überspringen.

skipper ['skipə] ♣ Schiffer m; ♣, ✕, Sport: Kapitän m.

skirmish ['skə:miʃ] 1. ✕ Scharmützel n; 2. plänkeln.

skirt [skə:t] 1. (Damen)Rock m; (Rock)Schoß m; oft ~s pl. Rand m, Saum m; 2. umsäumen; (sich) entlangziehen (an dat.); entlangfahren; ~ing-board ['skə:tiŋbɔ:d] Scheuerleiste f.

skit [skit] Stichelei f, Satire f; ~tish □ ['skitiʃ] ungebärdig.

skittle ['skitl] Kegel m; play (at) ~s Kegel schieben; ~alley Kegelbahn f. [Gemeinheit f.)

skulduggery Am. F [skʌl'dʌgəri]

skulk [skʌlk] schleichen; sich verstecken; lauern; sich drücken; ~er ['skʌlkə] Drückeberger m.

skull [skʌl] Schädel m.

sky [skai] oft skies pl. Himmel m; ~lark ['skaila:k] 1. orn. Feldlerche f; 2. Ulk treiben; ~light Oberlicht n; Dachfenster n; ~line Horizont m; Silhouette f; ~rocket F emporschnellen; ~scraper Wolkenkratzer m; ~ward(s) ['skaiwəd(z)] himmelwärts.

slab [slæb] Platte f; Scheibe f; Fliese f.

slack [slæk] 1. schlaff; locker; (nach)lässig; ♣ flau; 2. ♣ Lose n (loses Tauende); ♣ Flaute f; Kohlengrus m; 3. ■ = slacken; ■ = slake; ~en ['slækən] schlaff machen od. werden; verringern; nachlassen; (sich) lockern; (sich) entspannen; (sich) verlangsamen; ~s pl. (lange) Hose.

slag [slæg] Schlacke f.

slain [slein] p.p. von slay.

slake [sleik] Durst, Kalk löschen; fig. stillen.

slam [slæm] 1. Zuschlagen n; Knall m; 2. Tür etc. zuschlagen, zuknallen; et. auf den Tisch etc. knallen.

slander ['sla:ndə] 1. Verleumdung f; 2. verleumden; ~ous □ [~rəs] verleumderisch.

slang [slæŋ] 1. Slang *m*; Berufssprache *f*; lässige Umgangssprache; 2. *j-n* wüst beschimpfen.

slant [slɑ:nt] 1. schräge Fläche; Abhang *m*; Neigung *f*; *Am.* Standpunkt *m*; 2. schräg legen *od.* liegen; sich neigen; ~**ing** *adj.*, ◻ ['slɑ:ntiŋ], ~**wise** *adv.* [⸗twaiz] schief, schräg.

slap [slæp] 1. Klaps *m*, Schlag *m*; 2. klapsen; schlagen; klatschen; ~**jack** *Am.* ['slæpdʒæk] *Art* Pfannkuchen *m*; ~**stick** (Narren)Pritsche *f*; *a.* ~ *comedy thea.* Posse *f*, Burleske *f*.

slash [slæʃ] 1. Hieb *m*; Schnitt *m*; Schlitz *m*; 2. (auf)schlitzen; schlagen, hauen; verreißen (*Kritiker*).

slate [sleit] 1. Schiefer *m*; Schiefertafel *f*; *bsd. Am.* Kandidatenliste *f*; 2. mit Schiefer decken; heftig kritisieren; *Am.* F *für e-n Posten* vorschlagen; ~**pencil** ['sleit'pensl] Griffel *m*.

slattern ['slætə(:)n] Schlampe *f*.

slaughter ['slɔ:tə] 1. Schlachten *n*; Gemetzel *n*; 2. schlachten; niedermetzeln; ~**house** Schlachthaus *n*.

Slav [slɑ:v] 1. Slaw|e *m*, -in *f*; 2. slawisch.

slave [sleiv] 1. Sklav|e *m*, -in *f* (*a. fig.*); 2. F sich placken, schuften.

slaver ['slævə] 1. Geifer *m*, Sabber *m*; 2. (be)geifern, F (be)sabbern.

slav|ery ['sleivəri] Sklaverei *f*; F Plackerei *f*; ~**ish** ◻ [⸗viʃ] sklavisch.

slay *rhet.* [slei] [*irr.*] erschlagen; töten.

sled [sled] = *sledge* 1.

sledge[1] [sledʒ] 1. Schlitten *m*; 2. Schlitten fahren.

sledge[2] [⸗] *a.* ~**hammer** Schmiedehammer *m*.

sleek [sli:k] 1. ◻ glatt, geschmeidig; 2. glätten; ~**ness** ['sli:knis] Glätte *f*.

sleep [sli:p] 1. [*irr.*] *v/i.* schlafen; ~ (*up*)*on od.* over *et.* beschlafen; *v/t. j-n* für die Nacht unterbringen; ~ away *Zeit* verschlafen; 2. Schlaf *m*; go to ~ einschlafen; ~**er** ['sli:pə] Schläfer(in); 🚆 Schwelle *f*; Schlafwagen *m*; ~**ing** [⸗piŋ] schlafend; Schlaf...; **2ing Beauty** Dornröschen *n*; ~**ing-car(riage)** 🚆 Schlafwagen *m*; ~**ing partner** † stiller Teilhaber; ~**less** ◻ [⸗plis] schlaflos; ~**walker** Schlafwandler(in); ~**y** ◻ [⸗pi] schläfrig; verschlafen.

sleet [sli:t] 1. Graupelregen *m*; 2. graupeln; ~**y** ['sli:ti] graupelig.

sleeve [sli:v] Armel *m*; ⊕ Muffe *f*; ~**link** ['sli:vliŋk] Manschettenknopf *m*.

sleigh [slei] 1. (*bsd.* Pferde)Schlitten *m*; 2. (im) Schlitten fahren.

sleight [slait]: ~**of-hand** Taschenspielerei *f*; Kunststück *n*.

slender ◻ ['slendə] schlank; schmächtig; schwach; dürftig.

slept [slept] *pret. u. p.p. von sleep* 1.

sleuth [slu:θ], ~**hound** ['slu:θhaund] Blut-, Spürhund *m* (*a. fig.*).

slew [slu:] *pret. von slay.*

slice [slais] 1. Schnitte *f*, Scheibe *f*, Stück *n*; Teil *m, n*; 2. (in) Scheiben schneiden; aufschneiden.

slick F [slik] 1. *adj.* glatt; *fig.* raffiniert; 2. *adv.* direkt; 3. *a.* ~ *paper Am. sl.* vornehme Zeitschrift; ~**er** *Am.* F ['slikə] Regenmantel *m*; gerissener Kerl.

slid [slid] *pret. u. p.p. von slide* 1.

slide [slaid] 1. [*irr.*] gleiten (lassen); rutschen; schlittern; ausgleiten; geraten (*into* in *acc.*); let things ~ die Dinge laufen lassen; 2. Gleiten *n*; Rutsche *f*; ⊕ Schieber *m*; Diapositiv *n*; *a. land~* Erdrutsch *m*; ~**rule** ['slaidru:l] Rechenschieber *m*.

slight [slait] 1. ◻ schmächtig; schwach; gering, unbedeutend; 2. Geringschätzung *f*; 3. geringschätzig behandeln; unbeachtet lassen.

slim [slim] 1. ◻ schlank; dünn; schmächtig; dürftig; *sl.* schlau, gerissen; 2. e-e Schlankheitskur machen.

slim|e [slaim] Schlamm *m*; Schleim *m*; ~**y** ['slaimi] schlammig; schleimig.

sling [sliŋ] 1. Schleuder *f*; Tragriemen *m*; 𝕏 Schlinge *f*, Binde *f*; Wurf *m*; 2. [*irr.*] schleudern; auf-, umhängen; *a.* ~ *up* hochziehen.

slink [sliŋk] [*irr.*] schleichen.

slip [slip] 1. [*irr.*] *v/i.* schlüpfen, gleiten, rutschen; ausgleiten; ausrutschen; *oft* ~ *away* entschlüpfen; sich versehen; *v/t.* schlüpfen *od.* gleiten lassen; loslassen; entschlüpfen, entgleiten (*dat.*); ~ *in* Bemerkung dazwischenwerfen; ~ *into* hineinstecken *od.* hineinschieben in (*acc.*); ~ *on* (*off*) *Kleid* über-, (ab)streifen; have ~**ped** *s.o.'s* memory *j-m* entfallen sein; 2. (Aus)Gleiten *n*; Fehltritt *m* (*a. fig.*); Versehen *n*; (Flüchtigkeits)Fehler *m*; Verstoß *m*; Streifen *m*; Zettel *m*; Unterkleid *n*; *a.* ~**way** ⚓ Helling *f*; (Kissen)Überzug *m*; ~**s** *pl.* Badehose *f*; give *s.o.* the ~ *j-m* entwischen; ~**per** ['slipə] Pantoffel *m*, Hausschuh *m*; ~**pery** ◻ [⸗əri] schlüpfrig; ~**shod** [⸗ʃɔd] schlampig, nachlässig; ~**t** [slipt] *pret. u. p.p. von slip* 1.

slit [slit] 1. Schlitz *m*; Spalte *f*; 2. [*irr.*] (auf-, zer)schlitzen.

sliver ['slivə] Splitter *m*.

slobber ['slɔbə] 1. Sabber *m*; Gesabber *n*; 2. F (be)sabbern.

slogan ['slougən] Schlagwort *n*, Losung *f*; (Werbe)Slogan *m*.

sloop ⚓ [slu:p] Schaluppe *f*.

slop [slɔp] 1. Pfütze *f*; ~s *pl.* Spül-, Schmutzwasser *n*; Krankenspeise *f*; 2. *v/t.* verschütten; *v/i.* überlaufen.

slope [sloup] 1. (Ab)Hang *m*; Neigung *f*; 2. schräg legen; ⊕ abschrägen; abfallen; schräg verlaufen; (sich) neigen.

sloppy ['slɔpi] naß, schmutzig; schlampig; F labb(e)rig; rührselig.

slops [slɔps] *pl.* billige Konfektionskleidung; ⚓ Kleidung *f* u. Bettzeug *n*.

slot [slɔt] Schlitz *m*.

sloth [slouθ] Faulheit *f*; *zo.* Faultier *n*.

slot-machine ['slɔtməʃiːn] (Waren- *od.* Spiel)Automat *m*.

slouch [slautʃ] 1. faul herumhängen; F herumlatschen; 2. schlaffe Haltung; *hat* Schlapphut *m*.

slough[1] [slau] Sumpf(loch *n*) *m*.

slough[2] [slʌf] Haut abwerfen.

sloven ['slʌvn] unordentlicher Mensch; F Schlampe *f*; ~ly [~nli] liederlich.

slow [slou] 1. ˈ langsam (*of* in *dat.*); schwerfällig; lässig; *be* ~ nachgehen (*Uhr*); 2. *adv.* langsam; 3. *oft* ~ *down od. up od. off v/t.* verlangsamen; *v/i.* langsam(er) werden *od.* gehen *od.* fahren; ~**coach** ['sloukoutʃ] Langweiler *m*; altmodischer Mensch; ~**motion picture** Zeitlupenaufnahme *f*; ~**worm** *zo.* Blindschleiche *f*.

sludge [slʌdʒ] Schlamm *m*; Matsch *m*.

slug [slʌg] 1. Stück *n* Rohmetall; *zo.* Wegschnecke *f*; *Am.* F (Faust-) Schlag *m*; 2. *Am.* F hauen.

slugg|ard ['slʌgəd] Faulenzer(in); ~**ish** [~giʃ] träge, faul.

sluice [sluːs] 1. Schleuse *f*; 2. ausströmen (lassen); ausspülen; waschen.

slum [slʌm] schmutzige Gasse; ~s *pl.* Elendsviertel *n*, Slums *pl.*

slumber ['slʌmbə] 1. *a.* ~s *pl.* Schlummer *m*; 2. schlummern.

slump [slʌmp] *Börse* 1. fallen, stürzen; 2. (Kurs-, Preis)Sturz *m*.

slung [slʌŋ] *pret u. p.p. von* sling 2.

slunk [slʌŋk] *pret u. p.p. von* slink.

slur [sləː] 1. Fleck *m*; *fig.* Tadel *m*; ♪ Bindebogen *m*; 2. *v/t. oft* ~ *over* übergehen, ♪ *Töne* binden.

slush [slʌʃ] Schlamm *m*; Matsch *m*; F Kitsch *m*.

slut [slʌt] F Schlampe *f*; Nutte *f*.

sly [ ] [slai] schlau, verschmitzt; hinterlistig; *on the* ~ heimlich.

smack [smæk] 1. (Bei)Geschmack *m*; Prise *f* Salz *etc.*; *fig.* Spur *f*; Schmatz *m*; Schlag *m*, Klatsch *m*, Klaps *m*; 2. schmecken (*of* nach); e-n Beigeschmack haben; klatschen, knallen (mit); schmatzen (mit); *j-m* e-n Klaps geben.

small [smɔːl] 1. *allg.* klein; unbe-

deutend; *fig.* kleinlich; niedrig; wenig; *feel* ~, *look* ~ sich gedemütigt fühlen; *the* ~ *hours* die frühen Morgenstunden *f/pl.*; *in a* ~ *way* bescheiden; *a.* dünner Teil; ~s *pl.* F Leibwäsche *f*; ~ *of the back anat.* Kreuz *n*; ~**arms** ['smɔːlɑːmz] *pl.* Handfeuerwaffen *f/pl.*; ~**change** Kleingeld *n*; *fig.* triviale Bemerkungen *f/pl.*; ~**ish** [~liʃ] ziemlich klein; ~**pox** ✞ [~lpɔks] Pocken *f/pl.*; ~ **talk** Plauderei *f*; ~**time** *Am.* F unbedeutend.

smart [smɑːt] 1. ☐ scharf; gewandt; geschickt; gescheit; gerissen; schmuck, elegant, adrett; forsch; ~ *aleck Am.* F Neunmalkluge(r) *m*; 2. Schmerz *m*; 3. schmerzen; leiden; ~**money** ['smɑːtmʌni] Schmerzensgeld *n*; ~**ness** [~tnis] Klugheit *f*; Schärfe *f*; Gewandtheit *f*; Gerissenheit *f*; Eleganz *f*.

smash [smæʃ] 1. *v/t* zertrümmern; *fig.* vernichten; (zer)schmettern; *v/i.* zerschellen; zs.-stoßen; *fig.* zs.-brechen; 2. Zerschmettern *n*; Krach *m*; Zs.-bruch *m* (*a.* ✝); *Tennis* Schmetterball *m*; ~**up** ['smæʃʌp] Zs.-stoß *m*; Zs.-bruch *m*.

smattering ['smætəriŋ] oberflächliche Kenntnis.

smear [smiə] 1. (be)schmieren; *fig.* beschmutzen; 2. Schmiere *f*; Fleck *m*.

smell [smel] 1. Geruch *m*; 2. [*irr.*] riechen (*of* nach *et.*); *a.* ~ *at* riechen an (*dat.*); ~**y** ['smeli] übelriechend.

smelt[1] [smelt] *pret. u. p.p. von* smell 2.

smelt[2] [~] schmelzen.

smile [smail] 1. Lächeln *n*; 2. lächeln.

smirch [sməːtʃ] besudeln.

smirk [sməːk] grinsen.

smite [smait] [*irr.*] schlagen; heimsuchen; *schwer* treffen; quälen.

smith [smiθ] Schmied *m*.

smithereens ['smiðə'riːnz] *pl.* Stücke *n/pl.*, Splitter *m/pl*, Fetzen *m/pl.*

smithy ['smiði] Schmiede *f*.

smitten ['smitn] 1. *p.p. von* smite; 2. *adj.* ergriffen; betroffen; *fig.* hingerissen (*with* von).

smock [smɔk] 1. [veraltet] 2. Kittel *m*; ~**frock** ['smɔkˈfrɔk] Bauernkittel *m*.

smog [smɔg] Smog *m*, Gemisch *n* von Nebel und Rauch.

smoke [smouk] 1. Rauch *m*; *have a* ~ (eine) rauchen; 2. rauchen; dampfen; (aus)räuchern; ~**dried** ['smoukdraid] geräuchert; ~**r** [~kə] Raucher *m*; 🚃 F Raucherwagen *m*, -abteil *n*; ~**stack** ⚓ Schornstein *m*.

smoking ['smoukiŋ] Rauchen *n*; *attr.* Rauch(er)...; ~**compartment** 🚃 Raucherabteil *n*.

smoky □ ['smouki] rauchig; verräuchert. *[der.]*

smolder *Am.* ['smoulde] = *smoul-*

smooth [smu:ð] 1. □ glatt; *fig.* fließend; mild; schmeichlerisch; 2. glätten; ebnen (a. *fig.*); plätten; mildern; a. ~ over, ~ away *fig.* wegräumen; **~ness** ['smu:ðnis] Glätte *f.*

smote [smout] *pret. von* smite.

smother ['smʌðe] ersticken.

smoulder ['smoulde] schwelen.

smudge [smʌdʒ] 1. (be)schmutzen; (be)schmieren; 2. Schmutzfleck *m.*

smug [smʌg] selbstzufrieden.

smuggle ['smʌgl] schmuggeln; **~r** [ʌle] Schmuggler(in).

smut [smʌt] Schmutz *m.*; Ruß(fleck) *m.*; Zoten *f/pl.*; 2. beschmutzen.

smutty □ ['smʌti] schmutzig.

snack [snæk] Imbiß *m*; **~bar** ['snækbɑ:], **~counter** Snackbar *f*, Imbißstube *f.*

snaffle ['snæfl] Trense *f.*

snag [snæg] (Ast-, Zahn)Stumpf *m*; *fig.* Haken *m*; *Am.* Baumstumpf *m* (*bsd. unter Wasser*).

snail *zo.* [sneil] Schnecke *f.*

snake *zo.* [sneik] Schlange *f.*

snap [snæp] 1. Schnappen *n*, Biß *m*; Knack(s) *m*; Knall *m*; *fig.* Schwung *m*, Schmiß *m*; Schnappschloß *n*; *phot.* Schnappschuß *m*; *cold* ~ Kältewelle *f*; 2. *v/i.* schnappen (at nach); zuschnappen (*Schloß*); krachen; knacken; (zer)brechen; knallen; schnauzen; ~ at s.o. j-n anschnauzen; ~ into it! *Am. sl.* mach schnell, Tempo!; ~ out of it! *Am. sl.* hör auf damit!; komm, komm!; *v/t.* (er)schnappen (zu)schnappen lassen; *phot.* knipsen; zerbrechen; ~ out *Wort* hervorstoßen; ~ up wegschnappen; **~fastener** ['snæpfɑ:sne] Druckknopf *m*; **~pish** □ [ʌpiʃ] bissig; schnippisch; **~py** [ʌpi] bissig; F flott; **~shot** Schnappschuß *m*, Photo *n*, Momentaufnahme *f.*

snare [snɛe] 1. Schlinge *f*; 2. fangen; *fig.* umgarnen.

snarl [snɑ:l] 1. knurren; murren; 2. Knurren *n*; Gewirr *n.*

snatch [snætʃ] 1. schneller Griff; Ruck *m*; Stückchen *n*; 2. schnappen; ergreifen; an sich reißen; nehmen; ~ at greifen nach.

sneak [sni:k] 1. *v/i.* schleichen; F petzen; *v/t.* F stibitzen; 2. Schleicher *m*; F Petzer *m*; **~ers** ['sni:kez] *pl.* F leichte Segeltuchschuhe *m/pl.*

sneer [snie] 1. Hohnlächeln *n*; Spott *m*; 2. hohnlächeln; spotten; spötteln.

sneeze [sni:z] 1. niesen; 2. Niesen *n.*

snicker ['snike] kichern; wiehern.

sniff [snif] schnüffeln, schnuppern; riechen; die Nase rümpfen.

snigger ['snige] kichern.

snip [snip] 1. Schnitt *m*; Schnipsel

m, n; 2. schnippeln, schnipseln; knipsen

snipe [snaip] 1. *orn.* (Sumpf-) Schnepfe *f*; 2. ✗ aus dem Hinterhalt (ab)schießen; **~r** ✗ ['snaipe] Scharf-, Heckenschütze *m.*

snivel ['snivl] schniefen; schluchzen; plärren

snob [snɔb] Großtuer *m*; Snob *m*; **~bish** ['snɔbiʃ] snobistisch.

snoop *Am.* [snu:p] 1. *fig.* (herum-) schnüffeln; 2. Schnüffler(in).

snooze F [snu:z] 1. Schläfchen *n*; 2. dösen

snore [snɔ:] schnarchen.

snort [snɔ:t] schnauben, schnaufen.

snout [snaut] Schnauze *f*; Rüssel *m.*

snow [snou] 1. Schnee *m*; 2. (be-) schneien, *be ~ed under fig.* erdrückt werden, **~bound** ['snoubaund] eingeschneit, **~capped**, **~clad**, **~covered** schneebedeckt; **~drift** Schneewehe *f*; **~drop** ♀ Schneeglöckchen *n*, **~y** □ ['snoui] schneeig; schneebedeckt, verschneit; schneeweiß.

snub [snʌb] 1. schelten, anfahren; 2. Verweis *m*; **~nosed** ['snʌbnouzd] stupsnasig

snuff [snʌf] 1. Schnuppe *f* e-r *Kerze*; Schnupftabak *m*; 2. *a. take* ~ schnupfen, *Licht* putzen; **~le** ['snʌfl] schnüffeln; näseln.

snug [snʌg] geborgen; behaglich; eng anliegend; **~gle** ['snʌgl] (sich) schmiegen *od* kuscheln (to an *acc.*).

so [sou] so; deshalb; also; *I hope* ~ ich hoffe es, *are you tired?* ~ *I am* bist du müde? Ja; *you are tired*, ~ *am I* du bist müde, ich auch; ~ *far* bisher.

soak [souk] *v/t.* einweichen; durchnässen; (durch)tränken; auf-, einsaugen, *v/i* weichen; durchsickern.

soap [soup] 1. Seife *f*; *soft* ~ Schmierseife *f*; 2. (ein)seifen; **~box** ['soupbɔks] Seifenkiste *f*; improvisierte Rednertribüne; **~y** □ ['soupi] seifig; *fig.* unterwürfig.

soar [sɔ:] sich erheben, sich aufschwingen; schweben; ⊁ segelfliegen.

sob [sɔb] 1. Schluchzen *n*; 2. schluchzen.

sober ['soube] 1. □ nüchtern; 2. (sich) ernüchtern; **~ness** [ʌnis], **sobriety** [sou'braieti] Nüchternheit *f.*

so-called ['sou'kɔ:ld] sogenannt.

soccer F ['sɔke] (Verbands)Fußball *m* (*Spiel*).

sociable ['souʃebl] 1. □ gesellig; gemütlich; 2. geselliges Beisammensein

social ['souʃel] 1. □ gesellschaftlich; gesellig; sozial(istisch), Sozial...; ~ *insurance* Sozialversicherung *f*; ~ *services pl.* Sozialeinrichtungen *f/pl.*; 2. geselliges Beisammensein;

~ism [~lizəm] Sozialismus *m*;
~ist [~ist] 1. Sozialist(in); 2. *a.*
~istic [souʃə'listik] (~ally) soziali-
stisch; **~ize** ['souʃəlaiz] soziali-
sieren; verstaatlichen.

society [sə'saiəti] Gesellschaft *f*;
Verein *m*, Klub *m*.

sociology [sousi'ɔlədʒi] Sozialwis-
senschaft *f*.

sock [sɔk] Socke *f*; Einlegesohle *f*.

socket ['sɔkit] (Augen-, Zahn)Höhle
f; (Gelenk)Pfanne *f*; ⊕ Muffe *f*;
≠ Fassung *f*; ≠ Steckdose *f*.

sod [sɔd] 1. Grasnarbe *f*; Rasen
(-stück *n*) *m*; 2. mit Rasen bedecken.

soda ['soudə] Soda *f*, *n*; **~fountain**
Siphon *m*; *Am.* Erfrischungshalle
f, Eisdiele *f*.

sodden ['sɔdn] durchweicht; teigig.

soft [sɔft] 1. *allg* weich; *engS.*:
mild; sanft; sacht, leise; zart, zärtlich; weichlich; F einfältig; **~drink**
F alkoholfreies Getränk; 2. *adv.*
weich; 3. F Trottel *m*; **~en** ['sɔfn]
weich machen; (sich) erweichen;
mildern; **~headed** schwachsinnig;
~hearted gutmütig.

soggy ['sɔgi] durchnäßt; feucht.

soil [sɔil] 1. Boden *m*, Erde *f*; Fleck
m; Schmutz *m*; 2. (be)schmutzen;
beflecken.

sojourn ['sɔdʒə:n] 1. Aufenthalt *m*;
2. sich aufhalten.

solace ['sɔləs] 1. Trost *m*; 2. trösten.

solar ['soulə] Sonnen...

sold [sould] *pret. u. p.p. von sell.*

solder ['sɔldə] 1. Lot *n*; 2. löten.

soldier ['souldʒə] Soldat *m*; **~like**,
~ly [~li] soldatisch; **~y** [~əri] Militär *n*.

sole[1] □ [soul] alleinig, einzig; ~
agent Alleinvertreter *m*.

sole[2] [~] 1. Sohle *f*; 2. besohlen.

solemn □ ['sɔləm] feierlich; ernst;
~ity [sə'lemniti] Feierlichkeit *f*;
Steifheit *f*; **~ize** ['sɔləmnaiz] feiern; feierlich vollziehen.

solicit [sə'lisit] (dringend) bitten;
ansprechen, belästigen; **~ation**
[sɔlisi'teiʃən] dringende Bitte; **~or**
[sə'lisitə] ≠≠ Anwalt *m*; *Am.* Agent
m, Werber *m*; **~ous** □ [~təs] besorgt; ~ of begierig nach; ~ to inf.
bestrebt zu *inf.*; **~ude** [~tju:d]
Sorge *f*, Besorgnis *f*, Bemühung *f*.

solid ['sɔlid] 1.] fest; dauerhaft;
haltbar; derb; massiv; A körperlich, Raum...; *fig.* gediegen; solid;
triftig; solidarisch; *a* ~ hour e-e
volle Stunde; 2. (fester) Körper;
~arity [sɔli'dæriti] Solidarität *f*;
~ify [sə'lidifai] (sich) verdichten;
~ity [~iti] Solidität *f*; Gediegen-
heit *f*.

soliloquy [sə'liləkwi] Selbstge-
spräch *n*, Monolog *m*.

solit|ary □ ['sɔlitəri] einsam; ein-
zeln; einsiedlerisch; **~ude** [~tju:d]

Einsamkeit *f*; Verlassenheit *f*;
Öde *f*.

solo ['soulou] Solo *n*; ✈ Alleinflug
m; **~ist** [~ouist] Solist(in).

solu|ble □ ['sɔljubl] löslich; (auf)lös-
bar; **~tion** [sə'lu:ʃən] (Auf)Lösung
f; ⊕ Gummilösung *f*.

solve [sɔlv] lösen; **~nt** ['sɔlvənt]
1. (auf)lösend; ✝ zahlungsfähig;
2. Lösungsmittel *n*.

somb|re, *Am.* **~er** □ ['sɔmbə]
düster.

some [sʌm, səm] irgendein; etwas;
einige, manche *pl.*; *Am.* F prima;
~ 20 miles etwa 20 Meilen; in ~
degree, to ~ extent einigermaßen;
~body ['sʌmbədi] jemand; **~day**
eines Tages; **~how** irgendwie; ~ or
other so oder so; **~one** jemand.

somersault ['sʌməsɔ:lt] Salto *m*;
Rolle *f*, Purzelbaum *m*; turn a ~
e-n Purzelbaum schlagen.

some|thing ['sʌmθiŋ] (irgend) et-
was; ~ like so etwas wie, so ungefähr; **~time** 1. einmal, dereinst;
2. ehemalig; **~times** manchmal;
~what etwas, ziemlich; **~where**
irgendwo(hin).

somniferous □ [sɔm'nifərəs] einschläfernd.

son [sʌn] Sohn *m*.

song [sɔŋ] Gesang *m*; Lied *n*; Gedicht *n*; for a mere od. an old ~
für e-n Pappenstiel; **~bird** ['sɔŋ-
bə:d] Singvogel *m*; **~ster** ['sɔŋstə]
Singvogel *m*; Sänger *m*.

sonic ['sɔnik] Schall...

son-in-law ['sʌninlɔ:] Schwieger-
sohn *m*.

sonnet ['sɔnit] Sonett *n*.

sonorous □ [sə'nɔ:rəs] klangvoll.

soon [su:n] bald; früh; gern; as
od. so ~ as sobald als od. wie; **~er**
['su:nə] eher; früher; lieber; no ~
... than kaum ... als; no ~ said than
done gesagt, getan.

soot [sut] 1. Ruß *m*; 2. verrußen.

sooth [su:θ]: in ~ in Wahrheit, für-
wahr; **~e** [su:ð] beruhigen; mildern; **~sayer** ['su:θseiə] Wahr-
sager(in).

sooty □ ['suti] rußig.

sop [sɔp] 1. eingeweichter Brocken;
fig. Bestechung *f*; 2. eintunken.

sophist|icate [sə'fistikeit] verdre-
hen; verfälschen; **~icated** kultiviert, raffiniert; intellektuell; bla-
siert; hochentwickelt, kompliziert;
~ry ['sɔfistri] Spitzfindigkeit *f*.

sophomore *Am.* ['sɔfəmɔ:] Student
m im zweiten Jahr.

soporific [soupə'rifik] 1. (~ally) einschläfernd; 2. Schlafmittel *n*.

sorcer|er ['sɔ:sərə] Zauberer *m*;
~ess [~ris] Zauberin *f*; Hexe *f*; **~y**
[~ri] Zauberei *f*.

sordid □ ['sɔ:did] schmutzig,
schäbig (*bsd. fig.*).

sore [sɔ:] 1. □ schlimm, entzündet;

wund; weh; empfindlich; ~ throat Halsweh n; 2. wunde Stelle; ~head Am. F ['sɔːhed] 1. mürrischer Mensch; 2. enttäuscht.

sorrel ['sɔrəl] 1. rötlichbraun (bsd. Pferd); 2. Fuchs m (Pferd).

sorrow ['sɔrou] 1. Sorge f; Kummer m, Leid n; Trauer f; 2. trauern; sich grämen; ~ful □ ['sɔrəful] traurig, betrübt; elend.

sorry □ ['sɔri] betrübt, bekümmert; traurig; (I am) (so) ~I es tut mir (sehr) leid; Verzeihung!; I am ~ for him er tut mir leid; we are ~ to say wir müssen leider sagen.

sort [sɔːt] 1. Sorte f, Art f; what ~ of was für; of a ~ of ~ F so was wie; ~ of F gewissermaßen; out of ~s F unpäßlich; verdrießlich; 2. sortieren; ~ out (aus)sondern.

sot [sɔt] Trunkenbold m.

sough [sau] 1. Sausen n; 2. rauschen.

sought [sɔːt] pret. u. p.p. von seek.

soul [soul] Seele f (a. fig.).

sound [saund] 1. □ allg. gesund; ganz; vernünftig; gründlich; fest; ✝ sicher; ♫ gültig; 2. Ton m, Schall m, Laut m, Klang m; ♪ Sonde f; Meerenge f; Fischblase f; 3. (er)tönen, (er)klingen; erschallen (lassen); sich gut etc. anhören; sondieren; ♫ loten; ♫ abhorchen; ~film ['saundfilm] Tonfilm m; ~ing ♫ [~diŋ] Lotung f; ~s pl. lotbare Wassertiefe; ~less □ [~dlis] lautlos; ~ness [~dnis] Gesundheit f; ~proof schalldicht; ~track Film: Tonspur f; ~wave Schallwelle f.

soup¹ [suːp] Suppe f.

soup² Am. sl. mot. [~] 1. Stärke f; 2. ~ up Motor frisieren.

sour ['sauə] 1. □ sauer; fig. bitter; mürrisch; 2. v/t. säuern; fig. ver-, erbittern; v/i. sauer (fig. bitter) werden.

source [sɔːs] Quelle f; Ursprung m.

sour|ish □ ['sauəriʃ] säuerlich; ~ness ['sauənis] Säure f; fig. Bitterkeit f.

souse [saus] eintauchen; (mit Wasser) begießen; Fisch etc. einlegen, einpökeln.

south [sauθ] 1. Süd(en m); 2. Süd...; südlich; ~east ['sauθ'iːst] 1. Südosten m; 2. a. ~eastern [sauθ-'iːstən] südöstlich.

souther|ly ['sʌðəli], ~n [~ən] südlich; Süd...; ~ner [~nə] Südländer(in), Am. Südstaatler(in).

southernmost ['sʌðənmoust] südlichst.

southpaw Am. ['sauθpɔː] Baseball: Linkshänder m.

southward(s) adv. ['sauθwəd(z)] südwärts, nach Süden.

south|-west ['sauθ'west] 1. Südwesten m; 2. südwestlich; ~wester [sauθ'westə] Südwestwind

m; ♫ Südwester m; ~westerly, ~western südwestlich.

souvenir ['suːvəniə] Andenken n.

sovereign ['sɔvrin] 1. □ höchst; unübertrefflich; unumschränkt; 2. Herrscher(in); Sovereign m (20-Schilling-Stück); ~ty [~rənti] Oberherrschaft f, Landeshoheit f.

soviet ['souviet] Sowjet m; attr. Sowjet...

sow¹ [sau] zo. Sau f, (Mutter-)Schwein n; ⊕ Sau f, Massel f.

sow² [sou] [irr.] (aus)säen, ausstreuen; besäen; ~n [soun] p.p. von sow².

spa [spaː] Heilbad n; Kurort m.

space [speis] 1. (Welt)Raum m; Zwischenraum m; Zeitraum m; 2. typ sperren; ~craft ['speiskraːft], ~ship Raumschiff n; ~suit Raumanzug m.

spacious □ ['speiʃəs] geräumig; weit, umfassend.

spade [speid] Spaten m; Kartenspiel Pik n.

span¹ [spæn] 1. Spanne f; Spannweite f; Am. Gespann n; 2. (um-, über)spannen; (aus)messen.

span² [~] pret. von spin 1.

spangle ['spæŋgl] 1. Flitter m; 2. (mit Flitter) besetzen; fig. übersäen.

Spaniard ['spænjəd] Spanier(in).

Spanish ['spæniʃ] 1. spanisch; 2. Spanisch n.

spank F [spæŋk] 1. verhauen; 2. Klaps m; ~ing ['spæŋkiŋ] 1. □ schnell, scharf; 2. F Haue f, Tracht f Prügel

spanner ⊕ ['spænə] Schraubenschlüssel m.

spar [spaː] 1. ♫ Spiere f; ✕ Holm m; 2. boxen; fig. sich streiten.

spare [speə] 1. □ spärlich, sparsam; mager, überzählig; überschüssig; Ersatz...; Reserve...; ~ hours Mußestunden f/pl.; ~ room Gastzimmer n; ~ time Freizeit f; 2. ⊕ Ersatzteil m, n; 3. (ver)schonen; erübrigen; entbehren; (übrig)haben für; (er)sparen; sparen mit.

sparing □ ['speəriŋ] sparsam.

spark [spaːk] 1. Funke(n) m; fig. flotter Kerl; Galan m; 2. Funken sprühen; ~(ing)-plug mot. ['spaːk(iŋ)plʌg] Zündkerze f.

sparkle ['spaːkl] 1. Funke(n) m; Funkeln n; fig. sprühendes Wesen; 2. funkeln; blitzen; schäumen; sparkling wine Schaumwein m.

sparrow orn. ['spærou] Sperling m, Spatz m; ~hawk orn. Sperber m.

sparse [spaːs] spärlich, dünn.

spasm ♪ ['spæzəm] Krampf m; ~odic(al □) ♪ [spæz'mɔdik(əl)] krampfhaft, -artig; fig. sprunghaft.

spat¹ [spæt] (Schuh)Gamasche f.

spat² [~] pret. u. p.p. von spit² 2.

spatter ['spætə] (be)spritzen.

spawn [spɔːn] **1.** Laich *m*; *fig.*
contp. Brut *f*; **2.** laichen; *fig.* aus-
hecken.

speak [spiːk] [*irr.*] *v/i.* sprechen;
reden; ~ *out*, ~ *up* laut sprechen;
offen reden; ~ *to j-n od.* mit *j-m*
sprechen; *v/t.* (aus)sprechen; äußern; **~easy** *Am. sl.* ['spiːkizi]
Flüsterkneipe *f* (*ohne Konzession*);
~er [~kə] Sprecher(in), Redner(in);
parl. Vorsitzende(r) *m*; **~ing-
trumpet** [~kiŋtrʌmpit] Sprachrohr *n*.

spear [spiə] **1.** Speer *m*, Spieß *m*;
Lanze *f*; **2.** (auf)spießen.

special ['speʃəl] **1.** ⌐ besonder;
Sonder...; speziell; Spezial...;
2. Hilfspolizist *m*; Sonderausgabe *f*;
Sonderzug *m*; *Am.* Sonderangebot
n; *Am.* (Tages)Spezialität *f*; **~ist**
[~list] Spezialist *m*; **~ity** [speʃiˈæliti]
Besonderheit *f*; Spezialfach *n*; †
Spezialität *f*; **~ize** ['speʃəlaiz] besonders anführen; (sich) speziali-
sieren; **~ty** [~lti] *s* speciality.

specie ['spiːʃiː] Metall-, Hartgeld *n*;
~s [~iːz] *pl. u. sg.* Art *f*, Spezies *f*.

speci|fic [spiˈsifik] (**~ally**) spezi-
fisch; besonder; bestimmt; **~fy**
['spesifai] spezifizieren, einzeln angeben; **~men** [~imin] Probe *f*,
Exemplar *n*.

specious ⌐ ['spiːʃəs] blendend, be-
stechend; trügerisch; Schein...

speck [spek] **1.** Fleck *m*; Stückchen
n; **2.** flecken; **~le** ['spekl] **1.** Fleck-
chen *n*; **2.** flecken, sprenkeln.

spectacle ['spektəkl] Schauspiel *n*;
Anblick *m*; (*a pair of*) **~s** *pl.* (eine)
Brille.

spectacular [spekˈtækjulə] **1.** ☐
eindrucksvoll; auffallend, spekta-
kulär; **2.** *Am.* F Galarevue *f*.

spectator [spekˈteitə] Zuschauer *m*.

spect|ral ['spektrəl] gespenstisch;
~re, *Am.* **~er** [~tə] Gespenst *n*.

speculat|e ['spekjuleit] grübeln,
nachsinnen; † spekulieren; **~ion**
[spekjuˈleiʃən] theoretische Betrachtung; Grübelei *f*; † Spekulation *f*; **~ive** ['spekjulətiv] grüb-
lerisch; theoretisch; † spekulie-
rend; **~or** [~leitə] Denker *m*; †
Spekulant *m*.

sped [sped] *pret. u. p.p. von* speed 2.

speech [spiːtʃ] Sprache *f*; Rede *f*;
Ansprache *f*; make a ~ e-e Rede
halten; **~day** ['spiːtʃdei] *Schule:*
(Jahres)Schlußfeier *f*; **~less** ☐
[~ʃlis] sprachlos.

speed [spiːd] **1.** Geschwindigkeit *f*;
Schnelligkeit *f*; Eile *f*; ⊕ Drehzahl
f; **2.** [*irr.*] *v/i.* schnell fahren, rasen;
~ *up* (*pret. u. p.p. ~ed*) die Geschwindigkeit erhöhen; *v/t.* j-m
Glück verleihen; befördern; ~ *up*
(*pret. u. p.p. ~ed*) beschleunigen;
~limit ['spiːdlimit] Geschwindig-
keitsbegrenzung *f*; **~ometer** *mot.*

[spiˈdɔmitə] Geschwindigkeitsmes-
ser *m*, Tachometer *n*; **~way** Motor-
radrennbahn *f*; *bsd. Am.* Schnell-
straße *f*; **~y** ☐ [~di] schnell.

spell [spel] **1.** (Arbeits)Zeit *f*, ⊕
Schicht *f*; Weilchen *n*; Zauber
(-spruch) *m*; **2.** abwechseln mit *j-m*;
[*irr.*] buchstabieren; richtig schreiben; bedeuten; **~binder** *Am.*
['spelbaində] fesselnder Redner;
~bound *fig.* (fest)gebannt; **~er**
bsd. Am. [~lə] Fibel *f*; **~ing** [~liŋ]
Rechtschreibung *f*; **~ing-book**
Fibel *f*.

spelt [spelt] *pret. u. p.p. von*
spell 2.

spend [spend] [*irr.*] verwenden;
(*Geld*) ausgeben; verbrauchen;
verschwenden; verbringen; ~ *o.s.*
sich erschöpfen; **~thrift** ['spend-
θrift] Verschwender *m*.

spent [spent] **1.** *pret. u. p.p. von*
spend; **2.** *adj.* erschöpft, matt.

sperm [spəːm] Same(n) *m*.

spher|e [sfiə] Kugel *f*; Erd-, Him-
melskugel *f*; *fig.* Sphäre *f*; (Wir-
kungs)Kreis *m*; Bereich *m*; *fig.*
Gebiet *n*; **~ical** ☐ ['sferikəl] sphä-
risch; kugelförmig.

spice [spais] **1.** Gewürz(e *pl.*) *n*; *fig.*
Würze *f*; Anflug *m*; **2.** würzen.

spick and span ['spikən'spæn]
frisch u. sauber; schmuck; funkel-
nagelneu.

spicy ☐ ['spaisi] würzig; pikant.

spider *zo.* ['spaidə] Spinne *f*.

spiel *Am. sl.* [spiːl] Gequassel *n*.

spigot ['spigət] (Faß)Zapfen *m*.

spike [spaik] **1.** Stift *m*; Spitze *f*;
Dorn *m*; Stachel *m*; *Sport:* Lauf-
dorn *m*; *mot.* Spike *m*; ♣ Ähre *f*;
2. festnageln; mit *eisernen* Stacheln
versehen.

spill [spil] **1.** [*irr.*] *v/t.* verschütten;
vergießen; F *Reiter etc.* abwerfen;
schleudern; *v/i.* überlaufen; **2.** F
Sturz *m*.

spilt [spilt] *pret. u. p.p. von* spill 1;
cry over ~ *milk* über et. jammern,
was doch nicht zu ändern ist.

spin [spin] **1.** [*irr.*] spinnen (*a.fig.*);
wirbeln; sich drehen; *Münze* hoch-
werfen; sich et. ausdenken; erzählen; ✗ trudeln; ~ *along* dahinsau-
sen; ~ *s.th. out* et. in die Länge
ziehen; **2.** Drehung *f*; Spritztour *f*;
✗ Trudeln *n*.

spinach ♣ ['spinidʒ] Spinat *m*.

spinal *anat.* ['spainl] Rückgrat...; ~
column Wirbelsäule *f*; ~ *cord*, ~
marrow Rückenmark *n*.

spindle ['spindl] Spindel *f*.

spin-drier ['spindraiə] Wäsche-
schleuder *f*.

spine [spain] *anat.* Rückgrat *n*;
Dorn *m*; (Gebirgs)Grat *m*; (Buch-)
Rücken *m*.

spinning|-mill ['spiniŋmil] Spin-
nerei *f*; **~wheel** Spinnrad *n*.

spinster ['spinstə] unverheiratete Frau; (alte) Jungfer.

spiny ['spaini] dornig.

spiral ['spaiərəl] 1. □ spiralig; ~ staircase Wendeltreppe f; 2. Spirale f; fig. Wirbel m.

spire ['spaiə] Turm-, Berg- etc. Spitze f; Kirchturm(spitze f) m.

spirit ['spirit] 1. allg. Geist m; Sinn m; Temperament n, Leben n; Mut m; Gesinnung f; Spiritus m; Sprit m, Benzin n; ~s pl. Spirituosen pl.; high (low) ~s pl. gehobene (gedrückte) Stimmung; ~ away od. off wegzaubern; ~ed □ geistvoll; temperamentvoll; mutig; ~less □ [~tlis] geistlos; temperamentlos; mutlos.

spiritual □ ['spiritjuəl] geistig; geistlich; geistvoll; ~ism [~lizəm] Spiritismus m.

spirituous ['spiritjuəs] alkoholisch.

spirt [spə:t] (hervor)spritzen.

spit¹ [spit] 1. Bratspieß m; Landzunge f; 2. aufspießen.

spit² [~] 1. Speichel m; F Ebenbild n; 2. [irr.] (aus)spucken; fauchen; sprühen (fein regnen).

spite [spait] 1. Bosheit f; Groll m; in ~ of trotz (gen.); 2. ärgern; kränken; ~ful □ ['spaitful] boshaft, gehässig.

spitfire ['spitfaiə] Hitzkopf m.

spittle ['spitl] Speichel m, Spucke f.

spittoon [spi'tu:n] Spucknapf m.

splash [splæʃ] 1. Spritzfleck m; P(l)atschen n; 2. (be)spritzen; p(l)atschen; planschen; (hin)klecksen.

splay [splei] 1. Ausschrägung f; 2. auswärts gebogen; 3. v/t. ausschrägen; v/i. ausgeschrägt sein; ~foot ['spleifut] Spreizfuß m.

spleen [spli:n] anat. Milz f; üble Laune, Ärger m.

splend|id □ ['splendid] glänzend, prächtig, herrlich; ~o(u)r [~də] Glanz m, Pracht f, Herrlichkeit f.

splice [splais] (ver)spleißen.

splint [splint] 1. Schiene f; 2. schienen; ~er ['splintə] 1. Splitter m; 2. (zer)splittern.

split [split] 1. Spalt m, Riß m; fig. Spaltung f; 2. gespalten; 3. [irr.] v/t. (zer)spalten; zerreißen; (sich) et. teilen; ~ hairs Haarspalterei treiben; ~ one's sides with laughter sich totlachen; v/i. sich spalten; platzen; ~ting ['spliting] heftig, rasend (Kopfschmerz).

splutter ['splʌtə] s. sputter.

spoil [spoil] 1. oft ~s pl. Beute f, Raub m; fig. Ausbeute f; Schutt m; ~s pl. pol. bsd. Am. Futterkrippe f; 2. [irr.] (be)rauben; plündern; verderben; verwöhnen; Kind verziehen; ~sman Am. pol. ['spoilzmən] Postenjäger m; ~sport Spielver-derber(in); ~s system Am. pol. Futterkrippensystem n.

spoilt [spoilt] pret. u. p.p. von spoil 2.

spoke [spouk] 1. pret. von speak; 2. Speiche f; (Leiter)Sprosse f; ~n ['spoukən] p.p. von speak; ~sman ['ksmən] Wortführer m.

sponge [spʌndʒ] 1. Schwamm m; 2. v/t. mit e-m Schwamm (ab)wischen; ~ up aufsaugen; v/i. schmarotzen; ~cake ['spʌndʒ'keik] Biskuitkuchen m; ~r F fig. [~dʒə] Schmarotzer(in).

spongy ['spʌndʒi] schwammig.

sponsor ['sponsə] 1. Pate m; Bürge m; Förderer m; Auftraggeber m für Werbesendungen; 2. Pate stehen bei; fördern; ~ship [~ʃip] Paten-, Gönnerschaft f.

spontane|ity [spontə'ni:iti] Freiwilligkeit f; eigener Antrieb; ~ous □ [spon'teinjəs] freiwillig, von selbst (entstanden); Selbst...; spontan; unwillkürlich; unvermittelt.

spook [spu:k] Spuk m; ~y ['spu:ki] geisterhaft, Spuk...

spool [spu:l] 1. Spule f; 2. spulen.

spoon [spu:n] 1. Löffel m; 2. löffeln; ~ful ['spu:nful] Löffelvoll m.

sporadic [spə'rædik] (~ally) sporadisch, verstreut.

spore ♦ [spɔ:] Spore f, Keimkorn n.

sport [spɔ:t] 1. Sport m; Spiel n; fig. Spielball m; Scherz m; sl. feiner Kerl; ~s pl. allg. Sport m; Sportfest n; 2. v/i. sich belustigen; spielen; v/t. F protzen mit; ~ive □ ['spɔ:tiv] lustig; scherzhaft; ~sman ['~tsmən] Sportler m.

spot [spot] 1. allg. Fleck m; Tupfen m; Makel m; Stelle f; ♂ Leberfleck m; ♂ Pickel m; Tropfen m; a ~ of F etwas; on the ~ auf der Stelle; sofort; 2. sofort liefer- od. zahlbar; 3. (be)flecken; ausfindig machen; erkennen; ~less □ ['spotlis] fleckenlos; ~light thea. Scheinwerfer (-licht n) m; ~ter [~tə] Beobachter m; Am. Kontrolleur m; ~ty [~ti] fleckig.

spouse [spauz] Gatte m; Gattin f.

spout [spaut] 1. Tülle f; Strahlrohr n; (Wasser)Strahl m; 2. (aus)spritzen; F salbadern.

sprain ♂ [sprein] 1. Verstauchung f; 2. verstauchen.

sprang [spræŋ] pret. von spring 2.

sprat ichth. [spræt] Sprotte f.

sprawl [sprɔ:l] sich rekeln, ausgestreckt daliegen; ♦ wuchern.

spray [sprei] 1. zerstäubte Flüssigkeit; Sprühregen m; Gischt m; Spray m, n; = sprayer; 2. zerstäuben; et. besprühen; ~er ['spreiə] Zerstäuber m.

spread [spred] 1. [irr.] v/t. a. ~ out ausbreiten; (aus)dehnen; verbreiten; belegen; Butter etc. aufstreichen; Brot etc. bestreichen; ~ the *table* den Tisch decken; *v/i.* sich aus- *od.* verbreiten; 2. Aus-, Verbreitung *f;* Spannweite *f;* Fläche *f; Am. Bett- etc.* Decke *f; Brot-*Aufstrich *m;* F Festschmaus *m.*

spree F [spri:] Spaß *m,* Jux *m;* Zechgelage *n;* Orgie *f; Kauf- etc.* Welle *f.*

sprig [sprig] Sproß *m,* Reis *n* (*a. fig.*); ⊕ Zwecke *f,* Stift *m.*

sprightly ['spraitli] lebhaft, munter.

spring [spriŋ] 1. Sprung *m,* Satz *m;* (Sprung)Feder *f;* Federkraft *f,* Elastizität *f;* Triebfeder *f;* Quelle *f; fig.* Ursprung *m;* Frühling *m;* 2. [*irr.*] *v/t.* springen lassen; (zer-)sprengen; *Wild* aufjagen; ∼ *a leak* ⚓ leck werden; ∼ *a surprise on s.o.* j-n überraschen; *v/i.* springen; entspringen; ⚘ sprießen; ∼ *up* aufkommen (*Ideen etc.*); ∼**board** ['spriŋbɔ:d] Sprungbrett *n;* ∼ **tide** Springflut *f;* ∼**tide,** ∼**time** Frühling(szeit *f*) *m;* ∼**y** □ [∼ŋi] federnd.

sprinkl|e ['spriŋkl] (be)streuen; (be)sprengen; ∼**er** [∼lə] Berieselungsanlage *f;* Rasensprenger *m;* ∼**ing** [∼liŋ] Sprühregen *m; a* ∼ *of* ein wenig, ein paar.

sprint [sprint] *Sport:* 1. sprinten; spurten; 2. Sprint *m;* Kurzstreckenlauf *m;* Endspurt *m;* ∼**er** ['sprintə] Sprinter *m,* Kurzstreckenläufer *m.*

sprite [sprait] Geist *m,* Kobold *m.*

sprout [spraut] 1. sprießen, wachsen (lassen); 2. ⚘ Sproß *m;* (*Brussels*) ∼*s pl.* Rosenkohl *m.*

spruce[1] □ [spru:s] schmuck, nett.

spruce[2] ⚘ [∼] *a.* ∼ *fir* Fichte *f,* Rottanne *f.*

sprung [sprʌŋ] *pret.* (⚘) *u. p.p. von* spring 2.

spry [sprai] munter, flink.

spun [spʌn] *pret. u. p.p. von* spin 1.

spur [spə:] 1. Sporn *m* (*a. zo.,* ⚘); *fig.* Ansporn *m;* Vorsprung *m,* Ausläufer *m e-s Berges; on the* ∼ *of the moment* der Eingebung des Augenblicks folgend; spornstreichs; 2. (an)spornen.

spurious □ ['spjuəriəs] unecht, gefälscht.

spurn [spə:n] verschmähen, verächtlich zurückweisen.

spurt [spə:t] 1. alle s-e Kräfte zs.-nehmen; *Sport* spurten; *s. spirt;* 2. plötzliche Anstrengung, Ruck *m; Sport:* Spurt *m.*

sputter ['spʌtə] 1. Gesprudel *n;* 2. (hervor)sprudeln; spritzen.

spy [spai] 1. Späher(in); Spion(in); 2. (er)spähen; erblicken; spionieren; ∼**glass** ['spaiglɑ:s] Fernglas *n;* ∼**hole** Guckloch *n.*

squabble ['skwɔbl] 1. Zank *m,* Kabbelei *f;* 2. (sich) zanken.

squad [skwɔd] Rotte *f,* Trupp *m;* ∼**ron** ['skwɔdrən] ✕ Schwadron *f;* ✕ Staffel *f;* ⚓ Geschwader *n.*

squalid □ ['skwɔlid] schmutzig, armselig.

squall [skwɔ:l] 1. ⚓ Bö *f;* Schrei *m;* ∼*s pl.* Geschrei *n;* 2. schreien.

squalor ['skwɔlə] Schmutz *m.*

squander ['skwɔndə] verschwenden.

square [skwɛə] 1. □ viereckig; quadratisch; rechtwinklig; eckig; passend, stimmend; in Ordnung; direkt; quitt, gleich; ehrlich, offen; F altmodisch, spießig; .. *measure* Flächenmaß *n;* ∼ *mile* Quadratmeile *f;* 2. Quadrat *n;* Viereck *n; Schach-*Feld *n; öffentlicher* Platz; Winkelmaß *n;* F altmodischer Spießer; 3. *v/t.* viereckig machen; einrichten (*with* nach), anpassen (*dat.*); ♦ be-, ausgleichen; *v/i.* passen (*with* zu); übereinstimmen; ∼**built** ['skwɛə'bilt] vierschrötig; ∼**dance** Quadrille *f;* ∼**toes** *sg.* F Pedant *m.*

squash[1] [skwɔʃ] 1. Gedränge *n;* Fruchtsaft *m;* Platsch(en *n*) *m;* Rakettspiel *n;* 2. (zer-, zs.-)quetschen; drücken.

squash[2] ⚘ [∼] Kürbis *m.*

squat [skwɔt] 1. kauernd; untersetzt; 2. hocken, kauern; ∼**ter** ['skwɔtə] *Am.* Schwarzsiedler *m; Australien:* Schafzüchter *m.*

squawk [skwɔ:k] 1. kreischen, schreien; 2. Gekreisch *n,* Geschrei *n.*

squeak [skwi:k] quieken, quietschen.

squeal [skwi:l] quäken; gell schreien; quieken.

squeamish □ ['skwi:miʃ] empfindlich; mäkelig; heikel; penibel.

squeeze [skwi:z] 1. (sich) drücken, (sich) quetschen; auspressen; *fig.* (be)drängen; 2. Druck *m;* Gedränge *n;* ∼**r** ['skwi:zə] Presse *f.*

squelch F [skweltʃ] zermalmen.

squid *zo.* [skwid] Tintenfisch *m.*

squint [skwint] schielen; blinzeln.

squire ['skwaiə] 1. Gutsbesitzer *m;* (Land)Junker *m; Am.* F (Friedens-)Richter *m;* 2. *e-e Dame* begleiten.

squirm F [skwə:m] sich winden.

squirrel *zo.* ['skwirəl, *Am.* 'skwə:rəl] Eichhörnchen *n.*

squirt [skwə:t] 1. Spritze *f;* Strahl *m;* F Wichtigtuer *m;* 2. spritzen.

stab [stæb] 1. Stich *m;* 2. *v/t.* (er)stechen; *v/i.* stechen (*at* nach).

stabili|ty [stə'biliti] Stabilität *f;* Standfestig-, Beständigkeit *f;* ∼**ze** ['steibilaiz] stabilisieren (*a.* ✈).

stable[1] □ ['steibl] stabil, fest.

stable[2] [∼] 1. Stall *m;* 2. einstallen.

stack [stæk] 1. ∕ (Heu-, Stroh-, Getreide)Schober *m;* Stapel *m;* Schornstein(reihe *f*) *m;* Regal *n;* ∼*s pl. Am.* Hauptmagazin *n e-r*

Bibliothek; F Haufen *m;* 2. aufstapeln.

stadium ['steidjəm] *Sport:* Stadion *n;* Sportplatz *m;* Kampfbahn *f.*

staff [staːf] 1. Stab *m* (*a.* ✕); Stock *m;* Stütze *f;* ♪ Notensystem *n;* Personal *n;* Belegschaft *f;* Beamten-, Lehrkörper *m;* 2. (mit Personal, Beamten *od.* Lehrern) besetzen.

stag *zo.* [stæg] Hirsch *m.*

stage [steidʒ] 1. Bühne *f,* Theater *n; fig.* Schauplatz *m;* Stufe *f,* Stadium *n;* Teilstrecke *f,* Etappe *f;* Haltestelle *f;* Gerüst *n,* Gestell *n;* 2. inszenieren; **~coach** ['steidʒkoutʃ] Postkutsche *f;* **~craft** dramatisches Talent; Theatererfahrung *f;* **~direction** Bühnenanweisung *f;* **~fright** Lampenfieber *n;* **~manager** Regisseur *m.*

stagger ['stægə] 1. *v/i.* (sch)wanken, taumeln; *fig.* stutzen; *v/t.* ins Wanken bringen; staffeln; 2. Schwanken *n;* Staffelung *f.*

stagna|nt ['stægnənt] stehend (*Wasser*); stagnierend; stockend; träg; ♱ still; **~te** [~neit] stocken.

staid [steid] gesetzt, ruhig.

stain [stein] 1. Fleck(en) *m* (*a. fig.*); Beize *f;* 2. fleckig machen; *fig.* beflecken; beizen, färben; **~ed glass** buntes Glas; **~less** ['steinlis] ungefleckt; *fig.* fleckenlos; rostfrei.

stair [steə] Stufe *f;* **~s** *pl.* Treppe *f,* Stiege *f;* **~case** ['steəkeis], **~way** Treppe(nhaus *n*) *f.*

stake [steik] 1. Pfahl *m;* Marterpfahl *m;* (Spiel)Einsatz *m* (*a. fig.*); **~s** *pl.* Pferderennen: Preis *m;* Rennen *n; pull up* **~s** *Am.* F abhauen; *be at* **~** auf dem Spiel stehen; 2. (um)pfählen; aufs Spiel setzen; **~ out,** **~ off** abstecken.

stale □ [steil] alt; schal, abgestanden; verbraucht (*Luft*); fad.

stalk [stɔːk] 1. Stengel *m,* Stiel *m;* Halm *m; hunt.* Pirsch *f;* 2. *v/i.* einherstolzieren; heranschleichen; *hunt.* pirschen; *v/t.* beschleichen.

stall [stɔːl] 1. (Pferde)Box *f;* (Verkaufs)Stand *m,* Marktbude *f; thea.* Sperrsitz *m;* 2. *v/t.* einstallen; *Motor* abwürgen; *v/i. mot.* aussetzen.

stallion ['stæljən] Hengst *m.*

stalwart □ ['stɔːlwət] stramm, stark.

stamina ['stæminə] Ausdauer *f.*

stammer ['stæmə] 1. stottern, stammeln; 2. Stottern *n.*

stamp [stæmp] 1. (Auf)Stampfen *n;* ⊕ Stampfe(r *m*) *f;* Stempel *m* (*a. fig.*); (Brief)Marke *f;* Gepräge *n;* Art *f;* 2. (auf)stampfen; prägen; stanzen; (ab)stempeln (*a. fig.*); frankieren.

stampede [stæm'piːd] 1. Panik *f,* wilde Flucht; 2. *v/i.* durchgehen; *v/t.* in Panik versetzen.

stanch [staːntʃ] 1. hemmen; stillen; 2. □ fest; zuverlässig; treu.

stand [stænd] 1. [*irr.*] *v/i. allg.* stehen; sich befinden; beharren; *mst* **~ still** stillstehen, stehenbleiben; bestehen (bleiben); **~** *against j-m* widerstehen; **~** *aside* beiseite treten; **~** *back* zurücktreten; **~** *by* dabeistehen; *fig.* (fest) stehen zu; helfen; bereitstehen; **~** *for* kandidieren für; bedeuten; eintreten für; F sich *et.* gefallen lassen; **~** *in* einspringen; *in with* sich gut stellen mit; **~** *off* zurücktreten (von); **~** *off!* weg da!; **~** *on* (*fig.* be)stehen auf; **~** *out* hervorstehen; sich abheben (*against* gegen); standhalten (*dat.*); **~** *over* stehen *od.* liegen bleiben; **~** *pat Am.* F stur bleiben; **~** *to* bleiben bei; **~** *up* aufstehen; sich erheben; **~** *up for* eintreten für; **~** *up to* sich zur Wehr setzen gegen; standhalten (*dat.*); **~** *upon* (*fig.* be)stehen auf (*dat.*); *v/t.* (hin)stellen; aushalten, (v)ertragen; über sich ergehen lassen; F spendieren; 2. Stand *m;* Standplatz *m;* Bude *f;* Standpunkt *m;* Stillstand *m;* Ständer *m;* Tribüne *f; bsd. Am.* Zeugenstand *m; make a od. one's* **~** *against* standhalten (*dat.*).

standard ['stændəd] 1. Standarte *f,* Fahne *f;* Standard *m,* Norm *f,* Regel *f;* Maßstab *m;* Niveau *n;* Stufe *f;* Münzfuß *m;* Währung *f;* Ständer *m,* Mast *m;* 2. maßgebend; Normal...; **~ize** [~daiz] norm(ier)en.

stand-by ['stændbai] Beistand *m.*

standee [stæn'diː] Stehende(r) *m; Am.* Stehplatzinhaber *m.*

standing ['stændiŋ] 1. □ stehend; fest; (be)ständig; **~** *orders pl. parl.* Geschäftsordnung *f;* 2. Stellung *f,* Rang *m,* Ruf *m;* Dauer *f; of long* **~** alt; **~room** Stehplatz *m.*

stand|off *Am.* ['stændɔf] Unentschieden *n;* Dünkel *m;* **~offish** [~d'ɔːfiʃ] zurückhaltend; **~patter** *Am. pol.* [stænd'pætə] sturer Konservativer; **~point** ['stændpoint] Standpunkt *m;* **~still** Stillstand *m;* **~up:** **~** *collar* Stehkragen *m.*

stank [stæŋk] *pret. von* stink 2.

stanza ['stænzə] Stanze *f;* Strophe *f.*

staple[1] ['steipl] Hauptterzeugnis *n,* Hauptgegenstand *m; attr.* Haupt...

staple[2] [~] Krampe *f;* Heftklammer *f.*

star [staː] 1. Stern *m; thea.* Star *m;* **~s** *and Stripes pl. Am.* Sternenbanner *n;* 2. mit Sternen schmücken; *thea., fig.* die Hauptrolle spielen.

starboard ♄ ['staːbəd] 1. Steuerbord *n;* 2. *Ruder* steuerbord legen.

starch [staːtʃ] 1. (Wäsche)Stärke *f; fig.* Steifheit *f;* 2. stärken.

stare [steə] 1. Starren *n;* Staunen *n;* starrer Blick; 2. starren, staunen.

stark [stɑːk] **1.** *adj.* starr; bar, völlig (*Unsinn*); **2.** *adv.* völlig.
starlight ['stɑːlait] Sternenlicht *n.*
starling *orn.* ['stɑːliŋ] Star *m.*
starlit ['stɑːlit] sternenklar.
star|ry ['stɑːri] Stern(en)...; gestirnt; **~-spangled** ['stɑːspæŋgld] sternenbesät; ♀ *Banner Am.* Sternenbanner *n.*
start [stɑːt] **1.** Auffahren *n*, Stutzen *n*; Ruck *m*; *Sport:* Start *m*; Aufbruch *m*; Anfang *m*; *fig.* Vorsprung *m*; get the ~ of s.o. j-m zuvorkommen; **2.** *v/i.* aufspringen, auffahren; stutzen; *Sport:* starten; abfahren; aufbrechen; *mot.* anspringen; anfangen (*on* mit; *doing* zu tun); *v/t.* in Gang bringen; *mot.* anlassen; *Sport:* starten (lassen); aufjagen; *fig.* anfangen; veranlassen (*doing* zu tun); **~er** ['stɑːtə] *Sport:* Starter *m*; Läufer *m*; *mot.* Anlasser *m.*
startl|e ['stɑːtl] (er-, auf)schrecken; **~ing** [.liŋ] bestürzend, überraschend, aufsehenerregend.
starv|ation [stɑː'veiʃən] (Ver)Hungern *n*, Hungertod *m*; *attr.* Hunger...; **~e** [stɑːv] verhungern (lassen); *fig.* verkümmern (lassen).
state [steit] **1.** Zustand *m*; Stand *m*; Staat *m*; *pol. mst* ♀ Staat *m*; *attr.* Staats...; *in ~* feierlich; **2.** angeben; darlegen, darstellen; feststellen; melden; *Regel etc.* aufstellen; ~ **Department** *Am. pol.* Außenministerium *n*; **~ly** ['steitli] stattlich; würdevoll; erhaben; **~ment** [.tmənt] Angabe *f*; Aussage *f*; Darstellung *f*; Feststellung *f*; Aufstellung *f*; ♱ (~ *of account* Konto-) Auszug *m*; **~room** Staatszimmer *n*; ♣ Einzelkabine *f*; **~side** *Am.* F **1.** *adj.* USA-..., Heimat...; **2.** *adv.* go ~ heimkehren; **~sman** [.smən] Staatsmann *m.*
static ['stætik] statisch, Ruhe...
station ['steiʃən] **1.** Stand(ort) *m*; Stelle *f*; Stellung *f*; ⚔, ♣, ⚒ Station *f*; Bahnhof *m*; Rang *m*, Stand *m*; **2.** aufstellen, postieren, stationieren; **~ary** ☐ [.ʃnəri] stillstehend; feststehend; **~ery** [.] Schreibwaren *f/pl.*; **~-master** ♣ Stationsvorsteher *m*; **~ wagon** *Am. mot.* Kombiwagen *m.*
statistics [stə'tistiks] *pl.* Statistik *f.*
statu|ary ['stætjuəri] Bildhauer(-kunst *f*) *m*; **~e** [.juː] Standbild *n*, Plastik *f*, Statue *f.*
stature ['stætʃə] Statur *f*, Wuchs *m.*
status ['steitəs] Zustand *m*; Stand *m.*
statute ['stætjuːt] Statut *n*, Satzung *f*; (Landes)Gesetz *n.*
staunch [stɔːntʃ] *s.* **stanch.**
stave [steiv] **1.** Faßdaube *f*; Strophe *f*; **2.** [*irr.*] *mst ~ in* ein Loch schlagen in (*acc.*); ~ *off* abwehren.
stay [stei] **1.** ♣ Stag *n*; ⊕ Strebe *f*;

Stütze *f*; Aufschub *m*; Aufenthalt *m*; **~s** *pl.* Korsett *n*; **2.** bleiben; wohnen; (sich) aufhalten; Ausdauer haben; hemmen; aufschieben; *Hunger* vorläufig stillen; stützen; **~er** [steiə] *Sport:* Steher *m.*
stead [sted] Stelle *f*, Statt *f*; **~fast** ☐ ['stedfəst] fest, unerschütterlich; standhaft; unverwandt (*Blick*).
steady ['stedi] **1.** ☐ (be)ständig; stetig; sicher; fest; ruhig; gleichmäßig; unerschütterlich; zuverlässig; **2.** stetig *od.* sicher machen *od.* werden; (sich) festigen; stützen; (sich) beruhigen; **3.** *Am.* F feste Freundin, fester Freund.
steal [stiːl] **1.** [*irr.*] *v/t.* stehlen (*a. fig.*); *v/i.* sich stehlen *od.* schleichen; **2.** *Am.* Diebstahl *m.*
stealth [stelθ] Heimlichkeit *f*; *by ~* heimlich; **~y** ☐ ['stelθi] verstohlen.
steam [stiːm] **1.** Dampf *m*; Dunst *m*; *attr.* Dampf...; **2.** *v/i.* dampfen; ~ *up* beschlagen (*Glas*); *v/t.* ausdünsten; dämpfen; **~er** ♣ ['stiːmə] Dampfer *m*; **~y** ☐ [.mi] dampfig; dampfend; dunstig.
steel [stiːl] **1.** Stahl *m*; **2.** stählern; Stahl...; **3.** (ver)stählen.
steep [stiːp] **1.** steil, jäh; F toll; **2.** einweichen; einlegen; eintauchen; tränken; *fig.* versenken.
steeple ['stiːpl] Kirchturm *m*; **~-chase** *Sport:* Hindernisrennen *n.*
steer¹ [stiə] junger Ochse.
steer² [.] steuern; **~age** ♣ ['stiəridʒ] Steuerung *f*; Zwischendeck *n*; **~ing-wheel** [.riŋwiːl] Steuerrad *n*; *mot.* Lenkrad *n*; **~sman** ♣ [.əzmən] Rudergänger *m.*
stem [stem] **1.** (Baum-, Wort-) Stamm *m*; Stiel *m*; Stengel *m*; ♣ Vordersteven *m*; **2.** *Am.* (ab)stammen (*from* von); sich stemmen gegen, ankämpfen gegen.
stench [stentʃ] Gestank *m.*
stencil ['stensl] Schablone *f*; *typ.* Matrize *f.* [graph(in).]
stenographer [ste'nɔgrəfə] Steno-
step¹ [step] **1.** Schritt *m*, Tritt *m*; *fig.* Strecke *f*; Fußstapfe *f* (Treppen)Stufe *f*; Trittbrett *n*; **~s** *pl.* Trittleiter *f*; **2.** *v/i.* schreiten; treten, gehen; ~ *out* ausschreiten; *v/t.* ~ *off*, ~ *out* abschreiten; ~ *up* ankurbeln.
step² [.] *in Zssgn* Stief...; **~father** ['stepfɑːðə] Stiefvater *m*; **~mother** Stiefmutter *f.*
steppe [step] Steppe *f.*
stepping-stone *fig.* ['stepiŋstoun] Sprungbrett *n.*
steril|e ['sterail] unfruchtbar; steril; **~ity** [ste'riliti] Sterilität *f*; **~ize** ['sterilaiz] sterilisieren.
sterling ['stəːliŋ] vollwertig, echt; gediegen; ♱ Sterling *m* (*Währung*).
stern [stəːn] **1.** ☐ ernst; finster, streng, hart; **2.** ♣ Heck *n*; **~ness**

['stə:nnis] Ernst *m*; Strenge *f*; **∼-post** ⚓ Hintersteven *m*.

stevedore ⚓ ['sti:vidɔ:] Stauer *m*.

stew [stju:] **1.** schmoren, dämpfen; **2.** Schmorgericht *n*; F Aufregung *f*.

steward [stjuəd] Verwalter *m*; ⚓, ⚔ Steward *m*; (Fest)Ordner *m*; **∼ess** ⚓, ⚔ ['stjuədis] Stewardeß *f*.

stick [stik] **1.** Stock *m*; Stecken *m*; Stab *m*; (Besen- *etc.*)Stiel *m*; Stange *f*; F Klotz *m* (*unbeholfener Mensch*); **∼s** *pl.* Kleinholz *n*; the **∼s** *pl. Am.* F die hinterste Provinz; **2.** [*irr.*] *v/i.* stecken (bleiben); haften; kleben (*to an dat.*); **∼** *at nothing* vor nichts zurückscheuen; **∼** *out*, **∼** *up* hervorstehen; F abstehen; **∼** *to* bleiben bei; *v/t.* (ab)stechen; (an)stecken; (an)heften; (an)kleben; F ertragen; **∼ing-plaster** ['stikiŋplɑ:stə] Heftpflaster *n*.

sticky ☐ ['stiki] kleb(e)rig; zäh.

stiff ☐ [stif] steif; starr; hart; fest; mühsam; stark (*Getränk*); *be bored* **∼** F zu Tode gelangweilt sein; *keep a* **∼** *upper lip* die Ohren steifhalten; **∼en** ['stifn] (sich) (ver)steifen; **∼-necked** [∼'nekt] halsstarrig.

stifle ['staifl] ersticken (*a. fig.*).

stigma ['stigmə] (Brand-, Schand-) Mal *n*; Stigma *n*; **∼tize** [∼ətaiz] brandmarken.

stile [stail] Zauntritt *m*, Zaunübergang *m*.

still [stil] **1.** *adj.* still; **2.** *adv.* noch (immer); **3.** *cj.* doch, dennoch; **4.** stillen; beruhigen; **5.** Destillierapparat *m*; **∼-born** ['stilbɔ:n] totgeboren; **∼ life** Stilleben *n*; **∼ness** Stille *f*, Ruhe *f*.

stilt [stilt] Stelze *f*; **∼ed** ['stiltid] gespreizt, hochtrabend, geschraubt.

stimul|ant ['stimjulənt] **1.** ⚕ stimulierend; **2.** ⚕ Reizmittel *n*; Genußmittel *n*; Anreiz *m*; **∼ate** [∼leit] (an)reizen; anregen; **∼ation** [stimju-'leiʃən] Reizung *f*, Antrieb *m*; **∼us** ['stimjuləs] Antrieb *m*; Reizmittel *n*.

sting [stiŋ] **1.** Stachel *m*; Stich *m*; Biß *m*; *fig.* Schärfe *f*; Antrieb *m*; **2.** [*irr.*] stechen; brennen; schmerzen; (an)treiben.

sting|iness ['stindʒinis] Geiz *m*; **∼y** ☐ ['stindʒi] geizig; knapp, karg.

stink [stiŋk] **1.** Gestank *m*; **2.** [*irr.*] *v/i.* stinken; *v/t.* verstänkern.

stint [stint] **1.** Einschränkung *f*; Arbeit *f*; **2.** knausern mit; einschränken; *j-n* knapp halten.

stipend ['staipend] Gehalt *n*.

stipulat|e ['stipjuleit] *a.* **∼** *for* ausbedingen, ausmachen, vereinbaren; **∼ion** [stipju'leiʃən] Abmachung *f*; Klausel *f*, Bedingung *f*.

stir [stə:] **1.** Regung *f*; Bewegung *f*; Rühren *n*; Aufregung *f*; Aufsehen *n*; **2.** (sich) rühren; umrühren, bewegen; aufregen; **∼** *up* aufrühren; aufrütteln.

stirrup ['stirəp] Steigbügel *m*.

stitch [stitʃ] **1.** Stich *m*; Masche *f*; Seitenstechen *n*; **2.** nähen; heften.

stock [stɔk] **1.** (Baum)Strunk *m*; Pfropfunterlage *f*; Griff *m*, Kolben *m* *e-s Gewehrs*; Stamm *m*, Herkunft *f*; Rohstoff *m*; (Fleisch-, Gemüse)Brühe *f*; Vorrat *m*, (Waren)Lager *n*; (Wissens)Schatz *m*; *a. live∼* Vieh(bestand *m*) *n*; ⚓ Stammkapital *n*; Anleihekapital *n*; **∼s** *pl.* Effekten *pl.*; Aktien *f/pl.*; Staatspapiere *n/pl.*; **∼s** *pl.* ⚓ Stapel *m*; *in* (*out of*) **∼** (nicht) vorrätig; *take* **∼** F Inventur machen; *take* **∼** *of fig.* sich klarwerden über (*acc.*); **2.** vorrätig; ständig; gängig; Standard...; **3.** versorgen; *Waren* führen; ⊕ vorrätig haben.

stockade [stɔ'keid] Staket *n*.

stock|-breeder ['stɔkbri:də] Viehzüchter *m*; **∼broker** ⊕ Börsenmakler *m*; **∼ exchange** ⊕ Börse *f*; **∼-farmer** Viehzüchter *m*; **∼holder** ⊕ Aktionär(in).

stockinet [stɔki'net] Trikot *n*.

stocking ['stɔkiŋ] Strumpf *m*.

stock|jobber ⊕ ['stɔkdʒɔbə] Börsenmakler *m*; **∼-market** ⊕ Börse *f*; **∼still** unbeweglich; **∼taking** Inventur *f*; **∼y** ['stɔki] stämmig.

stog|ie, ∼y *Am.* ['stougi] billige Zigarre.

stoic ['stouik] **1.** stoisch; **2.** Stoiker *m*.

stoker ['stoukə] Heizer *m*.

stole [stoul] *pret. von* steal 1; **∼n** ['stoulən] *p.p. von* steal 1.

stolid ☐ ['stɔlid] schwerfällig; gleichmütig; stur.

stomach ['stʌmək] **1.** Magen *m*; Leib *m*, Bauch *m*; *fig.* Lust *f*; **2.** verdauen, vertragen; *fig.* ertragen.

stomp *Am.* [stɔmp] (auf)stampfen.

stone [stoun] **1.** Stein *m*; (Obst-) Kern *m*; *Gewichtseinheit von 6,35 kg*; **2.** steinern; Stein...; **3.** steinigen; entsteinen; **∼-blind** ['stoun'blaind] stockblind; **∼-dead** mausetot; **∼ware** [∼nwɛə] Steingut *n*.

stony ['stouni] steinig; *fig.* steinern.

stood [stud] *pret. u. p.p. von* stand 1.

stool [stu:l] Schemel *m*; ⚕ Stuhlgang *m*; **∼-pigeon** *Am.* ⚕ ['stu:l-pidʒin] Lockvogel *m*; Spitzel *m*.

stoop [stu:p] **1.** *v/i.* sich bücken; sich erniedrigen *od.* herablassen; krumm gehen; *v/t.* neigen; **2.** gebeugte Haltung; *Am.* Veranda *f*.

stop [stɔp] **1.** *v/t.* anhalten; hindern; aufhören; *a.* **∼** *up* (ver)stopfen; *Zahn* plombieren; (ver)sperren; *Zahlung* einstellen; *Lohn* einbehalten; *v/i.* stehenbleiben; aufhören; halten; F bleiben; **∼** *dead*, **∼** *short* plötzlich anhalten; **∼** *over* haltmachen; **2.** (Ein)Halt *m*; Pause *f*; Hemmung *f*; ⊕ Anschlag *m*; Aufhören *n*, Ende *n*; Haltestelle *f*; *mst* *full* ~ *gr.* Punkt *m*; ~**gap** ['stɔpgæp] Notbehelf *m*; ~**page** [‿pidʒ] Verstopfung *f*; (Zahlungs- *etc.*)Einstellung *f*; Sperrung *f*; (Lohn)Abzug *m*; Aufenthalt *m*; ⊕ Hemmung *f*; Betriebsstörung *f*; (Verkehrs-) Stockung *f*; ~**per** [‿pə] Stöpsel *m*; ~**ping** ✠ [‿piŋ] Plombe *f*.

storage ['stɔːridʒ] Lagerung *f*, Aufbewahrung *f*; Lagergeld *n*.

store [stɔː] 1. Vorrat *m*; *fig.* Fülle *f*; Lagerhaus *n*; *Am.* Laden *m*; ~**s** *pl.* Kauf-, Warenhaus *n*; *in* ~ vorrätig, auf Lager; 2. *a.* ~ *up* (auf)speichern; (ein)lagern; versorgen; ~**house** Lagerhaus *n*; *fig.* Schatzkammer *f*; ~**keeper** Lagerverwalter *m*; *Am.* Ladenbesitzer *m*.

stor(e)y ['stɔːri] Stock(werk *n*) *m*.

storeyed ['stɔːrid] mit ... Stockwerken, ...stöckig.

storied [‿] *s.* storeyed.

stork [stɔːk] Storch *m*.

storm [stɔːm] 1. Sturm *m*; Gewitter *n*; 2. stürmen; toben; ~**y** ['stɔːmi] stürmisch.

story ['stɔːri] Geschichte *f*; Erzählung *f*; Märchen *n*; *thea.* Handlung *f*; F Lüge *f*; *short* ~ Kurzgeschichte *f*.

stout [staut] 1. □ stark, kräftig; derb; dick; tapfer; 2. Starkbier *n*.

stove [stouv] 1. Ofen *m*; Herd *m*; 2. *pret. u. p.p. von* stave 2.

stow [stou] (ver)stauen, packen; ~**away** ⚓ ['stouəwei] blinder Passagier.

straddle ['strædl] (die Beine) spreizen; rittlings sitzen auf (*dat.*); *Am.* *fig.* es mit beiden Parteien halten; schwanken.

straggle ['strægl] verstreut *od.* einzeln liegen; umherstreifen; bummeln; *fig.* abschweifen; ⚘ wuchern; ~**ing** □ [‿liŋ] weitläufig, lose.

straight [streit] 1. *adj.* gerade; *fig.* aufrichtig, ehrlich; glatt (*Haar*); *Am.* pur, unverdünnt; *Am. pol.* hundertprozentig; *put* ~ in Ordnung bringen; 2. *adv.* gerade(wegs); geradeaus; direkt; sofort; ~ *away* sofort; ~ *out* rundheraus; ~**en** ['streitn] gerade machen *od.* werden; ~ *out* in Ordnung bringen; ~**forward** □ [streit'fɔːwəd] gerade; ehrlich, redlich.

strain [strein] 1. Abstammung *f*; Art *f*; ⊕ Spannung *f*; (Über)Anstrengung *f*; starke Inanspruchnahme (*on gen.*); Druck *m*; ✠ Zerrung *f*; Ton *m*; *mst* ~**s** *pl.* ♪ Weise *f*; Hang *m* (*of zu*); 2. *v/t.* (an)spannen; (über)anstrengen; überspannen; ⊕ beanspruchen; ✠ zerren; durchseihen; *v/i.* sich spannen; sich anstrengen; sich abmühen (*after um*); zerren (*at an dat.*); ~**er** ['streinə] Durchschlag *m*; Filter *m*; Sieb *n*.

strait [streit] (*in Eigennamen* ~**s** *pl.*)

Meerenge *f*, Straße *f*; ~**s** *pl.* Not (-lage) *f*; ~ *jacket* Zwangsjacke *f*; ~**ened** ['streitnd] dürftig; in Not.

strand [strænd] 1. Strand *m*; Strähne *f* (*a. fig.*); 2. auf den Strand setzen; *fig.* stranden (lassen).

strange □ [streindʒ] fremd (*a. fig.*); seltsam; ~**r** ['streindʒə] Fremde(r) *m*.

strangle ['stræŋgl] erwürgen.

strap [stræp] 1. Riemen *m*; Gurt *m*; Band *n*; 2. an-, festschnallen; mit Riemen peitschen. [List *f*.]

stratagem ['strætidʒəm] (Kriegs-)

strateg|ic [strə'tiːdʒik] (~**ally**) strategisch; ~**y** ['strætidʒi] Kriegskunst *f*, Strategie *f*.

strat|um *geol.* ['straːtəm], *pl.* ~**a** [‿ə] Schicht *f* (*a. fig.*), Lage *f*.

straw [strɔː] 1. Stroh(halm *m*) *n*; 2. Stroh...; ~ *vote Am.* Probeabstimmung *f*; ~**berry** ['strɔːbəri] Erdbeere *f*.

stray [strei] 1. irregehen; sich verirren; abirren; umherschweifen; 2. *a.* ~**ed** verirrt; vereinzelt; 3. verirrtes Tier.

streak [striːk] 1. Strich *m*, Streifen *m*; *fig.* Ader *f*, Spur *f*; kurze Periode; ~ *of lightning* Blitzstrahl *m*; 2. streifen; jagen, F flitzen.

stream [striːm] 1. Bach *m*; Strom *m*; Strömung *f*; 2. *v/i.* strömen; triefen; flattern; *v/t.* strömen lassen; ausströmen; ~**er** ['striːmə] Wimpel *m*; (fliegendes) Band; Lichtstrahl *m*; *typ.* Schlagzeile *f*.

street [striːt] Straße *f*; ~**car** *Am.* ['striːtkaː] Straßenbahn(wagen *m*) *f*.

strength [streŋθ] Stärke *f*, Kraft *f*; *on the* ~ *of* auf ... hin, auf Grund (*gen.*); ~**en** ['streŋθən] *v/t.* stärken; kräftigen; bestärken; *v/i.* erstarken.

strenuous □ ['strenjuəs] rührig, emsig; eifrig; anstrengend.

stress [stres] 1. Druck *m*; Nachdruck *m*; Betonung *f* (*a. gr.*); *fig.* Schwergewicht *n*; Ton *m*; *psych.* Stress *m*; 2. betonen.

stretch [stretʃ] 1. *v/t.* strecken; (aus)dehnen; *mst* ~ *out* ausstrecken; (an)spannen; *fig.* überspannen; *Gesetz* zu weit auslegen; *v/i.* sich (er-)strecken; sich dehnen (lassen); 2. Strecken *n*; Dehnung *f*; (An-) Spannung *f*; Übertreibung *f*, Überschreitung *f*; Strecke *f*, Fläche *f*; ~**er** ['stretʃə] Tragbahre *f*; Streckvorrichtung *f*.

strew [struː] [*irr.*] (be)streuen; ~**n** [‿uːn] *p.p. von* strew.

stricken ['strikən] 1. *p.p. von* strike 2; 2. *adj.* ge-, betroffen.

strict [strikt] streng; genau; ~**ly** *speaking* strenggenommen; ~**ness** ['striktnis] Genauigkeit *f*; Strenge *f*.

stridden ['stridn] *p.p. von* stride 1.

stride [straid] 1. [*irr.*] *v/t.* über-, durchschreiten; 2. (weiter) Schritt.

strident □ ['straidnt] kreischend.

strife [straif] Streit *m*, Hader *m*.

strike [straik] 1. Streik *m*; (Öl-, Erz)Fund *m*; *fig.* Treffer *m*; ✗ (Luft)Angriff *m* auf *ein Einzelziel*; *Am. Baseball:* Verlustpunkt *m*; be on ~ streiken; 2. [*irr.*] *v/t.* treffen, stoßen; schlagen; gegen *od.* auf (*acc.*) schlagen *od.* stoßen; stoßen *od.* treffen auf (*acc.*); *Flagge etc.* streichen; *Ton* anschlagen; auffallen (*dat.*); ergreifen; *Handel* abschließen; *Streichholz, Licht* anzünden; *Wurzel* schlagen; *Pose* annehmen; *Bilanz* ziehen; ~ up ♩ anstimmen; *Freundschaft* schließen; *v/i.* schlagen; ⚓ auf Grund stoßen; streiken; ~ home (richtig) treffen; ~r ['straikə] Streikende(r) *m*.

striking □ ['straikiŋ] Schlag...; auffallend; eindrucksvoll; treffend.

string [striŋ] 1. Schnur *f*; Bindfaden *m*; Band *n*; *Am.* F Bedingung *f*; (Bogen)Sehne *f*; ♩ Faser *f*; ♩ Saite *f*; Reihe *f*, Kette *f*; ~s *pl.* ♩ Saiteninstrumente *n/pl.*, Streicher *m/pl.*; pull the ~s der Drahtzieher sein; 2. [*irr.*] spannen; aufreihen; besaiten (*a. fig.*), bespannen; (ver-, zu)schnüren; *Bohnen* abziehen; *Am. sl. j-n* verkohlen; be strung up angespannt *od.* erregt sein; ~band♩ ['striŋbænd] Streichorchester *n*.

stringent □ ['strindʒənt] streng, scharf; bindend, zwingend; knapp.

stringy ['striŋi] faserig; zäh.

strip [strip] 1. entkleiden (*a. fig.*); (sich) ausziehen; abziehen; *fig.* entblößen, berauben; ⊕ auseinandernehmen; ⚓ abtakeln; *a.* ~ off ausziehen, abstreifen; 2. Streifen *m*.

stripe [straip] Streifen *m*; ✗ Tresse *f*.

stripling ['stripliŋ] Bürschchen *n*.

strive [straiv] [*irr.*] streben; sich bemühen; ringen (for um); ~n ['strivn] *p.p. von* strive.

strode [stroud] *pret. von* stride 1.

stroke [strouk] 1. Schlag *m* (*a.* ✗); Streich *m*; Stoß *m*; Strich *m*; ~ of luck Glücksfall *m*; 2. streiche(l)n.

stroll [stroul] 1. schlendern; umherziehen; 2. Bummel *m* Spaziergang *m*; ~er ['stroulə] Bummler(in), Spaziergänger(in); *Am.* (Falt)Sportwagen *m*.

strong □ [strɔŋ] *allg.* stark; kräftig; energisch, eifrig; fest; schwer (*Speise etc.*); ~box ['strɔŋbɔks] Stahlkassette *f*; ~hold Festung *f*; *fig.* Bollwerk *n*; ~room Stahlkammer *f*; ~willed eigenwillig.

strop [strɔp] 1. Streichriemen *m*; 2. *Messer* abziehen.

strove [strouv] *pret. von* strive.

struck [strʌk] *pret. u. p.p. von* strike 2.

structure ['strʌktʃə] Bau(werk *n*) *m*; Struktur *f*, Gefüge *n*; Gebilde *n*.

struggle ['strʌgl] 1. sich (ab)mühen; kämpfen, ringen; sich sträuben; 2. Kampf *m*; Ringen *n*; Anstrengung *f*.

strung [strʌŋ] *pret. u. p.p. von* string 2.

strut [strʌt] 1. *v/i.* stolzieren; *v/t.* ⊕ abstützen; 2. Stolzieren *n*; ⊕ Strebe(balken *m*) *f*; Stütze *f*.

stub [stʌb] 1. (Baum)Stumpf *m*; Stummel *m*; *Am.* Kontrollabschnitt *m*; 2. (aus)roden; sich *den Fuß* stoßen.

stubble ['stʌbl] Stoppel(n *pl.*) *f*.

stubborn □ ['stʌbən] eigensinnig; widerspenstig; stur; hartnäckig.

stuck [stʌk] *pret. u. p.p. von* stick 2; ~up ['stʌk'ʌp] F hochnäsig.

stud [stʌd] 1. (Wand)Pfosten *m*; Ziernagel *m*; Knauf *m*; Manschetten-, Kragenknopf *m*; Gestüt *n*; 2. beschlagen; besetzen; ~book ['stʌdbuk] Gestütbuch *n*.

student ['stju:dənt] Student(in).

studied □ ['stʌdid] einstudiert; gesucht; gewollt.

studio ['stju:diou] Atelier *n*; Studio *n*; *Radio:* Aufnahme-, Senderaum *m*.

studious □ ['stju:djəs] fleißig; bedacht; bemüht; geflissentlich.

study ['stʌdi] 1. Studium *n*; Studier-, Arbeitszimmer *n*; *paint. etc.* Studie *f*; be in a brown ~ versunken sein; 2. (ein)studieren; sich *et.* genau ansehen; sich bemühen um.

stuff [stʌf] 1. Stoff *m*; Zeug *n*; *fig.* Unsinn *m*; 2. *v/t.* (voll-, aus)stopfen; ~ed shirt *Am. sl.* Fatzke *m*; *v/i.* sich vollstopfen; ~ing ['stʌfiŋ] Füllung *f*; ~y □ [~fi] dumpf(ig), muffig, stickig; *fig.* verärgert.

stultify ['stʌltifai] lächerlich machen, blamieren; *et.* hinfällig machen.

stumble ['stʌmbl] 1. Stolpern *n*; Fehltritt *m*; 2. stolpern; straucheln; ~ upon stoßen auf (*acc.*).

stump [stʌmp] 1. Stumpf *m*, Stummel *m*; 2. *v/t.* F verblüffen; *Am.* F herausfordern; ~ the country als Wahlredner im Land umherziehen; *v/i.* (daher)stapfen; ~y ['stʌmpi] gedrungen; plump.

stun [stʌn] betäuben (*a. fig.*).

stung [stʌŋ] *pret. u. p.p. von* sting 2.

stunk [stʌŋk] *pret. u. p.p. von* stink 2.

stunning □ F ['stʌniŋ] toll, famos.

stunt¹ F [stʌnt] Kraft-, Kunststück *n*; (Reklame)Trick *m*; Sensation *f*.

stunt² [~] im Wachstum hindern; ~ed ['stʌntid] verkümmert.

stupefy ['stju:pifai] *fig.* betäuben; verblüffen; verdummen; ~endous □ [stju(:)'pendəs] erstaunlich; ~id □ ['stju:pid] dumm, einfältig, stumpfsinnig; blöd; ~idity [stju(:)'piditi] Dummheit *f*; Stumpfsinn *m*; ~or ['stju(:)pə] Erstarrung *f*, Betäubung *f*.

sturdy ['stə:di] derb, kräftig, stark; stämmig; stramm; handfest.

stutter ['stʌtə] 1. stottern; 2. Stottern n.

sty¹ [stai] Schweinestall m, Koben m.

sty², **stye** ✲ [ˌ] Gerstenkorn n am Auge.

style [stail] 1. Stil m; Mode f; Betitelung f; 2. (be)nennen, betiteln.

stylish □ ['staili∫] stilvoll; elegant; **~ness** [ˌ∫nis] Eleganz f.

stylo F ['stailou], **~graph** [ˌ∫əgrɑ:f] Tintenkuli m.

suave □ [swɑ:v] verbindlich; mild.

sub... [sʌb] mst Unter..., unter...; Neben...; Hilfs...; fast ...

subdeb Am. F [sʌb'deb] Backfisch m, junges Mädchen.

subdivision ['sʌbdiviʒən] Unterteilung f; Unterabteilung f.

subdue [səb'dju:] unterwerfen; bezwingen; bändigen; unterdrücken; verdrängen; dämpfen.

subject ['sʌbdʒikt] 1. unterworfen; untergeben, abhängig; untertan; unterliegend (to dat.); ~ to neigen zu; 2. adv. ~ to vorbehaltlich (gen.); 3. Untertan m, Staatsangehörige(r m) f; phls., gr. Subjekt n; a. ~ matter Thema n, Gegenstand m; 4. [səb'dʒekt] unterwerfen; fig. aussetzen; **~ion** [ˌkʃən] Unterwerfung f. [chen.)

subjugate ['sʌbdʒugeit] unterjo-)

subjunctive gr. [səb'dʒʌŋktiv] a. ~ mood Konjunktiv m.

sub|lease ['sʌb'li:s], **~let** [irr. (let)] untervermieten.

sublime □ [sə'blaim] erhaben.

submachine-gun ['sʌbmə'ʃi:ŋgʌn] Maschinenpistole f.

submarine ['sʌbməri:n] 1. unterseeisch; 2. ⚓ Unterseeboot n.

submerge [səb'mə:dʒ] untertauchen; überschwemmen.

submiss|ion [səb'miʃən] Unterwerfung f; Unterbreitung f; **~ive** □ [ˌisiv] unterwürfig.

submit [səb'mit] (sich) unterwerfen; anheimstellen; unterbreiten, einreichen; fig. sich fügen od. ergeben (to in acc.).

subordinate 1. □ [sə'bo:dnit] untergeordnet; untergeben; ~ clause gr. Nebensatz m; 2. [ˌ] Untergebene(r m) f; 3. [ˌdineit] unterordnen.

suborn gʒ [sʌ'bo:n] verleiten.

subscribe [səb'skraib] v/t. Geld stiften (to für); Summe zeichnen; s-n Namen setzen (to unter acc.); unterschreiben mit; v/i. ~ to Zeitung etc. abonnieren; e-r Meinung zustimmen, et. unterschreiben; **~r** [ˌbə] (Unter)Zeichner(in); Abonnent(in); teleph. Teilnehmer(in).

subscription [səb'skripʃən] (Unter-) Zeichnung f; Abonnement n.

subsequent □ ['sʌbsikwent] folgend; später; **~ly** hinterher.

subservient □ [səb'sə:vjənt] dienlich; dienstbar; unterwürfig.

subsid|e [səb'said] sinken, sich senken; fig. sich setzen; sich legen (Wind); ~ into verfallen in (acc.); **~iary** [ˌ'sidjəri] 1. □ Hilfs...; Neben...; untergeordnet; 2. Tochtergesellschaft f; Filiale f; **~ize** ['sʌbsidaiz] mit Geld unterstützen; subventionieren; **~y** [ˌdi] Beihilfe f; Subvention f.

subsist [səb'sist] bestehen; leben (on, by von); **~ence** [ˌtəns] Dasein n; (Lebens)Unterhalt m.

substance ['sʌbstəns] Substanz f; Wesen n; fig. Hauptsache f; Inhalt m; Wirklichkeit f; Vermögen n.

substantial □ [səb'stænʃəl] wesentlich; wirklich; kräftig; stark; solid; vermögend; namhaft (Summe).

substantiate [səb'stænʃieit] beweisen, begründen, dartun.

substantive gr. ['sʌbstəntiv] Substantiv n, Hauptwort n.

substitut|e ['sʌbstitju:t] 1. an die Stelle setzen od. treten (for von); unterschieben (for statt); 2. Stellvertreter m; Ersatz m; **~ion** [sʌbsti'tju:ʃən] Stellvertretung f; Ersatz m.

subterfuge ['sʌbtəfju:dʒ] Ausflucht f.

subterranean □ [sʌbtə'reinjən] unterirdisch.

sub-title ['sʌbtaitl] Untertitel m.

subtle □ ['sʌtl] fein(sinnig); subtil; spitzfindig; **~ty** [ˌlti] Feinheit f.

subtract gʒ [səb'trækt] abziehen, subtrahieren.

subtropical ['sʌb'trɔpikəl] subtropisch.

suburb ['sʌbə:b] Vorstadt f, Vorort m; **~an** [sə'bə:bən] vorstädtisch.

subvention [səb'venʃən] 1. Subvention f; 2. subventionieren.

subver|sion [sʌb'və:ʃən] Umsturz m; **~sive** [ˌə:siv] zerstörend (of acc.); subversiv; **~t** [ˌə:t] (um-) stürzen; untergraben.

subway ['sʌbwei] (bsd. Fußgänger-) Unterführung f; Am. Untergrundbahn f.

succeed [sək'si:d] Erfolg haben; glücken, gelingen; (nach)folgen (dat.); ~ to übernehmen; erben.

success [sək'ses] Erfolg m; **~ful** □ [ˌsful] erfolgreich; **~ion** [ˌeʃən] (Nach-, Erb-, Reihen)Folge f; Nachkommenschaft f; in ~ nacheinander; **~ive** □ [ˌesiv] aufeinanderfolgend; **~or** [ˌsə] Nachfolger(in). [fen.)

succo(u)r ['sʌkə] 1. Hilfe f; 2. hel-)

succulent □ ['sʌkjulənt] saftig.

succumb [sə'kʌm] unter-, erliegen.

such [sʌtʃ] solch(er, -e, -es); derartig; so groß; ~ a man ein solcher Mann; ~ as die, welche.

suck [sʌk] **1.** (ein)saugen; saugen an (*dat.*); aussaugen; lutschen; **2.** Saugen *n*; **~er** ['sʌkə] Saugorgan *n*; ♀ Wurzelsproß *m*; *Am.* Einfaltspinsel *m*; **~le** ['sʌkl] säugen, stillen; **~ling** [~liŋ] Säugling *m*.

suction ['sʌkʃən] (An)Saugen *n*; Sog *m*; *attr.* Saug...

sudden □ ['sʌdn] plötzlich; *all of a ~* ganz plötzlich.

suds [sʌdz] *pl.* Seifenlauge *f*; Seifenschaum *m*; **~y** *Am.* ['sʌdzi] schaumig, seifig.

sue [sjuː] *v/t.* verklagen; **~ out** erwirken; *v/i.* nachsuchen (*for* um); klagen.

suède [sweid] (feines) Wildleder.

suet [sjuit] Nierenfett *n*; Talg *m*.

suffer ['sʌfə] *v/i.* leiden (*from* an *dat.*); *v/t.* erleiden, erdulden, (zu-)lassen; **~ance** [~ərəns] Duldung *f*; **~er** [~rə] Leidende(r *m*) *f*; Dulder(in); **~ing** [~riŋ] Leiden *n*.

suffice [sə'fais] genügen; *~ it to say* es sei nur gesagt.

sufficien|cy [sə'fiʃənsi] genügende Menge; Auskommen *n*; **~t** [~nt] genügend, ausreichend.

suffix *gr.* ['sʌfiks] **1.** anhängen; **2.** Nachsilbe *f*, Suffix *n*.

suffocate ['sʌfəkeit] ersticken.

suffrage ['sʌfridʒ] (Wahl)Stimme*f*; Wahl-, Stimmrecht *n*.

suffuse [sə'fjuːz] übergießen; überziehen.

sugar ['ʃugə] **1.** Zucker *m*; **2.** zukkern; **~basin**, *Am.* **~bowl** Zuckerdose *f*; **~cane** ♀ Zuckerrohr *n*; **~coat** überzuckern, versüßen; **~y** [~əri] zuckrig; zuckersüß.

suggest [sə'dʒest] vorschlagen, anregen; nahelegen; vorbringen; *Gedanken* eingeben; andeuten; denken lassen an (*acc.*); **~ion** [~tʃən] Anregung *f*; Rat *m*, Vorschlag *m*; Suggestion *f*; Eingebung *f*; Andeutung *f*; **~ive** [~tiv] anregend; andeutend (*of acc.*); gehaltvoll; zweideutig.

suicide ['sjuisaid] **1.** Selbstmord *m*; Selbstmörder(in); **2.** *Am.* Selbstmord begehen.

suit [sjuit] **1.** (Herren)Anzug *m*; (Damen)Kostüm *n*; Anliegen *n*; (Heirats)Antrag *m*; *Karten*: Farbe *f*; ⚖ Prozeß *m*; **2.** *v/t.* passen, zusagen, bekommen; *j-n* kleiden; *j-m* stehen, passen zu (*Kleidungsstück etc.*); *~ oneself* tun, was e-m beliebt; *~ s.th. to et.* anpassen (*dat.*); *be ~ed* geeignet sein (*for* für), passen (*to* zu); *v/i.* passen; **~able**] ['sjuːtəbl] passend, geeignet; entsprechend; **~case** (Hand)Koffer *m*; **~e** [swiːt] Gefolge *n*; (Reihen)Folge *f*; ♪ Suite *f*; *a. ~ of rooms* Zimmerflucht *f*; Garnitur *f*, (Zimmer)Einrichtung *f*; **~or** ['sjuːtə] Freier *m*; ⚖ Kläger(in).

sulk [sʌlk] schmollen, bocken; **~iness** ['sʌlkinis] üble Laune; **~s** *pl.* = sulkiness; **~y** ['sʌlki] **1.** verdrießlich; launisch; schmollend; **2.** *Sport:* Traberwagen *m*, Sulky *n*.

sullen □ ['sʌlən] verdrossen, mürrisch.

sully ['sʌli] *mst fig.* beflecken.

sulphur 🜍 ['sʌlfə] Schwefel *m*; **~ic** [sʌl'fjuərik] Schwefel...

sultriness ['sʌltrinis] Schwüle *f*.

sultry □ ['sʌltri] schwül; *fig.* heftig, hitzig.

sum [sʌm] **1.** Summe *f*; Betrag *m*; *fig.* Inbegriff *m*, Inhalt *m*; Rechenaufgabe *f*; *do ~s* rechnen; **2.** *mst ~ up ~* zs.-rechnen; zs.-fassen.

summar|ize ['sʌməraiz] (kurz) zs.-fassen; **~y** [~ri] □ kurz (zs.-gefaßt); ⚖ Schnell...; **2.** (kurze) Inhaltsangabe, Auszug *m*.

summer ['sʌmə] Sommer *m*; *resort* Sommerfrische *f*; **~ school** Ferienkurs *m*; **~ly** [~əli], **~y** [~əri] sommerlich.

summit ['sʌmit] Gipfel *m* (*a. fig.*).

summon ['sʌmən] auffordern; (be-)rufen; ⚖ vorladen; *Mut etc.* aufbieten; **~s** Aufforderung *f*; ⚖ Vorladung *f*.

sumptuous □ ['sʌmptjuəs] kostbar.

sun [sʌn] **1.** Sonne *f*; *attr.* Sonnen...; **2.** (sich) sonnen; **~bath** ['sʌnbɑːθ] Sonnenbad *n*; **~beam** Sonnenstrahl *m*; **~burn** Sonnenbräune *f*; Sonnenbrand *m*.

Sunday ['sʌndi] Sonntag *m*.

sun|-dial ['sʌndaiəl] Sonnenuhr *f*; **~down** Sonnenuntergang *m*.

sundr|ies ['sʌndriz] *pl. bsd.* ✝ Verschiedene(s) *n*; Extraausgaben *f/pl.*; **~y** [~ri] verschiedene.

sung [sʌŋ] *pret. u. p.p. von sing.*

sun-glasses ['sʌnglɑːsiz] *pl.* (*a pair of ~ pl.* eine) Sonnenbrille *f*.

sunk [sʌŋk] *pret. u. p.p. von sink* 1.

sunken ['sʌŋkən] **1.** *p.p. von sink* 1; **2.** *adj.* versunken; *fig.* eingefallen.

sun|ny □ ['sʌni] sonnig; **~rise** Sonnenaufgang *m*; **~set** Sonnenuntergang *m*; **~shade** Sonnenschirm *m*; **~shine** Sonnenschein *m*; **~stroke** ⚕ Sonnenstich *m*.

sup [sʌp] zu Abend essen.

super F ['sjuːpə] erstklassig, prima, super.

super|... ['sjuːpə] Ober..., über...; Ober..., ober...; Groß...; **~abundant**] [sjuːpərə'bʌndənt] überreichlich; überschwenglich; **~annuate** [~'rænjueit] pensionieren; **~d** ausgedient; veraltet (*S.*).

superb □ [sjuː(:)'pəːb] prächtig; herrlich.

super|charger *mot.* ['sjuːpətʃɑːdʒə] Kompressor *m*; **~cilious** [sjuːpə-

'silios] hochmütig; ~ficial □ [~ə'fi-ʃəl] oberflächlich; ~fine ['sju:pə-'fain] extrafein; ~fluity [sju:pə-flu(:)iti] Überfluß m; ~fluous □ [sju(:)'pəːfluəs] überflüssig; ~heat ⊕ [sju:pə'hiːt] überhitzen; ~human [~'hjuːmən] übermenschlich; ~impose ['sjuːpərim'pouz] darauf-, darüberlegen; ~induce [~rin'djuːs] noch hinzufügen; ~intend [sju:prin'tend] die Oberaufsicht haben über (acc.); überwachen; ~intendent [~dənt] 1. Leiter m, Direktor m, (Ober)Aufseher m, Inspektor m; 2. aufsichtführend.

superior [sju(·) piəriə] 1. ꞁ ober; höher(stehend), vorgesetzt; besser, hochwertiger, überlegen (to dat.); vorzüglich, 2. Höherstehende(r m) f, bsd. Vorgesetzte(r m) f; eccl. Obere(r) m; mst Lady ♀, Mother ♀ eccl. Oberin f; ~ity [sju(:)piəri'oriti] Überlegenheit f

super|lative [sju(:)'pəːlətiv] 1. □ höchst, überragend, 2. a. ~ degree gr. Superlativ m, ~market Supermarkt m, ~natural [sju:pə'nætʃ-rəl] übernatürlich; ~numerary [~'njuːmərəri] 1. überzählig; 2. Überzählige(r m) f; thea. Statist (-in), ~scription [~ə'skripʃən] Über-, Aufschrift f; ~sede [~'siːd] ersetzen; verdrängen, absetzen; fig. überholen, ~sonic phys. ['sjuːpə'sɔnik] Überschall...; ~stition [sju:pə'stiʃən] Aberglaube m; ~~stitious [~ʃəs] abergläubisch; ~vene [~'viːn] noch hinzukommen; unerwartet eintreten; ~vise ['sjuːpəvaiz] beaufsichtigen, überwachen; ~vision [sjuːpə'viʒən] (Ober)Aufsicht f; Beaufsichtigung f; ~visor ['sjuːpəvaizə] Aufseher m, Inspektor m

supper ['sʌpə] Abendessen n; the (Lord's) ♀ das Heilige Abendmahl.

supplant [sə'plaːnt] verdrängen.

supple ['sʌpl] geschmeidig (machen).

supplement 1. ['sʌplimənt] Ergänzung f, Nachtrag m; (Zeitungs-etc.)Beilage f, 2. [~ment] ergänzen; ~al [~sʌpli'mentl], ~ary [~təri] Ergänzungs..; nachträglich; Nachtrags.

suppliant ['sʌpliənt] 1. □ demütig bittend, flehend, 2. Bittsteller(in).

supplicat|e ['sʌplikeit] demütig bitten, anflehen; ~ion [sʌpli'keiʃən] demütige Bitte

supplier [sə'plaiə] Lieferant(in).

supply [sə'plai] 1. liefern; e-m Mangel abhelfen, e-e Stelle ausfüllen; vertreten, ausstatten, versorgen; ergänzen; 2. Lieferung f; Versorgung f; Zufuhr f; Vorrat m; Bedarf m; Angebot n; (Stell)Vertretung f; mst supplies pl. parl. Etat m.

support [sə'pɔːt] 1. Stütze f; Hilfe f; ⊕ Träger m; Unterstützung f; Lebensunterhalt m; 2. (unter)stützen; unterhalten, sorgen für (Familie etc.); aufrechterhalten; (v)ertragen.

suppose [sə'pouz] annehmen; voraussetzen; vermuten; he is ~d to do er soll tun; ~ we go gehen wir; wie wär's, wenn wir gingen

supposed □ [sə'pouzd] vermeintlich; ~ly [~zidli] vermutlich.

supposition [sʌpə'ziʃən] Voraussetzung f; Annahme f; Vermutung f.

suppress [sə'pres] unterdrücken; ~ion [~eʃən] Unterdrückung f.

suppurate ['sʌpjuəreit] eitern.

suprem|acy [sju'preməsi] Oberhoheit f; Vorherrschaft f; Überlegenheit f; Vorrang m; ~e □ [sju(:)'priːm] höchst; oberst; Ober...; größt.

surcharge [səː'tʃaːdʒ] 1. überladen; Zuschlag od. Nachgebühr erheben von j-m; 2. ['səːtʃaːdʒ] Überladung f; (Straf)Zuschlag m, Nachgebühr f; Überdruck m auf Briefmarken.

sure □ [ʃuə] allg. sicher, to be ~!, ~ enough!, Am. ~! F sicher(lich)!; ~ly ['ʃuəli] sicherlich; ~ty ['ʃuəti] Bürge m.

surf [səːf] Brandung f.

surface ['səːfis] 1. (Ober)Fläche f; ✈ Tragfläche f; 2. ♦ auftauchen (U-Boot).

surf|-board ['səːfbɔːd] Wellenreiterbrett n; ~boat Brandungsboot n.

surfeit ['səːfit] 1. Übersättigung f; Ekel m; 2. (sich) überladen.

surf-riding ['səːfraidiŋ] Sport: Wellenreiten n.

surge [səːdʒ] 1. Woge f; 2. wogen.

surg|eon ['səːdʒən] Chirurg m; ~ery ['~əri] Chirurgie f; Sprechzimmer n; ~ hours pl. Sprechstunde(n pl.) f.

surgical □ ['səːdʒikəl] chirurgisch.

surly □ ['səːli] mürrisch, grob.

surmise 1. ['səːmaiz] Vermutung f; Argwohn m; 2. [səː'maiz] vermuten; argwöhnen.

surmount [səː'maunt] übersteigen; überragen; fig. überwinden.

surname ['səːneim] Zu-, Nachname m.

surpass fig. [səː'paːs] übersteigen, übertreffen; ~ing [~siŋ] überragend.

surplus ['səːpləs] 1. Überschuß m, Mehr n; 2. überschüssig, Über...

surprise [sə'praiz] 1. Überraschung f; ✕ Überrump(e)lung f; 2. überraschen; ✕ überrumpeln

surrender [sə'rendə] 1. Übergabe f, Ergebung f; Kapitulation f; Aufgeben n; 2. v/t. übergeben; aufgeben; v/i. a. ~ o.s. sich ergeben.

surround [sə'raund] umgeben; ✕

umzingeln; **~ing** [~diŋ] umliegend;
~ings pl. Umgebung f.

surtax ['sɔ:tæks] Steuerzuschlag
m.

survey 1. [sə'vei] überblicken;
mustern; begutachten; **surv.** vermessen; **2.** ['sə:vei] Überblick m
(a. fig.); Besichtigung f; Gutachten
n; **surv** Vermessung f; **~or** [sə(:)-
'veiə] Land-, Feldmesser m.

surviv|al [sə vaivəl] Über-, Fortleben n; Überbleibsel n; **~e** [~aiv]
überleben; noch leben; fortleben;
am Leben bleiben; bestehen
bleiben; **~or** [~və] Überlebende(r
m) f.

suscept|ible [~'septəbl], **~ive**
[~tiv] empfänglich (of, to für); empfindlich (gegen); **be ~ of** et. zulassen.

suspect 1. [səs'pekt] (be)argwöhnen;
in Verdacht haben, verdächtigen;
vermuten, befürchten; **2.** ['sʌspekt]
Verdächtige(r m) f; **3.** [~] = **~ed**
[səs'pektid] verdächtig

suspend [səs'pend] (auf)hängen;
aufschieben, in der Schwebe lassen; Zahlung einstellen, aussetzen;
suspendieren, sperren, **~ed** schwebend; **~er** [~də] Strumpf-, Sockenhalter m; **~s** pl. Am. Hosenträger
m/pl.

suspens|e [səs'pens] Ungewißheit f;
Unentschiedenheit f; Spannung f;
~ion [~nʃən] Aufhängung f; Aufschub m; Einstellung f; Suspendierung f, Amtsenthebung f; Sperre f;
~ion bridge Hängebrücke f; **~ive**
□ [~nsiv] aufschiebend.

suspici|on [səs'piʃən] Verdacht m;
Argwohn m, fig. Spur f; **~ous** □
[~ʃəs] argwöhnisch; verdächtig.

sustain [səs'tein] stützen, fig. aufrechterhalten, aushalten; erleiden;
ʒʒ anerkennen, **~ed** anhaltend; ununterbrochen

sustenance ['sʌstinəns] (Lebens-)
Unterhalt m, Nahrung f.

svelte [svelt] schlank (Frau).

swab [swɔb] **1.** Aufwischmop m;
♂ Tupfer m; ♂ Abstrich m; **2.** aufwischen

swaddl|e ['swɔdl] Baby wickeln;
~ing-clothes mst fig. [~liŋklouðz]
pl. Windeln f/pl.

swagger ['swægə] **1.** stolzieren;
prahlen, renommieren; **2.** f elegant.

swale Am. [sweil] Mulde f, Niederung f.

swallow ['swolou] **1.** orn. Schwalbe
f; Schlund m; Schluck m; **2.** (hinunter-, ver)schlucken; fig. Ansicht
etc. begierig aufnehmen.

swam [swæm] pret. von swim 1.

swamp [swomp] **1.** Sumpf m;
2. überschwemmen (a. fig.); versenken; **~y** ['swompi] sumpfig.

swan [swon] Schwan m.

swank sl. [swæŋk] **1.** Angabe f,

Protzerei f; **2.** angeben, protzen;
~y ['swæŋki] protzig, angeberisch.

swap F [swɔp] **1.** Tausch m;
2. (ver-, aus)tauschen.

sward [swɔ:d] Rasen m.

swarm [swɔ:m] **1.** Schwarm m;
Haufe(n) m, Gewimmel n; **2.**
schwärmen; wimmeln (with von).

swarthy □ ['swɔ:ði] dunkelfarbig.

swash [swɔʃ] plan(t)schen.

swat [swɔt] Fliege klatschen.

swath ♂ [swɔ:θ] Schwade(n m) f.

swathe [sweið] (ein)wickeln

sway [swei] **1.** Schaukeln n; Einfluß m; Herrschaft f; **2.** schaukeln;
beeinflussen; beherrschen.

swear [swɛə] [irr.] (be)schwören;
fluchen; **~ s.o.** in j-n vereidigen.

sweat [swet] **1.** Schweiß m; by the
~ of one's brow im Schweiße seines
Angesichts; all of a **~** F in Schweiß
gebadet (a. fig.); **2.** [irr.] v/i.
schwitzen; v/t. (aus)schwitzen; in
Schweiß bringen; Arbeiter ausbeuten; **~er** ['swetə] Sweater m, Pullover m; Trainingsjacke f; fig. Ausbeuter m; **~y** [~ti] schweißig; verschwitzt.

Swede [swi:d] Schwed|e m, -in f.

Swedish ['swi:diʃ] **1.** schwedisch;
2. Schwedisch n.

sweep [swi:p] **1.** [irr.] fegen (a.fig.),
kehren; fig. streifen; bestreichen
(a. ✕); (majestätisch) (dahin)rauschen; **2.** (fig. Dahin)Fegen n;
Kehren n; Schwung m; Biegung f;
Spielraum m, Bereich m; Schornsteinfeger m; **make a clean ~** reinen Tisch machen (of mit); **~er**
['swi:pə] (Straßen)Feger m; Kehrmaschine f; **~ing** □ [~piŋ] weitgehend; schwungvoll; **~ings** pl.
Kehricht m, Müll m.

sweet [swi:t] **1.** □ süß; lieblich;
freundlich; frisch; duftend; have
a **~ tooth** ein Leckermaul sein;
2. Liebling; Süßigkeit f, Bonbon
m, n; Nachtisch m; **~en** ['swi:tn]
(ver)süßen; **~heart** Liebling m,
Liebste(r m) f; **~ish** [~tiʃ] süßlich;
~meat Bonbon m, n; kandierte
Frucht; **~ness** [~tnis] Süßigkeit f;
Lieblichkeit f; **~ pea** ♀ Gartenwicke f.

swell [swel] **1.** [irr.] v/i. (an)schwellen; sich blähen; sich (aus)bauchen;
v/t. (an)schwellen lassen; aufblähen; **2.** F fein; sl. prima; **3.** Anschwellen n; Schwellung f; ♃ Dünung f; F feiner Herr; **~ing** ['sweliŋ] Geschwulst f.

swelter ['sweltə] vor Hitze umkommen.

swept [swept] pret. u. p.p. von
sweep 1.

swerve [swə:v] **1.** (plötzlich) abbiegen; **2.** plötzliche Wendung.

swift □ [swift] schnell, eilig, flink;
~ness ['swiftnis] Schnelligkeit f.

swill [swil] 1. Spülicht n; Schweine-
trank m; 2. spülen; saufen.
swim [swim] 1. [irr.] (durch-)
schwimmen; schweben; my head
~s mir schwindelt; 2. Schwimmen
n; be in the ~ auf dem laufenden
sein; ~ming ['swimiŋ] 1. Schwimmen n; 2. Schwimm...; ~bath
(bsd. Hallen)Schwimmbad n; ~pool
Schwimmbecken n; ~suit Badeanzug m.
swindle ['swindl] 1. (be)schwin-
deln; 2. Schwindel m.
swine [swain] Schwein(e pl.) n.
swing [swiŋ] 1. [irr.] schwingen,
schwanken; F baumeln; (sich)
schaukeln; schwenken; sich drehen;
2. Schwingen n; Schwung m;
Schaukel f; Spielraum m; in full ~
in vollem Gange; ~door ['swiŋdɔ:]
Drehtür f.
swinish □ ['swainiʃ] schweinisch.
swipe [swaip] 1. aus vollem Arm
schlagen; 2. starker Schlag.
swirl [swə:l] 1. (herum)wirbeln,
strudeln; 2. Wirbel m, Strudel m.
Swiss [swis] 1. schweizerisch,
Schweizer...; 2. Schweizer(in); the
~ pl. die Schweizer m/pl.
switch [switʃ] 1. Gerte f; ⚡ Weiche
f; ⚡ Schalter m; falscher Zopf;
2. peitschen; ⚡ rangieren; ⚡ (um-)
schalten; fig. wechseln, überleiten;
~ on (off) ⚡ ein- (aus)schalten; ~
board ⚡ ['switʃbɔ:d] Schaltbrett n,
-tafel f.
swivel ⊕ ['swivl] Drehring m; attr.
Dreh...
swollen ['swoulən] p.p. von swell 1.
swoon [swu:n] 1. Ohnmacht f;
2. in Ohnmacht fallen.
swoop [swu:p] 1. ~ down on od. upon
(herab)stoßen auf (acc.) (Raub-
vogel); überfallen; 2. Stoß m.
swop F [swɔp] s. swap.
sword [sɔ:d] Schwert n, Degen
m.
swordsman ['sɔ:dzmən] Fechter m.

swore [swɔ:] pret. von swear.
sworn [swɔ:n] p.p. von swear.
swum [swʌm] p.p. von swim 1.
swung [swʌŋ] pret. u. p.p. von
swing 1.
sycamore ♣ ['sikəmɔ:] Bergahorn
m; Am. Platane f.
sycophant ['sikəfənt] Kriecher m.
syllable ['siləbl] Silbe f.
syllabus ['siləbəs] (bsd. Vorlesungs-)
Verzeichnis n; (bsd. Lehr)Plan m.
sylvan ['silvən] waldig, Wald...
symbol ['simbəl] Symbol n, Sinnbild n; ~ic(al □) [sim'bɔlik(əl)]
sinnbildlich; ~ism ['simbəlizəm]
Symbolik f.
symmetr|ical □ [si'metrikəl] eben-
mäßig; ~y ['simitri] Ebenmaß n.
sympath|etic [simpə'θetik] (~ally)
mitfühlend; sympathisch; ~ strike
Sympathiestreik m; ~ize ['sim-
pəθaiz] sympathisieren, mitfühlen;
~y [~θi] Sympathie f, Mitgefühl n.
symphony ♪ ['simfəni] Symphonie f.
symptom ['simptəm] Symptom n.
synchron|ize ['siŋkrənaiz] v/i.
gleichzeitig sein; v/t. als gleichzeitig
zs.-stellen; Uhren auf-ea. abstimmen; Tonfilm: synchronisieren;
~ous [~nəs] gleichzeitig.
syndicate 1. ['sindikit] Syndikat n;
2. [~keit] zu e-m Syndikat verbinden.
synonym ['sinənim] Synonym n;
~ous] [si'nɔniməs] sinnverwandt.
synop|sis [si'nɔpsis], pl. ~ses [~si:z]
zs.-fassende Übersicht.
syntax gr. ['sintæks] Syntax f.
synthe|sis ['sinθisis], pl. ~ses [~si:z]
Synthese f, Verbindung f; ~tic(al
□) [sin'θetik(əl)] synthetisch.
syringe ['sirindʒ] 1. Spritze f;
2. (be-, ein-, aus)spritzen.
syrup ['sirəp] Sirup m.
system ['sistim] System n; Organismus m, Körper m; Plan m, Ordnung f; ~atic [sisti'mætik] (~ally)
systematisch.

T

tab [tæb] Streifen m; Schildchen n;
Anhänger m; Schlaufe f, Aufhänger
m; F Rechnung f, Konto n.
table ['teibl] 1. Tisch m, Tafel f;
Tisch-, Tafelrunde f; Tabelle f,
Verzeichnis n; Bibel Gesetzestafel
f; s. ~land; at ~ bei Tisch; turn
the ~s den Spieß umdrehen (on
gegen); 2. auf den Tisch legen;
tabellarisch anordnen.
tableau ['tæblou], pl. ~x [~ouz]
lebendes Bild.
table|-cloth ['teiblklɔθ] Tischtuch
n; ~land Tafelland n, Plateau n,

Hochebene f; ~linen Tisch-
wäsche f; ~spoon Eßlöffel m.
tablet ['tæblit] Täfelchen n; (Gedenk)Tafel f; (Schreib- etc.)Block
m; Stück n Seife; Tablette f.
table-top ['teibltɔp] Tischplatte f.
taboo [tə'bu:] 1. tabu, unantastbar;
verboten; 2. Tabu n; Verbot n;
3. verbieten.
tabulate ['tæbjuleit] tabellarisch
ordnen.
tacit □ ['tæsit] stillschweigend;
~urn □ [~tə:n] schweigsam.
tack [tæk] 1. Stift m, Zwecke f;

Heftstich *m*; ♠ Halse *f*; ♠ Gang *m*
beim *Lavieren*; *fig.* Weg *m*; 2. *v/t.*
(an)heften; *fig.* (an)hängen; *v/i.* ♠
wenden; *fig.* lavieren.

tackle ['tækl] 1. Gerät *n*; ♠ Takel-,
Tauwerk *n*; ⊕ Flaschenzug *m*;
2. (an)packen; in Angriff nehmen;
fertig werden mit; *j-n* angehen (for
um).

tacky ['tæki] klebrig; *Am.* F schäbig.

tact [tækt] Takt *m*, Feingefühl *n*;
~**ful** □ ['tæktful] taktvoll.

tactics ['tæktiks] Taktik *f*.

tactless □ ['tæktlis] taktlos.

tadpole *zo.* ['tædpoul] Kaulquappe*f*.

taffeta ['tæfitə] Taft *m*.

taffy *Am.* ['tæfi] ~ toffee; F Schmus
m, Schmeichelei *f*.

tag [tæg] 1. (Schnürsenkel)Stift *m*;
Schildchen *n*, Etikett *n*; Redensart
f, Zitat *n*; Zusatz *m*; loses Ende;
Fangen *n* (*Kinderspiel*); 2. etikettieren, auszeichnen, anhängen (to,
onto an *acc.*); ~ *after* herlaufen hinter (*dat.*); ~ *together* an-ea.-reihen.

tail [teil] 1. Schwanz *m*; Schweif *m*;
hinteres Ende, Schluß *m*; ~**s** *pl.*
Rückseite *f* e-r *Münze*; F Frack *m*;
turn ~ davonlaufen; ~**s** *up* in Hoch-
stimmung; 2. ~ *after s.o.* j-m nach-
laufen; ~ *s.o. Am.* j-n beschatten; ~
away, ~ *off* abflauen, sich verlieren;
zögernd enden; ~**-coat** ['teil'kout]
Frack *m*; ~**-light** *mot. etc.* ['teillait]
Rück-, Schlußlicht *n*.

tailor ['teilə] 1. Schneider *m*;
2. schneidern; ~**-made** Schneider..., Maß...

taint [teint] 1. Flecken *m*, Makel *m*;
♣ Ansteckung *f*; *fig.* krankhafter
Zug; Verderbnis *f*; 2. beflecken;
verderben; ♣ anstecken.

take [teik] 1. [*irr.*] *v/t.* nehmen; an-,
ab-, auf-, ein-, fest-, hin-, wegnehmen; (weg)bringen; *Speise* (zu
sich) nehmen; *Maßnahme*, *Gelegenheit* ergreifen; *Eid*, *Gelübde*, *Examen* ablegen; *phot.* aufnehmen; *et.
gut etc.* aufnehmen; *Beleidigung*
hinnehmen; fassen, ergreifen; fangen; *fig.* fesseln; sich *e-e Krankheit*
holen; erfordern, brauchen; *Zeit*
dauern; auffassen; halten, ansehen
(for für); *I* ~ *it that* ich nehme an,
daß; ~ *breath* verschnaufen; ~ *comfort* sich trösten; ~ *compassion on*
Mitleid empfinden mit; sich erbarmen (*gen.*); ~ *counsel* beraten; ~ *a
drive* e-e Fahrt machen; ~ *fire* Feuer
fangen; ~ *in hand* unternehmen; ~
hold of ergreifen; ~ *pity on* Mitleid
haben mit; ~ *place* stattfinden;
spielen (*Handlung*); ~ *a seat* Platz
nehmen; ~ *a walk* e-n Spaziergang
machen; ~ *my word for it* verlaß
dich drauf; ~ *about* herumführen; ~
along mitnehmen; notieren; ~ *for* halten für; ~ *from j-m* wegnehmen;

abziehen von; ~ *in* enger machen;
Zeitung halten; aufnehmen (*als
Gast etc.*); einschließen; verstehen;
erfassen; F *j-n* reinlegen; ~ *off* ab-,
wegnehmen; *Kleid* ausziehen, *Hut*
abnehmen; ~ *on* an-, übernehmen;
Arbeiter etc. einstellen; *Fahrgäste*
zusteigen lassen; ~ *out* heraus-, entnehmen; *Fleck* entfernen; *j-n* ausführen; *Versicherung* abschließen;
~ *to pieces* auseinandernehmen; ~
up aufnehmen; sich *e-r S.* annehmen; *Raum*, *Zeit* in Anspruch nehmen; *v/i.* wirken, ein-, anschlagen;
gefallen, ziehen; ~ *after j-m* nachschlagen; ~ *off* abspringen; ⚛ aufsteigen, starten; ~ *on* F Anklang
finden; ~ *over* die Amtsgewalt übernehmen; ~ *to* liebgewinnen; *fig.*
sich verlegen auf (*acc.*); Zuflucht
nehmen zu; sich ergeben (*dat.*); ~
up F sich bessern (*Wetter*); ~ *up
with* sich anfreunden mit; *that
won't* ~ *with me* das verfängt bei
mir nicht; 2. Fang *m*; *Geld*-Ein-
nahme *f*; *Film*: Szene(naufnahme)
f; ~**-in** F ['teik'in] Reinfall *m*; ~**n**
['teikən] *p.p. von* take 1; *be* ~ *besetzt sein*; *be* ~ *with* entzückt sein
von; *be* ~ *ill* krank werden; ~**-off**
['teiko:f] Karikatur *f*; Absprung *m*;
⚛ Start *m*.

taking ['teikiŋ] 1. □ F anziehend,
fesselnd, einnehmend; ansteckend;
2. (An-, Ab-, Auf-, Ein-, Ent-,
Hin-, Weg- *etc.*)Nehmen *n*; Inbe-
sitznahme *f*; ⚔ Einnahme *f*; F Aufregung *f*; ~**s** *pl.* ✝ Einnahmen *f/pl.*

tale [teil] Erzählung *f*, Geschichte *f*;
Märchen *n*, Sage *f*; *it tells its own* ~
es spricht für sich selbst; ~**-bearer**
['teilbɛərə] Zuträger(in).

talent ['tælənt] Talent *n*, Begabung
f, Anlage *f*; ~**ed** [~tid] talentvoll,
begabt.

talk [to:k] 1. Gespräch *n*; Unterredung *f*; Plauderei *f*; Vortrag *m*;
Geschwätz *n*; 2. sprechen, reden
(*von et.*); plaudern; ~**ative** □ ['to:-
kətiv] gesprächig, geschwätzig; ~**er**
['to:kə] Schwätzer(in); Sprechen-
de(r *m*) *f*.

tall [to:l] groß, lang, hoch; F übertrieben, unglaublich; *that's a* ~
order F das ist ein bißchen viel
verlangt.

tallow ['tælou] *ausgelassener* Talg.

tally ['tæli] 1. Kerbholz *n*; Gegenstück *n* (of zu); Kennzeichen *n*;
2. übereinstimmen.

talon *orn.* ['tælən] Kralle *f*, Klaue
f.

tame [teim] 1. □ zahm; folgsam;
harmlos; lahm, fad(e); 2. (be)zäh-
men, bändigen.

Tammany *Am.* ['tæməni] New
Yorker Demokraten-Vereinigung.

tamper ['tæmpə]: ~ *with* sich (unbefugt) zu schaffen machen mit;

j-n zu bestechen suchen; *Urkunde* fälschen.

tan [tæn] **1.** Lohe *f;* Lohfarbe *f;* (Sonnen)Bräune *f;* **2.** lohfarben; **3.** gerben; bräunen.

tang [tæŋ] Beigeschmack *m; scharfer* Klang; ♧ Seetang *m.*

tangent ['tændʒənt] Ⱥ Tangente *f; fly od. go off at a ~* vom Gegenstand abspringen.

tangerine ♧ [tændʒə'ri:n] Mandarine *f.*

tangible □ ['tændʒəbl] fühlbar, greifbar (*a. fig.*); klar.

tangle ['tæŋgl] **1.** Gewirr *n;* Verwicklung *f;* **2.** (sich) verwirren, verwickeln.

tank [tæŋk] **1.** Zisterne *f,* Wasserbehälter *m;* ⊕, ✕ Tank *m;* **2.** tanken.   [(Bier)Krug *m.*\

tankard ['tæŋkəd] Kanne *f, bsd.*\

tanner ['tænə] Gerber *m; ~y* [~əri] Gerberei *f.*

tantalize ['tæntəlaiz] quälen.

tantamount ['tæntəmaunt] gleichbedeutend (mit).

tantrum F ['tæntrəm] Koller *m.*

tap [tæp] **1.** leichtes Klopfen; (Wasser-, Gas-, Zapf)Hahn *m;* Zapfen *m;* Schankstube *f;* F Sorte *f; ~s pl. Am.* ✕ Zapfenstreich *m,* **2.** pochen, klopfen, tippen (auf, *an,* gegen *acc.);* an-, abzapfen; *~***dance** ['tæpda:ns] Stepptanz *m.*

tape [teip] schmales Band; *Sport:* Zielband *n; tel.* Papierstreifen *m;* Tonband *n; red ~.* Bürokratismus *m; ~***measure** ['teipmeʒə] Bandmaß *n.*

taper ['teipə] **1.** dünne Wachskerze; **2.** *adj.* spitz (zulaufend); schlank; **3.** *v/i.* spitz zulaufen; *v/t.* zuspitzen.

tape| recorder ['teiprikɔ:də] Tonbandgerät *n; ~ recording* Tonbandaufnahme *f.*

tapestry ['tæpistri] Gobelin *m.*

tapeworm['teipwə:m] Bandwurm *m.*

tap-room ['tæprum] Schankstube *f.*

tar [ta:] **1.** Teer *m;* **2.** teeren.

tardy □ ['ta:di] langsam; spät.

tare ✝ [tɛə] Tara *f.*

target ['ta:git] (Schieß)Scheibe *f; fig.* Ziel(scheibe *f) n;* Ziel(leistung *f) n;* Soll *n; ~ practice* Scheibenschießen *n.*

tariff ['tærif] (Zoll)Tarif *m.*

tarnish ['ta:niʃ] **1.** *v/t.* ⊕ trüb *od.* blind machen; *fig.* trüben; *v/i.* trüb werden, anlaufen; **2.** Trübung *f;* Belag *m.*

tarry[1] *lit.* ['tæri] säumen, zögern; verweilen.

tarry[2] ['ta:ri] teerig.

tart [ta:t] **1.** □ sauer, herb; *fig.* scharf, schroff; **2.** (Obst)Torte *f; sl.* Dirne *f.*

tartan ['ta:tən] Tartan *m;* Schottentuch *n;* Schottenmuster *n.*

task [ta:sk] **1.** Aufgabe *f;* Arbeit *f; take to ~* zur Rede stellen; **2.** beschäftigen; in Anspruch nehmen.

tassel ['tæsəl] Troddel *f,* Quaste *f.*

taste [teist] **1.** Geschmack *m;* (Kost)Probe *f;* Lust *f* (*for* zu); **2.** kosten, schmecken; versuchen; genießen; *~***ful** □ ['teistful] geschmackvoll; *~***less** □ [~tlis] geschmacklos.

tasty F ['teisti] schmackhaft.

ta-ta ['tæ'ta:] auf Wiedersehen!

tatter ['tætə] **1.** zerfetzen; **2.** *~s pl.* Fetzen *m/pl.*

tattle ['tætl] **1.** schwatzen; tratschen, **2.** Geschwätz *n;* Tratsch *m.*

tattoo [tə'tu:] **1.** ✕ Zapfenstreich *m;* Tätowierung *f; fig.* trommeln; tätowieren.

taught [tɔ:t] *pret. u. p.p. von* teach.

taunt [tɔ:nt] **1.** Stichelei *f,* Spott *m;* **2.** verhöhnen, verspotten.

taut ⊕ [tɔ:t] steif, straff; schmuck.

tavern ['tævən] Schenke *f.*

tawdry) ['tɔ:dri] billig; kitschig.

tawny ['tɔ:ni] lohfarben.

tax [tæks] **1.** Steuer *f,* Abgabe *f; fig.* Inanspruchnahme *f* (*on, upon gen.*); **2.** besteuern; *fig.* stark in Anspruch nehmen; **t⅔** *Kosten* schätzen; auf *e-e* harte Probe stellen; *~ s.o. with s.th.* j-n e-r S. beschuldigen; *~***ation** ['tæk'sei∫ən] Besteuerung *f;* Steuer(n *pl.) f; bsd.* **t⅔** Schätzung *f.*

taxi ['tæksi] **1.** — *~cab;* **2.** mit e-m Taxi fahren; ✈ rollen; *~***cab** Taxi *n,* (Auto)Droschke *f.*

taxpayer ['tækspeiə] Steuerzahler *m.*

tea [ti:] Tee *m; high ~, meat ~* frühes Abendbrot mit Tee.

teach [ti:t∫] [*irr.*] lehren, unterrichten, *j-m et.* beibringen; *~***able** □ ['ti:t∫əbl] gelehrig; lehrbar; *~***er** [~∫ə] Lehrer(in); *~***in** [~∫'in] (politische) Diskussion *als Großveranstaltung.*

tea|-cosy ['ti:kouzi] Teewärmer *m; ~***cup** Teetasse *f; storm in a ~ fig.* Sturm *m* im Wasserglas; *~***kettle** Wasserkessel *m.*

team [ti:m] Team *n,* Arbeitsgruppe *f;* Gespann *n; bsd. Sport* Mannschaft *f; ~***ster** ['ti:mstə] Gespannführer *m; Am.* LKW-Fahrer *m; ~***work** Zusammenarbeit *f,* Teamwork *n;* Zusammenspiel *n.*

teapot ['ti:pɔt] Teekanne *f.*

tear[1] [tɛə] **1.** [*irr.*] zerren, (zer)reißen; rasen, stürmen; **2.** Riß *m.*

tear[2] [tiə] Träne *f.*

tearful □ ['tiəful] tränenreich.

tea-room ['ti:rum] Tearoom *m,* Teestube *f,* Café *n.*

tease [ti:z] **1.** necken, hänseln; quälen; **2.** Necker *m;* Quälgeist *m.*

teat [ti:t] Zitze *f;* Brustwarze *f;* (Gummi)Sauger *m.*

technic|al □ ['teknikəl] technisch; gewerblich, Gewerbe...; fachlich, Fach...; **~ality** [tekni'kæliti] technische Eigentümlichkeit od. Einzelheit; Fachausdruck m; **~ian** [tek-'niʃən] Techniker(in).

technique [tek'niːk] Technik f, Verfahren n.

technology [tek'nɔlədʒi] Gewerbekunde f; *school of* ~ Technische Hochschule.

teddy boy F ['tedibɔi] Halbstarke(r) m.

tedious □ ['tiːdjəs] langweilig, ermüdend; weitschweifig.

tee [tiː] *Sport* Mal n, Ziel n; *Golf:* Abschlagmal n.

teem [tiːm] wimmeln, strotzen (*with* von).

teens [tiːnz] pl. Lebensjahre n/pl. von 13—19.

teeny F ['tiːni] winzig.

teeth [tiːθ] pl. *von* tooth; **~e** [tiːð] zahnen.

teetotal(l)er [tiː'toutlə] Abstinenzler(in).

telecast ['telikɑːst] **1.** Fernsehsendung f; **2.** [*irr.* (cast)] im Fernsehen übertragen.

telecourse *Am.* F ['telikɔːs] Fernsehlehrgang m.

telegram ['teligræm] Telegramm n.

telegraph ['teligrɑːf] **1.** Telegraph m; **2.** Telegraphen...; **3.** telegraphieren; **~ic** [teli'græfik] (*~ally*) telegraphisch; telegrammäßig (*Stil*); **~y** [ti'legrəfi] Telegraphie f.

telephon|e ['telifoun] **1.** Telephon n, Fernsprecher m; **2.** telephonieren; anrufen; **~e booth** Telephonzelle f; **~ic** [teli'fɔnik] (*~ally*) telephonisch; **~y** [ti'lefəni] Fernsprechwesen n.

telephoto *phot.* ['teli'foutou] *a.* ~ *lens* Teleobjektiv n.

teleprinter ['teliprintə] Fernschreiber m.

telescope ['teliskoup] **1.** *opt.* Fernrohr n; **2.** (sich) ineinanderschieben.

teletype ['telitaip] Fernschreiber m.

televis|e ['telivaiz] im Fernsehen übertragen; **~ion** [~viʒən] Fernsehen n; *watch* ~ fernsehen; **~ion set, ~or** [~vaizə] Fernsehapparat m.

tell [tel] [*irr.*] v/t. zählen; sagen, erzählen; erkennen; ~ *s.o. to do s.th.* j-m sagen, er solle et. tun; ~ *off* abzählen; auswählen; F abkanzeln; v/i. erzählen (*of, about* von); (aus)plaudern; sich auswirken; sitzen (*Hieb etc.*); **~er** [ˈtelə] (Er)Zähler m; **~ing** [ˈteliŋ] wirkungsvoll; **~tale** [ˈteltéil] **1.** Klatschbase f; ⊕ Anzeiger m; **2.** *fig.* verräterisch.

temerity [ti'meriti] Unbesonnenheit f, Verwegenheit f.

temper ['tempə] **1.** mäßigen, mildern; *Kalk etc.* anrühren; *Stahl* anlassen; **2.** ⊕ Härte(grad m) f;

(Gemüts)Ruhe f, Gleichmut m; Temperament n, Wesen n; Stimmung f; Wut f; *lose one's* ~ in Wut geraten; **~ament** [~rəmənt] Temperament n; **~amental** □ [tempərə'mentl] anlagebedingt; launisch; **~ance** ['tempərəns] Mäßigkeit f; Enthaltsamkeit f; **~ate** [~rit] gemäßigt; zurückhaltend; maßvoll; mäßig; **~ature** [~pritʃə] Temperatur f.

tempest ['tempist] Sturm m; Gewitter n; **~uous** □ [tem'pestjəs] stürmisch; ungestüm.

temple ['templ] Tempel m; *anat.* Schläfe f.

tempor|al □ ['tempərəl] zeitlich; weltlich; **~ary** □ [~əri] zeitweilig; vorläufig; vorübergehend; Not...; **~ize** [~raiz] (Aus)Hilfs..., Behelfs...; Zeit zu gewinnen suchen.

tempt [tempt] *j-n* versuchen; verleiten; verlocken; **~ation** [temp'teiʃən] Versuchung f; Reiz m; **~ing** □ ['temptiŋ] verführerisch.

ten [ten] **1.** zehn; **2.** Zehn f.

tenable ['tenəbl] haltbar (*Theorie etc.*); verliehen (*Amt*).

tenaci|ous □ [ti'neiʃəs] zäh; festhaltend (*of an dat.*); gut (*Gedächtnis*); **~ty** [ti'næsiti] Zähigkeit f; Festhalten n; Verläßlichkeit f *des Gedächtnisses*.

tenant ['tenənt] Pächter m; Mieter m.

tend [tend] v/i. (*to*) gerichtet sein (auf *acc.*); hinstreben (zu); abzielen (auf *acc.*); neigen (zu); v/t. pflegen; hüten; ⊕ bedienen; **~ance** ['tendəns] Pflege f; Bedienung f; **~ency** [~si] Richtung f; Neigung f; Zweck m.

tender ['tendə] **1.** □ zart; weich; empfindlich; heikel (*Thema*); zärtlich; **2.** Angebot n; Kostenanschlag m; 📷, 🚂 Tender m; *legal* ~ gesetzliches Zahlungsmittel; **3.** anbieten; *Entlassung* einreichen; **~foot** *Am.* F Neuling m, Anfänger m; **~loin** *bsd. Am.* Filet n; *Am.* berüchtigtes Viertel; **~ness** [~nis] Zartheit f; Zärtlichkeit f.

tendon *anat.* ['tendən] Sehne f.

tendril ♀ ['tendril] Ranke f.

tenement ['tenimənt] Wohnhaus n; (*bsd.* Miet)Wohnung f; ~ *house* Mietshaus n.

tennis ['tenis] Tennis(spiel) n; **~ court** Tennisplatz m.

tenor ['tenə] Fortgang m, Verlauf m; Inhalt m; ♪ Tenor m.

tens|e [tens] **1.** *gr.* Zeit(form) f, Tempus n; **2.** □ gespannt (*a. fig.*); straff; **~ion** ['tenʃən] Spannung f; Zweck m.

tent [tent] **1.** Zelt n; **2.** zelten.

tentacle *zo.* ['tentəkl] Fühler m; Fangarm m *e-s Polypen.*

tentative □ ['tentətiv] versuchend; Versuchs...; **~ly** versuchsweise.

tenth [tenθ] **1.** zehnte(r, -s); **2.** Zehntel *n*; **~ly** ['tenθli] zehntens.

tenuous □ ['tenjuəs] dünn; zart, fein; dürftig.

tenure ['tenjuə] Besitz(art *f*, -dauer *f*) *m*.

tepid □ ['tepid] lau(warm).

term [tə:m] **1.** (bestimmte) Zeit, Frist *f*, Termin *m*; Zahltag *m*; Amtszeit *f*; ½½ Sitzungsperiode *f*; Semester *n*, Quartal *n*, Trimester *n*, Tertial *n*; Å, *phls.* Glied *n*; (Fach-)Ausdruck *m*, Wort *n*, Bezeichnung *f*; Begriff *m*; **~s** *pl.* Bedingungen *f/pl.*; Beziehungen *f/pl.*; be on good (bad) **~s** with gut (schlecht) stehen mit; come to **~s**, make **s** sich einigen; **2.** (be)nennen; bezeichnen (als).

termagant ['tə:məgənt] **1.** □ zanksüchtig; **2.** Zankteufel *m* (*Weib*).

termina|l ['tə:minl] **1.** □ End...; letzt; **~ly** terminweise; **2.** Endstück *n*; ∮ Pol *m*; *Am.* ☏ Endstation *f*; **~te** [~neit] begrenzen; (be)endigen; **~tion** [tə:mi'neifən] Beendigung *f*; Ende *n*; *gr.* Endung *f*.

terminus ['tə:minəs] Endstation *f*.

terrace ['terəs] Terrasse *f*; Häuserreihe *f*; **~house** Reihenhaus *n*; **~d** [~st] terrassenförmig.

terrestrial □ [ti'restriəl] irdisch; Erd...; *bsd. zo.*, ⚘ Land...

terrible □ ['terəbl] schrecklich.

terri|fic [tə'rifik] **1.** schrecklich, fürchterlich, schrecklich; F ungeheuer, großartig; **~fy** ['terifai] *v/t.* erschrecken.

territor|ial [teri'tɔ:riəl] **1.** □ territorial; Land...; Bezirks...; ⚔ Army, ⚓ Force Territorialarmee *f*; **2.** ⚔ Angehörige(r) *m* der Territorialarmee; **~y** ['teritəri] Territorium *n*, (Hoheits-, Staats)Gebiet *n*.

terror ['terə] Schrecken *m*, Entsetzen *n*; **~ize** [~əraiz] terrorisieren.

terse □ [tə:s] knapp; kurz u. bündig.

test [test] **1.** Probe *f*; Untersuchung *f*; (Eignungs)Prüfung *f*; Test *m*; ⚗ Reagens *n*; **2.** probieren, prüfen, testen.

testament ['testəmənt] Testament *n*.

testicle *anat.* ['testikl] Hode(n *m*) [*m*, *f*.]

testify ['testifai] (be)zeugen; (als Zeuge) aussagen (on über *acc.*).

testimon|ial [testi'mounjəl] (Führungs)Zeugnis *n*; Zeichen *n* der Anerkennung; **~y** ['testiməni] Zeugnis *n*; Beweis *m*.

test-tube ⚗ ['testtju:b] Reagenzglas *n*.

testy □ ['testi] reizbar, kribbelig.

tether ['teðə] **1.** Haltestrick *m*; *fig.* Spielraum *m*; at the end of one's **~** *fig.* am Ende **s**-r Kraft; **2.** anbinden.

text [tekst] Text *m*; Bibelstelle *f*;

~book ['tekstbuk] Leitfaden *m*, Lehrbuch *n*.

textile ['tekstail] **1.** Textil..., Web...; **2.** **~s** *pl.* Webwaren *f/pl.*, Textilien *pl.*

texture ['tekstʃə] Gewebe *n*; Gefüge *n*.

than [ðæn, ðən] als.

thank [θæŋk] **1.** danken (*dat.*); **~** you, bei Ablehnung no, **~** you danke; **2.** **~s** *pl.* Dank *m*; **~s!** vielen Dank!; danke (schön)!; **~s to** dank (*dat.*); **~ful** □ ['θæŋkful] dankbar; **~less** □ [~klis] undankbar; **~sgiving** [~ksgivin] Danksagung *f*; Dankfest *n*; ♀ (*Day*) *bsd. Am.* (Ernte)Dankfest *n*.

that [ðæt, ðət] **1.** *pl.* those [ðouz] *pron.* jene(r, -s); der, die, das; der-, die-, das(jenige); welche(r, -s); **2.** *cj.* daß; damit.

thatch [θætʃ] **1.** Dachstroh *n*; Strohdach *n*; **2.** mit Stroh decken.

thaw [θɔ:] **1.** Tauwetter *n*; (Auf-)Tauen *n*; **2.** (auf)tauen.

the [ði; *vor Vokalen* ði; *vor Konsonanten* ðə] **1.** *art.* der, die, das; **2.** *adv.* desto, um so; **~ ... ~ ...** je ... desto ...

theat|re, *Am.* **~er** ['θiətə] Theater *n*; *fig.* (Kriegs)Schauplatz *m*; **~ric(al** □) ['θi'ætrik(əl)] Theater...; theatralisch.

thee *Bibel, poet.* [ði:] dich; dir.

theft [θeft] Diebstahl *m*.

their [ðeə] ihr(e); **~s** [~z] der (die, das) ihrige *od.* ihre.

them [ðem, ðəm] sie (*acc. pl.*); ihnen.

theme [θi:m] Thema *n*; Aufgabe *f*.

themselves [ðem'selvz] sie (*acc. pl.*) selbst; sich selbst.

then [ðen] **1.** *adv.* dann; damals; da; by **~** bis dann; inzwischen; every now and **~** alle Augenblicke; there and **~** sogleich; now **~** nun denn; **2.** *cj.* denn, also, folglich; **3.** *adj.* damalig.

thence *lit.* [ðens] daher; von da.

theolog|ian [θiə'loudʒən] Theologe *m*; **~y** [θi'ɔlədʒi] Theologie *f*.

theor|etic(al □) [θiə'retik(əl)] theoretisch; **~ist** ['θiərist] Theoretiker *m*; **~y** [~ri] Theorie *f*.

therap|eutic [θerə'pju:tik] **1.** (**~ally**) therapeutisch; **2.** **~s** *mst. sg.* Therapeutik *f*; **~y** ['θerəpi] Therapie *f*, Heilbehandlung *f*.

there [ðeə] da, dort; darin; dorthin; na!; **~** is, **~** are es gibt, es ist, es sind; **~about(s** ['θeərəbaut(s)] da herum; so ungefähr...; **~after** [θeər'ɑ:ftə] danach; **~by** ['ðeə'bai] dadurch; damit; **~fore** ['ðeəfɔ:] darum, deswegen; deshalb, daher; **~upon** ['θeərə'pɔn] darauf(hin); **~with** [ðeə'wiθ] damit.

thermal ['θə:məl] **1.** □ Thermal...; *phys.* Wärme...; **2.** Aufwind *m*.

thermo|meter [θə'mɔmitə] Thermometer *n*; 2s ['θəːmɔs] *a.* ~ **flask**, ~ **bottle** Thermosflasche *f.*

these [ðiːz] *pl von* this.

thes|is ['θiːsis], *pl.* ~es ['θiːsiːz] These *f*; Dissertation *f.*

they [ðei] sie (*pl.*)

thick [θik] 1. [*allg.* dick; dicht; trüb; legiert (*Suppe*); heiser; dumm; *pred.* ᴲ dick befreundet; ~ *with* dicht besetzt mit; 2. dickster Teil; *fig.* Brennpunkt *m*; *in the* ~ *of* mitten in (*dat.*); ~**en** ['θikən] (sich) verdicken; (sich) verstärken; legieren; (sich) verdichten; ~**et** ['θikit] Dickicht *n*; ~**-headed** dumm; ~**ness** ['θiknis] Dicke *f*, Stärke *f*; Dichte *f*; ~**-set** dicht (gepflanzt); untersetzt; ~**-skinned** *fig.* dickfellig.

thief [θiːf], *pl.* **thieves** [θiːvz] Dieb(in); **thieve** [θiːv] stehlen.

thigh [θai] (Ober)Schenkel *m.*

thimble ['θimbl] Fingerhut *m.*

thin [θin] 1. [*allg.* dünn; leicht; mager; spärlich, dürftig; schwach; fadenscheinig (*bsd. fig.*); 2. verdünnen; (sich) lichten, abnehmen.

thine *Bibel, poet.* [ðain] dein; der (die, das) deinige *od.* deine.

thing [θiŋ] Ding *n*; Sache *f*; Geschöpf *n*; ~**s** *pl.* Sachen *f/pl.*; die Dinge *n/pl.* (*Umstände*); *the* ~ ᴲ das Richtige; richtig; die Hauptsache; ~**s** *are going better* es geht jetzt besser.

think [θiŋk] [*irr.*] *v/i.* denken (*of an acc.*); nachdenken; sich besinnen; meinen, glauben, gedenken (*to inf. zu inf.*); *v/t.* (sich) *et.* denken; halten für; ~ *much etc.* of viel *etc.* halten von; ~ *s.th. over* (sich) *et.* überlegen, über *et.* nachdenken.

third [θəːd] 1. dritte(r, -s); 2. Drittel *n*; ~**ly** ['θəːdli] drittens; ~**-rate** ['θəːd'reit] drittklassig.

thirst [θəːst] 1. Durst *m*; 2. dürsten; ~**y** [['θəːsti] durstig; dürr (*Boden*).

thirt|een ['θəː'tiːn] dreizehn; ~**eenth** [~nθ] dreizehnte(r, -s); ~**ieth** ['θəːtiiθ] dreißigste(r, -s); ~**y** ['θəːti] dreißig.

this [ðis], *pl.* **these** [ðiːz] diese(r, -s); ~ *morning* heute morgen.

thistle 🜊 ['θisl] Distel *f.*

thong [θɔŋ] (Leder-, Peitschen-) Riemen *m.*

thorn 🜊 [θɔːn] Dorn *m*; ~**y** ['θɔːni] dornig, stach(e)lig; beschwerlich.

thorough [['θʌrə] vollkommen; vollständig; vollendet; gründlich; ~**ly** *a.* durchaus; ~**bred** Vollblüter *m*; *attr.* Vollblut...; ~**fare** Durchgang *m*, Durchfahrt *f*; Hauptverkehrsstraße *f*; ~**-going** gründlich; tatkräftig.

those [ðouz] *pl. von* that 1.

thou *Bibel, poet.* [ðau] du.

though [ðou] obgleich, obwohl,

wenn auch; zwar; aber, doch; freilich; *as* ~ als ob.

thought [θɔːt] 1. *pret. u. p.p. von* think; 2. Gedanke *m*; (Nach)Denken *n*; *on second* ~s nach nochmaliger Überlegung; ~**ful** ⫿ ['θɔːtful] gedankenvoll, nachdenklich; rücksichtsvoll (*of gegen*); ~**less** ⫿ ['θɔːtlis] gedankenlos; unbesonnen; rücksichtslos (*of gegen*).

thousand ['θauzənd] 1. tausend; 2. Tausend *n*; ~**th** [~ntθ] 1. tausendste(r, -s); 2. Tausendstel *n.*

thrash [θræʃ] (ver)dreschen, (ver-) prügeln, (hin und her) schlagen; *s. thresh*, ~**ing** ['θræʃiŋ] Dresche *f*, Tracht *f* Prügel; *s. threshing.*

thread [θred] 1. Faden *m* (*a. fig.*); Zwirn *m*, Garn *n*; ⊕ (Schrauben-) Gewinde *n*; 2. einfädeln; sich durchwinden(durch); durchziehen; ~**bare** ['θredbɛə] fadenscheinig.

threat [θret] Drohung *f*; ~**en** ['θretn] (be-, an)drohen; ~**ening** [~niŋ] bedrohlich.

three [θriː] 1. drei; 2. Drei *f*; ~**fold** ['θriːfould] dreifach; ~**pence** ['θrepəns] Dreipence(stück *n*) *m/pl.*; ~**score** ['θriː'skɔː] sechzig.

thresh [θreʃ] 🖊 (aus)dreschen; *s. thrash*; ~ *out fig.* durchdreschen; ~**er** ['θreʃə] Drescher *m*; Dreschmaschine *f*; ~**ing** [~ʃiŋ] Dreschen *n*; ~**ing-machine** Dreschmaschine *f.*

threshold ['θreʃhould] Schwelle *f.*

threw [θruː] *pret. von* throw 1.

thrice [θrais] dreimal.

thrift [θrift] Sparsamkeit *f*, Wirtschaftlichkeit *f*; ~**less** ⫿ ['θriftlis] verschwenderisch; ~**y** ⫿ [~ti] sparsam; *poet.* gedeihend.

thrill [θril] 1. *v/t.* durchdringen, durchschauern; *fig.* packen, aufwühlen, aufregen; *v/i.* er)beben; 2. Schauer *m*; Beben *n*; aufregendes Erlebnis; Sensation *f*; ~**er** ᴲ ['θrilə] Reißer *m*, Thriller *m*, Schauerroman *m*, Schauerstück *n*; ~**ing** [~ʃiŋ] spannend.

thrive [θraiv] [*irr.*] gedeihen; *fig.* blühen; Glück haben; ~**n** ['θrivn] *p.p. von* thrive.

throat [θrout] Kehle *f*; Hals *m*; Gurgel *f*; Schlund *m*; *clear one's* ~ sich räuspern.

throb [θrɔb] 1. pochen, klopfen, schlagen; pulsieren; 2. Pochen *n*; Schlagen *n*; Pulsschlag *m.*

throes [θrouz] *pl.* Geburtswehen *f/pl.* [Thrombose *f.*)

thrombosis 🝆 [θrɔm'bousis]

throne [θroun] Thron *m.*

throng [θrɔŋ] 1. Gedränge *n*; Menge *f*, Schar *f*; 2. sich drängen (in *dat.*); anfüllen mit.

throstle *orn.* ['θrɔsl] Drossel *f.*

throttle ['θrɔtl] 1. erdrosseln; ⊕ (ab)drosseln; 2. ⊕ Drosselklappe *f.*

through [θruː] 1. durch; 2. Durchgangs...; durchgehend; ~out [θruː(ː)'aut] 1. *prp.* überall in (*dat.*); 2. *adv.* durch u. durch, ganz und gar, durchweg.

throve [θrouv] *pret. von* thrive.

throw [θrou] 1. [*irr.*] (ab)werfen, schleudern; *Am.* F *Wettkampf etc.* betrügerisch verlieren; ~ürfeln; ⊕ schalten; ~ *off* (die Jagd) beginnen; ~ *over* aufgeben; ~ *up* in die Höhe werfen; erbrechen; *fig.* hinwerfen; 2. Wurf *m*; ~n [θroun] *p.p. von* throw 1.

thru *Am.* [θruː] = through.

thrum [θrʌm] klimpern (auf *dat.*).

thrush *orn.* [θrʌʃ] Drossel *f*.

thrust [θrʌst] 1. Stoß *m*; Vorstoß *m*; ⊕ Druck *m*, Schub *m*; 2. [*irr.*] stoßen; ~ *o.s. into* sich drängen in (*acc.*); ~ *upon s.o.* j-m aufdrängen.

thud [θʌd] 1. dumpf aufschlagen, F bumsen; 2. dumpfer (Auf)Schlag, F Bums *m*.

thug [θʌg] Strolch *m*.

thumb [θʌm] 1. Daumen *m*; Tom ♀ Däumling *m im Märchen*; 2. Buch *etc.* abgreifen; ~ *a lift* per Anhalter fahren; ~tack *Am.* ['θʌmtæk] Reißzwecke *f*.

thump [θʌmp] 1. F Bums *m*; F Puff *m*; 2. *v/t.* F bumsen *od.* pochen auf (*acc.*) *od.* gegen; F knuffen, puffen; *v/i.* F (auf)bumsen.

thunder ['θʌndə] 1. Donner *m*; 2. donnern; ~bolt Blitz *m u.* Donner *m*); ~clap Donnerschlag *m*; ~ous □ [~rəs] donnernd; ~storm Gewitter *n*; ~struck wie vom Donner gerührt.

Thursday ['θəːzdi] Donnerstag *m*.

thus [ðʌs] so; also, somit.

thwart [θwɔːt] 1. durchkreuzen; hintertreiben; 2. Ruderbank *f*.

thy *Bibel, poet.* [ðai] dein(e).

tick[1] *zo.* [tik] Zecke *f*.

tick[2] [~] 1. Ticken *n*; (Vermerk-) Häkchen *n*; 2. *v/i.* ticken; *v/t.* anhaken; ~ *off* abhaken.

tick[3] [~] Inlett *n*; Matratzenbezug *m*.

ticket ['tikit] 1. Fahrkarte *f*, -schein *m*; Flugkarte *f*; Eintrittskarte *f*; (Straf)Zettel *m*; (Preis- *etc.*)Schildchen *n*; *pol.* (Wahl-, Kandidaten-) Liste *f*; 2. etikettieren, *Ware* auszeichnen; ~machine Fahrkartenautomat *m*; ~ office, ~ window *bsd. Am.* Fahrkartenschalter *m*.

tickl|e ['tikl] kitzeln (*a. fig.*); ~ish □ [~liʃ] kitzlig; heikel.

tidal ['taidl]: ~ *wave* Flutwelle *f*.

tide [taid] 1. Gezeit(en *pl.*) *f*; Ebbe *f* und Flut *f*; *fig.* Strom *m*, Flut *f*; *in Zssgn*: *rechte* Zeit; *high* ~ Flut *f*; *low* ~ Ebbe *f*; 2. ~ *over fig.* hinwegkommen *od.* j-m hinweghelfen über (*acc.*).

tidings ['taidiŋz] *pl. od. sg.* Neuigkeiten *f/pl.*, Nachrichten *f/pl.*

tidy ['taidi] 1. ordentlich, sauber, reinlich; F ganz schön, beträchtlich (*Summe*); 2. Behälter *m*; Abfallkorb *m*; 3. *a.* ~ *up* zurechtmachen; ordnen; aufräumen.

tie [tai] 1. Band *n* (*a. fig.*); Schleife *f*; Krawatte *f*, Schlips *m*; Bindung *f*; *fig.* Fessel *f*, Verpflichtung *f*; *Sport*: Punkt-, *parl.* Stimmengleichheit *f*; *Sport*: Entscheidungsspiel *n*; ⚏ *Am.* Schwelle *f*; 2. *v/t.* (ver)binden; ~ *down fig.* binden (*to an acc.*); ~ *up* zu-, an-, ver-, zs.-binden; *v/i. Sport*: punktgleich sein.

tier [tiə] Reihe *f*; Rang *m*.

tie-up ['taiʌp] (Ver)Bindung *f*; ⚡ Fusion *f*; Stockung *f*; *bsd. Am.* Streik *m*.

tiffin ['tifin] Mittagessen *n*.

tiger ['taigə] *zo.* Tiger *m*; *Am.* F Beifallsgebrüll *n*.

tight [tait] 1. □ dicht; fest; eng; knapp (sitzend); straff, prall, knapp; F beschwipst; *be in a* ~ *place od. corner* F in der Klemme sein; 2. *adv.* fest; *hold* ~ festhalten; ~en ['taitn] *a.* ~ *up* (sich) zs.-ziehen; *Gürtel* enger schnallen; ~-fisted knick(e)rig; ~ness ['taitnis] Festigkeit *f*, Dichtigkeit *f*; Straffheit *f*; Knappheit *f*; Enge *f*; Geiz *m*; ~s [taits] *pl.* Trikot *n*.

tigress ['taigris] Tigerin *f*.

tile [tail] 1. (Dach)Ziegel *m*; Kachel *f*; Fliese *f*; 2. mit Ziegeln *etc.* decken; kacheln; fliesen.

till[1] [til] Laden(tisch)kasse *f*.

till[2] [~] 1. *prp.* bis (zu); 2. *cj.* bis.

till[3] ✗ [~] bestellen, bebauen; ~age ['tilidʒ] (Land)Bestellung *f*; Ackerbau *m*; Ackerland *n*.

tilt [tilt] 1. Plane *f*; Neigung *f*, Kippe *f*; Stoß *m*; Lanzenbrechen *n* (*a. fig.*); 2. kippen; ~ *against* anrennen gegen.

timber ['timbə] 1. (Bau-, Nutz-) Holz *n*; Balken *m*; Baumbestand *m*, Bäume *m/pl.*; 2. zimmern.

time [taim] 1. Zeit *f*; Mal *n*; Takt *m*; Tempo *n*; ~ *and again* immer wieder; *at a* ~ zugleich; *for the being* einstweilen; *have a good* ~ es gut haben; sich amüsieren; *in* ~, *on* ~ zur rechten Zeit, rechtzeitig; 2. zeitlich festsetzen; zeitlich abpassen; die Zeitdauer messen; ~hono(u)red ['taimɔnəd] altehrwürdig; ~ly ['taimli] (recht)zeitig; ~piece Uhr *f*; ~sheet Anwesenheitsliste *f*; ~table Terminkalender *m*; Fahr-, Stundenplan *m*.

tim|id □ ['timid], ~orous □ ['timərəs] furchtsam; schüchtern.

tin [tin] 1. Zinn *n*; Weißblech *n*; (Konserven)Büchse *f*; 2. verzinnen; in Büchsen einmachen, eindosen.

tincture ['tiŋktʃə] 1. Farbe *f*; Tinktur *f*; *fig.* Anstrich *m*; 2. färben.

tinfoil ['tin'fɔil] Stanniol *n*.

tinge [tindʒ] 1. Färbung *f*; *fig.* Anflug *m*, Spur *f*; 2. färben; *fig.* e-n Anstrich geben (*dat.*).

tingle ['tiŋgl] klingen; prickeln.

tinker ['tiŋkə] basteln (*at an dat.*).

tinkle ['tiŋkl] klingeln (mit).

tin|-opener ['tinoupnə] Dosenöffner *m*; **~plate** Weißblech *n*.

tinsel ['tinsəl] Flitter(werk *n*) *m*; Lametta *n*.

tin-smith ['tinsmiθ] Klempner *m*.

tint [tint] 1. Farbe *f*; (Farb)Ton *m*, Schattierung *f*; 2. färben; (ab-)tönen.

tiny ['taini] winzig, klein.

tip [tip] 1. Spitze *f*; Mundstück *n*; Trinkgeld *n*; Tip *m*, Wink *m*; leichter Stoß; Schuttabladeplatz *m*; 2. mit e-r Spitze versehen; (um-)kippen; *j-m* ein Trinkgeld geben; *a.* **~** off *j-m* e-n Wink geben.

tipple ['tipl] zechen, picheln.

tipsy ['tipsi] angeheitert.

tiptoe ['tiptou] 1. auf Zehenspitzen gehen; 2. on **~** auf Zehenspitzen.

tire¹ ['taiə] (Rad-, Auto)Reifen *m*.

tire² [~] ermüden, müde machen *od.* werden; **~d** ◊ müde; **~less** □ ['taiəlis] unermüdlich; **~some** □ ['taiəsəm] ermüdend; lästig.

tiro ['taiərou] Anfänger *m*.

tissue ['tisju:, *Am.* 'tiʃu:] Gewebe *n*; **~paper** Seidenpapier *n*.

tit¹ [tit] = teat.

tit² *orn.* [~] Meise *f*.

titbit ['titbit] Leckerbissen *m*.

titillate ['titileit] kitzeln.

title ['taitl] 1. (Buch-, Ehren)Titel *m*; Überschrift *f*; ⚖ Anspruch *m*; 2. betiteln; **~d** *bsd.* ad(e)lig.

titmouse *orn.* ['titmaus] Meise *f*.

titter ['titə] 1. kichern; 2. Kichern *n*.

tittle ['titl] Pünktchen *n*; *fig.* Tütelchen *n*; **~-tattle** [~'tætl] Schnickschnack *m*.

to [tu:, tu, tə] *prp.* zu (*a. adv.*); gegen, nach, an, in, auf; bis zu, bis an (*acc.*); um zu; für; **~** me *etc.* mir *etc.*; I weep **~** think *of* it ich weine, wenn ich daran denke; here's **~** you! auf Ihr Wohl!, Prosit!

toad *zo.* [toud] Kröte *f*; **~stool** ['toudstu:l] (größerer Blätter)Pilz; Giftpilz *m*; **~y** ['toudi] 1. Speichellecker *m*; 2. *fig.* vor *j-m* kriechen.

toast [toust] 1. Toast *m*, geröstetes Brot; Trinkspruch *m*; 2. toasten, rösten; *fig.* wärmen; trinken auf (*acc.*).

tobacco [tə'bækou] Tabak *m*; **~nist** [~kənist] Tabakhändler *m*.

toboggan [tə'bɔgən] 1. Toboggan *m*, Rodelschlitten *m*; 2. rodeln.

today [tə'dei] heute. [teln.]

toddle ['tɔdl] unsicher gehen; zot-]

toddy ['tɔdi] *Art* Grog *m*.

to-do F [tə'du:] Lärm *m*, Aufheben *n*.

toe [tou] 1. Zehe *f*; Spitze *f*; 2. mit den Zehen berühren.

toff|ee, ~y ['tɔfi] Sahnebonbon *m, n*, Toffee *n*.

together [tə'geðə] zusammen; zugleich; nacheinander.

toil [tɔil] 1. schwere Arbeit; Mühe *f*, F Plackerei *f*; 2. sich plagen.

toilet ['tɔilit] Toilette *f*; **~-paper** Toilettenpapier *n*; **~-table** Frisiertoilette *f*. [*n*.]

toils [tɔilz] *pl.* Schlingen *f/pl.*, Netz]

toilsome □ ['tɔilsəm] mühsam.

token ['toukən] Zeichen *n*; Andenken *n*, Geschenk *n*; **~** money Notgeld *n*; in **~** of zum Zeichen (*gen.*).

told [tould] *pret. u. p.p. von* tell.

tolera|ble □ ['tɔlərəbl] erträglich; **~nce** [~əns] Duldsamkeit *f*; **~nt** □ [~nt] duldsam (*of* gegen); **~te** [~reit] dulden; ertragen; **~tion** [tɔlə'reiʃən] Duldung *f*.

toll [toul] 1. Zoll *m* (*a. fig.*); Wege-, Brücken-, Marktgeld *n*; *fig.* Tribut *m*; **~** of the road die Verkehrsopfer *n/pl.*; 2. läuten; **~-bar** ['toulba:], **~-gate** Schlagbaum *m*.

tomato ◊ [tə'ma:tou, *Am.* tə'meitou], *pl.* **~es** Tomate *f*.

tomb [tu:m] Grab(mal) *n*.

tomboy ['tɔmbɔi] Range *f*.

tombstone ['tu:mstoun] Grabstein *m*.

tom-cat ['tɔm'kæt] Kater *m*.

tomfool ['tɔm'fu:l] Hansnarr *m*.

tomorrow [tə'mɔrou] morgen.

ton [tʌn] Tonne *f* (*Gewichtseinheit*).

tone [toun] 1. Ton *m*; Klang *m*; Laut *m*; out *of* **~** verstimmt; 2. e-n Ton geben (*dat.*); stimmen; *paint.* abtönen; **~** down (sich) abschwächen, mildern.

tongs [tɔŋz] *pl.* (a *pair of* **~** *pl.* eine) Zange.

tongue [tʌŋ] Zunge *f*; Sprache *f*; Landzunge *f*; (Schuh)Lasche *f*; hold one's **~** den Mund halten; **~-tied** ['tʌŋtaid] sprachlos; schweigsam; stumm.

tonic ['tɔnik] 1. (~*ally*) tonisch; ♪ stärkend; 2. ♪ Grundton *m*; ♪ Stärkungsmittel *n*, Tonikum *n*.

tonight [tə'nait] heute abend *od.* nacht.

tonnage ⚓ ['tʌnidʒ] Tonnengehalt *m*; Lastigkeit *f*; Tonnengeld *n*.

tonsil *anat.* ['tɔnsl] Mandel *f*; **~litis** ♪ [tɔnsi'laitis] Mandelentzündung *f*.

too [tu:] zu, allzu; auch, noch dazu.

took [tuk] *pret. von* take 1.

tool [tu:l] Werkzeug *n*, Gerät *n*; **~-bag** ['tu:lbæg], **~-kit** Werkzeugtasche *f*.

toot [tu:t] 1. blasen, tuten; 2. Tuten *n*.

tooth [tu:θ] *pl.* **teeth** [ti:θ] Zahn *m*; **~ache** ['tu:θeik] Zahnschmerzen *pl.* **~-brush** Zahnbürste *f*; **~less** □

['tu:θlis] zahnlos; ~-paste Zahn-
pasta f; ~pick Zahnstocher m;
~some □ ['tu:θsəm] schmackhaft.

top [tɔp] 1. oberstes Ende; Ober-
teil n; Gipfel m (a. fig.); Wipfel m;
Kopf m e-r Seite; mot. Am. Verdeck n; fig. Haupt n, Erste(r) m;
Stiefel-Stulpe f; Kreisel m; at the
~ of one's voice aus voller Kehle;
on ~ obenauf; obendrein; 2. ober(er,
-e, -es); oberst; höchst; 3. oben
bedecken; fig. überragen; vorangehen in (dat.); als erste(r) stehen
auf e-r Liste; ~boots ['tɔp'bu:ts]
pl. Stulpenstiefel m/pl.

toper ['toupə] Zecher m.

tophat F ['tɔp'hæt] Zylinderhut m.

topic ['tɔpik] Gegenstand m, Thema
n; ~al □ [~kəl] lokal; aktuell.

topmost ['tɔpmoust] höchst, oberst.

topple □ ['tɔpl] (um)kippen.

topsyturvy □ ['tɔpsi'tə:vi] auf den
Kopf gestellt; das Oberste zuunterst; drunter und drüber.

torch [tɔ:tʃ] Fackel f; electric ~
Taschenlampe f; ~light ['tɔ:tʃlait]
Fackelschein m; ~ procession Fak-
kelzug m.

tore [tɔ:] pret. von tear[1]1.

torment 1. ['tɔ:ment] Qual f,
Marter f; 2. [tɔ:'ment] martern,
quälen.

torn [tɔ:n] p.p. von tear[1] 1.

tornado [tɔ:'neidou], pl. ~es Wirbelsturm m, Tornado m.

torpedo [tɔ:'pi:dou], pl. ~es 1. Torpedo m; 2. ⚓ torpedieren (a. fig.).

torp|id □ ['tɔ:pid] starr; apathisch;
träg; ~idity [tɔ:'piditi], ~or ['tɔ:pə]
Erstarrung f, Betäubung f.

torrent ['tɔrənt] Sturz-, Gießbach
m; (reißender) Strom; ~ial □
[tɔ'renʃəl] gießbachartig; strömend;
fig. ungestüm.

torrid ['tɔrid] brennend heiß.

tortoise zo. ['tɔ:təs] Schildkröte f.

tortuous □ ['tɔ:tjuəs] gewunden.

torture ['tɔ:tʃə] 1. Folter f, Marter f,
Tortur f; 2. foltern, martern.

toss [tɔs] 1. Werfen n, Wurf m;
Zurückwerfen n (Kopf); 2. a.
~ about (sich) hin und her werfen;
schütteln; (mit adv.) werfen; a. ~
up hochwerfen; ~ off Getränk hin-
unterstürzen; Arbeit hinhauen; a.
~ up losen (for um); ~-up ['tɔsʌp]
Losen n; fig. etwas Zweifelhaftes.

tot F [tɔt] Knirps m (kleines Kind).

total ['toutl] 1. □ ganz, gänzlich;
total; gesamt; 2. Gesamtbetrag m;
3. sich belaufen auf (acc.); sum-
mieren; ~itarian [toutæli'tɛəriən]
totalitär; ~ity [tou'tæliti] Gesamtheit f.

totter ['tɔtə] wanken, wackeln.

touch [tʌtʃ] 1. (sich) berühren; anrühren, anfassen; stoßen an (acc.);
betreffen; fig. rühren; erreichen; ♪
anschlagen; a bit ~ed fig. ein biß-

chen verrückt; ~ at ⚓ anlegen in
(dat.); ~ up auffrischen; retuschieren; 2. Berührung f; Gefühl(s-
sinn m) n; Anflug m, Zug m; Fertigkeit f; ♪ Anschlag m; (Pinsel-)
Strich m; ~-and-go ['tʌtʃən'gou]
gewagte Sache; it is ~ es steht auf
des Messers Schneide; ~ing [~ʃiŋ]
rührend; ~stone Prüfstein m;
~y [~ʃi] empfindlich; heikel.

tough [tʌf] zäh (a. fig.); schwer,
hart; grob, brutal, übel; ~en ['tʌfn]
zäh machen od. werden; ~ness
[~nis] Zähigkeit f.

tour [tuə] 1. (Rund)Reise f, Tour
(-nee) f; conducted ~ Führung f;
Gesellschaftsreise f; 2. (be)reisen;
~ist ['tuərist] Tourist(in); ~ agency,
~ bureau, ~ office Reisebüro n;
~ season Reisezeit f.   [n.]

tournament ['tuənəmənt] Turnier]

tousle ['tauzl] (zer)zausen.

tow [tou] 1. Schleppen n; take in
~ ins Schlepptau nehmen; 2. (ab-)
schleppen; treideln; ziehen.

toward(s) [tə'wɔ:d(z)] gegen; nach
... zu, auf ... (acc.) zu; (als Beitrag)
zu.

towel ['tauəl] 1. Handtuch n; 2. abreiben; ~-rack Handtuchhalter m.

tower ['tauə] 1. Turm m; fig. Hort
m, Bollwerk n; 2. sich erheben;
~ing [['tauəriŋ] (turm)hoch; rasend (Wut).

town [taun] 1. Stadt f; 2. Stadt...;
städtisch; ~ clerk Stadtsyndikus m;
~ council Stadtrat m (Versammlung); ~ councillor Stadtrat m
(Person); ~ hall Rathaus n; ~sfolk
['taunzfouk] pl. Städter pl.; ~ship
['taunʃip] Stadtgemeinde f; ~ gebiet n; ~sman ['taunzmən]
(Mit)Bürger m; ~speople [~zpi:pl]
pl. = townsfolk.

toxic(al □) ['tɔksik(əl)] giftig;
Gift...; ~n [~in] Giftstoff m.

toy [tɔi] 1. Spielzeug n; Tand m;
~s pl. Spielwaren f/pl.; 2. Spiel-
(zeug)...; Miniatur...; Zwerg...;
3. spielen; ~-book ['tɔibuk] Bilder-
buch n.

trace [treis] 1. Spur f (a. fig.);
Strang m; 2. nachspüren (dat.); fig.
verfolgen; herausfinden; (auf-)
zeichnen; (durch)pausen.

tracing ['treisiŋ] Pauszeichnung f.

track [træk] 1. Spur f; Sport: Bahn
f; Rennstrecke f; Pfad m; Gleis
n; ~ events pl. Laufdisziplinen f/pl.;
2. nachspüren (dat.); verfolgen; ~
down, ~ out aufspüren.

tract [trækt] Fläche f, Strecke f,
Gegend f; Traktat n, Abhandlung f.

tractable □ ['træktəbl] lenk-, füg-
sam.

tract|ion ['trækʃən] Ziehen n, Zug
m; ~ engine Zugmaschine f; ~or ⊕
[~ktə] Trecker m, Traktor m.

trade [treid] 1. Handel *m*; Gewerbe *n*; Handwerk *n*; *Am.* Kompensationsgeschäft *n*; 2. Handel treiben; handeln; ~ on susnutzen; ~ **mark** ♣ Warenzeichen *n*, Schutzmarke *f*; ~ **price** Händlerpreis *m*; ~**r** ['treidə] Händler *m*; ~**sman** [~dzmən] Geschäftsmann *m*; ~ **union** Gewerkschaft *f*; ~ **wind** ⌘ Passatwind *m*.

tradition [trə'diʃən] Tradition *f*, Überlieferung *f*; ~**al** □ [~nl] traditionell.

traffic ['træfik] 1. Verkehr *m*; Handel *m*; 2. handeln (*in* mit); ~ **jam** Verkehrsstauung *f*; ~ **light** Verkehrsampel *f*.

traged|ian [trə'dʒiːdjən] Tragiker *m*; *thea.* Tragöd|e *m*, -in *f*; ~**y** ['trædʒidi] Tragödie *f*.

tragic(al □) ['trædʒik(əl)] tragisch.

trail [treil] 1. *fig.* Schweif *m*; Schleppe *f*; Spur *f*; Pfad *m*; 2. *v/t.* hinter sich (her)ziehen; verfolgen; *v/i.* (sich) schleppen; ♣ kriechen; ~ **blazer** *Am.* Bahnbrecher *m*; ~**er** ['treilə] (Wohnwagen)Anhänger *m*; ♣ Kriechpflanze *f*; *Film:* Vorschau *f*.

train [trein] 1. (Eisenbahn)Zug *m*; *allg.* Zug *m*; Gefolge *n*; Reihe *f*, Folge *f*, Kette *f*; Schleppe *f am Kleid*; 2. erziehen; schulen; abrichten; ausbilden; trainieren; (sich) üben; ~**ee** [trei'niː] in der Ausbildung Begriffene(r) *m*; ~**er** ['treinə] Ausbilder *m*; Trainer *m*.

trait [trei] (Charakter)Zug *m*.

traitor ['treitə] Verräter *m*.

tram [træm] *s.* ~**-car**, ~**way**; ~**-car** ['træmkɑ:] Straßenbahnwagen *m*.

tramp [træmp] 1. Getrampel *n*; Wanderung *f*; Tramp *m*, Landstreicher *m*; 2. trampeln, treten; (durch)wandern; ~**le** ['træmpl] (zer)trampeln.

tramway ['træmwei] Straßenbahn *f*.

trance [trɑːns] Trance *f*.

tranquil □ ['træŋkwil] ruhig; gelassen; ~**(l)ity** [træŋ'kwiliti] Ruhe *f*; Gelassenheit *f*; ~**(l)ize** ['træŋkwilaiz] beruhigen; ~**(l)izer** [~zə] Beruhigungsmittel *n*.

transact [træn'zækt] abwickeln, abmachen; ~**ion** [~kʃən] Verrichtung *f*; Geschäft *n*, Transaktion *f*; ~**s** *pl.* (Tätigkeits)Bericht(e *pl.*) *m*.

transalpine ['trænz'ælpain] transalpin(isch).

transatlantic ['trænzət'læntik] transatlantisch, Transatlantik...

transcend [træn'send] überschreiten, übertreffen; hinausgehen über (*acc.*); ~**ence**, ~**ency** [~dəns, ~si] Überlegenheit *f*; *phls.* Transzendenz *f*.

transcribe [træn'skraib] abschreiben; *Kurzschrift* übertragen.

transcript ['trænskript], ~**ion**

[træns'kripʃən] Abschrift *f*; Umschrift *f*.

transfer 1. [træns'fəː] *v/t.* übertragen; versetzen, verlegen; *v/i.* übertreten; *Am.* umsteigen; 2. ['trænsfə(ː)] Übertragung *f*; ♣ Transfer *m*; Versetzung *f*, Verlegung *f*; *Am.* Umsteigefahrschein *m*; ~**able** [træns'fəːrəbl] übertragbar.

transfigure [træns'figə] umgestalten; verklären.

transfix [træns'fiks] durchstechen; ~**ed** *fig.* versteinert, starr (*with* vor *dat.*).

transform [træns'fɔːm] umformen; um-, verwandeln; ~**ation** [trænsfə'meiʃən] Umformung *f*; Um-, Verwandlung *f*.

transfus|e [træns'fjuːz] ♣ *Blut etc.* übertragen; *fig.* einflößen; *fig.* durchtränken; ~**ion** [~uːʒən] (*bsd.* ♣ Blut)Übertragung *f*, Transfusion *f*.

transgress [træns'gres] *v/t.* überschreiten; übertreten, verletzen; *v/i.* sich vergehen; ~**ion** [~eʃən] Überschreitung *f*; Übertretung *f*; Vergehen *n*; ~**or** [~esə] Übertreter *m*.

transient ['trænziənt] 1. ~ *transitory*; 2. *Am.* Durchreisende(r *m*) *f*.

transit ['trænsit] Durchgang *m*; Durchgangsverkehr *m*.

transition [træn'siʒən] Übergang *m*.

transitive □ *gr.* ['trænsitiv] transitiv.

transitory □ ['trænsitəri] vorübergehend; vergänglich, flüchtig.

translat|e [træns'leit] übersetzen; übertragen; überführen; *fig.* umsetzen; ~**ion** [~eiʃən] Übersetzung *f*, Übertragung *f*; *fig.* Auslegung *f*; ~**or** [~eitə] Übersetzer(in).

translucent [trænz'luːsnt] durchscheinend; *fig.* hell.

transmigration [trænzmai'greiʃən] (Aus)Wanderung *f*; Seelenwanderung *f*.

transmission [trænz'miʃən] Übermittlung *f*; *biol.* Vererbung *f*; *phys.* Fortpflanzung *f*; *mot.* Getriebe *n*; *Radio:* Sendung *f*.

transmit [trænz'mit] übermitteln; übersenden; übertragen; senden; *biol.* vererben; *phys.* fortpflanzen; ~**ter** [~tə] Übermittler(in); *tel. etc.* Sender *m*.

transmute [trænz'mjuːt] um-, verwandeln.

transparent □ [træns'peərənt] durchsichtig (*a. fig.*).

transpire [træns'paiə] ausdünsten, ausschwitzen; *fig.* durchsickern.

transplant [træns'plɑːnt] um-, verpflanzen; ~**ation** [trænsplɑːn'teiʃən] Verpflanzung *f*.

transport 1. [træns'pɔːt] fortschaffen, befördern, transportieren; *fig.* hinreißen; 2. ['trænspɔːt] Fort-

35*

schaffen *n*; Beförderung *f*; Transport *m*; Verkehr *m*; Beförderungsmittel *n*; Transportschiff *n*; Verzückung *f*; **be in** ~**s** außer sich sein; ~**ation** [trænspɔːˈteiʃən] Beförderung *f*, Transport *m*.

transpose [træns'pouz] versetzen, umstellen; ♪ transponieren.

transverse □ ['trænzvəːs] quer laufend; Quer...

trap [træp] **1.** Falle *f* (*a. fig.*); Klappe *f*; **2.** (in e-r Falle) fangen, in die Falle locken; *fig.* ertappen; ~**door** ['træpdɔː] Falltür *f*; *thea.* Versenkung *f*.

trapeze [trə'piːz] *Zirkus:* Trapez *n*.

trapper ['træpə] Trapper *m*, Fallensteller *m*, Pelzjäger *m*.

trappings *fig.* ['træpiŋz] *pl.* Schmuck *m*, Putz *m*.

traps F [træps] *pl.* Siebensachen *pl.*

trash [træʃ] Abfall *m*; *fig.* Plunder *m*; Unsinn *m*, F Blech *n*; Kitsch *m*; ~**y** □ ['træʃi] wertlos, kitschig.

travel ['trævl] **1.** *v/i.* reisen; sich bewegen; wandern; *v/t.* bereisen; **2.** *das* Reisen; ⊕ Lauf *m*; ~**s** *pl.* Reisen *f/pl.*; ~(l)er [~lə] Reisende(r) *m*; ~**'s cheque** (*Am.* check) Reisescheck *m*.

traverse ['trævə(ː)s] **1.** Durchquerung *f*; **2.** (über)queren; durchqueren; *fig.* durchkreuzen.

travesty ['trævisti] **1.** Travestie *f*; Karikatur *f*; **2.** travestieren; verulken.

trawl [trɔːl] **1.** (Grund)Schleppnetz *n*; **2.** mit dem Schleppnetz fischen; ~**er** ['trɔːlə] Trawler *m*.

tray [trei] (Servier)Brett *n*, Tablett *n*; Ablage *f*; *pen*~ Federschale *f*.

treacher|ous □ ['tretʃərəs] verräterisch, treulos; (heim)tückisch; trügerisch; ~**y** [~ri] Verrat *m*, Verräterei *f*, Treulosigkeit *f*; Tücke *f*.

treacle ['triːkl] Sirup *m*.

tread [tred] **1.** (*irr.*) treten; schreiten; **2.** Tritt *m*, Schritt *m*; Lauffläche *f*; ~**le** ['tredl] Pedal *n*; Tritt *m*; ~**mill** Tretmühle *f*.

treason ['triːzn] Verrat *m*; ~**able** [~nəbl] verräterisch.

treasure ['treʒə] **1.** Schatz *m*, Reichtum *m*; ~ **trove** Schatzfund *m*; **2.** *Schätze* sammeln, aufhäufen; ~**r** [~ərə] Schatzmeister *m*, Kassenwart *m*.

treasury ['treʒəri] Schatzkammer *f*; (*bsd.* Staats)Schatz *m*; ♀ **Bench** *parl.* Ministerbank *f*; ♀ **Board**, *Am.* ♀ **Department** Finanzministerium *n*.

treat [triːt] **1.** *v/t.* behandeln; betrachten; ~ *s.o.* **to** *s.th.* j-m et. spendieren; *v/i.* ~ **of** handeln von; ~ **with** unterhandeln mit; **2.** Vergnügen *n*; *school* ~ Schulausflug *m*; **it is my** ~ F es geht auf meine Rechnung; ~**ise** ['triːtiz] Abhandlung *f*;

~**ment** [~tmənt] Behandlung *f*; ✗ Kur *f*; *follow-up* ~ ✗ Nachkur *f*; ~**y** [~ti] Vertrag *m*.

treble ['trebl] **1.** □ dreifach; **2.** Dreifache(s) *n*; ♪ Diskant *m*, Sopran *m*; **3.** (sich) verdreifachen.

tree [triː] Baum *m*.

trefoil ♀ ['trefɔil] Klee *m*.

trellis ['trelis] **1.** ✗ Spalier *n*; **2.** vergittern; ✗ am Spalier ziehen.

tremble ['trembl] zittern.

tremendous □ [tri'mendəs] schrecklich, furchtbar; F kolossal, riesig.

tremor ['tremə] Zittern *n*, Beben *n*.

tremulous □ ['tremjuləs] zitternd, bebend.

trench [trentʃ] **1.** (Schützen)Graben *m*; Furche *f*; **2.** *v/t.* mit Gräben durchziehen; ✗ umgraben; ~ (*up*)*on* eingreifen in (*acc.*); ~**ant** □ ['trentʃənt] scharf.

trend [trend] **1.** Richtung *f*; *fig.* Lauf *m*; *fig.* Strömung *f*; Tendenz *f*; **2.** sich erstrecken, laufen.

trepidation [trepi'deiʃən] Zittern *n*, Beben *n*; Bestürzung *f*.

trespass ['trespəs] **1.** Übertretung *f*; **2.** unbefugt eindringen (*on, upon* in *acc.*); über Gebühr in Anspruch nehmen; ~**er** ⚖ [~sə] Rechtsverletzer *m*; Unbefugte(r *m*) *f*.

tress [tres] Haarlocke *f*, -flechte *f*.

trestle ['tresl] Gestell *n*, Bock *m*.

trial ['traiəl] Versuch *m*; Probe *f*, Prüfung *f* (*a. fig.*); Plage *f*; ⚖ Verhandlung *f*, Prozeß *m*; **on** ~ auf Probe; vor Gericht; **give** *s.o.* *a* ~ es mit j-m versuchen; ~ **run** Probefahrt *f*.

triang|le ['traiæŋgl] Dreieck *n*; ~**ular** □ [trai'æŋgjulə] dreieckig.

tribe [traib] Stamm *m*; Geschlecht *n*; *contp.* Sippe *f*; ♀, *zo.* Klasse *f*.

tribun|al [trai'bjuːnl] Richterstuhl *m*; Gericht(shof *m*) *n*; ~**e** ['tribjuːn] Tribun *m*; Tribüne *f*.

tribut|ary ['tribjutəri] **1.** □ zinspflichtig; *fig.* helfend; Neben...; **2.** Nebenfluß *m*; ~**e** [~juːt] Tribut *m* (*a. fig.*), Zins *m*; Anerkennung *f*.

trice [trais]: **in** *a* ~ im Nu.

trick [trik] **1.** Kniff *m*, List *f*, Trick *m*; Kunstgriff *m*, -stück *n*; Streich *m*; Eigenheit *f*; **2.** betrügen; herausputzen; ~**ery** ['trikəri] Betrügerei *f*.

trickle ['trikl] tröpfeln, rieseln.

trick|ster ['trikstə] Gauner *m*; ~**y** □ [~ki] verschlagen; F heikel; verzwickt, verwickelt, schwierig.

tricycle ['traisikl] Dreirad *n*.

trident ['traidənt] Dreizack *m*.

trifl|e ['traifl] **1.** Kleinigkeit *f*; Lappalie *f*; *a* ~ ein bißchen, ein wenig, etwas; **2.** *v/i.* spielen, spaßen *f*; ~ *away* verschwenden; ~**ing** □ [~liŋ] geringfügig; unbedeutend.

trig [trig] **1.** hemmen; **2.** schmuck.

trigger ['trigə] Abzug *m am Ge-wehr*; *phot.* Auslöser *m*.

trill [tril] **1.** Triller *m*; gerolltes R; **2.** trillern; *bsd.* das R rollen.

trillion ['triljən] Trillion *f*; *Am.* Billion *f*.

trim [trim] **1.** □ ordentlich; schmuck; gepflegt; **2.** (richtiger) Zustand; Ordnung *f*; **3.** zurecht-machen; (~ *up* aus)putzen, schmük-ken; besetzen; stutzen, beschnei-den; ⚓, ⚙ trimmen; **~ming** ['tri-miŋ] *mst* **~s** *pl.* Besatz *m*, Garnie-rung *f*.

Trinity *eccl.* ['triniti] Dreieinigkeit *f*.

trinket ['triŋkit] wertloses Schmuck-stück; **~s** *pl.* F Kinkerlitzchen *pl.*

trip [trip] **1.** Reise *f*, Fahrt *f*; Aus-flug *m*, Spritztour *f*; Stolpern *n*, Fallen *n*; Fehltritt *m* (*a. fig.*); *fig.* Versehen *n*, Fehler *m*; **2.** *v/i.* trip-peln; stolpern; e-n Fehltritt tun (*a. fig.*); *fig.* e-n Fehler machen; *v/t.* *a.* ~ *up* j-m ein Bein stellen (*a. fig.*).

tripartite ['trai'pɑːtait] dreiteilig.

tripe [traip] Kaldaunen *f/pl.*

triple □ ['tripl] dreifach; **~ts** [~lits] *pl.* Drillinge *m/pl.*

triplicate 1. ['triplikit] dreifach; **2.** [~keit] verdreifachen.

tripod ['traipod] Dreifuß *m*; *phot.* Stativ *n*.

tripper F ['tripə] Ausflügler(in).

trite □ [trait] abgedroschen, platt.

triturate ['tritjureit] zerreiben.

triumph ['traiəmf] **1.** Triumph *m*, Sieg *m*; **2.** triumphieren; **~al** [trai-'æmfəl] Sieges..., Triumph...; **~ant** □ [~ənt] triumphierend.

trivial □ ['triviəl] bedeutungslos; unbedeutend; trivial; alltäglich.

trod [trod] *pret. von* tread **1**; **~den** ['trodn] *p.p. von* tread **1**.

troll [troul] (vor sich hin)trällern.

troll(e)y ['troli] Karren *m*; Draisine *f*; Servierwagen *m*; ⚡ Kontaktrolle *f* e-s *Oberleitungsfahrzeugs*; *Am.* Straßenbahnwagen *m*; **~bus** O(ber-leitungs)bus *m*. [Hure *f.*]

trollop ['troləp] F Schlampe *f*;/

trombone ♪ ['trom'boun] Posaune *f*.

troop [truːp] **1.** Truppe *f*, Schar *f*; ✕ (Reiter)Zug *m*; **2.** sich scharen, sich sammeln; ~ *away*, ~ *off* abzie-hen; **~ing** *the colour(s)* ✕ Fahnen-parade *f*; **~er** ['truːpə] Kaval-lerist *m*.

trophy ['troufi] Trophäe *f*.

tropic ['tropik] Wendekreis *m*; **~s** *pl.* Tropen *pl.*; **~(al** □) [~k(ə)l] tropisch.

trot [trot] **1.** Trott *m*, Trab *m*; **2.** traben (lassen).

trouble ['trʌbl] **1.** Unruhe *f*; Stö-rung *f*; Kummer *m*, Not *f*; Mühe *f*; Plage *f*; Unannehmlichkeit *f/pl.*; *ask od. look for* ~ sich (selbst) Schwierigkeiten machen; das

Schicksal herausfordern; *take* (the) ~ sich (die) Mühe machen; **2.** stö-ren, beunruhigen, belästigen; quä-len, plagen; Mühe machen (*dat.*); (sich) bemühen; ~ *s.o. for* j-n be-mühen um; **~man**, **~shooter** *Am.* F Störungssucher *m*; **~some** □ [~lsəm] beschwerlich, lästig.

trough [trof] (Futter)Trog *m*; Back-trog *m*, Mulde *f*.

trounce F [trauns] j-*n* verhauen.

troupe *thea.* [truːp] Truppe *f*.

trousers ['trauzəz] *pl.* (*a pair of* ~ *pl.* eine) (lange) Hose; Hosen *f/pl.*

trousseau ['truːsou] Aussteuer *f*.

trout *ichth.* [traut] Forelle(n *pl.*) *f*.

trowel ['trauəl] Maurerkelle *f*.

truant ['truː(ə)nt] **1.** müßig; **2.** Schul-schwänzer *m*; *fig.* Bummler *m*.

truce [truːs] Waffenstillstand *m*.

truck [trʌk] **1.** (offener) Güter-wagen; Last(kraft)wagen *m*, Lkw *m*; Transportkarren *m*; Tausch (-handel) *m*; Verkehr *m*; Natural-lohnsystem *n*; *Am.* Gemüse *n*; **2.** (ver)tauschen; **~farm** *Am.* ['trʌkfɑːm] Gemüsegärtnerei *f*.

truckle ['trʌkl] zu Kreuze kriechen.

truculent □ ['trʌkjulənt] wild, roh.

trudge [trʌdʒ] wandern; sich (da-hin)schleppen, mühsam gehen.

true [truː] wahr; echt, wirklich; treu; genau; richtig; *it is* ~ gewiß, freilich, zwar; *come* ~ sich bewahr-heiten; in Erfüllung gehen; ~ *to na-ture* naturgetreu.

truism ['truː(:)izm] Binsenwahr-heit *f*.

truly ['truːli] wirklich; wahrhaft; aufrichtig; genau; treu; *Yours* ~ Hochachtungsvoll.

trump [trʌmp] **1.** Trumpf *m*; **2.** (über)trumpfen; ~ *up* erdichten; **~ery** ['trʌmpəri] Plunder *m*.

trumpet ['trʌmpit] **1.** Trompete *f*; **2.** trompeten; *fig.* ausposaunen.

truncheon ['trʌntʃən] (Polizei-) Knüppel *m*; Kommandostab *m*.

trundle ['trʌndl] rollen.

trunk [trʌŋk] (Baum)Stamm *m*; Rumpf *m*; Rüssel *m*; *großer* Koffer; **~call** *teleph.* ['trʌŋkɔːl] Fernge-spräch *n*; **~exchange** *teleph.* Fern-amt *n*; **~line** 🖅 Hauptlinie *f*; *teleph.* Fernleitung *f*; **~s** [trʌŋks] *pl.* Turnhose *f*; Badehose *f*; Her-renunterhose *f*.

trunnion ⊕ ['trʌnjən] Zapfen *m*.

truss [trʌs] **1.** Bündel *n*, Bund *n*; 🌾 Bruchband *n*; △ Binder *m*, Ge-rüst *n*; **2.** (zs.-)binden; △ stützen.

trust [trʌst] **1.** Vertrauen *n*; Glaube *m*; Kredit *m*; Pfand *n*; Verwahrung *f*; 🏛 Treuhand *f*; ✝ Ring *m*, Trust *m*; ~ *company* Treuhandgesellschaft *f*; ~ *in* ... zu treuen Händen; **2.** *v/t.* (ver)trauen (*dat.*); anvertrauen, übergeben (*s.o. with s.th.*, *s.th. to s.o.* j-m et.); zuversichtlich hoffen;

v/i. vertrauen (*in*, to auf *acc.*); ~ee [trʌs'tiː] Sach-, Verwalter *m*; ⚖ Treuhänder *m*; ~ful □ ['trʌstful], ~ing □ [~tiŋ] vertrauensvoll; ~worthy [~twɔːði] vertrauenswürdig; zuverlässig.

truth [truːθ], *pl.* ~s [truːðz] Wahrheit *f*; Wirklichkeit *f*; Wahrhaftigkeit *f*; ~ful □ ['truːθful] wahrhaft(ig).

try [trai] 1. versuchen; probieren; prüfen; ⚖ verhandeln über *et. od.* gegen *j-n*; vor Gericht stellen; aburteilen; *die Augen etc.* angreifen; sich bemühen *od.* bewerben; ~ **on** *Kleid* anprobieren; 2. Versuch *m*; ~ing □ ['traiiŋ] anstrengend; kritisch.

Tsar [zɑː] Zar *m*.

T-shirt ['tiːʃəːt] kurzärmeliges Sporthemd.

tub [tʌb] 1. Faß *n*, Zuber *m*; Kübel *m*; Badewanne *f*; F (Wannen)Bad *n*.

tube [tjuːb] Rohr *n*; (*Am. bsd.* Radio)Röhre *f*; Tube *f*; (Luft-) Schlauch *m*; Tunnel *m*; F (Londoner) Untergrundbahn *f*.

tuber ♀ ['tjuːbə] Knolle *f*; ~culosis [tjuː(:)bəːkjuˈlousis] Tuberkulose *f*.

tubular □ ['tjuːbjulə] röhrenförmig.

tuck [tʌk] 1. Falte *f*; Abnäher *m*; 2. ab-, aufnähen; packen, stecken; ~ **up** hochschürzen, aufkrempeln; *in e-e Decke etc.* einwickeln.

Tuesday ['tjuːzdi] Dienstag *m*.

tuft [tʌft] Büschel *n*, Busch *m*; (Haar)Schopf *m*.

tug [tʌg] 1. Zug *m*, Ruck *m*; ⚓ Schlepper *m*; *fig.* Anstrengung *f*; 2. ziehen, zerren; ⚓ schleppen; sich mühen.

tuition [tjuˈ(ː)iʃən] Unterricht *m*; Schulgeld *n*.

tulip ♀ ['tjuːlip] Tulpe *f*.

tumble ['tʌmbl] 1. *v/i.* fallen, purzeln; taumeln; sich wälzen; *v/t.* werfen; zerknüllen; 2. Sturz *m*, Wirrwarr *m*; ~down baufällig; ~r [~lə] Becher *m*; *orn.* Tümmler *m*.

tumid □ ['tjuːmid] geschwollen.

tummy F ['tʌmi] Bäuchlein *n*, Magen *m*.

tumo(u)r ⚕ ['tjuːmə] Tumor *m*.

tumult ['tjuːmʌlt] Tumult *m*; ~uous □ [tjuˈ(ː)mʌltjuəs] stürmisch.

tun [tʌn] Tonne *f*, Faß *n*.

tuna *ichth.* ['tuːnə] Thunfisch *m*.

tune [tjuːn] 1. Melodie *f*, Weise *f*; ♪ Stimmung *f* (*a. fig.*); in ~ (gut-) gestimmt; out of ~ verstimmt; 2. stimmen (*a. fig.*); ~ **in** *Radio*: einstellen; ~ **out** *Radio*: ausschalten; ~ **up** die Instrumente stimmen; *fig. Befinden etc.* heben; *mot.* die Leistung erhöhen; ~ful □ ['tjuːnful] melodisch; ~less □ [~nlis] unmelodisch.

tunnel ['tʌnl] 1. Tunnel *m*; ⚒

Stollen *m*; 2. e-n Tunnel bohren (durch).

tunny *ichth.* ['tʌni] Thunfisch *m*.

turbid ['təːbid] trüb; dick.

turb|ine ⊕ ['təːbin] Turbine *f*; ~o-jet ['təːbouˈdʒet] Strahlturbine *f*; ~o-prop [~ouˈprɔp] Propellerturbine *f*.

turbot *ichth.* ['təːbət] Steinbutt *m*.

turbulent □ ['təːbjulənt] unruhig; ungestüm; stürmisch, turbulent.

tureen [təˈriːn] Terrine *f*.

turf [təːf] 1. Rasen *m*; Torf *m*; Rennbahn *f*; Rennsport *m*; 2. mit Rasen bedecken; ~y ['təːfi] rasenbedeckt.

turgid □ ['təːdʒid] geschwollen.

Turk [təːk] Türk|e *m*, -in *f*.

turkey ['təːki] *orn.* Truthahn *m*, -henne *f*; Pute(r *m*) *f*; *Am. sl. thea., Film:* Pleite *f*, Versager *m*.

Turkish ['təːkiʃ] türkisch.

turmoil ['təːmɔil] Aufruhr *m*, Unruhe *f*; Durcheinander *n*.

turn [təːn] 1. *v/t.* drehen; (um)wenden, umkehren; lenken; verwandeln; abbringen; abwehren; übertragen; bilden; drechseln; verrückt machen; ~ **a corner** um eine Ecke biegen; ~ *s.o.* **against** *j-n* aufhetzen gegen; ~ **aside** abwenden; ~ **away** abwenden; abweisen; ~ **down** umbiegen; *Gas etc.* kleinstellen; *Decke etc.* zurückschlagen; ablehnen; ~ **off** ableiten (*a. fig.*); hinauswerfen; wegjagen; ~ **off** (**on**) ab- (an)drehen, ab- (ein)schalten; ~ **out** hinauswerfen; *Fabrikat* herausbringen; *Gas etc.* ausdrehen; ~ **over** umwenden; *fig.* übertragen; ⚓ umsetzen; überlegen; ~ **up** nach oben richten; hochklappen; umwenden; *Hose etc.* auf-, umschlagen; *Gas etc.* aufdrehen; *v/i.* sich (um)drehen; sich wenden; sich verwandeln; umschlagen (*Wetter etc.*); *Christ, grau etc.* werden; *a.* ~ **sour** sauer werden (*Milch*); ~ **about** sich umdrehen; ⚔ kehrtmachen; ~ **back** zurückkehren; ~ **in** einkehren; F zu Bett gehen; ~ **off** abbiegen; ~ **on** sich drehen um; ~ **out** ausfallen, ausgehen; sich herausstellen als; ~ **to** sich zuwenden (*dat.*), sich wenden an (*acc.*); werden zu; ~ **up** auftauchen; ~ **upon** sich wenden gegen; 2. (Um)Drehung *f*; Biegung *f*; Wendung *f*; Neigung *f*; Wechsel *m*; Gestalt *f*, Form *f*; Spaziergang *m*; Reihe(nfolge) *f*; Dienst(leistung *f*) *m*; F Schreck *m*; at every ~ auf Schritt und Tritt; by *od.* in ~s der Reihe nach, abwechselnd; it is my ~ ich bin an der Reihe; take ~s mit-ea. abwechseln; does it serve your ~? entspricht das Ihren Zwecken?; ~coat ['təːnkout] Abtrünnige(r) *m*; ~er ['təːnə] Drechsler *m*; ˌery [ˌəri] Drechslerei *f*; Drechslerarbeit *f*.

turning ['tə:niŋ] Drechseln *n*; Wendung *f*; Biegung *f*; Straßenecke *f*; (Weg)Abzweigung *f*; Querstraße *f*; ˌpoint *fig.* Wendepunkt *m*.

turnip ♃ ['tə:nip] (*bsd.* weiße) Rübe.

turn|key ['tə:nki:] Schließer *m*; ˌout ['tə:n'aut] Ausstaffierung *f*; Arbeitseinstellung *f*; ✦ Gesamtproduktion *f*; ˌover ['tə:nouvə] ✦ Umsatz *m*; Verschiebung *f*; ˌpike Schlagbaum *m*; (gebührenpflichtige) Schnellstraße; ˌstile Drehkreuz *n*. [pentin *n.*] turpentine ♃ ['tə:pəntain] Terturpitude ['tə:pitju:d] Schändlichkeit *f*.

turret ['tʌrit] Türmchen *n*; ⚓, ⚔ Panzerturm *m*; ⚔ Kanzel *f*.

turtle ['tə:tl] *zo.* Schildkröte *f*; *orn. mst* ˌdove Turteltaube *f*.

tusk [tʌsk] Fangzahn *m*; Stoßzahn *m*; Hauer *m*.

tussle ['tʌsl] 1. Rauferei *f*, Balgerei *f*; 2. raufen, sich balgen.

tussock ['tʌsək] Büschel *n*.

tut [tʌt] ach was!; Unsinn!

tutelage ['tju:tilidʒ] ⚖ Vormundschaft *f*; Bevormundung *f*.

tutor ['tju:tə] 1. (Privat-, Haus-) Lehrer *m*; *univ.* Tutor *m*; *Am. univ.* Assistent *m mit* Lehrauftrag; ⚖ Vormund *m*; 2. unterrichten; schulen, erziehen; *fig.* beherrschen; ˌial [tju(:)'tɔ:riəl] *univ.* Unterrichtsstunde *f* ✦ *Tutors*; *attr.* Lehrer...; Tutoren...

tuxedo *Am.* [tʌk'si:dou] Smoking *m*.

TV ['ti:'vi:] Fernsehen *n*; Fernsehapparat *m*; *attr.* Fernseh...

twaddle ['twɔdl] 1. Geschwätz *n*; 2. schwatzen, quatschen.

twang [twæŋ] 1. Schwirren *n*; *mst nasal* ˌ näselnde Aussprache *f*; 2. schwirren (lassen); klimpern; näseln.

tweak [twi:k] zwicken.

tweet [twi:t] zwitschern.

tweezers ['twi:zəz] *pl.* (*a pair of* ˌ *pl.* eine) Pinzette.

twelfth [twelfθ] 1. zwölfte(r, -s); 2. Zwölftel *n*; 2ˌnight ['twelfθnait] Dreikönigsabend *m*.

twelve [twelv] zwölf.

twent|ieth ['twentiiθ] 1. zwanzigste(r, -s); 2. Zwanzigstel *n*; ˌy [ˌti] zwanzig.

twice [twais] zweimal.

twiddle ['twidl] (sich) drehen; mit *et.* spielen.

twig [twig] Zweig *m*, Rute *f*.

twilight ['twailait] Zwielicht *n*; Dämmerung *f* (*a. fig.*).

twin [twin] 1. Zwillings...; doppelt; 2. Zwilling *m*; ˌengined ⚔ ['twinendʒind] zweimotorig.

twine [twain] 1. Bindfaden *m*,

Schnur *f*; Zwirn *m*; 2. zs.-drehen; verflechten; (sich) schlingen *od.* winden; umschlingen, umranken.

twinge [twindʒ] Zwicken *n*; Stich *m*; bohrender Schmerz.

twinkle ['twiŋkl] 1. funkeln, blitzen; huschen; zwinkern; 2. Funkeln *n*, Blitzen *n*; (Augen)Zwinkern *n*, Blinzeln *n*.

twirl [twə:l] 1. Wirbel *m*; 2. wirbeln.

twist [twist] 1. Drehung *f*; Windung *f*; Verdrehung *f*; Verdrehtheit *f*; Neigung *f*; (Gesichts)Verzerrung *f*; Garn *n*; Kringel *m*, Zopf *m* (*Backwaren*); 2. (sich) drehen *od.* winden; zs.-drehen; verdrehen, verziehen, verzerren.

twit *fig.* [twit] *j-n* aufziehen.

twitch [twitʃ] 1. zupfen (an *dat.*); zucken; 2. Zupfen *n*; Zuckung *f*.

twitter ['twitə] 1. zwitschern; 2. Gezwitscher *n*; *be in a* ˌ zittern.

two [tu:] 1. zwei; *in* ˌ entzwei; *put* ˌ *and* ˌ *together* sich et. zs.-reimen; 2. Zwei *f*; *in* ˌ*s* zu zweien; ˌbit *Am.* F ['tu:bit] 25-Cent...; *fig.* unbedeutend, Klein...; ˌedged ['tu:'edʒd] zweischneidig; ˌfold ['tu:fould] zweifach; ˌpence ['tʌpəns] zwei Pence; ˌpenny ['tʌpni] zwei Pence wert; ˌpiece ['tu:'pi:s] zweiteilig; ˌseater *mot.* ['tu:'si:tə] Zweisitzer *m*; ˌstorey ['tu:'stɔ:ri], ˌstoried zweistöckig; ˌstroke *mot.* Zweitakt...; ˌway Doppel...; ˌ *adapter* ✦ Doppelstecker *m*; ˌ *traffic* Gegenverkehr *m*.

tycoon *Am.* F [tai'ku:n] Industriekapitän *m*, Industriemagnat *m*.

tyke [taik] Köter *m*; Kerl *m*.

type [taip] Typ *m*; Urbild *n*; Vorbild *n*; Muster *n*; Art *f*; Sinnbild *n*; *typ.* Type *f*, Buchstabe *m*; *true to* ˌ artecht; *set in* ˌ setzen; ˌwrite ['taiprait] [*irr.* (*write*)] (mit der) Schreibmaschine schreiben; ˌwriter Schreibmaschine *f*; ˌ *ribbon* Farbband *n*.

typhoid 🕮 ['taifoid] 1. typhös; ˌ *fever* = 2. (Unterleibs)Typhus *m*.

typhoon [tai'fu:n] Taifun *m*.

typhus 🕮 ['taifəs] Flecktyphus *m*.

typi|cal □ ['tipikəl] typisch; richtig; bezeichnend, kennzeichnend; ˌfy [ˌifai] typisch sein für; versinnbildlichen; ˌst ['taipist] *a. shorthand* ˌ Stenotypistin *f*.

tyrann|ic(al □) [ti'rænik(əl)] tyrannisch; ˌize ['tirənaiz] tyrannisieren; ˌy [ˌni] Tyrannei *f*.

tyrant ['taiərənt] Tyrann(in).

tyre ['taiə] *s. tire* 1.

tyro ['taiərou] *s. tiro*.

Tyrolese [tirə'li:z] 1. Tiroler(in); 2. tirolisch, Tiroler...

Tzar [zɑ:] Zar *m*.

U

ubiquitous □ [ju(:)'bikwitəs] allgegenwärtig, überall zu finden(d).

udder ['Λdə] Euter *n*.

ugly □ ['Λgli] häßlich; schlimm.

ulcer ✗ ['Λlsə] Geschwür *n*; (Eiter-) Beule *f*; ~ate ✗ [~əreit] eitern (lassen); ~ous ✗ [~rəs] geschwürig.

ulterior [Λl'tiəriə] jenseitig; *fig.* weiter; tiefer liegend, versteckt.

ultimate ['Λltimit] letzt; endlich; End..; ~ly [~tli] zu guter Letzt.

ultimat|um [Λlti'meitəm], *pl. a.* ~a [~tə] Ultimatum *n*.

ultimo ✦ ['Λltimou] vorigen Monats.

ultra ['Λltrə] übermäßig; Ultra...; ultra..; ~fashionable ['Λltrə'fæʃənəbl] hypermodern; ~modern hypermodern

umbel ♀ ['Λmbəl] Dolde *f*.

umbrage ['Λmbridʒ] Anstoß *m* (Ärger); Schatten *m*

umbrella [Λm'brelə] Regenschirm *m*; *fig.* Schirm *m*, Schutz *m*; ✗ Abschirmung *f*

umpire ['Λmpaiə] 1. Schiedsrichter *m*; 2. Schiedsrichter sein.

un... [Λn] un , Un. .; ent...; nicht...

unabashed [Λnə'bæʃt] unverfroren; unerschrocken

unabated ['Λnə'beitid] unvermindert. [stande.\

unable ['Λn'eibl] unfähig, außer-\

unaccommodating ['Λnə'kɔmədeitiŋ] unnachgiebig

unaccountable ['Λnə'kauntəbl] unerklärlich, seltsam; nicht zur Rechenschaft verpflichtet

unaccustomed ['Λnə'kΛstəmd] ungewohnt, ungewöhnlich

unacquainted ['Λnə'kweintid]: ~ with unbekannt mit, e-r S unkundig.

unadvised ['Λnəd'vaizd] unbedacht; unberaten.

unaffected ['Λnə'fektid] unberührt; ungerührt; ungekünstelt.

unaided ['Λn'eidid] ohne Unterstützung; (ganz) allein, bloß (Auge).

unalter|able [Λn'ɔ:ltərəbl] unveränderlich, ~ed ['Λn'ɔ:ltəd] unverändert

unanim|ity [ju:nə'nimiti] Einmütigkeit *f*; ~ous [ju:(:)'næniməs] einmütig, einstimmig.

unanswer|able [Λn'ɑ:nsərəbl] unwiderleglich; ~ed ['Λn'ɑ:nsəd] unbeantwortet

unapproachable □ [Λnə'proutʃəbl] unzugänglich.

unapt [Λn'æpt] ungeeignet.

unashamed □ ['Λnə'ʃeimd] schamlos.

unasked ['Λn'ɑ:skt] unverlangt; ungebeten.

unassisted □ ['Λnə'sistid] ohne Hilfe *od.* Unterstützung.

unassuming □ ['Λnə'sju:miŋ] anspruchslos, bescheiden.

unattached ['Λnə'tætʃt] nicht gebunden; ungebunden, ledig, frei.

unattractive ['Λnə'træktiv] wenig anziehend, reizlos; uninteressant.

unauthorized ['Λn'ɔ:θəraizd] unberechtigt, unbefugt.

unavail|able ['Λnə'veiləbl] nicht verfügbar; ~ing [~liŋ] vergeblich.

unavoidable □ [Λnə'vɔidəbl] unvermeidlich.

unaware ['Λnə'weə] ohne Kenntnis; *be* ~ *of et.* nicht merken; ~s [~əz] unversehens, unvermutet; versehentlich.

unbacked ['Λn'bækt] ohne Unterstützung; ungedeckt (*Scheck*).

unbag ['Λn'bæg] aus dem Sack holen *od.* lassen.

unbalanced ['Λn'bælənst] nicht im Gleichgewicht befindlich; unausgeglichen; geistesgestört.

unbearable □ [Λn'bɛərəbl] unerträglich.

unbeaten ['Λn'bi:tn] ungeschlagen; unbetreten (*Weg*).

unbecoming [['Λnbi'kΛmiŋ] unkleidsam; unziemlich, unschicklich.

unbeknown F ['Λnbi'noun] unbekannt.

unbelie|f ['Λnbi'li:f] Unglaube *m*; ~vable [Λnbi'li:vəbl] unglaublich; ~ving ['Λnbi'li:viŋ] ungläubig.

unbend ['Λn'bend] [*irr.* (*bend*)] (sich) entspannen; freundlich werden, auftauen; ~ing [~diŋ] unbiegsam; *fig.* unbeugsam

unbias(s)ed ['Λn'baiəst] vorurteilsfrei, unbefangen, unbeeinflußt.

unbid(den) ['Λn'bid(n)] ungeheißen, unaufgefordert; ungebeten.

unbind ['Λn'baind] [*irr.* (*bind*)] losbinden, befreien; lösen.

unblushing □ [Λn'blΛʃiŋ] schamlos. [boren.\

unborn ['Λn'bɔ:n] (noch) unge-\

unbosom [Λn'buzəm] offenbaren.

unbounded ['Λn'baundid] unbegrenzt; schrankenlos.

unbroken □ ['Λn'broukən] ungebrochen; unversehrt; ununterbrochen.

unbutton ['Λn'bΛtn] aufknöpfen.

uncalled-for [Λn'kɔ:ldfɔ:] ungerufen; unverlangt (*S.*); unpassend.

uncanny □ [Λn'kæni] unheimlich.

uncared-for ['Λn'kɛədfɔ:] unbeachtet, vernachlässigt.

unceasing □ [Λn'si:siŋ] unaufhörlich.

unceremonious □ ['Λnseri'mounjəs] ungezwungen; formlos.

uncertain □ [ʌn'səːtn] unsicher; ungewiß; unbestimmt; unzuverlässig; ~ty [~nti] Unsicherheit f.

unchallenged ['ʌn'tʃælindʒd] unangefochten

unchang|eable □ [ʌn'tʃeindʒəbl] unveränderlich, unwandelbar; ~ed ['ʌn'tʃeindʒd] unverändert; ~ing [ʌn'tʃeindʒiŋ] unveränderlich

uncharitable [ʌn'tʃæritəbl] lieblos; unbarmherzig, unfreundlich.

unchecked ['ʌn'tʃekt] ungehindert.

uncivil ['ʌn'sivl] unhöflich; ~ized [~vilaizd] unzivilisiert

unclaimed ['ʌn'kleimd] nicht beansprucht; unzustellbar (bsd. Brief).

unclasp ['ʌn'klɑːsp] auf-, loshaken, auf-, losschnallen, aufmachen.

uncle ['ʌŋkl] Onkel m

unclean ['ʌn'kliːn] unrein.

unclose ['ʌn'klouz] (sich) öffnen.

uncomely ['ʌn'kʌmli] reizlos; unpassend.

uncomfortable □ [ʌn'kʌmfətəbl] unbehaglich, ungemütlich; unangenehm.

uncommon □ [ʌn'kɔmən] ungewöhnlich

uncommunicative □ ['ʌnkə'mjuːnikətiv] wortkarg, schweigsam.

uncomplaining ['ʌnkəm'pleiniŋ] klaglos; ohne Murren, geduldig.

uncompromising ['ʌn'kɔmprəmaiziŋ] kompromißlos

unconcern ['ʌnkən'səːn] Unbekümmertheit f; Gleichgültigkeit f; ~ed □ [~nd] unbekümmert; unbeteiligt.

unconditional [['ʌnkən'diʃənl] unbedingt, bedingungslos

unconfirmed ['ʌnkən'fəːmd] unbestätigt; eccl nicht konfirmiert.

unconnected ['ʌnkə'nektid] unverbunden

unconquer|able □ [ʌn'kɔŋkərəbl] unüberwindlich; ~ed ['ʌn'kɔŋkəd] unbesiegt

unconscionable □ [ʌn'kɔnʃnəbl] gewissenlos; F unverschämt, übermäßig.

unconscious [[ʌn'kɔnʃəs] unbewußt; bewußtlos; ~ness [~snis] Bewußtlosigkeit f

unconstitutional ['ʌnkɔnsti'tjuːʃənl] verfassungswidrig

uncontroll|able [ʌnkən'trouləbl] unkontrollierbar, unbändig; ~ed ['ʌnkən'trould] unbeaufsichtigt; fig. unbeherrscht

unconventional [['ʌnkən'venʃənl] unkonventionell; ungezwungen.

unconvinc|ed ['ʌnkən'vinst] nicht überzeugt; ~ing [~siŋ] nicht überzeugend.

uncork ['ʌn'kɔːk] entkorken.

uncount|able ['ʌn'kauntəbl] unzählbar; ~ed [~tid] ungezählt.

uncouple ['ʌn'kʌpl] loskoppeln.

uncouth □ [ʌn'kuːθ] ungeschlacht.

uncover [ʌn'kʌvə] aufdecken, freilegen; entblößen.

unct|ion ['ʌŋkʃən] Salbung f (a. fig.); Salbe f; ~uous [['ʌŋktjuəs] fettig, ölig; fig. salbungsvoll.

uncult|ivated [['ʌn'kʌltiveitid], ~ured [~tʃəd] unkultiviert.

undamaged ['ʌn'dæmidʒd] unbeschädigt.

undaunted □ [ʌn'dɔːntid] unerschrocken

undeceive ['ʌndi'siːv] j-n aufklären.

undecided □ ['ʌndi'saidid] unentschieden; unentschlossen.

undefined [['ʌndi'faind] unbestimmt; unbegrenzt

undemonstrative [['ʌndi'mɔnstrətiv] zurückhaltend.

undeniable [[ʌndi'naiəbl] unleugbar; unbestreitbar.

under ['ʌndə] 1. adv. unten; darunter; 2. prp. unter; 3. adj. unter; in Zssgn: unter.., Unter.., mangelhaft ...; ~bid [~'bid] [irr (bid)] unterbieten; ~brush [~brʌʃ] Unterholz n; ~carriage ✈ (Flugzeug)Fahrwerk n; mot Fahrgestell n; ~clothes, ~clothing Unterkleidung f, Unterwäsche f; ~cut [~'kʌt] Preise unterbieten; ~dog [~dɔg] Unterlegene(r) m; Unterdrückte(r) m, ~done ['dʌn] nicht gar; ~estimate [~'estimeit] unterschätzen; ~fed [~'fed] unterernährt; ~go [ʌndə'gou] [irr (go)] erdulden; sich unterziehen (dat.); ~graduate [~'grædjuit] Student (-in); ~ground [~'ʌndəgraund] 1. unterirdisch; Untergrund...; 2. Untergrundbahn f; ~growth Unterholz n; ~hand unter der Hand; heimlich, ~lie [ʌndə'lai] [irr. (lie)] zugrunde liegen (dat.); ~line [~'lain] unterstreichen; ~ling ['ʌndəliŋ] Untergeordnete(r) m; ~mine [ʌndə'main] unterminieren; fig. untergraben, schwächen; ~most ['ʌndəmoust] unterst; ~neath [ʌndə'niːθ] 1. prp unter (-halb); 2. adv. unten, darunter; ~pin [~'pin] untermauern, ~plot ['ʌndəplɔt] Nebenhandlung f; ~privileged [~'privilidʒd] benachteiligt, ~rate [ʌndə'reit] unterschätzen; ~secretary ['ʌndə'sekrətəri] Unterstaatssekretär m; ~sell ↑ [~'sel] [irr (sell)] j-n unterbieten; Ware verschleudern; ~signed [~'saind] Unterzeichnete(r) m; ~sized [~'saizd] zu klein; ~staffed [ʌndə'stɑːft] unterbesetzt; ~stand [~'stænd] [irr (stand)] allg. verstehen; sich verstehen auf (acc.); (als sicher) annehmen, auffassen; (sinngemäß) ergänzen, make o.s. understood sich verständlich machen; an understood thing e-e abgemachte Sache; ~standable [~dəbl] verständlich; ~standing [~diŋ]

Verstand *m*; Einvernehmen *n*; Verständigung *f*; Abmachung *f*; Voraussetzung *f*; ~state ['ʌndə'steit] zu gering angeben; abschwächen; ~statement Unterbewertung *f*; Understatement *n*, Untertreibung *f*; ~take [ʌndə'teik] [*irr* 'take)] unternehmen; übernehmen, sich verpflichten; ~taker ['ʌndəteikə] Bestattungsinstitut *n*, ~taking [ʌndə'teikiŋ] Unternehmung *f*; Verpflichtung *f*; ['ʌndəteikiŋ] Leichenbestattung *f*; ~tone leiser Ton; ~value [ʌ'vælju:] unterschätzen; ~wear [~'weə] Unterkleidung *f*, Unterwäsche *f*; ~wood Unterholz *n*; ~write [*irr* (write)] *Versicherung* abschließen; ~writer Versicherer *m*.

undeserv|ed ['ʌndi'zɜːvd] unverdient; ~ing [~viŋ] unwürdig.

undesigned ['ʌndi'zaind] unbeabsichtigt, absichtslos.

undesirable ['ʌndi'zairəbl] 1. □ unerwünscht; 2. unerwünschte Person.

undeviating □ [ʌn'di:vieitiŋ] unentwegt.

undignified □ [ʌn'dignifaid] würdelos.

undisciplined [ʌn'disiplind] zuchtlos, undiszipliniert; ungeschult.

undisguised □ ['ʌndis'gaizd] unverkleidet; unverhohlen.

undisputed □ ['ʌndis'pju:tid] unbestritten.

undo ['ʌn'du:] [*irr*. (do)] aufmachen; (auf)lösen; ungeschehen machen, aufheben; vernichten; ~ing [~u(:)iŋ] Aufmachen *n*; Ungeschehenmachen *n*; Vernichtung *f*; Verderben *n*; ~ne ['ʌn'dʌn] erledigt, vernichtet.

undoubted □ [ʌn'dautid] unzweifelhaft, zweifellos.

undreamt [ʌn'dremt]: ~of ungeahnt.

undress ['ʌn'dres] 1. (sich) entkleiden *od.* ausziehen; 2. Hauskleid *n*; ~ed unbekleidet; unangezogen; nicht zurechtgemacht.

undue □ ['ʌn'dju:] ungebührlich; übermäßig; † noch nicht fällig.

undulat|e ['ʌndjuleit] wogen; wallen; wellig sein; ~ion [ʌndju'leiʃən] wellenförmige Bewegung.

undutiful □ ['ʌn'dju:tiful] ungehorsam, pflichtvergessen.

unearth ['ʌn'ɜːθ] ausgraben; *fig*. aufstöbern; ~ly [ʌn'ɜːθli] überirdisch.

uneas|iness [ʌn'i:zinis] Unruhe *f*; Unbehagen *n*; ~y □ [ʌn'i:zi] unbehaglich; unruhig; unsicher.

uneducated ['ʌn'edjukeitid] unerzogen; ungebildet.

unemotional □ ['ʌni'mouʃənl] leidenschaftslos; passiv; nüchtern.

unemploy|ed ['ʌnim'plɔid] 1. unbeschäftigt; arbeitslos; unbenutzt; 2.: the ~ *pl*. die Arbeitslosen *pl*.; ~ment [~'plɔimənt] Arbeitslosigkeit *f*.

unending □ [ʌn'endiŋ] endlos.

unendurable □ ['ʌnin'djuərəbl] unerträglich.

unengaged ['ʌnin'geidʒd] frei.

unequal □ ['ʌn'i:kwəl] ungleich; nicht gewachsen (*to dat.*); ~(l)ed [~ld] unvergleichlich, unerreicht.

unerring □ ['ʌn'ɜːriŋ] unfehlbar.

unessential □ ['ʌni'senʃəl] unwesentlich, unwichtig (*to* für).

uneven □ ['ʌn'i:vən] uneben; ungleich(mäßig); ungerade (*Zahl*).

uneventful □ ['ʌni'ventful] ereignislos; ohne Zwischenfälle.

unexampled [ʌnig'zɑ:mpld] beispiellos.

unexceptionable □ [ʌnik'sepʃnəbl] untadelig; einwandfrei.

unexpected □ ['ʌniks'pektid] unerwartet.

unexplained ['ʌniks'pleind] unerklärt.

unfading □ [ʌn'feidiŋ] nicht welkend; unvergänglich; echt (*Farbe*).

unfailing □ [ʌn'feiliŋ] unfehlbar; nie versagend; unerschöpflich; *fig*. treu.

unfair □ ['ʌn'feə] unehrlich; unfair; ungerecht.

unfaithful □ ['ʌn'feiθful] un(ge)treu, treulos; nicht wortgetreu.

unfamiliar ['ʌnfə'miljə] unbekannt; ungewohnt.

unfasten ['ʌn'fɑːsn] aufmachen; lösen; ~ed unbefestigt, lose.

unfathomable □ [ʌn'fæðəməbl] unergründlich.

unfavo(u)rable □ ['ʌn'feivərəbl] ungünstig.

unfeeling □ [ʌn'fi:liŋ] gefühllos.

unfilial □ ['ʌn'filjəl] respektlos, pflichtvergessen (*Kind*).

unfinished ['ʌn'finiʃt] unvollendet; unfertig.

unfit 1. □ ['ʌn'fit] ungeeignet, unpassend; 2. [ʌn'fit] untauglich machen.

unfix ['ʌn'fiks] losmachen, lösen.

unfledged ['ʌn'fledʒd] ungefiedert; (noch) nicht flügge; *fig*. unreif.

unflinching □ [ʌn'flintʃiŋ] fest entschlossen, unnachgiebig.

unfold ['ʌn'fould] (sich) entfalten *od.* öffnen; [ʌn'fould] klarlegen; enthüllen.

unforced □ ['ʌn'fɔːst] ungezwungen.

unforeseen ['ʌnfɔː'si:n] unvorhergesehen.

unforgettable □ ['ʌnfə'getəbl] unvergeßlich.

unforgiving ['ʌnfə'giviŋ] unversöhnlich.

unforgotten ['ʌnfə'gɔtn] unvergessen.

unfortunate [ʌn'fɔːtʃnit] 1. □ unglücklich; 2. Unglückliche(r m) f; ~ly [~tli] unglücklicherweise, leider.

unfounded □ ['ʌn'faundid] unbegründet; grundlos.

unfriendly ['ʌn'frendli] unfreundlich; ungünstig.

unfurl [ʌn'fəːl] entfalten, aufrollen.

unfurnished ['ʌn'fəːniʃt] unmöbliert.

ungainly [ʌn'geinli] unbeholfen, plump.

ungenerous □ ['ʌn'dʒenərəs] unedelmütig; nicht freigebig.

ungentle □ ['ʌn'dʒentl] unsanft.

ungodly □ [ʌn'gɔdli] gottlos.

ungovernable □ [ʌn'gʌvənəbl] unlenksam; zügellos, unbändig.

ungraceful □ ['ʌn'greisful] ungraziös, ohne Anmut; unbeholfen.

ungracious □ ['ʌn'greiʃəs] ungnädig; unfreundlich.

ungrateful □ [ʌn'greitful] undankbar.

unguarded □ ['ʌn'gɑːdid] unbewacht; unvorsichtig; ungeschützt.

unguent ['ʌngwənt] Salbe f.

unhampered ['ʌn'hæmpəd] ungehindert. [schön.]

unhandsome □ [ʌn'hænsəm] un-

unhandy □ [ʌn'hændi] unhandlich; ungeschickt; unbeholfen.

unhappy □ [ʌn'hæpi] unglücklich.

unharmed ['ʌn'hɑːmd] unversehrt.

unhealthy □ [ʌn'helθi] ungesund.

unheard-of [ʌn'həːdɔv] unerhört.

unheed|ed [ʌn'hiːdid] unbeachtet, unbewacht; ~ing [~diŋ] sorglos.

unhesitating □ [ʌn'heziteitiŋ] ohne Zögern; unbedenklich.

unholy [ʌn'houli] unheilig; gottlos.

unhono(u)red ['ʌn'ɔnəd] ungeehrt; uneingelöst (Pfand, Scheck).

unhook ['ʌn'huk] auf-, aushaken.

unhoped-for [ʌn'houptfɔː] unverhofft.

unhurt ['ʌn'həːt] unverletzt.

unicorn ['juːnikɔːn] Einhorn n.

unification [juːnifi'keiʃən] Vereinigung f; Vereinheitlichung f.

uniform ['juːnifɔːm] 1. □ gleichförmig, gleichmäßig; einheitlich; 2. Dienstkleidung f; Uniform f; 3. uniformieren; ~ity [juːni'fɔːmiti] Gleichförmigkeit f, Gleichmäßigkeit f.

unify ['juːnifai] verein(ig)en; vereinheitlichen.

unilateral □ ['juːni'lætərəl] einseitig.

unimagina|ble □ [ʌni'mædʒinəbl] undenkbar; ~tive □ ['ʌni'mædʒinətiv] einfallslos.

unimportant □ ['ʌnim'pɔːtənt] unwichtig.

unimproved ['ʌnim'pruːvd] nicht kultiviert, unbebaut (Land); unverbessert.

uninformed ['ʌnin'fɔːmd] nicht unterrichtet.

uninhabit|able ['ʌnin'hæbitəbl] unbewohnbar; ~ed [~tid] unbewohnt.

uninjured ['ʌn'indʒəd] unbeschädigt, unverletzt.

unintelligible □ ['ʌnin'telidʒəbl] unverständlich.

unintentional □ ['ʌnin'tenʃənl] unabsichtlich.

uninteresting □ ['ʌn'intristiŋ] uninteressant.

uninterrupted □ ['ʌnintə'rʌptid] ununterbrochen.

union ['juːnjən] Vereinigung f; Verbindung f; Union f, Verband m; Einigung f; Einigkeit f; Verein m, Bund m; univ. (Debattier)Klub m; Gewerkschaft f; ~ist [~nist] Gewerkschaftler m; 2 Jack Union Jack m (britische Nationalflagge); ~ suit Am. Hemdhose f.

unique □ [juː'niːk] einzigartig, einmalig.

unison ♪ u. fig. ['juːnizn] Einklang m.

unit ['juːnit] Einheit f; ⚔ Einer m; ~e [juː'nait] (sich) vereinigen, verbinden; ~ed vereinigt, vereint; ~y ['juːniti] Einheit f; Einigkeit f.

univers|al □ [juːni'vəːsəl] allgemein; allumfassend; Universal..., Welt...; ~ality [juːnivəː'sæliti] Allgemeinheit f; umfassende Bildung, Vielseitigkeit f; ~e ['juːnivəːs] Weltall n, Universum n; ~ity [juːni'vəːsiti] Universität f.

unjust □ ['ʌn'dʒʌst] ungerecht; ~ifiable □ [ʌn'dʒʌstifaiəbl] nicht zu rechtfertigen, unverantwortlich.

unkempt ['ʌn'kempt] ungepflegt.

unkind □ [ʌn'kaind] unfreundlich.

unknow|ing □ ['ʌn'nouiŋ] unwissend; unbewußt; ~n [~oun] 1. unbekannt; unbewußt; ~ to me ohne mein Wissen; 2. Unbekannte(r m, -s n) f.

unlace ['ʌn'leis] aufschnüren.

unlatch ['ʌn'lætʃ] aufklinken.

unlawful □ ['ʌn'lɔːful] ungesetzlich; weitS. unrechtmäßig.

unlearn ['ʌn'ləːn] [irr. (learn)] verlernen.

unless [ən'les] wenn nicht, außer wenn; es sei denn, daß.

unlike ['ʌn'laik] 1. adj. □ ungleich; 2. prp. anders als; ~ly [ʌn'laikli] unwahrscheinlich.

unlimited [ʌn'limitid] unbegrenzt.

unload ['ʌn'loud] ent-, ab-, ausladen; Ladung löschen.

unlock ['ʌn'lɔk] aufschließen; Waffe entsichern; ~ed unverschlossen.

unlooked-for [ʌn'luktfɔː] unerwartet.

unloose, ~n ['ʌn'luːs, ʌn'luːsn] lösen, losmachen.

unlov|ely ['ʌn'lʌvli] reizlos, unschön; ~ing □ [~viŋ] lieblos.

unlucky □ [ʌn'lʌki] unglücklich.

unmake ['ʌn'meik] [*irr.* (*make*)] vernichten; rückgängig machen; umbilden; *Herrscher* absetzen.

unman ['ʌn'mæn] entmannen.

unmanageable □ [ʌn'mænidʒəbl] unlenksam, widerspenstig.

unmarried ['ʌn'mærid] unverheiratet, ledig.

unmask ['ʌn'mɑːsk] (sich) demaskieren; *fig.* entlarven.

unmatched ['ʌn'mætʃt] unerreicht; unvergleichlich.

unmeaning □ [ʌn'miːniŋ] nichtssagend.

unmeasured [ʌn'meʒəd] ungemessen; unermeßlich.

unmeet ['ʌn'miːt] ungeeignet.

unmentionable [ʌn'menʃnəbl] nicht zu erwähnen(d), unnennbar.

unmerited ['ʌn'meritid] unverdient.

unmindful □ [ʌn'maindful] unbedacht; sorglos; ohne Rücksicht.

unmistakable □ ['ʌnmis'teikəbl] unverkennbar; unmißverständlich.

unmitigated [ʌn'mitigeitid] ungemildert; richtig; *fig.* Erz...

unmolested ['ʌnmou'lestid] unbelästigt.

unmounted ['ʌn'mauntid] unberitten; nicht gefaßt (*Stein*); unaufgezogen (*Bild*); unmontiert.

unmoved □ ['ʌn'muːvd] unbewegt, ungerührt.

unnamed ['ʌn'neimd] ungenannt.

unnatural □ [ʌn'nætʃrəl] unnatürlich. [nötig.\]

unnecessary □ [ʌn'nesisəri] un-\]

unneighbo(u)rly ['ʌn'neibəli] nicht gutnachbarlich.

unnerve ['ʌn'nəːv] entnerven.

unnoticed ['ʌn'noutist] unbemerkt.

unobjectionable □ ['ʌnəb'dʒekʃnəbl] einwandfrei.

unobserv|ant □ ['ʌnəb'zəːvənt] unachtsam; ~ed □ [~vd] unbemerkt.

unobtainable ['ʌnəb'teinəbl] unerreichbar.

unobtrusive □ ['ʌnəb'truːsiv] unaufdringlich, bescheiden.

unoccupied ['ʌn'ɔkjupaid] unbesetzt; unbewohnt; unbeschäftigt.

unoffending ['ʌnə'fendiŋ] harmlos.

unofficial □ ['ʌnə'fiʃəl] nichtamtlich, inoffiziell.

unopposed ['ʌnə'pouzd] ungehindert.

unostentatious □ ['ʌnɔstən'teiʃəs] anspruchslos; unauffällig; schlicht.

unowned ['ʌn'ound] herrenlos.

unpack ['ʌn'pæk] auspacken.

unpaid ['ʌn'peid] unbezahlt; unbelohnt; ⚭ unfrankiert.

unparalleled [ʌn'pærəleld] beispiellos, ohnegleichen.

unperceived □ ['ʌnpə'siːvd] unbemerkt.

unperturbed ['ʌnpə(ː)'təːbd] ruhig, gelassen.

unpleasant □ [ʌn'pleznt] unangenehm; unerfreulich; ~ness [~tnis] Unannehmlichkeit *f.*

unpolished ['ʌn'pɔliʃt] unpoliert; *fig.* ungebildet.

unpolluted ['ʌnpə'luːtid] unbefleckt.

unpopular □ ['ʌn'pɔpjulə] unpopulär, unbeliebt; ~ity ['ʌnpɔpju'læriti] Unbeliebtheit *f.*

unpracti|cal □ ['ʌn'præktikəl] unpraktisch; ~sed, *Am.* ~ced [ʌn'præktist] ungeübt.

unprecedented □ [ʌn'presidəntid] beispiellos; noch nie dagewesen.

unprejudiced □ [ʌn'predʒudist] unbefangen, unvoreingenommen.

unpremeditated □ ['ʌnpri'mediteitid] unbeabsichtigt.

unprepared □ ['ʌnpri'pɛəd] unvorbereitet.

unpreten|ding □ ['ʌnpri'tendiŋ], ~tious ⊐ [~nʃəs] anspruchslos.

unprincipled [ʌn'prinsəpld] ohne Grundsätze; gewissenlos.

unprivileged [ʌn'privilidʒd] sozial benachteiligt; arm.

unprofitable □ [ʌn'prɔfitəbl] unnütz.

unproved ['ʌn'pruːvd] unerwiesen.

unprovided ['ʌnprə'vaidid] nicht versehen (*with* mit); ~ *for* unversorgt, mittellos.

unprovoked □ ['ʌnprə'voukt] ohne Grund.

unqualified ['ʌn'kwɔlifaid] ungeeignet; unberechtigt; [ʌn'kwɔlifaid] unbeschränkt.

unquestion|able□[ʌn'kwestʃənəbl] unzweifelhaft, fraglos; ~ed [~nd] ungefragt; unbestritten.

unquote ['ʌn'kwout] *Zitat* beenden.

unravel [ʌn'rævəl] (sich) entwirren; enträtseln.

unready □ ['ʌn'redi] nicht bereit *od.* fertig; unlustig, zögernd.

unreal ['ʌn'riəl] unwirklich; ~istic ['ʌnriə'listik] (~ally) wirklichkeitsfremd, unrealistisch.

unreasonable □ [ʌn'riznəbl] unvernünftig; grundlos; unmäßig.

unrecognizable □ [ʌn'rekəgnaizəbl] nicht wiederzuerkennen(d).

unredeemed □ ['ʌnri'diːmd] unerlöst; uneingelöst; ungemildert.

unrefined ['ʌnri'faind] ungeläutert; *fig.* ungebildet. [dankenlos.\]

unreflecting □['ʌnri'flektiŋ] ge-\]

unregarded ['ʌnri'gɑːdid] unbeachtet; unberücksichtigt.

unrelated ['ʌnri'leitid] ohne Beziehung (*to* zu).

unrelenting □ ['ʌnri'lentiŋ] erbarmungslos; unerbittlich.

unreliable ['ʌnri'laiəbl] unzuverlässig.

unrelieved □ ['ʌnri'liːvd] ungelindert; ununterbrochen.

unremitting □ [ʌnri'mitiŋ] unablässig, unaufhörlich; unermüdlich.

unrepining □ ['ʌnri'painiŋ] klaglos; unverdrossen.

unrequited □ ['ʌnri'kwaitid] unerwidert; unbelohnt.

unreserved □ ['ʌnri'zəːvd] rückhaltlos; unbeschränkt; ohne Vorbehalt.

unresisting □ ['ʌnri'zistiŋ] widerstandslos.

unresponsive ['ʌnris'pɔnsiv] unempfänglich (to für).

unrest ['ʌn'rest] Unruhe f.

unrestrained □ ['ʌnris'treind] ungehemmt; unbeschränkt.

unrestricted □ ['ʌnris'triktid] uneingeschränkt.

unriddle ['ʌn'ridl] enträtseln.

unrighteous □ ['ʌn'raitʃəs] ungerecht; unredlich.

unripe ['ʌn'raip] unreif.

unrival(l)ed ['ʌn'raivəld] unvergleichlich, unerreicht, einzigartig.

unroll ['ʌn'roul] ent-, aufrollen.

unruffled ['ʌn'rʌfld] glatt; ruhig.

unruly [ʌn'ruːli] ungebärdig.

unsafe ['ʌn'seif] unsicher.

unsal(e)able ['ʌn'seiləbl] unverkäuflich.

unsanitary ['ʌn'sænitəri] unhygienisch.

unsatisf|actory □ ['ʌnsætis'fæktəri] unbefriedigend; unzulänglich; ~ied ['ʌn'sætisfaid] unbefriedigt; ~ying □ [~aiiŋ] = unsatisfactory.

unsavo(u)ry □ ['ʌn'seivəri] unappetitlich (a. fig.), widerwärtig.

unsay ['ʌn'sei] [irr. (say)] zurücknehmen, widerrufen.

unscathed ['ʌn'skeiðd] unversehrt.

unschooled ['ʌn'skuːld] ungeschult; unverbildet.

unscrew ['ʌn'skruː] v/t. ab-, los-, aufschrauben; v/i. sich abschrauben lassen.

unscrupulous □ [ʌn'skruːpjuləs] bedenkenlos; gewissenlos; skrupellos.

unsearchable □ [ʌn'səːtʃəbl] unerforschlich; unergründlich.

unseason|able □ [ʌn'siːznəbl] unzeitig; fig. ungelegen; ~ed ['ʌn'siːznd] nicht abgelagert (Holz); fig. nicht abgehärtet; ungewürzt.

unseat ['ʌn'siːt] des Amtes entheben; abwerfen.

unseemly [ʌn'siːmli] unziemlich.

unseen ['ʌn'siːn] ungesehen; unsichtbar.

unselfish □ ['ʌn'selfiʃ] selbstlos, uneigennützig; ~ness [~ʃnis] Selbstlosigkeit f.

unsettle ['ʌn'setl] in Unordnung

bringen; verwirren; erschüttern; ~d nicht festgesetzt; unbeständig; † unbezahlt; unerledigt; ohne festen Wohnsitz; unbesiedelt.

unshaken ['ʌn'ʃeikən] unerschüttert; unerschütterlich.

unshaven ['ʌn'ʃeivn] unrasiert.

unship ['ʌn'ʃip] ausschiffen.

unshrink|able ['ʌn'ʃriŋkəbl] nicht einlaufend (Stoff); ~ing □ [ʌn'ʃriŋkiŋ] unverzagt.

unsightly [ʌn'saitli] häßlich.

unskil(l)ful □ ['ʌn'skilful] ungeschickt; ~ed [~ld] ungelernt.

unsoci|able [ʌn'souʃəbl] ungesellig; ~al [~əl] ungesellig; unsozial.

unsolder ['ʌn'sɔldə] los-, ablöten.

unsolicited ['ʌnsə'lisitid] nicht gefragt (S.); unaufgefordert (P.).

unsolv|able [ʌn'sɔlvəbl] unlösbar; ~ed [~vd] ungelöst.

unsophisticated ['ʌnsə'fistikeitid] unverfälscht; ungekünstelt; unverdorben, unverbildet.

unsound □ ['ʌn'saund] ungesund; verdorben; wurmstichig; morsch; nicht stichhaltig (Beweis); verkehrt.

unsparing □ [ʌn'spɛəriŋ] freigebig; schonungslos, unbarmherzig.

unspeakable □ [ʌn'spiːkəbl] unsagbar; unsäglich.

unspent ['ʌn'spent] unverbraucht; unerschöpft.

unspoil|ed, ~t ['ʌn'spɔilt] unverdorben; unbeschädigt; nicht verzogen (Kind).

unspoken ['ʌn'spoukən] ungesagt; ~of unerwähnt.

unstable □ ['ʌn'steibl] nicht (stand)fest; unbeständig; unstet(ig); labil.

unsteady □ ['ʌn'stedi] unstet(ig), unsicher; schwankend; unbeständig; unsolid; unregelmäßig.

unstrained ['ʌn'streind] unfiltriert; fig. ungezwungen.

unstrap ['ʌn'stræp] los-, abschnallen.

unstressed ['ʌn'strest] unbetont.

unstring ['ʌn'striŋ] [irr. (string)] Saite entspannen.

unstudied ['ʌn'stʌdid] ungesucht; ungekünstelt, natürlich.

unsubstantial □ ['ʌnsəb'stænʃəl] wesenlos; gegenstandslos; inhaltlos; gehaltlos; dürftig.

unsuccessful □ ['ʌnsək'sesful] erfolglos, ohne Erfolg.

unsuitable □ ['ʌn'sjuːtəbl] unpassend; unangemessen.

unsurpassed ['ʌnsə(ː)'paːst] unübertroffen.

unsuspect|ed ['ʌnsəs'pektid] unverdächtig; unvermutet; ~ing □ [~tiŋ] nichts ahnend; arglos.

unsuspicious □ ['ʌnsəs'piʃəs] nicht argwöhnisch, arglos.

unswerving □ [ʌn'swəːviŋ] unentwegt.

untangle ['ʌn'tæŋgl] entwirren.

untarnished ['ʌn'taːniʃt] unbefleckt; ungetrübt.

unteachable ['ʌn'tiːtʃəbl] unbelehrbar (P.); unlehrbar (S.).

untenanted ['ʌn'tənəntid] unvermietet, unbewohnt.

unthankful □ ['ʌn'θæŋkful] undankbar.

unthink|able [ʌn'θiŋkəbl] undenkbar; ~ing □ ['ʌn'θiŋkiŋ] gedankenlos.

unthought ['ʌn'θɔːt] unbedacht; ~-of unvermutet.

unthrifty □ ['ʌn'θrifti] verschwenderisch; nicht gedeihend.

untidy □ [ʌn'taidi] unordentlich.

untie ['ʌn'tai] aufbinden, aufknüpfen; Knoten etc. lösen; j-n losbinden.

until [ən'til] 1. prp. bis; 2. cj. bis (daß); not ~ erst wenn od. als.

untimely [ʌn'taimli] unzeitig; vorzeitig; ungelegen.   [lich.)

untiring □ [ʌn'taiəriŋ] unermüd-)

unto ['ʌntu] = to.

untold ['ʌn'tould] unerzählt; ungezählt; unermeßlich, unsäglich.

untouched ['ʌn'tʌtʃt] unberührt; fig. ungerührt; phot. unretuschiert.

untried ['ʌn'traid] unversucht; unerprobt; ⚖ noch nicht verhört.

untrod, ~den ['ʌn'trɔd, ~dn] unbetreten.

untroubled ['ʌn'trʌbld] ungestört.

untrue ['ʌn'truː] unwahr; untreu.

untrustworthy □ ['ʌn'trʌstwəːði] unzuverlässig, nicht vertrauenswürdig.

unus|ed ['ʌn'juːzd] ungebraucht; [~uːst] nicht gewöhnt (to an acc.; zu inf.); ~ual [ʌn'juːʒuəl] ungewöhnlich; ungewohnt.

unutterable □ [ʌn'ʌtərəbl] unaussprechlich.

unvarnished fig. ['ʌn'vaːniʃt] ungeschminkt.

unvarying □ [ʌn'vɛəriiŋ] unveränderlich.

unveil [ʌn'veil] entschleiern, enthüllen.

unversed ['ʌn'vəːst] unbewandert, unerfahren (in in dat.).

unvouched ['ʌn'vautʃt] a. ~-for unverbürgt, unbezeugt.

unwanted ['ʌn'wɔntid] unerwünscht.

unwarrant|able □ [ʌn'wɔrəntəbl] unverantwortlich; ~ed [~tid] unberechtigt; ['ʌn'wɔrəntid] unverbürgt.

unwary □ [ʌn'wɛəri] unbedachtsam.

unwelcome [ʌn'welkəm] unwillkommen.

unwholesome ['ʌn'houlsəm] ungesund; schädlich.

unwieldy □ [ʌn'wiːldi] unhandlich; ungefüge; sperrig.

unwilling □ ['ʌn'wiliŋ] un-, widerwillig, abgeneigt.

unwind ['ʌn'waind] [irr. (wind)] auf-, loswickeln; (sich) abwickeln.

unwise) ['ʌn'waiz] unklug.

unwitting □ ['ʌn'witiŋ] unwissentlich; unbeabsichtigt.

unworkable ['ʌn'wəːkəbl] undurchführbar; ⊕ nicht betriebsfähig.

unworthy □ [ʌn'wəːði] unwürdig.

unwrap ['ʌn'ræp] auswickeln, auspacken, aufwickeln.

unwrought ['ʌn'rɔːt] unbearbeitet; roh; Roh...

unyielding □ [ʌn'jiːldiŋ] unnachgiebig.

up [ʌp] 1. adv. (her-, hin)auf; aufwärts, empor; oben; auf(gestanden); aufgegangen (Sonne); hoch; abgelaufen, um (Zeit); Am. Baseball: am Schlag; ~ and about wieder auf den Beinen; be hard ~ in Geldschwierigkeiten sein; ~ against a task e-r Aufgabe gegenüber; ~ to bis (zu); it is ~ to me to do es ist an mir, zu tun; what are you ~ to there? was macht ihr da? what's ~? sl. was ist los? 2. prp. hinauf; ~ the river flußaufwärts; 3. adj.: ~ train Zug m nach der Stadt; 4.: the ~s and downs das Auf und Ab, die Höhen und Tiefen des Lebens; 5. F (sich) erheben; hochfahren, hochtreiben.

up|-and-coming Am. F ['ʌpən'kʌmiŋ] unternehmungslustig; ~braid [ʌp'breid] schelten; ~bringing ['ʌpbriŋiŋ] Erziehung f; ~country [ʌp'kʌntri] landeinwärts (gelegen); ~heaval [ʌp'hiːvl] Umbruch m; ~hill ['ʌp'hil] bergan; mühsam; ~hold [ʌp'hould] [irr. (hold)] aufrecht(er)halten; stützen; ~holster [ʌp'houlstə] Möbel (auf)polstern; Zimmer dekorieren; ~holsterer [~ərə] Tapezierer m, Dekorateur m, Polsterer m; ~holstery [~ri] Polstermöbel n/pl.; Möbelstoffe m/pl.; Tapezierarbeit f.

up|keep ['ʌpkiːp] Instandhaltung(skosten pl.) f; Unterhalt m; ~land ['ʌplənd] Hoch-, Oberland n; ~lift 1. [ʌp'lift] (empor-, er)heben; 2. ['ʌplift] Erhebung f; fig. Aufschwung m.

upon [ə'pɔn] = on.

upper ['ʌpə] ober; Ober...; ~most oberst, höchst.

up|raise [ʌp'reiz] erheben; ~rear [ʌp'riə] aufrichten; ~right 1. □ ['ʌp'rait] aufrecht; ~ piano ♩ Klavier n; fig. ['ʌprait] rechtschaffen; 2. Pfosten m; Ständer m; ~rising [ʌp'raiziŋ] Erhebung f, Aufstand m.

uproar ['ʌprɔː] Aufruhr m; ~ious □ [ʌp'rɔːriəs] tobend; tosend.

up|root [ʌp'ruːt] entwurzeln; (her-) ausreißen; ~set [ʌp'set] [irr. (set)] umwerfen; (um)stürzen; außer Fassung od. in Unordnung bringen; stören; verwirren; be ~ außer sich sein; ~shot ['ʌpʃɒt] Ausgang m; ~side ['ʌpsaid] adv.: ~ down das Oberste zuunterst; verkehrt; ~stairs ['ʌp'stɛəz] die Treppe hinauf, (nach) oben; ~start ['ʌpstaːt] Emporkömmling m; ~state Am. ['ʌp'steit] Hinterland n e-s Staates; ~stream ['ʌp'striːm] fluß-, stromaufwärts; ~-to-date ['ʌptə'deit] modern, neuzeitlich; ~town ['ʌp'taun] im od. in den oberen Stadtteil; Am. im Wohn- od. Villenviertel; ~turn [ʌp'təːn] nach oben kehren; ~ward(s) ['ʌpwəd(z)] aufwärts (gerichtet).

uranium [juə'reinjəm] Uran n.

urban ['əːbən] städtisch; Stadt...; ~e □ [əː'bein] höflich; gebildet.

urchin ['əːtʃin] Bengel m.

urge [əːdʒ] 1. oft ~ on j-n drängen, (an)treiben; dringen in j-n; dringen auf et.; Recht geltend machen; 2. Drang m; ~ncy ['əːdʒənsi] Dringlichkeit f; Drängen n; ~nt □ [~nt] dringend; dringlich; eilig.

urin|al ['juərinl] Harnglas n; Bedürfnisanstalt f; ~ate [~neit] urinieren; ~e [~in] Urin m, Harn m.

urn [əːn] Urne f; Tee- etc. Maschine f.

us [ʌs, əs] uns; of ~ unser.

usage ['juːzidʒ] Brauch m, Gepflogenheit f; Sprachgebrauch m; Behandlung f, Verwendung f; Gebrauch m.

usance ✝ ['juːzəns] Wechselfrist f.

use 1. [juːs] Gebrauch m; Benutzung f; Verwendung f; Gewohnheit f, Übung f; Brauch m; Nutzen m; (of) no ~ unnütz, zwecklos; have no ~ for keine Verwendung haben

für; Am. F nicht mögen; 2. [juːz] gebrauchen; benutzen, ver-, anwenden; behandeln; ~ up ver-, aufbrauchen; I ~d to do ich pflegte zu tun, früher tat ich; ~d [juːzd] ge-, verbraucht; [juːst] gewöhnt (to an acc.); gewohnt (to zu od. acc.); ~ful □ ['juːsful] brauchbar; nützlich; Nutz...; ~less □ ['juːslis] nutz-, zwecklos, unnütz.

usher ['ʌʃə] 1. Türhüter m, Pförtner m; Gerichtsdiener m; Platzanweiser m; 2. mst. ~ in (hin)einführen, anmelden; ~ette [ʌʃə'ret] Platzanweiserin f.

usual □ ['juːʒuəl] gewöhnlich; üblich; gebräuchlich.

usurer ['juːʒərə] Wucherer m.

usurp [juː'zəːp] sich et. widerrechtlich aneignen, an sich reißen; ~er [~pə] Usurpator m.

usury ['juːʒuri] Wucher(zinsen pl.) m.

utensil [ju(ː)'tensl] Gerät n; Geschirr n.

uterus anat. ['juːtərəs] Gebärmutter f.

utility [ju(ː)'tiliti] 1. Nützlichkeit f, Nutzen m; public ~ öffentlicher Versorgungsbetrieb; 2. Gebrauchs..., Einheits...

utiliz|ation [juːtilai'zeiʃən] Nutzbarmachung f; Nutzanwendung f; ~e ['juːtilaiz] sich et. zunutze machen.

utmost ['ʌtmoust] äußerst.

Utopian [juː'toupjən] 1. utopisch; 2. Utopist(in), Schwärmer(in).

utter ['ʌtə] 1. □ fig. äußerst; völlig, gänzlich; 2. äußern; Seufzer etc. ausstoßen, von sich geben; Falschgeld etc. in Umlauf setzen; ~ance ['ʌtərəns] Äußerung f; Ausdruck m; Aussprache f; ~most ['ʌtmoust] äußerst.

uvula anat. ['juːvjulə] Zäpfchen n.

V

vacan|cy ['veikənsi] Leere f; leerer od. freier Platz; Lücke f; offene Stelle; ~t □ [~nt] leer (a. fig.); frei (Zeit, Zimmer); offen (Stelle); unbesetzt, vakant (Amt).

vacat|e [və'keit, Am. 'veikeit] räumen; Stelle aufgeben; aus e-m Amt scheiden; ~ion [və'keiʃən, Am. vei'keiʃən] 1. (Schul)Ferien pl.; bsd. Am. Urlaub m; Räumung f; Niederlegung f e-s Amtes; 2. Am. Urlaub machen; ~ionist Am. [~nist] Ferienreisende(r m) f.

vaccin|ate ['væksineit] impfen;

~ation [væksi'neiʃən] Impfung f; ~e ['væksiːn] Impfstoff m.

vacillate ['væsileit] schwanken.

vacu|ous □ ['vækjuəs] fig. leer, geistlos; ~um phys. [~uəm] Vakuum n; ~ cleaner Staubsauger m; ~ flask, ~ bottle Thermosflasche f.

vagabond ['vægəbənd] 1. vagabundierend; 2. Landstreicher m.

vagary ['veigəri] wunderlicher Einfall, Laune f, Schrulle f.

vagrant ['veigrənt] 1. wandernd; fig. unstet; 2. Landstreicher m, Vagabund m; Strolch m.

vague □ [veig] unbestimmt; unklar.

vain □ [vein] eitel, eingebildet; leer; nichtig; vergeblich; *in* ~ vergebens, umsonst; **~glorious** □ [vein'glɔːriəs] prahlerisch.

vale [veil] *poet. od. in Namen:* Tal *n.*

valediction [væli'dikʃən] Abschied(sworte *n/pl.*) *m.*

valentine ['vælэntain] Valentinsschatz *m,* -gruß *m* (*am Valentinstag, 14. Februar, erwählt, gesandt.*).

valerian ⚕ [vэ'liэriэn] Baldrian *m.*

valet ['vælit] **1.** (Kammer)Diener *m;* **2.** Diener sein bei *j-m; j-n* bedienen.

valetudinarian ['vælitjuːdi'neэriэn] **1.** kränklich; **2.** kränklicher Mensch; Hypochonder *m.*

valiant □ ['væljэnt] tapfer.

valid □ ['vælid] triftig, richtig, stichhaltig; (rechts)gültig; *be* ~ gelten; **~ity** [vэ'liditi] Gültigkeit *f;* Triftig-, Richtigkeit *f.*

valise [vэ'liːz] Reisetasche *f;* ✕ Tornister *m.*

valley ['væli] Tal *n.*

valo(u)r ['vælэ] Tapferkeit *f.*

valuable ['væljuэbl] **1.** □ wertvoll; **2.** ~*s pl.* Wertsachen *f/pl.*

valuation [vælju'eiʃэn] Abschätzung *f;* Taxwert *m.*

value ['væljuː] **1.** Wert *m;* Währung *f; give* (*get*) *good* ~ (*for one's money*) † reell bedienen (bedient werden); **2.** (ab)schätzen; *fig.* schätzen; **~less** [~julis] wertlos.

valve [vælv] Klappe *f;* Ventil *n; Radio:* Röhre *f.*

vamoose *Am. sl.* [vэ'muːs] *v/i.* abhauen; *v/t.* räumen (*verlassen*).

vamp [væmp] **1.** Vamp *m* (*verführerische Frau*); **2.** neppen.

vampire ['væmpaiэ] Vampir *m.*

van [væn] Möbelwagen *m;* Lieferwagen *m;* 🚃 Pack-, Güterwagen *m;* ✕ Vorhut *f.*

vane [vein] Wetterfahne *f;* (Windmühlen-, Propeller)Flügel *m.*

vanguard ✕ ['vængaːd] Vorhut *f.*

vanilla ⚕ [vэ'nilэ] Vanille *f.*

vanish ['væniʃ] (ver)schwinden.

vanity ['væniti] Eitelkeit *f,* Einbildung *f;* Nichtigkeit *f;* ~ *bag* Kosmetiktäschchen *n.*

vanquish ['væŋkwiʃ] besiegen.

vantage ['vɑːntidʒ] *Tennis:* Vorteil *m;* **~ground** günstige Stellung.

vapid □ ['væpid] schal; fad(e).

vapor|ize ['veipэraiz] verdampfen, verdunsten (lassen); **~ous** [~rэs] dunstig; nebelhaft.

vapo(u)r ['veipэ] Dunst *m;* Dampf *m.*

varia|ble □ ['veэriэbl] veränderlich; **~nce** [~эns] Veränderung *f;* Uneinigkeit *f; be at* ~ uneinig sein; (sich) widersprechen; *set at* ~ entzweien; **~nt** [~эnt] **1.** abweichend; **2.** Variante *f;* **~tion** [veэri'eiʃэn]

Abänderung *f;* Schwankung *f;* Abweichung *f;* ♪ Variation *f.*

varicose ⚕ ['værikous] Krampfader(n)...; ~ *vein* Krampfader *f.*

varie|d □ ['veэrid] verschieden, verändert, mannigfaltig; **~gate** [~igeit] bunt gestalten; **~ty** [vэ'raiэti] Mannigfaltigkeit *f,* Vielzahl *f; biol.* Abart *f;* † Auswahl *f;* Menge *f;* ~ *show* Varietévorstellung *f;* ~ *theatre* Varieté(theater) *n.*

various ⊐ ['veэriэs] verschiedene, mehrere; mannigfaltig; verschiedenartig. [Racker.\]

varmint *sl.* ['vɑːmint] *kleiner*

varnish ['vɑːniʃ] **1.** Firnis *m,* Lack *m; fig.* (äußerer) Anstrich; **2.** firnissen, lackieren; *fig.* beschönigen.

vary ['veэri] (sich) (ver)ändern; wechseln (*mit et.*); abweichen.

vase [vɑːz] Vase *f.*

vassal ['væsэl] Vasall *m; attr.* Vasallen...

vast □ [vɑːst] ungeheuer, gewaltig, riesig, umfassend, weit.

vat [væt] Faß *n;* Bottich *m;* Kufe *f.*

vaudeville *Am.* ['voudэvil] Varieté *n.*

vault [vɔːlt] **1.** Gewölbe *n;* Wölbung *f;* Stahlkammer *f;* Gruft *f; bsd. Sport:* Sprung *m;* **wine~** Weinkeller *m;* **2.** (über)wölben; *bsd. Sport:* springen (*über acc.*).

vaulting-horse ['vɔːltiŋhɔːs] *Turnen:* Pferd *n.*

vaunt *lit.* [vɔːnt] (sich) rühmen.

veal [viːl] Kalbfleisch *n; roast* ~ Kalbsbraten *m.*

veer [viэ] (sich) drehen.

vegeta|ble ['vedʒitэbl] **1.** Pflanzen..., pflanzlich; **2.** Pflanze *f; mst* ~*s pl.* Gemüse *n;* **~rian** [vedʒi'teэriэn] **1.** Vegetarier(in); **2.** vegetarisch; **~te** ['vedʒiteit] vegetieren; **~tive** □ [~tэtiv] vegetativ; wachstumfördernd.

vehemen|ce ['viːimэns] Heftigkeit *f;* Gewalt *f;* **~t** □ [~nt] heftig; ungestüm.

vehicle ['viːikl] Fahrzeug *n,* Beförderungsmittel *n; fig.* Vermittler *m,* Träger *m;* Ausdrucksmittel *n.*

veil [veil] **1.** Schleier *m;* Hülle *f;* **2.** (sich) verschleiern (*a. fig.*).

vein [vein] Ader *f* (*a. fig.*); Anlage *f;* Neigung *f;* Stimmung *f.*

velocipede [vi'lɔsipiːd] *Am.* (Kinder)Dreirad *n; hist.* Veloziped *n.*

velocity [vi'lɔsiti] Geschwindigkeit *f.*

velvet ['velvit] **1.** Samt *m; hunt.* Bast *m;* **2.** Samt...; samten; **~y** [~ti] samtig.

venal ['viːnl] käuflich, feil.

vend [vend] verkaufen; **~er**, **~or** ['vendэ, ~dɔː] Verkäufer *m,* Händler *m.*

veneer [vi'niэ] **1.** Furnier *n;* **2.** furnieren; *fig.* bemänteln.

venera|ble □ ['venərəbl] ehrwürdig; **~te** [~reit] (ver)ehren; **~tion** [venə'reiʃən] Verehrung f.

venereal [vi'niəriəl] Geschlechts...

Venetian [vi'ni:ʃən] 1. venetianisch; **~ blind** (Stab)Jalousie f; 2. Venetianer(in).

vengeance ['vendʒəns] Rache f; **with a ~** F und wie, ganz gehörig.

venial ['vi:njəl] verzeihlich.

venison ['venzn] Wildbret n.

venom ['venəm] (bsd. Schlangen-)Gift n; fig. Gift n; Gehässigkeit f; **~ous** □ [~məs] giftig.

venous ['vi:nəs] Venen...; venös.

vent [vent] 1. Öffnung f; Luft-, Spundloch n; Auslaß m; Schlitz m; **give ~ to** s-m Zorn etc. Luft machen; 2. fig. Luft machen (dat.).

ventilat|e ['ventileit] ventilieren, (be-, ent-, durch)lüften, fig. erörtern; **~ion** [venti'leiʃən] Ventilation f, Lüftung f; fig. Erörterung f; **~or** ['ventileitə] Ventilator m.

ventral anat. ['ventrəl] Bauch...

ventriloquist [ven'triləkwist] Bauchredner m.

ventur|e ['ventʃə] 1. Wagnis n; Risiko n; Abenteuer n; Spekulation f; **at a ~** auf gut Glück; 2. (sich) wagen; riskieren; **~esome** □ [~əsəm], **~ous** □ [~ərəs] verwegen, kühn.

veracious □ [ve'reiʃəs] wahrhaft.

verb gr. [və:b] Verb(um) n, Zeitwort n; **~al** □ ['və:bəl] wörtlich; mündlich; **~iage** ['və:biidʒ] Wortschwall m; **~ose** □ [və:'bous] wortreich. [reif.]

verdant □ ['və:dənt] grün; fig. un-]

verdict ['və:dikt] ½ (Urteils-)Spruch m der Geschworenen; fig. Urteil n; **bring in** od. **return a ~ of** guilty auf schuldig erkennen.

verdigris ['və:digris] Grünspan m.

verdure ['və:dʒə] Grün n.

verge [və:dʒ] 1. Rand m, Grenze f; **on the ~ of** am Rande (gen.); dicht vor (dat.); 2. sich (hin)neigen; **~ (up)on** grenzen an (acc.).

veri|fy ['verifai] (nach)prüfen; beweisen; bestätigen; **~similitude** [verisi'militju:d] Wahrscheinlichkeit f; **~table** □ ['veritəbl] wahr(-haftig).

vermic|elli [və:mi'seli] Fadennudeln f/pl.; **~ular** [və:'mikjulə] wurmartig.

vermilion [və'miljən] 1. Zinnoberrot n; 2. zinnoberrot.

vermin ['və:min] Ungeziefer n; hunt. Raubzeug n; fig. Gesindel n; **~ous** [~nəs] voller Ungeziefer.

vernacular [və'nækjulə] 1. **~** einheimisch; Volks...; 2. Landes-, Muttersprache f; Jargon m.

versatile ['və:sətail] wendig.

verse [və:s] Vers(e pl.) m; Strophe f; Dichtung f; **~d** [və:st] bewandert.

versify ['və:sifai] v/t. in Verse bringen; v/i. Verse machen.

version ['və:ʃən] Übersetzung f; Fassung f, Darstellung f; Lesart f.

versus bsd. ½ ['və:səs] gegen.

vertebra anat. ['və:tibrə], pl. **~e** [~ri:] Wirbel m.

vertical □ ['və:tikəl] vertikal, senkrecht.

vertig|inous □ [və:'tidʒinəs] schwindlig; schwindelnd (Höhe); **~o** ['və:tigou] Schwindel(anfall) m.

verve [veəv] Schwung m, Verve f.

very ['veri] 1. adv. sehr; **the ~ best** das allerbeste; 2. adj. wirklich; eben; bloß; **the ~ same** ebenderselbe; **in the ~ act** auf frischer Tat; gerade dabei; **the ~ thing** gerade das; **the ~ thought** der bloße Gedanke; **the ~ stones** sogar die Steine; **the veriest rascal** das größte Schuft.

vesicle ['vesikl] Bläs-chen n.

vessel ['vesl] Gefäß n (a. anat., ♀, fig.); ♣ Fahrzeug n, Schiff n.

vest [vest] 1. Unterhemd n; Weste f; 2. v/t. bekleiden (with mit); j-n einsetzen (in in acc.); et. übertragen (in s.o. j-m); v/i. verliehen werden.

vestibu|le ['vestibju:l] Vorhof m (a. anat.); Vorhalle f; Hausflur m; bsd. Am. ⓖ Korridor m zwischen zwei D-Zug-Wagen; **~ train** D-Zug m.

vestige ['vestidʒ] Spur f.

vestment ['vestmənt] Gewand n.

vestry ['vestri] eccl. Sakristei f; Gemeindevertretung f; Gemeindesaal m; **~man** Gemeindevertreter m.

vet F [vet] 1. Tierarzt m; Am. ⓧ Veteran m; 2. co. verarzten; gründlich prüfen.

veteran ['vetərən] 1. ausgedient; erfahren; 2. Veteran m.

veterinary ['vetərinəri] 1. tierärztlich; 2. a. **~ surgeon** Tierarzt m.

veto ['vi:tou] 1. pl. **~es** Veto n; 2. sein Veto einlegen gegen.

vex [veks] ärgern; sich schikanieren; **~ation** [vek'seiʃən] Verdruß m; Ärger(nis n) m; **~atious** □ [~ʃəs] ärgerlich.

via [vaiə] über, via.

viaduct ['vaiədʌkt] Viadukt m, Überführung f.

vial ['vaiəl] Phiole f, Fläschchen n.

viand ['vaiənd] mst. **~s** pl. Lebensmittel n/pl.

vibrat|e [vai'breit] vibrieren; zittern; **~ion** [~eiʃən] Schwingung f, Zittern n, Vibrieren n, Erschütterung f.

vicar ['vikə] eccl. Vikar m; **~age** [~əridʒ] Pfarrhaus n.

vice[1] [vais] Laster n; Fehler m; Unart f; ⊕ Schraubstock m.

vice[2] prp. ['vaisi] an Stelle von.

vice[3] [vais] F Stellvertreter m; attr. Vize..., Unter...; **~roy** ['vaisrɔi] Vizekönig m.

vice versa ['vaisi'vɔːsə] umgekehrt.

vicinity [vi'siniti] Nachbarschaft f; Nähe f

vicious ['viʃəs] lasterhaft; bösartig; boshaft, fehlerhaft.

vicissitude [vi sisiti̯uːd] Wandel m, Wechsel m; ~s pl. Wechselfälle m/pl.

victim ['viktim] Opfer n; ~ize [~maiz] (hin)opfern; fig. j-n hereinlegen

victor ['viktə] Sieger m; 2ian hist. [vik'tɔːriən] Viktorianisch; ~ious □ [~iəs] siegreich; Sieges...; ~y ['viktəri] Sieg m

victual ['vitl] 1. (sich) verpflegen od. verproviantieren, 2. mst ~s pl. Lebensmittel n/pl, Proviant m; ~(l)er [~lə] Lebensmittellieferant m.

video ['vidiou] Fernseh...

vie [vai] wetteifern.

Viennese [viə niːz] 1. Wiener(in); 2. Wiener, wienerisch.

view [vjuː] 1. Sicht f, Blick m; Besichtigung f, Aussicht f (of auf acc.); Anblick m, Ansicht f (a. fig.); Absicht f, at first ~ auf den ersten Blick; in sichtbar, zu sehen; in ~ of im Hinblick auf (acc.); fig. angesichts (gen), on ~ zu besichtigen; with a to inf od of ger. in der Absicht zu inf, have (keep) in ~ im Auge haben (behalten); 2. ansehen, besichtigen, fig betrachten; ~er ['vjuːə] Betrachter(in), Zuschauer (-in); ~less ['vjuːlis] ohne eigene Meinung, poet unsichtbar; ~point Gesichts Standpunkt m.

vigil ['vidʒil] Nachtwache f; ~ance [~ləns] Wachsamkeit f; ~ant □ [~nt] wachsam

vigo|rous ['vigərəs] kräftig; energisch, nachdrücklich; ~u)r ['vigə] Kraft f, Vitalität f; Nachdruck m.

viking ['vaikiŋ] 1. Wiking(er) m; 2. wikingisch, Wikinger...

vile [[vail] gemein; abscheulich.

vilify ['vilifai] verunglimpfen.

village ['vilidʒ] Dorf n; ~ green Dorfanger m, -wiese f; ~r [~dʒə] Dorfbewohner(in).

villain ['vilən] Schurke m, Schuft m, Bösewicht m, ~ous □ [~nəs] schurkisch; F scheußlich; ~y [~ni] Schurkerei f

vim F [vim] Schwung m, Schneid m.

vindicat|e ['vindikeit] rechtfertigen (from gegen), verteidigen; ~ion [vindi'keiʃən] Rechtfertigung f.

vindictive [[vin'diktiv] rachsüchtig.

vine ♀ [vain] Wein(stock) m, Rebe f; ~gar ['vinigə] (Wein)Essig m; ~growing ['vaingrouiŋ] Weinbau m; ~yard ['vinjəd] Weinberg m.

vintage ['vintidʒ] 1. Weinlese f; (Wein)Jahrgang m; 2. klassisch; erlesen; altmodisch; ~ car mot. Veteran m; ~r [~dʒə] Winzer m.

viola ♪ [vi'oulə] Bratsche f.

violat|e ['vaiəleit] verletzen; Eid etc. brechen; vergewaltigen, schänden; ~ion [vaiə'leiʃən] Verletzung f; (Eid- etc.)Bruch m, Vergewaltigung f, Schändung f

violen|ce ['vaiələns] Gewalt(samkeit, -tätigkeit) f, Heftigkeit f; ~t □ [~nt] gewaltsam; gewalttätig; heftig.

violet ♀ ['vaiəlit] Veilchen n.

violin ♪ [vaiə'lin] Violine f, Geige f.

V.I.P., VIP ['viːai'piː] F hohes Tier.

viper zo. ['vaipə] Viper f, Natter f.

virago [vi'raːgou] Zankteufel m.

virgin ['vəːdʒin] 1. Jungfrau f; 2. a. ~al [[~nl] jungfräulich, Jungfern...; ~ity [vəː'dʒiniti] Jungfräulichkeit f.

viril|e ['virail] männlich; Mannes...; ~ity [vi'riliti] Männlichkeit f.

virtu [vəː'tuː]: article of ~ Kunstgegenstand m; ~al [['vəːtjuəl] eigentlich; ~ally [~li] praktisch; ~e ['vəːtjuː] Tugend f, Wirksamkeit f; Vorzug m, Wert m, in od by ~ of kraft, vermöge (gen.), make a ~ of necessity aus der Not e-e Tugend machen; ~osity [vəːtju'ɔsiti] Virtuosität f; ~ous [['vəːtjuəs] tugendhaft.

virulent □ ['virulənt] giftig; ✎ virulent; fig. bösartig.

virus ['vaiərəs] Virus n; fig. Gift n.

visa ['viːzə] Visum n, Sichtvermerk m; ~ed [~əd] mit e-m Sichtvermerk od. Visum versehen

viscose ⚗ ['viskous] Viskose f; ~ silk Zellstoffseide f

viscount ['vaikaunt] Vicomte m; ~ess [~tis] Vicomtesse f

viscous [['viskəs] zähflüssig.

vise Am. [vais] Schraubstock m.

visé ['viːzei] = visa.

visib|ility [vizi'biliti] Sichtbarkeit f; Sichtweite f; ~le [['vizəbl] sichtbar; fig. (er)sichtlich, pred. zu sehen (S.); zu sprecher (P.).

vision ['viʒən] Sehvermögen n, Sehkraft f; fig. Seherblick m; Vision f, Erscheinung f; ~ary ['viʒnəri] 1. phantastisch; 2. Geisterseher(in); Phantast(in)

visit ['vizit] 1. v/t. besuchen; besichtigen; fig. heimsuchen; et. vergelten, v/i. Besuche machen; Am. sich unterhalten, plaudern (with mit); 2. Besuch m; ~ation [vizi'teiʃən] Besuch m; Besichtigung f; fig. Heimsuchung f; ~or ['vizitə] Besucher(in), Gast m; Inspektor m.

vista ['vistə] Durchblick m Rückod. Ausblick m.

visual [['vizjuəl] Seh...; Gesichts ...; ~ize [~laiz] (sich) vor Augen stellen, sich ein Bild machen von

vital □ ['vaitl] 1. Lebens...; lebenswichtig, wesentlich; lebensgefährlich; ~ parts pl. = 2. ~s pl. lebenswichtige Organe n/pl.; edle Teile m/pl.; ~ity [vai'tæliti] Lebenskraft f; Vitalität f; ~ize ['vaitəlaiz] beleben.

vitamin(e) ['vitəmin] Vitamin n.

vitiate ['viʃieit] verderben; beeinträchtigen; hinfällig (g'z ungültig) machen.

vitreous □ ['vitriəs] Glas.. ; gläsern.

vituperate [vi'tju:pəreit] schelten; schmähen, beschimpfen.

vivaci|ous □ [vi'veiʃəs] lebhaft; ~ty [vi'væsiti] Lebhaftigkeit f.

vivid □ ['vivid] lebhaft, lebendig.

vivify ['vivifai] (sich) beleben.

vixen ['viksn] Füchsin f; zänkisches Weib.

vocabulary [vɔ'kæbjuləri] Wörterverzeichnis n; Wortschatz m.

vocal □ ['voukəl] stimmlich; Stimm...; gesprochen, laut; ♪ Vokal..., Gesang...; klingend; gr. stimmhaft; ~ist [..list] Sänger(in); ~ize [..laiz] (gr. stimmhaft) aussprechen; stimmen.

vocation [vou'keiʃən] Berufung f; Beruf m; ~al □ [..nl] beruflich; Berufs...

vociferate [vou'sifəreit] schreien.

vogue [voug] Beliebtheit f; Mode f.

voice [vɔis] 1. Stimme f; active (passive) ~ gr. Aktiv n (Passiv n); give ~ to Ausdruck geben (dat.); 2. äußern, ausdrücken; gr. stimmhaft aussprechen.

void [vɔid] 1. leer; g'z ungültig; ~ of frei von; arm an (dat.); ohne; 2. Leere f; Lücke f; 3. entleeren; ungültig machen, aufheben.

volatile ['vɔlətail] ♫ flüchtig (a. fig.); flatterhaft.

volcano [vɔl'keinou] pl. ~es Vulkan m.

volition [vou'liʃən] Wollen n; Wille(nskraft f) m.

volley ['vɔli] 1. Salve f; (Geschoßetc.)Hagel m; fig. Schwall m; Tennis: Flugball m; 2. mst out e-n Schwall von Worten etc von sich geben; Salven abgeben, fig. hageln; dröhnen; ~ball Sport. Volleyball m, Flugball m.

volt ⚡ [voult] Volt n; ~age ⚡ ['voultidʒ] Spannung f; ~meter ⚡ Volt-, Spannungsmesser m.

volub|ility [vɔlju'biliti] Redegewandtheit f; ~le □ ['vɔljubl] (rede)gewandt.

volum|e ['vɔljum] Band m e-s Buches; Volumen n; fig. Masse f,

große Menge; (bsd. Stimm)Umfang m; ~ of sound Radio: Lautstärke f; ~inous □ [və'lju:minəs] vielbändig; umfangreich, voluminös.

volunt|ary □ ['vɔləntəri] freiwillig; willkürlich; ~ary n □ 1. Freiwillige(r m) f; attr. Freiwilligen...; 2. v/i. freiwillig dienen; sich freiwillig melden; sich erbieten; v/t. anbieten; sich e-e Bemerkung erlauben.

voluptu|ary [və'lʌptjuəri] Wolllüstling m; ~ous □ [~uəs] wolllüstig; üppig.

vomit ['vɔmit] 1. (sich) erbrechen; fig. (aus)speien, ausstoßen; 2. Erbrochene(s) n; Erbrechen n.

voraci|ous □ [vɔ'reiʃəs] gefräßig; gierig; ~ty [vɔ'ræsiti] Gefräßigkeit f; Gier f.

vort|ex ['vɔ:teks], pl. mst ~ices ['vɔ:tisi:z] Wirbel m, Strudel m (mst fig.).

vote [vout] 1. (Wahl)Stimme f; Abstimmung f; Stimmrecht n; Beschluß m, Votum n; ~ of no confidence Mißtrauensvotum n; cast a ~ (s)eine Stimme abgeben; take a ~ on s.th. über et. abstimmen; 2. v/t. stimmen für; v/i. (ab)stimmen; wählen; ~ for stimmen für; F für et. sein; et. vorschlagen; ~r ['voutə] Wähler(in).

voting ['voutiŋ] Abstimmung f; attr. Wahl...; ~ machine Stimmenzählmaschine f; ~paper Stimmzettel m; ~power Stimmrecht n.

vouch [vautʃ] verbürgen; ~ for bürgen für; ~er ['vautʃə] Beleg m, Unterlage f; Gutschein m; Zeuge m; ~safe [vautʃ'seif] gewähren; geruhen.

vow [vau] 1. Gelübde n; (Treu)Schwur m; 2. v/t. geloben.

vowel gr. ['vauəl] Vokal m, Selbstlaut m.

voyage ['vɔidʒ] 1. längere (See-, Flug)Reise; 2. reisen, fahren; ~r ['vɔidʒə] (See)Reisende(r m) f.

vulgar ['vʌlgə] 1. □ gewöhnlich, gemein, vulgär, pöbelhaft; ~ tongue Volkssprache f; 2.: the ~ der Pöbel; ~ism [~ərizəm] vulgärer Ausdruck; ~ity [vʌl'gæriti] Gemeinheit f; ~ize ['vʌlgəraiz] gemein machen; erniedrigen; populär machen.

vulnerable □ ['vʌlnərəbl] verwundbar; fig. angreifbar.

vulpine ['vʌlpain] Fuchs...; fuchsartig; schlau, listig.

vulture orn. ['vʌltʃə] Geier m.

vying ['vaiiŋ] wetteifernd.

W

wacky *Am. sl.* ['wæki] verrückt.
wad [wɔd] 1. (Watte)Bausch *m*; Polster *n*, Pfropf(en) *m*; Banknotenbündel *n*. 2. wattieren; polstern; zs.-pressen zustopfen; **~ding** ['wɔdiŋ] Wattierung *f*, Watte *f*.
waddle [wɔdl] watscheln, wackeln.
wade [weid] *v/i.* waten; *fig.* sich hindurcharbeiten, *v/t.* durchwaten.
wafer ['weifə] Waffel *f*; Oblate *f*; *eccl.* Hostie *f*.
waffle ['wɔfl] 1. Waffel *f*; 2. F quasseln
waft [wɑːft] 1. wehen, tragen; 2. Hauch *m*
wag [wæg] 1. wackeln (mit); wedeln (mit), 2. Schütteln *n*; Wedeln *n*; Spaßvogel *m*
wage[1] [weidʒ] *Krieg* führen.
wage[2] [~] *mst* ~s *pl.* Lohn *m*; **~earner** ['weidʒəːnə] Lohnempfänger *m*
wager ['weidʒə] 1. Wette *f*; 2. wetten.
waggish ['wægiʃ] schelmisch.
waggle [wægl] wackeln (mit).
wag(g)on [wægən] (Roll-, Güter-) Wagen *m* **~er** [~nə] Fuhrmann *m*.
wagtail *orn* ['wægteil] Bachstelze *f*.
waif [weif] herrenloses Gut; Strandgut *n*, Heimatlose(r *m*) *f*.
wail [weil] 1. (Weh)Klagen *n*; 2. (weh)klagen
wainscot ['weinskət] (Holz)Täfelung *f*
waist [weist] Taille *f*; schmalste Stelle, ♈ Mitteldeck *n*; **~coat** ['weiskout] Weste *f*; **~line** ['weistlain] *Schneiderei*: Taille *f*.
wait [weit] 1. *v/i* warten (*for* auf *acc.*); *a* ~ *at* (*Am.* on) table bedienen, servieren, ~ (*up*)on *j-n* bedienen; *j-n* besuchen; ~ *and see* abwarten; *v/t* abwarten; *mit dem Essen* warten (*for* auf *j-n*); 2. Warten *n*, Aufenthalt *m*; lie in ~ *for* s.o. *j-m* auflauern, **~er** ['weitə] Kellner *m*; Tablett *n*
waiting ['weitiŋ] Warten *n*; Dienst *m*; *in* ~ dienstuend; **~room** Wartezimmer *n*, ♈ *etc.* Wartesaal *m*.
waitress ['weitris] Kellnerin *f*.
waive [weiv] verzichten auf (*acc.*), aufgeben; **~r** r'z [weivə] Verzicht *m*.
wake [weik] 1. ♈ Kielwasser *n* (*a. fig.*); Totenwache *f*; Kirmes *f*; 2. [*irr.*] *v/i. a* ~ *up* aufwachen; *v/t. a.* ~ *up* (auf)wecken; erwecken; *fig.* wachrufen; **~ful** □ ['weikful] wachsam; schlaflos; **~n** ['weikən] *s.* wake 2.
wale *bsd. Am.* [weil] Strieme *f*.
walk [wɔːk] 1. *v/i.* (zu Fuß) gehen; spazierengehen; wandern; Schritt gehen; ~ *out* F streiken; ~ *out on sl.*

im Stich lassen; *v/t.* führen; *Pferd* Schritt gehen lassen; begleiten; (durch)wandern, umhergehen *v/t. od.* in (*dat.*); 2. (Spazier-)Gang *m*; Spazierweg *m*; ~ *of life* Lebensstellung *f*, Beruf *m*, **~er** ['wɔːkə] Fuß-, Spaziergänger(in)
walkie-talkie ⚔ [wɔːki'tɔːki] tragbares Sprechfunkgerät
walking ['wɔːkiŋ] Spaziergehen *n*, Wandern *n*; *attr* Spazier , Wander...; ~ *papers pl Am* ' Entlassung(spapiere *n/pl*) *f*; Laufpaß *m*; **~stick** Spazierstock *m*; **~tour** (Fuß)Wanderung *f*.
walk-out *Am.* ['wɔːkaut] Ausstand *m*; **~over** Kinderspiel *n*, leichter Sieg.
wall [wɔːl] 1. Wand *f*; Mauer *f*; 2. mit Mauern umgeben; ~ *up* zumauern.
wallet ['wɔlit] Ränzel *n*; Brieftasche *f*.
wallflower *fig.* ['wɔːlflauə] Mauerblümchen *n*.
wallop F ['wɔləp] *j-n* verdreschen.
wallow ['wɔlou] sich wälzen.
wall|-paper ['wɔːlpeipə] Tapete *f*; **~socket** ⚡ Steckdose *f*
walnut ♀ ['wɔːlnʌt] Walnuß(baum *m*) *f*.
walrus *zo.* ['wɔːlrəs] Walroß *n*.
waltz [wɔːls] 1. Walzer *m*; 2. Walzer tanzen.
wan □ [wɔn] blaß, bleich, fahl.
wand [wɔnd] (Zauber)Stab *m*.
wander ['wɔndə] wandern, umherschweifen, umherwandern, *fig.* abschweifen; irregehen, phantasieren.
wane [wein] 1. abnehmen (*Mond*); *fig.* schwinden; 2. Abnehmen *n*.
wangle *sl.* ['wæŋgl] *v/t* deichseln, hinkriegen; *v/i.* mogeln
want [wɔnt] 1. Mangel *m* (*of an dat.*); Bedürfnis *n*; Not *f*; 2. *v/i.:* be ~*ing* fehlen; es fehlen lassen (*in an dat.*); unzulänglich sein; ~ *for* Not leiden an (*dat.*), *it* ~*s of* es fehlt an (*dat.*); *v/t.* bedürfen (*gen.*), brauchen; nicht haben, wünschen, (haben) wollen; *it* ~*s* es fehlt an et. (*dat.*); he ~*s energy* es fehlt ihm an Energie; ~*ed* gesucht; **~ad** F ['wɔntæd] Kleinanzeige *f*; Stellenangebot *n*, -gesuch *n*.
wanton ['wɔntən] 1. [geil; üppig; mutwillig; 2. Dirne *f*; 3. umhertollen.
war [wɔː] 1. Krieg *m*; *attr.* Kriegs...; make ~ Krieg führen (*upon gegen*); 2. (ea. wider)streiten
warble ['wɔːbl] trillern; singen.
ward [wɔːd] 1. Gewahrsam *m*; Vormundschaft *f*; Mündel *n*; Schützling *m*; Gefängniszelle *f*; Abteilung *f*, Station *f*, Krankenzimmer *n*;

(Stadt)Bezirk *m*; ⊕ Einschnitt *m im Schlüsselbart*; 2. ~ off abwehren; ~en ['wɔ:dn] Aufseher *m*; (Luftschutz)Wart *m*; *univ* Rektor *m*; ~er ['wɔ:də] (Gefangenen)Wärter *m*; ~robe ['wɔ:droub] Garderobe *f*; Kleiderschrank *m*; ~ trunk Schrankkoffer *m*.

ware [weə] Ware *f*; Geschirr *n*.

warehouse 1. ['weəhaus] (Waren-) Lager *n*; Speicher *m*; 2. [~auz] auf Lager bringen, einlagern.

war|fare ['wɔ:feə] Krieg(führung*f*) *m*; ~head ⚔ Sprengkopf *m* e-r *Rakete etc.*

wariness ['weərinis] Vorsicht *f*.

warlike ['wɔ:laik] kriegerisch.

warm [wɔ:m] 1. ☐ warm (*a. fig.*); heiß; *fig.* hitzig; 2. ⌐ Erwärmung *f*; 3. *v/t. a.* ~ up (auf-, an-, er)wärmen; *v/i. a.* ~ up warm werden, sich erwärmen; ~th [wɔ:mθ] Wärme *f*.

warn [wɔ:n] warnen (*of. against* vor *dat.*); verwarnen; ermahnen; verständigen; ~ing ['wɔ:niŋ] (Ver-) Warnung *f*; Mahnung *f*; Kündigung *f*.

warp [wɔ:p] *v/i.* sich verziehen (*Holz*); *v/t. fig.* verdrehen, verzerren; beeinflussen; *j-n* abbringen (*from* von).

warrant ['wɔrənt] 1. Vollmacht *f*; Rechtfertigung *f*; Berechtigung *f*; ⚖ (Vollziehungs)Befehl *m*, Berechtigungsschein *m*; ~ of arrest ⚖ Haftbefehl *m*; 2. bevollmächtigen; *j-n* berechtigen; *et* rechtfertigen; verbürgen; ✝ garantieren; ~y [~ti] Garantie *f*; Berechtigung *f*.

warrior ['wɔriə] Krieger *m*.

wart [wɔ:t] Warze *f*; Auswuchs *m*.

wary ☐ ['weəri] vorsichtig, behutsam; wachsam.

was [wɔz, wəz] *1 und 3. sg. pret.* von be; *pret. pass von* be; he ~ *to have come er hätte kommen sollen.*

wash [wɔʃ] 1. *v/t.* waschen (um-) spülen; ~ up abwaschen, spülen; *v/i.* sich waschen (lassen), waschecht sein (*a. fig.*); spülen, schlagen (*Wellen*); 2. Waschen *n*, Wäsche *f*; Wellenschlag *m*; Spülwasser *n*; *contp.* Gewäsch *n*, *mouth-* Mundwasser *n*; ~able [' wɔʃəbl] waschbar; ~basin Waschbecken *n*; ~cloth Waschlappen *m*, ~er ['wɔʃə] Wäscherin *f*; Waschmaschine *f*; ⊕ Unterlagscheibe *f*, ~erwoman Waschfrau *f*; ~ing ['wɔʃiŋ] 1. Waschen *n*; Wäsche *f*; *s pl* Spülicht *n*; 2. Wasch...; ~ing-up Abwaschen *n*; ~rag *bsd. Am.* Waschlappen *m*; ~y ['wɔʃi] wässerig.

wasp [wɔsp] Wespe *f*.

wastage ['weistidʒ] Abgang *m*, Verlust *m*; Vergeudung *f*.

waste [weist] 1. wüst, öde; unbebaut; überflüssig; Abfall...; *lay* ~ verwüsten; ~ *paper* Altpapier *n*;

2. Verschwendung *f*, Vergeudung *f*; Abfall *m*; Einöde *f*, Wüste *f*; 3. *v/t.* verwüsten; verschwenden; verzehren; *v/i.* verschwendet werden; ~ful ☐ ['weistful] verschwenderisch; ~paper-basket [weist'peipəba:skit] Papierkorb *m*; ~pipe ['weistpaip] Abflußrohr *n*.

watch [wɔtʃ] 1. Wache *f*; Taschenuhr *f*; 2. *v/i.* wachen; ~ for warten auf (*acc.*); ~ out F aufpassen; *v/t.* bewachen, beobachten; achtgeben auf (*acc.*); *Gelegenheit* abwarten; ~dog ['wɔtʃdɔg] Wachhund *m*; ~ful ☐ [~ʃful] wachsam, achtsam; ~maker Uhrmacher *m*; ~man (Nacht)Wächter *m*; ~word Losung *f*.

water ['wɔ:tə] 1. Wasser *n*; Gewässer *n*; *drink the* ~s Brunnen trinken; 2. *v/t.* bewässern; (be-) sprengen; (be)gießen; mit Wasser versorgen; tränken; verwässern (*a. fig.*); *v/i.* wässern (*Mund*); tränen (*Augen*); Wasser einnehmen; ~closet (Wasser)Klosett *n*; ~colo(u)r Aquarell(malerei *f*) *n*; ~course Wasserlauf *m*; ~cress ⚜ Brunnenkresse *f*; ~fall Wasserfall *m*; ~front Ufer *n*, *bsd. Am. städtisches* Hafengebiet; ~ga(u)ge ⊕ Wasserstands(an)zeiger *m*; Pegel *m*.

watering ['wɔ:təriŋ]: ~can Gießkanne *f*; ~place Wasserloch *n*; Tränke *f*; Bad(eort *m*) *n*; Seebad *n*; ~pot Gießkanne *f*.

water|-level ['wɔ:tələvl] Wasserspiegel *m*; Wasserstand(slinie *f*) *m*; ⊕ Wasserwaage *f*; ~man Fährmann *m*; Bootsführer *m*; Ruderer *m*; ~proof 1. wasserdicht; 2. Regenmantel *m*; 3. imprägnieren; ~shed Wasserscheide *f*; Stromgebiet *n*; ~side 1. Fluß-, Seeufer *n*; 2. am Wasser (gelegen); ~tight wasserdicht; *fig.* unangreifbar; ~way Wasserstraße *f*; ~works *oft sg.* Wasserwerk *n*; ~y [~əri] wässerig.

watt ⚡ [wɔt] Watt *n*.

wattle ['wɔtl] 1. Flechtwerk *n*; 2. aus Flechtwerk herstellen.

wave [weiv] 1. Welle *f*; Woge *f*; Winken *n*; 2. *v/t.* wellig machen, wellen; schwingen; schwenken; ~ *s.o. aside* j-n beiseite winken; *v/i.* wogen; wehen, flattern; winken; ~length *phys.* ['weivleŋθ] Wellenlänge *f*.

waver ['weivə] (sch)wanken; flakkern.

wavy ['weivi] wellig; wogend.

wax[1] [wæks] 1. Wachs *n*; Siegellack *m*; Ohrenschmalz *n*; 2. wachsen; bohnern.

wax[2] [~] *irr.* zunehmen (*Mond*).

wax|en *fig.* ['wæksən] wächsern; ~y ☐ [~si] wachsartig; weich.

way [wei] 1. *mst* Weg *m*; Straße *f*;

Art u. Weise *f; eigene* Art; Strecke *f;* Richtung *f;* F Gegend *f;* ⚓ Fahrt *f; fig.* Hinsicht *f;* Zustand *m;* ⚓ Helling *f;* ~ in Eingang *m;* ~ out Ausgang *m; fig.* Ausweg *m; right of* ~ 🚃 Wegerecht *n; bsd. mot.* Vorfahrt(srecht *n)* **f;** *this* ~ hierher, hier entlang; *by the* ~ übrigens; *by* ~ *of* durch; *on the* ~, *on one's* ~ unterwegs; *out of the* ~ ungewöhnlich; *under* ~ in Fahrt; *give* ~ zurückgehen; *mot.* die Vorfahrt lassen (*to dat.*); nachgeben; abgelöst werden (*to* von); sich hingeben (*to dat.*); *have one's* ~ s-n Willen haben; *lead the* ~ vorangehen; **2.** *adv.* weit; **~bill** ['weibil] Frachtbrief *m;* **~farer** ['weifɛərə] Wanderer *m;* **~lay** [wei'lei] [*irr. (lay*)] *j-m* auflauern; **~side 1.** Wegrand *m;* **2.** am Wege; ~ **station** Am. Zwischenstation *f;* ~ **train** Am. Bummelzug *m;* **~ward** ['weiwəd] starrköpfig, eigensinnig.

we [wi:, wi] wir.

weak [wi:k] schwach; schwächlich; dünn (*Getränk*); **~en** ['wi:kən] *v/t.* schwächen, *v/i.* schwach werden; **~ling** ['wi:kliŋ] Schwächling *m;* **~ly** [~li] schwächlich; **~-minded** ['wi:k'maindid] schwachsinnig, **~ness** ['wi:knis] Schwäche *f.*

weal [wi:l] Wohl *n;* Strieme *f.*

wealth [welθ] Wohlstand *m;* Reichtum *m, fig* Fülle *f;* **~y** □ ['welθi] reich; wohlhabend.

wean [wi:n] entwöhnen; ~ *s.o. from s.th.* j-m et abgewöhnen.

weapon ['wepən] Waffe *f.*

wear [wɛə] **1.** [*irr.*] *v/t. am Körper* tragen, zur Schau tragen; *a.* ~ *away*, ~ *down*, ~ *off*, ~ *out* abnutzen, abtragen, verbrauchen; erschöpfen; ermüden; zermürben; *v/i.* sich gut *etc.* tragen *od* halten; *a.* ~ *off od.* out sich abnutzen *od.* abtragen; *fig.* sich verlieren, ~ *on* vergehen; **2.** Tragen *n;* (Be)Kleidung *f;* Abnutzung *f; for hard* ~ strapazierfähig; *the worse for* ~ abgetragen; ~ *and tear* Verschleiß *m.*

wear|iness ['wiərinis] Müdigkeit *f;* Ermüdung *f, fig* Überdruß *m;* **~some** [~səm] ermüdend; langweilig; **~y** ['wiəri] **1.** □ müde; *fig.* überdrüssig ermüdend; anstrengend; **2.** ermüden.

weasel zo ['wi:zl] Wiesel *n.*

weather ['weðə] **1.** Wetter *n,* Witterung *f,* **2.** *v/t* dem Wetter aussetzen, ⚓ *Sturm* abwettern; *fig.* überstehen *v/i* verwittern; **~beaten** von Wetter mitgenommen; **~bureau** Wetteramt *n;* **~chart** Wetterkarte *f;* **~forecast** Wetterbericht *m,* -vorhersage *f;* **~worn** verwittert.

weav|e [wi:v] [*irr.*] weben; wirken; flechten; *fig.* ersinnen, erfinden;

sich schlängeln; **~er** ['wi:və] Weber *m.*

weazen ['wi:zn] verhutzelt.

web [web] Gewebe *n; orn.* Schwimmhaut *f;* **~bing** ['webiŋ] Gurtband *n.*

wed [wed] heiraten; *fig.* verbinden (*to* mit); **~ding** ['wediŋ] **1.** Hochzeit *f;* **2.** Hochzeits. , Braut...; Trau...; **~ring** Ehe-, Trauring *m.*

wedge [wedʒ] **1.** Keil *m,* **2.** (ver)keilen; *a.* ~ in (hin)einzwängen.

wedlock ['wedlɔk] Ehe *f*

Wednesday ['wenzdi] Mittwoch *m.*

wee [wi:] klein, winzig; *a* ~ *bit* ein klein wenig.

weed [wi:d] **1.** Unkraut *n;* **2.** jäten; säubern (*of* von); ~ *out* ausmerzen; **~killer** ['wi:dkilə] Unkrautvertilgungsmittel *n;* **~s** *pl mst widow's* ~ Witwenkleidung *f;* **~y** ['wi:di] voll Unkraut, verkrautet; *fig.* lang aufgeschossen.

week [wi:k] Woche *f; this day* ~ heute in *od.* vor e-r Woche; **~day** ['wi:kdei] Wochentag *m;* **~end** ['wi:k'end] Wochenende *n;* **~ly** ['wi:kli] **1.** wöchentlich; **2.** *a.* ~ *paper* Wochenblatt *n,* Wochen(zeit)schrift *f.*

weep [wi:p] [*irr.*] weinen; tropfen; **~ing** ['wi:piŋ] Trauer...; ~ *willow* ♣ Trauerweide *f.*

weigh [wei] *v/t.* (ab)wiegen, *fig.* ab-, erwägen; ~ *anchor* ⚓ den Anker lichten; **~ed down** niedergebeugt; *v/i.* wiegen (*a. fig.*); ausschlaggebend sein; ~ (*up*)on lasten auf (*dat.*).

weight [weit] **1.** Gewicht *n* (*a. fig.*); Last *f* (*a. fig.*); *fig* Bedeutung *f,* Wucht *f;* **2.** beschweren; *fig.* belasten; **~y** □ ['weiti] (ge)wichtig, wuchtig.

weir [wiə] Wehr *n;* Fischreuse *f.*

weird [wiəd] Schicksals. .; unheimlich; F sonderbar, seltsam

welcome ['welkəm] **1.** willkommen; *you are* ~ *to inf* es steht Ihnen frei, zu *inf.*; (*you are*) ~! gern gescheheni, bitte sehr!; **2.** Willkomm(en *n*) *m;* **3.** willkommen heißen; *fig.* begrüßen.

weld ⊕ [weld] (zs-)schweißen.

welfare ['welfɛə] Wohlfahrt *f;* ~ **centre** Fürsorgeamt *n;* ~ **state** Wohlfahrtsstaat *m,* ~ **work** Fürsorge *f,* Wohlfahrtspflege *f;* ~ **worker** Fürsorger(in)

well¹ [wel] **1.** Brunnen *m; fig.* Quelle *f;* ⊕ Bohrloch *n;* Treppen-, Aufzugs-, Licht-, Luftschacht *m;* **2.** quellen.

well² [~] **1.** wohl; gut; ordentlich, gründlich; gesund; ~ *off* in guten Verhältnissen, wohlhabend; *I am not* ~ mir ist nicht wohl; **2.** *int.* nun!, F na!; **~being** ['wel'bi:iŋ] Wohl(sein) *n;* **~born** von guter

Herkunft; ~bred wohlerzogen; ~defined deutlich, klar umrissen; ~-favo(u)red gut aussehend; ~intentioned wohlmeinend; gut gemeint; ~ known, ~ known bekannt; ~mannered mit guten Manieren; ~nigh beinah; ~ timed rechtzeitig, ~-to-do ['weltə'du:] wohlhabend; ~-wisher Gönner m, Freund m, ~-worn abgetragen; fig. abgedroschen.

Welsh [welʃ] 1. walisisch, 2. Walisisch n; the ~ pl. die Waliser pl.; ~ rabbit überbackene Käseschnitte.

welt [welt] ⊕ Rahmen m, Schuh-Rahmen m; Einfassung f; Strieme f.

welter ['weltə] 1. rollen, sich wälzen; 2. Wirrwarr m, Durcheinander n.

wench [wentʃ] Mädchen n; Dirne f.

went [went] pret von go 1.

wept [wept] pret. u. p.p. von weep.

were [wɔ:, wə] 1. pret. pl. u. 2. sg. von be; 2. pret. pass. von be; 3. subj. pret. von be.

west [west] 1. West(en m); 2. West...; westlich; westwärts, ~erly ['westəli], ~ern [~ən] westlich, ~erner [~nə] Am. Weststaatler(in); Abendländer(in); ~ward(s) [~twəd(z)] westwärts.

wet [wet] 1. naß, feucht; Am. den Alkoholhandel gestattend; 2. Nässe f; Feuchtigkeit f; 3. [irr.] naß machen, anfeuchten.

wetback Am. sl. ['wetbæk] illegaler Einwanderer aus Mexiko.

wether ['weðə] Hammel m.

wet-nurse ['wetnə:s] Amme f.

whack F [wæk] 1. verhauen; 2. Hieb m.

whale [weil] Wal m; ~bone ['weilboun] Fischbein n; ~-oil Tran m; ~r ['weilə] Walfischfänger m.

whaling ['weiliŋ] Walfischfang m.

wharf [wɔ:f], pl. a. wharves [wɔ:vz] Kai m, Anlegeplatz m.

what [wɔt] 1. was; das, was; know ~'s ~ Bescheid wissen; 2. was?; wie?; wieviel?; welch(er, -e, -es)?; was für ein(e)?; ~ about ..? wie steht's mit ...?; ~ for? wozu?; ~ of it? was ist denn dabei?; ~ next? was sonst noch?; iro. was denn noch alles?; ~ a blessing! was für ein Segen!; 3. ~ with ... ~ with ... teils durch ... teils durch ...; ~ (so)ever [wɔt(sou)'evə] was od. welcher auch (immer).

wheat ❦ [wit] Weizen m.

wheedle ['wi:dl] beschwatzen; ~ s.th. out of s.o. j-m et. abschwatzen.

wheel [wi:l] 1. Rad n; Steuer n; bsd. Am. F Fahrrad n; Töpferscheibe f; Drehung f; ⚔ Schwenkung f; 2. rollen, fahren, schieben; sich drehen; sich umwenden; ⚔ schwenken; F radeln, ~barrow

['wi:lbærou] Schubkarren m; ~ chair Rollstuhl m; ~ed mit Rädern; fahrbar; ...räd(e)rig.

wheeze [wiz] schnaufen, keuchen.

whelp [welp] 1. zo. Welpe m; allg. Junge(s) n; F Balg m, n (ungezogenes Kind); 2. (Junge) werfen.

when [wen] 1. wann?; 2. wenn; als; während od. da doch; und da.

whence [wens] woher, von wo.

when(so)ever [wen(sou)'evə] immer od. jedesmal wenn; sooft (als).

where [wɛə] wo; wohin; ~about(s) 1. ['wɛərə'bauts] wo herum; 2. [~əbauts] Aufenthalt m; ~as [~r'æz] wohingegen, während (doch); ~at [~'æt] wobei, worüber, worauf; ~by [wɛə'bai] wodurch; ~fore ['wɛəfɔ:] weshalb; ~in [wɛər'in] worin; ~of [~r'ɔv] wovon; ~on [~r'ɔn] worauf(hin); ~ver [~r'evə] wo(hin) (auch) immer; ~withal ['wɛəwiðɔ:l] Erforderliche(s) n; Mittel n/pl.

whet [wet] wetzen, schärfen; anstacheln.

whether ['weðə] ob; ~ or no so oder so.

whetstone ['wetstoun] Schleifstein m.

whey [wei] Molke f.

which [witʃ] 1. welche(r, -s)?; 2. der, die, das; was; ~ever [~'evə] welche(r, -s) (auch) immer.

whiff [wif] 1. Hauch m; Zug m beim Rauchen; Zigarillo n; 2. paffen.

while [wail] 1. Weile f; Zeit f; for a ~ e-e Zeitlang; worth ~ der Mühe wert; 2. mst ~ away Zeit verbringen; 3. a. whilst [wailst] während.

whim [wim] Schrulle f, Laune f.

whimper ['wimpə] wimmern.

whim|sical ⚬ ['wimzikəl] wunderlich; sy ['wimzi] Grille f, Laune f.

whine [wain] winseln; wimmern.

whinny ['wini] wiehern.

whip [wip] 1. v/t. peitschen; geißeln (a. fig.); j-n verprügeln; schlagen (F a. fig.); umsäumen; werfen; reißen; ~ in parl. zs.-trommeln; ~ on Kleidungsstück überwerfen; ~ up antreiben; aufraffen; v/i. springen; flitzen; 2. Peitsche f; Geißel f.

whippet zo. ['wipit] Whippet m (kleiner englischer Rennhund).

whipping ['wipiŋ] Prügel pl.; ~top Kreisel m.

whippoorwill orn. ['wippuəwil] Ziegenmelker m.

whirl [wə:l] 1. wirbeln; (sich) drehen; 2. Wirbel m, Strudel m; ~pool ['wə:lpu:l] Strudel m; ~wind Wirbelwind m.

whir(r) [wə:] schwirren.

whisk [wisk] 1. Wisch m; Staubwedel m; Küche: Schneebesen m; Schwung m; 2. v/t. (ab-, weg)wischen; (ab-, weg)fegen; wirbeln (mit); schlagen; v/i. huschen,

flitzen; ~er ['wiskə] Barthaar *n*;
mst ~*s pl.* Backenbart *m*.

whisper ['wispə] 1. flüstern; 2. Geflüster *n*

whistle ['wisl] 1. pfeifen; 2. Pfeife*f*;
Pfiff *m*; F Kehle *f*; ~**stop** *Am.*
🅰 Haltepunkt *m*; *fig.* Kaff *n*; *pol.*
kurzes Auftreten *e-s Kandidaten im
Wahlkampf*

Whit [wit] *in Zssgn*: Pfingst...

white [wait] 1. *allg.* weiß; rein; F
anständig, Weiß...; 2. Weiß(e) *n*;
Weiße(r *m*) *f* (*Rasse*); ~**collar**
['wait'kɔlə] geistig, Kopf...; Büro...;
~ **workers** *pl* Angestellte *pl.*; ~ **heat**
Weißglut *f*; ~ **lie** fromme Lüge;
~**n** ['waitn] weiß machen *od.* werden; bleichen; ~**ness** [~nis] Weiße
f; Blässe *f*; ~**wash** 1. Tünche *f*;
2. weißen, *fig.* rein waschen.

whither *lit* ['wiðə] wohin.

whitish ['waitiʃ] weißlich.

Whitsun ['witsn] Pfingst...; ~**tide**
Pfingsten *pl*

whittle ['witl] schnitze(l)n; ~ **away**
verkleinern, schwächen.

whiz(z) [wiz] zischen, sausen.

who [hu:, hu] 1. welche(r, -s); der,
die, das, 2. wer?

whodun(n)it *sl* [hu:'dʌnit] Krimi
(-nalroman, -nalfilm) *m*.

whoever [hu(:)'evə] wer auch immer.

whole [houl] 1. □ ganz; heil, unversehrt, *made out of* ~ *cloth Am.*
F frei erfunden; 2. Ganze(s) *n*;
(*up*)*on the* ~. im ganzen; im allgemeinen, ~**hearted** □ ['houl'hɑː-
tid] aufrichtig, ~**meal bread**
['houlmi:l bred] Vollkorn-, Schrot-
brot *n*; ~**sale** 1. *mst* ~ *trade* Groß-
handel *m*; 2. Großhandels...; En-
gros...; *fig* Massen...; ~ *dealer* =
~**saler** [~lə] Großhändler *m*; ~**some**
□ [~səm] gesund

wholly ['houlli] ganz, gänzlich.

whom [hu:m, hum] *acc. von* who.

whoop [hu:p] 1. Schrei *m*, Geschrei
n; 2. laut schreien; ~ *it up Am. sl.*
laut feiern, ~**ee** *Am.* F ['wupi:]
Freudenfest *n*; *make* ~ auf die
Pauke hauen, ~**ing-cough** 🅰 ['hu:-
piŋkɔf] Keuchhusten *m*.

whore [hɔ:] Hure *f*.

whose [hu:z] *gen. von* who.

why [wai] 1. warum, weshalb; ~
so? wieso?; 2. ei!, ja!; (je) nun.

wick [wik] Docht *m*.

wicked ['wikid] *moralisch* böse,
schlimm; ~**ness** [~dnis] Bosheit *f*.

wicker ['wikə] aus Weide geflochten; Weiden...; Korb...; ~ *basket*
Weidenkorb *m*; ~ *chair* Korbstuhl
m.

wicket ['wikit] Pförtchen *n*; *Kricket*:
Dreistab *m*, Tor *n*; ~**keeper** Torhüter *m*.

wide [waid] *a.* □ *u. adv.* weit; ausgedehnt; weitgehend; großzügig;

breit; weitab; ~ *awake* völlig (*od.*
hell)wach; aufgeweckt (*schlau*);
3 feet ~ *3 Fuß breit*; ~**n** ['waidn]
(sich) erweitern; ~**open** ['waid'ou-
pən] weit geöffnet; *Am sl.* großzügig *in der Gesetzesdurchführung*;
~**spread** weitverbreitet, ausgedehnt.

widow ['widou] Witwe *f*; *attr.*
Witwen...; ~**er** [~ouə] Witwer *m*.

width [widθ] Breite *f*, Weite *f*.

wield *lit.* [wi:ld] handhaben.

wife [waif], *pl* **wives** [waivz] (Ehe-)
Frau *f*; Gattin *f*; Weib *n*; ~**ly**
['waifli] fraulich.

wig [wig] Perücke *f*.

wigging F ['wigiŋ] Schelte *f*.

wild [waild] 1. | wild; toll; un-
bändig; abenteuerlich; planlos;
run ~ *wild* (auf)wachsen; *talk* ~
(wild) darauflos reden, ~ *for od.*
about (ganz) verrückt nach; 2. *mst*
~*s pl.* Wildnis *f*, ~**cat** ['waildkæt]
1. *zo.* Wildkatze *f*; *Am* Schwindel-
unternehmen *n*, *bsd Am* wilde Öl-
bohrung; 2. wild (*Streik*); Schwindel...; ~**erness** ['wildənis] Wildnis
f, Wüste *f*; Einöde *f*; ~**fire**: *like* ~
wie ein Lauffeuer.

wile [wail] List *f*; *mst* ~*s pl.* Tücke *f*.

wil(l)ful □ ['wilful] eigensinnig;
vorsätzlich.

will [wil] 1. Wille *m*; Wunsch *m*;
Testament *n*; *of one's own free* ~
aus freien Stücken; 2. [*irr.*] *v/aux.*:
he ~ *come er wird kommen*; *er*
kommt gewöhnlich; *I* ~ *do it* ich
will es tun; 3. wollen; durch Willens-
kraft zwingen; entscheiden; *ž* vermachen.

willing □ ['wiliŋ] willig, bereit
(-willig); *pred.* gewillt (*to inf.* zu);
~**ness** [~nis] (Bereit)Willigkeit *f*.

will-o'-the-wisp ['wiləðwisp] Irr-
licht *n*.

willow ♀ ['wilou] Weide *f*.

willy-nilly ['wili'nili] wohl oder
übel.

wilt [wilt] (ver)welken.

wily □ ['waili] schlau, verschmitzt.

win [win] 1. [*irr.*] *v/t* gewinnen;
erringen; erlangen, erreichen; *j-n*
dazu bringen (*to do* zu tun); ~ *s.o.*
over j-n für sich gewinnen; *v/i.*
gewinnen; siegen; 2. *Sport:* Sieg *m*.

wince [wins] (zs.-)zucken.

winch [wintʃ] Winde *f*; Kurbel *f*.

wind[1] [wind, *poet. a* waind] 1. Wind
m; Atem *m*, Luft *f*; 🅰 Blähung *f*;
♪ Blasinstrumente *n/pl.*; 2. wittern;
außer Atem bringen; verschnaufen
lassen.

wind[2] [waind] [*irr.*] *v/t.* winden;
wickeln; *Horn* blasen; ~ *up Uhr*
aufziehen; *Gesellschaft* abwickeln; ↑
liquidieren; *v/i.* sich winden; sich
schlängeln.

wind|bag ['windbæg] Schwätzer *m*;
~**fall** Fallobst *n*; Glücksfall *m*.

winding ['waindiŋ] 1. Windung *f*; 2. □ sich windend; ~ stairs *pl.* Wendeltreppe *f*; ~-sheet Leichentuch *n*.

wind-instrument ♪ ['windinstrumənt] Blasinstrument *n*.

windlass Ⓔ ['windləs] Winde *f*.

windmill ['winmil] Windmühle *f*.

window ['windou] Fenster *n*; Schaufenster *n*, ~-dressing Schaufensterdekoration *f*, *fig* Aufmachung *f*, Mache *f*; ~-shade *Am.* Rouleau *n*; ~-shopping Schaufensterbummel *m*

wind|pipe windpaip] Luftröhre *f*; ~-screen *Am.* ~-shield *mot.* Windschutzscheibe *f*; ~ wiper Scheibenwischer *m*

windy ['windi] windig (*a. fig. inhaltlos*), geschwätzig

wine [wain] Wein *m*; ~press ['wainpres] Kelter *f*

wing [wiŋ] 1. Flügel *m* (*a.* ⚔ *u.* ✈); Schwinge *f*, *f co* Arm *m*, *mot.* Kotflügel *m*, ⚔ Tragfläche *f*; ⚔, ⚔ Geschwader *n*, ~ *s pl* Kulissen *f/pl.*; take ~ weg, auffliegen; on the ~ im Fluge, 2. *fig* befügeln; fliegen

wink [wiŋk] 1. Blinzeln *n*, Zwinkern *n*; not get *a* ~ of sleep kein Auge zutun; *s* forty, 2. blinzeln, zwinkern (mit), *at* ein Auge zudrücken bei *et* , *j-m* zublinzeln.

winn|er ['winə] Gewinner(in); Sieger(in), ~ing ['winiŋ] 1. Ⓔ einnehmend, gewinnend; 2. ~s *pl.* Gewinn *m*

winsome ['winsəm] gefällig, einnehmend

wint|er ['wintə] 1. Winter *m*; 2. überwintern, ~ry ['wintri] winterlich; *fig* frostig

wipe [waip] (ab , auf)wischen; reinigen; (ab)trocknen, ~ out wegwischen, (aus)löschen, *fig.* vernichten, tilgen

wire ['waiə] 1. Draht *m*, Leitung *f*; *F* Telegramm *n*, pull the ~s der Drahtzieher sein, ~ Beziehungen spielen lassen 2. (ver)drahten; telegraphieren, ~drawn ['waiədrɔn] spitzfindig, ~less ['waiəlis] 1. □ drahtlos; Funk , 2. *a* set Radio (-apparat *n*), *on* the ~ im Rundfunk; 3. funken ~-netting ['waiə'netiŋ] Drahtgeflecht *n*

wiry [['waiəri] drahtig, sehnig

wisdom ['wizdəm] Weisheit *f*; Klugheit *f*; ~ tooth Weisheitszahn *m*.

wise [waiz] 1. Ⓔ weise, verständig; klug; erfahren; ~ guy *Am. sl.* Schlauberger *m*; 2. Weise *f*, Art *f*.

wise-crack F ['waizkræk] 1. witzige Bemerkung, 2. witzeln.

wish [wiʃ] 1. wünschen; wollen; ~ for (sich) *et.* wünschen; ~ well (ill) wohl- (übel)wollen; 2. Wunsch *m*;

~ful □ ['wiʃful] sehnsüchtig; ~ thinking Wunschdenken *n*.

wisp [wisp] Wisch *m*, Strähne *f*.

wistful □ ['wistful] sehnsüchtig.

wit [wit] 1. Witz *m*, *a* ~s *pl.* Verstand *m*; witziger Kopf, be at one's ~'s end the ~s-r Weisheit zu Ende sein; keep one's ~s about one e-n klaren Kopf behalten; 2.: to ~ nämlich, das heißt.

witch [witʃ] Hexe *f*, Zauberin *f*; ~craft ['witʃkraft], ~ery ['witʃəri] Hexerei *f*; ~hunt *pol* Hexenjagd *f* (*Verfolgung politisch verdächtiger Personen*).

with [wið] mit; nebst; bei; von; durch; vor (*dat.*); ~ it *sl.* schwer auf der Höhe.

withdraw [wið'drɔ] [*irr.* (draw)] *v/t.* ab-, ent-, zurückziehen; zurücknehmen; Geld abheben; *v/i.* sich zurückziehen, abtreten, ~al [~ɔəl] Zurückziehung *f*; Rückzug *m*.

wither ['wiðə] *v/i.* (ver)welken; verdorren; austrocknen; *v/t.* welk machen.

with|hold [wið'hould] [*irr.* (hold)] zurückhalten; *et* vorenthalten, ~in [wi'ðin] 1. *adv* lit im Innern, drin(nen); zu Hause, 2. *prp* in(nerhalb); ~ doors im Hause, call in Rufweite; ~out [wi'ðaut] 1. *adv. lit.* (dr)außen; äußerlich, 2. *prp* ohne; *lit.* außerhalb, ~stand [wið stænd] [*irr.* (stand)] widerstehen (*dat.*).

witness ['witnis] 1. Zeuge *m*, -in *f*; bear ~ Zeugnis ablegen (to für; of von); in ~ of zum Zeugnis (*gen.*); 2. (be)zeugen; Zeuge sein von *et.*; ~-box, *Am.* ~ stand Zeugenstand *m*.

wit|ticism ['witisizəm] Witz *m*; ~ty □ ['witi] witzig, geistreich.

wives [waivz] *pl von* wife

wiz *Am. sl.* [wiz] Genie *n*; ~ard ['wizəd] Zauberer *m*, Genie *n*.

wizen(ed) ['wizn(d)] schrump(e)lig.

wobble ['wɔbl] schwanken, wackeln.

woe [wou] Weh *n*, Leid *n*, ~ is me! wehe mir!; ~begone ['woubigɔn] jammervoll; ~ful □ ['wouful] jammervoll, traurig, elend.

woke [wouk] *pret u p p von* wake 2; ~n ['woukən] *p.p von* wake 2.

wold [would] (hügeliges) Heideland.

wolf [wulf] 1. *zo pl* wolves [wulvz] Wolf *m*, 2. verschlingen; ~ish □ ['wulfiʃ] wölfisch, Wolfs...

woman ['wumən], *pl* women ['wimin] 1. Frau *f*; Weib *n*; 2. weiblich; ~ doctor Ärztin *f*; ~ student Studentin *f*; ~hood [~nhud] die Frauen *f/pl.*; Weiblichkeit *f*, ~ish □ [~niʃ] weibisch, ~kind [~n'kaind] Frauen(welt *f*) *f/pl.*; ~like [~nlaik] fraulich; ~ly [~li] weiblich.

womb [wum] *anat.* Gebärmutter *f*; Mutterleib *m*; *fig.* Schoß *m*.

women ['wimin] *pl. von* **woman**; **~folk(s)**, **~kind** die Frauen *f/pl.*; F Weibervolk *n*.

won [wʌn] *pret. u. p.p. von* **win 1**.

wonder ['wʌndə] **1.** Wunder *n*; Verwunderung *f*; **2.** sich wundern; gern wissen mögen, sich fragen; **~ful** [~ful] wunderbar, -voll; **~ing** [~əriŋ] staunend, verwundert.

won't [wount] - *will not*.

wont [~] **1.** *pred* gewohnt; *be* **~** *to* *inf.* pflegen zu *inf*; **2.** Gewohnheit *f*; **~ed** ['wountid] gewohnt.

woo [wu:] werben um; locken.

wood [wud] Wald *m*, Gehölz *n*; Holz *n*; Faß *n*; ♪ Holzblasinstrument (-e *pl.*) *n*; *touch* **~** unberufen!; **~chuck** *zo.* [~wudt[k] Waldmurmeltier *n*; **~cut** Holzschnitt *m*; **~cutter** Holzfäller *m*, Kunst Holzschneider *m*; **~ed** [~wudid] gewaldet; **~en** ['wudn] hölzern (a fig.); Holz...; **~man** Förster *m*, Holzfäller *m*; **~pecker** *orn.* [~wudpekə] Specht *m*; **~sman** wudzmən] *s* woodman; **~wind** Holzblasinstrument *n*; *oft* **~s** *pl.* ♪ Holzbläser *m/pl.*, **~work** Holzwerk *n*; **~y** ['wudi] waldig; holzig.

wool [wul] Wolle *f*; **~gathering** ['wulgæðəriŋ] Geistesabwesenheit *f*; **~(l)en** ['wulin] **1.** wollen; Woll...; **2.** **~s** *pl* Wollsachen *f/pl.*; **~(l)y** ['wuli] **1.** wollig, Woll...; belegt (*Stimme*); verschwommen; **2.** **woollies** *pl* Wollsachen *f/pl.*

word [wə:d] **1.** *mst* Wort *n*; *engS.*: Vokabel *f*; Nachricht *f*; ⚔ Losung(swort *n*) *f*; Versprechen *n*; Befehl *m*; Spruch *m*; **~s** *pl.* Wörter *n/pl.*; Worte *n/pl.*, *fig.* Wortwechsel *m*; Text *m* **~s** *Liedes*; *have a* **~** *with* mit *j-m* sprechen; **2.** (in Worten) ausdrücken, (ab-) fassen; **~ing** [~wə:diŋ] Wortlaut *m*, Fassung *f*; **~-splitting** Wortklauberei *f*.

wordy [~'wə:di] wortreich; Wort...

wore [wɔ:] *pret von* **wear 1**.

work [wə:k] **1.** Arbeit *f*; Werk *n*; *attr.* Arbeits...; **~s** *pl.* ⊕ (Uhr-, Feder)Werk *n*; ⚔ Befestigungen *pl.*; **~s** *sg.* Werk *n*, Fabrik *f*; **~** *of art* Kunstwerk *n*; *at* **~** bei der Arbeit; *be in* **~** Arbeit haben; *be out of* **~** arbeitslos sein, *set to* **~**, *set od.* go *about one's* **~** an die Arbeit gehen; **~s** *council* Betriebsrat *m*; **2.** [*a. irr.*] *v/i.* arbeiten (a. fig.); wirken; gären; sich *hindurch-* etc. arbeiten; **~** *at* arbeiten an (*dat.*); **~** *out* herauskommen (*Summe*); *v/t* (be)arbeiten; arbeiten lassen; betreiben; *Maschine etc* bedienen; (be)wirken; ausrechnen, *Aufgabe* lösen; **~** *one's way* sich durcharbeiten; **~** *off* abarbeiten; *Gefühl* abreagieren; ↑ abstoßen; **~** *out* ausarbeiten; lösen;

ausrechnen; **~** *up* hochbringen; aufregen; verarbeiten (*into* zu).

work|able [~wə:kəbl] bearbeitungs-, betriebsfähig; ausführbar; **~aday** [~ədei] Alltags...; **~day** Werktag *m*; **~er** [~wə:kə] Arbeiter (-in); **~house** Armenhaus *n*; *Am.* Besserungsanstalt *f*, Arbeitshaus *n*.

working ['wə:kiŋ] **1.** Bergwerk *n*; Steinbruch *m*; Arbeits-, Wirkungsweise *f*; **2.** arbeitend; Arbeits...; Betriebs...; **~-class** Arbeiter...; **~day** Werk-, Arbeitstag *m*; **~hours** *pl.* Arbeitszeit *f*.

workman ['wə:kmən] Arbeiter *m*; Handwerker *m*; **~like** [~nlaik] kunstgerecht; **~ship** [~nʃip] Kunstfertigkeit *f*.

work|out *Am.* F [~wə:kaut] *mst Sport:* (Konditions)Training *n*; Erprobung *f*; **~shop** Werkstatt *f*; **~woman** Arbeiterin *f*.

world [wə:ld] *allg* Welt *f*; *a* **~** *of* e-e Unmenge (von); *bring* (*come*) *into the* **~** zur Welt bringen (kommen); *think the* **~** *of* alles halten von; **~ling** [~wə:ldliŋ] Weltkind *n*.

worldly [~wə:ldli] weltlich; Welt...; **~-wise** [~i'waiz] weltklug.

world|-power *pol.* [~wə:ldpauə] Weltmacht *f*; **~-wide** weltweit; weltumspannend; Welt...

worm [wə:m] **1.** Wurm *m* (a. fig.); **2.** *ein Geheimnis* entlocken (*out of* dat.); **~ o.s.** sich schlängeln; *fig.* sich einschleichen (*into* in acc.); **~-eaten** [~wə:mi:tn] wurmstichig.

worn [wə:n] *p.p. von* **wear 1**; **~-out** ['wɔ:naut] abgenutzt, abgetragen; verbraucht (a. fig.); müde, erschöpft; abgezehrt; verhärmt.

worry ['wʌri] **1.** (sich) beunruhigen; (sich) ärgern; sich sorgen; sich aufregen; bedrücken, zerren, (ab-) würgen, plagen, quälen; **2.** Unruhe *f*; Sorge *f*; Ärger *m*; Qual *f*, Plage *f*; Quälgeist *m*.

worse [wə:s] schlechter, schlimmer; **~** *luck!* leider!; *um so schlimmer!*; *from bad to* **~** vom Regen in die Traufe; **~n** ['wə:sn] (sich) verschlechtern.

worship ['wə:ʃip] **1.** Verehrung *f*; Gottesdienst *m*; Kult *m*; **2.** verehren; anbeten; den Gottesdienst besuchen; **~(p)er** [~pə] Verehrer (-in); Kirchgänger(in).

worst [wə:st] **1.** schlechtest; ärgst; schlimmst; **2.** überwältigen.

worsted ['wustid] Kammgarn *n*.

worth [wə:θ] **1.** wert; **~** *reading* lesenswert; **2.** Wert *m*; Würde *f*; **~less** [~wə:θlis] wertlos, unwürdig; **~while** ['wə:θ'wail] der Mühe wert; **~y** [~wə:ði] würdig.

would [wud] [*pret. von* **will 2**] wollte; würde, möchte; pflegte; **~-be** ['wudbi:] angeblich, sogenannt; möglich, potentiell; Pseudo...

wound[1] [wu:nd] 1. Wunde *f*, Verwundung *f*, Verletzung *f*; *fig.* Kränkung *f*; 2. verwunden, verletzen (*a. fig.*).

wound[2] [waund] *pret. u. p.p. von* **wind** 2.

wove [wouv] *pret. von* **weave**; **~n** ['wouvən] *p.p. von* **weave**.

wow *Am.* [wau] 1. *int.* Mensch!; toll!; 2. *sl.* Bombenerfolg *m*.

wrangle ['ræŋgl] 1. streiten, (sich) zanken; 2. Streit *m*, Zank *m*.

wrap [ræp] 1. *v/t.* (ein)wickeln; *fig.* einhüllen; *be ~ped up in* gehüllt sein in (*acc.*); ganz aufgehen in (*dat.*); *v/i.* ~ *up* sich einhüllen; 2. Hülle *f*; *engS.:* Decke *f*; Schal *m*; Mantel *m*; **~per** ['ræpə] Hülle *f*, Umschlag *m*; *a. postal* ~ Streifband *n*; **~ping** ['ræpiŋ] Verpackung *f*.

wrath *lit.* [rɔ:θ] Zorn *m*, Grimm *m*.

wreak [ri:k] *Rache* üben, *Zorn* auslassen (*upon an j-m*).

wreath [ri:θ], *pl.* **~s** [ri:ðz] (Blumen)Gewinde *n*; Kranz *m*; Girlande *f*; Ring *m*, Kreis *m*; Schneewehe *f*; **~e** [ri:ð] [*irr.*] *v/t.* (um-)winden; *v/i.* sich ringeln.

wreck [rek] 1. ⚓ Wrack *n*; Trümmer *pl.*; Schiffbruch *m*; *fig.* Untergang *m*; 2. zum Scheitern (⚓ Entgleisen) bringen; zertrümmern; vernichten; *be ~ed* ⚓ scheitern; Schiffbruch erleiden; **~age** ['rekidʒ] Trümmer *pl*, Wrackteile *n/pl.*; **~ed** schiffbrüchig, ruiniert; **~er** ['rekə] ⚓ Bergungsschiff *n*, -arbeiter *m*; Strandräuber *m*; Abbrucharbeiter *m*; *Am.* mot Abschleppwagen *m*; **~ing** ['rekiŋ] Strandraub *m*; **~ company** *Am.* Abbruchfirma *f*; ~ *service Am.* mot. Abschlepp~, Hilfsdienst *m*.

wren *orn.* [ren] Zaunkönig *m*.

wrench [rentʃ] 1. drehen; reißen; entwinden (*from s.o.* j-m); verdrehen (*a. fig.*); verrenken; ~ *open* aufreißen; 2. Ruck *m*; Verrenkung *f*; *fig.* Schmerz *m*; ⊕ Schraubenschlüssel *m*.

wrest [rest] reißen; verdrehen; entreißen; **~le** ['resl] ringen (mit); **~ling** [.liŋ] Ringkampf *m*, Ringen *n*.

wretch [retʃ] Elende(r *m*) *f*; Kerl *m*. **wretched** □ ['retʃid] elend.

wriggle ['rigl] sich winden *od.* schlängeln; ~ *out of* sich drücken von *et.*

wright [rait]...macher *m*,...bauer *m*.

wring [riŋ] [*irr.*] *Hände* ringen; (aus)wringen; pressen; *Hals* umdrehen; abringen (*from s.o* j-m); ~ *s.o.'s heart* j-m zu Herzen gehen.

wrinkle ['riŋkl] 1. Runzel *f*; Falte *f*; Wink *m*; Trick *m*; 2. (sich) runzeln. **wrist** [rist] Handgelenk *n*; ~ *watch* Armbanduhr *f*; **~band** ['ristbænd] Bündchen *n*, (Hemd)Manschette *f*. **writ** [rit] Erlaß *m*; (gerichtlicher) Befehl; *Holy* ♀ Heilige Schrift.

write [rait] [*irr.*] schreiben; ~ *down* auf-, niederschreiben; ausarbeiten; hervorbringen; **~r** ['raitə] Schreiber (-in); Verfasser(in); Schriftsteller (-in).

writhe [raið] sich krümmen.

writing ['raitiŋ] Schreiben *n*; Aufsatz *m*; Werk *n*; Schrift *f*; Schriftstück *n*; Urkunde *f*; Stil *m*; *attr.* Schreib...; *in* ~ schriftlich; **~case** Schreibmappe *f*; **~desk** Schreibtisch *m*; **~paper** Schreibpapier *n*.

written ['ritn] 1. *p.p. von* **write**; 2. *adj.* schriftlich.

wrong [rɔŋ] 1. □ unrecht; verkehrt, falsch; *be* ~ unrecht haben; in Unordnung sein; falsch gehen (*Uhr*); *go* ~ schiefgehen; *on the* ~ *side of sixty* über die 60 hinaus; 2. Unrecht *n*; Beleidigung *f*; 3. unrecht tun (*dat.*); ungerecht behandeln; **~doer** ['rɔŋ'du:ə] Übeltäter(in); **~ful** □ ['rɔŋful] ungerecht; unrechtmäßig.

wrote [rout] *pret. von* **write**. **wrought** [rɔ:t] *pret. u. p.p. von* **work** 2; ~ *iron* Schmiedeeisen *n*; **~iron** ['rɔ:t'aiən] schmiedeeisern; **~up** erregt.

wrung [rʌŋ] *pret. u. p.p. von* **wring**. **wry** □ [rai] schief, krumm, verzerrt.

X, Y

Xmas ['krisməs] = **Christmas**.

X-ray ['eks'rei] 1. **~s** *pl.* Röntgenstrahlen *m/pl.*; 2. Röntgen...; 3. durchleuchten, röntgen.

xylophone ♪ ['zailəfoun] Xylophon *n*.

yacht ⚓ [jɔt] 1. (Motor)Jacht *f*; Segelboot *n*; 2. auf e-r Jacht fahren; segeln; **~club** ['jɔtklʌb] Segel-, Jachtklub *m*; **~ing** ['jɔtiŋ] Segelsport *m*; *attr.* Segel...

Yankee F ['jæŋki] Yankee *m* (*Amerikaner, bsd. der Nordstaaten*).

yap [jæp] kläffen; F quasseln.

yard [ja:d] Yard *n*, *englische Elle* (= 0,914 *m*); ⚓ Rah(e) *f*; Hof *m*; (Bau-, Stapel)Platz *m*; *Am.* Garten *m* (*um das Haus*); **~-measure**

['jɑːdmeʒə], ~stick Yardstock *m*,
-maß *n*.

yarn [jɑːn] 1. Garn *n*; F Seemanns-
garn *n*; abenteuerliche Geschichte;
2. F erzählen.

yawl ⚓ [jɔːl] Jolle *f*.

yawn [jɔːn] 1. gähnen; 2. Gähnen *n*.

ye †, *poet.*, *co.* [jiː] ihr.

yea †, *prov.* [jei] 1. ja; 2. Ja *n*.

year [jəː] Jahr *n*; ~ly ['jəːli] jährlich.

yearn [jəːn] sich sehnen, verlangen;
~ing ['jəːniŋ] 1. Sehnen *n*, Sehnsucht *f*; 2. 〕 sehnsüchtig.

yeast [jiːst] Hefe *f*; Schaum *m*.

yegg(man) *Am. sl.* ['jeg(mən)]
Stromer *m*; Einbrecher *m*.

yell [jel] 1. (gellend) schreien; auf-
schreien; 2. (gellender) Schrei; an-
feuernder Ruf.

yellow ['jelou] 1. gelb; F hasen-
füßig (*feig*); Sensations...; Hetz...;
2. Gelb *n*; 3. (sich) gelb färben;
~ed vergilbt; ~ fever ⚕ Gelb-
fieber *n*; ~ish [~ouiʃ] gelblich.

yelp [jelp] 1. Gekläff *n*; 2. kläffen.

yen *Am. sl.* [jen] brennendes Verlangen.

yeoman ['joumən] freier Bauer.

yep *Am.* F [jep] ja.

yes [jes] 1. ja; doch; 2. Ja *n*.

yesterday ['jestədi] gestern.

yet [jet] 1. *adv.* noch; bis jetzt;
schon; sogar; *as* ~ bis jetzt; *not* ~
noch nicht; 2. *cj.* (je)doch, dennoch, trotzdem.

yew ♀ [juː] Eibe *f*, Taxus *m*.

yield [jiːld] 1. *v/t.* hervorbringen,
liefern; ergeben; *Gewinn* (ein)brin-
gen; gewähren; übergeben; zugestehen; *v/i.* ✎ tragen; sich fügen;
nachgeben; 2. Ertrag *m*; ~ing □
['jiːldiŋ] nachgebend; *fig.* nachgiebig.

yip *Am.* F [jip] jaulen.

yodel, ~le ['joudl] 1. Jodler *m*;
2. jodeln.

yoke [jouk] 1. Joch *n* (*a. fig.*); Paar
n (Ochsen); Schultertrage *f*; 2. an-,
zs.-spannen; *fig.* paaren (to mit).

yolk [jouk] (Ei)Dotter *m*, *n*, Eigelb *n*.

yon [jɔn], ~der *lit.* ['jɔndə] 1. je-
ne(r, -s); jenseitig; 2. dort drüben.

yore [jɔː]: *of* ~ ehemals, ehedem.

you [juː, ju] ihr; du, Sie; man.

young [jʌŋ] 1. 〕 jung; *von Kindern*
a. klein; 2. (Tier)Junge(s) *n*;
(Tier)Junge *pl.*; *with* ~ trächtig;
~ster ['jʌŋstə] Junge *m*.

your [jɔː] euer(e); dein(e), Ihr(e);
~s [jɔːz] der (die, das) eurige, deinige, Ihrige; euer; dein, Ihr;
~self [jɔː'self], *pl.* ~selves [~lvz]
(du, ihr, Sie) selbst; dich, euch,
Sie (selbst), sich (selbst); *by* ~
allein.

youth [juːθ], *pl.* ~s [juːðz] Jugend *f*;
Jüngling *m*; ~ hostel Jugendher-
berge *f*; ~ful □ ['juːθful] jugendlich.

yule *lit.* [juːl] Weihnacht *f*.

Z

zeal [ziːl] Eifer *m*; ~ot ['zelət]
Eiferer *m*; ~ous □ [~əs] eifrig;
eifrig bedacht (*for* auf *acc.*); innig,
heiß.

zebra *zo.* ['ziːbrə] Zebra *n*; ~ crossing Fußgängerüberweg *m*.

zenith ['zeniθ] Zenit *m*; *fig.* Höhepunkt *m*.

zero ['ziərou] Null *f*; Nullpunkt *m*.

zest [zest] 1. Würze *f* (*a. fig.*); Lust
f, Freude *f*; Genuß *m*; 2. würzen.

zigzag ['zigzæg] Zickzack *m*.

zinc [ziŋk] 1. *min.* Zink *n*; 2. ver-
zinken.

zip [zip] Schwirren *n*; F Schwung *m*;
~-fastener ['zipfɑːsnə], ~per ['zipə]
Reißverschluß *m*.

zodiac *ast.* ['zoudiæk] Tierkreis *m*.

zone [zoun] Zone *f*; *fig.* Gebiet *n*.

Zoo F [zuː] Zoo *m*.

zoolog|ical □ [zouə'lɔdʒikəl] zoo-
logisch; ~y [zou'ɔlədʒi] Zoologie *f*.

Alphabetical List of the German Irregular Verbs

Infinitive — Preterite — Past Participle

backen - backte (buk) - gebacken
bedingen - bedang (bedingte) - bedungen (*conditional*: bedingt)
befehlen - befahl - befohlen
beginnen - begann - begonnen
beißen - biß - gebissen
bergen - barg - geborgen
bersten - barst - geborsten
bewegen - bewog - bewogen
biegen - bog - gebogen
bieten - bot - geboten
binden - band - gebunden
bitten - bat - gebeten
blasen - blies - geblasen
bleiben - blieb - geblieben
bleichen - blich - geblichen
braten - briet - gebraten
brauchen - brauchte - gebraucht (*v/aux.* brauchen)
brechen - brach - gebrochen
brennen - brannte - gebrannt
bringen - brachte - gebracht
denken - dachte - gedacht
dreschen - drosch - gedroschen
dringen - drang - gedrungen
dürfen - durfte - gedurft (*v/aux.* dürfen)
empfehlen - empfahl - empfohlen
erlöschen - erlosch - erloschen
erschrecken - erschrak - erschrocken
essen - aß - gegessen
fahren - fuhr - gefahren
fallen - fiel - gefallen
fangen - fing - gefangen
fechten - focht - gefochten
finden - fand - gefunden
flechten - flocht - geflochten
fliegen - flog - geflogen
fliehen - floh - geflohen
fließen - floß - geflossen
fressen - fraß - gefressen
frieren - fror - gefroren
gären - gor (*esp. fig.* gärte) - gegoren (*esp. fig.* gegärt)
gebären - gebar - geboren
geben - gab - gegeben
gedeihen - gedieh - gediehen
gehen - ging - gegangen
gelingen - gelang - gelungen
gelten - galt - gegolten
genesen - genas - genesen
genießen - genoß - genossen
geschehen - geschah - geschehen
gewinnen - gewann - gewonnen

gießen - goß - gegossen
gleichen - glich - geglichen
gleiten - glitt - geglitten
glimmen - glomm - geglommen
graben - grub - gegraben
greifen - griff - gegriffen
haben - hatte - gehabt
halten - hielt - gehalten
hängen - hing - gehangen
hauen - haute (hieb) - gehauen
heben - hob - gehoben
heißen - hieß - geheißen
helfen - half - geholfen
kennen - kannte - gekannt
klingen - klang - geklungen
kneifen - kniff - gekniffen
kommen - kam - gekommen
können - konnte - gekonnt (*v/aux.* können)
kriechen - kroch - gekrochen
laden - lud - geladen
lassen - ließ - gelassen (*v/aux.* lassen)
laufen - lief - gelaufen
leiden - litt - gelitten
leihen - lieh - geliehen
lesen - las - gelesen
liegen - lag - gelegen
lügen - log - gelogen
mahlen - mahlte - gemahlen
meiden - mied - gemieden
melken - melkte (molk) - gemolken (gemelkt)
messen - maß - gemessen
mißlingen - mißlang - mißlungen
mögen - mochte - gemocht (*v/aux.* mögen)
müssen - mußte - gemußt (*v/aux.* müssen)
nehmen - nahm - genommen
nennen - nannte - genannt
pfeifen - pfiff - gepfiffen
preisen - pries - gepriesen
quellen - quoll - gequollen
raten - riet - geraten
reiben - rieb - gerieben
reißen - riß - gerissen
reiten - ritt - geritten
rennen - rannte - gerannt
riechen - roch - gerochen
ringen - rang - gerungen
rinnen - rann - geronnen
rufen - rief - gerufen
salzen - salzte - gesalzen (gesalzt)
saufen - soff - gesoffen

saugen - sog - gesogen
schaffen - schuf - geschaffen
schallen - schallte (scholl) - geschallt (*for erschallen a.* erschollen)
scheiden - schied - geschieden
scheinen - schien - geschienen
schelten - schalt - gescholten
scheren - schor - geschoren
schieben - schob - geschoben
schießen - schoß - geschossen
schinden - schund - geschunden
schlafen - schlief - geschlafen
schlagen - schlug - geschlagen
schleichen - schlich - geschlichen
schleifen - schliff - geschliffen
schließen - schloß - geschlossen
schlingen - schlang - geschlungen
schmeißen - schmiß - geschmissen
schmelzen - schmolz - geschmolzen
schneiden - schnitt - geschnitten
schrecken - schrak - geschrocken
schreiben - schrieb - geschrieben
schreien - schrie - geschrie(e)n
schreiten - schritt - geschritten
schweigen - schwieg - geschwiegen
schwellen - schwoll - geschwollen
schwimmen - schwamm - geschwommen
schwinden - schwand - geschwunden
schwingen - schwang - geschwungen
schwören - schwor - geschworen
sehen - sah - gesehen
sein - war - gewesen
senden - sandte - gesandt
sieden - sott - gesotten
singen - sang - gesungen
sinken - sank - gesunken
sinnen - sann - gesonnen
sitzen - saß - gesessen
sollen - sollte - gesollt (*v/aux.* sollen)
spalten - spaltete - gespalten (gespaltet)
speien - spie - gespie(e)n
spinnen - spann - gesponnen
sprechen - sprach - gesprochen

sprießen - sproß - gesprossen
springen - sprang - gesprungen
stechen - stach - gestochen
stecken - steckte (stak) - gesteckt
stehen - stand - gestanden
stehlen - stahl - gestohlen
steigen - stieg - gestiegen
sterben - starb - gestorben
stieben - stob - gestoben
stinken - stank - gestunken
stoßen - stieß - gestoßen
streichen - strich - gestrichen
streiten - stritt - gestritten
tragen - trug - getragen
treffen - traf - getroffen
treiben - trieb - getrieben
treten - trat - getreten
triefen - triefte (troff) - getrieft
trinken - trank - getrunken
trügen - trog - getrogen
tun - tat - getan
verderben - verdarb - verdorben
verdrießen - verdroß - verdrossen
vergessen - vergaß - vergessen
verlieren - verlor - verloren
verschleißen - verschliß - verschlissen
verzeihen - verzieh - verziehen
wachsen - wuchs - gewachsen
wägen - wog (*** wägte) - gewogen (*** gewägt)
waschen - wusch - gewaschen
weben - wob - gewoben
weichen - wich - gewichen
weisen - wies - gewiesen
wenden - wandte - gewandt
werben - warb - geworben
werden - wurde - geworden (worden*)
werfen - warf - geworfen
wiegen - wog - gewogen
winden - wand - gewunden
wissen - wußte - gewußt
wollen - wollte - gewollt (*v/aux.* wollen)
wringen - wrang - gewrungen
ziehen - zog - gezogen
zwingen - zwang - gezwungen

* only in connexion with the past participles of other verbs, *e.g. er ist gesehen worden* he has been seen.

Alphabetical List of the English Irregular Verbs

Infinitive — Preterite — Past Participle

Irregular forms marked with asterisks (*) can be exchanged for the regular forms.

abide (*bleiben*) - abode* - abode*
arise (*sich erheben*) - arose - arisen
awake (*erwachen*) - awoke - awoke*
be (*sein*) - was - been
bear (*tragen; gebären*) - bore - getragen: borne - *geboren*: born
beat (*schlagen*) - beat - beat(en)
become (*werden*) - became - become
beget (*zeugen*) - begot - begotten
begin (*anfangen*) - began - begun
bend (*beugen*) - bent - bent
bereave (*berauben*) - bereft* - bereft*
beseech (*ersuchen*) - besought - besought
bet (*wetten*) - bet* - bet*
bid ([*ge*]*bieten*) - bade, bid - bid(den)
bide (*abwarten*) - bode* - bided
bind (*binden*) - bound - bound
bite (*beißen*) - bit - bitten
bleed (*bluten*) - bled - bled
blend (*mischen*) - blent* - blent*
blow (*blasen; blühen*) - blew - blown
break (*brechen*) - broke - broken
breed (*aufziehen*) - bred - bred
bring (*bringen*) - brought - brought
build (*bauen*) - built - built
burn (*brennen*) - burnt* - burnt*
burst (*bersten*) - burst - burst
buy (*kaufen*) - bought - bought
cast (*werfen*) - cast - cast
catch (*fangen*) - caught - caught
chide (*schelten*) - chid - chid(den)*
choose (*wählen*) - chose - chosen
cleave ([*sich*] *spalten*) cleft, clove* - cleft, cloven*
cling (*sich* [*an*]*klammern*) - clung - clung
clothe ([*an-*, *be*]*kleiden*) - clad* - clad*
come (*kommen*) - came - come
cost (*kosten*) - cost - cost
creep (*kriechen*) - crept - crept
crow (*krähen*) - crew* - crowed
cut (*schneiden*) - cut - cut
deal (*handeln*) - dealt - dealt
dig (*graben*) - dug - dug
do (*tun*) - did - done
draw (*ziehen*) - drew - drawn
dream (*träumen*) - dreamt* - dreamt*
drink (*trinken*) - drank - drunk
drive (*treiben; fahren*) - drove - driven
dwell (*wohnen*) - dwelt - dwelt

eat (*essen*) - ate, eat - eaten
fall (*fallen*) - fell - fallen
feed (*füttern*) - fed - fed
feel (*fühlen*) - felt - felt
fight (*kämpfen*) - fought - fought
find (*finden*) - found - found
flee (*fliehen*) - fled - fled
fling (*schleudern*) - flung - flung
fly (*fliegen*) - flew - flown
forbid (*verbieten*) - forbade - forbidden
forget (*vergessen*) - forgot - forgotten
forsake (*aufgeben; verlassen*) - forsook - forsaken
freeze ([*ge*]*frieren*) - froze - frozen
get (*bekommen*) - got - got, *Am.* gotten
gild (*vergolden*) - gilt* - gilt*
gird ([*um*]*gürten*) - girt* - girt*
give (*geben*) - gave - given
go (*gehen*) - went - gone
grave ([*ein*]*graben*) - graved - graven*
grind (*mahlen*) - ground - ground
grow (*wachsen*) - grew - grown
hang (*hängen*) - hung - hung
have (*haben*) - had - had
hear (*hören*) - heard - heard
heave (*heben*) - hove* - hove*
hew (*hauen, hacken*) - hewed - hewn*
hide (*verbergen*) - hid - hid(den)
hit (*treffen*) - hit - hit
hold (*halten*) - held - held
hurt (*verletzen*) - hurt - hurt
keep (*halten*) - kept - kept
kneel (*knien*) - knelt* - knelt*
knit (*stricken*) - knit* - knit*
know (*wissen*) - knew - known
lay (*legen*) - laid - laid
lead (*führen*) - led - led
lean ([*sich*] [*an*]*lehnen*) - leant* - leant*
leap ([*über*]*springen*) - leapt* - leapt*
learn (*lernen*) - learnt* - learnt*
leave (*verlassen*) - left - left
lend (*leihen*) - lent - lent
let (*lassen*) - let - let
lie (*liegen*) - lay - lain
light (*anzünden*) - lit* - lit*
lose (*verlieren*) - lost - lost
make (*machen*) - made - made
mean (*meinen*) - meant - meant
meet (*begegnen*) - met - met
mow (*mähen*) - mowed - mown*

pay (*zahlen*) - paid - paid
pen (*einpferchen*) - pent - pent
put (*setzen, stellen*) - put - put
read (*lesen*) - read - read
rend ([*zer*]*reißen*) - rent - rent
rid (*befreien*) - rid* - rid*
ride (*reiten*) - rode - ridden
ring (*läuten*) - rang - rung
rise (*aufstehen*) - rose - risen
rive ([*sich*] *spalten*) - rived - riven*
run (*laufen*) - ran - run
saw (*sägen*) - sawed - sawn*
say (*sagen*) - said - said
see (*sehen*) - saw - seen
seek (*suchen*) - sought - sought
sell (*verkaufen*) - sold - sold
send (*senden*) - sent - sent
set (*setzen*) - set - set
sew (*nähen*) - sewed - sewn*
shake (*schütteln*) - shook - shaken
shave ([*sich*] *rasieren*) - shaved - shaven*
shear (*scheren*) - sheared - shorn
shed (*ausgießen*) - shed - shed
shine (*scheinen*) - shone - shone
shoe (*beschuhen*) - shod - shod
shoot (*schießen*) - shot - shot
show (*zeigen*) - showed - shown*
shred ([*zer*]*schnitzeln, zerfetzen*) - shred* - shred*
shrink (*einschrumpfen*) - shrank - shrunk
shut (*schließen*) - shut - shut
sing (*singen*) - sang - sung
sink (*sinken*) - sank - sunk
sit (*sitzen*) - sat - sat
slay (*erschlagen*) - slew - slain
sleep (*schlafen*) - slept - slept
slide (*gleiten*) - slid - slid
sling (*schleudern*) - slung - slung
slink (*schleichen*) - slunk - slunk
slip (*schlüpfen, gleiten*) - slipt* - slipt*
slit (*schlitzen*) - slit - slit
smell (*riechen*) - smelt* - smelt*
smite (*schlagen*) - smote - smitten, smote
sow ([*aus*]*säen*) - sowed - sown*
speak (*sprechen*) - spoke - spoken
speed (*eilen*) - sped* - sped*
spell (*buchstabieren*) - spelt* - spelt*
spend (*ausgeben*) - spent - spent

spill (*verschütten*) - spilt* - spilt*
spin (*spinnen*) - spun - spun
spit ([*aus*]*spucken*) - spat - spat
split (*spalten*) - split - split
spoil (*verderben*) - spoilt* - spoilt*
spread (*verbreiten*) - spread - spread
spring (*springen*) - sprang - sprung
stand (*stehen*) - stood - stood
stave (*den Boden einschlagen*) - stove* - stove*
steal (*stehlen*) - stole - stolen
stick (*stecken*) - stuck - stuck
sting (*stechen*) - stung - stung
stink (*stinken*) - stank - stunk
strew ([*be*]*streuen*) - strewed - strewn*
stride (*über-, durchschreiten*) - strode - stridden
strike (*schlagen*) - struck - struck
string (*spannen*) - strung - strung
strive (*streben*) - strove - striven
swear (*schwören*) - swore - sworn
sweat (*schwitzen*) - sweat* - sweat*
sweep (*fegen*) - swept - swept
swell ([*an*]*schwellen*) - swelled - swollen
swim (*schwimmen*) - swam - swum
swing (*schwingen*) - swung - swung
take (*nehmen*) - took - taken
teach (*lehren*) - taught - taught
tear (*ziehen*) - tore - torn
tell (*sagen*) - told - told
think (*denken*) - thought - thought
thrive (*gedeihen*) - throve* - thriven*
throw (*werfen*) - threw - thrown
thrust (*stoßen*) - thrust - thrust
tread (*treten*) - trod - trodden
wake (*wachen*) - woke* - woke(n)*
wax (*zunehmen*) - waxed - waxen*
wear ([*Kleider*] *tragen*) - wore - worn
weave (*weben*) - wove - woven
weep (*weinen*) - wept - wept
wet (*nässen*) - wet* - wet*
win (*gewinnen*) - won - won
wind (*winden*) - wound - wound
work (*arbeiten*) - wrought* - wrought*
wreathe ([*um*]*winden*) - wreathed - wreathen*
wring ([*aus*]*wringen*) - wrung - wrung
write (*schreiben*) - wrote - written

German Proper Names

Aachen ['ɑːxən] *n* Aachen, Aix-la-Chapelle.

Adenauer ['ɑːdənauər] *first chancellor of the German Federal Republic.*

Adler ['ɑːdlər] *Austrian psychologist.*

Adria ['ɑːdria] *f* Adriatic Sea.

Afrika ['ɑːfrika] *n* Africa.

Ägypten [ε'gyptən] *n* Egypt.

Albanien [al'bɑːnjən] *n* Albania.

Algerien [al'geːrjən] *n* Algeria.

Algier ['alʒiːr] *n* Algiers.

Allgäu ['algɔʏ] *n* Al(l)gäu (*region of Bavaria*).

Alpen ['alpən] *pl.* Alps *pl.*

Amerika [a'meːrika] *n* America.

Anden ['andən] *pl. the* Andes *pl.*

Antillen [an'tilən] *f/pl.* Antilles *pl.*

Antwerpen [ant'verpən] *n* Antwerp.

Apenninen [ape'niːnən] *m/pl. the* Apennines *pl.*

Argentinien [argen'tiːnjən] *n* Argentina, the Argentine.

Ärmelkanal ['ermɔlkanɑːl] *m* English Channel.

Asien ['ɑːzjən] *n* Asia.

Athen [a'teːn] *n* Athens.

Äthiopien [eti'oːpjən] *n* Ethiopia.

Atlantik [at'lantik] *m* Atlantic.

Australien [au'strɑːljən] *n* Australia.

Bach [bax] *German composer.*

Baden - Württemberg ['bɑːdən-'vyrtəmberk] *n Land of the German Federal Republic.*

Barlach ['barlax] *German sculptor.*

Basel ['bɑːzəl] *n* Bâle, Basle.

Bayern ['baɪərn] *n* Bavaria (*Land of the German Federal Republic*).

Becher ['beçər] *German poet.*

Beckmann ['bɛkman] *German painter.*

Beethoven ['beːthoːfən] *German composer.*

Belgien ['belgjən] *n* Belgium.

Belgrad ['belgrɑːt] *n* Belgrade.

Berg [berk] *Austrian composer.*

Berlin [ber'liːn] *n* Berlin.

Bermuda-Inseln [ber'muːdaʔinzəln] *f/pl.* Bermudas *pl.*

Bern [bern] *n* Bern(e).

Bismarck ['bismark] *German statesman.*

Bloch [blɔx] *German philosopher.*

Böcklin ['bœkliːn] *German painter.*

Bodensee ['boːdənzeː] *m* Lake of Constance.

Böhm [bøːm] *Austrian conductor.*

Böhmen ['bøːmən] *n* Bohemia.

Böll [bœl] *German author.*

Bonn [bɔn] *n capital of the German Federal Republic.*

Brahms [brɑːms] *German composer.*

Brandt [brant] *German politician.*

Brasilien [bra'ziːljən] *n* Brazil.

Braunschweig ['braunʃvaɪk] *n* Brunswick.

Brecht [brɛçt] *German dramatist.*

Bremen ['breːmən] *n Land of the German Federal Republic.*

Bruckner ['bruknər] *Austrian composer.*

Brüssel ['brysəl] *n* Brussels.

Budapest ['buːdapest] *n* Budapest.

Bukarest ['buːkarest] *n* Bucharest.

Bulgarien [bul'gɑːrjən] *n* Bulgaria.

Calais [ka'lε] *n:* Straße von ~ Straits of Dover.

Calvin [kal'viːn] *Swiss religious reformer.*

Chile ['tʃiːlə] *n* Chile.

China ['çiːna] *n* China.

Christus ['kristus] *m* Christ.

Daimler ['daɪmlər] *German inventor.*

Dänemark ['dεːnəmark] *n* Denmark.

Deutschland ['dɔʏtʃlant] *n* Germany.

Diesel ['diːzəl] *German inventor.*

Döblin [dø'bliːn] *German author.*

Dolomiten [dolo'miːtən] *pl. the* Dolomites *pl.*

Donau ['doːnau] *f* Danube.

Dortmund ['dortmunt] *n industrial city in West Germany.*

Dresden ['dreːsdən] *n capital of Saxony.*

Dublin ['dʌblin] *n* Dublin.

Dünkirchen ['dyːnkirçən] *n* Dunkirk.

Dürer ['dyːrər] *German painter.*

Dürrenmatt ['dyrənmat] *Swiss dramatist.*

Düsseldorf ['dysəldorf] *n capital of North Rhine-Westphalia.*

Ebert ['eːbərt] *first president of the Weimar Republic.*

Egk [ek] *German composer.*

Eichendorff ['aɪçəndorf] *German poet.*

Eiger ['aɪgər] *Swiss mountain.*

Einstein ['aɪnʃtaɪn] *German physicist.*

Elbe ['elbə] *f German river.*

Elsaß ['elzas] *n* Alsace.

Engels ['eŋəls] *German philosopher.*

England ['ɛŋlant] *n* England.
Essen ['ɛsən] *n* *industrial city in West Germany.*
Europa [ɔʏ'roːpa] *n* Europe.

Feldberg ['fɛltbɛrk] *German mountain.*
Finnland ['finlant] *n* Finland.
Florenz [floˈrɛnts] *n* Florence.
Fontane [fɔn'taːnə] *German author.*
Franken ['fraŋkən] *n* Franconia.
Frankfurt ['fraŋkfurt] *n* Frankfort.
Frankreich ['fraŋkraiç] *n* France.
Freud [frɔʏt] *Austrian psychologist.*
Frisch [friʃ] *Swiss author.*

Garmisch ['garmiʃ] *n* *health resort in Bavaria.*
Genf [gɛnf] *n* Geneva; ~er See *m* Lake of Geneva.
Genua ['geːnua] *n* Genoa.
Gibraltar [gi'braltər] *n* Gibraltar.
Goethe ['gøːtə] *German poet.*
Grass [gras] *German author.*
Graubünden [grau'byndən] *n* the Grisons.
Griechenland ['griːçənlant] *n* Greece.
Grillparzer ['grilpartsər] *Austrian dramatist.*
Grönland ['grøːnlant] *n* Greenland.
Gropius ['groːpjus] *German architect.* [Great Britain.]
Großbritannien [groːs'britanjən] *n*
Großglockner [groːs'glɔknər] *Austrian mountain.*
Grünewald ['gryːnəvalt] *German painter.*

Haag [haːk]: Den ~ The Hague.
Habsburg *hist.* ['haːpsburk] *n* Hapsburg (*German dynasty*).
Hahn [haːn] *German chemist.*
Hamburg ['hamburk] *n* Land of the German Federal Republic.
Händel ['hɛndəl] Handel (*German composer*).
Hannover [ha'noːfər] *n* Hanover (*capital of Lower Saxony*).
Hartmann ['hartman] *German composer.*
Harz [haːrts] *m* Harz Mountains *pl.*
Hauptmann ['hauptman] *German dramatist.*
Haydn ['haidən] *Austrian composer.*
Hegel ['heːgəl] *German philosopher.*
Heidegger ['haidegər] *German philosopher.*
Heidelberg ['haidəlbɛrk] *n* *university town in West Germany.*
Heine ['hainə] *German poet.*
Heinemann ['hainəman] *president of the German Federal Republic.*
Heisenberg ['haizənbɛrk] *German physicist.*
Heißenbüttel ['haisənbytəl] *German poet.*
Helgoland ['hɛlgolant] *n* Heligoland.

Helsinki ['hɛlziŋki] *n* Helsinki.
Henze ['hɛntsə] *German composer.*
Hesse ['hɛsə] *German poet.*
Hessen ['hɛsən] *n* Hesse (*Land of the German Federal Republic*).
Heuß [hɔʏs] *first president of the German Federal Republic.*
Hindemith ['hindəmit] *German composer.*
Hohenzollern *hist.* [hoːən'tsɔlərn] *n German dynasty.*
Hölderlin ['hœldərliːn] *German poet.*
Holland ['hɔlant] *n* Holland.

Indien ['indjən] *n* India.
Inn [in] *m affluent of the Danube.*
Innsbruck ['insbruk] *n* *capital of the Tyrol.*
Irak [i'raːk] *m* Iraq, *a.* Irak.
Irland ['irlant] *n* Ireland.
Island ['iːslant] *n* Iceland.
Israel ['israel] *n* Israel.
Italien [i'taːljən] *n* Italy.

Japan ['jaːpan] *n* Japan.
Jaspers ['jaspərs] *German philosopher.*
Jesus ['jeːzus] *m* Jesus.
Jordanien [jɔr'daːnjən] *n* Jordan.
Jugoslawien [jugo'slaːvjən] *n* Yugoslavia.
Jung [juŋ] *Swiss psychologist.*
Jungfrau ['juŋfrau] *f* *Swiss mountain.*

Kafka ['kafka] *Czech poet.*
Kanada ['kanada] *n* Canada.
Kant [kant] *German philosopher.*
Karajan ['kaːrajan] *Austrian conductor.*
Karlsruhe [karls'ruːə] *n* *city in South-Western Germany.*
Kärnten ['kɛrntən] *n* Carinthia.
Kassel ['kasəl] *n* Cassel.
Kästner ['kɛstnər] *German author.*
Kiel [kiːl] *n capital of Schleswig-Holstein.*
Kiesinger ['kiːziŋər] *German politician.*
Klee [kleː] *German painter.*
Kleist [klaist] *German poet.*
Klemperer ['klɛmpərər] *German conductor.*
Koblenz ['koːblɛnts] *n* Coblenz, Koblenz.
Kokoschka [ko'kɔʃka] *German painter.*
Köln [kœln] *n* Cologne.
Kolumbien [ko'lumbjən] *n* Columbia.
Kolumbus [ko'lumbus] *m* Columbus.
Königsberg ['køːniçsbɛrk] *n capital of East Prussia.*
Konstanz ['kɔnstants] *n* Constance.
Kopenhagen [kopən'haːgən] *n* Copenhagen.
Kordilleren [kɔrdil'jeːrən] *f/pl.* the Cordilleras *pl.*

Kreml ['kre:məl] *m the* Kremlin.

Leibniz ['laibnits] *German philosopher.*
Leipzig ['laiptsiç] *n* Leipsic.
Lessing ['lɛsiŋ] *German poet.*
Libanon ['li:banon] *m* Lebanon.
Liebig ['li:biç] *German chemist.*
Lissabon ['lisabon] *n* Lisbon.
London ['lɔndon] *n* London.
Lothringen ['lo:triŋən] *n* Lorraine.
Lübeck ['ly:bek] *n city in West Germany.*
Luther ['lutər] *German religious reformer.*
Luxemburg ['luksəmburk] *n* Luxemb(o)urg.
Luzern [lu'tsern] *n* Lucerne.

Maas [ma:s] *f* Meuse.
Madrid [ma'drit] *n* Madrid.
Mahler ['ma:lər] *Austrian composer.*
Mailand ['mailant] *n* Milan.
Main [main] *m German river.*
Mainz [maints] *n* Mayence (*capital of Rhineland-Palatinate*).
Mann [man] *name of three German authors.*
Marokko [ma'roko] *n* Morocco.
Marx [marks] *German philosopher.*
Matterhorn ['matərhorn] *Swiss mountain.*
Meißen ['maisən] *n* Meissen.
Meitner ['maitnər] *German female physicist.*
Memel ['me:məl] *f frontier river in East Prussia.*
Menzel ['mentsəl] *German painter.*
Mexiko ['mɛksiko] *n* Mexico.
Mies van der Rohe ['mi:sfandər'ro:ə] *German architect.*
Mittelamerika ['mitəlʔa'me:rika] *n* Central America.
Mitteleuropa ['mitəlʔɔy'ro:pa] *n* Central Europe.
Mittelmeer ['mitəlme:r] *n* Mediterranean (Sea).
Moldau ['mɔldau] *f Bohemian river.*
Mörike ['møːrikə] *German poet.*
Mosel ['mo:zəl] *f* Moselle.
Mössbauer ['mœsbauər] *German physicist.*
Moskau ['mɔskau] *n* Moscow.
Mozart ['mo:tsart] *Austrian composer.*
München ['mynçən] *n* Munich (*capital of Bavaria*).

Neapel [ne'a:pəl] *n* Naples.
Neisse ['naisə] *f German river.*
Neufundland [nɔy'funtlant] *n* Newfoundland.
Neuseeland [nɔy'ze:lant] *n* New Zealand.
Niederlande ['ni:dərlandə] *n/pl. the* Netherlands *pl.*
Niedersachsen ['ni:dərzaksən] *n* Lower Saxony (*Land of the German Federal Republic*).

Nietzsche ['ni:tʃə] *German philosopher.*
Nil [ni:l] *m* Nile.
Nordamerika ['nɔrtʔa'me:rika] *n* North America.
Nordrhein-Westfalen ['nɔrtrainvest'fa:lən] *n* North Rhine-Westphalia (*Land of the German Federal Republic*).
Nordsee ['nɔrtze:] *f* German Ocean, North Sea.
Norwegen ['nɔrve:gən] *n* Norway.
Nürnberg ['nyrnberk] *n* Nuremberg.

Oder ['o:dər] *f German river.*
Orff [ɔrf] *German composer.*
Oslo ['ɔslo] *n* Oslo.
Ostasien ['ɔst'a:zjən] *n* Eastern Asia.
Ostende [ɔst'ɛndə] *n* Ostend.
Österreich ['øːstəraiç] *n* Austria.
Ostsee ['ɔstze:] *f* Baltic.

Palästina [palɛ'sti:na] *n* Palestine.
Paris [pa'ri:s] *n* Paris.
Persien ['pɛrzjən] *n* Persia.
Pfalz [pfalts] *f* Palatinate.
Philippinen [fili'pi:nən] *f/pl.* Philippines *pl.*, Philippine Islands *pl.*
Planck [plaŋk] *German physicist.*
Polen ['po:lən] *n* Poland.
Pommern ['pomərn] *n* Pomerania.
Portugal ['portugal] *n* Portugal.
Prag [pra:g] *n* Prague.
Preußen *hist.* ['prɔysən] *n* Prussia.
Pyrenäen [pyre'nɛ:ən] *pl.* Pyrenees *pl.*

Regensburg ['re:gənsburk] *n* Ratisbon.
Reykjavik ['raikjavi:k] *n* Reykjavik.
Rhein [rain] *m* Rhine.
Rheinland-Pfalz ['rainlant'pfalts] *n* Rhineland-Palatinate (*Land of the German Federal Republic*).
Rilke ['rilkə] *Austrian poet.*
Rom [ro:m] *n* Rome.
Röntgen ['rœntgən] *German physicist.*
Ruhr [ru:r] *f German river;* Ruhrgebiet ['ru:rgəbi:t] *n industrial centre of West Germany.*
Rumänien [ru'mɛ:njən] *n* Ro(u)mania.
Rußland ['ruslant] *n* Russia.

Saale ['za:lə] *f German river.*
Saar [za:r] *f affluent of the Moselle;* Saarbrücken [za:r'brykən] *n capital of the Saar;* Saarland ['za:rlant] *n* Saar (*Land of the German Federal Republic*).
Sachsen ['zaksən] *n* Saxony.
Scherchen ['ʃerçən] *Swiss conductor.*
Schiller ['ʃilər] *German poet.*
Schlesien ['ʃle:zjən] *n* Silesia.
Schleswig-Holstein ['ʃle:sviç'hɔl

ʃtaɪn] n Land of the German Federal Republic.
Schönberg [ˈʃøːnberk] Austrian composer.
Schottland [ˈʃɔtlant] n Scotland.
Schubert [ˈʃuːbərt] Austrian composer.
Schumann [ˈʃuːman] German composer.
Schwaben [ˈʃvaːbən] n Swabia.
Schwarzwald [ˈʃvartsvalt] m Black Forest.
Schweden [ˈʃveːdən] n Sweden.
Schweiz [ʃvaɪts] f: die ~ Switzerland.
Sibirien [ziˈbiːrjən] n Siberia.
Siemens [ˈziːməns] German inventor.
Sizilien [ziˈtsiːljən] n Sicily.
Skandinavien [skandiˈnaːvjən] n Scandinavia
Sofia [ˈzɔfja] n Sofia.
Sowjetunion [zɔˈvjɛtʔunjoːn] f the Soviet Union.
Spanien [ˈʃpaːnjən] n Spain.
Spitzweg [ˈʃpitsveːk] German painter.
Spranger [ˈʃpraŋər] German philosopher.
Steiermark [ˈʃtaɪərmark] f Styria.
Stifter [ˈʃtiftər] Austrian author.
Stockholm [ˈʃtɔkhɔlm] n Stockholm.
Storm [ʃtɔrm] German poet.
Strauß [ʃtraʊs] Austrian composer.
Strauss [ʃtraʊs] German composer.
Stresemann [ˈʃtreːzəman] German statesman.
Stuttgart [ˈʃtutgart] n capital of Baden-Württemberg.
Südamerika [ˈzyːtʔaˈmeːrika] n South America.
Sudan [zuˈdaːn] m S(o)udan.
Syrien [ˈzyːrjən] n Syria.

Themse [ˈtɛmzə] f Thames.
Thoma [ˈtoːma] German author.
Thüringen [ˈtyːriŋən] n Thuringia.
Tirana [tiˈraːna] n Tirana.
Tirol [tiˈroːl] n the Tyrol.
Trakl [ˈtraːkəl] Austrian poet.
Tschechoslowakei [tʃɛçɔslovaˈkaɪ] f: die ~ Czechoslovakia.
Türkei [tyrˈkaɪ] f: die ~ Turkey.

Ungarn [ˈuŋgarn] n Hungary.
Ural [uˈraːl] m Ural (Mountains pl.).

Vatikan [vatiˈkaːn] m the Vatican.
Venedig [veˈneːdiç] n Venice.
Vereinigte Staaten [vərˈainiçtə ˈʃtaːtən] m/pl. the United States pl.
Vierwaldstätter See [fiːrˈvaltʃtɛtər ˈzeː] m Lake of Lucerne.

Wagner [ˈvaːgnər] German composer.
Wankel [ˈvaŋkəl] German inventor.
Warschau [ˈvarʃaʊ] n Warsaw.
Weichsel [ˈvaɪksəl] f Vistula.
Weiß [vaɪs] German dramatist.
Weizsäcker [ˈvaɪtszekər] German physicist.
Werfel [ˈverfəl] Austrian author.
Weser [ˈveːzər] f German river.
Westdeutschland pol. [ˈvestdɔrtʃlant] n West Germany.
Wien [viːn] n Vienna.
Wiesbaden [ˈviːsbaːdən] n capital of Hesse.

Zeppelin [ˈtsɛpəliːn] German inventor.
Zuckmayer [ˈtsukmaɪər] German dramatist.
Zweig [tsvaɪg] Austrian author.
Zürich [ˈtsyːriç] n Zurich.
Zypern [ˈtsyːpərn] n Cyprus.

German Abbreviations

a. a. O. *am angeführten Ort* in the place cited, *abbr.* loc. cit., l. c.

Abb. *Abbildung* illustration.

Abf. *Abfahrt* departure, *abbr.* dep.

Abg. *Abgeordnete* Member of Parliament, *etc.*

Abk. *Abkürzung* abbreviation.

Abs. *Absatz* paragraph; *Absender* sender.

Abschn. *Abschnitt* paragraph, chapter. [dept.]

Abt. *Abteilung* department, *abbr.*

a. D. *außer Dienst* retired.

Adr. *Adresse* address.

AG *Aktiengesellschaft* joint-stock company, *Am* (stock) corporation.

allg. *allgemein* general.

a. M. *am Main* on the Main.

Ank. *Ankunft* arrival.

Anm. *Anmerkung* note.

a. O. *an der Oder* on the Oder.

a. Rh. *am Rhein* on the Rhine.

Art. *Artikel* article.

atü *Atmosphärenüberdruck* atmospheric excess pressure.

Aufl. *Auflage* edition.

b. *bei* at; with; *with place names*: near, *abbr.* nr; care of, *abbr.* c/o.

Bd. *Band* volume, *abbr* vol.; **Bde.** *Bände* volumes, *abbr.* vols.

beil. *beiliegend* enclosed.

Bem. *Bemerkung* note, comment, observation.

bes. *besonders* especially.

betr. *betreffend, betrifft, betreffs* concerning, respecting, regarding.

Betr. *Betreff, betrifft letter:* subject, re. [reference to.]

bez. *bezahlt* paid; *bezüglich* with

Bez. *Bezirk* district.

Bhf. *Bahnhof* station.

bisw. *bisweilen* sometimes, occasionally.

BIZ *Bank für Internationalen Zahlungsausgleich* Bank for International Settlements.

Bln. *Berlin* Berlin.

BRD *Bundesrepublik Deutschland* Federal Republic of Germany.

BRT *Bruttoregistertonnen* gross register tons.

b. w. *bitte wenden* please turn over, *abbr.* P.T.O.

bzw. *beziehungsweise* respectively.

C *Celsius* Celsius, *abbr.* C.

ca. *circa, ungefähr, etwa* about, approximately, *abbr.* c.

cbm *Kubikmeter* cubic met|re, *Am.* -er.

ccm *Kubikzentimeter* cubic centimet|re, *Am.* -er, *abbr.* c.c.

CDU *Christlich-Demokratische Union* Christian Democratic Union.

cm *Zentimeter* centimet|re, *Am.* -er.

Co. *Kompagnon* partner; *Kompanie* Company.

CSU *Christlich-Soziale Union* Christian Social Union.

d. Ä. *der Ältere* senior, *abbr.* sen.

DB *Deutsche Bundesbahn* German Federal Railway.

DDR *Deutsche Demokratische Republik* German Democratic Republic.

DGB *Deutscher Gewerkschaftsbund* Federation of German Trade Unions.

dgl. *dergleichen, desgleichen* the like.

d. Gr. *der Große* the Great.

d. h. *das heißt* that is, *abbr.* i. e.

d. i. *das ist* that is, *abbr.* i. e.

DIN, Din *Deutsche Industrie-Norm* (-en) German Industrial Standards.

Dipl. *Diplom* diploma.

d. J. *dieses Jahres* of this year; *der Jüngere* junior, *abbr.* jr, jun.

DM *Deutsche Mark* German Mark.

d. M. *dieses Monats* instant, *abbr.* inst.

do. *dito* ditto, *abbr.* do.

d. O. *der (die, das) Obige* the abovementioned.

dpa, DPA *Deutsche Presse-Agentur* German Press Agency.

Dr. *Doktor* Doctor, *abbr.* Dr; ~ *jur. Doktor der Rechte* Doctor of Laws (LL.D.); ~ *med. Doktor der Medizin* Doctor of Medicine M.D.); ~ *phil. Doktor der Philosophie* Doctor of Philosophy D ph[il]., Ph. D.); ~ *theol. Doktor der Theologie* Doctor of Divinity (D. D.).

DRK *Deutsches Rotes Kreuz* German Red Cross.

dt(sch). *deutsch* German.

Dtz., Dtzd. *Dutzend* dozen.

d. Verf. *der Verfasser* the author.

ebd. *ebenda* in the same place.

ed. *edidit* ~ *hat (es) herausgegeben.*

eig., eigtl. *eigentlich* properly.

einschl. *einschließlich* including, inclusive, *abbr.* incl.

entspr. *entsprechend* corresponding.

Erl. *Erläuterung* explanation, (explanatory) note.

ev. *evangelisch* Protestant.

e. V. *eingetragener Verein* registered association, incorporated, *abbr.* inc.

evtl. *eventuell* perhaps, possibly.
EWG *Europäische Wirtschaftsgemeinschaft* European Economic Community, *abbr.* EEC.
exkl. *exklusive* except(ed), not included.
Expl. *Exemplar* copy.

Fa. *Firma* firm; *letter*: Messrs.
FDGB *Freier Deutscher Gewerkschaftsbund* Free Federation of German Trade Unions.
FDP *Freie Demokratische Partei* Liberal Democratic Party.
FD(-Zug) *Fernschnellzug* long-distance express
ff. *sehr fein* extra fine; *folgende Seiten* following pages.
Forts. *Fortsetzung* continuation.
Fr. *Frau* Mrs.
frdl. *freundlich* kind.
Frl. *Fräulein* Miss.

g *Gramm* gram(me).
geb. *geboren* born; *geborene ...* née; *gebunden* bound
Gebr. *Gebrüder* Brothers.
gef. *gefällig(st)* kind(ly).
gegr. *gegründet* founded.
geh. *geheftet* stitched
gek. *gekürzt* abbreviated.
Ges. *Gesellschaft* association, company; *society* [registered.]
ges. gesch. *gesetzlich geschützt)*
gest. *gestorben* deceased
gez. *gezeichnet* signed, *abbr.* sgd.
GmbH *Gesellschaft mit beschränkter Haftung* limited liability company, *abbr.* Ltd., *Am.* closed corporation under German law.

ha *Hektar* hectare.
Hbf. *Hauptbahnhof* central *or* main station.
Hbg. *Hamburg* Hamburg.
h. c. *honoris causa* — *ehrenhalber academic title* honorary.
Hr., Hrn. *Herr(n)* Mr
hrsg. *herausgegeben* edited, *abbr.* ed.
Hrsg. *Herausgeber* editor, *abbr.* ed.

i. *im, in* in.
i. A. *im Auftrage* for, by order, under instruction
i. allg. *im allgemeinen* in general, generally speaking
i. Durchschn. *im Durchschnitt* on an average.
inkl. *inklusive, einschließlich* inclusive.
i. J. *im Jahre* in the year.
Ing. *Ingenieur* engineer.
Inh. *Inhaber* proprietor.
Interpol *Internationale Kriminalpolizei-Kommission* International Criminal Police Commission, *abbr.* ICPC.
i. V. *in Vertretung* by proxy, as a substitute.

Jb. *Jahrbuch* annual.
jr., jun. *junior, der Jüngere* junior *abbr.* jr, jun.

Kap. *Kapitel* chapter.
kath. *katholisch* Catholic.
Kfm. *Kaufmann* merchant.
kfm. *kaufmännisch* commercial.
Kfz. *Kraftfahrzeug* motor vehicle.
kg *Kilogramm* kilogram(me).
KG *Kommanditgesellschaft* limited partnership.
Kl. *Klasse* class; *school*: form.
km *Kilometer* kilomet|re, *Am.* -er.
'Kripo *Kriminalpolizei* Criminal Investigation Department, *abbr.* CID.
Kto. *Konto* account, *abbr.* a/c.
kW *Kilowatt* kilowatt, *abbr.* kw.
kWh *Kilowattstunde* kilowatt hour.

l *Liter* lit|re, *Am.* -er.
LDP *Liberal-Demokratische Partei* Liberal Democratic Party.
lfd. *laufend* current, running.
lfde. Nr. *laufende Nummer* consecutive number.
Lfg., Lfrg. *Lieferung* delivery; instalment, part.
Lit. *Literatur* literature.
Lkw. *Lastkraftwagen* lorry, truck.
lt. *laut* according to.

m *Meter* met|re, *Am.* -er.
m. A. n. *meiner Ansicht nach* in my opinion.
M. d. B. *Mitglied des Bundestages* Member of the Bundestag.
m. E. *meines Erachtens* in my opinion.
MEZ *mitteleuropäische Zeit* Central European Time.
mg *Milligramm* milligram(me[s]), *abbr.* mg.
Mill. *Million(en)* million(s).
mm *Millimeter* millimet|re, *Am.* -er.
möbl. *möbliert* furnished.
MP *Militärpolizei* Military Police.
mtl. *monatlich* monthly.
m. W. *meines Wissens* as far as I know.

N *Nord(en)* north.
nachm. *nachmittags* in the afternoon, *abbr.* p. m.
n. Chr. *nach Christus* after Christ, *abbr.* A. D.
n. J. *nächsten Jahres* of next year.
n. M. *nächsten Monats* of next month.
No., Nr. *Numero, Nummer* number, *abbr.* N°.
NS *Nachschrift* postscript, *abbr.* P. S.

O *Ost(en)* east.
o. B. *ohne Befund* ♂ without findings.
od. *oder* or.

OEZ *osteuropäische Zeit* time of the East European zone.

OHG *Offene Handelsgesellschaft* ordinary partnership.

o. J. *ohne Jahr* no date.

p. Adr. *per Adresse* care of, *abbr.* c/o.

Pf *Pfennig German coin* pfennig.

Pfd. *Pfund German weight* pound.

PKW, Pkw. *Personenkraftwagen* (motor) car.

P. P. *praemissis praemittendis* omitting titles, to whom it may concern.

p.P., p.pa., *ppa. per procura* per proxy, *abbr* per pro.

Prof. *Professor* professor.

PS *Pferdestärke(n)* horse-power, *abbr* H.P., h.p., *postscriptum*, *Nachschrift* postscript, *abbr.* P.S.

qkm *Quadratkilometer* square kilomet|re, *Am.* -er. [*Am.* -er.]

qm *Quadratmeter* square met|re,]

Reg. Bez. *Regierungsbezirk* administrative district.

Rel. *Religion* religion.

resp. *respektive* respectively.

S *Süd(en)* south.

S. *Seite* page.

s. *siehe* see, *abbr.* v., vid. (= *vide*).

s. a. *siehe auch* see also.

Sa. *Summa, Summe* sum, total.

s. d. *siehe dies* see this.

SED *Sozialistische Einheitspartei Deutschlands* United Socialist Party of Germany.

sen. *senior, der Ältere* senior.

sm *Seemeile nautical* mile.

s. o. *siehe oben* see above.

sog. *sogenannt* so-called.

SPD *Sozialdemokratische Partei Deutschlands Social* Democratic Party of Germany.

St. *Stück piece, Sankt* Saint.

St(d)., Stde. *Stunde* hour, *abbr.* h.

Str. *Straße street, abbr.* St.

s. u. *siehe unten* see below.

s. Z. *seinerzeit* at that time.

t *Tonne* ton.

tägl. *täglich* daily, per day.

Tel. *Telephon* telephone; *Telegramm* wire, cable.

TH *Technische Hochschule* technical university *or* college.

u. *und* and.

u. a. *und andere(s)* and others; *unter anderem or anderen* among other things, *inter alia.*

u. ä. *und ähnliche(s)* and the like.

U.A.w.g. *Um Antwort wird gebeten* an answer is requested, *répondez s'il vous plaît, abbr.* R.S.V.P.

u. dgl. (m.) *und dergleichen (mehr)* and the like.

u. d. M. *unter dem Meeresspiegel* below sea level; **ü. d. M.** *über dem Meeresspiegel* above sea level.

UdSSR *Union der Sozialistischen Sowjetrepubliken* Union of Soviet Socialist Republics.

u. E. *unseres Erachtens* in our opinion. [following.]

u. f., u. ff. *und folgende* and the]

UKW *Ultrakurzwelle* ultra-short wave, very high frequency, *abbr.* VHF.

U/min. *Umdrehungen in der Minute* revolutions per minute, *abbr.* r.p.m.

urspr. *ursprünglich* original(ly).

US(A) *Vereinigte Staaten (von Amerika)* United States (of America).

usw. *und so weiter* and so on, *abbr* etc. [stances permitting.]

u. U. *unter Umständen* circum-]

v. *von, vom* of; from; by.

V *Volt* volt; *Volumen* volume.

V. *Vers* line, verse.

v. Chr. *vor Christus* before Christ, *abbr* B.C.

VEB *Volkseigener Betrieb* People's Own Undertaking.

Verf., Vf. *Verfasser* author.

Verl. *Verlag* publishing firm; *Verleger* publisher.

vgl. *vergleiche* confer, *abbr.* cf.

v.g.u. *vorgelesen, genehmigt, unterschrieben* read, confirmed, signed.

v. H. *vom Hundert* per cent.

v. J. *vorigen Jahres* of last year.

v. M. *vorigen Monats* of last month.

vorm. *vormittags* in the morning, *abbr* a. m.; *vormals* formerly.

Vors. *Vorsitzender* chairman.

v. T. *vom Tausend* per thousand.

VW *Volkswagen* Volkswagen, People's Car.

W *West(en)* west; *Watt* watt(s).

WE *Wärmeeinheit* thermal unit.

WEZ *westeuropäische Zeit* Western European time (Greenwich time).

WGB *Weltgewerkschaftsbund* World Federation of Trade Unions, *abbr.* WFTU.

Wwe. *Witwe* widow.

Z. *Zahl* number; *Zeile* line.

z. *zu, zum, zur* at; to.

z. B. *zum Beispiel* for instance, *abbr.* e. g.

z. H(d). *zu Händen* attention of, to be delivered to, care of, *abbr.* c/o.

z. S. *zur See* of the navy.

z. T. *zum Teil* partly.

Ztg. *Zeitung* newspaper.

Ztr. *Zentner* centner.

Ztschr. *Zeitschrift* periodical.

zus. *zusammen* together.

zw. *zwischen* between; among.

z. Z(t). *zur Zeit* at the time, at present, for the time being.

American and British Proper Names

Aberdeen [æbə'di:n] *Stadt in Schottland.*

Africa ['æfrikə] Afrika *n.* [U.S.A.]

Alabama [ælə'bæmə] *Staat der* U.S.A.

Alaska [ə'læskə] *Staat der U.S.A.*

Albania [æl'beinjə] Albanien *n.*

Alberta [æl'bə:tə] *Provinz in Kanada.* [U.S.A.]

Alleghany ['æligeini] *Gebirge in*

Alsace ['ælsæs] Elsaß *n*

America [ə'merikə] Amerika *n.*

Antilles [æn'tili:z] *die Antillen.*

Appalachians [æpə'leifjənz] *die Appalachen Gebirge U.S.A.).*

Arizona [æri'zounə] *Staat der* U.S.A. [U.S.A.]

Arkansas ['a:kənsɔ:] *Staat der*

Arlington ['a:liŋtən] *Nationalfriedhof bei Washington*

Ascot ['æskət] *Stadt in England.*

Asia ['eifə] Asien *n.*

Athens ['æθinz] Athen *n.*

Australia [ɔ'treiljə] Australien *n.*

Austria ['ɔstriə] Österreich *n.*

Avon ['eivən] *Fluß in England.*

Azores [ə'zɔ:z] *die Azoren.*

Bacon ['beikən] *eng. Philosoph.*

Bahamas [bə'ha:məz] *die Bahamainseln.*

Balmoral [bæl'mɔrəl] *Königsschloß in Schottland*

Bedford(shire) bedfəd(fiə) *Grafschaft in England* [Biskaya.]

Belfast [bel'fa:st] *Hauptstadt von Nordirland*

Belgium ['beldʒəm] Belgien *n.*

Belgrade [bel'greid] Belgrad *n.*

Ben Nevis [ben nevis] *höchster Berg in Großbritannien*

Berkshire ['ba:kfiə] *Grafschaft in England*

Bermudas [bə'mju:dəz] *die Bermudainseln*

Bern(e) [bə:n] Bern *n*

Birmingham ['bə:miŋəm] *Industriestadt in England* [Biskaya.]

Biscay ['biskei] *Bay of Golf m von)*

Boston ['bɔstən] *Stadt in U.S.A.*

Bournemouth ['bɔ:nməθ] *Seebad in England*

Brighton ['braitn] *Seebad in England.* [land.]

Bristol ['bristl] *Hafenstadt in Eng-)*

Britten ['britn] *engl Komponist.*

Brooklyn ['bruklin] *Stadtteil von New York*

Brussels ['brʌslz] Brüssel *n.*

Bucharest ['bju:kərest] Bukarest *n.*

Buckingham(shire) ['bʌkiŋəm(fiə)] *Grafschaft in England.*

Budapest ['bju:də'pest] Budapest *n.*

Bulgaria [bʌl'gɛəriə] Bulgarien *n.*

Burns [bə:nz] *schott Dichter.*

Byron ['baiərən] *engl. Dichter.*

California [kæli'fɔ.njə] Kalifornien *n (Staat der U.S.A.).*

Cambridge ['keimbridʒ] *engl. Universitätsstadt; Stadt in U.S.A.; a.* ~shire ['~fiə] *Grafschaft in England.*

Canada ['kænədə] Kanada *n.*

Canary Islands [kə'nɛəri 'ailəndz] *die Kanarischen Inseln.*

Canberra ['kænbərə] *Hauptstadt von Australien.* [England.]

Canterbury ['kæntəbəri] *Stadt in)*

Capetown ['keiptaun] Kapstadt *n.*

Cardiff ['ka:dif] *Hauptstadt von Wales.*

Carinthia [kə'rinθiə] Kärnten *n.*

Carlyle [ka:'lail] *engl Autor.*

Carolina [kærə'lainə] *North ~ Nordkarolina n (Staat der U.S.A.); South ~ Südkarolina n (Staat der U.S.A.)*

Ceylon [si'lɔn] Ceylon *n.*

Chamberlain ['tfeimbəlin, ~lein] *Name mehrerer brit. Staatsmänner.*

Cheshire ['tfefə] *Grafschaft in England.*

Chicago [fi'ka:gou, Am. fi'kɔ:gou] *Industriestadt in U.S.A*

China ['tfainə] China *n.* [mann.]

Churchill ['tfə:tfil] *brit Staats-)*

Cleveland ['kli:vlənd] *Industrie- und Hafenstadt in U.S.A*

Clyde [klaid] *Fluß in Schottland.*

Coleridge ['koulridʒ] *engl. Dichter.*

Colorado [kɔlə'ra:dou] *Staat der* U.S.A.

Columbia [kə'lʌmbiə] *Fluß in U.S.A.; Bundesdistrikt der U.S.A.*

Connecticut [kə'netikət] *Staat der* U.S.A.

Constance ['kɔnstəns]: *Lake of ~ Bodensee m.*

Cooper ['ku:pə] *amer. Autor.*

Copenhagen [koupn'heigən] Kopenhagen *n.* [dilleren.]

Cordilleras [kɔ:di'ljeərəz] *die Kor-)*

Cornwall ['kɔ:nwəl] *Grafschaft in England.*

Coventry ['kɔvəntri] *Industriestadt in England.* [mann.]

Cromwell ['krɔmwəl] *engl. Staats-)*

Cumberland ['kʌmbələnd] *Grafschaft in England.*

Cyprus ['saiprəs] Zypern *n.*

Czecho-Slovakia ['tfekouslou'væːkiə] *die Tschechoslowakei.*

Dakota [də'koutə]: North ~ Nord-
dakota n (Staat der U.S.A.); South
~ Süddakota n (Staat der U.S.A.).
Defoe [də'fou] engl. Autor.
Delaware ['deləwɛə] Staat der
U.S.A.
Denmark ['denmɑːk] Dänemark n.
Derby(shire) ['dɑːbi(ʃə)] Graf-
schaft in England.
Detroit [də'trɔit] Industriestadt in
U.S.A.
Devon(shire) ['devn(ʃiə)] Graf-
schaft in England.
Dickens ['dikinz] engl. Autor.
Dorset(shire) ['dɔːsit(ʃiə)] Graf-
schaft in England   [land.]
Dover ['douvə] Hafenstadt in Eng-
Downing Street ['dauniŋ 'striːt]
Straße in London mit der Amts-
wohnung des Prime Minister.
Dublin ['dʌblin] Hauptstadt von Ir-
land.
Dunkirk [dʌn'kəːk] Dünkirchen n.
Durham ['dʌrəm] Grafschaft in
England.

Edinburgh ['edinbərə] Edinburg n.
Edison ['edisn] amer Erfinder.
Egypt ['iːdʒipt] Ägypten n.
Eire ['ɛərə] Republik Irland.
Eisenhower ['aizənhauə] Präsident
der U.S.A
Eliot ['eljət] engl. Dichter.
Emerson ['eməsn] amer Philosoph.
England ['iŋglənd] England n.
Epsom ['epsəm] Stadt in England.
Erie ['iəri] Lake Eriesee m.
Essex ['esiks] Grafschaft in England.
Eton ['iːtn] berühmte Public School.
Europe ['juərəp] Europa n.

Falkland Islands ['fɔːlklənd 'ai-
ləndz] die Falklandinseln.
Faulkner ['fɔːknə] amer Autor.
Finland ['finlənd] Finnland n.
Florida ['flɔridə] Staat der U.S.A.
Flushing ['flʌʃiŋ] Vlissingen n.
France [frɑːns] Frankreich n.
Franklin ['fræŋklin] amer. Staats-
mann und Physiker.

Galsworthy ['gɔːlzwəːθi] engl. Au-
tor.
Geneva [dʒi'niːvə] Genf n; Lake of ~
Genfer See m.
Georgia ['dʒɔːdʒə] Staat der U.S.A.
Germany ['dʒəːməni] Deutschland
n.   [nist.]
Gershwin ['gəːʃwin] amer. Kompo-
Gibraltar [dʒi'brɔːltə] Gibraltar n.
Glasgow ['glɑːsgou] Hafenstadt in
Schottland
Gloucester ['glɔstə] Stadt in Eng-
land; a. ~shire ['.ʃiə] Grafschaft in
England.
Great Britain ['greit 'britn] Groß-
britannien n.
Greece [griːs] Griechenland n.

Greene [griːn] engl. Autor.
Greenland ['griːnlənd] Grönland n.
Greenwich ['grinidʒ] Vorort von
London.
Guernsey ['gəːnzi] Kanalinsel.

Hague [heig]: The ~ Den Haag.
Hampshire ['hæmpʃiə] Grafschaft
in England.
Harlem ['hɑːlem] Stadtteil von New
York.
Harrow ['hærou] berühmte Public
School.
Harvard University ['hɑːvəd juː-
ni'vəːsiti] amer Universität
Harwich ['hæridʒ] Hafenstadt in
England.
Hawaii [hɑː'waiiː] Staat der U.S.A.
Hebrides ['hebridiːz] die Hebriden.
Helsinki ['helsiŋki] Helsinki n
Hemingway ['hemiŋwei] amer. Au-
tor.
Hereford(shire) ['herifəd(ʃiə)]
Grafschaft in England
Hertford(shire) ['hɑːtfəd(ʃiə)]
Grafschaft in England
Hollywood ['hɔliwud] Filmstadt in
Kalifornien, U.S.A
Houston ['juːstən] Stadt in U.S.A.
Hudson ['hʌdsn] Fluß in U.S.A
Hull [hʌl] Hafenstadt in England
Hume [hjuːm] engl Philosoph
Hungary ['hʌŋgəri] Ungarn n
Huntingdon(shire) ['hʌntiŋdən
(-ʃiə)] Grafschaft in England [m.]
Huron ['hjuərən] Lake ~ Huronsee
Huxley ['hʌksli] engl. Autor.

Iceland ['aislənd] Island n.
Idaho ['aidəhou] Staat der U.S.A.
Illinois [ili'nɔi] Staat der U.S.A.
India ['indjə] Indien n
Indiana [indi'ænə] Staat der U.S.A.
Iowa ['aiouə] Staat der U.S.A.
Irak, Iraq [i'rɑːk] Irak m.
Iran [i'rɑːn] Iran m
Ireland ['aiələnd] Irland n.
Irving ['əːviŋ] amer. Autor.
Italy ['itəli] Italien n.

Jefferson ['dʒefəsn] Präsident der
U.S.A., Verfasser der Unabhängig-
keitserklärung von 1776.
Johnson ['dʒɔnsn] 1. engl. Autor;
2. Präsident der U.S.A.

Kansas ['kænzəs] Staat der U.S.A.
Kashmir [kæʃ'miə] Kaschmir n.
Keats [kiːts] engl Dichter
Kennedy ['kenidi] Präsident der
U.S.A.; ~ Airport Flughafen von
New York.
Kent [kent] Grafschaft in England.
Kentucky [ken'tʌki] Staat der
U.S.A.
Kipling ['kipliŋ] engl. Dichter.
Klondike ['klɔndaik] Fluß und Land-
schaft in Kanada und Alaska.
Kremlin ['kremlin] der Kreml.

Labrador ['læbrədɔ:] *Halbinsel Nordamerikas.*
Lancashire ['læŋkəʃiə] *Grafschaft in England.*
Lancaster ['læŋkəstə] *Name zweier Städte in England und U.S.A.; s. Lancashire.* [land.]
Leeds [li:dz] *Industriestadt in Eng-]*
Leicester ['lestə] *Stadt in England; a. ~shire ['~ʃiə] Grafschaft in England.*
Lincoln ['liŋkən] 1. *Präsident der U.S.A.; 2. a. ~shire ['~ʃiə] Grafschaft in England.*
Lisbon ['lizbən] *Lissabon n.*
Liverpool ['livəpul] *Hafen- und Industriestadt in England.*
Locke [lɔk] *engl. Philosoph.*
London ['lʌndən] *London n.*
Los Angeles [lɔs 'ændʒili:z] *Stadt in U.S.A.*
Louisiana [lu:izi'ænə] *Staat der]*
Lucerne [lu:'sə:n]: *Lake of ~ Vierwaldstätter See m.*
Luxemburg ['lʌksəmbə:g] *Luxemburg n.*

Madrid [mə'drid] *Madrid n.*
Maine [mein] *Staat der U.S.A.*
Malta ['mɔ:ltə] *Malta n.*
Manchester ['mæntʃistə] *Industriestadt in England.*
Manhattan [mæn'hætən] *Stadtteil von New York.* [Kanada.]
Manitoba [mæni'toubə] *Provinz in]*
Maryland ['mɛərilənd, Am. 'merilənd] *Staat der U.S.A.*
Massachusetts [mæsə'tʃu:sits] *Staat der U.S.A.*
Melbourne ['melbən] *Stadt in Australien.*
Miami [mai'æmi] *Badeort in Florida, U.S.A.*
Michigan ['miʃigən] *Staat der U.S.A.; Lake ~ Michigansee m.*
Middlesex ['midlseks] *Grafschaft in England.*
Miller ['milə] *amer. Dramatiker.*
Milton ['miltən] *engl. Dichter.*
Milwaukee [mil'wɔ:ki:] *Stadt in U.S.A.*
Minneapolis [mini'æpəlis] *Stadt in U.S.A.* [U.S.A.]
Minnesota [mini'soutə] *Staat der]*
Mississippi [misi'sipi] *Strom und Staat der U.S.A.*
Missouri [mi'zuəri] *Fluß und Staat der U.S.A.*
Monmouth(shire) ['mɔnməθ(ʃiə)] *Grafschaft in England.*
Monroe [mən'rou] *Präsident der U.S.A.* [U.S.A.]
Montana [mɔn'tænə] *Staat der]*
Montgomery [mənt'gɔməri] *brit. Feldmarschall.*
Montreal [mɔntri'ɔ:l] *Stadt in Kanada.*
Moore [muə] *engl. Bildhauer.*
Moscow ['mɔskou] *Moskau n.*

Nebraska [ni'bræskə] *Staat der U.S.A.*
Nelson ['nelsn] *engl. Admiral.*
Netherlands ['neðələndz] *die Niederlande.*
Nevada [ne'vɑ:də] *Staat der U.S.A.*
New Brunswick [nju: 'brʌnzwik] *Provinz in Kanada.*
Newcastle ['nju:kɑ:sl] *Hafenstadt in England.* [von Indien.]
New Delhi [nju: 'deli] *Hauptstadt]*
New England [nju: 'iŋglənd] *Neuengland n.* [Neufundland n.]
Newfoundland [nju:fənd'lænd]]
New Hampshire [nju: 'hæmpʃiə] *Staat der U.S.A.*
New Jersey [nju: 'dʒə:si] *Staat der U.S.A.*
New Mexico [nju: 'meksikou] *Neumexiko n (Staat der U.S.A.).*
New Orleans [nju: 'ɔ:liəns] *Hafenstadt in U.S.A.*
Newton ['nju:tn] *engl. Physiker.*
New York ['nju: 'jɔ:k] *Stadt und Staat der U.S.A.*
New Zealand [nju: 'zi:lənd] *Neuseeland n.*
Niagara [nai'ægərə] *Niagara m.*
Nixon ['niksn] *Präsident der U.S.A.*
Norfolk ['nɔ:fək] *Grafschaft in England.*
Northampton [nɔ:'θæmptən] *Stadt in England; a. ~shire ['~ʃiə] Grafschaft in England.*
Northumberland [nɔ:'θʌmbələnd] *Grafschaft in England.*
Norway ['nɔ:wei] *Norwegen n.*
Nottingham ['nɔtiŋəm] *Stadt in England; a. ~shire ['~ʃiə] Grafschaft in England.*
Nova Scotia ['nouvə 'skouʃə] *Provinz in Kanada.*

Ohio [ou'haiou] *Staat der U.S.A.*
O'Neill [ou'ni:l] *amer. Dramatiker.*
Ontario [ɔn'tɛəriou] *Provinz in Kanada; Lake ~ Ontariosee m.*
Oregon ['ɔrigən] *Staat der U.S.A.*
Orkney Islands ['ɔ:kni 'ailəndz] *die Orkneyinseln.*
Osborne ['ɔzbən] *engl. Dramatiker.*
Oslo ['ɔzlou] *Oslo n.*
Ostend [ɔs'tend] *Ostende n.*
Ottawa ['ɔtəwə] *Hauptstadt von Kanada.*
Oxford ['ɔksfəd] *engl. Universitätsstadt; a. ~shire ['~ʃiə] Grafschaft in England.*

Pakistan [pɑ:kis'tɑ:n] *Pakistan n.*
Paris ['pæris] *Paris n.*
Pearl Harbour ['pə:l 'hɑ:bə] *Hafenstadt auf Hawaii.*
Pennsylvania [pensil'veinjə] *Pennsylvanien n (Staat der U.S.A.).*
Philadelphia [filə'delfjə] *Stadt in U.S.A.*
Philippines ['filipi:nz] *die Philippinen.*

Pittsburg(h) ['pitsbə:g] *Stadt in U.S.A.*

Plymouth ['pliməθ] *Hafenstadt in England.*

Poe [pou] *amer. Autor.*

Poland ['poulənd] *Polen n.*

Portsmouth ['pɔːtsməθ] *Hafenstadt in England.*

Portugal ['pɔːtjugəl] *Portugal n.*

Prague [prɑːg] *Prag n.*

Purcell ['pəːsl] *engl. Komponist.*

Quebec [kwi'bek] *Provinz und Stadt in Kanada.*

Reykjavik ['reikjəviːk] *Reykjavik n.*

Rhode Island [roud 'ailənd] *Staat der U.S.A*

Rocky Mountains ['rɔki 'mauntinz] *Gebirge in U S.A.*

Rome [roum] *Rom n.*

Roosevelt ['rouzəvelt] *Name zweier Präsidenten der U.S.A* [School.]

Rugby ['rʌgbi] *berühmte Public*

Rumania [ru meinjə] *Rumänien n.*

Russell ['rʌsl] *engl Philosoph.*

Russia ['rʌfə] *Rußland n.*

Rutland(shire) ['rʌtlənd(fiə)] *Grafschaft in England.*

San Francisco [sænfrən'siskou] *Hafenstadt in U.S.A.*

Saskatchewan [səs'kætfiwən] *Provinz von Kanada.*

Scandinavia [skændi'neivjə] *Skandinavien n*

Scotland ['skɔtlənd] *Schottland n.*

Shakespeare ['feikspiə] *engl. Dichter.*

Shaw [fɔː] *engl Dramatiker.*

Shelley ['feli] *engl Dichter.*

Shetland Islands ['fetlənd 'ailəndz] *die Shetlandinseln*

Shropshire ['fropfiə] *Grafschaft in England.*

Snowdon ['snoudn] *Berg in Wales.*

Sofia ['soufjə] *Sofia n.*

Somerset(shire) ['sʌməsit(fiə)] *Grafschaft in England.*

Southampton [sauθ'æmptən] *Hafenstadt in England*

Spain [spein] *Spanien n.*

Stafford(shire) ['stæfəd(fiə)] *Grafschaft in England*

Stevenson ['sti vnsn] *engl. Autor.*

St. Lawrence [snt'lɔrəns] *der St. Lorenz-Strom*

St. Louis [snt'luis] *Industriestadt in U.S.A.* [n.]

Stockholm ['stɔkhoum] *Stockholm*

Stratford ['strætfəd]: ‿on-Avon *Geburtsort Shakespeares.*

Suffolk ['sʌfək] *Grafschaft in England.* [rer See m.]

Superior [sju:'piəriə]: *Lake ‿ Obe-*

Surrey ['sʌri] *Grafschaft in England.*

Sussex ['sʌsiks] *Grafschaft in England.*

Sweden ['swiːdn] *Schweden n.*

Swift [swift] *engl. Autor*

Switzerland ['switsələnd] *die Schweiz.* [tralien.]

Sydney ['sidni] *Hafenstadt in Aus-*

Tennessee [tene'si] *Staat der U.S.A.*

Tennyson ['tenisn] *engl. Dichter.*

Texas ['teksəs] *Staat der U.S.A.*

Thackeray ['θækəri] *engl. Autor.*

Thames [temz] *Themse f.*

Tirana [ti'rɑːnə] *Tirana n.* [nada.]

Toronto [tə'rɔntou] *Stadt in Ka-*

Toynbee ['tɔinbi] *engl. Historiker.*

Trafalgar [trə'fælgə] *Vorgebirge bei Gibraltar.* [U.S.A.]

Truman ['truːmən] *Präsident der*

Turkey ['təːki] *die Türkei.*

Twain [twein] *amer. Autor.*

Tyrol ['tirəl] *Tirol n.*

United States of America [ju:'naitid 'steitsəvə'merikə] *die Vereinigten Staaten von Amerika.*

Utah ['juːtɑː] *Staat der U.S.A.*

Vancouver [væn'kuːvə] *Stadt in Kanada.*

Vermont [vəː'mɔnt] *Staat der*

Vienna [vi'enə] *Wien n.* [U.S.A.]

Virginia [və'dʒinjə] *Virginien n (Staat der U.S.A.); West ‿ Staat der U.S.A.*

Wales [weilz] *Wales n.*

Warsaw ['wɔːsɔː] *Warschau n.*

Warwick(shire) ['wɔrik(fiə)] *Grafschaft in England.*

Washington ['wɔfiŋtən] **1.** *Präsident der U.S.A.;* **2.** *Staat der U.S.A.;* **3.** *Bundeshauptstadt der U.S.A.*

Wellington ['weliŋtən] *Hauptstadt von Neuseeland.*

Westmoreland ['westmələnd] *Grafschaft in England.*

White House ['wait 'haus] *das Weiße Haus.*

Whitman ['witmən] *amer. Dichter.*

Wilson ['wilsn] **1.** *Präsident der U.S.A.;* **2.** *brit. Premier.*

Wiltshire ['wiltfiə] *Grafschaft in England.*

Wimbledon ['wimbldən] *Vorort von London.* [Kanada.]

Winnipeg ['winipeg] *Stadt in*

Wisconsin [wis'kɔnsin] *Staat der U.S.A.*

Worcester ['wustə] *Industriestadt in England; a. ‿shire [‿fiə] Grafschaft in England.*

Wordsworth ['wəːdzwəːθ] *engl. Dichter.*

Yale University ['jeil juːni'vəːsiti] *amer. Universität.*

York [jɔːk] *Stadt in England; a. ‿shire [‿fiə] Grafschaft in England.*

Yugoslavia ['juːgou'slɑːvjə] *Jugoslawien n.*

American and British Abbreviations

abbr. *abbreviated* abgekürzt; *abbreviation* Abk., Abkürzung *f.*

A.B.C. *American Broadcasting Company* Amer. Rundfunkgesellschaft *f.* [strom *m.*]

A.C. *alternating current* Wechsel-]

A.E.C. *Atomic Energy Commission* Atomenergie-Kommission *f.*

AFL-CIO *American Federation of Labor & Congress of Industrial Organizations (größter amer. Gewerkschaftsverband).*

A.F.N. *American Forces Network (Rundfunkanstalt der amer. Streit-)*

Ala. *Alabama.* [kräfte).]

Alas. *Alaska.*

a.m. *ante meridiem (lateinisch = before noon)* vormittags.

A.P. *Associated Press (amer. Nachrichtenbüro).* [Rotes Kreuz.)

A.R.C. *American Red Cross* Amer.)

Ariz. *Arizona.*

Ark. *Arkansas.*

arr. *arrival* Ank., Ankunft *f.*

B.A. *Bachelor of Arts* Bakkalaureus *m* der Philosophie.

B.B.C. *British Broadcasting Corporation* Brit. Rundfunkgesellschaft *f.*

B.E.A. *British European Airways* Brit.-Europäische Luftfahrtge-]

Beds. *Bedfordshire.* [sellschaft.)

Benelux *Belgium, Netherlands, Luxemburg (Zollunion).*

Berks. *Berkshire.*

B.F.N. *British Forces Network (Sender der brit. Streitkräfte in Deutschland).* [m des Rechts.)

B.L. *Bachelor of Law* Bakkalaureus)

B.M. *Bachelor of Medicine* Bakkalaureus *m* der Medizin.

B.O.A.C. *British Overseas Airways Corporation* Brit. Übersee-Luftfahrtgesellschaft *f.*

B.R. *British Railways.*

Br(it). *Britain* Großbritannien *n*; *British* britisch.

B.S. *Bachelor of Science* Bakkalaureus *m* der Naturwissenschaften.

Bucks. *Buckinghamshire.*

C. *Celsius, centigrade.*

c. *cent(s)* Cent *m*; *circa* ca., ungefähr, zirka; *cubic* Kubik...

Cal(if). *California.*

Cambs. *Cambridgeshire.*

Can. *Canada* Kanada *n*; *Canadian* kanadisch.

cf. *confer* vgl., vergleiche.

Ches. *Cheshire.*

C.I.C. *Counter Intelligence Corps (Spionageabwehrdienst der U.S.A.).*

C.I.D. *Criminal Investigation Department (brit. Kriminalpolizei).*

Co. *Company* Gesellschaft *f*; *County* Grafschaft *f*, Kreis *m.*

c/o *care of* p.A., per Adresse, bei.

Col(o). *Colorado.*

Conn. *Connecticut.*

cp. *compare* vgl., vergleiche.

Cumb. *Cumberland.* [ner *m.*)

cwt. *hundredweight (etwa 1)* Zent-)

d. *penny, pence.*

D.C. *direct current* Gleichstrom *m*; *District of Columbia (mit der amer. Hauptstadt Washington).*

Del. *Delaware.*

dep. *departure* Abf., Abfahrt *f.*

Dept. *Department* Abt., Abteilung *f.*

Derby. *Derbyshire.*

Devon. *Devonshire.*

Dors. *Dorsetshire.*

Dur(h). *Durham.*

dz. *dozen* Dutzend *n od. pl.*

E. *east* Ost(en *m*); *eastern* östlich; *English* englisch.

E.C. *East Central (London)* Mitte-Ost *(Postbezirk).*

ECOSOC *Economic and Social Council* Wirtschafts- und Sozialrat *m (U.N.).*

Ed., ed. *edition* Auflage *f*; *edited* hrsg., herausgegeben; *editor* Hrsg., Herausgeber *m.*

E.E.C. *European Economic Community* EWG, Europäische Wirtschaftsgemeinschaft.

E.F.T.A. *European Free Trade Association* EFTA, Europäische Freihandelsgemeinschaft *od.* -zone.

e.g. *exempli gratia (lateinisch = for instance)* z.B., zum Beispiel.

Enc. *enclosure(s)* Anlage(n *pl.) f.*

Ess. *Essex.*

F. *Fahrenheit.*

f. *fathom(s)* Faden *m*, Klafter *f, m, n*; *feminine* weiblich; *foot, pl. feet* Fuß *m od. pl.*; *following* folgend.

F.A.O. *Food and Agricultural Organization* Organisation *f* für Ernährung und Landwirtschaft *(U.N.).*

FBI *Federal Bureau of Investigation (Bundeskriminalamt der U.S.A.).*

fig. *figure(s)* Abb., Abbildung(en) [pl.) f.)

Fla. *Florida.*

F.O. *Foreign Office brit.* Auswärtiges)

fr. *franc(s)* Frank(en *pl.) m.* [Amt.)

ft. *foot, pl. feet* Fuß *m od. pl.*

g. *gramme* g, Gramm *n*; *guinea* Guinee *f* (*21 Schilling*).
Ga. *Georgia.*
gal. *gallon* Gallone *f*.
G.A.T.T. *General Agreement on Tariffs and Trade* Allgemeines Zoll- und Handelsabkommen.
G.B. *Great Britain* Großbritannien *n*.
G.I. *government issue* von der Regierung ausgegeben; Staatseigentum *n*; *fig der* amer Soldat.
Glos. *Gloucestershire*
G.P.O. *General Post Office* Haupt-}
gr. *gross* brutto   [postamt *n*.}
Gt.Br. *Great Britain* Großbritannien *n*.

h. *hour(s)* Std., Stunde(n *pl*.) *f*.
Hants. *Hampshire*
H.C. *House of Commons* Unterhaus *n*.
Heref. *Herefordshire.*
Herts. *Hertfordshire.*
hf. *half* halb
H.I. *Hawaiian Islands.*
H.L. *House of Lords* Oberhaus *n*.
H.M. *His (Her) Majesty* Seine (Ihre) Majestät
H.M.S. *His (Her) Majesty's Service* Dienst *m*, & Dienstsache *f*; *His (Her) Majesty's Ship* Seiner (Ihrer) Majestät Schiff *n*
H.O. *Home Office brit.* Innenministerium *n*   [stärke *f*.}
H.P., h.p. *horse-power* PS, Pferde-}
H.Q., Hq. *Headquarters* Stab(squartier *n*) *m*, Hauptquartier *n*.
H.R. *House of Representatives* Repräsentantenhaus *n* (*der U.S.A.*).
H.R.H. *His (Her) Royal Highness* Seine (Ihre) Königliche Hoheit *f*.
Hunts. *Huntingdonshire.*

Ia. *Iowa.*
I.C.B.M. *intercontinental ballistic missile* interkontinentaler ballistischer Flugkörper
I.D. *Intelligence Department* Nachrichtenamt *n*
Id(a). *Idaho*   [d.h., das heißt.}
i.e. *id est* (*lateinisch = that is to say*)}
Ill. *Illinois*
I.M.F. *International Monetary Fund* Weltwährungsfonds *m*.
in. *inch(es)* Zoll *m od. pl.*   [gen.}
Inc. *Incorporated* (amtlich) eingetra-}
Ind. *Indiana*
I.O.C. *International Olympic Committee* Internationales Olympisches Komitee
Ir. *Ireland* Irland *n*; *Irish* irisch.
I.R.C. *International Red Cross* Internationales Rotes Kreuz.

J.P. *Justice of the Peace* Friedensrichter *m*.

Kan(s). *Kansas.*
k.o. *knock(ed) out Boxen:* k.o. (ge-) schlagen; *fig.* erledigen (erledigt).
Ky. *Kentucky.*

£ *pound sterling* Pfund *n* Sterling.
La. *Louisiana.*
Lancs. *Lancashire.*   [wicht).}
lb. *pound(s)* Pfund *n od. pl.* (Ge-}
L.C. *letter of credit* Kreditbrief}
Leics. *Leicestershire.*   [m.}
Lincs. *Lincolnshire.*
LP *long-playing* Langspiel...(*Platte*).
L.P. *Labour Party* (*brit. Arbeiterpartei*).   [tung.}
Ltd. *limited* mit beschränkter Haf-}

m. *male* männlich; *metre* m, Meter *n*, *m*; *mile* Meile *f*; *minute* Min., Minute *f*.   [Philosophie.}
M.A. *Master of Arts* Magister *m der*}
Mass. *Massachusetts.*
M.D. *Medicinae Doctor* (*lateinisch = Doctor of Medicine*) Dr. med., Doktor *m* der Medizin.
Md. *Maryland.*
Me. *Maine.*
mi. *mile* Meile *f*.
Mich. *Michigan.*
Middx. *Middlesex.*
Minn. *Minnesota.*
Miss. *Mississippi.*
Mo. *Missouri.*
M.O. *money order* Postanweisung *f*.
Mon. *Monmouthshire.*
Mont. *Montana.*
MP, M.P. *Member of Parliament* Parlamentsabgeordnete *m*; *Military Police* Militärpolizei *f*.
m.p.h. *miles per hour* Stundenmei-}
Mr *Mister* Herr *m*.   [len *pl*.}
Mrs *Mistress* Frau *f*.
Mt. *Mount* Berg *m*.

N. *north* Nord(en *m*); *northern* nörd-}
n. *noon* Mittag *m*.   [lich.}
NASA *National Aeronautics and Space Administration* (*amer. Luftfahrt- und Raumforschungsbehörde*)
NATO *North Atlantic Treaty Organization* Nordatlantikpakt-Organisation *f*.
N.C. *North Carolina.*
N.D(ak). *North Dakota.*
Neb(r). *Nebraska.*
Nev. *Nevada.*
N.H. *New Hampshire.*
N.H.S. *National Health Service* Nationaler Gesundheitsdienst (*brit. Krankenversicherung*).
N.J. *New Jersey.*
N.M(ex). *New Mexico.*
Norf. *Norfolk.*
Northants. *Northamptonshire.*
Northumb. *Northumberland.*
Notts. *Nottinghamshire.*
nt. *net* netto.
N.Y. *New York.*   [York.}
N.Y.C. *New York City* Stadt *f* New}

O. *Ohio*; *order* Auftrag *m*.
O.A.S. *Organization of American States* Organisation *f* amerikanischer Staaten.

O.E.E.C. *Organization of European Economic Co-operation* Organisation *f* für europäische wirtschaftliche Zusammenarbeit.

Okla. *Oklahoma.*

Ore(g). *Oregon.*

Oxon. *Oxfordshire.*

Pa. *Pennsylvania.*

P.A.A. *Pan-American Airways* Panamer. Luftfahrtgesellschaft *f.*

P.C. *police constable* Schutzmann *m.*

p.c. *per cent* %, Prozent *n od. pl.*

pd. *paid* bezahlt.

P.E.N., *mst* **PEN Club** *Poets, Playwrights, Editors, Essayists, and Novelists* Pen-Club *m*, *(Internationale Vereinigung von Dichtern, Dramatikern, Redakteuren, Essayisten und Romanschriftstellern).*

Penn(a). *Pennsylvania.*

Ph.D. *Philosophiae Doctor (lateinisch = Doctor of Philosophy)* Dr. phil., Doktor *m* der Philosophie.

p.m. *post meridiem lateinisch = after noon)* nachmittags, abends.

P.O. *Post Office* Postamt *n*; *postal order* Postanweisung *f.*

P.O.B. *Post Office Box* Postschließfach *n.*

P.S. *Postscript* P.S., Nachschrift *f.*

P.T.O., **p.t.o.** *please turn over* b.w., bitte wenden.

PX *Post Exchange (Verkaufsläden der amer. Streitkräfte).*

R.A.F. *Royal Air Force* Königlich-Brit. Luftwaffe *f.*

Rd. *Road* Straße *f.*

ref(c). *(In) reference (to)* (in) Bezug *m* (auf); Empfehlung *f.*

regd. *registered* eingetragen; & eingeschrieben. [tonne *f.*)

reg. tn. *register ton* RT, Register-)

resp. *respective(ly)* bzw., beziehungsweise.

ret. *retired* i.R., im Ruhestand.

Rev. *Reverend* Ehrwürden.

R.I. *Rhode Island.* Marine *f.*)

R.N. *Royal Navy* Königlich-Brit.)

R.R. *Railroad Am* Eisenbahn *f.*

Rutland. *Rutlandshire.*

Ry. *Railway* Eisenbahn *f.*

S. *south* Süd(en *m*); *southern* südlich.

s. *second(s)* Sek., Sekunde(n *pl.) f*; *shilling(s)* Schilling *m od. pl.*

$ *dollar* Dollar *m.*

S.A. *South Africa* Südafrika *n*; *South America* Südamerika *n.*

Salop *Shropshire.*

S.C. *South Carolina*; *Security Council* Sicherheitsrat *m (U.N.).*

S.D(ak). *South Dakota.*

SEATO *South East Asia Treaty Organization* Südostasienpakt-Organisation *f.*

sh. *shilling(s)* Schilling *m od. pl.*

Soc. *society* Gesellschaft *f*; Verein *m.*

Som. *Somersetshire.*

Sq. *Square* Platz *m.*

sq. *square* ... Quadrat...

Staffs. *Staffordshire.*

St(.) *Saint* ... Sankt ...; *Station* Bahnhof *m*; *Street* Straße *f.*

Suff. *Suffolk.*

suppl. *supplement* Nachtrag *m.*

Sur. *Surrey.*

Suss. *Sussex.*

t. *ton(s)* Tonne(n *pl.) f.*

Tenn. *Tennessee.*

Tex. *Texas.*

T.M.O. *telegraph money order* telegraphische Geldanweisung.

T.O. *Telegraph (Telephone) Office* Telegraphen- (Fernsprech)amt *n*

T.U. *Trade(s) Union(s)* Gewerkschaft(en *pl.) f.*

T.U.C. *Trade(s) Union Congress brit.* Gewerkschaftsverband *m.*

U.K. *United Kingdom* Vereinigtes Königreich *(England, Schottland, Wales und Nordirland).*

U.N. *United Nations* Vereinte Nationen *pl.*

UNESCO *United Nations Educational, Scientific, and Cultural Organization* Organisation *f* der Vereinten Nationen für Wissenschaft, Erziehung und Kultur.

U.N.S.C. *United Nations Security Council* Sicherheitsrat *m* der Vereinten Nationen.

U.P.I. *United Press International (amer. Nachrichtenagentur).*

U.S.(A.) *United States (of America)* Vereinigte Staaten *pl.* (von Ame-)

Ut. *Utah.* [rika.))

Va. *Virginia.*

vol(s). *volume(s)* Band *m* (Bände)

Vt. *Vermont.* [*pl.).*)

V.T.O.(L.) *vertical take-off (and landing) (aircraft)* Senkrechtstart(er) *m.*

W. *west* West(en *m*); *western* west-)

War. *Warwickshire.* [lich.)

Wash. *Washington.*

W.C. *West Central* (London) Mitte-West *(Postbezirk).*

W.F.T.U. *World Federation of Trade Unions* Weltgewerkschaftsbund *m.*

W.H.O. *World Health Organization* Weltgesundheitsorganisation *f (U.N.).*

W.I. *West Indies* Westindien *n.*

Wilts. *Wiltshire.*

Wis. *Wisconsin.*

Worcs. *Worcestershire.*

wt. *weight* Gewicht *n.*

W.Va. *West Virginia.*

Wyo. *Wyoming.*

yd. *yard(s)* Elle(n *pl.) f.*

Yorks. *Yorkshire.*

German Weights and Measures

I. Linear Measure

1 mm   *Millimeter* millimet|re, *Am.* -er = 0.039 inch

1 cm   *Zentimeter* centimet|re, *Am.* -er = 10 mm = 0.394 inch

1 m   *Meter* met|re, *Am.* -er = 100 cm = 1.094 yards = 3.281 feet

1 km   *Kilometer* kilomet|re, *Am.* -er = 1000 m = 0.621 mile

1 sm   *Seemeile* nautical mile = 1852 m

II. Square Measure

1 mm²   *Quadratmillimeter* square millimet|re, *Am.* -er = 0.002 square inch

1 cm²   *Quadratzentimeter* square centimet|re, *Am.* -er = 100 mm² = 0.155 square inch

1 m²   *Quadratmeter* square met|re, *Am.* -er = 10000 cm² = 1.196 square yards = 10.764 square feet

1 a   *Ar* are = 100 m² = 119.599 square yards

1 ha   *Hektar* hectare = 100 a = 2.471 acres

1 km²   *Quadratkilometer* square kilomet|re, *Am.* -er = 100 ha = 247.11 acres = 0.386 square mile

III. Cubic Measure

1 cm³   *Kubikzentimeter* cubic centimet|re, *Am.* -er = 1000 mm³ = 0.061 cubic inch

1 m³   *Kubikmeter* cubic met|re, *Am.* -er = 1000000 cm³ = 35.315 cubic feet = 1.308 cubic yards

1 RT   *Registertonne* register ton = 2,832 m³ = 100 cubic feet

IV. Measure of Capacity

1 l   *Liter* lit|re, *Am.* -er = 1.760 pints = *U.S.* 1.057 liquid quarts *or* 0.906 dry quart

1 hl   *Hektoliter* hectolit|re, *Am.* -er = 100 l = 2.75 bushels = *U.S.* 26.418 gallons

V. Weight

1 g   *Gramm* gram(me) = 15.432 grains

1 Pfd.   *Pfund* pound (German) = 500 g = 1.102 pounds avdp.

1 kg   *Kilogramm* kilogram(me) = 1000 g = 2.205 pounds avdp. = 2.679 pounds troy

1 Ztr.   *Zentner* centner = 100 Pfd. = 0.984 hundredweight = 1.102 *U.S.* hundredweights

1 dz   *Doppelzentner* = 100 kg = 1.968 hundredweights = 2.204 *U.S.* hundredweights

1 t   *Tonne* ton = 1000 kg = 0.984 long ton = *U.S.* 1.102 short tons

American and British Weights and Measures

1. Linear Measure

1 inch (in.) = 2,54 cm
1 foot (ft)
  = 12 inches = 30,48 cm
1 yard (yd)
  = 3 feet = 91,439 cm
1 perch (p.)
  = 5¹/₂ yards = 5,029 m
1 mile (m.)
  = 1,760 yards = 1,609 km

2. Nautical Measure

1 fathom (f., fm)
  = 6 feet = 1,829 m
1 nautical mile
  = 6,080 feet = 1853,18 m

3. Square Measure

1 square inch (sq. in.)
  = 6,452 cm²
1 square foot (sq. ft)
  = 144 square inches
  = 929,029 cm²
1 square yard (sq. yd)
  = 9 square feet = 8361,26 cm²
1 square perch (sq. p.)
  = 30¹/₄ square yards = 25,293 m²
1 rood
  = 40 square perches = 10,117 a
1 acre (a.) = 4 roods = 40,47 a
1 square mile
  = 640 acres = 258,998 ha

4. Cubic Measure

1 cubic inch (cu. in.)
  = 16,387 cm³
1 cubic foot (cu. ft)
  = 1,728 cubic inches = 0,028 m³
1 cubic yard (cu. yd)
  = 27 cubic feet = 0,765 m³
1 register ton (reg. ton)
  = 100 cubic feet = 2,832 m³

5. Measure of Capacity
Dry and Liquid Measure

1 British or imperial gill (gl, gi.)
  = 0,142 l
1 British or imperial pint (pt)
  = 4 gills = 0,568 l
1 British or imperial quart (qt)
  = 2 pints = 1,136 l
1 British or imp. gallon (imp. gal.)
  = 4 imperial quarts = 4,546 l

Dry Measure

1 British or imperial peck (pk)
  = 2 imperial gallons = 9,092 l
1 Brit. or imp. bushel (bu., bus.)
  = 8 imperial gallons = 36,366 l

1 Brit. or imp. quarter (qr)
  = 8 imperial bushels = 290,935 l

Liquid Measure

1 Brit. or imp. barrel (bbl, bl)
  = 36 imperial gallons = 163,656 l

*

1 U.S. dry pint = 0,551 l
1 U.S. dry quart
  = 2 dry pints = 1,101 l
1 U.S. dry gallon
  = 4 dry quarts = 4,405 l
1 U.S. peck
  = 2 dry gallons = 8,809 l
1 U.S. bushel
  = 8 dry gallons = 35,238 l
1 U.S. gill = 0,118 l
1 U.S. liquid pint
  = 4 gills = 0,473 l
1 U.S. liquid quart
  = 2 liquid pints = 0,946 l
1 U.S. liquid gallon
  = 8 liquid pints = 3,785 l
1 U.S. barrel
  = 3¹/₂ liquid gallons = 119,228 l
1 U.S. barrel petroleum
  = 42 liquid gallons = 158,97 l

6. Avoirdupois Weight

1 grain (gr.) = 0,065 g
1 dram (dr.)
  = 27,344 grains = 1,772 g
1 ounce (oz.)
  = 16 drams = 28,35 g
1 pound (lb.)
  = 16 ounces = 453,592 g
1 quarter (qr)
  = 28 pounds = 12,701 kg
  (U.S.A. 25 pounds
  = 11,339 kg)
1 hundredweight (cwt.)
  = 112 pounds
  = 50,802 kg (U.S.A. 100 pounds
  = 45,359 kg)
1 ton (t.)
  (a. long ton) = 20 hundredweights = 1016,05 kg (U.S.A.,
  a. short ton, = 907,185 kg)
1 stone (st.) = 14 pounds = 6,35 kg

7. Troy Weight

1 grain = 0,065 g
1 pennyweight (dwt.)
  = 24 grains = 1,555 g
1 ounce
  = 20 pennyweights = 31,103 g
1 pound = 12 ounces = 373,242 g